LET'S GO

PAGES PACKED WITH ESSENTIAL INFORMATI[ON]

"Value-packed, unbeatable, accurate, and comp[...]

—*The Los Angeles Times*

"The guides are aimed not only at young budget trav[...] [ind]ependent traveler; a sort of streetwise cookbook for traveling alone."

—*The New York Times*

"Unbeatable; good sight-seeing advice; up-to-date info on restaurants, hotels, and inns; a commitment to money-saving travel; and a wry style that brightens nearly every page."

—*The Washington Post*

THE BEST TRAVEL BARGAINS IN YOUR BUDGET

"All the dirt, dirt cheap."

—*People*

"Let's Go follows the creed that you don't have to toss your life's savings to the wind to travel—unless you want to."

—*The Salt Lake Tribune*

REAL ADVICE FOR REAL EXPERIENCES

"The writers seem to have experienced every rooster-packed bus and lunar-surfaced mattress about which they write."

—*The New York Times*

"[Let's Go's] devoted updaters really walk the walk (and thumb the ride, and trek the trail). Learn how to fish, haggle, find work—anywhere."

—*Food & Wine*

"A world-wise traveling companion—always ready with friendly advice and helpful hints, all sprinkled with a bit of wit."

—*The Philadelphia Inquirer*

A GUIDE WITH A SPIRIT AND A SOCIAL CONSCIENCE

"Lighthearted and sophisticated, informative and fun to read. [Let's Go] helps the novice traveler navigate like a knowledgeable old hand."

—*Atlanta Journal-Constitution*

"The serious mission at the book's core reveals itself in exhortations to respect the culture and the environment—and, if possible, to visit as a volunteer, a student, or a teacher rather than a tourist."

—*San Francisco Chronicle*

LET'S GO PUBLICATIONS

TRAVEL GUIDES
Australia
Austria & Switzerland
Brazil
Britain
California
Central America
Chile
China
Costa Rica
Eastern Europe
Ecuador
Egypt
Europe
France
Germany
Greece
Hawaii
India & Nepal
Ireland
Israel
Italy
Japan
Mexico
New Zealand
Peru
Puerto Rico
Southeast Asia
Spain & Portugal with Morocco
Thailand
USA
Vietnam
Western Europe

ROADTRIP GUIDE
Roadtripping USA

ADVENTURE GUIDES
Alaska
Pacific Northwest
Southwest USA

CITY GUIDES
Amsterdam
Barcelona
Boston
Buenos Aires
London
New York City
Paris
Rome
San Francisco
Washington, DC

POCKET CITY GUIDES
Amsterdam
Berlin
Boston
Chicago
London
New York City
Paris
San Francisco
Venice
Washington, DC

LET'S GO

ROADTRIPPING
USA

THE COMPLETE COAST-TO-COAST GUIDE TO AMERICA

JUSTINE LESCROART EDITOR
SAM WALSH ASSOCIATE EDITOR
MATT ZIMMERMAN ASSOCIATE EDITOR

RESEARCHER-WRITERS
BEN COSGROVE   **JUSTIN KEENAN**
BENEDICT CUDDON   **PAUL MCMURRY**
LAURA JARAMILLO   **SARAH MOLINOFF**
MEGHAN JOYCE   **ALEXANDRA
PERLOFF-GILES**

REBECCA SMITH MAP EDITOR
NATHANIEL RAKICH MANAGING EDITOR

ST. MARTIN'S PRESS 🕊 NEW YORK

HELPING LET'S GO. If you want to share your discoveries, suggestions, or corrections, please drop us a line. We read every piece of correspondence, whether a postcard, a 10-page email, or a coconut. Visit Let's Go at **http://www.letsgo.com** or send email to:

feedback@letsgo.com
Subject: "Let's Go: Roadtripping USA"

Address mail to:

Let's Go: Roadtripping USA
67 Mt. Auburn St.
Cambridge, MA 02138
USA

In addition to the invaluable travel advice our readers share with us, many are kind enough to offer their services as researchers or editors. Unfortunately, our charter enables us to employ only currently enrolled Harvard students.

CONTENTS

HOW TO USE THIS BOOK

ORGANIZATION. This book is organized into eight distinct routes. Follow just one of them, create your own custom roadtrip by combining two or more, or freestyle it, only checking in with *Let's Go* when your and our destinations coincide. Each of our chapters begins with a **Top 5** box to help you pinpoint the best that a route has to offer. To find the right route in a hurry, let the black tabs on the side of the book guide you.

MAPS. In addition to city maps, *Let's Go: Roadtripping USA* includes vertical route maps that will help you navigate. Each map plots approximately 200 mi. The maps are oriented along your path; we've angled the text for easy reading if you rotate the book north.

SPECIAL FEATURES. *Let's Go: Roadtripping USA* includes special features to highlight the road's sights and stories in a way that standard coverage can't. **From the Road** captures a researcher's first-person moment of epiphany. **Local Story** and **Local Legend** take a closer look at regional culture, both real and surreal. **No Work, All Play** will help you to crash the area's best festivals and celebrations. Whet your appetite for local cuisine with **On the Menu.** We know you're on a budget, so we've incorporated **The Big Splurge** to tell you when an extravagance is worth the sticker shock and **The Hidden Deal** to help your pennies go further.

RANKINGS. Let's Go lists establishments in order of value, starting with the best. Places and things that we absolutely love, sappily cherish, generally obsess over, and wholeheartedly endorse are denoted by the all-empowering **⚑Let's Go thumbs-up.**

PHONE CODES AND TELEPHONE. After each town's name, you'll find its area code. Phone numbers in this guide are marked with the ☎ icon. All include the area code and local number. In many cities, all 10 digits are required even for local calls; often, in more remote areas, only the final seven are needed for local calls.

WHEN TO USE THIS BOOK

ONE YEAR BEFORE. Some national parks', cities' (think San Diego), and towns' summer accommodations and campgrounds fill up many months in advance. Plan ahead and secure your spot.

ONE MONTH BEFORE. Take care of insurance and write down a list of emergency numbers and hotlines. Make a list of packing essentials (see **Packing**). Make sure you understand the logistics of your itinerary (ferries, distance between gas and rest stops, etc.). Make any reservations if necessary.

TWO WEEKS BEFORE. Leave an itinerary and a photocopy of important documents with someone at home. Check all of the fluids in the vehicle you are planning on taking and make sure the tires are in good shape. It's a good idea to have a tune-up, just in case.

ON THE ROAD. The **Appendix** contains metric conversion tables and a basic introduction to French and Spanish terms, which may come in handy in eastern Canada and Mexico.

A NOTE TO OUR READERS. The information for this book was gathered by Let's Go researchers from May through August of 2008. Each listing is based on one researcher's opinion, formed during his or her visit at a particular time. Those traveling at other times may have different experiences since prices, dates, hours, and conditions are always subject to change. You are urged to check the facts presented in this book beforehand to avoid inconvenience and surprises.

RESEARCHER-WRITERS

Ben Cosgrove
Great North

This New Hampshire native and sometime roving troubadour set out for the Great North equipped in style, guitar in hand and convertible in tow. Ben's friendly inquisitiveness helped him charm shopkeepers, mechanics, four-legged critters, and probably even the good people of the UP. Whether awed by stunning mountain vistas or frustrated by needlessly ensnarled traffic, Ben's articulate writing let those in the office adventure vicariously.

Benedict Cuddon
Route 66

This British wizard quickly fell in love with the Rte. 66 culture and kitsch. His bold research and even bolder marginalia kept his editors alternately splitting their sides and biting their nails. Ben's gregarious personality and embrace of Americana kept the romance of the "Mother Road" ablaze.

Laura Jaramillo
East Coast

Not even a flash flood could damper the fiery disposition of this Colombian powerhouse. With determination and dedication she researched the party scene of Key West and hunkered down for the long drive north. Laura's editors cherish her frequent artwork and kind notes. Travel well!

Meghan Joyce
Pacific Coast

This Let's Go vet's sunny disposition and technical expertise made her a Roadtripping USA star. Meghan always wrote cleanly and clearly; her editors looked forward to her sparkling copy. Meghan showed a particular aptitude for including excellent new coverage. Neither forest fires nor Napa's wineries distracted her from her task; she finished her route weeks ahead of schedule.

Justin Keenan
Oregon Trail

Last seen tracking the elusive jackalope, Justin used his Southern sensibilities, caustic humor, and reflective nature to grind a new lens through which to view America. This literary gambit wooed us with his lyricism and awed us with a level of snarkiness heretofore unknown to man. May the diligent reader forever laze within his prose.

RESEARCHER-WRITERS

Paul McMurry
Southern Border

Paul drove, camped, hiked, and even—one night in N'awlins—line danced his way along the Southern Border route. His editors appreciated this New York native's laid-back personality, carpe diem mentality, and genuine interest in just about everything (local art museums excluded). Paul's copy reflects his thorough and highly entertaining research; he completed this long, hot, difficult route as easily as he made friends in hostels.

Sarah Molinoff
National Road

Whether Rocky Mountain peaks or Salt Lake City record store basements, Sarah doggedly traveled wherever her copy led her. As the researcher on the National Road, the longest route in the book, Sarah always went the extra mile. By the end of the summer, her detailed and colorful copy had her editor sighing with contentment. Sarah, a recent graduate, is now off to Europe, where she'll continue to explore new frontiers.

Alexandra Perloff-Giles
Deep South

Hailing from San Francisco, Lexie (and her car) was willing to go the distance to traverse the Deep South. Able to turn up both grits and granola, Elvis and Ellsworth Kelly, Lexie's encyclopedic copy showed us all a new side of Southern culture. From Hotlanta to Nashvegas and beyond, Lexie carried herself with characteristic grace and style, charming locals and her editors along the way.

CONTRIBUTING WRITERS

Noel Barlow   *Boston*

Grace Gu   *Boston*

Laura James   *Boston*

Lingbo Li   *Boston*

Yifan Zhang   *Boston*

Frank DeSimone   *New York City*

Joaquin Terrones   *New York City*

Charlie Schaub   *New York City*

Mike Marriner crossed the country in a neon-green RV, interviewing self-made men and women for his book *Roadtrip Nation: A Guide to Discovering Your Path in Life.*

ACKNOWLEDGMENTS

TEAM ROAD THANKS:

Nathaniel Rakich, ☎617-ALT-0151. 67 Mt. Auburn Street, SpadThai. Though questionably quaffable, 🖂edits undoubtedly increase sexy time surface area. A small birdcage. 🖂Redsox. Available 365/24/7.

Our 8 RWs, who braved hell, high water, bears, and bouncers to bring you this book. Our love for you is as inexhaustible as your itineraries. Mission control, for loving the black sheep of the Let's Go family—and, of course, for sheer natural athleticism. Last but by no means least, Mapland. Wat's up.

JUSTINE THANKS: First, of course, the pod: Pat, for metaphysical musings; Matt, who can have the whole cookie; and Sam, who's on my heart just like a tattoo. Nathaniel, for always demanding our best and giving us his. Sarah, Paul, and Meghan—for a rich vicarious life. Ronan: head nod. Gretch, for all those LGHQ early mornings and roommate late nights. 10-32, for a home that felt like one. AK47: HUG. B—por todo. S—just 'cause. And finally, M, D, and J, as ever, je t'aime.

SAM THANKS: Mom; for not summoning me home, yet. Justine; we started with Bleeding Love and ended... well, we'll find out. Matt; a good beer and friendship, that's life. Pat; for love from the top bunk. Diana; for all the balcony love. RJ; just because. Mamma Mia; for the soundtrack of my life. The Family; for dinners and memories. Dina and Brian; support and love from afar. Ben, Justin, and Laura; you complete me.

MATT THANKS: Ben and Lexie, who made my job a breeze; Justine for an inspiring imagination, 8:55am smiles, and the Go's finest musical taste; Sam, who I'm pretty sure did most of the real work; Ronan and Anna, for sharing the Garden of Eternity; C. Alex for making it seem so easy; and of course, all who attended Monday night dinners, for partaking in one of life's more gracious pleasures; Oh heyyyyy Pat, you too.

Editor
Justine R. Lescroart
Associate Editors
Sam Walsh, Matt Zimmerman
Managing Editor
Nathaniel Rakich
Map Editor
Rebecca Smith
Typesetter
C. Alexander Tremblay

LET'S GO

Publishing Director
Inés C. Pacheco
Editor-in-Chief
Samantha Gelfand
Production Manager
Jansen A. S. Thurmer
Cartography Manager
R. Derek Wetzel
Editorial Managers
Dwight Livingstone Curtis, Vanessa J. Dube, Nathaniel Rakich
Financial Manager
Lauren Caruso
Publicity and Marketing Manager
Patrick McKiernan
Personnel Manager
Laura M. Gordon
Production Associate
C. Alexander Tremblay
Director of IT & E-Commerce
Lukáš Tóth
Website Manager
Ian Malott
Office Coordinators
Vinnie Chiappini, Jenny Wong
Director of Advertising Sales
Nicole J. Bass
Senior Advertising Associates
Kipyegon Kitur, Jeremy Siegfried, John B. Ulrich
Junior Advertising Associate
Edward C. Robinson Jr.

President
Timothy J.J. Creamer
General Manager
Jim McKellar

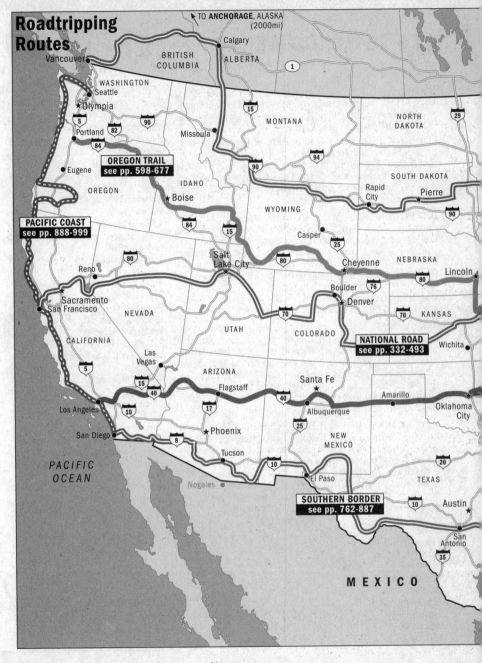

Roadtripping Routes

TO **ANCHORAGE**, ALASKA
(2000mi)

Vancouver

Calgary

BRITISH COLUMBIA

ALBERTA

1

WASHINGTON

★ Seattle

★ Olympia

5

Portland

82

90

Missoula

MONTANA

15

NORTH DAKOTA

29

OREGON TRAIL
see pp. 598–677

Eugene

IDAHO

OREGON

84

★ Boise

84

15

WYOMING

SOUTH DAKOTA

Rapid City

Pierre

90

PACIFIC COAST
see pp. 888–999

Casper

25

Cheyenne

NEBRASKA

Lincoln

Reno

80

Salt Lake City
★

80

80

Boulder

76

Denver

Sacramento

San Francisco

NEVADA

UTAH

70

70

COLORADO

NATIONAL ROAD
see pp. 332–493

Wichita

KANSAS

CALIFORNIA

Las Vegas

ARIZONA

Flagstaff

Santa Fe
★

Amarillo

Oklahoma City

5

15

40

17

40

Los Angeles

10

Albuquerque

25

★ Phoenix

NEW MEXICO

20

San Diego

8

Tucson

TEXAS

10

Austin

PACIFIC OCEAN

Nogales

10

El Paso

SOUTHERN BORDER
see pp. 762–887

San Antonio

35

M E X I C O

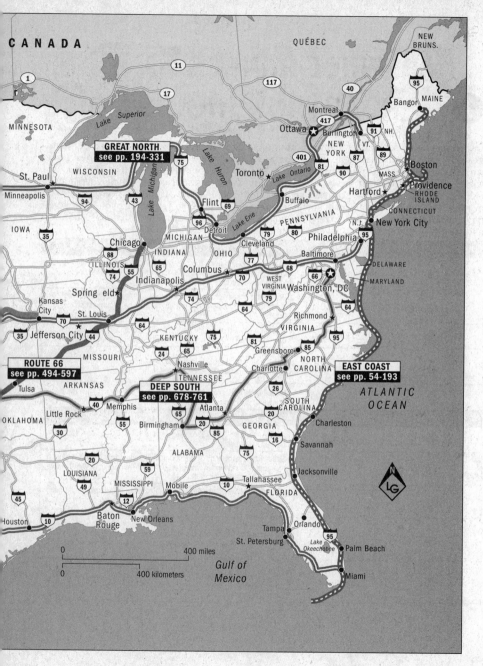

CANADA

QUÉBEC

NEW BRUNS.

MINNESOTA

Lake Superior

95

Bangor   MAINE

GREAT NORTH.
see pp. 194-331

Montreal

417

Ottawa

Burlington   91   N.H.

WISCONSIN

75

NEW YORK   VT.

St. Paul

Toronto   Lake Ontario

87   89

401

MASS.

Minneapolis

94

43

Flint   69

Buffalo

81   90

Hartford   Providence
RHODE ISLAND

Boston

IOWA

35

Lake Michigan

MICHIGAN   96   Detroit   Lake Erie

PENNSYLVANIA

CONNECTICUT

N.J.   New York City

Chicago   79   Cleveland   80   Philadelphia   95

88

INDIANA   OHIO

DELAWARE

ILLINOIS   55

65   Columbus   77   Baltimore   68   66

MARYLAND

74

Indianapolis   70   WEST VIRGINIA   Washington, DC

Spring eld   74   79

Kansas City   64   64

35   70   St. Louis   64   Richmond   95

Jefferson City   44   KENTUCKY   75   VIRGINIA

MISSOURI   24   65   81   Greensboro   85

ROUTE 66
see pp. 494-597

Nashville   NORTH CAROLINA

Charlotte

EAST COAST
see pp. 54-193

Tulsa   ARKANSAS   TENNESSEE   26   SOUTH CAROLINA

ATLANTIC OCEAN

OKLAHOMA   40   Memphis

DEEP SOUTH
see pp. 678-761

Atlanta   20

Little Rock   55   Birmingham   85   GEORGIA   Charleston

30   20   ALABAMA   16   Savannah

59   75

LOUISIANA   49   MISSISSIPPI   Mobile   Tallahassee   Jacksonville

45   10   12   FLORIDA

Houston   10   Baton Rouge   New Orleans   Tampa   Orlando

N
LG

St. Petersburg   Lake Okeechobee   95   Palm Beach

| 0 | | 400 miles |

| 0 | | 400 kilometers |

Gulf of Mexico   Miami

XI

❷ PRICE RANGES ❸ ❹
❶ # ROADTRIPPING USA ❺

Our researchers list establishments in order of value from best to worst, honoring our favorites with the Let's Go thumbs-up (🖒). Because the best value is not always the cheapest price, we have incorporated a system of price ranges based on a rough expectation of what you will spend. For **accommodations,** we base our range on the cheapest price for which a single traveler can stay for one night. For **restaurants** and other dining establishments, we estimate the average amount one traveler will spend in one sitting. The table below tells you what you'll typically find in the US at the corresponding price range, but keep in mind that no system can allow for the quirks of individual establishments.

ACCOMMODATIONS	RANGE	WHAT YOU'RE *LIKELY* TO FIND
❶	under $30	Campgrounds and dorm rooms, both in hostels and universities. Expect bunk beds and a communal bath. You may have to provide or rent towels and sheets.
❷	$30-50	Upper-end hostels or lower-end hotels. You may have a private bathroom, or there may be a sink in your room and a communal shower in the hall.
❸	$51-70	A small room with a private bath. Should have decent amenities, such as phone and TV. Breakfast may be included in the price of the room.
❹	$71-100	Should have bigger rooms than a ❸, with more amenities or in a more convenient location. Breakfast probably included.
❺	above $100	Large hotels or upscale chains. If it's a ❺ and it doesn't have the perks you want, you've paid too much.
FOOD	RANGE	WHAT YOU'RE *LIKELY* TO FIND
❶	under $7	Mostly sandwich shops, greasy spoons, or cafes. Don't worry about tucking in your shirt.
❷	$7-12	Sandwiches, appetizers at a bar, or low-priced entrees. Most ethnic eateries are a ❷. Either takeout or a sit-down meal, but only slightly more fashionable decor than a ❶.
❸	$13-17	Mid-priced entrees, possibly with soup or salad. More upscale ethnic eateries. Since you'll have the luxury of a waiter, tip will set you back a little extra.
❹	$18-24	A somewhat fancy restaurant. Entrees tend to be heartier or more elaborate, but you're really paying for decor and ambience. Few restaurants in this range have a dress code, but some may look down on T-shirts and sandals.
❺	above $24	Your meal might cost more than your room, but there's a reason—it's something fabulous, famous, or both. Slacks and dress shirts may be expected. Offers foreign-sounding food and a decent wine list. Don't order a PB&J!

the road

HISTORY

THE FIRST ROADTRIP

To win a $50 bet, Horatio Nelson Jackson vowed to cross the country by car in 90 days, challenging the belief that the newfangled "horseless carriage" was an impractical and unreliable means of travel. Jackson left San Francisco for New York City on May 23, 1903, in a newly purchased two-cylinder, 20-horsepower Winton Touring Car named the *Vermont*. Perhaps because Jackson had almost no driving experience, he hired a mechanic to travel with him. A tire blowout 15 mi. into the journey was the first of many mechanical setbacks encountered along the unmarked and often unpaved route, but Jackson and his mechanic persevered, winning the hearts of the public and acquiring a goggle-sporting bulldog named Bud along the way. Sixty-three days, 12 hours, and 30 minutes after departing, the triumphant trio crossed the Harlem River into Manhattan. The media raved about the trip's success, and Americans began to reconsider the possibilities of the automobile. Thus, the great American roadtrip was born.

HISTORY OF THE ROAD

MOLASSES AND SEASHELLS. At the turn of the 20th century, America's roads were haphazardly placed and unreliably maintained. Because roads were commissioned locally, their prevalence and quality varied considerably from region to region. Most roads, if paved at all, had surfaces of **macadam** (compacted stones ground with clay) or gravel. While these roads held up fine under horses' hooves and the iron wheels of wagons—in dry weather, that is—car tires and rain would quickly reduce them to rubble and mud.

In the inevitable attempt to better the quality of roads, early road builders experimented with a wide variety of paving materials. In 1870, the city of Charleston, West Virginia, laid brick roads that were attractive and easy to maintain but prohibitively expensive. In 1908, the just-born **US Office of Roads** introduced pavement of blackstrap molasses and quicklime in a petroleum binder. Although the road held up well under traffic, it was, as one reporter put it, "somewhat soluble in water." In 1911, the town of Gouverneur, New York, paved its roads with crushed marble and asphalt. (The asphalt cost $500 per carload; the marble $1.) Other towns tried out streets of wood blocks and rubber with pavements of seashells, coal tar, burnt clay, compressed straw, and a variety of other materials.

Although the first American concrete pavement was laid in Bellefontaine, Ohio, in the 1890s, for the next several decades concrete lagged behind asphalt, brick, and wood in popularity as a paving material. One reason for this may have been the poor workmanship of early concrete contractors, who gave the material a bad rap. After the advent of the automobile, however, concrete rapidly gained in popularity due to its moderate cost, low maintenance demands, durability, and smoothness.

In recent decades, however, asphalt roadways have regained popularity. Although some claim that asphalt is less durable than concrete, the material is unquestionably more cost-effective and can in many cases be repaired with a simple overlay—advantages that have won over many a road builder.

To lay a modern road, a contractor first covers a gravel subbase with asphalt or concrete, then lays a steel mesh over this subbase to absorb stress, and finally pours a second layer of asphalt or concrete on top.

GOOD ROADS. As an increasing number of drivers hit the road, ever more attention was paid to roads' quality. Motorists founded the **American Automobile Association (AAA)** in 1902 in order to lobby for safe and efficient roadways that would facilitate travel by car. In 1908, the association held its first annual National Good

1

Roads Convention to bolster the **Good Roads Movement,** which pushed for raised, graded, and ditched highways that wouldn't flood or wash out with every rain. The country's first mile of concrete highway appeared in 1909 outside Detroit, Michigan (not coincidentally the birthplace of the Model T).

In 1913, industrialists Carl Fischer, Frank Seiberling, and Henry Joy envisioned a paved road from coast to coast, and by 1915 their dream had been realized. The **Lincoln Highway,** as it was known, became the first transcontinental American road, stretching almost 3400 mi. from New York to California. The **Federal Aid Highway Act** of 1916 created a system of federal funding for local construction, while the Federal Aid Highway Act of 1921 established the Bureau of Public Roads to lay down a numbered system of paved, two-lane highways throughout the states.

JOBS AND MISSILES. Serious interest in a major system of interstate highways didn't arise, however, until the Great Depression, when the construction of divided multilane interstate highways was seen as a public works effort that would create jobs. In 1938 the Senate considered (but eventually rejected) a plan for an $8 billion network of toll highways. During WWII, the US directed its attention abroad, and road construction was moved to the back burner.

During the war, Dwight D. Eisenhower observed the strategic advantages of Germany's Autobahn in armed conflict. Experience showed that it was more difficult to permanently damage highways than railroads. During the Cold War, then-President Eisenhower championed a national system of interstate highways as a means of military defense. The Federal Aid Highway Act of 1944, and later the Federal Aid Highway Act of 1956, created the **National System of Interstate Highways,** an interregional network of high-speed routes that reflected a nationwide preoccupation with strategic defense. Clearances above any roadway on this interstate system were built high enough to allow the passage of 1950s-era trailer-drawn military missiles. Contrary to urban legend, however, interstates were never intended to serve as emergency airstrips for military landings.

The interstate program was touted as the greatest public works and defense program in history and promised to connect all of the country's principal cities. Designed to reach a length of 42,500 mi. when finished, the highway system would be 30 times as long as the Great Wall of China and would pave a surface area the size of West Virginia. It was a fitting project for post-war America and, in conjunction with the older Federal Aid and state-run highway projects, was the capstone of a national effort to make the continent accessible by car.

UNDER OUR WHEELS. In 1966, the **Department of Transportation** was formed to organize, maintain, and (when necessary) expand America's existing roadways. The Bureau of Public Roads was absorbed into this new department as the **Federal Highway Administration (FHWA).** During the 70s and 80s, interstate construction reached a state of virtual completion.

In 2002, the **National Highway System (NHS)** consolidated interstates, other arterial roadways, the strategic highway network (roads considered essential to national defense), the major strategic highway network connectors, and intermodal connectors into one road system. Although the 256,000 mi. of the NHS include only 4% of the nation's roads, they carry more than 40% of all highway traffic. Ninety-eight percent of all intended roads in this system are already constructed.

The future of America's highways is uncertain. In 2008, the FHWA expressed concern that its funding from the federal gasoline excise tax was dwindling following the nationwide decrease in driving caused by skyrocketing gas prices. (Between 2006 and 2008, America's number of cumulative vehicle miles traveled fell by 17.3 billion.) As transportation technology evolves, however, roads will no doubt keep pace.

ROAD NOSTALGIA. Eisenhower's dream of a well-organized interstate highway system has been realized—a comprehensive, well-maintained, and efficient network connects the cities and states of the US. Although originally intended to coexist with the new routes, classic two-lane highways drifted into disuse as interstates became America's primary arteries. On old highway maps, two-lane highways were colored in blue ink and interstates in red. Thanks to this, classic roads became known as **Blue Highways.**

The Blue Highways of America now represent an alternative to the commerce, congestion, anonymity, and pollution of the interstate system. They embody all that is central to the experience of the American roadtrip: the romance of the road, road culture, vintage diners, and 50s motels with large neon signs.

Several of the Blue Highways have become legendary. **US Route 66,** which runs from Chicago to Los Angeles, is today synonymous with American road culture. Created by a congressional act in 1925 and completely paved by 1938, Rte. 66 saw the Depression-era migration of thousands of families from the Dust Bowl of the Midwest to the greener fields of California, the subject of John Steinbeck's novel The Grapes of Wrath (1939). Rte. 66 would facilitate the movement of thousands more westward-bound, adventure-seeking travelers as well as the development of the modern service station and motel. Although officially decommissioned by 1985, the "Main Street of America" remains a standard roadtripping route.

US Route 40, the "National Road," spans the 3200 miles from Atlantic City to San Francisco. Sometimes called the "Golden Highway," Rte. 40 loosely follows the old Lincoln Highway and was the transcontinental route of choice for many travelers in the 1950s. Like other classic highways, Rte. 40 has largely been eclipsed by the interstate system, but it retains much of its neon-light and roadside-diner glory.

Recently, the US Department of Transportation has begun recognizing roads with special historic, scenic, or cultural significance through its **Scenic Byways Program.** Since 1992, the program has funded the preservation of almost 144 byways in 44 states. Famous byways include (in addition to parts of Rte. 66 and 40) the **Blue Ridge Parkway** through the southern Appalachian mountains, the **San Juan Skyway** in southern Colorado, and the **Pacific Coast Highway.**

FOR MORE INFORMATION.
See www.americanheritage.com.

HISTORY OF THE CAR

AND THEY'RE OFF. The automobile that made Horatio Jackson's journey a reality was the product of centuries of development. In 1769, French engineer Nicolas-Joseph Cugnot invented the world's first **self-propelled vehicle,** a steam-powered military tractor. (Two years later, Cugnot also became the first person to experience a motor-vehicle accident, when he drove one of his contraptions into a stone wall.) Other early inventors used coal oil, batteries, and even electrified rails to propel their novel machines. In the mid-1830s, Scottish inventor Robert Davidson constructed a battery-powered **electric carriage,** which managed to travel at a blazing 4 mph. Concerned with the new dangers of the road, the British Parliament's **Locomotive Act of 1865** mandated that all "road locomotives" be manned by a crew of three: a driver, a stoker, and a flag man to travel 60 yd. ahead on foot to warn passing horses. Speed was limited to 2 mph in cities, stifling automotive innovation in Britain for decades.

By the 1890s, the essential elements of the modern car began to emerge from the many experimental models. The German inventors Karl Benz and Gottlieb Daimler, working concurrently, produced the world's first vehicles powered by internal combustion engines, allowing for fuel-efficient operation and easy production. In 1891, the French car manufacturer Panhard and Levassor perfected the **Systeme Panhard,** the predominant automotive layout until the mid-1970s. Panhard's cars featured four wheels, a front-mounted internal combustion engine, rear-wheel-drive, and a clutch pedal. Piloting one of his vehicles, Emile Levassor drove his way to victory in the first automotive **Grand Prix,** the Paris-Bordeaux-Paris Rally of 1895, finishing in only 48hr., 6hr. ahead of his closest competitor.

COMING TO AMERICA. Gasoline-powered automobiles were not manufactured in the US until 1893, when brothers Charles and Frank Duryea, bicycle mechanics from Springfield, Massachusetts, started constructing a small number of expensive cars. The brothers' **Ladies Phaeton,** essentially a carriage equipped with a one-cylinder gasoline engine, managed to traverse several blocks of downtown Springfield. The first American car to be mass-produced, the four-horsepower **Curved Dash Oldsmobile,** sold for $650. Eventually, over 19,000 such cars were produced.

In 1903, **Henry Ford** joined Oldsmobile in Detroit, opening a plant that hand-assembled vehicles at the rate of two or three per day. Ford's breakthrough came in 1909, the first full year of production for the **Model T.** After opening a new factory equipped with a fully developed assembly line, Ford cut the average production time for the Model T from 12 man-hours to 93 minutes, revolutionizing industrial production in the process. Between 1909 and 1923, over 15 million cars rolled off the line. Although its debut marked the beginning of America's love affair with the automobile, the Ford Model T was soon to be superceded. Its simple, no-frills design rapidly gave way to bigger, fancier, and faster models, culminating in Cadillac's regal **V-16** of 1930, which was powered by a 16-cylinder engine. As engines grew more powerful, it became possible to build heavier cars with completely enclosed passenger space, allowing for greater comfort in all weather. In 1919, 90% of cars featured open cabs; by 1929, 90% were enclosed.

POST-WAR. Following WWII, American car manufacturers faced increasing competition from abroad. From the ruins of defeated Germany, the Volkswagen **Beetle** would go on to be one of the world's bestselling cars. Likewise, Toyota, Datsun, and Honda began importing a new type of fuel-efficient economy car, offering an alternative to Detroit's large engines and heavy car bodies. In the 60s, the classic American **muscle car** and its little sibling the **pony car** captured the nation's attention. These large two-door vehicles, like the **Ford Mustang** and **Pontiac GTO,** were equipped with massive eight-cylinder engines designed for drag racing. These glamorous vehicles captured the attention of youth nationwide.

Besides reflecting fashion, these vehicles were also indications of the changing place of the car in American culture. The early Fords were primarily farmers' cars, designed to be efficient and practical. By 1950, however, car ownership extended across broad cross-sections of society, with 60% of American households owning at least one car, despite their astronomical prices (half of the average household income). Teenagers, in particular, began to own automobiles, and the acquisition of a driver's license became a rite of passage and sign of independence.

In the 70s, world events dramatically affected American driving habits. Numerous Middle Eastern nations began curtailing oil shipments to the US due to political turmoil, leading to shortages across the country. The price of oil quadrupled in 1974 alone, while **rationing** at the pump began for the first time since WWII. To reduce fuel consumption, the federal government capped the speed limit at **55 mph** nationwide, and the first **Corporate Average Fuel Economy** standards, enacted by Congress in 1975, required manufacturers to increase the average fuel efficiency of their fleets of passenger vehicles to 27.5 miles per gallon. By the end of the decade, the major American manufacturers had reduced the size and power of most of their vehicles and introduced new **compact** and **subcompact cars** with efficient four-cylinder engines. Despite Detroit's response, foreign manufacturers like Toyota and Honda still saw increased sales.

Combined with an extensive road network, the wide availability of cars helped enable the growth of the **suburb,** transforming the American city from a residential center into a place of industry. America's love affair with the car also gave rise to new forms of roadside establishments. The **fast-food** joint, today an American icon, evolved to its present form in the 50s, when long roadtrips made eating on the go a necessity, while **motels** (from motor-hotel) sprung up to serve long-distance travelers. The popularity of the **drive-in movie theater,** a favored spot for many a hot-rodding suburbanite, peaked during the early 60s.

OUR CARS. Today, driving and car culture have evolved into a massive industry. The road continues to shape the American imagination, influencing art, film, literature, and personal identity. In 2006, there were 202 million drivers out of 299 million American citizens, who owned almost 251 million motor vehicles. Americans now drive over three trillion miles a year, and, even though the days of the hot rod and the muscle car are over, individuals still spend vast amounts of time and money on their automobiles. Meanwhile, the local, state, and federal governments continue to pump resources into road infrastructure, spending over $130 billion each year on the highway system.

Indeed, it is fair to say that cars are an American obsession. AAA is currently second only to the Catholic Church in membership in the US, with more than 45 million members and over 1100 offices. Magazines devoted to automobiles, like the popular *Car and Driver*, abound, and radio stations feature car-themed shows such as National Public Radio's *Car Talk*. Clubs like the **Antique Automobile Club of America** (which has over 400 chapters and 60,000 members nationwide) host conferences, shows, festivals, and "meets," at which old-car enthusiasts congregate by the thousands. Established in 1977, the **Society for Commercial Archaeology (SCA)** devotes itself to preserving the sights and symbols of 20th-century roadside culture, publishing a journal and hosting annual conferences and tours.

Nonetheless, the future of the classic roadtrip is uncertain. Increasing demand for fuel and declining oil supplies across the world drive gasoline prices ever higher, while environmental concerns necessitate cutting carbon emissions. As gas prices climbed above $4 per gallon for the first time in 2008, new technologies allowed **hybrid electric vehicles** to achieve previously unthinkable fuel efficiency. (Hybrid vehicles combine an internal combustion engine with on-board batteries recharged by the car's braking.) Whether alternative energy sources and advanced technology will keep the roadtrip of previous generations within the economic reach of most Americans remains to be seen.

LIFE ON THE ROAD

ROADTRIP ATTITUDE

And if you find her poor, Ithaca has not
deceived you / Wise as you have become,
with so much experience, / You must already
have understood what Ithacas mean.
- Constantine Cavafy

What is it that makes a roadtrip different from an ordinary vacation? Like the car and the open road, the roadtrip has acquired a specific meaning. The type of roadtrip ingrained in American tradition revolves around the road, not the destination.

At one extreme, a roadtrip can be a marathon, a test of endurance, a major undertaking. Visiting a certain category of sight is a popular way of planning a trip—taking a tour of America's historic battlefields, hitting up all of the missions in California, or visiting all of the lobster shacks on the East Coast, for example. Event-based trips are also popular—baseball roadtrips from one stadium to the next are an American institution. Pilgrimages to rock concerts (ask your parents about Woodstock), Shakespeare festivals, and historical tours, like the Lewis and Clark Trail, are all fair game.

At the other end of the spectrum, a roadtrip can also evolve with only a vague direction and a desire for knowledge and experience. Exploring a specific region or driving a historic two-lane highway are both good ways to start out, as is following one of the cardinal directions. This kind of trip revolves around discovering the lives and culture of the people who live along the way—seeing every historic site, stopping at every diner, mingling at every bar. It's all about the digression, all about the culture, and all about the detour.

ROADTRIP TRADITIONS

FRIENDS. From Bonnie and Clyde to Thelma and Louise, roadtrippers have traditionally traveled in pairs; roadtrip culture is oriented around the experience of a shared journey. Picking the right friend or friends to bring along requires care, but a trusty companion in the front seat makes the miles go by faster. Bringing a friend also means you have an extra navigator—unless your travel companion of choice, like John Steinbeck's, happens to be a dog.

CAR GAMES. Miles of uninterrupted soybean fields have inspired an extensive collection of road games to alleviate interstate boredom blues. "I Spy" and "20 Questions" are just the beginning.

Sweet and Sour. Whenever a car goes by the window, each player waves and smiles. If a person

THE ROAD

waves and smiles back, you get a point. If the person frowns or ignores you (sour), no points.

Howdy Doody. 1 player says a name, and the next player uses either the 1st or last name to create another one. Example: Will Smith to Will Rogers to Mister Rogers.

Alphabet Game. Players try to complete the alphabet in order from A to Z by spotting letters on road signs.

Car Bingo. Before setting out, players agree on a bingo board with squares featuring expected regional sights (for example, a cactus in the Southwest). You can take it from there.

WHO TO TAKE ALONG:

The Adventurer: Adventurers are outgoing and unafraid to deviate from pre-arranged plans to see a sight recommended by a complete stranger. When traveling with an adventurer, you're sure to reach a great destination—just maybe not *your* destination. The adventurer's motto is "It's just around the next bend."

The Navigator: These godsends couldn't get lost if you blindfolded them and left them in the middle of an Iowa cornfield. They have lodestones in their foreheads, Google maps on their BlackBerries, and the uncanny ability to refold the map on the first try. The navigator's motto is, "See? Here we are!"

The Optimist: These positive individuals can somehow make changing a tire in the snow on the New Jersey Turnpike feel like a rousing good time. They take adversity with a grain of salt and keep the big picture in mind. The optimist's motto is, "Good thing the radiator overheated; otherwise, we would never have seen this sunrise."

Ghost. You spell out words: the 1st person says a letter, the next person has to add a letter, and players continue adding letters in order. If you add a letter that completes a word, you lose. If you add a letter that could not form a word and the next player challenges you, you also lose.

Counting Cows. Teams count cows throughout the day on their side of the car (while trying to distract the other team). If you pass a cemetery on your side of the car, you lose all your cow points.

The Quiet Game (a.k.a. Dead Fish). Shut up, kids. Mom and Dad are having a conversation.

WHO NOT TO TAKE ALONG:

The Whiner: For whiners, the grass is always greener in the other lane. Any bump in the road or fly on the windshield will set them off, and there is nothing worse than a whiner's tirade, especially when you're changing a tire in the snow on the New Jersey Turnpike. The whiner's motto is, "Are we there yet?"

The Backseat Driver: With their constant driving critiques, multiple maps, and squeaks at every less-than-perfect turn, backseat drivers were your better friends before this roadtrip. The backseat driver's motto is a gasp.

The Crush: Unless you want to witness the plot development, conflict, resolution, and denouement of a relationship on fast-forward, leave your crush behind. After you find out that he or she is not only an avid Disney fan but also tone deaf, trust us, the romance will fade. The crush's motto is, "If you like me, you'll..."

CAR RITUALS. Details vary by region, but standard **roadtrip superstitions** include holding your breath while driving past graveyards, across state lines, or through tunnels, making wishes when you see a hay wagon or at the end of a tunnel, raising your feet while crossing bridges or railroad tracks, and touching the ceiling of your car when driving through a yellow traffic light. Another common ritual is the "punchbug" game, in which the first person to see a Volkswagen Beetle shouts "punchbug!" and punches the ceiling or (in a more aggressive or enthusiastic version, depending on your point of view) the arm of the person next to him. Variations of this classic (if somewhat violent) ritual, taken very seriously by the finest of roadtrippers, include extending it to include pink cars, limousines, or cars with one headlight and shouting "p-diddle!" instead of punchbug.

ROAD ETIQUETTE

The population of the US has nearly doubled since the 50s, when most interstates were designed. With a rising number of cars on the road, our highways and byways have become increasingly congested. Bumper-to-bumper traffic, parents rushing to get their children to soccer practice, and the erratic habits of new drivers can result in serious incidents of road rage. Tailgating, gratuitous horn-honking, driving with high beams on when approaching or following other cars, eye contact with aggressive drivers, and obscene language and gestures are all road taboos. On highways with two or more lanes, the left-hand lane (the "fast lane") is for passing, and, on any road, it is standard courtesy to let faster cars pass. Laws governing turns differ by state, but correct use of blinkers is (like wearing your seat belt) not just a good idea but the law. One of the most offensive gestures in the US is extending the middle finger of either hand. Known as "giving someone the finger" or "flipping the bird," this gesture is only appropriate when that canary-yellow Hummer won't get the &*$% off your tail.

Roadtrips mean long times in cramped quarters, and things can get a little "Lord of the Flies" if you're not careful. Play nice, share the candy, and don't talk without the conch shell. If tribes start dividing, try alleviating tension by exploring some of this book's many recommended hikes and trails or hit up a local gym.

ROAD DINING

Today, although most interstates and many highways are lined with fast-food joints, real American road food is best found at local, non-chain diners, delis, barbeque pits, hot-dog stands, and ice-cream parlors. Although it may seem difficult to find fresh produce while roadtripping, in reality many regions have roadside farmers' stands that sell affordable, local, seasonal fruits and vegetables.

Diners have historically been places where entire communities congregate to enjoy homestyle meals and swap gossip. The first roadside diner (established in 1872) was a horse-drawn wagon. Later diners included Art Deco eateries (in the 30s) and stainless-steel restaurants (in the 50s). The classic diner, a modular, prefabricated structure, still appears along many roadsides and usually promises considerate service, a hot cup of coffee, and warm (if greasy) food. Biscuits with gravy and apple pie a la mode—served by a waitress who calls you "honey"—have long been the roadtripper's weakness.

REGIONAL TREATS

Some claim that America has no national cuisine. While it's true that the US lacks France's or Italy's culinary history, roadtrippers will discover that the country boasts a national menu varied and flavorful enough to satisfy even the most jaded food critic. One of roadtripping's joys is tasting a spectrum of regional dishes and sauces. Whether you're a turkey-and-gravy type or more into jellied, lye-soaked fish, America will leave you thoroughly satisfied.

NORTHEAST. English pilgrims landed in the Northeast and combined their standard (tasteless) native meats and vegetables with uniquely American (tasty) foodstuffs such as turkey, lobster, clams, corn, cranberries, and maple syrup. Every year, Americans celebrate the bounty of a North American fall harvest—and the last time that the settlers and Native Americans dined together without reservations—with a Thanksgiving dinner of turkey, mashed potatoes, and cranberry sauce.

SOUTHEAST. If *Gone With the Wind*'s dinner parties left you hungry, this is the region for you. The highlights of Southeastern cuisine include fried chicken, biscuits, grits, sweet potato pie, collard greens, and okra. Virginia ham is ubiquitous; ham biscuits provide a savory supplement to any meal. More adventurous roadtrippers can try this region's celebrated animal byproducts (a.k.a. "soul food"): pig's knuckles and ears, hog maws, and chitterlings (boiled or fried pig intestines). Strong African and West Indian influences in this region's sauces and spices make dishes particularly mouthwatering. With food this good, it's not surprising that over 25% of the population is obese.

LOUISIANA. Cajun or Creole cooking is arguably the country's best. Recently, chefs have been heading to New Orleans as fast as FEMA heads to a flood. (Oh wait...) Jambalaya (rice cooked with ham, sausage, shrimp, and herbs), gumbo (a stew made from a roux with okra, meat, and vegetables), crawfish étouffée and fried catfish are delicacies. Be warned, however: this is not the region for the faint of heart. Spicy Cajun and Creole dishes can set off fireworks.

TEXAS. From juicy tenderloins to luscious baby back ribs to whole pig roasts, Texans like to slow-cook their meats over an open fire, flavoring the meat with smoke from burning mesquite or hickory. Eat at any of the state's many barbecue joints, though, and they'll tell you that the real secret is in the tangy sauce. Sauce recipes are meticulously kept secrets passed from generation to generation. In this border state, Tex-Mex is also always a good option. Burritos, fajitas, and *chiles rellenos* are never hard to come by here.

MIDWEST. Influenced by the Scandinavian and German influence of 19th-century settlers, Midwestern cuisine is hearty, simple, and abundant. Scandinavia contributed *lefse* (potato bread) and *lutefisk* (fish jellied through a process of soaking in lye) to regional cuisine, while German settlers popularized the bratwurst, a pork sausage that invariably surfaces at every ballgame and church picnic in the region. Breads include Swedish *limpa* rye and German *Stollen*, both of which complement an assortment of meats, cheeses, soups, and relishes.

CALIFORNIA. The world's fifth-largest supplier of food and agriculture commodities, California is known for its fresh fruits and vegetables. Avocado and citrus fruits are trademark favorites; a ripe avocado sliced in half and seasoned with a little salt makes a great quick bite. Asian influence in California has given rise to fusion cuisine, including dishes such as seared tuna with wasabi and honey-glazed walnut shrimp. Mexican food, too, is popular here. Last but not least, California is home to the spiritual mother of all road stops, **In-N-Out Burger,** where you can get a simple and cheap 50s-style burger that has been nowhere near a microwave, heat lamp, or freezer. Ask about the secret menu.

SOUTHWEST. Mexican staples such as rice, beans, and chili are the essential components of Southwestern grub. Salsa made from tomatoes, chilies, and cilantro adds a spicy kick to nearly all dishes and varies greatly in intensity and flavor from brand to brand and restaurant to restaurant. At most Southwestern roadside stops, you can get a side of green chili with just about anything you want.

PACIFIC NORTHWEST. Northwestern waters are no place to live if you're a salmon or a halibut. Many cities in the Pacific Northwest boast this-morning-fresh seafood in dishes ranging from chowder to tacos. Juicy apples and bursting huckleberries abound in Washington's wet weather, and, if you're not that kind of thirsty, Oregon is the microbrewery capital of North America. British Columbia is known for bannock, a biscuit-like cake made from flour, lard, and honey.

CANADA. As in the US, Canadian specialties vary by region. Newfoundland boasts food with rather unusual names, including bangbelly (salt pork in a spiced bun), toutons (salt pork with white raisin bread), figgy duff (a raisin pudding), and Jigg's dinner (a large meal prepared in a pot containing salted beef, cabbage, turnips, carrots, and potatoes). Smoked salmon is a favorite in British Columbia, and Quebec is well known for its maple syrup (served on everything from pancakes to omelets to meats) and for varieties of *poutine*, a tasty combination of french fries, cheese curds, and a thick, dark gravy sauce.

ROADTRIP CULTURE

LITERATURE

"Afoot and light-hearted, I take to the open road... From this hour, freedom!"
—Walt Whitman, 1856

Today, many roadtrips take shape in the daydreams of library-bound college students, small-town natives itching to get out, and foreigners whose curiosity about America has been whetted by Hollywood films. Perhaps the quintessentially American urge to move is grounded in the country's history of westward migration. Generations of writers have found inspiration for their greatest works in the promise of wide horizons and open roads. Audio books, CDs, and MP3s can put roadtrippers in touch with past travelers who share their need for spontaneity and room to breathe.

FICTION

Around the World in Eighty Days (1872) by Jules Verne. Phileas Fogg's madcap quest to circumnavigate the world and win a £20,000 bet.

Roughing It (1872) by Mark Twain. Semi-autobiographical journal of Twain's journeys through the "Wild West" and disillusionment with the American dream.

Adventures of Huckleberry Finn (1884) by Mark Twain. A boy's misadventures along the Mississippi River typify the American roadtrip spirit.

Free Air (1919) by Sinclair Lewis. Claire Boltwood travels from New York City to the Pacific Northwest in the early 20th century, falls in love with a down-to-earth young man, and gives up her cosmopolitan mannerisms.

The Grapes of Wrath (1939) by John Steinbeck. A Depression-era journey westward and one of American literature's angriest works.

The Adventures of Augie March (1953) by Saul Bellow. An expansive, overabundant chronicle of a Chicago youth's quest for fulfillment.

Lolita (1955) by Vladimir Nabokov. Famous and controversial. Humbert Humbert is a classic antihero.

On the Road (1957) and just about everything else written by Jack Kerouac. A beatnik's odyssey and the seminal text of road literature.

The Getaway (1958) by Jim Thompson. 2 bank robbers flee across the country and cut a violent swath through America.

Rabbit Run (1960) by John Updike. The story of Harry "Rabbit" Angstrom's flight from his former life and search for new meaning.

Travels with Charley: In Search of America (1962) by John Steinbeck. A veteran writer takes to the road with his dog (Charley) to rediscover his homeland.

In Cold Blood (1966) by Truman Capote. An analysis of a crime and the mystery as to why 2 men would drive over 400 mi. to kill 4 people whom they did not know.

Another Roadside Attraction (1971) by Tom Robbins. A story of comedic genius and 1960s counterculture recounting how a troupe of carnies comes into the possession of the embalmed body of Jesus Christ.

Zen and the Art of Motorcycle Maintenance (1974) by Robert Pirsig. A cross-country roadtrip both physical and philosophical.

A Thousand Acres (1991) by Jane Smiley. Winner of the Pulitzer Prize. A retelling of Shakespeare's *King Lear* on a 1000-acre farm in Iowa.

Interstate (1995) by Steven Dixon. The telling and retelling of a father's search for the perpetrators of a seemingly random act of road violence.

America (The Book) (2004) by Jon Stewart. A citizen's comedic guide to democracy "inaction."

NON-FICTION AND POETRY

A Hoosier Holiday (1916) by Theodore Dreiser. A precursor to the "road novel," this work documents a roadtrip Dreiser took with fellow artist Franklin Booth.

The Wasteland (1922) by TS Eliot. Commentary on the spiritually barren nature of modern existence and inquiry into the possibility of rebirth.

The Air-Conditioned Nightmare (1945) by Henry Miller. An account of Henry Miller's 1940-41 journey through America and his criticism of American culture.

The Electric Kool-Aid Acid Test (1968) by Tom Wolfe. Documents Ken Kesey and the band of Merry Pranksters' drug-fueled journey through America.

Blue Highways: A Journey into America (1983) by William Least Heat-Moon. A trip through the backroads of small-town America.

Out West (1987) by Dayton Duncan. The narrative of a man and his Volkswagen's trip westward, following the trail of Lewis and Clark.

The Lost Continent: Travels in Small Town America (1990) by Bill Bryson. A search across 38 states for the essence of small-town life.

American Nomad (1997) by Steve Erickson. The account of Erickson's road journey after covering the 1996 presidential election for *Rolling Stone*.

Songs for the Open Road: Poems of Travel and Adventure (1999) by The American Poetry & Literacy Project. Collection of 80 poems by 50 British and American poets about travel and journeys.

Driving Visions (2002) by David Laderman. Discusses the cultural roots of the road movie and analyzes its role in literary tradition.

Ridge Route: The Road That United California (2002) by Harrison Irving Scott. An in-depth look at highway construction over the grapevine.

RV Traveling Tales: Women's Journeys on the Open Road (2003) edited by Jaimie Hall and Alice Zyetz. An anthology of women writers' stories about their experiences living on the road.

MOVIES

Counterculture, existential, visionary, or just slapstick, road movies tell the story of rebels, outlaws, and nomads. If you want to learn just about everything there is to know about the genre, pick up a copy of David Laderman's in-depth study, *Driving Visions*.

North by Northwest (1959). Cary Grant crosses the country to try to reclaim his identity in one of Hitchcock's best. Look for the famed crop-dusting scene.

Bonnie and Clyde (1967). The world's most notorious and romanticized bank robbers, played by Warren Beatty and Faye Dunaway, drive across the Midwest robbing banks during the Great Depression.

Easy Rider (1969). Peter Fonda and Dennis Hopper play 2 non-conformist bikers searching for America on a motorcycle trek from L.A. to New Orleans.

Two-Lane Blacktop (1971). James Taylor and Dennis Wilson, as "The Driver" and "The Mechanic," drag race their way across the US.

The Blues Brothers (1980). On a mission from God to save the orphanage they were raised in from financial ruin, Jake and Elwood Blues travel the Midwest to reassemble their mythic band.

Back to the Future (1985). A car can take you farther than cross-country.

Rainman (1988). Selfish yuppie Charlie Babbitt travels cross-country with his autistic brother Raymond.

My Own Private Idaho (1991). Gus Van Sant directs this gay interpretation of *Henry IV*, in which River Phoenix and Keanu Reeves search across the country and across the Atlantic for maternal support.

Thelma and Louise (1991). A housewife and a waitress shoot a rapist and make their getaway in a 1966 Thunderbird.

Bottle Rocket (1996). Luke and Owen Wilson look to become thieves and go on the lam in a movie Martin Scorsese called one of the 10 best films of the 90s.

The Straight Story (1999). An elderly man hits the road in a tractor in David Lynch's heartfelt tale of fraternal reconciliation.

O Brother, Where Art Thou? (2000). A loose adaptation of Homer's *Odyssey*, this story of escape and Southern life is a modern classic.

Road Trip (2000). 4 college students hop in a car and travel cross-country to retrieve a mistakenly mailed, incriminating videotape.

Rat Race (2001). 6 strangers dash across the desert to reach a $2 million cash prize first. A no holds barred comedy with an all-star cast.

Y Tu Mamá También (2001). 2 amorous teenage boys, ditched by their girlfriends, travel by car through Mexico with an older woman in search of a hidden beach.

About Schmidt (2002). After retirement and his wife's death, Jack Nicholson sets out in a Winnebago to crash his daughter's wedding.

Horatio's Drive: America's First Road Trip (2003). Directed by Ken Burns, the story of Horatio Jackson, America's first roadtripper.

Harold and Kumar Go to White Castle (2004). 2 best friends hit the road in a do-or-die quest for late-night grub.

The Motorcycle Diaries (2004). A dramatization of the motorcycle roadtrip Che Guevara took during his youth that inspired his life's work.

Transamerica (2005). A pre-operative, male-to-female transsexual embarks on an unexpected journey after discovering she has fathered a son.

Cars (2006). The animated saga of Lightning McQueen, a hot-shot car who gets stranded in Radiator Springs.

No Country for Old Men (2007). A hunter stumbles upon the site of a drug deal gone bad. A look into the darker side of American culture.

ROAD TUNES

Even the most zealous roadtripper can fall victim to driving ennui. Like playing road games and sharing life stories, listening to music can greatly improve a roadtripper's experience on seemingly interminable stretches of American highway. Whether the volume is turned up (to drown out screaming children) or down (to facilitate deep thoughts), music enables roadtrippers to immerse themselves in national history and culture without ever leaving the comfort of the A/C. From bluegrass to indie rock, each region has its own sound. Our recommended playlists account for subject, genre, artist origination, and downright necessary tunes.

PLAYLISTS

EAST COAST

Augustana, "Boston"
Boston, "More Than a Feeling"
Bruce Springsteen, "Born to Run"
Dispatch, "The General"
Jackopierce, "Vineyard"
Jimmy Buffett, "Margaritaville"
John Mayer, "No Such Thing"
Kenny Chesney, "Please Come to Boston"
Paul Simon, "Diamonds on the Soles of Her Shoes"
Talking Heads, "And She Was"

DEEP SOUTH

Buddy Jewell, "Sweet Southern Comfort"
The Charlie Daniels Band, "The Devil Went Down to Georgia"
Elvis Presley, "Hound Dog"
James Taylor, "Carolina on My Mind"
Joan Baez, "The Night They Drove Old Dixie Down"
John Mayer, "Why Georgia"
Limbeck, "Comin' from Tuscon"
Lynyrd Skynyrd, "Sweet Home Alabama"
Marc Cohn, "Walking in Memphis"
Paul Simon, "Graceland"
Reba McEntire, "The Night the Lights Went Out in Georgia"

GREAT NORTH

Bob Dylan, "Tangled Up and Blue"
Creedence Clearwater Revival (CCR), "Bad Moon Rising"
Decemberists, "July, July!"
Gordon Lightfoot, "Second Cup of Coffee"
The Hold Steady, "Stuck Between Stations"
John Denver, "Wild Montana Skies"
Laura Bradley, "O Canada"
Shania Twain, "Man! I Feel Like a Woman!"
Shania Twain, "You're Still the One"
Steppenwolf, "Born to Be Wild"

NATIONAL ROAD

82nd Airborne All-American Chorus, "The Star-Spangled Banner"
Bob Dylan, "On the Road Again"
Bruce Springsteen, "Born in the U.S.A."
David Ball, "Riding With Private Malone"
Don McLean, "American Pie"
John Denver, "Take Me Home Country Roads"
Phil Vassar, "American Child"
Reuben's Accomplice, "America, You Look Good"
Saves the Day, "The Vast Spoils of America"
Will Smith, "Wild Wild West"

ROUTE 66

Audioslave, "I Am the Highway"
The Beatles, "Drive My Car"
Frank Sinatra, "My Way"
Frank Sinatra, "Route 66"
The Hold Steady, "Chicago Seemed Tired Last Night"
The Killers, "This River Is Wild"
Limbeck, "Sin City"
Tom Cochrane, "Life Is a Highway"
Tracy Chapman, "Fast Car"
Woody Guthrie, "Hard Traveling"

OREGON TRAIL

Bob Dylan, "Like a Rolling Stone"
Count Basie, "Jumping at the Woodside"
Doobie Brothers, "Rockin' Down the Highway"
Jimi Hendrix, "All Along the Watch Tower"

Kansas, "Carry on My Wayward Son"
Modest Mouse, "Little Motel"
Modest Mouse, "Tiny Cities Made of Ashes"
Nirvana, "Smells Like Teen Spirit"
Sawyer Brown, "I'll Take the Dirt Road"
Woody Guthrie, "Oregon Trail"

SOUTHERN BORDER

Blake Shelton, "Austin"
Britney Spears, "You Drive Me Crazy"
The Doobie Brothers, "China Grove"
George Strait, "Run"
Jamie O'Neil, "There Is No Arizona"
Johnny Cash, "City of New Orleans"
Tina Turner, "Proud Mary"
Toby Keith, "New Orleans"
Tracy Chapman, "She's Got Her Ticket"
Van Halen, "Runnin' With the Devil"

PACIFIC COAST

The Beach Boys, "California Girls"
The Beach Boys, "Fun Fun Fun"
The Beach Boys, "Surfin' USA"
Cake, "Short Skirt Long Jacket"
Cake, "Stick Shifts and Safety Belts"
Death Cab for Cutie, "Why You'd Want to Live Here"
The Distillers, "City of Angels"
Eagles, "Hotel California"
The Mamas and the Papas, "California Dreamin'"
Phantom Planet, "California"
Red Hot Chili Peppers, "Californication"

ON THE WEB

These websites are useful for trip planning, on-road troubleshooting, and staying current with national news.

www.aaa.com. For all your automobile needs, membership information, and a thorough history of the organization.

www.chicagotribune.com. The website of the newspaper the *Chicago Tribune*.

www.dallasnews.com. The website of the newspaper the *Dallas Morning News*.

www.fhwa.dot.gov. The website of the FHWA with current highway-related news.

www.fws.gov/refuges. A list of all National Wildlife Refuges. Useful for planning hiking and bird-watching trips.

www.latimes.com. The website of the newspaper the *Los Angeles Times*.

www.mapquest.com. The authoritative website for driving directions.

www.maps.google.com. By zooming in in "Satellite" mode, you can see your house. The "Street View" mode allows you to visually navigate urban areas.

www.nps.gov/parks. The website of the US National Park Service. Useful for planning camping and backcountry hiking trips.

www.nytimes.com. The website of the newspaper *The New York Times*.

HOLIDAYS

WHAT	WHEN
New Year's Day (US)	January 1
Martin Luther King, Jr., Day (US)	Third Monday in January
Presidents Day (US)	Third Monday in February
Easter weekend	Sometime in April
Victoria Day (ÇAN)	Monday before or on May 24
Memorial Day (US)	Last Monday in May
Canada Day (CAN)	July 1
Independence Day (US)	July 4
Labor Day	First Monday in September
Columbus Day (US); Thanksgiving (CAN)	Second Monday in October
Veterans Day (US); Remembrance Day (CAN)	November 11 or closest weekday
Thanksgiving (US)	Fourth Thursday in November
Christmas Day	December 25
Boxing Day (CAN)	December 26

FESTIVALS

WHAT AND WHEN	WHERE
Tournament of Roses *December 29 to January 1*	Pasadena, CA *Pacific Coast*
Mardi Gras *Sometime in February or early March*	New Orleans, LA *Southern Border*
Daytona 500 *Second or third Sunday in February*	Daytona Beach, FL *East Coast*
Houston Livestock Show & Rodeo *First three weeks of March*	Houston, TX *Southern Border*
South by Southwest *One week in mid-March*	Austin, TX *Southern Border*
St. Patrick's Day Celebration *March 17*	Savannah, GA *East Coast*
Cinco de Mayo *May 5*	Los Angeles, CA *Pacific Coast*
Memphis in May *All of May*	Memphis, TN *Deep South*
Gullah Festival *Memorial Day weekend*	Beaufort, SC *East Coast*
Rose Festival *June*	Portland, OR *Oregon Trail*
CMA Music Festival *June*	Nashville, TN *Deep South*
San Francisco Pride *Late June*	San Francisco, CA *Pacific Coast*
Taste of Chicago *Last week of June and first week of July*	Chicago, IL *Route 66*

WHAT AND WHEN	WHERE
Colorado Shakespeare Festival *Mid-June to mid-August*	Boulder, CO *National Road*
Freedom Fest *Week leading up to July 4*	Philadelphia, PA *National Road*
Cheyenne Frontier Days *Last full week of July*	Cheyenne, WY *Oregon Trail*
Kansas City Blues and Jazz Festival *July*	Kansas City, MO *Oregon Trail and National Road*
Wild Pony Roundup *Last consecutive Wednesday and Thursday in July*	Assateague Island, VA *East Coast*
Ohio State Fair *Early August*	Columbus, OH *National Road*
Newport Jazz Festival *August*	Newport, RI *East Coast*
Bumbershoot *Labor Day Weekend*	Seattle, WA *Pacific Coast*
Monterey Jazz Festival *Third full weekend in September*	Monterey, CA *Pacific Coast*
Austin City Limits *September*	Austin, TX *Southern Border*
Great American Beer Festival *Early October*	Denver, CO *National Road*
International Balloon Fiesta *Early October*	Albuquerque, NM *Route 66*
Head of the Charles Regatta *Third full weekend in October*	Boston, MA *East Coast*
Helldorado Days *Third full weekend in October*	Tombstone, AZ *Southern Border*

MAKING FRIENDS ON THE ROAD

Roadtripping takes many forms and serves many purposes. When my buddy Nathan and I graduated from college, our form was a 31 ft. long neon-reen funky RV from 1984, and our purpose was to go out and interview people from all walks of life to learn how they got to where they are today. What started out as a roadtrip to figure out what we wanted to do with our lives soon became a documentary on PBS, a nationally released book with Random House, and a program on college campuses across the country that puts other students on their own roadtrips.

While creating Roadtrip Nation in the last few years, we've logged more than 14 months on the road, traveled at least 45,000 mi., been to every contiguous state, and met more amazing, eccentric, and brilliant people than we could have ever met inside our comfort zones. And we discovered that when you boil everything down—the photo ops, the scenic drives, the endless cheeseburgers—you discover the real beauty of roadtripping comes from the people you meet along the way.

Without those people, a roadtrip becomes, well, a mere trip. People give your expedition texture. They push you to a deeper level—a level that makes your roadtrip not just a fun vacation, but a change-your-life-forever experience.

Here's the difference. Imagine a roadtrip in Maine. Some drivers will just coast through, only stopping to eat lobster at some cheeseball restaurant with a big neon sign. Those people miss the chance to meet Manny the lobsterman on the docks. Through him, we were able to spend a day out on his boat, the Jarvis Bay. On that boat, we weren't just in Maine; we were living Maine. We helped bring in the day's catch, downed a few shipyard brews as we watched the sun slip into the Atlantic, and retired to Manny's pad to cook up a few lobster tails. The meal was the best we've ever had, but what we remember the most is Manny.

It might seem tough to find interesting characters on the road, but opportunities pop up with every twist and turn of the journey. Say you get a flat tire on the Texas/Louisiana state line. You pull into the most classic truck stop you've ever seen, and out comes a tattooed 60-year-old man with a cigarette plastered to his mouth, Vietnam vet medals pinned to the mesh on his trucker's hat, and a rough beard grown to cover the scars on his face. Do you sit in the waiting room reading a three-year-old issue of Entertainment Weekly until your tire is neatly primped, or do you hang with "Doc" as he puts the tire back on, learning a bit about him and going out to coffee with him afterward? If you choose the latter option, you will learn, over a 3hr. cup of coffee at a typical Louisiana diner, that he flew helicopters in Vietnam, sat in a POW camp for months, survived to go on and get his PhD in electrical engineering from MIT, and now runs his own truck stop because fixing trucks (and big green RVs) is his passion.

Yep, meeting people on the road is where it's at, but HOW do you meet them?

The first rule is carpe diem—seize the day. It's not just a rule; it's also a roadtrip philosophy, a perspective thwack on how you live your life, and an elevation of intensity that milks the experience out of every day. To live the rest of your life at this high pace would be not only tiring, but also it would be impossible. But, while you're on the road for that finite amount of time, you really have nothing to lose. If Manny offers you a day on his boat, you put off your plans to go to Boston. If the founder of Starbucks, who also owns the Seattle Supersonics, offers you tickets to the basketball game that night, you have a quiet, relaxing evening some other time. If the guy who decoded the human genome wants to have coffee with you the next morning, and you're an 8hr. roadtrip away, fire up the engine and drive all night. You can sleep when you get home. Carpe diem, roadtrip-style.

Second, leave your prejudices at home. On the road, nothing is as it seems. The moment you start judging people is the moment you close yourself off from an authentic connection. If we would have seen Doc as some low-level mechanic not worth our time, we would have missed out on one of the best cups of coffee of our lives.

Third, make a project out of it. Wrapping your roadtrip in some creative framework gives you the excuse to get in doors you wouldn't normally be able to open and meet people you wouldn't normally be able to meet. Our excuse was to film an independent documentary about learning how people got to where they are today. So we interviewed the lobsterman on his boat, we captured the story of the founder of Starbucks, and we learned where the guy who decoded the human genome was when he was our age. Your project could be doing a coffee-table book on the best bakeries in the Pacific Northwest, taking photos of the best breakfast burritos in every state, surfing the northernmost point break in Maine, or finding the best concert venues down the Eastern Seaboard. Get creative. Open your mind. Put a little twist on things to wrap a mission around your expedition.

The degree of commitment to achieving "the mission" ranges from slacker to obsessive, but by thinking differently about your journey you'll meet people you would have never imagined. And who knows where it could go? I thought I would be in medical school right now.

Mike Marriner crossed the country in a neon-green RV, interviewing self-made men and women from the CEO of National Geographic to the head stylist for Madonna. He is a founder of www.roadtripna-tion.com and an author of Roadtrip Nation: A Guide to Discovering Your Path In Life.

essentials

PLANNING YOUR TRIP

TOURIST INFORMATION

AMERICAN CONSULAR SERVICES ABROAD

Australia: Moonah Place, Yarralumla, Australian Capital Territory 2600 (☎+61 2 6214 5970). **Consulates:** 553 St. Kilda Rd., Melbourne, Victoria 3004 (☎+61 3 9526 5900). 4th fl., 16 St. George's Terrace, Perth, Western Australia 6000 (☎+61 8 9202 1224). MLC Centre, Level 59, 19-29 Martin Pl., Sydney, New South Wales 2000 (☎+61 2 9373 9184).

Ireland: 42 Elgin Rd., Ballsbridge, Dublin 4 (☎+353 1 668 9612).

New Zealand: 29 Fitzherbert Terr., Thorndon, Wellington (☎+64 4 462 6000). **Consulate:** 3rd fl., Citigroup Building, 23 Customs St. E., Auckland (☎+64 9 303 2724, ext. 2842/2848/2856), at Commerce St.

UK: 24 Grosvenor Sq., London, W1A 2LQ (☎+44 20 7499 9000). **Consulates:** Danesfort House, 223 Stanmillis Rd., Belfast BT9 5GR (☎+44 28 9038 6100). 3 Regent Terr., Edinburgh, Scotland, EH7 5BW (☎+44 131 556 8315).

CONSULAR SERVICES IN THE US

Most foreign countries have consulate offices in major American cities such as Boston, Chicago, Denver, Houston, Los Angeles, New York City, and San Francisco. Country-specific information can be found on the Internet and should be checked before planning your trip to the US.

Australia: 123 N. Wacker Dr., Ste. 1330, Chicago, IL 60606 (☎312-419-1480). 150 E. 42nd St., 34th fl., New York, NY 10017 (☎212-351-6500). 575 Market St., Ste. 1800, San Francisco, CA 94105 (☎415-536-1970).

ENTRANCE REQUIREMENTS

Passport (see next page). All individuals entering the US, including US citizens, are required to present a valid passport upon entry. Non-American visitors will experience the newest aspect of US Homeland Security—the collection of biometric data such as fingerprints and digital images. As of early January 2008, Canadian and Bermudian citizens must present documentation proving both identity and citizenship. Oral declaration of citizenship is no longer accepted at the border for citizens of Canada or Bermuda.

Visa (see next page). Generally required of all visitors who are not citizens of the US or Canada, but the requirement can be waived for residents of certain countries (including Australia, New Zealand, Ireland, and the UK) if staying fewer than 90 days. See www.travel.state.gov and the following section on visas for more specific information.

Driver's License (p. 18). US citizens need a state-issued driver's license to legally drive on public roads. Foreign-issued licenses are accepted, though an International Driver's permit is also a good idea.

Ireland: 400 N. Michigan Ave., Chicago, IL 60611 (☎312-337-1868). 345 Park Ave., 17th fl., New York, NY 10154 (☎212-319-2555). 100 Pine St., Ste. 3350, San Francisco, CA 94111 (☎415-392-4214).

New Zealand: 8600 Bryn Mawr Ave., Ste. 550 N., Chicago, IL 60631 (☎773-714-8669). 2425 Olympic Blvd., Santa Monica, CA 90404 (☎310-566-6555). 222 E. 41st St., Ste. 2510, New York, NY 10017 (☎212-832-4038).

UK: 400 N. Michigan Ave., 13th fl., Chicago, IL 60611 (☎312-970-3800). 845 3rd Ave., New

15

York, NY 10022 (☎212-745-0200). 1 Sansome St., Ste. 850, San Francisco, CA 94104 (☎415-617-1300).

TOURIST OFFICES

Many cities have tourist offices which provide information on transport, events, sites of interest, and accommodations for visitors. When available, *Let's Go* provides the address, hours, and phone number for these offices (much of the information provided at these offices is also available in this book). See www.towd.com for specific city listings.

DOCUMENTS AND FORMALITIES

PASSPORTS

REQUIREMENTS

Anyone entering the US (including US citizens returning from abroad) needs a valid passport. Passports must be valid for at least six months (for visitors to the US) or one day (for visitors to Canada) beyond the intended stay. Trying to leave the country with an expired passport is illegal and will either force you to stay here longer (not too grim) or pay a hefty fine (grim). Your passport will prove your most convenient method of identification and, if the photo was taken long ago, may also prove a source of humorous conversation.

NEW PASSPORTS

Citizens of Australia, Canada, Ireland, New Zealand, the UK, and the US can apply for a passport at any passport office or at selected post offices and courts of law. Citizens of these countries may also download passport applications from the official website of their country's government or passport office. Any new passport or renewal applications must be filed well in advance of the departure date, though most passport offices offer rush services for a very steep fee. Note, however, that even "rushed" passports can take up to two weeks to arrive. Because of new laws requiring US citizens to present passports when traveling within North America, the US passport office has been heavily backlogged.

PASSPORT MAINTENANCE

Photocopy the page of your passport with your photo as well as your visas, traveler's check serial numbers, and any other important documents. Carry one set of copies in a safe place, apart from the originals, and leave another set at home (preferably in a place where your mother can quickly find it). Consulates also recommend that you carry an expired passport or an official copy of your birth certificate in a part of your baggage separate from other documents.

If you lose your passport, immediately notify the local police and your home country's nearest embassy or consulate. To expedite its replacement, you must show ID and proof of citizenship; it also helps to know all information previously recorded in the passport. In some cases, a replacement may take weeks to process, and it may only be valid for a limited time only. Any visas stamped in your old passport will be lost forever. In an emergency, ask for emergency temporary traveling papers that will permit you to re-enter your home country.

VISAS AND WORK PERMITS

VISAS

Foreign travelers seeking to enter the US will need a nonimmigrant visa and passport (there is a non-refundable application fee of $131 for a visa). However, visas are not required if you are a citizen from one of 27 countries with Visa Waiver Programs (VWP), which include Canada, Australia, Ireland, the UK, New Zealand, and most other European countries (a small fee may apply). Visitors from VWP countries qualify for a waiver if they are traveling only for business or pleasure (not work or study), are staying for fewer than 90 days, have proof of intent to leave (e.g., a return plane ticket), and possess an I-94W form, which is available on board most flights or at border entry points (for more specifics, see http://travel.state.gov).

Visitors in the VWP must possess a machine-readable passport to be admitted to the US without a visa. Most countries in the VWP have been issuing such passports for some time, and many travelers will not need new ones (though if you are looking for an excuse for a new passport photo, here it is). Children from these countries who normally travel on a parent's passport will also need to obtain their own machine-readable passports. See http://travel.state.gov/visa or contact your consulate for a list of countries participating in the VWP.

Upon entering the US, nearly everyone except American citizens will be asked to submit to certain biometric testing (for the most part, this includes digital photos and fingerprints). Your request for entrance will be denied if you refuse to submit to these tests.

For stays of longer than 90 days in the US (including individuals of VWP countries), all foreign travelers, except Canadians, must obtain a visa. Travelers eligible to waive their visas who wish to stay for more than 90 days must receive a visa before entering the US. In Canada, citizens of some non-English-speaking countries need a visitor's visa if they're not traveling with a valid green card. Citizens of Australia, Ireland, New Zealand, the UK, the US, and many other countries do not need a visa. See http://www.cic.gc.ca/english/visit/visas.asp for a list of countries whose citizens are required to hold visas or call your local Canadian consulate. Visitor's visas cost CDN$75 and can be purchased from the Canadian Embassy (☎202-682-1740) in Washington, DC.

WORK PERMITS

Admittance to a country as a traveler does not include the right to work, which is authorized only by a work permit. Certain individuals, such as foreign students, fiancés or fiancées of American citizens, and refugees, can apply for a permit to work in the US. See www.uscis.gov for more information.

IDENTIFICATION

When you travel, always carry at least two forms of identification on your person, including a photo ID. A passport and a driver's license or birth certificate will usually suffice. Never carry all of your IDs together; split them up in case of theft or loss and keep photocopies in your luggage and at home.

STUDENT, TEACHER, AND YOUTH IDENTIFICATION

The **International Student Identity Card (ISIC)**, the most widely accepted form of student ID, provides discounts on some sights, accommodations, food, and transportation; access to a 24hr. emergency help line; and insurance benefits for US cardholders (see **Insurance**, next page). To find specific discounts in cities, visit http://www.myisic.com/MyISIC/DiscountFinder/Home.aspx. Applicants must be full-time secondary- or post-secondary-school students at least 12 years old. Because of the proliferation of fake ISICs, some services (particularly airlines) require additional proof of student identity.

The **International Teacher Identity Card (ITIC)** offers teachers the same insurance coverage as the ISIC and similar but limited discounts. To qualify for the card, teachers must be currently employed and have worked a minimum of 18hr. per week for at least one school year. For travelers who are under 26 years old but are not students, the **International Youth Travel Card (IYTC)** also offers many of the same benefits as the ISIC.

Each of these identity cards costs $22. ISICs, ITICs, and IYTCs are valid for one year from the date of issue. To learn more about ISICs, ITICs, and IYTCs, try www.myisic.com. Many student travel agencies (p. 28) issue the cards; for a list of issuing agencies or more information, see the **International Student Travel Confederation (ISTC)** website (www.istc.org). The **International Student Exchange Card (ISE Card)** is a similar identification card available to students, faculty, and children aged 12 to 26. The card provides discounts, medical benefits, access to a 24hr. emergency help line, and the ability to purchase student airfares. An ISE Card costs $25; call ☎800-255-8000 (in North America) or ☎480-951-1177 (from all other continents) for more info or visit www.isecard.com.

CUSTOMS

If you are a roadtripper entering the US or Canada from abroad, you must declare certain articles and pay a duty on them if they exceed the allowance established by the US's or Canada's customs service. Goods and gifts purchased at duty-free shops abroad are not exempt from duty or sales tax; "duty-free" means that you won't pay tax in the country of purchase. Upon returning home, you must likewise declare all articles acquired abroad and pay a duty on the value of articles in excess of your home country's allowance. In order to expedite your return, make a list of any valuables brought from home and register them with customs before traveling abroad. It's a good idea to keep receipts for all goods acquired abroad.

PERMITS AND INSURANCE

INTERNATIONAL DRIVING PERMIT

If you do not have a license issued by a US state or Canadian province or territory, you might want an **International Driving Permit (IDP).** While the US and Canada accept foreign licenses for up to a year, it will ease interaction with police if your license is written in English. You must carry your home license with your IDP at all times. IDPs are valid for a year and must be issued in the country from which your license originates. To apply, contact the national or local branch of your automobile association.

CAR INSURANCE

While the minimum level varies by state, insurance is required throughout the US; proof of insurance must be kept in the car at all times. Insurance costs depend on type of coverage and how big of a "risk" the driver poses. Cost may vary depending on age, sex, driving record, and credit history. Common types of coverage include **liability insurance,** the standard and most often required type, which protects against the cost of damage to other people or property; **uninsured** or **underinsured motorist insurance** protects against damages to you caused by those driving illegally without insurance or without sufficient coverage; **collision insurance** protects against the cost of damage caused to your vehicle in a collision in which you are at fault. Most US insurance policies cover drivers in Canada as well; check with your provider before departure to obtain proof of coverage. For helpful info about the different types of insurance and statistics on which are required in each state, consult www.autoinsuranceindepth.com.

RENTAL INSURANCE

If you are renting a car for your roadtrip, it is still necessary to have adequate insurance. Much of the time your personal car insurance (if you have it) will suffice to cover the rental requirement. However, if you do not have car insurance, you will need to purchase one of the insurance packages offered by the rental company. These can cost anywhere between $15-70 per day. Cost depends on the amount and type of insurance you want (as described above). Just as a reminder, if you are driving a rental car on an unpaved road, you are almost never covered by insurance.

MONEY

CURRENCY AND EXCHANGE

The currency chart below is based on August 2008 exchange rates between US dollars ($) and Australian dollars (AUS$), Canadian dollars (CDN$), European Union euro (EUR€), New Zealand dollars (NZ$), and British pounds (UK£). Check the currency converter on websites like www.xe.com or www.bloomberg.com for the latest rates.

US DOLLARS ($)		
AUS$1 = US$0.94	US$1 = AUS$1.06
CDN$1 = US$0.98	US$1 = CDN$1.02
EUR€1 = US$1.55	US$1 = EUR€0.64
NZ$1 = US$0.75	US$1 = NZ$1.32
UK£1 = US$1.95	US$1 = UK£0.51

As a general rule, it's cheaper to convert money in the US than at home. While currency exchange will probably be available in your arrival airport, it's wise to bring enough foreign currency to last for at least 24-72hr.

When changing money abroad, try to go only to banks or bureaux de change that have at most a 5% margin between their buy and sell prices. Since you lose money with every transaction, it makes sense to convert large sums at one time (unless the currency is depreciating rapidly).

If you use traveler's checks or bills, carry some in small denominations (the equivalent of $50 or less) for times when you are forced to exchange money at poor rates, but bring a range of denominations since charges may be applied per check cashed. Store your money in a variety of forms; ideally, at any given time you will be carrying some cash, some traveler's checks, and an ATM and/or credit card.

TRAVELER'S CHECKS

Traveler's checks are one of the safest and most convenient means of carrying funds. American Express and Visa are the best-recognized brands. Many banks and agencies sell them for a small commission. Check issuers provide refunds if the checks are lost or stolen, and many provide additional services, such as toll-free refund hotlines abroad, emergency message services, and assistance with lost and stolen credit cards or passports. Traveler's checks are readily accepted in most establishments. Ask about toll-free refund hotlines and the location of refund centers when purchasing checks and always carry emergency cash.

American Express: Checks available with commission at select banks, at all AmEx offices, and online (www.americanexpress.com; US residents only). AmEx cardholders can also purchase checks by phone (☎800-528-4800). Checks available in American, Australian, British, Canadian, European, and Japanese currencies, among others. AmEx also offers the Travelers Cheque Card, a prepaid reloadable card. Cheques for Two can be signed by either of 2 people traveling together. For purchase locations or more information, contact AmEx's service centers: in Australia ☎+61 2 9271 8666, in New Zealand +64 9 367 4567, in the UK +44 1273 696 933, in the US and Canada 800-221-7282; elsewhere, call the US collect at 336-393-1111.

Travelex: Visa TravelMoney prepaid cash card and Visa traveler's checks available. For information about Thomas Cook MasterCard in Canada and the US, call ☎800-223-7373, in the UK +44 0800 622 101; elsewhere, call the UK collect at +44 1733 318 950. For information about Interpayment Visa in the US and Canada, call ☎800-732-1322, in the UK +44 800 515 884; else-

where, call the UK collect at +44 1733 318 949. For more information, visit www.travelex.com.

Visa: Checks available (generally with commission) at banks worldwide. For the location of the nearest office, call the Visa Travelers Cheque Global Refund and Assistance Center: in the UK ☎+44 800 895 078, in the US 800-227-6811; elsewhere, call the UK collect at +44 20 7937 8091. Checks available in American, British, Canadian, European, and Japanese currencies, among others. Visa also offers TravelMoney, a prepaid debit card that can be reloaded online or by phone. For more information on Visa travel services, see http://usa.visa.com/personal/using_visa/travel_with_visa.html.

CREDIT, DEBIT, AND ATM CARDS

For foreigners, credit cards often offer superior exchange rates—up to 5% better than the retail rate used by banks and other currency-exchange establishments. Credit cards may also offer services such as insurance or emergency help and are sometimes required to reserve hotel rooms or rental cars. **MasterCard** and **Visa** are the most frequently accepted; **American Express** cards work at some ATMs and at AmEx offices and major airports.

ATMs can be found in nearly all convenient stores and at least one on every major city street. Depending on the system that your bank uses, you can most likely access your personal bank account from the road. ATMs get the same wholesale exchange rate as credit cards, but there is often a limit on the amount of money you can withdraw per day (usually around $500). There is also typically a surcharge of $1-5 per withdrawal.

Debit cards are as convenient as credit cards but withdraw money directly from the holder's checking account. A debit card can be used wherever its associated credit-card company (usually MasterCard or Visa) is accepted. Debit cards often function as ATM cards and can be used to withdraw cash from associated banks and ATMs throughout the US and Canada.

The two major international money networks are **MasterCard/Maestro/Cirrus** (for ATM locations ☎800-424-7787 or www.mastercard.com) and **Visa/PLUS** (for ATM locations ☎800-847-2911 or www.visa.com).

Most ATMs charge a transaction fee that is paid to the bank that owns the ATM.

GETTING MONEY FROM HOME

If you run out of money while traveling, the easiest and cheapest solution is to have someone back home make a deposit to your bank account. Otherwise, consider the following.

WIRING MONEY

It is possible to arrange a **bank money transfer,** which means asking a bank back home to wire money to a bank in the US. This is the cheapest way to transfer cash, but it's also the slowest, usually taking several days or more. Note that some banks may only release your funds in local currency, potentially sticking you with a poor exchange rate; inquire about this in advance. Money transfer services like **Western Union** are faster and more convenient than bank transfers—but also much pricier. Western Union has many locations worldwide. To find one, visit www.westernunion.com or call in Australia ☎1800 173 833, in Canada and the US 800-325-6000, or in the UK 0800 833 833. To wire money using a credit card, call in Canada and the US ☎800-CALL-CASH, in the UK 0800 833 833. Money transfer services are also available to **American Express** cardholders and at selected **Thomas Cook** offices.

COSTS

The cost of your trip will vary considerably, depending on where you go, how you travel, and where you stay. Significant expenses will include food, lodging, car maintenance, and gasoline. Before you go, spend some time calculating a reasonable daily budget.

STAYING ON A BUDGET

To give you a general idea, a bare-bones day on the road (camping or sleeping in hostels/guesthouses, buying food at supermarkets) would cost about $25; a slightly more comfortable day (sleeping in hostels/guesthouses and the occasional budget hotel, eating one meal per day at a restaurant, going out at night) would cost $50-65; and, for a luxurious day, the sky's the limit. Don't forget to factor in emergency reserve funds (at least $200) when planning how much money you'll need.

TIPS FOR SAVING MONEY

Some simple ways to save include searching out free entertainment options, splitting accommodation and food costs with trustworthy fellow travelers, and buying food in supermarkets rather than eating out. Bring a **sleepsack** to save on sheet charges in hostels and do your **laundry** in the sink (unless you're explicitly prohibited from doing so). Museums often have certain days once a month or once a week when admission is free; plan accordingly. If you are eligible, consider getting an ISIC or an IYTC (p. 17); many sights and museums offer reduced admission to students and youths. Drinking at bars and clubs quickly becomes expensive. It's cheaper to buy alcohol at a supermarket and imbibe before going out. That said, don't go overboard. Though staying within your budget is important, don't do so at the expense of your health or a great travel experience.

GASOLINE

Gas prices have risen steeply over the past few years. A gallon of gas now costs about $4 ($1.05 per L), but prices vary widely according to state gasoline taxes. In Canada, gas costs as much as CDN$1.50 per L (CDN$5.66 per gallon). It is more than worth your while to shop around for the best price. Gas prices fluctuate quickly, but there are a number of websites entirely devoted to helping you find good gas prices. For average gas prices by state, check out www.fuelgaugereport.com. There's also a gas cost calculator: enter the start and end points of your trip, and the make, model, and year of your car to get approximate fuel costs for your roadtrip. Two websites, www.fuelmeup.com and www.gasbuddy.com, let travelers enter a zip code and then provide high, low, and average gas prices for that zip code as well as the gas stations at which those prices can be found. However, because both rely on info submitted by other consumers, coverage can be spotty, especially in rural areas.

In general, it is a good idea to fill up your car before entering urban areas. Gas tends to be more expensive in cities, and you never know when you will get stuck in a traffic jam with the fuel needle flirting with empty.

Similarly, fill up before entering a large rural stretch of road where there may not be a gas station when you need it.

In some cities, and at night, gas stations require you to pay before you pump. At most gas stations in the US, you'll be able to pay with a credit card, either inside the station or at the pump; however, at some rural stations, you may only be able to pay by cash or check, so carry enough cash to fill up, just in case.

TIPPING AND BARGAINING

In the US and Canada, it is customary to tip waitstaff and cab drivers 15-20% (at your discretion). Tips are usually not included in restaurant bills unless you are in a party of six or more. In hotels, porters expect a tip of at least $1 per bag to carry your luggage. In general, anyone who offers a service and then waits around afterward expects a tip. In restaurants, waiters are tipped based on quality of service; good service deserves at least 15%.

TAXES

In the US, sales tax is usually 4-10%, depending on the item and the place. Usually, taxes are not included in the prices of items. In many states, groceries are not taxed. In Canada, you'll quickly notice the 6% **goods and services tax (GST)** and an additional sales tax in some provinces. Visitors can claim a rebate of the GST they pay on accommodations during stays of less than one month and on most goods they buy and take home, so save your receipts and pick up a GST rebate form while in Canada. To qualify for a rebate, total purchases must reach CDN$200, and the rebate application must be made within 11 months of the date of the purchase. A brochure detailing restrictions is available from tourist offices.

PACKING

Pack lightly: lay out only what you absolutely need, then take half the clothes and twice the money. The **Travelite FAQ** (www.travelite. org) is a good resource for tips on traveling light. The online **Universal Packing List** (http://upl.codeq.info) will generate a customized list of suggested items based on your trip length, the expected climate, your planned activities, and other factors. Consider what

you'll be doing along the way; pack comfortable clothes and shoes for driving and, if you plan to do a lot of hiking or camping, consult the **The Great Outdoors** section (p. 43). Some frequent travelers keep a bag packed with all the essentials: passport, money belt, hat, socks, etc. Then, when they decide to leave, they know they haven't forgotten anything.

Luggage: In addition to your main pieces of luggage, a daypack (a small backpack or courier bag) is useful for storing essentials like your water bottle and copy of Let's Go for on-foot exploration.

Clothing: No matter when you're traveling, it's a good idea to bring a warm jacket or wool sweater, a rain jacket (Gore-Tex® is both waterproof and breathable), sturdy shoes or hiking boots, and thick socks. Flip-flops or waterproof sandals are must-haves for grubby hostel showers, and extra socks are always a good idea. You may also want one outfit for going out and maybe a nicer pair of shoes. If you plan to visit religious or cultural sites, remember that you will need modest and respectful dress.

Sleepsack: Some hostels require that you either provide your own linen or rent sheets from them. Save by making your own sleepsack: fold a full-size sheet in half the long way, then sew it closed along the long side and one of the short sides.

Converters and Adapters: In the US and Canada, electricity is 120 volts AC. Appliances from anywhere outside of North America will need an adapter (which changes the shape of the plug; $5) and a converter (which changes the voltage; $20-30). Don't make the mistake of using only an adapter (unless appliance instructions state otherwise). For more on all things adaptable, check out http://kropla.com/electric.htm.

Toiletries: Condoms, deodorant, razors, tampons, and toothbrushes are often available, but it may be difficult to find your preferred brand; bring extras. Also bring your glasses and a copy of your prescription in case you need emergency replacements.

First-Aid Kit: For a basic first-aid kit, pack bandages, a pain reliever, antibiotic cream, a thermometer, a multifunction pocketknife, tweezers, moleskin, decongestant, motion-sickness remedy, diarrhea or upset-stomach medication (Pepto Bismol® or Imodium®), an antihistamine, sunscreen, insect repellent, and burn ointment.

ESSENTIALS

Other Useful Items: For safety purposes, you should bring a **money belt** and a **small padlock.** Basic **outdoors equipment** (plastic water bottle, compass, waterproof matches, pocketknife, sunglasses, sunscreen, hat) may also be handy. Quick repairs of torn garments can be done on the road with a needle and thread; also consider bringing electrical tape for patching tears. Other things you're liable to forget include an umbrella, sealable **plastic bags** (for damp clothes, soap, food, shampoo, and other spillables), an **alarm clock,** safety pins, rubber bands, a flashlight, earplugs, garbage bags, and a small calculator. A **cell phone** can be a lifesaver (literally) on the road; see p. 38 for information on acquiring one that will work in the US.

Important Documents: Don't forget your driver's license, proof of insurance, passport, traveler's checks, ATM and/or credit cards, adequate ID, and photocopies of all of the aforementioned in case these documents are lost or stolen. Also check that you have any of the following that might apply to you: a hosteling membership card (p. 41); a driver's license (p. 18); travel insurance forms (p. 18); and/or your ISIC (p. 17).

For Your Car: When traveling in the summer or in the desert, bring substantial amounts of water (1 gallon per person per day) for drinking and for the radiator. It is also a good idea to carry extra food. Make sure you take good maps and sunglasses. A compass and a car manual can also be useful (though most interstates do point in a cardinal direction). You should always carry a spare tire and jack, jumper cables, extra oil, flares, a flashlight, and heavy blankets (in case your car breaks down at night or in the winter). An empty gas container in your trunk can come in handy if you need to carry fuel to your car from a distant gas station (most will only sell you one, not lend it out). For more essentials, see **Car Care on the Road,** p. 33.

SAFETY AND HEALTH

GENERAL ADVICE

In any type of crisis, the most important thing to do is **stay calm.** For foreigners, your country's **embassy** abroad (p. 15) is usually your best resource in an emergency; registering with that embassy upon arrival in the country is a good idea.

LAWS OF THE ROAD

Calling for emergency assistance, ☎911 on any phone, will result in police, fire, and ambulance emergency response. Calling 911 works both in the US and Canada and is toll free from all phones, including coin pay phones and cell phones. For vehicle-related assistance, see p. 37. Instructions from law enforcement officers should be followed at all times. In case of a natural or national disaster, follow the instructions of emergency response teams. Tune to the emergency broadcasting system on your radio for information.

It is a felony to leave the scene of an accident. Should you be the victim of an automobile accident, dial ☎911 for highway patrol.

DRUGS AND ALCOHOL

In the US, the drinking age is 21; in Canada, it is 19, except in Alberta, Manitoba, and Québec, where it is 18. Most localities restrict where and when alcohol can be sold. Sales usually stop at a certain time of night and are often prohibited entirely on Sundays. Drinking restrictions are particularly strict in the US. The youthful should expect to be asked to show government-issued identification when purchasing any alcoholic beverage.

Driving under the influence is a serious crime in the US and Canada. Don't do it. All 50 states, the District of Columbia, and all Canadian provinces have laws which make it a crime to drive with a **blood-alcohol concentration (BAC)** above a certain level (in most cases, 0.08%), which can be achieved with as little as two drinks in one hour. A DUI conviction usually results in license suspension or revocation, and, in 30 states, repeat offenders may have their cars taken away. Most states have zero-tolerance laws for those under 21, with severe consequences for those found to have consumed any amount of alcohol. In many states, open containers of alcoholic beverages in the passenger compartment of a car will result in heavy fines; a failed breathalyzer test will mean fines, a suspended license, imprisonment, or all three. Drivers under 21 should be aware that they may be convicted of underage possession if any alcohol is present in their vehicle.

Narcotics, such as heroin and cocaine, are highly illegal in the US and Canada. Though it may be partially decriminalized in some areas of Canada, **marijuana** is still illegal in most provinces and throughout the US. If you carry **prescription drugs** while you travel, keep a copy of the prescription with you, especially at border crossings. A letter from your doctor is advisable if you carry large amounts of prescription drugs.

SPECIFIC CONCERNS

NATURAL DISASTERS

EARTHQUAKES. Earthquakes occur frequently in certain parts of the US, particularly California, but most are too small to be felt. If a strong earthquake does occur, it will last at most 1-2min. Open a door to provide an escape route and protect yourself by moving underneath a sturdy doorway or table. If you are outside, move to an open area free from buildings, trees, and power lines.

TORNADOES AND HURRICANES. Tornadoes have been reported in every US state, though they are most common in the Midwest during the spring and summer. If you are inside during a tornado, move to a basement or interior location away from windows. If you are outside, lie flat on the ground in a low place away from power lines. Hurricanes are most common on the coasts of the Atlantic and the Gulf of Mexico. These areas are evacuated in anticipation of particularly severe hurricanes. If you are not advised to evacuate, stay inside, away from windows.

FOREST FIRES. Dry spells are common in the western US, which suffers from annual droughts. In 2003, forest fires ravaged much of the eastern Cascades as well as parts of California and Oregon. If you are hiking or camping and smell smoke, see flames, or hear fire, leave the area immediately. To prevent forest fires, always make sure campfires are completely extinguished; during high lev-

els of fire danger, campfires will most likely be prohibited. Before you go hiking or camping, be sure to check with local authorities for the level of fire danger in the area.

> **! TRAVEL ADVISORIES.** The following government offices provide travel information and advisories by telephone, by fax, or via the web:
> **Australian Department of Foreign Affairs and Trade:** ☎+61 2 6261 1111; www.dfat.gov.au.
> **Canadian Department of Foreign Affairs and International Trade (DFAIT):** ☎800-267-8376; www.dfait-maeci.gc.ca. Call for their free booklet, *Bon Voyage...But*.
> **New Zealand Ministry of Foreign Affairs:** ☎+64 4 439 8000; www.mfat.govt.nz.
> **United Kingdom Foreign and Commonwealth Office:** ☎+44 20 7008 1500; www.fco.gov.uk.
> **US Department of State:** ☎888-407-4747; http://travel.state.gov. Visit the website for the booklet, *A Safe Trip Abroad*.

TERRORISM

In light of the September 11, 2001, terrorist attacks, there is an elevated threat of terrorist activity in the US. Terrorists often threaten to target landmarks popular with tourists; however, the threat of an attack is generally not specific or great enough to warrant avoiding certain places or modes of transportation. Keep aware of developments in the news and watch for alerts from federal, state, and local law enforcement officials. Also, due to heightened security, allow for extra time at border crossings, and be sure you have the appropriate documents. For more info on security threats to the US, visit the US Department of Homeland Security's website at www.dhs.gov. The box below lists offices to contact and webpages to visit to get the most updated list of your home country's government advisories about travel.

PERSONAL SAFETY

EXPLORING AND TRAVELING

To avoid unwanted attention, try to blend in as much as possible. Respecting local customs (in many cases, dressing more conservatively than you would at home) may ward off would-be hecklers. Familiarize yourself with your surroundings before setting out and carry yourself with confidence. Check maps in shops and restaurants rather than on the street. If you are traveling alone, be sure someone at home knows your itinerary and never tell anyone you meet that you're by yourself. When walking at night, stick to busy, well-lit streets and avoid dark alleyways. If you ever feel uncomfortable, leave the area as quickly and directly as you can.

There is no surefire way to avoid all the threatening situations that you might encounter while traveling, but a good **self-defense course** will give you concrete ways to react to unwanted advances. **Impact, Prepare,** and **Model Mugging** can refer you to local self-defense courses in Australia, Canada, Switzerland, and the US. Visit www.modelmugging.org for a list of nearby chapters.

It is important to learn local driving signals and wear a seat belt. Children under 40 lb. should ride only in specially designed car seats, available for a small fee from most car-rental agencies. Study route maps before you hit the road and bring spare parts. For long drives in desolate areas, invest in a cell phone and a **roadside assistance program** (p. 37). Park your vehicle in a garage or well-traveled area and use a steering-wheel locking device in larger cities. Sleeping in your car is the most dangerous way to get your rest, and it's also illegal in many areas.

POSSESSIONS AND VALUABLES

Never leave your belongings unattended; crime can occur in even the most safe-looking hostel or hotel. Bring your own padlock for hostel lockers and don't ever store valuables in a locker. Be particularly careful on **buses** and **trains;** horror stories abound about determined thieves who wait for travelers to fall asleep. Carry your bag or purse in front of you where you can see it.

When out of the car, make sure that you do not leave your possessions within sight of anyone who might be interested in nabbing them. Underneath the rug, beneath the seat, and inside the glove box or trunk are places you might consider hiding items you cannot take with you. Make sure to lock your doors and roll up the windows.

There are a few steps you can take to minimize the financial risk associated with traveling. First, **bring as little with you as possible.** Second, buy a few combination **padlocks** to secure your belongings either in your pack or in a hostel or train-station locker. Third, **carry as little cash as possible.** Keep your traveler's checks and ATM/credit cards in a money belt—not a "fanny pack"—along with your passport and ID cards. Fourth, **keep a small cash reserve separate from your primary stash.** This should be about $50 sewn into or stored in the depths of your pack, along with your traveler's check numbers, photocopies of your passport, your birth certificate, and other important documents.

In large cities, **con artists** often work in groups and may involve children. Beware of certain classics: sob stories that require money, rolls of bills "found" on the street, mustard spilled (or saliva spit) onto your shoulder to distract you while they snatch your bag. **Never let your passport and your bags out of your sight.** Beware of **pickpockets** in city crowds, especially on public transportation. Also, be alert in public telephone booths: if you must say your calling-card number, do so very quietly; if you punch it in, make sure no one can look over your shoulder.

If you will be traveling with electronic devices, such as a laptop computer or a PDA, check whether your homeowner's insurance covers loss, theft, or damage when you travel. If not, you might consider purchasing a low-cost separate insurance policy. **Safeware** (☎800-800-1492; www.safeware.com) specializes in covering computers and charges $90 for 90-day comprehensive international travel coverage up to $4000.

PRE-DEPARTURE HEALTH

In your passport, write the names of any people you wish to be contacted in case of a **medical emergency** and list any allergies or medical conditions. Matching a prescription to a foreign equivalent is not always easy, safe, or possible, so, if you take **prescription drugs**, consider carrying up-to-date prescriptions or a statement from your doctor stating the medication's trade name, manufacturer, chemical name, and dosage. While traveling, be sure to keep all medication with you in your carry-on luggage. For tips on packing a **first-aid kit** and other health essentials, see this page.

IMMUNIZATIONS AND PRECAUTIONS

Travelers over two years old should make sure that the following vaccines are up to date: MMR (for measles, mumps, and rubella); DTaP or Td (for diphtheria, tetanus, and pertussis); IPV (for polio); Hib (for *haemophilus influenzae* B); and HepB (for Hepatitis B). For recommendations on immunizations and prophylaxis, consult the Centers for Disease Control and Prevention (CDC; below) in the US or the equivalent in your home country and check with a doctor for guidance.

MEDICAL INSURANCE

Travel insurance covers four basic areas: medical/health problems, property loss, trip cancellation/interruption, and emergency evacuation. Though regular insurance policies may well extend to travel-related accidents, you may consider purchasing separate travel insurance if the cost of potential trip cancellation, interruption, or emergency medical evacuation is greater than you can absorb. Prices for travel insurance purchased separately generally run about $50 per week for full coverage, while trip cancellation/interruption may be purchased separately at a rate of $3-5 per day, depending on length of stay.

Medical insurance (especially university policies) often covers costs incurred abroad; check with your provider. **Homeowners' insurance** (or your family's coverage) often covers theft and loss of travel documents (passport, plane ticket, etc.) up to $500.

ISIC and **ITIC** (p. 17) provide basic insurance benefits to US cardholders, including $100 per day of in-hospital sickness for up to 100 days and $10,000 of accident-related medical reimbursement (see www.isicus.com for details). Cardholders have access to a toll-free 24hr. help line for medical, legal, and financial emergencies overseas. **American Express** grants most cardholders automatic collision and car-rental theft insurance on rentals made with the card.

USEFUL ORGANIZATIONS AND PUBLICATIONS

The American **Centers for Disease Control and Prevention** (**CDC**; ☎877-FYI-TRIP; www.cdc.gov/travel) maintains an international travelers' hotline and an informative website. Consult the appropriate government agency of your home country for consular information sheets on health, entry requirements, and other issues for various countries (see the listings in the box on **Travel Advisories**, p. 23). For quick information on health and other travel warnings, contact a passport agency, embassy, or consulate abroad. For information on medical evacuation services and travel insurance firms, see the US government's website at http://travel.state.gov/travel/abroad_health. html or the **British Foreign and Commonwealth Office** (www.fco.gov.uk). For general health information, contact the **American Red Cross** (☎202-303-4498; www.redcross.org).

STAYING HEALTHY

Common sense is the simplest prescription for good health while you travel. Drink lots of fluids to prevent dehydration and constipation and wear sturdy, broken-in shoes and clean socks.

ON THE ROAD

ENVIRONMENTAL HAZARDS

Altitude Sickness: Many mountainous areas are high enough for altitude sickness to be a concern. Symptoms may include headache, dizziness, and

ESSENTIALS

sleep disruption. To minimize effects, avoid rapid increases in elevation, allow your body a couple of days to adjust to a new elevation before exerting yourself, and take special care when driving. Note that alcohol is more potent and UV rays stronger at high elevations.

Heat exhaustion and dehydration: Heat exhaustion, characterized by dehydration and salt deficiency, can lead to fatigue, headaches, and wooziness. Avoid it by drinking plenty of fluids, eating salty foods (e.g., crackers), and abstaining from dehydrating beverages (e.g., alcohol, coffee, tea, and caffeinated soda). Continuous . heat stress can eventually lead to heat stroke, with symptoms that include rising body temperature, severe headache, and cessation of sweating. Victims should be cooled off with wet towels and taken to a doctor. The risk of heat exhaustion is greatest while traveling through desert areas, where the combination of heat and dryness can result in rapid water loss.

Hypothermia and frostbite: A rapid drop in body temperature is the clearest sign of overexposure to cold. Victims may also shiver, feel exhausted, have poor coordination or slurred speech, hallucinate, or suffer amnesia. Do not let hypothermia victims fall asleep. To avoid hypothermia, keep dry, wear layers, and stay out of the wind. When the temperature is below freezing, watch out for frostbite. If skin turns white or blue, waxy, and cold, do not rub the area. Drink warm beverages, stay dry, and slowly warm the area with dry fabric or steady body contact until a doctor can be found.

Sunburn: Always wear sunscreen (SPF 30 or higher) when outdoors. If you are planning on spending time near water, in the desert, or in the snow, you are at a higher risk of getting burned, even on a cloudy day. If you get sunburned, drink more fluids than usual and apply an aloe-based lotion. Severe sunburns can lead to sun poisoning, a condition that affects the entire body, causing fever, chills, nausea, and vomiting. Sun poisoning should be treated by a doctor.

INSECT-BORNE DISEASES

Many diseases are transmitted by insects—mainly mosquitoes, fleas, ticks, and lice. Be aware of insects in wet or forested areas, especially while hiking and camping. Wear long pants and long sleeves, tuck your pants into your socks, and use a mosquito net. Use insect repellents such as DEET and soak or spray your gear with permethrin (licensed in the US only for use on clothing). **Mosquitoes** can be particularly abundant in the wet, swampy, or wooded areas of the Southeast, Northeast, and Pacific Northwest. **Ticks**—which can carry Lyme and other diseases—are also prevalent in these areas.

Lyme disease: A bacterial infection carried by ticks and marked by a circular bull's-eye rash of 2 in. or more. Later symptoms include fever, headache, fatigue, and aches and pains. Antibiotics are effective if administered early. Left untreated, Lyme can cause problems in joints, the heart, and the nervous system. If you find a tick attached to your skin, grasp the head with tweezers as close to your skin as possible and apply slow, steady traction. Removing a tick within 24hr. greatly reduces the risk of infection. Do not try to remove ticks with petroleum jelly, nail polish remover, or a hot match. Ticks usually inhabit moist, shaded environments and heavily wooded areas. If you are going to be hiking in these areas, wear long clothes and DEET.

West Nile Virus: West Nile Virus has been detected in all 48 continental states and is transmitted through the bite of an infected mosquito. Most victims do not show symptoms, but some develop a mild flu-like condition; less than 1% of cases involve more severe complications, including meningitis or encephalitis. Those at highest risk are the elderly and those with compromised immune systems, but people of all ages can develop a serious illness. To minimize the risk of infection, limit outdoor activity in dawn, dusk, and early evening, wear long clothes, and use DEET.

FOOD- AND WATER-BORNE DISEASES

Although hygienic standards in the US are high, prevention is the best cure: be sure that your food is properly cooked and the water you drink is clean. Watch out for food from markets or street vendors that may have been cooked in unhygienic conditions. If camping, buy bottled water or purify your own water by bringing it to a **rolling boil** or treating it with **iodine tablets;** note, however, that boiling is more reliable.

Giardiasis: Transmitted through parasites and acquired by drinking untreated water from streams or lakes. Symptoms include diarrhea, cramps, bloating, fatigue, weight loss, and nausea. If untreated, it can lead to severe dehydration. Giardiasis occurs worldwide.

Gastroenteritis/stomach flu: Caused by a class of viruses called Noroviruses and spread via contact with the bodily fluids of infected people, including exposure to contaminated food, touching contaminated objects and then placing the hands in or near the mouth, and direct contact with infected persons. Symptoms appear within 48hr. of infection and include vomiting, nausea, chills, diarrhea, and abdominal cramping. Though the symptoms usually pass within a few days, the disease can be contagious for several weeks and a doctor should be consulted if any of these symptoms develop.

OTHER INFECTIOUS DISEASES

The following diseases exist all over the world. Travelers should know how to recognize them and what to do if they suspect they have been infected.

AIDS and HIV: For detailed information on Acquired Immune Deficiency Syndrome (AIDS) in the US, call the 24hr. National AIDS Hotline at ☎800-342-2437.

Hepatitis B: A viral infection of the liver transmitted via blood or other bodily fluids. Symptoms, which may not surface until years after infection, include jaundice, appetite loss, fever, and joint pain. It is transmitted through unprotected sex and unclean needles. A 3-shot vaccination sequence is recommended for sexually active travelers and anyone planning to seek medical treatment abroad; it must begin 6 months before you start off on your trip.

Hepatitis C: Like Hepatitis B, but the mode of transmission differs. IV drug users, those with occupational exposure to blood, hemodialysis patients, and recipients of blood transfusions are at the highest risk, but the disease can also be spread through sexual contact or sharing items like razors and toothbrushes that may have traces of blood on them. No symptoms are usually exhibited. If left untreated, Hepatitis C can lead to liver failure.

Sexually transmitted infections (STIs): Gonorrhea, chlamydia, genital warts, syphilis, herpes, HPV, and other STIs are easier to catch than HIV and can be just as serious. Though ▨ **condoms** may protect you from some STIs, oral or even tactile contact can lead to transmission. If you think you may have contracted an STI, see a doctor immediately.

OTHER HEALTH CONCERNS

MEDICAL CARE ON THE ROAD

Medical care in the US and Canada is about as good as it gets. In case of medical emergency, call ☎**911** from any phone and an operator will dispatch paramedics, a fire brigade, or the police as needed. Emergency care is also readily available at any emergency room on a walk-in basis. If you do not have insurance, you will have to pay for medical care following treatment. Appointments are required for non-emergency medical services.

If you are concerned about obtaining medical assistance while traveling, you may wish to employ special support services. The **Med-Pass** from **GlobalCare, Inc.**, 6875 Shiloh Rd. E., Alpharetta, GA 30005 (☎800-860-1111; www.globalcare.net), provides 24hr. international medical assistance, support, and medical evacuation resources. The **International Association for Medical Assistance to Travelers (IAMAT;** US ☎716-754-4883, Canada 519-836-0102; www.iamat.org) has free membership, lists English-speaking doctors worldwide, and offers details on immunization requirements and sanitation. If your regular insurance policy does not cover travel abroad, you may wish to purchase additional coverage.

Those with medical conditions (such as diabetes, allergies to antibiotics, epilepsy, or heart conditions) may want to obtain a **MedicAlert** membership ($40 per year), which includes among other things a stainless-steel ID tag and a 24hr. collect-call number. Contact the MedicAlert Foundation International, 2323 Colorado Ave., Turlock, CA 95382 (☎888-633-4298, outside US 209-668-3333; www.medicalert.org).

WOMEN'S HEALTH

Unsanitary conditions and even stretching the distance between pit stops can contribute to **urinary tract (including bladder and kidney) infections.** Over-the-counter medicines can sometimes alleviate symptoms, but if they persist, see a doctor. **Vaginal yeast infections** may flare up in hot and humid climates. Wearing loose-fitting trousers or a skirt and cotton underwear will help, as will over-the-counter remedies like Monistat® or Gynelotrimin®, which should only be used if you have been previously diagnosed with a yeast infection and have exactly the same symptoms. **Tampons, sanitary pads,** and **contraceptive devices** are available in the US and Canada. **Abortion** is legal in the US and Canada.

GETTING TO THE US

BY PLANE

When it comes to airfare, a little effort can save you a bundle. The key is to hunt around, be flexible, and ask about discounts. Students, seniors, and those under 26 should never pay full price for a ticket.

AIRFARES

Airfares to the US peak between June and August; holidays are also expensive. The cheapest times to travel are in the winter. Midweek (M-Th morning) round-trip flights run $40-50 cheaper than weekend flights, but they are generally more crowded and less likely to permit frequent-flier upgrades. Not fixing a return date ("open return") or arriving in and departing from different cities ("open-jaw") can be pricier than round-trip flights. Patching one-way flights together is the most expensive way to travel. Flights to major hubs will tend to be the cheapest. These vary by airline but include New York, Washington, Chicago, Atlanta, Dallas, and Los Angeles.

Fares for round-trip flights to the East Coast from Europe cost $800-1400, $400-900 in the low season (Sept.-May); round-trip flights from Australia or New Zealand to the West Coast usually cost $1100-1800.

BUDGET AND STUDENT TRAVEL AGENCIES

While knowledgeable agents specializing in flights to the US can make your life easier, they may not spend the time to find you the lowest possible fare—they get paid on com-

mission. Travelers holding **ISICs** and **IYTCs** (p. 17) qualify for big discounts from student travel agencies. Most flights from budget agencies are on major airlines, but in peak season some may sell seats on less reliable chartered aircraft.

FLIGHT PLANNING ON THE INTERNET. The Internet may be the budget traveler's dream when it comes to finding and booking bargain fares, but the array of options can be overwhelming. Many airline sites offer special last-minute deals on the web. **STA** (www.statravel.com) and **StudentUniverse** (www.studentuniverse. com) provide quotes on student tickets, while **Orbitz** (www.orbitz.com), **Expedia** (www.expedia.com), and **Travelocity** (www.travelocity.com) offer full travel services. **Airfare Watchdog** (www.airfarewatchdog.com) scours the Internet for sale prices, both foreign and domestic. **Priceline** (www. priceline.com) lets you specify a price and obligates you to buy any ticket that meets or beats it. **Hotwire** (www. hotwire.com) offers bargain fares but won't reveal the airline or flight times until you buy. Other sites that compile deals include www.bestfares.com, www.flights.com, www.lowestfare.com, www.onetravel.com, and www.travelzoo.com. **SideStep** (www.sidestep. com), **Booking Buddy** (www.bookingbuddy.com), **Kayak** (www.kayak.com), and **Qixo** (www.qixo.com) are online tools that can help sift through multiple offers; these let you enter your trip information once and search multiple sites. **Air Traveler's Handbook** (www. faqs.org/faqs/travel/air/handbook) is an indispensable resource on the Internet; it has a comprehensive listing of links to everything you need to know before you board a plane.

The Adventure Travel Company, 124 MacDougal St., New York City, NY 10021 (☎800-467-4595; www.theadventuretravelcompany.com). Offices across the US and Canada, including New York City, San Diego, San Francisco, and Seattle.

STA Travel, 5900 Wilshire Blvd., Ste. 900, Los Angeles, CA 90036 (24hr. reservations and info ☎800-781-4040; www.statravel.com). A student and youth travel organization with over 150 offices worldwide (check their website for a listing of all their offices), including US offices in Boston, Chicago, Los Angeles, New York City, Seattle, San Francisco, and Washington, DC. Ticket booking, travel insurance, railpasses, and more. Walk-in offices are located throughout Australia (☎+61 3 9207 5900), New Zealand (☎+64 9 309 9723), and the UK (☎+44 8701 630 026).

Travel CUTS (Canadian Universities Travel Services Limited), 187 College St., Toronto, ON M5T 1P7, Canada (☎888-592-2887; www.travelcuts. com). Offices across Canada and the US including Los Angeles and New York City.

USIT, 19-21 Aston Quay, Dublin 2, Ireland (☎+353 1 602 1906; www.usit.ie). Ireland's leading student/budget travel agency has 20 offices throughout the island. Offers programs to work, study, and volunteer worldwide.

COMMERCIAL AIRLINES

The commercial airlines' lowest regular offer is the **APEX (Advance Purchase Excursion)** fare, which provides confirmed reservations and allows "open-jaw" tickets. Generally, reservations must be made seven to 21 days ahead of departure, with seven- to 14-day minimum-stay and up to 90-day maximum-stay restrictions. These fares carry hefty cancellation and change penalties (fees rise in summer). Book peak-season APEX fares early. Use **Expedia** (www.expedia.com) or **Travelocity** (www.travelocity.com) to get an idea of the lowest published fares, then use the resources outlined here to try to beat those fares. Low-season fares should be appreciably cheaper than the high-season (from mid-June to Aug.) ones listed here.

TRAVELING FROM IRELAND AND THE UK

Round-trip fares from the UK and Ireland to the East Coast range $500-1000, with flights from London usually cheapest. Legacy carriers like **Delta** (☎800-221-1212; www.delta. com) and **American** (☎800-433-7300; www. aa.com) will probably offer the most convenient flights, but they may not be the cheapest. Also try **Lufthansa** (☎800-399-5838; www.lufthansa.com) and **British Airways** (☎800-247-2929; www.britishairways.com).

TRAVELING FROM AUSTRALIA AND NEW ZEALAND

Check **Air New Zealand** (☎800-262-1234; www.airnewzealand.com) and **Quantas Airways** (☎800-227-4500; www.qantas.com) for tickets from Australia and New Zealand.

TICKET CONSOLIDATORS

Ticket consolidators, or **"bucket shops,"** buy unsold tickets in bulk from commercial airlines and sell them at discounted rates. The best place to look is in the Sunday travel section of any major newspaper, where many bucket shops place tiny ads. Call quickly, as availability is extremely limited. Not all bucket shops are reliable, so insist on a receipt that gives full details of restrictions, refunds, and tickets and pay by credit card (in spite of the 2-5% fee) so you can stop payment if you never receive your tickets. For more info, see www.travel-library.com/air-travel/consolidators.html.

BORDER CROSSINGS

FROM CANADA

Crossing into the US from Canada is usually an easy process. There are many crossing points on the US-Canada border, most of which accept both commercial and and private traffic. Delays are usually negligible, but the busiest checkpoints can be backed up for 20min. or more. For required documents, see **Documents and Formalities,** p. 16. Although inspections at the border are normally perfunctory, border guards can search your vehicle. In an effort to decrease the risk of terrorism, both the US and Canada are tightening border security, which means more random searches.

FROM MEXICO

As with the US-Canada border, there are numerous crossing points along the US-Mexico border. Mexican citizens entering the US are required to present both a passport and nonimmigrant visa upon entry. US citizens returning to the US are not technically required to present a passport at this time, but they must show documentation proving citizenship. Delays in crossing the US-Mexico are generally short but can be longer depending on traffic conditions. Border guards claim the right to conduct random searches.

GETTING AROUND

NAVIGATING

On most road signs and maps, "I" (as in "I-90") refers to interstate highways, "US" (as in "US 1") to US highways, and "Rte." (as in "Rte. 7") to state and local highways. For Canadian highways, "TCH" refers to the **Trans-Canada Highway,** while "Hwy." or "Autoroute" refers to standard routes.

Most US roads are named with an intuitive **numbering system.** Even-numbered interstates run east-west, and odd run north-south, decreasing in number toward the south and the west. Except for a few cases, primary (2-digit) interstates have unique numbers nationwide. North-south routes begin on the West Coast with I-5 and end on the East Coast with I-95. The southernmost east-west route is I-4 in Florida. The northernmost east-west route is I-94, stretching from Montana to Wisconsin. Three-digit numbers signify branches of other interstates that often skirt large cities and generally are numbered by adding a multiple of 100 to the number of its parent interstate (as in I-285, a branch of I-85). Traditionally, if an interstate has three digits that start with an even number, then it is bounded on both ends by other interstates, and, if it begins with an odd digit, it meets another interstate at only one end.

A good **map** is a roadtripper's best friend; make sure you have one before starting your journey. *Rand McNally's Road Atlas*, covering all of the US and Canada, is one of the best commercial guides (available at bookstores, gas stations, and online at www.randmcnally.com; $9). Free maps of the interstate and national highway systems can be found online from the US Department of Transportation at www.fhwa.dot.gov/planning/nhs.

YOUR WHEELS

For a life-changing, classic American road-trip, any car will do. If you already own one, drive it. In truth, most of America's roads are paved and navigable by any car.

CAR RENTAL

National car-rental agencies usually allow you to pick up a car in one city and drop it off in another for a hefty charge, sometimes in excess of $1000. The drawbacks of car rentals include high prices (a compact car rents for $30-50 per day) and high minimum ages (usually 25). Some branches rent to drivers age 21-24 for an additional (often steep) charge, but policies vary from agency to agency. **Alamo** (☎800-462-5266; www.alamo.com), **Dollar** (☎800-800-3665; www.dollar.com), **Enterprise** (☎800-736-8222; www.enterprise.com), and **Thrifty** (☎800-367-2277; www.thrifty.com) all rent to ages 21-24 for varying surcharges. **Rent-A-Wreck** (☎800-944-7501; www.rent-a-wreck.com) specializes in supplying vehicles that are past their prime for lower-than-average prices; a bare-bones compact less than eight years old rents for around $20-25 per day. There may be an additional charge for a **collision and damage waiver (CDW)**, which usually comes to about $12-15 per day. Major credit cards (including Visa, MasterCard, and AmEx) will sometimes cover the CDW if you use their card to rent a car; call your credit-card company for specifics.

Because it is mandatory in all states, check that you are covered by **insurance.** Be sure to ask whether the price includes insurance against theft and collision. Some credit cards cover standard insurance. If you rent, lease, or borrow a car and you are not from the US or Canada, you will need a **green card,** or **International Insurance Certificate,** to certify that you have liability insurance that applies abroad. Green cards can be obtained at car-rental agencies, car dealerships, and some travel agents and border crossings. Driving a con-

ventional rental on an unpaved road is almost never covered by insurance.

Instead of a traditional rental, **Adventures on Wheels,** 42 Hwy. 36, Middletown, NJ 07748 (☎800-943-3579 or 732-495-0959; www.wheels9.com), will sell you a motor home, minivan, station wagon, or compact car, organize its registration and insurance, and guarantee that they will buy it back after your travels. Cars with a buy-back guarantee start at $2500. Buy a camper van for $6500, use it for six months, and sell it back for $3000-4000. The main office is in New Jersey; there are others in L.A., San Francisco, Las Vegas, Denver, and Miami. Vehicles can be picked up at one office and dropped off at another.

CAR TRANSPORT SERVICES

Car transport services match drivers with car owners who need cars moved from one city to another. Would-be travelers give the company their desired destination and the company finds a car that needs to go there. Expenses include gas, tolls, and your own living expenses. Some companies insure their cars; with others, your security deposit covers any breakdowns or damage. You must be over 21, have a valid license, and agree to drive about 400 mi. per day on a fairly direct route. More info on auto transport options (including overseas and listings by state) can be found at www.movecars.com. **Auto Driveaway Co.,** 310 S. Michigan Ave., Chicago, IL 60604 (☎800-346-2277; www.autodriveaway.com) is one such company.

CAMPERS AND RVS

Much to the chagrin of purist outdoorsmen, the US and Canada are havens for the home-and-stove on wheels known as the **recreational vehicle (RV).** Most national parks and small towns cater to RV travelers, providing campgrounds with large parking areas and electrical outlets ("full hookup"). The costs of RVing compare favorably with the price of staying in hotels and renting a car, and the convenience of bringing along your own bedroom, bathroom, and kitchen makes it an attractive option. **Renting** is also a possibility. **Cruise America,** 11 W. Hampton Ave., Mesa, AZ 85210 (☎800-671-8042; www.cruiseamerica.com)

rents and sells RVs in the US and Canada. Rates vary widely by region, season (July and Aug. are most expensive), and type, but prices for a standard RV are around $800 per week.

MOTORCYCLES

The revving engine, worn leather, and wind-in-your-face thrill of motorcycling have built up a cult following, but motorcycling is one of the most dangerous ways to experience the open road. ⬛**Helmets** are required in many states and always recommended; wear the best one you can find. Those considering long trips should contact the **American Motorcyclist Association**, 13515 Yarmouth Dr., Pickerington, OH 43147 (☎800-262-5646; www.ama-cycle. org), the linchpin of US biker culture. And, of course, take a copy of Robert Pirsig's *Zen and the Art of Motorcycle Maintenance.*

CAR SAFETY

ROAD RULES

While driving, be sure to buckle up. ⬛**Seat belts** are required by law in many regions of the US and Canada. *Let's Go* does not recommend hitchhiking under any circumstances; it is particularly dangerous for women and solo travelers. It is *never* a good idea to pick up hitchhikers.

The **speed limit** in the US varies considerably from region to region. Most urban highways have a limit of 55 mph (89km per hr.), while rural routes range from 65 mph (104km per hr.) to 75 mph (120km per hr.). Heed the speed limit; not only does it save gas, but most local police forces and state troopers make use of radar to catch speed demons. The speed limit in Canada is 50km per hr. (31 mph) in cities and 80km per hr. (49 mph) on highways. On rural highways, the speed limit may be 100km per hr. (62 mph).

Don't tailgate. Most rear-end collisions are a result of following too closely, so use the **two-second rule** to determine a safe following distance—choose a fixed object ahead of you on the road and start counting slowly when the vehicle in front of you passes it. If you reach the object before two seconds, you're following too closely.

Driving at night requires extra caution. Switch from your brights to normal lights so as not to blind any oncoming drivers and stay alert. Be aware of **weather conditions** and drive appropriately. Try to avoid **driving in fog,** but, if you must, go slowly and keep your headlights on dim or use fog lights. In the **rain,** roads get slippery, so it's a good idea to slow down and allow extra time for braking, especially right after it has started raining and roads are slick with dust and oil. In most states, drivers are required to keep their headlights on while it's raining, even during the day.

Finally, **winter driving** can be especially hazardous; be aware of the temperature and of road conditions. It can be hard to tell if roads are icy (bridges and overpasses can be icy even when the rest of the road is clear), and braking can take extra time.

BEFORE YOU LEAVE

It's a good idea to have your car checked over by a mechanic a few weeks before you depart to allow time to fix any problems. Things like worn brakes or strained shocks, while not always in need of immediate replacement, may fail after you've put them through a rigorous, long-distance roadtrip.

Fuel-injected vehicles may benefit from a few doses of **fuel system cleaner** both before you go and while on the road—though it might cost you $10-15 per bottle (typically, 1 bottle is dumped into 1 tank of gas), it is cheaper than having the fuel system overhauled. At the same time, don't consider cleaner a substitute for necessary repairs uncovered during a pre-departure inspection.

In order to make minor repairs to your car or to keep it moving after a problem, you will need to carry several tools, including **wrenches** (an adjustable wrench can handle many sizes of bolts but may be too large for small spaces), a **flashlight** or two (a larger flashlight for illuminating things at night and a smaller pen light for slim crevices), a few good **screwdrivers** with both Phillips and flat-head ends (these should range in size from small to large and should be long enough to reach down into concealed engine spaces—if your vehicle has star, square, or other special types of screw, make sure that you have the correct screwdriver on hand), and a couple of different kinds of **pliers** (one for gripping larger items and a narrower needle-nosed pair for reaching into tight spaces).

Other vital items include extra oil, extra coolant, a jack, a tire iron, a full-size spare tire, a tire pressure gauge, road flares, hose sealant, a first-aid kit, jumper cables, extra windshield washer fluid, plastic sheeting, string or rope, a larger tow rope, duct tape, an ice scraper, rags, a funnel, a spray bottle filled with glass cleaner, a compass, matches, blankets, and food. Even if you don't have a tow hitch or are traveling alone, be sure to carry along a tow rope. Having a tow rope on hand will make it that much easier for others to help get you out of your jam.

CAR CARE ON THE ROAD

TIRE CARE

Check your **tire pressure** periodically throughout your trip. Most tires are stamped with the pressure to which they should be inflated. If not, look at the inside of your driver's side door or in your vehicle's owner's manual. The pressure is represented in pounds per square inch (PSI). You can use a **tire pressure gauge** to determine the PSI of your tires—this small tool is often shaped like a pen with a metal bulb at one end and will cost $10-40, depending on the model (digital models are typically priced higher). **Overinflation** and **underinflation** are both dangerous and can contribute to skidding, flats, and blowouts in addition to reducing your gas mileage.

Be aware that temperature shifts can have a large impact on tire PSI—make sure to check it after periods of changing temperature. Since hot temperatures will give you inaccurate readings, check the PSI after your tires have cooled down from driving. Regular tire maintenance should also include **tire rotations** every 6000 mi. If your tires are worn or bald, consider having them replaced entirely before taking a roadtrip. Tires that are dangerously worn can cause the car to start vibrating, producing lots of noise.

FLUID, HOSE, AND FILTER CARE

Long days of driving mean that you will need to change your **oil** and **oil filter** more frequently

than you would normally. Three thousand miles (4800km) should be the absolute maximum distance you drive before changing your oil. If conditions are extremely dusty, it may be necessary to change your oil even more frequently. You should check your oil level every few days by taking your vehicle's **dipstick** and sliding it into the engine's oil level test tube. The dipstick will often be resting in this tube, but, to get an accurate measurement, wipe it off first and then plunge it in and out of the tube, checking the actual oil level against the level recommended on the dipstick or in your vehicle's owner's manual. Test the level after your vehicle has been at rest for several minutes. If your level is low, add more oil.

Dust can also collect in your **air filter** and clog it. Though air filter replacements are normally recommended every 20,000 mi. (32,300km), you will want to have yours inspected during each oil change. Replacement air filters may cost $15-40, but, if your filter is dirty, the money will be well spent—your air filter doesn't just strain the junk out of your air. It also protects your fuel system.

Other essentials to have inspected before your journey and after hard driving include your **brake fluid, transmission fluid, fuel filter, automatic transmission filter,** and **spark plugs.** It is cheaper to replace these beforehand than to fix a single catastrophe caused by ignoring one of them.

Hoses and **belts** are extremely important to monitor for wear and damage—even very small problems with vacuum hoses, for instance, will prevent your vehicle from starting. **Fan belts** are notorious for snapping in the most remote places. It is worthwhile to carry along a few extra fan belts, but it is better to get failing belts replaced early. Replace any fan belt if it looks loose, cracked, glazed, or shiny. In an emergency, **panty hose** can serve as a temporary yet sultry substitute.

CHANGING A FLAT TIRE

To change a tire, you will need a **jack,** a sturdy **tire iron** capable of withstanding a couple hundred pounds of pressure, and a **full-size spare tire.** Park your vehicle securely on level ground with the emergency brake applied. Turn on your **emergency flashers** to alert other vehicles. At night, it may be helpful to light a couple **road flares,** especially if your vehicle is not entirely off of the road. Place the jack on smooth ground (you may need to lay down a flat board for the jack) and locate the place underneath the vehicle where the jack will do its lifting. These are usually flat panels close to each wheel. Locate this area and align it with the jack. Don't pump the jack yet—you will need to loosen the tire's **lugnuts.** If you have a **hubcap,** remove it and set it aside.

Practice changing your tire before you leave—if the lugnuts are fastened too tightly, they may be difficult or impossible for you to loosen on your own. Choose a lugnut to loosen, place the tire iron against it, and loosen it until it spins freely. After loosening the first lugnut, loosen the opposite lugnut. The third lugnut you loosen should be next to the first. The fourth will be opposite the third. Repeat this pattern until each one is loose.

Before jacking up the car, make sure your spare tire is on the ground outside of the car. Raise the jack slowly and carefully, making sure that your vehicle is stable. Never place anything else underneath the vehicle or reach under the vehicle while it is propped up by a jack. Use the jack to raise your vehicle far enough for your tire to rotate freely. Once the vehicle is raised, remove the loosened lugnuts and place them in your hubcap or another secure area. Carefully remove the tire.

Take the spare tire and align its holes with the tire studs on the wheel hub. If you can't see the tire's air valve facing you, the tire is probably on backwards. Once the spare tire is resting against the wheel hub, replace the lugnuts in the same order you removed them and tighten them down with your fingers. Do not use the tire iron yet. Slowly lower your vehicle, remove the jack, and use the tire iron to tighten the lugnuts. As with loosening, tighten the lugnuts in opposite pairs. Drive slowly for a few hundred feet to make sure that the tire is on correctly. Gradually increase your speed and make your way down to the next service station to buy yourself another spare.

OVERHEATING

In the US and some parts of Canada, summer days can be scorchingly hot. Take **several gallons of clean water** with you—this can be used for drinking or for pouring into your radiator

if you experience overheating or loss of coolant. Dedicate at least one gallon of water per person per day solely for drinking and carry a few additional gallons for your radiator. The water should be clean to prevent damage, though it is possible to use impure stream or lake water to top off your radiator. Just be sure to have the radiator flushed afterward. Also carry a gallon of coolant along with you. Coolant needs to be mixed with water after being poured into the radiator, so don't substitute water with more coolant.

On a hot day, you can help prevent overheating by turning off your **air-conditioning** system. This would seem to be exactly the time when you need air-conditioning the most, but it takes a toll on your vehicle's cooling mechanisms. If your car has a temperature gauge, check it frequently. If not, stop periodically and check for signs of overheating—any sort of boiling noise coming from under your hood is a strong indicator that you need to let the vehicle cool down for a while—and check your hoses for leaks. Turning the **heater** on full blast will also help cool the engine. If your car overheats, pull off the road and turn on the heater to let the engine blow off its steam. If radiator fluid is steaming or bubbling, turn off the car for 30min. or more. If not, run the car in neutral at about 1500 rpm for a few minutes, allowing the coolant to circulate. Never pour water over the engine and never try to lift a searingly hot hood. Be warned that, if you turn on the heater, the heat may actually be enough to melt the plastic fins that cover your car's vents—put them in an open and loose position in case they become trapped.

If you need to open your radiator cap, always wait 45min. or more, until the coolant inside of the radiator loses its heat—otherwise, you may be spattered with boiling coolant. Even after waiting, you may still be spattered with warm coolant, so stand to the side whenever opening the cap. Remember that "topping off" your radiator does not mean filling it completely. Instead, there is probably a tank or reservoir with a filling indicator somewhere near the radiator. Pour a small amount of water and coolant into the radiator (in a 50-50 mixture) and wait for it to work its way into the system and raise the reservoir. Some vehicles need the engine running in order to draw in the coolant.

Coolant leaks are sometimes just the product of pressure from overheating, which forces coolant out of the gaps between the hoses and their connections to the radiator. If, however, there are other holes in the hose, it helps to have hose sealant on hand. Many hose sealants also double as temporary gas-tank sealants and cost between $7-15. If you apply sealant, treat it as a very short-term solution and get the vehicle to a service station as soon as possible. Drive slowly and keep your heater on to avoid stressing the seal. Always put the radiator cap back on—coolant will erupt from your vehicle if you don't.

BATTERY FAILURES AND FLUBS

If you turn the key in the ignition and nothing happens or if the engine refuses to start, you may have a dead battery. Recharging the battery at a service station may be your only option if your battery is too drawn down. It helps to have the tools on hand to remove your battery (and often the accompanying battery cover) from your vehicle. A **screwdriver** and **wrench** are usually required for this task. However, your first option should be to try to **jump-start** your car. This may require waiting on the side of the road with your hood raised waiting for a helpful passerby, and it is one of the reasons why you should always have jumper cables on hand. Since many batteries are run down through simple carelessness (forgetting to turn off headlights, etc.), it's a good idea to devise a simple system to help you remember to turn off all your lights when leaving the vehicle. Also, many vehicles have lights in places that are not obvious, such as below the rearview mirror. Check these periodically to make sure that they are not on.

To safely jump-start your vehicle, position the two cars close to each other while making sure that there is no contact between them. Set the emergency brakes, turn off both engines, and take out the keys before you open the hoods. If the battery looks damaged or cracked, do not attempt to jump-start; you'll need to call for a tow. Identify the positive posts on both batteries and attach the red cable to the positive post of the dead battery, then to the positive post of

the working battery. Do not let the red clips contact the clips on the black cable. Attach one clip on the black cable to the negative post on the working battery, and then attach the other clip to bare metal on the disabled vehicle's engine frame (or another part of the disabled car with exposed, unpainted metal) as far as possible from the battery—otherwise, the battery's hydrogen gas could ignite. Start the working vehicle and rev it for a few moments before starting the disabled vehicle. Once both vehicles are running, disconnect the cables in reverse order, starting with the black cable attached to the bare metal. Do not kill the engines or allow the cables to contact each other until they are completely disconnected. Afterward, drive around for 30min. to allow the alternator to recharge the battery.

LEAVING YOUR KEYS IN THE CAR

Lockouts can be particularly troublesome in remote areas, since locksmiths are uncommon and often expensive. Prevent lockouts by keeping a **spare copy** of your vehicle's door key somewhere on your person at all times, perhaps in a money belt. If you do happen to find yourself locked out, it may be possible to get assistance from local police services. Though they may be reluctant to provide assistance if there are other options in the area, in some towns the police are the only agency with locksmithing equipment. Be prepared to prove your ownership of the vehicle afterward.

As a very last resort, if you simply cannot wait for the police, many vehicles have **small triangular windows** next to the main roll-down windows, especially in the rear. If you can reach the lock from this window, use a stone or other blunt object to break the glass. Take care not to cut yourself—wrap a cloth around your hand and arm before reaching for the lock. You can temporarily patch the damage with a **plastic sheet** or **tarp,** folded over several times until it is quite thick and taped to the car with **duct tape** on every edge. Keep it taut to resist the wind.

ROAD HAZARDS

SKIDDING

Avoid skids by reducing your speed if driving in wet or icy conditions. If you find yourself in a skid, **do not apply the brakes.** This will only make things worse and may cause your vehicle to roll over. Instead, at the beginning of a skid, ease off both the brake and gas. The most important thing to do is to control the steering wheel. Grip the wheel firmly with both hands. **Steer into the skid.** If you are skidding to the right, take the wheel and firmly turn it to the right. Once you feel the vehicle straightening out, carefully tug the wheel back toward a straight position. At this point, you may need to press down on the gas pedal a bit to push the vehicle onto its new course.

Afterward, slow down—you were probably skidding because you were traveling faster than you could safely handle. You may want to pull over and inspect your vehicle for damage. Prioritize a **brake inspection.** Your skid probably sapped a few months off the life of your brake pads.

BLOWOUTS

You should become familiar with the feel of your car under normal driving conditions— the first sign of a tire rupture will probably involve a change in the way the vehicle feels while you are driving. A deflating tire may not be obvious at first, especially if you have the windows rolled up or are playing loud music. You might notice that the car doesn't turn as easily, or it might feel a bit more wobbly than usual. Pull over to a safe place at the first sign of trouble—make sure that you stop somewhere off the road, away from blind corners, and on level ground. You will feel a tire blowout (or tread separation) right away—the car will suddenly become much more difficult to steer, especially on turns, and you may be tugged in a particular direction.

To handle a tire blowout, absolutely **do not slam on the brakes,** even though this may be your first instinct. A blown tire (especially a blown front tire) will reduce your braking capability, and slamming on the brakes will just send you into an uncontrolled skid—at worst, the car may even roll over. The same advice applies to steering—even though your vehicle may be pulled out of its original direction, don't compensate by wrenching the wheel forcefully the other way around. Instead, grip the wheel firmly while you take your foot off the gas, steering only enough to keep the vehicle

in a straight line or away from obstructions. Let the vehicle come to a complete stop— don't worry about damaging the wheel of the blown tire, since a blowout is an emergency situation, and your safety is more important.

CRITTERS

One of the dangers of driving in rural areas is that long distances and straight roads tend to lull you into complacency. You might not check the speedometer as often as you should, or you might be tempted to gaze at the scenery instead of the road. This may seem safe for stretches at a time, but don't do it—some areas of the US are rife with wildlife that like to play in the road, such as deer, moose, elk, opossums, raccoons, turtles, or bears. If you aren't paying attention, you could find yourself poised to collide with any one of these creatures. (And don't forget to make way for ducklings.)

TRUCKS AND GRAVEL

Roads are repaired in sections, so you may find yourself cruising comfortably on a smooth road when the pavement suddenly ends and your excessive speed sends you slamming into deep potholes and roadside brush. One useful indicator of potential road trouble is the presence of **black tire marks**—these are created by the tag axles of large trucks as they hit dips in the road. If you see these markings, reduce your speed dramatically.

The large number of RVs and trucks on the road means that you could easily suffer a chipped or cracked windshield from flying debris—if you see a large vehicle trundling toward you on the road, pull as far away from the center as possible and slow down. Hopefully, stones flung in your direction will just bounce off your windshield if you keep it slow. You can take other measures to reduce the risk of rock damage. Consider having **protective covers** placed on your headlights.

STEEP GRADES

Some parts of the road ascend **steep grades.** Make sure that your **brake system** is in good order before you set out and particularly that your brake pads aren't worn. Don't attempt to run up steep hills too quickly—it might cause your car to overheat or your transmission to blow. On downhill grades, go slower than you typically would, since controlling a skid on a downhill slope is one of the hardest things you should never have to do. Travel slowly in case you meet an oncoming truck—flung gravel will punish reckless speeders. Finally, if you blow a tire on a slope (much more likely if you speed), you will need to keep going until you find a flat and level place to stop, meaning that you might have to absorb damage to your wheels.

INCIDENTS AND ACCIDENTS

If you see flashing lights in your rearview mirror, you're being **pulled over.** Slow down and move onto the shoulder as soon as you can. Turn off the engine, keep your hands on the wheel, and wait for an officer to come to your window. Don't fumble for your license and registration until you're asked for it. Excuses usually won't get you out of a ticket, but respect and courtesy go a long way.

If you're involved in an **accident,** even a minor fender-bender, stay calm and call the police. Never move an injured person unless he or she is in danger, but do move your car out of traffic if you can. Exchange info with the other driver involved; get the driver's license number, insurance company info, address, phone number, and license-plate number as well as the names and contact information of any witnesses. You may need to file an accident report and contact your insurance company.

CAR ASSISTANCE

In addition to ☎**911** service in the US and Canada, most **automobile clubs** offer free towing, emergency roadside assistance, travel-related discounts, and random goodies in exchange for a modest membership fee. Travelers should strongly consider membership in one if planning an extended roadtrip.

▨ **American Automobile Association (AAA;** ☎800-222-4357; www.aaa.com). Emergency assistance, free trip-planning services, maps, guidebooks, and 24hr. emergency road service anywhere in the US. Free towing and commission-free AmEx Travelers Cheques from over 1000 offices across the country. Discounts on Hertz car rental (5-20%) and various motel chains and theme parks. Basic membership $48, each extra person $24. To sign up, call ☎800-564-6222.

Canadian Automobile Association (CAA), 1145 Hunt Club Rd., #200, Ottawa, ON K1V 0Y3 (☎800-222-4357; www.caa.ca). Affiliated with AAA (above), the CAA provides the same membership benefits, including 24hr. emergency roadside assistance, free maps and tourbooks, route planning, and various discounts. Basic membership CDN$70-90. Call ☎800-564-6222 for membership services.

KEEPING IN TOUCH

BY INTERNET

GETTING ONLINE

WIRELESS

Increasingly, travelers find that taking their **laptop computers** on the road is a convenient way to stay connected. Many accommodations and restaurants now offer Wi-Fi. Travelers who own wireless-enabled computers (almost all modern laptops are wireless-enabled) can take advantage of an ever-increasing number of Internet "hot spots" and get online for free or for a small fee. Newer computers can detect these hot spots automatically; otherwise, websites like www.jiwire.com, www.wififreespot.com, and www.wi-fihotspotlist.com can help you find them. "Stealing" wireless Internet from an open private network is sometimes an option but is not endorsed by *Let's Go* (below).

WARY WI-FI. Wireless hot spots make Internet access possible in public and remote places. However, they also pose **security risks.** Hot spots are public, open networks that use unencrypted, unsecured connections. They are susceptible to hacks and "packet sniffing"—ways of stealing passwords and other private information. To prevent problems, disable ad hoc mode, turn off file sharing and network discovery, encrypt your email, turn on your firewall, beware of phony networks, and watch for over-the-shoulder creeps.

ETHERNET

Local area networks (LAN) connect computers within a building or a small group of buildings. The most common LAN design since the mid-70s has been **ethernet.** Today, some accommodations and restaurants offer patrons the chance to hook into a LAN through an ethernet cable. These cables can often be rented at a hostel, motel, or hotel front desk, or occasionally it is permitted to use one's own cable. Traveling with an ethernet cable, while certainly not necessary, might be a convenient alternative to Wi-Fi for roadtrippers.

SOMEONE ELSE'S COMPUTER

There are many opportunities in the US to access the Internet from a computer other than your own laptop. Accommodations, particularly hostels and hotels, often have a computer in the lobby for visitors' convenience. Many **public libraries** have computers that are open to the public. Nearly every US town has its own **Internet cafe;** *Let's Go* lists the locations of these cybercafes in the **Vital Stats** sections of major cities.

ONLINE

EMAIL

Free **web-based email accounts** (e.g., ✉**www. gmail.com** and **www.hotmail.com**) allow roadtrippers to access their Internet accounts from any computer, anywhere. Web-based email sends instantly and archives old mail; it is a great method for communicating with loved ones from a distance.

SOCIAL NETWORKING

Many travelers find that social networks such as **Facebook** (www.facebook.com) and **MySpace** (www.myspace.com) are a convenient and low-key way to maintain relationships with friends back home while far away. **Blogging** has grown in popularity among travelers as a less intrusive alternative to the mass update email. Social networking websites and blogs often permit users to upload photos to the Internet, where they can be viewed by friends and family members back home.

SKYPE, ETC.

Programs such as ✉**Skype** (www.skype.com) and **Google Talk** (www.google.com/talk) have begun to offer free computer-to-computer voice calls. Such programs are often offered in conjunction with older instant-messaging technology and with newer video technology. Some software allows users to purchase minutes (available in monthly or pay-as-you-go plans), which can be used to make computer-to-landline calls—even overseas—at a low cost. **Webcams** are built into many new computers and can be attached to old computers through a USB port. Voice-and-video calls are lifelike and can help combat homesickness when it strikes.

BY TELEPHONE

CELL PHONES

Cell phones are ubiquitous in the US; on first dates, in business meetings, and in lecture halls across the country, individuals shamefacedly regret choosing R. Kelly ring tones. There are two basic ways to pay for a cell phone: in advance or through monthly bills. In either case, you must first buy your own cell phone ($40-400) with a **Subscriber Identity Module (SIM) card,** a thumbnail-size chip that gives you a local phone number and plugs the phone into the local network. Cell phones are sold at retail stores run by major service providers, as well as at electronics stores like RadioShack and big-box stores like Best Buy, Costco, and Wal-Mart. After purchasing a phone, you can, through a service provider such as AT&T, Sprint Nextel, Verizon, or T-Mobile, either purchase a prepaid number of minutes, or enter into a longer (often 2-year) billing arrangement, in which you'll be billed monthly. For those traveling for fewer than two years, a prepaid plan is almost certainly preferable to a two-year contract—the latter is notoriously difficult to get out of early. The company **Cellular Abroad** (www.cellularabroad. com) rents cell phones that work in a variety of destinations around the world, useful for the roadtripper coming from another country or for an American roadtripper considering jaunts into Canada and Mexico.

PAY PHONES

The simplest way to make domestic calls is to use a coin-operated phone. Carry quarters. Prepaid calling cards (available at mini-marts, big-box stores, grocery stores, newspaper kiosks, and tobacco stores) also work from a pay phone and can save time and money in the long run.

CALLING CARDS

Another option is to purchase a **calling card**, linked to a major telecommunications service. Calls are billed collect or to your account. To call home with a calling card, contact the operator for your service provider in the US by dialing the appropriate toll-free access number (listed below in the third column).

COMPANY	TO OBTAIN A CARD:	TO CALL OVERSEAS:
AT&T (US)	www.att.com	☎800-364-9292
Canada Direct	www.infocanadadirect.com	☎800-561-8868
MCI (US)	www.minutepass.com	☎800-777-5000
Telecom New Zealand Direct	www.telecom.co.nz	☎+64 3 374 0253
Telstra Australia	www.telstra.com	☎+61 1800 065 908

INTERNATIONAL CALLS

Prepaid phone cards are a common and relatively inexpensive means of calling abroad. Each one comes with a Personal Identification Number (PIN) and a toll-free access number. You call the access number and then follow the directions for dialing your PIN. To purchase prepaid phone cards, check online for the best rates; www.callingcards.com is a good place to start. Online providers generally send your access number and PIN via email, with no actual "card" involved.

> **PLACING INTERNATIONAL CALLS.** To call abroad from home or to call home from abroad, dial:
> 1. The **international dialing prefix**. To call from **Australia**, dial 0011; **Canada** or the **US**, 011; **Ireland, New Zealand**, or the **UK**, 00.
> 2. The **country code** of the country you want to call. To call **Australia**, dial 61; **Canada** or the **US**, 1; **Ireland**, 353; **New Zealand**, 64; the **UK**, 44.
> 3. The **city/area code**.
> 4. The **local number**.

Placing a collect call through an international operator can be expensive but may be necessary in case of an emergency. You can frequently call collect without even possessing a company's calling card just by calling its access number and following the instructions.

TIME DIFFERENCES

In the continental US, there are four different time zones: **Eastern Standard Time (EST)**, which comprises roughly the states on the Atlantic coast and the eastern two thirds of the Ohio Valley, **Central Standard Time (CST)**, which comprises the Gulf Coast, Tennessee Valley, and Great Plains, **Mountain Standard Time (MST)**, which comprises the Rocky Mountains, and **Pacific Standard Time (PST)**, which comprises the states on the Pacific coast, plus Nevada.

Each US state has officially chosen to apply one of the following two rules regarding **Daylight Saving Time (DST)** to its entire territory. Most use the standard time for their zone but do use DST during the summer months. DST begins on the second Sunday in March and ends on the first Sunday in November. Note, that Indiana didn't begin to observe DST until 2006, and Arizona and Hawaii still don't.

5AM	6AM	7AM	8AM	1PM	11PM*
Seattle L.A. Las Vegas	Denver Boise	Chicago Graceland	Toronto Boston Miami	London	Sydney Melbourne

*Note that Australia observes Daylight Saving Time from October to March, the opposite of the Northern Hemisphere. Therefore, it is 14hr. ahead of Boston from March to October and 16hr. ahead from November to March, for an average of 15hr. ahead.

BY SNAIL MAIL

SENDING MAIL

Within the US, the **United States Postal Service (USPS)** is the most affordable mail carrier. Nearly every town has a post office. *Let's Go* lists post offices in the **Vital Stats** section for each city and most towns. Rates vary with type of parcel (postcard, letter, large envelope, package, or large package), speed of delivery, and destination. Large postcards and letters, in general, cost $0.42 to send at standard speed to any domestic destination. Exhaustive information on rates can be found at the USPS's user-friendly website, www.usps.com. Private mail carriers include **DHL, Federal Express (FedEx),** and the **United Parcel Service (UPS).** These carriers, while at times more expensive than the USPS, are very reliable.

INTERNATIONAL MAIL

SENDING IT

To ensure timely delivery of mail that you're sending abroad, mark envelopes "airmail." In addition to the standard postage system whose rates are listed below, FedEx (Australia ☎ +61 13 26 10, Canada and the US 800-463-3339, Ireland +353 800 535 800, New Zealand +64 800 733 339, the UK +44 8456 070 809; www.fedex.com) handles express mail services from the US to most countries.

International surface mail is by far the cheapest and slowest way to send mail. It takes one to two months to cross the Atlantic and one to three to cross the Pacific—good for heavy items you won't need for a while, such as your keepsake replica of the world's largest hairball. These are standard rates for mail from the US to:

- **Australia:** Allow 6-10 days for regular airmail. Postcards cost $0.94. Letters up to 1 oz. cost $0.94; packages up to 5 lb. $40.50, up to 10 lb. $59.25.
- **Canada:** Allow 6-10 days for regular airmail. Postcards cost $0.72. Letters up to 1 oz. cost $0.72; packages up to 5 lb. $22.60, up to 10 lb. $30.10. Note that the shipment of "used or secondhand hives or bee supplies" is prohibited.
- **UK:** Allow 6-10 days for regular airmail. Postcards cost $0.94. Letters up to 1 oz. cost $0.94; packages up to 5 lb. $37.50, up to 10 lb. $52.50.

RECEIVING IT

There are several ways to arrange pickup of letters sent from abroad. Mail can be sent via **General Delivery** to almost any city or town in the US with a post office, and it is very reliable. Address General Delivery letters like:

Thomas PYNCHON
General Delivery
Humptulips, WA 98552
USA

The mail will go to a special desk in the central post office unless you specify a specific post office by street address or postal code. It's best to use the largest post office, since mail may be sent there regardless. It is usually safer and quicker, though more expensive, to send mail express or registered. Bring your passport (or other photo ID) for pickup; there may be a small fee. If the clerks insist that there is nothing for you, ask them to check under your first name as well.

American Express's travel offices throughout the world offer a free **Client Letter Service** (mail held up to 30 days and forwarded upon request) for cardholders who contact them in advance. Some offices provide these services to non-cardholders (especially AmEx Travelers Cheque holders), but call ahead to make sure; for a complete list, call ☎ 800-528-4800 or visit www.americanexpress.com/travel.

ACCOMMODATIONS

GET A BED

HOSTELS

Many hostels are laid out dorm-style, often with large single-sex rooms and bunk beds, although private rooms that sleep two to four are becoming more common. Hostels sometimes have kitchens and utensils for your use, bike rentals, storage areas, transportation to airports, breakfast and other meals, laundry facilities, and Internet. However, there can be drawbacks: some hostels close during certain daytime "lockout" hours, have a curfew, don't accept reservations, impose a maximum stay, or, less frequently, require that you do chores. In the US, a dorm bed in a hostel will average around $25 per night and a private room around $50. Hostels and other types of establishments that offer similar sleeping arrangements (universities, YMCAs and YWCAs) are a great (and usually not too sketchy) place to meet other travelers.

> **A HOSTELER'S BILL OF RIGHTS.** There are certain standard features that we do not include in our hostel listings. Unless we state otherwise, you can expect that every hostel has no lockout, no curfew, free hot showers, some system of secure luggage storage, and no key deposit.

HOSTELLING INTERNATIONAL

Joining the youth hostel association in your own country (listed below), be it the US or elsewhere, automatically grants you membership privileges with **Hostelling International (HI),** a federation of national hosteling associations. Non-HI members may be allowed to stay in hostels, but they will have to pay extra to do so. HI hostels are scattered throughout the US and may or may not be less expensive than private hostels. HI's umbrella organization's website (www.hihostels.com), which lists the web addresses and phone numbers of all national associations, can be a great place to begin researching hosteling in a specific region. Other comprehensive hosteling websites include www.hostels.com.

Most HI hostels also honor **guest memberships**—you'll get a blank card with space for six validation stamps. Each night you'll pay a nonmember supplement (one-sixth the membership fee) and earn one guest stamp; six stamps make you a member. This system works well in most of Western Europe, but in the US you will most likely need to remind the hostel reception about HI. A new membership benefit is the FreeNites program, which allows hostelers to gain points toward free rooms. Most student travel agencies (p. 28) sell HI cards, as do all of the national hosteling organizations listed below. All prices listed below are valid for one-year memberships unless otherwise noted.

Australian Youth Hostels Association (AYHA), 422 Kent St., Sydney, NSW 2000 (☎+61 2 9261 1111; www.yha.com.au). AUS$52, under 18 AUS$19.

Hostelling International-Canada (HI-C), 205 Catherine St., Ste. 400, Ottawa, ON K2P 1C3 (☎613-237-7884; www.hihostels.ca). CDN$35, under 18 free.

Hostelling International Northern Ireland (HINI), 22-32 Donegall Rd., Belfast BT12 5JN (☎+44 28 9032 4733; www.hini.org.uk). UK£15, under 25 UK£10.

Youth Hostels Association of New Zealand Inc. (YHANZ), Level 1, 166 Moorhouse Ave., P.O. Box 436, Christchurch (☎+64 3 379 9970, in NZ 0800 278 299; www.yha.org.nz). NZ$40, under 18 free.

Youth Hostels Association (England and Wales), Trevelyan House, Dimple Rd., Matlock, Derbyshire DE4 3YH (☎+44 8707 708 868; www.yha.org.uk). UK£16, under 26 UK£10.

Hostelling International-USA, 8401 Colesville Rd., Ste. 600, Silver Spring, MD 20910 (☎301-495-1240; www.hiayh.org). $28, under 18 free.

UNIVERSITY DORMS

Many **colleges** and **universities** open their residence halls to travelers when school is not in session; some do so even during term time. Getting a room may demand advance planning and several patient phone calls, but rates tend to be low and many student residences offer free local calls and Internet access.

YMCAS AND YWCAS

Young Men's Christian Association (YMCA) and **Young Women's Christian Association (YWCA)** lodgings are usually more expensive than a hostel but cheaper than a hotel. Not all locations offer lodging; those that do are often located in urban areas. Many YMCAs accept women and families; some will not lodge those under 18 without parental permission.

YMCA of the USA, 101 N. Wacker Dr., Chicago, IL 60606 (☎800-872-9622; www.ymca.net). Provides a listing of the nearly 1000 Ys across the US and Canada as well as info on prices and services.

YWCA of the USA, 1015 18th St. NW, Ste. 1100, Washington, DC 20036 (☎202-467-0801; www.ywca.org). Provides a directory of YWCAs across the US.

YMCA Canada, 42 Charles St. E., 6th fl., Toronto, ON M4Y 1T4 (☎416-967-9622; www.ymca.ca). Offers info on Ys in Canada.

GET A ROOM

HOTELS AND MOTELS

Hotels and motels, especially those catering to budget travelers, may not differ much. In general, hotels are slightly more expensive than motels, have common spaces, and offer basic amenities. Motels, by contrast, consist of little more than an office, a row of bedrooms with plain walls and inexpensive double beds, and a parking lot. In a small hotel, you may share a bathroom; in most motels, however, each room has its own bathroom. Rates at hotels and motels are often comparable. In the US, budget hotel and motel rooms cost about $50-100 per night. If you make **reservations** in writing, indicate your night of arrival and the number of nights you plan to stay. The hotel or motel will send you a confirmation and may request payment for the first night.

It is often convenient to book a hotel or motel in advance online. Websites such as **Expedia** (www.expedia.com) and **HotelReservations.com** (www.hotelreservations.com) offer easy Internet booking and (at times) special discount rates.

BED AND BREAKFASTS (B&BS)

For a cozy alternative to impersonal hotel and motel rooms, B&Bs (private homes with rooms available to travelers) range from acceptable to sublime. Rooms in B&Bs generally cost $100-200. Many websites provide listings for B&Bs; check out **Bed & Breakfast Inns Online** (www.bbonline.com), **InnFinder** (www.inncrawler.com), **InnSite** (www.innsite.com), **BedandBreakfast.com** (www.bedandbreakfast.com), or **BNB-Finder.com** (www.bnbfinder.com).

HOME EXCHANGES AND HOSPITALITY CLUBS

Home exchanges, in which two individuals or groups of people trade houses for any length of time, offer travelers various types of homes (houses, apartments, condominiums, and villas), plus the opportunity to live like natives and to cut down on accommodation fees. While home exchanges and roadtripping may not usually go hand-in-hand, a home base can make for easy and comfortable day outings, particularly when traveling with children or with adults who act like them. For more information, contact **HomeExchange.com Inc.,** P.O. Box 787, Hermosa Beach, CA 90254 (☎310-798-3864 or toll-free 800-877-8723; www.homeexchange.com) or **Intervac International Home Exchange** (www.intervac.com).

Hospitality clubs link their members with individuals or families abroad who are willing to host travelers for free or for a small fee to promote cultural exchange and general good karma. In exchange, members usually must be willing to host travelers in their own homes; a small fee may also be required. **The Hospitality Club** (www.hospitalityclub.org) is a good place to start. **Servas** (www.servas.org) is an established, more formal, peace-based organization and requires a fee and an interview to join. An Internet search will find many similar organizations, some of which cater to special interests (e.g., women, GLBT travelers, or members of certain professions). As always, use common sense when planning to stay with or host someone you do not know.

LONG-TERM ACCOMMODATIONS

Travelers planning to stay in the US for extended periods of time may find it most cost-effective to **rent an apartment.** A basic one-bedroom (or studio) apartment in Manhattan (New York City, not Kansas) costs as much as $1000-4000 per month. In smaller cities, though, rent is more affordable; in Austin, Texas, a studio apartment runs $500-1500 per month. Besides the rent itself, prospective tenants are usually also required to front a security deposit (frequently 1 month's rent).

ESSENTIALS

Another, possibly less expensive option is subletting an apartment or renting it from a renter. Subletting is particularly common in college and university towns during the summer months. The websites www.sublet.com and www.subletsearch.com list many subletting options in different cities.

When renting or subletting an apartment, one can either go through a real-estate agent or deal with the renter or subletter directly. Websites such as www.craigslist.org or Google's housing search (http://base.google.com) can make the apartment-search process easier by putting individuals directly in contact with one another.

GET OUT

CAR CAMPING

The roadtripper will find that car camping is a great way to travel for cheap as well as an opportunity to experience America's outdoors. By carrying basic camping equipment (see **Camping and Hiking Equipment,** p. 46) you can take advantage of ready-made drive-up campgrounds nationwide. Campgrounds often have basic amenities, including a fire pit, outhouses, picnic tables, potable water, utility hookups such as gas, water, electricity, plumbing, and trash cans. In high-traffic national parks, camping elsewhere than in a designated campground is often illegal. In high-traffic parks and urban areas, spontaneous camping is thought by some to be damaging to the environment and is associated with vagrancy. Many less trafficked campgrounds, however, particularly those with few sites, often require reservations.

BACKCOUNTRY CAMPING

If your car's cramped conditions have you aching to stretch your legs, perhaps the time is right for a night of backcountry camping. **Backpacking** combines hiking with camping; it is both free (or nearly free) and great exercise. In many national and state parks and forests, in order to backpack and camp you need a wilderness permit (free)—available at the park or forest's ranger station. For popular destinations like the Tuolumne Meadows

trailhead in Yosemite National Park, permits may need to be booked several months in advance. For more information on outdoor activities, see **The Great Outdoors,** below.

THE GREAT OUTDOORS

The **Great Outdoor Recreation Page** (www.gorp.com) provides excellent general information for travelers planning on camping or enjoying the outdoors.

 LEAVE NO TRACE. Let's Go encourages travelers to embrace the "Leave No Trace" ethic, minimizing their impact on natural environments and protecting wilderness for future generations. Trekkers and wilderness enthusiasts should set up camp on durable surfaces, use cookstoves instead of campfires, bury human waste away from water supplies, pack out trash, and respect wildlife and natural objects. For more detailed information, contact the **Leave No Trace Center for Outdoor Ethics,** P.O. Box 997, Boulder, CO 80306 (☎800-332-4100 or 303-442-8222; www.lnt.org).

USEFUL RESOURCES

A variety of publishing companies offer guidebooks to meet the needs of novice or expert hikers. For information about camping, hiking, and biking, write or call the publishers listed below to receive a free catalog.

The Mountaineers Books, 1001 SW Klickitat Way, Ste. 201, Seattle, WA 98134 (☎206-223-6303; www.mountaineersbooks.org). Over 600 titles on hiking, biking, mountaineering, natural history, and conservation.

Sierra Club Books, 85 2nd St., 2nd fl., San Francisco, CA 94105 (☎415-977-5500; www.sierraclub.org). Publishes general books on hiking and camping as well as specific guides by region.

Woodall Publications Corporation, 2575 Vista Del Mar Dr., Ventura, CA 93001 (☎877-680-6155; www.woodalls.com). Annually updates campground directories.

NATIONAL PARKS

National parks protect the most spectacular scenery in North America. Their primary purpose is preservation, but the parks also host recreational activities such as ranger talks, guided hikes, skiing, and snowshoe expeditions. For more info, contact the **National Park Service,** 1849 C St. NW, Washington, DC 20240 (☎202-208-6843; www.nps.gov).

The larger and more popular parks charge a $20-30 entry fee for cars. The **America the Beautiful Annual Pass** ($80), available at park entrances, allows the pass holder's party entry into all national parks for one year. National parks passes can also be bought through the **National Park Foundation,** 1201 Eye St. NW, Ste. 550B, Washington, DC 20005 (☎202-354-6460; www.nationalparks.org). Senior citizens aged 62 and older qualify for the **America the Beautiful Senior Pass** ($10), a lifetime pass that entitles the holder's party to free park entry, a 50% discount on camping, and reductions on various recreational fees. People eligible for federal disability benefits can enjoy the same privileges with the free **America the Beautiful Access Pass** (this page).

Most national parks have both backcountry and developed camping. Some welcome RVs, and a few offer grand lodges. At the more popular parks, reservations are essential and available through a user-friendly website hosted by the **National Recreation Reservation Service** (☎877-444-6777, outside US 518-885-3639; www.recreation.gov). You can book up to one year in advance at many campgrounds. Smaller campgrounds often observe policies of first come, first served, and many fill up by late morning.

NATIONAL FORESTS

Often less accessible and less crowded than national parks, national forests (www.fs.fed.us) are a purist's alternative. While some have recreation facilities, most are equipped only for primitive camping—pit toilets and non-potable water are the norm. When charged, entrance fees are $10-20, but camping is generally $3-4 or free. Necessary wilderness permits for backpackers can be obtained at the US Forest Service field offices in the area. The **Guide to Your National Forests** is available at all Forest Service branches and the main office at 1400 Independence Ave. SW, Washington, DC 20250. (☎202-205-1760.) This booklet includes a list of all national forest addresses; request maps and other info directly from the forests you plan to visit. Reservations are available for most forests with a $9 service fee, but they are usually only needed during high season at the more popular sites. Call the **National Recreation Reservation Service** (see above) up to one year in advance.

STATE PARKS

State parks are maintained by (you guessed it) states; most states operate comprehensive websites that introduce their parks and allow visitors to make camping reservations and obtain backpacking permits.

WILDERNESS SAFETY

Staying **warm, dry,** and **well hydrated** is key to a happy and safe wilderness experience. For any hike, prepare yourself for an emergency by packing a first-aid kit, a reflector, a whistle, high-energy food, extra water, raingear, a hat, mittens, and extra socks. For warmth, wear wool or insulating synthetic materials designed for the outdoors.

Check weather forecasts often and pay attention to the skies when hiking, as weather patterns can change suddenly. Always let someone—a friend, your hostel, or a park ranger—know when and where you are headed. See **Safety and Health,** p. 22, for information on outdoor medical concerns.

MAN VERSUS NATURE

BEARS

If you are hiking in an area frequented by bears, sing or make noise as you walk to warn them of your approach. If you see a bear, keep your distance. Steer clear of bear cubs; their moms are usually nearby and tend to be aggressive when they sense danger (you) between themselves and their cubs. No matter how cute bears may appear, don't be fooled—they are powerful and dangerous animals. If you see a bear at a distance, calmly walk (don't run) in the other direction. If the bear pursues you, back away slowly while speaking in low, firm tones. If you are attacked by a bear, get in a fetal position to protect yourself, put your arms over your neck, and play dead. Remain calm and don't make any loud noises or sudden movements. Don't leave food or other scented items (e.g., trash, toiletries, Cheerios, the clothes that you cooked in) near your car or tent. Putting these objects into canisters is now mandatory in some national parks. **Bear-bagging**—hanging edibles and other good-smelling objects far from camp in a tree out of reach of hungry paws—is the best way to keep your toothpaste from becoming a condiment. Bears are also attracted to any perfume, as are bugs; cologne, scented soap, deodorant, and hairspray should stay at home.

MOOSE

Mountainous regions are stomping grounds for moose. These big, antlered animals have been known to charge humans, so never feed, walk toward, or throw anything at a moose. If a moose charges, get behind a tree. If it attacks, get on the ground in a fetal position and stay still.

MOUNTAIN LIONS

In the American Southwest, you'll find no moose, but you may encounter a mountain lion. When it comes to mountain lions, preventing an encounter really is your best survival strategy; the cats are naturally shy, so when hiking make a lot of noise. If confronted by a mountain lion, do not move. Instead, try to make your body appear as large as possible by raising your hands above your head. Never start running or stoop to pick up rocks, as this will cause you to look more like a deer, the mountain lion's prey of choice. Throwing rocks at a mountain lion

can make it skitter away, however, so it is not a bad idea to plan in advance and fill your pockets with small nuggets—just in case. If you've done this, when you raise your hands above your head, you can hurl a few rocks in the mountain lion's direction.

SNAKES

Poisonous snakes are hazards in many areas of North America and should be avoided. The two most dangerous are coral snakes and rattlesnakes. **Coral snakes** reside in the American Southwest and Mexico and can be identified by black, yellow, and red bands. **Rattlesnakes** live in desert and marsh areas and will shake the rattle at the end of their tail when threatened. Don't attempt to handle or kill a snake; if you see one, back away. If you are bitten, wash the wound with soap and water, apply a dry dressing (but not a tourniquet), immobilize the limb, and keep it below the level of the heart. Do not apply ice, as this may worsen the bite. Contrary to what *The Oregon Trail* computer game might lead you to believe, any sort of physical movement and, particularly, stringent exercise is *not* recommended for someone with a poisonous snakebite, as a faster heart rate will pump blood (and poison) more quickly through one's arteries. Seek immediate medical attention for any snakebite.

POISONOUS LIZARDS

In the desert areas of the American Southwest and Mexico, travelers should also be on the lookout for poisonous lizards. Two dangerous types of lizards are Gila monsters and Mexican beaded lizards. **Gila monsters** are large lizards (around 12-18 in.) with dark, highly textured skin marked by pinkish mottling and thick, stumpy tails. The **Mexican beaded lizard** resembles the Gila monster, but with uniform spots rather than bands of color. Both are poisonous, though they are docile in nature and unlikely to bite unless antagonized.

SCORPIONS

Not just desert dwellers, scorpions can be found throughout the grasslands, savannahs, jungles, and forests of North America. The coloration of these arachnids (8 legs, not 6) varies greatly, though they are generally brown or black. Scorpions range from the typical 1 in. to the more impressive (and scary) 8 in. and are active mostly at night. Scorpions usually sting in self-defense, and stings are usually excruciatingly painful but not life-threatening. Nevertheless, if stung, you should seek immediate medical attention.

MOSQUITOES

Mosquitoes will be your main source of agony during the summer. The volume of mosquitoes after spring thaw can be unbearable without some sort of protection. Though these creatures start cropping up in spring, peak season runs from June through August before tapering off at the approach of fall. Mosquitoes can bite through thin fabric, so cover up with thicker materials. Products with DEET are useful, but the mosquitoes sometimes can be so ravenous that nothing short of a mosquito hood and netting will stop the worst jabs. See **Staying Healthy,** p. 25.

CAMPING AND HIKING EQUIPMENT

WHAT TO BUY

Good camping equipment is both sturdy and light. North American suppliers tend to offer the most competitive prices.

Sleeping Bags: Most sleeping bags are rated by season; "summer" means 30-40°F (around 0°C) at night; "4-season" or "winter" often means below 0°F (-17°C). Bags are made of **down** (warm and light, but expensive, and miserable when wet) or of **synthetic** material (heavy, durable, and warm when wet). Prices range from $50-250 for a summer synthetic to $200-300 for a good down winter bag. **Sleeping bag pads** include foam pads ($10-30), air mattresses ($15-50), and self-inflating mats ($30-120). Bring a **stuff sack** to store your bag and keep it dry.

Tents: The best tents are freestanding (with their own frames and suspension systems), set up quickly, and only require staking in high winds. Low-profile dome tents are the best all around.

Worthy 2-person tents start at $100, 4-person tents at $160. Make sure your tent has a rain fly and seal its seams with waterproofer. Other useful accessories include a **battery-operated lantern**, a plastic **ground cloth**, and a nylon **tarp.**

Backpacks: Internal-frame packs mold well to your back, keep a lower center of gravity, and flex adequately to allow you to hike difficult trails, while **external-frame** packs are more comfortable for long hikes over even terrain, as they carry weight higher and distribute it more evenly. Make sure your pack has a strong, padded hip belt to transfer weight to your legs. There are models designed specifically for women. Any serious backpacking requires a pack of at least 4000 cu. in. (65,000cc), plus 500 cu. in. for sleeping bags in internal-frame packs. Sturdy backpacks cost anywhere from $125 to $420—your pack is an area where it doesn't pay to economize. On your hunt for the perfect pack, fill up a prospective model with something heavy, strap it on correctly, and walk around the store to get a sense of how the model distributes weight. Either buy a rain cover ($10-20) or store all of your belongings in plastic bags inside your pack.

Boots: Be sure to wear hiking boots with good **ankle support.** They should fit snugly and comfortably over 1-2 pairs of **wool socks** and a pair of thin **liner socks.** Break in boots over several weeks before you go to spare yourself blisters.

Other Necessities: Synthetic layers, like those made of polypropylene or polyester, and a pile jacket will keep you warm even when wet. A **space blanket** ($5-15) will help you to retain body heat and doubles as a **ground cloth.** Plastic **water bottles** are vital; look for shatter- and leak-resistant models. Carry **water-purification tablets** for when you can't boil water. Although most campgrounds provide campfire sites, you may want to bring a small **metal grate** or **grill.** For those places that forbid fires or the gathering of firewood, you'll need a **camp stove** (starts at $50) and a fuel bottle to operate it. Also bring a **first-aid kit, pocketknife, insect repellent,** and **waterproof matches** or a **lighter.**

WHERE TO BUY IT

The online and mail-order companies listed below offer lower prices than many retail stores. A visit to a local camping or outdoors store will give you a good sense of the look and weight of certain items before you buy.

Campmor, 400 Corporate Dr., P.O. Box 680, Mahwah, NJ 07430 (☎800-525-4784; www.campmor.com).

Eastern Mountain Sports (EMS), 1 Vose Farm Rd., Peterborough, NH 03458 (☎888-463-6367; www.ems.com).

L.L.Bean, Freeport, ME 04033 (US and Canada ☎800-441-5713, UK 0800 891 297; www.llbean.com).

Recreational Equipment, Inc. (REI), Sumner, WA 98352 (US and Canada ☎800-426-4840, elsewhere 253-891-2500; www.rei.com).

ORGANIZED ADVENTURE TRIPS

Organized adventure tours offer another way of exploring the wild. Activities include hiking, biking, skiing, canoeing, kayaking, rafting, climbing, photo safaris, and archaeological digs. Tourism bureaus can often suggest parks, trails, and outfitters. Organizations that specialize in camping and outdoor equipment, like REI and EMS (above), are also good sources for info.

Specialty Travel Index, P.O. Box 458, San Anselmo, CA 94979 (☎888-624-4030, elsewhere 415-455-1643; www.specialtytravel.com).

TrekAmerica, P.O. Box 189, Rockaway, NJ 07866 (☎ US 800-221-0596 or 973-983-1144, elsewhere +44 870 444 8735; www.trekamerica.com). Operates tours in the US, Canada, and Mexico.

Outward Bound, 100 Mystery Point Rd., Garrison, NY 10524 (☎854-424-4000). A nonprofit educational travel organization.

SPECIFIC CONCERNS

SUSTAINABLE TRAVEL

As the number of travelers on the road rises, environmental impact is increasingly a concern. *Let's Go* promotes the philosophy of **sustainable travel** with this in mind. Through sensitivity to ecology and sustainability, today's travelers can be a powerful force in preserving and restoring the places they visit.

Ecotourism, a rising trend in sustainable travel, focuses on the conservation of natural habitats—mainly, how to use them to build up the economy without exploitation or overdevelopment. Travelers can make a difference by doing advance research, by supporting organizations and establishments that pay attention to their **carbon footprint,** and by patronizing establishments that strive to be environmentally friendly.

Roadtripping is not the most eco-friendly means of travel. This means that roadtrippers should put extra effort into making their trips green. Carpooling is a great way to reduce the number of cars on the road and to get the most out of your gasoline. For those with the option, driving a hybrid is good for both the environment and the wallet. Roadtrippers can buy carbon credits from companies like **Carbon Fund** (www.carbonfund.org) and **Terrapass** (www.terrapass.com) that seek to offset carbon emissions by investing in carbon-reducing projects such as renewable energy, energy efficiency, and reforestation projects.

Other environmentally friendly options include using public transportation while within a city, choosing between air-conditioning and rolling the windows down, not littering, and saving recyclables until reaching a recycling bin. Roadtrippers should never throw anything, but especially glass or cigarettes, out of the window, as doing so can damage other cars or start a wildfire. Being aware of your eco-footprint (by turning off lights, not taking long showers, etc.) is a good idea not only while roadtripping but also in normal life.

RESPONSIBLE TRAVEL

Your tourist dollars can make a big impact on the destinations you visit. The choices you make during your trip can have powerful effects on local communities—for better or for worse. Travelers who care about the destinations and environments they explore should make themselves aware of the social and cul-

tural implications of their choices. Simple decisions such as buying local products and paying fair prices for products or services can have a strong, positive effect on the community.

Community-based tourism aims to channel tourist dollars into the local economy by emphasizing tours and cultural programs that are run by members of the host community. This type of tourism also benefits the tourists themselves, as it often takes them beyond the traditional tours of the region. *The Ethical Travel Guide* (UK£13), a project of **Tourism Concern** (☎+44 20 7133 3330; www.tourismconcern.org.uk), is an excellent resource for information on community-based travel, with a directory of 300 establishments.

The **Center for a New American Dream** (www.newdream.org) and the pocket-sized book *The Better World Shopping Guide* (www.betterworldshopper.org) give consumers information about different companies' records with human rights, the environment, animal protection, community involvement, and social justice. Supporting local businesses preserves the regional "flavor" that makes roadtripping an adventure.

> **ECO-RESOURCES.** For more information on environmentally responsible tourism, contact one of the organizations below:
>
> **Conservation International,** 2011 Crystal Dr., Ste. 500, Arlington, VA 22202 (☎800-406-2306 or 703-341-2400; www.conservation.org).
>
> **International Ecotourism Society,** 1333 H St. NW, Ste. 300E, Washington, DC 20005 (☎202-347-9203; www.ecotourism.org).
>
> **United Nations Environment Program (UNEP),** 39-43 Quai André Citroën, 75739 Paris Cedex 15, France (☎+33 1 44 37 14 50; www.unep-tie.org/pc/tourism).

ROADTRIPPING SOLO

Traveling alone can be extremely beneficial, providing a sense of independence and great opportunities to connect with locals. On the other hand, solo travelers are more vulnerable to harassment and street theft. If you are traveling alone, look confident, try not to stand out as a tourist, and be especially careful in deserted or very crowded areas. Stay away from areas that are not well lit. If questioned, never admit that you are traveling alone. Maintain regular contact with someone at home who knows your itinerary and always research your destination before traveling. For more tips, pick up *Traveling Solo* by Eleanor Berman (Globe Pequot Press; $18), visit www.travelaloneandloveit.com, or subscribe to **Connecting: Solo Travel Network**, 689 Park Rd., Unit 6, Gibsons, BC V0N 1V7 (☎604-886-9099; www.cstn.org; membership $30-48).

WOMEN ROADTRIPPERS

Women exploring on their own inevitably face some additional safety concerns. Single women might consider staying in hostels that offer single rooms that lock from the inside or in religious accommodations with single-sex rooms. It's a good idea to stick to centrally located accommodations and to avoid solitary late-night treks or metro rides.

Always carry extra cash for a phone call, bus, or taxi. Hitchhiking is never safe for lone women or even for two women traveling together. Look as if you know where you're going and approach older women or couples for directions if you're lost or feeling uncomfortable in your surroundings. The less you look like a tourist, the better off you'll be. Dress conservatively, especially in rural areas. Wearing a conspicuous **wedding band** sometimes helps to prevent unwanted advances.

Your best answer to verbal harassment is no answer at all; feigning deafness, sitting motionless, and staring straight ahead at nothing in particular will usually do the trick. The extremely persistent can sometimes be dissuaded by a firm, loud, and very public "Go away!" Don't hesitate to seek out a police officer or a passerby if you are being harassed. Consider carrying a whistle on your keychain. A **self-defense course** will both prepare you for a potential attack and raise your level of awareness of your surroundings. It might be a good idea to talk with your doctor about the **health concerns** that women face when traveling.

GLBT ROADTRIPPERS

Attitudes towards GLBT roadtrippers will vary greatly from region to region within the US. California, New England, and major cities tend to be more GLBT-friendly than the South, Midwest, and small towns. Consult *The Spartacus Guide* (www.spartacusworld.com) for information about many different travel destinations and their local attitudes towards GLBT travelers. Listed below are contact organizations, mail-order catalogs, and publishers that offer materials addressing some specific concerns. **Out and About** (www.planetout.com) offers a weekly newsletter and a comprehensive site addressing gay travel concerns. The online newspaper **365gay.com** also has a travel section (www.365gay.com/travel/travelchannel.htm).

> ▼ **ADDITIONAL GLBT RESOURCES:**
> *Spartacus International Gay Guide 2008* ($33).
> *Damron Men's Travel Guide, Damron Road Atlas, Damron Accommodations Guide, Damron City Guide,* and *Damron Women's Traveller* ($18-24). For info, call ☎800-462-6654 or visit www.damron.com.
> *The Gay Vacation Guide: The Best Trips and How to Plan Them,* by Mark Chesnut. Kensington Books ($15).
> *Gayellow Pages USA/Canada,* by Frances Green. Gayellow Pages ($20). They also publish regional editions. Visit Gayellow pages online at http://gayellowpages.com.

Gay's the Word, 66 Marchmont St., London WC1N 1AB, UK (☎+44 20 7278 7654; http://freespace.virgin.net/gays.theword). The largest GLBT bookshop in the UK, with both fiction and non-fiction titles. Mail-order service available.

Giovanni's Room, 345 S. 12th St., Philadelphia, PA 19107 (☎215-923-2960; www.queerbooks.

com). An international lesbian and gay bookstore with mail-order service (carries many of the publications listed below).

International Lesbian and Gay Association (ILGA), Avenue des Villas 34, 1060 Brussels, Belgium (☎+32 2 502 2471; www.ilga.org). Provides political information, such as homosexuality laws of individual countries.

ROADTRIPPERS WITH DISABILITIES

Roadtripping can be a great option for those with disabilities because the US is considerably more accessible than many other countries. Under the federal **Americans with Disabilities Act of 1990,** new public and private business construction must employ "accessible design" that permits the passage of wheelchairs. Nonetheless, those with disabilities should inform airlines and hotels of their disabilities when making reservations; some time may be needed to prepare special accommodations. Call ahead to find out if restaurants, museums, and other facilities are wheelchair-accessible. In all areas of the US, guide dogs are legally allowed on public transit and in all "public establishments," including hotels, restaurants, and stores.

In the US, both Amtrak and major airlines will accommodate disabled passengers if notified in advance. **Amtrak** (☎800-872-7245; www.amtrak.com) offers a discount to physically disabled travelers. **Greyhound** buses may provide a 50% discount for a companion if the ticket is purchased at least one day in advance. If you are without a fellow traveler, call Greyhound (☎800-752-4841) at least two days before you plan to leave, and they will make arrangements to assist you. For information on transportation availability in individual US cities, contact the local chapter of the **Easter Seal Society** (☎800-221-6827; www.easter-seals.org).

If you are planning to visit a national park or attraction in the US run by the **National Park Service** (☎888-467-2757; www.nps.gov), obtain a free **America the Beautiful Access Pass,** which is available at park entrances. The pass entitles disabled travelers and their families

to free park admission and provides a lifetime 50% discount on all campsite and parking fees. Federal lands have varying levels of accessibility. Bigger parks like Yosemite and Yellowstone have many wheelchair-accessible vistas, campsites, and even trails, while smaller parks may not. Similarly, bigger parks have more features that cater to the vision- and hearing-impaired than smaller parks do. If planning to visit a park or camp, call ahead to check on a specific locale's accessibility.

USEFUL ORGANIZATIONS

Accessible Journeys, 35 W. Sellers Ave., Ridley Park, PA 19078 (☎800-846-4537; www.disabilitytravel.com). Designs tours for wheelchair users and slow walkers. The site has tips and forums for all travelers.

The Guided Tour, Inc., 7900 Old York Rd., Ste. 114B, Elkins Park, PA 19027 (☎800-783-5841; www.guidedtour.com). Organizes travel programs for persons with developmental and physical challenges.

Mobility International USA (MIUSA), P.O. Box 10767, Eugene, OR 97440 (☎541-343-1284; www.miusa.org). Provides a variety of books and other publications containing information for travelers with disabilities.

Society for Accessible Travel and Hospitality (SATH), 347 5th Ave., Ste. 610, New York, NY 10016 (☎212-447-7284; www.sath.org). An advocacy group that publishes free online travel information. Annual membership $49, students and seniors $29.

MINORITY ROADTRIPPERS

Attitudes toward minority citizens vary widely in different regions of the US. Some states are considerably more diverse than others, and minority roadtrippers may feel more comfortable in these than elsewhere. Over half of America's African-American, Asian-American, and Hispanic citizens live in California, Texas, New York, Florida, and Illinois. Cities tend to be more diverse than small towns.

Even in these places, however, roadtrippers may encounter blatant or, more often, subtle discrimination or harrassment. Verbal harassment is now less common than unfair pricing, false info on accommodations, or unfriendly service at restaurants. Remain calm and report discriminating individuals to the **Better Business Bureau** (www.bbb.org); contact the police in extreme cases. *Let's Go* always welcomes reader input regarding discriminating establishments. Be aware that racial tensions do exist, even in large, ostensibly progressive areas, and try to avoid confrontations.

In towns along the US-Mexico border, the Department of Homeland Security's US **Customs and Border Protection (CBP)'s** border patrol agents remain on a constant lookout for Mexican nationals who have crossed the border illegally. In border towns, the agents may pull over anyone who looks suspicious, search his or her vehicle for smuggled goods or people, and ask for identification.

FURTHER RESOURCES
United States Department of Justice (www.usdoj.gov).

Go Girl! The Black Woman's Book of Travel and Adventure, Elaine Lee. Eighth Mountain Press ($18).

The African-American Travel Guide, Wayne C. Robinson. Hunter Publishing ($16).

DIETARY CONCERNS

Most major US and Canadian cities are vegetarian-friendly, especially those on the West Coast. While vegetarians should have no trouble finding suitable cuisine as they travel, vegans may still meet with some blank stares, especially along routes through small-town America. *Let's Go* often indicates vegetarian options in restaurant listings; other places to look for vegetarian and vegan cuisine are local health-food stores or large national food chains such as **Trader Joe's** (www.traderjoes. com) and **Whole Foods** (www.wholefoodsmarket.com). The travel section of **The Vegetarian Resource Group's** website, at www.vrg.org/travel, has a comprehensive list of organizations and websites that are geared toward helping vegetarians and vegans traveling abroad. They also provide an online restaurant guide. Check out *The Vegetarian Journal's Guide to Natural Food Restaurants in the US and Canada* (the book is in its 4th edition!) for listings of vegetarian-friendly restaurants, accommodations, travel companies, and more. For additional information, consult *The Vegetarian Traveler: Where to Stay if You're Vegetarian, Vegan, Environmentally Sensitive,* by Jed and Susan Civic (Larson Publications; $16) or pick up *Vegetarian United States,* by John Howley (available at www.vegetarianguides.co.uk/products/vegetarianusa.shtml; $20). Vegetarians will also find numerous resources at the plethora of websites that address vegetarian concerns; try www.vegdining.com, www.happycow.net, and www.vegetariansabroad.com.

Travelers who keep **kosher** should contact synagogues in larger cities for information on kosher restaurants. Your own synagogue or college Hillel should have access to lists of Jewish institutions across the nation. If you are strict in your observance, you may have to prepare your own food on the road. Alternatively, the online worldwide kosher restaurant database at http://shamash.org/kosher might prove useful. A good resource is the *Jewish Travel Guide,* edited by Michael Zaidner (Valentine Mitchell; $18). Travelers looking for **halal** restaurants may find www.zabihah.com a useful resource.

OTHER RESOURCES

Let's Go tries to cover all aspects of budget travel, but we can't put everything in our guides. Listed below are books and websites that can serve as jumping-off points for your own research.

USEFUL PUBLICATIONS

America Bizarro: A Guide to Freaky Festivals, Groovy Gatherings, Kooky Contests, and Other Strange Happenings Across the USA, by Nelson Taylor ($15).

Colman National Forest Campground & Recreation Directory. Our Forests ($20).

The Economist. A weekly magazine about international and US political affairs.

A History of the US, by Joy Hakim. 11-volume set ($111).

A People's History of the United States, by Howard Zinn ($13).

Rand McNally Road Atlas: United States/Canada/ Mexico. Rand McNally ($12). For more info, visit www.randmcnally.com.

WORLD WIDE WEB

Almost every aspect of budget travel is accessible via the web. In 10min. at the keyboard, you can make a hostel reservation, get advice on travel hot spots from other travelers, or find out how much a train from Buffalo to Reno costs. Listed here are some regional and travel-related sites to start off your surfing; other relevant websites are listed throughout the book. Because website turnover is high, use search engines (e.g., www.google.com) to strike out on your own.

LET'S GO ONLINE. Plan your next trip on our newly redesigned website, **www.letsgo.com.** It features the latest travel info on your favorite destinations as well as tons of interactive features: make your own itinerary, read blogs from our researcher-writers, browse our photo library, watch exclusive videos, check out our newsletter, find travel deals, and buy new guides. We're always updating and adding new features, so check back often!

THE ART OF TRAVEL

Backpacker's Ultimate Guide: www.bugamerica. com. Tips on packing, transportation, and where to go. Also tons of country-specific travel information.

BootsnAll.com: www.bootsnall.com. Resources for independent travelers, from planning your trip to reporting on it when you get back.

How to See the World: www.artoftravel.com. A compendium of travel tips, from cheap flights to self-defense to interacting with local culture.

Travel Intelligence: www.travelintelligence.net. A large collection of travel writing by distinguished travel writers.

Travel Library: www.travel-library.com. A fantastic set of links for general information and personal travelogues.

INFORMATION ON THE US

CIA World Factbook: www.odci.gov/cia/publications/factbook/index.html. Tons of vital statistics on the US's geography, government, economy, and people.

Geographia: www.geographia.com. Highlights, culture, and people of the US.

PlanetRider: www.planetrider.com. A subjective list of links to the "best" websites covering the culture and tourist attractions of the US.

The Splendid Table Restaurant Guide: www. splendidtable.publicradio.org/whereweeat/ index.shtml. A guide to the best in American food, cross country.

HI WALDO WATCHERS! I've been on the road for 21 years...at the beach, on the ski slopes, at sports stadiums, and more! As you embark on your travels, see if you can spot me... who knows where I'll pop up next?

JOIN THE SEARCH!

Waldo

Visit FindWaldo.com

the east coast

TOP 5

1. Discover the party that won't quit in **Key West** (p. 56).
2. Whip up a mint julep, find yourself a porch, and soak up **Savannah's** quiet charm (p. 85).
3. Make haste to the limitless fun in **New York City** (p. 121).
4. Follow in the footsteps of the Founding Fathers in **Boston** (p. 159).
5. Blaze your way up the spectacular Precipice Trail in **Acadia National Park** (p. 188).

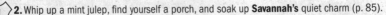

EAST COAST

The East Coast route is a testament to the breadth and diversity of America; from the proud South to historic New England, it's one nation. This is where the country began, and American history, runs deep along the coastline. You will encounter the homes and works of some of the country's famed literary, political, scientific, and philosophical luminaries. For those more inclined to loud beats than historic feats, the East Coast provides—in abundance. Key West, Savannah, New York City, and Boston alone hold more than enough for any reveler, hipster, or historian.

You'll set off in idyllic **Key West** (p. 56), home to some of the best nightlife in the country and hordes of Ernest Hemingway look-alikes. The road will pass through **Key Largo** (p. 60) before plunging into the **Everglades** (p. 61). Alligators and mosquitoes give way to all-night bacchanalia in **South Beach, Miami** (p. 63). The rest of Florida hosts a bevy of landmark sights, from the Kennedy Space Center in **Cape Canaveral** (p. 73) to the International Speedway at **Daytona Beach** (p. 76) to the Fountain of Youth in **Saint Augustine** (p. 78). After the **Cumberland Island National Seashore** (p. 83), you'll reach **Savannah** (p. 85), one of the route's true highlights. The historic homes and plantations keep coming in **Charleston** (p. 89). Past **Myrtle Beach** and the **Grand Strand** (p. 94), you'll steel your nerves and brave **Cape Fear** (p. 97). The road will coast through North Carolina's **Outer Banks** on its way to **Kitty Hawk** (p. 104), where the Wright Brothers are inescapable—on signs, storefronts, even license plates. **Virginia Beach** (p. 106) will be your last stop in the present before the road visits the smithies and taverns of **Colonial Williamsburg** (p. 109). **Chincoteague Wildlife Refuge** (p. 111) will ease you back into the present, and **Assateague** **Island National Seashore** (p. 111) features free-ranging wild horses. The road then leaves Maryland for Delaware, where the Lewes-Cape May Ferry heads into New Jersey. **Lucy the Elephant** (p. 120), in Margate, is the finest example of zoomorphic architecture in New Jersey, and its surreal quality is a good prelude to **Atlantic City** (p. 121), where the streets of the Monopoly board lead to gaudy casinos and wide beaches. Up the **Garden State Expressway**, the road hits **New York City** (p. 121). The best pizza on the coast is tucked away in **New Haven, Connecticut** (p. 144).

Providence, Rhode Island (p. 148), home of **Brown University**, the **Rhode Island School of Design**, and a spectacular public art installation, is a roadtripper's paradise. **Newport** (p. 152) follows, and its mansions, embodying giddy absurdity, are jaw-dropping sights. Then it's off to **Cape Cod** (p. 154), where the lighthouses nearly outnumber the Nantucket Reds. At **Plimoth Plantation**, you'll find that **Plymouth Rock** (p. 158) is smaller than you thought. Then it's off to the East Coast's apotheosis of colonial history: **Boston** (p. 159).

Heading into northern Massachusetts, the road enters **Salem** (p. 173), either the scari-

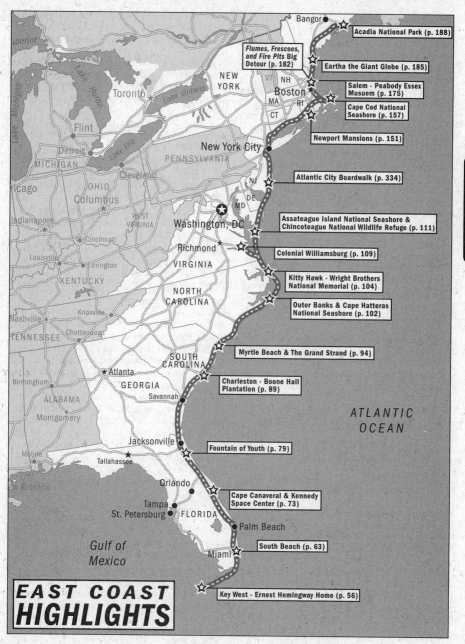

Bangor

Acadia National Park (p. 188)

Flumes, Frescoes, and Fire Pits Big Detour (p. 182)

NEW YORK

VT NH

Eartha the Giant Globe (p. 185)

Boston

MA RI

Salem - Peabody Essex Musuem (p. 175)

CT

Cape Cod National Seashore (p. 157)

New York City

Newport Mansions (p. 151)

PENNSYLVANIA

Toronto

Lake Ontario

Flint

Detroit

Lake Erie

MICHIGAN

Cleveland

icago

OHIO

Columbus

Indianapolis

WEST VIRGINIA

Washington, DC

Richmond

Louisville

Lexington

VIRGINIA

Cincinnati

KENTUCKY

NJ

DE

MD

Atlantic City Boardwalk (p. 334)

Assateague Island National Seashore & Chincoteague National Wildlife Refuge (p. 111)

Colonial Williamsburg (p. 109)

Kitty Hawk - Wright Brothers National Memorial (p. 104)

NORTH CAROLINA

Nashville

Chattanooga

Knoxville

TENNESSEE

SOUTH CAROLINA

Outer Banks & Cape Hatteras National Seashore (p. 102)

Myrtle Beach & The Grand Strand (p. 94)

Atlanta

Charleston - Boone Hall Plantation (p. 89)

Birmingham

GEORGIA

Savannah

ALABAMA

Montgomery

ATLANTIC OCEAN

Mobile

Jacksonville

Fountain of Youth (p. 79)

Tallahassee

New Orleans

Orlando

Cape Canaveral & Kennedy Space Center (p. 73)

Tampa

St. Petersburg

FLORIDA

Palm Beach

Gulf of Mexico

Miami

South Beach (p. 63)

EAST COAST
HIGHLIGHTS

Key West - Ernest Hemingway Home (p. 56)

est place on the coast or the most hilarious, depending on your disposition. If the salty sea air is getting to you, the **Flumes, Frescoes, and Family Camping Big Detour** (p. 182) is the perfect inland distraction. **Yarmouth, Maine** is home to **Eartha** (p. 184), the largest rotating globe in the world. Soon afterward the route enters **Mount Desert Island** (p. 187), the end of the road.

So whether you prefer sucking down piña coladas in a straw hat or swirling the finest brandy with Boston brahmins, the East Coast route will take you through some of the most fascinating and varied parts of the country. Don't forget the sunscreen!

ROUTE STATS
Miles: c. 2000
Route: Key West, FL, to Bar Harbor, ME.
States: 14; Florida, Georgia, South Carolina, North Carolina, Virginia, Maryland, Delaware, New Jersey, New York, Connecticut, Rhode Island, Massachusetts, New Hampshire, Maine.
Driving Time: You could drive it in 4 days, but what fun would that be? Take 3 weeks to sample the diverse environments of the Atlantic coast.
When To Go: Anytime, though winter brings snow to New England and late summer brings the danger of hurricanes to the South.
Crossroads: National Road in Atlantic City, NJ (p. 121); **Southern Border** in the Everglades, FL (p. 764).

The Sunshine State
FLORIDA
Welcomes You

KEY WEST   ☎ 3 0 5

This tiny island was once the wealthiest city per capita in the US, depending at different times on shipwrecks, cigars, and even natural sponges as the source of its wealth. These days, the last of the Florida Keys is a tourist haven, welcoming cruise ships, families with small children, spring-breakers, and a sizable gay population. Key West's popularity makes it an expensive stay, but, with hundreds of

bars and tropical breezes, it's well worth a visit. Hooked on the so-called "Key West lifestyle," Henry Flagler, Ernest Hemingway, Tennessee Williams, Truman Capote, and Jimmy Buffett have all called it home. Key West is as far south as you can get in the continental US. Make sure to take a picture next to the iconic mile marker "0" on US 1; this is truly where the road begins.

VITAL STATS
Population: 25,811
Tourist Office: Key West Chamber of Commerce, 402 Wall St. (☎305-294-2587 or 800-527-8539; www.keywestchamber.org), in old Mallory Sq. Open M-F 8am-6:30pm, Sa-Su 9am-6pm.
Library and Internet Access: Key West Library, 700 Fleming St. (☎305-292-3595). Open Tu and Th-F 9:30am-6pm, W 9:30am-8pm, Sa 10am-6pm.
Post Office: 400 Whitehead St. (☎305-294-9539), 1 block west of Duval St. Open M-F 8:30am-5pm, Sa 9:30am-noon. **Postal Code:** 33040.

✴ ORIENTATION

Key West lies at the end of **Overseas Highway (US 1),** 155 mi. southwest of Miami. The island is divided into two sections; the eastern part, known as **New Town,** harbors tract houses, chain motels, strip malls, and the airport. The distinctive architecture of the beautiful old houses that fill **Old Town** west of White St., with their white wood facades, is imitated throughout the country. **Duval Street** is the main north-south thoroughfare in Old Town and the heart of all the action; **Truman Avenue (US 1)** is a major east-west route. The historic seaport is located on the northwestern tip of the island, where grand old schooners and tour boats alike can be found by the dozen and where many bars and restaurants welcome hungry tourists and local seamen. Driving in town can be difficult; traversing Key West by bike, foot, or moped is more fun and very safe given the low-speed roads on the island.

⚑ ACCOMMODATIONS

Key West is packed from January through March, so reserve rooms far in advance. During the summer, prices drop and many places have vacancies. **Pride Week** (www.pridefestkeywest.

com) in June and **Fantasy Fest** (www.fantasty-fest.net) on Halloween are particularly busy. In Old Town, B&Bs dominate, and "reasonably priced" still means over $60. Rates decrease as you move farther south and away from Duval St. Some of the guesthouses in Old Town are exclusively for gay men or gay women.

Angelina Guesthouse, 302 Angela St. (☎305-294-4480; www.angelinaguesthouse.com), 2 blocks from Duval St. This 1920s bordello is now a haven for budget-conscious travelers. It has welcoming common spaces and the name of the woman who once worked in each room hanging from the door. A/C, communal fridge, beautiful pool surrounded by tropical vegetation, and hammocks. No TVs or phones. No spring break parties allowed. Breakfast included. Wi-Fi. Rooms Dec.-Apr. $99-199; May-Dec. $69-139. D/MC/V. ❸

Key West Youth Hostel and Seashell Motel, 718 South St. (☎305-296-5719). While the hostel is not the most comfortable or welcoming option, it's the cheapest game in town. Common bathroom and kitchen. Linen included. Dorms $34; private rooms in summer $95-150. MC/V. ❷

Casablanca Hotel, 900 Duval St. (☎305-296-0815). In the center of town. This basic B&B once hosted Humphrey Bogart and James Joyce. Pool, cable TV, and large bathrooms. Breakfast included. Rooms Dec.-May $225-255; June-Nov. $125-155. AmEx/D/MC/V. ❺

Boyd's Campground, 6401 Maloney Ave. (☎305-294-1465; www.boydscampground.com). Take a left off US 1 onto MacDonald Ave., which becomes Maloney. Sprawls over 12 oceanside acres with full facilities. Sites in summer $50, with water and electricity $60, with full hookup $75; in winter $60/70/60-85. MC/V. ❸

🍴 FOOD

Expensive restaurants line Duval St. Side streets offer lower prices and fewer crowds.

Schooner Wharf Bar and Galley, 202 William St. (☎305-292-9520; www.schoonerwharf.com). On the Harborwalk. Laid-back open-air restaurant and bar offers a million-dollar view of the historic seaport and marina with the purchase of a blackened mahi melt ($13). Live music, cigar bar, and cartoonist available. MC/V. ❷

El Siboney, 900 Catherine St. (☎305-296-4184; www.elsiboneyrestaurant.com). This authentic establishment has been voted Key West's favorite Cuban restaurant 15 years in a row. Entrees, like half a roasted chicken ($9.50), come with rice, black beans, and plantains. Save room for sangria and flan (both $3). Open daily 11am-9:30pm. D/MC/V. ❷

Camille's Restaurant, 1202 Simonton St. (☎305-296-4811; www.camilleskeywest.com). It's always time for breakfast at Camille's, where you can get Belgian waffles ($3) or buttermilk pancakes ($5) all day long. The bustling establish-

UNTIL DEATH (AND BEYOND) DO US PART

Key West's warm air and magnificent sunsets have led many a soul to fall in love, yet none as madly as Count Carl Von Cosel. The middle-aged doctor, whose real name was Georg Karl Tanzler, met his soul mate in 1930. Elena Milagro Hoyos was his 20-year-old patient, a dark-haired Cuban beauty afflicted by tuberculosis. Despite his desperate attempts to win her heart—and save her life—the frail Elena stubbornly rejected his advances as her health continued to deteriorate. The young girl died in October of 1931, and Von Cosel, refusing to let her body rot in a common grave, built her a mausoleum that he visited nightly. Soon, the short visits were insufficient to satisfy his desire to be near his beloved. He quietly stole the body and carried it to his house on Flagler Ave., where he concentrated all his efforts in salvaging her remains from the unrelenting decay of death. He dressed her in a white wedding gown, perfumed her rotting body, and covered her skin with wax. For seven years, the doctor slept with his otherworldly bride until he was finally discovered. Legend has it that Elena's soul never left the cemetery she was stolen from, so, as you take a stroll among the historic white tombstones,

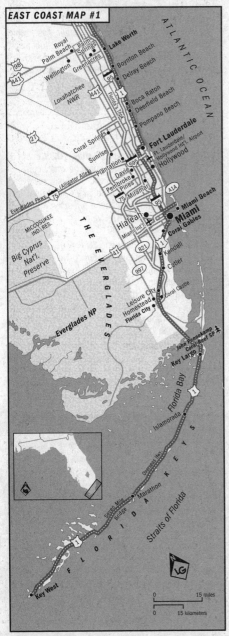

EAST COAST MAP #1

ment also serves chicken-salad sandwiches ($7) with a pickle on the side. Open daily 8am-10pm. AmEx/D/MC/V. ❷

Blue Heaven, 729 Thomas St. (☎305-296-8666; www.blueheavenkw.com). Feast on homemade pecan pancakes ($7.50) for breakfast or Caribbean lunches like the Jamaican jerk chicken sandwich ($9). Outdoor courtyard dining. Open in summer M-Tu and Th-Sa 8am-3pm and 6-10:30pm, Su 8am-2pm and 6-10:30pm; in winter M-Sa 8am-3pm and 6-10:30pm, Su 8am-2pm. AmEx/D/MC/V. ❷

◎ SIGHTS

⬛ERNEST HEMINGWAY HOME. No one should leave Key West without visiting this Caribbean-style mansion where "Papa" wrote *For Whom the Bell Tolls* and had some nasty fights with the second of his four wives. Take a tour with hilarious guides who relate strange-but-true Hemingway history, then enjoy the garden with 51 descendants of Hemingway's cat, half of which have six toes. *(907 Whitehead St. ☎305-294-1136; www.hemingwayhome.com. Open daily 9am-5pm. $12, ages 6-12 $6.)*

⬛FORT ZACHARY TAYLOR HISTORIC STATE PARK. Although Key West is better known for its nightlife than the beauty of its beaches, the park is a sight not to be missed. Fort Zachary Taylor offers the unique opportunity to see live coral, colorful tropical fish, and even the occasional sea turtle by snorkeling just a few feet off the beach. In addition, its Civil War-era fortress will transport you to a time when cannons were more common than drag shows. *(End of Southard St. on Truman Annex. ☎305-292-6213; www.floridastateparks.org/forttaylor. Open daily 8am-sundown. Pedestrians $1.50, vehicle with 1 person $3.50, with 2 people $6; $0.50 per additional person. Snorkeling gear available for rent.)*

⬛SUNSET CELEBRATION. Even in pricey Key West, the best things in life are free. As the sun sinks in the water, head to the Mallory Sq. Dock to partake in the nightly Sunset Celebration, where daring street performers work the crowd and local artisans sell handmade souvenirs. *(☎305-292-7700; www.sunsetcelebration.org. 2hr. before sunset.)*

HARRY S. TRUMAN LITTLE WHITE HOUSE MUSEUM. Originally built in 1890 as naval quarters, the museum provides a fascinating look at both President Truman and his get-away in Key West. Don't expect to explore this simple, relaxing house on your own, as it is still a presidential site and can only be visited in guided tours by order of the Secret Service. The Little White House has been used at times by six presidents, including John F. Kennedy and Bill Clinton. (*111 Front St. ☎305-294-9911; www.trumanlittlewhitehouse.com. Open daily 9am-5pm. Grounds open 8am-6pm. House $15, children $5. Grounds free.*)

MEL FISHER MARITIME HERITAGE SOCIETY MUSEUM. The museum showcases the discovery and salvaging of the Spanish galleon *Nuestra Señora de Atocha*, which sank off the Keys in 1622 and was uncovered after a 16-year search. Look at the endless piles of silver and jewels that Mel Fisher finally found on the sea bottom and even lift a real gold bar. (*200 Greene St. ☎305-294-2633; www.melfisher.org. Open daily 9:30am-5pm. $12, ages 6-12 $6.*)

KEY WEST SHIPWRECK HISTOREUM MUSEUM. Here lie the remains of the *Isaac Allerton*, the 594-ton cargo ship that sank in 1856. Entertain your inner kid by watching one of the shows presented every 20min. The museum's Lookout Tower, which stands 65 ft. tall, offers one of the best views of the island. (*1 Whitehead St., in Mallory Sq. ☎305-292-8990; www.shipwreckhistoreum.com. Open daily 9:40am-5pm. $12, ages 4-12 $5, under 4 free.*)

SOUTHERN POINT. At the opposite end of Duval St., on the corner of Whitehead and South St., you'll come to the southernmost point in the continental US. A large red-and-black cement buoy marks the spot: "90 Miles to Cuba." The glass-bottom boat *Fury* cruises to the reefs and back. (*☎305-296-6293; www.furykeywest.com. 2hr. cruises daily 11:30am, 3:30, 6pm. $35, ages 5-12 $16.*)

📷 NIGHTLIFE

Nightlife in Key West revs up in the early evening and winds down in the wee hours of the morning, though it's not uncommon to find bars full in the middle of the afternoon. The action centers on upper Duval St. Key West nightlife reaches its peak in the third week of October's **Fantasy Fest** (☎305-296-1817; www.fantasyfest.net), when decadent floats filled with drag queens, pirates, and wild locals take over Duval St. Known for its wild, outspoken gay community, Key West hosts more than a dozen fabulous drag lounges, nightclubs, and private bars that cater to a gay clientele. No one, gay or straight, should leave without experiencing one of the drag shows. Most gay clubs welcome straight couples and lesbians, but check with the bouncer. Gay clubs line **Duval Street** south of Fleming Ave.

▨ **Capt. Tony's Saloon,** 428 Greene St. (☎305-294-1838; www.capttonyssaloon.com). The oldest bar in Key West and the location of Jimmy Buffett's 1st paid gig. Bras and business cards festoon the ceiling, and the city's old hanging tree still grows right through the bar. Live music nightly. Open M-Sa 10am-2am, Su 10am-1am. D/MC/V.

▨ **The Green Parrot,** 601 Whitehead St. (☎305-294-6133; www.greenparrot.com). Though away from the wild Duval St., this bar warranted a nod from *Playboy* as one of the best bars in America in 2000. A real area hangout; stop by and meet a crowd of local characters. Open M-Sa 10am-4am, Su noon-4am. Cash only.

The Bourbon Street Pub, 724 Duval St. (☎305-294-9354; www.bourbonstreetpub.com). A mainstay of Key West's gay scene. If the boys in very tiny undies dancing to the nightly lineup of music videos aren't raunchy enough for you, head to the clothing-optional pool out back (only men allowed until 6pm). Open M-Sa 11am-4am, Su noon-4am. Sister club **T,** 801 Duval St. (☎305-294-4737). Hosts 2 nightly cabaret drag shows at 9 and 11pm. Open M-Sa 11am-4am, Su noon-4am. Cover $5.

Sloppy Joe's, 201 Duval St. (☎305-294-5717; www.sloppyjoes.com). The most famous bar in Key West and Hemingway's favorite hangout. Prepare to be blown away by the house specialty, the Sloppy Rita ($7.50). 3 live bands play blues in the afternoon and rock at night. 21+. Open M-Sa 9am-4am, Su noon-4am. AmEx/D/MC/V.

Rick's, 202 Duval St. (☎305-296-5513). This trendy entertainment complex boasts a bar with live music downstairs, a dance floor upstairs, and a strip club around back. $3 domestic beers in souvenir cup, $2 refills. Open M-Sa 11am-4am, Su noon-4am. AmEx/D/MC/V.

Aqua, 711 Duval St. (☎305-294-0555; www. aquakeywest.com). Cabaret shows by the Aqua-nettes (9pm) play to a mixed crowd of tourists at this GLBT nightspot. Dancing after the show. Cover after 8:30pm $12. Happy hour 3-8pm daily. Open daily 3pm-last customer. MC/V.

KWEST MEN, 705 Duval St. (☎305-292-8500). By day, it's a mild-mannered gay bar. By night, it's a male strip club. Happy hour 3-8pm. Strip show 9pm. Amateur strip contest Sa midnight. Open daily 3pm-4am. AmEx/D/MC/V.

⌕ THE ROAD TO KEY LARGO: 99 MI.

From Key West, follow **US 1 North** into town.

KEY LARGO ☎305

Over half a century ago, Hollywood stars Humphrey Bogart and Lauren Bacall immortalized the name "Key Largo" with their hit movie. The quick-thinking locals of Rock Harbor, where some scenes were shot, decided to take advantage, changing the name of their town to Key Largo to attract tourists. The plan worked. While some visitors still come to see the relics of the moviemaking past, more are drawn to Key Largo's greatest natural assets: miles of coral reefs and incredible fishing.

VITAL STATS
Population: 16,000
Tourist Office: Key Largo Chamber of Commerce/Florida Keys Visitors Center, 106000 US 1 (☎305-451-1414 or 800-822-1088; www.keylargo. org), at mi. 106. Open daily 9am-6pm.
Library and Internet Access: Key Largo Library Branch, 101485 Overseas Hwy. (☎305-451-2396), in the Tradewinds Shopping Center. Open Tu and Th-F 9:30am-6pm, W 9:30am-8pm, Sa 10am-6pm.
Post Office: 101000 US 1 (☎305-451-3155), at mi. 100. Open M-F 8am-4:30pm, Sa 10am-1pm.
Postal Code: 33037.

◼ ORIENTATION

The **Overseas Highway (US 1)** bridges the Keys and the southern tip of Florida, stitching the islands together. Mile markers section the

highway and replace street addresses beginning with mi. 0 in Key West. In Key Largo, US 1 is a divided highway, and establishments are labeled "oceanside" (east of US 1) or "bayside" (to the west).

◼ ACCOMMODATIONS

The Pelican, mi. 99.5 bayside (☎305-451-3576; www.thepelican-keylargo.com). Features tropical flowers and cozy rooms with double beds, fridges, and cable TV. Guests have access to a small private beach, a dock, paddle boats, canoes, and hammocks. Rooms with kitchen and waterfront suites available. Laundry. Free Internet. Rooms $60-185. AmEx/D/MC/V. ❸

Ed and Ellen's Lodgings, mi. 103 oceanside (☎305-451-9949 or 888-333-5536; www.ed-ellens-lodgings.com). Large, clean rooms with cable TV, A/C, mini-fridges, and microwaves. Ed and Ellen, the cheerful owners, live out back and are eager to help. Doubles in winter $59-79; in summer $49-59. Suites also available. MC/V. ❸

Key Largo House Boatel, mi. 103.5 oceanside (☎305-766-0871; www.keylargohouseboatel. com). These floating boat houses come complete with A/C, cable TV, and full kitchens as well as a sun deck to enjoy the spectacular waterfront view. Rooms $75-150. AmEx/D/MC/V. ❹

John Pennekamp State Park Campground, mi. 102.5 (☎305-451-1202; www.pennekamppark. com). The 47 sites are clean, convenient, and worth the effort required to obtain them. The sites are available through advance registration and fill a year in advance for the winter. During the summer, call a few months in advance for weekends. While outdoors, beware of the pesky insects that descend at nightfall in Key Largo. Showers. Laundry. Open 8am-sunset. Sites with electricity $28.50. AmEx/D/MC/V. ❶

◼ FOOD

Seafood restaurants of varying price and specialty line the Overseas Hwy.

Mrs. Mac's Kitchen, mi. 99.4 bayside (☎305-451-3722). Serves bowls of chili ($4) and a truly divine homemade key lime pie ($3.25) to a mix of locals and tourists. The windows feature neon beer signs, and every surface is adorned with hundreds of license plates. Open M-Sa 7am-9:30pm. AmEx/D/MC/V. ❶

The Hideout Restaurant, mi. 103.5 oceanside (☎305-451-0128), at the end of Transylvania Ave. With bright pink walls and trophies over the mantle, The Hideout keeps locals happy with large homestyle breakfasts and fresh fish. Their blueberry pancakes ($4.25) will keep you truckin' all day. Open daily 7am-2pm. Cash only. ❶

Hobo's, mi. 101.7 oceanside (☎305-451-5888). Families take a break from the outdoors and cool down in the air-conditioned Hobo's. Happy hour features $0.40 clams, shrimp, and wings (M-F 3-6pm). For something a little more substantial, try the Hobo's Fish Sandwich ($8.50). Open daily 11am-10pm. MC/V. ❷

The Fish House, mi. 102.5 oceanside (☎305-451-4665; www.fishhouse.com). For a bit of a splurge, you can be served fish caught daily by local fishermen. Enjoy the catch of the day ($20) after a long day in the sun. Open daily 11:30am-10pm. AmEx/D/MC/V. ❺

🎵 NIGHTLIFE

Key Largo, unlike its sister to the south, isn't known for its nightlife. If you can't get enough of the great outdoors, try **Coconuts,** behind the Holiday Inn at mi. 100 oceanside. There's a tiki bar outside—inside, bands play Friday and Saturday nights. (☎305-453-9794. W ladies night. Su karaoke. Open 11am-2am. AmEx/D/MC/V.) Scuba divers and fishermen relax at **Sharkey's Pub and Galley,** mi. 100 oceanside, after a long day at sea; turn on Laguna Ave. (oceanside), take a left at Caribbean Dr., and follow the bend. The pub is tucked away in the side of the building facing the canal. The pool tables, darts, and $1.50 drafts keep the local crowd happy. (☎305-453-0999. Open noon-2am. MC/V.)

🏞️ OUTDOORS

Key Largo is the self-proclaimed "Dive Capital of the World," and diving instructors advertise on highway billboards. The ⚑**John Pennekamp Coral Reef State Park,** mi. 102.5 oceanside, is the nation's first underwater sanctuary and the best place to dive. The park extends 3 mi. into the Atlantic Ocean, safeguarding the only living coral reef in the continental US.

While Pennekamp's reefs are its main attraction, the park also has miles of mangroves reaching like fingers into the salt water. Stop by the park's **visitors center** for maps, boat and snorkeling tour info, an aquarium, and films about the park's habitat. (☎305-451-1202; www.pennekamppark.com. $3.50 per vehicle, $6 for two people; $0.50 per additional person.) To see the reefs, visitors must take their own boats or rent. (For boat reservations call ☎305-451-6325. 18 ft. motorboat $160 per 4hr., $259 per day. Canoes and kayaks $12-17 per hr. Deposit required. Open daily 8am-5pm.) **Scuba trips** depart from the visitors center. (☎305-451-6322. 9:30am, 1:30pm. 2-tank dive $50. Equipment rental surcharge. Deposit required. Certification required. Classes available.) A **snorkeling tour** allows non-certified visitors to experience the reefs. (☎305-451-6300. Tours 9am, noon, 3pm. Equipment $6. Deposit required. $29, under 18 $24.) The park also rents snorkeling equipment ($10) for use in the beach area. **Glass-bottom boat tours** provide a crystal-clear view of the reefs without wetting your feet. (☎305-451-1621. Tours 9:15am, 12:15, 3pm. $22, under 12 $15.) Head to any local marina to charter a spot on a fishing boat. At mi. 100 oceanside, the Holiday Inn Hotel's **marina** also hosts a number of companies that provide scuba, snorkel, and boat trips. The best known is the **Key Largo Princess,** which offers 2hr. glass-bottom boat tours. (☎305-451-4655; www.keylargoprincess.com. Tours 10am, 1, 4pm. $30, children $15.) The marina has become a tourist destination in its own right; it houses the **African Queen,** the boat from the 1952 film starring Humphrey Bogart and Katharine Hepburn.

🚩 THE ROAD TO THE EVERGLADES: 29 Mi.

Drive north on **US 1** until Florida City. Turn right onto **Palm Drive,** and follow the signs into the park.

THE EVERGLADES ☎239

Encompassing the entire tip of Florida and dipping into Florida Bay, Everglades National Park (the country's second-largest national park) spans 1.6 million acres and includes nine unique and fragile ecosystems. Vast prairies of sawgrass cut through broad expanses of shallow water, creating the park's famed

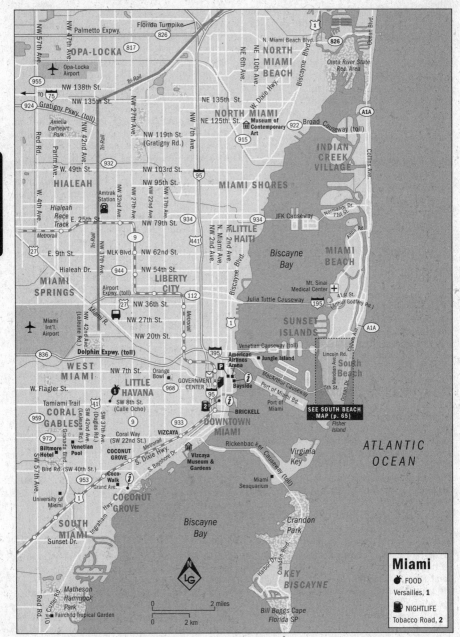

NW 57th Ave.
NW 47th Ave.
Palmetto Expwy.
826
Florida Turnpike
N. Miami Beach Blvd.
826
817
OPA-LOCKA
NE 6th Ave.
NORTH MIAMI BEACH
NE 10th Ave.
Biscayne Blvd.
Oleta River State Rec. Area
955
Opa-Locka Airport
75
TO
NW 138th St.
Tri-Rail
NW 135th St.
924
Gratigny Pkwy. (toll)
NE 135th St.
W. Dixie Hwy.
NORTH MIAMI
A1A
Amelia Earheart Park
NW 27th Ave.
NW 7th Ave.
NE 125th St.
Museum of Contemporary Art
922
Broad Causeway (toll)
Collins Ave.
Red Rd.
NW 42nd Ave.
NW 119th St. (Gratigny Rd.)
915
INDIAN CREEK VILLAGE
932
NW 103rd St.
Palmm Ave.
W. 49th St.
95
Normandy Dr. 71st St.
HIALEAH
NW 95th St.
MIAMI SHORES
W. 4th Ave.
NW 32nd Ave.
NW 22nd Ave.
NW 17th Ave.
934
JFK Causeway
934
Alton Rd.
Hialeah Race Track
Amtrak Station
E. 25th St.
NW 79th St.
N. Miami Ave.
LITTLE HAITI
MIAMI BEACH
Metrorail
Tri-Rail
9
441
NE 2nd Ave.
Biscayne Bay
27
E. 9th St.
MLK Blvd.
NW 62nd Ave.
N. Miami Ave.
NW 2nd Ave.
Mt. Sinai Medical Center
41st St.
Hialeah Dr.
944
NW 54th St.
LIBERTY CITY
112
Biscayne Blvd.
Julia Tuttle Causeway
195
(Arthur Godfrey Rd.)
MIAMI SPRINGS
Airport Expwy. (toll)
27
NW 36th St.
Miami R.
NW 27th St.
Metrorail
A1A
NW 42nd Ave. (Lejeune Rd.)
Miami Int'l. Airport
NW 20th St.
SUNSET ISLANDS
Ollie Ave.
836
Dolphin Expwy. (toll)
395
Venetian Causeway (toll)
Lincoln Rd.
SEE SOUTH BEACH MAP (p. 65)
WEST MIAMI
NW 7th St.
Orange Bowl
American Airlines Arena
Jungle Island
Meridian Ave.
SOUTH BEACH
W. Flagler St.
GOVERNMENT CENTER
P
MacArthur Causeway
5th St.
Ocean Dr.
LITTLE HAVANA
968
95
Bayside
Port of Miami Bd.
Tamiami Trail
SW 8th St. (Calle Ocho)
Port of Miami
41
SW 37th Ave.
SW 42nd Ave. (Lejeune Rd.)
SW 22nd Ave.
9
933
VIZCAYA
DOWNTOWN MIAMI
SEE SOUTH BEACH MAP (p. 65)
959
CORAL GABLES
Coral Way (SW 22nd St.)
BRICKELL
Fisher Island
972
Granada Blvd.
Venetian Pool
Metrorail
COCONUT GROVE
Rickenbacker Causeway (toll)
ATLANTIC OCEAN
Biltmore Hotel
Bird Rd. (SW 40th St.)
Vizcaya Museum & Gardens
Virginia Key
SW 57th Ave.
Coco-Walk
Grand Ave.
S. Dixie Hwy.
S. Bayshore Dr.
953
1
Miami Seaquarium
University of Miami
COCONUT GROVE
Crandon Park
SOUTH MIAMI
Ingraham Hwy.
Sunset Dr.
Biscayne Bay
Crandon Blvd.
Harbor Dr.
KEY BISCAYNE
N LG
Matheson Hammock Park
Fairchild Tropical Garden
Cutler Rd.
Red Rd.
0   2 miles

0   2 km
Bill Baggs Cape Florida SP

Miami
🍎 FOOD
Versailles, **1**
🍸 NIGHTLIFE
Tobacco Road, **2**

"river of grass," and tangled mazes of mangrove swamps wind up and down the western coast. To the south, delicate coral reefs lie below the shimmering blue waters of the bay. Keep your eyes open for American alligators, dolphins, sea turtles, birds, and fish—and particularly for the endangered American crocodile, Florida manatee, and Florida panther.

 PAGE TURN. See p. 764 in the **Southern Border** for complete coverage of the Everglades.

See p. 764 in the **Southern Border**

🝔 THE ROAD TO MIAMI: 43 MI.

Follow signs to **SR 821 North.** Get on **SR 824 North** and head into downtown Miami.

MIAMI ☎305

No longer purely a vacation spot for "snowbirds" (wealthy East Coasters escaping harsh winters), Miami's heart pulses to a beat all its own, fueled by the largest Cuban population this side of Havana. Appearance rules in this city, and nowhere is this more clear than on the shores of South Beach, where visual delights include Art Deco hotels and tanned beach bodies. South Beach (SoBe) is also host to a nightclub scene that attracts some of the world's most beautiful people. But it's not all bikinis and glitz—Miami is the entry point for one of America's great natural habitats, the Everglades, as well as the gateway to the Florida Keys and the Caribbean.

VITAL STATS

Population: 360,000

Tourist Offices: Miami Beach Visitors Center, 1920 Meridian Ave. (☎305-674-1300). Open M-F 9am-6pm, Sa-Su 10am-4pm. **Coconut Grove Chamber of Commerce,** 2820 McFarlane Rd. (☎305-446-9900). Open M-F 9am-5pm.

Library and Internet Access: Miami Public Library, 101 W. Flagler St. (☎305-375-2665). Open M and W-Th 9am-8pm, Tu and F-Sa 9am-5pm, Su 1-5pm.

Post Office: 500 NW 2nd Ave. (☎305-639-4284), downtown. Open M-F 8am-5pm, Sa 9am-1:30pm. **Postal Code:** 33101.

🝔 ORIENTATION

Three highways crisscross the Miami area. **I-95,** which runs along the east side of the city and is the most direct north-south route, merges into **US 1 (Dixie Highway)** just south of downtown. **Route 836 (Dolphin Expressway),** the east-west artery through town, connects I-95 to **Florida's Turnpike,** which circles the city in the west. Downtown Miami has a systematic street layout: streets run east-west, avenues run north-south, and both are numbered. Miami is divided into northeast, northwest, southeast, and southwest quadrants by **Flagler Street** and **Miami Avenue.**

The heart of **Little Havana** lies on **Calle Ocho (Southwest 8th Street)** between SW 12th and SW 27th Ave. **Coconut Grove,** south of Little Havana, centers on the shopping and entertainment district on **Grand Avenue** and **Virginia Street. Coral Gables,** an upscale residential area, is around the intersection of **Coral Way** and **Le Jeune Road (Southwest 42nd Avenue).** The **Tri-Rail,** an above-ground subway system, as well as a comprehensive bus network (☎305-770-3131; www.miamidade.gov/transit) provide safe and reliable public transportation, but it's still difficult to get around without a car in downtown Miami. Blocks are long, and pedestrians (the few and the proud) often have to cross many-laned roads with no crosswalks.

 LET'S NOT GO. When you're visiting Miami, it's best to avoid Liberty City, which is considered an unsafe area and has little to offer tourists.

Several causeways connect Miami to **Miami Beach.** The most useful is **MacArthur Causeway,** which becomes **Fifth Street.** Numbered streets run east-west across the island, increasing as you go north. In **South Beach (SoBe), Collins Avenue (Route A1A)** is the main north-south drag and runs parallel to club-filled **Washington Avenue** and beachfront **Ocean Drive.** The commercial district sits between Sixth and 23rd St. One-way streets, traffic jams, and limited parking make driving around South Beach frustrating. Tie on your most stylish sneakers, park the car, and enjoy the small island at your leisure or hop on the South Beach Local

($0.25) a bus service that runs every 10-15 min. around SoBe. (☎305-770-3131. Runs M-Sa 7:45am-1am, Su 10am-1am.)

ACCOMMODATIONS

Nothing comes cheap in South Beach, and rooms are no exception. Even so, choosing a place to stay is all about attitude. If young bohemian isn't your thing, cruise down Collins Ave. to hot-pink Art Deco hotels. In general, high season for Miami Beach runs from late December to mid-March; during the low season, hotel clerks are often quick to bargain. The **Miami Beach Visitors Center** (previous page) can help you find a place. Camping is not allowed on Miami Beach.

The Clay Hotel and International Hostel (HI-AYH), 1438 Washington Ave. (☎305-534-2988; www.theclayhotel.com). This historic Mediterranean-style building was once the center of Al Capone's Miami gambling syndicate and now hosts an international crowd. Kitchen and A/C. Lockers $1 per day. Laundry $1. Internet $4 per hr. Key deposit $10. Reservations required. In winter dorms $27, members $25; private rooms $60-160. In summer dorms $24, members $23; private rooms $48-78. MC/V. ❶

Hotel Shelley, 844 Collins Ave. (☎305-531-3341; www.hotelshelley.com). Its plush white lounge chairs, chic decor, loud music and dark hallways make Hotel Shelley feel more like a SoBe nightclub than an affordable place to spend the night. Complimentary mixed drinks and VIP passes to nearby clubs make it the perfect stay for partiers. Continental breakfast included. Free Internet and cable TV. Rooms M-F from $75, Sa-Su from $115. AmEx/MC/V. ❹

The Tropics Hotel/Hostel, 1550 Collins Ave. (☎305-531-0361; www.tropicshotel.com), across the street from the beach. This quiet refuge from the intense SoBe scene offers large, comfortable rooms and access to a lovely patio, pool, and outdoor kitchen. Linen included. Laundry $1. Free Internet. Key deposit $20. Reservations required Feb.-Apr. Dorms $27-34; private doubles $90-150. MC/V. ❷

Miami Beach International Travelers Hostel (HI-AYH), 236 9th St. (☎305-534-0268). Right in the heart of SoBe's club scene. Common room with TV and fridge. Storage room and safe-deposit boxes are strongly recommended. Laundry $1. Internet $5 per hr. Dorms $21, members $19; singles $67-111. MC/V. ❷

FOOD

Miami has a wide variety of restaurants, and most don't come cheap. For less expensive fare, check out **Little Havana** and **Little Haiti** or head to the open-air snack counters in South Beach and along **Calle Ocho.** In South Beach, restaurants can be found up and down **Ocean Drive** and along **Lincoln Road,** west of Washington St. and Espanola Way. Go one block inland from the beach to find cheaper prices.

David's Cafe, 1058 Collins Ave. (☎305-672-8707). In the 1940s, David opened an American-style diner. When it was bought by Cuban owners in the early 1960s, they changed the food but kept the name and the decor. An institution in SoBe, David's has open-air counters where you can get churros ($3), Cuban espresso ($0.75), or *batido* (fruit shakes; $3) on the go. Lunch specials $5. Open 24hr. AmEx/MC/V. ❶

News Cafe, 800 Ocean Dr. (☎305-538-6397). Though the food is outstanding, you're really paying for one of the best people-watching locations on Ocean Dr. Go in the evening for dessert (chocolate fondue for 2 $13) and gaze at the stylish bodies strolling by. Open 24hr. AmEx/MC/V. ❷

Macarena, 1334 Washington Ave. (☎305-531-3440). This festive eatery serves up Spanish delights alongside wine from its own vineyards. Live flamenco dancing F night. Cover after 10pm $10-20. Open M-Tu 7pm-midnight, W-Su 7pm-4am. AmEx/MC/V. ❸

Flamingo Cafe, 1454 Washington Ave. (☎305-673-4302). Overwhelming amounts of delicious food for staggeringly low prices. Breakfast plate with eggs, toast, and meat $3. Beef tacos $4. *Frijoles con queso* $2.75. Open M-Sa 7am-9:30pm. Cash only. ❶

Versailles, 3555 SW 8th St. (☎305-444-0240), in Little Havana. Miami Cuban to the core. Sit in the company of power brokers as you enjoy classic Cuban dishes like *ropa vieja* with sweet plantains ($10.50). Entrees $8-24. AmEx/MC/V. ❸

👁 SIGHTS

SOUTH BEACH

The hot bodies, Art Deco design, and sparkling sand of South Beach make these 17
blocks seem like their own universe. Ocean
Dr. is part fashion show and part raging party,
and it's the place for Miami's hottest to see and
be seen. Along Espanola Way and Lincoln Rd.,
pedestrian walkways feature outdoor dining,
tourist shops, and overpriced boutiques while
the Miami Beach Visitors Center offers free
maps and advice.

HOLOCAUST MEMORIAL. A series of sculptures and monuments erected over the course
of four years by sculptor Kenneth Treister.
Guided tours are sometimes offered free
by Holocaust survivors, a large population
of which immigrated to Miami Beach after
WWII. *(1933-1945 Meridian Ave. ☎305-538-1663.
www.holocaustmmb.org. Open daily 9am-9pm. Free.)*

MIAMI BEACH BOTANICAL GARDEN. Next to
the memorial, the gardens are a tropical paradise you can wander around for free. *(2000
Convention Center Dr. ☎305-673-7256; www.mbgarden.
com. Open daily 9am-5pm. Tours Tu-Su 11am. Free.)*

WOLFSONIAN MUSEUM. The museum examines the cultural impact of art and design from
1885 to 1945, exhibiting over 70,000 pieces. It
includes an exhaustive look at propaganda
from WWII, an array of political cartoons,
and a series of original Norman Rockwell
paintings. *(1001 Washington Ave. ☎305-531-1001;
www.wolfsonian.org. Open M-Tu and Sa-Su noon-6pm,
Th-F noon-9pm. $7.50, students and seniors $5. F after
6pm free.)*

JUNGLE ISLAND. Since 1936, visitors to Jungle Island have walked among orangutans
and free-flying parrots and flamingos. Other
attractions include an albino alligator and
parrot or reptile shows throughout the day.
*(1111 Parrot Jungle Trail. From downtown Miami, take the
MacArthur Causeway to Watson Island. Look for signs for
Parrot Jungle Trail. ☎305-258-6453; www.jungleisland.
com. Open daily 10am-6pm. $28, ages 3-10 $23, under
3 free.)*

COCONUT GROVE. A stroll through the streets
of Coconut Grove reveals an unlikely combi-

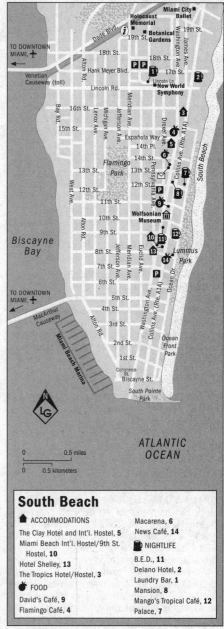

EAST COAST

South Beach

🛏 **ACCOMMODATIONS**

The Clay Hotel and Int'l. Hostel, **5**
Miami Beach Int'l. Hostel/9th St.
  Hostel, **10**
Hotel Shelley, **13**
The Tropics Hotel/Hostel, **3**

🍴 **FOOD**

David's Café, **9**
Flamingo Café, **4**

Macarena, **6**
News Café, **14**

🍸 **NIGHTLIFE**

B.E.D., **11**
Delano Hotel, **2**
Laundry Bar, **1**
Mansion, **8**
Mango's Tropical Café, **12**
Palace, **7**

nation of upscale boutiques and tacky tourist traps. The open-air mall, CocoWalk, along Grand Ave., presents ample opportunities for people-watching.

VIZCAYA MUSEUM AND GARDENS. As you walk around this 70-room 1916 Italian villa, it is easy to forget that you are still in sunny Florida. It has also been featured in numerous rap videos. *(3251 S. Miami Ave. On the bayfront between Coconut Grove and downtown. ☎305-250-9133; www. vizcayamuseum.com. Open daily 9:30am-4:30pm. $12, students $9, ages 6-12 $5. Gardens free.)*

BAYSIDE MARKETPLACE. Miami's outdoor, oceanfront shopping center caters to cruiseship guests and tourists with money to burn. Stores and restaurants are mainly chains or tourist boutiques. The free concerts held most nights and some afternoons are a redeeming feature. *(Off Biscayne Blvd., between NE 4th St. and NE 6th St. www.baysidemarketplace.com. Open M-Th 10am-10pm, F-Sa 10am-11pm, Su 11am-9pm.)*

MILLIONAIRES' ROW. From Bayside, you can take a boat tour with Island Queen Cruises to see mansions built on exclusive islands that can only be seen from the water. Ogle Enrique Iglesias's palatial mansion and Al Capone's former abode from afar. *(☎305-379-5119; www. islandqueencruises.com. Departures daily every hr. 11am-7pm. $22, ages 6-12 $16.)*

NORTH MIAMI

THE MUSEUM OF CONTEMPORARY ART (MOCA). MOCA is known for its often eccentric exhibits and displays. Having played host to Versace dresses and steel drummers alike, MOCA supports uncommon means of artistic expression. *(770 NE 125th St. ☎305-893-6211; www.mocanomi.org. Open Tu-Sa 11am-5pm, Su noon-5pm. $5, students and seniors $3, under 12 free.)*

CORAL GABLES. Dade County Commissioner George Merrick began building his "perfectly designed" city in 1921 to counter the sprawl of an emerging Miami. Merrick's city, now called the Coral Gables neighborhood, is replete with fountains, tree-lined esplanades, and Mediterranean-style houses. A drive down Granada Blvd. gives a taste of true Miami glamor. At the roundabout, stop to check out the imposing **Biltmore Hotel,** where Esther Williams once made aquatic movie masterpieces.

Those who can afford the hefty price tag for a room may enjoy a complimentary carriage ride through Coral Gables. *(1200 Anastasia Ave. ☎305-445-1926; www.biltmorehotel.com.)* For a more wallet-friendly but equally grandiose activity, check out the **Venetian Pool,** a beautiful Spanish-inspired swimming pool built in 1924. Even if you're not into swimming, the 820,000 gal. oasis deserves a quick look, if only for its role in the first Hollywood Tarzan movie. *(2701 De Soto Blvd. ☎305-460-5306; www. venetianpool.com. Open June-July M-F 11am-7:30pm, Sa-Su 10am-4:30pm; Aug. M-F 11am-5:30pm, Sa-Su 10am-4:30pm; Sept.-Oct. Tu-F 11am-5:30pm, Sa-Su 10am-4:30pm; Nov.-Mar. Tu-Su 11am-4:30pm; Apr.-May Tu-F 11am-5:30pm, Sa-Su 10am-4:30pm. Nov.-Mar. $6.25, ages 3-12 $3.25; Apr.-Oct. $9.50/5.25.)*

♫ ENTERTAINMENT

For the latest on Miami entertainment, check out the "Living Today," "Lively Arts," and Friday's "Weekend" section of the *Miami Herald. Weekly Oceandrive, New Times, Street,* and *Sun Post* also list local happenings. *TWN* and *Miamigo,* the major gay papers, are available free in paper boxes along Ocean Dr. Events occur regularly at the **Orange Bowl** (☎305-643-7100; www.orangebowlstadium.com.) and the **American Airlines Arena** (☎786-777-1000; www.aaarena.com); the latter is home to the **Miami Heat** NBA team. Football's **Miami Dolphins** (☎888-346-7849; www. miamidolphins.com) and, for now, baseball's **Florida Marlins** (☎877-627-5467; www.marlins. com) play at **Dolphin Stadium,** 2267 Dan Marino Blvd. (☎305-623-6100). Look for concerts at the **New World Symphony Orchestral Academy,** 541 Lincoln Rd. (☎305-673-3331; www.nws. edu. Tickets from $36.) **The Miami City Ballet,** 2200 Liberty Rd., and its performance school, known for cutting-edge ballet, also has performances throughout the year. (☎305-929-7000; www.miamicityballet.org. Tickets from $25. Student discounts up to 50%.) **Carnaval Miami** (☎786-444-3445; www.carnavalmiami.com), the nation's largest Hispanic festival, fills 23 blocks of Calle Ocho in early March with salsa dancing and the world's longest conga line.

🚇 NIGHTLIFE

Nightlife in the Art Deco district of South Miami Beach starts late and continues until well after sunrise. Clubs are centered on **Ocean Drive, Collins Avenue,** and **Washington Avenue,** between Seventh and 18th St. The scene is transient; what's there one week may not be there the next, so call in advance before heading out. Many clubs don't demand cover until after midnight, and the $20+ door charge can include an open bar. However, willingness to pay a steep cover is no guarantee of admission. Difficult doormen can prove impossible after 1am, so show up early and dress to impress. Many clubs have dress codes, and everyone always dresses to the nines, even on so-called "casual" nights. For a chance to experience a variety of clubs without breaking the bank, consider the Nightlife Pass, which will get you into 12 different clubs for only $25. (☎786-444-3445; www.nightlifepass.com.) Most nightclubs in Miami are 21+. South Beach's gay scene may be somewhat diminished since its heyday, but the gay and mixed clubs are still dance-club staples, attracting partiers of every inclination. Check out the unofficially gay portion of the beach, known as "muscle beach," around 12th St. and Ocean, across from Palace.

- 🏛 **Delano Hotel,** 1685 Collins Ave. (☎305-672-2000). What happens when a $3500 per night hotel sets up a lounge in its lobby and courtyard? Jaw-dropping decor and the poshest atmosphere in SoBe—and maybe the continent. Splurge for a $1300 bottle of champagne or, more realistically, dress in your finest and head over for a mixed drink ($15). No cover. Open daily noon-1 or 2am. AmEx/D/MC/V.

- 🏛 **Mansion,** 1235 Washington Ave. (☎305-532-1525; www.mansionmiami.com). An assault on all the senses, the lavish Mansion features a strange mix of extravagant chandeliers and oil paintings with bar dancers in lingerie. Mostly known as a bumping club with lines around the corner. The VIP section is littered with celebrities sipping Cristal. Cover $25. Open daily 11pm-5am. AmEx/D/MC/V.

- 🏛 **Laundry Bar,** 721 Lincoln Ln. N. (☎305-531-7700; www.thelaundrybar.com). Small street just north of Lincoln Rd. In wild South Beach, even doing your chores is an occasion to party in style. Men and women alike flock to the GLBT Laundry Bar, a casual hangout spot where you can play pool, grab a drink, and do a load of laundry ($2.75). Yes—really. 21+ after 10pm. No cover. Open daily 8am-5am. AmEx/D/MC/V.

- 🏛 **Palace,** 1200 Ocean Dr. (☎305-531-9077). Offers a glimpse of what Ocean Dr. was like in the 80s. A laid-back gay bar with wild dancing and impromptu drag shows. Music can vary depending on the nightly theme. Passersby are often pulled off the street to join the party. No cover. Open daily 10am-11pm. AmEx/MC/V.

- **Mango's Tropical Cafe,** 900 Ocean Dr. (☎305-673-4422; www.mangostropicalcafe.com). All that noise you hear while walking up Ocean Dr. is coming from here. Mango's is the main Latin-inspired venue in SoBe and is always filled with tourists. Order a stiff and delicious CoCo-Loco ($8) and stay for a set of live music, ending with a bar-top dance extraordinaire by alluring waitresses and buffed-up waiters. Not for the faint of heart. 21+ after 6pm. Cover $5-20. Open daily 11am-5am. AmEx/D/MC/V.

- **BED,** 929 Washington Ave. (☎305-532-9070). The acronym stands for Beverage, Entertainment, and Dining, which pretty much sums up the attraction of this venue. Patrons lounge on sexy beds as they enjoy dinner, drinks, and the atmosphere of silky seduction that oozes from every corner of this SoBe favorite. No cover.

- **Tobacco Road,** 626 S. Miami Ave. (☎305-374-1198), at SW 7th St. Fun, laid-back, and the oldest bar in Miami. Munch on killer burgers ($6-9) to the rhythm of local bands belting out the blues and old-fashioned rock and roll. Shows ($5) often held on the top floor. Open daily 11:30am-5am. AmEx/D/MC/V.

🚗 THE ROAD TO FORT LAUDERDALE: 53 MI.

From Florida City, follow **US 1 North** until it becomes **I-95 North.** Follow signs to Fort Lauderdale.

FORT LAUDERDALE ☎954

Over the past two decades, Fort Lauderdale has transformed from a city known as a beer-stained, spring-break mecca to the largest yachting center in North America. City streets and highways may be fine for the commoner's transportation needs, but Fort Lauderdale adds another option: canals. Intricate waterways connect ritzy homes with the intracoastal waterway, and even mere mortals can cruise the canals via the **Water Taxi,** an on-the-water bus system. "The Venice of America" also has 23 mi. of beaches where spring-break mayhem still reigns supreme, making Fort "Liquordale" fun even for those who can't afford a yacht.

Population: 167,000

Tourist Office: Greater Fort Lauderdale Convention and Visitors Bureau, 100 E. Broward Blvd., Ste. 200 (☎954-765-4466; www.sunny.org). Open M-F 8:30am-5pm.

Library and Internet Access: Broward County Library, 100 S. Andrews Ave. (☎954-357-7444). Open M-Th 9am-9pm, F-Sa 9am-5pm, Su noon-5:30pm.

Post Office: 1900 W. Oakland Park Blvd. (☎954-765-5720). Open M-F 7:30am-7pm, Sa 8:30am-2pm. **Postal Code:** 33310.

ORIENTATION

Fort Lauderdale is bigger than it looks. The city extends westward from its 23 mi. stretch of beach to encompass nearly 450 sq. mi. Streets and boulevards run east-west and avenues run north-south. All are labeled "NW," "NE," "SW," or "SE" according to quadrant. The two major roads in Fort Lauderdale are **Broward Boulevard** and **Andrews Avenue.** The brick-and-mortar downtown centers on **US 1 (Federal Highway)** and **Las Olas Boulevard,** about 2 mi. west of the oceanfront. Yachts fill the inlets of the **Intracoastal Waterway** between downtown and the waterfront. **The Strip** (a.k.a. Rte. A1A, Fort Lauderdale Beach Blvd., 17th St. Causeway, Ocean Blvd., or Seabreeze Blvd.) runs 4 mi. along the beach between **Oakland Park Boulevard** to the north and **Las Olas Boulevard** to the south. North-south **I-95** connects West Palm Beach, Fort Lauderdale, and Miami. **Route 84/I-75 (Alligator Alley)** runs 100 mi. west from Fort Lauderdale across the Everglades to small cities on Florida's Gulf Coast. **Florida's Turnpike** runs parallel to I-95.

ACCOMMODATIONS

Thank decades of spring-breakers for the abundant hotels lining the beachfront. Motels just north of the strip and a block west of Rte. A1A are the cheapest. Generally, it's easy to find a room at any time of the year. High season runs from mid-February to early April, and many hotels offer low-season deals. The *Fort Lauderdale News* and the *Miami Herald* occasionally publish listings from local residents who rent rooms to tourists in spring. Sleeping on the patrolled beaches is illegal.

Tropi-Rock Resort, 2900 Belmar St. (☎954-564-0523 or 800-987-9385), 2 blocks west of Rte. A1A at Birch Rd. This brightly colored and eclectically decorated yellow-and-orange hotel provides personalized attention by the owners, unique decorations in every room, and a pool set in a lush tropical garden. Gym, tiki bar, tennis courts, BBQ grills, free local calls, and refrigerators. No parties allowed. Free Internet. Rooms from mid-Dec. to Apr. $112-128; from Apr. to mid-Dec. from $75. AmEx/D/MC/V. ❹

Fort Lauderdale Beach Hostel, 2115 N. Ocean Blvd. (☎954-567-7275; www.fortlauderdale-hostel.com), off NE 21st St. After a long day at the beach, backpackers mingle in the tropical courtyard. A/C, a pool table, 2 lounges with TVs, and coin-operated washer and dryer. Breakfast included. Free lockers. Free Internet. Key deposit $10. Free parking. Reception 8am-noon. Reservations recommended. Dorms $20; private rooms $39-59. AmEx/D/MC/V. ❶

The Bridge II, 506 SE 16th St. (☎954-522-6350). Sunburned travelers take a break from the beach by jumping in this hostel's pool. A/C and kitchens. Linen deposit $10. Laundry. Free Internet. Reception 8:30-11:30am and 4:30-9pm. 4-bed dorms for ages 18-35 $25. MC/V. ❶

Floyd's Hostel/Crew House, 445 SE 16th St. (☎954-462-0631; www.floydshostel.com). A homey hostel catering to international travelers and boat crews. Lockers. Linen deposit $10. Laundry. Internet. Passport or American driver's license required. No FL residents. 4-bed dorms $23. Private rooms $50. AmEx/D/MC/V. ❶

FOOD

Locals and tourists alike flock to **Las Olas Boulevard** for a mix of casual and upscale restaurants and great people-watching.

- **The Floridian,** 1410 E. Las Olas Blvd. (☎954-523-8636). A low-key local favorite whose walls are covered with photos of celebrities taken by the owner's good friend, a photographer for the *Sun-Sentinel*. Try the burger platter, served with a heaping mound of fries ($7.60), with one of the excellent milkshakes ($4), and you might never want to leave. Free Wi-Fi. Open 24hr. AmEx. ❷

- **Big City Tavern,** 609 E. Las Olas Blvd. (☎954-727-0307). An elegant eatery in the heart of the Las Olas strip serving patrons beneath art and a finely paneled ceiling. Enjoy chicken rigatoni ($17) or almond crusted trout ($21) in the brick-lined interior or on the bustling patio. Open daily 11:30am-2:30pm and 5pm-midnight. AmEx/D/MC/V. ❹

- **Squiggy's NY Style Pizza,** 207 SW 2nd St. (☎954-522-6655), in Old Town. Whether you're between bars or looking for a treat before heading home, Squiggy's is the place for those late-night munchies. This no-nonsense pizza shop serves gooey slices of Sicilian pie ($2.25, after 8pm $3) and $3 domestic beers long into the night. Open M-Tu 11am-11pm, W-Su 11am-5am. AmEx/D/MC/V. ❶

SIGHTS

Fort Lauderdale Beach doesn't have a dull spot on it, but most of the action is between Las Olas Blvd. and Sunrise Blvd. Alongside the canal system is the Las Olas waterfront, where people stroll and enjoy the clubs, restaurants, shopping, and bars.

WATER TAXI. Sure, these boats are a relaxing way to beat rush-hour traffic and maneuver through town, but they're also an attraction in their own right. The friendly captains will steer right up to any Las Olas restaurant or drop you off at any of the 11 stops along the Intracoastal Waterway or New River. Alternatively, ride the entire route for an intimate view of the colossal houses along the canal. *(651 Seabreeze Blvd., on Rte. A1A. ☎954-467-6677; www.watertaxi.com. Runs daily 11am-midnight. 1-day pass $13, under 12 $10. $7 after 7pm; 3-day pass $12. Purchase tickets on board. Cash only.)*

DANIA JAI-ALAI. It's a bird! It's a plane! No, it's **jai alai.** This fast-paced game—with players hurling balls at up to 180 mph—is relatively unknown to most Americans; think of it as racquetball on steroids. Place your bets on a match at Dania, which sports one of the largest frontons (courts) in the state. *(301 E. Dania Beach Blvd., off US 1, 10min. south of Fort Lauderdale. ☎954-927-2841; www.dania-jai-alai.com. Games Tu and Sa noon and 7pm, W-F 7pm, Su 1pm. Tickets from $2.)*

ECOLOGICAL "BREAKTHROUGH" BACKFIRES

One hundred and twelve successful artificial reefs around Fort Lauderdale, generated using materials such as sunken ships, oil rigs, and concrete, have many ecological benefits. They provide new habitats for marine life and relieve the pressure of tourism and fishing from the fragile natural reefs. However, in 1972, in an enlightened attempt to both recycle cumbersome material and create a huge new habitat, an estimated two million used tires were dumped into the ocean. The tires, which are too light to stay at the bottom, have created what the *Washington Post* called a "spectacular disaster." Strong currents and hurricanes have spread the tires over 35 acres of ocean bottom, often slamming them against the natural reefs. The cleanup of this well-intentioned underwater dump is a colossal task that will cost the county millions. Yet, even in this dire situation, a government partnership has been reached that will make the task a feasible one. Over the next few years, divers of the US Army, Navy, and Coast Guard will recover tires from the sea bottom as part of their military training. This unprecedented agreement will help the county, the military, and, most importantly, the vulnerable

FISHING HALL OF FAME AND MUSEUM. Cast your line at the International Game Fishing Association's Hall of Fame and Museum, where life-size mounts of record fish finally settle the long-standing question, "How big was it?" Interactive fishing simulations allow visitors to feel the bite, while exhibits describe the technology and history of fishing. The museum also hosts the largest fishing library in the world. (*300 Gulf Stream Way, off I-95 at Griffin Rd., Exit 23. ☎ 954-922-4212; www.igfa.org. Open M-F 10am-6pm, Su noon-6pm. $6, seniors and children $5. Free parking.*)

INTERNATIONAL SWIMMING HALL OF FAME AND MUSEUM. For a different kind of high-seas adventure, dog-paddle over to the Swimming Hall of Fame, where exhibits on the sport, its greatest athletes, and sequined bathing costumes await. Check out the collection of Olympic medals and the $550 bathing suit in which swimmers have broken 36 world records. (*1 Hall of Fame Dr., off E. Rte. A1A. ☎ 954-462-6536; www.ishof.org. Open daily 9am-5pm. $8, students $4, under 12 free.*)

MUSEUM OF ART FORT LAUDERDALE. The museum is home to an extensive collection of American Impressionist painter William Glacken's work. There are also remarkable temporary exhibits, which showcase everything from laser shows to photojournalism. (*1 E. Las Olas Blvd. ☎ 954-525-5500; www.moafl.org. Open M and W-Su 11am-7pm. Tours Sa-Su 1:30pm. $10, ages 6-17 and seniors $7. Free Th 4-7pm.*)

🎭 NIGHTLIFE

As any local will tell you, the real Fort Lauderdale nightlife action is in Old Town. Two blocks northwest of Las Olas Blvd. on Second St. near the Riverwalk district, the 300 ft. stretch of Old Town is packed with raucous bars, steamy clubs, cheap eats, and a stylish crowd. Considerably more expensive and geared specifically toward tourists, the Strip, along Rte. A1A and across from the beach, is home to several popular nightspots.

Tarpon Bend, 200 SW 2nd St. (☎ 954-523-3233). Always the busiest place on the block, it feels like an upscale version of a raucous beach party. Live, loud rock music most nights. Happy hour daily 4-7pm with 2-for-1 drinks. Open M-Sa 11:30am-4am, Su noon-4am. AmEx/D/MC/V.

Elbo Room, 241 S. Fort Lauderdale Beach Blvd., (☎ 954-463-4615), at the corner of Rte. A1A and Las Olas Blvd. This booming sidewalk bar has one of the most packed scenes on the Strip. Casual, fun, and perfect for wandering in off the beach. Nightly live rock. Domestic beers $3. Imported beers $4. Open M-F 11am-2am, Sa 11am-3am, Su noon-2am. Cash only.

The Voodoo Lounge, 111 SW 2nd St. (☎ 954-522-0733). With 18,000 sq. ft. of dance floors, plush, roped-off VIP tables, and its own clothing line, the Voodoo Lounge is Fort Lauderdale's answer to South Beach. The party doesn't get going until midnight or later; come too early and you'll be grinding under the black lights all alone. Drag shows Su midnight, 2am. Cover for men $10, for women Sa $5. Open W-Su 10pm-4am. AmEx/D/MC/V.

🏞 OUTDOORS

WATER

Aloha Watersports, 301 Seabreeze Blvd. Rte. A1A. (☎ 954-462-7245). The best known beach spot for watersport equipment rentals and trips. Charter a sailboat or enjoy the serene blue water from above on a parasailing trip. Speedboats and waverunners are also available. Parasailing $75 per hr. Single kayak $20 per hr. Waverunner $65 per 15min. Open daily 9am-5pm.

LAND

Hugh Taylor Birch State Park, 3109 E. Sunrise Blvd. (☎ 954-564-4521), west off Rte. A1A. In the midst of Fort Lauderdale's urban sprawl; the park is an enclave of subtropical trees and animals. Bike, jog, or drive through the 2 mi. stretch of mangroves and royal palms or canoe through the freshwater lagoon filled with herons, gophers, tortoises, and marsh rabbits. Areas for picnicking, fishing, birding, and swimming. Open daily 8am-sunset. Gate on Rte. A1A open 9am-5pm. $4 per vehicle, $1 per pedestrian. Canoes $5.30 per hr. Cabins and primitive sites available by reservation; call ahead.

🚗 THE ROAD TO PALM BEACH AND WEST PALM BEACH: 45 MI.

From Fort Lauderdale, follow **US 1 North** into town.

PALM BEACH AND WEST PALM BEACH ☎561

Nowhere else in Florida is the line between the "haves" and the "have-nots" as visible as the intracoastal waterway dividing the aristocratic vacationers of Palm Beach Island from the residents of West Palm Beach. Five-star resorts and mansions reign over the "Gold Coast" island, while auto-repair shops and fast-food restaurants characterize the mainland. Budget travel may be difficult here, but the region still offers some unique museums and stunning houses.

VITAL STATS
Population: 10,000/88,932
Tourist Office: Palm Beach County Convention and Visitors Bureau, 1555 Palm Beach Lakes Blvd., Ste. 800 (☎561-233-3000; www.palmbeachfl.com), in West Palm Beach. Open M-F 8:30am-5:30pm.
Library and Internet Access: West Palm Beach Public Library, 100 Clematis St. (☎561-868-7701; www.wpbpl.com). Open M-Th 9:30am-8:30pm, F-Sa 9am-5pm, Su noon-5pm.
Post Office: 640 Clematis St. (☎561-833-0929), in West Palm Beach. Open M-F 8:30am-5pm. **Postal Code:** 33401.

ORIENTATION

I-95 runs north-south through the center of West Palm Beach and then continues north to Daytona and Jacksonville. The more scenic coastal highway **Route A1A** also travels north-south, crossing over Lake Worth at the **Flagler Memorial Bridge** to run along the beach in Palm Beach. Large highways cut through urban areas and residential neighborhoods; finding your way around can be a bit confusing. Stick to major roads like north-south **US 1** (which turns into **South Dixie Highway**), Rte. A1A, east-west **Palm Beach Lakes Boulevard,** and **Belvedere Road.** The heart of downtown West Palm Beach is **Clematis Street,** across from the Flagler Memorial Bridge, and the nearby outdoor mall **CityPlace,** 700 Rosemary Ave.; both contain affordable restaurants and wild nightclubs. **Molly's Trolleys** offer free transportation in the downtown area of Clematis St. and CityPlace. (☎561-838-9511; www.mollystrol-

leys.com. Open M-W and Su 11am-9pm, Th-F 11am-11pm.)

ACCOMMODATIONS

Catering to the rich and famous who flock to Palm Beach during the winter months, extravagant resorts and hotels are arguably the most notable attraction lining the Gold Coast. Many reasonably priced B&Bs are booked far in advance; reserve a room before you arrive. West Palm Beach is the best bet for an affordable room near the action, but the absolute cheapest options are the chain hotels near the highway.

Hibiscus House Downtown Bed & Breakfast, 213 S. Rosemary Ave. (☎561-833-8171 or 866-833-8171; www.hibiscushousedowntown. com), just down the block from CityPlace. Large, airy rooms, each individually named and tastefully decorated in 2 historic 1919 homes. After a late night at the house bar, wake up to a complimentary gourmet breakfast. Free Internet. Rooms in winter $140-280; in summer $120-240. AmEx/D/MC/V. ⑤

Hibiscus House Bed & Breakfast, 501 30th St. (☎561-863-5633 or 800-203-4927; www. hibiscushouse.com), at the corner of Spruce St. Flanked by historic houses, the sister establishment to the downtown Hibiscus is a quiet, antique-filled home with a heated pool, tropical gardens, and fishpond. Call ahead for reservations in winter. Rooms Dec.-Apr. $150-210; May.-Nov. $89-125. AmEx/D/MC/V. ⑤

Hotel Biba, 320 Belvedere Rd. (☎561-832-0094; www.hotelbiba.com), in West Palm Beach. Fun, funky, and eclectic. Don't be fooled by its turquoise exterior; Hotel Biba, with quirky furniture and an elegant courtyard, is a haven for travelers with a sense of style. Beautiful bodies lounge on the pool deck and gather in the garden bar for drinks in the evening. Champagne party and live DJ at the bar W-Th. Live jazz F. Breakfast included. Free Internet. Rooms Dec.-Mar. $215-325; Apr.-Nov. $110-200. AmEx/MC/V. ⑤

FOOD

Clematis St., in downtown West Palm Beach, offers lively options for budget travelers.

Pizza Girls, 114 Clematis St. (☎561-833-4004; www.pizzagirls.com). The slices here put ordinary

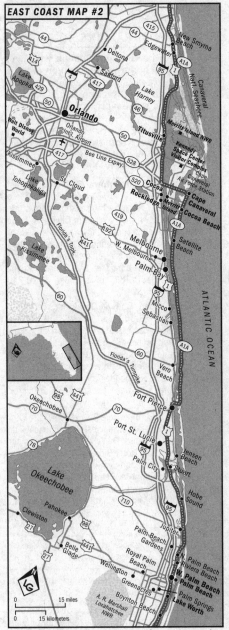

EAST COAST MAP #2

pizza to shame. Try an enormous slab ($2.50) with garlic bread ($3), and they'll have to roll you out the door. For a vegetarian option, go for the New Yorker ($4). Open M-W 11am-10pm, Th-Sa 11am-11pm, Su noon-9pm. MC/V. ❶

Sloan's, 112 Clematis St. (☎561-833-3335; www.sloansonline.com). Though this bright-pink ice-cream store looks more like a toy store than anything else, don't be surprised to find candy underwear for sale on the counter. Silly, perhaps, but the 34 flavors of ice cream ($4.60) are no joke. Open M-W 1-10pm, Th-Sa 11am-11pm, Su noon-10pm. D/MC/V. ❶

Maison Carlos, 207 Clematis St. (☎561-659-6524; www.maisoncarlos.com). This elegant French and Italian bistro serves a fantastic grilled artichoke with house hollandaise ($12) under indoor umbrellas and low-hanging lights. Open Oct.-May M-F 11:30am-2:30pm and 5:30-10pm, Sa 5:30-10pm; June-July Tu-F 11:30am-2:30pm and 5:30-10pm, Sa 5:30-10pm. AmEx/MC/V. ❹

👁 📷 SIGHTS AND BEACHES

To the east, in Palm Beach, just walking around is one of the most enjoyable (and affordable) activities. Known as the "Rodeo Dr. of the South," **Worth Avenue,** between S. Ocean Blvd. and Coconut Row, outfits Palm Beach's rich and famous in the threads of fashion heavyweights. Drive along Ocean Blvd. to gawk at spectacular mansions owned by celebrities and millionaires.

RAGTOPS. For a true roadtripper, a stop at Ragtops is a must, and not just because it's the only place where you'll see a gas pump advertising $0.45 a gallon. This 1927 Cadillac dealership is now a museum of sorts, housing over 50 beautiful classic cars as well as old road signs, traffic lights, drive-in diners, and all kinds of car-culture relics. Most of the cars are actually for sale. *(2119 S. Dixie Hwy. ☎561-655-2836; www.ragtopsmotorcars.com. Open M-Sa 10am-6pm. $5.)*

NORTON MUSEUM OF ART. The museum is well known for its collection of European, American, contemporary, and Chinese art. The museum displays works by Picasso, Warhol, Rubens, and Matisse. Stop by the central garden, which features its own fountain of youth, and make sure to take at look at the stunning Chihuly ceiling.

(1451 S. Olive Ave. ☎561-832-5196; www.norton.org. Open Nov.-Apr. M-Sa 10am-5pm, Su 1-5pm; May-Oct. Tu-Sa 10am-5pm, Su 1-5pm. Tours F-Su 2pm. $12, ages 13-21 $5. Special exhibits $10/4.)

ROGER DEAN STADIUM. If you're visiting in early spring, catch the training seasons of the **Saint Louis Cardinals** and **Florida Marlins,** who hold training camp at Roger Dean Stadium in Jupiter, 15 mi. to the north. During the rest of the season, the Jupiter Hammerheads and the Palm Beach Cardinals single-A minor-league teams play nightly. *(4751 Main St., Jupiter. Take I-95 N. to Exit 73. ☎561-966-3309; www.rogerdeanstadium.com. Spring training $12-27; minor league $8.50.)*

PALM BEACH ZOO. For a glimpse of lions and tigers and bears, check out the Palm Beach Zoo, where you'll watch with envy as kids frolic in the interactive fountain. *(1301 Summit Blvd. ☎561-547-9453; www.palmbeachzoo.org. Open daily 9am-5pm. $13, ages 3-12 $9.)*

THE BREAKERS. One particularly remarkable complex is The Breakers, a sprawling Italian Renaissance-style resort with a regal driveway flanked by tall palms. If you can't afford the bare-minimum $300 price tag for a night of luxury, live vicariously though a guided tour. *(1 S. County Rd. ☎561-655-6611 or 888-273-2537. Tours Tu 2pm. $15. Call ahead for reservations, ext. 7690.)*

SEASIDE. A trip to Palm Beach County is incomplete if you don't take the time to relax on one of its picturesque beaches. Although most of the beachfront property in Palm Beach is private, more public beaches can be found in West Palm Beach. Good options on Palm Beach include the popular **Midtown Beach** and **Phipps Ocean Park,** which has tennis courts for public use. *(Midtown 400 S. Ocean Blvd. Phipps 2185 S. Ocean Blvd. ☎561-585-9203. Open 8am-8pm. Tennis courts open M-F 8am-12:30pm and 2-7:30pm, Sa-Su 8am-12:30pm.)*

🎵 NIGHTLIFE

West Palm Beach's nightlife centers on Clematis St. and nearby CityPlace. Clematis St. in downtown West Palm Beach offers a lively option for travelers on the cheap, with a Thursday-to-Saturday nightlife scene that rivals any college town.

Dr. Feelgoods Bar and Grill, 219 Clematis St. (☎561-833-6500; www.drfeelgoodsbar.com). Big motorcycles, a huge mural, and a life-like green 🐉**dragon** climbing up a pillar adorn Dr. Feelgoods, where rock fans young and old dance and drink the night away. 21+. No cover Tu-W or before 10pm. Open Tu-W 8pm-3am, Th-F 5pm-3am, Sa 8pm-4am.

O'Shea's Irish Pub and Restaurant, 531 Clematis St. (☎561-833-3865; www.osheaspub.com), at Rosemary St. With tasty meals like shepherd's pie ($13), O'Shea's is a perfect place to have a few beers, play some pool, and watch the game. Free Wi-Fi. Open M-F 10am-3am, Sa-Su 10am-4am. AmEx/D/MC/V.

🚗 **THE ROAD TO COCOA BEACH AND CAPE CANAVERAL: 140 MI.**

From West Palm Beach, take **US 1 North** to Fort Pierce and take **Route A1A North** into Cocoa Beach.

COCOA BEACH AND CAPE CANAVERAL ☎321

Cape Canaveral and the surrounding "Space Coast" were hot spots during the Cold War. Once the great Space Race began, the area took off, becoming the base of operations for every major space exploration, from the Apollo moon landings to the current International Space Station effort. During summer launch dates, tourists pack the area and hotel prices skyrocket. The town of Cocoa Beach is a popular spring-break destination, full of beach bums and surfers; make sure to catch a wave while in the area.

🔳 ORIENTATION

The Space Coast, 50 mi. east of Orlando, consists of mainland Cocoa and Rockledge, oceanfront Cocoa Beach and Cape Canaveral, and Merritt Island. Both **I-95** and **US 1** run north-south on the mainland, while **Route A1A (North Atlantic Avenue)** is the beach's main drag. East-west **Route 520** connects Cocoa Beach with the mainland, while **Route 528** connects Cape Canaveral to Merritt Island.

EAST COAST

VITAL STATS

Population: 12,588

Tourist Offices: Cocoa Beach Chamber of Commerce, 400 Fortenberry Rd. (☎321-459-2200; www.cocoabeachchamber.com), on Merritt Island. Open M-F 9am-4pm. **Convention and Visitor's Bureau,** 8501 Astronaut Blvd. (Rte. A1A), Ste. 4. (☎321-454-2022; www.visitcocoabeach.com), on Cape Canaveral. Open daily 9am-4pm. **Space Coast Office of Tourism,** 530 Brevard Ave., Ste. 150 (☎321-433-4470; www.space-coast.com). Open M-F 8am-5pm.

Library and Internet Access: Cocoa Beach Public Library, 550 N. Brevard Ave. (☎321-868-1104; www.cocoabeachpubliclibrary.org), in Cocoa Beach. Free. Open M-W 9am-9pm, Th 9am-6pm, F-Sa 9am-5pm, Su 1-5pm.

Post Office: 500 N. Brevard Ave. (☎321-783-2544), in Cocoa Beach. Open M-F 9am-5pm, Sa 9am-noon. **Postal Code:** 32931.

ACCOMMODATIONS

Wary of wild teenagers, some hotels in Cocoa Beach rent rooms only to those 21+.

Dixie Motel, 301 Forrest Ave. (☎321-632-1600). From A1A, take Rte. 528 W. In Cocoa proper, the Dixie Motel is a family-owned establishment with clean rooms, A/C, cable TV, and a swimming pool. No parties allowed. Laundry available. Rooms $66. 21+. AmEx/MC/V. ❸

Fawlty Towers Resort, 100 E. Cocoa Beach Causeway (☎321-784-3870 or 800-887-3870; www.fawltytowersresort.com), off Rte. A1A. Along wtih the hot-pink decor comes a heated 24hr. pool, a tiki bar, and the entire video collection of *Fawlty Towers.* Rooms in winter $130-160; in summer $60-80. AmEx/MC/V. ❹

Motel 6, 3701 N. Atlantic Ave. (☎321-783-3103; www.motel6.com). Across from the beach, Motel 6 offers clean, comfortable rooms at cheaper rates than most accommodations in the area. A/C, pool, shuffleboard, and laundry. Wi-Fi $3 per 24hrs. Rooms $50-70. AmEx/D/MC/V. ❸

Jetty Park Campgrounds, 400 E. Jetty Rd. (☎321-783-7111; www.jettypark.org). Follow Rte. A1A N. 100s of sites, which include hookup, a playground, a swimming beach, a volleyball court, and a dump site. Showers and laundry.

Reserve 3 months ahead. Sites Jan.-Apr. $30, with water and electricity $35, with full hookup $40; May-Dec. $20/25/30. MC/V. ❶

FOOD

Coconuts on the Beach, 2 Minutemen Causeway (☎321-784-1422; www.coconutsonthebeach.com), at Rte. A1A. Prime beachside real estate and live music make the pastel-colored Coconuts on the Beach a popular hangout for folks of all ages. Try the classic crab cake ($7.45) for lunch or the coconut-crusted mahi-mahi ($15) for dinner while chilling on the deck and watching surfers. Open daily 11am-10pm. AmEx/D/MC/V. ❸

The Sunrise Diner, 365 W. Cocoa Beach Causeway (☎321-783-5647), at Rte. 520. Serves Greek food alongside typical diner fare. Don't let the fake plants discourage you; the gyro ($5) and corned beef ($5.50) are both delicious, and be sure to save room for pie ($2), baked fresh daily. Open daily 6am-9pm. AmEx/D/MC/V. ❶

Roberto's Little Havana, 26 N. Orlando Ave. (☎321-784-1868). For an authentic Cuban meal, try Roberto's Little Havana, where fried green plantains ($2.25) or the Classic Cuban Sampler ($12) will give you a taste of Havana that Fidel himself would crave. Open Tu-Th and Su 7am-3pm and 5-9pm, F-Sa 7am-3pm and 5-10pm. AmEx/D/MC/V. ❷

Cafe Unique, 607 Florida Ave. (☎321-504-0823; www.uniquecreationscourtyard.com/cafe), in Cocoa Village. An Amish deli and coffee shop that serves up farmers' cheeses and meats on freshly baked Amish bread. For a vegetarian treat, order the Village Veggie Delight ($6) and try 1 of more than 20 flavors of ice cream ($2). Open M-F 7:30am-6pm, Sa 7:30am-4pm. ❶

SIGHTS

KENNEDY SPACE CENTER. All of NASA's shuttle flights take off from the Kennedy Space Center, 18 mi. north of Cocoa Beach on Rte. 3. The **Kennedy Space Center Visitors Complex (KSC)** provides a huge welcome center, complete with two 3D IMAX theaters, a Rocket Garden, the brand new Shuttle Launch Experience simulator, and exhibits on the latest in space exploration. *(Follow Rte. A1A N. as it joins Rte. 528 W. onto Merritt Island, then to Rte. 3 N.*

☎321-452-2121 or 449-4444; www.kennedyspace-center.com. Open daily 9am-7pm. Tours 9am-2:45pm every 15min.) The KSC offers three tours of its 220 sq. mi. grounds. The **Kennedy Space Center Tour** features the three main attractions: the **LC 39 Observation Gantry,** where visitors can see the launch pads and assembly buildings; the **Apollo/Saturn V Center,** which houses a 363 ft. rocket; and the **International Space Station Center.** It also includes access to the **Astronaut Hall of Fame** as well as all of the movies, exhibits, and shows. (Open daily 9am-6pm. $38, ages 3-11 $28.) Meet a real space pioneer face to face at the daily **Lunch with an Astronaut,** in which astronauts of the past and present discuss their otherworldly experiences. ($23, ages 3-11 $16.) The **NASA Up Close Tour** provides access to facilities that are restricted on the standard tour. Guides take you to the shuttle launch pad, the gigantic VAB building (where the shuttle is put together), and the Crawler Transporter. ($21, ages 3-11 $15.) Check NASA's launch schedule—you may have a chance to watch *Endeavor, Atlantis,* or *Discovery* thunder off into the blue yonder above the cape. A combo package will get you admission to the visitors complex and transportation to a viewing area to watch the fiery ascension. The **Cape Canaveral: Then and Now Tour** goes to the first launch site, the **Air Force Space and Missile Museum,** and the **Cape Canaveral Lighthouse.** ($25, ages 3-11 $15.)

MERRITT ISLAND NATIONAL WILDLIFE REF-UGE. Surrounding the NASA complex, the 140,000-acre Merritt Island National Wildlife Refuge teems with sea turtles, manatees, 21 endangered species, and over 300 species of birds. Spot wildlife from your car on the 7 mi. Black Point Wildlife Drive or hike the 5 mi. Cruickshank Trail for a closer look at the marshes. (Take Rte. A1A/528 off Cape Canaveral, over Merritt Island, onto the mainland, and take US 1 N. through Titusville. Turn east onto Rte. 406 and bear right on Rte. 402. ☎321-861-0667; www.merrittislandwildlife. org. Open daily sunrise-sunset. Visitors center open M-F 8am-4:30pm, Sa-Su 9am-5pm. Free.)

CANAVERAL NATIONAL SEASHORE. The seashore, on the northeastern shore of the refuge, covers 67,000 acres of undeveloped beach and dunes. Launch boats at nearby **Playalinda Beach** or swim under lifeguards'

supervision from June to September. Go well supplied, as there are no phones, food, showers, or drinking water available. (Take Rte. 406 E. off US 1, in Titusville. ☎321-867-0677. Open daily Apr.-Oct. 6am-8pm; Nov.-Mar. 6am-6pm. Closed 3 days before and 1 day after NASA launches and on the day of shuttle landings. $3 per person.)

🎵 NIGHTLIFE

Bars line **Route A1A** by the ocean, each with outdoor patios to catch the cool night breezes. One of the best is **Coconuts on the Beach,** 2 Minutemen Causeway (opposite page), which has live rock music from Tuesday to Saturday 8:30-11pm. Take Rte. A1A N. to Port Canaveral at Exit B to find a row of brightly lit bars. At the end of the row, **Grills,** 505 Glen Cheek Dr., has live rock and reggae several times a week on a patio. (☎321-868-2226; www. visitgrills.com. Open M-Th 11am-10pm, F-Su 11am-midnight or later. AmEx/D/MC/V.)

🏖 BEACHES

Aside from the Space Center, Cocoa Beach's main attraction is out-of-this-world beaches. By the Atlantic, you'll find windswept surfers and sunbathers galore. For volleyball, fishing, and a boardwalk that extends over the Atlantic, there's the **Cocoa Beach Pier,** 401 Meade Ave., off Rte. A1A. Four restaurants and five bars will be waiting for you when the waves and the sun finally drain all of your energy. (☎321-783-7549; www.cocoabeachpier.com. Free.) Those low on essentials like surf wax and sunscreen will find them at **Ron Jon Surf Shop,** 4275 N. Atlantic Ave. This enormous glorified souvenir shop sells surfboards as well as T-shirts, shot glasses, postcards, and the Ron Jon stickers you'll inevitably see on the bumper of every surfer girl's car. The store has, oddly enough, attracted a large tourist following. (☎321-799-8840. Open 24hr.)

🔀 DETOUR

DISNEY WORLD

Take **I-4 West** to **Exit 64** for the Magic Kingdom and MGM Studios. Take **Exit 65** for the Animal Kingdom and **Exit 67** for EPCOT Center.

Disney World is the Rome of central Florida: all roads lead to it. Within this Never-Never-Land, theme parks, resorts, theaters, restaurants, and nightclubs all work together to form the "happiest place on earth." The four main parks are the Magic Kingdom, EPCOT, MGM Studios, and Animal Kingdom, but Disney offers innumerable other attractions with different themes and—of course—separate admissions. (☎407-939-6244; www.disneyworld.com. 1 park $71, ages 3-9 $60; 4-day Park Hopper Pass $212/178.)

THE ROAD TO DAYTONA BEACH: 79 MI.

From Cocoa Beach, take **Route A1A/528 North.** Take **US 1 North** until Daytona Beach.

DAYTONA BEACH ☎386

When locals first started auto racing on the hard-packed shores of Daytona Beach more than 60 years ago, they combined two aspects of life that would come to define the city's entire mentality: speed and sand. Daytona played an essential role in the founding of the **National Association of Stock Car Auto Racing (NASCAR)** in 1947, and the Daytona International Speedway still hosts several big races each year. Though races no longer occur on the sand, 23 mi. of Atlantic beaches still pump the lifeblood of the community.

VITAL STATS
Population: 64,422
Tourist Office: Daytona Beach Area Convention and Visitors Bureau, 126 E. Orange Ave. (☎800-854-1234 or 386-255-0415; www.daytonabeachcvb.org), on City Island. Open M-F 9am-5pm.
Library and Internet Access: Volusia County Library Center, 105 E. Magnolia Ave. (☎386-257-6036; www.vcpl.lib.fl.us). Free. Open M-Th 9am-7pm, F 9am-5pm, Sa 9am-3pm, Su 1-5pm.
Post Office: 220 N. Beach St. (☎386-226-2618). Open M-F 8:30am-5pm, Sa 10am-noon. **Postal Code:** 32115.

ORIENTATION

US 1 parallels the coast and the barrier island. **Atlantic Avenue (Route A1A)** is the main drag along the shore. **International Speedway Boulevard (US 92)** runs east-west from the ocean through the downtown area to the racetrack. Daytona Beach is a collection of smaller towns; many street numbers are not consecutive, and navigation can be difficult, so stick to the main roads. To avoid gridlock around the beach, arrive early (8am) and leave early (around 3pm). Visitors can drive and park on the beach itself but must pay $5; police enforce the 10 mph speed limit. Free parking is plentiful during most of the year but sparse during spring break (usually from mid-Feb. to Apr.), **Speedweek, Bike Week, Biketoberfest,** and the **Coke Zero 400.**

ACCOMMODATIONS

Almost all of Daytona's accommodations cluster on **Atlantic Avenue (Route A1A),** either on the beach or across the street; those off the beach offer the best deals. Spring break and race events drive prices to absurdly high levels, but low-season rates are more reasonable. Almost all of the motels facing the beach cost around $59 for a low-season single; on the other side of the street, it's $39. Reservations are recommended for all stays.

The Camellia Motel, 1055 N. Atlantic Ave./Rte. A1A (☎386-252-9963), across the street from the beach. An especially welcoming retreat with 12 cozy, bright rooms, cable TV, and A/C. All rooms are nonsmoking. Rooms $43-70, up to $100 during special events. MC/V. ❷

Daytona Shore Inn, 805 N. Atlantic Ave. (☎386-253-1441). A clean motel with cable TV. Some rooms have fridges and microwaves. Singles $40. AmEx/D/MC/V. ❷

Tomoka State Park, 2099 N. Beach St. (☎386-676-4050, reservations 800-326-3521). From Rte. A1A N., take Granada Blvd. West to N. Beach St. 8 mi. north of Daytona in Ormond Beach, the park has 100 sites under a tropical canopy. Enjoy saltwater fishing, ½ mi. of nature trails, and a sculpture museum with many Native American artifacts. Unfortunately, no swimming is allowed. Open daily 8am-sunset. Entrance fee $4 per vehicle. Sites $20. AmEx/D/MC/V. ❶

FOOD

The Dancing Avocado Kitchen, 110 S. Beach St. (☎386-947-2022). Glass bottles and funny signs line the walls. Welcomes vegans and carnivores alike. Enjoy the "dancer" sandwich (avocado, cheese, sprouts, and tomato; $6.25) or the portobello veggie panino ($6.25) while people-watching from the patio. Open M-Sa 8am-4pm. AmEx/D/MC/V. ❷

Pasha's Middle East Cafe, 919 W. International Speedway Blvd. (☎386-257-7753). Arabic music plays in Pasha's, where you'll find plenty of healthful and vegetarian options. Have some fresh falafel ($4.75) or shish tawook ($5.25). After you eat, stock up on dates and freshly baked pita bread in the attached grocery. Open M-Sa 10am-7pm, Su noon-6pm. AmEx/MC/V. ❶

👁 SIGHTS

THE MUSEUM OF ARTS AND SCIENCES. Exhibits combine traditional and decorative art, natural history, and science in the displays. The museum complex includes several miniature museums, two trains, and nature trails. Check out the Cuban Museum, donated by President Batista just two years before his overthrow, for a look into the country's artistic and historical past. Visit the enormous giant sloth or see the Root Family Museum, which has classic cars, Coke paraphernalia, and hundreds of teddy bears on display. (352 S. Nova Rd. ☎386-255-0285; www.moas.org. Open M-Sa 9am-5pm, Su 11am-5pm. $13, students and seniors $11, ages 6-17 $7, under 6 free.)

DAYTONA INTERNATIONAL SPEEDWAY. The center of the racing world, the Daytona International Speedway hosts the Daytona 500 every February. Speedweek precedes the legendary race, while the Coke Zero 400 heats up the track in early July. (☎386-947-6530, NASCAR tickets ☎800-748-7467; www.daytonainternationalspeedway.com. Open daily 9am-7pm.) The **Speedway Tour** is a chance to see the garages, grandstands, and 31° banked turns up close; you can even take a photo on Victory Lane. The **Richard Petty Driving Experience** puts fans in a stock car for a 150 mph drive or ride-along. (☎800-237-3889. 14+ to ride; $135. 18+ to drive; call for prices.)

HALIFAX HISTORICAL MUSEUM. To learn about the origins of the race, go to the Halifax Historical Museum, which also displays Spanish artifacts, old cameras, and a Victrola. Upstairs, play with a spinning wheel and antique toys to your inner child's content. (252 S. Beach St. ☎386-255-6976; www.halifaxhistorical.org. Open Tu-Sa 10am-4pm. $4, ages 3-12 $1. Free on Th afternoon.)

JACKIE ROBINSON BALLPARK. Daytona Beach was the only place to allow young Jackie Robinson to suit up for his AAA spring training in 1946. During the summer, check out the single-A Daytona Cubs on the diamond where he played. (105 E. Orange Ave. ☎386-257-3172; www.daytonacubs.com. Games Apr.-Aug. Tickets $5, VIP $7.)

IN THE FAST LANE

The National Association of Stock Car Racing, or NASCAR, has the most live spectators of any sport in America and is second in television viewers only to the National Football League. NASCAR claims 40 million so-called "hard-core fans," who spend 9hr. per week on NASCAR-related media and spend $900 a year on NASCAR products. Though the sport was originally made popular in the South, its popularity has spread across the country and internationally. Stock-car racing is a sport that gained popularity relatively recently; NASCAR fans may not be aware of its unconventional origins. NASCAR was born during Prohibition, when bootleggers ran alcohol from their workshops to thirsty clients. "Coppers" were, of course, in hot pursuit, so bootleggers had to be fast, and they worked hard to make their vehicles faster and faster. The bootleggers tested (and showed off) new car designs by driving around long ovals—the precursors of the NASCAR tracks we see today. It was only a matter of time before they started competing with one another and until promoters realized they had a viable spectator sport on their hands. The races moved from empty fields to the beaches of Daytona, and NASCAR was officially formed in 1947. The association's first race was held in Charlotte, North Carolina, in 1949. Though NASCAR's drivers are no longer fleeing the law, they still drive with a lead

NIGHTLIFE

When spring break hits, concerts, hotel-sponsored parties, and other events answer the call of students. News travels fastest by word of mouth, but the *Calendar of Events* and *SEE Daytona Beach* make good starting points for planning a night out. On mellow nights, head to the boardwalk to play volleyball or shake your groove-thang to rock or jazz at the **Oceanfront Bandshell,** an open-air amphitheater. Dance clubs thump along Seabreeze Blvd., just west of N. Atlantic Ave.

Ocean Deck, 127 S. Ocean Ave. (☎386-253-5224; www.oceandeck.com), behind the Wendy's. Stands out among the clubs because of its live music on the beach, amazing ocean view, and laid-back atmosphere. Sip the house specialty Red Tide ($5) while grooving to reggae, jazz, and calypso. Nightly live music 9:30pm-last customer. 21+ after 9pm. Open daily 11am-2:30am. Kitchen open until 2am. AmEx/D/MC/V.

Razzle's, 611 Seabreeze Blvd. (☎386-257-6236). A fixture in Daytona for 20 years. Its high-energy dance floors, flashy light shows, and popular ladies' nights (W-F) keep locals and tourists happy. 18+. Cover $10. Open M 8pm-midnight, Tu-Sa 8pm-3am. AmEx/D/MC/V.

Aqua, 640 N. Grandview Ave. (☎386-248-8243). Hip hop oriented club in a bright blue building behind Razzle's. Industrial-looking locale plays insanely loud music all night long, as the bartenders hand out drinks from behind a bar with a waterfall. 18+. Cover $5-20. Open Th-F and Sa 9pm-3am. AmEx/D/MC/V.

THE ROAD TO ST. AUGUSTINE: 43 MI.

Continue following **Route A1A** to St. Augustine.

ST. AUGUSTINE ☎904

In 1513, Spaniard Ponce de León came to these shores in search of the legendary Fountain of Youth. Fifty-two years later, Pedro Menéndez de Aviles founded St. Augustine in 1565, making it the first European colony in North America and the oldest continuous settlement in the US. Though Wal-Marts and drive-throughs have sprung up alongside buildings made of coquina shell, St. Augustine's historic district and Spanish flavor remain intact. This city's pride lies in its provincial cobblestone streets, coquina-rock walls, and antique shops rather than in its token beaches. Most consider the Fountain of Youth a legend, but don't be too sure—St. Augustine sure looks good for its age.

ORIENTATION

Narrow streets and frequent one-ways can make driving in St. Augustine unpleasant. Free parking is scarce—park at your accommodation or be prepared to pay a fee. The city's major east-west routes, **King Street** and **Cathedral Place,** run through downtown and become the **Bridge of Lions** that leads to the beaches. **San Marco Avenue,** or **Avenida Menendez,** runs north-south. **Castillo Drive** diverges from San Marco Ave. near the center of town. **Saint George Street,** a north-south pedestrian route, contains most of the shops and many of the sights in town.

VITAL STATS
Population: 12,157
Tourist Office: St. Augustine Visitors Center, 10 Castillo Dr. (☎904-825-1000; www.oldcity.com), at San Marco Ave. Open daily 8:30am-5:30pm.
Library and Internet Access: St. Johns County Public Library, 1960 N. Ponce de Leon Blvd. (☎904-827-6940). Free. Open M-W 9:30am-9pm, Th-F 9:30am-6pm, Sa 9:30am-5pm, Su 1-5pm.
Post Office: 99 King St. (☎904-825-0628). Open M-F 8:30am-5pm, Sa 9am-1pm. **Postal Code:** 32084.

ACCOMMODATIONS

Pirate Haus Inn and Hostel, 32 Treasury St. (☎904-808-1999; www.piratehaus.com), just off St. George St. From Rte. A1A N., take Cordoba to Charlotte St. Hands-down the best place to stay in town, with spotless dorms, themed private rooms, and a great location. Most sights are a 10-15min. walk. Weary travelers are pampered by a fun common room, full kitchen, and pancake breakfast. Lockers. Linen deposit $5. Wi-Fi $3. Key deposit $5. Dorms $20; private rooms $70-80. D/MC/V. ●

Seabreeze Motel, 208 Anastasia Blvd. (☎904-829-8122; www.seabreezemotel.com). Clean rooms with fridges and pool access. A/C, cable TV, and free local calls. The 2 nonsmoking rooms available are booked early. Free Internet. Singles $45; doubles $55. D/MC/V. ❸

Anastasia State Park, 1340 Rte. A1A (☎904-461-2033; www.floridastateparks.org/anastasia), 4 mi. south of the historic district. Nearby Salt Run and the Atlantic provide great windsurfing, swimming, and hiking. Within the park are the coquina quarries used to build the Castillo de San Marco. Reception 8am-sunset. Reservations recommended. Sites with water and electricity but no sewer $25. Day use $5 per vehicle, $3 for 1 person in a vehicle, $1 per pedestrian. AmEx/D/MC/V. ❶

🍴 FOOD

The bustle of daytime tourists and the abundance of budget eateries make lunch in St. Augustine's historic district a delight, especially among the cafes and bars of **Saint George Street.**

☒ **Bunnery Bakery Cafe,** 121 St. George St. (☎904-829-6166). A casual cafe that offers hearty, Southern-style breakfasts. Try the eggs, biscuits, gravy, and grits ($6) or a hulking stack of pancakes ($5), and you'll be drawling in no time. In the afternoon, the Bunnery offers veggie panini and salads. Open daily 8am-3pm. Cash only. ❶

☒ **Pizzalley's,** 117 St. George St. (☎904-825-2627). Scarf down a slice of pizza ($2.50) or chicken tropical salad ($4.25) in this inviting eatery. Open daily from 11am; closing time varies, usually around 9pm. MC/V. ❶

Cafe del Hidalgo, 35 Hypolita St. (☎904-823-1196). St. Augustine may have been founded by Spaniards, but this restaurant honors Italy. Patrons line up for gelato ($4) and cannoli ($3.25), then relax at the huge wood tables. Free Internet. Open M-Th and Su 9:30am-9pm, F-Sa 9:30am-10pm. AmEx/D/MC/V. ❶

Scarlett O'Hara's, 70 Hypolita St. (☎904-824-6535; www.scarlettoharas.com), at Cordova St. Veggie wraps ($7) and full slabs of ribs ($17.45) are consumed by patrons who will never go hungry again. Live music, usually classic or Southern rock, entertains Tu and F-Sa out on the porch. 80s day Th. Karaoke M and Su. Happy hour M-F 4-7pm with 2-for-1 drinks. Open daily 11am-1am. AmEx/D/MC/V. ❸

👁 SIGHTS

▨FLAGLER COLLEGE. Visitors can take a spirited student-led tour through Flagler College, a small liberal-arts institution housed in the restored Spanish Renaissance-style **Ponce de León Hotel.** Constructed by railroad and Standard Oil tycoon Henry Flagler in 1888, the hotel served as a luxurious playground for America's social elite. Celebrity heavyweights such as John Rockefeller and Will Rogers once strolled through the gorgeous interior, much of which was designed by Louis Comfort Tiffany. (☎904-819-6383; www.flagler.edu. Tours daily from mid-May to mid-Aug. every hr. 10am-3pm; during the school year 10am, 2pm. $6, under 12 $1.)

FOUNTAIN OF YOUTH. Forget L.A.'s pricey plastic surgeons; eternal youth comes cheap around these parts—$7.50, to be exact, in the form of admission to the famed Fountain of Youth. With animatronic Spanish figures and brightly painted dioramas, it's the ultimate in tacky fun. To sample the historical significance of the place, take a swig of the sulfurous libation and try to ignore the fact that the water now runs through a pipe. Other attractions are included with admission, such as the Spring House and planetarium. (11 Magnolia Ave. Take a right right on Williams St. from San Marco Ave. and continue until it ends at Magnolia Ave. ☎904-829-3168 or 800-356-8222; www.fountainofyouthflorida.com. Open daily 9am-5pm. $7.50, ages 6-12 $4.50.)

CASTILLO DE SAN MARCOS. The oldest masonry fortress in the continental US, Castillo de San Marcos National Monument has 14 ft. thick walls built of coquina, a material chosen because the shell rock does not shatter under cannon fire. The fort, a four-pointed star complete with drawbridge and moat, contains a museum, a large courtyard, garrison quarters, a jail, a chapel, and the original cannon brought overseas by the Spanish. (1 Castillo Dr., off San Marco Ave. ☎904-829-6506; www.nps.gov/casa. Monument open daily 8:45am-5:15pm. Last entry 4:45pm. Grounds open 5:30am-midnight. Ranger-led tours every hr. from 10am. $6, under 16 free.)

EAST COAST

SHRINE OF OUR LADY OF LA LECHE. One of the most significant religious sights in the US is the Shrine of Our Lady of la Leche and Mission of Nombre de Dios, where the first mass in the US was held over 400 years ago. A 208 ft. cross commemorates the city's founding, and the shaded lawns and view of Matanzas Bay make for a lovely stroll. Casual visitors should be respectful of those visiting for religious purposes. (27 Ocean St., off San Marco Ave. ☎904-824-2809. Open M-F 8am-5pm, Sa 9am-5pm, Su 9:30am-5pm. Mass M-F 8am, Sa 5pm, Su 7, 9, 11am, 6pm. Donation suggested.)

LIGHTNER MUSEUM. In 1947, Chicago publisher and art lover Otto Lightner converted the Alcazar Hotel into the Lightner Museum to hold a collection of cut, blown, and burnished glass as well as old clothing and oddities. Today, the museum houses everything from antique musical instruments to a Russian bath steam room. (75 King St., across the street from Flagler College. ☎904-824-2874; www.lightnermuseum.org. Open daily 9am-5pm. Last entry 4pm. $10, ages 12-18 $5.)

SAINT AUGUSTINE LIGHTHOUSE. For the best view of the nation's oldest city and its surrounding waters, climb the 219 stairs of the black-and-white-striped St. Augustine Lighthouse and Museum, Florida's oldest lighthouse. Tour the 19th-century tower and keeper's house to learn about marine archaeological studies in the area waters. (81 Lighthouse Ave., off Rte. A1A. ☎904-829-0745; www.staugustinelighthouse.com. Open daily 9am-6pm. Tower, house, and grounds $8, ages 6-11 $6; house and grounds $6/4.)

GONZALEZ-ALVAREZ HOUSE. The 300-year-old settlement contains some of the nation's oldest artifacts. The Gonzalez-Alvarez House was constructed in the early 18th century. It now serves as a tourist attraction, containing exhibits on the Spanish, British, and American heritage of the area, a museum, and gardens. (14 St. Francis St. ☎904-824-2569; www.oldesthouse.org. Open daily 9am-5pm. Tours every 30min. Last tour 4:30pm. $8, students $4, under 6 free; families $18.)

ALLIGATOR FARM. The St. Augustine Alligator Farm allows visitors to get up close and personal with some of nature's finest reptiles, including 15 ft. long Maximo. The park, which has been delighting visitors since 1893, is the only place in the world where all 23 known crocodilian species live. Check out the white alligator from the Louisiana bayou, who, according to legend, bestows good luck on viewers. (On Rte. A1A S. ☎904-824-3337. Open daily 9am-6pm. Presentations every hr. Feeding daily noon, 2, 3pm. $22, ages 5-11 $11.)

MARINELAND. The world's original oceanarium, Marineland, was once the premier attraction in Florida, drawing thousands for its dolphin show. A hurricane later, Marineland is rebuilding with an emphasis on close dolphin interactions. While the extravagant dolphin shows are no more, visitors can now play with the dolphins (10min., $75), swim with them (75min., $179), or even be a trainer for a day ($500). And, of course, adults and kids can still watch Flipper cruise through the 1.3 million-gallon tank while enjoying a breathtaking view of the beach. (9600 Oceanshore Blvd., off Rte. A1A, 14 mi. south of St. Augustine. ☎904-471-1111 or 888-279-9194; www.marineland.net. Open daily 8:30am-4:30pm. $6, under 12 $3.)

◙ NIGHTLIFE

St. Augustine supports a variety of bars, many on Rte. A1A and St. George St. *Folio Weekly* contains event listings.

- **The Milltop,** 19 St. George St. (☎904-829-2329; www.milltop.com). Local string musicians play on 2 stages in a tiny yet illustrious bar above an 1888 mill in the restored district. Sip a tall draft for $2 and enjoy the acoustic crooners and the majestic view of the Castillo. Music daily 1pm-midnight. Cover F-Sa $3. Open daily 11:30am-midnight. D/MC/V.

  Oasis Deck and Restaurant, 4000 Rte. A1A S. (☎904-471-3424; www.worldfamousoasis.com), at Ocean Trace Rd. Up a flight of rickety stairs, there's frequent live rock and reggae. Happy hour daily 4-7pm with $1.50 drafts. Open daily 6am-1am. AmEx/D/MC/V.

◪ THE ROAD TO JACKSONVILLE: 40 MI.

From St. Augustine, take **US 1 North** into town.

JACKSONVILLE ☎904

At almost 850 sq. mi., Jacksonville is geographically the largest city in the continental US. Because Jacksonville lacks top-draw tourist attractions, it's often overshadowed by cities to the south. However, Jacksonville's beautiful beaches, big-city museums, and revitalized downtown make it an undiscovered treat. While Jacksonville rolls up its carpets at 10pm, during the day visitors will find much to enjoy, though it may be difficult to see much of the city in one day.

✴ ORIENTATION

Three highways intersect in Jacksonville, forming a cross with a C around it. Because Jacksonville is so large, it can take over an hour to get from one end to the other; be sure to set aside 30min. for transportation between most points. **I-95** runs north-south, while **I-10** starts downtown and heads west. **I-295** forms the giant "C" on the western half of the city, and **Arlington Expressway** becomes **Atlantic Boulevard (Route 10)** heading to the beach. The **Saint Johns River** snakes through the city.

VITAL STATS

Population: 777,000

Tourist Offices: Visit Jacksonville, 550 Water St., Ste. 1000 (☎904-798-9111 or 800-733-2668; www. visitjacksonville.com). Open M-F 8am-5pm. **Visitor's Center at Jacksonville Landing,** 2 Independent Dr. (☎904-791-4305). Open M-Sa 10am-7pm.

Library and Internet Access: Jacksonville Main Public Library, 303 N. Laura St. (☎904-630-2665). Free. Open M-Th 9am-8pm, F-Sa 9am-6pm, Su 1-6pm.

Post Office: 311 W. Monroe St. (☎904-353-3445). Open M-F 8:30am-5pm, Sa 9am-1pm. **Postal Code:** 32202.

♟ ACCOMMODATIONS

Inexpensive hotels lie along I-95 and on the Arlington Expy. The cheapest options are the chains north of the city off I-95.

Fig Tree Inn Bed and Breakfast, 185 4th Ave. S. (☎904-246-8855 or 877-217-9830; www.figtree-inn.com). Just steps from the sands of Jacksonville Beach, the Fig Tree offers 6 tastefully decorated, themed rooms such as the "nautical room" and the "garden room." All rooms include TVs, VCRs, and private baths. Some rooms include hot tubs, fireplaces, or ocean views. Enjoy your breakfast or afternoon tea on the front porch of this beach-style shingle cottage. Free Wi-Fi. Rooms M-F $145-165, Sa-Su $155-175. AmEx/D/MC/V. ❺

Kathryn Abbey Hanna Park, 500 Wonderwood Dr. (☎904-249-4700), in Mayport. Has 293 wooded sites near the beach, all with full hookup, and 4 cabins with A/C. 20 mi. of bike paths and a water playground. 2-night min. stay in cabins. Reception 8am-5pm. Reservations recommended. Tent sites $18; RV sites $30. Cabins $30-50. Cash or check deposit for cabins. MC/V. ❶

♨ FOOD

🍴 **The Metro Diner,** 3302 Hendricks Ave. (☎904-398-3701; www.metrodinerjax.com). Even a city as large as Jacksonville has a small-town diner, where locals gather for brunch. Enjoy the friendly banter over cinnamon raisin pecan French toast ($6) or the daily specials. Open daily 7am-2:30pm. AmEx/D/MC/V. ❶

Beachside Seafood Market and Restaurant, 120 S. 3rd St./Rte. A1A (☎904-241-4880; www. beachsideseafood.info), by 2nd Ave. Beach bums take a break from the rays while the cooks fry up fish baskets ($7) and perch sandwiches ($5) made from their own fresh catches. Open M-W 10am-7pm, Th-Su 10am-9pm. MC/V. ❶

La Nopalera, 1629 Hendricks Blvd. (☎904-399-1768). Spray-painted murals welcome patrons to La Nopalera, where you can get platters of tacos and enchiladas for $7-9. Open M-Th 11am-10pm, F-Sa 11:30am-10:30pm, Su 11:30am-9pm. AmEx/MC/V. ❷

👁 SIGHTS

One of the nicest things to do in Jacksonville—weather permitting, of course—is to walk. **San Marco,** across the bridge from downtown, offers restaurants, shops, and people-watching. **Five Points,** near the Cummer Museum, has an edgier mix of tattoo parlors and coffee shops. The **Riverwalk** along both banks of the river allows joggers and strollers alike to enjoy the view for almost 5 mi.

JACKSONVILLE ZOO AND GARDENS. The zoo has been largely redone in the last few years and now features lovely gardens and world-class exhibits. The award-winning "Range of the Jaguar" features big cats, while another

EAST COAST

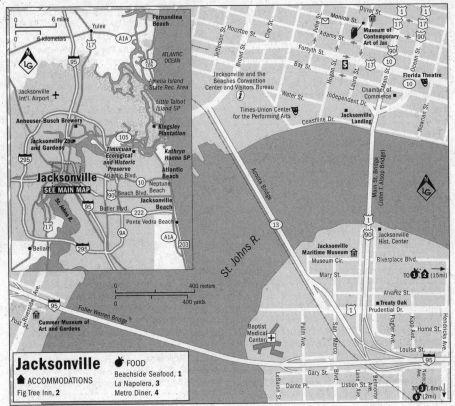

Jacksonville

ACCOMMODATIONS
Fig Tree Inn, **2**

FOOD
Beachside Seafood, **1**
La Napolera, **3**
Metro Diner, **4**

area allows visitors to pet giraffes. *(Take I-95 to Exit 358A to Heckscher Dr. E.* ☎ *904-757-4463; www.jax-zoo.org. Open Mar.-Sept. M-F 9am-5pm, Sa-Su 9am-6pm; Oct.-Feb. daily 9am-5pm. $12, ages 3-12 $7.50.)*

JESSIE BALL DUPONT PARK. For a cool escape from the asphalt downtown, climb into the Treaty Oak, a 200-year-old tree more than 70 ft. tall. Conservationists falsely said that the oak was the site of a settler-Indian treaty in order to save it from the axe. *(Corner of Prudential Dr. and Main St., on the south bank of the river. Open daily sunrise-sunset. Free.)*

TIMUCUAN ECOLOGICAL AND HISTORIC PRE-SERVE. This preserve contains 46,000 serene acres of saltwater marshes and tidal creeks teeming with fish, dolphins, and eagles. The 2

mi. **Willie Browne Trail** is a biker's paradise and meanders through salt marshes and maritime hammocks. *(Take I-95 N. to Rte. 105 E., off Exit 124A. Signs point to the major sights and the visitors center.* ☎ *904-641-7155; www.nps.gov/timu. Open daily 8am-sunset. Free.)* One of the park's two historical sights is the **Ribault Monument,** which marks the spot where, in 1562, French Huguenot Jean Ribault claimed the land for King Charles IX. Near the visitors center, **Fort Caroline National Memorial** was the site of a 1565 battle between Spanish and French Huguenot forces—the first armed conflict between European powers over a New World settlement. Today, visitors can try their hand at storming a replica of the fort while the less aggressive peruse the museum's Native American and French artifacts. *(12713 Fort Caroline Rd. ☎ 904-641-7155. Open daily 9am-5pm. Free.)*

🏛 MUSEUMS

CUMMER MUSEUM OF ART AND GARDENS. The beautiful gardens and reflecting pools behind the Cummer Museum of Art and Gardens line the St. Johns River south of downtown. Indoors, Baroque, modern, and American colonial exhibits impress art connoisseurs while children and adults delight in "Art Connections," the exciting, high-tech, hands-on art education center. *(829 Riverside Ave. ☎ 904-356-6857; www.cummer.org. Open Tu 10am-9pm, W–Sa 10am-5pm, Su noon-5pm. Free tours Tu 7pm, Su 3pm. $10, students and seniors $6, under 6 free. Tu 4-9pm free. Tu-F 1:30-4:30pm college students with ID free.)*

MUSEUM OF CONTEMPORARY ART OF JACKSONVILLE. Jacksonville's newest museum, the Museum of Contemporary Art of Jacksonville, known to locals as "MOCA," is next door to the fountains of Hemming Plaza. Displays include a rotating collection of eclectic pieces, ranging from photography to interactive mechanical statues. *(333 N. Laura St. ☎ 904-366-6911; www.mocajacksonville.org. Open Tu and Th-Sa 10am-4pm, W 10am-9pm, Su noon-4pm. $8, students $5. W 5-9pm free. Su free for families with children under age 18.)*

JACKSONVILLE MARITIME MUSEUM. Model-ship enthusiasts may enjoy the Jacksonville Maritime Museum, which displays antique navigation tools and models of ships that once docked on the St. Johns. *(1015 Museum Cir., Unit 2, Southbank Riverwalk Main St. ☎ 904-398-9011; www.jacksonvillemaritimemuseum.org. Open M-F 10:30am-3pm, Sa-Su 1-4pm. Free.)*

🎭 ENTERTAINMENT

Acts ranging from Ringo Starr to the Dixie Chicks to Gilbert and Sullivan theater companies have performed at the historic **Florida Theatre**, 128 E. Forsyth St., built in 1927. The theater hosts more than 300 performances per year; check out it's website for upcoming shows and pricing. (☎ 904-355-2787; www.floridatheatre.com.) The **Times-Union Center for Performing Arts**, 300 W. Water St. (☎ 904-633-6110), offers traveling Broadway shows, the **Jacksonville Symphony,** and local college productions. A

different kind of popular culture thrives at the **Jacksonville Municipal Stadium** (☎ 904-633-2000), at E. Duval and Haines St., home to the NFL's **Jaguars**. The **Jacksonville Baseball Grounds**, 301 A. Philip Randolph Blvd., offers AA minor-league baseball from April through August for mere peanuts. (☎ 904-358-2846. Tickets $6-20.) Much of Jacksonville's nightlife centers on **Jacksonville Landing**, at Main St. and Independent Dr., a riverfront area packed with restaurants, shops, and live entertainment. (☎ 904-353-1188. Open M-Th 10am-8pm, F-Sa 10am-9pm, Su noon-5:30pm.)

🏖 BEACHES

Miles of uncrowded white sands can be found at **Jacksonville Beach.** Fishermen stake out spots on the Pier while golfers take advantage of the more than 70 golf courses in northeastern Florida. Free parking lots run along the beach, but they fill up quickly and there are no bathrooms. The **Jacksonville Beach Pier** is abuzz with activity, from music festivals to sandcastle-building contests. Surfing and volleyball tournaments take place in May. (☎ 904-241-1515. Open 6am-10pm. $4 to fish, $1 per pedestrian.) Those looking for a less crowded stretch of sand should try **Atlantic Beach** to the north. Staple Florida attractions are nearby, minigolf, go-carts, and a water park. To reach the Atlantic Ocean, take Rte. 90/Beach Blvd. or Rte. 10/Atlantic Blvd. heading east from downtown for about 30min.

🏝 THE ROAD TO CUMBERLAND ISLAND: 65 MI.

From Jacksonville, take **Route A1A North** to the **Saint Johns River Ferry.** Take the ferry (every 30min. M-F 6am-7pm, Sa-Su 7am-8:30pm; $3) and continue on A1A N. Just over the ferry is the Kingsley Plantation. When her husband died, former slave Anna Kingsley took over control of the plantation, including the slaves that worked it. Today, visitors can see the remains of the slave quarters, house, and barn. (☎ 904-251-3537. Open daily 9am-5pm. Free.) In Fernandina Beach, take **A1A/200 West** to **I-95 North.** Get off at **Exit 29** and take **Route 40 East** to the town of St. Mary's.

CUMBERLAND ISLAND ☎ 912

Off the coast of southeastern Georgia, near the tiny town of St. Mary's, **Cumberland Island**

National Seashore remains an astoundingly untouched piece of nature, with herds of wild horses roaming the 36,500 acres of the park. Up to 300 visitors per day can wander on near-deserted beaches, but be sure to pack a lunch, as only limited water and no stores are available on the island. The park is only accessible by a ferry that leaves twice a day, often fully booked in advance, or by private boat, so plan your visit ahead of time. Ferries leave from St. Mary's to two docks on the island. Tickets are sold at the visitors center on the mainland daily 8am-6pm in summer and 8am-4:30pm in winter. (☎912-882-4335 or 877-860-6787. Ferries depart from St. Mary's Mar.-Nov. daily 9, 11:45am; Dec.-Feb. M and Th-Su 9, 11:45am. Return from Cumberland Island Mar.-Sept. 10:15am, 2:45, 4:45pm; Oct.-Feb. 10:15am, 4:45pm. $17, under 13 $12, seniors $15. Park admission $4.) On the southern end of the island stands **Dungeness,** the eerie ruins of the former mansion of Carnegie sibling Thomas and his wife Lucy. A tour leaves from the Sea Camp dock 15min. after the ferry arrives. The **Ice House Museum,** located in the Carnegies' old ice house, documents the history of the island beginning with Native American settlers. (Open daily 8am-4pm. Free.) In St. Mary's, the **Cumberland Island Mainland Museum,** 169 Osborne St., displays artifacts on the history of Cumberland. (☎912-882-4335. Open daily 1-4pm. Free.) If you wish to spend the night on the island, come prepared—aside from water, all provisions must be carried in and out. The only developed campground, **Sea Camp ❶,** is a 15min. walk from the Sea Camp dock and has cold-water showers and bathrooms. Sites are fully booked up to two months in advance. (Primitive sites $2; developed sites $4.)

▓ THE ROAD TO ST. SIMONS ISLAND: 26 MI.

Take **Route 40 West** back to **I-95 North.** Exit at **Route 17/25** and follow signs to St. Simons Island.

ST. SIMONS ISLAND ☎912

Though it can be rather vacant in the winter, St. Simons Island has long been a popular resort and summer vacation destination. The beach is always busy by the pier and lighthouse; visitors can rent kayaks and sailboats.

The Village, along Mallery St., is a fun, funky strip of restaurants and shops. **Neptune Park** is home to the **Saint Simons Island Lighthouse.** The second lighthouse built on the island (the first was destroyed during the Civil War by retreating Confederate soldiers who did not want the Union to use it to their advantage), it dates from 1872 and rises 104 ft. Climb 129 steps to the top for a breathtaking view of the area. (☎912-638-4666; www.saintsimonslighthouse.org. Open M-Sa 10am-5pm, Su 1:30-5pm. $6, ages 6-12 $3.) A drive north on Frederica Rd. leads to **Fort Frederica,** a military stronghold established by Georgia founder James Oglethorpe. A movie explains the settlement's history, and a walking tour leads visitors through the meager remains of the town to the fort itself. (☎912-638-3639; www.nps.gov/fofr. Open daily 8:30am-5pm. Visitors center open daily 9am-5pm. 7-day access $3.) Just before the fort on Frederica Rd. lies **Christ Episcopal Church,** the second-oldest Episcopal church in the state. Built by shipbuilders, the ceiling of the tiny structure looks like the hull of a ship, and the rare stained-glassed windows fill it with multicolored light. The church is still active, so be respectful of those visiting for religious purposes. (☎912-638-8683. Visiting hours daily 2-5pm. Free.) Across the street, the **Wesley Memorial Monument** celebrates Reverend Charles Wesley, who conducted the parish's first services in 1736. Off Demere Rd. lies the frighteningly named **Bloody Marsh,** where Oglethorpe's men ambushed Spanish troops fighting to retake the island in 1742. The marsh didn't really run red with blood—there were only 12 deaths—but the Spanish returned to St. Augustine and never again tried to take Georgia. (Open daily 8:30am-4pm. Free.)

The least expensive accommodations on the island are available at **Epworth by the Sea ❸,** 100 Arthur J. Moore Dr., a Methodist center that mostly hosts large groups for retreats and other events. Guests of all faiths are welcome. (☎912-638-8688; www.epworthbythesea.org. Free Wi-Fi. Reservations required. Rooms $64-121. MC/V.) The local favorite, **Dressner's Village Cafe ❶,** 223 Mallery St., serves basic Southern fare, three-egg veggie omelets (with grits and biscuits, of course; $5), and delectable French toast ($4) with pecans and raisins.

(☎912-634-1217. Open M-F 7:30am-2:30pm, Sa-Su 8am-2:30pm.) **Zuzu's ❷**, 119 Mallery St., is an old-fashioned ice-cream shop with vegetarian meal options. Relax with a portobello mushroom sandwich ($6.50) and a milkshake ($3.50) after a day at the beach. (☎912-638-8655. Open daily 11am-9pm. MC/V.)

▓ THE ROAD TO SAVANNAH: 65 MI.

Take **US 17 North** to Savannah.

The Peach State

GEORGIA

Welcomes You

SAVANNAH ☎912

General James Oglethorpe and his band of 120 vagabonds founded Savannah in 1733, designing the city around more than 20 beautiful green squares. Oglethorpe's design escaped Sherman's March to the Sea—as it did modern-day expansion. It now remains Georgia's greatest treasure. This is a walking city, with tree-lined roads and park benches so that tired travelers can "set for a spell." Be sure to strike out on foot and enjoy the streets that Sherman found too pretty to burn.

VITAL STATS
Population: 130,000
Tourist Office: Savannah Visitors Center, 301 Martin Luther King, Jr., Blvd. (☎912-944-0455; www.savannahgeorgia.com), at Liberty St. Open M-F 8:30am-5pm, Sa-Su 9am-5pm.
Internet Access: Gallery Espresso, 234 Bull St. (☎912-233-5348). Free Wi-Fi.
Post Office: 2 N. Fahm St. (☎912-235-4619), at Bay St. Open M-F 7am-6pm, Sa 9am-3pm. **Postal Code:** 31402.

▓ ORIENTATION

Savannah rests on the coast of Georgia at the mouth of the **Savannah River,** which runs north of the city along the border with South Carolina. The city stretches south from bluffs overlooking the river. The restored 2 sq. mi.

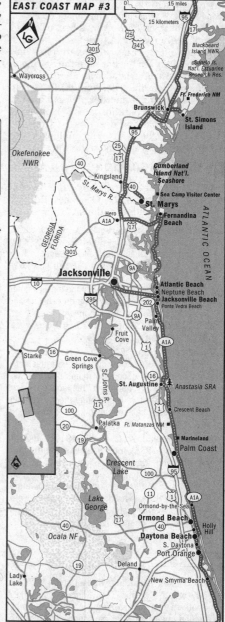

EAST COAST MAP #3

0 — 15 miles
0 — 15 kilometers

Waycross

Blackbeard Island NWR

Sapelo Is. Nat'l. Estuarine Research Res.

Ft. Frederica NM

Brunswick

St. Simons Island

Okefenokee NWR

Kingsland

St. Marys R.

Cumberland Island Nat'l. Seashore

Sea Camp Visiter Center

St. Marys

Hero

Fernandina Beach

GEORGIA / FLORIDA

Jacksonville

Atlantic Beach
Neptune Beach
Jacksonville Beach
Ponte Vedra Beach

Palm Valley

Fruit Cove

Starke

Green Cove Springs

St. Johns R.

St. Augustine

Anastasia SRA

Crescent Beach

Palatka   Ft. Matanzas NM

Marineland
Palm Coast

Crescent Lake

Lake George

Ocala NF

Ormond-by-the-Sea

Ormond Beach

Holly Hill

Daytona Beach

S. Daytona
Port Orange

Deland

Lady Lake

New Smyrna Beach

ATLANTIC OCEAN

EAST COAST

downtown historic district, bordered by **East Broad Street, Martin Luther King, Junior, Boulevard, Gwinnett Street,** and the river, is best explored on foot. Do not stray outside these borders; the historic district quickly deteriorates into an unsafe area. On the banks of the Savannah River, **River Street** is lined with shops, restaurants, and nightlife. The nearby **City Market,** by **Franklin Square,** is another pleasant area to stroll and shop. A parking pass ($8), obtained at the public parking desk across from the visitors center, allows two-day unlimited use of all metered parking, city lots, and garages.

ACCOMMODATIONS

Downtown motels cluster near the historic area and visitors center. Ogeechee Rd. (US 17) has several budget options.

The Eliza Thompson House, 5 W. Jones St. (☎912-236-3620 or 800-348-9378; www. elizathompsonhouse.com). The premier B&B in Savannah, located in the heart of downtown and minutes from the city's beautiful, bustling squares. Built in 1847, this historic inn welcomes guests with complimentary wine and cheese and breakfast served in the courtyard. Free Internet. Rooms in summer $179-219; in winter $179-209. AmEx/D/MC/V. ❺

Thunderbird Inn, 611 W. Oglethorpe Ave. (☎912-232-2661; www.thethunderbirdinn.com). Offers large, well-decorated rooms near the visitors center. Fridge, hair dryer, free local calls, and cable. Be careful walking around the surrounding area, as it may become unsafe after dark. Rooms M-F $99, Sa-Su $129. AmEx/D/MC/V. ❺

Skidaway Island State Park (☎912-598-2300 or 800-864-7275), 6 mi. southeast of downtown off Diamond Causeway. Follow Liberty St. east from downtown until it becomes Wheaton St.; turn right on Waters Ave. and follow it to Diamond Causeway. 88 sites with bathrooms, hot-water showers, electricity, and water as well as miles of hiking trails. Open daily 7am-10pm. Reservations recommended. Sites $22, with hookup $24. ❶

FOOD

Mrs. Wilkes' Boarding House, 107 W. Jones St. (☎912-232-5997; www.mrswilkes.com). A Southern institution where friendly folks gather around large tables for soul food served home-style. The dining room fills up quickly with strangers uniting over fried chicken, okra, greens, and cornbread. All-you-can-eat $16, under 13 $8. Open M-F 11am-2pm. Cash only. ❸

Clary's Café, 404 Abercorn St. (☎912-233-0402; www.claryscafesavannah.com). Savannah's best breakfasts since 1903. Blueberry pancakes ($5), sourdough French toast ($5), and free Wi-Fi; you might never want to leave. Open M-Th 7am-4pm, F-Sa 8am-5pm, Su 8am-4pm. AmEx/D/MC/V. ❶

Angel's BBQ, 21 W. Oglethorpe Ln. (☎912-495-0902), hidden in an alley off Whitaker and Hull. It doesn't look like much inside, but you won't mind when you taste the grub. Try one of the huge pork sandwiches with coleslaw on top ($5.50). Open Tu 11:30am-3pm, W-Sa 11:30am-6pm. AmEx/D/MC/V. ❶

SIGHTS

Most of Savannah's 21 squares contain some distinctive centerpiece, such as a monument or fountain. Elegant antebellum houses and drooping, vine-entangled trees often cluster around the squares, contributing to the classic Southern aura. Simply visiting Savannah's squares is an excellent way to appreciate the beauty of the city. Bus and horse carriage tours leave from the visitors center, but walking can be more rewarding.

HISTORIC HOUSES

Savannah is known for its beautiful early-19th-century homes, which have been preserved thanks to a vocal preservation movement. Though all the historic homes are lovely, unless you have a particular interest in architecture, pick one tour as a representative of the genre.

DAVENPORT HOUSE. Built in 1820, the Davenport House Museum was the first home to be saved from the wrecking ball by the seven women of the Savannah Historical Foundation. Docents show visitors the cantilevered staircase, beautiful marble fireplaces, and truly hideous 1820s wallpaper. (☎912-236-8097; www.davenporthousemuseum.org. 324 E. State St., on Columbia Sq. Open M-Sa 10am-4pm, Su 1-4pm. Tours every 30min.; last tour 4pm. $8, ages 7-18 $5.)

OWENS-THOMAS HOUSE. An example of English Regency architecture, the Owens-Thomas House includes three false doors,

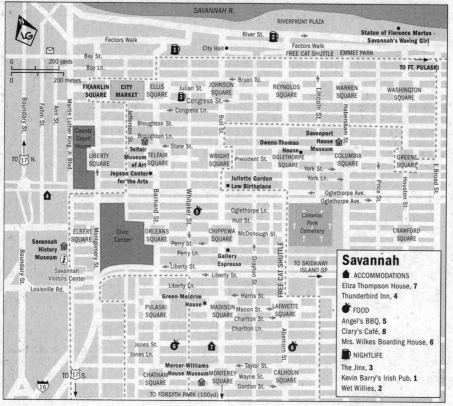

Savannah R.

RIVERFRONT PLAZA

Factors Walk

River St. 2️⃣

■ Statue of Florence Martus -
Savannah's Waving Girl

City Hall ■

Factors Walk
FREE CAT SHUTTLE   EMMET PARK

1️⃣

Bay St.
Bay Ln.

TO FT. PULASKI

0   200 yards
0   200 meters

Bryan St.

FRANKLIN   CITY   ELLIS   Julian St.   JOHNSON   REYNOLDS   WARREN   WASHINGTON
SQUARE   MARKET   SQUARE   SQUARE   SQUARE   SQUARE   SQUARE

3️⃣ Congress St.→

← Congress Ln.

Boundary St.
Fahm St.
Ann St.
Martin Luther King, Jr. Blvd.

Broughton St.

Broughton Ln.

Jefferson St.

County
Court
House

Davenport
House
Museum

Habersham St.
Lincoln St.

TO 17 N.

Telfair
Museum
of Art

Telfair
← State St.

Owens-Thomas
House
Museum

LIBERTY
SQUARE

TELFAIR
SQUARE

WRIGHT
SQUARE   President St.   OGLETHORPE
SQUARE

COLUMBIA
SQUARE

GREENE
SQUARE

E. Broad St.

Jepson Center
for the Arts

York St.
York Ln.

Price St.
Houston St.

Juliette Gordon
■ Low Birthplace

Oglethorpe Ave.
Oglethorpe Ave.

4️⃣

Oglethorpe Ln.
Hull St.

CRAWFORD
SQUARE

Whitaker St.
Barnard St.

5️⃣

Colonial
Park
Cemetery

Savannah
History
Museum

ELBERT
SQUARE

Civic
Center

ORLEANS
SQUARE

CHIPPEWA
SQUARE   McDonough St.

Montgomery St.

Perry St. →

Perry Ln.

Savannah
Visitors Center

← Liberty St.

Gallery
Espresso

Drayton St.
FREE CAT SHUTTLE

TO SKIDAWAY
ISLAND SP

Louisville Rd.

Liberty St.

Liberty Cn.

Harris St. →

Savannah
▲ ACCOMMODATIONS
Eliza Thompson House, 7
Thunderbird Inn, 4
🍴 FOOD
Angel's BBQ, 5
Clary's Café, 8
Mrs. Wilkes Boarding House, 6
🍷 NIGHTLIFE
The Jinx, 3
Kevin Barry's Irish Pub, 1
Wet Willies, 2

Green-Meldrim
House

PULASKI
SQUARE

MADISON
SQUARE

Macon St.   LAFAYETTE
SQUARE

Charlton St.

Charlton Ln.

Jones St.
Jones Ln.

6️⃣

7️⃣

Abercorn St.

8️⃣

TO 17 S.

Mercer-Williams
House Museum

CHATHAM
SQUARE

MONTEREY
SQUARE

← Taylor St.

Wayne St.
Gordon St.

CALHOUN
SQUARE

16

TO FORSYTH PARK (100yd) ▼

E A S T   C O A S T

a bridge connecting two areas of the house, and an emphasis on symmetry. The Marquis de Lafayette stayed here in 1825. (124 Abercom St., on Oglethorpe Sq. ☎912-233-9743. Open M noon-5pm, Tu-Sa 10am-5pm, Su 1-5pm. Tours every 30min.; last tour 4:30pm. $9, students $6, ages 6-12 $4.)

GREEN MELDRIM HOUSE. This Gothic Revival mansion served as General Sherman's Savannah headquarters following his famed March to the Sea. It was from this house that Sherman wrote a telegram to President Lincoln, giving him the city as a gift. (14 W. Macon St., on Madison Sq. ☎912-232-1251. Open Tu and Th-F 10am-4pm, Sa 10am-1pm. Tours every 30min. $7, students $2.)

MERCER-WILLIAMS HOUSE MUSEUM. Built in 1868 and restored in 1969, this museum

is filled with fantastic artwork. (429 Bull St. ☎912-236-6352 or 877-430-6352; www.nps.gov/fopu. Open M-Sa 10:30am-4pm, Su 12:30-4pm. Tours every 40min. $12.50, students and ages 6-12 $8.)

OTHER SIGHTS

FORT PULASKI NATIONAL MONUMENT. Savannah's four forts once protected the city's port from Spanish, British, and other invaders. The most intriguing of these, Fort Pulaski National Monument, marks the Civil War battle where Union forces first used rifled cannons to decimate the Confederate opposition. (15 mi. east of Savannah on US 80 E. and Rte. 26. ☎912-786-5787. Open daily in summer 8:30am-6pm; in winter 8:30am-5:15pm. $3, under 16 free.)

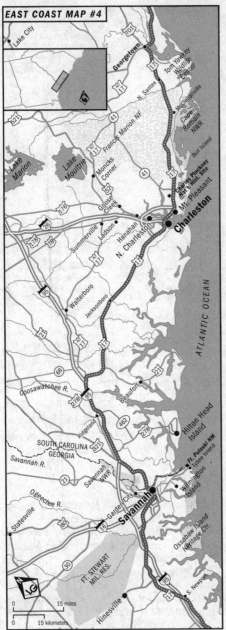

EAST COAST MAP #4

SAVANNAH HISTORY MUSEUM. Conveniently located in the same building as the visitors center, the Savannah History Museum has displays on Savannah history, a cotton gin, a steam locomotive, and memorabilia such as **Forest Gump's bench.** *(303 Martin Luther King, Jr. Blvd. ☎912-651-6825. Open M-F 8:30am-5pm, Sa-Su 9am-5pm. $4.25, students and ages 6-11 $3.75.)*

TELFAIR MUSEUM OF ART. The oldest art museum in the South, the Telfair Museum of Art was once a Regency-style mansion. Now it houses major works of the Ashcan School and the statue *Bird Girl*, depicted on the cover of *Midnight in the Garden of Good and Evil. (121 Barnard St. ☎912-232-1177; www. telfair.org. Open M, W, F-Sa 10am-5pm, Th 10am-8pm, Su noon-5pm. $8, students $5, ages 6-12 $4.)* The **Jepson Center for the Arts** is the new contemporary wing of the Telfair and houses photographic, abstract, and modern pieces. The most stunning artistic feat is the building itself—with grand staircases, airy exhibit halls, and an outdoors sculpture garden, it's an architectural triumph well worth visiting. *(207 W. York St., on Telfair Sq. ☎912-790-8800. Hours and prices are the same as for the Telfair Museum.*

ENTERTAINMENT

Green is the theme of the **Saint Patrick's Day Celebration** on the river (☎912-234-0295), a five-day reenactment of your college days that packs the streets and warms celebrants up for the annual St. Patrick's Day Parade (☎912-233-4804; www.savannahsaintpatricks-day.com), the second-largest in the US. During the annual NOGS Tour of the **Hidden Gardens of Historic Savannah** (☎912-961-4805), in late April, private walled gardens are opened to the public, who can join in a Southern tea. **First Friday for the Arts** (☎912-232-4903) occurs on the first Friday of each month in City Market, when art galleries open their doors to visitors. **First Saturday on the River** (☎912-234-0295) brings arts, entertainment, and food to historic River St. each month. The free *Connect Savannah*, found in restaurants and stores, has the latest in news and entertainment.

NIGHTLIFE

The waterfront area on River St. is one of the five places in the nation where you can walk with an open container of alcohol, but don't be fooled; not all laws regarding alcohol are lax in this old city. All nightclubs and bars are 21+ by law, as are all restaurants with a bar after 10pm. The area brims with endless dining opportunities, street performers, and a friendly pub ambience.

Wet Willies, 101 E. River St. (☎912-233-5650; www.wetwillies.com). If sugary drinks are your pleasure, this is the place for you. Try the trademark Call a Cab ($5-7), the strongest drink in the house (and do make sure to call a cab afterward). Karaoke M-Tu. DJ F-Sa. Open M-Th 11am-1am, F-Sa 11am-2am, Su 12:30pm-1am. Cash only.

Kevin Barry's Irish Pub, 117 W. River St. (☎912-233-9626; www.kevinbarrys.com). Home to a laid-back crowd that relaxes over Guinness and Irish folk music. Nightly live music after 8:30pm. 21+ after 7pm. Open M-Sa noon-3am, Su 12:30pm-2am. AmEx/D/MC/V.

The Jinx, 127 W. Congress St. (☎912-236-2281), located downtown off Barnard St. A favorite with local college students, this hot spot has been voted the best place in town to hear live music. It sells earplugs ($1) for those who can't handle the pounding hip hop, metal, and indie rock. Open M-Sa 4pm-3am. AmEx/D/MC/V.

THE ROAD TO CHARLESTON: 108 MI.

From Savannah, take **US 17 North.** Carefully observe all posted speed limits—the smaller towns between the two cities are notorious speed traps. Once in Charleston, get off at **Calhoun Street** and follow signs to parking, major attractions, and the visitors center.

The Palmetto State
SOUTH CAROLINA
Welcomes You!

CHARLESTON ☎843

During the early 1800s, Charleston was the richest city in the nation, topping even Boston and New York City. The vast riches generated by rice and cotton plantations were used to build stately town-houses and intricate furniture. Charleston today is a funky mix of old and new, plantations and college culture. So sit back with a mint julep and experience the capital of the old South.

ORIENTATION

Old Charleston lies at the southernmost point of the 1 mi. wide peninsula below **Calhoun Street.** The major north-south routes through the city are **Meeting Street, King Street,** and **East Bay Street.** The area north of Spring St. and under the highway has little to offer travelers, as it is run-down, uninviting, and possibly unsafe. **Savannah Highway (US 17)** cuts across the peninsula, heading south to Savannah and north across two towering bridges to Mt. Pleasant and Myrtle Beach.

VITAL STATS
Population: 115,540
Tourist Office: Charleston Visitors Center, 375 Meeting St. (☎843-853-8000 or 800-868-8118; www.charlestoncvb.com), across from the Charleston Museum. Open daily 8:30am-5:30pm.
Library and Internet Access: Charleston Public Library, 68 Calhoun St. (☎843-805-6801). Open M-Th 9am-9pm, F-Sa 9am-6pm, Su 2-5pm.
Post Office: 83 Broad St. (☎843-577-0690). Open M-F 9am-5pm. **Postal Code:** 29402.

TRANSPORTATION

Charleston is a great walking city, but, when the heat is oppressive, visitors may want to make use of alternative means of transportation. The **Downtown Area Shuttle (DASH)** is made up of trolley routes that circle downtown. (Operates daily 8am-11pm; schedule and hours vary by route. $1.50, seniors $0.75; 1-day pass $5; 3-day $11.) **The Bicycle Shoppe,** 280 Meeting St., between George and Society St., offers bike rentals and even delivers the bike to your hotel free of charge. (☎843-722-8168; www.thebicycleshoppecharleston.com. $5 per hr., $20 per day; deposit required. Open M-F 9am-7pm, Sa 9am-6pm, Su 1-5pm.)

ACCOMMODATIONS

Motel rooms in historic downtown Charleston are expensive. Cheap motels can be found a few miles out of the city, around Exits 209-211 on I-26 W. in North Charleston, or across the Ashley River, on US 17 in Mt. Pleasant.

- **Charleston's NotSo Hostel,** 156 Spring St. (☎843-722-8383; www.notsohostel.com). Use Ashley Ave. to get to downtown and avoid the west side of Spring St., as it borders an unsafe neighborhood. A scrupulously clean hostel near the bright lights of downtown Charleston. 2 fully equipped kitchens, a wraparound porch with hammocks, and a make-your-own waffle breakfast. BYO padlock. Coin-op laundry. Free Wi-Fi. Parking. Reception daily 5-10pm. Dorms $21; private rooms $60. AmEx/D/MC/V. ❶

- **Bed, No Breakfast,** 16 Halsey St. (☎843-577-2821). This charming 2-bedroom inn offers guests an affordable way to stay in the heart of the city. Shared bathroom. Reservations recommended. Rooms $95-125. Cash only. ❹

- **Campground at James Island County Park,** 871 Riverland Dr. (☎843-795-4386 or 800-743-7275). Take US 17 S. to Rte. 171 and turn left onto Riverland Dr. Spacious, open sites. The spectacular park features 16 acres of lakes, bicycle and walking trails, a climbing wall, and a small water park. Round-trip shuttle service to Charleston $7. Bike and boat rental. Primitive sites $21; tent sites $31, with hookup $35. Day use $1. AmEx/D/MC/V. ❶

FOOD

Charleston has some of the best food in the country. While restaurants in high-traffic areas cater to big-spending tourists, there are plenty of budget options. Step off the main drag to find the Southern cooking, barbecue, and fresh seafood that have made the Low Country famous, and oh so delicious.

- **Gaulart & Maliclet (Fast and French),** 98 Broad St. (☎843-577-9797; www.fastandfrench.org). Strangers bond over shared countertops and veggie "croq" baguettes (grilled cheese with tomato, zucchini, and mustard; $4). From the paintings to the chocolate croissants ($3), it's all French, and all *magnifique*. Open M 8am-4pm, Tu-Th 8am-10pm, F-Sa 8am-10:30pm. AmEx/D/MC/V. ❶

- **Hominy Grill,** 207 Rutledge Ave. (☎843-937-0930; www.hominygrill.com). With low lights and white tablecloths, this is down-home cooking gone slightly upscale. Stop by for 2 eggs and hominy grits ($4.50) in the morning or sesame-crusted catfish ($13) in the evening. Open M-F 7:30am-8pm, Sa-Su 9am-3pm. AmEx/MC/V. ❷

- **Jestine's Kitchen,** 251 Meeting St. (☎843-722-7224). Serving up some of the best Southern food in Charleston, Jestine's has become a local favorite for its fried green tomatoes ($5), chicken livers, and okra and greens ($3). There must be something in the food—Jestine herself lived to be 112. Open M-Th 11am-9:30pm, F-Sa 11am-10pm, Su 11am-9pm. MC/V. ❷

- **Hyman's Seafood Company,** 215 Meeting St. (☎843-723-6000; www.hymanseafood.com). This restaurant has offered 15-25 kinds of fresh fish daily ($7-15), served in 8 styles by 5 generations of the same family since 1890. Get started with some stuffed mushrooms ($5.50) and request some complimentary boiled peanuts to munch on as you decipher the complicated menu. No reservations; expect long waits. Open Apr.-Oct. daily 11am-11pm; Nov.-Feb. M-Th 11am-9pm, F-Su 11am-9pm. AmEx/D/MC/V. ❸

- **Andolini's Pizza,** 82 Wentworth St. (☎843-722-7437; www.andolinis.com), just west of King St. Perfectly hidden from the ubertrendy King St. shoppers, Andolini's is fabulously funky, with statues, lightbulb signs, and a loft. Amazing pizza at unbeatable prices (large slice with any topping, a salad, and a drink; $6). Cheese pizza $14. Calzones from $6.50. Open M-Th 10:30am-10pm, F-Su 10:30am-11pm. AmEx/D/MC/V. ❷

SIGHTS

Charleston's historic homes, monuments, churches, galleries, and gardens can be seen by foot, car, bus, boat, trolley, horse-drawn carriage, or one of the several ghost tours that leave from City Market (around $16). **City Market,** downtown at **Meeting Street,** stays abuzz in a restored 19th-century building. (Open daily about 6am-11:30pm.)

BOONE HALL PLANTATION. This 738-acre, still-working plantation in Mt. Pleasant features a plantation house, slave cabins, and the gorgeous **Avenue of Oaks,** a much-photographed half-mile drive of oaks draped in Spanish moss. A fun, interactive Gullah presentation teaches visitors about slave culture through storytelling and dance. Tours of the grounds and of the 1936 Colonial Revival plantation home are included with admission. *(1235 Long Point Rd., off US 17. ☎843-884-4371; www.boonehall-plantation.com. Open Apr.-Aug. M-Sa 8:30am-6:30pm, Su 1-5pm. Sept.-Mar. M-Sa 9am-5pm, Su 1-4pm. $17.50, ages 6-12 $7.50, seniors and military $15.)*

SOUTH CAROLINA AQUARIUM. With waterfalls and towering tanks, the aquarium has become Charleston's most prominent attraction. Exhibits showcase aquatic life from the region's swamps and oceans. Stare down the fishies at the 330,000 gal. Great Ocean Tank, which rises two full stories. *(At the end of Calhoun St., on the Cooper River, overlooking the harbor. ☎843-720-1990; www.scaquarium.org. Open from Apr. to mid-Aug. M-Sa 9am-6pm, Su noon-6pm; from mid-Aug. to Apr. M-Sa 9am-5pm, Su noon-5pm. $17, ages 3-11 $10.)*

MAGNOLIA PLANTATION. The 300-year-old Magnolia Plantation and Gardens is the most majestic of Charleston's plantations, with fabulous gardens and miles of walking paths along the marsh. Guided tours lead groups through the plantation home, rice fields, and surrounding flora, but even without taking a tour visitors will enjoy stopping to smell the flowers. *(On Rte. 61, 10 mi. northwest of town off US 17. ☎843-571-1266 or 800-367-3517. Open Mar.-Oct. daily 8am-5:30pm; Nov.-Feb. call for hours. Gardens $15, ages 6-12 $10, seniors $14. House tour, nature train, nature boat, and swamp garden each $7, seniors $4.)*

MIDDLETON PLACE. A bit farther down the road, Middleton Place is a manicured plantation with working stables, gardens, a house, a restaurant, and an inn as well as demonstrations of 18th- and 19th-century crafts. *(4300 Ashley River Rd. on Rte. 61, 14 mi. northwest of downtown. ☎843-556-6020 or 800-782-3608; www.middletonplace.org. Open daily 9am-5pm. Gardens $25, under 16 $5. House tour $10.)*

CYPRESS GARDENS. The long trek out to Cypress Gardens may be worth it to visitors who wish to paddle boats out onto eerie, gator-filled swamps. You may recognize some of the landscape, as it was part of the set for the movie *The Notebook*. *(3030 Cypress Gardens Rd., off Rte. 52. ☎843-553-0515; www.cypressgardens.info. Open daily 9am-5pm. Last entry 4pm. $10, ages 6-12 $5, seniors $9.)*

CHARLESTON MUSEUM. Across the street from the visitors center stands the Charles-

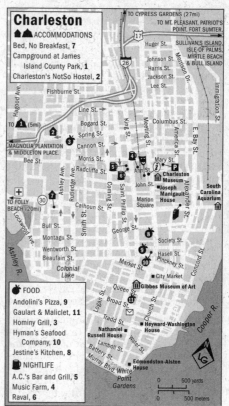

Charleston

▲▲ ACCOMMODATIONS
Bed, No Breakfast, **7**
Campground at James Island County Park, **1**
Charleston's NotSo Hostel, **2**

🍎 FOOD
Andolini's Pizza, **9**
Gaulart & Maliclet, **11**
Hominy Grill, **3**
Hyman's Seafood Company, **10**
Jestine's Kitchen, **8**

NIGHTLIFE
A.C.'s Bar and Grill, **5**
Music Farm, **4**
Raval, **6**

ton Museum, the country's oldest museum, founded in 1773. The museum contains outstanding exhibits on the Revolutionary War and the Civil War and takes an exhaustive look into the cultural history of the South Carolina Low Country. Take a picture next to the replica of the first succesful battle submarine outside. *(360 Meeting St. ☎843-722-2996; www.charlestonmuseum.org. Open M-Sa 9am-5pm, Su 1-5pm. $10, ages 3-12 $5.)*

PATRIOTS POINT. Climb aboard four naval ships, including a submarine and the aircraft carrier *Yorktown*, in Patriots Point Naval and Maritime Museum, the world's largest naval museum. Exhibits include a Congressional Medal of Honor display, several aircraft, and the *USS Laffey*, known as the "Ship That

Would Not Die." *(40 Patriots Point Rd., across the Cooper River in Mt. Pleasant. ☎866-831-1720; www. patriotspoint.org. Open daily 9am-6:30pm. $15, ages 6-11 $8, seniors and military $13.)*

FORT SUMTER. Boat excursions are available to the national historic site where the Civil War began in April 1861. Tours leave from Patriot's Point in Mt. Pleasant and Liberty Sq. in Charleston. *(☎843-883-3123; www.nps.gov/fosu. No park entrance fee for those arriving by private boats. Ferry ☎800-789-3678; www.fortsumtertours.com. $15, ages 6-11 $5, seniors and military $14.50.)*

CHARLES PINCKNEY NATIONAL HISTORIC SITE. The site lies on what was once the property of Charles Pinckney, a South Carolina delegate to the 1787 Constitutional Convention and former state governor. The grounds cover 28 acres and feature a half-mile-long nature trail, an 1828 Low Country cottage, and a museum with exhibits on rice agriculture, plantation life, the Gullah, and the American Revolution. *(1254 Long Point Rd., 6 mi. north of Charleston, off US 17, in Mt. Pleasant. ☎843-881-5516; www.nps.gov/chpi. Open daily 9am-5pm. Free.)*

BULL ISLAND. To get away from human civilization, take a 30min. ferry to Bull Island, a 6 mi. long island off the coast of Charleston. The island is home to several endangered species, including the loggerhead turtle and red wolf. On the island there are 16 mi. of hiking trails popular with birdwatchers. *(Ferries depart from Garris Landing, off Seewee Rd., 16 mi. north of Charleston off US 17. ☎843-884-7684; www. coastalexpeditions.com. Departs Mar.-Nov. Tu and Th-Sa 9am, 12:30pm; returns noon, 4pm; Dec.-Feb. Sa 10am; returns 3pm. Round-trip $30, under 12 $15.)*

GIBBES MUSEUM OF ART. The museum features portraits and miniatures, as well as an extensive collection of Japanese block prints. Rotating exhibits highlight local and regional artists. *(135 Meeting St. ☎843-722-2706; www.gibbesmuseum.org. Open Tu-Sa 10am-5pm, Su 1-5pm. Tours Tu and Sa 2:30pm. $9; students, military, and seniors $7, ages 6-12 $5.)*

OTHER SIGHTS. Charleston has a number of beautiful late-18th- and early-19th-century homes, so, unless you particularly adore cabinets and cantilevered staircases, choose just one of the tours. The **Nathaniel Russell House** features a unique free-flying spiral staircase, a geometric floor plan, and exceptional guides. *(51 Meeting St. ☎843-724-8481. Open M-Sa 10am-5pm, Su 2-5pm. $10, ages 6-16 $6, under 6 free.)* George Washington rented the **Heyward-Washington House** during his trip through the South in 1791. Home to Thomas Heyward, Jr., a signer of the Declaration of Independence, the house features timeless American furniture and a lush garden. *(87 Church St. ☎843-722-2996. Open M-Sa 10am-5pm, Su 1-5pm. $10, ages 3-12 $3.)* Built in 1803, The **Joseph Manigault House** is a stunning example of Federal or Adam-style architecture. Be sure to check out the Gate Temple, a gorgeous outdoor vestibule that stays cool in the muggy summer months. *(350 Meeting St. ☎843-722-2996. Open M-Sa 10am-5pm, Su 2-5pm. $10, ages 3-12 $5.)*

NIGHTLIFE

Thanks to nearby colleges and a constant tourist presence, Charleston's nightlife thrives. Free copies of *City Paper*, available in stores and restaurants, lists events.

AC's Bar and Grill, 467 King St. (☎843-577-6742). Hipsters and The Man mingle at this loud, friendly neighborhood dive. Locals come for the beer of the month ($2), pool tables, and Frogger. Su brunch 11am-4pm with $1 mimosas. Open daily 11am-2am. AmEx/D/MC/V.

Music Farm, 32 Ann St. (☎843-722-8904; www.musicfarm.com, tickets www.etix.com). From hippie jam bands to bluegrass, Music Farm is *the* place for live music in Charleston. Housed in what was once a train station, Music Farm seats 1000 for the big-name acts that come through town. Tickets $5-20; $3 surcharge for patrons under 21. Shows start between 7pm and 9pm. Box office open Tu-Th 1-4pm. AmEx/MC/V.

Raval, 453 King St. (☎843-853-8466; www.ravalwinebar.com). Named after a famous neighborhood in Barcelona, this is one funky tapas bar. It may seem like a typical wine bar, but in the back a DJ spins house and hip hop F-Sa. Tapas $4-12. Open M-Sa 5pm-2am. AmEx/D/MC/V.

BEACHES

Folly Beach, over the James Bridge and US 171, about 20 mi. southeast of Charleston, is popular with students from the Citadel, College of Charleston, and University of South Carolina. (☎843-588-2426. Open daily 9am-6pm.) The more exposed **Isle of Palms,** across the Cooper Bridge, drive 10 mi. down US 17 N. and turn right onto the Isle of Palms Connector, extends for miles down toward the less crowded Sullivan's Island. (☎843-886-3863. Open daily 9am-7pm.)

☝ THE ROAD TO GEORGETOWN: 60 MI.

Follow **US 17 North;** as you enter Georgetown it becomes **Church Street**.

GEORGETOWN ☎843

Don't plan on hurrying through Georgetown. In this decidedly Southern town, everyone takes their time. Stroll through the downtown area or along the waterfront and take a moment to enjoy the peace and quiet. It might not be the most happening place along the route, but it gives visitors a chance to while away an afternoon.

✦ ORIENTATION

From **US 17,** turn right onto **Front Street** to reach downtown Georgetown. US 17 (Church St.) bends to run parallel to the waterfront and Front St. **Swamp Fox Tours** gives narrated tram rides through the historic district, highlighting points of interest and local stories. Tours leave from 624 Front St. (☎843-527-1112; www.swampfoxtours.com. Tours every hr. M-Sa 10am-4pm. $7.50, ages 6-12 $4.)

VITAL STATS

Population: 9000

Tourist Office: Georgetown County Chamber of Commerce, 531 Front St. (☎843-546-8436; www.georgetownchamber.com). Open M-Sa 9am-5pm.

Library and Internet Access: Georgetown County Library, 405 Cleland St. (☎843-545-3300). Open June-Aug. M-Th 9am-8pm, F-Sa 9am-5pm; Sept.-May M-Th 9am-8pm, F-Sa 9am-5pm, Su 2-5pm.

Post Office: 1101 Charlotte St. (☎843-546-5515). Open M-F 8:30am-5pm, Sa 9am-noon. **Postal Code:** 29440.

☝ ACCOMMODATIONS

Downtown Georgetown is peppered with B&Bs, but for budget options visitors will have to resort to generic hotels and motels.

Carolinian Inn, 706 Church St. (☎800-722-4667; www.carolinianinn.com). Has standard amenities, some rooms with incredibly high beds. Don't be frightened by the deer head in the lobby. Free Wi-Fi. Rooms from $80. AmEx/D/MC/V. ❹

The Budget Inn, 412 James St. (☎843-546-4117), just off US 17. Offers cable TV, fridge, microwave, and phone. Ask for 1 of the newly renovated rooms. Rooms $45. AmEx/D/MC/V. ❷

🍴 FOOD

Front Street Deli, 809 Front St. (☎843-546-2008; www.frontstreetdeli.com). The owners of Front Street Deli left corporate America to open a small-town sandwich shop with large, tasty sandwiches like chicken cordon bleu ($5.50). Open M-Sa 10am-4pm. Cash only. ❶

The Thomas Cafe, 703 Front St. (☎843-546-7776). A no-frills restaurant that focuses on what matters—the food. They serve up Low Country favorites like shrimp and grits ($8.75) and coastal gumbo ($3.75). Open M-F 7am-2pm, Sa 7am-1pm. AmEx/D/MC/V. ❷

👁 SIGHTS

KAMINSKI HOUSE MUSEUM. Located right next to the chamber of commerce, the museum is a 1769 house decorated with period English and American furnishings, including examples of Charleston's finest cabinet-making. Friendly tour guides lead visitors through the home, explaining its particular history and satirizing its inhabitants. (*1003 Front St. ☎843-546-7706 or 888-233-0383. Tours every hr. M-Sa 10am-4pm, Su 1-4pm. $7, ages 6-12 $3, under 6 free, seniors $5.*)

RICE MUSEUM. This museum presents the history of rice culture in the county and illustrates how dependence on a single agricultural product shaped the era. The museum also contains the hull of the oldest boat manufactured in the colonies. (*633 Front St. ☎843-546-7423; www.ricemuseum.org. Open M-Sa 10am-4:30pm. $7, ages 6-21 $3, seniors $5.*)

HAMPTON PLANTATION STATE HISTORIC SITE. The plantation focuses on Low Country rice culture. The tour of the white, stately plantation house uses cutaway sections of wall and ceiling to show its evolution from farmhouse to grand manor. (*1950 Rutledge Rd. in McClellanville, off US 17 south of Georgetown.* ☎843-546-9361. Park grounds open daily 9am-6pm. Mansion tours every hr. Apr.-Oct. Tu-Su noon-4pm; Nov.-Apr. Th-Su noon-4pm. Last tour 3pm. Tours $4, ages 6-16 $3.)

⚲ THE ROAD TO MURRELLS INLET: 20 MI.
Take **US 17 North** to **Business US 17** and follow it until hitting Murrells Inlet.

MURRELLS INLET   ☎843

Ten miles south of Myrtle Beach lies tiny Murrells Inlet, which stretches along Bus. US 17. The town is famous as a fishing village and provides day access to its multiple marinas for a reasonable fee. The Huntingtons built the sprawling 🅑**Brookgreen Gardens,** US 17, opposite **Huntington Beach State Park** south of Murrells Inlet, to showcase Anna Hyatt Huntington's sculpture. Over 1200 sculptures now preside over the beautiful gardens and reflecting pools. Tours of the gardens and wildlife trails are available in addition to summer drama, music, and food programs. (☎843-235-6000; www.brookgreen.org. Open daily from mid-June to mid-Aug. 9:30am-9pm; from mid-Aug. to mid-June 9:30am-5pm. 7-day pass $12, ages 13-18 $10, ages 6-12 $5.)

The family-owned **Brookwood Inn ❸,** off Bus. US 17, offers travelers a quiet, shady place to hang their hats. There are hammocks and a pool under elegant oak trees, along with standard fridges and TV sets in each room. (☎843-651-2550. Rooms in summer $65-85; in winter $45-65. AmEx/D/MC/V.) **Huntington Beach State Park Campground ❶,** 16148 Ocean Hwy., 3 mi. south of Murrells Inlet on US 17, is located in an environment that includes lagoons, salt marshes, and a beach. Take advantage of the boat access and nature trails. Be careful: gators come within yards of the sites. (☎843-237-4440. Open Apr.-Oct. daily 6am-10pm; Nov.-Mar. M-Th and Sa-Su 6am-6pm, F 6am-8pm. 2-night min. stay. Sites with water and electricity $23-25, with full hookup $25-28. Day use $5, ages 6-15 $3.)

AmEx/D/MC/V.) Decorated with Mardi Gras beads and memorabilia, 🅑**Flo's Place ❸,** 3797 Bus. US 17, serves up authentic Cajun cuisine. Make sure to sample the alligator nuggets ($7.25) for a real taste of the swamp. (☎843-651-7222; www.flosplace.com. Live New Orleans jazz Su at 4pm. Open daily 11:30am-10pm. AmEx/MC/V.) For 60 years, **Lee's Inlet Kitchen ❺,** 4460 Bus. US 17, has served fresh, local seafood, like crab-stuffed flounder ($24). It's expensive, but it's definitely worth the splurge. Be sure to get here early—the place fills up fast. (☎843-651-2881; www.leesinletkitchen.com. Open M-Sa 5-10pm. AmEx/MC/V.)

⚲ THE ROAD TO MYRTLE BEACH: 10 MI.
Follow **US 17 North** to **Business US 17,** which becomes **Kings Highway.**

MYRTLE BEACH   ☎843

A long time ago, one restaurant must have put up the gaudy sign that ignited an advertising arms race. As you drive through Myrtle Beach, neon and pastel assault the senses, and you're never far from an elaborately decorated minigolf course. While lovers of the absurd will adore Myrtle Beach, those seeking to escape its incessant tackiness will find lovely beaches and excellent state parks farther along the Grand Strand.

VITAL STATS
Population: 23,000
Tourist Office: Myrtle Beach Chamber of Commerce, 1200 N. Oak St. (☎843-626-7444 or 800-356-3016; www.mbchamber.com), at 12th Ave. N. Open M-F 8:30am-5pm, Sa 9am-5pm, Su 10am-2pm.
Library and Internet Access: Chapin Memorial Library, 400 14th Ave. N. (☎843-918-1275; www.chapinlibrary.org). Free. Open June-Aug. M and W 9am-6pm, Tu and Th 9am-8pm, F 9am-5pm, Sa 9am-1pm; Sept.-May M and W 9am-6pm, Tu and Th 9am-8pm, F-Sa 9am-5pm.
Minigolf: Absolutely everywhere.
Post Office: 505 N. Kings Hwy. (☎843-626-9533), at 5th Ave. N. Open M-F 8:30am-5pm, Sa 9am-1pm. **Postal Code:** 29577.

✈ ORIENTATION

US 17 splits into a business route and a bypass 4 mi. south of Myrtle Beach and comes back together before the town of North Myrtle Beach (not to be confused with north Myrtle Beach). Most attractions are on **Kings Highway**, a.k.a. **Business US 17.** Parallel to Kings Hwy. is **Ocean Boulevard,** which follows the shoreline, flanked on either side by cheap motels. Cross streets are numbered, but the town is split into a southern half and a northern half. **Route 501** runs west toward **Conway** and **I-95.**

🏠 ACCOMMODATIONS

There are hundreds of motels lining Ocean Blvd., with those on the ocean fetching higher prices. Cheap motels also dot US 17. From October to March, prices plummet as low as $25-35 per night for one of the luxurious hotels right on the beach, and many of the hotels close down.

Coastal Breeze Motel, 2010 S. Ocean Blvd. (☎843-626-3531 or 888-487-5762). Big, newly renovated rooms with microwaves, fridges, and TVs. The motel also has a pool and hot tub and is right across the street from the beach. Rooms in summer $90-120; in winter $40. 18+. $50-100 deposit if under 21. AmEx/D/ MC/V. ❸

Coral Sands Motel, 301 N. Ocean Blvd. (☎843-448-3584 or 800-248-9779). Standard rooms and laundry facilities. Free Wi-Fi. In summer singles $60; doubles $70. In winter singles $25; doubles $35. AmEx/D/MC/V. ❸

Myrtle Beach State Park, 4401 S. Kings Hwy. (☎843-238-5325 or 866-345-7275), a few miles south of Myrtle Beach. Offers over 300 sites along a gorgeous beach. The park also includes picnic areas, laundry facilities, a general store, and miles of bike trails. Apr.-Oct. sites with water and electricity M-Th and Su $26, F-Sa $29; full hookup $29/32. Rates vary in winter. Day use $4, ages 6-15 $1.50. AmEx/D/MC/V. ❶

🍴 FOOD

The **Grand Strand** tempts hungry motorists with over 1900 restaurants serving every

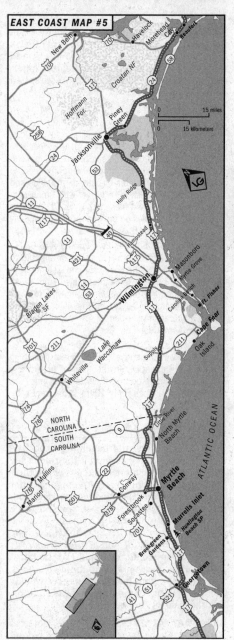

EAST COAST MAP #5

type of food in every imaginable setting. Massive all-you-can-eat joints beckon from beneath the glow of traffic lights. US 17 offers countless steakhouses, seafood buffets, and fast-food restaurants. Dinner theaters entertain guests with elaborately choreographed shows.

River City Cafe, 404 21st Ave. N. (☎843-448-1990; www.rivercitycafe.com). With license plates covering the walls and ceiling and discarded peanut shells crunching underfoot, the River City Cafe celebrates a brand of American informality bordering on delinquency. Peruse the enthusiastic signatures of patrons on tables and walls as you polish off a burger with Cajun seasoning ($5.29) and fries ($2) while sitting at one of the picnic tables on the front porch. Open daily 11am-10pm. D/MC/V. ❶

Manny's, 1701 S. Kings Hwy. (☎843-946-6817) off 17th Ave. S. Be sure to bring an appetite to Manny's, where deli sandwiches come stuffed with meat and cheese. The atmosphere is not much to speak of, but the pastrami sandwich ($5.75) or the Vegetarian Delight ($5) really make up for its shortcomings. Open M-Sa 11am-8pm, Su 11am-4pm. Cash only. ❶

Goodberry's, 1205 Celebrity Dr. (☎843-448-8000; www.goodberrys.com). Offers a refreshing taste of authenticity in the form of frozen custard. Customers polish off old favorites and new concoctions. Open daily 10am-11pm. AmEx/D/MC/V. ❶

🅢 SIGHTS

The boulevard and the beach are both "the strand," and while you're on it the rule is see and be seen. Fashionable teens strut their stuff, lowriders cruise the streets, and older beachgoers showcase their sunburns. Coupons are everywhere—never pay full price for any attraction. Pick up a free copy of the *Monster Coupon Book, Sunny Day Guide, Myrtle Beach Guide,* or *Strand Magazine* at any visitors center or hotel. For the latest information on events, attractions, festivals, and more, get your hands on the free weekly *Kicks,* available in most hotels, gas stations, and the visitors center.

BROADWAY AT THE BEACH. The colossal Broadway at the Beach is a sprawling complex designed to stimulate and entertain with theaters, a water park, minigolf, 20 restaurants, nightclubs, 100 shops, and other attractions. Of course, it's decorated with buildings shaped like pyramids or topped with enormous frogs. The info centers and booths sell tickets for major attractions at a discount. *(At US 17 Bypass and 21st Ave. N. ☎843-444-3200 or 800-386-4662. Open in summer daily 10am-11pm.)*

FAMILY KINGDOM. Several amusement parks line the beach, with unapologetically tacky decor and carnival games. One such park is Family Kingdom, which includes a wood roller coaster, a merry-go-round, and pastels galore. *(300 4th Ave. S. ☎843-946-9821; www.family-kingdom.com. Open M-F and Su 4pm-midnight, Sa 1pm-midnight. Single rides $2-6, unlimited rides $23.)*

ALLIGATOR ADVENTURE. The reptile capital of the world is Alligator Adventure, on US 17 in North Myrtle Beach at Barefoot Landing, where visitors are mesmerized by snakes, lizards, frogs, and, obviously, alligators. Watch alligators leap 4 ft. for raw chicken at hourly feedings starting at 10am. The park's enormous resident, Utan, is the largest crocodile ever exhibited in the US. *(☎843-361-0789; www.alligatoradventure.com. Open daily 9am-7pm. $17, ages 4-12 $11, seniors $15.)*

HARD ROCK PARK. For music lovers and thrill seekers, the brand-new Hard Rock Park is a bit of heaven on earth. With wild roller coasters and daily entertainment, the theme park is sure to delight those who can afford the hefty admission price. *(211 George Bishop Pkwy. off Main St. 3.5 mi. west of the beach. ☎843-236-7625; www.hardrockpark.com. Open daily June-Aug. 10am-1am; Sept.-Dec. and Apr.-May most days from 10am, closing times vary. $50, military $40. $5 discount for reservations made online 2 days in advance.)*

> **?**
>
> **DID YOU KNOW?** The state dance of both North and South Carolina is 🅢 **the shag.** The shag is a form of swing dancing that originated on the strands between Myrtle Beach, South Carolina, and Wilmington, North Carolina, in the 1940s.

NIGHTLIFE

The New Orleans-style nightclub district of Celebrity Sq., at **Broadway at the Beach,** facilitates stepping out with 10 clubs, ranging in theme from classic rock to Latin. One cover gains you access to four neighboring clubs ($5-10; www.celebrationsnitelife.com). With karaoke every night at 9pm, **Broadway Louie's** allows your inner diva to take the stage. (☎843-445-6885. 21+ after 7pm. Happy hour 4-7pm. Open daily Mar.-Nov. noon-2am; Dec.-Feb. 4pm-2am. AmEx/D/MC/V.) **Club Boca** is a dance club playing Latin and house. (☎843-444-3500. Open Th-Sa 10pm-3am. AmEx/D/MC/V.) Revelers sip fishbowl drinks ($8-10) at **Froggy Bottomz** while listening to live music, usually Top 40. (☎643-444-3500. Live music Tu-Sa 9pm. Open daily 9:45pm-2:30am. AmEx/D/MC/V.) **Malibu's** is a surf bar where locals cruise on in. (☎843-444-3500. Open daily 9pm-the party ends. AmEx/D/MC/V.)

THE ROAD TO CAPE FEAR: 67 MI.

From Myrtle Beach, take **US 17 North.** To bypass North Myrtle Beach traffic, take **Route 31** to **Route 9** and then rejoin US 17.

WILMINGTON AND CAPE FEAR ☎910

Situated on the Carolina coast at the mouth of the Cape Fear River and only a few miles from the beaches of the Atlantic, Wilmington has long been an important center for shipping and trade. Home to the largest film production facility east of L.A., the city is sometimes referred to as "Wilmywood" and "Hollywood East." Over 400 feature films and TV projects have been shot along the picturesque Cape Fear coast since 1983, including the hit TV series *Dawson's Creek* and, more recently, *One Tree Hill.* Even if you don't glimpse a celebrity, the historic downtown has plenty to offer, from memorials and excellent restaurants to picturesque views of the waterfront.

ORIENTATION

Wilmington proper is north of Cape Fear. In town, **Business US 17** is called **Market Street** and runs midway through downtown. Downtown is bounded by **Red Cross Street** to the west, **Castle Street** to the east, and **Front Street** along the water. The streets running parallel to Front St. are all numbered and form a grid. **US 421** runs the length of Cape Fear. A free trolley, the **Wave** (☎910-343-0106), runs downtown every 20min. There are three parking decks—two on **Second Street** and one on **Water Street.** (M-F $1 per hr., $5 per day; Sa-Su free.)

VITAL STATS

Population: 76,000

Tourist Office: Cape Fear Coast Convention and Visitors Bureau, 24 N. 3rd St. (☎910-341-4030 or 800-222-4757), in the 1892 courthouse. Open M-F 8:30am-5pm, Sa 9am-4pm, Su 1-4pm.

Library and Internet Access: New Hanover County Public Library, 201 Chestnut St. (☎910-798-6302). Open M-W 9am-8pm, Th-Sa 9am-5pm, Su 1-5pm.

Post Office: 152 Front St. (☎910-313-3293). Open M-F 8am-5pm, Sa 8am-noon. **Postal Code:** 28401.

ACCOMMODATIONS

Wilmington's best lodging comes in the form of B&Bs; you'll find most of them in the historic downtown area. Though rooms usually cost $100-200 per night, the personalized experience, breakfasts, unique rooms, and riverfront views make them worth the extra cash. Those seeking less expensive lodging will find nearly every budget chain on Market St., between **College Road** and **23rd Street.** Rates generally run $60 during the summer and $40 in winter, with weekend rates $5-10 higher than weekday prices.

Travel Inn, 4401 Market St. (☎910-763-8217). Provides basic rooms. Pool and cable TV. Rooms in summer M-F $50, Sa-Su $55; in winter from $35. AmEx/D/MC/V. ❸

Carolina Beach State Park (☎910-458-8206) about 18 mi. south of the city on US 421. Offers campsites as well as hiking, picnic areas, and a marina. You'll find hungry Venus flytraps growing in the park, so guard your *Nematocera* and *Brachycera* well. Restrooms, water, and grills. No RV hookups. Hot showers. No reservations. Sites $15, seniors $10. Day-use free. MC/V. ❶

🍴 FOOD

Wilmington's downtown is flush with trendy cafes, many of which have outdoor seating.

Caffé Phoenix, 9 S. Front St. (☎910-343-1395). Has a chic, European feel with abundant greenery and colorful art on the walls. Try the pear and fennel salad ($5.50) or the *spinaci con prosciutto* ($12)—both served with freshly baked bread. Open M-Sa 11:30am-10pm, Su 11am-4pm. AmEx/D/MC/V. ❷

Bella's, 19 Market St. (☎910-762-2777). With funky chairs, a shelf of poetry, and free Wi-Fi, Bella's draws young locals and tourists. The Mediterranean Harvest sandwich (hummus and veggies; $6) and smoothies ($4) will appeal to anyone. Open daily 8am-midnight. MC/V. ❶

The Caprice Bistro, 10 Market St. (☎910-815-0810; www.capricebistro.com). Serves upscale French cuisine at intimate tables. After savoring a *feuillete monsieur* ($9) for dinner, head up to the sofa bar to relax with mixed drinks. Open M-W and Su 5-10pm, Th 5-10:30pm, F-Sa 5pm-midnight. Bar open to 2am. AmEx/MC/V. ❷

👁 SIGHTS

CAPE FEAR MUSEUM. The museum documents and celebrates all aspects of Cape Fear life—political, cultural, and scientific. The interactive habitat exhibits and the lit diorama of the battle of Fort Fisher are particularly interesting. For basketball fans, there's also an exhibit on hometown hero Michael Jordan. (*814 Market St. ☎910-341-4350; www.capefearmuseum.com. Open from Memorial Day to Labor Day M-Sa 9am-5pm, Su 1-5pm; from Labor Day to Memorial Day Tu-Sa 9am-5pm, Su 1-5pm. $6, students, seniors, and military $5; ages 3-17 $3.*)

BELLAMY MANSION MUSEUM. Once the residence of planter John D. Bellamy, this mansion is a terrific example of antebellum architecture and one of the few urban slave quarters still standing in the country. The 22 rooms have been restored, and, unlike in most historic homes, visitors are free to wander through the empty rooms at their own leisure. (*503 Market St. ☎910-251-3700; www.bellamymansion.org. Open Tu-Sa 10am-5pm, Su 1-5pm. $10, ages 5-12 $4.*)

CAPE FEAR SERPENTARIUM. With red lighting and in-depth descriptions of death by snakebite, the Serpentarium doesn't shy away from shocking its visitors. Snakes and crocodiles are rated on a scale of deadliness, from one to five skull and crossbones. If you aren't frightened yet, just listen to the eerie background music or take a look at the massive 340 lb. anaconda. (*20 Orange St. ☎910-762-1669; www.capefearserpentarium.com. Open M-F and Su 11am-5pm, Sa 11am-6pm; in summer W-F and Su 11am-5pm, Sa 11am-6pm, but hours vary. Snake feedings Sa-Su 3pm. $8, under 2 free.*)

LOUISE WELLS CAMERON ART MUSEUM. Dedicated to North Carolina's artistic heritage, the Louise Wells Cameron Art Museum displays the work of artists such as Mary Cassatt. Traditional media are supplemented by exhibits on commercial design and computer-generated art. (*3201 S. 17th St. ☎910-395-5999; www.cameronartmuseum.com. Open Tu-W and F-Su 11am-5pm, Th 11am-9pm. $8, students $5, ages 6-18 $3.*)

BATTLESHIP NORTH CAROLINA. With its crew of 2300, the *North Carolina* served in every major naval battle of WWII. Visitors can climb inside the bowels of this floating city, which includes barber and ice-cream shops. The museum provides insight into the lives of WWII sailors and the ship's battles. (*Off US 17, south of Wilmington. ☎910-350-1817; www.battleshipnc.com. Open daily from Memorial Day to Labor Day 8am-8pm; from Labor Day to Memorial Day 8am-5pm. Last entry 1hr. before closing. $12, ages 6-11 $6, under 6 free, seniors and military $10.*)

WILMINGTON RAILROAD MUSEUM. For over 150 years, Wilmington was home to the Atlantic Coast Line Railroad, and the old transportation headquarters now houses the Wilmington Railroad Museum. In addition to pictures and models, it also contains a refurbished freight warehouse, a steam engine, a boxcar, and a caboose. (*505 Nutt St. ☎910-763-2634; www.wrrm.org. Open Apr.-Sept. M-Sa 10am-5pm, Su 1-5pm; Oct.-Mar. M-Sa 10am-4pm. $6, ages 2-12 $3.*)

FORT FISHER. Fort Fisher was one of the Confederacy's last major strongholds. The fort was able to withstand the shock of torpedo shells and other blasts because it consisted almost entirely of sand and dirt, but it was finally captured in January 1865. The visitors center has exhibits on the Civil War, including cannons and rifles, while the recreation site has a crowded beach and a number of nature-oriented programs. *(On US 421, 20 mi. south of Wilmington. ☎910-458-5538. Historic site open Apr.-Sept. M-Sa 9am-5pm, Su 1-5pm; Oct.-Mar. Tu-Sa 10am-4pm. Recreation area open in summer daily 6am-9pm. Free.)* The **North Carolina Aquarium**, also at Fort Fisher, allows visitors to view and interact with the state's aquatic life. Visitors can touch the animals in the Touch Tanks and see the staff feed the fishies. *(☎910-458-8257. Open daily 9am-5pm. $8, ages 6-17 $6 , seniors $7.)*

LATIMER HOUSE. Built in the popular Italianate style, this 1852 home contains period furnishings and artwork, including portraits of the wealthy Latimer family. Be sure to check out the clothing and hair wreath. *(126 S. 3rd St. ☎910-762-0492; www.latimerhouse.org. Open M-F 10am-3:30pm, Sa noon-5pm. Walking tours W and Sa 10am. $10, under 13 $5.)*

⛟ THE ROAD TO BEAUFORT: 98 MI.

Take **US 17 North** to Jacksonville, then take **Route 24 East.** Rte. 24 will become **Route 70 East.**

BEAUFORT   ☎252

A tiny town near Morehead City, Beaufort is home to a beautiful, quaint downtown with a celebrated history. It may be small, but Beaufort offers a relaxed weekend of window-shopping and strolling by the waterfront.

VITAL STATS
Population: 4000
Tourist Office: Beaufort Historic Site (☎252-728-5225; www.beauforthistoricsite.org), at Turner St. Open Mar.-Nov. M-Sa 9:30am-5pm, Su noon-4pm; Dec.-Feb. M-Sa 10am-4pm.
Library and Internet Access: Carteret County Public Library, 210 Turner St. (☎252-728-2050). Open M-Th 8:30am-9pm, F 8:30am-6pm, Sa 8:30am-5pm.
Post Office: 701 Front St. (☎252-728-4821). Open M-F 10am-1:30pm and 2:35-4pm, Sa 10am-noon. **Postal Code:** 28516.

◪ ORIENTATION

Turner Street leads south from US 70 to the main part of Beaufort, including the historic downtown. **Front Street** runs along the water and is home to shops and restaurants.

⛉ ACCOMMODATIONS

Beaufort is happily devoid of chain accommodations. Unfortunately, it isn't cheap.

▨ **Inlet Inn,** 601 Front St. (☎252-728-3600; www.inlet-inn.com). Has 35 enormous rooms with porches on the first 2 floors, fridges, and fireplaces. Rooms are very attractive and have fantastic views. Continental breakfast. Rooms Mar.-Dec. $85-145 Jan.-Feb. $75-95. Waterfront rooms $20 more. AmEx/D/MC/V. ❹

⛾ FOOD

Downtown Beaufort has a generous array of tasty, elegant restaurants.

Beaufort Grocery Co., 117 Queen St. (☎252-728-3899; www.beaufortgrocery.com). Serves delicious sandwiches for lunch, like the "fuhgeddaboudit" (turkey, red pepper, greens, bacon; $9) and the "sonnamabeach" (ham, *capicolla*, salami, and cheeses; $10) in a casual cafe setting. Dinner is a bit pricier, with main courses going for $25-37. Open from Memorial Day to Labor Day M and W-Sa 11:30am-3pm and 5:30-10pm, Su 5:30-9:30pm; from Labor Day to Memorial Day M and W-Su 11:30am-2:30pm and 5:30-9:30pm. AmEx/D/MC/V. ❸

The Spouter Inn, 218 Front St. (☎252-728-5190; www.thespouterinn.com). Makes superb sandwiches, like the Islander (veggies in pita with balsamic vinaigrette; $7) and the One Eye Terrible (ham, salami, and swiss; $8.25). The restaurant overlooks the calm waters of Taylor's Creek. Open 11:30am-2:30pm and 5-9pm. AmEx/MC/V. ❷

Royal James Cafe, 117 Turner St. (☎252-728-4573). Part pool hall, part casual restaurant, the cafe offers a refreshing break from the expensive eateries downtown and serves cheeseburgers ($2.25) and draft beers ($1.50) to a young, local crowd. Make sure to get your burgers "all the way" with chili, mustard, and onions. Open daily 9am-2am. Cash only. ❶

SIGHTS

HISTORIC DOWNTOWN. The **Beaufort Historical Association** gives narrated double-decker bus tours to the nearly 100 historic buildings throughout town. (*☎252-728-5225. Tours M, W, F-Sa 11am and 1:30pm. $8, ages 6-12 $4.*) The **Beaufort Historic Site** is composed of nine historic buildings owned by the Beaufort Historic Society. (*100 Turner St.*) The **Mattie King Davis Art Gallery** features rotating paintings and sculptures by local artists as well as several restored buildings. Be sure to visit the **Apothecary Shop** and **Doctor's Office,** built in 1859, for a glimpse of dusty bottles and grisly medical instruments. Visitors can also tour the **Carteret County Courthouse,** the oldest wood-framed courthouse in the state, the **Josiah Bell House,** and the **Old Jail,** among other historic buildings. (*☎252-728-5225; www.beauforthistoricsite. org. Art Gallery open M-Sa 10am-4pm. Tours M-Sa 11:30am, 1, 3pm. Tours $8, ages 6-12 $4.*) A block away lies the **Old Burying Ground,** a cemetery deeded to the town in 1731. The site has a pamphlet for a self-guided walking tour with stories about the interred. Legend has it that most of the graves face east because those buried wanted the sun on their faces on the morning of Judgment Day. (*☎252-728-5225. Open daily 8am-5pm. Tours June-Sept. Tu-Th 2:30pm. $8, children $4.*)

NORTH CAROLINA MARITIME MUSEUM. The North Carolina Maritime Museum features exhibits on Blackbeard, who met his end just miles from Beaufort, along with model ships and an underwater observation chamber that you can climb inside. Those who haven't yet satisfied their nautical cravings can head across the street to the **Harvey W. Smith Watercraft Center,** an extension of the museum, and see small watercraft being handbuilt by experts as well as displays of tools and the "half-models" used to design ships. (*315 Front St. ☎252-728-7317; www.ncmaritime.org. Open M-F 9am-5pm, Sa 10am-5pm, Su 1-5pm. Free.*)

FORT MACON STATE PARK. The park lies a few miles south of Beaufort at Atlantic City Beach. Constructed between 1826 and 1834, the fort is a pentagonal structure that was used in both the Civil War and the Spanish-American War. Check out the soldiers' quarters, the commissary, and the "hot shot furnace," which heated non-explosive cannonballs that were used to destroy wood marine vessels. (*Take Rte. 70 S., then head east over the Highrise Bridge and take a left on E. Fort Macon Rd., which heads to the fort. ☎252-726-3775. Swimming area open daily 10am-5:45pm. Fort open daily 9am-5:30pm. Tours daily every hr. 10am-3pm. Free.*)

NIGHTLIFE

The Backstreet Pub, 124 Middle Ln. (*☎252-728-7108; www.thebackstreetpub.com*). In the building of an 1880s bakery, hidden behind the shops and restaurants of Front St., the pub is decorated with tattered flags and life preservers. Climb the easy-to-miss red spiral staircase to listen to live bands (Sa 9pm-1am) or borrow a book from the library. Open daily noon-2am. Cash only.

The Dock House, 500 Front St. (*☎252-728-4506*). The place to go for a beer and live music, usually classic rock or beach. Sit outside and enjoy the breeze coming off the water. Open daily 11:30am-2am. Kitchen open until 10pm. MC/V.

THE ROAD TO OCRACOKE: 61 MI.

The only way to reach Ocracoke is by **ferry,** which departs from Cedar Island. From Beaufort, take **Route 70 East** to **Route 12 North** to Cedar Island. (*☎252-225-3551 or 800-856-0343. Reservations required. $15 per vehicle, $1 per pedestrian, $3 per cyclist.*)

OCRACOKE   ☎252

Tiny Ocracoke was once extremely isolated, allowing for the development of a unique dialect. Now easily accessible by ferry, Ocracoke has come to rely increasingly on tourism. As a result of this influx in visitors, the brogue—and the natives' way of life—is fading. For visitors, the town still represents a magical escape from the hustle of mainland life.

VITAL STATS
Population: 800
Tourist Office: Ocracoke Visitors Center (☎252-928-4531; www.nps.gov/caha or www.ocracokevillage.com), located off Rte. 12 by the ferry. Open daily May-Sept. 9am-6pm; Oct.-Apr. 9am-5pm.
Library and Internet Access: Ocracoke Public Library, on Back Rd. (☎252-928-4436). Open M and Th noon-4pm and 7-9pm, Tu-W and F noon-4pm, Sa 9am-1pm.
Post Office: Off Rte. 12, at the northern end of town (☎252-928-4771). Open M-F 9am-2pm and 3-5pm, Sa 10am-1pm. **Postal Code:** 27960.

◧ ORIENTATION

The entire island, with the exception of **Ocracoke Village,** is owned by the US National Park Service. **Route 12,** also called the **Irvin Garrish Highway,** stretches the length of the island and forms the major road in Ocracoke. Be patient; the speed limit is 25 mph around the island, and traffic can be even slower. Pedestrians and bikers abound; if you choose to stay on your four wheels, do make sure to keep them in mind. It's hard to get lost in Ocracoke; there are few roads, and most lead back to Rte. 12.

> **TIP**
>
> **DROPPED CALLS.** Most cellphone companies have no reception in Ocracoke or Cedar Island. Plan accordingly and bring plenty of quarters for the expensive pay phones.

⌂ ACCOMMODATIONS

Blackbeard's Lodge, 111 Back Rd. (☎252-928-3421, reservations 800-892-5314; www.blackbeardslodge.com). Offers shipshape wood-paneled rooms. If the life-size pirate in the lobby gives you a scare, worry not; there is also a grand piano whose music will most certainly soothe you. A/C, cable TV, and pool. Standard rooms from Memorial Day to Labor Day $99-$125. Prices are 30-60% lower the rest of the year. AmEx/D/MC/V. ❺

Sand Dollar Motel, 70 Sand Dollar Rd. (☎252-928-5571 or 866-928-5571). Well-kept rooms at a good price. Refrigerators, microwaves, A/C, cable TV, pool, and breakfast included. Open from Apr.-Nov. Rooms May-Aug. from $99; Sept.-Nov. from $89; Apr. $69. AmEx/D/MC/V. ❹

Cape Hatteras National Seashore (☎800-365-2267). There are plenty of places to camp just steps from the beach. Camping on the beach itself is prohibited. The campground has water and restrooms, but no electricity or heated showers. The 136 sites may be reserved Mar.-Oct.; the rest of the year, they're 1st come, 1st served. Sites $23. MC/V. ❶

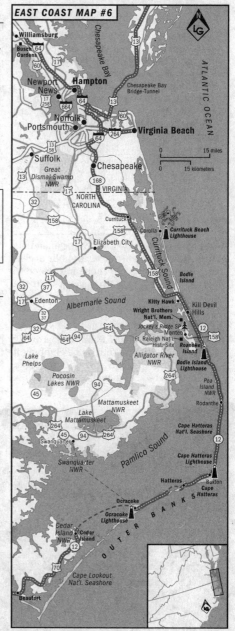
EAST COAST MAP #6

EAST COAST

FOOD

Flying Melon Cafe (☎252-928-2533), on Rte. 12 and Ocean View. Decorated with brightly colored roosters. While you wait for your eggs, biscuit, and grits ($4.25), or fried oysters at dinnertime ($15), test your artistic abilities coloring on the tablecloth. The best drawings are saved on a special wall. Open Mar.-Nov. Tu-Sa 9am-2pm and 5-9pm, Su 9am-2pm. MC/V. ❷

Howard's Pub, 1175 Irvin Garrish Hwy. (☎252-928-4441; www.howardspub.com). During the day, enjoy hush puppies ($5) or a cheeseburger ($7.30). When night falls, drink up to the strains of live acoustic guitar. Music begins 9 or 10pm. Open daily 11am-midnight. D/MC/V. ❷

SIGHTS

Most people come to Ocracoke for unending, white beaches; there are several public access points along the island. Those interested in watersports need look no further than the booths lining Rte. 12 in town, and many visitors also rent bikes to pedal about the island.

OCRACOKE LIGHTHOUSE. The lighthouse was built in 1823 and stands 75 ft. tall. A boardwalk leads to the lighthouse, but, alas, climbing it is generally prohibited. Speak with a ranger; sometimes there are special entrance hours. *(On Lighthouse Rd.)*

OCRACOKE PRESERVATION SOCIETY MUSEUM. The museum has artifacts from life on Ocracoke Island, including a parlor with a cast-iron stove and a kitchen with a handpump that represents the recent installation of running water in 1970. The museum also has a room devoted to the **Ocracoke brogue,** including a video illustrating the pronunciation, grammar, and vocabulary— "dingbatters" are non-natives of the island, as any true "O'cocker" would know. *(Near the ferry terminal. ☎252-928-7375. Open M-F 10am-5pm, Sa 11am-4pm. Free.)*

THE ROAD TO CAPE HATTERAS: 60 MI.
Free **ferries** run between Ocracoke and Cape Hatteras (www.ncferry.org; 40min., daily 5am-midnight). Arrive early to avoid a wait during rush-hour.

CAPE HATTERAS ☎252
Hatteras Island, covered almost entirely by the **Cape Hatteras National Seashore,** stretches 70 mi. and includes several small towns. Gorgeous, duned public access beaches line Rte. 12, many of which are deserted save for a lonely swimmer or fisherman. While heading up the coast, drivers can look out to the ocean to marvel at the feared **Graveyard of the Atlantic,** the cause of more than 600 shipwrecks. Storms uncover the remains of unlucky vessels. A few miles north of the ferry, the **Frisco Native American Museum and Natural History**

SPEAKING LIKE AN O'COCKER

Ocracoke was founded in the 1700s and, until recently, has been fairly isolated from the rest of North Carolina. The island developed its own dialect that sounds completely different from that of the mainland. Speakers pronounce the long "i" sound (as, for example, in the word high) as "oy." On the mainland, the sound has changed to an "ah" sound (as in "ah'm tahrd" for "I'm tired"). Similarly, Ocracoke residents pronounce ending "r" sounds, as in the words "car" or "near," while mainland North Carolinans often use a soft "r," pronouncing those words as "cah" or "neuh." In addition to the different pronunciation, speakers of the Ocracoke brogue have a specialized vocabulary, some of which was originally used in 18th-century England.

So you think you can talk like a native? Try some of these phrases on for size: **haint**—a ghost; **mommick**—to bother; **O'cocker**—a native of Ocracoke; **quamish**—sick to the stomach; **pizer**—porch. Now put it all together: the haint on the pizer mommicked the O'cocker until he was quamish. And if

Center is an interactive museum about the history of the island's first inhabitants. The museum consists mostly of local artifacts, such as baskets, beadwork, and a Hopi kiva drum. (☎252-995-4400. Open M by appointment, Tu-Su 11am-5pm. $5, seniors $3.) At the southern end of Hatteras Island on Rte. 12 lies the **Cape Hatteras Lighthouse.** As the rangers proudly proclaim, the 210 ft. structure is the tallest brick lighthouse in the country, and the climb in the hot, narrow spiral staircase is not for the faint of heart. While you wait for your chance to climb the 248 steps to the top, visit the old keeper's quarters, now a museum with displays on the lighthouse. (☎252-995-4474. Open from late April to Columbus Day daily 9am-5:30pm. Museum free. Lighthouse $7, children and seniors $3.50.) The top half of the island consists of the **Pea Island National Wildlife Refuge,** established in 1938 to preserve the island's unique barrier island habitat. The visitors center has info about local wildlife and marks the beginning of the **North Pond Wildlife Trail,** which stretches a half mile to the sound. More intrepid explorers can bike or walk the 4 mi. of service road that encircle the pond and connect back to Rte. 12. (☎252-987-2394. Open daily in summer 9am-5pm; in winter 9am-4pm.)

⚲ THE ROAD TO ROANOKE ISLAND: 17 MI.

Take **Route 12 North** to **US 64 West.**

ROANOKE ISLAND   ☎252

Roanoke Island was the location of the first (failed) English settlement in the New World. A second settlement on the island was established in 1587 and mysteriously disappeared sometime during the following three years. Though it is most famous for its role as the earliest English settlement on the continent, the island also features parks, gardens, and inexpensive food.

✴ ORIENTATION

US 64 is the largest road on Roanoke Island. It serves as the main thoroughfare of Manteo at the northern end of the island. Roanoke Sound in the east, Wanchese in the south, and Manteo in the north are the main towns. Manteo is where most attractions are located; the waterfront is the center of activity.

VITAL STATS
Population: 6000
Tourist Office: Outer Banks Visitors Bureau, 1 Visitors Center Cir. (☎252-473-2138). Open daily 9am-6pm.
Library and Internet Access: Manteo Public Library, on the corner of Burnside Rd. and Hwy. 64 (☎252-473-2372), in Manteo. Open M and Th 10am-7pm, Tu-W and F 9am-5:30pm, Sa 10am-4pm.
Post Office: 212 Hwy. 64, Ste. B (☎252-473-2534). Open M-F 9am-4:30pm, Sa 10am-noon. **Postal Code:** 27954.

⚑ ACCOMMODATIONS

Duke of Dare Motor Lodge, 100 S. US 64 (☎252-473-2175). Offers a no-nonsense place to rest your head. Large, clean rooms. Pool access. Rooms in summer $68; in winter $54. MC/V. ❸

Dare Haven Motel, US 64/264 (☎252-473-2322; www.darehaven.com). With flowerbeds, a basketball hoop, and wood-paneled rooms, the motel has the personal touch of a family-owned hotel. Doubles Apr.-Oct. $80-90; Sept.-Mar. $50-60. AmEx/D/MC/V. ❸

🍴 FOOD

Poor Richard's Sandwich Shop & Pub, 305 Queen Elizabeth Ave. (☎252-473-3333; www.poorrichardsmanteo.com). Serves up reuben sandwiches and burgers ($6.50). Live folk and 60s rock on the weekends 8-11pm. Sandwich shop open M-Sa 8am-3pm. Bar open M-Sa 5pm-midnight, Su noon-midnight. MC/V. ❷

🎟 SIGHTS

◪THE LOST COLONY. Roanoke's vanished colony is the inspiration for *The Lost Colony*, a musical theatrical extravaganza performed throughout the summer. *(1409 National Park Rd., on the Fort Raleigh National Historic Site. ☎252-473-3414; www.thelostcolony.org. Shows June-Aug. M-F and Su 8:30pm. $16, under 11 $8, seniors $15.)*

FORT RALEIGH VISITORS CENTER. Fort Raleigh has information about the famed lost colony and daily programs explaining and reenacting pieces of its history. (☎252-473-2111; www.nps.gov/fora. Visitors center open daily June-Aug. 9am-6pm; Sept.-Mar. 9am-5pm. Grounds open daily sunrise-sunset. Free.)

ELIZABETHAN GARDENS. Flowers perfume the air of the romantic gardens where visitors can wander among fountains, finely tended gardens, and a statue of Virginia Dare, the first English child born in the New World. (1411 National Park Dr. ☎252-473-3234; www.elizabethangardens.org. Hours vary, call for information. $8, ages 6-18 $5, under 5 free.)

ROANOKE ISLAND FESTIVAL PARK. Facing the Manteo Waterfront, the 25-acre park, staffed largely by accented actors in 16th-century garb, features the *Elizabeth II* and a replica of a 16th-century English merchant ship. It also includes a settlement site with craft demonstrations, an art gallery, an interactive museum, and a film depicting the native reaction to the European arrival. During the summer, students from the **North Carolina School of the Arts** perform theater and ballet at the park's outdoor pavilion. (Follow signs from the highway. ☎252-475-1500; www.roanokeisland.com. Open daily May-Oct. 9am-6pm; Nov.-Dec. and Feb.-Apr. 9am-5pm daily. $8, students $5, under 6 free. For theater and ballet, call ☎252-475-1506. Free.)

THE ROAD TO BODIE AND KITTY HAWK: 18 MI.

From Roanoke Island, take **US 64 East** to **US 158**.

BODIE AND KITTY HAWK ☎252

Bodie Island is composed of four towns, with Nags Head at the southern end and Kitty Hawk to the north. The island is the most trafficked of the Outer Banks, due to easy access from the mainland and the Wright brothers' historic flight in 1903. Despite crowds in the summertime, there are more than enough beaches, restaurants, and kites to go around.

VITAL STATS

Population: 3000

Tourist Office: Aycock Brown Welcome Center, mi. 1.5 on US 158 (☎252-261-4644; www.outerbanks.org), in Kitty Hawk. Open daily 9am-6pm.

Library and Internet Access: Dare County Library, 400 Mustian St. (☎252-441-4331), mi. 8.5 in Kill Devil Hills, 1 block west of US 158. Open M and Th-F 9am-5:30pm, Tu-W 10am-7pm, Sa 10am-4pm.

Post Office: 3841 N. Croatan Hwy. (☎252-261-2211), in Kitty Hawk. Open M-F 9am-4:30pm, Sa 10am-noon. **Postal Code:** 27949.

ORIENTATION

Bodie is the northernmost of the Outer Banks islands. It is joined to the mainland by **US 158** and serves as a major point of entry to the Outer Banks for travelers coming south over the **Wright Memorial Bridge.** For much of Bodie Island, **Route 12 (Virginia Dare Trail)** parallels US 158 (called the Bypass), with Rte. 12 east of the Bypass along the beach. Directions on Bodie Island are usually given in terms of distances in miles from the bridge. Traffic calls for extra travel time on weekends.

ACCOMMODATIONS

Most visitors stay in houses rented by the week (weekend rentals are sometimes available in the low season), which range from cottages to oceanfront mansions.

Outer Banks Motor Lodge, 1509 S. Virginia Dare Trail (☎252-441-77404 or 877-625-6343; www.obxmotorlodge.com), at mi. 9.5. Large, inexpensive rooms by the ocean. Cable, fridge, microwave, and pool. Laundry. Rooms in summer from $69; in winter from $39. D/MC/V. ❸

Outer Banks Adventure Bound, 1004 W. Kitty Hawk Rd. (☎252-255-1130). Offers tent camping 1 mi. inland. The campground has volleyball, shuffleboard courts, grills, and picnic tables. Boogie boards and beach chairs available at no charge. Hot showers. Sites $20. Cash only. ❶

FOOD

Tortuga's Lie (☎252-441-7299; www.tortugaslie.com), mi. 11 on Beach Rd. in Nags Head. Serves

($15) and Creole Crawdad Fett ($13) in a low-key, beachy setting. Sandwiches, burgers, and vegetarian options available. Sushi night W. Open daily 11:30am-10:30pm. AmEx/D/MC/V. ❸

Chilli Peppers (☎252-441-8081), mi. 5.5 on US 158. Specializes in top-notch Tex-Mex, like shrimp quesadillas ($8) and veggie burritos in sun-dried tomato wraps ($7). Happy hour 3-5pm daily with $0.25 wings. Open daily 11am-10pm. Bar open 11am-2am. AmEx/D/MC/V. ❷

Stack 'em High (☎252-261-8221. www.stackemhigh.com), at mi. 9 on the Bypass. The food is by-the-book Southern. Have a short stack of pancakes ($4) or eggs, grits, and toast ($4.50) in the dining room. Open daily 7am-1pm. MC/V. ❶

🜚 SIGHTS

▨WRIGHT BROTHERS NATIONAL MEMORIAL. The memorial marks the spot where bicycle mechanics Orville and Wilbur Wright took to the skies. Exhibits in the visitors center document the brothers' triumph over gravity and display a full-size replica of the plane the brothers used. Outside, stone markers show the distance of the four flights taken the morning of December 17, 1903. The Centennial Pavilion contains a recreation of the Wrights' camp and a timeline of developments in aviation. *(Mi. 8 on US 158. ☎252-441-7430; www.nps.gov/wrbr. Open daily June-Aug. 9am-6pm; Sept.-May 9am-5pm. $4, under 16 free.)*

JOCKEY'S RIDGE STATE PARK. The park includes the East Coast's largest naturally occurring sand dune, around 100 ft. high and containing some 30 million tons of sand. Bring a kite or a sandboard and enjoy this über-beach. The museum at the visitors center explains the origins of the formation. *(Mi. 12 on US 158. ☎252-441-7132; www.jockeysridgestatepark.com. Open daily June-Aug. 8am-9pm; Sept.-Oct. and Mar.-May 8am-8pm; Nov.-Feb. 8am-6pm. Free.)*

CURRITUCK BEACH LIGHTHOUSE. The 158 ft. lighthouse on the northern tip of the island was completed in 1875 to fill the final "dark spot" on the state's coast. Visitors can climb the 214 steps to the top of the unpainted brick structure. *(20 mi. north of Kitty Hawk on Rte. 12. ☎252-453-4939. Open for climbing Mar.-Nov. daily 10am-6pm. $7, under 8 free. Cash only.)*

BODIE ISLAND LIGHTHOUSE. At the southernmost tip of the island is the Bodie Island Lighthouse, first lit in 1872. Standing 150 ft. high, the lighthouse is painted with a distinctive white and black striped pattern, each stripe 22 ft. thick. Climbing the lighthouse is not permitted because it is still in use, but the old keeper's house serves as a museum. *(☎252-441-5711. Open daily 9am-6pm.)*

WALDO WISDOM. Pirates in the Outer Banks used to tie lanterns around their horses' heads to simulate boats bobbing at anchor to lure passing ships onto the sandbars. This practice resulted in the name Nags Head.

🜚 NIGHTLIFE

During the summer, tourists flood Bodie Island, and bars respond in kind with nightly music and dancing.

Kelly's Restaurant and Tavern (☎252-441-4116; www.kellysrestaurant.com), mi. 10.5 on the Bypass. Has 2 bars, a large dance floor, and pool tables. Bands play dance music nightly for a friendly, casual crowd. Music in summer Tu-Su 10pm-1 or 2am; hours vary in winter. Cover $2-5. Open M and W-Sa 4:30pm-2am, Tu and Su 4:30pm-1am. AmEx/D/MC/V.

Outer Banks Brewing Station (☎252-449-2739; www.obbrewing.com), mi. 8.5 on the bypass. Winner of the bronze medal at the World Beer Competition. Has 6 of its own beers on tap (16 oz. $4.50). On weekends, regional acts play everything from rock to hip hop. Music 10:30pm-2am. Ladies night W. Open mike Su. Cover $5. Open 11:30am-2am. AmEx/D/MC/V.

▨ THE ROAD TO VIRGINIA BEACH: 88 MI. From Bodie and Kitty Hawk, take **US 158 West** to **US 168 North.** There is a $2 toll after you enter Virginia. After 60 mi., take **I-64 West** to **I-264 East,** which splits into **21st** and **22nd Streets** downtown.

VIRGINIA BEACH ☎757

This boardwalk-centered town overflows with all-you-can-eat buffets, age-old motels, and cheap discount stores: the hallmarks of

The Old Dominion State

VIRGINIA

Welcomes You

VIRGINIA BEACH ☎ 757

This boardwalk-centered town overflows with all-you-can-eat buffets, age-old motels, and cheap discount stores: the hallmarks of seemingly every resort town in America. Load up on saltwater taffy, homemade fudge, and tacky T-shirts, because the best part of a Virginia Beach vacation is not getting wrapped up in the stuffiness that plague more pretentious resort towns.

VITAL STATS
Population: 430,000
Tourist Office: Virginia Beach Visitors Center, 2100 Parks Ave. (☎757-437-4919 or 800-822-3224; www.vbfun.com), at 22nd St. Open daily June-Aug. 9am-7pm; Sept.-May 9am-5pm.
Library and Internet Access: Virginia Beach Public Library, 4100 Virginia Beach Blvd. (☎757-219-2640). Open June-Sept. M-Th 10am-9pm, F-Sa 10am-5pm; Oct.-May M-Th 10am-9pm, F-Sa 10am-5pm, Su 1-5pm.
Post Office: 201 Virginia Beach Blvd. (☎757-463-5925). Open M-F 7:30am-7pm, Sa 10am-3pm.
Postal Code: 23452.

▚ ORIENTATION

In Virginia Beach, east-west streets are numbered while north-south avenues, running parallel to the beach, have ocean names. The main east-west thoroughfares are **Virginia Beach Boulevard, I-264,** and **Laskin Ave.** Prepare to feel like a thimble on a Monopoly board: **Atlantic** and **Pacific Avenues** are the main drags. **Arctic, Baltic,** and **Mediterranean Avenues** are farther inland. Free parking close to the boardwalk is practically nonexistent. There are plenty of parking lots and garages, which charge around $7 per day.

▟ ACCOMMODATIONS

▨ **Angie's Guest Cottage, Bed and Breakfast, and HI-AYH Hostel,** 302 24th St. (☎757-428-4690;

www.angiescottage.com). Flowers welcome guests to an old house with a fantastic location. Kitchen, sun deck, barbecue grill, ping-pong, and boogie boards. No A/C in dorms. Linen $2. Street parking 1st come, 1st served with a $20 deposit. 2-night min. stay, 3-night during holidays. Reception 8:30am-9pm. Check-out 10am. Reservations recommended. Open Apr.-Oct. 4- to 9-bed dorms May-Sept. $21, members $17; Oct. and Apr. $17/14. Private singles $38. MC/V. ❶

The Castle Motel, 2700 Pacific Ave. (☎757-425-9330). Spacious, clean rooms come with cable TV, refrigerators, and outdoor pool access. The beach is just 2 blocks away. Rooms in summer M-F from $80-90, Sa-Su from $130-170; in winter around $50. AmEx/D/MC/V. ❹

First Landings, 2500 Shore Dr. (☎757-412-2300 or 800-933-7275; www.dcr.state.va.us), about 8 mi. north of town on Rte. 60. Picnic areas, a sprawling beach, a bathhouse, and boat-launching areas. Cabins include full kitchens, furnishings, fireplaces, and A/C. Call several months ahead for reservations. Sites $24, with hookup $30. Cabins May-Sept. $126; Sept.-Nov. and Apr.-May $90; Dec.-Mar. $68. AmEx/D/MC/V. ❶

▚ FOOD

▨ **The Jewish Mother,** 3108 Pacific Ave. (☎757-422-5430; www.jewishmother.com). Don't be deceived by the crazy graffiti art on the facade. Heal what ails you with some aptly named "Penicillin soup" (chicken soup with matzah ball; $4). The restaurant also offers some decidedly un-kosher options, like a bacon cheeseburger ($9)—oy, gevalt! Live music on occasion; call for details. Open daily 8am-2am. AmEx/D/MC/V. ❷

▨ **Cuisine and Company,** 3004 Pacific Ave. (☎757-428-6700; www.cuisineandcompany. com). This sophisticated eatery serves gourmet lunches and rich desserts in a sleek, clean environment. Take your vegetarian sandwich (avocado, mushrooms, sprouts, Swiss; $4.25) to a cafe armchair and be sure to save room for a slab of killer chocolate cake ($4.25). Open M-Sa 9am-7pm, Su 9am-6pm. AmEx/D/MC/V. ❶

Chicho's, 2112 Atlantic Ave. (☎757-422-6011), at 29th St. The glorious combination of pizza ($3 per slice) and beer makes Chicho's one of the most popular spots for locals and tourists alike. Live music some weekends, starting around

10pm. Open M-Th and Su 11:30am-midnight, F-Sa 11:30am-2am. AmEx/D/MC/V. ❶

🏖️ 🏞️ SIGHTS AND OUTDOORS

🖼️**CONTEMPORARY ART CENTER OF VIRGINIA.** These constantly changing galleries showcase photography, installations, and video. Would-be collectors are in luck—many of the works featured are for sale. *(2200 Parks Ave. ☎757-425-0000; www.cacv.org. Open Tu-F 10am-5pm, Sa 10am-4pm, Su noon-4pm. 5, students, seniors, and military $3.)*

VIRGINIA BEACH. Toned and tanned bods drag surfboards through the thick, heavy sand of Virginia Beach. Your mother might have said staring is impolite, but it's a pastime here. The boardwalk, with lanes for walking and biking, runs 3 mi. past a pier and amusement park. For a less crowded beach and free parking, drive north of the boardwalk; you can park in a residential neighborhood and use one of the many public beach access points.

BACK BAY NATIONAL WILDLIFE REFUGE. Composed of islands, dunes, forests, marshes, ponds, and beaches, this remote national refuge is a sanctuary for an array of endangered species and other wildlife—not to mention tourists tired of Virginia Beach's joyful tackiness. The natural wonderland, home to nesting bald eagles and peregrine falcons, is open to the public for camping, hiking, fishing, and photography—but only on foot. Driving is prohibited beyond the **Visitor Contact Station.** The **Back Bay Tram** is available to transport visitors around the refuge. *(Take General Booth Blvd. to Princess Anne Dr.; turn left, then take Sandbridge Rd. and continue approximately 6 mi. Turn right on Sandpiper Rd., which leads to the visitors center. ☎757-721-2412; www.backbay.fws.gov. Open daily sunrise-sunset. May-Oct. $5 per vehicle. Tram ☎757-721-7666 or 426-3643; www.bbrf.org. From Memorial Day to Labor Day departs 9am, returns 12:45pm; from Labor Day to Memorial Day departs 1pm, returns 3pm. $8, under 12 and seniors $6.)* Also in the refuge, **False Cape State Park** got its name because ships used to touch shore here in the 17th century, mistakenly thinking that they had landed at the nearby Cape Henry (where America's first English settlers landed in 1607). False Cape State Park is located 4 mi. within the refuge and can only be reached by foot, bicycle, or the tram. *(4001 Sandpiper Rd. ☎757-426-7128, tours 480-1999; www.dcr.state.va.us/parks. No hookups available.)*

VIRGINIA AQUARIUM AND MARINE SCIENCE CENTER. Virginia's largest aquarium is home to hundreds of species of sea creatures, including crowd-pleasing sharks and sea turtles. A wood boardwalk connects the main building with the Marsh Pavilion. The museum also houses a six-story IMAX theater and offers excursions for dolphin observation in summer and whale watching in winter. *(717 General Booth Blvd., 1 mi. drive or 30min. walk south down Pacific Ave., which becomes General Booth Blvd. ☎757-425-3474, excursions 437-2628; www.vmsm.com. Open daily May-Aug. 9am-7pm; Sept.-Apr. 9am-5pm. $12, ages 3-11 $8, seniors $11. With IMAX $17/13/16.)*

🍸 NIGHTLIFE

Peabody's, 209 21st St. (☎757-422-6212; www.peabodysvirginiabeach.com), at Pacific Ave. This venerable club offers something for everyone—pounding dance music, pool tables, and occasional live music. Fierce dodgeball matches on the dance floor every F before the music starts (sign up by 8:30pm). 21+ F-Sa. Cover $5; Th ladies get in free, F students free. Open Th-Sa 7pm-2am. AmEx/D/MC/V.

Mahi Mah's, 615 Atlantic Ave. (☎757-437-8030; www.mahimahs.com), at 7th St., inside the Ramada Hotel. Watch tanned in-line skates zoom by as you enjoy the band M-Th and Su 6-10pm, F-Sa 7-11pm, with music ranging from bluegrass to 70s R&B. Seafood, sushi, and an extensive wine list. Karaoke W. Happy hour daily 3-7pm. Open daily 7am-2am. AmEx/D/MC/V.

Harpoon Larry's, 216 24th St. (☎757-422-6000; www.harpoonlarrys.com). Serves tasty fish in an everyone-knows-your-name atmosphere. The amicable staff welcomes 20- and 30-somethings to the loud, friendly bar. Open May-Sept. daily noon-2am; hours vary in winter. AmEx/MC/V.

🚗 THE ROAD TO HAMPTON: 30 MI.

From Virginia Beach, take **I-264 West** to **I-64 West.** Take **Exit 267** to Hampton.

HAMPTON ☎757

The town's relaxed, uncommercialized approach to tourism makes it a refreshing break from East Coast beach resorts. Plenty of free parking and several free attractions make it easy on the pocket.

VITAL STATS
Population: 150,000
Tourist Office: Hampton Visitors Center, 120 Hampton Ln. (☎757-727-1102 or 800-800-2202; www.hamptoncvb.com). Open daily 9am-5pm.
Library and Internet Access: Hampton Public Library, 4207 Victoria Blvd. (☎757-727-1312; www.hamptonpubliclibrary.org). Open M-Th 9am-9pm, F-Sa 9am-5pm, Su 1-5pm.
Post Office: 809 Aberdeen Rd. (☎757-826-0299). Open M-F 8am-7pm, Sa 9am-3pm. **Postal Code:** 23670.

✴ ORIENTATION

Off the highway, take a left onto **Settlers Landing Road,** the main drag through downtown. The Hampton River runs between downtown and the Hampton University campus.

🏠 ACCOMMODATIONS

Most accommodations in Hampton are generic hotel chains.

Magnolia House, 232 S. Armistead Ave. (☎757-722-9888; www.maghousehampton.com). Provides 3 luxurious rooms in a historic home. Those who can afford it will wake up to a full breakfast and all kinds of goodies in the guest pantry. Free Wi-Fi. Rooms $135-195. AmEx/D/MC/V. ❺

Sandy Bottom Nature Park (☎757-825-4657; www.hampton.gov/sandybottom), bounded by I-64, Big Bethel Rd., and Hampton Road Center Pkwy. 9 sites with picnic tables and barbecue, but no electricity or water. Quiet hours 10pm-7am. No reservations. Sites $10. Cabins $40; $60 deposit. AmEx/D/MC/V. ❶

🍴 FOOD

Most of Hampton's restaurants are downtown, and pricier options are on Queens Way.

La Bodega Hampton, 22 Wine St. (☎757-722-8466; www.labodegahampton.com). Inexpensive sandwiches on freshly baked bread like the Navigator (turkey, sun-dried tomatoes, and Gouda; $6). La Bodega also sells gourmet food and a variety of wines, specializing in local vineyards. Open M-F 7:30am-6pm, Sa 10am-3pm. Breakfast served until 10:30am. AmEx/D/MC/V. ❶

Grey Goose Tearoom, 101 W. Queens Way (☎757-723-7978). You'll find Virginia ham croissants ($6.50) and Brunswick stew for only $4. Open M-Sa 11am-3pm. AmEx/D/MC/V. ❶

Marker 20, 21 E. Queens Way (☎757-726-9410; www.marker20.com). Offers microbrews and fresh seafood in a pub atmosphere. Try the signature crab dip ($8.50) or a thick 10 oz. burger for $5.50. Open daily 11am-2am. AmEx/MC/V. ❷

👁 🏛 SIGHTS AND OUTDOORS

A great way to save if you want to see many of the attractions in Hampton is to get your hands on a **Day Pass,** which includes admission to the best attractions and even a cruise through the harbor. ($31, ages 4-12 $21; available at the visitors center and the Space Center.) Also available at the visitors center is the Value Card, which provides discounts and special offers at many restaurants and stores around town. (Free; valid for 1 year.)

VIRGINIA AIR AND SPACE CENTER. With simulators, build-your-own paper airplanes, and a B-24, the museum will have even the stodgiest visitor shouting, "I want to be a fighter pilot!" The flight simulators let visitors step into the cockpit of a number of different jets. The enormous IMAX theater plays films on everything from volcanoes to space travel. (600 Settlers Landing Rd. ☎757-727-0900 or 800-296-0800; www.vasc.org. Open from Memorial Day to Labor Day M-W 10am-5pm, Th-Su 10am-7pm; from Labor Day to Memorial Day M-Sa 10am-5pm, Su noon-5pm. $9.50, students and ages 3-18 $7.50, seniors and military $8.50. IMAX $8/6.75/7.)

HAMPTON UNIVERSITY MUSEUM. The **Emancipation Proclamation** was first read at Hampton University in 1863; the university's museum is dedicated to African-American history, containing over 9000 artifacts and works of art. (In the Huntington Bldg., on the Hampton University campus. Follow Settlers Landing Rd. over the Hampton River and take a right into the Hampton University campus. ☎757-727-5308; www.museum.hamptonu.edu. Open M-F 8am-5pm, Sa noon-4pm. Free.)

SANDY BOTTOM NATURE PARK. Visitors can rent boats and canoes to explore the lake, learn about the local animals and habitats at the Nature Center, or go birding at the observation tower. Ten trails run through the park, all marked and most fairly level. (1255 Big Bethel Rd. From I-64, take Exit 261A. ☎757-825-4657; www.hampton.gov/sandybottom. Park open daily sunrise-sunset. Nature Center open M-Th 9am-6pm, F-Su 9am-7:30pm. Free. Canoes $4 per hr., $15 per day. Free.)

HAMPTON CAROUSEL. From 1921 until the mid-80s, this antique carousel was located at the Buckroe Beach Amusement Park. Nowadays, it belongs to the city and is one of only 70 such carousels still functioning in the US. In addition to being a great ride for kids, it's also an unexpected example of American folk art; the horses and oil paintings are all originals. (On Settlers Landing Rd., by the Virginia Air and Space Center. ☎757-727-0900. Open M-W noon-5pm, Th-Su noon-7pm. $1.50, 5 rides $5.)

COUSTEAU SOCIETY. The US headquarters for the Cousteau Society, the building hosts a small museum about the life and work of underwater explorer Jacques-Yves Cousteau. Although maybe best appreciated by those already somewhat familiar with Cousteau's work, it has several nifty pieces, including the remains of a mechanical, remote-controlled shark named Allison and one of the claustrophobia-inducing mini-subs Cousteau used to explore the depths from the deck of the *Calypso*. (710 Settlers Landing Rd. ☎757-722-9300 or 800-441-4395. Open in summer daily 9:30am-4pm; in winter W-Su 9:30am-4pm. Free.)

◣ DETOUR
BUSCH GARDENS

Located 30 mi. west of Hampton, off **I-64.**

Busch Gardens puts its own spin on Williamsburg's colonial theme. The park is divided into themed sections such as "Italy," "Germany," and "New France," with appropriate restaurants and rides. A train runs around the park's perimeter from the entrance to New France on the other side, and a skyride provides a view of the park and quicker journey from England to France and from France to Germany. The park features five roller coasters to get your adrenaline flowing: the Alpengeist, the hurtling Apollo's Chariot, the tamer Big Bad Wolf, the thrilling ◪**Griffon,** and the Loch Ness Monster. There are also many activities and entertaining shows for the not-so-adventurous. If you get hungry, expect to find the usual amusement park fare and unamusing prices. (☎800-343-7946; www.buschgardens.com. Hours vary greatly by season but are available on the website. Restaurants open 11:30am-8:30 or 9:30pm. $57, ages 3-6 $50. Parking $10.)

◥ THE ROAD TO WILLIAMSBURG: 2 MI.
From Busch Gardens, take **I-64 West** to Williamsburg.

WILLIAMSBURG ☎757

Colonial Williamsburg manages to recreate the world of colonial America faithfully, appealing to tourists but not pandering to them. The result is a town where men in wigs and tights hardly draw a glance. A few blocks away from the historical madness, the College of William and Mary provides great cafes, bookstores, and nightlife. Travelers who visit in late fall or early spring avoid the crowds but miss the special summer programs.

VITAL STATS
Population: 12,000
Tourist Office: Colonial Williamsburg Visitors Center, 100 Visitors Center Dr. (☎757-229-1000 or 800-447-8679; www.colonialwilliamsburg.com). Open daily 8:45am-9pm.
Library and Internet Access: Williamsburg Library, 7770 Croaker Rd. (☎757-259-4040). Open M-Th 10am-9pm, F 10am-6pm, Sa 10am-5pm, Su 1-5pm.
Post Office: 425 N. Boundary St. (☎757-229-0838). Open M-F 8am-5pm, Sa 9am-2pm. **Postal Code:** 23185.

✦ ORIENTATION

The **Colonial Parkway** enters Williamsburg from the east, curving south to intersect with **Route 5** and **Francis Street. Duke of Gloucester Street,** the focal point of Colonial Williamsburg's sights, runs parallel to Francis St., one block north. Cars are not permitted within the historic area. A shuttle runs from the visitors center to the colonial area (free with admission), though a short walking path is also available. The **Orientation Walking Tour,** included with admission, begins at the shuttle stop and introduces visitors to the town's main sights.

ACCOMMODATIONS

There are many chain hotels and motels along Rte. 60. Make reservations in advance in the summer, but during quieter times you can get major discounts as a walk-in at the Lodging and Dining desk in the visitors center.

Bassett Motel, 800 York St. (☎757-229-5175; www.bassettmotel.com). Large, standard rooms 3 blocks from the historic area. Rooms in summer $59; lower in winter. MC/V. ❸

Liberty Rose, 1022 Jamestown Rd. (☎757-253-1260 or 800-545-1825; www.libertyrose.com). A romantic Victorian B&B with 4 lavishly decorated rooms. Rooms M-Th from $185, F-Su $195. AmEx/D/MC/V. ❺

FOOD

The Cheese Shop (☎757-220-0298), in Merchants Sq. A popular stop for a quick, tasty meal. Doubling as a gourmet food store, the restaurant sells fresh sandwiches like veggie focaccia ($5.50) and prosciutto ($6), perfect for eating on the patio out front. Go early or late to avoid the lunchtime rush, or else you may have to wait a while for your sandwich. Open M-Sa 10am-8pm, Su 11am-6pm. AmEx/D/MC/V. ❶

Aromas, 431 Prince George St. (☎757-221-6676; www.aromasworld.com). Caters to the college crowd. Though the food is yummy and vegetarian-friendly, the real attractions are the many exotic teas and coffees (Prince George's green mint mocha $2.75). Free Wi-Fi. Open M-Th 7am-10pm, F-Sa 8am-11pm, Su 8am-8pm. MC/V. ❶

Old Chickahominy House, 1211 Jamestown Rd. (☎757-229-4689; www.oldchickahominy.com). Serves plantation breakfasts with ham, bacon, sausage, eggs, grits, and biscuits ($9.50) in a down-home setting. Open daily 8:30-10:15am and 11:30am-2:30pm. MC/V. ❷

SIGHTS

COLONIAL WILLIAMSBURG. Welcome to the world's largest living history museum; you'll see drummer boys and bayonet-wielding soldiers walking alongside visitors on cell phones. Many of the costumed interpreters have spent years learning their craft, and one of the most interesting ways to experience Williamsburg is to see a wigmaker, brickmaker, or silversmith at work. Children who want to dress the part can rent costumes inside the visitors center. *($20; $75 deposit.)* There are over 80 original 18th-century buildings in the historic area, and 500 more have been reconstructed. The **Public Gaol** (pronounced "jail") on Market Sq. shows what happened to those colonists who stole a horse or failed to honor the Sabbath. The **Governor's Palace,** at the head of the village green, housed seven colonial governors (as well as Patrick Henry and Thomas Jefferson). Five hundred swords and guns festoon the walls of the building, which has been restored to its appearance in the days of Governor Dunmore, the last of the British colonial governors. At the **Raleigh Tavern,** on Duke of Gloucester St., tours explain the significance of the tavern in town life. Tours of the **Capitol** focus on the events and philosophies that led up to the American Revolution. Performances occur throughout the day at the reconstructed **Play Booth Theater.** The original was an indoor theater, but this incarnation was built to resemble open-air English theaters of the colonial era. Those interested in the painstaking process that transformed a sleepy 1920s town into Colonial Williamsburg will enjoy touring **Bassett Hall.** Multimillionaire John D. Rockefeller financed the initial venture, and his home is preserved as it looked when he lived there in the 1930s. *(☎757-229-1000 or 800-447-8679; www. history.org. Most exhibits open daily 9am-5pm. Capital City pass $37, ages 6-17 $18; includes access to over 40 sites and orientation walk but not to the Governor's Palace or Bassett Hall. Access to the Governor's Palace and 2nd day of access to all exhibits $6 each.)*

NIGHTLIFE

Though Williamsburg rolls up the welcome mat early in the evening, the nearby College of William and Mary provides plenty of great nightlife options for the young at heart.

Paul's Deli, 761 Scotland St. (☎757-229-8976; www.paulsdelirestaurant.com). Has a young, laid-back bar scene. Have a pitcher of Budweiser ($7) and watch a sports game on the 52 in. TV. Open daily 10:30am-2am. AmEx/D/MC/V.

Green Leafe, 765 Scotland St. (☎757-220-3405; www.greenleafe.com). Appeals to college kids, townies, and anyone in need of a good beer. 30 beers on tap and over 150 bottled brews; try something new. Open daily 10:30am-2am. AmEx/D/MC/V.

THE ROAD TO ASSATEAGUE AND CHINCOTEAGUE: 145 MI.

From Williamsburg, take **I-64 East** to **US 13 North.** Just after switching to **US 13,** pay a $12 toll and continue to **Route 175 East,** which takes you over bridges and through tunnels all the way to Chincoteague.

ASSATEAGUE AND CHINCOTEAGUE ☎757

Crashing waves, windswept dunes, wild ponies galloping free—if it sounds like the stuff of a childhood fantasy, that's because it is. Local legend has it that ponies first came to Assateague Island by swimming ashore from a sinking Spanish galleon. A less romantic and likelier theory is that miserly colonial farmers put their horses out to graze on Assateague to avoid mainland taxes. Whatever their origins, the famous ponies now roam free across unspoiled beaches and picturesque forests.

VITAL STATS
Population: 4300
Tourist Office: Chincoteague Chamber of Commerce, 6733 Maddox Blvd. (☎757-336-6161; www.chincoteaguechamber.com), in Chincoteague. Open M-Sa 9am-4:30pm.
Library and Internet Access: Island Library, 4077 Main St. (☎757-336-3460), in Chincoteague. Open M-Tu 10am-5pm, W and F-Sa 1-5pm, Th 4-8pm.
Post Office: 4144 Main St. (☎757-665-7412). Open M-F 8am-4:30pm, Sa 8:30am-noon. **Postal Code:** 23336.

ORIENTATION

Assateague Island is a long barrier island composed entirely of parkland. The island is shared by Maryland and Virginia and is divided into three parts: **Assateague State Park** (in Maryland), **Assateague National Seashore** (also in Maryland), and **Chincoteague Wildlife Refuge** (in Virginia). Driving the length of the island is neither permitted nor possible: there aren't any roads. Nestled between Assateague and the mainland is Chincoteague, which is a smaller, developed island where you will find restaurants, hotels, and shops. **Main Street** and **Maddox Boulevard** are the main roads here.

ACCOMMODATIONS

Visitors eat and sleep on Chincoteague. Camping is not permitted on the Virginia side of Assateague; you can camp at Assateague State Park in Maryland (see, p. 113).

Sea Hawk Motel, 6520 Maddox Blvd. (☎757-336-6527). Across the street from Chincoteague Bay. Large rooms with microwaves, refrigerators, and pool access. Free Wi-Fi. Rooms from late May to Sept. $85-89, from Oct. to early May $59-69. AmEx/D/MC/V. ❹

Maddox Family Campground (☎757-336-3111), across from the visitors center. A sprawling, 500-site complex with a grocery store, pool, and bathhouse. Open Mar.-Nov. Tent sites $38.50; RV sites with full hookup $44. AmEx/D/MC/V. ❷

FOOD

Sea Star, 4121 Main St. (☎757-336-5442). Serves carry-out from a brightly painted booth. Specialties include the Harv ($5.50), with roast beef and Havarti cheese on sourdough, and the Super Veggie ($5.25), with avocado, other veggies, and Swiss. Open M-Sa 11am-6pm, Su 11am-4pm. Cash only. ❶

AJ's on the Creek, 6585 Maddox Blvd. (☎757-336-5888). Proffers treats like artichoke hearts stuffed with crab ($12) and salty oyster sandwiches ($6). The restaurant has an island approach to elegance, and pairs white tablecloths and napkins with a laid-back atmosphere. Open M-Sa 11:30am-10pm. AmEx/D/MC/V. ❷

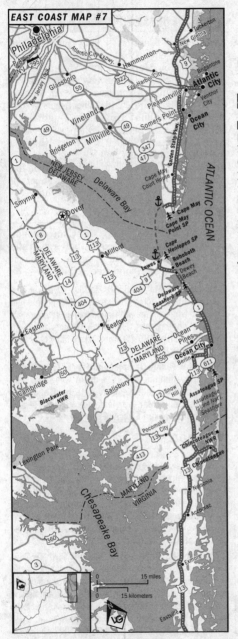

EAST COAST MAP #7

Main Street Shop & Coffee House, 4288 Main St. (☎757-336-6782; www.mainstreet-shop.com). Stop by for coffee and scones. The shop also sells quirky clothes, jewelry, and housewares in rainbow colors. Open June-Sept. daily 8:30am-5pm. AmEx/D/MC/V. ❶

👁 🏛 SIGHTS AND OUTDOORS

🐎**CHINCOTEAGUE NATIONAL WILDLIFE REFUGE.** The refuge stretches across the Virginia side of the island. Avid birdwatchers flock here to see rare species such as peregrine falcons, snowy egrets, and black-crowned night herons. During the annual **Pony Swim,** held the last consecutive Wednesday and Thursday in July, local firemen herd the ponies together for a swim from Assateague to Chincoteague Island, where they are auctioned off. Head to the visitors center, located just inside the refuge, to learn about biking, hiking, walking, and bird and nature tours. Guided wildlife bus tours are also available. *(Tours from Memorial Day to Labor Day daily 10am, 1, 4pm. $12, children $5, seniors $10.)* Trails include the 3 mi. pony-populated **Wildlife Loop,** the 1 mi. **Woodland Trail,** and the quarter-mile **Lighthouse Trail.** *(Open 3pm-sunset for vehicles; 24hr. for pedestrians and bicyclists.)* The last leads to the **Assateague Lighthouse,** which visitors can climb. *(Open Easter-Thanksgiving F-Su 9am-3pm. $4, ages 2-12 $2.)* Park rangers request that visitors resist the urge to feed the ponies, who, if overfed by guests, could starve in the winter months when visitors have left the islands. Gawk from a safe distance—the ponies may appear to be harmless, but they can be temperamental. *(8231 Beach Rd., off Maddox Blvd. ☎757-336-6122; http://chinco.fws.gov. Park open daily May-Sept. 5am-10pm; Oct. and Apr. 6am-8pm; Nov.-Mar. 6am-6pm. Visitors center open daily from Memorial Day to Labor Day 9am-5pm; from Labor Day to Memorial Day 8am-4:30pm. No pets permitted. $5 per vehicle, 7-day pass $15 per vehicle.)*

CHINCOTEAGUE PONY CENTRE. Capitalizing on the famous children's book and subsequent movie set in Chincoteague, the center has a museum dedicated to all things "Misty"—including quite a few of her descendants. The center also offers pony rides and showcases veteran ponies of the yearly swim in shows every night at 8pm. *(6417 Carriage Dr. Heading north on Main St., turn right on Church St., left on Chicken City Rd., and right on Carriage Dr. ☎ 757-336-2776. Open in summer M-Sa 9am-10pm. Rides M-Sa 9am-1pm and 3:30-6pm. $6. Museum $5. Shows $8, children $5.)*

OYSTER AND MARITIME MUSEUM. Originally focused on the seafood industry, the museum has turned its attention to local history. Don't miss the 1865 Barbier & Fenestre first-order Fresnel lens from the old Assateague Lighthouse, one of only 21 in the US. Its light could be seen from 23 mi. away. *(7125 Maddox Blvd. ☎ 757-336-6117. Open May-Sept. M-Sa 10am-5pm, Su noon-5pm. Hours vary in spring and fall. Free.)*

THE ROAD TO OCEAN CITY: 51 MI.

The road from Chincoteague to Ocean City is slightly confusing; look for signs along the way. From Chincoteague, take **Route 175 West** to **US 12 North.** Take **US 113 North,** then **Route 376 East** to **Route 611 South** for Assateague State Park. Take **Route 50** from US 113 for Ocean City.

The Old Line State

MARYLAND

Welcomes You

OCEAN CITY ☎ 410

Ocean City is like an all-you-can-eat buffet—at first, you're overwhelmed by all the choices, but then you look closer and realize there's nothing there worth eating. The city features a strip of Atlantic beach crowded with tourists looking for fun in the form of garish amusement parks, minigolf, and crowded boardwalks. From June to August, the city is packed and hotel rates skyrocket; the low season allows travelers to enjoy the beaches for reasonable prices.

ORIENTATION

Within Ocean City, numbered streets run east-west across the narrow strip of land linking the ocean to the bay. Numbers increase from south to north. Avenues run north-south through town, as does the **Coastal Highway.** The **Boardwalk** parallels the ocean, running from

the southern tip to **27th Street.** Most hotels are in the lower numbered streets near the ocean, while most clubs and bars are uptown toward the bay. Parking downtown can be extremely difficult during the summer; the city offers a $1 park-and-ride service off Rte. 50 just west of town. (May-Oct. every 15min. 6am-3am.)

VITAL STATS

Population: 7200

Tourist Office: Ocean City Visitors and Convention Center, 4001 Coastal Hwy. (☎800-626-2326; www.ococean.com), at 40th St., in the Convention Center. Open daily 9am-5pm.

Library and Internet Access: Ocean City Public Library, on Coastal Hwy., between 14th and 15th St. Open M, W, F 10am-6pm, Tu and Th 10am-8pm, Sa 10am-2pm.

Post Office: 7101 Coastal Hwy. (☎410-524-7611). Open M-F 9am-5pm, Sa 9am-noon. **Postal Code:** 21842.

ACCOMMODATIONS

In July and August, it's almost impossible to find a room in town for under $100. After the crowds subside in September, prices are much more reasonable.

Maridel Motel, 101 42nd St. (☎410-289-7665 or 800-333-1734; www.maridelmotel.com). Not as close to the neon lights of downtown as some might like. Has clean rooms with all the standard amenities and pool access. Free Wi-Fi. Rooms July-Aug. M-Th and Su $100, F-Sa $140; Sept.-Oct. and Mar.-June $40/70. D/MC/V. ❺

Atlantic House Bed & Breakfast, 501 N. Baltimore Ave. (☎410-289-2333; www.atlantichouse.com), at 5th St. Offers a full breakfast buffet, a great location, and a wholesome change of pace. The 1920s house has a hot tub, a front porch, and even complimentary beach chairs, umbrellas, and towels. Off-street parking. Open May-Oct. Rooms with shared bath $180, with private bath $225. D/MC/V. ❺

Assateague State Park, 7307 Stephen Decatur Hwy. (☎410-641-2918, reservations 888-432-2267; www.reservations.dnr.state.md.us), off Rte. 611 a few miles south of town. Sharing a campsite with wild horses can be a great experience, but watch out for "presents"

EAST COAST

they may leave behind. Open Apr.-Oct. Sites $30, with water and electricity $40. AmEx/D/MC/V. ❷

FOOD

Ocean City's cuisine is plentiful and cheap, but don't expect gourmet quality.

Brass Balls Saloon & Bad Ass Cafe (☎410-289-0069; www.brassballssaloon.com), on the Board-walk between 11th and 12th St. Known for its drinks. The Oreo waffles ($5.25) and cheeseburg-ers with waffle fries ($8) are worth the wait. Live music nightly. ½-price house drinks, $1 Miller Lite M-F and Su 4pm-6pm. Open Mar.-Oct. M-F 8:30am-2am. D/MC/V. ❶

Kitchen Restaurant, 106 Wicomico St. (☎410-289-2244). Stands out from the cluttered offerings of the Boardwalk with its down-home atmosphere. Try its specialty, french toast ($5.50), or experiment with the creamed chipped beef ($8.50) served on a biscuit. Open M-Tu and Su 7am-2pm, W-Th 7am-2pm and 5-11pm, F-Sa 7am-11pm. MC/V. ❷

SIGHTS

Ocean City's star attraction is its beautiful beach. The wide stretch of surf and sand runs the entire 10 mi. of town and can be accessed by turning east onto any side street off **Phila-delphia** and **Baltimore Avenues.** At the inlet, **Trimper's Amusements** has a Ferris wheel, a cen-tury-old Herschell carousel, and a tilt-a-whirl. (☎410-289-8617. Open M-F 1pm-midnight or later, Sa-Su noon-midnight or later. Unlim-ited rides 1-6pm $22.) For a larger park, try the **Jolly Roger Amusement Park,** 2901 Coastal Hwy., which includes multiple go-cart tracks, minigolf, rides, and the huge **Splash Mountain water park.** (☎410-289-4902; www.jollyroger-park.com. Rides open from Memorial Day to Labor Day daily 2pm-midnight. Splash Moun-tain open from Memorial Day to Labor Day daily 10am-8pm. Unlimited rides $16. Splash Mountain day pass $35, under 42 in. $12.) The **Ocean City Life-Saving Station Museum,** at the southern tip of the Boardwalk, contains artifacts from the history of the United States Life-Saving Service, as well as over a hundred different "sands of the world," antique swim-suits, and an all-things-mermaid collection. (☎410-289-4991; www.ocmuseum.org. Open June-Sept. daily 10am-10pm; Oct. and May daily 10am-4pm; Nov.-Dec. and Apr. Sa-Su 10am-4pm; Jan.-Mar. call for hours. Free pro-grams in summer 10:30am. $3, ages 6-12 $1.)

NIGHTLIFE

Seacrets (☎410-524-4900; www.seacrets.com), on 49th St. An entertainment complex that works a tiki-bar-gone-wild motif. This oasis features 17 bars. Barefoot partygoers wander from bar to bar, sipping the Pain in the Ass—a frozen rum runner mixed with piña colada ($6)—to the strains of live bands. Shoes and shirt required after 6pm. 21+

THE WILD, WILD EAST

The small barrier island of Chincoteague, with its windswept dunes and sandy beaches, is not the setting you'd usually associate with the lawless horsemen that made the Old West the stuff of many a Hollywood movie. Yet quaint Chincoteague is the home of the world-renowned Saltwater Cowboys. In a yearly tradition that started in 1925 as a fundraiser for the island's volunteer fire company, the cow-boys (mainly local firemen) round up the herd of wild ponies on Assateague and swim them across the channel at low tide. Thousands of delighted visitors and locals watch the unlikely spectacle, as the close to 90 ponies are herded through the narrow streets of the town. If your visit to Chincoteague awakened your childhood's burning desire to have your very own pony, you don't have to leave broken-hearted: the foals are auctioned to the highest bidder after being examined by a vet. But be advised: these ponies are wild and hard to train, and they go for an average of $2000, sometimes reaching up to $19,000. After the auction, spectators head for the carnival, where they enjoy attractions and live entertainment as well as the chance to win King or Queen Neptune, the first pony to come ashore.

after 10pm. Cover $5-10. Open daily 11am-2am. AmEx/D/MC/V.

Fager's Island (☎410-524-5500), at 60th St. in the bay. Has hordes walking the plank to its island location. During the summer, modern rock bands play nightly. Cover Th-Sa $5-10. Open daily 11am-2am. AmEx/D/MC/V.

THE ROAD TO REHOBOTH BEACH: 27 MI. Take **Coastal Highway North,** which becomes **US 1.**

REHOBOTH BEACH ☎302

Rehoboth Beach treads the line between neon insanity and inactivity. The small downtown area has great shops and restaurants, and when the sun sets there are plenty of low-key places to relax with a drink. Along with families and young professionals, Rehoboth Beach hosts a sizable gay population.

ORIENTATION

The town's main drag is **Rehoboth Avenue,** which heads straight for the water. The downtown area is small and packed with shops and restaurants. The Boardwalk runs for 17 blocks along the water.

VITAL STATS

Population: 1500

Tourist Office: Rehoboth Beach Chamber of Commerce, 501 Rehoboth Ave. (☎302-227-2233 or 800-441-1329; www.beach-fun.com). Open M-F 9am-5pm, Sa-Su 9am-1pm.

Library and Internet Access: Rehoboth Beach Public Library, 226 Rehoboth Ave. (☎302-227-8044). Free Wi-Fi. Open M and F 10am-5pm, Tu and Th noon-8pm, W 10am-8pm, Sa 10am-3pm.

Post Office: 179 Rehoboth Ave. (☎302-227-8406), at 2nd St. Open M-F 9am-5pm, Sa 8:30am-12:30pm.
Postal Code: 19971.

TRANSPORTATION

Atlantic Cycles, 18 Wilmington Ave., offers bike rentals, complete with helmets, locks, and maps. (☎302-226-2543; www.atlanticcycles. net. Open daily May-Sept. 7am-7pm; Oct. and Apr. 9am-5pm. $6 per hr., $18 per day.)

ACCOMMODATIONS

Like other resort towns on the coast, rates skyrocket during the summer months and drop off sharply as the weather cools.

High Seas Motel, 12 Christian St. (☎302-227-2022; www.highseasde.com). Just a block south of the main drag. Serves free doughnuts in the morning. Rooms June M-F $65, Sa-Su $130; July-Sept. $100/130; Oct. and Apr. $45/60. AmEx/D/MC/V. ❺

Big Oaks Family Campground (☎302-645-6838; www.bigoakscamping.com), a few miles north of town, off US 1 on Rte. 270. Offers a cheaper alternative to town lodging. A swimming pool and game room on the grounds as well as shuttle service to the beach. Open May-Oct. Tent sites $38; RV sites $47, with full hookup $53. Cash only. ❷

FOOD

Rehoboth is known for high-quality beach cuisine at bargain prices.

Cafe Papillon, 42 Rehoboth Ave. (☎302-227-7568), in the Penny Lane Mall. Offers light, authentic French fare. Chefs serve fresh Nutella crepes ($4.50) and croissants ($5.50) on a small outdoor patio. Open May-Sept. daily 8am-11pm. Cash only. ❶

Royal Treat, 4 Wilmington Ave. (☎302-227-6277). Serves up stacks of pancakes ($4) and oxy-moronic Italian french toast ($4.25). Ice cream sold in the afternoon. Open June-Aug. daily 8-11:30am and 1-11:30pm. Cash only. ❶

SOB's Deli, 56 Baltimore Ave. (☎302-226-2226). Assembles classic sandwiches and creatively named "specialty hoagies" like the Soprano Combo with ham, salami, and provolone for $7. Open May-Sept. daily 11am-10pm. AmEx/D/MC/V over $10. ❷

👁 〰 SIGHTS AND BEACHES

Coming from Ocean City, you'll first encounter **Bethany Beach,** which is popular with families. Navigate through ongoing construction to find the **Delaware Seashore State Park,** with opportunities for swimming in the ocean or bay and crabbing and clamming. There is also a marina packed with fishing boats and concession stands. (☎302-227-2800; www. destateparks.com. Open daily 8am-sunset. $8.) Slightly north of the park is the **Indian River Life-Saving Station Museum and Historic Site,** 130 Coastal Hwy., in one of six life-saving stations built along Delaware's coast to rescue shipwreck victims. Thirty minute tours describe the methods used to save sailors from the sea and the rescuers from boredom. (☎302-227-6991; www.destateparks.com/ irlss. Open Apr.-Sept. daily 8:30am-4:30pm; hours vary in winter. $4, ages 6-12 $2, seniors $3.) Just south of Rehoboth lies **Dewey Beach,** a favorite with the younger crowd and home to plenty of hotels, motels, and food.

🎷 NIGHTLIFE

Rehoboth partygoers head out early to maximize their time before 1am last calls.

🍺 **Dogfish Head Brewings & Eats,** 320 Rehoboth Ave. (☎302-226-2739; www.dogfish.com). Brews its own beer on-site and in a larger brewery nearby. Live music 10pm-1am F-Sa. No cover. Open M-Th and Su noon-midnight, F-Sa noon-1am. AmEx/MC/V.

Summer House Saloon, 228 Rehoboth Ave. (☎302-227-3895; www.summerhousesaloon. com). Ideal for meeting friends for a beer ($3) and a relaxed night out. Open M-Sa 11:30am-1am, Su 11am-1am. AmEx/D/MC/V.

🛣 THE ROAD TO LEWES: 8 MI.

From Rehoboth Beach, take **US 1 North** to **US 9,** which becomes **Kings Highway.**

LEWES ☎302

Explored by Henry Hudson and founded in 1613 by the Dutch, Lewes (LEW-iss) was the first town in the first state in America. Today, year-rounders populate the town's Victorian homes, and savvy tourists come for the beach in the summer months. While it isn't exactly happening, it's a beautiful area in which to spend a calm weekend.

VITAL STATS

Population: 2900

Tourist Office: Fisher-Martin House Info Center, 120 Kings Hwy. (☎302-645-8073 or 877-465-3937; www.leweschamber.com), off Savannah Rd. Open M-F 10am-4pm, Sa 9am-3pm, Su 10am-2pm.

Library and Internet Access: Lewes Public Library, 111 Adams Ave. (☎302-645-2733; www.leweslibrary.org), at Kings Hwy. Open M-Th 10am-8pm, F 10am-5pm, Sa 10am-2pm.

Post Office: 116 Front St. (☎302-645-0235). Open M-F 8:30am-5pm, Sa 8am-12:30pm. **Postal Code:** 19958.

✳ ORIENTATION

Cape Henlopen Drive (Route 19) runs along the coast into **Cape Henlopen State Park. Kings Highway (US 9)** runs out from the city and intersects with US 1. Most restaurants and shops are on or around **Second Street.**

🏠 ACCOMMODATIONS

Hotel Rodney, 142 2nd St. (☎302-645-6466; www.hotelrodneydelaware.com). Sits between shops and restaurants on the main thoroughfare. The beautiful, newly remodeled rooms include flatscreen TVs, hardwood floors, and black and white marble bathrooms. Rooms Jun.-Sept. M-Th and Su $140, F-Sa $190; Sept.-Dec. $95/150; Jan.-Feb. $80/$105; Mar.-May $90/125; May-June $115/175. AmEx/D/MC/V. ❺

Cape Henlopen State Park (☎302-645-8983, reservations 877-987-2757). Just a short hike from the beach. Has an amazing view of the dunes. There are 150 wooded sites with water but no electricity. Campground open Apr.-Nov. Sites $27, with water $29. AmEx/D/MC/V. ❶

🍽 FOOD

🍴 **Cafe Azafran,** 109 Market St. (☎302-644-4446; www.cafeazafran.com). Serves gourmet Mediterranean dishes such as tapas. Try the La Mancha Plate ($9), which comes with Manchego cheese, chorizo, Serrano ham, and romesco. The cafe's walls are decorated with art for sale, and on sunny days patrons enjoy the outdoor patio. Free Wi-Fi. Open daily Apr.-Oct. 7am-3:30pm and 6-10pm; Nov.-Mar. 7am-3:30pm. MC/V. ❷

Second Street Grille, 115 W. 2nd St. (☎302-644-4121; www.secondstreetgrille.com). Has a chic, European feel. Sandwiches and salads for lunch as well as fried calamari ($12). Live piano M 5-7pm. Open W-Sa 11am-9pm, Su 11am-2pm. MC/V. ❸

Books by the Bay Cafe, 111 Bank St. (☎302-644-6571). Serves omelets ($6.50) and waffles ($5.25) in the morning. Sandwiches like the Pilgrim's Feast panino (turkey, stuffing, cranberries; $6.75) available in the afternoon. While you wait for your sandwich, browse through the small bookshop. Open daily 7am-5pm. MC/V. ❷

Kings Homemade Ice Cream Shop, 201 2nd St. (☎302-645-9425). Always full of lactose lovers. Try a scoop of Oh! Cookie for $3.50. Open May-Oct. M-Sa noon-11pm. Cash only. ❶

👁 🔺 SIGHTS AND OUTDOORS

CAPE HENLOPEN STATE PARK. Against the backdrop of the Atlantic Ocean, this 4000-acre park swells with sand dunes and scrub pines. In addition to its beach, the park is home to a fishing pier, sparkling white "walking dunes," and a 2 mi. paved trail ideal for biking or in-line skating. *(1 mi. east of Lewes. From the south, follow US 9 E. toward the ferry. ☎302-645-8983; www.destateparks.com/chsp. Park open daily 8am-sunset. Day use $8 per car.)* Bike rentals are free at the **Seaside Nature Center,** the park's museum on beach and ocean wildlife, which also hosts weekly lectures and leads hikes. *(☎302-645-6852. Bike rental 9am-3pm; 2hr. limit. Open daily July-Aug. 9am-5pm; Sept.-June 9am-4pm.)*

ZWAANENDAEL MUSEUM. A bright two-story space filled with relics of maritime history and exhibits on the settlement of Delaware, lighthouses, and shipwrecks. The building itself is a replica of the old town hall in Hoorn, the Netherlands. *(102 Kings Hwy. ☎302-645-1148. Open Tu-Sa 10am-4:30pm, Su 1:30-4:30pm. Free.)*

🚗 THE ROAD TO CAPE MAY: 5 MI.

A **ferry** runs between Lewes, Delaware, and Cape May, New Jersey, cutting 2-3hr. off the drive. From Lewes, take **Route 9 East** and follow the signs. The ferry often sells out during the summer, so call ahead for reservations. (☎800-643-3779; www.capemaylewesferry.com. Call ahead for schedule.) From the ferry terminal, take US 9 (Ferry Rd.) to **Route 626 (Seashore Road),** which turns into **Broadway Road** and leads to **Beach Avenue** and the ocean.

The Garden State **NEW JERSEY** *Welcomes You*

CAPE MAY   ☎609

At the southern end of New Jersey's coast, Cape May is the oldest seashore resort in the US, and the money here is no younger. Once the summer playground of Upper East Side New Yorkers, the town still shows signs of affluence in the elegant restaurants of Beach Ave. However, Cape May is a steal for budget travelers, with sparkling beaches, cheap accommodations, and a boardwalk and downtown that invite strolling.

⚔ ORIENTATION

The **Garden State Parkway** leads into Cape May from the north, culminating at **Cape May Harbor.** Parallel to the parkway are **US 9** and **Route 626.** As Rte. 626 heads south toward the tip of the cape, it becomes **Seashore Road** and then **South Broadway,** running parallel to **Lafayette Street (Route 633).**

VITAL STATS
Population: 4000
Tourist Office: Welcome Center, 609 Lafayette St. (☎609-884-9562). Open daily 9am-4:30pm.
Library and Internet Access: Cape May County Library, 30 Mechanic St. (☎609-463-6350). Open in summer M-Th 8:30am-9pm, F 8:30am-4:30pm, Sa 9am-4:30pm; in winter M-F 8:30am-9pm, Sa 9am-4:30pm, Su 1-5pm.
Post Office: 700 Washington St. (☎609-884-3578). Open M-F 9am-5pm, Sa 8:30am-12:30pm.
Postal Code: 08204.

ACCOMMODATIONS

Cape May's streets are lined with pricey, beautiful Victorian B&Bs, but budget accommodations are available too. Prices drop farther from the shore. Campgrounds line US 9, just north of Cape May.

Hotel Clinton, 202 Perry St. (☎609-884-3993), at S. Lafayette St. Breezy, homey rooms, 2 porches overlooking a busy street, and charismatic Italian proprietors. Truly fantastic. Reservations recommended. Open from mid-June to Sept. Singles with shared bath M-F $35, Sa-Su $40; doubles $45/50. Cash only. ❷

Poor Richard's Inn, 17 Jackson St. (☎609-884-3536; www.poorrichardsinn.com). There's nothing poor about this inn's period furniture and beautiful 1882 national landmark. Cat on the premises. Rooms July-Aug. $120-180, Sept.-June $110-150. AmEx/D/MC/V. ❺

Seashore Campsites, 720 Seashore Rd./Rte. 626 (☎609-884-4010 or 800-313-2267; www.seashorecampsite.com). Connected to Cape May by the Seashore Line. Wooded campground with minigolf, pool, lake, playground, store, and laundry facilities. June-Sept. tent sites $37; RV sites $40, with full hookup $44. AmEx/D/MC/V. ❷

FOOD

Cape May's cheapest food is found in generic pizza and ice-cream shops along Beach Ave. Tastier (but more expensive) options can be found on side streets.

George's Place, 301 Beach Ave. (☎609-884-6088; www.georgesplacecapemay.com), at Beach Dr. and Perry St. This diner blends all-American favorites with Greek cuisine, serving pancakes ($6.50) alongside spanakopita (phyllo dough with spinach and feta; $7). Show up early and expect long waits. Open daily 7am-3pm and 5-9pm. Cash only. ❷

Freda's Cafe, 210 Ocean St. (☎609-884-7887), by Washington St. Mall. This pleasant little restaurant serves up big flavor. Try the stuffed chicken *en croute* ($18) and finish off with a baked brie Lisa ($8). Open in summer daily 11:15am-5pm; in winter M and F-Su 11:15am-5pm. MC/V. ❷

The Mad Batter, 19 Jackson St. (☎609-884-5970; www.madbatter.com). Start the morning right with orange-and-almond french toast ($7.50) or a 3-egg omelet ($7.50). For lunch, try a Maryland crab-cake sandwich ($13.50) on the beautiful porch. Live jazz W 7pm, Su 5:30pm; acoustic guitar F 7pm. Open daily 8am-3pm and 5-10pm. AmEx/D/MC/V. ❸

SIGHTS

CAPE MAY POINT STATE PARK. Three clearly marked trails feature excellent birdwatching in the marsh and oceanside dunes. The behemoth bunker right in the water is a WWII gun emplacement, used to scan the shore for German U-boats. The bunker was originally built 900 ft. inland, but, due to beach erosion, it is now touching the ocean. There's a sandy beach, too, but swimming is not allowed. Right by the entrance of the state park is the **Cape May Lighthouse.** The 157½ ft. lighthouse was first lit in 1859, and the 1893 oil house now serves as a combined gift shop and visitors center. *(Lighthouse and museum ☎609-884-5404; www.njparksandforests.org. Visitors center ☎609-884-2159. Lighthouse open in summer daily 9am-8pm; hours vary in winter. Visitors center and museum open July-Aug. M-Tu and Su 8:30am-5pm, W-F 8:30am-4pm, Sa 8:30am-6pm; Sept.-June daily 8:30am-3:30pm. Lighthouse $5. Park free.)*

MID-ATLANTIC CENTER FOR THE ARTS (MAC). The MAC runs walking and 30min. trolley tours of the city's major historic sites, including the Emlen Physick Estate, a Victorian mansion that showcases the luxury of the upper classes and the living conditions of their servants. Trolley tours run throughout the city and along the beachfront. The MAC also runs unique cultural events such as Sherlock Holmes Weekends (early Mar. and Nov.) and Victorian Week in early October. *(1048 Washington St. ☎609-688-5404 or 800-275-4278; www.capemaymac.org. Physick Estate $10, ages 3-12 $5. Trolley tour $10/7.)*

NIGHTLIFE

Cabana's, 429 Beach Ave. (☎609-884-4800; www.cabanasonthebeach.com). Filled with a young crowd. Alternative and blues bands play Tu-Sa 10pm, with original acts on Th. 21+ after

OCEAN CITY • 119

pm. Cover F-Sa $5. Happy hour 4-7pm. Open daily 11:30am-2am. AmEx/D/MC/V.

Martini Beach, 429 Beach Ave. (☎609-884-1925; www.martinibeachcapemay.com). Serves martinis in an intimate, unpretentious environment. Sit back with a Red Door martini ($12) and enjoy the live jazz. Karaoke M. DJ Sa. No cover. Open daily 3pm-2am. AmEx/D/MC/V.

BEACHES

Cape May's sands, which are studded with famous "Cape May diamonds" (quartz pebbles), actually do sparkle. Beach tags, available from roaming vendors, are required for beachgoers over 11. You can also purchase tags at the **Beach Tag Office,** at Grant and Beach Dr. (☎609-884-9522. Open daily 6am-10pm; for swimming 10:30am-5pm. Tags required from Memorial Day to Labor Day. $4 per day, $13 per week.) The **South End Surf Shop,** 311 Beach Ave., rents beach necessities. (☎609-898-0988; www.southendsurfshop.com. Soft-top surfboards $25 per day, $80 per week. Driver's license required. Open Apr.-Sept. daily 9am-10pm.) **Beach Drive,** which runs parallel to the ocean, makes for a beautiful walk. In the summer, artists sell their work on the street. Crawling with pedestrians hunting for heavenly fudge and saltwater taffy, Washington St. supports several popular eateries.

WILDLIFE

Due to the close proximity of fresh and saltwater, migratory birds flock to Cape May for a break from the long southbound flight. Sneak a peek at over 300 types of feathered vacationers at the **Cape May Bird Observatory,** 701 E. Lake Dr., on Cape May Point, a birdwatcher's paradise. Bird maps, field trips, and workshops are available, along with advice about where to go for the best birdwatching. (☎609-884-2736; www.njaudubon.org. Open daily Apr.-May and Sept.-Nov. 9am-4:30pm, June-Aug. and Dec.-Mar. M-Tu and Th-Su 9am-4:30pm.) For a look at some larger creatures, hop on the **Cape May Whale Watcher.** (☎800-786-5445; www.capemaywhalewatcher.com. 3hr. tours Mar.-Dec. 1pm. $38, ages 7-12 $23.)

☞ THE ROAD TO OCEAN CITY: 32 MI.
From Cape May, take the **Garden State Parkway North** to **Exit 25.** There is a $0.70 toll.

OCEAN CITY ☎609

Billing itself as "America's greatest family resort," Ocean City features a busy boardwalk and beachside minigolf. A few blocks from the shore, the beach attractions give way to a calmer downtown area with cafes and stores. The family-oriented atmosphere means that there's not much to do after dark, so it's best to take advantage of the daytime activities.

VITAL STATS

Population: 15,500

Tourist Offices: Ocean City Regional Chamber of Commerce (☎609-399-2629 or 800-232-2465), on the Howard Stainton Memorial Causeway. Open M-Sa 9am-5pm, Su 10am-3pm. **Information booth** on the boardwalk at 8th Ave.

Library and Internet Access: Ocean City Free Public Library, 1735 Simpson Ave. (☎609-399-2434 or 399-2143; www.ocnj.us), off 17th St. Open M-F 9am-9pm, Sa 9am-5pm, Su 1-5pm.

Post Office: 859 Ocean Ave. (☎609-399-0475). Open M-F 8:30am-5pm, Sa 9am-1pm. **Postal Code:** 08226.

ORIENTATION

The boardwalk stretches 2 mi. along the beach toward the north end of the island. **Bay Street** runs parallel to the ocean on the west. Most hotels lie between the beach and **Ocean Avenue** between **First** and **Ninth Streets.** Downtown centers on Asbury Ave. between Sixth and 14th St. Free parking can be found in some residential areas, but all parking fills up quickly in summer.

ACCOMMODATIONS

Ocean City has plenty of pricey B&Bs.

Glen Nor Inn, 1015 Central Ave. (☎609-399-4138 or 800-320-4138; www.glennorinn.com). Accommodations are pretty standard, but the family-owned inn feels a bit more personal than most motels. Most rooms 2-night min. stay. Open from Memorial Day to Labor Day. Rooms from June

EAST COAST

to Labor Day $85-$110; Sept. and May-June $75-85. MC/V. ❹

Homestead Hotel, 805 E. 8th St. (☎609-391-0200; www.homesteadhotel.info). Offers more distinctive accommodations in a European-style building with views of the city and the ocean. Rooms include stovetops, fridges, microwaves, and flat-screen TVs. Open June-Sept. Rooms June $140-250; Jul-Aug. $160-275; Sept. $100-150. AmEx/D/MC/V. ❺

🍴 FOOD

Ocean City's boardwalk is lined with storefronts that provide the cheapest, if not the best-rounded, meals in town, selling pizza and South Jersey favorites like Italian ice (also, redundantly, called "water ice"), funnel cakes, and custard. Downtown, streets are lined with a number of casual, inexpensive eateries.

Kibbitz Down the Shore, 846 Central Ave. (☎609-398-0880). A New York-style deli dishing out massive portions—the Reubens (half $8.50, whole $12) have a full pound of corned beef. For something a bit lighter, feed your soul with some matzah ball soup for $4.25. Open daily 11am-8pm. AmEx/D/MC/V. ❷

The Chatterbox (☎609-399-0113), at 9th St. and Central Ave. Has been serving buttermilk pancakes ($4) and "chatter burgers" ($7) for 70 years. During peak times, there's a line out the door. Open daily 7am-11pm. AmEx/D/MC/V. ❶

The Panini Grill, 953 Asbury Ave. (☎609-391-1111). Serves the Capri (tomato, mozzarella, balsamic vinaigrette; $6) and 10 other types of panini. If you're all sandwiched out, there's also pizza ($12) and a variety of breakfast options. Open M-Th and Su 8am-8:30pm, F-Sa 8am-9pm. AmEx/MC/V. ❶

👁 SIGHTS

Once a month, the **Second Friday Art Walk** showcases local artists on Asbury Ave. (☎609-814-0308; www.2ndfridayartwalk.com.)

BAYSIDE CENTER. Bayside contains an environmental center with exhibits on local animals, a lifeguard museum, and models of local buildings. During the summer, the center also offers guided beach walks, starting at 59th St.

and Central Ave. *(520 Bay Ave. ☎609-525-9244. Open daily 10am-6pm. Free.)*

OCEAN CITY HISTORICAL MUSEUM. Displays remnants of the *Sindia*, a large barque that ran aground in Ocean City in 1901, an old-fashioned telephone switchboard, and a taffy machine. *(1735 Simpson Ave. ☎609-399-1801. Open May-Oct. M-F 10am-4pm, Sa 11am-2pm; Nov.-Apr. Tu-F 10am-4pm, Sa 10am-2pm. Free.)*

🏖 BEACHES

In the summer, Ocean City's beaches are its best attraction. Those over 11 must wear beach tags, available on the boardwalk at the end of Eighth Ave. and from beach-tag checkers who work around the beach. (☎609-525-9333. Open from June to Labor Day daily 6am-10pm; swimming 9:30am-5:30pm. Beach tag $5 per day, $10 per week.) **Surf Buggy Centers**, at Eighth Ave. and Broadway, rents bikes and surreys for seashore exploration. (☎800-976-5679; www.surfbuggycenters.com. Bikes $5 per hr., $15 per day; surreys $15 per hr. Open daily 8am-8pm.) The **7th Street Surf Shop**, 654 Boardwalk, rents surfboards and offers lessons in surfing and gnarly lingo. (☎609-391-1700; www.7thstreetsurfshop.com. Surfboards $10 per hr., $30 per day; $50 deposit. Credit card or driver's license required. Lessons daily 8, 10:30am. $35 for 2hr., surfboard and wetsuit included. Advance registration recommended. Open daily 7:30am-11:30pm.) If you are looking for a thrill, ride the chutes at **Gillian's Island**, at Plymouth Place on the Boardwalk. (☎609-399-0483; www.gillianswaterpark.com. Open daily from June to Labor Day 9:30am-6pm. Day pass $24, under 48 in. $20.)

✂ DETOUR
LUCY THE ELEPHANT

9200 Atlantic Avenue, in Margate City, off the **Garden State Parkway** at **Exit 36.** Follow signs to Lucy.

Originally built in 1881 by land developer James Lafferty as a marketing gimmick, Lucy has always been a sight for the public. It's no wonder; at 65 ft. and 90 tons, she's hardly the average pachyderm. After she fell into disrepair in the 1960s, the Save Lucy Committee convinced the city to donate land for a site and raised $62,000 to move her down the beach to her present location. (☎609-823-6473; www.

lucytheelephant.org. Open from mid-June to Labor Day M-Sa 10am-8pm, Su 10am-5pm; from Labor Day to Oct. and from May to mid-June M-F 11am-4pm, Sa-Su 10am-5pm; Nov.-Dec. W-F 11am-4pm, Sa-Su 10am-5pm. Tours every 30min. $6, children $3.)

 THE ROAD TO ATLANTIC CITY: 5 MI.
From Margate, take **Atlantic Avenue** west into town.

ATLANTIC CITY ☎609

Atlantic City was once a premier getaway, but lately even Miss America has taken flight. It's easy to see why. During a 1970s refurbishment effort, giant casino-resorts were built over the rubble of the old Boardwalk, sacrificing the city's old-time charm in hopes of attracting tourist dollars with glitz and glamor. Today, the Boardwalk is the safest and most interesting part of the city, but poverty and crime lurk around the fringes of downtown. Still, tourists stream into the city hoping to win big, and visitors can enjoy themselves if they avoid leaving the labyrinthine casinos.

PAGE TURN. See p. 334 in **National Road** for complete coverage of Atlantic City.

 THE ROAD TO NEW YORK CITY: 53 MI.
Follow **I-95** to the **Lincoln Tunnel** ($6), which leads you to Midtown. To bypass the city, skip ahead to p. 144; otherwise, sit back and enjoy the ride.

The Empire State
NEW YORK
Welcomes You!

NEW YORK CITY ☎212

The self-proclaimed "Capital of the World" puts its money where its mouth is. Eight million New Yorkers pack themselves into the city limits, and each one—but especially taxi drivers—can tell you exactly why theirs is the greatest city on earth. This is where the legendary Yankees hold court, the lights of Broadway never dim, and every street corner promises a hot dog and a pretzel. Towering skyscrapers form the hub of American business by day, and the pounding beats of legendary clubs thump forth from neon-tinged shadows by night. When an act of terrorism destroyed the twin towers of the World Trade Center on September 11, 2001, New Yorkers were awakened to horror and heroism. The city has moved on, but it hasn't forgotten. For more info, check out ▩**Let's Go: New York City.**

VITAL STATS
Population: 8,100,000
Tourist Office: NYC & Company, 810 7th Ave. (☎212-484-1222; www.nycvisit.com). Open M-F 8:30am-6pm, Sa-Su 9am-5pm. Also in Grand Central and Penn Station.
Post Office: 421 8th Ave. (☎212-330-2902), at W. 32nd St. Open 24hr. **Postal Code:** 10001.

✦ ORIENTATION

NYC is comprised of five boroughs: the Bronx, Brooklyn, Manhattan, Queens, and Staten Island. Flanked on the east by the East River (actually a strait) and on the west by the Hudson River, Manhattan is an island, measuring 13 mi. long and 2 mi. wide. Queens and Brooklyn are on the other side of the East River. Staten Island, southwest of Manhattan, is the most residential borough. North of Manhattan sits the Bronx, the only borough connected by land to the rest of the US.

MANHATTAN

Above 14th St., Manhattan is an organized grid of avenues running north-south and streets running east-west. Street numbers increase as you travel north. Avenues are slightly less predictable: some are numbered while others are named. The numbers of the avenues increase as you go west. **Broadway** defies the pattern, cutting diagonally across the island. **Central Park** and **Fifth Avenue** (south of 59th St., north of 110th St.) separate the city into the East Side and West Side. **Washington Heights** is located north of 155th St.; **Morningside Heights** (above 110th St. and below 125th St.) is sandwiched between **Harlem** (110th St. to the 150s) and the **Upper West Side** (59th to 110th St., west of Central Park). The museum-heavy **Upper East Side** is across Central Park, above 59th St. on Fifth Ave. **Midtown** (42nd to 59th St.) includes Times Sq. and the **Theater District.** **Lower Midtown** (14th to 41st St.) includes Herald Sq., Chelsea, and Union Sq. Below 14th St., the city dissolves into a confusing tangle of old, narrow streets that aren't numbered south of Houston St. The bohemian **East Village** and Alphabet City are grid-like, with alphabetized avenues from Ave. A to Ave. D, east of First Ave. Intellectual Greenwich Village, to the west, is especially complicated west of Sixth Ave. As you move South, trendy **SoHo** (South of Houston St.) and **TriBeCa** (Triangle Below Canal St.) are just west of historically ethnic enclaves **Little Italy, Chinatown,** and the **Lower East Side.** The **Financial District/Wall Street** area, at the tip of Manhattan, was set over the original Dutch layout and is full of narrow, winding, one-way streets.

BROOKLYN

The **Brooklyn-Queens Expressway (BQE)** links to the **Belt Parkway** and circumscribes Brooklyn. Ocean Pkwy., Ocean Ave., Coney Island Ave., and diagonal Flatbush Ave., running from the beaches of southern Brooklyn (Coney Island and Brighton Beach) to the heart of the borough in **Prospect Park.** The streets of western Brooklyn, including **Park Slope,** are aligned with the western shore and intersect central Brooklyn's main arteries at a 45° angle. In northern Brooklyn (including **Williamsburg, Greenpoint,** and **Downtown Brooklyn**), several avenues—Atlantic Ave., Eastern Pkwy., and Flushing Ave.—travel east into Queens.

QUEENS

The streets of Queens resemble neither the orderly grid of Upper Manhattan nor the haphazard angles of Greenwich Village. Streets generally run north-south and are numbered from west to east, from First St. in **Astoria** to 271st St. in **Glen Oaks.** Avenues run perpendicular to streets and are numbered from north to south, from Second to 165th Ave. Pick up the useful **Queens Bus Map,** free and available on most Queens buses.

THE BRONX

Major highways divide the Bronx. The **Major Deegan Expressway (I-87)** runs up the western border, next to the Harlem River. The **Cross-Bronx Expressway (I-95)** runs across the borough, turning north on its easternmost edge. Up the center of the borough runs the **Bronx River Parkway.** Many avenues run north-south, including **Jerome Avenue** on the western side and White Plains and Boston Rd. to the east. East-west streets include Tremont Ave., Fordham Rd., and the Pelham Pkwy.

STATEN ISLAND

Sometimes referred to as New York's "forgotten borough," quiet Staten Island is very spread out. It has a limited tourist infrastructure, making a vehicle necessary. Pick up bus route maps at the chamber of commerce, 130 Bay St. (☎718-727-1900).

🖃 TRANSPORTATION

The **Metropolitan Transit Authority (MTA)** runs the city's subways, buses, and trains. The subway system is open 24hr.; once inside, a passenger may transfer onto any other train without restrictions. The subway is much more useful for traveling north-south than east-west, but crosstown shuttle buses run on several streets, including 14th, 23rd, 34th, 42nd, 57th, 79th, and 86th St. Maps are available in any station. **Buses,** often slower than subways, stop roughly every two blocks and run throughout the city. Blue signposts announce bus numbers; glass-walled shelters display schedules and route maps. Be sure to grab a borough bus map. **MetroCards** for subways and buses have a pre-set value (12 rides for the price of 10) and allow free bus and subway transfers within 2hr. The one-day ($7), seven-day ($24), and 30-day ($76) "Unlimited Rides" MetroCards (as opposed to $2 "Pay-Per-Ride" cards) are good for tourists.

🖍 ACCOMMODATIONS

Accommodations in New York City are Very expensive, with a capital "V." You can expect a dorm room in a hostel to cost around $35, with private rooms closer to $50. Hotel singles start around $60, with the upper limit around the highest number you can think of, plus three—zeroes, that is.

HOSTELS

⬛ **Central Park Hostel,** 19 W. 103rd St. (☎212-678-0491; www.centralparkhostel.com), between Manhattan Ave. and Central Park W. This 5-story brownstone boasts hand-painted murals in the lobby, a funky tiled floor, spotless rooms with A/C, and a nice downstairs TV lounge. Shared bathrooms. Lockers available. Linen and towels included. Key deposit $2. Reservations recommended. Dorms $26-35; private doubles $85-95. Cash only. ❶

⬛ **New York International HI-AYH Hostel,** 891 Amsterdam Ave. (☎212-932-2300; www.hinewyork.org), at 103rd St. Large youth hostel. 96 dorm-style rooms. 624 beds. Soft carpets, tight security, spotless bathrooms, and A/C. Kitchens, dining rooms, communal TV lounges, and large outdoor garden. Linen and towels. Internet access $2 per 20min. Check-in after 4pm. Check-out 11am. 10- to 12-bed dorms $33; 6- to 8-bed $35-38; 4-bed $38. AmEx/MC/V. ❷

Jazz on Harlem, 104 W. 128th St. (☎212-222-5773; www.jazzonthepark.com), near Lenox (6th) Ave. This new hostel from the owners of the Jazz on the Park hostel was recently converted from a brownstone apartment complex and offers clean, secure lodging in the heart of Harlem. Sparkling hardwood floors, new furniture, and A/C make for a comfortable stay. TV lounge, lockers, and luggage storage. Reception 24hr. 10- to 14-bed dorms $24; 4- to 6-bed $28. Private rooms from $85. MC/V. ❷

Big Apple Hostel, 119 W. 45th St. (☎212-302-2603; www.bigapplehostel.com), between 6th and 7th Ave. This hostel provides a clean and safe place to sleep in a great location. Kitchen with refrigerator, luggage room, big deck with grill, common rooms, and laundry. Internet $1 per 8min. Check-in and check-out 11am. Aug.-Sept. reservations accepted on website only. 4-bed dorms $28; private rooms $77. MC/V. ❷

Chelsea International Hostel, 251 W. 20th St. (☎212-647-0010; www.chelseahostel.com), between 7th and 8th Ave. Full of funky (mostly European) travelers, this hostel has rooms at unbeatable prices. The neighborhood is safe

(there's a police station right across the street). Free pizza W night. Kitchens and TV rooms. Passport required. Internet access $1 per 8min. Key deposit $10. Reception 24hr. Reservations recommended. Rooms $28, with private bath $32. AmEx/D/MC/V. ❶

Jazz on the Park, 36 W. 106th St./Duke Ellington Blvd. (☎212-932-1600; www.jazzonthepark.com), between Manhattan Ave. and Central Park W. A brightly colored hostel with fun decor. 255 beds. Live jazz on weekends. Internet access $1 per 9min. Check-in 11am. Check-out 1pm. Reservations required June-Oct. 10- to 12-bed dorms $27; 6- to 8-bed dorms $29; 4-bed dorms $32; private rooms from $75. MC/V. ❶

HOTELS AND GUEST HOUSES

⬛ **Gershwin Hotel,** 7 E. 27th St. (☎212-545-8000; www.gershwinhotel.com), between Madison and 5th Ave. This budget boutique hotel sports a stunning red facade ornamented with sculpted glass, giving its modern lobby a Warhol vibe. Rooms have bathrooms, cable TV, A/C, and phones. Wi-Fi $10 per day, $35 for 5 days. Reception 24hr. Check-in 3pm. Check-out 11am. Dorms $33-45; singles and doubles $109-249. ❸

⬛ **Thirty Thirty,** 30 E. 30th St. (☎212-689-1900 or 800-497-6028; www.thirtythirty-nyc.com), between Park Ave. S. and Madison Ave. This upscale hotel has chic minimalist style, a prime location, and rooms with A/C, cable TV, hair dryers, irons, and phones. There's also an attached restaurant and evening bar. As an added bonus, bring your pet along for no additional charge. Wi-Fi $10 per day. Check-in 3pm. Check-out 11am. Singles and doubles $169-299. ❺

The Pod Hotel, 230 E. 51st St. (☎212-355-0300 or 800-742-5945; www.thepodhotel.com), between 2nd and 3rd Ave. Formerly the Pickwick Arms, this recently made-over hotel marries Manhattan chic with out-of-town prices. The small but efficient bedrooms all feature iPod docks, A/C, flatscreen TVs, phones, and voicemail. The roof garden facilitates socializing among guests. Wi-Fi. Check-in 2pm. Check-out 1pm. Singles and twin bunks with shared bath $149-169; double and queen with private bath $199-269. ❺

Hotel Stanford, 43 W. 32nd St. (☎212-563-1500 or 800-365-1114; www.hotelstanford.com), between 5th Ave. and Broadway. This Herald Sq.

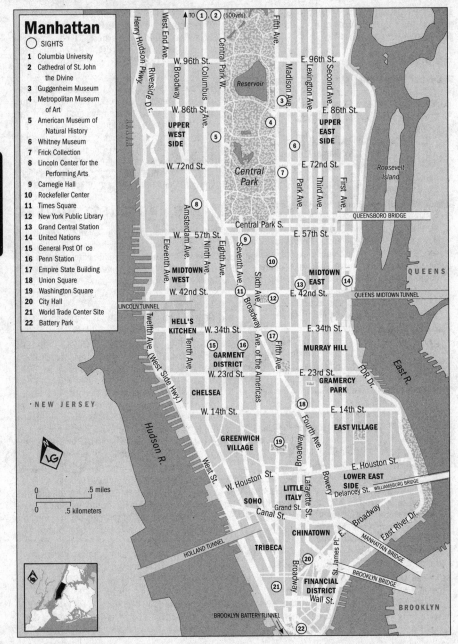

Manhattan

○ SIGHTS

1 Columbia University
2 Cathedral of St. John
  the Divine
3 Guggenheim Museum
4 Metropolitan Museum
  of Art
5 American Museum of
  Natural History
6 Whitney Museum
7 Frick Collection
8 Lincoln Center for the
  Performing Arts
9 Carnegie Hall
10 Rockefeller Center
11 Times Square
12 New York Public Library
13 Grand Central Station
14 United Nations
15 General Post Of ce
16 Penn Station
17 Empire State Building
18 Union Square
19 Washington Square
20 City Hall
21 World Trade Center Site
22 Battery Park

EAST COAST

TO ①.② (500yds)

Henry Hudson Pkwy.
West End Ave.
West Broadway
Riverside Dr.
Central Park W.
Fifth Ave.

W. 96th St.
E. 96th St.

Madison Ave.
Lexington Ave.
Second Ave.

Reservoir

W. 86th St.
E. 86th St.

③

④

UPPER
WEST
SIDE

UPPER
EAST
SIDE

Columbus Ave.

⑤

⑥

W. 72nd St.
Central Park
E. 72nd St.

⑦

Park Ave.
Third Ave.
First Ave.

Roosevelt
Island

Amsterdam Ave.

⑧

QUEENSBORO BRIDGE

Central Park S.

Eleventh Ave.

W. 57th St.
E. 57th St.

⑨

QUEENS

Ninth Ave.
Eighth Ave.
Seventh Ave.
Sixth Ave.
Broadway

⑩

MIDTOWN
WEST

MIDTOWN
EAST

⑭

⑬

W. 42nd St.
⑪
⑫
E. 42nd St.

LINCOLN TUNNEL

QUEENS MIDTOWN TUNNEL

HELL'S
KITCHEN

E. 34th St.

Twelfth Ave. (West Side Hwy.)
Tenth Ave.

W. 34th St.
⑮ ⑯
⑰

MURRAY HILL

Fifth Ave.

GARMENT
DISTRICT

Ave. of the Americas

W. 23rd St.
E. 23rd St.

GRAMERCY
PARK

CHELSEA

FDR Dr.

East R.

W. 14th St.
⑱
E. 14th St.

NEW JERSEY

EAST VILLAGE

Fourth Ave.

GREENWICH
VILLAGE

⑲

Broadway

Hudson R.

E. Houston St.

West St.

W. Houston St.

LOWER EAST
SIDE

LITTLE
ITALY

Lafayette St.

Bowery

Delancey St.

WILLIAMSBURG BRIDGE

0 .5 miles

SOHO
Grand St.
Canal St.

Broadway

East River Dr.

0 .5 kilometers

HOLLAND TUNNEL

CHINATOWN

St. James Pl.

MANHATTAN BRIDGE

TRIBECA

⑳

BROOKLYN BRIDGE

Broadway

㉑

FINANCIAL
DISTRICT
Wall St.

BROOKLYN

BROOKLYN BATTERY TUNNEL

㉒

hotel's lobby has sparkling ceiling lights, a polished marble floor, and a front desk with great service. Rooms have comfortable beds with A/C, private bathrooms, cable TV, phones, hair dryers, safes, and fridges. The hotel also houses a Korean bakery and a bustling 24hr. Korean eatery. Multilingual concierges. Continental breakfast included. Wi-Fi $12 per day. Check-in 3pm. Check-out noon. Twins and doubles from $189; queen from $199; king deluxe from $239. ❺

Hotel Newton, 2528 Broadway (☎212-678-6500 or 888-468-3558; www.newyorkhotel.com), between 94th and 95th St. One of the best values in Manhattan, this classy, recently renovated hotel boasts clean and spacious rooms with A/C, TVs, and private baths. Wi-Fi $1 per 9min. Check-in 2pm. Check-out noon. Singles and doubles from $170. Prices lowest on weekdays. ❺

Larchmont Hotel, 27 W. 11th St. (☎212-989-9333; www.larchmonthotel.com), between 5th and 6th Ave. Clean, European-style rooms on a quiet block that is still close to everything. A/C, closets, desks, phones, TVs, and wash basins in all rooms. Wear your cotton robe and slippers to the shared bath. Continental breakfast included. Check-in 3pm. Check-out noon. Reserve 4-6 weeks ahead. Singles $90-125; doubles $119-145; queens $149-165. ❸

🍴 FOOD

CHINATOWN

🏮 **Joe's Shanghai,** 9 Pell St. (☎212-233-8888; www.joeshanghairestaurant.com), between the Bowery and Mott St. From fried turnip cakes ($4) to crispy whole yellowfish ($14), the Shanghai specialties served here draw huge crowds. Joe's is well known for its *xiao long bao* (soup dumplings; $7). Made to order and absolutely delicious. Expect long lines on weekends. Be sure to check out Joe's original Queens location, 13621 37th Ave., Flushing. Open daily 11am-11pm. Cash only. ❸

Fried Dumpling, 106 Mosco St. (☎212-693-1060), between Mulberry and Mott St. For half the price of a subway ride, you can get either 5 dumplings or 4 pork buns ($1). Delicious, dirt-cheap food from a tiny hole in the wall with no A/C and a tiny counter with about 4 stools; most people eat at Columbus Park, right next door. Other available

items include soy milk ($1) and a very good hot-and-sour soup ($1). When you buy $5 worth of dumplings, there's a slight discount (as if you needed one). Cash only. ❶

LITTLE ITALY AND NOLITA

🏮 **Lombardi's Coal Oven Pizza,** 32 Spring St. (☎212-941-7994; www.firstpizza.com), between Mott and Mulberry St. Recognized as the nation's oldest pizzeria (established in 1905), Lombardi's can be forgiven for its checkered tablecloths and clichéd atmosphere. A large pizza ($20) feeds 2. Try to visit during off-peak hours; otherwise, the line is invariably out the door. Open M-Th 11:30am-11pm, F-Sa 11:30am-midnight, Su 11:30am-10pm. Cash only. ❷

Rice, 292 Elizabeth St. (☎212-226-5775; www.riceny.com), at Houston St. Rice offers every permutation of its namesake you could imagine—and others that you probably couldn't—served in a subdued, chic atmosphere. Sauces range from mango chutney to Aleppo yogurt. The menu offers a variety of original items you won't find elsewhere, such as butternut squash chowder ($5) and warm pear cider ($2). Salads are also a treat; Asian slaw salad $7. Rice entrees $4-9.50. Open daily noon-midnight. Cash only. ❷

La Mela, 167 Mulberry St. (☎212-431-9493; www.lamelarestaurant.com), between Broome and Grand St. Enormous La Mela is old-school Little Italy at its best, with family-style portions, long communal tables, chummy staff, and heaps of pasta drenched in red sauce. It's a great choice for a rowdy evening with a large group. 4-course dinner $28 per person, 3-course $19; 2-person min. 1.5L house wine $26. Pasta $11-16. House's huge dessert concoction (ice cream, cake, coconut, glazed bananas) $6 per person. After 6pm, dinner served only family-style. Open M-Th and Su noon-2am, F-Sa noon-3am. ❷

GREENWICH VILLAGE

🏮 **Sacred Chow,** 227 Sullivan St. (☎212-337-0863; www.sacredchow.com), between W. 3rd St. and Bleeker St. This delightful vegan restaurant serves creative and delicious cuisine—without any animal products, refined sugar, or white flour. Mix and match from the tapas selection (3 for $15), or go for one of the heaping hero sandwiches ($9.75). There's a big selection of smoothies, energy drinks, and organic beer and wine. Desserts like triple-chocolate brownies, nougatines, and the Sacred Sundae make for guilt-free treats ($3-9). Open M-Th 11am-10pm, F-Sa 11am-11pm. ❷

Arturo's Pizza, 106 W. Houston St. (☎212-677-3820), at Thompson St. Arturo's has provided the Village with outstanding pizza for decades. Many consider it the best pizza in the city. Big cheesy pies $15-22. Classic Italian entrees like veal parmigiana and shrimp scampi $16-25. Open M-Th 4pm-1am, F-Sa 4pm-2am, Su 3pm-midnight. ❸

MEATPACKING DISTRICT

🖾 **Spice Market,** 403 W. 13th St. (☎212-675-2322), at 9th Ave. A worthwhile splurge. The latest effort of celebrity chef Jean-Georges Vongerichten, who, despite his French roots, pays homage to Asian street food here. Vongerichten's updates on Asian appetizers, like mushroom-stuffed egg rolls and chicken samosas in a cilantro yogurt sauce, may be the best part of the meal. Entrees $16-36. Open M-F noon-3pm and 5:30pm-midnight, Sa-Su noon-4pm and 5:30pm-midnight. ❹

Pastis, 9 9th Ave. (☎212-929-4844; www.pastisny.com), at 12th St. One of the cornerstones of the Meatpacking District's rebirth, always-mobbed Pastis recreates the atmosphere of a classic Parisian brasserie with a slight New York edge. It's one of the best brunch spots in the city, and it's a hip scene at night. Brioche french toast $16. *Croque-monsieur* $13. Pork chop with honey and lavender $24. Pan-seared organic salmon $27. Open M-Th 9am-2am, Sa-Su 9am-2:30am. ❹

CHELSEA

🖾 **Le Zie 2000,** 172 7th Ave. (☎212-206-8686; www.lezie.com), between 20th and 21st St. This candlelit trattoria is a Chelsea standby. The Venetian-style cuisine changes seasonally, but some dishes, like delicious baked goat cheese with tomato sauce and garlic croutons ($7), are always available. Entrees $13-18. Wines $6-11. Mixed drinks in the adjoining lounge $10-11. Open daily noon-11:30pm. ❸

Rosa Mexicano, 9 E. 18th St. (☎212-533-3350; www.rosamexicano.com), between 5th Ave. and Broadway. Extraordinary Mexican cuisine in a romantic setting. The signature dish is guacamole, prepared tableside ($14). *Flautas de pollo* (crispy rolled chicken tacos; $9.50). Entrees

$19-28. Open M-F noon-1am, Sa 11am-1am, Su 11am-11pm. ❸

THEATER DISTRICT

🖾 **Empanada Mama,** 763 9th Ave. (☎212-698-9008), between 51st and 52nd St. Empanadas are an artery-clogging Latin American specialty—some combination of meat, cheese, and/or vegetables wrapped in dough and fried. This narrow, always-jammed Hell's Kitchen find offers over 40 variations, from the Pizza (mozzarella and cheese; $2) to the Viagra (crab meat, scallops, and shrimp; $3). There's a smaller selection of baked empanadas for a healthful treat. Don't miss the dessert empanadas, like the Elvis (peanut butter and bananas; $2). Beer, wine, and sangria $4.25. Open daily 10am-midnight. ❶

🖾 **Becco,** 355 W. 46th St. (☎212-397-7597; www.becconyc.com), between 8th and 9th Ave. This Restaurant Row standby serves huge portions of Italian food and offers 70 wines priced at $25 per bottle. The $18 fixed-price lunch (dinner $23) gets you a gourmet antipasto platter or caesar salad and unlimited servings of the 3 pastas of the day. Min. lunch $14, dinner $18. Try the mesclun salad with Tuscan beans and ripe tomatoes, tossed with an aged Chianti vinaigrette ($8) or the *pollo al limone* (chicken breast with lemon, olives, and capers; $17 lunch, $20 dinner). Open daily noon-3pm and 5pm-midnight. ❹

UPPER EAST SIDE

🖾 **Barking Dog Luncheonette,** 1678 3rd Ave. (☎212-831-1800), at 94th St. A haven for Upper East Siders and their 4-legged friends (who eat on the patio), the Barking Dog is known for its tasty American comfort food, served in a homey, dog-festooned setting. Try the buttermilk-battered ½ chicken ($13), which comes with mashed potatoes, gravy, and homemade biscuits. Daily sunset specials (M-F 5-7pm; $13-17) include soup or salad and dessert. Sandwiches $6-8. Takeout and delivery available. Open daily 8am-11pm. (☎212-861-3600). Cash only. ❷

🖾 **Mon Petit Café,** 801 Lexington Ave. (☎212-355-2233) at 62nd St. This welcoming and unpretentious Parisian-style bistro is a perfect place to relax after a day of shopping. While dinner entrees ($17-28) aren't cheap, breakfast and lunch make a delicious value. Omelets

$7.25-11. Escargot $8. *Mousse de foie gras au portoil* $11. *Steak frites* $28. *Fondant au chocolat* $9. Some nights feature live music. Open M-Sa 8am-11pm, Su 11am-6pm. ❸

UPPER WEST SIDE

Good Enough to Eat, 483 Amsterdam Ave. (☎212-496-0163; www.goodenoughtoeat. com), between 83rd and 84th St. Vermont cabin-style decor, complete with miniature white picket fences, quilts, and mismatched cow-motif dishware. Try the traditional turkey dinner ($18.50) or the macaroni and cheese ($12). Brunch is a mob scene, but it's worth the wait. All desserts, ice creams, and bread are made on-site. Cakes $5-6.50. Pies $5.50-6. 2 scoops of ice cream $5. Full bar. Open M-Th 8am-4pm and 5:30-10:30pm, F 8am-4pm and 5:30-11pm, Sa 9am-4pm and 5:30-11pm, Su 9am-4pm and 5:30-10:30pm. ❷

Barney Greengrass, 541 Amsterdam Ave. (☎212-724-4707; www.barneygreengrass.com), between 86th and 87th St. This classic family-run deli, in business since 1908, proclaims itself the "Sturgeon King" of New York City. Weekend crowds flock for homemade matzah ball soup ($5), lox scrambled with eggs and onions ($14), and hot pastrami sandwiches ($9.50). Open Tu-Su 8am-6pm. Cash only. ❷

LOWER EAST SIDE

Freeman's, at the end of Freeman Alley (☎212-420-0012; www.freemansrestaurant. com), off Rivington St., between the Bowery and Chrystie St. Finding this restaurant, tucked away at the end of a narrow alley, is nearly as fun as eating here. Nosh on traditional American cuisine in what looks like a hunting lodge, complete with antlers and stuffed geese. 3-cheese macaroni $13. Whole grilled trout with thyme, garlic, and lemon $18. Brunch specialties like poached eggs, lamb sausage, and watercress ($12) are crowd-pleasers. Open M-F 6:30-11:30pm, Sa-Su 11am-4pm and 6:30-11:30pm. ❸

Schiller's Liquor Bar, 131 Rivington St. (☎212-260-4555; www.schillersny.com), at Norfolk St. Schiller's owner, also responsible for popular Balthazar and Pastis, sought to create his own "low-life restaurant and bar" on the Lower East Side. The result is somewhere between a dive bar and a French bistro housed in an old-time New York City diner. Cheesesteak $12.50-16. Brunch, available Sa-Su 10am-5pm, features hazelnut waffles ($9) and huevos rancheros ($10). The wine list is divided by budget: cheap ($6), decent ($7), and good ($8). Free Wi-Fi. Open M-Tu 11am-1am, W-Th 11am-2am, F 11am-3am, Sa 10am-3am, Su 10am-1am. ❷

HARLEM AND MORNINGSIDE HEIGHTS

Miss Maude's Spoonbread Too, 547 Lenox (6th) Ave. (☎212-690-3100; www.spoonbreadinc. com), between 137th and 138th St. Heaping portions of delicious, down-home soul food. The restaurant is famous for spoonbread (similar to cornbread) and sweet potato pie ($3.50), and the macaroni and cheese ($4) is to die for. Entrees include Louisiana catfish ($15), Southern fried chicken ($13), and Jamaican jerk chicken ($14); all come with 2 sides. Delivery available; $15 min. Open M-Th noon-9:30pm, F-Sa noon-10:30pm, Su 11am-9:30pm. ❷

Tom's Restaurant, 2880 Broadway (☎212-864-6137; www.toms-diner.com), at 112th St. Tom's famous sign was featured in Seinfeld, but despite the souvenirs this diner remains surprisingly untouristy and undeniably cheap. Tom's forte is breakfast, when locals and students fill up on huge pancakes ($5.65) and 3-egg omelets (from $7). Lunch and dinner also served (burgers from $4.25; entrees with sides from $9). Open M-Th and Su 6am-1:30am, F-Sa 24hr. Cash only. ❶

BROOKLYN

Grimaldi's, 19 Old Fulton St. (☎718-858-4300; www.grimaldis.com), between Front and Water St. A favorite of Frank Sinatra, Grimaldi's serves classic brick-oven New York-style pizza, with wonderfully fresh mozzarella. The line outside is more an indication of quality than narrow tourist appeal. Small pies $12, large $14. Toppings from $2 each. Wine by the glass $4. Open M-F 11:30am-10:45pm, Sa 11:30am-11:45pm, Su noon-11:45pm. Cash only. ❷

DuMont Restaurant, 432 Union Ave. (☎718-486-7717; www.dumontrestaurant.com), at Devoe St. One of the best of Williamsburg's many brunch spots, DuMont is a magnet for locals looking to drink mimosas ($8) and munch on favorites like huevos rancheros ($10) and smoked trout salad ($9) in the early afternoon. At dinner, the signature DuMac and Cheese ($14) and seasonal specials (pan-roasted ahi tuna; $24) are fresh and delicious. The service is excellent, the wine list is solid, and the garden areas in back couldn't be more pleasant when the weather's warm. Open M-Th and Su 11am-3pm, F-Sa 11am-3pm and 6pm-midnight. ❷

QUEENS

🦪 **Elias Corner,** 2402 31st St. (☎718-932-1510). A fantastic seafood restaurant with a distinctly Greek character, Elias Corner has an ever-changing selection of fish caught the morning before your dinner. Try the *marides* (small fish), calamari, or grilled octopus as *mezedes* (appetizers). Prices depend on the catch of the day, with meals $10-25. Open daily 4-11pm. Cash only. ❷

🎯 SIGHTS

NEW YORK HARBOR

STATUE OF LIBERTY. The Statue of Liberty, long a symbol of hope for immigrants, stands at the entrance to New York Harbor. In 1886, the French government presented Frederic-Auguste Bartholdi's sculpture to the US as a sign of goodwill. The statue's crown and torch were closed in September 2001; views are limited to the 150 ft. concrete pedestal. (☎212-363-3200; www.statueofliberty.org. *Liberty Island open daily 9am-5pm. Ferries leave for Liberty Island from the piers at Battery Park every 30min. M-F 9:15am-3:30pm, Sa-Su 9am-4pm. Tickets for ferry with access to Liberty Island and Ellis Island $12, ages 4-12 $5, under 4 free.)*

ELLIS ISLAND. Accessible via the same ferry as the Statue of Liberty, Ellis Island was the processing point for millions of immigrants from 1897 to 1938. Each day, as many as 5000 immigrants would wait in the main building's vaulted Registry Room until they were called forward to be questioned by inspectors. Despite the long wait and the often harrowing medical exams that they were forced to undergo, only 1-2% of immigrants failed inspection. Of those that were granted entry to the US, one-third

settled in New York City. (☎212-363-3200; www. ellisisland.org. *45min. guided tours throughout the day. Free. Audio tour $5, under 17 $4.)*

DOWNTOWN

FINANCIAL DISTRICT. Once the northern border of the New Amsterdam settlement, Wall St. is named for the wall built in 1653 to shield the Dutch colony from British invasion. By the early 19th century, the area was the financial capital of the US. On the southwest corner of Wall and Broad St. stands the **New York Stock Exchange.** This 1903 temple to capitalism sees billions of dollars change hands daily. The exchange, founded in 1792 at 68 Wall St., is now off-limits to tourists. Around the corner, at the end of Wall St., stands the seemingly ancient **Trinity Church,** with its delicately crafted steeple. (*74 Trinity Pl.* ☎212-602-0800; www. trinitywallstreet.org. *Open M-F 7am-6pm, Sa 8am-4pm, Su 7am-4pm.)* With a fence erected in 1771, **Bowling Green** is Manhattan's oldest park. It was restored in the 1970s following decades of neglect. (*Intersection of Battery Pl., Broadway, and Whitehall St.)* The **Custom House** was completed in 1907, when the city still derived most of its revenue from customs. The magnificent Beaux-Arts building, designed by Cass Gilbert, is fronted by sculptures of four women representing America, Europe, Africa, and Asia. (*1 Bowling Green St.)*

WORLD TRADE CENTER SITE (GROUND ZERO). The site where the World Trade Center once stood is sobering. The poignancy of the vastly empty landscape can only really be understood in person. However, it won't be empty for long. Construction for the memorial, Reflecting Absence, began in the summer of 2006 and is scheduled for completion by the eighth anniversary of the attacks, September 11, 2009. (*On the corner of Liberty and West St. The Tribute Center, 120 Liberty St., between Church and Greenwich St., is scheduled to open in September 2008 and will feature exhibits and an education center.* ☎212-422-3520; www.tributenyc.org. *Open M and W-Sa 10am-6pm, Tu and Su noon-6pm. 1hr. walking tours of the site, led by those affected by the attacks, M-F 1, 3pm; Sa-Su noon, 1, 2, 3pm. $10, under 12 free; reserve at www.telecharge.com.)*

CIVIC CENTER. The city's center of government is located north of its financial district. The New York City mayor's office is in **City Hall;** around it are courthouses, civic buildings, and federal buildings. The building's interior is closed indefinitely to the public. *(Broadway at Murray St., off Park Row.)* The **Woolworth Building,** a 1913 Neo-Gothic skyscraper built for $15.5 million to house the offices of FW Woolworth's five-and-dime store empire, looms south of City Hall. *(233 Broadway, between Barclay St. and Park Pl. Closed to the public.)* A block and a half south on Broadway lies ◪**Saint Paul's Chapel.** Inspired by the design of London's St. Martin-in-the-Fields, this modest chapel was built between 1764 and 1766 and is Manhattan's oldest church—George Washington prayed here regularly. *(Between Vesey and Fulton St. ☎212-233-4164; www.stpaulschapel.org. Chapel open M-F 9am-3pm, Su 7am-3pm. Free.)*

SOUTH STREET SEAPORT. The shipping industry thrived here for most of the 19th century, when New York City was the most important port city in the US. In the 20th century, shipping was replaced by bars, brothels, and crime. Now a 12-block "museum without walls," the seaport displays old schooners, sailboats, and houses. Sadly, it is also a monument to unimaginative consumerism: **Pier 17** houses a three-story mall full of chain stores. A gigantic Pizzeria Uno is the most visible dining option in the area. Still, kids and nautical history buffs may enjoy a visit. *(Bounded by FDR Dr., Water St., Beekman St., and John St. Visitors center: 12 Fulton St. ☎212-748-8600; www.southstseaport. org. Open daily 10am-5pm. Admission to ships, shops, and tours $8, students and seniors $6, under 12 free. Walking around the museum is free.)* Built in 1911 by a Hamburg-based company, the *Peking* is the second-largest sailing ship ever launched. An intensive 12-year restoration has returned this four-masted barque to her former glory. For information on the ship's rich history, catch the 15min. 1929 film of the ship's passage around Cape Horn, shown daily 10am-6pm. *(On the East River, off Fulton St., next to Pier 16. Open daily 10am-5pm. Free with Seaport Museum admission from visitors center.)* In addition to the *Peking*, there are seven ships open to the public. Some are stationary, like the 325 ft. iron-hulled, full-rigged *Wavertree* (1885; currently undergoing restoration) and the *Ambrose*, a floating lighthouse built in 1908 to mark the entrance to New York Harbor. Others take to the open seas: the *Pioneer* (1885) offers 2hr. and 3hr. tours.

GREENWICH VILLAGE

WASHINGTON SQUARE. Washington Sq. Park is at the center of Village life. On the north side of the park is **The Row,** a stretch of 1830s brick residences that were once populated by writers, dandies, and professionals. Use caution here late at night. During the day, you'll find a motley mix of musicians, misunderstood teenagers, homeless people, and romping children in the park. At the north end of the park stands the **Washington Memorial Arch,** built in 1889 to commemorate the centennial of George Washington's inauguration. Until 1964, Fifth Ave. actually ran through the arch. Residents complained about the noisy traffic, so the city cut the avenue short.

NEW YORK UNIVERSITY. With 48,000 students in 14 schools, NYU is the country's largest private university. On the southeast side of the park looms the rust-colored **Elmer Holmes Bobst Library,** NYU's central library and one of the largest in the country. On the same block stands NYU's Reuben Nakian-designed **Loeb Student Center,** which is garnished with pieces of scrap metal, supposedly meant to represent birds in flight. An enormous concrete monolith, known simply as the **Picasso,** sits in a green square at the center of NYU's three 30-story Silver Towers. Proclaimed by *The New York Times* to be the city's ugliest piece of public art, the 36 ft., 60-ton structure made of black stone and concrete is Norwegian artist Carl Nesjar's adaptation of Picasso's 24 in. *Bust of Sylvette*. **Gould Plaza,** which houses an aluminum sculpture by Dadaist Jean Arp, sits a few steps east on W. Fourth St., in front of NYU's Stern School of Business and the Courant Institute of Mathematical Sciences.

CHRISTOPHER PARK AND ENVIRONS. The intersection of Seventh Ave., Christopher St., and W. Fourth St. forms a green triangle, home to one statue, two sculptures, and a few benches, known (mistakenly) as Sheridan Sq. and (correctly) as **Christopher Park.**

The park owes its common misidentification to the statue of General Sheridan that stands at the triangle's eastern tip. The 1969 Stonewall Riots, arguably the beginning of the modern gay-rights movement, took place here. Off 10th St. and Sixth Ave., you'll see an iron gate and street sign marking **Patchin Place.** Theodore Dreiser, EE Cummings, and Djuna Barnes lived in the 145-year-old buildings that line this path. The Village's narrowest building, **75 Bedford Street,** only 9 ft. in width, housed writer Edna St. Vincent Millay in the 1920s. Anthropologist Margaret Mead and actors Lionel Barrymore and Cary Grant each lived at 75 Bedford after Millay's departure. *(Near the corner of Commerce St.)*

LOWER MIDTOWN

UNION SQUARE. At the intersection of Fourth Ave. and Broadway, Union Sq. and the surrounding area sizzled with high society before the Civil War. At the nexus of a number of neighborhoods, Union Sq. has become the crossroads of downtown. In the square itself, the scent of herbs and fresh bread wafts through the air, courtesy of the ⬛**Union Square Greenmarket.** Farmers, fishermen, and bakers from all over the region come to sell fresh produce, jellies, and baked goods. In late November, the south end of Union Sq. is transformed into the Union Sq. Holiday Market. *(Between Broadway and Park Ave. S., between 14th and 17th St. Greenmarket open M, W, and F-Sa 8am-6pm.)* New York's first skyscraper over 20 stories high, the **Flatiron Building** was also one of the first buildings in which exterior walls were hung on a steel frame. This photogenic building (originally the Fuller Building) was named for its resemblance to the clothes-pressing device. Constructed in 1902, its triangular shape produced wind currents that made women's skirts billow; police coined the term "23 skidoo" to shoo gapers from the area. The building is now all commercial space. *(175 5th Ave., off the southwest corner of Madison Sq. Park.)*

HOTEL CHELSEA. Hotel Chelsea is hallowed literary ground. Some 150 books have been penned here, including works by Arthur Miller, Mark Twain, Vladimir Nabokov, Thomas World, and O. Henry. *(222 W. 23rd St., between 7th and 8th Ave. ☎ 212-243-3700; www.hotelchelsea.com.)*

GENERAL THEOLOGICAL SEMINARY. Founded in 1817, General Theological Seminary is the oldest Episcopal seminary in America. Hidden behind a rather unfortunate 1960s exterior is a compound of ivy-covered Gothic Revival brick buildings, home to about 100 seminarians. The grounds are open to the public year-round, and, if you're lucky, you may catch some aspiring priests playing tennis. *(175 9th Ave., between 20th and 21st St. ☎ 212-243-5150; www.gts.edu. Gardens open daily 11am-3pm.)*

HERALD SQUARE. Herald Sq. is located between 34th and 35th St., between Broadway and Sixth Ave., and is a mecca for shopping. Ever since King Kong first climbed the **Empire State Building** in 1933, the skyscraper has attracted scores of tourists. The limestone and granite structure stretches 1454 ft. into the sky, and its 73 elevators run through 2 mi. of shafts. *(350 5th Ave., at 34th St. ☎ 212-736-3100. Open daily 8am-midnight; last elevator up at 11:15pm. $18, under 12 $12, seniors $16.)* East on 34th St. stands department store Goliath **Macy's,** which sprawls over 10 floors and houses two million sq. ft. of merchandise ranging from designer clothes to housewares. The store sponsors the **Macy's Thanksgiving Day Parade,** a NYC tradition buoyed by 10-story Snoopys, marching bands, and floats. *(151 W. 34th St., between Broadway and 7th Ave. ☎ 212-695-4400. Open M-F 10am-9pm, Sa 10am-10pm, Su 11am-8pm.)*

MIDTOWN

FIFTH AVENUE. A monumental research library in the style of a classical temple, the main branch of the ⬛**New York Public Library,** between 40th and 42nd St., contains the world's seventh-largest research library and an immense reading room. Featured in the film *Ghostbusters,* two marble lions representing patience and fortitude guard the library against illiteracy—and ghosts. *(42nd St. and 5th Ave. ☎ 212-869-8089; www.nypl.org. Open Tu-W 11am-7:30pm, Th-Sa 10am-6pm. Free.)* Behind the library, **Bryant Park** features free summertime cultural events, like classic film screenings and live comedy. *(☎ 212-768-4242; www.bryantpark.org. Open daily 7am-9pm.)* Designed by

James Renwick, the twin spires of **Saint Patrick's Cathedral** stretch 330 ft. into the air, making it the largest Catholic cathedral in the US. *(51st St. ☎ 212-753-2261. Open daily 7am-10pm.)* The **Plaza Hotel,** on 59th St., at the southeast corner of Central Park, was constructed in 1907 at an astronomical cost. Its 18-story, 800-room French Renaissance interior flaunts five marble staircases, ludicrously named suites, and a grand ballroom.

ROCKEFELLER CENTER. Rockefeller Center got its start in the Roaring 20s, when tycoon John D. Rockefeller, Jr., wanted to move the Metropolitan Opera to Midtown. The plans fell through when the Great Depression struck in 1929, so Rockefeller made the center a media hub instead. The main entrance is on Fifth Ave. between 49th and 50th St. **The Channel Gardens,** so named because they sit between the **Maison Française** on the left and the **British Empire Building** on the right, usher pedestrians toward **Tower Plaza.** This sunken space, topped by the gold-leafed statue of Prometheus, is surrounded by the flags of over 100 countries. During spring and summer, an ice-skating rink lies dormant beneath an overpriced cafe. The rink, which is better for people-watching than for skating, re-opens in winter in time for the annual Christmas tree lighting, one of New York City's greatest traditions. Behind Tower Plaza is the **General Electric Building,** a 70-story skyscraper. **NBC,** which makes its home here, offers an hourlong tour that traces the history of the network, from its first radio broadcast in 1926 through the heyday of TV programming in the 1950s and 60s to today's sitcoms. The tour visits six studios, including the infamous 8H studio, home of *Saturday Night Live,* and 6A studio, home of *Late Night with Conan O'Brien. (☎212-664-3700. Departs from the NBC Experience Store in the GE Building M-Th every 30min. F-Su every 15min. M-Sa 8:30am-5:30pm, Su 9:30am-4:30pm. No children under 6. $18.50, seniors and ages 6-16 $15.50.)*

RADIO CITY MUSIC HALL. After narrowly escaping demolition in 1979, this Art Deco landmark received a complete interior restoration. Radio City's main attraction is the Rockettes, a high-stepping, long-legged dance troupe whose annual Christmas and Easter extravaganzas are legendary. The Stage

Door Tour takes you through the Great Stage and various rehearsal halls. *(50th St. at 6th Ave. ☎ 212-247-4777; www.radiocity.com. Departs daily every 30min. 11am-3pm. $17, under 12 $10.)*

PARK AVENUE. A luxurious boulevard with greenery running down its center, Park Ave., between 45th and 59th St., is lined with office buildings and hotels. Completed in 1913, the **Grand Central Terminal** is a train station of monumental proportions. On the classical facade on 42nd St., you'll find a beautiful sculpture of Mercury, the Roman god of transportation. An information booth sits in the middle of the commuter-filled concourse. For a dizzying array of chocolates, cheeses, breads, meats, and pastries, swing by the **Grand Central Market,** located on the main level. *(Between 42nd and 45th St.)* Several blocks uptown is the *crème de la crème* of Park Ave. hotels, the **Waldorf-Astoria.** Cole Porter's piano sits in the front lounge, and every US president since Hoover has spent a night or two here. *(301 Park Ave., between 49th and 50th St.)* The dark and gracious **Seagram Building,** the only building in the city designed by Ludwig Mies van der Rohe, stands a few blocks uptown. *(375 Park Ave., between 52nd and 53rd St.)*

UNITED NATIONS. Founded just after WWII to serve as a "center for harmonizing the actions of nations," the **United Nations** is located in international territory along what would be First Ave. The UN complex consists of the Secretariat Building (the skyscraper), the General Assembly Building, the Hammarskjöld Library, and the Conference Building. The only way into the General Assembly Building is by guided tour. *(1st Ave., between 42nd and 48th St. ☎ 212-963-4475, tours 963-3242; www. un.org. 1hr. tours depart from the UN visitors' entrance at 1st Ave. and 46th St. every 15min. M-F 9:15am-4:45pm, Sa-Su 9:30am-4:45pm. $12, students $8.)*

CHRYSLER BUILDING. One of New York's most iconic buildings, the Chrysler Building is a monument to the car. The building's spire is meant to evoke a 1930 Chrysler's radiator grill. Other motoring mementos include gargoyles styled after hood ornaments and hubcaps. *(On 42nd St. and Lexington Ave.)*

TIMES SQUARE. At the intersection of 42nd St., Seventh Ave., and Broadway, Times Sq.

EAST COAST

is a nonstop, neon-lit, overcrowded, over-stimulating feast of excess. The square was once the epicenter of New York City seediness, filled with peep shows, prostitutes, and drug dens. Today the smut has been replaced by 30 ft. tall video screens, Disney musicals, and nearly 40 million tourists per year. This is techno-commercial postmodernity at its most apocalyptic. Stop by the **Times Square Information Center,** in the restored Embassy Movie Theatre on Seventh Ave., between 46th and 47th St., for free bathrooms, free Internet access, and a theater ticketing service. *(☎212-869-1890; www.timessquarenyc.org. Open daily 8am-8pm.)*

THEATER DISTRICT. New York City's theater district, centered on Broadway just north of Times Sq., is home to approximately 40 theaters, of which 22 have been declared historic landmarks. **Shubert Alley,** half a block west of Broadway, between 44th and 45th St., was originally built as a fire exit between the Booth and Shubert Theaters and is now a pedestrian zone where theater groupies cluster after shows to get their playbills signed by their favorite actors. *(From 41st to 54th St., between 6th and 8th Ave.)*

CARNEGIE HALL. Amid 57th St.'s galleries and stores, New York City's musical center is Carnegie Hall. Since hosting Tchaikovsky's American debut in 1891, Carnegie Hall has featured such classical icons as Caruso, Toscanini, and Bernstein, jazz greats like Dizzy Gillespie, Ella Fitzgerald, and Thelonious Monk, and even rock and rollers such as The Beatles and The Rolling Stones. *(881 7th Ave., at W. 57th St. ☎212-247-7800, tours 903-9765; www.carnegiehall.org. 1hr. tours M-F 11:30am, 2, 3pm. $9, students and seniors $6, under 12 $3.)*

CENTRAL PARK. Central Park was founded in the mid-19th century when wealthy New Yorkers advocated the creation of a park in the style of the public grounds of Europe. Frederick Law Olmsted and Calvert Vaux designed the park in 1858; their Greensward plan took 15 years and 20,000 workers to implement. With 58 mi. of pedestrian paths lined by 26,000 trees, it's a great place to escape Manhattan's traffic, pollution, and noise. Expansive fields like the **Sheep Meadow,** from 66th to 69th St., and the **Great Lawn,** from 80th to 85th St., complement developed spaces such as the **Mall,** between 66th and 71st St., the **Shakespeare Garden,** at 80th St., and the **Imagine Mosaic,** commemorating the music of John Lennon, on the western side of the park at 72nd St. Don't miss free summer shows at Central Park SummerStage and Shakespeare in Central Park. *(☎212-310-6600; www.centralparknyc.org.)*

UPPER EAST SIDE

TEMPLE EMANU-EL. The largest synagogue in the world, Temple Emanu-El was completed in 1929 for its German-American congregation.

TURKEY, THE CAT IN THE HAT, AND ... COMAS?

The Macy's Thanksgiving Day Parade, like football and turkey, is an essential Thanksgiving tradition. New Yorkers have reveled in the parade since 1924, when 250,000 people showed up for the inaugural festivities. Today, over two million people attend each year.

The parade is famous for its procession of massive balloons, which collectively are filled with over 400,000 cu. ft. of helium. Most balloons are between five and six stories tall. Up to 3000 volunteers wrangle the balloons through the canyons of Manhattan while navigating around marching bands, dance teams, and motorized floats. It's not an easy job, and accidents have occurred in recent years, such as when a giant Cat in the Hat balloon collided with a lamppost and put one bystander in a month-long coma. In the distant past, the balloons were released into the sky at the end of the parade but exploded just above street level. Then for a while the balloons were marked with a return address and a written statement promising the person who returned the balloon a gift from Macy's.

The night before the parade, crowds gather at the American Museum of Natural History, where the balloons are inflated. At 9am, the balloons and the parade travel down Central Park West, through Columbus Cir., down Broadway and to Herald Sq. They no longer release the balloons into the sky, but the parade still has a ceremonial finish, marked by the arrival of Santa Claus and the accompanying

Its 65th St. entrance features an intimidating Romanesque limestone facade trimmed with archways representing the 12 tribes of Israel. Tours are available after morning services and on Saturdays at noon. *(1 E. 65th St., at 5th Ave. ☎ 212-744-1400; www.emanuelnyc.org. Open daily 10am-5pm. Services M-Th and Su 5:30pm; call for service schedule F-Sa.)*

CARL SCHURZ PARK AND GRACIE MANSION. The 15-acre park, built in 1896, overlooks the turbulent waters of the East River. Gracie Mansion, at the northern end of the park, has been the official "home" of the mayor of New York City since 1942. Almost all of the objects in the recently restored mansion were made in New York, and many of the paintings and prints depict scenes of the city. The privately funded Gracie Mansion Conservancy was established in 1981 to preserve, maintain, and enhance the mansion and its surroundings. *(Between 84th and 90th St. Park open sunrise-1am. ☎ 212-570-4751. 50min. tours from Mar. to mid-Nov. W 10, 11am, 1, 2pm by reservation only. $7, students free, seniors $4.)*

UPPER WEST SIDE

LINCOLN CENTER. Inspired by John D. Rockefeller's belief that "the arts are not for the privileged few, but for the many," this 15-acre center for the performing arts is home to 12 facilities that can accommodate nearly 18,000 spectators in all. A reinterpretation of the public plazas in Rome and Venice, Lincoln Center was initially dismissed by *The New York Times* as "a hulking disgrace." Since then, its spare and spacious architecture and the performances it hosts have made Lincoln Center one of New York City's beloved public spaces. *(Between 62nd and 66th St.)*

OTHER SIGHTS. Perhaps Manhattan's most famous apartment building, the **Dakota Apartments** counts Lauren Bacall, Leonard Bernstein, Roberta Flack, and Boris Karloff as former residents. The Dakota provided the eerie setting for Roman Polanski's New York City horror classic, *Rosemary's Baby*, and the sidewalk outside was the site of resident John Lennon's tragic shooting on December 8, 1980. The interior is closed to the public. *(1 W. 72nd St., at the corner of Central Park W.)* The upscale *Ansonia Apartments* complex, completed in 1904, was once the grande dame of Beaux-Arts apartments. While the inside is closed to the public, the building's exterior—complete with weathered stone ornaments and rounded corner towers—is still worth a look. Soundproof walls and thick floors once enticed musically inclined tenants like Enrico Caruso, Arturo Toscanini, and Igor Stravinsky. *(2109 Broadway, between 73rd and 74th St.)*

COLUMBIA UNIVERSITY. This world-famous university was chartered in 1754 as King's College, but it lost its original name in the American Revolution. The campus, designed by prominent New York architects, is urban—don't come looking for leafy quads. Its centerpiece, the majestic Roman Classical **Low Library,** looms over **College Walk,** the school's central promenade, which bustles with academics and students. Just to the east of Low Library stands **Saint Paul's Chapel,** a small but beautiful space with magnificent acoustics, which holds free choral and chamber concerts on Tuesdays and Saturdays. **Morningside Park,** where Meg Ryan discussed her sexual fantasies in *When Harry Met Sally*, is just east of the campus along Morningside Dr. *(Morningside Dr. and Broadway, from 114th to 120th St. ☎ 212-854-1754; www.columbia.edu. Group tours from late fall to spring; no regularly scheduled public tours.)*

CATHEDRAL OF SAINT JOHN THE DIVINE. The still-unfinished Cathedral of St. John the Divine, under construction since 1892, is the largest in the world. It features altars and bays dedicated both to the sufferings of Christ and to the experiences of immigrants, victims of genocide, and AIDS patients. *(Amsterdam Ave., between 110th and 113th St. ☎ 212-316-7540, tours 932-7347; www.stjohndivine.org. Open M-Sa 7am-6pm, Su 1pm. Tours Tu-Sa 11am, Su 1pm. $5, students $4.)*

RIVERSIDE CHURCH. Inspired by the Chartres Cathedral, Riverside Church has an observation deck in its tower and an amazing view, as well as the world's largest carillon (74 bells), a gift of John D. Rockefeller, Jr. *(490 Riverside Dr., at 120th St. ☎ 212-870-6792; www.theriversidechurch.org. Open daily 7am-10pm. Tours Su 12:30pm, after services, and upon request. Free.)*

LOWER EAST SIDE

SUNG TAK BUDDHIST ASSOCIATION. The Sung Tak Buddhist Association occupies a former synagogue. Look for the two imposing stone staircases on either side of a Chinese emporium, with a giant, white Buddha at the top. The interior reflects the building's multicultural past in its juxtaposition of Middle Eastern and Asian architectural styles. Services are held daily. *(15 Pike St., between E. Broadway and Henry St. ☎ 212-587-5936. Open daily 9am-6pm. Free.)*

ELDRIDGE STREET SYNAGOGUE. The Moorish-style Eldridge St. Synagogue was built in 1886 as the first synagogue for New York City's Eastern European Jews. It now presides over a crowded, noisy block of Chinatown. The synagogue hosts community events almost every Sunday, including lectures, concerts, and festivals. *(12 Eldridge St., south of Canal St. ☎ 212-219-0888; www.eldridgestreet.org. Tours Tu-Th and Su 11am-4pm. Tours $5, students and seniors $3.)*

HARLEM

SUGAR HILL. African-Americans with "sugar" (that is, money) moved here in the 1920s and 30s. Musical legends Duke Ellington and WC Handy lived in the neighborhood, while leaders WEB DuBois and Thurgood Marshall inhabited apartments at 409 Edgecombe Ave. Some of the city's most notable gangsters also operated here. The area was the birthplace of Sugarhill Records, the rap label that created the Sugarhill Gang. Their 1979 single "Rapper's Delight" became the first hip-hop song to enter the Top 40. Today, skyrocketing real-estate prices in Manhattan have made Sugar Hill's beautiful brownstones prized possessions once more. *(From 143rd to 155th St., between St. Nicholas and Edgecombe Ave.)*

SCHOMBURG CENTER FOR RESEARCH IN BLACK CULTURE. This research branch of the **New York Public Library** houses the city's vast archives, manuscripts, and rare books on black history and culture. Scholar Arturo Schomburg collected some five million photographs, oral histories, and pieces of art. The center also houses the American Negro Theater, famous during the 1940s, and the Langston Hughes Auditorium. *(515 Malcolm X Blvd./Lenox Ave., at 135th St. ☎ 212-491-2200; www.schomburgcenter.org. Research and reference open Tu-W noon-8pm, Th-F noon-6pm, Sa 10am-6pm. Exhibition house open Tu-Sa 10am-6pm.)*

CITY COLLEGE. City College was the nation's first public college and the alma mater of Woody Allen, Colin Powell, Edward Koch, and Walter Mosley. Architect George Brown Post employed the Gothic style associated with Oxford and Cambridge, but, seeking to identify the college as a "workingman's school," he insisted on rust-streaked and iron-spotted schist instead of marble or ivory. *(Admissions office at 138th St. and Convent Ave.; campus from 130th to 140th St. Enter at 138th St. ☎ 212-650-7000, tours 650-6977; www.ccny.cuny.edu.)*

WASHINGTON HEIGHTS

FORT TRYON PARK. Fort Tryon Park has one of the most majestic landscapes in the city. Inside are the crumbling remains of Fort Tryon, a Revolutionary War bulwark captured by the British in 1776, and the well-tended Heather Garden. The ▧**Cloisters,** the Met's palatial sanctuary of medieval art, overlooks the park from its perch. Fragments of 12th- and 13th-century French monasteries are incorporated into the building's own medievalist architecture; the building is as much of an attraction as the artwork it houses. *(☎ 212-923-3700; www.metmuseum.org. Open Tu-Su Mar.-Oct. 9:30am-5:15pm; Nov.-Feb. 9:30am-4:45pm. Tours Mar.-Oct. Tu-F 3pm, Su noon. $20, students and seniors $10, under 12 free.)*

MORRIS-JUMEL MANSION. The Morris-Jumel Mansion is Manhattan's oldest free-standing house, built in 1765, and has famous bedchambers, Napoleonic ornaments, and regal furniture. The gardens afford a great view of the Harlem River. Ring the doorbell for admission, even if the museum looks closed. *(65 Jumel Terr., between 160th and 162nd St. ☎ 212-923-8008; www.morrisjumel.org. Open W-Su 10am-4pm. $3, students and seniors $2, under 12 free. 1hr. tour of building $3.50, under 12 $2.50; 1hr. tour of building, grounds, and neighborhood $7.)*

BROOKLYN

FULTON LANDING. Fulton Landing is reminiscent of the days when the ferry—not the subway or the car—was the primary means of transportation between Brooklyn and Manhattan. Completed in 1883, the nearby ▓**Brooklyn Bridge**—spanning the gap between lower Manhattan and Brooklyn—is the product of elegant calculation, careful design, and human exertion. A walk across the bridge at sunrise or sunset is one of the most beautiful strolls New York City has to offer.

PROSPECT PARK. Central Park designers Frederick Law Olmsted and Calvert Vaux also designed Brooklyn's Prospect Park. While Manhattan's park incorporated existing swamps and bluffs, Prospect Park's "nature" was constructed entirely from scratch. Supposedly, the two designers liked Prospect Park better. The 80 ft. tall **Soldiers and Sailors Arch,** in the middle of **Grand Army Plaza,** was built in the 1890s to commemorate the Union's Civil War victory. The park also contains a children's museum, tennis courts, a carousel, and a zoo. *(Bounded by Prospect Park W., Flatbush Ave., Ocean Ave., Parkside Ave., and Prospect Park SW. ☎ 718-965-8951; www.prospectpark.org.)*

BROOKLYN BOTANIC GARDEN. This 52-acre oasis was founded in 1910 by the Brooklyn Institute of Arts and Sciences on a reclaimed waste dump. The artificial scenery is so convincing that water birds flock to the site. Favorite spots include the Discovery Garden, the discovery center in the Steinhardt Conservatory; the Fragrant Garden with mint, lemon, violet, and other aromatic flora, and the Japanese Hill-and-Pond Garden. *(1000 Washington Ave.; other entrances on Eastern Pkwy. and Flatbush Ave. ☎ 718-623-7000, events hotline 623-7333; www.bbg.org. Open Apr.-Sept. Tu-F 8am-6pm, Sa-Su 10am-6pm; Oct.-Mar. Tu-F 8am-4:30pm, Sa-Su 10am-4:30pm. $5, students and seniors $3, under 16 free. Tu and Sa 10am-noon free.)*

BROOKLYN PUBLIC LIBRARY. The striking Art Deco main branch of the Brooklyn Public Library stands majestically on Grand Army Pl. Its front doors are flanked by two large pillars with gold engravings and the words, "Here are enshrined the longings of great hearts." The library has spawned 53 branches and contains 1,600,000 volumes. Temporary exhibitions are on the Second floor. *(Corner of Eastern Pkwy. and Flatbush Ave. ☎ 718-230-2100. Open M and F 9am-6pm, Tu-Th 9am-9pm, Sa 10am-6pm.)*

CONEY ISLAND. An elite resort until the subway made it accessible to the masses, Coney Island is now a rickety slice of Americana. The legendary **Cyclone,** built in 1927, was once the most terrifying roller coaster in the world. The National Register has designated it a historic place, and couples have even been married on it. *(At Astroland, 1000 Surf Ave. Open M-Th 10am-10pm, F noon-6pm, Sa-Su noon-4pm. Individual rides $2.50-6; M-F 6hr. unlimited-ride pass $23.)* Meet sharks and other beasties at the **New York Aquarium.** *(At Surf and W. 8th St. ☎ 718-265-3474; www.nyaquarium.com. Open May-Oct. M-F 10am-6pm, Sa-Su 10am-7pm; Nov.-Apr. daily 10am-4:30pm. $12, ages 2-12 $8.)*

QUEENS

SOCRATES SCULPTURE PARK. Led by sculptor Mark di Suvero, artists transformed this former landfill into an artistic exhibition space with 35 stunning Day-Glo and rusted-metal abstractions. On Wednesday evenings in August, stop by the **Summer Solstice Celebration,** which screens a variety of independent and foreign films beginning at sunset. *(At the end of Broadway, across the Vernon Blvd. intersection. ☎ 718-956-1819; www.socratessculpturepark.org. Open daily 10am-sunset. Free.)*

STEINWAY PIANO FACTORY. The Steinway company has manufactured world-famous pianos here ever since it moved from its original location in the Village during the 1860s. The 12,000 parts of a typical Steinway piano, which weighs anywhere 750-1365 lb., include a 340 lb. plate of cast iron and tiny bits of Brazilian deer skin. If you're interested in visiting, make plans in advance to take the tour, which takes you through the process of construction. *(1 Steinway Pl., at 19th Rd. and 77th St. ☎ 718-721-2600; www.steinway.com/factory. Free tours every other Th; call ahead for info.)*

FLUSHING MEADOWS. Formerly a 1255-acre swamp nestled between Corona and Flushing, **Flushing Meadows-Corona Park** was a huge rubbish dump until city planners decided to turn the area into fairgrounds for the 1939 and

1964 World's Fairs. The park now holds **Citi Field** (home of the Mets), the **USTA National Tennis Center** (where the US Open is played), and the simple but interesting **New York Hall of Science**. *(4701 111th St., at 48th Ave. ☎ 718-699-0005; www.nyhallsci.org. Open July-Aug. Tu-Su 9:30am-5pm; Sept.-June Tu-W 9:30am-2pm, Th-Su 9:30am-5pm. $9, students and ages 5-17 $6, 2-4 $2.50, under 2 free.)* The **Unisphere,** a 380-ton globe in front of the New York City Building, is the structure featured in the 1997 movie *Men In Black*.

THE BRONX

BRONX ZOO. The Bronx Zoo/Wildlife Conservation Park is the largest urban zoo in the US. It houses over 4000 animals in a 265-acre expanse of recreated natural habitats. Grab a free map at the entrance. The **World of Reptiles** is home to a poison dart frog, a timber rattlesnake, and Samantha the python, the largest snake in the US. More benign beasts wander free in the park's "protected sanctuary," allowing for interactions between inhabitants and visitors. If you get tired of all the kids, work out your aggression at the crocodile feedings Mondays and Thursdays at 2pm. *(☎ 718-367-1010; www.bronxzoo.com. Open daily M-F 10am-5pm, Sa-Su 10am-5:30pm. Parts of the zoo closed Nov.-Apr. $12, ages 2-12 and seniors $9. W free.)*

NEW YORK BOTANICAL GARDEN. Across from the zoo, the 250-acre New York Botanical Garden, created in 1891, serves as a research laboratory and plant museum, with rare specimens, like the Japanese pagoda tree, the Kobus magnolia, and the Daybreak Yoshino cherry. The 50-acre native forest is the last of the woodlands that once covered the city. Although it costs a few extra dollars to enter, the gorgeous domed **Conservatory** is worth a visit. *(Bronx River Pkwy. Exit 7W and Fordham Rd. ☎ 718-817-8700; www.nybg.org. Open Tu-Su Apr.-Oct. 10am-6pm; Nov.-Mar. 10am-5pm. $13, students and seniors $11, ages 2-12 $5. Call for tour info.)*

BELMONT. Arthur Ave. is the center of this uptown Little Italy, where you'll find wonderful homestyle southern Italian cooking. *(Centered on Arthur Ave. and E. 187th St., near the Southern Blvd. entrance to the Bronx Zoo.)* To get a concentrated sense of the area, stop into **Arthur Avenue Retail Market,** an indoor market

with a cafe, butcher, grocer, cheese shop, and deli. *(2334 Arthur Ave., between 186th and Crescent St. ☎ 718-295-5033. Open M-Sa 6am-6pm.)*

EDGAR ALLEN POE COTTAGE. Poe lived in this cottage from 1846 to 1849 with his tubercular cousin and wife, Virginia. The writer married her when he was 26 and she 13. It was in this cottage that Poe wrote "Annabel Lee," "Eureka," and "The Bells," which refers to the bells of nearby Fordham University. The museum, a small clapboard structure, displays a slew of Poe's manuscripts and macabre effects, including the bed in which his young bride died. *(E. Kingsbridge Rd. and Grand Concourse, 5 blocks west of Fordham University. ☎ 718-881-8900. Open Sa 10am-4pm, Su 1-5pm. $3, students and seniors $2.)*

STATEN ISLAND

Staten Island has a limited tourist infrastructure and is quite difficult to traverse without a car. The **Staten Island Ferry** is itself a sight not to be missed; it offers the best and cheapest (free) tour of NYC's harbor. It departs from South Ferry.

■**SNUG HARBOR CULTURAL CENTER.** Founded in 1801, Sailors' Snug Harbor served as a home for retired sailors for 175 years. The iron fence kept old mariners from quenching their thirst at nearby bars. Purchased by the city and opened in 1976 as a cultural center, this national landmark now includes 28 historic buildings scattered over 83 acres of parkland. In the restored Main Hall, one of the center's most breathtaking buildings, the **Newhouse Center for Contemporary Art** shows temporary exhibits. *(1000 Richmond Terr. Bus S40. ☎ 718-448-2500; www.snug-harbor.org. Free tours of the grounds Apr.-Nov. Sa-Su 2pm, starting at the visitors center. Newhouse Center ☎ 718-448-2500, ext. 508. Open Tu-Su; hours vary. $3, under 12 $2.)*

🏛 MUSEUMS

Whether you're looking to examine medieval armor, dinosaur fossils, or abstract paintings, New York City has a museum for you. For listings of current and upcoming exhibits, consult *The New Yorker, New York* magazine, or the Friday *New York Times*'s "Weekend" section. Beware: most museums are closed on Mondays and packed elbow-tight on weekends. Many request a donation in place of an admission fee—don't be embarrassed to give as little as a dollar.

UPPER WEST SIDE

⬛AMERICAN MUSEUM OF NATURAL HISTORY. For generations of New York school-children, future paleontologists, and pretty much anyone with a pulse, the Natural History Museum has been a can't-miss opportunity to marvel at dinosaur skeletons, stargaze at the Hayden Planetarium, or buy mineral slabs and rubber snakes at the gift shop. The undisputed champion of the museum's exhibits is the fourth-floor **⬛dinosaur hall,** which displays real fossils in most exhibits. *(Central Park W., between 77th and 81st St. ☎212-769-5100; www. amnh.org. Open daily 10am-5:45pm. Suggested donation $14, students and seniors $10.50, ages 2-12 $8.)*

NEW YORK HISTORICAL SOCIETY. Founded in 1804, this block-long Neoclassical building houses a library and New York City's oldest continuously operating museum. The society's extensive, six-million-object collection, displayed in the **Henry Luce III Center** on the fourth floor, includes 132 Tiffany lamps, an array of children's toys, George Washington's bed, Napoleon's chair, 435 Audubon watercolors, and a display about September 11, 2001. *(2 W. 77th St., at Central Park W. ☎212-873-3400; www. nyhistory.org. Open Tu-Su 10am-6pm. $10, students and seniors $5, children free.)*

UPPER EAST SIDE

⬛METROPOLITAN MUSEUM OF ART. Founded in 1870 by a group of distinguished philanthropists and artists, the Met has more than two million works of art spanning over 5000 years. You could camp out here for a month and still not see everything the museum has to offer. Highlights are the fully intact Temple of Dendur, given to the US by Egypt in 1965, and the European paintings collection. The Costume Institute houses over 75,000 costumes and accessories from the 17th century to the present. *(1000 5th Ave., at 82nd St. ☎212-879-5500; www. metmuseum.org. Open Tu-Th and Su 9:30am-5:30pm, F-Sa 9:30am-9pm. Suggested donation $15, students and seniors $10, under 12 free.)*

⬛GUGGENHEIM MUSEUM. The Guggenheim's most famous exhibit is the building itself. Frank Lloyd Wright's inverted white, ridged shell was hailed as a modern masterpiece. Though critics feared that the design would overshadow the art housed within, the collection of modern and postmodern paintings has put those concerns to rest. *(1071 5th Ave., at 89th St. ☎212-423-3500; www.guggenheim.org. Open M-W and Sa-Su 10am-5:45pm, F 10am-8pm. $18, students and seniors $15, under 12 free. F 6-8:30pm "pay what you wish.")*

FRICK COLLECTION. Built in the style of an 18th-century mansion, the magnificent former residence of industrialist Henry Clay Frick was transformed into an art connoisseur's museum in 1935. The collection, two-thirds of which belonged to Frick himself, includes impressive Western masterpieces from the early Renaissance through the late 19th century. Frick's favorite organ music sometimes plays in the relaxing Garden Court. *(1 E. 70th St., at 5th Ave. ☎212-288-0700; www.frick.org. Open Tu-Sa 10am-6pm, Su 11am-5pm. $15, students $5. No children under 10 admitted, under 16 must be accompanied by an adult.)*

MUSEUM OF THE CITY OF NEW YORK. This fascinating museum recounts the history of the Big Apple through a vast, 1,500,000 object collection. Highlights include an extensive photography exhibit documenting New York City's evolution during the first half of the 20th century, a toy gallery, a fascinating theater exhibit, and a collection of 19th-century vehicles used by the police and fire departments. Cultural history of all varieties is on parade; don't miss the model ships, hot pants, and the Yankees' World Series trophies—if you can stomach the sight of them. *(1220 5th Ave., at 103rd St. ☎212-534-1672; www.mcny.org. Open Tu-Su 10am-5pm. Suggested donation $9, students, children and seniors $5, under 12 free.)*

JEWISH MUSEUM. The museum's permanent exhibits span two floors and 4000 years of Jewish art, beginning with ancient biblical artifacts and ceremonial objects and moving to contemporary masterpieces by Marc Chagall, Frank Stella, and George Segal. Culminating in postmodernism, the museum includes a deconstructivist mezuzah and an interactive Talmud exhibit. *(1109 5th Ave., at 92nd St. ☎212-423-3200; www.jewishmuseum.org. Open M-W and Su 11am-5:45pm, Th 11am-9pm, F 11am-5pm. $10, students and seniors $7.50, under 12 free. Th 5-9pm "pay what you wish.")*

WHITNEY MUSEUM OF AMERICAN ART. In 1929, the Metropolitan Museum declined a donation of over 500 works from the Greenwich Village sculptor and collector Gertrude Vanderbilt Whitney, so she founded her own museum instead. This museum, unique in its aim to champion the work of living American artists, has assembled a 12,000-object collection of 20th- and 21st-century American art, the largest in the world. *(945 Madison Ave., at 75th St. ☎212-570-3676; www.whitney.org. Open W-Th and Sa-Su 11am-6pm, F 1-9pm. $15, students and seniors $10, under 12 free. F 6-9pm "pay what you wish.")*

LOWER EAST SIDE

LOWER EAST SIDE TENEMENT MUSEUM. This museum, dedicated to the experience of New York City's immigrants in the early 20th century, offers one of the most personal and fascinating approaches to New York City history around. The museum can only be seen by guided tour, so it's best to reserve ahead. One tour focuses on the lives of two Depression-era families, one German-Jewish, another Sicilian-Catholic. A second tour focuses on the hardships of turn-of-the-century garment workers. A third, focusing on the life of a Sephardic Jewish family, is led by a costumed guide. *(108 Orchard St., between Broome and Delancey St. ☎212-431-0233, tickets 866-811-4111; www.tenement.org. Tours limited to 15. Buy tickets online at least 24hr. in advance. $15, students and seniors $11.)*

MIDTOWN

✦MUSEUM OF MODERN ART (MOMA). In the 1920s, when the conservative Met Museum refused to display modernist work, scholar Alfred Barr responded by holding the first exhibit of what would become the MoMA. As the groundbreaking works of the 20th century have gone from shockers to masterpieces, the contemporary MoMA has shifted from revolution to institution. Still, it's one of the best museums of its kind in the world, with over 100,000 paintings, 2000 videos, and 25,000

photographs. *(11 W. 53rd St. ☎212-708-9400. Open M, W-Th, and Sa-Su 10:30am-5:30pm, F 10:30am-8pm. $20, students $12.)*

MUSEUM OF TELEVISION AND RADIO. More an archive than a museum, this shrine to modern media contains over 200,000 TV and radio programs donated by the major networks. You can watch *I Love Lucy* episodes, listen to the original announcement of the Pearl Harbor attacks, or wonder at the popularity of the *Newlywed Game*. Most shows arrive with their original commercials intact. *(25 W. 52nd St., between 5th and 6th Ave. ☎212-621-6800; www.mtr.org. Open Tu-W and F-Su noon-6pm, Th noon-8pm. $10, students and seniors $8, under 14 $5.)*

BROOKLYN

✦BROOKLYN MUSEUM OF ART (BMA). If it weren't for the Met, the BMA would be NYC's most magnificent museum. Oceanic and New World art collections reside on the first floor; ancient Greek, Roman, Middle Eastern, and Egyptian galleries are on the Third floor. Free tours of the museum are offered most weekends around 1:30pm, but call or check the website for times. *(200 Eastern Pkwy., at Washington Ave. ☎718-638-5000; www.brooklynmuseum.org. Open W-F 10am-5pm, Sa-Su 11am-6pm; 1st Sa of each month 11am-11pm. $8, students and seniors $4, under 12 free. 1st Sa of each month free.)*

NEW YORK TRANSIT MUSEUM. Embrace your inner subway nerd. This museum, housed in the now-defunct Court St. subway station (yes, the entrance is, in fact, a subway stop), details the birth and evolution of New York City's mass-transit system. Exhibits include old subway maps, turnstiles, and restored trains as well as an in-depth look at how the subway was constructed. The museum is also home to one of the best tourist shops in New York City—souvenirs include subway-emblem-emblazoned socks ($6.50), T-shirts ($20), and MetroCard playing cards ($4.50) for all those poker cravings along the road. *(Corner of Schermerhorn St. and Boerum Pl. ☎718-694-1600; www.mta.info/museum. Open Tu-F 10am-4pm, Sa-Su noon-5pm. $5, children and seniors $3. W seniors free.)*

QUEENS

AMERICAN MUSEUM OF THE MOVING IMAGE. This museum, dedicated to the art of film and television production, features fascinating exhibits explaining television and film production, along with cool movie memorabilia. Check out the Yoda puppet from *The Empire Strikes Back*, the chariot from *Ben Hur*, and the jowl-enhancing mouthpiece worn by Marlon Brando in *The Godfather*. *(35th Ave., at 36th St. Walk 1 block down Steinway St. and turn right onto 35th Ave. ☎ 718-784-0077; www. movingimage.us. Open W-Th 11am-5pm, F noon-8pm, Sa-Su 11am-6:30pm. $10, students and seniors $7.50, ages 5-18 $5, under 4 free. F 4-8pm free.)*

ISAMU NOGUCHI GARDEN MUSEUM. The stunning, recently restored home of the Noguchi Museum showcases over 240 works by the celebrated sculptor Isamu Noguchi, whose works probe the relationship between the natural and the manmade. The building, a converted factory, encircles a climate-controlled garden. *(32-37 Vernon Blvd., at 10th St. and 33rd Rd., in Long Island City, Queens. ☎ 718-204-7088; www. noguchi.org. Open W-F 10am-5pm, Sa-Su 11am-6pm. $10, students and seniors $5.)*

⌂ GALLERIES

New York City's galleries provide a riveting—and free—introduction to the contemporary art world. To get started, pick up a free copy of *The Gallery Guide* at any major museum or gallery. Most galleries are open Tuesday through Saturday from 10 or 11am to 5 or 6pm. In the summer, galleries are usually only open on weekend afternoons, and many are closed from late July to early September.

Artists Space, 38 Greene St., 3rd fl. (☎212-226-3970; www.artistsspace.org), at Grand St. Nonprofit gallery founded in 1972. Champions work by emerging and unaffiliated artists as well as work in digital media. The gallery presents works in all media, but the focus is on works in architecture and design. The Irving Sandler Artists File, containing slides and digitized images of works by more than 3000 artists, is open F-Sa to critics, curators, and the public by appointment. Open Sept.-July Tu-Sa 11am-6pm.

The Drawing Center, 35 Wooster St. (☎212-219-2166; www.drawingcenter.org), between Grand and Broome St. Specializing in original works on paper, this nonprofit space sets up high-quality rotating exhibits. Open Sept.-July Tu-F 10am-6pm, Sa 11am-6pm. There is a suggested donation of $3.

525 West 22nd Street, between 10th and 11th Ave. Houses a handful of excellent, petite galleries of contemporary art in 1 space, including the **303 Gallery** (☎212-255-1121; www.303gallery.com). Many galleries cater to art students. Call for hours.

529 West 20th Street, between 10th and 11th Ave. This 11-floor colossus houses over 20 contemporary art galleries, including the **ACA Galleries** (☎212-206-8080; www.acagalleries.com) and the **Dorfman Projects** (☎212-352-2272; www.dorfmanprojects.com). Call for hours.

Leo Castelli, 59 E. 79th St., Apartment 3A (☎212-249-4470; www.castelligallery.com), between Park and Madison Ave. Founded in 1957 by Leo Castelli, a highly influential art dealer known for showcasing the early efforts of Frank Stella and Andy Warhol. A selection of both established and up-and-coming artists. Open from mid-Aug. to late June Tu-Sa 10am-6pm.

🎵 ENTERTAINMENT

Publications with noteworthy entertainment and nightlife sections are the *Village Voice*, *New York* magazine, and the Sunday edition of *The New York Times*. *The New Yorker* has the most comprehensive theater survey.

MUSIC

JAZZ

The **JVC Jazz Festival** comes into the city from June to July. All-star performances from past series have included Elvin Jones, Ray Charles, Tito Puente, and Mel Torme. Tickets go on sale in early May, but many events take place outdoors in the parks and are free. Check the newspaper for listings. An old-school jazz club, the **Village Vanguard,** 178 Seventh Ave., serves its music straight up—no food and no talking during sets. The club is in a windowless, wedge-shaped basement 70 years thick with the memories of John Coltrane, Lenny Bruce, Leadbelly, Miles Davis, and Sonny Rollins. (☎212-255-4037; www.villagevanguard. net. Cover M-Th and Su $20, F-Sa $25. $10 drink min. $10 discount with student ID for M-Th and Su 11pm set. Sets M-Th and Su 9, 11pm, F-Sa 9, 11pm, sometimes 12:30am.) The **Cotton Club**, 656 W. 125th St., on the corner of Riverside Dr., has been around since 1923 and has seen jazz greats like Lena Horne, Ethel Waters, and Cab Calloway. (☎212-663-7980 or 800-640-7980; www.cottonclub-newyork.com. Swing/big band M. Buffet dinner and jazz show Th-Sa evening. M and Th-Sa evening 21+; call for age restrictions at other events. Su brunch and gospel show $30; dinner jazz show $38. Call 2 weeks ahead for reservations.)

ROCK, POP, PUNK, AND FUNK

New York City has a long history of producing bands on the forefront of popular music and performance. **Music festivals** provide the opportunity to see tons of bands at a (relatively) low price. The **CMJ Music Marathon** (☎917-606-1908; www.cmj.com) runs for four nights in the fall and includes over 400 bands and workshops on the alternative music scene. The **Macintosh New York Music Festival** presents over 350 bands over a weeklong period in July.

SOBs (Sounds of Brazil), 204 Varick St., at W. Houston St., is a dinner-dance club that has some of NYC's best live music and hip hop's best talents, including Talib Kweli and the Black Eyed Peas. Monday nights begin with a 1hr. Latin dance class at 7pm ($5); Latin bands play at 9pm. (☎212-243-4940; www. sobs.com. Samba Sa 6:30pm-4am $20. Usually 21+, occasionally 18+. Box office at 200 Varick St. open M-F 11am-6pm, Sa noon-6pm. Open M-Sa 6:30pm.) The **Knitting Factory**, 74 Leonard St., between Broadway and Church St., is a multilevel performance space featuring several shows each night. There are two shows per night—one at the bar, one on the main stage—ranging from avant-garde and indie rock to jazz and hip hop. (☎212-219-3006; www.knittingfactory.com. Cover $5-25. Tickets from $8. Box office open M-Sa 10am-2am, Su 2pm-2am. Bar open 6pm-4am.)

CLASSICAL

Lincoln Center has the greatest selection in its halls. The **Great Performers Series** packs the Avery Fisher and Alice Tully Halls and the Walter Reade Theater from October until May with quality classical music, films, and world premieres. (☎212-875-5456; www.lincolncenter.org. Tickets $20-60.) Avery Fisher Hall presents the annual **Mostly Mozart Festival**, which features Mozart along with some Schubert, Beethoven, and Haydn. Show up early; there are usually recitals 1hr. before the main concert that are free to ticket holders. (☎212-875-5456; www.lincolncenter.org. July-Aug. Tickets $25-70.) The **New York Philharmonic** begins its regular season in mid-September. Students and seniors can sometimes get $10 tickets on the day of performances; call ahead. (☎212-875-5656; www.newyorkphilharmonic. org. Tickets $20-80.) For a few weeks in late June, the philharmonic holds **free concerts** (☎212-875-5709) on the Great Lawn in Central Park, at Prospect Park in Brooklyn, at Van Cortlandt Park in the Bronx, and elsewhere.

Music schools promise low-cost, high-quality music—a gift for the weary budget traveler. Except for opera and ballet productions ($5-12), concerts at the following schools are free and frequent, especially during the school year (Sept.-May). The best options are the **Juilliard School of Music**, Lincoln Center (☎212-769-7406; www.juilliard.edu), the **Mannes College of Music**, 150 W. 85th St. (☎212-580-0210; www.mannes.edu), and the **Manhattan School of Music**, 120 Claremont Ave. (☎212-749-2802; www.msmnyc.edu).

SPORTS

Most cities are content to have one major team in each big-time sport. New York City has two baseball teams, two hockey teams, NBA and WNBA basketball teams, two football teams, and one lonely soccer squad. The beloved **New York Mets** bat at **Citi Field** in Queens. (☎718-507-6387. Tickets $5-70.) The **Yankees** play ball at the new **Yankee Stadium** in the Bronx. (☎718-293-4300. Tickets $12-115.) Both the **Giants** and the **Jets** play football across the river at **Giants Stadium** in East Rutherford, New Jeresey. The **New York/ New Jersey Metrostars** play soccer in the same venue. (☎201-935-3900. Tickets from $25.) The NBA's **Knickerbockers** (that's the Knicks to you), the WNBA's **Liberty,** and the NHL's **Rangers** play at **Madison Square Garden,** the "World's

Most Famous Arena." (☎212-465-5800. Tickets from $22, $8, and $25, respectively.)

THEATER

Broadway tickets are pricey, starting at around $45. **TKTS,** Duffy Sq., at 47th St. and Broadway, sells tickets for many Broadway and some larger off-Broadway shows at a 25-50% discount on the day of the performance. The lines begin to form an hour or so before the booths open, but they move fairly quickly. (☎212-768-1818. Tickets sold M-Sa 3-8pm for 8pm performances, W and Sa 10am-2pm for matinees, Su 11am-7pm for matinees and evening performances.) **Shakespeare in Central Park** (☎212-539-8750; www.publictheater.org) is a New York City summer tradition. From June through August, two plays are presented at the outside Delacorte Theater in Central Park, near the 81st St. entrance on the Upper West Side, just north of the main road. Tickets are free, but lines form extremely early.

OPERA

The **Metropolitan Opera Company's** premier outfit performs on a Lincoln Center stage as big as a football field. You can stand in the orchestra for $16 or all the way back in the Family Circle for $12. (☎212-362-6000; www.metopera. org. Season Sept.-May M-Sa. Upper balcony around $65. Student rush tickets M-Th $25, F-Sa $35. Box office open M-Sa 10am-8pm, Su noon-6pm.) It may not be the juggernaut that the Met is, but the smaller **New York City Opera** has gained a reputation for inventive programming and reasonable prices. (☎212-870-5630; www.nycopera.com. Tickets $12-105. Student rush tickets $10 day of performance. Box office open M 10am-7:30pm, Tu-Sa 10am-8:30pm, Su 11:30am-7:30pm.) **Dicapo Opera Theatre,** 184 E. 76th St., between Third and Lexington Ave., is a small company that garners standing ovations after almost every performance. (☎212-288-9438; www. dicapo.com. Shows Th-Sa 8pm, Su 4pm. Tickets around $40.)

DANCE

The **New York State Theater** in Lincoln Center is home to the late George Balanchine's ▧**New York City Ballet.** Tickets for *The Nutcracker* in December sell out almost immediately.

(☎212-870-5570; www.nycballet.com. Season Nov.-Mar. Tickets from $30. Student rush tickets $12; call ☎212-870-7766.) The **American Ballet Theatre** troupe dances at the Metropolitan Opera House. (☎212-477-3030, box office 362-6000; www.abt.org. Tickets from $25.) **City Center,** 131 W. 55th St. (☎212-581-1212; www. citycenter.org), has the city's best dance, from modern to ballet, including the ▧**Alvin Ailey American Dance Theater** (☎212-767-0590; www.alvinailey.org). **De La Guarda** (think disco in a rainforest) performs at 20 Union Sq. E. (☎212-239-6200. Standing room only. $65; rush tickets $20 2hr. before show. Box office open Tu-Th 1-8:15pm, F 1-10:30pm, Sa 1-10pm, Su 1-7:15pm.) Other dance venues include **Dance Theater Workshop,** 219 W. 19th St. (☎212-924-0077; www.dtw.org), between Seventh and Eighth Ave.; **Joyce Theater,** 175 Eighthth Ave. (☎212-242-0800; www. joyce.org), between 18th and 19th St., and **Thalia Spanish Theatre,** 4117 Greenpoint Ave. (☎718-729-3880), in Queens.

▧ NIGHTLIFE

Whether you prefer a Chelsea nightclub or a Harlem jazz club, a smoky Brooklyn bar or a Lower East Side be-seen-ery, New York City has it all. Try the *Village Voice, New York* magazine, The *New York Press,* and *The New York Times* (particularly the Sunday edition) for daily, weekly, and monthly nightlife calendars. Gay nightlife in New York City is centered in Chelsea, especially along Eighth Ave. in the 20s, and in Greenwich Village.

LOWER EAST SIDE

▧ **The Back Room,** 102 Norfolk St. (☎212-228-5098), between Rivington and Delancey St. Housed in an ordinary-looking apartment building, this faithful rendition of a Prohibition-era speakeasy even recreates their secretive nature. Go through the iron gate by the "Lower East Side Toy Company" sign. Head to the back of the courtyard and go up the stairs to your right. You'll find yourself in a classy parlor-like space, where 20- and 30-somethings drink hard-liquor concoctions out of teacups and beer from bottles wrapped in paper bags. A sliding bookcase gives way to a "secret" 2nd bar. A fireplace blazes in the winter. Large groups, especially of men, could have trouble at the door. Some patrons under 25 report being turned away at the door as well. Beer $6-8. Wine $8. Open Tu-Sa 7:30pm-2am.

Happy Ending, 302 Broome St. (☎212-334-9676; www.happyendinglounge.com), between Eldridge and Forsyth St. This bar and club was converted from a massage parlor (yes, that kind). Mirrors etched with naked women remain, and the saunas have become semi-private booths, their waist-high shower heads left intact. There's a DJ every night downstairs. The canopy outside still reads "Xie He Health Club"; you're in the right place. Beer $3-6. Mixed drinks $7-10. Specialty drinks $12. Popular W 8pm reading series; the 3rd W of each month is erotica-themed. Every other Th 10pm "Something Tight" gay dance party. Open Tu-Sa 10pm-4am, Su 7pm-4am.

SOHO AND TRIBECA

☒ **Lucky Strike,** 59 Grand St. (☎212-941-0772), at W. Broadway. France meets the Wild West at this stylishly worn hangout that is part bistro, part saloon. At meal times, it serves tasty and unpretentious food (most entrees $12-18), and it's a great place for a late-night drink. Wine and mixed drinks from $7. Open M-W and Su noon-1am, Th noon-2am, F-Sa noon-2:30am.

☒ **Grand Bar and Lounge,** 310 W. Broadway (☎212-963-3588), 2nd fl. of the SoHo Grand Hotel. If you want a full dose of downtown cool in 1 location, pony up some cash for a drink at this über-hip hotel bar. The mixed drinks ($14) are outstanding; try the Honeysuckle (Cruzan rum and maraschino liqueur), Perfect 10 (Stoli vanilla, pineapple, lemon, and lime), or the signature drink, the Grand Kir (champagne, ginger syrup, and cream). Open M-W and Su 6pm-1am, Th-Sa 6pm-3am.

GREENWICH VILLAGE

☒ **Employees Only,** 510 Hudson St. (☎212-242-3021; www.employeesonlynyc.com), between W. 10th and Christopher St. In this classy bar with a 20s feel, skilled bartenders in chef's uniforms mix up some of the best vintage mixed drinks in the city. Try the Mata Hari (Courvoisier with chai-infused vermouth and fresh-squeezed pomegranate; $13). The name derives from the establishment's goal of mixing drinks so good

that other bars' employees come here for their own libations. There's no sign other than the neon "Psychic" in the window; one is often on hand. Enclosed garden open year-round. Open daily 6pm-4am. Kitchen open until at 3am.

Henrietta Hudson, 438 Hudson St. (☎212-924-3347; www.henriettahudsons.com), between Morton and Barrow St. A young, primarily lesbian crowd, along with an assortment of gay and straight males, frequents this friendly Greenwich Village institution. Cover F-Sa $10. Open M-F 4pm-4am, Sa 1pm-4am, Su 3pm-4am.

MEATPACKING DISTRICT

☒ **Flatiron Lounge,** 37 W. 19th St. (☎212-727-7741; www.flatironlounge.com), between 5th Ave. and Ave. of the Americas (6th Ave.). Candlelight and tinkling jazz provide respite from the neighborhood's frenetic nightlife. The 30 ft. mahogany bar was salvaged from The Ballroom, which hosted the likes of Frank Sinatra. Today, it provides the setting for a 30s-inflected menu of classic mixed drinks. Try the NY Sour (rye whiskey, fresh lemon juice, a dash of orange, and a float of dry red wine; $12). Open M-W and Su 5pm-2am, Th-Sa 5pm-4am. AmEx/MC/V.

Cielo, 18 Little W. 12th St. (☎212-645-5700), between Washington and Greenwich St. A proudly exclusive and surprisingly intimate dance club centered on a sunken dance floor. DJs spin electronica, Nu-jazz, future soul, and deep house every night. The clientele is stylish and the door is tightly guarded; plan your outfit well. Cover $10-20. Open W-Sa 10pm-4am. MC/V.

EAST VILLAGE

☒ **Angel's Share,** 8 Stuyvesant St., between 9th St. and St. Mark's Pl. Hidden behind an unmarked door in the back of a bustling Korean restaurant, this secluded nightspot with soft jazz is a great choice for a romantic night out. To ensure the genuinely serene atmosphere, the house rules here are strictly enforced: no parties larger than 4, no shouting, and no standing. This nirvana is complemented by a heavenly menu of mixed drinks. Try the Lady in Satin (sake, violet liqueur, and vodka; $10) or the Sophisticated Lady (plum wine, Campari, and grapefruit juice; $10). Excellent selection of whiskeys and brandies. 1-drink min. Mixed drinks $8-12. Open 6pm-2:30am.

d.b.a., 41 1st Ave. (☎212-475-5097; www.drink-goodstuff.com), between E. 2nd and 3rd St. A sophisticated choice by the standards of even the most demanding alcohol connoisseur, this bar has 19 always-changing premium beers on tap, well over 100 bottled imports and microbrews, 50 kinds of bourbon, 130 single-malt whiskeys, and 45 different tequilas. To accompany your drink, classic rock, grunge, and 90s tunes play unobtrusively, and conversations fill the air. Outdoor beer garden open until 10pm; space heaters keep it toasty even on cold winter nights. Happy hour 1-7:30pm; $1 off drinks. Open daily 1pm-4am.

CHELSEA

Splash Bar New York, 50 W. 17th St. (☎212-691-0073; www.splashbar.com), between 5th and 6th Ave. One of the most popular gay mega-bars. The main floor is devoted to dancing and drinking, while the basement lounge provides a place to rest. Both floors drip with neon lights and industrial-chic decor. Nightly theme parties: Th is college night. Cover after 11pm M-W $5, Th $10, F $20; often increases after midnight. Happy hour M-Sa 4-9pm; 2-for-1 beer and mixed drinks. Open M-Th and Su 4pm-4am, F-Sa 4pm-5am.

g, 223 W. 19th St. (☎212-929-1085; www.glounge.com), between 7th and 8th Ave. A lounge that is comfortable enough for actual lounging. Set in an unadorned brick building, g offers plenty of couches as well as a more lively bar area. Draws a diverse crowd of gay men; on Su nights the scene is younger. Happy hour M-F 4-9pm. Open daily 4pm-4am. Cash only.

UPPER EAST SIDE

Metropolitan Museum Roof Garden, 1000 5th Ave. (☎212-535-7710). On the 5th fl. of the Met, this lovely patio bar (open only in summer) affords spectacular views of Central Park and the Manhattan skyline. It's an ideal place to start the evening with a glass of wine ($9), a beer ($7), or a martini ($10). Enter at the main entrance and take the elevator from the 1st fl. Open May-Oct., weather permitting, Tu-Th 10am-4:30pm, F-Sa 10am-8:15pm, Su 10am-4:30pm.

The Stumble Inn, 1454 2nd Ave. (☎212-650-0561), at 76th St. Stumble in to this bar on any day of the week, and you'll find amazing drink specials and an after-work crowd looking

to blow off steam with foosball and beer pong. Daily happy hour 11:30am-7pm, ½-off entire bar. Open daily 11:30-4am.

UPPER WEST SIDE

Dive 75, 101 W. 75th St. (☎212-362-7518; www.divebarnyc.com), between Columbus and Amsterdam Ave. This cozy bar offers all the joys of your favorite dive without the unusable bathroom. Locals lounge on comfy couches watching TV, enjoying the pop-rock jukebox, eating from the bowl of candy on every table, and pondering the eerily glowing fish tank. A stack of board games sits in the corner, and people take games like Scrabble seriously. Happy hour 5-7pm; Bud $2.50, $1 off mixed drinks. Open M-Th 5pm-4am, F 2:30pm-4am, Sa-Su noon-4am.

Shalel Lounge, 65 W. 70th St. (☎212-873-2300), between Central Park W. and Columbus Ave. This subterranean jewel, beneath eatery Metsovo, oozes romance. Bead-draped nooks, lightly tinkling waterfalls, dim votive lighting, and a chic international crowd create a definite mystique. Wine $9. Martinis $12. On weekends, a Moroccan band plays softly in the background. Open M-Th and Su 6pm-2am, F-Sa 6pm-3am.

BROOKLYN

Pete's Candy Store, 709 Lorimer St. (☎718-302-3770; www.petescandystore.com), between Frost and Richardson St. This soda shop turned bar hosts live music every night at 9pm and a quirky assortment of activities beforehand. M 7:30pm alternates between spelling bees and stand-up comedy. Bingo night Tu 7:30-9pm. Every other Th 7:30pm prose and poetry readings. Jay Bakker, Tammy Faye's son, preaches to the tattooed and pierced masses during the Revolution Church service at 4pm Su; also Su in summer 5-9pm barbecue in the backyard. Happy hour 5-7pm; $2 Yuengling, $3 Brooklyn, $3 well drinks. Open M-Tu and Su 5pm-2am, W-Sa 5pm-4am.

Union Pool, 484 Union Ave. (☎718-609-0484; www.myspace.com/unionpool), off Skillman Ave. Converted from an old swimming pool supply depot, this bar hosts a variety of whimsical events, from circus performances to film festivals. Barbecues are frequent in the recently renovated backyard. Live DJ or music nearly every night, usually at 9pm; cover $5-10. Beer $3-8. Mixed drinks from $5. Happy hour daily 5-8pm; Bud with a shot of Jim Beam $6. Open 5pm-4am.

⚑ THE ROAD TO NEW HAVEN: 80 MI.
To leave **New York City**, get on **I-95 North**. Take **Exit 47** to get on **Route 34 West** and head into downtown.

NEW HAVEN   ☎ 203

Despite a bad reputation that has proven hard to shake, New Haven is growing from the inside out. The center of the city is home to the solid stone foundations of Yale University, a shining academic light that continues to expand into the dangerous areas of the city. Today, the "new" New Haven, especially the area immediately around Yale's campus, sustains a healthy assortment of ethnic restaurants, art galleries, pizza joints, and coffee shops filled with both students and townies.

VITAL STATS
Population: 124,000
Tourist Offices: Greater New Haven Convention and Visitors Bureau, 169 Orange St. (☎203-777-8580; www.newhavencvb.org). Open M-F 8:30am-5pm. **Info New Haven,** 1000 Chapel St. (☎203-773-9494; www.infonewhaven.com). Open M-Th 10am-9pm, F-Sa 10am-10pm, Su noon-5pm.
Library and Internet Access: New Haven Public Library, 133 Elm St. (☎203-946-8130). Open from June to mid-Sept. M noon-8pm, Tu-W 10am-6pm, Th 10am-8pm, F noon-5pm; from mid-Sept. to May M noon-8pm, Tu-W 10am-6pm, Th 10am-8pm, Sa 10am-5pm.
Post Office: 50 Brewery St. (☎203-782-7104). Open M-F 8am-6pm, Sa 8am-1pm. **Postal Code:** 06510.

⚑ ORIENTATION

New Haven lies at the intersection of **I-95** and **I-91** and is laid out in nine squares. The main northwest-southeast routes, **Chapel Street** and **Elm Street,** run one-way in opposite directions

along the Yale campus and border New Haven Green. Cross streets **College** and **Temple Streets** frame the green's other edges and are bordered by restaurants and bars. At night, don't wander too far from the downtown and campus areas; surrounding neighborhoods, especially south of the green, can be unsafe.

⚑ ACCOMMODATIONS

Inexpensive lodgings are sparse in New Haven, especially around Yale Parents' Weekend (mid-Oct.) and commencement (early June). For a variety of budget-friendly options, head 10 mi. south on I-95 to Milford.

⚐ **Hotel Duncan,** 1151 Chapel St. (☎203-787-1273), in the heart of the Yale campus. This century-old building has the most affordable rates in the downtown area. Guests enjoy spacious rooms and ride in the oldest manually operated elevator in the state. Reservations recommended. Singles $50; doubles $90. AmEx/D/MC/V. ❸

Mayflower Motel, 219 Woodmont Rd. (☎203-878-6854 or 888-800-6854; www.milford-motel.com), just off the highway at Exit 40. Offers very large rooms with HBO and access to a laundromat. Free Wi-Fi. Key deposit $4. Singles $57; doubles $67. AmEx/D/MC/V. ❸

⚑ FOOD

New Haven supports an enviable variety of cheap, high-quality cafes, including several all-vegetarian eateries. For authentic Italian cuisine, work your way along Wooster St. in Little Italy, 10min. east of downtown off Chapel St. Indian restaurants dominate the neighborhood southwest of downtown.

⚐ **Frank Pepe's Pizzeria Napoletana,** 157 Wooster St. (☎203-865-5762). Claims to be the inventor of the American pizza, originally known as "tomato pie" (large $13.60). If you're really starving, try the "Special" with mozzarella, sausage, pepper, onion, salami, bacon, mushroom and pepperoni (large $21.40). Be prepared to wait for a table. Open M-Th and Su 11:30am-10pm, F-Sa 11:30am-10:30pm. AmEx/D/MC/V. ❸

Tandoor, 1226 Chapel St. (☎203-776-6620). Though from outside it looks more like a 50s diner than anything else, this authentic eatery serves up some delicious Indian fare. Try the perfect *keema naan,* stuffed with ground lamb and spices ($4.25), or one of the cheap, delicious lunch specials (11:30am-3pm). Those unfamiliar with Indian cuisine or just really hungry may prefer to try the enormous Tandoori Dinner, which includes soup, appetizer, dessert, and 3 mini entrees for $20. Open daily 11:30am-10:30pm. AmEx/D/MC/V. ❶

Libby's Italian Pastries, 139 Wooster St. (☎203-772-0380). Serves 10 types of cannoli and 8 flavors of delicious gelato ($2.25). Open M and Su 11:30am-9pm, W-Th 11:30am-10pm, F-Sa 11:30am-11pm. Cash only. ❶

⬛ SIGHTS

The majority of the sights and museums in New Haven are located on or near the **Yale University** campus. Most of the campus buildings were designed in the English Gothic or Georgian Colonial styles, many of them with intricate moldings and a few with ⬛**gargoyles.** Bordered by **Chapel, College, Grove,** and **High Streets,** the charming **Old Campus** contains **Connecticut Hall,** which is the university's oldest remaining building. The **Yale Visitors Center,** 149 Elm St., faces the New Haven Green and is the starting point for campus tours. (☎203-432-2300; www.yale.edu. Open M-F 9am-4:30pm, Sa-Su 11am-4pm. 1hr. tours M-F 10:30am, 2pm, Sa-Su 1:30pm. Free.)

⬛YALE UNIVERSITY ART GALLERY. The Yale gallery holds over 100,000 pieces from around the world, including works by Monet, Van Gogh, Matisse, and Picasso. The sheer density of stunning artwork will have you seeing starry nights. *(1111 Chapel St., at York St. ☎203-432-0600; www.artgallery.yale.edu. Open Tu-W and F-Sa 10am-5pm, Th 10am-8pm, Su 1-6pm. Free.)*

PEABODY MUSEUM OF NATURAL HISTORY. The Peabody Museum houses Rudolph F. Zallinger's Pulitzer Prize-winning mural depicting the "Age of Reptiles" in a room containing dinosaur skeletons. Be sure to check out the prehistoric skulls and Egyptian mummy. The Discovery Room is fantastic for children. *(170 Whitney Ave., at Exit 3 off I-91. ☎203-432-5050; www.peabody.yale.edu. Open M-Sa 10am-5pm, Su noon-5pm. $7, students and ages 3-18 $5. Highlight tours Sa-Su 12:30, 1:30pm. Free.)*

YALE CENTER FOR BRITISH ART. The Center for British Art is housed in the last building designed by architect Louis I. Kahn. The museum contains 2000 paintings, the most complete collection of British art outside the UK. *(1080 Chapel St. ☎203-432-2800; www.yale.edu/ycba. Open Tu-Sa 10am-5pm, Su noon-5pm. Free.)*

STERLING MEMORIAL LIBRARY. Sterling Memorial Library is designed to resemble a monastery—even the telephone booths are shaped like confessionals. The design is not without a sense of humor, though—the Cloister Hall has carved stone corbels portraying students sleeping, lounging, and smoking. *(120 High St., 1 block north of the Yale Visitors Center. ☎203-432-1818. Open daily 8:30am-5pm.)*

BEINECKE RARE BOOK AND MANUSCRIPT LIBRARY. Paneled with 900 lb. sheets of Vermont marble cut thin enough to be translucent, the Beinecke Rare Book and Manuscript Library is a massive modern structure containing 600,000 rare books and manuscripts. The building protects one of the five Gutenberg Bibles in the US as well as an extensive collection of John James Audubon's prints. *(121 Wall St. ☎203-436-1254. Open M-Th 8:30am-8pm, F 8:30am-5pm, Sa 10am-5pm. Free.)*

⬛ NIGHTLIFE

The **Yale Repertory Theatre,** 1120 Chapel St., hosts productions with professionals and students at the Yale School of Drama. (☎203-432-1234; www.yalerep.org.) The **New Haven Symphony Orchestra,** 247 College St., performs at the **Shubert Theater** year-round. (☎203-562-5666; www.shubert.com. Tickets $25-50. Box office open M-F 9:30am-5:30pm, Sa 10am-2pm.)

⬛ **Toad's Place,** 300 York St. (☎203-562-5589; www.toadsplace.com). Has hosted the likes of Bob Dylan, the Rolling Stones, and George Clinton. Toad's also features huge dance parties Sa nights during the school year. Cover $5-35 for shows, $10 for dance nights; discount with college ID. Open on show nights around 7pm-2am. Open on dance nights from 9:30pm. Box office open M-F 11am-6pm. AmEx/D/MC/V.

Bar, 254 Crown St. (☎203-495-1111; www.bar-nightclub.com). A hip, industrial-looking hangout with a pool table, lounge room, dance floor/theater, 5 homemade beers ($5) at the bar, and brick-oven pizza. Party every Tu night attracts a large gay crowd. College night Th with $1 drafts. Live indie rock Su. Cover Tu $5, F-Sa $6. Open M-Tu and Su 4pm-1am, W-Th 11:30am-2:30am, F 11:30am-2am, Sa 4pm-2am. AmEx/D/MC/V.

Alchemy, 223 College St. (☎203-777-9400; www.alchemynightclub.com). 3 levels of dancing, including 1 dance floor with a 30 ft. wide waterfall. Live music W. Th-Sa 9-11:30pm penny wells. Cover W $12 for open bar upstairs. Open M-Th 9pm-1am, F-Sa 9pm-2am. AmEx/D/MC/V.

Playwright, 144 Temple St. (☎203-752-0450; www.playwrightirishpub.com). Looks more Su morning than Sa night—the facade and interior were cobbled together from parts of abandoned Irish and British churches, and it caters to an older crowd. Live music F 5-7pm during happy hour, with ½-price drinks. $0.25 wings Th. DJ F-Sa. Open M-Th and Su noon-1am, F-Sa noon-2am. AmEx/D/MC/V.

◤ THE ROAD TO OLD SAYBROOK: 33 MI.

Continue on **US 1 North.**

OLD SAYBROOK ☎401

The small town of Old Saybrook has an amazing array of historic homes. The quaint downtown doesn't cater to tourists, but there are a variety of excellent places to eat, and the local attractions make it a pleasant stroll. Staying in Old Saybrook is expensive, and cheaper rooms can be found elsewhere. Most attractions in Old Saybrook celebrate the town's rich history. Don't miss the ◪**Florence Griswold Museum,** 96 Lyme St., in nearby Old Lyme. In the late 19th century, Florence Griswold opened her home to boarders, including artist Harry Ward Ranger, who founded an art colony there. Over 200 artists, mostly Impressionists, eventually came and painted at the estate, inspired by their surroundings. Today, visitors can see both the grounds and much of the art that was created on-site, including several paintings on the home's doors. (☎860-434-5542; www.flogris.org. Open Tu-Sa 10am-5pm, Su 1-5pm. $8, students and seniors $7, ages 6-12 $4.)

In downtown Old Saybrook, ◪**Caffe Toscana ❷,** 25 Main St., serves fantastic mozzarella sandwiches ($7) on the sunny outside porch. Patrons can also take advantage of the

pile of newspapers. (☎860-388-1270. Open M-F 7am-4pm, Sa 8am-4pm, Su 8am-noon. Cash only.) **Savory ❷,** 254 Main St., serves a rotating selection of gourmet choices, like the onion and chevre tart ($4), in a crisp, modern storefront. Side dishes and entrees are sold by weight, while sandwiches, like the mango shrimp wrap ($9), are individually priced. (☎860-395-0755. Open daily 10am-6pm. AmEx/D/MC/V.)

◤ THE ROAD TO MYSTIC: 27 MI.

From Old Saybrook, take **US 1 North** into town, where it becomes **Main Street.**

MYSTIC ☎860

When Herman Melville's white whale, Moby Dick, became a legend, Connecticut's coastal towns were busy seaports full of dark, musty inns and tattooed sailors. Today, there's nothing mystical about this bright town overlooking the water. With history, a cute downtown, and natural beauty, Mystic has something for everyone—even Julia Roberts fans.

VITAL STATS
Population: 4000
Tourist Office: Mystic Tourist and Information Center (☎860-536-1641; www.visitmystic.com), Bldg. 1D in Old Mystick Village, off Rte. 27. Open from mid-June to Sept. M-Sa 9:30am-5:30pm, Su 10am-5pm; from Oct. to early June M-Sa 9:30am-5pm, Su 10am-4pm.
Library and Internet Access: Mystic & Noank Library, 40 Library St. (☎860-536-7721; www.mysticnoanklibrary.com). $0.25 per 15min. Open from mid-June to early Sept. M-W 10am-9pm, Th-Sa 10am-5pm; from late Sept. to early June M-W 10am-9pm, Th-F 10am-5pm, Sa 9am-1pm.
Post Office: 23 E. Main St. (☎860-536-8143). Open M-F 8:30am-5pm, Sa 8:30am-12:30pm. **Postal Code:** 06355.

◢ ORIENTATION

Downtown Mystic lies along **US 1,** which becomes **Main Street** between **Greenmanville Avenue (Route 27)** to the east and the **Mystic River** to the west. **Route 184** runs north-south to Groton. Most attractions lie along Rte. 27 south of **I-95,** which roughly parallels US 1.

ACCOMMODATIONS

It's almost impossible to find budget-friendly lodgings in Mystic.

Windsor Motel, 345 Gold Star Hwy./Rte. 184 (☎860-445-7474), 6 mi. out of town in Groton. Large rooms with standard amenities. Singles M-Th and Su $45, F-Sa $60-65; doubles $50/70. AmEx/D/MC/V. ❸

Seaport Campground (☎860-536-4044; www. seaportcampground.com). Take Rte. 27 west 3 mi. to Rte. 184. Has a pool, minigolf course, fishing pond, and laundromat. Free Wi-Fi. Open from mid-Apr. to mid-Nov. Sites with water and electricity $41, on holiday weekend $48; with full hookup $45/53. D/MC/V. ❷

FOOD

Rice Spice Noodles, 4 Roosevelt Ave. (☎860-572-8488; www.ricespicenoodles.com), on US 1 just north of Main St. Serves Thai favorites with a twist, like wonton pad thai ($12) and curry puffs ($7). Open M-F 11:30am-2:45pm and 5-9:30pm, Sa 11:30am-10pm, Su 11:30am-9:30pm. AmEx/D/MC/V. ❷

Bartleby's, 46 W. Main St. (☎860-245-0017). Delicious sandwiches along with a wide array of coffees and teas. Give the veggie burger ($5.50) a try. The tables double as chessboards. Open M-Sa 7am-8:30, Su 7am-9pm. MC/V. ❶

Cove Fish Market (☎860-536-0061; www. covefish.com), in a shack on Old Stonington Rd., 1 mi. east of downtown. Excellent seafood. They serve more than 200 gal. of their amazing clam chowder a week; don't leave without trying a cup. Open M-Th and Su 11am-8pm, F-Sa 11am-9pm. Fish market open daily 10am-6:30pm. MC/V. ❷

SIGHTS

MYSTIC SEAPORT. The port offers a depiction of 19th-century whaling culture and industry. In 17 acres of recreated village, visitors explore old drugstores, schoolhouses, original whaling ships, and a functioning shipyard. Interactive exhibits let the curious learn to tie knots and play with period toys. *(Located along the Mystic River off Rte. 27. ☎860-973-2767; www.mys-*

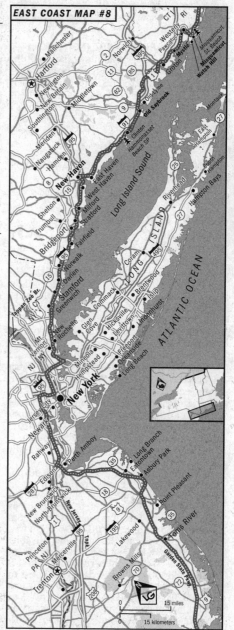

EAST COAST MAP #8

EAST COAST

ticseaport.org. Open daily Apr.-Oct. 9am-5pm; Nov.-Mar. 10am-4pm. $18.50, students and seniors $16.50, ages 6-12 $13.)

MYSTIC AQUARIUM AND INSTITUTE FOR EXPLORATION. The exhibits take visitors underwater through video feeds from marine sanctuaries around the US. The aquarium features an impressive collection of seals, penguins, sharks, and beluga whales. (55 Coogan Blvd., north of Rte. 27 off US 1. ☎ 860-572-5955; www. mysticaquarium.org. Open daily 9am-6pm. Tickets sold until 5pm. $23, ages 3-17 $17, seniors $20.)

⌁ THE ROAD TO MISQUAMICUT AND WATCH HILL: 17 MI.
From Mystic, take **US 1 North** to Misquamicut.

MISQUAMICUT AND WATCH HILL   ☎ 401

The town of Westerly is split into several fire districts, two of which are Misquamicut and Watch Hill. The towns are connected to US 1 by US 1A, which loops toward them. While Misquamicut is a fun, crowded beach town, Watch Hill caters to more affluent tourists. Far west on the Rhode Island coast lies **Misquamicut State Beach,** a half-mile stretch of crowded sand. (☎401-596-9097. Lifeguards on duty 9am-6pm. Park open 9am-sunset. Parking $6.) Farther down the coast, **Watch Hill Beach** is a favorite with locals. (Open M-F 10am-7pm, Sa-Su 9am-6pm. $6, ages 13-17 $4, under 13 $1. Parking $10. Umbrella rentals $5.) Watch Hill is also home to many beautiful old houses and the **Flying Horse Carousel,** the country's oldest merry-go-round. (Open M-F 11am-9pm, Sa-Su 10am-9pm. Ages 2-12 only. Outside horse $1.50, inside horse $1.)

Accommodations are cheaper in Misquamicut than in Watch Hill and cheaper still as you move away from the beach. Just down the road from Misquamicut Beach, the **Tradewinds Motel ❹,** 4 Rabbit Run, has rooms with air-conditioning and fridges. (☎401-596-5557; www. tradewindsmotel.com. Rooms from late June to Sept. M-Th and Su $90, F-Sa $105; from Sept. to late June $60/70. AmEx/D/MC/V.) Take US 1 a few miles north to Charlestown, home to **Burlingame State Camp Ground ❶,** 1 Burlingame Park Rd. The park has 750 sites as well as bathroom facilities, a playground, swimming in Watchaug Pond, and hiking trails. (☎401-

322-7994 or 322-7337. Reservations at www. rhodeislandstateparks.reserveamerica.com. Open from mid-Apr. to Oct. Sites $20. Cabins $35.) Hungry beachgoers get off the sand to get down at **Paddy's ❷,** 159 Atlantic Ave. Sandy patrons chow on Kahuna burgers ($11) during the day, then dance to live bands every weekend evening. They have free Wi-Fi, but you won't want to work or study with the ocean breeze distracting you. (☎401-596-2610; www. paddysbeach.com. Open daily 11am-1am. Live music starts at 10pm. MC/V.) **The Bay Street Deli ❷,** 112 Bay St., has creatively christened sandwiches like the Carousel (turkey, cheese, sprouts; $9). Just don't eat it right before riding its namesake. (☎401-596-6606. Open daily 8am-8pm. MC/V.)

⌁ THE ROAD TO PROVIDENCE: 47 MI.
From Watch Hill, take **US 1 North** to **Route 108 South** to visit the **Point Judith Lighthouse,** on Point Judith Rd. Visitors can explore the small park surrounding the lighthouse, but the building itself belongs to the Coast Guard and is off-limits. (☎401-789-0444. Free.) Take US 1 N. until it becomes **Broad Street** in Providence.

PROVIDENCE   ☎ 401

Providence manages to blend its colorful history as the birthplace of the American Industrial Revolution with its current status as home to two world-class universities. The cobblestone streets are crowded with cheap, funky places to eat, and the young, artsy inhabitants support a multitude of performance spaces. When the bonfires of WaterFire are aflame, it feels like the best place on earth—or at least on the East Coast—to hang your hat.

◼ ORIENTATION

I-95 and the **Providence River** run north-south and split Providence into three sections. West of I-95 is **Federal Hill,** between I-95 and the Providence River is **Down City,** and east of Providence is **College Hill,** home to **Brown University** and the **Rhode Island School of Design (RISD).** I-195 cuts across

Providence, running east-west, and connects it to Seekonk, Massachusetts. A jaunt down **Benefit Street** in College Hill reveals notable historic sights and art galleries, and **Westminster Street** provides a pleasant array of unique shops.

VITAL STATS

Population: 174,000

Tourist Offices: Providence/Warwick Convention and Visitors Bureau, 1 Sabin St. (☎800-233-1636; www.goprovidence.com). Open M-Sa 9am-5pm. **Roger Williams National Memorial Information Center,** 282 N. Main St. (☎401-521-7266). Open daily 9am-4:30pm.

Library and Internet Access: Providence Public Library, 225 Washington St. (☎401-455-8000). Open M and Th noon-8pm, Tu-W 10am-6pm, F-Sa 9am-5:30pm.

Post Office: 2 Exchange Terr. (☎401-421-5214). Open M-F 8am-5pm, Sa 8am-2pm. **Postal Code:** 02903.

TRANSPORTATION

Providence Link, run by the Rhode Island Public Transit Authority (RIPTA), has trolleys ($1.75; $5 per day) that run through the city with stops at major sights. (www.ripta.com. M-F 6:30am-9pm, Sa 8am-6:30pm, Su 11am-6:30pm. Trolleys every 20 min.) If you have the stamina to go up and down the city's hills, walking is really the best way to see the city during daylight hours.

ACCOMMODATIONS

Steep downtown motel rates make Providence an expensive place to stay. Rooms fill up far in advance for graduation in May and early June. Head 10 mi. south on I-95 to Warwick or Cranston or to Seekonk, Massachusetts on US 6 for cheaper motels.

■ **International House of Rhode Island,** 8 Stimson Ave. (☎401-421-7181; www.members.cox.net/internationalhouse), off Hope St. near the Brown campus. Catering largely to international visitors, this house has 6 unique rooms and stained-glass windows. Fridge, bath, and TV in each room. Shared kitchen and laundry. Free Wi-Fi. Reception June-July M-F 9am-4pm; Aug.-May M-F 9am-5pm. Reservations required. Singles $75, students $60; doubles $90/75. ❸

Motel 6, 821 Fall River Ave. (☎508-336-7800; www.motel6.com), on Rte. 144A, just off I-195. 10min. from downtown Providence. Clean rooms with TVs and tables. Laundry facilities. Wi-Fi $3 per 24hr. Rooms M-Th and Su $50, F-Sa $60. AmEx/D/MC/V. ❸

Colwell's Campground, 119 Peckham Ln. (☎401-397-4614), in Coventry. From Providence, take I-95 S. to Exit 10, then head west 8 mi. on Rte. 117 to Peckham Ln. A perfect place to swim. Hookups for sites along a lake. Showers. Sites $20-22. Cash only. ❶

FOOD

Providence has a wide variety of delicious, inexpensive culinary options for the budget traveler. Atwells Ave., on Federal Hill just west of downtown, has a distinctly Italian flavor. Thayer St., on College Hill to the east, is home to offbeat student hangouts and ethnic restaurants. Wickenden St., in the southeast corner of town, also has a diverse selection of inexpensive eateries.

■ **Spike's Junkyard Dogs,** 273 Thayer St. (☎401-454-1459). Frequented by Brown students, Spike's serves pizza and subs along with their hot dog specialties like the Pizza Dog (pizza sauce, mozzarella, and Italian spices; $3) and the German Shepherd (sauerkraut and mustard; $2.60). Open M-W and Su 11am-midnight, Th-Sa 11am-2am. AmEx/D/MC/V. ❶

Geoff's Superlative Sandwiches, 163 Benefit St. (☎401-751-2248), in College Hill. Attracts a mixed crowd with about 85 creatively named sandwiches, like the Dead Head (provolone and veggies; $5.50) and the Kevorkian (pastrami, bacon, cheddar, hot sauce; $7). Grab a green treat (or 2) from the huge pickle barrel to complement your meal. Open M-F 8am-9pm, Sa-Su 9:30am-9pm. AmEx/D/MC/V. ❶

Roma Gourmet, 310 Atwells Ave. (☎401-331-8620). Gourmet grocery serves delicious subs (prosciutto and mozzarella; $8.50), but its specialty are pastas sold by the pound (lasagna $7). Open M-Th 8:30am-6pm, F-Sa 8am-7pm, Su 8:30am-5pm. AmEx/MC/V. ❷

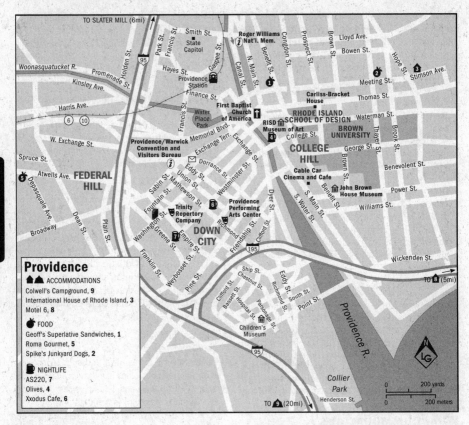

Providence

🏠🏔 ACCOMMODATIONS
Colwell's Campground, **9**
International House of Rhode Island, **3**
Motel 6, **8**

🍎 FOOD
Geoff's Superlative Sandwiches, **1**
Roma Gourmet, **5**
Spike's Junkyard Dogs, **2**

🌃 NIGHTLIFE
AS220, **7**
Olives, **4**
Xxodus Cafe, **6**

👁 SIGHTS

RISD MUSEUM OF ART. The world-renowned Rhode Island School of Design (RISD) occasionally shows the work of its students and professors at the RISD Museum of Art. The museum's three-floor maze of galleries also exhibits Egyptian, Indian, Impressionist, medieval, and Roman artwork as well as a gigantic 12th-century Japanese Buddha. (*224 Benefit St. ☎401-454-6500; www.risd.edu/museum.cfm. Open Tu-Su 10am-5pm. $8, students and ages 5-18 $3, seniors $5. Su 10am-1pm and 3rd Th of each month free.*)

BROWN UNIVERSITY. Established in 1764, Brown boasts several 18th-century buildings, including the Carliss-Brackett House, now the Admission Office. (*45 Prospect St. ☎401-863-2378; www.brown.edu/admission. Open M-F 8am-4pm. 1hr. walking tours M-F 9am-3pm. Free.*)

RHODE ISLAND STATE CAPITOL HOUSE. The stunning marble dome of the Rhode Island State Capitol is visible from nearly every vantage point in the city. Visitors can take free 50min. tours; book at least two weeks in advance and get there early to get through security. (*☎401-222-3983; www.state.ri.us. Open M-F 8:30am-4:30pm. Tours every hr. M-F 9am-1pm. Free.*)

SLATER MILL. The factory that started the American Industrial Revolution is preserved in Pawtucket at the Slater Mill Historic Site. Situated by the rushing Blackstone River, the site has a large water wheel and working water-powered machinery from the early 19th century. *(67 Roosevelt Ave., in Pawtucket, north of the city on I-95. ☎401-725-8638; www.slatermill.org. Open July-Sept. Tu-Su 10am-5pm; Oct.-Nov. Tu-Su 11am-3pm; Mar.-Apr. Sa-Su 11am-3pm; May-June Tu-Su 11am-3pm. 1hr. tours. $9, ages 6-12 $7, seniors $8. $1 discount coupon for admission available online.)*

BAPTIST CHURCH. In addition to founding Rhode Island, in 1638 Roger Williams founded the first First Baptist Church of America. Visitors should register with the church office. *(75 N. Main St. ☎401-454-3418; www.fbcia.org. Open M-F 9am-3:30pm. $1.)*

JOHN BROWN HOUSE MUSEUM. The building is a prime example of Georgian style, with symmetry and squirrel-printed French wallpaper. The 1hr. tour includes a brief video introducing the house and the Brown family, who endowed Brown University. Those less enamored of furniture may prefer the walking tours of Benefit St., which start from the house. *(52 Power St. ☎401-331-8575; www.rihs.org. Open Tu-Sa 10am-4pm. $8, students and seniors $6, ages 7-17 $4.)*

CULINARY ARTS MUSEUM. Make sure you don't come hungry to browse through the museum's yummy collection, which includes 4000 menu options, rare cookbooks, Roman eating utensils, and myriad kitchen gadgets old and new. *(315 Harborside Blvd. on the Providence and Cranston city line. ☎401-598-2805; www.culinary. org. Open Tu-Su 10am-5pm. $7, students $4, ages 5-18 $2, seniors $6.)*

🎵 ENTERTAINMENT

Stationary bonfires spanning the entire length of the downtown rivers are set ablaze during ▓**WaterFire,** a public art exhibition and festival held every few weeks from May to October. *(☎401-272-3111; www.waterfire.org. Free.)* From March through November, the third Thursday of each month is **Gallery Night,** when 24 galleries across the city open their doors for free, with free parking in eight designated lots. *(☎401-490-2042; www.gallerynight.info.)* The **Cable Car Cinema and Cafe,** 204 S. Main St., shows art-house and foreign films in a small theater with comfy couches. A friendly staff serves up veggie wraps, vegan baked goods,

ice cream, and beverages. *(☎401-272-3970; www.cablecarcinema.com. 3 shows during the day, 2 shows in the evening; times vary. $8.50; M-W students $6.50. Cafe open M-F 7:30am-11pm, Sa-Su 9am-11pm.)* The regionally acclaimed **Trinity Repertory Company,** 201 Washington St., typically offers $15 student rush tickets the day of performances. *(☎401-351-4242; www.trinityrep.com. Tickets $40-50. Box office open M-F noon-5pm.)* The **Providence Performing Arts Center,** 220 Weybosset St., hosts high-end productions like Broadway musicals. *(☎401-421-2787; www. ppacri.org. Tickets $18-80. Box office open M-Th 10am-3pm.)*

🍸 NIGHTLIFE

Brownies, townies, and RISDs rock the night away at several hot spots throughout town. For nightlife listings, read the "Weekend" section of the *Providence Journal* or pick up a free *Providence Phoenix.*

▓ **Xxodus Cafe,** 276 Westminster St. *(☎401-351-0353; www.blackrep.org).* Serves up mixed drinks in a sleek lounge and hosts regular poetry readings, musical performances, and battling MCs. The cafe is also home to the Providence Black Repertory Company, which puts up more formal theatrical performances celebrating black creativity. Theater tickets $20, seniors $10, Su matinees pay what you can. Open M-Th 9pm-1am, F-Sa 9pm-2am. AmEx/D/MC/V.

AS220, 115 Empire St. *(☎401-831-9327; www. as220.org),* between Washington and Westminster St. A taqueria, bar, gallery, and performance space wrapped into one. This self-proclaimed "anti-institutional institution" is nonprofit and totally uncensored. The chalkboard outside lists the acts and times for upcoming performances and events. Cover under $10. Open M and Su 6pm-1am, Tu-F 5pm-1am, Sa noon-1am.

Olives, 108 N. Main St. *(☎401-751-1200; www. olivesri.com).* Martinis are their game; throw one back for $7-9. Live rock music F-Sa. DJ Th and Su. Cover F-Sa $5. Open W-Th 5pm-1am, F-Sa 5pm-2am, Su 8pm-1am. AmEx/D/MC/V.

🚗 THE ROAD TO NEWPORT: 34 MI.

From Providence, take **I-195 East** to **Route 24 South,** which becomes **Route 114 South.**

NEWPORT ☎401

Money has always found its way into Newport. Once a center of transatlantic shipping, the coastal town later became the summer escape for the elite of the elite. Today, the awe-inspiring mansions of big-business tycoons remain, but they are only a part of this high-priced tourist town—world-famous music festivals and the beautiful landscape are now the big draws.

VITAL STATS

Population: 26,000

Tourist Office: Newport County Convention and Visitors Bureau, 23 America's Cup Ave. (☎401-845-9123 or 800-976-5122; www.gonewport.com), 2 blocks from Thames St., in the Newport Gateway Center. Open from Memorial Day to Labor Day daily 9am-5pm, F-Sa 9am-6pm.

Internet Access: Public Library, 300 Spring St. (☎401-847-8720). Open in summer M 11am-8pm, Tu-Th 9am-8pm, F-Sa 9am-6pm; in winter M 12:30-9pm, Tu-Th 9:30am-9pm, F-Sa 9:30am-6pm.

Post Office: 320 Thames St. (☎401-847-0700). Open M-F 8:30am-6pm, Sa 9am-1pm. **Postal Code:** 02840.

✴ ORIENTATION

Running parallel to the shore, **Thames Street** is home to the tourist strip and wharves, while **Bellevue Avenue** is lined with many of Newport's mansions. Walking is the best way to navigate the downtown area. The mansions are a mile or two away from downtown, so you may wish to drive or take RIPTA buses.

▐ ACCOMMODATIONS

With over 250 guesthouses and inns scattered throughout the city, small, private lodgings abound in Newport. During the summer, it's hard to find anything for under $100, and weekends are even pricier. Many hotels and guesthouses book solid two months in advance for summer weekends, especially during festivals. For less expensive lodging, it's best to head out of town. Rte. 114 (W. Main Rd.) hosts a variety of chain motels about four miles from Newport.

Newport International Hostel, 16 Howard St. (☎401-369-0248; www.newporthostel.com). Located in a historic home and conveniently near the waterfront. Kitchen and common room. Free parking. Reception 8:30-10:30am and 5-7pm. Dorms from $35. MC/V. ❷

Newport Gateway Hotel, 31 W. Main Rd. (☎401-847-2735 or 800-427-9444), in Middletown. Large rooms with pullout beds, A/C, and cable TV. Continental breakfast included. Open Mar.-Nov. Rooms M-Th and Su $89, F-Sa $179. AmEx/D/MC/V. ❹

▐ FOOD

While many Newport restaurants are pricey, cheap food can be found with a little extra effort. Your best bet for inexpensive eateries and ice-cream parlors are on Thames St.

Panini Grill, 186 Thames St. (☎401-847-7784; www.thepaninigrill.com). Creative twists on old favorites, like the Greek panini (red peppers, cucumbers, feta, hot peppers, olives; $5) and turkey portobello melts ($6). This funky shop attracts a young crowd in search of free Wi-Fi and late night eats. Open M-Th and Su 11am-10pm, F-Sa 11am-2am. MC/V. ❶

Franklin Spa, 229 Spring St. (☎401-847-3540; www.franklinspa.us). Good, hearty breakfasts ($7-8) like the Portuguese Sailor (chorizo sausage and eggs) are prepared right before your eyes. Open M-W 6am-2pm, Th-Sa 6am-3pm, Su 7am-1:30pm. Cash only. ❷

Roll Your Own, 408 Thames St. (☎401-846-4411). Though the walls are plain and the dining room is just a bunch of chairs, Roll Your Own has no trouble luring in burrito fans. Sadly, you can't actually make your own—but you can dictate just what goes on your chicken ($9) or veggie ($8) burrito. Open daily 11:30am-2am. AmEx/D/MC/V. ❷

◉ SIGHTS

George Noble Jones built the first "summer cottage" in Newport in 1839, thereby kicking off the creation of an extravagant string of palatial summer estates. Most of the **mansions** lie south of downtown on Bellevue Ave. Self-guided tours and tours led by the **Preservation Society of Newport,** 424 Bellevue Ave., provide a chance to ogle the decadence. (☎401-847-

EAST COAST

1000; www.newportmansions.org. Open daily in summer 10am-5pm; in winter 10am-4pm.) The five largest mansions are **The Elms,** 367 Bellevue Ave., **Chateau-sur-Mer,** 474 Bellevue Ave., **Rosecliff,** 548 Bellevue Ave., the **Marble House,** 596 Bellevue Ave., and **The Breakers,** 44 Ochre Point Ave. Of these, The Breakers, once owned by the Vanderbilts, is the largest and most popular, with 70 rooms of unchecked opulence. Also well worth checking out is the Marble House, which cost $11 million to build in 1892. The mansion features over 500,000 cu. ft. of marble, silk walls, and more gold leaf than you can shake a monocle at. (☎401-847-1000. Open daily 10am-5pm. $11-17 per house, ages 6-17 $4.)

OCEAN DRIVE. In the Fort Adams area, Ocean Drive winds along the coast with startling views of the rocky beach, tide pools, and luxurious inns and mansions lining Newport's shoreline. There are plenty of places to pull over to walk along the coast or take a dip, but watch out—private owners do not appreciate trespassing. Stop at **Brenton Point State Park** to take in the view or play on the fields. (☎401-847-2400. Open sunrise-sunset. Free.)

FORT ADAMS STATE PARK. Fort Adams State Park has a 19th-century fort, a small (but free) beach, and picnicking areas galore. (South of town on Ocean Dr., 2 mi. from the visitors center. ☎401-841-0707; www.fortadams.org. Park open daily sunrise-sunset. Tours daily every hr. 10am-4pm. Free. Tours $10, students and ages 5-17 $5.) The park also features the **Museum of Yachting,** but your time is better spent watching the boats circling on Narragansett Bay. (☎401-847-1018; www.moy.org. Open from mid-May to Oct. M and W-Su 10am-6pm. $8, students and under 18 free.)

OTHER SIGHTS. The oldest synagogue in the US, the restored **Touro Synagogue,** dates back to 1763. George Washington sent a letter to the synagogue in 1790, pledging his support for religious freedom. (85 Touro St. ☎401-847-4794; www.tourosynagogue.org. Tours July-Aug. every 30min. M-F and Su 10am-5pm; Sept.-June call for times. $5, under 12 free.) The **Tennis Hall of Fame** celebrates the history of the sport with displays on champions like Arthur Ashe, Althea Gibson, and Billie Jean King. A colorful exhibit on tennis-ball canisters through history rounds

out the collection. (194 Bellevue Ave. ☎401-849-3990 or 800-457-1144; www.tennisfame.com. Open daily 9:30am-5pm. $10, students and seniors $8, under 16 $5.) The **Newport Historical Society** celebrates Newport's colonial history and its emergence as a resort town with the **Museum of Newport History.** The organization also owns the **Great Friends Meeting House,** the state's oldest place of worship, and two colonial-era buildings. Tours of **Colony House** depart every 30min. from 11:30am to 2pm, while tours of the meetinghouse and **Wanton-Lyman-Hazard House** depart at 3pm and 4pm, respectively, on Monday, Wednesday, Friday, and Saturday. All of the properties are open for 30min. tours from late June to August. (Newport Historical Society 82 Touro St. ☎401-846-0813; www.newporthistorical. org. Museum of Newport History 127 Thames St. ☎401-841-8770. Open June-Sept. daily 10am-4pm; Sept.-Dec. Th-Sa 10am-4pm, Su 1-4pm. $4, ages 5-18 $2. Great Friends Meeting House at Farewell and Marlborough St. Tours $5, children $2.)

NIGHTLIFE

Pubs and clubs line Thames St., Newport's liveliest nighttime drag. Be sure to bring proper ID, as area clubs are very strict, and almost all of them are 21+.

Rhino Bar and Grille and Mamba Room, 337 Thames St. (☎401-846-0707). Rhino Bar has everything from game night M with Wii and Rock Band to reggae Th, while the Mamba Room always has a DJ spinning hip hop and Top 40. Try the Rough Rider, a 72 oz. fishbowl ($22) designed for 4. Cover F-Sa $5, good for both establishments. Rhino open M-F 4pm-1am, Sa-Su noon-1am. Mambo open F-Sa 9pm-1am. AmEx/D/MC/V.

One Pelham East, 270 Thames St. (☎401-847-9460). Doesn't bother with the slick look of many Newport clubs. Live rock, cover, and acoustic sets draw a crowd of faithful regulars. Drinks $4.50-5.50. Live music daily 10pm. Cover M-Sa $5-20. Open daily 3pm-1am. Cash only.

The Newport Blues Cafe, 286 Thames St. (☎401-841-5510; www.newportbluescafe.com). Hosts live music ranging from blues to rock to jazz. Previous acts include the Allman Brothers and Sugar Daddy. Drinks $4-6.50. Live music nightly 10pm. Tickets $5-30. Open daily 6pm-1am. Kitchen open until 10pm. AmEx/D/MC/V.

✺ FESTIVALS

Newport gives lovers of classical, folk, jazz, and film each a festival to call their own from June to August. Festival tickets, as well as accommodations, are claimed months ahead of time, so start looking early. The **Newport Music Festival** brings in classical musicians from around the world for over 60 concerts during two weeks in July. (☎401-846-1133, box office 849-0700; www.newportmusic. org. Tickets $25-45. Box office open M-F 10am-6pm, Sa 10am-1pm.) Bring a picnic to Fort Adams State Park and partake in the festivities at one of the oldest and best-known jazz festivals in the world, the **Newport Jazz Festival.** In early August, guitars replace saxophones at the **Newport Folk Festival.** Former acts include Bob Dylan, Joan Baez, and the Indigo Girls.(☎401-847-3700; www.festivalproductions.net. Jazz festival $69 per day, under 12 $15. Folk festival $69/15.) Over the course of six days in June, the **Newport International Film Festival** screens over 70 feature, documentary, and short films in the **Jane Pickens Theater** and the **Opera House Cinema,** both on Truro St. (☎401-846-9100; www.newportfilmfestival. com. Tickets $10.)

> **TIP** **CLOGGED ARTERIES.** Cape Cod is one of New England's premier vacation destinations, attracting tourists with small towns, sandy beaches, sundrenched landscapes, and ▧**cranberry bogs.** It resembles a bent arm, with Hyannis at the biceps, Chatham at the elbow, Cape Cod National Seashore tattooed onto the forearm, and Provincetown at the clenched fist. Rte. 6 is your best bet if you're in a hurry, but those with time should take Rte. 6A and Rte. 28 along the cape's inner and outer coasts, respectively.

⌒ BEACHES

Newport's gorgeous beaches are frequently as crowded as its streets. The most popular sandy spot is **Easton's Beach,** on Memorial Blvd., also known as First Beach. (☎401-845-5810.) Starting at Easton's Beach or Bellevue Ave., the ▧**Cliff Walk** traverses Newport's eastern shore as a 3 mi. walking trail. The Cliff Walk is a must, especially if you're not shelling out for the mansion tours. The path follows the rocky coastline, with a cliff and crashing waves on one side and huge mansions on the other. Access and parking are available along a number of roads that intersect with Bellevue Ave. (www.cliffwalk.com. Open 24hr.)

⇗ THE ROAD TO PROVINCETOWN: 120 MI. Take **Route 114 North** to **Route 24 North.** Take **I-195 East** to **Route 25 North,** then switch to **Route 6.**

The Bay State MASSACHUSETTS *Welcomes You*

PROVINCETOWN ☎508

Provincetown has changed quite a bit since the Pilgrims landed here briefly in 1620. In the early 20th century, the town's popularity soared with resident artists and writers like Norman Mailer and Edward Hopper. Provincetown's tradition of open-mindedness has attracted a large gay community, making it a premier destination for gay vacationers, who fill the town to capacity in summer. Although far from cheap, P-town has better options for outdoor activities, dining, and nightlife than the rest of Cape Cod.

VITAL STATS
Population: 3400
Tourist Office: Provincetown Chamber of Commerce, 307 Commercial St. (☎508-487-3424; www.ptownchamber.com), on MacMillian Wharf. Open June-Sept. M-Sa 9am-5pm, Su 10am-4pm; hours vary in winter.
Internet Access: Provincetown Public Library, 356 Commercial St. (☎508-487-7094; www.ptownlib. com). Open M and F 10am-5pm, Tu and Th noon-8pm, W 10am-8pm, Sa 10am-2pm, Su 1-5pm.
Post Office: 219 Commercial St. (☎508-487-0368). Open M-F 8:30am-5pm, Sa 9am-noon. **Postal Code:** 02657.

⚜ ORIENTATION...?

P-town's main drag, **Commercial Street,** runs along the harbor, centered on **MacMillian Wharf. Standish Street** divides the town into the East and West Ends. The **East End** is crowded with galleries. It's easy to navigate Provincetown by foot, but it's a bit of a trek out to the beaches.

🅟 ACCOMMODATIONS

Provincetown teems with expensive places to rest your head, mainly found on Bradford St.

Somerset House, 378 Commercial St. (☎508-487-0383 or 800-575-1850; www.somerset-houseinn.com). A 12-room guesthouse with sleek, stylish rooms and art on the walls. All rooms include fridges, DVD players, and A/C, and hosts Bob and Dan serve mixed drinks every afternoon. Sa barbecue in summer. Some rooms have fireplaces. Free Internet. 4-night min. stay in high season. Doubles from late June to Aug. $150-295; Sept.-Oct. and May-June $110-225; Nov.-Apr. $85-175. AmEx/D/MC/V. ❺

Outermost Hostel, 28 Winslow St. (☎508-487-4378; www.outermosthostel.com), just steps from the heart of town. 5 cottages and kind management. Key deposit $10. Reception 8am-9:30am and 5:30-9:30pm. Open from May to mid-Oct. Dorms $25. Cash only. ❶

Cape Codder Guests, 570 Commercial St. (☎508-487-0131; www.capecodderguests.com). It may be a 15min. walk to downtown, but the Cape Codder is easy on the wallet. Rooms with shared bath are small but bright, and there's a peaceful garden in the front as well as access to a private beach accross the street. Breakfast included. Free parking. Rooms June-Aug. $37-75; Sept.-May $30-60. AmEx/D/MC/V. ❸

Dunes' Edge Campground, 386 Rte. 6 (☎508-487-9815; www.dunes-edge.com), just outside downtown. 100 wooded sites that border Cape Cod National Seashore. Open May-Sept. Sites $30-40. MC/V. ❷

🍴 FOOD

Sit-down meals in Provincetown tend to be expensive. Fast-food joints selling footlong hot dogs and lobster rolls line the Commercial St. extension (next to MacMillian Wharf) and the Aquarium Mall, farther west on Commercial St.

Karoo Kafe, 338 Commercial St. (☎508-487-6630; www.karookafe.com). The self-titled "fast-food safari" serves up falafel ($7.25) and chicken sosatie ($7.75), a South African dish. Open daily June-Aug. 11am-9pm; Sept.-Nov. and Mar.-May hours vary. AmEx/D/MC/V. ❷

Cafe Edwidge, 333 Commercial St. (☎508-487-4020). Though the cafe is open for dinner, the breakfast dishes, like fruit-topped french toast ($11), draw the crowds. Open in summer 8:30am-1pm and 6-11pm; hours vary in winter. AmEx/D/MC/V. ❸

Angel Foods, 467 Commercial St. (☎508-487-6666). Grilled veggie sandwiches ($7) in a grocery store lined with dried fruit and organic juice. Entrees are sold by the pound: the Mediterranean chicken pasta ($10 per lb.) and curried chicken salad ($10 per lb.) are 2 of the best. Open M-Sa 7am-8pm, Su 8am-8pm. AmEx/D/MC/V. ❷

👁 SIGHTS

PROVINCETOWN ART ASSOCIATION AND MUSEUM. The museum has an eclectic collection of art, tied together only by the fact that it all relates somehow to Provincetown. The museum showcases mainly 20th-century art, though exhibits are ever-rotating. *(460 Commercial St. ☎508-487-1750; www.paam.org. Open M-Th 11am-8pm, F 11am-10pm, Sa-Su 11am-5pm. $5, under 12 free. F after 5pm free.)*

PILGRIM MONUMENT AND PROVINCETOWN MUSEUM. The monument, the tallest all-granite structure in the US at 253 ft., and the Provincetown Museum commemorate the Pilgrims' first landing. Hike up to the top of the tower for stunning views of the cape and the Atlantic; unfortunately, you have to gaze through wire fencing. *(On High Pole Hill just north of the center of town. ☎508-487-1310. Open daily July-Aug. 9am-7pm; Sept.-Oct. and Apr.-June 9am-5pm. Last entry 45min. before close. $7, students and seniors $5, ages 4-14 $3.50.)*

🍸 NIGHTLIFE

Nightlife in P-town is almost totally GLBT.

Crown & Anchor, 247 Commercial St. (☎508-487-1430; www.onlyatthecrown.com). A massive complex with a restaurant, an inn, 2 cabarets, the chill Wave video bar, the Vault leather bar, and the Paramount dance club. Cabaret shows $18-25. Cover $10; no cover for Wave. Open in summer daily 5pm-1am. Paramount open F-Sa 9pm-1am. AmEx/D/MC/V.

Atlantic House, 6 Masonic Pl. (☎508-487-3821; www.ahouse.com), just off Commercial St. Founded in 1798 by gay whalers, the "A-house" still attracts its fair share of seamen. Choose from 3 different scenes: the low-key "little bar" with sing-along jukebox, the Leather & Levis "macho bar," and the "big room," where you too can be a dancing queen. Cover for big room $5-10. Little bar open daily noon-1am. Macho bar and big room open daily 10pm-1am.

Governor Bradford, 312 Commercial St. (☎508-487-2781). Don't be fooled by the traditional decor; the Governor hosts drag karaoke nightly at 9:30pm. Ladies as well as gents sing along as a wigged beauty cavorts behind them. Drinks around $5. 21+. No cover. Open M-Sa 11am-1am, Su noon-1am.

❄ FESTIVALS

P-Town's gay community comes out in droves for **Carnival,** a "Gay Paree!" held every August. Be sure to book rooms well in advance, as visitors flood into town for the weeklong celebration and colorful parade (☎800-761-0182; www.ptown.org). On the first weekend in November, gay singles gather for **Meet Your Man** in Provincetown, a whirlwind weekend of speed dating and clubbing (☎800-637-8696; www.ptown.org).

⚠ OUTDOORS

P-town's miles of shoreline provide spectacular scenery and more than enough space to catch some sun. At the west end of Commercial St., the 1 mi. ⬛**Breakwater Jetty** stretches into the bay, providing fantastic views of marsh, sand, and Provincetown. Follow it all the way to the end to find a secluded peninsula with empty beaches, two working lighthouses, and the remains of a Civil War fort. At **Race Point Beach,** waves roll in from the Atlantic, while **Herring Cove Beach,** at the west end of town, offers calm, protected waters. Directly across from Snail Rd., on US 6, an unlikely path leads to a world of rolling sand dunes; look for shacks where writers such as Tennessee Williams, Norman Mailer, and John

Dos Passos spent their days. To spare yourself a long walk, get a rental bike at **Arnold's,** 329 Commercial St. (☎508-487-0844. Bikes $4 per hr., $21 per day.)

Those not content just looking at Cape Cod Bay can rent a kayak from **Venture Athletics,** 237 Commercial St. The shop also offers 2-3hr. guided tours of the harbor. (☎508-487-2395; www.ventureathletics.com. Single kayaks $25 per 4hr.; double kayaks $45 per 4hr. Guided tours $45-65. Open daily 9am-6pm.) Today, Provincetown seafarers have traded harpoons for cameras, but they still pursue the same beast—whale-watching cruises rank among P-town's most popular attractions. Most companies guarantee sightings. (3hr. tour $30-35. Coupons at the chamber of commerce.) **Dolphin Fleet** (☎508-240-3636 or 800-826-9300) and **Portuguese Princess** (☎508-487-2651 or 800-422-3188) both leave from MacMillian Wharf.

⛰ THE ROAD TO CAPE COD NATIONAL SEASHORE: 20 MI.

From Provincetown, take **US 6 West.** Cape Cod National Seashore runs nearly the entire length of the Cape's inner forearm.

CAPE COD NATIONAL SEASHORE ☎508

As early as 1825, the cape had suffered so much erosion that the town of Truro required locals to plant beach grass and keep their cows off the dunes. These conservation efforts culminated in 1961, when President Kennedy and the National Park Service created the Cape Cod National Seashore. Park rangers at the **Salt Pond Visitors Center,** at Salt Pond, off US 6 in Eastham, provide maps, schedules for guided tours, and additional information about the park. (☎508-255-3421. Open daily July-Aug. 9am-5:30pm; Sept. and June 9am-5pm; Oct.-May 9am-4:30pm.) At the northern end of the cape, the **Province Lands Visitors Center,** off US 6 in Provincetown, provides similar assistance. (☎508-487-1256. Open May-Oct. daily 9am-5pm.) The seashore spans Lower and Outer Cape Cod from Provincetown to Chatham, comprising six beaches. Of the six, **Marconi,** in Wellfleet, is a favorite of surfers, while **Race Point,** in Provincetown, offers more secluded waters if you keep walking about half a mile from the parking lot. Parking at the beaches is expensive, costing up to $15 per day. Among the best of the seashore's 11 self-guided nature trails is the **Great Island Trail**, in Wellfleet. It traces an 8 mi. loop through pine forests and grassy marshes and has views of the bay and Provincetown.

Camping in the national seashore is illegal, but there are commercial campgrounds just off parkland. 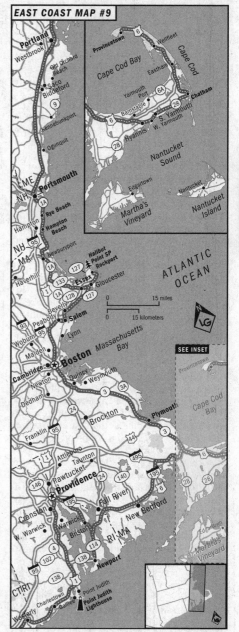**Truro Hostel (HI) ❶**, 111 N. Pamet Rd., in Truro, sits high atop a bluff overlooking the ocean and offers a large kitchen, a porch, and access to Ballston Beach. The building is a turn-of-the-century Coast Guard station, located on the national seashore, so walking and biking trails abound. From US 6, take the Pamet Rd. exit, which becomes N. Pamet Rd. (☎508-349-3889 or 888-901-2086. Key deposit $10. Open June-Sept. 6- to 8-bed dorms $35. MC/V.) Eastham's **Mid-Cape Hostel (HI-AYH) ❶**, 75 Goody Hallet Dr., features communal bungalow living in a woodsy location. You don't have to go far to do some birdwatching—the spacious kitchen has a great view of birds perched in the front yard. From Provincetown, follow US 6 and take the Rock Harbor exit at the Orleans Center rotary. Turn left onto Bridge Rd., then left again onto Goody Hallet Dr. (☎508-255-2785 or 888-901-2085. All-you-can-eat pancake and waffle breakfast $4. Open May-Sept. Dorms $35. MC/V.)

⚐ THE ROAD TO CHATHAM: 35 MI.

Take **US 6 West** to **Route 137 South,** which deadends into Rte. 28. Take **Route 28 East** into town, where it becomes **Main Street.**

CHATHAM
☎**508**

Chatham is an expensive stay, popular with an affluent family crowd. Though budget travelers may not want to spend the money to stay the night in Chatham, it's a pleasant stop for an afternoon, with a quaint downtown and historically relevant museums. One of the best (and cheapest) things to do in Chatham is walk along **Main Street,** which is home to shops, restaurants, and galleries. Run by the Chatham Historical Society, the 250-year-old **Atwood House Museum,** 347 Stage Harbor Rd., has artifacts and pieces of art documenting over two centuries of life in Chatham. Be sure to check out

Chatham resident Alice Stahlknecht's haunting Depression-era paintings of townspeople, including one with untied shoelaces. (☎508-945-2493; www.chathamhistoricalsociety.org. Open July-Aug. Tu-Sa 10am-4pm; June and Sept.-Oct. Tu-Sa 1-4pm. $5, students $3, under 12 free.) The **Chatham Fish Pier,** on Shore Rd. north of the intersection with Main St., attracts many summer tourists. In the afternoon (2-4pm), visitors can watch the fishing fleet bring in haddock, cod, lobster, and halibut that can be purchased in local fish markets later the same day. You can also see the **Fisherman's Monument,** built to honor the town's fishing industry. The monument, called the Provider, is a little unusual: an abstraction of an upturned hand is supported by a structure of poles over a base of fish and shellfish in relief. The **Josiah Mayo House,** 540 Main St., was built from 1818 to 1820 by the town postmaster for his bride to be. It is now maintained as an accurate representation of a home from that era. Guides conduct tours, highlighting period architecture and furniture. (☎508-945-4084. Open July-Sept. Tu-Th 11am-4pm. Free.) The **Old Grist Mill** is a small windmill built in the late 18th century to grind corn. The mill itself is locked, but it is surrounded by a small park. From the rotary, take Main St. toward the water, take a right on Cross St., and hang a left on Shattuck.

Main St. has tasty, inexpensive options for hungry diners. **Chatham Cookware Cafe ❷,** 524 Main St., might sound like Martha Stewart's favorite store, but it's actually a cafe with a bakery in the front and a soup-and-sandwich counter in the back. The sandwiches are creative reincarnations of old favorites like the "hungry pilgrim" (smoked turkey, cranberries, and stuffing; $7) and the BLAT ($6), a BLT with avocado. (☎508-945-1250. Open daily 6:30am-4pm. MC/V.) The **Anytime Cafe ❸,** 512 Main St., serves sophisticated pizzas like the Blanco (olive oil, garlic, chèvre, and sun-dried tomatoes; $19) alongside deep-fried cheese sticks ($8). If the giant Einstein painted on the wall makes you want to eat smart, the cafe serves vegetable wraps and panini, with plenty of veggie options. (☎508-945-4080. Open M-W and Su 11am-10pm, Th-Sa 11am-11pm. AmEx/D/MC/V.)

THE ROAD TO PLYMOUTH: 51 MI.

From Chatham, take **Route 28 West.** The road provides a glimpse of the quintessential Middle of Cape Cod, crossing shallow tidal rivers and wide salt marshes while passing countless cottages, ice-cream shops, clam shacks, and minigolf courses. From Hyannis, follow **Route 132 North** to **US 6 West** to **Route 3 North.** Take **Exit 6** for downtown Plymouth.

PLYMOUTH ☎508

Your textbook may say otherwise, but the Pilgrims' first step onto the New World was not at Plymouth. They stopped first at Provincetown (p. 154), then promptly left because the soil was inadequate.

VITAL STATS

Population: 52,000

Tourist Office: Waterfront Tourist Information Center (☎508-747-7525 or 800-872-1620), on Water St. Open daily from June to Labor Day 8am-8pm; from Labor Day to Nov. and Apr.-May 9am-5pm.

Library and Internet Access: Plymouth Public Library, 132 South St. (☎508-830-4250; www.plymouthpubliclibrary.org). Open M-W 10am-9pm, Th 10am-6pm, F-Sa 10am-5:30pm.

Post Office: 6 Main St. (☎508-746-8175). Open M-F 9am-1:30pm and 2:30-5pm, Sa 9am-noon. **Postal Code:** 02360.

ACCOMMODATIONS

Blue Anchor Motel and Guest Rooms, 7 Lincoln St. (☎508-746-9551; www.theblueanchormotel.com). Roomy, well-decorated digs and a comfortable front porch. Open June-Sept. Rooms $75-95. AmEx/D/MC/V. ❸

Whispering Oaks Motel, 517 State Rd. 3A (☎508-224-2500), a few miles south of Plymouth. Large standard rooms. Rooms M-Th and Su $68, F-Sa $79. 21+. AmEx/D/MC/V. ❸

Myles Standish State Forest (☎508-866-2526, reservations 877-422-6762) on Cranberry Rd. Take Rte. 3 N. to Exit 3 and make a left, then a right onto Long Pond Rd. 400 sites in a forested area alongside 16 ponds. The park also has miles of hiking and biking trails. Open from mid-Apr. to mid-Oct. Sites $17. MC/V. ❶

FOOD

Jubilee, 22 Court St. (☎508-747-3700). Serves gourmet sandwiches like the veggie hummus roll-up ($6.75) and ham and brie ($6.25). Open M-F 10am-3pm. AmEx/MC/V. ❶

SIGHTS

Plymouth is extremely proud of its place in American history.

PLYMOUTH ROCK. This piece of geology is actually a small stone that has been dubiously identified as the rock on which the Pilgrims disembarked the second time. A symbol of liberty during the American Revolution, it has since moved three times before ending up beneath a portico on Water St., at the foot of North St. After several vandalizations and one dropping (in transit), it's cracked and under "tight" security.

PLIMOTH PLANTATION. The historical park recreates the Pilgrims' early settlement. In the Pilgrim Village, costumed actors play the roles of villagers carrying out their daily tasks, while Hobbamock's Homesite represents a Native American village of the same period. (*A few miles south of town on Rte. 3.* ☎508-746-1622; www.plimoth.org. Open Apr.-Nov. daily 9am-5pm. $24, ages 6-12 $14.)

MAYFLOWER II. Docked off Water St. in Plymouth, the *Mayflower II* is a 1950s scale replica of the Pilgrims' vessel, staffed by actors who recapture the atmosphere of the original ship. (Open Apr.-Nov. daily 9am-5pm. $10, ages 6-12 $7. Combined admission with Plimoth Plantation $28/18.)

OTHER SIGHTS. The **Pilgrim Hall Museum** contains objects owned by the Pilgrims, including a hat stained with Pilgrim sweat. (*75 Court St.* ☎508-746-1620; www.pilgrimhall.org. Open Feb.-Dec. daily 9:30am-4:30pm. $7, ages 5-17 $4.) Atop a hill on Allerton St., the **National Monument to the Forefathers,** erected in 1889 to pay homage to the Pilgrims, is the largest solid granite statue in the nation. Take Samoset St. west to Allerton St. The **1749 Court House** has a museum on the first floor and a real courtroom on the second. The courthouse was the Plymouth court for over 70 years, hosting young attorneys like John Adams and James Otis. (In Town Sq.

☎508-830-4075. Open from late June to Columbus Day M-Sa 10:30am-4:30pm, Su noon-4:30pm. Free.)

THE ROAD TO BOSTON: 40 MI.

Take **Route 44 West** out of town to **Route 3 North.**

BOSTON ☎617

Founded in 1630 by Puritan colonists fleeing England, this "City Upon a Hill" soon became the New World's largest. Boston was first a vital trading center of the British Empire. Later, the city played a starring role in America's fight for independence—from the Boston Tea Party to the Battle of Bunker Hill. In the 19th century, some of America's most influential doers and thinkers called Boston home, leading famed resident Oliver Wendell Holmes to dub the State House the "Hub of the Solar System." In the 20th century, Boston experienced its share of growing pains, including immigration booms, civil-rights battles, and problems with urban expansion and renewal. Today, Boston is a stew of distinct communities, cultural attractions, and urban parks as well as home to over 250,000 college students and four world-class sports teams. Wandering around Boston's many districts, jumble of streets, and rarely square squares will give you a meaningful glimpse of this evolving metropolis. The **Freedom Trail** is a nice place to start. For more comprehensive coverage of the Boston area, see ▓**Let's Go: Boston.**

ORIENTATION

Boston is situated on a peninsula jutting into Massachusetts Bay. **I-93/US 1/Route 3** runs north-south along the city's eastern edge. The **Charles River** divides Boston and its neighbor to the north, Cambridge; **Storrow** and **Memorial Drives** run along its southern and northern banks, respectively.

Boston's heart is the grassy **Boston Common,** sandwiched between **Beacon Hill** to the north, downtown to the south and east, and **Back Bay** to the west. Back Bay is Boston's most navigable area. Major avenues **Beacon Street, Commonwealth Avenue, Newbury Street,** and **Boylston Street** run parallel to Storrow Dr.; alternating one-way cross streets are named alphabetically from Arlington to Hereford as you head west. Elsewhere, driving is more complicated.

Completed in 2007 after decades of construction, **The Big Dig** once wreaked havoc on the roads of the waterfront but now eases the flow of traffic at the intersection of I-93 and **I-90 (Mass Pike),** which divides the city going east-west. The labyrinthine cobblestone paths of Boston's colonial downtown and the **North End** are difficult to navigate and will leave you wishing for flaxen thread or wax wings.

VITAL STATS

Population: 600,000

Tourist Offices: Greater Boston Convention and Visitors Bureau, 2 Copley Pl., Ste. 105 (☎617-536-4100; www.bostonusa.com), has a booth at Boston Common, at ⓣ Park St. Open M-F 8:30am-5pm. Downtown's **National Historic Park Visitor Center,** 15 State St. (☎617-242-5642; www.nps.gov/bost), has Freedom Trail info and tours. ⓣ State. Open daily 9am-5pm.

Library and Internet Access: Boston Public Library, 700 Boylston St. (☎617-536-5400; www.bpl.org). ⓣ Copley. Open M-Th 9am-9pm, F-Sa 9am-5pm. Free.

Post Office: 25 Dorchester Ave. (☎617-654-5302), behind South Station at ⓣ South Station. Open 24hr. **Postal Code:** 02205.

▣ TRANSPORTATION

For sightseeing in Boston's compact center, it makes sense to park and walk. Parking garages are pricey ($20 per day and up) but are often the only option; metered parking is limited, and ticketing is relentless. Resident parking permits are required for street parking in many neighborhoods.

Subway: MBTA (☎617-222-5000; www.mbta. com). Luckily for out-of-towners, Boston's subway system is clean, efficient, and cheap. Known as the ⓣ , the subway has 5 colored lines—Red, Blue, Orange, Green (which breaks into lines B-E), and Silver—that radiate from Downtown. **"Inbound"** trains head toward ⓣ Park St., ⓣ Government Center, ⓣ State, or ⓣ Downtown Crossing; **"outbound"** trains head away from those stops. All ⓣ stops have maps and schedules. Lines run daily 5:30am-12:30am. Fare $2, with Charlie Card $1.70.

Buses: Holes in the ⓣ 's coverage are filled by an extensive (though sometimes sluggish) bus system, which links to the subway lines. Many buses use **Harvard Square** as their home base, leaving from the underground hub in the Harvard ⓣ station or from Johnston Gate. Buses cost $1.50, with Charlie Card $1.25. There is no free transfer between buses and the subway. Most buses run from M-Sa about 5am-1am, Su 6am-1am.

▣ ACCOMMODATIONS

With so many colleges in and around Boston, the cheapest housing option for youthful travellers is unquestionably to crash with a long-lost high-school classmate. Cheap accommodations are rare and even scarcer in summer and during college-rush times in September, late May, and early June. Reservation services promise to find discounted rooms. Try **Boston Reservations** (☎617-332-4199) or **Central Reservation Service** (☎800-332-3026). Listed prices do not include Boston's 12.45% room tax.

▨ **Oasis Guest House,** 22 Edgerly Rd. (☎617-267-2262; www.oasisgh.com), at Stoneholm St. ⓣ Hynes/ICA. Though its name and logo might hint at an exotic lodging experience, Oasis is still closer to Symphony Hall than the Sahara. Its 16 rooms, all outfitted with TVs, are clean and homey. Reservations recommended. Rooms from May to mid-Nov. $69-99; from mid-Nov. to Apr. $90-150. AmEx/MC/V. ❸

▨ **Newbury Guest House,** 261 Newbury St. (☎617-437-7666; www.newburyguesthouse.com), between Fairfield and Gloucester St. ⓣ Copley or Hynes/ICA. A blend of colonial and cosmopolitan located in the heart of the Back Bay neighborhood. Victorian architecture and 21st-century amenities make for a comfortable stay in spacious rooms. Queen-size beds, desks, and fireplaces. Cable TV. Breakfast included. Free Wi-Fi. Parking $15 per day; reserve ahead. Wheelchair-accessible rooms available. Singles $130-170; doubles $155-195; tack on $20 for commencement season. AmEx/D/MC/V. ❺

American Youth Hostels, 12 Hemenway St. (☎617-536-9455; www.hiayh.org), in Back Bay. From ⓣ Hynes/ICA, walk down Massachusetts Ave., turn right on Boylston St., then swing a left onto Hemenway St. AYH in Boston is the US headquarters of Hostelling International (HI), the world-wide hosteling syndicate with 4500 hostels in 71 countries. Reception 24hr. Check-in noon. Check-out 11am. Dorms $35-38, members $32-35. AmEx/MC/V. ❷

Copley House, 239 W. Newton St. (☎617-236-8300; www.copleyhouse.com). ⓉPrudential. A small studio and 1-bedroom apartment complex in Back Bay, Copley House offers fully equipped studios for short-term residents. Each of the 55 rooms includes a kitchenette, private bath, cable TV, and local phone access. Limited parking $10 per night. Daily rates $95-150 in summer, $85-135 in winter $95-150; weekly $525-925 in summer, $475-775 in winter. AmEx/D/MC/V. ❹

Greater Boston YMCA, 316 Huntington Ave. (☎617-927-8040). At only $46 per bunk, Greater Boston YMCA offers many perks, including a swimming pool, track, racquetball and squash courts, and coin-op laundry. A good last-minute bet, since reservations are taken up to 2 weeks in advance. Key deposit $5. 10-night max. stay. Singles with bath $66; double $66; triples $81; quads $96. Men only Sept.-May. 18+. Discount with HI membership. Another location at 150 3rd Avenue, Charlestown. ❷

🍴 FOOD

Whether your car is loaded down with twin teenage daughters looking at colleges or a pack of recent Stanford grads jealously hobnobbing at Harvard, Boston's dining establishments are a gastronomic playground for all passengers. Filled with plenty of trendy, ethnic, and locally owned eateries, Boston has come a long way since the days of baked beans and chowder (though if these are what you crave, never fear, both are readily available). The city recently prohibited the use of trans fats in all dining establishments, and organic and local options are common.

DOWNTOWN

Though downtown does not offer the most unique eating in Boston, its history and locale are difficult to beat. Budget options are not the standard here; however, the sandwich shops on almost every corner and the diverse food court inside Quincy Market (p. 164) are

affordable. Fresh seafood shops line Boston's Waterfront district.

No Name, 15 Fish Pier (☎617-338-7539). ⓉSouth Station. Famous for its delicious seafood chowder ($3-5), No Name has been serving Boston reasonably priced seafood since 1917. No awards here for snazzy presentation, but the seafood can't be beat. Entrees $8-14. Open M-Sa 11am-10pm, Su 11am-9pm. D/MC/V. ❷

Fajitas and 'Ritas, 25 West St. (☎617-426-1222). ⓉPark St. This laid-back restaurant offers (surprise!) delicious fajitas ($7.50-13.50) and the perfect drink to wash them down. The bar stocks 24 different kinds of tequila (margaritas $4+, pitchers $12+). Try the tequila-marinated wings ($7-13), a smoked barbecue platter ($10), or build your own nachos ($3+). Should José Cuervo bring out your artistic impulses, feel free to doodle on the tables and walls (crayons provided). Takeout also available. AmEx/D/MC/V. ❷

Zuma's Tex-Mex Grill, 7 N. Market St. (☎617-367-9114). ⓉGovernment Center. Zuma's is reasonably priced, colorful, and even rowdy—everything you could want from a Tex-Mex restaurant. Entrees $8-13. Open M-Th 11:30am-midnight, F-Sa 11:30am-1am, Su noon-11pm. AmEx/D/MC/V. ❷

Durgin Park, 340 Fanueil Hall Marketplace (☎617-227-2038). ⓉGovernment Center. Established in 1826, Durgin Park has been serving up local favorites for longer than you, your parents, and even your grandparents have been around. This legendary tourist hot spot doubles as a belly-busting New England family-style restaurant and a good watering hole for the after-work crowd. Entrees $7-30. Open M-Sa 11:30am-10pm, Su 11:30am-9pm. AmEx/MC/V. ❹

NORTH END

Boston's Italian-American enclave is the place to go for authentic Italian fare, with over 100 restaurants packed into 1 sq. mi. With narrow streets and dim lighting, it is the perfect spot for a cutsie date or girls night out. Most establishments line Hanover St., accessible from ⓉHaymarket. After dinner, try the cannoli ($2-4) and other Italian sweets at 🏛Mike's Pastry, 300 Hanover St. (☎617-742-3050), or **Modern Pastry,** 257 Hanover St. (☎617-523-3783).

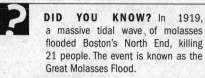

DID YOU KNOW? In 1919, a massive tidal wave of molasses flooded Boston's North End, killing 21 people. The event is known as the Great Molasses Flood.

Taranta, 210 Hanover St. (☎617-720-0052). Ⓣ Haymarket. If the North End date seems like a tired cliche, you clearly haven't been to Peruvian-influenced Taranta. The menu is nothing short of inspired, yielding such treats as *gnocci di yuca*, or cassava-root gnocchi with lamb ($24). For dessert, share the delicate hazelnut mousse drizzled in dulce de leche ($7) with your date and you'll be gazing into each other's eyes in no time. Reservations recommended. M-Th 5:30-10pm, F-Sa 5:30-11pm, Su 5:30-9pm. AmEx/MC/V. ❹

Trattoria Il Panino, 11 Parmenter St. (☎617-720-1336). Ⓣ Haymarket. Unquestionably one of the finest North End restaurants for food service and value, Trattoria Il Panino serves up Italian delicacies to the crowds that gather anxiously in front of the door every night. You won't look back after 1 bite of the *gnocchi alla sorrentina* (potato dumplings with tomato, basil, and mozzarella; $14). Open daily 11am-11pm. AmEx/D/MC/V. ❸

L'Osteria, 104 Salem St. (☎617-723-7847). Ⓣ Haymarket. A lively, family-owned restaurant, L'Osteria has been serving a variety of Italian favorites for over 20 years. The restaurant features a straightforward but fabulous selection of pastas, veal, chicken, and seafood. Entrees $10-24. Open M-Th and Su noon-10pm, F-Sa noon-11pm. AmEx/MC/V. ❸

Dolce Vita, 221 Hanover St. (☎617-720-0422). Ⓣ Haymarket. From the moment you enter the radiant dining room of this North End establishment, owner Franco Graceffa will cajole you into having a good time. Servers recommend traditional Sicilian dishes (the kitchen's forte) or you can adapt dishes to individual tastes. Seating for large groups is also available. Open daily 11am-11pm. AmEx/MC/V. ❸

CHINATOWN

Boston's Chinatown doesn't throw any curveballs. A destination for cheap, filling Asian food at nearly anytime of the day, Chinatown is the closest you can get to Beijing or Hong Kong in New England. Stuck between the skyscrapers of the Financial District and the Theater District, the neighborhood is slightly grimy and run-down, but the prices are unbeatable and most places stay open late (3-4am). Most establishments are accessible from Ⓣ Chinatown.

Ocean Wealth, 8 Tyler St. (☎617-423-1338). Ocean Wealth claims the loyalty of Greater Boston's Chinese residents with its unbeatable lobster special: $10 for 2 lobsters lightly fried in your choice of seasoning. Your server will bring the live creature out in a bucket to let you see it move, and then it's into the pot and out of the world. Delicious crustaceans aside, Ocean Wealth serves up Chinatown's best Cantonese cuisine. Open daily 11am-3am. MC/V. ❸

East Ocean City, 25-29 Beach St. (☎617-542-2504). Attentive service and a varied menu make this a great spot to eat out in Chinatown. Standard Chinese fare and vegetarian options are available, but East Ocean's real attraction is its wide range of seafood, as evidenced by tanks of giant crustaceans in the front window. Consider sauteed sea conch with vegetables ($15.50) and, although there are no chickens in the front window tanks, fried chicken fingers ($6.25). Rice and noodle dishes are cheaper ($7.50-8.50), as are weekday lunch specials (M-F 11am-3pm excluding holidays; $5-8). Min. dinner purchase $10. Open M-Th 11:30am-10pm, F 11:30am-11pm, Sa noon-11pm, Su noon-10pm. AmEx/MC/V. ❷

Ginza, 16 Hudson St. (☎617-338-2261). Ginza's mouthwatering sushi doesn't come cheap, but the sake bombs will ease the pain that your bill inflicts. Entrees $17-46. Open M-Th 11:30am-2:30pm and 5-11pm, F 11:30am-2:30pm and 5pm-3:30am, Sa noon-3:30am, Su noon-11pm. AmEx/MC/V. ❸

BACK BAY

The diverse eateries of the Back Bay line elegant Newbury St., accessible from Ⓣ Hynes/ICA or Back Bay. Though Newbury is known as Boston's most expensive shopping district, affordable restaurants do exist here.

Parish Café, 361 Boylston St. (☎617-247-4777). Ⓣ Arlington. Draws crowds not only because of its huge windows perfect for people-watching but also because the list of creators of its specialty sandwich menu reads like a who's who of Boston chefs. At $10-12, they're both delicious and big enough to be worth the price tag, but—there are no substitutions—not great for picky eaters. "Would you change the Mona Lisa?" asks their plucky website. Open M-Sa 11:30am-2am, Su noon-2am. Kitchen closes 1am. AmEx/MC/V. ❸

Kashmir, 279 Newbury St. (☎617-536-1695), at Gloucester St. ⓣ Hynes/ICA. Marble floors, traditional carpets, and plush red seats create a setting as light and exotic as Kashmir's subtle Indian curries and vegetarian dishes. Your cheapest bet is the all-you-can-eat buffet M-F 11:30am-3pm ($9), Sa-Su noon-3pm ($12). Open daily 11:30am-11pm. AmEx/D/MC/V. ❷

Island Hopper, 91 Massachusetts Ave. (☎617-266-1618). ⓣ Hynes/ICA. Brings authentic Southeast Asian spices from Malaysia, Indonesia, the Philippines, and Singapore to the Boston University masses. Try the delicious curry chicken ($13) and finish with fried ice cream ($6). Lunch combos $7.50. Large portions. Open M-Th 11:30am-11pm, F-Sa 11:30am-midnight, Su noon-11pm. AmEx/MC/V. ❸

SOUTH END

The long waits and hefty bills at these establishments are worth the expense. The South End's upscale restaurants meld flavors and techniques from around the world with amazing results. Most eateries line Tremont St., accessible from ⓣ Back Bay.

Addis Red Sea, 544 Tremont St. (☎617-426-8727). ⓣ Back Bay. The straw tables and low, stool-like chairs bring back the days of childhood tea parties, and the freedom to eat with one's hands can bring out even the most mature adult's inner kindergartener. The combination plates ($15+) are the perfect way to try different entrees, but most options are already a steal at $7-11. Try the cardamom-infused honey wine ($5 per glass, $20 per bottle), a regional specialty. Entrees $7-16. Takeout available. Open M-F 5-11pm, Sa-Su noon-11pm. Reservations accepted for 5 or more. AmEx/D/MC/V. ❸

Sibling Rivalry, 525 Tremont St. (☎617-338-5338). Head chefs Bob and David Kinkead duel it out over the stove to see who can create the more delicious dishes from the same fresh and seasonal ingredients. Appetizers $10-15; entrees

$25-35. M night 3-course *prix-fixe* menu $35. M-Th 5:30-10pm, F 5:30-11pm, Sa 5-11pm, Su 11am-3pm and 4-9pm. AmEx/D/MC/V. ❺

Flour, 1595 Washington St. (☎617-267-4300; www.flourbakery.com). ⓣ Prudential, Mass. Ave., or Back Bay. Sandwiches like roasted lamb with tomato chutney and goat cheese ($7) lure the lunchtime crowd, which can't resist picking up a slice of hazelnut-almond dacquoise ($3) on the way out. Weekly dinner specials (M-F $8-11); check website for the current menu. Baked goods $1-4. Cakes $22+, slices $5. Open M-F 7am-9pm, Sa 8am-6pm, Su 9am-3pm. D/MC/V. ❶

Franklin Cafe, 278 Shawmut Ave. (☎617-350-0010; www.franklincafe.com). ⓣ Back Bay. Hidden away in a residential area of the South End, this trendy dinner-and-drinks spot is clearly the place to be for locals in the know. The food justifies the long wait on weekend nights. Salads $5-9. Entrees $17-19. Open daily 5:30pm-1:30am. AmEx/D/MC/V. ❸

👁 SIGHTS

FREEDOM TRAIL

The 2½ mi. **Freedom Trail** passes the landmarks that put Boston on the map and is a great introduction to the city's history. Following the Freedom Trail on your own is fairly simple (just follow the faded red line painted on or paved into the sidewalk), but the National Park Service does offer free 1½hr. tours from April to November, departing from its **visitors center** (*15 State St., opposite Old State House.)* Bring a bit of cash ($10) if you want to visit the historical sites, since some have entrance fees. (ⓣ *State.* ☎*617-242-5642; www.nps.gov/bost. Tours June 21-Aug. daily 10, 11am, 2pm; April 19-June 20 and Sep.-Nov. weekdays 2pm and weekends 10, 11am, 2pm. Arrive 30min. before tour to get a ticket.)*

BEACON HILL. The trail first runs uphill to the **Robert Gould Shaw Memorial,** which honors the first black regiment of the Union Army in the American Civil War and its Bostonian leader. On July 19, 1863, Shaw led the Massachusetts 54th in an assault on Fort Wagner, South Carolina, where he and 62 members of his regiment were killed. The larger-than-life, high-relief bronze sculpture of Gould (by Augustus

Saint-Gaudens, a sculptor of the "American Renaissance") was dedicated on May 31, 1897, in a ceremony attended by surviving soldiers of the 54th as well as prominent activists and thinkers of the era. Opposite the memorial is the gold-domed **Massachusetts State House.** *(Tours ☎617-727-3676. Open M-F 10am-4pm. 40min. tours depart every 20min.; tour pamphlet available at tourist desk. Free.)*

DOWNTOWN. Passing the **Park Street Church,** the trail reaches the **Granary Burial Ground,** where John Hancock, Samuel Adams, Elizabeth Goose ("Mother Goose"), and Paul Revere rest. **Kings Chapel and Burying Ground** is America's oldest Anglican church; the latest inhabitants are Unitarian. The city's first cemetery, next door, is the final resting place of that other midnight rider, William Dawes. *(64 Beacon St. Chapel ☎617-227-2155. Chapel open Memorial Day to Labor Day M 10am-4pm, Tu-W 10-11:15am and 1:30-4pm, Th-Sa 10am-4pm, Su 1:30-4pm. Burying Ground open daily June-Oct. 8am-3pm; Nov.-May 9am-3pm. Chapel $1-3. Burying Ground free.)* Within the walls of the **Old South Meeting House,** Ben Franklin was baptized and Samuel Adams gave the speech that led to the **Boston Tea Party.** *(310 Washington St. ☎617-482-6439; www.oldsouthmeetinghouse.org. Open daily Apr.-Oct. 9:30am-5pm; Nov.-Mar. 10am-4pm. $5, students and seniors $4, ages 6-18 $1.)* Formerly the seat of the British colonial government, the **Old State House** is the oldest public building in Boston. Preserved and run by the Bostonian Society as a museum of the history of Boston, the Old State House is perhaps the most interesting and well organized of the stops along the Freedom Trail. *(206 Washington St. ☎617-720-1713. Open daily July-Aug. 9am-6pm; Sept.-Dec. and Feb.-June 9am-5pm; Jan. 9am-4pm. $5, students and seniors $4, ages 6-18 $1.)* Stand under the Old State House balcony and look right for the ring of cobblestones; this marks the site of the **Boston Massacre.** The **Faneuil Hall** and **Quincy Market** complex, a former meeting hall and current mega-mall, houses a food court and carts selling kitschy items. *(☎617-523-1300. Open M-Sa 10am-9pm, Su noon-6pm.)*

NORTH END. Heading into the heavily Italian-American North End, the trail passes through recently constructed parkland (over The Big Dig) to the **Paul Revere House,** where a self-guided tour helps visitors navigate meticulously recreated 18th-century rooms. *(19 North Sq. ☎617-523-2338; www.paulreverehouse.org. Open June-Oct. daily 9-am-6pm; Nov.-Dec. daily 10am-5pm; Jan. Tu-Su 10am-4pm; Mar.-May daily 9am-5pm. $3, students and seniors $2.50, ages 5-17 $1.)* The **Old North Church** is where Robert Newman was instructed by Revere to hang lanterns— "one if by land, two if by sea"—warning patriots in Charlestown that the British were coming. The church still houses such Revolutionary relics as George Washington's wig and tea from the Boston Tea Party. *(193 Salem St. ☎617-523-6676. Jan. Su and Tu-Sa 10am-4pm, Mar.-May daily 9am-5pm, June-Oct. 9am-6pm, Nov. and Dec. 10am-5pm. Suggested donation $3.)*

CHARLESTOWN. The **Battle of Bunker Hill** is the focus of much of the rest of the trail, which heads across the Charles River to the USS Constitution (a.k.a. "Old Ironsides") and its companion museum. *(☎617-426-1812; www.ussconstitutionmuseum.org. Ship open Apr.-Oct. Tu-Su 10am-6pm; Nov.-Mar. Th-Su 10am-4pm. Museum open daily May-Oct. 9am-6pm; Nov.-Apr. 10am-5pm. Free.)* The trail winds through residential Charlestown toward the Bunker Hill Monument, which is actually on Breed's Hill—where the entire Battle of Bunker Hill was fought. A grand view awaits at the top of the obelisk's 294 steps. *(Monument Sq. Visitor Lodge open daily 9am-5pm. Monument open daily 9am-4:30pm. Free.)*

DOWNTOWN

In 1634, colonists designated **Boston Common** a grazing ground for their cattle. Today, street vendors, runners, and tourists roam the green and congregate near **Frog Pond,** a wading pool in summer and a skating rink in winter. *(Ⓣ Park St.)* Across Charles St. from the Common is the lavish **Public Garden,** the nation's first botanical garden. Bronze versions of the title characters from the children's book **Make Way for Ducklings** point the way to the **Swan Boats,** graceful paddle boats that float around a quiet willow-lined pond. *(☎617-522-1966. Park open daily sunrise-sunset. Boats open Apr.-June daily 10am-4pm; from June 20 to Labor Day daily 10am-5pm; Sept. M-F noon-4pm, Sa-Su 10am-4pm. 15min. ride $2.75, ages 2-15 $1.25, seniors $2, ages 2-15 $1.25.)* Steps from the Common is the frenzied pedestrian mall at **Downtown Crossing,**

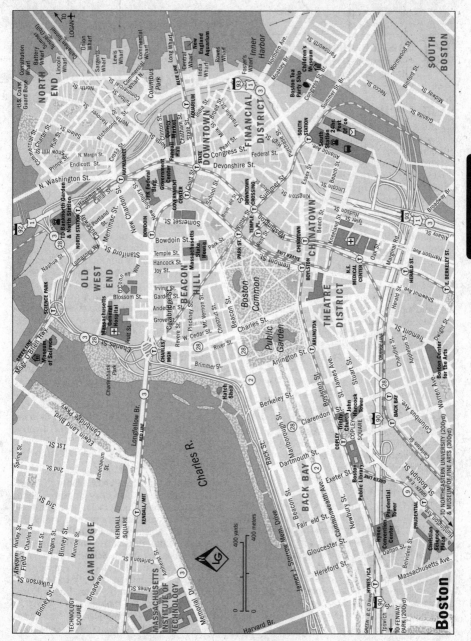

EAST COAST

Boston

the city's biggest budget shopping district and department store mecca.

 DID YOU KNOW? The first football game in America was played on Boston Common in 1862.

BEACON HILL

Looming over the Common is aristocratic Beacon Hill, an exclusive residential neighborhood located on the first spot on the Shawmut Peninsula settled by Puritans. Antique shops, pricey cafes, and ritzy boutiques line narrow **Charles Street,** the neighborhood's main artery. For generations, the hill was home to Boston's intellectual, political, and social elite, christened the "Boston Brahmins." For a taste of Brahmin life, visit the **Nichols House Museum,** restored to its 19th-century state. (55 Mt. Vernon St., off Charles St. ⓣ Charles/MGH. ☎617-227-6993. Open Apr.-Oct. Tu-Sa noon-4pm; Nov.-Mar. Th-Sa noon-4pm. $7, under 12 free. Entrance by tour only.) Boston was the first city in the US to outlaw slavery, and many African-Americans moved to the Beacon Hill area after the Civil War. The **Black Heritage Trail** is a free 2hr., 1½ mi. walk through important Beacon Hill sights of Boston's abolitionist era (☎617-742-5415. Tours daily from Memorial Day to Labor Day 10am, noon, 2pm; from Labor Day to Memorial Day by appointment. Free.) The tour begins at the foot of Beacon Hill, near the Shaw Memorial, and ends at the **Museum of Afro-American History.** (46 Joy St. ☎617-725-0022; www.afroammuseum.org. Museum open M-Sa 10am-4pm. Suggested donation $5.) Also at the foot of the hill is the **Bull & Finch Pub,** 84 Beacon St., the inspiration for the bar in Cheers.

WATERFRONT

The Waterfront district refers to the wharves along Boston Harbor from South Station to the North End. The extensive **New England Aquarium** features cavorting penguins, an animal infirmary, and briny beasts in a four-story tank. (On Central Wharf at ⓣ Aquarium. ☎617-973-5200; www.neaq.org. Open Sept.-June M-F 9am-5pm, Sa-Su 9am-6pm; July-Aug. M-Th 9am-6pm, F-Su 9am-7pm. $20, students and seniors $18, ages 3-11 $12.) The Long Wharf, north of Central Wharf, is **Boston Harbor Cruises's** departure point for sightseeing

cruises and whale watching. (☎617-227-4321; www.bostonharborcruises.com. Open Apr.-Oct. 45min. cruises depart every 30min. 10:30am-4:30pm. $14, students and seniors $12, under 12 $10. 3hr. whale watches $35/32/29. Reservations recommended.)

BACK BAY

Back Bay was initially an uninhabitable tidal flat tucked into the "back" corner of the bay until it was filled in at the end of the 19th century. Today, elegant Back Bay's stately brownstones and shady promenades are laid out in an easily navigable grid. Running through Back Bay, fashionable **Newbury Street,** accessible from ⓣ Hynes/ICA, is where Boston's trendiest strut their stuff and empty their wallets.

COPLEY SQUARE. Named for painter John Singleton Copley, Copley Sq. is popular with both lunching businessmen and Newbury St. tourists. The square is dominated by HH Richardson's Romanesque **Trinity Church,** reflected in the 14 acres of glass used in IM Pei's stunning John Hancock Tower, now closed to the public. (206 Clarendon St. ⓣ Copley. ☎617-536-0944. Open daily M-Sa 9am-6pm, Su 1-6pm. $6, students and seniors $4, under 16 free.) Facing the church, the dramatic **Boston Public Library** is an art museum in disguise; don't miss John Singer Sargent's Triumph of Religion murals or the hidden courtyard. (☎617-536-5400; www.bpl.org. Open M-Th 9am-9pm, F-Sa 9am-5pm.) The 50th floor of the **Prudential Center** next door to Copley Sq. is home to the **Prudential Skywalk,** which offers a 360° view of Boston from a height of 700 ft. (ⓣ Prudential. ☎617-859-0648. Open daily Mar.-Oct. 10am-10pm, Nov.-Feb. 10am-8pm. $11, seniors $9, under 12 $7.50.)

CHRISTIAN SCIENCE PLAZA. Down Massachusetts Ave. from Newbury St., the 14-acre Christian Science Plaza is an epic expanse of concrete, centered on a smooth reflecting pool. The Byzantine-revival "Mother Church" serves as the administrative headquarters of the **First Church of Christ, Scientist,** (not to be confused with the Church of Scientology) a Christian denomination of faith-based healing founded in Boston by Mary Baker Eddy. (175 Huntington Ave. ⓣ Symphony. ☎617-450-2000. 30min. tours Tu noon-4pm, W 1-4pm, Th-Sa noon-5pm, Su 11am-3pm. Free.) The adjacent **Mary Baker Eddy**

Library, another of Boston's library/museum hybrids, has exhibits on Eddy's life and a surreal "Hall of Ideas," where holographic words bubble out of a fountain. Step inside the **Mapparium,** a three-story stained-glass globe that depicts the world as it was in 1934 and details the changes that have occurred since then. The globe's perfect acoustics let you whisper in the ear of Pakistan and hear it in Suriname. *(200 Massachusetts Ave. ☎617-450-7000. Open Tu-Su 10am-4pm. $6, students and seniors $4.)*

JAMAICA PLAIN

Jamaica Plain offers everything quintessentially un-Bostonian: ample parking and Mother Nature. Although it's one of Boston's largest green spaces (over 265 acres), many Boston residents never make it to the lush **Arnold Arboretum,** which has flora and fauna from all around the world. *(Ⓣ Forest Hills. ☎617-524-1718. Visitors center open M-F 9am-4pm, Sa 10am-4pm, Su noon-4pm. Arboretum open daily sunrise-sunset. Free.)* Nearby, **Jamaica Pond** is a popular—but officially forbidden—skinny-dipping spot and a great place for a quiet sail. Naked sailing has yet to catch on. To conclude your JP junket, salute beer-guzzling patriots at the **Sam Adams Brewery.** At the end of the tour, experts teach you how to "taste" beer. *(30 Germania St. Ⓣ Stony Brook. ☎617-368-5080. Tours every 45min. Tu-Th noon-3pm, F noon-5:30pm, Sa 10am-3pm. Tastings 21+. Suggested donation $2.)*

🏛 MUSEUMS

If you're planning a museum binge, consider a **CityPass** (www.citypass.com), which covers the MFA, the Museum of Science, Harvard's Museum of Natural History (p. 172), the Aquarium (opposite page), and the Prudential Center Skywalk (opposite page). Passes, available at museums or online, are valid for nine days. ($44, ages 3-17 $24.)

🖼MUSEUM OF FINE ARTS. The museum hosts one of the world's finest collections of Asian art with exceptional exhibits of Classical, Egyptian, European, and American works. Enter at the Huntington Ave. entrance to experience the museum's traditional grandeur, or arrive through the soaring granite-and-glass West Wing. *(465 Huntington Ave. in* Fenway. *Ⓣ Museum. ☎617-267-9300; www.mfa.org. Open M-Tu 10am-4:45pm, W-F 10am-9:45pm, Sa-Su 10am-5:45pm. $17, students, ages 7-17 $6.50.)*

🖼ISABELLA STEWART GARDNER MUSEUM. This astounding private collection remains exactly as the eccentric Gardner arranged it in her Venetian palazzo over a century ago, not least because her will stipulates that the collection be donated to Harvard if a piece is ever moved. In 1990, 13 major works were stolen in the largest art robbery in US history. The as-yet unclaimed $5 million reward might be incentive enough to test out your sleuthing skills. The mansion still houses some remarkable works of art and is built around a lush, 4-story glass-roofed garden courtyard. *(280 The Fenway. Ⓣ Museum. ☎617-566-1401; www.gardnermuseum.org. Open Tu-Su 11am-5pm. $12, seniors $10, students $5, under 18 and those named "Isabella" free with ID.)*

INSTITUTE OF CONTEMPORARY ART. Recently relocated, the ICA's new building offers an avant-garde take on the waterfront's industrial past. The museum has established a permanent collection, culling the most important works from its array of rotating exhibits by top contemporary artists. Concerts, screenings, and performances of all sorts are held throughout the year. *(100 Northern Ave. Ⓣ Courthouse. ☎617-478-3100; www.icaboston.org. Open Tu-W and Sa-Su 10am-5pm, Th-F 10am-9pm. $12, students and seniors $10, 17 and under free.)*

MUSEUM OF SCIENCE. Make your way through a sea of wide-eyed, field-tripping 4th graders to get a look at the museum's over 400 exhibits, 5-story dome Omnimax Theater, and planetarium. *(Science Park. Ⓣ Science Park. ☎617-723-2500; www.mos.org. Open M-Th and Sa-Su 9am-5pm, F 9am-9pm. $17, ages 3-11 $14, seniors $15, . Omnimax $9/7/8.)*

THE MUSEUM OF BAD ART (MOBA). Located in the basement of the Dedham Community Theater in suburban Dedham, the gallery rotates through exhibits of 20-25 of the worst paintings of all time. The museum's curators discover their disaster pieces at garage sales, in garbage piles, or through word of mouth, then usually title the finds themselves—for example, "In the Cat's Mouth." *(580 High St.*

☎ *781-444-6757; www.museumofbadart.org. Open M-Th and Su 2-9pm, F-Sa 1-10pm. Free.)*

JFK LIBRARY AND MUSEUM. Dedicated to "all those who through the art of politics seek a new and better world" and designed by IM Pei, this enormous oceanside edifice contains 21 exhibits that chronicle the lives of President John F. Kennedy and First Lady Jacqueline Onassis. It's worth a visit just for the building's dramatic views of the harbor. *(Columbia Pt. Ⓣ JFK/UMass. ☎617-514-1600; www.jfklibrary.org. Open daily 9am-5pm. $10, students and seniors $8, ages 13-17 $7.)*

🎵 ENTERTAINMENT

The best publications for entertainment listings are the weekly *Boston Phoenix* and *Dig* (both free from street-side boxes), and the *Boston Globe's* Thursday *Calendar* section.

Bostix, Faneuil Hall and Copley Sq. (☎617-723-5181; www.bostix.org). In addition to selling tickets to most major theater shows, Bostix sells ½-price, day-of-show tickets (after 11am) from their 2 booths. Open M-Sa 10am-6pm, Su 11am-4pm. Cash only.

The Charles Playhouse, 74 Warrenton St. (☎617-426-6912; www.broadwayinboston.com). Ⓣ Boylston. The Charles hosts the famous and energetic Blue Man Group. Tickets from $46. Box office open M-Tu 10am-6pm, W-Th 10am-7pm, F-Sa 10am-9pm, Su noon-6pm.

Boston Lyric Opera, 265 Tremont St., (☎617-542-4912) at the Shubert Theater. Ⓣ Park or Boylston. Tickets $34-159. Box office open 10am-6pm M-Sa.

Fenway Park, 4 Yawkey Way (☎617-482-4769). Ⓣ Kenmore. Diehard fans cheer on their 2004 and 2007 World Series Champion 🧦 **Red Sox** in this fabled stadium. The nation's oldest, smallest, and most expensive baseball park, Fenway is home to the Green Monster, the towering left-field wall. If you can find them, tickets $12-125. Box office M-F 9am-5pm.

TD Banknorth Garden, 50 Causeway St. (Bruins ☎617-624-2327, Celtics 854-8000). Ⓣ North Station. The Gardens host both Boston's basketball, **Celtics,** and hockey, **Bruins,** teams.Celtic tickets $10-140, Bruins $19-99. www.ticektmaster.com for tickets.

🎭 NIGHTLIFE

Youthful and party-prone, Boston residents like to enjoy a few good drinks and the resulting revelry. Be warned: Boston bars and clubs are notoriously strict about age requirements (usually 21+), so bring backup ID. Puritanical (literally) zoning laws require that all nightlife shuts down by 2am. The Ⓣ stops running at 12:30am, so bring extra cash for a taxi ride home.

DANCE CLUBS

Boston is a town for pubbers, not clubbers. The city's few clubs are on or near Kenmore's Lansdowne St., near Ⓣ Kenmore.

The Modern, 48 Winter St. (☎617-536-2100). From its beginnings as a rock and roll bar co-owned by Aerosmith, the Modern has evolved into the classiest member of the Lansdowne trio. Sister clubs Embassy and Avalon are better options for those who want to dance, but here loungers will find lots of black-clad barmates to ogle. The popular martinis come in every flavor from chocolate to apple, though more generic mixed drinks are also available ($10). F-Sa cover $15. Call ahead for DJ schedules. Open M-Sa 10pm-2am.

Europa/Buzz, 51-67 Stuart St. (☎617-267-8969). Ⓣ Boylston. Which face and name you get depends on the night, but this club is usually filled with good-looking fashionable types. 2 dance floors, numerous lounges, and a pool room. On Sa the club is called Buzz. Ladies free Th before 11pm. $10 cover; $15 for ages 19-20.

BARS AND PUBS

Boston's large student and Irish populations mean the city has numerous stops for libations. Most tourists stick to the Irish pubs around downtown, while the Theater District is the premier after-dark destination for the city's international elite. The Back Bay's Boylston St. is a shameless yuppie hangout.

The Littlest Bar, 47 Province St. (☎617-523-9766). Ⓣ Downtown Crossing. No shamrock-flaunting imitation. The Littlest Bar is a true Irish pub, sandwiched into a room the size of your closet. The convivial space packs in about 38 drinkers—a mix of tourists, locals, and visiting Irish students. $4 pints. No cover. Open daily 8:30am-1:30am. Cash only.

Vox Populi, 755 Boylston St. (☎617-424-8300). ⓉCopley. Serving 15 of the most creative martinis in Boston in a hip but unpretentious milieu, this swanky bar is Boylston's "It" spot. A mostly 20 and 30 something crowd on the prowl (the bar was voted Boston's "best place to find a relationship of limited duration") downs $10 drinks. Open M-Sa 11:30am-1am, Su 11:30am-midnight. Kitchen open M-Th and Su until 10pm, F-Sa until 11pm. AmEx/D/MC/V.

Daisy Buchanan's, 240 Newbury St. (☎617-247-8516). ⓉHynes/ICA. Newbury St. may have plenty in common with East Egg, but somehow Daisy Buchanan's has skipped the ostentation and become a gem of a bar. It's home to cheap beer ($3-6), shots ($6), and mixed-drinks ($6) as well as a notably un-Newbury crowd. Open daily 11am-2am. Kitchen open M-Sa until 10pm, Su until 7pm. Cash only.

Purple Shamrock, 1 Union St. (☎617-227-2060). ⓉGovernment Center. Just across the way from Quincy Market, the Purple Shamrock attracts an older crowd of regulars relaxing after work, while a younger crowd drops by this combination restaurant, nightclub, and Irish pub on weekends. A selection of draft beers and specialty drinks (chocolate cake martini $8) are available. 21+ after 9pm. Cover Th-Sa $5. Open daily 11:30am-2am. AmEx/D/MC/V.

GLBT NIGHTLIFE

For listings of GLBT nightlife, pick up a free copy of *Bay Windows*, a gay weekly available everywhere, or check the free *Boston Phoenix* and *Improper Bostonian*. Many of the South End's bars and late-night restaurants, accessible from ⓉBack Bay, are all gay-friendly (sorry ladies, these are mostly for the boys). Lesbians flock to Jamaica Plain's bookstores and cafes, many of which are queer-owned. Of late, the gay community has started "guerrilla" gay-night, a coup of otherwise heterosexual clubs and bars (1st F of every month; http://bostonguerrilla.googlepages.com).

Ramrod and Machine, 1254-1256 Boylston St. (☎617-266-2986; www.ramrodboston.com). ⓉHynes/ICA. A gay institution for 25 years, Ramrod and Machine offers the full range of nightlife

experience, from friendly drinking to kinky fetishism. Ramrod is a traditional bar: video machines, pool tables, and Th karaoke. Machine's club nights (cover $5-8) offer blisteringly loud house and scantily clad male models gyrating on platforms. M 19+. Open daily noon-2am. Cash only.

Chaps, 100 Warrenton St. (☎617-695-9500). ⓉNE Medical Center. A young, attractive male crowd moves in time to urban beats at Chaps, one of Boston's most popular gay bars and dance clubs. Renowned theme nights (W Latino night, Th "Music Factory," and Sa "Evolution") attract throngs of partygoers, especially W and Sa when a younger crowd turns out in droves. Drinks $3-5. W and Su 19+. Cover usually $4-10. Open M-Sa 3pm-2am, Su noon-2am. AmEx/D/MC/V.

Club Café, 209 Columbus Ave. (☎617-536-0966; www.clubcafe.com). ⓉArlington. Atop a glass-roofed fitness club, this restaurant-cafe and bar caters to the South End's "guppie" (gay-yuppie) crowd. Regulars know that the "club" moniker is deceiving: Club Café is more restaurant than bar and certainly not so much club, making it a good place to have actual conversations. Bar open daily 11:30am-2am. Club open M-W 11:30am-2:30pm and 5:30-10pm, Th-F 11:30am-2:30pm and 5:30-11pm, Sa 5:30-11pm, Su 11am-3pm and 5:30-10pm. AmEx/D/MC/V.

◸ THE ROAD TO CAMBRIDGE: 3 MI.

Head northwest on **Congress Street** and bear left onto **Merrimac Street.** Bang a left onto **New Chardon Street** and then turn right onto **Cambridge Street.** Continue onto **Route 3 North,** turning right on the ramp to stay on Rte. 3. Across the river, get onto **Memorial Drive** and take a right onto **Massachusetts Avenue** to head into Cambridge. Alternatively, and to avoid high parking fees in Cambridge, you can park your car in Boston and take the Red Line to ⓉHarvard.

CAMBRIDGE   ☎617

While world-renowned universities Harvard (founded 1636) and MIT (1861) do lovingly co-habitate in Cambridge, they don't exhaustively define the city's culture. Sure, in the vicinity of these old-style private institutions you're likely to see popped collars aplenty—but it's equally probable that you'll observe dreadlocks and protest signs. Perhaps Cambridge's biggest tourist draw, however, is the headquarters of ⧉**Let's Go Publications,** also known as the headquarters of cool.

VITAL STATS
Population: 125,000
Tourist Office: Cambridge Office for Tourism (☎617-441-2884; www.cambridge-usa.org), in Harvard Sq. The office runs a booth outside ⓣ Harvard with plenty of maps and info. Call for hours.
Internet Access: Free public Wi-Fi in **Harvard Sq.** Also free at **Boloco** 71 Mt. Auburn St. (☎617-354-5838), in Harvard Sq., with any purchase.
Post Office: 770 Massachusetts Ave. (☎617-275-8777), in Central Sq. Open M-F 7am-7pm, Sa 7:30am-2pm. **Postal Code:** 02139.

▮ ORIENTATION

"The People's Republic" of Cambridge is a 10min. ride down the **MBTA Red Line** from Boston. ⓣ **Kendall/MIT** is just across the river from Boston, near MIT's campus. The subway continues to **Central Square,** a barhopper's paradise; **Harvard Square,** the city's heart; and largely residential **Porter Square.** Cambridge's main traffic and pedestrian roadway is **Massachusetts Avenue ("Mass. Ave."),** which follows the same route as the Red Line, but aboveground. Harvard Sq. sits at the intersection of Mass. Ave., **Brattle, JFK,** and **Dunster Streets.**

▮ ACCOMMODATIONS

Cambridge Bed and Muffin, 267 Putnam Ave. (☎617-576-3166; www.bedandmuffin.com). ⓣ Harvard. Offers 5 clean, private bedrooms, 1 muffin room (kitchen), and 2 shared bathrooms. Owner cheerfully provides extra quilts and daily continental breakfast. Rooms $80, with 2-night stay $65. Cash only. ❹

Cambridge Gateway Inn, 211 Concord Tnpk, (☎617-661-7800; www.cambridgegatewayinn. com). ⓣ Alewife. Right by the highway, but one of the best deals around. Free Internet. Singles from $90. AmEx/D/MC/V. ❹

The Irving House, 24 Irving St. (☎617-547-4600), less than a 10min. walk from Harvard Sq. ⓣ Harvard. Has 44 rooms. Complimentary drinks, teacakes, and brownies provided until

10pm. Free Internet. Singles $75-185, with private bath $90-265. AmEx/D/MC/V. ❺

▮ FOOD

Cambridge's restaurants can be roughly divided into two categories: where students eat and where students eat when their parents are in town. Though everyone loves dinner at Chez Henri, when on your own dollar you're best off sticking to the numerous tasty options in the first category.

▨ Pinocchio's, 74 Winthrop St. (☎617-876-4897). ⓣ Harvard. Has survived rampant commercialization and doesn't seem to be going anywhere. Students flock to "Noch's" late at night for its famous crispy-gooey Sicilian pizza ($2.25 per slice, 2 for $4). Open M-W 11am-1am, Th-Sa 11am-2am, Su 1pm-midnight. MC/V over $10. ❶

Café Pamplona, 12 Bow St. (☎617-492-0352). ⓣ Harvard. Harvard's hidden Bohemian treasure. Home to students who scribble in black moleskin notebooks and avidly discuss topics like consumerist identity over espresso. Bright yellow cellar walls, small semi-subterranean windows, and geraniums in flowerpots. Dining options limited but excellent. Garlic soup $4. *Tortilla española* $7. Open M-Sa 11am-midnight, Su 2pm-midnight. AmEx/D/MC/V. ❶

Darwin's Ltd., 148 Mt. Auburn St. (☎617-354-5233; www.darwinsltd.com), 2min. past the Post Office from Harvard Sq. 2nd location at 1629 Cambridge St. ⓣ Harvard. (☎617-492-2999). This specialty store's deli serves creative sandwiches ($6-7.50) named for local streets intersecting Brattle, like the Sparks (roast beef with horseradish mayonnaise) and the Hubbard Park (hummus, avocado, green apple, carrots, tomato, and sprouts). Has an extensive collection of coffees and teas and low plush couches for lounging. Open M-Sa 6:30am-9pm, Su 7am-9pm. AmEx/D/MC/V over $10. ❷

Punjabi Dhaba, 225 Hampshire St. (☎617-547-8272), in Inman Sq. An "Indian Highwayside Cafe" with a fast-food feel that serves customers metal cafeteria trays of Indian food. Delicious. Entrees $5-11. Cash only. ❷

The Middle East, 472-480 Mass. Ave. (☎617-864-3278; www.mideastclub.com). ⓣ Central. Located above the nightclub of the same name, this restaurant's *baba ghanoush* ($4.50) and couscous ($9.75-11.50) will take you straight to Rabat. Free Wi-Fi. Brunch Sa and Su 11am-3pm (18+). Open M-W and Su 11am-midnight, Th-Sa 11am-1am. ❷

Dalí, 415 Washington St. (☎617-661-3254; www.dalirestaurant.com), in Inman Sq. Gilded walls, blue fairy lights, and disembodied mannequin legs. As unconventional and charming as the artist himself. Serves the best tapas in town, with 40+ dishes to choose from ($5-10). Sausage with figs $8. Paella $24. Vegetarian options available. Drink menu includes sangria, Spanish wines, and ports. Open daily 5:30pm-12:30am. Reservations accepted M-Th before 6:30pm and F-Sa before 6pm. AmEx/D/MC/V. ❸

Chez Henri, 1 Shepard St. (☎617-354-8980; www.chezhenri.com), between Ⓣ Harvard and Ⓣ Porter. Warm, red walls, antique French posters, and wrought-iron and red glass lamps. Classically French with an offbeat Cuban twist. An inventive menu that tends toward seafood with specials like ceviche ($14) and rice-crusted tuna ($28). Appetizers $11-19. Entrees $24-32. Open M-Th 6-10pm, F-Sa 5:30-10:30pm, Su 5:30-9:30pm. Reservations accepted for 6 or more. ❺

Christina's Homemade Ice Cream, 1255 Cambridge St. (☎617-492-7021), in Inman Sq. Ⓣ #69 bus. Over 40 exotic flavors, including Mexican *cajeto,* Indian cardamom, and pistachio-infused *khulfi.* Ambrosial. Ice cream and frozen yogurt $2.57 for 1 scoop, $3.37 for 2, $4 for 3. Sundaes $4.52-5.65. Pint $4.65. Cash only. ❶

BerryLine, 1 Arrow St. (☎617-868-3500; www.theberryline.com), Ⓣ Harvard. Line out the door nightly. This froyo ($2.40-4.30), served with a selection of fruits, nuts, and sweet toppings, has gained cult status among Harvard undergraduates. Open M-W and Su noon-11pm, Th-Sa noon-midnight. AmEx/D/MC/V. ❶

◎ SIGHTS

HARVARD UNIVERSITY
Tours of Harvard University come in many flavors. The official Crimson Key Tours, given by Harvard Events and Information (and led by good-looking undergrads) offer a dignified look into the university's past. Leaves from Holyoke Center Arcade, across Dunster St. from the Ⓣ *.* ☎*617-495-1573; www. harvard.edu. Open M-Sa 9am-5pm. Tours from Sept. to mid-May M-F 10am, 2pm, Sa 2pm; June to mid-Aug. M-Sa 10, 11:15am, 2, 3:15pm. Unofficial Tours*

offers a sensationalized, but wholly entertaining, version of Harvard's history. Outside Out of Town News, Ⓣ *Harvard. www.harv.unofficialtours.com. Daily 10:30, 11:30am, 12:30, 1:30, 2:30, 3:30pm. 90min. Free. Gratuity discretionary.*

Just off Mass Ave., **Harvard Yard** is the center of undergraduate life at Harvard University. Look out for plump squirrels—and for the foreign tourists who photograph them.

JOHN HARVARD STATUE. The most photographed monument in the Yard is known as "The Statue of the Three Lies" because the statue depicts not John Harvard, but one of Harvard college's first students; Harvard did not found the college but only donated his library to it; and the college was founded in 1636, not 1638 as the statue indicates.

WIDENER MEMORIAL LIBRARY. Widener houses three million of Harvard's more than 15 million books, making it the world's largest university library. Unfortunately, even the most persistent tourists are denied entry.

MASSACHUSETTS HALL. Harvard's oldest standing building (built in 1720) once housed Revolutionary-era troops and is now home to the president's offices. The building was occupied in 2001 for three weeks by student protesters who sought a higher minimum wage for Harvard employees.

UNIVERSITY HALL. Designed by Charles Bulfinch, this hall was Harvard College's dining room until 1849. Today, "U Hall" houses administrative offices.

> **?** **DID YOU KNOW?** The first book printed in the US, the *Bay Psalm Book*, was printed in Cambridge in 1640.

MIT
Campus tours begin at the MIT Info Center and include visits to the Chapel and the Kresge Auditorium, which touches the ground in only 3 places. 77 Mass. Ave. In Lobby 7/Small Dome building. ☎*617-253-1000; www.mit.edu.* Ⓣ *Kendall/MIT. Tours M-F 10:45am and 2:45pm.*

The Massachusetts Institute of Technology, the world's leading institution in the study of science, is also home to some dangerously good poker players.

MIT MUSEUM. The museum features technological wonders in dazzling multimedia exhibitions. Highlights include a gallery of "hacks" (elaborate, if nerdy, pranks) and the world's largest hologram collection. *(265 Mass. Ave. Bldg. N51. ☎617-253-4444. Open daily 10am-5pm. Closed major holidays. $7.50; students, seniors, and ages 5-18 $3. Su 10am-noon free.)*

OTHER SIGHTS

HARVARD BOOK AND BINDING SERVICE. This small locale is easy to miss but claims a devoted following. Robert Marshall, the friendly Renaissance man who runs the shop, will proudly take customers on a tour of his collection, which includes an original copy of *Paradise Lost* and an impressive collection of Greek and Roman coins ($10-750). Aside from the rare and ancient books that rival the cost of a college education, most of the shop's used books go for $2. *(5 JFK St., 3rd fl. ⓣ Harvard. ☎617-233-6756. Open daily 9am-5pm.)*

LONGFELLOW HOUSE. This lemon-yellow house was the home of famous 19th-century American poet Henry Wadsworth Longfellow, who lived here for over 40 years until his death in 1882. *(105 Brattle St. ☎617-876-4491; www.nps. gov/long. Accessible by guided tour only. Tours May-June Th-Sa 10:30, 11:30am, 1, 2, 3, 4pm; June-Sept. W-Su. Gardens and grounds open daily dawn to dusk.)*

TORY ROW. Until the Revolutionary War began, tree-lined Brattle St. was referred to as Tory Row because the stately mansions along the street were home to British sympathizers, known as Loyalists or Tories. Nearly 300 years later, the homes still house Cambridge's most blue-blooded families. *(ⓣ Harvard.)*

🏛 MUSEUMS

HARVARD MUSEUM OF NATURAL HISTORY. The museum's most famous holding is its spectacular glass-flower display, which includes over 3000 incredibly lifelike, life-size or magnified glass models of plants. Other museum exhibits include a narwhal skeleton, a 1600 lb. amethyst geode, and a popular 42 ft. **Kronosaurus.** *(26 Oxford St. ☎617-495-3045; www.hmnh. harvard.edu. Ticket includes admission to the Peabody. Open daily 9am-5pm. $9, seniors and students $7, children $6. MA residents free W 3-5pm, Su 9am-noon.)*

PEABODY MUSEUM OF ARCHAEOLOGY AND ETHNOLOGY. Founded in 1866, the Peabody is one of the oldest museums in the world devoted to anthropology. *(11 Divinity Ave. ☎617-496-1027; www.peabody.harvard.edu. Ticket includes admission to the Museum of Natural History. Open daily 9am-5pm. $9, seniors and students $7, children $6. MA residents free W 3-5pm, Su 9am-noon.)*

HARVARD SEMITIC MUSEUM. Founded in 1889, the Harvard Semitic Museum was moved to its present location in 1903 and has since become the Harvard Department of Near Eastern Languages and Civilizations The museum's most prominent exhibit is a recreation of a house from ancient Israel. *(6 Divinity Ave. ☎617-495-4631. Open M-F 10am-4pm, Su 1-4pm. Free.)*

> **TIP**
>
> **HARVARD ART MUSEUMS.** Harvard's celebrated art museums, the Fogg, Busch-Reisinger, and Sackler, will be undergoing renovation until 2013. During the five-year project, a limited selection of works from the collections will be on display at the current Sackler Museum, 485 Broadway (☎617-495-9400; www.artmuseums. harvard.edu).

🍸 NIGHTLIFE

On weekend nights, Harvard Sq. is equal parts gathering place, music hall, and three-ring circus; locals, students, pierced suburban punks, and tourists enjoy a variety of street performances. Bars abound in Harvard Sq., but Cambridge's best nightlife options are in Central Sq., a barhopper's heaven.

- **Charlie's Kitchen,** 10 Eliot St. (☎617-492-9646). ⓣ Harvard. A vinyl oasis of greasy goodness. Upstairs, sports TV and a loud, laid back ambiance. Friendly waitstaff. 16 beers on tap. Double cheeseburger $5. Lobster rolls with fries $11. Appetizers $4-7.50, entrees $4-11. Live music on M, karaoke on Tu. Appetizers $4-7.50, entrees $4-11. Open M-W 10:30am-12:45am, Th-Sa 10:30am-1:45am and Su 11:30am-12:45am. Kitchen open until last call.

- **The People's Republik,** 878 Mass. Ave. (☎617-491-6969). ⓣ Central. Keeps the proletariat happy with cheap beer and cheeky chalkboards with adages like "Drink beer—it's cheaper than gasoline." 21+. No cover. Open M-W, Su noon-1am, Th-Sa noon-2am. Cash only.

Grendel's Den, 89 Winthrop St. (☎617-491-1160). ⊤ Harvard. Subterranean venue with small wood tables and limited outdoor seating. Gets busy during happy hour, when all menu items are ½-price with a $3 min. drink purchase. Bar food $3.50-10. Open daily 11:30am-1am.

Daedalus, 45 Mt. Auburn St. (☎617-349-0071). ⊤ Harvard. 2 floors (and 2 bars) mean room for both intimate couples and gregarious groups. Outdoor deck upstairs. Calamari $10. Flank steak $22. 12 beers on tap and specialty cocktails ($8-10). Open M-W 11am-1am, Th-Sa 11am-2am, Su 10am-1am. Expect a wait during prime dinner hours. AmEx/D/MC/V.

The Cantab Lounge, 738 Mass. Ave. (☎617-354-2685; www.cantab-lounge.com). ⊤ Central. Eclectically fuses arcade games, live entertainment, music, and heaping nachos ($4-6). Diane Blue and the Fatback Band play every F and Sa starting at 9pm. Open-mike folk session (M 8pm), bluegrass (Tu 8:30pm), and acclaimed poetry slam (W 8pm) round out the entertainment options. Cover Th-Sa varies but is less than $10. Open M-W 8am-1am, Th-Sa 8am-2am, Su noon-1am. Kitchen temporarily closed; check website for re-opening.

Enormous Room, 567 Mass. Ave. (☎617-491-5550; www.enormous.tv). ⊤ Central. This bar is so exclusive that it doesn't even have a sign on the door. Look for the door with an elephant on it and head up the stairs to an avant-garde haven. Hummus and grape leaves $4. La Perla (tequila, strawberry puree, and champagne) $9. 21+. F-Sa cover $3 after 9:30pm. Open M-F and Su 5:30pm-1am, Th-Sa 5:30pm-2am.

🚩 THE ROAD TO SALEM: 16 MI.

From Boston, take **I-93 North** to **I-95 North,** which splits into I-95 and Rte. 128. Take **Route 128 North** to **Route 114 East,** which leads into town.

SALEM ☎978

Salem can't seem to get over 1692, the year in which witch hysteria gripped the town. Although Salem has more to offer than witch kitsch, its infamous past has spawned a Halloween-based tourist trade that culminates in the month-long Haunted Happenings festival in October. The town also has a fantastic art museum and a legacy as the birthplace of author Nathaniel Hawthorne. So whether you're into the paranormal, tacky tourist traps, or great literature, you'll likely find Salem to be a wicked cool little town.

VITAL STATS

Population: 40,400

Tourist Office: Salem Visitors Center, 2 New Liberty St. (☎978-740-1650). Open daily 9am-5pm.

Tours: Like everything else in Salem, walking tours of the city focus on witchcraft, hangings, and the supernatural. Expect tours to be over the top. If you're into the witch mania, you may as well go all-out. The **Spellbound Tour,** 192 Essex St., (☎978-745-0138; www.spellboundtours.com), led by a licensed ghost hunter, takes visitors on a quest for Salem's spectral undead. Tours Mar.-Oct. 8pm; Nov. 5:30pm. $13, students and seniors $10, under 13 $7. **Salem Trolley Tours** (☎978-744-5469) provides a more historical view of the city. The tour takes visitors through the city to several non-witch-related sites. Tours Apr.-Oct. daily 10am-5pm. $12, seniors $10, ages 5-14 $5.

Library and Internet Access: Salem Public Library, 370 Essex St. (☎978-744-0860). Open M-Th 9am-9pm, F-Sa 9am-5pm, Su 1-5pm.

Post Office: 2 Margin St. (☎978-744-4671). Open M-F 8am-5pm, Sa 8am-1pm, Su 8am-3pm. **Postal Code:** 01970.

🧭 ORIENTATION

Most of Salem's attractions center on **Essex Street** and **Derby Street,** which run east-west parallel to **Route 107** (leading to Beverly). **Washington Street** runs north-south, becoming **Route 114** (leading to Danvers) south of Derby St. **US 1A** runs parallel to Washington St. Taking Derby St. north leads to the waterfront.

🏨 ACCOMMODATIONS

Salem has a large number of B&Bs and quaint inns in historic houses, most outside the price range of the budget traveler.

Clipper Ship Inn, 40 Bridge St. (☎978-745-8022; www.clippershipinn.com), off US 1A. 60 larger-than-average rooms have A/C and cable TV, but guests have to drive into the downtown area—

E A S T   C O A S T

or take a long walk–to reach the most famous attractions. Rooms M-Th and Su $75-105, F-Sa $85-115. AmEx/D/MC/V. ❹

Days Inn, 152 Endicott St. (☎978-774-8045). Take Rte. 114 W. to Rte. 128 N. Exit 24. Large rooms with fridges, microwaves, and irons. Continental breakfast included. Wi-Fi. Rooms M-Th and Su $70, F-Sa $80. AmEx/D/MC/V. ❸

🍴 FOOD

Fuel, 196 Essex St. (☎978-741-0850). Serves creative fare such as apple-and-strawberry salad ($5.25) and the Green Monster wrap (lettuce, broccoli, snow peas, sprouts, pine nuts, cheese; $5.50). Design your own wrap or salad from a list of ingredients: choose wisely, for with great power comes great responsibility. Free Wi-Fi. Open M-F 11am-5pm, Sa-Su 8am-5pm. Cash only. ❶

Derby Deli Cafe, 245 Derby St. (☎978-741-2442). Deli options like smoked turkey ($4.50) as well as panini and salads. Open M-Sa 9am-9pm, Su 9am-6pm. MC/V. ❶

👁 SIGHTS

PEABODY ESSEX MUSEUM. The Peabody houses an enormous collection of attractively displayed Asian art from China, Japan, and India. The museum also has collections of maritime and contemporary art; a highlight is the Yin Yu Tang house, which was dismantled, shipped from China, and reassembled for display. (*East India Sq. ☎978-745-9500 or 866-745-1876; www.pem.org. Open daily 10am-5pm. $15, students and under 16 $11. Yin Yu Tang $4 more.*)

HOUSE OF THE SEVEN GABLES. The so-called "second most famous house in America," the Turner-Ingersoll Mansion became famous as Nathaniel Hawthorne's House of the Seven Gables. Many changes were made to the home in 1910 to make it more closely resemble the house in the book, including the addition of a secret passageway to the second floor and a recreation of the Cent Shop from the novel. (*54 Turner St. ☎978-744-0991; www.7gables.org. Open daily July-Sept. 10am-7pm, Oct. 9:30am-7pm; Nov.-June 10am-5pm. $12, ages 5-12 $7.25.*)

SALEM MARITIME NATIONAL HISTORICAL SITE. Down the waterfront from the witch-

oriented section of town, the site is dedicated to Salem's colonial and maritime history. The Orientation Center shows a film entitled *To the Farthest Part of the Rich East* every 30min. throughout the day. Guides lead tours of the 1817 Custom House, where Hawthorne worked, the 1762 Derby House, and the 1672 Narbonne House, once owned by wealthy Salem residents. Visitors can also tour the *Friendship*, a three-masted ship constructed in the late 18th century. (*193 Derby St. ☎978-740-1660; www.nps.gov/sama. Orientation Center open daily 9am-5pm. Tour times vary; call ahead. $5, ages 6-15 and seniors $3.*)

WITCH HOUSE. Salem certainly doesn't try to hide the most infamous event in its history. Most of the museums that have opened to capitalize on the witch craze are overwrought, tacky, and not worth the price of admission. The Witch House, once home to witch-trial judge Jonathan Corwin, is the only home with legitimate historical ties to the trials. The museum focuses on everyday life in the 17th century, turning only briefly to its role in the trials. (*310 Essex St. ☎978-744-8815; www.salem-web.com/witchhouse. Open May-Nov. daily 10am-5pm. Guided tours every hr. $8, ages 6-14 $4.*)

SALEM WITCH TRIALS MEMORIAL. The memorial consists of stones with the names and dates of the 20 individuals killed during the hysteria. (*Next to the graveyard. Free.*)

SALEM WITCH MUSEUM. The museum tells the story of the trials from the perspective of those involved through life-size figures and recorded narration. (*Washington Sq. ☎978-744-1692; www.salemwitchmuseum.com. Open daily July-Aug. 10am-7pm; Sept.-June 10am-5pm. $8, ages 6-14 $5.50.*)

BIG DETOUR. Explore the kooky side of New Hampshire on the **Flumes, Frescoes, and Fire Pits Big Detour,** p. 182.

THE ROAD TO ROCKPORT: 22 MI. Take **Route 128 North** to **Route 127.**

ROCKPORT ☎978

Cape Ann, on which Rockport is located, claims to be the "home of the perfect vacation." While that's up for debate, Rockport is well worth a visit. With historic and offbeat sights and a beautiful waterfront, it's got something for everyone. The area can be an expensive stay, but luckily budget travelers will be content just walking the streets of Bearskin Neck.

VITAL STATS

Population: 7300

Tourist Office: Rockport Chamber of Commerce, 3 Whistlestop Mall, off Rte. 127 N. (☎978-546-6575; www.rockportusa.com). Open M-F 9am-5pm.

Library and Internet Access: Rockport Public Library, 17 School St. (☎978-546-6934). Open M and W-Th 1-8pm, Tu 1-5pm, Sa 10am-5pm, Su 1-6pm.

Post Office: 39 Broadway (☎978-546-2667). Open M-F 9am-5pm, Sa 8:30am-noon. **Postal Code:** 03870.

◈ ORIENTATION

Route 127 leads into **Main Street** and **Broadway,** two of the town's central streets. Main St. turns to run along the water and leads into **Mount Pleasant Street** to the southeast and **Beach Street** to the northwest. This stretch along the beach is the main commercial and tourist section of town and has numerous restaurants, shops, and accommodations. The intersection of Main St., Mt. Pleasant St., and Bearskin Neck forms **Dock Square,** the center of the downtown.

⚑ ACCOMMODATIONS

Like many towns along the New England coast, Rockport has a plethora of accommodations, most of which are hard on the pocketbook. During the summer, there's nothing in the area for under $100.

> **Bearskin Neck Motor Lodge,** 64 Bearskin Neck (☎978-546-6677). Porches with fantastic views of the harbor and ocean. 8 rooms just steps from the area attractions. Rooms June-Sept. $159; Oct.-Nov. and May $109. AmEx/D/MC/V. ❺

> **The Peg Leg Inn,** 18 Beach St. (☎978-546-2352 or 800-346-2352; www.thepegleginn.com), across the street from Front Beach. 14 colonial-style rooms with beautiful views of the water. Rooms are spacious and have TVs, refrigerators, and microwaves. Breakfast included. Open Apr.-Dec. Rooms $150-235. AmEx/MC/V. ❺

▤ FOOD

Rockport was formerly a dry town, and even now few restaurants sell alcohol. Some allow you to bring your own, but you'll have to carry it from afar: there are no liquor stores in Rockport.

> **Roy Moore Lobster Company** (☎978-546-6696), on Bearskin Neck. The morning's catch is boiled and buttered for lunch. Take your lobster (price varies, usually $10-12 per lb.), clam chowder ($4), or baked stuffed clams ($1 each) to the back deck, which overlooks the water. Open daily 7:30am-6pm. MC/V. ❷

> **Top Dog** (☎978-546-0006; www.topdogrockport. com), on Bearskin Neck. Serves a wide array of dogs—hot dogs, that is—such as the Chihuahua (jalapeño peppers, salsa, and cheese; $3.50) and the Golden Retriever (macaroni and cheese; $3.50). Diners get a free meal if they are ordering when the Red Sox hit a home run. Open May-Oct. daily 11am-9pm. Cash only. ❶

◖ SIGHTS

BEARSKIN NECK. One of the country's oldest artist colonies, Bearskin Neck is now also one of Rockport's most tourist-oriented areas, featuring gift shops, ice-cream stores, and, of course, galleries aplenty. Most of the galleries highlight painting, but a few display sculpture and jewelry. Though the area is certainly geared toward tourists, it avoids kitsch, making it an enjoyable area for walking and window-shopping. (At the center of town, off Dock Sq. From Broadway, take a left onto Mt. Pleasant St., then a right onto Bearskin Neck. There is not a lot of space to drive, so parking and walking is easiest.)

MOTIF NO. 1. A sort of little fish shack that could, Motif No. 1 is still just a fish shack, but it is perhaps the most famous fish shack in the world. At the end of Bradley Wharf in

Bearskin Neck, the red fish shack is the most-often-painted building in America. Legend has it that the building received its name when artist Lester Hornby saw yet another student's drawing featuring this popular subject—or motif—and christened it "Motif no. 1." Visitors can try their hand at painting, but the building itself is locked.

PAPER HOUSE. In 1922, Elis F. Stenman, a mechanical engineer from Cambridge, was experimenting with newspapers as an insulation material for his summer cottage. After the walls survived a harsh New England winter with minimal damage, Stenman decided to leave them exposed, and the paper house was born. While it has a wood frame and a normal roof, the walls and the furniture that Stenman continued to add until his death in 1942 are made entirely of newspapers. About 100,000 newspapers were used to construct the home, a grandfather clock, a radio cabinet, and even a piano. *(52 Pigeon Hill. Follow Rte. 127 north to Pigeon Cove, take a left onto Curtis St., and make a left onto Pigeon Hill. The house is on the right; there are signs marking the way. ☎ 978-546-2629; www.paperhouse-rockport.com. Open Apr.-Oct. daily 10am-5pm. $1.50.)*

HALIBUT POINT STATE PARK. Occupying the land around the Babson Farm Quarry off Rte. 127, Halibut Point State Park features a half-mile, self-guided walking tour around the 60 ft. deep quarry. Brochures detailing the tour and its sights are available at the visitors center, which highlights the history and natural habitat of the park and the artifacts left over from the quarry. Visitors can also follow a path down to a beach of huge rocks, but wear shoes suitable for climbing over stones and exploring tide pools. *(On Gott Ave. Take Rte. 127 N. out of downtown Rockport and turn right on Gott Ave. ☎ 978-546-2997; www.mass.gov/dcr. Open from Memorial Day to Labor Day 8am-8pm; from Labor Day to Memorial Day sunrise-sunset. Free.)*

⚑ THE ROAD TO ESSEX: 11 MI.
From Rockport, take **Route 127 South** to Gloucester, then switch to **Route 133 West,** which leads into Essex.

ESSEX ☎ 978

Tiny Essex—without even a traffic light to its name—is known for two distinctive features: its many antique shops and flea markets and Lawrence "Chubby" Woodman, who, in 1916, dipped the clam in vegetable oil and cornmeal and invented the fried clam. The **White Elephant,** 32 Main St., and **RC Schonick Antiques,** 67 Main St., are among the town's endless stores devoted to serious antiquing. On the weekends, deal hunters flock to **Todd Farm,** a few miles north on Rte. 1A in Rowley, for anything that can be sold. *(☎ 978-948-3300; www.todd-farm.com. Open Su 5am-3pm.)* **Essex Shipbuilding Museum and Store,** 66 Main St., has exhibits on schooners, dories, Chebacco boats, and privateers. *(☎ 978-768-7541; www.essexship-buildingmuseum.org. Open W-Su 10am-5pm. $7, students and seniors $6, ages 6-12 $5.)*

Visitors can stay at the town's only hotel, the **Essex River House Motel ❺,** 132 Main St., where each room has a name, like the Puritan or the Tattler. The rooms are smallish but nicely decorated. *(☎ 978-768-6800; www.essexriverhousemotel.com. Rooms $99-130. D/MC/V.)* To experience Essex's clamming history, head to **Woodman's ❺,** 121 Main St., for fried clams ($20) served the way Chubby liked 'em. Proud of its history, Woodman's has a black-and-white picture of the shop dating from 1919. *(☎ 978-768-7541; www.woodmans.com. Open daily in summer 11am-10pm; in winter 11am-9pm. Cash only.)* Across the street is **Tom Shea's ❸,** 122 Main St., which offers a formal dining experience and serves seafood delicacies like clam chowder ($6), Tuscan catfish ($20), and the Essex clam plate (market price). Enjoy the view of the Essex River. *(☎ 978-768-6931; www.tomsheas.com. Open daily 11:30am-10pm. AmEx/D/MC/V.)*

⚑ THE ROAD TO RYE AND HAMPTON BEACH: 42 MI.
From Essex, take **Route 133 North.** Switch to **US 1A North** in Rowley, then change to **US 1 North** in Newburyport. As you approach Hampton, switch back to US 1A, which becomes **Ocean Boulevard.**

RYE AND HAMPTON BEACH ☎603

New Hampshire may not have much shoreline, but it certainly tries to make the most of it. Unfortunately, that means crowded beaches, gaudy boardwalks, and motels everywhere. Hampton Beach is packed with tourists during the summer; drive farther north, and you'll find more peaceful shores.

VITAL STATS
Population: 5200/15,000
Tourist Office: Hampton Beach Chamber of Commerce (☎603-926-8717; www.hamptonbeach.org), on Ocean Blvd. Open 9:30am-9pm.
Library and Internet Access: Rye Public Library, 581 Washington Rd. (☎603-964-8401), off US 1A near Wallis Sands State Beach, in Rye. Open M, W, F 9am-5pm, Tu and Th 9am-8pm, Sa 9am-3pm.
Post Office: 25 Stickney Terr. (☎603-926-6413), in Hampton Beach. Open M-F 8:30am-5pm, Sa 8:30am-noon. **Postal Code:** 03870.

⊞❋ ORIENTATION

US 1A runs along the shore in both towns. In Hampton Beach, it becomes one-way heading north, so southbound drivers must take **Ashworth Avenue** and double back. Parking is tight in Hampton during high season, especially on summer weekends. Beach meters charge $1.50 per hour if paid with quarters or $5 for 4hrs. if you purchase a token by the visitors center; lots are $5-10 for all-day parking on weekdays but can be as much as $20 on the weekends. Expect slow- moving traffic.

🛏 ACCOMMODATIONS

Hampton Beach is filled to the brim with hotels and motels that are close to the beach. The farther you go from the ocean, the less you'll pay.

Regal Inn, 162 Ashworth Ave. (☎603-926-7758 or 800-445-6782; www.regalinn.com). Offers large, clean rooms within walking distance of Hampton Beach as well as a large outdoor pool. Rooms $69-109. AmEx/D/MC/V. ❹

Janmere Motel, 52 Ashworth Ave. (☎603-926-3925). Has some of the best prices around. Some rooms don't have A/C, but all are clean and have TVs and access to a pool. Rooms without A/C $90, with A/C $135. Cash only. ❹

⊞ FOOD

Along with the henna tattoo stands and arcades, **Ocean Boulevard** is crowded with fast-food joints, burger stands, and pizza parlors.

Purple Urchin, 167 Ocean Blvd. (☎603-929-0800; www.purpleurchin.net), right across from the visitors center. The view alone is well worth climbing up the stairs; consider it VIP seating for the beach concerts on the stage across the street. The menu mainly features seafood, like the fried-haddock sandwich ($11), but also includes a good selection of salads, including one topped with crumbled blue cheese and bacon ($6). Open daily noon-10pm. AmEx/D/MC/V. ❷

Ray's Seafood, 1677 Ocean Blvd. (☎603-436-2280; www.raysseafoodrestaurant.com), just past Rye Harbor State Park. Serves only lobster it catches itself. Try the lobster quesadilla ($9) or baked mushrooms ($8), stuffed with lobster. You can even mail loved ones back home their very own live lobster. Open daily 11am-10pm. AmEx/D/MC/V. ❷

◔ SIGHTS

Stands sell whale watching tours and trips around the **Isles of Shoals,** nine islands off the coast that were once popular resort communities. **The Granite State Whale Watch** tours last 4-5hr. and are led by a naturalist. (☎603-964-5545 or 800-962-5364; www.granitestatewhale-watch.com. Whale watching from mid-June to Aug. daily 8:30am, 1:30pm; from mid-Sept. to mid-Oct. and from late May to mid-June Sa-Su 1pm; from mid-June to Aug. daily 8:30am, 1:30pm. $29, ages 4-17 $20, seniors $24.) **Atlantic Queen II** also organizes half-day fishing tours as well as whale-watching tours. (☎603-

964-5220. Fishing tour 8am. Whale watching 1pm. Fishing $32, ages 4-16 $22, seniors $24. Whale watching $29/22/27.)

ODIORNE STATE PARK. Odiorne State Park consists of open fields and a rocky beach more suitable for looking at than for swimming. It features the **Seacoast Science Center,** with exhibits on aquaculture, radar, and a shipwreck off the coast. Visitors can play a 3D underwater video game and pick up a free 1hr. audio tour of the seven distinct natural habitats featured in the park. *(570 Ocean Blvd. North of Rye along US 1A. ☎603-436-8042; www.seacentr.org. Open Apr.-Oct. daily 10am-5pm; Nov.-Mar. M and Sa-Su 10am-5pm. $4, ages 3-12 $2, under 3 free.)* Along with meandering trails, the park also includes the remains of WWII's **Fort Dearborn,** built in response to Pearl Harbor. *(☎603-436-7406. Open sunrise-sunset. $4, ages 6-11 $2, under 12 free.)*

SEASHELL STAGE. If you want something fun to do after nightfall, head to the Seashell Stage by the visitors center and rock out to rock and roll, country, polka, blues, and more in the nightly concert series in the summer. *(June-July 7-8pm and 8:30-9:30pm. Free.)* From May to October, there are weekly fireworks shoots. *(W and holidays at 9:30pm, rain date Th.)*

BEACHES

Entering town, you'll first come upon the crowded sands and arcades of **Hampton Beach.** The downtown area is saturated with motels and storefronts full of tried tourist staples. **North Hampton State Beach** is a thin strip of sandy beach far less crowded than Hampton Beach itself. Head north on Rte. 1A. *(☎603-436-1552. Open 24hr. Lifeguards on duty from mid-June to Aug. daily 10am-4:45pm.)* Between **Odiorne State Park** and **Rye Beach** lies **Wallis Sands State Beach,** the prettiest of the beaches between Hampton and Rye. *(☎603-436-9404. Open from mid-June to Labor Day M-Th 8am-6pm, F-Su 8am-7pm. Gates close at 8pm. $15 per vehicle.)*

THE ROAD TO PORTSMOUTH: 11 MI.
From Rye, take **Route 1A North** into town.

PORTSMOUTH ☎603

Portsmouth was once a center of New England, home to signers of the Declaration of Independence. The town has undergone a rebirth, focusing on tourism, but it has avoided the temptation of tackiness and maintains a vibrant, funky downtown.

ORIENTATION

State Street (US 1) and **Congress Street** are the two major roads that run northeast-southwest through town. The central intersecting road is **Market Street,** which runs southeast-northwest. The town is best navigated by foot; drivers will miss the cafes and shops that line the streets. **Seacoast Trolley** has 11 stops around Portsmouth and surrounding areas. *(☎603-431-6975. Runs in M-Th and Su every hr. 11am-3pm. Partial loop $3.50, full loop with reboarding privileges $7.)*

VITAL STATS
Population: 21,000
Tourist Offices: Discover Portsmouth, 108 Maplewood Ave. (☎603-436-8433). Open from Memorial Day to Oct. daily 10am-5pm. **Greater Portsmouth Chamber of Commerce,** 500 Market St. (☎603-436-5526; www.portcity.org). Open daily 9am-5pm. **Info kiosk** in Market Sq. Open from May to mid-Oct. daily 10am-5pm.
Library and Internet Access: Portsmouth Public Library, 8 Islington St. (☎603-427-1540), at the corner of Middle and State St. Open M-Th 9am-9pm, F 9am-5:30pm, Sa 9am-5pm.
Post Office: 80 Daniel St. (☎603-431-1301). Open M-F 7:30am-5:30pm, Sa 8am-12:30pm. **Postal Code:** 03801.

ACCOMMODATIONS

Portsmouth isn't budget-friendly when it comes to finding a place to hang your hat. Cheaper options can be found at the rotary where US 1, I-95, and Rte. 4 meet.

Motel 6 (☎603-334-6606; www.motel6.com). A 5min. drive from Portsmouth. Take Maplewood Ave. north to the rotary and make a right onto Rte. 4. Get off at Exit 1; the motel is on your right.

Offers clean rooms and an outdoor pool. Singles M-Th and Su $70, F-Sa $90. AmEx/D/MC/V. ❹

Camp Eaton (☎207-363-3424; www.campeaton. com), in York Harbor, about 10 mi. north of Portsmouth off US 1. Take US 1 N. into York village. Make a right onto York St. and follow it to the beach. The wooded sites are expensive for a campground but have immaculate bathrooms and well-kept grounds. Open May-Oct. Sites $40-59. MC/V. ❷

🍴 FOOD

Portsmouth supports a number of offbeat cafes, with an emphasis on fresh, local, and vegetarian fare.

◼ Friendly Toast, 121 Congress St. (☎603-430-2154). Cluttered with ghastly artifacts of the 1950s: mannequin limbs, pulp novels, Formica, and bad art. French toast ($4.50 for 1 slice), made with thick, homemade bread, is heavenly, while massive items like the mission burrito ($9.25) are a tasty struggle to finish. Breakfast served all day. Open M-Th 7am-10pm, F-Sa 24hr., Su until 9pm. AmEx/D/MC/V. ❷

Gilley's Lunchcart, 175 Fleet St. (☎603-431-6343). The place is tiny—it was once hauled into town each day as a lunchcart—but the food makes up for the squeeze. Heavenly burgers ($2.60) and cheese fries ($2.60). It may look closed; just slide the door and climb right in. Open daily 11am-2am. Cash only. ❶

Juicery 2, 51 Hanover St. (☎603-431-0693). Serves an entirely organic, vegetarian menu that points out the health benefits of each item. Grab your juice or Peaches & Cream smoothie ($5) and head to the streets; the restaurant doesn't have much seating. Open M-Sa 10am-5pm, Su 10am-4pm. AmEx/D/MC/V. ❶

🔵 SIGHTS

STRAWBERY BANKE MUSEUM. Modern Portsmouth sells itself with its past, and the Strawbery Banke Museum is a prime example. Each building has been restored to illustrate life in the region in various time periods, from a Revolutionary War-era tavern to an early-20th-century Russian immigrant's home. Guided tours begin in the visitors center on the hour 11am-2pm. *(At the corner of Marcy and Hancock St. Follow the signs that lead toward the harbor. ☎603-433-1100; www.strawberybanke.org. Open May-Oct. daily 10am-5pm; call for winter hours. $15, ages 5-17 $10; valid for 2 consecutive days.)*

PRESCOTT PARK. Across the street from the Strawbery Banke Museum, Prescott Park runs along the bank of the Piscataqua River. The small, well-tended gardens and lawns offer a pleasant respite with an amazing view. *(Open daily sunrise-midnight.)*

USS ALBACORE. The *USS Albacore* was a research submarine used to test brakes, sonar equipment, and escape mechanisms. Visitors

[the local story]

OLD MAN DEAD AT 12,000

Lincoln, NH, May 3, 2003—A medical examiner announced today that the Old Man of the Mountain, a Lincoln native, passed away during the night. Said one crying child, "I'm so sad. He rocked." The 12,000-year-old had been a fixture in the community. A neighbor first realized something was amiss when he did not see Mr. Mountain on his morning stroll. "I always wave good morning to the Old Man," reported the 65-year-old, "but today I was just waving at air." Further investigation revealed that the Old Man had fallen to his death during the night. The autopsy concluded that the proximal cause of Mr. Mountain's fall was water damage, which caused his center of gravity to shift. Residents of Lincoln expressed grief at Mr. Mountain's untimely end. Said neighbor Bald Mountain, "I'll truly miss seeing the Old Man's face every day—that regal nose, that jutting chin." The Old Man's friend Eagle Cliff added, "Though his profile is gone, I know that he's still looking down on us somehow." The Old Man of the Mountain is survived by his father, the Man in the Moon, as well as his four siblings, who reside on Mount Rushmore. Unfortunately, they were unable to attend his funeral. Those wishing to pay their respects may purchase a New Hampshire state quarter for $0.25. Proceeds go to the Old Man in the Mountain Foundation, which helps young granite slabs achieve the goal of becoming

can explore a small museum before navigating the cramped sub. You don't have to be a Navy buff to find looking through the spyglass exciting. *(600 Market St. ☎603-436-3680. Open May-Oct. daily 9:30am-5pm; Nov.-Apr. M and Th-Su 9:30am-4pm. $5, ages 7-17 $3, seniors and military with ID $4.)*

JOHN PAUL JONES HOUSE. The famous captain, known as the "father of the US Navy," stayed here for a few months in 1781; in 1905, his mummified body was found under the streets of Paris and reburied in the US. The museum serves as a historical catchall, with furniture, tar-dipped fire buckets, and china galore. The house also has an exhibit on the Portsmouth peace treaty that ended the Russo-Japanese war. *(At the corner of Middle and State St. ☎603-436-8420; www.portsmouthhistory.org. Open from mid-May to Oct. daily 11am-5pm. $6, under 14 free with adult, seniors $5.)*

MUSIC HALL. The Music Hall, a 125-year-old theater, shows mainstream, independent, and foreign films during the summer and hosts live musical and dance performances during the winter. Visitors can tour the newly renovated lobby and the horseshoe balcony, which has witnessed performances by Suzanne Vega, Buffalo Bill, and Patti LuPone. Schedules of movies and events are available outside the theater and on its website. *(28 Chestnut St. ☎603-436-2400; www.themusichall.org. Box office open M-Sa noon-6pm or until 30min. after shows. Live acts $20-35. Movies $8.50, students and seniors $6.50. Cash only. Tours June-Sept. F 2pm. $6.)*

NEWCASTLE SCENIC DRIVE. Drive, bike, or jog this scenic loop onto the nearby island of Newcastle. From Portsmouth, take Rte. 1B and follow the 5 mi. loop over bridges, past beautiful homes, and through the trees. Return to Portsmouth by taking Rte. 1A east into town.

NORTH CEMETERY. One of Portsmouth's oldest graveyards, the North Cemetery is the resting place for some of the city's most prominent citizens, including William Whipple, a signer of the Declaration of Independence, and John Langdon, who signed the US Constitution. *(On Maplewood Ave., near Deer St. Free.)*

🚗 THE ROAD TO PORTLAND: 51 MI.
From Portsmouth, follow **I-95 North** to Portland. There is a $1.75 toll just after you enter Maine. **Exit 7** takes you into downtown Portland.

The Pine Tree State

MAINE

Welcomes You!

PORTLAND ☎207

Tucked between forested land and a wild sea, Portland is the largest port town in Maine. The city thrives as an urban center in an otherwise rural area, with a mixture of industry, arts, and well-preserved relics of colonial times. In summer, the streets fill with the exuberant sounds of parades and festivals. Meanwhile, laughter can be heard long into the night in the old port district, where pubs beckon the city's spirited youth to set even the coldest night aflame.

VITAL STATS

Population: 64,000

Tourist Offices: Visitor Information Center, 245 Commercial St. (☎207-772-5800; www.visitportland.com), between Union and Cross St. Open M-F 8am-5pm, Sa 10am-5pm. **Deering Oaks Information Center,** 356 State St. (☎207-828-0149). Open M-Sa 10am-4pm; extended hours in summer.

Library and Internet Access: Portland Public Library, 5 Monument Sq. (☎207-871-1700). Open M, W, F 9am-6pm, Tu and Th noon-9pm, Sa 9am-5pm.

Post Office: 400 Congress St. (☎207-871-8464). Open M-F 8am-7pm, Sa 9am-1pm. **Postal Code:** 04101.

🧭 ORIENTATION

Downtown Portland rests in the middle of a peninsula jutting into Casco Bay, along **Congress Street,** between **State** and **Pearl Streets.** A few blocks south of Congress St. along the waterfront lies the Old Port, between **Commercial** and **Middle Street.** These two districts contain most of the city's sights and attractions. **I-295** (off I-95) forms the northwestern boundary of the city. The peninsula is only about 4 mi. by three quarters of a mile, so it's best to park your car and navigate the downtown area on foot.

ACCOMMODATIONS

Portland has some inexpensive accommodations during the winter, but prices jump steeply during the summer, especially on weekends. Standard chain motels can be found off Rte. 25 about 10min. west of town.

The Inn at St. John, 939 Congress St. (☎207-773-6481 or 800-636-9127; www.innatstjohn.com). Surrounded by fast-food joints and gas stations, but its old-fashioned upscale decor makes it elegant nonetheless. Victorian rooms come in several styles, from comfy kings with jetted tubs to twin beds with shared hall bathrooms. Rooms include fridges. Continental breakfast included. Free Wi-Fi. Rooms in summer $75-159, in winter $60-105. AmEx/D/MC/V. ❺

Wassamki Springs, 56 Saco St. (☎207-839-4276; www.wassamkisprings.com), in Scarborough. Take I-95 to Exit 7A, then take Rte. 22 W. to Saco St. The closest campground to Portland. Over 100 sites clustered around a lake encircled by sandy beaches. Volleyball and basketball courts and free weekend activities. Coin-op laundry. Reservations recommended July-Aug. Open from May to mid-Oct. Sites from mid-June to Sept. $43-47, with hookup $45-50; Sept.-Oct. and from May to mid-June. $29/32. MC/V. ❷

FOOD

Portland's harbor overflows with the fruits of the ocean, but non-aquatic and vegetarian fare isn't hard to find.

Gilbert's Chowder House, 92 Commercial St. (☎207-871-5636). This restaurant may have swordfish on the walls, but it's another aquatic animal that gets the praise. Make sure to try the clam chowder (small $4.50; medium $5.50; large $6.50; bread bowl $7.75), and, if you're still hungry, the clam cakes ($2.50), clam strips ($7), and, well, clam everything. Open daily 11am-11pm. AmEx/D/MC/V. ❷

Federal Spice, 225 Federal St. (☎207-774-6404; www.federalspice.com), just off Congress St. Serves up delicious Jamaican specialties as well as many vegetarian and vegan options. The small shop also features local brewskies and

paintings by local artists. Open M-F 11am-9pm, Sa 11am-6pm. D/MC/V. ❶

Flatbread Company, 72 Commercial St. (☎207-772-8777). Organic pizza is the specialty, and the view is a combination of ocean and parking garage. The sun-dried tomato flatbread (half $9.75, whole $16.75), baked in a wood-fired clay oven, is ample distraction. Take a minute to notice the original art on each menu, made with crayons by Flatbread's youngest costumers. Open M-Th 11:30am-10pm, F-Sa 11:30am-10:30pm, Su 9:30am-10pm. AmEx/MC/V. ❸

SIGHTS

PORTLAND MUSEUM OF ART. Along with several galleries of temporary exhibits, the museum has an excellent collection of Impressionist and Post-Impressionist art, mostly by local artists, but with some works by Degas, Monet, and Picasso. *(7 Congress Sq. ☎207-775-6148; www.portlandmuseum.org. Open from Memorial Day to Columbus Day M-Th and Sa-Su 10am-5pm, F 10am-9pm; from Columbus Day to Memorial Day Tu-Su 10am-5pm. Tours M-Th and Sa-Su 2pm, F 2, 6:30pm. $10, students and seniors $8, ages 6-17 $4. F 5-9pm free.)*

VICTORIA MANSION. Built in 1860 by a luxury hotelier, this mansion has a free-flying staircase, chairs with cloven hooves, and a portrait of Cupid that looks suspiciously like the owner. Guides lead 45min. tours through the home, which still has 90% of its original furnishings. *(109 Danforth St., off High St. ☎207-772-4841; www.victoriamansion.org. $12.50, ages 6-17 $3, seniors $11. Open May-Oct. M-Sa 10am-4pm, Su 1-5pm; from late Nov.-Dec. Tu-Su 11am-5pm. Tours every 30min.)*

PORTLAND OBSERVATORY. Not only is it the last maritime signal tower in the US, but at 86 ft. it's also the best view in town. Tours provide a history and an enthusiastic explanation of signaling. *(138 Congress St. ☎207-774-5561; www.portlandlandmarks.org. Open daily from May to Columbus Day 10am-5pm. Tours every 30min. Last tour 4:40pm. $7, ages 6-16 $4, under 6 free.)*

SHIPYARD BREWING CO. While it takes about eight days to brew a batch of beer at the Shipyard Brewing Co., it will only take 20min. to

FLUMES, FRESCOES, & FIRE PITS

EASTERN NEW HAMPSHIRE

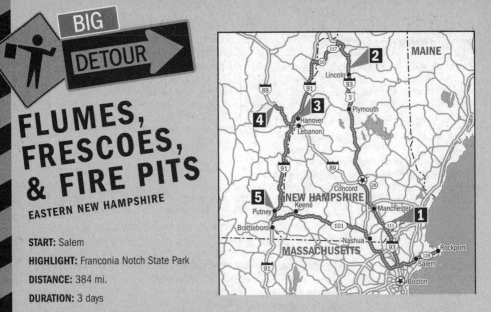

START: Salem

HIGHLIGHT: Franconia Notch State Park

DISTANCE: 384 mi.

DURATION: 3 days

From Salem, take Rte. 128 S. to I-93 N. Cross the border into New Hampshire and take Rte. 111 E. for 4½ mi., past the North Salem Village Shops. Make a right at the traffic light and follow the road 1 mi.

1. AMERICA'S STONEHENGE. Step within an ordinary New Hampshire forest to find a maze of stone structures, supposedly constructed 4000 years ago. It's unclear who built the structures—Native Americans, seafaring Europeans, or rascally kids—but there are a number of chambers and the frighteningly named "sacrificial table." If you can't decide whether it's all true or an elaborate hoax, ask the alpaca out back. They know everything, but, unfortunately, they aren't talking. (☎603-893-83000; www.stonehengeusa.com. $9.50, ages 6-12 $6.50, seniors $8.50. Open daily 9am-5pm.)

From America's Stonehenge, take I-93 N. to Exit 34A toward the Gilman Visitors Center.

2. FRANCONIA NOTCH STATE PARK. In the heart of the White Mountains, Franconia Notch State Park offers rushing waterfalls, fantastic views of miles upon miles of trees, and a glacially formed lake. The rangers at the **Gilman Visitors Center,** at Exit 34A off I-93, suggest trails and provide maps of the area. (☎603-745-8391. Open daily 9am-5pm.) The entire park is gorgeous, but the **Flume Gorge** is a must-see. A walking loop (2 mi.) takes visitors up a series of wood stairs to the top of the 800 ft. gorge, surrounded by lichen-covered walls of Conway granite. (☎603-271-3556. Open daily May-June and Sept.-Oct. 9am-5:30pm. $10, ages 6-12 $7.) Formed by glacial melting 25,000 years ago, **Glacier Basin** is a 20 ft. deep pothole fed by the Pemigewasset River. The waterfall produces a cool spray, covering the basin in a fine mist. The **Old Man of the Mountain,** a rock formation that looked like a face, once looked out over Profile Lake. The old man's visage collapsed in 2003, but a historical site and museum remain to pay homage to New Hampshire's trademark. **Echo Lake Beach** offers overheated hikers a place to cool off. Visitors can also rent canoes and kayaks for $10 per hour. (☎603-823-8800. Lifeguards from mid-June to Aug. daily 10am-5pm. $4, ages 6-11 $2.) Campers can pitch their tents at **Lafayette Campground ❶,** centrally located within the park. The sites are heavily wooded and are located at the heads of several trails. The campground is very busy on the weekends—make reservations a few weeks in advance. To reach them, take I-93 to Exit 34B and head south to the pull-off. (☎603-823-9513. Open from mid-May to mid-Oct.; no water Jan.-May. Sites $24. D/MC/V.)

From Franconia Notch State Park, take I-93 N. to Rte. 117 W. Then follow Rte. 10 S. to I-91 S.

3. DARTMOUTH COLLEGE. Located in the heart of New Hampshire, Hanover is almost entirely subsumed by Dartmouth College. Wheelock St. and Main St., home to restaurants and shops, are the main thoroughfares of the town. The lower level of the **Baker-Berry Library** houses the **Orozco Frescoes,** 24 panels tracing American civilization. Beware: Orozco's vision of American history is not a sunny one. (☎603-646-2560; www.dartmouth.edu/~library/orozco. Call ahead for hours. Free.) Visitors can tour Dartmouth's campus on student-led tours, which leave from the **Office of Admissions,** 6016 McNutt Hall. (☎603-646-2560. Tours M-F 10am, 12:30, 3pm, Sa noon. Free.) The **Dirt Cowboy Cafe ❶**, 7 S. Main St., serves baguette sandwiches to hungry students. The cafe has a wide selection of coffees and beans for sale. (☎802-643-1323; www.dirtcowboycafe.com. Free Wi-Fi. Open daily 7am-6pm. MC/V.)

From Hanover, take I-89 N. to Rte. 14 at Exit 2. Follow Rte. 14 about 5 mi. toward South Royalton, then make a right on Dairy Hill Rd. There's a sign for the monument on your right.

4. JOSEPH SMITH BIRTHPLACE MONUMENT. Mormons believe that there are two holy sites in the world: Bethlehem and Sharon, Vermont, birthplace of the religion's founder, Joseph Smith. Step out of your car to hear otherworldly music mysteriously emanating from the hills. Missionary tour guides lead you through a museum detailing the prophet's life, including a 9min. video. The monument itself is 38½ ft. granite shaft. (☎802-763-7742; www.lds.org/placestovisit. Open May-Oct. M-Sa 9am-7pm, Su 1:30-6pm; Nov.-Apr. M-Sa 9am-5pm, Su 1:30-5pm. Free.)

From the Joseph Smith Birthplace Monument, take I-89 S. Take Exit 4 and make a left onto Rte. 5 headed toward Putney. The smoke will be visible to your right just after exiting the highway.

5. CURTIS' BARBEQUE ❹. Hard to believe, but it's true—Curtis' Barbeque has been cooking up ribs in New England for 40 years. Curtis Tuff started selling his slabs on the side of the road but has since made his permanent residence in a couple of bright blue school buses in Putney. Tuff cooks the ribs ($25 per slab) and chicken ($7 per ½ chicken) on a wood-fired open pit. If you're lucky, you may even catch a glimpse of pet pig CJ running around. Here's to hoping he never strays too close to the flames. (☎802-387-5474; www.curtisbbqvt.com. Open Apr.-Oct. Th-Su 10am-sunset. Cash only.)

Back to the route. From Putney, head south on I-91, then east on Rte. 9. Near the town of Keene, get onto Rte. 101. Stay on Rte. 101A past Milford, then get on US 3 S. Switch to I-95 N. at Woburn, then take Rte. 128 N. To finish the drive in style, take Rte. 127A into Rockport.

tour the brewery and try the free sample. If you're driving (or too young) take advantage of their several sodas in fun flavors. *(86 Newbury St. ☎207-761-0807; www.shipyard.com. Open daily noon-4pm. Tours every hr. Free.)*

OFFSHORE ISLANDS. These rocky islands are ideal for an afternoon of hiking or biking. Casco Bay Lines, on State Pier near the corner of Commercial and Franklin St., runs ferries daily from June to September to Long Island, where waves crash on an unpopulated beach, and Peaks Island, home to tide pools and wooded areas. The Sunset Cruise takes travelers past several islands as night falls. *(☎207-774-7871; www.cascobaylines.com. Long Island M-F 5am-9:30pm, Sa-Su 6:30am-9:30pm; round-trip $10, ages 5-9 and seniors $5. Peaks Island M-Sa 5:45am-11:30pm, Su 7:45-11:30; round-trip $8, ages 5-9 and seniors $4.)*

OTHER SIGHTS. It's worth your time to take the scenic detour to the functioning **Portland Head Light** in **Fort Williams Park.** Families play on the large green spaces of the park, which offers numerous views of the rocky shoreline and nearby islands, including a lighthouse off the coast. Inside is the **Port Head Light Museum** with a timeline that documents the history of the lighthouse. Unfortunately, there is no access to the tower. *(From State or York St., go south along Rte. 77 to Cape Elizabeth, turn left at the flashing signal onto Shore Rd., and proceed to the park. Open sunrise-sunset. Museum open June-Oct. daily 10am-4pm; Nov.-Dec. and Apr.-May Sa-Su 10am-4pm. $2, ages 6-18 $1.)* Across the Casco Bay Bridge, **Two Lights State Park** is a great place to picnic or walk along the shimmering ocean. *(From State or York St., go south along Rte. 77 to Cape Elizabeth. ☎207-799-5871; www.state.me.us/doc/parks. Open 9am-sunset. $3, ages 5-11 $1, under 5 and over 64 free.)*

🎵 ENTERTAINMENT

Signs for theatrical productions are ubiquitous, and schedules are available at the visitors center. Info on Portland's jazz, blues, and club scene packs the *Casco Bay Weekly* (www.cascobayweekly.com) and *FACE*, both of which are free. Traditionally held the first Sunday in June, the **Old Port Festival** (☎207-772-6868) fills the blocks from Federal to Commercial St. with as many as 50,000 people enjoying free public entertainment, including a battle of the bands and parade. Every Thursday afternoon in summer, the **Alive at Five** music series in Monument Sq. offers working people a reason to make it through the day. (☎207-772-6828. July-Aug. Th 5-7:30pm.) On Friday afternoons in summer, the **Weekday Music Series** (☎207-772-6828; July-Aug. F noon) has a more low-key selection of bands that play at noon in Post Office Sq. between Middle and Exchange St.

🍷 NIGHTLIFE

The Old Port area, known as "the strip"—especially Fore St. between Union and Exchange St.—livens up after dark.

Brian Ború, 57 Center St. (☎207-780-1506; www.brianboruportland.com). Hard to miss since its bright red building has a giant Guinness toucan painted on the side wall. The mellow Irish pub features live bands Th-Sa 10pm-1am, mainly rock, reggae, and cover bands. Irish sessions on Su 3-6pm. $2.50 pints Su. 21+ after kitchen closes. Open daily 11am-1am. AmEx/D/MC/V.

Gritty MacDuff's, 396 Fore St. (☎207-772-2739; www.grittys.com). Brews its own beer (pints $4) and entertains a largely local crowd with live jazz, blues, and rock Th and Sa 9 or 10pm. Pitchers $9 Th. Open daily 11:30am-1am. AmEx/D/MC/V.

Úna Wine Bar & Lounge, 505 Fore St. (☎207-828-0300). Mixes speciality martinis ($7-12) for an older, sophisticated crowd. The nightclub section opens at 9pm and often features live entertainment. The bar also serves tapas in a bit more upscale environment. Open M-Sa 4:30pm-1am, Su 6pm-1am. AmEx/MC/V.

🢔 DETOUR.
EARTHA
2 Delorme Drive, in Yarmouth, off **I-295.**

The world's largest rotating globe and the largest printed representation of the earth, Eartha was finished in July of 1998, stealing the title of world's largest from a globe in Wellesley, Massachusetts. Forty two feet in diameter and weighing 5600 lb., the globe has a circumference of 130 ft. and rotates on an axis at 23.5°, just like the real thing. Every inch on Eartha is about 16 mi.; how many inches have you roadtripped? (☎207-846-7100 and 800-642-0970; www.delorme.com. Open M-Th and Su 9:30am-6pm, F-Sa 9:30am-7pm. Free.)

THE ROAD TO CAMDEN: 80 MI.

Take **I-295 North** for 22 mi. to **Exit 28** toward **US 1**. Head left on US 1. Make a left onto **Camden Road** and head into town.

CAMDEN ☎207

Camden is chock-full of Teva-clad hikers, bikers, and kayakers taking advantage of the nearby outdoor attractions. The town's outdoor activities are its largest draw, but the downtown area, full of restaurants, shops, and T-shirt vendors, makes for an enjoyable afternoon.

VITAL STATS
Population: 5200
Tourist Office: Camden-Rockport-Lincolnville Chamber of Commerce (☎207-236-4404; www.visitcamden.com), at the public landing. Open from Memorial Day to Christmas M-F 9am-5pm and Sa 10am-5pm; from Christmas to Memorial Day M-F 9am-5pm.
Library and Internet Access: Camden Public Library, 55 Main St. (☎207-236-3440; www.camden.lib.me.us). Open M, W, F-Sa 9:30am-5pm, Tu and Th 9:30am-8pm, Su 1-5pm.
Post Office: 28 Chestnut St. (☎207-236-3570). Open M-F 8:30am-5pm, Sa 9am-noon. **Postal Code:** 04843.

ORIENTATION

US 1 heads right into town, becoming **Main Street.** Most restaurants and shops lie around Main St. and **Elm Street,** near the public green.

ACCOMMODATIONS

The downtown area is full of expensive B&Bs, but less expensive options are available on US 1, just outside of town.

Beloin's on the Maine Coast, 254 Belfast Rd. (☎207-236-3262; www.beloins.com), about 1½ mi. north of Camden. Offers travelers spacious rooms in a quiet area close to the state park. They have shore cottages and rooms with a view as well as beach access. Many rooms have kitchenettes, and all have microwaves, refrigerators, and coffeemakers. Open from mid-May to mid-Oct. Non-waterfront rooms July-Sept. $80; from Sept. to mid-Oct. $64; from mid-May to June $56. MC/V. ❸

Camden Hills State Park (☎207-236-3109, reservations 287-3824; www.campwithme.com), 1 mi. north of town on US 1. Almost always full in summer. Be sure to make a reservation for 1 of the 106 wooded sites. Reception 7am-10pm. Open from mid-May to mid-Oct. Sites $27, with water and electricity $38. MC/V. ❶

FOOD

Cappy's Chowder House, 1 Main St. (☎207-236-2254; www.cappyschowder.com). Patrons wait outside for a chance to try the clam chowder served in a mug (small $7; large $8). Open daily 11am-11pm. MC/V. ❷

Camden Deli, 37 Main St. (☎207-236-8343). Patrons enjoy gourmet sandwiches like the meaty Islander (roast beef, turkey, cheddar, and horseradish; $7.50) and the artichoke-and-spinach wrap ($6.25). 2 spacious seating areas offer gorgeous ocean views. Open daily 7am-9pm. AmEx/D/MC/V. ❷

SIGHTS AND OUTDOORS

CAMDEN HILLS STATE PARK. The park is home to **Mount Battie,** an 800 ft. hill popular with hikers for its gorgeous view. The park includes 25 mi. of trails as well as a scenic road up Mt. Battie. (☎207-236-3109. Open 7am-sunset. $3, ages 5-11 $1, over 63 free.)

OTHER SIGHTS. Intrepid paddlers can also kayak in the harbor or take a tour offered by **Maine Sport Outfitters.** The company rents boats out of its store off US 1, south of town in Rockport, while tours leave from Camden Harbor. (☎207-236-7120 or 800-722-0826. Single kayaks $25-40 per day; tandems $30-50. Canoes $30 per day. 2hr. tour $35, ages 10-15 $30; 4hr. tour $75/60. Open daily 9am-8pm.) **Day tours** are available on a variety of boats at the public dock and range $20-30. Most boat owners sit at the public landing displaying their signs. *(Schooner Olad ☎ 207-236-2323. Betselma ☎ 207-236-4446. Surprise ☎ 207-236-4687.)* The **Maine State Ferry Service** runs to quaint and residential Islesboro Island. *(5 mi. north of Camden in Lincolnville. ☎ 207-789-5611. 30min. 5-9 per day; last return trip 4:30pm. Round-trip $8.50; with bike $16, car and driver $30.)* The ferry also runs trips to Vinalhaven and North Haven. *(517A Main St., on US 1 in Rockland. ☎ 207-596-2202. Round-trip $16, with bike $31, car and driver $47.)*

THE ROAD TO BELFAST: 20 MI.

From Camden, take **US 1 North** into Belfast.

BELFAST ☎ 207

This small town has a funky feel, with a co-op, countless cafes, and a gallery-filled downtown area. Like Camden, it pushes its outdoor opportunities, but it also celebrates its history as a shipbuilding center. You'll wake up one morning and Belfast will have won you over—without even trying that hard.

VITAL STATS

Population: 6400

Tourist Office: Belfast Information Center, 15 Main St. (☎207-338-5900; www.belfastmaine.org). Open from Memorial Day to Labor Day M-F 10am-6pm, Sa-Su 10am-8pm; hours vary in winter.

Library and Internet Access: Belfast Public Library, 106 High St. (☎207-338-3884; www.belfast.lib.me.us). Open M 9:30am-8pm, Tu and Th-F 9:30am-6pm, W noon-8pm, Sa 10am-2pm.

Post Office: 1 Franklin St. (☎207-338-1820). Open M-F 8am-5pm, Sa 8am-noon. **Postal Code:** 04915.

ORIENTATION

Belfast sits at the mouth of the **Passagasswakeag River**, on **Penobscot Bay. Main Street** and **High Street** are the main commercial and shopping streets in downtown Belfast; their intersection forms the center of town.

ACCOMMODATIONS

Belfast's historic B&Bs occupy the gorgeous houses downtown, but rates are over $100 in summer. An accommodations pamphlet is available at the visitors center downtown.

Seascape Motel and Cottages, 2202 Searsport Ave. (☎207-338-2130 or 800-477-0786; www.seascapemotel.com), 3 mi. from downtown off Rte. 1. Provides one of the best deals in the area. The well-furnished rooms include use of the heated pool. Continental breakfast included. Wi-Fi $2 per 24hr. Rooms July-Aug. $85-139; Sept.-Oct. $75-94; May-June $65-75. MC/V. ❸

Searsport Shores Camping Resort, 209 W. Main St. (☎207-548-6059; www.campocean.com), in Searsport. Has miles of gorgeous beach, as well as laundry facilities and a video arcade. Free Wi-Fi. Tent sites $38-49; RV sites $46-65; cabins $65. MC/V. ❷

FOOD

Belfast Co-op, 123 High St. (☎207-338-2532). Has delicious organic fare like the Greek salad ($7) and grilled-chicken pesto sandwich ($8). The store attracts an outdoorsy, relaxed crowd of locals who mingle in the cafe. Open daily 7:30am-8pm. AmEx/D/MC/V. ❷

Lookout Bar and Grill, 37B Front St. (☎207-388-8900; www.thelookoutpub.com). Sports a marine theme and a casual bar atmosphere. Try the onion teriyaki burger ($8) or shoot pool with locals. Open M-Sa 11:30am-1am, Su noon-11pm. Kitchen open until 10pm. MC/V. ❷

SIGHTS

PENOBSCOT MARINE MUSEUM. The museum includes four historic homes, several boats, and a large collection of nautical paintings. Be sure to check out "lobstah," an exhibit dedicated to Maine's favorite crustacean. *(At US 1 and Church St. in Searsport. ☎207-548-2529; www.penobscotmarinemuseum.org. Open from Memorial Day to late Oct. M-Sa 10am-5pm, Su noon-5pm. Last entry 4pm. $8, ages 7-15 $3, seniors $6.)*

EAST COAST

FORT KNOX. Constructed in the mid-1800s using granite from nearby Mt. Waldo, the first and least famous Fort Knox was part of a plan to protect the Penobscot River against British invasion. Info panels guide visitors through the Fort Knox State Historic Site, from the storage vaults to the powder magazine. Visitors can also take an elevator to the 🅰**Penobscot Narrows Bridge Observatory,** which sits on top of the impressive new bridge almost 450 ft. above the river. *(Take US 1 N. to Rte. 178; the fort is the 1st right. ☎207-469-6553; www.fortknox.maineguide.com. Fort open May-Oct. daily 8:30am-sunset. Grounds open year-round. Observatory open July-Aug. 9am-5pm. Fort $3, ages 5-12 $1. Fort and observatory $5/3.)*

🅰 THE ROAD TO ELLSWORTH: 27 MI.
From Belfast, take **US 1 North** to Ellsworth.

ELLSWORTH ☎207

Fuel and stock up here—this town, the largest between Bar Harbor and Bangor, is more of a pit stop than an attraction, but the short stretch of **Main Street** is pleasant for a stroll. **Birdsacre, Stanwood Wildlife Sanctuary,** 289 High St., was built in 1958 as a memorial to Cordelia J. Stanwood, a leading ornithologist and wildlife photographer. The homestead on the property was placed on the National Register of Historic Places in 1973, ensuring that no urban expansion would ever invade the area. The 165 acres of woodland are home to wild birds. (☎207-667-8460; www.birdsacre.com. Sanctuary open daily sunrise to sunset. Homestead open June-Sept. daily 10am-4pm. Donations accepted.)

Those in need of a good night's sleep should consider the **Ellsworth Motel ❸,** 24 High St., an affordable place to stay on the main road. The cheerful yellow main house has been around since the mid-1800s. The rooms are comfortable and have brand-new microwaves and refrigerators. (☎207-667-4424; www.ellsworthmotel.com. Rooms $45-75. MC/V.) On your right as you drive uphill out of town, **China Hill ❷,** 301 High St., has an extensive menu, including a meaty, delicious fried rice—get the dark one ($7.50). It also has a small American selection, including steak ($13.75) and a hamburger ($7.50) served with fries or fried rice. The lunch ($6-7) specials include an entree, egg roll, and fried rice. (☎207-667-5308. All-you-can-eat buffet $11. Open M-Th and Su 11am-9pm, F-Sa 11am-10pm. AmEx/D/MC/V.)

🅢 DETOUR
GREAT MAINE LUMBERJACK SHOW
In Trenton, off **Route 3.**

In the 1870s, Maine was one of America's important logging centers. Lumberjacks used to challenge each other to the "Olympics of the Forest," an event the **Great Maine Lumberjack Show** reenacts nightly during the summer. As seen on ESPN, the 14 events include axe-throwing, logrolling, and crosscut sawing. The show also offers hands-on activities for kids to try. Don't miss the **LumberJills,** a group of women who keep up with (and sometimes outlast) their male counterparts. (☎207-667-0067; "log" onto www.mainelumberjack.com. Shows from mid-June to Labor Day daily 7pm. $8.25, ages 4-11 $6.25, seniors $7.75. Box office opens 6pm.)

🅰 THE ROAD TO MT. DESERT ISLAND: 47 MI.
From Ellsworth, head south on **High Street** for nearly 3 mi. This will turn into **Bar Harbor Road,** which you can follow to the island.

MOUNT DESERT ISLAND

There's no better place to end your roadtrip than Mt. Desert Island, where gorgeous sights meet a hopping small town. Acadia National Park is easily the most beautiful place on the East Coast and allows roadtrippers to stretch their legs on trails overlooking lakes and mountains. Mt. Desert Island is shaped roughly like a lobster claw, 16 mi. long and 13 mi. wide. The claw reaches from the north to the south and is dotted with small towns. The island's only links to the mainland are **Route**

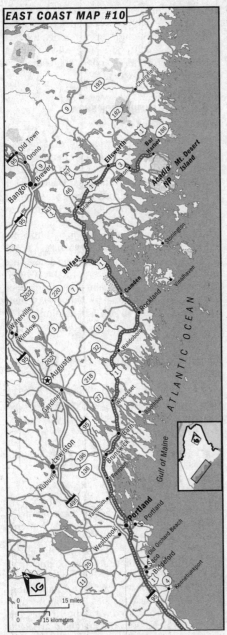

EAST COAST MAP #10

3, which runs down the arm of the claw from the north, and the vehicle **ferry** to Yarmouth, Nova Scotia, which leaves from Bar Harbor. (☎888-249-7245; www.catferry.com. $69, ages 5-14 $47.) The island's main roads are Rte. 3 and **Route 102,** which traces the western coast. To the east, on Rte. 3, lies **Bar Harbor,** the island's largest town. **Seal Harbor,** also on Rte. 3, sits on the southeast corner of the island. South on Rte. 198, near the cleft of the claw, is **Northeast Harbor.** Across Somes Sound on Rte. 102 is ruggedly scenic **Southwest Harbor.** At the southern tip of the island, on the west half of the claw, sits the town of **Bass Harbor,** and up the western coast on Rte. 102 lie the hamlets of **Seal Cove, Pretty Marsh,** and **Somesville.**

ACADIA NATIONAL PARK ☎207

Roughly half of Mt. Desert Island, plus several other small islands, constitutes Acadia, New England's only national park. The park has activities that appeal to a wide range of visitors. Park Loop Rd. allows you to see vistas from the safety and comfort of your own car, while challenging trails allow intrepid hikers to climb cliffs. Whether you're a hiker, biker, runner, or watcher, Acadia is a sublimely beautiful place to visit.

❖ ORIENTATION

Though visitors are welcome to drive into Acadia, most of the beauty of the place is off-limits to cars, thanks to John D. Rockefeller. Fearing the island would one day be overrun by automobiles, millionaire Rockefeller funded the creation of 51 mi. of carriage roads, which are now accessible only to hikers, mountain bikes, and horse-drawn carriages, of course. The one-way **Park Loop Road** is the only car access to the park's eastern zone. The **Island Explorer** is a free shuttle system consisting of eight different routes that runs from late June to October and allows you to dump the car and explore the island.

VITAL STATS

Area: 48,000 acres

Tourist Offices: Hulls Cove Visitors Center (☎207-288-3338; www.nps.gov/acad), off Rte. 3. Open from mid-June to late Aug. daily 8am-6pm; from mid-Sept. to Oct. daily 8am-4:30pm and from mid-May to mid-June. **Park Headquarters** (☎207-288-3338), on Rte. 233., 3 mi. west of Bar Harbor, near Eagle Lake. Provides visitor info during the low season. Open M-F 8am-4:30pm.

Gateway Town: Bar Harbor (next page).

Fees: 7-day pass $20 per vehicle, $5 per motorcycle.

🏕 CAMPING

While solid-roof accommodations cluster in Bar Harbor, quality camping is all over the park, especially on Rte. 102 and Rte. 198. Backcountry camping is not allowed anywhere in the park.

Blackwoods (☎800-365-2267), on Rte. 3. Has 306 wooded sites 5 mi. from Bar Harbor and a 10min. walk from the ocean. No hookups. Coin-operated showers. Call 5 months ahead to assure a spot. Open year-round for primitive camping; all facilities available from mid-Mar. to Oct. Sites $20; call for rates Nov.-Apr. No hookups. D/MC/V. ❶

Seawall (☎800-365-2267), off Rte. 102A on the western side of the island, 4 mi. south of Southwest Harbor. 214 sites. More secluded than most island campgrounds, with widely spaced sites and deep woods. No hookups. No reservations, so come early in the day to assure a spot. Open from late May to Sept. Sites $20. D/MC/V. ❶

📷 SIGHTS

PARK LOOP ROAD AND ATTRACTIONS. A good way to see Acadia is to drive the Park Loop Rd. About 4 mi. south of Bar Harbor on **Route 3,** Park Loop Rd. runs along the shore of the island, where waves crash against vertical cliffs. The road eventually makes a 27 mi. circuit of the eastern section of the island and passes by several premier hiking trails. Begin your drive on Park Loop Rd. at the **Hulls Cove Visitors Center** by going straight on the four-way stop right after coming out

of the parking lot onto the one-way road to Sand Beach. The first stop is **Sieur de Monts Spring,** where over 300 floral species thrive in the **Wild Gardens of Acadia.** The original **Abbe Museum,** built in honor of the native Wabanaki people, is also here, though it pales in comparison to the newer branch in Bar Harbor. (☎207-288-3519. Open from late May to mid-Oct. 9am-4pm. $2, children $1.) The next stop is **Sand Beach,** the only sandy beach in the otherwise rocky park. The water may look enticing, but the Atlantic can be 50° even in late summer. From here, you can also take a short but very difficult hike to see the **Beehive,** a 520 ft. hill sculpted by glaciers to resemble a honeycomb. Next, the road passes **Thunder Hole,** where, at three-quarters tide, the air trapped in the narrow granite hollow emits a thunderous howl. At **Wildwood Stables,** a mile south of **Jordan Pond,** tourists can explore Rockefeller's carriage roads via horse and carriage. (☎207-276-3622. 1hr. tour $18, ages 6-12 $9, ages 2-5 $5.) Farther along the road is Jordan Pond, surrounded by 3 mi. of trails; unfortunately, no swimming is allowed. Near the end of Park Loop Rd. is 🏔**Cadillac Mountain;** try the detour to the top of the mountain for an effortless yet absolutely breathtaking view of the island.

🥾 HIKING

Getting out of the car is the only way to see Acadia in full; the park is full of short, rewarding scenic hikes. Rangers at the visitors center provide maps and advice on the best trails as well as a handout that lists them by difficulty level and length.

🗻 **Precipice Trail** (1 mi.; difficult). A popular and strenuous hike. Iron rungs and ladders allow hikers to make their way up the sheer cliffs to the summit. Peregrine falcons circle overhead; the trail is often closed due to nesting, especially Mar.- Aug.

Mt. Champlain/Bear Brook (2 mi.; moderate). Provides dramatic views of the Atlantic coast. A relatively easy 1 mi. amble along the Bowl trail from the summit of Mt. Champlain rewards hikers with views of Sand Beach and Otter Point.

Jordan Pond Loop (3 mi.; moderate). Offers views of lakes, mountains, and forests.

BAR HARBOR ☎207

Bar Harbor serves as a gateway town for visitors to Acadia, but is a worthy destination in and of itself. During the summer, the downtown area is crowded with visitors licking ice-cream cones and checking out the terrific galleries. Though Bar Harbor is full of B&Bs, a hostel makes the town accessible to the budget traveler as well. It's a small town, to be sure, but Bar Harbor has plenty of museums, shops, and bars to keep visitors happy—especially those at the end of the road.

VITAL STATS
Population: 4800
Tourist Offices: Bar Harbor Area Chaber of Commerce, 1201 Bar Harbor Rd., in Trenton on Rt. 3. (☎207-664-2940; www.barharbormaine.org). Open from Memorial Day to Columbus Day daily 8am-6pm; from Columbus Day to Memorial Day M-F 8am-5pm. **Visitor Information Center,** 1 West St., by the town pier. Open from Memorial Day to Columbus Day M-F 8am-5pm.
Library and Internet Access: Jesup Memorial Library, 34 Mt. Desert St. (☎207-288-4245). Open Tu and Th-Sa 10am-5pm, W 10am-7pm.
Post Office: 55 Cottage St. (☎207-288-3122). Open M-F 8am-4:30pm, Sa 9am-noon. **Postal Code:** 04609.

✦ ORIENTATION

Bar Harbor's streets are all state highways, most of which are known by other names within town. **Route 3** runs through Bar Harbor, becoming **Mount Desert Street,** and then runs along the water as **Main Street.** On the waterfront, **Cottage** and **West Streets** run parallel to Mt. Desert St. Both Mt. Desert and Cottage St. are home to shops, restaurants, and bars.

⌐ ACCOMMODATIONS

Lodging is easy to find in Bar Harbor—it seems that every other building is an inn or a B&B. Affordable accommodations, on the other hand, are another story; grand hotels and even grander prices recall the island's exclusive resort days. Cheaper establishments assemble on Rte. 3 north of Bar Harbor. Book as early as possible to get the best deal.

▨ **Bar Harbor Hostel,** 321 Main St. (☎207-288-5587; www.barharborhostel.com). This spotlessly clean old house is right in the heart of downtown Bar Harbor, 2 mi. from Acadia. The fun colors will make you feel like a kid again. Movie nights and coffee in the mornings. Free Wi-Fi. Reception 8-10am and 5-10pm. Lockout 10am-5pm. No curfew. Open May-Nov.; call about winter availability. In summer dorms $25; private rooms $80. In winter dorms $20; private rooms $50. MC/V. ❶

Llangolan Inn & Cottages, 865 Rte. 3 (☎207-288-3016; www.llangolan.com). Lovely B&B 5 mi. north of the park. Clean rooms are tastefully decorated. Inn with 5 rooms (shared bath for 2 rooms) open year-round; 8 cottages with stove, pots, and pans

TOP 10 MAKE-OUT SPOTS ON THE EAST COAST

10. Sunset Celebration, Key West, Florida. There's nothing more romantic than snuggling with your honey as an Elvis impersonator shakes his butt.

9. WaterFire, Providence, Rhode Island. You think candlelight is romantic? Try 100 bonfires.

8. Rockport, Massachusetts. As you overlook Motif No. 1, shack up and form a motif of your own.

7. Breakwater Jetty, Provincetown, Massachusetts. The wind blows through your hair, salty water laps at the jetty, and you might even catch a glimpse of a speedo-clad swimmer.

6. John Pennekamp State Park, Key Largo, Florida. Coral reefs and brilliant blue skies make this a gorgeous spot. Though dusk is popular with lovers, it's also when the bugs come out for love bites.

5. Savannah, Georgia. Savannah's 21 squares provide green, secluded spots for a midday tête-a-tête. Beware the camera-laden trolley tours.

4. Mystic, Connecticut. Julia Roberts did it, so it must be good.

3. Assateague Island, Virginia. Wild horses roam free along the coast, and chicks totally dig that, you stud. Watch out, though; they bite.

2. Kitty Hawk, North Carolina. Feel like you're walking on the clouds at the spot where the Wright brothers took to the sky.

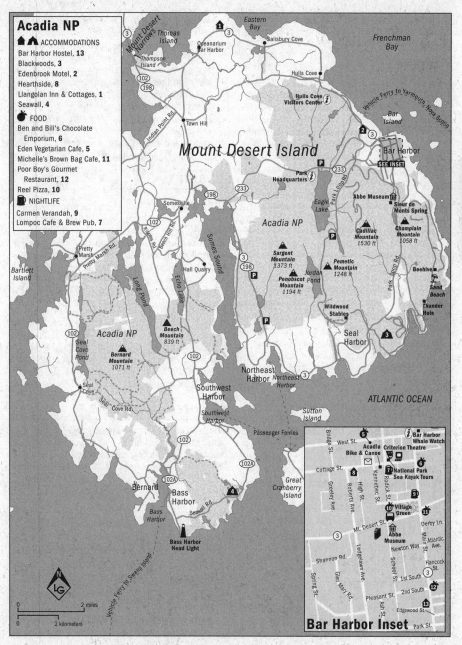

Acadia NP

🏠🏕 ACCOMMODATIONS
Bar Harbor Hostel, **13**
Blackwoods, **3**
Edenbrook Motel, **2**
Hearthside, **8**
Llangolan Inn & Cottages, **1**
Seawall, **4**

🍎 FOOD
Ben and Bill's Chocolate
 Emporium, **6**
Eden Vegetarian Cafe, **5**
Michelle's Brown Bag Cafe, **11**
Poor Boy's Gourmet
 Restaurant, **12**
Reel Pizza, **10**

🍷 NIGHTLIFE
Carmen Verandah, **9**
Lompoc Cafe & Brew Pub, **7**

EAST COAST

Eastern Bay
Mount Desert Narrows
Thomas Island
Thompson Island
Oceanarium Bar Harbor
Salisbury Cove
Frenchman Bay
Hulls Cove
Vehicle Ferry to Yarmouth, Nova Scotia
Hulls Cove Visitors Center
Indian Point Rd.
Town Hill
Bar Island
Bar Harbor
SEE INSET
Mount Desert Island
Park Headquarters
Abbe Museum
Sieur de Monts Spring
Eagle Lake
Cadillac Mountain 1530 ft
Champlain Mountain 1058 ft
Acadia NP
Somesville
Ridges Rd.
Beech Hill Rd.
Hall Quarry
Somes Sound
Sargent Mountain 1373 ft
Pemetic Mountain 1248 ft
Beehive
Pretty Marsh
Pretty Marsh Rd.
Bartlett Island
Long Pond
Echo Lake
Penobscot Mountain 1194 ft
Jordan Pond
Sand Beach
Thunder Hole
Wildwood Stables
Acadia NP
Beech Mountain 839 ft
Bernard Mountain 1071 ft
Seal Harbor
Seal Cove Pond
Seal Cove
Seal Cove Rd.
Northeast Harbor
Northeast Harbor
Southwest Harbor
Southwest Harbor
ATLANTIC OCEAN
Sutton Island
Passenger Ferries
Bernard
Bass Harbor
Bass Harbor
Seawall Rd.
Great Cranberry Island
Bass Harbor Head Light
Vehicle Ferry to Swans Island

0 — 2 miles
0 — 2 kilometers

Bar Harbor Inset
West St.
Bridge St.
Bar Harbor Whale Watch
Acadia Bike & Canoe
Criterion Theatre
Cottage St.
Greeley Ave.
High St.
Roberts Ave.
Kennebec St.
Rodick St.
National Park Sea Kayak Tours
Village Green
Mt. Desert St.
Abbe Museum
Newton Way
Main St.
Derby Ln.
Atlantic Ave.
Shannon Rd.
Legeelawn Ave.
School St.
Hancock St.
Spring St.
Glen Mary Rd.
Pleasant St.
1st South
2nd South
Ash St.
Edgewood St.
Park St.
Atlantic Ave.

open from May to mid-Oct. Home-cooked continental breakfast for those staying in the inn. July-Aug. rooms $75-85; cottages $90. From Sept. to mid-Oct. rooms $70-80; cottages $70. May-June rooms $50-60; cottages $65. AmEx/D/MC/V. ❸

Edenbrook Motel, 96 Eden St. (☎207-288-4975 or 800-323-7819; www.edenbrookmotelbh.com). Located between Bar Harbor and Acadia's entrance. Has clean, welcoming rooms. Open from mid-May to mid-Oct. Rooms in summer $80; fall $55; spring $48. AmEx/D/MC/V. ❸

Hearthside, 7 High St. (☎207-288-4533; www.hearthsideinn.com). A comfortable B&B on a back street a short walk from downtown. A/C and private bath; some rooms have fireplaces. Free afternoon tea. Rooms from June to mid-Oct. $120-$170, from May to mid-June and Oct. $75-$110. AmEx/D/MC/V. ❺

🍴 FOOD

Only vegetarians have a good excuse to leave Bar Harbor without eating lobster.

Reel Pizza, 33 Kennebec Pl. (☎207-288-3828; www.reelpizza.com), at the end of Rodick Pl. off Main St. Combination movie theater and pizzeria shows 2 films each evening for $6 and serves up creative pies, such as the "Hawaii 5-O," with ham, pineapple, green pepper, and macadamia nuts (large $18.50). Open daily from 4:30pm to last screening. MC/V. ❸

Ben and Bill's Chocolate Emporium, 66 Main St. (☎207-288-3281; www.benandbills.com), near Cottage St. Scoops out 72 flavors of homemade ice cream, including—no kidding—lobster. Come hungry; the small ($4.50) is 2 gigantic scoops. Open May-Sept. daily 8:30am-11pm. MC/V. ❶

Eden Vegetarian Cafe, 78 West St. (☎207-288-4422; www.barharborvegetarian.com). This stylish cafe is pricey but worth every penny. Everything on the menu is vegan, and many of the ingredients are organic and locally grown. The portobello mushroom vindaloo ($17.50) and the pesto pasta ($16.50) are chlorophyll-rich. Open May-Oct. M-Sa 5-9pm. Reservations recommended. D/MC/V. ❹

Michelle's Brown Bag Cafe, 154 Main St. (☎207-288-5858). The eatery serves up light, fresh sandwiches. Village Green (greens, cucumbers, tomatoes, sprouts, and hummus; $7). ½

sandwich and small salad or soup $8. Open daily 9am-5pm. AmEx/D/MC/V. ❷

Poor Boy's Gourmet Restaurant, 300 Main St. (☎207-288-4148). Local favorite for good food at great prices. The extensive menu features lobster in no fewer than 10 incarnations, with a section of the menu called "Lobster, lobster, lobster." Catch the early-bird special before 7pm, with 9 entrees and all-you-can-eat pasta for $10. Lobster meal ($21) includes bisque, lobster, baked potato, and dessert. Open daily 4:30-10pm. Reservations recommended. AmEx/D/MC/V. ❸

👁 SIGHTS

ABBE MUSEUM. The Abbe is a museum especially for those interested in the Wabanaki, Maine's first Native American inhabitants. The museum showcases all types of creative expression, from paintings and beaded purses to arrowheads. (*26 Mt. Desert St. ☎207-288-3519; www.abbemuseum.org. Open daily May-Oct. 10am-6pm; Oct.-May 10am-4pm. $6, ages 6-15 $2.*)

HISTORIC CRITERION THEATRE. The historic theater hosts main stream feature length films. Constructed in 1937, it has a floating balcony complete with bar. (*35 Cottage St. ☎207-288-3441. 2 movie showings nightly. Box office opens 30min. before show. $7.50, under 12 $5.50, seniors $6.50; balcony seats $8.50.*)

🎵 ENTERTAINMENT

The historic Criterion Theatre, 35 Cottage St., hosts mainstream films. Constructed in 1937, it has a floating balcony complete with bar. (☎207-288-3441. Box office opens 30min. before show. 2 movie showings per night. $7.50, under 12 $5.50, seniors $6.50; balcony seats $8.50.)

🍺 NIGHTLIFE

Although the surrounding scenery is the town's best offering, roadtrippers looking for nightlife won't be disappointed here.

Lompoc Cafe & Brew Pub, 36 Rodick St. (☎207-288-9392), off Cottage St. Live music in a relaxed setting. Locals adore this evening haunt, where you can sip a pint of ◢**Dark and Stormy** ($6) while playing bocce on the porch. Open-mike Th.

Live music—mainly rock, acoustic, and indie—F-Sa nights at 9:30pm. Th open mike. No cover. 21+. Open May-Oct. daily 11:30am-1am. MC/V.

Carmen Verandah, 119 Main St. (☎207-288-2766; www.carmenverandah.com). Has a cool, relaxed atmosphere with lively peach walls and a comfy lounge area. That all changes at 9:30pm, when the night's entertainment kicks in. Karaoke M, Jam-on Tu, DJ W, rotating live entertainment Th including the occasional drag show, House party DJ F, live band Sa, Reggae DJ Su. 21+ after 9:30. Cover $2-5. AmEx/D/MC/V.

▲ OUTDOORS

Along the **Shore Path** are some of the area's largest waterfront "cottages," most dating from the late 1800s or early 1900s. These homes recall the gilded age of Bar Harbor, when only the rich and famous inhabited the island. Those on foot can head to Bar Island at low tide, when a gravel path with tidepools, accessible via Bridge St., is exposed for 2-3hr. Take Bridge St. from West St. For those who want to bike in the park or navigate the harbor, **Acadia Bike & Canoe,** 48 Cottage St., has

the goods. The company also leads day and overnight sea-kayaking tours. (☎207-288-9605 or 800-526-8615. Mountain bikes $22 per day; 2½hr. kayak tours $38, 4hr. $48. Open May-Oct. daily 8am-6pm.) **National Park Sea Kayak Tours,** 39 Cottage St., specializes in ecological tours, pointing out local birds and marine life. (☎207-288-0342 or 800-347-0940. 4hr. tours $45-48. Open daily 7:30am-8:30pm.) **Bar Harbor Whale Watch,** 1 West St., sets sail several times a day for 3-4hr. tours and offers a refund if no whales are sighted. (☎207-288-238. $53, ages 6-14 $26, under 6 $8.)

THE END OF THE ROAD

Acadia National Park's beauty is unmatched on the Eastern Seaboard. Set up camp, take a relaxing trek through the wilderness, and taste the fruits of the ocean with a tall blueberry ale. Congratulations on a journey well done. But don't head back home yet—the rugged **Great North** is just around the corner. Who knows what adventures await off US 1?

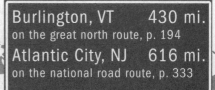

EXIT TO

Burlington, VT   430 mi.
on the great north route, p. 194
Atlantic City, NJ   616 mi.
on the national road route, p. 333

the great north

TOP 5

1. Sip *café au lait* or catch the **Festivale Internationale de Jazz** (p. 203) in Montréal, Québec.
2. See a housing project turned installation art at the **Heidelberg Project** (p. 234) in Detroit.
3. Get caught in a **bison jam** (p. 274) in one of earth's largest calderas, Yellowstone National Park.
4. Relax at the **Vandusen Botanical Gardens** (p. 321) after eating well in Vancouver's Chinatown.
5. Take **high tea** (p. 329) at the Empress Hotel in Victoria, British Columbia.

The Great North route is a many-splendored thing: the first half of the trip is marked by some of the most vibrant cities in the US and Canada, while the second half travels through many of the largest and most beautiful national parks in North America. The Great North offers the best of both worlds, whether you enjoy sipping espresso in the coffee shops of Montréal and Minneapolis or backcountry camping in the serene wilderness of Yellowstone, Grand Teton, and Banff National Parks. So don your raccoon skin cap and grab your rifle—the rugged North awaits.

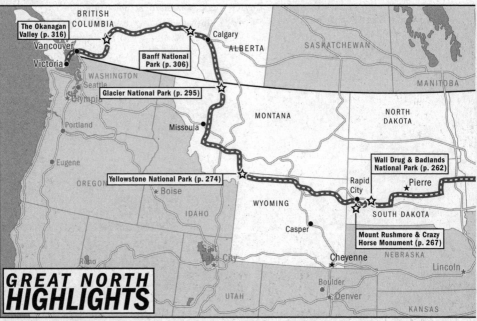

GREAT NORTH
HIGHLIGHTS

The road begins in youthful **Burlington,** bordered by the waters of Lake Champlain and Vermont's tranquil farmland. The route then heads north across the border into Canada, to francophone **Montréal** (p. 203), home to McGill University and the "Underground City," which makes pedestrian travel in the winter much more pleasant. The road continues through Ontario, where you'll see Parliament Hill in **Ottawa** (p. 213) before passing into New York, home of the **Thousand Island Seaway** (p. 218) and the **Jell-O Museum** of LeRoy (p. 221). Continue on to **Niagara Falls** (p. 222), where, in a bizarre reversal, the American side of the falls has serene parks and wilderness while the Canadian side features bright lights and rampant consumerism. Next, the route travels south around the shore of Lake Erie, offering the opportunity to sample the original buffalo wings at the **Anchor Bar** in **Buffalo** (p. 225). The road along the lake hits small towns and big cities, visiting the **Rock and Roll Hall of Fame** in **Cleveland** (p. 228) and the **Motown Historical Museum** in **Detroit** (p. 234) before crossing to

Michigan's Upper Peninsula over the spectacular **Mighty Mac** bridge (p. 242).

From there, the road travels past the cheese factories of **Wisconsin** on its way to the Twin Cities, **Minneapolis** and **Saint Paul,** home of the **Mall of America** (p. 256) and its indoor roller coaster. Leaving the Twin Cities, the road shifts from big cities and Great Lakes to the oddities of the Midwest. Beginning with the **Jeffers Petroglyphs** (p. 260) in western Minnesota, the road abounds with unusual sights, from the bizarre landscape of the **Badlands** (p. 262) to the kitschy animatronic dinosaurs of **Wall Drug** (p. 264) to the manmade wonders of **Mount Rushmore** (p. 267). From there, the road strikes out to the natural wonders of **Wind Cave** (p. 268) and **Jewel Cave** (p. 269), then north to the **Crazy Horse Memorial** (p. 269) and the shootouts and casinos of **Deadwood** (p. 269)—what more could a roadtripper ask for?

After leaving South Dakota, the road continues toward the vast expanses of some of North America's most majestic lands. The road travels by the geysers and mudpots of

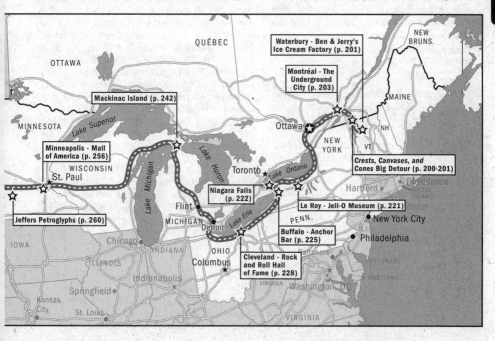

Yellowstone National Park (p. 274), the granite peaks of **Grand Teton National Park** (p. 279), the alpine lakes of the **Waterton-Glacier Peace Park** (p. 296), the mineral springs and backcountry beauty of **Banff National Park** (p. 307), and the Continental Divide at **Yoho National Park** (p. 311) before rediscovering civilization in **Vancouver** (p. 321). Finally, feed your inner scone fiend in self-consciously British **Victoria** (p. 329) as you gaze out over the harbor and ponder that eternal roadtripper question: "Exactly how far away am I from Wall Drug?

ROUTE STATS

Miles: c. 3500

Route: Burlington, VT, to Victoria, BC.

States and Provinces: 14; Vermont, Québec, Ontario, New York, Pennsylvania, Ohio, Michigan, Wisconsin, Minnesota, South Dakota, Wyoming, Montana, Alberta, and British Columbia.

Driving Time: 2-3 weeks minimum; allow 4 to appreciate the natural beauty of the north.

When To Go: While the snow of winter may make camping and driving much more difficult, those who brave the cold can take on some of the best skiing in North America. Depart in mid-Sept. to watch the leaves change all along the route.

Crossroads: A near-miss with **The Pacific Coast** at Vancouver, BC; just jot on down to Seattle, WA.

The Green Mountain State
VERMONT
Welcomes You!

BURLINGTON ☎ 802

Tucked between Lake Champlain and the Green Mountains, Burlington offers spectacular views of New York's Adirondack Mountains across the sailboat-studded waters of the lake. Several colleges, including Champlain College and the University of Vermont (UVM), give the area a youthful, progressive flair. If the weather is nice, stroll along the waterfront or try the Burlington Bike Path, which runs along the side of the lake. Alternatively, walk down Church St., where numerous cafes, bookstores, and boutiques (most of

them locally owned) offer a taste of the hip and laid-back Vermont atmosphere.

VITAL STATS

Population: 39,000

Tourist Office: Lake Champlain Regional Chamber of Commerce, 60 Main St. (☎802-863-3403; www.vermont.org). Open May to mid-Oct. M-F 8am-5pm, Sa-Su 10am-5pm; mid-Oct.-Apr. M-F 8am-5pm.

Library and Internet Access: Fletcher Free Library, 235 College St. (☎802-864-7146). Free. Open M-Tu and Th-F 8:30am-6pm, W 8:30am-9pm, Sa 9am-5pm, Su noon-6pm.

Post Office: 11 Elmwood Ave. (☎802-863-6033), at Pearl St. Open M-F 8am-5pm, Sa 9am-1pm. **Postal Code:** 05401.

⚑ ORIENTATION

In Burlington, **US 2,** known as **Main Street,** cuts an east-west route across downtown. The major north-south streets downtown are **Saint Paul Street, Pine Street,** which is one block to the west of St. Paul, and **Battery Street,** which runs next to the lake. **Church Street** also runs north-south but is mainly a pedestrian thoroughfare, lined with restaurants and shops. Major east-west streets are (from south to north) **Main Street, College Street, Cherry Street,** and **Pearl Street.** Parking is generally cheap and easy to find. Nothing is outside walking distance, so park anywhere. At the end of Lake St. by the waterfront, parking is free after 6pm all week, and drivers get 2hr. of free parking in all city-owned garages every day. Parking is free on Sundays.

❓ DID YOU KNOW? In 1981, Burlington elected (and subsequently re-elected 3 times) a socialist mayor, Bernie Sanders. Now, after serving 16 years in the House of Representatives, Sanders was elected to the United States Senate in 2006.

⚐ ACCOMMODATIONS

Downtown Burlington has very few accommodations. Reasonably priced hotels and guesthouses line **Shelburne Road (Route 7),** south of

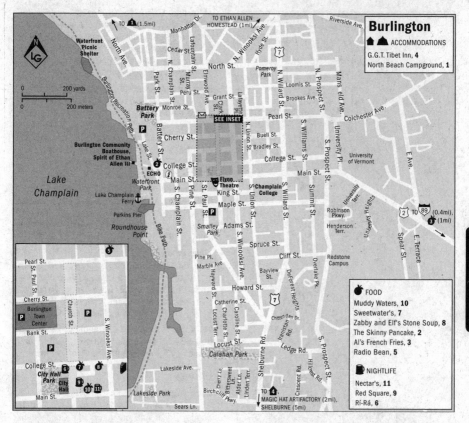

Burlington

♠ ▲ ACCOMMODATIONS

G.G.T. Tibet Inn, **4**
North Beach Campground, **1**

🍎 FOOD

Muddy Waters, **10**
Sweetwater's, **7**
Zabby and Elf's Stone Soup, **8**
The Skinny Pancake, **2**
Al's French Fries, **3**
Radio Bean, **5**

🍷 NIGHTLIFE

Nectar's, **11**
Red Square, **9**
Rí-Rá, **6**

downtown, and **Main Street (Route 2),** east of downtown. The motels on Rte. 7 tend to be a generation older and family-run, and are slightly cheaper (singles from $40) than the corporate chain options on Rte. 2 (from $80). Be warned: rates vary wildly here, almost on a day-to-day basis, depending on local festivals, weather conditions, and day of the week. Call ahead to guarantee the most affordable visit.

G.G.T. Tibet Inn, 1860 Shelburne Rd. (☎802-863-7110; www.ggttibetinn.com). Greets visitors with a large picture of the Dalai Lama and prayer flags. Excellent value and rates. Pool, TV, A/C, fridges, and microwaves. Breakfast included. Call ahead for rates. AmEx/MC/V. ❹

North Beach Campground, 60 Institute Rd. (☎802-862-0942 or 800-571-1198). 1.5 mi.

north of town by North Ave. 137 sites with access to a pristine, sandy beach on Lake Champlain. Beach open to non-campers and stellar for picnics. Beach open 9am-9pm; beach parking closes 9pm. $5 parking fee for non-campers. Lifeguards on duty mid-June to Aug. daily 10am-5:30pm. Showers $0.50 per 5min. Campgrounds open May to mid-Oct. Sites $24, with water and electricity $29, with full hookup $33. ❶

🍴 FOOD

With approximately 85 restaurants in the Church St. Marketplace and adjacent streets, Burlington is a haven for hungry travelers. In warm weather, the restaurants spill out onto patios in the marketplace, making for a truly vibrant dining experience.

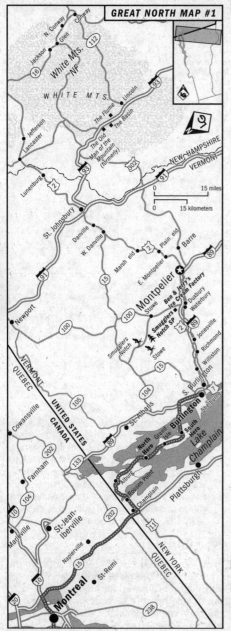

GREAT NORTH MAP #1

15 miles

15 kilometers

GREAT NORTH

Zabby and Elf's, 211 College St. (☎802-862-7616). Mostly vegetarian cafe specializing in hefty meals from hot and cold bars ($8.50 per lb.) and sandwiches on freshly baked bread ($7-8). Open M 7am-7pm, Tu-F 7am-9pm, Sa 9am-7pm. Cash only. ❷

American Flatbread's Burlington Hearth, 115 St. Paul St. (☎802-861-2999). Wood-fired pizzas are covered with local, organic ingredients ($12-17). Try some of the award-winning in-house brews as well as the extensive selection of rare draft beers. Open M-Th and Su 5-10pm, F-Sa 11:30am-2:30pm and 5-11pm. Taproom open 2hr. past dining room. AmEx/MC/V. ❸

Sweetwater's, 120 Church St. (☎802-864-9800). High ceilings and vast murals create an airy atmosphere in which to enjoy your meal. Delicious sandwiches $7-10. Dinner entrees $11-16. Open daily 11:30am-midnight. AmEx/D/MC/V. ❸

Skinny Pancake, 60 Lake St. (☎802-540-0188; www.skinnypancake.com). On the corner of Lake and College St. Offers crepes ($4.50-9) of all kinds featuring local ingredients. Patio with lake view. Open M 8am-2:30pm, Tu-W and Su 8am-9pm, Th-Sa 8am-midnight. ❷

The Radio Bean, 8 N. Winooski Ave (☎802-660-9346; www.radiobean.com). Artsy cafe. Hip, dimly lit atmosphere. Bar and live music of all genres most days. Open daily 8am-1:30am. MC/V. ❶

Muddy Waters, 184 Main St. (☎802-658-0466). The hippest of Burlington's hippie cafes. Features woodsy decor and organic menu. Coffee drinks $3; smoothies $4.25. Open M 7:30am-6pm, Tu-F 7:30am-midnight, Sa 8:30am-midnight, Su 8:30am-10pm. Cash only. ❶

Al's French Frys, 1251 Williston Rd. (☎802-862-9203). On Rte. 2 just past the I-89 interchange. Serves affordable fare including burgers, shakes, and fries (available by the cup, pint, or quart) unaltered since the 1940s. Open M-Th 10:30am-11pm, F-Sa 10:30am-midnight, Su 11am-11pm. Cash only. ❶

☉ SIGHTS

SHELBURNE MUSEUM. Seven miles south of Burlington on Rte. 7, the Shelburne houses an impressive and diverse collection of Americana, including the enormous paddleboat

Ticonderoga and paintings by Degas, Cassatt, Manet, Monet, Rembrandt, and Whistler collected by the museum's founder. Numerous meticulously restored historic buildings contain well-curated exhibits, making the museum easily worth the price of admission. *(☎ 802-985-3346; www.shelburnemuseum.org. Open May-Oct. daily 10am-5pm. Tickets valid for 2 days. $18, ages 6-18 $9; after 3pm $10/5.)*

ETHAN ALLEN HOMESTEAD. In the 1780s, Allen and his Green Mountain Boys forced the surrender of Fort Ticonderoga in New York, and were later instrumental in establishing Vermont's statehood. Today, 1hr. tours tell the story of Vermont's favorite son. *(Northeast of Burlington on Rte. 127 in the Winooski Valley Park. ☎ 802-865-4556; www.ethanallenhomestead.org.)*

MAGIC HAT ARTIFACTORY. The brewery offers free tours, tastings, and an array of Magic Hat swag at its industrial-punk-themed headquarters, three miles south of Burlington off Rte. 7. *(5 Bartlett Bay Rd. ☎ 802-658-2739; www.magichat. net. Tours W-F 3, 4, 5pm; Sa noon, 1, 1:30, 2, 3pm.)*

SHELBURNE FARMS. Built in 1886, the complex is now a nonprofit environmental education center for sustainable agriculture as well as a scenic 1400-acre working farm. Don't miss the majestic **Inn at Shelburne Farms.** *(1611 Harbor Rd. ☎ 802-985-8686; www.shelburnefarms.org. Welcome center open daily May-Oct. 9am-5:30pm; Nov.-*

Apr. 10am-5pm. Wagon tours mid-May to mid-Oct. $6, ages 3-17 $4, seniors $5.)

ECHO. Visitors have the opportunity to discover ecology, culture, and history at this science center and aquarium built in a former naval station. Though designed for a younger crowd, the exhibits are nonetheless filled with fascinating information. Check out the display on "Champ," Lake Champlain's own Loch Ness Monster, first sighted by Samuel de Champlain himself. *(1 College St. ☎ 802-864-1848; www.echovermont.org. Open daily 10am-5pm. $9, students and seniors $8, ages 3-17 $7.)*

THE SPIRIT OF ETHAN ALLEN III. Lake Champlain's largest cruise ship runs narrated scenic cruises for up to 500 passengers at a time. It departs from the boathouse at the bottom of College St. *(☎ 802-862-8300; www.soea.com. Cruises late May to mid-Oct. daily 10am, noon, 2, 4pm. $15, children $6. Sunset cruise $20/13.)*

OTHER SIGHTS. Architecture buffs can take delight in **South Willard Street,** where **Champlain College** occupies many of the Victorian houses that line the street. The pastoral **City Hall Park,** in the heart of downtown, and **Battery Street Park,** on Lake Champlain near the edge of downtown, provide an escape into the cool shade on hot summer days. With an amazing view across the lake, the **Burlington Community Boathouse,** at the base of College St., operates a small snack bar and offers observation decks

MAPLE SUGAR

Maple sugar is a big deal in the Northeast. Almost all of the world's maple syrup comes from Quebec and Vermont, and many locals argue that the region's true heart and soul only comes out in the sugaring season. During the warm days and freezing nights of March and April, grizzled farmers, huge manufacturers, and amateurs all spend time huddled in front of stoves, boiling sap to make maple syrup. It's no small task, either—40 gal. of sap are needed for every gallon of syrup. The sap is traditionally harvested from a sugar bush (a stand of maple trees) using a simple tap and metal bucket, but industrial farms often employ elaborate systems of hoses.

Vermonters in particular are very attached to their product and use it liberally: maple sugar has been known to appear as an ingredient in everything from fudge, cookies, and pie to applesauce, chicken glaze, and baked beans. A favorite treat, Sugar on Snow, combines what might be Vermont's two most readily available ingredients and is made at community events throughout the state. Syrup is boiled to 242°F, then dribbled onto tightly packed snow and eaten as it cools down, often (and

BIG DETOUR

CRESTS, CANVASES, & CONES

VERMONT

START: Burlington

HIGHLIGHT: Ben and Jerry's Factory

DISTANCE: 360 mi.

DURATION: 2 days

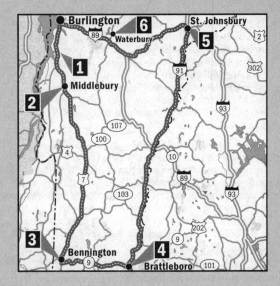

From Burlington, take US 7 S. to Charlotte. Turn left on State Park Rd. and follow it for about 1 mi. Go straight across the intersection with Mt. Philo Rd. and enter the park.

1. MOUNT PHILO STATE PARK. The centerpiece of Vermont's oldest state park, Mt. Philo is a quick and easy hike that ends with a gratifying view of the Lake Champlain Valley and the Adirondack Mountains from its 968 ft. summit. For those who would rather drive, a narrow road also winds to the top. A few **campsites ❶** are available. (Open from Memorial Day to mid-October sunrise-sunset. Sites $14-16. Day use $3.)

Get back on US 7 S. and proceed to Middlebury.

2. MIDDLEBURY. The town of Middlebury, nestled in the valleys of west-central Vermont, was built on the countryside's ample marble supply and is now home to the aptly named Middlebury College. The quiet village abuts the campus and surrounds Otter Creek. While much of the downtown is aimed at thicker wallets, several small, comfy, and affordable bookstores, galleries, and cafes are tucked in along Main St. Try **Carol's Hungry Mind Café ❶**, 24 Merchant's Row, with a large window in the back overlooking the river and local artwork displayed on the walls. (☎802-388-0101. Open M-F 7am-6pm, Sa-Su 9am-6pm.) Nearby, at the campus edge, **Sama's Cafe ❷**, 54 College St., occupies a rustic wood building and serves everything from coffee and ice cream to panini and wood-fired pizza. (☎802-388-6408. Open M-Th 7am-7:30pm, F 7am-8:30pm, Sa-Su 7:30am-5pm.) On campus, the **Middlebury College Museum of Art** has a broad collection with art from four millennia. (☎802-443-5007. Open Tu-F 10am-5pm, Sa-Su noom-5pm. Free.)

Continue south on US 7 to Bennington.

3. BENNINGTON. Anchoring the southwest corner of the state, Bennington was the sight of a noted Revolutionary War battle, at which General John Stark of New Hampshire (of "Live Free or Die" fame) led the successful rout of two detachments of the British army. In commemoration of the event, a large obelisk, the **Bennington Battle Monument,** 15 Monument Cir., was erected during the 19th century. At 306 ft., it is the tallest structure in Vermont. (☎802-447-0550. Open from mid-Apr. to Oct. daily 9am-5pm. $2, ages 6-14 $1.) West of downtown on Rte. 9, the **Ben-**

nington Museum, 75 Main St., displays fine art and historic artifacts from New England history. The collection highlights the work of folk artist Grandma Moses, a one-time Bennington resident whose one-room schoolhouse now comprises a wing of the museum. (☎802-447-1571. Open daily 10am-5pm. $9, students and children free). A lively downtown centers on the junction of US 7 and Rte. 9 and has galleries, restaurants, and cafes catering to Bennington's student population.

Take Rte. 9 out of downtown and proceed east to Brattleboro.

4. BRATTLEBORO. The spirit of Vermont is clearly on display here; the psychedelic progressivism and traditional rural values infuse Brattleboro with excitement. The hillside town looks out over the Connecticut River to New Hampshire that beautiful scenery frames bustling Main St. **Brattleboro Books,** 34 Elliot St., has an immense collection of over 75,000 old and out-of-print books. (☎802-257-7777. Open M-Sa 10am-6pm, Su 11am-5pm.) The subterranean café **Mocha Joe's ❶,** 183 Main St., serves coffee brewed with beans from around the world. (☎802-257-5637. Open M-Th 7am-8pm, F-Sa 7:30-10pm, Su 7:30am-7pm.)

From Brattleboro, take Rte. 9 W. to I-91 N. Exit at St. Johnsbury.

5. SAINT JOHNSBURY. In a comfortable position at the nexus of four highways and two railroads, St. Johnsbury is the flagship town of Vermont's famed Northeast Kingdom. Along Main St., just off US 2 after it dives downhill, sits the **Saint Johnsbury Athenaeum,** 1171 Main St., a beautiful public library with an attached art gallery containing a massive landscape painting by Albert Bierstadt. (☎802-748-8291. Open M and W 10am-8pm, Tu and Th-F 10am-5:30pm, Sa 9:30am-4pm. $5.) The **Fairbanks Museum and Planetarium,** 1302 Main St., opened in 1891, displays wealthy philanthropist Franklin Fairbanks's "cabinet of curiosities" in a gorgeous Victorian building. The collection includes over 170,000 objects ranging from animals to totem poles to fossils. The building also houses Vermont's only public planetarium. (☎802-748-2372. Open Tu-Sa 9am-5pm, Su 1-5pm. $6, children and seniors $5.) **Maple Grove Farms,** 1052 Portland St., is the country's largest producer of maple syrup. Take your photo next to the world's largest can of maple syrup (over 10 ft. tall) and buy as many maple-related products as you can in the gift shop. (☎802-748-5141. Tours M-F 8am-2pm. $1, under 13 free.)

Take US 2 W. to Waterbury and go north 1 mi. on Rte. 100 until you see the Ben and Jerry's factory on your left.

6. BEN AND JERRY'S. Round off your tour of Vermont with a stop at Ben and Jerry's headquarters in Waterbury. The factory, which produces the state's most beloved export, offers regular 30min. tours of the facility that begin with a short "moo-vie" about the company's origins, proceed through a large room where visitors can watch the ice cream being made and packaged, and conclude with tastings of one of many "euphoric flavors." Outside the factory, a "flavor graveyard" pays homage to ice-cream varieties such as "Ethan Almond" or "Peanut Butter and Jelly" that the company has (often wisely) retired. To the amusement of visitors, tombstones for each flavor are inscribed with little rhyming epitaphs. (☎866-258-6877. Open daily from July to mid-Aug. 9am-9pm; from mid-Aug. to Oct. 9am-7pm; Nov.-June 10am-6pm. $3.)

Back to the route. Take Rte. 100 S. back to US 2. Follow US 2 E. back to Burlington.

and seating for those who want to enjoy the stunning sunsets over Lake Champlain. (☎802-865-3377. Open mid-May to mid-Oct.)

 DID YOU KNOW? Burlington was the home of Horatio Nelson Jackson, the first person to cross the US by automobile (p. 1).

◙ NIGHTLIFE

Several colleges in the area keep Burlington's nightlife scene alive and kicking.

Nectar's, 188 Main St. (☎802-658-4771). Where the band Phish played while its members were UVM students. Inexpensive food, including locally acclaimed gravy fries ($4). Nightly live tunes—check the monthly schedule. Saturday 80s nights. Open daily 10am-2:30am. AmEx/MC/V.

Red Square, 136 Church St. (☎802-859-8909). Live music nightly. Bands play in the alley if the crowd gets large. No kitchen. Open M-Sa 4pm-2am, Su 8pm-2am. AmEx/MC/V.

Rí-Rá, 123 Church St. (☎802-860-9401; www.rira.com) Traditional Irish pub with live Celtic music Su 5-8pm. Beer $2-4.50. Open M-W 11:30am-1am, Th-Sa 11:30am-2am, Su 11:30am-midnight. AmEx/D/MC/V.

◪ THE ROAD TO THE CHAMPLAIN ISLANDS: 20 MI.

From **Main Street** in Burlington, turn left on **US 2/US 7 (Ethan Allen Highway).** Merge with **I-89 North** for about 6 mi. Take **Exit 17** for **US 2 West.**

CHAMPLAIN ISLANDS ☎802

US 2 heads north through the rural Champlain Islands. Nestled between the Adirondacks and Green Mountains, these mostly flat islands of "New England's West Coast" have avoided exploitation despite the allure of their natural beauty and prime location between Montréal and Burlington. Residents still devote their land to farms, orchards, vineyards, and sandy beaches. North of Winooski, the Sandbar Causeway connects to the south end of the Champlain Islands. The northern end is connected to New York by Rouses Point Bridge, west of Alburg.

The town of South Hero is known as the "Garden Spot of Vermont" due to an especially long agricultural season. **Grand Isle State Park ❶,** 36 E. Shore Rd. S., 2 mi. north of town on the east side of the road, offers near-perfect camping, accompanied by the lapping waves of Lake Champlain. Because South Hero is less marshy, there are fewer bugs in this campground than on North Hero. (☎802-372-4300; www.vtstateparks.com. 36 lean-tos and 117 sites. Showers, RV sites, swimming, fishing, boat ramp, volleyball courts, and playground. Dump station; no hookups. Rowboat and kayak rentals $7.50 per hr., $20 per half-day, $35 per day. Reception 2-9pm. Quiet hours 10pm-7am. Sites $16-18; lean-tos $23-25; cabins $42. Day use $3, $2 per child. MC/V.)

Called the "Finest General Store on the Planet" by *Yankee Magazine,* **Hero's Welcome ❶,** 3537 US 2 in North Hero, stocks anything you could ever (or never) need, from Slinkies to DVDs, fish bait to film. The store includes a bakery and deli, specializing in delicious sandwiches ($4-7) named after famous locals ranging from Ethan Allen to "Champ," the Loch Ness Monster-like denizen of Lake Champlain. (☎802-372-4121. Open in summer daily 6:30am-8pm; in winter M-Sa 6:30am-6pm, Su 8am-6pm. D/MC/V.) North Hero offers a few other restaurants and shops, almost entirely along Rte. 2, but they tend to be expensive, especially during the summer months. The **Lake Champlain Islands Chamber of Commerce,** near Hero's Welcome, offers more information. (☎802-372-8400 or 800-262-5226; www.champlainislands.com. Open M-F 9am-4pm.)

◪ THE ROAD TO MONTRÉAL: 47 MI.

From the islands, it's a quick 8 mi. jaunt through New York to the US-Canada border. Get on **I-87 (Adirondack Northway)** heading north, which will almost immediately bring you to customs and turn into **Autoroute 15.** Just east of Montréal, Autoroute 15 merges with **Autoroutes 10 and 20** to cross the St. Lawrence River via the **Pont Champlain (Champlain Bridge).** Right after you cross the massive river, take the exit for Centre-Ville (Downtown) along the **Autoroute Bonaventure (Highway 10).** Follow the expressway to the end, where it becomes **rue Université.**

GREAT NORTH

Bienvenue à

QUÉBEC

La Belle Province

MONTRÉAL ☎ 514

This island city has been coveted territory for over 300 years. War and sieges dominated Montréal's early history as British forces strove to wrest it from French control. Today's invaders are not French, British, or American generals but rather visitors eager to experience a diverse, cosmopolitan city, and perhaps to brush up on their *français québécois.* Despite being located only an hour from the US border, Montréal is the second-largest French-speaking city in the world. Fashion that rivals Paris, a nightlife comparable to London, and international cuisine all attest to the city's prominent European legacy. With its global flavor and large student population, it is hard not to be swept up by the energy coursing through the *centre-ville.*

✤ ORIENTATION

The one-way **Boulevard Saint-Laurent** (also called **"la Main,"** or **"The Main"**) runs north through the city, splitting Montréal and its streets east-west. The Main also serves as the unofficial French/English divider; English-speaking **McGill University** lies to the west, while **Saint-Denis,** a street running parallel to St-Laurent, lies to the east and defines the French student quarter (also called the Quartier Latin). **Rue Sherbrooke,** which is parallel to **de Maisonneuve** and **Sainte-Catherine** downtown, runs east-west almost the entire length of Montréal. The **Underground City,** a network of shops and restaurants, runs north-south, stretching from rue Sherbrooke to **rue de la Gauchetière** and **rue Saint-Antoine.** Pick up a free (and helpful) map from the tourist office.

VITAL STATS
Population: 1,600,000
Tourist Office: Infotouriste, 1001 rue de Square-Dorchester (☎877-266-5687; www.tourisme-montreal.org), on N. Ste-Catherine between rue Peel and rue Metcalfe. Open daily July-Aug. 8:30am-8pm; Sept.-June 9am-6pm.
Currency Exchange: Custom House, 905 blvd. Maisonneuve (☎514-844-1414). Open M-F 8:30am-6pm, Sa 9am-4pm. **Calforex,** 1250 rue Peel (☎514-392-9100). Flat $2.75 fee. Open in summer M-W 8:30am-7pm, Th-Sa 8:30am-9pm, Su 10am-6pm.
Library and Internet Access: Bibliothèque Nationale du Québec, 1700 rue St-Denis (☎514-873-1100). Open daily 10am-midnight for limited access.
Post Office: 1250 rue Université (☎800-267-1177). Open M-F 8am-5:45pm. **Postal Code:** H3B 3B0.

When first founded, Montréal was limited to the riverside area of present-day **Vieux Montréal,** but it has since evolved from a settlement of French colonists into a cosmopolitan metropolis. A stroll along rue Ste-Catherine, the flashy commercial avenue, is a must. European fashion is all the rage, conversations mix English and French, and upscale retail shops are intermingled with tacky souvenir stores and debaucherous clubs. The street's assortment of peep shows and neon-lit sex shops has earned it the nickname "Saint-Vitrine" (holy windows).

A small **Chinatown** lines rue de la Gauchetière. At the northern edge of the city's center, **Little Italy** occupies the area north of rue Beaubien between rue St-Hubert and Louis-Hémon. Rue St-Denis, home to the city's elite at the turn of the century, still serves as the **Quartier Latin's** main street. Restaurants of all types are clustered along **rue Prince Arthur.** Nearby, **Square Saint-Louis** hosts a beautiful fountain and sculptures. **Boulevard Saint-Laurent,** north of Sherbrooke, is perfect for walking or biking. Many attractions between **Mont-Royal** and the **Fleuve Saint-Laurent** (St. Lawrence River) are free. **Le Village,** the gay village, is located along rue Ste-Catherine Est between rue St-Hubert and Papineau.

Montréal Overview

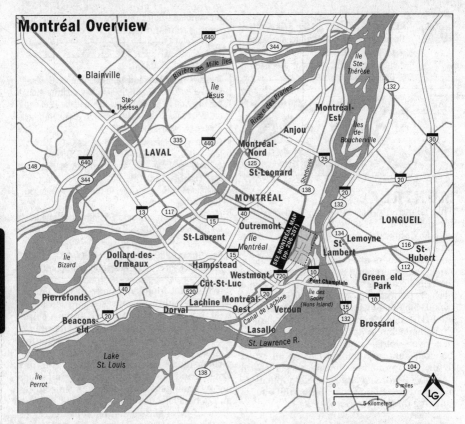

▤ TRANSPORTATION

Parking can be a miserable experience, often extremely expensive and very difficult to find along the streets. Try lots on the city's outskirts for reasonable prices and consider using the convenient **STM Métro and Bus** (☎514-288-6287; www.stm.info). The four Métro lines and most buses run daily 5:30am-12:30am ($2.75, 6 tickets $12, weekly pass $19.25). Alternatively, **Ça Roule,** 27 rue de la Commune Est, rents bicycles and rollerskates starting at $8 per hr. during the summer. (☎514-866-0633; www.caroulemontreal.com. Open daily 9am-8pm.) Reasonable parking is available at the McGill Residences ($14 per day, $30 per week) or the Université de Montréal ($10 per day) for those who stay in the dorms.

⌂ ACCOMMODATIONS

The **Infotouriste** (☎877-266-5687) is the best resource for info about hostels, hotels, and *chambres touristiques* (rooms in private homes or small guesthouses). Inquire about B&Bs at the **Downtown Bed and Breakfast Network,** 3458 av. Laval, near Sherbrooke; the managers run their own modest hideaway and maintain a list of 80 other homes downtown. (☎800-267-5180; www.bbmontreal.qc.ca. Open daily 9am-9pm. Singles $75-85; doubles $85-95. AmEx/MC/V.) **Canada Day** and the **Grand Prix** in June make accommodations scarce and expensive.

▨ **Auberge de Jeunesse, Montréal Youth Hostel (HI-C),** 1030 rue MacKay (☎514-843-3317;

www.hostellingmontreal.com). M: Lucien-L'Allier; from the station exit, cross the street and head right. The hostel is on the 1st real street on the left, across from the parking lot. Bath in every room, kitchen, laundry, pool tables, Internet, and a cafe with bar. Pub crawls, bike tours, improv nights, and other activities several times per week. Linen $2.30; no sleeping bags. 1-week max. stay. Reception 24hr. Check-in 1pm. Check-out 11am. The 250+ beds fill quickly in summer; reservations strongly recommended. Dorms $35, members $30; doubles $90/80. MC/V. ❷

☒ **La Maison du Patriote**, 169 rue St-Paul Est. (☎514-866-0855; www.lamaisondupatriote.ca). Cozy hostel and B&B in a stone house. 7 private rooms and a 12-person dorm. A/C in summer. The bars and clubs on Rue St. Paul can make the street-facing rooms somewhat noisy on weekends. Continental breakfast included. Free Internet. Dorms $33.50; private rooms $60-170. ❷

McGill University, Bishop Mountain Hall, 3935 rue de l'Université (☎514-398-5200; www. mcgill.ca/residences/summer). M: McGill. Follow Université along the edge of campus; when the road seems to end in a parking lot at the top of the steep hill, bear right—reception is in the circular stone building with lots of windows. Kitchenettes on each floor. 1000 beds. Common room with TV. Towels and linens provided. Laundry facilities. Free Internet. Check-in 3pm. Check-out noon. Open mid-May to mid-Aug. Singles $45, students and seniors $40. MC/V. ❷

Université de Montréal, Residences, 2350 rue Edouard-Montpetit (☎514-343-8006; www.stu-diohotel.ca). M: Edouard-Montpetit or Université-de-Montréal. Follow the signs up the steep hill. Located in a tranquil, remote neighborhood on the edge of a beautiful campus, the East Tower affords a great view. Free local calls. TV lounge. Continental breakfast $5 per person. Cafe open M-F 7:30am-2:30pm. Laundry facilities. TV lounge. Internet $5 per day. Parking $10. Reception 24hr. Check-in 3pm. Check-out noon. Open mid-May to early Aug. Singles $40; doubles $50. 10% student discount. MC/V. ❷

Hôtel de Paris, 901 rue Sherbrooke Est (☎514-522-6861 or 800-567-7217; www.hotel-montreal. com). M: Sherbrooke. This European-style 19th-century apartment building houses pleasant hotel rooms with private bath, TV, telephone, and A/C.

Some rooms contain kitchenettes. Linen $3. Single-sex dorms $23; rooms $74-155. AmEx/MC/V. ❶

Camping Alouette, 3449 rue de l'Industrie (☎450-464-1661 or 888-464-7829; www. campingalouette.com), 30km from the city. Follow Autoroute 20 south, take Exit 105, and follow the signs. The campground is a secluded alternative to Montréal's bustling hostels. Nature trail, pool, laundry facilities, a small store, volleyball courts, a dance hall, and a daily shuttle to and from Montréal (30min., $12). Sites for up to 2 $32, with hookup $37. MC/V. ❶

🍴 FOOD

In Montréal, chic restaurants rub shoulders with funky cafes. Stop by **Chinatown** or **Little Italy** for outstanding examples of their respective culinary heritages. The western half of **Sainte-Catherine** and the area around **Boulevard Saint-Laurent** north of Sherbrooke offer a large range of choices. By far the best and most affordable restaurants cluster on **rue Saint-Denis**. Many restaurants, even upscale ones, have no liquor license; head to the nearest *dépanneur* or **SAQ** (*Societé des alcools du Québec*) to buy wine. For further guidance, consult the free *Restaurant Guide*, published by the **Greater Montréal Convention and Tourism Bureau** (☎514-844-5400), which lists over 130 restaurants by type of cuisine.

☒ **Jardin Nelson**, 407 Pl. Jacques Cartier (☎514-861-5731; www.jardinnelson.com), near the waterfront. Classy courtyard dining at reasonable prices, immersed in the historic ambiance of Vieux Montréal. Live jazz daily. Entrees range from crepes to pizza and salads ($14-17). Open Apr.-Oct. daily 11:30am-2am. AmEx/MC/V. ❸

☒ **La Crème de la Crème Bistro Café**, 21 rue de la Commune Est (☎514-874-0723), in Vieux Montréal. A brick cafe on the waterfront that combines Greek cuisine and Provençal decor. Dimly lit interior offers expansive views of nearby quays. Serves tasty baguette sandwiches (with salad; $9-11) and slices of cake ($4). Open 11am-midnight. Closed Jan.-Mar. MC/V. ❷

☒ **Brûlerie St-Denis**, 3967 rue St-Denis (☎514-286-9158). M: Sherbrooke. A fun student cafe where the food and coffee are excellent, the waiters are friendly, and the patrons seem to

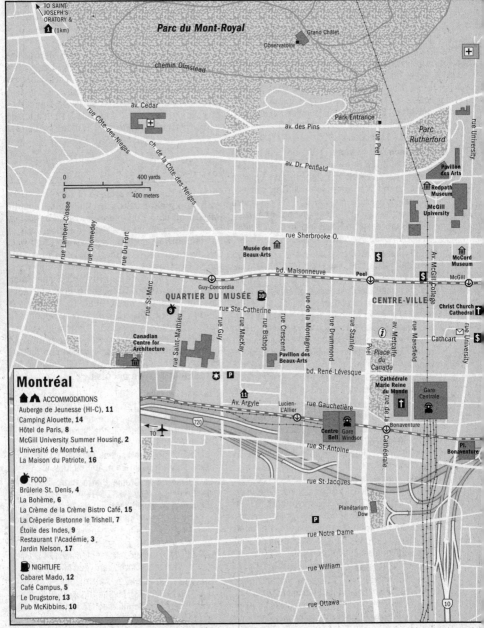

TO SAINT-
JOSEPH'S
ORATORY &
(1km)

Parc du Mont-Royal

Grand Châlet

Observatoire

chemin Olmstead

av. Cedar

Park Entrance

av. des Pins

Parc Rutherford

rue Peel

rue University

av. Dr. Penfield

Pavillon des Arts

rue Côte-des-Neiges

ch. de la Côte-des-Neiges

Redpath Museum

McGill University

0   400 yards

0   400 meters

rue Sherbrooke O.

McCord Museum

rue Lambert-Closse

rue Chomedey

rue Du Fort

rue St-Marc

Musée des Beaux-Arts

bd. Maisonneuve

Peel

McGill

Av. McGill College

Christ Church Cathedral

Guy-Concordia

QUARTIER DU MUSÉE

rue Ste-Catherine

CENTRE-VILLE

Cathcart

rue University

rue Saint-Mathieu

rue Guy

rue MacKay

rue Bishop

rue Crescent

rue de la Montagne

rue Drummond

rue Stanley

Peel

av. Metcalfe

rue Mansfield

Place du Canada

Canadian Centre for Architecture

Pavillon des Beaux-Arts

bd. René-Lévesque

Cathédrale Marie Reine du Monde

Gare Centrale

Av. Argyle

Lucien-L'Allier

rue Gauchetière

rue de la Cathédrale

Bonaventure

Montréal

ACCOMMODATIONS
Auberge de Jeunesse (HI-C), **11**
Camping Alouette, **14**
Hôtel de Paris, **8**
McGill University Summer Housing, **2**
Université de Montréal, **1**
La Maison du Patriote, **16**

FOOD
Brûlerie St. Denis, **4**
La Bohème, **6**
La Crème de la Crème Bistro Café, **15**
La Crêperie Bretonne le Trishell, **7**
Étoile des Indes, **9**
Restaurant l'Académie, **3**
Jardin Nelson, **17**

NIGHTLIFE
Cabaret Mado, **12**
Café Campus, **5**
Le Drugstore, **13**
Pub McKibbins, **10**

720

TO

Centre Bell

Gare Windsor

rue St-Antoine

Pl. Bonaventure

rue St-Jacques

Planétarium Dow

rue Notre Dame

rue William

rue Ottawa

10

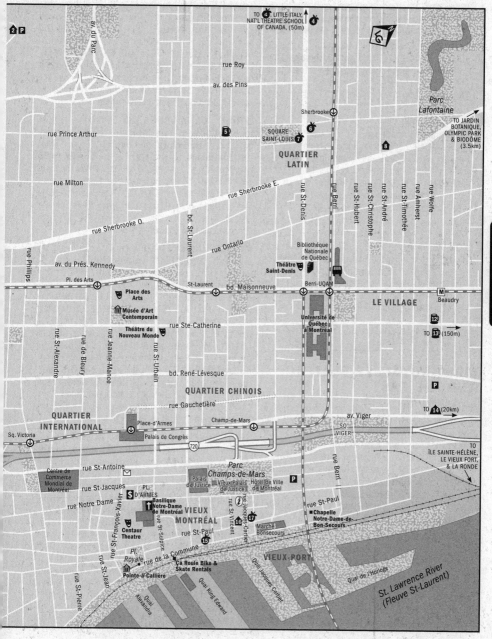

TO LITTLE ITALY,
NAT'L THEATRE SCHOOL
OF CANADA, (50m)

rue Roy

av. des Pins

Sherbrooke

rue Prince Arthur

SQUARE
SAINT-LOUIS

QUARTIER
LATIN

rue Milton

rue Sherbrooke E.

rue Sherbrooke O.

rue Ontario

av. du Prés. Kennedy

bd. St-Laurent

rue St-Denis

rue Berri

rue St-Hubert

rue St-Christophe

rue St-André

rue St-Timothée

rue Wolfe

rue Amherst

Parc
Lafontaine

TO JARDIN
BOTANIQUE,
OLYMPIC PARK
& BIODÔME
(3.5km)

Bibliothèque
Nationale
de Québec

Théâtre
Saint-Denis

Pl. des Arts

St-Laurent

bd. Maisonneuve

Berri-UQAM

Place des
Arts

Musée d'Art
Contemporain

Théâtre du
Nouveau Monde

rue Ste-Catherine

Université de
Québec
à Montréal

LE VILLAGE

Beaudry

TO (150m)

rue St-Alexandre

rue de Bleury

rue Jeanne-Mance

rue St-Urbain

bd. René-Lévesque

QUARTIER CHINOIS

rue Gauchetière

Champ-de-Mars

av. Viger

SQ
VIGER

TO (20km)

QUARTIER
INTERNATIONAL

Sq. Victoria

Place-d'Armes

Palais de Congrès

TO
ÎLE SAINTE-HÉLÈNE,
LE VIEUX FORT,
& LA RONDE

Centre de
Commerce
Mondial de
Montréal

rue St-Antoine

rue St-Jacques

PL.
D'ARMES

rue Notre Dame

Basilique
Notre-Dame
de Montréal

VIEUX
MONTRÉAL

rue St-François-Xavier

rue St-Sulpice

Centaur
Theatre

rue St-Vincent

rue St-Paul

Parc
Champs-de-Mars

Palais
de Justice

Vieux-Palais
de Justice

Hôtel de Ville
de Montréal

rue Jacques-Cartier

Marché
Bonsecours

Chapelle
Notre-Dame-de-
Bon-Secours

rue St-Paul

rue Berri

PL.
Royale

rue de la Commune

Ça Roule Bike &
Skate Rentals

VIEUX-PORT

Pointe-à-Callière

rue St-Jean

rue St-Pierre

Quai
Alexandra

Quai King Edward

Quai Jacques-Cartier

Quai de l'Horloge

St. Lawrence River
(Fleuve St-Laurent)

know each other already. Beans roasted in house. Other locations throughout Montréal. *Café du jour* $1.50. Open daily 9am-11pm. AmEx/MC/V. ➋

La Crêperie Bretonne le Trishell, 3470 rue St-Denis (☎514-281-1012). M: Sherbrooke. Montréalers have been known to line up for a taste of le Trishell's melt-in-your-mouth crepes and fondues. Strawberry crepe $7.25. Open M-Th 11:30am-11pm, F 10:30am-11:30pm, Sa-Su noon-11:30pm. AmEx/MC/V. ➌

Restaurant l'Académie, 4051 rue St-Denis (☎514-849-2249; www.lacademie.ca), at the corner of av. Duluth. M: Sherbrooke. Dine with white linen without breaking the bank. Lunch offers the best deals on French standards. For something unique, try the frogs' legs ($17). Open daily noon-10pm. AmEx/D/MC/V. ➍

Étoile des Indes, 1806 Ste-Catherine Ouest (☎514-932-8330), near St-Mathieu. A local favorite for Indian food. Spicy Bangalore *phal* dishes are only for the brave, but the homemade cheese paneer plates are for everyone. The butter chicken ($11) is also phenomenal. Dinners $5-15. Open M-Sa 11:30am-2:30pm and 5-11pm, Su 5-11pm. AmEx/MC/V. ➌

⬤ SIGHTS

MONT-ROYAL, LE PLATEAU, AND THE EAST

◼BIODÔME. The fascinating Biodôme is the most recent addition to Olympic Park. Housed in the former Olympic Vélodrome, the Biodôme is a "living museum" of four complete ecosystems: a tropical forest, a Laurentian forest, a St-Laurent marine ecosystem, and a polar world. (*4777 av. Pierre-de-Coubertin. M: Viau.* ☎*514-868-3000; www.biodome.qc.ca. Open daily in summer 9am-6pm; in winter 9am-5pm. $16, students and seniors $12, ages 5-17 $8.*)

◼PARC DU MONT-ROYAL. Designed by Frederick Law Olmsted, designer of New York City's Central Park and Boston's Emerald Necklace, the 127-year-old Parc du Mont-Royal surrounds and includes Montréal's namesake mountain. Though the hike from rue Peel up the mountain is longer and steeper than it looks (5.5km by the gradual Olmsted Trail, 0.6km by staircase), the jaw-dropping view of the city from the observation deck is more than worth it. The 30m cross at the summit is a replica of the cross placed there in 1643 by Maisonneuve, the founder of Montréal. (*M: Mont-Royal or bus #11.* ☎*514-844-4928, tour info 843-8240. Open daily 6am-midnight. Tours M-F 9am-5pm from Smith House, 1260 ch. Remembrance, between Beaver Lake and Chalet du Mont-Royal. Free.*)

◼TOUR OLYMPIQUE. The world's tallest inclined tower, built for the 1976 summer games, is the glory of Olympic Park. Take the **Funiculaire** to the top of the tower for a breathtaking view. (*3200 rue Viau. M: Viau or Pie-IX.* ☎*514-252-4737; www.rio.gouv.qc.ca. Funiculaire open daily mid-June to early Sept. 9am-7pm; early Sept. to mid-June 9am-5pm. Guided tours every hr. French and English. Tours $8, with tower admission $17. $14, students and seniors $10.50, ages 5-17 $7.*)

MCGILL UNIVERSITY. One of Canada's premier educational institutions, the McGill University campus extends up Mont-Royal and is made up mostly of stately Victorian buildings on pleasant greens. Stop by the **McGill Welcome Center** for a tour. (*Burnside Hall Bldg., 805 rue Sherbrooke, Room 115.* ☎*514-398-6555; www.mcgill.ca/ visiting. Tours available M-F, usually 10:30am, 2:30pm. Call 48hr. in advance for reservations.*) The campus includes the **Redpath Museum of Natural History,** housed in the oldest building in North America to be built specifically as a museum. (*859 rue Sherbrooke; main gate at rue McGill and Sherbrooke. M: McGill.* ☎*514-398-4086; www.mcgill.ca/redpath. Open M-F 9am-5pm, Su 1-5pm. Free.*)

SAINT JOSEPH'S. The dome of St-Joseph's Oratory is the second-highest dome in the world (after St. Peter's Basilica in Rome). An acclaimed religious site that attracts pilgrims from all over the globe, St-Joseph's is credited with a long list of miracles and unexplained healings. The **Votive Chapel,** where the crutches and canes of thousands of healed devotees hang for all to see, stays warm with the heat of 10,000 candles. On display nearby, the heart (seriously) of founder Brother Andre sits in an ornate reliquary. The heart was stolen in 1973 but recovered from a Montreal basement by police two years later. (*3800 ch. Queen Mary. M: Côte-des-Neiges.* ☎*514-733-8211; www.saint-joseph. org. Open daily 9am-8pm. Museum open 10am-5pm.*)

BOTANICAL GARDENS AND INSECTARIUM. The Japanese and Chinese landscapes at the Jardin Botanique showcase the largest bonsai and penjing collections outside of Asia. The gardens also harbor an insectarium of exotic bugs, including more than a dozen fist-size spiders. *(4101 rue Sherbrooke Est. M: Pie-IX. ☎514-872-1400; www.ville.montreal.qc.ca/jardin. Open daily Nov.-May 9am-5pm; May-Aug. 9am-6pm; Sept.-Oct. 9am-9pm. Parking $8 per day. $16, students and seniors $12, ages 5-17 $8.)*

CATHÉDRALE MARIE REINE DU MONDE. A scaled-down replica of St. Peter's basilica in Rome, this Roman Catholic cathedral stirred tensions when it was built in the heart of Montréal's Anglo-Protestant area. *(At René-Lévesque and Cathédrale. ☎514-866-1661. Open daily 6am-6:30pm. Free.)*

THE UNDERGROUND CITY

Montréal residents don't let the winter weather freeze their *joie de vivre* but rather flock underground, where 30km of tunnels link Métro stops and form an ever-expanding "prototype city of the future" that includes restaurants, cinemas, theaters, hotels, two universities, two department stores, 1700 businesses, 1615 housing units, and 2000 boutiques. Here, residents bustle through the hallways of this mall-like "sub-urban" city. At the McGill stop lie some of the Underground City's finest and most navigable offerings.

SHOPS. To find the shopping wonderland **Place Bonaventure,** follow signs marked "Restaurants et Commerce" through the maze of shops under rue de la Gauchetière Ouest. The visitors center supplies maps of the tunnels and underground attractions. *(900 rue de la Gauchetière Ouest. M: Bonaventure. ☎514-397-2325. Shops open daily 9am-9pm.)* The **Promenades de la Cathédrale** take their name from their above-ground neighbor, **Christ Church Cathedral.** *(635 rue Ste-Catherine Ouest. Church ☎514-843-6577. Open daily 8am-6pm. Promenades ☎514-849-9925.)*

VIEUX MONTRÉAL

In the 17th century, Montréal's citizens, struggling with Iroquois tribes for control of the area's lucrative fur trade, erected walls to encircle the settlement. Today, the remnants of those ramparts delineate the boundaries of Vieux Montréal, the city's first settlement, on the stretch of river bank between **rue McGill, Notre-Dame,** and **Berri.** The fortified walls that once protected the quarter were torn down long ago in the interest of expansion, but the beautiful 17th- and 18th-century mansions of politicos and merchants have retained their splendor. **Guidatour** leads walking tours of Vieux Montréal, departing from the Basilique Notre-Dame-de-Montréal. *(☎514-844-4021 or 800-363-4021; www.guidatour.qc.ca. 1hr. tours mid-June to late Sept. daily 11am in French, 1:30pm in English; late May to mid-June and early Oct. Sa-Su 11am in French, 1:30pm in English. $17.50, students $15.50, ages 6-12 $8.50; includes admission to church.)*

▓BASILIQUE NOTRE-DAME DE MONTRÉAL. Towering above the Place d'Armes and its memorial to Maisonneuve is the most beautiful church in Montréal. One of North America's largest churches and a historic center for the city's Catholic population, the neo-Gothic Basilique Notre-Dame de Montréal has hosted everyone from Québec separatists to the pope. Don't miss the Sacred Heart Chapel's bronze altarpiece and the sound-and-light spectacular *Et la lumière fut*—"And then there was light." *(110 rue Notre-Dame Ouest. M: Place-D'Armes. ☎514-842-2925; www.basiliquenddm.org. Open M-F 8am-4:30pm, Sa 8am-4:15pm, Su 12:30-4:15pm. Light show Tu-Th 6:30pm, F 6:30 and 8:30pm, Sa 7 and 8:30pm. $10, under 18 $5, seniors $9. $5, ages 7-17 $4.)*

🏛 MUSEUMS

MCCORD MUSEUM. The McCord's exhibits range from toys to wedding gowns, lawn ornaments to photographs. Displays chronicle Montréal's development and quirks. *(690 rue Sherbrooke Ouest. ☎514-398-7100; www.musee-mccord.qc.ca. M: McGill or bus #24. Open June-Sept. M-F 10am-6pm, Sa-Su 10am-5pm; Oct.-May Tu-F 10am-6pm, Sa-Su 10am-5pm. $13, students $7, ages 6-12 $5, seniors $10.)*

MUSÉE DES BEAUX-ARTS. The museum's small permanent collection, displayed in galleries on both sides of the street, features art ranging from ancient to contemporary. Don't miss the collection of decorative arts, which includes an 18th-century French sleigh and a cactus-shaped hat stand. *(1380 and 1379 rue Sherbrooke Ouest. ☎514-285-2000; www.mmfa.qc.ca. Open Tu 11am-6pm, W-F 11am-9pm, Sa-Su 10am-5pm. Tours W and Su 1:30 (French), 2:30pm (English). $15, students and seniors $7.50, children under 13 free.)*

POINTE-À-CALLIÈRE: MONTRÉAL MUSEUM OF ARCHAEOLOGY AND HISTORY. Built on the footprint of a 19th-century customs house, this museum uses the products of 10 years of archaeological digs to give an informative tour of the city's past. *(350 Pl. Royale. ☎514-872-9150; www.pacmusee.qc.ca. Open in summer M-F 10am-6pm, Sa-Su 11am-6pm; in winter Tu-F 10am-5pm, Sa-Su 11am-5pm. $13, students $7.50, ages 6-12 $5, under 5 free, seniors $9.)*

CANADIAN CENTRE FOR ARCHITECTURE. The Centre houses one of the world's most important collections of architectural prints, drawings, photographs, and books. The 1874 Shaughnessy House, now incorporated into the design of the modern building, is attached. *(1920 rue Baile. M: Guy-Concordia or Atwater. ☎514-939-7026; www.cca.qc.ca. English tours in summer Sa-Su 10:30am, 1:30pm; in winter Sa-Su 1:30pm. Open Tu-W and F-Su 11am-6pm, Th 11am-9pm. $10, students $5, under 12 $3, seniors $7.)*

MUSÉE D'ART CONTEMPORAIN. Canada's premier modern art museum concentrates on the work of Canadians. It's full of prints, drawings, photographs, and books. *(185 rue Ste-Catherine Ouest. M: Place-des-Arts. ☎514-847-6226; www.macm.org. Open in summer M-Tu and Th-Su 11am-6pm, W 11am-9pm; in winter Tu and Th-Su 11am-6pm, W 11am-9pm. $8, students $4, under 12 free, seniors $6. W free after 6pm.)*

♫ ENTERTAINMENT

Like much of the city, Vieux Montréal is best seen at night. Street performers, artists, and *chansonniers* in various *brasseries* set the tone for lively summer evenings of clapping, stomping, and singing along. For a sweet Sunday afternoon during the summer, **Parc Jeanne-Mance** teems with bongos, dancing, handicrafts, and people.

SPORTS

Montréal has its share of sporting events. Between October and April, hockey's **Canadiens** (a.k.a. Les Habitants—"the locals"—or Les Habs) play at the **Centre Bell,** 1250 rue de la Gauchetière Ouest. (☎514-989-2841, tickets 514-790-1245. $23-150.) Spin to victory during the one-day **Tour de l'Île,** an amateur cycling event with over 45,000 participants. (☎514-521-8356.)

THEATER

Montréal lives up to its cultured reputation with a vast selection of theater in French and English. **Admission Ticket Network** has tickets throughout Québec. (☎514-790-1245 or 800-678-5440; www.admission.com. Open daily 8am-midnight.)

> **Théâtre du Nouveau Monde,** 84 rue Ste-Catherine Ouest (☎514-878-7878, tickets 514-866-8668; www.tnm.qc.ca). Stages French productions. M: Place-des-Arts. Tickets from $18.

> **National Theatre School of Canada,** 5030 rue St-Denis (☎514-842-7954; www.ent-nts.qc.ca). Stages excellent "school plays." Most shows free.

> **Théâtre Saint-Denis,** 1594 rue St-Denis (☎514-849-4211; http://theatrestdenis.com). Hosts Broadway-style productions. Peruse the *Calendar of Events,* available at tourist offices and newspaper stands, or call **Tel-Spec** for ticket info. (☎514-790-2222; www.tel-spec.com. Open M-Sa 9am-9pm, Su noon-6pm.)

DANCE AND MUSIC

The city's exciting **Place des Arts,** 260 Blvd. de Maisonneuve Ouest (☎514-842-2112; www.pda.qc.ca;), at rue Ste-Catherine Ouest and Jeanne Mance, houses the **Opéra de Montréal** (☎514-985-2258; www.operademontreal), the **Montréal Symphony Orchestra** (☎514-842-9951; www.osm.ca), and **Les Grands Ballets Canadiens** (☎514-849-0269; www.grandsballets.qc.ca).

◗ NIGHTLIFE

Combine a drinking age of 18 with thousands of taps flowing unchecked until 3am and the result is the unofficially titled "nightlife capital of North America." Most pubs and bars offer a happy hour (usually 5-8pm) when bottled drinks may be two for one and cocktails may be double their usual potency. In summer, restaurants often spill over onto outdoor patios. The bars of Vieux Montreal, along rue St-Paul, see lots of activity on the weekends, though mostly from tourists. For a taste of the local scene, head over to the Quartier Latin, where the pubs along rue St-Denis north of Ste-Catherine and the clubs and restaurants in the pedestrian-only section of rue Prince Arthur at rue St-Laurent spill over with students and young Montrealers. In recent years, Montréal has reached out to the GLBT community, making it one of the most popular gay travel destinations in the world. The ideological capital of the first province in North America to allow gay marriage, the city also hosted the world's first **Outgames** in 2006. Most of Montréal's gay and lesbian hot spots can be found in the gay village, one of the world's largest and safest, along rue Ste-Catherine between St-Hubert and Papineau. While most of the village's establishments cater to men, there are a few lesbian-friendly locales.

🍸 **Café Campus,** 57 rue Prince Arthur (☎514-844-1010; www.cafecampus.com). Unlike the more touristy meat-market discothèques, this hip club gathers a friendly student and 20-something crowd regularly. Tu retro, Th "Hits-Moi" (Top Ten), Su French music. Drinks $3.50-5.50. Cover $3-6. Open Tu and Th-Su 8:30pm-3am. Cash only.

Pub McKibbins, 1426 rue Bishop (☎514-288-1580). Fine drinks are served in this warmly lit Irish pub. Trophies ornament the walls and dartboards entertain the crowds while a fieldstone fireplace warms the room in winter. Live music nightly around 9 or 10pm, including Irish bands. Open daily 11:30am-3am. Kitchen closes 10pm. AmEx/MC/V.

Le Drugstore, 1366 rue Ste-Catherine Est (☎514-524-1960). M: Beaudry. One of the biggest and oldest gay bars in Canada, Le Drugstore, established in 1908, is a 3-story megaplex bar basking in the glow of colored lights. The crowd is usually mixed sex, though the crowd is mostly female on F. Open daily 8am-3am. Cash only.

Cabaret Mado, 1115 Ste-Catherine Est (☎514-525-7566). M: Beaudry. This GLBT cabaret is the home of the wildest drag shows in town. Come Tu for "le Mardi à Mado." Straight-friendly, especially weekends. Drinks $4-5. Cover $5-10. Open daily 11am-3am. AmEx/MC/V.

🌺 FESTIVALS

On any given day, you're likely to find a festival somewhere in Montréal. To keep track of the offerings, pick up a copy of *Mirror* (English) or *Voir* (French) in any theater and in many bars and cafes. In summer, keep your eyes peeled for *ventes-trottoirs*, "sidewalk sales" that shut down major streets.

Mondial de la Bière (☎514-722-9640; www.festivalmondialbiere.qc.ca), in late May. Crowds from all over the world come for to taste more than 300 brands of beer, port, and whiskey. Tasting coupons $1.

Fringe Festival (☎514-849-3378; www.montrealfringe.ca), during mid-June. Theater, dance, and musical events at various spots throughout the Plateau Mont-Royal.

Fête Nationale (☎514-849-2560; www.cfn.org), on St-Jean-Baptiste Day, June 24. A celebration of Québecois pride through performances of local music and other cultural events.

Montréal International Jazz Festival (☎514-871-1881; www.montrealjazzfest.com), during the 1st week of July. Jazz fiends take over the city, bringing together over 300 performers.

Divers/Cité (☎514-285-4011; www.diverscite.org), during early August. In Émilie-Gamelin Park. Gay pride week.

🚗 THE ROAD TO SAINT-EUSTACHE: 21 MI.

Getting out of Montréal to the west can be a harrowing experience. To avoid traffic, try leaving in the morning. The easiest way to reach St-Eustache is to take **rue Saint-Antoine,** which merges onto **Highway 720 West.** Take Hwy. 720 2.5km west to **Highway 15,** then take Hwy. 15 22km to the northwest until it connects with **Highway 344** at **Exit 19.** Continue west on Hwy. 344 for about 6 mi. to St-Eustache.

SAINT-EUSTACHE ☎450

The area of St-Eustache near the highway brims with chain restaurants and strip malls, but **Old Saint-Eustache,** the heart of the town established in the 18th century, is worth seeing. If you're hungry, try **La Chitarra ❸,** 168 rue

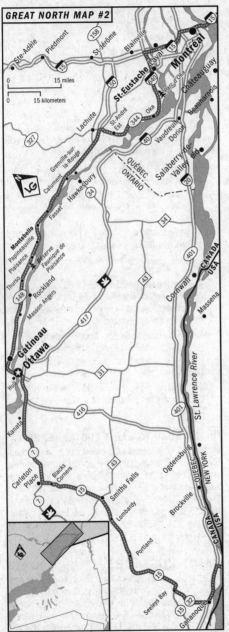

GREAT NORTH MAP #2

St-Louis, which lists an extensive selection of *cuisine Italienne*, including pasta, steak, and seafood. Try *ombria* (lamb with goat cheese; $16), a regional specialty. (☎450-974-2727. Entrees $9-19. Open M-Tu and Sa-Su 4:30-10pm, W-F 11am-10pm. AmEx/MC/V.)

THE ROAD TO MONTEBELLO: 57 MI.
Follow **Highway 344** west. Between Grenville and St-Andre-Est, Hwy. 344 merges with Hwy. 148, continuing to the west as **Highway 148.**

MONTEBELLO ☎819

In the town of Montebello, be sure to check out **Fairmont le Château Montebello,** 392 rue Notre Dame, (Hwy. 148). Château Montebello may just be the world's largest log building; trying to squeeze the whole star-shaped marvel into one photograph is challenging. Built out of 10,000 red cedar logs in just three months, the château has hosted movie stars, athletes, and even summits of world leaders on its riverfront grounds. You can wander around the property yourself or call to reserve a tour. To stay at the château is incredibly pricey, however, starting at $160 per person per night and fluctuating wildly. (☎819-423-6341 or 800-441-1414; www.fairmont.com.) If you don't want to pay $5 per hour to park, leave your car at the Info Touristique and take a pleasant 15min. trail through the historic **Manoir Papineau** to get to the château. The Manoir itself is a Canadian National Historic Site and is worth exploring in its own right. (500 Notre Dame St (Hwy. 148), ☎819-423-6455) Be sure not to wash your car before a visit to **Parc Omega,** Hwy. 323 N., since deer slobber will inevitably ruin the effort. Turn onto Hwy. 323 in Montebello; the park is 4km north on the left. Majestic elk, buffalo, ducks, and boars roam freely throughout the park and will walk right up to your car and lick the windows in hopes of a treat. The 1500-acre enclosed area has a 10km driving loop and walking trails. ☎819-423-5487; www.parc-omega.com. Open daily June-Oct. 9:30am-6pm; Nov.-May 10am-5pm. June-Oct. $16, ages 6-15 $11, ages 2-5 $6; Nov.-May $13/9/5.) For more info on Montebello and the surrounding area, swing by **Info**

Touristique, 502 rue Notre Dame (☎819-423-5602), constructed with logs left over from the château.

🏠**Le Zouk ❸**, 530 rue Notre Dame (Hwy. 148), looks like a wood cabin inside, but the terrace feels like a Caribbean resort, with colorful umbrellas, beach music, and plants. On its eclectic pub and cafe menu, you'll find mountainous salads and grilled panini, like the baguette des Alpes ($10), with Black Forest ham, asparagus, and cheese. (☎819-423-2080. Breakfast $3-6. Entrees $10-19. Open daily 11am-9pm. AmEx/MC/V.)

🔺 THE ROAD TO GATINEAU: 41 MI.
Enter Gatineau from the east on **Highway 148.**

GATINEAU   ☎819
As of January 1, 2002, the city of Gatineau was formed out of the cities Aylmer, Buckingham, Masson-Angers, Gatineau, and Hull, part of a recent trend toward Canadian metropolitan areas' reincorporation into regional entities. Housed in a striking, sand-dune-like structure across from the National Gallery, the **Canadian Museum of Civilization,** 100 Laurier St., the most visited museum in Canada, has life-size dioramas and architectural re-creations exploring 1000 years of Canadian history. (☎819-776-7000; www.civilization.ca. Open July-Aug. M-W and Sa-Su 9am-6pm, Th-F 9am-9pm; May-June and Sept. M-W and F-Su 9am-6pm, Th 9am-9pm; Oct.-Apr. daily 9am-6pm. $10, students $6, ages 2-12, $4 seniors $8. Th after 4pm free. Su ½-price.)

Occupying 361 sq. km northwest of Ottawa, **Gatineau Park** is worth visiting for its spectacular autumn foliage. Bikes and a variety of boats are available at Lac Philippe and Lac la Pêche. (☎819-827-2020, rentals 456-3016; www.canadascapital.gc.ca/gatineau. Bikes $8 per hr., $36 per day; campers only. Boats $10/38. Open daily sunrise-sunset.) There are three rustic campgrounds within the park: **Lac Philippe Campground ❶,** which offers 248 sites with facilities for family camping, trailers, and campers; **Lac Taylor Campground ❶,** which has 33 semi-rustic sites; and **Lac la Pêche Campground ❶,** with 36 sites accessible only by canoe. Take Hwy. 5 N. and exit at Old

Chelsea. (Reservations ☎819-456-3016; www.gatineau-park-camping.ca. Sites $27. MC/V.)

🔺 THE ROAD TO OTTAWA: 1 MI.
Cross the **Alexandra Bridge,** which will take you into the Parliament Hill area of the city.

OTTAWA   ☎613
Legend has it that in the mid-19th century Queen Victoria chose Ottawa as Canada's capital by closing her eyes and pointing a finger at a map. In reality, perhaps political savvy rather than blind chance guided her to this once-backwater logging town known for saloons and bar fights. Settled by neither the French nor the English colonists, Ottawa was the perfect compromise. Forced to try to forge national unity while preserving local identities, Ottawa continues to play cultural diplomat to the rest of Canada.

🔶 ORIENTATION

The **Rideau Canal** divides Ottawa into the eastern **lower town** and the western **upper town** and is lined with bike paths and walkways. The canal is a major access route and the world's longest skating rink during the winter. West of the canal, Parliament buildings and government offices line **Wellington Street,** a major east-west artery, which runs directly into the heart of downtown. **Laurier Avenue** and the Mackenzie King Bridge are the only other east-west streets permitting traffic from one side of the canal to the other. East of the canal, Wellington St. becomes **Rideau Street** and is surrounded by a fashionable shopping district. North of Rideau St., the Byward Market hosts a summertime open-air market and most of Ottawa's nightlife. **Elgin Street** runs north-south from Hwy. 417 (the Queensway) to the War Memorial just south of Wellington near Parliament Hill. **Bank Street,** which runs parallel to Elgin St. three blocks to the west, leads to the town's older shopping area. Parking downtown is hard to find, and Ottawa is notorious for relentless ticketing.

VITAL STATS
Population: 850,000
Tourist Office: National Capital Commission Information Center, 90 Wellington St. (☎613-239-5000; www.canadascapital.gc.ca), opposite the Parliament bBuilding. Open daily early May to early Sept. 9am-9pm; early Sept. to early May 9am-5pm.
Currency Exchange: Accu-Rate Foreign Exchange, 111 Albert St. (☎613-596-0612; www.accurate.com).
Library and Internet Access: Ottawa Public Library, 120 Metcalf St. (☎613-580-2945). Free. Open M-Th 10am-9pm, F 10am-6pm, Sa 10am-5pm, Su 1-5pm.
Post Office: 59 Sparks St. (☎613-844-1545). Open M-F 8am-6pm. **Postal Code:** K1P 5A0.

ACCOMMODATIONS

In downtown Ottawa, the only way to stick to your budget is to avoid the expensive hotels. Reservations are recommended, especially if you're staying through Canada Day (July 1). **Ottawa Bed and Breakfast** represents 10 B&Bs in the Ottawa area. (☎613-563-0161. Singles $70-100; doubles $90-110.)

Ottawa International Hostel (HI-C), 75 Nicholas St. (☎613-235-2595; www.hihostels.ca/ottawa), in downtown Ottawa. The site of Canada's last public hanging, the former Carleton County Jail now hosts travelers. Jail tours nightly 7pm; $12.50, guests $8.50. A friendly atmosphere with kitchen, internet access, and laundry. Parking $5 per day. Reception in summer 24hr.; in winter 7am-2am. Check-in 1pm. Check-out 11am. Dorms $35, members $30; single jail cells $59/53. AmEx/MC/V. ❷

University of Ottawa Residences, 90 University St. (☎613-564-5400 or 877-225-8664), in the center of campus, an easy walk from downtown. Clean dorms in a concrete landscape. Free Internet (bring an ethernet cable). Parking $11 per day. Check-in 4:30pm. Check-out 10:30am. Open early May to late Aug. Singles $40, students $30; doubles $60/45. MC/V. ❷

FOOD

Ottawa's **Byward Market,** on Byward St. between York and George St., is full of tables displaying produce, plants, and sweet maple syrup. (☎613-562-3325; www.byward-market.com. Open in warmer weather daily 8am-5pm.) **York, George,** and **Clarence Streets** are packed with cafes, great restaurants, and bars.

Byward Cafe, 55 Byward Market (☎613-241-2555), at George St. A friendly atmosphere and a huge array of baked goods and savory deli dishes bring both young and old to eat, drink, and relax on the covered patio. Panini $4.50. Open daily in summer 8am-11pm; in winter 8am-6pm. AmEx/MC/V. ❶

Mamma Grazzi's Kitchen, 25 George St. (☎613-241-8656; www.mammagrazzis.com). This Italian hideaway in one of the oldest parts of Ottawa is tucked away in a stone building. Thin-crust pizza ($10-16), hand-rolled to order, is worth the wait. Open M-Th and Su 10:30am-10pm, F-Sa 10:30am-11pm. AmEx/MC/V. ❸

The Highlander Pub, 115 Rideau St. (☎613-562-2011; www.highlanderpub.ca). A bastion of Scottish culture in the heart of the Byward Market, the Highlander boasts a kilted waitstaff, a comprehensive selection of entrees, and over 150 single-malt scotches. The brave might try "A Wee Taste O' the Haggis" for $10. Open M-F 11am-2am, Sa-Su 9am-2am. ❷

D'Arcy McGee's Irish Pub, 4 Sparks St. (☎613-230-4433; www.darcymcgees.ca). Whether lured in by the traditional Celtic music or chased in by the traditional Canadian weather, visitors to D'Arcy are never sorry they came. Hearty pub food and Irish dishes $6-19. Live music W. Open M-Tu and Su 11am-1am, W-Sa 11am-2am. AmEx/MC/V. ❸

SIGHTS

PARLIAMENT HILL. Parliament Hill, on Wellington at Metcalfe St., towers over downtown with its distinguished neo-Gothic architecture. The **Centennial Flame** at the south gate was lit in 1967 to mark the 100th anniversary of Confederation. The prime minister can be spotted at the central Parliament structure, **Centre Block,** which contains the House of

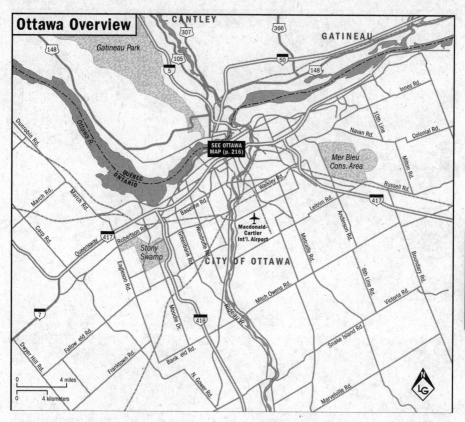

Ottawa Overview

Commons, Senate, and Library of Parliament. Tours of Centre Block depart every 30min. from the white **Infotent** by the visitors center. (☎613-992-4793. *Infotent open daily mid-May to mid-June 9am-5pm; mid-June to Labor Day 9am-8pm. Tours in French and English mid-May to Sept. M-F 9am-8pm, Sa-Su 9am-5pm; Sept. to mid-May daily 9am-3:30pm. In winter, go straight to entrance just to the right of the main door of the Centre Block. Free.*) When Parliament is in session, you can watch Canada's officials debate. (☎613-992-4793; www.parl.gc.ca. *In session mid-Sept. to Dec. and Feb. to mid-June M-Th 2:15-3pm, F 11:15am-noon. Arrive about 2hr. in advance to obtain passes.*) Behind the Library of Parliament, the bell from Centre Block is one of few remnants of the original 1859-66 structure that survived a 1916 fire. According to legend,

the bell crashed to the ground after chiming at midnight the night of the blaze. Today, daily concerts chime from 53 bells hanging in the **Peace Tower.** An observation deck remains open until 30min. before the last tour of the day. (*1hr. concerts June-Sept. M-F 2pm. 15min. concerts Sept.-June M-F noon.*) Those interested in trying to make a statuesque soldier smile should attend the 30min. **Changing of the Guard** on the broad lawns in front of Centre Block. (☎613-993-1811. *Late June to late Aug. daily 10am, weather permitting.*) At dusk, Centre Block and its lawns transform into the background for **Sound and Light,** which relates the history of the Parliament buildings and the nation. (☎613-239-5000. *Shows July to early Sept.*)

GATINEAU

Alexandra Bridge

TO RIDEAU HALL, ACCU-RATE
FOREIGN EXCHANGE (700yds)

0   200 yards
0   200 meters

Parent Ave.

Dalhousie St.

Bruyere St.

St. Andrew St.

Gulguee Ave.

St. Patrick St.

Parent Ave.

Royal
Canadian
Mint

Nepean
Point

Riverside Path

Ottawa R.

Nat'l.
Gallery

Peacekeeping
Monument

Murray St.

Clarence St.

Majors Hill
Park

MacKenzie Ave.

US Embassy

York St.

GREAT NORTH

Sussex Dr.

**BYWARD
MARKET**

**Byward
Market**

George St.

Riverside Path

Supreme
Court

Centre
Block

Infotent

PARLIAMENT
BUILDINGS

Château
Laurier

3

2

4

Canadian Museum
of Contemporary
Photography

Rideau St.

5

Centennial
Flame

Wellington St.

TO CANADIAN WAR
MUSEUM (0.6mi)

Nat'l. War
Memorial

CONFEDERATION
SQ.

Rideau
Centre

Nicholas St.

Waller St.

Sparks St. Mall

6

Queen St.

Nat'l.
Arts
Centre

Congress
Centre

7

Albert St.

MacKenzie King Bridge

Kent St.

Bank St.

O'Connor St.

Metcalfe St.

Elgin St.

Colonel Dr.

TO LAURIER
HOUSE (500yds)

Slater St.

Ottawa
Public
Library

Laurier Ave.

Laurier Bridge

Gloucester St.

Ontario Courthouse

8

Queen Elizabeth Dr.

Rideau Canal

UNIVERSITY
OF OTTAWA

Nepean St.

City Hall

Université St.

Ottawa

⌂ ACCOMMODATIONS
Ottawa International Hostel (HI-C), **7**
University of Ottawa Residences, **8**

🍎 FOOD
Byward Café, **3**
D'Arcy McGee's Irish Pub, **6**
Mamma Grazzi's Kitchen, **2**

🍸 NIGHTLIFE
The Honest Lawyer, **4**
The Highlander Pub, **5**
Zaphod, **1**

Lisgar St.

Cooper St.

Somerset St.

TO (0.5mi),
DOW'S LAKE (4mi)

MacLaren St.

TO CANADIAN MUSEUM OF
NATURE (400yds)

CONFEDERATION SQUARE. East of the Parliament buildings at the junction of Sparks, Wellington, and Elgin St. stands Confederation Sq. and the enormous **National War Memorial,** dedicated by King George VI in 1939. The structure, a life-size representation of Canadian troops marching under the eye of the angels of liberty, symbolizes the eventual triumph of peace over war.

RIDEAU HALL. The governor general, the queen's representative in Canada, resides at Rideau Hall. Take a tour of the house, gardens, and art collection—many visitors even run into the governor general herself. (1 Sussex Dr. ☎ 613-991-4422 or 866-842-4422; www.gg.ca. Free 45min. guided tours May-June Sa-Su 10am-4pm; July-Aug. daily 1-5pm; Sept.-Oct. Sa-Su noon-4pm. Self-guided tours July-Aug. 10am-1pm.)

OTHER SIGHTS. Several blocks west along Wellington St. stand the **Supreme Court of Canada,** the **National Archives,** and the **Federal Court.** (☎613-995-5361; www.scc-csc.gc.ca. Open June-Aug. daily 9am-5pm; Sept.-May hours vary. Free tours every 30min. except Sa-Su noon-1pm. Tours alternate between French and English.) At **Nepean Point,** several blocks northwest of Rideau Centre and the Byward Market, visitors can share a panoramic view of the capital or watch the sun set over Gatineau with a statue of explorer Samuel de Champlain. See the production of collectors' "loonies" ($1 coins) at the **Royal Canadian Mint.** (320 Sussex Dr. ☎613-993-8990 or 800-276-1871; www.mint.ca. Guided tours M-F 9am-7pm, Sa-Su 9am-4:30pm. Reservations recommended. M-F $5, Sa-Su $3.50.)

MUSEUMS

NATIONAL GALLERY. A glass-towered building adjacent to Nepean Pt. holds the world's most comprehensive collection of Canadian art. The facade is a reinterpretation of the nearby neo-Gothic Library of Parliament. Don't miss Rideau Chapel, a church reconstructed inside the Gallery. (380 Sussex Dr. ☎613-990-1985; www.gallery.ca. Open M-W and F-Su 10am-5pm, Th 10am-8pm. $9, students and seniors $7, ages 12-19 $4. Th after 5pm free.)

CANADIAN MUSEUM OF CONTEMPORARY PHOTOGRAPHY. Closed for renovations as of summer 2008, the museum usually showcases an impressive rotation of temporary photography exhibits. (1 Rideau Canal, located between the Château Laurier and the Ottawa Locks. ☎613-990-8257; http://cmcp.gallery.ca. Open May-Sept. M-W and F-Su 10am-5pm, Th 10am-8pm; Oct.-Apr. W and F-Su 10am-5pm, Th 10am-8pm. $4, students and seniors $3, ages 12-19 $2. Th after 5pm free.)

CANADIAN WAR MUSEUM. This museum traces the history of the Canadian armed forces, from colonial skirmishes to UN peacekeeping missions. See Hitler's armored car and walk through a mock WWI trench. (1 Vimy Pl., west on Wellington St., past Parliament and the National Archives. ☎819-776-8600; www.warmuseum.ca. Open May-June and Sept.-Oct. M-W and F-Su 9am-6pm, Th 9am-9pm; July-Aug. M-W and Sa-Su 9am-6pm, Th-F 9am-9pm; Oct.-Apr. Tu-W and F-Su 9am-5pm, Th 9am-9pm. $10, seniors and students $8, ages 3-12 $4. Th after 4pm free.)

CANADIAN MUSEUM OF NATURE. This comprehensive and kid-friendly exploration of the natural world is housed in a recently-renovated building at the end of Metcalfe St. (240 McLeod St. ☎613-566-4700; www.nature.ca. Open May-Aug. M-W and F-Su 9am-6pm, Th 9am-8pm; Sept.-Apr. Tu and Su 9am-5pm, Th 9am-8pm. $5, under 4 free.)

FESTIVALS

Ottawans celebrate everything, even the bitter Canadian cold. During the first three weekends of February, **Winterlude** (☎800-465-1867; www.canadascapital.gc.ca/winterlude) lines the Rideau Canal. Ice sculptures and a working ice cafe illustrate how it feels to be an Ottawan in the winter—frozen. In early May, the **Tulip Festival** (☎613-567-4447 or 800-668-8547; www.tulipfestival.ca) showcases more than a million buds around Dow's Lake, while pop concerts and other events center on Major's Hill Park. Flying feet fill the air during the **Dance Festival** (☎613-947-7000; www.canadadance.ca) in late June. The city explodes for the all-important **Canada Day,** July 1, which involves fireworks, partying in Major's Hill Park, and concerts. The **Jazz Festival** (☎613-241-2633; www.ottawajazzfestival.com) brings numerous world class musicians to Ottawa at the end of July.

NIGHTLIFE

Many of Ottawa's nightspots are located, unsurprisingly, in or around the Byward Market, whose numerous bars and pubs attract a decent crowd each night.

The Honest Lawyer, 141 George St. (☎613-562-2262), near Dalhousie St. If you were to mix an arcade, a college library, and a law office, this cavernous sports bar is what you'd end up with. A bowling alley, foosball tables, and billiards attract a more mature crowd. The 130 oz. "Beerzooka" is, well, a lot of beer ($30). Specials every night, including M all-you-can-eat wings ($13). F-Sa 21+. Cover $3 after 11pm. Open M-W and Sa 3pm-2am, Th-F 11:30am-2am, Su 6pm-2am. AmEx/MC/V.

Zaphod, 27 York St. (☎613-562-1010; www.zaphodbeeblebrox.com), in Byward Market. Named for a character in the classic sci-fi spoof *The Hitchhiker's Guide to the Galaxy,* this popular alternative rock club showcases local musicians. Serves drinks from the book, like Pangalactic Gargle Blasters ($6.75). Live music most nights. Cover $3-20. Open daily 4pm-2am. AmEx/MC/V.

OUTDOORS

Ottawans take advantage of the miles of trails at their disposal, many of which run along the river and are easily accessible from downtown. The artificial **Dow's Lake,** 1001 Queen Elizabeth Dr., extends off the Rideau Canal south of Ottawa. **Dow's Lake Pavilion** rents pedal boats ($13 for 1st hr., $8 thereafter), canoes ($15 for 1st hr., $8 thereafter), and kayaks ($10 for 1st hr., $8 thereafter) in summer and ice skates and sleighs (both $12 for 1st hr., $7.50 thereafter) during the winter. (1001 Queen Elizabeth Driveway, near Preston St. ☎613-232-1001. Open in summer daily 11:30am-8:30pm; in fall and spring M-F 4pm-sunset, Sa-Su 11am-sunset; in winter M-F 9:30am-9pm, Sa 9am-9pm, Su 9am-8pm.)

THE ROAD TO WELLESLEY ISLAND: 103 MI.

From Ottawa, take **Highway 417 (Queensway)** west to **Highway 7,** which will meet **Highway 15** 17 mi. before Smiths Falls. Hwy. 15 enters Smiths Falls as **Union Street** from the north at a T-junction with **Cor-**nelia Street. Turn right on Cornelia St., then take a left onto **Elmsley Street.** From Smiths Falls, take **Route 29** south to **Route 401,** the **Trans-Canada Highway.** Follow this highway until **Exit 661** and **I-81** on the American side of the border.

> **LEAVING CANADA.** See **Vital Documents** (p. 16) for information on passport and visa requirements. From here, prices return to American dollars unless otherwise indicated.

The Empire State
NEW YORK
Welcomes You!

WELLESLEY ISLAND   ☎315

Wellesley Island is part of the **Thousand Island Seaway,** which spans 100 mi. from the mouth of Lake Ontario to the first of the many locks on the St. Lawrence River. Surveys conducted by the US and Canadian governments determined that there are 1864 "islands" in the seaway, where an island is defined as having at least 1 sq. ft. of land above water year-round and two trees growing on it. The islands are famously picturesque, and the **Thousand Islands Skydeck,** on Hill Island just before the border in Lansdowne, provides visitors with a chance to view them in a 360° panorama from atop a 400 ft. tower. (☎613-659-2335; www. 1000islandsskydeck.com. Open daily 9am-8pm. $9, ages 6-13 $5.)

After the tower, the road carries you straight over the border into New York and onto **Wellesley Island,** home to **Wellesley Island State Park** and 2600 acres of marshes and woodland for hiking, cross-country skiing, boating, or **camping ❶.** The beach in the park hosts swimmers in the summer and ice fishermen in the winter. (☎315-482-2722. 438 sites plus cabins. Sites $13-19, with electricity $19, with full hookup $25.

THE ROAD TO CAPE VINCENT: 24 MI.

From **I-81,** exit immediately onto **Route 12** (the first exit after the visitors center, right after you hit the mainland) and continue straight to Clayton. The road hugs the shore all the way to Cape Vincent.

CAPE VINCENT   ☎315

For roadtrippers with time, Cape Vincent makes a nice base from which to explore the region. The town of **Alexandria Bay**, 26 mi. to the north, offers boat tours of the islands and tells the romantic story surrounding **Boldt Castle**. The **Tibbetts Point Lighthouse Hostel (HI-AYH) ❶**, 33439 County Rte. 6, provides maritime-themed accommodations in an old keeper's quarters. Go west on Broadway and follow the shore for 3 mi. (☎315-654-3450. 36 beds; family rooms available. Check-in 5-10pm. Reservations recommended July-Aug. Open from mid-May to mid-Oct. Dorms $18, members $15. Cash only.) **Burnham Point State Park ❶**, on Rte. 12 E., 4 mi. east of Cape Vincent, has a wonderful view of the water and 51 sites but lacks a beach. However, the admission fee grants entrance to any park in the system, so you can drive to any of the nearby beaches. (☎315-654-2324. Reception from late May to early Sept. daily 7am-9pm. Sites $13-19, with electricity $19-23. Day use $6 per car, after 4pm $4. AmEx/D/MC/V.) **Aubrey's Inn ❶**, 126 S. James St., serves up some of the best deals in the seaway next to an indoor mural of the Tibbetts Point Lighthouse. (☎315-654-3754. Giant breakfasts $2-6. Lunch $3-6. Dinner $6-7. Open M-Sa 7am-9pm, Su 7am-8pm. AmEx/D/MC/V.)

◤ THE ROAD TO OSWEGO: 74 MI.

Continue south on **Route 12 East.** In the village of Limerick, turn right onto **Route 180 South.** Take a right on **Route 3 West.** Follow Rte. 3 until merging onto **Route 104 West,** which becomes **Bridge Street** as it enters central Oswego.

OSWEGO   ☎315

This small city offers a wealth of historical attractions. Because of Oswego's strategic location, it became a hotbed of military activity during the War of 1812. Rebuilt time and time again by Britain and the US after attacks, the **Fort Ontario State Historic Site**, 1 E. Fourth St., was established as a historical site in 1949. Today, it has been restored to its 1867-72 appearance, and costumed interpreters host

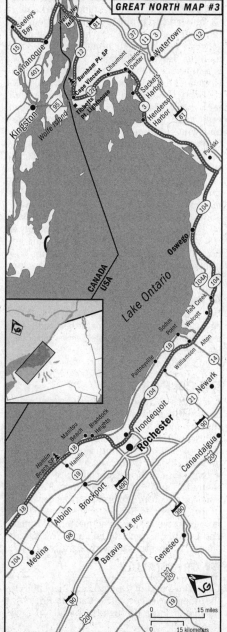

GREAT NORTH MAP #3

demonstrations. (☎315-343-4711. Open May-Oct. Tu-Su 10am-5pm. $4, students and seniors $3, under 12 free.) In 1944, 982 refugees fled the Nazi regime from 18 war-torn countries; Oswego became their home for the next 18 months. **Oswego Safe Haven,** 2 E. Seventh St., is a museum that documents the lives of the Holocaust refugees who found sanctuary at the Fort Ontario Emergency Refugee Shelter. (☎315-342-3003; www.oswegohaven. org. Open Tu-Su in summer 11am-5pm; in fall and winter 11am-4pm.) West of the bridge, Oswego has a hip downtown, full of locally owned shops and restaurants. **Zonie's ❶,** 182 W. First St., serves only calzones ($5.80) but takes them seriously. Offerings range from the traditional (pepperoni) to the daring, like mac and cheese. (☎315-342-9664. Open M-Th 4pm-3am, F-Sa 11am-4am, Su noon-3am. MC/V.) Stop in the **Port City Cafe and Bakery ❶,** 209 W. First St., for gelato or homemade granola. (☎315-343-2412. Panini and wraps $5-7; also serves breakfast. Open M-F 6:30am-9pm, Sa 8am-6pm, Su 8am-5pm. MC/V.)

◪ THE ROAD TO ROCHESTER: 74 MI.

Take **Route 104** to **I-590** to **I-490,** which leads into downtown Rochester. For a longer but more scenic route along the lake, follow the Seaway signs along Rte. 104 until it meets I-590.

ROCHESTER ☎585

Rochester is New York's third-largest urban area and has an inventive metropolitan feel that enhances its historic past. Few American cities its size have had such a lasting social and political impact; both Susan B. Anthony and Frederick Douglass spent their most active years in Rochester and are buried in Rochester's Mt. Hope Cemetery. The presence of two top universities, the University of Rochester and Rochester Institute of Technology, as well as the headquarters of Bausch and Lomb, Eastman Kodak, and Xerox, have shaped Rochester's modern identity.

✈ ORIENTATION

I-490 forms part of the **Inner Loop** that encircles the downtown core. The **Genesee River** runs north and south through the middle of town,

paralleled on the west by **State Street** and on the east by **South Avenue** and **Clinton Avenue.** Cutting through the Inner Loop east-west is **Main Street.** Affordable lodging near Rochester can be found at chain motels in Henrietta, Webster, and other suburbs.

VITAL STATS

Population: 220,000

Tourist Office: Greater Rochester Visitors Association, 45 East Ave., Ste. 400 (☎800-677-7282; www.visitrochester.com). Open from Memorial Day to Labor Day M-F 8:30am-5pm, Sa 9am-5pm, Su 10am-3pm; from Labor Day to Memorial Day M-F 8:30am-5pm.

Library and Internet Access: Central Library of Rochester and Monroe County, 115 South Ave. (☎585-428-7300). Open July-Aug. M and Th 9am-9pm, Tu-W and F 9am-6pm; Sept.-May M and Th 9am-9pm, Tu-W and F 9am-6pm, Sa 9am-5pm, Su 1-5pm; June M and Th 9am-9pm, Tu-W and F 9am-6pm, Sa 9am-5pm.

Post Office: 216 Cumberland St. (☎585-546-6425). Open M-F 8:30am-5pm, Sa 9am-noon. **Postal Code:** 14603.

⬛ FOOD

Rochester is famous for its local take on hot dogs, or "white hots," which are unsmoked to maintain a white color. You can try them in equally famous "garbage plates," a customizable mountain of sides, sauces, condiments, and meat, throughout Rochester.

▧ **Dinosaur BBQ,** 99 Court St. (☎585-325-7090; www.dinosaurbarbque.com). A dazzling array of BBQ meats, including the Big Ass Pork Plate ($13), awaits at this popular hangout. Live music most nights. Open M-Th 11am-midnight, F-Sa 11am-1am, Su noon-10pm. AmEx/D/MC/V. ❸

Nick Tahou Hots, 320 Main St. W. or 2260 Lyell Ave. (☎585-436-0184/429-6388). Specializes in enormous garbage plates ($6) and local cooking. Open daily 8am-8pm. Lyell Ave. location open 24hr. Cash only. ❶

Charlie's Frog Pond, 652 Park Ave. (☎585-271-1970). Funky, colorful straw sculptures and paintings complement eclectic dinner options, including the Horny Toad: ground beef, an English muffin, chili, and cheese. Breakfast $4-8.

Sandwiches $3-8. Open M-Th 7am-9pm, F-Sa 8am-10pm, Su 8am-3pm. AmEx/MC/V. ❷

👁 SIGHTS

🎞GEORGE EASTMAN HOUSE. In 1888, George Eastman produced a flexible camera that launched an amateur photography company later known as Eastman Kodak. His mansion, now restored, holds works by over 10,000 photographers and the world's largest collection of American cameras, including the first Kodak Brownie and a camera that belonged to Ansel Adams. Check out the conservatory (complete with elephant head), which the perfectionist Eastman literally sawed in half to expand to a suitable size. Frustrated with the irregularity of the traditional calendar, Eastman devised a new system, with 13 months (the new one fell between June and July and was called "Sol") of exactly 28 days each. Though it never caught on, it was actually enforced in the Eastman Kodak factory until (ready?) 1989. *(900 East Ave. ☎ 585-271-3361; www.eastman.org. Open Tu-Sa 10am-5pm, Th 10am-8pm, Su 1-5pm. Tours M-Sa 10:30am, 2pm; Su 10:30am. $8, students $5, ages 5-12 $3, under 5 free, seniors $6.)*

SUSAN B. ANTHONY HOUSE. Once the home of women's rights pioneer Susan B. Anthony, the house is now a museum. It was in this red-brick house that Anthony was arrested for voting in 1872. *(17 Madison St. From Main St., head west ½ mi. and turn right onto Madison St. ☎ 585-235-6124; www.susanbanthonyhouse.org. Open Tu-Su 11am-5pm. Last tour 1hr. before close. $6, students and children $3.)*

STRONG NATIONAL MUSEUM OF PLAY. A reproduction of Sesame St. has helped make this museum the nation's leading hands-on history center for the young and young at heart. The building contains the largest collection of toys and dolls in the world in addition to Americana. *(1 Manhattan Sq. From Main St., turn south onto S. Clinton Ave. Turn left onto Woodbury Ave. At the next light, cross Chestnut St. into the parking lot. ☎ 585-263-2700; www.strongmuseum.org. Open M-Th and Sa 10am-6pm, F 10am-8pm, Su noon-6pm. $9, ages 2-17 $7, seniors $8.)*

HIGH FALLS ENTERTAINMENT DISTRICT. Check out the dazzling laser light show projected on the walls of the river gorge, nightclubs, restaurants, and shops. High Falls is also a National Register historic district with old mills and factories from Rochester's glory days. The 850 ft. Pont de Rennes pedestrian bridge sits across the High Falls waterfall. *(60 Browns Race. ☎ 585-325-2030. Laser shows in summer most Th-Sa 9:30pm.)*

↘ DETOUR
JELL-O MUSEUM

23 East Main Street. Take **I-490 West** from Rochester, merge onto **I-90 West (New York State Thruway),** and exit onto Rte. 19 southbound. LeRoy is 4 mi. south of the interstate. The museum is located directly behind the historic LeRoy House.

The Jell-O factory offers tours with a guided introduction. Get your fill of Jell-O memorabilia, souvenirs, and trivia—did you know that the citizens of Salt Lake City consume more lime Jell-O per year than any other city?—and receive a free package of the world's wiggliest dessert. *(☎585-768-7433; www.jellomuseum.com. Open Apr.-Dec. M-Sa 10am-4pm, Su 1-4pm; Jan.-Mar. M-F 10am-4pm. $4, ages 6-11 $1.50, under 6 free.)*

🚗 THE ROAD TO YOUNGSTOWN: 88 MI.
At the end of **I-390 North,** veer left onto the **Lake Ontario State Parkway,** which becomes **Route 18 (Lake Road).** Forty miles after the parkway ends, turn right onto **Route 18F** to enter Youngstown. Look across the lake to see the impressive skyline of **Toronto** and the **CN Tower,** once the world's tallest freestanding structure. There are no services on this stretch, but they can be found throughout the Erie Canal corridor roughly 10 mi. south.

YOUNGSTOWN ☎716
Although Youngstown is sleepy today, its past is surprisingly violent. Strategically located at the mouth of the Niagara River, control of Youngstown was key to securing commerce on Lake Ontario. In 1678, René-Robert Cavelier, Sieur de La Salle, built the first fortifications at **◆Old Fort Niagara.** For the next 150 years, four nations fought desperately for it. It remained an active military post until 1963, when it was converted into a museum. The "French Castle," a stone fortress disguised as a château to catch the Iroquois off-guard,

[from the road]

is especially impressive. July brings reenactments with over 1000 living-history demonstrators. (☎716-745-7611; www.oldfortniagara.org. Open Sept.-June M-F 9am-5pm, July-Aug. daily 9am-7pm. $10, ages 6-12 $6, seniors $9.) **Whirlpool Jet Boat Tours,** S. Water St., in nearby Lewiston, sends visitors racing through the perilous Devil's Hole rapids of the Niagara Gorge to the massive whirlpool in the Lower Niagara River. (☎888-438-4444. Trips Apr.-Oct. $56, ages 6-13 $47.)

Campers can stay among great blue herons at **Four Mile Creek State Park ❶,** 1 Four Mile Creek Dr., 4 mi. east of Youngstown via Rte. 18F or the Robert Moses Pkwy., which has 275 campsites, including 21 on a bluff overlooking Lake Ontario. (☎716-745-3802, reservations 800-456-2267. Store and hiking trails. Showers. Check-in 3pm. Check-out 11am. Open from mid-Apr. to mid-Oct. Tent sites $13-16, with electricity $19-22; waterfront sites $17-20/25-28. AmEx/D/MC/V.)

THE ROAD TO NIAGARA FALLS: 13 MI.

Continue south along **Route 18F (Lower River Road).** In Lewiston, 18F becomes **Center Street.** Turn right onto the **Robert Moses Parkway** heading toward Niagara Falls. Keep an eye out; along the way you'll drive over the famous **Niagara Power Project.**

NIAGARA FALLS   ☎716

Niagara Falls is flat-out spectacular. The Ontario side of Niagara is full of flashy Vegas-style attractions—a trend that has horrified residents over the past few decades—while the New York side's best feature is parkland. The giant falls are best viewed from the Canadian side of the Niagara River, but prices tend to be more reasonable on the American side.

VITAL STATS
Population: New York 56,000, Ontario 79,000
Tourist Offices: US: Orin Lehman Visitors Center (☎716-278-1796), on Prospect St., in front of the observation deck. Open M-F 8am-7pm, Sa-Su 10am-6pm. **Canada: Niagara Falls Tourism,** 5515 Stanley Ave. (☎905-356-6061 or 800-563-2557; www.discoverniagara.com). Open daily 8am-8pm.
Library and Internet Access: Niagara Falls Public Library, 1425 Main St. (☎716-286-4894; www.niagarafallspubliclib.org). Open June- Aug. M-W 9am-9pm, Th-F 9am-5pm; Sept.-May M-W 9am-9pm, Th-Sa 9am-5pm.
Post Office: 615 Main St. (☎716-285-7561). Open M-F 8:30am-5pm, Sa 8:30am-2pm. **Postal Code:** 14302.

ORIENTATION

Niagara Falls cuts across the US-Canadian border. The **Robert Moses Parkway** runs along the river to the sights on the US side of the

HOOK, LINE, AND SINKER

When you're out on the open road, it can be tempting to ignore your bank account's activity. After all, who wants to pore over online bank reports when there's a great big world out there? The problem is that you're most vulnerable to identity theft when you're traveling and using your card frequently. There are plenty of opportunities for ill-intentioned people to overhear your card number and try to use it themselves. Would-be thieves will initially make a small charge to your account. They're fishing for a person who isn't paying attention, and, if they see that you don't close out the card, they'll quickly reel you in—by cleaning out your account. Fraudulent charges generally stand out, even though they are so tiny, because they tend to come from overseas. If you notice unauthorized activity on your account, close out the card as soon as possible by calling your bank's security number. Closing the card presents a problem for the roadtripper, because the bank will mail a new card to your permanent address, which is probably miles away. However, you don't need to end your roadtrip early. Many banks will issue temporary ATM cards so that you can still access your account while traveling. Just go to a local branch of your bank and ask for a temporary ATM card to use until you return home.

—Annie Levenson

falls. On the US side, **Niagara Street** is the main street, ending in the west at the **Rainbow Bridge** to Canada (pedestrians $1, cars $3.75; fee includes return). In Canada, **Roberts Street (Route 420)** is the main east-west street and **Stanley Avenue** is the main north-south street, but **Clifton Hill** is where the attractions are. Slightly downriver, the **Whirlpool Bridge** also joins the two countries.

ACCOMMODATIONS

Niagara is a popular honeymoon destination. In Canada, cheap motels (from $35) advertising free wedding certificates line **Lundy's Lane**, while moderately priced B&Bs (from $50) overlook the gorge on **River Road** between the Rainbow Bridge and the Whirlpool Bridge. In New York, cheap motels line **Niagara Falls Boulevard (Route 62)** from I-190 eastward. Excellent camping is also available 14 mi. away at **Four Mile Creek State Park** (p. 221).

Hostelling International–Niagara Falls (HI-AYH), 4549 Cataract Ave. (☎905-357-0770 or 888-749-0058; www.hihostels.ca), just off Bridge St., in Ontario. A well-equipped hostel with a laid-back atmosphere and convivial, rainbow-colored interior. Lockers $1. Linen included. Internet $3 per hr. Free Wi-Fi. Reception in summer 24hr.; in winter 8am-midnight. Check-out 11am. Dorms CDN$30, members CDN$25; singles CDN$52/48. AmEx/D/MC/V. ❶

Backpacker's International Hostel, 4219 Huron St. (☎905-357-1266 or 800-891-7022; www.backpackers.ca), at Zimmerman Ave., in Ontario. A well-maintained hostel in a historic home with clean dorm rooms. Family-owned and run. Breakfast and linens included. Free Internet access. Reception 24hr. with reservation. Dorms CDN$25; doubles CDN$50-60. Cash only. ❶

FOOD

Restaurants and nightclubs line the **Clifton Hill** entertainment district, and more affordable places can be found west of **Victoria Avenue.**

Simon's Restaurant, 4116 Bridge St. (☎905-356-5310), in Ontario, 1 block from the HI hostel. The oldest restaraunt in in town is still a local favorite, thanks to its huge breakfasts ($6), giant homemade muffins ($1), and homestyle

dinners for $6-10. Open M-Sa 5:30am-7pm, Su 5:30am-2pm. Cash only. ❶

Red Coach Inn, 2 Buffalo Ave. (☎716-282-1459; www.redcoach.com), in New York across from the Goat Island car bridge. A lovely dining experience overlooking the Upper Rapids. Lunches for $9-13 and steak and seafood dinners for $22-34. Open daily 11:30am-10pm. AmEx/D/MC/V. ❹

SIGHTS

The **Niagara Scenic Trolley** is the easiest way to travel between the numerous sights on the American side of the falls. (☎716-278-1730. Runs May-Aug. daily 9am-10pm every 10-20min. $2, children $1.)

AMERICAN SIDE

The **Master Pass,** available at the visitors center, covers admission to the Maid of the Mist, the Cave of the Winds Tour, and the trolley ($30, ages 6-12 $23).

NIAGARA FALLS STATE PARK. Most attractions center on this, the oldest state park in America. Don't miss the surprisingly serene Three Sisters Islands off Goat Island in the Upper Rapids. (☎716-278-1796.)

MAID OF THE MIST. For over 150 years, this boat tour has inspired kings and commoners alike with awe-inspiring (and wet) views from the foot of the falls. (☎716-284-8897. Open daily 9:30am-5:45pm; extended hours in summer. Tours depart from base of observation deck every 15min. in summer. $12.50, ages 6-12 $7.30. Observation deck $1.)

CAVE OF THE WINDS TOUR. Grab a souvenir (read: ineffective) yellow raincoat and sandals for a drenching hike to the base of Bridal Veil Falls, including an optional walk to the Hurricane Deck where waves slam down from above. (☎716-278-1730. Open from May to mid-Oct. daily 9am-7:30pm. Trips depart every 15min. from Goat Island. Must be at least 42 in. tall. $8, ages 6-12 $7.)

NIAGARA GORGE DISCOVERY CENTER. Located in Prospect Park, the center offers a simulated elevator ride through the geological history of the falls and a hiking trail through the gorge. (☎716-278-1780. Open daily 9am-6:30pm. $5, children $3.)

AQUARIUM OF NIAGARA. The endangered Peruvian penguin is housed alongside 1500 other aquatic animals. *(701 Whirlpool St., directly across from the Discovery Center. ☎716-285-3575; www.aquariumofniagara.org. Open daily 9am-5pm. $9, children $6, seniors $6.50.)*

niagara power authority. The visitors center offers spectacular views of both the gorge and the power project, which supplies nearly a quarter of New York's power. It includes displays on electricity and hydropower. *(Take the Robert Moses Pkwy. north 4 mi. to the Power Vista exit. Turn left onto Rte. 104 for 1 mi. ☎716-285-3211. Open daily 9am-5pm. Free.)*

CANADIAN SIDE

QUEEN VICTORIA PARK. The park provides the best views of **Horseshoe Falls.** The **Niagara River Recreation Trail** runs through the park for over 33km from Fort Erie to Fort George. At 10pm on Fridays and Sundays during the summer, a fireworks display lights up the sky.

SKYLON TOWER. Check out the falls from 520 ft. above the ground. The tower's observation deck offers a calming, unobstructed view. *(5200 Robinson St. ☎716-356-2651. Open daily 8am-midnight. CDN$12, children CDN$7.)*

SPANISH AERO CAR. Take an aerial cable ride over the whirlpools and rapids. *(3850 Niagara River Pkwy. ☎905-354-5711. Open daily 10am-8pm. CDN$11, children CDN$6.50.)*

JOURNEY BEHIND THE FALLS. The tour takes visitors behind spectacular Horseshoe Falls. *(☎905-354-1551. Open daily 9am-5:30pm. CDN$12, children CDN$7.)*

BUTTERFLY CONSERVATORY. Over 2000 butterflies await visitors on the grounds of the world-famous Niagara Parks Botanical Gardens. *(☎905-358-0025. Open daily 9am-6:30pm. CDN$13, children CDN$7.50.)*

NIAGARA PARKWAY. Called the "prettiest Sunday afternoon drive in the world" by Winston Churchill, this 10 mi. drive leads north through the heart of the Niagara wine region to the town of Niagara-on-the-Lake. Across from Youngstown, Niagara-on-the-Lake is filled with gorgeous Victorian homes and inns. Every summer, the town hosts the Shaw Festival, which features performances of plays by George Bernard Shaw and his con-

temporaries. *(☎905-468-2172; www.shawfest.com. Mar.-Nov. Tickets CDN$25-86.)*

⚑ THE ROAD TO BUFFALO: 26 MI.

Continue on the **Robert Moses Parkway.** Exit as if for I-190 N. but instead continue on **Route 384** (Buffalo Ave.) toward Buffalo. Rte. 384 will become **River Road** as it heads into **North Tonawanda.** Continue south on Rte. 384, which will become **Delaware Avenue** and lead you downtown in **Niagara Square.**

BUFFALO ☎716

At the turn of the 19th century, Buffalo—the "Queen City of the Lake"—was the playground of Gilded Age grandeur, home to more millionaires than any other American city. When the steel industry collapsed and the Erie Canal became obsolete, those glory days became a thing of the past. Still, don't underestimate a city that easily shrugs off 7 ft. of snow in one storm. Buffalo's past has given it a cultural and architectural legacy that is equal to much larger and pricier cities. From the downtown skyline to funky Elmwood Village, Buffalo balances small-town warmth with big-city culture.

VITAL STATS
Population: 280,000
Tourist Office: Visitors Center, 617 Main St. (☎716-852-2356 or 800-283-3256; www.visitbuffaloniagara.com), in the Theater District. Open M-F 10am-4pm, Sa 10am-2pm.
Library and Internet Access: Buffalo and Erie County Public Library, 1 Lafayette Sq. (☎716-858-8900), at Washington St. $1. Open in summer M-W and F-Sa 8:30am-6pm, Th 8:30am-8pm; in winter M-W and F-Sa 8:30am-6pm, Th 8:30am-8pm, Su 1-5pm.
Post Office: 701 Washington St. (☎716-856-4603). Open M-F 8:30am-5:30pm, Sa 8:30am-1pm. **Postal Code:** 14203.

🔁 ORIENTATION

Buffalo is one of the few American cities with a radial layout like Washington, DC; **Niagara Square** forms its center. The principal spokes, in a clockwise direction, are **Niagara Street (Route 266), Delaware Avenue (Route 384), Main Street (Route 5), Genessee Street, Broadway, Clin-**

ton Street, and Seneca Street (Route 16). Buffalo's expressways are rarely called by their posted names, so if asking for directions from locals, I-290 is the "Youngman," Rte. 198 is the "Scajaquada," and Rte. 33 is the "Kensington."

ACCOMMODATIONS

Budget lodgings are a rarity in downtown Buffalo, but chain motels can be found near the airport and off I-90. Family-run independent motels (under $50 per night) line "the Boulevard" (Route 62), 15min. from downtown.

Hostel Buffalo (HI-AYH), 667 Main St. (☎716-852-5222; www.hostelbuffalo.com). A bright, clean 50-bed facility in a centrally located neighborhood. The friendly staff makes travelers feel at home and offers free nightly movies. Common rooms, a kitchen, a pool table. Free linen, laundry facilities. Free Internet, and Wi-Fi. Reception 8-10:45am and 5-10pm. Check-out 10am. Reservations recommended. Dorms $28, members $25; rooms $60-81. AmEx/MC/V. ❶

Lenox Hotel & Suites, 140 North St. (☎716-884-1700; www.lenoxhotelandsuites.com), at Delaware Ave. The large and luxurious rooms at this historic hotel are only 5min. from Elmwood Village nightlife. Singles $89; studio suites $99. AmEx/D/MC/V. ❸

FOOD

Elmwood Village, up Elmwood Ave. between Virginia and Forest Ave., and **Allentown,** which runs the length of Allen St., are full of funky coffee shops and ethnic restaurants.

Anchor Bar, 1047 Main St. (☎716-886-8920; www.anchorbar.com). On a busy night in 1964, Teressa Bellissimo cooked up an unusual midnight snack, and Buffalo wings were born. Try 10 wings for $10 or a bucket of 50 for $30. The Anchor Bar is fully aware of its historic significance and features an attached gift shop that sells giant foam hats shaped like buffalo wings for $25. Live jazz F-Sa 9pm-midnight. Open M-Th 11am-11pm, F 11am-1am, Sa noon-1am, Su noon-11pm. AmEx/D/MC/V. ❷

Gabriel's Gate, 145 Allen St. (☎716-886-0602). A friendly saloon-like restaurant with rustic furniture, mounted animal heads, and a big chandelier. Enjoy a famous "Richmond Ave." burger ($6) or a vegetarian portobello sandwich ($6)

on the comfy shaded patio. Open M-W and Su 11:30am-midnight, Th 11:30am-1am, F-Sa 11:30am-2am. AmEx/MC/V. ❷

Club 59, 59 Allen St. (☎716-883-1880). A comfortable, hip cafe on the corner of Franklin St. Sandwiches ($6-8) include salmon, portobello, and "Queen City Eggplant." Specialty drinks ($4) include the Nutty Devil, steamed milk, chocolate, espresso, coffee, and hazelnut syrup. Open M-F 8am-6pm, Sa 10am-5pm. AmEx/MC/V. ❷

Broadway Market, 999 Broadway St. (☎716-893-0705). A bit of a hike from downtown, but well worth it. Over 40 vendors have served German, Polish, and Eastern European foods here for more than a century. Open M-F 8am-5pm. AmEx/MC/V. ❸

SIGHTS

Architecture buffs can take a 2hr. self-guided walking tour of historic downtown Buffalo. Pick up the free guide, *Walk Buffalo,* at the visitors center. Buffalo has stunning examples of 20th-century architecture. Don't miss **City Hall,** in Niagara Sq., Buffalo's Art Deco masterpiece. Other highlights are the **Guaranty Building,** 28 Church St., the *piece de resistance* of American skyscraper pioneer Louis Sullivan; the creepy Gothic towers of the **Richardson Complex** at Buffalo State College; the former **Buffalo Psychiatric Center,** 400 Forest Ave., designed by HH Richardson; the **Liberty Building,** topped by massive twin replicas of the Statue of Liberty; and the Gilded Age mansions of **Millionaires Row,** along Delaware Ave., between Summer and Bryant St. The area also showcases the largest number of Prairie School works by Frank Lloyd Wright outside of Chicago, including the **Darwin D. Martin House Complex,** 125 Jewett Pkwy., an estate of five buildings by the architectural master. (☎716-856-3858; www.darwinmartinhouse.org. Call for tour schedules and reservations. $12, students $8.) Buffalo is also home to Frederick Law Olmsted's first public park system, an interconnected series of green gems linked by tree-lined parkways, at the heart of which lies **Delaware Park.**

ALBRIGHT-KNOX ART GALLERY. The Albright-Knox Art Gallery houses an internationally recognized collection of over 6000 modern

GREAT NORTH

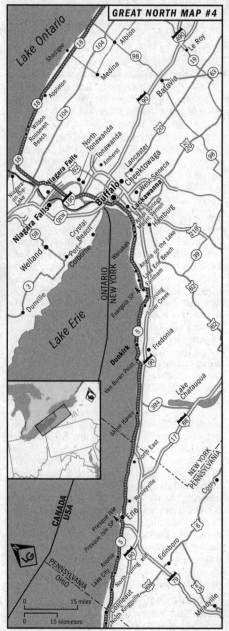

GREAT NORTH MAP #4

and contemporary pieces, including works by Picasso and Rothko. *(1285 Elmwood Ave. ☎716-882-8700; www.albrightknox.org. Open W and and Sa-Su 10am-5pm, Th-F 10am-10pm. $10, students and seniors $8, under 13 free. F 3-10pm free.)*

BUFFALO ZOO. At the Buffalo Zoo, over 23 acres shelter 1500 exotic and domestic animals in the country's third-oldest zoo. Hands-on summer activities include feeding giraffes and washing elephants, but by far the best attraction is Surapa, the painting elephant. *(300 Parkside Ave. ☎716-837-3900; www.buffalozoo.org. Open daily July-Aug. 10am-5pm; Sept.-June 10am-4pm. $9.50, students and seniors $7, ages 2-14 $6.)*

♫ ENTERTAINMENT

PERFORMING ARTS

Buffalo has a thriving **Theatre District,** with many different venues right in the heart of downtown and several more sprinkled throughout the city.

Shea's Performing Arts Center, 646 Main St. (☎716-847-0850, box office 852-5000; www.sheas.org), is a beautifully restored 1920 vaudeville theater that features the best Broadway musicals, concerts, and a free film series. Box office open M-F 10am-5pm. Tours Tu and Th 10am, 1pm. $8, seniors $4.

The Studio Arena, 710 Main St. (☎716-856-5650; www.studioarena.org). This large venue has hosted the likes of Glenn Close and Jon Voight. Box office open M-F 10am-5pm.

Kleinhans Music Hall, 71 Symphony Cir. (☎716-885-5000; www.bpo.org), is home to the Buffalo Philharmonic Orchestra and was recognized as a national historic landmark before it was even 50 years old. Box office open M-F 9am-6pm. Tickets $18-60.

SPORTS

The success of local sports franchises is a testament to the fervor of Buffalo's fans. Tailgating is elevated to an art form before **Bills** football games at **Ralph Wilson Stadium,** 1 Bills Dr., just south of town in Orchard Park. (☎716-648-1800.) **HSBC Arena,** 1 Seymour H. Knox III Plaza (☎716-855-4100), downtown, is home to hockey's **Sabres** and Buffalo's professional lacrosse team, the **Bandits.**

NIGHTLIFE

Downtown bars and clubs are concentrated on **Chippewa Street** and **Franklin Street,** but live music can be found at numerous establishments throughout the city. From Thursday to Saturday, the bars are open until 4am across Erie County, and thousands of Western New Yorkers stay out all night. Pick up a copy of *Artvoice* for event listings.

Nietzsche's, 248 Allen St. (☎716-886-8539; www.nietzsches.com). Music is burned into the walls at this legendary club where Ani DiFranco and the 10,000 Maniacs got their big breaks. Beer from $2.75. Live bands every night. 21+. Open M-Th 1pm-4am, F and Su noon-4am, Sa 3pm-4am. Cash only.

D'Arcy McGee's Irish Pub and Sky Bar, 257 Franklin St. (☎716-853-3600; www.darcymcgees.com). An authentic Irish pub on the 1st fl. and an open-air rooftop lounge on top. Patrons can ride a glass elevator up to the sky bar to relax above the bustling scene below. Cover for sky bar Th-Sa after 9pm $2-5. Open M-W 11am-midnight, Th-Su 11am-4am. AmEx/D/MC/V.

◪ THE ROAD TO DUNKIRK: 12 MI.
Take **Route 5 West** towards Dunkirk.

DUNKIRK ☎716
The **Dunkirk Historical Lighthouse and Veterans Park Museum** is located at the end of Point Dr. The keeper's quarters house a museum of war memorabilia as well as various lighthouse paraphernalia. (☎716-366-5050; www.dunkirklighthouse.com. Open M-Tu and Th-Sa May-June and Sept.-Oct. 10am-2pm; July-Aug. 10am-4pm. Access to grounds $1. Tours $5, ages 4-12 $2.) If you haven't gotten your daily dose of ◪giant carvings of Native American heads, drive along Lakeshore Dr., on the west side of town, to see a gnarly 15 ft. giant (Ong-Gwe-Ohn-Weh) carved into an existing tree trunk. In the 1970s and 80s, Peter Wolf Toth traveled the country carving these wood heads as part of his "Trail of Whispering Giants" project, which now reaches across the country.

Lodging on beautiful Lake Erie is desirable but expensive. The **Pines Motel** ❸, 10684 W. Lake Rd., south of town in Ripley, has a half-mile of private lake access. The rooms feature knotty pine walls. (☎716-736-7463 or 800-736-8850; www.thepineslakeerie.com. Rooms from mid-May to mid-Sept. $50-70; from mid-Sept. to mid-Nov. and from mid-Apr. to mid-May $45-50. AmEx/D/MC/V.)

◪ THE ROAD TO GENEVA-ON-THE-LAKE: 103 MI.
Continue along on **Route 5** westbound. In Conneaut, take **US 20** to **Route 7 North.** From Rte. 7, turn onto **Route 531 West** along Lake Rd. **Route 531** leads through tiny Ashtabula and into Geneva-on-the-Lake.

GENEVA-ON-THE-LAKE ☎440
By the end of WWII, Geneva-on-the-Lake was widely known as the playground of Lake Erie. Today, the resort town retains a 1950s ambience but caters to modern visitors. Chain hotels still haven't discovered Geneva-on-the-Lake, where go-carts coexist with vintage kiddy rides along "the Strip." **Woody's World,** 5483 Lake Rd., allows you to enjoy old-fashioned amusement with an arcade and rides. (☎440-466-8650. Open M-Th and Su 2-9pm, F-Sa 2-10pm. 1 ticket $2; full-day pass $15.) Located just down the street, **Adventure Zone,** 5600 Lake Rd., offers go-carts, bumper boats, games, and an arcade. (☎440-466-3555. Go-cart rides $6. Bumper boat $4. Open M-Th 11am-10pm, F-Su 11am-11pm.)

The **Anchor Motel** ❹, 5196 Lake Rd. (Rte. 531), features a friendly staff, clean rooms, and some of the best rates on the Strip. The grounds have free Wi-Fi, gas grills, and a shaded picnic area. (☎440-466-0726 or 800-642-2978; www.anchormotelandcottages.com. Reservations recommended. Singles $65-75; doubles $85.) You can enjoy a complete vacation without leaving the boundaries of the **Indian Creek Camping Resort** ❷, 4710 Lake Rd. E. (Rte. 531). The 110-acre campground right on the Strip features a game room, a grocery store, a restaurant, swimming pools, mini golf, fishing lakes, and laundromats. Planned activities include volleyball, basketball, hayrides, and shuffleboard. (☎440-466-8191; www.indiancreekresort.com. Sites with hookup $47. AmEx/D/MC/V.)

Overlooking Lake Erie, the village's first fire station now houses the **Old Firehouse Winery ❸**, 5499 Lake Rd. (Rte. 531), which is decorated with fire-engine memorabilia and serves barbecue ribs (½-rack $13, full $17) that pack a punch. (☎440-466-9300 or 800-862-6751; www.oldfirehousewinery.com. Sandwiches $6.50. Mexican dishes $8-13. Open M-Th and Su noon-9pm, F-Sa noon-midnight. D/MC/V.)

⚲ THE ROAD TO CLEVELAND: 24 MI.
Head south on **Route 531** out of Geneva. Rte. 531 turns into **US 20 West.** Take US 20 W. to **Route 306 North.** Get onto **Route 2 West** and follow it along the coast of Lake Erie into downtown Cleveland. Exit and make a left onto **East Ninth Street,** then make a right onto **Euclid Avenue** to go into **Public Square.**

CLEVELAND ☎216
Ridiculed for having a river so polluted it caught fire (twice) and even branded the "Mistake on the Lake," Cleveland has gone to great lengths over the past decade to correct its beleaguered image. The industrial ooze that once lapped up on its shores is now gone, and Cleveland has made valiant efforts to spruce up its civic center. Yet the city is still struggling to reinvent itself. Hip coffee shops and music venues fill the eastern and western edges of Cleveland, and residents are hopeful that these enclaves will become increasingly integrated with the invigorated museums and playhouses downtown.

❈ ORIENTATION

Terminal Tower, in **Public Square,** at the intersection of **Detroit Avenue** and **Ontario Street,** forms the center of downtown and splits the city east and west. Street numbers correspond to the distance of the street from Terminal Tower. To reach Public Sq. from **I-90** or **I-71,** take the Ontario St./Broadway exit. While the downtown area and **University Circle** are relatively safe, the area between the two around 55th St. can be rough and should be avoided

at night. **Ohio City,** across the Cuyahoga River from downtown, and **Coventry Road,** in Cleveland Heights, are the best spots for food and nightlife. Bars also line the **Flats,** which runs along both banks of the Cuyahoga.

VITAL STATS

Population: 480,000

Tourist Office: Cleveland Convention and Visitors Bureau, 100 Public Sq. (☎216-875-6680; www.travelcleveland.com), in the rotunda of the Terminal Tower. Open in summer M-F 9am-5pm, Sa-Su 10am-3pm; in winter M-F 9am-5pm.

Library and Internet Access: Cleveland Public Library, 325 Superior Ave. (☎216-623-2800; http://cpl.org). Open in summer M-Sa 9am-6pm; in winter M-Sa 9am-6pm, Su 1-5pm.

Post Office: 2400 Orange Ave. (☎216-443-4494). Open M-F 7am-8:30pm, Sa 8:30am-3:30pm. **Postal Code:** 44101.

⚲ ACCOMMODATIONS

Cheap lodging is difficult to find in Cleveland, not least because of hotel taxes as high as 14.5%. Prices tend to be lower in the suburbs or near the airport.

❖ Cuyahoga Valley Stanford Hostel (HI-AYH), 6093 Stanford Rd. (☎330-467-8711; www.stanfordhostel.org), in Peninsula, 22 mi. south of Cleveland in Cuyahoga Valley National Park. Housed in a 19th-century farmhouse, this idyllic hostel offers cozy dorms and nightly cricket serenades. Kitchen, living room, and access to trails along the old Ohio & Erie Canal towpath. Reception 8-10am and 5-10pm. May-Oct. $19, under 18 $8.50; Nov.-Apr. $15/7. Cash only. ❶

Danes Guest House, 2189 West Blvd. (☎216-961-9444). Follow I-90 west of downtown to the West Blvd. exit, go straight off the ramp, and then turn right onto West Blvd. The unmarked B&B will be on your right. 2 rooms in a 1920s colonial revival house are a particularly good deal for travelers in groups. Homemade breakfast included. Singles range $55-70; doubles $65-80. Cash only. ❸

🍴 FOOD

Colorful cafes grace **Coventry Road** in **Cleveland Heights** between Mayfield Rd. and Euclid

Heights Blvd. The sounds of Italian crooners fill the sidewalks of **Little Italy,** around **Mayfield Road.** Over 100 vendors hawk fresh produce, meat, and cheese at the Old World-style **West Side Market,** 1979 W. 25th St., at Lorain Ave. (☎216-664-3387; www.westsidemarket.com. Open M and W 7am-4pm, F-Sa 7am-6pm.)

Tommy's, 1824 Coventry Rd. (☎216-321-7757; www.tommyscoventry.com), in Cleveland Heights. This bright, spacious cafe stays busy throughout the day serving vegetarian fare like falafel ($5), although meat-eaters get in on the action with juicy burgers ($4). Open M-Th and Su 9am-9pm, F 9am-10pm, Sa 7:30am-10pm. MC/V. ❶

Lelolai Bakery and Cafe, 1889 W. 25th St. (☎216-771-9956), in Ohio City. Revered for its velvety flan ($2) and sandwiches slathered with garlic mayonnaise ($4-6), this Hispanic bakery also offers buttery breakfast pastries ($1.50) that are absolutely perfect with a steaming cup of *café con leche.* Open M-W 8am-5pm, Th-Sa 8am-6pm. MC/V. ❶

Mama Santa's, 12305 Mayfield Rd. (☎216-231-9567), in Little Italy, just east of University Cir. Mama Santa's has kept hordes of college students and courting couples happy for over 40 years with its sumptuous Sicilian pizzas and welcoming atmosphere. Cheese pizzas $5.50-6.50. Open M-Th 11am-10pm, F-Sa 11am-11:30pm. MC/V. ❷

Panini's Bar and Grille, 840 Huron Rd. (☎216-522-1510). One of several locations in the Cleveland area. Panini's is famous for its overstuffed sandwiches, prepared in an open kitchen behind the bar. Seating spills out onto the patio, especially before Indians games. Open daily 11am-2:30am. AmEx/MC/V. ❷

👁 SIGHTS

DOWNTOWN

Cleveland's aspirations are revealed in its new downtown—a self-declared and far improved "Remake on the Lake."

▧ROCK AND ROLL HALL OF FAME. The museum is the centerpiece of IM Pei's glass pyramid. Blaring music invites visitors into a dizzying retrospective of rock music. Take a tour through rock history on the "Mystery Train," listen to the "500 Songs that Shaped

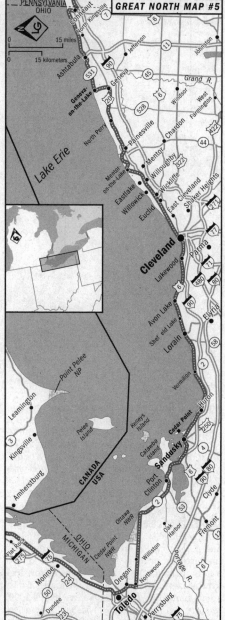

GREAT NORTH MAP #5

GREAT NORTH

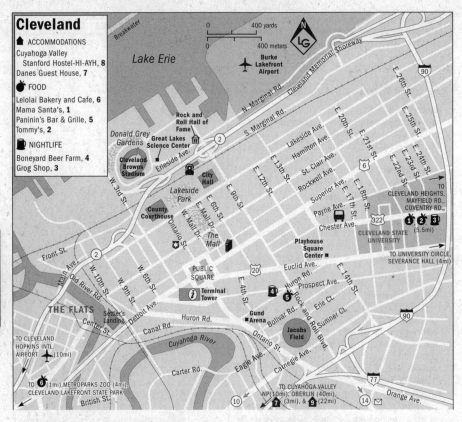

Cleveland

ACCOMMODATIONS
Cuyahoga Valley
  Stanford Hostel-HI-AYH, **8**
Danes Guest House, **7**

FOOD
Lelolai Bakery and Cafe, **6**
Mama Santa's, **1**
Paninin's Bar & Grille, **5**
Tommy's, **2**

NIGHTLIFE
Boneyard Beer Farm, **4**
Grog Shop, **3**

Rock and Roll," and ogle memorabilia including Elvis's jumpsuits, Jimi Hendrix's guitar, John Lennon's glasses, and relics from modern bands like Modest Mouse and Franz Ferdinand. (*1100 Rock and Roll Blvd.* ☎*216-781-7625 or 888-764-ROCK; www.rockhall.com. Open in summer M-F and Su 10am-5:30pm, Sa 10am-9pm; in winter M-Tu and Th-Su 10am-5:30pm, W 10am-9pm. $22, ages 9-12 $13, under 9 free, seniors $17.*)

GREAT LAKES SCIENCE CENTER. The center trots out high-tech toys like infrared cameras and a solar car to create interactive exhibits that are fun for all ages. Stick your hand into a mini-tornado, play with a series of musical synthesizers, and even control the flight of a small blimp. (*601 Erieside Ave.* ☎*216-694-2000; www.glsc.org. Open daily 9:30am-5:30pm. Science Cen-*ter or OMNIMAX $9.50, students and seniors $8.50, ages 3-17 $7.50. Both $15/12/10.*)

THE WILD SIDE

Nearly 20,000 acres of undeveloped land comprise the **Cleveland Metroparks,** perfect for biking, horseback riding, swimming, and hiking; the trail along the northern edge of Big Creek Reservation's Lake Isaac is a great place to listen for songbirds.

CLEVELAND LAKEFRONT STATE PARK. The park, near downtown, provides 14 mi. of beaches, bike trails, and great picnic areas. The soft sand at Edgewater Beach beckons sunbathers and swimmers. (*8701 Lakeshore Blvd. NE.* ☎*216-881-8141; www.clevelandlakefront.org. Open daily 6am-11pm. Free.*)

CLEVELAND METROPARKS ZOO. The zoo, 5 mi. south of Cleveland on I-71 at the Fulton Rd. exit, offers a more manicured look at Mother Nature, from North America's largest primate collection to the Australian Adventure Walk. Along the African Savannah and the Northern Trek, you can catch glimpses of Siberian tigers, red pandas, and hissing cockroaches. *(3900 Wildlife Way. ☎ 216-661-6500; www.clemetzoo.com. Open from Memorial Day to Labor Day M-F 10am-5pm, Sa-Su 10am-7pm; from Labor Day to Memorial Day daily 10am-5pm. Apr.-Oct. $10, ages 2-11 $6, under 2 free; Nov.-Mar. $7/5.)*

CUYAHOGA VALLEY NATIONAL PARK. Scenic Cuyahoga Valley National Park lies just 10 mi. south of Cleveland. The **Cuyahoga River** forms the park's heart, winding 30 mi. through dense forests and open farmland, passing stables, aqueducts, and mills along the way. The best way to see the park is to hike or bike its long trails. The **Ohio & Erie Canal Towpath Trail** runs through shaded forests and past the numerous locks used during the canal's heyday, when it served as a vital link between Cleveland and the Ohio River. The park's visitors center has maps and information on the canal. *(To reach the park, take I-77 S. to Rockside Rd. Take a left after the exit, continue to Canal Rd., and make a right into the park. ☎ 800-445-9667; www.nps.gov/cuva. Visitors center open daily 10am-4pm. Park open daily sunrise-sunset.)*

UNIVERSITY CIRCLE

While much has been made of Cleveland's revitalized downtown, the city's cultural nucleus still lies in University Circle, a part of Case Western University's campus, four miles to the east of the city.

CLEVELAND MUSEUM OF ART. Although under renovation until 2011, the museum has recently re-opened several galleries. *(11150 East Blvd. ☎ 614-421-7340; www.clevelandart.org. Open Tu, Th, Sa-Su 10am-5pm, W and F 10am-9pm.)*

CLEVELAND MUSEUM OF NATURAL HISTORY. The museum showcases a menagerie of animals preserved by taxidermists, while live deer, bobcats, and great horned owls populate the Wildlife Center outside. *(1 Wade Oval Dr. ☎ 216-231-4600; www.cmnh.org. Open M-Tu and Th-Sa 10am-5pm, W 10am-10pm, Su noon-5pm. $9; students, seniors, and ages 7-18 $7; ages 3-6 $6.)*

CLEVELAND BOTANICAL GARDEN. The garden provides a peaceful respite from urban life with traditional Victorian and Japanese gardens both indoors and out. The Eleanor Armstrong Smith Glasshouse recreates a Costa Rican cloud forest and the spiny desert of Madagascar. *(11030 East Blvd. ☎ 216-721-1600; www.cbgarden.org. Open Apr.-Oct. M-Sa 10am-5pm, Su noon-5pm; Nov.-Mar. Open Tu-Sa 10am-5pm, Su noon-5pm. $7.50, children 3-12 $3.)*

♪ ENTERTAINMENT

The **Cleveland Orchestra** performs at **Severance Hall,** 11001 Euclid Ave. (☎216-231-7300 or 800-686-1141; www.clevelandorch.com. Box office open M-F 9am-5pm. Tickets from $25.) **Playhouse Square Center,** 1519 Euclid Ave., a 10min. walk east of Terminal Tower, is the second-largest performing arts center in the US. (☎614-771-4444; www.playhousesquare.org. Box office open daily 11am-6pm.) Inside, the **State Theater** hosts the **Cleveland Opera** (☎614-575-0900; www.clevelandopera.org) and the **Cleveland Ballet** (☎614-426-2500; www.clevelandballet.com). Football reigns supreme in Cleveland, where the **Browns** grind it out at **Cleveland Browns Stadium.** (☎216-241-5555. Tickets from $25.) Baseball's **Indians** hammer the hardball at **Progressive Field,** 2401 Ontario St. (☎216-420-4200. Tickets from $5.) If you can't catch a game, the best way to see the field is on a 1hr. **stadium tour.** (☎216-420-4385. Tours Apr.-June and Sept. M-F 1, 2pm, and Sa when the Indians are away every hr. 10am-2pm; from mid-June to Aug. M-Sa every hr. 10am-2pm. $6.50, under 16 and seniors $4.50.) The **Cavaliers** play basketball at the **Gund Arena,** 1 Center Ct. (☎216-420-2000). In summer, the WNBA's **Rockers** (☎216-263-7625) play in the same building.

☕ NIGHTLIFE

A few pubs and music venues stay open at major hotels downtown. The **Warehouse District** features upscale clubs, while edgier crowds favor nightspots along **Coventry Road** in Cleveland Heights or along W. 25th St. in Ohio City. For more info on clubs and concerts, pick up a free copy of *Scene* or the *Free Times.* The *Gay People's Chronicle* and *OUTlines* are available at gay clubs, cafes, and bookstores.

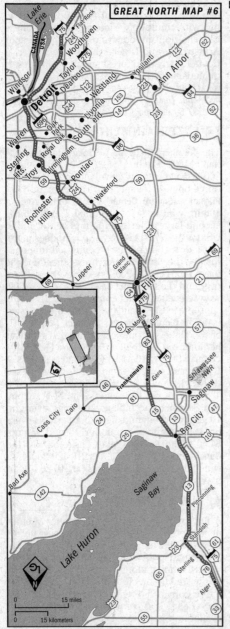

GREAT NORTH MAP #6

GREAT NORTH

Grog Shop, 2785 Euclid Heights Blvd. (☎216-321-5588), at Coventry Rd. in Cleveland Heights. A mainstay of Cleveland's alternative music scene. A move to a larger, less dingy location in the summer of 2003 had purists waxing nostalgic about a lost era, but the Grog continues to host the best in underground rock and hip hop. Cover varies. Open M-F 7pm-2:30am, Sa-Su 1pm-2:30am. AmEx/D/MC/V.

Boneyard Beer Farm, 748 Prospect Ave. (☎216-575-0226), in the Gateway District. Serves over 120 beers from around the world for brew lovers. Skull and crossbones decor, faux-cowskin chairs, and barrels of peanuts make this a great place to enjoy a brew. Beer $3-6.50. Open M-F 4pm-2:30am, Sa 7pm-2:30am.

⊠ DETOUR
OBERLIN

Take **1-90 West** to **Exit 140,** then follow **Route 53** for six miles into Oberlin.

Two young missionaries from the East Coast founded the Oberlin Collegiate Institute in 1833. Their commitment to coeducation and racial integration left its imprint on the small town of Oberlin; three years before the Civil War broke out, local abolitionists swarmed the nearby village of Wellington to rescue a fugitive slave who was being returned to captivity. Progressive politics are still alive and well in Oberlin, as Birkenstocked students from **Oberlin College** pad around S. Main St. and dream of a free Tibet. The college's **Conservatory of Music** (☎440-775-8044; www.oberlin.edu/com) is one of the finest in the nation, and free recitals are open to the public year-round. The **Allen Memorial Art Museum,** 87 N. Main St., features a strong collection of 17th-century Dutch and Flemish canvases, although its modern holdings are also vast. (☎440-775-8665; www.oberlin.edu/allenart. Open Tu-Sa 10am-5pm, Su 1-5pm. Free.) Town-gown relations are at their rosiest during the **Big Parade,** held on the first Saturday in May, while mid-June's **Juneteenth** celebration commemorates the signing of the Emancipation Proclamation in 1865.

⛏ THE ROAD TO SANDUSKY: 58 MI.

From Cleveland, take **US 6 West,** which enters downtown Sandusky from the east along **Cleveland Road** and then turns into **Washington Street.**

SANDUSKY   ☎419

Consistently ranked the "best amusement park in the world" by *Amusement Today,* ■**Cedar Point Amusement Park,** 1 Cedar Point Dr., off US 6, has many of the world's highest and fastest roller coasters. The towering **Top Thrill Dragster** takes the cake in both categories, launching thrill-seekers 420 ft. before plummeting down at 120 mph. Fifteen other coasters, including the enormous **Millennium Force** (310 ft., 93 mph), offer a grand adrenaline rush. (☎800-237-8386; www.cedarpoint. com. Open June-Aug. daily. Hours vary, so call ahead. $43, seniors and under 4 ft. tall $16. Parking $10.) Though most visit Sandusky for Cedar Point, the waterfront business district, established in 1818, has one of the most beautiful collections of historic architecture in the Midwest. **Washington Park,** along Washington St. between Wayne St. and Jackson St., contains a lovely floral park and the historic "Boy with the Boot" statue and fountain.

The **Mecca Motel ❸,** 2227 Cleveland Rd. (US 6), has lower rates than the chain hotels surrounding Cedar Point plus a free nine-hole minigolf course and swimming pool. (☎800-986-3222. Rooms $50-73. D/MC/V.)

A devoted staff serves customers at **Markley's ❶,** 160 Wayne St., on the corner of Market St., downtown. For lunch, try the Little Sister sandwich platter (bacon cheeseburger, fries, and cole slaw; $5), the house specialty for 45 years. Breakfast, including fresh doughnuts and pies, is served all day. Try a slice of "bumbleberry pie" for $2.50. (☎419-627-9441. Open M-Th and Su 6am-2pm, F-Sa 6am-7pm. MC/V.) Nearby, **Mr. Smith's Coffeehouse ❶,** 140 Columbus Ave., serves standard cafe fare amid comfy couches and large pieces of local artwork. The musically inclined will find a guitar with which to entertain fellow customers. (☎419-625-6885. Open M-F 7am-7pm, Sa 9am-7pm, Su 10am-5pm. MC/V.)

⛏ THE ROAD TO TOLEDO: 53 MI.

Take **US 6 East** to **US 2.** Proceed through Port Clinton and Oregon to reach Toledo.

TOLEDO   ☎419

The ■**Toledo Zoo** is home to over 4700 animals and 700 species, including polar bears, seals, primates, and elephants. Visit the **Hippoquarium,** with underwater viewing of Nile River hippos, or go nose to nose with wolves in the Arctic Encounter Wolf Exhibit. From downtown, take N. Michigan St. south past I-75 until it becomes Anthony Wayne Trail. The zoo is 2 mi. ahead. (☎419-385-5721; www.toledozoo. org. Open daily May to Labor Day 10am-5pm; Labor Day to Apr. 10am-4pm. $10, ages 2-11 and seniors $7, under 2 free.) The **Toledo Museum of Art,** 2445 Monroe St., has exhibits spanning the centuries from ancient Egypt to the present. (☎800-644-6862; www.toledomuseum.org. Open Tu-Th and Sa 10am-4pm, F 10am-10pm, Su 11am-5pm. Free.)

There are few affordable motels in downtown Toledo, but several chain motels are clustered to the south near I-475 and I-80/90. The **Classic Inn ❷,** 1821 E. Manhattan Blvd., near the junction of I-75 and I-280, has standard motel rooms with access to an outdoor swimming pool and free doughnuts and coffee in the morning. (☎419-729-1945. Singles $35; doubles $45. MC/V.)

■**Tony Packo's Cafe ❷,** 1902 Front St., was made famous by *M*A*S*H* star Jamie Farr, whose character Klinger frequently craved a Packo's dog. The wieners are even part of the decor; celebrity-autographed buns line the walls. Try the M*O*A*D ($8), also known as the "mother of all dogs" and pronounced "mo-ay-ad." (☎419-691-6054; www.tonypackos.com. Open M-Th 11am-10pm, F-Sa 11am-11pm, Su noon-9pm. AmEx/D/MC/V.) The **Maumee Bay Brewing Company ❸,** 27 Broadway St., runs a restaurant and the Toledo Brewing Hall of Fame. Try a huge burger ($9) or the pizzas ($7-9) with your brew. (☎419-243-1302. Open M-F 11am-10pm, Sa 1:30-11pm. AmEx/D/MC/V.)

GREAT NORTH

THE ROAD TO DETROIT: 58 MI.
From downtown, take **Summit Street (Route 65 East)** to **I-280,** which connects to I-75 north of town. Take **I-75** to **Grand River Avenue.**

DETROIT ☎ 313

Heavyweight champ Joe Louis is one of Detroit's best-known native sons and a fitting icon for the city; Detroit resembles an aging slugger, caught up on the ropes in the seventh round but determined to stay standing until the final bell. Violent race riots in the 1960s spurred a massive exodus to the suburbs, while the decline of the auto industry in the late 1970s chiseled away at the city's industrial base and left behind a weary, crumbling shell of Motown's glory days. Detroit continues to shrink with each succeeding census, and yet the stalwarts who have stayed behind love their city with an almost cultish ferocity. With a generation of young DJs reinventing the Detroit sound, this plucky town won't go down without a fight.

VITAL STATS
Population: 870,000
Tourist Office: Convention and Visitors Bureau, 211 W. Fort St., 10th fl. (☎313-202-1800 or 800-338-7648; www.visitdetroit.com). Open M-F 9am-5pm.
Library and Internet Access: Detroit Public Library, 5201 Woodward Ave. (☎313-833-1000). Open Tu-W noon-8pm, Th-Sa 10am-6pm.
Post Office: 1401 W. Fort St. (☎313-226-8075). Open 24hr. **Postal Code:** 48233.

✳ ORIENTATION

Detroit lies on the **Detroit River,** which connects Lake Erie and Lake St. Clair. Across the river to the south, the town of Windsor, Ontario, can be reached by a tunnel just west of the Renaissance Center (toll $3.50) or by

the **Ambassador Bridge** ($2.75). Those planning to make the crossing should expect delays because of heightened border security. Detroit can be a dangerous town, but it is generally safe during the day; expect to be approached by panhandlers and avoid walking alone at night. Office buildings and sports venues dominate the downtown, while neighborhoods like **Corktown** open out to the west. Detroit is spread out, so driving is the best way to get around town.

Detroit's streets form a grid, though, annoyingly, streets tend to end suddenly and reappear several blocks later. The numbered **Mile Roads** run east-west and measure the distance away from downtown. **Eight Mile Road** is the city's northern boundary. **Woodward Avenue** (Rte. 1) is the city's main north-south artery and divides both city and suburbs into "east side" and "west side." **Gratiot Avenue** flares out northeast from downtown, while **Grand River Avenue** shoots west. **I-94** and **I-75** also pass through downtown. For a particularly helpful map, check *Visit Detroit*, available at the Detroit Visitors Bureau.

⚑ ACCOMMODATIONS

Staying in downtown Detroit often leaves travelers with the choice of high-end hotels or questionable dives. There are a few options along **East Jefferson Avenue,** near downtown, but it may be easier to find chain motels in the suburbs or across the border in **Windsor.** For a mix of convenience and affordability, look along **Michigan Road** in Dearborn or **Telegraph Road** off I-94, both west of the city.

Victory Inn, 23730 Michigan Rd. (☎313-565-7250), in Dearborn. Located straight down Michigan Ave. from downtown, 1½ mi. past the Henry Ford, near Telegraph Rd. Convenient and affordable rooms with outdoor pool. Breakfast included. Free Wi-Fi and parking. Singles $59; doubles $79. ❸

University of Windsor, 401 Sunset Ave. (☎519-253-3000, ext. 7041), in Windsor, Ontario. The university rents both bunks and private rooms. Use of university facilities is available at an additional charge, and private rooms come equipped with free Internet access. Open from early May to late Aug. Dorms CDN$31; private rooms CDN$81. AmEx/MC/V. ❷

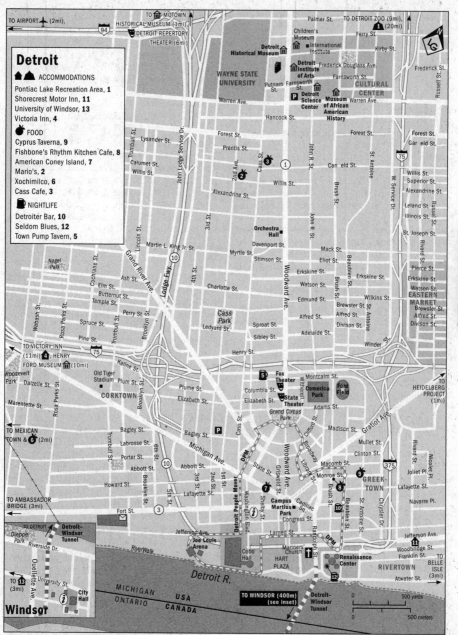

Detroit

▲▲ ▲ ACCOMMODATIONS

Pontiac Lake Recreation Area, **1**
Shorecrest Motor Inn, **11**
University of Windsor, **13**
Victoria Inn, **4**

🍎 FOOD

Cyprus Taverna, **9**
Fishbone's Rhythm Kitchen Cafe, **8**
American Coney Island, **7**
Mario's, **2**
Xochimilco, **6**
Cass Cafe, **3**

🍷 NIGHTLIFE

Detroiter Bar, **10**
Seldom Blues, **12**
Town Pump Tavern, **5**

Pontiac Lake Recreation Area, 7800 Gale Rd. (☎248-666-1020), in Waterford, 45min. northwest of downtown. Take I-75 to Rte. 59 W., turn right on Will Lake N., and hang a left onto Gale Rd. Follow the signs. 176 wooded sites with electricity and showers line the lake. Vehicle permit $8. Sites $18. AmEx/D/MC/V. ❶

🍴 FOOD

Gourmet restaurants may have cast their lot with the northern suburbs, but city dwellers continue to dine in the city's ethnic neighborhoods. At **Greektown**, Greek restaurants and bakeries line one block of Monroe St., east of Beaubien St. To snag a pierogi, cruise Joseph Campau Ave. in **Hamtramck** (ham-TRAM-eck), a Polish neighborhood northeast of Detroit. **Mexican Town**, just west of downtown, is packed with restaurants, markets, and nightspots. No one should miss the **Eastern Market,** just north of the corner of Gratiot Ave. and Russell St., an 11-acre produce-and-goodies festival. (☎313-833-1560. Open M-Sa 7am-5pm.)

American Coney Island, 114 W. Lafayette Blvd. (☎313-961-7758), on the delta. The oldest and most beloved family-owned restaurant in Detroit. Doles out coney dogs ($2.50) and chili fries ($3) to loyal customers. Engaged in a bitter rivalry with Lafayette Coney Island next door, owned by another relative. Open daily 24hr. MC/V. ❶

Xochimilco, 3409 Bagley St. (☎313-843-0129). Draws the biggest crowds in Mexican Town with delicious enchiladas and burrito platters ($5-9). Murals, warm chips, a tiled ceiling, and evocative lighting are just a few of the details that separate Xochimilco (so-she-MIL-co) from its competition. Open daily 11am-2am. AmEx/MC/V. ❷

Fishbone's Rhythm Kitchen Cafe, 400 Monroe St. (☎313-965-4600, www.fishbonesusa.com), in Greektown. Fishbone's brings Mardi Gras to the Motor City with zydeco music and Cajun dishes like deep-fried alligator ($10) and seafood gumbo ($7), in addition to an extensive sushi menu ($2-5.25 per piece.). Live jazz F-Sa nights. Open M-Th and Su 11am-midnight, F-Sa 11am-2am. AmEx/D/MC/V. ❸

Cass Cafe, 4620 Cass St. (☎313-831-1400; www.casscafe.com). A hip cafe and art gallery near the museums and university. Features skylights and balcony seating in addition to the impressive art gallery that takes up half the cafe. Sandwiches $5-6. Open M-Sa 11am-2am, Su 5pm-midnight. AmEx/D/MC/V. ❶

Cyprus Taverna, 579 Monroe St. (☎313-961-1550). Serves moussaka (eggplant casserole; $9) and other delicious Greek specialties in the heart of Greektown. Lunch specials are a great deal from $8. Entrees start at $10. Open M-Th and Su 10:30am-1:30am, F-Sa 10:30am-4am. AmEx/D/MC/V. ❸

Mario's, 4222 2nd St. (☎313-832-6464). An elegant, old-fashioned Italian eatery. All meals include antipasto platters, salad, and soup. Live bands and ballroom dancing take over on the weekends. Entrees from $18; lobster dinner $12 on Tu. Open M-Th 11:30am-11pm, F 11:30am-midnight, Sa noon-midnight, Su noon-10pm. AmEx/D/MC/V. ❺

👁 SIGHTS

DETROIT ZOO. Exotic animals like tigers and red pandas roam the suburban grounds of the Detroit Zoological Park. The **National Amphibian Conservation Center** allows visitors to get up close and personal with enormous salamanders, while the Arctic Ring of Life exhibit showcases polar bears and offers a trek through the tundra. (*8450 W. 10 Mile Rd., just off the Woodward exit of Rte. 696 in Royal Oak.* ☎*248-398-0900; www.detroitzoo.org. Open M-Tu and Th-Su 10am-5pm, W 10am-8pm. $11, ages 2-12 $7.*)

CAMPUS MARTIUS PARK. The same firm that gave the Bellagio casino in Las Vegas its famous fountains designed the centerpiece of Detroit's newest public space. The park borrows its name from an 18th-century military drill ground and has already emerged as a center for activity with its shaded gardens and a skating rink during the winter months. (*800 Woodward Ave., between Fort St. and Michigan Ave.* ☎*313-962-0101. Open M-Th 7am-10pm, F 7am-midnight, Sa 9am-midnight, Su 9am-8pm.*)

CRANBROOK. Founded by Detroit philanthropists in 1922, Cranbook Schools gives more than 1600 students a world-class education in the posh suburb of Bloomfield Hills. The public gardens, several museums, and house designed by Eliel Saarinen are well worth a look. Far and away the best of the lot is the

Cranbrook Institute of Science, with a planetarium and exhibits emphasizing educational fun. The new Bat Zone area houses bats, sloths, and other creatures that go bump in the night. *(39221 N. Woodward Ave. ☎ 877-462-7262; www.cranbrook.edu. Open M-Th and Sa-Su 10am-5pm, F 10am-10pm. $9, ages 2-12 $7. Planetarium shows $4, under 2 free. Bat Zone $4/1.)*

HEIDELBERG PROJECT. Drawing on the imagery of painters like Dubuffet and Basquiat, Tyree Guyton has spent the better part of two decades transforming a row of crack houses and abandoned lots on Detroit's Near East Side into installation art. The project began as a building painted with pink polka dots, and it now includes such artistic oddities as rows of vacuum cleaners lined up in waist-high weeds and a building strewn with hundreds of stuffed animals. *(Heidelberg St., between Ellery and Mt. Elliott; pick up Gratiot St. downtown and follow it north for 1 mi. ☎ 313-267-1622; www.heidelberg.org. Free.)*

🏛 MUSEUMS

🖼HENRY FORD MUSEUM. The astonishing eight acres of exhibit space in the Henry Ford Museum include iconic artifacts like the bus where Rosa Parks stood her ground, the convertible in which JFK was assassinated, the chair in which Lincoln was shot, Thomas Edison's last breath (in a glass jar), and the Wright brothers' flight shop. In addition to chronicling the history of transportation in America, the museum gives a taste of popular culture through the 20th century; sit for a few minutes to play with a vintage Mr. Potato Head. Next door, the Greenfield Village outdoor museum features a collection of historic American buildings, including Edison's Menlo Park laboratory. *(20900 Oakwood Blvd., off Michigan Rd. in Dearborn. Take a left onto Oakwood Blvd. 10 mi. from downtown on Michigan. ☎ 313-271-1620; www.the-henryford.org. Museum open daily 9:30am-5pm. Village open from mid-Apr. to Oct. daily 9:30am-5pm; Nov.-Dec. F-Su 9:30am-5pm. Museum $14, ages 5-12 $10, seniors $13. Village $20/14/19. Both $26/20/24.)*

🖼MOTOWN HISTORICAL MUSEUM. The Motown Historical Museum is housed in the apartment where entrepreneur and producer Berry Gordy founded Hitsville, USA, and created the Motown sound. Knowledgeable guides lead visitors on thorough tours past the hat and glove donned by Michael Jackson when he introduced the world to the moonwalk before descending to the legendary Studio A, where the Jackson 5, Marvin Gaye, Smokey Robinson, and countless others cut their soulful tracks. *(2648 W. Grand Blvd. ☎ 313-875-2264; www.motownmuseum.com. Open Tu-Sa 10am-6pm. $8, under 12 $5.)*

DETROIT INSTITUTE OF ARTS (DIA). Six years of renovation added a new wing and 77,000 sq. ft. to the DIA's already impressive footprint. The vast museum features encyclopedic collections that include Diego Rivera's famous *Detroit Industry* fresco cycle and a Vincent van Gogh self-portrait, the first Van Gogh to enter any US museum. *(5200 Woodward Ave. ☎ 313-833-7900; www.dia.org. Open W-Th 10am-5pm, F 10am-10pm, Sa-Su 10am-6pm. $8, children $4, seniors $6. 1st F of each month free.)*

NEW DETROIT SCIENCE CENTER. The museum features an extensive series of interactive exhibits that manage to be both educational and fun. Play the stringless laser harp or take virtual trips through the rings of Saturn in the planetarium. Don't miss the immense Erector Set model of the Mackinac Bridge, weighing in at over a ton! *(5020 John R. St. ☎ 313-577-8400; www.sciencedetroit.org. Open M-F 9am-5pm, Sa-Su 10am-6pm. $13, ages 2-12 $12; with IMAX $17/$15.)*

DETROIT HISTORICAL MUSEUM. The Detroit Historical Museum explores the region's transformation from "frontiers to factories." Visitors can tour a streetscape of old-time-Detroit and gawk at a working piece of the Cadillac assembly line. *(5401 Woodward Ave. ☎ 313-833-1805; www.detroithistorical.org. Open W-F 9:30am-3pm, Sa 10am-5pm, Su noon-5pm. $6, students and ages 5-18 $4.)*

🎵 ENTERTAINMENT

SPORTS

Baseball's **Tigers** round the bases at **Comerica Park,** 2100 Woodward Ave. (☎313-471-2255. Tickets $5-60.) Football's **Lions** hit the gridiron at **Ford Field,** 2000 Brush St. (☎800-616-7627. Tickets $40.) Inside the **Joe Louis Arena,** 600 Civic Center Dr., the highly regarded **Red Wings** play NHL hockey, and zealous fans traditionally chuck octopuses onto the ice. (☎313-645-6666. Tickets $20-40.) Basketball's **Pistons** hoop it up at **The Palace at Auburn Hills,** 2 Championship Dr., in Auburn Hills. (☎248-377-0100. Tickets $10-80.)

THEATER

Though the era of Motown has come and gone, a vibrant music scene lives on in the Motor City. The **Detroit Symphony Orchestra** performs at **Orchestra Hall,** 3711 Woodward Ave., at Parsons St. (☎313-576-5111; www.detroitsymphony.com. Open M-F 10am-6pm. Tickets start at $20. ½-price student and senior rush tickets 1hr. prior to show.) Dramatic works are performed in the restored **Theater District,** around Woodward Ave. and Columbia St. The **Fox Theatre,** 2211 Woodward Ave., near Grand Circus Park, features dramas, comedies, and musicals in a 5000-seat theater. (☎313-983-3200. Tickets $25-100. Box office open M-F 10am-6pm.) The **State Theatre,** 2115 Woodward Ave. (☎313-961-5450, tickets 248-645-6666), hosts concerts, while the acclaimed **Detroit Repertory Theatre,** 13103 Woodrow Wilson Ave., shakes things up with a commitment to race-transcendent casting. (☎313-868-1347; www.detroitreptheatre.com. Tickets from $17. Shows Th-F 8:30pm, Sa 3, 8:30pm, Su 2, 7:30pm.)

NIGHTLIFE

For info on the trendiest hot spots, pick up a free copy of *Orbit* in record stores and restaurants. The *Metro Times* also has complete entertainment listings. *Between the Lines,* also free, has GLBT entertainment info. Bars abound in the area around the stadiums, though their popularity peaks on game nights. Many more bars are sprinkled throughout Greektown and Bricktown, the most pedestrian-friendly section of town. Avoid walking alone downtown at night.

Town Pump Tavern, 100 Montcalm St. (☎313-961-1929; www.thetownpumptavern. com), behind the Fox Theatre. Good pints and atypical bar fare like roasted turkey and gouda sandwiches ($6) and pizzas ($10). Pints $3.75-5. "Beer and a burger" combo $5 except on game nights. Open M-Sa 11am-2am, Su noon-2am. Kitchen open until 11pm. AmEx/D/MC/V.

Detroiter Bar, 655 Beaubien St. (☎313-963-3355), in Bricktown, at the corner of Fort St. Catch the Lions or Tigers game alongside locals in this old-fashioned American pub. Burgers $5.75-7.75. Sandwiches $4.25-6.75. Open daily 10am-2am. AmEx/D/MC/V.

Seldom Blues, 400 Renaissance Center (☎313-567-7301). The food is pricey ($8-35), but this joint is well known among Detroiters for frequent jazz performances and the view over the Detroit River. Open M-Th 11:30am-10pm, F 11:30am-midnight, Sa 5pm-midnight, Su 11:30am-4pm. AmEx/D/MC/V.

FESTIVALS

Detroit's festivals draw millions of visitors. Most outdoor events take place at **Hart Plaza,** a downtown oasis that hugs the Detroit River. A recent and successful downtown tradition, the **Detroit Electronic Music Festival** (☎313-393-9200; www.demf.org) lures over a million ravers to Hart Plaza on Memorial Day weekend. Jazz fans jet to the riverbank during Labor Day weekend for the **Ford Detroit International Jazz Festival** (☎313-963-7622; www. detroitjazzfest.com), which features more than 70 acts on three stages. The international **Freedom Festival** (☎313-923-7400), a week long extravaganza in late June, celebrates the friendship between the US and Canada. The continent's largest fireworks display ignites the festivities on both sides of the border. Detroit's **African World Festival** (☎313-494-5853) fills Hart Plaza on the third weekend in August for free reggae, jazz, and gospel concerts. The nation's oldest state fair, the **Michigan State Fair** (☎313-369-8250), at Eight Mile Rd. and Woodward Ave., beckons with art and livestock two weeks before Labor Day.

THE ROAD TO FRANKENMUTH: 94 MI.

Take **I-75 North.** At Exit 136 take **Route 83,** which leads into Frankenmuth.

FRANKENMUTH ☎989

Frankenmuth was founded in 1845 by a band of Bavarian missionaries who came to Michigan to convert the Chippewa Indians to Christianity. Since then, Frankenmuth has decided to market itself as "Michigan's Little Bavaria" and proudly displays an entirely Bavarian-themed downtown and some of the most authentic Bavarian architecture found anywhere in the country (the Bavarian-themed McDonald's excepted.)

VITAL STATS

Population: 4800

Tourist Office: Frankenmuth Visitors Center, 635 S. Main St. (☎989-652-6106 or 800-386-8696; www.frankenmuth.org). Open May-Aug. M-W 8am-6pm, Th-F 8am-8pm, Sa 10am-8pm, Su noon-6pm; Sept.-Dec. M-F 8am-6pm, Sa 10am-6pm; Jan.-May M-F 8am-5pm, Sa 10am-5pm, Su noon-5pm.

Library and Internet Access: Wickson James E. Memorial Library, 359 S. Franklin St. (☎989-652-8323). Open June-Aug. M-Th 9am-9pm, F 9am-5pm, Sa 10am-5pm; Sept.-May M-Th 9am-9pm, F 9am-5pm, Sa 10am-5pm, Su 1-4pm.

Post Office: 119 N. Main St. (☎989-652-6751). Open M-F 8:30am-5pm, Sa 9am-noon. **Postal Code:** 48734.

ORIENTATION

Route 83 enters Frankenmuth from the south and becomes **Main Street** in town. The main intersections with Main St. are at **Curtis Road** and **Genesee Street.**

ACCOMMODATIONS

Frankenmuth Motel, 1218 Weiss St. (☎800-821-5362). One of the most affordable options. Rooms in summer $75-99, in winter $49-90. AmEx/D/MC/V. ❸

Bavarian Inn Lodge, 1 Covered Bridge Ln. (☎888-775-6343 or 989-652-7200; www.bavarianinn.com), across the covered bridge on Cass River. 7-acre building features 5 pools, indoor minigolf, 4 tennis courts, 2 lounges, and nightly entertainment. The lodge runs continuous shuttle service to the restaurant, 300 ft. away. Rooms in summer $135-165, in winter $105-$165. AmEx/D/MC/V. ❺

FOOD

The streets of Frankenmuth are lined with multitudes of candy, fudge, and taffy shops. Frankenmuth's downtown is packed with Bavarian-themed restaurants and shops. Visit **Rau's Country Store,** 656 S. Main St (☎989-652-8388), the self-proclaimed "Michigan's Most Unusual Country Store," which sells everything from bulk candy ($4.50 per lb.) to massive pickles ($0.50) and enormous wood Indian sculptures.

Bavarian Inn , 713 S. Main St. (☎989-652-9941; www.bavarianinn.com). If you're famished, try the family-style dinner ($20), a Frankenmuth tradition that includes platters of Frankenmuth Chicken, baked dressing, mashed potatoes, *gemuese* (hot vegetable), chicken *nudelsuppe*, *Stollen* (fruit and nut bread), *krautsalat* (cole slaw), and homemade ice cream. If you haven't had enough, the lederhosen-clad wait staff will cheerfully bring you additional German wienerschnitzel, *kasseler rippchen*, *sauerbraten*, or bratwurst. Open M-Th and Su 11am-9:30pm, F-Sa 11am-9pm. AmEx/D/MC/V. ❹

Zehnders, 730 S. Main St. (☎800-863-7999; www.zehnders.com). All-you-can-eat deal with chicken, dressing, noodle soup, cabbage salad, chicken liver *pâté*, cheese spread with garlic toast, freshly baked bread, mashed potatoes, egg noodles, and ice cream for $19. A gift shop, specialty grocery, cafe, and pretty serious bakery are located downstairs. Open Apr.-Dec. daily 11am-9:30pm; Jan.-Mar. M-Th and Su 11am-8pm, F-Sa 11am-9:30pm. D/MC/V. ❹

SHOPPING

Bronner's Christmas Wonderland, 25 Christmas Ln. (☎989-652-9931; www.bronners.com). The world's largest Christmas store. The European-style marketplace is the size of 1½ football fields, and the landscaped grounds cover 27 acres. You can see 400 Nativity scenes from around the world, 200 types of nutcrackers, a replica of the Silent Night Memorial Chapel in Oberndorf, Austria, and over 10,000 twinkling lights on Christmas Ln. at night. Open June-Dec. M-Sa 9am-9pm, Su noon-7pm; Jan.-May M-Th and Sa 9am-5:30pm, F 9am-9pm, Su noon-5:30pm.

Frankenmuth River Place Shopping Area, 925 S. Main St. (☎800-600-0105; www.frankenmuthriverplace.com). Built as a miniature European style village and features a "Lights Fantastic" laser show most nights.

GREAT NORTH

⌖ THE ROAD TO ROSCOMMON: 105 MI.

Continue on **Route 83** heading north. Rte. 83 becomes **Route 15** as it reaches Bay City. In Bay City, take **Center Avenue (Route 15/25)** across the bridge onto **Jenny Street.** From Jenny St., turn north onto **Euclid Avenue (Route 13),** which becomes **Huron Road.** Huron Rd. becomes **Main Street** as it enters the town of Standish to the north. Take **Old Route 76** northwest toward the town of Sterling. Taking Rte. 76 instead of the freeway between Standish and West Branch is worth it. Giant pine trees line the stick-straight road, allowing you to see for miles through tunnel-like greenery. Hop on I-75 and take **Exit 239** for Roscommon.

ROSCOMMON   ☎ 989

Roscommon is a small village on the banks of the Au Sable River's South Branch, known for its clear blue waters. Born a typical lumber town when the railroad made its way through, Roscommon now has one main business: tourism. The **Firemen's Memorial,** 1 mi. south of Roscommon, half a mile east of Rte. 18 on County Rd. 103, stands 12 ft. tall. During the third weekend in September, the **Michigan Firemen's Memorial Festival** (☎989-275-5880; www. firemensmemorial.org) brings thousands of visitors from all over the US to honor the valiant firefighters who lost their lives protecting their communities.

The **Spruce Motor Lodge ❷,** 900 Lake St., offers reasonably priced rooms in a historic building. The lodge occupies the Pioneer House, a building used in the 1870s as lodging for lumberjacks. (☎989-275-5781. Rooms $35-41.) **North Higgins Lake State Park ❶,** 11747 N. Higgins Lake Dr., and **South Higgins Lake State Park ❶,** 106 State Park Dr., both have campgrounds and sandy beaches. North Higgins Lake (most easily accessed by heading up I-75 for 1 more exit) also contains the **Civilian Conservation Corps (CCC) Museum,** which describes the successful New Deal program that reforested much of northern Michigan. (☎800-447-2757. Open daily 8am-10pm. Entrance fee $4 per vehicle. Sites $29.)

⊠ DETOUR
HARTWICK PINES STATE PARK

4216 Granger Rd. Located on **Route 93** in Grayling, at **Exit 259** off **I-75.**

The 9762 acres of Hartwick Pines are home to 49 acres of one of Michigan's last and largest stands of old-growth pine forest as well as a campground ❶. The 1 mi. **Old Growth Forest Foot Trail** leads to the **Logging Museum,** a recreated logging camp. (☎989-348-7068. Grounds open daily 8am-10pm. Museum open May-Oct. daily 10am-6pm. Tours 11am, 1, 3pm. Free. Sites $16, with full hookup $37. Day use $6.)

⌖ THE ROAD TO GAYLORD: 28 MI.

Continue north on **I-75** and take **Exit 282** toward **Gaylord/Alpena.** Turn right onto **West Main Street.**

GAYLORD   ☎ 989

In the 1960s, Gaylord recreated itself as an alpine village to attract tourists. These days the town's main attractions are its Swiss architecture and its status as the ski capital of Michigan. In 1965, Gaylord chose Pontresina, Switzerland, as its sister city, and Pontresina sent a boulder from the Swiss Alps as a gift to the town. You can see the **Pontresina Stone** on the corner of the courtyard lawn at S. Otsego Ave. and W. Main St.

The **Cross in the Woods,** 7078 Rte. 68, is one of Michigan's best-known roadside monuments. The cross was inspired by Kateri Tekakwitha, a Native American woman who erected crosses in the woods around the area. This particular cross was crafted from a redwood tree, and its crucified Jesus was created by renowned Michigan sculptor Marshall M. Fredericks. The cross—55 ft. high and 22 ft. wide—is among the world's largest. The **Museum of the Cross in the Woods** keeps the largest collection of nun dolls in the US but (amazingly) fails to include any of those punching-nun puppets. Halfway between Gaylord and Mackinaw City, take Exit 310 from I-75 north of town and follow Rte. 68 W. (☎231-238-8973; www.crossinthewoods.com. Cross open 24hr. Museum open daily in summer 9am-6pm; in winter 10am-3pm. Free.)

The **Downtown Motel ❸,** 208 S. Otsego Ave., is conveniently located near Gaylord's commercial center and offers "squeaky-clean rooms." The architecture is quaintly in keeping with the town's alpine theme. (☎989-732-5010. Free Wi-Fi. Rooms in summer $40-70; in winter $36-56. AmEx/D/MC/V). **Diana's Delights ❶,**

143 W. Main St., serves omelets ($6.35) all day alongside healthful smoothies ($4) and hearty sandwiches ($7-9), too. (☎989-732-6564. Open M-Sa 7am-3:30pm.)

⚑ THE ROAD TO MACKINAW CITY: 58 MI.
Continue north on **I-75.** Take **Exit 337 (Old US 31/M-108/Nicolet)** into downtown Mackinaw City.

MACKINAW CITY ☎231

First things first: Mackinac is pronounced "MACK-i-naw," so curb the urge to rhyme your syllables by saying "MACK-i-nack" to avoid the rolled eyes of the locals. The Mackinac Bridge ("Mighty Mac") soars over the intersection of Lake Michigan and Lake Huron, connecting Mackinaw City to St. Ignace in the Upper Peninsula (UP). Measuring 950 ft. longer than the Golden Gate Bridge, the 5 mi. span makes the suspension bridge the sixth-longest in the world.

VITAL STATS

Population: 860

Tourist Office: Michigan Department of Transportation Welcome and Travel Information Center (☎231-436-5566), on Nicolet St., off I-75 at Exit 338. Open daily from mid-June to Aug. 8am-6pm; from Sept. to mid-June 9am-5pm.

Library and Internet Access: Mackinaw Area Public Library, 528 W. Central Ave. (☎231-436-5451). Open M-Tu and Th-F 11am-5pm, W 1-9pm.

Post Office: 306 E. Central Ave. (☎231-436-5526). **Postal Code:** 49701.

✴ ORIENTATION

I-75 runs through town and across the **Mackinac Bridge** (toll $3). **US 23** enters Mackinaw City from Cheboygan to the east. **Nicolet Street** and **Huron Street** are the main north-south thoroughfares. **Central Avenue,** the main east-west street, leads west to **Wilderness State Park.**

⛺ ACCOMMODATIONS

Lakeshore lodging options abound on **US 23,** south of the city. Budget and chain motels line nearly every major street in town, but the best deals lie on **Old US 31** and across the Macki-

nac Bridge on **Business I-75** in St. Ignace. For an outdoor escape, try one of the 600 sites at **Mackinac Mill Creek Campground ❶,** 3 mi. south of town on US 23. The grounds provide beach access, fishing, and trails. (☎231-436-5584. Pool, showers, and Internet. Sites $19-41; cabins $30-170. AmEx/D/MC/V.)

🍴 FOOD

Family-oriented restaurants cluster around Central St., near Shepler's Dock.

▨ Mackinaw Pastie & Cookie Co., 516 S. Huron St. (☎231-436-5113). Serves variations of the pastie, the U.P.'s favorite meat pie, for $5.50. Only open in summer, but another location on 117 W. Jamet St. is open year-round. Open daily 8:30am-9pm. Nearby James St. location open in winter 9am-7pm. MC/V. ❶

Cunningham's, 312 E. Central St. (☎231-436-8821). Serves homemade pasties ($7), pies, and fresh fish. Dinner specials $8.50. Open daily in spring 8am-8pm; in summer 8am-10pm; in fall 8am-9pm. AmEx/D/MC/V. ❷

👁 SIGHTS

The annual **Labor Day Bridge Walk,** at which Michigan's governor leads over 50,000 people north across the bridge to St. Ignace, is a tradition not to be missed. Chain motels and tacky gift shops dominate the town, although the **Mackinac State Historic Parks** are well worth a look. Colonial enthusiasts should buy a combination ticket, good for seven days from date of purchase, for unlimited admission to any three of the four historic parks. (www.mackinacparks.com. $22, ages 6-17 $13.50. Available at all 4 sights.) Just west of the Mackinac Bridge's southern landfall, **Colonial Michilimackinac Fort** guards the straits between Lake Michigan and Lake Huron. The site features a fort built in 1715 by French fur traders. (☎231-436-4100. Open daily from mid-June to late Aug. 9am-6pm; from late Aug. to mid-Oct. and from early May to early June 9am-4pm. $9.50, ages 6-17 $6.) A 5min. walk away, the **Old Mackinac Point Lighthouse** opened in 2005 as a restoration project in progress. Warped wood and cracked plaster walls give visitors a sense of the work that remains to be done, although the four-story climb to the tower already offers a sweeping view of the surrounding straits. (Open daily from mid-June to mid-Aug. 9am-5pm; from mid-Aug. to mid-Oct. and mid-May to early June 9am-4pm. $6, ages 6-17 $3.50, under 6 free.) **Fort Mackinac** (on Mackinac Island; see below) and **Old Mill Creek Historic State Park,** a complex with a working sawmill and nature trails located three miles south of Mackinaw City on US 23, round out the impressive list of Mackinac State Historic Parks. (☎231-436-4100. Open daily from mid-July to late Aug. 9am-5pm; from Sept. to mid-Oct. and from early May to early July 9am-4pm. $7.50, ages 6-17 $4.50.)

▶ THE ROAD TO MACKINAC ISLAND: 7 MI.
Ferries leave from Mackinaw City (in summer every 30min. 7:30am-9pm). Shepler's offers the fastest service. (☎800-828-6157; www.sheplersferry.com. Round-trip $19, ages 5-12 $9.50. Bikes $7.50.) Catamarans operated by Arnold Transit Co., Shepler's chief competitor, are another fun way to get to the island. (☎800-542-8528. Round-trip $25, ages 5-12 $10.)

MACKINAC ISLAND ☎906

Mackinac Island, a 16min. ferry ride from the mainland, has been a destination for summer vacationers since the 1870s. Railroad barons lined the south-facing bluffs with elegant Victorian homes and, by banning automobiles from the island in 1896, tried to guarantee that Mackinac would retain its genteel, unhurried atmosphere for years to come. The slew of shops pressing Mackinac fudge on daytrippers proves that the early inhabitants weren't entirely successful, although there are still quiet corners of the island to explore. Walk off the ferry landing, cross the garish strip that is Main St., and never look back.

▣ ORIENTATION

Travel on the island is limited to foot, bicycle, and horse-drawn carriage. **Michigan State Highway M-185,** one of the few US highways without motorized vehicles, encircles the island as **Lake Shore Drive** and **Huron Street.**

VITAL STATS
Population: 500
Tourist Office: Mackinac Island Tourism Bureau (☎906-847-3783; www.mackinacisland.org.), on Main St. Open June-Sept. daily 9am-5pm; Oct.-May M-F 10am-4pm.
Tours: Mackinac Island Carriage Tours, 7278 Main St. (☎906-847-3307; www.mict.com). Sends horse-drawn buggies on a 2hr. trot around the southern half of the island. Tours daily from Sept. to mid-Oct. and from early May to June 9am-3pm; July-Aug. 9am-5pm. $23.50, ages 5-12 $9.
Post Office: 35 Market St. (☎906-847-3821). Open M-F 9am-4pm, Sa 9-11am. **Postal Code:** 49757.

PASTY BUSINESS

Pasties, originally a Cornish dish best described as a cross between a potpie and a calzone, are traditionally a staple for residents of Michigan's Upper Peninsula. While hardly anyone in most parts of the country has even heard of a pasty, stands selling the savory treats line nearly every major road in the Upper Peninsula. The region's fascination with these meat-and-veggie-filled pastries can be traced to a mid-19th-century influx of Cornish miners, who brought the dish with them from across the pond. Pasties were found to be an ideal food for miners because they could be filled with anything, were reasonably portable, and could stay warm for almost 8hr. More than just a favorite dish, the pasty is a cultural phenomenon, and pasty likenesses appear on everything from postcards to T-shirts across the region. The town of Calumet even hosts an annual Pasty Fest in early July, featuring a parade, games, and a bake-off, where pasty chefs compete fiercely for the coveted Copper Pasty Award.

[on the menu]

TOUR DE MACKINAC. Bike rental shops are nearly as common as fudge shops on Main St., and rentals generally begin at $5 per hr. for a single-speed bike. Prices for rentals are generally uniform across the island.

ACCOMMODATIONS

Hotel rates on the island generally reach into the stratosphere, but **McNally Cottage ❸** offers a haven for thrifty travelers. Situated about 50 ft. from the ferry docks in the heart of downtown, this B&B has been owned and operated by the same family every summer since its construction in the 1880s. (☎906-847-3565; www.mcnallycottage.net. Reservations highly recommended. Open May-Sept. Rooms $55-175. Cash or check only.)

FOOD

Take your cue from the locals and "shop across" in Mackinaw City for food; everything is more expensive on the island, whether you buy it in a restaurant or a convenience store. **Mighty Mac ❶**, 7315 Main St., keeps it cheap, serving quarter-pound burgers for $4.60. (☎906-847-8039. Open daily 8am-8pm.) The **Pink Pony ❸**, 105 Main St., serves handmade pastas, fresh salads, and fish under the watchful eyes of the pink horses on the wall. (☎906-847-3341. Entrees from $9-26. Live music nightly. Open daily 8am-10pm.)

SIGHTS AND OUTDOORS

Escape the touristy Main St. for a quiet look at what made the island popular in the first place—its beautiful flora and rolling hills.

FORT MACKINAC. Commanding a lofty view of the island's southern harbor, Fort Mackinac was a hotly contested piece of military architecture during the War of 1812. Today, cannon firings, carefully restored buildings, and the sounds of fifes and drums lure a steady stream of tourists up the bluffs. Tickets to the fort also allow access to four museums on island history that are housed in refurbished period buildings. (☎231-436-4100. Open daily

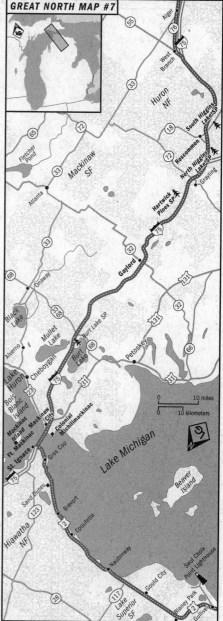

GREAT NORTH MAP #7

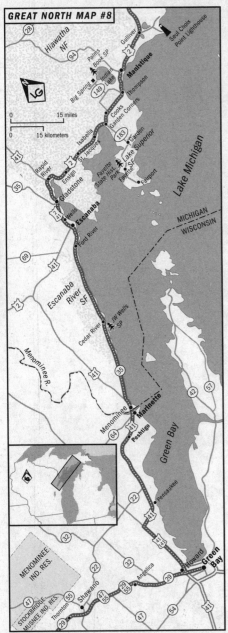

GREAT NORTH MAP #8

from mid-June to late Aug. 9:30am-6pm; from late Aug. to mid-Oct. 9:30am-4:30pm; from early Aug. to mid-June 9am-4:30pm. $9.50, ages 6-17 $6, under 6 free.)

OTHER SIGHTS. The **Grand Hotel** is something of a sight. It features a 660 ft. front porch (the world's longest), an unmatched view over the straits, and, accordingly, a pretty severe price tag (a single can range $375-675 per night!). Keep an eye out for weepy devotees of the 1980 Christopher Reeve film *Somewhere in Time*, which was set at the hotel and filmed all over the island. For those who would like to take the reins themselves, **Jack's Livery Stable** rents saddle horses and buggies. (331 Mahoney Ave., off Cadotte Ave. ☎906-847-3391. Saddle horses $35 per hr., 2-person horse and buggy $54 per hr., 4-person $66 per hr. Open daily in summer 8am-6pm; in winter 9am-5pm.) Encompassing 80% of the island, **Mackinac Island State Park** features a circular 8 mi. road that takes an hour by bike.

🚗 THE ROAD TO MANISTIQUE: 81 MI.

From the mainland, hop onto **I-75** and cross the **Mackinac Bridge** ($3). Take the first exit onto **US 2 East** to enter St. Ignace. Head out on **US 2 West**. Just after St. Ignace, encounter the unusual at Michigan's unabashedly tourist **Mystery Spot,** 150 Martin Lake Rd., 5 mi. west of St. Ignace off US 2, where "the laws of physics and gravity do not apply." For fun with optical illusions, this classic tourist trap has tours, but don't fret if you miss it—there's an identical attraction in Montana, a thousand miles down the road. (☎906-643-8322; www.mysteryspotstignace.com. Open daily from mid-May to mid-June 9am-8pm; from mid-June to Labor Day 8am-9pm; from Labor Day to late Oct. 9am-7pm. Return to **US 2,** which becomes **Lakeshore Drive.**

MANISTIQUE   ☎906

The restored iron-smelting village of Manistique is now a popular tourist destination on Lake Michigan. The city's central location makes it a great base for the many outdoor activities in the Upper Peninsula. The wood and cement **Manistique Boardwalk** lines 2 mi. of Lake Michigan shoreline. In front of the Chamber of Commerce, on the north side of Rte. 2, is yet another Paul Bunyan statue. It's usually crowded inside **Marley's Bar & Grill ❶,** 127 Walnut St., which has served basic bar fare under the same pressed-tin ceiling for 116 years. Try the chicken cordon bleu sandwich on homemade bread for $6. (☎906-341-8297. Open M-Th 11am-12:30am, F-Sa 11am-2:30am, Su noon-midnight. AmEx/D/MC/V.)

⬛ DETOUR
PICTURED ROCKS NATIONAL LAKESHORE

From Manistique, head west on **Route 94.** In Shingleton, some 35 mi. later, continue straight onto **County Road H-15.** Make a left onto **County Road H-58** and a right onto **Miners Castle Road** a few miles later.

With the largest surface area of any freshwater lake in the world and an average depth of 500 ft., Lake Superior contains enough water to fill the other four Great Lakes. The Pictured Rocks National Lakeshore hugs Lake Superior's wild shoreline for 40 mi., offering spectacular views of the colorfully striated sandstone cliffs along with sand dunes, waterfalls, forests, lakes, and a lighthouse. From Miners Castle, a rock formation mentioned in Henry Wadsworth Longfellow's *The Song of Hiawatha,* you can see grand views of the cliffs in either direction. A pleasant 1 mi. hike along the **Lakeshore Trail** leads down the cliffs through blueberry patches to **Miners Beach,** a beautiful sand beach on frigid waters. (☎906-387-3700; www.nps.gov/piro. Free.)

⬛ THE ROAD TO ESCANABA: 55 MI.

If you skip the Pictured Rocks National Seashore, it's a straight 55 mi. shot down **US 2 West/Route 35** to Escanaba. From Pictured Rocks, take **Miners Castle Road** and make a right onto County Road H-58 toward Munising. In Munising, make a left onto **Route 28,** then follow **Route 94 West** to **Route 67 South.** Turn onto **US 41 South** in Trenary, which will merge with US 2 W./ Rte. 35 to bring you to Escanaba.

ESCANABA   ☎906

A pleasant town on the southern side of the Upper Peninsula, Escanaba has a few noteworthy sights. Set in picturesque Ludington Park, one of the largest city parks in Michigan, the **Sand Point Lighthouse** was built in 1867 and operated until 1939, when it was closed because the changing contour of Escanaba Harbor no longer necessitated its use. After that, the lens and lantern were removed and the tower shortened. You can visit the lighthouse and the **Delta County Historical Museum** next door, which houses 50 years of memo-

rabilia ranging from vintage costumes to a blacksmith shop. From US 2, turn east onto Ludington St. (☎906-789-6790. Open in summer daily 10:30am-5:30pm. $3, children $1.) The arrival of the first cold front in early September marks the departure of thousands of ⬛**monarch butterflies** from their summer home near Escanaba. Each year, the butterflies fly over 1900 mi. from Michigan to their winter home near Zitácuaro, Mexico. The dates of migration are unpredictable, but good viewing locations include Point Peninsula and Stonington Peninsula.

The Hiawatha Motel ❷, 2400 Ludington St., at US 2 and Rte. 41., has comfy beds, movie rentals, and some rooms with kitchenettes. (☎800-249-2216. Continental breakfast included. Singles from $40. AmEx/D/MC/V.)The **Swedish Pantry ❷,** 819 Ludington St., is consistently packed with locals enjoying Swedish specialties. (☎906-786-9606. Open in summer M-F and Su 8am-8pm, Sa 8am-4pm; in winter M-F and Su 8am-7pm, Sa 8am-3pm. AmEx/D/MC/V.)

> ⏱ **TIME CHANGE.** Upon entering Michigan's Menominee County, Rte. 35 enters the Central Time Zone, where it is 1hr. earlier.

⬛ THE ROAD TO MARINETTE: 55 MI.

Continue southwest on **Route 35 (Lakeshore Drive)** to the junction with **US 41** and cross the **Interstate Bridge.** In downtown Marinette, US 41 becomes the main drag and is known as **Marinette Avenue.**

The Badger State
WISCONSIN
Welcomes You!

MARINETTE   ☎715

Named in honor of a 19th-century Native American trading post owner known as Queen Marinette, Marinette County is the waterfall capital of Wisconsin, with over 14 waterfalls located within a one-day drive. Most are located within the county park system. (☎715-732-7530; www.marinettecounty. com. Day use $3.) Between Menominee and

Marinette, the Menominee River flows into Green Bay. The surrounding bodies of water provide Menominee and Marinette with boating, fishing, swimming, and even ice fishing in the winter. Exhibits at the **Marinette County Historical Society Logging Museum,** on Stephenson Island, between Menominee and Marinette, include a logging camp in miniature and the Evancheck log cabin. Special exhibits honor Queen Marinette and the Menominee Indians. (☎715-732-0831. Open from Memorial Day to Labor Day M-F 10am-4:30pm, Sa 9am-noon. $3, ages 13-18 $1.) For information on Marinette and the surrounding area, cross the pedestrian bridge from the museum to the **Wisconsin Welcome Center,** 1680 Bridge St., where you just might be offered crackers and Wisconsin cheese. (☎715-732-4333; http://travelwisconsin.com. Open daily 8am-4pm.)

The **Brothers Three ❸**, 1302 Marinette Ave., is famous for its thin-crust pizza made with Wisconsin cheese. (☎715-735-9054. Large $14.50. Open M-W and Su 11am-10pm, Th-Sa 11am-11pm. AmEx/D/MC/V.) To satisfy your dairy cravings, **◪Seguins House of Cheese,** W. 1968 US 41, offers Wisconsin cheeses, cheese curds, spreads, sausages, and a slew of north country themed gifts from moccasins to flannel jackets. (☎800-338-7919; www.seguin-scheese.com. Open daily 8am-8pm. MC/V.)

◪ **THE ROAD TO PESHTIGO: 7 MI.**
Take **US 41 South.**

PESHTIGO   ☎715

Peshtigo was the site of the deadliest forest fire in US history. At least 1200 people perished and 1.2 million acres of timber were destroyed in Northern Wisconsin on Oct. 8, 1871—coincidentally, the same day as the Great Chicago Fire—when a nearby prairie fire fueled by strong winds suddenly swept through the town. It took less than 1hr. for Peshtigo to burn to the ground. The **◪Peshtigo Fire Museum,** 400 Oconto Ave., showcases period life and the few items that survived the inferno, including the Catholic church's tabernacle, saved by a priest who flung it into the river in desperation. (☎715-582-3244. Open

from late May to Oct. 8 daily 10am-4:30pm. Donation suggested.)

◪ **THE ROAD TO GREEN BAY: 48 MI.**

US 41 enters Green Bay from the north and borders the city along the west side. To enter downtown, head from the highway onto **Dousman Street** or **Shawano Street** and head east.

GREEN BAY   ☎920

Green Bay is the oldest settlement in the Midwest, established in 1634 when French fur trappers explored the area. Today, the city is well known for its rowdy, cheese-headed football fans, who crowd the city to get a seat in the revered Lambeau Field, home of the NFL's Packers. Winter brings hockey season, when the popular Green Bay Gamblers play at the Resch Center.

VITAL STATS
Population: 101,000
Tourist Office: Packer Country Regional Tourism Office, 1901 S. Oneida St. (☎920-494-9507 or 888-867-3342; www.packercountry.com). Open M-F 8am-4:30pm.
Library and Internet Access: Brown County Library, 515 Pine St. (☎920-448-4400). Open from Memorial Day to Labor Day M-Th 9am-8pm, F 9am-5pm, Sa 9am-1pm; from Labor Day to Memorial Day M-Th 9am-9pm, F-Sa 9am-5pm, Su noon-4pm.
Post Office: 300 Packer Land Dr. (☎920-498-3849). Open M-F 7:30am-6:30pm, Sa 8am-3pm. **Postal Code:** 54303.

⚐ ORIENTATION

Downtown Green Bay is surrounded by a rectangular loop of freeways. **US 41** runs north-south along the western edge of Green Bay, while **I-43** borders the city to the north and east. **Route 172** flanks Green Bay to the south. Downtown consists of the area on both sides of the river around **Dousman Street, Shawano Avenue** (called Walnut St. on the eastern side), and **Mason Street,** and businesses cluster on **Broadway** and **Washington Street.** The stadiums are best approached via **Lombardi Avenue,** southwest of downtown.

ACCOMMODATIONS

Be warned that room prices in Green Bay soar on game weekends.

Motel 6, 1614 Shawano Ave. (☎920-494-6730) Closer to the stadium. Singles $36-42; doubles $42-48. AmEx/D/MC/V. ❷

The Bay Motel, 1301 S. Military Ave. (☎920-494-3441). Clean rooms located close to Lambeau Field. Singles $42-52; doubles $49-59. AmEx/D/MC/V. ❷

FOOD

Titletown Brewing Company, 200 Dousman St. (☎920-437-2337; www.titletownbrewing.com). Walls lined with historical photographs of Green Bay. Specialty brews on tap include Johnny "Blood" McNally Red Ale, Dousman St. Wheat, and Grandma's root beer. Open M-F 11am-10pm, Sa-Su 11am-11pm. Bar open until 2am. ❹

Kroll's, 1990 S. Ridge Rd. (☎920-468-4422), in the shadow of Lambeau Field. A long-time local favorite. Open M-Th and Su 10:30am-midnight, F-Sa 10:30am-1am. D/MC/V. ❶

SIGHTS AND OUTDOORS

NATIONAL RAILROAD MUSEUM. At the museum, there are more than 70 trains on display, including one that will take you on a ride around the block. Take a break and sit in the cab of the world's largest steam locomotive, "Big Boy." (2285 S. Broadway. ☎920-437-7623; www.nationalrrmuseum.org. Open M-Sa 9am-5pm, Su 11am-5pm. Rides May-Oct. daily 10, 11:30am, 1, 2:30, 4pm. May-Sept. $9, ages 4-12 $6.50; Oct.-Apr. $8/5.)

LAMBEAU FIELD. Of course, no trip through Green Bay would be complete without a visit to historic Lambeau Field. Visit the Hall of Fame, which recounts decades of Packers history, or call ahead for a stadium tour. (1265 Lombardi Ave. ☎920-569-7500. Open daily 9am-6pm. Hall of Fame $10, ages 6-11 $5, seniors $8. Tours $11/8/10. Combination ticket $19.)

HERITAGE HILL STATE PARK. The park has managed to fit four periods of Wisconsin history into 48 acres. Barter with a fur trader (1672-1825), march alongside soldiers at Fort Howard (1836), get your horse shod at a blacksmith shop (1871), or churn butter with the farmers at the Belgian Farm (1905) in one of the 25 historic buildings. (2640 S. Webster Ave., off Rte. 172. ☎800-721-5150; www.heritagehillgb.org. Open from late May to early Sept. W-Sa 10am-4:30pm, Su noon-4:30pm. Guided tours M-Tu 10:15am-2:15pm. W-Th $8, ages 5-17 $6, seniors $7; F-Su $10/6/7.)

BAY BEACH AMUSEMENT PARK. The park is your ticket to the days before Six Flags and $60 admission fees. Free admission to the park includes 16 old-fashioned rides as well as concessions, volleyball and softball facilities, and games. The tallest rides offer unbeatable views of the bay. (1313 Bay Beach Rd., off the Webster Ave. exit on I-43, on the Green Bay waterfront. ☎920-391-3671. Open from late May to mid-Aug. daily 10am-9pm; from mid-Aug. to late Aug. daily 10am-6pm; Sept. and early May Sa-Su 10am-6pm.)

THE ROAD TO WAUSAU: 93 MI.

Leaving Green Bay, head west through residential areas on **Shawano Street,** which becomes **Route 29 West** outside of town. Continue on Rte. 29 for 86 mi. To get to the visitors center, take **Exit 171** to **Business US51 South;** to go downtown, take Exit 171 to Bus. US 51 N. through Schofield for 3 mi. into Wausau.

WAUSAU ☎715

Wausau was founded in 1845 as Big Bull Falls. At the request of the postmaster, the name was changed to something more appropriate for ladies to write on envelopes, and Wausau was chosen. Today, Marathon County is the world's leading producer of medicinal ginseng. White water canoeing and kayaking on the Wisconsin River are also big attractions.

ORIENTATION

Route 29 enters Wausau from the south, between Schofield and Rothschild. Southwest of Wausau, Rte. 29 connects with **US 51.** At the north side of town, Rte. 29 continues to the west and US 51 continues north.

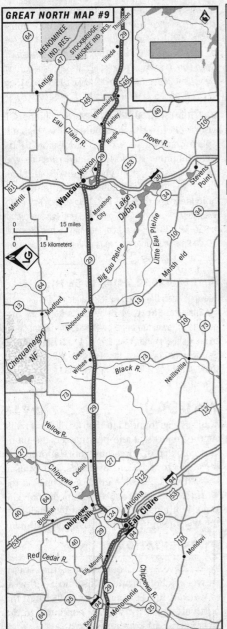

GREAT NORTH MAP #9

GREAT NORTH

VITAL STATS

Population: 42,000

Tourist Office: Wausau/Central Wisconsin Convention & Visitors Bureau, 10204 Park Plaza, Ste. B (☎715-355-8788 or 888-948-4748; www.wausaucvb.com), off Exit 185 on I-39/US 51 in Mosinee. Open M-F 8am-5pm, Sa-Su 9am-5pm.

Library and Internet Access: Marathon County Public Library, 300 N. 1st St. (☎715-261-7200). Open M-Th 9am-8:30pm, F 9am-5pm, Sa 9am-1pm.

Post Office: 235 Forest St. (☎715-261-4200). Open M-F 8am-6pm, Sa 8am-2pm. **Postal Code:** 54403.

ACCOMMODATIONS

Rooms at the **Nite Inn ❷**, 425 Grand Ave., in Schofield, are available with kitchenettes. (☎715-355-1641; www.theniteinn.com. Singles $32; doubles $59. AmEx/D/MC/V.) Visit **Rib Mountain State Park ❶** for excellent camping options. (Sites $10-22.)

FOOD

Wausau Mine Company, 3904 W. Stewart Ave. (☎715-845-7304). Turn north on I-39/US 51, and exit at Sherman St. Turn left on Sherman St., then right on 28th St., and continue 1 mi. Discover the Mother Lode Eatery and Rusty Nail Saloon, which has been carved to resemble the caverns within the mine, complete with original mining artifacts. Belly up to the bar next to perennial barfly Virgil, a dummy dressed as a miner, and tear into a burger ($6.50), topped with a snowy cap of sour cream. Open M-Th and Su 11am-10pm, F-Sa 11am-11pm. AmEx/MC/V. ❸

Hudson's Classic Grill, 2200 W. Stewart Ave. (☎715-849-8586; www.hudsongrillonline.com). A 50s bar and grill where the walls are lined with Burma Shave signs. Choose between booths and the outdoor patio and beer garden. Try the "lugnuts" (breaded cheddar curds; $6.50) for a warm-up. Open M-Th and Su 11am-11pm, F-Sa 11am-midnight. AmEx/D/MC/V. ❸

SIGHTS AND OUTDOORS

LEIGH YAWKEY WOODSON ART MUSEUM. Changing exhibits at the Leigh Yawkey Woodson Art Museum display artwork from around the world. The museum is home to permanent painting and decorative arts collections as well as "Birds in Art," a world-class collection of avian art. (700 N. 12th St., at Franklin and McLellan St. ☎ 715-845-7010; www. lywam.org. Open Tu-F 9am-4pm, Sa-Su noon-5pm. Free.)

HSU GINSENG ENTERPRISES. The company specializes in all things ginseng. It seems that Wisconsin's cool summers and soil are perfect for producing the roots for food and medicinal products. (T6819 County Rd. W. ☎ 800-388-3818; www.hsuginseng.com. Open M-F 8:30am-5pm.)

ARTSBLOCK. The complex was built around the historic Grand Theater, adding 75,000 sq. ft. of performance space. The three buildings connected by the new space—the **Grand Theater**, the **Center for the Visual Arts**, and the **Great Hall**—host events ranging from Broadway productions to staged spectaculars. (401 N. Fourth St., bordered by Scott, 4th, Jefferson, and 5th St. ☎ 715-842-0988; www.onartsblock.org. Tickets $19-97. Box office open M-F 8:30am-5pm.)

GRANITE PEAK. The peak is home to one of America's oldest ski resorts and one of the Midwest's most popular. (3605 N. Mountain Rd. ☎ 715-845-2846; www.skigranitepeak.com. Open from mid-Nov. to Mar. daily 9am-9pm. Lift tickets from mid-Dec. to mid-Mar. $48, ages 6-12 $36; from mid-Nov. to mid-Dec. $38/26.)

◻ DETOUR
RIETBROCK GEOLOGICAL MARKER

From **Route 29 West,** take a right onto **Cardinal Road,** between mile markers 150 and 149. When Cardinal Rd. ends in a T intersection 2 mi. north of the highway, turn left onto **County Road U.** After 1.5 mi. you will reach the town of Poniatowski. Take a left at the stop sign and then a right a half mile later onto (appropriately) **Meridian Road.** The marker will be on your right about 900 ft. from the intersection.

If you're interested in this sort of thing (or just want a break from driving in a straight line through hundreds of miles of farmland), take a detour off Rte. 29 to the **geographic center of the northwest quadrant.** The point lies exactly halfway between Greenwich and the International Date Line and between the equator and North Pole. It falls in a field in the tiny town of Poniatowski, Wisconsin. Visitors are encouraged to become a member of the "45x90" club

by signing the logbook at the Wasau/Central Wisconsin Visitor Center. Those who do even get a commemorative medallion (no joke).

◪ THE ROAD TO CHIPPEWA FALLS: 90 MI.

Head west on **Stewart Avenue** from downtown and merge onto **Route 29 West,** which takes you through the heart of dairy country. Take **Exit 79** toward Chippewa Falls, merge onto **Route 124 North,** and cross the bridge over the Chippewa River into downtown.

CHIPPEWA FALLS ☎ 715

Chippewa Falls was named one of the top 10 small towns in the US in 1997 by *Time Magazine*, and it's easy to see why: museums, gardens, and the Chippewa River make this picturesque city worth visiting. The industrial area is full of historic buildings, including the Chippewa Shoe Factory, which started out making shoes for lumberjacks and rivermen.

VITAL STATS
Population: 13,000
Tourist Office: Chippewa Falls Area Visitors Center, 10 S. Bridge St. (☎715-723-0331 or 888-723-0024; www.chippewachamber.org). Open in summer M-F 8am-5pm, Sa 10am-3pm; in winter M-F 8am-5pm.
Library and Internet Access: Chippewa Falls Public Library, 105 W. Central St. (☎715-723-1146). Open M and Th 10am-8pm, Tu-W and F 10am-5:30pm, Sa 10am-12:30pm.
Post Office: 315 N. Bridge St. (☎715-723-5805). **Postal Code:** 54729.

◪ ORIENTATION

Route 29 borders Chippewa Falls to the south. **Route 124** becomes **Bridge Street** as it comes from the south and crosses the river. It curves north on the other shore, intersecting with Rte. 29 and **Route 178,** eventually becoming **North High Street** and **Jefferson Street.**

◪ ACCOMMODATIONS

Indianhead Motel, 501 Summit Ave. (☎715-723-9171 or 800-306-3049; www.indianheadmotelchippewa.com), off Rte. 29 S., east of town. Simple rooms with desks, clean beds,

G R E A T   N O R T H

and little decoration. Singles $43-65; doubles $55-85. AmEx/D/MC/V. ❷

🍴 FOOD

Olson's Ice Cream Parlor & Deli, 611 N. Bridge St. (☎715-723-4331). Serves over 20 different "homaid" ice creams made daily in flavors ranging from chocolate-chip cookie dough to orange-pineapple. Sandwiches ($4-5), soups ($2-4), and salads ($3-6) are served in the deli. Open daily 10am-9pm. Cash only. ❶

Lucy's Delicatessen, 117 N. Bridge St. (☎715-720-9800; www.foreign5.com). Bills itself as "the real deal deli" and is a favorite of even the mayor. Sandwiches include the M&P ($6.30), featuring muenster and portobello. Pizza $7.30. Open M-F 8am-7pm, Sa 8am-4pm. ❶

⛰️ 🧗 SIGHTS AND OUTDOORS

OLD ABE STATE TRAIL. The trail connects Chippewa Falls to Cornell and is open year-round for biking, horseback riding, and cross-country skiing. (711 N. Bridge St. ☎800-866-6264; www.wiparks.net. Day use $4.)

LEINENKUGEL'S BREWERY. The brewery is Chippewa Falls' oldest business and has been brewing German-style beer in the Northwoods of Wisconsin since 1867. Tours offer a firsthand look at the Leinenkugel family history and brewing process. After the tour, hang out in the Leinie Lodge next door, where you can sip two free beer samples, whether or not you've been on the tour. (1 Jefferson Ave. ☎715-723-5557 or 888-534-6437; www.leinie.com. Open M-Th and Sa 9am-5pm, F 9am-8pm, Su 11am-4pm. 45min. tours every 30min.; last tour 60-90min. before close. Reservations strongly recommended. Free.)

CHIPPEWA FALLS MUSEUM OF INDUSTRY AND TECHNOLOGY. The history of manufacturing and processing in Chippewa Falls dates back to the 1840s. In the 1950s, the town was the site of Seymour Cray's invention of the supercomputer, which set the benchmark for speed. The Chippewa Falls Museum of Industry and Technology has interactive exhibits on regional industries, photos, and documents from Cray's collection. (21 E. Grand Ave. ☎715-720-9206; www.cfmit.com. Open Tu-F 11am-4pm, Sa 10am-4pm. $3, children $1.)

🚗 THE ROAD TO EAU CLAIRE: 12 MI.

Take **Route 124 South.** Merge with **US 53 South** to get to **Birch Street,** which will take you downtown.

EAU CLAIRE ☎715

Eau Claire (French for "clear water") was one of Wisconsin's busiest lumber towns in the 1800s, thanks to its location at the junction of the Eau Claire and Chippewa Rivers. Today, Eau Claire might have been named "Routes Encombrées" for its perpetual, ever-changing road construction, which confuses tourists and locals alike. The **Paul Bunyan Logging Camp,** 1110 Carson Park Dr., welcomes visitors with the Henry O. Strand Interpretive Center, a hands-on introduction to Wisconsin's logging industry with—of course—a giant Paul Bunyan statue. The camp's restored log cabins duplicate the rugged conditions faced by early settlers. Follow Main St. until it ends at Graham Ave. Turn left on Graham Ave., go two blocks, and turn right on Lake St. (☎715-835-6200. Open May-Sept. daily 10am-4:30pm. $4, children $2.) Beneath the towering pines of Carson Park next door, the exhibits at the **Chippewa Valley Museum** begin with the arrival of the Ojibwa Native Americans and continue through the days of European settlers and the changing social roles of farm life. It includes the 1882 Sunnyville Schoolhouse standing next door and a mock cow for milking practice. (☎715-834-7871; www.cvmuseum.com. Open daily M and W-Sa 10am-5pm, Tu 10am-8pm, Su 1-5pm. $4, children $2. Combo ticket with camp $7/2.50.)

🛏️Maple Manor Motel ❷, 2507 S. Hastings Way, after a left onto Storr Dr. from Rte. 12 W., is an ordinary motel on the outside, but inside it's a quaint B&B. Each room has its own unique flavor; the Wisteria is a vision in purple. Rose Memories (Room 139) has a floral theme and is decorated with 1950s wedding photos. (☎715-834-2618 or 800-624-3763; www.themaplemanor.com. Singles $40-50; doubles $50-65. AmEx/D/MC/V.) The **Highlander Inn ❷,** 1135 W. MacArthur Ave., has large rooms and a great location off Rte. 12. (☎715-835-2261 or 877-568-0773. Rooms $44-60. AmEx/D/MC/V.)

"Let no one hunger for lack of a better sandwich" is the motto at the **Acoustic Cafe ❶,** 505 S. Barstow St. The food is excellent, and the atmosphere makes up for the limited choices. (☎715-832-9090. Soup and sandwich $5. Nightly live music. Open M-Th 8am-10pm, F-Sa 8am-midnight, Su 11am-9pm. MC/V.)

THE ROAD TO THE TWIN CITIES: 94 MI.
Follow **US 12** to downtown Menomonie. Take **Route 25 South** for 35 mi., then make a right on **Route 35 (Great River Road)** heading toward Pepin. Continue along **Route 35**, which winds through ■ **Mississippi River Bluff Country**, with scenic and historic pull-offs along the way. In Prescott, follow **US 10 West** over the St. Croix River into Minnesota, and alongside the Mississippi River toward St. Paul.

MINNEAPOLIS AND ST. PAUL ☎612

Native Garrison Keillor wrote that the "difference between St. Paul and Minneapolis is the difference between pumpernickel and Wonder bread." For years St. Paul, viewed as a conservative, Irish-Catholic town, contrasted sharply with its young, metropolitan neighbor. Remnants of this distinction are evident in Minneapolis's big venues and bigger skyscrapers and St. Paul's traditional capitol and cathedrals, but it is impossible to typecast the cities' diverse residents.

VITAL STATS

Population: 380,000/290,000

Tourist Offices: Minneapolis Convention and Visitors Association, 250 Marquette Ave. S. (☎612-335-6000; www.minneapolis.org), in a kiosk at the Convention Center. Open M-Sa 8am-4:30pm, Su noon-5pm. **St. Paul Convention and Visitors Bureau,** 175 W. Kellogg Blvd., Ste. 502 (☎651-265-4900; www.visitstpaul.com), in the River Centre. Open M-F 8am-4:30pm.

Library and Internet Access: Minneapolis Public Library, 300 Nicollet Mall (☎612-630-6000; www.mplib.org). Open M and Th 10am-8pm, Tu-W 10am-6pm, F-Sa 10am-5pm.

Post Office: 100 S. 1st St. (☎612-349-4713), at Marquette Ave. on the river. Open M-F 7am-8pm, Sa 9am-1pm. **Postal Code:** 55401.

ORIENTATION

Downtown Minneapolis lies about 10 mi. west of downtown St. Paul via **I-94. I-35** splits in the

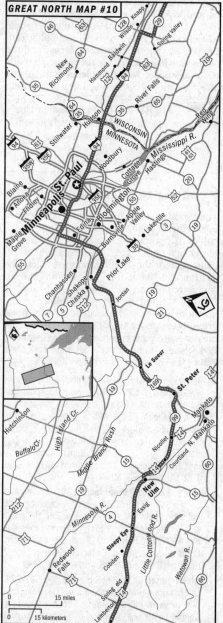

GREAT NORTH MAP #10

Twin Cities, with **I-35 West** serving Minneapolis and **I-35 East** serving St. Paul. **I-494** runs to the airport and the Mall of America, while **I-394** heads to downtown Minneapolis from the western suburbs. **Hennepin Avenue** and the pedestrian **Nicollet Mall** are the two main roads in Minneapolis; **Kellogg Boulevard** and **Seventh Street** are the main thoroughfares in St. Paul.

LIGHT RAIL. The **Hiawatha Line** runs from the Mall of America to Hennepin Ave. Tickets are good for 2½hr. after the time of purchase. ($2; off-peak $1.50; day pass $3.50.)

ACCOMMODATIONS

The Twin Cities are filled with unpretentious, inexpensive accommodations. Minneapolis caters to a younger crowd and consequently has cheaper hotels; St. Paul offers finer establishments for those with thicker wallets. The section of I-494 at Rte. 77, near the Mall of America, is lined with budget chain motels from $55. Similarly priced options dot the northern suburbs. The nearest private campgrounds are about 15 mi. outside the city; the closest state park camping is in the **Hennepin Park** system, 25 mi. away. Call **Minnesota State Parks** (☎651-296-6157 or 888-646-6367).

Minneapolis International Hostel, 2400 Stevens Ave. S. (☎612-522-5000; www.minneapolishostel.com), south of downtown, near the Institute of Arts. Clean hostel with a strong community atmosphere and friendly staff. Living room, porch, patio, and free Internet. Reception June-Aug. 8am-midnight; Sept.-May 8am-10pm. Check-in 1pm. Check-out 11am. Dorms $26; singles $39-125. AmEx/D/MC/V. ❶

Evelo's Bed and Breakfast, 2301 Bryant Ave. S. (☎612-374-9656; evelosbandb@comcast.net), in south Minneapolis, just off Hennepin Ave. Owner rents out 3 lovingly tended rooms in this 1897 Victorian home. Flowers in each room. Continental breakfast. Reservations and deposit required. Rooms $75-95. AmEx/D/MC/V. ❸

Saloon Hotel, 828 Hennepin Ave. (☎612-288-0459; www.gaympls.com), in downtown Minneapolis, between 8th and 9th St. Located above the Saloon nightclub, this hotel offers food, lodging,

and entertainment geared toward the GLBT community. "The inn that's out" has a colorful lounge with TV, laundry facilities, and free Internet. Reception 24hr. Reservations recommended. Singles $55-65; queens $70; suites $80. MC/V. ❷

FOOD

In the Twin Cities, many forgo restaurants for area cafes (p. 254). For cook-it-yourselfers, pick up fresh produce at the **Minneapolis Farmers Market,** off I-94 W. at E. Lyndale Ave. and Third Ave. N. The market offers over 450 booths of fruits, vegetables, flowers, and crafts that claim to make up the "largest open-air market in the upper Midwest." (☎612-333-1737. Open from late Apr. to late Dec. daily 6am-1pm.)

MINNEAPOLIS

Uptown Minneapolis, near Lake St. and Hennepin Ave., has funky restaurants where the Twin Cities' young socialites meet after work. In downtown Minneapolis, the **Warehouse District,** on First Ave. N. between Eighth St. and Washington Ave., and Nicollet Mall, a 12-block pedestrian stretch of Nicollet Ave., have eateries ranging from burgers to Tex-Mex. South of downtown, Nicollet turns into **Eat Street,** a 17-block stretch of international cuisine.

Chino Latino, 2916 Hennepin Ave. (☎612-824-7878; www.chinolatino.com), at Lake St., Uptown. Drinks like the "Citroen My Face" ($10) characterize this Latin-Asian fusion restaurant. With a chic satay bar ($7-9) and unusual dishes that often require instructions from the waitstaff, Chino Latino is for the hip. Entrees $13-40. Open M-Th and Su 4:30pm-1am, F-Sa 4:30pm-2am. AmEx/MC/V. ❹

Bryant-Lake Bowl, 810 W. Lake St. (☎612-825-3737; www.bryantlakebowl.com), at Bryant St., near Uptown. Built in the 1930s, this funky bowling alley, bar, and theater serves quality food at friendly prices. The breakfast "BLB Scramble" (eggs and vegetables; $5.75), ravioli, soups, and sandwiches ($5-11) ensure that the stylish patrons throw strikes (or whatever) on full stomachs. Bowling $3.75 per game, shoe rental $1.50. Entrees $9-12. Happy hour 3-6pm. Open daily 8am-1am. AmEx/D/MC/V. ❸

Figlio, 3001 Hennepin Ave. S. (☎612-822-1688), at W. Lake St. in the Calhoun Sq. complex,

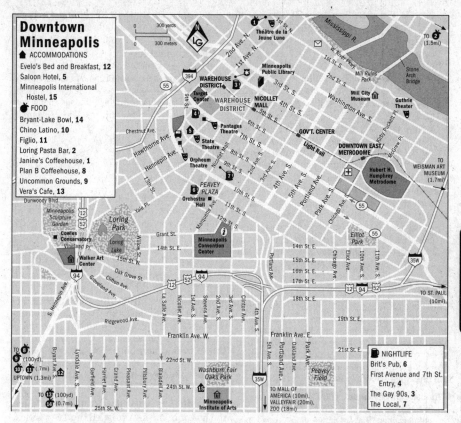

Downtown Minneapolis

ACCOMMODATIONS

Evelo's Bed and Breakfast, **12**
Saloon Hotel, **5**
Minneapolis International
Hostel, **15**

FOOD

Bryant-Lake Bowl, **14**
Chino Latino, **10**
Figlio, **11**
Loring Pasta Bar, **2**
Janine's Coffeehouse, **1**
Plan B Coffeehouse, **8**
Uncommon Grounds, **9**
Vera's Cafe, **13**

NIGHTLIFE

Brit's Pub, **6**
First Avenue and 7th St.
Entry, **4**
The Gay 90s, **3**
The Local, **7**

Uptown. Italian fare with flair. Residents have awarded Figlio the title of "Best Late-Night Dining" for years. Scrumptious sandwiches from $10. Pizzas from $12. Family-style meals ($9 per person) offered Su. Open M-Th and Su 11:30am-1am, F-Sa 11:30am-2am. AmEx/D/MC/V. ❹

ST. PAUL

In St. Paul, the upscale **Grand Avenue,** between Lexington and Dale, is lined with laid-back restaurants and bars, while **Lowertown,** along Sibley St. near Sixth St. downtown, is a popular nighttime hangout. Near the University of Minnesota (U of M) campus between the downtowns, **Dinkytown,** on the east bank of the river, and the **Seven Corners** area of the west

bank, on Cedar Ave., cater to student appetites—including late-night cravings.

Mickey's Diner, 36 W. 7th St. (☎651-222-5633), at St. Peter St. A diner on the National Register of Historic Places, Mickey's offers food that manages to outshine its 1939 chrome-and-vinyl decor. Take a spin at one of the counter stools or groove to some oldies on the jukebox at each booth. Cheeseburger $3. Buttermilk pancakes $4.30-$5.25. Open 24hr. AmEx/D/MC/V. ❶

Cafe Latte, 850 Grand Ave. (☎651-224-5687), at Victoria St. More substantial than a cafe and more gourmet than its prices and cafeteria-style setup would suggest. This cafe, bakery, pizzeria, and wine bar combo is also famous for its desserts. Chicken-salsa chili $5. Turtle cake $4.

GREAT NORTH

Open M-W and Su 9am-10pm, Th 9am-11pm, F-Sa 9am-midnight. AmEx/D/MC/V. ❶

Cossetta, 211 W. 7th St. (☎651-222-3476). Began as an Italian market in 1911. Now serves eat-in specialities. Try the veal parmigiana ($7) or the pizza ($12-22). Open M-Th 11am-9pm, F-Sa 11am-10pm, Su 11am-8pm. MC/V. ❸

Loring Pasta Bar, 327 14th Ave. SE (☎612-378-4849; www.loringcafe.com), in Dinkytown, near the U of M campus. A whimsical restaurant with dishes ranging from tasty pot stickers ($8) to pasta ($12-16). Live music. Tango DJ Su night. Open M-F 11:30am-10pm, Sa noon-11pm, Su 11am-2pm and 4:30-10pm. MC/V. ❸

Day By Day Cafe, 477 W. 7th St. (☎651-227-0654; www.daybyday.com). An unpretentious restaurant started in 1975 serves the community all-day breakfast ($5-9), lunch, and dinner specials ($8.75-10) in its library-like dining room. Live music F 7-10pm. Open M-F 6am-8pm, Sa 6am-3pm, Su 7am-3pm. Cash only. ❷

🍴 CAFES

Cafes are an integral part of the Twin Cities' social life. Particularly in Uptown Minneapolis, quirky coffeehouses caffeinate the masses and draw crowds as large as those at any bar. Most of these creatively-decorated coffeehouses complement their java with some of the cheapest food in town.

🖾 Uncommon Grounds, 2809 Hennepin Ave. S. (☎612-872-4811), at 28th St., Uptown. The self-described "BMW of coffee shops" uses secret ingredients to make the tastiest coffees ($2-5) and teas around. With velour booths and relaxing music in a Victorian house, this coffeehouse lives up to its name. Free Wi-Fi. Open M-F 5pm-1am, Sa 10am-1am, Su noon-1am. Cash only. ❶

Plan B Coffeehouse, 2717 Hennepin Ave. (☎612-872-1419), between 27th and 28th St., Uptown. Animated conversation and mismatched furniture in a laid-back earth-tone atmosphere. Try the "tripper's revenge" ($3.85). Patio seating. Free Wi-Fi. Open M-Th and Su 9am-midnight, F-Sa 9am-1am. D/MC/V. ❶

Vera's Cafe, 2901 Lyndale Ave. (☎612-822-3871; www.verascafe.com), between 29th and Lake St., Uptown. The "vintage cafe for the hip and saucy," Vera's serves a mixed gay and straight crowd its signature "White Zombie" ($4.60) and

all-day breakfast ($5-6). Occasional events on the patio and live music most weekend nights. Free Wi-Fi. Open daily 7am-midnight. MC/V. ❶

Janine's Coffeehouse, 119 1st St N. (☎612-630-5188; www.janinescoffeehouse.net), located near Theatre de la Jeune Lune, in the Warehouse District. Exquisite cafe serves coffee, espresso, and baked goods in addition to daily soups, salads, and sandwiches ($5). Free Wi-Fi. Open M-F 7am-6pm, Sa-Su 8am-2pm. ❶

👁 SIGHTS

MINNEAPOLIS

🖾WALKER ART CENTER. A few blocks southwest of downtown, the world-renowned Walker Art Center counts daring exhibits by Lichtenstein, Rothko, and Warhol among its collections of contemporary art. *(725 Vineland Pl., at Lyndale Ave. ☎612-375-7622; www.walkerart.org. Open Tu-W and Sa-Su 11am-5pm, Th-F 11am-9pm. $10, students $6, seniors $8.)*

MINNEAPOLIS SCULPTURE GARDEN. Rotating exhibits join the iconic, postcard-friendly *Spoonbridge and Cherry* sculpture in the largest sculpture garden in the US. The adjacent **Cowles Conservatory** houses an array of plants and an impressive Frank Gehry fish sculpture. *(Garden open daily 6am-midnight. Conservatory open Tu-Sa 10am-8pm, Su 10am-5pm. Free.)*

WEISMAN ART MUSEUM. Gehry also holds the honor of having designed the Twin Cities' most unique and controversial structure: the Weisman Art Museum, on the east bank of the U of M campus. The undulating metallic building was his first museum building in America and served as the rough draft for the famous Guggenheim in Bilbao. The museum hosts an inspired collection of modern art, including works by O'Keeffe, Warhol, and Kandinsky. The thought-provoking apartment replica, by Edward and Nancy Reddin Kienholz, engages all the senses by asking viewers to eavesdrop at each door. *(333 E. River Rd. ☎612-625-9494; www.weisman.umn.edu. Open Tu-W and F 10am-5pm, Th 10am-8pm, Sa-Su 11am-5pm. Free.)*

MINNEAPOLIS INSTITUTE OF ARTS. The Minneapolis Institute of Arts, south of downtown, showcases more than 100,000 art objects spanning 5000 years, including windows by Frank Lloyd Wright, Rembrandt's *Lucretia*, and the world-famous *Doryphoros*, Polykleitos's perfectly-proportioned man. *(2400 3rd Ave. S. ☎612-870-3131; www.artsmia.org. Open Tu-W and F-Sa 10am-5pm, Th 10am-9pm, Su 11am-5pm. Free.)*

MILL CITY MUSEUM. The museum is a national historic landmark and takes visitors on a tour of Minneapolis's manufacturing history. *(704 S. 2nd St. ☎612-341-7555; www. millcitymuseum.org. Open Tu-W and F-Sa 10am-5pm, Th 10am-9pm, Su noon-5pm.)*

ST. PAUL

◪SUMMIT AVENUE. History and architecture define stately St. Paul. Nowhere is this more evident than along Summit Avenue, the nation's longest continuous stretch of Victorian houses, including the childhood home of novelist **F. Scott Fitzgerald** and the Minnesota **Governor's Mansion.** *(Fitzgerald: 599 Summit Ave. Currently a private residence. Governor's Mansion: 1006 Summit Ave. ☎651-297-8177. Tours June-Aug. first three Th of each month 1-3pm. Free.)* The magnificent home of railroad magnate **James J. Hill**—the largest and most expensive home in the state when it was completed in 1891—offers 1hr. tours. *(240 Summit Ave. ☎651-297-2555. Open W-Sa 10am-3:30pm, Su 1-3:30pm. Reservations recommended. $8, ages 6-17 $5, seniors $6.)* **Walking tours** of Summit Ave. depart from the Hill House and explore the architectural and social history of the area. *(☎651-297-2555. 1hr. tours May-Sept. Sa 11am and 2pm, Su 2pm. $10, seniors and students $8, ages 6-17 $6.)*

◪MINNESOTA HISTORY CENTER. The innovative and exciting Minnesota History Center houses nine interactive, hands-on exhibit galleries on Minnesota history that entertain young and old alike. Learn how Minnesotans cope with their extreme seasons, ogle Prince's "Purple Rain" attire, or admire action figures of pro-wrestler-turned-Minnesota-governor Jesse Ventura. *(345 Kellogg Blvd. W. ☎651-296-6126; www.mnhs.org. Open Tu 10am-8pm, W-Sa 10am-5pm, Su noon-5pm. $10, students and seniors $8, ages 6-17 $5.)*

SCIENCE MUSEUM OF MINNESOTA. The Science Museum of Minnesota includes a

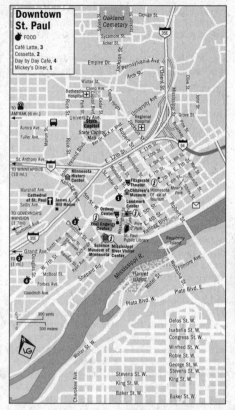

beautiful atrium overlooking the Mississippi, an exhibit on the human body, and a paleontology hall. The **Mississippi River Visitor Center,** housed in the same building, provides a wealth of information about America's longest and most famous river. *(120 W. Kellogg Blvd. ☎651-221-9444; www.smm.org. Open mid-June to early Sept. M-Sa 8:30am-11pm; early Sept. to mid-June M-W 9:30am-5pm, Th-Sa 9:30am-9pm, Su noon-7pm. $11, children and seniors $8.50.)*

SUBURBS

MINNESOTA ZOO. Located on 500 wooded acres in suburban Apple Valley, the Minnesota Zoo houses over 2,000 local and exotic animals in their natural habitats, including 22 endangered and threatened species, a tiger

GREAT NORTH

lair exhibit, and native beavers, lynx, and wolverines. *(13000 Zoo Blvd. Take Rte. 77 S. to the Zoo exit and follow signs.* ☎ *952-431-9500 or 800-366-7811; www.mnzoo.org. Open June-Aug. daily 9am-6pm; Sept. and May M-F 9am-4pm, Sa-Su 9am-6pm; Oct.-Apr. daily 9am-4pm. $15, ages 3-12 $8, seniors $9.)*

VALLEYFAIR. In Shakopee, even the most daring thrill-seekers can get their jollies at Valleyfair, a quality amusement park with six roller coasters, a water park, and the heart-stopping Power Tower, which drops over 10 stories. *(1 Valleyfair Dr. Take I-35 W. south to Rte. 13 W.* ☎ *800-386-7433; www.valleyfair.com. Open June-Aug. daily; Sept. and May hours vary. Call or check website for hours, usually 10am-10pm during summer; water park closes earlier. $37, over 60 and under 48 in. $15, under 3 free; after 5pm, $19/15/free.)*

MALL OF AMERICA. Welcome to the largest mall in America. With more than 520 specialty stores and 60 restaurants extending for over 2 mi., the "MoA" is the consummation of an American love affair with all that is obscenely gargantuan. Don't settle for just shopping and eating; the complex also boasts a movie megaplex, an aquarium, a casino, an adventure golf course, and the largest indoor amusement park in the world. *(60 E. Broadway, in Bloomington. From St. Paul, take I-35 E. south to I-494 W. and exit at 24th Ave.* ☎ *952-883-8800; www.mallofamerica.com. Open M-Sa 10am-9:30pm, Su 11am-7pm.)*

Other Sights. Golden horses top the ornate **State Capitol,** the world's largest unsupported marble dome. *(75 Reverend Dr. Martin Luther King, Jr., Blvd.* ☎ *651-296-3962. Open M-F 9am-4pm, Sa 10am-3pm, Su 1-4pm. Tours every hr. Last tour 1hr. before close. Free.)* A scaled-down version of St. Peter's in Rome, the **Cathedral of Saint Paul,** at the end of Summit Ave., overlooks the capitol. *(239 Selby Ave.* ☎ *651-228-1766. Open M-Th 7am-5:30pm, F 7am-4pm, Sa 7am-7pm, Su 7am-5pm. Tours M, W, F 1pm. Donations accepted.)*

ENTERTAINMENT

MUSIC
The Twin Cities' vibrant music scene offers everything from opera and polka to hip hop and alternative. For more info, read the free *City Pages* (www.citypages.com), available at libraries, most cafes, and newsstands around town. **Sommerfest,** a month-long celebration of Viennese music put on by the Minnesota Orchestra, is the best of the cities' classical options during July. **Orchestra Hall,** 1111 Nicollet Ave., in downtown Minneapolis, hosts the event. (☎ 612-371-5656 or 800-292-4141; www. minnesotaorchestra.org. Tickets $15-43. Student rush tickets available 30min. before show; $10. Box office open M-F 10am-5pm, Sa 1-5pm.) Nearby, **Peavey Plaza,** on Nicollet Mall, holds free nightly concerts and occasional film screenings. The **Saint Paul Chamber Orchestra,** the **Schubert Club,** and the **Minnesota Opera Company** all perform at St. Paul's glass-and-brick **Ordway Center For The Performing Arts,**

A REALLY COOL CELEBRATION

In January 1885, a visiting reporter from New York City described Minnesota's capital city as "another Siberia, unfit for human habitation." The local chamber of commerce decided to show East Coasters how wonderful their icy city was by throwing a giant outdoor festival in the middle of winter, thus initiating the annual St. Paul Winter Carnival. The festival revolves around a concocted feud between King Boreas, ruler of the winds and lover of all things cold, and his arch-nemesis, Vulcanus Rex, the god of fire. Each year, the members of the king's court reside within a massive ice castle constructed from 27,000 bathtub-size bricks of ice carved from Lake Phalen. In Mardi Gras fashion, elaborate floats are outfitted for the festival's opening and closing parades. The celebration includes activities like ice-carving contests, snow sculpting, curling, ice skating, and car races on ice. For the past half-century, one of the festival's highlights has been a treasure hunt organized by the local *St. Paul Pioneer Press,* which publishes cryptic daily clues to the location of a medallion hidden in an unnamed public park. The medallion's finder wins up to $10,000. Previous hiding places have included a White Castle box, a baby diaper, an Oreo cookie, and—of course—a block of ice.

345 Washington St., which also hosts touring productions. (☎651-224-4222; www.ordway. org. Tickets $30-60. Box office open M-F 10am-6pm, Sa-Su 11am-3pm.) The **Current,** 89.3FM, plays an eclectic mix and very often features local music. For those looking to buy some, **Cheapo,** 1300 W. Lake St., has an impressively vast collection of new and used CDs, tapes, and records, all reasonably priced. The "local" section contains over 1000 titles and is a great way to find out about upcoming shows. (☎612-827-8238; www.cheapodiscs. com/mn.htm. Open daily 9am-midnight.)

SPORTS

The puffy **Hubert H. Humphrey Metrodome,** 900 S. Fifth St., in downtown Minneapolis, hosts baseball's **Minnesota Twins** (☎612-375-7454; www.twinsbaseball.com) and football's **Vikings** (☎612-338-4537; www.vikings.com). The NBA's **Timberwolves** (☎612-337-3865; www.timberwolves.com) and WNBA's **Lynx** (☎612-673-8400; www.wnba.com/lynx) play at the **Target Center,** 601 First Ave., between Sixth and Seventh St., in downtown Minneapolis. The cities' NHL team, the **Wild,** takes the ice at **St. Paul's Xcel Energy Center.** (☎651-222-9453.)

THEATER

Rumored to be second only to New York City in number of theaters per capita, the Twin Cities are alive with drama and music. The renowned ⬛**Guthrie Theater,** 818 S. Second St., located in its recently completed Minneapolis venue, draws praise for its mix of daring and classic productions. (☎612-377-2224; www. guthrietheater.org. Shows Aug.-June. Tickets $16-60. Rush tickets 10min. before show $15; line starts 1-1½hr. before show. Box office open daily 10am-8pm.) The historic **State Theatre,** 805 Hennepin Ave., the **Orpheum Theatre,** 910 Hennepin Ave. N., and the **Pantages Theatre,** 710 Hennepin Ave., comprise the **Hennepin Theater District** in downtown Minneapolis. (☎612-339-7007; www.hennepintheaterdistrict.com. Broadway shows $30-80; concerts $25-50. Box office open M-F 10am-6pm, Sa noon-3pm.) The tongue-in-cheek public-radio variety show ⬛**A Prairie Home Companion** is broadcast live from the Fitzgerald Theater, 10 E. Exchange St., in St. Paul. (☎651-290-1200, tickets 290-1221; www.fitzgeraldtheater.org;

http://prairiehome.publicradio.org. Tickets $32-42. Rush tickets available 30min. before shows, but line starts several hours earlier; $15. Box office open Tu-F noon-6pm, Sa 10am-2pm. Shows Sa 4:45pm.) **Brave New Workshop,** 2605 Hennepin Ave., in Uptown, stages comedy shows and improv in an intimate club. (☎612-332-6620; www.bravenewworkshop. com. Tickets $14-27. Box office open M-Th 9:30am-5pm, F 9:30am-8pm, Sa 10am-11pm.)

⬛ NIGHTLIFE

Minneapolis's vibrant youth culture feeds the Twin Cities' nightlife. Anchored by strong post-punk influences, the area's thriving music scene has spawned, among others, Prince, Soul Asylum, Hüsker Dü, and the Replacements. A cross-section of the diverse nightlife options can be found in the downtown **Warehouse District** on Hennepin Ave., in **Dinkytown,** by U of M, and across the river on the west bank (bounded on the west by I-35 W. and to the south by I-94), especially on Cedar Ave. Even the top floor of the Mall of America invites barhopping until the wee hours. The Twin Cities card hard, however, even for cigarettes.

Brit's Pub, 1110 Nicollet Mall (☎612-332-3908; www.britspub.com), between 11th and 12th St. Patrons can play a game of lawn bowling on the rooftop garden ($5 per hr.). 18 different beers, a Stilton burger ($12), and fish and chips ($11.50-16.50) add to the English flavor. Open daily 11am-2am. AmEx/D/MC/V.

The Local, 931 Nicollet Mall (☎612-904-1000; www.the-local.com), at 10th St., in Mineapolis. Irish pub that doubles as a restaurant and bar. Outdoor patio and dark interior make for a mellow and intimate night out. Signature drinks include the famed "Big Ginger" ($6). Open M-F 11am-2am, Sa-Su 9am-2am. AmEx/D/MC/V.

First Ave. and the 7th St. Entry, 701 1st Ave. N. (☎612-332-1775; www.first-avenue.com), in downtown Minneapolis. Rocks with the area's best live music several nights a week, including concerts with the hottest rock bands in the nation. Music from grunge to world beat. Cover $6-30. Open daily 5pm-3am. AmEx/MC/V.

The Gay 90s, 408 Hennepin Ave. (☎612-333-7755; www.gay90s.com), at 4th St. This gigantic complex hosts gay and lesbian revelers in its 8 bars, though the straight crowd is also sizable. 2-for-1 drinks M 9pm-1am. Drag shows W-Su 9:15pm. M-Tu and F-Sa 21+, W-Th and Su 18+. Cover after 9pm $3-5. Open M-Sa 8am-2am, Su 10am-2am.

OUTDOORS

In the land of 10,000 lakes Minneapolis boasts many of its own: the city contains 22 lakes, along with 150 parks and 100 golf courses. **Lake Calhoun,** on the west end of Lake St., is the largest of the bunch and a recreational paradise. Scores of in-line skaters, bicyclists, and runners loop the lake on all but the coldest days. Encircled by stately mansions, the serene **Lake of the Isles** has lovely views but no public access to the water. Just southeast of Lake Calhoun on Sheridan St., **Lake Harriet** lures the locals with tiny paddle boats and a band shell with free concerts on summer nights. The city maintains 28 mi. of lakeside trails around the three lakes for strolling and biking. **Calhoun Rentals,** 1622 W. Lake St., three blocks east of Lake Calhoun, rents out bikes for exploring the paths. (☎612-827-8231; www.calhounrental.com. $25-40 per day. Credit card and driver's license required. Open daily in summer 9am-7pm, in winter 10am-6pm.) At the northeast corner of Lake Calhoun, the **Tin Fish,** 3000 Calhoun Pkwy. E., offers canoe, kayak, and paddle-boat rentals on the side of the restaurant pavilion. (☎612-555-1234; www.thetinfish.com. All boats $10 per hr. $20 deposit and driver's license or credit card required. Open M-Sa 11am-9pm, Su 11am-7pm.) **Minnehaha Park** offers striking views of the impressive **Minnehaha Falls,** immortalized in Longfellow's *Song of Hiawatha.* The falls are located off Minnehaha Ave. at Minnehaha Pkwy.

FESTIVALS

In late January and early February, the **Saint Paul Winter Carnival,** near the state capitol, cures cabin fever with ice sculptures, ice fishing, skating contests, and a giant ice palace. On July 4, St. Paul celebrates the **Taste of Minnesota** with fireworks, concerts, and regional and ethnic cuisine from local vendors. The **Minneapolis Riverfront Fourth of July Celebration and Fireworks** is a day for the family with trolley rides, concerts, food, and fireworks. (☎612-378-1226; www.minneapolis-riverfront.com.) On its coattails rides the 10-day **Minneapolis Aquatennial,** which has concerts and art exhibits glorifying the lakes. (☎612-518-3486; www.aquatennial.org.) In the two weeks prior to Labor Day, everyone heads to the nation's largest state fair, the **Minnesota State Fair,** at Snelling and Como St., in St. Paul. (☎651-288-4427; www.mnstatefair.org. $9, ages 5-12 $8, under 5 free.)

THE ROAD TO LE SUEUR: 57 MI.

From Minneapolis, take **I-35 West** south to **I-494 West.** Continue along **US 169 South** to Le Sueur.

LE SUEUR ☎507

Entering Le Sueur along US 169, drivers are greeted by a monstrous billboard cutout of the **Jolly Green Giant** and Sprout (his diminutive pea-pod pal) standing guard over the valley, much like in the commercials. The valley is just as you'd expect, with rolling green hills covered in bushy trees and farmland. The **Le Sueur Museum,** 709 N. Second St., documents the history of the Green Giant. Exhibits, videos, and jolly green statues tell the history of the canning company, from its start in 1903 under CN Cosgrove to its purchase in 1979 by the Pillsbury Company. (☎507-665-2050. Open Memorial Day to Labor Day Tu-F 10am-4:30pm, Sa 1-4:30pm. Free.) The **WW Mayo House,** 118 N. Main St., is where Dr. William Worrall Mayo set up his medical practice in 1859. Tours of the house given by costumed interpreters relate the lives of the two famous families who called it home. (☎507-665-3250; www.mayohouse.org. Open June-Aug. Tu-F 10am-4:30pm; Sept.-Nov. and late May Sa 1-4:30pm. $3, children $1, seniors $2.)

THE ROAD TO ST. PETER: 11 MI.

Continue along **US 169,** which enters St. Peter from the north as **North Minnesota Avenue.**

ST. PETER ☎507

St. Peter lures visitors with the beauty of the Minnesota River Valley and surrounding bluffs. One of Minnesota's oldest cities, St. Peter is built on the rich black soil that makes the surrounding area some of the most fertile farmland in the country. **Gustavus Adolphus College** was founded here in 1876, and the 2500-student college is one of the best private liberal-arts colleges in the Midwest. It hosts the annual **Nobel Conference** on the first Tuesday and Wednesday of October, the first ongoing educational conference in the US to earn official authorization from the Nobel Foundation. The **Treaty Site History Center,** 1851 N. Minnesota Ave., has exhibits on the treaty in which the Sioux transferred much of the Dakota Territory to the US. It's located 1 mi. north of St. Peter at the intersection of US 169 and Rte. 22 W. (☎507-934-2160. Open Tu-Sa 10am-4pm, Su 1-4pm. $3, ages 13-18 $0.50, under 13 free.) The adjacent **Traverse des Sioux State Historic Site** is a short trail with interpretive signs leading to the site of the signing, an ancient Minnesota River crossing. (Open May-Oct. daily dawn-dusk.) At **Whiskey River ❸,** on Rte. 99, just east of town over the bridge, you can stick to the classic Whiskey River burger ($10) or expand your horizons with the beer-cheese soup ($4), made from Wisconsin cheese. (☎507-934-5600; www.riversp. com. Live music F. Open M-Th 11am-9:30pm, F 11am-10:30pm, Sa 7am-10:30pm, Su 9am-9:30pm. AmEx/D/MC/V.)

> **PHOTO OP.** Before you leave St. Peter, get your picture taken at the **Pearly Gates,** located next to the Chamber of Commerce, 101 S. Front St., at Rte. 99.

◪ THE ROAD TO NEW ULM: 28 MI.

Take **US 169** out of St. Peter. Turn onto **Route 99 West** headed toward Nicollet. In Nicollet, Rte. 99 meets **US 14** and continues west to New Ulm. Follow **County Road 37** into the southeastern section of New Ulm and turn right onto **Broadway,** the main drag in town.

NEW ULM ☎ 507

German heritage is still evident in this small city full of manicured yards and well-kept homes. New Ulm's **August Schell's Brewery,** 1860 Schells Rd., founded in 1860, is the second-oldest family-owned brewery in the US. Today, the fifth generation of Schells crafts the acclaimed beer in the original brewery.

Head south on Broadway and turn west on 18th St. (☎507-354-5528 or 800-770-5020; www.schellsbrewery.com. Open in summer daily 11am-5pm; in winter Sa-Su noon-3pm. Tours in summer M-F 2:30, 4pm, Sa-Su 1, 2, 3, 4pm; in winter Sa-Su 1, 2:30pm. $3, under 13 free.) The **New Ulm Glockenspiel,** at Fourth St. N. and Minnesota St., guards the city center. Three times each day (noon, 3, 5pm) the stage door slides up and entertains viewers with wood carvings that move mechanically to the chiming bells. The 45 ft. tall clock is one of the world's only freestanding carillon clock towers. The enormous **Hermann Monument,** at Center and Monument St., honors the hero Hermann, who liberated Germany from the Romans. (☎507-359-8344. Open from Memorial Day to Labor Day daily 10am-7pm. $1.25 to climb to the top.) The **Heritage Tree,** at First and Minnesota St., was planted in 2004 to celebrate New Ulm's 150th anniversary. These are common decorations in German villages that tell local history in a public manner.

The small **Colonial Inn ❸,** 1315 N. Broadway, west of town, has 24 basic units with air conditioning and refrigerators. (☎507-354-3128. Rooms start at $49. AmEx/D/MC/V.) **Veigel's Kaiserhoff ❸,** 221 N. Minnesota St., has been a New Ulm institution and "home to those famous barbecue ribs" for over 65 years. Its first order of barbecue ribs sold for $0.45, but today you'll have to fork over $9-17. Jukeboxes sit by each table, so you can impose your musical taste on everyone in the dining room for just a quarter. (☎507-359-2071. Open daily 11am-9pm. D/MC/V.)

◪ THE ROAD TO SLEEPY EYE: 14 MI.

From Broadway, take **US 14 West.** Just after leaving New Ulm, you will see your first Wall Drug sign, one of many on the trip toward Wall, South Dakota. The landscape also loses its rolling green hills and settles into flatness as you prepare to cross the Great Plains. US 14 passes through Sleepy Eye as **Main Street.**

SLEEPY EYE ☎ 507

Sleepy Eye is named after a Dakota chief with droopy eyelids, Ish Tak Ha Ba. The **Sleepy Eye Depot Museum,** 100 Oak St. NW, displays artifacts from the Sleepy Eye area, including a permanent display about the state-champion drum-and-bugle corps. Next to the Depot Museum is a granite obelisk erected in honor of Chief Sleepy Eye. Turn right one block before the main intersection downtown. (☎507-794-5053. Open May-Dec. Tu-Sa 10am-4pm. Free.) **Sleepy Eye Lake** features swimming beaches, parks, picnic areas, boat landings, and a new 3 mi. bike path around the lake. As you're driving out of town, don't miss the **Linus Statue** in front of the Dyckman Library on US 14. Linus Mauer, a Sleepy Eye native and friend of Charles Schulz, the creator of the Peanuts comic, was the inspiration for Charlie Brown's highly intelligent and blanket-loving best friend. Info is available at the Sleepy Eye **Chamber of Commerce**, 115 Second Ave NE. (☎507-794-4731 or 800-290-0588. Open M-F 9am-4pm.)

◨ DETOUR
JEFFERS PETROGLYPHS

27160 County Road 2. Take **US 14 West** to **US 71 South.** Go 3 mi. east on Cottonwood **County Road 10** and travel 1 mi. south on **County Road 2.**

The Jeffers Petroglyphs are some of Minnesota's most intriguing artifacts. Native Americans carved records into these islands of exposed rock nearly 5000 years ago. The rock outcroppings feature bison, turtles, thunderbirds, human figures, and other images frozen in time. (☎507-628-5591. Open from Memorial Day to Labor Day M-F 10am-5pm, Sa 10am-8pm, Su noon-5pm; Sept. and May F-Sa 10am-5pm, Su noon-5pm; Oct.-Apr. by appointment. $6, ages 6-12 $4, seniors $5.)

⛟ THE ROAD TO PIPESTONE: 91 MI.
Continue west on **US 14** until it intersects with **Route 23** 7 mi. past Balaton. Take Rte. 23 S. to Pipestone.

PIPESTONE   ☎507
The historic downtown of Pipestone has a decidedly different flavor than any other Midwestern town; many of the buildings were crafted from the Sioux Quartzite mined in the town quarries. The **Pipestone National Monument,** 36 Reservation Ave., provides relief from the surrounding plains. The monument is a Native American quarry, where visitors can watch pipes and carvings being crafted. The **Circle Tour** (¾ mi.) leads past Winnewissa Falls,

Leaping Rock, and a marker from the Nicollet expedition. (☎507-825-5464; www.nps.gov/pipe. Open daily in summer 8am-6pm; in winter 8am-5pm. $3, under 16 free.) Constructed in 1888, the **Calumet Inn ❹,** 104 West Main St., is now a historical landmark. (☎507-825-5871 or 800-535-761. Rooms in summer $72-103; in winter $82-133. AmEx/D/MC/V.)

⛟ THE ROAD TO MADISON: 43 MI.
Follow **Route 30** to **Route 34.**

MADISON   ☎605
Madison's proximity to Lake Madison and Lake Herman, the second-most-visited state park in South Dakota, makes it ideal for a stop. The city is also home to the 1800-student **Dakota State University.** Two miles west of Madison, the **Prairie Village,** at Rte. 34 and Rte. 81, is a living history museum built as a pioneer town. Over 50 buildings have been moved into the village and restored in their original decor. Attractions include a steam carousel, a sod house, and a working railroad. (☎605-256-3644 or 800-693-3644; www.prairievillage.org. Open from late May to Sept. M-Sa 10am-5pm, Su 11am-6pm. $5, ages 6-12 $2, under 5 free, seniors $4.50.)

Since any lake in South Dakota is a welcome sight, **Lake Herman State Park ❶,** 23409 State Park Dr., has been a popular camping area for hundreds of years. Before settlers arrived, it was a stopover for Native Americans traveling to nearby quarries. The grounds boast fishing, boating, swimming, hiking, and 72 campsites with electricity, showers, and dump stations. (☎605-256-5003, reservations 800-710-2267; www.campsd.com. Open for day use May-Sept. 6am-11pm; Oct.-Apr. 6am-9pm. Sites $10, with electricity $14. Cabins $32. Day use $5 per vehicle. Cash only.)

⛟ THE ROAD TO CHAMBERLAIN: 142 MI.
Continue on **Route 34/US 81.** Just past Howard, fields of corn become untamed grassland—the real

backbone of the plains that stretch across the Midwest. Drive west on **Route 34** until you hit **Route 45.** Turn left to go south on Rte. 45 until you reach **I-90** and head west.

CHAMBERLAIN ☎ 605

Nearly 200 years ago, the Lewis and Clark expedition spent three days at Camp Pleasant watching thousands of bison graze on the nearby bluffs. The **Lewis and Clark Information Center**, off I-90 at mile marker 264, is accessible from both the east and west. It offers information on these early "rivertrippers" and offers panoramic views of the Missouri River Valley. (☎605-895-2188. Open May-Oct. daily 8am-6pm. Free.) One of Chamberlain's main sights is the **Akta Lakota Museum,** 1301 N. Main St., at St. Joseph's Indian School. Akta Lakota means "to honor the people," and the museum honors the Lakota people, offering a living lesson on how their culture has changed over the past few centuries. (☎605-234-3452 or 800-798-3452; www.aktalakota.org. Open from Memorial Day to Labor Day M-Sa 8am-6pm, Su 9am-5pm; from Labor Day to Memorial Day M-F 8am-5pm.)

The **Derby Cafe ❶,** 138 S. Main St., is a relatively new addition to Chamberlain. On Friday and Saturday evenings the cafe has steak dinners ($11-17); the rest of the week it serves up breakfast, sandwiches ($5), soups, and the best espresso within 100 mi. (☎605-234-1380. Open M-Th 7am-6pm, F-Sa 7am-9pm. D/MC/V.) Just across the river in Oacoma lies the "largest stop for 200 mi.," the immense and sprawling **Al's Oasis,** Exit 260 off I-90, which features, for starters, a general store, bakery, bank, grocery store, motel, campground, and restaurant. Despite its questionable quaffability, the $0.05 coffee is still a deal. (☎605-234-6054; www.alsoasis.com.)

🚗 **THE ROAD TO MURDO: 73 MI.**
Continue west on **I-90** to **Exit 192.**

MURDO ☎ 605

At the **Pioneer Auto Museum,** Exit 192 off I-90, there are over 275 vehicles and an eclectic mix of Americana, including the only surviving "General Lee" from *The Dukes of Hazzard.*

GREAT NORTH MAP #11

GREAT NORTH

Recent acquisitions include a car made entirely from wood, but the museum's pride and joy remains Elvis's '76 Harley. (☎605-669-2691; www.pioneerautoshow.com. Open from Memorial Day to Labor Day 7am-10pm; hours vary in winter. $9, ages 6-13 $4.50, under 6 free.)

 TIME CHANGE. Just after Murdo, I-90 enters the Mountain Time Zone, where it is 1hr. earlier.

◪ **THE ROAD TO MIDLAND: 24 MI.**
Continue west on **I-90** to **Exit 170.**

MIDLAND ☎ 605

As you pass into the Mountain Time Zone and set your watch back, you may think you've gone a little too far when you see the statue of Lulu, the *T. rex* guarding Exit 170 near the **1880 Town and Longhorn Ranch.** The town showcases a collection of transplanted buildings from an early South Dakota town. The buildings range from Indian relics to a 14-sided barn built in 1919. A museum houses more valuable collections, including Buffalo Bill memorabilia, a tribute to Casey Tibbs, the 19-time world champion rodeo cowboy, and movie props from *Dances with Wolves.* (☎605-344—2387. Open daily June-Aug. 6am-sunset; Sept. 7am-sunset; Oct. and May 8am-sunset. $8, ages 13-18 $5, ages 6-12 $4, under 5 free, seniors $7.)

◪ **THE ROAD TO THE BADLANDS: 69 MI.**
Continue west on **I-90** until you reach **Exit 131.** Follow **Route 240 West** toward Badlands National Park.

THE BADLANDS ☎ 605

When they first saw these mountainous rock formations rising out of the prairie, early explorers were less than enthusiastic. General Alfred Sully called the arid and treacherous formations "Hell with the fires out," and the French translated the Sioux name for the area, *mako sica,* as *les mauvaises terres,* meaning "bad lands." Late spring and fall in the Badlands offer pleasant weather that can be a relief from the extreme temperatures of mid-summer and winter; however, even at

their worst, the Badlands are worth a visit. Deposits of iron oxide lend layers of marvelous red and brown hues to the land, and the moods of the Badlands change with the time, season, and weather. According to geologists, they erode about 2 in. every year. At that rate they will disappear in 500,000 years—hurry and visit before it's too late.

VITAL STATS

Area: 244,000 acres

Tourist Offices: The Ben Reifel Visitors Center (☎605-433-5361; www.nps.gov/badl), 5 mi. inside the park's northeastern entrance. Open daily from June to mid-Aug. 7am-7pm; from mid-Aug. to mid-Oct. and from mid-Apr. to May 8am-5pm; from mid-Oct. to mid-Apr. 9am-4pm. **White River Visitors Center** (☎605-455-2878), 55 mi. to the southwest, off Rte. 27, in the park's less visited southern section. Open in summer daily 10am-4pm.

Gateway Towns: Wall (p. 264), **Kadoka,** and **Interior.**

Fees: $15 per vehicle.

◪ **ORIENTATION**

Badlands National Park lies just south of I-90. The highlight of the park is the amazing drive along the 31 mi. long ◪**Badlands Loop Scenic Byway (Route 240),** between Exit 131 and Exit 110, off I-90. The road winds in and out of the rock formations of the North Unit, offering stunning vistas of the White River drainage area. Go during the evening for your best chance to beat the summer heat and crowds, see wildlife, and catch the colorful hues of the sunset against the rocks. The gravel **Sage Creek Rim Road,** west of Rte. 240, has fewer people and more animals, although it can be tough on your car. Highlights include the Roberts Prairie Dog Town and the park's herds of bison and antelope; across the river from Sage Creek campground lies another prairie-dog town and popular bison territory.

◪ **ACCOMMODATIONS**

In addition to standard lodging and camping, backcountry camping allows an intimate introduction to this austere landscape, but be sure to bring water. Campers are strongly urged to contact one of the rangers at the visitors center before heading out and to be careful of bison, which can be extremely dangerous. Sleeping under the stars is a significantly more wallet-friendly option around the Badlands.

Badlands Motel & Campground, 900 Rte. 377 (☎605-433-5335 or 800-388-4643), south of the park in Interior. Open May to mid-Oct. Campsites from $16. Rooms from $56. ❸

Cedar Pass Lodge, 1 Cedar St. (☎605-433-5460; www.cedarpasslodge.com), next to the Ben Reifel Visitors Center. Cabins with A/C and showers. Reservations recommended. Open from mid-Apr. to mid-Oct. Cabins with private bath $79-110; 2-bedroom with shared bath $94-150; cottages $105-157. AmEx/D/MC/V. ❸

Cedar Pass Campground, south of the Ben Reifel Visitors Center. Sites with water and flush toilets but no showers. It's best to get there before 6pm in summer, since sites fill before evening. At this National Park service campground, no reservations are accepted. Sites $10. Cash only. ❶

Sage Creek Campground, 13 mi. from the Pinnacles entrance south of Wall. Take Sage Creek Rim Rd. off Rte. 240. Lies on a flat open field in the prairie with pit toilets and no water. No reservations taken. Free. ❶

🔥 FOOD

Cuny Table Cafe (☎605-455-29578), 8 mi. west of the White River Visitors Center, on Rte. 2. Truly in the middle of nowhere. The restaurant is packed at lunchtime. Try the Indian Tacos (fry bread piled with veggies, beans, and beef) for $5. Open daily 5:30am-5:30pm. Cash only. ❶

Cedar Pass Lodge Restaurant (☎605-433-5460), near the Ben Reifel Visitors Center. Buffalo burgers ($4.95), fry bread ($2.50), and fantastic views to the north. Open daily in summer 7am-9pm; in fall 8am-4:30pm. AmEx/D/MC/V. ❶

🧭 HIKING

The 244,000-acre park protects large tracts of prairie and stark rock formations. **Hiking** is permitted throughout the entire park, although officials discourage climbing on the formations and request that you stick to high-use trails. The south unit is mostly uncharted territory, and the occasional path is most likely the tracks of wildlife. Five hiking trails begin off Loop Rd. near the Ben

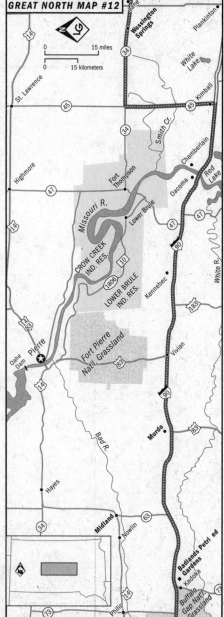

GREAT NORTH MAP #12

GREAT NORTH

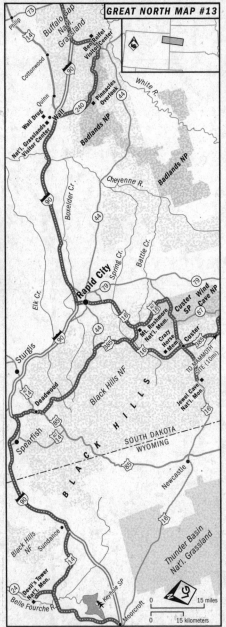

GREAT NORTH MAP #13

Reifel Visitors Center. The **Notch Trail** (1½ mi., 1-2hr.) demands sure-footedness and the will to climb a shaky ladder at a 45° angle. Not for the faint of heart, the trail traverses narrow ledges before making its way to the grand finale: an unbelievable view of the Cliff Shelf and White River Valley. The moderate **Cliff Shelf Nature Trail** (½ mi., 30min.) consists of stairs, a boardwalk, and unpaved paths. It is your best bet for coming face to face with wildlife. The **Door Trail** (¾ mi., 20min.) cuts through buttes and crevices for spectacular views of the countryside. The **Window Trail** (¼ mi., 10min.), more of a scenic overlook than an actual hike, consists of a wheelchair-accessible ramp that leads to a splendid overlook.

PHOTO OP. The Ranch Store, off Exit 131 on the eastern entrance to the Badlands Loop, has the **World's Largest Prairie Dog.** And no, it won't dig tunnels in your backyard or eat your flowers—it's a six-ton statue. Out back behind the gift shop, they have the real thing; a maze of prairie-dog tunnels populated by hungry dogs. For $0.50 you can buy a bag of peanuts to keep 'em satisfied. (☎605-433-5477. Open June-Sept. daily 7:30am-8pm.)

THE ROAD TO WALL: 39 MI.
Head out of the park on **Route 240 West** to Wall.

WALL ☎605

Wall is world famous for the presence of ⬛**Wall Drug**, 510 Main St. You absolutely can't miss it, because the highway is lined for hundreds of miles in either direction with Wall Drug billboards and Wall Drug signs, most of them erected by enterprising individuals. Signs have been seen on the Paris Métro, the buses of London, and rail lines in Kenya, at the Taj Majal, the Great Wall of China, and both poles. At the actual store, you can purchase nearly anything, especially if it's useless and has your name on it. Opened in 1931 as a small-town drug store, it has turned into a sprawling complex that includes innumerable novelty shops, an arcade, an 80 ft. dinosaur, and a guitar and banjo played by a machine.

Stop by, if only for the free ice water or exceptionally quaffable ▨$.05 coffee. (☎605-279-2175; www.walldrug.com. Open daily 6:30am-10pm.) Two blocks south of Wall Drug is the **Buffalo Gap National Grassland Visitors Center,** 708 Main St., whose slogan is, "Anyone can love the mountains, but it takes soul to love the prairie." The 591,000-acre grassland is one of 20 national grasslands and includes intermingled bits of the Badlands. There are no established hiking trails, but you can mountain bike, ATV, hunt, fish, and birdwatch in designated areas. (☎605-279-2125. Open M-F 8am-4:30pm. Free.) The **Sunshine Inn ❸,** 608 Main St., offers basic rooms with air conditioning and cable TV. (☎605-279-2178; www.sunshineinnatwallsd.com. Rooms in summer $57-67; in winter $47-57. AmEx/D/MC/V.)

◪ THE ROAD TO RAPID CITY: 56 MI.

From Wall, travel west on **I-90** to Rapid City. Downtown Rapid City is located off **Exit 57.**

RAPID CITY   ☎605

Rapid City's location makes it a convenient base from which to explore the surrounding attractions; Mount Rushmore, Crazy Horse, the Black Hills, and the Badlands are all within an hour's drive of downtown. As the second-largest city in South Dakota, Rapid City also offers the most amenities in the region. The area welcomes three million tourists each summer—over 50 times the city's population.

✦ ORIENTATION

Rapid City's roads are laid out in a sensible grid, making driving along its wide streets easy. **Saint Joseph Street** and **Main Street** are the main east and west thoroughfares, respectively, and **Omaha Street** is two-way. **Mount Rushmore Road (US 16)** is the main north-south route. Many north-south roads are numbered, and numbers increase from east to west, beginning at **East Boulevard.**

7000 MILES TO WALL DRUG

Buying a tiny drugstore in the middle of South Dakota during the depths of the Great Depression might not have been the most auspicious beginning for a world-famous enterprise, but Ted Hustead, founder of Wall Drug, succeeded nonetheless. Nearly 80 years after its establishment, Wall Drug has grown to immense proportions. The giant Western-themed complex now includes a wedding chapel, an 80 ft. dinosaur, and an art museum. When Ted and his wife Dorothy purchased Wall Drug in 1931, they believed that they had received divine instructions to set up shop in Wall. After five years with only an unreliable trickle of customers, however, even they were began to doubt the future of their store. The tide turned almost immediately, however, when Dorothy had an idea. By putting up signs advertising free ice water, she hoped to lure some potential customers out of the heat. Within hours, the plan had worked—little by little, thirsty travelers began to swing by, and the rest is history. Amid the hoopla, the store still serves thousands of glasses of ice water each summer afternoon. Wall Drug has built its fortune on Dorothy's idea of highway advertising, and its catchy billboards can be seen for hundreds of miles around and across the world.

ACCOMMODATIONS

Rapid City accommodations are expensive in summer, and motels often fill weeks in advance, especially during the **Sturgis Motorcycle Rally** in mid-August. Budget motels surround the junction of I-90 and Rte. 59 by the Rushmore Mall. Camping is available at **Badlands National Park** (p. 262), **Black Hills National Forest**, and **Custer State Park** (p. 268).

Big Sky Lodge, 4080 Tower Rd. (☎605-348-3200 or 800-318-3208), 5min. south of town on a service road, off Mt. Rushmore Rd. The rooms are clean and the doubles have great views of Rapid City and the surrounding valley. Free Wi-Fi. From mid-June to mid-Aug. singles from $79; doubles from $95. Call ahead in winter. D/MC/V. ❹

FOOD

Millstone Family Restaurant, 2010 W. Main St. (☎605-343-5824), at Mountain View Rd. Cooks up large portions of chicken for $7-9, spaghetti and meatballs for $8, and pork ribs for $10. Open daily 6am-11pm. AmEx/D/MC/V. ❷

Black Hills Bagels, 913 Mt. Rushmore Rd. (☎605-399-1277; www.blackhillsbagels.com), south of downtown. Over 20 varieties of homemade bagels, sandwiches ($8), and free Wi-Fi. Open M-F 6am-3pm, Sa-Su 7am-3pm. ❶

Firehouse Brewing Company, 610 Main St. (☎605-348-1915; www.firehousebrewing.com). The company brews several beers and serves sandwiches, burgers, and salads ($7.50-11) in a restored 1915 firehouse. Smokejumper Stout ($3.75). Nightly live music. Open M-Sa 11am-2am, Su 11am-midnight. AmEx/MC/V. ❷

SIGHTS

Much in South Dakota during tourist season can be expensive, but Rapid City abounds in free attractions. Try a jaunt up **Skyline Drive** for a bird's-eye view of the city or check out the seven concrete dinosaurs of **Dinosaur Park**. In **Memorial Park,** see America's largest **Berlin Wall exhibit,** featuring two 12 ft. pieces of the wall. The **Journey Museum,** 222 New York St., traces the history of the Black Hills, detailing the geology, archaeology, and people of the region, with skull castings of a *Tyran-*

nosaurus rex, a holographic story tent, and a mercantile trading post. (☎605-394-6923; www.journeymuseum.org. Open daily in summer 9am-5pm; in winter M-Sa 10am-5pm, Su 1-5pm. $7, ages 11-17 $5, seniors $6.) Just in case the 39 who missed the cut for Mt. Rushmore feel slighted, the **City of Presidents** is an ongoing project to place life-size bronze statues of every president at intersections in Rapid City. Tip your hat at James Monroe in front of the **Presidents Information Center,** 631 Main St., as you pick up your free map. The center also offers presidentially-themed books, ice cream, and sodas, making this the only place in the world where you can buy a Richard M. Nixon Root Beer. (☎605-484-2162. Open June-Sept. M-Sa noon-9pm. Free.) The 8 mi. **Rapid City Recreational Path** runs along Rapid Creek. Park at the Civic Center and pick up the path in Memorial Park.

> **TIP**
>
> **HOG HEAVEN.** Unless you've got a Harley underneath you, the Black Hills are best avoided during the first two weeks in August, when the Sturgis Rally takes over the area. Nearly 500,000 motorcyclists roar through the hills, filling up campsites and motels and bringing traffic to a standstill.

DETOUR
REPTILE GARDENS

On **US 16,** 5 mi. south of Rapid City. Look for a huge dome on the right side of the street.

Reptile Gardens was opened in the winter of 1937 (4 years before Mt. Rushmore was completed) by Earl Brockelsby, who noted that the biggest draw at other attractions was the thrill of seeing a rattlesnake close up. Reptile Gardens is more fun than your average zoo: an enormous Australian croc named "Maniac," giant tortoises, komodo dragons, and exhibits like "death row," which is filled with the world's most poisonous snakes, keep visitors on their toes. Non-reptiles aren't ignored; the herpetarium features a bald eagle, prairie dogs, and a large exhibit of enormous bugs. (☎605-342-5873 or 800-335-0275; www.reptilegardens.com. Open Apr.-Dec. daily 8am-7pm;

GREAT NORTH

hours vary in spring and fall. $13.50, ages 5-12 $8.50, under 5 free, seniors $12.)

◼ DETOUR
BLACK HILLS NATIONAL FOREST

US 16 snakes toward Custer through the Black Hills.

The Lakota called this region "Paha Sapa," meaning Black Hills, for the hue that the Ponderosa pines take on from a distance. The region was considered to be so sacred that the Lakota would visit but never settle. The Treaty of 1868 gave the Black Hills and the rest of South Dakota west of the Missouri River to the tribe, but, when gold was discovered here in the 1870s, the US government snatched back 6000 sq. mi. Today, the area attracts millions of visitors with a trove of natural treasures and is protected by an assortment of state and national parks, monuments, and forests. Mining, logging, ranching, and recreation all take place in close proximity. The forest itself provides opportunities for backcountry hiking, swimming, biking, and camping, as do park-run campgrounds and tent sites. **Forest Service Visitor Centers** are available on US 385 at Pactola Lake (☎605-343-8755. Open from late May to early Sept. daily 8am-5pm) and in Rapid City (p. 265). **Backcountry camping ❶** in the national forest is free and allowed 1 mi. away from any campground or visitors center and at least 200 ft. from the side of the road. Leave your car in a parking lot or just pull off. Open fires are prohibited, but fires in provided grates are allowed. Campgrounds include: **Pactola ❶**, on the Pactola Reservoir just south of the junction of Rte. 44 and US 385; **Sheridan Lake ❶**, 5 mi. northeast of Hill City on US 385; and **Roubaix Lake ❶**, 14 mi. south of Lead on US 385. All three have some sites in winter. All national forest campgrounds are quiet and wooded and offer fishing, swimming, and pit toilets. (☎877-444-6777; www.reserveusa.com. No hookups. Sites $17-20. Cash only.) The Wyoming side of the forest permits campfires and horses and draws fewer visitors.

◪ THE ROAD TO MT. RUSHMORE: 23 MI.

Traveling from Rapid City through the Black Hills along **US 16,** you'll pass the town of Keystone. Just after Keystone, turn west (right) onto **Route 244,** which will lead to Mt. Rushmore after 2 mi.

MOUNT RUSHMORE ☎605

◪**Mount Rushmore National Memorial** boasts the faces that launched a thousand minivans. Historian Doane Robinson originally conceived of this "shrine of democracy" in 1923 as a memorial for frontier heroes; sculptor Gutzon Borglum chose four presidents instead. In 1941, the 60 ft. heads of Washington, Jefferson, Theodore Roosevelt, and Lincoln were "finished" due to Borglum's death. The **Info Center** details the monument's history and has ranger tours every hour on the half-hour. A state-of-the-art **visitors center** chronicles the local history and the lives of the featured presidents. (Info center ☎605-574-3198, visitors center 574-3165. Both open daily in summer 8am-10pm; in winter 8am-5pm. Parking $10.) From the visitors center, it's half a mile along the wood boardwalk of the **Presidential Trail** to **Borglum's Studio.** (Open in summer daily 9am-6pm. Ranger talks every hr.) In summer, the **Mount Rushmore Memorial Amphitheater** hosts a patriotic speech and film nightly at 9pm, and lights flood the monument 9:30-10:30pm. (☎605-574-2523; www.nps.gov/moru. Trail lights extinguished at 11pm.)

Horsethief Campground ❶ lies between Mt. Rushmore and Custer State Park on Hwy. 87 in the Black Hills National Forest. President George HW Bush fished here in 1993; rumor has it that the lake was overstocked with fish to guarantee presidential success. (☎605-574-2668, reservations 800-657-5802; www.horsethief.com. Water and flush toilets. Reservations recommended on weekends. Sites from late May to early Sept. $18, with electricity $24.50, with full hookup $33.50-37. Cash only.) The commercial **Mount Rushmore KOA/Palmer Gulch Lodge ❷,** 7 mi. west of Mt. Rushmore, on Rte. 244, has campsites, cabins, two pools, a spa, nightly movies, a small strip mall, pancake breakfasts, and $3 shuttles to Mt. Rushmore. (☎605-574-2525 or 800-562-8503; www.palmergulch.com. Free Wi-Fi. Reservations recommended. Open May-Sept. Tent sites $33-61. AmEx/D/MC/V.)

◪ THE ROAD TO CUSTER STATE PARK: 20 MI.

From Mt. Rushmore, backtrack on **Route 244** to **US 16A/Iron Mountain Road** and head south to Custer State Park. Large RVs (greater than 13 ft., 5 in. wide or 12 ft., 4 in. tall) will need to continue west on Rte. 244

GREAT NORTH

to follow US 16 into the town of Custer and then head east on US 16A to enter the park.

CUSTER STATE PARK ☎ 605

Peter Norbeck, governor of South Dakota in the late 1910s, loved to hike among the thin, towering rock formations that haunt the area south of Sylvan Lake and Mt. Rushmore. In order to preserve the land, he created Custer State Park. The spectacular **Needles Highway (Route 87)** follows his favorite hiking route—Norbeck designed this road to be especially narrow and winding so that newcomers could experience the pleasures of discovery. For those who love roller-coaster freeways, **Iron Mountain Road (US 16A)** from Mt. Rushmore to near the Norbeck Visitors Center (below) takes drivers through a series of one-lane tunnels, "pigtail" curves, and alpine meadows. The park's **Wildlife Loop Road** twists past prairie-dog towns, bison wallows and corrals, and wilderness areas near prime hiking and camping territory. Pronghorns, elk, deer, and burros loiter by the side of the road, and traffic will often stop while some of Custer's 1500 bison cross the road. Don't get out—bison are dangerous. At 7242 ft., **Harney Peak** is the highest point east of the Rockies and west of the Pyrenees. An ascent requires a strenuous 6 mi. round-trip hike. The 3 mi. **Sunday Gulch Trail** offers the most amazing scenery of all the park's hikes. The park also provides 30 lower-altitude trails. At **Sylvan Lake,** on Needles Hwy., you can hike, fish, boat, or canoe. (☎605-575-2561. Paddle boats $5 per 30min.) Fishing is allowed anywhere in the park, but a South Dakota fishing license is required. ($16 per day, $34 per 3 days.)

The **Peter Norbeck Visitors Center,** on US 16A, half a mile west of the State Game Lodge (where Eisenhower and Coolidge stayed), serves as the park's info center. (☎605-255-4464; www.custerstatepark. info. Open daily June-Aug. 8am-8pm; Sept. 8am-6pm; Oct.-Nov. and Apr.-May 9am-5pm. Weekly entrance pass May-Oct. $5 per person, $12 per vehicle; Nov.-Apr. $2.50/6.) The visitors center offers info about walk-in primitive camping, which is available for $2 per night in the **French Creek Natural Area ❶**. Eight additional **campgrounds ❶** have sites with showers and restrooms. No hookups are provided. (☎800-710-2267; www.campsd.com. Over 200 of the 400+ sites can be reserved; the entire park fills in summer by 3pm. Open daily 7am-9pm. Sites $13-18.) The **Legion Lake Resort,** on US 16A, 6 mi. west of the visitors center, rents mountain bikes. (☎605-255-4521. $10 per hr., $25 per ½-day, $40 per day.) The strong granite of the Needles makes for great rock climbing. For more info, contact **Sylvan Rocks,** in Hill City, 20 mi. north of Custer City. (☎605-484-7585; www.sylvanrocks.com. Open in summer M-Tu and Th-Su 8-10am.)

⚑ DETOUR
MAMMOTH SITE

1800 US 18 Bypass, in Hot Springs. From Custer, take **US 89 South** to **US 18 West.**

The Mammoth Site is the only in situ (bones left as found) mammoth fossil display in America. Remains of more than 50 mammoths have been found among other prehistoric animals that were trapped in a spring-fed sinkhole. The first remains were discovered in 1974 when excavation began for a housing project. (☎605-745-6017; www.mammoth-site.com. Open from mid-May to mid-Aug. daily 8am-8pm; from mid-Aug. to early Sept. daily 8am-6pm; from mid- to late Sept. daily 8am-5pm; Oct. daily 9am-5pm; Nov.-Feb. M-Sa 9am-3:30pm, Su 11am-3:30pm; from Mar. to mid-May daily 8am-5pm. $7.50, ages 5-12 $5.50, seniors $7.) The Mammoth Site is located in the town of Hot Springs, which also boasts a waterfall, a pretty downtown, and a slew of shops, services, and affordable lodging. Even if you're not that into mammoths, the town itself is worth a look.

⚑ DETOUR
WIND CAVE NATIONAL PARK

From Custer, take **Route 89 South** to **US 385 South.** The park is about 18 mi. from Custer.

In the cavern-riddled Black Hills, the subterranean scenery often rivals the sights above ground. After the Black Hills formed from shifting plates of granite, warm water filled the cracked layers of limestone, eroding it to form the fourth-largest cave in the world, discovered in 1821. Bring a sweater on all tours—Wind Cave remains a constant 53°F, while Jewel Cave is 49°F. Scientists estimate that only 5% of the cave's volume has been explored. Wind Cave houses over 95% of the world's "boxwork"—a honeycomb-like lattice of calcite crystals. Five different tours are offered, ranging from a brief scenic walk through the cave to the elite "Wild Cave Tour," which involves 4hr. of "strenuous crawling." (☎605-745-4600. Tours June-Aug. daily 8:40am-6pm; in winter call ahead. Tours $7-23.) The **Wind Cave National Park Visitors Center,** in Hot Springs, can provide more info. (☎605-745-4600; www.nps.gov/wica. Open daily from mid-June to mid-Aug. 8am-7pm; from mid-Aug. to late Sept. and from mid-Apr. to mid-June 8am-6pm; from late Sept. to mid-Oct. 8am-5pm; from Oct. to Apr. hours vary.)

◪ DETOUR
JEWEL CAVE NATIONAL MONUMENT
From Custer, take **US 16** west for 13 mi.

Distinguishing itself from nearby Wind Cave's boxwork, the walls of Jewel Cave are covered with a layer of calcite crystal. Enticed by the cave's twinkling walls, the cave's discoverers filed a mining claim for "jewels" only to realize that giving tours would be more profitable. The popular **Jewel Cave Discovery Tour** gives you a quick peek at the main room of the caverns. ($4, with National Parks Pass free.) The **Scenic Tour** (½ mi., 1¼ hr., 723 stairs) highlights chambers with the most interesting formations. (In summer every 20min. 8:20am-6pm; in winter call ahead. $8, ages 6-16 $4, under 6 free.) The **Lantern Tour** is an illuminating journey that lasts 1¾hr. (In summer every hr. 9am-5pm; in winter call ahead. $8, ages 6-16 $4.) The **Visitors Center,** next to the parking lot, has more information. (☎605-673-2288. Open daily from June to mid-Aug. 8am-7:30pm; from Oct. to mid-May 8am-4:30pm.) The short **Roof Trail** behind the visitors center provides a memorable introduction to the Black Hills through a trek across the "roof" of Jewel Cave.

◪ DETOUR
▓CRAZY HORSE MEMORIAL
Take a left off **Route 385/US 16,** 17 miles to the southwest of Mt. Rushmore.

In 1947, Lakota Chief Henry Standing Bear commissioned sculptor Korczak Ziółkowski to sculpt a memorial to Crazy Horse, a famed warrior who garnered respect by refusing to sign treaties or live on a government reservation. Crazy Horse was stabbed in the back by a white soldier in 1877. At its completion, the Crazy Horse Memorial will be the **world's largest sculpture.** The first blast rocked the hills on June 3, 1948, taking off 10 tons of rock. On the memorial's 50th anniversary, the completed face (all four of the Rushmore heads could fit inside it) was unveiled. With admissions funding 85% of the cost, Ziółkowski's wife Ruth and seven of their 10 children carry on his work, currently concentrating on the horse's head, which will be 219 ft. high. Part of Crazy Horse's arm is also visible, and eventually his entire torso and head, as well as part of his horse, will be carved into the mountain. The memorial includes the **Indian Museum of North America,** the **Sculptor's Studio-Home,** and the **Native American Educational and Cultural Center,** where artisans' works are displayed and sold. The orientation center shows a video entitled "Dynamite and Dreams." (☎605-673-4681; www.crazyhorse.org. Open daily in summer 7am-sunset; in winter 8am-5pm. $10, under 6 free; $27 per vehicle with 3 or more.)

◪ THE ROAD TO DEADWOOD: 66 MI.
Take **US 16 West** towards Custer. In Custer, continue on **US 385 North/16** toward Hill City. Go north on US 385 until you reach Deadwood, making a right onto **US 85 North** to enter downtown.

DEADWOOD ☎ 605
Gunslingers Wild Bill Hickok and Calamity Jane sauntered into Deadwood during the height of the gold rush in the summer of 1876. Bill stayed just long enough—three weeks—to spend eternity here. At her insistence, Jane and Bill now lie side by side in the **Mount Moriah Cemetery,** just south of downtown, off Cemetery St. ($1, ages 5-12 $0.50. Open May-Sept 8am-6pm.) Gambling takes center stage in this authentic western town—casinos line **Main Street,** and many innocent-looking establishments have slot machines and poker tables waiting in the wings. There's live music outside the **Stockade** at the **Buffalo-Bodega Complex,** 658 Main St. (☎605-578-1300), which is packed with throngs of 24hr. gambling spots.

Saloon #10, 657 Main St., was forever immortalized by Wild Bill's murder. Hickok was shot holding black aces and eights, thereafter known as the "dead man's hand." The chair in which he died is on display, and every summer the shooting is reenacted on location. (☎605-578-3346 or 800-952-9398; www.saloon10.com. Open daily 8am-2am. Reenactments in summer daily 1, 3, 5, 7pm.) Onlookers follow the scene outdoors as shootouts happen along Main St. as traffic is rerouted by signs reading "Whoa There, Pardner. Gunfight In Progress." Listen for gunshots and the sound of Calamity Jane's whip.

The chain motels in town are all much more expensive than the **Thunder Cove Inn ❸,** 311 Cliff Ave., off US 85 south of town, which has 30 large rooms with free Wi-Fi and some with reclining chairs. The inn is located at a Deadwood trolley stop. (☎605-578-3045 or 800-209-7361. Rooms $59-99. D/MC/V.) The **Whistler Gulch Campground ❷,** off US 85, has a pool, trolley service to downtown, and showers. (☎605-578-2092 or 800-704-7139; www.whistlergulch.com. Open May-Sept. Sites $22, with full hookup $36. D/MC/V.)

⚑ THE ROAD TO DEVILS TOWER: 77 MI.
Take **US 85 North** to **I-90 West.** Exit I-90 at Sundance. Devils Tower is a short 21 mi. drive from Sundance along **US 14 West.** Turn north onto **Route 24,** and follow it 9 mi. to the visitors center.

DEVILS TOWER NATIONAL MONUMENT ☎307

The massive column that figures so prominently in Native American myths, geological studies, and space alien movies is the centerpiece of ⚑**Devils Tower National Monument,** the nation's first national monument. The tower was formed when molten rock pushed up into the area's existing sedimentary rock. The cooling igneous rock formed a tall mass ribbed with hexagonal columns, and when the surrounding sedimentary rock was eroded by the elements, the tower was exposed. Read about the rock and register to climb it at the **Devils Tower Visitors Center,** 3 mi. from the entrance. (☎307-467-5283; www.nps.gov/deto. Open late May to early Sept. daily 8am-7pm; Mar. to late May and Sept.-Nov. usually 9am-5pm. Entrance fee $10 per vehicle or $5 per person, good for 7 days.) The most popular of the several hiking trails, the paved **Tower Trail** (1¼ mi., 45 min.), loops the monument and provides terrific views of the multi-faceted columns of the tower. The **Red Beds Trail,** a 3 mi., 2 hr. loop, takes hikers up and around the bright red banks of the Belle Fourche River. Hikers can connect with the shorter **Valley View Trail** (½ mi.) for a flat walk through the prairie-dog town and the **South Side Trail** (½ mi.), which climbs back to the bluffs of the Red Beds Trail. The **Joyner Ridge Trail** (1½ mi.) traverses the top of the ridge, providing unique views of the tower from the north and west. The park maintains a **campground ❶** near the Belle Fourche River. (☎307-467-5283. Water, bathrooms, grills, picnic tables, and lots of noisy prairie dogs; no showers. Open roughly Apr.-Oct.; call ahead. Sites $12. Cash only.) For hookups, the **Fort Devils Tower ❶** campground, 601 Rte. 24, just outside the park at the intersection of Rte. 24 and 112, is your cheapest option. (☎307-467-5655. Tent sites $18-28; RV sites $18-28. MC/V.)

⚑ THE ROAD TO GILLETTE: 61 MI.
Take **Route 24 South** to **US 14 West.** Drive past the scenic Keyhole State Park and Reservoir on your way to the interstate; when you get to **I-90** in Moorcroft, go west until you reach Gillette.

GILLETTE ☎307

Gillette is Wyoming's fourth-largest city and proudly calls itself the "Energy Capital of the Nation." Gillette is the commercial hub for the oil, gas, and coal industries, as evinced by the factories outside the city to the east. If it were a country of its own, Campbell County would be the sixth-largest coal-producing nation in the world. The free **Rockpile Museum,** 900 W. Second St., rises above the landscape as a symbol of Gillette's history. One hundred years ago, it marked the end of the cattle drive for weary cowboys, and today it has exhibits on ranching life. The saddles, rifles, and artifacts are impressive, as is the video presentation of explosive surface coal mining. (☎307-682-5723. Open June-Aug. M-Sa 9am-7pm, Su 1-5pm; Sept.-Mar. M-Sa 9am-5pm. Free.)

Lula Belle's Cafe ❶, 101 N. Gillette Ave., offers no-frills eatin' alongside folks in cowboy hats. Breakfast gets no more basic than "Meat and Eggs" ($6.25). Try the burgers for $5-7 or the chicken-fried steak for $8.75. (☎307-682-9798. Open daily 5am-3pm. MC/V.)

⚐ THE ROAD TO BUFFALO: 70 MI.
Between Gillette and Buffalo, jump on **I-90 West.**

BUFFALO   ☎307

Buffalo has a historic main street dating back to 1804, complete with bronze sculptures, murals, and an old-fashioned soda fountain. The city is home to one of the west's premier frontier history museums. The **Jim Gatchell Museum**, 100 Fort St., overflows with 15,000 artifacts from Native Americans, soldiers, and settlers, most of them accumulated by Gatchell himself, a turn-of-the-century pharmacist and confidant of local Indian chiefs. The museum features carefully crafted dioramas of local battles and other historical scenes. (☎307-684-9331; www.jimgatchell.com. Open from mid-Apr. to Sept. daily 9am-6pm. $5, ages 6-17 $3, under 6 free.) Before leaving Buffalo, swing by the **Bighorn National Forest Ranger Office**, 1415 Fort St., where you can obtain maps and information before continuing through the forest to Ten Sleep. (☎307-684-7806. Open M-F 8am-4:30pm.) From the outside, **Grandma's ❷**, 845 Fort St., looks like a motel, but inside it is a rustic restaurant that serves comfort food ($8-9), sandwiches ($6-7), and large breakfasts for $5-7. (☎307-684-0713. Open M 6-11am, W-Sa 6am-3pm, Su 6am-2pm. MC/V.)

⚐ THE ROAD TO TEN SLEEP: 64 MI.
Take the amazingly scenic **US 16 West,** otherwise known as the Cloud Peak Skyway. Make sure your brakes are in good shape before attempting the descent into the stunning Ten Sleep Canyon, wherein rests the hamlet of Ten Sleep.

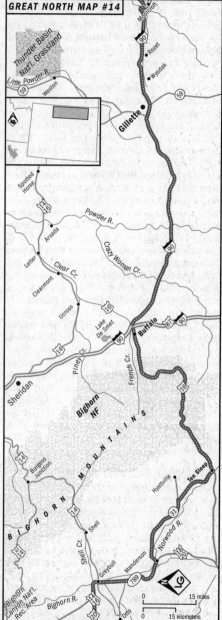

GREAT NORTH MAP #14

GREAT NORTH

TEN SLEEP ☎307

Don't rush to get to Ten Sleep; the town is nothing more than a bit of civilization on the far edge of the **Bighorn National Forest** and the **Bighorn Mountains.** Ten Sleep earned its name because it took the Sioux 10 "sleeps" to travel from there to their main winter camps. The mountains erupt from the hilly pasture land of northern Wyoming, providing a dramatic backdrop for grazing cattle, sprawling ranch houses, and valleys full of wildflowers. Visitors can hike through the woods or follow **US 16** in the south to waterfalls, layers of prehistoric rock, and views above the clouds. Within the forest is the **Cloud Peak Wilderness,** which offers utter solitude. Registration at major trailheads is required to enter the Cloud Peak area. The most convenient access to the wilderness area is from the trailheads off US 16, around 20 mi. west of Buffalo. To get to the top of 13,175 ft. Cloud Peak, most hikers enter at **West Ten Sleep Trailhead,** accessible from Ten Sleep. Thirty-five campgrounds (☎877-444-6777; www.reserve-usa.com) fill the forest. There is no fee to camp at the uncrowded **Elgin Park Trailhead,** 16 mi. west of Buffalo off US 16, which promises good fishing along with parking and toilets. **Doyle Campground ❶,** near a fish-filled creek, has 19 sites with toilets and water. Drive 26 mi. west of Buffalo on US 16, then south 6 mi. on Hazelton Rd./County Rd. 3—it's a rough ride. (☎307-684-7981. Sites $10. Cash only.) Many other campgrounds line US 16. Campgrounds rarely fill up in the Bighorns, but, if they do, free **backcountry camping ❶** is permitted. Contact the Bighorn National Forest's Tongue District for more information (☎307-674-2600).

⚑ THE ROAD TO CODY: 111 MI.

From Ten Sleep, continue on **US 16** for 25 mi. to Worland. Turn right on **North 10th Street,** which is actually US 16 in disguise. Continue heading northwest for 30 mi. through Manderson to the town of Basin. In Basin, turn left onto **C Street,** which becomes **State Route 30** as you head west out of town. Follow SR 30 for 26 mi.; it will bend sharply to the north (right) at the intersection with County Rd. 8 and 40, but stay on SR 30 as it passes through Burlington. When the road ends, turn west (left) on **US 14/16/20 (Greybull Highway)** and proceed 30 mi. to Cody.

CODY ☎307

Cody is named for famed showman Buffalo Bill Cody, who agreed to be buried in the town under the condition that it be renamed in his honor. The town seems to have gotten the better part of the deal, and Buffalo Bill's name and face now adorn a startling number of Cody's businesses, museums, parks, sites, and streets. To this day, as numerous billboards proclaim, Cody is rodeo—a visit to this cowboy town is your best chance to catch the sport.

VITAL STATS

Population: 8800

Tourist Office: Chamber of Commerce Visitors Center, 836 Sheridan Ave. (☎307-587-2777; www.codychamber.org). Open M-F 8am-5pm.

Library and Internet Access: Cody Public Library, 1157 Sheridan Ave. (☎307-527-8820). Open in summer M 9am-8pm, Tu-F 9am-5:30pm, Sa 9am-4pm; in winter M and Th 9am-8pm, Tu-W and F 9am-5:30pm, Sa 9am-4pm.

Post Office: 1301 Stampede Ave. (☎307-527-7161). Open M-F 8am-5:30pm, Sa 9am-noon. **Postal Code:** 82414.

✈ ORIENTATION

Cody is 54 mi. from Yellowstone National Park along the **Buffalo Bill Cody Scenic Byway,** at the junction of **Route 120, US 14A,** and **US 14/16/20.** The town's main drag is **Sheridan Avenue,** which turns into **Yellowstone Avenue** west of town.

⛰ ACCOMMODATIONS

Room rates go up in the summer; the most reasonably priced motels (from around $70 in summer) line W. Yellowstone Ave. **Buffalo Bill State Park** offers two campgrounds on the Buffalo Bill Reservoir. The **North Shore Bay Campground ❶** is located 9 mi. west of town on US 14/16/20. (☎307-527-6274. Sites $12. Day-use $4. Cash only.)

Rainbow Park Motel, 1136 17th St. (☎307-587-6251; www.rainbowparkmotel.com). Wood-paneled rooms. Open Mar.-Nov. In summer singles $60-75; doubles $75-90. Late-fall singles $38-45; doubles $45-60. AmEx/D/MC/V. ❸

GREAT NORTH

Gateway Motel and Campground, 203 Yellowstone Ave. (☎307-587-2561; www.gatewayc-amp.com). 4 one-bed cabins with bath, A/C, cable, and free Wi-Fi. Cabins from $69. ❹

🍴 FOOD

Irma Hotel, 1192 Sheridan Ave. (☎307-587-4221; www.irmahotel.com), at the corner of Sheridan Ave. and 12th St. "Buffalo Bill's Hotel in the Rockies" includes a few restaurants and bars. Grab a bison burger ($6-10) with Irma fries and you'll find yourself suddenly in touch with your inner cowboy. Open daily 6am-10pm. ❷

Beta, 1132 12th St. (☎307-587-7707). Serves affordable cafe fare amid changing displays of local artwork. Open M-F 7am-6pm, Sa-Su 7am-4pm. Cash only. ❶

Peter's Cafe and Bakery (☎307-527-5040), at 12th St. and Sheridan Ave. Cheap breakfasts (three buttermilk pancakes $4.75), pastries ($1), and thick subs from $3.75. Open daily 6:45am-10pm. MC/V. ❶

👁 🏔 SIGHTS AND OUTDOORS

Praised for its breathtaking scenery and Western charm, Cody is home to the longest-running rodeo in the US. For 63 straight years, the **Cody Nite Rodeo** has thrilled audiences every night in summer with bucking broncos, fearless bull riders, steer wrestlers, and more. (☎307-527-9453. Shows June-Aug. 8pm; grounds open at 7pm. $17, ages 7-12 $8.) Over July 4 weekend, the town attracts the country's cowboys when the **Buffalo Bill Cody Stampede** rides into town. (☎307-587-5155 or 800-207-0744; www.codystampederodeo.com. $18. Reservations recommended.) There are street gunfights every afternoon, when 12th St., in front of the Irma Hotel, is blocked off and actors in period attire fire blanks at each other in a noisy, smoky skit. (Daily 6pm.) The **Cody Trolley Tour** offers a 1hr. tour of the city, visiting frontier sites and portraying the Old West. (☎307-527-7043; www.codytrolley-tours.com. Tours depart from the Irma Hotel June-Sept. M-Sa 11am, 3, 6pm, Su 11am, 3pm. $18, ages 5-17 $8, under 5 free, seniors $16.) The highlight of town is the ◪**Buffalo Bill Historical Center,** 720 Sheridan Ave., a complex of five museums with innovative exhibits and

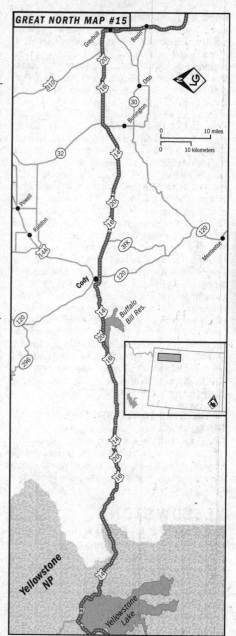

GREAT NORTH MAP #15

Greybull, Basin, Otto, Burlington, Powell, Ralston, Meeteetse, Cody, Buffalo Bill Res., Yellowstone NP, Yellowstone Lake

0 — 10 miles
0 — 10 kilometers

GREAT NORTH

displays. The **Buffalo Bill Museum** showcases local history, while the **Whitney Gallery of Western Art** includes pieces by Paxson, Bierstadt, Moran, and Sitting Bull. The complex also includes the **Plains Indian Museum,** the **Draper Museum of Natural History,** and the **Cody Firearm Museum,** which houses over 2700 guns. (☎307-587-4771; www.bbhc.org. Open from May to mid-Sept. daily 8am-8pm; from mid-Sept. to Oct. daily 8am-5pm. Nov.-Mar. Tu-Su 10am-3pm; Apr. daily 10am-5pm. $22, students $20, ages 5-12 $10. Combined admission with trolley tour $32/20/16.) Six miles west of Cody on US 14/16/20, just after an impressive tunnel, the **Buffalo Bill Dam** affirms man's ability to control the flow of water. Built between 1904 and 1910, it measures 350 ft. in height. (☎307-527-6076. Visitors center open June-Aug. M-F 8am-8pm, Sa 8am-6pm, Su 10am-6pm. Free.) West of the dam, strange rock formations, created millions of years ago by volcanic eruptions in the Absarokas, dot the dusty hillsides.

Rafting trips on the Shoshone are livelier diversions. To make arrangements, call **Wyoming River Trips,** 233 Yellowstone Hwy./Rte. 14. (☎307-587-6661 or 800-586-6661; www.wyomingrivertrips.com. Open May-Sept. 2hr. trip $26-36, ½-day trip $65.) For equine adventures, try **Cedar Mountain Trail Rides,** east of town, near the KOA campground, on your right as you travel toward Cody. (☎307-527-4966.)

THE ROAD TO YELLOWSTONE NATIONAL PARK: 52 MI.

Follow the **Buffalo Bill Cody Scenic Byway (US 14/16/20)** westbound to the **East Entrance** of Yellowstone. Along the way, you'll pass Shoshone Canyon and drive through the Shoshone National Forest.

YELLOWSTONE NATIONAL PARK ☎307

Established in 1872, Yellowstone National Park has the distinction of being the first national park in the world. Yellowstone also happens to be the largest active volcano in the world, with over 300 geysers and more than 10,000 geothermal features spewing steam and boiling water—as well as less-than-savory sulfur gases—from beneath the earth's crust.

The park's hot springs are popular among local wildlife; bison and elk gather around the thermal basins for warmth and easier grazing during the winter months. Today, Yellowstone is still recovering from extensive wildfires that burned over a third of the park in 1988. The effects are especially evident in the western half of the park, where young saplings rise through a graveyard of charred tree stumps. Despite the fires, Yellowstone retains its rugged beauty. Now that wolves have been reintroduced, all the animals that lived in the Yellowstone area before the arrival of Europeans, with the exception of the black-footed ferret, still roam the landscape.

VITAL STATS

Area: 2.2 million acres

Tourist Offices: Most regions of the park have their own visitors centers. All centers offer general info and backcountry permits, but each has distinct hiking and camping regulations and features special regional exhibits. The main visitors center, **Albright** (☎307-344-2263; www.nps.gov/yell), at Mammoth Hot Springs, features exhibits on the history of Yellowstone and the origins of America's national parks, along with stuffed examples of wildlife. Open daily from late May to early Sept. 8am-7pm; from early Sept. to May 9am-5pm. The closest visitors center to the East Entrance is **Fishing Bridge** (☎307-242-2450). Open daily from late May to Aug. 8am-7pm; Sept. 9am-6pm.

General Park Information: ☎307-344-7381. **Weather:** ☎307-344-2113. **Road Report:** ☎307-344-2117. **Radio Info:** 1610AM.

Gateway Towns: Pahaska (WY) to the east, West Yellowstone (MT) to the west (p. 286), Gardiner (MT) to the north, and Cooke City (MT) to the northeast.

Fees: $25 per vehicle.

✈ ORIENTATION

Yellowstone is huge; Delaware could fit within its boundaries. Allow yourself a few days to make the most of your experience here. Just getting from one side of the park to the other can take hours, so plan accordingly. Yellowstone's roads form a figure eight, with side roads leading to park entrances and some lesser-known attractions. The natural wonders that make the park famous are scattered along the **Upper** and **Lower Loops.** Construction and renovation of roads is ongoing; call ahead (☎307-344-7381) or consult the extremely helpful *Yellowstone Today*, available at the entrances and visitors centers, to find out which sections will be closed during your visit. Travel through the park can be slow regardless of construction. The speed limit is at most 45 mph and is closely radar-patrolled; steep grades, tight curves, and frequent animal crossings can also cause delays.

The bulk of Yellowstone National Park lies in the northwest corner of Wyoming, with slivers in Montana and Idaho. There are five entrances to the park; **West Yellowstone, Montana** and **Gardiner, Montana** are the most developed entrance points, as they are closest to I-15 and I-90. The East Entrance to the park is 53 mi. west of Cody along **US 14/16/20.** The southern entrance to the park is bordered by **Grand Teton National Park.** The only road within the park that is open year-round is the northern strip between the North Entrance and Cooke City. All other roads are only open from May through late October.

ACCOMMODATIONS

The park's high season extends from mid-June to mid-September. Lodging within the park can be hard to come by on short notice but is sometimes a better deal than the motels along the outskirts of the park. **Xanterra** controls all accommodations within the park, employing a code to distinguish between cabins: "Roughrider" means no bath and no facilities; "Budget" offers a sink; "Pioneer" has a shower, toilet, and sink; "Frontier" is bigger and more plush; and "Western" is the biggest and most comfortable. Public facilities are available near cabins that lack private baths. (☎307-344-7311; www.travelyellowstone.com. Reservations strongly recommended. AmEx/D/MC/V.) In-park accommodations can be very expensive, however, particularly in summer; camping (below) is a much easier way to stay in the park without going broke.

▨ **Old Faithful Inn,** 30 mi. southeast of the West Yellowstone entrance, between Madison and Grant on the lower loop. In the heart of key attractions and a masterpiece unto itself. Admire the 6-story central lobby and stone fireplace from numerous balconies and stairways, all built from tree trunks. Constructed in 1904 by architect Robert Reamer as an embodiment of the natural surroundings, it is the quintessential example of "parkitecture." Open from mid-May to mid-Sept. Budget cabins $68; hotel rooms from $98, with bath from $125; Frontier cabins $112. ❸

Roosevelt Lodge, in the northeast portion of the upper loop, 19 mi. north of Canyon Village. A favorite of Teddy Roosevelt, who seems to have frequented every motel and saloon west of the Mississippi. Provides scenic accommodations located in a relatively isolated section of the park. Open from June to early Sept. Roughrider cabins with wood-burning stoves $67; Frontier cabins $112. ❸

Canyon Lodge and Cabins, in Canyon Village, overlooking the Grand Canyon of Yellowstone. Less authentic than Roosevelt's cabins, but centrally located and more popular with tourists. Open from early June to mid-Sept. Pioneer cabins $74; Frontier cabins $101; Western cabins $156. ❸

Mammoth Hot Springs, on the northwest part of the upper loop near the north entrance. A good base for early-morning wildlife-viewing excursions in the Lamar Valley to the east. Open from early May to mid-Oct. Budget cabins $75; hotel rooms $89, with bath $112; Frontier cabins (some with porches) from $112. ❸

Lake Lodge Cabins, 4 mi. south of Fishing Bridge, southeast corner of the lower loop. A cluster of cabins from the 1920s and 50s, close to Yellowstone Lake. Open from mid-June to late Sept. Pioneer cabins $74; Western cabins $145-156. ❸

CAMPING

Campsites fill quickly during the summer months. Call **Park Headquarters** (☎307-344-7381) for info on campsite vacancies. Permits for backcountry camping must be obtained in person no more than 48hr. in advance from a ranger station. You can reserve a permit beginning in April of the year in question by filling out a "trip planning worksheet" and mailing it, along with a $20 fee, to the **Central Backcountry Office,** P.O. Box 168, Yellowstone National Park, WY 82190. (☎307-344-2160. Open daily 8am-5pm.)

National Park Service campgrounds. No reservations. During summer, sites usually fill by 10am.

Stunning locations are well worth the effort required to secure a spot. Cash only. ❶

Slough Creek Campground, 10 mi. northeast of Tower Jct. 29 sites with vault toilets. Open June-Oct. $12.

Pebble Creek Campground, in the northeast corner of the park, between Tower Falls and the Northeast Entrance. 32 isolated sites with good fishing. Vault toilets. No RVs. Open from early June to late Sept. $12.

Lewis Lake, halfway between West Thumb and the South Entrance. Walk-in tent sites often tend to fill late in the day. 85 rugged sites with vault toilets. Open from mid-June to early Nov. $12.

Tower Falls, between the Northeast Entrance and Mammoth Hot Springs. 32 sites situated atop a hill with fine views. Vault toilets. Open from May to Sept. $12.

Norris. 116 sites. Water and flush toilets. Open from late May to late Sept. $12.

Indian Creek, between the Norris Geyser Basin and Mammoth Hot Springs. 75 sites. Vault toilets. Open from mid-June to mid-Sept. $12.

Mammoth. 85 sites with water and flush toilets. $14.

Xanterra (reservations ☎307-344-7311, same-day 344-7901). 5 campgrounds in the park. Flush toilets, water, and dump stations. Open from mid-May to early Oct., except Canyon. Grant Village and Bridge Bay are best for last-minute reservations. All sites $18. AmEx/D/MC/V. ❶

Canyon. 272 spacious sites on forested hillsides. Showers $3.25. Coin laundry. Open mid-June to mid-Sept.

Madison. 277 sites on the banks of the Firehole River. In the heart of the park's western attractions.

Grant Village. 425 open sites near Yellowstone Lake. Showers $3.25. Coin laundry.

Bridge Bay. 432 sites near Yellowstone Lake.

Fishing Bridge. RVs only. Densely packed parking spots for the large motor homes. Full hookups. Showers $3.25. Coin laundry.

🍴 FOOD

Buying food in the park can be expensive; stick to general stores at each lodging location, though even these can be pricey. The stores at Fishing Bridge, Lake Village, Grant Village, and Canyon Village sell lunch counter-style food. (Open daily 7:30am-9pm, but times may vary.) For other restaurants, see coverage of **West Yellowstone** (p. 286).

K-Bar Restaurant (☎406-848-9995), on US 89 just in Gardiner. Wash down meat-laden pizzas ($7.25) with cheap pints ($2-3). Don't let the rustic exterior fool you; this is one of the tastiest

and most filling places to enjoy dinner after a day in the park. Open daily 11am-2am. MC/V. ❶

Helen's Corral Drive-In (☎406-848-7627), in Gardiner, a few blocks north on US 89. Serves up super ½ lb. buffalo burgers and pork-chop sandwiches ($5-8) in a lively atmosphere. Open in summer daily 11am-10pm. Cash only. ❶

👁 SIGHTS

Xanterra (☎307-344-7311) organizes tours ($26, under 17 $13), horseback rides (1hr. $33, 2hr. $52), and chuckwagon dinners ($51, ages 5-11 $41). These outdoor activities are expensive, however, and Yellowstone is best explored on foot. Visitors centers give out self-guided tour pamphlets with maps for each of the park's main attractions ($0.50). Trails to these sights are accessible from the road via walkways, usually extending ¼-1¾ mi. from the road.

Yellowstone is set apart from other national parks and forests in the Rockies by its **geothermal features**—the park protects the largest geothermic area in the world. The bulk of these wonders can be found on the western side of the park between Mammoth Hot Springs in the north and Old Faithful in the south. The most dramatic thermal fissures are the **geysers.** Hot liquid magma close to the surface of the earth superheats water from snow and rain until it boils and bubbles, eventually building up enough pressure to burst violently through the cracks.

While **bison jams** and **bear gridlock** may make wildlife seem more of a nuisance than an attraction, they afford a unique opportunity to see a number of native species in their natural environment. The best times for viewing are early morning and just before dark, as most animals nap during the hot midday. The road between Tower-Roosevelt and the northeast entrance, in the untamed **Lamar River Valley,** often called the "Serengeti of Yellowstone," is where most of Yellowstone's wolf packs roam. Bison are best spotted between Fishing Bridge and Canyon, elk between Norris and Canyon. Roadside parking is limited, so get there early if you want a spot. Some species take to the higher elevations in the heat of summer, so travel earlier or later in the season (or hike to higher regions) to increase your chances for good viewing.

GRAND CANYON. The east side's featured attraction, the Grand Canyon of the Yellowstone, wears rusty red and orange hues created by hot water running over the rock. The canyon is 800-1200 ft. deep and 1500-4000 ft. wide. For a close-up view of the mighty **Lower Falls** (308 ft.), hike down the short, steep **Uncle Tom's Trail** (over 300 steps). **Artist Point,** on the southern rim, and **Lookout Point,** on the northern rim, offer broader canyon vistas and are accessible from the road between Canyon and Fishing Bridge. Keep an eye out for bighorn sheep along the canyon's rim.

> **BEWARE!** Yellowstone can be dangerous. While roadside wildlife may look tame, these large beasts are unpredictable and easily startled. Stay at least 75 ft. from any animal and keep at least 300 ft. between yourself and bears. Both black bears and grizzly bears inhabit Yellowstone; consult a ranger about proper precautions before entering the backcountry. If you should encounter a bear, inform a ranger. Bison, sometimes naively regarded as overgrown cows, can run up to 30 mph; visitors are gored every year. Finally, "widow makers"—dead trees that can fall over at any time, especially during high winds—are always a threat in forests but are especially common in burn areas.

OLD FAITHFUL AREA. Yellowstone's trademark attraction, **Old Faithful,** is no longer the most predictable or largest of the large geysers, but its high frequency has consistently pleased audiences since its discovery in 1870. Eruptions usually shoot 100-190 ft. in the air and occur every 45min. to 2hr. The average is 90min., though geologists speculate that intervals will grow longer. Predictions for the next eruption, usually accurate to within 10min., are posted at the **Old Faithful Visitors Center.** *(Open from late May to early Nov. 8am-7pm; from late Apr. to late May daily 9am-5pm.)* Old Faithful lies in the **Upper Geyser Basin,** 16 mi. south of the Madison area and 20 mi. west of Grant Village. This area has the largest concentration of geysers in the world, and boardwalks connect them all. The spectacular rainbow spectrum of **Morning Glory Pool** is an easy 1 mi. hike from Old Faithful and provides up-close-and-personal views of hundreds of hydrothermal features along the way, including the tallest predictable geyser in the world, **Grand Geyser,** and the graceful **Riverside Geyser,** which spews at a 60° angle across the Firehole River. Between Old Faithful and Madison, along the Firehole River, lie the **Midway Geyser Basin** and the **Lower Geyser Basin.** The **Excelsior Geyser Crater,** a large, steaming lake created by a powerful geyser blast, and the **Grand Prismatic Spring,** the largest hot spring in the park, are both located in the Midway Geyser Basin. The basin is about 5 mi. north of Old Faithful and worth the trip. Two miles north is the less developed but still thrilling **Firehole Lake Drive,** a 2 mi. side loop through hot lakes, springs, and dome geysers. Eight miles north of Old Faithful gurgles the **Fountain Paint Pot,** a bubbling pool of hot milky-white, brown, and gray mud. Four types of geothermal activity present in Yellowstone (geysers, mudpots, hot springs, and fumaroles) are found along the trails of the Firehole River. There's a temptation to wash off the grime of camping, but swimming in the hot springs is prohibited. You can swim in the Firehole River, near Firehole Canyon Dr., south of Madison Junction, though prepare for chilly water; the name of the river is deceptive.

NORRIS GEYSER BASIN. Fourteen miles north of Madison and 21 mi. south of Mammoth, the colorful Norris Geyser Basin is both the oldest and the hottest active thermal zone in the park. The geyser has been spewing water and steam at temperatures up to 459°F for over 115,000 years. The area has a half mile northern **Porcelain Basin** loop and a 1½ mi. southern **Back Basin** loop. **Echinus,** in the Back Basin, is the largest known acidic geyser, with a pH similar to vinegar; it erupts 40-60 ft. every 1-4hr. Its neighbor, **Steamboat,** is the tallest active geyser in the world, erupting over 300 ft. for anywhere 3-40min. Steamboat's eruptions, however, are entirely unpredictable; the last eruption occurred in 2002, after two years of inactivity.

> **! WARNING: CONTENTS ARE HOT.** The crust around many of Yellowstone's thermal basins, geysers, and hot springs is thin, and boiling, acidic water lies just beneath the surface. Stay on the marked paths and boardwalks at all times. In the backcountry, keep a good distance from hot springs and fumaroles.

MAMMOTH HOT SPRINGS. The hot-spring terraces resemble huge wedding cakes at Mammoth Hot Springs, 21 mi. to the north of the Norris Basin and 19 mi. west of Tower in the northwest corner of the upper loop. Shifting water sources, malleable travertine limestone deposits, and temperature-sensitive, multicolored bacterial growth create the most rapidly changing natural structure in the park. The **Upper Terrace Drive,** 2 mi. south of Mammoth Visitors Center, winds 1 mi. through colorful springs and rugged travertine limestone ridges and terraces. When visiting, ask a ranger where to find the most active springs, as they vary in intensity from year to year. Some go dormant for decades, their structures gradually crumbling, only to revive unexpectedly to build new domes and cascades. **Canary Spring,** on the south side of the main terrace, has been expanding into virgin forest, killing trees and bushes in its path. Inquire at ranger stations about area trails that provide wildlife viewing. Swimming is permitted in the **Boiling River,** 2½ mi. north, where a hot spring flows into the Gardner River.

YELLOWSTONE LAKE AREA. Situated in the southeast corner of the park, **Yellowstone Lake** is the largest high-altitude lake in North America and is a protective sanctuary for cutthroat trout. While the surface of the lake may appear calm, geologists have found geothermal features at the bottom. Geysers and hot springs in **West Thumb** dump 3100 gal. of water into the lake per day. Notwithstanding this thermal boost, the temperature of the lake remains quite cold, averaging 45°F during the summer. Visitors to the park once cooked trout on fishing lines in the boiling water of the **Fishing Cone** in the West Thumb central

basin, but this is no longer permitted. Along the same loop on the west side of the lake, check out the **Thumb Paint Pots,** a field of puffing miniature mud volcanoes and chimneys. On the northern edge of the lake is the rustic **Fishing Bridge,** where fishing has been prohibited in an effort to help the endangered native trout. The sulfurous odors of **Mud Volcano,** 6 mi. north of Fishing Bridge, can be distinguished from miles away, but the turbulent mudpots, caused by the creation of hydrogen sulfide gas by bacteria working on the naturally occurring sulfur in the spring water, are worth the assault on your nose. The unusual geothermal mudpots, with their rhythmic belching, acidic waters, and cavernous openings, have appropriately medieval names, such as **Dragon's Mouth, Sour Lake,** and **Black Dragon's Cauldron.**

OUTDOORS

HIKING

Most visitors to Yellowstone never get out of their cars and therefore miss hiking any of the 1200 mi. of trails in the park. Options for exploring Yellowstone's more pristine areas range from short day hikes to long backcountry trips. When planning a hike, pick up a **topographical trail map** ($9-10 at any visitors center or general store) and ask a ranger to describe the network of trails. Visitors centers also have day-hike pamphlets for each major park area. Some trails are poorly marked, so be sure of your skill with a map and compass before setting off on more obscure paths. Fires in 1988 scarred over a third of the park; hikers should consult rangers and maps about which areas were damaged. Burned areas have less shade, so pack hats, extra water, and sunscreen. In addition to the self-guided trails at major attractions, many worthwhile sights are only a few miles off the main road. There are dozens of extended backcountry trips in the park, including treks to the Black Canyon of the Yellowstone, in the north-central region, and to isolated Heart Lake in the south.

Fairy Falls Trail (5 mi., 2hr. round-trip), 3 mi. north of Old Faithful. Provides a unique perspective on the Midway Geyser Basin and up-close views of 200 ft. high Fairy Falls. This easy round-trip trail begins in the parking lot marked Fairy Falls just south of Midway Geyser Basin.

Twin Buttes, beyond Fairy Falls. A 650 ft. elevation gain, which turns this trail into a moderate, 4hr. round-trip hike.

Mount Washburn (5 mi., 4hr. round-trip; 1380 ft. elevation gain). Trail is enhanced by an enclosed observation area with sweeping views of the park's central environs, including the patchwork of old and new forests and herds of bighorn sheep. Begins at Chittenden Rd. parking area, 10 mi. north of Canyon Village, or Dunraven Pass, 6 mi. north of Canyon Village.

Avalanche Peak (4 mi., 4hr.; final elevation 10,568 ft.), starts 8 mi. west of the East Entrance on East Entrance Rd. A steep ascent up several switchbacks opens to stunning panoramas out over Yellowstone Lake and the southern regions of the park, west to the Continental Divide and east to Shoshone National Forest. Wildlife-viewing opportunities in this area are superb.

BOATING AND FISHING

Boating and Fishing are both allowed within the park. Permits are required for fishing, which is catch-and-release only. (Fishing permits $15 per 3 days, $20 per week; under 15 free.) In addition to Yellowstone Lake, popular fishing spots include the Madison and Firehole Rivers; the Firehole is available for fly-fishing only. To go boating or even floating on the lake, you'll need a boating permit, available at backcountry offices (check *Yellowstone Today*), Bridge Bay Marina, and the South, West, and Northeast Entrances to the park. **Xanterra** rents rowboats, outboards, and dock-slips at Bridge Bay Marina. (☎307-344-7311. Open from mid-June to early Sept. Rowboats $9.50 per hr., $43 per 8hr. Outboards $45 per hr. Dockslips $15-20 per night.)

⚑ THE ROAD TO GRAND TETON NATIONAL PARK: 10 MI.

Follow **US 89/191/287** south from Yellowstone into the Grand Teton National Park.

GRAND TETON NATIONAL PARK ☎307

The Teton Range is the youngest in the entire Rocky Mountain system. Glaciers more than 2000 ft. thick sculpted the jagged peaks, carved U-shaped valleys, and gouged out Jenny, Leigh, and Phelps Lakes. Though the Shoshone Indians called the range the "hoary-headed fathers," French trappers dubbed the three most prominent peaks—South Teton, Grand Teton, and Middle Teton—*Les trois tetons*, meaning "the three breasts," giving some clue as to what desperately lonely men these trappers must have been. Grand Teton National Park delights hikers with miles of both easy and strenuous trails as well as steep rock faces along the range's eastern face.

FLOUR POWER

Passing by the many lakes and streams in the Rockies, you may notice that they have an unusual color. When looking at the swimming-pool turquoise or glowing blue of the water, you might wonder if this is some kind of gimmick perpetuated by the park wardens to bring in the tourists. Many years ago, a visitor to Lake Louise claimed that he had solved the mystery of the beautiful water: it had obviously been distilled from peacock tails. It turns out he was a bit off the mark. The actual cause of the color is "rock flour." This fine dust is created by the pressure exerted by the glacier upon rocks trapped in the ice; the resulting ground rock is washed into streams and lakes in the glacial melt-water. Suspended particles trap all colors of the spectrum except for the blues and greens, which are reflected back for your visual pleasure. The glacially fed lakes are too cold to grow murky algae, and the water is free from the dirt sediment that would interfere with its color. This means, however, that the water is usually free of large populations of fish as well—it's pleasing to the eye but not so pleasing to the touch. The floury water is just as safe as any other water in the mountains as long as you filter it first, but only try it as a last resort: you'll have to go through plenty of clogged filters

VITAL STATS

Area: 309,760 acres

Tourist Offices: Craig Thomas Discover and Information Center (☎307-739-3300), on Teton Park Rd., at the southern part of the park, ½ mi. west of Moose Jct. Open daily from early June to early Sept. 8am-7pm; from early Sept. to late May 8am-5pm.

Jenny Lake Visitors Center (☎307-739-3392), next to the Jenny Lake Campground at South Jenny Lake. Open daily from early June to early Sept. 8am-7pm; from mid-May to early June and Sept. 8am-4:30pm.

Colter Bay Visitors Center (☎307-739-3594), on Jackson Lake in the northern part of the park. Open daily from June to early Sept. 8am-7pm; Sept. and May 8am-5pm.

Internet Access: Jackson Lake Lodge (☎307-543-3100), off US 89 5 mi. west of Moran.

Post Office: Next to Park Headquarters (☎307-733-3336), in Moose. Open M-F 9am-1pm and 1:30-5pm, Sa 10:30-11:30am. **Postal Code:** 83012.

Gateway Town: Jackson (p. 284) to the south.

ORIENTATION

Grand Teton's roads consist of a scenic loop through the park with approach roads coming from Jackson in the south, Dubois in the east, and Yellowstone in the north. There are three entrances to the park: **Moose, Moran Junction,** and **Teton Village.** The east side of the main loop, **US 89,** from Jackson to Moran Jct. entrance, offers excellent views of the Tetons. US 89 in the park is open year-round.

Visitors centers and campgrounds have free copies of *Teewinot*, the park's newspaper, which contains news and info on special programs, hiking, and camping. For general info and a visitor's packet or to make back-country camping reservations, contact **Park Headquarters** (☎307-739-3300; www.nps.gov/grte) or write Grand Teton National Park, P.O. Drawer 170, Moose, WY 83012.

At high elevations, snow often remains into July, and the weather can become dangerous any time of the year, so severe weather gear is strongly advised. Bears are active in the park, so be sure to follow all food storage guidelines and other precautions.

ACCOMMODATIONS

The **Grand Teton Lodge Company** runs several accommodations in the park. (Reservations ☎800-628-9988; www.gltc.com. Or write to the Reservations Manager, Grand Teton Lodge Co., P.O. Box 250, Moran, WY 83013. Deposit required.) Lodges are pricey, but there are several options for relatively affordable cabins at Colter Bay.

Signal Mountain Lodge, (☎307-543-2831 or 800-672-6012; www.signalmountainlodge.com). Scenic lodging on the shores of Jackson Lake. Options include rustic log cabins with private bath (doubles $127), lodge-style rooms (quads $151), and lakefront retreats with living areas and kitchenettes (6 people $222). ❹

Colter Bay Village Cabins (☎800-628-9988). 166 log cabins near Jackson Lake. A cabin with shared bath is one of the best deals in the area; book early. Open from late May-late Sept. 2-person cabins with shared bath from $49; 1-room with private bath $89-135; 2-rooms with connecting bath $149-179. ❷

Colter Bay Tent Cabins ❷ (☎800-628-9988). Primitive log and canvas tents with cement floors, wood-burning stoves, and bunks. Sleeping bags, cots, and blankets are available for rent. 66 cabins. Open from early June to early Sept. 2-person tents $43. Each additional person $6. ❷

CAMPING

To stay in the Tetons without emptying your wallet, find a tent and pitch it. There are seven campgrounds in the park, five of which are operated on a first come, first served basis. (Info ☎307-739-3603. Sites generally open from early May to late Sept.) All sites have cold water, fire rings, picnic tables, and restrooms; Signal Mountain, Gros Ventre, and Colter Bay have dump stations. The maximum stay is 14 days, except for Jenny Lake sites, where it is seven days. There is a maximum of six people and one vehicle per site; Colter Bay and Gros Ventre accept larger groups for $3 per person plus a $15 reservation fee. (☎307-543-3100 or 800-628-9988. Reservations required.)

Permits are required for all **backcountry camping** ❶ and are free if reserved in person within 24hr. of the trip. Reservations made more than 24hr. in advance require a $25 non-refundable fee. Requests are accepted by mail or online from January 1 to May 15; write to Grand Teton National Park, Backcountry Permits, P.O. Box 170, Moose, WY 83012 or visit www.nps.gov/grte. For more info, contact the Moose Visitor Center. (☎307-739-3309). Advance reservations are recommended for sites in the popular mountain canyons or near lakes. After May 15, two-thirds of all backcountry spots are available on a first come, first served basis; the park staff can help plan routes and find campsites.

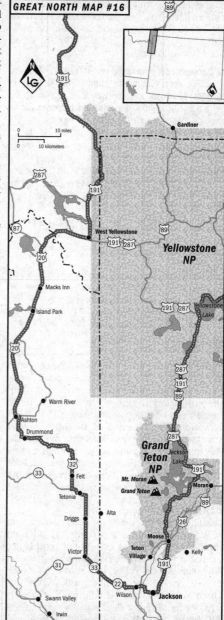

GREAT NORTH MAP #16

Jenny Lake, in the shadow of towering Mt. Teewinot, within walking distance of Jenny Lake. Offers 50 scenic sites that usually fill by 10am, so get there early. No RVs. Open from mid-May to late Sept. Bicycle sites $5, Vehicle sites $19. ❶

Signal Mountain, along the southeastern shore of Jackson Lake. The 81 sites, situated on a hillside overlooking the water, are a little more secluded than at Colter Bay and have the best views and lake access of any of the campgrounds. Usually full by noon. Open from early May to mid-Oct. Sites $18, with full hookup $45. ❶

Lizard Creek, closer to Yellowstone. Has 60 spacious, secluded sites along the northern shore of Jackson Lake. Fills by 2pm. Open from June to early Sept. Vehicle sites $18. ❶

Colter Bay, on the shores of Jackson Lake. With 350 crowded sites, a grocery store, laundromat, showers, and 2 restaurants, Colter is more suburb than wilderness. Sites rarely fill. Showers open 7:30am-9pm; $3.50. Open from late May to late Sept. Vehicle sites $18, with full hookup $49. ❶

Gros Ventre, along the bank of the Gros Ventre River, close to Jackson. The biggest campground, with 350 sites and 5 group sites. The Tetons, however, are hidden from view by Blacktail Butte. Rarely fills and is the best bet for late arrivals. Open from early May to late Sept. Sites $18. ❶

🍴 FOOD

The best way to eat on a budget in the Tetons is to bring your own food. Non-perishables are available at the surprisingly comprehensive **Trading Post Grocery,** in the Dornan's complex near the Moose Visitors Center, and the deli makes hefty subs for $6-7. (☎307-733-2415, ext. 201. Open daily May-Sept.

8am-8pm; Oct.-Apr. 8am-6pm. Deli closes 1hr. earlier.) Jackson has an **Albertson's supermarket,** 105 Buffalo Way, at the intersection of W. Broadway and Rte. 22. (☎307-733-5950. Open daily 6am-midnight.)

▨ **Dornan's Chuckwagon** (☎307-733-2415, ext. 203), across from the Trading Post Grocery in Moose. Locals and tourists alike gather 'round pots of ribs, stew, and mashed potatoes for an authentic Old West dinner. Breakfast $8.50. Lunch $5.50-10. Chuckwagon dinner $16. ❷

Trapper Grill (☎307-543-2831), inside Signal Mountain Lodge. Top off a day of hiking with a heaping mound of nachos ($8.25-13.75) If you've still got room, the elk chili burgers ($10.25) are unbeatable. Breakfasts $6.70-8.75. Open from early May to mid-Oct. daily 7am-10pm. ❸

John Colter Cafe Court (☎307-543-2811), in Colter Bay. Serves burgers, burritos, and other cross-cultural fare. Entrees $5-8.25. Open daily 11am-10pm. ❷

Blue Heron Lounge (☎307-543-3100), inside the Jackson Lake Lodge. If you want a peek at wild moose and elk while nursing a mojito this is the place. Free Wi-Fi. Live music most nights. Huckleberry margarita $6.50. Drafts $4.75. ❷

⚠ OUTDOORS

While Yellowstone captivates visitors with geysers and mudpots, the Tetons boast some of the most scenic mountains in the US, if not the world. Only 13 million years old, the ▨Teton **Range** rises between 10,000 and 13,770 ft. in elevation. The absence of foothills creates spectacular mountain vistas that accentuate the range's steep rock faces. Dramatic rock draws scores of climbers, while thousands of seasoned hikers flock here to experience the beauty of the Teton backcountry.

BIKING

Biking is a particularly popular activity on roads in the park, but is strictly forbidden on hiking trails. Outdoor equipment rentals are available in the Dornan's complex in Moose. **Adventure Sports** rents bikes and provides advice on the best trails. (☎307-733-3307. Open May-Oct. daily 9am-6pm. Bike rentals $10 per hr., $32 per day. Kayaks and canoes $10 per hr., $46 per day. Deposit required.)

BOATING

Getting out onto the water provides an entirely different perspective on the surrounding landscape. Non-motorized boating and hand-powered crafts are permitted on a number of lakes; motorboats are allowed only on Jackson, Jenny, and Phelps Lakes. Boating permits can be obtained at any visitors center and are good in Yellowstone National Park as well. (Motorized boat pass $20 per week, $40 per year; non-motorized craft $10/20. Jet skis prohibited on all park waterways.)

Grand Teton Lodge Company (☎307-543-1097). Rents boats at Colter Bay. Scenic cruises of Jackson Lake leave from Colter Bay Marina. 1hr. cruises $21, ages 3-11 $10. Canoes $13 per hr. Motorboats $27 per hr.; 2hr. min. Rentals available daily May-Aug. 8am-3pm.

Jenny Lake Marina (☎307-739-9227). A peaceful experience on the smaller, quieter lake. Canoes and kayaks $12 per hr. Scenic cruise $14.

Signal Mountain Marina (☎307-543-2831), on Jackson Lake. Large pontoon boats $65 per hr. Motorboats $29 per hr. Canoes $13.50 per hr. Kayaks $12 per hr. Rentals available May-Aug.

CLIMBING

Two companies offer more extreme backcountry adventures, including four-day packages that let beginners work their way up the famed Grand Teton.

▨ **Exum Mountain Guides** (☎307-733-2297; www. exumguides.com), located near the Jenny Lake Visitors Center. Offers classes for all levels of climbers. Founded by early Teton mountaineer and local legend Glenn Exum. 1-day beginner rock-climbing course $130. Guided 1- to 2-day climbs $250-375. 2-day Grand Teton ascents $645-935. Reservations required.

Jackson Hole Mountain Guides and Climbing School, 165 N. Glenwood St. (☎307-733-4979 or 800-239-7642; www.jhmg.com), in Jackson. 1-day beginner course for $135. 1-day guided climbing course for $225. More advanced programs are available, including 4-day Grand Teton ascents ($1780). Open daily 8:30am-5:30pm. Reservations required.

Moosely Seconds (☎307-739-1801), in Moose. Rents mountaineering and camping equipment. Open in summer daily 8am-7pm. Climbing shoes

$5 per day, $25 per week; crampons $8/40; ice axes $6/30; trekking poles $4/20.

FISHING

Fishing is permitted within the park with a Wyoming license, available at Moose Village Store, Signal Mountain Lodge, and Colter Bay Marina. ($10.50 Wyoming Conservation stamp required with all annual fishing licenses. $11 per day; $76 per season, ages 14-18 $15.) Women interested in learning how to fly-fish can learn with **Reel Women Fly Fishing Adventures,** an Idaho-based company developed to introduce women to this traditionally male-dominated sport. (☎208-351-6410; www.reel-women.com. Full-day float trips $450, 2-day basic fly-fishing school $595. Reservations required.) **Jack Dennis Fishing Trips** also has float fishing trips on the Snake River in the park. (☎307-733-3270 or 800-570-3270; www.jackdennis.com. $425 for 2 people.) **Solitude Float Trips** sends raft floats down the scenic Snake River. (☎307-733-2871 or 888-704-2800; www.solitudefloattrips.com. 10 mi. trip $50, under 13 $30.) **Snake River Angler** has advice and rents rods. (☎307-733-3699; www.snakeriverangler.com. Open May-Oct. daily 8am-6pm. Rods $15-25 per day.)

HIKING

All visitors centers provide pamphlets about day hikes and sell guides and maps ($3-10). Rangers also lead informative hikes; check the *Teewinot* or the visitors centers for details. Before hitting the trail or planning extended hikes, be sure to check in either at a visitors center or at the ranger station; trails at higher elevations may still be snow-covered and thus require ice axes and experience with icy conditions. During years with heavy snowfall, prime hiking season does not begin until well into July. Getting an "alpine start" very early in the day helps to avoid crowds. Recently, bears have become more active in the park; be sure to educate yourself on bear safety.

Cunningham Cabin Trail (¾ mi., 1hr. round-trip; 20 ft. elevation gain; easy). Relives the history of early homesteading in the valley. Trailhead lies 6 mi. south of Moran Jct.

Taggart Lake (3 mi., 2hr. round-trip; 277 ft. elevation gain; moderate). Passes through the 1000-acre remains of the 1985 Beaver Creek fire, which removed most of the tree cover to allow an open view of the Tetons and Taggart lakeshore; look out for ▨**marmots** sunning themselves.

Bradley Lake (4 mi., 3hr. round-trip; 397 ft. elevation gain; moderate). Begins at Taggart Lake trailhead and proceeds up a glacial moraine to the more secluded Bradley Lake. For a longer trek, follow the trail another 1 mi. along the eastern shore, over another moraine, and along a meadow before joining Amphitheater Lake Trail 1 mi. above the Lupine Meadows trailhead.

Hermitage Point (8 mi., 4hr. round-trip; 100 ft. elevation gain; easy), beginning at Colter Bay, is a gentle hike along gently rolling meadows and streams and past Swan Lake and Heron Pond. The trail provides a unique perspective on Jackson Lake, which it approaches at several points, and is a prime spot for observing wildlife.

▨ **Cascade Canyon Trail** (round-trip with boat ride 14 mi., 8hr.; without boat ride 18½ mi., 10hr.; 2252 ft. elevation gain; very challenging.) Beware: trail begins easy to moderate but becomes more difficult. The hike begins on the far side of tranquil Jenny Lake and follows Cascade Creek through a U-shaped valley carved by glaciers. The Hidden Falls Waterfall is located ½ mi. up; views of Teewinot, Mt. Owen, and Grand Teton are to the south. Hikers with more stamina can continue another ½ mi. up toward Inspiration Point (elevation 7200 ft.), which has stunning views eastward across Jackson Hole and the Gros Ventre Range. For some of the most spectacular hiking, trek 6 mi. farther to Lake Solitude (elevation 9024 ft.). Ranger-led trips to Inspiration Point depart from Jenny Lake Visitors Center every morning June-Aug. 8:30am. Hikers can reach the Cascade Canyon Trail by way of the 2 mi. trail around the south side of Jenny Lake or by taking one of the boat shuttles offered by Jenny Lake Boating. (☎307-734-9227. Boats leave Jenny Lake boat dock every 20min. daily 8am-6pm. $5, ages 4-12 $4; round-trip $9/5.) Most hikers, including many families, choose one of these options. An alternative route begins at String Lake trailhead and traverses the isolated north side of Jenny Lake for 1 mi.

Surprise and Amphitheater Lakes (9 mi., 8hr. round-trip; 2958 ft. elevation gain; very challenging), originating just south of Jenny Lake at the Lupine Meadows parking lot. A strenuous trek with a significant elevation change along several switchbacks. 3 mi. into the trail, a fork directs hikers either to Garnet Canyon to the left or Surprise Lake and Amphitheater Lake to the right. Garnet Canyon is 1 mi. from the fork and provides access to several mountaineering routes up South, Middle, and Grand Teton. Camping at the trail's end requires a permit. Climbers should consult with park rangers for info on routes. The lakes are another 1 mi. from the fork; both are stunning examples of high alpine tarns gouged out by glaciers long since melted. Lupines, the purple flowers visible all along the roads in the park, bloom June-July along the trail.

WINTER ACTIVITIES

In the winter, all hiking trails and the unplowed sections of Teton Park Rd. are open to cross-country skiers and snowshoers. Sign up for a free, ranger-led snowshoe hike at the Craig Thomas Visitors Center. (☎307-739-3300. 2hr. hikes depart Jan.-Mar. 2-4pm. Days and times vary; call for details.) **Snowmobiling** is only allowed on the Continental Divide Snowmobile Trail and Grassy Lake Rd.; pick up a $15 permit at the Craig Thomas Visitors Center and a map and guide at the Jackson Chamber of Commerce. **Grand Teton Park Snowmobile Rental**, in Moran at GTP RV Resort, rents snowmobiles. (☎307-733-1980 or 800-563-6469. $99 per ½-day, $139 per day; includes clothing, helmet, boots, and snowmobile instruction.) The Colter Bay and Moose parking lots are available for parking in the winter. All campgrounds close in winter, but backcountry snow camping (only for those with experience) is allowed with a permit obtained from the Moose Visitors Center. Before making plans, consider that wind chills regularly drop below negative 30°F. Be sure to carry extreme weather clothing and check with a ranger station for current weather and avalanche updates.

THE ROAD TO JACKSON: 5 MI.

Follow **US 89/189/191** south into Jackson.

JACKSON ☎307

The southern gateway to both Grand Teton and Yellowstone National Parks, the town of Jackson teems with hordes of tourists in sum-

mer. However, the area is equally renowned for its skiing. When in Jackson, you are also in Jackson Hole, the valley that separates the Teton and Gros Ventre mountain ranges. A glamorous playground for the rich and famous, Jackson walks a fine line between staying chic enough for the *nouveau riche* who come to ski and Western enough for the old-time cowboys who have always been around. Regardless of how it presents itself, the town can't be beat as a base for hiking, biking, rafting, fishing, and exploring the Tetons and Snake River.

ORIENTATION

Downtown Jackson is centered on the intersection of **Broadway** (east-west) and **Cache Street** (north-south) and marked by **Town Square Park**, which is itself marked by the four enormous arches of antlers that frame each corner. Most shops and restaurants are within a four-block radius of this intersection. South of town, at the intersection with **Route 22 West**, Broadway becomes **US 191/89/26**. To get to **Teton Village**, take Rte. 22 to **Route 390 (Teton Village Road)** just before the town of Wilson. Winding backroads, unpaved at times, with close underbrush and frequent wildlife spottings, connect Teton Village to Moose and the southern entrance of the national park. North of Jackson, Cache St. turns into **Route 89**, leading directly into the park.

VITAL STATS
Population: 8700
Tourist Office: Jackson Hole and Greater Yellowstone Information Center, 532 N. Cache St. (☎307-733-3316). Open from early June to Sept. daily 8am-7pm; from Oct. to early June M-F 9am-5pm.
Library and Internet Access: Teton County Library, 125 Virginian Ln. (☎307-733-2164). Free. Open M-Th 10am-9pm, F 10am-5:30pm, Sa 10am-5pm, Su 1-5pm.
Post Office: 1070 Maple Way (☎307-733-3650), at Powderhorn Ln. Open M-F 8:30am-5pm, Sa 10am-1pm. **Postal Code:** 83002.

ACCOMMODATIONS

Jackson draws hordes of visitors year-round, making rooms outrageously expensive and difficult to find without reservations. The primitive campgrounds in Grand Teton National Park and the 4.4 million-acre **Bridger-Teton National Forest** offer the area's absolute cheapest accommodations. The park's **Gros Ventre campground ❶** (p. 281) is only a 15min. drive north of the town of Jackson on Rte. 89. There are exactly 37 developed **campgrounds ❶** in the Bridger-Teton National Forest, including several along US 26 east of Jackson. **Backcountry camping ❶** is free in the forest; campers must stay at least 200 ft. from water and 100 ft. from trails. Ask ranger beforehand; some areas may be restricted.

Hostel X, 3315 McCollister Dr. (☎307-733-341), 12 mi. northwest of Jackson in Teton Village. Lets skiers and others stay slopeside for cheap. The hostel has a lounge with TVs, ping-pong and pool tables, and shelves of puzzles and games, a ski-waxing room, and a convenient location just a close stumble from the Mangy Moose (below). Rooms are private with either four twin beds or one king-size bed. Free Wi-Fi. Singles and doubles $80; triples and quads $95. MC/V. ❸

The Bunkhouse, 215 N. Cache St. (☎307-733-3668; www.anvilmotel.com). Though the bunks in the basement of the Anvil Motel might not be the most appealing beds in town, they certainly are the cheapest. Free coffee. Showers included for guests, $6 for non-guests; includes towel. Laundry. Bunks $25. D/MC/V. ❶

Alpine Motel, 70 S. Jean St. (☎307-739-3200), 2 blocks from the town square. One of the few lodgings in Jackson with rooms under $100 during high season. Provides basic rooms with cable TV, free local calls, and an outdoor pool. June-Sept. singles $68; doubles $80. ❸

Kudar Motel, 260 N. Cache St. (☎307-733-2823). Offers snug log cabins and motel-style rooms with cable TV, fridges, and microwaves. Open May-Oct. Singles $85; cabins from $95-120. D/MC/V. ❹

FOOD

Jackson has dozens of restaurants, but few are suited to the budget traveler.

Jedediah's House of Sourdough, 135 E. Broadway (☎307-733-5671). Serves up authentic breakfasts and lunches ranging from famous sourdough flapjacks ($6) to Rocky Mountain spring trout and eggs ($11) in a log building building listed on the National Register of Historic Places. Open daily 7am-2pm. ❷

Bubba's Bar-B-Que, 515 W. Broadway (☎307-733-2288). A family restaurant that serves generous portions of Western comfort food for breakfast, lunch, and dinner. Most meals come with Bubba's famous barbecued beans. Lunch specials $7-10. Spare-rib dinner $14. Open daily June-Aug. 6:30am-10pm; in winter 6:30am-8:30pm. AmEx/D/MC/V. ❸

The Bunnery, 130 N. Cache St. (☎307-734-0075 or 800-349-0492; www.bunnery.com). Makes delicious breakfasts and baked goods, including omelets ($8-10) and the special OSM (oats, sunflower, and millet) bread. Breakfast $4-8. Sandwiches $7-8. Pie slices $4-5. Open daily in summer 7am-9pm; in winter 7am-3pm. D/MC/V. ❷

Mountunes, 265 W. Broadway (☎307-733-4514). An akternative-feeling combination tattoo parlor, music store, and Internet cafe. Coffee drinks run $2-3. Open M-Sa noon-"6ish." ❶

SIGHTS

THE NATIONAL MUSEUM OF WILDLIFE ART. If inclement weather has fouled your outdoor plans, don't miss The National Museum of Wildlife Art boasts an extraordinary collection of diverse artwork chronicling the relationship between man and beast. *(2820 Rungius Rd., on Rte. 89. heading south into Jackson. ☎307-733-5771 or 800-313-9553; www.wildlifeart.org. Open daily 9am-5pm. $10, students $9, under 18 free.)*

NIGHTLIFE

The Mangy Moose (☎307-733-4913, entertainment hotline 733-9779; www.mangymoose.net), in Teton Village at the base of Jackson Hole Ski Resort. A quintessential après-ski bar, featuring an enormous stuffed moose hanging from the ceiling. Cover $5-15. Open daily 11am-2am. Kitchen open daily 11am-10pm.

Snake River Brewery, 265 S. Millward St. (☎307-739-2337; www.snakeriverbrewing.com). Award-winning "Zonkers Stout" and pub favorite bratwursts ($9) are worth a trip. Pints $3.50, pitchers $11. Happy hour 4-6pm. Open daily 11:30am-1am. Kitchen open until at 11pm.

OUTDOORS

World-class **skiing** and **climbing** lie within minutes of Jackson, and whitewater **rafting** on the legendary Snake River is an adrenaline rush. Rafting is best in June, before the Jackson Dam flow is cut down in order to improve the **fishing**, which peaks in late July and August. **Barker-Ewing,** 45 W. Broadway, provides tours of varying lengths and difficulty levels, led by a highly experienced staff. (☎307-733-1000 or 800-448-4202; www.barker-ewing.com. 8 mi. tour on a 14-person raft $55, ages 6-12 $45; on a more agile 8-person raft $60/50. Gentle 13 mi. scenic trip $50/35. Overnight 16 mi. adventure $200/170. 16 mi. 14-person tour with breakfast $85/65; 8-person $90/70.) **Leisure Sports,** 1075 Rte. 89, has **boating** and fishing equipment and the best deals on camping and backpacking rentals. (☎307-733-3040; www.leisuresportsadventure.com. Open daily in summer and winter 8am-6pm; in fall and spring 8am-5pm. 2-person tents $5 per day. 6-person tents $15 per day. Sleeping bags $4 per day. Backpacks $4 per day. Canoes and kayaks $35-65 per day. rafts $65-125 per day.)

Jackson Hole Mountain Resort, located 12 mi. north of Jackson in the even smaller town of Teton Village, has some of the best runs in the entire US, including the infamous, jaw-droppingly steep ▓**Corbet's Couloir.** (☎307-733-2292 or 888-333-7766; www.jacksonhole.com. Open from early Dec. to Apr. Lift tickets $77 per day, ages 15-21 $63, under 14 and seniors $39. ½ day $58/48/29.) Even after the snow melts, the aerial tram whisks eager tourists to the top of Rendezvous Mountain (elevation 10,450 ft.) for a view of the valley. Jackson Hole is a prime locale for cross-country skiing. **Skinny Skis,** 65 W. Delorney Ave., in downtown Jackson, rents gear. (☎307-733-6094. Open daily June-Aug. and Dec.-Feb. 9am-8pm; in low season 9am-6pm. Equipment rental $18 per day.)

▓ THE ROAD TO WEST YELLOWSTONE: 127 MI.

From Jackson, follow **Route 22 West** over the Teton Pass. The road enters Idaho as **Highway 33** and passes through Driggs. After the town of Tetonia, turn north onto **Highway 32** and follow it to Ashton. In Ashton, you can either jump on **Route 20 North** and follow it straight into West Yellowstone or take a small detour via **Highway 45 North,** the **Mesa Falls Scenic Byway,** which joins back up with Rte. 20 just south of the Montana border. It adds 30min. and spectacular waterfall views to the trip.

Big Sky Country
MONTANA
Welcomes You

WEST YELLOWSTONE   ☎406

Much of West Yellowstone is, unsurprisingly, park-oriented. The **Yellowstone Historic Center,** 104 Yellowstone Ave., on the corner of Canyon St., has extensive exhibits on park flora and fauna, earthquakes, fires, and historical development. See old "Snaggletooth," a favorite former grizzly resident and a series of 100-year-old stagecoaches. (☎406-646-7461. Open from mid-May to mid-Oct. daily 9am-9pm. $5, students and children $3, seniors $4.) In the likely event that you didn't see them in the park, the **Grizzly and Wolf Discover Center,** 201 S. Canyon St., gives visitors an opportunity to view the legendary grizzly bear and gray wolf. The center is home to animals that are unable to survive on their own in the wild. The animals are most active early and late in the day, so plan your visit accordingly. (☎406-646-7001 or 800-257-2570; www.grizzlydiscoverctr.org. Open daily 8am-dusk. $9.75, ages 5-12 $5, under 5 free, seniors $9.)

The ▓**West Yellowstone International Hostel ❶,** 139 Yellowstone Ave., at the Madison Hotel, provides some of the best indoor budget accommodations around the park. The friendly staff, rustically themed rooms, and welcoming lobby make travelers feel right at home. (☎800-838-7745. Internet $5 per hr. Open from late May to mid-Oct. Dorms $28; private rooms $45-79. AmEx/D/MC/V.) The **Lazy G Motel ❸,** 123 Hayden St., has 15 spacious 1970s-style rooms with queen-size beds, refrigerators, cable TV, and Wi-Fi. (☎406-646-7586. Reservations recommended. Open May-Mar. Singles $61; doubles $74. D/MC/V.) The ▓Timberline Cafe ❸, 135 Yellowstone Ave., prepares travelers for a day tromping through the park with a large soup-and-salad bar ($9.25) as well as homemade pies ($4 per slice). For a high-energy meal with all the fixings, chow down on the homestyle country-fried steak with soup and salad for $16.25. (☎406-646-9349. Breakfast $5-10. Lunch $6-10. Dinner $15-30. Open daily 6:30am-10pm. AmEx/D/MC/V.) At the **Gusher Pizza & Sandwich Shoppe** ❷, at the corner of Madison and Dunraven, food is only half the fun—partake of the full video-game room, pool tables, and casino. (☎406-646-9050. Open daily 11:30am-10:30pm. D/MC/V.)

◥ DETOUR
BIG SKY

1 Lone Mountain Trail. Located off of **US 191** 45 miles south of Bozeman.

A world-class ski area, Big Sky has over 150 trails and short lift lines. The **Lone Peak** trams reach an altitude of 11,166 ft. for extreme skiing options. (☎800-548-4486; www.bigskyresort.com. Open from mid-Nov. to mid-Apr. daily 9am-4pm. Lift tickets $78, ages 14-21 $58, seniors $68. Ski rentals $30; snowboards $44.) In summer, scenic lift rides soar up Big Sky. (Open from mid-June to early Oct. daily 9:45am-4pm. Full suspension mountain-bike rentals are available and include lift ride to summit ($43 per hr., $87 for 8hr.).

◥ THE ROAD TO BOZEMAN: 89 MI.

From West Yellowstone, take **US 191/287 North** to Bozeman through Yellowstone's northwestern corner and the Gallatin National Forest.

BOZEMAN ☎406

Surrounded by world-class hiking, skiing, and fishing, Bozeman has recently become a magnet for outdoor enthusiasts. Equal parts college town and gateway to the outdoors, Bozeman gives off a hip Western vibe.

VITAL STATS

Population: 36,000

Tourist Office: Bozeman Chamber of Commerce (☎406-586-5421; www.bozemanchamber.com), 1003 N. 7th Ave. Open daily 9am-6pm.

Library and Internet Access: Bozeman Public Library, 220 E. Lamme St. (☎406-582-2400). Open M-Th 10am-8pm, F-Sa 10am-5pm.

Post Office: 32 E. Babcock St. (☎406-586-2373). Open M-F 9am-5pm. **Postal Code:** 59715.

◧ ORIENTATION

I-90/US 191 enters Bozeman from the southeast, and US 191 splits off to become **Main Street** in town. Main St. runs east-west and has major intersections with **Route 86, Seventh Avenue,** and **19th Avenue (Route 412).**

◤ ACCOMMODATIONS

Budget motels line Main St. and Seventh Ave. north of Main.

Bozeman Backpacker's Hostel, 405 W. Olive St. (☎406-586-4659; www.bozemanbackpackershostel.com). Has a kitchen, a dog, and the cheapest beds in town. Dorms $20; private rooms with shared bath $42. ❶

Imperial Inn (☎406-586-3354; www.innbozeman.com). In the heart of downtown. Offers rooms with A/C, cable TV, computers, and free Wi-Fi. In summer singles $59; doubles $69. In winter $10 less. AmEx/D/MC/V. ❸

Bear Canyon Campground (☎800-438-1575), 4 mi. east of Bozeman at Exit 313 off I-90. Great views of the surrounding mountain ranges. Pool, showers, and laundry. Open from May to mid-Oct. Sites $20, with water and electricity $28, with full hookup $33. D/MC/V. ❶

◩ FOOD

Affordable eateries aimed at the college crowd line W. College St. near the university.

MacKenzie River Pizza Co., 232 E. Main St. (☎406-587-0055; www.mackenzieriverpizza.com). Offers gourmet pizzas at decidedly non-gourmet prices. The Sequoia features pesto, tomatoes, artichokes, and almonds. Pizzas $6.25-16;

sandwiches $9. Open M-Th 11am-10pm, F-Sa 11am-11pm, Su noon-9pm. ❸

Pickle Barrel, 809 W. College St. (☎406-587-2411). Enormous sandwiches with fresh ingredients and free pickles have drawn MSU students for years. Hefty 9 in. sandwiches $5.25-6. Open daily in summer 10:30am-10pm; in winter 11am-10:30pm. MC/V. ❶

Cateye Cafe, 23 N. Tracy Ave. (☎406-587-8655). Popular among locals and the college crowd. Serves an eclectic melange of sandwiches and entrees ($7-16). Try the Melazane Sammy, with eggplant and mozzarella ($7.75). Open M and W 7am-2:30pm, Th-F 7am-2:30pm and 5-9pm, Sa 7am-2pm and 5-9pm, Su 7am-2pm. MC/V. ❷

🅖 SIGHTS

🅜MUSEUM OF THE ROCKIES. Get friendly with dinosaurs and other artifacts from Rocky Mountain history at the Museum of the Rockies. Dr. Jack Horner (the model for *Jurassic Park*'s Alan Grant) and other paleontologists make this their base for excavating prehistoric remains throughout the West. See the **largest dinosaur skull ever found.** It's the size of a small car and part of one of the world's most up-to-date dinosaur collections. A host of other exhibits emphasizing local history. *(600 W. Kagy Blvd. ☎406-994-2551; www.museumoftherockies.com. Open in summer daily 8am-8pm; in winter M-Sa 9am-5pm, Su 12:30-5pm. $10, ages 5-18 $7.)*

PIONEER MUSEUM. Standing on the site of the old county jail, the Pioneer Museum offers a look at gallows and jail cells along with artifacts from Bozeman's history. *(317 W. Main St. ☎406-522-8122; www.pioneermuseum.org. Open from mid-May to mid-Sept. M-Sa 10am-5pm; from mid-Sept. to mid-May Tu-Sa 11am-4pm. $3, under 12 free.)*

🅒 NIGHTLIFE

Get the lowdown on music and nightlife from the weekly *Tributary* or *The BoZone.*

Montana Ale Works, 601 E. Main St. (☎406-587-7700). Often voted the best bar in Bozeman. Offers over 30 microbrews. Open daily 4pm-midnight. AmEx/D/MC/V.

Zebra Cocktail Lounge, 320 E. Main St. (☎406-585-8851), in the basement at Rouse Ave. Locals and travelers thirsty for good beer and great live music head over for the large selection of beers. The hipster atmosphere always draws a young, cool crowd. DJ or bands W-Sa. Open daily 8pm-2am. AmEx/D/MC/V with $10 min.

Rocking R Bar, 211 E. Main St. (☎406-587-9355). Offers hot drink specials every night. . Happy hour Tu-Th 5-9pm. Open daily 10:30am-1:40am.

🅝 OUTDOORS

The warm, shallow **Madison River** makes tubing a popular, relaxing, and cheap way to pass long summer days. Rent tubes at **Big Boys Toys,** 28670 Norris Rd. (☎406-587-4747; www.bigboystoysrentals.com. Tubes $7-17 per day. Canoes $35 per day. Open daily 8am-6pm.) **Montana Whitewater** shoots the rapids of the Gallatin River, 7 mi. north of the Big Sky area on US 191. Trips meet at the office, between mileposts 55 and 56 on US 191. (☎800-348-4376; www.montanawhitewater.com. ½-day $49, children $39; full day $81/66.)

🅝 DETOUR
LIVINGSTON

Off **I-90,** 26 mi. east of Bozeman.

Surrounded by three renowned trout-fishing rivers—Yellowstone, Madison, and Gardner—the small town of Livingston is an angler's heaven; the film *A River Runs Through It* was shot here and in Bozeman. Livingston's Main St. features a strip of early 20th-century buildings, including bars (with gambling), restaurants, and fishing outfitters. If fishing is your thing, **Dan Bailey's,** 209 W. Park St. in Livingston, sells licenses and rents gear. (☎406-222-1673 or 800-356-4052. Open in summer M-Sa 7am-7pm, Su 7am-noon; in winter M-Sa 8am-6pm, Su 8am-noon. 2-day fishing license $25. Rod and reel $20; waders and boots $15. AmEx/D/MC/V.)

🅝 DETOUR
LEWIS AND CLARK CAVERNS

On **Route 2,** 20 mi. from Three Fork.

At Lewis and Clark Caverns, visitors can take a tour of the extensive limestone and calcite caves. The 2 mi. tour has steep grades, and stooping and bending are required to descend the 600 steps into the caverns. Be sure to dress warmly; temperatures in the caverns hover around 50°F year-round. Above ground camping is also available. (☎406-287-3541. Tours May-Sept. daily 9:15am-6:30pm. $10, ages 6-11 $5. MC/V.)

⚑ THE ROAD TO BUTTE: 91 MI.

Take **I-90 West** about 30 mi. to the Three Forks exit and continue west along **Route 2.**

BUTTE   ☎406

An old mining town, Butte is popularly described as being "a mile high, a mile deep, and a mile wide." The city is spread over a literal butte, 1 mi. high in the Rocky Mountains. One nearby mine reaches 1 mi. deep, and another, the Berkeley Pit, is 1 mi. wide. The ▧**World Museum of Mining,** 155 Museum Way, presents a realistic look at a mining camp in the 1880s. Located on the site of the silver, lead, and zinc **Orphan Girl Mine,** the 44-acre museum presents the history of mining in exhibits like Hell Roarin' Gulch, a town lined with over 50 reconstructed mining camp businesses. Daily tours circle the museum on the Orphan Girl Express, a train pulled by a 1911 tram engine. Also available is a 1½hr. underground tour into the mine itself with a professional miner who demonstrates mining techniques. (☎406-723-7211; www.miningmuseum.org. Open in summer M-W and Su 9am-5:30pm, Th-Sa 9am-9pm; in winter daily 9am-5:30pm. $7, ages 13-18 $5, ages 5-12 $2, seniors $6. Mine tour $10, students and seniors $8.) The **Mineral Museum,** 1300 W. Park St., located on the Montana Tech campus, displays classic mineral specimens from Butte's underground mines as well as a 27-troy-ounce gold nugget and a 400 lb. smoky quartz crystal called "Big Daddy." (☎406-496-4414. Open from mid-June to mid-Sept. daily 9am-5pm; from mid-Sept. to mid-June M-F 9am-4pm. Free.) The **Mai Wah Museum,** 17 W. Mercury St., was built to honor the Chinese miners who came to Butte to work the mines. (☎406-723-3231; www.mai-wah.org. Open from Memorial Day to Labor Day Tu-Sa 11am-5pm.) Looming over Butte from the east, **Our Lady of the Rockies,** seated on the Continental Divide, is the tallest Madonna statue in America at 90 ft.; her gaze overlooks peaks and valleys for nearly 100 mi. Bus tours to her base leave daily from the Butte Plaza Mall, 3100 Harrison Ave., at 10am and 2pm.

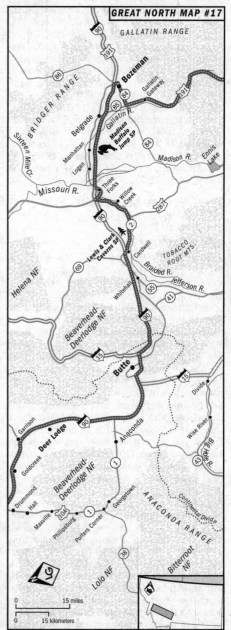

GREAT NORTH MAP #17

GREAT NORTH

10am and 2pm. (☎800-800-5239; www.ourla-dyoftherockies.org. 2hr. tours June-Sept. $15, ages 13-17 $11, under 13 $7, seniors $13.)

Located in historic Uptown Butte, the **Finlen Hotel and Motor Inn ❸**, 100 E. Broadway, was opened in 1923 and has been in constant operation ever since. These hotel rooms once housed copper kings; they now provide lodging for nostalgic visitors. (☎800-729-5461; www.finlen.com. Singles $52-58; doubles $62-68. AmEx/D/MC/V.) What mining town would be complete without pasties? Get the meat-filled pastries at **Park Street Pasties ❶**, 800 W. Park St., for $4. (☎406-782-6400. Open M-F 8am-6pm. AmEx/D/MC/V.)

⚑ THE ROAD TO DEER LODGE: 37 MI.

Hop on **I-90 West** to Deer Lodge.

DEER LODGE   ☎607

Nestled in a sheltered valley, Deer Lodge has always offered gold seekers, ranchers, and settlers the opportunity for a good life. The trout-filled waters of the Clark Fork, Little Blackfoot, and Blackfoot rivers all flow through the area. Today, the town is home to the ⬛**Old Prison Museums** complex, 1106 Main St., a collection of four museums plus other free exhibits. The **Frontier Museum**, 1153 Main St., has the largest display of cowboy collect-ibles between Cody and Calgary and the larg-est collection of (empty) whiskey bottles this side of Kentucky. While still a territory, Mon-tana chose Deer Lodge to hold its prison and very slowly constructed it by inmate labor. Today, you can incarcerate yourself in the **Old Montana Prison**, 1160 Main St. The fortress held at least one member of Butch Cassidy's Wild Bunch and is the final resting place of the "galloping gallows," Montana's official mobile gallows until the state outlawed hang-ing in the late 1990s. The **Montana Auto Museum**, 1160 Main St., showcases over 120 classic cars in chronological order. The collection is sure to make a motorhead drool; offer-ings include Model Ts, Model As, V8 Fords, a DeSoto Airflow, a 1929 Hudson, a 1903 Ford, and an impressive quantity of Burma Shave signs. Across the street from the prison, the **Yesterday's Playthings Museum** is Montana's fore-most doll and toy museum. (☎406-846-3111;

www.pcmaf.org. Prison and Auto Museum open daily in summer 8am-8pm; in winter 8:30am-5pm. Frontier and Playthings Museum open daily in summer 9am-6pm; in winter 8:30am-5pm. 1hr. tours daily in summer 10am, 2pm. Admission to all $9, ages 10-15 $5.)

◥ DETOUR
GARNET GHOST TOWN

From **I-90,** turn right at **Exit 138.** Go east for 10 mi. on **Frontage Road** and then north on **Bear Gulch Road.** The road is steep and unpaved, so be careful!

Montana's history claims more than 600 min-ing camps and towns, many of which vanished as quickly as they appeared when inhabitants fled, following rumors of other strikes. Visit Garnet to see Montana's best-preserved ghost town, once a mining camp. (☎406-522-3856; www.montana.com/ghosttown. Open daily May-Sept. $3, under 16 free.)

> 🏆 **WALDO WISDOM.** The tiny town of Ismay (pop. 26) temporarily changed its name to Joe, Montana, in 1993 to honor the professional football player.

⚑ THE ROAD TO MISSOULA: 81 MI.

Take **I-90/US 12 West** toward Missoula.

MISSOULA   ☎406

A liberal haven in a largely conservative state, Montana's second-largest city attracts new residents every day with its revitalized down-town and bountiful outdoor opportunities. Home to the University of Montana, down-town Missoula is lined with bars and coffee-houses that cater to the large student popula-tion. Four different mountain ranges and five major rivers surround Missoula, supporting skiing during the winter and fly fishing, hik-ing, and biking during the summer.

◨ ORIENTATION

The **Clark Fork River** divides Missoula into northern and southern halves. From west to east, the city's principal routes are **Reserve Street** (portions of which are US 93), **Orange Street,** and **Higgins Avenue.** The principal east-west route is **Broadway Street (Business I-90/**

Route 200). Downtown lies north of the river, around the intersection of N. Higgins Ave. and Broadway St. The **University of Montana** lies southeast of downtown, accessible by heading south on Madison St. from Broadway. Businesses outside of downtown have parking lots, and meters are readily available in the downtown area during business hours.

VITAL STATS

Population: 57,000

Tourist Office: Missoula Convention and Visitors Bureau, 1121 E. Broadway, Ste. 103. (☎406-532-3250). Open M-F 8am-7pm, Sa-Su 10am-2pm.

Library and Internet Access: Missoula Public Library, 301 E. Main St. (☎406-721-2665; www. missoulapubliclibrary.com). Open M-Th 10am-9pm, F-Sa 10am-6pm, Su 1-5pm.

Post Office: 200 E. Broadway St. (☎406-329-2222). Open M-F 8am-5:30pm. **Postal Code:** 59801.

ACCOMMODATIONS

There are no hostels in Missoula, but there are plenty of inexpensive options on Broadway.

Aspen Motel, 3720 Rte. 200 E. (☎406-721-9758), in East Missoula. Take I-90 E. to Exit 107 and travel ½ mi. east. The motel has spacious rooms with A/C, cable TV, coffee, and breakfast included. Free Wi-Fi. Singles $45. ❷

Missoula/El-Mar KOA Kampground, 3450 Tina Ave. (☎406-549-0881 or 800-562-5366), just south of Broadway off Reserve St. One of the best KOAs around, providing shaded tent sites apart from RVs as well as a pool, hot tub, minigolf course, and 24hr. laundry facilities. Tent sites $25-30. Cabins $42-48. AmEx/D/MC/V. ❶

FOOD

Missoula, the culinary capital of Montana, has a number of innovative, delicious, and inexpensive eating establishments. Head downtown, north of the Clark Fork River along Higgins Ave., and check out the array of restaurants and coffeehouses that line the road.

Butterfly Herbs, 232 N. Higgins Ave. (☎406-728-8780; www.butterflyherbs.com). Walk through the gift shop/pharmacy to find exciting alternatives to diner fare like the hummus sandwich ($4), chai milkshake ($3), and organic green salad ($2.50). Open M-F 7am-7pm, Sa-Su 9am-5:30pm. MC/V. ❶

Tipu's Tiger, 115 S. 4th St. W. (☎406-542-0622). One of the only vegetarian establishments and the first Indian restaurant in Montana. All-you-can-eat lunch buffet ($7) is available until 4:30pm. Open Tu-Th and Su 11am-8:30pm, F-Sa 11am-9:30pm. AmEx/D/MC/V. ❷

Taco del Sol, 422 N. Higgins Ave. (☎406-240-3480; www.tacodelsol.com). Get a Mission Burrito and other Mexican favorites for under $5. Tacos from $2.50. Open M-Sa 11am-10pm, Su noon-9pm. MC/V. ❶

SIGHTS

Pick up the *Missoula Gallery Guide* brochure at the tourist office for a self-guided tour of Missoula's art galleries.

SMOKEJUMPER CENTER. Missoula's hottest sight is the nation's largest training base for aerial firefighters who parachute into flaming forests. *(5765 Rte. 10. Just past the airport, 7 mi. northwest of town on Broadway. ☎406-329-4934. Open from Memorial Day to Labor Day daily 8:30am-5pm; from Labor Day to Memorial Day by appointment. 4-5 tours per day 10am-4pm. Free.)*

CAROUSEL. Located in Caras Riverfront Park, the Carousel is a hand-carved merry-go-round. *(☎406-549-8382. Open daily June-Aug. 11am-7pm; Sept.-May 11am-5:30pm. $1.50.)*

HISTORICAL MUSEUM AT FORT MISSOULA. The museum displays 22,000 artifacts from Missoula's past. *(In Bldg. 322 at Fort Missoula, on South Ave. 1 block west of Reserve St. ☎406-728-3476; www.fortmissoulamuseum.org. Open from Memorial Day to Labor Day M-Sa 10am-5pm, Su noon-5pm; from Labor Day to Memorial Day Tu-Su noon-5pm. $3, students $1, seniors $2.)*

ROCKIN' RUDY'S. Signs and bumper stickers all over town read "Keep Missoula Weird," and no business better exemplifies this sentiment than does Rudy's. Much more than just a record store, this enormous outfitter of strange ephemera sells everything from inflatable moose heads and Hawaiian shirts to some surprisingly nice jewelry. *(237 Blaine St. ☎406-542-0077; www.rockinrudys.com. Open M-Sa 9am-9pm, Su 11am-6pm.)*

LOLO HOT SPRINGS. The 103-105°F springs were a meeting place for local Native Americans and were frequented by Lewis and Clark in 1806. Today, you can swim in a pool fed by the springs. *(35 mi. southwest of Missoula on Rte. 12 in Lolo National Forest. ☎406-273-2290 or 800-273-2290; www.lolohotsprings.com. Open daily 10am-10pm. $7, under 13 $5.)*

🕯 NIGHTLIFE

The *Independent* and *Lively Times*, available at newsstands and cafes, offer the lowdown on the Missoula music scene, while the *Entertainer*, in the Friday *Missoulian*, has movie and event schedules. *Out Words*, another free publication available in most cafes, supplies information for Montana's GBLT scene. College students swarm the downtown bar area around Front St. and Higgins Ave. during the school year. Bars have a more relaxed atmosphere in summer.

Charlie B's, 428 N. Higgins Ave. (☎406-549-3589). Draws an eclectic clientele of bikers, farmers, students, and hippies. Framed photos of longtime regulars cover the walls—park at the bar for 10 or 20 years and join them. Hungry boozers can weave their way to the **Dinosaur Cafe** at the back of the room for creole delights. Bowl of jambalaya $5.25. Open daily 8am-2am.

Iron Horse Brew Pub, 501 N. Higgins Ave. (☎406-728-8866; www.ironhorsebrewpub.com). Always packs a crowd. The relaxed patio fills up during summer. Pints $2.50-4. Open daily 11am-2am. AmEx/D/MC/V.

The Kettle House Brewing Co., 602 Myrtle (☎406-728-1660; www.kettlehouse.com), 1 block west of Higgins between 4th and 5th. Follow the advice of the "beer coaches" and "support your local brewery." Serves an assortment of beers, including its hemp beer, Fresh Bongwater Pale Ale. Pints $3.75. Open M-Sa noon-9pm; no beer served after 8pm. D/MC/V.

🏔 OUTDOORS

Nearby parks, recreation areas, and surrounding wilderness areas make Missoula an outdoor enthusiast's dream.

BIKING

Bicycle-friendly Missoula is located along both the Transamerica and the Great Parks bicycle routes, and all major streets have designated bike lanes. Pick up a free bike map from the visitors center. **Open Road Bicycles and Nordic Equipment,** 517 S. Orange St., has bike rentals. (☎406-549-2453. $3.50 per hr., $17.50 per day. Open M-F 9am-6pm, Sa 10am-5pm, Su 11am-3pm.) The national **Adventure Cycling Association,** 150 E. Pine St., is the place to go for info about local trails, including the Transamerica and Great Parks routes. (☎406-721-1776 or 800-755-2453; www.adventurecycling.org. Open from spring to fall M-F 8am-5pm.) The **Rattlesnake Wilderness National Recreation Area,** 11 mi. northeast of town off the Van Buren St. exit on I-90, and the **Pattee Canyon Recreation Area,** 3 mi. east of Higgins on Pattee Canyon Dr., are highly recommended for their biking trails.

HIKING

As might be expected in a town surrounded by mountains, hiking opportunities also abound in the Missoula area. The relatively easy 30min. hike to the "M" (for the U of M, not Missoula) on **Mount Sentinel** has a tremendous view of Missoula and the surrounding mountains. The Rattlesnake Wilderness National Recreation Area, named for the river's shape (there are no rattlers for miles), is 11 mi. northeast of town, off the Van Buren St. exit from I-90, and makes for a great day of hiking. Other popular areas include **Pattee Canyon** and **Blue Mountain,** south of town. Maps ($7) and info on longer hikes in the Bitterroot and Bob Marshall areas are at the **US Forest Service Information Office,** 200 E. Broadway; the entrance is at 200 Pine St. (☎406-329-3511. Open M-F 8am-4pm.) For rentals, stop by **Trailhead,** 221 E. Front St. (☎406-543-6966; www.trailheadmontana.com. Tents $8-14. Open M-F 9:30am-8pm, Sa 9am-6pm, Su 11am-6pm.)

SKIING

Alpine and Nordic skiing keep Missoulians busy during winter. With a 1500 ft. vertical drop, three lifts, and 23 runs, **Marshall Mountain** is a great place to learn how to ski and has night skiing. (☎406-258-6000. Lift tickets $24, children $19.) Experienced skiers should check out the extreme **Montana Snowbowl,** 12 mi. northwest of Missoula, with a vertical drop of 2600 ft., an average annual snowfall of 300 in., and over 35 trails. (☎406-549-9777 or 800-728-2695; www.montanasnowbowl.com. Open Nov.-Apr. daily 9:30am-4pm. Lift tickets $36, children $16. Rentals $14.)

WATER ACTIVITIES

The **Blackfoot River,** along Rte. 200 east of Bonner, is an excellent place to tube or raft on a hot day. Call the **Montana State Regional Parks and Wildlife Office,** 3201 Spurgin Rd., for info about rafting locations. (☎406-542-5500. Open M-F 8am-5pm.) Rent tubes or rafts from the **Army and Navy Economy Store,** 322 N. Higgins. Ave. (☎406-721-1315; www.armynavyeconomy.com. Tubes $4 per day. Rafts $60 per day. Open M-F 9am-7:30pm, Sa 9am-5:30pm, Su 10am-5:30pm. AmEx/D/MC/V.)

Western Montana is fly-fishing country, and Missoula is at its heart. Fishing licenses are required and can be purchased from the **Department of Fish, Wildlife, and Parks,** 3201 Spurgin Rd. (☎406-542-5500), or from sporting-goods stores. **Kingfisher,** 926 E. Broadway, offers licenses ($25-70) and fishing trips. (☎406-721-6141; www.kingfisherflyshop.com. Trips from $345. Open in summer daily 7am-7pm; hours vary in winter.)

◪ DETOUR
NATIONAL BISON RANGE

Take **I-90 West** out of town and exit in Ravalli. Take **Route 200 West.** Follow the signs and take a right onto **Route 212** 5 mi. after Ravalli. The entrance to the park is 5 mi. north, on your right.

The National Bison Range was established in 1908 to save bison from extinction. At one time, 30-70 million bison roamed the plains, but after years of hunting the population dropped to less than 1000. Today the range is home to 350-500 bison as well as deer, pronghorn, elk, bighorn sheep, and mountain goats. The **Red Sleep Mountain** self-guided tour offers a view of the Flathead Valley and the best chance for wildlife observation, but shorter routes exist. Early morning and evening are the best wildlife viewing times. The Wild West comes alive the first Monday and Tuesday of October during the **Roundup,** in which

wranglers gather the bison together to do checkups and herd-size management. (☎406-644-2211. Visitors center open from mid-May to Oct. M-F 8am-6pm, Sa-Su 9am-6pm; from Nov. to mid-May M-F 8am-4:30pm. Red Sleep Mountain Dr. open mid-May to mid-Oct. daily 7am-sunset. $5 per vehicle.)

◪ THE ROAD TO ST. IGNATIUS: 41 MI.
Follow **US 93** into the quiet mountain country.

ST. IGNATIUS ☎406

Named for the Jesuit mission for which it is best known, St. Ignatius sits just east of US 93 at the foot of the Mission Mountains on the Flathead Indian Reservation. While there's not much to see in town, **Saint Ignatius Catholic Mission,** the brick building just off the highway, is worth a look. Founded in 1854 at the request of the local Salish and Kootenai tribes, the mission's 1891 church features 58 frescoes and murals painted by the mission cook, Brother Carignano. (☎406-745-2768. Open daily 9am-8pm. Donations accepted.) Across the highway from town, Colonel Doug Allard's mini-empire constitutes most of the services offered in St. Iggy's, starting with **Colonel Doug Allard's Indian Museum and Trading Post.** Visitors can see traditional native clothing and artifacts as well as a small display of stuffed (read: dead) animals. An attached gallery includes works by local artists. (☎406-745-2951. Open daily 9am-5pm. Free.) Head to **The Malt Shop ❶,** 101 First St., for burgers, hot dogs, and tasty sandwiches ($1-5). The huckleberry milkshake ($3.25) is delightful. (☎406-745-3501. Open M-Sa 10:30am-10pm, Su 11:30am-9pm. MC/V.)

◪ THE ROAD TO POLSON AND FLATHEAD LAKE: 28 MI.
Follow **US 93 (Main Street)** through town, around the courthouse rotary, and out to the west shore of beautiful Flathead Lake, which the highway follows straight to Polson.

POLSON AND FLATHEAD LAKE ☎406

On the southern side of Flathead Lake, Polson has a small town's share of outdoor activities and art, but the real reason to stop here is

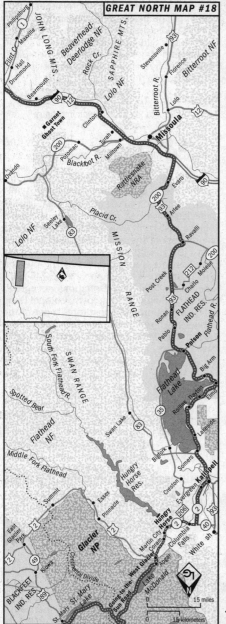

GREAT NORTH MAP #18

the **Miracle of America Museum,** 36094 Memory Ln., off US 93 just before town. With displays of old posters, uniforms, motorcycles, and weapons, the museum is the life's work of proprietor Gil Mangels. A recreated general store, saddlery, barber shop, soda fountain, and gas station sit among such oddities as an 1898 sheep-powered treadmill. The museum celebrates **Live History Day** the third weekend in July. (☎406-883-6804. Open June-Sept. daily 8am-8pm; Oct.-May M-Sa 8am-5pm, Su 1:30-5pm. $4, ages 3-12 $1.) Fresh-fruit stands line Flathead Lake. Renowned for its fish and adjacent cherry trees, the lake is skirted by US 93 between Polson and Kalispell. The largest island you'll see as you drive along the shore is the 2000-acre **Wild Horse Island,** accessible only by boat, where the Salish-Kootenai Indians used to pasture their horses to prevent theft by neighboring tribes. Today, Montana allows a few neutered and vaccinated "wild" horses to roam free. The waters near Polson have some of the best Class II and Class III rafting around, and the **Flathead Raft Company,** 1501 US 93, prepares visitors for the experience. (☎406-883-5838 or 800-654-4359; www. flatheadraftco.com. Open M-F 9am-7pm, Sa-Su 9am-6pm. ½-day trips $42, ages 8-12 $34, seniors $36.) The famous **Buffalo Rapids** of the Lower Flathead River are especially good at folding your raft in half and tossing your shipmates overboard. A local secret, **Blacktail Mountain Ski Resort,** in Lakeside, is one of the newest ski areas in the country. The lone ski lodge is a welcome break from the crowded ski resorts scattered throughout the Rocky Mountains—you won't find any lift lines here. (☎406-844-0999; www.blacktailmountain. com. Lift tickets $36, ages 13-17 $25.)

Most lodging on the lake is expensive, but there are some affordable options. **Edgewater Motel** ➍, 7140 US 93, in Lakeside, has rooms with kitchenettes, some facing the lake. (☎406-844-3644 or 800-424-3798. Open in summer. RV sites $34. Singles from $70. Cabins $120. AmEx/D/MC/V.) The **Cherry Hill Motel** ➌, 1810 US 93, in Polson, offers clean and comfortable rooms just north of the museum. (☎406-883-2737. Singles $63; doubles $67. MC/V.) **M&S Meats** ➊, 86755 US 93, just after Dayton, is worth a stop for some of the best jerky you'll ever taste ($12-25 per lb.).

Jerky and sausage are made with either beef or bison meat. (☎406-844-3414 or 800-454-3414. Open daily 7:30am-6pm. D/MC/V.)

⚐ THE ROAD TO KALISPELL: 51 MI.
Drive along the western shore of the lake via **US 93 North** to reach Kalispell.

KALISPELL ☎406
Nestled between the ski haven Big Mountain and gorgeous Flathead Lake, Kalispell mixes an outdoor orientation with the art and culture of the largest urban center of northwestern Montana. While it may not take long to get a feel for the town proper, Kalispell is a gateway to the wild Montana countryside.

✴ ORIENTATION
Kalispell is laid out in a grid centered on the intersection of **Main Street (US 93)** and **Idaho Street (Route 2),** the older highway around which the town's businesses first developed. Numbered avenues flank Main St., increasing in number as they move out in both directions, with "East" and "West" designating their orientation. Numbered streets count southward from **Center Street,** while streets north of Center bear state names.

VITAL STATS
Population: 15,000
Tourist Office: Chamber of Commerce, 15 Depot Park (☎406-758-2800), on Main St. at Center St. Open M-F 8am-5pm.
Library and Internet Access: Flathead County Library, 247 1st Ave. E. (☎406-758-5819), 1 block off Main St. (US 93). Open M-Th 10am-8pm, F 10am-5pm, Sa 11am-5pm.
Post Office: 350 N. Meridian Rd. (☎406-755-6450), right off US 2 west of Main St., at 3rd St. Open M-F 8:30am-5:30pm, Sa 10am-2pm. **Postal Code:** 59904.

⚑ ACCOMMODATIONS
A few chain motels dot the sides of Main St. on the south side of town, just past the courthouse. Older, privately run establishments crop up along Idaho St. as you head east.

The Kalispell Grand Hotel, 100 Main St. (☎800-858-7422; www.kalispellgrand.com), at 1st St., has provided the finest that "frontier hotels" have to offer since 1912. Vintage architecture blends seamlessly with jetted bathtubs and high-speed Internet access. Singles $92-133; doubles $99-140. AmEx/D/MC/V. ❹

Blue & White Motel, 640 E. Idaho St. (Rte. 2), (☎800-382-3577), 6 blocks east of Main St. Spruces up the motel experience with an indoor swimming pool, a sauna, and a hot tub. Singles $77; doubles $83-94. D/MC/V. ❸

⬛ FOOD
A variety of chain restaurants line US 93 and US 2, but a few local eateries can be found.

Bojangles Diner, 1319 US 2 W. (☎406-755-3222). A 50s-style throwback replete with a jukebox. Breakfasts $3.50-12. Burgers and sandwiches $6-8. Open daily 7am-3pm. AmEx/D/MC/V. ❷

DG Barley's Brewhouse & Grill, 285 N. Main St. (☎406-756-2222), at the junction of US 93 and US 2. Serves up Southwestern fare in a kitschy, glam-ranch atmosphere. Steaks $15-24. Salads $7-13. Burgers $7-12. Open M-Th 11:30am-10pm, F-Sa 11:30am-10:30pm, Su noon-10pm. AmEx/D/MC/V. ❸

◉ SIGHTS
Museums, small stores, and galleries give the downtown area around Main St. more character than most towns of this size.

HOCKADAY MUSEUM OF ART. The museum houses a collection of art inspired by Glacier National Park along with rotating exhibits of nationally renowned and emerging artists. (*302 2nd Ave. E. ☎406-755-5268. Open Tu-F 10am-6pm, Sa 10am-5pm, Su noon-4pm. $5, students $2, ages 6-18 $1, seniors $4.*)

CONRAD MANSION NATIONAL HISTORIC SITE MUSEUM. The mansion shows 26 beautifully furnished rooms in their original 1895 condition along with pleasant gardens and a Victorian gift shop. (*6 blocks east of Main St. on 4th St. E. ☎406-755-2166. Open in summer Tu-Su 10am-5pm. Tours every hr. until 4pm. $8, under 12 $3.*)

⚐ THE ROAD TO HUNGRY HORSE: 27 MI.
Head east on **East Idaho Street (US 2).**

HUNGRY HORSE ☎406

Named after two starving horses, Tex and Jerry, who survived the bitter winter of 1900, Hungry Horse advertises itself as the "friendliest dam town in the West." The impressive Hungry Horse Dam controls the flow of the Flathead River. Stop by **The Huckleberry Patch ❶**, 8868 US 2, which specializes in Montana's local berry, a tart, blueberry-like fruit. For a treat, try the huckleberry milkshakes ($3.50-5). The restaurant serves pancake breakfasts ($4-8) made with, of course, huckleberries. (☎406-387-5000 or 800-527-7340; www.huckleberrypatch.com. Open in summer daily 8am-10pm. AmEx/D/MC/V.)

🚶 THE ROAD TO GLACIER NATIONAL PARK: 11 MI.

Continue on **US 2 East** for a few more miles to bring you to West Glacier. Turn left onto **Going-to-the-Sun Road,** which brings you into the park.

GLACIER NATIONAL PARK ☎406

Glacier National Park makes up most of the Waterton-Glacier Peace Park; although technically one park, Waterton-Glacier is actually two distinct areas: the small Waterton Lakes National Park in Alberta and the enormous Glacier National Park in Montana. Waterton-Glacier transcends international boundaries to encompass one of the most strikingly beautiful portions of the Rockies. The massive Rocky Mountain peaks span both parks, providing sanctuary for endangered bears, bighorn sheep, moose, mountain goats, mountain lions, and gray wolves—it's the only area in the lower 48 states with its historical predators intact. Perched high in the Northern Rockies, Glacier is sometimes called the "Crown of the Continent," and the alpine lakes and glaciers shine like jewels.

◼ ORIENTATION

Linking **West Glacier** and **Saint Mary,** ◼**Going-to-the-Sun Road,** the only road through the park, is a spectacular 52 mi. scenic drive climbing 3000 ft. through cedar forests, mountain passes, and arctic tundra. (Allow 2-3hr. or more. Closed in winter.) **US 2** skirts the southern border of the park. At **Goat Lick,** about halfway between East and West Glacier, mountain goats traverse steep cliffs to lick up natural salt deposits. **US 89** heads north along the east edge of the park through St. Mary.

🏠 ACCOMMODATIONS

Staying indoors within Glacier is expensive, but several affordable options lie just outside the park boundaries. On the west side of the park, the small, electricity-less town of **Polebridge** provides access to Glacier's remote and pristine northwest corner. From Apgar, take Camas Rd. north and take a right onto the poorly marked gravel North Fork Rd., just past a bridge over the North Fork of the Flathead River. (Avoid Inside North Fork Rd.—your shocks will thank you.) From Columbia Falls, take Rte. 486 northbound. To the east, inexpensive lodging is just across the park border in **East Glacier.** The distant offices of park concessioner **Glacier Park, Inc.** (☎406-756-2444; www.glacierparkinc.com), handle reservations for all in-park lodging.

🏠 **Brownies Grocery (HI-AYH),** 1020 Rte. 49 (☎406-226-4426), in East Glacier Park. Check in at the grocery counter and head up to the spacious hostel. Kitchen, showers, and a view of the Rockies. Linen and laundry. Internet $1.75 per 15min. Key deposit $5. Check-in by 9pm. Reservations recommended; credit card required. Open from mid-May to Sept., weather permitting. Tent sites $10. Dorms $16; private singles $21; doubles $29; family rooms $41. MC/V. ❶

North Fork Hostel, 80 Beaver Dr. (☎406-888-5241), in Polebridge. The wood walls and kerosene lamps are reminiscent of a hunting lodge. Showers and a beautiful, fully equipped kitchen, but no flush toilets. During the winter, old-fashioned wood stoves warm frozen fingers. Linen $3. Canoe rentals $20 per day; mountain bikes free. Check-out noon. Call ahead. Open Apr.-Oct. Dorms $15; tipis $30 per person; cabins $35; log homes $70. AmEx/D/MC/V. ❶

Backpacker's Inn Hostel, 29 Dawson Ave. (☎406-226-9392), in East Glacier, at Serrano's, the Mexican restaurant. 8 clean beds in a co-ed cabin. Sleeping bags $1. Hot showers. Open May-Sept. Dorms $12; singles $30; doubles from $40. AmEx/D/MC/V. ❶

GREAT NORTH

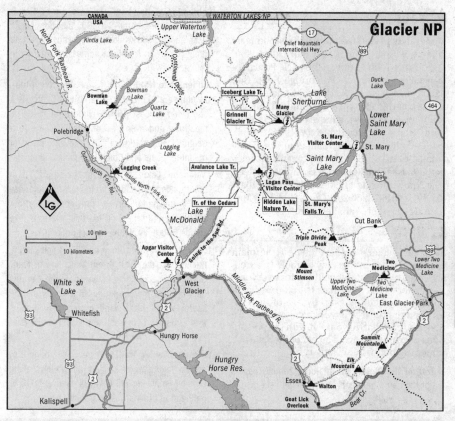

Glacier NP

Swiftcurrent Motor Inn (☎406-732-5531), in Many Glacier Valley. One of the few budget motels in the area. Most cabins have shared bath. Open from early June to early Sept. 1-bedroom cabins $55; 2-bedroom $65; cottage with private bath $80; motel rooms $107-124. AmEx/D/MC/V. ❸

🏕 CAMPING

Visitors planning overnight backpacking trips must obtain the necessary backcountry permits. With the exception of the Nyack/Coal Creek camping zone, all **backcountry camping** must be done at designated campsites equipped with pit toilets, tent sites, food preparation areas, and food-hanging devices. (June-Sept. $5 per person, ages 9-16 $2.50; Oct.-May free. For an additional $30, reserva-

tions are accepted beginning in mid-Apr. for trips between June 15 and Oct. 31. AmEx/D/MC/V.) Pick up a free and indispensable *Backcountry Camping Guide* from a visitors center or the **Backcountry Permit Center,** next to the visitors center in Apgar, which also has valuable info for those seeking to explore Glacier's less traveled areas. (Open daily from July to mid-Sept. 7am-4pm; from mid-Sept. to Oct. and May-June 8am-4pm.) The park also maintains 13 campgrounds (8 with flush toilets), ranging $6-17 per night. The largest and closest to the West Glacier entrance is **Apgar Campground ❶**, with 192 wooded sites just off Lake McDonald. (Open from May to mid-Oct. Sites $15. AmEx/D/MC/V.)

FOOD

Moderately priced restaurants exist in major villages within the park, but more affordable options are found outside the park. **Polebridge Mercantile Store ❶**, on Polebridge Loop Rd., half a mile east of N. Fork Rd., has homemade pastries ($1-4) as splendid as the surrounding peaks. Gas, gifts, groceries, and pay phones are also available. (☎406-888-5105. Open daily June-Sept. 8am-9pm; Oct.-May 8am-6pm. MC/V.) Sample Montanan delicacies at the **Whistle Stop Restaurant ❷**, in East Glacier, best known for its huckleberry French toast ($7.50). (☎406-226-9292. Open from mid-May to mid-Sept. daily 7am-9pm. AmEx/D/MC/V.)

HIKING

Most of Glacier's scenery lies off the main roads and is accessible only by foot. An extensive trail system has something for everyone, from short, easy day hikes to rigorous backcountry expeditions. Stop by one of the visitors centers for free day-hike guides. Beware of bears. Familiarize yourself with the precautions necessary to avoid an encounter and ask rangers about wildlife activity.

Trail of the Cedars (½ mi. loop, 20min.) begins at the same trailhead as Avalanche Lake and is an easy walk.

Saint Mary Falls (1 mi., 1hr. round-trip). Beginning on Going-to-the-Sun Rd. between Logan Pass and St. Mary, this trail descends 260 ft. to bring you to an small but impressive cataract in the St. Mary River.

Hidden Lake Nature Trail (3 mi., 2hr. round-trip), beginning at the Logan Pass Visitors Center, is a short and modest 460 ft. climb through alpine meadows and over the Continental Divide to a beautiful view of Hidden Lake. A favorite place for mountain goats and Columbian ground squirrels.

Avalanche Lake (4 mi., 3hr. round-trip) is a breathtaking trail and by far the most popular day hike in the park. Starting north of Lake McDonald on Going-to-the-Sun Rd., this moderate hike climbs 500 ft. to picture-perfect panoramas.

Iceberg Lake (7 mi., 5hr. round-trip) begins at the trailhead at the Swiftcurrent Motor Inn in Many Glacier. The trail climbs steeply for the 1st mi., then inclines more gradually. The lake rivals the beauty of any in the world, circled by mountains with turquoise blue water and icebergs that float in the lake year-round.

Grinnell Glacier Trail (11 mi., 7hr. round-trip) passes near several glaciers and follows along Grinnell Point and Mt. Grinnell, gaining 1600 ft. Trailhead at the Many Glacier Picnic Area.

BLASTING THE PASS

When the Canadian Pacific Railway was plotting routes for its trans-Canada line in the 1880s, it was faced with the decision of heading north, through the Yellowhead Pass, or south, over a steeper pass in the Rockies and an as-yet-undiscovered pass through the Selkirk range, where Glacier National Park sits today. The railroad decided (against the advice of its engineers) to take the southern route, in order to prevent US railroads from making a land grab in southern British Columbia. To find a pass through Selkirk, Canadian Pacific hired AB Rogers, an American engineer, offering him a $5000 bonus if he actually found a pass. Rogers was known for three things: an immense mustache, superhuman endurance, and an uncontrollable temper resulting in a constant stream of profanity. The men who had ventured into the unknown wilderness with him were kept in constant fear of their boss's unpredictable anger. Rogers did find his pass, a narrow slot that today bears his name. The Canadian Pacific was completed in 1882 and Rogers received his $5000. He was more interested in glory than money, however, and had the check framed. His check lasted longer than his pass—avalanches closed the route so frequently in winter that the Connaught Tunnel bypassed the area in 1916.

⚠ OTHER OUTDOORS

Opportunities for **cycling** are limited and confined to roadways and designated bike paths; cycling on trails is strictly prohibited. Although the **Going-to-the-Sun Road** is a popular route, only experienced cyclists with appropriate gear and legs of titanium should attempt this grueling ride; the sometimes nonexistent road shoulder can create hazardous situations. The **Inside North Fork Road,** which runs from Kintla Lake to Fish Creek on the west side of the park, is good for mountain biking, as are the old logging roads in the **Flathead National Forest.** Equestrian explorers should check that trails are open; there are steep fines for using closed trails. Two-hour trail rides from **Swan Mountain Outfitters** are available at Many Glacier, Apgar, and Lake McDonald. (☎406-387-4405; www.swanmountainoutfitters.com. From May to early Sept. daily 8:30, 10:45am, 1:15, 3:30pm. $50.)

The **Glacier Park Boat Company** (☎406-257-2426) runs boat tours ($12-16) that explore Glacier's lakes. **Glacier Raft Company,** in West Glacier, leads trips down the middle fork of the Flathead River. (☎800-235-6781. ½-day $46, under 13 $36; full day with lunch $78/55.) You can rent rowboats, kayaks, and canoes (all $14 per hr.) and outboards ($24 per hr.) at Lake McDonald, Two Medicine, and Apgar.

No permit is needed to fish in the park, and limits are high in the main lakes. Some areas, however, are severely restricted, and certain species may be catch-and-release. Pick up *Fishing Regulations*, available at visitors centers, for info.

⌁ DETOUR
CATTLE BARON SUPPER CLUB

At the intersection of **US 89** and the road to Many Glacier, in **Babb.**

The **Cattle Baron Supper Club** ⑤ might just be the nicest surprise you'll ever find in the middle of nowhere; inside the immense and beautiful dining room, complete with murals, a buffalo jump sculpture, and an enormous pine tree that grows right through the mid-

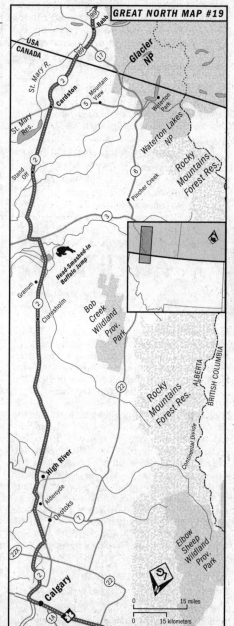

GREAT NORTH MAP #19

dle of the building, waiters in tuxedos serve amazing steaks ($24-29) and seafood entrees ($20-30). The food may be expensive, but the Cattle Baron has been known to convert vegetarians. (☎406-732-4033. Open daily 5-10pm. Bar open until midnight. D/MC/V.)

⚑ THE ROAD TO CARDSTON: 35 MI.

From St. Mary, take **US 89 North** to the **Piegan/Carway border crossing** (open daily 7am-11pm). In Canada, US 89 becomes **Highway 2.**

> **LEAVING THE US.** See **Vital Documents** (p. 16) for info on passport, visa, and identification requirements. From here, all prices are listed in **Canadian dollars.**

The Sunshine Province

ALBERTA

Welcomes You!

CARDSTON ☎403

Cardston, located in the Lee Creek Valley where the foothills of the Rockies meet the Great Plains, became the center of the Canadian Mormon Church after some of Brigham Young's descendents migrated here. There are several worthwhile attractions in town, including the **Fay Wray Fountain,** just over the bridge past the visitors center, which honors the hometown girl who was hoisted to fame by King Kong. The **⬛Remington Carriage** Museum, 623 Main St., houses over 250 horse-drawn vehicles, the largest collection in the New World. Watch master craftsmen at work in the restoration shop or take a carriage ride. (☎403-653-5139; www.remington-centre.com. Open daily from mid-May to mid-Sept. 9am-6pm; from mid-Sept. to mid-May 10am-5pm. $9, ages 7-17 $5, seniors $8.)

⬛ DETOUR
HEAD-SMASHED-IN BUFFALO JUMP

Located 11 mi. from Fort MacLeod on **Route 785.**

For over 10,000 years, Native Americans stampeded buffalo off sandstone cliffs. Legend has

it that this particular buffalo jump got its name from a young brave who wanted to witness the falling buffalo. Standing in the shelter of an overhanging ledge, he was trapped by the mounting bodies. When his people came to collect the buffalo, they found him with his skull crushed and named the place "Head-Smashed-In." Today you can visit the jump that was used for at least 5700 years. The 650 ft. **Cliff Top Trail,** accessible from the interpretive center, overlooks the kill site. (☎403-553-2731; www.head-smashed-in.com. Open daily from mid-May to mid-Sept. 9am-6pm; from mid-Sept. to mid-May 10am-5pm. $9, ages 7-17 $5, under 7 free.)

> **❓ DID YOU KNOW?** The United Nations named Head-Smashed-In a **UNESCO World Heritage Site;** 30 ft. deep beds of bone and tools make this one of the best-preserved buffalo jumps in North America.

⚑ THE ROAD TO HIGH RIVER: 107 MI.

From Cardston, **Highway 2** is a straight shot all the way to Calgary. The road north from Cardston might just be flatter than South Dakota. Prepare for locusts dive-bombing your car and delicate little white butterflies launching themselves to a gruesome demise on your bumper. Just before you arrive, you'll pass Canada's largest wind farm. Continue north on **Route 2** toward downtown High River.

HIGH RIVER ☎403

The best way to see High River is to follow the 9 mi. **Happy Trails** pathway system, which winds by a number of murals that transform the concrete walls of downtown shops into works of art. Exhibits rotate at the **Museum of the Highwood,** 406 First St. SW. Past exhibits have focused on themes in local history ranging from music to furniture and ladies' hairstyles. Local history and reference material is also archived here. (☎403-652-7156. Open from mid-May to Sept. M-Sa 10am-4pm, Su noon-4pm. $3, students and seniors $2, under 16 free.) The food is as unique as the atmosphere at the **⬛Whistle Stop Cafe ❷,** 406 First St. SW, adjacent to the Museum of the

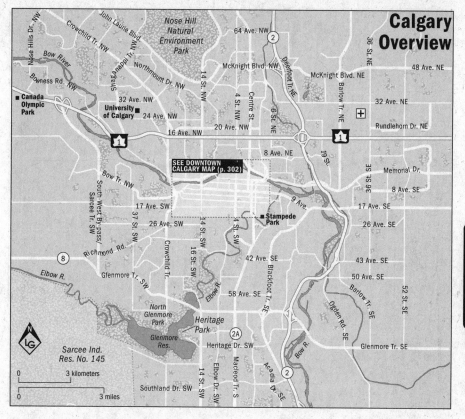

Calgary Overview

SEE DOWNTOWN CALGARY MAP (p. 302)

GREAT NORTH

Highwood, in the dining car of an old train. Try the shrimp and avocado sandwich ($9.25) or a slice of the amazing Donna's Homemade Bread for $0.95. (☎403-652-7156. Open Tu-Sa 10am-4pm, Su 10am-3pm. MC/V.)

THE ROAD TO CALGARY: 41 MI.

Continue north on **Route 2** toward Calgary.

CALGARY   ☎403

Mounties founded Calgary in the 1870s to control Canada's flow of illegal whiskey, but oil made the city what it is today. Petroleum fuels Calgary's economy and explains why the city hosts the largest number of corporate headquarters in Canada outside Toronto. As the host of the 1988 Winter Olympics, Calgary's dot on the map grew larger; already Alberta's largest city, this thriving young metropolis is the fastest-growing in all of Canada.

ORIENTATION

Calgary is 78 mi. east of Banff along the **Trans-Canada Highway (Highway 1)**, which becomes 16th Ave. in town. The city is divided into quadrants: **Centre Street** is the east-west divider, while the **Bow River** splits the city north and south. Avenues run east-west, streets north-south. The light-rail **C-Train** runs in a zigzag across downtown, from the northwest to the southeast. Ride for free along **Seventh Avenue** ($1.60 elsewhere).

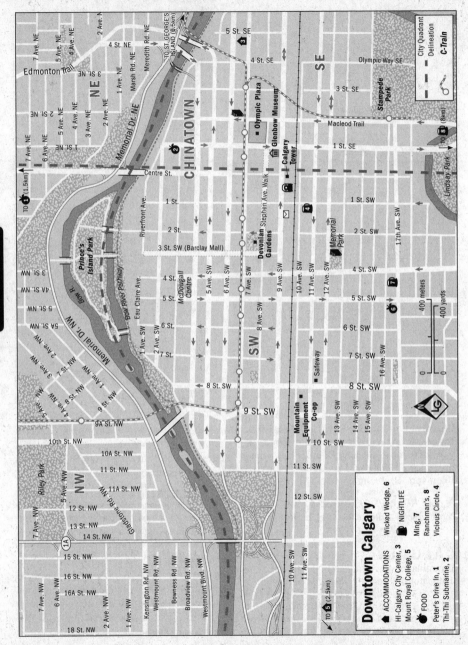

Edmonton Trail

NE

CHINATOWN

SE

Olympic Way SE

Stampede Park

Macleod Trail

5 St. SE

4 St. SE

3 St. SE

1 St. SE

TO ST. GEORGE'S ISLAND (0.5km)

Olympic Plaza

Glenbow Museum

Calgary Tower

Devonian Gardens

Stephen Ave. Walk

Centre St.

1 St.

2 St.

3 St. SW (Barclay Mall)

4 Ave. SW

5 Ave. SW

6 Ave. SW

7 Ave. SW

8 Ave. SW

9 Ave. SW

10 Ave. SW

11 Ave. SW

12 Ave. SW

SW

1 St. SW

2 St. SW

17th Ave. SW

Memorial Park

3 St. SW

4 St. SW

5 St. SW

6 St. SW

7 St. SW

8 St. SW

13 Ave. SW

14 Ave. SW

15 Ave. SW

16 St. SW

Mountain Equipment Co-op

Safeway

9 St. SW

10 Ave. SW

11 Ave. SW

12 Ave. SW

Lindsay Park

McDougall Centre

Prince's Island Park

Bow River Pathway

Memorial Dr. NW

Bow R.

Riverfront Ave.

Eau Claire Ave.

1 Ave. SW

2 Ave. SW

7 St.

6 St.

5 St.

4 St.

Riley Park

NW

Kensington Rd. NW

Gladstone Rd. NW

9A St. NW

10th St. NW

10A St. NW

11 St. NW

11A St. NW

12 St. NW

13 St. NW

14 St. NW

15 St. NW

16 St. NW

16A St. NW

18 St. NW

7 Ave. NW

6 Ave. NW

2 Ave. NW

1 Ave. NW

Westmount Rd. NW

Bowness Rd. NW

Broadview Rd. NW

Westmount Blvd. NW

10 Ave. SW

11 Ave. SW

TO (2.5km)

TO (1.5km)

TO (1.5km)

TO (8km)

400 meters

400 yards

Downtown Calgary

▲ ACCOMMODATIONS
HI-Calgary City Center, 3
Mount Royal College, 5

🍴 FOOD
Peter's Drive In, 1
Thi-Thi Submarine, 2

Wicked Wedge, 6

🍸 NIGHTLIFE
Ming, 7
Ranchman's, 8
Vicious Circle, 4

City Quadrant Delineation

C-Train

GREAT NORTH

VITAL STATS

Population: 990,000

Tourist Office: Tourism Calgary (☎403-263-8510; www.tourismcalgary.ca), in the base of the Calgary Tower, behind the gift shop. Open M-F 8am-8pm, Sa-Su 9am-5pm.

Library and Internet Access: Calgary Public Library, 616 Macleod Trail SE (☎403-260-2600). $2 per hr. Open June-Aug. M-Th 10am-9pm, F-Sa 10am-5pm, Su noon-5pm; Sept.-May M-Th 10am-9pm, F-Sa 10am-5pm.

Post Office: 207 9th Ave. SW (☎403-974-2078). Open M-F 8am-5:45pm. **Postal Code:** T2P 2G8.

ACCOMMODATIONS

Mount Royal College (☎403-440-6275; www. mtroyal.ab.ca/residence). From 16th Ave. NW, take Crowchild Trail S. to Mt. Royal Gate W. Make a left at the end of Mt. Royal Gate; it's on your left. MRC offers visitors modern apartment complexes with linens, Internet, and free parking. From mid-May to mid-Aug. bedrooms in 4-bedroom apartment with 2 baths, kitchen, and living room $46; singles $90. MC/V. ❷

HI-Calgary City Centre, 520 7th Ave. SE (☎403-269-8239; www.hihostels.ca/calgary), downtown. Kitchen, lounge areas, and backyard with barbecue. 120 beds. Laundry. Free Wi-Fi. Dorms from $31; private rooms $76. MC/V. ❷

FOOD

Thi-Thi Submarine, 209 1st St. SE (☎403-265-5452). Manages to pack in 2 plastic seats, toaster ovens, and the finest Vietnamese submarines in Calgary. Most subs cost around $6; the veggie sub is an unreal $3.75. Open M-F 11am-7pm, Sa 11:30am-7pm. Cash only. ❶

Peter's Drive In, 219 16th Ave. NE (☎403-277-2747). One of the city's last remaining drive-ins. Hordes of chummy patrons attest to the swell quality. Drive in or walk to the service window. Famous milkshakes cost $4.50. Burgers $3-5. Open daily 9am-midnight. Cash only. ❶

Wicked Wedge, 618 17th Ave. SW (☎403-228-1024). Serves large, topping-heavy pizza ($4.20 per slice) to Calgary's post-party scene. Open

M-W 11am-midnight, Th-Sa 11am-3am, Su noon-8pm. MC/V. ❶

SIGHTS

CALGARY TOWER. To get your bearings quickly, take a trip up the Calgary Tower. The 626 ft. tower, built in 1967, was the first of its kind. Now the tower has a grill, observation deck, and revolving dining room. (101 9th Ave. SW. ☎403-266-7171; www.calgarytower.com. Open daily in summer 7:30am-10pm; in winter 9am-9:30pm. $13, ages 5-17 $10, under 5 $10, seniors $11.)

OLYMPIC HALL OF FAME. For two glorious weeks in 1988, the world's eyes were on Calgary for the Winter Olympics. Almost 20 years later, the world has moved on, but the city still clings relentlessly to its Olympic stardom. The Olympic Hall of Fame honors Olympic achievements with displays, films, and a hockey simulator. (10min. northwest of downtown on Hwy. 1. ☎403-247-5452. Open daily July-Sept. 9am-5pm; Oct.-June 10am-4pm. $6. Tours $16; includes chairlift and entrance to ski-jump buildings, Hall of Fame, and icehouse.)

OLYMPIC OVAL. The Olympic Oval, an enormous indoor speed-skating track on the University of Calgary campus, remains a major international training facility. Speed skaters work out in the early morning and late afternoon; sit in the bleachers to observe the action for free. (☎403-220-7890; www.oval.ucalgary.ca. Public skating hours vary. $4.75, children and seniors $2.75. Skate rental $3.75.)

GLENBOW MUSEUM. The Glenbow Museum is the self-proclaimed spot "where the world meets the West." Far more than a local history museum, the Glenbow boasts several engaging collections spanning four floors. Check out the "Mavericks: An Incorrigible History of Alberta" exhibit, honoring some of the province's spunkier characters. (130 9th Ave. SE. ☎403-268-4100; www.glenbow.org. Open M-W and F-Su 9am-5pm, Th 9am-8pm. $14, students $12, ages 7-17 $9, under 6 free, seniors $10.)

DEVONIAN GARDENS. One of the world's largest indoor parks, the gardens span three levels of the Toronto Dominion Square and house 20,000 plants. A visit to the peaceful gardens will reveal waterfalls and fountains

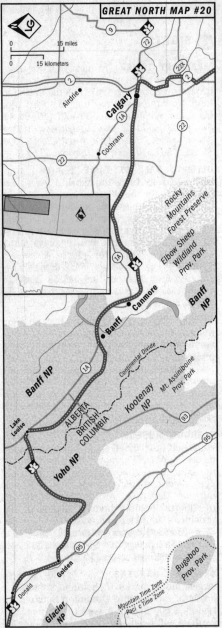

GREAT NORTH MAP #20

GREAT NORTH

in the Sun Garden, flower-banked pathways in the Quiet Garden, or fish and turtles to feed. *(317 7th Ave. SW. ☎403-268-5207. Open M-W and Sa-Su 9:30am-6pm, Th-F 9:30am-8pm. Free.)*

PRINCE'S ISLAND PARK. Footbridges stretch from either side of the Bow River to Prince's Island Park, a natural refuge only blocks from the city center. In July and August, Mount Royal College performs Shakespeare in the Park. *(☎403-240-6908. Call for shows and times.)*

★ NIGHTLIFE

Vicious Circle, 1011 1st St. SW (☎403-269-3951; www.viciouscircle.ca). Offers a solid menu, colored mood lights, and a disco ball, plus pool tables, couches, eclectic art, and a TV. Kick back on the summer patio seating and try 1 of the 141 different martinis for $9.50. Happy hour M-Sa 4-7pm. Open M-Th 11:30am-1am, F 11:30am-2am, Sa noon-2am, Su noon-1am. AmEx/MC/V.

Ming, 520 17th Ave. SW (☎403-229-1986). Though a little smoky, ultra-hip Ming offers modern decor and original martinis like the Jane Goodall or Mother Teresa along with an equally creative menu. Open daily 4pm-2am. MC/V.

Ranchman's, 9615 Macleod Trail (☎403-253-1100). Do-si-do to your heart's content. Open M-Sa 10:30am-2am. MC/V.

❋ FESTIVALS

The more cosmopolitan Calgary becomes, the more tenaciously it holds on to its frontier roots. The **Stampede** draws two million cowboys and tourists each July for world-class steer wrestling, bareback and bull riding, and pig races. The festival spills into the streets from early in the morning (free pancakes for all) through the night. Stampede Park, featuring the architecturally impressive Saddledome, is just southeast of downtown, bordering the east side of Macleod Trail between 14th Ave. SE and the Elbow River. (☎800-661-1767; www.calgarystampede.com. $13, ages 7-12 and seniors $7, under 7 free.)

⚑ THE ROAD TO CANMORE: 62 MI.

From Calgary, take **Route 1 West** (marked by the Maple Leaf sign) all the way to Lake Louise.

CANMORE ☎403

Canmore got its start over 100 years ago, when miners were lured to the valley by rich coal deposits. Worldwide attention turned to the sleepy town in 1988, when the Nordic skiing events of the Winter Olympic Games were held here. A charming downtown offers a walk past family shops and homey restaurants. The **Canmore Museums,** 902 Seventh Ave., include a Geoscience Center with ancient stones and bones, the historic North West Mounted Police Barracks, and artifacts from local mines. (☎403-678-2462; www.cmags. org. Open M-Tu noon-5pm, W-Su 10am-6pm. $3, students and seniors $2.)

HI Canmore ❶, on Indian Flats Rd., offers plush accommodations, but the beds are closely packed. (☎403-678-3200. Linens, sauna, and firepit. Reservations required. Laundry. Internet. Coed dorms $36-41, private rooms from $81. MC/V.)

⚑ THE ROAD TO BANFF TOWNSITE: 15 MI.

Continue west on **Highway 1** to **Banff National Park.** All traffic will be forced to stop to pay the entrance fee to the park. Your pass will get you into any of the other national parks in the area (Jasper, Yoho, Kootenay, Glacier, and Mt. Revelstoke), so purchase as many days as you want to explore them.

BANFF TOWNSITE ☎403

Less townsite than chic resort, Banff provides the weary traveler with fine dining and luxury lodgings just below majestic, snow-capped peaks. A stroll downtown reveals decadent candy shops and jewelry boutiques alongside sports outfitters and equipment rental. The chilly weather hasn't affected the people—Banff residents are warm and welcoming.

⚛ ORIENTATION

The Banff townsite is located off the **Trans-Canada Highway (Highway 1). Banff Avenue** leads to downtown, where restaurants, shops, and bars reside. Parallel to and west of Banff Ave. is **Bear Street,** where the movie theater and the Whyte Museum are located. Accommodations are scattered across the downtown area, with pricier options clustered closer to the center of town. Parking is ample an and around the downtown area.

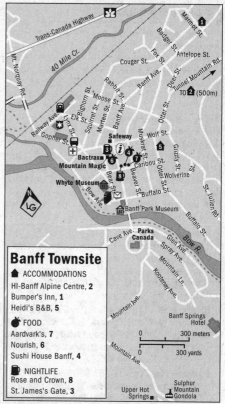

Banff Townsite

▲ ACCOMMODATIONS
HI-Banff Alpine Centre, **2**
Bumper's Inn, **1**
Heidi's B&B, **5**

🍴 FOOD
Aardvark's, **7**
Nourish, **6**
Sushi House Banff, **4**

🎵 NIGHTLIFE
Rose and Crown, **8**
St. James's Gate, **3**

VITAL STATS

Population: 8000

Tourist Offices: Banff Visitor Centre, 224 Banff Ave. (☎403-762-8421; www.banfflakelouise.com), and **Parks Canada** (☎403-762-1550). Open daily July-Aug. 8am-8pm; from early to mid-Sept. and mid-May to June 8am-6pm; from late Sept. to mid-May 9am-5pm.

Library and Internet Access: Banff Library, 101 Bear St. (☎403-762-2611). Sign up in advance. Open June-Aug. M-Th 10am-8pm, F-Sa 10am-6pm; Sept.-May daily 10am-8pm.

Post Office: 204 Buffalo St. (☎403-762-2586). Open M-W 8:30am-5:30pm, Th-F 8:30am-7pm, Sa 9am-5pm. **Postal Code:** TOL 0C0.

GREAT NORTH

ACCOMMODATIONS

Finding a cheap place to stay in Banff has become exceedingly difficult; the number of visitors soars into the millions every year. Residents offer rooms in their homes, occasionally at reasonable rates ($75-140; in winter $60-100). Check the list at the back of the *Banff and Lake Louise Official Visitor Guide*, available free at the visitors centers. The hostel does provide an alternative to camping, and several inns in town run on the not-so-expensive-compared-to-everything-else side. For more options, stop by the Banff tourist office, which supplies free accommodations guides with general price rankings. For options inside the park, see opposite page.

HI-Banff Alpine Centre (☎403-762-4122), 3km uphill from Banff Townsite on Tunnel Mountain Rd. This monster hostel sleeps 215 and has 3 lounges and kitchens. Hot showers and laundry. Internet $6 per hr. Check-in 3pm. Check-out 11am. Dorms $38, members $34. MC/V. ❶

Heidi's B&B, 214 Otter St. (☎403-762-3806), between Wolf and Caribou St., 3 blocks from downtown. Comfortable rooms have private baths and tubs with jets. Rooms in summer $70-85; in winter $50. Cash only. ❹

Bumper's Inn (☎403-762-3386 or 800-661-3518; www.bumpersinn.com), at the corner of Banff Ave. and Marmot St. This cozy, quiet inn is ½ mi. from downtown and offers comfortable suites and an outdoor courtyard. Rooms $101-150. AmEx/MC/V. ❺

FOOD

Like everything else in town, Banff's restaurants tend to be expensive, although the hostels serve cheap meals ($5-9) in their cafes.

Sushi House Banff, 304 Caribou St. (☎403-762-4353). Sushi chefs make a variety of dishes before your eyes and place them on a model train, which carries them around the long, round table. Take what you want, and the bill is calculated at the end of your meal. Each dish $2-5. Open daily noon-10pm. MC/V. ❸

Nourish, 215 Banff Ave. (☎403-760-3933). A relaxed vegetarian cafe hidden upstairs in a touristy mall—try the *spanakopita* for $8. Tapas $6-12. Open daily noon-3pm and 5-9pm. High tea 3-4:30pm by reservation. MC/V. ❸

Aardvark's, 304A Caribou St. (☎403-762-5500). Does big business selling pizza after the bars close. It's often standing room only as hungry revelers jostle for a spot. Slices $3. Small pie $8-10; large $17-24. Subs $5-8. Open daily 10am-4am. MC/V. ❶

SIGHTS

There are numerous outdoor activities in **Banff National Park** (below), but a quiet day in the townsite can prove rewarding as well. The **Whyte Museum of the Canadian Rockies,** 111 Bear St., explores the history and culture of the Canadian Rockies over the last two centuries in its Heritage Gallery, while temporary exhibits focus on the natural history of the region. Displays include works by Canadian painters. (☎403-762-2291; www.whyte.org. Open daily 10am-5pm. $6, students $3.50, under 6 free.)

NIGHTLIFE

For some real wildlife, check out Banff's bars. Ask at the visitors center to find out which nightspots are having "locals' night," featuring cheap drinks. Banff Ave. hosts a ton of bars, restaurants, kitschy gift shops, and banks.

Rose and Crown, 202 Banff Ave. (☎403-762-2121; www.roseandcrown.ca), upstairs at the corner of Caribou St. Ample room for dancing and billiards ($1.50; free Tu), even on busy nights. Living room for watching sports and a rooftop patio with unparalleled views. Pints $6-8. Live music daily at 10pm. Cover Sa $2-3. Jam Night Su with happy hour 9pm-last customer. Open daily 11am-2am. AmEx/MC/V.

St. James's Gate, 207 Wolf St. (☎403-762-9355). A laid-back Irish pub. Ask the bartenders to recommend 1 of 32 beers on tap. Live jigs F-Sa. Happy hour daily 7-9pm. Open M-Th and Su 11am-1am, F-Sa 11am-2am. AmEx/MC/V.

OUTDOORS

There are countless outdoor opportunities in Banff National Park (below). Before you head out, however, you'll need to rent equipment in town. Here are several options:

Mountain Magic Equipment, 224 Bear St. (☎403-762-2591). One of the few places in Banff to rent mountaineering packages ($40 per day). Also offers ski (from $30 per day) and cross-country (from $15 per day) rentals. Open M-Sa 9am-9pm, Su 9am-6pm.

Bactrax Rentals, 225 Bear St. (☎403-762-8177). Rents mountain bikes ($9-13 per hr., $32-44 per day). Bike tours $20-60. Ski packages from $23 per day; snowboard packages $31. Camping equipment rentals $4-26 per day. Open daily Apr.-Oct. 8am-8pm; Nov.-Mar. 7am-9pm.

Wilson Mountain Sports (☎403-522-3636), in the Lake Louise Samson Mall. Rents bikes ($15 per hr., $39 per day) and camping and fishing gear. Mountaineering ($49 per day) and rock-climbing packages ($27 per day). Open daily from mid-June to Oct. 9am-8pm; from Nov. to mid-June 8am-8pm.

THE ROAD TO BANFF NATIONAL PARK: 0 MI.

Don't move. You're already in the park.

BANFF NATIONAL PARK ☎403

Banff is Canada's best-loved and best-known natural park, with 2500 sq. mi. of peaks, forests, glaciers, and alpine valleys. It became Canada's first national park only days after the Canadian Pacific Railway's completion in 1885. The park's name comes from Banff-shire, Scotland, the birthplace of two Canadian Pacific Railway financiers who convinced Canada's first prime minister that a "large pecuniary advantage" might be gained from the region, telling him that "since we can't export the scenery, we shall have to import the tourists." Banff's natural beauty, along with the laid-back attitude it fosters, has attracted hordes of young people to Banff Townsite (previous page).

VITAL STATS	
Area: 1,600,000 acres	
Visitor Info: Banff Visitor Centre, 224 Banff Ave. (p. 305).	
Gateway Towns: Banff, Lake Louise	
Fees: $9.80, ages 6-16 $4.90, seniors $8.30.	

ORIENTATION

Banff National Park hugs the Alberta side of the Alberta/British Columbia border, 80 mi. west of Calgary. The **Trans-Canada Highway (Highway 1)** runs east-west through the park, connecting it to **Yoho National Park** (p. 311) in the west. The **Icefields Parkway (Highway 93)** connects Banff with **Jasper National Park** to the north and **Kootenay National Park** to the south-west. Civilization in the park centers on the towns of **Banff** and **Lake Louise,** 36 mi. apart on Hwy. 1. The more serene **Bow Valley Parkway (Highway 1A)** parallels Hwy. 1 from Lake Louise to 5 mi. west of Banff, offering excellent camping, hosteling, sights, and wildlife. The southern portion of Hwy. 1A is restricted at night in late spring and early summer to accommodate wildlife. Parking in Banff National Park is plentiful.

ACCOMMODATIONS

Enormous, modern hostels in Banff and Lake Louise anchor a chain of cozier hostels from Calgary to Jasper. Rustic hostels provide more of a wilderness experience (read: no electricity or flush toilets) and often have some of the park's best hiking and cross-country skiing right in their backyards. Wait-list beds become available at 6pm, and the larger hostels try to save a few standby beds for shuttle arrivals. Beds go quickly, especially during the summer, so make reservations as early as possible. Reservations can be made through the southern Alberta HI administration (☎866-762-4122; www.hihostels.ca). Free reservations are held until 6pm but can be guaranteed until later with a credit card.

Rampart Creek Wilderness Hostel (HI), 21 mi. south of the Icefield Centre. Close to several world-famous ice climbs (including Weeping Wall, 11 mi. north), this hostel is a favorite for winter mountaineers and anyone who likes a rustic sauna after a hard day's hike. Wood-burning sauna, full-service kitchen. Reservations recommended. Open from mid-May to mid-Oct. and from mid-Nov. to mid-Apr. 12-bed co-ed dorms $27, members $23. MC/V. ●

Castle Mountain Wilderness Hostel (HI), in Castle Jct., 1 mi. east of the junction of Hwy. 1 and Hwy. 93 south, between Banff and Lake

Louise. One of the hardest hostels to find. A quieter alternative to the hubbub of its big brothers. Comfortable common area with huge bay windows. A friendly staff, kitchen, electricity, and volleyball. Hot showers. Free laundry. Check-in 5-10pm. Check-out 10am. Dorms June-Aug. and Oct. $23-27; Sept. $27. MC/V. ●

Mosquito Creek Wilderness Hostel (HI), 64 mi. south of the Icefield Centre and 16 mi. north of Lake Louise. Across the creek from the Mosquito Creek campground. Close to the Wapta Icefield. Enormous living room with wood stove, wood-burning sauna, kitchen, and pump water. Check-in 5-10pm. Check-out 11am. 16-bed co-ed dorms $27; private rooms $66. MC/V. ●

⛺ CAMPING

A chain of campgrounds stretches between Banff and Jasper. Extra-large, fully hooked-up grounds lie closer to the townsites; for more trees and fewer vehicles, try more remote sites farther from Banff and Lake Louise. If you feel like warming up, be prepared to spend some cash: at park campgrounds that allow fires, a campfire permit costs an additional $9.80, including firewood. Sites are first come, first served; arrive early. The sites are listed from south to north and have pit toilets but no showers, unless otherwise noted.

Tunnel Mountain Village, 2 mi. from Banff Townsite on Tunnel Mountain Rd. With nearly 1200 sites, this is a camping metropolis. Trailer/RV area has 321 full RV sites, Village 2 has 188 sites, and Village 1 houses a whopping 618. Fires allowed in Village 1 only; all villages have showers. Village 2 open year-round; Village 1 and 3 open from mid-May to Sept. Sites in Village 1 $27.40; in Village 2 $32.30; RV sites $38.20. AmEx/MC/V. ●

Two Jack, 8 mi. northeast of Banff, across Hwy.1. 381 main sites with no showers. 80 lakeside sites with showers. Open from mid-May to Aug. Main sites $21.50; lakeside $27.40. AmEx/MC/V. ●

Johnston Canyon, 16 mi. northwest of Banff on Bow Valley Pkwy. 132 sites. Access to Johnston Canyon Trail. Showers. Open from Memorial Day to mid-Sept. Sites $27.40. AmEx/MC/V. ●

Protection Mountain, 9 mi. east of Lake Louise and 7 mi. west of Castle Jct. on the Bow Valley Pkwy. (Hwy. 1A). 89 spacious, basic sites and 14

RV sites. Open from late June to early Sept. Sites $21.50. AmEx/MC/V. ●

Lake Louise, 2 mi. southeast of the visitors center on Fairview Rd. On Bow River, not the lake. Plenty of hiking and fishing awaits. Showers. 189 trailer sites with electricity open year-round. 206 tent sites open from mid-May to Sept. Tent sites $27.40; RV sites $32.30. AmEx/MC/V. ●

Mosquito Creek, 35 mi. south of the Icefield Centre and 16 mi. north of Lake Louise. 32 sites with hiking access. Sites $15.70. AmEx/MC/V. ●

Rampart Creek, 91 mi. north of Banff, 21 mi. south of the Icefield Centre, across from Rampart Creek Hostel and amazing ice climbing. 50 sites. Open June-Sept. Sites $15.70. AmEx/MC/V. ●

👁 SIGHTS

BANFF PARK MUSEUM NATIONAL HISTORIC SITE. The museum is western Canada's oldest natural history museum, with rooms of stuffed specimens dating from the 1860s. (92 Banff Ave. ☎ 403-762-1558. Open daily from mid-May to Sept. 10am-6pm; from Oct. to mid-May 1-5pm. Tours in summer daily 3pm; in winter Sa-Su 3pm. $4, seniors $3.50, children $2.)

CAVE AND BASIN NATIONAL HISTORIC SITE. Banff National Park would not exist if not for the Cave and Basin mineral springs, once rumored to have miraculous healing properties. The Cave and Basin National Historic Site, a refurbished bath house built circa 1914, is now a small museum detailing the history and science of the site. Access to the low-ceilinged cave containing the original spring is inside the building. Five of the pools are the only home of the park's most endangered species: the small Banff Springs snail, *Physella johnsoni*. (☎ 403-762-1566. Open in summer daily 9am-6pm; in winter M-F 11am-4pm, Sa-Su 9:30am-5pm. Tours daily 11am. $4, children $2.)

UPPER HOT SPRINGS POOL. For a dip in the hot water, follow the smell to the Upper Hot Springs pool, a 104°F sulfurous cauldron. (Southwest of the city on Mountain Ave. ☎ 403-762-1515; www.hotsprings.ca. Open daily from mid-May to early Sept. 9am-11pm; from early Sept. to mid-May M-Th and Su 10am-10pm, F-Sa 10am-11pm. Swimsuits $2, towels $2, lockers $1. $7.50, children and seniors $6.50.)

OUTDOORS

A visitor sticking to paved byways will see a tiny fraction of the park and the majority of the park's visitors. Those interested in the endless outdoor options can hike or bike on more than 1000 mi. of trails. Grab a free copy of the *Mountain Biking and Cycling Guide* or *Dayhikes in Banff* and peruse trail descriptions at information centers. For still more solitude, pick up *The Banff Backcountry Experience* and an overnight camping permit at a visitors center and head out to the backcountry. ($9.80 per person per day. AmEx/MC/V.) Be sure to check with the rangers at the information center for current weather, trail, and wildlife updates.

BIKING

Biking is permitted on public roads, highways, and certain trails in the park. Spectacular scenery and a number of hostels and campgrounds make the **Bow Valley Parkway (Highway 1A)** and the **Icefields Parkway (Highway 93)** perfect for extended cycling trips. Every other store downtown seems to rent bikes; head to Bactrax (p. 307) for HI discounts. Parks Canada publishes a free *Mountain Biking and Cycling Guide* that describes trails and roadways where bikes are permitted; pick up a copy at bike-rental shops or visitors centers.

HIKING

Two easy trails are within walking distance of Banff Townsite, but longer, more rigorous trails abound farther away. The best escapes are found in the backcountry. Restaurants are few and far between, so, unless you plan to throttle elk with your bare hands, bring your own food on hikes.

Fenland (1 mi., 1hr.). Follow Mt. Norquay Rd. to the outskirts look for signs across the tracks on road's left side. This flat, easy trail crosses area inhabited by beavers, muskrats, and waterfowl, but it is closed for elk calving in late spring.

Tunnel Mountain (1.5 mi., 2hr.). Follow Wolf St. east from Banff Ave. and turn right on St. Julien Rd. to reach the head of the steep, moderately difficult trail. After a rise of 850 ft., there is a dramatic view of the Bow Valley and Mt. Rundle.

Tunnel Mountain has the distinction of being the Rockies' smallest mountain.

Sulphur Mountain (3.5 mi., 2hr.). Winds along a well-trodden trail to the peak, where a spectacular view awaits; the Sulphur Mountain Gondola charges ½-price for the 8min. downhill trip if you buy your ticket at the top. Round-trip $23.50, ages 6-15 $11.75, under 6 free.

Johnston Canyon (3 mi., 2hr.). West of the Norquay Interchange on Hwy. 1, then 11 mi. along the Bow Valley Pkwy. (Hwy. 1A). A popular moderate-to-strenuous day hike. A catwalk along the edge of the deep limestone canyon runs ½ mi. over the thundering river to the canyon's lower falls and another mile to the upper falls. The trail continues for a rugged 2 mi. to 7 blue-green cold-water springs, known as the Inkpots, in a valley above the canyon. More than 26 mi. of trails beyond the Inkpots are blissfully untraveled and punctuated with campgrounds roughly every 6 mi.

Aylmer Pass (16.5 mi., 8hr. round-trip). Leaves from the shore of Lake Minnewanka on Lake Minnewanka Rd. (the extension of Banff Ave. across the Trans-Canada from town). Parking just above tour boat area. A steep climb to the summit yields a panoramic view of the lake and surrounding scenery. The trail can be abridged by hiking only the 7 mi. to the lookout, cutting the final ascent.

 BACKWOODS BANFF. Backcountry trekking is the way to see Banff. The wild backcountry, replete with mind-boggling scenery, belies the civilized tourist trap that the townsite has become. Amateurs and experts alike should beware of dangerous and changing conditions on strenuous trails that do not receive as much maintenance as more popular routes; consult park rangers for information.

WATERSPORTS

Fishing is legal in most of the park during specific seasons, but natural bait and lead weights are not. Get a permit and check out regulations at the info center. (Permits $9 per day; season pass $30.) **Bourgeau Lake**, a 4 mi. hike, is home to a particularly feisty breed of brook trout. Closer to the road, try **Herbert**

Lake, off the Icefields Pkwy., or **Lake Minnewanka,** on Lake Minnewanka Rd. northeast of Banff. Lake Minnewanka Rd. passes Johnson Lake, where shallow warm water makes for a perfect swimming hole.

Hydra River Guides runs rafting trips along the Kicking Horse River. (☎403-762-4554 or 800-644-8888; www.raftbanff.com. Up to Class V rapids. $95; includes lunch, transportation, and gear.) **Blast Adventures** leads half-day inflatable kayak trips on the rowdy Kananaskis River. (☎403-609-2009 or 888-802-5278; www.blastadventures.com. $72; includes transportation, gear, and snacks.)

⚲ THE ROAD TO LAKE LOUISE: 35 MI.
Continue on **Highway 1 West** to Lake Louise.

LAKE LOUISE TOWNSITE ☎403

The highest community in Canada (5000 ft.), Lake Louise and the surrounding glaciers have often passed for Swiss scenery in movies and are the emerald in the Rockies' tiara of tourism. The lake was named in 1884 in honor of Queen Victoria's daughter, and its beauty is nothing short of royal.

VITAL STATS
Population: 1200
Tourist Office: Lake Louise Visitor Centre (☎403-522-3833), at Samson Mall on Village Rd. Open daily in summer 9am-8pm; in spring and fall 9am-5pm; in winter 9am-4pm.
Internet Access: The Depot (☎403-522-3870), in the Samson Mall. $8 per hr. Open M-F 7am-6pm, Sa-Su 7am-5pm.
Post Office: Mail services at **The Depot** (above). **Postal Code:** TOL 1E0.

◪ ORIENTATION

Lake Louise is still part of Banff National Park, so be sure to keep your pass. The townsite's center, to the right off **Highway 1/ Highway 93,** is literally that—a small shopping center with a few restaurants and a market. Parking is ample in the city center and at the motels and campsites around the lake.

⬗ ACCOMMODATIONS

There are several campsites near Lake Louise and one hostel in town.

▨ **Lake Louise International Hostel (HI)** (☎403-522-2200). West of the visitors center, on Village Rd. toward the park warden's office. More like a resort than a hostel—it boasts a reference library, a stone fireplace, 2 full kitchens, a sauna, and a cafe with Wi-Fi. 184 beds. Internet access $2 per 20min. Check-in 24hr. Check-out 11am. Reservations recommended. Dorms $29-42. Private rooms $93-117. MC/V. ❶

▨ FOOD

There are more food options in Banff than Lake Louise, so if you plan to dine out it's best to stay in the city. The town's main shopping center, however, has a grocery and a few restaurant options. The **Village Market,** in the Samson Mall, has fresh produce and the basics. (☎403-522-3894. Open 7am-10pm. MC/V.)

▨ **Laggan's Deli** (☎403-522-2017), in Samson Mall. Always crowded. Thick sandwiches ($3-7.50) and fresh-baked loaves ($3.20) are perennial favorites. Open daily June-Sept. 6am-8pm; Oct.-May 6am-7pm. Cash only. ❶

Lake Louise Village Grill & Bar Family Restaurant & Lounge (☎403-522-3879), in the Samson Mall. Versatile menu with steaks ($12-24), breakfast options, sandwiches, and Chinese food. Salads $5-13. Sandwiches and burgers $9-13. Chinese entrees $16-19. Open daily 11am-10pm. Bar open until 2am. MC/V. ❹

⛰ OUTDOORS

The **Lake Louise Sightseeing Lift,** up Whitehorn Rd. and across the Trans-Canada Hwy. from Lake Louise, cruises up Mt. Whitehorn. (☎403-522-3555; www.lakelouisegondola.com. Open daily from May to mid-June and Sept. 9am-4:30pm; from mid-June to Aug. 9am-6pm. $25, ages 6-15 $12.50.)

HIKING

You can view the water and its surrounding splendor from several hiking trails that begin in the neighborhood and climb along the surrounding ridgelines. Be warned: with beauty comes crowds, so expect masses of tourists.

Lake Agnes Trail (3 mi., 2hr. round-trip) and the **Plain of 6 Glaciers Trail** (3 mi., 4hr. round-trip) both end at teahouses and make for lovely, if sometimes crowded, day hikes with views down to the lake. Open in summer daily 9am-6pm.

Moraine Lake, 9 mi. from the village, at the end of Moraine Lake Rd. and off Lake Louise Dr. (no trailers or long RVs). Moraine lies in the awesome Valley of the 10 Peaks, opposite glacier-encrusted Mt. Temple. Join the multitudes on the **Rockpile Trail** for an eye-popping view of the lake and valley and a lesson in ancient ocean bottoms (10min. walk to the top). To escape the camera-wielding hordes, try one of the lake's more challenging trails, either **Sentinel Pass** via Larch Valley (4 mi., 5-6hr. one-way), with stunning views from flower-studded meadows, or **Wenkchemna Pass** via Eiffel Lake (6 mi., 1 day one-way), which carries hikers the length of the Valley of the 10 Peaks with incredible views in both directions. Be sure to arrive before 10am or after 4pm to see the view instead of the crowds.

Paradise Valley, depending on how you hike it, can be an intense day hike or a relaxing overnight trip. From the Paradise Creek Trailhead, 1.5 mi. up Moraine Lake Rd., the loop through the valley runs 11 mi. through subalpine and alpine forests and along rivers (7hr.; elevation gain 2900 ft.). One classic backpacking route runs from Moraine Lake up and over Sentinel Pass, joining the top of the Paradise Valley loop after 5 mi. A backcountry campground marks the midpoint from either trailhead. Grizzly activity often forces the park wardens to close the area in summer; check with them before hiking in this area.

WINTER SPORTS

Winter activities in the park range from world-class ice climbing to ice fishing. Those 1000 mi. of hiking trails make for exceptional **cross-country skiing.** Moraine Lake Rd. is closed to vehicle traffic in the winter and is used for cross-country skiing, as are the backcountry trails. Three allied resorts offer a range of skiing and snowboarding opportunities from early November to mid-May. All have terrain parks for snowboarders. Shuttles to the following three resorts leave from most big hotels in the townsites, and Banff and

Lake Louise hostels typically have ticket and transportation discounts available for guests. Multi-day passes good for all three resorts are available at the **Ski Banff/Lake Louise office,** 225 Banff Ave. (☎403-762-4561), in Banff, at all resorts, and online (www.skibig3.com). Passes include free shuttle service and an extra night of skiing at Mt. Norquay (3-day passes $198-225).

Sunshine Mountain (☎403-762-6500, snow report 760-7669; www.skibanff.com). 3168 acres on 3 mountains, with the most snowfall (33 ft.) in the area. Attracts loyal followers.

Lake Louise (☎403-522-3555, snow report 762-4766; www.skilouise.com). The 2nd-largest ski area in Canada (4200 skiable acres), with amazing views, over 3300 ft. of vertical drop, and the best selection of expert terrain. Some simpler slopes cover plenty of the mountain.

Mt. Norquay (☎403-762-4421; www.banff-norquay.com). A locals' mountain: small and located close to town. Has the Canadian Rockies' only night skiing on F.

⚑ THE ROAD TO YOHO NATIONAL PARK: 16 MI. From Lake Louise, continue west on **Highway 1.** When you cross the Continental Divide, you enter British Columbia and Yoho National Park. Descend the **Kicking Horse Canyon** toward Field, the gateway town to Yoho National Park.

The Pacific Province
BRITISH COLUMBIA
Welcomes You!

YOHO NATIONAL PARK ☎403

A Cree expression for awe and wonder, Yoho is the perfect name for this park. It sports some of the most engaging names in the Rockies, such as Kicking Horse Pass, named after Captain John Hector, who was kicked in the chest by his horse. Driving down Yoho's narrow pass on Hwy. 1, visitors can see geological forces at work: massive bent and tilted sedimentary rock layers exposed in sharply eroded cliff faces and rock bridges formed by water that has carved away the stone.

Beneath these rock walls, Yoho overflows with other natural attractions, including the largest waterfall in the Rockies—Takakkaw Falls—and 500-million-year-old fossils.

VITAL STATS
Area: 325,000 acres
Tourist Office: Yoho National Park Visitor Centre (☎250-343-6783; www.pc.gc.ca/yoho), in Field on Hwy. 1. Open daily in summer 9am-7pm; in fall and spring 9am-5pm; in winter 9am-4pm.
Gateway town: Field.
Fees: $9.80, children $4.90.

ORIENTATION

The park lies on the **Trans-Canada Highway (Highway 1),** next to Banff National Park. Within Yoho is the town of Field, 17 mi. west of Lake Louise on Hwy. 1. Parking is available at campsites, lookout points, and trailheads.

ACCOMMODATIONS

Whiskey Jack Hostel (☎403-762-4122), 9 mi. off Hwy. 1 on the Yoho Valley Rd. Blurs the line between civilization and nature. Offers a kitchen, plumbing, propane light, access to Yoho's best high-country trails, and the splendor of the Takakkaw Falls from the porch. Check-in 5-10pm. Reserve through the Banff Hostel. Open from late June to Sept., depending on snow. Dorms $27, members $23. MC/V. ❶

Takakkaw Falls Campground, situated beneath mountains, glaciers, and the magnificent falls 9 mi. up curvy Yoho Valley Rd. Offers only pump water and pit toilets, and campers must park in the falls lot and haul their gear ½ mi. to the 35 peaceful sites. Open from late June to Sept. Sites $17.60. AmEx/MC/V. ❶

Kicking Horse. By far the most popular and extensively outfitted campground in the park. 88 sites. Flush toilets and hot showers. Open from mid-May to mid-Oct. Sites $27.40. AmEx/MC/V. ❶

FOOD

The most convenient food stop in Yoho is **Chercher un Vache,** a cafe, general store, and craft shop on Stephen Ave. in Field, which sells foodstuffs, coffee, microbrews, wine, and camping supplies. Crafts line the walls, and the owners peddle sandwiches ($7-10), breakfast ($2-9), and delicious dinners ($9-24). You may end up staying all day. The restaurant has the area's only ATM. (☎250-343-6462. Open in summer daily 8am-10pm; in winter M-Sa 10am-7pm. AmEx/MC/V.)

SIGHTS

The Continental Divide is both the boundary between Alberta and British Columbia and the Atlantic and Pacific watersheds. Here a stream forks, with one arm flowing to the Pacific Ocean and the other flowing to the Atlantic via the Hudson Bay. It is also the site of **Burgess Shale,** a layer of sedimentary rock containing imprints of the insect-like, soft-bodied organisms that inhabited the world's oceans prior to the Cambrian explosion. Discovered in 1909, the unexpected complexity of these 505-million-year-old specimens changed the way paleontologists thought about evolution. Larger, clumsier animals known as humans have since lobbied to protect the shale from excessive tourism: educational hikes led by the **Yoho-Burgess Shale Foundation** are the only way to see it. (☎800-343-3006. From July to mid-Sept. Call ahead. Full-day 12 mi. hike $70, under 12 $27.) A steep 4 mi. loop to the equally old and trilobite-packed **Mount Stephen Fossil Beds** costs $48, children $16. For easier sightseeing, follow the 8 mi. of the Yoho Valley Rd. to views of the Takakkaw Falls, Yoho's most splendid waterfall, and the highest-altitude major falls in the Canadian Rockies.

HIKING

The park's six backcountry campgrounds and 250 mi. of trail make for an intense wilderness experience, with countless quickly accessed trails exhibiting scenery equal to that of the larger parks. Before setting out, pick up camping permits ($9.80 per person per day), maps, and the free *Backcountry Guide to Yoho National Park* at the visitors center. Whiskey Jack Hostel is also well stocked with trail info. The park's finest terrain is in the Yoho Valley, accessible only after the snow melts in mid- to late summer.

Wapta Falls (3 mi. round-trip; 100 ft. elevation change). The trailhead is not marked on Hwy. 1

for westbound traffic, as there is no left-turn lane. Continue 2 mi. to the west entrance of the park and come back east. Highlights include the Kicking Horse River's 100 ft. drop. The least ambitious of the hikes and the least spectacular.

Mt. Hunter Lookout to Upper Lookout (7 mi. one-way; 1400 ft. elevation change). Cuts through lower altitudes, with a nice view of Kicking Horse and Beaverfoot valleys, leading to 2 fire towers.

Iceline Trail (via Little Yoho 13 mi., via Celeste Lake 11 mi.; 2300 ft. elevation change). Starts at the hostel. Takes hikers through forests of alder, spruce, and fir before leading them above the treeline, over glacial moraines, and past the striated rock and pools of Emerald Glacier.

Emerald Triangle (12 mi. round-trip; 2900 ft. elevation change). The route travels through the Yoho Pass to the Wapta Highline trail, Burgess Pass, and back to the start. Most of the journey is above the treeline with breathtaking views over diverse landscapes.

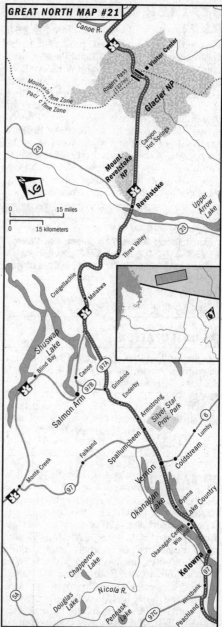 THE ROAD TO GOLDEN: 35 MI.

From Yoho, haul keel west on **Highway 1**. Golden is a bit south of the intersection with **Highway 95**. The drive through the Kicking Horse Canyon is stunning but dangerous—watch out for impatient drivers attempting ridiculous passing feats on this two-lane road. This stretch is BC's top priority for expansion, so construction will be ongoing for the next few years.

GOLDEN ☎ 250

Surrounded by six national parks (Glacier, Yoho, Banff, Jasper, Kootenay, and Mt. Revelstoke), Golden is a convenient base for regional exploration and outdoor activities. At the foot of Kicking Horse Ski Mountain, the **Kicking Horse Hostel ❶**, 518 Station Ave., matches its location with ski-lodge decor, complete with skis and snowshoes hanging from the walls. Exit for the city center off Hwy. 1, then make an immediate left onto Station Ave. (☎250-344-5071; www.kicking-horsehostel.com. Kitchen. Linen included. Co-ed dorms $30. Cash only.)

THE ROAD TO GLACIER NATIONAL PARK: 52 MI.

Take **Highway 95 North** to **Highway 1 West**.

GLACIER NATIONAL PARK ☎250

This aptly named national park (not to be confused with Glacier National Park in Montana) is home to over 400 monolithic ice floes that cover one-tenth of its 520 sq. mi. area. The jagged peaks and steep, narrow valleys of the Columbia Range not only make for breathtaking scenery but also prevent development in the park. In late summer, brilliant explosions of mountain wildflowers offset the deep green of the forests. In the winter, more literal explosions shake the calm of the valleys—scientists fire 105mm shells into mountainsides to create controlled avalanches.

VITAL STATS

Area: 333,000 acres

Tourist Office: Rogers Pass Information Centre (☎250-837-7500), on Hwy. 1 in Glacier. Open daily in summer 7:30am-8pm; in early fall and late spring 8:30am-4:30pm; Dec.-Apr. 7am-5pm.

Gateway Town: Rogers Pass

Fees: $7.80, under 16 $3.90.

⊕ ORIENTATION

Glacier is 220 mi. west of Calgary and 450 mi. east of Vancouver. The only road in the park is the **Trans-Canada Highway (Highway 1).**

TIME CHANGE. Just before Glacier National Park, you'll enter the Pacific Time Zone, where it is 1hr. earlier.

⚑ CAMPING

Glacier has two recently rebuilt campgrounds: **Illecillewaet ❶** (ill-uh-SILL-uh-way-et), 2 mi. west of Roger's Pass (60 sites; open from late June to early Oct.; sites $21.50; MC/V), and smaller **Loop Brook ❶**, another 1.5 mi. west on Hwy. 1 (20 sites; open from July to early Sept.; sites $21.50; MC/V). Both offer flush toilets, kitchen shelters with cook stoves, and firewood. The park has no vehicle-accessible sites until late June; Canyon Hot Springs is the closest alternative for drivers. Backcountry campers must purchase a backcountry pass from the Parks Canada office in Revelstoke (☎205-837-7500; $9.80 per day; MC/V) or from the **Rogers Pass Information Centre.**

◈ HIKING

More than 87 mi. of rough, often steep trails lead from the highway, inviting mountaineers to attempt the unconquerable. While the highway works its way through the park's lush valleys, a majority of the area in the parkland lies above the treeline, providing for incredibly steep, high-altitude, highly beautiful hikes. Leaving from the info center, the easy **Abandoned Rails Trail** (1 mi., 1hr. one-way) follows the 1885 Canadian Pacific Railway bed over the top of historic Rogers Pass. Free guided tours are available during July and August from the visitors center. From the Beaver River Trailhead, **Copperstain Trail** (9 mi., 6hr., one-way; 1500 ft. elevation change) leads uphill through alpine meadows. This trail is often combined with the longer **Beaver Valley Trail** to create a four-day backpacking loop. The challenging **Balu Pass Trail** (6 mi., 4hr., round-trip; 2500 ft. elevation change) begins at the west edge of Rogers Centre parking lot, near Rogers Pass Information Centre, and rises to the Ursus Major and Ursus Minor peaks. As their names might suggest, they provide an excellent opportunity to see bears. This trail is prime bear habitat; check with park wardens before embarking, and exercise caution on the trails. Just east of the information center, **Hermit Trail** (1.7 mi., 2hr. one-way) climbs nearly 2600 ft. into the Hermit Glacier, hanging over Rogers Pass.

◈ DETOUR
CANYON HOT SPRINGS

On **Highway 1.**

At Canyon Hot Springs, two spring water swimming pools simmer at 86°F and 104°F to ease aching muscles. (☎250-837-2420; www.canyonhotsprings.com. Firewood $7. Swim pass $8.50, ages 4-14 $7.50, under 4 free. Open daily July-Aug. 9am-10pm; Sept. and May-June 9am-9pm. Sites $29, with water and electricity $39. Day use $12.50, ages 4-14 $10.50.)

⚑ THE ROAD TO REVELSTOKE: 39 MI.

Follow **Highway 1 West** to Revelstoke.

REVELSTOKE   ☎ 205

Located on both the Columbia River and the Canadian Pacific Railway, Revelstoke was born as a transfer station for boats and trains. A laid-back social life complements the physical rigors of the area's activities. Excellent hostels and surprisingly lively outdoor entertainment in the town center make Revelstoke a welcoming destination.

✈ ORIENTATION

Revelstoke is on the **Trans-Canada Highway (Highway 1)**, 177 mi. west of Banff. The town is easily navigated on foot or by bike—hence the lack of traffic and abundance of parking spaces downtown. **Mount Revelstoke National Park** lies just east of town on Hwy. 1. Most of the town is on the east bank of the river, and **Victoria Road** is the main street that curves parallel to the highway.

VITAL STATS

Population: 7500

Tourist Offices: Visitors Centre (☎205-837-3522; www.revelstokecc.bc.ca), at the junction of Mackenzie and Victoria Rd. Open daily July-Aug. 8:30am-9:30pm; May-June 9am-5pm. **Parks Canada** (☎205-837-7500), at Boyle Ave. and 3rd St. Open M-F 8:30am-noon and 1-4:30pm.

Library and Internet Access: Revelstoke Public Library, 600 Campbell Ave. (☎205-837-5095). Open Tu noon-8pm, W noon-7pm, Th 10am-4pm, F-Sa 10am-5pm.

Post Office: 307 W. 3rd St. (☎205-837-3228). Open M-F 8:30am-5pm. **Postal Code:** V0E 2S0.

🛏 ACCOMMODATIONS

Nearby Mt. Revelstoke National Park has two campgrounds, **Eva Lake,** a 3 mi. hike, and **Jade Lake,** a 6 mi. hike. (Each has 4 sites. No pumped water. Jade Lake is equipped with a bear pole. Open July-Sept. Contact park office for fee information.)

▨ **SameSun Backpacker Lodge,** 400 2nd St. W. (☎877-562-2783; www.samesun.com). The friendly hostel fosters a lively youth scene and a more sedate older crowd in the private rooms. Several kitchens, full bathrooms, living room with TV, and a constant mellow soundtrack. Pool table

and backyard barbecue. Internet $3 per 30min. Free Wi-Fi. Reception 8am-noon and 2-10pm. Dorms $25; singles $56. MC/V. ❶

Martha Creek Provincial Park, 1224 Stanley St. (☎250-825-4212), in Nelson, 12 mi. north of Revelstoke on Hwy. 23. Beach and a boat launch. The campground tends to be full of RVs, so get there early if you want a good spot. Open May-Sept. Sites $15. Cash only. ❶

Williamson's Lake Campground, 1818 Williamson Lake Rd. (☎888-676-2267; www.williamsonlakecampground.com), 3 mi. southeast of town on Airport Way. Farther from the highway than competitors, next to a peaceful swimming hole. Free showers. Laundry. Reception 8am-9pm. Open from mid-Apr. to Oct. Tent sites $16; RV sites $21.50. MC/V. ❶

➡ FOOD

The town's market is **Cooper's Supermarket,** 555 Victoria St. (☎205-837-4372. Open daily 8am-9pm.) Revelstoke's streets, especially Mackenzie Ave., are lined with wonderful cafes, restaurants, and bars, including a collection of Chinese-Western hybrids.

Chalet Deli and Bakery, 415B Victoria St. (☎205-837-5552), across the parking lot from Cooper's. This bakery is also a lunch spot with a hot deli, freshly baked bread (loaves $3-3.50), and sandwiches ($5.75). Open M-W 5am-5pm, Th-Sa 5am-6pm. MC/V. ❶

The Modern Bakeshop and Cafe, 212 Mackenzie Ave. (☎250-837-6886). Serves European-style coffee, sweets, and pastries at great prices in a pleasant space decorated with local artwork. Try the brie and baguette sandwich for just $4. Other sandwiches on fresh-baked bread $4-7. Open M-Sa 7am-5pm. ❶

☉ ❀ SIGHTS AND FESTIVALS

Canada's only mechanical music museum can be found downtown at the ▨**Revelstoke Nickelodeon Museum,** 111 First St. W., which houses an immense collection of automated music makers ranging from player pianos and jukeboxes to wonders like a combination piano-violin from 1929, which plays a duet with itself, and an enormous dance organ, featuring a saxophone, accordion, organ, light show, and full drum set. A 1hr.

tour given by the friendly owners lets you see about 20 of the machines. (☎250-837-5250; www.revelstokenickelodeon.com. Open in summer daily 10am-6pm; in spring and fall Tu-Sa 11am-4pm. Tours $10.) By now, you've undoubtedly seen several Canadian-Pacific trains, whose route was later shared by the Trans-Canada Highway. The **Revelstoke Railway Museum,** 719 W. Track St., off Victoria Rd., tells of the construction of the Trans-Canada line, which was completed a few miles from Revelstoke in 1885. Other exhibits include a steam engine and a passenger car. (☎877-837-6060; www.railwaymuseum.com. Open July-Aug. daily 9am-8pm; Sept.-Oct. and May-June daily 9am-5pm; Nov.-Feb. M-Tu and F-Su 11am-4pm; Mar.-Apr. M-Tu and Th-Su 9am-5pm. $8, ages 7-16 $4, under 7 free.) **Revelstoke Dam** is one of North America's largest hydroelectric developments. (☎205-814-6697. Open from mid-Apr. to mid-Oct. daily 9am-5pm. $5, ages 7-17 $3.) The town also hosts a blues festival during the third weekend in June, a lumberjack competition in early July, and a railroad festival in August.

◤ OUTDOORS

SUMMER ACTIVITIES

The **Revelstoke Adventure Centre** provides many exciting aquatic and outdoor experiences. Kayaking trips on the Columbia River start at $119, tours on the river and on Lake Revelstoke from $145. The center also offers 2-3hr. mountain-bike tours ($59-79) and ATV tours ($79). Rent a full suspension bike, two- to four-person canoe, or sea kayak for $45 per day or $35 per half-day. (☎877-837-9594.) The **Apex Raft Company,** 112 First St. E., offers exciting rafting trips up and down the river for $85. (☎888-232-6666. Open June-Labor Day.)

Adjacent to town, **Mount Revelstoke National Park** has astounding scenery and furnishes convenient access to nature. It is a favorite of mountain bikers and hikers. The park requires a **National Parks Permit** ($7.80, under 16 $3.90) that can be purchased at the Parks Canada Office in Revelstoke or at the gate. Two boardwalks off Hwy. 1, on the east side of the park, provide access to the trails. **Skunk Cabbage Trail** (1 mi., 30min.) leads through acres of stinking perfection: skunk cabbage plants tower at

heights of over 9 ft. **Giant Cedars Trail** (¼ mi., 15min.) showcases majestic, 600-year-old trees growing around babbling brooks. **Meadows in the Sky Parkway** (Summit Rd.) branches off Hwy. 1 between the town's two exits, leading 16 mi. up 16 switchbacks. From there, you can take a half-mile hike up Mt. Revelstoke to subalpine meadows.

WINTER ACTIVITIES

Winter in Revelstoke brings 60-80 ft. of powder and excellent downhill skiing. **Powder Springs Resort,** 3 mi. outside town, maintains one chairlift and 21 trails with a 1000 ft. vertical drop on the bottom third of Mt. MacKenzie. (☎800-991-4455; www.catpowder.com. Lift tickets $28-32.) The **Powder Springs Inn,** 200 Third St. W., offers reasonable hotel and skiing packages and rents skis. (☎205-837-5151; www.catpowder.com.) **Parks Canada** has excellent advice and brochures on area Nordic trails and world-class backcountry skiing. They also provide info on area snowmobiling, as does **Great Canadian Snowmobile Tours,** by Frisby Ridge, 4 mi. north of town on West Side Rd. (☎205-837-5030 or 877-837-9594; www.snowmobilerevelstoke.com. Snowmobiles $190-295 per day. $2500 credit-card deposit required. 22+. Reservations recommended.)

PHOTO OP. On Hwy. 1 at Craigellachie, the **Last Spike Monument** stands in honor of the completion of the transcontinental Canadian Pacific Railway; the last spike was pounded in here on November 7, 1885.

◤ THE ROAD TO SICAMOUS: 48 MI.
Follow **Highway 1 West** to Sicamous.

SICAMOUS   ☎250

The houseboat capital of Canada and gateway to the nearby Shuswap Lakes, Sicamous is also home to the **D Dutchmen Dairy ❶,** 1321 Maeir Rd. Savor over 40 flavors of ice cream (1 scoop $3, 2 scoops $4) and wander around the petting zoo to see llamas, cows, donkeys, and more. Follow the signs to the left of Hwy. 1 after entering town. (☎250-836-4304. Open daily 8am-9pm. Cash only.)

THE ROAD TO KELOWNA: 77 MI.

Continue south on **Route 97A** through the Okanagan Valley. Just before Vernon, merge onto **Route 97 South,** and continue through the Okanagan Valley on to the picturesque town of Kelowna.

KELOWNA   ☎250

In the heart of the Okanagan Valley, Kelowna (kuh-LOW-nuh) is one of Canada's richest agricultural regions and a popular tourist destination. The town's fruit stands, wineries, and independent shops draw thousands every summer. In winter, those not skiing in Whistler find the slopes of Big White Ski Resort equally rewarding.

VITAL STATS

Population: 105,000

Tourist Office: Tourism Kelowna, 544 Harvey Ave. (☎250-861-1515; www.tourismkelowna.org). Open May-Sept. daily 8am-7pm; Oct.-Apr. M-F 8am-5pm, Sa-Su 10am-3pm.

Library and Internet Access: Okanagan Regional Library Kelowna Branch, 1380 Ellis St. (☎250-762-2800). Open Apr.-Sept. M and F-Sa 10am-5:30pm, Tu-Th 10am-9pm; Oct.-Mar. M and F-Sa 10am-5:30pm, Tu-Th 10am-9pm, Su 1-5pm.

Post Office: 571 Bernard Ave. (☎250-868-8480). Open M-F 8:30am-5:30pm, Sa 9am-5pm. **Postal Code:** V1Y 7G0.

ORIENTATION

At the eastern shore of **Okanagan Lake,** Kelowna lies on **Highway 97 (Harvey Avenue),** which runs east-west across the lake and bisects the town. In the east, Hwy. 97 becomes the **Okanagan Highway** and curves north, intersecting **Highway 33** by the golf course. The floating bridge across the lake is unique in Canada. Traffic is notoriously terrible in Kelowna, as the bridge creates a massive bottleneck.

ACCOMMODATIONS

Warm, dry summer days attract thousands, so make reservations, even at campgrounds. If everything is full, there are inns and chain hotels along Lakeshore Dr. and Hwy. 97 in either direction. Kelowna has a plethora of B&Bs—stop by the visitors center for a list.

SameSun Backpacker's Lodge, 245 Harvey Ave. (☎877-562-2783; www.samesun.com), right before the floating bridge. This lively hostel features barbecues, pub crawls, movie nights, and other activities almost every night in summer. Key deposit $20. Dorms $26; private rooms $69-80. Credit card and ID required. MC/V. ❶

Kelowna International Hostel, 2343 Pandosy St. (☎250-763-6024; www.kelowna-hostel.bc.ca). 1 block from the beach in a colorful home. This laid-back hostel features super-friendly hosts, a comfortable lounge, and daily activities. Pancake breakfast included. Internet $1 per 30min. Reception 7am-11pm. Dorms $20; private doubles $50. MC/V. ❶

Bear Creek Provincial Park (☎800-689-9025 or 800-494-6500), 6 mi. north of Hwy. 97 on Westside Rd. Day-use area and camping. Shaded lakeside sites, boat launch, and a walking trail along the waterfront. Sites $24. Cash only. ❶

FOOD

Kelowna overflows with fresh produce. Find juicy delights at the stands outside town along Benvoulin Rd. and KLO Rd. or head south on Lakeshore Dr. to the pick-your-own cherry orchards. Bernard Ave. is lined with restaurants and cafes.

The Bohemian Bagel Cafe, 524 Bernard Ave. (☎250-862-3517; www.vtours.com/boh). Rich offerings in a colorful atmosphere on the main drag. The soup-salad-sandwich special is a steal at $12. Open W-F 7:30am-3pm, Sa 8:30am-3pm, Su 8:30am-2pm. AmEx/MC/V. ❶

Le Triskell Creperie, 467 Bernard Ave. (☎250-763-5151). This long, narrow restaurant with Parisian artwork captures the essence of a sidewalk bistro. Open M-W 9am-2pm, Th-Sa 9am-2pm and 5-9pm. MC/V. ❷

The Mad Mango Cafe, 551 Bernard St. (☎250-762-8588). Serves an eclectic variety of menu options, from full breakfasts ($2-5.50) to Chinese food ($3.50-7), all for cheap. Sandwiches $4-5. Open daily 7am-6pm. MC/V. ❶

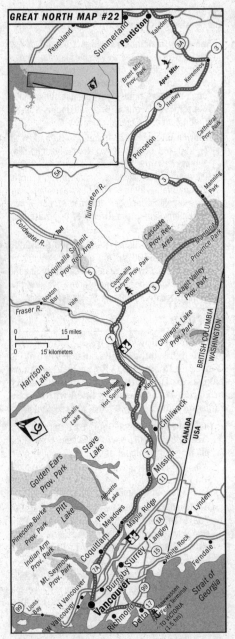

GREAT NORTH MAP #22

GREAT NORTH

SIGHTS

KELOWNA MUSEUMS. This set of four museums deals with local history from various perspectives, including military and agricultural. The **Okanagan Heritage Museum** houses regional artifacts, particularly those of the Okanagan and other First Nations, as well as rotating temporary exhibits. (*470 Queensway Ave.* ☎ *250-763-2417; www.kelownamuseum.ca. Open M-F 10am-5pm, Sa 10am-4pm. $2, children $1.*)

MISSION HILL. Over the past few years, the Okanagan Valley has become the center of the Canadian wine industry. Kelowna and the surrounding area are home to 12 of the valley's wineries, all of which offer tastings. Mission Hill is one of Kelowna's most respected wineries, offering tours of an underground wine cavern, bell tower, and outdoor amphitheater, with tastings of four wines. Cross the bridge west of town, turn left on Boucherie Rd., and follow the signs. (*1730 Mission Hill Rd., overlooking the west bank of Okanagan Lake.* ☎ *250-768-6448; www.missionhillwinery.com. Open daily July-Sept. 10am-7pm; Oct.-June 10am-5pm. Tours daily July-Aug. every 30min. 10am-5pm; Sept. and May-June every hr. 11am-4pm; Oct.-Apr. 11am, 1, 3pm. $5.*)

KELOWNA LAND AND ORCHARD. The town's oldest family-owned farm offers a 45min. hayride that explains farming techniques. The tour finishes at the orchard's farm stand. (*3002 Dunster Rd. Take KLO Rd. to E. Kelowna Rd., then make a left.* ☎ *250-763-1091; www.k-l-o.com. Open Apr.-Oct. daily 9am-4pm; call for winter hours. Tours Apr.-Oct. 1pm. $7.50, students $4, under 12 free.*)

OUTDOORS

Equipment rental is available at **Sports Rent,** 2936 Pandosy St. (☎250-861-5699; www.sportsrentkelowna.com. Bikes from $29 per day; in-line skates $11 per day; kayaks $30 per day. Ski packages from $24 per day. Open daily May-Sept. 9am-6pm; Oct.-Apr. 9am-8pm.)

BEACHES AND PARKS

The sun is Kelowna's main attraction, warming Okanagan parks and beaches for an average of 2000hr. per year. City Park and Waterfront Park, on the west end of downtown, are popular hangouts. Boyce Gyro Park, on Lakeshore Rd. south of the Okanagan Bridge, features beach volleyball. **Kelowna Parasail Adventures,** 1310 Water St., transforms patrons into living kites, floating them high above the lake. (☎250-868-4838; www.parasailcanada.com. Open May-Sept. daily 9am-sunset. $67.) Take a sail around the lake with **Go With the Wind Cruises,** on Waterfront Walkway. (☎250-763-5204; www.gowiththewind.com. $25 per hr., min. 2hr. Reservations recommended. Open May-Oct. daily 9am-6pm.)

BIKING AND HIKING

While Kelowna's main attraction is **Okanagan Lake,** surrounding areas offer excellent opportunities for off-road fun. Ponderosa pines dominate this hot, dry landscape. **Knox Mountain,** just north of the city, features many hiking trails as well as a paved road to the summit. Hike, bike, or drive to the top for a spectacular view of Kelowna and Okanagan. While you're there, don't pass up a chance to check out one of the city's natural secrets, **Paul's Tomb.** A secluded gravel beach named for the grave of one of Kelowna's early settlers, it's only a 1 mi. walk or bike from either the trailhead at the base of the mountain or the one at the lookout halfway up. **Bear Creek Regional Park's** 12 mi. of trails include a challenging hike that ascends to the canyon rim to view the city and lake. Much of the large and popular **Okanagan Mountain Provincial Park** was ravaged by a wildfire in 2003, leaving portions of the park scarred. Though the park has long since re-opened, ask at the visitors center for updates on trail conditions.

The **Kettle Valley Railbed (KVR),** another biking trail, passes through scenic **Myra-Bellevue Provincial Park,** the stunning **Myra Canyon,** and the only desert in western Canada. The rail bed through Myra Canyon stretches 7 mi., but the bike trail continues all the way to Penticton.

In addition, there are 18 regional parks within a 25 mi. radius of Kelowna that provide everything from picnic areas to swim spots and, in some cases, nature and hiking trails. Highlights include the **Mission Creek Regional Park,** with over 7 mi. of hiking trails and a connection to the **Mission Creek Greenway,** with 5 mi. of trails leading to the waterfront, and **Glen Canyon Regional Park,** which offers hikes along the old concrete flume and the cliff edges.

CLIMBING

The area around Kelowna boasts numerous spots for climbers. Along the Kettle Valley Railway in the Myra-Bellevue Provincial Park are the **Boulderfields,** with six main areas and 25 independent walls, almost all of advanced difficulty. **Idabel Lake,** lying near Okanagan Falls on Rte. 33 off Hwy. 97, boasts the best bouldering routes in the area. The most popular climbing in the area can be found at **Kelowna Crags,** by **Chute Lake Mountain Park.** The area offers climbs of a range of difficulties as well as a trail to the top for spectators to see the lake vista and relax in well-worn chairs constructed from stones. Follow Lakeshore Ave. to Chute Lake Rd. Follow the road for 2 mi. after it becomes a dirt road, 1 mi. after the sign marking the edge of Kelowna.

WINTER SPORTS

In the winter, downhill skiing is the most popular outdoor activity in the Okanagan Valley. **Big White Ski Resort** offers 15 lifts serving over 100 trails throughout 7355 acres of terrain. The resort completed a $130 million expansion at the beginning of the 2004 season, adding two new chairlifts and a state-of-the-art terrain park. The resort is located on a clearly marked access road off Hwy. 33, east of town. (☎250-765-3101; www.bigwhite.com. Open from mid-Nov. to late Apr. Lift tickets $68, ages 13-18 $56, ages 6-12 $33. Ski or snowboard rental $36.) Those preferring a smaller, less crowded mountain should head to **Crystal Mountain,** with 22 trails and an 800 ft. drop located at the top of Glenrosa Rd., 10min. from the Westbank overpass of Hwy. 97. (☎250-768-5189; www.crystalresort.com. Open from mid-Nov. to mid-Dec. Sa-Su 9am-3:30pm; from mid-Dec. to mid-Jan. daily 9am-3:30pm; from mid-Jan. to Mar. Th-Su 9am-3:30pm. Lift tickets $41, ages 13-18 $35. Ski or snowboard rental $31.)

⚐ THE ROAD TO PENTICTON: 40 MI.

Continue south on scenic **Highway 97** to Penticton.

PENTICTON ☎250

Indigenous peoples named the region between Okanagan and Skaha Lakes Pen-tak-tin, "a place to stay forever." Today, Penticton is known more commonly as the "Peach City," complete with a giant peach that would make Roald Dahl proud. Penticton is more than an agricultural mecca, however; the city bustles with tourists during the summer.

ORIENTATION

Penticton lies at the junction of **Highway 3** and **Highway 97,** at the southern extreme of the Okanagan Valley. **Okanagan Lake** borders the north end of town, while smaller **Skaha Lake** lies to the south. **Main Street** bisects the city from north to south, turning into **Skaha Lake Road** as it approaches the lake.

VITAL STATS
Population: 31,000
Tourist Office: Penticton Wine and Information Center, 533 Railway St. (☎800-663-5052; www.penticton.org), at Power and Eckhardt St. Free Internet and Wi-Fi. Open July-Sept. daily 8am-8pm; Oct.-June M-F 9am-6pm, Sa-Su 10am-5pm.
Internet Access: At the tourist office (above).
Post Office: 56 W. Industrial Ave. (☎250-492-5769). Open M-F 8:30am-5pm. **Postal Code:** V2A 6J8.

ACCOMMODATIONS

Penticton is a resort city year-round; cheap beds are few and far between. It's essential to make reservations in summer. If possible, avoid the hotels that lurk along Skaha Lake Rd. and take advantage of the beautiful hostel. Campgrounds along Skaha Lake are costly and often tightly packed.

The Penticton Hostel (HI), 464 Ellis St. (☎250-492-3992). A large, well-maintained hostel only 10min. from the beach. Relax in the comfy lounge or enjoy the hot water, powered by rooftop solar panels. Laundry $2. Reception 8am-noon and 5-10pm. Dorms $24-28, members $20-24; private rooms $59-67/51-58. MC/V. ❶

Okanagan Lake Provincial Park (☎250-494-6500 or 800-689-9025). North of town on Hwy. 97. 168 sites on 2 campgrounds. The north park is more spacious, with a good swimming beach.

Free firewood and showers. Reservations recommended. Sites $24. Cash only. ❶

FOOD

The Penticton **farmers' market** ❶, 100 Block Main St., in Gyro Park, sells local produce and baked goods. (☎250-770-3276. Open June-Oct. Sa 8:30am-noon.) You can't miss fruits and vegetables at family stands (look for signs on the side of the road) both north and south of town on Hwy. 97 and 3A.

Il Vecchio Delicatessen, 317 Robinson St. (☎250-492-7610), off Main St. Delicious sandwiches at incredibly cheap prices. Open M-Sa 9am-6pm. Cash only. ❶

The Dream Cafe, 67 Front St. (☎250-490-9012). An organic oasis with light sandwiches and dinners; try the spring rolls ($8.50) or the mango-roasted chicken sandwich ($10). Open Tu 9am-4pm, W-Su 9am-9pm. AmEx/MC/V. ❷

Isshin Japanese Deli, 449 Main St. (☎250-770-1141). A local favorite, serving affordable, fresh sushi ($2-13 per roll) and heaping noodle dishes ($6-17). Open M-F 11:30am-2:30pm and 5-8:30pm, Sa noon-2pm and 5-8:30pm. AmEx/MC/V. ❸

SIGHTS

SS SICAMOUS AND SS NARAMATA. While lounging on the beachfront, meander over to the *SS Sicamous* and *SS Naramata,* restored steel-hulled ships from 1914 that transported goods and passengers to the communities along the Okanagan. Tours offer a window into the leisure and luxury of the early Okanagan Valley; for those who are truly intrigued, the *Sicamous* also hosts a musical about life on the ship. Just adjacent is the small but fragrant and calming Rose Garden in which to sit or stroll. (*1099 Lakeshore Dr.* ☎250-492-0403; www.sssicamous.com. Open daily June-Sept. 9am-9pm; from Oct. to mid-Dec. and Apr.-May 9am-6pm; from mid-Jan. to Mar. 9am-5pm. $5, students $4, ages 5-12 $1.)

SUMMERLAND. Just 12 mi. north of Penticton on Hwy. 20, the town of Summerland is home to ornamental gardens and the preserved portion of the 1910 Kettle Valley Steam Railway, today operating as a tourist attraction. The 1hr. tour provides views of vineyards and the highest bridge on the original railway. *(Take Hwy. 97 to the Summerland exit. Follow Prairie Valley Rd. and turn right on Doherty Ave. ☎877-494-8424; www.kettlevalleyrail.org. Tours July-Sept. M and Th-Su 10:30am, 1:30pm; Oct. and from late May to June M and Sa-Su 10:30am, 1:30pm. $21, ages 13-17 $17, ages 3-12 $13.)*

PENTICTON MUSEUM. The museum chronicles the history of Penticton's gold trails and the Kettle Valley Railway, as well as First Nations history, with over 8000 artifacts. *(785 Main St., in the same building as the library. ☎ 250-490-2451. Open Tu-Sa 10am-5pm. Suggested donation $2, children $1.)*

◪ OUTDOORS

BIKING AND HIKING

Although the lakes are the star attractions, those looking for land-based adventures will not be disappointed. Visit **Munson Mountain,** an extinct volcano with "PENTICTON" spelled out in letters 50 ft. high and 30 ft. wide, for a bird's-eye view of the valley. Take Vancouver Ave. north of town and turn right on Tupper Ave., then left on Middle Bench Rd., to Munson Mountain Rd. The road ends just below the summit. Bikers, walkers, and runners will enjoy dozens of pathways and trails in the city and surrounding hills, many of which offer panoramic views of the lakes. The abandoned tracks of the Kettle Valley Railway run through Penticton and along both sides of Okanagan Lake and are the site of the **Trans-Canada Trail** in this area. Traveling north, you'll pass through orchards, vineyards, and wineries, all with a fantastic view of the lake. Those looking for a daytrip from Penticton can make the 12 mi. gradual ascent to Glenfir or go the 24 mi. to Chute Lake. For a short, moderate hike, follow the trail on the western side of the river channel to **Sage Mesa** for stunning views. Take Vancouver Ave. north to the intersection with Vancouver Pl. *(☎250-496-5220.)*

CLIMBING

The **Skaha Bluffs,** southeast of town on Valley View Rd., feature some of Canada's best rock climbing. For hikers and spectators, there are trails throughout the park. Check out *Skaha Rock Climbs,* by Howie Richardson, for detailed info on climbs. **Skaha Rock Adventures,** 437 Martin St., offers guide and instructional services. *(☎250-493-1765; www.skaharock-climbing.com. Open M-F 9am-5pm. Guided climbing and lessons from $110.)*

LAKEFRONT

In the summer, the Penticton tourist trade revolves around **Lake Okanagan** and **Lake Skaha.** Youths head toward **Skaha Lake Park** to the south for tubing down the **Okanagan River. Coyote Cruises,** 215 Riverside, rents tubes for $11 and provides a free shuttle for the return trip. *(☎250-492-2115. Open daily from late June to Sept. 10am-6pm.)* **Pier Water Sports,** 45 N. Martin St., just beyond the peach on the beach pier, rents water vessels for those with an active spirit and a few extra bucks. *(☎250-493-8864. Open daily 9am-8pm. Jet skis $85 per hr.; kayaks and pedal boats $18 per hr. Banana-boat rides $13.)*

SKIING

Apex Mountain Resort, off Green Mountain Rd., west of Penticton on Hwy. 3, offers the best downhill skiing in the area. Apex has downhill, cross-country, and night skiing on over 60 runs with a 2000 ft. vertical drop. They also boast a halfpipe and terrain park for boarders and an extensive glade area for the adventurous. In the summer, ski slopes become a dream come true for mountain bikers. *(☎877-777-2739; www.apexresort.com. Night skiing F-Sa 4:30-9:30pm. Lift tickets $60, ages 13-18 $49.50, ages 8-12 $37.50. Ski rentals $35/22/13. Night skiing $18.)*

⚐ THE ROAD TO VANCOUVER: 258 MI.

In Kaleden, turn west on **Highway 3A.** In Keremeos, turn west onto the **Crowsnest Highway (Highway 3).** From Hope, head west to Vancouver along **Highway 7.**

VANCOUVER ☎604

Even more so than most cities in North America, Vancouver boasts a thriving multicultural populace; the Chinese influence is so strong that it is commonly joked that Cantonese will soon become Canada's third national language. You'll find Asian flavor in everything from the peaceful manicured gardens to the raucous annual festivals in one of the largest

Vancouver Overview

ACCOMMODATIONS
Capilano RV Park, 1
Vancouver Hostel Jericho
Beach (HI), 2

FOOD
Benny's Bagels, 8
Montri's Thai Restaurant, 4
The Naam, 5
Sophie's Cosmic Cafe, 6
Uncle Fatih's Pizza, 10
WaaZuBee Cafe, 9

NIGHTLIFE
The King's Head, 3
Koerner's Pub, 7

Chinatowns in North America. Surrounded on three sides by water and closely hemmed in by the Pacific Coast Range, Vancouver never strays far from its logging-town roots. From the hip neighborhood of Gastown to walks in Stanley Park, Vancouver's diversity, location, and worldly atmosphere keep its residents friendly and the tourist influx constant.

ORIENTATION

Vancouver lies in the southwestern corner of mainland British Columbia. It is divided into distinct regions, mostly by waterways. South of the city flows the **Fraser River,** and to the west lies the **Georgia Strait,** which separates the mainland from **Vancouver Island.** Downtown juts north into the **Burrard Inlet,** and **Stanley Park**

goes even farther north. The **Lions Gate** suspension bridge over **Burrard Inlet** links Stanley Park with **North** and **West Vancouver** (West Van), known collectively as the **North Shore;** the bridges over **False Creek** south of downtown link downtown with **Kitsilano** ("Kits") and the rest of the city. West of Burrard St. is the **West End. Gastown** and **Chinatown** are just east of downtown. The **University of British Columbia (UBC)** lies to the west of Kitsilano on **Point Grey. Highway 99** runs north-south from the US-Canada border through the city along **Oak Street,** through downtown and Stanley Park, then over the Lions Gate bridge. It temporarily joins with the **Trans-Canada Highway (Highway 1)** before splitting off again and continuing north to Whistler. Roadtrippers may want to consider using the **Park 'n' Ride** system (☎604-

953-3333; www.translink.bc.ca) or making the use of free parking lots at major transit hubs.

VITAL STATS

Population: 2,000,000

Tourist Office: 200 Burrard St. (☎604-683-2000; www.tourismvancouver.com), on the plaza level near Canada Place. Open daily 8:30am-6pm.

Library and Internet Access: Vancouver Public Library, 350 W. Georgia St. (☎604-331-3600). Open M-Th 10am-9pm, F-Sa 10am-6pm, Su 1-5pm.

Post Office: 349 W. Georgia St. (☎604-662-5725). Open M-F 8am-5:30pm. **Postal Code:** V6B 3P7.

▐ ACCOMMODATIONS

Vancouver B&Bs are a good deal for couples or small groups, with singles generally from $45 and doubles from $55. Check out www. bedsandbreakfasts.ca/vancouver_area.htm for more information. HI hostels are good for clean and quiet rooms.

HOSTELS

▣ **Vancouver Hostel Downtown (HI),** 1114 Burnaby St. (☎604-684-4565 or 888-203-4302), in the West End. Sleek, clean 225-bed facility in a quiet neighborhood surrounded by downtown, the beach, and Stanley Park. Library, kitchen, and patio. Free pub crawls M and W; frequent tours of Granville Island. Breakfast included. Lockers. Laundry $3. Internet $3 per hr. Reception 24hr. Reservations recommended June-Sept. Dorms $30-34, members $26-30; doubles $70-88/62-80. MC/V. ❶

▣ **SameSun Hostel,** 1018 Granville St. (☎604-682-8226 or 877-972-6378; www. samesun.com), at the corner of Nelson, next to the Ramada Inn. Funky, laid-back, colorful hangout in an area with great nightlife. Backpackers bar downstairs. Pool table. 250 beds. Laundry $2. Internet $1 per 30min. Dorms $28-30, members $25-28; doubles $80/70. MC/V. ❶

C&N Backpackers Hostel, 927 and 1038 Main St. (☎604-682-2441 or 888-434-6060; www. cnnbackpackers.com). At the 1038 location, cheap meal deals with the Ivanhoe Pub ($2.50 breakfast) make living above the bar a bargain, but across the street is a quieter location. Laundry

$2. Bikes $10 per day. Reception 8am-10:30pm. Dorms $20; doubles $50. AmEx/MC/V. ❶

Seymour Cambie Hostel, 515 Seymour St. (☎604-684-7757 or 877-395-5535; www. cambiehostels.com), in Gastown. The quieter of 2 downtown Cambie hostels. Movie nights (M and Su), soccer games (July-Sept.), and free tours of Granville Island Brewery (Tu noon, 2, 4pm). Breakfast $2.50. Laundry $2. Internet $4 per hr. Dorms $26-28; private rooms $56-70. MC/V. ❶

Cambie International Hostel, 300 Cambie St. (☎877-395-5335; www.cambiehostels.com), in Gastown. The Cambie offers easy access to the busy sights and sounds of Gastown (including those of the bar downstairs) in one of the neighborhood's older buildings. Can be noisy at night. Breakfast included at the bakery next door. Laundry $2. Internet $4 per hr. Reception 24hr. Dorms $21-30; singles $60. MC/V. ❶

Vancouver Hostel Jericho Beach (HI), 1515 Discovery St. (☎888-203-4303), in Jericho Beach Park. Follow 4th Ave. west past Alma and bear right at the fork. Practically on the beach, with a great view across English Bay. Homey. Attracts guests of all ages. 280 beds in 14-person dorm rooms. 10 4-bed family rooms. Kitchen, TV, cafe (breakfast $8; dinner $8-10). Laundry $2.50. Parking $5 per day. Open May-Sept. Dorms $28, members $24; family rooms $60. ❶

Pacific Spirit Hostel at UBC Lodgings, Place Vanier Residence, 1935 Lower Mall (☎604-822-1000; www.ubcconferences. com). Private rooms with access to TV lounges, microwave and fridge, and campus pubs. Linen included. Laundry $2.50. Internet $10. Open May-Aug. Singles $33; doubles $66. ❶

CAMPING

Capilano RV Park, 295 Tomahawk Ave. (☎604-987-4722; www.capilanorvpark.com), at the foot of Lions Gate Bridge in North Van. By far the most convenient camping location, with pool, hot tub, and laundry facilities. Reception 8am-11pm. Tent sites $35; RV sites $45. ❶

ParkCanada, 4799 Hwy. 17 (☎604-943-5811), in Delta, near the Tsawwassen ferry terminal. Take Hwy. 99 S. to Hwy. 17, then go east for 1.5 mi. The campground is next to a water park and has a pool. Tent sites $24; RV sites from $27-32. ❶

🖎 FOOD

From Vietnamese noodle shops to Italian cafes, Vancouver has your corner of the globe covered. Vancouver's **Chinatown** and the **Punjabi Village** along Main and Fraser, around 49th St., both serve cheap, authentic food. Restaurants in downtown compete for the highest prices in the city. The **West End** caters to diners seeking a variety of ethnic cuisines (check out the globe-spanning lineup on Denman St.), while **Gastown** has funky coffee shops. Many cheap establishments along Davie and Denman St. stay open around the clock. Dollar-a-slice, all-night pizza joints pepper downtown and Commercial Ave. to the east.

WEST END, DOWNTOWN, AND GASTOWN

🖎 **Subeez Cafe,** 891 Homer St. (☎604-687-6107), downtown. Serves a hipster crowd with delicious upscale dishes like the chicken and brie baguette ($13) or vegetable and pasta frittata ($10). Lengthy wine list, large bar, and home-spun beats. DJs W and F-Sa 9pm-midnight. Open M-F 11:30am-1am, Sa 11am-1am, Su 11am-midnight. MC/V. ❸

La Luna Cafe, 117 Water St. (☎604-687-5862), in Gastown. Loyal patrons swear by the coffee, roasted onsite. Satisfying sandwiches ($6-7). Internet $1 per 15min. Open M-F 7:30am-5pm, Sa 10am-5pm. MC/V. ❶

The Dish, 1068 Davie St. (☎604-689-0208). This longtime Vancouver staple prides itself on large portions and creative, healthy dishes. Vegetarian sandwiches and entrees are available, including the roasted veggie wrap ($5.15) and the lentil stew on rice ($7). Carnivores will not be disappointed by the deli-style sandwiches ($5.30) and entrees like curry chicken on rice ($6.50). Open M-Sa 7am-10pm, Su 9am-9pm. MC/V. ❷

Samurai Sushi House, 1108 Davie St. (☎604-609-0078). A range of cheap, not-so-dainty sushi options makes this Japanese restaurant a backpackers' favorite. Virtually nothing on the menu is over $9. Open M-Th and Su 11am-midnight, F-Sa 11am-1am. MC/V. ❷

COMMERCIAL DRIVE

WaaZuBee Cafe, 1622 Commercial Dr. (☎604-253-5299), at E. 1st St. Sleek, metallic decoration, ambient music, huge murals, and an enormous wine list. Entrees such as spinach and ricotta pasta or Thai prawns run $11-23. Chicken, lamb, beef, tuna, and veggie burgers $11-12. Open M-F 10:30am-1am, Sa 10am-1am, Su 10am-midnight. AmEx/D/MC/V. ❹

Uncle Fatih's Pizza, 1685 E. Broadway (☎604-707-0744; www.unclefatihspizza.com). A local favorite, Uncle Fatih's stands out among pizza joints in the area, offering high-quality pizza for incredible prices. Small 3-topping pizzas only $5; 2 jumbo slices and a soda for $3.80. Open M-Th 10am-1am, F-Su 10am-3am. ❷

KITSILANO

🖎 **Sophie's Cosmic Cafe,** 2095 W. 4th Ave. (☎604-732-6810). Colorful walls decorated with lunch boxes and antique hats make Sophie's homey place to enjoy a big breakfast or a diner-style lunch. Omelets, waffles, hot cereal, sandwiches, and hearty entrees are done with flair and old-fashioned charm. Entrees $5-10. Open daily 8am-8:45pm. AmEx/D/MC/V. ❷

The Naam, 2724 W. 4th Ave. (☎604-738-7151; www.thenaam.com), at MacDonald St. One of the most diverse vegetarian menus around, with great prices to boot. Beautifully presented entrees such as Crying Tiger Thai stir-fry ($11) and several kinds of veggie burgers for under $9. Tofulati dairy-free ice cream $5. Live music daily 7-10pm. Open 24hr. MC/V. ❷

Montri's Thai Restaurant, 3629 W. Broadway (☎604-738-9888). Voted the best Thai restaurant 6 years running by *Vancouver Magazine*. It's worth sampling the Thai Gai-Yang (chicken in coconut milk; $14) along with the traditional but perfectly done pad thai ($11). Open Tu-Su 5-10pm. AmEx/MC/V. ❸

Benny's Bagels, 2505 W. Broadway (☎604-731-9730). Benny's can start, end, or continue your day with bagels ($1), sandwiches ($4-7), and beer ($3). Free Wi-Fi. Open M-Th and Su 7am-1am, F-Sa 7am-3am. MC/V. ❶

CHINATOWN

🖎 **Hon's Wun-Tun House,** 268 Keefer St. (☎604-688-0871). This award-winning Cantonese noodle house is the place to go for great Chinese. Pick from over 300 options—reading the menu

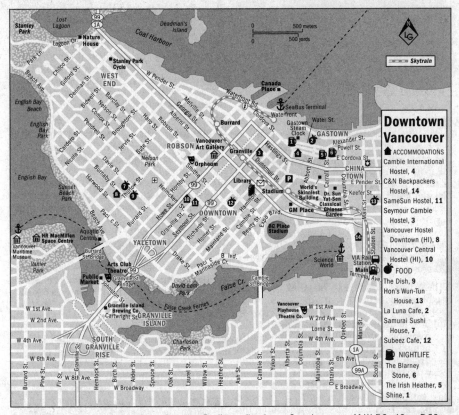

Downtown Vancouver

▲ ACCOMMODATIONS
Cambie International
Hostel, **4**
C&N Backpackers
Hostel, **14**
SameSun Hostel, **11**
Seymour Cambie
Hostel, **3**
Vancouver Hostel
Downtown (HI), **8**
Vancouver Central
Hostel (HI), **10**
🍴 FOOD
The Dish, **9**
Hon's Wun-Tun
House, **13**
La Luna Cafe, **2**
Samurai Sushi
House, **7**
Subeez Cafe, **12**
🍸 NIGHTLIFE
The Blarney
Stone, **6**
The Irish Heather, **5**
Shine, **1**

might take as long as eating what you finally order. Noodle bowls $8. Open M-Th 9am-9pm, F-Su 9am-10pm. Cash only. **❷**

MyLite Soya Foods, 163 Keefer St. (☎604-682-8867). If you're down with the soybean, you'll be in heaven. This deli-style vegetarian restaurant's menu incorporates tofu or soy milk into all of its veggie dishes. Entrees $3-5. Open daily 9:30am-6pm. MC/V. **❶**

👁 SIGHTS

🟦**VANCOUVER ART GALLERY.** This gallery hosts fantastic temporary exhibitions and houses a permanent collection of contemporary art and design from the West Coast. (*750 Hornby St., in Robson Sq. ☎604-662-4700; www.vanart-gallery.bc.ca. Open in summer M, W, F-Su 10am-5:30pm, Tu and Th 10am-9pm; hours vary in winter. $19.50, students $14, ages 5-12 $6.)*

🟦**VANDUSEN BOTANICAL GARDEN.** Fifty five tranquil acres purchased from the Canadian Pacific Railway in 1966 are the site of the stunning Vandusen Botanical Garden, which showcases 7500 species from six continents. A nice place for a picnic or an evening stroll, the grounds also feature an international sculpture collection, while more than 60 species of birds can be seen in areas such as the Fragrance Garden, Children's Garden, Bonsai House, Chinese Medicinal Garden, and Elizabethan Maze, which is planted with 3000 pyramidal cedars. Daily tours are given at 2pm and on Wednesday at 11am. If you'd rather stroll the garden on your own, follow a self-guided tour tailored to show the best of the season. *(5251 Oak St., at W. 37th Ave. ☎604-878-9274; www.vandusengarden.org. Open daily from June to mid-Aug. 10am-9pm; from mid-Aug. to Sept. 10am-7pm; Oct. and Mar. 10am-5pm; Nov.-Feb. 10am-4pm; Apr. 10am-6pm; May 10am-8pm. Apr.-Sept. $8.50, ages 13-18 $6.50, ages 6-12 $4.25, under 6 free; Oct.-Mar. $6.25/4.50/4.75/3.)*

◪VANCOUVER AQUARIUM. If you've never seen a white whale, head here for the must-see version of Melville's muse. A visit to the aquarium, on Stanley Park's eastern side not far from the entrance, is like spending time at the British Columbia coastline. You'll see **◪playful otters,** white beluga whales (a huge tank allows for outdoor and underwater viewing), dolphins, and smaller, more delicate species. *(☎604-659-3474; www.vanaqua.org. Open daily July-Aug. 9:30am-7pm; Sept.-June 10am-5:30pm. Shows every 30 min. 10am-5:30pm. $25, students and seniors $20, ages 4-12 $17, under 4 free.)*

CHINATOWN. Southeast of Gastown, the neighborhood bustles with restaurants, shops, bakeries, and the world's narrowest building, **8 West Pender Street.** In 1912, the city expropriated all but a 1.8m (6 ft.) strip of Chang Toy's property in order to expand the street; he built on the land anyhow, and today the building is a symbol of Chinatown's perseverance. The serene **Doctor Sun Yat-Sen Classical Chinese Garden** maintains imported plants, carvings, and rock formations in the first full-size garden of its kind outside China. The neighboring park is free but lacks the ornate beauty of the actual gardens. *(578 Carrall St. ☎604-662-3207; www.vancouverchinesegarden. com. Open daily from mid-June to Aug. 9:30am-7pm; Sept. and from May to mid-June 10am-6pm; Oct.-Apr. 10am-4:30pm. Tours every hr. 10am-6pm. $10, students $9, seniors $8.)* Don't miss the sights, sounds, smells, and tastes at the night market, where vendors set up stands selling nearly anything along Keefer St. east of Main. *(F-Su 6:30-11pm.)* Chinatown is relatively safe, but surrounding areas are some of Vancouver's less savory sections and should be avoided.

BLOEDEL FLORAL CONSERVATORY. Go from the tropics to the desert in 100 paces inside this 130 ft. diameter dome, constructed of Plexiglas bubbles and aluminum tubing. The conservatory, which is maintained at a constant 65°F, is home to 500 varieties of exotic plants and 150 birds. The conservatory is located inside beautiful Queen Elizabeth Park, whose elevation also affords views of downtown. *(1 block east of Cambie St. and 37th Ave. ☎604-257-8584. Open daily Apr.-Sept. 10am-5pm; Oct. and Feb.-Mar. 10am-5:30pm; Nov.-Jan. 10am-5pm. $4.60, ages 13-18 $3.45, ages 6-12 $2.30.)*

UNIVERSITY OF BRITISH COLUMBIA (UBC). The high point of a visit to UBC is the breathtaking **◪Museum of Anthropology.** The high-ceilinged glass-and-concrete building houses totems and carvings, highlighted by Bill Reid's depiction of Raven discovering the first human beings in a giant clamshell. *(6393 NW Marine Dr. ☎604-822-5087; www.moa.ubc.ca. Open May-Sept. M and W-Su 10am-5pm, Tu 10am-9pm; Sept.-May Tu 10am-9pm, W-Su 10am-5pm. $9, students and seniors $7, under 6 free. Tu after 5pm free.)* Across the street, caretakers tend to the **Nitobe Memorial Garden,** rated as one of the finest classical Shinto gardens outside of Japan. *(☎604-822-9666; www.nitobe.org. Open daily from mid-May to Aug. 10am-6pm; Sept.-Oct. and from mid-Mar. to mid-May 10am-5pm. $6, students $3, ages 13-17 $2.)* The **Botanical Gardens** are a collegiate Eden, encompassing eight gardens in the central campus. The garden includes the largest collection of rhododendrons in North America. *(6804 SW Marine Dr. ☎604-822-9666; www.ubcbotanicalgarden. org. Open daily from mid-May to Aug. 10am-6pm; Sept.-Oct. and from mid-Mar. to mid-May and 10am-5pm. $8, students $6, under 6 free.)*

STANLEY PARK. Established in 1888 at the tip of the downtown peninsula, the 1000-acre Stanley Park is a testament to the foresight of Vancouver's urban planners. The thickly wooded park is laced with cycling and hiking trails and surrounded by a 6 mi. seawall promenade popular with cyclists, runners, and in-line skaters. *(☎778-257-8400. A free shuttle runs between major destinations throughout the park from late June to Sept. every 30min. 10am-6:30pm.)* On the south side of the park, the **Lost Lagoon** brims with fish, birds, and the odd trumpeter swan and provides a utopian escape from the skyscrapers. Nature walks start from the Nature House, underneath the Lost Lagoon bus loop at the west side of Alberni St. *(☎604-*

257-8544. Walks Su 1pm. $10, under 12 free. Nature House open June-Aug. F-Su 11am-7pm.) The park's edges feature restaurants, tennis courts, a running track, swimming beaches staffed by lifeguards, and an outdoor theater, the **Malkin Bowl.** *(☎604-687-0174.)*

DID YOU KNOW? Think that the totem poles in Stanley Park are fake? Think again. They are actually authentic and among the most valuable totems in the world.

HR MACMILLAN SPACE CENTRE. The space center runs a motion-simulator ride, a planetarium, a solar observatory, an exhibit gallery, and laser-light rock shows. *(1100 Chestnut St. ☎604-738-7827; www.hrmacmillanspacecentre. com. Open July-Aug. daily 10am-5pm; Sept.-June Tu-Su 10am-5pm. Laser shows F-Sa 9:45, 10:30pm. $15, students and seniors $10.75, ages 5-10 $10.75, under 5 free. Laser-light show $10.50.)*

GRANVILLE ISLAND. This hidden gem, underneath the Granville St. bridge, has shops ranging from umbrella designers to silversmiths, a market with fresh produce and seafood, and a waterfront location with frequent musical performances. *(1689 Johnston St. ☎604-666-5784; www.granvilleisland.bc.ca. Open daily 9am-7pm.)*

🎵 ENTERTAINMENT

MUSIC AND THEATER

The renowned **Vancouver Symphony Orchestra** (☎604-876-3434; www.vancouversymphony. ca; tickets $25-78) plays from September to May in the refurbished **Orpheum Theatre** (☎604-665-3050), at the corner of Smithe and Seymour St. The VSO often joins forces with other groups, such as the **Vancouver Bach Choir.** (☎604-921-8012; www.vancouverbachchoir. com. Tickets $35-90.) The **Vancouver Playhouse Theatre Company** (☎604-873-3311), at Dunsmuir and Georgia St., and the **Arts Club Theatre** (☎604-687-1644; www.artsclub.com), on Granville Island, stage low-key shows, often including local work. **Theatre Under the Stars** puts on outdoor musicals in the summer in Stanley Park's Malkin Bowl. (☎604-687-0174; www.tuts.bc.ca. Tickets $20-30.) The world-famous improvisational theater company **Theatresports League** performs competitive improv, comedies, and improv jam sessions at the **Arts Club New Revue Stage** on Granville Island. (☎604-687-1644; www.vtsl.com. Tickets $10-18.) The **Ridge Theatre,** 3131 Arbutus St., shows art-house, indie, European, and vintage film double features. (☎604-738-6311; www.ridgetheatre.com. $5, children and seniors $4.) The **Hollywood Theatre,** 3123 W. Broadway, shows indie films, documentaries, and second-run, mainstream double features for less than other theaters downtown. (☎604-515-5864; www.hollywoodtheatre.ca. Films $6, under 14 and seniors $3.50.)

SPORTS

One block south of Chinatown on Main St. is **BC Place Stadium**, 777 S. Pacific Blvd., home to the CFL's **BC Lions** and the world's largest air-supported dome. (☎604-669-2300; www.bcplacestadium.com. Tickets from $20.) The NHL's **Vancouver Canucks** (www.canucks.com/gm) call nearby **GM Place** home. The **Vancouver Canadians** play AAA baseball in **Nat Bailey Stadium,** at 33rd. Ave. and Ontario St., opposite Queen Elizabeth Park. For tickets and info, call Ticketmaster at ☎604-280-4400 or visit www.ticketmaster.ca.

ⓝ NIGHTLIFE

Vancouver's nightlife centers on dance clubs, with lively beats and DJs spinning every night. Pubs are scattered through the city's neighborhoods. The weekly *Georgia Straight* (www.straight.com) publishes comprehensive event listings, restaurant reviews, and coupons. *Discorder* (http://discorder.citr.ca) is the monthly publication of the university radio station CITR.

ⓝ **The Irish Heather,** 217 Carrall St. (☎604-688-9779; www.irishheather.com). The 2nd-highest seller of Guinness in BC, this true Irish pub and bistro serves up nostalgia of the Emerald Isle to a clientele of regulars. 20 oz. drafts ($8), mixed drinks ($5), and bangers and mash will keep those eyes smiling. Live music Tu-Th 8pm-last customer. Open M-Sa noon-midnight. AmEx/D/MC/V.

Shine, 364 Water St. (☎604-408-4321; www.shinenightclub.com), in the basement. Named the "sexiest club in Canada" in 2001 by *Flare Magazine,* this ultra-hip club draws in crowds with its sleek decor and nightly specials. Beer $6-8. Cover M-Th and Su $3, F-Sa $7. Open daily 9pm-4am. AmEx/MC/V.

The Blarney Stone, 216 Carrall St. (☎604-687-4322). For a more raucous Irish experience, join the university crowd for music 4 nights a week by Killarney, a Celtic rock band that has played

here for 20 years. Cover F-Sa $8. Open W-Sa 7pm-2am. MC/V.

The King's Head, 1618 Yew St. (☎604-738-6966), at York Ave. Cheap drinks, cheap food, relaxing atmosphere, and a great location near the beach. Bands play acoustic sets Th-Sa nights at 9pm on a tiny stage. Breakfast $3.50 before 11am. Daily drink specials. $4 pints. Open M-Sa 8am-1am, Su 8am-midnight. AmEx/MC/V.

Koerner's Pub, 6371 Crescent Rd. (☎604-822-0983), in the basement of the Graduate Student Bldg. on UBC's campus. Owned and operated by the Graduate Student Society, this is the place to meet sexy brains. Mellow M with live music and open jam. Pints $5. Open M-F noon-10pm. Kitchen open until 7pm.

⚠ OUTDOORS

BEACHES

Follow the western side of the Stanley Park seawall south to **Sunset Beach Park,** a strip of grass and beach extending all the way along English Bay to the Burrard Bridge. **Kitsilano Beach,** across Arbutus St. from Vanier Park, is a favorite for tanning and beach volleyball, but the water is a bit cool for swimming. For smaller crowds, more kids, and free showers, visit **Jericho Beach.** Head west along Fourth Ave. and follow signs. A cycling path at the side of the road leads uphill to the westernmost end of the UBC campus. West of Jericho Beach is the quieter **Spanish Banks;** at low tide the ocean retreats almost 1 mi., allowing long walks on the flats. Most of Vancouver's 19 mi. of beaches are patrolled by lifeguards from late May to Labor Day between 11:30am and 9pm. For information on beaches, call the **Parks and Recreation department.** (☎604-738-8535, from mid-Sept. to mid-May ☎604-665-3424; www.city.vancouver.bc.ca/parks/rec/beaches.)

SKIING

Grouse Grind is the ski hill closest to downtown Vancouver and has the crowds to prove it. The very steep and well-traveled 2 mi. **Grouse Grind Trail,** also known as "Mother Nature's Stairmaster," is a popular hiking trail among Vancouverites in the summer. It charges straight up 2800 ft. to the top of the mountain but rewards hikers with a beautiful view of downtown. (☎604-984-0661; www.grousemountain.com. Slopes lit for skiing from mid-Nov. to mid-Apr. daily 9am-10pm. Lift tickets $47, ages 13-18 $37, ages 5-12 $21. Tramway $35, ages 13-18 $21, ages 5-12 $13, seniors $33.) **Cypress Bowl** in West Vancouver provides a less-crowded skiing alternative to Grouse Mountain. It boasts the most advanced terrain of the local mountains on its 23 runs at prices comparable to Grouse Mtn. The 10 mi. of groomed trails at **Hollyburn cross-country ski area** are open to the public. In summer, the cross-country trails have hiking and berry-picking. Go west on Hwy. 1, and take Exit 8/Cypress Bowl Rd. (☎604-922-0825; www.cypressmountain.com. Open daily Dec. 9am-4pm; Dec.-Mar. 9am-10pm.) At **Mount Seymour Provincial Park**, trails leave from Mt. Seymour Rd. and a paved road winds 7 mi. to the top. The Mt. Seymour ski area has the cheapest skiing around. Its marked terrain is also the least challenging, although the spectacular backcountry is preferred by many pro snowboarders. (☎604-986-2261; www.mountseymour.com. Call ahead for seasonal hours. Lift tickets $34, ages 13-18 $28, ages 6-13 $18, under 6 free, seniors $24.)

⛏ THE ROAD TO VICTORIA: 68 MI.

From Vancouver, take **Highway 99 South** until the junction with **Highway 17**. Follow Hwy. 17 heading southwest until you reach the **Tsawwassen Ferry Terminal.** (☎888-223-3779; www.bcferries.com. 8-16 per day; $14.25, cars $47.15.) You will need to take the 1hr. ferry trip across to Vancouver Island. On Vancouver Island, head south on **Highway 17**.

VICTORIA ☎250

A fitting place to end the Great North roadtrip, Victoria is the proper British counterpart to cosmopolitan Vancouver, complete with perfectly groomed gardens and polite society tea. Many tourist operations would have you believe that Victoria fell off Great Britain in a neat little chunk, but the truth is that Victoria's British flavor was created in the 1950s to attract tourists. Today, double-decker buses motor past art galleries, countless "English" pubs, and waterfront cafes. Victoria lies within easy distance of Vancouver Island's outdoor paradise, making it a destination for both leisure and adventure.

VITAL STATS
Population: 330,200
Tourist Office: Tourism Victoria, 812 Wharf St. (☎250-953-2033), at Government St. Open daily July-Aug. 8:30am-6:30pm; Sept.-June 9am-5pm.
Library and Internet Access: Central Library, 735 Broughton St. (☎250-382-7241). Open M and F-Sa 9am-6pm, Tu-Th 9am-9pm, Su 1-5pm.
Post Office: 706 Yates St. (☎250-267-1177). Open M-F 8am-5pm. **Postal Code:** V8W 2L9.

⚡ ORIENTATION

Victoria surrounds the **Inner Harbour,** a boulevard meant for pedestrians. The main north-south streets are **Government Street** and **Douglas Street.** To the north, Douglas St. becomes **Highway 1,** which runs to **Nanaimo. Blanshard Street,** one block to the east, becomes **Highway 17.**

📷 ACCOMMODATIONS

A number of flavorful hostels and B&B-hostel hybrids make a night in Victoria an altogether pleasant experience. More than a dozen campgrounds lie in the greater Victoria area.

Ocean Island Backpackers Inn, 791 Pandora St. (☎250-385-1788 or 888-888-4180; www.oceanisland.com), downtown. This hostel boasts a better lounge than most clubs, tastier food than most restaurants, and accommodations comparable to many hotels. Lockers and linen included. Internet access $1 per 15min. Parking $6. Reception 24hr. Dorms $25-27, members $23-25; private rooms from $33. MC/V. ❶

Victoria International Hostel (HI), 516 Yates St. (☎250-385-4511). Colorful barracks-style dorms and private rooms in downtown. Laundry $3.50. Dorms $27, members $23; private rooms $69/61. MC/V. ❶

Paul's Motor Inn, 1900 Douglas St. (☎866-333-7285; www.paulsmotorinn.com), just past Chinatown. Offers hotel rooms with TVs, fridges, and queen beds. Rooms $64-109. ❹

Goldstream Provincial Park, 2930 Trans-Canada Hwy. (☎250-391-2300 or 800-689-9025), 10 mi. northwest of Victoria. Offers tent sites in a forested riverside area with great hiking trails and swimming in the Goldstream River. Toilets and showers. Sites $22. ❶

🍴 FOOD

🍴 **Rebar,** 50 Bastion Sq. (☎250-361-9223; www.rebarmodernfood.com). Perhaps the most healthful, best-tasting cuisine around. Mosaic walls, an eclectic menu of organic breakfast treats, salads, and pastas will make even the pickiest of diners happy. Dishes $5-13. Open M-Th 8:30am-9pm, F-Sa 8:30am-10pm, Su 8:30am-3:30pm. ❸

John's Place, 723 Pandora St. (☎250-389-0711; www.johnsplace.ca). Dishes up Canadian fare with a spicy Mediterranean and Asian twist. Fluffy omelets ($6.25), salmon with pecans and maple syrup ($15), and chicken souvlaki ($9) are a few examples of what awaits. Open M-Th 7am-9pm, F 7am-10pm, Sa 8am-4pm and 5-10pm, Su 8am-4pm and 5-9pm. AmEx/MC/V. ❷

James Bay Tea Room and Restaurant, 332 Menzies St. (☎250-382-8282), at Superior St., behind the Parliament Bldg. A trip to Victoria is not complete without a spot of tea. Sa and Su High Tea ($19.25) is delightful and significantly less expensive than the famous High Tea at the Empress Hotel. Open M-Sa 7am-5pm, Su 8am-5pm. AmEx/MC/V. ❷

Blue Carrot Cafe, 188 Bastion Sq. (☎250-381-8722). A tucked-away little cafe with a cozy seating area and exposed brick walls. Sandwiches $7-8. Offers delicious breakfast options ($7-8). Open daily 8am-4pm. MC/V. ❷

🔆 SIGHTS

If you don't mind becoming one with the flocks of tourists heading to the shores of Victoria, wander along the **Inner Harbour.** You'll see boats come in and admire street performers on the Causeway as the sun sets behind neighboring islands.

BUTCHART GARDENS. The elaborate and world-famous Butchart Gardens sprawl across 55 acres 13 mi. north of Victoria, off Hwy. 17. Immaculate landscaping includes the magnificent Sunken Garden (a former limestone quarry), the Rose Garden, Japanese and Italian gardens, and fountains. The gardens sparkle with live entertainment and lights at night, while Saturday-evening fire-

works shows in July and August draw out the locals. *(Bus #75 from downtown. ☎250-652-4422; www.butchartgardens.com. Open daily from mid-June to Aug. 9am-11:30pm; call ahead for winter hours. $23, ages 13-17 $11.50, ages 5-12 $2.50, under 5 free.)*

VANCOUVER ISLAND BREWERY. After a few days of hiking, biking, and museum-going, unwind with a tour of the Vancouver Island Brewery. The 1hr. tour includes 20min. of touring and 40min. of drinking. *(☎250-361-0007; www.vanislandbrewery.com. Tours M and Th 1pm, F 1, 3pm, Sa 3pm. 19+ to taste. $6.)*

ROYAL BRITISH COLUMBIA MUSEUM. This thorough museum houses exhibits on the biological, geological, and cultural history of the province. Step into a coastal ecosystem, temperate forests, and an ice age, complete with woolly mammoth. *(675 Belleville St. ☎250-356-7226; www.royalbcmuseum.bc.ca. Open daily 9am-5pm. $15, ages 6-18 $9.50, under 6 free. IMAX and Museum $23, students $19, ages 6-18 $18.25, under 6 $5.)*

OTHER SIGHTS. The **Parliament Buildings** light up Victoria's skyline in the evenings and majestically preside over the Inner Bay during the day. Stroll through the buildings and admire the late-19th-century architecture of Francis Rattenbury. *(501 Belleville St. ☎250-387-3046; www.legis.gov.bc.ca. Open daily 8:30am-5pm. Tours in summer daily 9am-5pm; hours vary in winter, so call ahead. Free.)* The **Fairmont Empress Hotel** is one of Victoria's most popular icons, with ivy-covered brick and regal flair. Staying the night is pricey, but a free visit to the tea room and grounds is well worth the stop. *(721 Government St. ☎250-384-8111.)*

🎵 NIGHTLIFE

English pubs, watering holes, and clubs abound throughout town. Live music is available practically every night, and the free weekly *Monday Magazine* (www.mondaymag.com) will keep you updated on who's playing when and where.

Irish Times Pub, 1200 Government St. (☎250-383-7775). For a cheap and swanky time, head here. Pizza and pints $13 W. Live Irish music daily. Happy hour daily 3-6pm with $1 oysters. Open daily 11am-1am. AmEx/D/MC/V.

Upstairs Cabaret, 15 Bastion Sq. (☎250-385-5483). The college venue for live music and dancing. DJs bring a crowd F-Sa nights. Doors open 9pm. AmEx/D/MC/V.

Darcy's Pub, 1127 Wharf St. (☎250-380-1322; www.darcyspub.ca), just below Upstairs. Caters to a drinking, people-watching, lively-without-dancing crowd and doubles as the Victoria Rock and Roll Music Hall of Fame. Outdoor seating right on the square makes it a prime spot in summer. Beer-battered prawns $11. Open M-W and Su 11am-midnight, Th-Sa 11am-1am. AmEx/MC/V.

OUTDOORS

The flowering oasis of **Beacon Hill Park,** off Douglas St., south of the Inner Harbour, pleases walkers, bikers, and picnickers; it borders the gorgeous Dallas Rd. scenic drive and even features a petting zoo. Mountain bikers can tackle the **Galloping Goose,** a 62 mi. trail beginning downtown and continuing to the west coast of the island through rainforests and canyons. **Ocean River Sports,** 1824 Store St., offers kayak rentals, tours, and lessons. (☎250-381-4233 or 800-909-4233; www.oceanriver.com. Open M-W 9:30am-6pm, Th-F 9:30am-8pm, Sa 9:30am-6pm, Su 10am-5pm. Single kayak $40 per day; double $60.)

THE END OF THE ROAD

You've braved wild animals, giant cities, forbidding mountain passes, and that dreaded Canadian "eh" for nearly 4000 miles across North America. Take a moment to revel in your success—clamber onto a double-decker bus, indulge in some crumpets and Earl Grey tea, and explore British Columbia's outdoor paradise. You've conquered the Great North, and nothing can stop you now. Head south for the **Pacific Coast** or **Oregon Trail** to continue the adventure.

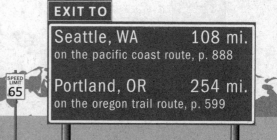

EXIT TO

Seattle, WA   108 mi.
on the pacific coast route, p. 888

Portland, OR   254 mi.
on the oregon trail route, p. 599

the national road

TOP 5

1. Find hoodoos (and that ever-elusive lost cow) in **Bryce Canyon National Park** (p. 440), Utah.
2. Gag in awe at the **world's biggest hairball** (p. 398) in Garden City, Kansas.
3. Get messy eating a **cheesesteak** (p. 339) in Philadelphia, Pennsylvania.
4. Hike (or, better yet, ski) the Rocky Mountains in **Vail, Colorado** (p. 424).
5. Kneel in the shadow of the **world's biggest cross** (p. 376) in Effingham, Illinois.

For roadtrippers who don't want to mess around, the 3000 mile National Rd. puts all others to shame. This route cuts across the middle of the country, from sea to shining sea. For the first stretch, you'll follow the Old National Rd., much of which is today's US 40. Construction on this road began in 1811, and the road reached its original terminus, Wheeling, West Virginia, in 1818. By 1833, it had been extended to Vandalia, Illinois; from the start of the route to Vandalia, Old National Rd. markers, as well as Madonna of the Trail statues, are still visible on the road.

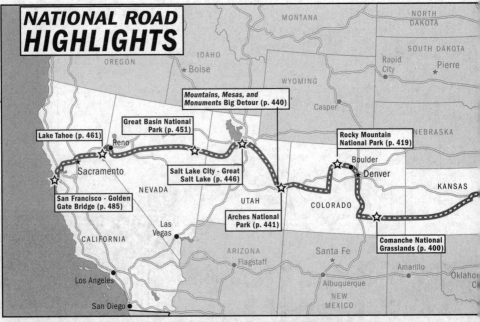

NATIONAL ROAD HIGHLIGHTS

Start your trip in **Atlantic City, NJ**—check out **Lucy the Elephant** (p. 338), but don't spend all your quarters at the slots here; save some for **Reno, NV** (p. 456), still 2700 mi. down the road. From here, continue on to **Philadelphia** (p. 339), revered by some as the birthplace of the nation and revered by more as the birthplace of the cheesesteak sandwich, before passing through **Baltimore** (p. 349). Soon enough you'll enter the foothills of the **Blue Ridge Mountains.** Stop at scenic **Harpers Ferry National Historic Park** (p. 355) before rolling through Ohio and into Indiana, home of the world-famous **Indianapolis Motor Speedway** (p. 373). Pass into the West under the arch at **St. Louis** (p. 379) and then through Missouri, home state of ragtime legend **Scott Joplin** in Sedalia, MO (p. 389). Next is Kansas, home of the **world's largest hairball** (p. 398). By now, you'll be on **US 50,** another famous continent-crosser, paralleling the historic **Lincoln Highway.** It's a long, straight shot to Colorado, and then to **Denver** (p. 408) up into the mountains, winding through the **Rocky Mountains National Park** (p. 419), and passing by some of the nation's best skiing at **Vail** (p.

424). This area also hosts unparalleled opportunities for summertime activities, including rafting and mountain biking.

The stunning scenery continues into Utah; our route takes you through **Moab** (p. 436), gateway to the spectacular **Mountains, Monuments, and Mesas Big Detour** (p. 440), and then north to **Salt Lake City** (p. 446) and its namesake Great Salt Lake. From there, it's on to northern Nevada, where US 50 is known as **"The Loneliest Road."** The road here is a black ribbon winding across the desert, broken by the occasional cow, cactus, or mining town. You'll pass **Great Basin National Park (p. 451)** and then Reno—"the biggest little city in the world"—before the welcome blue oasis of **Lake Tahoe** (p. 461), which somehow offers pristine wilderness and casino-sponsored debauchery side-by-side. Continuing west, you'll come down from the **Sierra Nevada** through California's Central Valley. **Berkeley** (p. 472) is a bibliophile's dream and home to **Chez Panisse** (p. 473), the birthplace of California cuisine. Go west, young roadtripper, until you can go west no more, ending your journey in

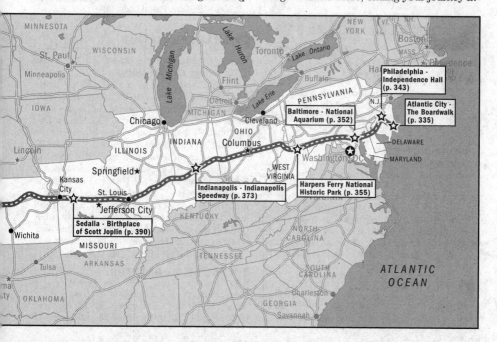

San Francisco (p. 477). Watch the sun set over the Golden Gate Bridge (p. 485), a grand end to a grand transcontinental roadtrip.

ROUTE STATS
Miles: c. 3000
Route: Atlantic City, NJ to San Francisco, CA.
States: 14; New Jersey, Pennsylvania, Delaware, Maryland, West Virginia, Ohio, Indiana, Illinois, Missouri, Kansas, Colorado, Utah, Nevada, and California.
Driving Time: Give yourself at least 3-4 weeks to experience what the road has to offer.
When To Go: Almost any time you feel like taking off for California. Go in winter and ski in Colorado (but keep in mind that driving conditions can be treacherous) or go in summer and explore the wilderness along the way (but keep in mind that prices and temperatures are higher). The bottom line? Just go.
Crossroads: The East Coast in Atlantic City, NJ (p. 121); **Route 66** in St. Louis, MO (p. 518); **The Oregon Trail** in Independence, MO (p. 600); **The Pacific Coast** in San Francisco, CA (p. 948).

The Garden State
NEW JERSEY
Welcomes You

ATLANTIC CITY ☎609

For 70 years, board-game enthusiasts have been wheeling and dealing with Atlantic City geography, famously depicted on the Monopoly game board. Meanwhile, the opulence of the original Boardwalk and Park Pl. faded first into neglect and then into casino-driven tackiness. Gambling, legalized in the 1970s, brought mega-dollar casinos to the Boardwalk and restored a steady flow of tourists, but the casinos appear to have done little for the city aesthetically. Highlights center on the Boardwalk, where announcements invite pedestrians to step into the casinos and try their luck at blackjack or slots. Venues feature Top 40 hits and 80s classics, which makes for an energizing and upbeat environment.

✦ ORIENTATION

Attractions cluster on and around the **Boardwalk**, which runs northeast-southwest along

the Atlantic Ocean. Parallel to the Boardwalk, **Pacific Avenue** and **Atlantic Avenue** offer cheap restaurants, hotels, and convenience stores. Atlantic Ave. and Pacific Ave. can be unsafe after dark, and areas past the Boardwalk's flurry of activity are desolate and unsafe. Transport is easy on foot on the Boardwalk.

VITAL STATS
Population: 41,000
Tourist Offices: Atlantic City Visitors Welcome Center (☎609-383-2727), on the Atlantic Expwy., 1 mi. after the Pleasantville Toll Plaza, at mile marker 3.5 out of Atlantic City. Open M-Th and Su 9am-5pm, F-Sa 9am-8pm. **Atlantic City Boardwalk Info Center** (☎888-228-4748; www.atlanticcitynj.com), on the Boardwalk at Mississippi Ave. Open daily from Labor Day to Memorial Day 9:30am-5:30pm; from Memorial Day to Labor Day M-W 9:30am-5:30pm, Th-Su 9:30am-8pm.
Library and Internet Access: Atlantic City Library, 1 N. Tennessee Ave. (☎609-345-2269). Open M-W 10am-8pm, Th-Sa 9am-5pm, Su noon-5pm.
Post Office: 1701 Pacific Ave. (☎609-345-5583), at Illinois Ave. Open M-F 8:30am-5:30pm, Sa 8:30am-12:30pm. **Postal Code:** 08401.

⌐ TRANSPORTATION

Jitneys, or small shuttle buses, run to all the casinos and most major points of interest. You can find the stops mainly along Pacific Ave. (☎609-344-8642; www.jitneys.net.) **Rolling Chair Rides** appear along the Boardwalk as frequently as yellow cabs in Manhattan. (☎609-347-7500. $5 for up to 5 blocks.) Free parking is available on some residential streets, but you're only likely to find spots in unsafe areas. You can also try **Oriental Avenue** at **New Jersey Avenue** near the Garden Pier Historic Museum for free 3hr. parking at an easy walking distance from the Boardwalk. Be careful at night: this area is more desolate than other parts of the city. **B&K Bike Rental** provides two-wheelers at locations on the Boardwalk and North Carolina and Iowa Ave.

⌂ ACCOMMODATIONS

Motels are located 2-6 mi. out of town on US 40 and US 30 as well as in Absecon, 8 mi. west of town on US 30. Some of the side streets

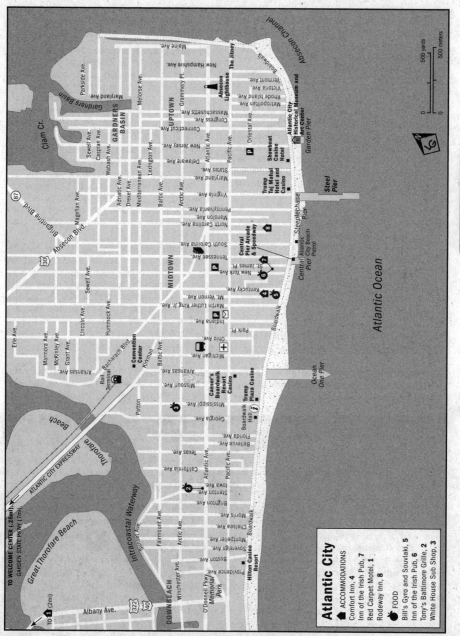

Atlantic City

ACCOMMODATIONS
Comfort Inn, 4
Inn of the Irish Pub, 7
Red Carpet Motel, 1
Rodeway Inn, 8

FOOD
Bill's Gyro and Souvlaki, 5
Inn of the Irish Pub, 6
Tony's Baltimore Grille, 2
White House Sub Shop, 3

connecting Atlantic Ave. and the Boardwalk have plenty of cheap places to stay, particularly between South Carolina Ave. and Indiana Ave. Rates may vary wildly between weekdays and weekends, so call ahead.

Inn of the Irish Pub, 164 St. James Pl. (☎609-344-9063; www.theirishpub.com), between New York Ave. and Tennessee Ave. About 60 spacious, clean rooms near the Boardwalk. Enjoy the porch's rocking chairs and refreshing Atlantic breeze. The downstairs bar offers lively entertainment and a friendly atmosphere. Key deposit $5. No parking affiliated with the inn, but unmetered parking on adjacent streets. Singles with shared bath M-Th and Su $25, F-Sa $40. Doubles with shared bath $40/55; with private bath $55/90. AmEx/D/MC/V. ❷

Rodeway Inn, 124 S. North Carolina Ave. (☎609-345-0155), across from the Resorts Casino. Rooms have standard amenities (TV, A/C) with an excellent location just off the Boardwalk to boot. Free parking. Rooms in summer M-Th and Su $95, F-Sa $160-270; Jan.-Feb. rooms may be as low as $45. AmEx/D/MC/V. ❹

🍴 FOOD

Although not recommended by nutritionists, $0.75 hot dogs and $1.50 pizza slices are readily available on the Boardwalk, and there is no shortage of ice-cream parlors here. Some of the best deals in town await at the casinos, where all-you-can-eat lunch ($7) and dinner ($11) buffets abound. Tastier, less tacky fare can be found farther from the seashore.

Inn of the Irish Pub, 164 St. James Pl. (☎609-344-9063; www.theirishpub.com). Locals lounge downstairs, joined by the foreign students and hostelers staying upstairs at this hostel-and-bar combo. Serving hearty pub-style food all night, it's packed with carousers at all hours. Wash down a liverwurst and onion sandwich ($3) with a domestic pint ($2). Dinner specials $6.50. Domestic drafts $1. Open 24hr. Cash only. ❶

White House Sub Shop, 2301 Arctic Ave. (☎609-345-1564), at Mississippi Ave. According to rumor, Sinatra had these immense subs (half $6, whole $12) flown to him while on tour. Pictures of sublovers Joe DiMaggio, Wayne Newton, and Mr. T overlook the team making each sandwich to order. Open M-Th 10am-9pm, F-Sa 10am-9:30pm. Cash only. ❷

Tony's Baltimore Grille, 2800 Atlantic Ave. (☎609-345-5766), at Iowa Ave. It's hard to resist the Grille's old-time Italian-American atmosphere—defined by personal jukeboxes and cheap prices. Pizza $8.25. Seafood platter with shrimp, crab cakes, and scallops $13.45. Salads from $4. Kitchen open daily 11am-3am. Bar open 24hr. Cash only. ❸

Bill's Gyro and Souvlaki, 1607 Boardwalk (☎609-347-2466), near Kentucky Ave. 1000s of customer-signed dollar bills adorn the walls, stools, cash registers, and counter at this airy, well-lit establishment. The menu offers all-day

HOW'S MY (KID) DRIVING?

During a roadtrip, "How's My Driving?" bumper stickers are a common sight. Plastered to the back of 18-wheelers, these stickers prominently display a toll-free number that private drivers can call to report commercial vehicles' traffic violations. As you drive through New Jersey, Delaware, and Pennsylvania, however, you might see these stickers somewhere unexpected: on privately owned cars. Inspired by the trucks' stickers, Delaware residents James Pugh and Kevin Brown started a teen-monitoring service from their homes, charging $25 per year. In return for membership, parents receive a simple black-and-white bumper sticker bearing the company name (howsmykiddrivingtoday. com), a toll-free number, and an identification code. Thanks to these stickers, other drivers can then share the (perhaps ugly) truth—via email—of how the teen in question is really driving. Many other similar companies exist, including the Chicago-based myteen.com and Wisconsin's tell-my-mom. com. These services cater to parental paranoia, sure, but Mom and Dad's fears may be warranted. Car crashes are the leading cause of death for teens, and drivers from ages 16 to 19 have the highest average annual crash and traffic violation rates of any age group. Reactions to "How's My Driving?" services have been mixed; embarrassment at sporting such a bumper sticker can lead to teen-parent conflict. The stickers' perceived safety advantage, however, has lead to their increased

breakfast (omelet $4.25) and gyros ($5). Open 7am-midnight or later. AmEx/D/MC/V. ❶

🔊🌊 SIGHTS AND BEACHES

THE BOARDWALK

This area is a flurry of activity and seagulls, lined with gift shops, food stalls selling pizza, funnel cakes, stromboli, and ice cream, and, of course, casinos (see next page). There's often live music playing, usually paid for by casinos trying to attract gamblers. Visitors can walk, ride bikes between 6-10am, or take advantage of the ubiquitous rolling chairs. Most of the action along this 8 mi. stretch takes place south of the Showboat.

CENTRAL PIER ARCADE AND SPEEDWAY. Those under 21 play for prizes at the many arcades that line the Boardwalk, including Central Pier Arcade and Speedway. It feels like real gambling, but instead of winning money (lame) you can pick up a new iPod or Wii, along with more typical carnival prizes like stuffed animals and sports jerseys. The pier also has go-carts and paintball. *(At the Boardwalk and Tennessee Ave. ☎ 609-345-5219. Open M-Th and Su 10am-midnight, F-Sa 10am-2am. Single go-cart $8; double $13. Must be at least 12 years old and 54 in. tall to ride alone. Paintball $5 per 30 shots.)*

STEEL PIER. The historic Steel Pier juts into the coastal waters with a Ferris wheel that spins riders over the Atlantic. It also offers a smorgasbord of amusement park attractions: a roller coaster, a carousel, and games of skill. *(On the Boardwalk at Virginia Ave. ☎ 609-345-4893; www. steelpier.com. Open M-F 3pm-midnight, Sa-Su noon-1am. Tickets $0.75, 35 for $25.)*

ELSEWHERE

ATLANTIC CITY ART CENTER. If you're seeking a quiet way to spend the afternoon (and can ignore the noise from casinos under construction), wander through the Atlantic City Art Center, which displays the work of local and regional artists. *(On Garden Pier at New Jersey Ave. and the Boardwalk. ☎ 609-347-5837; www.acart-center.org. Open daily 10am-4pm. Free.)*

ATLANTIC CITY HISTORICAL MUSEUM. Also on Garden Pier, the Atlantic City Historical Museum contains memorabilia that docu-

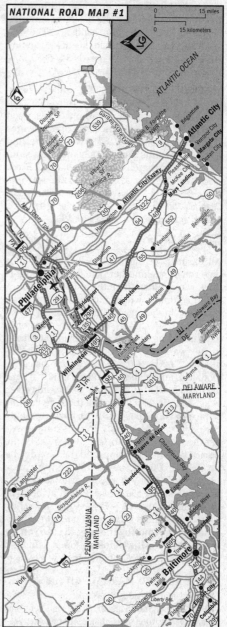

ments the history of the "Queen of Resorts," and includes displays on the Miss America Pageant, Monopoly, and sand art. The displays successfully turn old, seemingly gaudy objects into works of art. (☎609-347-5839; www.acmuseum.org. Open daily 10am-4pm. Free.)

ABSECON LIGHTHOUSE. The tallest lighthouse in New Jersey and the third-tallest in the nation, Absecon Lighthouse has been painted with several different color schemes since it was built in 1857. Now white and black, it contains a small museum and a stunning view of the city and ocean. (31 S. Rhode Island Ave. Drive northeast on Pacific Ave. from midtown. ☎609-449-1360; www.absecon lighthouse.org. Open July-Aug. daily 10am-5pm; in winter M and Th-Su 11am-4pm. $7, ages 4-12 $4, seniors $5.)

🏛 CAINO

All casinos on the Boardwalk fall within a dice roll of one another. The farthest south is the swanky **Hilton** (its interior decor includes white columns, white marble, and mirrors), between Providence and Boston Ave. (☎609-347-7111 or 800-257-8677; www.hiltonac.com), and the farthest north is the gaudy **Showboat**, at Delaware Ave. and Boardwalk (☎609-343-4000 or 800-621-0200; www.harrahs.com). Donald Trump's glittering **Trump Taj Mahal Hotel and Casino,** 1000 Boardwalk, at Virginia Ave., is an Atlantic City landmark too ostentatious to be missed. (☎609-449-1000; www.trumptaj. com.) In true Monopoly form, Trump owns another hotel casino on Boardwalk: the **Trump Plaza,** at Mississippi and the Boardwalk. (☎609-441-6000 or 800-677-7378; www.trump-plaza.com.) Many a die is cast at **Caesar's Boardwalk Resort and Casino,** 2100 Pacific Ave., at Arkansas Ave. (☎800-443-0104; www.har-rahs.com), which is connected to three other casinos, all owned by Harrahs, in case you get bored at one. All casinos are open 24hr. and are dominated by slot machines.

🛣 THE ROAD TO MARGATE CITY: 5 MI.

From the Atlantic City Boardwalk, take any side street to **Pacific Avenue.** Stay to the left as the road turns onto **Albany Avenue,** then turn left onto **Atlantic Avenue.**

MARGATE CITY ☎609

Trim beachfront houses and condos replace the glitz and grit of the Atlantic City Boardwalk. If you didn't get your fill of over-the-top there, check out **Lucy the Elephant,** 9200 Atlantic Ave. Originally built in 1881 as a marketing gimmick, Lucy has always been in the public eye. It's no wonder—at 60 ft. and 100 tons, she's hardly the average pachyderm. (☎609-823-6473; www.lucytheelephant.org. Open mid-June to Labor Day M-Sa 10am-8pm, Su 10am-5pm; from Apr. W-F 11am-4pm, Sa-Su 10am-5pm; May to mid-June M-F 11am-4pm, Sa-Su 10am-5pm. Tours every 30min. $6, children $3.) If you've grown too attached to Lucy to leave and decide to stay for a meal, head to **I Love Lucy's Beach Grille ❶,** the all-outdoors, laid-back restaurant right in front of her trunk. (☎609-822-7268. Burgers $5. Open from Memorial Day to Labor Day M-Tu 10am-5pm, W-Su 10am-5pm and 5:30-10pm. Guests are welcome to BYOB. Cash only.)

🛣 THE ROAD TO MAYS LANDING: 18 MI.

Leaving Margate City, take **Ventnor Avenue** back toward Atlantic City and make a left onto **Albany Avenue (US 40).** Stay right to stay on **US 40** when it splits from **US 322** to become the **Harding Highway.** Continue on it for 5 mi. The countryside is a welcome change from the skyscrapers of Atlantic City.

MAYS LANDING ☎609

When you enter well-maintained Mays Landing, be sure to note the **American Hotel** on your left and the **courthouse** on your right, both built in the late 1830s. The American Hotel has replaced its beds with bookshelves and now forms part of the **Atlantic County Library,** 40 Farragut Ave. (☎609-625-2776. Free Internet. Open M-Th 9am-9pm, F-Sa 9am-5pm.) Homier than your typical diner, **Main Street Cafe ❷,** 6033 W. Main St., has $7 lunch specials with savory french fries. (☎609-625-5500. Breakfast $1.50-8. Sandwiches $5-9. Open M-Sa 8am-3pm, Su 8am-2pm. AmEx/MC/V.)

🛣 THE ROAD TO PHILADELPHIA: 66 MI.

Turn onto **Cape May Avenue/Harding Highway,** which is **US 40.** Follow US 40 until you hit Woodstown. From Woodstown, turn right at **North Main Street (Route 45 North)** which becomes **Woodstown Road** after 7 mi.

Turn left on **Commissoners Road** to follow **Route 45 North.** Take **Route 295 North** to **I-76** and follow signs to **I-676.** Take **Exit 2** on **I-676 North** to **Camden/Ben Franklin Bridge.** Take the bridge to the exit for **Independence Hall** to access the central attractions.

The Keystone State

PENNSYLVANIA

Welcomes You!

PHILADELPHIA ☎215

With his band of Quakers, William Penn founded the City of Brotherly Love in 1682. It was Benjamin Franklin, however, who planted the seeds of the metropolis it is today. Franklin, the ingenious American ambassador, inventor, and womanizer, almost single-handedly built Philadelphia into an American colonial capital. Today, sightseers will eat up Philly's historic attractions, world-class museums, and architectural accomplishments—not to mention the city's native cheesesteaks and other culinary offerings.

VITAL STATS
Population: 1,500,000
Tourist Office: Independence Visitors Center and National Park Service Visitors Center (☎215-965-7676), on Market St. between 5th and 6th St. inside the welcome center. Open daily in summer 8:30am-7pm; in winter 8:30am-5pm.
Library and Internet Access: Free Library of Philadelphia, 1901 Vine St. (☎215-686-5322). Open M-W 9am-9pm, Th-Sa 9am-5pm, Su 1-5pm.
Post Office: 2970 Market St. (☎215-895-8980), at 30th St., across from the Amtrak station. Open 7am-10pm, Su 7:30am-10pm. **Postal Code:** 19104.

▪ ORIENTATION

The construction of **I-676** and **I-95** through Philadelphia's center has made navigating the already challenging grid of one-way streets and alleys even more difficult. I-676 runs east-west through the **Center City** area, which is bordered by I-95 on the east and

I-76 just across the **Schuylkill River.** Within the city, numbered north-south streets ascend in value from the **Delaware River** on the east past the Schuylkill River on the west and serve as good reference points. The first street is **Front Street;** the others follow consecutively from Second to 69th.

▣ TRANSPORTATION

Seeing attractions in the historic district is best done on foot. There is no shortage of expensive parking lots (about $11 per day) in **Center City.** Outside of the area around the convention center and Independence Hall, lot prices get somewhat cheaper, and many lots offer day-long specials if you are in by 9 or 10am and out by 6pm. There is a somewhat cheaper lot ($5-11) on Race St. between Ninth and Tenth St. Metered spots ($1 per hr.) also exist throughout the city except in the immediate area of **Independence Mall.** Also, while most Center City meters give you 2hr., the spots at the Delaware River end of Chestnut and Market St. above **Penn's Landing** sometimes offer 4hr. time slots. Meters in **University City** offer 3hr. slots. If you've parked your car and want to ride to the attractions that are harder to walk to, consider using the **Philly Phlash,** a cheap, purple shuttle service that runs to most of the major attractions, including many museums and down Market St. (☎215-389-8687; www.phillyphlash.com. $2 per ride. Day pass $5. Runs May-Oct. daily 10am-6pm.) The **Southeastern Pennsylvania Transportation Authority (SEPTA)** is Philadelphia's public transportation organization, with bus, subway, and regional rail service. (☎215-580-7800; www.septa.com. Tokens $1.45; cash fare $2.)

▮ ACCOMMODATIONS

Aside from the two hostels, inexpensive lodging in Philadelphia is uncommon. If reserved a few days in advance, comfortable rooms close to Center City can be found for around $70. The motels near the airport at Exit 9A on I-95 sacrifice location for affordable rates. **Bed and Breakfast Connections/Bed and Breakfast of Philadelphia,** in Devon, books rooms in Philadelphia and southeastern Pennsylvania;

NATIONAL ROAD

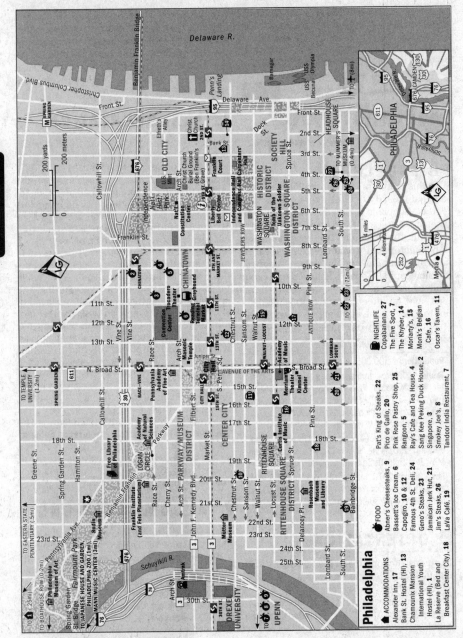

you can search the website by geographic location. (☎610-644-8790; www.bnbphiladelphia.com. Open M-F 9am-5pm. Singles $70-90; doubles $75-250.) Most accommodations lack packing; park in a lot or plan to pay meters.

◪ **Chamounix Mansion International Youth Hostel (HI-AYH),** 3250 Chamounix Dr. (☎215-878-3676; www.philahostel.org), in W. Fairmount Park. Ride I-76 W. to Exit 339 and take a left on Belmont, a left on Ford Rd., and a left on Chamounix Rd. An energetic staff maintains this lavish hostel. Kitchen, piano, TV/VCR, and bikes. Laundry $3. Free Internet kiosk and Wi-Fi. Free parking. Check-in 8-11am and 4:30pm-midnight. Lockout 11am-4:30pm. Curfew midnight. Dorms $23, members $20. MC/V. ❶

Apple Hostel (HI-AYH), 32 S. Bank St. (☎215-922-0222; www.applehostels.com), between Chestnut and Market St. Social hostel in an alleyway in the historic district. Organizes walking tours and pub crawls for guests. Kitchen, A/C, TV, and pool table. Laundry $3. Internet $1 per 10min.; free Wi-Fi. Dorms $27-31. MC/V. ❶

Alexander Inn, 12th and Spruce St. (☎215-923-3535; www.alexanderinn.com). 48 spacious rooms with Wi-Fi, cable TV, A/C, breakfast buffet, access to a fitness room, and very helpful staff, located in the heart of a GLBT neighborhood (with rainbow street signs aplenty). Check-in 3pm. Check-out noon. Singles $110; doubles from $120. AmEx/D/MC/V. ❺

La Reserve (Bed and Breakfast Center City), 1804 Pine St. (☎215-735-1137; www.lareservebandb.com). A stately house with a Steinway in the entryway. 12 rooms with 19th-century decor. All rooms have A/C; some have kitchens. Full breakfast. Rooms $130-180. AmEx/D/MC/V. ❺

Timberlane Campground, 117 Timberlane Rd. (☎856-423-6677; www.timberlanecampground.com), in Clarksboro, NJ. Take US 295 S. to the first turnoff for Exit 18A, follow the campground signs, and turn right on Friendship Rd. Timberlane is 1 block down on the right. Hot showers, toilets, fishing pond, pool, and batting cages. Reservations recommended. Tent sites $30-33; RV sites $38-40. MC/V. ❷

◪ FOOD

Street vendors are at the heart of Philadelphia culinary tradition, hawking cheesesteaks, hoagies, cashews, and soft pretzels. Ethnic eateries cluster in several specific areas: hip **South Street,** between Front and Seventh St.; **18th Street** around Sansom St.; and **Second Street,** between Chestnut and Market St. Chinatown is bounded by 11th, Eighth, Arch, and Vine St. Philadelphia's original farmers market (since 1893), the ◪**Reading Terminal Market,** at 12th and Arch St., across from the Pennsylvania Convention Center, is the largest indoor market in the US. A food court on steroids, the market is home to a variety of venues that range from traditional Amish meat mongers to trendy Asian fusion stalls. (☎215-922-2317; www.readingterminalmarket.org. Open M-Sa 8am-6pm, Su 9am-4am. Amish merchants open W-Th 8am-3pm, F-Sa 8am-5pm.)

HISTORIC DISTRICT

◪ **Famous 4th Street Delicatessen,** 700 S. 4th St. (☎215-922-3274), at Bainbridge St. This deli rivals New York City's finest. A landmark since 1923, this delicatessen has acquired a cult following for its hot corned-beef sandwiches ($12.50). The best cookies in the city ($1.35). Open daily 8am-9pm. AmEx/MC/V. ❸

Jim's Steaks, 400 South St. (☎215-928-1911; www.jimssteaks.com), at 4th St. Customers arrive in droves, clamoring for the authentic hoagies ($5-7.50). Pass the time in line by inspecting the wall of fame, which includes Pat Sajak and Kobe Bryant. Open M-Th 10am-1am, F-Sa 10am-3am, Su 11am-10pm. Cash only. ❶

Pink Rose Pastry Shop, 630 S. 4th St. (☎215-592-0565; www.pinkrosepastry.com). Serves up homemade delicacies at tables graced with fresh flowers. Grandmotherly decorations like pink tablecloths and floral prints. Breakfast and lunch $4-8. Open M-Th 8am-10:30pm, F 8am-11:30pm, Sa 9am-11:30pm, Su 9am-10:30pm. AmEx/D/MC/V. ❷

Red Hook Coffee and Tea, 765 S. 4th St. This community-minded coffee shop hosts art openings on the 4th F of each month. Wide range of coffees, teas, and smoothies ($1.50-6), and sandwiches ($4-8), including a banana-Nutella panino. Cash only. ❶

CHINATOWN

Rangoon, 112 9th St. (☎215-829-8939), between Cherry and Arch St. Pink and plastic decor complements the spicy scent of Burmese cuisine. Noodle dishes $6-9. Open M-Th and Su 11:30am-9pm, F-Sa 11:30am-10pm. MC/V. ❷

Sang Kee Peking Duck House, 238 9th St. (☎215-925-7532), near Arch St. Locals pack in for the extensive menu. If you're eating in-house, the duck requires lengthy in-house preparation. Alternatively, takeout duck costs $16. Entrees $5-10. Open M-Th and Su 10am-10:45pm, F-Sa 10am-11:45pm. Cash only. ❷

CENTER CITY

Pico de Gallo, 1501 South St., (☎215-772-3003), on the corner of South and 15th St. This fun Mexican place makes no attempt at authenticity, but every meal is a fiesta. The plantain, roasted pork, and organic black-bean burrito ($8) will challenge even the hungriest roadtripper. Freshly squeezed juices $3.25. Open daily noon-11pm or later. Cash only. ❷

Jamaican Jerk Hut, 1436 S. St. (☎215-545-8644). While chefs jerk ½ chickens ($13) to perfection, Bob Marley tunes blast in the veranda. Live music F-Sa 7pm. Movies Th 8:45pm. Cover $2. Open M-Th 11am-10pm, F-Sa 11am-11pm, Su 5-10pm. Cash only. ❸

Bassett's Ice Cream (☎215-925-4315), in Reading Terminal Market at 12th and Arch St. Founded in 1861, Bassett's is the oldest creamery in the state, and some say the best in the nation. Originals like pumpkin ice cream may be throwbacks to the olden days, but modern concoctions—moose tracks, mocha chip, and rum raisin—also await. 2 scoops $3.15. Open M-F 9am-6pm, Sa 8am-6pm, Su 9am-4pm. Cash only. ❶

Capogiro, 119 S. 13th St. and 117 S. 20th St. (☎215-351-0900; www.capogirogelato.com), both at Sansom. The gelato artisans at Capogiro have over 300 flavors at their fingertips. Sample the cactus pear, mojito, and lavender or try a more normal but equally delicious flavor. Unlimited free samples. Open in summer M-Th 7:30am-11:30pm, F 7:30am-1am,

Sa 8am-1am, Su 10am-11:30pm; in winter M-Th 7:30am-10pm, F 7:30am-midnight, Sa 8am-midnight, Su 10am-10pm. AmEx/MC/V. ❶

UNIVERSITY CITY

▨ **Tandoor India Restaurant,** 106 S. 40th St. (☎215-222-7122). Cheap Indian restaurants are a dime a dozen on college campuses, but this is a highlight. Lunch buffet ($6) daily 11:30am-3:30pm. Dinner buffet ($9) daily 4-10pm. Student discount 20%. Open daily 11:30am-10pm. AmEx/D/MC/V. ❷

Smokey Joe's, 210 S. 40th St. (☎215-222-0770), between Locust and Walnut St. Hearty meals at student-friendly prices make Joe's popular with a UPenn crowd. Sandwiches from $6.75. Pints $2. Open daily 11:30am-2am. AmEx/D/MC/V. ❶

Abner's Cheesesteaks, 3813 Chestnut St. (☎215-662-0100; www.abnerscheesesteaks. com), at 38th St. This bright, spacious, and sparkling-clean joint is a local favorite with the professional set and UPenn students. Cheesesteak, large soda, and fries $6.20. Open M-Th 11am-midnight, F-Sa 11am-3am, Su 11am-11pm. AmEx/D/MC/V. ❶

◉ SIGHTS

OLD CITY

INDEPENDENCE NATIONAL HISTORICAL PARK

A small green framed by Market, Walnut, 2nd, and 7th St., the park is home to several historic buildings. Instead of wandering blindly through the park, begin your trip down American history's memory lane at the impressive **Independence Visitors Center.** *It dispenses detailed maps and brochures, offers a small exhibit detailing each historic site, and provide guides and trip-planners. On Chestnut St. ☎800-537-7676 or 215-925-6101. Open daily 9am-5pm. An elaborate audio program narrates a 1hr., half-mile tour through the park. On summer nights, the* **Lights of Liberty Show**—*a walking tour with an impressive soundtrack and light display—relates the story of the* ▨ **American Revolution.** *☎215-542-3789 or 877-462-1776; www.lightsofliberty.org. Light show starts at the PECO Energy Liberty Center at 6th and Chestnut St. Tu-Sa sun-*

set. *Reservations required. $19.50, students and seniors $16.50, ages 6-12 $13.*

INDEPENDENCE HALL. Revolutionary history abounds at Independence Hall, one of the most popular of Philadelphia's historic landmarks. Delegates signed the Declaration of Independence here in 1776 and reconvened in 1787 to endorse the US Constitution. Today, knowledgeable park rangers lead visitors on a brief but informative tour through the nation's first capitol building. *(Free tours every 15min. Tickets distributed at the visitors center.)*

CONGRESSIONAL SIGHTS. Capitol of the fledgling nation, Philadelphia's **Congress Hall** was host to the first assembly of Congress from 1790 to 1800. While soaking up years of history, visitors can rest in plush Senate chairs. *(At Chestnut and 6th St. Open daily 9am-5pm. Free.)* The First Continental Congress in 1774 united against the British in **Carpenters' Hall,** now a small museum heralding such architectural achievements as Old City Hall and the Pennsylvania State House. *(320 Chestnut St. ☎ 215-925-0167. Open Mar.-Dec. Tu-Su 10am-4pm; Jan.-Feb. W-Su 10am-4pm. Free.)*

LIBERTY BELL CENTER. While freedom still rings at the Liberty Bell Center, the Liberty Bell does not (inauspiciously, it cracked). The stately bell is also visible—at a slight distance, through a glass wall—from Chestnut St. *(On Market St., between 5th and 6th St. ☎ 215-965-2305. Open in summer M-Th and Su 9am-5pm, F-Sa 9am-6pm; in winter daily 9am-5pm. Free.)*

NATIONAL CONSTITUTION CENTER. The stunning National Constitution Center invites visitors to become "delegates" as they learn about the history of the Constitution and the ideas for which it stands. A 17min. presentation called "Freedom Rising" on the history of the Constitution wows visitors—touchscreens and monitors replace dusty artifacts here. The museum can seem imposing, but it is well organized and free of overdone flag-waving. *(525 Arch St. ☎ 215-409-6600; www.constitutioncenter.org. Open M-F 9:30am-5pm, Sa 9:30am-6pm, Su noon-5pm. Last presentation 4pm. $12, seniors $11, under 4 and active military free, under 12 $8.)*

OTHER SIGHTS. The rest of the park preserves residential and commercial buildings of the Revolutionary era. On the northern edge of the mall, a white building replicates the size and location of Benjamin Franklin's home in **Franklin Court.** His original abode was unceremoniously razed by the statesman's heirs in order to erect an apartment complex. The home features an underground museum, a 20min. movie, a replica of Franklin's printing office, and a working post office—the first post office in the nation and the only one not to fly the American flag, since there wasn't one in 1775. *(318 Market St., between 3rd and 4th St. ☎ 215-965-2305. Courtyard open in summer daily 9am-5pm. Building open W-Su 1-2pm. Free.)* On a more somber note, a statue of the first American president and army general presides over the **Tomb of the Unknown Soldier,** in Washington Sq., where an eternal flame commemorates the fallen heroes of the Revolutionary War.

SOCIETY HILL

South and east of Independence Mall, between Walnut and Lombard St. and Front and 17th St, the Society Hill neighborhood is rich with history. The area boasts century-old townhouses and cobblestone paths under electric gaslights. America's oldest firehouse, historic **Head House Square,** *at Second and Pine St., now houses restaurants and boutiques. Bargain hunters can test their skills at the outdoor crafts fair. (☎ 215-790-0782. Open June-Aug. Crafts fair 10am-10pm. Free.) Each January, sequin- and feather-clad participants join in a rowdy New Year's Day Mummers Parade, which began in celebration of the masked festival actors known as mummers. The streets fill up quickly with 750,000 spectators, so get your seat early, or just visit the* **Mummers Museum,** *which swells with glamorous old costumes. (1100 S. 2nd St., at Washington Ave., south of Head House Sq. ☎ 215-336-3050; www.mummersmuseum.com. Open Tu-Sa 9:30am-4:30pm. Free concerts Th 8pm. $3.50; students, seniors, and under 12 $2.50.)*

CENTER CITY

Center City is the financial hub of Philadelphia and has barely enough room to accommodate the professionals who cram into the area bounded by 10th, 23rd, Vine, and South St. Though rife with activity during the day, the region retires early at night.

ACADEMY OF FINE ART. The country's first art museum and school, the Pennsylvania

Academy of Fine Art has displays of artwork by Winslow Homer and Mary Cassatt. Each May, the academy exhibits work by current students and alumni. *(118-128 N. Broad St., at Cherry St. ☎215-972-7600; www.pafa.org. Open Tu-Sa 10am-5pm, Su 11am-5pm. 1hr. tours Tu-F 11:30am, 12:30pm, Sa-Su noon, 1pm. Admission to both buildings $15, students and seniors $12, ages 5-18 $8.)*

CITY HALL. Presiding over Center City, the granite and marble City Hall took 30 years to build. At 548 ft., it remains the nation's largest working municipal building and, until 1908, it reigned as the tallest building in the US—including, that is, the 37 ft. statue of William Penn at its peak. A "gentlemen's agreement" prohibited building anything higher than Penn's hat until entrepreneurs overturned it in 1987. A commanding view of the city still awaits visitors in the tower. *(At Broad and Market St. ☎215-686-2840. Visitors center open M-F 9:30am-5pm. Tower tour daily every 15min. 9:30am-4:15pm. Reservations recommended. $5, children $4, seniors $3. City Hall tour daily 12:30pm; ends at the tower at 2pm. $10, children and seniors $8.)*

MASONIC TEMPLE. Notoriously secretive, the Freemasons of Philadelphia may or may not rule the world. It's obvious to all, though, that their Temple, just north of City Hall, is stunning. *(1 N. Broad St. ☎215-988-1917; www.pagrand-lodge.org. Tours July-Aug. M-F 10, 11am, 2, 3pm; Sa 10, 11am. Sept.-June Tu-F 10, 11am, 2, 3pm; Sa 10 and 11am. $8, students $6, under 12 and over 64 $5.)*

MÜTTER MUSEUM. Digest lunch completely before viewing the often gory medical abnormalities displayed at the Mütter Museum. Among the potentially unsettling exhibits are a wall of human skulls and a collection of preserved body parts of famous people, including John Marshall's bladder stones and a cancerous section of John Wilkes Booth's neck. The museum also contains a Level 4 biohazard suit, a medicinal herb garden, and a bizarre gift shop. *(19 S. 22nd St. ☎215-563-3737, ext. 211; www.collphyphil.org. Open daily 10am-5pm. $12; students, ages 6-18 and seniors $8.)*

ROSENBACH MUSEUM AND LIBRARY. Just south, the nondescript exterior of the Rosenbach Museum and Library hides an enormous, must-see collection of rare books and manuscripts, from the original manuscript of James Joyce's *Ulysses* to Lewis Carroll's copy of *Alice in Wonderland*. *(2010 Delancey St. ☎215-732-1600; www.rosenbach.org. Open Tu and Th-Su 10am-5pm, W 10am-8pm. 1hr. tours Tu-Su 11am-4pm. $10, students $5, seniors $8.)*

PARKWAY AND MUSEUM DISTRICT

Once nicknamed "America's Champs-Élysées," the Benjamin Franklin Pkwy. has one of the best art museums in the country but has seen better days. Of the city's five original town squares, **Logan Circle** was the sight of public executions until 1823. It now delights hundreds of children who frolic and splash about in its **Swann Memorial Fountain.** Designed by Alexander Calder, the fountain represents the Wissahickon Creek and the Schuylkill and Delaware Rivers—the three bodies of water that surround the city.

SCIENCE MUSEUMS. A modern assemblage of everything scientific, the interactive **Franklin Institute** would make the old inventor proud. A skybike allows the most daring of visitors to pedal across a tightrope suspended nearly four stories high. *(222 N. 20th St., at Race St. ☎215-448-1200; www.fi.edu. Open daily 9:30am-5pm. $14.25, ages 4-11 $11.50, seniors $13.25. IMAX $9. Museum and IMAX $19.75/18.75/17.)* Part of the institute, the newly renovated **Fels Planetarium** flashes laser shows on Saturday nights. *(222 N. 20th St. ☎215-448-1388.)* Opposite Fels, the **Academy of Natural Sciences** allows budding archaeologists to try their hand digging up fossils. The animal center is home to over 100 beasties awaiting your visit. *(1900 Ben Franklin Pkwy., at 19th St. ☎215-299-1000; www.acnatsci.org. Open M-F 10am-4:30pm, Sa-Su 10am-5pm. $9, ages 3-12 $8, seniors and military $8.25.)*

PHILADELPHIA MUSEUM OF ART. Sylvester Stallone may have etched the sight of the Philadelphia Museum of Art into the minds of movie buffs everywhere when he bolted up its stately front steps in *Rocky*, but it is the artwork within that has earned the museum its fine reputation. The collections of Impressionist, northern Renaissance, and American works are particularly strong, and the Japanese tea house provides peaceful respite from the busy city. The opening of the Perelman Building gave the museum even more exhibition space for its costume and design collections. *(At Benjamin Franklin Pkwy. and 26th St. The Perelman Building is located at Fairmount and Pennsylvania Ave.; free shuttle bus between the 2 buildings. ☎ 215-763-8100; www.philamuseum.org. Open Tu-Th and Sa-Su 10am-5pm, F 10am-8:45pm. Introductory tours 11am, 2pm. $14, students and ages 13-18 $10, seniors $12. Su "pay what you wish.")*

RODIN MUSEUM. A cast of *The Gates of Hell* outside the Rodin Museum guards the portal of human passion, anguish, and anger in the most extensive collection of the sculptor's works this side of the Seine. One of the original casts of *The Thinker* (1880) at the head of a beautiful courtyard marks the museum entrance. *(At Benjamin Franklin Pkwy. and 22nd St. ☎ 215-568-6026; www.rodinmuseum.org. Open Tu-Su 10am-5pm. Suggested donation $3.)*

FAIRMOUNT PARK. Philly's finest outdoor opportunities can be found in the resplendent Fairmount Park. The faux-Greek ruins by the waterfall behind the Museum of Art are the abandoned **Waterworks,** built between 1819 and 1822. Free tours of the Waterworks' Romantic architecture, technology, and social history meet on Aquarium Dr., behind the art museum. *(☎ 215-685-0722; www.fairmountwaterworks.org. Open Tu-Sa 10am-5pm, Su 1-5pm.)* Farther down the river, the line of crew clubs forming historic **Boathouse Row** make Philadelphia's place in the rowing world clear. The Museum of Art hosts tours of Boathouse Row on Wednesday and Sunday as well as trolley tours to mansions in Fairmount Park. The area near Boathouse Row is also the city's most popular in-line-skating spot. In the northern arm of Fairmount Park, trails follow the secluded Wissahickon Creek for 5 mi. The **Japanese House and Garden** is designed in the style of a 17th-century *shoin;* the authentic garden offers the utmost tranquility. Some neighborhoods surrounding the park are not safe, and the park is not safe at night. *(Off Montgomery Dr., near Belmont Ave. ☎ 215-878-5097; www.shofuso.com. Open May-Oct. Tu-F 10am-4pm, Sa-Su 11am-5pm; hours vary in winter. 30-45min. tour not included with ticket. $4; students, ages 6-17 and seniors $3.)*

🎵 ENTERTAINMENT

The part of Old City framed by Chestnut, Vine, Front and 4th St., comes alive for the **First Friday** celebration, when art galleries, museums, and restaurants open their doors to entice visitors with free food. *(☎ 215-440-7000; www.oldcity.org. The 1st F of every month.)* The **Academy of Music,** at Broad and Locust St., was modeled after Milan's La Scala and hosts the **Pennsylvania Ballet.** *(☎ 215-551-7000; www.paballet.org. Tickets $20-140. $10 rush tickets 2½hr. before show.)* The **Philadelphia Orchestra** performs from September to May at the **Kimmel Center,** 260 S. Broad St. at Spruce St. *(☎ 790-5800 or 215-893-1999; www.kimmelcenter.org. Box office open daily 10am-6pm. Tickets from $10. $10 student rush tickets Tu and Th 30min. before show.)*

With 5000 seats under cover and 10,000 on outdoor benches and lawns, the **Mann Music Center,** on George's Hill near 52nd and Parkside Ave. in Fairmount Park, hosts big-name entertainers like Tony Bennett and Willie Nelson as well as jazz and rock concerts. *(☎ 215-546-7900, tickets 893-1999; www.mann-center.org. Lawn seats $10-32.)* The **Trocadero,** 1003 Arch St., is the oldest operating Victorian theater in the US and hosts local as well as big-name bands. *(☎ 215-922-5483; www.thetroc.com. Advance tickets through Ticketmaster. Box office open M-F 11:30am-6pm, Sa 11:30am-5pm. Tickets from $7 for small events.)* The **Robin Hood Dell East,** on Ridge Ave. near 33rd St. in Fairmount Park, brings in top names in pop, jazz, and gospel in July and August. Check its website (www.delleast.org/index) for updates. During the school year, the students of the **Curtis Institute of Music,** 1726 Locust St., give free concerts *(☎ 215-893-5252; www.curtis.edu).*

Baseball's **Phillies** *(☎ 215-463-1000; www.phillies.com)* play at the new **Citizens Bank Park,** on Citizens Bank Park Way off Pattison Ave. between 11th and Darien St. Football's **Eagles** *(☎ 215-463-5500; www.philadelphiaeagles.com)* play at **Lincoln Financial Field,** at Broad St. and Pattison Ave. Across the street, fans fill the **First Union Center** to watch the NBA's **76ers** *(☎ 215-339-7676; www.sixers.com)* and the NHL's **Flyers** *(☎ 215-755-9700; www.philadelphiaflyers.com).*

NATIONAL ROAD

NIGHTLIFE

Check the Friday *Philadelphia Inquirer* for entertainment listings. The free Thursday *City Paper* and the Wednesday *Philadelphia Weekly* have weekly listings. A diverse club crowd jams to live music on weekends along **South Street.** Many upscale pubs line **Second Street** near Chestnut St. and Market St., close to the Apple Hostel. Continuing south to Society Hill, especially near **Head House Square,** an older crowd fills dozens of streetside bars and cafes. **Delaware Avenue** and **Columbus Boulevard,** running along Penn's Landing, have become a hot spot full of nightclubs and restaurants that attract droves of yuppies and students. Gay and lesbian weeklies *Au Courant* (free) and *PGN* (free) list events. Most bars and clubs that cater to a gay clientele are along **Camac, South 12th,** and **South 13th Streets.** While buying alcohol is difficult thanks to Philadelphia's complicated liquor laws, getting a cheap drink has become much easier with the many happy-hour specials at bars around the city. These specials are usually available 5-7pm and often include deals on appetizers.

Monk's Belgian Cafe, 626 S. 16th St. (☎215-545-7005; www.monkscafe.com), in Rittenhouse Sq. Don't let the simple exterior fool you—Monk's carries 200-225 beers, and its expert staff promises to find the right brew for you. Domestic beers $4.50. Belgian drafts $6-7. Open M-Sa 11:30am-2am, Su 11am-2am. Kitchen open until 1am. AmEx/D/MC/V.

Oscar's Tavern, 1524 Sansom St. (☎215-972-9938), at 15th St. This dark bar gets packed with students and locals at night. The $3 23 oz. drafts are available all day long. Burgers $4-5. Open M-Sa 11am-2am. Cash only.

The Copabanana, 344 South St. (☎215-923-6180), at South and 4th St. The hottest club north of Havana—the place to start off your night. Tangy margaritas and lighter fare than the nearby cheesesteak joints. Happy hour M-F 4-7pm with $2 off mixed drinks and $5 appetizers. Open daily 11:30am-2am. AmEx/D/MC/V.

The Khyber, 56 S. 2nd St. (☎215-238-5888; www.thekhyber.com). A speakeasy during Prohibition, the Khyber now gathers a young crowd to listen to a range of punk and heavy metal at volumes that will make your socks hurt. The ornate wood bar was built in Philly around 1876. Nightly live music M-W and Su 8pm, Th-Sa 9pm. Cover $5-10. Open daily 11am-2am. Cash only.

THE ROAD TO MEDIA: 13 MI.

Take **I-76 West** to **Exit 339** for **City Avenue/US 1 South.** Continue down **US 1** toward Media. Once you get to Media, turn right on **West Baltimore Avenue,** right on **South Monroe,** and left on **State Street.**

MEDIA ☎610

Architecturally eclectic restaurants and shops, many of which date from the 19th century, line State St., Media's main drag. As you enter town, notice the **armory** on State St. just after Monroe St., still used by the Army National Guard. A large stone bank marks the center of town at **Veterans Square.** Two blocks to the north stands Media's **courthouse,** its most significant architectural attraction, built in four stages from 1851 to 1929.

Restaurants in Media are not overly expensive, but don't come expecting cheap eats. For a light bite, head to the **Coffee Club ❶,** 214 W. State St., near Orange St., which offers coffee, pastries, smoothies, wraps, sandwiches, and several vegetarian selections in addition to free Wi-Fi. (☎610-891-6600. Sandwiches $3-6. Open M-Th 7am-7pm, F-Sa 7am-10pm, Su 8am-3pm. AmEx/D/MC/V.) The glass and wood of **Iron Hill Brewery and Restaurant ❸,** 30 E. State St., stand out among the old buildings of Media. Sample the selection of homemade brews. (☎610-627-9000. Lunch $8-12. Pizza $10-13. Happy hour M and Th 5-7pm. Open M-W 11:30am-10pm, Th-Sa 11:30-midnight, Su 11am-10pm. AmEx/D/MC/V.)

THE ROAD TO CHADDS FORD: 12 MI.

Take **Baltimore Avenue,** which becomes **Baltimore Pike** and merges onto **US 1** 1 mi. from town. Follow **US 1.**

CHADDS FORD ☎610

Located 3 mi. after US 202 on US 1, the **Brandywine Battlefield Park** is on a small section of the 10 sq. mi. area where a critical Revolutionary War battle took place. A ticket grants access to the two houses on the site, inhabited by "living historians" on special occasions throughout the year—men costumed as the Marquis de Lafayette and George Washington, who adopt accents and tell their life stories. (☎610-459-3342; www.ushistory.org/brandywine. Open Tu-Sa 9am-5pm, Su noon-5pm. $5, ages 6-17 $2.50, seniors $3.50.) Further west on US 1, the ⬛**Brandywine River Museum** displays an extensive collection of works by N.C., Andrew, and Jaime Wyeth in a restored mill house. (Rte. 1, in Chadds Ford, PA. From Wilmington, take Rte. 52 N. to Rte. 1 and follow it east. ☎610-388-2700; www.brandywinemuseum.org. Open daily 9:30am-4:30pm. $8; seniors, students, and ages 6-12 $5.)

🏕 THE ROAD TO WILMINGTON: 10 MI.

Continue on **US 202 (Concord Pike)** and turn right onto **North Market Street.**

The First State
DELAWARE
Welcomes You

WILMINGTON ☎302

In 1683, a Swedish ship, the *Kalmar Nyckel*, sailed from Europe to the banks of what was then called the South River, leaving its passengers to establish the colony of New Sweden. These days, the city of Wilmington might as well be named DuPontville, because, from the grand Hotel DuPont downtown to the DuPont mills along the Brandywine River, there's no escaping the name.

🔲 ORIENTATION

In the city's center, numbered streets run east-west, starting at the southern end with **Lancaster Avenue** and running from Second to 15th St., then continuing with 16th St. on the other side of the Brandywine River. Major north-south roads in the downtown area include **Walnut Street, King Street,** and **Market Street.** To the west, north-south **Union Street** and **Lincoln Streets** boast a number of restaurants. Take **Pennsylvania Avenue** from the city center for easy access to these streets.

Population: 73,000

Tourist Office: Greater Wilmington Convention and Visitors Bureau, 100 W. 10th St. (☎302-652-4088; www.visitwilmingtonde.com), at Orange St. Open M-F 9am-5pm.

Library and Internet Access: Wilmington Library (☎302-571-7400), at 10th and Market St., downtown. Free. Open M-Th 9am-8pm, F-Sa 9am-5pm.

Post Office: 500 Delaware Ave. (☎302-656-0228). Open M-F 7am-5:30pm, Sa 5am-3pm. **Postal Code:** 19801.

🛏 ACCOMMODATIONS

Chain hotels and motels dominate the northern portion of the city; some cheaper motels lie south of the city on **Dupont Highway (Route 13)** in **New Castle,** but the neighborhood is uninteresting. You can find clean rooms with microfridges and HBO at the **Budget Motor Lodge ❸,** 140 S. Dupont Hwy., 3 mi. south of I-95. (☎302-322-1800. Singles $55; doubles $65. AmEx/D/MC/V with driver's license.)

🍴 FOOD

Restaurants can be found in two areas: **Union** and **Lincoln Streets,** and the **Trolley Square District,** up Delaware Ave.

Mrs. Robino's, 520 N. Union St. (☎302-652-9223; www.mrsrobinos.com). A great family-run restaurant in Wilmington's Little Italy which serves delicious homemade pasta and sauces. Pasta $8-11. Entrees $8-19. Open M-Th 11am-9pm, F-Sa 11am-10pm, Su noon-9pm. D/MC/V. ❷

Kelly's Logan House, 1701 Delaware Ave. (☎302-652-9493; www.loganhouse.com), in Trolley Sq. Irish pub fare. Appetizers ($7-9) include loaded fries with cheese, bacon, jalapeños, and ranch dressing. Burgers $9-11. Happy hour daily 4-7pm. Open M-Sa 11am-1am, Su noon-6pm. AmEx/D/MC/V. ❸

👁 SIGHTS

HAGLEY MUSEUM AND LIBRARY. The DuPont estates are numbered among Wilmington's most popular tourist attractions. Closest to downtown, the museum emphasizes the home and work life of the DuPonts, with tours of the original family mansion and black powder works. Mechanical minds will love the enormous stone mills, water turbines, steam engines, and powder testers. Brace yourself when the guide demonstrates the power of blasting powder. *(Take Rte. 202 N. for 1 mi., turn onto Rte. 141 S. for 2 mi., turn right onto the bridge, and look for the main entrance on the right.* ☎ *302-658-2400; www.hagley.lib.de.us. Mar.-Dec. daily 9:30am-4:30pm; Jan.-Mar. M-F tour at 1:30pm, Sa-Su open 9:30am-4:30pm. $11, students and seniors $9, ages 6-14 $4.)*

NEMOURS MANSION AND GARDENS. This ritzy estate shows a glamorous side of DuPont. *(Rte. 141 and Alapocas Rd.* ☎ *302-651-6912. Tours May-Dec. Tu-Sa 9, 11am, 1, 3pm; Su 11am, 1, 3pm. $12.)*

⚑ THE ROAD TO HAVRE DE GRACE: 41 MI.
Follow signs to **Route 13 South** in the south-central area of the city. **US 13** joins **US 40 West.** Stay on US 40 to Havre de Grace. Turn left on **Otsego Road** to reach the waterfront attractions.

The Old Line State
MARYLAND
Welcomes You

HAVRE DE GRACE   ☎410
Located where the Susquehanna River meets the Chesapeake Bay, Havre de Grace is home to residents who once made their living by building boats and fishing. Both industries remain, though more for the benefit of tourists than for commercial purposes. At the corner of Lafayette and Concord St. in the southeast corner of town is the **Concord Point Lighthouse.** Short and stubby, this lighthouse was officially decommissioned in 1975 but still illuminates the port. You can brave the granite spiral stairs and metal ladder for a free view of the bay. Next door, you'll find the small **Havre de Grace Maritime Museum.** (☎410-939-4800. Open June-Aug. daily 11am-5pm; Sept.-May M, W, F-Su 10am-5pm. Boat building Tu 6-9:30pm. $3, students and seniors $2.)

A local favorite, **La Cucina ❷,** 103 N. Washington St., is a combination pizza parlor and gourmet Italian restaurant with a romantic feel and an accordion player on Sunday evenings. Identity crisis aside, it's a good place for either a quick bite or a relatively inexpensive meal. (☎410-939-1401. Pizzas $8-15. Pastas $8.50-11. Open Tu-Th 10:30am-10pm, F-Sa 10:30am-11pm, Su noon-9pm. AmEx/D/MC/V.)

⚑ THE ROAD TO ABERDEEN: 4 MI.
Continue down **US 40** for 4 mi. to reach Aberdeen.

ABERDEEN   ☎410
Just 4 mi. past Havre de Grace lies the town of Aberdeen, which Baltimore Orioles fans know as the hometown of their beloved **Cal Ripken Jr.,** who broke Lou Gehrig's record for most consecutive baseball games ever played. "Real" is the best word to describe the **◉US Army Ordnance Museum,** on the Aberdeen Proving Ground. There are few photos or replicas—just real guns, real mortars, and real tanks. The M65 cannon by the parking lot is as tall as the trees around it. To get there, take Rte. 715 E., and follow the signs. After passing the checkpoint, take a left at the fourth light, and a right into the parking lot in front of the tanks. In 2011 the Museum will be relocating to Fort Lee, Virginia. (☎410-278-3602. Open daily 9am-4:45pm. Free.)

Two quirky, nostalgic roadside diners occupy the Aberdeen area. The **New Ideal Diner ❸,** on US 40 just past Bel Air Ave., is a prettied-up railway car. The diner specializes in seafood; the prices are on the high side, but items like burgers ($4.50-5) are yummy and affordable. (☎410-272-1880. Seafood up to $23. Open daily 5:30am-9pm. D/MC/V.) The 17-page menu at the chrome-and-neon **White Marsh Double T Diner ❸,** 10741 Pulaski Hwy. (US 40), at the corner of Ebenezer Rd. in White Marsh, is sure to have something you want. This is one of the better diners on this stretch of US 40. (In White Marsh, at the corner of Ebenezer Rd. ☎410-344-1020. Burgers $5-8. Open 24hr. AmEx/D/MC/V.)

⚑ THE ROAD TO ROSEDALE: 20 MI.
Cross the **Baltimore Beltway** and follow **US 40.**

ROSEDALE   ☎410
Diners and motels abound on this stretch of the road, but tiny Rosedale is home to a pleas-

ing pair. **Duke's Motel** ❸, 7905 Pulaski Hwy., has some of the cheapest accommodations around, but the service leaves something to be desired. (☎410-686-0400. Key deposit $5. Singles $56; doubles $61. D/MC/V.) The chrome **Happy Day Diner** ❷, 8302 Pulaski Hwy., has a limited selection, but the food is delicious and cheap. A plate of French toast, two eggs, bacon, and sausage is $5.50. (☎410-687-2129; www.happydaydiner.com. Open M-Th and Su 6am-10pm, F-Sa 24hr. AmEx/D/MC/V.)

⛏ THE ROAD TO BALTIMORE: 6 MILES

Stay on **US 40** as it crosses **I-895/I-95.** About 1 mi. past the beltway, veer right, following signs for **US 40/ Orleans Street.**

BALTIMORE   ☎410

Nicknamed "Charm City" for its mix of small-town hospitality and big-city flair, Baltimore impresses visitors with its lively restaurant and bar scene, first-class museums, and devotion to history. The pulse of the city lies beyond its star attraction, the glimmering Inner Harbor, in Baltimore's overstuffed markets, coffee shops, and diverse citizenry. The city's Southern heritage is evident in Roland Park, where friendly neighbors greet you from front porches in a "Bawlmer" accent.

◫ ORIENTATION

Baltimore lies 35 mi. north of Washington, DC, and about 150 mi. west of the Atlantic Ocean. **Baltimore Street** (east-west) and **Charles Street** (north-south) divide the city. **US 40** runs east-west through the northern end of downtown, while the **Jones Falls Expressway (I-83)** cuts into Baltimore from the north. The **Baltimore Beltway (I-695)** and a series of other ring roads circle the city, which lies just off I-95. The main arteries serving the Inner Harbor and downtown Baltimore are mostly one-way and include Charles St. and **Saint Paul Street/Light Street,** which runs south (both intersect US 40). **Pratt Street** runs east, **Lombard Street** runs west, and both end at **Frederick Road (Route 144).** Some neighborhoods in Baltimore, like around Orleans St. and west of Martin Luther King, Jr., Blvd., are not safe at night.

VITAL STATS
Population: 650,000
Tourist Office: Baltimore Area Visitors Center, 401 Light St. (☎877-225-8466; www.baltimore.org). Open M-Th, Su 9am-7pm, F-Sa 9am-8pm.
Library and Internet Access: Enoch Pratt Free Library, 400 Cathedral St. (☎410-396-5430). Open June-Aug. M-W 10am-8pm, Th 10am-5:30pm, F-Sa 10am-5pm; Sept.-May M-W 10am-8pm, Th 10am-5:30pm, F-Sa 10am-5pm, Su 1-5pm.
Post Office: 900 E. Fayette St. (☎410-347-4202). Open M-F 8:30am-9pm, Sa 8:30am-5pm. **Postal Code:** 21233.

⯃ TRANSPORTATION

Your best bet for parking is to bring a roll of quarters, as meters are plentiful but hungry (generally $1 per hr.). Parking for longer than 24hr. is not permitted. Garages are easy to find throughout downtown and are most expensive near the Inner Harbor (up to $12 per day). A long stretch of 4hr. parking meters lies along Key Hwy. just south of the Inner Harbor; take St. Paul St. south past the Inner Harbor and turn left on Key Hwy. In **Little Italy,** there are many options on Albemarle St., just north of Eastern St. Baltimore sights cluster together, so it's smart to park and walk.

⛰ ACCOMMODATIONS

Hotels dominate the Inner Harbor, and budget lodgings elsewhere are hard to find. There are motels on **Washington Boulevard,** 4-10 mi. south of the downtown area. Take Light St. west to Conway St. Turn left to get on I-395 S.; following it to I-95 S.. Take Exit 50A onto Caton Ave. and turn right on Washington Blvd.

▨ **Aunt Rebecca's B&B,** 106 E. Preston St. (☎410-625-1007), in the Mt. Vernon district. Decor is typified by gilded mirrors and chandeliers. Only 3 bedrooms, but if you book one you'll save big over the downtown hotels. Breakfast included. Free parking. Singles $110; doubles $135. AmEx/D/MC/V. ❺

▨ **Baltimore Hostel (HI),** 17 W. Mulberry St. (☎410-576-8880; www.baltimorehostel.org), between Charles and Cathedral St. Fun building with gilded moldings, eclectic local artwork, and

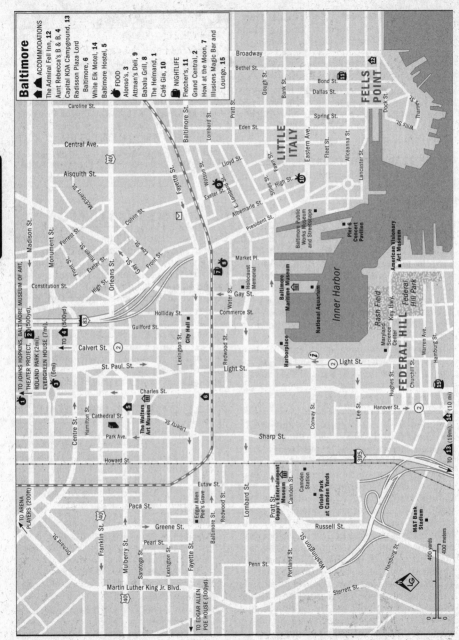

Baltimore

▲ ACCOMMODATIONS
The Admiral Fell Inn, **12**
Aunt Rebecca's B & B, **4**
Capital KOA Campground, **13**
Radisson Plaza Lord
  Baltimore, **6**
White Elk Motel, **14**
Baltimore Hostel, **5**

● FOOD
Alonso's, **3**
Attman's Deli, **9**
Babalu Grill, **8**
The Helmand, **1**
Café Gia, **10**

■ NIGHTLIFE
Fletcher's, **11**
Grand Central, **2**
Howl at the Moon, **7**
Illusions Magic Bar and
  Lounge, **15**

NATIONAL ROAD

karaoke. 44 beds. Th $3 dinner specials. Pancake breakfast included. Free Internet and Wi-Fi. $25-30. MC/V. ❶

The Admiral Fell Inn, 888 S. Broadway (☎410-522-7377 or 866-583-4162; www.harbormagic.com), at Thames St. Blast to the past with themed rooms that include canopied beds and armoires. Amenities fee including Internet access $10 per day. Valet parking $29 per night. Rooms $189-309. AmEx/D/MC/V. ❺

White Elk Motel, 6195 Washington Blvd. (☎410-796-5151), in Elkridge, 10 mi. south of downtown. While a bit out of the way, a landscaped entrance and 27 cottage-inn-style rooms with bathtubs make this a comfy place. Singles $55; doubles $60. AmEx/D/MC/V. ❸

🍴 FOOD

If you're blowing through Baltimore with some cash to burn, forget the overpriced eateries that crowd the Inner Harbor and head to some of Baltimore's more upscale choices, scattered throughout the city. Be sure not to leave without a taste of the region's famous crab cakes.

🦀 **The Helmand,** 806 N. Charles St. (☎410-752-0311; www.helmand.com). The best Afghan restaurant in town, with famous dishes like *kaddo borani* (pan-fried and baked pumpkin in a yogurt-garlic sauce; $5). Plenty of vegetarian options and enough dessert to satisfy even the most die-hard sweet tooth. Open M-Th and Su 5-10pm, F-Sa 5-11pm. AmEx/D/MC/V. ❸

Attman's Deli, 1019 E. Lombard St. (☎410-563-2666), on Baltimore's "Corned Beef Row." Made a name for itself serving hot pastrami ($6) and corned-beef sandwiches ($6) just like you'd find in New York City. The reuben ($7.50) was voted Baltimore's best. Open M-Sa 8am-7pm, Su 8am-5pm. AmEx/D/MC/V. ❷

Babalu Grill, 32 Market Pl. (☎410-234-9898; www.babalugrill.com), specializing in Cuban and Nuevo Latino dishes. Popular appetizers include grilled tuna with mango salsa ($8). Entrees $16-36. Babalu turns into a hot and zesty salsa club at night. Cover after 11pm $10. Open Tu-F 5-10pm, Sa 5-11pm. Club open Th-Sa 11pm-2am. AmEx/D/MC/V. ❹

Alonso's, 415 W. Cold Spring Ln. (☎410-235-3433), in the Roland Park neighborhood. Take Exit 9A from I-83 N. Famous for 1 lb. burgers ($14). The vegetable panino ($8) and crab-cake sandwiches ($15) are more manageable. Open M-Th and Su 11am-10pm, F-Sa 11am-11pm. AmEx/D/MC/V. ❸

👁 SIGHTS

Commercial shopping and restaurants frequented by tourists crowd the **Inner Harbor,** home to the National Aquarium. An excursion to the Johns Hopkins University campus and nearby **Druid Hill Park** escapes the glitz (and grime) of the city.

AMERICAN VISIONARY ART MUSEUM (AVAM). An art museum unlike any other, the AVAM contains powerful art by those who have no formal training. Some of them have had recognition elsewhere, but many have not. Although some themes, such as religion and mysticism, reappear throughout, many pieces are unique and unexpected, such as a neurosurgeon's CAT scans, paintings by farmers' wives, and rag-doll sculptures of artists with Down syndrome and kleptomania. *(800 Key Hwy. ☎410-244-1900; www.avam.org. Open Tu-Su 10am-6pm. $12, students and seniors $8.)*

WALTERS ART MUSEUM. With over 50 centuries of art in three buildings, the Walters Art Museum houses one of the largest private art collections in the world, and, thanks to a large recent gift, admission is now free. The ancient art collections include sculpture, jewelry, and metalwork from Egypt, Greece, and Rome, the museum's pride and joy. Byzantine, Romanesque, and Gothic art are also on display. The **Hackerman House** displays art from China, Korea, Japan, and India among dark wood furniture, patterned rugs, and plush velvet curtains. *(600 N. Charles St. ☎410-547-9000; www.thewalters.org. Open W-Su 11am-5pm. Tours Sa 11:30am, Su 2pm. Free.)*

JOHNS HOPKINS UNIVERSITY. Approximately 3 mi. north of the harbor, prestigious Johns Hopkins University (JHU) radiates out from 33rd St. JHU was the first research university in the country and is currently a world leader in medicine, public health, and engineering. The campus was originally the Homewood estate of Charles Carroll, Jr., the son of the longest-lived signer of the Declaration of Independence. One-hour campus tours begin at the **Office of Admissions** in Mason Hall. *(3400 N. Charles St. ☎410-516-8171; www.jhu.edu. Tours Sept.-May M-F 11am, 2pm. Call ☎410-516-5589 for summer hours.)* One mile north of the main campus, the **Evergreen House** is an exercise in excess—even the bathroom of this elegant mansion is plated in 23-carat gold. Purchased in 1878 by railroad tycoon John W. Garret, the house, along with its collections of fine porcelain, impressive artwork, Tiffany silver, and rare books, was bequeathed to JHU in 1942. *(4545 N. Charles St. ☎410-516-0341. Open Tu-F 11am-4pm, Sa-Su noon-4pm. Tours every hr. 10am-3pm. $6, students $3, seniors $5.)*

GEPPI'S ENTERTAINMENT MUSEUM. Located right on top of the Sports Legends Museum, Geppi's explores American history through the lens of pop culture from 1776 to today. All of America's favorite characters are here, like Elvis, Superman, and Punch and Judy. Less familiar faces surface, too, in the museum's extensive collection of original comics, cartoons, toys, posters, and games grouped by era, from "Pioneer Spirit" to "Going Global." While today's material seems comparatively normal at first glance, by the end of your visit you'll be struck by just how bizarre American culture can be. *(301 W. Camden St. ☎410-625-7060; www.geppismuseum.com. Open Apr.-Sept. daily 10am-6pm; Oct.-Mar. Tu-Su 10am-5pm. $10, seniors $9, students $7. Tu tickets ½-price.)*

EDGAR ALLAN POE HOUSE. Gothic author Poe lived in this now-preserved historical landmark from 1833 to 1835. Between taking doses of opium, Poe penned famous stories such as "The Tell-Tale Heart" and "The Pit and the Pendulum" as well as macabre poems like "The Raven" and "Annabel Lee." The house contains period furniture and exhibits relating to Poe, maintained by a staff eager to regale visitors with Poe stories. Steer clear of the neighborhood at night; you'll find darkness there, and nothing more. *(203 N. Amity St., near Saratoga St. ☎410-396-7932; www.eapoe.org. Open Apr.-Nov. W-Sa noon-3:30pm. $4, under 12 free.)*

NATIONAL AQUARIUM. The National Aquarium is perhaps the one thing (besides Baltimore's murder rate) that sets the city apart from all other major American cities. The eerie **Wings in the Water** exhibit showcases 50 species of stingrays in an immense pool. In the **Tropical Rainforest,** parrots and a pair of two-toed sloths peer through the dense foliage in a 157 ft. glass pyramid. At the **Marine Mammal Pavilion,** dolphins perform most hours on the half-hour. *(501 E. Pratt St., Pier 3. ☎410-576-1084; www.aqua.org. Open M-Th 9am-5pm, F-Sa 9am-8pm, Su 9am-6pm. $22, ages 3-11 $13, seniors $21.)*

🎵 ENTERTAINMENT

At **Harborplace,** street performers are constantly amusing tourists with magic acts and juggling during the day. On weekend nights, dance, dip, and dream to the sounds of anything from country to calypso.

The Baltimore Museum of Art, 10 Art Museum Dr. (☎443-573-1701). Offers summer jazz concerts with award-winning musicians in its sculpture garden. May-Sept. Sa 7pm. Tickets $25.

Pier 6 Concert Pavilion, 731 Eastern Ave. (☎410-783-4192). Jazz May-Oct. in this canvas-topped pavilion. Tickets $15-30.

The Theatre Project, 45 W. Preston St. (☎410-752-8558), near Maryland St. Experiments with theater, poetry, music, dance. Box office open 1hr. before shows. Tickets $15.

The Arena Players, 801 McCullough St. (☎410-728-6500), at Martin Luther King, Jr., Blvd. The 1st black theater group in the country performs comedy, drama, and dance. Box office open M-F 10am-2pm. Tickets from $15.

The Showcase of Nations Ethnic Festivals (☎877-225-8466). These festivals celebrate Baltimore's ethnic neighborhoods during summer and showcase a different culture each week.

Baltimore Orioles, 333 W. Camden St. (☎410-685-9800; www.orioles.mlb.com). The Orioles play ball at Camden Yards, at the corner of Russell and Camden St. Tickets $8-80.

Baltimore Ravens, 1101 Russell St. (☎410-481-7328; www.ravenszone.net). The city's football team plays in the M&T Bank Stadium.

⚑ NIGHTLIFE

Neighborhood bars in **Mount Vernon** know their middle-aged patrons by name, while the loud and sweaty dance floors of **Fells Point** and **Power Plant Live** cater to a college and 20-something crowd. Be prepared for a 1:30am last call. If you make it through the dozens of bars in Fells Point, you can head to **Canton** and will find a similarly youthful scene.

Howl At The Moon, 22 Market Pl. (☎410-783-5111; www.howlatthemoon.com). A dueling-piano bar where the crowd runs the show, with frequent sing- (or "howl-") alongs. Crowd ranges from just-barely-adult to could-be-your-parents. Cover $3-10. Happy hour F 5-8pm, Sa 5:30-9pm with free buffet. Open W-Th 7pm-2am, F 5pm-2am, Sa 5:30pm-2am. Piano showtimes W-Th 7:45pm, F-Sa 5:45pm. AmEx/MC/V.

Grand Central, 1001-1003 N. Charles St. (☎410-752-7133; www.centralstationpub.com), at Eager St. Chill under chandeliers from the set of *A Few Good Men* and *Batman* or play some pool with a mixed gay and straight crowd. $5 flavored martinis. The disco club next door is the spot for bumping and grinding W-Su 9pm-2am. Dance club 18+. Cover for dance club $6. Happy hour daily 4-8pm with $1 off beer. Open daily 4pm-2am. AmEx/D/MC/V.

Illusions Magic Bar, 1025 S. Charles St. (☎410-727-5811; www.illusionsmagicbar.com). The magician Spencer Horsman escapes from his straitjacket here every F and Sa night as the bar fills up with locals. Beers from $3. Magical Margarita $8. Posters from the 20s and 30s decorate the cherry walls, and you can buy your own tricks at the attached magic store. Open W-Sa 5pm-1am. AmEx/D/MC/V.

Fletcher's, 701 S. Bond St. (☎410-558-1889; www.fletchersbar.com). Food, drinks, and live bands several nights a week. Alternative, blues, rap, rock and more. Fletcher's has "discovered" bands including the Black Eyed Peas and Cake—a good venue for getting a sense of the up and coming. Be careful at night; the neighborhood is not safe. Concert tickets usually around $10. Happy hour daily 6-8pm. Kitchen open 6-11pm. AmEx/D/MC/V.

⚑ THE ROAD TO ELLICOTT CITY: 10 MI.

The route out of Baltimore follows the old **National Road,** or **Route 144,** not US 40. From downtown, get on **Lombard Street** heading west, take a soft left, and proceed on **Route 144 West.** Ten miles from Baltimore, Frederick Ave. (Rte. 144) becomes **Main Street** as it crawls into Ellicott City, an old Quaker mill town nestled in an idyllic hillside.

ELLICOTT CITY   ☎410

The most memorable experience of your stop here may be marveling at the city's physical location on the descending Patapsco River. Today, antique shops in equally antique buildings line the brick sidewalks along Main St.

Housed in the oldest railroad terminal in America, the **B&O Railroad Station Museum,** 2711 Maryland Ave., at Main St., discusses the role that the area's railroad played in the civil war. (☎410-461-1945; www.ecborail.org. Open W-Su 11am-4pm. $5, children $3, seniors $4.)

Sweet: Bakery & Cafe ❶, 8143 Main St., bakes up specialty cakes that seem almost too beautiful to cut into. The cafe has breakfast offerings ranging from bagels with butter ($1.30) to Belgian waffles ($5). The cafe's lunch menu consists mostly of sandwiches and wraps ($5.50-7.50) such as the classic roast beef for $6.50. (☎410-461-9275; www.sweetbakery-cafe.com. Open Tu-Th and Su 8am-5pm, F-Sa 8am-6pm. MC/V.) **La Palapa Grill & Cantina ❸,** 8307 Main St., features burritos ($10-12), fajitas ($13-15), and seafood specialties ($15-17) in a colorful dining room. (☎410-465-0070; www.lapalapagrill.com. Open M-Th and Su 11:30am-9:30pm, F-Sa 11:30am-10:30pm. MC/V.) **The Trolley Stop ❸,** 6 Oella Ave., lies at the bottom of the hill on the east side of town. The stone building was built in 1833; a trolley once stopped outside. The extensive menu features fresh seafood (Maryland crab cakes—$19) and a large selection of sandwiches ($7-8) such as a reuben and a french dip. (☎410-465-8546; www.thetrolleystop.com. Lunch entrees $8-12. Open M-Th 8am-10pm, F 8am-1:30am, Su 8am-9:30 pm. MC/V.)

NATIONAL ROAD

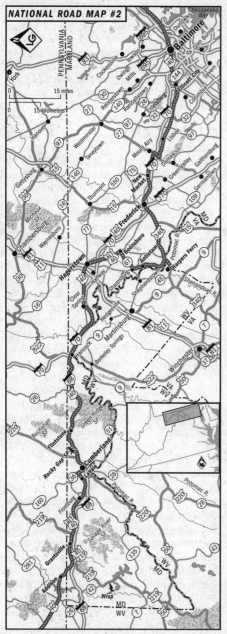

NATIONAL ROAD MAP #2

The **Ellicott City Visitors Center,** 8267 Main St., has info on self-guided walking tours of the town's historical sites, including ghost tours on F-Sa and every summer night with a full moon. It's in the basement of the post office; enter from Hamilton St. (☎410-313-1900. Open Apr.-Nov. M-Th and Su 10am-5pm, F-Sa 10am-8:30pm; Dec.-Mar. daily 10am-5pm.

THE ROAD TO NEW MARKET: 30 MI.

The road continues to be two-lane and rural, with few lights or services. The gradual hills signal the approach of the Appalachian Mountains. **Route 144 (Frederick Avenue)** flirts with US 40 after leaving Baltimore; at one point you must take **US 40 West** before turning left back onto Rte. 144. Proceed around the rotary and pass through the small town of Lisbon. After Lisbon, Rte. 144 curves and stops at a T intersection. Turn right onto **Route 27,** following signs for Mt. Airy. Turn left on **East Ridgeville Boulevard,** which becomes the **Old National Pike** after about 1 mi.

NEW MARKET ☎301

New Market is the self-proclaimed "antiques capital of Maryland." The town has several buildings dating from the 1700s and has become a center for antique shops, each with its own area of expertise. Shopkeepers here seem to have found the good life; most stores open only on weekends. During the week, you can find fudge, jams, and other touristy products at the **General Store,** 26 W. Main St. (☎301-865-2350. Open M-Sa 10am-5pm, Su 1-5pm; hours vary in winter. MC/V.) If you're in a rush, you can pick up a personal pizza ($7, slices on weekends $2) at **Mom's Pizza and Grill ❶,** located in the back of the General Store. (☎301-865-0808; www.momspizzaonline.com. Open Tu-Su 11am-9pm. AmEx/MC/V.)

THE ROAD TO HARPERS FERRY: 33 MI.

Leave on **Main Street.** About 3 mi. past New Market, take the right fork at the sign for "To West 40." Stay west on **Route 144,** which is W. Patrick St. in Frederick. Proceed to the intersection with Jefferson St. and make a soft left at the sign for **US 340 West.** Continue west on US 340, ignoring signs that warn of the freeway ending. At the sign for Harpers Ferry, turn left to enter the National Historic Park or right to enter the town of Harpers Ferry on **Washington Street.**

The Mountain State
WEST VIRGINIA
Welcomes You!

HARPERS FERRY ☎304

A pastoral hillside town overlooking the Shenandoah and Potomac Rivers, Harpers Ferry was thrown into the national spotlight in 1859, when a band of abolitionists led by John Brown raided the US Armory. Although Brown was captured and executed, the raid brought the issue of slavery to public attention and, according to some, started a chain of events that led to the Civil War. (Brown's adamant belief that violence was the only means to overcome the problem of slavery gained considerable popular support.) The town was a major theater of conflict and changed hands no fewer than eight times during the Civil War. Today, Harpers Ferry's violent history is a thing of the past; mild-mannered outdoors enthusiasts and field trippers take in the park's natural beauty and rich history.

VITAL STATS

Population: 300

Tourist Offices: Jefferson County Convention and Visitors Bureau (☎304-535-2627; www.jeffersoncountycvb.com), on Washington St., just off US 340. Open daily in summer 9am-6pm; in winter 9am-5pm. **Cavalier Heights Visitors Center** (☎304-535-6298; www.harpersferryhistory.org), off US 340, inside Harpers Ferry National Historic Park. Open daily 8am-5pm.

Library and Internet Access: Harpers Ferry-Bolivar Library, 151 Polk St. (☎304-535-2301). Open M-Tu and F-Sa 10am-5:30pm, W-Th 10am-8pm.

Post Office: 1010 Washington St. (☎304-535-2479). Open M-F 8am-4pm, Sa 9am-noon. **Postal Code:** 25425.

✳ ORIENTATION

Harpers Ferry lies just south of the **Potomac River** and is surrounded on three sides by **Harpers Ferry National Historic Park**. **US 340** runs just south of town; most attractions are located on **Washington Street,** which runs east-west through town. Parking is generally free at Washington St. establishments but is not permitted on the streets of the **Lower Town** area of the national historic park; visitors must park at the **Cavalier Heights Visitors Center** unless they are staying at accommodations with parking within walking distance of town. **Free shuttles** run between the lot and the upper town every 10min.; the last pickup is at 6:45pm.

🛏 ACCOMMODATIONS

There are B&Bs in town and in nearby Charles Town (west of Harpers Ferry on US 340). Within the park, there's also a campsite.

Harpers Ferry Lodge, 19123 Sandy Hook Rd. (☎301-834-7652; www.harpersferryhostel.org). Fully-equipped kitchen, lounge, showers and laundry machines. Lockout 9am-6pm. Reservations recommended. Tent sites $10. Dorms $23, members $20. D/MC/V. ❶

Hillside Motel, 19105 Keep Tryst Rd. (☎301-834-8144), 3 mi. from town in Knoxville. 19 clean rooms inside a beautiful stone motel. Singles $45; doubles $50. AmEx/D/MC/V. ❷

Anglers Inn, 867 W. Washington St. (☎304-535-1239; www.theanglersinn.com). Fans of extreme fishing might appreciate this inn's fly-fishing packages available May-Oct. Guides are fully trained to take people out on the (often dangerous) river. All rooms with private bath. Rooms $95-165. AmEx/D/MC/V. ❺

Greenbrier State Park, on US 40 E. (☎301-791-4767 or 888-432-2267; http://reservations.dnr.state.md.us), off Rte. 66. 165 campsites and a recreation area near a lake. Reservations required. Open Apr.-Oct. Sites $25, with hookup $30. MC/V. ❶

🍴 FOOD

The historic area of Harpers Ferry, especially around High and Potomac Sts., caters to a lunch crowd with burgers, salads, and steaks but is vacant at dinnertime. There are few budget options, however. US 340, fortunately, has many fast-food and chain restaurants.

Cindy Dee Restaurant, 19112 Keep Tryst Rd. (☎301-695-8181), at US 340, across the street from the Hillside Motel and down the street from the Harper's Ferry Lodge. Fries enough chicken ($7) to clog all of your arteries. The apple dumplings ($4.50) and homemade bread pudding ($3.50) are delectable. Open in summer M-Th and Su 6am-10pm, F-Sa 6am-11pm; in winter M-Th and Su 6am-9pm, F-Sa 6am-10pm. ❷

The Anvil, 1290 Washington St. (☎304-535-2582). Serves delightfully non-greasy pub food for lunch, and fresh fish and beef at dinnertime. Try your luck at the slot machines in the "gaming room" behind the door that's opposite the bar. Pasta $13, other dishes $15-25. Open W-Su 11am-9pm. AmEx/D/MC/V. ❸

SIGHTS

Harpers Ferry National Historic Park comprises most of historic Harpers Ferry and includes several museums, admission to all of which is included in the cost of general admission to the park. (☎304-535-6029. Vehicles $6, individuals on bike or foot $4.) Museums close at 5:45pm. The park also offers occasional reenactments of Harpers Ferry's history.

SHENANDOAH STREET. The shuttle from the park's parking lot stops at Shenandoah St., where a phalanx of replicated 19th-century shops greets visitors. The **Dry Goods Store** displays clothes, hardware, liquor, and groceries, complete with an 1850s price list. The **Harpers Ferry Industrial Museum** describes the methods used to harness the powers of the Shenandoah and Potomac Rivers and details the town's status as the terminus of the nation's first successful rail line. At the **African American History Museum,** at the corner of High and Shenandoah St., visitors can listen to audio clips of the memoirs of fettered and freed slaves expressing their opinions of John Brown and his raid. The **John Brown Museum,** on Shenandoah St., just beyond High St., is the town's most captivating historical site. A 30min. video chronicles Brown's raid of the armory with a special focus on the moral and political implications of his actions.

HIGH STREET AND UPPER HARPERS FERRY. A daunting, steep staircase hewn into the hillside off High St. follows the **Appalachian Trail** to Upper Harpers Ferry, which has fewer sights but is laced with interesting historical tales. Allow 45min. to ascend past **Harper's House,** the restored home of town founder Robert Harper, and **Saint Peter's Church,** where a pastor flew the Union Jack during the Civil War to protect the building. Just a few steps uphill from St. Peter's lie the ruins of **St. John's Episcopal Church,** which was built in 1852 and used as a hospital and barracks during the Civil War before being abandoned in 1895.

OUTDOORS

Pick up trail maps at the park's visitors center before setting off into the wilderness.

INFORMATION

Appalachian Trail Regional Headquarters and Information Center, 799 Washington St. (☎304-535-6331; www.appalachiantrail.org). Here, a 10 ft. relief map shows the whole trail, and less exercise-prone visitors can educate themselves about the trail digitally, on a computer monitor. Open Apr.-Oct. M-F 9am-5pm, Sa-Su 9am-4pm; Nov.-Apr. M-F 9am-5pm.

OUTFITTERS

River & Trail Outfitters, 604 Valley Rd. (☎301-695-5177; www.rivertrail.com), 2 mi. out of Harpers Ferry, off US 340, in Knoxville, MD. River & Trail rents canoes, kayaks, inner tubes, and rafts. The outfitter also organizes excursions ranging from scenic day trips to placid rides down tranquil parts of the Shenandoah River ($45) to more extreme overnight trips. Tubing $32 per day. Canoes $55 per day. Raft trips $60.

Butt's Tubes, Inc. (☎800-836-9911; www.butts-tubes.com), on Rte. 671, off US 340. Butt's drives shuttles to and from the river and provides inner tubes and life jackets—all you have to do is show up. Open M-F 10am-3pm, Sa-Su 9am-4pm. Last pickup 2hr. after close. $19-30.

TRAILS

Bolivar Heights Trail. History dominates this ¾ mi. trail that starts at the northern end of Whitman Ave.

Chesapeake & Ohio Canal Towpath. This 4.2 mi. path at the end of Shenandoah St. and over the railroad bridge serves as a reminder of the town's industrial roots and is the departure point for a day's bike ride to Washington, DC.

Maryland Heights Trail. This moderately difficult trail, located across the railroad bridge in the Lower Town of Harpers Ferry, winds 4 mi. through the steep Blue Ridge Mountains along precipitous cliffs and passes crumbling Civil War-era forts.

Loudon Heights Trail. Get a good workout on this difficult 8 mi. trail. It starts in Lower Town, off the Appalachian Trail, and leads to Civil War infantry trenches and scenic overlooks.

THE ROAD TO ANTIETAM: 18 MI.

Head east on **US 340** for about 4 mi., passing into Virginia and then Maryland. Cross **Harpers Ferry Road,** and turn right on **Keep Tryst Road.** Take the first right onto **Sandy Hook Road,** which becomes Harpers Ferry Rd. This section of road is narrow, and there are unsigned sharp curves. Exercise caution and avoid driving this stretch at night or in snowy conditions, and be wary of road signs that have shifted over the years. Continue on Harpers Ferry Rd. until it becomes **Mechanic Street** in Sharpsburg. Take **Mechanic Street** to **Main Street** and turn right. After 1 mi., take a left onto **South Church Street (Route 65).**

ANTIETAM ☎301

September 17, 1862, the day of the Battle of Antietam in the Civil War, was the bloodiest day in US history. Nearly 25,000 soldiers died at Antietam, more than in the American Revolution, War of 1812, and Mexican-American War combined. Though neither side won decisively, the Union Army did manage to stop General Lee's advance toward Harrisburg. Inside the park, a stone observation tower offers a view of expansive fields and nearby farmhouses. There are several fairly flat hiking trails in the area. Be sure to stick to them to avoid nettles, snakes, and ticks. A driving tour leads past the major sites of the battle. The **Antietam National Battlefield Visitors Center** distributes a driving guide, and a short film plays every 30min. except between noon and 1pm. Ranger tours of the battlefield (around 2hr.) run daily at 1:30pm from the visitors cen-

ter and are preceded by a 1hr. documentary narrated by James Earl Jones. (☎301-432-5124. Open daily in summer 8am-7pm; in winter 8:30am-5pm. $4, families $6.)

THE ROAD TO GETTYSBURG NATIONAL MILITARY PARK: 17 MI.

Take **East Main Street** out of Sharpsburg, where it becomes **Route 34.** In the town of Boonsboro, turn left onto **Alternate US 40,** which becomes **Frederick Street.** You'll come into Hagerstown. From town head east on **Jefferson Boulevard** (**Route 64/804**) to Smithsburg. Turn right on **Foxville Road,** which becomes **Route 77.** After passing through **Catoctin Mountain Park,** get on **US 15 North** toward Gettysburg, watching for signs that direct you to the visitors center (between SR 134 and Taneytown Rd.).

GETTYSBURG NATIONAL MILITARY PARK ☎717

In the heat of July 1-3, 1863, Union and Confederate forces clashed spectacularly at Gettysburg. Though the Union ultimately prevailed, its victory came at the cost of more than 50,000 casualties. Four and a half months later, President Abraham Lincoln arrived in Gettysburg to dedicate the **Gettysburg National Cemetery,** where he delivered the Gettysburg Address on November 19, 1863. Today, the **Soldiers' National Monument** stands on the spot where Lincoln delivered his speech. A good place to start is the **Gettysburg National Military Park Visitors Center,** 1195 Baltimore Pike, which distributes free driving tour maps and houses the **Gettysburg Museum of the Civil War.** The museum's 100-year-old **cyclorama** (a cylindrical mural intended to give its viewer a 360° view of the scene depicted) recently underwent restoration. (☎717-334-1124; www.nps.gov/gett. Open daily June-Aug. 8am-7pm; Nov.-Mar. 8am-5pm. Sept.-Oct. and Apr.-May 8am-6pm; Free.) The information desk at the visitors center can set you up with a licensed battlefield guide on a first come, first served

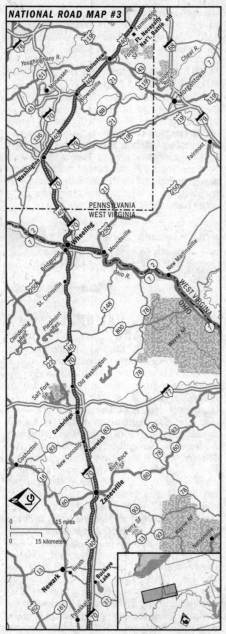

NATIONAL ROAD MAP #3

basis, so arrive early. (☎877-874-2478. 1-6 people in a vehicle $55.)

◤ THE ROAD TO CUMBERLAND: 58 MI.

Head back to Hagerstown. There, turn left on **Franklin Street** and head out of town. About 3 mi. down, merge onto **I-70.** 60 mi. from Hagerstown off Exit 50, you'll find idyllic **Rocky Gap State Park.** To get to Cumberland, take **I-68 West** and get off at **Exit 43C.**

The Old Line State

MARYLAND

Welcomes You

CUMBERLAND ☎301

Cumberland is the site of the C&O Canal and several railroads and accordingly once served as the gateway to the west. The **C&O Canal National Historic Park Visitors Center,** 13 Canal St., explains the significance of the waterway. (☎301-722-8226. Open daily sunrise-sunset. 3-day pass $5.) The same building houses the visitors center and the restored **Western Maryland Scenic Railroad,** which attracts train lovers to its old diesel and steam locomotives and runs daily excursions to Frostburg. (☎301-759-4400 or 800-872-4650; www.wmsr. com. Schedule varies greatly with season: check website.)

Rocky Gap State Park (see **The Road to Cumberland,** above) offers fishing, boating, and swimming in blue Lake Habeeb as well as **camping ❶** nearby. (☎888-432-2267; http:// reservations.dnr.state.md.us. May-Oct. reservations required; from Nov. to mid-Dec. and Apr. first come, first served. Sites $25. 4-bed cabins $50; 6-bed $65. MC/V.)

◤ THE ROAD TO LA VALE: 6 MI.

Head west on **Centre Street,** which becomes **Alternate US 40 West;** take 40 out of town toward La Vale.

LA VALE ☎301

In La Vale there's not a whole lot to do, but you can catch a few winks at the clean **Slumberland Motel ❸,** 1262 National Hwy. (☎301-729-2880. Singles $57; doubles $60. AmEx/D/MC/V.) Maryland's only surviving **tollhouse** is perched above the road. (Open Sa-Su 1:30-4:30pm. Free.)

🚗 THE ROAD TO GRANTSVILLE: 23 MI.
Continue on **Alternate US 40 West/National Highway** out of town and into Frostburg. Stay on Alt. US 40 W. and keep heading toward Grantsville.

The Keystone State
PENNSYLVANIA
Welcomes You!

GRANTSVILLE   ☎ 301
Pretty much the only attraction in Grantsville is the **Penn Alps,** 125 Casselman Rd., a village that offers a selection of local arts and showcases local history. In the village, **Stanton's Mill** looks rickety for a reason; it has stood here since 1797 and still mills flour today. The nearby **Casselman River Bridge** is under construction and cannot be viewed. The bridge dates back to the beginning of the 19th century and was in use from 1813 to 1932. Adjacent to the bridge, a collection of old buildings houses artists in residence at the **Spruce Forest Artisanal Village.** Artists undergo a rigorous selection process to win a coveted spot in the village. Drop-ins are welcome. (☎301-895-3332; www.spruceforest.org. Mill open by appointment.) The **Penn Alps Restaurant ❸,** 125 Casselman Rd., was built largely by volunteers as the Penn Alps expanded to bring visitors in from the highway. The German-inspired restaurant serves hearty and affordable meals. A smoked sausage sandwich with sauerkraut runs $5. (☎301-895-5985; www.pennalps.com. Entrees $11-21. Open M-F 11am-7pm, Sa 8am-7pm, Su 11am-3pm. AmEx/D/MC/V.)

🚗 THE ROAD TO FORT NECESSITY: 26 MI.
Keep to the **National Pike (US 40),** and turn left at the sign for Fort Necessity.

FORT NECESSITY
NATIONAL BATTLEFIELD   ☎ 724
Leave those Civil War sites behind and jump back in time to the French and Indian War.

This battlefield, much more tranquil and less crowded than Gettysburg, includes a reproduction of the original stockade fort, the **Mount Washington Tavern,** and **General Edward Braddock's Grave.** While the notion of entering the West in Pennsylvania seems a bit farfetched, the stockade bears witness to the fact that this wooded area was once the frontier. The tavern has an exhibit on the National Rd. along with period furnishings. (☎724-329-5512. Visitors center open daily 9am-5pm. Grounds open sunrise-sunset. $5.)

🔀 DETOUR
KENTUCK KNOB AND FALLINGWATER
Turn right at the sign for Kentuck Knob onto **Farmington-Ohiopyle Road.** The house is 12 mi. down the road, after you pass through Ohiopyle State Park.

Contemporary architect Frank Lloyd Wright chose a beautiful site at Kentuck Knob to construct a house three years before his death. Part of an 1000-acre estate, the home is Modernist architecture writ large. Tours explore the house and sculpture garden. A little-known bonus is that the house holds the original owners' impressive collections of modern furniture, ninth-century Buddhist art, and dinosaur vertebrae. (☎724-329-1901; www.kentuckknob.com. Tours Mar.-Dec. at 11am, 1, 3pm; Jan.-Feb. by reservation only. $16, ages 6-12 $10. In-depth tour including Wright's drawings and the house's basement $55.) Down the way, **Fallingwater,** the most famous private residence ever built, exemplifies Wright's organic architecture. Though from some angles the house does actually seem to be falling into the water, what strikes you most is how fluidly Wright's architecture and nature interact. The grounds around the house offer good views and tranquil walking paths. (☎724-329-8501; www.fallingwater.org. Open Mar.-Nov. M-Tu and Th-Su 10am-4pm; Jan.-Feb. M-Tu and Th-Su 11am-3pm, Dec. Sa-Su 11am-3pm. $16, ages 6-12 $10. Grounds pass $6.) In non-architectural news, **Ohiopyle State Park** provides some of the best rafting in the eastern US and 79 mi. of trails for hiking, horseback riding, and biking. There are plenty of park outfitters, most located right on Rte. 381 S. (Farmington-Ohiopyle Rd.).

THE ROAD TO SCENERY HILL: 33 MI.

Follow **US 40** around Uniontown; take the exit for **US 40 West.** Follow the signs indicating the original National Road. Continue following the **National Road** markers across the **Monongahela River** and rejoin **US 40** after about 3 mi. Eight miles from Brownsville, check out the **Madonna of the Trail,** US 40. This 16 ft. statue is one of 12 (the 1st of 5 along the National Rd.) erected in 1928 by the **Daughters of the American Revolution** in honor of "pioneer mothers of the covered-wagon days."

SCENERY HILL ☎ 724

Scenery Hill has little to offer besides the **Hill's Tavern at Century Inn ❹,** 2175 E. National Pike (US 40). Once host to Andrew Jackson, this tavern, built in 1794, remains active as an elegant B&B and restaurant and has been in continuous operation since 1794. The rooms are richly decorated with antiques and prints. (☎724-945-6600; www.centuryinn.com. Rooms $80-150. MC/V. If you head inside the actual **tavern ❸,** check out the flag from the Whiskey Rebellion to the right of the entrance. Lunch offerings include American, but unorthodox, entrees such as peanut soup made from Thomas Jefferson's recipe ($5), Welsh rarebit ($8), and rainbow trout ($12).

THE ROAD TO WASHINGTON: 9 MI.

Continue on **US 40** to Washington.

WASHINGTON ☎ 724

When entering Washington, be sure to check out the majestic US Capitol-style **County Courthouse** at the corner of Main and Beau St. At the family-friendly and kitschy **Pennsylvania Trolley Museum,** 1 Museum Rd., an earlier era lives on. Visitors can ride restored vintage streetcars down a 3 mi. track. Head east on W. Maiden St./US 40 toward Brownson Ave. Turn left at S. Main St., then right at Museum Rd., and follow the blue signs for the museum. (☎724-228-9256; www.pa-trolley.org. Open June-Aug. M-Th 10am-4pm, F 11am-8:30pm, Sa-Su 11am-5pm; Sept.-May M-F 10am-4pm, Sa-Su 11am-5pm. Tours start 15min. after the hr., rides start 35min. after the hr. $8, ages 2-15 $5, seniors $7.) Visitors to the **LeMoyne House,** 49 E. Maiden St. (US 40), can see where runaway slaves hid and learn about Dr. LeMoyne,

the staunch abolitionist who ran this stop on the Underground Railroad. (☎724-225-6740; www.wchspa.org. Open Tu-F 11am-4pm, Sa-Su by appointment only. $5, students $3.)

Washington has very few motels, but the chains that cluster on W. Chestnut St. (US 40) at the exits for I-70, 2 mi. west of town, offer rooms for as low as $46 per night. Just east of the city, the **Washington KOA ❶,** 7 KOA Rd., has campsites with a game room, a pool, and laundry. Follow signs from US 40/19. (☎724-225-7590 or 800-562-0254. Free Wi-Fi. Sites $34. Cabins $44. D/MC/V.)

The **New Tower Restaurant and Lounge ❷,** 680 W. Chestnut St. (US 40), caters to locals and travelers looking for a no-fuss bite to eat. Sandwiches cost $5-6, sirloin strip steak is $10.50, and fried chicken runs $9.50. (☎724-222-5952. Breakfast $3-6. Dinner with 2 sides and salad $8-10. Open Tu-Th 7am-10pm, F-Sa 7am-11pm, Su 7am-8pm. D/MC/V.)

For visitor info, see the **Washington County Tourism Promotion Agency,** 273 S. Main St., north of the railroad tracks. (☎866-927-4969; www.washpatourism.org. Open M-F 9am-4:30pm.)

THE ROAD TO WHEELING: 26 MI.

Chestnut Street becomes **US 40** 7 mi. from Washington. The odd **S-bridge** is visible on the north side of US 40. The bridge was built in an S-shape because the river was at an angle to the road, and it was easier to construct straight arches over the river. Seventeen miles from Washington, the road leaves Pennsylvania and enters West Virginia; 9 mi. later, US 40 turns right to head into Wheeling. On your way into town, notice the next **Madonna of the Trail** monument on the right. From here, US 40 takes a long, scenic route around the hills to downtown Wheeling. The fastest way to get into Wheeling, however, is on **I-70 West.**

The Mountain State **WEST VIRGINIA** *Welcomes You!*

WHEELING ☎ 304

Once the thriving economic and political center of West Virginia, Wheeling today remains proud of its history. The **Kruger Street Toy and**

Train Museum, 144 Kruger St., displays 30,000 toys in a gorgeous restored Victorian-era schoolhouse. (☎304-242-8133; www.toy-andtrain.com. Open from Memorial Day to Jan. daily 9am-5pm; from Jan. to Memorial Day Sa-Su 9am-5pm. $9.75, seniors $8, ages 6-17 $5.30, under 6 free.) The answer to that eternal question, "Why does West Virginia exist?", can be found at the **West Virginia Independence Hall,** 1528 Market St., which narrates the history of the division between the regions of Richmond and Wheeling. The building marks the site where West Virginia became a state. Proceed south on Main St. to 16th St. and turn left. (☎304-238-1300. Open M-Sa 10am-4pm. Free.) From Main St., at 10th St., you can view the **Wheeling Suspension Bridge,** just south of the current I-70/US 40 bridge. Built in 1849 to carry the National Rd. across the Ohio River, this 1010 ft. suspension bridge opened 34 years before the Brooklyn Bridge. **Coleman's Fish Market ❶,** at 22nd and Market St., in Centre Market, serves up fried and steamed delicacies from the sea. Most items, including the shrimp and the fish sandwich, are around $5. (☎304-232-8510. Open M-Th and Sa 10am-5:30pm, F 10am-6pm. Cash only.) **Michael's Beef House ❶,** in the same market, sells hot roast beef ($4) and other affordable sandwiches. Vegetarians beware: you will find little here. (☎304-232-2231. Open M-Th and Sa 11am-4pm, F 11am-7pm. Cash only.)

⬛ DETOUR

FORMER WEST VIRGINIA PENITENTIARY

818 Jefferson Avenue. From downtown Wheeling, take **Route 2 South,** which turns into **Main Street/Chapline Street** in Wheeling, for 12 mi. to Moundsville, and then turn left on **Eighth Street.** Continue and you'll find the penitentiary two blocks ahead.

If you can't wait until Alcatraz (2586 mi. down the road), tour this grim, castle-like Civil War-era structure where West Virginia still conducts its mock prison riot training. With reservations, you can even spend the night; just watch out for the ghosts. (☎304-845-6200; www.wvpentours.com. Open Apr.-Nov. Tu-Su 10am-4pm. $10, seniors $8, ages 6-12 $5.)

◪ THE ROAD TO BRIDGEPORT: 4 MI.

Follow signs in the downtown area for **US 40.** Continue west on 40 through Bridgeport.

The Buckeye State
OHIO
Welcomes You!

BRIDGEPORT ☎740

Bridgeport doesn't have much going on, but the air smells good in this mountain town, and the friendly and scenic **Hillside Motel ❷,** 54481 National Rd. (US 40), is an excellent place to spend the night. A room comes with HBO, free Wi-Fi, and free long-distance domestic calls. Camper hookups are also available. (☎740-635-9111; www.hillside-motel.com. Singles $45; doubles $52. D/MC/V.)

◪ THE ROAD TO CAMBRIDGE: 46 MI.

US 40 merges with **I-70** 22 mi. from Wheeling. Take it and get off at Ohio **Exit 178.** Make a right at **Southgate Parkway** and take it into Cambridge.

CAMBRIDGE ☎740

Cambridge was and still is at the heart of a glass-producing region. **Mosser Glass Inc.,** 9279 Cadiz Rd. (US 22 E.), is the largest operational glass factory in Cambridge. (☎740-439-1827. Open M-F 8am-4pm. Tours 8-10am and 11:15am-2:30pm.) Inside **Boyd's Crystal Art Glass,** 1203 Morton Ave., on the corner of Woodlawn Ave., workers are busy producing specialty glass. From US 40, turn left onto 11th St., which becomes Morton Ave. (☎740-439-2077. Open M-F 8am-4pm.) The **Degenhart Paperweight and Glass Museum,** 65323 Highland Hills Rd., at Cadiz Rd. (US 22) and I-77, has glass samples from different companies and eras, each with informative explanations. From town, take US 22 E.; the museum is on the left just before the I-77 exit. (☎740-432-2626. Open Apr.-Oct. M-Sa 10am-5pm; Nov.-Mar. M-F 10am-4pm. $1.50, under 12 free, seniors $1.)

The rooms of the cozy, family-run **Budget Inn ❷,** 6405 Glenn Hwy. (US 40), 2 mi. west of town, have green-and-red floral comforters on the beds and innocuous watercolors on the walls. The rooms are generic but comfortable. (☎740-432-2304. Singles $32; doubles $40. D/MC/V.) **Theo's Restaurant ❷,** 632 Wheeling Ave. (US 40), serves delightfully cheap and

**NATIONAL
ROAD**

non-greasy food. Theo's specialty is the Coney Island Hot Dog ($1.25), which is perfectly accompanied by a wedge of freshly baked pie for $2. (☎740-432-3878. Barbecue $6-7. Steak sandwich $4.25. Open M-Sa 10am-9pm. AmEx/D/MC/V.)

▓ THE ROAD TO NORWICH: 11 MI.
Follow **US 40 West** to New Concord. Continue on US 40 toward Norwich, passing an S-bridge on the right.

NORWICH ☎740

Norwich is a small town whose welcome sign proclaims it to be the sight of the first fatal traffic accident in Ohio—an overturned stagecoach in 1835. The town's less macabre claim to fame is the fantastic ▓**National Road/ Zane Grey Museum**, 8850 E. Pike (US 40). All the bits and pieces of National Rd. history and America's love affair with the car come together at this museum—along with exhibits of sights you've already passed and some yet to come. Check out the displays on Zane Grey, a pulp author widely recognized as the father of the "adult" Western novel The title is perhaps misleading; by today's standards, Grey's books are far from scandalous. From US 40, look for the large sign for Baker's Motel and turn left into the museum. (☎740-872-3143. Open Memorial Day to Labor Day W-Sa 9:30am-5pm, Su noon-5pm; winter hours vary. $7, students $3, under 6 free.) **Baker's Motel ❷**, 8855 E. Pike, has a convenient location and comfortable, simple rooms. (☎740-872-3232; www.bakersmotel.com. Singles $34-50; doubles $50-70. AmEx/D/MC/V.)

▓ THE ROAD TO ZANESVILLE: 13 MI.
Follow **US 40** to Zanesville.

ZANESVILLE ☎740

Amelia Earhart described Zanesville as the "most recognizable city in the country" due to its **Y-shaped bridge.** The current Y-bridge is the fifth of its kind since 1814. On the opposite side of town, your best bet for a glimpse of the bridge is on your way out. As you leave town on US 40, just after the Y-bridge, take the first left on Pine St. and then turn left on Grandview Ave., following signs for "Y-Bridge Overlook." From **Zane's Landing Park**, roadtrip-

pers can ride the **Lorena Sternwheeler** down the Muskingum River. There are four different cruise options. The dinner cruise ($30) is accompanied by on-board entertainment, the twilight cruise ($8) provides a sunset view of the river, the lunch cruise ($15) serves lunch, and the simple public ride ($8) offers only the opportunity for you and your lover to straddle the boat's stern and throw your arms back a la Titanic. Take Market St. west until it ends at the park. (☎740-455-8282 or 800-743-2303. Call for cruise schedule.)

Hotels in Zanesville are surprisingly expensive and cluster around the US 40 junction with I-70, though there are a number of other chains downtown. Your best bet is to head back to Cambridge to spend the night. The original incarnation of a roadside favorite, ▓**Classic Denny's ❷**, 10 Airport Rd., 6 mi. east of Zanesville and just off Rte. 40, has a regular Denny's menu. However, the venue's sparkly red and silver leather seats—whose crome finishing makes them look like they came right out of your grandfather's Chevy—and extra-jolly staff will remind you that this is something a little bit more extravagant than your average Denny's. If you love classic cars, try to drop in on a Friday between June and August; Denny's hosts classic car shows that pack the parking lot with the area's best cars and their proud owners. (☎740-450-8387. Open 24hr. AmEx/D/MC/V.) At **Nicol's Restaurant ❶**, 730 Putnam Ave., homestyle entrees with two sides are $7 and up, while the medium James Dean Pizza (for meat lovers) is $12. Don't forget Nicol's homemade ice cream ($2) or pie ($3) for dessert. From Main St. or Market St., turn left onto Fourth St. or Fifth St., turn left at Canal St., and take the first right onto Sixth St., which becomes Putnam Ave. (☎740-452-2577. Open M-Th 8am-10pm, F-Su 7am-10pm. MC/V.)

▓ THE ROAD TO NEWARK: 30 MI.
Take **Main Street (US 40)** out of town, bearing left on the Y-bridge to stay on US 40. Take a right on **Route 13/Jacksontown Road Southeast** toward Newark.

NEWARK ☎740

A visit to Newark requires a brief detour from US 40, but the 1000+ acres of **Dawes Arboretum,**

7770 Jacksontown Rd. SE., provide plenty of scenic walks through landscaped grounds, perfect for the road-weary. The highlight is the "all-season garden," which features different plants depending on the month. Turn right onto Rte. 13 and head north; the arboretum is just a few hundred yards on the left. (☎740-323-2355 or 800-443-2937; www.dawesarb.org. Open daily sunrise-sunset. Free.)

🚗 THE ROAD TO BUCKEYE LAKE: 15 MI.

Return on **Route 13** back to **US 40 West;** get off at **Route 79 South/Hebron Road.** Hebron Rd. will turn into **Walnut Road Southeast.** Voila! You've arrived.

BUCKEYE LAKE ☎ 740

The well-maintained **Buckeye Lake/Columbus East KOA ❷,** 4460 Walnut Rd., offers shaded tent sites, a pool, miniature golf course, and laundry. (☎740-928-0706. Open Apr.-Oct. Tent sites $29-55; RV sites $35-84. Cabins $55-94. AmEx/D/MC/V.) If you're hungry, don't miss the pizza at **Catfish Charley's ❷,** 11048 Hebron Rd. (Rte. 79), in Buckeye Lake Village. Charley's has both plain and gourmet pizzas as well as other Italian fare. (☎740-928-7174. All-you-can-eat lunch buffet M-F $5.50, Sa-Su $6. Dinner buffet M, W, F $6. Open M-Th and Su 11am-10pm, F-Sa 11am-11pm. D/MC/V.)

🚗 THE ROAD TO COLUMBUS: 30 MI.

Return to **US 40** via **Route 79 South.** In Bexley, US 40 strays from Main St. The sign for US 40 is small and hard to see; if you miss the turn, **Main Street** will also take you into downtown, albeit on a less scenic path.

COLUMBUS ☎ 614

Less a single, coherent metropolis than a collection of freeway exits, Columbus crept past Cleveland in 1990 as Ohio's most populous city. White-collar workers hit the freeways at 5pm and make for the inner-ring suburbs, while immigrants and young artists keep parts of downtown aglow after dark. The capitol's museums and galleries are well worth a day or two of exploration. Although many residents in Columbus have a strong sense of pride associated with their neighborhoods, everyone unites in support of the Buckeyes (Ohio State football).

VITAL STATS
Population: 711,000
Tourist Office: Visitors Center, 277 W. Nationwide Blvd., Ste. 125. (☎614-221-6623 or 866-397-2657; www.experiencecolumbus.com), at the corner of Neil Blvd. and Nationwide Ave. Open M-F 8am-5pm, Sa-Su 10am-4pm.
Library and Internet Access: Columbus Metropolitan Library, 96 S. Grant Ave. (☎614-645-2275). Open M-Th 9am-9pm, F-Sa 9am-6pm, Su 1-5pm.
Post Office: 850 Twin Rivers. (☎614-469-4541). Open M-F 8am-7pm, Sa 8am-2pm. **Postal Code:** 43215.

🔁 ORIENTATION

The city is laid out in a simple grid, and its low speed limits help when navigating unfamiliar territory. **High Street,** running north-south, and **Broad Street (US 40),** running east-west, are the main thoroughfares. High St. heads north from the towering office complexes downtown to the lively galleries and restaurants in the **Short North,** continuing on to **Ohio State University (OSU).** South of downtown lies historic **German Village.** There is little free parking available in Columbus except on evenings and weekends at certain meters. There is free parking available in German Village and some of the more residential areas. Lots downtown tend to be expensive ($12 per day). Meters proliferate on almost every street, but time limits and prices vary widely.

⛰ ACCOMMODATIONS

Those under 21 will have a hard time finding accommodations in Columbus; a city ordinance prevents hotels from renting to underage visitors. Nearby suburbs are your best bet to dodge the ban and catch your Zs.

The Homestead Motel, 4182 E. Main St./US 40 (☎614-235-2348), 7 mi. from downtown Columbus. Located near the beginnings of suburbia. Exceedingly spacious, clean, and well-lit rooms. Singles and doubles $45. MC/V. ❷

German Village Inn, 920 S. High St. (☎614-443-6506). The newly remodeled inn offers clean, well-appointed rooms (think green floral bedspreads and faux-leather chairs) with cable

NATIONAL ROAD

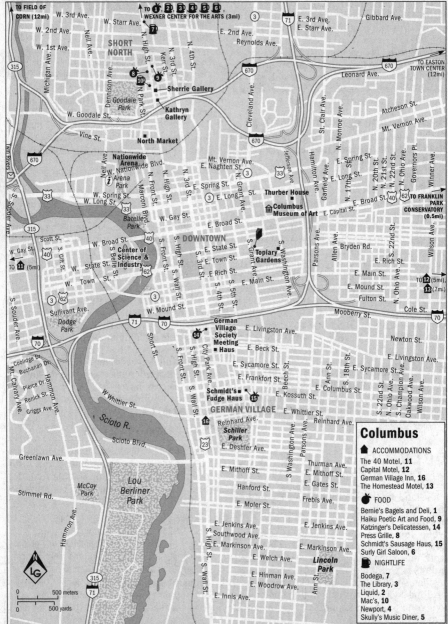

TO FIELD OF CORN (12mi)

W. 3rd Ave.
W. 2nd Ave.
W. 1st Ave.

W. Starr Ave.

SHORT NORTH

N. High St.
Kerr St.
N. 3rd St.
N. 4th St.

TO WEXNER CENTER FOR THE ARTS (3mi)

E. 3rd Ave.
E. Starr Ave.
Gibbard Ave.

E. 2nd Ave.
Reynolds Ave.

Michigan Ave.
Neil Ave.
Dennison Ave.

N. Park St.

Sherrie Gallery

Kathryn Gallery

Goodale Park

W. Goodale St.

Vine St.

North Market

Cleveland Ave.
Leonard Ave.

St. Clair Ave.
N. Monroe Ave.
Atcheson St.
Mt. Vernon Ave.

TO EASTON TOWN CENTER (12mi)

Nationwide Arena
Nationwide Blvd.
Arena Park

Mt. Vernon Ave.
E. Naghten St.

Jefferson Ave.
Hamilton Ave.
Garfield Ave.

E. Spring St.
E. Long St.

N. 17th St.
N. 20th St.
N. 21st St.
N. 22nd St.
N. Ohio Ave.

Winner Ave.
Governors Pl.

TO FRANKLIN PARK CONSERVATORY (0.5mi)

W. Spring St.
W. Long St.

Maroni Blvd.

Battelle Park

W. Gay St.

E. Spring St.
N. Grant Ave.
E. Long St.

Thurber House

Columbus Museum of Art

E. Broad St.
E. Capital St.

DOWNTOWN

Scott St.
W. Broad St.

Center of Science & Industry

W. Gay St.
TO (5mi)

W. State St.
W. Town St.

S. Gift St.
S. Belle St.

S. High St.
S. Front St.
S. 3rd St.
S. 4th St.
S. 5th St.

E. State St.
E. Town St.
E. Rich St.
E. Main St.

Topiary Gardens

S. Grant Ave.
S. Washington Ave.

Parsons Ave.
Allen Ave.
Bryden Rd.

E. Rich St.
E. Main St.
E. Mound St.
Fulton St.

S. 22nd Ave.
N. Ohio Ave.
Wilson Ave.
Cole St.

TO (5mi)
(7mi)

Sullivant Ave.
Dodge Park

S. Souder Ave.

W. Mound St.

Mooberry St.

Newton St.

E. Livingston Ave.

Coolidge Dr.
Buchanan Dr.
Pierce Dr.
Renick St.
Griggs Ave.

W. Whittier St.

German Village Society Meeting Haus

City Park Ave.
S. High St.
S. Front St.

E. Livingston Ave.
E. Beck St.
E. Sycamore St.
E. Frankfort St.
E. Columbus St.

Beech St.
Ann St.
S. 18th St.

E. Sycamore St.
E. Livingston Ave.

S. 22nd St.
N. Ohio Ave.
N. Champion Ave.
Oakwood Ave.
Wilson Ave.

Scioto R.

Schmidt's Fudge Haus

Schiller Park

GERMAN VILLAGE

Reinhard Ave.
E. Deshler Ave.
E. Mithoff St.
Hanford St.
E. Moler St.

E. Kossuth St.
E. Whittier St.

S. Washington Ave.
Parsons Ave.
Reinhard Ave.

Thurman Ave.
E. Mithoff St.
E. Gates St.
Frebis Ave.

Mt. Calvary Ave.
Hammon Ave.

Greenlawn Ave.
Stimmel Rd.

McCoy Park

Lou Berliner Park

Scioto Blvd.

Hammon Ave.

E. Jenkins Ave.
E. Southwood Ave.
E. Markinson Ave.
E. Welch Ave.
E. Hinman Ave.
E. Woodrow Ave.
E. Innis Ave.

S. High St.
S. Wall St.

E. Jenkins Ave.
E. Markinson Ave.

Ann St.

Lincoln Park

Columbus

ACCOMMODATIONS

The 40 Motel, **11**
Capital Motel, **12**
German Village Inn, **16**
The Homestead Motel, **13**

FOOD

Bernie's Bagels and Deli, **1**
Haiku Poetic Art and Food, **9**
Katzinger's Delicatessen, **14**
Press Grille, **8**
Schmidt's Sausage Haus, **15**
Surly Girl Saloon, **6**

NIGHTLIFE

Bodega, **7**
The Library, **3**
Liquid, **2**
Mac's, **10**
Newport, **4**
Skully's Music Diner, **5**

NATIONAL ROAD

0   500 meters
0   500 yards

TV, A/C, and free local phone calls. The most important meal of the day included. Singles $54; doubles $59. 21+. AmEx/D/MC/V. ❸

The 40 Motel, 3705 W. Broad St./US 40 (☎614-276-2691), 5 mi. from downtown Columbus. This motel has generously sized rooms and the largest neon sign in the city of Columbus. Singles $42; doubles $44. AmEx/D/MC/V. ❷

🍴 FOOD

By far the best place for budget eats in Columbus is the **North Market**, 59 Spruce St., in the Short North Arts District. From every corner of this restored marketplace, vendors offer a variety of wines, meats, cheeses, fruits, and prepared ethnic foods from sushi to barbecue. On the first Sunday of each month from May to October, there is also an artisan's market here. Take High St. north to Spruce St. and turn left. (☎614-463-9664; www.northmarket.com. Open Tu-F 9am-7pm, Sa 8am-5pm, Su noon-5pm. Some merchants open M 9am-5pm.) High St. is lined with a variety of cafes and coffee shops, all of which are reasonably good and reasonably affordable.

🍴 **Katzinger's Delicatessen,** 475 S. 3rd St. (☎614-228-3354; www.katzingers.com). Charges a whopping $11.25 for its incredible ½ lb. reuben. But with Black Angus corned beef shipped down from Detroit and Bill Clinton's personal approval, Katzinger's can't be beat for sandwiches ($9-12) or Su morning bagels and lox. Special vegetarian and vegan menu. Open M-F 8:30am-8:30pm, Sa-Su 9am-8:30pm. AmEx/MC/V. ❸

🍴 **Surly Girl Saloon,** 1126 N. High St. (☎614-294-4900; www.surlygirlsaloon.com). A Western-style saloon with a feminine punk twist, with lots of skulls, figurines of Indians, and crystal chandeliers. Oldies and rock music complete the mood. Mixed drinks include the Surly Temple ($3), and the spicy PB&J stands out among the sandwiches. Ask for the daily cupcake specials. Open daily 11am-2am. Bar open until 2:30am.

Schmidt's Sausage Haus, 240 E. Kossuth St. (☎614-444-6808; www.schmidthaus.com). Serves Bavarian specialties like sausage platters ($10-11) and vanilla cream puffs ($5.25), while traditional oompah bands lead polkas (W-Th 7pm, F-Sa 8pm). Some traditions seem newer, like the Bahama Mama sausage. Dinner entrees

$11-15. Open M-Th and Su 11am-10pm, F-Sa 11am-11pm. AmEx/D/MC/V. ❸

Haiku Poetic Art and Food, 800 N. High St. (☎614-294-8168). Sushi chefs produce their edible art amid earth-colored Japanese decor. The pan-Asian focus includes sushi and noodle dishes ($10-13), such as udon tempura, lo mein, or pad thai, that might just inspire poetry. Open M-Th 11am-11pm, F-Sa 11am-midnight, Su 4-10pm. AmEx/D/MC/V. ❸

Press Grille, 741 N. High St. (☎614-298-1014), in the Short North District. Serves a variety of modern foods to a crowd of locals and OSU students in a laid-back setting. Reubens $6.75. Cheeseburgers $4. Pizzas with the works $14. Open M-Sa 11:30am-2:30am, Su 11:30am-1am. Kitchen open until 1am. AmEx/MC/V. ❷

Bernie's Bagels and Deli, 1896 N. High St. (☎614-291-3448). Serves healthful sandwiches ($3-5) and all-day breakfast in a subterranean joint. Nightly live punk, rock, indie, or hip-hop music. Open M-Sa 11am-2:30am, Su 11am-5pm. Kitchen open M-Sa until 5pm. MC/V. ❶

👁 SIGHTS

WEXNER CENTER FOR THE ARTS. This was the first public building designed by controversial Modernist Peter Eisenman. The center now sports a five-story "permanent scaffold," an aesthetic of unfinished construction that matches its commitment to avant-garde visual art and performance. (*1871 N. High St. ☎614-292-3535; www.wexarts.org. Open Feb.-June Tu-W and Su 11am-6pm, Th-Sa 11am-8pm. Free. Films $7, students and seniors $5, under 12 $3.*)

COLUMBUS MUSEUM OF ART. The museum has a strong permanent collection of early modern canvases by European luminaries like Matisse and Klee as well as lesser-known Americans like George Bellows. Highlights include a collection of local folk art and fun exhibits created for kids but open to all ages. Don't miss the giant "ART" sign towering right behind the museum. (*480 E. Broad St. ☎614-221-6801; www.columbusmuseum.org. Open Tu-W and F-Su 10am-5:30pm, Th 10am-8:30pm. $8, students, ages 6-18 and seniors $5. Su free.*)

CENTER OF SCIENCE AND INDUSTRY (COSI). The submarine-shaped center allows visitors to explore space from the safety of an armchair, create their own short stop-animation films, and watch school groups go crazy with their love of science. A seven-story **Extreme Screen** shows action-packed films. *(333 W. Broad St. Take Broad St./US 40 W. past High St.; the museum is on the left just after the river. ☎614-228-2674; www.cosi.org. Open M-Sa 10am-5pm, Su noon-6pm. $12.50, seniors $10.50, ages 2-12 $7.50. Extreme Screen $7.50. Combination ticket $18.50/16.50/13.50.)*

THURBER HOUSE. James Thurber's childhood home showcases major events of the famous *The New Yorker* writer's life. It's also a literary center that hosts seminars with authors like John Updike and ◼literary picnics in the summer. *(77 Jefferson Ave., off E. Broad St. From Broad St., turn right on Jefferson Ave., just past I-71, and circle around. ☎614-464-1032; www.thurberhouse.org. Open daily 1-4pm. Free. Tours Su $2.50, students $2.)*

SHORT NORTH ARTS DISTRICT. The Short North Arts District is rife with galleries to browse *(☎614-299-8050; www.shortnorth.org)*. On the first Saturday of each month from 6 to 10pm, the district fills with an eclectic crowd for the free **Gallery Hop Night,** in which artists, purveyors, and appreciators come together and watch street performances, nibble hors d'oeuvres, and sip champagne. **Sherrie Gallerie** sells funky local art jewelry and features contemporary American painting and ceramics. *(694 N. High St. ☎614-221-8580. Open Tu-F 11am-6pm, Sa 11am-5pm, Su 1-5pm. Free.)* The **Kathryn Gallery** features contemporary American and European artists and has a backroom for private viewing of individual works. *(642 N. High St. ☎614-222-6801; www.kathryngallery.com. Open Tu-Sa 11am-6pm, Su noon-5pm. Free.)*

GERMAN VILLAGE. For some good Germanica, march down to the German Village, south of Capitol Sq. This area, settled in 1843, is now the largest privately-funded restoration in the US and is full of stately homes and beer halls. The **German Village Society Meeting Haus** provides info on local happenings like summertime performances of **Shakespeare in Schiller Park**—don't tell them he was English. *(588 S. 3rd St. ☎614-221-8888. Open M-F 9am-4pm, Sa 10am-2pm; hours vary in winter.)* **Schmidt's Fudge Haus** concocts tasty chocolate delicacies named for local celebrities. Schmidt's fudge is made in

shop, and its other chocolates all come from Ohio. *(220 E. Kossuth St. ☎614-444-2222. Truffles and other candies $12-17 per lb. Open June-Aug. M and W-Sa noon-9pm, Tu noon-4pm, Su noon-8pm; Sept.-May daily noon-4pm. AmEx/D/MC/V.)*

OTHER SIGHTS. The **Franklin Park Conservatory and Botanical Garden** cultivates lush greenery from various parts of the world and is a good break from the variable Ohio weather. In the park's own words, "We nurture plants and people." Flora from the Himalayan Mountains, the tropical rainforest, and the desert all live here. *(1777 E. Broad St. ☎614-645-8733; www.fpconservatory.org. Open Tu and Th-Su 10am-5pm, W 10am-8pm. $7.50, students and seniors $6, ages 2-12 $4.)* About 10 mi. north of downtown, the surreal **Field of Corn** contains 109 7 ft. concrete ears of corn that pay homage to the town's agrarian roots. *(4995 Rings Rd., in Dublin. From Columbus, take I-70 W. to I-270 N.; take Exit 15 and turn right on Tuttle Crossing Blvd. Turn left onto Frantz Rd. The field is visible at the intersection of Frantz Rd. and Rings Rd. Open 24hr. Free.)* The **Topiary Park,** 480 E. Town St., at Washington, is modeled after Georges Seurat's *A Sunday Afternoon on the Isle of La Grande Jatte.* It is the only topiary garden (a garden of sculpted bushes) in the world that is based on a work of art and provides a peaceful, bizarre sanctuary in the middle of downtown. *(☎614-645-0197; www.topiarygarden. org. Open daily from dawn to dusk.)*

🎵 ENTERTAINMENT

Two free weekly papers available in shops and restaurants, *The Other Paper* and *Columbus Alive*, list arts and entertainment options. In early August, the **Ohio State Fair** rolls into town, as it has for 150 years, with competitions, rides, concerts, and fluffy cotton candy. *(☎888-646-3976; www.ohiostatefair. com. $10, ages 5-12 and seniors $8, under 5 free.)* The always formidable **Ohio State Buckeyes** play football in the historic horseshoe-shaped Ohio Stadium. *(☎614-292-6446.)* Major League Soccer's **Columbus Crew** kicks off at Crew Stadium. *(☎614-447-2739; www.crewstadium.com. Tickets $12-40.)* Columbus's NHL hockey team, the **Blue Jackets,** plays in Nationwide Arena. *(☎614-246-3350; www.bluejackets.nhl.com. Tickets $6-10.)* The **Clippers,** a minor-league affiliate of baseball's

Washington Nationals, play games from April to early September. (☎614-462-5250; http://clippersbaseball.com. Tickets $6-10.)

NIGHTLIFE

Cleveland might have been the birthplace of rock and roll, but "bar bands" are a Columbus mainstay, and it's hard to find a bar that doesn't have live music on the weekend. South from Union Station is the **Brewery District,** where barley and hops have replaced coal and iron in the once industrial area. The **Short North** district, on N. High St., has a large selection of bars and restaurants; the following is a by no means exhaustive sampling.

Bodega, 1044 N. High St. (☎614-299-9399). The largest selection of beers on tap in Ohio. Attracts a fun crowd of students and young professionals. Open daily 11am-2:30am. M-Tu may close early if night is slow. AmEx/D/MC/V.

Mac's, 693 N. High St. (☎614-221-6227). Scottish culinary specialties like Forfar bridie probably don't attract the crowds as much as the bar's warm, casual environment, but they do make it a fun change from your usual Irish pub. Open M-Sa 11am-2:30am, Su noon-2:30am. AmEx/MC/V.

Newport, 1722 N. High St. (☎614-294-1659; www.promowestlive.com). National acts of all shapes and sizes stop here to strut their stuff. Cover $5-40. Cash only.

The Library, 2169 N. High St. (☎614-299-3245). A local watering hole that also attracts students where beer-chugging and pool-playing replace "traditional" study techniques. Beer $2-3. Happy hour M-Sa 3-9pm, Su 7-9pm. Open M-Sa 3pm-2:30am, Su 7pm-2:30am. MC/V.

Skully's Music Diner, 1151 N. High St. (☎614-291-8856). Diner decorated with guitars and leopard print with a stage in the back, where locally and nationally known bands perform. Fun dance club. Burgers from $6. Some healthy options like the portobello mushroom sandwich from $5. Open M-F 11am-2:30am, Sa noon-2:30am, Su 1pm-2:30am. Kitchen open M-W until 11pm, Th-Su until midnight.

Liquid, 1100 N. High St. (☎614-298-3000; www.liquidhotspot.com). The electric-blue liquid running down the bar provides a cool mood for trying the Malibu Barbie and her sour sister, the Malibu Bitch (rum with grenadine and pineapple or grapefruit; $6.25). Make-your-own pizza from $5. Various DJs spin F-Sa after 10pm. Brunch Su 11am-3pm. Open daily 11am-2am.

🎆 THE ROAD TO SPRINGFIELD: 44 MI.

From **Broad Street,** proceed west out of the downtown area on **US 40.** US 40 mostly bypasses the tiny towns; you can take Old US 40 for brief stretches to pass through Summerford and South Vienna, and (don't worry), you'll still end up back on US 40.

SPRINGFIELD ☎937

A town proud of its manufacturing heritage, Springfield is the proud home of Wittenberg University, the seat of Clark County, and the gateway to Buck Creek State Park. In 1983, Newsweek dubbed Springfield the "Most Typical City in the USA"—when we say all-American here, we mean it!

VITAL STATS
Population: 64,000
Tourist Office: Springfield Area Convention and Visitors Bureau, 20 S. Limestone St. #100 (☎937-325-7621 or 800-803-1553; www.greater-springfield.com). Open M-F 8am-5pm.
Library and Internet Access: Clark County Public Library, 201 S. Fountain Ave. (☎937-328-6903). Open M-F 9am-9pm, Sa 9am-6pm, Su 1-5pm.
Post Office: 150 N. Limestone St. (☎937-323-6498). Open M-F 8am-6pm, Sa 8am-1pm. **Postal Code:** 45501.

💥 ORIENTATION

In Springfield, **US 40 West** becomes **North Street** and runs one-way through town. One block south, **US 40 East** runs the other way as **Columbia Street.** The two are intersected by **Limestone Street,** which runs one-way north, and **Fountain Avenue,** which runs one-way south.

🏠 ACCOMMODATIONS

The Executive Inn, 325 W. Columbia St. (☎937-324-5601). Luxurious red and gold bedspreads in otherwise simple rooms. One of the most affordable options in town. Key deposit $5. Singles $40; doubles $45. D/MC/V. ❷

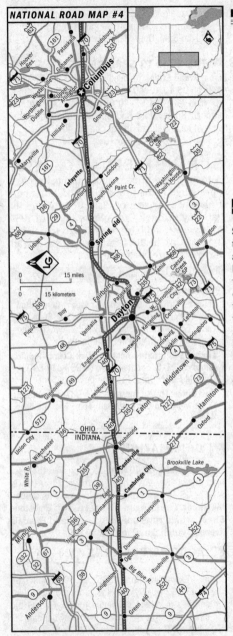

NATIONAL ROAD MAP #4

FOOD

Station One, 325 N. Fountain Ave. (☎937-324-3354). Locals flock to this neighborhood bar for its scrumptious sandwiches ($3-5), subs ($4-7), and pizza ($5-7). Hot dogs $2. Open M-Sa 11am-2:15am, Su 3pm-2:15am. Kitchen open until 9pm. AmEx/D/MC/V. ❶

Joe's US 40 Grille, 1205 W. North St. (☎937-323-3383; www.eatatjoes40.com). On your way out of town, watch for the retro neon lights. Comfort foods like meatloaf and mashed potatoes $7-8. Open M-F 8am-9pm, Sa 7am-9pm, Su 7am-7pm. AmEx/D/MC/V. ❷

SIGHTS

SPRINGFIELD MUSEUM OF ART. A collection of paintings by mostly American artists adorns the pastel-toned walls of the **Springfield Museum of Art.** The museum also exhibits the work of local high-school students and offers classes on everything from sculpture to photography. Check out the political popular culture room, with a huge statue of Uncle Sam and slippers shaped like President George HW and Barbara Bush. *(107 Cliff Park Rd. From North St., turn right on Fountain Ave., cross the small bridge, and take an immediate left onto Cliff Park Rd. ☎937-325-4673; www.spfld-museum-of-art.org. Open M-F 7am-4:30pm, Sa 7am-5pm, Su noon-4:30pm. $5, students and seniors $3. Galleries also open when the school is open; call in advance.)*

FRANK LLOYD WRIGHT WESTCOTT HOUSE. The large, prairie-style house is now open for guided tours. *(1340 E. High St., From North St., head south 2 blocks to High St. ☎937-327-9291; www. westcotthouse.org. Tours W-F 11am, 1, 3pm, Sa every hr. 11am-4pm, Su every hr. 1-4pm. Reservations recommended. $8.50, seniors $7, students $6.)*

THE ROAD TO DAYTON: 30 MI.

In Springfield, continue on **North Street,** following signs for **US 40 West,** which merges with **Route 4 South.** Stay on Rte. 4, which merges with **I-70 West.** Take I-70 W. 2 mi. to **I-675 South.** Continue to Exit 13 for **US 35 West.** Follow **US 35** to the exit for **Main Street/Jefferson Street/Route 48** and then watch for signs for Rte. 48 N. Follow Rte. 48 N. into town.

DAYTON ☎937

Nicknamed the "Gem City" and known as "the birthplace of aviation," Dayton has much to offer the passing roadtripper. Originally the home of the Wright brothers, Dayton's economy still revolves around the sprawling Wright-Patterson Air Force Base, but the city has attempted to take advantage of the recent centennial of the first human flight to reinvent itself as a tourist destination. While the city may at times seem aviation-obsessed, there are other diversions for those less interested in the history of air travel.

VITAL STATS
Population: 166,000
Tourist Office: Dayton/Montgomery County Convention and Visitors Bureau, 1 Chamber Plaza, Ste. A (☎937-226-8211), at 5th and Main St. Open M-F 8am-5:30pm.
Library and Internet Access: Dayton Metro Library, 215 E. 3rd St. (☎937-227-9500), at the corner of St. Clair. Open June-Aug. M-Th 9am-9pm, F-Sa 9am-5pm; Sept.-May M-Th 9am-9pm, F-Sa 9am-5pm, Su 1-5pm.
Post Office: 1111 E. 5th St. (☎937-227-1122). Open M-F 7am-6pm, Sa 8am-noon. **Postal Code:** 45401.

⚑ ORIENTATION

I-75 runs north-south through the city just west of downtown. **US 35**, a controlled-access highway for much of its length, runs east-west near downtown. **Route 48** runs primarily on **Main Street** north-south through the center of downtown. Numbered streets run east-west perpendicular to Main St., and **Monument Avenue** is one block north of **First Street**.

⚑ ACCOMMODATIONS

Econolodge, 2140 Edwin C. Moses Blvd. (☎937-222-9929), just west of Exit 51, on I-75. Some of the cheapest rooms in town. Continental breakfast included. Singles $59. MC/V. ❸

⚑ FOOD

⚑ Smokin Bar-B-Que, 200 E. 5th St. (☎937-586-9790; http://smokinbarbque.com).

Makes the entire intersection smell tantalizingly like hickory—your mouth will water from blocks away. Its ½ lb. burgers ($4) are slow smoked for hours. Open M-Th 10:30am-10pm, F-Sa 10:30am-4am. AmEx/D/MC/V. ❶

Flanagan's Pub, 101 E. Stewart St. (☎937-228-5776), near Broad St. For standard Irish fare, try this pub, where a lunch crowd gathers to enjoy burgers ($4-5) and beer. Drafts $2.75. Open M-Sa 11am-2:30am. Kitchen open until 8pm. AmEx/D/MC/V. ❶

⚑ SIGHTS

⚑UNITED STATES AIR FORCE MUSEUM. On the Wright-Patterson Air Force Base, visitors pour through the museum to see 300-odd aircrafts dating from the beginning of human flight. Also on site is the **National Aviation Hall of Fame.** View recent enshrinees or sign up to see the Presidential Aircraft Hangars. (*1100 Spaatz St. Follow I-70 E. to I-675, take Exit 15 for the Colonel Glenn Hwy., and follow the signs.* ☎937-255-3286; www.wpafb.af.mil. Open daily 9am-5pm. Free.)

WRIGHT BROTHERS AVIATION CENTER. At this center in **Carillon Historical Park,** the history of the Wright brothers is told in intricate detail. The center shows items that belonged to the Wright brothers, including their 1905 plane. (*☎937-293-2841. Open Tu-Sa 9:30am-5pm, Su noon-5pm. $8, seniors $7, ages 3-17 $5.*)

DAYTON ART INSTITUTE. Those tired of aviation paraphernalia will appreciate the castle-like Dayton Art Institute. In addition to some contemporary pieces, the institute displays Peter Rothermel's magnificent *King Lear,* created in 1858. Some smaller collections of Asian, African, European, and Native American art are also on display. One of the few mentions of the Wright brothers is a silver spiral sculpture outside, dedicated to their spirit, which seems to fly away. (*456 Belmonte Park N. Take Monument Ave. across the bridge and turn right onto Riverview Ave., then head left on Belmonte Park N.* ☎937-223-5277; www.daytonartinstitute.org. Open Tu-W and F-Su 10am-4pm, Th 10am-8pm. Free.)

SUNWATCH PREHISTORIC INDIAN VILLAGE. Archaeologists have reconstructed a Native American village that dates back 800 years. (*2301 W. River Rd. From Edwin C. Moses Blvd.*

downtown, turn left and head southwest under the I-75 exits. After 3 lights, turn left onto W. River Rd. ☎937-268-8199; www.sunwatch.org. Open Tu-Sa 9am-5pm, Su noon-5pm. $5, ages 6-17 $3.)

⚑ THE ROAD TO CENTERVILLE: 49 MI.

Head north on **Route 48**, which joins **US 40 West** for a brief stretch, and then take a left at the **National Road/US 40** sign. Fill up your tank at the Indiana border; there are few gas stations for the next 28 mi. Then continue on **US 40** for another 5 mi. toward Centerville. The stretch of US 40 from Richmond to Knightstown, including Centerville and Cambridge City, forms part of Indiana's so-called Antique Alley.

The Hoosier State
INDIANA
Welcomes You!

NATIONAL ROAD

CENTERVILLE ☎765

As you enter Centerville, venture to **Webb's Antique Mall**, 200 W. Union St., which hosts an 85,000 sq. ft. collection of antique merchants. At the traffic light, turn right on Morton St., then take a left on Union St. (☎765-855-5551; www.webbsantiquemalls.com. Open daily Mar.-Nov. 8am-6pm; Dec.-Feb. 9am-5pm.)

Rooms are small but clean at the **Richmond Motel ❷**, 793 E. Main St., US 40 E., 5 mi. from Richmond. (☎765-855-5616. Rooms $34. MC/V.) The **City View Motel ❷**, 5149 US 40, 3 mi. from Richmond, also has small and affordable rooms with more character than most rooms in chain motels. (☎765-962-2943. Doubles $30. AmEx/D/MC/V.) The antique mall is also home to the **Station Stop Restaurant ❶**, a well-located eatery with kitschy decor. (☎765-855-5551. Sandwiches $4-8. Pie $3. Open M-F 11am-2:30pm, Sa-Su 11am-3:30pm. D/MC/V.) While the Station Stop is open daily as part of the antique mall, other restaurants in Centerville are open only on the weekends (to serve antique-hunters).

⚑ THE ROAD TO CAMBRIDGE CITY: 10 MI.

Continue west on **US 40** toward Cambridge City, where US 40 becomes **East Main Street**.

CAMBRIDGE CITY ☎765

Six native sisters of Cambridge City helped turn pottery into an American art form. A small collection of their vaunted work is on display at the **Museum of Overbeck Art Pottery**, 33 W. Main St. (US 40), in the Cambridge City Public Library. (☎765-478-3335. Open M-Sa 10am-noon and 2-5pm or by appointment. Free.) The **Hilltop Drive-In ❶**, 705 W. Main St., offers cheap and casual meals on a scenic hilltop, with limited seating on park benches. It boasts nine flavors of milkshakes for $2.50, hamburgers for $2.25, and other sandwiches for $2-4. (☎765-478-5880. Open M-Sa 11am-9pm, Su noon-9pm. Cash only.)

⚑ THE ROAD TO NEW CASTLE: 8 MI.

Take **US 40** to **Route 3 North**.

NEW CASTLE ☎765

New Castle is home to the **Indiana Basketball Hall of Fame**, 1 Trojan Ln., which glorifies hoops and the best Hoosiers to play the game, including Larry Bird, George McGinnis, and Kent Benson. Turn right on Trojan Ln. as you go north on Rte. 3; the museum is on the left. (☎765-529-1891. Open M-Sa 10am-5pm, Su 1-5pm. $5, children $3.) The **New Castle Inn ❷**, 2005 S. Memorial Dr., has big rooms and a great location—right next to the Basketball Hall of Fame. (☎765-529-1670. Rooms $41. Cash only.) The **Steve Alford All-American Inn ❸**, 21 E. Executive Dr., off Memorial Dr. (Rte. 3), offers cozy rooms adorned with lots of basketball memorabilia and has two hoops in the parking lot. (☎765-593-1212. Free Wi-Fi. Singles $55; doubles $60. MC/V.)

⚑ THE ROAD TO INDIANAPOLIS: 48 MI.

Take **Route 3 South** to **US 40 West**. When you reach the beltway, head north on **I-465** to the exit for **I-70**. Follow **I-70 West** to **East Ohio Street**.

INDIANAPOLIS ☎317

Surrounded by flat farmland, Indianapolis feels like a model Midwestern city. Locals shop and work all day among downtown's skyscrapers before returning to sprawling suburbia. Life ambles here—until May, that is, when 250,000 spectators invade the city and the road warriors of the Indianapolis 500 claim the spotlight. Historically, Indianapolis's nicknames "Napville" and "India No Place" have seemed merited; however, the state government recently resolved to build a cultural infrastructure that would outlast the seasonal boom of the Indianapolis 500.

VITAL STATS
Population: 785,000
Tourist Office: Indianapolis Convention and Visitors Association, 30 S. Meridian St., Ste. 410 (☎317-639-4282; www.indy.org). Open M-F 8:30am-5pm.
Library and Internet Access: Indianapolis/Marion County Interim Public Library, entrances at 40 E. St. Clair St. and 1 Library Plaza (☎317-275-4100). Open M-Th 9am-9pm, F 9am-6pm, Sa 9am-5pm, Su 1-5pm.
Post Office: 125 W. South St. (☎317-262-1870). Open M 7:30am-4:30pm, Tu-F 8:30am-4pm. **Postal Code:** 46204.

ORIENTATION

While most attractions are within several miles of city center, Indianapolis lends itself more to driving than to walking. The only areas of the city that are pedestrian-friendly are **Market Street** and **Monument Circle.** The downtown, called **Center City,** is marked by a dense cluster of skyscrapers. **Washington Street** divides the city north-south; **Meridian Street** divides it east-west. The two meet just south of Monument Cir. downtown. **I-465** circles the city, while **I-70** cuts through the city east-west. Outside the beltway (I-465) both east and west of the city, Washington St. is **US 40.** Metered parking is abundant almost everywhere along Indianapolis's wide, straight streets, including downtown and near **Circle Centre Mall.**

ACCOMMODATIONS

Budget motels line I-465, 5 mi. from downtown. Make reservations up to a year in advance for the Indy 500. Smaller budget hotels line US 40 both east and west of town.

All Nations Bed and Breakfast, 2164 N. Capitol Ave. (☎317-923-2622), 1.5 mi. north of downtown. Large, tastefully decorated rooms with themes stemming from various countries, including China, Zimbabwe, and Ireland. Attracts a fun international crowd. The staff has been known to make brownies for guests. Each reasonably priced room has a private bath, and some have sofa beds. Free Wi-Fi. Rooms $75-100. ❹

FOOD

Ethnic food stands, produce markets, and knick-knack vendors fill the spacious **City Market,** 222 E. Market St., a renovated 19th-century building. (☎317-634-9266; www.indianapoliscm.com. Open M-F 6am-6pm, Sa 8am-4pm.) Moderately priced restaurants cluster in Indianapolis's newly constructed **Circle Centre,** 49 W. Maryland St. (☎317-681-8000). **Massachusetts Avenue** is home to some of the liveliest restaurants and bars in town; in the summer, outdoor patios hum with restaurant-goers' dinner table conversation.

Bazbeaux Pizza, 334 Massachusetts Ave. (☎317-636-7662). Other locations at 111 W. Main St. in Carmel and 811 E. Westfields Blvd. Hugely popular pizza joint, where you can specify thick or thin crust and construct your own masterpiece ($7.25) from 54 toppings, including Cajun shrimp and hearts of palm. Open M-Th and Su 11am-10pm, F-Sa 11am-11pm. MC/V. ❷

The Bosphorous, 935 S. East St. (☎317-974-1770; www.bosphorouscafe.com). Authentic Turkish and Mediterranean food at reasonable prices. Plenty of intriguing choices like the stuffed eggplant ($12). The real *doner kebab* is better than your local street stand's. Lunch specials $8.50. Open M-Th 11am-9pm, F 11am-10pm, Sa noon-10pm, Su noon-8pm. AmEx/D/MC/V. ❸

Shapiro's, 808 S. Meridian St. (☎317-631-4041; www.shapiros.com). Head south on Meridian St. past South St. When it diverts onto Madison St., take a quick right on Henry St. and then a quick left to get back on Meridian St. Shapiro's is a large and pleasant cafeteria-style restaurant with huge sandwiches ($7-10). Features Jewish comfort food like matzah ball soup ($4) and pastries like rugelach and elephant ears. Open daily 6:30am-8pm. AmEx/D/MC/V. ❷

Union Jack Pub, 6225 W. 25th St. (☎317-243-3300) and 924 Broad Ripple Ave. (☎317-257-4343). From I-465, take Exit 16A and head east on Crawfordsville Rd. Turn left onto High School Rd., then right onto 25th St. Despite the pub's name, about the only British item on the menu is fish and

NATIONAL ROAD

TO SPEEDWAY, (4mi)

16th St.

TO (.5mi)

TO INDIANAPOLIS CHILDREN'S MUSEUM (6.3mi)

TO INDIANAPOLIS MUSEUM OF ART (2.5mi)

TO (4mi), BROAD RIPPLE (6mi)

15th St.
14th St.
Cora St.
Smith St.
13th St.
12th St.

Fall Creek Pkwy. East Dr.
Ransom St.
13th St.
Drake St.
12th St.
11th St.
10th St.

Brooks St.

Crispus Attucks Museum

Dr. Martin Luther King Jr. St.
California St.
Fayette St.

University Blvd.
Indiana Ave.
Brackford St.

9th St.
St. Clair
Walnut St.

Walker Theater
North St.
Michigan St.

West St.
Senate Ave.
Roanoke St.
Indiana Ave.

CANAL WALK DISTRICT

Indiana University Purdue University Indianapolis

Vermon St.
Tippecanoe St.

New York St.

Military Park

Allegheny St.

Capitol Ave.
Illinois St.
Pierson St.
Meridian St.

University Park

Ohio St.

St. Joseph St.
Sahm St.

MASSACHUSETTS AVENUE ARTS DISTRICT

St. Clair

Fort Wayne St.
Alabama St.
New Jersey St.
Massachusetts Ave.
East St.
Park Ave.
Fulton St.
Spring St.

North St.

Hudson St.
Michigan St.

15th St.
14th St.
13th St.

College Ave.

11th St.
10th St.
Puryear St.

New York St.

Talbott St.
Delaware St.
Pennsylvania St.

Cleveland St.
Miami St.

College Ave.

Wabash St.

Market St.
Monument Circle

State House

Court St.

Hilbert Circle Theater

City Market
Market St.

Washington St.
Pearl St.

Pine St.

NCAA Hall of Champions
Washington Ave.

Eiteljorg Museum

Indiana State Museum
Washington St.

Circle Centre Mall

WHOLESALE DISTRICT

WHITE RIVER STATE PARK

Maryland St.

Scioto St.

Davidson St.
Concordia St.

TO INDIANAPOLIS ZOO (3.4mi)

Chesapeake St.
Georgia St.

Conseco Fieldhouse

Virginia Ave.

Louisiana St.
Lord St.

RCA Dome

Jackson Pl.

Fletcher Ave.
Lexington Ave.
Elm St.

Union Station

Calvary St.

West St.

South St.

Henry St.

Madison Ave.

South St.
Empire St.
Henry St.

Merrill St.

Stevens St.

Meridian St.

McCarty St.
Wyoming St.

Delaware St.

McCarty St.

Buchanan St.

Ray St.

200 yards
200 meters

Virginia Ave.

Prospect St.

Morris St.
Kansas St.

Morris St.
Sanders St.

Indianapolis

▲ ▲ ACCOMMODATIONS
All Nations Bed and Breakfast, **3**
Indiana State Fair Campgrounds, **6**
Motel 6, **1**

🍎 FOOD
Bazbeaux Pizza, **8**
The Bosphorous, **11**
Shapiro's, **10**
Union Jack Pub, **2** & **5**

🍸 NIGHTLIFE
The Jazz Cooker, **7**
The Slippery Noodle, **9**
Vogue, **4**

chips ($10). In reality, this cozy spot showcases American sports; decorations include race memorabilia, rows of drivers' helmets, and even an Indy racecar. Chicago-style pizzas $16-20. Mile-high cheesecake $5.30. Domestic drafts from $2.50. Open M-W 11am-11pm, Th-Sa 11am-midnight, Su noon-11pm. AmEx/D/MC/V. ❸

🖸 SIGHTS

EITELJORG MUSEUM OF AMERICAN INDIANS AND WESTERN ART. Near the entrance to the White River State Park, this museum features an impressive collection of art depicting the Old West, including works by Georgia O'Keeffe, Frederick Remington, Thomas Hart Benton, and Andy Warhol. The museum also highlights a collection of Native American artifacts. The works and the eloquent texts accompanying them address the West's promise of adventure, romance and glory. *(500 W. Washington St. ☎317-636-9378; www.eiteljorg.org. Open M-Sa 10am-5pm, Su noon-5pm. Tours daily 1pm. $8, students, ages 5-17 $5, seniors $7.)*

INDIANAPOLIS MUSEUM OF ART (IMA). Not far from downtown, the IMA showcases American, African, Asian, and Neo-Impressionist works along with 152 acres of nature trails, a historic 1930s home, botanical gardens, a greenhouse, and a theater. The IMA is the fifth-largest general collection in the country and has a variety of interesting, well-curated exhibits. The **Art and Nature Park,** a facility for emerging artists, will open in 2009. Fashionistas will enjoy the collection of women's costumes from 19th and 20th-century Europe and America. *(4000 Michigan Rd. ☎317-923-1331; www.imamuseum.org. Open Tu-W and Sa 11am-5pm, Th-F 11am-9pm, Su noon-5pm. Free.)*

CRISPUS ATTUCKS MUSEUM. This museum chronicles the history of the Crispus Attucks High School, formed in 1927 to educate African-Americans in Indianapolis. *(1140 Dr. Martin Luther King, Jr., St., on the Crispus Attucks Medical Magnet High School campus. Look for the visitor entrance; enter the office and ask to be let in. ☎317-226-2432. Open M-F 9am-4pm. Free.)*

INDIANAPOLIS MOTOR SPEEDWAY. The country's passion for fast cars peaks during the **500 Festival,** an entire month of parades and hoopla

leading up to race day at the Indianapolis Motor Speedway. The festivities begin with time trials in mid-May and culminate with the "Gentlemen, start your engines" of the Indianapolis 500 the Sunday before Memorial Day. Tickets for the race go on sale the day after the previous year's race and usually sell out within a week. In quieter times, buses full of tourists drive around the 2 mi. track at tamer speeds for a nominal charge. *(4790 W. 16th St., off I-465 at the Speedway exit. ☎317-481-8500 or 492-8500; www.indy500.com. Track tours daily 9am-4:40pm. $3, ages 6-15 $1.)* The **Speedway Museum,** at the south end of the infield, includes the Indy 500 Hall of Fame and a collection of cars that have tested their mettle on the track. *(☎317-492-6784. Open daily 9am-5pm. $3, ages 6-15 $1.)*

🎵 ENTERTAINMENT

The **Walker Theatre,** 617 Indiana Ave., used to house the headquarters of African-American entrepreneur Madame CJ Walker's beauty enterprise. Today, the landmark hosts arts programs, including the monthly **Jazz on the Avenue** event. (☎317-236-2099. Open M-F 9am-5pm. Tours by appointment. Jazz 4th F of every month 6-10pm. $10.) The **Indianapolis Symphony Orchestra** performs from late June to August in the **Hilbert Circle Theater** on Monument Cir. (☎317-639-4300; www.indyorch.org. Box office open M-F 9am-5pm, Sa 10am-2pm; also and 2hr. prior to events.) Basketball lovers watch the **Pacers** hoop it up at the **Conseco Fieldhouse,** 125 S. Pennsylvania St. (☎317-917-2500. Tickets from $10.) The WNBA's **Indiana Fever** take over in the summer. (☎317-239-5151. Tickets $8-90.) Football's **Colts** hit the gridiron at the **RCA Dome,** 100 S. Capitol Ave. (☎317-239-5151.)

🖸 NIGHTLIFE

Although somewhat bland by day, the Broad Ripple area, 7 mi. north of downtown at College Ave. and 62nd St., transforms into a center for nightlife after dark. Revelers fill the clubs and bars and spill out onto the sidewalks until about 1am on weekdays and usually 3am on weekends.

The Jazz Cooker, 925 E. Westfield Blvd. (☎317-253-2883; www.thejazzcooker.com). Heats up when the live bands begin jamming.

NATIONAL ROAD

The attached Monkey's Tale is a nice, relaxed bar. Check website for shows. Live music F-Su 7-10pm. Bar open M-Sa until 3am, Su until 12:30am. AmEx/D/MC/V.

Vogue, 6259 N. College Ave. (☎317-254-2727). Midsize venue hosts rock and indie concerts for mostly-young audiences. Not-quite-daily shows start between 7-9pm; call for schedule. Ladies free Sa until 11:30pm. Regional acts F. Cover $3-5. Bar open W and F-Sa 10pm-3am. MC/V.

⚑ THE ROAD TO TERRE HAUTE: 71 MI.

Head west on **Washington Street;** it becomes **US 40** after crossing the beltway **(I-465).** US 40 becomes **Wabash Avenue** toward **Terre Haute.**

TERRE HAUTE ☎812

Terre Haute was once called the "crossroads of America" by virtue of its existence at the junction of US 40 and US 41, which runs north-south. Deceptively large, the city today retains only a shadow of its former importance. Industry powers the area close to downtown, but outlying areas have become a little more run-down. Further outside are the flat fields of the Midwest.

✴ ORIENTATION

US 40 and **US 41** (locally 3rd Street) intersect in downtown Terre Haute. US 40 heads east-west, while US 41 heads north-south. The **Wabash River** borders town to the west.

VITAL STATS
Population: 60,600
Tourist Office: Terre Haute Visitors Center, 2155 Rte. 46 (☎812-234-5555). From US 40 W., turn left on Rte. 46. Open M-F 8am-4pm.
Library and Internet Access: Vigo County Public Library, 1 Library Sq. (☎812-232-1113). Open M-Th 9am-9pm, F 9am-6pm, Sa 9am-5pm, Su 1-5pm.
Post Office: 70 Rose Ave. (☎812-232-9133). Open M-F 7:30am-4:30pm, Sa 8:30am-noon. **Postal Code:** 47803.

⌂ ACCOMMODATIONS

Regency Inn & Suites, 400 S. 3rd St. (☎812-232-0383). Comfortable, spacious, and close to both US 40 and the center of town. Singles $38; doubles $48. D/MC/V. ❷

The Woodbridge Motel, 4425 Wabash Ave. (☎812-877-1571). A great alternative to the chain motels a few miles away. Singles $40; doubles $45. D/MC/V. ❷

🍴 FOOD

Gerhardt's Bierstube, 1724 Lafayette Ave. (☎812-466-9249). From downtown, head north on 7th St. to Lafayette Ave. and turn right. The eatery's founder was a German immigrant whose ghost is still blamed for dropped glasses. German music and beer complement menu items like sausage (4 kinds, $8 each). Lunch specials include hot sandwiches with wurst for $6.50. Open Tu-Th 11am-2pm and 4-9pm, F 11am-2pm and 4-10pm, Sa 4-10pm. AmEx/D/MC/V. ❸

Coffee Cup Family Restaurant, 1512 Lafayette Ave. and 2919 S. 3rd St. (☎812-466-7200). Serves typical, cheap American fare like hamburgers ($3.50) and sandwiches ($3.50-6) as well as some classier options like the Alpine burger with sauteed mushrooms, bacon, and Swiss cheese ($5). Open daily 6am-9pm. MC/V. ❶

Bella Rossa, 669 Wabash Ave. (☎812-234-3663). Downtown. Serves Italian sandwiches with huge portions of mozzarella. Has several vegan and vegetarian options. Half-portions go for $3.50, whole $5.50. Open M-F 11am-6pm, Sa 10am-4pm. AmEx/D/MC/V. ❶

👁 SIGHTS

SWOPES ART MUSEUM. The Swopes museum includes works by artists such as Edward Hopper, Grant Wood (of *American Gothic* fame), Andy Warhol, and Robert Motherwell. (*25 S. 7th St. ☎812-238-1676. Open Tu-F 10am-5pm, Sa noon-5pm. Free.*)

CLABBER GIRL MUSEUM. Quite a bit of self-glorification goes on at this museum, which waxes poetic about all that Hulman & Co. has done for the American homemaker. The museum's founder, the museum informs visitors, "helped organize and was a member of the Terre Haute Telephone Exchange." A demonstration illustrates the process of manufacturing baking powder, but stay seated; even more thrilling are the museum's collection of old telephones and telegraphs, a display of an early-20th-century kitchen, and World War II-era posters and goods. *(900 Wabash Ave., at 9th St. ☎812-478-7223; www.clabbergirl.com. Open M-F 10am-6pm, Sa 9am-3pm. Free tours by appointment. Tour plus sugar cookie and milk $5.)*

🖪 THE ROAD TO MARSHALL: 15 MI.

Hop on **US 40 West** 1 mi. past **Third Street.** There is an unlabeled curve—follow it around to the left and merge with **I-70.** Rejoin US 40 in about 2 mi. Fourteen miles from Terre Haute, turn left at the sign for **Marshall/Historic National Road.**

 TIME CHANGE. Set your clocks back 1hr. once you cross the border into Illinois; you are now in the Central Time Zone.

The Land of Lincoln
ILLINOIS
Welcomes You!

MARSHALL   ☎217

The small town of Marshall is home to the inviting **Lincoln Trail State Park.** This 1000-acre enchanting beech wood offers fishing, picnicking, and inexpensive **camping ❶** around a 146-acre lake. Two kinds of wildflowers can be found here that, unlike most plants, have no chlorophyll. From the center of town, head south on Rte. 1 for 3 mi. *(☎217-826-2222. No swimming. Sites $20-30.)* For a good night's rest indoors, an affordable option with clean, simple rooms is the **Relax Inn ❷,** 107 E. Trefz Dr. The rooms are lovely and large, with maroon bedspreads, refrigerators, and microwaves. *(☎217-826-3031. Singles $45; doubles $58. AmEx/D/MC/V.)*

The **Lincoln Trail Restaurant ❷,** 16985 1350th Rd., is a convenient spot for a hot meal while you're exploring the park or camping. The restaurant serves up BLTs ($4.50), cod filet ($4.50), and more. Follow the signs from inside the park. *(☎217-826-8831. Homemade pastries $2. Open daily 6am-8pm. AmEx/D/MC/V.)* **Bishop's Cafe ❶,** 710 Archer Ave., is the

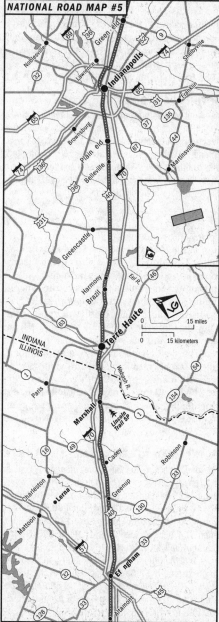

NATIONAL ROAD MAP #5

NATIONAL ROAD

home cooking that you've been hungering for. Locals come for the baskets ($6), which include sandwiches with fries and slaw. Breakfast ($3-5) is served until 10:30am, and one pancake costs $1.75—but, really, who eats one pancake? (☎217-826-9933. Open M-Sa 5am-1:30pm, Su 6am-2pm. Cash only.)

THE ROAD TO LERNA: 53 MI.

Head out of town on **Archer Avenue**; it rejoins **US 40**. Continuing west, follow the sign for the **National Road** heading into Greenup. Take **Route 130 North** to Lerna. For the log cabin, turn left on **Route 16** in Charleston, take another left on **Fourth Street**, and follow Fourth St. as it curves to the right to become **Lincoln Highway**. The log cabin will be on the left.

LERNA ☎217

Lerna's most noteworthy (read: only) attraction is the **Lincoln Log Cabin State Historic Site**, 400 S. Lincoln Hwy. Rd. At this living history museum and working 1840s farm, first-person interpreters become members of the Lincoln family and their wealthy neighbors, the Sargents, complete with 1845 twangy accents. They maintain the farm using techniques from the period and answer questions in character. The wonderfully friendly staff members run a 10min. movie inside the visitors center, which is decorated with valuable quilts. (☎217-345-1845; www.lincolnlogcabin.org. Open daily 8am-dusk. Living history program operates Apr.-Oct. W-Su 9am-5pm; Nov.-Mar. W-Su 9am-4pm. Free.)

THE ROAD TO EFFINGHAM: 50 MI.

The road from Lerna to Effingham is notoriously confusing. Leaving the log cabin, head north on **North County Road 1420 East** toward **East County Road 80 North**. Make a slight left at **East County Road 80 North**. After 2 mi., turn left at **North County Road 1200 East**. Soon after, turn right at **East County Road 000 North/County Road 1400 North/Trilla Road**. Continue for 7 mi. and then turn left at **US 45**. After 5 mi., turn left to merge onto **I-57 South**. Take **Exit 162** for US 45 toward Sigel/Effingham. Turn left at **US 45 South** and, after 2 mi., turn left at **East Fayette Avenue/Route 33/US 40**. Follow US 40 to **Route 33**.

EFFINGHAM ☎217

Effingham is surprisingly cosmopolitan considering its rural location. Locals hang out in the proud shadow of a 198 ft. tall steel cross that stands on the outskirts of town.

VITAL STATS
Population: 12,400
Tourist Office: Convention and Visitors Bureau, 210 E. Jefferson Ave. (☎217-342-5310 or 800-772-0750), 2nd fl. of City Hall, at the corner of 3rd St.
Library and Internet Access: Helen Matthes Library, 100 E. Market Ave. (☎217-342-2464). Take N. 3rd St. from Fayette Ave. and turn left at the sign. Open M-Th 9am-8pm, F-Sa 9am-5pm.
Post Office: 210 N. 3rd St. (☎217-342-6016). Open M-F 7:30am-5:30pm, Sa 8:30am-12:30pm. **Postal Code:** 62401.

ORIENTATION

Main east-west streets in Effingham include **Fayette Avenue (US 40), Jefferson Avenue,** and **Washington Avenue,** each of which is lined with shops and restaurants. Jefferson Ave. runs one-way east between Banker St. and Third St., while Washington Ave. runs one-way west. The main north-south thoroughfare through the center of town is **Third Street (Route 45).** At the western edge of downtown is **Keller Drive** (which is named Henrietta St. on the other side of Fayette Ave.), another main drag. There is free 2hr. street parking in the downtown area; most establishments have parking lots. Parking is almost never a problem.

ACCOMMODATIONS

Paradise Inn, 1000 W. Fayette Ave./US 40 (☎217-342-2165). Offers large, well-maintained rooms not far from downtown. Singles $37; doubles $47. D/MC/V. ❷

Abe Lincoln Motel, 1108 W. Edgar Ave. (☎217-342-4717). The cheapest rates in town. Singles $32; doubles $35. ❷

FOOD

El Rancherito, 1313 Keller Dr. (☎217-342-4753). Take W. Fayette Ave. heading west out of downtown and turn right on Keller Dr. Huge portions of sizzling hot, authentic, and non-greasy Mexican food are guaranteed to stuff and satisfy even the hungriest roadtripper. Try a skillet of mouthwatering fajitas ($10) or one of the combination dinners ($7)—any 3 of *chile relleno*, burrito, taco, tostado, chalupa, tamal, or enchilada. The painted booths add a festive touch. Lunch $3.50-6. Open M-Th 11am-9:30pm, F-Su 11am-10pm. D/MC/V. ❷

Niemerg's Steak House, 1410 W. Fayette Ave. (☎217-342-3921). Steak, steak, steak, and more steak. A smattering of other options includes fish dinner specials ($7-9), eggs ($2), and the special "country-fried chicken dinner" for $6. Try to save room for a slice of homemade pie (choose from 17 flavors, including peanut butter and cherry cheesecake; $2) for dessert. Su brunch buffet $4.60. Open daily 6am-2am. AmEx/D/MC/V. ❸

🄖 SIGHTS

◪CROSS AT THE CROSSROADS. It's visible from US 40 on the way out of town, but, for the full experience, you have to drive up close to the Cross at the Crossroads. On the outskirts of Effingham, this gargantuan 181-ton steel cross stands a whopping 198 ft. tall and 113 ft. across, surrounded by black stone monuments representing each of the 10 commandments. Quite simply, this "world's biggest" has to be seen to be believed. There is also a 10min. movie about how the cross was built, complete with New Age music. *(Off Pike Ave. Take W. Fayette St. out of downtown turn left on Raney St., then right on Pike Ave. ☎ 217-347-2846; www.cross-susa.org. Visitors center open daily Apr.-Oct. 10am-7pm; Nov.-Mar. 10am-4pm.)*

◪MIKE YAGER MID-AMERICA DESIGNS CORVETTE MUSEUM. The 20-odd pristine Corvettes at the Mike Yager Mid-America Designs Corvette Museum is enough to make any car buff drool. The walls are almost as fun as the cars; the airplane-hangar-size garage is set up with 1950s and 60s-style wall decorations and storefronts. Ask about Funfests, at which thousands of cars descend on the town for some serious partying. The **Volkswagon Funfest** takes place the first weekend of June, and the much larger **Corvette Funfest** takes place around the third weekend of September. *(17082 N. US 45. Take N. 3rd St.; the museum is on your right. ☎ 217-540-4277; www.mamotorworks.com. Open M-Sa 8am-5pm. Free.)*

🄖 THE ROAD TO VANDALIA: 33 MI.

Follow **US 40** out of Effingham. The big Effing cross is to the left after you turn right off **Henrietta Street** and onto the **Old National Road.** US 40 turns right in Vandalia; proceed straight at the National Rd. sign for one block on **Gallatin Avenue** until you reach the **Madonna of the Trails Statue.** This statue marks the original end of the former National Rd. that ran from Cumberland, Maryland, to Vandalia, Illinois.

VANDALIA   ☎618

It's hard to believe that tiny Vandalia was once the capital of Illinois. The **Vandalia Statehouse State Historic Site,** 315 W. Gallatin St., at the corner of Third St., however, manifests the city's rich history. The imposing white-painted brick building was the Illinois State House from 1836 to 1839 and was where Abraham Lincoln first served as a state representative. The building is now open for tours. (☎618-283-1161. Open Tu-Sa 9am-5pm. Suggested donation $4, under 17 $2.) Across the street is tiny **Lincoln Park,** complete with a statue of a young Abraham Lincoln sitting on a bench. Two blocks from the State House, the **Evans Public Library,** 215 S. Fifth St., houses a reproduction of artist Leonard Volk's life mask of Abraham Lincoln. The real (and eerie) thing sits in the Lincoln Room at the State House. (☎618-283-2824. Free Internet. Open M-Th 9am-7pm, F-Sa 9am-5pm.) You'll find what you're thirsting for at the **Something Special Soda Fountain and 50s Cafe ❶**, on the corner of Fourth and Gallatin St. You'll need to suck hard to get one of its thick milkshakes ($3.75) through the straw. (☎618-283-1810. Open M-F 9am-5pm, Sa 9am-noon. MC/V.)

🄖 THE ROAD TO GREENVILLE: 20 MI.

Follow **US 140 West/Historic National Road** out of town; at first it's called **West Saint Louis Avenue.** Turn right to go north on **Route 127,** toward Greenville.

GREENVILLE   ☎618

This small town—the county seat of Bond County and home to picturesque Greenville College—calls itself a "Norman Rockwell town." The description is apt. The hamlet pre-

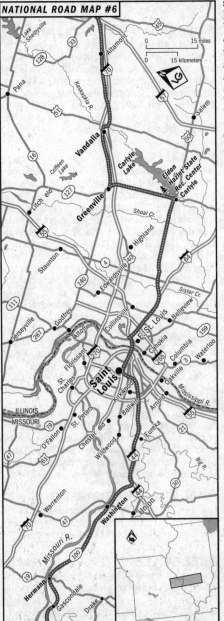

NATIONAL ROAD MAP #6

serves the work of Illinois sculptor Richard Bock, who worked closely with Frank Lloyd Wright, in the **Richard W. Bock Sculpture Museum,** on E. College Ave., just before the intersection with Spruce St. The museum houses around 300 of Bock's sculptures, plasters, and bronzes as well as 500 of his sketches. (☎618-664-6724; www.greenvilleusa.org/bock.htm. Open by appointment only. Free.) You'll find large and affordable rooms at the **Budget Host Inn ❷,** 1525 S. Rte. 127, near US 40. The inn has 50 rooms that have bedspreads of a green and white floral design, desks, and chairs. (☎618-664-1950. Singles $36; doubles $48. AmEx/D/MC/V.) Close to the museum, the **Bakery Nook ❶,** 303 W. Main St., offers delicious pastries and breakfast food. (☎618-664-3797. Large cinnamon rolls $1.60. Omelets from $3.70. Open W-Su 5am-2pm. MC/V.)

THE ROAD TO CARLYLE LAKE: 21 MI.
Take **Route 127 South** until you reach Carlyle.

CARLYLE LAKE ☎618

Carlyle Lake is second only to Chicago as the most visited place in Illinois. The visitors center shows a 10min. (and rather biased) video about how the lake was made and the beauty of controlling nature. State parks and campsites operated by the US Army Corps of Engineers encircle the 26,000-acre manmade lake, each with its own combination of camping, sailing, fishing, hunting, boating, and swimming facilities. Strong winds make for especially challenging sailing on the lake. The small county seat of Carlyle, at the southwest corner of the lake, serves park users.

VITAL STATS
Population: 3500
Tourist Office: Carlyle Lake Visitors Center, 801 Lake Rd. (☎618-594-5253), east off Rte. 127. Open in summer daily 10am-6pm.
Library and Internet Access: Case-Halstead Library, 571 Franklin St. (☎618-594-5210), at 6th St. Open M-Th noon-8pm, F-Sa 9am-2pm.
Post Office: 1080 Fairfax St. (☎618-594-3322), at 11th St. Open M-F 9am-5pm, Sa 9am-11pm. **Postal Code:** 62231.

✴ ORIENTATION

Carlyle Lake occupies three counties; primary access points include those near the towns of **Carlyle, Keyesport,** and **Boulder. Eldon Hazlet State Park** is 4 mi. north of Carlyle off Rte. 127. The **Dam West, Dam East,** and **McNair** areas lie just north of the town of Carlyle, while the **Coles Creek** facility and **South Shore State Park** both lie on the southeastern shore of the lake between Carlyle and Boulder.

In the town of Carlyle, **Route 127** runs north-south through downtown as **12th Street;** getting to most places requires turning off Rte. 127 before this point, so check out directions in advance to avoid having to backtrack. All north-south streets in town are numbered, from **First Street** in the east to **24th Street** in the west. **US 50** joins with Rte. 127 and runs north-south above **Franklin Street,** meeting it on the way out of town. Most restaurants and services are concentrated along Franklin St. or **Fairfax Street,** one block north. If you take Fairfax St. all the way east to the river, you'll get a nice view from the wobbly suspension bridge, built in 1859 and used for 70 years. You can still walk across it and read about its history and one-time collapse.

⚑ ACCOMMODATIONS

Campsites ❶ are mostly scattered near the lake, with a few abutting the lakefront directly; these offer shady trees and gorgeous views across the water. Only 65 sites allow reservations; the rest are first come, first served. Sites are often booked solid on summer weekends in June and July. (☎618-594-3015. Sites $8, with hookup $20. Cabins $35. Cash only.) Two campgrounds here are run by the US Army Corps of Engineers. **Coles Creek ❶** has 148 campsites, a beach, showers, and laundry. (Sites $14-24. Cash only, or reserve ahead of time with AmEx/D/MC/V.) **McNair ❶**, has 32 sites and a beach. (☎877-444-6777. Sites $14. Cash only.) The **Sunset Motel ❷**, 1631 Franklin St., at 16th, has indoor accommodations, which, unlike the campgrounds, make it extremely difficult to watch the sunset. (☎618-594-2888. Singles $40. AmEx/D/MC/V.)

🍴 FOOD

Lighthouse Grill, 5 Resort Dr. (☎618-594-8411). The grill has a good view of the boats moored in the nearby lake. With a log-cabin exterior and simple interior, the diner was built to accommodate the growing tourist crowd. The varied dinner menu includes pasta (from $9), ¼ fried chicken ($8), and walleye ($8.50). Open M-Th and Su 6am-9pm, F-Sa 6am-10pm. AmEx/D/MC/V. ❷

Fifties Cruiser's Diner, 911 Fairfax St. (☎618-594-5940). The diner takes you back to a time when life was no less complicated but rock and roll was a lot more fun. Famous for its walleye ($8) and crispy fried chicken salad ($6). Specials with 2 sides from $6-9. Open M-Th 10:30am-8pm, F-Sa 10:30am-9pm, Su 7am-8pm. AmEx/D/MC/V. ❷

Patrick's, 870 Franklin St. (☎618-594-8115), at 9th St. More elegant than your average Irish pub. Dishes like pork chops, prime rib, and baked roughy fill the menu. Open M-Th and Su 4-9pm, F-Sa 4-10pm. AmEx/D/MC/V. ❸

⚠ OUTDOORS

Eldon Hazlet State Park (☎618-594-3015 or 594-2484). From Rte. 127, head east on Hazlet Park Rd. Attracts families for summer lakeside getaways. Park day use is free, and the lake is stocked with farm-raised fish. Hunting is permitted in winter. Swimming pool $4. Visitors center open daily 10am-6pm.

⚑ THE ROAD TO ST. LOUIS: 50 MI.

Take **US 50 West;** at the large highway split, stay left towards **I-64** to St. Louis. Take the first exit for the **Martin Luther King, Jr., Memorial Bridge** toward the center of downtown St. Louis.

The Show - Me State
MISSOURI
Welcomes You!

ST. LOUIS ☎314

Lying directly south of the junction of the Mississippi, Missouri, and Illinois Rivers, St. Louis gained prominence in the 18th and 19th centuries as the US expanded west. The Gateway Arch rises above the sprawling city, framing it against the river that nurtured its growth.

Combining Southern hospitality, Midwestern pragmatism, and Western optimism, St. Louis offers a fusion of fast-paced urban frenzy and Midwestern "chill."

VITAL STATS
Population: 348,000
Tourist Office: Visitors Center, inside America's Convention Center (☎314-342-5160), at the corner of 7th St. and Washington Ave. Open M-F 9am-5pm, Sa 9am-2pm.
Library and Internet Access: St. Louis Central Library, 1301 Olive St. (☎314-241-2288). Open M 10am-9pm, Tu-F 10am-6pm, Sa 9am-5pm.
Post Office: 1720 Market St. (☎314-436-4114). Open M-F 8:30am-8pm, Sa 8:30am-1pm. **Postal Code:** 63101.

■ ORIENTATION

St. Louis has highways running through almost every neighborhood. Watch out—roads that seem normal turn into ramps without much notice. **US 40/I-64** runs east-west through the center of the metropolitan area, while **I-70, I-44 (US 50),** and **I-55** all head downtown from other outlying areas. Downtown is defined as the area east of **Tucker Boulevard** between **Martin Luther King Street** and **Market Street,** which divides the city north-south. Numbered streets parallel the **Mississippi River,** with addresses increasing to the west. St. Louis's neighborhoods are well defined, with attractions and restaurants concentrated in several distinct areas. The historic **Soulard** district borders the river south of downtown. **Forest Park** and **University City,** home to **Washington University** and old, stately homes, lie west of downtown. **The Hill,** an Italian neighborhood, lies south of these. St. Louis is very much a driving town; parking comes easily along the wide streets, and traffic moves quickly along interstates, except downtown during and right after the Cardinals play at Busch Stadium.

■ ACCOMMODATIONS

Most budget lodging is far from downtown. For chain motels, try **Lindbergh Boulevard (US 67)** near the airport or the area north of the **I-70** junction with **I-270** in **Bridgeton,** 5 mi. beyond the airport. **Watson Road** near Chippewa is littered with cheap motels. Take **I-64** or **I-44 West** to **Hampton Boulevard South,** turn right on **Chippewa Street,** and cross the **River des Peres** to **Watson Road (Route 366).**

Huckleberry Finn Youth Hostel (HI-AYH), 1908 S. 12th St. (☎314-241-0076), at Tucker Blvd. Take Broadway/7th St. S. toward Soulard, turn right just past Geyer Ave. onto Allen Ave., and then take a right on 12th St.; it's on the right. The hostel's full kitchen, nice ivy-covered buildings, and proximity to Soulard bars make it a great option. Dorms $20. Cash only. ❶

Congress Airport Inn, 3433 N. Lindbergh Blvd. (☎314-739-5100), 1 mi. south of I-70. This clean, no-frills hotel puts you close to the Loop. Singles $37; doubles $44. AmEx/D/MC/V. ❸

Royal Budget Inn, 6061 Collinsville Rd. (☎618-874-4451), in Fairmont City, IL, 20min. east of the city, off I-55/I-70 at Exit 6. Clean rooms with a Taj Mahal flavor make for a fun budget option. Rooms $45. Cash only. ❷

The Mayfair, 806 St. Charles St. (☎314-421-2500). Constructed at the height of the Jazz Age, the Mayfair has hosted famous musicians and politicians from Irving Berlin to Harry Truman. Standard rooms are spacious, with marble-topped sinks and soft beds. Rooms from $109; suites from $119. AmEx/D/MC/V. ❺

Dr. Edmund A. Babler Memorial State Park, 800 Guy Park Dr. (☎636-458-3813 or 877-422-6766), located in Wildwood 20 mi. west of downtown. Tent and RV sites and showers and toilets. Tent sites $9; RV sites with hookup $16. Cash only. ❶

■ FOOD

In St. Louis, the difference of a few blocks can mean a culinary transformation. The area surrounding Union Station, on Washington and Market St. downtown, is being revamped with hip restaurants and bars. The **Central West End** offers coffeehouses and outdoor cafes. A slew of impressive restaurants awaits just north of Lindell Blvd. along Euclid Ave. St. Louis's historic Italian neighborhood, **The Hill,** southwest of downtown and just northwest of Tower Grove Park, produces plenty of pasta. Cheap **Thai, Philippine,** and **Vietnamese** restaurants spice the South Grand area, at Grand Blvd., just south of **Tower Grove Park.** Coffee

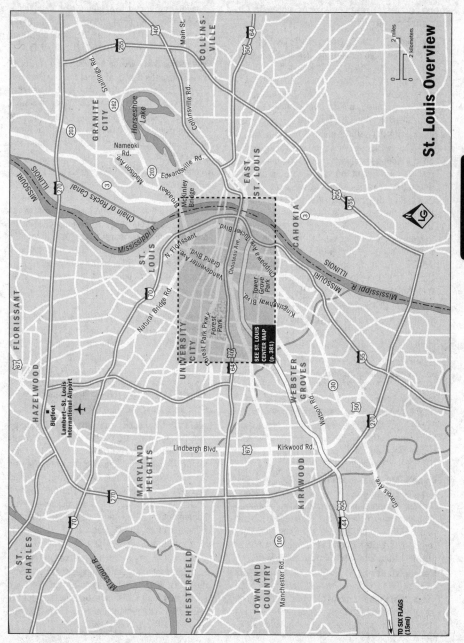

St. Louis Overview

NATIONAL
ROAD

SEE ST. LOUIS CENTER MAP (p. 381)

shops and restaurants cluster on **University City Loop,** on Delmar Blvd.

▨ **City Diner,** 3139 S. Grand Blvd. (☎314-772-6100; www.citydiner.us), at Arsenal St. A fabulous 50s diner. The eatery is known for its meatloaf platter ($8.50) and its Cuban sandwich (with pork, chicken, Gouda, and MoJo sauce; $7.75). Open M-W 7am-11pm, Th from 7am, F-Sa 24hr., Su until 10pm. AmEx/D/MC/V. ❸

▨ **Blueberry Hill,** 6504 Delmar Blvd. (☎314-727-4444; www.blueberryhill.com), at Westgate St., on the Loop. An eclectic rock and roll restaurant with 9 different rooms, each with a different decorative scheme—think life-size centaurs and pop culture display cases. Call ahead to find out if Chuck Berry is playing; he usually jams in the Duck Room the 1st W of each month. Big, juicy burgers $6. Live bands F-Sa and some weeknights 9:30pm. 21+ after 9pm. Tickets for shows $5-25, depending on the band. Table service daily 11am-9pm; bar menu available M-Sa until midnight, Su until 11pm. AmEx/D/MC/V. ❸

In Soo, 8423 Olive Blvd. (☎314-997-7473), at 82nd St. Home to the best pot stickers ($5) and vegetable moo shu ($16) you'll ever taste. Wonderful service and even better food. Open M-Sa 5-10pm, Su 5-9pm. Cash only. ❸

Ted Drewes Frozen Custard, 4224 S. Grand Blvd. (☎314-352-7376). The St. Louis summertime experience since 1929 and an integral part of Rte. 66 history. There may be a line, but the Fox Treat—with hot fudge, raspberries, macadamia nuts, and no fox ($3.50-5.75)—is worth the wait. Open May-Aug. M-Th and Su 11am-11:30pm, F-Sa 11am-midnight. D/MC/V. ❶

Chava's Mexican Restaurant, 925 Geyer Ave. (☎314-241-5503, www.chavasmexican.com). Serves Guadalajaran specialties in a relaxed, family-friendly environment. Deep-fried cheesecake $4.50. Happy hour M-F 4-6pm, with 16oz. margaritas $3.50. Open M-Th 11am-10pm, F-Sa 11am-11pm, Su 1-9pm. AmEx/D/MC/V. ❷

Mangia Italiano, 3143-3145 S. Grand Blvd. (☎314-664-8585; www.dineatmangia.com). Fresh pasta made on-site ($7-17), which Mangia also distributes to Whole Foods and other restaurants. Also serves gourmet sandwiches. Newly

renovated: your choice of intimate or bright, cafe-like ambience. Karaoke M. Jazz F. Open M-Th and Su 11:30am-10pm, F-Sa 11:30am-10:30pm. Bar open daily until 3am. AmEx/D/MC/V. ❷

Amighetti's, 5141 Wilson Ave. (☎314-776-2855; www.amighettis.com), at Marconi St. Probably the city's most famous sandwich joint, Amighetti's has served its "special sandwich" (small $3.85, large $6.50) for 3 generations. Open in summer M 8am-3pm, Tu-F 8am-7pm, Sa 8am-5:30pm; in winter M 8am-3pm, Tu-F 8am-6pm, Sa 8am-5:30pm. MC/V. ❷

Arcelia, 2001 Park Ave. (☎314-231-9200; www.arcelias.com). Big combination platters ($5.50-10.25) feature the usual suspects like burritos and enchiladas, but this bustling Mexican eatery also offers more suspicious characters: dishes like *nopales* (stir-fried cactus with tomato, onion, eggs, and chorizo; $9) and *menudo* ($7). Open Tu-Th 11am-2pm and 5-9pm, F-Sa 11am-10pm, Su noon-10pm. AmEx/D/MC/V. ❸

Everest Cafe and Bar, 4145 Manchester Ave. (☎314-531-4800; www.everestcafeandbar. com). Indian, Nepalese, Tibetan, and Korean specialties like a delicious lentil soup ($6), Tibetan dumplings ($9), and kimchi pancakes ($7.50). The owner has a PhD in public health and tries to serve only healthful food in this city of fried foods. Tibetan prayer flags line the interior. Lunch buffet $8. Open M-Th 11:30am-2:30pm and 5-9pm, F-Sa 11:30am-2:30pm and 5-10pm. ❷

Kaldi's Coffeehouse and Roasting Company, 700 De Mun Ave. (☎314-727-9955), in Clayton. From downtown, take I-64 W. to Exit 34B: Clayton Rd./Skinker Blvd. Proceed straight to Clayton Rd. and take a right onto De Mun Ave. An eclectic crowd sips espresso drinks and munches on freshly baked goods, including deliciously soft homemade cookies and vegetarian delights. Hummus plate $4.50. Open M-Sa 7am-11pm, Su 7am-9pm. AmEx/D/MC/V. ❶

Imo's, 8437 Olive Blvd. (☎314-997-1444). Numerous locations. Imo's makes the city's favorite St. Louis-style thin-crust pizza and receives shout-outs from rap superstar Nelly. Lasagna $6. Open M-Th 10am-midnight, F-Sa 10am-1:30am, Su 11am-midnight. AmEx/MC/V. ❷

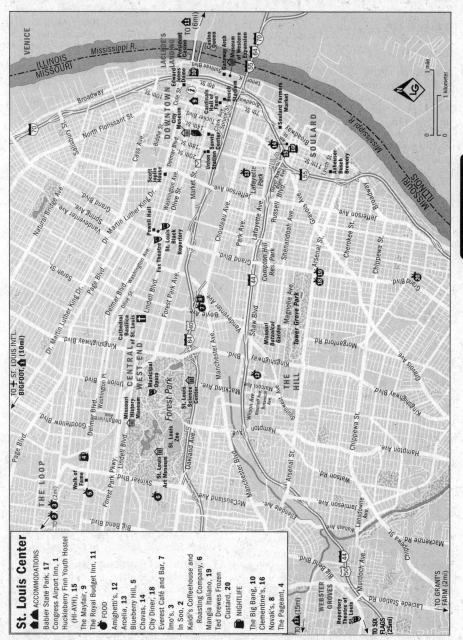

St. Louis Center

St. Louis Center

🔺▲ **ACCOMMODATIONS**

Babler State Park, **17**
Congress Airport Inn, **1**
Huckleberry Finn Youth Hostel
  (HI-AYH), **15**
The Mayfair, **9**
The Royal Budget Inn, **11**

🍴 **FOOD**

Amighetti's, **12**
Arcelia, **13**
Blueberry Hill, **5**
Chavas, **14**
City Diner, **18**
Everest Café and Bar, **7**
Imo's, **3**
In Soo, **2**
Kaldi's Coffeehouse and
  Roasting Company, **6**
Mangia Italiano, **19**
Ted Drewes Frozen
  Custard, **20**

🎵 **NIGHTLIFE**

The Big Bang, **10**
Clementine's, **16**
Novak's, **8**
The Pageant, **4**

SIGHTS

DOWNTOWN

GATEWAY ARCH. At 630 ft., the nation's tallest monument towers gracefully over all of St. Louis and southern Illinois and testifies to the city's historical role as the gateway to the West. The ground-level view is impressive, and the arch frames downtown beautifully from the Illinois side, but the high point of your visit is sure to be the 4min. tram ride to the top in a quasi-futuristic elevator module. Waits are shorter in mornings and evenings but are uniformly long on Saturday. Beneath the arch, the underground **Museum of Westward Expansion** adds to the appeal of the grassy 92-acre park complex known as the **Jefferson Expansion Memorial.** The museum radiates in a semi-circle from a statue of Jefferson that celebrates the Louisiana Purchase, the gold rush, and unstoppable Westward expansion. (☎314-655-1700; www.gatewayarch.com. Open daily in summer 8am-10pm; daily in winter 9am-6pm. Free. Tram $10, ages 13-15 $7, ages 3-12 $3.)

ST. LOUIS CARDINALS HALL OF FAME MUSEUM. The museum exhibits memorabilia from the annals of St. Louis hardball. (111 Stadium Plaza. ☎314-231-6340. Open Apr.-Sept. daily 9am-5pm, game days until 6:30pm; Oct.-Mar. Tu-Sa 11am-4pm. $7.50, ages 5-12 $4.)

UNION STATION. Just west of downtown, the station houses a shopping mall, food court, and entertainment center in a magnificent building that was once the nation's busiest railroad terminal. (At 18th and Market St. ☎314-421-6655; www.stlouisunionstation.com. Open M-Sa 10am-9pm, Su 10am-6pm.)

SCOTT JOPLIN HOUSE. "The Entertainer" lives on at this house, where the ragtime legend tickled the ivories and penned classics from 1900 to 1902. The 45min. tour delves into Joplin's influence on American music. (2658 Delmar Blvd. ☎314-340-5790. Tours Mar.-Oct. M-Sa every 30min. 10am-4pm, Su noon-4pm; Nov.-Feb. Tu-Sa every 30min. 10am-4pm. $2.50, ages 6-12 $1.50.)

SOULARD

In the early 1970s, the city proclaimed this area, bounded by I-55 and Seventh St., a historic district due to its former populations of German and Eastern European immigrants, many of whom worked in the breweries. Today, it is an attractive tree-lined neighborhood where you'll find many 19th-century brick townhouses.

SOULARD FARMERS MARKET. The district surrounds this bustling market (est. 1779), known for its fresh, inexpensive produce. (730 Carroll St. ☎314-622-4180. Open W-F 8am-5pm, Sa 6am-5pm; hours vary among merchants.)

ANHEUSER-BUSCH BREWERY. The largest brewery in the world produces the "King of Beers." The 1hr. tour includes a glimpse of the famous Clydesdales, two beer samples, and dozens of fun factoids for both beer and history lovers. (1127 Pestalozzi St., at 12th and Lynch St. Take bus #40 "Broadway" south from downtown. ☎314-577-2626; www.budweisertours.com. Tours June-Aug. M-Sa 9am-5pm, Su 11:30am-5pm; Sept.-May M-Sa 9am-4pm, Su 11:30am-4pm. Free.)

MISSOURI BOTANICAL GARDEN. Open since 1959, this internationally acclaimed 79-acre garden thrives north of **Tower Grove Park** on grounds that once belonged to entrepreneur Henry Shaw. The Japanese Garden and numerous fountain plazas are guaranteed to soothe the weary traveler. (4344 Shaw Blvd. From downtown, take I-44 W. ☎800-642-8842; www.mobot.org. Open daily 9am-5pm. Free tours June-Aug. daily 10am. $8, under 12 free.)

FOREST PARK

Forest Park contains three museums, a zoo, a 12,000-seat amphitheater, a canal as well as picnic areas, pathways, and flying golf balls.

SAINT LOUIS ZOO. Marlin Perkins, the late host of TV's *Wild Kingdom*, turned the St. Louis Zoo into a world-class institution, with black rhinos, Asian elephants, and a top-notch penguin and puffin habitat. (☎314-781-0900; www.stlzoo.org. Open daily June-Aug. 8am-7pm; Sept.-May 9am-5pm. Free. Children's zoo $4, under 2 free.)

ST. LOUIS ART MUSEUM. Atop Art Hill, a statue of King Louis IX, the city's namesake, raises his sword in front of the St. Louis Art Museum, which contains works by the likes of Rothko and Pollock. Strong collections include Oceanic, pre-Columbian, and ancient Chinese art and artifacts as well as 20th-century European—particularly, German—painting. The building itself is interesting; it is the only surviving one from the 1904 World's Fair. (☎314-721-0072; www.slam.org. Open Tu-Th and Sa-Su 10am-5pm, F 10am-9pm. Tours W-Su 10:30 and 1:30pm. Free. Special exhibits usually $10, students and seniors $8, ages 6-12 $6. F special exhibits free.)

MISSOURI HISTORY MUSEUM. This museum explores (drumroll, please) Missourian history and cultural heritage. Includes an exhibit on the pivotal 1904 World's Fair. (Located at Lindell and DeBaliviere St. ☎314-454-3124; www.mohistory.org. Open M and W-Su 10am-6pm, Tu 10am-8pm. Free. Special exhibits usually $10, students and seniors $8. Tu 4-8pm free.)

SAINT LOUIS SCIENCE CENTER. The center features an Omnimax theater, a planetarium, and over 700 interactive exhibits. (5050 Oakland Ave. ☎314-289-4444; www.slsc.org. Open June-Aug. M-Th and Sa 9:30am-5:30pm, F 9:30am-9:30pm, Su 11:30am-5:30pm; Sept.-May M-Th and Sa 9:30am-4:30pm, F 9:30am-9:30pm, Su 11:30am-4:30pm. Free. Omnimax $8, ages 2-12 $7. Planetarium $6/5.)

CENTRAL WEST END

From Forest Park, head east to gawk at the Tudor homes of the Central West End.

CATHEDRAL BASILICA OF SAINT LOUIS. The vast cathedral boasts intricate ceilings and mosaics that depict Missouri church history. (4431 Lindell Blvd. ☎314-373-8200. Open M-F 6am-5pm, Sa-Su 7am-6pm. Tours M-F 10am-3pm, Su afternoon mass 1pm. Call to confirm hours.)

BIGFOOT. At a shrine of a different sort, monster-truck enthusiasts pay homage to Bigfoot, the "Original Monster Truck," who lives with his descendants in a hanger near the airport. (6311 N. Lindbergh St. ☎314-731-2822. Open M-F 9am-5pm, Sa 9am-3pm. Free.)

WALK OF FAME. Northwest of the Central West End, the sidewalks of the Loop are studded with gold stars on the St. Louis Walk of Fame, which features local luminaries including Maya Angelou and Ike and Tina Turner. (6504 Delmar Blvd. ☎314-727-7827; www.stlouiswalkoffame.org.)

OTHER SIGHTS

CITY MUSEUM. The slightly surreal museum is constructed from salvaged parts of area buildings and is a wonderful amalgam of architectural styles. The outdoor "Monstrocity," made entirely of recycled parts, includes two planes, a fire truck, a Ferris wheel, sky tunnels, and a gothic tower with gargoyles. It's a killer playground for kids as well as adults who act like them. (701 N. 15th St. ☎314-231-2489; www.citymuseum.org. Open Mar.-Oct. M-Th 9am-5pm, F 9am-1am, Sa 10am-1am. $12, under 3 free. F-Sa after 5pm $10.)

SIX FLAGS SAINT LOUIS. This park reigns supreme in the kingdom of amusement parks and now features a water park and the 230 ft. "Tower of Power." (30min. southwest of St. Louis on I-44 at Exit 261. ☎636-938-4800. Call ahead for hours. $35, if reserved online or under 48 in. $30.)

🎵 ENTERTAINMENT

GAMBLING

Gambling is permitted on the river for those over 21. The **President Casino on the Admiral** floats below the Arch on the Missouri side. (☎314-622-1111 or 800-772-3647; www.presidentscasino.com. Open M-Th 8am-4am, F-Su 24hr. Entry $2.) On the Illinois side, the **Casino Queen** lays claim to "the loosest slots in town." (☎618-874-5000 or 800-777-0777; www.casinoqueen.com. Open daily 8am-6pm.)

MUSIC

Founded in 1880, the **Saint Louis Symphony Orchestra** is one of the country's finest orchestral ensembles. **Powell Hall,** 718 N. Grand Blvd., holds concerts. (☎314-534-1700. Tickets $16-110, students ½-price. Performances from late Sept. to early May F-Sa 8pm, Su 3pm. Box office open from late May to mid-Aug. M-F 9am-5pm; from mid-Aug. to late May M-Sa 9am-5pm and before performances.)

SPORTS

The **Saint Louis Cardinals** swing away at Busch Stadium. (☎314-345-9000. Tickets $9-55.) The **Rams** toss the pigskin at the Edward Jones Dome. (☎314-425-8830. Tickets $40-49.) The **Blues** hockey team plays at the Savvis Center at 14th St. and Clark Ave. (☎314-421-4400. Tickets from $15.)

THEATER

St. Louis offers theatergoers many options. The outdoor **Municipal Opera**, also known as the "Muny," presents hit musicals on summer nights in Forest Park. (☎314-361-1900. Tickets $8-54. Box office open from June to mid-Aug. daily 9am-9pm.) Productions are also regularly staged by the **St. Louis Black Repertory**, 3610 Grandel Sq. (☎314-534-3810), and by the **Repertory Theatre of Saint Louis**, 130 Edgar Rd. (☎314-968-4925). The brassy **Fox Theatre**, 527 N. Grand Blvd., was originally a 1930s movie palace, but it now hosts Broadway shows, classic films, and country and rock music stars. (☎314-534-1111; www.fabulousfox.com. Open M-F 10am-6pm, Sa 10am-2pm. Tours Tu, Th, Sa 10:30am. Tu $5, Th and Sa $8; under 12 $3. Call for reservations.) **Metrotix** (☎314-534-1111) has tickets to most area events.

▣ NIGHTLIFE

The music scene rules the night in St. Louis. The *Riverfront Times* (free at many bars and clubs) and the *Get Out* section of the *Post-Dispatch* list weekly entertainment. For a summary of the gay scene, find a copy of *EXP*, available in many shops and clubs. The *St. Louis Magazine*, published monthly, lists seasonal events. **Laclede's Landing,** a collection of restaurants, bars, and dance clubs housed in 19th-century industrial buildings north of the Arch on the riverfront, is almost always happening. In the summer, bars take turns sponsoring "block parties," with food, drink, music, and dancing in the streets. (☎314-241-5875. Generally open 9pm-3am, with some places open for lunch and dinner.) The bohemian **Loop** along Delmar Blvd. hops with revelers at night.

▨ **Novak's,** 4121 Manchester St. (☎314-531-3699; www.novaksbar.com). This favorite of the St. Louis GLBT community attracts gay and straight party-goers alike with mega-amplified karaoke (W, F, Su), extensive patio seating, and a plethora of games. Whether you're dancing or just hanging out, Nancy Novak might take your picture. The staffers all have $4 shots suggestively named

after them, such as Ricki's Panties, Karla's Klimax, and Jack Off Jill. Open M-F 11am-3am, Sa-Su noon-3am. AmEx/D/MC/V.

The Big Bang, 807 N. 2nd St. (☎314-241-2264), at Laclede's Landing. Dueling pianists in a massive brick room lead the enthusiastic crowd in a rock and roll sing-along. Cover F-Sa $6. Open Tu-Th 8pm-3am, F-Sa 5pm-3am. AmEx/D/MC/V.

The Pageant, 6161 Delmar Blvd. (☎314-726-6161). Line up early for a spot in the fantastic 33,000 sq. ft. nightclub and major concert venue, which hosts acts like Modest Mouse and Nas. 18+. Call ahead for ticket and cover prices. Doors usually open 7pm. The much classier Halo Bar is open W-Sa 7pm-3am, Su 10pm-3am. AmEx/MC/V.

Clementine's, 2001 Menard St. (☎314-664-7869), in Soulard. St. Louis's oldest gay bar (est. 1978) also houses the crowded **Oh My Darlin' Cafe.** Open M-F 10am-1:30am, Sa 8am-1:30am, Su 11am-midnight. AmEx/MC/V.

◪ THE ROAD TO WASHINGTON: 66 MI.

Head west out of St. Louis on **I-44/US 50.** I-44 entrance ramps can be accessed from **Tucker Boulevard** or **South Jefferson Avenue** south of downtown. From I-44, take **Exit 251** for **Route 100 West.** Curve to the right and continue straight at the light onto Rte. 100 toward Washington. After about 8 mi., turn right at the light onto **South Point Road,** which becomes **Fifth Street;** cross **Route 47** and head into the center of town on **Fifth Street** by turning right on **Lafayette.**

WASHINGTON   ☎636

Washington and its neighbor Hermann were both settled in the early to mid-19th century by Catholic German families; the area's greenery and rolling hills reminded them of Germany's Rhine Valley. Today, some industry in Washington continues, including the manufacture of corncob pipes at the very old and very large Missouri Meerschaum Company. Washington is also home to the **Washington Historical Society Museum,** at the corner of E. Fourth and Market St. The museum has three main areas of focus: founding German families' shoes and instruments, objects belonging to the city's important beer-producing families, and prehistoric Native American artifacts. Although they seem wholly unrelated to one another, the three do paint an interesting picture of the region's history. (☎636-239-0280; www. washmohistorical.org. Open Mar.-Dec. Tu-Sa 10am-4pm, Su noon-4pm. Free.)

La Dolce Vita ❺, 4 Lafayette St., a beautiful B&B overlooking the river, has two lovely rooms. (☎636-390-8180. Rooms $120, both for $190. AmEx/MC/V.) The colorfully painted **American Inn** ❷, 1715 E. Fifth St., on the way into town, offers modestly-sized but clean and comfortable rooms. (☎636-239-3172. Singles $45; doubles $55. AmEx/MC/V.) The best place to eat in town is **Cowan's** ❷, 114 Elm St. The eatery's wood tables and floors and black chairs make it feel like a very large and comfortable kitchen (with free Wi-Fi). The spaghetti and meatball dinner ($8) comes bottomless with salad and toast. Finish up with a wedge of homemade pie for $3; flavors include strawberry rhubarb and chocolate banana meringue. Take Market St. to Second St. and turn left. (☎636-239-3213. Sandwiches $5.50-7. Open M and W-Sa 6am-8pm, Su 6am-7pm.) **La Dolce Vita Restaurant** ❷, which is in the same building as the B&B, offers a selection of light salads ($8), sandwiches, wraps, quiches, and pizzas. Outdoor seating overlooking the river is plentiful. (☎636-390-8180; www.ladolcevitawinery.com. Open M-Th 11am-6pm, F-Su 11am-8pm. AmEx/MC/V.) You can stock up on regional produce at the **Washington Farmer's Market**, 317 W. Main St. Local arts and crafts are also sold here frequently in summer. (Open W 3-6pm, Sa 8am-2pm.)

🚩 **THE ROAD TO HERMANN: 27 MI.**

Take **Jefferson Street** to **Route 100 West** and follow it as it curves into Hermann. **Route 100** becomes **First Street** before joining with **Route 19** and turning south onto **Market Street.**

HERMANN ☎573

Surrounded by Missouri wineries, Hermann depends heavily on tourism for revenue; tourist-oriented development (centered on the area's German heritage) of this picturesque valley has made it the B&B capital of Missouri. The artifacts on display at the **Historic Hermann Museum**, 312 Schiller St., chronicle the history of early German immigrants in this area, and the **Deutsch Market** inside sells works by local artisans. To get to the museum, take Market St. to Fourth St. and turn left; it's in the old German school on the corner of Fourth. (☎573-486-2017; www.historichermann.com. Open Apr.-Oct. Tu-Sa 10am-4pm, Su noon-4pm. $12.) On the way out of Hermann is the **Stone Hill Winery**, the oldest winery in Missouri. Stone Hill lets visitors explore the grounds and caves where the wine ages; tours relate the history of the winery and the story of Hermann. Visitors can taste samples of wine and grape juice at the end of the tour. The friendly owners only add to the winery's welcoming atmosphere. (☎573-486-2221 or 800-909-9463; www.stonehillwinery.com. Hours vary by day; call ahead. $2.50, under 12 $1.) Not much farther is **Adam Puchta Winery**, 1947 Frene Creek Rd. The current winemakers are the sixth generation. Among the 15 different vintages, many of them national prizewinners, you're likely to find a new favorite. The winery doesn't offer tours, but during the free wine tastings vintners will happily gossip with you about whatever you want to know regarding the winery or the family's history. (☎573-486-5596. Open May-Oct. M-Sa 9am-6pm, Su 11am-6pm, Nov.-Apr.; M-Su 9am-5pm, Su 11am-5pm.)

To find a B&B, call or stop by the **Hermann Visitors Center**, 312 Market St. (☎573-486-2744 or 800-932-8687; www.hermannmo.info. Open Apr.-Oct. M-Sa 9am-5pm, Su 11am-4pm; Nov.-Mar. M-Sa 9am-4:30pm, Su 11am-4pm.) The **Hermann Motel** ❸, 112 E. 10th St., has pleasant rooms (with TVs) but unpleasant service. (☎573-486-3131. Continental breakfast included. Singles $50; doubles up to $129. AmEx/D/MC/V.) On Rte. 100, the **Rivertown Restaurant** ❷, 222 E. First St., offers ravenous roadtrippers old-fashioned cooking amid kitschy trinkets, black-and-white photos of Hermann, and assorted old trophies. True to the town's history, there's plenty of German cuisine. An all-you-can-eat salad bar costs $5.50, and dinner plates, like roast beef, go for about $7. (☎573-486-3298. Sandwiches $1.60-5. Steaks $8-12. Open M 7am-2pm, Tu-Sa 7am-8pm, Su 7am-1pm. MC/V.)

🚩 **THE ROAD TO JEFFERSON CITY: 43 MI.**

From Hermann, **Route 100** winds along the scenic Missouri River, passing wineries. Forty-two miles from Hermann, the road rejoins **US 50** near the town of Linn;

NATIONAL ROAD

turn right here to head west on US 50. US 50 becomes the **Whitton Expressway** in downtown Jefferson City.

JEFFERSON CITY ☎573

As one might expect from the capital of Missouri, Jefferson City is relaxed and low-key. Because there's virtually no industry, government is the main business in town, and it operates at a slow pace—the Missouri legislature has been known to spend seven years on the passage of a bill. The tall capitol building is situated above the Missouri River and is the focal point of downtown.

VITAL STATS
Population: 40,000
Tourist Office: Jefferson County Convention and Visitors Bureau, 100 E. High St. (☎573-632-2820 or 800-769-4183; www.visitjeffersoncity.com). Open M-F 8am-5pm.
Library and Internet Access: Missouri River Regional Library, 214 Adams St. (☎573-634-2464), off High St. Open M-Th 9am-9pm, F-Sa 9am-6pm, Su 1-5pm.
Post Office: 131 W. High St. (☎573-636-4186), across from the capitol building. Open M-F 8am-5:30pm, Sa 9am-noon. **Postal Code:** 65101.

✳ ORIENTATION

Jefferson City is surprisingly easy to navigate, especially with a good map from the visitors center. **Whitton Expressway (US 50)** runs northwest to southeast just south of the downtown area. **McCarty Street, High Street,** and **Main Street/Capitol Avenue** are north of US 50 and run parallel to it. North-south streets through downtown are named for the first six US presidents, though unfortunately not in order. **Missouri Boulevard (Business US 50),** a major thoroughfare, runs parallel to US 50 west of downtown and north-south within the downtown area itself. **US 54** runs southwest to northeast through the entire area. Street parking is available and sometimes metered.

▰ ACCOMMODATIONS

Most accommodations, including many chain motels, lie on US 54 just south of downtown.

Budget Inn, 1309 Jefferson St. (☎573-636-6167). The inn's comfortable beds, clean rooms, and powerful showers make for a pleasant stay. Singles $42; doubles $45. AmEx/D/MC/V. ❷

Hotel DeVille, 319 W. Miller St. (☎573-636-5231; www.devillehotel.com). This popular, upscale hotel has well-furnished rooms in a wide range of sizes. About 30 state senators, representatives, and lobbyists stay here when the Missouri Congress is in session. Free Wi-Fi. Rooms $45-100. AmEx/D/MC/V. ❸

▰ FOOD

Chain restaurants line Missouri Blvd.

Central Dairy, 610 Madison St. (☎573-635-6148). If you do nothing else while passing through town, indulge in a scoop of freshly made ice cream. 52 flavors. Waffle cones $2. Open M-Sa 8am-6pm, Su 10am-6pm. Cash only. ❶

Hotel DeVille, 319 W. Miller St. (☎573-636-5231). Hotel's restaurant employs 2 classically trained chefs who make delicious sandwiches ($6-8). Open M 11am-2pm and 5-10pm, Tu-Sa 7am-2pm and 5-10pm. AmEx/D/MC/V. ❷

Bone's Lounge, 210 Commercial Ave. (☎573-636-8955), is really 2 restaurants in 1; the carpeted ground floor serves hearty meals in an unusually intimate sports-bar environment, while the bar and patio upstairs are characterized by neon decorations, plastic furnishings, and a young clientele. Sandwiches $5-7. Open M-F and Su 11am-1am. AmEx/D/MC/V. ❸

◉ SIGHTS

MISSOURI STATE CAPITOL BUILDING. This building overlooks the Missouri River from High St. Informative tours explain Missouri's government and showcase the plush legislative floor (when the legislature is not in session). The highlight of the tour is a visit to the influential and expansive Thomas Hart Benton mural on the third floor, which illustrates Missouri's history. (☎573-751-4127. Open daily 8am-5pm. Tours M-Sa every hr. 8-11am and 1-4pm, Su at 10, 11am, 2, 3pm. Free.)

VETERINARY MUSEUM. Five centuries of veterinary medicine are on display at the museum that calls itself "The Little Museum That's the Cat's Meow." Visitors can learn about instruments, animal specimens, diseases, surgery, and the roles veterinarians play in NASA. The Siamese piglets, calf fetuses, and warthog skull make this museum a unique experience. *(2500 Country Club Dr. Take US 50 W. to the exit for Rte. 179; turn right at the bottom of the ramp and take the next right onto Country Club Dr. ☎573-636-8737. Open M-F 9am-4pm, Sa by appointment. Free.)*

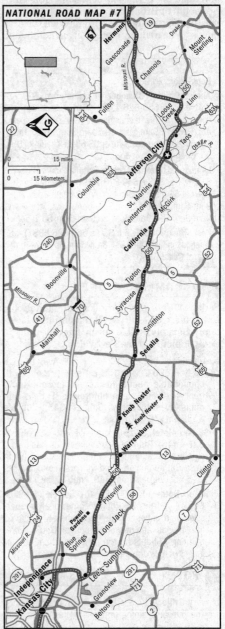 THE ROAD TO CALIFORNIA: 23 MI.

From downtown, take Broadway or Jefferson St. south to **Whitton Expressway (US 50)** and turn right to head west. Push that pedal down and head for California.

CALIFORNIA   ☎573

California is one of the many towns in this region that feature attractive centers, river overlooks, and residential areas. US 50 is lined with fast food and gas stations, but the good stuff—like **Burger's Smokehouse ❶**, 32819 Rte. 87—is just a little way off the road. Burger's cures ham and other meats and ships them all around the world. If a full ham won't fit in your car, settle for a simple sandwich ($2.50-4) packed with the same signature meats. Take Rte. 87 south for two miles and turn left at the sign. (☎573-796-3134 or 800-203-4244; www.smokehouse.com. Open Jan.-Aug. M-F 8am-5pm; Sept.-Dec. M-Sa 8am-5pm. AmEx/D/MC/V.)

THE ROAD TO SEDALIA: 38 MI.

Take **US 50** into town. Turn right on **Ohio Avenue** to reach the downtown historic district.

SEDALIA   ☎660

Sedalia is a quiet, well-to-do city with a graceful feel. Home of the Missouri State Fair for 11 days every August, Sedalia livens up, welcoming city and country dwellers numbering over 345,000 who fill the town's hotels, bars, and restaurants.

✦ ORIENTATION

US 50 is known as **Broadway Boulevard** and runs east-west through the entire area (where 8th St. would otherwise be). North of Broadway on Ohio Ave. and the surrounding streets lies the scenic and well-maintained downtown historic district. The **Missouri State Fairgrounds**

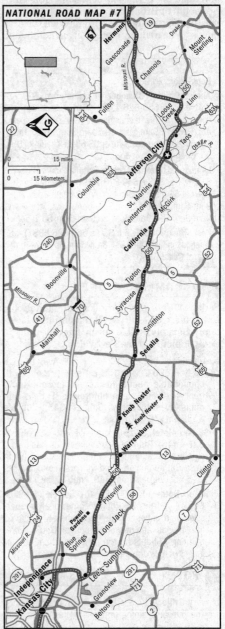

NATIONAL ROAD

and **State Fair Community College** lie along 16th St. (south of Broadway) to the west. **Limit Avenue (US 65)** runs north-south through the area and is home to many motels, chain hotels, and chain restaurants.

VITAL STATS

Population: 20,000

Tourist Offices: Chamber of Commerce, 600 E. 3rd St. (☎660-826-2222; www.visitsedaliamo. com), inside the reconstructed Katy Depot. Open Apr.-Dec. M-F 9am-5pm, Sa 10am-3pm. **Visitor Info Caboose,** on the west side of US 65, just south of US 50. Open M-F 10am-3pm.

Library and Internet Access: Sedalia Public Library, 311 W. 3rd St. (☎660-826-1314), at Kentucky St. Internet $1 per hr. Open May-Aug. M 9am-8pm, Tu-F 9am-6pm, Sa 9am-5pm, Su 1-5pm; Sept.-May M-W 9am-9pm, Th-F 9am-6pm, Sa 9am-5pm, Su 1-5pm.

Post Office: 405 E. 5th St. (☎660-826-8887), at Washington Ave. Open M-F 8am-6pm, Sa 8am-4pm. **Postal Code:** 65301.

ACCOMMODATIONS

Sedalia offers a range of accommodations, but some aren't very well maintained. Rates approximately double during fair time and the Scott Joplin Ragtime Festival.

American Inn, 1217 S. Limit Ave./US 65 (☎660-826-2488). Has extra large rooms with comfortable beds and tasteful artwork above each bed, and clean bathrooms. Fridges and microwaves. Laundry. Singles $45; doubles $53. AmEx/D/MC/V. ❷

Sunset Motel, 3615 S. Limit Ave./US 65 (☎660-826-1446). The motel's rooms are as basic as it gets but are also some of the most affordable in town. Bathrooms are lined with green tile.. Singles $36-45; doubles from $40. AmEx/D/MC/V. ❷

Hotel Bothwell, 103 E. 4th St. (☎660-826-5588), at Ohio St. Rooms come in all shapes, sizes, and prices. Ornately furnished with carved bedspreads and reproductions of Dutch flower paintings. Sheets have a high thread count. Singles $74-84; doubles $95. AmEx/D/MC/V. ❹

FOOD

Ivory Grille, 317 S. Ohio St. (☎660-829-0060). The elegant dining room of Hotel Bosworth. Serves food that is downright delicious. Lunch entrees ($5-7) are more affordable than dinner ($13-30)—but dinner portions are generous. Dishes are named for Scott Joplin songs and albums. Open M and Sa 5-9pm, Tu-F 11am-2pm and 5-9pm. AmEx/D/MC/V. ❸

McGrath's, 2901 W. Broadway/US 50 (☎660-826-9902). White tablecloths and wood-and-brick walls. The restaurant dishes out meat-oriented pub fare. Decorations include tasteful pictures and heraldry signs of Ireland. McGrath's has a regular menu, but there are no set recipes—each dish is cooked to customer specifications. Steak, chicken, and fish $7.50-26. Open M-Sa 5-10pm. AmEx/D/MC/V. ❸

Eddie's Drive-In, 115 W. Broadway/US 50 (☎660-826-0155). The squat structure of this eatery is a holdover from the glory days of automobile travel. Don't be fooled by the restaurant's name—you do have to get out of your car. The guberburger ($3.10), a burger with peanut butter, is an area specialty. Dinner specials 4-7:30pm $5.75. Steakburgers $2.40-4. Open M-Sa 7:30am-8pm. AmEx/D/MC/V. ❶

Kehde's Barbeque (☎660-826-2267), at 20th and Limit. Seats its customers in an old dining car, complete with vintage baggage overhead. The scent of ribs ($14) makes them hard to resist. 7 kinds of baked potatoes ($6.50). Open M and W-Su 11am-9pm. AmEx/D/MC/V. ❷

SIGHTS

DAUM MUSEUM OF CONTEMPORARY ART. The museum has an excellent permanent collection of modern paintings and sculptures. *(3201 W. 16th St. From US 50, go south on US 65 to 16th St., then head west just past the fairgrounds. ☎660-530-5888. Open Tu-F 11am-5pm, Sa-Su 1-5pm; call ahead. Free.)*

BOTHWELL LODGE STATE HISTORIC SITE. Here is where John Homer Bothwell, an influential (and eccentric) Sedalia resident and politician, originally built a 12,000 sq. ft. castle as his vacation residence. Tours run through the house, disclosing Bothwell's secret hiding places and his system of cooling the house, which involved air from underground caves. Hiking trails take you to great views of the mountains and fields. *(19349 Bothwell State Park Rd. From US 50, head north on US 65 for 6 mi. until you* *reach the right turn for Bothwell Lodge.* ☎ 660-827-0510. *Open in summer daily 9am-4pm; hours vary in winter. Tours begin on the hr. M-Sa 10am-4pm, Su 11am-5pm. Tours $2.50, ages 6-12 $1.50.)*

KATY DEPOT RAILROAD HERITAGE SITE. This site highlights its role as a railroad junction, home to the shops and stockyards of the MKT (Missouri-Kansas-Texas) and Missouri Pacific Railroads. *(600 E. 3rd St. ☎ 660-826-2222. Open M-F 9am-5pm, Sa 10am-3pm. Free.)*

❈ FESTIVALS

Ragtime was born and bred in Sedalia thanks to native son Scott Joplin. People relive his memory each year at the **Scott Joplin Ragtime Festival,** a series of concerts held each June. The rest of the time, pick up ragtime music and memorabilia at the **Scott Joplin Ragtime Store,** 321 S. Ohio St. (☎ 660-826-2271 or 866-818-6258; www.scottjoplin.org. Open M-F 9am-4pm. Call ahead.)

🚗 THE ROAD TO KNOB NOSTER: 19 MI.

Take **Broadway Boulevard (US 50 West)** out of town.

KNOB NOSTER ☎ 660

While in Knob Noster, venture to **Knob Noster State Park,** a 3567-acre park that caters to naturalists and equestrians alike with its mixture of prairie and second-growth forest. From US 50, take the exit for Rte. 23. At the top of the ramp, turn left and proceed straight for 1 mi. to the park entrance. Trails run from half a mile to 7 mi. **Camping ❶** is available; reserve sites at the **Missouri Centralized Reservation System.** (☎ 877-422-6766; www.mostateparks. com. Open daily 7-10am. Visitors center open M-F 9am-4:30pm, Sa-Su 10am-4pm. Apr.-Oct. sites $9, with electricity $16; Nov.-Mar. $8/14.) Knob Noster's **Hometown Cafe ❶,** 111 N. State St., is a patriotic local diner whose colorful mural celebrates the B-2 Spirit stealth bombers stationed nearby at the Whitman Air Force Base. The friendly staff serves basic sandwiches ($5.50-8.25) and breakfast items, including breakfast sandwiches ($2-3) on toast or a biscuit. From US 50, turn onto McPherson St. and turn left onto N. State St. (☎ 660-563-7482. Open M-F 6am-2pm, Sa-Su 7am-2pm. MC/V.) The **Panther Steak House ❷,** 506 W. McPherson St., serves steaks, hot dogs,

and hamburgers in a red and black panther-themed drive-in. (☎ 660-563-3930. Sirloin $8; monster chili dog $5. Open M-F 11am-9pm, Sa-Su 7am-9pm. MC/V.)

🚗 THE ROAD TO WARRENSBURG: 9 MI.

Take **US 50 West** and take the exit for **Route 13.** Turn left at the top of the ramp to go south, then turn right at **Young Street (Business US 50).** To reach the town center, proceed two blocks to the light at **Holden Street** and turn left.

WARRENSBURG ☎ 660

A speech given at the **Old Warrensburg Courthouse,** 300 N. Holden St., as part of the 1870 Trial of Old Drum gave rise to the phrase "Man's best friend is his dog." A statue of Old Drum himself tops a monument here; on the monument, the pathos-filled speech has been faithfully inscribed for all to read. Comfortable beds can be found at the **Camel Crossing Bed and Breakfast ❸,** 210 E. Gay St., built in 1906. The friendly owners rent out four lavishly decorated rooms and serve full breakfast. (☎ 660-429-2973. Rooms $60-80. MC/V.) **Java Junction ❶,** 112 N. Holden St., has exposed interior bricks, plenty of seating, and all the caffeine that a downtown worker could crave. (☎ 660-747-0725. Coffee $1.40. Muffins and cake $1.40-3.75. Open M-F 7am-6pm, Sa 8am-midnight. D/MC/V.) Farther away from downtown is **Mary Jane's Cafe ❷,** 1042 S. Maguire St., which serves dishes like meatloaf sandwich for $7 and tuna salad for $4.80 in a homey atmosphere. (☎ 660-429-1596. Open daily 6am-2pm. D/MC/V.)

⬗ DETOUR
POWELL GARDENS

1609 Northwest **US 50,** On the north side of US 50, 19 mi. from Warrensburg. Follow the signs.

Colorful, carefully sculpted flower beds surround bridges and mini-waterfalls at Powell Gardens. The grounds are concentrated into four small sites and include wildflowers, a perennial garden, and a rock and waterfall garden. A free garden trolley drives weary visitors around. Take a break at Cafe Thyme. Driving is not permitted in the gardens. (☎ 816-697-2600; www.powellgardens.org.

Open daily Apr.-Oct. 9am-6pm; Nov.-Mar. 9am-5pm. $8, seniors $7, ages 5-12 $3.)

THE ROAD TO INDEPENDENCE: 50 MI.

Take **US 50** and get off at **I-470 East/Route 291 North**. At the **23rd Street** light, turn left. Drive 2 mi. and turn right onto **South Main Street**.

INDEPENDENCE ☎816

Now overshadowed by Kansas City, Independence was once more exciting. During the era of westward expansion, this city stood on the edge of a vast wilderness and was the last waystation for pioneers seeking a new life. Today, the city is home to century-old businesses and modern estates.

> **PAGE TURN.** See **Oregon Trail** (p. 599) for complete coverage of Independence, Kansas City, Lawrence, Topeka, and Manhattan.

THE ROAD TO JUNCTION CITY: 20 MI.

Take **Route 18 West** out of Manhattan. Eight miles from town, Rte. 18 exits to the right. Follow it south to rejoin **I-70** heading west and take **Exit 300** for Junction City attractions.

JUNCTION CITY ☎785

There is one reason that you absolutely have to stop in Junction City, and it is to see the show titled "Undercover Story" at the **Geary County Historical Society Museum,** 530 N. Adams St. The museum will dazzle—or, perhaps, stun—you with this live demonstration of historic undergarments, in which middle-aged and elderly women parade in period undergarments dating from the 1880s through the 1920s. The museum director narrates. (☎785-238-1666. Open Tu-Su 1-4pm. Call museum director Gaylynn Childs in advance. Free.) While you're in town, be sure to check out **Freedom Park** and the **Atomic Cannon,** just south of I-70 at Exit 301. A climb up a shadeless switchback trail leads to the cannon—one of 20 designed during the Cold War to launch nuclear shells. (Seven survived.) Across the Kansas River in **Fort Riley,** visitors can learn about the cavalry's role in war and in the expansion of the American frontier at the **US Cavalry Museum.** You can

also drive around the rest of the 19th-century buildings of the fort, some of which were used by General Custer in the Civil War. Entrance to the museum requires passing through a military police checkpoint—bring photo ID and proof of car registration and insurance. (☎785-239-2737. Open M-Sa 9am-4:30pm, Su noon-4:30pm. Free.)

THE ROAD TO ABILENE: 30 MI.

From **I-70**, take **Exit 275** and turn left onto **Route 15,** which becomes **Buckeye Street** in Abilene.

ABILENE ☎785

The birthplace of President Dwight D. Eisenhower began as a small cow town but remains prosperous today thanks to the industries on its outskirts. With a small but entertaining collection of sights and museums as well as excellent food and motels, Abilene is a good place for a brief stopover.

VITAL STATS
Population: 6500
Tourist Office: Abilene Convention and Visitors Bureau, 201 NW 2nd St. (☎785-263-2231; www.abilenekansas.org). Open M-Sa 9am-5pm, Su noon-4pm.
Library and Internet Access: Abilene Public Library, at NW 4th St. and Broadway. Open M-W 9am-6pm, Th 9am-7pm, F 9am-5pm, Sa 9am-4pm.
Post Office: 217 N. Buckeye St. (☎785-263-2691), at 3rd St. Open M-F 8am-4:30pm, Sa 9am-11:30am. **Postal Code:** 67410.

ORIENTATION

Buckeye Street (Route 15) is the major north-south axis stretching from I-70 into town. Numbered streets run east-west and count up in both directions from **First Street**.

ACCOMMODATIONS

Diamond Motel, 1407 NW 3rd St. (☎785-263-2360). Large and well-decorated rooms in a quiet, relaxed residential area. Each room has a velvet couch or easy chair. Refrigerators, microwaves and A/C. Continental breakfast included. Free Wi-Fi. Singles $26; doubles $37. AmEx/D/MC/V. ❶

Abilene's Victorian Inn, 820 NW 3rd St. (☎785-263-7774; www.abilenesvictorianinn. com). Occupies the same house (built in 1887) where Eisenhower used to play as a child. There is a piano that was played by Nat King Cole in the living room. Rooms $79-129. ❹

Budget Lodge Inn, 101 NW 14th St. (☎785-263-3600). Has clean rooms with large bathrooms and pastel bedspreads. TVs, fridges, and microwaves in all rooms. Pleasant owners. Singles $30; doubles $40. AmEx/D/MC/V. ❷

🍴 FOOD

Brookville Hotel, 105 E. Lafayette Dr. (☎785-263-2244; www.brookvillehotel.com). Take Buckeye 1 block north of I-70 to Lafayette Dr. and turn right. There is only 1 item on the menu at this Midwestern restaurant: "One-Half Skillet Fried Chicken," served family style with cottage cheese, sweet-and-sour cole slaw, mashed potatoes, creamed corn, biscuits, and ice cream ($13.50, ages 3-11 $8, under 3 $3). Open Tu-F 5-7:30pm, Sa 11:30am-2pm and 4:30-7:30pm, Su 11:30am-2:30pm and 5-7pm. Reservations recommended. AmEx/D/MC/V. ❸

Kirby House Restaurant, 205 NE 3rd St. (☎785-263-7336; www.kirby-house). Serves Midwestern fare in a former Victorian home, distinctively painted pink. Rib night F ($19-20). Sandwiches and salads $7-8. Open M-Sa 11am-2pm and 5-8pm; espresso bar open M-Sa 8:30am-8pm. AmEx/D/MC/V. ❹

👁 SIGHTS

EISENHOWER CENTER. The center focuses on Eisenhower's military and presidential careers as well as the work of his wife, Mamie. Newly revised and updated, the museum still glorifies Ike's presidency, but some newer exhibits question elements of his legacy. Other attractions include the family's 19th-century home and a visitors center that shows a film every hour. *(200 SE 4th St., at Buckeye. ☎877-746-4453; www.eisenhower.archives.gov. Visitors center open daily 8am-5:45pm; museum, library, and boyhood home open daily 9am-4:45pm. $8, under 16 $1, under 8 free, seniors and military $6.)*

COUNTY HISTORY MUSEUM AND MUSEUM OF INDEPENDENT TELEPHONY. Housed inside the former, the Museum of Independent Telephony has telephone technology dating from the 1880s, including switchboards, switching stations, and some foreign equipment. *(412 S. Campbell St. From Buckeye, turn left on SE 3rd St. and proceed past the Eisenhower Center. Follow Campbell St. around to the right. ☎785-263-2681. Open from Memorial Day to Labor Day M-Sa 10am-6pm, Su 1-5pm; from Labor Day to Memorial Day M-F 9am-4pm, Sa 10am-5pm, Su 1-5pm. $4, seniors $3, under 15 $2.)*

GREYHOUND HALL OF FAME. Live specimens greet visitors here, where you can learn about greyhounds (the dog, not the bus) and dog racing. *(407 S. Buckeye Ave. ☎800-932-7881 or 785-263-3000; www.greyhoundhalloffame.com. Open daily 9am-5pm. Free.)*

FASHION MUSEUM. This entertaining museum focuses on the 100 years of style from 1870 to 1970. The collection includes antique wedding dresses. *(212 Broadway St. ☎785-263-7997. Open in summer Tu-Sa 10am-4pm; in winter Th-Sa 10am-4pm. $5, under 13 free.)*

🚗 THE ROAD TO SALINA: 26 MI.

Take **Buckeye (Route 15)** north. Turn left on **Northwest 14th Street** or **2300 Avenue.** Follow as it curves first left, then right, then becomes **US 40;** turn left on **North Santa Fe Avenue.**

SALINA   ☎785

Salina is a midsize town with offbeat sights and good food. The educational **Smoky Hill Museum,** 211 W. Iron Ave., presents the history of the Smoky Hill region, which spans central Kansas from Salina to the south. The first items on display are rocks, but the rest is more exciting and hands-on. (☎785-309-5776; www.smokyhillmuseum.org. Open Tu-F noon-5pm, Sa 10am-5pm, Su 1-5pm. Free.) The **Yesteryear Museum,** 1100 Diamond Dr., off Exit 252 from I-70, has an impressive collection of old farming tools, cigarette paraphernalia from the 1800s to 1900s, ancient radios, and a display on George Washington Carver. (☎785-825-8473; www.yesteryearmu-

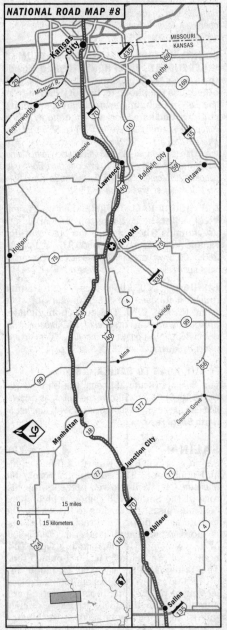

NATIONAL ROAD MAP #8

seum.com. Open Tu-Sa 9am-5pm. Suggested donation $4.) At the **Rolling Hills Zoo**, 625 N. Hedville Rd., 65 acres of Kansas prairie have been transformed into the naturalistic habitats of exotic animals. Although there don't seem to be that many animals, the grounds are pretty. Pay the extra $3 for the tram, or be prepared to walk across the un-shaded park. Follow I-135 or 9th St. north to I-70 and take Exit 244 and head south 2 mi. to the zoo. (☎785-827-9488; www.rollinghillswildlife. com. Open daily from Memorial Day to Labor Day 8am-5pm; in winter 9am-5pm. $11, ages 3-12 $6, seniors $10.)

For accommodations, the **Travelers Lodge ②**, 245 S. Broadway, offers clean, comfortable rooms not far from downtown. (☎785-827-9351. Outdoor pool. Free Wi-Fi. Singles $42; doubles $45-50. AmEx/D/MC/V.) Nearby, the **Village Inn ②**, 453 S. Broadway, has basic rooms with green bedspreads. The lobby is well equipped with a TV, a computer, and magazines. (☎785-827-4040. Outdoor pool. Singles $36; doubles $46. AmEx/D/MC/V.) At Exit 252 off I-70, the large **Salina Inn ②**, 222 E. Diamond Dr., has 90 clean rooms, a children's play area, a pet walk, and laundry facilities. (☎785-827-0292. Singles from $40; doubles from $50. D/MC/V.) Located at the same exit, **KOA campgrounds ①**, 1109 W. Diamond Dr., offers convenient sites with free swimming, fishing, and Wi-Fi. (☎785-827-3182. Sites $28, with full hookup $33.)

Locals chill in the large red and blue rooms at **Mokas Bakery and Bistro ②**, 109 N. Santa Fe Ave., where the menu has items like a turkey and artichoke panino ($6.50) and a chipotle burger ($7). The joint pours free refills on coffee ($1.40) and serves breakfast ($2-5) all day. (☎785-404-6941; www.mokascoffee.com. Open M-Sa 7am-5pm, Su 8am-2pm. AmEx/D/MC/V.) It may look like a deli, but **Martinelli's Little Italy ③**, 158 S. Santa Fe Ave., between Walnut St. and E. Iron Ave., is actually a great Italian restaurant with red and white checkered tablecloths and lots of seating. (☎785-826-9190. Open M-Sa 11am-10pm, Su 11am-9pm. MC/V.)

⚐ THE ROAD TO ELLSWORTH: 38 MI.

From **Broadway**, take **State Street West** and follow it as it becomes **Route 140**. From Rte. 140, take **Route 156** into town and bear right on **Eighth Street.**

ELLSWORTH ☎785

Texas Longhorn cattle were once herded through the lawless streets of Ellsworth, and the town's main street, **Douglas Avenue,** has purposefully preserved itself as it was in the 1870s. To equip yourself with contemporary cowboy gear, start at **Drovers Mercantile,** 119 N. Douglas Ave., which sells hats, boots, and spurs. It also gives out information on historic walking tours around Ellsworth and publishes a newspaper that records Kansas cowboy history and culture. (☎785-472-4703; www.droversmercantile.com. Open M-Sa 10am-5pm.) At the **Hodgden House Museum Complex,** 104 W. Main St., off Douglas Ave., a set of preserved buildings and displays of pistols and bullets recall Ellsworth's dusty, turbulent history. (☎785-472-3059. Hours vary, but usually open Tu-Sa 9am-5pm. $3, ages 6-12 $1.)

◪ DETOUR
◪MUSHROOM ROCK STATE PARK

200 Horsethief Rd. From Salina, take **Route 140 West** for 19 mi., then turn onto **Route 141 South** for 3 mi. Turn west onto the dirt road at the sign and follow it for 2 mi.

The huge, creviced, mushroom-shaped rocks at Mushroom Rock State Park resemble petrified UFOs on top of stone landing posts. (☎785-546-2565. Free.)

⬕ THE ROAD TO GREAT BEND: 40 MI.
Leave Ellsworth on **Route 156.** Outside of Great Bend, turn right to get on **US 56 West.** US 56 runs straight through the area; head north on **Main Street** to reach downtown shops and businesses or continue west on US 56 to reach chain motels.

GREAT BEND ☎620

Great Bend serves as a support city for the region's dominant industry, agribusiness. Despite, or perhaps because of, this the downtown area is mostly dead. The **Kansas Quilt Walk,** 1400 Main St., in Courthouse Sq., surrounds the courthouse on the sidewalk and showcases Kansan quilt patterns from the late 19th and early 20th centuries. **Baltzell Motel ❷,** 620 E. 10th St., offers 19 affordable rooms. All rooms have fridges, microwaves, and Wi-Fi. (☎620-792-4395. Singles $29-33; doubles $40. AmEx/D/MC/V.) The rooms at **Travelers Bud-**

get Inn ❷, 4200 W. 10th St., are decorated in a contemporary style that makes use of many shades of brown. (☎620-793-5448. Singles $37; doubles $42. AmEx/D/MC/V.)At **Delgado's Restaurant ❷,** 2210 10th St., you'll find Mexican fare and festive murals. (☎620-793-3786. Open M-F 11am-2pm and 5-8:30pm.) Across from Courthouse Sq., the lively **Home Field Bar and Grille ❶,** 2017 Forest Ave., lays claim to the best burgers ($3.50-7) in Great Bend. (☎620-793-6420. Open M-Th 11am-2pm and 4:30-10pm, F 11am-2pm and 4:30pm-midnight, Sa 11am-10pm. D/MC/V.) The small **visitors center,** 3111 10th St., just west of downtown, is around the rear side of the Convention Center through an unmarked doorway. (☎620-792-2750; www.visitgreatbend.com. Open M-F 8:30am-noon and 1-5pm.)

◪ DETOUR
PAWNEE ROCK STATE PARK

In Pawnee Rock, turn right onto **Centre Street.**

The bizarrely large Pawnee Rock was once a major landmark on the Santa Fe Trail, rising high above this flat area. It served as both a lookout point and a signpost for frontiersmen and was a rallying point during Native American wars. Erosion and development have shortened what was once the only interruption in this vast, uncultivated landscape. An observation deck set as high as the original height of the rock allows visitors to view the area from the same perspective as travelers did ages ago. Some graffiti remain from visitors in the 1800s, though they are faint and barely legible. (☎785-272-8681. Open daily 8am-sunset. Free.)

⬕ THE ROAD TO LARNED: 24 MI.
Follow **US 56 West** from Great Bend to Kinsley. US 56 is aligned with the **Santa Fe Trail.** Stay straight to remain on **Route 156.**

LARNED ☎620

Fort Larned once defended the mail and commerce of the Santa Fe Trail against "hostile Indians." The **Fort Larned National Historic Site** consists of nine 1860s-era stone buildings. The officers' quarters have been recreated, and the visitors center has informational displays on life and death at the fort for fron-

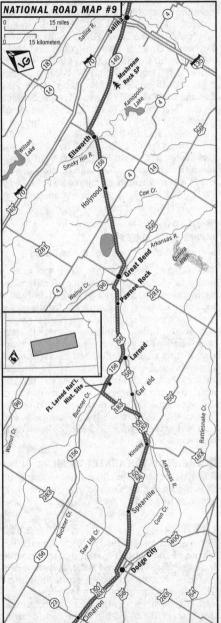

NATIONAL ROAD MAP #9

tiersmen and Native Americans, including old toys, guns, and a peace medal awarded by President Monroe that was strung on a necklace of buffalo teeth. (☎620-285-6911. Open daily 8:30am-5pm. Free.) At the **Santa Fe Trail Center,** 1349 Rte. 156, exhibits explore this ancient transportation route and the way it blended Native, American, and Spanish cultures. (☎620-285-2054. Open from Memorial Day to Labor Day daily 9am-5pm; from Labor Day to Memorial Day Tu-Su 9am-5pm. $4, students $2.50, children $1.50.)

▶ THE ROAD TO DODGE CITY: 70 MI.

Continue along **Route 156** until the junction with **Route 183;** take Rte. 183 S. to **US 56.** Follow US 56 through Kinsley, where it merges with **US 50.** On the outskirts of Dodge City, head left to get on **Business US 50 West,** the main drag of Dodge City—known in town as **Wyatt Earp Boulevard.**

PHOTO OP. The **middle of the US** is in Kinsley, where a large road sign on US 50 east of the Rte. 56 interchange features two arrows pointing in opposite directions; New York City 1561 mi., San Francisco 1561 mi.

DODGE CITY   ☎620

Dodge City was and still is one of the West's most famous cow towns. Silhouettes of cowboys on horses welcome visitors driving into town, and the smell of beef hangs in the air. This is the dusty heart of meat-packing country, and, though it's been 125 years since Dodge City served as a frontier post, the factories still provide the town with its economic base. While it can be hard to separate what's real from what's just for show, you'll find that local residents display a pride in Dodge that is independent of all the cowboy hoopla.

✦ ORIENTATION

Dividing the city east and west at Central Ave., **Wyatt Earp Boulevard (Business US 50)** runs east-west through the entire area and is the reference point for most directions. **Downtown Dodge** lies north of Wyatt Earp Blvd. between Central Ave. and Fifth Ave.; **Boot Hill** lies on

Front St., next to Wyatt Earp Blvd., between Third and Fifth Ave.

ACCOMMODATIONS

Thunderbird Motel, 2300 W. Wyatt Earp Blvd. (☎620-225-4143). Clean, spacious rooms off thickly carpeted halls. The greenhouse-style lobby has plants and a fish tank. Free Wi-Fi. Singles $31-35; doubles $40-44. AmEx/D/MC/V. ❷

Bel Air Motel, 2000 E. Wyatt Earp Blvd. (☎620-227-7155). The exterior is turquoise and white, making it easy to spot. A clean single-level motel with basic rooms. Singles $27; doubles $32-35. MC/V. ❷

Dodge House Hotel and Convention Center, 2408 W. Wyatt Earp Blvd. (☎620-225-9900; www.dodgehousehotel.com). This is a fun (albeit gimmicky) option; the inner courtyard is lined with silhouettes of cowboys and oversized pastel murals of Western scenes. Indoor pool. Attached saloon. All rooms $85. AmEx/D/MC/V. ❹

Holiday Motel, 2100 W. Wyatt Earp Blvd. (☎620-227-2169). Offers simple rooms with clean bathrooms and matching red, green, and brown beds and curtains. Singles $35; doubles $40. AmEx/D/MC/V. ❷

FOOD

Dodge City is dominated by chain restaurants, but the steakhouses here in cow country are certainly worth a look.

Casey's Cowtown, 503 E. Trail St. (☎620-227-5225). Take 1st St. south across the railroad tracks and turn left on to Trail St. Place settings here always include a steak knife, but in addition to steak ($10-20) Casey's also offers chicken, seafood, and salads ($6-8). The huge denim buffalo sculpture in the lobby makes for a great photo op. Open M-Sa 11am-10pm. AmEx/D/MC/V. ❸

Casa Alvarez, 1701 W. Wyatt Earp Blvd. (☎620-225-7164). Authentic Mexican food. Fajitas $12. Combo plates $6-8.50. Open M-Th 10:30am-2pm and 5-9pm, F-Sa 11am-9pm, Su 10am-8pm. Cash only. ❸

Central Station, 207 E. Wyatt Earp Blvd. (☎620-225-1176). A converted railway station. The most popular dish, the Central Station Rib-Eye ($16), uses its signature sauce. Open M-F 11am-2pm and 5-10pm, Sa 4-10pm. Bar open M-Sa until 2am M-Sa. AmEx/D/MC/V. ❸

SIGHTS

BOOT HILL MUSEUM. This museum is a 1950s-era recreation of Dodge City's legendary frontier and is Dodge's main attraction. For $20, you can dress up in old-fashioned clothing and take an "antique" picture. There is also a display on the "guns that won the West," including those used by outlaws, lawmen, buffalo hunters, gamblers, and frontiersmen. Farther up the hill, the old cemetery preserves the hill as it looked before the town was settled. (*On Front St., between 3rd and 5th Ave.* ☎620-227-8188; www.boothill.org. *Open in summer daily 8am-8pm; in winter M-F 9am-5pm, Su 1-5pm. In summer $8, students and seniors $7.50, families $30; in winter $7/6.50/20.*)

KANSAS TEACHERS' HALL OF FAME AND GUN-FIGHTERS WAX MUSEUM. In an odd twist of fate, these two museums ended up in the same building. The Hall of Fame honors Kansas's best teachers and showcases early school desks, inkwells, and textbooks that might make you surprisingly nostalgic. Upstairs, life-size figures of fighters like Calamity Jane, Buffalo Bill, Jesse James, and John F. Kennedy (who once visited Dodge City) await in cases illuminated by a black-light. There's also the grisly decapitated (wax) head of Joaquin Murrieta. (*603 5th St.* ☎620-225-7311. *Open M-Sa 10am-5pm, Su 1-5pm. Call ahead in winter. Free.*)

NATIONAL ROAD

WOOD CORONADO CROSS AND FORT DODGE. This cross marks the spot where the Spanish explorer Coronado supposedly crossed the Arkansas River in 1541 in search of the mythical "Cities of Gold." On your way back, check out Fort Dodge, which once guarded the Santa Fe Trail. (*Located 4 mi. east of town on US 400.*)

◪ THE ROAD TO GARDEN CITY: 50 MI.
Wyatt Earp Boulevard (Business US 50) rejoins **US 50/US 400 West** outside of town. Take US 50 toward Garden City. During the 50-year period when this area was part of the **Santa Fe Trail,** continuous use by wagons scarred the land with deep ruts. Check them out off the side of **US 50/400** on your way out of Dodge City. Twenty eight miles west of the city, pull off at the marked overlook for a good view of cattle, farms, and lots of grass. US 50 turns north just outside of Garden City; head straight into town on **Fulton Street.**

GARDEN CITY   ☎ 620

Though it has a large population, Garden City doesn't cater much to tourists except for a few attractions and a large number of hotels. The **Finney County Historical Museum,** 403 S. Fourth St., is home to the world's largest hairball as well as other displays, including an excellent exhibit on the Santa Fe Trail. The exhibits on sugar-beet production, notable Kansans, and recent immigrants are interesting—but the hairball is the museum's real tourist draw. (☎620-272-3664. Open in summer M-Sa 10am-5pm, Su 1-5pm; in winter daily 1-5pm. Free.) The **Sandsage Bison Range and Wildlife Area,** south of town on Rte. 83, is where the buffalo roam; call ahead for a driving tour to see the beasts in their natural home. The refuge also protects other native animals, including quail, ground squirrels, jackrabbits, and deer. Unluckily for the critters, portions of the area are open to limited hunting—not much "protection" there. (☎620-276-9400; www.gardencity.net/fofgr.)

The **Continental Inn ❷,** 1408 Buffalo Jones Ave., has comfortable rooms whose walls are hung with nostalgic prints of Native Americans and also a heated outdoor pool. (☎620-276-7691. Singles from $50; doubles from $55. AmEx/D/MC/V.) The **Garden City Inn ❸,** 1202 W. Kansas Ave., at the corner of Taylor and Kansas Ave., has an indoor pool and a hot tub. (☎620-276-7608; www.gardencityinnkansas.com. Continental breakfast included. Free Wi-Fi. Singles from $70; doubles from $80. AmEx/D/MC/V.) The **National 9 Inn ❷,** 123 Honeybee Ct., has photos of wildlife in the lobby. The rooms are spacious and well cooled and have comfortable beds. (☎620-275-0677 or 800-333-4264. Singles $48; doubles $53. AmEx/D/MC/V.) **Hanna's Corner Restaurant ❶,** 2605 N. Taylor Ave., is a neighborhood hangout (think friendly, floral tablecloths) in the shadow of a beef-packing plant. Besides a large breakfast selection and cheap sandwiches ($3-6), Hanna's also offers meaty dinners for $7-14. (☎620-276-8044. Open M-F 5:30am-8:30pm, Sa 5:30am-9pm, Su 6am-1:30pm. MC/V.) Mexican restaurants are a dime a dozen here, but the local population opts for **Marisco's ❷,** 1107 N. Taylor Ave., which sets itself apart from the competition with aquatic decor, seafood dishes, an all-in-Spanish menu, and 🔥**burn-your-mouth-hot salsa.** A burrito is $3.75; seafood soup is $11. (☎620-275-7723. Open M-Th and Su 8am-midnight. Cash only.)

> **PHOTO OP.** The world's largest hairball weighs 20 lb. (it weighed 55 lb. when it was first removed in 1993) and is nearly 36 in. in circumference. Ripley's Believe It or Not reportedly offered the museum a letter of certification in exchange for the hairball, but the Finney County Historical Museum rejected the bid and keeps the ball on a stand by the information desk.

◪ THE ROAD TO HOLCOMB: 5 MI.
Take **North Taylor Avenue** or **North Main Street** north to **Mary Street.** Turn left on Mary St., which turns into **Old US 50,** and follow it into Holcomb. Follow **Jones Avenue** as it curves right and head to US 50.

HOLCOMB   ☎ 620

This town became infamous as the site of the grisly murders depicted in Truman Capote's *In Cold Blood.* The house where the murders took place is on the outskirts of town; you may be able to find it, but people live there, and they don't want to be disturbed. Pay attention to the "NO TRESPASSING" signs. Holcomb is also home to the world's largest beef-packing plant, a Tyson plant formerly known as IBP. It sits at 3105 N. IBP Rd.; turn left from US 50 W. at the sign. (☎620-277-4234. Some tours available. Call ahead.) *Let's Go* does not recommend murder or trespassing, but, if you feel like beef-packing, go for it.

🚗 THE ROAD TO SYRACUSE: 49 MI.

Follow **US 50,** which becomes **East Avenue A.**

> 🕐 **TIME CHANGE.** After Holcomb, US 50 passes from the Central Time Zone to the Mountain Time Zone, where it is 1hr. earlier.

SYRACUSE ☎620

Sixteen miles from the border of Colorado, Syracuse is the last cow town in Kansas and a convenient place to fill up on gas before leaving the state. While in Syracuse, check out the **Hamilton County Museum,** at Gates St. and US 50. The museum's unassuming exterior may underwhelm you, but its spacious interior is impressive and showcases everything from a 50s pinball machine to a picture of a tree made from the human hair of one family to the vintage quilts and guns. Also, don't miss the gigantic mammoth tusk, discovered just outside of town. (☎620-384-7496. Open May-Oct. Tu-Sa 9am-noon and 1-4pm; call ahead for hours in winter. Free.)

The Syracuse Inn ❷, 612 US 50, just west of town, has compact rooms with fridges and clean bathrooms. (☎620-384-7411. Singles $38; doubles $47. AmEx/D/MC/V.) **The Syracuse Pizzeria ❸,** 208 N. Main St., is not far from the museum and offers freshly baked pizzas ($8-15) in a country-style diner decorated with American flags. (☎620-384-5928. Open M-F 11am-1:30pm and 4-5:30pm, Sa 11am-1:30pm and 4-9:30pm. AmEx/D/MC/V.)

🚗 THE ROAD TO LAMAR: 50 MI.

Continue west on **US 50/US 400;** it becomes a major thoroughfare in Lamar and changes names first to **Olive Street** and then to **Main Street.**

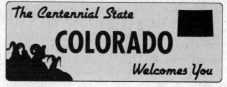

The Centennial State
COLORADO
Welcomes You

LAMAR ☎719

Lamar may be in Colorado, but, at only 32 mi. inside the state border, it doesn't resemble the mountainous terrain depicted on postcards and license plates so much as it looks like, well, Kansas. As the buzzing flies constantly remind you, Lamar is a land of cows. This region is known as "Big Timbers" after the giant cottonwood trees that once stood on the banks of the Arkansas River. The **Big Timbers Museum,** 7517 US 50, focuses on settlement in the area. (☎719-336-2472; www.bigtimbersmuseum.org. Open June-Aug. M-Sa 10am-5pm, Su 1-5pm; Sept.-May daily 1-5pm. Free.) Drive by a building made of 150-year-old petrified wood on Main St., at Sherman, which was constructed in the hopes that it would bring tourists to southeast Colorado (and, look, here you are). The car shop next door, **Stagners** (☎719-336-3462), gives short tours of the edifice by request, but its insides are disappointingly empty. At the northwest corner of Main and Beech St. by the Welcome Depot, the familiar **Madonna of the Trail** (p. 360) is visible once again. (☎719-336-3483. Visitors center open daily from Memorial Day to Labor Day 8am-6pm; from Labor Day to Memorial Day daily 8am-5pm.)

The clean rooms of the **Midtown Motel ❷,** 215 E. Third St., are located two blocks south of US 50 in a residential area. (☎719-384-7741. Singles $40; doubles $50. AmEx/D/MC/V.) Rooms at the **Passport Inn ❷,** 113 N. Main St., are a solid bet. (☎719-336-7746. Free Wi-Fi. Singles $31.50; doubles $41.50. AmEx/D/MC/V.) The **Blue Spruce ❷,** 1801 S. Main St., has large, clean rooms with colorful Western decorations. Some come with kitchenettes. (☎719-336-7454. Pool and fountain in courtyard. Breakfast included. Singles $42; doubles $50-60. AmEx/D/MC/V.) If your insides are disappointingly empty, find sustenance at the colorfully painted **Caffeine Coffee House and Sandwich Board ❶,** 117 W. Elm St. The extensive menu of wraps and panini ($3.75-5) rotates daily; coffee and espresso drinks are

NATIONAL ROAD

$1.50-5. The eatery's furniture is comfortably squishy. Heading north, turn left onto Elm St. from Main St. (☎719-336-1070. Open Tu-Th 6:30am-3:30pm, F 6:30am-8pm, Sa 8am-2pm. MC/V.) For a heartier meal, you may consider **Hickory House ❸**, 1115 N. Main St. The restaurant is decorated with paintings of Rocky Mountain scenes and serves stick-to-your-ribs classics like chicken-fried steak for $10. (☎719-336-5018. Open in summer M-Th and Su 5:30-9pm, F-Sa 5:30-10pm; in winter M-Th and Su 5:30-8pm, F-Sa 5:30-9pm. D/MC/V.)

⚐ THE ROAD TO LA JUNTA: 56 MI.
Follow **US 50 West** through Las Animas.

LA JUNTA ☎719
The ▣**Koshare Indian Museum,** 115 W. 18th St., is the reason to stop in La Junta. The museum celebrates all things Native American and includes exhibits ranging from modern fine arts to ancient artifacts. You'll even find a kiva, a log-roofed theater built in 1949. Today's traditional Koshare Indian Dancers perform on weekends and some weekdays in June and July. (☎719-384-4411; www.koshare.org. Open May-Sept. daily 10am-5pm; Oct.-Apr. Tu-Su 12:30-4:30pm. $5, students and seniors $3. Shows $8/5.)

The crowded and kitschy **Copper Kitchen ❶**, 116 Colorado Ave., offers a large variety of breakfast and lunch options. Daredevils can try a meal of Rocky Mountain oysters ($6.75), while the merely brave will prefer the large and spicy chili burger ($5.75), with two burger patties and red or green chili. (☎719-384-7508. Breakfast $1-5. Open M-Sa 6am-2pm, Su 6am-12:30pm. MC/V.)

⚐ THE ROAD TO COMANCHE NATIONAL GRASSLANDS: 0 MI.
Look around you. You're in 'em.

COMANCHE NATIONAL GRASSLAND ☎719
The sandy, cactus-filled Comanche Grasslands are a spectacularly surreal 435,000 acres—a welcome change from the monotonous land-scape of Kansas and eastern Colorado. The name "grasslands" is somewhat misleading, because the area also includes canyons and hills; there is without doubt enough wilderness here to occupy adventurers for days.

The US government founded Comanche and 19 other grasslands after the Dust Bowl of the 1930s as part of a land-use reform movement. Perhaps because they are remote and difficult to reach, the grasslands remain largely undiscovered by tourists.

The grasslands are divided into two units. The **Carrizo Unit** is south of Springfield, Colorado, and quite a ways off-route, while the **Timpas Unit** is just south of La Junta and, as such, less of a jaunt off the National Rd. (Coverage here focuses on the latter.) For those who don't feel like finding the units on their own, the **Forest Service,** 1420 E. Third St., La Junta, leads **auto tours** of the canyons, and the guides know where to find the best ruins, rock art, and tracks. Visitors who wish to take such a tour must provide their own four-wheel-drive high-clearance vehicle with a full a tank of gas, at least two quarts of drinking water, good high-top hiking shoes, river shoes, lunch, and sunscreen. The Forest Service also offers a checklist for **birdwatching,** with information as to which species of birds (there are 264 that live or pass through here) are visible during each season. (☎719-384-2181. Tours run about 8am-4pm. $15, ages 6-12 $7.50. Open M-F 8am-noon and 1-5pm.)

◤ DETOUR
TIMPAS AND PICKET WIRE CANYONS
Head west on **US 50** toward La Junta. From La Junta, just west of the Forest Service office, take **Route 109 South** for 13 mi. Turn right (west) on **County Road 802** and continue for 8 mi. At this point, you are in open range; watch for cows on the road. Turn left (south) on **County Road 25** and follow it for 6 mi. Turn left at **Picket Wire Corrals** onto **Forest Service Road 500A** and drive for 3 mi., following the signs to **Withers Canyon Trailhead.** Park at the Withers Canyon Trailhead parking loop, where there are a few campsites and an acceptable toilet.

Picket Wire Canyon is the highlight of the Timpas Unit. A group of 17th-century Spaniards died in the canyon while searching for treasure; the river became known as El Rio de las Perdidas en Purgatorio, or the River of

Souls Lost in Purgatory. French settlers came along soon after and simplified this name to Purgatoire. Eventually, the pronunciation shifted to Picket Wire. There's no reason that you will share the Spaniards' fate, provided you bring enough drinking water.

In Picket Wire Canyon, the **Withers Canyon Trailhead** loops around the top of the canyon, and plaques list flora and fauna that you may encounter. Not far away, you can make the relatively steep climb down to the canyon.

The first major site along this path is the abandoned **Dolores Mission and Cemetery,** an early Catholic Church, 3¾ mi. from the trailhead. The mission was built sometime between 1871 and 1889 by some of the first permanent Mexican settlers.

The next major landmark is a **dinosaur track site,** 5¼ mi. from the start of the trail. The tracks were discovered in 1935, but the area was too remote to sustain scientists' interest, and only in the 80s were the findings studied in detail. The site is the largest continuously mapped site in all of North America; it has over 1300 footprints in four layers of earth that date from the late-Jurassic Morrison Formation (about 150 million years ago). About 40% are *Apatosaurus* tracks, and 60% are carnivorous *Allosaurus* dinosaurs. In the track patterns, scientists observe a recognizable kind of teenage angst; a group of juvenile apatosaurs left a separate group of tracks as they gregariously traveled west along what was then a shoreline.

As you make your way along the trail, watch for wagon ruts and smaller ruins from more than 100 years ago, when the Santa Fe Trail was the best way to reach the West. In addition, throughout the zone in unmarked areas, some **rock art** is visible. The fragile rock art dates from 375-4500 years ago and should not be touched. Because the area is so remote, historians know very little about the canyon's Native Americans, except that they were nomadic hunter-gatherers. The Forest Service office has information about **archaeoastronomy** (the study of ancient astronomy) and suggests that the vertical and horizontal lines of the rock art may have recorded the passage of days and kept track of celestial movements. Wheels, spirals, circles, scratches and plus marks could mark specific objects in

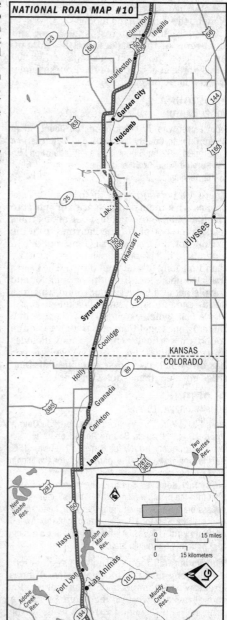

NATIONAL ROAD MAP #10

the sky, like important stars, constellations, planets, the sun, and the moon.

The third site of interest is the adobe and jacal ruins of the **Rourke Ranch,** 8¾ mi. out. At its peak, the ranch encompassed 52,000 acres; three generations of the Rourke family worked here for about 100 years.

⬐ DETOUR
VOGEL CANYON

From Picket Wire, drive back north on **County Road 25** for 6 mi. to **County Road 802** and right (east) on Country Rd. 802 for 6.5 mi. Take a left (south) on **Forest Service Road 505A** and drive for another 1.5 mi. to the parking lot.

There are two springs at the bottom of **Vogel Canyon.** Visit them during sunrise or sunset to catch a glimpse of wildlife. Four hiking trails lead to the bottom of the canyon. From the parking lot, the **Overlook Trail** (1 mi. round-trip) extends to the **Mesa Trail,** which is a bit more than 1 mi. long (2¼ mi. round-trip). The **Canyon Trail** also heads out from the parking lot and travels about 1 mi. (1¾ mi. round-trip) to a spring and four small ruins. It connects to the **Prairie Trail,** which extends 1½ mi. farther into the canyon. Vogel Canyon's rock art is often found on vertical rock faces and includes abstract designs and symbols. Vogel Canyon has one toilet, two horse hitching rails, and three covered picnic tables with grills.

⬐ DETOUR
TIMPAS CREEK: 19 MI.

From Picket Wire Corrals, head back north on **County Road 25** for 11 mi. to **County Road North.** Turn left (west) on County Rd. N. for 8 mi. to **Highway 350.** Turn left on Hwy. 350. The parking lot for the picnic area will be immediately on the right just off Hwy. 350 on **County Road 16.5.** Cross the railroad and turn right into the picnic parking area. Timpas Creek is also accessible from La Junta. From the town, head southwest on Hwy. 350 for 16 mi. and turn right (northwest) on County Rd. 16.5. Just after the railroad crossing, turn right into the picnic area.

The **Nature Trail** loop to Timpas Creek is half a mile long and not too strenuous. Timpas Creek was an important water source for those traveling west on the Santa Fe Trail. A longer (7½ mi. round-trip) trail leads to the scenic **Sierra Vista Overlook.** The Timpas Creek

area has one toilet and a total of six picnic tables with grills.

⬐ THE ROAD TO PUEBLO: 65 MI.

About 58 mi. from La Junta, **US 50** and **Route 96** join. When they split 3 mi. later, take the exit for Rte. 96 (4th St.) and turn left at the top of the ramp.

PUEBLO ☎719

A one-time steel town and once Colorado's second-largest city, Pueblo has in the recent past been denigrated by residents of mountainous regions for its flatness and supposed lack of sophistication. Today, however, the city is reinventing itself; artists are moving into downtown warehouse spaces, funky restaurants are opening, and museums are doing more than ever to attract visitors. The **Rosemount Museum,** 419 W. 14th St., four blocks west of Santa Fe Ave. at Greenwood St., is one of the city's best sights. More a castle than a home, this 37-room, 24,000 sq. ft. restored Victorian mansion is decked out with an elegant original interior. Hourlong tours explain the architecture and furnishings of the house, from its 10 English tile fireplaces to its Tiffany chandeliers to its Art Deco Grand Steinway—one of only 200 ever made. (☎719-545-5290; www.rosemount.org. Open Feb.-Dec. Tu-Sa 10am-4pm. $6, ages 6-18 $4.) The **El Pueblo History Museum,** 301 N. Union Ave., includes many exhibits that treat the settlement of the area from the 1780s to the 1860s; here, you'll see Native American artifacts, old saddles, and silver. (☎719-583-0453. Open Tu-Sa 10am-4pm. $4, students, children, and seniors $3.)

The **Bramble Tree Inn ❷,** 115 E. Eighth St., at Santa Fe Ave., has small rooms in good condition, with standard amenities including TVs with cable, fridges, and microwaves. (☎719-542-1061. Rooms $35. MC/V.) The **Traveler's Motel ❷,** 1012 N. Santa Fe Ave., is a bare-bones motel with white cinderblock walls and airy, pink-tiled bathrooms. The furniture is rustic but comfortable, and walls are adorned with posters from circa 1980. (☎719-543-5451. Singles $35; doubles $40. AmEx/D/MC/V.) Restaurants abound in the arts and antique district, just south of downtown. The hip, yellow-painted **Hopscotch Bakery ❶,** 333 S. Union Ave., makes great quiches ($2.50) and panini like the smoked turkey with red pepper mayo, applewood-smoked bacon, and Swiss ($7). The homemade ice cream ($2.75) can't be beat. (☎719-542-4467; www.hop-scotchbakery.net. Open M-F 7am-5:30pm, Sa 8am-4pm. AmEx/D/MC/V.) **Angelo's Pizza Parlor and More ❷,** 105 E. Riverwalk, serves very cheesy pizza slices ($2.85) and pasta dishes for $8-10. (☎719-544-0092. Open M-Th and Su 11am-10pm, F-Sa 11am-11pm. AmEx/D/MC/V.) The **City Diner ❶,** 1002 N. Santa Fe Ave., has scenic pictures of the Rockies that hang above its old-fashioned booths. The diner offers a large breakfast menu ($4-7) as well as a daytime menu that includes Mexican dishes ($5-9), fried chicken, and steak. (☎719-545-2152. Open M-Sa 6am-6pm, Su 6am-1pm. D/MC/V.)

⚑ THE ROAD TO CAÑON CITY: 39 MI.

Head north on **Elizabeth Street** and turn left on **US 50 West.** Proceed 35 mi. to Cañon City, where US 50 becomes **Royal Gorge Avenue.** Note the junction with **Route 115 North** 11 mi. east of Cañon City; you will be returning here later.

CAÑON CITY   ☎719

Millions of years before *Homo sapiens* arrived in these parts, Cañon City was dinosaur territory. Many sets of fossilized remains have been discovered, especially in the area of Florissant National Monument. For human Coloradans, however, the mountain town of Cañon City will always be associated with prisons; Colorado's first territorial prison was here, and there are still several correctional facilities in the area. Today, Cañon City (at 5300 ft. above sea level) lays claim to being the (relatively warm) "climate capital of Colorado" and is a great base for exploring the surrounding wilderness.

✦ ORIENTATION

US 50 runs east-west through the entire area and is known as **Royal Gorge Avenue.** The town itself mostly lies north of US 50 in an easily navigable downtown area; numbered streets head north from US 50. **Royal Gorge** is about 10 mi. west of Cañon City on US 50.

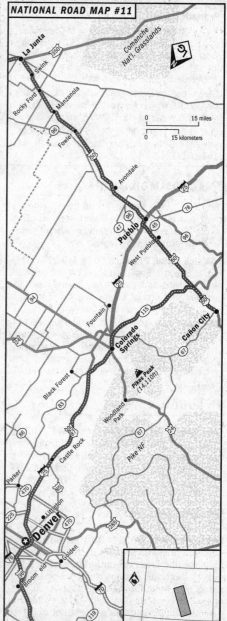

NATIONAL ROAD MAP #11

Population: 16,000

Tourist Office: Cañon City Chamber of Commerce, 403 Royal Gorge Blvd. (☎719-275-2331; www.canyoncitycolorado.com), at 4th St. Dinosaur-shaped info center just north of US 50 on the way into town, on Fremont St. Open M-F 8am-5pm.

Library and Internet Access: Cañon City Public Library, 516 Macon Ave. (☎719-269-9020). Open M-Th 9:30am-7pm, F-Sa 9:30am-5pm.

Post Office: 1501 Main St. (☎719-275-6877). Open M-F 8:30am-5:30pm, Sa 9am-noon. **Postal Code:** 81212.

ACCOMMODATIONS

There are a few motels on **US 50** near downtown as well as on **East Main Street,** south of US 50. It's a good idea to reserve ahead, especially on summer weekends.

Skyline Motel, 219 Main St. (☎719-275-5814). Has 6 rooms. Small and charming. The presence of kitchens and mismatched towels make the rooms feel homey. Rooms May-Oct. $40; from Nov.-Apr. weekly rates only. Cash only. ❷

Colorado Inn, 1031 Royal Gorge Blvd. (☎719-275-2463 or 719-275-9601). Classy and clean rooms with romantic Western prints, pastel beds, and small but very nicely arranged bathrooms. Wi-Fi. Singles $40-58; doubles $60-78. AmEx/D/MC/V. ❸

FOOD

GoodThyme Cafe, 412 Main St. (☎719-275-0222). Spacious. Has a menu of fresh sandwiches and salads ($5-6). Save room for a slice of one of their homemade cakes and pies. Breakfast $3-7. Lunch specials $8. Open M-F 7am-2pm, Sa 7am-1pm, Su 8am-1pm. D/MC/V. ❶

SIGHTS

MUSEUM OF COLORADO PRISONS. The museum presents a series of informative cell displays that treat execution methods, disciplinary methods, famous riots, prison breaks, gangs and their tattoos, and individual prisoners. Also on display is a great collection of contraband, such as a chess set made of toilet paper, and prisoners' artwork, including a wood plaque made for a staff member that reads, "I paid a convict a buck for this sign." Ghost walks in Cañon City (1½hr.) meet at the museum. *(201 N. 1st St., at the western edge of downtown. ☎719-269-3015; www.prisonmuseum.org. Open daily from Memorial Day to Labor Day 8:30am-6pm; from Labor Day to mid-Oct. 10am-5pm; from mid-Oct. to Memorial Day 8:30am-6pm. Includes audio tour. Ghost walks from Memorial Day to Labor Day M and F-Su 6:30pm. $7, children $5, seniors $6. Ghost walks $8, children and seniors $5.)*

ROYAL GORGE ROUTE TRAIN RIDE. This is a 2hr., 24 mi. train ride through the Royal Gorge. It may not be cheap, but the luxury train is a good way to kick back and enjoy the canyon. Select trains serve wine while en route. *(401 Water St. Take 3rd St. south to Santa Fe Depot at Water St., behind the Dinosaur Depot. ☎719-276-4000 or 888-724-5748; www.royalgorgeroute.com. Dinner, mystery, and wine trains select evenings. Call for hours. Reservations recommended. Coach $33, children $21.50; first class $58/47. Dinner train $85 for a 3 hr. ride. Locomotive ride $99.)*

DINOSAUR DEPOT MUSEUM. The museum has the world's most complete *Stegosaurus* and other significant Colorado paleontological findings. *(330 Royal Gorge Blvd. #A. ☎719-269-7150. Open from mid-May to mid-Aug. daily 10am-5pm; from mid-Aug to Sept. daily 10am-4pm. From Sept. to mid-May W-Su 10am-4pm. $4, ages 4-12 $2.)*

ROYAL GORGE BRIDGE. Years ago, it was free to walk over this, the world's highest suspension bridge, but today they charge an exorbitant price at the Royal Gorge Park. Admission for the amusement-park-style area includes a trip on the world's steepest incline railway or the world's longest single-span aerial tram above it. The scenery from the air is spectacular, but to see the bridge for free, park in the parking lot and take the short trail down to an overlook. Some visitors report getting discounts just before the park closes. *(Take US 50 W. 10 mi. from Cañon City. ☎719-275-7507 or 888-333-5597; www.royalgorgebridge.com. Bridge open from Memorial Day to Labor Day 7am-sunset; from Labor Day to Memorial Day daily 10am-4:30pm. $23, ages 4-11 $19, seniors $21.)*

⚠ OUTDOORS

Tunnel Drive Trail, a 2 mi. trail through three tunnels, offers views of the Arkansas River. It's best explored in early morning when the reflections off the river are brilliant. Head west on US 50 past the prison; it's on the left. The **Arkansas River** reaches a hilly point around Cañon City where it produces some fantastic rapids. Four companies based in and around the city offer rafting excursions: **Raft Masters,** 2315 E. Main St. (☎800-568-7238; www.raftmasters. com); **Whitewater Adventure Outfitters,** 50905 US 50 W. (☎719-275-5344 or 800-530-8212; www. waorafting.com); **Echo Canyon River Expeditions,** 45000 US 50 W. (☎800-755-3246; www. raftecho.com); and **Raven Adventure Trips,** 43659 US 50 W. (☎800-332-3381; www.ravenraft. com). All trips are around $55-110 per person, depending on duration.

⚲ THE ROAD TO COLORADO SPRINGS: 45 MI.

A bit of backtracking is required here—from Cañon City, follow **Royal Gorge Boulevard (US 50)** back east 11 mi. out of town to the junction with **Route 115 North,** which becomes **Nevada Avenue** in Colorado Springs.

COLORADO SPRINGS ☎719

When early gold seekers discovered bizarre red rock formations here, they named the region "Garden of the Gods," in part due to a Ute legend that the rocks were petrified bodies of enemies hurled down from the sky. Today, the name remains appropriate: the US Olympic team trains here, and jets from the US Air Force Academy roar overhead. Colorado Springs is a thriving metropolis and the second-largest city in Colorado.

◢ ORIENTATION

Colorado Springs is laid out in a grid of broad thoroughfares. **Nevada Avenue** is the main north-south strip from which named and numbered streets ascend, moving westward. **I-25** cuts through downtown, dividing Old Colorado City from the residential eastern sector of the town. **Colorado Avenue** and **Pikes Peak Avenue** run east-west across the city. Just west of Old Colorado City lie **Manitou Springs** and the Pikes Peak area. Colorado Ave., the main street through town, becomes Manitou Ave. as it extends into Manitou Springs.

VITAL STATS
Population: 370,000
Tourist Office: Colorado Springs Convention and Visitors Bureau, 515 S. Cascade Ave. (☎719-635-7506). Open May-Sept. daily 8am-6pm; in winter M-F 8:30am-5pm.
Library and Internet Access: Penrose Public Library, 20 N. Cascade Ave. (☎719-531-6333). Open M-Th 10am-9pm, F-Sa 10am-6pm, Su 1-5pm.
Post Office: 201 E. Pikes Peak Ave. (☎719-570-5336), at Nevada Ave. Open M-F 7:30am-5:30pm, Sa 8am-1pm. **Postal Code:** 80903.

◤ ACCOMMODATIONS

Motels line **Nevada Avenue** near downtown, but the best options can be found farther west in Manitou Springs. **Campgrounds ❶** clutter Rte. 67, 5-10 mi. north of Woodland Park, which lies 18 mi. northwest of Colorado Springs on US 24. Try Colorado, Painted Rocks, or South Meadows, near Manitou Park. (Generally open May-Sept. Sites $13-15. MC/V accepted online, cash only on-site.) Unless otherwise posted, you can camp on national or forest property for free if you are at least 500 ft. from a road or stream. The **Pikes Peak Ranger District Office,** 601 S. Weber St., has maps. (☎719-636-1602. Open M-F 8am-4:30pm.)

Mecca Motel, 3518 W. Colorado Ave. (☎800-634-2442). Well-kept rooms with pastel beds and clean bathrooms. Microwaves and fridges. Heated pool—with a slide! Singles $65, with hot tub $150; doubles $80-90. MC/V. ❷

Maverick Motel, 3620 W. Colorado Ave. (☎719-634-2852 or 800-214-0264). Expect an explosion of different styles the moment you walk in, from zebra-print pillows to fuschia-and-green beds to Western pastel-colored walls. Pleasantly shaded courtyard. Fridge and microwave. Singles from $35; doubles from $45. MC/V. ❷

Beckers Lane Lodge, 115 Beckers Ln. (☎719-685-1866), at the south entrance of the Garden of the Gods. Microwaves and fridges.

NATIONAL ROAD

Heated outdoor pool and barbecue. Pets allowed. Rooms $55, with kitchenette $90. Cash only. ❷

Rocky Top Motel and Campground, 10090 W. Hwy. 24 (☎719-684-9044 or 866-900-9044; www.rockytopco.com). Close to the Rampart Reservoir, which offers fishing, hiking, and the Waldo Canyon Trail. In summer primitive tent sites $18.50; RV sites with full hookup $22-29; motel rooms $59-129. In winter primitive tent sites $16; RV sites with full hookup $19-26; motel rooms $49-119. AmEx/D/MC/V. ❶

🍴 FOOD

Students fill the outdoor tables in front of the cafes and restaurants lining **Tejon Avenue.** Old Colorado City, west of town on **Colorado Avenue,** is also a great place for independent and friendly restaurants.

🅱 **Poor Richard's Restaurant,** 324 N. Tejon St. (☎719-632-7721). A popular local hangout with great New York-style pizza (slices from $3.65; pizzas from $14), healthy sandwiches ($7), and salads ($5-8) as well as a good selection of microbrews from in and around Colorado ($3-3.50). The plain brick walls and comfortable chairs make this restaurant a pleasant, offbeat space to hang out. Open M-W and Sa-Su 11am-9pm, Th-F 11am-10pm. AmEx/D/MC/V. ❶

🅱 **Savelli's,** 301 Manitou Ave. (☎719-685-3755). Cheery waitresses serve quality Italian food at this friendly restaurant. The pasta ($5-10) is tasty, but the specialty here is the pizza ($7-20). Open daily in summer 11am-9pm; winter 11am-8:30pm. AmEx/D/MC/V. ❷

Henri's by Jorge's, 2427 W. Colorado Ave. (☎719-634-9031). Brightly colored Mexican restaurant with fun music. Fajitas $11.50. Margarita happy hour (M-F 4-6pm). Open Tu-Sa 11am-9pm, Su 11am-8pm. AmEx/D/MC/V. ❷

Manitou Pancake and Steak House, 26 Manitou Ave. (☎719-685-9225). Feels like a pleasant country home. Enjoy a filling country-style breakfast or lunch in the breezy dining room under the open rafters. Most lunch items $5-9; all-you-can-eat breakfast buffet $9. Open daily 6am-2pm. AmEx/D/MC/V. ❷

Wild Ginger Thai Restaurant, 3020 W. Colorado Ave. #A (☎719-634-5025; www.wildgingerthai. com). As they themselves say: a spicy alternative to Southwestern cuisine. Lunch includes dishes like lemongrass shrimp ($6.75); dinner specialties include ginger stir-fried beef ($9). Thai art decorates the walls alongside beer ads. Open M 5-9pm, Tu-Th 11am-3pm and 5-9pm, F-Sa 11am-3pm and 5-10pm, Su noon-9pm. AmEx/D/MC/V. ❷

📷 SIGHTS

PIONEER'S MUSEUM. The museum recounts the settling of the city and has plenty of artifacts that bring to mind cowboys and Native Americans, like the spurs of local outlaws. The museum is the only one in the world to have had a homicide take place inside, and the ghost of the murdered janitor is said to haunt the second floor and the shaft of the birdcage elevator. (215 S. Tejon Ave. ☎719-385-5990; www.cspm.org. Open Tu-Sa 10am-5pm. Free.)

US OLYMPIC COMPLEX. Olympic hopefuls train at this complex. The best times to get a glimpse of athletes in training are 10-11am and 3-4pm. The rest of the time, the Hall of Fame provides entertaining tales of rags to riches. (1750 E. Boulder St., at the corner of Union St. ☎719-866-4618 or 888-659-8687. Tours M-Sa June-Aug. every 30 min. 9-11:30am and 12:30-4pm; Sept.-May every hr. 9am-4pm. Free.)

SEVEN FALLS. Seven Falls promises the grandest mile of scenery in Colorado, seen from a 14-story elevator. The falls are beautiful at any time of day but are especially pretty at night from September to May when they are lit up. There are also two moderately difficult hiking trails here. (2850 S. Cheyenne Canyon Rd. ☎719-632-0765; www.sevenfalls.com. Call for hours. Day $9, night $10.50; ages 6-17 $5.50/6.50.)

VAN BRIGGLE POTTERY. Here, potters demonstrate their skill during free tours through the studio and showroom. Witness the spinning, casting, and etching process that has produced pieces displayed in museums throughout the world. (600 S. 21st St. ☎719-633-7729; www.vanbriggle.com. Open M-Sa 8:30am-5pm. Tours M-Tu and Th-Sa 9am-4pm. Free.)

CANDY MOGUL PATSY'S. The factory offers 30-45min. tours that include tasting chocolate, taffy, gelato, and whatever else Patsy's is making that day. (1540 S. 12th St. ☎719-633-7215

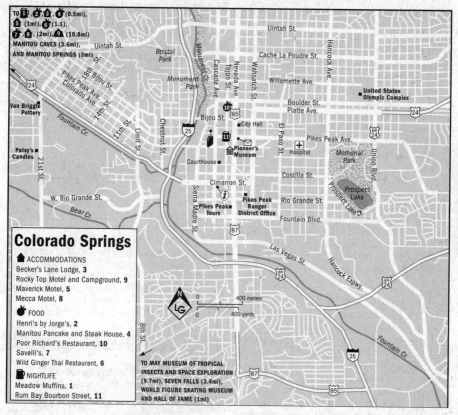

Colorado Springs

🏠 ACCOMMODATIONS
Becker's Lane Lodge, 3
Rocky Top Motel and Campground, 9
Maverick Motel, 5
Mecca Motel, 8

🍎 FOOD
Henri's by Jorge's, 2
Manitou Pancake and Steak House, 4
Poor Richard's Restaurant, 10
Savelli's, 7
Wild Ginger Thai Restaurant, 6

🍸 NIGHTLIFE
Meadow Muffins, 1
Rum Bay Bourbon Street, 11

or 866-372-8797. Store open M-F 9am-5:30pm, Sa 10am-5pm. Tours May 15-Sept. 15 M-F 11am, 2pm.)

MAY MUSEUM OF TROPICAL INSECTS AND SPACE EXPLORATION. The May Museum provides a somewhat bizarre educational experience. Look for the giant insect off the highway. (710 Rock Creek Canyon Rd. Take Hwy. 115 south 5 mi., turn right at the insect, and follow the road 1 mi. ☎719-576-0450 or 800-666-3841; www.maymuseum-camp-rvpark.com. Open May-Oct. daily 9am-6pm; in winter by appointment only. $6, ages 6-12 $3, seniors $5; includes both museums.)

MANITOU CAVES. These 700-year-old Anasazi buildings are distinct in that you can walk around in and touch them as much as you want. The buildings naturally reject

heat and provide a cool break from the sun. An attached museum displays Anasazi artifacts. Dancers perform somewhat irregularly between June and August; call ahead. (10 Cliff Dwelling Rd. ☎719-685-5242 or 800-354-9971. Open daily May-Sept. 9am-6pm; Oct.-Nov. and Mar.-Apr. 9am-5pm; Dec.-Feb. 10am-4pm. $9.50, children ages 7-11 $7.50, seniors $8.50.)

WORLD FIGURE SKATING MUSEUM AND HALL OF FAME. The museum traces the history, art, and science of skating through film and photos. It boasts an extensive collection of medals and skating outfits. (20 1st St., just north of Lake St. ☎719-635-5200; www.worldskatingmuseum. org. Open Apr.-Oct. M-Sa 10am-4pm; Nov.-Mar. M-F 10am-4pm. $3, ages 6-12 and seniors $2.)

⚑ NIGHTLIFE

Bars in Colorado Springs stay filled with students until late into the night.

Rum Bay Bourbon Street, 20 N. Tejon St. (☎719-634-3522; www.csnightclubs.com). A multilevel bar and club complex with 8 clubs included under 1 cover charge ($5, F-Sa after 10pm $10). The main Rum Bay Club features Top 40. Masquerade is a disco club, Copy Cats is a karaoke bar, Blondies does remixes, and Pipeline plays rock and roll. Drinks $6-7. Open bar Th; cover men $10, women $5. Rum Bay open Th-Sa 7pm-2am; the other clubs generally open 4pm-2am. AmEx/MC/V.

Meadow Muffins, 2432 W. Colorado Ave. (☎719-633-0583). Wagons hanging from the ceiling were used in *Gone With The Wind,* and the windmill-style fan was in *Casablanca.* Live music Tu and F. Karaoke Th and Sa. Ladies night Sa. Open daily 11am-2am. AmEx/D/MC/V.

PHOTO OP. Sam's, a bar at Rum Bay Bourbon Street in Colorado Springs, is officially the world's smallest bar according to the *Guinness Book of World Records.* You will barely have room to turn around with your drink; Sam's has a diminutive 109.57 sq. ft. of space and a maximum occupancy of five people—a bartender and one person at each of the bar's four pint-sized seats.

⚑ OUTDOORS

If you want to do serious hiking anywhere in the Colorado Springs/Pikes Peak region, buy the *Pikes Peak Discovery Atlas,* which contains detailed topographical maps of the whole region. **Pikes Peak Tours,** 132 E. Las Animas St., offers occasional whitewater rafting trips on the Arkansas River as well as a combo tour of the US Air Force Academy and the Garden of the Gods. They also offer tours of Pikes Peak and the Royal Gorge. (☎719-633-1181 or 800-345-8197. Open daily 8am-5pm. Tours $35-90.)

⚑ THE ROAD TO DENVER: 70 MI.

Take **West Cimarron Street (US 24)** west from downtown or east from Old Colorado City to **I-25 North.** For the first part of the drive, an unbroken chain of the **Rocky Mountains** greets drivers on the left, while plains can be seen on the right. Proceed about 68 mi. north to Denver. For downtown and sights, take **Exit 210A** for **US 40/Colfax Avenue.**

DENVER   ☎303

In 1858, the discovery of gold in the Rocky Mountains brought a rush of eager miners to northern Colorado. After an excruciating trek through the plains, the desperados set up camp before heading west into "them thar hills." Overnight, Denver became a flourishing frontier town. Recently named the number-one sports town in America, Denver boasts the nation's largest city park system, brews the most beer of any metropolitan area, and has a high percentage of high-school and college graduates compared to the rest of the country. Arguably, though, the city's best characteristic is its atmosphere—a unique combination of Western grit and cosmopolitan urban sophistication.

VITAL STATS
Population: 565,000
Tourist Office: Denver Visitors Bureau, 1600 16th St., Unit 6 (☎303-892-1505; www.denver.org), at the 16th St. Mall. Open May-Oct. M-F 9am-6pm, Sa 9am-5pm, Su 11am-3pm; Nov.-Apr. M-F 9am-6pm.
Library and Internet Access: Denver Public Library, 10 W. 14th Ave. (☎720-865-1111). Open M-Tu 10am-8pm, W-F 10am-6pm, Sa 9am-5pm, Su 1-5pm.
Post Office: 951 20th St. (☎303-296-4692). Open M-F 7am-7pm, Sa 8am-7pm. **Postal Code:** 80202.

⚑ ORIENTATION

Broadway runs north-south and slices Denver in half. About 2 mi. east of Broadway, **Colorado Boulevard** is another north-south thoroughfare. Running east-west, **Colfax Avenue (US 40)** is the main north-south dividing line. Both named and numbered streets run diagonally in the downtown area; east of Broadway and west of **Downing Avenue,** only streets above 14th St. run diagonally. In the rest of the city, numbered avenues run east-west, increasing as you head north. Named streets run north-south. Many of the avenues on the eastern side of the city become numbered streets downtown. **Downtown,** specifically the **16th Street Mall,** is the social, culinary, and entertainment center. At night, avoid the **West End** (Colfax Avenue, Federal Boulevard, S. Santa Fe Boulevard.), the **Capitol Hill** area (on the east side of town beyond the capitol), and **25th-34th Streets** on the west side of the barrio.

🔓 ACCOMMODATIONS

Inexpensive hotels line **East Colfax Avenue** as well as **Broadway** and **Colorado Boulevard.**

Hostel of the Rocky Mountains, 1717 Race St. (☎303-861-7777), off E. Colfax Ave. Take E. Colfax Ave. east of the capitol and turn left on Race St. The best value in Denver. Saturday night barbecue in the backyard ($4), weather permitting. Linen $2.50. Laundry. Free Internet. Reception 8am-10pm. Dorms $24; private rooms $35 either in the same building or in a Victorian-era house 5 blocks away. MC/V. ❶

Broadway Plaza Motel, 1111 Broadway (☎303-893-0303), south of the Capitol. Clean, spacious rooms near downtown. Prints of the Rockies hang above tan and blue beds. Singles $65; doubles $95. AmEx/D/MC/V. ❷

Budget Host Inn, 2747 Wyandot St. (☎303-458-5454), on the corner of 27th St. and Wyandot St. Comfortable rooms conveniently located near Elitch Gardens and offers $15 off tickets. Singles from $30; doubles from $55. AmEx/D/MC/V. ❷

Cherry Creek State Park, 4201 S. Parker Rd. (☎303-699-3860), in Aurora, an urban area situated around Cherry Creek Lake. Take I-25 to Exit 200, then head north for about 3 mi. on I-225 and take the Parker Rd. Exit to Lehigh St. Pine trees provide some shade. Boating, fishing, swimming, hiking, biking trails, shooting range, jet-ski rental, and 🔓**horseback riding** available. Arrive early. Sites $14, with electricity $22. MC/V. ❶

🔓 FOOD

Denver offers a full range of cuisines, from traditional Southwestern to Russian. Alfresco dining and people-watching are available along the **16th Street Mall.** Gourmet eateries

are located southwest of the Mall on **Larimer Street.** Sports bars and trendy restaurants occupy **LoDo.** Outside of downtown, **Colorado Boulevard** and **Sixth Avenue** also have some posh restaurants. **East Colfax Avenue** has a number of reasonably priced ethnic restaurants.

🔓 **Mercury Cafe,** 2199 California St. (☎303-294-9281), at 22nd St. Decorated with bright red walls, Christmas lights, and political posters, the Merc specializes in home-baked bread, vegan desserts, and veggie specials. The soulful crowd is multigenerational. Salads $4-16. Enchiladas $9-12. Live local bands play in the dining room, while the upstairs dance area hosts tango lessons W and F and swing lessons Tu, Th, Su. Dancing Tu-Th and Su until 1am, F-Sa until 2am. Open Tu-Th 5:30-11pm, F 5:30pm-2am, Sa-Su 9am-3pm and 5:30-11pm. Cash only. ❸

🔓 **Domo,** 1365 Osage St. (☎303-595-3666; www.domorestaurant.com). Take Colfax Ave. to Osage St. (east of I-25) and head south 1 block. Traditional dishes ($15-22) served in an outdoor Japanese garden or airy, rustic interior, where tables are simple slabs of stone. Lunch $6-9.Open M-Sa 11am-2pm and 5-10pm. MC/V. ❺

Benny's Restaurante y Tequila Bar, 301 E. 7th Ave. (☎303-894-0788; www.bennysrestaurant. com). A local favorite for cheap, tasty Mexican food. *Huevos rancheros* $6.75 and fish tacos $8. Open M 11am-10pm, Tu-F 11am-11pm, Sa 9am-11pm, Su 9am-10pm. AmEx/D/MC/V. ❷

Wazee Lounge & Supper Club, 1600 15th St. (☎303-623-9518), in LoDo. The Lounge & Supper Club's black-and-white tile floor, stained glass, Depression-era wood paneling, and bleached mahogany create a unique bohemian ambience. Award-winning pizza $7-9. Stromboli $9. Happy hour M-F 4-6pm. Open M-Sa 11am-2am, Su noon-midnight. AmEx/MC/V. ❷

Pete's Kitchen, 1962 E. Colfax Ave. (☎303-321-3139; www.petesrestaurants.com). Pete's serves hamburgers ($6) and award-winning breakfast burritos with eggs, hash browns, and almost every kind of meat. Casual diner setting. Chili $7.75. Open 24hr. AmEx/D/MC/V. ❷

The Buckhorn Exchange, 1000 Osage St. (☎303-534-9505; www.buckhorn.com). Take Colfax Ave. to Osage St. and head south 3 blocks. Denver's oldest restaurant, famous for its hunting-themed walls. Gourmets will delight in the Buckhorn's mammoth steaks (as would saber-toothed tigers). Try the rattlesnake appetizer ($16). Lunch $10-21. Dinner $22-49. Open M-Th 11am-2pm and 5:30-9pm, F 11am-2pm and 5-10pm, Sa 5-10pm, Su 5-9pm. AmEx/D/MC/V. ❹

Trattoria Stella, 3470 W. 32nd Ave. (☎303-458-1128). Popular, small restaurant with lots of outdoor seating and dishes like walnut chicken with gorgonzola ($11) and creative pasta dishes ($9-15) like truffle-asparagus spaghetti ($14). Open M and W-Sa 11am-2pm and 5-10pm, Su 10am-2pm and 5-10pm. ❸

Gallop Cafe, 2401 W. 32nd Ave. (☎303-455-5650; www.gallopcafe.com), at Zuni. Tasty sandwiches ($6-9) in a quiet neighborhood with limited outdoor seating in summer. Breakfast $5-9. Open M-W 6:30am-3pm, Th-F 6:30am-10pm, Sa 7am-10pm, Su 7am-3pm. AmEx/D/MC/V. ❷

ⓢ SIGHTS

Many of Denver's best sights are downtown, which makes touring on foot easy.

COLORADO STATE CAPITOL. The beautiful capitol building is a sensible place to start a visit to the Mile High City. Marked by a small engraving, one step leading to the building's entrance sits exactly one mile above sea level. (Mad points for creativity if this is where you join the club.) Free tours show visitors the governor's office and the House and Senate chambers. (200 E. Colfax Ave. ☎303-866-2604. Open M-F 7am-5:30pm. 45min. tours June-Aug. M-F 9am-3:30pm; Sept.-May M-F 9:15am-2:30pm. Tours of the dome available by reservation only; reserve 2 weeks in advance. Free.)

DENVER ART MUSEUM (DAM). Near the capitol stands the Denver Art Museum. Recently overhauled, the museum includes the original seven-story building and a new, uniquely shaped annex next door. The DAM houses a world-class collection of Native American art and pre-Columbian artifacts. (100 W. 14th Ave. Pkwy. ☎720-865-5000; www.denverartmuseum.org. Tours daily of special exhibits; call for times. Open Tu-Th and Sa 10am-5pm, F 10am-10pm, Su noon-5pm. $13, students and seniors $10, ages 6-18 $5.)

ELITCH GARDENS. Make a splash at the Island Kingdom water park at Elitch Gardens, across the freeway from Mile High Stadium. The Boomerang, EXLR8R, Halfpipe, and Tower of Doom keep thrill-seekers screaming, as do concerts by artists like Smash Mouth on Saturdays from June to August. (2000 Elitch Cir., at Speer Blvd. ☎303-595-4386. Open in summer daily 10am-9pm; in early fall and spring Sa-Su, hours vary. $35, under 4 ft. $20.)

DENVER MUSEUM OF NATURE AND SCIENCE. This gigantic museum hosts a variety of fun exhibits, including the Hall of Life and the Prehistoric Journey room. Many are region-specific and focus on areas like South America, Botswana, and Colorado. Others investigate a specific topic (like minerals) or time period (like ancient Egypt). The museum also has a planetarium. (2001 Colorado Blvd., at Montview St. ☎303-322-7009 or 800-925-2250; www.dmns.org. Open daily 9am-5pm. $11, children and seniors $6. IMAX or planetarium and museum $16/10.)

BLACK AMERICAN WEST MUSEUM. Denver resident Paul W. Stewart had a lifelong desire to tell the public about a fact that was "not recorded in history books"—that one out of every three cowboys was black. This small museum, which includes both a collection of photos (with captions) and cowboy paraphernalia, details the role African-Americans played in settling the Wild West. There are also exhibits about Justina Ford, whose house the museum occupies; he was an early-20th-century physician to Denver's poor and minority residents. (3091 California St. ☎303-482-2242. Open Tu-Sa June-July 10am-5pm; Sept.-May Tu-Sa 10am-2pm. $8, ages 5-12 $6, seniors $7.)

KIRKLAND MUSEUM OF FINE AND DECORATIVE ARTS. Though small, the Kirkland Museum houses an impressive collection of modernist decorative art and painting, and the *Sunday Denver Post* has even called it Denver's most interesting museum. The curators believe in Colorado artist Vance Kirkland's mission of supporting talented locals, so the collection continues to grow. Highlights include collections of Bauhaus and pop art. (1311 Pearl St. ☎303-832-8576; www.kirklandmuseum.org. Open Tu-Sa 11am-5pm, Su 1-5pm. Tours W-Sa 1:30pm. $6, students, seniors, and teachers $5.)

OCEAN JOURNEY DOWNTOWN AQUARIUM. Denver's brand-new aquarium guides visitors through spectacular underwater

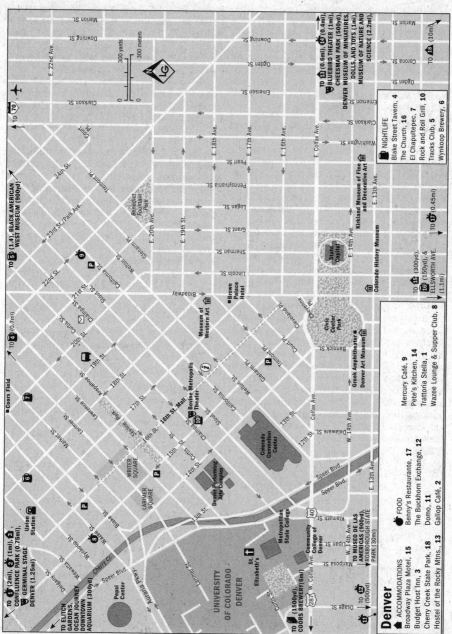

NATIONAL ROAD

Denver

▲ ACCOMMODATIONS
Broadway Plaza Motel, 15
Budget Host Inn, 3
Cherry Creek State Park, 18
Hostel of the Rocky Mtns, 13

● FOOD
Benny's Restaurante, 17
The Buckhorn Exchange, 12
Domo, 11
Gallop Café, 2

Mercury Café, 9
Pete's Kitchen, 14
Trattoria Stella, 1
Wazee Lounge & Supper Club, 8

📖 NIGHTLIFE
Blake Street Tavern, 4
The Church, 16
El Chapultepec, 7
Rock and Roll Grill, 10
Tracks Club, 5
Wynkoop Brewery, 6

exhibits. Highlights include the In the Desert, Sunken Temple, Shipwreck, and Rainforest exhibits. The aquarium houses over 15,000 exotic marine creatures, including several species of sharks, sea otters, and the magnificent Napoleon wrasse. *(700 Water St. ☎303-561-4450; www.aquariumrestaurants.com/downtownaquariumdenver. Open M-Th and Su 10am-9pm, F-Sa 10am-9:30pm. $13.75, ages 3-12 $8.25, seniors $13.)*

OTHER SIGHTS. Located in nearby Golden, the **Coors Brewery** is the world's largest one-site brewery. Free tours take visitors through the brewing process and provide free samples: *(Take I-70 W. to Exit 264, head west on 32nd Ave. for 4 mi., turn right on Ford St., and follow the signs. ☎866-812-2337. 1hr. tours every 30min. M and Th-Sa 10am-4pm, Su noon-4pm.)* At the **Colorado History Museum,** interesting exhibits document Colorado's multifaceted history, including a series of intricate historical dioramas made by the WPA in the 1930s. *(1300 Broadway, at 13th St. ☎303-866-3682;- www.colorado.org. Open M-Sa 10am-5pm, Su noon-5pm. $7, students and seniors $6, ages 6-12 $5.)* The **Museo de Las Americas** exhibits its work by Latin American artists, including photographers, painters, and fabric makers. *(861 Santa Fe Dr., between 8th and 9th Ave., south of downtown. ☎303-571-4401; www.museo.org. Open Tu-F 10am-5pm, Sa-Su noon-5pm. $4, students and seniors $3.)* The **Denver Museum of Miniatures, Dolls, and Toys** has an impressive and surprising collection displayed around a house dating from 1899. The items date from as far back as 1680 through the present. *(1880 Gaylord St. ☎303-322-1053; www.dmmdt.org. Open W-Sa 10am-4pm, Su 1-4pm. $6, ages 5-16 $4, seniors $5.)*

PHOTO OP. Forty miles west of Denver, the road to the top of Mt. Evans (14,240 ft.) is the **highest paved road** in North America. Take I-70 W. to Rte. 103 in Idaho Springs. (☎303-567-3000. Open from late May to early Sept. $10.)

🎵 ENTERTAINMENT

SPORTS

Denver's baseball team, the **Colorado Rockies,** plays at **Coors Field,** at 20th and Blake St.

(☎303-762-5437 or 800-388-7625). Football's **Denver Broncos** play at the **Invesco Field at Mile High** at the intersection of I-25 and Colfax Ave. (☎720-258-3333). Denver's soccer team, the **Colorado Rapids,** play at **Dick's Sporting Goods Park,** 6000 Victory Way (☎303-727-3500) during the spring and summer. The NBA's **Denver Nuggets** and the NHL's **Colorado Avalanche** share the state-of-the-art **Pepsi Center,** 1000 Chopper Cir. (☎303-405-1100).

THEATER

The **Denver Performing Arts Complex (DPAC),** at Speer Blvd. and Arapahoe St., is the largest arts complex in the nation. DPAC is home to the **Denver Center for the Performing Arts, Colorado Symphony, Colorado Ballet,** and **Opera Colorado.** (☎303-893-4100 or 800-641-1222. Tickets M-Sa 10am-6pm.) The **Denver Center Theater Company** (☎303-446-4895) offers student discounts on matinees. In the intimate **Germinal Stage Denver,** 2450 W. 44th Ave., every seat is a good one. (☎303-455-7108. Shows F-Su. $14-18.) The **Bluebird Theater,** 3317 E. Colfax Ave. (☎303-377-1666), is an old theater turned music venue. The **Bovine Metropolis Theater,** 1527 Champa St., offers improv comedy shows five to six nights a week, including Tuesday's "Battle Royale" smackdown starting at 7:30pm. (☎303-758-4722; www.bovinemetropolis.com. $5-16.)

🌙 NIGHTLIFE

Downtown Denver, in and around the 16th St. Mall, is an attraction in itself. The weekly *Westword* gives the lowdown on LoDo, where much of the action begins after dark.

- **El Chapultepec,** 1962 Market St. (☎303-295-9126), at 20th St. A beboppin' jazz holdover from the Beat era of the 50s with a menu of cheap Mexican food ($3-9). The regulars are often a mix of older and younger locals who come for the live music nightly 9pm-1am. No cover; 1-drink minimum per set. Open daily 8am-2am. Cash only.

- **The Church,** 1160 Lincoln St. (☎303-832-3528; www.the-church.com). In a remodeled chapel complete with stained-glass windows and an elevated altar area, the Church offers 4 full bars, a cigar lounge, and a sushi bar Sa-Su. Music ranges from jazz to Top 40 to nationally known DJs. Free cover on some nights; check schedule. 18+ Th,

21+ F-Su. Cover after 10pm $5-15. Open Th-Sa 9pm-2am, Su 9pm-midnight. AmEx/D/MC/V.

Wynkoop Brewery, 1634 18th St. (☎303-297-2700; www.wynkoop.com), in LoDo. Colorado's first brewpub serves fresh beer ($3.75-4.50) and homemade root beer along with full lunch and dinner dishes ($8-21) in a fun, airy setting with brick walls and wood furniture. Free brewery tour Sa 1-5pm. An independent improv troupe, Impulse (☎303-297-2111), performs downstairs Th-Sa . Happy hour M-F 3-6pm. Kitchen open M-Th 11am-11pm, F-Sa 11am-midnight, Su 11am-10pm. Brunch Sa-Su 11am-3pm. Bar open M-Sa 11am-2am, Su 11am-midnight. AmEx/D/MC/V.

Rock & Roll Grill, 1531 Champa St. (303-333-6373; www.myspace.com/rockandrollgrill). They don't serve alcohol, but you could meet the nerd of your dreams at this rock venue that doubles as a computer repair center and cafe by day. Sandwiches named after musicians, like the Kurt Cobain Chicken Salad, are $5. Smaller sandwiches like PBJ $2. Cheesecake of the week $3. F and Sa nights, 8 bands play (4 bands per floor). Open M-Th 9am-5pm, F 9am-midnight, Sa 5am-midnight. AmEx/D/MC/V.

Tracks Club, 3500 Walnut St. (☎303-863-7326; www.tracksdenver.com). A GLBT-friendly nightclub that sometimes hosts fun events like Madonna tributes. Several DJs keep things exciting on the weekends. Women's Party 1st F of each month 6pm-2am. 21+ Sa. Cover Th ages 18-20 $7; over 20 9-11pm free, 11pm-2am $5. Cover Sa 9-10pm free, 10-11pm $5, 11pm-2am $10. Open Th and Sa 9pm-2am.

Blake Street Tavern, 2401 Blake St. (☎303-675-0505; www.blakestreettavern.com). Sports bar with a classy twist. Moderately priced burgers, sandwiches, wraps, and hot dogs, made extra large. ½ lb. burger $9. ¼ lb. hot dog $7. Thai tuna salad $11.50. Open daily 11am-2am. Opens earlier for NFL and college games. Kitchen open M-W and Su 11am-10:30pm, Th-Sa 11am-midnight. AmEx/D/MC/V.

FESTIVALS

Every January, Denver hosts the nation's largest livestock show and one of its biggest rodeos, the **National Western Stock Show & Rodeo,** 4655 Humboldt St. Cowboys compete for prize money while over 10,000 head of cattle, horses, sheep, and rabbits compete for "Best of Breed." Between big events, all sort of oddball fun takes place, including Western battle recreations, monkey sheep herders, and rodeo clowns. (☎303-295-6124; www.nationalwestern.com. Tickets $10-20.) The whole area vibrates during the **Denver March Powwow,** at the Denver Coliseum, when over 1000 Native Americans from all over North America dance in full costume to the beat of the drums. (☎303-934-8045; www.denvermarchpowwow.org. $7.) During the first full week of June, the **Capitol Hill People's Fair** is one of the largest arts and crafts festivals in Colorado. (☎303-830-1651; www.peoplesfair.com.) Originally named to celebrate Denver's dual personalities as the Queen City of the Plains and the Monarch Metropolis of the Mountains, the **Festival of Mountain and Plain: A Taste of Colorado** (☎303-295-6330; www.atasteofcolorado.com) packs Civic Center Park on Labor Day weekend. Free live music is the name of the game at **Confluence Concerts,** along the banks of the South Platte at 15th and Little Raven St.

OUTDOORS

Denver has more public parks per square mile than any other city—if you want to bicycle, walk, or play capture the flag, you've come to the right place. **Cheesman Park,** at Eighth Ave. and Humboldt St., offers picnic areas, manicured flower gardens, and a view of snow-capped peaks. **Confluence Park,** at Cherry Creek and the South Platte River, lures bikers and hikers with paved riverside paths. (☎303-358-6696. From mid- to late July. Th 6:30-8pm.) One of the best parks for sporting events, **Washington Park,** at Louisiana Ave. and Downing St., hosts impromptu volleyball and soccer games on summer weekends. Wide paths for biking, jogging, and in-line skating encircle the park, and the two lakes in the middle are popular fishing spots. At **Roxborough State Park** in Littleton, visitors can hike among rock formations and Native American ruins along the Dakota Hogback ridge. Take US 85 S., turn right on Titan Rd., and follow it 6 mi. (☎303-973-3959. Open sunrise-sunset.)

THE ROAD TO BOULDER: 30 MI.

Take **I-25 North** to **Exit 217** for **US 36 West**, the Denver-Boulder Turnpike.

BOULDER ☎303

The 1960s have been slow to fade in Boulder. A liberal haven in an otherwise conservative region, the city brims with fashionable coffee shops, teahouses, and juice bars. Boulder is home to both the central branch of the University of Colorado (CU) and Naropa University, the only accredited Buddhist university in the US. Seek spiritual enlightenment through meditation workshops at Naropa or pursue a physical awakening through Boulder's incredible outdoor activities, including biking, hiking, and rafting along Boulder Creek.

VITAL STATS

Population: 95,000

Tourist Office: Boulder Chamber of Commerce and Visitors Service, 2440 Pearl St. (☎303-442-1044; www.boulderchamber.com), at Folsom St. Open M-F 8:30am-5pm.

Library and Internet Access: Boulder Public Library, 1000 Canyon Blvd. (☎303-441-3100), at Broadway. Open M-Th 10am-9pm, F-Sa 10am-6pm, Su noon-6pm.

Post Office: 1905 15th St. (☎303-938-3704), at Walnut St. Open M-F 7:30am-5:30pm, Sa 10am-2pm. **Postal Code:** 80302.

ORIENTATION

Boulder is a small, manageable city. The most developed area lies between **Broadway (Route 7/Route 93)** and **28th Street (Route 36),** two busy north-south streets. Broadway, 28th St., **Arapahoe Avenue,** and **Baseline Road** border the **University of Colorado (CU)** campus. The area around the school is known as the **Hill** and is home to plenty of shops, bars, and cafes. The pedestrian-only **Pearl Street Mall,** between Ninth and 15th St., is lined with cafes, restaurants, and posh shops. Be alert for bicyclists and careless pedestrians. Avoid meandering around the Hill alone after dark.

ACCOMMODATIONS

There are few budget hotels and motels in and around Boulder. Camping options, however, abound. The **Boulder Ranger District,** 2140 Yarmouth Ave., just off Rte. 36 to the north of town, has information on local campsites. (☎303-541-2500, reservations 877-444-6777. Open from mid-May to early Sept. M-F 8am-4:30pm, Sa 7am-3:30pm; from early Sept. to mid-May M-F 8am-4:30pm.)

Boulder International Hostel, 1107 12th St. (☎303-442-0522; www.boulderhostel.com), at College Ave. The best deal in town. Youthful travelers fill the spacious lobby to watch cable TV and surf the Internet ($4 per day). Linen $7. Laundry. Key deposit $10. 3-night max. stay in dorms in summer. Reception 8am-11pm. Lockout 10am-5pm. Dorms $27; singles $49; doubles $55. AmEx/MC/V. ❶

Boulder Mountain Lodge, 91 Four Mile Canyon Dr. (☎303-444-0882 or 800-458-0882), 2 mi. west of Boulder off Canyon Blvd./Hwy. 119. It may be in the mountains, but it's also just 5min. from downtown. Guests are treated to clean and elegant rooms as well as a hot tub by the stream. Cookies in each room. Check-in 2pm. Check-out 10am. Singles $77-89; doubles with full kitchen $87-109. AmEx/MC/V. ❸

Arapahoe/Roosevelt National Forest (☎303-541-2500, reservations 877-444-6777). Information available at Boulder Ranger District (above). Most sites have water; none have electric hookups. Open from mid-May to Oct. Sites $10-19. Cash only. ❶

Kelly Dahl (☎303-541-2500, reservations 877-444-6777), 17 mi. west on Hwy. 119. The closest campground to Boulder. 46 sites lie among pine trees and picnic tables with open views of the mountainous Continental Divide. Sites $16. Cash only. ❶

Rainbow Lakes (☎303-541-2500, reservations 877-444-6777), 6 mi. north of Nederland off Hwy. 72; turn at the Mountain Research Station (Country Rd. 116) and follow the dirt road for 5 mi. A primitive, quiet camping experience. No water. Sites $10. Cash only. ❶

FOOD

The streets on the **Hill,** which surround CU, as well as those along the **Pearl Street Mall,** burst with eateries, natural food markets, and colorful bars. Twice a week from April through October, Boulder shuts down 13th St. between Canyon Blvd. and Arapahoe Ave. for a lively **farmers' market.** Most produce and other foods sold are organic; samples are widely available. (Open Apr.-Oct. W 4-8pm, Sa 8am-2pm.)

Dushanbe Teahouse, 1770 13th St. (☎303-442-4993). Everything from the intricately carved pillars to the teahouse's mosaics were built by artists in Tajikistan and then mailed piece by piece from Boulder's sister city of Dushanbe. Lays out a scrumptious spread from cultures spanning the globe, focusing on Persia and East and Southeast Asia. Specialties include the lamb burger with mint chutney ($10), Indonesian peanut noodles ($9.50), and Tajikistan *plov* sirloin ($13). Breakfast $5-11. Lunch $7-15. Dinner $11-19. Brunch Sa-Su 8am-3pm. Open daily 8am-9pm. AmEx/D/MC/V. ❸

Half Fast Subs, 1215 13th St. (☎303-449-0404). A standout among sandwich shops. Over 90 oven-baked subs. Delicious cheesesteak, stuffed, and vegetarian subs galore go for ridiculously inexpensive prices ($3.50-5). Happy hour M-F 5-7pm with 7 in. subs for $4. Open M-W 10:30am-11pm, Th-F 10:30am-midnight, Sa 11am-midnight, Su 11am-10pm. AmEx/D/MC/V. ❶

Rio Grande, 1101 Walnut St. (☎303-444-3690). Fresh Mexican fare served to a lively crowd in several large dining areas painted a festive yellow. Express lunch items ($5.75-6.50) are filling. Great collection of premium tequilas. Fajitas $12-16. Enchiladas $9-13. Happy hour daily 3-5pm with $1 off house margaritas, $2 Coronas, and ½-price quesadillas. Brunch Sa-Su 11am-4pm. Open May-Nov. M-W and Su 11am-10pm, Th-Sa 11am-10pm; Dec.-Apr. daily 11am-10pm. AmEx/D/MC/V. ❷

Pasta Jay's, 1001 Pearl St. (☎303-444-5800). Crowded Italian restaurant decorated with vintage pasta ads. Massive portions are served on red-checkered tablecloths. Outdoor seating available in the summer. Pizza $7-17. Entrees $11-15. Open M-Th 11am-11pm, F-Sa 11am-midnight, Su 11am-10pm. AmEx/MC/V. ❸

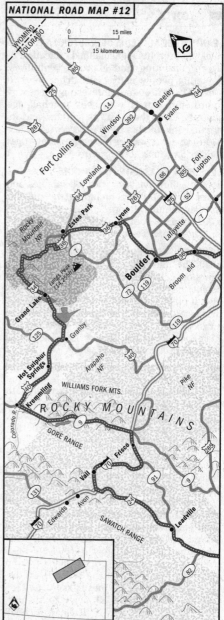

NATIONAL ROAD MAP #12

SIGHTS

LEANIN' TREE MUSEUM OF WESTERN ART. The museum presents an acclaimed collection of over 200 paintings and 80 bronze sculptures, depicting people and scenes from the Old West. There are some interesting pieces by unorthodox artists who seek to challenge stereotypes of the West, its settlers, and its original inhabitants. (6055 Longbow Dr. ☎303-530-1442, ext. 0; www.leanintreemuseum.com. Open M-F 8am-5pm, Sa-Su 10am-5pm. Free.)

CELESTIAL SEASONINGS TEA COMPANY. The company lures visitors with tea samples and tours of the factory, including the delightful Peppermint Room. (4600 Sleepytime Dr. ☎303-530-5300. Open M-F 10am-4pm, Sa 10am-3pm, Su 11am-3pm. Tours every hr. Free.)

BOULDER MUSEUM OF CONTEMPORARY ART. The museum, located in a converted warehouse, has no permanent collection but usually has three or four solo shows on display. It offers free tours and admission during the **farmers' market.** (1750 13th St. ☎303-443-2122; www.bmoca.org. Open Tu and Th-F 11am-5pm, W 11am-8pm, Sa 9am-4pm, Su noon-3pm. Free tours Sa 11am. $5, students and seniors $4.)

ENTERTAINMENT

An exciting street scene bumps through both the **Mall** and the **Hill;** the university's kiosks have the lowdown on happenings. From June to August, find live music and street performances on **Pearl Street Mall.** (Tu and Th-F noon-1:30pm.) From late June to early August, the **Colorado Shakespeare Festival** draws over 50,000 people, making it about the third-largest festival of its kind. (☎303-492-0554; www.coloradoshakes.org. Box office open Tu-F 10am-6pm, Sa-Su noon-6pm. Weekday tickets from $14, weekends $18.) The **Colorado Music Festival** performs at Chautauqua Park from late June through August. (☎303-449-1397; www.coloradomusicfest.org. Tickets from $12.) The local indie music scene is on display at the popular **Fox Theatre and Cafe,** 1135 13th St. (☎303-443-3399; www.foxtheatre.com. Shows usually 8pm. Call ahead or check online for schedule and prices.

NIGHTLIFE

The city overflows with nightlife hot spots, each catering to a young crowd with its own spin. At **Pearl Street** and the **Hill** (around Broadway and 13th) you'll find bars, restaurants, and cafes that stay open late.

Mountain Sun Pub and Brewery, 1535 Pearl St. (☎303-546-0886). The place to go for bluegrass, funk, and the best brews in town. Try the "kind crippler." Acoustic music Su 10pm-1am. $2.75 pints M-F 4-6pm and 10pm-1am. Open M-Sa 11:30am-1am, Su noon-1am. Cash only.

The Sink, 1165 13th St. (☎303-444-7465; www.thesink.com). A Boulder classic, the Sink still awaits the return of its one-time janitor, Robert Redford, who quit his job and headed to California in the late 1950s. Students fill the place for late-night drinking, great pizzas ($5-18), and famous burgers ($7.50) amid wild graffiti and low ceilings. Open daily 11am-2am. Kitchen open until 10pm. AmEx/D/MC/V.

Bookcliff Vineyards, 1468 Pearl St. #120 (☎303-449-9462; www.bookcliffvineyards.com). Entrance on 15th St. Plenty of comfortable sofas. F offers tasting of local Colorado wines—and live jazz. Open M-Th 2-8pm, F 1-10pm, Sa 1-8pm, Su 1-7pm. MC/V. Attached is the **Belvedere Belgian Chocolate Shop** (☎303-447-0336; www.belvedereboulder.com)—sheer brilliance. Whoever thought of this should get a Nobel. A decadent experience. Hot chocolate soup $4.50. Truffles $1.25. Frozen hot chocolate $4.75-5. Open M-Th 9am-8pm, F 9am-9pm, Sa 10am-8pm, Su noon-7pm. AmEx/D/MC/V.

Sundown Saloon, 1136 Pearl St. (☎303-449-4987). No windows in this basement bar, but free pool daily until 10:30pm. Snapshots of customers (everyone from sorority girls to cowboys) crowd the brick walls. $1 "mystery can" M. Open daily 2pm-2am. MC/V.

The West End Tavern, 926 Pearl St. (☎303-444-3535). Has a rooftop bar with an inspiring view of downtown and the Flatirons and a moderately priced menu. Draft beers $4-5. Open daily 11am-11:30pm. Bar open daily until 1:30am. AmEx/MC/V.

Foundry, 1109 Walnut St. (☎303-447-1803). Large room downstairs for playing pool and generally relaxing. Rooftop bar has a full view of the Flatirons and uses misters and heaters for climate control. Occasional live blues and reggae; otherwise a DJ spins eclectic mixes. Free pool M. 80s night Tu. Bands play on the roof F. No cover. Happy hour daily until 7pm. Open daily 11am-2am. AmEx/D/MC/V.

Tonic Oxygen Bar, 2011 10th St. (☎303-544-0202; www.tonicbar.net), at Pearl St. Has a very relaxed, organic mood and caters to Boulder's granola crowd. 10min. of aroma-infused oxygen $10, 40min. $21. A good option is the 20min. oxygen session plus massage for $30. Herbal drinks $3-6. Alcohol comes in the form of local organic mead ($7). Open M 2-9pm, Tu-Th 1-9pm, F-Sa 2-10pm, Su 1-7pm. MC/V.

🏔 OUTDOORS

Boulder supports many outdoor activities in the nearby mountains. Starting at **Scott Carpenter Park,** hiking and biking trails follow Boulder Creek to the foot of the mountains. **Chautauqua Park,** south of the Hill, has many trails varying in length and difficulty that climb up and around the Flatirons. From the auditorium, the **Enchanted Mesa/McClintock Trail** (2 mi.) is an easy loop through meadows and ponderosa pine forests. A more challenging hike, **Greg Canyon Trail,** starts at the Baird Park parking lot and rises through the pines above Saddle Rock, winding back down the mountain past Amphitheater Rocks. Before heading into the wilderness, grab a map at the entrance to Chautauqua Park. Beware of mountain lions and dispose of garbage in the designated receptacles to avoid attracting bears. **University Bikes,** 839 Pearl St., rents out quality bikes and will share a wealth of knowledge about various biking trails. (☎303-444-4196. Day rentals $10-25. Open M-F 10am-7pm, Sa 10am-6pm, Su 10am-5pm.)

🛤 THE ROAD TO LYONS: 17 MI.
Head north on **28th Street** to **US 36 West.**

LYONS ☎303

Lyons is a cute town (pop. 1500) surrounded by red cliffs. The main reason that out-of-towners visit is for bluegrass concerts that take place throughout the summer. The **Chamber of Commerce** (☎303-823-5215) has information on when and where the concerts

occur. The **Aspen Leaf Motel ❸,** 338 Main St., has affordable rooms and flower gardens out back. (☎303-823-6181. Singles $64-70; doubles $74-80. MC/V.) Main St. is lined with local shops and cafes (with outdoor seating) where locals hang out. A good place for pizza is **Ma's Pizzeria ❶,** 430 Main St., which serves slices for $2.50 and cakes, ice cream, and cookies for $2. (☎303-823-6262; www.maspizza.net. Open M-Th and Su 11am-8pm, F-Sa 11am-9pm. MC/V.)

🛤 THE ROAD TO ESTES PARK: 21 MI.
Continue on **US 36 West.** Allow 45min. from Lyons to Estes Park and another 30min. to get into **Rocky Mountain National Park** itself. Gas gets even more expensive beyond the park (the next spot with decent prices is Kremmling), so fill up on this side.

> **❗ ROAD BLOCK.** The route through Rocky Mountain National Park from Estes Park to Grand Lake is closed from mid-October to Memorial Day, and, even during the summer, it is sometimes temporarily closed due to snowfall. If you are traveling during the winter, you will need to head back out to Estes Park and take **Route 7** to **Route 72** to **Route 119** down to **I-70.**

ESTES PARK ☎970

As the gateway town to Rocky Mountain National Park, Estes Park sits in the valley below the Front Range, the first of the Rockies. Although the town's prime location would make it a perfect tourist destination, quaint Estes Park has largely resisted the commercialization and glitz of nearby towns.

✴ ORIENTATION

Trail Ridge Road (US 34) runs from Estes Park through Rocky Mountain National Park; in Estes Park it is known as **Beaver Meadow Road, Fall River Road,** and **Big Thompson Avenue. US 36** (**North Saint Vrain Avenue** in the east) also runs east-west through town. **Route 7,** called both **South Saint Vrain Avenue** and **Peak to Peak Scenic Byway,** runs north-south. Getting from one side of downtown to the other can take a long time due to pedestrian and auto traffic, but free parking is available at the **visitors center,** which is within walking distance of the downtown area. From the end of June to Labor Day, four different free shuttles run from the visitors center into down town and to Rocky Mountain National Park.

VITAL STATS

Population: 5400

Tourist Office: Estes Park Visitors Center, 500 Big Thompson Ave. (☎970-577-9900). Open from mid-May to early Oct. daily 9am-8pm.

Library and Internet Access: Estes Public Library, 335 E. Elkhorn Rd. (☎970-586-8116). Open in summer M-Th 9am-9pm, F-Sa 9am-5pm, Su 1-5pm; in winter M-Sa 10am-5pm, Su 1-5pm.

Post Office: 215 W. Riverside Dr. (☎970-586-0170). Open M-F 9am-5pm, Sa 10am-1pm. **Postal Code:** 80517.

ACCOMMODATIONS

Colorado Mountain School, 341 Moraine Ave. (☎970-586-5758). Tidy, dorm-style rooms are open to travelers unless booked by mountain-climbing students. Befriend mountain guides ,and they'll show you the best routes. Reception June-Sept. M-Sa 8am-5pm, Su 8am-1pm; hours vary in winter. Dorms June-Sept. $35; Oct.-May $25. AmEx/D/MC/V. ❷

Saddle & Surrey Motel, 1341 S. St. Vrain Ave./ Rte. 7 (☎970-586-3326 or 800-204-6226; www.saddleandsurrey.com). Offers clean and comfy rooms with access to a heated outdoor pool and spa. Limited continental breakfast. Free Wi-Fi. Singles $89; doubles $99. D/MC/V. ❹

Baldpate Inn, 4900 S. St. Vrain Ave./Rte. 7 (☎970-586-6151 or 866-577-5397; www.baldpateinn.com). Although it's not cheap, it's located at the doorstep of Rocky Mountain National Park and has a great patio where you can watch gorgeous sunsets. 2-night min. stay for cabins. Reservations recommended. Lodge rooms $110-135; cabins $200. MC/V. ❺

FOOD

Dunraven Inn, 2470 Rte. 66 (☎970-586-6409). Take Moraine Ave. to Rte. 66. The staff here estimates that the restaurant has about $16,000 in dollar bills covering the walls. You can leave your own signed bill for good luck. Try the homemade lasagna ($12.25) or fried shrimp ($15.50). Once you've ordered a certain dish 15 times, your name gets mentioned with it on the menu. Steaks $18-26. Open from Memorial Day to mid-Oct. M-Th 5am-9:30pm, F-Sa 5am-10pm, Su 5am-9pm; from mid-Oct. to Memorial Day M-Sa 5am-9pm, Su 5am-8:30pm. AmEx/D/MC/V. ❸

Notchtop Bakery & Cafe, 459 E. Wonderview. (☎970-586-0272). In the upper Stanley Village Shopping Plaza, east of downtown off Rte. 34. Freshly baked breads, pastries, pies, and tapas such as fried artichokes ($5) and baked brie ($7). Sandwiches and wraps $4-8. Open in summer M-Sa 7am-9pm, Su 7am-2pm; in winter Tu-Sa 7am-8pm, Su 7am-2pm. D/MC/V. ❷

Sweet Basilico Cafe, 430 Prospect Village Rd. (☎970-586-3899; www.sweetbasilico.com). Well lit and simply decorated. Overflows with locals seeking focaccia-bread sandwiches ($7) and freshly made pastas ($7-13). Be prepared to wait, even during the week. Open June-Sept. daily 11am-10pm; Oct.-May Tu-Su 11:30am-9pm. AmEx/D/MC/V. ❷

Coffee on the Rocks, 510 Moraine Ave. (☎970-586-5181). Overlooks the river. Delicious sandwiches and salads ($5) named after local hikes. Coffee drinks and smoothies $1.50-4.50. Breakfast served all day. Free Wi-Fi. Open daily 6am-8pm. AmEx/D/MC/V. ❶

Smokin' Dave's BBQ and Taphouse, 820 Moraine Ave. (☎970-577-7427). Serves platters of meat ($10-19) cooked in Dave's special barbecue sauces. Meat sandwiches $8-10. Open in summer M-Th and Su 11am-9pm, F-Sa 11am-10pm; in winter daily 11am-8pm. AmEx/MC/V. ❷

Wheel Bar, 132 E. Elkhorn Ave. (☎970-586-9381). One of the few bars in town. Large outdoor patio gets crowded with both locals and tourists during the summer. The rustic interior has pool tables. Open daily 10am-2am. Cash only. ❶

SIGHTS

STANLEY HOTEL. This hotel found itself in the spotlight as the basis of the original Overlook Hotel in Stephen King's novel *The Shining*. Though the film wasn't shot here, the ABC film series adaptation was, and so were parts of several other movies, including *Dumb and Dumber*. Six ghosts are said to inhabit the building. Tours of the hotel discuss its connections to Stephen King and its other appearances in pop culture; ghost-storytelling sessions take place on weekends. Cookies are provided. *(333 Wonderview Ave. ☎970-586-3371 or 800-976-1377; www.stanleyhotel. com. Around 8 tours per day 10am-5pm; ghost stories F-Sa 9pm. Tours and ghost stories $10. For tour information, call ☎970-577-4110.)*

ESTES PARK AREA HISTORICAL MUSEUM. In its account of the area's culture and history, the museum focuses on local wildlife, Native American tribes, and the fur-trapping and gold-mining industries. Of particular interest is a display that treats Native American words that have become place names. *(200 4th St. ☎970-586-6256. Open May-Oct. M-Sa 10am-5pm, Su 1-5pm; Nov.-Apr. F-Sa 10am-5pm, Su 1-5pm. Free.)*

ESTES PARK THEATER. You can still catch a movie at this theater, which is the tallest building in Estes Park and the oldest running theater west of the Mississippi. *(130 Moraine Ave. ☎970-586-8904; www.historicparktheatre.com. Showtimes around 7 and 9pm. $7, ages 3-11 $5.)*

OUTDOORS

At the **Colorado Mountain School,** 314 Moraine Ave., good grades are a cinch, and some travelers report that the teachers are darn good-lookin'. The school teaches rock climbing and mountaineering. It offers a wide variety of half-, full-, and multi-day trips up Longs Peak and other local mountains from $170, with discounts for each additional person. (☎970-586-5758; www.totalclimbing.com.)

THE ROAD TO ROCKY MOUNTAIN NATIONAL PARK: 3 MI.

Take **Moraine Avenue West** to **US 36 West,** which goes by **Beaver Meadows Visitor Center** and into the park, where it hits **US 34 West (Trail Ridge Road).**

ROCKY MOUNTAIN NATIONAL PARK   ☎970

Of all the US national parks, Rocky Mountain National Park is closest to heaven; it has 72 peaks that exceed 12,000 ft. A third of the park lies above the treeline, and Longs Peak tops

off at 14,259 ft. Here among the clouds, granite boulders, and 150 crystal lakes, the alpine tundra ecosystem supports Arctic shrubs and dwarf wildflowers. Black bears, elk, mountain lions, mule deer, bighorn sheep, and marmots also call the park home.

VITAL STATS
Area: 266,000 acres
Tourist Office: Park Headquarters and Visitors Center (☎970-586-1206), 2 mi. west of Estes Park on Rte. 36, at the Beaver Meadows entrance to the park. Open daily from mid-June to mid-Sept. 8am-9pm; from Sept. to mid-June 9am-4:30pm.
Fees: 7-day pass $20 per vehicle, $10 per motorcycle, bike, or pedestrian.

ORIENTATION

US 36 and **US 34** both lead into Rocky Mountain National Park. US 34 is the main route through the park. Heading into the park, US 36 passes the **Beaver Meadows Visitors Center,** the campgrounds at **Moraine Park** and **Glacier Basin,** and the trailheads at **Sprague Lake** and **Bear Lake** before hitting US 34. The US 34 entrance, which is usually less crowded, passes the **Aspenglen** campground, provides access to **Old Fall River Road,** and goes by the smaller **Fall River Visitors Center.**

The park's most popular trails are all accessible from the **Bear Lake Trailhead** at the south end of Bear Lake Rd. Parking is available in several places along the road, and a shuttle bus leads from this parking area to the scenic (and very busy) trailhead.

CAMPING

Visitors can camp a total of seven days anywhere within the park. In the backcountry, the maximum stay increases to 14 days from October to May. Water spigots are available but are turned off during the winter. Reservations are taken at **Glacier Basin** and **Moraine Park** up to five months in advance, but the other sites are first come, first served and fill up quickly. Backcountry permits are available from the **Backcountry Permits and Trip Planning Building,** directly adjacent to the park headquarters at Beaver Meadows. (☎970-586-1242. Open daily 8am-5pm. $20.)

Timber Creek (☎877-444-6777), 10 mi. north of Grand Lake. The only national park campground on the western side of the park. Sites in summer $20; in winter $14. AmEx/D/MC/V. ❶

Arapaho National Forest (☎970-887-4100). Sites generally fill up in the summer by noon. Sites $14-19. Cash only. ❶

Stillwater Campground, 6 mi. west of Grand Lake on Lake Granby. 129 tranquil sites. 11 sites open year-round, with no facilities after Sept. Sites $19, with full hookup $21. AmEx/D/MC/V. ❶

Green Ridge Campground (☎877-444-6777; www.recreation.gov) is located on the south end of serene Shadow Mountain Lake. 78 sites. No electricity. Open from mid-May to mid-Nov. Sites $16. AmEx/D/MC/V. ❶

🔾 SIGHTS

MORAINE PARK VISITORS CENTER. The center has exhibits on the park's geology and ecosystem. Muse about glacier melt and tectonic shifting while rocking in one of the center's comfortable chairs that overlook the mountains. (*Off Bear Lake Rd., 1 mi. from the Beaver Meadows entrance.* ☎970-586-8842. Open from May to mid-Oct. daily 9am-5pm. Free.)

⚓ OUTDOORS

The star of the park is 🔲**Trail Ridge Road (US 34)**, which stretches 48 mi. and rises through a swath of frigid tundra to 12,183 ft. The drive takes roughly 3hr. by car (with traffic and a few stops), though it is possible to get to the other side of the park in 1½hr. Beware of slow-moving tour buses and people stopping to ogle wildlife. The road usually closes for the year in mid-October and re-opens Memorial Day weekend, but it is also sometimes closed or inaccessible due to icy conditions, even in June. Heading west, steal a view of the park from the boardwalk along the highway at **Many Parks Curve. Rainbow Curve** and the **Forest Canyon Overlook** offer impressive views of the tree-carpeted landscape. The **Tundra Communities Trail** provides a look at the fragile alpine tundra. Signposts along the paved trail explain local geology and wildlife. The **Lava Cliffs** attract crowds but are worth the annoyance. After reaching its high point between the Lava Cliffs and Gore Range, Trail Ridge

Rd. runs north to the **Alpine Visitors Center** and again west toward the **Continental Divide,** where a sign makes for a good photo op.

A wilder alternative to Trail Ridge Rd. is the **Old Fall River Road,** near the US 34 entrance into the park. This one-way 9 mi. dirt road leads uphill through part of the park and passes **Chasm Falls.** The road rejoins Trail Ridge Rd. behind the Alpine Visitors Center. RVs and trailers should not take Old Fall River Rd. because of steep hills. This road is closed in winter and does not usually open until July 4. **Bear Lake Road,** south of Trail Ridge Rd., leads to campgrounds and the most popular hiking trails within the park. **Flattop Mountain** (4½ mi., 3hr.), the most challenging and picturesque of the Bear Lake hikes, climbs 2900 ft. to a vantage point along the Continental Divide. **Nymph** (½ mi., 15min.), **Dream** (1 mi., 30min.), and **Emerald Lakes** (1¾ mi., 1hr.) are a series of three glacial pools whose waters reflect the surrounding peaks. Forking left from the trail, **Lake Haiyaha** (2 mi., 1hr.) includes switchbacks through dense subalpine forests and superb views of the mountains. A scramble over the rocks at the end of the trail grants a view of Lake Haiyaha. Numerous trailheads lie in the western half of the park, including the **Continental Divide** and its accompanying hiking trail. Several of these trails end at historic sites, such as abandoned mines and ghost towns.

⚓ THE ROAD TO GRAND LAKE: 4 MI.

Turn off **US 34** at the sign for **Grand Lake** and stay right at the fork in the road.

GRAND LAKE ☎970

Grand Lake, the "snowmobile capital of Colorado," offers spectacular cross-country routes and is the jumping-off point for hiking trails.

✴ ORIENTATION

Trail Ridge Road runs through **Grand Lake. Shadow Mountain Lake** and Grand Lake both border town. **Grand Avenue** is a main thoroughfare, and **Route 278 (West Portal Road)** runs parallel to Grand two blocks north.

VITAL STATS

Population: 450

Tourist Office: Grand Lake Chamber of Commerce, 14700 US 34 (☎970-627-3402; www.grandlake-chamber.com). Open from Memorial Day to Labor Day M-Sa 9am-7pm, Su 9am-6pm; from Labor Day to Memorial Day M-Tu and Th-Sa 9:30am-3:30pm.

Library and Internet Access: Juniper Library, 316 Garfield St. (☎970-627-8353). Free. Open in summer M and F 10am-6pm, W-Th 10am-8pm, Sa-Su noon-4pm; in winter M and F 10am-6pm, W-Th 10am-8pm, Sa noon-4pm.

Post Office: 520 Center Dr. (☎970-627-3340). Open M-F 8:30am-5pm. **Postal Code:** 80447.

ACCOMMODATIONS

Shadowcliff Hostel (HI-AYH), 405 Summerland Park Rd. (☎970-627-9220; www.shadowcliff.org). Perched on a cliff overlooking the Rockies. Hand-built and sure to delight. Friendly staff and magnificent view. Kitchen, showers, wood-burning stove. Linen included. Wi-Fi $5 per day. Reception daily 9am-9pm. 7-night min. stay for cabins. Reservations highly wrecommended. Open from Memorial Day to late Sept. Dorms $23; private rooms with shared bath $55; 6- to 8-bed cabins $125-175. AmEx/D/MC/V. ●

Sunset Motel, 505 Grand Ave. (☎970-627-3318). Boasts a yellow front and baby-blue trim. Cozy rooms and the only heated, indoor pool in Grand Lake. Nonsmoking rooms have fireplaces; smoking rooms are pet-friendly. Rooms in summer from $95; in winter from $45. MC/V. ●

Bluebird Motel, 30 River Dr. (☎970-627-9314), 2 mi. west of town on Rte. 34. Overlooks Shadow Mountain Lake and the Continental Divide and has green and blue colored rooms with microwaves and fridges. Singles in summer $85; in winter $45. MC/V. ●

FOOD

Pancho and Lefty's, 1120 Grand Ave. (☎970-627-8773), at the far end of town. Has an outdoor patio overlooking Grand Lake and a bar large enough to fit most of its residents. Try the *rellenos fritos* ($13-14) and wash it all down with a margarita ($7). Live music some weekends.

Open June-Sept. M-Th and Su 11am-9pm, F-Sa 11am-9:30pm; Sept.-June M-Th 11am-8pm, F-Sa 11am-9pm. D/MC/V. ●

Bear's Den, 612 Grand Ave. (☎970-627-3385; www.thebearsdenrestaurant.com). Serves hearty meals, like chicken-fried steak ($14.50) and box lunches ($8-9; call ahead) with chips, a pickle, and dessert—perfect for taking on the road. Restaurant is built like a log cabin and decorated with bears and Christmas lights. Breakfast $4-8. Open M-Th 6am-9pm, F-Sa 6am-10pm, Su 7am-9pm. D/MC/V. ●

Sagebrush Bar and Grill, 1101 Grand Ave. (☎970-627-1404). Serves barbecue, steaks, burgers, and sandwiches ($8-23). Peanut shells on the floor add to a laid-back ambience. Breakfast $5-12. Open in summer daily 7am-10pm; in winter M-Th and Su 7am-9pm, F-Sa 7am-10pm. AmEx/D/MC/V. ●

OUTDOORS

Lake Verna (7 mi., 3hr. round-trip) starts at the **North Inlet Trailhead** at the east end of Grand Lake. This moderate hike gains a total of 1800 ft. in elevation as it passes Adams Falls and Lone Pine Lake and rewards hikers with open views of Mt. Craig before re-entering the forest. Turn off US 34 at the sign for Grand Lake and stay left at the fork for W. Portal Rd. The North Inlet Trailhead is off a dirt road to the left. The East Inlet Trailhead lies at the end of the road; proceed straight onto County Rd. 339, and the trailhead is to the left. **Deer Mountain** (6 mi., 3hr. round-trip), leaving from **Deer Mountain Trailhead,** is a moderate hike with a 1000 ft. rise. The light foliage affords views of the Rockies all the way up. For fun in the snow, the **Lone Eagle Lodge,** 720 Grand Ave., offers unguided snowmobile rentals that include suits, helmets, boots, fuel, oil, and a helpful map. (☎970-627-3310 or 800-282-3311; www.loneeaglelodge.com. 1hr. deposit required. 4hr. single rental $125, double $145; 8hr. rental $190/210.)

THE ROAD TO HOT SULPHUR SPRINGS: 25 MI.

Continue west on **US 34** to **US 40 West.**

HOT SULPHUR SPRINGS ☎970

For years, Hot Sulphur Springs has attracted a stream of tourists who can't get enough of scalding water that smells like rotten eggs. Treat yourself to a soak at the **Hot Sulphur Springs Resort and Spa ❸**, 5609 County Rd. 20. The natural mineral hot springs that flow through this tranquil spot range 98-112°F in temperature. Signs exhort you to preserve a sense of tranquillity (read: be quiet). Dining options are limited, so pack a lunch. For those who can't drag their relaxed muscles away, the motel-style rooms are small but clean and have log-style wood furniture. (☎970-725-3306. Open daily 8am-10pm. Hot springs $17.50, ages 6-11 $11.50. Private bath $13 per hr. 18+. 30min. massage $50-70. Rooms $98-108. D/MC/V.)

⚑ THE ROAD TO KREMMLING: 17 MI.

Continue on **US 40 West** for 17 mi.; it becomes **West Park Avenue** in Kremmling.

KREMMLING ☎970

Forty two miles from Grand Lake, Kremmling offers few cultural attractions or restaurants; the area serves primarily as a regional base for outdoor sports. **Mad Adventures,** on US 40, east of town, will outfit you for Class I-III rafting on the Colorado River. (☎970-726-5290; www.madadventures.com. Advance reservations recommended. ½-day trips $47, ages 4-12 $41; full-day $67/57.) Before leaving Kremmling, consider taking a ride down **Trough Road,** 2 mi. south of town. It ascends gradually for 8 mi. to a turnoff at **Inspiration Point,** providing a stupendous view of the steep Gore Canyon and the headwaters of the Colorado River, which slices through the canyon far below.

The prices at **Hotel Eastin ❷**, 105 S. Second St., off W. Park Ave., can't be beat. Some rooms still have original antique furnishings from 1906. (☎970-724-3261; www.hoteleastin.net. Free Wi-Fi. Reception 7am-10pm. Rooms $30-55. MC/V.) **Bob's Western Motel ❸**, 110 W. Park Ave., has spacious rooms with richly finished wood-paneled walls, comfortable beds, and clean white bathrooms. (☎970-724-3266. Singles $55; doubles $66. AmEx/D/MC/V.)

The wonderful owners of **Big Shooters Coffee ❶**, 311 Park Ave., have a great selection of coffee drinks ($1.25-4), ice cream ($1.50-5.50), and pastries ($2) baked fresh daily. Look for the sign with a cow drowning in coffee. (☎970-724-3735. Open daily May-Sept. 6:30am-6pm; Nov.-Apr. 6:30am-5pm. MC/V.) The **Moose Cafe ❶**, 115 W. Park Ave., serves all-day breakfast and lunch. Try the moose scramble ($7), which is made of lots of things—but no moose. The moose latte ($4.50) is an espresso milkshake with chocolate and caramel sauce—but still no moose. (☎970-724-9987. Breakfast $3.50-9.25. Hot sandwiches $6-7.50. Open daily 6am-2pm. MC/V.) The family-friendly **Quarter Circle Saloon ❷**, 106 W. Park Ave., serves bar food like burgers (beef, not moose; $5.50) and Mexican dishes ($7-9.50) in a quiet, Western-themed setting. (☎970-724-9601. Open daily 11am-10pm. MC/V.)

⚐ DETOUR
LOWER CATARACT LAKE TRAIL AND WHITE RIVER NATIONAL FOREST

Take **Route 9 South** for 12 mi. and turn right onto **Heeney Road 30.** After 5 mi., turn right on **Cataract Creek Road.** The campground is 2 mi. along the road, and the trailhead is farther. This route is not recommended in wintertime.

The lake is magnificent, surrounded by sloping hills on all sides and higher rocky peaks off in the distance to the south. The highlight of the area is the **Lower Cataract Loop Trail** and neighboring **Cataract Creek Campsite** (entrance fee $5). There are seven mostly sunny lakeside **campgrounds ❶**, operated by the National Forest Service (sites $9-13), several of which are accessible from Rte. 9 and Heeney Rd. 30. There are also four primitive drive-in camping sites ($10), perfect for fulfilling your sleep-under-the-stars fantasy.

⚑ THE ROAD TO FRISCO: 42 MI.

Take **Route 9 South** until it joins with **I-70 West.** Follow I-70 for 3 mi. to **Exit 203** for **Route 9 South/Frisco.**

FRISCO ☎970

The mountains stare down from all sides at the droves of tourists who come to Frisco to bike the mountain trails or ski. Downtown, expensive restaurants and sport shops cater to seasonal visitors.

ORIENTATION

The layout of Frisco is darn easy to grasp. **I-70** borders the town to the northwest. **Summit Boulevard (Route 9),** home to motels, Wal-Mart, Safeway, and other large stores, runs north-south along the eastern edge of town from I-70 to Main St. before heading southeast. **Main Street,** the town's principal commercial street, runs east-west from I-70 in the west to Summit Blvd. in the east and is home to restaurants, lodgings, and local stores.

VITAL STATS

Population: 2400

Tourist Office: Summit County Visitors Center, 300 Main St. (☎800-424-1554; www.townoffrisco.com), on the corner of 3rd St. Open June-Aug. M-Sa 9am-8pm, Su 9am-5pm; Sept.-May daily 9am-5pm.

Library and Internet Access: Frisco-Summit County Library, 37 County Rd. 1005 (☎970-668-5555). Take Summit Blvd. south of Main St. Open M-Th 9am-9pm, F-Sa 9am-5pm, Su 1-5pm.

Post Office: 35 W. Main St. (☎970-668-0610), at Madison. Open M-F 8:30am-5pm, Sa 9am-12:30pm. **Postal Code:** 80443.

ACCOMMODATIONS

Fireside Inn (HI-AYH), 114 N. French St. (☎970-453-6456; www.firesideinn.com). South of Frisco, in Breckenridge, 2 blocks east of Main St., at the corner of Wellington Rd. The wonderful owners exemplify Breckenridge's claim to be a real town with real people. Set in a mining cottage that dates back to 1870, the beautiful inn is well maintained and has an indoor hot tub great for après-ski. Dorms were modeled after the railway cars in the Marilyn Monroe classic *Some Like it Hot.* Breakfast $3-6. Reception daily 8am-8pm. Dorms in summer $28; in winter $30-43. Private rooms $66-190. MC/V. ❷

Frisco Lodge, 321 Main St. (☎970-668-0195 or 800-279-6000). 18 well-decorated Victorian rooms in the middle of downtown. The building was originally a stagecoach stop dating from 1885. Outdoor hot tub. Full breakfast. Singles $39-59; doubles from $79. AmEx/D/MC. ❷

New Summit Inn, 1205 N. Summit Blvd. (☎970-668-3220). Off Dillon Dam Rd. Take Summit Blvd. 1 block south from I-70. Tidy rooms with refrigerators and mountain views. Continental breakfast. Free Wi-Fi. Rooms in summer $50-84; in winter $99-220. AmEx/D/MC/V. ❹

Snowshoe Motel, 521 Main St. (☎970-668-3444). In town. Modern rooms, some with kitchenettes. Hot tub, sauna, and free Wi-Fi. On winter weekends, 2- to 3-night min. stay. Rooms in summer $55-75; in winter $75-125. AmEx/D/MC/V. ❹

Heaton Bay Campground, on Dillon Dam Rd. (☎877-444-6777; www.recreation.gov). 72 shaded spots northwest of the reservoir with water and outhouse-style toilets. D loop is the quietest, but C loop has hookups. Some 1st come, 1st served sites during low season. Weekends 2-night min. stay. 10-day max. stay. Sites $16, with electricity $21. AmEx/D/MC/V. ❶

FOOD

Pika Bagel Bakery and Cafe, 401 Main St. (☎970-668-0902). Proudly bakes its pastries at an elevation of 9100 ft. The "Cool One" sandwich ($3.25) features cucumbers and herb cream cheese. Sandwiches $3.50-6.50, Bagels $2-7. Open daily 7:21am-3:08pm or until the bagels run out. D/MC/V. ❶

Backcountry Brewpub and Pizzeria, 720 Main St. (☎970-668-2337; www.backcountrybrewery.com). Although this restaurant offers light items like a smoked-turkey-club wrap with chipotle ranch dressing ($10), pizza (from $10) is their specialty. Pints $4. Open daily 11am-1am. Kitchen open until 10pm. AmEx/MC/V. ❷

Boatyard Pizzeria and Grill, 304 Main St. (☎970-668-4728). Sandwiches from $8.75. Gourmet pizzas starting at $12. Open daily 11am-10pm. AmEx/D/MC/V. ❸

Himalayan Cuisine, 409 Main St. (☎970-668-3330). Filling asian dishes. M-Sa lunch buffet $8. Dinner $11-19. Open daily 11:30am-2:30pm and 5-9pm. ❸

OUTDOORS

In the summer Frisco, Breckenridge, and surrounding Summit County are a biking haven, with some 70 mi. of paved trails and many more mountain paths. A popular moderate route circles **Dillon Reservoir** (18 mi., 2hr.). Biking the easy route to Breckenridge along the **Blue River Bikeway** (9½ mi., 1hr.) is also popular. Each of these trails can be accessed near the parking lot by the Frisco Bay marina, at the end of Main St. Bike rentals are available at **Wilderness Sports,** 400 Main St. (☎970-668-8804. Bikes $15-40 per ½day, $25-50 per day. Open daily 8:30am-6:30pm.) Miles of hiking trails crisscross the area and go into the mountains. The fun, moderate climb up to 10,502 ft. **Mount Royal** (4 mi., 2-3hr. round-trip) offers great views of Lake Dillon and Frisco. To get to the trailhead, take Main St. heading west. Just before the entrance to I-70, turn left into the parking lot for the Tenmile Canyon Trailhead. Park and follow the bike path a half-mile southeast along the mountain's base. **Tenmile Meadows** (12 mi., 5-6hr. round-trip), off W. Main St. after the entrance to I-70, is considered one of the most difficult and rewarding trails in the area, passing a series of meadows and a view of the Swan River Valley. **Blue River Anglers,** 281 Main St., offers equipment and guides for fishing trips along the Colorado, South Platte, Blue, and Arkansas Rivers, among others. (☎970-668-2583 or 888-453-9171. ½-day $200, each additional person $75. Full day $275/85.)

Summit County offers some of Colorado's best skiing. **Breckenridge** (☎970-453-5000 or 800-789-7669; www.breckenridge.com) is 9 mi. south of Frisco on Rte. 9. One of the most popular ski resorts in the country, Breckenridge has a 3400 ft. vertical drop, plenty of hiking trails, one of the best halfpipes in North America, and 2358 acres of skiable terrain accessible by 30 lifts. In the summer, most mountains offer hiking, biking, and other outdoor activities; consult thestaff at the **Breckenridge Activities Center,** 203 S. Main St., at Washington St., for details. (☎970-453-5579 or 877-864-0868. Open daily June-Sept. and Dec.-Mar. daily 9am-9pm; Apr.-May and Sept.-Nov. daily 9am-6pm.)

THE ROAD TO VAIL: 36 MI.
Follow **Main Street** to **I-70 West.** Take **Exit 176.**

VAIL ☎970

Lord Gore discovered the Vail area in 1854, and it was swarmed by prospectors during the 1870s gold rush. Although that era has passed, Vail remains glitzy. What Tiffany is to silver, Vail is to skiing; this, the largest one-mountain ski resort in all of North America, is where every skier hopes to go when he dies. In the winter, the mountain dazzles with its famed powder and black-diamond bowls, and in the summer wildflowers bloom in abundance. The resort town's employees and visitors come from around the world; street signs and directions are even translated into several European languages. *C'est fantastique!*

VITAL STATS

Population: 4500

Tourist Office: Vail Visitors Center, S. Frontage Rd. (☎970-476-4941), in Vail Village. Open daily July-Sept. 9am-8pm; Nov.-June 9am-5pm.

Library and Internet Access: Vail Public Library, 292 W. Meadow Dr. (☎970-479-2184). Open M-Th 10am-8pm, F-Su 11am-6pm.

Post Office: 1300 N. Frontage Rd. W. (☎970-476-5217). Open M-F 8:30am-5pm, Sa 8:30am-noon. **Postal Code:** 81657.

ORIENTATION

Vail consists of **East Vail, Vail Village, Lionshead Village, Cascade Village,** and **West Vail.** Vail Village and Lionshead Village, which are the main centers of action, are pedestrian-only. Free shuttle buses run to all the villages, and free summer parking is available at the visitors center in Vail Village and the other visitors center in Lionshead.

ACCOMMODATIONS

Cheap lodging is not part of Vail's mentality. Rooms rarely dip below $175 per night in winter, and summer lodging can be as pricey. A bit out of town, prices may be lower.

Lionshead Inn, 705 W. Lionshead Cir. (☎970-476-2050 or 800-283-8245; www.lionsheadinn.com). Has good deals on luxury accommodations in the summer. In addition to an exercise room, game room, hot tub, and fireplace lounge the Inn offers plush robes, down comforters, and balconies in every room. Continental breakfast included. Free Internet. Singles in summer from $99-119; in winter from $199. AmEx/D/MC/V. ❺

The Minturn Inn, Holy Cross Ranger District 1, 24747 US 24 (☎970-827-5715), in Minturn. Provides info on summer campgrounds near Vail. Most sites are primitive with picnic tables and fire grates. Ranger District 1 open M-F 8am-5pm. Sites $10-15. MC/V. ❶

🍴 FOOD

Eating cheaply in Vail is like a double black diamond (read: really hard), but at some local hot spots you can still make it happen.

Little Diner, 616 W. Lionshead Cir. (☎970-476-4279), on the west end of Lionshead Village. You'll never need to cook breakfast in Vail as long as the griddle is hot at this diner. During the winter, locals and visitors alike ski in around the clock to warm up with DJ's sweet and savory crepes ($8-12), like Joe's Special (ground beef, spinach, onions, and parmesan) or the Chunky Monkey (chocolate and banana), both $10. Burgers $9-13. Open May-Sept. daily 7am-2pm; in winter 24hr. MC/V. ❷

Moe's Original BBQ, 675 W. Lionshead Cir. (☎970-479-7888). Describes itself as "A Southern Soulfood Revival." The $10 meat platter, with 2 sides and cornbread, is a good deal. Call ahead for useful and tasty boxed lunches. Open M-Sa 11am-9pm. D/MC/V. ❷

The Red Lion, Hanson Ranch Rd. and Bridge St. (☎970-476-7676). Right in the heart of Vail Village. Was built by its owners as a hotel, but they had so many children that there were no rooms left for guests. The barbecue brisket platter ($13) is made with special barbecue sauce. Open daily in summer 11am-midnight; in winter 11am-2am. Kitchen open until 10pm. AmEx/D/MC/V. ❹

The Tap Room, 333 Bridge St. (☎970-479-0500), in Vail Village. 2 bars and 7 decks. Caters to an après-ski crowd looking for good, rowdy fun. Wash down one of the Tap Room's famous burgers ($6-12) with your drink of choice and breathe in the clean, cold mountain air. Known for serving margaritas ($6) and lunch specials ($7) until 3pm. Open daily in ski season 11am-1:30am; in off season 11am-11pm. Kitchen open until 10pm. AmEx/D/MC/V. ❷

Garfinkel's, 536 E. Lionshead Cir. (☎970-476-3789). Draws a young crowd with a good beer selection and generous portions. The popular Monte sandwich is made of turkey, pastrami, bacon, Swiss, and coleslaw. Ribs, steaks, chicken, and fish $16-26. Open June-Sept. and from Nov. to mid-Apr. daily 11am-2am. Kitchen open until 10pm. D/MC/V. ❸

👁 SIGHTS

SKI HALL OF FAME. The Ski Hall of Fame is housed in the **Colorado Ski Museum.** One gripping exhibit focuses on the 10th Mountain Division and its training in the Rockies for the rigors of fighting in the mountains of Italy during WWII. Check out the fun, if overpriced, vintage posters of Vail in the gift shop. *(231 S. Frontage Rd. E., on the 3rd level of the Vail Transportation Center. ☎970-476-1876. Open daily from mid-Apr. to mid-Nov. 10am-6pm; from mid-Nov. to mid-Apr. daily 10am-8pm. Free.)*

BETTY FORD ALPINE GARDENS. Stroll through the peaceful meditation and rock gardens. *(☎970-476-0103. Open from Memorial Day to Labor Day sunrise-sunset. Tours M, Th, Sa 10:30am. Free.)*

🎵 ENTERTAINMENT

In the summer, the **Gerald R. Ford Amphitheater,** at the less frequented east edge of Vail Village, presents a number of outdoor concerts, dance festivals, and theater productions. (☎970-476-2918. Box office open June-Sept. daily 11am-5pm. Lawn seats $19-23.) The **Vilar Center for the Arts,** in Beaver Creek, at I-70 at Exit 267, hosts performances of everything from Shakespeare to Broadway. (☎970-845-8497 or 888-920-2787; www.vilarcenter.org. Box office open M-Sa 11am-5pm.)

🏔 OUTDOORS

The mountain's 193 trails, 32 lifts, 5289 skiable acres, and seven legendary back bowls are certainly worth the expense. (☎970-476-5601 or 888-605-7573; www.vail.com.) Before slaloming, visit the outfitters that line Vail's streets. **Ski Base,** 610 W. Lionshead Cir., rents ski equipment in the winter and bikes in the summer, when the store becomes **Wheel Base Bike Shop.** (☎970-476-5799; www.vailskibase.com. Skis, poles, and boots from $19 per day. Snowboard and boots from $24 per day. Bikes from #11 per ½-day, $17 per day. Open daily June-Aug. 9am-6pm; in winter 8am-9pm.) The **Eagle Bahn Gondola** in Lionshead and the **Vista Bahn Chairlift,** part of Vail Resort, whisk hikers and bikers to the top of the mountains. On Fridays at 5:30pm, there are free concerts at the top of the gondola, where drinks are served. Tickets and passes can be purchased at the **Vail Snow Sports School,** located by **Garfinkel's Restaurant** (see below) near the base of the Gondola, or at the **Vail Village Pass Office.** (☎970-476-9090. Eagle Bahn open Jan.-Aug. M-W and Su 10am-4pm, Th-Sa 10am-9pm; Sept.-Dec. daily 9am-3pm. Day pass $20, under 12 free with adult, seniors $13; with lunch $25. Bike haul $25. Vista Bahn open from mid-July to early Sept. F-Su 10am-4pm.)

⚑ THE ROAD TO LEADVILLE: 32 MI.

Take **I-70 West** to **Exit 171** for **US 24 East,** which becomes **Poplar Street** in Leadville.

LEADVILLE ☎719

Leadville has a rich and at times tragic history as a mining town. Fortunes were made and lost overnight as 13 major minerals, including gold, silver, lead, zinc, and molybdenum, were mined here. The mining history is documented in the town's six museums; Leadville has the highest per capita number of museums of any city in Colorado. At an elevation of 10,152 ft., it is the highest incorporated city in the US and also marks the beginning of a cluster of "14ers" (mountain peaks over 14,000 ft.), which attract hikers and thrill-seekers from far and wide. The town's pride is evinced by its commonplace souvenir T-shirts that read "Got Pb?" (the chemical slogan for lead) and "I think this whole town is high."

▦ ORIENTATION

Front Street, Poplar Street, Harrison Avenue, Mountain View Drive, Mount Massive Drive, and **McWethy Drive** form a loop around downtown. Within this, **Sixth Street** is the main thoroughfare.

VITAL STATS

Population: 2800

Tourist Office: Leadville Chamber of Commerce, 809 Harrison Ave. (☎719-486-3900). Open from Memorial Day to Labor Day daily 9am-4pm; from Labor Day to Memorial Day Tu-Sa 10am-4pm.

Library and Internet Access: Lake County Public Library, 1115 Harrison Ave. (☎719-486-0569). Open M and W 10am-8pm, Tu and Th 10am-5pm, F-Su 1-5pm.

Post Office: 130 W. 5th St. (☎719-486-9397). Open M-F 8am-5pm, Sa 9am-noon. **Postal Code:** 80461.

⌂ ACCOMMODATIONS

Hotels dot the landscape along US 24 north and south of town.

Leadville Hostel, 500 E. 7th St. (☎719-486-9334; www.leadvillehostel.com). Quiet. Climbers and bikers will find colorful quilted beds, clean bathrooms, and a comfortable living room with a fireplace—i.e., everything you ever wanted to go with a cup of hot chocolate. (And fortunately...) Full kitchen available. Dorms $18-30; private rooms $35-100. MC/V. ❶

Delaware Hotel, 700 Harrison Ave. (☎719-486-1418 or 800-748-2004; www.delawarehotel.com). In downtown Leadville. Clean and nicely decorated Victorian rooms with period furnishings. Flower patterns everywhere. Continental breakfast. Rooms May-Oct. from $85; Nov.-Apr. from $79. AmEx/D/MC/V. ❹

▥ FOOD

Quincy's, 416 Harrison Ave. (☎719-486-9765). This restaurant's menu is limited yet manages to fill all of the restaurant's dark and intimate green pleather booths—and then some. M-Th and Su the dish is filet mignon (various sizes $8-14), and F-Sa it's prime rib ($10-17). There is also vegetable lasagna ($8) for vegetarians. House margaritas $3.50. Open daily June-Sept. 5-9:30pm; Oct.-May 5-9pm. ❸

El Mexicano (☎970-376-1358). Parked next to the Stop 'n Save store just north of town on US 24. Go out of your way to go here (many people from Vail do); it's hailed as the best Mexican food for miles around. Though essentially a food wagon, this eatery reportedly passes health inspections with higher marks than some restaurants in town. Open W-Su noon-9pm. Cash only. ❶

Golden Burro, 710 Harrison Ave. (☎719-486-1239). Try the signature breakfast item, the Golden Breakfast Burrito ($9) with green chili. Chcken-fried steak ($10) is popular. Open daily June-Aug. 6:30am-9pm; Sept.-May 6:30am-8pm. AmEx/D/MC/V. ❷

👁 SIGHTS

NATIONAL MINING HALL OF FAME AND MUSEUM. The museum showcases the mining techniques and culture of the Colorado '49 gold rush. The best part of the museum is the second floor, which features three recreated mines and a set of dioramas. The mines have motion-sensor noises that are creepily realistic. The crystal room is also worth a look, and so is the exhibit about how coal mining is, in fact, safe and environmentally friendly. *(120 W. 9th St. ☎719-486-1229; www.mininghalloffame.org. Open daily July-Nov. 9am-5pm; Dec.-June 11am-4pm. $7, ages 6-12 $3, seniors $6.)*

MINERAL BELT TRAIL. This 11mi. all-season paved loop circles the town, following old railroad rights of way and paths through the California and Slaughterhouse Gulches. Along the way, it passes the remnants of several old mines, tunnels, and shafts. The trail is closed to motor vehicles but is popular with bikers.

�️ THE ROAD TO BUENA VISTA: 34 MI.
Follow **US 24 East,** heading south.

BUENA VISTA ☎719

Buena Vista may lack the cultural opportunities of the larger town Salida down the road, but it offers easy access to the 14ers, hot springs, and rafting in the summer and snowmobiling and cross-country skiing in the winter. One of the best-located resorts in Colorado, the spiritually minded **Cottonwood Hot Springs Inn and Spa ❷,** 18999 County Rd. 306, steams the stress away with soaking pools of varied sizes, shapes, and temperatures, a 108° hot tub, and cold pools. Yoga and belly-dancing classes are available for $12-15; call ahead for the schedule. From US 24, turn right onto Main St., which becomes County Rd. 306. Watch for the surreal abandoned drive-in movie theater on the left. (☎719-395-6434; www.cottonwood-hot-springs.com. Open daily 8am-midnight. No children after dark. From mid-May to Sept. $15, under 16 $10; from Oct. to mid May M-Th and Su $10/7.50, F-Sa $15/10. 2-night min. stay for cabins. Dorms in summer $50; in winter $40; for 2 people $65. Cabins $97-165.) The drive-through **Pancho's ❶,** 215 N. US 24, has great inexpensive Mexican (and some American) food. (☎719-395-2863.

EARTH, WIND, AND FIRE

"Vail is entirely wind-powered." The restaurant worker was proud of her employer, but, unfortunately, her statement was not quite correct. Vail Resorts is the second-largest corporate buyer of wind energy credits in America. What, exactly, does that mean? It does not quite mean that they are wind-powered, but rather that they are using a system of offsetting environmental costs that is based on the idea of supporting progressive energy sources instead of actually using them. In 2006, *USA Today* reported that Vail Resorts (comprising Vail, Breckenridge, and other resorts) uses about the same amount of electricity as 14,000 homes. To "make up" for that energy consumption, Vail purchased a large number of credits, not directly from the energy producers, but from a broker who uses those companies. The wattage comes to about 152,000 megawatts. More impressively, Vail CEO Rob Katz notes that this is the equivalent of taking 18,000 cars off the road.

The rules of energy credits and the entire system of "offsetting" are difficult to understand for non-specialists. It seems easy to click a link when buying a plane ticket, knowing that you are "making up" for the carbon footprint of your flight, but the very newness of this system makes some wary. Furthermore, critics argue that the entire system is faulty and provides a false sense of being relieved of environmental responsibility. There is no easy answer, only hard questions—especially for the road-

[the local story]

Burritos $2.25-6. Hamburgers $2.25-5.30. Open daily 6am-10pm. MC/V.)

⚑ THE ROAD TO SALIDA: 25 MI.

About 2 mi. south of Buena Vista, get on **US 285 South** and turn left onto **Route 291**.

SALIDA
☎**719**

Residents are proud of what they consider to be Colorado's last unspoiled mountain town. Though tourists have yet to discover Salida, artists have already done so; there are excellent galleries on several streets. Salida's downtown is made up of galleries, eateries, and outlets catering to outdoor enthusiasts.

✈ ORIENTATION

Route 291 runs along the northeastern edge of town, along the **Arkansas River**. It is called **Grand Avenue** as it approaches town, **First Street** in downtown, and **Oak Street** as it heads south to **Rainbow Boulevard (US 50)**, which runs east-west at the southern edge of town. Lettered streets run northeast-southwest between US 50 and the Arkansas River, while numbered streets parallel the river, starting with First St., which runs northwest-southeast.

VITAL STATS
Population: 5600
Tourist Office: Salida Chamber of Commerce, 406 W. US 50 (☎719-539-2068; www.salidachamber.org). Open M-Sa 9am-5pm.
Library and Internet Access: Salida Regional Library, 405 E St. (☎719-539-4826). Open M-F 9am-8:30pm, Sa 9am-5:30pm, Su 1-5pm.
Post Office: Salida Main Post Office, 310 D St. (☎719-539-2548), at 3rd St. Open M-F 7:30am-5pm, Sa 8:30am-noon. **Postal Code:** 81201.

⚑ ACCOMMODATIONS

▨ **Simple Lodge and Hostel,** 224 E. 1st St. (☎719-650-7381; www.simplelodge.com). Hardwood floors, red walls, yellow velvet chairs. Clean, beautiful, and has a full kitchen to boot. Almost every piece of the building has an interesting story behind it. The community-minded owners offer Su afternoon brunch as an opportunity for guests and locals to intermingle. Free coffee and pancakes. Linen $2. Free Wi-Fi. Dorms $21; private rooms $50. D/MC/V. ❶

Budget Lodge, 1146 E. US 50 (☎719-539-6695 or 877-909-6695). The owner is friendly, and the price is right. Some rooms with kitchenettes. Singles $39; doubles $54. MC/V. ❷

🍴 FOOD

Laughing Ladies, 128 W. 1st St. (☎719-539-6209). This elegant restaurant's name comes from the term for old frontier prostitutes. Here, Napa Valley-trained chefs serve California-inspired cuisine; it's a high-end downtown fixture. Dinner entrees ($18-24) include dishes like chile-roasted duck with a carnitas tamal, poblano mole, avocado, and pico de gallo ($23) and orange-roasted free-range chicken with almond quinoa and basil sauce ($19.50). The fish is always fresh. Lunch $7-10. Open M and Th-Sa 11am-2pm and 5-8:30pm, Su 9am-2pm and 5-8:30pm. D/MC/V. ❺

Los Girasoles, 10035 W. US 50 (☎719-539-3990). Serves great Mexican food just 4 mi. west of Salida. Chairs are carved and painted like sunflowers. Lunch $5.75-7.50. Large combination plates with rice and beans $8-11. Open daily 8am-9:30pm. AmEx/D/MC/V. ❷

Country Bounty, 413 W. US 50 (☎719-539-3546; www.countrybounty.net). Old-fashioned country cooking. Dishes include the elk burger, marinated in rosemary and juniper berries (lunch $10, dinner $11). Breakfast $6-8. Sandwiches $8-13. Entrees $11-19. Open daily from Memorial Day to Labor Day 6:30am-9pm; from Labor Day to Memorial Day 7am-8pm. AmEx/D/MC/V. ❸

Cowgirl Coffee Company, 105 F St. (☎719-539-4377). Pastries ($1-1.50), smoothies ($4), and more than 20 flavors of lattes and Italian cream sodas. Coffee drinks $1.50-3. Open in summer M-F 7am-8pm, Sa 7am-9pm, Su 8am-9pm; in winter M-F 7am-5pm, Sa 7am-6pm, Su 8am-6pm. AmEx/D/MC/V. ❶

Mama D's, 140 N. F St. (☎719-539-2228). Quick no-frills fun. 6 in. tacos $2.50. Cup of mashed Fritos with chili, cheese, and onions $2.25. Open May-Oct. M-Sa 11am-9pm, Su 11am-5pm; Nov.-Apr. M-Sa 11am-7pm. MC/V. ❶

👁 SIGHTS

In the last decade, Salida has seen a new gallery or two open each year, leading some locals to wonder if it might be on its way to becoming the best little art town in America. Salida's 15 or so downtown galleries concentrate on First St. between E and G St.

🏔 OUTDOORS

A number of hiking trails run through the Salida area, and it's a good base for hiking 14ers. Check www.salida.com/html/hiking.htm for excellent hiking tips and directions to several of the trailheads.

MOUNTAIN BIKING

Bike rentals and information on bike trails are available at **Otero Cyclery,** 248 W. US 50. (☎719-539-6704. Open M-F 10am-6pm, Sa 9am-6pm, Su 10am-5pm. Full-suspension bikes $25-75.) **Subculture Cyclery,** 246½ E. First St., offers cruisers (ideal for exploring downtown) from $12 per day; mountain and road bikes are available on request. (☎719-539-5329. Open M and F-Sa 9am-5pm; call ahead on other days. MC/V.)

> **Midland Trail** (8 mi., 1hr.). An intermediate ride, with minimal rock climbing and great views of the Sawatch Range.
>
> **Monarch Crest Trail** (28 mi., 4hr.). Salida is a stopping point on this grueling ride. The trail, which runs from Salida to Monarch Pass, includes 14 mi. along the Continental Divide and a spectacular view of the Rockies.

RAFTING

Canyon Marine Whitewater, 10015 W. US 50, leads rafting trips several times per day. In the winter, it becomes **Wilderness Ski and Snowboard Shop.** It resides in Poncha Springs, 4 mi. west of Salida on US 50. (☎719-539-4444 or 800-539-4447; www.canyonmarine.com. Brown's Canyon ½-day trip $45, under 12 $35; full-day $78/68. Royal Gorge ½-day trip $58, full-day $91. Open daily 8am-5pm.) While there are rafting companies located all along the Arkansas River, Salida is conveniently located next to **Brown's Canyon,** a relaxing section of the river. Thrill-seekers also use Salida

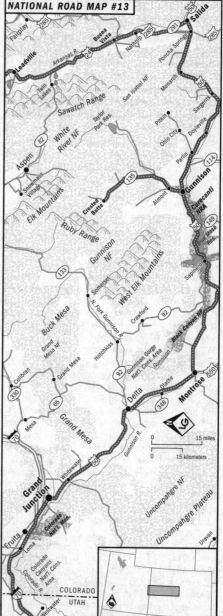

NATIONAL ROAD MAP #13

as a jumping-off point for boating on the challenging **Royal Gorge.**

◪ THE ROAD TO GUNNISON: 65 MI.

From downtown, head to **US 50** and turn right. About 5 mi. west of town, fork right and turn left to stay on **US 50 West.** There are lots of bikers here; pay careful attention. Twenty three miles from Salida, US 50 crosses the **Continental Divide** at **Monarch Pass** (11,312 feet) and then becomes **Tomichi Avenue** in downtown Gunnison.

GUNNISON   ☎970

Gunnison is ideal for an afternoon rest stop. The **Pioneer Museum,** 801 E. Tomichi Ave. (US 50), has a large collection of Western hats and about 50 antique cars. There's also a gun room, a music room, antique jewelry and clothes, and luxurious hair clippings of old Gunnison residents. (☎970-641-4530. Open from mid-May to Sept. M-Sa 9am-5pm, Su 11am-5pm. $7, ages 6-12 $3.) If you'd rather steer clear of hair clippings, the **Gunnison National Forest Office,** 216 N. Colorado Ave., has info on area forest service lands. (☎970-641-0471. Open M-F 7:30am-4:30pm.) As US 50 curves left at the western edge of town, look left for the giant white "W" carved into W Mountain—the "W" is for **Western State College.**

Accommodations in Gunnison are easy to find but somewhat expensive during the summer. The **Gunnison Inn ❸,** 412 E. Tomichi Ave., has good-size rooms with blue carpets and red and green beds. (☎970-641-0700 or 866-641-0700. Laundry and free Wi-Fi. Singles in summer from $75; in winter from $65. AmEx/D/MC/V.) At **QT Cabins ❶,** 12 mi. east of Gunnison in Parlin at 1 Earl Ave. off US 50, each of the comfortable and clean wood cabins is named and decorated like a particular cowboy gone bad. Each comes with a kitchen. (☎970-641-0485. 2 RV sites available. Open from May to mid-Nov. 3-person cabin $59; 6-person cabin $90. AmEx/D/MC/V.) You can experience modern ranch life at the 500-acre **Kreugers Ranch ❷,** 6794 US 114, about 15 mi. southeast of Gunnison. Kreugers runs cattle and rents out cabins. (☎970-210-0600 or 254-381-7561. Cabins from $45-60. Cash only.) The **Gunnison Chamber of Commerce** (☎970-641-1501) also has info on **campgrounds ❶** in the area. ◪**Farrells'**

Restaurant ❷, 310 N. Main St., serves sandwiches ($7-8) and fresh breads to patrons on an airy and shady back patio. The deliciously fiery chili is $3.25. Everything is made from scratch, even salad dressings. (☎970-641-2655. Open M-F 7am-3pm. MC/V.) The **Blue Iguana ❶,** 303 E. Tomichi Ave., is housed in a wood cabin. The friendly folks here serve up tasty Mexican food. A three-quarter-pound burrito with five fillings is only $4.50. (☎970-641-3403. Open M-Sa 11am-9pm. AmEx/D/MC/V.)

◪ DETOUR
CRESTED BUTTE

Take **Route 135** 27 mi. north of Gunnison.

Crested Butte was settled by miners in the 1870s. The coal was exhausted in the 1950s, but a few years later the steep powder fields began attracting skiers. Thanks to strict zoning rules, the historic downtown is a throwback to early mining days. Three miles north of town, **Crested Butte Mountain Resort,** 12 Snowmass Rd., offers over 800 acres of bowl skiing with a vertical drop of 2775 ft. (☎800-544-8448; www.skicb.com. Open mid-Dec. to mid-Apr. From mid-Nov. to mid-Dec., free skiing with lodging. From mid-Dec. lift tickets $74.) In summer, Crested Butte becomes the mountain-biking capital of Colorado. In 1976, a group of cyclists rode from Crested Butte to Aspen, starting the **Pearl Pass Tour,** which is now the oldest mountain-biking event in the world. Every September, experienced bikers repeat the trek over the 12,705 ft. pass to Aspen and back. The tour is organized by the **Mountain Biking Hall of Fame,** 331 Elk Ave.; on the premises, the hall relates the short history of the sport. (☎970-349-1880. Museum open daily from Memorial Day to Sept. noon-8pm; from Thanksgiving to mid-Apr., or whenever lifts are running, noon-6pm. $3.) During June, the town hosts the **Fat Tire Bike Festival** (www.ftbw.com), four days of biking, racing, and fraternizing.

The **Crested Butte Hostel ❶,** 615 Teocalli Ave., is next to the laundry service. Vintage postcards of the region line the otherwise classically decorated hallways. (☎970-349-0588; www.crestedbuttehostel.com. Dorms $29-31; private rooms $85-95. AmEx/D/MC/V.) At the

Ruby Bed and Breakfast ❺, 624 Gothic Ave., each room is uniquely decorated. There's a fireplace (and a good collection of DVDs) in the living room as well as an indoor hot tub. (☎800-390-1338; www.therubyofcrestedbutte. com. Fresh-baked cookies every afternoon. Rooms $200-300. AmEx/D/MC/V.)

At **Sunshine Deli ❷**, 214 Elk Ave., you can sit at a varnished wood table while you eat homemade Belgian waffles ($7.75) for "brekkie" or one of the signature sandwiches ($8-9) for lunch. The Joker sandwich, with turkey, Muenster cheese, red peppers, and curry mayonnaise ($8.50), can't exactly make a pencil disappear, but it will certainly stun your taste buds. (☎970-349-6866. Open daily 8am-4pm. MC/V.) **Teocalli Tamale Fresh Burrito Bar ❷**, 311½ Elk Ave., lives up to its name with freshly-made burritos. The Thai Veggie is served with ginger marinade and peanut sauce and costs $8. (☎970-349-2005. Open daily 11am-9pm. MC/V.) The **Princess Wine Bar ❷**, 218 Elk Ave., serves coffee ($2) and cookies ($3) at a beautiful gold and black bar (with a marble top and classy leather stools). Decadent desserts like the molten chocolate cake and Menage a Trois (chocolate cups filled with liqueurs) run $6-10. (☎970-349-0210; www.princesscb. com. Live acoustic music nightly around 8:30pm; Su is bluegrass night. Happy hour daily 5-7pm, with ½-price wine and tapas. Open daily 10am-midnight. AmEx/D/MC/V.)

⚑ THE ROAD TO CURECANTI NATIONAL RECREATION AREA: 74 MI.

The Curecanti National Recreation Area begins along **US 50,** 6 mi. from Gunnison.

CURECANTI NATIONAL RECREATION AREA ☎970

You wouldn't know it by looking, but the large bodies of water in this area are manmade, created by dams on the **Gunnison River.** Curecanti gets crowded in the summer when it provides opportunities for fishing, boating, sailing, and horseback riding. The moderately strenuous **Dillon Pinnacles Trail** (4 mi. round-trip) ascends 600 ft. through sagebrush and conifers to an up-close view of the large set of spires. The trailhead is off US 50, 6 mi. west of the Elk Creek Visitor Center. For those with time, the strenuous **Curecanti Creek Trail** (4 mi., 2-3hr. round-trip) goes down into the upper Black Canyon and then along the tumbling Curecanti Creek, with an elevation change of 900 ft. At the end, look across the Morrow Point Reservoir to view the 700 ft. Curecanti Needle, a granite spire. Eleven miles west of Elk Creek Visitors Center, turn right onto Rte. 92. Continue 5¾ mi. to the Pioneer Point Trailhead. The most challenging hike in the area is **Hermit's Rest** (6 mi., 3-4hr. round-trip, 1800 ft. elevation change), which passes through oaks, pines, and firs into the campsites at Morrow Point Reservoir. Eleven miles west of Elk Creek Visitor Center, turn right onto Rte. 92 and continue for 17 mi. **Morrow Point Boat Tours** leave from Pine Creek Boat Dock, 12 mi. west of Elk Creek Visitors Center, and rush through the upper Black Canyon. For 1hr., park rangers discuss the area's geology, wildlife, history, and the dams and reservoirs. (☎970-641-2337, ext. 205. Tours in summer M and W-Su 10am, 12:30pm. Reservations required. $15, under 13 $7.50.) **Elk Creek Marina** has boat rentals and guided fishing trips. (☎970-641-0707. Boat rentals $40-45 per hr., $145-165 per ½-day, $200-230 per day. Guided fishing trips start at $350.)

⚑ THE ROAD TO BLACK CANYON NATIONAL PARK: 48 MI.

Turn right at the sign for **Route 347/Black Canyon** and go 6 mi. to Black Canyon National Park.

BLACK CANYON NATIONAL PARK ☎970

In an unorthodox twist on "Rapunzel," Native American parents used to tell their children that the light-colored strands of rock streaking through the walls of the 53 mi. Black Canyon were hairs of a blonde woman—if they got too close to the edge, they would get tangled and fall. Visitors today should remember this lesson—the beautiful canyon can be very dangerous to the unwary. At 2250 ft., the Painted Wall cliff face is taller than the Empire State Building (1250 ft.) and the Sears Tower (1454 ft.).

VITAL STATS

Area: 30,000 acres

Tourist Office: South Rim Visitors Center (☎970-249-1914, ext. 423; www.nps.gov/blca), on South Rim Dr. Open daily in summer 8am-6pm; in winter 8:30am-4pm.

Gateway Town: Montrose (see opposite page).

Fees: $15 per vehicle, $7 per individual on foot or bicycle. Free wilderness permits are mandatory for inner canyon use.

ORIENTATION

The **South Rim** is easily accessible by a 6 mi. drive off **US 50** at the end of **Route 347;** the wilder **North Rim** can only be reached by an 80 mi. detour around the canyon followed by a gravel road from Crawford off **Route 92.** This road is closed in winter. The **East Portal Road,** accessed from South Rim Rd. near the park entrance, takes you down to the East Portal, inside the canyon at the side of the river. East Portal Rd. is closed in winter, and vehicles over 22 ft. long are prohibited. Stay in first gear. Be advised that both North and South Rim Rd. are dead ends, and driving around the canyon takes 2-3hr.

CAMPING

South Rim Campground (☎970-641-2337 or 249-1914, ext. 423). Access from entrance station. 102 sites with pit toilets, charcoal grills, and water. Sites $12, with hookup $18. Cash only. ❶

East Portal (☎970-240-5300), located 2 mi. below Crystal Dam at the bottom of Black Canyon. Take Rte. 347 6 mi. north from the junction of 347 and US 50 to the entrance of Black Canyon of the Gunnison National Park. Turn right just past the entrance station and follow East Portal Rd. 5 mi. down to the campground. 2 camping loops: 1 drive-in and 1 walk-in, with toilets available. 15 sites open spring-fall. Sites $12. ❶

Gunnison Gorge National Conservation Area (☎970-240-5300). Northwest of Montrose. 11 primitive hike-in campsites are available. Sites are 1st come, 1st served; pay at the trailhead. Pit toilets at 3 of the trails. 2-night maximum stay. $10 per person, 2nd night $5 per person. Day use $3. Cash only. ❶

OUTDOORS

HIKING

The spectacular 6 mi. ◪**South Rim Road** traces the edge of the canyon and boasts a jaw-dropping vista of Chasm View, where you can peer down a 1850 ft. drop to the streaked Painted Wall. For an even better view of the Painted Wall—arguably the most impressive in the park—head to the **Painted Wall View overlook.**

Hiking routes into the canyon follow unmarked drainage gullies. The Park Service discourages inexperienced hikers from taking these steep and strenuous routes; consult a park ranger at the visitors center before attempting one. A drainage is by nature wide at the top and narrow at the bottom, so it can be very difficult to find your way back. Setting up cairns (piles of rocks) is permitted but discouraged, so knock down your cairns on your return. Park rangers recommend taking mental notes of the terrain. Leave early in the morning to avoid the afternoon heat and bring at least one gallon of water per person per day. A few hiking routes skirt the edge of the canyon and provide a more in-depth experience than the short overlooks do. A free **wilderness permit** (from the South Rim Visitors Center) is required for inner-canyon routes, and you must checkout upon return.

The moderate **Oak Flat Loop Trail** (2 mi.) begins near the visitors center and gives a good sense of the terrain below the rim. From the South Rim, you can scramble down the **Gunnison Route,** which drops 1800 ft. over the course of 1 mi. Allow 1-2hr. for the descent and even longer for the climb out. Three campsites are located along the trail. If you're feeling courageous and have adjusted to the elevation, tackle the difficult **Tomichi Route** or **Warner Route,** both of which make good overnighters. The Tomichi Route includes a 1 mi., 1960 ft. descent and passes two campsites, while the Warner Route takes 2 3/4 mi. to descend 2722 ft. and passes five campsites.

CLIMBING

The sheer walls of the Black Canyon make for a rock-climbing paradise. This rock is not for beginners or the faint of heart; some of the best climbers in the world travel here to

NATIONAL ROAD

tackle the difficult walls. All climbers must carry a full rack of gear and register at the visitors center. The National Park Service recommends researching your climb ahead of time with *Black Canyon Rock Climbs* (by Robbie Williams) or *Rock Climbing, Colorado* (by Stewart Green).

FISHING

Anglers from all over Colorado trek to the Black Canyon for fly-fishing. A Colorado **fishing license** is required. Regulations apply to certain fish; rainbow trout, for example, must always be released. **Gunnison River Expeditions** runs fly-fishing float trips in the gorge and walk-wade trips on the Gunnison. (☎970-874-8184. Walk-wades from $75 including lunch. Float trips from $900 for a boat with 5 people.)

⚐ THE ROAD TO MONTROSE: 15 MI.
Take **Route 347 South** to **US 50 West**, following the signs pointing to Montrose.

MONTROSE   ☎970

The quiet community of Montrose serves as both the center of a farming region and a gateway to the spectacular beauty of southwest Colorado. Amid the sounds of "nature music" at the **Ute Indian Museum**, 17253 Chipeta Dr., you can learn the history of the Ute people. Though they once inhabited much of present-day Colorado and Utah, the Utes now have only a small reservation at the southern end of the state. In April, the museum organizes the **Chipeta Walk,** a 3 mile hike culminating in a gathering at the museum. Take Townsend/US 550 South; the museum is located on your right. (☎970-249-3098. Open July-Sept. M-Sa 9am-4pm, Su 11am-4pm; Oct.-June hours vary, so call in advance. $3.50, students $1.50, seniors $3.)

The family-owned **Canyon Trails Inn ❸**, 1225 E. Main St., has small and clean single rooms with access to an outdoor hot tub. (☎970-249-3426 or 800-858-5911; www.canyontrailsinn.com. Breakfast included. Free Wi-Fi. From May to mid-Sept. singles $60-65; doubles $75-80. From mid-Sept. to Apr. singles $52-55; doubles $65-70. AmEx/D/MC/V.) The **Western Motel ❸**, 1200 E. Main St., offers 27 tidy rooms, a pool, hot tub, and continental breakfast. (☎970-249-3481 or 800-445-7301.

Reception 24hr. Check-out 10am. From Memorial Day to Sept. singles $55; doubles $78. From Sept. to Memorial Day singles $48; doubles $65. AmEx/D/MC/V.) For tasty sandwiches and delightful omelets ($7), head to the **Daily Bread Bakery and Cafe ❶**, 346 Main St. Vegetarians will love the Garden Delight ($7), with avocado, mushrooms, sprouts, tomatoes, and cheese. (☎970-249-8444. Pastries $2. Muffins $1. Open daily 6am-4pm. D/MC/V.) The spacious, well-lit **Gigi and Ann's Marketplace and Cafe ❷**, 309 E. Main St., serves American food like cajun-seared chicken pasta ($15) and panini and burgers for lunch ($7-12). Brunch includes green eggs and ham (eggs with spinach, cilantro pesto, cream cheese, and ham; $7). Happy hour (M-F 4:30-6:30pm) often has live music. Mimosas at brunch are $2. (☎970-240-4339. Dinner $9-23. Open Tu-Sa 11am-9pm, Su 10am-2:30pm. Bar open until midnight or later. D/MC/V.) **Camp Robber Cafe ❹**, 1515 Ogden Rd. off Townsend (US 550), caters to locals with its cheerful yellow walls and contemporary Southwestern flavors. Dishes include green chili chicken potato soup for $3.75. (☎970-240-1590. Dinner entrees $19-22. Open M-Th 11am-9pm, F-Sa 11am-10pm, Su 9am-2pm. AmEx/D/MC/V.)

⚐ THE ROAD TO GRAND JUNCTION: 61 MI.
US 50 becomes **Fifth Street** entering Grand Junction.

GRAND JUNCTION   ☎970

The city takes its name from its position at the junction of the Colorado and Gunnison Rivers. The name aptly describes the town—a transportation hub for the masses heading to southern Utah and the Colorado Rockies. If you need big-city services, Grand Junction is the place to stop; the next stop with a population over 10,000 is Salt Lake City.

▣ ORIENTATION

Grand Junction lies on the **Colorado River** near I-70. In town, streets run north-south, increasing in number from west to east, and avenues run east-west. **Grand Avenue** runs one block north of **Main Street** and contains many hotels

NATIONAL ROAD

and restaurants. **North Avenue (US 6)** runs one block north of Grand Ave.

VITAL STATS

Population: 48,000

Tourist Office: Grand Junction Visitors Bureau, 740 Horizon Dr. (☎970-256-4060; www.grandjunction. net). Head east to 7th St., turn left, and turn right on Horizon Dr. Open May-Sept. M-Sa 8:30am-8pm, Su 9am-8pm; Oct.-Apr. daily 8:30am-5pm.

Library and Internet Access: Mesa County Library, 530 Grand Ave. (☎970-243-4442). Open June-Aug. M-Th 9am-9pm, F 9am-6pm, Sa 9am-5pm; Sept.-May M-Th 9am-9pm, F 9am-6pm, Sa 9am-5pm, Su 1-5pm.

Post Office: 241 N. 4th St. (☎970-244-3400). Open M-F 7:45am-5:15pm, Sa 10am-1:30pm. **Postal Code:** 81501.

ACCOMMODATIONS

Mesa Inn, 704 Horizon Dr. (☎970-245-3080 or 888-955-3080), very close to the visitors center. Offers small but clean rooms with green beds, red carpets, and nice bathrooms. Unexpectedly sloping hallways are similar to those at Hogwarts. Rooms in summer $65-95; rooms in winter $45-65. AmEx/D/MC/V. ❸

The Columbine Inn, 2824 North Ave. (☎970-241-2908). Not far from downtown. In summer singles $56; doubles $65. In winter singles $46; doubles $56. AmEx/D/MC/V. ❸

James M. Robb Colorado River State Park, Fruita Section 1 (☎970-858-9188), 10 mi. west of town, off Exit 19 from I-70. 57 sites; 44 have electric hookups. Entrance fee $6 per vehicle. Sites $14-22. MC/V. ❶

FOOD

Thursday nights in summer, Main St. between Third and Seventh transforms into the **Farmers' Market Festival,** with local produce, live music, and extended Main St. restaurant hours. (☎970-245-9697. June-Aug. Th 5-8pm.)

Crystal Cafe, 314 Main St. (☎970-242-8843). Massive, mouthwatering breakfasts ($5.50-7.25) are the cafe's specialty, but hot lunches and decadent baked goods like an enormous caramel pecan roll ($3) will also satisfy. Sandwiches

($8-12) include a massive ¼ lb., sushi-grade tuna sandwich with onion, feta, and kalamata relish on fresh bread. Open M-F 7am-2pm, Sa 8am-noon. AmEx/D/MC/V. ❷

The Rockslide Restaurant and Brew Pub, 401 S. Main St. (☎970-245-2111). Crowded and fun. Modern brewpub atmosphere. The fish and chips ($12) are popular, as are the mahi mahi tacos ($9). The Big Bear Stout comes in a ½ gal. growler for $8.50. Happy hour M-F 4-6pm and 10pm-midnight with discounted appetizers. Open M-Th and Su 11am-midnight, F-Sa 11am-2am. Kitchen open until 10pm. AmEx/D/MC/V. ❹

SIGHTS

DINOSAUR RIDING A BICYCLE. There are lots of sidewalk sculptures in downtown Grand Junction; don't miss the dinosaur riding a bicycle. *(At 3rd and Main St.)*

MUSEUM OF WESTERN COLORADO. The museum has several excellent exhibits, including some information on the infamous Alfred Packer, tried and convicted of cannibalism. See Bill Cody's gun from 1881, learn about Teddy Roosevelt's hunting trip, and head up the Educational Tower for a 360° view of the surrounding area. If you like recreations, you're in luck; the museum has an opera house, mine, saloon, and schoolhouse. *(462 Ute Ave., at 5th St. ☎970-242-0971. Open May-Sept. M-Sa 9am-5pm, Su noon-4pm; Oct.-Apr. Tu-Sa 10am-3pm. $5.50, ages 3-12 $3, seniors $4.50.)*

NIGHTLIFE

Weaver's Tavern, 103 N. 1st St. (☎970-241-4010). A sports bar with gads of drink specials. Happy hour F 4-8pm with $1.50 well wine; daily 10pm-midnight $3 you-call-its. Open daily 11am-2am. AmEx/D/MC/V.

The Mesa Theater, 538 Main St. (☎970-241-1717; www.mesatheater.com). Live music summer weekends. Hours and cover vary. MC/V.

OUTDOORS

HIKING

The best hiking around Grand Junction awaits in the **McInnis Canyons National Conservation Area** just west of Colorado National Monument. **Pollock, Rattlesnake,** and **Knowles Canyons** all feature beautiful hikes ranging from easy to strenuous. Take I-70 to Exit 19 and head south 1 mi. to Kings View Estates subdivision. Follow the Kings View Rd. westbound, and after 6 mi. look for signs to the trailhead. The **Mount Garfield Trail** (4 mi., 4hr round-trip.) leads to amazing views of this otherworldly rock-scape. Wild horses are sometimes visible from the top during winter and early spring. Take Exit 42 from I-70 and travel south on 37 Three-Tenths Rd. to G Seven-Tenths Rd. Take the first right and stay to the right.

MOUNTAIN BIKING

The **Kokopelli Area,** the **18-Mile Road Area,** and the **Tabeguache Area** each attract mountain bikers in search of adventure. A bevy of mountain-bike shops offer advice and rent bikes. **Ruby Canyon Cycles,** 301 Main St., is a bike shop with full-day rentals. (☎970-241-0141. Open M-F 9am-6pm, Sa 9am-5pm. Mountain bikes $50 per day. Enduros $50 per day. Street bikes $25 per day.) Near the visitors center on North Ave., **Board and Buckle Ski and Cyclery,** 2822 North Ave., rents bikes, snowboards, and skis from a fun shop decorated with antique ski paraphernalia. (☎970-242-9285. Bikes $35 per day. Skis $15 per day. Snowboards $18-20 per day. Open in summer M-F 9am-6pm, Sa 9am-5pm; in winter daily 9am-6pm.)

THE ROAD TO COLORADO NATIONAL MONUMENT: 4 MI.

Proceed north on **Fifth Street** three blocks past **Main Street** to **Grand Avenue** and turn left. At the intersection with **First Street,** head straight onto **Broadway/Route 340.** After about 1 mi., turn left onto **Monument Road** at the sign for the monument.

COLORADO NATIONAL MONUMENT ☎970

On the outskirts of Grand Junction, Colorado National Monument is a 32 sq. mi. sculpture of steep cliff faces, canyon walls, and obelisk-like spires wrought by the forces of gravity, wind, and water. The monument was established in 1911, largely due to the efforts of John Otto, who blazed many of the trails used today and badgered the government to

protect this dream world of rock. After the government finally complied, Otto happily became the caretaker of the park for a salary of $1 per month until 1927.

ORIENTATION

For those without time to explore on foot, the 23 mi. **Rim Rock Drive** runs from Grand Junction to Fruita along the edge of red canyons and across the mesa top.

VITAL STATS
Area: 20,500 acres
Tourist Office: Colorado National Monument Visitors Center (☎970-858-3617; www.nps.gov/colm), 4 mi. south of the western entrance. Open daily in summer 8am-6pm; in winter 9am-5pm.
Gateway Towns: Fruita, Grand Junction (p. 433).
Fees: $7 per vehicle.

CAMPING

Backcountry camping ❶ is allowed anywhere a quarter-mile from the road and 150 ft. from any trail. A free **wilderness permit** is required and available at the visitors center. **Saddlehorn Campground ❶,** a quarter-mile north of the visitors center, offers 80 beautiful, secluded sites on the mesa's edge. Sites are first come, first served. (☎970-858-3617. Water and bathrooms. No showers. Sites $10. Cash only.)

OUTDOORS

Rim Rock Drive provides views of awe-inspiring rock monoliths, the Book Cliffs, Grand Mesa, and the city of Grand Junction. Grand View offers a panoramic look back into the canyon's multiple layers. At the **Independence Monument View** overlook, visitors can glimpse the park's icon, a free-standing rock formation.

While driving affords great views, the hiking trails that crisscross the monument are the only way to fully appreciate the scope and scale of this canyon country. There are a number of short walks that get hikers away from the road and immerse them in the terrain. The **Window Rock Trail** (½ mi. round-trip) leaves from a trailhead on the Saddlehorn campground road and offers expansive vistas through piñon-juniper woodland over the

Grand Valley as well as views of Monument Canyon, Wedding Canyon, and many of the monument's major rock formations. **Otto's Trail** (1 mi. round-trip), which runs south from Rim Rock Dr. to Pipe Organ, is easy and offers good views of monoliths. The **Coke Ovens Trail** (1 mi. round-trip), a few miles down Rim Rock Dr. from the visitors center toward Coke Ovens, ambles to a scenic overlook. The **Devil's Kitchen Trail** (1½ mi. round-trip) begins off Rim Rock Dr. just past the east entrance and leads into Devil's Kitchen, a formation surrounded by enormous upright boulders.

There are a number of primitive trails good for long or overnight hikes. The moderately strenuous **Monument Canyon Trail** (12 mi. round-trip) allows hikers to view eerie, skeletal rock formations up close. The upper trail descends 600 ft. from the mesa top to the canyon floor and then wanders amid giant rocks, including Coke Ovens, Kissing Couple, and Independence Monument, before emerging on Rte. 340 (Broadway/Redlands Rd.). The **Ute Canyon Trail** (7 mi., 4hr. round-trip) and **Liberty Cap Trail** (7 mi., 4hr. round-trip) are also scenic backcountry hikes ideal for overnight trips. John Otto called **Serpents Trail** (1¾ mi., 1½ hr. round-trip) "the crookedest road in the world" because of its 50+ switchbacks. The most isolated, primitive hike is through **No Thoroughfare Canyon** (8½ mi., 8hr.), which starts with a maintained trail but continues on an undeveloped trail through two waterfalls and the canyon in which the sides rise more than 400 ft. and finishes at the **Devils Kitchen Trail** near the eastern entrance. At points, the trail is marked with cairns. To find the trailhead, exit the monument at the east entrance, drive 4 mi., turn left (south) on East Glade Park Rd., continue 6.5 mi. and turn left on Little Park Rd., and finally drive 1½ mi. until you see a small pullout on the left.

THE ROAD TO MOAB: 102 MI.

Leave the monument from the west entrance and turn left at the T onto **Route 340**. Go 2 mi. to **I-70 West**. Take **Exit 204** for **Route 128 South** to **Route 128 West**. After rounding a corner about 4 mi. past the bridge, you will see the first of the area's hallmark red spires. Rte. 128 dead-ends at **US 191**; from here, turn left toward downtown Moab.

The Beehive State
UTAH
Welcomes You!

MOAB ☎435

Moab, about 70 mi. from the Colorado/Utah border, first flourished in the 1950s, when uranium miners rushed to the area and transformed the town into a gritty desert outpost. Today, the Nalgene bottle has replaced the Geiger counter, as outdoors enthusiasts rush into town eager to bike the slick rock, raft whitewater rapids, and explore Arches and Canyonlands National Parks.

VITAL STATS
Population: 7500
Tourist Office: Moab Information Center, 3 Center St. (☎435-259-8825 or 800-635-6622), at the corner of Main St. Open in summer M-Sa 8am-9pm, Su 9am-7pm; in winter daily 9am-5pm.
Library and Internet Access: Grand County Library, 257 E. Center St. (☎435-259-1111). Open M-F 9am-8pm, Sa 9am-5pm.
Post Office: 50 E. 100 N. (☎435-259-7427). Open M-F 8am-5pm, Sa 9am-1pm. **Postal Code:** 84532.

ORIENTATION

Moab is the only incorporated town in Grand County. It sits 31 mi. south of **I-70** on **US 191**, just south of the junction with **Route 128**. The town center is 6 mi. south of the entrance to **Arches National Park** and 38 mi. north of the turn-off to the Needles section of **Canyonlands National Park**. US 191 becomes **Main Street** for 5 mi. through downtown.

ACCOMMODATIONS

The Moab area features 433 **campsites ❶** managed by the Bureau of Land Management —and plenty more in Arches and Canyonlands National Parks and Manti-La Sal National Forest—so finding a place to sleep shouldn't be a problem. **Goose Island, Negro Bill, Drinks Canyon, Hal Canyon, Oak Grove,** and **Big Bend Campgrounds,** all on Rte. 128, sit on the banks of the Colorado River, 3-8 mi. northeast of downtown Moab. Big Bend takes reservations. (☎435-259-2100. Fire pits and toilets but no hookups or showers. Sites $8-12.) Chain motels cluster along **Main Street,** but rooms in Moab are not cheap and fill up fast from April through October.

Lazy Lizard International Hostel, 1213 S. US 191 (☎435-259-6057). 1 mi. south of Moab. The kitchen, VCR, and hot tub draw a mix of college students and backpackers, and the owners will give you the lowdown on the area. While not the cleanest place in town, it is cheaper and more comfortable than most campsites. Laundry. Reception 8am-11pm. Check-out 11am. Reservations recommended. Tent sites $6. Dorms $9; private rooms from $23; cabins for up to 6 people $28-48. AmEx/D/MC/V. ❶

The Silver Sage Inn, 840 S. Main St. (☎435-259-4420; www.silversageinn.com). On the southern edge of downtown. Small, clean rooms. Free Wi-Fi. Open Mar.-Oct. Singles $55-70; doubles $60-80. AmEx/D/MC/V. ❸

The Adventure Inn Moab, 512 N. Main St. (☎435-259-6122 or 866-662-2466; www. adventureinnmoab.com). Inn offers visitors basic rooms that have earth-colored beds and nice bathrooms. Open May-Oct. Singles $60; doubles $72. AmEx/D/MC/V. ❸

🍴 FOOD

🍴 **Moab Diner and Ice Cream Shoppe,** 189 S. Main St. (☎435-259-4006). Retro booths take you to the 1950s. The Sweetwater Skillet ($6.50) includes fried potatoes, bacon, green onions, bell peppers, 2 eggs, and cheese. Open M-Th 6am-10pm, F-Sa 6am-11pm. AmEx/D/MC/V. ❷

🍴 **Eclectica Coffee,** 352 N. Main St. (☎435-259-6896). Offers coffee, breakfast, lunch specialties M-Sa ($4.50-9), and delicious pastries. Free Wi-Fi. Open M-Sa 7:30am-2:30pm, Su 7:30am-1pm. MC/V. ❷

Peace Tree Juice Cafe, 20 S. Main St. (☎435-259-8503). Serves smoothies ($3.25-5.25) and juice. The wraps are also good energy boosters, especially the peanut butter wrap (with granola and berries; $6). Full Breakfasts $2.50-8. Open daily 8am-6:30pm. AmEx/D/MC/V. ❷

Milt's Stop and Eat, 356 Millcreek Dr. (☎435-259-7424). Close to the entrance to Slickrock Trail. Sandwiches $4-5.50. Cheeseburger $3.30. Mushroom Swiss burger $4. Ice cream $1. Open Tu-Sa in summer 11am-9pm; in winter Tu-Su 11am-7pm. AmEx/D/MC/V. ❶

Miguel's Baja Gril, 51 N. Main St. (☎435-259-6546). Serves fresh Mexican food in a small but pleasant courtyard garden. The MOAB (Mother Of All Burritos) is $10-14 depending on fillings. Tacos $11-15. Open daily 5-10pm. ❸

🄢 SIGHTS

DAN O'LAURIE CANYON COUNTRY MUSEUM. The museum focuses on the area's geology, the Native Americans who once lived here, and the 1950s mining boom. One noteworthy item is a geological balsam wood model of the region surrounding Moab, carved by hand over a period of 20 years by a park ranger. Three light switches show the region at sunrise, noon, and sunset. *(118 E. Center St. ☎435-259-7985. Open in summer M-F 10am-6pm, Sa noon-6pm; open in winter M-F 10am-3pm, Sa noon-5pm. $3, under 12 free.)*

HOLE 'N THE ROCK. It's not exactly what the name purports. In 1932, a couple blasted a set of cozy, cavernous rooms for themselves out of Entrada Sandstone, and you can tour the unique, naturally climate-controlled home. *(11037 S. US 191. Take US 191 South 13 mi. from Moab. ☎435-686-2250. Open daily 9am-5pm. 12min. tours every 12-15min. $5, ages 6-12 $3.50.)*

SCENIC BYWAY 279. Stretching along the Colorado River for about 17 mi. west out of Moab, Scenic Byway 279 passes several noteworthy sites, including prehistoric petroglyphs on the side of the canyons, Jaycee Park (where a 1½ mi. hike leads to a scenic overlook), and a series of dinosaur tracks seen from afar. As always, do not touch the rock art. The road ends with a series of three arches near a dirt road entrance into Canyonlands National Park. **Corona Arch** and **Bow Tie Arch** sit at the end of a 1½ mi. trail, and **Jug Handle Arch** is found next to the highway. *(From Moab, head north on US 191 and turn left on 279.)*

⬛ OUTDOORS

MOUNTAIN BIKING

The popular **Slickrock Trail** (10½ mi. one-way), commonly acknowledged as the most difficult trail in Moab, rolls up and down the slick rock (which is actually sandstone) outside of town. The trail doesn't have a big vertical gain, but the level of technical skill required makes it an expert-level trail, and temperatures often reach 100°F. Take Center St. to 400 E. and make a left on Millcreek Dr. The **Porcupine Rim Trail** (14 mi. one-way), a local favorite of moderate difficulty, offers great views of Castle Valley and starts near two metal stack tanks on the north side of Sand Flats Rd., 11 mi. from Moab. **Poison Spider** (5¾ mi. one-way; moderate), with an 860 ft. elevation change, is another popular route, though only skilled bikers should take the Portal Trail portion of the route, as it has exposure to dangerous cliffs. The trailhead is on Potash Rd. (Rte. 279), at the Dinosaur Tracks sign. **Rim Cyclery**, 94 W. 100 N., rents bikes and has trail info. (☎435-259-5333; www.rimcyclery.com. Bikes $35 per day, subsequent days and ½-days $35, children's bikes $25-30; includes helmet, pump, and water bottle. Open M-Sa 8am-7pm, Su 8am-6pm.)

RAFTING

Numerous rafting companies are based in Moab. The **Moab Adventure Center**, 225 S. Main St., offers good deals on rafting trips and also arranges helicopter, Hummer, jeep, motorboat, horseback, and rock-climbing expeditions that cover the entire area, including Canyonlands and Arches National Park. (☎435-259-7019 or 800-453-7450. ½-day river trips $45-55, full-day $55-155, 2-day $225. Canyonlands scenic flight $135. Canyoneering or rock climbing $99.)

> ➦ **BIG DETOUR.** To explore the stunning scenery in Utah, take the **Mountains, Mesas, and Monuments Big Detour** (p. 440).

⬛ THE ROAD TO GREEN RIVER: 53 MI.

Take **US 191 North** until it merges with **I-70 West**; get off at **Exit 164 (Route 19)** toward Green River.

GREEN RIVER ☎435

The town of Green River straddles the calm section of the waterway famous for its raging rapids to the north and south. An oasis in the vast desert traversed by the interstate, Green River once acted as a remote desert hideout for the Wild Bunch and other outlaws. Robber rumors aside, today Green River is known as a base for rafting the Green and Colorado Rivers and for its flourishing melon industry. If you're in town for the August harvest or the September festival, don't miss the watermelon and cantaloupe.

VITAL STATS
Population: 900
Tourist Office: Green River Visitors Center, 885 E. Main St. (☎435-564-3526), in the John Wesley Powell Museum. Open daily June-Aug. 8am-8pm; Sept.-May 8am-5pm.
Library and Internet Access: Green River City Library, 85 S. Long St. (☎435-564-3349). Open M-F 10am-6pm.
Post Office: 80 E. Main St. (☎435-564-3329). Open M-F 8:30am-noon and 1-4:30pm, Sa 8:30-11:30am. **Postal Code:** 84525.

⬛ ORIENTATION

Picturesque Green River lies along **I-70** just east of its intersection with **US 191,** 185 mi. southeast of Salt Lake City. **Main Street** runs between two exits off I-70.

⬛ ACCOMMODATIONS

Free **Backcountry camping** is usually allowed, but check with the Bureau of Land Management in advance. Developed sites are available at Goblin Valley State Park, about 30min. from the Green River State Park, south of the swell, near Temple Mountain and Crack Canyon, just off Rte. 24.

  Budget Inn, 60 E. Main St. (☎435-564-3441), across the street from the Green River Community Park. The distinctive white and teal inn offers large rooms with comfy queen-size turquoise or purple beds, cable TV, and A/C. Reception 24hr. Singles $35; doubles $40. AmEx/D/MC/V. ❷

Robbers Roost Motel, 325 W. Main St. (☎435-564-3452; www.rrmotel.com). Have your getaway car drop you off here. Offers tidy, basic rooms with wood walls, pink beds, blue carpets, and few decorations. Free Wi-Fi. Reception M-F 9am-1am, Sa 10am-midnight. Check-out 10:30am. Singles $31; doubles $40. AmEx/D/MC/V. ❷

Green River State Park, 450 S. Green River Blvd. (☎435-564-3633, 564-8379, or 800-322-3770; www.reserveamerica.com). 40 grassy sites and 2 showers, 1 with temperature control and 1 where you "wait and see what you get." No hookups. Check-in 3pm. Check-out 2pm. Sites $16. AmEx/MC/V. ❶

🍴 FOOD

During August, look for stands along Main St., where fresh watermelon and cantaloupe (Why can't melons marry? 'Cause they can't elope!) cost only $0.17 per pound.

West Winds, 1095 E. Main St. (☎435-564-8240). Enjoy a piping hot breakfast alongside hungry truckers. Generous helpings of country-fried steak ($10) and 2-patty chili burgers ($9) keep people rolling back for more. Breakfast $3.50-10. Open 24hr. AmEx/D/MC/V. ❷

Ben's Cafe, 115 W. Main St. (☎435-564-3352). Ample portions of Mexican and American fare. Breakfast $2.25-9.50. Sandwiches $4.25-9. Dinners $8-13. Open daily Feb.-Sept. 7am-11pm; Oct.-Jan. 8am-10pm. AmEx/D/MC/V. ❷

Ray's Tavern, 25 S. Broadway (☎435-564-3511). Rafting T-shirts on the walls and diners helping themselves to ½ lb. burgers ($7.25), chicken teriyaki, and pizzas ($14-17) at tree-trunk tables. Open daily in summer 11am-10pm; in winter 11am-9pm. AmEx/D/MC/V. ❷

Green River Coffee Company, 25 E. Main St. (☎435-564-3411). Comfortable red sofas, rock-and-roll paraphernalia, and signs that read "Friends Don't Let Friends Drink Starbucks" everywhere. Free Internet and a good assortment of books. Build-your-own breakfast $4.75. Sandwiches $5-6. Gourmet mini pizzas $6. Open 6am-9pm. D/MC/V. ❶

👁 SIGHTS

JOHN WESLEY POWELL MUSEUM. Outdoor activities steal the show in Green River, but this museum captivates history buffs with Colorado River lore and a slideshow with narrated excerpts from Powell's journals. Artifacts from his expedition, including a replica of his boat, the *Emma Dean*, are on display. (*885 E. Main St. ☎435-564-3427. Open daily June-Aug. 8am-8pm; Sept.-May 8am-5pm. $4, ages 3-12 $1.*)

SCENIC DRIVES

The visitors center in Green River provides info on road conditions and a free guide to the San Rafael Desert Loop Drive, which begins just south of town and follows the river to Horseshoe Canyon, an extension of Canyonlands National Park. It then links with Rte. 24 to skirt the edge of the sawtooth ridge that marks the eastern rim of the swell, called San Rafael Reef, before intersecting with I-70. To see the terrain from the banks, try the **Green River Scenic Drive** along Hastings Rd., off Main St. This drive traces the river through Gray Canyon for almost 20 mi., offering access to biking, hiking, and swimming. The drive starts from Hastings Rd., off Main St., east of downtown and the Powell Museum. Turn north on Hastings Rd. 8 mi. out at Swasey Beach; the pavement ends, and the road stays above the river for the rest of the drive, ending at a rock formation that resembles Queen Nefertiti.

⚔ OUTDOORS

RAFTING

From late spring to early fall, visiting Green River is all about getting wet. Two reputable rafting outfitters are **Moki Mac River Expeditions,** 100 S. Sillman Ln. (☎435-564-3361 or 800-284-7280; www.mokimac.com), and **Holiday Expeditions,** 1055 E. Main St. (☎435-564-3273 or 800-624-6323; www.bikeraft.com), whose employees, are, incidentally smokin' hot. Both companies offer daytrips on the Green River for about $55-60 as well as multi-day trips on the Green, the Colorado, Cataract Canyon, and other area rivers.

NATIONAL ROAD

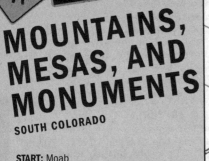

BIG DETOUR

MOUNTAINS, MESAS, AND MONUMENTS

SOUTH COLORADO

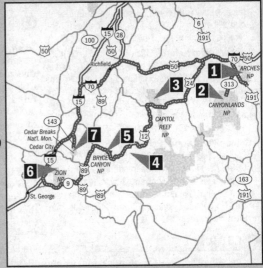

START: Moab

HIGHLIGHT: Bryce Canyon National Park

DISTANCE: 800 mi.

DURATION: 5 days

From Moab, head north on US 191, passing Rte. 128. The park entrance is 5 mi. north of Moab.

1. ARCHES NATIONAL PARK. Here, thousands of sandstone arches, spires, pinnacles, and fins tower above the desert floor with overwhelming grandeur. Some arches are so perfect that early settlers believed they were constructed by a lost civilization. Green piñon pines, gray dead trees, red rock, silver brush, and a striking blue sky combine in an unforgettable color palette. While most visitors come in the summer, 100°F temperatures make hiking difficult; bring at least one gallon of water per person per day. The weather is best in spring and fall, when temperate days and nights provide a more comfortable stay. Winter snows contrast brilliantly with the red arches. While the striking red rock around Arches may seem worthy enough, the park's real points of interest lie off the paved road. Load up on water and sunscreen and seek out the park's thousands of natural arches, each one pinpointed on the free pamphlet distributed at the entrace. The most popular hike in the park leads to the oft-photographed **Delicate Arch.** The unshaded trail (3 mi., 2½hr.) leaves from the Wolfe Ranch parking area and climbs 480 ft. To view the spectacular Delicate Arch without the 3 mi. hike, take the paved **Delicate Arch Lower Viewpoint Trail** (300 ft., 10min.), which starts at the Viewpoint parking area, 14 mi. from the park's entrance. **Tower Arch** (3½ mi., 2-3hr.) can be accessed from the trailhead at the Klondike Bluffs parking area via Salt Valley Rd. This moderate hike explores one of the remote regions of the park and is a good way to escape the crowds. Salt Valley Rd. is often washed out—check at the visitors center before departing. (☎435-719-2299. Open daily 8am-4:30pm; extended hours in summer. Entrance fee $10 per vehicle, $5 per pedestrian or biker.)

To get from Arches to Canyonlands, take US 191 N. for 6 mi. to Hwy. 313 S. Follow Hwy. 313 for 21 mi.

2. CANYONLANDS NATIONAL PARK. Canyonlands is a vast, rugged park of red sandstone sculpted by the Green and Colorado Rivers. Its stone canyons, mesas, arches, and spires are divided into three districts: **Island in the Sky** ("I-Sky"), the **Needles,** and the **Maze.** It is nearly impossible to see more than one or two of them in a single trip; they are not directly connected, and it takes roughly 2-3hr. to travel between them. Island in the Sky is the most popular and accessible district, drawing the majority of the park's visitors, while the Needles and Maze entice those more interested in backcountry trips. Canyonlands, like much of the surrounding area, is very hot and dry in the summer; bring at least one gallon of water per person per day and sunscreen. The **visitors center** near Needles is the only place in the park where water is available. (Needles visitors center ☎435-259-4711, Island in the Sky 259-4712. Both open daily in summer 8am-6pm; in winter 9am-4:30pm. Entrance fee $10 per vehicle, $5 per pedestrian.)

For vehicles with four-wheel drive, the scenic **White Rim Road** follows the border of Island in the Sky for about 100 mi. Once out of your car, note that trails in Canyonlands are marked with cairns (small rock piles); do not disturb them or build new ones. The **Mesa Arch** is a popular destination in Island in the Sky, lying a quarter-mile uphill from its trailhead, 6 mi. from the visitors center. The rocky but easy trail is a loop, passing many outcroppings of slick rock. The arch itself lies on a cliff edge 2200 ft. above the Colorado River; the sweeping view from the arch is unforgettable. You won't regret waking up early to watch the sunrise, but take caution around the cliff edge. **Grand View Point** (2 mi., 1½hr. round-trip), 13 mi. from the visitors center, provides a gorgeous panoramic view of the mighty rivers that carved the canyons. The rocky, moderate **Upheaval Dome Trail** (¾-1¾ mi., 1-1½hr. round-trip) leads to the mysterious Upheaval Dome, a circular rock deformation nearly 3 mi. across. Geologists are still not sure how this structure formed. The signs in front of the dome explain two popular theories: one states that an ancient "salt bubble" rose through layers of dense rock above it, shaping the rock into a circular form, while the other states that the area is a crater left by a meteorite 500-1000 ft. in diameter. In either case, the enormous phenomenon is unlike anything else in the park and has fantastic viewpoints. **Backcountry hiking** is permitted in the park; a permit ($5) is required and is available at the visitors centers—consult with a ranger before heading out. **Rock climbing** is popular in Island in the Sky; the other park districts lack hard stone and established routes. Permits are not required unless trips include overnight stays in the backcountry. As with most parks, changing or defacing the rock is prohibited; consult a park ranger for more details on technical climbing routes and regulations.

To get from Canyonlands to Capitol Reef, take Rte. 313 N. to US 191 N. to I-70 W. From I-70, take Exit 149 for Rte. 24 southwest for 88 mi. In Caineville, consider stopping at the ◼ **Mesa Farm Market,** a small shop with coffee ($2) brewed fresh by the cup, artisan bread, and fresh, certified organic fruits and veggies. (☎435-456-9146. Open Easter-Oct. sunrise-sunset. Cash only.)

3. CAPITOL REEF NATIONAL PARK. Capitol Reef is an oasis in the desert. With about 2700 fruit trees bearing antique and heirloom varieties of cherries, peaches, apricots, apples, and pears, Capitol Reef has the largest orchard system of any national park. The **Fruita Orchards** lie off the roads near the visitors center; visitors are welcome to eat as much ripe fruit as they like while in the orchards, but there is a nominal fee for taking fruit out of the orchards. The flooding of the Fremont River helps to irrigate the orchards that Mormon settlers started planting around 1880. A one-room Mormon schoolhouse still stands near the park entrance. Mormons were not the only ones who favored this area—Native Americans who settled in the area long ago left ancient petroglyphs on rock walls near the park entrance. From May to September, the park offers many free ranger-guided programs, providing lessons about the Fruita Schoolhouse, historic Gifford farm, the park's geology, and more at the campground amphitheater. More information can be found at the **visitors center,** nine miles to the west of the park entrance. (☎435-425-1791, ext. 111. Open daily 8am-6pm.)

You can see Capitol Reef's towering and colorful landforms from your car on the 25 mi. **scenic drive,** 1hr. round-trip, that wiggles around the cliffs, washes, and canyon floors on paved and improved dirt roads. The easy **Capitol Gorge Trail** (1 mi.) runs off the scenic drive. Another easy trail, the **Grand Wash** (2¼ mi.), on Rte. 24, 4 mi. east of the visitors center, leads visitors along sheer canyon walls. These and other canyon trails can become inundated with water during flash floods, common in late summer and early fall; check at the visitors center for weather and flood information. The park's premier hike is a backcountry route, the **Halls Creek Narrows** (22 mi. round-trip). Marked with cairns but not otherwise maintained, the steep trail leads down to the Halls Creek drainage and then south to the Narrows themselves. It begins near the Halls Creek overlook. Some hiking experience and a topographic map (available at the visitors center) are required.

Continue on Rte. 24 for 6¼ mi. to Rte. 12 in Torrey, which leads through the monument and toward the small towns of Escalante and Cannonville.

4. GRAND STAIRCASE-ESCALANTE NATIONAL MONUMENT. Big, wild, and best suited to backcountry adventures, Grand Staircase was the last place in the continental US to be mapped. No main roads run through the monument. **Route 12** provides a dizzying view of the monument's cliffs and plateaus as you approach Escalante, but be sure to keep your eyes on the road—it can be treacherous. The staircase itself is comprised of exposed rock layers rising in a series of cliffs from Lake Powell to Bryce Canyon; the forms continue all the way to the Grand Canyon. Information can be found at the **Escalante Interagency Visitor Center,** 755 W. Main St., in Escalante. (☎435-826-5499. Open in summer daily 7:30am-5:30pm; in winter M-F 8am-4:30pm.)

Some relatively easy routes along the canyon floors exist, but much of the monument is extremely dangerous for the careless and unprepared. **Hiking** most routes without a guide is not advised unless you have a firm grasp of the landscape and geographical organization. Two beautiful, narrow slot canyons, **Spooky** and **Peek-A-Boo** (3-4 mi., 3-5hr.), are suitable for hikers with some experience and require no climbing gear. To get to the trailheads, head 26 mi. down **Hole-In-The-Rock Road,** 5 mi. east of Escalante, and turn left at **Dry Fork.** The moderate **Calf Creek Falls Trail** (6 mi., 3-5hr. round-trip) is the main developed trail in the monument and leads to a beautiful 126 ft. waterfall and crystal-clear swimming hole. It is accessible from the **Calf Creek Recreation Area,** 15 mi. east on Rte. 12 (day use $2). **Excursions of Escalante,** 125 E. Main St., in Escalante, offers guided trips through the most pristine, unvisited canyons in the monument; guides say that they have never seen anyone else on their trips. The owner, Rick Green, has been exploring the region for 20 years and only shares his knowledge of the unnamed, unpublished canyons he has found with his staff and customers. (☎800-839-7567; www.excursionsofescalante.com. $115-150; includes full gear, lunch, and transportation. Cash only.)

Take Rte. 12 W. through the town of Tropic to Bryce Canyon.

5. BRYCE CANYON. One of the West's most striking landscapes, Bryce Canyon brims with haunting, slender rock pinnacles known as hoodoos. What it lacks in Grand Canyon-esque magnitude, Bryce makes up for in intricate beauty, especially early in the morning when the rising sun illuminates the Bryce amphitheater. As Ebenezer Bryce, a Mormon carpenter with a penchant for understatement, once said, the canyon is "one hell of a place to lose a cow." (Bryce's descendents insist that he never would have used the word "hell," but the general meaning remains true.) To limit park traffic, the Park Service has a free, air-conditioned shuttle service that takes visitors to the visitors center, lodge, and scenic overlooks of the northern parts of the park. You can pick up the shuttle at the huge Ruby Inn just outside the park. (Shuttle runs from Memorial Day to Sept. daily every 12min. 9am-6pm. Free.) Private vehicles can travel park roads, but the Park Service urges visitors to leave their cars outside the park. The **visitors center** is located just inside the park. (☎435-834-5322; www.nps.gov/brca. Open daily May-Sept. 8am-8pm; Oct.-Nov. and Apr. 8am-6pm; Nov.-Mar. 8am-4:30pm. Entrance fee $25 per vehicle, $12 per pedestrian or biker.)

The park is best viewed in the early morning, especially right at sunrise. Bryce's 18 mi. main road winds past spectacular lookouts, with **Bryce and Inspiration Points** providing quintessential postcard-worthy views of the canyon. One oft-missed viewpoint is **Fairyland Point,** at the north end of the park, 1 mi. off the main road, which has some of the best sights in the park; here you can see the hoodoos up close. A range of hiking trails lures visitors from their cars. The **Rim Trail** can be accessed anywhere along the rim and has very little elevation change (11 mi., 4-6hr.). The moderate **Navajo/Queen's Garden Loop** (3 mi., 2-3hr.) is an excellent way to experience the canyon and see some of the park's most famous vistas. A less traveled trail with great views of hoodoos and wildflowers in the summer is the **Tower Bridge Trail** (3 mi., 3-4hr.). A more challenging option is the **Peek-A-Boo Loop** (5½ mi., 3-4hr.), which starts at Bryce Point and winds in and out of hoodoos. A word to the wise: the air is thin. If you start to feel short of breath, take a rest. Very sturdy hiking shoes are a must. The visitors center notes that every instance of a broken ankle occurred when the patient was wearing street or running shoes. Campgrounds are available in the park; ask at the visitors center.

To get from Bryce Canyon to Zion, take Route 12 West to its end at the US 89 interchange. Get on US 89 South and take Exit 149 for Route 9, which leads into the park.

6. ZION NATIONAL PARK.   Zion is Utah's most developed and popular national park, with over 2.5 million visitors exploring its wonders per year. The sandstone cliffs are among the world's highest, and the Virgin River is stunning. The park stands as a refuge for at least five rare or endangered species, including the peregrine falcon, Mexican spotted owl, and Zion snail, found only at the park. The park's expansive **visitors center,** near the south entrance, 14 mi. from the east entrance, offers park information and backcountry permits. (☎435-772-3256, backcountry information 772-0170. Open daily 8am-8pm.) The long, dark **Zion-Mount Carmel Tunnel** connects the east side of the park to Zion Canyon. Built in the 1920s, it was never intended for very large vehicles, which means that lines can build up and cause delays. Any vehicle 7 ft. 10 in. or more in width or 11 ft. 4 in. or more in height will require traffic control to get through the tunnel and must pay a fee of $15.

Most of the park's attractions are found in and around Zion Canyon. Rte. 9 intersects with the **Zion Canyon Scenic Drive** 4¾ mi. from the east entrance. The scenic drive is closed to private vehicles and only accessible by a **shuttle bus,** which stops at all the trailheads and points of interest. (Runs in summer daily 5:45am-11pm; in winter F-Sa 6:45am-10pm. Frequency varies, but can run as often as every 6min. Free.) Park at the visitors center if you can find a spot or try parking in Springdale and riding the free town shuttle to the park. The easy **Riverside Walk** (2 mi., 1½hr. round-trip), a paved walk following the Virgin River into a narrow canyon, is the park's most popular trail. Here, you can see a unique "desert-swamp" environment, a wet home to plant life. The trailhead is at the **Temple of Sinawava** shuttle stop. If you are feeling intrepid, get your feet wet and continue beyond the end of the path through the **Zion Narrows** (1-5hr. round-trip). Wear sturdy shoes and carry a light jacket. The trails leading to the algae-rich Emerald Pools are also popular. You can usually see a small waterfall here. The easy **Lower Emerald Pool Trail** (1¼ mi., 1hr. round-trip) and the moderate **Middle-Emerald Pools Trail** (2 mi., 2hr. round-trip) connect with each other; the trailhead is at the **Zion Lodge** stop.

To get from Zion to Cedar Breaks, Take Rte. 9 to Rte. 17 N., then take I-15 N. for 29 mi. and take Exit 57 for Rte. 14. Follow Rte. 14 for 17 mi. to Rte. 148 N.

7. CEDAR BREAKS NATIONAL MONUMENT.   The landscape in Cedar Breaks changes abruptly from forested hills to colorful fields of flowers, cliffs, spires, arches, and canyons. Try to come in mid- to late July for the wildflower festival; contact the **visitors center** for exact dates. (☎435-586-0787. Open from June to late Sept. daily 8am-6pm. In winter, park open only to winter sports, including cross-country skiing and snowmobiles.) There are two high-country trails. Easy **Alpine Pond Trail** (2 mi. round-trip) leads to a forest glade and pond. Strenuous **Ramparts Trail** ends at a viewpoint overlooking the whole amphitheater.

Continue on Rte. 143 N. to Rte. 148 N. for 21 mi. to I-15. Take I-15 N. for 55 mi. to I-70 E. and follow I-70 for 158 mi. to Green River. Gas is scarce, so fill up when you can.

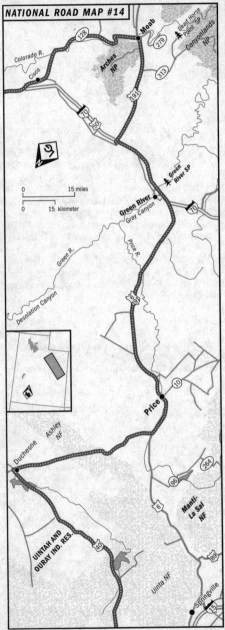

NATIONAL ROAD MAP #14

HIKING AND BIKING

The spectacular valleys, canyons, gorges, mesas, and buttes of the 75 mi. by 40 mi. **San Rafael Swell** (created by a plate uplift 40-60 million years ago and the subsequent forces of erosion) make this area a wonderland for hikers, backpackers, and bikers. The unusual, kidney-shaped area, located off I-70 and 19 mi. west of Green River, has been designated a Wilderness Study Area (WSA) by the Bureau of Land Management (BLM).

GEYSERS

Crystal Geyser, about 7½ mi. southeast of town, erupts about twice a day at irregular times, shooting a jet of water 80-100 ft. high. Environmental purists may be surprised to learn that the phenomenon owes its origin to the oil-extraction industry; the geyser formed in 1936 after a petroleum test well was drilled on the riverbank. To reach the geyser, drive east on Main St. over I-70 and turn left onto the frontage road. After 2 mi., turn right and continue 4 mi. to the geyser.

⚐ THE ROAD TO PRICE: 63 MI.
Take **I-70 West** to **US 191 North/US 6 West.**

PRICE   ☎435
If you feel like getting in touch with your primitive (i.e., prehistoric) self, then head to Price. The **College of Eastern Utah's Prehistoric Museum,** 155 E. Main St., displays fossils and skeletons from the Cleveland-Lloyd Quarry and has exhibits on Nine-Mile Canyon and prehistoric life in Utah. The enormous Huntington mammoth skeleton is the most complete of its kind in the world. Exhibits explain what we can learn from teeth, claws, eggs, footprints, and even fossilized dino droppings. (☎435-613-5060; www.museum.ceu.edu. Open Apr.-Sept. daily 9am-6pm; Oct.-May M-Sa 9am-5pm. $5, ages 2-12 $2, seniors $4.) Next door, in the lobby of **Price City Hall,** 185 E. Main St., you can see a WPA mural, by artist Lynn Fausett, depicting the history of the area. (☎435-636-5010. Open M-F 8am-5pm.) The wilderness surrounding the city will make you feel like you traveled back in time to a more pristine age.

   Price's Budget Host Inn Motel and RV Park ❸, 145 N. Carbonville Rd., has large, clean, quality rooms with blue carpets and earth-toned linens. (☎435-637-2424. Tent-sites $15; RV sites $30. Singles $53, doubles $70. AmEx/D/MC/V.) **Grogg's ❷**, 1652 N. Carbonville Rd., has hardwood floors and antique farming equipment by way of decoration. The eatery serves gourmet sandwiches ($7.25-9.25) and burgers to a local crowd. (☎435-637-2974. Open M-Th 11am-9pm, F-Sa 11am-10pm, Su 1-9pm. AmEx/D/MC/V.) The **Greek Streak ❷**, 84 S. Carbon Ave., is a good stop for satisfying plates of souvlaki ($6-10), Greek salad ($5-9), and dreams of Crete without leaving Utah. (☎435-637-1930. Open M-F 9am-9pm, Sa 11am-9pm. AmEx/MC/V.)

⚑ THE ROAD TO HEBER CITY: 125 MI.

Head west on **East First Street.** After crossing over the viaduct, merge right with **US 6 West/US 191 North** through Helper and follow **US 191 North** as it forks off to the right. A designated scenic byway, this section starts off near factories but later runs through the **Ashley National Forest** and the **Uintah** and **Ouray Indian Reservations.** At **Duchesne,** take a right off US 191 and follow **US 40 West** left to Heber City.

HEBER CITY   ☎435

This small farming community lies in the shadow of its wealthier neighbor, Park City. Despite (or perhaps because of) its diminutive size, it still manages to charm those passing through. Heber City is home to the **Heber Valley Historic Railroad,** 450 S. 600 W. This scenic

railroad goes into **Provo Canyon** (3hr. round-trip; Tu-Sa 11am, 2pm, Su 11am), though the shorter trip to **Soldier Hollow** (1½hr.; F-Sa 11am, 3pm) and one-way trips are also available. (☎435-654-5601. Provo Canyon $30, children $20, seniors $23. Soldier Hollow $24/18/16.)

The colorfully mismatched and friendly **Vista Grande Motel ❷**, 1891 S. Main St., has soft, worn beds and small kitchenettes. (☎435-671-1979. Rooms $40.) **Mac's Motel ❸**, 670 S. Main St., has rooms with microwaves and free Wi-Fi. (☎435-654-0612 or 671-5952; www.macmotel.net. Reception M-F 10am-11pm, Sa 10am-midnight, Su noon-10pm. Singles $60; doubles $70. AmEx/D/MC/V. Slough your budget-travel skin and indulge in something gourmet at the **Snake Creek Grill ❺**, 650 W. 100 S. The grill seems somewhat out of place in Heber City, but the restaurant's gourmet dishes are a welcome change from diner fare. Eclectic entrees ($13-31) include the honey and rosemary glazed lamb, risotto with red-wine-roasted mushrooms, and Moroccan spiced salmon with couscous. (☎435-654-2133; www.snakecreekgrill.com. Open W-Sa 5:30-9:30pm, Su 5:30-8:30pm. AmEx/D/MC/V.) The **Hub Cafe ❷**, 1165 S. Main St., has standard fare like ham steak ($11) and club sandwiches ($7.50). The delicious biscuits and gravy ($5.75) are served until noon. (☎435-654-5463. Open daily in summer 6am-10pm; in winter 6am-9pm. MC/V.)

THE TWO FESTIVALS OF TORREY, UTAH

The population of Torrey, Utah, is about 120, but, judging from the level of town spirit, one would think the town was a major metropolitan center. Locals are quick to boast about the town's two festivals, both of which happen in July. The entire town comes together to participate in these two traditions. First is Apple Days, the local version of July 4. Apple Days features what is claimed to be the world's fastest parade, which travels by car at a speed of 55 mph. It is also the only parade in the world that completes its route twice: the town is too small to make a bigger loop, so they compensate by driving it a second time. Torrey's second trademark is the Bicknell International Film Festival (BIFF), which occurs in mid- to late July (technically held in nearby Bicknell). Rarely does a film festival attract such boisterous attention from locals and visitors alike. Viewers often dress up in the theme of the festival. In 2008 the theme was "Wild Wild Worst," showcasing B-list Westerns (including *The Outlaw* from 1943, which starred Jane Russell's breasts and was censored repeatedly), and in 2007 the theme was Christmas in July. Two restaurants kindly host the often-rowdy after-parties: on Friday night, **Café Diablo,** 599 W. Main St. (☎435-425-3070; www.cafediablo.net), does the honor, and Saturday night the **Rim Rock Inn,** 2523 E. Hwy. 24 (☎435-435-3388), is the host. To contact the BIFF, call the Wayne Theatre (☎435-425-3123). For Apple Days, call Capitol Reef Country/Wayne County Travel Council (☎800-858-7951 or 435-425-3365).

THE ROAD TO SALT LAKE CITY: 43 MI.

Follow **US 40** to **I-80 West** directly to Salt Lake City.

SALT LAKE CITY ☎801

Tired from five months of travel across the plains, Brigham Young looked out across the Great Salt Lake (a vast, otherworldly salt flat) and said, "This is the place." He believed that in this desolate valley his band of Mormon pioneers had finally found a haven where they could practice their religion freely—and, in retrospect, he was right. Temple Sq. is still the focal point of downtown Salt Lake City, and the Church of Jesus Christ of Latter-day Saints (LDS) continues to hold tremendous sway over the city. As the only American city with world-class skiing within 30min. of downtown, Salt Lake City also serves as a home base for visitors to the seven surrounding ski meccas and was selected to host the 2002 Winter Olympics. Whether you come seeking salvation or just some great slalom, the city won't disappoint.

VITAL STATS
Population: 180,000
Tourist Office: Salt Palace Convention Center and Salt Lake City Visitors Bureau, 90 S. West Temple (☎801-534-4902; www.visitsaltlake.com), in Salt Palace Convention Center. Open in summer daily 9am-6pm; call for winter hours.
Library and Internet Access: Salt Lake Public Library, 210 E. 400 S. (☎801-524-8200). Open M-Th 9am-9pm, F-Sa 9am-6pm, Su 1-5pm.
Post Office: 230 W. 200 S. (☎801-532-2906). Open M-F 8am-5:30pm, Sa 9am-2pm. **Postal Code:** 84101.

ORIENTATION

Like most in cities in Utah, Salt Lake City's streets follow a grid system. Brigham Young designated **Temple Square** as the heart of downtown. Street names increase in increments of 100 and indicate how many blocks east, west, north, or south they lie from Temple Sq.; the "0" points are **Main Street** (north-south) and **South Temple** (east-west). **State Street, West Temple,** and **North Temple** are 100-level streets. Occasionally, streets are referred to as 13th South or 17th N., which are the same as 1300 S. or 1700 N. Local address listings often include two cross streets. For example, a building on 13th S. (1300 South) might be listed as 825 E. 1300 S., meaning the address is on 1300 S. between 800 E. (8th E.) and 900 E. (9th E.). The streets are wide but can become congested during rush hour. Metered parking is available. Garages frequently offer specials with 2hr. free parking.

ACCOMMODATIONS

Affordable chain motels cluster at the southern end of downtown, around **200 West** and **600 South,** and on **North Temple.**

The Avenues Hostel (HI-AYH), 107 F St. (☎801-359-3855), a 15min. walk from Temple Sq., in a nice residential area. Keep an eye out—there is no sign marking the hostel. A new entertainment system, 2 kitchens, laundry, and free Wi-Fi make the hostel one of the best budget options around. Key deposit $10. Free parking. Reception 24hr. by phone or at office. Reservations recommended July-Aug. and Jan.-Mar. Dorms $15-17; private rooms $30-45. MC/V. ●

Ute Hostel (AAIH/Rucksackers), 21 E. Kelsey Ave. (☎801-595-1645 or 888-255-1192), near the intersection of 1300 S. and Main St. Young domestic and international travelers crash at this cozy, friendly hostel. Free tea and coffee. Linen included. Free Wi-Fi. Reservations recommended July-Sept. and Jan.-Mar. Dorms $20; private rooms $30-45. Cash only. ●

City Creek Inn, 230 W. North Temple (☎801-533-9100; www.citycreekinn.com), a stone's throw from Temple Sq. *Let's Go* does not recommend casting stones. This solid family-owned and operated motel has 33 immaculate, ranch-style rooms. Free coffee and Wi-Fi. In summer singles $54; doubles $64. In winter singles $58; doubles $68. AmEx/D/MC/V. ●

Scenic Motel, 1345 Foothill Dr. (☎801-582-1527), near the University. Small fowl sing in the lobby. Colorful queen-size beds in cozy, clean rooms near the university of Utah's museums. Singles $47; doubles $55. AmEx/D/MC/V. ●

FOOD

Cheap restaurants are sprinkled around the city. If you're looking for calories straight up, **ZCMI Mall** and **Crossroads Mall,** both across from Temple Sq., have standard food courts. (Open M-F 10am-7pm, Sa 10am-5pm.)

▨ **Ruth's Diner,** 2100 Emigration Canyon Rd. (☎801-582-5807; www.ruthsdiner.com). The best breakfasts in town. Originally run out of a trolley car, Ruth's is the 2nd-oldest restaurant in Utah and has been a Salt Lake landmark for 70 years. Huge omelets like the "Rutherino" ($7-8.50) and brownie sundaes ($5.50). Open daily 8am-10pm. AmEx/D/MC/V. ❷

▨ **Sage's Cafe,** 473 E. 300 S. (☎801-322-3790). They call themselves "culinary astronauts," and the talented chefs at this classy eatery do indeed produce dishes that are out of this world. Try the basil and walnut pesto pasta ($15.50) or the Rabbit's Pick sandwich (carrot butter, avocado, and other veggies; $7.75). Open M-Th 11:30am-2:30pm and 5-10pm, F 11:30am-2:30pm and 5-11pm, Sa 9am-11pm, Su 9am-10pm. AmEx/D/MC/V. ❸

Red Iguana, 736 W. North Temple (☎801-322-1489; www.rediguana.com), in the bright-orange building with bumper stickers covering the door. Most famous for mole ($13.50-14). Serves authentic Mexican food and has a fun ambience. Burritos, enchiladas, and tacos $7-8. Open M-Th 11am-10pm, F 11am-11pm, Sa 10am-11pm, Su noon-9pm. AmEx/D/MC/V. ❷

Nobrow Coffee and Tea, 315 E. 300 S. (☎801-364-3448; www.nobrowcoffee.com). A spacious, airy warehouse building that was once an auto shop for Model Ts in the 20s. Decorated with local art. Serves good coffee (from $1.75), pastries, and cupcakes ($2-4). Free Wi-Fi. Open M-Th 7am-9pm, F 7am-10pm, Sa 9am-10pm, Su 9am-7pm. D/MC/V. ❶

🅖 SIGHTS

LATTER-DAY SIGHTS. The center of the Mormon religion, **Temple Square** encloses the seat of the highest Mormon authority and the central temple. The square has two visitors centers. *(50 E. North Temple and 50 W. South Temple* ☎*801-240-1245. Open daily 9am-9pm.)* Visitors can wander around the 10-acre square, but the temple is not open to the public. Tours leave from the north and south gates every 15min. *Joseph Smith,* a film about the life of the church's founding prophet, are screened

at the **Joseph Smith Memorial Building.** *(15 E. South Temple* ☎*800-537-9703; www.lds.org/events. Open M-Sa 9am-9pm. Tours upon request. Free.)* Temple Sq. is also home to the **Mormon Tabernacle** and its famed choir. Weekly rehearsals and performances are free. In the summer, there are frequent free concerts at **Assembly Hall,** next door. *(*☎*800-537-9703 or 801-240-3323. Organ recitals from Memorial Day to Labor Day M-Sa noon-12:30pm and 2-2:30pm, Su 2-2:30pm, 2nd show held in Conference Center across the street; from Labor Day to Memorial Day M-Sa noon-12:30pm, Su 2-2:30pm. Choir rehearsals most Th 7:30-9:30pm. Choir broadcasts Su 9:30am. Arrive at least 15min. early.)* The **Church of Jesus Christ of Latter Day Saints Office Building** is the tallest skyscraper in town. Take the elevator to the 26th floor for a view of the Great Salt Lake to the west. *(40 E. North Temple* ☎*801-240-3789. Observation deck open M-F 9am-5pm, Sa noon-5pm. Free.)* The church's genealogical materials are accessible at the **Family Search Center,** in the Joseph Smith Memorial Building *(15 E. South Temple* ☎*800-537-9703. Open M-Sa 9am-9pm.)* The collection is housed in the **Family History Library,** which is free for visitors to browse. *(35 N. West Temple.* ☎*801-240-6535. Open M 8am-5pm, Tu-Sa 8am-9pm.)*

> **?** **DID YOU KNOW?** The site for the Salt Lake City Temple was selected in just four days, but the temple took 40 years to build.

PIONEER MEMORIAL MUSEUM. In Salt Lake City, "pioneer" refers to those who came to Utah with Joseph Smith and in the 22 years thereafter (1847-69) to help found the Mormon Church. This huge museum has hundreds of photographs and handcrafted personal items, including several sets of sometimes racist "character dolls" and a 1902 horse-drawn steam fire engine. There is also a case full of items made with human hair. *(300 N. Main St., directly across from the State Capitol building.* ☎*801-532-6479. Open June-Aug. M-Sa 9am-5pm, Su 1-5pm; Sept.-May M-Sa 9am-5pm. Free.)*

MUSEUM OF CHURCH HISTORY AND ART. The museum recounts early Mormon history. The building contains an original 1830 *Book of Mormon,* Brigham Young's famous prayer

can wander around the 10-acre square, but the temple is not open to the public. Tours leave from the north and south gates every 15min. *Joseph Smith*, a film about the life of the church's founding prophet, are screened at the **Joseph Smith Memorial Building.** *(15 E. South Temple ☎800-537-9703; www.lds.org/events. Open M-Sa 9am-9pm. Tours upon request. Free.)* Temple Sq. is also home to the **Mormon Tabernacle** and its famed choir. Weekly rehearsals and performances are free. In the summer, there are frequent free concerts at **Assembly Hall,** next door. *(☎800-537-9703 or 801-240-3323. Organ recitals from Memorial Day to Labor Day M-Sa noon-12:30pm and 2-2:30pm, Su 2-2:30pm, 2nd show held in Conference Center across the street; from Labor Day to Memorial Day M-Sa noon-12:30pm, Su 2-2:30pm. Choir rehearsals most Th 7:30-9:30pm. Choir broadcasts Su 9:30am. Arrive at least 15min. early.)* The **Church of Jesus Christ of Latter Day Saints Office Building** is the tallest skyscraper in town. Take the elevator to the 26th floor for a view of the Great Salt Lake to the west. *(40 E. North Temple ☎801-240-3789. Observation deck open M-F 9am-5pm, Sa noon-5pm. Free.)* The church's genealogical materials are accessible at the **Family Search Center,** in the Joseph Smith Memorial Building *(15 E. South Temple ☎800-537-9703. Open M-Sa 9am-9pm.)* The collection is housed in the **Family History Library,** which is free for visitors to browse. *(35 N. West Temple. ☎801-240-6535. Open M 8am-5pm, Tu-Sa 8am-9pm.)*

> **WALDO WISDOM.** The site for the Salt Lake City Temple was selected in just four days, but the temple took 40 years to build.

PIONEER MEMORIAL MUSEUM. In Salt Lake City, "pioneer" refers to those who came to Utah with Joseph Smith and in the 22 years thereafter (1847-69) to help found the Mormon Church. This huge museum has hundreds of photographs and handcrafted personal items, including several sets of sometimes racist "character dolls" and a 1902 horse-drawn steam fire engine. There is also a case full of items made with human hair. *(300 N. Main St., directly across from the State Capitol building. ☎801-532-6479. Open June-Aug. M-Sa 9am-5pm, Su 1-5pm; Sept.-May M-Sa 9am-5pm. Free.)*

MUSEUM OF CHURCH HISTORY AND ART. The museum recounts early Mormon history. The building contains an original 1830 *Book of Mormon*, Brigham Young's famous prayer bell, and even Joseph Smith's death mask. *(45 N. West Temple St. ☎801-240-4620. Open M-F 9am-9pm, Sa-Su 10am-7pm. Free.)*

STATE CAPITOL. At the northern end of State St. stands Utah's beautiful State Capitol. Free 30min. tours run year-round and address the history of the building and local government. Call ahead to meet the architect. *(350 N. State St. ☎801-538-1800. Open M-F 9am-4pm.)*

CLARK PLANETARIUM. The planetarium will leave you starry-eyed with its exhibits on black holes and the International Space Station. The planetarium also has laser and IMAX shows. *(☎801-456-7827. Open M-Th 10:30am-8pm, F-Sa 10:30am-midnight, Su 10:30am-6pm. Laser shows M-Sa 8pm-close. Free. Shows and IMAX $8, ages 3-12 $6. All shows before 5pm $6.)*

UTAH MUSEUM OF FINE ARTS. Exhibits wow art enthusiasts at this expanded museum on the University of Utah campus. The museum includes pieces from around the world and has a notable Japanese collection. *(410 Campus Center Dr. ☎801-581-7332. Open Tu and Th-Su 9:30am-5:30pm, W 9:30am-8pm. $5, students $3.)*

MUSEUM OF NATURAL HISTORY. Also located on the University of Utah's campus, this museum has displays on the history of the Wasatch Front, with an emphasis on anthropology, biology, and paleontology. Observe a working paleontology lab through a glass wall. A different exhibit lets you shake things up with your own mini earthquake. The black-and-white photo booth produces fun souvenirs. *(1390 E. Presidents Cir. ☎801-581-6927. Open M-Sa 9:30am-5:30pm, Su noon-5pm. $6, ages 3-12 and seniors $3.50, under 3 free.)*

RED BUTTE GARDEN AND ARBORETUM. In the hills above the city, this outdoor arboretum offers 4 mi. of hiking and paved trails that almost guarantee encounters with local wildlife. The arboretum includes the Red Butte Canyon, herb and fragrance gardens, and wildflowers aplenty. The garden has an outdoor summer concert series with blues, folk, jazz, and R&B, entertaining attendees

Salt Lake City

⌂ ACCOMMODATIONS

The Avenues Hostel (HI-AYH), **3**
City Creek Inn, **2**
Scenic Motel, **11**
Ute Hostel (AAIH/Rucksackers), **14**

🍴 FOOD

nobrow coffee and tea, **9**
Red Iguana, **1**
Ruth's Diner, **12**
Sage's Cafe, **10**
Thai Lotus, **13**

🍸 NIGHTLIFE

Circle Lounge, **7**
Totem's, **4**
Squatter's Pub Brewery, **5**
Tavernacle Social Club, **8**
W Lounge, **6**

with musicians like KT Tunstall, Al Green, and Wilco. (*300 Wakara Way, at the University of Utah. ☎801-581-4747; www.redbuttegarden.org. Open May-Aug. M-Sa 9am-9pm, Su 9am-5pm; Sept. and Apr. M-Sa 9am-7:30pm, Su 9am-5pm; Oct.-Mar. daily 10am-5pm. $6, students, children, and seniors $4.*)

🎭 ENTERTAINMENT

Salt Lake City's sweltering summer months are jammed with evening concerts. The **Temple Square Concert Series** presents free outdoor concerts in Brigham Young Historic Park, with music ranging from string quartets to acoustic guitar. (*☎801-240-2534. Concerts June-July 8pm; Aug.-Apr. Tu 7:30pm. Free.*) The **Utah Symphony Orchestra** performs in **Abravanel Hall**, 123 W. South Temple. (*☎801-533-*

6683; www.utahsymphony.org. Tickets $15-58. Office open M-F 10am-6pm, Sa 10am-2pm.*) The **Frosty Darling Cupcake Social**, 177 E. 300 S., occurs the last Friday of July from 6-9pm. (*☎801-532-4790. Suggested donation $1.*)

🎵 NIGHTLIFE

The free *City Weekly* lists events and is available at bars, clubs, and restaurants. Famous teetotalers, the early Mormon theocrats made it illegal to serve alcohol in public places. Hence, all liquor-serving institutions are "private clubs," serving only members and "sponsored" guests. To get around this law, most bars and clubs charge a "temporary membership fee"—essentially a cover charge. Under this system, Salt Lake City has an active night-

⊠ DETOUR
GREAT SALT LAKE

From downtown, follow **600 North** west to **I-15 South** and take the first exit for **I-80 West**. Take **Exit 104** for access to the south shore; there is also a scenic overlook from the highway about 3 mi. past the exit, near mi. 101. To get to the island, take **Exit 335** from **I-15** and follow signs to the causeway.

The Great Salt Lake is *really* salty; only blue-green algae, brine shrimp, and Utahans can survive in it. The salt content varies from 5% to 27%, providing the unusual buoyancy credited with keeping the lake free of drownings. Decaying organic material on the shore gives the lake its pungent odor, which locals prefer not to discuss and visitors wish they didn't smell. **Antelope Island State Park**, in the middle of the lake 1½ mi. from the south shore, is a popular destination. There, you have a fair chance of spotting the island's namesake species as well as deer, bobcats, and coyotes. Although roughly the size of Manhattan, the island is home only to animals, a sole park ranger, and his family.

On the south shore, **Saltair**, just across from Exit 104, has a souvenir shop that promises ⧫**one free piece of saltwater taffy** per visitor, free restrooms, and showers. The beach itself is nearly nonexistent, but many tourists use this spot to access the water. The space doubles as a rock concert venue in the winter and holds concerts about once a week. (☎801-250-4388. Open May-Sept. daily 9am-6pm.)

⧫ THE ROAD TO DELTA: 135 MI.

Follow **I-80 West** to **Route 36** toward **Tooele**. Rte. 36 runs across a sparsely populated area of the state, ending about 88 mi. from Salt Lake City. Follow signs for **US 6 West** to Delta. If you need to fill up before cutting to the western part of the state, pump some gasoline in the tiny town of **Lynndyl**. The dunes are open at the **Little Sahara Recreation Area**, just over 100 mi. from Salt Lake City. Primitive **camping ❶** is available and drinking water is available year-round at the visitors center. Turn off US 6 and head about 6 mi. on a dirt road. Follow signs to the visitors center. (☎435-433-5960. Visitors center open M and Th-Su 8am-4:30pm; call ahead in winter. Day use $8.) In Delta, **US 6** and **US 50 West** become **Main Street.**

DELTA   ☎435

Delta is the largest in a cluster of desert towns near a wide section of the Sevier River and is your last taste of civilization until Ely, Nevada, 170 mi. west. Rock hunting—prowling the desert for minerals—is a popular activity here. The **Great Basin Museum**, 328 W. 100 N., has a collection of local memorabilia as well as exhibits on beryllium mining and geology. Ask a volunteer to operate the black light in the mineral fluorescence display. Outside is an exhibit and building from the **Topaz Internment Camp**, where Japanese-Americans were held during WWII. Don't miss the 3D map, which shows the roadtrip route from Green River to the Nevada border. (☎435-864-5013. Open M-Sa 10am-4pm. Free.)

The **Diamond D Motor Lodge ❷**, 234 W. Main St., is clean. During the summer, it hosts special wagon dinner shows; call ahead for details. (☎435-864-2041. Laundry. Free Wi-Fi. Singles $37; doubles $40-45. AmEx/D/MC/V.) The **Budget Motel ❷**, 75 S. 350 E., offers rooms with eye-pleasing abstract prints. (☎435-864-4533. Singles $32; doubles $36. MC/V.) Small but homey, the **Delta Inn Motel ❷**, 347 E. Main St., has well-maintained rooms with standard amenities and free Wi-Fi. (☎435-864-5318. Singles $34.50; doubles $42.25. AmEx/D/MC/V.) Locals drink from their own mugs (or sometimes a really good friend's) at **Top's City Cafe ❸**, 313 W. Main St. The "Big Daddy" burger ($8) with Swiss cheese and mushrooms is a house specialty. (☎435-864-2148. Entrees $8-17. Open daily in summer 6am-10pm; in winter 6am-9pm. D/MC/V.) The **Pizza House ❷**, 69 S. 300 E., serves filling Italian and American food and claims to have the "best pizza in the West." (☎435-864-2207. Open in summer M-Th 11am-9:30pm, F-Sa 11am-10pm; in winter M-Th 11am-9pm, F-Sa 11am-10pm. AmEx/D/MC/V.)

⧫**TIP** | **FILL 'ER UP.** Fill up on gas before leaving Delta—there are many miles between here and the next pump!

⧫ THE ROAD TO GREAT BASIN: 101 MI.

Head west on **Main Street (US 6/50)**, following the signs for Ely. The last gas station is 6 mi. west of Delta, in Hinckley. West of Delta, there is a **trilobite quarry** where you can find your own 550-million-year-old fossils; turn right at the sign—32 mi. west of Delta, between mile markers 56 and 57—and travel about 20 mi. on dirt roads to the quarry. (☎435-864-3638. Open Apr.-Nov., M-Sa 9am-6pm. 2hr. session $28, ages 7-16 $16; ½-day $42/28; full day $70/42.) Just after the cattle guard, exactly 3 mi. after you cross the Nevada state border, turn left at the sign for **Great Basin National Park.** Turn left at the stop sign onto **Route 487** and right at the junction with **Route 488** in the town of **Baker.** The park lies 5 mi. down the road.

>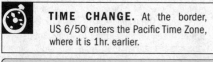
>
> **TIME CHANGE.** At the border, US 6/50 enters the Pacific Time Zone, where it is 1hr. earlier.

GREAT BASIN NATIONAL PARK ☎775

Established in 1986, Great Basin National Park preserves ancient glaciers, diverse flora and fauna, and miles of unmaintained trails. The park's prehistoric bristlecone pine trees are said to be the world's oldest living organisms, or at least its oldest living trees; take a moment to reflect on the ephemeral nature of human existence. The basin area extends through much of Nevada and is so named because no precipitation falling in the region reaches the ocean. Eastern Nevada's Snake Range forms the spine of the park; its various creeks, lakes, and forest spread out from its peaks. Despite the desolation of this vast desert area, the towering ranges also make for high alpine zones with considerable ecological diversity. If you're very lucky (or very unlucky), you may spot a mountain lion among the pines.

ORIENTATION

Route 488 is the only paved road that enters the park; it runs west to the visitors center. **Wheeler Peak Scenic Drive** is paved, begins just after the park entrance, and provides access to three of the park's four developed camp-grounds. Improved gravel roads grant access to the park's northern reaches and central drainage, while a high-clearance dirt road ventures into the park's southern mountains. The town of **Ely** (p. 454) bills itself as a gateway to the park and offers the requisite creature comforts; **Baker** (5 mi. from the visitors center) shares Ely's gateway-town niche.

VITAL STATS
Area: 77,100 acres
Tourist Offices: Lehman Caves Visitors Center (☎775-234-7331; www.nps.gov/grba), at the end of Rte. 488. Open daily 8am-4:30pm; extended hours in summer. **Great Basin Visitors Center** (☎775-234-7331), on Rte. 487, just north of Baker. Open daily 8am-4:30pm; extended hours in summer.
Gateway Towns: Baker, Ely (p. 454).

ACCOMMODATIONS

There are a few budget inns and motels in the area in addition to campgrounds.

Border Inn (☎775-234-7300). Straddles the Utah/Nevada border along US 6 and US 50. Boasts sizable wood-paneled rooms with small TVs. Rooms $42-49. MC/V. ❷

Silver Jack Motel, 14 Main St. (☎775-234-7323; www.silverjackinn.com), in Baker. Simple rooms close to the mountains. Campsites with full hookup $22; private rooms $49-75. MC/V. ❸

CAMPING

Four developed campgrounds, several primitive sites along Snake and Strawberry Creeks, and nearly unlimited backcountry camping accommodate Great Basin visitors. All four developed campgrounds are first come, first served, and reservations are not allowed. Developed campgrounds have water only in the summer. Both the **Wheeler Peak** and **Upper Lehman** campgrounds (see listings below) host evening ranger talks during summer months. Scenic primitive camping, which offers pre-dug fire pits, rewards those willing to travel gravel roads. **Snake Creek Road,** 5 mi. south of Baker along Rte. 487, follows the fertile Snake Creek watershed area and allows easy access to six primitive sites. **Strawberry Creek Road,** 3 mi. north of the US 6/50 and Rte. 487

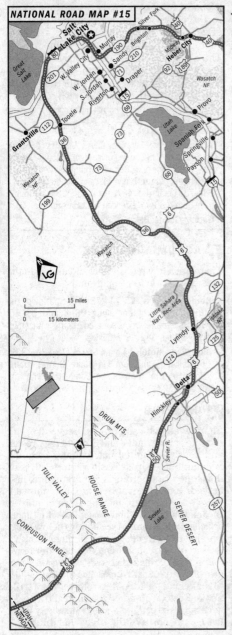

NATIONAL ROAD

junction, leads to four primitive sites along Strawberry Creek. (☎775-234-7331. Both campgrounds have tables and pit toilets but no potable water. Free.)

Wheeler Peak Campground (9890 ft.). Scenic sites nestled among aspen groves and alpine meadows in the shadow of Wheeler Peak. Access to the sites is at the end of the serpentine Wheeler Peak Scenic Drive, which is closed to vehicles over 24 ft. in length. 37 sites. Pit toilets and water. Open June-Sept. Sites $12.❶

Baker Creek Campground (7530 ft.), south down the graded gravel road from Rte. 488. Serene spots right on the banks of Baker's creek. 34 sites. Pit toilets and potable water. Open May-Oct. Sites $12. Cash only. ❶

Upper and Lower Lehman Creek Campgrounds, close to the visitors center and Lehman Caves. Guards the banks of Lehman Creek along the 1st 3 mi. of the Wheeler Mountain Scenic Drive Both campgrounds crowd quickly, so arrive early. Sites are removed and spacious. Both campgrounds have pit toilets and potable water. Upper Lehman open May-Oct.; lower Lehman open year-round. Sites $12. Cash only. ❶

FOOD

Lehman Caves Cafe (☎775-234-7221), at the end of Rte. 488. Caters to those unwilling to trek to Baker or pack their own grub. Serves breakfast ($2-4), hot dogs ($3.75), and ice cream ($1.50-3) and also peddles standard park memorabilia. Open from mid-Apr. to mid-Oct. daily 8am-4pm. D/MC/V. ❶

SIGHTS AND OUTDOORS

HIKING AND BIKING
Because much of the park remains undeveloped, exploring its far reaches requires good hiking boots, a jacket, plenty of water, several days' worth of food, and strong legs. Luckily, for those not enthusiastic about hauling a heavy pack through the backcountry, the park's other notable features, **Lehman Cave, Lexington Arch,** and **Bristlecone Groves** (below) are accessible via shorter excursions, though the route to Lexington Arch requires a high-clearance four-wheel-drive. Several trails

along the Wheeler Peak Scenic Drive grant ample opportunities to stretch weary legs. For a less crowded jaunt, try the longer trails departing from the **Baker Creek Trailhead**. The **Mountain View Nature Trail** (30min.; easy) begins at the Rhodes Cabin next to the visitors center and is a brief glimpse of park ecology and geology that is just right for those pressed for time. Stop by the visitors center for a trail guide and watch for the signs along the way. The only day hike flagged for winter use, the **Lehman Creek Trail** (7 mi., 4-6hr. round-trip) passes through a range of habitats over its 2200 ft. elevation change. It departs from the end of Wheeler Peak Scenic Drive or the Lehman Creek campgrounds.

Although bicycling in the park is restricted to roads (including the 4WD roads), mountain bikers will relish excellent riding at the **Sacramento Pass Recreation Site,** northeast of the park along US 6/50. Some of the best trails in the area explore **Black Horse Canyon,** accessible off US 6/50 via the unmarked forest road, north of Sacramento Pass.

LEHMAN CAVES. Absalom Lehman came across these splendid caves in 1885, and soon he was charging visitors to explore them by candlelight. The caves have truly fantastic formations. The Park Service prohibits self-guided tours but offers two guided-tour options: a 1hr. tour of the Gothic Palace, Lodge Room, and Inscription Room and a 1½hr. tour of the entire cave, including the spectacular Grand Palace Room. The cave remains at 50°F all year, a refreshing break from the intensely hot sun in the summer months; just be sure to bring an extra layer. (☎775-234-7331, ext. 242. *Hours vary, so call ahead. 1hr. tour $8, ages 5-15 $4, under 5 free; 1½hr. tour $10, children $5; under 5 not permitted.*)

LEXINGTON ARCH. This is a mammoth, six-story limestone sculpture in the wild southeast section of the park. A moderate 3 mi. round-trip hike switches back and forth up several hundred feet through meadows and a canyon before paralleling a drainage ditch back to the base of the arch. The majority of the trail, which ascends a total of 830 ft., sits on Forest Service land. (*Drive south 11 mi. on Rte. 487 from the intersection of Rte. 487 and 488 through Garrison, UT. At the sign for Lexington Arch, follow the rough, high-clearance dirt road 12 mi. to the trailhead.*)

BRISTLECONE GROVE. The Great Basin bristlecones, gnarled but beautiful trees, are the world's oldest living organisms, according to common definitions of "life" (your guess is as good as ours). Bristlecones survive on high mountain slopes by deadening themselves until more hospitable times allow them to flourish again. The oldest trees are found in some of the most inhospitable locations and can be 4000-5000 years old. Although there are several bristlecone groves throughout the park, the grove below Wheeler Peak is the most accessible. To get there, follow the **Wheeler Peak Scenic Drive** to the end and take the trail (2 mi.; moderate) from Bristlecone Trailhead to the trees. The **Alpine Lakes Loop Trail** (2 mi.; 1-3hr. round-trip) is a highly trafficked trail that has a trailhead at the end of Wheeler Peak Scenic Drive (at 10,000 ft. above sea level). The trail allows quick access to two scenic lakes, **Lake Stella** and **Lake Teresa.**

SCENIC DRIVES

Just down the hill from the visitors center, the paved **Wheeler Peak Scenic Drive** (1hr. round-trip) winds 12 mi. up to an elevation of 10,000 ft. Full of sharp curves and switchbacks, the road demands either constant vigilance or James Bond's good luck. As the road climbs, it passes first through grease bush and sagebrush, then piñon pines and junipers, then ponderosa pines, white fir, and mountain mahogany, and finally through spruce, limber pine, and high alpine aspen groves. As late as June, snowbanks line the summit area and make the warm desert weather at the base a pleasant memory. **Mather Overlook** features an awe-inspiring view of jagged Wheeler Peak and Jeff Davis; in the other direction, the road stretches across the flat basin you crossed on your way west to the park. For a closer view of the peak, stop at Wheeler Peak Overlook. No vehicles over 24 ft. long are allowed on the scenic drive past Lehman Creek.

⚑ THE ROAD TO ELY: 52 MI.

Continue northwest on **US 6/US 50.** Entering Ely, US 6 heads left; stay on US 50.

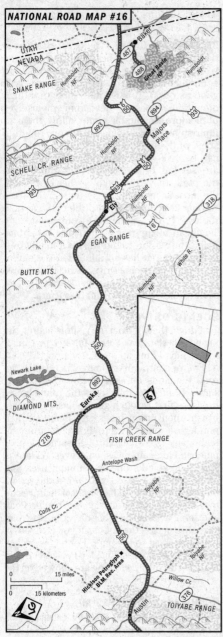

NATIONAL ROAD MAP #16

ELY ☎ 775

This mining town hardly fits the profile of a typical "gateway" city. Yet its barren surroundings and the convergence of several highways make Ely (rhymes with "really") a hub for much trans-Nevadan traffic. In the early 20th century, development of the area's copper resources brought an influx of residents and a railroad system. Today Ely is but a shadow of its former self, but glitzy remnants of past glory remain—like the stately Nevada Hotel and Casino, once the state's tallest building.

VITAL STATS

Population: 4000

Tourist Office: White Pine County Chamber of Commerce, 636 Aultman St. (☎775-289-8877). Open M-F 9am-5pm.

Library and Internet Access: White Pine County Library, 900 Campton St. (☎775-289-3737), 1 block south of Aultman St. Open M-Th 9am-6pm, F 9am-1pm, 1st and 3rd Sa of each month 10am-2pm.

Post Office: 2600 Bristlecone Ave. (☎775-289-9276). Open M-F 8:30am-5pm, Sa 10am-2pm.

Postal Code: 89301.

✦ ORIENTATION

US 6, US 50, and **US 93** meet in Ely and radiate toward Reno, Las Vegas, Utah, Idaho, and California. Approaching the town from the southeast, US 50 runs along Great Basin Blvd. before turning west onto **Aultman Street,** Ely's main drag. Lettered streets run east-west, east of **Great Basin Boulevard.**

🛏 ACCOMMODATIONS

Many of Ely's hotels and motels are located on **Aultman Street.**

Hotel Nevada, 501 Aultman St. (☎775-289-6665 or 888-406-3055). A relic from another era. Sometimes unreliable water temperature, but the rooms are spacious, comfortable, and elegant. A third of the rooms are shrines to celebrities who have stayed here, like Mickey Rooney and Wayne Newton. 24hr. cafe. Texas hold 'em F-Sa. Laundry. Wi-Fi. Rooms $35-55. AmEx/D/MC/V. ❷

The Deser-est Motel, 1425 Aultman St. (☎775-289-8885). Large rooms with wood-paneled walls, colorful floral beds, and bathrooms. Singles $35; doubles $51. AmEx/D/MC/V. ❷

White Pine Motel, 1301 Aultman St. (☎775-289-4600). Basic rooms with mini-fridges, microwaves, and free Wi-Fi. Rooms $40-50. AmEx/D/MC/V. ❷

🍴 FOOD

Aultman St. has several steak-and-potatoes chophouses, including restaurants in the downtown casinos.

The Silver State Restaurant, 1204 Aultman St. (☎775-289-8866). Popular with locals who come for sandwiches ($5.50-9), burgers ($6.80-9.60), and meat dishes ($10-18). Open daily 6am-9pm. AmEx/D/MC/V. ❸

Twin Wok, 700 Great Basin Blvd. (☎775-289-3699). Chinese. Try Mandarin entrees ($8-11) like pineapple chicken. Open M-Sa 11am-9:30pm. D/MC/V. ❷

👁 SIGHTS

NEVADA NORTHERN RAILWAY MUSEUM. In 1983, the railroad through East Ely shut down, leaving behind an office and a depot full of equipment and records. Relics from the depot are on display at this museum in East Ely. A tour goes through the restored office building, and well-informed guides share their knowledge of the railroad, town, and surrounding region. There's also a train ride on the old line, pulled by a 94-year-old coal-fired locomotive. You can also drive a locomotive 14 mi. yourself—it justs costs $695 for the steam locomotive or $495 for the diesel. *(1100 Ave. A. Where US 50 turns left on Aultman St., turn right and then left onto 11th St. E. ☎775-289-2085 or 866-407-8326; www.nnry.com. Museum hours vary. Gift shop open M and W-Sa 8am-7pm, Su 8am-4pm. Tours $4, ages 4-12 $2. For train schedule, see website or call. $24, ages 4-12 $15, specialty trains on Sa night $28-46.)*

WHITE PINE PUBLIC MUSEUM. The museum displays a hodgepodge of artifacts ranging from stuffed birds to telegraph equipment. *(2000 Aultman St. ☎775-289-4710. Usually open Tu-Sa noon-4pm. $4, ages 4-12 $2, seniors $3.)*

🚩 **THE ROAD TO EUREKA: 77 MI.**
Follow **Aultman Street (US 50 West)** out of downtown. Don't forget to fill up before leaving Ely—the next chance is 77 mi. down the road.

EUREKA ☎775

Eureka boomed in population and wealth after the discovery of silver. The mine quickly busted, however, leaving behind a smattering of late-1870s buildings and little else. A bit of mining remains, but Eureka has never regained its 19th-century prosperity. US 50, known as Main St., runs straight through the center of town. The **Eureka County Sentinel Museum,** 10 N. Monroe St., contains the printing press that produced the local *Eureka Sentinel,* a daily from 1871 to 1960. The wall is papered with decaying posters from the Opera House and old news stories. (☎775-237-5010. Open May-Oct. daily 10am-6pm; Nov.-Apr. Tu-Sa 10am-6pm. Free.) The **Eureka Courthouse,** 10 S. Main St., is restored and elegant. Ask someone to show you the old jail out back. (☎775-237-5263. Open M-F 8am-noon and 1-5pm. Free.) Nevadan artists display their work at the **Opera House,** 31 S. Main St. The vintage screen in the auditorium is worth checking out, and so are the photographs of ancient opera stars downstairs, many of whom could easily be confused with modern country singers. (☎775-237-6006. Open M-F 8am-noon and 1-5pm. Free.)

The **Sundown Lodge ❷,** 60 N. Main St., offers three floors of clean rooms organized around a small courtyard. (☎775-237-5334. Singles $44-48; doubles $52-64. AmEx/D/MC/V.) **D.J.'s Drive-In and Diner ❷,** 509 S. Main St., is a burger-and-sandwich joint that serves sandwiches ($3-7), pizza, and chicken/rib/seafood dinners ($8.50-11.50), alongside pool tables and a connected movie rental store. (☎775-237-5356. Open daily 10am-10pm. AmEx/D/MC/V.)

🚗 **DETOUR**
HICKISON PETROGLYPH RECREATION AREA
Off **US 50 West,** 45 mi. from Eureka. Turn right on a dirt road to reach the site.

A free interpretive guide discusses a short loop trail, which leads to prehistoric designs carved into rock faces. The designs, which are somewhat harder to see than those at Grimes

Point, consist mostly of curved lines. There are also 16 free campsites with no water. (☎775-635-4000. Free.)

◄ DETOUR
SPENCER HOT SPRINGS

Turn left on **Route 376** and then make another immediate left at the sign onto a dirt road. After about 2½ mi., make a left up a hill for about a quarter mile.

Surrounded by jagged mountains and isolated from civilization, Spencer Hot Springs is worth a stop. The springs are well known to locals and legal to use, but there are not any signs pointing the way to these rock-lined pools. (Open 24hr. Free.)

↗ THE ROAD TO AUSTIN: 70 MI.

Continue on **US 50 West** toward Austin.

AUSTIN   ☎775

Like Ricky Martin, Austin is not what it once was. Although the town has dwindled significantly since its days as a major mining camp, it does remain the only evidence of civilization for miles around. It is a good 2hr. drive from Austin to Fallon (the next town), so do at least get out of the car. A developed network of mountain-biking trails goes through the nearby **Toiyabe National Forest**, just south of town. Trails range in difficulty and length; pick up a trail guide and Forest Service map at the **Austin Ranger District Office**, just west of town (☎775-964-2671, open M-F 8am-4:30pm), or at the **Chamber of Commerce**, on the second floor of the **Austin Courthouse** (☎775-964-2200; open M-F 9am-5pm). Based on an Italian design, the three-story **Stokes Castle** was built as a luxury summer home for Ansen Stokes, a mine developer and railroad magnate. Today, it lies in ruin, just west of the Chevron station and left on Castle Rd. (Free.)

Austin's motels line US 50. The **Pony Canyon Motel ❷**, 30 Main St., has nice and spacious rooms with fans and satellite TV. (☎775-964-2605. Singles $42; doubles $52. AmEx/D/MC/V.) **Lincoln Motel ❷**, 60 N. Main St., provides minimalist rooms with satellite TV. (☎775-964-2698. Singles $33; doubles $42. AmEx/D/MC/V.) The **International Cafe and Bar ❶**, 59 N. Main St., is a good call for nosh. (☎775-964-1225. Breakfast $3-12. Sandwiches

and burgers $6-9. Pizza $6-12. Open daily 6am-9:30pm. MC/V.) The **Toiyabe Cafe ❷**, 150 Main St., serves basic sandwiches ($5.25-12) and other normal diner fare. (☎775-964-2220. Open daily in summer 6am-9pm; in winter 6am-9pm. AmEx/D/MC/V.)

> **PHOTO OP.** In the last 25 mi. before Fallon, watch for Navy jets overhead; Fallon is the home of the Naval Fighters Weapons School, a.k.a. "Top Gun."

↗ THE ROAD TO FALLON: 110 MI.

Continue on **US 50** into downtown Fallon.

FALLON   ☎775

The self-proclaimed "Oasis of Nevada," Fallon is at the center of a fertile farming region, which was created when the Newlands Project built two dams and a canal, bringing water to the desert. While artifacts are few at the **Churchill County Museum**, 1050 S. Maine St., this local history museum has scintillating displays on the natural history of northwestern Nevada. Highlights include a display on the Hidden Cave as well as a large mineral and rock collection. (☎775-423-3677. Open Mar.-Nov. M-Sa 10am-5pm, Su noon-5pm; Dec.-Feb. M-Sa 10am-4pm, Su noon-4pm.)

The **Value Inn ❷**, 180 W. Williams Ave., has large rooms with comfortable beds and nice bathrooms. (☎775-423-5151. Free Wi-Fi. Singles $42; doubles $49. AmEx/D/MC/V.) At **La Fiesta ❸**, 60 W. Center St., friendly waiters in tuxedo shirts and bow ties serve delicious Mexican food in this spotlessly clean restaurant. From US 50, head south one block on Maine St. and turn right. (☎775-423-1605. Open daily 11am-10pm. D/MC/V.)

↗ THE ROAD TO RENO: 63 MI.

Head west out of Fallon on **US 50.** Nine miles west of town, the road divides; take **Alternate US 50 (Reno Highway)** to **I-80** and Reno. Take **Exit 13** off I-80 and turn left onto **Virginia Street** to reach the casinos.

RENO   ☎775

With decadent casinos only a throw of the dice away from snow-capped mountains,

Reno embodies both the opportunist frenzy and the natural splendor of the West. Catering to those interested in making a fast buck or saying a quick vow, the self-proclaimed "biggest little city in the world" has earned a reputation for gritty glamor, crazed gamblers, and delirious lovers.

VITAL STATS

Population: 207,000

Tourist Office: Reno-Sparks Convention and Visitors Authority, 4001 S. Virginia St. (☎800-367-7366; www.visitrenotahoe.com). Open M-F 8am-5pm.

Library and Internet Access: Washoe County Library-Downtown Reno Branch, 301 S. Center St. (☎775-327-8300). Open M-F 9am-5pm, Sa-Su 11am-3pm.

Post Office: 2000 Vassar St. (☎775-788-0785). Open M-F 7:30am-5:30pm, Sa 9am-3pm. **Postal Code:** 89510.

✈ ORIENTATION

Most major casinos are downtown between **West** and **Center Streets** and **Second** and **Sixth Streets.** The neon-lit streets are heavily patrolled, but don't stray far east of the city center at night. **Virginia Street** is Reno's main drag; south of the **Truckee River** there are cheaper accommodations, outlying casinos, and strip mall after strip mall. The town of **Sparks,** a few miles northeast along I-80, has several casinos frequented by locals. The *Reno/Tahoe Visitor Planner,* available at info kiosks throughout the city, has a local map and is a helpful city guide.

🛏 ACCOMMODATIONS

While weekend prices at casinos are usually high, weekday rates and low-season discounts make for great deals. Rates can vary widely, however, so call ahead. Across the board, prices peak during festivals like **Hot August Nights,** Reno's antique car festival.

🏨 **Harrah's Reno,** 219 N. Center St. (☎800-427-7247 or 775-786-5700), between E. 2nd St. and Commercial Row. 2 towers of luxurious rooms, 7 restaurants, a pool, and a health club leave little to be desired—except, of course, a straight flush. The 65,000 sq. ft. casino has some of Reno's highest table limits. Sammy's Showroom and the Plaza host top performers. Free valet parking. Rooms from $49. AmEx/D/MC/V. ❷

Grand Sierra Resort, 2500 E. 2nd St. (☎800-648-5080 or 775-789-2000), off US 395. More than 2000 elegant rooms, a mall, a health club and spa, go-carts, a driving range, and a 50-lane bowling alley make this casino one of Reno's most gargantuan. Try your luck at the slots or check out the Ultimate Rush reverse bungee for something even more stomach-churning. Rooms $59-350. AmEx/D/MC/V. ❸

Davis Creek Park (☎775-849-0684), 18 mi. south on US 395 to Rte. 429. Follow the signs 1 mi. west. Volleyball courts and trout-packed Ophir Creek Pond. 1st come, 1st served. Showers and toilets on-site. Sites $19. Cash only. ❶

Grand Sierra RV Park, 2500 E. 2nd St. (☎800-258-7366 or 775-789-2147), next to the Grand Sierra Resort. There's no grass, but campers have access to the pool, tennis courts, and fitness center. Showers, restrooms, and full hookups. Sites $25-50. AmEx/D/MC/V. ❷

🍴 FOOD

The cost of eating out in Reno is low, but the food quality doesn't have to be. Casinos offer long all-you-can-eat buffets, but if size doesn't matter to you, then try a local venue with a shorter but more specialized menu.

Blue Moon Gourmet Pizza, 190 California St. (☎775-324-2828). Cool local hangout with blue walls. Pizzas with a range of gourmet toppings, including goat cheese, sun-dried tomatoes, and roasted garlic ($17). A good selection of beers and wines rounds out the menu. Open M-Sa 11am-9pm, Su noon-8pm. MC/V. ❹

Java Jungle, 246 W. 1st St. (☎775-329-4484). Decorated with urban jungle graffiti. Serves coffee and pastries ($1.50-3.50), smoothies ($4.25), and hand-rolled pizzas ($10). Connected to Jungle Vino, which serves wines by the glass ($6-15). Free Wi-Fi. Cafe open daily 6am-midnight. Wine bar open M-Th Su 3pm-midnight, F-Sa noon-midnight. AmEx/D/MC/V. ❶

Bangkok Cuisine, 55 Mt. Rose St. (☎775-322-0299), near S. Virginia St. Wood lattice walls and beaded Buddha paintings. Delicious Thai dishes include soups ($4-12), noodles ($9-12), and

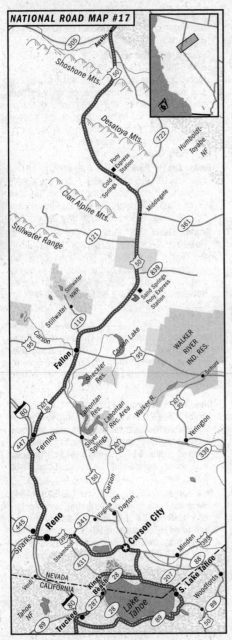

NATIONAL ROAD MAP #17

curries ($9-11). Open M-Sa 11am-10pm, Su 4-10pm. AmEx/D/MC/V. ❸

Victorian Buffet, 407 N. Virginia St. (☎775-329-4777), inside the Silver Legacy. The huge domed ceiling with replica mining tower makes this casino feel more like Las Vegas than anywhere else in Reno. Long buffet with carving station, seafood, pizza, desserts, and tons of fresh fruit. Extensive breakfast buffet M-F $9, Sa-Su $13. Dinner buffet M-F $16, Sa-Su $21.50. Open M-Th and Su 7:30am-2pm and 4:30-9pm, F-Sa 7:30am-2pm and 4:30-10pm. AmEx/D/MC/V. ❺

La Strada, 345 N. Virginia St. (☎775-329-4777), in the Eldorado Hotel. Award-winning northern Italian cuisine in the heart of the Eldorado. Carbo-load before skiing or snowboarding with pastas made fresh daily ($15-20), or load up on protein with beef and fish entrees ($23-39). ❹

The Prime Rib Grill, 345 N. Virginia St. (☎775-786-5700, ext. 7328), in the Eldorado Hotel. Worthwhile specials include the 8 oz. prime rib for $15 5-6pm. Open M-Th and Su 5-9pm, F-Sa 5-10pm. AmEx/D/MC/V. ❹

👁 SIGHTS

🚗 NATIONAL AUTOMOBILE MUSEUM. By far the best car collection along the route, the museum boasts rare cars, early model years, and one-of-a-kind prototypes from the private collection of the late gambling magnate Bill Harrah. One definite highlight is the Thomas Flyer, which drove from New York City to Paris (with water crossings) in 1907. (*10 Lake St. S. ☎775-333-9300. Open M-Sa 9:30am-5:30pm, Su 10am-4pm. 1hr. tours M-Sa 10:30am, 1:30pm, Su 12:30pm. $10, ages 6-18 $4, seniors $8.*)

NEVADA MUSEUM OF ART. This museum is in a striking structure inspired by the Black Rock Desert. Rotating exhibits feature artists like Diego Rivera, Edward Hopper, and Dennis Oppenheim. (*160 W. Liberty St. ☎775-329-3333. Open Tu-W and F-Su 10am-5pm, Th 10am-8pm. $10, students and seniors $8, ages 6-12 $1, under 6 free.*)

🎵 ENTERTAINMENT

Almost all casinos offer live nighttime entertainment, but few shows are worth the steep admission prices. **Harrah's,** 219 N. Center St., is an exception; the casino has several nightly comedy shows in Sammy's Showroom. (☎775-786-3232. Tickets from $30.) At **Circus Circus**, 500 N. Sierra St., a small circus on the midway above the casino floor performs "big top" circus shows. (☎775-329-0711. Every 40min. daily 11:15am-11:45pm. Free.)

NIGHTLIFE

Tonic Lounge, 231 W. 2nd St. (☎775-337-6868). Hip. Mixed drinks $6-8, ½-proce F-Sa 8-10pm. Has live music Th-Sa, with everything from hip hop to hard rock, dance rock, and trance. Happy hour M-Sa 5-9pm with ½-price beers. Open M-Sa 5pm-5am. Cash only.

5 Star Saloon, 132 West St. (☎775-329-2878; www.5starsaloon.net). GLBT-friendly. An excellent place for dancing in to the night and chatting with locals. Open 24hr. MC/V.

Se7en Teahouse and Bar, 100 N. Arlington Ave., Ste. 102 (☎775-348-9526; www.seenatse7en. com). You're sure to eventually find peace here, if not because of the tranquil mountain setting, variety of gourmet teas, and pastries, then because of the full bar. Pots of tea $1.50-10. Quiche of the day $5. Movie screenings W around 8pm. Bar open M-Th 10am-midnight, F 10am-2am, Sa noon-2am. AmEx/MC/V.

THE ROAD TO CARSON CITY: 33 MI.

Head east from **Virginia Street** to **US 395 South.** Bear right on **North Carson Street** in Carson City.

CARSON CITY   ☎775

At the crossroads of traffic bound for Lake Tahoe and home to three large casinos, this former mint town lacks the quaint, homey feel of other capital cities. Thirty miles from Reno and only 10 mi. from Lake Tahoe, Carson City's main claim to fame (other than that capital thing) is that it's a good overnight stop before a day of outdoor exploration.

ORIENTATION

Route 50 runs east-west in the eastern half of Carson City. When it runs into **US 395,** Rte. 50 turns 90° and follows US 395 north-south through the center of the city. A few blocks east, **North Roop Street** runs parallel to US 395.

VITAL STATS

Population: 53,000

Tourist Office: Carson City Convention and Visitors Bureau, 1900 S. Carson St. (☎775-687-7410; www.carsoncity.com). Open M-F 9am-4pm, Sa-Su 10am-3pm.

Library and Internet Access: Carson City Library, 900 N. Roop St. (☎775-887-2244; www.carsoncitylibrary.org). Open M 10am-6pm, Tu-Th 10am-8pm, F noon-6pm, Sa 10am-4pm.

Post Office: 1111 S. Roop St. (☎775-884-2300). Open M-F 8:30am-5pm, Sa 10am-1pm. **Postal Code:** 89701.

ACCOMMODATIONS

Carson City has the usual set of casino hotels and motels, but rooms fill fast on weekends, especially during events. Motels line Carson St. throughout town. Call ahead to check rates, which change frequently.

The Best Value Inn, 2731 S. Carson St. (☎775-882-2007; www.bestvaluecarsoncity. com). Offers rooms with comfy chairs, refrigerators, coffeemakers, and free Wi-Fi. Singles $39-79; doubles $49-99. AmEx/D/MC/V. ❸

Desert Hills Motel, 1010 S. Carson St. (☎775-882-1932 or 800-652-7785). Decorated with different themes. Access to an outdoor hot tub. Rooms from $55. AmEx/D/MC/V. ❸

FOOD

Red's Old 395 Grill, 1055 S. Carson St. (☎775-887-0395). Covered wagons, horses, and sleighs hang suspended from the ceiling. Patrons devour delicious, home-smoked barbecue or sip one of the 101 beers next to an old Carson City DPW steam roller, one of two left that paved New York City's Wall St. Sandwiches $7.25-9. Wood-fired pizzas $7.50. Dinner entrees $11.50-27.50. Happy hour daily 3-6pm with $2 select drafts and wines. Open M-Th 11am-9:30pm, F-Su 11am-10:30pm. AmEx/MC/V. ❹

B'Sghetti's, 318 N. Carson St. (☎775-887-8879). Attracts locals with its upbeat service, easygoing atmosphere, and savory pasta dishes. The gnocchi ($12.50) with your choice of sauce are especially tasty. Soups, salads, and sandwiches

NATIONAL ROAD

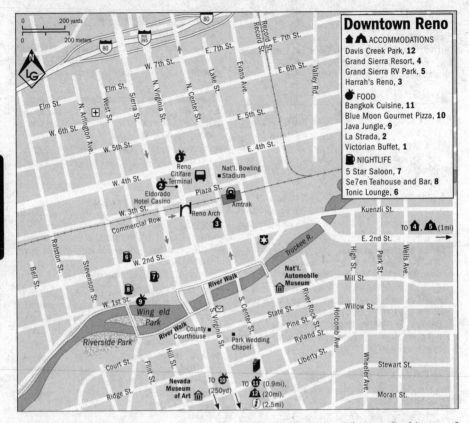

Downtown Reno

♠♦ ACCOMMODATIONS
Davis Creek Park, **12**
Grand Sierra Resort, **4**
Grand Sierra RV Park, **5**
Harrah's Reno, **3**

🍴 FOOD
Bangkok Cuisine, **11**
Blue Moon Gourmet Pizza, **10**
Java Jungle, **9**
La Strada, **2**
Victorian Buffet, **1**

🍸 NIGHTLIFE
5 Star Saloon, **7**
Se7en Teahouse and Bar, **8**
Tonic Lounge, **6**

$7-11. Pasta $9-15. Open M-Sa 11am-9pm, Su 4-9pm. AmEx/D/MC/V. ❸

🔆 SIGHTS

NEVADA STATE MUSEUM. Occupying part of the building that once contained a US Mint, this museum highlights aspects of Nevada's past and present with displays on silver mining, the old Carson City coin mint, ghost towns, animal and plant life of the desert, and the Native Americans that inhabited the area. Many state museums might be content with just that, but this one has higher ambitions: you'll find an emphasis on prehistory here,

and even a good exhibit on the history of Earth. (*600 N. Carson St. ☎ 775-687-4810. Open daily 8:30am-4:30pm. $5, under 18 free, seniors $3.*)

NEVADA STATE RAILROAD MUSEUM. This museum showcases a collection of cars and engines from the historic Virginia & Truckee Railroad. True enthusiasts might also enjoy the museum's annual railroad symposium. (*2180 S. Carson St. ☎ 775-687-6953. Open daily 8:30am-4:30pm. $4, under 18 free, seniors $3.*)

🚗 THE ROAD TO LAKE TAHOE: 30 MI.

US 50 merges with **Route 28** on the eastern edge of the lake. You can take Rte. 28 South to South Shore or Rte. 28 North to North Shore.

The Golden State
CALIFORNIA
Welcomes You!

VITAL STATS

Population: 34,000

Tourist Office: South Lake Tahoe Creek Visitors Center, 3066 Lake Tahoe Blvd. (☎530-543-2674 or 544-5050), in the middle of South Lake Tahoe. Open daily 9am-5pm.

Library and Internet Access: South Lake Tahoe Branch Library, 1000 Rufus Allen Blvd. (☎530-573-3185). Open Tu-W 10am-8pm, Th-Sa 10am-5pm.

Post Office: 1046 Al Tahoe Blvd. (☎530-544-5867). Open M-F 8:30am-5pm, Sa noon-2pm. **Postal Code:** 96151.

▓LAKE TAHOE ☎775

As roadtrippers come over the Sierra Nevada Mountains from Carson City, the green-blue of Lake Tahoe is a welcome sight indeed. Every visitor will leave half in love with the lake itself; after all, it's the second-deepest lake in North America and has water so clean that it's crystal clear. The water is surrounded by rugged peaks whose beauty, if not size, puts the Rockies and even the Alps to shame. In this town with no low season, visitors can try everything from keno to kayaking. South Lake Tahoe caters to visitors with a plethora of casinos, restaurants, and outdoors shops. North Lake Tahoe is the South Shore's nerdy little sibling; right now, it's less glamorous, but in twenty years it will probably be the one you want to move in with.

✦ ORIENTATION

Lake Tahoe is divided into two main regions: **South Lake Tahoe** (or, as the locals say, "South Shore") and **North Lake Tahoe.** Starting at the city of **Incline Village,** Nevada, on the North Shore and moving counter-clockwise around the oval-shaped lake, you'll hit **Kings Beach,** Califronia, and **Tahoe City,** California, both on the North Shore, and then **South Lake Tahoe,** California, and **Stateline,** Nevada, both on the South Shore. **Lake Tahoe Boulevard (US 50)** is the main drag in South Lake Tahoe, and major streets include **Ski Run Boulevard, Wildwood Avenue,** and **Park Avenue.** Route 89 traces the lake's western shore. If you want to ▓**loop the lake** (2-4hr.), much as is described above, circumnavigate the shore by heading north on **Route 28** to **Route 89 South** and back to **US 50** in South Lake Tahoe. This 72 mi. long route, once named the "Most Beautiful Drive in America," provides spectacular views and bypasses the busiest section of the lake.

▓ ACCOMMODATIONS

SOUTH SHORE

On the South Shore, the blocks bordering US 50 on the California side of the border support the bulk of the area's motels. Glitzy and cheap, motels in South Shore cost next to nothing in the middle of the week.

▓ **Tahoe Valley Lodge,** 2241 Lake Tahoe Blvd. (☎800-669-7544 or 530-541-0353; www.tahoevalleylodge.com). Immaculate rooms take the mountain motif to an extreme, with alpine-themed bedspreads and wallpaper. Fireplaces in every room make it worth every penny. DVD players. Free Wi-Fi. Reception 24hr. Rooms from $125. AmEx/D/MC/V. ❺

Tahoe Retreat, 2446 Lake Tahoe Blvd. (☎530-544-6776). Although its on the South Shore's busiest street, it's downright peaceful here. The basic rooms vary in size but are clean and near local attractions. Some rooms have kitchenettes. Rooms from $59. MC/V. ❸

Doug's Mellow Mountain Retreat, 3787 Forest Ave. (☎530-544-8065). Coming from the north, turn left onto Wildwood Rd., west of downtown Stateline, and take a left on Forest Ave. It's the 6th house on the left. Doug's supplies a modern kitchen, barbecue, and fireplace in this woodsy house in a residential neighborhood. Linen included. Dorms $25. Cash only. ❷

Best Tahoe West Inn, 4107 Pine Blvd. (☎800-700-8246 or 530-544-6455), off Park Ave. Located within walking distance of the casinos but also close to the beach. Modern rooms are chock-full of amenities, and some have kitchenettes. Pool, hot tub, and sauna. Reception 7am-11pm. Rooms in summer from $60; in winter from $43. AmEx/D/MC/V. ❸

NORTH SHORE

Most of the North Shore is residential, not touristy. Accommodations tend to be expensive, affiliated either with ski resorts like **Northstar,** or with casinos like the **Hyatt.** Most rooms at both run over $125 a night.

Tahoe Inn, 9937 N. Lake Blvd. (☎530-546-3341 or 800-648-2324; www.staynorthtahoe.com), in Tahoe City on the east side of the city. Decent rooms during the week $39-69, on weekends $69-99. AmEx/D/MC/V. ❸

Fire Lite Lodge, 7035 N. Lake Blvd. (☎800-934-7222 or 530-546-7222), in Tahoe City. Clean and elegant rooms arranged around a small courtyard with a pool. Outdoor hot tub. Free breakfast. Wi-Fi.In summer singles $78-108; doubles $88-136. In winter singles $68-104; doubles $82-128. AmEx/D/MC/V. ❹

! KNOW THY SHORE. South Shore and North Shore are distant from one another; it takes at least an hour to drive between the two. If you stay at South Shore, make sure to budget extra time into your day to get to North Shore before the lifts open.

CAMPING

In the summer, you'll be hard-pressed to find any room as beautiful as the Sierra Nevada wilderness. During winter, however, it's smarter to take a cue from the local black bears and hole up inside. The visitors center provides up-to-date info on camping. Rte. 89 is rife with campgrounds between South Lake Tahoe and Tahoe City. Sites can be full on weekends in July and August, so it pays to reserve in advance; call the **California State Parks Reservation Center** (☎800-444-7275) or the **National Recreation Reservation System** (☎877-444-6777; www.recreation.gov). **Backcountry camping** is allowed in designated wilderness areas with a permit from the Forest Service.

Nevada Beach (☎775-588-5562). South Shore. Off US 50, 10 mi. south of the junction with Rte. 28. 54 sites near a calm yet family-friendly beach. Water, but no showers. Sites $25-29. MC/V. ❶

Fallen Leaf Lake (☎530-544-0426). South Shore. Take US 50 to Rte. 89 and head 3 mi. north; turn left on Fallen Leaf Rd. 206 sites on the shores of Fallen Leaf Lake. Reservations recommended. Sites $25. D/MC/V. ❶

DL Bliss State Park (☎530-525-7277). South Shore. Off Rte. 89, 10 mi. north of US 50. Has access to Lester Beach and is near the trailheads for the Rubicon and Lighthouse Trails. Grills, water, flush toilets, and showers. Open from late May to Sept. Sites $15-35. MC/V. ❶

🍴 FOOD

SOUTH SHORE

Sprouts Natural Foods Cafe, 3123 Harrison Ave. (☎530-541-6969), at Alameda Ave. Natural foods in large portions. Everything is done just right. Try the breakfast burrito with avocados ($7), one of the smoothies and fresh juices ($3.50-4.25), or a shot of wheatgrass ($1.75). Open daily 8am-9pm. Cash only. ❶

The Red Hut Cafe, 2723 Lake Tahoe Blvd. (☎530-541-9024). A friendly staff has been dishing out homestyle cooking since 1959 at this Tahoe original. Waffles piled with fruit and whipped cream $7. Avocado burgers $7.50. Open daily 6am-2pm. Cash only. ❷

Lakeside Beach Grill, 4081 Lakeshore Blvd. (☎530-544-4050), on the beach between Park and Stateline Ave. The real draw is the spectacular view as you enjoy your meal outside overlooking the lake. Try one of the inventive lunch entrees ($8-16) like the calamari steak sandwich ($12). Garlic lovers will love the garlic fries ($6). Open June-Sept. M and W-Su 11am-4pm and 5-8:30pm. AmEx/D/MC/V. ❹

Sno-Flake Drive In, 3059 Harrison Blvd. (☎530-544-6377), on the corner of US 50. Laid-back, retro drive-in with good ice cream ($2-3) and burgers ($4). Chicken and fish dinners $5-6. Open daily in summer 11am-9pm; in winter 11am-8pm. D/MC/V. ❶

NORTH SHORE

Wild Alaskan Cafe, 930 Tahoe Blvd. (☎775-832-6777). In Incline Village, just across the Nevada border. Has a good selection of healthful yet flavorful dishes. **Thai seafood soup** ($4.50-6.50) will hit the spot. Open daily 11am-9pm. MC/V. ❷

Wildflower Cafe, 869 Tahoe Blvd. (☎775-831-8072). Can't be beat for a full breakfast. Unremarkable decor, but, when it's packed full of friendly locals and you're gobbling down delicious home fries, you will thank the powers-that-be that you decided to come. Open M-Sa 7am-2:30pm, Su 8am-2pm. ❷

The Blue Agave, 425 N. Lake Blvd. (☎530-583-8113). Good, filling Mexican standards like fajitas ($13-16) as well as dishes like roast pork with oranges, garlic, and guacamole ($14.50). Open daily 11:30am-9pm. AmEx/D/MC/V. ❸

NIGHTLIFE

Nightlife in Lake Tahoe centers on casinos, which are busy at all hours.

McP's Pub, 4093 Lake Tahoe Blvd. (☎530-542-4435). South Shore. Nightly live music, usually rock or folk. Downstairs has a pool table, but the outdoor seating on the top floor draws the locals. The ribs ($15.50) are a good bet. Open daily 11:30am-2am. AmEx/MC/V.

The Brewery, 3542 Lake Tahoe Blvd. (☎530-544-2739). South Shore. Stop in and try 1 of the 7 microbrews on tap, including favorites like the Bad Ass Ale and Alpine Amber (pints $4.75, pitchers $14). Pizzas (starting at $14) come full of toppings. A laid-back atmosphere makes this spot a favorite with numerous locals. Open M-Th and Su 11am-10pm, F-Sa 10:30am-11pm. AmEx/D/MC/V.

HIKING

Hiking is a great way to explore the Tahoe Basin. Always bring a jacket and drinking water. Ask where the snow has (or has not) melted—it's usually not all gone until July. After decades of work, the 165 mi. **Tahoe Rim Trail** has finally been completed. The trail, which circles the lake along the ridge tops of Lake Tahoe Basin, welcomes hikers, equestrians, and mountain bikers. **Camping ❶**

is allowed on most of the trail, though permits for camping and hiking are required in the Desolation Wilderness ($5 per person). The visitors center has information on many separate sections of the trail. On the western shore, the route comprises part of the **Pacific Crest Trail.** Popular trailheads include **Spooner Summit,** at the US 28/50 junction, and **Tahoe City,** off Rte. 89 on Fairway Dr.

SOUTH SHORE

The southern region of the basin offers moderate to strenuous hiking trails; stop by the visitors center for maps and info. For many visitors, picturesque **Emerald Bay** is an essential stop. This crystal-clear pocket of the lake is home to Tahoe's only island and most photographed sight—tiny, rocky Fannette, which is accessible by boat. **Emerald Bay State Park,** from which you can access the **Bayview Trail** into the Desolation Wilderness, offers trails of varying difficulty, along with camping and rock climbing. (☎530-541-3030. Entrance fee $3.) Possibly the most popular South Shore trail, the **Eagle Falls Trail** (1 mi.) offers a moderate hike into the Desolation Wilderness to Eagle Lake. A strenuous trail continues past Eagle Lake several miles to the Velma Lakes, a series of lakes surrounded by the nearby mountains. Accessible from DL Bliss State Park and ending at Vikingsholm is one of the best hikes in Tahoe, the **Rubicon Trail** (5 mi.), which wraps around Emerald Bay. If you make it the full distance, you can take a shuttle back to DL Bliss; inquire at the park visitors center for details. Those looking for a more leisurely excursion can enjoy the nature trails around the visitors center. The **Lake of the Sky Trail** (1½ mi.) is dotted with informative signs about the lake's origins, its early inhabitants, and current wildlife.

NORTH SHORE

At 10,200 ft., **Mount Rose** is one of the tallest mountains in the region as well as one of the best climbs. The panoramic view from the summit offers views of the lake, Reno, and the Sierra Nevadas. The 12 mi. round-trip trek starts out as an easy dirt road but ascends switchbacks for the last couple of miles. Take Rte. 431 N. from Incline Village to reach the trailhead. The **Granite Chief Wilderness,** west of

Squaw Valley, is a spectacular outdoor destination; its hiking trails and mountain streams wind through secluded forests in 5000 ft. valleys to the summits of 9000 ft. peaks. The **Alpine Meadows Trailhead,** at the end of Alpine Meadows Rd. off Rte. 89 between Truckee and Tahoe City, and the **Pacific Crest Trailhead,** at the end of Barker Pass Rd. (Blackwood Canyon Rd.), grant further access to the wilderness.

OTHER OUTDOORS

BEACHES

Many beaches dot Lake Tahoe; the water is almost uncomfortably cold even in summer, but the gorgeous scenery compensates. On the North Shore, **Sand Harbor Beach,** US 28, 2 mi. south of Incline Village, has granite boulders and clear waters that attract swimmers, rock-jumping enthusiasts, sunners, and boaters to its marina. **Tahoe City Commons Beach,** just off North Lake Blvd., in the heart of the city, contains a playground for kids, a sandy beach for sunbathing, and pristine lake waters for swimming. Boats, jet skis, wakeboards, kayaks, and water skis can be rented at **Tahoe Water Adventures,** 120 Grove St. (☎530-583-3225). The western shore offers family-oriented **Meeks Bay,** equipped with picnic tables, volleyball courts, barbecue pits, campsites, and a store. DL Bliss State Park, on Rte. 89, 17 mi. south of Tahoe City, is home to **Lester Beach** and **Calawee Cove Beach,** on striking Rubicon Bay. It's also the trailhead for the Rubicon Trail. **Baldwin Beach** and neighboring **Pope Beach,** near the southernmost point of the lake off Rte. 89, are shaded expanses of shoreline popular with South Lake Tahoe crowds. **Nevada Beach,** off US 50, 3 mi. north of South Lake Tahoe, is close to the casinos and offers a sandy sanctuary with a view of sun-kissed mountains. **Zephyr Cove Beach,** US 50, 8 mi. south of the intersection with Rte. 28, hosts a young crowd keen on beer and bikinis. This beach offers boat rentals, jet skis, parasailing, and towel-side drink service.

BIKING

Miles of excellent trails and killer views make Tahoe a hot spot for mountain biking. For rentals in South Lake Tahoe, check out **South Shore Bike & Skate,** 1056 Ski Run Blvd. (☎530-544-7433. Bikes $25-35 per day. Open Tu-Sa 10am-6pm, Su 10am-4pm.) Cyclists can cover parts of the Lake Tahoe loop; the **Pope-Baldwin Bike Path** on the South Shore runs parallel to Rte. 89 for over 3 mi. past evergreen forests until it joins the South Lake Tahoe Bike Path, which goes through South Lake Tahoe and into Nevada.

The lake's premier ride is the **Flume Trail,** in Nevada State Park, which begins near the picnic area at Spooner Lake. This 23 mi. single-track loop has magnificent views of the lake from 1500 ft. off the deck. **Flume Trail Mountain Biking,** at Spooner Lake, rents bikes and runs

STUCK IN A BLIZZARD? GOOD THING YOU MADE ANZAC BISCUITS.

The name ANZAC comes from Australia and New Zealand Army Corps. According to the popular version of the cookies' story, during World War I, folks would send ANZAC biscuits to the soldiers so that they would have something healthy to munch on in Gallipoli. The cookies become hard as rocks (so hard, in fact, that some opted to grind them up to eat like porridge), but this is good—they survive, effectively, forever. The recipe is very useful and can be adapted to suit the needs of modern roadtrippers. Avoid the fate of the Donner Party; bring some. The following is an official popular recipe.

1 cup flour
1 cup sugar
1 cup rolled oats
1 cup coconut
4 oz. butter
1 tablespoon treacle or golden syrup (available in specialty stores or large food stores with international sections; maple syrup is an OK second choice)
2 tablespoons boiling water
1 teaspoon baking soda
Mix together and bake at 350°F until golden

shuttles to popular trails. (☎775-749-5349. Bikes $40 per day. Shuttles $10-12.50. Open daily 9am-5:30pm.) Other tire trails include **Mr. Toad's Wild Ride,** a 3 mi., 2200 ft. descent south of South Lake Tahoe off Rte. 89, and **McKinney/Rubicon Road,** a loop ride to difficult peaks from Rte. 89, north of Tahoma.

CLIMBING
There are many climbs in Lake Tahoe, but proper safety precautions and equipment are a must. Inexperienced climbers can try bouldering in **DL Bliss State Park.** A host of popular climbing spots are scattered along the South Shore; the super-popular, beginner-friendly **Ninety-Foot Wall** at Emerald Bay, **Twin Crags** at Tahoe City, and **Big Chief,** near Squaw Valley, are some of the more famous area climbs. **Lover's Leap,** in South Lake Tahoe, is an incredible (and crowded) route spanning two giant cliffs. East of South Lake Tahoe, off US 50, the **Phantom Spires** have amazing ridge views, while **Pie Shop** offers serious exposure.

LAKES
Many small lakes are accessible from hiking routes and may offer more privacy than Tahoe. **Angora Lakes,** a pair of mountain lakes accessible by car except for a final half-mile walk, are popular with families. Take Rte. 89 N. from South Lake Tahoe for 3 mi. Turn left onto Fallen Leaf Rd. and left again onto Tahoe Mountain Rd. Continue and turn right onto Forest Service Rd. #1214. (Open daily 6am-10pm. Free.)

SKIING
With its world-class alpine slopes and notorious California sun, Tahoe is a skier's mecca. There are 15 ski resorts in the Tahoe area. Visitors centers provide info, coupons, maps, and free publications like *Ski Tahoe* and *Sunny Day*. All the major resorts offer lessons and rent equipment. For the best slopes, try **Squaw Valley,** site of the 1960 winter Olympic Games. (☎530-583-6985 or 888-766-9321; www.squaw. com. Lift tickets $60.) **Heavenly** also offers great powder. (☎775-586-7000; www.skiheavenly.com. Lift tickets $55-80.) While families might want to cruise the groomers at **Northstar** (☎530-562-1010 or 800-466-6784; www. northstarattahoe.com; lift tickets from $74),

experienced skiers will find the sweet chutes they're seeking at **Sugar Bowl** (☎530-426-9000; www.sugarbowl.com). One of the best ways to enjoy Tahoe's pristine snow-covered forests is to cross-country ski. **Spooner Lake,** at the junction of US 50 and Rte. 28, offers 80 mi. of machine-groomed trails and incredible views. (☎775-749-5349. Lift tickets $21.) Snowshoeing is easier to pick up than cross-country skiing, and equipment is available at many sporting-goods stores for about $15 per day. Check local ranger stations for ranger-guided winter snowshoe hikes.

⚐ THE ROAD TO AUBURN: 80 MI.
On the northwest shore of the lake, take **Route 89 North** to **I-80 West** for 66 mi. Exit at **Nevada Road** to get to Auburn's Old Town.

AUBURN   ☎530
Auburn's Old Town is a good place to stop for lunch or an afternoon snack. Despite the hilly streets, the area is pleasant to explore on foot. The **Placer County Historical Museum,** 101 Maple St., in the 1898 courthouse, has a typical collection of local historical objects and Native American art; what sets it apart from other local history museums is the million-dollar display of gold in the gift shop. (☎530-889-6500. Open daily 10am-4pm. Free.)

Accommodations in Auburn are not cheap, but the **Motel 6 ❸,** 1819 Auburn Ravine Rd., 2 mi. east of the historic district off I-80, has standard rooms. (☎530-888-7829. Singles $58; doubles $62. AmEx/D/MC/V.) Every traveler's first stop in Auburn should be at **Ikeda's California Country Market ❷,** 13500 Lincoln Way. Locals know this burger joint/market mostly as *the* place to stop when jamming from North Lake Tahoe to the Central Valley; its burgers and pies are legendary. (☎530-885-4243. Open M-Th and Sa-Su 8am-9pm, F 8am-10pm. MC/V.) The modestly named **Awful Annies ❷,** 160 Sacramento St., is actually the opposite: very good. Annie's is a local favorite for creative and healthful sandwiches like the turkey avocado BLT ($8.75). Try the "awful waffles," such as the strawberry, banana, and macadamia nut waffle, for $8. (☎530-888-9857. Open M-Th and Su 8am-3pm, F-Sa 8am-8:30pm. AmEx/MC/V.) **Cafe Delicious ❷,** 1591 Lincoln

Way, serves Mexican food like beef enchiladas ($6.25) and *chile verde* burritos ($7.50). Lunch specials cost $6-8.50. (☎530-885-2050. Open daily 9am-9pm. AmEx/D/MC/V.)

⚐ THE ROAD TO SACRAMENTO: 33 MI.

Take **I-80 West** to **I-5 South**. Exit at **J Street** for Old Sacramento and Downtown.

SACRAMENTO ☎530

Sacramento is the indistinct capital of a highly distinctive state; the city's somewhat desperate-looking palm trees and a garish yellow suspension bridge over the river, however, remind roadtrippers that you have indeed reached the Golden State. In 1848, Swiss emigré John Sutter, fleeing debtor's prison, purchased 48,000 dusty acres from the Miwok tribe for a few trinkets. His trading fort became the central pavilion for the influx of gold miners in the 1850s. Over the next century, mansions and suburban bungalows gradually changed the landscape, paving the way for future residents Ronald Reagan and the Brady Bunch. Sacramento balances the nonstop bustle of San Francisco to the west with the tranquility of the mountains to the east, remaining as slow-paced as any small town, especially in the summer, when temperatures can easily soar to 115°F. Like your parents' bedroom, Sacramento is inviting and innocuous by day but someplace to be wary of at night.

✴ ORIENTATION

Sacramento is at the center of the Sacramento Valley. Five major highways converge on the capital: **I-5** and **Route 99** run north-south, with I-5 to the west, **I-80** runs east-west between San Francisco and Reno, and **US 50** and **Route 16** bring traffic westward from Gold Country. **Downtown,** numbered streets run north-south and lettered streets run east-west in a grid. The street number on a lettered street corresponds to the number of the cross street (2000 K St. is near the corner of 20th St.). The capitol building, parks, and endless cafes and restaurants occupy the area around 10th St. and Capitol Ave. **Old Sacramento** is located just west of downtown, along the Sacramento River, down Second St.

VITAL STATS
Population: 460,000
Tourist Office: Old Sacramento Visitors Center, 1002 2nd St. (☎916-442-7644). Open daily 10am-5pm.
Library and Internet Access: Sacramento Public Library, 828 I St. (☎916-264-2920), between 8th and 9th St. Open Tu-Th 10am-8pm, F 10am-6pm, Sa 10am-5pm, Su noon-5pm.
Post Office: 801 I St. (☎916-556-3415). Open M-F 8am-5pm. Postal Code: 95814.

♜ ACCOMMODATIONS

Sacramento has many hotels, motels, and B&Bs, but advance reservations are always a good idea. W. Capitol Ave. has many cheap hotels. Within Sacramento proper, 16th St. has hotels and motels. Rates fluctuate, but standard chain hotel and motel rooms usually go for $50-150 per night.

◪ **Sacramento Hostel (HI-AYH),** 925 H St. (☎916-443-1691, reservations 800-909-4776, ext. 40), at 10th St. Built in 1885, this pastel Victorian mansion looks more like a B&B than a hostel. Huge modern kitchen, 3 lounges, library, TV/VCR, and a selection of free videos. Parking $5 per night. Check-in 2-10:30pm. Check-out 11am. Dorms $28.75, members $25.75; private rooms $45-81.50. AmEx/D/MC/V. ❷

Vagabond Inn Midtown, 1319 30th St. (☎916-454-4400; www.vagabondinn.com), at N St. Moderately sized, well-kept rooms, with extra perks. Rooms have cable TV, phones, and free newspapers. Pool and spa available. Continental breakfast included. Internet. Rooms from $58. AmEx/D/MC/V. ❸

▧ FOOD

Food in Sacramento is plentiful and good thanks to hip midtown, immigrant populations and Californian culinary ingenuity. Many eateries are concentrated on J St. or Capitol Ave., between 19th and 29th St. The stretch of Fair Oaks Blvd. between Howe and Fulton St. is home to restaurants of all price ranges. Old Sacramento is home to many an expensive and gimmicky restaurant, but there are also a few cheap finds.

Zelda's Pizza, 1415 21st St. (☎916-447-1400), at N St. Posters of Italy and Christmas lights enliven this windowless joint. The Chicago-style pizzas are loaded with everything from standard pepperoni and mushrooms to feta and spinach. Open M-Th 11:30am-2pm and 5-10pm, F 11:30am-2pm and 5-11:30pm, Sa 5-11:30pm, Su 5-9:30pm. Cash only. ❷

Ernesto's, 1901 16th St. (☎916-441-5850; www.ernestosmexicanfood.com), at the corner of S St. Dishes out upscale Mexican food. Huge burritos ($7.50-10.50), quesadillas ($7), and salads ($7.50-10.50). Open M-W 11am-10pm, Th 11am-11pm, F 11am-midnight, Sa 9am-midnight, Su 9am-10pm. AmEx/MC/V. ❸

Cafe Bernardo, 2726 Capitol Ave. (☎916-443-1180; www.cafebernardo.com), at 28th St. Decorated in earth tones and stainless steel. Breakfast pancakes will help you through existential crises. Sandwiches ($7-8.50), soups ($2-4), and salads ($3-7) with freshly baked bread. Open M-Th and Su 7am-10pm, F-Sa 7am-11pm. MC/V. ❷

The Fox and Goose, 1001 R St. (☎916-443-8825; www.foxandgoose.com), at 10th St. Situated in a brick factory, the Fox and Goose blends English public house with American alternative culture. Primarily a brunch spot with sandwiches, fish and chips ($8.50), and pasties ($7.50). Open-mike M nights. Live music W-Sa. Open M-F 7am-midnight, Sa-Su 8am-2am. AmEx/MC/V. ❷

Annabelle's, 200 J St. (☎916-448-6239). The dinner buffet is $7 at this Old Sacramento highlight, which also serves sandwiches and pizza ($6.50-15). Open daily 11am-4pm. All-you-can-eat Italian lunch buffet $6. D/MC/V. ❶

Beach Hut, 2406 J St. (☎916-442-1400). A fun beach-obsessed spot; don't tell them the shore is still 3hr. away. The Surfin' Cow sandwich ($7.50) has roast beef, avocado, bacon, and cream cheese. Domestic drafts $3.25-5.25. Open M-Sa 10am-10pm, Su 11am-8pm. AmEx/MC/V. ❷

👁 SIGHTS

CAPITOL PARK. Colonnades of palm trees and grassy lawns transform Capitol Park into a shaded oasis in the middle of downtown's busy bureaucracy. Debates about the

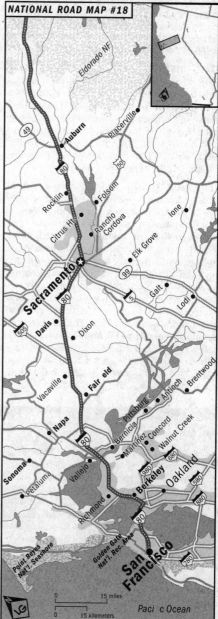

budget and water shortages take place daily in the elegant **state capitol**, stomping ground of none other than current Governor Arnold Schwarzenegger. *(At 10th and L St. ☎ 916-324-0333 or 866-240-4655. 1hr. tours daily 9am-4pm. Free.)*

STATE HISTORIC PARK GOVERNOR'S MANSION. The mansion was built in 1877, and its faded, weathered exterior makes it look not a year younger. The mansion served as the residence of California's governor and his family until then-governor Ronald Reagan opted to rent his own pad. *(At 16th and H St. ☎ 916-653-6995. Open daily 10am-5pm. Tours every hr. 10am-4pm. $4, ages 6-17 $2, under 6 free.)*

OLD SACRAMENTO. This 28-acre town of mid-19th-century buildings attracts nearly five million visitors per year. Tourists tread wooden-planked sidewalks, browse gift shops, or eat at restaurants. Attractions include a restored riverboat, California's first theater, and a military museum. The 100,000 sq. ft. ⊠**California State Railroad Museum** exhibits 21 historic locomotives and railroad cars, five of which you can walk through, and is regarded by many as the finest railroad museum in North America. The sleeping car simulates speeds of 60 mph—quite realistically. *(125 I St. ☎ 916-323-9280; www.csrmf.org. Open daily 10am-5pm. $8, ages 6-17 $3, under 6 free. 40min. train rides from the train depot in Old Sacramento Apr.-Sept. Sa-Su. $8, ages 6-17 $3.)*

CALIFORNIA STATE MUSEUM FOR HISTORY, WOMEN, AND THE ARTS. At this museum dedicated to the history of women in California, multimedia exhibits include a virtual trip on a 1936 bus and a video documenting immigrants' California stories, hopes, and dreams. *(1020 O St. ☎ 916-653-0560; www.californiamuseum. org. Open Tu-Sa 10am-5pm, Su noon-5pm. $7.50, seniors $6, under 6 free, ages 6-13 and students $5.)*

SUTTER'S FORT. Sutter's Fort was the only remaining property of John Sutter after the rest were overrun by gold-seekers. These days, busloads of tourists and local schoolchildren come to see the restored fort and its educational exhibits. *(2701 L St., between 26th and 28th St. ☎ 916-445-4422. Open daily 10am-5pm. $4, ages 6-17 $2, under 6 free.)*

CROCKER ART MUSEUM. This small museum packs in excellent art with permanent works by Brueghel, Renoir, and David, as well as rotating exhibits. What makes the Crocker stand out, however, is its contemporary Californian art, including pieces by local artist Robert Arneson. *(216 O St. ☎ 916-808-7000; www. crockerartmuseum.org. Open Tu-Sa 10am-5pm; 1st and 3rd Th of the month, open until 9pm. $6, ages 7-17 $3. Su 10am-1pm free. Jazz concerts on 3rd Th 5:30pm.)*

LELAND STANFORD MANSION STATE HISTORIC PARK. The extravagant mansion of former governor Leland Stanford was recently restored and is open for guided tours, dur-

WINETASTING 101

While European wines are often known by their region of origin, California wines are generally known by the type of grape from which they are made. California white wines include Chardonnay, Riesling, and Sauvignon Blanc; reds include Pinot Noir, Merlot, Cabernet Sauvignon, and Zinfandel, which is indigenous to California. Blush or rosé wines come from red grapes that have their skins removed during fermentation, leaving just a kiss of pink. Dessert wines, such as Muscat, are made with grapes that have acquired the "noble rot" (botrytis) at the end of picking season, giving them an extra-sweet flavor. When tasting, be sure to follow the proper procedure. Always start with a white, moving from dry to sweet. Proceed through the reds, which range from lighter to more full-bodied, depending on tannin content. Ideally, you should cleanse your palate between wines with a biscuit, cheese, or fruit.

Tasting proceeds thus: stare, sniff, swirl, swallow. You will probably encounter tasters who slurp their wine and make concerned faces. These are serious tasters who are aerating the wine into their mouths to better bring out the flavor. Keywords to help you seem more astute during tasting sessions include dry, sweet, buttery, light, crisp, fruity, balanced, rounded, subtle, rich, woody, and complex.

ing which visitors can learn about his life and times. *(800 N St. ☎916-324-9266. Open daily 9:30am-5pm. Tours 10am-4pm. $8, ages 6-17 $3.)*

SACRAMENTO ZOO. Chimps, giraffes, lions, white tigers, and an albino alligator are among the nearly 400 critters at the Sacramento Zoo. The zoo sits in a eucalyptus-filled park and emphasizes protection of endangered species and the restoration of natural habitats. *(On William Land Park Dr., off I-5 at the Sutterville exit. ☎916-808-5888; www.saczoo.com. Open daily Feb.-Oct. 9am-4pm, Nov.-Jan. 10am-4pm. On weekdays $8.50, ages 3-12 $6, seniors $7.75; on weekends $9/6.50/8.25.)*

🎵 ENTERTAINMENT

In summer, Sacramento bustles with free afternoon concerts and cheap food. The Fri-day *Sacramento Bee* contains a supplement called "Ticket," which gives a rundown of events. For music and activities, check free weeklies such as *Sacramento News and Review* and *Inside the City. Alive and Kicking* has music and arts schedules.

If you're visiting Sacramento in the spring, scream alongside **Sacramento Kings** fans, reputed to be the loudest in the NBA, at the **Arco Arena,** 1 Sports Pkwy. (☎916-649-8497). Dedicated minor-league baseball fans catch the ▧**Sacramento Rivercats** at **Raley Field,** 400 BallPark Ln., in West Sacramento. (☎916-376-4700; www.rivercats.com. Lawn seats $5. Season runs Apr.-Sept.)

On the second Saturday of each month, art galleries stay open late for the **Second Satur-**

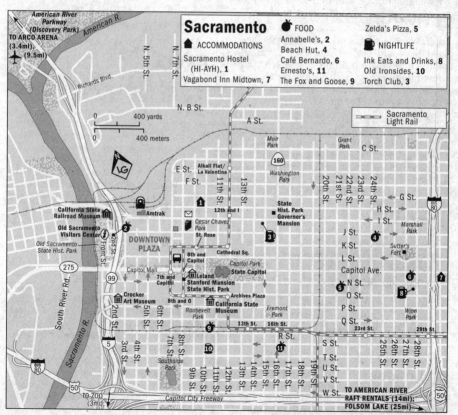

Sacramento

🍎 **FOOD**
Annabelle's, **2**
Beach Hut, **4**
Café Bernardo, **6**
Ernesto's, **11**
The Fox and Goose, **9**

🏠 **ACCOMMODATIONS**
Sacramento Hostel (HI-AYH), **1**
Vagabond Inn Midtown, **7**

Zelda's Pizza, **5**

🍷 **NIGHTLIFE**
Ink Eats and Drinks, **8**
Old Ironsides, **10**
Torch Club, **3**

day Art Walk. Art lovers wander and check out the scene. (www.2nd-sat.com. Open 6-10pm. Free.) The **Friday Night Concert Series,** in César Chávez Park, at 10th and I St., has live bands (rock, blues, jazz, folk, and pop), food stands, and beer gardens. Local bars often offer post-concert specials. (☎916-442-8575; www.downtownsac.org. From 1st F in May to 3rd F in Aug. 5-9pm. Free.) Over 100 bands attract thousands every Memorial Day weekend at the **Dixieland Jazz Jubilee,** in Old Sacramento. (☎916-372-5277; www.sacjazz.com.)

The **California State Fair,** which runs mid-August to early September, doesn't skimp on spinning rides, fair food, or pig races. The fairgrounds can be scorchingly hot, so take water, a hat, and sunscreen. (☎916-263-3000; www.bigfun.org. $8, children $5, seniors $6.)

☻ NIGHTLIFE

Capital-dwellers hang in brass and mahogany-lined bars and coffeehouses. Sacramento's midtown venues entertain a clientele with a few more body piercings than their representatives in the government. Nightclubs are scattered around Sacramento's periphery.

Old Ironsides, 1901 10th St. (☎916-443-9751; www.theoldironsides.com), at S St. The 1st bar to get its liquor license after Prohibition, Old Ironsides has 2 rooms, 1 for grooving and 1 for boozing. Drafts $2-4. Lipstick DJ spins indie and Britpop Tu. Open-mike W. Live music Th-Sa. Cover Tu after 9:30pm and Th-Sa $3-10. Open M-F 8am-1:30am, Sa 6pm-1:30am. MC/V.

Torch Club, 904 15th St. (☎916-443-2797; www.torchclub.net), at I St. A swell blues venue, voted "Best Place To Hear Blues" by *Sacramento News* and *Review Readers Choice Awards.* Cover varies. Open Tu-Su noon-2am. AmEx/D/MC/V.

Ink Eats and Drinks, 2730 N St. (☎916-456-2800; www.inkeats.com). The walls are adorned with strangely classy designs straight from a tattoo parlor. Small plates $6.75-9.75. Gourmet sandwiches and burgers $7.75-11.50. Open M-Tu 11:30am-1am, W-F 11:30am-3am, Sa 9am-3am, Su 9am-1am. AmEx/D/MC/V.

⚠ OUTDOORS

The **American River** winds through Sacramento, and its rushing waters make river rafting an opportunity for those seeking adventure. Rent rafts at **American River Raft Rentals,** 11257 S. Bridge St., in Rancho Cordova, 14 mi. east of downtown on US 50. Exit on Sunrise Blvd. and take it north 1 mi. to the American River. (☎916-635-6400. 4-person rafts $48; kayaks $33-50. Launch fee $2. Return shuttle $4 per person. Open daily 9am-6pm; rentals available until 1pm.) The **American River Recreation Trail and Parkway,** spanning 23 mi. from Discovery Park to Folsom Lake, is a nature preserve with a view of the downtown skyline. Hundreds of people cycle, jog, swim, fish, hike, and ride horses along the paths every day. You can enter the trail in Old Sacramento or at designated points off US 50 or along the river.

⚐ THE ROAD TO DAVIS: 15 MI.

Hop on **I-80 West** and cross the **Yolo Causeway.**

⬛ DAVIS   ☎530

Davis prides itself on higher education, agriculture, and two-wheeled transportation. Residents fancy themselves to be living in the model eco-conscious town—and their self-image is certainly substantiated. All of Davis is linked by well-manicured greenbelts, its streets sport as many bikes as residents (more per capita than any other US city), and the town even built a "toad tunnel" built to prevent resident amphibians from meeting untimely deaths while crossing the Pole Line Overpass. The inviting character of the city is shaped largely by the attitude of students at the University of California at Davis (UCD): progressive and playful.

▓ ORIENTATION

UC Davis lies in the southwest corner of the city, bounded by **I-80** and **Route 113.** Vic Fazio Highway (Route 113), Anderson Road, F Street, and **Pole Line Road** are all major north-south thoroughfares. **West Covell Boulevard** runs east-west until F St., where its name changes to **East Covell Boulevard.** (Don't confuse it with the similarly named Cowell Blvd., or you'll end up on the wrong side of town.) **Russell Boulevard** runs east-west, and at **A Street** it suddenly turns into **Fifth Street.**

VITAL STATS

Population: 64,000

Tourist Offices: Davis Visitors Bureau, 105 E St., Ste. 300 (☎530-297-1900; www.yolocvb.org.com). Open M-F 8:30am-4:30pm. **UC Davis Information Center** (☎530-752-2222), at Memorial Union. Open in summer M-F 9am-4pm; term time M-F 8am-5pm.

Library and Internet Access: Yolo County Library, 315 E. 14th St. (☎530-757-5593). Open M 1-9pm, Tu-Th 10am-9pm, F-Sa 10am-5:30pm, Su 1-5pm.

Post Office: 2020 5th St. (☎530-753-0428). Open M-F 8am-5:30pm, Sa 10am-2pm. **Postal Code:** 95616.

ACCOMMODATIONS

Motels in Davis don't come cheap, and rooms are scarce during university events.

University Park Inn & Suites, 1111 Richards Blvd. (☎530-756-0910; www.universityparkinn.com), off I-80 at the Richards Blvd. exit, just 6 blocks from campus. 45 spotless rooms with cable TV, refrigerators, A/C, and a pool. Breakfast included. Rooms from $99. AmEx/D/MC/V. ❹

The Aggie Inn, 245 1st St. (☎530-756-0352; www.aggieinn.com). Near the UCD campus. Pleasant rooms with refrigerators and microwaves. Guests also have access to a fitness room and computer station. Continental breakfast included. Free Wi-Fi. Singles $105; doubles $115. AmEx/D/MC/V. ❹

FOOD

Wednesday nights in summer bring locals to Central Park (at 4th and C St.) for fresh produce, live music, and face painting at the **Davis Farmers' Market.** A more sedate version of the market takes place Saturday mornings. (☎530-756-1695; www.davisfarmersmarket.org. Open Mar.-Nov. W 4:30-8:30pm, Sa 8am-1pm; Dec.-Apr. Sa 8am-1pm.)

Dos Coyotes, 1411 W. Covell Blvd. (☎530-753-0922; www.doscoyotes.net). Inventive Tex-Mex. Addiction is guaranteed; you'll won't be able to stop upping your Dos. Try the enchilada plate or paella burrito. Open M-Th and Su 11am-9:30pm, F-Sa 11am-10pm. MC/V. ❷

Fuji's Sushi Buffet, 213 G St. (☎530-753-3888). Oh so fresh. A popular choice for students and locals; the lunch buffet line regularly stretches down the street and around the corner. All-you-can-eat lunch $13, dinner $16. Open daily 11am-2pm and 5-9pm. MC/V. ❸

Redrum Burger, 978 Olive Dr. (☎530-756-2142). Right off the Olive Dr. exit on I-80 W. An institution. Delights true carnivores with full 1 lb. burger meals ($11.50). Super-thick milkshakes ($4-6) come in a wide variety of flavors. *Let's Go* recommends butterscotch or peach. Open daily 10am-midnight. AmEx/D/MC/V. ❶

Davis Food Co-op, 620 G St. (☎530-758-2667; www.daviscoop.com). What Whole Foods might have been before it went corporate. Organic produce, fresh deli foods, and international wines. 15min. of free Internet access. Open daily 8am-10pm. AmEx/D/MC/V. ❶

SIGHTS

UNIVERSITY OF CALIFORNIA AT DAVIS (UCD). Of the UC schools, the University of California at Davis tops the list in agriculture. It is also one of only a handful of schools in the country with a department specializing in viticulture (vine cultivation) and enology (wine making). Who wouldn't want to attend a school famous for winemaking? Step into nature at the **UCD Arboretum,** which features trees and plants from Mediterranean climates around the world. *(Take Russell Blvd. to LaRue Rd.* ☎*530-752-4880. Open 24hr. Free.)*

NIGHTLIFE

For cultural entertainment, check out the recently opened **Mondavi Center for the Arts,** 9399 Old Davis Rd. . Built for UCD by wine tycoon Robert Mondavi, this striking sandstone performance center draws cultural heavyweights such as Joshua Redman, Ladysmith Black Mambazo, and Salman Rushdie. (☎530-754-2787; www.mondaviarts.org. Box office open M-F 10am-6pm, Sa noon-6pm, and 1hr. before performances.)

Bistro 33, 226 F St. (☎530-756-4556). This hot spot occupies the building that used to be the police station and is where the residential half of Davis (and some students too) goes for a night out; dishes include Ahi Tuna Poke ($13) and

Chop Chop salad ($11). Live music F 8pm. Open M-W 11:30am-10pm, Th-F 11:30am-midnight, 8am-midnight, Su 8am-10pm. AmEx/MC/V. ❸

The Graduate, 805 Russell Blvd. (☎530-758-4723; www.davisgrad.com), in the University Mall. Where UCD students have partied since your parents were in college. The walls usually reverberate with mainstream pop and hip hop, but "The Grad" occasionally hosts country dance nights. Check the website's calendar for events and specials. F evenings attract swarms with drink specials. Happy hour 3-6pm. Open daily 11am-2am. AmEx/D/MC/V.

🏔 OUTDOORS

Davis is marked by more than 40 mi. of bike trails. For trail maps and ratings, stop by the visitors bureau or a bike shop in town. **Ken's Bike and Ski,** 650 G St., rents bikes and gives advice about biking around the city. (☎530-758-3223; www.kensbikeski.com. Open M-F 9am-8pm, Sa 9am-7pm, Su noon-5pm. City bikes $7 per ½-day, $14 per day; road bikes $16/29.) For some practice before hitting the rocks, check out the **Rocknasium,** 720 Olive Dr., Ste. Z., in a warehouse just past Redrum Burger, which offers climbing at all levels. (☎530-757-2902; www.rocknasium.com. Open M-F 11am-11pm, Sa 10am-9pm, Su 10am-6pm. $12, students $10. Equipment rental $8/6.)

🚗 THE ROAD TO FAIRFIELD: 30 MI.

Take **I-80** and exit at **North Texas Street;** follow it south until it turns west onto Texas St.

FAIRFIELD   ☎707

Fairfield's most roadtrip-worthy attraction is the **Jelly Belly Factory,** 1 Jelly Belly Ln. While waits can be unbearably long in summer, the 40min. tour, an artful mix of observation of the factory floor and video presentations, leaves you sugar-high and jellybean-enlightened. They even sweeten the deal with a small bag of free jellybeans. Don't miss the opportunity to buy "Belly Flops"—irregularly sized jellybeans—which are sold at the factory store. From downtown, take Pennsylvania Ave. south to Rio Vista Rd., also known as Rte. 12. Then, turn right, exit at Beck Rd., and follow the signs. (☎800-953-5592. Open daily 9am-5pm. Free.)

Joe's Buffet ❶, 834 Texas St., near Jackson St., offers food that's a little less sugary. When you order a sandwich at this old-style delicatessen, the fresh meat is sliced right onto it; the messy result is fantastic. (☎707-425-2317. Sandwiches from $5.50. Open M-Sa 10am-4:30pm. Cash only.)

🚗 THE ROAD TO BERKELEY: 35 MI.

Continue straight onto **West Texas Street** to get back on **I-80** toward Berkeley. About 15 mi. past the **Carquinez Bridge,** take the **University Avenue exit** to downtown Berkeley and the UC Berkeley (Cal) campus.

BERKELEY   ☎510

Famous as an intellectual center and a haven for iconoclasts, Berkeley lives up to its reputation. Although the peak of its political activism occurred in the 1960s and 70s—when students attended more protests than classes—UC Berkeley continues to foster an alternative atmosphere. The vitality of the population infuses the streets, which overflow with hip cafes and top-notch bookstores. Telegraph Ave., with its street-corner soothsayers, hirsute hippies, and itinerant musicians, remains one of the main draws.

VITAL STATS
Population: 105,000
Tourist Office: Berkeley Convention and Visitor Bureau, 2015 Center St. (☎510-549-7040; www.visitberkeley.com), between Milvia St. and Shattuck Ave. Open M-F 9am-1pm and 2-5pm. **UC Berkeley Visitors Center,** 101 University Hall (☎510-642-5215; www.berkeley.edu), at the corner of University Ave. and Oxford St. Open M-F 8:30am-4:30pm.
Library and Internet Access: Berkeley Public Library, 2090 Kittredge St. (☎510-981-6100). Open M noon-8pm, Tu 10am-8pm, W-Sa 10am-6pm, Su 1-5pm.
Post Office: 2000 Allston Way (☎510-649-3114), at Milvia St. Open M-F 9am-5pm, Sa 9am-3pm. **Postal Code:** 94704.

🏛 ORIENTATION

To prevent people from using residential streets as cutoffs to bypass traffic-filled main streets, Berkeley installed rows of planters that interrupt many streets. Use main streets to navigate as close to your destination as possible before cutting in. The heart of town, **Telegraph Avenue**, runs south from the UC Berkeley Student Union, while the **Gourmet Ghetto** north of campus hosts some of California's finest dining. Beware of bicycles and unwary pedestrians.

ACCOMMODATIONS

There are few cheap accommodations in Berkeley. The **Berkeley-Oakland Bed and Breakfast Network** (☎510-547-6380; www.bbonline.com/ca/berkeley-oakland) coordinates great East Bay B&Bs with a range of rates. No-frills motels line University Ave. between Shattuck and Sacramento St.; ritzier joints are downtown, especially on Durant Ave. **UC Berkeley Summer Visitor Housing,** at Stern Hall, has simple dorms, shared baths, and free Internet access. (☎510-642-5925. Parking $13 per day. Rooms $59. Open from June to mid-Aug. MC/V.)

YMCA, 2001 Allston Way (☎510-848-6800; www.baymca.org). A communal kitchen, shared bath, computer room, TV lounge, pool, and fitness center. 10-night max. stay. Reception daily 8am-9:30pm. Free Wi-Fi. Singles from $45; doubles from $78. 18+. MC/V. ❷

Capri Motel, 1512 University Ave. (☎510-845-7090), at Sacramento St. Tasteful rooms with cable TV, A/C, and fridges. Free coffee. Rooms from $75-105. 18+. AmEx/D/MC/V. ❸

FOOD

Berkeley's **Gourmet Ghetto,** at Shattuck Ave. and Cedar St., is the birthplace of California cuisine. The north end of Telegraph Ave. caters to student appetites and wallets, with late-night offerings along Durant Ave. A growing number of international establishments are helping to diversify the area. Solano Ave. is great for Asian cuisine, while Fourth St. is home to more upscale eats.

Chez Panisse, 1517 Shattuck Ave. (☎510-548-5525, cafe 548-5049; www.chezpanisse.com). If you're going to splurge once on this route, do it here. Dishes like grilled quail and Alaskan salmon with salsa verde have made Chez Panisse famous across the world. *Prix-fixe* dinners $60-75. Cafe entrees $18-28. Restaurant open M-Sa; call well in advance. Cafe open M-Th 11:30am-3pm and 5-10:30pm, F-Sa 11:30am-3:30pm and 5-11:30pm. ❺

Café Intermezzo, 2442 Telegraph Ave. (☎510-849-4592). A veggie lover's paradise. Serves salads ($4.25-7.50), sandwiches on just-baked bread ($6.25), and tasty soups ($3.50-4.25), all at deliciously low prices. Open daily 8am-9:30pm. Cash only. ❶

César, 1515 Shattuck Ave. (☎510-883-0222), north of Cedar St., in the Gourmet Ghetto. Great for drinks and a light meal, with savory tapas ($4.75-11.75), *bocadillos* (small sandwiches on French bread; $9.75-10.75), and desserts

THE PLAY

The Bay Area is known for its intense sports rivalries, but none inspire the fiery devotion of the California-Stanford football game, known simply as "The Big Game." The most famous Big Game occurred on November 20, 1982, at the University of California. Down by one at the last minute, the Stanford Cardinal managed to kick a desperate field goal to make the score 20-19. It looked as though the game was over. With only three seconds left on the clock, Bears fans were a deflated bunch. Stanford kicked off, certain they had an easy tackle and a historic win ahead. The Cal Bears caught the ball and started to run, taking advantage of the fact that until the ball was dead, the game couldn't be over. The Bears started passing the football back and forth like a hot potato, and out of a tangle of bodies a Cal player emerged with the ball. The Stanford football team was confused, but not as confused as the Stanford marching band. Not realizing that the game wasn't over, the band marched on to the field, blaring the Stanford fight song with celebratory enthusiasm. With only a marching band between them and the victory, the Cal team charged through the horde of trumpets and trombones, flattening a drum major in the endzone for good measure and winning the game 25-20. It has since lived on in California history as "The Play."

($5.75-6.75). Open daily noon-midnight. Kitchen open M-Th and Su noon-11pm, F-Sa noon-11:30pm. AmEx/D/MC/V. ❸

Cheese Board Pizza, 1504 Shattuck Ave. (☎510-549-3055; www.cheeseboardcollective. coop). Wood floors, wood tables. Open and spacious. There's only one kind of pizza per day, but it's always good. Open Tu-Sa 11:30am-3pm and 4:30-8pm. Cash only. ❷

Yogurt Park, 2433 Durant Ave. (☎510-549-2198), just west of Telegraph Ave. A mainstay of Berkeley gastronomic life, serving huge portions of frozen yogurt ($2.50-3) made fresh daily. Open daily 11am-midnight. Cash only. ❶

🔟 📐 SIGHTS AND OUTDOORS

⬛BERKELEY ART MUSEUM (BAM). The museum is most respected for its 20th-century American and Asian art. BAM is also associated with the Pacific Film Archive, which screens selections from its Asian, European, and American holdings. (2626 Bancroft Way. ☎510-642-0808; www.bampfa.berkeley.edu. Open W-Su 11am-5pm. $8, students, ages 12-17, and seniors $5.)

TELEGRAPH AVENUE. You haven't really visited Berkeley until you've strolled the first five or so blocks of Telegraph Ave. The action is close to the university, where Telegraph Ave. is lined with a motley assortment of cafes, bookstores, and secondhand clothing and record stores. Businesses come and go at the whim of the marketplace, but the scene—a rowdy jumble of 60s and 90s counter-culture—persists. Vendors push tie-dye, tarot readings, and jewelry, the disenfranchised hustle for change, and characters looking like Old Testament prophets carry on hyper-dimensional conversations, transmitting knowledge accrued through hard years of Berkeley experience.

UNIVERSITY OF CALIFORNIA AT BERKELEY. In 1868, the private College of California and the public Agricultural, Mining, and Mechanical Arts College united as the University of California. The 178-acre university in Berkeley was the first of nine U of C campuses, so by seniority it has sole right to the nickname "Cal." The campus is bounded on the south by Bancroft Way, on the west by Oxford St., on the north by Hearst Ave., and on the east by

Tilden Park. Enter through Sather Gate into Sproul Plaza, site of both celebrated sit-ins and bloody confrontations with police. Weekend tours leave from **Sather Tower,** the tallest building on campus; its observation level offers a great view. Weekday tours leave from the visitors center at **University Hall.** (Tours M-Sa 10am, Su 1pm. $3.)

LAWRENCE HALL OF SCIENCE. This fine science museum has one of the most stunning views in the Bay Area. Its ever-changing exhibits stress hands-on science activities catering to children but fun for all ages. Visit the renowned **planetarium** (planetariums are fun!) and check out the outdoor "Forces that Shape the Bay" display. (On Centennial Dr. ☎510-642-5132; www.lawrencehallofscience.org. Open daily 10am-5pm. $11. Planetarium shows $3.)

OTHER SIGHTS. For off-campus fun, check out ⬛Takara Sake USA, Inc., where visitors can learn the history and science of sake-making and sample 13 different types of Japan's firewater and plum wine. (708 Addison St. ☎510-540-8250; www.takarasake.com. Open daily noon-6pm. Free.) When you're ready to get out of town, Berkeley is happy to oblige. In the pine and eucalyptus forests east of the city lies the beautiful anchor of the East Bay park system, **Tilden Regional Park.** Hiking, biking, running, and riding trails crisscross the park and provide impressive views of the Bay Area. (Take Spruce St. to Grizzly Peak Blvd. to Canon Ave. ☎510-635-0135; www.ebparks.org. Open daily 5am-10pm.) Also inside the park, the small, sandy beach at **Lake Anza** is a popular swimming spot during the hot summer days. (☎510-843-2137. Open in summer daily 11am-6pm. $3.50, children and seniors $2.50.)

🔲 NIGHTLIFE

Jupiter, 2181 Shattuck Ave. (☎510-843-8277). Features a beer garden, live blues and jazz, and pizza ($7.50-15). The bartender juggles lemons. Open M-Th 11:30am-1am, F 11:30am-2am, Sa noon-2am, Su noon-midnight. MC/V.

Caffè Strada, 2300 College Ave. (☎510-843-5282), at Bancroft Way. A glittering jewel of the caffeine-fueled intellectual scene. Open daily June-Aug. 6am-11pm; Sept.-May 6am-midnight. Cash only.

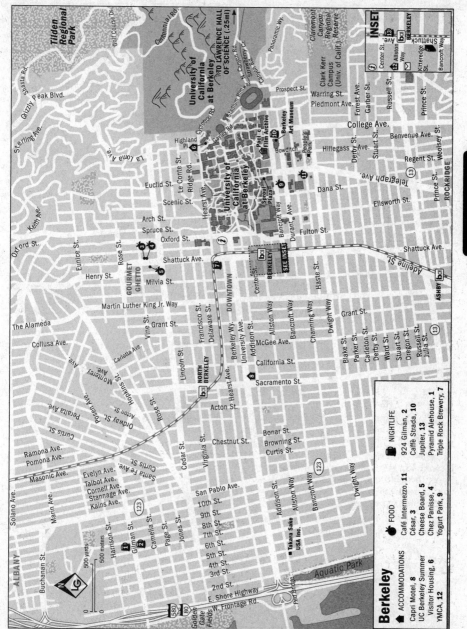

INSET

Berkeley

ACCOMMODATIONS
Capri Motel, 8
UC Berkeley Summer
Visitor Housing, 6
YMCA, 12

FOOD
Café Intermezzo, 11
César, 3
Cheese Board, 5
Chez Panisse, 4
Yogurt Park, 9

NIGHTLIFE
924 Gilman, 2
Caffè Strada, 10
Jupiter, 13
Pyramid Alehouse, 1
Triple Rock Brewery, 7

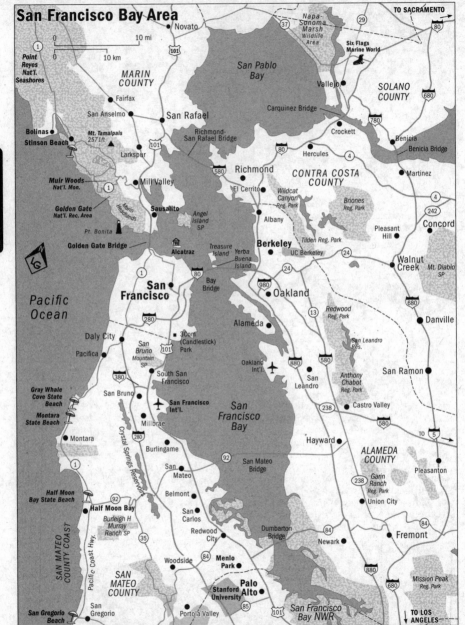

San Francisco Bay Area

Pyramid Alehouse, 901 Gilman St. (☎510-528-9880). Has meals designed to complement its gold-medal-winning beers. Burgers $8-10. Open M-Th and Su 11:30am-10:30pm, F-Sa 11:30am-11:30pm. Brewery tours M-F 5:30pm, Sa-Su 4pm. AmEx/D/MC/V.

924 Gilman, 924 Gilman St. (☎510-524-8180; www.924gilman.org). A legendary all-ages club and a staple of California punk. Maintained by volunteers, the venue is nonprofit and dedicated to non-corporate music and community service and is alcohol- and drug-free. Cover $5-9. Shows F-Sa and occasionally Su. Cash only.

Triple Rock Brewery, 1920 Shattuck Ave. (☎510-843-2739; www.triplerock.com), north of Berkeley Way. Boisterous and friendly. The 1st (and to many the best) of Berkeley's numerous brewpubs. Pull up a chair to the antique wood bar and try the award-winning Red Rock Ale. Pints $4.75-5.50. Open M-W and Su 11:30am-midnight, Th-Sa 11:30am-1:30am. Rooftop garden open until 10pm. MC/V.

▥ THE ROAD TO SAN FRANCISCO: 14 MI.

Head south on **Shattuck Avenue,** past downtown Berkeley. Just after crossing Derby St., Shattuck forks right onto **Adeline Street;** follow that fork and turn right half a mile later at the light onto **Ashby Street.** Proceed down Ashby St. 2 mi. to **I-80 West.**

SAN FRANCISCO ☎415

If California is a state of mind, then San Francisco is euphoria. Welcome to the city that will take you to new highs, leaving your mind spinning, your taste buds tingling, and your calves aching. The dazzling views, daunting hills, one-of-a-kind neighborhoods, and laid-back, friendly people fascinate visitors. Though smaller than most "big" cities, the city manages to pack an incredible amount of vitality into its 47 sq. mi., from its thriving art communities and bustling shops to the pulsing beats in some of the country's hippest nightclubs and bars.

▦ ORIENTATION

San Francisco sits at the junction of several major highways, including **I-280, US 101, Highway 1,** and **I-80.** From the east, I-80 runs across the **Bay Bridge** (westbound-only toll $5) into the **South of Market (SoMa)** area and then connects with US 101 just before it runs into **Van Ness Avenue. Market Street,** one of the city's main thoroughfares, runs on a diagonal from the Ferry Building near the bay through downtown and to The Castro in the southwest.

Neighborhood boundaries get a bit confusing; a good map is a must. Touristy **Fisherman's Wharf** sits at the northeast edge of the city. Just south of the wharf is **North Beach,** a historically Italian area, and south of North Beach lies **Chinatown.** Wealthy **Nob Hill** and **Russian Hill** round out the northeast of the city. Municipal buildings cluster in the **Civic Center,** which lines Market St. and is bounded on the west by Van Ness Ave. On the other side of Van Ness Ave. is hip **Hayes Valley.** Retail-heavy **Union Square** is north of Market St. and gives way in the west to the rougher **Tenderloin,** which, incidentally, is not the meatpacking district.

The Golden Gate Bridge stretches over the bay from **The Presidio** in the city's northwest corner. Just south of The Presidio, **Lincoln Park** reaches westward to the ocean, while vast **Golden Gate Park** dominates the western half of the peninsula. Near Golden Gate Park sits the former hippie haven of **Haight-Ashbury.** The trendy **Mission** takes over south of 14th St. The diners and cafes of the "gay mecca" of **The Castro** dazzle on Castro and Market St., northwest of the Mission. On the opposite side of the city, the skyscrapers of the **Financial District** crowd down to the **Embarcadero.**

VITAL STATS
Population: 740,000
Tourist Office: California Welcome Center (☎415-956-3493; www.sfvisitor.org), on Pier 39 at the Great San Francisco Adventure. Open M-Th and Su 9am-9pm, F-Sa 9am-10pm.
Internet Access: At the **California Welcome Center** (above). Free. For complete listings of Internet cafes, check www.surfandsip.com.
Post Office: 170 O'Farrell St. (☎415-956-0131), at Powell St., in the basement of Macy's. Open M-Sa 10am-5:30pm, Su 11am-5pm. **Postal Code:** 94108.

NATIONAL ROAD

TIP

PARKING. When parking facing uphill, turn front wheels away from the curb, and, if driving a standard, leave the car in first gear. If your car starts to roll, it will stop when the tires hit the curb. When facing downhill, turn the wheels toward the curb and leave the car in reverse. Always set the emergency brake.

ACCOMMODATIONS

For those who don't mind sharing a room with strangers, many San Francisco hostels are homier and cheaper than budget hotels. Book in advance if at all possible, but, since many don't take reservations for summer, you might have to just show up or call early on your day of arrival. B&Bs are often the most comfortable and friendly, albeit expensive, options. Beware that some of the cheapest budget hotels may be located in areas requiring extra caution at night.

HOSTELS

Adelaide Hostel and Hotel, 5 Isadora Duncan Ln. (☎877-359-1915; www.adelaidehostel.com), at the end of a little alley off Taylor St., between Geary and Post St. in Union Sq. The bottom 2 floors, recently renovated with fresh paint and new furniture, entice a congenial international crowd. Laundry $1. Soap $1. Breakfast, linens, towels, and Wi-Fi included. Check-out 11am. Reservations recommended. Dorms $25-31; private rooms from $70. AmEx/D/MC/V. ❶

San Francisco International Guesthouse, 2976 23rd St. (☎415-641-6173), in the Mission. Look for the blue Victorian with yellow trim near the corner of Harrison St. With hardwood floors, tapestries festooning the walls, and comfortable common areas, this hostel feels like the well-designed room of your tree-hugger college roommate. There are only 4 bunk beds, all in 1 room. Free Internet access. 7-night min. stay. No reservations, but chronically filled to capacity. All you can do is try calling a few days ahead of time. Dorms $20. Passport with international stamps required. Cash only. ❶

Green Tortoise Hostel, 494 Broadway (☎415-834-1000; www.greentortoise.com), off Columbus Ave., in North Beach. A ballroom preceded this super-mellow, friendly pad, allowing today's fun-seeking young travelers to hang out amid abandoned finery in the spacious common room. There's even a sauna. Breakfast (daily) and dinner (M, W, F) included. Coin-operated laundry machines. Th free beer and beer pong tournaments. Free Wi-Fi. Key deposit $20. Reception 24hr. Check-out 11am. Dorms $26-29; private rooms $58-70. MC/V. ❶

Fort Mason Hostel (HI-AYH), Bldg. #240 (☎415-771-7277), at the corner of Funston and Pope St., in Fort Mason. Beautiful surrounding forest and wood bunks provide a campground feel. Not a place for partiers—strictly enforced quiet hours (11pm) and no smoking or alcohol. Cafe with organic and vegan options open daily 7:30am-4pm and 5:30-10:30pm. Huge kitchen. Overnight storage $3. Laundry. Breakfast included. Free Wi-Fi. Check-in 2:30pm. Reservations recommended. Dorms $23-28; private rooms $75-85. AmEx/D/MC/V. ❶

City Center Hostel (HI-AYH), 685 Ellis St. (☎415-474-5721), between Larkin and Hyde. This newly renovated 1920s hotel is located near many art and theater activities. 167 dorm beds and 10 private rooms. Linens and towels included. Free Wi-Fi. Reception 24 hr. Dorms $29; private rooms $85-100. AmEx/D/MC/V. ❶

HOTELS AND GUESTHOUSES

The San Remo Hotel, 2237 Mason St. (☎415-776-8688; www.sanremohotel.com), between Chestnut and Francisco St., in Russian Hill. Built in 1906, this pension-style hotel features small but elegantly furnished rooms with antique armoires, bedposts, lamps, and complimentary back-scratchers. If your back needs more than scratching, settle into one of the shared massage chairs. Shared bathrooms are fancy and spotless. Check-out 11am. Reservations recommended. Rooms $65-95. AmEx/D/MC/V. ❷

Hayes Valley Inn, 417 Gough St. (☎415-431-9131, reservations 800-930-7999; www.hayes-valleyinn.com), in Hayes Valley. European-style B&B with small, clean rooms, shared bath, and lace curtains. Bedrooms range from charming singles to extravagant turret rooms with wraparound windows and comfy queen-size beds. All rooms have cable TV, phones, and sinks. Breakfast, afternoon tea, and cookies included. Check-in 3pm. Check-out 11am. Singles $69-97; doubles $76-112. AmEx/D/MC/V. ❹

The Red Victorian Bed, Breakfast, and Art, 1665 Haight St. (☎415-864-1978; www.redvic. com), west of Belvedere St., in the Upper Haight. Continental breakfast included downstairs in the attached cafe. Reception 9am-9pm. Check-in 3-6pm. Check-out 11am. Reservations recommended. Rooms $89-122. MC/V. ❹

San Francisco Zen Center, 300 Page St. (☎415-863-3136; www.sfzc.org), near Laguna St. in the Lower Haight. Even if rigorous soul-searching is not for you, the Zen Center offers breezy, homelike rooms and impossibly comfortable beds. Courtyard views are sure to evoke a meditative peace of mind. Breakfast included; lunch $6; dinner $7. All meals included in the discounted weekly (10% off) or monthly (25% off) rates. Rooms $72-114. MC/V. ❸

Golden Gate Hotel, 775 Bush St. (☎415-392-3702 or 800-835-1118; www.goldengatehotel. com), between Mason and Powell St., in Union Sq. A positively charming B&B, with a staff as kind and solicitous as the rooms are plush and inviting. Continental breakfast and afternoon tea (4-6:30pm) included. Parking $22. Reservations recommended. Doubles $95, with bath $150. AmEx/D/MC/V. ❹

🍽 FOOD

For the most up-to-date listings of restaurants in town, try the *Examiner*, the *S.F. Bay Guardian*, and the *Bay Area Vegetarian*. **Chinatown** is filled with cheap restaurants, the sheer number of which can baffle even the savviest of travelers. Some locals claim that Chinese restaurants in **Richmond** are better than those in Chinatown. In **North Beach's** tourist-friendly restaurants, California cuisine merges with the bold palate of Italy. In the **Financial District,** corner cafes vend Mediterranean grub at rock-bottom prices. The dominance of Mexican specialties and gigantic burritos is clear in the **Mission.** Be prepared to change the way you think about enchiladas.

FISHERMAN'S WHARF

Pat's Café, 2330 Taylor St. (☎415-776-8735; www.patscafe.com), between Chestnut and Francisco St. With playful yellow swirls on the building's facade, Pat's bright decor welcomes diners to a hearty home-cooked meal like Mom would make. Burgers, sandwiches, and big breakfasts $5-10. Open daily 7:30am-3pm. D/MC/V. ❷

CHINATOWN

🏯 **Chef Jia,** 925 Kearny St. (☎415-398-1626), at Pacific St. Insanely cheap and delicious food. A local crowd comes for lunch and dinner specials ($5.25) or the celebrated signature dishes like prawns with peanut butter sauce ($9). Open M-Th 11:30am-10pm, F 11:30am-11pm, Sa-Su 5-10:30pm. Cash only. ❷

Golden Gate Bakery, 1029 Grant Ave. (☎415-781-2627). This tiny bakery sells moon cakes, noodle puffs, and vanilla cream buns (all $0.65-1.50) in a tiny enclave amid the bustle of the surrounding streets. Open daily 8am-8pm. ❶

NORTH BEACH

🏯 **L'Osteria del Forno,** 519 Columbus Ave. (☎415-982-1124), between Green and Union St. Italian roasted and cold foods, plus homemade breads. Terrific thin-crust pizza (slices $3-4) and focaccia sandwiches ($5-7). Open M-Th and Su 9am-10pm, F-Sa 9am-11pm. Cash only. ❷

Mario's Bohemian Cigar Store Café, 566 Columbus Ave. (☎415-362-0536), at the corner of Washington Sq. The Beats frequented this laidback cafe, which still serves 1st-rate chow along with beer and coffee. Panini $6-8. Open daily 10am-11pm. MC/V. ❷

NOB AND RUSSIAN HILLS

Zarzuela, 2000 Hyde St. (☎415-346-0800), at Union St. Tapas and Spanish homestyle cooking in a festive upscale setting make *chorizo al vino* (sausage in wine sauce; $6.75) the highlight of the evening. Entrees $9-20. Open Tu-Th 5:30-10pm, F-Sa 5:30-10:30pm. D/MC/V. ❸

Sushigroove, 1916 Hyde St. (☎415-440-1905), between Union and Green St. This chic sushisake joint (sushi and maki $3-7) serves up a lot of rolls but nothing that has seen the inside of

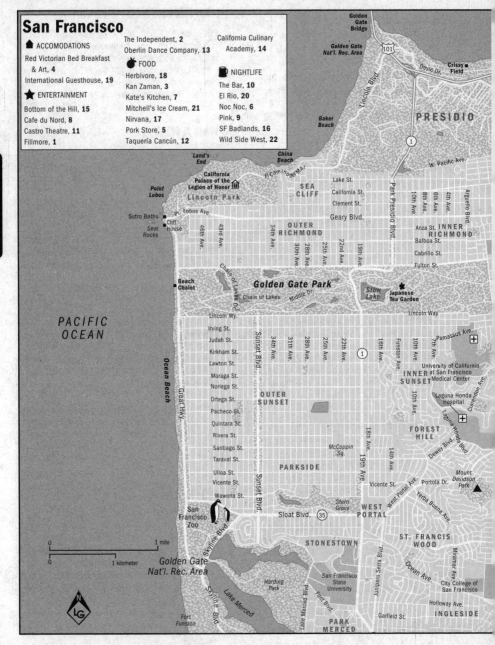

San Francisco

ACCOMODATIONS
Red Victorian Bed Breakfast & Art, **4**
International Guesthouse, **19**

ENTERTAINMENT
Bottom of the Hill, **15**
Cafe du Nord, **8**
Castro Theatre, **11**
Fillmore, **1**

The Independent, **2**
Oberlin Dance Company, **13**

FOOD
Herbivore, **18**
Kan Zaman, **3**
Kate's Kitchen, **7**
Mitchell's Ice Cream, **21**
Nirvana, **17**
Pork Store, **5**
Taquería Cancún, **12**

California Culinary Academy, **14**

NIGHTLIFE
The Bar, **10**
El Rio, **20**
Noc Noc, **6**
Pink, **9**
SF Badlands, **16**
Wild Side West, **22**

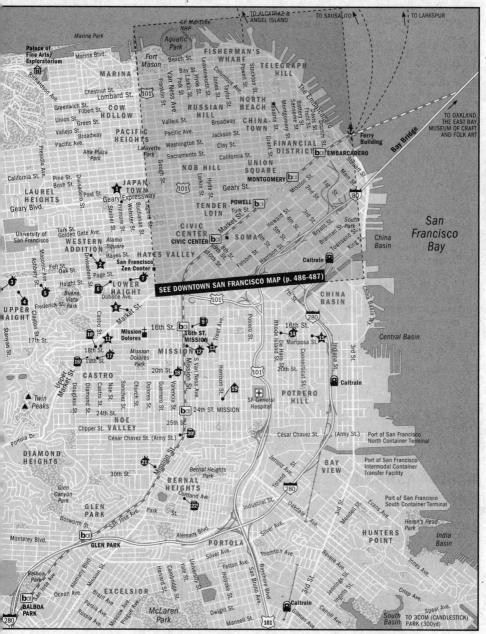

SEE DOWNTOWN SAN FRANCISCO MAP (p. 486–487)

NATIONAL ROAD

TO ALCATRAZ & ANGEL ISLAND

TO SAUSALITO

TO LARKSPUR

TO OAKLAND, THE EAST BAY, MUSEUM OF CRAFT AND FOLK ART

Palace of Fine Arts/ Exploratorium

Marina Park

Marina Blvd.

Richardson Ave.

Chestnut St.

Lombard St.

Greenwich St.

Filbert St.

Union St.

Green St.

Vallejo St.

Broadway

Pacific Ave.

Presidio Ave.

Pine St.

Bush St.

California St.

MARINA

COW HOLLOW

PACIFIC HEIGHTS

Alta Plaza Park

Lafayette Park

SF Maritime NHP

Aquatic Park

Fort Mason

Beach St.

Bay St.

FISHERMAN'S WHARF

TELEGRAPH HILL

NORTH BEACH

RUSSIAN HILL

Vallejo St.

Broadway

Pacific Ave.

Washington St.

Sacramento St.

CHINA TOWN

Clay St.

California St.

Jackson St.

The Embarcadero

FINANCIAL DISTRICT

Ferry Building

EMBARCADERO

Bay Bridge

San Francisco Bay

LAUREL HEIGHTS

Geary Blvd.

University of San Francisco

JAPAN-TOWN

Geary Expressway

Post St.

Turk St.

Golden Gate Ave.

WESTERN ADDITION

Alamo Square

HAYES VALLEY

NOB HILL

UNION SQUARE

MONTGOMERY

TENDER-LOIN

POWELL

Geary St.

Turk St.

Market St.

CIVIC CENTER

CIVIC CENTER

SOMA

China Basin

San Francisco Bay

Masonic Ave.

Ashbury St.

Fell St.

Oak St.

Haight St.

LOWER HAIGHT

Duboce Ave.

San Francisco Zen Center

Page St.

Hayes St.

Howard St.

Folsom St.

Harrison St.

Bryant St.

Brannan St.

Townsend St.

King St.

Caltrain

CHINA BASIN

China Basin W.

UPPER HAIGHT

Frederick St.

Clayton St.

Stanyan St.

17th St.

Buena Vista Park

Market St.

16th St.

Mission Dolores

16th ST. MISSION

MISSION

Mission Dolores Park

Potrero St.

16th St.

Mariposa St.

Indiana St.

3rd St.

Central Basin

Twin Peaks

CASTRO

Noe St.

Castro St.

Sanchez St.

Church St.

Dolores St.

Guerrero St.

Valencia St.

Mission St.

18th St.

19th St.

20th St.

Harrison St.

24th ST. MISSION

25th St.

POTRERO HILL

20th St.

De Haro St.

Rhode Island St.

Connecticut St.

Indiana St.

Caltrain

Diamond St.

24th St.

NOE VALLEY

Clipper St.

SF General Hospital

César Chavez St. (Army St.)

Port of San Francisco North Container Terminal

DIAMOND HEIGHTS

Portola Dr.

Glen Canyon Park

30th St.

BERNAL HEIGHTS

Bernal Heights Park

Cortland Ave.

BAY VIEW

Jerrold Ave.

Toland St.

Port of San Francisco Intermodal Container Transfer Facility

Port of San Francisco South Container Terminal

GLEN PARK

Bosworth St.

San Jose Ave.

Park St.

Alemany Blvd.

GLEN PARK

Monterey Blvd.

PORTOLA

Industrial St.

Oakdale Ave.

Evans Ave.

Mendell St.

HUNTERS POINT

Heron's Head Park

India Basin

Balboa Park

Ocean Ave.

Alemany Blvd.

Mission St.

EXCELSIOR

Brazil Ave.

Persia Ave.

Russia Ave.

Moscow St.

Prague St.

McLaren Park

Silver Ave.

Felton Ave.

Burrows St.

Dwight St.

Mansell St.

Bayshore Blvd.

San Bruno Ave.

Silver Ave.

Revere Ave.

Carroll Ave.

Gilman Ave.

Caltrain

Jennings St.

Ingalls St.

Crisp Ave.

Spear Ave.

South Basin

TO 3COM (CANDLESTICK) PARK (300yd)

BALBOA PARK

an oven. Open M-Th and Su 5:30-10pm, F-Sa 5:30-10:30pm. AmEx/MC/V. ❷

UNION SQUARE AND THE TENDERLOIN

▨ **Le Colonial,** 20 Cosmo Pl. (☎415-931-3600; www.lecolonialsf.com), off Post St., between Taylor and Jones St. Exquisite French-Vietnamese cuisine in a stunning French-inspired building. The veranda, with its high, white adobe walls, ivy-clad lattice, and overhead heating lamps, offers the best opportunity to revel in the architecture and sip a signature mojito ($8). Entrees $12-40. Open M-W and Su 5:30-10pm, Th-Sa 5:30-11pm. AmEx/D/MC/V. ❺

The California Culinary Academy, 350 Rhode Island St. (☎888-897-3222). Academy students cook up delicious and affordable main lunch courses like butter poached salmon (with black rice and asparagus $13) and dinner courses like maple syrup slow-braised beef short ribs ($15). Wine with each course is a steal at $5. Grand buffet lunch ($22) and dinner ($38) Th-F draws large crowds; reserve 1 week ahead. Open Tu-F 11:30am-1pm and 6-8pm. AmEx/D/MC/V. ❹

SOMA

▨ **The Butler and the Chef Cafe,** 155A S. Park Ave. (☎415-896-2075; www.thebutlerandthechef. com). Advertising itself as San Francisco's only authentic French bistro, this stellar reproduction of a Parisian street cafe serves organic buckwheat breakfast crepes ($4-14) and baguette sandwiches ($12). Open Tu-Sa 8am-3pm, Su 10am-3pm. AmEx/D/MC/V. ❷

HAIGHT-ASHBURY

▨ **Pork Store Cafe,** 1451 Haight St. (☎415-864-6981; www.porkstorecafe.com), between Masonic Ave. and Ashbury St. A breakfast joint that strives to help your inner fat kid blossom—they proudly stock only whole milk. The 2 delicious healthful options—"Tim's Healthy Thursdays" ($7.50) and "Mike's Low Carb Special" ($7.25)—pack enough spinach, avocado, and salsa to hold their own against the Piggy Special (2 eggs with your choice of 2 pancakes or french toast; $6.25). Open M-F 7am-3:30pm, Sa-Su 8am-4pm. AmEx/MC/V. ❷

Kan Zaman, 1793 Haight St. (☎415-751-9656), at Schrader St. Delicious Middle Eastern fare like falafel sandwiches ($4). Top it off with a hookah session ($10-14) and some Arabic tea. Belly dancing W and Su 9pm, F-Sa 9, 10:30pm. Open M-Th 5pm-midnight, F 5pm-2am, Sa noon-2am, Su noon-midnight. MC/V. ❷

Kate's Kitchen, 471 Haight St. (☎415-626-3984), near Fillmore St. Start your day off right with one of the best breakfasts in the neighborhood (served all day), like the Farmer's Breakfast ($5.50) or the French Toast Orgy (with fruit, yogurt, granola, and honey; $8.50). Often packed. Open M 9am-2:45pm, Tu-F 8am-2:45pm, Sa-Su 8:30am-3:45pm. Cash only. ❷

MISSION AND THE CASTRO

▨ **Taquería Cancún,** 2288 Mission St. (☎415-252-9560), at 19th St. Delicious burritos (grilled chicken $4) and scrumptious egg dishes with chips and salsa, small tortillas, and choice of sausage, ham, or salsa ($5). Open M-Th and Su 9am-1:45am, F-Sa 9am-3am. Cash only. ❶

▨ **Mitchell's Ice Cream,** 688 San Jose Ave. (☎415-648-2300), at 29th St. This takeout parlor gets so busy that you have to take a number at the door. Mitchell's boasts a list of awards almost as long as the list of flavors (from caramel praline to Thai iced tea) and will chocolate-dip any scoop. Cone $2.65. Pint $6.20. Open daily 11am-11pm. Cash only. ❶

Herbivore, 983 Valencia St. (☎415-826-5657; www.herbivorerestaurant.com). If you are unfamiliar with vegan cuisine, the sandwiches are a safe and tasty bet ($9.50) and come with potatoes and salad. Pastas and wraps vary from Thai to shawarma. Open M-Th and Su 9am-10pm, F-Sa 9am-11pm. MC/V. ❸

Nirvana, 544 Castro St. (☎415-861-2226), between 18th and 19th St. Playfully concocted mixed drinks such as "nirvana colada" and "phat margarita" ($9-9.50) complement Burmese cuisine (from $8) with a twist. Open M and W 11:30am-10pm, Tu and Th 4:30-10pm, F-Sa 11:30am-11pm, Su noon-10pm. MC/V. ❸

⊚ SIGHTS

FISHERMAN'S WHARF AND THE BAY

ALCATRAZ. In its 29 years as a maximum-security federal penitentiary, Alcatraz Prison harbored a menacing cast of characters, including Al "Scarface" Capone and George "Machine Gun" Kelly. There were 14 separate escape attempts, but only one man is known to have survived crossing the bay—unfortunately for him, he was recaptured. On the Rock the cell-house audio tour immerses visitors in the infamous days of Alcatraz. A **park ranger tour** can take you around the island and discuss its history. Over the past 200 years, the island has been a hunting and fishing ground for Native Americans, a Civil War outpost, a military prison, a federal prison, and the birthplace of the Native American civil-rights movement. Now part of the **Golden Gate National Recreation Area,** Alcatraz is home to diverse plants and birds. *(Take the Blue and Gold Fleet from Pier 41. ☎415-773-1188, tickets 705-5555. Departures every 30min. beginning at 9am; arrive 20min. early. $24.50, ages 5-11 $15.25. Reservations recommended. Park ranger tours free. Evening tour $31.50, ages 12-17 $30.50, ages 5-11 $18.75; call for times and availability.)*

GHIRARDELLI SQUARE. Ghirardelli Sq. is a mall in what used to be a chocolate factory. No golden ticket is required to gawk at the Ghirardelli Ice Cream and Chocolate Shop's vast selection of goodies and bountiful free samples. *(900 N. Point St. Mall ☎415-775-5500. Stores open M-Sa 10am-9pm, Su 10am-6pm. Shop ☎415-474-1414. Open M-Th 8:30am-9pm, F 8:30am-10pm, Sa 9am-10pm, Su 9am-9pm.)*

MARINA AND FORT MASON

◫PALACE OF FINE ARTS. With its open-air domed structure and curving colonnades, the Palace of Fine Arts was originally built to commemorate the opening of the Panama Canal, testifying to San Francisco's recovery from the 1906 earthquake. It serves today as a monument to all artistic endeavors. The Palace of Fine Arts Theater, located directly behind the rotunda, hosts dance and theater performances and film festivals. *(On Baker St., between Jefferson and Bay St., next to the Exploratorium. ☎415-563-6504. Open daily 6am-9pm. Free.)*

FORT MASON CENTER. The area around Fort Mason Center is free from the crowds that dominate much of the area, making it a great choice for a picnic. The grounds are also the headquarters of the Golden Gate National Recreation Area and offer convenient, inexpensive parking. *(☎415-441-3400; www.fortmason.org.)*

SAN FRANCISCO MUSEUM OF MODERN ART ARTISTS GALLERY. Over 1200 Bay Area artists show, rent, and sell work here. Monthly curated exhibits are downstairs, while most other pieces are sold upstairs. Every May, the gallery hosts a benefit sale at which works are half-price. *(In Bldg. A, on the 1st fl. ☎415-441-4777; www.sfmoma.org. Open Tu-Sa 11:30am-5:30pm. Free.)*

NORTH BEACH

◫COIT TOWER. At the top of Telegraph Hill (also built by Lillie Hitchcock Coit), the Coit Tower stands 210 ft. high and commands a spectacular view of the bay. During the Great Depression, the government's Works Progress Administration employed artists to paint the colorful and distinctly leftist murals in the lobby. *(☎415-362-0808. Open daily 10am-7pm. Elevator $3.75, ages 6-12 $1.50, under 6 free.)*

WASHINGTON SQUARE. Washington Sq., bordered by Union, Filbert, Stockton, and Powell St., is North Beach's *piazza,* a pretty, not-quite-square, tree-lined lawn. The wedding site of Marilyn Monroe and Joe DiMaggio, the park fills every morning with tai chi enthusiasts. By noon, sunbathers, picnickers, and bocce players take over. St. Peter and St. Paul Catholic Church beckons sightseers to its dark nave. Ten stained-glass windows on the upper walls depict the Ten Commandments, though the real highlight is the rose window. *(666 Filbert St. ☎415-421-0809.)* Turn-of-the-century San Francisco philanthropist and party girl Lillie Hitchcock Coit donated the **Volunteer Firemen Memorial** in the middle of the square.

CITY LIGHTS BOOKSTORE. Beat writers came to national attention when Lawrence Ferlinghetti's City Lights Bookstore published Allen Ginsberg's *Howl,* which was banned in

1956 and then subjected to an extended trial. The judge found the poem "not obscene," and City Lights has been a landmark ever since. It has expanded since its Beat days and now stocks a wide selection of fiction and poetry, but it remains committed to publishing young poets and writers under its own label. *(261 Columbus Ave. ☎ 415-362-8193; www.citylights.com. Open daily 10am-midnight.)*

CHINATOWN

WAVERLY PLACE. Find this little alley and you'll want to spend all day gazing at the incredible architecture. The fire escapes are painted in pinks and greens and held together by railings cast in intricate Chinese patterns. *(Between Sacramento and Washington St. and between Stockton St. and Grant Ave.)* **Tien Hou Temple** is the oldest Chinese temple in the city. *(125 Waverly Pl. Open daily 10am-5pm.)*

ROSS ALLEY. Once lined with brothels and opium dens, today's Ross Alley has the look and feel of old Chinatown. The narrow street has stood in for the Orient in such films as *Big Trouble in Little China*, *Karate Kid II*, and *Indiana Jones and the Temple of Doom*. Squeeze into the doorway to see fortune cookies being shaped at the ◪**Golden Gate Cookie Company.** *(56 Ross Alley. ☎ 415-781-3956. Bag of cookies $3.50, with "funny," "sexy," or "lucky" fortunes $4.50. Open daily 10am-8pm.)*

NOB AND RUSSIAN HILLS

CROOKEDEST STREET IN THE WORLD. The famous curves of Lombard St.—installed in the 1920s so that horse-drawn carriages could negotiate the extremely steep hill—serve as an icon of San Francisco. From the top, pedestrians and passengers enjoy the view of city and harbor. The view north along Hyde St. isn't too shabby either. *(Between Hyde and Leavenworth St. at the top of Russian Hill.)*

GRACE CATHEDRAL AND HUNTINGTON PARK. The largest Gothic edifice west of the Mississippi, Grace Cathedral is Nob Hill's stained-glass crown. Inside, modern murals mix San Franciscan and national historical events with saintly scenes. The cathedral is particularly famous for the Ghiberti doors that replicate the *Doors of Paradise*. The

altar of the AIDS Interfaith Memorial Chapel celebrates the church's "inclusive community of love." *(1100 California St., between Jones and Taylor St. ☎ 415-749-6300; www.gracecathedral.org. Open M-Sa 8am-6pm, Su 7am-7pm. Tours M-F 1-3pm, Sa 11:30am-1:30pm, Su 1:30-2pm. $5.)*

UNION SQUARE AND THE TENDERLOIN

MAIDEN LANE. When the Barbary Coast (now the Financial District) was down and dirty, Union Sq.'s Morton Alley was dirtier. Around 1900, murders here averaged one per week and prostitutes waved to customers from second-story windows. After the 1906 earthquake and fires destroyed most of the brothels, merchants moved in and renamed the area Maiden Ln. in hopes of changing the street's image. It worked. Today, the pedestrian-only street is the place to sip espresso while sporting your new Gucci shades.

THE PRESIDIO

When Spanish settlers forged their way up the San Francisco peninsula from Baja California in 1769, they established presidios, or military outposts, as they went. San Francisco's presidio, the northernmost point of Spanish territory in North America, was dedicated in 1776. Today The Presidio is home to many nonprofit organizations as well as residential housing. **Baker Beach** offers sunbathing and views of the Golden Gate and lies at the northwest end of The Presidio. Unfortunately, undertow and rip currents make it unsafe for swimming. **Crissy Field** is another popular recreation area, where people head for a picnic or a game of Frisbee. Head to the **Coastal Bluffs** to explore gun batteries from the 1890s, abandoned after WWII, as well as rare plants that have adapted to the serpentine soil and cool, foggy conditions of the bay.

LINCOLN PARK

COASTAL TRAIL. The Coastal Trail loops around the interior of Lincoln Park for a scenic and sometimes hard-core coastal hike. The entrance to the trail is not well marked, so be careful not to mistakenly tackle a much more difficult cliffside jaunt. The path leads first into **Fort Miley,** a former army post. Near the picnic tables rests the **USS San Francisco Memorial.** The *USS San Francisco* sustained 15 major hits during the Battle of Guadalcanal in November 1942. Nearly 200 men died in the clash, but the ship survived and went on to fight in later battles. The Coastal Trail continues for a 3 mi. hike into **Land's End,** famous for its views of both the Golden Gate Bridge and the "sunken ships" that signal treacherous waters below. Biking is permitted on the trail, although parts contain stairs and bumpy terrain better suited for mountain bikes. From Land's End, onlookers can hike an extra 6 mi. into The Presidio and on to the arches of the Golden Gate Bridge. *(Begins at Point Lobos and 48th Ave.)* For hikers and bikers who aren't so inclined, the walk along **El Camino Del Mar** originates close to the Coastal Trail but runs farther in from the shore. Enjoy the forested views of the Palace of the Legion of Honor before finishing "The Path of the Sea" at China Beach. *(Begins at Point Lobos and Sea Rock Dr.)*

BEACHES. Swimming is permitted but dangerous at scenic **China Beach,** at the end of Seacliff Ave. on the eastern edge of Lincoln Park. Once the camping grounds of Chinese fisherman, this beach is somewhat hidden down a long flight of stairs. Adolph Sutro's 1896 bathhouse lies in ruins on the cliffs. Cooled by ocean water, the baths were capable of packing in 25,000 occupants at a time. **Ocean Beach,** the largest and most popular of San Francisco's beaches, begins south of Point Lobos and extends down the northwestern edge of the city's coastline. The undertow along the point is dangerous, but diehard surfers brave the treacherous currents and the ice-cold water anyway. **Bakers Beach,** a local favorite, is located in The Presidio west of the Golden Gate Bridge. Its proximity to the Golden Gate makes it a popular sunbathing spot on the city's nice summer days.

GOLDEN GATE SIGHTS

GOLDEN GATE BRIDGE. When Captain John Fremont coined the term "Golden Gate" in 1848, he meant to name the harbor entrance to the San Francisco Bay after the mythical Golden Horn port of Constantinople. In 1937, however, the colorful name became per-

manently associated with Joseph Strauss's copper-hued engineering masterpiece—the Golden Gate Bridge. Built for $35 million, the bridge stretches across 1 mi. of ocean, its towers looming 966 ft. above the bay. On sunny days, hundreds of people take the 30min. walk across. Only the adventurous would attempt the trek on windy days, when the bridge can sway up to 27 ft. in each direction. The views from the bridge are amazing, as they are from the **Vista Point** in Marin County just after the bridge. To see the bridge itself, it's best to get a bit farther away; **Fort Point** and **Fort Baker** in The Presidio, **Land's End** in Lincoln Park, and **Mount Livermore** on Angel Island all offer spectacular views on clear days.

GOLDEN GATE PARK. Take your time to enjoy this park. Museums (p. 489) and cultural events pick up where the lush flora and fauna leave off, and athletic opportunities abound. The park has a municipal golf course, an equestrian center, sports fields, tennis courts, and a stadium. On Sundays, park roads close to traffic, and bicycles and in-line skates come out in full force. The **Golden Gate Park Visitors Center** is in the Beach Chalet on the western edge of the park. *(☎415-751-2766. Open daily 9am-5pm.)* **Surrey Bikes and Blades,** in Golden Gate Park, rents equipment. *(50 Stow Lake Dr.☎415-668-6699. Bikes from $6-8 per hr., $20-25 per day. In-line skates $6/15. Open daily 10am-sunset.)*

GARDENS. The **Garden of Fragrance** is designed especially for the visually impaired; all labels are in Braille, and the plants are chosen specifically for their textures and scents. Salvia, rosemary, lemon verbena, lavender, and Grecian laurel are prime examples of the plants growing in this warm, secluded area. *(In the Botanical Gardens. www.sfbotanicalgarden.org. Open M-F 8am-4:30pm, Sa-Su 10am-5pm. Free guided walks daily at 1:30pm.)* Near the Music Concourse off South Dr., the **Shakespeare Garden** contains almost every flower and plant ever mentioned by the Bard. *(Open in summer daily sunrise-sunset; in winter Tu-Su sunrise-sunset. Free.)* The **Japanese Cherry Orchard,** at Lincoln Way and South Dr., blooms in the first week of April. Created for the 1894 Mid-Winter Exposition, the elegant **Japanese Tea Garden** is a serene collection of wood buildings, small pools, graceful footbridges, carefully pruned trees, and lush

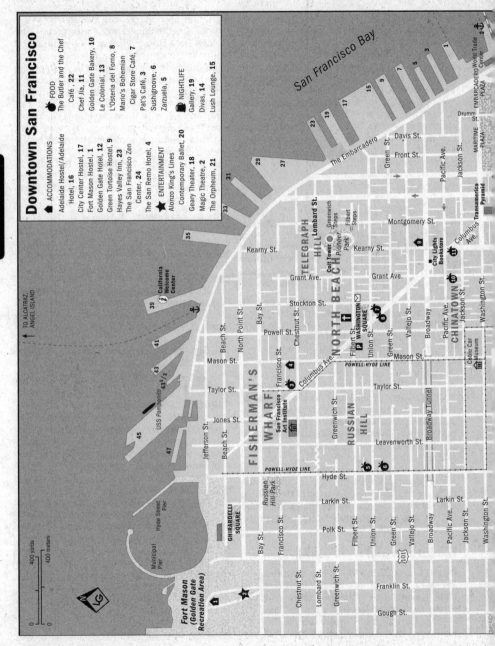

Downtown San Francisco

◀ ACCOMMODATIONS
Adelaide Hostel/Adelaide Hotel, **16**
City Center Hostel, **17**
Fort Mason Hostel, **1**
Golden Gate Hotel, **12**
Green Tortoise Hostel, **9**
Hayes Valley Inn, **23**
The San Francisco Zen Center, **24**
The San Remo Hotel, **4**

★ ENTERTAINMENT
Alonzo King's Lines Contemporary Ballet, **20**
Geary Theater, **18**
Magic Theatre, **2**
The Orpheum, **21**

● FOOD
The Butler and the Chef Café, **22**
Chef Jia, **11**
Golden Gate Bakery, **10**
Le Colonial, **13**
L'Osteria del Forno, **8**
Mario's Bohemian Cigar Store Café, **7**
Pat's Café, **3**
Sushigroove, **6**
Zarzuela, **5**

■ NIGHTLIFE
Gallery, **19**
Divas, **14**
Lush Lounge, **15**

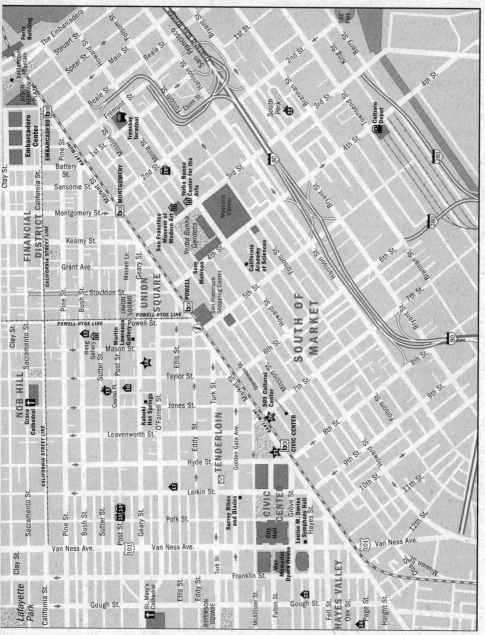

plants. Don't leave without trying the tea. (☎415-752-4227. *Open daily in summer 8:30am-6pm; in winter 8:30am-5pm. $3.50, ages 6-12 and seniors $1.25. Free in summer 8:30-9:30am and 5-6pm; in winter 8:30-9:30am and 4-5pm.*)

FINANCIAL DISTRICT

TRANSAMERICA PYRAMID. Certain areas of the Financial District's architectural landscape rescue it from the otherwise banal functionality of the business area. The leading lady of the city's skyline, the Transamerica Pyramid, is, by all descriptions, impressive: a four-sided pyramid with two wing-like protrusions, it stands at 850 ft. Though its shape may be architecturally awkward, its individuality makes it stand out. Planned as an architect's joke and co-opted by one of the leading architectural firms in the country, the building has earned disdain from purists and reverence from city planners. (*600 Montgomery St., between Clay and Washington St.*)

JAPANTOWN AND PACIFIC HEIGHTS

SAINT DOMINIC'S ROMAN CATHOLIC CHURCH. Churchgoers and architecture buffs appreciate the towering altar of St. Dominic's, carved in the shape of Jesus and the 12 apostles. With its imposing stone and Gothic architecture, St. Dominic's is a must-see, especially its renowned ⬛**shrine of Saint Jude.** (*2390 Bush St. ☎415-567-7824. Open M-F 6:30am-5:30pm, Sa 8am-5:30pm, Su 7:30am-9pm. Mass M-F 6:30, 8am, 5:30pm, Sa 8am and 5:30pm, Su 7:30, 9:30, 11:30am, 1:30, 5:30, 9pm.*)

FUJI SHIATSU AND KABUKI HOT SPRINGS. After a rigorous day hiking the hills, reward your weary muscles with an authentic massage at Fuji Shiatsu. (*1721 Buchanan Mall, between Post and Sutter St. ☎415-346-4484; www.fujishiatsusf.com. Massage $45-72. Open M-F 9am-8:30pm, Sa 9am-6:30pm, Su 10am-6:30pm.*) Alternatively, head to the bathhouse at Kabuki Hot Springs to relax in the sauna and steam room or enjoy the *reiki* (light touching) treatment to heal, rejuvenate, and restore balance. (*1750 Geary Blvd. ☎415-922-6000; www.kabukisprings. com. Open daily 10am-9:45pm. M-F $20, Sa-Su $25. Men only M, Th, Sa; women only W, F, Su; co-ed Tu.*)

CIVIC CENTER

Referred to as the "Crown Jewel" of American classical architecture and with a dome to rival St. Paul's Cathedral and an area of over 500,000 sq. ft., **City Hall,** 1 Dr. Carlton B. Goodlett Pl., at Van Ness Ave., reigns supreme over the nearby Civic Center. (☎415-554-4000. *Open M-F 8am-8pm. Free.*)

THE MISSION

MISSION DOLORES. Completed in 1791, the Mission Dolores is thought to be the city's oldest building. Father Francisco Palou, one of Father Serra's coworkers, celebrated the first mass here on June 29, 1776. The 1906 earthquake destroyed the parish church, and the current building was completed in 1918; look for the stained-glass depiction of St. Francis of Assisi, patron of the Mission and of the city of San Francisco, at the rear of the church. Bougainvillea, poppies, and birds of paradise bloom in its cemetery, which was featured in Hitchcock's *Vertigo.* (*3321 16th St., at Dolores St. ☎415-621-8203. Open daily May-Oct. 9:30am-4:30pm; Nov.-Apr. 9:30am-4pm. $5, ages 5-12 $3.*)

MISSION MURALS. A walk east or west along 24th St. takes you past magnificent murals. Continuing the Mexican mural tradition made famous by Diego Rivera and José Orozco, the murals have been a source of pride for Mexican-American artists and community members since the early 1980s. Standout examples include the political murals of Balmy Alley, off 24th St., between Harrison and Folsom St., a three-building tribute to guitar god Carlos Santana at 22nd St. and Van Ness Ave., the face of St. Peter's Church at 24th and Florida St., and the murals that cover the life skills center on 19th St.

THE CASTRO

For a tour of The Castro that includes sights other than ripped biceps and eight-pack abs, check out **Cruisin' the Castro.** Once run by resident Trevor Hailey, the tour has recently taken on a new leader whose 3hr. walking tours cover Castro life and history from the Gold Rush to today. (☎415-550-8110; www.cruisinthecastro.com. Tours Tu-Sa 10am. $35, ages 3-12 $25. Leaves from the rainbow flag at the corner of Castro and Market St. Reservations required.)

CASTRO STREET. Stores throughout the area cater to gay-mecca pilgrims, with everything from rainbow flags and pride wear to the latest in GLBT books, dance music, and trinkets of the unmentionable variety. Many local shops, especially on colorful Castro St., also double as novelty galleries. Discover just how anatomically correct Gay Billy is at **Does Your Father Know?,** a one-stop kitsch and camp overdose. To read up on gay history and culture, try at **A Different Light Bookstore.** (489 Castro St. ☎415-431-0891; www.adlbooks.com.)

HAIGHT-ASHBURY

Put on your tie-dye and bake your best brownies; since the 60s, when the influence of the Beat generation turned then-affordable Haight-Ashbury into the nation's epicenter of counter-culture, this neighborhood has been a hippie's mecca. The area's funky stores and laid-back coffee shops retain the vibe of its not-so-distant alternative past.

FORMER CRIBS. The former homes of counter-culture legends still attract visitors. From the corner of Haight and Ashbury St., walk just south of Waller St. to check out the house occupied by the Grateful Dead when they were still the Warlocks. (710 Ashbury St.) Look across the street for the Hell's Angels house. If you walk back to Haight St., go right three blocks, and make a left on Lyon St., you can check out Janis Joplin's abode. (122 Lyon St., between Page and Oak St.) Cross the Panhandle, continue three blocks to Fulton St., turn right, and wander seven blocks toward the park to see where the Manson "family" planned murder and mayhem at the Charles Manson mansion. (2400 Fulton St., at Willard St.)

SAN FRANCISCO ZEN CENTER. Appropriately removed from the havoc of the Haight, the San Francisco Zen Center offers a peaceful retreat. The temple is called Beginner's Mind Temple, so don't worry if you don't know

where to begin looking for your chi. The best option for most is the Saturday morning program, which includes a meditation lecture at 8:45am followed by activities and lunch. (300 Page St., at Laguna St. ☎415-863-3136. Open M-F 9:30am-12:30pm and 1:30-5pm, Sa 8:30am-noon. Call ahead for schedule. Sa morning program $6.)

🏛 MUSEUMS

▨SAN FRANCISCO MUSEUM OF MODERN ART (SFMOMA). This black-and-white cylindrical museum houses five spacious floors of photography, painting, media, and sculpture, with an emphasis on architecture and design. It houses the largest selection of 20th-century American and European art this side of New York City. (151 3rd St., between Mission and Howard St. ☎415-357-4000; www.sfmoma.org. Open June-Sept. M-Tu and F 10am-5:45pm, Th 10am-9:45pm, Sa-Su 10am-7:45pm; Sept.-May M-Tu and F-Su 11am-5:45pm, Th 11am-8:45pm. 4 free gallery tours per day. $12.50, students $7, under 13 free, seniors $8.)

▨EXPLORATORIUM. Over 4000 people can visit the Exploratorium at one time, and when admission is free it usually fills up. Over 650 displays—including miniature tornadoes, computer planet-managing, and giant bubble-makers—explain the wonders of the world. Heighten your sense of touch in the Tactile Dome, a dark maze of tunnels, slides, and crevices. (3601 Lyon St. ☎415-563-7337; www.exploratorium.edu. Open Tu-Sa 10am-5pm. $14; students and ages 13-17 $11; ages 4-12 $9, under 4 free. 1st W of each month free. Tactile Dome $17.)

CALIFORNIA PALACE OF THE LEGION OF HONOR. Outside the museum, a copy of Rodin's *The Thinker* beckons visitors into the courtyard, where a glass pyramid recalls the Louvre. A thorough catalogue of great masters, from the medieval to the modern, hangs inside, and extensive statuary and decorative art collections are spread throughout. Just outside the palace, a Holocaust memorial depicts a single, hopeful survivor looking out through a barbed-wire fence to the beauty of the Pacific. (In the middle of Lincoln Park.

NATIONAL ROAD

☎ 415-863-3330; www.legionofhonor.org. Open Tu-Su 9:30am-5:15pm. $10, ages 13-17 $6, under 12 free, seniors $7. 1st Tu of each month free.)

CALIFORNIA ACADEMY OF SCIENCES. The California Academy of Sciences houses multiple museums specializing in different fields of science. The **Steinhart Aquarium**, home to over 600 aquatic species, is livelier than the natural history exhibits. Watch the food chain do its thing at animal feedings throughout the week. At the **Natural History Museum,** the Hotspot exhibit features live animals and endangered species. (875 Howard St. ☎ 415-750-7145; www.calacademy.org. Snake feeding F 1pm; fish feeding M and W 2pm; penguin feeding daily 11am, 3:30pm. Open M-Sa 9:30am-5pm, Su 11am-5pm. $25, ages 12-17 $20, ages 7-11 $15, under 7 free. 3rd W each month free.)

YERBA BUENA CENTER FOR THE ARTS. The center includes an excellent theater and gallery space with programs emphasizing performance, film, viewer involvement, and local multicultural work. It is surrounded by the **Yerba Buena Rooftop Gardens,** a vast expanse of concrete, fountains, and foliage. Also on the grounds is a restored 1906 carousel. (701 Mission St. on the corner of 3rd St. ☎ 415-978-2787; www.ybca.org. Open Tu-W and F-Su noon-5pm, Th noon-8pm. $5, students and seniors $5.)

MUSEUM OF CRAFT AND FOLK ART (MOCFA). The art doesn't just hang on walls at the MOCFA. The museum brings together a fascinating collection of crafts and functional art (clothing, furniture, jewelry) from past to present, near and far. Highlights include 19th-century Chinese children's hats and unorthodox war-time commentary. (51 Yerba Buena Ln. ☎ 415-227-4888; www.mocfa.org. Open Tu-F 11am-6pm, Sa-Su 11am-5pm. $5, under 18 free. Tu free.)

CABLE CAR POWERHOUSE AND MUSEUM. After the steep journey up Nob Hill, you'll understand the importance of the vehicles celebrated at the Cable Car Powerhouse and Museum. The building is the working center of San Francisco's extensive cable-car system. Look down on 57,300 ft. of cable whizzing by or learn about the cars, some of which date back to 1873. (1201 Mason St. ☎ 415-

474-1887; www.cablecarmuseum.org. Open daily Apr.-Sept. 10am-6pm; Oct.-Mar. 10am-5pm. Free.)

⬛ GALLERIES

LUGGAGE STORE AND 509 CULTURAL CENTER. The Luggage Store and its annex, the 509, present exhibitions, performances, and education initiatives, though the often-graphic art exhibits probably won't be Grandma's favorites. Regular events include open-mike comedy, improv music concerts, and a theater festival each June. (1007 Market St. ☎ 415-865-0198; www.luggagestoregallery.org. Open-mike Tu 9pm. Concerts Th 8pm. Suggested donation $6-10.) Next door to 509, the **Cohen Alley** houses a third venue for the area's creative talent; the alley is leased to the Luggage Store, which has made it an artistic showcase.

SAN FRANCISCO ART INSTITUTE. Before he set off across the country to create some of America's most iconic images, Ansel Adams got his start at the San Francisco Art Institute. The oldest art school west of the Mississippi, the institute is lodged in a converted mission and has produced a number of American greats including Mark Rothko, Imogen Cunningham, Dorothea Lange, and James Weeks. To the left as you enter is the Diego Rivera Gallery, one wall of which is covered by a huge 1931 Rivera mural. (800 Chestnut St. ☎ 415-771-7020 or 800-345-7324; www.sfai.edu. Open daily 9am-9pm. Free.)

MARTIN LAWRENCE GALLERY. The gallery displays works by pop artists like Warhol and Haring, who once distributed his work for free to New York City commuters in the form of subway station graffiti; his playful works now command upward of $13,000 in print form. The gallery also houses studies by Picasso and America's largest collection of work by Marc Chagall. (366 Geary St. ☎ 415-956-0345; www.martinlawrence.com. Open M and Su 10am-6pm, Tu-Sa 10am-8pm. Free.)

HANG. Artistic works hang from the exposed ceiling beams of this aptly named chrome warehouse. An annex recently opened directly across the street at 567 Sutter St. (556

Sutter St. ☎*415-434-4264; www.hangart.com. Open M-Sa 10am-6pm, Su noon-5pm. Free.)*

🎭 ENTERTAINMENT

DANCE, FILM, AND THEATER

Downtown, Mason St. and Geary St. constitute Theater Row, the city's center for theatrical entertainment. **TIX Bay Area,** located in a kiosk in Union Sq., at the corner of Geary and Powell St., is a Ticketmaster outlet and sells half-price tickets the day of performances. (☎415-433-7827; www.theaterbayarea.org. Open Tu-Th 11am-6pm, F-Sa 11am-7pm, Su 10am-3pm.) **Magic Theatre,** in Fort Mason Center, stages international and American premieres. (☎415-441-8822; www.magictheatre. org.) A famous landmark, **The Orpheum,** 1192 Market St., at Hyde St., near the Civic Center, hosts big Broadway shows. (☎415-512-7770.) **Geary Theater,** 415 Geary St., is home to the renowned **American Conservatory Theater,** at Mason St. in Union Sq., one of the best theater companies in the country. (☎415-749-2228; www.act-sfbay.org.) The 🎬**Castro Theatre,** 429 Castro St., near Market St., shows eclectic films, festivals, and double features. Some feature live organ music. (☎415-621-6350; www.thecastrotheatre.com.) The 🎭**Oberlin Dance Company,** 3153 17th St., between S. Van Ness Ave. and Folsom St., in the Mission, mainly stages dance performances, but it also has theatrical productions and art exhibitions. (☎415-478-2787; www.odctheater.org. Box office open W-Sa 2-5pm.) At **Alonzo King's Lines Contemporary Ballet,** 26 Seventh St., in Hayes Valley, dancers combine elegant classical moves with athletic flair to the music of great living jazz and world-music composers. (☎415-863-3040; www.linesballet.org. Open M-F 9am-10pm, Sa-Su 9am-6pm.)

MUSIC

CLASSICAL AND OPERA

The seating in the $33 million glass-and-brass **Louise M. Davies Symphony Hall,** 201 Van Ness Ave., was designed to give audience members a close-up view of performers. The resident **San Francisco Symphony** is highly esteemed. Rush tickets available at the box office (during business hours) the day of performances. (☎415-552-8000. Open M-F 10am-6pm, Sa noon-6pm. Rush tickets $20.) The recently renovated **War Memorial Opera House,** 301 Van Ness Ave., between Grove and McAllister St., hosts the **San Francisco Opera Company** and the **San Francisco Ballet.** (☎415-864-3330. Open M-F 10am-6pm and 2hr. before each show.)

POP

The distinction between bars, clubs, and live music venues is hazy in San Francisco. Almost all bars will occasionally have bands, and small venues have rock and hip-hop shows. Look for the latest live music listings in *San Francisco Weekly* and *The Guardian.* Hard-core concertgoers might snag a copy of *Bay Area Music (BAM).*

🎵 **Café du Nord,** 2170 Market St. (☎415-861-5016; www.cafedunord.com), between Church and Sanchez St., in the Castro. One of San Francisco's best music venues. Live music—from pop and groove to garage rock—plays every night, and the Monday Night Hoot showcases local singing and songwriting. 21+. Cover $15. Shows at 9:30pm; doors open at 8:30pm.

The Independent, 628 Divisadero St. (☎415-771-1422; www.independentsf.com), at Hayes St., in the Lower Haight. Live performances nearly every night feature genres as diverse as reggae, indie rock, and hip hop. 2-drink min. Open daily 11am-6pm.

Bottom of the Hill, 1233 17th St. (☎415-626-4455; www.bottomofthehill.com), between Missouri and Texas St., in Potrero Hill. The best place to see up-and-coming artists before they move to bigger venues. Most Su afternoons feature local bands and 🍖**all-you-can-eat barbecue.** 21+; some shows open to all ages. Cover $7-12. Happy hour F 4-7pm. Open M-Tu and Sa 8:30pm-2am, W-F 4pm-2am.

Fillmore, 1805 Geary Blvd. (☎415-346-6000; www.thefillmore.com), at Fillmore St., in Japantown. Bands that pack stadiums may play this club legendary for its history, but the venue's bread and butter is still midsize groups like Jurassic 5 and The Black Keys. The Fillmore was the foundation of San Francisco's 1960s music scene, and performers like Janis Joplin, The Grateful Dead, and Jefferson Airplane all performed here. Box office open Su 10am-4pm.

SPORTS

Baseball's **Giants** play at **AT&T Park,** 24 Willie Mays Plaza, in SoMa. (☎415-972-2000 or 888-464-2468; www.sfgiants.com. Tickets $13-68.) **Candlestick Park** is home to the NFL's storied **49ers.** (☎415-464-9377, tickets 656-4900; www.sf49ers.com. Tickets $49-94.)

◪ NIGHTLIFE

Nightlife in San Francisco is as varied as the city's personal ads—everyone from the "shy first-timer" to the "bearded strap daddy" can find places to go at night. The spots listed below are divided into bars and clubs, but the lines get blurred in San Francisco after dark, and even cafes hop at night. Check out the nightlife listings in the *S.F. Weekly, S.F. Bay Guardian,* and *Metropolitan.* San Francisco is not particularly friendly to those under 21.

BARS

◪ **Noc Noc,** 574 Haight St. (☎415-861-5811; www. nocnocs.com), near Fillmore St., in the Lower Haight. This lounge, creatively outfitted as a modern cavern, seems like the only happening place before 10pm—neo-hippies mingle at bar stools or relax on the padded floor cushions. With a "No Bud, No Miller, No Coors" mantra, Noc Noc favors unique drinks. Happy hour daily 5-7pm with $3 pints. Open daily 5pm-2am. MC/V.

◪ **111 Minna Gallery,** 111 Minna St. (☎415-974-1719), at 2nd St., in SoMa. Funky gallery by day, trendy hipster groove spot by night. The bar turns club W 5-10pm for a crowded night of progressive house music. Cover $5-15. Gallery open Tu-F noon-5pm. Bar open Tu 5-9pm, W 5-11pm, Th-F 5pm-2am, Sa 10pm-2am. AmEx/D/MC/V.

Lush Lounge, 1092 Post St. (☎415-771-2022; www.thelushlounge.com), in Nob Hill. Oh so lush, with ample vegetation and sassy classic Hollywood throwback decor. Kick back as the best of the 80s, from ABBA to Madonna, streams through the speakers. Raspberry cosmos $6. Watermelon martinis $4. Open daily 4pm-2am. Cash only.

CLUBS

◪ **El Rio,** 3158 Mission St. (☎415-282-3325; www. elriosf.com), between César Chavez and Valencia St., in the Mission. Each area in this sprawling club has its own bar, but the patio is center stage for the young urbanites who play cards. Diverse queer and straight crowd. Live local bands Tu-W and Sa-Su. Live salsa Su 3-8pm; salsa lessons 3-4pm. Pool table and jukebox in the bar area. Open M-Th 5pm-2am, F 4pm-2am, Sa-Su 3pm-2am. Cash only.

Pink, 2925 16th St. (☎415-431-8889; www. pinksf.com), at S. Van Ness Ave., in the Mission. Filled with the scent of gardenias, this venue plays it *très chic.* Pink satin and gossamer draperies lend a lounge feel on weekdays, but expect a throng of clubbers F-Sa. DJs spin a mix of world music, soulful house, Cuban jazz, and Afro beats. Cover $12 after midnight. Open Tu-Th and Su 10pm-2am, F-Sa 10pm-3am. MC/V.

GLBT NIGHTLIFE

Politics aside, nightlife alone is enough to earn San Francisco the title of "gay mecca." Generally, the boys hang in The Castro, while the girls gravitate to the Mission, around Valencia St. All frolic along Polk St. (several blocks north of Geary Blvd.) and in SoMa.

◪ **Divas,** 1081 Post St. (☎415-474-3482; www. divassf.com), at Polk St., in the Tenderloin. With a starlet at the door and a savvy madame working the bar, this transgender nightclub is simply fabulous. Talent night Tu. Drag show F-Sa. Cover $7-10. Open daily 6am-2am. Cash only.

◪ **The Bar,** 456 Castro St. (www.thebarsf.com), between Market and 18th St. An urbane Castro staple with padded walls and dark plush couches perfect for eyeing the stylish young crowd or scoping the techno-raging dance floor. Happy hour M-Th 5-8pm, F 6-8pm with $2 drinks. Open M-F 5pm-2am, Sa-Su 1pm-2am. Cash only.

SF Badlands, 4121 18th St. (☎415-626-0138), near Castro St. This swanky club serves the "best cosmo in the Castro" for $5.25. Men of all ages bust a move on the circular dance floor late into the night. Drinks $4-5. Cover F-Sa $2. 2 for 1 happy hour daily 2-8pm. Open daily 2pm-2am.

Wild Side West, 424 Cortland Ave. (☎415-647-3099), at Wool St., in Bernal

Heights. The oldest lesbian bar in the city has been a favorite of women and men since 1962. The backyard jungle has fountains, statues, and benches hidden in nooks. Pink Sa and Pride Su parties at 2pm. Open daily 1pm-2am. Cash only.

FESTIVALS

If you can't find a festival going on in San Francisco, well, you just aren't trying hard enough. Cultural, ethnic, and queer events take place year-round. There's no better place to explore your every curiosity.

Japanese Cherry Blossom Festival (☎415-563-2313). For 2 consecutive weekends in Apr., this festival lights up the streets of Japan-town with 100s of ethnic performers.

San Francisco International Film Festival (☎415-561-5000; www.sffs.org). The oldest film festival in North America shows more than 100 international films of all genres over 2 weeks in Apr. Films are shown at 12 venues throughout the city, but the Kabuki Theatre, 1881 Post St., and the Castro Theatre, 429 Castro St., are 2 main venues. $10.50, students $7.50.

San Francisco International Gay and Lesbian Film Festival (☎415-703-8650). California's 2nd-largest film festival and the world's largest gay and lesbian media event. Takes place during the 11 days leading up to Pride Day.

Pride Day (☎415-864-3733; www.sfpride.org). Celebrated the last weekend in June with a parade and events downtown starting on Market St. at Davis St. at 10:30am.

San Francisco Shakespeare Festival (☎415-558-0888; www.sfshakes.org). Every Sa and Su in Sept. in The Presidio. Shows Sa 7:30pm, Su 2:30pm.

San Francisco Blues Festival (☎415-979-5588). Held the 3rd weekend in September, this is the oldest blues festival in America and attracts some of the biggest names in the business.

THE END OF THE ROAD

Navigate the crookedest street in the world, plan your escape from Alcatraz, walk across the Golden Gate Bridge, and head to the beach to contemplate the Pacific. You've finished a colossal coast-to-coast trek, the National Road. But don't rest on your laurels—the road awaits. **Route 66** and the **Pacific Coast** are only a few highway exits away.

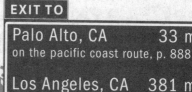

EXIT TO

Palo Alto, CA   33 mi.
on the pacific coast route, p. 888

Los Angeles, CA   381 mi.
on route 66, p. 495

route 66

TOP 5

1. Get a rabbit autograph at **Henry's Route 66 Emporium and Rabbit Ranch** (p. 517).
2. Learn about the atomic bomb at Los Alamos, site of the **Manhattan Project** (p. 552).
3. Indulge your **Elvis** passion and sleep in his favorite room in Clinton, Oklahoma (p. 534).
4. Discover what Rte. 66 means to the people who lived on it at **Shea's gas station** (p. 512).
5. Bust a move at one of America's legendary honky tonks, the **Museum Club**, Flagstaff (p. 565).

Rte. 66 is *the* roadtrip. Born of America's love affair with the automobile, Rte. 66 is the final resting place of classic car culture, known variously as the "Main Street of America," the "Mother Road," and the "Will Rogers Highway." Decommissioned in 1985, this hallmark of Americana retains its neon signs, kitschy themes, and the tire tread of millions. Whether you're searching for yourself or just a good burger and a cheap motel room, Rte. 66, in all its neon-lit glory, delivers.

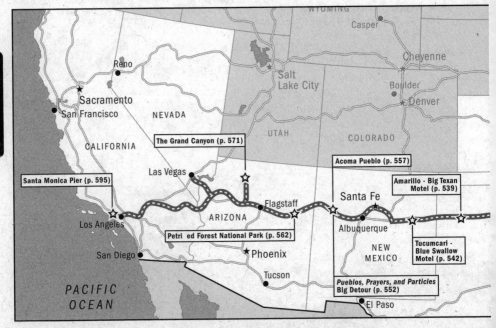

Continuously paved by 1938, Rte. 66 saw the westward migration of thousands of families heading to California, looking to escape the dust and poverty of the Great Depression. It also spawned the motel, the drive-through, and, of course, the assortment of mom-and-pop businesses that sprang up along the way. While Rte. 66 was eventually eclipsed by the many-laned sterility of the Interstate Highway System and officially decommissioned in 1985, the road is experiencing a revival in the form of thousands of modern-day migrants, who seek to re-create the classic journey of generations past. From its lakeside beginnings in **Chicago, Illinois** (see next page), which offers world-class architecture (not to mention deep-dish pizza), our route follows the original as closely as possible, through the rolling countryside of Illinois and Missouri, home to **Henry's Route 66 Emporium and Rabbit Ranch** (p. 517). From there, the next stop is **Meramec Caverns** (p. 517)—if the caverns' reputation as Missouri's biggest tourist attraction doesn't reach you, the sheer number of signs surely will. After passing the oddly

Gothic **Jasper County Courthouse** (p. 523), it's on to the lonely, dusty plains of Oklahoma, where traffic is sparse, cows are many, and almost every town has a street (or at least a park) named after **Will Rogers.** Rte. 66 passes through El Reno, OK, where **Johnnie's Grill** (p. 533) proudly prepares the **world's largest hamburger** each May, before traversing west **Texas** and entering the deserts of **New Mexico,** where you, too, can stay in "Tucumcari tonight" at the **Blue Swallow Motel** (p. 541).

Rte. 66 then cuts a magnificent swath across New Mexico, Arizona, and Nevada through miles and miles of scrubby desert, where skies are blue and sweeping, and colorful trading posts line the road, peddling Navajo crafts, road snacks, and, of course, Rte. 66 souvenirs. The road passes through **Santa Fe** (p. 546), where Spanish colonial architecture, Native American influence, and green chiles come together in one spicy, delicious mix, and then explores New Mexico on the **Pueblos, Prayers, and Particles Big Detour** (p. 552). The route continues on through charming **Albuquerque** (p. 551), the stunning and scenic

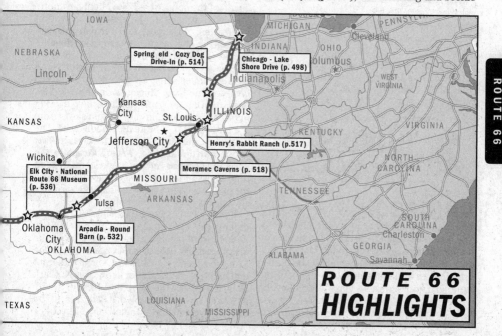

ROUTE 66

ROUTE 66 **HIGHLIGHTS**

pueblo country of Arizona, and the one and only **Petrified Forest National Park** (p. 562). Take it easy in **Winslow, Arizona** (p. 564) before reaching **Flagstaff,** where you can take a brief jaunt off 66 to visit the **Grand Canyon** (p. 571). Ponder the mind-boggling engineering of the 726 ft. **Hoover Dam** (p. 580), and play the tables in **Las Vegas** (p. 580) if you're feeling lucky. Or—if you really want to gamble—get hitched at the **Little White Wedding Chapel.** Continue across the punishing **Mojave Desert** toward **Los Angeles** (p. 595), the sprawling city of the stars. Finally, the near-perfect roadtrip reaches its near-perfect end at **Santa Monica** (p. 595). There's never been a better time to get your kicks, so pack your sunglasses and bring a camera—the journey has begun.

ROUTE STATS

Miles: c. 2400

Route: Chicago, IL, to Santa Monica, CA.

States: 8; Illinois, Missouri, Oklahoma, Texas, New Mexico, Arizona, Nevada, and California.

Driving Time: You could spend forever cruising the lonely backroads of the Southwest, but allow at least 3 weeks to savor Rte. 66.

When To Go: Summer in the desert is hot—very, very hot. Summertime highs in Needles, CA, can reach 120°F. We leave you with this; go when the urge hits.

Crossroads: The National Road in St. Louis, MO (p. 379); **The Deep South** in Oklahoma City, OK (p. 759), **The Pacific Coast** in Los Angeles, CA (p. 906).

The Land of Lincoln
ILLINOIS
Welcomes You!

CHICAGO   ☎ 312

Students in Hyde Park can ponder philosophy, and floor traders at the Board of Exchange can make millions, but at the end of the day Chicago places its trust in the tangible. Its heroes are builders and magnates; its version of the American dream raises a glass to anyone who can get ahead in this clamorous boomtown. Long a city of immigrants and underdogs, Chi-

cago knows how to rub elbows with sophistication and then hop on the wheezing, clanking El for the long ride home.

VITAL STATS

Population: 2,900,000

Tourist Offices: Visitor Information Center, 77 E. Randolph St. (☎312-744-2400), in the Chicago Cultural Center. Open M-Th 8am-7pm, F 8am-6pm, Sa 9am-6pm, Su 10am-6pm. **Water Works Visitor Center,** 163 E. Pearson St. (☎312-742-8811), at Michigan Ave. in the Water Tower. Open M-Th 8am-7pm, F 8am-6pm, Sa 9am-6pm, Su 10am-6pm.

Library and Internet Access: Chicago Public Library, Harold Washington Library Center, 400 S. State St. (☎312-747-4300), at Congress. Open M-Th 9am-9pm, F-Sa 9am-5pm, Su 1-5pm.

Post Office: 433 W. Harrison St. (☎800-275-8777). Open M-Sa 8am-5pm. **Postal Code:** 60607.

◪ ORIENTATION

Chicago dominates the entire northeastern corner of Illinois, running north-south along 29 mi. of the southwest Lake Michigan shoreline. The city sits at the center of a web of interstates, rail lines, and airplane routes. Chicago is the origin or terminus, depending on the direction in which you travel, of **Old Route 66.** The flat and sprawling city grid usually makes sense to drivers. At the city's center is the **Loop,** Chicago's downtown business district and the public-transportation hub. The block numbering system starts from the intersection of State and Madison St. The Loop is bounded loosely by the **Chicago River** to the north and west, **Wabash Avenue** to the east, and **Congress Parkway** to the south. A good map is essential for navigating; pick one up for free at the tourist office or any **Chicago Transit Authority (CTA)** station (below).

North of the Loop, LaSalle St. loosely defines the west edge of the posh **Near North** area; most of its activity is centered along the **Magnificent Mile** of **Michigan Avenue,** between the Chicago River and Oak St. A trendy restaurant and nightlife district, **River North** lines N. Clark St. just north of the Loop and west of Michigan Ave. The **Bucktown/Wicker Park** area, at the intersection of North, Damen, and Milwaukee

Chicago Overview

MOUNT
ROSPECT

W. Golf Rd.

W. Golf Rd.

EVANSTON

Dempster St.

Northwestern
University

SKOKIE

Green Bay Rd.

ROSEMONT

Chicago O'Hare
Int'l. Airport

Thorndale Ave.

Mannheim Rd.

NORRIDGE

W. Peterson Ave.

SCHILLER
PARK

Irving Park Rd.

FRANKLIN
PARK

OAK PARK

W. North   Ave.

ELMHURST

W. Lake St.

Harlem

HILLSIDE

Eisenhower Expwy.

CHICAGO

Lincoln
Park

SEE DOWNTOWN
CHICAGO MAP
p. (499)

Grant
Park

Lake Michigan

CICERO

W. 22nd St.

Tri-State Tollway

W. Ogden Ave.

Cermak Rd.

Burnham
Park

Archer Ave.

W. 47th St.

University
of Chicago

Stevenson Expwy.

N. Joliet Rd.

Chicago
Midway
Airport

*Marquette
Park*

W. 55th St.

W. Garfield Blvd

Jackson
Park

Ronald J. Rieglaal
Memorial Blvd.

BEDFORD PARK

BRIDGE-
VIEW

BURBANK

W. 79th St.

W. 79th St.

Rainbow
Park

87th St.

Calumet
Park

Archer Ave.

OAK
LAWN

W. 95th St

W. 95th St.

E. 95th St.

Kilbery Hwy.

Calumet Sag Channel

Indianapolis Blvd.

Alsip

CALUMET
PARK

Calumet R.

Wolf
Lake

Lake
George

Cline Ave.

ORLAND
PARK

W. 159th St.

E. 159th St.

W. 162nd St.

CALUMET
CITY

Southwest Hwy.

ROUTE 66

HAMMOND

Ave., is home to many artsy cafes and to the city's wildest/hippest nightlife venues. **Lincoln Park** revolves around the junction of N. Clark St., Lincoln Ave., and Halsted St. To the north, near the 3000 block of N. Clark St. and N. Halsted Sts., sits Lakeview, a gay-friendly area teeming with food and nightlife that becomes Wrigleyville in the 4000 block. **Andersonville,** 5 mi. farther up N. Clark St. north of Foster Ave., is the center of the Swedish-American community, though immigrants from Asia and the Middle East have recently settled here. It is a good idea to stay within the more active and populated areas as evening sets in; especially avoid the South Side neighborhood.

⊟ TRANSPORTATION

Parking your car in downtown Chicago may remind you of a reality TV show— the competition for spots and hourly prices are extreme. To avoid driving and parking in the city, daytrippers can leave their cars in one of the suburban park-and-ride lots ($1.75-10.75 per day, depending on station). In the city, the **CTA** runs subways and buses. The **elevated rapid-transit train system,** called the **El,** encircles the Loop. Late-night service is infrequent and unsafe in many areas. Helpful CTA maps are available at many stations and at the Tourist offices. (☎312-836-7000 or 888-968-7282; www.transitchicago.com. Runs 24hr. $2; day pass $5.)

Parking lots west of the southern Loop and across the canal from the **Sears Tower** generally have the best rates, but avoid parking in the Loop if possible. Also, beware the 45 mph speed limit on **Lake Shore Drive,** a scenic freeway that hugs Lake Michigan and offers "express" north-south connections.

⬕ ACCOMMODATIONS

It's easy to find a cheap, convenient place to rest your head at one of Chicago's many hostels. Motel chains off the interstates, about 1hr. from downtown, are out of the way and more expensive (from $40) but are an option for late arrivals. **At Home Inn Chicago** (☎800-375-7084) offers a reservation and referral service for many downtown B&Bs. Most have a two-night minimum stay, and

rooms start around $145. Chicago has a 15% tax on most accommodation rates.

⬕ Hostelling International-Chicago (HI-AYH), 24 E. Congress Pkwy. (☎312-360-0300; www.hichicago.org), off Wabash St. in the Loop. Great location offering easy access to major museums and the center of the city. Be aware of your surroundings at night—this is downtown. Foosball, pool tables, and fun organized outings give the hostel a lively social atmosphere to match its bright decor. Laundry. Internet $2 per 20min. Free Wi-Fi. Reception 24hr. Check-out 11am. Check-in 3pm. Reservations recommended. Dorms $31-37. HI members $3 less. MC/V. ❷

Arlington House, 616 W. Arlington Pl. (☎773-929-5380; www.arlingtonhouse.com), in Lincoln Park. A renovated nursing home, this hostel offers a nice alternative to the HI downtown. Situated in a quiet, leafy residential neighborhood. An attractive historic building with a light, airy communal area opening out onto the back. Free Internet. Wi-Fi $1 for 3 days. Key deposit $10. Reception 24hr. Reservations recommended. Dorms $33; private rooms with shared bath $66, with private bath $80. MC/V. ❷

International House, 1414 E. 59th St. (☎773-753-2270; www.ihouse.uchicago.edu), at the corner of 59th and Blackstone on the University of Chicago campus. Marble floors and ornate trim make the International House seem more like a snazzy hotel than a student residential hall. Guests must be affiliated with some institution of learning (being a "student of life" does not count). Laundry, coffee shop, game room, and weight room. Reservations recommended. Dorms $60; doubles $70. MC/V. ❸

The Write Inn, 211 N. Oak Park Ave. (☎708-383-4800; www.writeinn.com), in Oak Park. This historic building transports guests into the 1920s with select antique furnishings and quilt-laden box-frame beds. Free Wi-Fi. Reception 24hr. Reservations recommended. Rooms from $99. AmEx/MC/V. ❹

Ohio House Motel, 600 N. LaSalle St. (☎312-943-6000), at Ohio St. Keep your eyes peeled for this 2-story motel—it's dwarfed by the surrounding buildings and easy to miss. TV and private baths. Smoking and non-smoking rooms available. Free parking. Reservations recommended. Doubles $100. AmEx/MC/V. ❺

TO WRIGLEYA FIELD (3mi)
North Ave.
Second
City
Chicago Historical Society
TO LINCOLN PARK (1mi)
TO STEPPENWOLF THEATER (500yd), OAK PARK (7mi)
TO 1 (1mi)
2 (4.5mi), AND 3 (3mi)
International Museum of Surgical Science

Downtown Chicago

ACCOMMODATIONS

Arlington House, **1**
Hostelling International Chicago (HY-AYH), **14**
International House, **15**
Ohio House Motel, **8**

Gino's East of Chicago, **5**
Heaven on Seven, **12**
Lou Malnati's, **10**
Lou Mitchell's, **13**
Pizzeria Uno, **9**
Portillos Hotdogs, **6**

FOOD

Al's #1 Italian Beef, **7**
Billy Goat Tavern, **11**
Ed Debevic's, **4**

NIGHTLIFE

Berlin, **3**
The Green Mill, **2**

W. Schiller St.
Goethe St.
La Salle St.
Division St.
Elm St.
Cedar St.
Bellevue Pl.
Oak St. Beach
Rush St.
Walton St.
Delaware Pl.
E. Chestnut
Locust St.
Orleans St.
Sedgwick St.
Franklin St.
Wells St.
Oak St.
Larabee St.
Hudson Ave.
La Salle St.
Clark St.
Dearborn St.
Huron St.
Erie St.
Ontario St.
Ohio St.
Grand Ave.
Illinois St.
W. Hubbard St.

John Hancock Center
Water Tower Place
Pearson St.
Chicago Water Tower
Chicago Ave.
Superior St.
Museum of Contemporary Art

NEAR NORTH
St. Clair St.
Michigan Ave.
Northwestern Memorial Hospital

Outer Harbor
Olive Park
Navy Pier

4 5 6
7 8
9
10 **RIVER NORTH**
Merchandise Mart
Kinzie St.
Wrigley Building
Tribune Tower
E. North Water St.
Chicago R.
Wacker Dr.
S. Water St.
E. Lake St.

N. Kingsbury St.
Chicago R.
Clinton St.
Canal St.
Lake St.
Franklin St.
Wacker Dr.
State of Illinois Building

TO MUSEUM OF HOLOGRAPHY (1.1mi)
Randolph St.
Daley Plaza
City Hall
Goodman Theatre
12
Chicago Cultural Center
E. Randolph Dr.

Civic Opera House
Washington St.
Northwestern Station
Madison St.
Chicago Temple
Chase Tower Plaza
THE LOOP
Monroe St.
Union Station
Sears Tower and Observ.
Adams St.
Jackson Blvd.
Monadnock Building
Van Buren St.
13
290
Congress Pkwy.
Harrison St.
W. Polk St.

Symphony Center
Art Institute of Chicago
Petrillo Music Shell
Chicago Architecture Foundation
E. Jackson Dr.
Grant Park

Harold Washington Library Center
14
Auditorium Theater
Congress Dr.
Columbia College
E. Balbo Dr.

Field Bd.
Lake Shore Dr.
Millenium Park
Monroe Harbor
E. Monroe Dr.

Lake Michigan

Chicago Harbor

0   300 yards
0   300 meters

S. Wells St.
E. 8th St.
9th St.
E. 11th St.
Roosevelt Rd.
Wabash Ave.
Michigan Ave.
Indiana Ave.
E. 13th St.
Columbus Dr.
W. 14th St.
E. 14th St.
Clark St.
State St.
Canal St.
S. Branch Chicago R.
Lake Shore Dr.

Field Museum Of Natural History
John G. Shedd Aquarium
Solidarity Dr.
Adler Planetarium

TO 15, COMISKEY PARK, MUSEUM OF SCIENCE & INDUSTRY, HYDE PARK, U. OF CHICAGO (8mi)
Soldier Field
Burnham Park Harbor

ROUTE 66

◢ FOOD

Chicago's many culinary delights, from pizza to po' boy sandwiches, are among its main attractions. One of the best guides to city dining is the monthly *Chicago* magazine, which includes an extensive restaurant section indexed by price, cuisine, and quality. It can be found at tourist offices and newsstands throughout the city.

THE LOOP

◪ **Heaven on Seven,** 111 Wabash Ave. (☎312-263-6443; www.heavenonseven.com), in the Garland Bldg. Friendlier staff and tastier gumbo than one would imagine even in heaven. Nestled on the 7th floor of a rather nondescript office building, this folksy New Orleans-inspired eatery is a delight. Tuck into hearty southern-style gumbo amid the clatter of plates, lively lunchtime conversation, and hot, fragrant steam billowing from the open kitchen. Open M-F 9am-4pm Sa 10am-3pm. Cash only. ❷

Lou Mitchell's, 565 W. Jackson St. (☎312-939-3111), at the corner of Jefferson St., 2 mi. west of the start of Rte. 66. Recently inducted into the Restaurant Hall of Fame, this retro diner has been stuffing faithful customers for 80 years and lies on the path of the original Rte. 66. Start the day with "the world's finest cup of coffee" ($2) or end with a piece of homemade pie. Lines are long but move fast. Everyone gets free doughnut holes while they wait, and women and children get Milk Duds. Massive salads. Open M-Sa 5:30am-3pm, Su 7am-3pm. Cash only. ❷

NEAR NORTH

◪ **Ed Debevic's,** 640 N. Wells St. (☎312-644-1707; www.eddebevics.com). Valet parking ($8) or on-street metered parking. Half 1950s diner, half sassy spectacle, with the slogan "eat and get out," Ed Debevic's features poodle-skirted waitresses who dance on countertops and whose manner ranges from sulky to downright rude. Come here to get sworn at for dithering over your menu choice or for a thoroughly unheartfelt rendition of happy birthday. Appetizers from $5. Burgers $9. Shakes $5. Open M-Th and Su 11am-9pm, F-Sa 11am-11pm. AmEx/D/MC/V. ❸

Lou Malnati's, 439 N. Wells St. (☎312-828-9800; www.loumalnatis.com). A downtown mainstay for over 30 years. Lou used to be in business with the founders of Pizzeria Uno's, but in the mid-70s they irreconcilably divided over recipes. Today's rivalry remains fierce over whose pies are Chicago's finest. Pizzas from $5.40. Open M-Th 11am-11pm, F-Sa 11am-midnight, Su noon-10pm. AmEx/D/MC/V. ❷

Pizzeria Uno's, 29 E. Ohio St. (☎312-321-1000), at the corner of Wabash and Ohio St. It may look like any other Uno's, but this is where the legacy of deep-dish began in 1943. Most pizzas (large $22) take 45min. to prepare, but the wait only makes you crave the world-famous pies even more. Individual-sized pies ($7) only take 25min. Open M-F 11am-1am, Sa 11am-2am, Su 11am-11pm. AmEx/D/MC/V. ❷

Gino's East of Chicago, 633 N. Wells St. (☎312-943-1124; www.ginoseast.com), at Ontario, 7 blocks west of Michigan Ave. The writing on the wall proclaims this the best pizza around. Signs invite you to make your own mark on the already heavily decorated surfaces of the restaurant. Deep-dish or thin-crust pizza (from $14) and pasta (from $10). Lunch combos $6.25. Open M-Th 11am-9pm, F-Sa 11am-11pm, Su noon-9pm. MC/V. ❷

Billy Goat Tavern, 430 N. Michigan Ave (☎312-222-1525; www.billygoattavern.com). It's easy to miss this legendary institution, located down a flight of steps just under the main road. In 1945, owner William Sianis was refused entry to Wrigley Field because he was accompanied by his pet goat, prompting him to put a hex on the Cubs that would keep them from ever winning the pennant. Duck in here for a burger ($5) and to soak up Chicago history. Open M-F 6am-2am, Sa 11am-3am, Su 11am-2am. Cash only. ❶

Portillo's Hotdogs, 100 W. Ontario St. (☎312-587-8910; www.portillos.com), at Clark St. Portillo's won so many "Silver Platter" awards for its tasty hot dogs that it retired for 5 years to give the competition a chance. Try the famous hot dog on a poppy-seed bun ($2.45), best with a schooner of beer (from $3). Open M-W and Su 10am-midnight, Th-Sa 10am-1am. D/MC/V. ❶

Al's #1 Italian Beef, 169 W. Ontario St. (☎312-943-3222; www.alsbeef.com), at N. Wells St. You can get some of America's best sandwiches at this no-frills eatery. Sandwiches

$5. Burgers $4. Open M-Th 10am-midnight, F-Sa 10am-3am, Su 11am-9pm. AmEx/D/MC/V. ❶

SOUTH SIDE

Dixie Kitchen and Bait Shop, 5225A S. Harper St. (☎773-363-4943), in Hyde Park. Metered lot across the street. Tucked in a parking lot on 52nd St., Dixie looks like an exploded garage sale. You might want to eat with your eyes first—coffee cans, bottles, signs, and even a gas pump decorate the walls. Check out the oyster po' boy sandwich smeared with New Orleans remoulade ($9.50). Open M-Th and Su 11am-10pm, F-Sa 11am-11pm. AmEx/D/MC/V. ❷

Manny's Coffee Shop & Deli, 1141 S. Jefferson St. (☎312-939-2855; www.mannysdeli.com), 1 block east of I-90, off the Madison St. exit. Serving up "Chicago's best corned beef since 1942," this enormous and locally worshipped kosher coffee shop serves up huge and affordably priced servings, cafeteria-style. 2 eggs and corned beef hash $6. Open M-Sa 5am-8pm. ❶

LINCOLN PARK

Penny's Noodle Shop, 950 W. Diversey Pkwy. (☎773-281-8448). One of the best budget options in town, Penny's presents generous portions of Asian noodles (all under $7) in a bright, inviting setting. Open M-Th and Su 11am-10pm, F-Sa 11am-10:30pm. MC/V. ❷

Cafe Ba-Ba-Reeba!, 2024 N. Halsted St. (☎773-935-5000), just north of Armitage. With a rich and dark wood interior and artistic signs announcing upcoming wine tastings and cooking classes, Ba-Ba-Reeba has unbeatable tapas ($4-8) and frequent flamenco performances. Reservations recommended. Open M-Th 5-10pm, F 5pm-midnight, Sa 11am-midnight, Su 11am-10pm. AmEx/D/MC/V. ❷

BUCKTOWN/WICKER PARK

🌑 **The Smoke Daddy**, 1804 W. Division St. (☎773-772-6656), in Wicker Park. Pulled pork ($8.50) and finger-lickin' rib platters ($12.25-22) definitely justify the neon "WOW" sign dangling out front. Live blues and jazz daily 10pm. Open M-W and Su 11:30am-1am, Th-Sa 11:30am-11pm. AmEx/MC/V. ❸

Alliance Bakery & Cafe, 1736 W. Division St. (☎773-278-0366). When the owners of an 80-year-old Polish bakery scrape together the cash to buy an adjacent storefront next to their bakery, you might expect them to use it for storing flour. In Wicker Park, however, they have converted the space into a luminous coffeehouse where 20-somethings type away at their laptops. Open M-Sa 6am-9pm, Su 7am-9pm. AmEx/MC/V. ❶

Handlebar, 2311 W. North Ave. (☎773-384-9546). Launched in 2003 by a local brewer who loved bicycling, Handlebar features bar stools made out of the rims of bicycle wheels. Dive into a dish of West African groundnut stew ($8.75) or swing by for hearty brunch Sa-Su. Open M-W 11am-midnight, Th-F 11am-2am, Sa 10am-2am, Su 10am-midnight. AmEx/D/MC/V. ❷

🄶 SIGHTS

Tourist brochures, bus tours, and strolls through the downtown area reveal only a fraction of Chicago's eclectic attractions. Chicago's sights range from well-publicized museums to undiscovered back streets, from towering skyscrapers to sunny beaches and parks. Seeing it all requires some off-the-beaten-path exploration. Fortunately, Chicago is one of a growing number of cities worldwide to have a **Greeter** program (☎312-744-8000; www.chicagogreeter.com), whose volunteer staff of knowledgeable Chicagoans will show you around.

THE LOOP

When the Great Fire of 1871 razed Chicago's downtown, the burgeoning metropolis had an opportunity to start anew. Bounded by the river on one side and Lake Michigan on the other, the city was forced to build up rather than out. Drawing on new technologies, including steel-frame construction and the elevator brake, the Windy City assembled a daring skyline regarded today as one of America's most elegant. Visitors can take a crash course on columns and cornices through tours organized by the **Chicago Architecture Foundation**, 224 S. Michigan Ave. The foundation offers more than 80 different tours including river cruises, walking tours, and bus tours. Led by knowledgeable docents, the tours are an excellent introduction not only to Chicago's architectural history but also to its social and cultural past. Highlights include the stained-glass windows of the Marquette Building, the Art Deco flourishes of the Board of Trade, and the revolutionary aesthetics of Mies van der Rohe. (☎312-922-3432; www.architecture.org. Tickets start at $5 for walking tours, $28 for the river cruise.)

SEARS TOWER. The 1454 ft. tall **Sears Tower** is undoubtedly Chicago's most recognizable landmark. Early in 1997, the Petronas Towers in Malaysia edged out the Sears Tower as the tallest building in the world; however, the tower can still claim the highest occupied floor as well as its own zip code. The ear-popping elevator ride to the 103rd-floor skydeck earns visitors a view of four states on a clear day. *(233 S. Wacker Dr.; enter on Jackson St. ☎312-875-9696; www.theskydeck.com. Open daily Apr.-Sept. 10am-10pm; Oct.-Mar. 10am-8pm. Lines usually at least 1hr. $13, ages 3-11 $9.50)*

THE PLAZA. The **Chase Tower** (formerly the Bank One Building) is one of the world's largest bank buildings, luring longing gazes skyward with its diamond-shaped, diagonal slope. *(10 S. Dearborn St.)* Back on the ground, Marc Chagall's vivid mural *The Four Seasons* lines the block and defines a public space used for concerts and lunchtime entertainment. One block north, you'll find the Methodist **Chicago Temple,** once Chicago's tallest building. *(77 W. Washington St., at the corner of Clark and Washington St. ☎312-236-4548; www.chicagotemple.org. Free.)*

STATE STREET. State and Madison St., the most famous intersection of "State Street, that great street," is the focal point of the Chicago street grid as well as another architectural mecca. Louis Sullivan's signature **Carson Pirie Scott** store is adorned with ornate ironwork and wide Chicago windows. Sullivan's other masterpiece, the **Auditorium Building,** now a part of Roosevelt University, sits several blocks south at the corner of Congress St. and Michigan Ave. Once Chicago's tallest building, it typifies Sullivan's obsession with form and function, housing a hotel and an opera house that boasts the world's finest acoustics.

LAKESIDE. Grant Park, covering 14 lakefront blocks east of Michigan Ave., follows the 19th-century French park style: symmetrical and ordered, with corners, a fountain, and wide promenades. The Grant Park Concert Society hosts free summer concerts in the **Petrillo Music Shell.** *(520 S. Michigan Ave. ☎312-742-4763.)* Colored lights illuminate **Buckingham Fountain** 9-11pm. Just to the north, the new **Millennium Park** also hosts free concerts and performances as well as exercise and dance classes. *(☎312-742-1168; www.millenniumpark.org.)*

OTHER ARCHITECTURAL WONDERS. Burnham and Root's **Monadnock Building** deserves a glance for its alternating bays of purple and brown rock. *(53 W. Jackson Blvd.)* The $144 million **Harold Washington Library Center** is a researcher's dream come true as well as a postmodern architectural delight. *(400 S. State St. ☎312-747-4300. Open M-Th 9am-7pm, F-Sa 9am-4:30pm, Su 1-4:30pm.)* On the north side of the Loop, the glass **State of Illinois Building** offers an elevator ride to the top that gives a thrilling view of a sloping atrium, circular floors, and hundreds of employees.

NEAR NORTH

MAGNIFICENT MILE. Chicago counts Paris as one of its sister cities, and the Magnificent Mile must be the Windy City's answer to the Champs-Élysées. Expensive shopping on the order of Tiffany and Cartier lines the stretch of N. Michigan Ave. between the Chicago River and Oak St. Several of these retail stores were designed by the country's foremost architects and merit a look. At Pearson Ave., the squat **Chicago Water Tower** and **Pumping Station,** built in 1869, were the only buildings in the area to survive the Great Chicago Fire. One block north, the **John Hancock Center** has an exoskeleton of steel girders and glass that casts a stunning figure on the skyline. *(875 N. Michigan Ave. ☎312-751-3681. Observation deck open daily 9am-11pm. $15, ages 4-11 $9, seniors $13.)*

NAVY PIER. With a concert pavilion, dining options, nightspots, sightseeing boats, a spectacular Ferris wheel, a crystal garden with palm trees, and an IMAX theater, the mile-long pier is like Las Vegas, Mardi Gras, a Shakespeare festival, and a state fair all rolled into one. Explorers can rent bicycles to navigate the Windy City or hop on a free trolley to State St.; consider taking advantage of reasonable parking rates on the pier and ride in to get a close-up of downtown. *(600 E. Grand Ave. ☎ 312-595-7437 or 800-595-7437; www.navypier.com. Open daily May-Sept. M-Th and Su 10am-10pm, F-Sa 10am-midnight; Sept.-Apr. M-Th and Su 10am-8pm, F-Sa 10am-10pm.)*

LINCOLN PARK

⬛Lincoln Park proper extends across 5 mi. of lakefront on the north side, with winding paths and natural groves of trees. The **Lincoln Park Zoo** is usually filled with herds of children fascinated by the gorillas and lions. (☎312-742-2000; www.lpzoo.com. Open Nov.-Mar. daily 9am-5pm; Apr.-Oct. M-F 9am-6pm, Sa-Su 9am-7pm. Free.) Next door, the **Lincoln Park Conservatory** is a veritable glass palace of plants from various ecosystems. (☎312-742-7736. Open daily 9am-5pm. Free.) On the north side, Lake Michigan lures swimmers and sunbathers to **Lincoln Park Beach** and **Oak Street Beach.** Beware, though: the rock ledges are restricted areas, and swimming from them is illegal. Although the beaches are patrolled 9am-9:30pm, they can be unsafe after dark. The **Chicago Parks District** (☎312-742-7529) has further info.

OAK PARK

Gunning for the title of the most fantastic suburb in the US, Oak Park, 10 mi. west of downtown, is a must-see destination for any architecture aficionado—just take I-290 W. to Harlem St. **The Oak Park Visitors Center,** 158 N. Forest Ave., offers both metered parking and garage parking for $0.25 per hr. (☎708-848-1500 or 888-625-7275; www.visitoakpark.com. Open daily in summer 10am-5pm; in winter 10am-4pm.)

UNITY TEMPLE. When Frank Lloyd Wright designed this cubical church, his "jewel box," he declared it the beginning of modern architecture. It was a personal project for Wright, who was a member of the congregation that moved into the completed building. *(875 Lake St. 1 mi. north of I-290 on Harlem Ave., turn right on Lake St. and follow it ½ mi. to Kenilworth Ave. ☎ 708-383-8873; www.unitytemple.utrf.org. Open M-F 10:30am-4:30pm, Sa-Su 1-4pm. Tours M-F by appointment; Sa-Su 1, 2, 3pm. $8, students and seniors $6, under 5 free.)*

FRANK LLOYD WRIGHT HOME AND STUDIO. Frank Lloyd Wright's house showcases the evolution of his creative ideas, from conception to reality. Visitors can see not only the studio where he planned his work but also his house, which was the constantly evolving subject of his architectural experimentation. *(951 Chicago Ave. From I-290 and Harlem, go north to Chicago Ave. and head east for 3 blocks. ☎ 708-848-1976; www.gowright.org. Open daily 10am-5pm. 45min. tours M-F 11am, 1, 3pm; Sa-Su every 20min. 11am-3:30pm. $12, ages 11-18 and seniors $10, ages 4-10 $5.)*

ERNEST HEMINGWAY BIRTHPLACE AND MUSEUM. Throughout the year, fans flock to the Ernest Hemingway Birthplace and Museum to take part in the many events honoring the architect of the modern American novel. The museum features rare photos of Hemingway, his letters, and other memorabilia. *(Birthplace 339 N. Oak Park Ave. Museum 200 N. Oak Park Ave. ☎ 708-848-2222; www.ehfop.org. Open M-F and Su 1-5pm, Sa 10am-5pm. $8, students $6.)*

🏛 MUSEUMS

Chicago's museums range from some of the largest collections in the world to one-room galleries. The first five listings (known as the Big Five) provide a diverse array of exhibits, while a handful of smaller collections target specific interests. Lake Shore Dr. has been diverted around Grant Park, linking the Field Museum, Adler, and Shedd. This compound, known as **Museum Campus,** offers a free shuttle between museums. Visitors who plan on seeing the Big Five (not including the Art Institute of Chicago) plus the Hancock Observatory can save money by purchasing a **CityPass** that grants admission to the sights for nine days as well as discount coupons for some restaurants and shops. (☎888-330-5008; www.citypass.com. $59, ages 4-11 $49.)

⬛ART INSTITUTE OF CHICAGO. It's easy to feel overwhelmed in this expansive museum, with a collection spanning four millennia of art from Asia, Africa, Europe, and beyond. Make sure to see Chagall's stunning *America Windows*—the artist's stained-glass tribute to the country's bicentennial—as well as Grant Wood's *American Gothic*, Edward Hopper's *Nighthawks*, and Monet's *Wheat-*

stacks. *(111 S. Michigan Ave., at Adams St., in Grant Park. ☎312-443-3600; www.artic.edu/aic. Open M-W 10:30am-5pm, Th-F 10:30am-9pm, Sa-Su 10am-5pm. $12, students $7, under 12 free. Th-F 5-9pm free.)*

SHEDD AQUARIUM. The Shedd, the world's largest indoor aquarium, has over 6600 species of fish and marine life in 206 tanks. The Oceanarium features beluga whales, dolphins, seals, and penguins in a giant pool that appears to flow into Lake Michigan. See piranhas and tropical fish of the rainforest in the Amazon Rising exhibit or wave to sharks in the Caribbean Reef exhibit. *(1200 S. Lake Shore Dr., in Grant Park. ☎312-939-2438; www.sheddaquarium.org. Open May-Sept. daily 9am-6pm; Sept.-May M-F 9am-5pm, Sa-Su 9am-6pm. $25, ages 3-11 $18.)*

FIELD MUSEUM OF NATURAL HISTORY. Sue, the Field Museum's mascot and the largest *Tyrannosaurus rex* skeleton ever unearthed, towers over geology, anthropology, botany, and zoology exhibits. Other highlights include Egyptian mummies and an exhibit on the cultures and environments of the African continent. *(1400 S. Lake Shore Dr., at Roosevelt Rd. in Grant Park. ☎312-922-9410; www.fieldmuseum.org. Open daily 9am-5pm. Last entry 4pm. $14, students and seniors $11, ages 4-11 $9.)*

MUSEUM OF SCIENCE AND INDUSTRY. This museum features the Apollo 8 command module, a full-size replica of a coal mine, and a host of interactive exhibits on topics from DNA to the Internet. Stop by the Yesterday's Main Street exhibit for a scoop of ice cream at the 1920s-style parlor. *(57th St. and Lake Shore Dr., in Hyde Park. ☎773-684-1414; www.msichicago.org. Open June-Aug. M-Sa 9:30-5:30 and Su 11am-5:30pm; Sept.-May M-Sa 9:30am-4pm, Su 11am-4pm. $13, ages 3-11 $9, seniors $12.)*

ADLER PLANETARIUM. Traditional and digital sky shows bring you face to face with the awesome glory of the cosmos at America's first planetarium, now over 75 years old. Aspiring astronauts can learn their weight on Mars, read the news from space, and explore a medieval observatory. The more sedate can simply sit back and marvel at the breathtaking beauty of the night sky in the Sky Theater. *(1300 S. Lake Shore Dr., on Museum Campus, in Grant Park. ☎312-922-7827; www.adlerplanetarium.org. Open*

daily in summer 9:30-6pm; in winter 9:30am-4:30pm. $10, ages 4-17 $6, seniors $8.)*

MUSEUM OF CONTEMPORARY ART. The white-and-chrome immensity of this cutting-edge museum provides an ideal backdrop for the ambitious rotating exhibitions within. The beautiful view of Lake Michigan is the only unchanging feature in the MCA's ultramodern exhibition space. See Warhol's iconic Marilyn or a selection of Calder's mobiles. Call to see what is on display—the collection also includes works by Bruce Nauman, Francis Bacon, and Joseph Beuys. *(220 E. Chicago Ave., 1 block east of Michigan Ave. ☎312-280-2660; www.mcachicago.org. Open Tu 10am-8pm, W-Su 10am-5pm. $10, students and seniors $6, under 12 free. Tu free.)*

MUSEUM OF HOLOGRAPHY. This unconventional museum explores the wild world of holograms, and includes truly fantastic hologram pictures of famous people. *(1134 W. Washington Blvd., just west of the Loop. ☎312-226-1007; www.holographiccenter.com. Open W-Su 12:30-5pm. $4, under 12 $3, under 6 free.)*

INTERNATIONAL MUSEUM OF SURGICAL SCIENCE. This quirkily specific museum details the history of health care around the world, from a room filled with the original apparatus for X-rays to a fully tricked-out apothecary. If you've never seen a human skull, this is your chance. *(1524 N. Lake Shore Dr., at North Ave. ☎312-642-6502; www.imss.org. Open May-Sept. Tu-Su 9am-4pm; Oct.-Apr. Tu-Sa 10am-4pm. $9, students $5.)*

🎭 ENTERTAINMENT

The free weeklies *Chicago Reader* and *New City*, available in many bars, record stores, and restaurants, list the latest events. The *Reader* comes out each Thursday and reviews all major shows with times and ticket prices. *Chicago* magazine includes theater reviews alongside exhaustive club, music, dance, and opera listings. The *Chicago Tribune* includes an entertainment section every Friday. *Gay Chicago* provides info on the hottest scenes.

COMEDY AND THEATER

One of the foremost theater centers of North America, Chicago boasts more than 150 theaters featuring everything from blockbuster musicals to off-color parodies. Downtown, the recently formed **Theater District** centers on State and Randolph St. and includes the larger venues in the city. Smaller theaters are scattered throughout Chicago. Most tickets are expensive. Half-price tickets are sold on the day of performances at Hot Tix booths, including at 78 W. Randolph St. (open Tu-F 8:30am-6pm, Sa 10am-6pm, Su noon-6pm) and at the Water Works Visitor Center, 163 E. Pearson St. (☎312-559-1212; open Tu-Sa 10am-6pm, Su noon-5pm). **Ticketmaster** supplies tickets for many theaters; ask about discounts at all Chicago shows. (☎312-559-1212; www.broadwayinchicago.com).

The "Off-Loop" theaters on the North Side put on excellent original productions, with tickets usually under $18.

Steppenwolf Theater, 1650 N. Halsted St. (☎312-335-1650; www.steppenwolf.org). Both Gary Sinise and John Malkovich got their starts at the Steppenwolf, a company devoted to producing "dynamic and exciting theater."

Bailiwick Repertory, 1229 W. Belmont Ave. (☎773-883-1090; www.bailiwick.org). An experimental studio space.

Second City, 1616 N. Wells St. (☎312-664-4032; www.secondcity.com), at North Ave. The most famous comedy club in town, Second City spoofs Chicago life and politics. Alums include Bill Murray, John Candy, and John Belushi. Most nights, a free improv session follows the show.

Comedy Sportz, 929 W. Belmont Ave. (☎773-549-8080). Watch improv actors compete to bust your gut at Comedy Sportz, where 2 teams of comedians create sketches based on audience suggestions. Tickets $19. Shows Th 8pm, F 8, 10pm, Sa 6, 8, 10pm.

DANCE, MUSIC, AND OPERA

Auditorium Theatre, 50 E. Congress Pkwy. (☎312-922-2110; www.auditoriumtheatre.org). Ballet, comedy, live theater, and musicals are performed here. Box office open M-F noon-6pm.

Chicago Symphony Orchestra, 220 S. Michigan Ave. (☎312-294-3000; www.cso.org). You can hear the sounds of the world-famous Chicago Symphony Orchestra at Symphony Center.

Ballet Chicago (☎312-251-8838; www.balletchicago.org). The ballet performs regularly throughout theaters in Chicago.

Lyric Opera of Chicago, 20 N. Wacker Dr. (☎312-332-2244; www.lyricopera.org). Performs Sept.-Mar. at the Civic Opera House.

Grant Park Music Festival, Millennium Park (☎312-742-4763; www.grantparkmusicfestival.com). Chicago has figured out a way to encourage classical-music listening—free concerts. From mid-June through late Aug., the acclaimed Grant Park Symphony Orchestra plays a few free evening concerts per week. W-Su; schedule varies.

SPORTS

Cubs, Wrigley Field, 1060 W. Addison St. (☎773-404-2827; www.cubs.com). Chicago's National League baseball team. Tickets $17-60.

White Sox, US Cellular Field, 333 W. 35th St. (☎312-674-1000. www.chicago.whitesox.mlb.com). Chicago's storied American League baseball team. Tickets $14-55.

Bears, Soldier Field, 425 E. McFetridge Dr. (☎888-792-3277; www.chicagobears.com). Chicago's pro football team. Tickets $68+.

Bulls, United Center, 1901 W. Madison St. (☎312-943-5800; www.nba.com/bulls), just west of the Loop. Chicago's basketball team has won 3 NBA championships. Tickets $30-450.

Blackhawks (☎312-455-4500; www.blackhawks.nhl.com). Chicago's professional hockey team takes over the United Center when the Bulls aren't playing. Tickets $25-100.

NIGHTLIFE

Chicago is proud of the innumerable blues performers who have played here. Jazz, folk, reggae, and punk clubs groove, step, jam, and pogo all over the **North Side.** The **Bucktown/Wicker Park** area stays open late with bars and clubs. Some of the best dancing in town is at **Rush Street** and **Division Street.** Full of bars, cafes, and bistros, **Lincoln Park** is frequented by singles and young couples, both gay and straight. The center of gay culture is between 3000 and 4500 **North Halsted Street.** For more upscale raving and discoing, there are plenty of clubs near **River North,** in **Riverwest,** and on **Fullerton Street.**

BARS AND BLUES JOINTS

☒ **The Green Mill,** 4802 N. Broadway Ave. (☎773-878-5552; www.greenmilljazz.com). Once a Prohibition-era speakeasy favored by Al Capone, the Green Mill has phased out gangsters and gun-runners in favor of elegant live jazz and is said to be the oldest continuously run jazz club in the world. The jam sessions on weekends after main acts finish (no cover) are reason enough to chill until the wee hours. Cover $6-12. Open M-F noon-4am, Sa noon-5am, Su 11am-4am. AmEx.

The Matchbox, 770 N. Milwaukee Ave. (☎312-666-9292). Probably the slenderest bar in the world and certainly one of the most endearing drinking spots in the whole city. Come here if you need some lovin'—apparently the sheer intimacy of the place has led to many marriages. Mixed drinks and outdoor seating too. Open M-F and Su 4pm-2am, Sa 4pm-3am. AmEx/MC/V.

Kingston Mines, 2548 N. Halsted St. (☎773-477-4646). Mick Jagger and Bob Dylan have been known to frequent this venerable club, which has dueling blues acts alternating on 2 stages. Live blues daily from 9:30pm. Appetizers $5. Cover $8-15. Open M-F and Su 8pm-4am, Sa 8pm-5am. AmEx/D/MC/V.

The Hideout, 1354 W. Wabansia Ave. (☎773-227-4433; www.hideoutchicago.com). Tucked away in a municipal truck parking lot, this bar and performance space lures hipsters with indie rock shows and families with a late-Sept. block party. Cover Tu-F $5-10. Open M 8pm-2am, Tu-F 4pm-2am, Sa 7pm-3am. Cash only.

B.L.U.E.S., 2519 N. Halsted St. (☎773-528-1012). Chicago's oldest blues bar focuses on local blues acts and packs in patrons elbow to elbow on weekends. Albert King, Bo Diddley, Wolfman Washington, and Dr. John have played here. Live blues nightly 9:30pm-2am. Cover M-Th $6-8, F-Sa $8-10. Open M-F and Su 8pm-2am, Sa 8pm-3am. AmEx/D/MC/V.

DANCE CLUBS

Berlin, 954 W. Belmont Ave. (☎773-348-4975; www.berlinchicago.com), just off Halsted St. Anything goes at Berlin, a black-and-neon, gay-friendly mainstay of Chicago's nightlife. Crowds pulsate to house dance music and disco nights. 1st Su of each month hosts an ever-popular Madonna night. Ladies night W. Cover F-Sa $7. Open M-F 5pm-4am, Sa 7pm-5am, Su 10pm-4am. Cash only.

Funky Buddha Lounge, 728 W. Grand Ave. (☎312-666-1695). Trendy, eclectic dance club where hip hop and funk blend with leopard and velvet decor. Serves homemade organic aphrodisiac and energy drinks such as Kombucha, "the immortal elixir of ancient Asia." Cover $20. Open M-W 10pm-2am, Th-F 9pm-2am, Sa 9pm-3am, Su 6pm-2am. AmEx/MC/V.

The Apartment, 2251 N. Lincoln Ave. (☎773-348-5100). On a street packed with generic pubs, this heavily themed club stands out. Sit on sofas in front of the fireplace and play video games, lounge in the master bedroom, or chat in the faux kitchen. A duckie-curtained bathtub of beer satisfies most requests, but, if you have more mixed cravings, just head downstairs to the Lion's Head Pub. No cover. Open W-F 9am-2am, Sa 9am-3am. AmEx/D/MC/V.

Hydrate, 3458 N. Halsted St. (☎773-975-9244; www.hydratechicago.com). This red-lit club is a favorite of Halsted St. Smiling, heavily muscled male bartenders bring in, unsurprisingly, a smiling, heavily male crowd. $1 drinks M. Drag show W 9:30pm. Go-go dancers nightly. No cover.

Spin, 3200 Halsted St. (☎773-327-7711; www.spin-nightclub.com), at Belmont St. Themed nights and a fabulous disco ball make Spin a popular club on the gay scene in the Lincoln Park area. Free pool M. $1 drinks W. Shower contest F. Open M-Tu and Th-F 4pm-2am, W 8pm-2am, Sa 2pm-3am, Su 2pm-2am. Cash only.

☙ FESTIVALS

The city celebrates summer on a grand scale. During the first week in June, the **Blues Festival** celebrates the city's soulful music. The **Chicago Gospel Festival** takes place in late May or early June, and Nashville moves north for the **Country Music Festival** (date varies). In late June or early July, the **Taste of Chicago** festival cooks for eight days. Seventy-plus restaurants set up booths with endless samples in Grant Park, while crowds chow down to the blast of big-name bands. The Taste's fireworks are the city's biggest. The **¡Viva Chicago!** Latin music festival steams up in late August, while the **Chicago Jazz Festival** scats over Labor Day weekend. All festivals center on Grant Park's Petrillo Music Shell and Millennium Center. (Check the Mayor's Office's Special Events Hotline for more information: ☎312-744-3370; www.cityofchicago.com/specialevents.com.) Pick up an official visitor's guide at the visitors center for a list of upcoming events. The **Ravinia Festival**, in the Highland Park area, is the oldest outdoor music festival in the country. During the festival's 14-week season (June-Sept.), the Chicago Symphony Orchestra, ballet troupes, folk and jazz musicians, and comedians perform. On certain nights, the Orchestra allows free lawn admission with student ID. (☎847-266-5100; www.ravinia.org. Shows 8pm, occasionally 4:30 and 7pm; call ahead. Lawn seats $10-15, other seats $20-75.)

THE ROAD TO RIVERSIDE: 14 MI.

Just west of the Art Institute of Chicago on Adams St., an unimposing road sign marks the beginning of "The Mother Road," **Route 66.** To begin at the very beginning, follow **Lake Shore Drive** to **Jackson Street,** then turn west on **Adams Street.** Follow Adams St. 2 mi. west until you hit **Ogden Street,** angle left on Ogden St., and continue 10 mi. to **Harlem Avenue (Route 43).** Turn right on Harlem Ave. to reach Riverside.

RIVERSIDE   ☎ 708

Run by the Stanga family for over 20 years, the **Riverside Family Restaurant ❷**, 3422 S. Har-

lem Ave., serves giant portions of Czech food for cheap, cheap, cheap. Enormous plates of wienerschnitzel, duck, or pork come with delicious, warm rye bread, your choice of sauerkraut, applesauce, cabbage, or beets, plus dessert—all for an astounding $8-10. Be sure to try the apricot kolache ($1) for dessert. (☎708-442-6055. Open Tu-Sa 11am-8pm, Su 11am-7pm. Cash only.)

THE ROAD TO BERWYN: 3 MI.

From Riverside, continue north on **Harlem Avenue.**

BERWYN   ☎ 708

Nothing starts a roadtrip quite like a jolt of wry sobriety in the form of a 50 ft. tower of impaled cars in the middle of a parking lot. The **"Spindle,"** as the structure is named, is just one of several artistic statements scattered throughout the Cermak Plaza in the town of Berwyn. Don't miss the flattened VW as you enter from Harlem Ave. Find it on Harlem Ave., 1 mi. north of the Ogden St. intersection. Turn right after 26th St.

THE ROAD TO LEMONT: 20 MI.

Turn left on **Harlem Avenue** and drive 10 mi. south. Then turn right onto **Joliet Road.** Rte. 66 is well marked through these parts—look for the brown-and-white signs by the roadside leading you down "Historic Rte. 66." To follow the original Rte. 66 alignment, follow Joliet Rd. for 7 mi. until it merges with I-55 where Rte.

PRESERVING THE LEGACY OF THE MOTHER ROAD

"The Main Street of America" was always much more than simply a route heading west. In its day, Rte. 66 also nurtured an entire set of businesses that housed, fed, and supported hundreds of thousands of westward migrants over several decades. Since 1985, the year when Rte. 66 was decommissioned and replaced by I-44 as the main artery leading from the Midwest to California, many businesses along the road have fallen into decline. In rural areas, establishments have been abandoned, while in urban areas buildings have been threatened by new development. But in the face of these difficulties, courageous and dedicated souls have undertaken the task of preserving Rte. 66. All along the route, you will find preservation projects supported by a variety of different organizations and people, from the federal government right down to individual Rte. 66 diehards. Preservation projects can operate with various strategies. Sometimes buildings are preserved as they originally were, fossilized like museum exhibits. Elsewhere, they have been converted to new uses. Another, and more difficult option, is to convert a disused building back to its original use. It's not just buildings that are the focus of preservation efforts; in areas where a very old piece of the road still exists, the asphalt itself is being preserved and saved from being tarred over. (See www.historic66.com for a digest of all news

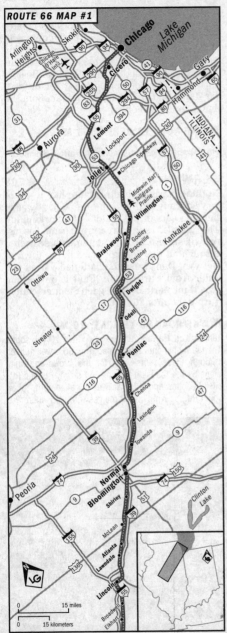

ROUTE 66 MAP #1

ROUTE 66

66 has been paved over. Continue on I-55 S./Rte. 66. Take Exit 271A for Lemont Rd. and drive south for 3 mi. Head west after crossing the bridge, where Lemont Rd. becomes State St., and turn left onto Main St.

LEMONT ☎ 630

Known locally as "the village of faith" due to the preponderance of churches, Lemont was a town born out of the canal-digging industry and used to be full of Irish, German, and Polish laborers (and the brothels and bars in which they spent their free time). This chapter of its history is gradually fading out of memory, but there are still some vestigial traces of its formative era. Almost out of place in its grandeur atop the hill overlooking Lemont, the lavishly carved **Hindu Temple of Greater Chicago,** 10915 Lemont Rd., 1 mi. north of downtown Lemont, is a religious and community center for the Hindus of Chicago. (☎630-972-0300. Open daily 9am-9pm.)

Tom's Place, 110 Stephen St., the oldest saloon bar in Lemont, was a watering hole for the canal diggers. (☎630-257-9875. Open daily 10am-2am. Cash only.) At the same location for 75 years in the various guises of pharmacy, garage sale, and convenience store, **Budnik's,** 400 Main St., sells everything from cigars to china and various local collectables. (☎630-257-6224.) Head to **Lemont Lanes Bowling Alley and Pizzeria,** 1015 State St., for some ball-hurling and excellent thin-crust pizza. (☎630-257-5426; www.vitoandnick.com.) **Nick's Tavern ❷,** 221 Main St., is the home of the Nickburger ($6) and features a cash register from 1908 and figurines that range from JFK to giant hamburgers. (☎630-257-6564. Open M-Sa 10am-midnight. Grill open until 10:30pm. Cash only.)

THE ROAD TO JOLIET: 14 MI.

Leave Lemont the only way you can: south on **I-55.** To continue following Rte. 66, exit I-55 8 mi. south of Lemont at **Exit 269.** Head south on **Joliet Road.** Joliet Rd. is marked as **Route 53,** but every mile or so you should see the easily distinguishable Historic Rte. 66 markers. Call it wild speculation, but 9 mi. south from picking up Joliet Rd. you'll find the **Ilinois State Police.** Hit the gas too hard here, and you might find yourself a quarter-mile down the road quicker than you expected, at one of Joliet's best known land-marks, the **Department of Corrections.**

JOLIET ☎815

For lunch or a tour of the Rte. 66 welcome center, stick to the north side of Joliet, though supermarkets, gas stations, and banks abound farther south. At the **Joliet Historical Museum and Welcome Center,** 204 N. Ottawa St., you can visit a drive-in movie and sit in a replica Corvette for the "Rte. 66 experience." (☎815-723-5201; www.jolietmuseum.org. Open Tu-Sa 10am-5pm, Su noon-5pm. $5, students and seniors $4, ages 4-17 $3.) A restored vaudeville theater guarded by massive two-story columns, the **Rialto Square Theatre,** 102 N. Chicago St., was designed to resemble the Hall of Mirrors at Versailles and is supposedly haunted. (☎815-726-6600. Box office open M-F 9am-5pm, Sa 9am-noon.) Three miles south of Joliet, racecar enthusiasts can watch the pros get their kicks at the **Chicagoland Speedway,** which sits on 930 acres and seats over 75,000. **Route 66 Raceway,** Chicagoland's sister track, is near. (☎815-727-7223; www.chicagolandspeedway.com.)

Follow the lunch crowd to the **Sandwich Shoppe ❶,** 79 N. Chicago St., for $5 subs or $4 salads. (☎815-723-8071. Open M-F 8am-2pm. Cash only.) The **Chicago Street Pub ❷,** 75 N. Chicago St., has classy beer ads and mirrors along with its reasonably priced fare. Try their flagship meal, the Guinness-braised beef stew ($8), while indulging in one of the 16 beers on tap. (☎815-727-7171; www.chicagost.com. Sandwiches $6.50. Live music M-Sa. Open M-F 11am-10pm, Sa 5-10pm, Su 1-8pm. MC/V.)

⚑ THE ROAD TO WILMINGTON: 16 MI.

Take **Ottawa Street** left. Follow signs for **Route 6 West, Route 53 South,** and **Route 66.** Expect to see a sea of corn stalks; they'll be "knee-high by the fourth of July."

WILMINGTON ☎815

From May to September, Mr. Van Duyne of the **Van Duyne Motel ❷,** 107 Bridge St., 1 mi. south of central Wilmington, offers canoe trips ($40) up the river and opens his Rte. 66 memorabilia-lined balcony for cookouts and socializing. The spotless rooms in the motel each come with mini-fridge, microwave, cable

TV, and bathroom in a beautiful and quiet spot overlooking the water. (☎815-476-2801. Singles $50. AmEx/D/MC/V.) Nothing says Rte. 66 like the 28 ft. tall **Gemini Giant,** the first of three giants you'll encounter along the way and the mascot of the **Launching Pad Drive-In ❶,** at the corner of Daniels St. and Rte. 66. Rte. 66 wallpaper and map-covered tabletops let you trace your path while enjoying tasty eats. (☎815-476-6535. Hamburgers $1.15. Shakes $2.10. Open daily 10am-9pm. Cash only.)

⚑ THE ROAD TO BRAIDWOOD: 4 MI.

Continue south on **Route 66.** Keep your eyes peeled for the fireflies that cavort through the fields at dusk.

BRAIDWOOD ☎815

Right by the tracks is the clean and comfortable **Braidwood Motel ❷,** 120 N. Washington St. Rooms have fridges, cable TV, microwave, and free Wi-Fi. (☎815-458-2321. Reception 24hr. Check-out 11am. Singles $35; doubles $45. AmEx/D/MC/V.) Elvis, Marilyn, James Dean, and Betty Boop welcome you to the parking lot of the **Polka Dot Drive-In ❶,** 222 N. Front St. Even without the celebrities, you could hardly miss the spinning, neon-pink sign of this chrome-and-checkered 50s diner, which was originally located in a white bus decorated with rainbow polka dots. Stop by on the first Saturday in August for the annual Rte. 66 roadster cruise. (☎815-458-3377. Burgers $2. Chicken $8.25. Open daily in summer 11am-9pm; in winter 11am-8pm. MC/V.)

⚑ THE ROAD TO GARDNER: 9 MI.

Continue south on **Route 66** for 6 mi. Turn right on **East Washington Street** to head into downtown Gardner.

GARDNER ☎815

From E. Washington St., follow the brown, historical directional signs to the **two-cell jail,** a local landmark. Built in 1906 and used through the 1960s, this tiny building holds an old cast-iron stove and just two small jail cells. Also on site are papers detailing the feats of the legendary Reverend Christiansen. (Open daily. Free.)

Find a haven of wall-scribbling at **Curley's,** 114 Depot St., an ancient beer-meets-arts-and-crafts establishment. (☎815-237-8060. Beer

$2. Open M 3pm-1:30am, Tu-Su 11am-1:30am. Cash only.) On your way into town, stop by the ▨**Riviera Restaurant ❷**, 5650 Rte. 53. "Al Capone passed gas here in 1932," proclaims the sign by the toilet in the bathroom, and Gene Kelly danced through the parking lot on his way to Hollywood. Watch out for resident ghost Charley. (☎815-237-2344. Kitchen open Tu-Th 5-9pm, F-Sa 5-10pm, Su 4-9pm. Bar opens Tu-Su at 1pm. MC/V.)

⚑ THE ROAD TO DWIGHT: 10 MI.

Heading south on **Route 66,** watch for turns in the road; they are all marked by familiar brown signs. Three miles south of Gardner, take a right onto **Route 53** and go over the railroad tracks, then follow the signs directing you left on **Route 66** 10 mi. later.

DWIGHT   ☎815

Another railroad town over the tracks, Dwight prides itself on its refurbished windmill. As you pass through the south end of town, the **Becker Marathon Gas Station** on the left dates back to 1932. To see downtown Dwight, head east toward the railroad tracks and turn right onto E. Main St. The massive Mother Road mural on the outside matches the part-"God Bless America," part-"God Bless Route 66" interior of the **Old 66 Family Restaurant ❷**, 105 S. Old 66, 2 mi. south of town. (☎815-584-2920. Burgers $4. Chicken bucket $10. Open M-Th and Su 5am-9pm, F-Sa 5am-10pm. D/MC/V.)

⚑ THE ROAD TO PONTIAC: 17 MI.

Continue south, following the brown **"Historic Route 66" signs.** Even where Rte. 66 has been paved over or routed under I-55, divergent rows of telephone poles peeling off into the distance reveal the old path of the Mother Road. Nine miles south of Dwight, you'll diverge from I-55 to follow the **railroad.** One mile into **Odell,** you'll see the **Standard Oil Company Gas Station** (with a sign proudly proclaiming "87 mi. from Chicago, 2361 from L.A."). This restored station was the recent winner of the "Best Preservation Project on All of Rte. 66" award in 2001. Don't roll in on an empty tank—you can fill up on 66 memorabilia, but not on gas.

PONTIAC   ☎815

Famed for its ornate courthouse and extensive veterans memorials, Pontiac has several elegant swinging bridges abutting the Chatauqua Recreation Area; the popular saying is: "Pontiac has three swinging bridges, and we're a swinging town!" The **Pontiac Route 66 Museum,** 110 W. Howard St., focuses on the outstanding individuals, couples, and families who have helped to define and shape Route 66 over the decades: those who helped build and preserve it, policemen who patrolled it, and the people who ran the businesses that housed and fed travellers who went along it. (☎815-844-4566. Apr.-Oct. M-F 9am-5pm, Sa-Su 10am-4pm; Nov.-Mar. M-F 11am-3pm, Sa-Su 10am-4pm. Free.)

When Rte. 66 was re-routed away from the railroad tracks, the whole **Old Log Cabin Food and Spirits** building, just off the northbound side of Rte. 66, was jacked up and turned around to keep it facing the road. Decorated with discarded telephone poles by the founding Selotis brothers in the early 1920s, today the log cabin is one of the route's dining highlights; it puts kitsch to shame with its genuine yet casual reverence for the old road and road-knowledgeable staff. (☎815-842-2908. Shockingly bright bottles of Rte. 66 pop $1.60. Open M-Sa 5am-8pm.)

⚑ THE ROAD TO BLOOMINGTON/NORMAL: 32 MI.

Continue south on **Route 66** with railroad tracks and stocky telephone poles to your left. After 7 mi., look to the right to see signs detailing a historic stretch of original 66 known as **Dead Man's Curve,** which was an accident-heavy right-angle turn until it was altered after WWII. Shortly afterwards, check out the six bright-orange original Burma Shave ads from 1927, spaced 100 paces apart and reading, "The wolf—is shaved—so neat and trim—Red Riding Hood—is chasing him—Burma Shave." Twenty-nine miles south of Pontiac, Rte. 66 is not a straight shot; pay close attention to signs.

BLOOMINGTON/NORMAL   ☎309

The "twin cities" of Bloomington and Normal, about 127 mi. from Chicago, are home to an array of food and lodging establishments as well as a significant student population, thanks to the presence of **Illinois State University** in Normal and **Illinois Wesleyan University** in Bloomington. If driving is already getting you down, take advantage of the **Constitution Trail,** a joint Bloomington/Normal recreational venture, including over 20 mi. of trails throughout the two cities. Built for Supreme Court Justice and longtime Lincoln associate David Davis, the **David Davis Mansion** displays the elegant home and lifestyle of one of Illinois's most celebrated politicians. Be sure to see the bathroom, the height of modernity in its day but amusingly old-fashioned from today's viewpoint. (☎309-828-1084. Tours W-Su 9am-4pm. Suggested donation $4, children $2.) The majestic **Ewing Manor,** 48 Sunset Rd., at the corner of Towanda Ave. and Emerson St., looms like a castle above the surrounding wooded area. Although visitors can tour the manor only by appointment, in the summer locals gather for a **Shakespeare festival** put on in the theater out back. The manor has two lovely gardens, one Japanese and the other Elizabethan. (☎309-829-6333; www. ewingmanor.ilstu.edu. Shakespeare festival ☎309-438-8974; www.thefestival.org. From $20, students from $16.)

Standard chain motels are found around Normal and Bloomington, particularly to the north near Normal. For a break from roadside digs, visit the stately, antique-laden **Davis Rose Inn ❸,** 1001 E. Jefferson St., across from the David Davis Mansion in Bloomington. (☎309-829-6854; www.davisroseinn. com. Rooms F-Su from $99, M-Th from $59.) Playboy ranked **Pub II ❶,** 102 N. Linden St., among its top 100 campus bars. Sports posters galore and video games ensure that Pub II doesn't disappoint its fun-loving patrons. (☎309-452-0699. Burgers $2.70. Open in summer M-Th 11am-1am, F-Sa 11am-2am, Su 4pm-1am; in winter M-Th 11am-1am, F-Sa 11am-2am, Su noon-1am. MC/V.)

◪ THE ROAD TO SHIRLEY: 9 MI.

From Bloomington, head south on **Center Street** through town, following the signs toward I-55. 4 mi. south of where Bloomington and Normal meet, things get tricky. Rte. 66 effectively doubles back on itself, finally heading south again on **Beich Road,** parallel to I-55. Just hold on tight and follow the signs.

SHIRLEY   ☎309

Signs advertise no services in Shirley, but keep going to the 18-acre **Funks Grove Nature Preserve.** Funks Grove produces some of the finest maple sirop in the Midwest. And, yes, they do mean "sirop"—according to the FDA, "sirop" with an "i" means it's 100% natural. To buy the sweet stuff, continue a half-mile south of Funk's Grove to the small store. (☎309-874-3360. Maple candy $1.75. Open by chance or appointment.) Follow the signs down Funks Grove Rd. to the **Funks Grove Church and Cemetery,** 1 mi. off Rte. 66. Behind the 1864 church is a modest monument to the more than 50 Irish immigrants who came to Illinois in the 1850s to help construct the Chicago and Alton Railroad. Across the road, in the **Church of the Templed Trees,** felled trunks form the pews and stumps the altar of an outdoor sanctuary. The friendly folks at the **Sugar Grove Nature Center** will show you everything you ever wanted to know about sugar. The center is closed in winter, but butterfly tours, firefly campfires, and other activities are free and open to the public May-Sept. (☎309-874-2174; www.funksgrove.org.)

At the junction of I-55 and US 36, 4 mi. farther down Rte. 66, the epic truck stop **Dixie Trucker's Home ❷** keeps its parking lot rumbling with rigs, gargantuan portions, and all-day breakfast. Also on-site is the **Route 66 Hall of Fame,** with Polaroid pictures of the hundreds of truckers who have passed through. (☎309-874-3399. Burgers $5. Open 24hr.)

◪ THE ROAD TO LINCOLN: 26 MI.

Continue south on **Route 66.** Just off the road is the small town of **Atlanta,** where you can see the **Hot Dog Giant,** the second of three iconic fiberglass **Muffler Men** on Rte. 66. A few yards away, Atlanta's three-in-one **1908 Clocktower, Library, and Museum** is definitely worth a glimpse. Twenty-three miles south of Bloomington, you'll pass **Lawndale** and enter Lincoln.

LINCOLN   ☎217

The only town to be named for Abraham Lincoln during his lifetime, the town of Lincoln is home to a gleaming white courthouse and refurbished movie theater. History buffs can visit the **Postville Courthouse,** a careful reproduction of the original courthouse Lincoln visited twice a year as a lawyer in 1840. (☎217-732-8930. Open Tu-Sa Mar.-Oct. noon-5pm; Nov.-Feb. noon-4pm. Suggested donation $2, children $1.)

Campsites at McMillan's **Camp-a-While ●**, 1779 1250 Ave., 1 mi. north of Lincoln and 2 mi. west of Rte. 66, have a great deal of privacy in a beautiful and shady location amid cornfields. Sites include hookups, hot showers, laundry, and laptop Internet connections. There's also a dump station. (☎217-732-8840. Tent sites $10; RV sites $22. Cash only.)

⛟ THE ROAD TO SPRINGFIELD: 29 MI.

Continue south on **Route 66**. As you pass through Broadwell, stop by the **Pig Hip Restaurant Museum**. Now retired after serving thousands of Pig Hip sandwiches from 1937 to 1991, Ernie, "the Old Coot on 66," still loves talking to travelers. Nine miles past Broadwell, turn right on **Elm Street**. About 1 mi. later, turn right, then turn right again. Follow **I-55** to **Exit 105**, passing through Sherman, to reach Springfield.

SPRINGFIELD   ☎217

Home of Abraham Lincoln and the corn dog, Springfield could not be any more American. Lincoln-mania is the tourist focus of the town, but, amid the dated storefronts of Fifth St. and under the domes of the stately legislative buildings, business—primarily the running of the state—gets done. Springfield also honors its portion of Rte. 66; the city is home to the **International Route 66 Mother Road Festival**, several classic diners, and historic Rte. 66 signs on portions of Second and Fifth St.

VITAL STATS
Population: 111,000
Tourist Office: Springfield Convention and Visitors Bureau, 109 N. 7th St. (☎217-789-2360). Open M-F 8am-5pm.
Library and Internet Access: Lincoln Public Library, 326 S. 7th St. (☎217-753-4900). Free. Open June-Aug. M-Th 9am-9pm, F 9am-6pm, Sa 9am-5pm; Sept.-May M-Th 9am-9pm, F 9am-6pm, Su noon-5pm.
Post Office: 411 E. Monroe St. (☎217-753-3432), at Wheeler St. Open M-F 7:45am-5pm. **Postal Code:** 62701.

✦ ORIENTATION

Getting around Springfield is fairly simple. **North Grand Avenue** is one of the city's main thoroughfares, running east-west through town. Streets run north-south and are numbered. Main arteries include **Fifth Street,** which borders the Lincoln Neighborhood and Oak Park Cemetery. North Grand Avenue is known as **North Grand Avenue West,** west of the intersection with 5th St., and **North Grand Avenue East** east of the intersection. The only real difficulty is the prevalence of one-way streets, but excellent downtown maps detailing the location of historic sights are available throughout the city. To enter downtown, take **Sixth Street;** to leave downtown, take Fifth St.

⛏ ACCOMMODATIONS

There are cheap lodgings off I-55 and US 36 on **Dirksen Parkway.** Rooms downtown should be reserved early for holiday weekends and the state fair in mid-August.

▩ **Henry Mischler House Bed and Breakfast,** 802 E. Edwards St. (☎217-525-2660; www.mischlerhouse.com). Proprietor Jane Murphy has infused this gorgeous Victorian house with welcoming sumptuousness. Wine and cheese is offered upon reception, and breakfast is served every morning. 8 rooms with private baths. Breakfast included. Rooms from $95. MC/V. ❹

Route 66 Hotel and Conference Center, 625 E. St. Joseph St. (☎217-529-6626; www.rt66hotel.com), just beyond the Cozy Dog. Heavily themed hotel decorated head to toe with Rte. 66 paraphanalia, including vintage vehicles in the lobby. 1950's-style diner on the premises and pool out front. Singles from $66; doubles from $72. AmEx/D/MC/V. ❸

The Pear Tree Inn, 3190 S. Dirksen Pkwy. (☎217-529-9100; www.druryhotels.com). Rooms slightly larger than a motel and prices slightly lower than an inn. Singles from $55; doubles from $70. AmEx/D/MC/V. ❸

Mr. Lincoln's Campground, 3045 Stanton Ave. (☎217-529-8206), off Stevenson Dr. RV hookups, tent sites, and a limited number of private cabins. Reception in summer 8am-7pm; in winter 8am-4pm. Make reservations, as this campground fills quickly with festival-goers and snowbirds. Cabins closed in winter. Sites $20, with hookup $29. Cabins with A/C $35. D/MC/V. ❶

KOA Campground, 5775 W. Farm 140 (☎217-498-7002). The sites are fairly close together,

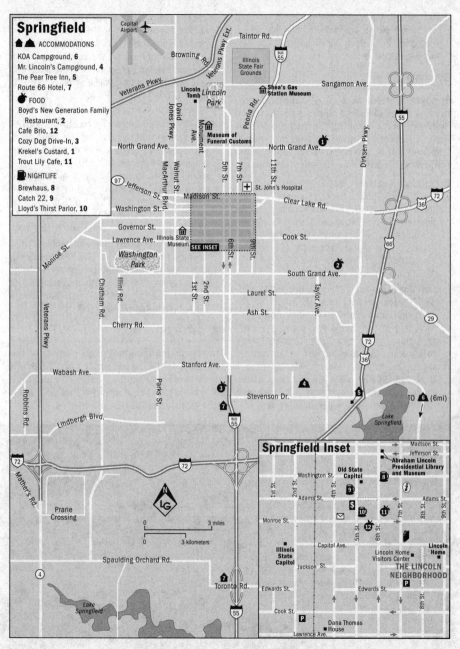

Springfield

🏕️ **ACCOMMODATIONS**

KOA Campground, **6**
Mr. Lincoln's Campground, **4**
The Pear Tree Inn, **5**
Route 66 Hotel, **7**

🍎 **FOOD**

Boyd's New Generation Family
  Restaurant, **2**
Cafe Brio, **12**
Cozy Dog Drive-In, **3**
Krekel's Custard, **1**
Trout Lily Cafe, **11**

🍸 **NIGHTLIFE**

Brewhaus, **8**
Catch 22, **9**
Lloyd's Thirst Parlor, **10**

Capital Airport

Taintor Rd.

Browning Rd.

Veterans Pkwy. Ext.

Veterans Pkwy.

Illinois State Fair Grounds

Sangamon Ave.

BUS 55

Lincoln Tomb

Lincoln Park

Shea's Gas Station Museum

Peoria Rd.

Dirksen Pkwy.

55

Museum of Funeral Customs

North Grand Ave.

North Grand Ave.

David Jones Pkwy.

Monument Ave.

Walnut St.

MacArthur Blvd.

5th St.

7th St.

11th St.

St. John's Hospital

72

36

66

97

Jefferson St.

Madison St.

Clear Lake Rd.

Washington St.

Governor St.

Lawrence Ave.

Illinois State Museum

6th St.

9th St.

Cook St.

SEE INSET

Washington Park

South Grand Ave.

Chatham Rd.

Illini Rd.

1st St.

2nd St.

Laurel St.

Ash St.

Taylor Ave.

29

Cherry Rd.

72

36

Monroe St.

Veterans Pkwy

Wabash Ave.

Robbins Rd.

Parks St.

Stanford Ave.

Stevenson Dr.

Lake Springfield

TO 6 (6mi)

Lindbergh Blvd.

BUS 55

72

Mather's Rd.

72

Prarie Crossing

N LG

0   3 miles

0   3 kilometers

Spaulding Orchard Rd.

4

Lake Springfield

Toronto Rd.

55

ROUTE 66

Springfield Inset

Madison St.

Jefferson St.

Abraham Lincoln Presidential Library and Museum

Washington St.

Old State Capitol

8

1st St.

2nd St.

4th St.

Adams St.

9

7th St.

8th St.

9th St.

Adams St.

$

Monroe St.

10

11

5th St.

6th St.

12

Illinois State Capitol

Capitol Ave.

Lincoln Home Visitors Center

Lincoln Home

Jackson St.

THE LINCOLN NEIGHBORHOOD

Edwards St.

Edwards St.

8th St.

Cook St.

Lawrence Ave.

Dana Thomas House

but the campground is removed from the road in the sweeping countryside south of Springfield. Reception 24hr. Open Apr.-Nov. Sites $18. Cabins $45. MC/V. ❶

FOOD

Springfield offers an array of dining options, ranging from classic American to Italian to Southern home cooking. Springfield is also home to several classic Rte. 66 diners and fast-food joints; even if you're just passing through, these are ones you shouldn't miss.

Krekel's Custard, 2121 N. Grand Ave. (☎217-525-4952). Eat-in, eat-out, or drive-through since 1949, the shakes and burgers here are legendary. The "concrete" milkshakes ($2.80) are only for those with ample jaw dexterity. Milkshakes from vanilla and chocolate to lemon and pineapple $2.55. Cheeseburgers $2. Open M-Sa 10:30am-9pm. Cash only. ❶

Cozy Dog Drive-In, 2935 5th St. (☎217-525-1992; www.cozydogdrivein.com). Run by the Waldmire family since 1949, Cozy Dog is the birthplace of the corn dog and one of the all-time greats of the road. You might be surprised to learn that the Cozy-Dog was almost called a Crusty Cur. Pick up postcards ($0.30), maps, a Cozy Dog ($1.85), a Rte. 66 root beer, bottled in Wilmington ($1.80), or other quick road food. Open M-Sa 8am-8pm. AmEx/D/MC/V. ❶

Trout Lily Cafe, 218 S. 6th St. (☎217-391-0101; www.troutlilycafe.com). A little girl's dream room meets a French cafe in this friendly establishment decorated with local art and colorful murals. An excellent selection of specialty and drip coffees including unusual treats such as blackberry and coconut. Live music M-F noon-1pm. Open M-F 7am-4:30pm, Sa 9am-3pm. MC/V. ❶

Cafe Brio, 524 E. Monroe St. (☎217-544-0574), at the corner of 6th St. High ceilings, wood chairs and tables, and plants trailing down the central columns make this one of the more sophisticated eating options in town. Stylized Mexican-influenced cuisine (habañero chicken $16; chimichanga $12) and a nice bar too (with 13 different margaritas). Open M-Th 11am-10pm, F-Sa 11am-11pm, Su 11am-3pm. AmEx/D/MC/ V. ❸

Boyd's New Generation Family Restaurant, 1831 S. Grand Ave. E. (☎217-544-9866). The South rises again in this homestyle eatery featuring whole catfish ($8) or catfish nuggets ($6) for the faint of heart. Open M-Th 7:30am-3pm, F 7:30am-7pm. AmEx/D/MC/V. ❷

SIGHTS

The sleepy state capital plays curator to the 16th president's legacy; many of Springfield's sights revolve around Lincoln's life and family. For variety, there are also Rte. 66-related attractions and oddball distractions.

FINDING THE MOTHER ROAD

Since Rte. 66 was decommissioned in 1985, various stretches of asphalt that made up the road have suffered different fates. Some parts of it were engulfed by the new highways, some parts survived intact, and some parts have fallen into disuse and have been abandoned.

This means that finding the original Route 66 is not always easy. In some places it is clearly signposted. But in others you will need to use your detective skills in order to find it. Here are some tips for tracking it down:

↳ First, and most obviously, look for the brown and white "Historic 66" signs.
↳ Be on the lookout for secondary roads that run directly parallel to the highway.
↳ The original road usually ran right next to the railroad, so, as a general rule, the closer to the railroad, the older the alignment.
↳ Pay attention to the nature of the road itself. The original route tended to follow the natural contours of the countryside and often used poured sectional concrete instead of continuously smooth

SHEA'S GAS STATION MUSEUM. Looking as though Rte. 66 exploded into one happy jumble of signs, car parts, and Mother Road memorabilia, this eclectic museum should be a priority for any roadtripper on Rte. 66. Three different Bill Sheas preside over this wonderful collection (the original founder plus his son and grandson), and any one of them will be more than happy to explain how it all began with an adding machine in 1955. This place, more than almost any other stop, helps explain how Rte. 66 defined the livelihoods of entire families. (*2075 Peoria Rd.* ☎ *217-522-0475. Open Tu-F 7am-4pm, Sa 7am-noon. Suggested donation $2.*)

LINCOLN NEIGHBORHOOD. Abraham Lincoln's old haunts have been turned into a pedestrian-only pilgrimage site called the Lincoln Neighborhood. The principal Lincoln site is the **Presidential Library and Museum,** which features movie presentations on the career of America's most liberating president, artifacts from his childhood, and other temporary exhibitions related to American history and politics. (*212 N. 6th St.* ☎ *800-610-2094; www.alplm.org. Open daily 9am-5pm. $10, students $7, ages 5-15 $4.*) Abe-o-philes can take 25min. tours of the fully restored **Lincoln Home,** which features his original writing desk in the parlor where he was offered the presidential nomination. (☎ *217-492-4241, ext. 244; www.nps.gov/liho. Open daily 8:30am-5pm; extended hours in summer. Tickets available at the visitors center. Free.*) The final resting place of Honest Abe, Mary Todd Lincoln, and three of the Lincoln children is outside Lincoln Neighborhood in the **Lincoln Tomb,** under an obelisk in the Oak Ridge Cemetery. (*1500 Monument Ave.* ☎ *217-782-2717. Open daily Mar.-Oct. 9am-5pm; Nov.-Feb. 9am-4pm. Free.*)

DANA-THOMAS HOME. Built in 1902, this stunning home was one of Frank Lloyd Wright's early experiments in his Prairie Style and features the largest collection of original furniture and art glass of any Wright structure. Tours describe the house and the eccentric millionaire who lived there. (*301 E. Lawrence Ave.* ☎ *217-782-6776; www.dana-thomas.org. Open W-Su 9am-4pm. Tours every 20min. $5, children $3.*)

OTHER SIGHTS. The **Museum of Funeral Customs** features a history of American embalming and funeral customs, including exhibits on Lincoln's funeral affairs and mourning jewelry, as well as the history of formaldehyde. Check out the massive Cadillac hearse and harmonica-size chocolate coffins. (*1440 Monument Ave.* ☎ *217-544-3480. Open Tu-Sa 10am-4pm, Su 1-4pm. $4, children $2.*) The **Illinois State Museum** has everything you ever wanted to know about Illinois. The highlight is the replica of an Alaskan Tlingit totem pole, complete with its own Lincoln tribute, outside the building. (*502 S. Spring St.* ☎ *217-782-7386; www.museum.state.il.us. Open M-Sa 8:30am-5pm, Su noon-5pm. Donations accepted.*) In 1858, Lincoln delivered his famous "House Divided" speech at the **Old State Capitol;** the building is open for guided tours. (☎ *217-785-7961. Open Mar.-Oct. daily 9am-5pm; Nov.-Feb. Tu-Sa 9am-4pm.*) Each September ,Springfield also hosts an International Rte. 66 Mother Road Festival with car parades and music. (*www.route66fest.com.*)

☕ NIGHTLIFE

Brewhaus, 617 E. Washington St. (☎217-525-6399). Locals crowd around the bar and wood booths at Brewhaus, one of the most popular nightspots around. Housed in an elegant 19th-century building. Beer $1.25+. Open M-Sa 3pm-1am, Su 5pm-1am. AmEx/D/MC/V.

Lloyd's Thirst Parlor, 212 S. 5th St. (☎217-522-2020). Catch it on a good night, and you'll rock the night away. Any other night it still has the requisite beer and spirits. Open M-Sa 3pm-1am. AmEx/D/MC/V.

Catch 22, 11 W. Capitol Plaza (☎217-522-5732). If you're feeling energetic and in the mood for a boogie, head to Catch 22, which plays mainstream pop and chart music to a college-age crowd. Jam-packed on weekends. New Orleans-style bar upstairs, dance floor downstairs. Beer $2-3. Cover $5. Open M-W 8pm-1am, Th-Sa 8pm-3am. AmEx/D/MC/V.

⛟ THE ROAD TO LITCHFIELD: 46 MI.

Take **Fifth Street** south to **I-55.** At **Exit 88,** you'll see signs for **Historic 66.** From Springfield, the towns on the way south to St. Louis pride themselves on their Rte. 66 status, and many host restaurants that hark back to the days of Mother Road glory. Directly south of Springfield, Glenarm (with an attractive restored

ROUTE 66

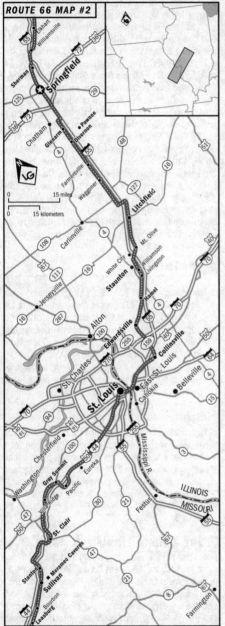

ROUTE 66 MAP #2

ROUTE 66

covered bridge), Pawnee, and Divernon are home to gas, mom-and-pop diners, and motels. Head left at the T and then back onto **I-55.** At Litchfield, drivers have the choice of heading straight through town on the 1940-77 alignment of Rte. 66 or diverging to the left on the older section, dating from 1930-40. The newer alignment leads to chain motels and fast food, while the older alignment passes the Skyview Drive-In and the Ariston Cafe.

 PHOTO OP. On your way to Litchfield, keep an eye out for a giant tribute to Abraham Lincoln—he's perched in a wagon and absorbed in a law book.

LITCHFIELD   ☎217

Litchfield is a town proud to be on Rte. 66. **The Sky View Drive-In,** on the Rte. 66 1930-40 alignment, just north of Union St., still shows movies for $2 in the summer months, just like in the old days. (☎217-324-4451. Films F-Su. Call for showtimes.) Numerous annual celebrations in Litchfield include an April reenactment of 1800s life and a July **International Chili Society** district cook-off. Nearby **Lake Lou Yaeger** offers beachfront, watersports, campgrounds, and playgrounds. Take Union Ave. heading east, then turn left on Yaeger Lake Trail. (☎217-324-4771.) **The Ariston Cafe ❸,** at the corner of Rte. 66 and Union St., on the 1930-40 alignment, has been serving roadies since the 1920s. (☎217-324-2023; www.ariston-cafe.com. Appetizers $6. Entrees $13+. Steak $22. Open M-F 11am-10pm, Sa 4-10pm, Su 11am-9pm. AmEx/D/MC/V.)

⌘ THE ROAD TO STAUNTON: 13 MI.

Take **I-16** back to the 1940-77 alignment of **Route 66.** After 7 mi., you'll pass through **Mount Olive,** the final resting place of Mary "Mother" Jones and "General" Alexander Bradley, both instrumental in the fight for the rights of mine workers, in the **Union Miners Cemetery.** One mile past the cemetery, look to the right to see the restored 1926 **Russel Soulsby Shell Gas Station.** Approximately 10 mi. south of central Litchfield, Rte. 66 reaches a T intersection; take a right to rejoin the old route, and continue on over **I-55.** The road forks in a number of places but is clearly marked and leads directly into downtown Staunton.

STAUNTON ☎618

"Hare it is!" proclaim the signs for **Henry's Route 66 Emporium and Rabbit Ranch,** 1107 Historic Rte. 66 Rd., as if you could miss the two giant tractor trailers out front with "Humpin' to Please" painted on them. Henry's Emporium embodies the joy of Rte. 66 culture—38 rabbits in the "Rabbit Ranch," 15 Volkswagen rabbits, and one Rte. 66 enthusiast extraordinaire hop among an ever-expanding collection of memorabilia. Rich Henry has worked and lived on Rte. 66 all his life, and he can talk a blue streak. Ask to pet Montana, the most famous of his rabbits, and she (yes, the rabbit) might even autograph a brochure for you. (☎618-635-5655; www.henrysroute66.com. Open daily 9am-4pm.)

ⵣ THE ROAD TO EDWARDSVILLE: 19 MI.
Continue on **Route 66** from Henry's Emporium for 10 mi. to hit the town of Hamel. Just north of Hamel, on the eastern side of I-55, is a repainted sign for the famous **Meramec Caverns** of Staunton, Missouri. Across Rte. 66 from the Meramec Barn is **Saint Paul's Church,** where the neon-blue cross at the top has been lighting roadtrippers' ways for years. Seven miles later, you'll reach the town of Edwardsville. The next manifestation of Rte. 66 is **East Vandalia Street,** which becomes **West Vandalia** after intersecting Main St.

EDWARDSVILLE ☎618

Edwardsville is home to the **Southern University of Illinois.** Gas and amenities, including a new library and some excellent eating and lounging options, are available. For a relaxing jaunt through nature, head to the **Watershed Nature Center,** 1591 Tower Rd., a 40-acre nature preserve with wetlands, forests, hiking trails, and a 3000 ft. walkway. From Main St., take Lincoln St. to Eberhart St. and then to Tower Rd. (☎618-692-7578. Open sunrise-sunset. Free.) If you're passing through on a Saturday between May and October, look out for the **Goshen Market** (a farmers' market), which takes place each week 8am-noon on Main St. next to the courthouse. **Sacred Grounds Cafe ❷,** 233 N. Main St., off E. Vandalia, is a student-friendly coffee shop offering ample space to relax with a book, spread out over a board game, or just gobble down some health food. (☎618-692-4150. Wraps, salads,

quiches, or panini $4. Open daily 7am-11pm. MC/V.) Chalkboards at the **Stagger Inn Again ❷,** 104 E. Vandalia St., are festooned with specials and quips, and the wood bar, checkered floors, and spacious dining area draw potential diners through the saloon doors for a night out or a lunch on the go. Try the Nightmare (a chili burger with jalapenos) for $6.50. (☎618-656-4221. Open M-W 11am-1am, Th-Sa 11am-2:30am, Su 3pm-1am. MC/V.)

ⵣ THE ROAD TO MITCHELL: 10 MI.
Five miles past **Main Street, West Vandalia** becomes **Chain of Rocks Road,** which takes you to Mitchell.

MITCHELL ☎618

Now a quiet town of metal yards and auto shops laced with old railroad tracks, Mitchell used to be the last big stop before St. Louis on Rte. 66. The **Apple Valley Motel ❷,** 701 and 709 E. Chain of Rocks Rd., offers basic but clean rooms in an attractive, green, and shady location. (☎618-931-6085. Singles $37; doubles $44. AmEx/MC/V.) You can still knock back brews with the local crowd at the **Luna Cafe ❶,** 201 E. Chain of Rocks Rd. Rumor has it that Al Capone used to come to this legendary old Rte. 66 bar, tucked under a blinking vintage neon sign, when he feared foul play in St. Louis. (☎618-931-3152. Hamburgers $3. Drinks $2-3. Open M-F 8am-2am, Sa 9am-3am, Su 10am-2am. Cash only.)

ⵣ THE ROAD TO COLLINSVILLE: 13 MI.
Take **I-55 South** to **Route 159 South** to get to downtown Collinsville. Head south on **Morrison Street** as your hamburger dreams materialize over the horizon.

COLLINSVILLE ☎618

Pick up your catsup postcards and catsup paraphernalia at **Ashmann's Drugs,** 209 E. Main St. (Open daily 9am-9:30pm.) As you head down Main St., keep an eye to the left for an ancient Bull Durham Tobacco sign painted on a brick wall. Outside of Collinsville, the **Cahokia Mounds** are the remnants of the prehistoric Native American city of Cahokia. Archaeologists are fairly certain that some were burial mounds. Monks Mound, the largest Indian mound north of Mexico, is named for Trappist monks who set up camp on top of the mound in the 1800s. Take I-55 S. to I-255 S. Take Exit 24 and turn left onto Collinsville Rd. (☎618-346-5160; www.cahokiamounds.com. Museum open W-Su 9am-5pm. Park open daily 8am-sunset. Suggested donation $2, children $1.)For cheap eats, stop into **Bert's Chuckwagon BBQ ❷**, 207 E. Clay St. On the outside of the A-frame building is a giant mural of biblical scenes (check out Mary's mirrored eyes) painted by the owner's sons. Inside is tasty barbecue and Tex-Mex. (☎618-344-7993. Rib tips $4. Full side $10. Open M-Th 10am-9pm, F-Sa 10am-10pm. AmEx/D/MC/V.)

◤ THE ROAD TO ST. LOUIS: 15 MI.

Take **Main Street** in Collinsville west to **Saint Louis Road**, which turns into **Collinsville Road**. Turn left to take **I-255 North** to **I-55 South/I-70 West**, which will take you toward St. Louis. There will be a number of exit options for St. Louis, each for a major street or intersection. It is best to decide which part of the city you want to see beforehand and look at a map to determine where to exit.

The Show - Me State
MISSOURI
Welcomes You!

ST. LOUIS ☎314

Directly south of the junction of three rivers—the Mississippi, Missouri, and Illinois—St. Louis marks the transition between the Midwest and the West. Known as the "Gateway to the West," a theme expressed by the soaring Gateway Arch, the sprawling city is also at the crossroads of Rte. 66 and the **National Road.** Stay on Rte. 66 to continue your classic roadtrip journey or take the other fork in the road, following I-40 straight to San Francisco.

> **PAGE TURN.** See the **National Road** (p. 379) for complete coverage of St. Louis.

◤ THE ROAD TO GRAY SUMMIT: 39 MI.

From downtown St. Louis, hop on **I-44 West.** On either side of the route, cliffs fall away sharply—be careful, as the route is narrow and frequently traveled by giant tractor-trailers. Continue on I-44 to **Exit 253,** turning right at **Route 100.**

GRAY SUMMIT ☎636

An extension of the Missouri Botanical Garden, the **Shaw Nature Reserve,** across from the Diamonds Restaurant signs, provides hiking trails, wildflower gardens, and horticultural exhibits in the former home of Confederate Colonel Thomas William Bouldin Crews. (☎636-451-3512; www.shawnature.org. Grounds open daily 7am-sunset. Visitors center open M-F 8am-4:30pm, Sa 9am-5pm. $3, under 12 free, seniors $2.)

◤ THE ROAD TO STANTON: 22 MI.

Continue along **Route 66,** crossing over the highway 6 mi. from Gray Summit and continuing parallel to the railroad tracks. Eleven miles south of Gray Summit on Rte. 66, the **Indian Harvest** store, in the two giant blue-and-white tipis, has bison sausage and jewelry made by the Navajo and the Zuni tribes of New Mexico. The $2 entrance fee is waived if you buy something. Continue southwest into St. Clair. Just past the intersection with **Route 30,** head north over I-44, then head left on the **Outer Road** and follow the signs for the Meramec Caverns into downtown Stanton.

STANTON ☎573

Stanton may be all about the Meramec Caverns, but, before heading to the caves, be sure to check out the **Jesse James Wax Museum,** at Exit 230 off I-44, just after the turnoff for the caverns. In this memorial to the legendary bandit, rooms are devoted to wax reenactments of key moments in James's life, including the first bank robbery on record in the US. (☎573-927-5233. Open June-Aug. daily 9am-6pm; Sept.-Oct. and Apr.-May Sa-Su 9am-5pm. $6, ages 5-11 $2.50, under 5 free.) **Meramec Caverns** can't be missed after the miles and miles of advertisements on barns and billboards that you just drove. Reputedly where Jesse James and his gang once hid their loot, the 26 mi. of caverns are now one of Missouri's biggest tourist draws and lie in a beautiful location along the banks of the river. If you want to take a break from the fast-paced life of the highway, come here to kick back, wind down, and wallow in a green and shady riverside idyll. Other cave-side attractions include riverboat and mining tours. (☎573-468-3166. Caverns open daily but hours vary, so call ahead. Tours every 30min. $17.50, ages 5-11 $8, under 5 free.) On your way back to Rte. 66, stop by the **Riverside Reptile Ranch and Wildlife Center.** Here you can stroke a snake, test the jaw strength of baby alligators with your finger, get wrapped up in a Burmese python, or watch the scaly creatures from behind glass—just keep an eye out for Zeus, the giant American alligator who paddles freely through the grounds. The owner may casually mention the lion and tigers he has out back. (☎573-927-6253. Open daily 10am-7pm. $8, ages 5-12 $6.)

The **Meramec Caverns Motel ❷**, in La Jolla Natural Park, provides riverfront lodging adjacent to the caves. (☎573-468-4215. Open Apr.-Oct. Singles $50; doubles $55. AmEx/D/MC/V.) Meramec Caverns's **La Jolla Natural Park ❶** has comfortable, shaded campsites along the river at the mouth of the caverns. Amenities include bathrooms, showers, a supply store, a concession stand, and canoe and raft rentals. (☎573-468-3166. Open Apr.-Oct. Sites $15, with hookup $19. Cash only.)

⚑ THE ROAD TO LEASBURG: 16 MI.

From Stanton, follow **Route 66** into Sullivan. Motels and gas stations are located along the west side while fast-food restaurants assemble to the east. To continue on Rte. 66, turn left, driving over **I-44,** then take the **Outer Road** south from Sullivan, driving with I-44 on your right. About 10 mi. later you'll hit Leasburg.

LEASBURG   ☎573

Located in Onondaga Caves State Park, just south of Leasburg, the **Onondaga Caves** feature a river, spring, and several hiking trails. Head left from Rte. 66 through Leasburg, following signs for the caves. (☎573-245-6576. Visitors center open daily 9am-5pm. Cave tours Mar.-Oct. daily 9am-5pm. $10, ages 6-12 $5, under 5 free, seniors $8.) Camping is permitted in the park at the **Onondaga Caves Campgrounds ❶**, which offer bathrooms, a general store, showers, and laundry. (☎877-422-6766. Call for availability and opening dates. Sites $8, with full hookup $17. Cash only.) Sometimes it seems like every car in town pulls up in front

of **Ike's Chat 'n' Chew ❷**, 2344 Rte. H, which serves breakfast, nosh, and sandwiches. (☎573-245-6268. Open Tu-Su 8am-4pm.)

⚑ THE ROAD TO CUBA: 6 MI.

Continue on **Route 66** to Cuba.

CUBA   ☎573

The Wagon Wheel Motel ❶, 901 E. Washington St., offers attractive rooms at prices for the proletariat—almost as low as they were when the motel first opened in 1934. (☎573-885-3411. Reservations recommended. Singles $15-18; doubles $20. Cash only.) ◪**Missouri Hick Barbecue ❷**, 913 E. Washington St., in a funky and distinctive wood building, is decorated with saddles and farm equipment and provides a welcome break from diner fare. Try the tasty and healthy smoked meats. (☎573-885-6791. Beef brisket $10. Sandwiches $7. Open in summer M-Th and Su 11am-9pm, F-Sa 11am-10pm; in winter M-Th and Su 11am-8pm, F-Sa 11am-9pm. AmEx/D/MC/V.)

⚑ THE ROAD TO ST. JAMES: 14 MI.

Roughly 14 mi. south of Cuba on **Route 66** is St. James. To get to the winery, turn right on **Jefferson Street (Route 68)** and then right onto **Route B** at the first lights after the bridge over the highway.

ST. JAMES   ☎573

The area south of Cuba is grape country, and St. James is no exception. The **Saintt. James Winery,** 540 Sidney St., has 15min. tours, daily wine tastings, and excellent grape juice for drivers. (☎800-280-9463. Open daily for tours 11am-4pm. Tasting room open M-Sa 8am-7pm, Su 9am-7pm. Free.)

⚑ THE ROAD TO ROLLA: 11 MI.

Head right at **Jefferson Street (Route 68),** crossing **I-44.** Go west on the **Outer Road** and turn left 8 mi. later on **Bishop Avenue (US 63)** into Rolla.

ROLLA   ☎573

Touted as Missouri's "center of everything," Rolla is home to quirky motels, a state university, and Rte. 66 trading posts and gift shops, as well as a convenient gateway to outdoor attractions. Rolla's stretch of Rte. 66 is truly unique; few places can transition from a likeness of Stonehenge at one end of town to the Totem Pole Trading Post at the other.

VITAL STATS
Population: 18,500
Tourist Office: Rolla Chamber of Commerce and Visitors Center, 1301 Kingshighway St. (☎573-364-3577; www.rollachamber.org). Open May-Oct. M-F 8am-5pm, Sa 9am-3pm, Su 1-4pm; Nov.-Apr. M-F 8am-5pm, Sa 9am-3pm.
Library and Internet Access: Rolla Public Library, 900 Pine St. (☎573-364-2604). Free. Open M-Th 9am-9pm, F-Sa 9am-5pm, Su 1:30-5pm.
Post Office: 501 W. 8th St. (☎573-364-1775). Open M-F 7:45am-5:15pm, Sa 8:30am-12:30pm.
Postal Code: 65401.

ORIENTATION

Rte. 66 cuts through town on **US 63,** which is known in town as **Bishop Avenue** and runs north-south. Numbered streets run east-west through downtown. To reach downtown, head east on **10th Street** or south on **Pine Street,** which runs parallel to Bishop Ave. a few blocks to the east. **Kingshighway Street** heads west from US 63, becoming **Martin Springs Drive** in the west and running parallel to I-44.

ACCOMMODATIONS

Motels cluster along **Martin Springs Drive** on the western edge of Rolla.

Zeno's Motel and Steakhouse, 1621 Martin Springs Dr. (☎573-364-1301). For a night of quirky elegance, Zeno's offers a motel-meets-antique-shop atmosphere and an adjoining steakhouse. Run by the Scheffer family since the 1950s. Entrees $12-25. Singles from $50; doubles from $62. AmEx/D/MC/V. ❸

Vernelle's Motel, Rte. 66 (☎573-762-2798), 8 mi. south of Rolla. Follow Martin Springs Dr., which becomes Sugartree Rd., and turn onto Arlington Rd. just before you get to I-44. Vernelle's offers wood-paneled rooms straight out of the glory days of Rte. 66. Built in the late 50s. Few other places carry such a tangible sense of the past. Just behind Vernelle's is one of the most fascinating sights on the route: the now-derelict John's Modern Cabins, untouched since they were abandoned in the last few decades. Singles from $30; doubles from $42. Cash only. ❷

Rustic Motel, 812 S. Bishop Ave. (☎573-364-6943). Family-owned with clean rooms and just a hint of rustic charm. Singles M-Th $45, F-Su $52. AmEx/D/MC/V. ❷

FOOD

Granny's Saw Mill (☎573-364-8383), at the corner of 9th and Pine St. Let Granny fill you up with giant pancakes ($2) or a burger ($4) made with ½ lb. of juicy ground beef. Open M-F 5am-2pm, Sa 5am-1:30pm. AmEx/MC/V. ❶

A Slice of Pie, 601 Kingshighway St. (☎573-364-6203). Everything is homemade, with fillings from Peanut Butter Lust to Tahitian Cream. Light lunches are also available. Open daily 10am-10pm. Cash only. ❷

Joe and Linda's Tater Patch, 103 Bridge School Rd. (☎573-368-3111). A convivial bar and restaurant that serves heaping plates of pasta. It's also a good spot to grab a drink and mix with local Rollans who come here to gamble and shoot pool. Entrees $8-10. Open M-Sa 7am-1:30am, Su 9am-9pm. AmEx/D/MC/V. ❷

SIGHTS

To fill any holes in your 66 memorabilia collection, head to the **Route 66 Nostalgia Gift Shop,** 12601 Old Hwy. 66. The adjoining **Route 66 Motors** showcases old cars; most are available for purchase. (☎573-265-5200. Hours are flexible—better to call in advance.) For a break from the automobile, head over to the **Stonehenge Replica,** at 14th St. and Bishop Ave., on the campus of the University of Missouri at Rolla. Approximately 160 tons of granite compose the giant rock structure. Though it's smaller than the original, the replica includes features the original lacked, such as a hole through which the North Star can be seen. (☎573-341-4111. Open daily sunrise-sunset. Free.) Don't miss the historic **Totem Pole Trading Post,** 1413 Martin Springs Dr. A well-known Rte. 66 landmark, the Totem Pole has been offering gas and souvenirs since 1933, including collector's items such as Wurlitzer jukeboxes. (☎573-364-3519. Open daily in summer 8am-8pm; in winter 8am-6pm.)

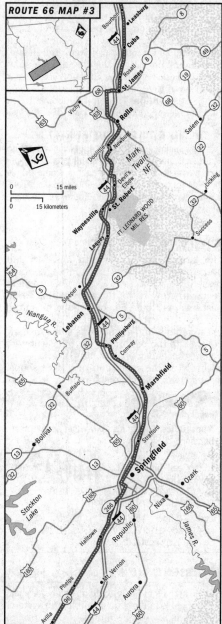 THE ROAD TO ST. ROBERT: 21 MI.

Veer southwest (left) off **Kingshighway Street** onto **Martin Spring Drive,** which runs parallel to **I-44.** Although the road becomes narrow and is relatively unmarked, follow its curves across the one-lane bridge until the sign for **Arlington Road** on your left. Here you will need to join I-44 West for 6 mi. before taking **Exit 169** (marked Historic 66). Turn left over I-44 and take the first right (unsigned). Here **Route 66** widens to two lanes, with a grassy verge in the middle. Follow this over the creek until you emerge in St. Robert.

ST. ROBERT ☎ 573

St. Robert sprawls on either side of the highway. The **Deville Motor Inn ❷**, 461 Old Rte. 66, is another Rte. 66 standard with a restaurant and clean cinder block rooms. (☎573-336-3113. Singles from $40; doubles from $48. AmEx/MC/V.) **Sweetwater BBQ ❷**, 14076 Hwy. Z, makes mouthwatering barbecue in a small cabin on a hill at the northeastern entrance to St. Robert. (☎573-336-8830. Pork plates $7.50-8.75. Open daily 11am-8pm. AmEx/MC/V.)

THE ROAD TO LEBANON: 31 MI.

Stay on **Route 66,** continuing through to Waynesville, passing over I-44, and veering left at the fork on the west edge of town. Follow **South Outer Road** from **Exit 153,** steering right on **Route 17** to the intersection with **Route P** and **Route NN.** two miles later, head right to **Laquey** on **Route P,** then left at the fork in town onto **Route AA.** Head right at **Route AB;** Hazelgreen is 9 mi. down the road. At the junction with **Route F** 13 mi. later, turn north and cross I-44.

LEBANON ☎ 417

Head to the **Peggy Palmer Summers Memorial Library,** 915 S. Jefferson Ave., to see the Rte. 66 museum with replicas of a diner and a 30s cabin-style motel room recreated with authentic furniture. Note that there are "no firearms inside the library." (☎417-532-2148. Free Internet and Wi-Fi. Open M-Th 8am-8pm, F-Sa 8am-5pm.) Next to the museum within the library is **Maria's Route 66 Cafe ❶**, where chrome and a piano key floor meet burritos and smoked brisket. (☎417-588-7922. Salads and sandwiches $5. Open M-Th 10am-6pm, F-Sa 10am-4pm. Cash only.) One of the best lodging options on this stretch of road is the **Munger Moss Motel ❷**, a holdout from the

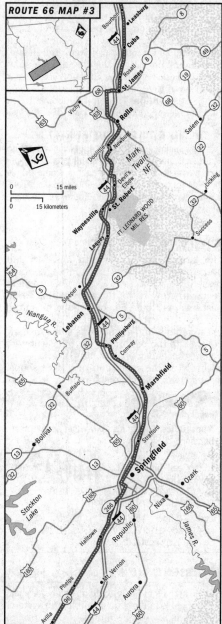

glory days of the old road. Pass through at night, and the glowing red, blue, yellow, and green blinking sign beckons like a siren. Each pleasantly furnished room has hand-quilted bedspreads, and many are decorated in Rte. 66 memorabilia, all for the cost of your standard roadside motel. The gift shop has a great selection of Rte. 66 memorabilia. (☎417-532-3111. Reservations recommended. Singles $42; doubles from $49. AmEx/MC/V.)

THE ROAD TO SPRINGFIELD: 47 MI.

Leaving Lebanon, turn right at the junction with **Route W,** then left onto the **Outer Road** 9 mi. later. In Phillipsburg, cross over I-44 then turn right on **Route CC,** so that I-44 is now on your right. Veer right in Marshfield, 12 mi. later and head left onto **Route OO.** Continue across the junction with **Route B.**

SPRINGFIELD   ☎417

The largest city in southern Missouri and hometown of hunky Brad Pitt (the only reason we went to see *Troy*), Springfield seems to grow out of the surrounding cattle pastures. As Route 66 enters town from the northeast, the stretch of fast-food restaurants, cheap motels, and gas stations stand in stark contrast to the old-time heart of downtown, where the ghost of **Wild Bill Hickock** seems as lively as the multitude of coffee shops, swanky bars, and hip restaurants.

VITAL STATS
Population: 150,000
Tourist Office: Springfield Convention and Visitors **Bureau,** 815 St. Louis St. (☎800-678-8767; www. springfieldmo.org). Open M-F 8am-5pm.
Library and Internet Access: Springfield-Greene County Library Center, 4653 S. Campbell St. (☎417-882-0714). Free. Open M-Sa 8:30am-9pm, Su 1-5pm.
Post Office: 500 W. Chestnut Expwy. (☎417-864-0199). Open M-F 7:30am-5:30pm and Sa 9am-2pm. **Postal Code:** 65801.

ORIENTATION

Rte. 66 arrives in Springfield as **Kearney Avenue.** Springfield is laid out on a simple grid system; Kearney is the northernmost of three principal roads that traverse the city from east to west; to the south of it are **Chestnut Expressway** and **Sunshine Avenue.** Running north to south through town are (from east to west) **Glendstone Avenue, National Avenue, Campbell Street,** and **Kansas Expressway.** As you drive into town along Kearney, head left down Campbell in order to get to the heart of downtown.

ACCOMMODATIONS

Walnut St. Inn, 900 E. Walnut St. (☎417-864-6346; www.walnutstreetinn.com), in the historic district. Bedside chocolate-chip cookies sum up the luxury of this Victorian inn. Reservations recommended. Rooms $89-169. AmEx/D/MC/V. ❹

Rail Haven Best Western, 203 S. Glenstone Ave. (☎417-866-1963). Just pretend not to see the blue hallmark of America's biggest hotel chain; this well-kept motel, dating from 1937, has ties to the motor courts of Old 66. Cool vintage gas pumps and a nice pool. Free Wi-Fi. Singles from $60; doubles from $80. AmEx/D/MC/V. ❸

Rest Haven Court, 2000 E. Kearney Ave. (☎417-869-9114). Look for the giant neon sign on the left side of Kearney as you drive into town. Clean rooms with a decent pool. Wi-Fi. Singles $40; doubles $45. AmEx/D/MC/V. ❷

Springfield KOA Campground, 5775 W. Farm Rd. 140 (☎800-562-1228 or 417-831-3645). Take Chestnut St. westbound and turn left on Hazeltine to reach Farm Rd. 140. Over 60 pleasant sites, some with hookup. Sites from $23, with hookup from $32. Cabins $50. AmEx/D/MC/V. ❶

FOOD

Springfield's streets are studded with quirky coffeehouses, hearty cafes, and a number of laid-back bars.

Mudhouse Downtown Coffeehouse, 323 S. B Ave. (☎417-832-1720). Mudhouse roasts its own beans (espresso $2), throws its own ceramics, and whips up smoothies ($4) and sandwiches ($6). Free Wi-Fi. Open M-Sa 7am-midnight, Su 8am-11pm. AmEx/D/MC/V. ❶

Nonna's Italian American Cafe, 306 South Ave. (☎417-831-1222), at McDaniel St. *Nonna* means grandma in Italian, and along the walls of this cheery bistro you will find photos of all the grannies of anyone who has worked there. Hosts live music and open-mike nights. Sandwiches $7-8. Entrees $8-9. Open M and Su 11am-9pm, Tu-Sa 11am-10pm. AmEx/D/MC/V. ❷

Crosstown Barbecue, 1331 E. Division St. (☎417-862-4646). This place has been serving Springfield's finest hickory-smoked meats for decades. Come here to shamelessly tuck away a huge plate of beef, pork, and ham, all cooked to perfection, and then spend the rest of the day digesting it. Full dinners $10 and up. Sandwiches $7 and up. Open M-Sa 11am-9pm. Drive-through open until 10pm. MC/V. ❷

Anton's Coffee Shop, 937 S. Glendstone Ave. (☎417-869-7681), at Grand. Unremarkable from the outside, on the inside Springfield's best breakfast bar is festooned with ancient pots and pans, menus from around the world, and 35 years of local history. Every omelet you could imagine ($7-8) plus sandwiches, salads, and burgers for lunch (all $6-8). Su brunch. Open M and W-Sa 6am-2pm, Su 8am-2pm. Cash only. ❷

◐ SIGHTS

More than just a retail store, **Bass Pro Shops,** 1935 S. Campbell Ave., is an outdoorsman's indoor amusement park. The store includes acres of merchandise plus a restaurant with a 20,000 gal. aquarium, a firing range, a four-story waterfall, a **taxidermy museum,** the **Archery Hall of Fame,** and thousands of stuffed animals, including two polar bears. (☎417-887-7334. Open M-Sa 7am-10pm, Su 9am-7pm.) **The American National Fish and Wildlife Museum,** 500 W. Sunshine St., usually features live animals swimming below and flying overhead but is closed until August 2009. (☎888-521-9497; www.wondersofwildlife.org. Open daily 9am-6pm.) For a relaxing walk, visit Springfield's "oasis of serenity," the **Mizumoto Japanese Stroll Garden,** 2400 S. Scenic Ave., in Nathanael Greene Park. (☎417-864-1049. Open Apr.-Oct. M and F-Sa 9am-7:30pm. $3, under 12 free.) Just north of Springfield, **Fantastic Caverns,** 4872 N. Farm Rd. 125, offers "America's Only Drive-Thru Cave" in caverns that were once owned by the Ku Klux Klan. (☎417-833-2010; www.fantasticcaverns.com. Open daily 8am-sunset. $21.50, ages 6-12 $13.50, under 6 free.) Trade in your road-worn paperbacks at the **Well-Fed Head,** 331 S. Campbell Ave., which

buys, sells, and trades books. (☎417-832-9333. Open Tu-Sa 11am-9pm.)

◪ NIGHTLIFE

The intersection of **Walnut Street** and **South Avenue** comes alive on the weekends, with lots of drinking options, live music, horse-pulled carriages, and bicycle rickshaws.

Ernie Biggs Dueling Piano Bar, 312 South Ave. (☎417-865-4782; www.erniebiggs.com). Get in early to find a table at this popular downtown joint with nightly acts. The performers are slick, but some of the best entertainment comes from the well-hydrated audience. Piano shows 8pm. $3 drinks Th. Cover $5. Open Tu-W 9pm-1:30am, Th-Sa 7pm-1:30am. AmEx/D/MC/V.

Patton Alley Pub, 313 S. Patton Ave. (☎417-865-1188). If you're sick of tasteless American beer, this is the spot for you; 42 beers from around the world on tap and a further 88 bottled. Live music 6 nights a week. Trivia Su. Open daily 2pm-1:30am. AmEx/D/MC/V.

⚲ THE ROAD TO CARTHAGE: 56 MI.

Leave Springfield on **West Chestnut Expressway.** This road becomes **Route 266;** follow it westward. The road from Springfield south to Carthage is one of the most untouched stretches of Missouri's Rte. 66; decrepit stone buildings with Rte. 66 signs stand amid functioning cattle ranches. Follow Rte. 66 straight where Rte. 96 diverges. Two miles later, cross Rte. 96 and head right over the creek and bridge, turning left when the back road crosses Rte. 96. Follow **Route 66/96** until it becomes **Central Avenue.** Turn left on **Main Street** and continue to Courthouse Sq. in Carthage.

CARTHAGE ☎417

Miles of cattle and little else give way to the chateau-like turrets of the Jasper County Courthouse in elegant but diminutive Carthage. Carthaginians proudly trace their history parallel to the rise and fall, and rise again, of ancient Carthage and pride themselves on being emblematic of Missouri's contentious position in the Civil War.

✳ ORIENTATION

Route 66/96 enters Carthage from the east and runs just north of downtown as **Central Avenue.**

Numbered streets, starting with **Second Street** one block south of Central Ave., run east-west through town. In the eastern section, east-west streets take the names of trees; **Oak Street** is two blocks south of Central Ave. **Route 571,** known as **Garrison Avenue,** is a main north-south drag.

VITAL STATS

Population: 13,000

Tourist Office: Chamber of Commerce, 402 S. Garrison St. (☎417-358-2373; www.visit-carthage.com). Open M-F 8:30am-5pm.

Library and Internet Access: Carthage Public Library, 612 S. Garrison Ave. (☎417-237-7040), at the corner of 7th St. Open M-W 9am-8pm, Th-F 9am-6pm, Sa 9am-4pm.

Post Office: 226 W. 3rd St. (☎417-358-2307). Open M-F 8am-4:30pm, Sa 8:30am-noon. **Postal Code:** 64836.

ACCOMMODATIONS

Grand Avenue B&B, 1615 Grand Ave. (☎888-380-6786). Each room is adorned in the style of a different 19th-century author; you'll hardly be roughing it in the Mark Twain room. Breakfast included. Rooms $74-109. ❸

Best Budget Inn, 13008 E. Hwy. 96 (☎417-358-6911). Offers comfy rooms overlooking a pond on the east side of Carthage as well as a pool, laundry, and free Wi-Fi. Singles $45; doubles $55. D/MC/V. ❸

FOOD

Carthage Deli, 301 S. Main St. (☎417-358-8820). A 50s-style diner with pink Cadillac booths. Features diner favorites as well as Italian sodas and espresso drinks. Sandwiches $3-4. Open M-F 7am-5pm, Sa 8am-4pm. MC/V. ❶

Carthage Family Restaurant, 125 N. Garrison Ave. (☎417-359-8411). Serves up just about anything your heart desires (the menu is large) for breakfast, lunch or dinner. Everything under $10. Open daily 6am-9pm. MC/V. ❷

Stone's Throw Dinner Theater, 796 S. Stone Ln. (☎417-358-9665). The relaxed theater presents comedies, mysteries, and dramas. Call ahead for hours. $20, under 16 $17, seniors $19. ❹

SIGHTS

As you leave town, don't miss the **Route 66 Drive-In,** 17231 Old 66 Blvd. Built in 1949, it is the last of the six original drive-in theaters named after the Mother Road. (☎417-359-5959. $5.)

JASPER COUNTY COURTHOUSE. Downtown Carthage centers on the spired, castle-like courthouse where historic cannons and exhibits on the county's past are on display. (☎417-358-0421. Open M-F 8:30am-4:30pm. Free.)

CARTHAGE CIVIL WAR MUSEUM. Down the street at the Carthage Civil War Museum, army figurines and mannequins explain the town's role in the Civil War and Missouri politics. (205 Grant St. ☎417-237-7060. Open M-Sa 8:30am-5pm, Su 1-5pm. Free.)

THE ROAD TO JOPLIN: 12 MI.

From **Central Avenue,** turn left on **Garrison Avenue,** then right on **Oak Street.** Bear left at the fork on the western edge of town, pass over the highway, and turn left again at the T in front of the Carterville, cemetery, at which point **Route 66** becomes **Pine Street.** When you get into Carterville turn right onto **Main Street,** go through Webb City, and veer left onto **Madison Street,** which leads to downtown Joplin.

JOPLIN ☎417

Joplin is noted for the mural in the **Municipal Building,** at Third St. and Broadway, painted by Thomas Hart Benton, a noted Missourian and an early mentor of Jackson Pollock. The **Joplin Museum Complex,** in Schifferdecker Park, at the corner of Old Rte. 66 and Schifferdecker Ave., contains a rock display, a cookie-cutter collection, and a salute to the area's mining past. (☎417-623-1180. Open Tu 10am-7pm, W-Sa 10am-5pm, Su 2-5pm. $2, under 5 free.) The **Red Onion Cafe** ❸, at the corner of Fourth and Virginia St., is an island of gourmet sandwiches ($6-8) in a sea of fast food. The Kentucky bourbon pecan pie ($4) is finger-lickin' good. (☎417-623-1004. Salads $5-7. Open M-Th 11am-8pm, F-Sa 11am-9pm. AmEx/MC/V.)

THE ROAD TO RIVERTON: 11 MI.

Take **Seventh Street** out of Joplin and turn right at the "Rte. 66 Next Right" sign onto an old alignment featuring white Rte. 66 shields on the narrow stretches of concrete. Be careful on the rises over railroad tracks, where oncoming traffic is difficult to see. Where bustling I-44 heads straight from Missouri to Oklahoma, Rte. 66 pays a 13 mi. tribute to southeastern Kansas. After passing by Galena, take Seventh St. for 3 mi.

The Sunflower State
KANSAS
Welcomes You!

RIVERTON ☎620

For any souvenir needs, be sure to stop at **Eisler Brothers Old Riverton Store.** Located in a red-and-white roadside shack right along Historic Rte. 66, Eisler Bros. is part deli, part grocery store, and part Rte. 66 souvenir shop. The store has been offering a little bit of everything since 1925. (☎620-848-3330. Open M-Sa 7:30am-8pm, Su noon-7pm. AmEx/MC/V.)

 THE ROAD TO BAXTER SPRINGS: 5 MI.

Cross over at the junction with Rte. 400, heading straight and then left, passing an old, white trussed bridge along the way. Entering town, turn left, then right on **Aron Lane,** which turns into **Military Avenue.**

BAXTER SPRINGS ☎620

This village can lay claim to two curious historical footnotes: baseball legend **Mickey Mantle** was playing here when he was spotted by the New York Yankees, and the **Eden Grocery Store,** at 12th St. and Wyandotte Ave., was twice robbed by Bonnie and Clyde. Check out **Angles on the Route,** 1143 Military Ave., for soups, sandwiches, and goodies like scones, brownies, and frozen custard. (☎620-856-2266. Free Wi-Fi. Open M-Tu and Th-F 7am-7pm, Sa 9am-5pm, Su 10am-3pm. Cash only.) Located in the Baxter National Bank, the **Cafe on the Route ❸,** 1101 Military Ave., is a long-standing Rte. 66 eatery, with upscale dining and downscale prices. The menu features delicious salads ($6), pasta ($6-8), and meat entrees for $8-14. (☎620-856-5646. Open M-Sa 11am-2:30pm and 4-9pm, Su 11am-2pm. AmEx/D/MC/V.) Upstairs, The **Little Brick Inn ❷** offers spacious rooms, each with bath. (☎620-856-5646. Rooms $50-75. D/MC/V.)

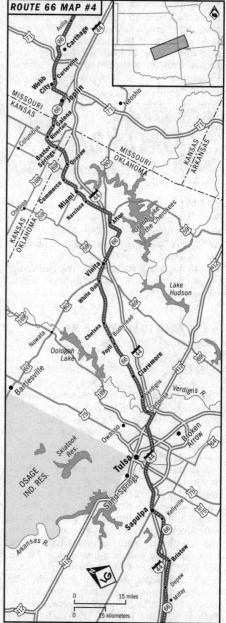

ROUTE 66 MAP #4

ROUTE 66

⚲ THE ROAD TO MIAMI: 16 MI.

Leaving town, head left on **Roberts Street,** swinging right to detour behind the businesses and then merging left again onto **US 69** as you head into Oklahoma. Go through Quapaw, 4 mi. over the border, then pass into Commerce, Mickey Mantle's hometown. Locals will be happy to point out the little house where Mickey, the Commerce Comet, grew up.

The Sooner State
OKLAHOMA
Welcomes You!

MIAMI ☎918

Don't blow your cover by mispronouncing Miami—properly said, it's "My-AM-uh." Check out **Waylan's Ku-Ku Hamburgers ❶,** 915 N. Main St., a 1960s chain whose yellow-and-green cuckoos are the last of their breed. The restaurant serves up burgers ($2.50-4.50), shakes, malts, and sundaes. (☎918-542-1696. Open M-Th and Su 10am-11pm, F-Sa 10am-midnight. MC/V.)

⚲ THE ROAD TO VINITA: 25 MI.

Continue on **US 69** into Vinita.

VINITA ☎918

As you enter Vinita from the north, the first major attraction is the **Will Rogers Rodeo Grounds** to the left. The Will Rogers Memorial Rodeo, which attracts some of the best cowboys in the country, takes place here over four days every August. (☎918-256-7133.) Instead of following Rte. 66 all the way through town, stop by the **World's Largest McDonald's** (though the title is heavily disputed). Spanning the Will Rogers Expwy., the giant glass monument to fast food includes McMeeting rooms, McGiftshops, and McBathrooms in addition to all your McFood needs. Turn left at the Rodeo, and follow the road for about half a mile. Turn right just before the overpass. (☎918-256-5571. Open daily 5:30am-midnight.) Each room in **The Relax Inn ❷,** 110 W. Dwain Wills Ave., has dark wood paneling, cable TV, and free Wi-Fi. (☎918-256-6492. Singles from $36; doubles from $47. AmEx/D/MC/V.) The **Clanton**

Cafe ❷, 319 E. Illinois St., is the oldest family-owned restaurant on Rte. 66 and has offered up unique meal options since 1927, including Vinita's famed "calf fries" (cow testicles; $6), as well as tamer cow-part options. (☎918-256-9053. Open M-F 6am-8pm, Sa 7am-2pm, Su 11am-2pm. D/MC/V.)

⚲ THE ROAD TO FOYIL: 27 MI.

In the heart of downtown Vinita, head left on **Wilson Street.** Leave town on **Route 66,** following it southwest through the small towns of White Oak and Chelsea until reaching Foyil.

FOYIL ☎918

One of the stranger attractions along the Oklahoma stretch of Rte. 66 is **Totem Pole Park.** Artist Ed Galloway's masterpiece is a meadow of brightly colored totem poles, including the **world's largest totem pole** (90 ft.), birdbaths, and an 11-sided "Fiddle House" that once held over 300 fiddles. The building now serves as the park's museum and visitors center. Turn east at the northern end of town on Rte. 28A, following the road for about 4 mi. to get to the park. (☎918-342-9149. Open M-Sa 11am-3pm, Su noon-4pm. Donation suggested.)

⚲ THE ROAD TO CLAREMORE: 10 MI.

Returning to **Route 66,** continue west for 8 mi.

CLAREMORE ☎918

What Abe Lincoln is to Illinois, cowboy/entertainer Will Rogers is to Oklahoma, and Claremore is the center of Rogers mania. The Will Rogers Memorial Museum sits on Will Rogers Blvd., next to Rogers State University, while Will Rogers sculptures and memorials line the streets. A number of antique stores line Will Rogers Blvd., which has a Sooner look.

▣ ORIENTATION

Route 65 runs northeast-southwest through Claremore as **Lynn Riggs Boulevard,** and streets are arranged in a navigable grid south of Rte. 65. Numbered streets run east-west through the city, while avenues run north-south. **Will Rogers Boulevard,** the city's main street, is one block southwest of **Fourth Street.**

VITAL STATS

Population: 16,000

Tourist Office: Claremore Convention and Visitors Bureau, 419 W. Will Rogers Blvd. (☎918-341-8688; www.claremore.org). Open M-F 8:30am-5pm.

Library and Internet Access: Will Rogers Library, 1515 N. Florence St. (☎918-341-1564). Open M-Tu 9:30am-8pm, W-Th 9:30am-6pm, F-Sa 9:30am-5pm.

Post Office: 400 W. 9th St. (☎918-343-5912). Open M-F 8am-5pm, Sa 9am-noon. **Postal Code:** 74017.

ACCOMMODATIONS

Claremore Motor Inn, 1709 N. Lynn Riggs Blvd. (☎918-342-4545; www.cmi66.com). Well-kept rooms. Singles from $50; doubles from $58. AmEx/D/MC/V. ❷

Hawthorn Bluff Campground (☎918-443-2319), 9 mi. north of Claremore. On the way to the Will Rogers Birthplace Ranch, Hawthorn Bluff Campground has swimming and basic sites. Sites $15, with electricity $18. AmEx/D/MC/V. ❶

FOOD

Hammett House, 1616 W. Will Rogers Blvd. (☎918-341-7333). Unusual variety characterizes the cooking. Pies ($4) come in flavors like lemon pecan and sour cream raisin, and their lamb and turkey fries (cousins to calf fries; See opposite page.) have a thankful resemblance to chicken. Sandwiches and salads $8. Entrees $10-25. Open Tu-Sa 11am-9pm. AmEx/D/MC/V. ❸

Dot's Cafe, 310 W. Will Rogers Blvd. (☎918-341-9718). Claremore's oldest restaurant. The homemade chili ($4) is a specialty, but the burgers ($2.50) are also delicious. Open M-W and F-Su 7am-2pm, Th 7am-8pm. Cash only. ❷

SIGHTS

WILL ROGERS MUSEUM. Fanfare for Will Rogers, the legendary trick roper, actor, and philanthropist, is everywhere in Claremore—if he was merely a name when you entered town, he'll seem like an old friend when you leave. At the Will Rogers Memorial Museum, the Will Rogers statue out front watches over Claremore from high on a hill to the northeast of town. Inside, video reels and a barrage of paintings, clippings, and photographs pay homage to the life of Oklahoma's favorite son. *(1720 W. Will Rogers Blvd. ☎800-324-9455; www.will-rogers.com. Open daily 8am-5pm. Tours by appointment. Suggested donation $4, children $3.)*

WILL ROGERS BIRTHPLACE. At the Will Rogers Birthplace Ranch, the white log cabin where Will Rogers grew up has largely been preserved. The view from atop the hill remains quietly breathtaking, interrupted only by the horses, goats, and peacock that wander the grounds. *(2 mi. east of Oologah. Head northwest on Will Rogers Blvd. and take Rte. 88 for 12 mi. north toward Oologah. ☎918-275-4201. Open daily 8am-5pm. Tours by appointment. Suggested donation $3-4.)*

LYNN RIGGS MEMORIAL. If you haven't found yourself spelling out "Oklahoma" in song yet, a visit to the Lynn Riggs Memorial will give you a jump-start. Riggs wrote *Green Grow the Lilacs,* upon which Rodgers and Hammerstein based their smash hit *Oklahoma!* (121 N. Weenonah St. ☎918-627-2716. Open M-F 9am-noon and 1-4pm. Suggested donation $3.)

JM DAVIS ARMS AND HISTORICAL MUSEUM. The museum features the 20,000-piece collection of JM Davis, making it the world's largest privately owned gun collection. The collection includes 1200 beer steins, Native American artifacts, and a 500-year-old Chinese hand cannon. *(333 N. Lynn Riggs Blvd. ☎918-341-5707. Open M-Sa 8:30am-5pm, Su 1-5pm. Free.)*

PHOTO OP. In Catoosa, about 11 mi. beyond Claremore, the main attraction is a **giant blue whale,** once a water slide and now merely a picnic area and roadside gawking point.

THE ROAD TO TULSA: 15 MI.

Leave town heading west on **Lynn Riggs Boulevard** and continue west on **Route 66.** Just past Catoosa, head right on **Ford Avenue,** 1 mi. past Spunky Creek, then left on **Cherokee Street** at the T intersection 2 mi. later. Head left under the interstate, continuing about 1 mi. to **11th Street.** Turn right on 11th St.

ROUTE 66

TULSA ☎918

Though Tulsa is not Oklahoma's political capital, it is in many ways the state's center of commerce and culture. First settled by Creek Native Americans arriving on the Trail of Tears and named for the old Alabama settlement "Tulsey Town," Tulsa's location on the banks of the Arkansas River made it an optimal trading outpost. It was once known as the oil capital of the world, but for roadtrippers it is most notable as the home of Cyrus Avery, the "Father of Rte. 66."

VITAL STATS

Population: 390,000

Tourist Office: Tulsa Convention and Visitors Bureau, 2 W. 2nd St., #150 (☎918-585-1201 or 800-558-3311; www.visittulsa.com). Open M-F 8am-5pm.

Library and Internet Access: Tulsa Public Library, 400 Civic Center (☎918-596-7977), at 4th St. and Denver Ave. Open M-Th 9am-9pm, F-Sa 9am-5pm, Su 1-5pm.

Post Office: 333 W. 4th St. (☎918-584-0489). Open M-F 7:30am-5pm. **Postal Code:** 74103.

✈ ORIENTATION

Tulsa is divided into quadrants. Downtown surrounds **Main Street** (north-south) and **Admiral Boulevard**. Numbered east-west streets ascend to the north and south of Admiral Blvd. Named avenues run north-south in alphabetical order; those named after western cities are west of Main St., while eastern cities lie to the east.

🛏 ACCOMMODATIONS

Decent budget accommodations are scarce downtown, but they are plentiful off **I-44** on the east and west sides of Tulsa.

Desert Hills Motel, 5220 E. 11th St. (☎918-834-3311). Look for the neon cactus sign. This motel offers clean rooms, although non-smoking options are limited. Free Wi-Fi. Singles $40; doubles $50. AmEx/D/MC/V. ❷

Western Inn, 5915 E. 11th St. (☎918-835-7640). Down the road from the Desert Hills. Basic but clean rooms run by a friendly family. Free Wi-Fi. Singles $40; doubles $45. AmEx/D/MC/V. ❷

Western Capri Motel, 5320 W. Skelly Dr. (☎918-446-2644). The vintage sign on this recently renovated motel proves that it's the cheapest option on the strip. There are few decorations in the rooms, but in a good, thank God they didn't bother kind of way. Free Wi-Fi. Singles $38; doubles $45. MC/V. ❶

Gateway Motor Hotel, 5600 W. Skelly Dr. (☎918-446-6611). Rooms with cable TV and DVD/VCR players. Free Wi-Fi. Singles $35; doubles $44. AmEx/D/MC/V. ❷

🍴 FOOD

Tulsa has the usual fast-food chains lining I-44, but if it's real food you're after, skip these and head for the more original establishments scattered around town. Upscale food is available downtown, but many restaurants cater to businesspeople and close at 2pm on weekdays and altogether on weekends.

Tally's Cafe, 1102 S. Yale St. (☎918-835-8039). It might appear to be simply another 1950s cafe with vinyl booths and a checkered floor, but Tally's offers something rarely found in a 66 diner: a "healthy corner" on its menu. If scurvy has begun to set in, duck in here for a remedy (seasonal fruit plate $6). If you don't care about your health, you can always just tuck into the famous chicken-fried steak for $7. Open daily 6am-10pm. AmEx/D/MC/V. ❷

Weber's Root Beer, 3817 S. Peoria Ave. (☎918-742-1082). A local classic housed in an unmistakable orange hut. A family-run business since the late 1800s. Weber's founder Oscar Weber Bilby was recently credited with having invented the hamburger. Root beer $1.25. Half-pound hamburger $5. Open M-Sa 11am-8pm, Su 11am-5pm. MC/V. ❶

Brook Restaurant & Bar, 3401 S. Peoria Ave. (☎918-748-9977), in an old movie theater. Classic Art Deco appeal with a menu of chicken, burgers, wraps, and salads ($8-9). Open M-Th 11am-midnight, F-Sa 11am-1am, Su 11am-11pm. AmEx/D/MC/V. ❸

Queenie's Cafe, 1834 Utica Sq. (☎918-749-3481). Caters to every need: a healthful breakfast, a light lunch, an indulgent afternoon tea, or a hasty burger dinner. Just be sure to try the cookies or a tasty slice of tart. Sandwiches $6-7. Bakery products $1.25 and up. Open M-F 7am-7pm, Sa 8am-6pm, Su 9am-2pm. MC/V. ❷

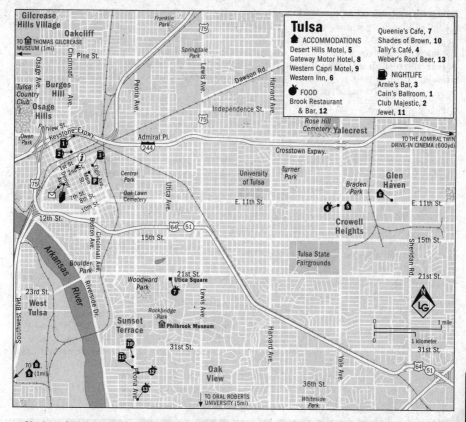

Tulsa

🏠 ACCOMMODATIONS
Desert Hills Motel, **5**
Gateway Motor Hotel, **8**
Western Capri Motel, **9**
Western Inn, **6**

🍎 FOOD
Brook Restaurant
& Bar, **12**

Queenie's Cafe, **7**
Shades of Brown, **10**
Tally's Café, **4**
Weber's Root Beer, **13**

🍺 NIGHTLIFE
Arnie's Bar, **3**
Cain's Ballroom, **1**
Club Majestic, **2**
Jewel, **11**

Shades of Brown, 3302 S. Peoria Ave. (☎918-747-3000). Bohemian student hangout with comfy sofas and shelves of books to sample. Lattes $2.80. Free Wi-Fi. Open M-Th 6:30am-midnight, F 6:30-1am, Sa 7am-1am, Su 9am-midnight. MC/V. ❶

👁 SIGHTS

🖼PHILBROOK MUSEUM. The museum houses an extensive collection of Renaissance paintings in a luxurious Italianate villa deep in one of Tulsa's swankiest neighborhoods. The beautifully manicured gardens alone are worth the visit. In the summer, the museum hosts films, lectures, and art classes. (*2727 S. Rockford Rd. Follow the signs from Utica Ave.* ☎800-324-7941; www.philbrook.org. Open Tu-W and F-Su 10am-5pm, Th 10am-8pm. $7.50, students.)

THOMAS GILCREASE MUSEUM. Perched amid the Osage Hills, 2 mi. from downtown, the Thomas Gilcrease Museum has the world's largest collection of Western American art as well as 250,000 Native American artifacts. See feather bonnets, cowboy sculptures, and wonderful themed gardens. (*1400 Gilcrease Museum Rd. Take the Gilcrease Rd. exit off I-244.* ☎918-596-2700; www.gilcrease.org. Open Tu-Su 10am-5pm. $8, students $5, under 18 free, seniors $6.*)

🍺 NIGHTLIFE

Check out the free *Urban Tulsa*, at local restaurants, and *The Spot* in the Friday *Tulsa*

World for up-to-date specs on arts and entertainment. Tulsa's nightlife is neatly situated in pockets around the city. In **Brookside**, along the southern sector of Peoria Ave., a cluster of bars and restaurants cater to young professionals. For a slightly more artsy and bohemian scene, head downtown.

Cain's Ballroom, 423 N. Main St. (☎918-584-2306; www.cainsballroom.com). Housed in an old garage. Tulsa's premier live music venue regularly hosts big-name acts. Ticket prices vary according to events. Box office open M-F 10am-noon and 1-4pm.

Arnie's Bar, 318 E. 2nd St. (☎918-812-6219). A delightful rough and ready interior with Oklahoma's oldest shuffleboard (operating since 1943) and a small beer garden. Arnie's is open 364 days a year—closed only the day after St. Patrick's Day for the requisite clean-up. Open daily 2pm-2am. AmEx/D/MC/V.

Jewel, 3340 S. Peoria Ave. (☎918-743-0600). To shake your booty with Tulsa's finest, head to Jewel, a martini lounge and champagne bar with a small dance floor. Dress casual Tu-Th, smart F-Sa. 21+ Tu-Th, 23+ F-Sa. Open Tu-Sa 9pm-2am.

Club Majestic, 124 N. Boston Ave. (☎918-584-949; www.clubmajestictulsa.com). Tulsa's principal gay venue. Hosts drag shows, pageants, and other events. Cover varies. Open Th-Su 9pm-2am. D/MC/V.

⚑ FESTIVALS

Tulsa thrives during the **International Mayfest** (☎918-582-6435) in mid-May. August brings both **Jazz on Greenwood,** which includes concerts at Greenwood Park, 300 N. Greenwood Dr., and the **Intertribal Powwow,** at the Tulsa Fairgrounds Pavilion. The Powwow attracts Native Americans and thousands of onlookers for a three-day festival of food, crafts, and nightly dance contests. (www.iicot.org. $5.)

⚐ THE ROAD TO SAPULPA: 11 MI.

Head southwest on **11th Street.** Curve left passing Denver Ave. as 11th St. turns into **12th Street.** Half a mile later, turn left and cross the river. Continue on **Southwest Boulevard** toward Sapulpa. Follow Southwest Blvd. until it becomes **Frankoma Road.** Rte. 66 heading into Sapulpa is also known as **Mission Street;** turn right on Mission St., following the railroad tracks.

SAPULPA   ☎918

Named for Chief Sapulpa, the Lower Creek Native American who established a trading post here in 1850, Sapulpa was once an oil and gas town. It is now known for **Frankoma Pottery,** 9549 Frankoma Rd., which has produced pieces made from Oklahoma clay since 1938. (☎918-224-5511; www.frankoma.com. Open M-Sa 9am-5pm, Su 1-5pm. Free.)

Al's Route 66 Cafe ❶, 219 E. Dewey Ave., is another of those rare diners that also has

WHO DRIVES ROUTE 66?

Rte. 66 holds most meaning for those who lived on its path and for the people whose lives were shaped and sustained by the steady stream of voyagers who passed along it. But there is also a strong interest in Rte. 66 from beyond the communities situated directly along the road: from elsewhere in America, from Europe, and beyond.

Indeed, many of those driving the route today are foreigners who come to the US to explore a lifelong interest in the legendary highway. Exposed to the ethos of classic American roadtrip culture in Europe, they come to get a taste of it for themselves. The custom is to fly into Chicago or LA, buy a Harley Davidson, drive the route, and then get the bike shipped back to one's home country.

There are also many non-American Rte. 66 support groups and fan clubs. The first website dedicated to Rte. 66 (www.historic66.com) was set up by a man from Belgium. And in February 2008 the first Czech Route 66 Association Convention was held, with more than 150 Rte. 66 aficionados from the Czech Republic and Slovakia gathering to celebrate the Mother Road.

Roadtripping USA raises a glass to all voyagers of this legendary route: may you find every diner

healthy options. Try the tuna salad ($4) or stuffed tomatoes. (☎918-224-4190. Open M-F 8am-8pm, Sa 8am-3pm. MC/V.)

⌐ THE ROAD TO BRISTOW: 21 MI.

One mile after turning onto **Mission Street** at the northeastern edge of Sapulpa, turn right onto **Dewey Street.** There is no Historic 66 sign at this turn, but you will see the signs for Rte. 66 and 33. Follow **Route 66** through Kelleyville, site of Oklahoma's worst train disaster in 1917, and on to Bristow.

BRISTOW   ☎918

Bristow was born in 1897 as a trading post for the Cherokee Nation, and a historic flavor is evident as you drive through; the streets are brick, and the buildings are old-fashioned. Rte. 66 is the main street of Bristow, where people seem relatively unconcerned with the Mother Road. **Russ's Ribs ❷**, 223 S. Main St., however, displays its Rte. 66 pride with hand-stenciled 66 shields and vintage signs as well as messages tacked on the walls from everyone who passes through. Sample some of the excellent barbecue like the rib sandwich ($4) or try the frog-legs basket for $7. (☎918-367-5656. All-you-can-eat ($9.50) F 6pm. Open Tu-Th 10:30am-7pm, F-Sa 10:30am-8pm. MC/V.)

⌐ THE ROAD TO STROUD: 16 MI.

Take a right on **Fourth Street.** The road bends to the left to become **Roland Street** and takes you into the heart of Stroud.

STROUD   ☎918

Home to the Sac and Fox Nation, one of Oklahoma's 39 Native American tribes, Stroud sports many buildings built prior to statehood. As you leave, stop by the **Stable Ridge Vineyard,** 2016 Hwy. 66 W. The tasting room is located in Stroud's historic Catholic church, and the wine, which has won international awards, is delicious. (☎800-359-3990; www.stableridgevineyards.com. Open M-Th 10am-5pm, F-Sa 10am-6pm, Su noon-5pm.)

Rooms at the **Skyliner Motel ❷**, 717 W. Main St., beneath the dazzling sign, are clean and cheap and come with fridges and microwaves. (☎918-968-9556. Singles from $45; doubles from $55. AmEx/D/MC/V.)

⌐ THE ROAD TO DAVENPORT: 8 MI.

Continue along **Route 66,** and don't miss the Burma Shave signs welcoming you to Davenport.

DAVENPORT   ☎918

Davenport is home to the first spherical oil tank, erected in 1925 to the northeast of town. **Garwooly's Game Room ❷**, 1023 Broadway, at the eastern side of town, covers the nightlife bases with a dim dining area, squeaky-clean chrome and tile ice-cream parlor, and adjoining checkered dance floor. (☎918-377-2230. Indian taco made with fry bread $4. Chicken-fried steak $7. Open M-Sa 10am-9pm, Su 11am-3pm. D/MC/V.)

⌐ THE ROAD TO CHANDLER: 4 MI.

Continue following **Route 66.**

CHANDLER   ☎405

In Chandler, you can see buildings that survived the 1897 tornado and some authentic ghost signs on the sides of old buildings. The town is also home to the **Lincoln County Historical Society Museum,** 719 Manvel St., which depicts Oklahoma pioneer history with period clothing, a 19th-century buggy, a buffalo skull, and a flush-toilet outhouse from 1902 (really, there wasn't much else). (☎405-258-2425. Open Tu-Sa 10am-4pm. Suggested donation $2.) The **Route 66 Interpretive Center,** 400 E. Hwy. 66, is housed in a magnificently restored former National Guard Armory. The place is ideal for those who suffer from museum fatigue: it supplies retro glitter beds to lie on while you watch video exhibits. (☎405-258-1300; www.route66interpretivecenter.org. Open Tu-Sa 10am-5pm. $5, students and seniors $4.) The **Lincoln Inn Motel ❸**, 740 E. First St., offers snug wood duplexes that have faced Rte. 66 for the last 62 years. (☎405-258-0200. Free Wi-Fi. Singles $45; doubles $55. AmEx/D/MC/V.)

⌐ THE ROAD TO LUTHER: 18 MI.

Follow **Manvel Street** as it curves left, heading west toward the town of Luther.

LUTHER   ☎705

South of the pecan grove at the west end of Luther, the **Tres Suenos Vineyards,** 19691 E.

ROUTE 66

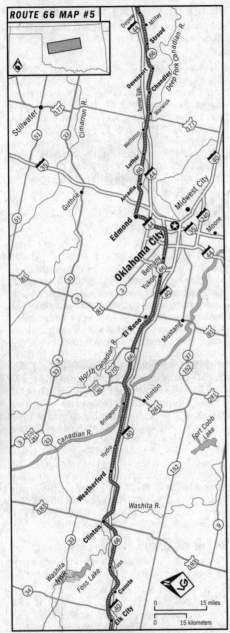

ROUTE 66 MAP #5

Charter Oak Rd., offers free tours and tastings, although it takes a 10min. drive on an unpaved, dusty road to get there. Twelve wines are bottled here; you can taste any of them, but be sure to try the Chenin, made from an American grape. (☎405-277-7089; www.tressuenos.com. Open Th-Sa noon-6pm or by appointment.)

THE ROAD TO ARCADIA: 8 MI.

Continue west on **Route 66.** As you enter Arcadia, look to see remnants of the **Rock of Ages** gas station.

ARCADIA ☎405

Arcadia's main attraction is the **Round Barn.** Originally built in 1898 and restored in 1992, the structure is now a historic landmark. The bottom level is a museum of round barns as they are found around the world, while upstairs is a venue for hosting events. Speak on the center platform and experience an acoustic phenomenon firsthand. (☎405-396-0824; www.arcadiaroundbarn.org. Open daily 10am-5pm. Free.)

THE ROAD TO EDMOND: 15 MI.

Continue on **Route 66** to reach Edmond.

EDMOND ☎405

The site of both the first church and the first school in the Oklahoma Territory, Edmond is now largely overrun with popular commercial establishments and looks like it was erected within the last 15 years. Lodging is plentiful in Edmond, and it is cheaper than the chain motel alternatives in Oklahoma City. **Stafford Inn ❸,** 1809 E. Second St., rents elegant brick-walled rooms, some with hot tubs and king-size beds. (☎405-340-8197. Continental breakfast included. Singles from $55; doubles from $59. AmEx/D/MC/V.) **Broadway Suites ❷,** 1305 S. Broadway, provides excellent value with suites or kitchenette units as well as VCRs ($10) and laundry. (☎800-200-3486. Singles $40; doubles $45. AmEx/D/MC/V.) Hidden among the plentiful food chains is **El Parian ❸,** 315 S. Broadway, serving authentic Mexican food in a colorful red and blue shack. The El Parian special (1 asada taco, 1 fajita quesadilla, and 1 fajita enchilada; $10) is delicious. (☎405-359-1068. Open M-Th and Su 10:30am-9pm, F-Sa 10:30am-9:30pm. MC/V.)

 THE ROAD TO OKLAHOMA CITY: 18 MI. Take **Route 66.** Turn left at **Broadway,** following the **Memorial Road exit.** Go left at the yield sign.

OKLAHOMA CITY ☎405

In the late 1800s, Oklahoma's capital was a major transit point on cattle drives from Texas to the north, and today its stockyards are a fascinating window into a world not often seen by outsiders. Lying along the Santa Fe Railroad, the city was swarmed by over 100,000 homesteaders when Oklahoma was opened to settlement in 1889, and it continues to celebrate American expansion at one of the largest museums devoted to the West.

> **PAGE TURN.** See the **Deep South** (p. 759) for complete coverage of Oklahoma City.

 THE ROAD TO EL RENO: 29 MI.
Continue west on **Route 66.** As you enter El Reno, 66 becomes **Rock Island Avenue.** Look to the right when you first enter to see the historic **Oasis Drive-In** sign, which promises five burgers for $1.

EL RENO ☎405

Located at the intersection of Rte. 66 and the old Chisholm Trail, El Reno has a rich history and the buildings to back it up. The city was the site of three land runs, events where tens of thousands of settlers made a mad dash over newly opened territory to stake the largest claim they could. Thousands of dead German and Italian POWs from WWII, whose remains were recently recovered from North Africa, also lie beneath Reno's red dirt. More recently, the 1988 film *Rain Man* was shot here, and Dustin Hoffman fever runs high.

ORIENTATION

El Reno is laid out in a simple grid; most streets run east-west, while most avenues run north-south. **US 40** runs just south of town, while **Business US 40** splits off to become **Sun-**set Drive** in town. **US 81** enters El Reno from the north, turning into **Choctaw Avenue** on its way through town; downtown is centered on the intersection of Choctaw Ave. and Sunset Dr. Parking is generally plentiful.

VITAL STATS

Population: 16,000

Tourist Office: El Reno Convention and Visitors Bureau, 206 N. Bickford St. (☎888-535-7366; www.elreno.org). Open M-F 9am-5pm.

Library and Internet Access: El Reno Carnegie Library, 215 E. Wade St. (☎405-262-2409). Open M-Th 9am-7pm, F 9am-5pm, Sa 9am-1pm.

Post Office: 203 N. Evans Ave. (☎405-262-5095). Open M-F 8:30am-5pm, Sa 9-11am. **Postal Code:** 73036.

ACCOMMODATIONS

Turn left onto US 81 S. as you enter town to reach a cluster of motels.

The Budget Inn, 1221 W. Sunset Dr. (☎405-262-0251). Conveniently located near the downtown. Lacy decor, cable TV, and laundry. Singles $35; doubles $45. AmEx/D/MC/V. ❷

The Economy Express, 2851 US 81 S. (☎405-262-1022). Has clean and basic rooms with fridges and microwaves. Small breakfast included, so wake up cheerful and hungry. Singles from $45; doubles from $48. AmEx/D/MC/V. ❷

FOOD

Sid's Diner, 300 S. Choctaw Ave. (☎405-262-7757), 1 block south of US 81. Check out the countertop at Sid's Diner for photos of Dustin Hoffman and hundreds of other historic shots. Enjoy the steak and shake special for $5.25. Open M-Sa 7am-8:30pm. Cash only. ❶

Johnnie's Grill, 301 S. Rock Island St. (☎405-262-4721). Grilled onions are pressed into the burger patty and cooked together. Onion fried burger $2.70. Open M-Sa 6am-9pm, Su 11am-8pm. Cash only. ❶

SIGHTS

In town, you can take the **Heritage Express Trolley**—the only rail-based trolley in Oklahoma—

which runs from Heritage Park into El Reno's historic downtown. (☎405-262-5121. Boards at 300 S. Grand St. Call for schedule.)

HEROES PLAZA. The plaza pays tribute to the 206 Canadian County men and women who were killed in 20th-century wars. *(206 N. Bickford Ave. ☎405-262-1188.)*

LAKE EL RENO. Outside of town, Lake El Reno has 4 mi. of shoreline and is perfect for recreational activities like water skiing, swimming, boating, and fishing. The lake is also home to a herd of buffalo.

> **PHOTO OP.** The truly lucky will pass through El Reno on the First Saturday in May for Onion Fried Burger Day, when Johnnie's cranks out the world's largest hamburger, an 800 lb. onion-fried burger bonanza.

🖼 THE ROAD TO WEATHERFORD: 53 MI.
Leave El Reno on **Sunset Drive**, which becomes **Business I-40 West.** Take the Fort Reno turnoff onto **Route 66.** Eleven miles later, turn right onto **US 281.** Spur for about 2 mi., then take a left at the top of the hill onto the old two-lane road. Watch carefully, because it's easy to miss. Turn left at the bottom of the hill to rejoin US 281. Continue on the frontage road through Bridgeport and on toward Weatherford. The stretch between Bridgeport and Weatherford is a vintage piece of road, the old segmented concrete gently rising and falling over the hills. As you drive past Hydro on Rte. 66, check out the structure sporting antique gas pumps on the right. It used to be **Lucille's,** a landmark filling station and market that was sold on eBay following Lucille's death in 2000. New owner Rich Koch is currently restoring the station and built Lucille's Roadhouse (below) in its honor.

WEATHERFORD ☎580
Weatherford is extremely proud of native son Thomas P. Stafford—the 18th man in space. The **Stafford Air and Space Museum,** 3000 E. Logan Rd., Exit 84 from I-40, includes replicas and artifacts of air and space travel from the Wright brothers' plane to the actual desk that responded to Apollo 13's infamous report, "Houston, we have a problem." (☎580-772-5871; www.staffordspacecenter.

com. Open M-Sa 9am-5pm, Su 1-5pm. $5, students and ages 6-18 $2.) ⧉**Lucille's Roadhouse ❷,** 1301 Airport Rd., in Weatherford, pays tribute to the Mother Road with some real food. (☎580-772-8808. Burger and fries $6. Open M-Sa 6am-10pm. AmEx/D/MC/V.)

🖼 THE ROAD TO CLINTON: 15 MI.
About a half mile after the space museum, turn left onto **Lyle Road** and follow it around as it becomes **Main Street.** Continue on Main St. through the center of town. The road bends to the left and you will see a Historic 66 sign indicating a right turn onto **Rainey Avenue,** then another for a left turn onto **Fourth Street.** This becomes the north frontage road. Take this 4 mi. before crossing over to the south side of the highway; cross to the north side again when you hit the end.

CLINTON ☎580
Deeded the land by the federal government, the Native Americans that had been relocated to the area were prohibited from selling more than half of their 160-acre allotments. Determined to found a town in the rich valley, JL Avant and EE Blake secretly bought half allotments from four different men, and in 1902 the amalgamated town was dubbed Clinton for Judge Clinton Irwin. As the headquarters of the **National Highway 66 Association** for almost three decades, Clinton has an abundance of Rte. 66 pride and the first state-sponsored Rte. 66 museum.

VITAL STATS
Population: 9000
Tourist Office: Clinton Chamber of Commerce, 101 S. 4th St. (☎580-323-2222; www.clintonok.org). Open M-F 9am-5pm.
Library and Internet Access: Clinton Public Library, 721 Frisco Ave. (☎580-323-2165). Open M and W 9am-6pm, Tu and Th 9am-8pm, F 9am-5pm, Sa 9am-1pm.
Post Office: 212 S. 11th St. (☎580-323-0712). Open M-F 8am-4:30pm, Sa 9-11am. **Postal Code:** 73601.

◤ ORIENTATION

Clinton is centered on the intersection of **Business I-40** and **US 183. I-40** runs just south of downtown. In town, US 183 is known as

Cox Street, and Bus. I-40 is called **Gary Boulevard,** one of the city's main drags. Numbered streets run north-south, starting with **First Street** in the east.

ACCOMMODATIONS

Best Western Trade Winds Courtyard Inn, 2128 Gary Blvd. (☎800-321-2209 or 580-323-2610). Check in for a little heartbreak and hang up your blue suede shoes where the King himself rocked around the clock each time he came through Clinton. Room 215, where Elvis stayed on 4 occasions, still contains much of the original furniture, and there are probably microscopic traces of his DNA on the surfaces. Singles $45; doubles $54; Elvis Suite $89. AmEx/D/MC/V. ❷

At the Glancy Motel, 217 Gary Blvd. (☎580-323-0112). The giant red vintage sign and the 70s-style wrought iron indicate the age of the motel, but rooms are comfortable enough. Singles $35; doubles $40. MC/V. ❷

FOOD

At the Cherokee **Trading Post Cafe** ❷, 6101 NE Service Rd., a juicy, enticing buffalo burger costs only $6. Take Exit 71 from I-40. (☎580-323-0001. Sandwiches $4-7. Open daily 7am-10pm. AmEx/D/MC/V.)

SIGHTS

OKLAHOMA ROUTE 66 MUSEUM. The state's tribute to Rte. 66 traces the road decade by decade. The museum includes a film narrated by Rte. 66 aficionado Michael Wallis with fascinating archive footage of the construction of the road and its earliest travelers. (*2229 W. Gary Blvd. ☎580-323-7866. Open from Memorial Day to Labor Day M-Sa 9am-7pm, Su 1-6pm; from Labor Day to Memorial Day M-Sa 9am-5pm, Su 1-5pm. $3, ages 6-18 $1, under 6 free, seniors $2.50.*)

CHEROKEE TRADING POST. On the way into Clinton, the much-advertised Cherokee Trading Post sells crafts of every variety, including beautiful jewelry, moccasins, cactuses, and postcards. (*6101 NE Service Rd. Take Exit 71 from I-40. ☎580-323-0001. Open daily 7am-10pm.*)

CHEYENNE CULTURAL CENTER. The center displays work by Cheyenne craftspeople and artists and exhibits on Cheyenne regional history and culture. (*2250 NE Rte. 66. ☎580-323-6224. Open Tu-F 10am-4:30pm. Free.*)

THE ROAD TO CANUTE: 20 MI.

To leave Clinton, head west along **Gary Boulevard.** Just after the Rte. 66 Museum on your right, turn left on **Jay Cee Lane.** Continue for five blocks, then turn right at the T onto **10th Street.** At the fork shortly afterward turn right onto **Neptune Drive.** Fourteen miles after Clinton, you will hit a stop sign: turn right, go over the highway, follow the road as it curves right, then left, and take a left by the large red shed. Continue with **I-40** on your left until you get to the KOA campground (below). For Canute, turn left after the KOA, pass over the interstate, turn right, and continue into Canute.

CANUTE   ☎580

Canute has few diversions to slow your cross-country progress, but Elvis fans can stop at **Kupka's Station,** a gas station where the King was known to stop and fuel up. It's the white building with green stripes on Main St. opposite Fourth St. A convenient spot for camping, the local **KOA Campground** ❶, Exit 50 off I-40, offers a general store, pool, and laundry facilities. (☎580-592-4409. Store open daily in summer 8am-9pm; in winter 8am-7pm. Tent sites $23,; RV sites $32. Cabins $40. D/MC/V.) If you're feeling peckish, head to **Debbie's Diner** ❷, 116 Ninth St. There is no legend of Elvis having taken luncheon here, but it's worth a stop nonetheless, with hearty homecooking to fuel the hungry road warrior. Daily lunch specials run $7.25. (☎580-472-3659. Open M-Sa 7am-3pm. AmEx/D/MC/V.)

THE ROAD TO ELK CITY: 9 MI.

Go straight through the four-way stop in Canute and take a right 1 mi. west to pass under the interstate. Turn left to take the service road into Elk City, following **Business I-40** as you enter town.

ELK CITY   ☎580

Although Elk City's biggest—in all senses—attraction is heralded by a giant neon Rte. 66 sign at the west end of town, the small historic downtown is relatively unconcerned with the tourist traffic just to the north and offers an assortment of homey dining and

ROUTE 66

loitering options in no-frills settings with no-frills prices. Meanwhile, the standard bevy of fast-food regulars lines Rte. 66.

VITAL STATS

Population: 10,500

Tourist Office: Elk City Chamber of Commerce, 1016 Airport Industrial Rd. (☎800-225-0207; www.elkcitychamber.com). Open M-F 9am-5pm.

Library and Internet Access: Elk City Carnegie Library, 221 W. Broadway (☎580-225-0136). Open M, W, F 10am-6pm, Tu and Th 10am-9pm, Sa 10am-2pm.

Post Office: 101 S. Adams Ave. (☎580-225-0294), at Broadway Ave. Open M-F 8:30am-4:30pm, Sa 9am-11am. **Postal Code:** 73644.

ORIENTATION

Streets in Elk City form a grid; avenues run north-south while streets are numbered and run east-west. An exception to this is **Broadway Avenue,** which runs east-west one block south of **Third Street,** both major Elk City thoroughfares. Parking is plentiful.

ACCOMMODATIONS

The Flamingo Inn, 2000 W. 3rd St. (☎580-225-1811). Has all sorts of nice touches that make a welcome change from the monotony of identical, bland motel rooms. 2-tone, colorful tiling in the bathrooms, 1920s cartoon wallpaper, a lovely swing set in the courtyard, and well-tended flower beds will all tickle your sensory organs. Rooms with fridges. Laundromat and park are nearby. Free Wi-Fi. Singles from $40; doubles from $55. AmEx/D/MC/V. ❷

FOOD

Country Dove Tea Room, 610 W. 3rd St. (☎580-225-7028). The French Silk Pie ($3.50) is glorious. If you feel the need to justify it with a meal, the soups and sandwiches ($6.50) are also local legends. Open M-Sa 11am-5pm. Kitchen open until 2pm. D/MC/V. ❶

The Olde Glory Cafe, 104 Meadow Ridge Dr. (☎580-225-4050). Head down S. Main St. past the Sugar Shack and continue over the bridge. Olde Glory serves up standard diner fare, plus

select items like frogs' legs, in an atmosphere that is a mixture of antique shop and restaurant. Dinners $10 and up. Open Tu-Sa 11am-9pm. AmEx/D/MC/V. ❷

The Sugar Shack, 521 S. Main St. (☎580-243-1670). Although its main gig is decorating cakes, the peanut butter fudge ($0.50) and enormous cinnamon rolls ($1.75) are also scrumptious. Open Tu-F 8:30am-5:30pm, Sa 9am-noon. AmEx/D/MC/V. ❶

SIGHTS

The **National Route 66 Museum,** 2717 W. Hwy. 66/W. Third St., right along Rte. 66, is Elk City's pride and joy. Part of a complex of four museums, it features a map of the road made out of T-shirts plus state-by-state displays on the history of Rte. 66. Two giant Kachina dolls guard the grounds, and the exterior of the museum recreates an Old West Rte. 66 townscape. Next door, the **Old Town Museum** features regional history, including a display on Elk City's own Miss America 1981, Susan Powell, and a rotating display of local collections. Also in the complex, the **Farm and Ranch Museum** has vintage machinery, and the **Transportation Museum** allows you to ring the bell on a 1917 fire truck. (☎580-225-6266. Open from Memorial Day to Labor Day M-Sa 9am-7pm, Su 1-5pm; from Labor Day to Memorial Day M-Sa 9am-5pm, Su 2-5pm. Any museum $3. Combination ticket $5, students, ages 6-16, and seniors $4, under 6 free.)

THE ROAD TO SAYRE: 19 MI.

From Elk City, follow **Third Street** out of town. Continue on **Route 66** 7 mi., then turn right onto the Two-lane north frontage road with **Business I-40** directly on your left. After 6 mi., turn left at the T, crossing over **I-40** onto the south side frontage road. One mile later, cross onto the north side again, continuing west. Two miles later, turn right at the stop sign onto Bus. I-40 (unmarked). Bus. I-40 becomes **Fourth Street** heading into downtown Sayre.

SAYRE ☎580

Worth a stop as you pass through Sayre is the **RS&K Railroad Museum,** 411 N. Sixth St. Like a railroad annex to Santa's workshop, Shirley and Ray Killian's garage whirs, whistles, toots, and chugs with hundreds of minia-

 ROUTE 66

ture trains and train-station paraphernalia. (☎580-928-3525. Open M-F 9am-9pm or when the Killians are home. Knock on the front door for a tour. Free.) **The Western Motel ❸,** 315 NE Rte. 66, on the eastern edge of town, rents unremarkable but clean rooms. Look for the vintage sign. (☎580-928-3353. Free Wi-Fi. Singles $56; doubles $70. AmEx/D/MC/V.)

☇ THE ROAD TO TEXOLA: 23 MI.

From **Fourth Street** cross the north fork of the Red River. One mile west of town, take a right just before the overpass onto **El Dorado Street.** Turn left at the stop sign onto **Old Route 66,** then bear right onto the frontage road where the road diverges. Fourteen miles later, take the exit for Texola.

TEXOLA   ☎580

Follow tumbleweeds through the ghost town of Texola. On the western edge of town, an ever-so-truthful sign reads, "There's no other place like this place anywhere near this place, so this must be the place." About nine families live in the main area of town, and it won't take much for you to drive past Texola without even noticing. Pull over for some delicious barbecue at **Windmill Restaurant ❷,** 21 Texola #A, pretty much the only place to eat for miles. Take a right just before the church. (☎580-526-3965. Sandwiches $6. Pork ribs $9.25. Open Tu-F 9am-9pm, Sa 8am-9pm, Su 8am-2:30pm. AmEx/D/MC/V.)

☇ THE ROAD TO SHAMROCK: 13 MI.

From the Oklahoma border, continue 13 mi. to Shamrock. The south service road turns into **Business I-40/ Old Route 66** entering town.

The Lone Star State
TEXAS
Welcomes You!

SHAMROCK   ☎806

Shamrock takes St. Patrick's Day seriously. All men are expected to grow a beard for the occasion. Those without beards are detained in a small jail that is wheeled around the town. The only way you can get around the rule is by pur-

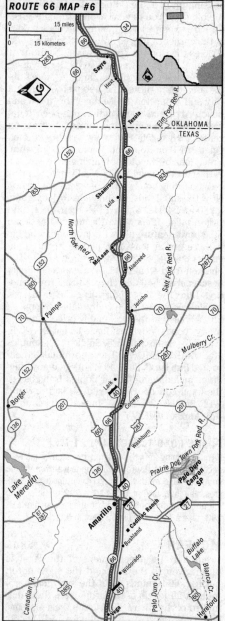

ROUTE 66 MAP #6

ROUTE 66

chasing a $1 "no-beard permit" in advance of the big day. (You needn't worry, though—visitors are exempt.) The historic **U-Drop Inn Cafe,** at the corner of Rte. 66 and US 83, was built in 1936 as the Conoco Tower Service Station. At the time, the cafe was said to be the "swankiest of swank eating places" and the "most up-to-date edifice of its kind between Oklahoma City and Amarillo." These days, the green and peach Art Deco construction has been renovated into a museum and tourist information center. (☎806-256-2501; www.shamrocktx.net. Open M-F 9am-noon and 1-5pm, Sa 10am-4pm. Free.) One of the oldest buildings in town, the **Pioneer West Museum,** 204 N. Madden St., used to be a boarding house for construction workers. Now the small museum hosts history exhibits. (☎806-256-3941. Open M-F 10am-noon and 1-3pm.) The **Texan Movie Theater,** 205 N. Main St., shows feature films Friday-Sunday nights if there are at least five people in the audience. (☎806-256-1212. $4, children $2.50.) The chicken-fried steaks ($8.75) at **Mitchell's Family Restaurant ❷,** I-40 and Hwy. 83 E., are legendary. Take the first right after the overpass. (☎806-256-2141. Open daily 6am-9:30pm. D/MC/V.) Sleep at the reasonably priced and formerly "cowboy owned" **Route 66 Inn ❷,** 800 E. Hwy. 66. (☎806-256-3225. Singles $32; doubles $38. AmEx/D/MC/V.) The enormous, green-roofed **Irish Inn ❸,** 301 I-40 E., offers many amenities including an indoor pool, a free pass to the local golf course, breakfast, laundry, and Wi-Fi. (☎806-256-2106. Singles $50; doubles $76. AmEx/D/MC/V.)

▥ THE ROAD TO MCLEAN: 21 MI.

If you're coming from the Irish Inn, jog left over the **I-40** access, following **Route 66** as you leave town on the south frontage road. Just over 14 mi. down the road, cross the interstate at **Exit 146,** and 2 mi. later, turn left on the north frontage road. At the stop sign at **Exit 143,** take a right onto **First Street** in McLean.

MCLEAN   ☎806

Credit for the development of the West is often given to the rifle and the six-shooter, but Rte. 66 reminds us of the significance of tools at all levels of function, from the windmill to barbed wire. The **Devil's Rope Museum,** dedicated jointly to barbed wire and Rte. 66,

features over 2550 different types of barbed wire. The museum is run by the Barbed Wire Symposium, whose mission, as stated on a plaque in the museum, is, "To present and discuss ideas, come to a consensus of opinion, and publish those ideas and suggestions in an effort to continue and promote the hobby of barbed wire collecting." The **Texas Old Route 66 Association and Museum** is in the same building. Entering town on Rte. 66, turn left on Kingsley St. (☎806-779-2225; www.barbwiremuseum. com. Open Mar.-Nov. 9am-5pm. Donations suggested.) Farther down Rte. 66, in the heart of McLean, the **McLean-Alanreed Area Museum** has an area ranching exhibit, a memorial to local veterans, and a history of McLean and Alanreed. (☎806-779-2731. Open Tu-F 10am-noon and 1-4pm. Free.) Leaving town, glance to the south to see a bright orange 1920s Phillip's 66 service station, the first Phillip's 66 station in Texas. The **Red River Steakhouse ❸,** 101 Rte. 66 West, is a blend of barn and saloon, with bandana napkins, mounted deer heads, doodles by patrons, and license plates along the walls. (☎806-779-8940. Cheeseburger $7. Catfish $12. Open Tu-Sa 11am-9pm. AmEx/D/MC/V.)

▥ THE ROAD TO AMARILLO: 73 MI.

One mile west of McLean, take a left before the overpass. You will briefly double back on yourself before joining the south frontage road with the interstate on your right. Continue on the south frontage road through Alanreed. Continue with the interstate on your right until **Exit 132,** where you need to join the highway. Follow the interstate westbound to **Exit 124** and cross to the south service road. Three miles later, turn left to stay on the frontage road passing through Jericho, Groom, Lark, and Conway, an uneventful stretch of road save for the **enormous cross** you'll see to the right in Groom. Seven miles beyond Conway, cross to the north side of the road and turn left on the north frontage road. Fifteen miles from Amarillo, this becomes **Northeast Avenue.** Follow the road as it makes a sharp turn right and passes an industrial park on the left. Go under the overpass, then take **Route 60 West** into town as **Amarillo Boulevard.**

AMARILLO   ☎806

Named for the yellow clay of nearby Lake Meredith, Amarillo began as a railroad construction camp in 1887 and evolved into a

Texas-size truck stop. Here, you'll find big steaks, bigger canyons, and horns affixed to just about everything. After years of seeing little more than a lot of cattle and oil, Amarillo is now the prime overnight stop for motorists en route from Dallas, Houston, or Oklahoma City to Denver and other Western destinations.

VITAL STATS
Population: 170,000
Tourist Offices: Amarillo Convention and Visitors Bureau, 401 S. Buchanan St. (☎806-374-8474; www.amarillo-cvb.org). Open May-Sept. M-F 9am-6pm, Sa-Su 10am-4pm. Oct.-Apr. M-F 8:30am-5:30pm, Sa noon-4pm. **Texas Travel Info Center,** 9700 I-40 E. (☎806-335-1441), at Exit 76. Open daily 8am-6pm.
Library and Internet Access: Amarillo Public Library, 413 E. 4th Ave. (☎806-378-3054). Internet card $5. Open M-Th 9am-9pm, Sa 9am-6pm, Su 2-6pm.
Post Office: 505 E. 9th Ave. (☎806-373-3192). Open M-F 8am-5pm. **Postal Code:** 79105.

ORIENTATION

Amarillo sprawls at the intersection of **I-27, I-40,** and **US 87/287. Route 335** (the Loop) encircles the city. **Route 66** runs east-west through town as **Amarillo Boulevard** parallel to I-40. Very much a driver's city, Amarillo is fairly easy to navigate, and parking is abundant.

ACCOMMODATIONS

Amarillo provides over 4000 beds for travelers to leave their boots under. Budget motels proliferate along the entire stretch of I-40, I-27, and US 87/287 near town. Prices rise near downtown, but grab a book of coupons at the visitors center to save a few dollars.

Big Texan Motel, 7701 I-40 E. (☎806-372-5000 or 800-657-7177; www.bigtexan.com). Heavily themed, but still rather fun with saloon doors to the bathrooms. Singles from $60; doubles from $70. AmEx/D/MC/V. ❸

Civic Center Inn, 715 S. Fillmore St. (☎806-376-4603). Right in the heart of downtown, with all services within easy walking distance. Offers comfortable, quiet rooms at great rates. Free Wi-Fi. Singles $35; doubles $40. AmEx/D/MC/V. ❷

KOA Kampground, 1100 Folsom Rd. (☎806-335-1792). Take I-40 to Exit 75, head north to Rte. 60, and go east 1 mi. Propane, cable TV, cafe, and swimming pool. Laundry. Free Wi-Fi. Reception daily June-Aug. 8am-9pm; Sept.-May 8am-6pm. Tent sites $26; RV sites with full hookup $37. ❷

FOOD

Dyer's BBQ (☎806-358-7104), on I-40 at Georgia. Expect heaping portions and a friendly vibe. The rib plate includes ribs, potato salad, cole slaw, baked beans, apricot sauce, and onion rings for $9—sharing is advised. Open M-Sa 11am-10pm, Su 11am-9pm. AmEx/D/MC/V. ❸

Tacos Garcia, 1100 S. Ross St. (☎806-371-0411), at 11th St. Try the *carne guisada* (stewed beef simmered with fresh vegetables served with beans, rice, guacamole, and tortillas; $9) and satisfy your sweet tooth with flaky, fresh *sopaipillas* (a pastry covered in sugar; 3 for $3). Open M 10:30am-9:30pm, Tu-Sa 10:30am-10pm, Su 10:30am-3:30pm. AmEx/D/MC/V. ❷

Big Texan Steak Ranch, 7701 I-40 E. (☎806-372-6000; www.bigtexan.com). Promises a free 72 oz. steak dinner if you can eat it in under 1hr. (if not, it'll cost you $72). 1 in 7 men and 1 in 2 women who try manage it! Call for a free limo pickup from any I-40 hotel, motel, or RV park. 8 oz. sirloin $16. AmEx/D/MC/V. ❸

SIGHTS

The recently re-opened **Amarillo Botanical Gardens,** 1400 Streit Dr., now includes a large entry court in addition to the tropical conservatory, fragrance gardens, and butterfly gardens. (☎806-352-6513; www.amarillobotanicalgardens.org. Open Mar.-Nov. Tu-F 9am-5pm, Sa 11am-4pm, Su 1-4pm; Dec.-Apr. Tu-F 9am-5pm. $4, ages 2-12 $2.) At **Cadillac Ranch,** Stanley Marsh III planted 10 Cadillacs—ranging from model year 1948 to 1963—at the same angle as the Great Pyramids in a wheat field west of Amarillo. Get off I-40 at the Hope Rd. exit (62A), 9 mi. west of Amarillo, cross to the south side of I-40, turn right at the end of the bridge, and drive half a mile down the highway access road. (Free.) Marsh is responsible for another quirky attraction in Amarillo. While in the city, keep an eye out for official-looking diamond-shaped signs with slightly

ROUTE 66

offbeat messages. They are scattered around the city and, according to Marsh, are intended as "a system of unanticipated rewards." One reads "What is a village without village idiots?" and another, rather enigmatically, "It's the same brick in the ice pack, it's the same trick with an ice pick."

NIGHTLIFE

Amarillo has a lively drinking scene, with several bars clustered along S. Polk St. in downtown. **Butler's Martini Bar,** 703 S. Polk St., is a pretty cool and swanky joint, with live jazz and blues several times a week. (☎806-376-8180. Bottled beers $2.50 and up. Martinis $6 and up. No cover. Open daily 4pm-2am. AmEx/MC/V.)

DETOUR
PALO DURO CANYON

Palo Duro is 23 mi. south of Amarillo; take **I-27** to **Exit 106** and head east on **Route 217.**

Palo Duro Canyon spans 20,000 acres, and, while it lacks the sheer scale of the Grand Canyon or the beauty of somewhere like Bryce Canyon, it certainly makes a pleasant detour from the route. The 16 mi. scenic drive through the park begins at the headquarters. Rangers allow backcountry hiking, but the majority of visitors stick to interconnected, marked trails. Temperatures in the canyon frequently climb to **100°F;** bring at least two quarts of water. The park headquarters, just inside the park, has trail maps and info on park activities. (☎806-488-2227. Open daily in summer 8am-10pm; in winter 8am-6pm. $4, under 12 free.) The official play of Texas, the musical ▓**Texas Legacies,** 1514 Fifth Ave., is performed in a spectacular outdoor amphitheater. With the canyon as its backdrop, the epic drama includes a tree-splitting lightning bolt and fireworks. (☎806-655-2181; www.texas-show.com. Shows June-Aug. Tu-Su 8:30pm. Tickets $11-27, under 11 $7-23. Barbecue dinner $16, under 11 $12.) **Old West Stables,** a quarter-mile farther along, rents horses and saddles. (☎806-488-2180. Rides June-Aug. 10am, noon, 2, 4, 6pm; Sept.-Oct. and Apr.-May 10am, noon, 2, 4pm. Reservations recommended. 1hr. horseback ride $35.) The largest history museum in the state of Texas,

the **Panhandle-Plains Historical Museum,** 2503 Fourth Ave., in nearby Canyon, displays an impressive collection of "cowboy" art as well as the popular Pioneer Town, a full-sized replica of a Panhandle settlement and working oil derrick. (☎806-651-2244; www.panhandle-plains.org. Open June-Aug. M-Sa 9am-6pm, Su 1-6pm; Sept.-May M-Sa 9am-5pm, Su 1-6pm. $7, ages 4-12 $3.)

THE ROAD TO VEGA: 36 MI.
Follow **Amarillo Boulevard** through Amarillo. For the original old **Route 66,** head right onto **Indian Hill Road** just before the **I-40** overpass into a residential neighborhood. Continue 4 mi. to the T, head left, then immediately right, following the north frontage road toward Wildorado. In Wildorado, cross to the north service road to stay on Rte. 66. Twelve miles past Wildorado on Rte. 66, head left on **Business I-40** after crossing over the road to enter Vega on **Vega Boulevard.**

VEGA   ☎806
The folks in Vega take great pride in being on an original alignment of Rte. 66. Dot Leavitt, proprietress of **Dot's Mini Museum,** 105 N. 12th St., has seen—and collected—it all. The outbuildings next to her house contain a voluminous and eclectic collection of memorabilia amassed since 1944, including a room full of cowboy hats and a boot tree. Self-professed to be "Rte. 66-obsessed," she'll gladly chat with passersby. (☎806-267-2367. Call ahead for hours. Free.) The historic Vega Motel has sadly closed down, but you can still find a bed at the **Bonanza Motel ❷,** 607 Vega Blvd. The spacious and well-furnished rooms come with fridges. (☎806-267-2128. Singles $35; doubles $40. AmEx/D/MC/V.) The **Boot Hill Saloon and Grill ❷,** 909 Vega Blvd., has a replica old Wild West-style bar with stuffed animals, beautiful carved wood furniture, and waitresses in period dress. (☎806-267-2904. Burgers $9-11. Entrees from $16. Open M-Sa 11:30am-midnight, Su 11am-10pm. MC/V.)

THE ROAD TO ADRIAN: 15 MI.
Continue west on **Vega Boulevard.**

ADRIAN   ☎806
Entering town from the east, look out for the **Antique Ranch.** Although abandoned, it is

a fascinating ruin; admire the rusting pickup truck outside with a star-spangled "66" sign on the back. As they say in Adrian, "When you're here, you're halfway there!" From the sign across from the **Midpoint Cafe ❷**, on Rte. 66, it's 1139 mi. to either end of the Mother Road. The decor is one part antique kitchen, two parts "we love Rte. 66." Take Exit 23A off I-40. (☎806-538-6379; www.midpointroute-66cafe.com. Sandwiches $7. Dessert $5. Open Mar.-Nov. daily 8am-4pm. MC/V.)

🏔 THE ROAD TO TUCUMCARI: 64 MI.

Take **I-40** from **Exit 18 (Gruhlkey Road)** 20 mi. to the New Mexico border, passing the ghost town of Glenrio, where an abandoned gas station is the only building for miles. As you enter from the interstate, the **New Mexico Visitors Center,** on the north side, has every map you could ever need. If you use the metal toilets, you can press a button on your way out approving or condemning the facilities. Continue on I-40 to **Exit 369,** heading right at the stop sign on the exit, then immediately left on the frontage road. Take **Exit 356** to cross the interstate in San Jon, then turn right and continue west through town. Continue on the south frontage road from San Jon. Twenty one miles down the road, head right under the interstate at **Exit 335** and enter Tucumcari on **Tucumcari Boulevard.**

 TIME CHANGE. At the border you cross into the **Mountain Time Zone,** where it is 1hr. earlier.

Land of Enchantment
NEW MEXICO
Welcomes You!

TUCUMCARI ☎575

The road between Amarillo and Albuquerque is a long one, and, in the heyday of Rte. 66, Tucumcari made its name as the town with 2000 rooms for weary travelers. "Tucumcari Tonight" became a popular slogan for travelers, and the wall-to-wall motels lining Tucumcari Blvd. do not disappoint. The strip of neon signs lights up the night—recent renovation and Rte. 66 preservation efforts have brought attention to signs like the Blue Swallow, the bluebird of happiness, to drivers for decades.

VITAL STATS
Population: 6000
Tourist Office: Tucumcari/Quay County Chamber of Commerce, 404 W. Tucumcari Blvd. (☎575-461-1694; www.tucumcarinm.com). Open M-F 8am-noon and 1-5pm.
Library and Internet Access: Tucumcari Public Library, 602 S. 2nd St. (☎575-461-0295). Open M 9:30am-7pm, Tu-F 9:30am-5:30pm, Sa 9am-1pm.
Post Office: 220 S. 1st St. (☎575-461-0370). Open M-F 8am-4:30pm, Sa 9:30-11:30am. **Postal Code:** 88401.

⊁ ORIENTATION

Tucumcari sits just north of **I-40; US 54** runs into town from the north. **Business US 54** is known as **Tucumcari Boulevard** in town and is home to the city's famous motel strip. Getting around is fairly simple; streets run north-south and are numbered, while avenues run east-west. Most establishments have parking lots; parking is plentiful almost everywhere.

🏠 ACCOMMODATIONS

▣ **Buckaroo Motel,** 1315 W. Tucumcari Blvd./Rte. 66 (☎575-461-1650). Run by a friendly family, the Buckaroo has a lovely green courtyard, immaculate rooms, and—not surprisingly at these rates—many loyal return guests. Singles $22; doubles $30. AmEx/D/MC/V. ❶

▣ **Blue Swallow Motel,** 815 E. Rte. 66 Blvd. (☎575-461-9849; www.blueswallowmotel.com). Just may be Rte. 66's most celebrated motel. Pink building with bright blue carports. Well-decorated rooms and, according to the sign under the neon swallow, "100% refrigerated air." Free Wi-Fi. Singles $50; doubles $70. AmEx/D/MC/V. ❸

🍴 FOOD

Del's Restaurant, 1202 E. Tucumcari Blvd. (☎575-461-1740; www.delsrestaurant.com). Hard to miss, considering the huge cow perched atop its sign. Del's features a great selection of American and Mexican foods as well as a fortune-telling machine. Red chili pork enchiladas $10. Open M-Sa 7am-9pm. AmEx/D/MC/V. ❷

Lena's Café, 112 E. Main St. (☎575-461-1610). Tucked away in the back streets of town away from the main drag. Enjoy cheap and filling homestyle Mexican cooking against a backdrop of wall murals depicting New Mexican rural life. *Chili relleno* plate with beans and rice $6. Open M-F 7am-6pm, Sa 7am-2pm. MC/V. ❶

Rubee's Diner, 605 W. Tucumcari Blvd. (☎575-461-1463). Burritos $4-7. Open M-F 7am-7pm, Sa 7am-4pm. Cash only. ❶

👁 🏔 SIGHTS AND OUTDOORS

TEE PEE TRADING POST. This stop has been peddling "damn fine stuff" to Rte. 66 travelers from inside a concrete tipi since the 1940s. Check out the colorful blankets from Mexico for only $8. *(924 E. Tucumcari Blvd. ☎575-461-3773. Open M-Sa 8:30am-6pm, Su 8:30am-7pm. D/MC/V.)*

MESALANDS DINOSAUR MUSEUM. Since Tucumcari is one of the world's foremost paleontological sites, its main attraction is a dinosaur museum featuring touchable bronze castings of beasts and bones as well as coprolites, also known as fossilized dino droppings. *(At 1st and Laughlin St. ☎575-461-3466; www.mesalands.edu. Open Tu-Sa from Mar. to Labor Day 10am-6pm; from Labor Day to Mar. noon-5pm. $6, students $4, ages 4-12 $3.50, seniors $5.)*

TUCUMCARI HISTORICAL MUSEUM. A 1903 schoolhouse overflowing with historical artifacts from the region. *(416 S. Adams Ave. ☎575-461-4201. Open in summer M-Sa 8am-6pm; in winter M-F 8am-5pm. $2.50.)*

ODEON THEATER. This lovely theater was built in the 1930s and still shows movies. *(123 S. 2nd St. ☎575-461-0100. $5.50, under 12 $4.50.)*

UTE LAKE STATE PARK. Just north of Tucumcari on US 54, the lake is a narrow, glistening strip of natural beauty with boating, fishing, and swimming. *(☎575-487-2284; www.emnrd.state. nm.us. Open 24hr. Free.)*

🗺 THE ROAD TO SANTA ROSA: 52 MI.

Head west on **Tucumcari Boulevard** as it joins **I-40** at **Exit 329.** Take I-40 to **Exit 321,** crossing to the south side of I-40 and taking the frontage road through

the tunnel 11 mi. later to Montoya. Cross to the south side of the interstate at **Exit 311** and continue through Newkirk and Cuervo, where you will rejoin I-40. Take the interstate to **Exit 277** for Santa Rosa. Turn right after exiting onto **Business I-40/Historic 66.**

> **TIP** **FILL 'ER UP.** There's gas in Cuervo, but it's best to fill up before leaving Tucumcari to avoid making inconvenient detours before Santa Rosa, 52 mi. from Tucumcari. Passersby are few and far between along some of the road, and the vultures would be only too happy for the company.

SANTA ROSA ☎575

Halfway between Albuquerque and Amarillo, Santa Rosa is an oasis amid the arid surroundings. The town got its start as a ranching community and grew under the propriety of Don Celso Baca, an officer in Kit Carson's brigade. Less gaudy than neighboring Tucumcari, the city has equal claim to Old 66, with a main drag lined with ancient motels, landmark billboards, and friendly diners. The train scene in the film *The Grapes of Wrath* features the Pecos River railroad bridge on the western side of town, though Santa Rosa's principal draw is its lakes; the Blue Hole and Perch Lake have great scuba diving.

VITAL STATS
Population: 2800
Tourist Office: Santa Rosa Visitors Center, 2445 4th St. (☎575-472-3763). Open M-F 9am-5pm.
Library and Internet Access: Moise Memorial Public Library, 208 5th St. (☎575-472-3101). Open M-F 10am-6pm, Sa 9am-noon.
Post Office: 120 S. 5th St. (☎575-472-3743), at Rte. 66. Open M-F 8:30am-5pm, Sa 9:45-11:45am. **Postal Code:** 88435.

🧭 ORIENTATION

Unlike many other cities along the route, Santa Rosa is not laid out in a grid. **Route 66,** also known as **Will Rogers Drive,** runs east-west through the city and is the principal road.

Streets are numbered starting in the west and run roughly northwest-southeast through town. Parking is readily available. Continue on Rte. 66 over the crest of the hill to get the full effect of Santa Rosa's magnificent perch.

 ## ACCOMMODATIONS

Like Tucumcari's, Santa Rosa's stretch of Rte. 66 is lined with vintage motels offering decent rooms at very reasonable rates.

Sun N' Sand Motel, 1120 Rte. 66 (☎505-472-5268). A big, sunny sign leads to comfortable rooms with fridges, TVs, and the ever-essential A/C. Free Wi-Fi. Singles $33; doubles $39. AmEx/D/MC/V. ❷

Santa Rosa Campground, 2136 Historic 66 (☎505-472-3126). 100 sites in a tree-shaded location off the main road. Facilities include outdoor pool (open May 15-Oct.), restaurant, and laundry. Tent sites $22; RV sites with full hookup $33. AmEx/D/MC/V. ❶

FOOD

Route 66 Restaurant, 1819 Rte. 66 (☎575-472-9925), at the top of the hill. Has been feeding roadies since the 1950s. The interior is a testimony to the town's roadfever. Entrees $8-12. Open daily 7am-9pm. MC/V. ❷

Joseph's Bar and Grill, 865 Rte. 66 (☎575-472-3361). Landmark Fat Man billboards (symbols of American prosperity during WWII and the Vietnam War) point to a Rte. 66 legend. Hungry folk look forward to it for miles, and weary travelers can relax with a margarita within easy walking distance of a bevy of motels. The *carne adovada* (pork marinated in spicy chili sauce; $8.50) is a favorite. Entrees $6-13. Open daily 7am-10pm. AmEx/D/MC/V. ❷

Silver Moon Cafe, 3701 Rte. 66 (☎575-472-3162). Has been serving Mother Road burgers (2 patties with all the trimmings; $7.50) since 1959. If you prefer to eat with a knife and fork they also have full entrees (fajitas $11) and serve beer and wine. Open daily 6am-10pm. D/MC/V. ❷

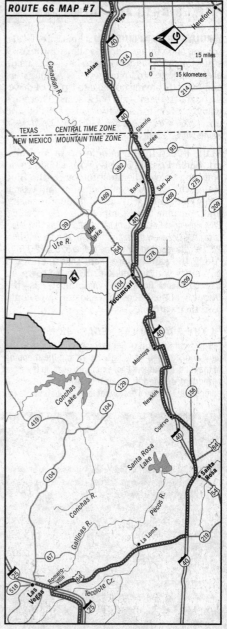

ROUTE 66 MAP #7

ROUTE 66

ⓢ 🏔 SIGHTS AND OUTDOORS

⬛ROUTE 66 AUTO MUSEUM. Fins, street rods, trucks, and vintage chrome shine at the awesome Santa Rosa Rte. 66 Auto Museum. Inside are a collection of lovingly restored roadsters and exhibits paying homage to a past of drive-throughs, cruisin', and back seats. There are usually a few for sale too—just $40,000 and up. *(2766 Rte. 66. ☎575-472-1966. Open M-Sa 8am-5pm, Su 10am-5pm. $5, under 12 $2.)*

BLUE HOLE. In the middle of an arid desert, Santa Rosa is blessed with 13 lakes and watering holes. The most famous is the Blue Hole, which draws scuba fanatics and casual swimmers alike with its 80 ft. depth, clarity, and constant 64°F temperature. *(To reach the Blue Hole from Rte. 66, turn left on 4th St. and left again onto Lake Dr. Follow the signs and turn left onto Blue Hole Rd. Permits required for diving. Call ☎575-472-3763.)* Along the same route, **Park Lake** features a two-story water slide. Northeast of town on Rte. 91, **Santa Rosa Lake** was built to ease the flooding of the Pecos River so cowboys could ford their cattle.

🚗 THE ROAD TO LAS VEGAS: 58 MI.

Follow **Route 66** out of Santa Rosa as it curves to the right and join **I-40** heading west. During the mapping of the road, an outgoing governor with rivals in the town of Moriarty decided to thwart the town by bypassing it completely with the extravagant loop through Santa Fe. Only later did alignments head in a gas-efficient, but far less interesting, straight line. Get off at **Exit 256** and take **US 84 North** through Dilia and Romeroville until you hit the junction with **I-25** just over 55 mi. from Santa Rosa. Although it isn't on Rte. 66, heading 3 mi. east from Romeroville on I-25 will bring you to the other Las Vegas—Las Vegas, New Mexico.

LAS VEGAS   ☎ 505

Though this Las Vegas won't chew you up and spit you out broke and hungover like its northern namesake, it will razzle and dazzle you with history. In 1899, Las Vegas was the biggest city in the New Mexico territory, and it flourished when the railroad was routed through town at the turn of the century. What remains today is a town frozen in time, with nine historic districts and 900 buildings on the National Register of Historic Places. The **City of Las Vegas Museum** and **Rough Riders Memorial Collection,** 727 Grand Ave., chronicle the history of Theodore Roosevelt's Rough Riders, a US Cavalry regiment involved in the Spanish-American War. In addition to Rough Riders artifacts and local history paraphernalia, the museum includes an annotated photo display on the hanging of the notorious Black Jack, reported to have said to the priest ministering to him: "Padre, make it snappy. I haven't much time. I have to be in Hell and eat dinner with the devil at noon." Due to a mistake with the rope tension, his head was "cut plumb

HEAT: IT'S WHAT'S FOR DINNER

When coffee loses its impact yet the road stretches on to California, the fiery chili pepper of New Mexico may be just the thing to jolt you awake and rekindle your dying flames. Chili pepper is used to flavor many popular dishes and salsas in the Southwest, and it is likely available at your next roadside stop. The pepper's spicy flavor comes from the chemical capsaicin, which is found not in the plant's seeds, as many believe, but rather in the pod's membranes and the soft tissue that supports the seeds. The chemical is thought to be an evolutionary adaptation to prevent mammals from eating the pods. Unable to taste capsaicin, birds eat but can't digest the seeds, thus helping with their dispersal; mammals, who can digest the seeds, taste the heat and avoid chilies entirely. Though human taste buds certainly respond to the spicy chemical, the proper preparation of chilies in cuisine provides a pleasant culinary heat. In the summer, farmers' markets brim with chili peppers of all kinds. All told, New Mexico produces about 100,000 tons of chilies each year, the most of any state in the US. Most common is the New Mexico green chili, with a 6 in. pod and a firm, crisp texture; other varieties include fat, orange habañeros, skinny red *de árboles*, and the stubby, green jalapeño. The habañero is the undisputed king of heat. Its orange variety has eight times the heat of a regular jalapeño, and its juice can actually blister bare skin. When a pepper's fiery flavor hits your tongue,

off." (☎505-454-1401. Open Tu-Sa 10am-4pm. Free.) Budget motels can be found all along Grand Ave., between I-25 Exits 343 and 347. The **Town House Motel ❷**, 1215 Grand Ave., has clean rooms with massive TVs, charming features, and Wi-Fi in the lobby. (☎505-425-6717. Singles from $40; doubles from $53. AmEx/D/MC/V.) Next door, the **Sunshine Motel ❷**, 1201 Grand Ave., also has pleasant rooms. (☎505-425-3506. Singles $36; doubles $44. AmEx/D/MC/V.) Slightly upmarket dining is available at the ⬛**El Rialto Restaurant ❸**, 141 Bridge St., housed in one of Las Vegas's many historic properties. Try the delicious Rainbow Trout Dinner for $14. (☎505-454-0037. Open Tu-Sa 10:30am-9pm. AmEx/D/MC/V.) **Estella's Cafe ❷**, 148 Bridge St., offers some of the best Northern New Mexican food in town. (☎505-454-0048. Entrees $5-9. Open M-W 11am-3pm, Th-F 11am-8pm, Sa 7am-2pm. Cash only.) **Dick's Deli ❷**, 705 Douglas Ave., has a liquor store, bar, and restaurant. The premises sprawl from the storefront deli area all the way back into a charming bistro. All your standard Mexican favorites are here, as is a huge range of sandwiches: order a gourmet option ($7-9) or build your own. (☎505-425-8261. Open M-F 10am-10pm, Sa 10am-11:30pm. AmEx/MC/V.) **Charlie's Spic and Span Bakery and Cafe ❸**, 715 Douglas Ave., has a full espresso bar and fresh baked goods daily. Breakfast is served all day, plus more substantial lunch and dinner options. (☎505-426-1921. Open M-F 6:30am-5:45pm, Sa 7am-5:45pm, Su 6:30am-3pm. AmEx/MC/V.)

⛟ THE ROAD TO PECOS: 41 MI.

Take **I-25** south from Las Vegas. Thirty five miles later, take the turn marked with the big "Historic 66" sign into Pecos, following the road another 5 mi. into the town. Turn left onto **Route 50** in the center of town.

PECOS   ☎505

The main attraction in Pecos is the **Pecos Wilderness Area and Historical Park.** The Pecos Wilderness protects 233,667 acres of high country in the heart of the Sangre de Cristo Mountains, punctuated by the second-highest point in New Mexico, the 13,103 ft. Trunchas Peak. Winters are long and snowy, but from late spring to early autumn this is an

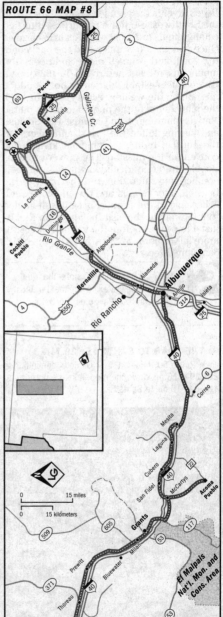

ROUTE 66 MAP #8

ROUTE 66

ideal spot for backcountry hiking. The upper Pecos River is the premier trout-fishing site in the Southwest, so don't be surprised to find campgrounds crowded with Texan fishermen. Once you get a few miles into the backcountry, you'll find yourself alone amid beautiful mountains, forests, and rivers. In 1625, Spanish colonists established an elaborate adobe mission on the wealthy **Pecos Pueblo.** In 1680, the inhabitants of the pueblo joined a united Native American force against the Spanish and, having killed the priest and destroyed the church, built a ceremonial kiva in the convent of the mission. The power of Pecos Pueblo gradually declined through disease, conflict, and migration, but the ruins of the mission, later rebuilt, and the pueblo are still accessible in the form of a 1 mi. self-guided tour. Stop in at the visitors center on Rte. 66 just a few miles before the town of Pecos for more information. (☎505-757-6414. Open M-F 8am-5pm. Free.)

BIG DETOUR. Explore the quirky side of New Mexico on the **Pueblos, Prayers, and Particles** Big Detour (p. 552).

THE ROAD TO SANTA FE: 20 MI.
From **Route 50,** rejoin **I-25** at Glorieta, continuing to **Exit 294,** 10 mi. down the road. Take the north frontage road 10 mi. to Santa Fe.

SANTA FE ☎505

Everyone who isn't selling something seems to be a tourist in this city where the winding streets, beautiful adobe buildings, exquisite museums, and smell of incense in the streets bring to life a time long forgotten in much of the rest of the region. Founded by the Spanish in 1608, Santa Fe's prime location at the convergence of the Santa Fe Trail, an old trading route running from Missouri, and the Camino Real ("Royal Road") has always brought commerce and bustle. In recent years, Santa Fe has skyrocketed in popularity; it's become one of the leading vacation destinations in the US and seen the arrival of many a gated community and California millionaire. In many spots, prices have risen accordingly, but Santa Fe's architecture, museums, and scenery make the bargain hunt well worth the time.

ORIENTATION

The streets of downtown Santa Fe seem to wind and wander without rhyme or reason. It is helpful to think of Santa Fe as a wagon wheel, with the **Plaza** in the center and roads leading outward like spokes. **Paseo de Peralta** forms a loop around the downtown area, and the main roads leading out toward **I-25** are **Cerrilos Road, Saint Francis Drive,** and **Old Santa Fe Trail.** Narrow streets make driving troublesome; park your car and pound the pavement. The downtown area is compact

OH, BILLY

Lawrence Murphy owned the only general store in Lincoln in the 1870s. When John Tunstall and Alexander McSween opened a rival store in 1878, Murphy saw red, and his assistant James Dolan had Tunstall killed. One of Tunstall's men, William H. Bonney, vowed to get revenge. Bonney, a.k.a. Billy the Kid, rounded up a posse called the Regulators who wreaked havoc in Lincoln, killing Tunstall's assassins along with the sheriff. Dolan's men fought back, burning McSween's house with his family inside. McSween himself was shot unarmed on the doorstep as he came out to propose a truce. Billy the Kid, then only a peach-fuzzed teenager, escaped and spent the next two years on the run. The new Lincoln sheriff, Pat Garrett, finally caught up with Billy in nearby Fort Sumner. Billy was subsequently put on trial for killing the sheriff. Sentenced to hang, Billy was in jail awaiting execution in Lincoln on April 28, 1881, when he made his famous escape. While in the outhouse, he grabbed a pistol hidden by an accomplice, burst out, and killed one of his two guards. Billy then killed the other guard with the man's own shotgun and fled on a horse. Less than three months later, Garret caught up with Billy again, and this time he did not give the slippery Kid a chance to escape. Garret shot him dead, and

and lined with interesting shops, restaurants, and sights, and the Plaza area is restricted to pedestrians. Parking lots are abundant, and closely monitored metered spaces line the streets near Plaza and **Canyon Road.** Public lots throughout town run $9-10 per day. The visitors center has free parking (M-F 2hr. free, Sa-Su free all day).

VITAL STATS

Population: 62,000

Tourist Offices: Visitor Info Center, 491 Old Santa Fe Trail (☎505-827-7336 or 800-545-2070; www.santafe.com). Open daily in high season 8am-6pm; in low season 8am-5pm. **Santa Fe Convention and Visitors Bureau,** 201 W. Marcy St. (☎800-777-2489). Open M-F 8am-5pm.

Library and Internet Access: Santa Fe Public Library, 145 Washington Ave. (☎505-955-6780). Open M-Th 10am-9pm, F-Sa 10am-6pm, Su 1-5pm.

Post Office: 120 S. Federal Pl. (☎505-988-2239), next to the courthouse. Open M-F 8am-5:30pm, Sa 9am-4pm. **Postal Code:** 87501.

ACCOMMODATIONS

Hotels in Santa Fe tend toward the expensive side. As early as May they become swamped with requests for rooms during **Indian Market** and **Fiesta de Santa Fe.** Make reservations early. In general, the motels along **Cerrillos Road** have the best prices, but even these places run $40-60 per night. Downtown, B&Bs and spa inns dot most corners, but, unless your budget is liberal, steer clear. Nearby camping is pleasant during the summer and easier on the wallet. Two sites for free primitive camping are **Big Tesuque ❶** and **Ski Basin Campgrounds ❶.** These campgrounds are both off Rte. 475 toward the Ski Basin and have pit toilets.

Santa Fe International Hostel and Pension, 1412 Cerrillos Rd. (☎505-988-1153). Offers far and away the cheapest beds in town. Run along strong community lines. Guests are responsible for the cleanliness of the place; you will be expected to pull your weight! Donations from local supermarkets mean the kitchen is often fully stocked with food to which guests can help themselves. Wi-Fi $2 per day. $10 key deposit. Dorm beds with chores $18; private rooms $25;

private rooms with no chores $35. Reception 7am-11pm. Cash only. ❶

Thunderbird Inn, 1821 Cerrillos Rd. (☎505-983-4397). Comfortable rooms with fridges around a courtyard in an adobe building. Singles $50; doubles $60. AmEx/D/MC/V. ❸

Kings Rest Court Motel, 1452 Cerrillos Rd. (☎505-983-8879). Look for the vintage sign. Clean rooms with fridges around a courtyard. Singles $50; doubles $60. AmEx/D/MC/V. ❸

Western Scene Motel, 1608 Cerrillos Rd. (☎505-983-7484). Spacious rooms in a shady, tree-lined courtyard set back from the main road. Singles $50; doubles $55. AmEx/MC/V. ❸

Hyde State Park Campground. (☎505-983-7175), 8 mi. from Santa Fe on Rte. 475. Over 50 sites with water, pit toilets, and shelters. Sites $10, with hookup $14. ❶

 DON'T GET HUNG UP. Handheld cell phones are illegal to use while driving in Santa Fe. Hands-free devices, however, are permitted.

FOOD

Even flybys through Santa Fe should take a time out to sample some of the best food the Southwest has to offer. Green chili is New Mexico's specialty, and most dishes come with the offer to have them smothered in the zesty sauce. Note that levels of spiciness can vary and you can order many dishes to taste. That said, only a wuss asks for "mild."

Maria's, 555 W. Cordova Rd. (☎505-983-7929; www.marias-santafe.com). This restaurant is known for serving the best margarita in Santa Fe, ($5.50) among 100 other delicious concoctions ($5-45). Entrees $11-15. AmEx/MC/V. ❸

Tia Sophia's, 210 W. San Francisco St. (☎505-983-9880). Looks unassuming, with a few decorative baskets and narrow walk space, but, long waits will testify to the food's exceptional quality. Most popular item is the Atrisco plate ($7.50)—chili stew, a cheese enchilada, beans, posole, and a sopaipilla. Open M-Sa 7am-2pm. MC/V. ❸

Bobcat Bite, 420 Old Las Vegas Hwy. (☎505-983-5319). Every car in town is generally

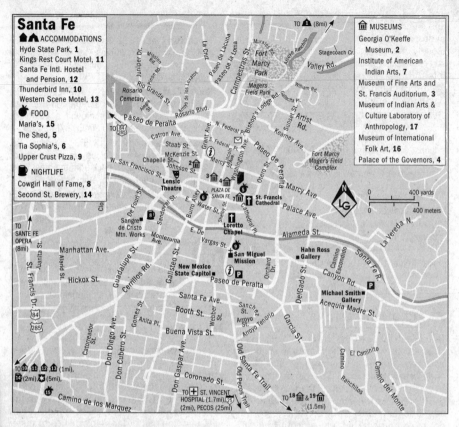

Santa Fe

🏠🏠🏔 ACCOMMODATIONS
Hyde State Park, **1**
Kings Rest Court Motel, **11**
Santa Fe Intl. Hostel
 and Pension, **12**
Thunderbird Inn, **10**
Western Scene Motel, **13**

🍎 FOOD
Maria's, **15**
The Shed, **5**
Tia Sophia's, **6**
Upper Crust Pizza, **9**

🍸 NIGHTLIFE
Cowgirl Hall of Fame, **8**
Second St. Brewery, **14**

🏛 MUSEUMS
Georgia O'Keeffe
 Museum, **2**
Institute of American
 Indian Arts, **7**
Museum of Fine Arts and
 St. Francis Auditorium, **3**
Museum of Indian Arts &
 Culture Laboratory of
 Anthropology, **17**
Museum of International
 Folk Art, **16**
Palace of the Governors, **4**

---

parked outside this pink adobe roadhouse constructed in 1954. If you've got a hankering for a hunk of meat or just a taste of New Mexico's finest green chilis, you're in the right place. Open W-Sa 11am-7:50pm. Cash only. ❸

The Shed, 113 E. Palace Ave. (☎505-982-9030), up the street from the Plaza. The beautiful vine-lined patio feels like a garden, so you won't notice the 15min. wait. Lots of vegetarian dishes, like quesadillas ($8) and excellent blue-corn burritos ($8.75). Meat-eaters will enjoy the red chile enchiladas ($8.75). Open M-Sa 11am-2:30pm and 5:30-9pm. AmEx/D/MC/V. ❸

Counter Culture, 930 Baca St. (☎505-995-1105). Serves a variety of breakfast, lunch, and dinner dishes in a hip and informal aluminum-interiored shack. Big communal tables, a massive

chalkboard with the day's choices, and healthful, eclectic cuisine with fruit in unexpected places. Big lunch salads $8-10. Dinner entrees $11-15. Free Wi-Fi. Open M 8am-3pm, Tu-Sa 8am-3pm and 5-9pm, Su 8am-2pm. Cash only. ❸

Upper Crust Pizza, 329 Old Santa Fe Trail (☎505-982-0000). This pizza place has won awards for the best pizza in Santa Fe nearly every year for the last decade. Small pizza $13. Open daily in summer 11am-11pm; in winter 11am-10pm. D/MC/V. ❸

🅖 SIGHTS

The grassy Plaza de Santa Fe is a good starting point for exploring the museums, sanctuaries, and galleries of the city. Since 1609, the

Plaza has been the site of religious ceremonies, military gatherings, markets, cockfights, and public punishments—now, it shelters ritzy shops and dozens of artisans selling their crafts. Historic walking tours leave from the blue doors of the Palace of the Governors on Lincoln St. (Apr.-Oct. M-Sa at 10:15am. $10.)

SAINT FRANCIS CATHEDRAL. Santa Fe's Catholic roots are evident in the Romanesque St. Francis Cathedral, built from 1869 to 1886 under the direction of Archbishop Lamy to help convert Westerners to Catholicism. The basilica features wide doors and a tintinnabulum, in case the pope needs to enter on horseback. (213 Cathedral Pl., 1 block east of the Plaza on San Francisco St. ☎505-982-5619. Open daily 7:30am-5:30pm. Free.)

LORETTO CHAPEL. This was the first Gothic-inspired building west of the Mississippi River and dates to the 1870s. The church is famous for its "miraculous" spiral staircase—architects still argue about how it was accomplished. (207 Old Santa Fe Trail, 2 blocks south of the cathedral. ☎505-982-0092. Open in winter M-Sa 9am-5pm, Su 10:30am-5pm; in summer M-Sa 9am-6pm, Su 10:30am-6pm. $2.50, children and seniors $2.)

SAN MIGUEL MISSION. About five blocks southeast of the plaza lies the San Miguel Mission. Built in 1610 by Tlaxcalan Native Americans, the mission is the oldest functioning church in the US and has a beautiful wood-ceiling. Also in the church is the San Jose Bell, the oldest bell in the US, made in Spain in 1356. You can ring the bell by hitting it with a small rubber mallet. (At the corner of DeVargas St. and the Old Santa Fe Trail. ☎505-988-9504. Open M-Sa 9am-5pm, Su 9am-4pm. Mass 5pm. $1.)

🏛 MUSEUMS

MUSEUM OF NEW MEXICO. Sante Fe is home to six imaginative, world-class museums. Four are run by the Museum of New Mexico. A worthwhile four-day pass includes admission to all four museums and can be purchased at any of them. (☎505-827-6463; www.museumofnewmexico.org. All museums have the same opening hours and rates. Open May-Sept. daily 10am-5pm; Sept.-May Tu-Su 10am-5pm. $8, under 12 free. 4-day pass $18. Museum of Fine Arts and Palace of the Governors are both free F 5-8pm.) Inhabiting a large adobe building on the northwest corner of the Plaza, the **Museum of Fine Arts** dazzles visitors with the works of major Southwestern artists as well as contemporary exhibits of controversial American art. (107 W. Palace Ave. ☎505-476-5072; www.mfasantafe.org.) The **Palace of the Governors** is the oldest public building in the US and was the seat of seven successive governments after its construction in 1610. The hacienda-style palace is now a museum with exhibits on Native American, Southwestern, and New Mexican history. (On the north side of the Plaza. ☎505-476-5100; www.palaceofthegovernors.org.) The fascinating **Museum of International Folk Art** houses the largest collection of folk art in the world, including over 10,000 handmade dolls, dollhouses, and other toys. Other galleries display ethnographic exhibits. (706 Camino Lejo. ☎505-476-1200; www.moifa.org.) Next door, the **Museum of Indian Arts and Culture Laboratory of Anthropology** displays Native American photos and over 10 million artifacts from New Mexico archaeological sites. (710 Camino Lejo. ☎505-476-1250.)

GEORGIA O'KEEFFE MUSEUM. This popular museum attracts the masses with the artist's famous flower paintings as well as some of her more abstract works. The collection, complemented by a brief biographical documentary, spans her entire life and is the first museum dedicated to an internationally acclaimed female artist. (217 Johnson St. ☎505-946-1000; www.okeeffemuseum.org. Open June-Oct. daily 10am-5pm; Nov.-May M-Tu and Th-Su 10am-5pm. $8, students $4, under 18 free; F 5-8pm free.)

INSTITUTE OF AMERICAN INDIAN ARTS MUSEUM. This downtown museum houses an extensive collection of contemporary Native American art with an intense political edge and many inviting interactive exhibits. (108 Cathedral Pl. ☎505-983-8900. Open M-Sa 10am-5pm, Su noon-5pm. $5, students and seniors $2.50, under 17 free.)

STATE CAPITOL. The New Mexico State Capitol was built in 1966 in the form of the Zia Sun Symbol. The House and Senate galleries are open to the public, and the building contains an impressive art collection. (5 blocks south of the Plaza on Old Santa Fe Trail. ☎505-986-4589. Open *in summer M-F 8am-6pm, Sa 8am-5pm; in winter M-F 8am-6pm. Free guided tours 10am, 2pm.)*

CANYON ROAD. Santa Fe's most successful artists live and sell their work along Canyon Rd. Pick up a map and guide to the businesses featured here at the visitors center or at any one of the galleries. On the first Friday of each month, many of the galleries keep their doors open late and offer free wine and cheese. *(To reach the galleries, depart the Plaza on San Francisco Dr. and take a left on Alameda St., a right on Paseo de Peralta, and a left on Canyon Rd.)* Most galleries are open 10am-5pm and contain interesting and often fantastically expensive collections. The Michael Smith Gallery is full of beautiful, intricately woven baskets. *(526 Canyon Rd. ☎505-995-1013. Open daily 10am-5pm.)* The Hahn Ross Gallery has hip, enjoyable, and pricey works. *(409 Canyon Rd. ☎505-984-8434.)*

🎵 ENTERTAINMENT

The **Santa Fe Opera,** on Opera Dr., 7 mi. north of Santa Fe on Rte. 84/285, performs outdoors against a mountain backdrop. Nights are cool; bring a blanket and someone to cuddle with. (☎800-280-4654 or 505-986-5900; www.santafeopera.org. Tickets $26-180; standing-room tickets $8-15. Shows July W and F-Sa; Aug. M-Sa. Performances begin 8-9pm.) The **Santa Fe Chamber Music Festival** celebrates the works of Baroque, Classical, Romantic, and 20th-century composers in the St. Francis Auditorium of the Museum of Fine Arts and the Lensic Theater. (☎505-983-2075, tickets 982-1890; www.sfcmf.org. From mid-July to mid-Aug. $16-40, students $10.) In the third week of August, the **Santa Fe Indian Market** floods the plaza. The **Southwestern Association for Indian Arts** (☎505-983-5220) has more info. Don Diego de Vargas's peaceful reconquest of New Mexico in 1692 marked the end of the 12-year Pueblo Rebellion, now celebrated in the three-day **Fiesta de Santa Fe** (☎505-988-7575), held in mid-September. Festivities begin with the burning of the Zozobra (a 50 ft. marionette) and include street dancing, processions, and political satires. The *New Mexican* publishes a guide and a schedule of events.

🎹 NIGHTLIFE

Santa Fe nightlife tends to be mellower than that of nearby Albuquerque.

Cowgirl Hall of Fame, 319 S. Guadalupe St. (☎505-982-2565). Live hoedowns that range from bluegrass to country. The place to get a drink in Santa Fe. 21+ after midnight. Cover $3-4. Happy hour 3-6pm and midnight-1am. Open M-F 11am-2am, Sa-Su 8:30am-2am. AmEx/D/MC/V.

Second Street Brewery, 1814 2nd St. (☎505-982-3030), at the railroad tracks. Caters to a hip, artsy crowd. Live music W-Sa 5:30-8:30pm. Open M-Sa 11am-midnight, Su noon-midnight. AmEx/D/MC/V.

STAIRWAY TO HEAVEN

The Loretto Chapel is one of the most intriguing tourist attractions in Santa Fe, primarily because of its "miraculous staircase," a 33-step helix-shaped construction that stands without any visible support. Architects are at a loss to explain the phenomenon, though the people of Santa Fe have their own speculations. The Sisters of Loretto first came to Santa Fe in 1852 and immediately began construction on a chapel. The chapel was nearing completion when builders realized that there was no way to get from the chapel to the choir loft, since it was too high for ordinary stairs. Carpenter after carpenter measured the space and announced that building a standard staircase was impossible. The sisters prayed for aid, and one day a man entered the chapel with only a hammer, a saw, and a T square. The stranger offered to build a stairway and finished his work in just three months, leaving before the nuns could pay him. The staircase that he built is a structure that the laws of physics say should have collapsed the moment someone stepped on it. The wood itself is of an unknown species and is held together by wood pegs. Many sisters believe that the mysterious carpenter was St. Joseph, the patron saint of craftsmen, though to this day the origin of the staircase and the identity of its creator remain a mystery. Though possibly of heavenly craftsmanship, the staircase now suffers

⚑ OUTDOORS

The nearby **Sangre de Cristo Mountains** reach heights of over 12,000 ft. and offer countless opportunities for hikers, bikers, skiers, and snowboarders. The **Pecos** and **Rio Grande Rivers** are playgrounds for kayakers, rafters, and canoers. Before heading into the wilderness, stop by the **Public Lands Information Center,** 1474 Rodeo Rd., near the intersection of St. Francis Rd. and I-25, to pick up maps, guides, and friendly advice. (☎505-438-7542; www.publiclands.org. Open in summer M-F 8am-5pm; in winter M-Sa 8am-5pm.) The Sierra Club guide to *Day Hikes in the Santa Fe Area* and Falcon Guides's to *Best Easy Day Hikes in Santa Fe* are good purchases for those planning to spend a few days hiking. You can buy them in **Travel Bug,** 839 Paseo de Parelta. (☎505-992-0418.) The closest hiking trails to downtown Santa Fe are along Rte. 475 on the way to the Santa Fe Ski Area. On this road, 10 mi. northeast of town, the **Tesuque Creek Trail** (4 mi., 2hr.) leads through the forest to a flowing stream. The best skiing is 16 mi. northeast of downtown, at **Ski Santa Fe.** In the towering Sangre de Cristo Mountains on Rte. 475, the ski area operates six lifts, servicing 43 trails on 600 acres of terrain with a 1650 ft. vertical drop. (☎505-982-4429. Open from late Nov. to early Apr. daily 9am-4pm. Lift tickets $58, ages 13-20 $46, under 13 $40. Rental packages from $22 per day. Lessons from $65.)

⛰ DETOUR
COCHITI PUEBLO

At **Exit 264** off the interstate, go west, turning right onto **Route 16.** Go 8 mi. and then right onto **Route 22.** Take a left into the **Cochiti Pueblo Reservation,** and then a right onto **Forest Route 266.** The parking area is 5 mi. from the turnoff.

An excellent spot for picnicking, The **Kasha-Katuwe Tent Rocks Natural Monument** has two easy trails through magnificent slot canyons and towering tent rock formations; one (20min. round-trip) leads up to a small cave, the other (40min. round-trip) includes a steep climb up a well-marked path but leads hikers to a spectacular view. (☎505-761-8700. Monument open daily in summer 7am-7pm; in winter 7am-6pm. $5 per vehicle.) Nearby, the

Cochiti Lake Campground ❶ is high on the mesa, with toilets, showers, cooking pits, and lake access. (☎505-465-0307; www.reserveusa.com. Sites $10, with hookup $12. MC/V.)

⚑ THE ROAD TO BERNALILLO: 47 MI.

Follow **Cerillos Road** out of Santa Fe, passing under **I-25** and turning right at **Route 599.** Turn left onto the frontage road and continue to Waldo. Join **I-25** and take the interstate to Algodones at **Exit 248.** Take a right from the off-ramp and a left at the stop sign, taking **Route 313 South** to Bernalillo.

BERNALILLO   ☎505

The **Coronado State Monument,** 485 Kuaua Rd., has recreated Indian ruins and a reconstructed kiva. A small attached museum has original murals from the kiva and town walls. (☎505-867-5351. Open daily 8:30am-5pm. $3, under 17 free.) The **Coronado Campground ❶,** on Hwy. 44 just west of Bernalillo along the Rio Grande, is a good place to sleep. (☎505-867-3311. Sites $14, with water and electricity $22. Cash only.) The **Range Cafe ❹,** 925 Camino del Pueblo, is an exhibition space for local artists that offers a mix of Mexican and American dishes. (☎505-867-1700. Sandwiches $9-11. Entrees $11-18. Open M-Th 7:30am-9:30pm, F-Su 7:30am-10pm. AmEx/D/MC/V.)

⚑ THE ROAD TO ALBUQUERQUE: 18 MI.

In Bernalillo, turn right onto **Camino del Pueblo** to find **I-25.** Continue through Alameda to Albuquerque.

ALBUQUERQUE   ☎505

At the crossroads of the Southwest, Albuquerque buzzes with history and culture, nurturing ethnic restaurants, offbeat galleries, quirky cafes, and raging nightclubs. Rte. 66 may no longer appear on maps, but it's alive and kicking here. The mythic highway radiates a palpable energy that gives shops, restaurants, and bars a distinctive spirit found nowhere else in the state. Downtown Albuquerque may lack East Coast elegance, but it has a cosmopolitan feel of its own, fed by a unique combination of students, cowboys, bankers, and government employees.

ROUTE 66

BIG DETOUR

PUEBLOS PRAYERS & PARTICLES

NEW MEXICO

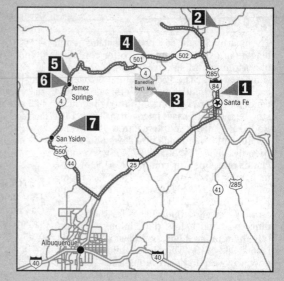

START: Santa Fe

HIGHLIGHT: Black Hole Surplus Store

DISTANCE: 160 mi.

DURATION: 2 days

From Santa Fe, take St. Francis Dr., a.k.a. US 84/285 N., to Tesque. Take Exit 168 and follow the signs to Tesque Village to reach the Shidoni Foundry.

1. SHIDONI FOUNDRY. The Shidoni Foundry encompasses a bronze-casting foundry, an art gallery, and eight acres of sculpture gardens. There's something to cater to every taste, from life-size bronze alligators to monks sitting in thoughtful repose. (☎505-988-8001; www.shidoni. com. Live bronze pourings Sa 1, 2:45, 4pm. Open M-Sa 9am-5pm. Free.)
Continue through Tesque village and rejoin US 84/285 N. at Exit 172. At Exit 175, take in the unique rock formation that resembles a camel. Continue to Espanola. Take Rte. 76 east to Chimayo.

2. EL SANCTURIO DE CHIMAYO. Built between 1814 and 1816, El Sancturio de Chimayo is known by locals as "Little Lourdes" and attracts over 30,000 worshippers every Good Friday to celebrate Easter. The chapel was privately owned until 1929, when it was transferred to the Archdiocese of Santa Fe. (Open May-Sept. 9am-6pm; Oct.-Apr. 9am-4pm.)
From Chimayo, return to US 84/285 N. and head south, branching off to Rte. 502 W. as you follow signs to Los Alamos. Turn left onto Rte. 4 and head south 12 mi. to Bandelier National Park.

3. BANDELIER NATIONAL MONUMENT. Bandelier National Monument features the remnants of over 2400 cliff dwellings and pueblos amid 50 sq. mi. of mesas and rugged canyons. The park centers on Frijoles Canyon, the site of many natural caves and settlements along the canyon floor that were occupied for roughly 500 years. The Main Loop Trail (1½ mi.) begins at the back porch of the visitors center and passes the ruins of Tyuonyi Trail and the Long House, an 800 ft. section of adjoining multistory stone homes. Those with more time should go half a mile farther to Alcove House, a kiva carved high above the canyon floor. (☎505-672-3861; www.nps. gov/band. Visitors center open daily 8am-6pm. Entrance fee $12 per vehicle.)
Continue on US 84 as it curves to the west. Turn right onto Rte. 501/W. Jemez Rd. 6 mi. later to enter Los Alamos. Turn left onto Diamond Dr. and right onto Canyon Rd., which becomes Central Ave.

4. LOS ALAMOS. In the early 20th century, all that existed in this tiny town, situated in the idyllic northern New Mexico mountains, was the famous **Ranch School,** where wealthy parents would send their effete and ailing boys in order to toughen them up. Then, in 1943, it was chosen as the location for the Manhattan Project, the top-secret enterprise to build an atomic bomb and bring a swift end to WWII. Since then, it has remained the United States's principal research center for nuclear technology, and the entire town basically consists of scientists and their families. The fascinating story behind the construction of the bomb is told in the **Bradbury Science Museum,** at 15th and Central Ave. Learn about the living conditions of the early researchers, the agonizing path to constructing the weapon, and the moral dilemmas over the eventual deployment of the bomb. (☎505-667-4444; www.bsm.lanl.gov. Open M and Su 1-5pm, Tu-Sa 10am-5pm. Free.) You can also take a walking tour of the town and see the beautiful main building of the Ranch School and the house of Robert Oppenheimer, the scientist chosen as civilian director of the Manhattan Project. For a fascinating look into the technology behind the construction of bombs, make a visit to the **Black Hole Surplus Store and Museum,** 4015 Arkansas Ave. From Central Ave, take a right onto Diamond Dr. and head up the hill; Arkansas Ave. will be on your left. Former lab scientist Ed Grothus has collected a treasure-trove of atomic paraphernalia including 50-year-old calculators, fiber-optic cables, time-mark generators, and bomb detonator cables (yours for $5). A passionate voice against nuclear proliferation, Ed is dedicated to channeling nuclear research away from bombs to civilian use and is erecting a enormous stone obelisk as part of this cause. (☎505-662-5053. Open M-Sa 10am-5pm.)

Return down Arkansas Ave. and turn right onto Diamond Dr. Follow the road around, then turn right onto W. Jemez Rd. and follow the extremely curvy road 33 mi. to Jemez Springs. You will pass through a number of natural preserves and have several chances to stop for a magnificent view of the Valle Grande. The state monument will come into view a few miles into Jemez Springs.

5. JEMEZ STATE MONUMENT AND SODA DAM. Over 600 years ago, the Jemez people built villages in the mountain valley and on top of mesas. In the 17th century, Spanish colonists built a Catholic mission directly in the middle of the valley, and the Jemez villages were soon abandoned. The ruins of the Church of San Jose de los Jemez are some of the most spectacular ruins in the Southwest. (Open M and W-Su 8:30am-5pm. $3, under 17 free.) Soda Dam, one of the many natural hot springs in the region, doesn't have a visitors center, but you can swim in the pool. It may smell like sulfur, but you won't mind when you're basking in the warm water amid thousands of years of minerals. If you're feelings adventurous, try the waterslide.

Follow Rte. 4 for a short way to reach downtown Jemez Springs.

6. LOS OJOS RESTAURANT AND SALOON. Los Ojos, 17596 Rte. 4, is a true Old West watering hole, with lots of dead animals, antlers, and guns mounted on the walls. Not only is it the best restaurant in town, but it also has an eclectic mix of New Mexican cuisine. Try the Jemez burger with Swiss cheese and black olives for $8.50. (☎505-829-3547. Open M-Th and Su 11am-8:30pm, F-Sa 11am-9:30pm. Bar open M-Sa until 2am, Su until midnight. MC/V.)

Continue along Rte. 4 for 12 mi., then turn left onto Rte. 290; 3 mi. later, you will reach the Ponderosa Winery.

7. PONDEROSA WINERY. Nestled in a scenic valley and situated on volcanic ash deposits, Ponderosa, 3171 Rte. 290, specializes in Riesling wines and has also recently added an award-winning Pinot Noir to its vineyards. Tour the premises and sample the wines in the tasting room. Don't forget to designate a driver! (☎505-834-7487; www.ponde-rosawinery.com. Open Tu-Sa 10am-5pm, Su noon-5pm.)

Back to the route. Return to Rte. 4. Fifteen miles past Jemez, turn onto US 550 to Bernalillo. You can either take I-25 N. back to Santa Fe or continue toward Albuquerque.

VITAL STATS

Population: 450,000

Tourist Offices: Albuquerque Convention and Visitors Bureau, 20 1st Plaza NW, Ste. 601 (☎505-842-9918 or 800-284-2282; www.itsatrip.org). Open M-F 8am-5pm. **Old Town Visitors Center,** 303 Romano St. NW (☎505-243-3215; www.itsatrip.org). Open daily Nov.-Mar. 10am-5pm; Apr.-Oct. 10am-6pm.

Library and Internet Access: Albuquerque Public Library, 501 Copper Ave. NW (☎505-768-5141). Free Wi-Fi. Open M and Th-Sa 10am-6pm, Tu-W 11am-7pm.

Post Office: 1135 Broadway NE (☎505-346-8052), at Mountain St. Open M-F 8am-5:30pm.

Postal Code: 87101.

✳ ORIENTATION

Route 66 is known in Albuquerque as **Central Avenue.** It is the main thoroughfare of the city and runs through all of its major neighborhoods. Central Ave. runs east-west, while **I-25** runs north-south; the two divide Albuquerque into quadrants. All downtown addresses come with a quadrant designation: northeast, northwest, southeast, or southwest. The campus of the **University of New Mexico (UNM)** spreads along Central Ave. from University Ave. to **Carlisle Street. Nob Hill,** the area of Central Ave. around Carlisle St., features coffee shops, bookstores, and galleries. **Downtown** lies on Central Ave., between **10th Street** and **Broadway. Old Town Plaza** sits between San Felipe, North Plaza, South Plaza, and Romero.

🏠 ACCOMMODATIONS

Cheap motels line Central Ave., even near downtown. Though many of them are worth their price, be sure to evaluate the quality before paying. During the October **Balloon Festival,** rooms are scarce, so be sure to plan ahead for reservations.

Route 66 Youth Hostel, 1012 Central Ave. SW (☎505-247-1813; www.rt66hostel.com), at 10th St. Friendly hostel located between downtown and Old Town. Dorm and private rooms are simple but clean. Each guest responsible for 1 of 10 easy chores. Free Wi-Fi. Reception 7:30am-1pm and 3-10pm. Dorms $20, private rooms $25, with bath $35. AmEx/D/MC/V. ❶

University Lodge, 3711 Central Ave. NE (☎505-266-7663). Bright and welcoming colors. Excellent value rooms come with TVs, fridges, microwaves, and use of the pool. Wi-Fi. Singles $30; doubles $45. AmEx/D/MC/V. ❷

Sandía Mountain Hostel, 12234 Rte. 14 N. (☎505-281-4117), in nearby Cedar Crest, 10 mi. from the Sandía Ski Area. Take I-40 E. to Exit 175 and go 4 mi. north on Rte. 14. Housed in a comfortable log cabin. An ideal spot to rest and recuperate after a long day on the road. A family of donkeys out back will keep you company. Hiking and biking trails across the street. Tent sites $8. Dorms $14; private cabins $32. MC/V. ❶

Coronado Campground, 106 Monument Rd. (☎505-980-8256), about 15 mi. north of Albuquerque. Take I-25 to Exit 242 and follow the signs. A pleasant campground on the banks of the Rio Grande. Adobe shelters offer respite from the heat. Toilets, showers, and water. Self-service pay station after hours. Office open M-F 9am-5pm. Tent sites with shelters and picnic tables $14, with full hookup $22. MC/V. ❶

🍴 FOOD

A diverse ethnic community, hordes of hungry interstate travelers, and a load of green chilis render the cuisine of Albuquerque surprisingly tasty. The area around UNM is the best bet for inexpensive eateries. A bit farther east, Nob Hill is a haven for yuppie fare, including avocado sandwiches and iced cappuccinos.

Annapurna Ayurvedic Cuisine & Chai House, 2201 Silver Ave. SE (☎505-262-2424), on the corner of Yale Blvd. Named after the Hindu goddess of food and abundance, Annapurna serves delicious South Indian vegetarian options designed to promote healing and balance. Determine which body type you have to maximize effects. Try the Masala Dosa ($8) or the Idli Sambhar ($6.25). Open M-W 7am-8pm, Th-Sa 7am-9pm, Su 10am-2pm. MC/V. ❷

Java Joe's, 906 Park Ave. SW (☎505-765-1514), 1 block south of Central Ave. This lively, casual restaurant has tasty wraps ($7) and great breakfast burritos ($3.50). Lots of vegetarian dishes and live music Sa-Su mornings. Free Wi-Fi. Open daily 6:30am-3:30pm. MC/V. ❶

66 Diner, 1405 Central Ave. NE (☎505-247-1421). Refuel your Rte. 66 mojo. Comes with all the

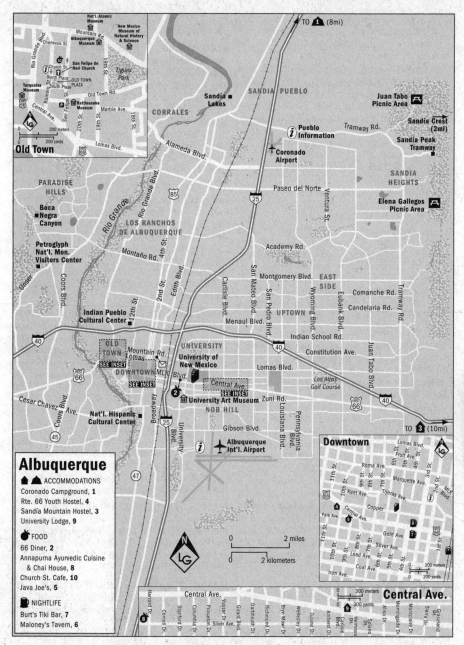

Old Town

Nat'l. Atomic Museum
Mountain Rd.
Albuquerque Museum
New Mexico Museum of Natural History & Science
Charlevoix St.
Rio Grande Blvd.
San Felipe de Neri Church
Church St.
North Plaza
OLD TOWN PLAZA
South Plaza
Tiguex Park
Turquoise Museum
Romero
Central Ave.
Rattlesnake Museum
Marble Ave.
Old Town Rd.
San Felipe
19th St.
20th St.
19th St.
18th St.
Lomas Blvd.
0 200 meters
0 200 yards

TO 1 (8mi)
SANDIA PUEBLO
Sandía Lakes
CORRALES
Alameda Blvd.
Pueblo Information
Coronado Airport
Juan Tabo Picnic Area
Sandía Crest (2mi)
Sandía Peak Tramway
Tramway Rd.

PARADISE HILLS
Rio Grande
Los Ranchos Blvd.
85
25
Paseo del Norte
Ventura St.
SANDIA HEIGHTS
Elena Gallegos Picnic Area

Boca Negra Canyon
LOS RANCHOS DE ALBUQUERQUE
Montaño Rd.
4th St.
Academy Rd.

Petroglyph Nat'l. Mon. Visitors Center
Unser
Coors Blvd.
2nd St.
Edith Blvd.
San Mateo Blvd.
Montgomery Blvd.
EAST SIDE
Comanche Rd.
Candelaria Rd.
Tramway Rd.

Indian Pueblo Cultural Center
12th St.
Carlisle Blvd.
San Pedro Blvd.
UPTOWN
Wyoming Blvd.
Eubank Blvd.

40
OLD TOWN
SEE INSET
Mountain Rd.
Lomas
DOWNTOWN
SEE INSET
Menaul Blvd.
Indian School Rd.
40
Juan Tabo Blvd.

66
Cesar Chavez Ave.
Coors Blvd.
Broadway
MLK Blvd.
UNIVERSITY
University of New Mexico
Central Ave.
SEE INSET
Lomas Blvd.
Constitution Ave.
Los Altos Golf Course
HIST 66
TO 3 (10mi)

45
Nat'l. Hispanic Cultural Center
25
University Blvd.
University Art Museum
NOB HILL
Zuni Rd.
Louisiana Blvd.
Pennsylvania Blvd.

47
Gibson Blvd.
Albuquerque Int'l. Airport

Albuquerque

ACCOMMODATIONS
Coronado Campground, 1
Rte. 66 Youth Hostel, 4
Sandía Mountain Hostel, 3
University Lodge, 9

FOOD
66 Diner, 2
Annapurna Ayurvedic Cuisine & Chai House, 8
Church St. Cafe, 10
Java Joe's, 5

NIGHTLIFE
Burt's Tiki Bar, 7
Maloney's Tavern, 6

N
0 2 miles
0 2 kilometers

Downtown
Lomas Blvd.
Fruit Ave.
Roma Ave.
11th St.
10th St.
9th St.
8th St.
7th St.
6th St.
5th St.
4th St.
3rd St.
2nd St.
MLK Blvd.
Marquette Ave.
66
Kent Ave.
Tijeras Ave.
Park Ave.
Copper
Central Ave.
11th St.
10th St.
9th St.
8th St.
7th St.
Gold Ave.
Silver Ave.
Lead Ave.
Coal Ave.
Iron Ave.
1st St.
0 200 meters
0 200 yards

Central Ave.
Central Ave.
Harvard Dr.
Cornell Dr.
Stanford Dr.
Columbia Dr.
Princeton Dr.
Vassar Dr.
Silver Ave.
Girard Blvd.
Dartmouth Dr.
Richmond Dr.
Bryn Mawr Dr.
Wellesley Dr.
Tulane Dr.
Amherst Dr.
Carlisle Blvd.
Hermosa Dr.
Solano Dr.
Aliso Dr.
Morningside Dr.
Sierra Dr.
Montclaire Dr.
Graceland Dr.
0 300 meters
0 300 yards

expected paraphernalia: jukebox, car licence plates, gas pumps, and lots of green chili. Sandwiches $5-9. Open M-F 11am-11pm, Sa 8am-11pm, Su 8am-10pm. AmEx/D/M/V. ❷

Church St. Cafe, 2111 Church St. NW (☎505-247-8522; www.churchstreetcafe.com), in Old Town. This eatery is in the Casa de Ruiz, which dates back to 1706, making it really freakin' old. Glass-topped wagon-wheel tables. Breakfasts $6-8. Entrees $11-13. Open M-Sa 8am-9pm, Su 8am-4pm. AmEx/D/MC/V. ❸

👁 🏔 SIGHTS AND OUTDOORS

▓TURQUOISE MUSEUM. To learn about the beautiful stone that is the lifeblood of so many New Mexican artisans, stop by the Turquoise Museum. The museum has been in a family of turquoise experts for generations, and lapidary demonstrations take place daily at 10am. The collection room features gorgeous stones from over 60 mines. You can also watch craftsmen applying their skills in the workshop, and there's lots of jewelry for purchase. (2107 Central Ave. NW. ☎505-247-8650. Open M-Sa 10am-4pm. $4, children $3.)

OLD TOWN. When the railroad cut through Albuquerque in the 19th century, it missed Old Town by almost 2 mi. As downtown grew around the railroad, Old Town remained untouched until the 1950s, when the city realized that it had a tourist magnet right under its nose. Just north of Central Ave. and east of Rio Grande Blvd., the adobe plaza looks today much like it did over 100 years ago, save for the ubiquitous restaurants, gift shops, and jewelry vendors. Sure, it's a tourist trap, but Old Town is an architectural marvel, and a stroll through is worthwhile. On the north side of the plaza, the quaint **San Felipe de Neri Church,** built in 1706, has stood the test of time. (Open daily 9am-5pm. Accompanying museum open M-Sa 10am-4pm. Free.) Walking tours of Old Town meet at the Albuquerque Museum. (1hr. tours Tu-Su 11am. Free with admission.)

NATIONAL ATOMIC MUSEUM. Though the difference between fusion and fission might be over your head, the museum features enthralling exhibits on nuclear physics, the social history of the Cold War, and the Manhattan Proj-

ect. (1905 Mountain Rd. NW. ☎505-245-2137. Open daily 9am-5pm. $6, ages 6-17 $4, under 6 free.)

ALBUQUERQUE MUSEUM. The museum showcases New Mexican art and history. The comprehensive exhibit on the conquistadors and Spanish colonial rule is especially impressive, with full suits of armor and weaponry as well as replicated New Mexican homes from the 18th century. Even if you choose not to go in, be sure to see the beautiful sculpture gardens outside. (2000 Mountain Rd. NW. ☎505-243-7255; www.cabq.gov/museum. Open Tu-Su 9am-5pm. Tours of the sculpture garden Tu-Su 10am. $4, ages 4-12 $1, seniors $2; Su 9am-1pm free.)

RATTLESNAKE MUSEUM. With over 30 species ranging from the deadly Mojave to the tiny pygmy, this is the largest collection of live rattlesnakes in the world. Spiders, scorpions, lizards, and venomous toads also call the museum home. It's not for the faint of heart. (202 San Felipe St. NW. ☎505-242-6569; www.rattlesnakes.com. Open M-Sa 10am-6pm, Su 1-5pm. $3.50, students $3, ages 3-12 $2.50.)

NEW MEXICO MUSEUM OF NATURAL HISTORY AND SCIENCE. Spike and Alberta, two statuesque dinosaurs, greet tourists outside. The museum features a five-story "dynatheater," a planetarium, and a *Diplodochus*, the longest dinosaur ever unearthed. (1801 Mountain Rd. NW. ☎505-841-2800; www.nmnaturalhistory.org. Open Feb.-Aug. and Oct.-Dec. daily 9am-5pm; Sept. and Jan. Tu-Su 9am-5pm. $7, ages 3-12 $4, seniors $6.)

UNIVERSITY ART MUSEUM. The University Art Museum features changing exhibits that focus on 20th-century New Mexican paintings and photography. (Near the corner of Central Ave. and Cornell St. ☎505-277-4001. Open Tu 9am-8pm, W-F 9am-4pm, Sa-Su 1-4pm. Free.)

MAXWELL MUSEUM OF ANTHROPOLOGY. This museum has excellent exhibits on the culture and history of Native American settlement in the Southwest. (On University Blvd., just north of Martin Luther King Ave. ☎505-277-4405. Open Tu-F 9am-4pm, Sa 10am-4pm. Free.)

INDIAN PUEBLO CULTURAL CENTER. The center has a commercial edge, but it still provides a good introduction to the history and culture of the 19 Native American Pueblo tribes of New Mexico. The center includes a museum, a store, and a restaurant. *(2401 12th St. NW. ☎505-843-7270; www.indianpueblo.org. Museum open daily 9am-4:30pm. Art demonstrations Sa-Su 11am-2pm. Indian dances Sa-Su 11am, 2pm. $6, students $1, seniors $5.50.)*

NATIONAL HISPANIC CULTURAL CENTER. The center features an art museum with exhibits that explore folk art and representations of Hispanic social and cultural life in America. *(1701 4th St. SW, at the corner of Bridge Blvd. ☎505-246-2261; www.nhccnm.org. Open Tu-Su 10am-5pm. $3, under 16 free, seniors $2.)*

PETROGLYPH NATIONAL MONUMENT. Just outside Albuquerque, the Petroglyph National Monument features more than 20,000 images etched into lava rocks by Pueblo Native Americans and Spanish settlers between 1300 and 1680. The park encompasses much of the 17 mi. West Mesa, a ridge of black basalt boulders formed by volcanic activity that occurred 130,000 years ago. The most accessible petroglyphs can be found via three short trails at **Boca Negra Canyon,** 2 mi. north of the visitors center. The **Rinconada Canyon Trail,** 1 mi. south of the visitors center, has more intricate rock art and is an easy 2 mi. desert hike along the base of the West Mesa. To see the nearby volcanos, take Exit 149 off I-40 and follow Paseo del Volcán to a dirt road. *(Take I-40 to Unser Blvd./ Exit 154. ☎505-899-0205. Park open daily 8am-5pm. $1 per vehicle on weekdays, $2 on weekends.)*

SANDÍA MOUNTAINS. Rising a mile above Albuquerque to the northeast, the sunset-pink crest of the Sandía Mountains gives the peaks their name, which means "watermelon" in Spanish. The crest draws thousands of visitors for its first-rate hiking and exploring. One of the most popular trails in New Mexico, **La Luz Trail** (7 mi. one-way) climbs the Sandía Crest, beginning at the Juan Tabo Picnic Area. *(From Exit 167 on I-40, drive north on Tramway Blvd. 10 mi. to Forest Rd. 333. Follow Trail 137 for 7 mi. and then take Trail 84 to the top.)* The mountains also have excellent biking trails. Warm up on the moderate **Foothills Trail** (7 mi.), which starts at the Elena Gallegos Picnic Area, off Tramway Blvd., and skirts along the bottom of the mountains. The most popular place for biking is at the **Sandía Peak Ski Area,** 6 mi. up Rte. 536 on the way to Sandía Crest. Bikers of all skill levels can take their bikes up the chairlift and then ride down on 15 mi. of mountain trails and rollers. *(☎505-856-6419; www.sandiapeak.com. Bikes $48 per day. Helmets required. Chairlifts run June Sa-Su 10am-4pm; July-Aug. F-Su 10am-4pm. Full-day lift ticket $18.)* In winter, the peak is also a serviceable ski area for those who can't escape north to Taos or south to Ruidoso. Six lifts service 25 short trails on 200 acres. The summit has a vertical drop of 1700 ft. *(☎505-242-9052; www. sandiapeak.com. Open Dec.-Mar. Full-day lift ticket $48, ages 13-20 $38, ages 6-12 $35. Rentals from $22.)*

🎷 NIGHTLIFE

Albuquerque is an oasis of interesting bars, jamming nightclubs, art-house cinemas, and university culture. Check flyers posted around the university area or pick up a copy of *Alibi*, the free local weekly, for info on live music. The most happening nightlife takes place on Central Ave., downtown, and near the university. Nob Hill establishments tend to be the most gay-friendly.

Maloney's Tavern, 325 Central Ave. NW (☎505-242-7422; www.maloneystavern.com). Decorated with black-and-white shots of classic moments from the silver screen. Burgers ($9-10) are available until 10pm. No cover. Open M-Sa 11am-2am, Su 11am-midnight. AmEx/D/MC/V.

Burt's Tiki Bar, 313 Gold St. SW (☎505-247-2878), 1 block south of the Central Ave. Friendly, laid-back. Surf and tiki paraphernalia line the walls and ceiling, while musicians that perform music ranging from funk to punk to hip hop take the stage. Live music Tu-Sa. No cover. Open Tu-Sa 9pm-2am. AmEx/D/MC/V.

🌿 FESTIVALS

During the Second week of October, hundreds of aeronauts take flight in hot-air balloons during the **Balloon Festival.** Beneath a surreal sky filled with the colorful giants, the entire city enjoys barbecues and musical events. (☎888-422-7277; www.balloonfiesta.com.)

🚩 THE ROAD TO ACOMA PUEBLO AND SKY CITY: 64 MI.

The old route joins the interstate; follow **Route 66 West** out of Albuquerque onto **I-40 West** all the way to Exit 117. In Mesita, turn left onto the **north service road** and follow it 5 mi. to the junction with **Route 124.** Turn right onto Rte. 124 and pass through the tiny towns of Paraje, Budville, Cubera, Villa de Cubero, and San Fidel. Cross to the I-40 south service road in McCartys, just after San Fidel **(Exit 96).** One mile past the exit you will see signs to the Acoma Pueblo and Sky City.

ACOMA PUEBLO AND SKY CITY ☎505

Arguably the oldest continuously inhabited area in North America, Sky City, or the Acoma Pueblo, peers over the edge of the high sandstone mesa on which it is built. Accessible only by a narrow staircase, Sky City avoided Spanish rule until 1599, when its residents were brutally enslaved by Don Juan de Onate. Between seven and 13 families live on the mesa, which lacks electricity and running water. Perched high above the rocky world below, the **San Esteban Rey Mission** is a gravity-defying architectural feat and a stunning example of Southwestern Pueblo architecture. Visitors must buy a bus pass at the visitors center to ride up up the mesa to the pueblo with a guide. Photographs are prohibited unless you buy a photography pass ($10), and video cameras are forbidden. Bring cash if you plan on ascending the pueblo, as resident native artists often lay out their renowned hand-painted pottery. All are welcome in September for the **Harvest Dance** and **Annual Feast of San Estevan** at Old Acoma. (☎505-552-7860; www.skycity.com. Open daily. Tours daily 8am-6:30pm. Last tour 5pm. $12, ages 6-17 $9, seniors $11.)

⚐ THE ROAD TO GRANTS: 37 MI.

From the service road leading from McCartys, pass under **I-40.** After 5 mi., RVs should go back to I-40 and take it to **Exit 89,** where they can rejoin **Old Route 66,** since there is a low and narrow tunnel on this stretch of the service road. Cross onto the north side 7 mi. later at the **Sky City turnoff** and turn right onto **Route 117** (marked Historic 66). Enter downtown Grants on **Santa Fe Avenue/Route 122.**

GRANTS ☎505

Grants first appeared on the map when three Canadian brothers were given a contract to build the Santa Fe railroad through the area.

After the railroad boom, Grants became a shoot-'em-up Old West town, and the population dipped as low as 350. The town rose to prominence again in 1950 when a Navajo named Paddy Martinez overheard some prospectors in a cafe discussing a valuable yellow mineral they called carnotite and found the rock near his sheep pastures outside of town. Grants became a mining town, and the uranium wealth made the town glow until the last of the mines was tapped out in the 1980s.

VITAL STATS

Population: 8800

Tourist Offices: Grants Chamber of Commerce, 100 N. Iron Ave. (☎505-287-4802; www.grants.org), in the New Mexico Mining Museum. Open M-F 9am-5pm. **El Malpais Info Center** (☎505-783-4774), 23 mi. south of I-40 on Rte. 53. Open daily 8:30am-4:30pm.

Library and Internet Access: Mother Whiteside Memorial Library, 525 High St. (☎505-287-4793). Open Tu-F 9am-6pm, Sa 9am-3:30pm.

Post Office: 816 W. Santa Fe Ave. (☎505-287-3143). Open M-F 8:50am-5pm, Sa 8:30am-noon. **Postal Code:** 87020.

✴ ORIENTATION

Although streets in Grants are laid out erratically, getting around is simple. **Route 66** runs through the center of town as **Santa Fe Avenue;** most attractions, restaurants, and accommodations can be found along this strip. **I-40** runs just south of town, parallel to Santa Fe Ave.

⚐ ACCOMMODATIONS

Entering town on Santa Fe Ave., look to the left for chain accommodations, which cluster near fast-food joints at the east end of town. As you continue west on Santa Fe Ave., Grants has a neon strip to rival Santa Rosa and Tucumcari. Several of the original Rte. 66 motels are still great budget options.

Sands Motel, 112 McArthur St. (☎505-287-2996; www.sandsmotelonroute66.com). A quiet location one block north of the main road; look for the big sign on the south side of the street. Comfortable rooms come with TVs, fridges, microwaves and Wi-Fi. Singles $33; doubles $45. D/MC/V. ❷

Desert Sun Motel, 1121 E. Santa Fe Ave. (☎505-287-7925). Rooms have old furnishings, but this lends them an enjoyable historical feel. Fridges and free coffee. Check-out 10am. Singles $20; doubles $31. AmEx/D/MC/V. ❶

FOOD

El Cafecito, 820 E. Santa Fe Ave. (☎505-285-6229). Hands down the best Mexican food in town. The great prices don't hurt either. Entrees $5-8. Open M-F 7am-9pm, Sa 7am-8pm. D/MC/V. ❶

La Ventana Steakhouse, 110½ Geis St. (☎505-287-9393). The local pick for an upscale meal. Terra-Cotta exterior. Dinner steak $9.25. Prime rib $15.50. Appetizers $4-9. Open daily 11am-11pm. AmEx/D/MC/V. ❸

Canton Cafe, 1212 W. Santa Fe Ave. (☎505-287-8314). Serves above-average, all-you-can-eat Chinese food. Dinner buffet $7. Open daily 11am-9pm. D/MC/V. ❶

SIGHTS

NEW MEXICO MINING MUSEUM. The museum will educate you on every aspect of mining uranium. You can take a tour of a restored mineshaft. *(100 N. Iron Ave. ☎505-287-4802. Open M-Sa 9am-4pm. $3, ages 7-18 $2, under 6 free.)*

MALPAIS NATIONAL MONUMENT. The volcanic past of the Grants area has created an abundance of interesting natural phenomena. The monument is home to 17 mi. of lava tube caves, ice caves, spatter cones, and generally rugged terrain. Miles of hiking trails lead to sandstone bluffs, natural arches, ancient Native American trade routes, and over 30 volcanic craters. Despite its spectacular landscape, the monument does not receive the traffic of some of its neighbors, making it a perfect spot to escape the crowds. *(South of town on Rte. 53. ☎505-285-4641.)*

ICE CAVES. These ice caves were formed by collapsed lava tubes and remain 31°F year-round. Admission to the ice caves also includes admission to the **Bandera Volcano,** once a gaping maw of fire, now just a hole. Tickets to the attractions can be purchased at the converted logging saloon and dance hall, now the **Old Time Trading Post.** *(12000 Ice Caves*

Rd. on Rte. 53. ☎888-423-2283. Open daily from 8am to 1hr. before sunset. $9, ages 5-12 $4.)

◪ THE ROAD TO THOREAU: 22 MI.
Follow **Route 122** through the suburb of Milan. Continue south 9 mi. through Prewitt.

THOREAU   ☎505

Although signs as far east as Albuquerque advertise a multitude of jewelry and souvenir stops, one of the best places to splurge is in the tiny town of Thoreau (THREW). Less blazingly publicized than the stores clustering around the Continental Divide, the **Navajo Cooperative Store,** 19 Paradise Ln., has jewelry, clothing, and other souvenirs. Profits from the store support The Gathering Place, a community-based organization run by the Navajo people. (☎505-862-8075. Open M-Th 9am-4pm. MC/V.) Five miles west of town is the **Continental Divide;** rain falling east of the line makes its way to the Atlantic, while rain falling on the west ends up in the Pacific.

◪ THE ROAD TO GALLUP: 25 MI.
Enter **I-40** at **Exit 47** and take it to **Exit 36,** 11 mi. later. Take the north service road 14 mi. to Gallup.

GALLUP   ☎505

Gallup lies at the intersection of Rte. 66 and US 666 and is the gateway to some of the more beautiful stretches of New Mexico. Native American vendors fill parking lots, and "trading posts" overflowing with silver and local turquoise line the downtown streets. If you can overlook the gaudy signs and ubiquitous turquoise vendors, the landscape and proximity to Petrified Forest National Park, Chaco Culture National Historic Park, Navajo Reservation, and El Morro National Monument make Gallup a worthwhile stop.

ORIENTATION

Almost all you need to know about getting around in Gallup is that **Route 66,** the city's main drag, runs parallel to and south of **I-40.** Numbered streets run roughly north-south; **Second Street** is also a main artery.

ROUTE 66

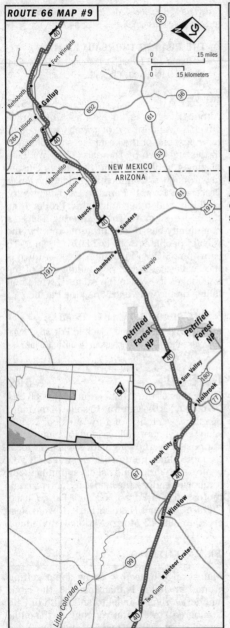

ROUTE 66 MAP #9

0   15 miles

0   15 kilometers

NEW MEXICO
ARIZONA

Petrified Forest NP

Petrified Forest NP

ROUTE 66

VITAL STATS

Population: 20,000

Tourist Office: Gallup Chamber of Commerce, 103 Rte. 66 (☎505-722-2228 or 800-242-4282). Open M-F 8:30am-5pm, Sa 10am-4pm.

Library and Internet Access: Octavia Fellin Library, 115 W. Hill St. (☎505-836-1291). Open M-Th 9am-8pm, F 10am-6pm, Sa 9am-6pm.

Post Office: 950 W. Aztec Ave. (☎505-863-3491). Open M-F 8:30am-5pm, Sa 10am-1:30pm. **Postal Code:** 87301.

🏠 ACCOMMODATIONS

At the east end of town, Rte. 66 is lined with dirt-cheap motels (in some cases, the emphasis is on the dirt).

Roadrunner Motel, 3012 Rte. 66 (☎505-863-3804). Offers clean rooms with fridges, microwaves, and free Wi-Fi in a quiet location. Singles $30; doubles $36. AmEx/D/MC/V. ❷

Capitan Motel, 1300 Rte. 66 (☎505-863-6828). Clean, well-maintained rooms with fridges and spacious bathrooms around a brightly painted orange and pink courtyard. Singles $36; doubles $41. AmEx/D/MC/V. ❷

El Rancho Hotel and Motel, 1000 Rte. 66 (☎505-863-9311). The motel has been the longtime lodging choice of celebrities passing through (such as Clark Gable and Katherine Hepburn), and most have had a room or a dish in the restaurant named after them. Singles from $74; doubles from $86. AmEx/D/MC/V. ❹

🍽 FOOD

Earl's Restaurant, 1400 Rte. 66 (☎505-863-4201 or 863-3285), at the east end of town. Has been a 1st stop for roadtrippers since the 1940s. Hand-pressed hamburgers $7-9. Steaks from $10. Open M-Sa 6am-9pm, Su 7am-4pm. AmEx/MC/V. ❷

Ranch Kitchen, 3001 Rte. 66 (☎505-722-2537), 2 mi. west of town on Rte. 66. Dishes up hearty portions of inventive Mexican and American cuisine, like the popular turkey sandwich with guacamole and green chili ($9) or Native American lamb stew ($8). Open daily 8:30am-10pm. AmEx/D/MC/V. ❷

Virgie's, 2720 Rte. 66 (☎505-863-5152). Topped with a splendid vintage Rte. 66 sign. Serves tasty Mexican dishes. Fajitas $8.50. Open M-Sa 7am-10pm. AmEx/D/MC/V. ❷

🄶 SIGHTS

NAVAJO CODE TALKER MUSEUM. The museum pays tribute to the over 400 Navajo whose "code" was never broken by enemy forces during WWII. The museum details the use of the Navajo language as a military code, the Navajo involvement in WWII, and Ronald Reagan's declaration of August 14 as National Navajo Code Talkers Day. *(103 Rte. 66, in the same building as the chamber of commerce. ☎505-722-2228. Open M-F 8:30am-5pm. Free.)*

GALLUP CULTURAL CENTER. The center houses the **Storyteller Museum, Kiva Cinema, Angela's Cafe con Leche,** the **Ceremonial Gallery,** the **Wisdom Keeper Book Store/Gift Shop,** and seasonal artist presentations. *(201 Rte. 66. ☎505-863-4131. Open M-F 9am-4pm. Free.)*

RICHARDSON'S TRADING COMPANY AND CASH PAWN, INC. The shop deals an amazing selection of turquoise jewelry and other locally produced goods. Most merchandise is purchased from local artists and citizens. *(222 Rte. 66. ☎505-722-4762. Open M-Sa 9am-6pm.)*

🄽 THE ROAD TO HOUCK: 34 MI.

Approximately 5 mi. out of town on **Route 66,** head left on **Route 118.** Go under the interstate and turn right onto the south frontage road. Follow this for 4 mi., under **I-40,** and then curve right over the railroad tracks. The tiny, old town of Manuelito is 15 mi. out of Gallup. The view leaving town is stunning and expansive; a riverbed cuts away on one side, and snow-capped mountains rise on the far side of the tracks. Attractions and gas stations are few and far between, although curio shops virtually wallpaper the strip. Just past the Arizona border, the **Painted Cliffs Welcome Center** will outfit roadtrippers with maps and info. (☎928-688-2448. Open daily 8am-5pm.) Just east of the welcome center, cross under I-40 to the south frontage road. Continue 5 mi. to join I-40. Take the interstate to **Exit 351** to reach Houck.

TIME CHANGE. Most of Arizona does not observe Daylight Saving Time, so, if you're traveling between April and October, set your clock back 1hr. as you enter the state. If you're traveling from November to March, there is no change.

The Grand Canyon State **ARIZONA** *Welcomes You!*

HOUCK ☎928

Houck is yet another town brimming with Ortega family stores. In addition to Ortega jewelry, you'll find **Indian City** (☎928-688-2691; open daily 7:30am-7pm) and **Chee's Indian Store** (☎928-688-2433; open M-Sa 8am-7:30pm, Su 1:30-7:30pm). The adjacent food stand is little more than a shack, but it has phenomenal tacos ($5) and fry bread ($2) with honey, sugar, or cheese. (Cash only.) Farther down the road is the **Fort Courage Trading Post,** in case you need to stock up on paraphernalia. The exit also includes a post office and a gas station. (☎928-688-2681. Post office open M-F 8:30am-noon and 1-5pm, Sa 9am-noon.)

🄽 THE ROAD TO SANDERS: 10 MI.

From Houck, follow the interstate 1 mi. to **Exit 346.** For the next 7 mi., original **Route 66** is a nasty piece of narrow dirt road, so you might want to stay on the interstate until **Exit 340.** Those who take the dirt road can find age-old **Querino Trading Post,** which stocks everything from shampoo to ice cream. (☎928-688-3047. Open daily 6am-10pm. Cash only.) Follow the dirt road 6 mi. or stay on I-40 to Exit 340. At Exit 340, follow the north frontage road 2 mi. to Sanders.

SANDERS ☎928

Sanders is home to the pink, white, and chrome **Route 66 Diner and Pizza Shack ❷,** on the south side of the interstate. This roadside classic serves shakes ($2.65), cobblers ($3), large breakfasts, sandwiches, and dinner plates—not to mention pizza. (☎928-688-2537. Open M-F 7am-8pm, Sa 9am-8pm. MC/V.)

◪ THE ROAD TO CHAMBERS: 6 MI.

Continue on the north frontage road. Chambers is at the junction of **I-40** and **Route 191.**

CHAMBERS   ☎928

Chambers has offered respite to many a traveler at the **Best Western Chieftain Motel ❸**, the only motel for miles. The adjacent restaurant provides non-fast-food meals. (☎928-688-2754. Restaurant open daily 6am-8pm. Singles $67; doubles $73. AmEx/D/MC/V.)

◪ THE ROAD TO PETRIFIED FOREST NATIONAL PARK: 28 MI.

Continue through Navajo. Take **Exit 311** from **I-40.**

PETRIFIED · FOREST NATIONAL PARK   ☎928

Spreading over 60,000 acres, Petrified Forest National Park looks like an overturned, psychedelic crayon box. Some 225 million years ago, when Arizona's desert was swampland, volcanic ash covered the logs, slowing their decay. Silica-infused water seeped through the wood, and the silica crystallized into quartz, combining with iron-rich minerals to produce rainbow hues. Colorful sediment was laid down in this floodplain, creating the stunning colors that stripe the park's badlands.

VITAL STATS

Area: 93,500 acres

Tourist Office: Painted Desert Visitors Center (☎928-524-6228), off I-40 at the north entrance to the park. Open daily June-Aug. 7am-7pm; Sept.-May 8am-5pm.

Gateway Towns: Gallup (p. 559), Sun Valley (see opposite page), Holbrook (see opposite page).

Fees: 7-day pass $10 per vehicle. $5 per bike.

◪ ORIENTATION

Roughly speaking, the park can be divided into two parts: the northern **Painted Desert** and the southern **Petrified Forest.** A 28 mi. road connects the two sections. With lookout points and trails at intervals along the road, driving from one end of the park to the other is a good way to take in the full spectrum of landscapes. An entrance station welcomes visitors

to both ends of the park, and a restaurant is located at the northern end.

◪ CAMPING

There are no campgrounds in the park, but **backcountry camping ❶** is allowed in the **Painted Desert Wilderness** with a free permit, available at the **Painted Desert Visitors Center and Rainbow Forest Museum.** Water is available at the visitors centers. In case of emergency, call the ranger dispatch (☎928-524-9726). No fires are allowed. Motels and diners line Rte. 66, but there aren't any right around the park. Gallup and Holbrook offer more options.

◎ ◪ SIGHTS AND OUTDOORS

Most travelers opt to drive the 28 mi. park road from north to south, which takes at least 45min. From the north, the first stop is **Tiponi Point.** From the next stop at **Tawa Point,** the **Painted Desert Rim Trail** (1 mi. one-way) skirts the mesa edge above the **Lithodendron Wash** and the **Black Forest** before ending at **Kachina Point.** The panoramas from Kachina Point are among the best in the park, and the point provides access to the **Painted Desert Wilderness,** the park's designated region for backcountry hiking and camping. As the road crosses I-40, it enters the Petrified Forest portion of the park. The next stop is the 100-room **Puerco Pueblo.** A short paved trail through the pueblo offers viewpoints of nearby petroglyphs. Hundreds of petroglyphs can be seen from a distance at **Newspaper Rock.** The road then wanders through the eerie moonscape of the **Tepees** before arriving at the 3 mi. **Blue Mesa Vehicle Loop.** The **Long Logs** and **Giant Logs Trails,** near the southern visitors center, are littered with fragments of petrified wood. Both trails are less than 1 mi. long and fairly flat, but they travel through the densest concentration of petrified wood in the world. Don't pick up the petrified wood; taking fragments is illegal and unlucky. One wall of the visitors center is covered with notes from people who took petrified wood and sent it back to the park with good riddance. At the southern end of the park near US 180, the **Rainbow Forest Museum** provides a look at petrified logs up close and serves as a visitors center. (☎928-524-6822. Open daily 7am-7pm. Free.)

⊠ DETOUR

STEWART'S PETRIFIED WOOD

Take **Exit 303** from **I-40**.

A number of curio shops west of the park hawk bits of the petrified wood. Some even offer "petrified rocks straight from the factory." The most entertaining of these shops is **Stewart's Petrified Wood**; keep an eye out for the giant dinosaurs munching on mannequins. If you get to the school bus perched on a cliff mannequin, poised to sail off the edge, you've gone just a bit too far. Charles and Gazell Stewart have used every kooky advertising ploy in the book to lure visitors into their rock shop—from the papier-mâché dinos to the ostrich pen next door. The store itself has fossils and rocks. (☎800-414-8533; www.petrifiedwood.com. Open daily 9am-5pm.)

⊼ THE ROAD TO SUN VALLEY: 24 MI.

Get back on **I-40** and take **Exit 294** for Sun Valley.

SUN VALLEY   ☎928

Between Stewart's rock haven and Holbrook is Sun Valley. Barring extreme need for pause, it's best to press on to Holbrook for food and service. The **Sun Valley RV Park ❶** sells petrified wood and has RV sites as well as shelters for tenters. (☎928-524-2972. Tent sites $12; RV sites $17. Cash or check only.)

⊼ THE ROAD TO HOLBROOK: 9 MI.

Continue on **I-40 West** and take **Exit 289** to enter Holbrook on **Historic 66**.

HOLBROOK   ☎928

All of the Rte. 66 attractions of the surrounding miles converge on tiny Holbrook. Every curio shop hawks petrified wood and Rte. 66 collectibles, and the town may have more giant plastic dinosaurs and Rte. 66 murals per capita than anywhere else on the planet. Founded in 1882, Holbrook has always been a tourist mecca, first as home to one of the first Fred Harvey railroad restaurants and later as a Rte. 66 stopping point, where tourists could hunker down in concrete tipis.

VITAL STATS

Population: 5000

Tourist Office: Holbrook Chamber of Commerce, 100 E. Arizona Ave. (☎800-524-2459). Open M-F 8am-noon and 1-5pm, Sa-Su 8am-4pm.

Library and Internet Access: Holbrook Public Library, 403 Park St. (☎928-524-3732). Open M 10am-5pm, Tu-Th 10am-7pm, F 1-5pm, Sa 10am-2pm.

Post Office: 100 W. Erie. St. (☎928-524-3311). Open M-F 9am-5pm, Sa 10am-noon. **Postal Code:** 86025.

⊁ ORIENTATION

Navajo Boulevard is Holbrook's main north-south thoroughfare. At the west end of town, **North Eighth Avenue** also runs north-south. **West Florida Street** and **West Hopi Drive** are the two main roads running east to west.

⚑ ACCOMMODATIONS

Wigwam Motel, 811 W. Hopi Dr. (☎928-524-3048). The concrete tipis are surprisingly comfortable, each with private bath, TV, A/C, and a glorious vintage vehicle parked outside. Singles from $48; doubles $54. MC/V. ❷

Holbrook Inn, 235 W. Hopi Dr. (☎928-524-3809). Standard rooms with fridges and microwaves within tipi eyeshot. Free Wi-Fi. Singles $30; doubles $38. AmEx/D/MC/V. ❷

🍴 FOOD

Joe and Aggie's Cafe, 120 W. Hopi Dr. (☎928-524-6540). A Holbrook institution since 1949 and locals' favorite for authentic Mexican cuisine. Cheese enchilada plates $7.50. Open M-Sa 6am-8pm. AmEx/D/MC/V. ❷

Romo's Cafe, 121 W. Hopi Dr. (☎928-524-2153). Serves up decent Mexican fare and Wi-Fi. $8-12. Open M-Sa 10am-8pm. AmEx/D/MC/V. ❷

⊙ SIGHTS

JULIEN'S ROADRUNNER SHOP. The shop has Rte. 66 trinkets galore as well as a great collection of signs and T-shirts amassed over the past 33 years. (*109 W. Hopi Dr.* ☎*928-524-2388. Open M-Sa 8am-5pm.*)

NAVAJO COUNTY COURTHOUSE AND MUSEUM. Capturing a sense of local history, the courthouse has a small museum including a claustrophobic jail cell embellished with murals. In summer the small performance space outside the courthouse features Navajo dancing with professional dancers and children in traditional garb. (*On Rte. 66 at the corner of E. Arizona St. and Navajo Blvd.* ☎ *928-524-6558. Open M-F 8am-5pm and 6-9pm, Sa-Su 8am-4pm. Navajo dance June-Aug. M-F 6:30-8:30pm. Free.*)

GERONIMO TRADING POST. The trading post, with geode pillars and a stand of tipis, has been luring travelers with postcards, jewelry, and petrified wood for years. (*A few miles west of Holbrook at Exit 290, off I-40.* ☎ *928-288-3241. Open daily in summer 7am-7pm; in winter 8am-4pm.*)

⚐ THE ROAD TO JOSEPH CITY: 11 MI.
Continue on **I-40 West** and take it to **Exit 269** in order to reach the **Jackrabbit Trading Post** in Joseph City.

JOSEPH CITY   ☎928

The giant "Here It Is" sign of the **Jackrabbit Trading Post,** 5 mi. down the road at Exit 269, should be familiar—remember Henry's Rte. 66 Emporium and Rabbit Ranch's "Hare it is!" sign (p. 517) back in Staunton, Illinois? The photo-op with the giant plastic rabbit is too good to miss. The store sells the usual Rte. 66 paraphernalia and trinkets. (☎928-288-3230. Open M-Sa 8am-6pm, Su noon-6pm.)

⚐ THE ROAD TO WINSLOW: 22 MI.
Rejoin **I-40,** take it to **Exit 255,** pass under the interstate, and continue on the south frontage road.

WINSLOW   ☎928

If you don't already know that Winslow was inspiration for the Eagles song "Take it Easy," the folks in Winslow will tell you. "Standing on a corner in Winslow, Arizona; such a fine sight to see" has been taken to the extreme, with an entire intersection and three out of the four corners dedicated to that happy moment. If you can get away from the Eagles-mania, Winslow is a small, leisurely paced town, with an amazing hotel and a few small restaurants.

✦ ORIENTATION

North Williamson Avenue and **North Berry Avenue** are two main arteries in Winslow. **Route 66** heads one-way west, and **West Second Street** runs one-way east.

VITAL STATS
Population: 9550
Tourist Office: Winslow Chamber of Commerce and Visitors Center, 101 E. 2nd St. (☎928-289-2434). Open M-F 9am-5pm, Sa 9am-4pm.
Library and Internet Access: Winslow Public Library, 420 W. Gilmore St. (☎928-289-4982). Open Tu and F 10am-5pm, W-Th 10am-7pm, Sa 11am-4pm.
Post Office: 223 N. Williamson Ave. (☎928-289-2131). Open M-F 9am-5pm, Sa 10am-1pm. **Postal Code:** 86041.

🏠 ACCOMMODATIONS

La Posada Hotel, 303 E. 2nd St. (☎928-289-4366; www.laposada.org). A sprawling hacienda of tiled elegance. Designed in the 1920s by the renowned architect Mary Jane Colter, in its day it was the finest hotel in the Southwest. At roughly the same price as some high-end motels, a stay here includes plush rooms (some with their own balconies), landscaped outdoor patios, decadent downstairs lounges, a game room, and a library. Visitors are free to roam the downstairs lounge area and admire the beautiful paintings and sculptures. The hotel also houses The Turquoise Room (☎928-0289-2888), an upscale restaurant with entrees from $20. Check-out noon. Rooms from $99. AmEx/D/MC/V. ❹

Motel 10, 725 W. 3rd St. (☎928-289-3211), at the west end of town. Decent rooms with fridges and microwaves. Cookies W night. Wi-Fi. Singles from $33; doubles from $37. AmEx/D/MC/V. ❷

Homolovi Ruins State Park (☎928-289-4106). See below. Hookups from Apr.-Oct. only. Tent sites $12, with hookup $19. Day use $5. MC/V. ❶

🍴 FOOD

Bojo's Grill and Sports Club, 117 W. 2nd St. (☎928-289-0616). Great sandwiches ($6-8) and decent Mexican options. Open M-Sa 11am-9pm. AmEx/D/MC/V. ❷

ROUTE 66

Falcon Family Restaurant, 113 E. 3rd St. (☎928-289-2628). A Rte. 66 historic family restaurant since 1955. Serves reasonably priced American and Mexican dishes with a bar next door. Green chili burger $7. Entrees $8. Open daily 6am-9pm. Bar open M-W and Su 2-10pm, Th-Sa 2pm-2am. AmEx/D/MC/V. ❷

🖝 SIGHTS

ROADWORKS GIFTS AND SOUVENIRS. What's that voice in the air? Is it God? No, it's Don Henley. The shop pumps Eagles music onto the infamous corner and sells a full variety of "standin' on the corner" memorabilia. *(101 W. 2nd St. ☎928-289-5423. Open daily 8:30am-6pm.)*

OLD TRAILS MUSEUM. "Winslow's Attic" is the repository for every sort of historical Winslow knick-knack, including Anasazi artifacts, souvenirs from the La Posada Hotel, and Santa Fe Railroad memorabilia. Run by the historical society, the museum is staffed by members willing and eager to talk about their town. *(212 N. Kinsley Ave. ☎928-289-5861. Open Tu-Sa 10am-4pm. Free.)*

HOMOLOVI RUINS STATE PARK. The park offers easy walks among pueblo ruins and a beautiful campground. *(2 mi. east of Winslow at Exit 257, off I-40. ☎928-289-4106. Open daily 8am-5pm.)*

�︎ DETOUR
METEOR CRATER

Turn right on **I-40 West** at the edge of town and follow it until you hit Meteor Crater, 18 mi. west of Winslow.

At Meteor Crater, visitors drive up the side of the first proven meteor impact site and hike the ridge of the crater, 2 mi. in diameter. A museum on the rim details the story of the crater, including how its moon-like terrain has made it a training ground for Apollo astronauts. (☎928-289-2362. Open daily from Memorial Day to Labor Day 7am-7pm; from Labor Day to Memorial Day 8am-5pm. Tours 15min. past each hr. Closed-toed shoes required. $15, ages 6-17 $7, seniors $13.) There is also an **RV park** ❶ near the park entrance. (☎928-289-4002. Sites with water and electricity $25, with sewer $27. AmEx/D/MC/V.)

🖝 THE ROAD TO FLAGSTAFF: 22 MI.

Continue on **I-40** heading west. At **Exit 211**, go north on the frontage road, **Townsend-Winona Road**, and follow it through Winona to the northeast end of Flagstaff. Turn left on **US 89**, 10 mi. after the turnoff, and follow it south into downtown Flagstaff.

FLAGSTAFF   ☎928

Born on the Fourth of July, Flagstaff began as a rest stop along the transcontinental railroad, its mountain springs providing precious refreshment on the long haul across the continent to the Pacific Ocean. These days, Flagstaff is still a major stopover on the way to the Southwest's must-sees. Trains plow through town 72 times a day, while travelers pass through on their way to the Grand Canyon, Sedona, and the Petrified Forest, all within a day's drive. The outdoorsman will never be bored here, but Flagstaff caters to fashionistas as well, with numerous outlet malls and great downtown boutiques.

✴ ORIENTATION

Downtown lies between **Leroux Street** and **Aspen Street,** one block north of **Route 66;** the visitors center, hostels, and inexpensive restaurants and bars are all within a half-mile of this spot. **South San Francisco Street,** a block east of Leroux St., hosts many outdoors shops. Split by Rte. 66, the touristy northern area of Flagstaff is the center of downtown. The area south of the tracks is less developed but has hostels and vegetarian eateries.

VITAL STATS
Population: 58,000
Tourist Office: Flagstaff Visitors Center, 1 E. Rte. 66 (☎928-774-9541; www.flagstaff.com), in the Amtrak station. Open M-Sa 8am-5pm, Su 9am-4pm.
Library and Internet Access: Cline Library (☎928-523-2171), on the NAU campus. Take Riordan Rd. east from Rte. 66. Open M-Th 7:30am-10pm, F 7:30am-6pm, Sa 10:30am-5pm, Su noon-10pm.
Post Office: 104 N. Agassiz St. (☎928-779-2371). Open M-F 9am-5pm, Sa 9am-1pm. **Postal Code:** 86001.

ROUTE 66

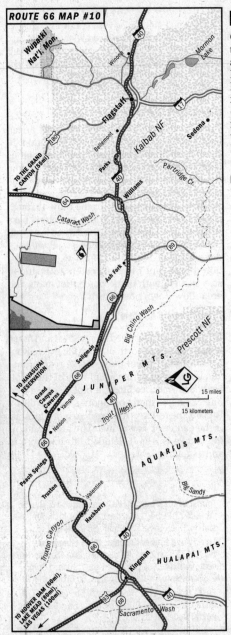

ROUTE 66 MAP #10

ACCOMMODATIONS

Cheap motels line Rte. 66 entering town, but there are great, inexpensive lodging deals for almost as cheap in the heart of downtown. Free **backcountry camping** ❶ is available around Flagstaff in designated areas. Pick up a map from the **Peaks Ranger Station,** 5075 N. US 89A (☎928-526-0866). All backcountry campsites must be located at least 200 ft. away from trails, waterways, wet meadows, and lakes. For more info, call the **Coconino National Forest.** (☎928-527-3600. Open M-F 8am-4:30pm.)

Du Beau Hostel, 19 W. Phoenix Ave. (☎928-774-6731; www.dubeauhostel.com). 1 block from Rte. 66 and downtown Flagstaff. The funky lounge space with leather futons, foosball, pool, and an electric jukebox sees a regular flow of international travelers. Breakfast included 7-10am. Laundry. Internet $2 per 30min. Free Wi-Fi. Key deposit $5. Dorms $18-20; private rooms (some with bath) $41-48. MC/V. ❶

Grand Canyon Hostel, 19 S. San Francisco St. (☎928-779-9421 or 888-442-2696; www.grandcanyonhostel.com). Du Beau's sister hostel with the same great value and friendly atmosphere. Du Beau is more popular for socializing, so this is a better option for those wanting a good night's sleep. Breakfast included. Laundry. Dorms $18-20; private rooms $38-48. D/MC/V. ❶

Western Hills Motel, 1580 E. Rte. 66 (☎928-774-6633). The sign outside reads "European Hostess," but don't worry, this isn't a brothel, it's just a motel run by a Polish woman. The sign is one of the best along the route, and inside it gets better; original vintage room furnishings, well-kept gardens, and a nice elevated position away from the main road. Free Wi-Fi. Singles $40; doubles $50. AmEx/D/MC/V. ❷

Weatherford Hotel, 23 N. Leroux St. (☎928-779-1919; www.weatherfordhotel.com). The oldest hotel in Flagstaff, dating from 1898, the Weatherford has 10 large rooms with balconies, antique furniture, and bay windows. Suites come with TVs and phones. Reservations recommended. Rooms $49-130. AmEx/D/MC/V. ❸

Pinegrove Campground (☎877-444-6777; www.recreation.gov), 5 mi. south of Lakeview at the other end of Upper Lake Mary. Set in a charming locale, with drinking water and flush toilets. $16 per vehicle. ❶

Ashurst/Forked Pine Campground (☎928-526-0866), on both sides of Ashurst Lake, a smaller, secluded lake on Forest Rd. 82 E. Turn left off Lake Mary Rd., across from Pinegrove Campground. Water and flush toilets on-site. The fishing is stupendous. 64 sites are available 1st come, 1st served. $14 per vehicle. ❶

🍴 FOOD

Flagstaff will make epicurean roadtrippers happy with its diverse selection of eateries. Vegetarian, organic, and just plain good food abounds in this area.

Mountain Oasis, 11 E. Aspen Ave. (☎928-214-9270; www.themenuplease.com). A genuinely up-market restaurant, but with prices that won't bankrupt you. Elegant plants, water fountains, and conscientious service make this an intimate and relaxing dining experience. Diverse menu with Middle Eastern, Mediterranean, and American options; try the sumptuous prime rib ($16), so tender you won't even need a knife. Appetizers $3-6. Entrees from $11. Open daily 11am-8:30pm. D/MC/V. ❸

Macy's European Coffee House and Bakery, 14 S. Beaver St. (☎928-774-2243), behind Du Beau Hostel. A cheery, earthy hangout serving only vegetarian food and excellent vegan selections. Specials ($7) change daily. Start the day with a bowl of granola ($4) and a cup of fresh-roasted coffee ($1.50-4). Free Wi-Fi. Open daily 6am-10pm. Kitchen open until 4pm. MC/V. ❶

Galaxy Diner, 931 W. Rte. 66 (☎928-774-2466). Cheerful Rte. 66 diner with the added bonuses of swing dancing Sa 7:30-10pm and the Rte. 66 Cruisers meeting every F night. Burgers from $6. Open daily 6am-9pm. AmEx/D/MC/V. ❶

Martanne's, 10 N. San Francisco St. (☎928-773-4701). Serves generous portions of tasty Mexican food in a cheerful, brightly painted little diner. Lunch combo plates $6-10. Open M-F 8am-1:30pm, Sa-Su 8:30am-1pm. Cash only. ❷

🅖 SIGHTS

LOWELL OBSERVATORY. In 1894, Percival Lowell chose Flagstaff as the site for an astronomical observatory. He spent the rest of his life here, devoting it to the study of heavenly bodies and culling data to support his theory that life exists on Mars. The Lowell Observatory, where Lowell discovered Pluto (which they also considered calling "Jean," "Peace," and even "Twelow"), is both a tribute to his genius and to this high-powered research center sporting five mammoth telescopes. During the day, admission includes tours of the telescope as well as entrance to a museum with hands-on astronomy exhibits. With nightfall, the unpolluted Arizona skies provide the perfect backdrop for a viewing of heavenly bod-

BURMA SHAVE

In 1927, a study emerged showing that the average person spent less than 18 seconds reading a billboard or magazine advertisement. Burma Shave decided to use this to its advantage and created a fantastic new advertising gimmick. Six red Burma Shave signs were spaced 300 ft. apart along a highway such that a car traveling 35 mph would take three seconds to travel between each post. Given this three-second approach, each advertisement experience would last 18 seconds. The number of Burma Shave ads multiplied steadily; at the height of their popularity, there were over 7000 Burma Shave ads across America. The last Burma Shave ads were placed in 1963, but many still flavor the roads today. Here are some classics:

🔽 To kiss / a mug / that's like a cactus / takes more nerve / than it does practice. / Burma Shave.

🔽 If you think / she likes your bristles / walk barefooted / through some thistles. / Burma Shave

🔽 Nobody likes / to dance or dine / accompanied by / a porcupine. / Burma Shave

🔽 The wolf is shaved / so neat and trim / Red Riding Hood / is chasing him. / Burma Shave

🔽 To steal / a kiss / he had the knack / but lacked the cheek / to get one back. / Burma Shave

ies. *(1400 W. Mars Hill Rd., 1 mi. west of downtown off Rte. 66. ☎928-233-3211; www.lowell.edu. Open daily Apr.-Oct. 9am-5pm; Nov.-Mar. noon-5pm. Guided tours every hr. 10am-4pm. Evening programs June-Aug. M-Sa 5:30-10pm; Sept.-May M, W, F-Sa 5:30-9:30pm. $6, students and seniors $5, ages 5-17 $3.)*

MUSEUM OF NORTHERN ARIZONA. The Museum of Northern Arizona details anything and everything about the land and peoples of the Colorado Plateau. The museum has a wonderful geology gallery, but most of its space is dedicated to the area's diverse cultures, traditions, and artistic works. It also hosts the annual Hopi (July 4 weekend), Navajo (first weekend in Aug.), and Hispanic (last weekend in Oct.) heritage marketplaces, celebrating each group's art and culture. *(3101 N. Fort Valley Rd., 3 mi. north of downtown Flagstaff on US 180. ☎928-774-5213; www.musnaz.org. Open daily 9am-5pm. $7, students $5, ages 7-17 $4, seniors $6.)*

SEDONA. A short drive from Flagstaff is a site that ranks as one of the physical highlights of the Southwest: the town of Sedona. Set in a beautiful location surrounded by stunning red sandstone rock formations, crumbling canyon walls, and picture-perfect blue skies, Sedona has become a popular site for a variety of visitors, from hikers to artists to New Age spiritualists. The town hosts various artistic and cultural festivals. *(29 mi. south of Flagstaff on US 89A. ☎800-288-7336; www.sedonaaz.gov.)*

🎵 ENTERTAINMENT

In the second weekend of June, the annual **Flagstaff Rodeo** comes to town with competitions, barn dances, a carnival, and a waitress race. Competitions and events go on from Friday to Sunday at the **Coconino County Fair Grounds,** on US 89A, just south of town; ask at the Flagstaff Visitors Center for details. On July 4, the town celebrates its birthday with street fairs, live music, barbecues, a parade, and, of course, fireworks. On Labor Day, the **Coconino County Fair** arrives with rides, animal competitions, and carnival games. **Theatrikos,** a local theater group, stages plays year-round at 11 W. Cherry Ave. (☎928-774-1662; www.theatrikos.com. Tickets $13-21. Box office open Tu-F noon-5pm.)

📢 NIGHTLIFE

🎵 **Museum Club,** 3404 E. Rte. 66 (☎928-526-9434). Flagstaff's premier spot for honky-tonk action. If you like dancing around in forests, then you'll love this place; there are 5 trees protruding up through the dance floor. Climb into the upper branches and perform complex maneuvers to impress the onlookers down below. Live country music F-Sa. Weekly karaoke and poker nights. Cover W and F-Sa $5. Happy hour daily 11am-7pm. Open daily 11am-2am. MC/V.

Charley's, 23 N. Leroux St. (☎928-779-1919). Plays live jazz and blues in the Weatherford Hotel, one of the classiest buildings in town. Happy hour 5-7pm. Open daily 11am-2am.

Collins Irish Pub, 2 N. Leroux St. (☎928-214-7363). Hands down the best dancing in town. The tables are swept aside F-Sa night and a DJ plays pop and R&B to a college-age crowd. Happy hour 4-7pm; $2.50 drinks. Open 11am-2am daily. AmEx/MC/V.

🏔 OUTDOORS

With the northern **San Francisco Peaks** and the surrounding **Coconino National Forest,** Flagstaff offers numerous options for the outdoorsman. Due to the 7000 ft. altitude, bring plenty of water, regardless of the season. In late spring and summer, rangers may close trails if the risk of fire gets too high. The mountains occupy national forest land, so backcountry camping is free and loosely regulated.

HIKING

In the summer, these peaks attract hikers and bikers aplenty. The **Coconino National Forest** has trails for hikers of all abilities. Consult the **Peaks Ranger Station,** 5075 N. US 89A (☎928-526-0866), for trail descriptions and possible closures. For the more energetic hiker, the **Elden Lookout Trail** is ideal for jaw-dropping, mountaintop views. The trail climbs 2400 ft. in only 3 mi.; it is demanding, but the view makes up for it. The trail begins at the Peaks Ranger station. The most popular trail in the area is the hike to **Humphrey's Peak,** Arizona's highest mountain. This 9 mi. round-trip hike begins in the first parking lot at the Snow Bowl ski area. For a longer hike, the moderate

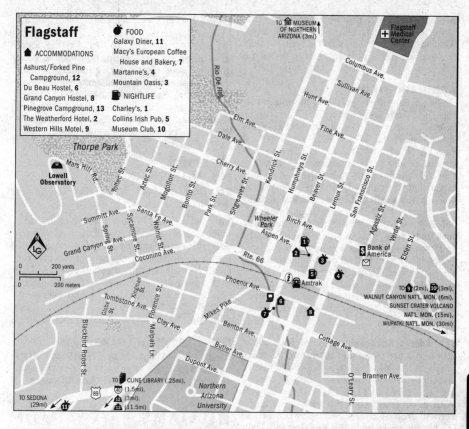

Flagstaff

🏕 ACCOMMODATIONS

Ashurst/Forked Pine
  Campground, **12**
Du Beau Hostel, **6**
Grand Canyon Hostel, **8**
Pinegrove Campground, **13**
The Weatherford Hotel, **2**
Western Hills Motel, **9**

🍎 FOOD

Galaxy Diner, **11**
Macy's European Coffee
  House and Bakery, **7**
Martanne's, **4**
Mountain Oasis, **3**

🍸 NIGHTLIFE

Charley's, **1**
Collins Irish Pub, **5**
Museum Club, **10**

to strenuous 17 mi. round-trip **Weatherford Trail** offers excellent opportunities for bird- and animal-spotting. The trailhead can be found next to **Schultz Tank,** about 7 mi. from Flagstaff. The 1000 ft. cinder cone of **Sunset Crater Volcano National Monument,** 12 mi. north of Flagstaff on US 89, is the result of nearly 200 years of periodic volcanic eruptions beginning in AD 1065. It may not be Pompeii, but it's still pretty cool. The easy **Lava Flow Nature Trail,** 1 mi. east of the visitors center, wanders 1 mi. through the rocky black terrain—tinged with yellow and red—that gave the formation its name. Hiking up **Sunset Crater** itself is not allowed, but the **Lenox Crater Trail** is a tough scramble up the loose cinders of a neighboring cone, followed by a quick slide down. The visitors center

has more information. (☎928-526-0502. Open daily May-Oct. 8am-5pm; Nov.-Apr. 9am-5pm. $5, under 16 free.) **Wupatki National Monument,** 30 mi. northeast of Flagstaff, off US 89, has gorgeous views of the Painted Desert and fascinating Pueblo sights. The Sinagua people moved here in the 11th century after a Sunset Crater eruption forced them to evacuate the land to the south, but archaeologists speculate that in less than 200 years, drought, disease, and over-farming led them to abandon these stone houses. The remnants of five pueblos form a loop off US 89. The largest and most accessible, **Wupatki,** on a 1 mi. loop trail from the visitors center, is three stories high. The spectacular **Doney Mountain Trail** rises 1 mi. from the picnic area to the summit. Get

ROUTE 66

info and trail guide brochures at the visitors center. Backcountry hiking is not permitted. (Visitors center ☎928-526-0502. Open daily in summer 8am-5pm; in winter Nov.-Apr. 9am-5pm. Monument open daily 8am-5pm.)

MOUNTAIN BIKING

Flagstaff also offers excellent mountain biking. The **Schultz Creek Trail** leads bikers into an extensive network of trails in the San Francisco Mountains. Take US 180 N. to Schultz Pass Rd. (Forest Service Rd. 420) and park in the dirt lot just as the road becomes unpaved. The trail climbs north along the bottom of a ravine and, after almost 4 mi., splits into **Sunset Trail** heading south and **Little Elden Trail** heading east. Sunset Trail climbs through the woods before cresting and descending along **Brookbank Trail** down glorious single-track dropoffs and switchbacks. This 4 mi. stretch spits out riders bearing big grins of satisfaction onto Forest Service Rd. 557. The road can either be used to ride 4 mi. back to the trailhead or to access the renowned and challenging **Rocky Ridge Trail,** which leads to the same trailhead.

SKIING

The **Arizona Snowbowl** operates four chairlifts and a tow rope and maintains 32 trails. Majestic Humphrey's Peak (12,633 ft.) is the backdrop for the Snowbowl, though the skiing takes place at 11,500 ft. on Agassiz Peak. With an average snowfall of 260 in. and a vertical drop of 2300 ft., the Snowbowl rivals the big-time resorts of the Rockies and easily outclasses its Arizona competition. Take US 180 about 7 mi. north to the Fairfield Snowbowl turnoff. (☎928-779-1951; www.arizonasnowbowl.com. Season runs from mid-Dec. to mid-Apr. Lift tickets $48, ages 8-12 and seniors $26.) Equipment rental is available on the mountain. (Ski package $25 per day; snowboards $30 per day.)

⚑ THE ROAD TO PARKS: 17 MI.

From Flagstaff, curve left on **Route 66** under the rail tracks, then swing right 1 mi. later. After 4 mi., join **I-40 West.** Follow I-40 for 5 mi., take **Exit 185** for Bellemont, and head north on the frontage road. After 2 mi., the road enters the **Kaibab National Forest** and, 1 mi. beyond that, turns to dirt; the pavement resumes 3 mi. later. Parks is 1 mi. beyond the paved road.

PARKS   ☎928

Just to the south of Rte. 66, the **Parks General Store,** 101 Parks Rd., is also the local gas station, antique shop, post office, hairdresser, massage parlor, gunsmith, chainsaw sharpening stop, real-estate office, and video-rental store. (☎928-635-1310. Open daily 6:30am-6:30pm.) Next door is the **Ponderosa Forest RV Park ❷,** which offers sites for RVs, with propane, showers, and laundry. (☎928-635-0456. Sites $37. AmEx/D/MC/V.)

◪ DETOUR
DEER FARM PETTING ZOO

6752 Deer Farm Road. At **Exit 171,** 6 mi. down the road from Parks, take a left on Deer Farm Rd.

The Deer Farm Petting Zoo gives friendly deer, donkeys, wallabies, llamas, and reindeer the opportunity to maul your pockets as you circulate among the animals and the small children feeding them. If you buy food in a cup instead of at the quarter machines, you get more food and a souvenir cup. (☎928-635-4073 or 800-926-3337. Open daily 9am-6pm. $8.50, ages 3-13 $5, seniors $7.50.)

⚑ THE ROAD TO WILLIAMS: 16 MI.

Backtrack to **I-40 West** from **Deer Farm Road** and take it to **Exit 165.** Turn left from the off-ramp into Williams, entering town on **Business I-40/Railroad Avenue.**

WILLIAMS   ☎928

The closest town to the South Rim of the Grand Canyon, Williams bills itself as the "Gateway to the Grand Canyon." This fortunate geography ensures a steady flow of tourists, and Williams offers small-town America with trees (instead of cactuses) and the leisurely pace of country living.

✈ ORIENTATION

Getting around in Williams is relatively easy, as **Route 66** runs through downtown. One block south of Rte. 66 is **Railroad Avenue,** another main drag. Streets in Williams are numbered and run north-south, while most avenues run east-west. Most of Williams's downtown is centered on Railroad Ave. and Rte. 66 between **First** and **Fourth Streets.**

Population: 3000

Tourist Office: Williams Visitors Center and Chamber of Commerce, 200 W. Railroad Ave. (☎928-635-4061). Open daily in summer 8am-6:30pm; in winter 8am-5pm.

Library and Internet Access: Williams Library, 113 S. 1st St. (☎928-635-2263). Open Tu-Th 9am-5pm and 6-8pm, F 9am-5:30pm, Sa 9am-1pm.

Post Office: 120 S. 1st St. (☎928-635-4572). Open M-F 9am-4:30pm. **Postal Code:** 86046.

ACCOMMODATIONS

Route 66 Inn, 128 E. Rte. 66 (☎928-635-4791). May not look like the most historic motel around, but it has been accommodating guests in cute pastel rooms since the 1930s. Rooms have TVs, microwaves, fridges, and elegant white wood furnishings. Singles M-Th and Su $49, F-Sa $55; doubles $60. MC/V. ❷

Williams Circle Pines KOA, 1000 E. Circle Pines Rd. (☎928-635-2626 or 800-562-9379). Has camping options with access to minigolf, game room, heated indoor pool and 2 hot tubs, nightly family movies, an outdoor cafe, and seasonal activities like horseback riding, Su evening hayrides, and Grand Canyon tours. Bike rental available. Tent sites $17-26; RV sites $29-50. 4-person cabins $40. AmEx/D/MC/V. ❶

FOOD

Twister's 50s Soda Fountain, 417 E. Rte. 66 (☎928-635-0266). A glittering chrome soda fountain and Rte. 66 gift shop with sparkling vintage cars out front. Ice cream $2-5. Burgers $7-8. Open M-Sa 8am-9pm. MC/V. ❶

Cruisers, 233 W. Rte. 66 (☎928-635-2445). A vintage signs verifies that it's one of the great Rte. 66 diners. Burgers $8-10. Pasta dishes $11-14. Open daily 11am-10pm. AmEx/D/MC/V. ❷

Pancho McGillicuddy's Mexican Cantina and Espresso Bar, 141 Railroad Ave. (☎928-635-4150). A curious Mexican-Irish blend, although the food seems to favor the south-of-the-border side of the family. The daily lunch specials ($6-7) are great deals. Come in the evening to enjoy the outside terrace and live music. Open daily 11am-10pm. AmEx/MC/V. ❷

SIGHTS

GRAND CANYON RAILROAD. The train departs from the Williams railroad depot for the Grand Canyon at 10am daily, arrives 2¼hr. later, and returns in the afternoon. (☎800-863-0546 or 928-635-4061. For reservations, call ☎800-843-8724. Tickets $65-175.) Grand Canyon National Park entrance tickets can be purchased here. For more info on the Grand Canyon, see below.

PETE'S ROUTE 66 GAS STATION MUSEUM. The museum has every kind of Rte. 66 car memorabilia crammed into a gas station. (101 E. Rte. 66. ☎928-635-2675. Open daily 9:30am-9pm.)

THE ROAD TO THE GRAND CANYON: 90 MI.

From Williams, take **I-40 East** to the junction with **I-64 North.** Turn left onto I-64 N., and follow it for 88 mi. to Grand Canyon National Park. To bypass the Grand Canyon, skip ahead to Peach Springs (p. 578).

GRAND CANYON ☎928

Skeptics often wonder if it deserves its grandiose reputation, but seeing one sunrise or sunset in the canyon is enough to make a believer out of even the most reluctant visitor. First, there's the space: 277 mi. long and over 1 mi. deep, the enormous crevasse overwhelms the human capacity for perception. Then there's the color: the shifts in hue translate to millions of years of geologic history and make the panoramic view even more awe-inspiring. Grand Canyon National Park is divided into three sections: the popular South Rim, the more serene North Rim, and the canyon gorge itself, which begins at Lake Powell, Arizona, and feeds into Lake Mead, Nevada. Between the national park area and Lake Mead are the Hualapai and Havasupai Reservations, which offer separate entrances into the canyon. Traveling between rims takes approximately 5hr. via the long drive to the Lee's Ferry bridge or even longer via a grueling 13 mi. hike.

VITAL STATS

Area: 1,200,000 acres

South Rim Tourist Office: Canyon View Information Plaza (☎928-638-7888; www.grandcanyon.com or www.nps.gov/grca), across from Mather Point by the park entrance. To get there, park at Mather Point, then walk 1 mi. to the info plaza.

North Rim Tourist Office: North Rim Visitors Center (☎928-638-7864), on Rte. 67 just before the lodge. Open May-Oct. daily 8am-6pm. **Kaibab Plateau Visitors Center** (☎928-643-7298), at Jacob Lake, next to the inn. Issues backcountry permits and has displays on the canyon and its ecosystem. Open daily 8am-5pm, but hours may vary.

Gateway Towns: Williams (p. 570), Flagstaff (p. 565), Kanab, UT.

Fees: 7-day pass $25 per car; $12 for travelers using other modes of transportation.

SOUTH RIM   ☎928

In the summer, everything on two legs or four wheels comes to this side of the Grand Canyon, primarily for the fantastic and easily accessible views from the rim. If you plan to visit at this time, be sure to make reservations for everything far in advance and prepare to battle crowds. A friendly park service staff, well-run facilities, and beautiful scenery generally make for enjoyable visits despite the high volume of people. Fewer tourists brave the canyon in the winter, so most hotels and facilities close during the low season.

ORIENTATION

Posted maps and signs in the park make navigation easy. Lodges and services concentrate in **Grand Canyon Village**, at the west end of **Park Entrance Road**. To the east lie the visitors center, campground, and general store, while most of the lodges and the **Bright Angel Trail** are in the west section. The **South Kaibab Trail** is off **Desert View Drive** east of the village. Free shuttle buses to eight rim overlooks run along **Hermit Road** (closed to private vehicles Feb.-Dec.) in the west. Avoid walking on the drive; the rim trails are safer and more scenic.

ACCOMMODATIONS

Indoor lodging within the park requires months of advance planning, but a few options exist just outside the park and even more within an hour's drive in neighboring Williams and Flagstaff. Summer rooms in the park should be reserved 11 months in advance (☎888-297-2757; www.xanterra.com). That said, there are frequent cancellations; if you arrive unprepared, check for vacancies or call the hotel switchboard (☎928-638-2631) and ask to be connected with the proper lodge.

Bright Angel Lodge (☎928-638-2631), in Grand Canyon Village. Sits in a historic building right on the rim. Close to Bright Angel Trail and shuttle buses. Singles and doubles with shared bath $56, with private bath $68; 1- to 2-person cabins $89. AmEx/D/MC/V. ❸

Maswik Lodge (☎928-638-2631), at the west end of Grand Canyon Village. Small, clean cabins with showers. Rooms with 2 queen-size beds also available. Rooms $86-162. AmEx/D/MC/V. ❹

Phantom Ranch (☎928-638-2631), on the canyon floor, a day's hike down the South Kaibab Trail or Bright Angel Trail. Reservations are necessary and can be made up to 13 months in advance. If you want to sleep on the canyon floor but have no reservation, go to the Bright Angel transportation desk at 6am on the day prior to your planned stay and try the waiting list. Single-sex dorms $36; 1- or 2-person cabins $97. AmEx/D/MC/V. ❷

Grand Canyon Inn (☎928-635-9203 or 800-635-9203; www.grand-canyon-inn.com), in Valle, at Hwy. 180, 25min. from the park entrance. Clean, spacious rooms and a pool. Reservations recommended in summer. Singles from $49; doubles from $99. AmEx/D/MC/V. ❸

CAMPING

Lodgings in the park are usually filled before you've even decided to visit the Grand Canyon, so camping is a good second option. Some reservations can be made through **SPHERICS** (☎800-365-2267). If you do run out of options, you can camp for free in the **Kaibab National Forest,** along the south border of the park, though no camping is allowed within a quarter-mile of US 64. Dispersed camping sits conveniently along the oft-traveled **North Long**

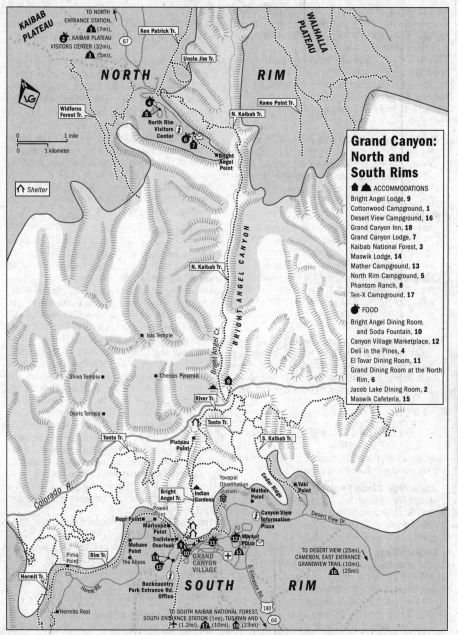

Grand Canyon: North and South Rims

🏠 🏕 ACCOMMODATIONS

Bright Angel Lodge, **9**
Cottonwood Campground, **1**
Desert View Campground, **16**
Grand Canyon Inn, **18**
Grand Canyon Lodge, **7**
Kaibab National Forest, **3**
Maswik Lodge, **14**
Mather Campground, **13**
North Rim Campground, **5**
Phantom Ranch, **8**
Ten-X Campground, **17**

🍎 FOOD

Bright Angel Dining Room
  and Soda Fountain, **10**
Canyon Village Marketplace, **12**
Deli in the Pines, **4**
El Tovar Dining Room, **11**
Grand Dining Room at the North
  Rim, **6**
Jacob Lake Dining Room, **2**
Maswik Cafeteria, **15**

ROUTE 66

Jim Loop Road—turn right about a mile south of the south entrance station. For quieter, more remote sites, follow signs for the **Arizona Trail** into the national forest between miles 252 and 253 on US 64. Fires are heavily restricted or even banned in some areas; make sure you know the rules. For more info, contact the **Tusayan Ranger Station,** Kaibab National Forest, P.O. Box 3088, Tusayan 86023 (☎928-638-2443).

Ten-X Campground (☎928-638-2443), in Kaibab National Forest, 10 mi. south of Grand Canyon Village, off Rte. 64. Away from the highway, Ten-X offers quality sites surrounded by pine trees. Toilets and water. 1st come, 1st served. Sites Mar.-Oct. $18; Nov.-Feb. $15. ●

Mather Campground (☎800-365-2267; http://reservations.nps.gov), in Grand Canyon Village, ½ mi. south of the Canyon Village Marketplace; follow signs from Yavapai Lodge. 327 shady, relatively isolated sites. Those on foot or bike can snag a spot in a communal hiker/biker site; they are usually available on a walk-up basis. 7-night max. stay. For Mar.-Oct. reserve up to 5 months in advance; Nov.-Feb. first come, first served. Nov.-Feb. sites $15, Mar.-Oct. $18. ●

Desert View Campground (☎928-638-7888), 25 mi. east of Grand Canyon Village. Far from the South Rim, but perfect for avoiding crowds. Sites with toilets. No hookups, campfires, or reservations. Open from mid-May to Oct. Sites $12. ●

FOOD

Fast food has yet to develop in the South Rim (the closest McDonald's is 7 mi. south in Tusayan), but, fortunately, you can find better-quality meals at fast-food prices.

Bright Angel Dining Room (☎928-638-2631), in Bright Angel Lodge. Serves breakfast, sandwiches, and Southwestern-style entrees. Breakfast $6-11. Hot sandwiches $8-11. Dinner $10-15. Open daily 6am-10pm. AmEx/D/MC/V. ●

Canyon Village Marketplace (☎928-638-2262), at Market Plaza, 1 mi. west of Mather Point on the main road. Has a deli counter with the cheapest eats in the park, groceries, camping supplies, and enough Grand Canyon apparel to clothe your extended family. Sandwiches $6.50. Open daily 7am-9pm. AmEx/D/MC/V. ●

Maswik Cafeteria (☎928-638-2631), in Maswik Lodge. Serves soups, salads, and Mexican dishes. Sandwiches $6-7. Hot entrees $7-10. Open daily 6am-10pm. AmEx/D/MC/V. ●

Soda Fountain (☎928-635-0266), just outside the dining room of the Bright Angel Lodge. 13 flavors of ice cream ($3) and snack-bar sandwiches ($5). Open daily 10am-8pm. AmEx/D/MC/V. ●

El Tovar Dining Room (☎928-638-2631, ext. 6432), in the El Tovar Hotel in the Grand Canyon Village. The classiest dining in the park. The grandly appointed dining room has a great view of the canyon and food that lives up to its surroundings. Lunch entrees $12-20. Dinner entrees $22-35. Open daily 6:30-10:45am, 11:15am-2pm, 4:30-10pm. Reservations recommended. AmEx/D/MC/V. ●

HIKING

Hikes in and around the Grand Canyon can be broken down into day hikes and overnight hikes. Confusing an overnight hike for a day-hike can be a dangerous mistake, so heed the warnings of rangers and don't attempt to get to the Colorado River and back in one day. All overnight trips require permits obtained from the **Backcountry Office,** located on the west side of Parking Lot E near Maswik Lodge (permit $10; camping fee $5). Permits often take up to four months to obtain, so request one as early as possible via the Internet (www.nps.gov/grca), via mail (P.O. Box 129, Grand Canyon, AZ 86023), or in person. For day hikes into the canyon, be prepared to retrace every footstep uphill on the way back. An enjoyable hike usually means beginning before 7am or after 4pm; it's best to consult a ranger at the **Canyon View Information Plaza** before leaving. National Park Service rangers also lead a variety of guided hikes; times and details are listed in *The Guide.*

The **Rim, Bright Angel, South Kaibab,** and **River Trails** are the only South Rim trails regularly maintained and patrolled by the National Park Service. While other trails do exist, they are only for experienced hikers and may contain steep chutes and technically challenging terrain. Consult a ranger before heading out.

Rim Trail (9 mi., 4-6hr. one-way). With only a slight elevation change (about 200 ft.) and the security of the nearby shuttle, the Rim Trail is an excellent way to see the canyon from several angles. The trail is wheelchair-accessible to Maricopa Point in the west and has 8 viewpoints along Hermit Rd. and 3 east of it. Convenient access to viewpoints makes this trail the most crowded, but toward the eastern and western ends hikers have a bit more room. Hopi Point's panoramic canyon views make it a great place to watch the sunset; *The Guide* lists sunrise and sunset times.

South Kaibab Trail (7 mi. to Phantom Ranch, 4-5hr. one-way). For those seeking a more challenging descent. Beginning at Yaki Point (7260 ft.), Kaibab is steep and tricky and lacks shade or water, but it rewards intrepid hikers with a better view of the canyon. The South Kaibab avoids the obstructed views and safety of a side-canyon route as it winds directly down the ridge, offering a panoramic look across the canyon. Day hikes to **Cedar Ridge** (3 mi. round-trip) and **Skeleton Point** (6 mi. round-trip) are reasonable only for experienced hikers due to the trail's steep grade. Kaibab meets up with Bright Angel at the Colorado River. Fewer switchbacks and a rapid descent make the South Kaibab Trail 1 mi. shorter than the Bright Angel to this point—guests staying at the Phantom Ranch or Bright Angel Campground can access them via either trail.

OTHER OUTDOORS

There are several more ways to explore the canyon. **Mule trips** from the South Rim are an option, but they're expensive and are often booked up to one year in advance. (☎303-297-2757; www.xanterra.com. Daytrip to **Plateau Point** 6 mi. down **Bright Angel Trail** $154, lunch included; overnight including lodging at Phantom Ranch and all meals $420.) The view of the Grand Canyon from a whitewater raft is another popular option but usually costs $1500-3500, depending on trip length. Trips into the Grand Canyon vary from seven to 18 days and generally require one-year advanced booking. The *Trip Planner* (available by request at the info center or online) lists several guides licensed to offer trips in the canyon. Most guides run out of Flagstaff or Page, Arizona. If the views from the rim fail to astound you, try the higher vantages provided by one of the park's many **flightseeing** companies, located at the Grand Canyon

Airport. **Grand Canyon Airlines** flies 45min. tours every hour in the summer. (☎866-235-9422; www.grandcanyonairlines.com. Reservations recommended. $99, children $79.)

> **!** **CAUTION.** Seeing the canyon from the inside is harder than it looks. Even the young of body and heart should recall that there are no easy trails, and what starts as a downhill stroll can become a nightmarish 50° incline on the way back. Also, note that the lower you go, the hotter it gets; when it's 85°F on the rim, it's around 100°F at Indian Gardens and around 110°F at Phantom Ranch. Heat stroke, the greatest threat to a hiker, is marked by a monstrous headache and dry, red skin. For a day hike, take at least a gallon of water per person; drink at least a quart per hour hiking uphill under the hot sun. Footwear with excellent tread is also necessary; the trails are steep, and every year careless hikers take what locals morbidly call "the 12-second tour." Parents should think twice about bringing children more than 1 mi. down any trail.

NORTH RIM   ☎928

If you're looking to avoid the South Rim's crowds, the park's North Rim is rugged and serene, with a view almost as spectacular as that from the South Rim. Unfortunately, it's hard to reach by public transit and is a long drive by car. From October 15 to November 30, the North Rim is open for day use only, and from December 1 to May 15 it closes entirely. In summer, sunsets from the Grand Canyon Lodge are spectacular and worth the trip.

ORIENTATION

To reach the North Rim from the South Rim, take **Route 64 East** to **US 89 North,** which runs into **Alternate 89;** from Alt. 89, follow **Route 67 South** to the edge but don't go over it. The drive is over 220 mi. long. Snow closes Rte. 67 from early December to mid-May, and park facilities (including the lodge) close from mid-October to mid-May. The visitor parking lot, 12 mi. south of the park entrance, is near the end of Rte. 67, close to both the visitors center and **North Rim Lodge.** Parking is also available at the **North Kaibab** and **Widforss** trails and at scenic points along the road to **Cape Royal.**

ACCOMMODATIONS

Staying inside on the North Rim is pricey and requires advance planning, but there are still many lodging options. If you can't find lodging within the park, many less-expensive accommodations can be found 80 mi. north in Kanab, Utah.

Grand Canyon Lodge (☎928-638-2611, reservations 888-297-2757), on the edge of the rim. This swank but rustic lodge is the only indoor lodging in the park. The overlook near the reception area is open to all and is a great place to relax on comfortable leather sofas. Reception 24hr. Reserve as early as 6 months in advance, or 2 years in advance for the 4 rim-view cabins. Open from mid-May to mid-Oct. Motel rooms $115; cabins $119-165. AmEx/D/MC/V. ❺

Kaibab National Forest (☎928-635-8200). Runs from north of Jacob Lake to the park entrance. You can camp for free, as long as you're ¼ mi. from the road, water, or official campgrounds and 1 mi. from any commercial facility. No fires. ❶

Cottonwood Campground, 7 mi. down the North Kaibab Trailhead. A good resting place for those doing an overnight hike into the canyon. Drinking water available May-Oct. Requires $5 camping permit from the Backcountry Office (p. 574). ❶

FOOD

Grand Dining Room at the North Rim (☎928-638-2612, ext. 160). On the edge of the canyon, the North Rim Lodge's dining room treats guests to sweeping views. The breakfast buffet ($10) and lunch buffet ($12) are generic but affordable. Dinners (entrees $10-20) do justice to the grand atmosphere. Open daily 6:30-10am, 11:30am-2:30pm, 4:45-9:45pm. Reservations required for dinner. AmEx/D/MC/V. ❸

Deli in the Pines (☎928-638-2611), at the North Rim Lodge. Specializes in no-frills dining on the go. Salads, sandwiches, and burgers $4-7. Open daily 7am-9pm. AmEx/D/MC/V. ❶

Jacob Lake Dining Room (☎928-643-7232; www.jacoblake.com), 30 mi. north of the park entrance. A good alternative to North Rim establishments. The old-fashioned diner counter, full restaurant, and tempting bakery offer a variety of options. Breakfast $5-10. Dinner $12-20. Open daily 6:30am-8pm. AmEx/D/MC/V. ❸

OUTDOORS

Hiking in the leafy **North Rim** seems like a trip to the mountains—the mountain just happens to be upside down. While the temptation to plunge down into the canyon is strong, it would be an extraordinarily bad idea. The North Rim is at a surprisingly high elevation, so the air is very thin, and there are no easy trails down into the canyon. You should never attempt to hike to the river and back in a single day. Info on trails can be found in the North Rim's version of *The Guide.*

Day hikes of various lengths beckon the active North Rim visitor. The **Bright Angel Point Trail** (½ mi., 30min. round-trip) departs from the lodge area, and the **Cape Royal Trail** (1 mi., 30min. round-trip) departs from the Cape Royal parking area. Both offer impressive views of the canyon and demand little physical effort. The **Widforss Trail** (10 mi., 6hr. round-trip) is a more challenging day hike but offers views of both canyon and forest and can be tailored into a shorter hike. The **North Kaibab Trail** (28 mi. round-trip) is the only maintained trail into the canyon on the North Rim and is for only the most experienced hikers. Consult rangers before beginning this hike. Pick up the invaluable *Official Guide to Hiking the Grand Canyon* ($12), available at any of the visitors centers and gift shops. Overnight hikers must get permits from the **Backcountry Office** in the ranger station, just north of the campground entrance, 11 mi. from the park entrance. ($10 permit plus $5 per person per night. Open daily 8am-noon and 1-5pm.) Park rangers run nature walks, lectures, and evening programs at the **North Rim Campground and Lodge.** The info desk or campground bulletin boards have schedules. Mule trips through **Canyon Trail Rides** circle the rim or descend into the canyon. (☎435-679-8665. 1hr. $30, ½ day $65, full day $125. Reservations recommended. Open May-Oct. daily 7:30am-5pm.)

THE ROAD TO ASH FORK: 76 MI.
Take I-40 West to Exit 146. Make a right for Ash Fork.

ASH FORK ☎928

Those in need of beautification need look no farther than the 1960 DeSoto (with Elvis inside) parked on the roof of the **DeSoto Salon,** 314 W. Lewis Ave. You'll look as glamorous as the giant rooftop hood ornament. (☎928-637-9886. Open W-Sa 9am-5pm.)

THE ROAD TO SELIGMAN: 21 MI.
In Ash Fork, you'll see a sign for Old Route 66. This doesn't actually lead anywhere. Instead, rejoin I-40 West for 4 mi. to Exit 139. Take a right on Crookton Road. Continue for 17 mi. to the Rte. 66 celebration that is Seligman and turn left at the T intersection.

SELIGMAN ☎928

The Rte. 66 enthusiasm in Seligman is hard to miss. The town was founded at the junction of the main line of the Santa Fe Railroad, and, when Rte. 66 was routed along the main street of the town, tourist accommodations flourished. When I-40 cut the town off the main road, local residents were quick to react; Seligman was where the Arizona Route 66 Association—the nation's first—was founded to bring fame back to the road as a destination rather than a thoroughfare. Rte. 66 through Seligman is crowded with outrageous kitsch, including Marilyn Monroe and James Dean cutouts leaning on antique cars lining the street. A semi-functioning barber shop, **Delgadillo's Route 66 Gift Shop, Museum, and Visitors Center,** 217 E. Rte. 66, is also lined with memorabilia from appreciative travelers world wide; add your business card to the wall. You can even get a trim ($15) from the iconic Angel Delgadillo if he has time. (☎928-422-3352; www.route66giftshop.com. Open daily 8am-6pm.) The **Rusty Bolt Gift Shop,** 115 E. Rte. 66, is hard to miss, with dressed-up mannequins perched on the second-floor balcony and Eagles cover tunes perpetually blasting in the otherwise quiet street. (☎928-422-0106. Open daily in summer 8am-6pm; in winter 9am-5pm.)

The **Supai Motel** ❷, 134 W. Chino St., has one of the best signs you'll see anywhere along the route, recently restored for $14,000. The rooms aren't bad either, with fridges, microwaves, TVs (170 channels), and Wi-Fi. (☎928-422-4153. Singles $45; doubles $53. AmEx/D/MC/V.) Juan Delgadillo's (brother to Angel) **Snow Cap Ice Cream Shop** ❶, 301 E. Chino St., is decorated year-round in holiday decorations and prides itself on serving "Dead Chicken" and great shakes ($3.50). Juan's sons Bob and John are a couple of world-class pranksters who are sure to entertain while they take your order. (Open daily 9am-6pm. Cash only.) The cuisine at the **Road Kill Cafe** ❸, 502 W. Rte. 66, may not be exactly true to the name, but the decor certainly seems to be. Enjoy a foot-high pile of onion rings ($8) or the meat of your choice ($11-20) in the company of an entire herd of dead animals. Try the "chicken that almost crossed the road" for $13. (☎928-422-3554. Open daily 10am-10pm. Kitchen open until 9pm. AmEx/D/MC/V.)

THE ROAD TO GRAND CANYON CAVERNS: 24 MI.
Head west on Route 66 out of Seligman to reach the Grand Canyon Caverns.

GRAND CANYON CAVERNS ☎928

A giant green plastic dinosaur guards the entrance to Grand Canyon Caverns, the largest registered dry cavern in the US. Tours of the enormous rooms, 210 ft. underground, are led by guides eager to point out the unique features of this one-time fallout shelter, including a mummified bobcat, a recreation of a giant 15 ft. tall sloth, and enough toilet paper for three weeks of nuclear fallout. (☎928-422-3223 or 713-2671; www.gccaverns.com. 45min. tours daily every 30min. $15, ages 5-12 $10. 25min. tours $12/8. Explorer's tour $50; reservations and deposit required.) The pink, 70s-inspired rooms at **Grand Canyon Caverns Inn** ❹, at the caverns' entrance, is the only option for miles in either direction. The motel also has bike rentals, a convenience store, and horseback riding. (☎928-422-3223. Bikes $5 per hr. Horseback riding $17 per 20min. Rooms Mar.-Oct. from $85; Nov.-Feb. from $75. AmEx/D/MC/V.) The **Grand Canyon Cavern**

ROUTE 66

Restaurant ❶, also conveniently located at the entrance to the caverns, serves diner cuisine cafeteria-style. (Open M-Th and Su 7am-7pm, F-Sa 7am-10pm. AmEx/D/MC/V.)

◩ DETOUR
HAVASUPAI RESERVATION

Follow signs for Supai and the Havasupai Reservation, 3 mi. from the Caverns on **Route 18.** Follow the road north approximately 60 mi., ending in a series of narrow turns down to the canyon rim and the trailhead down to the village of Supai and the Supai waterfalls.

The "people of the blue-green water," the Havasupai live in a protected enclave at the base of the canyon, bordered by Grand Canyon National Park. Ringed by dramatic sandstone faces, their village, Supai, rests on the shores of the Havasu River and is only accessible from a 10 mi. trail starting at the **Hualapai Hilltop.** Two miles down the path from the village are three crystal-clear waterfalls.

The village has a post office, general store, and cafe (☎928-448-2591). Prices are high because everything must be brought in by mule or helicopter; bringing your own food is advised. Reservations for the campground, lodge, and mules can be made by calling the **Havasupai Tourist Enterprise.** (☎928-448-2121. Mules leave from the Hualapai Hilltop daily 10am. One-way $75.)

Camping permits are required for overnight hiking, so reservations should be made far in advance. The Havasupai tribe operates the **Havasupai Campground ❶** and the **Havasupai Lodge,** both on the canyon floor. The campground, 2 mi. past Supai, lies between Havasu and Mooney Falls, bordering the Havasu River's blue-green water and swimmer-friendly lagoons. There are no showers or flush toilets. (☎928-448-2121; www.kaibab.org/supai. Register in the Supai tourist office. Entrance fee $35. Sites $17.) The trail from Supai to the campground extends to **Mooney Falls** (1 mi. from campground), **Beaver Falls** (3 mi.), and the **Colorado River** (8 mi.). The hike down to Mooney Falls is steep, so exercise caution— shoes with good tread are a must. Swimming and frolicking are both permitted and encouraged in the lagoons at the bottom of the falls.

◪ THE ROAD TO PEACH SPRINGS: 6 MI.
From Grand Canyon Caverns, continue west along **Route 66** to reach Peach Springs.

PEACH SPRINGS ☎928
The headquarters of the Hualapai Tribe and once the western terminus of the Santa Fe Railroad, Peach Springs is where you will find **River Runners,** a rafting outfitter offering day-trips on the Colorado River. (☎888-255-9550 or 928-769-2230. Trips Mar.-Oct. $351 per person; includes round-trip transport, food, helicopter uplift, and life jackets.) Peach Springs prides itself on having the only access road into the bottom of the Grand Canyon.

The adjoining **Hualapai Lodge ❹**, 900 Rte. 66, has comfortable, upscale rooms. (☎888-255-9550. Rooms $89-119. AmEx/D/MC/V.) The **Diamond Creek Restaurant ❸**, 900 Rte. 66, serves favorites like catfish baskets ($11) and Hualapai stew for $9. (☎928-769-2800. Open daily 6:30am-9pm. AmEx/D/MC/V.)

◪ THE ROAD TO TRUXTON: 8 MI.
Take **Route 66** west out of Peach Springs.

TRUXTON ☎928
In its heyday, Rte. 66 kept Truxton busy 24hr. a day and supported many businesses. Today, all that is a distant memory. All that remains are ruined gas stations and abandoned truck yards; Truxton is a place for those who really like to feel Rte. 66 history. Cars race through at 70 mph because technically Truxton isn't a town (it doesn't have a post office), but you'd do well to slow down and stop to take it in.

The **Frontier Motel ❸** has a vintage blue sign and old wood ceilings. The rooms don't have plush modern furnishings, but they more than make up for it in historical appeal. All rooms come with TVs and air-conditioning, and a couple have a fridges and microwaves. (☎928-769-2238. Singles $55; doubles $65. AmEx/D/MC/V.) There's also a shop with a small assortment of curios. The **Frontier Café ❸**, next door, has a great roadside diner vibe and is open for breakfast, lunch, and dinner. Try the tender baby-back ribs ($15) with a $3 root beer float. (☎928-769-2237. Dinner entrees $11-18. Open M-Sa 7am-9pm. AmEx/D/MC/V.)

THE ROAD TO HACKBERRY: 15 MI.

Take **Route 66** out of Truxton. The road is expansive.

HACKBERRY ☎928

The **Hackberry Visitor Center & General Store** is a must-see Rte. 66 roadside store. Once you get past the vintage cars outside, you'll find a recreated 50s diner, 1955 Marilyn Monroe calendars ($25), glass-bottled Cokes ($1.25), and other Rte. 66 memorabilia and souvenirs. (☎928-769-2605. Open daily in summer 9am-6pm; in winter 10am-5pm. MC/V.)

THE ROAD TO KINGMAN: 23 MI.

From Hackberry, continue on **Route 66.** The road winds though a magnificent landscape of dry, desolate mountains, and running alongside are freight trains that snake their way across the continent. Enter Kingman on **Andy Devine Avenue.**

KINGMAN ☎928

Kingman has always prided itself on being a transportation town; the railroad and Rte. 66 brought in voyagers aplenty, including Clark Gable and Carole Lombard, who were married in the Old Courthouse. The town is as Rte. 66 crazy as any and hosts the Rte. 66 Fun Run the first weekend in May.

VITAL STATS
Population: 20,000
Tourist Office: Powerhouse Visitors Center, 120 W. Rte. 66 (☎866-427-7866; www.kingmanchamber. org). Open daily 8am-5pm.
Library and Internet Access: Kingman Public Library, 3269 N. Burbank St. (☎928-692-2665). Open M and W 9am-6pm, Tu and Th 9am-8pm, F-Sa 9am-5pm.
Post Office: 1901 Johnson Ave. (☎928-753-2480). Open M-F 8:30am-5:30pm, Sa 9am-noon. **Postal Code:** 86401.

ORIENTATION

Most avenues in Kingman run east-west, while streets are numbered and run north-south, though just north of the downtown area some streets also run east-west. **Route 66** enters Kingman from the northeast and is known in town as **Andy Devine Avenue;** many of the city's sights and establishments lie along this road. Downtown centers on the area near **Fourth Street, Beale Street,** and Andy Devine Ave.

ACCOMMODATIONS

Hotel Brunswick, 315 E. Andy Devine Ave. (☎928-718-1800). Offers a variety of rooms, ranging from austere "cowboy rooms" with shared bathrooms to expansive suites. Breakfast included. Singles from $36. AmEx/D/MC/V. ❷

Hilltop Motel, 1901 E. Andy Devine Ave. (☎928-753-2198; www.hilltopmotelaz.com). Has an outstanding sign. Offers great views of the desert and mountains amid well-kept cactus gardens. Rooms have fridges, microwaves, and pool access. Wi-Fi. Reservations recommended. Singles $42; doubles $46. AmEx/D/MC/V. ❷

FOOD

Mr. D'z Route 66 Diner, 105 E. Andy Devine Ave. (☎928-718-0066), at 1st St. A pink, blue, and chrome tribute to the kitschy Rte. 66 diner. Serves breakfast, lunch, and dinner with the hoot of a train whistle. Try the classic cheeseburger ($6) with root-beer float ($2.75) or something less conventional, such as the seafood chimichanga ($11). Open daily 7am-9pm. AmEx/MC/V. ❶

El Palacio, 401 Andy Devine Ave. (☎928-718-0018). The local Mexican cantina of choice, with a comprehensive and exclusively Mexican menu. Salads $6-8. Entrees $9-12. Open daily 11am-9pm. AmEx/D/MC/V. ❷

Kingman Deli, 419 E. Beale St. (☎928-753-4151). Take 4th St. Any sandwich you can dream up and coffee to match. Sandwiches $4-6. Open M-F 9am-3pm, Sa 10am-2pm. AmEx/MC/V. ❶

SIGHTS

POWERHOUSE VISITORS CENTER. The center is a converted 1907 power station that hosts a decent Rte. 66 gift shop. The top floor houses an extensive, lovingly curated Rte. 66 transportation museum featuring exhibits on Burma Shave, *The Grapes of Wrath,* and Seligman's role in the development of Historic Rte. 66. Road buffs can while away the hours in the Rte. 66 Arizona Reading Room

ROUTE 66

upstairs. *(120 W. Rte. 66.* ☎*866-427-7866. Open daily 9am-4:30pm. Museum $4.)*

MOHAVE MUSEUM OF HISTORY AND ARTS. Exhibits focus on the area, Native American arts and culture, and the life and career of actor Andy Devine, a native of Kingman. An outdoor display highlights a 19th-century Santa Fe caboose as well as wagons, mining equipment, and farm machinery. *(400 W. Beale St.* ☎*928-753-3195; www.mohavemuseum.org. Open M-F 9am-5pm, Sa 1-5pm. $4, under 13 free.)*

⚑ THE ROAD TO HOOVER DAM: 71 MI.

Take **Andy Devine Avenue** through town until it becomes **Beale Avenue,** which becomes **US 93 North** at the edge of town. To bypass the Hoover Dam, Lake Mead, and the glitz and grime of Las Vegas, skip ahead to Oatman (p. 587).

HOOVER DAM ☎702

Built to subdue the flood-prone Colorado River and give vital water and energy to the Southwest, this ivory monolith took 5000 men five years to construct. By the time the dam was finished in 1935, 96 men had died. Their labor rendered a 726 ft. colossus that pumps more than four billion kilowatt-hours of power to Las Vegas and L.A. A lasting tribute to America's "think big" era, the dam is a spectacular feat of engineering, weighing 6,600,000 tons and measuring 660 ft. thick at its base and 1244 ft. across the canyon at its crest. Tours and an interpretive center explore the dam's history and future. (☎702-494-2517. Open daily 9am-5pm. Last tour 4:15pm. Self-guided tours $11, students and ages 4-16 $9.)

⚑ THE ROAD TO LAKE MEAD: 5 MI.

Continue on **US 93 North** to reach Lake Mead.

> ⏱ **TIME CHANGE.** If you're traveling between November and March, set your clock back 1hr. as you enter Nevada. If you're traveling between April and October and already set your clock when you entered Arizona, don't touch that dial.

LAKE MEAD ☎702

The largest reservoir in the US, Lake Mead was created when Hoover Dam was constructed

across the Colorado River in the 1930s. First-time visitors will benefit from a trip to the **Alan Bible Visitors Center,** 4 mi. east of Boulder City on Rte. 93, where the helpful staff has brochures and maps. (☎702-293-8990; www.nps.gov/lame. Open daily 8:30am-4:30pm. Entrance fee $3 per pedestrian, $5 per vehicle.) Falling water levels have left **Lake Mead** roughly half its usual depth, forcing boat ramps to close and exposing previously submerged hazards. Despite these conditions, Lake Mead is still a haven of water recreation. Park service-approved outfitters rent boats and more on the shores; www.funonthelake.com has more info. Popular **Boulder Beach,** the departure point for many water-based activities, is accessible from Lakeshore Dr., at the south end of the lake.

⚑ THE ROAD TO LAS VEGAS: 30 MI.

Head north on **Route 93.** Take **Exit 61** to **I-215 West.**

LAS VEGAS ☎702

Rising out of the Nevada desert, Las Vegas is a shimmering tribute to excess. Gambling, whoring, and mob muscle built this city and continue to add to its mystique. Those who embrace it find a mirage made real, an oasis of vice and greed, and one hell of a good time. Those not immediately enthralled by its frenetic pace may still find sleeping (and decision-making) nearly impossible, with sparkling casinos, cheap gourmet food, free drinks, and spectacular attractions at every turn. Nowhere else do so many shed inhibitions and indulge with such abandon. A word of caution: know thy tax bracket; walk in knowing what you want to spend and get out when you've spent it. In Las Vegas, there's a busted wallet and a broken heart for every garish neon light.

✸ ORIENTATION

Las Vegas has two major casino areas. The downtown area, around Second and **Fremont Steet,** has been converted into a pedestrian promenade; here, casinos cluster together beneath a shimmering space-frame structure covering over five city blocks. The other main area is the **Strip,** a collection of mammoth hotel-casinos along **Las Vegas Boulevard.** Parallel to the east side of the Strip and in its shadow is **Paradise Road,** also lined with casinos. Some areas of Las Vegas are unsafe, so remain on well-lit pathways and don't wander too far from major casinos and hotels. Valet parking your car at a major casino and sticking to Fremont St. are safe bets. The neighborhoods just north of Stewart St. and west of Main St. in the downtown vicinity are especially dangerous.

VITAL STATS

Population: 1,300,000

Tourist Office: Las Vegas Convention and Visitors Authority, 3150 Paradise Rd. (☎702-892-0711 or 877-847-4858; www.visitlasvegas.com), at the corner of Paradise Rd. and Convention Center Dr., 4 blocks from the Strip in the big pink convention center by the Hilton. Open daily 8am-5pm.

Library and Internet Access: Clark County Library, 1401 E. Flamingo Rd. (☎702-507-3400). Open M-Th 9am-9pm, F-Su 10am-6pm.

Post Office: 4975 Swenson St. (☎702-736-7649), near the Strip. Open M-F 8:30am-5pm. **Postal Code:** 89119.

ACCOMMODATIONS

Room rates in Las Vegas fluctuate greatly, and a room that normally costs $30 can cost hundreds during a convention weekend; www.vegas.com and casino websites often list some of the best rates. Free publications like *What's On In Las Vegas, Today in Las Vegas, 24/7,* and *Vegas Visitor* list discounts, coupons, general info, and schedules of events. Booking through a travel company online can also yield slightly cheaper quotes, and you should book two to three months in advance if a casino hotel is your plan. Hotels along the Strip are the center of the action and within walking distance of each other, but they sell out quickly and are much more expensive than comparable off-Strip hotels. A number of motels concentrate around Sahara Rd. and S. Las Vegas Blvd. Budget motels also stretch

along the southern end of the Strip across from Mandalay Bay. The 9% hotel tax (11% for downtown Fremont St.) is not included in the prices listed below.

CURFEW. Despite, or perhaps as a result of, its reputation for debauchery, Las Vegas has a curfew. Those under 18 are not allowed in public places at night (M-Th and Su 10pm-5am, F-Sa midnight-5am) unless accompanied by an adult. Laws are harsher on the Strip, where no one under 18 is allowed unaccompanied 9pm-5am—ever.

The Imperial Palace, 3535 Las Vegas Blvd. (☎800-634-6441; www.imperialpalace.com). Has some of the best value rooms in town, right at the heart of the Strip and within walking distance of many of the prime attractions. Free shuttles to other Harrah's casinos (such as Bally's and The Rio) and the added bonus of "dealertainers" (celebrity look-alike dealers). Rooms start at $60. AmEx/D/MC/V. ❸

Excalibur, 3850 S. Las Vegas Blvd. (☎702-597-7777; www.excalibur.com), at Tropicana Ave. The best value of all the major resort casinos. This King Arthur-themed castle features a moat and drawbridge, 2 pools, a modern spa and fitness center, a large casino and poker room, and a monorail station to Luxor and Mandalay Bay. Rooms M-Th and Su $51-80, F-Sa $79-129. AmEx/D/MC/V. ❸

USA Hostels Las Vegas, 1322 Fremont St. (☎702-385-1150 or 800-550-8958; www.usahostels.com). Though it's far from the Strip's action, this hostel's staff keeps guests entertained. Nightly organized events like champagne limo tours of the Strip ($27). Passport, proof of international travel, or out-of-state college ID required. Nice pool and hot tub in the courtyard. Breakfast included. Laundry, free Wi-Fi. Key deposit $10. 8-bed dorms $22; 6-bed $24; 4-bed $26. Private rooms from $60. MC/V. ❶

Sin City Hostel, 1208 S. Las Vegas Blvd. (☎702-868-0222; www.sincityhostel.com). North of the heart of the Strip but south of Fremont St., this new hostel balances the excitement of the city with a restful atmosphere, allowing the young crowd to sleep it off in peace after partaking of

·wild clubbing tours. International passport or student ID required. Breakfast included. Free Wi-Fi. Dorms $19-21; private rooms with shared bath $38-42. AmEx/D/MC/V. ❷

Aruba Hotel and Spa, 1215 Las Vegas Blvd. (☎702-383-3100; www.arubalasvegas.com). Conveniently located at the north end of the Strip, this hotel has an outdoor pool, exercise room, and theme nights at the affiliated bar that attract a local crowd. Massage $60 for 25min. Rooms from $35. AmEx/MC/V. ❷

Holiday Motel, 2205 Las Vegas Blvd. (☎702-735-6464). For fans of classic motels. Has a magnificent sign, nicely decorated rooms, and a decent, refreshing pool. Singles $43-49; doubles $54-63. MC/V. ❷

🍴 FOOD

From swanky eateries run by celebrity chefs to gourmet buffets, culinary surprises are everywhere in Las Vegas. Everyone comes to gorge at Vegas's gigantic buffets. The trick to buffet bliss is to find places that are more than glorified cafeterias, which can be difficult. Beyond buffets, Vegas has some of the world's best restaurants, though few have prices palatable to the budget traveler.

🍴 **Battista's Hole in the Wall,** 4041 Audrie St. (☎702-732-1424), behind the Flamingo. 3 decades worth of celebrity photos, an accordion player, mini liquor bottles, and the head of Moosolini (the Fascist moose) adorn the walls. Dinner ($21-38) includes all-you-can-drink wine. Reservations highly recommended. Open daily 5-10:30pm. AmEx/D/MC/V. ❹

🍴 **Le Village Buffet,** 3655 Las Vegas Blvd. (☎702-946-7000), in the Paris. French cuisine at 5 stations, each representing a different region. Begin with heaps of fresh shellfish and cheeses, and then order fresh fruit crepes. Beef and veal sit at carving stations, while a pastry chef prepares more than 40 *gateaux.* Lunch $18. Dinner $25. Open daily 7am-11pm. AmEx/D/MC/V. ❹

Firefly, 3900 Paradise Rd. (☎702-369-3971; www.fireflylv.com). Just far enough away from the Strip to feel like you're mingling with locals rather than the tourist hordes. Picasso-esque paintings help to evoke a convivial Southern Mediterranean atmosphere, and the tapas are authentic, tasty, and filling. Meat tapas $4-10, wine by the glass

$5-9. Open M-Th and Su noon-2am, F-Sa noon-3am. AmEx/D/MC/V. ❸

Peppermill, 2985 S. Las Vegas Blvd. (☎702-735-4177). A Vegas favorite straight from the 1970s, this Day-Glo purple restaurant serves up heaping plates of comfort food ($12-25). Open 24hr. AmEx/MC/V. ❷

Paymon's Mediterranean Cafe, 4147 S. Maryland Pkwy. (☎702-731-6030). Some of the best Mediterranean food in the city. Try the delicious combo plate with hummus, *tabouli,* falafel, *bourrani,* and stuffed grape leaves ($16) or a big falafel and hummus sandwich ($8-10). Open M-Th and Su 11am-1am, F-Sa 11am-2am. AmEx/D/MC/V. ❸

Nine Fine Irishmen (☎702-740-6463), in New York-New York. A bit too trendy to be a proper pub, but the Irish favorites are beautifully garnished. Steak and stout appetizer $11. Bangers and mash $19. Cover F-Sa men $5. Open daily 11am-11pm. Bar open until 3am. D/MC/V. ❹

Carnival World Buffet, 3700 W. Flamingo Rd. (☎702-777-7777), in the Rio. One of the most upscale international cafeterias you will see. The line can be long, but the 12 themed food stations, from sushi to Mexican, will delight those who wait. Breakfast $15. Lunch $17. Dinner $24. Open daily 7am-10pm. AmEx/D/MC/V. ❹

👁 SIGHTS

Before casinos suck you dry of greenbacks, explore the simpler oddities of the city.

LIBERACE MUSEUM. Fans of classical music and kitsch will be delighted by the Liberace Museum, which displays the showman's velvet, rhinestone, fur, and suede stage costumes. *(1775 E. Tropicana Ave. ☎702-798-5595; www.liberace.org. Open Tu-Sa 10am-5pm, Su noon-4pm. $15, students and seniors $10, under 11 free.)*

AUTO COLLECTIONS. Visitors can feast their eyes on 300 classic cars and dream of how they're going to spend their jackpot. *(3535 Las Vegas Blvd. S. Located on the 5th fl. of the Imperial Palace Casino. ☎702-794-3174; www.autocollections.com. Open daily 9:30am-9:30pm. Enter through the casino to get admission coupons. $7, under 12 and seniors $3.)*

LITTLE WHITE WEDDING CHAPEL. From 3min. drive-through whirlwinds to elaborate fantasy-themed extravaganzas, the Little White Wedding Chapel is a mainstay of the city's

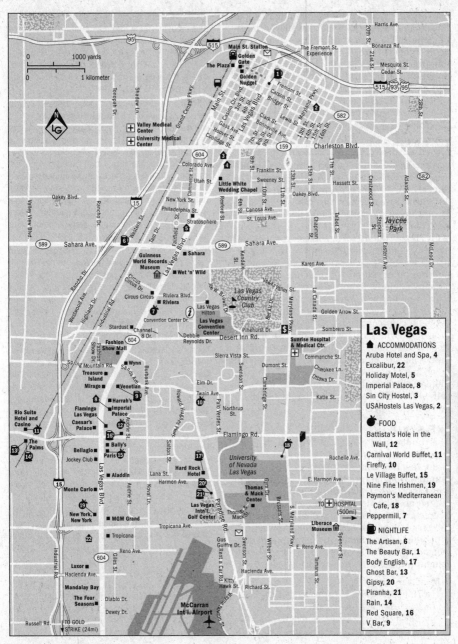

Las Vegas

ACCOMMODATIONS
Aruba Hotel and Spa, **4**
Excalibur, **22**
Holiday Motel, **5**
Imperial Palace, **8**
Sin City Hostel, **3**
USAHostels Las Vegas, **2**

FOOD
Battista's Hole in the
Wall, **12**
Carnival World Buffet, **11**
Firefly, **10**
Le Village Buffet, **15**
Nine Fine Irishmen, **19**
Paymon's Mediterranean
Cafe, **18**
Peppermill, **7**

NIGHTLIFE
The Artisan, **6**
The Beauty Bar, **1**
Body English, **17**
Ghost Bar, **13**
Gipsy, **20**
Piranha, **21**
Rain, **14**
Red Square, **16**
V Bar, **9**

matrimonial traditions. Vegas luminaries like Frank Sinatra and Liberace as well as celebrities Michael Jordan and Britney Spears have been hitched here. The drive-through wedding tunnel begins at a romantic $50 (plus a donation to the minister), and possibilities end only with the imagination. *(1301 Las Vegas Blvd. ☎702-382-5943 or 800-545-8111. No reservations required for drive-through services. Have your marriage license ready. Open 24hr.)*

🏛 CAINO

Casinos spend millions attracting big spenders to Las Vegas. Efforts to bring families to Sin City are evident everywhere, with arcades and thrill rides at every turn. Still, Vegas is no Disneyland—most attractions, including casinos, require all entrants to be 21 years old. With steamy nightclubs, topless revues, and scantily clad waitresses serving free liquor, it's clear that casinos' priorities center on the mature, moneyed crowd. Casinos, bars, and some wedding chapels are open 24hr., so, whatever your itch, Vegas can usually scratch it. Look for casino "funbooks" that feature deals on chips and entertainment. Cash goes in a blink when you're gambling, so it pays to have a budget. There are far more casinos harboring far more attractions than can be listed here; use the following as a compendium of the best, but explore Vegas for yourself—there are ways to fulfill fantasies where you'd least expect it.

THE STRIP

The undisputed locus of Vegas's surging regeneration, the Strip is a fantasyland of neon, teeming with people, casinos, and restaurants. The nation's 10 largest hotels line the legendary 3½ mi. stretch of Las Vegas Blvd., named an All-American Road and a National Scenic Byway. Despite the sparkling facade, the Strip's seedy underbelly still shows; porn is peddled behind family fun centers, and denizens of the night sporting open alcohol containers wander in search of elusive jackpots.

Mandalay Bay, 3950 S. Las Vegas Blvd. (☎702-632-7777; www.mandalaybay.com). Undoubtedly Vegas's hippest casino, Mandalay Bay tries to convince New York City and L.A. fashionistas they haven't left home. With swank restaurants and chichi clubs, gambling seems an afterthought. Shark Reef has aquatic beasts from all over the globe, including 15 species of shark. Afterwards you may or may not want to check out the surf and sand beach, complete with 6 ft. waves. Open daily 10am-11pm. Last entry 10pm. $17, ages 5-12 $11, under 5 free.

Bellagio, 3600 S. Las Vegas Blvd. (☎888-987-6667; www.bellagio.com). The world's largest 5-star hotel, made famous in the remake of *Ocean's Eleven.* Houses a gallery of fine art, the world's tallest chocolate fountain, and a floral conservatory that changes with the seasons. Check out the carefully choreographed dancing fountains in front of the casino and see the water leap several stories high. Shows M-F 3-8pm every 30min. and 8pm-midnight every 15min., Sa-Su noon-8pm every 30min. and 8pm-midnight every 15min. Free.

Venetian, 3355 S. Las Vegas Blvd. (☎702-414-1000; www.venetian.com). Singing gondoliers serenade passengers on the chlorinated "canal" that runs through this palatial casino. Madame Tussauds wax museum evokes a little bit of old Europe, Blue Man Group adds some edge, and the smash-hit musical *Jersey Boys* provides entertainment.

Caesar's Palace, 3570 S. Las Vegas Blvd. (☎866-227-5938; www.caesarspalace.com). At Caesar's, busts abound: some are plaster, and others are barely concealed by waitresses' low-cut get-ups. The 160 boutiques in the Forum provide posh opportunities to spend your winnings.

Wynn, 3131 S. Las Vegas Blvd. (☎877-321-9966; www.wynnlasvegas.com). This latest addition to the Strip more than competes with the Bellagio for classiest casino. The gambling floor is tastefully decorated, with flashing slot machine lights noticeably absent. Limits are high, but the dealers are friendly and the grounds are beautiful.

Luxor, 3900 S. Las Vegas Blvd. (☎877-386-4658; www.luxor.com). This architectural marvel recreates the majestic pyramids of ancient Egypt in opaque glass and steel. Popular with young adults but still family-friendly, Luxor has an IMAX theater, a replica of King Tut's tomb, and clubs.

Paris, 3655 S. Las Vegas Blvd. (☎877-603-4386; www.parislasvegas.com). From restaurants that resemble French cafes to replicas of the Arc de Triomphe and the Eiffel Tower, this resort adds a Parisian *je ne sais quoi* to Las Vegas's .

Mirage, 3400 S. Las Vegas Blvd. (☎702-791-7111; www.mirage.com). This tropical oasis is home to a 20,000 gal. aquarium, a lush indoor rainforest, and several rare white tigers and lions as well as a volcano that puts science fair projects to shame erupts every 15min.

Treasure Island (TI), 3300 S. Las Vegas Blvd. (☎702-894-7111; www.treasureisland.com). Catering to a younger crowd with raucous party clubs and chic loungers, the pirate's cove is the place to go for a big night out. See the Sirens of TI in one of Vegas's most scantily clad shows. Free shows daily 7, 8:30, 10, 11:30pm.

> **CASINO TIPPING.** While gambling, players are served free mixed drinks, and $1 is the standard tip for servers. Leave at least $1 per person for the drink server and bussers at a buffet. Many players reward a good table-game dealer with a $1 tip next to their main bet.

DOWNTOWN AND OFF-STRIP

The tourist frenzy that grips the Strip is less noticeable in "old" downtown Vegas. Glitter Gulch has smaller hotels, cheaper alcohol and food, and table limits as low as $1. Years of decline were reversed with Las Vegas's citywide rebound and the 1995 opening of the Fremont Street Experience. Now, a protective canopy of neon and a pedestrian promenade have aided the area's renaissance, making it almost as entertaining as the Strip and much more welcoming to the budget traveler.

Golden Gate, 1 Fremont St. (☎800-426-1906; www.goldengatecasino.com). Opened in 1906, Las Vegas's oldest hotel and casino now anchors the Fremont Street Experience and offers a thoroughly modern good time. Grab a famous $1 shrimp cocktail and sharpen your gambling skills in the relaxed atmosphere.

Golden Nugget, 129 E. Fremont St. (☎800-634-3454; www.goldennugget.com). An outpost of Strip-like class downtown, this 4-star hotel charms gamblers with marble floors, chandeliers, and high-end gambling.

Palms, 4321 W. Flamingo Rd. (☎866-942-7777; www.palms.com). The ultimate venue to spot celebrities and party with the young and beauti-

ful. The Skin Pool Lounge has swings and cabanas to enjoy before you hit the bars and clubs.

Hard Rock Hotel, 4455 Paradise Rd. (☎800-693-7625; www.hardrockhotel.com). The largest night scene in Vegas, the Hard Rock is furbished with all sorts of music memorabilia and often the stars to go along with it. Feels more like a giant lounge than a casino, especially thanks to The Joint, a small venue that attracts famous rockers for intimate concerts.

♫ ENTERTAINMENT

Vegas entertainment revolves around the casinos. Big bucks will buy you a seat at a made-in-the-USA phenomenon: the Vegas spectacular. These stunning, casino-sponsored productions feature waterfalls, explosions, fireworks, and casts of hundreds. You can also see Broadway plays and musicals, ice revues, and individual entertainers in concert. All hotels have citywide ticket booths in their lobbies. Check out some of the free show guides—*Showbiz, Today in Las Vegas, What's On*—for listings. For a more opinionated perspective, check out one of the independents—*Las Vegas Mercury, City Life, Las Vegas Weekly*—or the *Las Vegas Review-Journal's* weekly entertainment supplement, *Neon*. Some "production shows" are topless; many are tasteless, but there are a few exceptions. The ✪Cirque de Soleil's creative shows— O, Mystere, and the racy Zumanity, to name just a couple—are awe-inspiring displays of human agility and physical strength channeled as artistic expression at the Bellagio, Treasure Island, New York-New York, MGM, Mirage, and Luxor (from $69). "Limited view" tickets are discounted, and the view isn't that limited. **Blue Man Group** at the Venetian is a production that pushes the limits of stage entertainment with percussion sets and audience participation. (☎866-641-7469.)

For a show by one of the musical stars who haunt the city, such as Gladys Knight (Flamingo) or Wayne Newton (MGM), you'll have to fork over a minimum of $60. Incredible impersonator/singer/dancer Danny Gans entertains at the Mirage (about $100). The tricks of Lance Burton (a mainstay at the Monte Carlo) are good, old magic ($66-75), while Penn and Teller at the Rio are far darker (from $75). With a bit of everything, former street performer The Amazing Jonathan

ROUTE 66

stages one of Vegas's edgiest productions (from $65). Chicago's classic comedic institution The Second City also graces the stage at the Flamingo for a reasonable $45.

NIGHTLIFE

Nightlife in Vegas gets rolling around midnight and runs until everyone drops—or runs out of money. Dress codes at dance clubs are strictly enforced, so call ahead before heading out. In a city that never sleeps, inebriated club-hoppers bounce from one happening joint to the next to the next to the next..

BARS

Red Square, 3950 Las Vegas Blvd. (☎702-632-7407), in Mandalay Bay. Probably the sweetest bar on the Strip, this Miami Beach import pulls off post-communist chic with ease. Serves amazing martinis, frozen vodkas, and caviar. Red Square is the hippest way to celebrate the fall of the Soviet Union. Open M-Th and Su 5pm-2am, F-Sa 4pm-4am. AmEx/MC/V.

V Bar, 3355 Las Vegas Blvd. (☎702-414-3200). This elegant bar in the Venetian deftly recreates the New York City lounge scene. Minimalist design and mellow beats make V Bar equally suitable for hanging low or dancing. Open M-W and Su 5pm-2am, Th-Sa 5pm-3am. AmEx/D/MC/V.

The Artisan, 1501 W. Sahara Ave. (☎800-554-4092). Part of a small boutique hotel. Popular hangout for the city's theater performers. Come here if you want to escape the tourist crowds and experience a more chilled out, less frenetic ambience. Elegantly decorated with copies of paintings of the Old Masters and with naughty water statues. Happy hour daily 5-7pm. Open daily 5pm-1am. AmEx/D/MC/V.

The Beauty Bar, 517 Fremont St. (☎702-598-1965; www.beautybar.com). Located in historic downtown Vegas, the Beauty Bar serves as a refuge from casino culture for locals and visitors alike. Authentic late-50s interior and a manicurist on duty F night (except 1st F of the month). Open F-Sa 9pm-late. MC/V.

CLUBS

Ghost Bar and Rain, 4231 W. Flamingo Rd. (☎702-942-6832), at the Palms. Indisputably the hottest nightspots, drawing revelers in droves.

You may wait in line for hours, but once you're in, groove with Vegas's hottest bodies while DJs throw down. Ghost Bar is on the 55th fl., with a deck and 360° view of Vegas. Cover M-Th and Su $10, F-Sa $25. Open daily 8pm-late. Rain has over 25,000 sq. ft. of dance floor and intense displays of fire, fog, and, of course, rain. Cover $25. Open F-Sa 11pm-5am. AmEx/D/MC/V.

Body English, 4455 Paradise Rd. (☎702-693-4000), inside the Hard Rock Hotel. Imagine a European rock star's mansion, add lots of black leather, and you have it. World-class DJs spin mostly rock and hip hop. Cover men $30, women free. Open W and F-Su 10:30pm-4am. AmEx/D/MC/V.

Gipsy and Piranha, 4605 Paradise Rd. (☎702-731-1919). 2 venues but basically all part of the same club; this is the wildest GLBT option in the city. Labyrinthine inside, with a variety of dance floors, intimate sofa rooms, tanks full of Piranhas, and wacky hosts setting the mood. Liquor beer bust (all you can drink) M and Th. Cover for non-members $20. Open daily 9am-sunrise. Cash only.

THE ROAD TO OATMAN: 132 MI.

Take **US 93 South** back the way you came. all the way into Arizona toward Kingman. Bear left and continue on **Beale Avenue** and **Historic Route 66** to get back to Kingman. Bear right onto **Andy Devine Avenue,** and Historic 66 is on the right marked to Oatman and Needles. Follow the road as you turn right under the interstate and then left onto the Oatman highway. The last stretch between Kingman and Oatman is an intense series of hair-raising switchbacks along cliff sides in an otherworldly landscape of craggy peaks and undulating valleys. Check your gauges and make sure the sun won't be in your eyes; after dark, the unlit roads are downright treacherous. If you really want to recreate the authentic 66 experience, you'll need to turn around go up in reverse; back in the day many cars had to make this part of the journey backward because they had gravity-fed fuel systems.

TIME CHANGE. If you're traveling between November and March, set your clock ahead 1hr. as you return to Arizona. Since most of Arizona doesn't observe Daylight Saving Time, travelers between April and October don't have to do a thing.

ROUTE 66

The Grand Canyon State
ARIZONA
Welcomes You!

OATMAN   ☎928

Harleys and burros vie rather bizarrely for the right of way in Oatman, and leather-clad bikers stage mock gunfights in the heart of town during the week. (Daily noon, 1:30, 2:15, 3:15pm.) The town was originally founded to support the nearby mining interests of the present-day ghost town **Gold Road,** and it became the traditional last stop before venturing across the Mojave, but the road leading to the town was later bypassed in favor of a looping but flatter by-way. Oatman displays its own Wild West version of hospitality at the **Oatman Visitors Center,** an old, open-air outhouse. The display in the gold mine next door answers more questions about the town. Across the street, the **Oatman Jail** displays various instruments of imprisonment as well as photos and clippings about the town. Stop at the **Oatman post office,** 251 Main St., to have your mail marked with the special Oatman cancellation stamp, one of the few small-town cancellation stamps left in America. (☎928-768-3990. Open M-F 9am-4pm.) Three miles outside of Oatman proper, '49er wannabes can tour **Gold Road Mine's** now-defunct mine-

shafts that run directly under Rte. 66. Forty-five-minute tours are conducted throughout the day and take visitors deep into the old mine. When you're done, the gift shop stocks T-shirts proudly proclaiming, "Rte. 66—Been on it, been under it!" (☎928-768-1600. Open daily 10am-5pm. Tours $12.50, under 12 $6.)

The **Oatman Hotel,** 181 Main St., is famous as the location of Clark Gable and Carole Lombard's 1939 honeymoon. The hotel is also an informal museum where you can read about the history of the town and see the original 1920s rooms. Downstairs, the colorful bar is wallpapered in over 25,000 signed dollar bills. You can leave one behind, like Ronald Reagan did, if you can find a spot! (☎928-768-4408. Open M-Th and Su 10:30am-6:30pm, F-Sa 8am-6:30pm. Suggested donation $1.) Oatman was named in honor of the Oatmans, a family of pioneers who were ambushed by Native Americans on their way west. Two of the Oatman daughters, Olive and Mary, were taken captive, and their brother was left for dead. Mary died in captivity, but Olive was rescued by the US Army at age 14. The namesake **Olive Oatman Restaurant and Saloon ❷,** 171 Main St., has heaping Navajo tacos, fry bread, and live music on the weekends. (☎928-768-1891; www.oatmangold.com/olive. Entrees $6-8. Open daily 8:30am-4:30pm. AmEx/D/MC/V.)

DESERT WATERFALLS

Las Vegas is home to posh hotels, flashy casinos, and a whole lot of ... water? Despite the presence of springs beneath the city, Vegas has long been an arid city. Architects and financiers artificially transformed this desert city into an oasis of faux Venetian canals, gushing fountains, and elaborate water ballets. With more than half a million residents tapping into it, the city's water system swallows up 190 gal. of water per day per citizen. Amid the southern Nevada desert, Las Vegas's water supply is, not surprisingly, perpetually in short supply. Explosive urban sprawl, coupled with irresponsible use of water at big-name resorts and casinos, is rapidly using up the supply of water allotted to Nevada by the states (including Arizona) who share rights to the Colorado River. Experts are fearful that water restrictions may not solve the growing problem, and it seems unlikely that a population accustomed to gluttonous water use is willing to change its ways. With more than 5000 people moving to the area each month, the only conceivable solution to the water supply shortage may be to cut the city's ceaseless influx of residents. The expansion of Arizona's urban areas, however, make this solution less viable with each passing year. While other cities could work on tightening their leaky faucets, Las

THE ROAD TO GOLDEN SHORES: 18 MI.
Two miles beyond Oatman, bear left at the fork, following signs for Golden Shores.

GOLDEN SHORES ☎928

The town of Golden Shores has the basics for the traveler in need, but the hint of palm trees and the scent of impending California along the banks of the Colorado River impel most roadtrippers onward. Enjoy diner deals and a life-size Marilyn Monroe cutout at **Linda's Cafe ❷**, 12826 S. Hwy. 66. Try the chicken breast sandwich with tropical fruit mixed drink for $6. (☎928-768-8011. Open Tu-Sa 8am-6pm, Su 8am-2pm. Cash only.)

> **⏱ TIME CHANGE.** If you're traveling between November and March, set your clock back 1hr. as you enter California and the Pacific Time Zone (for good this time). If you're traveling between April and October there is no change. Thank you, Arizona state law.

THE ROAD TO MOABI REGIONAL PARK: 7 MI.
Five miles beyond Golden Shores at Topock (the Mojave word for "bridge"), take **Exit 1** to join **I-40** heading west into California, the promised land. About 2 mi. from the border, you will reach Moabi Regional Park.

MOABI REGIONAL PARK ☎760

The Moabi **campgrounds ❶**, Moabi Park Rd., offer a chance to cool off in the Colorado River and provides an alternative to the nondescript motels of nearby Needles. (☎760-326-3831. Sites $15-22, with hookup $25-35. D/MC/V.)

> **📷 PHOTO OP.** About 30 mi. southeast of Topock, near Lake Havasu City, is **London Bridge,** which was dismantled in the 1960s because it was unable to support London traffic. It was later moved and reassembled in Arizona. Take I-40 E. from Topock and head south on Rte. 95 to see for yourself.

THE ROAD TO NEEDLES: 11 MI.
Approaching Needles on **I-40,** take the **95 South/East Broadway** exit approximately 10 mi. from the border

into town, making a right onto Broadway and following as it swings into town. The original alignment of **Route 66** actually cuts away to the left of the interstate, then veers right again to enter town on Broadway.

The Golden State **CALIFORNIA** *Welcomes You!*

NEEDLES ☎760

Needles, famed for its unrelenting summer heat, has wide streets lined with dingy motels and truck stops. Needles was the birthplace of comic-strip artist Charles Schulz and the home of his character "Spike." The iconic **Route 66 Motel**, 91 Desnok St., might look familiar—it was the backdrop for several scenes of the film adaptation of *The Grapes of Wrath*. (☎760-326-3611.)

Clean rooms are available at the **Desert Mirage Inn and Suites ❷**, 1910 Needles Hwy. Rooms come with fridges, microwaves, and pool access, which you need to cool down in this town. (☎760-326-4205. Wi-Fi. Singles $36; doubles $42.) At **Route 66 Burger ❶**, 701 Broadway, you can pick up Mexican-American fast food at great prices. (☎760-326-2342. Roast beef sandwiches $6. Shakes $2.50. Open M-Th and Su 7am-9pm. Cash only.) The **Wagon Wheel ❷**, 2420 Needles Hwy., is the ultimate truck stop and has a half-pound burger for $7. (☎760-326-4305. Entrees $8-10. Open daily 5am-10pm. MC/V.) At **Lucy's Mexican Restaurant ❷**, 811 Front St., just off Rte. 66, Lucy herself serves up popular Mexican fare. Try the *chile relleno* dinner, with two *rellenos*, rice, beans, and a tortilla, for $7.50. (☎760-326-4461. Entrees $4-8. Open Th-Su 11am-8pm. Cash only.) The **Hungry Bear ❸**, 1906 Needles Hwy., is a classic, family-style diner with booths upholstered in Rte. 66-themed fabric. Entrees like halibut steaks run $12-18. (☎760-326-2988. Open M-Th and Su 5:30am-9pm, F-Sa 5:30am-9:30pm. AmEx/D/MC/V.)

THE ROAD TO AMBOY: 60 MI.
It's a lonely road across the desert; fill up on gas before leaving Needles. From **Broadway,** head left

onto **Needles Highway** after crossing the tracks. Continue until **Park Road,** then turn left and join **I-40** 1 mi. later. Eight miles down I-40, take the **US 95/Searchlight/Vegas exit** and make a right on **Route 66.** Six miles later, turn left onto **Goffs Road,** following signs for Goffs. Pass through Goffs 14 mi. later. The town of Fenner, another 9 mi. down the road, is even smaller than Goffs but has the only gas station for miles. Five miles past Fenner, head right at the T intersection. Another 2 mi. will bring you through Essex, which has little besides a small auto-repair shop. Twenty five miles past Essex is Amboy.

AMBOY   ☎760

Roy's Cafe and Motel is somewhere between comic and picturesque, with a bright 1950s-era sign vying for customer attention with what must be imaginary competition. The motel is now only a historical site (although it has been bought and there are plans to revive it), but you can stop for soda or water in the former cafe. (Gas also available 24hr. Open daily 7am-3pm. AmEx/D/MC/V.) As you head west from Amboy, the rising mountains on the north side of the road are countered by an equally surprising geological feature to the south—a volcanic crater set back from the road across a volcanic field. A hike up the walls of **Amboy Crater** affords a view not only of a depression of caked mud inside the crater but also the surrounding plains and mountains.

Ⓜ THE ROAD TO LUDLOW: 25 MI.

Continue on **Route 66** for a rather bumpy 15 mi. past Amboy Crater to the town of Ludlow.

LUDLOW   ☎760

As recently as 1988, Ludlow telephones had no dials so, residents had to dial an operator to place a call. Incoming calls were placed through an operator to numbers Ludlow 1, 2, 3, etc. Different extensions had distinctive rings, and it was up to residents to decipher their ring and determine when to pick up. Rooms are available at the **Ludlow Motel ❷**, 68315 Ludlow Rd. (☎760-733-4338. Singles $46; doubles $52. AmEx/MC/V.) A veritable metropolis in the desert hinterlands, Ludlow now offers a 24hr. gas station and mini-mart as well as the **Ludlow Cafe ❷**, which is a popu-

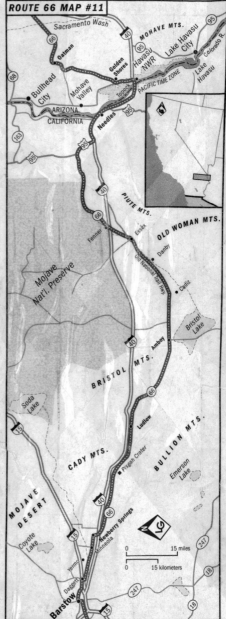

ROUTE 66

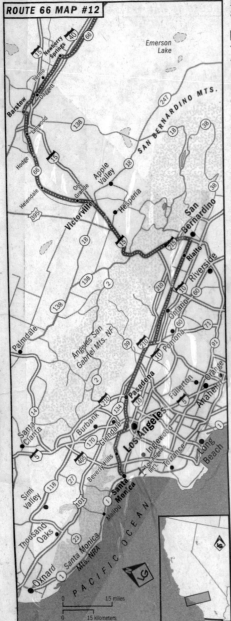

ROUTE 66 MAP #12

lar roadside pit stop. (☎760-733-4501. Entrees $9-11. Open daily 7am-9pm. MC/V.)

THE ROAD TO NEWBERRY SPRINGS: 27 MI.

Take a right on **Crucero Road** to head under **I-40,** then take a left to Newberry Springs.

NEWBERRY SPRINGS ☎760

The motel part of the **Newberry Mountain RV and Motel Park ❶**, 47800 National Trails Hwy., has yet to be resurrected, but the RV park is up and running, with a manmade lake full of catfish—a good place to test your hunter-gatherer skills. (☎760-257-0066. Showers, laundry. Reception 8am-10pm. RV sites $22. D/MC/V.) Newberry Springs is home to the now semi-famous **Bagdad Cafe ❷**, 46548 National Trails Hwy., which inspired a movie of the same title. (☎760-257-3101. Entrees $8-12. Open daily 7am-7pm. AmEx/MC/V.) For the wayfarer who happens to end up in Newberry Springs at nightfall, **The Barn**, 44560 National Trails Hwy., has dancing "every so often." Drinks are cheap (beer $2), and there's pool and darts to keep you entertained. (☎760-257-4110. Open daily 10am-9pm. Cash only.)

THE ROAD TO BARSTOW: 20 MI.

Take **Route 66** from Newberry Springs. After 13 mi., curve left onto the **Nebo Access Road,** then right onto the highway. At the **Marine Corps exit,** 2 mi. down the road, turn left under **I-40,** right on **East Main Street,** and right on **Montara Road** into Barstow.

BARSTOW ☎760

Barstow, a classic rest-stop town of inexpensive motels and fast-food chains, may be what the Joad family was hoping for as they crossed into California. Downtown streets are lined with small shops, and the Italian Renaissance-style railroad depot adds Old World grandeur to this gateway to the California desert.

■ ORIENTATION

Barstow sits at the junction of **I-15** and **I-40** and at the convergence of a number of California state routes. Most avenues run north-south; streets run east-west. Downtown centers on the intersection of **First Avenue** and

Main Street (Route 66). Main St. is known as W. Main St. or E. Main St. on the respective sides of First Ave. Barstow Rd. parallels First Ave. a few blocks east.

VITAL STATS

Population: 23,000

Tourist Office: Barstow Chamber of Commerce, 681 N. 1st Ave. (☎760-256-8617). Open M-F 10am-4pm.

Library and Internet Access: Barstow Public Library, 304 Buena Vista St. (☎760-256-4850). Open M and W noon-8pm, Tu and Th-F 10am-6pm, Sa 9am-5pm.

Post Office: 425 S. 2nd Ave. (☎760-256-9304) Open M-F 9am-5pm, Sa 10am-noon. **Postal Code:** 92311.

ACCOMMODATIONS

E. Main St. offers an endless line of motels. Prices fluctuate depending on the season, day, and whether Vegas accommodations are full.

The Desert Inn, 1100 E. Main St. (☎760-256-2146). A fantastic value; its big rooms come with fridges and microwaves. The large swimming pool out front is nicely secluded by well-tended bushes and trees. Wi-Fi. Singles $32; doubles $40. AmEx/D/MC/V. ❷

Route 66 Motel, 195 W. Main St. (☎760-256-7866). Built in 1922. Comfortable round beds inside stucco cottage-like units with vintage cars and signs decorating the outside. Singles $40; doubles $50. AmEx/D/MC/V. ❷

FOOD

Every restaurant chain imaginable has a branch on Main St., but Barstow's local cuisine is far more rewarding to the palate.

Rosita's Mexican American Food, 540 W. Main St. (☎760-256-9218). The aroma of savory dishes fills the festive dining room. Mexican combo plates $10-15. Lunch specials Tu-F $6. Open Tu-Sa 11am-9pm, Su 11am-8pm. D/MC/V. ❷

Firehouse Italian Eatery, 1358 E. Main St. (☎760-256-1094), just behind the Shell gas station. Traditional pizzeria fare is served in a refurbished firehouse, complete with the front of a fire engine and a fire pole. Pasta dishes $9-11.

Dinner entrees $11-15. Open M-Sa 11am-9 pm. AmEx/D/MC/V. ❸

Lola's Kitchen, 1244 E. Main St. (☎760-2?5-1007), in Lyon's Supermarket complex. Serves classic Mexican dishes, all for under $8. Open 4am-7.30pm, Sa 4am-4.30pm. Cash only. ❷

Starlight Donut Shop, 101 W. Main St. (☎760-256-597?). World-class doughnuts ($6.50 dozen) past the start. Offerings include ice cream, pies, hot dogs, burgers, and croissants. Open 24hr. Cash only. ❶

SIGHTS

ROUTE 66 MOTHER ROAD MUSEUM. Located in the Casa del Desierto train station, the museum focuses on Route 66's evolution from a collection of old trails to the epic Mother Road. (681 1st Ave. ☎760-255-1890. Open Apr.-Oct. F-Sa 10am-4pm, Nov.-Mar. F-Su 11am-4pm. Free.)

RAINBOW BASIN NATURAL AREA. Hikers investigate colorful canyon by day and gaze at unpolluted by city lights at night. Near Rainbow Basin Natural Area, **Owl Canyon Campground** offers primitive camping (sites $6). (8mi. of Barstow. Head north on N. 1st St., take a right Irwin Rd., continue for 7 mi., and turn left on Fed Rd. Follow the signs down this dirt-and-gravel for 3 mi. ☎760-252-6000.)

CALICO. ghost town of Calico is a collection of touristy craft stores and mini attractions like "Calico Woodworking" and the "? Shack." (On Ghost Town Rd., off I-15, 10mi. Barstow. ☎800-862-2542; www.calico-town... 9am-5pm. $6, ages 6-15 $3.)

ROAD TO VICTORVILLE: 30 MI.

Leaving Barstow, follow **Route 66** through Hodge. Head past Helendale and 15 mi. from Barstow for a forest of bottle trees on your right. Continue though Oro Grande, toward Victorville...

VICTORVILLE

Victorville offers little long-term diversion, but ... to a few excellent eateries as well as ... California Route 66 Museum, 16849 Rte. 66. ... stop, the museum holds an impressive collection of Rte. 66 memorabilia ... a refreshing array of modern artistic

ROUTE 66

takes on the Old Road. (☎760-951-0436. Open M and Th-Sa 10am-4pm, Su 11am-3pm. Free.) Inexpensive lodging options are scarce in Victorville, though chain motels are abundant at the west end of town and along I-15. The **New Corral Motel ❸,** 14643 Seventh St., has well-kept gardens and pretty paints on the walls of its rooms, all of which have Wi-Fi. (☎760-245-9378. Singles $45; doubles $53 AmEx/D/MC/V.) The new **Johnny Reb's ❷,** 15051 Seventh St., offers an entertaining break from fare. As the building instructs, "put south in your mouth." (☎760-955-3700. Sr beef brisket $9. Open M-Th 7am-8:30pm, am-9:30pm. AmEx/D/MC/V.)

🚗 THE ROAD TO SAN BERNO: 37 MI.

Take **Seventh Street** out of town; pick up **I-15 South.** Follow I-15 over the mo, Cajun Pass for 17 mi. Head right at the Cl road exit, then curve left 6 mi. farther on, headin the interstate. Almost 2 mi. beyond that right onto the ramp southbound — immediately he left lane for **Exit 215** to San Bernardino. he highway splits, exit for **Devore** and turn lef p sign onto **Cajun Boulevard.** Follow Cajun Bl. until you hit the **Mt. Vernon** traffic light and onto **Mount Vernon Avenue, which** takes you

SAN BERNARDINO ☎909

San Bernardino, the seat a's largest county, is a generic So California

It may call itself the hub of the smog ire, but the only real empires in Inland us city are the rampant corporate this s—the side benefit of which is cheap fran lodging for those en route to a more food destination. app

VITAL STATS	
Population: 182,000	
Post Office: San Bernardino **Convention Visitors Bureau,** 1955 Hunts Ln., Ste. 102 (☎800-867-8366). Open M-Th 7:30am-5:30pm, F 7:0am-4:30pm.	
Library and Internet Access: Norman F. Feldheim **Library,** 555 W. 6th St. (☎909-381-8201). Open M-W 10am-8pm, Th-Sa 10am-6pm.	
Post Office: 2160 N. Arrowhead Ave. (☎909-881-2523). Open M-F 9am-5pm, Sa 10am-3pm. **Postal Code:** 92405.	

🧭 ORIENTATION

Although traffic in San Bernardino may be a little overwhelming for roadtrippers used to open stretches of Arizona desert, getting around is relatively simple; the city is laid out in a grid, with numbered streets running north-south and lettered streets east-west. **Route 66** enters the city from the north on **I-15,** becoming **Mount Vernon Avenue** in town. The area along Mt. Vernon Ave. (Old Rte. 66) can be unsafe, especially at night, so stick to the

TH ND OUTS OF IN-N-OUT

From its begin n ing in 1948 a stand, IN-N-OUT Burger has come a long way. Its distinctive yellow-and-red sign is now ubi ross California, Nevada, and Arizona. Many first-time visitors are surprised to see a menu w e choic (hamburger, cheeseburger, double-double, fries, and shake), but IN-N-OUT also cret menu. These options aren't technically on the menu, but they're available at all loca

- **Animal Style:** Burger grilled in with lettuce, tomato, pickles, grilled on IN-N-OUT's special sandw ich spread.
- **Protein Style:** Burger of you pped in lettuce instead of a bun.
- **Double Me at:** Two beef patti se.
- **Flying Dutchman:** Two beef p slices of cheese, nothing else.
- **Wish Burger:** No meat.
- **MxC: Simple**—the number of ies you want by the number of slices and cheese. For example, a 10×20 (not recommend have 10 patties and 20 slices of cheese. It also comes with lettuce, to ato, and spread

north end of town or **Hospitality Lane,** which crosses **Waterman Avenue** just north of **I-10.**

ACCOMMODATIONS

Golden Star Motel, 668 W. 5th St. (☎909-885-6696). Has spacious rooms in a pretty southern-Mediterranean style building with a red-tiled roof. Free Wi-Fi. Singles $55; doubles $65. AmEx/D/MC/V. ❸

FOOD

Molly's, 350 N. D St. (☎909-888-1778), at Court St. Lined with tributes to James Dean and Elvis. Has healthful options with just enough creativity to draw in the out-of-towners. Sandwiches $6-8. Omelets $6-7. Open M-F 6am-6pm, Sa 7am-3pm, Su 8am-3pm. AmEx/D/MC/V. ❷

Mitla's, 602 Mt. Vernon Ave. (☎909-888-0460). Enormous Mexican specialties, many of them for rock-bottom prices. Taco, enchilada, and tamal plate $7.25. Open Tu-Th 9am-2pm and 4:30-8pm, F 9am-9pm, Sa-Su 9am-8pm. AmEx/D/MC/V. ❷

SIGHTS

CALIFORNIA THEATER. Will Rogers performed his final show here, and entertainers Buster Crabbe and Rita Hayworth have also appeared. Today, the theater is home to the **California Theater of Performing Arts,** which hosts popular musicals like *Cats* and *Phantom of the Opera.* Don't miss the giant Will Rogers mural outside. *(562 W. 4th St. ☎ 909-386-7361.)*

GOLDEN ARCHES. The original McDonald's, 1398 N. E St., was established by Richard and Maurice "Mac" McDonald in 1948, but don't expect $0.15 burgers anymore. The only thing offered at this halfhearted historic site is a growing display of Golden Arches memorabilia and Happy Meal toys. *(☎909-885-6324. Open M-F 8am-5pm, Sa-Su 10am-5pm.)*

FESTIVALS

Every September, San Bernardino hosts the **Route 66 Rendezvous Weekend** (www.route-66.org), a weekend open to all vehicles made

between 1900 and 1973 and any model Viper, Corvette, or Prowler.

THE ROAD TO RIALTO: 5 MI.

From San Bernardino, head out of town on **Fifth Street,** which turns into **Foothill Boulevard** toward Rialto, 2 mi. west of **Mount Vernon Avenue.**

RIALTO ☎909

The historic stop in Rialto is the **Wigwam Motel** ❸, 2728 W. Foothill Blvd. Situated around immaculate gardens with a jelly-bean-shaped swimming pool, the concrete structures are a blend of modern convenience and antique quirkiness, featuring TV, air-conditioning, fridges, and wagon-wheel headboards. (☎909-875-3005. Wi-Fi. Singles M-Th and Su $65, F-Sa $77; doubles $75. AmEx/D/MC/V.)

THE ROAD TO PASADENA: 35 MI.

In summer, juice-mongers operate from inside the giant orange on the south side of the road in Rancho Cucamonga. Just a few miles ago, towns were as hard to come by as water in the stretch of punishing Mojave Desert across eastern California. From San Bernardino to L.A., however, the urban sprawl of countless strip-mall towns blends together in one commercialized, brand-happy stretch of suburbia that might send east-west roadtrippers into population-density shock. Those with an itch for the ocean might consider taking **I-10** directly to the beach, bypassing the urban sprawl leading into Los Angeles. In upland, 16 mi. from San Bernardino, is the **Madonna of the Trail** statue, a statue that marks the end of the Mother Road and the Californian cousin to Illinois's Madonna of the Highway. From Upland, continue through Claremont, Laverne, San Dimas, and Glendora. Continue on **Foothill Boulevard** through Azusa, Duarte, Monrovia, and Arcadia. One mile after entering Arcadia, take a right onto **Colorado Boulevard** and follow it into Pasadena.

PASADENA ☎626

Nationally, Pasadena is known as the home of the Rose Bowl; for Californians, it's a serene, ritzy suburb. Old Town combines historic sights with a lively entertainment scene, and wide boulevards lined with trendy eating and shopping options, side streets with world-

ROUTE 66

class museums, and graceful architecture make Pasadena quite distinct from its noisy downtown neighbor.

ORIENTATION

Pasadena sits on the northeast edge of the sprawling metropolis that is L.A. **Route 66** approaches Pasadena from the west and runs through the city as **Colorado Boulevard. I-210** parallels Colorado Blvd. to the north; downtown Pasadena and many attractions, including Old Town Pasadena, lie between I-210 and Colorado Blvd. Avenues in Pasadena run north-south; streets and boulevards run east-west. On the west edge of the city, the **Arroyo Parkway (Route 110)** runs north-south. It turns into the **Pasadena Freeway** as it heads southwest toward L.A., serving as the major route between the cities.

VITAL STATS
Population: 134,000
Tourist Office: Convention and Visitors Bureau, 171 S. Los Robles Ave. (☎800-307-7977; www.pasadenacal.com). Open M-F 8am-5pm, Sa 10am-4pm.
Library and Internet Access: Pasadena Central Library, 285 E. Walnut St. (☎626-744-4066). Open M-Th 9am-9pm, F-Sa 9am-6pm, Su 1-5pm.
Post Office: 967 E. Colorado Blvd. (☎626-432-4835). Open M-F 9am-5pm. **Postal Code:** 91106.

ACCOMMODATIONS

Pasadena Motor Inn, 2097 E. Colorado Blvd. (☎626-796-3122). The narrow hallways may feel a bit like your college dorm, but the rooms are large and comfortable, with fridges and balconies. Free Wi-Fi. Singles $52; doubles $56. Cash deposit $20. AmEx/D/MC/V. ❷

Saga Motor Hotel, 1633 E. Colorado Blvd. (☎626-795-0431; www.thesagamotorhotel.com). This apartment-like hotel offers pleasant peach-colored rooms with shady gardens with a heated outdoor pool. Free Wi-Fi. Singles from $92; doubles from $99. AmEx/D/MC/V. ❹

Astro Motel, 2818 E. Colorado Blvd. (☎626-449-3370). Zany 70s bedspreads, floral wallpaper,

carved bedsteads, and antique glass lamps lend chaotic comfort to this colorful budget option. Singles $44; doubles $52. MC/V. ❷

FOOD

Eateries line Colorado Blvd. from Los Robles Ave. to Orange Grove Blvd. in Old Town. The restaurants and sights around the boulevard make it pleasant and walkable.

Fair Oaks Pharmacy and Soda Fountain, 1526 Mission St. (☎626-799-1414), at Fair Oaks Ave. in South Pasadena. From Colorado Blvd., go south 1 mi. on Fair Oaks Ave. to Mission St. This old-fashioned drugstore has been serving travelers since 1915. Hand-dipped shakes and malts $6. Sandwiches $6-10. Open M-Sa 9am-9pm, Su 9am-7pm. AmEx/D/MC/V. ❶

Pita! Pita!, 927 E. Colorado Blvd. (☎626-356-0106; www.citycent.com/pitapita), 1 block east of Lake Ave. Never has a flatbread deserved so many exclamation points. Free appetizers of green olives, yellow peppers, and toasted pita. Great salad options $5.50-7.25. Spicy chicken pita $6.50. Lamb kebab with salad, rice, and beans $9. Open M-Th and Su 9am-9pm, F-Sa 9am-10pm. AmEx/D/MC/V. ❷

Pie 'n' Burger, 913 E. California Blvd. (☎626-795-1123; www.pienburger.com), just east of S. Lake Ave. A classic 1963 diner, complete with Formica counters and plaid wallpaper. Burgers ($6.25) and pies (19 varieties; $3.50-4.50) are your best bets. Open M-F 6am-10pm, Sa 7am-10pm, Su 7am-9pm. Cash only. ❸

SIGHTS

Besides sports, Pasadena's main draw is Old Town, a series of trendy shops and restaurants bordered by Walnut St. and Del Mar Ave., between Pasadena Ave. and Arroyo Pkwy.

NORTON SIMON MUSEUM OF ART. This world-class private collection chronicles Western art from Italian Gothic to 20th-century abstract. The museum features paintings by Raphael, Van Gogh, Monet, and Picasso as well as rare etchings by Rembrandt and Goya. The Impressionist and Post-Impressionist hall, the Southeast Asian sculptures, and the 79,000 sq. ft. sculpture garden by California landscape artist Nancy Goslee Power are particularly impressive. (*411 W. Colorado Blvd., at*

Orange Grove Blvd. ☎626-449-6840; www.nortonsimon. org. Open M, W-Th, Sa-Su noon-6pm, F noon-9pm. $8, students with ID and under 18 free, seniors $4.)

ROSE BOWL. In the gorge that forms the city's western boundary stands Pasadena's most famous landmark. The sand-colored, 90,000-seat stadium is home to "the granddaddy of them all," the annual college football clash on January 1 between the champions of the Big Ten and Pac-10 conferences. The Bowl Championship Series comes every four years, and the UCLA Bruins play regular-season home games here as well. (1001 Rose Bowl Dr. ☎626-577-3101; www.rosebowlstadium.com.) The Rose Bowl also hosts an enormous monthly flea market that attracts upward of 2000 vendors selling close to one million items. (☎323-560-7469. 2nd Su of each month 9am-3pm.)

TIP SMELL THE ROSES. Pasadena has over 3500 jacaranda trees, which, when in bloom, create a violent sea of violet-blue blossoms. The best time of year to catch them is April, May, or June. Stop by Del Mar Blvd. for the best view of them.

PASADENA PLAYHOUSE. The playhouse fostered the careers of William Holden, Dustin Hoffman, and Gene Hackman. Founded in 1917 and restored in 1986, it offers some of L.A.'s finest theater. (39 S. El Molino Ave., between Colorado Blvd. and Green St. ☎626-356-7529.)

PASADENA MUSEUM OF CALIFORNIA ART. The museum proudly displays Californian art, architecture, and design from 1850 to the present. (490 E. Union St. ☎626-568-3665; www. pmcaonline.org. Open W-Su noon-5pm. $5, students and seniors $5. 1st F of each month free.)

CALIFORNIA INSTITUTE OF TECHNOLOGY (CALTECH). Some of the world's greatest scientific minds do their work here. Founded in 1891, Caltech has amassed a faculty that includes several Nobel laureates and a student body that prides itself on both its staggering intellect and its loony practical jokes. (1200 E. California Blvd., about 2 mi. southeast of Old

Town. ☎626-395-6811, tours 395-6341. Free student-led tours every weekday during term time.)

NASA JET PROPULSION LABORATORY. The lab impressively executed the journey of the *Mars Pathfinder*. Ask to see pictures of the face of Mars. (4800 Oak Grove Dr. About 5 mi. north of Old Town. ☎818-354-9314. Free tours by appointment.)

⚐ THE ROAD TO LOS ANGELES: 10 MI.
From **Colorado Boulevard,** turn left onto **Arroyo Parkway,** which immediately feeds into **Route-110.** Take Rte. 110 southwest into the heart of Los Angeles.

LOS ANGELES ☎213

In a city where nothing seems to be more than 30 years old, the latest trends command more respect than does tradition. People flock to this historical vacuum in an effort to live like the stars—and what better place? Bring your sense of style and an attitude; both are mandatory in this city of celebrities. Cruise through the city and watch the sun set over the Pacific in Santa Monica or stay to see the sights; either way, it's one hell of a show.

➤ PAGE TURN. See the Pacific Coast (p. 906) for complete coverage of Los Angeles.

⚐ THE ROAD TO SANTA MONICA: 16 MI.
Get on **Route 110 West.** Exit at **Sunset Boulevard** and turn left from the off-ramp, crossing the freeway. Bear right on **Figueroa Street** (following signs to Sunset Blvd.) and turn right. Three miles later, turn left onto **Manzanita Street,** which immediately turns into **Santa Monica Boulevard.** Follow Santa Monica Blvd. through West Hollywood, Beverly Hills, and West Los Angeles to reach Santa Monica. At the junction with **I-10,** turn left at **Lincoln Street** and follow it to **Olympic Street.** The intersection of Lincoln and Olympic is the official end of **Route 66,** but, to reach the famously eclectic Santa Monica Pier, continue west on Santa Monica Blvd.

SANTA MONICA ☎310

Finally—the Pacific! After mile upon mile of open road, from the shores of Lake Michigan across flat Oklahoma plains and through the Arizona desert, Santa Monica awaits on the edge of the dazzling blue expanse. But Santa Monica is known as much for its shore scene as its shore; the promenade and the pier are popular destinations.

ORIENTATION

Route 66 enters Santa Monica from the east on **Santa Monica Boulevard.** Just north of the boulevard, the **Santa Monica Freeway (I-10)** runs west from L.A. to the **Pacific Coast Highway.** Pedestrian **Third Street Promenade** heads north from Broadway to **Wilshire Boulevard.** Much of Santa Monica is best seen by foot or bike.

VITAL STATS
Population: 87,000
Tourist Office: Santa Monica Visitors Center, 1920 Main St., 2nd fl., Ste. B (☎310-393-7593). Open daily 9am-6pm.
Library and Internet Access: Santa Monica Public Library, 601 Santa Monica Blvd. (☎310-458-8600). Open M-Th 10am-9pm, F-Sa 10am-5:30pm, Su 1-5pm.
Post Office: 1248 5th St. (☎310-576-6786), at Arizona Blvd. Open M-F 9am-6pm, Sa 9am-3pm. **Postal Code:** 90401.

ACCOMMODATIONS

Accommodations in Santa Monica range from cheap oceanfront hostels to expensive oceanfront hotels. The closer you stay to the beach, the more you dish out. Depending on the hotel, the tax may be 8.5% or 14%.

Los Angeles/Santa Monica Hostel, 1436 2nd St. (☎310-393-9913). Prime access to the beach and Santa Monica hot spots. Sponsors tours and activities. The hostel has video games, nightly movie showings, library, self-service kitchen, and a travel store. Check-in 2pm-midnight. Laundry. Wi-Fi. Dorms $39, members $37; private rooms from $89; 4-person family room $145. MC/V. ❷

Ocean Lodge Hotel, 1667 Ocean Ave. (☎310-451-4146). Spacious and clean rooms with fridges. Close enough to smell the ocean. Parking $10. Rooms $165-275. AmEx/MC/V. ❺

Pacific Sands Motel, 1515 Ocean Ave. (☎310-395-6133). At the epicenter of what's happening. Has modest rooms and a large heated pool. Free Wi-Fi. Rooms from $149-229. AmEx/D/MC/V. ❺

FOOD

Take advantage of the sunny weather and catch a meal outside. Giant, colorful table umbrellas sprout from sidewalk patios along the Third St. Promenade and Ocean Ave., punctuating Santa Monica's upscale eating scene. Menus nod to deep-pocketed health buffs, offering organic and vegetarian choices.

Barney's Beanery, 1351 3rd St. (☎310-656-5777). A convivial bar and restaurant with a colossal menu (the length of a broadsheet newspaper), a colossal choice of beers, and a colossal number of televisions (98 to be precise). Burgers range $8-15. Happy hour M-F 4-7pm. Open daily 9am-2am. AmEx/D/MC/V. ❷

Fritto Misto, 601 Colorado Ave. (☎310-458-2829), at 6th St. The friendly waitstaff urges you to create your own pasta (from $8). Bring your own bottle (corkage $2 per person). Vegetarian entrees $10-15. Open M-Th 11:30am-10pm, F-Sa 11:30am-10:30pm, Su 11:30am-9:30pm. AmEx/D/MC/V. ❸

Big Dean's "Muscle-In" Cafe, 1615 Ocean Front Walk (☎310-393-2666). You don't need to venture far from the beach for the "burger that made Santa Monica famous." Burgers $5.50-7.50. Chili $6. Happy hour M-F 4-7pm. Open M noon-sunset, Tu-F 11am-sunset, Sa-Su 10:30am-sunset. AmEx/D/MC/V. ❶

Father's Office, 1018 Montana Ave. (☎310-736-2224). Emulating the rich bar culture of Europe, this upscale gastropub serves craft beers and esoteric small producer wines. It's also home to the Office Burger ($12; ideally eaten with sweet potato fries for $6); a complex taste sensation more sophisticated than your average beef patty. Open M-Th 5pm-1am, F 4pm-2am, Sa noon-2am, Su noon-midnight. MC/V. ❸

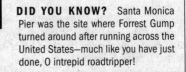

DID YOU KNOW? Santa Monica Pier was the site where Forrest Gump turned around after running across the United States—much like you have just done, O intrepid roadtripper!

SIGHTS

Filled with gawkers and hawkers, the area on and around the carnival pier is the hub of tourist activity. Farther inland, along Main St. and beyond, are galleries, design shops, and museums. Cars are prohibited on the ultra-popular Third St. Promenade, a three-block stretch of mosaic art tiles, fashionable stores, movie theaters, and lively restaurants.

THIRD STREET PROMENADE. The promenade truly heats up when the sun sets, the ocean breeze kicks in, and the ivy-lined mesh dinosaur sculptures spurt water into fountains. On Wednesday and Saturday mornings, the area becomes a farmers' market selling flowers and produce, with Saturdays featuring organic products. *(Between Broadway and Wilshire in downtown Santa Monica. Exit off 4th St. from I-10.)*

SANTA MONICA PIER. The pier is the heart of Santa Monica Beach and home to the carnival-esque **Pacific Park.** Adrenaline addicts over 4 ft. tall can twist and turn on the five-story West Coaster or soar 100 ft. above the ocean in the first solar-powered Ferris wheel. *(☎310-458-8900; http://santamonicapier.org. Pier open 24hr. Park open in summer M-Th and Su 11am-11pm, F-Sa 11am-12:30am; hours vary in winter.)*

THE END OF THE ROAD

Sink your toes into the sand, ride the Ferris wheel on the pier, take a picture next to the plaque on the grass at Ocean Ave. and Santa Monica Blvd., and dip your feet in the Pacific. You've finished "the Journey," the Mother Road, the Will Rogers Highway, the Main Street of America. Now that you've mastered Rte. 66, why stop the adventure? Replenish your stock of chocolate-covered coffee beans and head north for the Pacific Coast or meet up with the Southern Border in San Diego.

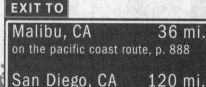

EXIT TO

Malibu, CA   36 mi.
on the pacific coast route, p. 888

San Diego, CA   120 mi.
on the southern border route, p. 887

oregon trail

TOP 5

1. Lick your chops and indulge in Kansas City **barbecue** (p. 603).
2. Ponder for a good long minute on the wonder of the **jackalope** in Douglas, Wyoming (p. 625).
3. Encounter **Carhenge,** in Alliance, Nebraska, and see your car in a whole new way (p. 620).
4. Take in the beauty of Oregon on your way to the **Ashland Shakespeare Festival** (p. 666).
5. Find inner peace at the end of your journey in the **Japanese gardens** of Portland (p. 669).

You learned about it in history class and maybe spent hours honing your bison-hunting, river-fording, and epitaph-writing skills on the computer game, but this is your chance to experience the real thing—and without dying of cholera or dysentery (hopefully). You will find all that is gorgeous about nature and all that is rewarding in small, hip towns along this 2000 mi. trek. So gather your oxen, pack your grain, and, above all, heed your inner Lewis and Clark.

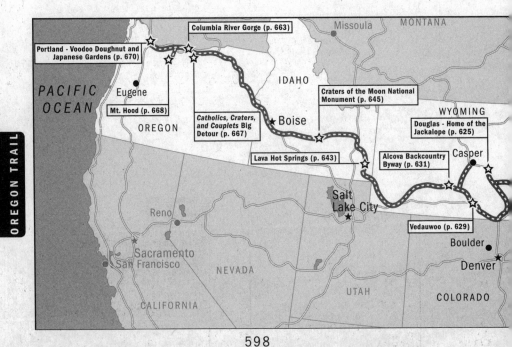

By the mid-1860s, over 300,000 pioneers had emigrated from the crowded East to the fertile valleys of the West Coast. While the original journey, a four to- six-month undertaking, offered settlers the opportunity to stake claims in new lands, it also posed great risks. One in 10 people traveling the trail died en route, many claimed by cholera. Wagons were full and space was limited; most travelers walked—barefoot. Today's travels are less treacherous, but reminders of pioneers past still line the way, including famous **Alcove Spring** (p. 611), **Chimney Rock** (p. 620), **Scotts Bluff** (p. 621), and, of course, **Independence Rock** (p. 633)—make it here by July 4, and you'll be in Oregon before the winter. The route also crosses the original **Pony Express** trails, pathways of daring young adventurers who embodied the roadtripping spirit. But the modern Oregon Trail offers far more than just historical sights. From sprawling **Kansas City** (p. 603) in the east, through laid-back **Boise** (p. 650), to funky **Portland** (p. 669) in the west, the cities that line the road are varied and vibrant. Many revel in their Wild West heritage; **Douglas, Wyoming** (p. 625) bills itself as the **"Jackalope Capital of the World,"** while **Cheyenne** (p. 626) celebrates **Frontier Days** with rodeos, parades, and square dances each July. Others take full advantage of their natural resources; **Hood River, Oregon** (p. 664) offers kiteboarding, **Enterprise** and **Joseph, Oregon** (p. 657) has mountain biking opportunities aplenty, and in **Lava Hot Springs, Idaho** (p. 642) you can soak away that in-the-car ache. Like the towns along the way, the Oregon Trail's landscape is just about as varied as it gets. From the sweeping prairies of Kansas and Nebraska, you'll climb into the towering Rocky Mountains of southern Wyoming—don't miss the **Scenic Alcova Backcountry Byway** (p. 630). Pass through the spectacularly bizarre rock formations of **Craters of the Moon National Monument** (p. 645) in Idaho, and follow the beautiful **Columbia River Gorge** (p. 662) along the waterfalls that line the **Historic Columbia River Highway** (p. 626).

The Oregon Trail isn't a big-city route by any stretch of the imagination, so don't expect mega-malls or cosmopolitan downtowns. Instead, prepare for the tiny hamlets

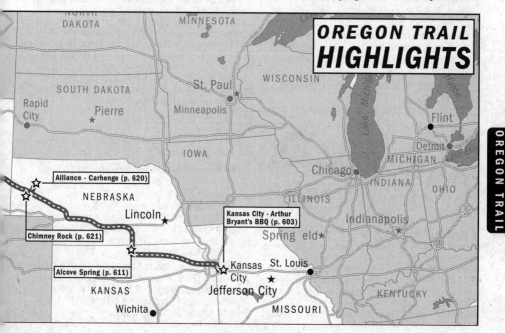

OREGON TRAIL HIGHLIGHTS

Alliance - Carhenge (p. 620)

Kansas City - Arthur Bryant's BBQ (p. 603)

Chimney Rock (p. 621)

Alcove Spring (p. 611)

that line the rural highways of the Great Plains and Rocky Mountains—places where motel rooms and ice-cream cones are cheap, owners are friendly, stoplights are few, and cows are plentiful. Fortunately, even the tiniest towns aren't completely devoid of attractions, and the open road between them has an appeal of its own. And, of course, near Alliance, Nebraska, you'll pass by what is perhaps the epitome of all roadtrip culture—delightfully wacky **Carhenge** (p. 620), modeled after England's famous Stonehenge but constructed entirely out of old automobiles.

It's a long, arduous road, but the views along the way are unparalleled: far better than what you'll find in any computer game or textbook. Get going. Oregon awaits!

ROUTE STATS

Miles: c. 2000

Route: Independence, MO to Oregon City, OR.

States: 7; Missouri, Kansas, Nebraska, Wyoming, Idaho, Washington, and Oregon.

Driving Time: At least 9 days; ideally, allow 2-3 weeks to appreciate the scenic drives and historic landmarks of the trail.

When To Go: Pioneers started in mid-spring. You, however, benefit from paved roads, so you could set off almost any time you want. Heed your forerunners; avoid the mountains in winter, when snow makes some stretches impassible. Watch for late-summer tornadoes in the plains.

Crossroads: National Road in Independence, MO (p. 392).

The Show - Me State
MISSOURI
Welcomes You!

INDEPENDENCE ☎816

Every authentic Oregon Trail trip begins in Independence, hometown of Harry S. Truman. During the era of westward expansion, this city stood on the edge of a vast wilderness, truly the last way station for pioneers. Modernized antebellum estates and 100-year-old businesses allow this suburb to remain a

trailhead to the West. Independence revels in its varied history, mixing the romantic frontier spirit of the 19th century with the small-town charm of the early 20th. Visitors can relax at the local soda fountain sipping on phosphates while watching mule-drawn carts pass through the square.

VITAL STATS

Population: 115,000

Tourist Office: Tourist Information Center and Truman Home Ticket Center, 223 N. Main St. (☎816-254-9929), at Main St. and Truman Rd. Open M-F 8:30am-5pm.

Library and Internet Access: Mid-Continent Public Library, South Independence Branch, 13700 E. 35th St. (☎816-461-2050). Open M-Th 9am-9pm, F 9am-6pm, Sa 9am-5pm.

Post Office: 301 W. Lexington Ave. (☎816-521-3608). Open M-F 8am-5pm, Sa 8am-noon. **Postal Code:** 64050.

■ ORIENTATION

Downtown Independence remains the practical center of the city. **Exit 12** from **I-70** leads to **Noland Road,** a busy strip of gas stations and fast-food joints. Follow this road for about three miles, then go left onto **Walnut Street.** A right onto either **Main** or **Liberty Street** will lead to the central square formed by Liberty, Lexington, Main, and Maple St. All four of these streets are lined with free parking and surround the Jackson County Courthouse, the historic center of Independence.

⌂ ACCOMMODATIONS

Hotels are cheaper and easier to find just outside of Independence.

The Serendipity Bed and Breakfast, 116 Pleasant Ave. (☎800-203-4299 or 816-833-4719; www.bbhost.com/serendipitybb). 3 blocks west of Liberty St. Victorian-era hospitality and candlelit breakfasts. Spend your afternoon relaxing amid the garden overrun by concrete statues and gazing balls. Check-in 4-9pm. Singles $45-80; doubles $90. MC/V. ❸

American Inn, Woods Chapel Rd. (☎816-228-1080). Off Exit 18 from I-70. 2nd location at 4141 S. Noland Rd. (☎816-373-8300). Rooms are clean and well maintained. Singles $40-50. AmEx/D/MC/V. ❷

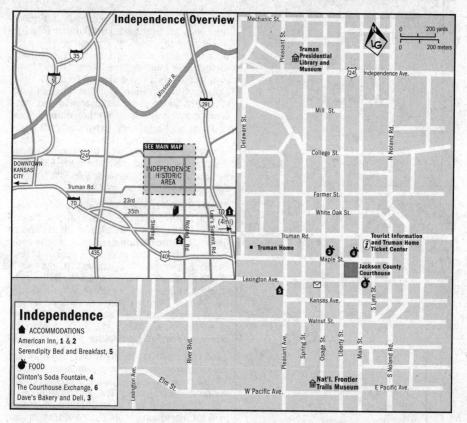

Independence Overview

Mechanic St.

Truman Presidential Library and Museum

Independence Ave.

Mill St.

College St.

Farmer St.

White Oak St.

Truman Rd.

■ Truman Home

Maple St.

Tourist Information and Truman Home Ticket Center

Jackson County Courthouse

Lexington Ave.

Kansas Ave.

Walnut St.

Nat'l. Frontier Trails Museum

W Pacific Ave.

E Pacific Ave.

DOWNTOWN KANSAS CITY

Truman Rd.

23rd

35th

TO (4mi)

SEE MAIN MAP

INDEPENDENCE HISTORIC AREA

Missouri R.

0   200 yards
0   200 meters

Independence

🏠 ACCOMMODATIONS
American Inn, **1** & **2**
Serendipity Bed and Breakfast, **5**

🍴 FOOD
Clinton's Soda Fountain, **4**
The Courthouse Exchange, **6**
Dave's Bakery and Deli, **3**

🍴 FOOD

The Courthouse Exchange, 113 Lexington Ave. (☎816-252-0344). Great home-cooked food served in the basement of a former pioneer trading post. The adventurous can begin with an order of gizzards and livers ($5.30) and finish with one of the Exchange's signature "Three Trails Burgers;" the Oregon comes with Swiss cheese, sour cream, and mushrooms ($8). Open M-Th 11am-9pm, F-Sa 11am-10pm. AmEx/D/MC/V. ❷

Clinton's Soda Fountain, 100 Maple St. (☎816-833-2046). Located right in Independence Sq., Clinton's (then a drug store) provided a teenage Harry Truman with his 1st job and now serves double duty as a historic site. Order a soup or sandwich for under $6. The real attractions are the soda-fountain phosphates ($1.50-2) and Harry's Favorite ($3.70), a butterscotch sundae with chocolate ice cream. Open M-F 8:30am-6pm, Sa 10am-6pm. D/MC/V. ❶

Dave's Bakery and Deli, 214 Maple St. (☎816-461-0756). A block west of Independence Sq. The deli's retro 50s theme feels more than slightly incongruous with historic downtown Independence, but the home-baked pastries and bread are still delicious. Doughnuts for $1.50. Freshly made deli sandwiches for $3.50. Open M-F 6am-5pm, Sa 7am-3pm. MC/V. ❶

👁 SIGHTS

TRUMAN PRESIDENTIAL LIBRARY AND MUSEUM. Travelers who just haven't had

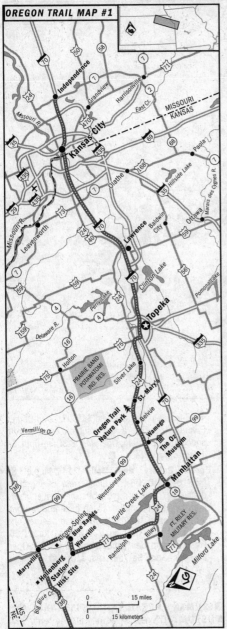

OREGON TRAIL MAP #1

OREGON TRAIL

enough Truman by this point should make their way to the extensive Truman Library. The graves of President Truman and his wife may be found in the courtyard. Attractions include the famous "The Buck Stops Here" sign as well as a recreation of Truman's Oval Office, with narration from the man himself. A lengthy video provides historical and contemporary perspectives on the controversies of Truman's presidency, particularly his decision to drop the atomic bomb. *(500 US 24. Head north up Liberty St., turn left at US 24, and follow the signs into the museum's parking lot. ☎816-833-1225; www.trumanlibrary.org. Open M-Sa 9am-5pm, Su noon-5pm. $8, ages 6-15 $3, seniors $7.)*

TRUMAN HOME. Back up Main St. at the corner of Truman Rd., the Truman Home Ticket Center houses the Tourist Information Center. Tours of Truman's home depart from the center following a video acknowledging that "few memorable events took place at 219 Delaware." While the tour allows for a nice walk through one of Independence's Victorian neighborhoods, real Truman enthusiasts will prefer his presidential library and museum. *(219 Delaware St. ☎816-254-9929. Tours from Labor Day to Memorial Day every 15min. Tu-Su 9am-4:45pm. $4.)*

JACKSON COUNTY COURTHOUSE. In the center of downtown stands the Jackson County Courthouse where a young Harry Truman worked as a judge. The building houses offices now, but its statue-filled courtyard is still an interesting stop. *(Main and Lexington St. ☎816-881-4431.)*

NATIONAL FRONTIER TRAILS MUSEUM. The museum is filled with exhibits and a few genuine artifacts from the days of manifest destiny. An interactive exhibit forces visitors to choose between coffee and ammunition while packing their wagon. Other attractions include a covered wagon, equipment used on the trail, and the original diaries and letters of the westward bound. *(318 W. Pacific St. ☎816-325-7575; www.frontiertrailsmuseum.org. Open M-Sa 9am-4:30pm, Su 12:30-4:30pm. $5, ages 6-17 $3.)*

PIONEER TRAILS ADVENTURES. These mule-drawn wagon rides provide a nice overview of downtown Independence and the surrounding area while the Wrangler, an in-character driver and storyteller, regales visitors with stories of the outlaw Frank James and Harry Truman's first job. *(Start on sidewalk outside of tourist center.* ☎*816-456-4991 or 254-2466; www.pioneertrailsadventures.com. $7-25.)*

⚐ THE ROAD TO KANSAS CITY: 13 MI.

From downtown Independence, return to **Noland Road** via **Walnut Street** and drive 3 mi. south. Ramps onto **I-70** are very well marked. I-70 passes through the northern part of Kansas City, close to downtown. **Exit 3A** feeds onto **The Paseo,** which is a large road parallel to, and a bit east of, **Main Street.**

KANSAS CITY   ☎816

With boulevards and fountains rivaling those of Paris and Rome, Kansas City looks and acts more European than one might expect from the "Barbecue Capital of the World." When Prohibition stifled the rest of the country's fun in the 1920s, Mayor Tom Pendergast used his party machinery to keep the good times rolling. The Kansas City of today maintains its blues-and-jazz reputation in a metropolis spanning two states: the highly suburbanized town in Kansas (KCKS) and the quicker-paced commercial metropolis in Missouri (KCMO).

VITAL STATS
Population: 150,000
Tourist Offices: Convention and Visitors Bureau of Greater Kansas City, 1100 Main St., Ste. 2200 (☎816-221-5242 or 800-767-7700; www.visitkc. com), on the 22nd fl. of the City Center Sq. Bldg. Open M-F 8:30am-5pm. **Missouri Tourist Information Center,** 4010 Blue Ridge Cutoff (☎816-889-3330 or 800-877-1234). Follow signs from Exit 9 off I-70. Open daily 8am-5pm.
Library and Internet Access: Kansas City Public Library, 14 10th St. (☎816-701-3414). Free. Open M-W 9am-9pm, Th 9am-6pm, F 9am-5pm, Sa 10am-5pm, Su 1-5pm.
Post Office: 315 W. Pershing Rd. (☎816-374-9100). Open M-F 8am-8pm, Sa 8:30am-3:30pm. **Postal Code:** 64108.

⊞ ORIENTATION

Though Kansas City is laid out in a relatively simple grid, car travel can be frustrating due to the tangle of one-way streets and turn-only lanes. East-west streets are numbered, with numbers increasing as one travels south. **Main Street,** which runs north-south and divides the city, is in fact two one-way streets located a block apart from each other. Traffic and the proximity of many sites to one another make parking and walking a viable option in the area around Crown Center as well as the Westport neighborhood. Besides, you can't dance in the fountains if you're stuck in traffic.

⚑ ACCOMMODATIONS

The least expensive lodgings lie near the interstates, especially **I-70,** and toward Independence and Blue Springs. Downtown hotels tend to be on the pricey side.

American Inn, 4141 S. Noland Rd. (☎816-373-8300; www.americaninn.com), off I-70 at Exit 12. Dominates the KC budget-motel market with locations throughout the city. The rooms are large and come with all the trimmings: A/C, cable TV, and access to the outdoor pool. Singles and doubles from $42. AmEx/MC/V. ❷

Lake Jacomo, (☎816-795-8200), 22 mi. southeast of downtown. From I-70, take Rte. 291 S. to Colbern Rd, go left (east) on Colbern Rd., and head 2 mi. down to Beach Rd. Lots of water activities, 33 forested campsites, and a marina. No swimming. 21+. Sites $12, with electricity $17, with electricity and water $18. Cash only. ❶

▧ FOOD

Kansas City's specialty is its unusually tangy barbecue. The **Westport** area, at Westport Rd. and Broadway St. just south of 40th St., has an array of cafes. Ethnic eateries cluster along **39th Street,** just east of the state line. The **City Market** area has Asian grocery stores and inexpensive open-air produce markets at the intersection of Fifth and Walnut St. (Open M-F and Su 9am-4pm, Sa 6am-4pm.)

▨ **Arthur Bryant's,** 1727 Brooklyn Ave. (☎816-231-1123). Not for the faint of heart, Arthur Bryant's serves up the tangiest barbecue sandwiches ($8) around. The no-frills approach is refreshing and authentic. Watch the cooks pile on the meat while you stand in line. Open M-Th 10am-9:30pm, F-Sa 10am-10pm, Su 11am-8:30pm. AmEx/D/MC/V. ❷

▨ **Oklahoma Joe's,** 3002 W. 47th Ave. (☎913-722-3366). Oklahoma Joe's began in a gas station

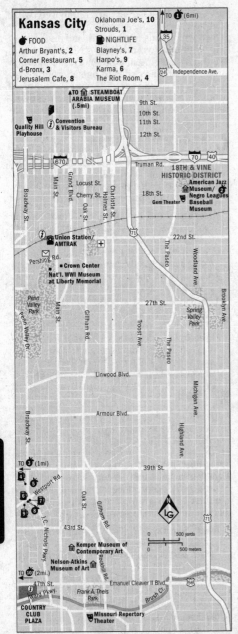

Kansas City

🍴 FOOD
Arthur Bryant's, **2**
Corner Restaurant, **5**
d-Bronx, **3**
Jerusalem Cafe, **8**

Oklahoma Joe's, **10**
Strouds, **1**

🍷 NIGHTLIFE
Blayney's, **7**
Harpo's, **9**
Karma, **6**
The Riot Room, **4**

and is probably the only place where you can enjoy a delicious barbecue sandwich ($5) while you pump gas. Cheaper than most barbecue around here. Open M-Th 11am-8:30pm, F-Sa 11am-9:30pm. MC/V. ❶

d-Bronx, 3904 Bell St. (☎816-531-0550), at 39th St. With pizza slices ($2.50) and an atmosphere straight out of New York, d-Bronx serves over 35 kinds of subs (half $4-6, whole $8-12), with powdered-sugar brownies ($1.50) for dessert. Open M-W 10:30am-9pm, Th 10:30am-10pm, F-Sa 10:30am-11pm. AmEx/D/MC/V. ❸

Jerusalem Cafe, 431 Westport Rd. (☎816-756-2770). A Mediterranean place in the heart of Westport, Jerusalem is an oasis for vegetarians in Kansas City. Patrons enjoy unusual appetizers like flaming cheese ($4.50) while playing backgammon and waiting for their pita sandwiches ($6-7). Open M-Sa 11am-10pm, Su noon-8pm. AmEx/D/MC/V. ❷

Strouds, 5410 NE Oak Ridge Dr. (☎816-454-9600). Situated on a lake and renowned for fried catfish ($15) and 2hr. waits for tables. On 18-acre grounds overlooking a pond. Entrees $15-25. Open M-Th 5-9:30pm, F 11am-10:30pm, Sa 11am-9:30pm, Su 2-10:30pm. AmEx/MC/V. ❹

👁 SIGHTS

STEAMBOAT ARABIA MUSEUM. A massive working paddle wheel greets visitors at the entrance to the largest intact collection of antebellum artifacts in the world. Recovered from the wreckage of a Missouri River steamboat, the pieces range from delicate china and glassware to thousands of shoes to pickles perfectly preserved in their original jars. Visitors can even sample French perfume replicated from a bottle found on board—it's cool, guys wore it back then, too. (400 Grand Blvd., next to the City Market. ☎816-471-4030; www.1856.com. Open M-Sa 10am-5:30pm, Su noon-5pm. $12.50, ages 4-12 $4.75, seniors $11.50.)

NATIONAL WORLD WAR I MUSEUM AT LIBERTY MEMORIAL. Adorned with modernist angles and surrounded by sphinxes, the Liberty Memorial dominates the hillside overlooking Union Station. Erected in 1926, the memorial pays tribute to America's service in WWI. The museum attempts to frame the war as a tragedy from all sides and includes several life-size dioramas depicting the horrors of trench warfare. The exhibits are filled with thousands of artifacts, including uniforms, artillery pieces, and a French tank. A film runs regularly explaining the causes of WWI and how nationalists "fought frantically for freedom" and the monarchs of Europe didn't see that they were "destined for disaster." An elevator ride to the top of the memorial provides an unbeatable view of the city. (*100 W. 26th St.* ☎ *816-784-1918; www.libertymemorialmuseum.com. Open Tu-Su 10am-5pm. $10, ages 6-11 $5.*)

COUNTRY CLUB PLAZA. The most "European-influenced" section of Kansas City is undoubtedly the Country Club Plaza, or just "the Plaza," the oldest and perhaps most picturesque shopping center in the US. Modeled after the architecture of Sevilla, Spain, the Plaza boasts fountains, sculptures, hand-painted tiles, gargoyles, luxury chain stores, an abundance of restaurants, and latte-sipping yuppies. The Plaza is also famous for its Christmas lights, lit annually on Thanksgiving eve. (*Along 47th St., between Main and Madison St. Free concerts May-Sept. Th 5-8pm, Sa-Su 2-5pm.*)

NELSON-ATKINS MUSEUM OF ART. The architecture alone is worth the visit, but tucked away in this marble-columned beauty is one of the best East Asian art collections in the world as well as a sculpture park with 13 pieces by Henry Moore. The Bloch Building houses more modern pieces, including photographs by Dorothea Lang and Ansel Adams. Live jazz plays on Friday 5:30-8:30pm inside the Rozzelle Court Restaurant. (*4525 Oak St., 3 blocks northeast of the Country Club Plaza.* ☎ *816-561-4000; www.nelson-atkins.org. Open Tu-Th 10am-4pm, F 10am-9pm, Sa 10am-5pm, Su noon-5pm. Free walking tours Sa 11am-2pm, Su 1:30-3pm.*)

KEMPER MUSEUM OF CONTEMPORARY ART. The Kemper Museum's high-ceilinged, sterile white galleries host rotating exhibitions of contemporary art. Visitors will either find themselves enraptured by the museum's often irreverant, always provocative works or infuriated by the death of high art. Their reactions to the enormous spiders that grace the museum's exterior should give them a pretty good idea of how they'll find the inside. (*4420 Warwick Blvd., off Main St., just north of the Country Club Plaza.* ☎ *816-753-5784; www.kemperart.org. Open Tu-Th 10am-4pm, F-Sa 10am-9pm, Su 11am-5pm. Free.*)

18TH AND VINE HISTORIC DISTRICT. During the day, it's difficult to imagine that the meek streets around 18th and Vine once throbbed with the rhythms of the jazz greats who played there. **The American Jazz Museum** tries to bring the music back with listening stations, neon dance-hall signs, and paraphernalia ranging from Ella Fitzgerald's eyeglasses to Louis Armstrong's lip salve. (*1616 E. 18th St.* ☎ *816-474-8463; www.americanjazzmuseum.com. Open Tu-Sa 9am-6pm, Su noon-6pm. $7, under 12 $3.*) The same building also houses the **Negro Leagues Baseball Museum.** Though less interactive than the jazz museum, the baseball museum uses artifacts and exhibits to celebrate the accomplishments of black athletes marginalized by white society. (*1616 E.18th St.* ☎ *816-474-8453; www.nlbm.com. Open Tu-Sa 9am-6pm, Su noon-6pm. $7, under 12 $3; both museums $9/5.*)

UNION STATION AND CROWN CENTER. In a city known for its spectacular fountains, the ▧**Bloch fountain** in front of **Union Station** is one of the finest. The station itself, built in 1914, is the second-largest train station in North America. The beautiful architecture is somewhat marred by the generic shops and restaurants that now fill the interior. (*30 W. Pershing Rd. Open daily 6am-midnight.*) It is linked by a skywalk to the elaborate **Crown Center,** an upscale shopping center. On the third floor of the Crown Center is the **Hallmark Visitors Center,** which chronicles the history and production of the famous greeting cards. Be sure to get a free bow from the bow-making machine and try not to disturb the artist at work. (*2405 Grand Ave.* ☎ *816-274-3613; www.hallmarkvisitorscenter. com. Open M-F 9am-5pm, Sa 9:30am-4:30pm. Free.*) The Hallmark Visitors Center is also home to the children's **Coterie Theatre,** which features games, a maze, and theater technology demonstrations. (☎ *816-474-6785. $9, under 18 $7.*)

ICE TERRACE. During the winter, the Ice Terrace is Kansas City's only public outdoor ice-skating rink. (☎ *816-274-8412. Open Nov.-Dec. M-Th and Su 10am-9pm, F-Sa 10am-11pm; Jan.-Mar. daily 10am-9pm. Skate rental $2.50.*)

♫ ENTERTAINMENT

JAZZ

The days of Count Basie and Charlie Parker might be over, but Kansas City's jazz scene still finds excuses to keep the music going late into the night. The restored **Gem Theater,** 1615 E. 18th St., stages old-time blues and jazz. From October to April, the Jammin' at the Gem concert series celebrates talent past and present. (☎816-474-6262. Box office open M-F 10am-4pm. Tickets from $30.) Across the street, the **Blue Room,** 1600 E. 18th St., cooks four nights per week with some of the smoothest local acts in town. (☎816-474-2929. Cover F-Sa $5. Open M and Th 5-11pm, F 5pm-1am, Sa 7pm-1am.)

SPORTS

Sports fans stampede into Arrowhead Stadium, at I-70 and Blue Ridge Cutoff, home to football's **Chiefs** (☎816-920-9400 or 800-676-5488; tickets $51-70) and soccer's **Wizards** (☎816-920-9300; tickets $12-17). Next door, Kauffman Stadium houses the **Royals,** Kansas City's baseball team. (☎816-921-8000 or 800-676-9257. Tickets $5-22.)

THEATER

From September to May, the **Missouri Repertory Theatre,** on the campus of the University of Missouri at Kansas City, at 50th and Oak St., stages American classics. (☎816-235-2700; www.missourirep.org. Tickets $15-50.) **Quality Hill Playhouse,** 303 W. 10th St., produces off-Broadway plays and revues from September to June. The box office is located at 912 Baltimore Ave., Ste. 200. (☎816-421-1700. Box office open M-F 9am-5pm. Tickets $20-22.) From late June to mid-July, the **Heart of America Shakespeare Festival,** in Southmoreland Park, at 47th and Oak St., puts on free shows. (☎816-531-7728; www.kcshakes.org.)

☺ NIGHTLIFE

For something besides jazz, bars and nightclubs of all stripes cluster in **Westport.**

Blayney's, 415 Westport Rd. (☎816-561-3747). A Westport standby for 35 years. Caters mostly to the over-30 crowd with its speakeasy atmosphere and live blues. Cover $2-6. Open Tu-Th 6pm-1:30am, F-Sa 4pm-3am. AmEx/MC/V.

The Riot Room, 4048 Broadway St. (☎816-442-8177). A haven for local musicians and art students who come for the Kaisermeisters (root-beer schnapps mixed with Jägermeister) and stay for the live music. Occasional ska and rockabilly acts mix up the normal indie and punk lineup. Rock-band tournaments (every M) and the occasional burlesque show keep the atmosphere fun. Open M-Sa 5pm-3am. MC/V.

Karma, 504 Westport Rd. (☎816-531-4111). 2-for-1 specials chase the Mondays away while guest DJs turn this rock-and-roll bar into an all-out dance party. Make time to chat up the super-friendly bartenders and try one of their trademark Porn Stars (Bacardi Peach Red, X-rated liqueur, cranberry, and pineapple). Open-air view of sidewalk when warm. Open M-Sa 8pm-3am. MC/V.

⬆ THE ROAD TO LAWRENCE: 40 MI.

The easiest way to leave Kansas City is to take **Broadway Street** north. Right before reaching the Missouri River, take the ramp to **I-70 West.** The road on the way to Lawrence is an uninspiring stretch of I-70 about 25 mi. long. Tollbooths are common, so keep quarters ready. Lawrence can be reached by either **Exit 202** or **204** off **I-70.** Exit 202 provides the more direct approach. Follow the exit through the tolls and straight through the intersection with **Second Street,** as the exit ramp becomes **McDonald Road.** Continue south until it intersects with **Sixth Street.** Turn left, and drive east to **Massachusetts Street.**

The Sunflower State
KANSAS
Welcomes You!

LAWRENCE   ☎785

Forty miles from Kansas City, Lawrence was founded in 1854 by anti-slavery advocates to ensure that Kansas became a free state. Now home to the flagship University of Kansas (KU), Lawrence is a college town that doesn't die when the students leave, fully equipped with excellent restaurants and a happening music scene.

VITAL STATS

Population: 80,000

Tourist Office: Lawrence Visitors Center, 402 N. 2nd St. (☎785-865-4499 or 888-529-5267; www.visitlawrence.com), at Locust St. Open M-Sa 8:30am-5:30pm, Su 1-5pm. Free Wi-Fi.

Library and Internet Access: Lawrence Public Library, 707 Vermont St. (☎785-843-3833; www. lawrencepubliclibrary.org). Free. Open M-F 9am-9pm, Sa 9am-6pm, Su 2-6pm.

Post Office: 645 Vermont St. (☎785-843-1681). Open M-F 8am-5:30pm, Sa 9am-noon. **Postal Code:** 66045.

ORIENTATION

Almost everything of interest is found along **Massachusetts Street** or on parallel **Vermont** and **New Hampshire Streets.** Numbered streets run east-west. Vermont and New Hampshire St. are full of free 2hr. parking lots.

ACCOMMODATIONS

Inexpensive motels are hard to come by in Lawrence. The best place to look is near Iowa and Sixth St., just west of the KU campus.

The Halcyon House Bed and Breakfast, 1000 Ohio St. (☎785-841-0314). Close to local attractions and provides good parking. The rooms are a little small but very comfortable, and the furnishings make up for the lack of space. Private bath available. Rooms $49. AmEx/MC/V. ❷

The Virginia Inn, 2903 W. 6th St. (☎785-843-6611). Right downtown, the inn offers large rooms with sparkling bathrooms and flatscreen TVs. What more could you ask for? Singles $49; doubles $59. AmEx/D/MC/V. ❷

The Eldridge Hotel, 701 Massachusetts St. (☎800-527-0909). The Eldridge combines violent history and modern luxury. The historic building and Lawrence landmark has burned down twice, once at the hand of William Quantrill and his raiders. Even if you aren't staying the night, its worth a stop. Staff and guests alike have reported a ghost in Room 506. Rooms $145-250. ❺

FOOD

Downtown Lawrence features both traditional barbecue joints and health-conscious venues to sate all palates.

The Free State Brewing Company, 636 Massachusetts St. (☎785-843-4555; www.freestatebrewing.com). The 1st legal brewery in Kansas; brews over 50 beers annually and always has at least 5 on tap. The turkey bacon focaccia sandwich ($6.50) goes well with a draft. Pasta $8-10. M $1.25 beer. Open M-Sa 11am-midnight, Su noon-11pm. AmEx/D/MC/V. ❷

Jefferson's, 743 Massachusetts St. (☎785-832-2000). A sports bar for the "bro's" with a modicum of class and local color. Jefferson's promotes "Peace, Love, and Hotwings" along with its entrees, all under $7. Massive burgers, including the Jefferson Burger (bacon, cheese, and barbecue sauce; $6.50), satisfy even the hungriest KU student. 1000s of decorated dollar bills line the walls; if you bring a marker, you too can deface your own piece of government property. Open M-W 11am-10pm, Th-Sa 11am-11pm, Su noon-10pm. AmEx/D/MC/V. ❶

Ingredient, 947 Massachusetts St. (☎785-832-0100; www.ingredientrestaurant.com). Soups and pizzas for $7-10; the main attraction is the build-your-own-salad ($8), which lets you pick from an array of vegetables, meats, and cheeses, including Gouda and hearts of palm. Open daily 11am-9pm. AmEx/D/MC/V. ❷

SIGHTS

Maps are available at the visitors center for two tours: **Quantrill's Raid** is a 1hr. driving tour that traces the events leading up to the slaughter of over 200 men by pro-slavery forces on August 21, 1863. **House Styles of Old West Lawrence** provides a look at 19th-century homes. There are walking (45min.) and driving (25min.) variations.

UNIVERSITY OF KANSAS WATKINS COMMUNITY MUSEUM OF HISTORY. The Wild West was in full swing in Lawrence during the "Bleeding Kansas" days, giving the city quite a bit of fascinating history. The Museum of History features several floors of Lawrence lore, including displays on Lawrence natives Langston Hughes and James Naismith (the inventor of basketball), as well as a fully-preserved Victorian-era playhouse. (*1047 Massachusetts St. ☎785-841-4109; www.watkinsmuseum. org. Open Tu-W 10am-6pm, Th 10am-9pm, F 10am-5pm, Sa 10am-4pm. Suggested donation $3.*)

SPENCER MUSEUM OF ART. The museum houses a collection of 18th- and 19th-century European art. The contemporary gallery experiments with different ways of presenting art, but the clutter may ruin the effect. *(1301 Mississippi St. ☎ 785-864-4710. Open Tu-W and F-Sa 10am-5pm, Th 10am-9pm, Su noon-5pm. Free.)*

KU NATURAL HISTORY MUSEUM. Visitors can see the stuffed remains of Comanche, the sole survivor of Custer's Last Stand. *(1345 Jayhawk Blvd. ☎ 785-864-4540. Open M-Sa 9am-5pm, Su noon-5pm. $5, ages 6-18 and seniors $3.)*

▣ NIGHTLIFE

Lawrence's rough-and-tumble days might be over, but that doesn't mean the town has forgotten how to have a good time. Almost every bar in Lawrence is also a venue, which keeps students and townies rocking late.

▨ **The Bottleneck,** 737 New Hampshire St. (☎ 785-841-5483). The professional sound engineers at The Bottleneck make sure that the music always sounds great. Local acts jam throughout the week while big-name touring artists bring the noise on weekends. Locals love 80s Dance Night on Th. Nightly drink specials. Cover $2-10. Open daily 3pm-2am. AmEx/MC/V.

Jazzhaus, 926 Massachusetts St. (☎ 913-749-3320). Live music and a neighborhood bar atmosphere keep this joint hoppin. No live music Tu. Cover after 9pm M and W-Su $2-8, Tu $1.50. Open daily 4pm-2am.

The Jackpot Saloon, 943 Massachusetts St. (☎ 785-832-1085). Live acts every night in a fun, sociable atmosphere. KU students and townies alike dig their signature North Lawrence Iced Tea (Hamm's on ice with lime). Shows daily. 18+. Open daily 4pm-2am. Cash only.

◥ THE ROAD TO TOPEKA: 27 MI.

Tollbooths are in effect all along **I-70,** so it's best to take **Sixth Street (US 40 West)** out of town. 22 mi. from Lawrence, exit to stay on US 40; it joins **Route 4** and I-70 toward Topeka.

TOPEKA ☎ 785

To the casual observer, Topeka might appear to be a vast wasteland of strip malls and fast-food chains. This is not entirely inaccurate.

Nevertheless, some diamonds in the rough may be found nestled amongst the billboards and parking lots. Closer to downtown, several historic sites commemorate the state's role in the abolition and civil-rights movements.

◢ ORIENTATION

Much of Topeka is a rough grid of four-lane roads—it's definitely a driver's city. **Topeka Boulevard** is the city's major north-south artery and is lined with numerous restaurants and hotels. **Gage Boulevard,** about 2 mi. west, is lined on both sides with gas stations and fast food. Though many east-west streets end in residential cul-de-sacs, **10th Avenue** to the north and **29th Street** to the south both span the breadth of the city.

VITAL STATS
Population: 122,000
Tourist Office: Topeka Convention and Visitors Bureau, 1275 Topeka Blvd. (☎ 800-235-1030; www.topekacvb.com). Open M-F 9am-5pm.
Library and Internet Access: Topeka and Shawnee County Public Library, 1515 10th Ave. (☎ 785-580-4400; www.tscpl.org), at the corner of Washburn Ave. Free. Open M-F 9am-9pm, Sa 9am-6pm, Su noon-9pm.
Post Office: 424 S. Kansas Ave. (☎ 785-295-9178). Open M-F 8am-5pm, Sa 9am-noon. **Postal Code:** 66603.

▛ ACCOMMODATIONS

Hotels cluster near the highway exits, but some of the nicest and least expensive accommodations are closer to downtown.

The Plaza Inn Hotel, 3810 Topeka Blvd. (☎ 785-266-4591). Located just south of 37th St. Though it looks like every other budget hotel on the outside, the rooms are exceptionally spacious, and the attached lounge might be your best bet for nightlife in Topeka. Singles $39; doubles $47. MC/V. ❷

Lake Shawnee Campground, 3435 E. Edge Rd. (☎ 785-267-1156). Follow 29th St. east to the edge of Topeka, then go south on Croco Rd.; E. Ridge Rd. is a short distance on the right. Road-weary travelers tired of the standard motel can spend the night toasting marshmallows and walk-

OREGON TRAIL

ing by the water's edge. The tent sites are kind of tricky to find, so grab a map from the registration office. Showers. From mid-Apr. to mid-Oct. tent sites $18; RV sites $20. From mid-Oct. to mid-Apr. Tentsites $14; RV sites $15. MC/V. ❶

FOOD

Topeka is home to several fine restaurants, though finding them can be a bit of challenge; like many things in this city, they are scattered across countless strip malls.

The Blind Tiger Brewery and Restaurant, 417 37th St. (☎785-267-2739; www.blindtiger.com), east of Topeka Blvd. Named for the stuffed tigers that once advertised Prohibition-era speakeasies. The Prohibition Float ($3), is made with root beer brewed in the building. Appetizers from $6. Pasta from $11. Grill entrees from $8. Restaurant open M-Th and Su 11am-9pm, F-Sa 11am-10pm. Lounge open M-Th and Su 11am-1am, F-Sa 11am-2am. AmEx/D/MC/V. ❷

Kiku Japanese Steak House, 5331 22nd Pl. (☎785-272-6633). In the Fairlawn Plaza. Food preparation is a spectacle at Kiku where Hibachi-style chefs cook traditional Japanese steak ($15-20) right at your table. Appetizers $3-10. Entrees $12-22. Reservations recommended. Open M-W 4-9:30pm, Th-Su 11:30am-1:30pm, and 4-9:30pm. AmEx/MC/V. ❹

SIGHTS

Points of interest are scattered throughout the city; expect to do a lot of driving.

STATE CAPITOL. In the center of Topeka is the city's architectural and political high point, the beautiful capitol building. *(At the corner of 10th Ave. and Jackson St. ☎785-296-3966. Tours M-F every hr. 8am-3pm, except noon. Free.)*

BROWN V. BOARD NATIONAL HISTORIC SITE. A memorial to the groundbreaking Supreme Court decision that ruled school segregation unconstitutional. Situated inside a former elementary school, the museum attempts to explain the significance of *Brown v. Board of Education* in the context of not just the American civil-rights movement but struggles for equality all over the world. The moving but potentially upsetting Hall of Courage exhibit places visitors in a narrow corri-

dor while scenes of jeering whites and effigy lynchings play all around them set to George Wallace's famous proclamation to defend segregation. *(At the intersection of Monroe and 15th St. Follow 10th Ave. to Topeka Blvd. and proceed south to 15th St. ☎785-354-4273. Open daily 9am-5pm. Free.)*

TOPEKA ZOOLOGICAL PARK. In addition to lions, giraffes, and other standard attractions, the zoo has an indoor rainforest where visitors can experience exotic bird droppings firsthand. *(635 Gage Blvd. ☎785-368-9143. Open daily 10am-5pm. $4.50, ages 3-12 $3, seniors $3.50.)*

THE ROAD TO ST. MARYS: 28 MI.

To leave the city, follow **Topeka Boulevard** north through downtown and over the Kansas River to **US 24.** As you make your way across the Kansas prairie, be prepared for sudden speed drops; the limit swings between 70 and 20 mph. This stretch of road stays close to the original Oregon Trail, so watch for big, brown **historical markers.** The markers vary in quality and significance, but some of them provide a bench with a scenic view of the prairie. Be grateful; your forerunners had to walk most of the way and would have killed for a place to sit down every once in a while.

ST. MARYS   ☎785

On the eastern outskirts of St. Marys, stop by **Froggy's ❶,** 311 W. Bertrand Ave., for delicious pancakes ($6.50) and Tex-Mex-style lunch specials for $7-9. (☎785-437-6733. Open M-Sa 8am-9pm, Su noon-3pm. D/MC/V.) **The Oregon Trail Nature Park,** just west of town off US 24, has a series of walking trails through the prairie and around a small pond. The longest trail takes you through the "Sea of Grass," which is exactly what it sounds like. A nice breeze ripples through the grass at the top of a hill that overlooks the deepest lake in Kansas. The park also has restrooms and an old silo painted with scenes from the prairie. (To get there from US 24, follow signs right down Schoeman Rd., just west of St. Marys. Turn left at the end onto Oregon Trail Rd. (☎785-456-2035. Open daily May-Sept. 7am-9pm; Oct.-Apr. 8am-6pm.)

THE ROAD TO WAMEGO: 14 MI.

Continue on **US 24** heading northwest to Wamego.

OREGON TRAIL

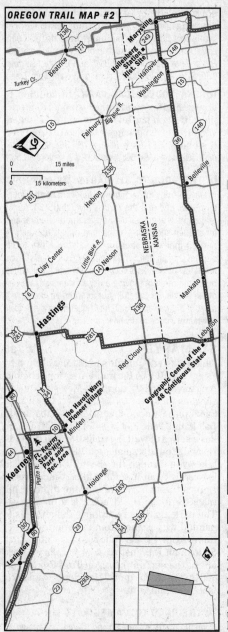

OREGON TRAIL MAP #2

WAMEGO ☎785

Wamego plays proud host to the **Oz Museum,** 511 Lincoln Ave; the museum recreates Dorothy's journey with costumes and props used in the movie. Also on display are first edition copies of L. Frank Baum's novel as well as hundreds of posters and other promotional materials used for the film. Concrete blocks immortalize the handprints of several Munchkinland inhabitants; turn left on Lincoln St., shortly after crossing into Wamego; the museum is six blocks up on the right. (☎866-458-8686; www.ozmuseum.com. Open M-Sa 10am-5pm, Su noon-5pm. $7, ages 4-12 $4.)

◪ THE ROAD TO MANHATTAN: 15 MI.

On the outskirts of Manhattan, **Poyntz Avenue** runs parallel to **US 24.** Entering the city is easiest if you get on this road as soon as possible.

MANHATTAN ☎785

Filled with Kansas State University students and a remarkable number of indoor shopping centers, Manhattan calls itself "the Little Apple." While it may seem like the Really Little Apple compared to its big brother, Manhattan stands on its own.

VITAL STATS
Population: 48,000
Tourist Office: Manhattan Convention and Visitors Bureau, 501 Poyntz Ave. (☎785-776-8829; www.manhattancvb.org). Open M-F 8am-5pm.
Library and Internet Access: Manhattan Public Library, 629 Poyntz Ave. (☎785-726-4741). Free. Open M-Th 9am-8:30pm, F 9am-6pm, Sa 9am-5:30pm, Su 1-5:30pm.
Post Office: 500 Leavenworth St. (☎785-776-8851). Open M-F 8:30am-4:30pm, Sa 9:30am-noon. **Postal Code:** 66502.

✦ ORIENTATION

Poyntz Avenue is the town's main drag, with curbside parking in front of most businesses and official buildings, but watch out—it degenerates into a mess of highway intersections to the east. Unfortunately, this area is the only way to reach the lodgings on **Tuttle Creek Boulevard (US 24). Anderson Avenue** runs parallel to and a few blocks north of Poyntz Ave. and is home to the **Kansas State University** campus.

ACCOMMODATIONS

Chain hotels are abundant in Manhattan.

Morning Star Bed and Breakfast, 617 Houston St. (☎785-587-9703). Weary travelers with cash to burn might try daintly decored and cozy Morning Star. The tea-themed suites are simple yet comfortable. Across the street from the library, the location provides good parking close to downtown. Rooms $99-139. MC/V. ❺

Motel 6, 510 Tuttle Creek Blvd. (☎785-537-1022). Outdoor pool. Singles M-Th and Su $44, F-Sa $50; doubles $50/56. AmEx/D/MC/V. ❸

FOOD

Though a number of restaurants lie within Manhattan's shopping centers, others are scattered throughout the downtown area.

4th St. Cafe, 106 S. 4th St. (☎785-539-2233). Turn onto 4th St. from Poyntz Ave. The sandwiches and salads here are a healthy and flavorful change from most cafes' lunch menus. Everything on the menu is $6 or less, including the delicious pesto turkey sandwich ($5). The full coffee bar sells pastries ($1-3) and coffee beans. Open M-F 7:30am-3pm, Sa 8am-2pm. D/MC/V. ❶

Village Inn, 204 Tuttle Creek Blvd. (☎785-537-3776). In addition to standard burger-and-fries fare, the Village Inn distinguishes itself with its pies ($1.50-4 per slice). The Brownie Pie and Caramel Pecan Silk Supreme (both $4) are worth the trip alone. Open M-Th and Su 6am-10pm, F-Sa 6am-1pm. AmEx/D/MC/V. ❷

SIGHTS

SUNSET ZOO. The prairie lives on in the city at the Sunset Zoo, which features an exhibit on native Kansas species like raccoons and prairie dogs as well as more exotic animals like the red panda, Siberian tigers, and a snow leopard. (*2333 Oak St. Follow Poyntz Ave. past Sunset Ave., and take a right on Oak St. ☎ 785-587-2737; www. sunsetzoo.com. Open daily Apr.-Oct. 9:30am-5pm; Nov.-Mar. noon-5pm. $4, ages 3-12 $2.*)

BEACH MUSEUM OF ART. Fields and clouds are a constant motif at the Beach Museum, which exhibits sculpture and painting from or about Kansas. (*701 Beach Ln. From Sunset Ave., turn left onto 17th St. ☎785-532-7718; www.k-state.edu/ bma. Open Tu-Sa 10am-5pm, Su noon-5pm. Free.*)

▶ THE ROAD TO ALCOVE SPRING: 43 MI.

To leave Manhattan, simply head north on **Tuttle Creek Boulevard.** Outside of the city, it drops the name and becomes **US 24** again. Switch to **US 77 North** after driving by Tuttle Creek Lake. Just past the towns of Waterville and Blue Rapids, **Tumbleweed Road** appears, leading west. This dirt road is marked only by a small sign pointing the way to Alcove Spring, so it is easy to miss; the **Alcove Spring Historic Marker,** 300 ft. south of the turn, is easier to spot than the road.

ALCOVE SPRING ☎785

Roadtrippers can still see the names of their forerunners carved into the rocks at Alcove Spring, a popular camping spot for those heading west, including Kit Carson and the doomed Donner Party. The area is serene, although, like the members of the Donner Party, the horseflies here will find you tasty. The spring itself can only be reached on foot, but the trail is well maintained, and the 5min. walk is nothing compared to the drive. Beware of horseflies. (Open daily sunrise-sunset. Free.)

▶ THE ROAD TO MARYSVILLE: 18 MI.

From Alcove Spring, **Tumbleweed Road** arcs through the wooded hills of the countryside, where wild turkeys are more plentiful than cars. Follow Tumbleweed for 15 mi. to **Linden Street** and take a right, which will lead you back to **US 77.** Follow US 77 to the intersection of **Broadway** and **Central Street (US 36).**

MARYSVILLE ☎785

Pretty and quiet, Marysville is the last outpost before the long haul to Hastings, Nebraska. Don't be fooled by its modest size; there's some unique history and good food to be found along the brick streets of downtown Marysville. Once the first major stop on the **Pony Express,** Marysville proudly remembers the daring of those western icons with a major road, statue, and museum. In the center of Marysville, the **Pony Express Museum,** 106 S. Eighth St., contains the barn that served as the first station where courierriders slept. The other half of the museum details the short history of overland mail service. Glass-enclosed displays depict scenes from the history of the Pony Express with lots of artifacts, including an early telegraph—the very invention that put the Pony Express out of business. (☎785-562-3825. Open May-Oct. M-Sa 10am-5pm, Su noon-4pm. $3, ages 6-12 $1.)

To the east, accommodations can be found on the section of Center St. renamed Pony Express Hwy. **The Oak Tree Inn ❸**, 1127 Pony Express Hwy. (US 36), has clean, well-furnished rooms. In addition to an exercise center and hot tub, it shares its lot with Penny's Diner, which offers breakfast discounts to Oak Tree guests. (☎785-562-1234. Rooms from $65. Cash only.) The **Best Western Surf Motel ❷**, 2105 Center St., offers comfortable rooms and amenities including an exercise room, hot tub, and game room. (☎785-562-2354. Wi-Fi. Rooms from $60. AmEx/D/MC.)

The Wagon Wheel ❷, 703 Broadway St., has a lot of local flavor and prices frugal roadtrippers will appreciate. Antique photographs from all over town line the wood-paneled interior. The brisket ($6) is a favorite of locals and visitors alike. (☎785-562-3784. Appetizers from $2. Sandwiches from $2. Entrees from $5.50. Open M-Sa 6am-9pm. AmEx/D/MC/V.)

The Marysville Chamber of Commerce, 101 N. 10th St., has more info for visitors. (☎785-562-3101. Open M-F 9am-5pm.)

⛰ THE ROAD TO HANOVER: 17 MI.

Head west on **Center Street** out of Marysville; it becomes **US 36 West.** Head north on **Route 148** for about 5 mi. to reach Hanover.

HANOVER ☎785

Hollenberg Pony Express Station State Historic Site, 2889 23rd Rd., was a store and rest stop for Oregon Trail travelers that also served as a Pony Express relay station. The visitors center has a gallery on pioneer life and opens onto a short trail lined with info stations. The path sometimes has demos on the art of trail cooking—a fine skill for roadtrippers past and present. Still standing after all these years, the station at the end of the trail is open for exploration, including the attic where Pony Express riders could rest on their dash westward. In Hanover, Rte. 243 will be on the right. (☎785-337-2635. Open Mar.-Nov. W-Sa 9am-5pm, Su 1-5pm; Dec.-Feb. by appointment only. $3, students and seniors $2.)

◗ DETOUR
GEOGRAPHIC CENTER OF THE US

Get back on **US 36 West.** At the town of Lebanon, the route turns north onto **US 281.** One mile after turning onto US 281 N., take a left onto **Route 191.**

A simple stone marker and flag announce the geographic center of the US. Established in 1898 by government surveyors, the site became the "historical" center of the contiguous states after Alaska and Hawaii joined the Union in 1959. A set of covered benches invite you have a picnic lunch as you contemplate the vastness of the surrounding cornfields.

⛰ THE ROAD TO HASTINGS: 60 MI.

Get back on **US 281.** From there, it's a 20 mi. journey across the Kansas-Nebraska border to the city of **Red Cloud**, then another 40 mi. to Hastings. The road is long, but at least a half-dozen historical markers help to break up the monotony of cows and corn. US 281 bends to the east after passing the Hastings city limits and then immediately takes a sharp turn to the left. At this point it changes its name to **Burlington Avenue;** this road runs through the center of Hastings.

HASTINGS ☎402

To those who don't look too hard, Hastings is a typical residential city, but beneath its suburban skin beats a funky heart. It's the birthplace of Kool-Aid, home to a great summer festival, and a haven of cheap hotels—it doesn't get much better than that in Nebraska.

VITAL STATS
Population: 25,000
Tourist Office: Adams County Convention and Visitors Bureau, 100 N. Shore Dr. (☎402-461-2370; www.visithastingsnebraska.com), off Burlington Ave. near the northern edge of the city. Open M-F 10am-5pm.
Library and Internet Access: Hastings Public Library, 517 W. 4th St. (☎402-461-2346). Open June-Aug. M-Th 9am-9pm, F 9am-6pm, Sa 9am-5pm; Sept.-May M-Th 9am-9pm, F 9am-6pm, Sa 9am-5pm, Su 1-5pm.
Post Office: 300 N. Kansas Ave. (☎402-463-3107). **Postal Code:** 68901.

⚜ ORIENTATION

Burlington Avenue is Hastings's main drag and runs north-south through the city. Numbered streets run east-west very close together, with free parking along most streets. Most sights are spread throughout the city, but the best restaurants are concentrated downtown.

⛏ ACCOMMODATIONS

Rainbow Motel, 1000 W. J St. (☎402-463-2989). The furnishings are better than you might expect. Free Wi-Fi. Singles $34. AmEx/D/MC/V. ❷

The Midlands Lodge, 910 W. J St. (☎402-463-2428). Has a heated outdoor pool and full-sized refrigerators, and continental breakfast. Singles $32; doubles $38. D/MC/V. ❷

🍴 FOOD

Big Dally's Deli, 801 2nd St. (☎402-463-7666). Serves delicious sandwiches that taste much more expensive than they are ($2-3 for a ½ sandwich, $4-6 for a whole). 50 varieties to choose from, including lots of vegetarian options. Open daily 7:30am-3:30pm. AmEx/D/MC. ❶

👁 SIGHTS

FISHER FOUNTAIN. The largest fountain between Chicago and Denver, it's impressive enough during the day, but every night between Mother's Day and Labor Day, colored lights turn the fountain into a beautiful array of illuminated water jets reaching up to 67 ft. high. *(At the corner of Denver and 12th St.)*

HASTINGS MUSEUM OF NATURAL AND CULTURAL HISTORY. can provide an entire day of amusement. The main floor is a hall of stuffed wildlife from all over the world, and the "Groundwater Discovery Adventure" educates while it entertains. Tucked away in the basement like the weird uncle at a family reunion, the **Kool-Aid** exhibit traces the history of the sugary, colorful beverage. The Kool-Aid Kid (a scarf-wearing nerd in knee socks) explains the development of the secret formula as well as the origins of the jolly anthropomorphic juice pitcher we all know and fear. *(1330 N. Burlington Ave., at 14th St. ☎402-461-4629 or 800-508-4629; www.hastingsmuseum.org. Open M-W*

9am-5pm, Th-Sa 9am-8pm, Su 10am-6pm. Museum and planetarium $6, ages 3-12 $4.)*

⊠ DETOUR
⊠HAROLD WARP PIONEER VILLAGE

138 East Highway 6. At the southern border of Hastings, **US 281 North** takes an abrupt right turn. Turn left at this intersection to reach **US 6.** The village is 30 mi. down US 6, at the intersection with **Route 10.**

Surreally wonderful and wonderfully surreal, this place, meant to provide a timeline of "mankind's progress since 1830," has everything from antique flying machines to a collection of 3000 unique pens and pencils. In the 26 buildings that compose the village proper, you'll find a firehouse, a Native American stockade, and a building devoted to those household appliances that "lessen women's work." As much a monument to encyclopedic obsession as to progress, Mr. Warp's collection is exactly the kind of oddity for which roadtrips were made. The **Pioneer Village Hotel** provides spacious and rustic rooms from $49 as well as campsites for true pioneers from $16. (☎308-832-1181; www.pioneervillage.org. Open daily May-Aug. 8am-6pm; Sept.-Apr. 8am-5pm. $10.50, ages 6-12 $6. MC/V.)

⊠ DETOUR
FORT KEARNY STATE HISTORICAL PARK AND RECREATION AREA

1020 V Road. Ten miles up **Route 10,** take **Link 50A** W. to the fort.

This historical park is a reconstruction of Fort Kearny, which evolved from a wilderness protection post into a busy rest stop for forty-niners and the Pony Express. The fort was abandoned after the Civil War, but the smithy, stockade, and powder magazine are open to visitors. **Campsites ❶** are available for people who want to take their time exploring the 150-acre grounds. Those stopping by on Memorial Day or July 4 will be treated to historical reenactments, but the best time to visit is in March and April, when sandhill cranes flock here on their way north. (☎308-865-5305. Visitors center open daily 9am-5pm. Requires a $4 Nebraska State Park permit. Primitive sites $11, with electricity $15.)

🚗 THE ROAD TO KEARNEY: 15 MI.
Immediately west of the Harold Warp Pioneer Village, the route to Kearney turns north along **Route 10**

toward **I-80.** From there, it's about 15 mi. to Kearney. Get off I-80 at **Exit 272,** which will lead to **Second Avenue** in southern Kearney.

KEARNEY   ☎308

It's pronounced "KAR-nee," like the confused-looking guy with nine fingers who ran the tilt-a-whirl. Notice the spelling discrepancy between the town and fort? When the town was founded, it took its name from the nearby fort, but a misspelled piece of official mail sidled the town with an extra "e" it never got around to correcting. Home to part of the University of Nebraska, Kearney is by no means a big city, but its tasty restaurants and lively bar scene give it a personality all of its own.

VITAL STATS
Population: 28,000
Tourist Office: Kearney Visitors Bureau, 1007 2nd Ave. (☎308-237-3178 or 800-652-9435; www.visitkearney.org). Open M-F 8am-6pm, Sa 9am-5pm, Su 1-4pm.
Library and Internet Access: Kearney Public Library, 2020 1st Ave. (☎308-233-3282; www.kearneylib.org). Open M-Th 9am-9pm, F-Sa 9am-5pm, Su 1-5pm.
Post Office: 2401 Ave. E (☎308-234-2051), at the corner of 23rd St. Open M-F 8am-5pm, Sa 9-11:30am. **Postal Code:** 68847.

✈ ORIENTATION

While Kearney has a logical layout, it can still be a little quirky. Avenues run north-south while streets run east-west. **Central Avenue** is the axis of the city. To the east of Central Ave., avenues are numbered, while to the west they are lettered. All streets are numbered.

⚑ ACCOMMODATIONS

Hotels line **Second Avenue,** which is Kearney's busiest thoroughfare.

   The Midtown Western Inn, 1401 2nd Ave. (☎308-237-3153; www.midtownwesterninn.com). Large, comfy recliners in each room allow for quality relaxation. The pool and deck overlooking the divided highway are also nice touches. Singles $50; doubles $55. AmEx/MC/V. ❷

   The Western Inn South Motel, 510 3rd Ave. (☎800-437-8457). For roadtrippers who don't need quite so many amenities at so high a price. Each room comes with a desk and recliner, and the hot tub is open 7am-11pm. Singles $60; doubles $70. AmEx/D/MC/V. ❸

🍴 FOOD

   The Cellar, 3901 2nd Ave. (☎308-236-6541). Watch for the sign leading to The Cellar, which lurks—surprise—under a cluster of businesses. Though the menu carries little more than stan-

---

A CAPITAL IDEA

Kearney, Nebraska, is a nice town, certainly. Its bustling nightlife and happening atmosphere give it a cozy, intimate sort of atmosphere. For one man, however, Kearney's greatest asset was its centralized location, 1733 mi. from both Boston and San Francisco. Moses Syndenham moved to nearby Fort Kearny in the 1860s, where he served as postmaster until the fort's closing in 1871. After that, he opened up a general store and started a newspaper, *The Kearney Herald.* In the aftermath of the Civil War, Syndenham decided that the nation's capital needed to be in a more centralized location, in order to more efficiently oversee the needs of a rapidly expanding country.

To this end, Syndenham embarked on a lengthy (though largely feeble) campaign to petition the government to move from the mosquito-infested swamps of Washington, DC, to the rolling plains of central Nebraska. He changed the name of his paper to *The Centorian* and even helped organize the National Removal Convention in St. Louis. Among his many proposals for making Kearney more suitable for national prominence were the creation of public buildings, parks, bridges, fountains, "and other public improvements." For reasons Syndenham never fully comprehended, the government chose to remain in the muggy swamps of Washington, DC.

Though his plans never came to fruition, Syndenham is still fondly remembered around town as a

dard Tex-Mex fare, diners can enjoy the rolling armchairs and peaceful, candlelit atmosphere. Enchiladas ($7) are a specialty. Entrees $7-18. Open M-Sa 11am-11pm. AmEx/D/MC/V. ❸

Come and Get It, 942 24th St. (☎308-233-5949). Road-weary travelers who find themselves missing that tangy Kansas City barbecue should visit here. Smother your sandwich ($3-5) in one of 7 homemade sauces ("lip-smackin'" is the best), then treat yourself to some homemade ice cream ($2-3). Entrees $5-10. Bottles of sauce $2.50. Open M-Sa 11am-9pm. AmEx/D/MC/V. ❷

🜨 SIGHTS

GREAT PLATTE RIVER ROAD ARCHWAY MONUMENT. While the monument may not be the quirkiest spectacle on the road, it's certainly one of the most grandiose. The archway spans all four lanes of I-80 just east of Kearney, and its towers spread huge metallic wings. After driving under it, continue a few more miles to Exit 272 and backtrack east on First St. to the parking lot. Visitors don headphones and ride up to the "trail" contained by the arch. Displays chronicle the evolution of I-80 from Oregon Trail to Union Pacific Railroad to modern highway, complete with lots of Ten Commandments-style fake thunder. *(3060 1st St. ☎877-511-2724; www.archway.org. Open from Memorial Day to Labor Day daily 9am-6pm; from Labor Day to Oct. and from Mar. to Memorial Day daily 9am-4pm; Nov.-Mar. F-Su 10am-3pm. $10, ages 11-15 $6, ages 6-10 $3, seniors $8.50.)*

MUSEUM OF NEBRASKA ART. The museum is dedicated to works and artists connected to Nebraska. Despite its modest size, the museum covers a wide range of styles and media, from contemporary sculpture and video art to a gallery of "Vivaporous Quadrupeds" by John James Audobon. *(2401 Central Ave. ☎308-865-8559. Open Tu-Sa 11am-5pm, Su 1-5pm. Free.)*

TRAILS AND RAILS MUSEUM. Though the title is a little misleading ("rails" refers to a single train and there are no real trails to speak of), this collection of historical buildings provides an interesting glimpse into the region's history. Be careful when ringing the bell on the fire engine; it's a lot louder than it looks. The town archives are also present, in case you think you have long-lost relatives here.

(710 W. 11th St. ☎308-234-3041; http://bchs.kearney. net/museum.html. Open June-Aug. M-Sa 10am-6pm, Su 1-5pm; Sept.-May M-F 1-5pm. $5, ages 5-12 $2.)

🜨 NIGHTLIFE

Thunderhead Brewing, 18 E. 21st St. (☎308-237-1558; www.thunderheadbrewing. com), just off Central Ave. A perennial gold-medal winner at the World Beer Cup. Patrons can down one of the signature Honeywheat brews while shooting some pool in the low-key atmosphere. They also serve several spicy varieties of pizza (10 in. $7.50-10), like the Thunderpie—a behemoth with pepper jack, chicken, bacon, jalapeños, white sauce, and ranch. $2-off pints W-Th. Open daily 10am-1am. AmEx/D/MC/V.

Copperfield's, 13 21st St. (☎308-233-5173). Serves up mixed drinks in a rustic setting. With a pick for a door handle and situated in a 100-year-old building, Copperfield's has a very distinct atmosphere. The weekend music leans toward honky-tonk and bluegrass. A favorite drink among regulars is a concoction called the "Chuck Norris Bomb." (☎308-237-9259. Open M-Sa 4pm-1am. AmEx/MC/V.)

⚑ THE ROAD TO LEXINGTON: 30 MI.

Follow **Second Avenue South,** then take the ramp onto **I-80** and pull into Lexington.

LEXINGTON   ☎308

Lying about 30 mi. northwest of Kearney, little Lexington is still the largest town around. In addition to WWII uniforms from local servicemen, the **Dawson County Historical Museum,** 805 N. Taft St., houses some highly irregular objects, including the remains of Big Al the mammoth and an elliptical-winged airplane built by a local high-school student that flew, defying the principles of aerodynamics. (☎308-324-5340; www.dchsmuseum.com. Open M-Sa 9am-5pm. Free.)

The few motels in Lexington are on **Plum Creek Parkway,** which links I-80 to town. Approaching from US 30, Plum Creek Pkwy. is the large road to the south that crosses the bridge over the Platte River. **The Gable View Inn ❷,** 2701 Plum Creek Pkwy., has good rates, clean bathrooms, and angular ceilings on second-story rooms. (☎308-324-5595. Singles $35; doubles $40. AmEx/D/MC/V.)

OREGON TRAIL

The townsfolk who frequent the **A&D Cafe ❷,** 604 N. Washington St., are a pretty insular bunch, but outsiders can still enjoy the home-style breakfast and lunch specials ($4.50-6). (Head north up Washington St. from US 30. ☎308-324-5990. Open daily 6am-3pm. MC/V.) For something quick, check out **Kirk's Nebraskaland Restaurant ❸,** off I-80 at Exit 237, south of town, on the opposite side of the highway. Kirk's serves a little bit of everything and might be the only place on the road where you can order a glass of Merlot or Zinfandel ($3.65 per glass) to go with your french toast and scrambled eggs ($3-4). (☎308-324-6641. Appetizers $4-7. Sandwiches $5.50-8. Entrees $8-10. Breakfast served all day. Open M-Th and Su 6am-midnight, F-Sa 6am-1am. AmEx/D/MC/V.)

THE ROAD TO NORTH PLATTE: 64 MI.

Hop back on **I-80** and take **Exit 177** into town.

NORTH PLATTE ☎308

As the place where Buffalo Bill Cody hung his hat, North Platte is invested in perpetuating the Wild West. Cody Park, Rodeo Rd., and the Wild West Arena all testify to the influence of the era over the whole town. Nothing, however, holds a candle to **Nebraskaland Days.** Over two weeks in early June, the entire state turns out for this strange mix of music festival, pageant, carnival, and rodeo.

VITAL STATS
Population: 24,000
Tourist Office: North Platte Convention and Visitors Bureau, 219 S. Dewey St. (☎308-532-4729 or 800-955-4528; www.visitnorthplatte.com). Open M-F 8am-5pm.
Library and Internet Access: North Platte Public Library, 120 W. 4th St. (☎308-535-8036). Open M and Th 9am-9pm, Tu-W and F-Sa 9am-6pm. Free.
Post Office: 300 E. 3rd St. (☎308-532-3346). Open M-F 7:30am-5:30pm, Sa 8:30am-noon. **Postal Code:** 69101.

ORIENTATION

The major roads of North Platte intersect downtown; **Fourth Street** runs east-west, and **Jeffers Street** runs north-south. Most accom-

modations are on Fourth St.; most food is on Jeffers or **Dewey Street,** which runs parallel to Jeffers St. one block west. A few sites lie to the northwest on **Buffalo Bill Avenue,** which joins Fourth St. on the city's western edge.

ACCOMMODATIONS

While food options might feel a little restrictive, North Platte does happen to be graced by a plethora of cheap motels. **Cody Park ❶** offers primitive campsites ($5).

The Blue Spruce Motel, 821 S. Dewey St. (☎308-534-2600). Downtown, has rooms that are unusually large and well furnished for the roadtripper friendly price. Free Wi-Fi. Singles $36; doubles $49. AmEx/D/MC/V. ❷

Traveler's Inn, 602 E. Fourth St. (☎308-534-4020; www.bestvalueinn.com). Comfy armchairs, full-length mirrors, and heated outdoor pool. Singles $50; doubles $60. AmEx/D/MC/V. ❷

FOOD

In the heart of steak country, North Platte is unabashedly a meat-eater's city. Steak shows up on most menus, even when it seems a little out of place. While you can certainly find chicken fried steak ($12) at **Little Mexico Restaurant ❷,** 104 N. Jeffers St., you're probably better off sticking to the more traditional entrees ($9-14) or the special for $6. (☎308-534-3052. Appetizers $6-10. Open daily 11am-10pm. AmEx/D/MC/V.)

SIGHTS

Despite the glut of attractions, most of the highlights can be hit pretty quickly.

CODY PARK. A carnival-esque combination of amusement park, zoo, city park, and memorial, Cody Park can provide some respite after a day's sightseeing. The gazebo at the entrance marks the site of the first spectator rodeo hosted by Cody in 1882. (*1400 N. Jeffers St., off US 30. ☎800-955-4528. Open daily sunrise-sunset. Free.*)

BUFFALO BILL STATE HISTORICAL PARK. Meticulously preserved, the park attempts to keep the ranch the way Cody left it while adding displays that perpetuate the Cody myths. The barn features a small theater that plays footage of Cody's famed Wild West show in action. *(2921 Scout's Rest Ranch Rd. ☎308-535-8035; www.nypc.state.ne.us/cody.html. Open from Memorial Day to Labor Day daily 9am-5pm; from Labor Day to Oct. 1 and from late Mar. to Memorial Day M-F 10am-4pm. Requires a $4 Nebraska State Park permit.)*

◤ THE ROAD TO PAXTON: 34 MI.

Take **Jeffers Street** south. Jeffers St. intersects **Rodeo Road,** which becomes **US 30** outside Paxton.

PAXTON   ☎217

Beef is the menu at ▧**Ole's Big Game Steakhouse ❸,** on Oak St., off US 30, but every other kind of animal is on the wall, often right over the table. Chat up your server; every piece on the wall—from the African elephant to the giraffe to the full-body polar bear to the elusive jackalope (p. 625) next to the bison—has a story behind it, and they know a lot of them. Be sure to ask about the propeller above the doorway. The food is great, too, once you get around to ordering. The burgers come in cow or buffalo ($6-8), while the larger steak options run $14-22. (☎308-239-4500; www.olesbiggame.com. Open daily 10am-midnight. AmEx/D/MC/V.)

 TIME CHANGE. Between North Platte and Paxton, US 30 passes into the Mountain Time Zone, where it is 1hr. earlier.

◤ THE ROAD TO OGALLALA: 20 MI.

US 30 becomes **First Street,** making the approach to Ogallala a straight shot.

OGALLALA   ☎308

Like most of the surrounding towns, Ogallala tries to capitalize on its Old West heritage, but the best parts are the farthest from downtown. Lake McConaughy has a lot to offer those who appreciate the outdoors, including a great view of western Nebraska's rolling hills and ravines. It might be tempting to skip Ogallala altogether, but a few sights and some good eating make a stop worthwhile.

◳ ORIENTATION

Ogallala's street layout undermines the brilliant simplicity of the grid with a nonsensical naming scheme. **First Street (US 30)** forms the central artery, running east-west through the city. Parallel streets increase sequentially as one travels north. **Spruce Street,** cutting north-south, is the other key route. Streets parallel to Spruce St. are lettered, but they come in pairs: one block east of Spruce is **East A Street,** one block west is **West A Street.** As a result, E. E St. and W. E St. are nowhere near each other—they're 10 blocks apart.

VITAL STATS
Population: 5000
Tourist Office: Ogallala Keith County Chamber of Commerce and Visitors Center, 204 E. A St. (☎308-284-4066; www.visitogallala.com). Open M-F 8am-5pm.
Library and Internet Access: Goodall City Library, 203 W. A St. (☎308-284-4354; www.goodallcitylibrary.com). Open M-Th 9am-8pm, F-Sa 9am-5pm.
Post Office: 301 N. Spruce St. (☎308-284-3251). Open M-F 8am-4:30pm, Sa 9am-11am. **Postal Code:** 69153.

◤ ACCOMMODATIONS

Those who prefer not to **camp ❶** at the lake (primitive sites $5, with camping pad $10, with full hookup $18; MC/V) will find options in town, including the usual clump of chain motels off I-80, at the south end of Spruce St.

The Western Paradise Motel, 221 E. 1st St. (☎308-284-8098). Has textured wallpaper and that wonderful air freshener smell in addition to microwaves and refrigerators in every clean room. Singles $35; doubles $40. MC/V. ❷

Grey Goose Lodge, 201 Chuckwagon Rd. (☎308-284-3623 or 800-573-7148). A fine hotel with comfortable rooms and karaoke on Th. Singles $65; doubles $70. AmEx/MC/V. ❸

◳ FOOD

Dining establishments in Ogallala are steeped in the character of the Old West.

Front Street Steakhouse, 519 E. 1st St. (☎308-284-6000). Serves 9 kinds of steak ($12-25) and sarsaparilla ($2.25) in an old saloon setting. The Crystal Palace Steak Sandwich ($14) slaps ribeye on Texas toast and calls it a day.

OREGON TRAIL

Sandwiches $6-14. Entrees $9-25. Open daily 11am-9pm. AmEx/D/MC/V. ❹

Homemade Heaven Sandwich Shoppe, 12 N. Spruce St. (☎308-284-4879). Offers the best variety and value to be found around here. Its menu boasts 3 different sandwiches ($4.50-8.50), including a shrimp sandwich and a guacamole burger, in addition to more traditional choices. Soups $2.50-3.50. Open M-F 8am-7pm, Sa 8am-4pm. MC/V. ❷

🕹 SIGHTS

LAKE MCCONAUGHY. As with all Nebraska state parks, visitors are required to have a Nebraska state parks sticker ($4) on their cars; they're available at the visitors center, 1475 Rte. 61, ¼ mi. before reaching the lake. Beyond the visitors center, the road leads over the enormous Kingsley Dam, affording a spectacular, if terrifying, view of the river below. From there, 5 mi.of shoreline present myriad possibilities: boating, fishing, swimming, camping, or just relaxing on the beach. There is even an eagle observation post, though the birds are only present during the winter months. If you decide to camp, be warned: Nebraska's ground is notoriously hard and dry. *(Rte. 61 runs northeast from town to the eastern end of the lake. ☎308-284-8800. For more info on eagle viewing, call ☎308-284-2332.)*

PETRIFIED WOOD GALLERY. The gallery contains a large collection of wood turned stone, much of it brightly colored and spectacularly patterned. *(525 E. 1st St. ☎308-284-9996 or 800-658-4390; www.petrifiedwoodgallery.com. Open from Memorial Day to Labor Day M-Sa 10am-7pm; Sept. and Apr. 1 to Memorial Day M-Sa 10am-4pm; Nov.-Dec. W-F 10am-4pm, Sa 10am-1pm.)*

BOOT HILL CEMETERY. For those more interested in real Western history, Boot Hill Cemetery contains the graves of cowboys and locals who died with their boots on. Several dozen graves are present, some dating back to 1875. A bronze statue commemorates those who died. Locals have occasionally reported strange sightings in the area after dark. *(At the corner of W. 10th and C St. ☎308-284-4066. Open daily sunrise-sunset. Free.)*

🚗 THE ROAD TO WINDLASS HILL/ASH HOLLOW: 12 MI.

Head north on **East A Street,** following signs toward Lake McConaughy until it merges into **Spruce Street.** Head north for several miles to the junction with **Route 61** and **US 26.** Turn left and go west on US 26.

WINDLASS HILL AND ASH HOLLOW ☎308

Windlass Hill derives its name from the legend that wagons had to be lowered down its steep slope with a special winch, though no evidence of such a device exists. The haul

NO COCK AND BULL STORY

Conventional wisdom holds that desert and mountainous regions should not be considered great sources of fresh seafood. But on bar and grill menus from Montana to Arizona appears a dish labeled "Rocky Mountain oysters." What's usually missing is the explanatory note; Rocky Mountain oysters are bull testicles. Traditionally coated in flour, pepper, and salt, occasionally pounded flat, and then deep-fried, this alleged delicacy is popular pub fare all over the Mountain Time Zone. Whatever its popularity among the locals, however, Rocky Mountain oysters are more often used as a practical joke. Convincing tourists to try out the regional delicacy—usually listed as an appetizer but occasionally more cruelly labeled as "seafood"—is a time-honored pasttime in some towns.

The dish's origins remain uncertain. Some claim it originated among cowboys as a way for them to assert their masculinity, while others claim that it comes from the old ranching tradition of using the teeth as the surgical instrument in castration. Not surprisingly, the oysters have become something of a popular novelty. "Rocky Mountain Oyster Feeds" are popular eating competitions found at state fairs and festivals all over the region. The annual feed at Eagle Fun Days in Eagle, Idaho, claims to be the world's largest, though it seems unlikely that many towns would be willing to challenge them

to the top is worth it for the view alone. The windswept ravines of Nebraska have an austere beauty to them. Also visible across the countryside are the scars of thousands of iron-wheeled wagons; at least eight distinct sets of wagon ruts are visible, in addition to a ravine made entirely by wagon traffic. Down the road about 2 mi. is **Ash Hollow.** The site contains a **visitors center** and a small museum situated in a nearby cave, which displays artifacts from the cave's prehistoric days. The walking trail to the spring itself takes about 10min., but the way can be steep, and signs warn of rattlesnakes in the area. Both sites require a $4 Nebraska state park permit, available at the visitors center by Ash Hollow. (☎308-778-5651. Open Tu-Su 10am-4pm.)

THE ROAD TO BRIDGEPORT: 50 MI.

Follow **US 26** to where it crosses the **North Platte River** into Bridgeport.

BRIDGEPORT ☎308

The first of the spectacular stone formations that dominate the rolling hills of western Nebraska, **Courthouse Rock** and **Jail Rock** may be less celebrated than the more iconic Chimney Rock or Scotts Bluff, but they're still impressive enough to merit a brief detour. Both are visible from a historical marker along Rte. 88, about 4 mi. south of town, but just a little farther down a dirt road marked Rd. 84 gives an unbeatable view of Jail Rock and leads to the base of Courthouse Rock. The adventurous may attempt the dirt trail that leads up Courthouse Rock, but watch out for rattlesnakes.

The Bridgeport Inn ❷, 517 Main St., is a star among budget motels. The rooms are huge and clean, with all the accommodations you would expect from a significantly more expensive place, including comfy rocking chairs. (☎760-932-7380. Free Wi-Fi. Singles $45; doubles $50. AmEx/D/MC/V.) **Karette's Drive-In ❶,** 409 Main St., has more options than you would expect from a roadside stop. Burgers of the single and double variety ($2-5) are an improvement from most fast-food places, while delicious milkshakes ($2-3) provide a satisfying end to every meal. (☎308-262-0790. Open daily 11am-10pm. Cash only.)

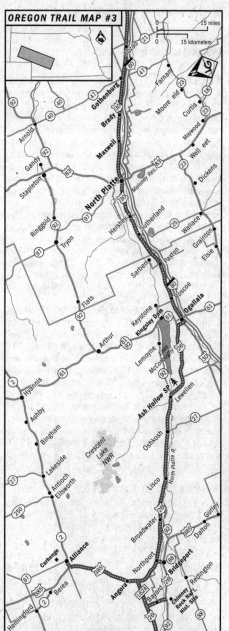

OREGON TRAIL MAP #3

OREGON TRAIL

⚲ THE ROAD TO ALLIANCE: 30 MI.

Returning up **Main Street** onto **US 26** and crossing the North Platte River leads to the junction with **US 385.** Take **US 385** to **Third Street.**

ALLIANCE   ☎308

Alliance is a quiet town with decent food and cheap lodging. Lurking under this placid surface, however, is one of the most awesome roadside stops on the haul westward. Combining past and present, stone and steel, druids and drive-ins, ⬛**Carhenge** is the quintessential roadtripper's monument. Built by a local man as a monument to his love of Stonehenge and America's love of cars, Carhenge accurately recreates the famed ruins in the middle of a Nebraska field. Other car-art decorates the fringes of the site, including a dinosaur and salmon. Carhenge T-shirts, license-plate covers, and bandanas can be purchased at the Carhenge Pitstop next door. Head east on Third St. for 3 mi. and turn north on Rte. 87. (Open daily sunrise-sunset. Gift shop open M-F 10am-5pm. Free.)

The **First Interstate Inn ❷**, 1207 W. Third St., maintains comfortable rooms with ottomans. (☎308-762-4040. Wi-Fi. Singles $40; doubles $50. AmEx/MC/V.) **The Rainbow Motel ❶**, 614 W. Third St., has nicer amenities than you'd expect from a budget motel, including big closets, recliners, and Wi-Fi. (☎308-762-4980. Singles from $32; doubles from $40. AmEx/MC/V.) **Ken & Dale's Restaurant ❷**, 123 E. Third St., serves diner fare in a comfortable atmosphere, though the leathery booths don't make up for the meager portions. (☎308-762-7252. Burgers $6-8. Entrees $8-12. Open M-Sa 6am-9:30pm, Su 6am-8pm. AmEx/MC/V.)

⚲ THE ROAD TO BAYARD: 39 MI.

Head west on **Third Street** to the junction with **Route 385** and return south. To take a shortcut to Chimney Rock, head west on **Link 62A**, just south of Angora. To get to Bayard, head south on **US 26.**

BAYARD   ☎308

Bayard serves as the jumping-off point for the **Oregon Trail Wagon Train,** 1 mi. east of Oregon Trail Rd. and 2 mi. south of Bayard. This service gives travelers with time and money a chance to experience life on the trail. Cov-

ered-wagon treks wind through the Chimney Rock area, where "pioneers" cook over campfires. The four-day trek includes horseback riding, riflery, a Pony Express delivery, and a Native American raid. For something less time-consuming, chuckwagon cookouts with a short wagon tour are also available. (☎308-586-1850; www.oregontrailwagontrain. com. Reservations required. 24hr. trek $200, children $175; 4-day trek $575/475; cookouts $19/9.50.) **Pizza Point ❶**, 106 E. Second St., is a hometown pizza joint offering personal pizzas ($3) for the solo roadtripper or large pizzas ($9.75) for entire families. (☎308-586-2255. Open M-Sa 11am-9pm, Su 4-8pm. Cash only.)

◪ DETOUR
CHIMNEY ROCK NATIONAL HISTORIC SITE

Head south on **US 26,** then turn west on **Route 92.** Follow the signs over dirt roads to the visitors center.

Western Nebraska was once a vast, high-elevation plain of clay and volcanic ash. As wind and water wore the surface down to present-day levels, caps of harder stone resisted erosion, protecting the ash underneath. Thus Chimney Rock, a delicate spire of vulcan material topped with stone, was formed. Visible for miles around, Chimney was one of the best-known landmarks along the Oregon Trail, mentioned in surviving diaries more than any other landmark. Unfortunately, the erosion that created Chimney Rock will likely destroy it. Made of little more than sandstone, the spire has lost an estimated 45 ft. of its original height to wind, water, and lightning strikes. Due to this and the omnipresent rattlesnake threat, the park forbids visitors from actually approaching the rock. A closer look is achieved by driving farther down the dirt road, which terminates close to the rock near a cemetery dedicated to pioneers who died on the trail. (☎308-586-2581; www.nps.gov/chro. Visitors center open from Memorial Day to Labor Day daily 9am-5pm; from Labor Day to Memorial Day Tu-Su 9am-5pm. Requires a $4 Nebraska state park permit.)

⚲ THE ROAD TO SCOTTSBLUFF: 24 MI.

From Chimney Rock, it's only 20 mi. west along **US 26** to Scottsbluff. To go straight to the city, stay on US 26, which runs through northwest Scottsbluff, connecting directly to **20th Street** in the eastern part of the city and **Avenue I** in the north.

SCOTTSBLUFF ☎ 308

Scottsbluff, Gering, and the intermediate region of Terrytown all lie in the shadow of Scotts Bluff, the towering rock formation that gives the largest of the cities its name. Originally a major milestone on the Oregon Trail and the gateway to the foothills of the Rocky Mountains, the bluff is now home to two cities where visitors can find a range of cheap and delicious food as well as a zoo and some decent lodging. It's the bluff itself, however, and the spectacular views that it affords, that keep drawing people in.

VITAL STATS
Population: 15,000
Tourist Office: Scotts Bluff County Tourism, 1517 Broadway (☎308-632-2133; www.visitscottsbluff. com). Open M-F 8am-5pm.
Library and Internet Access: Scottsbluff Public Library, 1809 3rd Ave. (☎308-630-6250; www. scotsbluff.org/lib). Open M-Th 9am-8pm, F-Sa 9am-6pm, Su 2-5pm.
Post Office: 112 W. 20th St. (☎308-635-1121). Open M-F 8:30am-4:30pm, Sa 9:15am-11am.
Postal Code: 69361.

✷ ORIENTATION

Scottsbluff is the biggest city in western Nebraska but shares many of its services and much of its bustle with the smaller city of Gering to the south. The two also share the same main street, which changes its name at the border. In Gering it's called **10th Street;** in Scottsbluff, **Broadway.** This road is the largest and most direct link between the two. Unless otherwise noted, all listings are in Scottsbluff. The north-south roads in Scottsbluff are avenues. To the west of Broadway they are lettered; to the east, they are numbered. The east-west roads are streets and are numbered. **First Street** is near the Gering border, and street numbers increase heading north. Don't confuse these with 10th St. in Gering.

⚑ ACCOMMODATIONS

Scottsbluff has a fair selection of hotels and motels, though they're scattered around town. Chain accommodations can be found along **East 20th Street** and **Avenue I,** near US 26.

Lamplighter American Inn, 606 E. 27th St. (☎308-632-7108). Comes with spacious rooms, an indoor pool, and Wi-Fi. Singles $56; doubles $63. AmEx/MC/V. ❸

Riverside Campground, 1600 S. Beltline Hwy. (☎308-632-6342), right next to the zoo. Provides a nice view of the bluff. Gates closed 11pm-5am. Primitive sites $8, with water and electricity $10, with full hookup $15. Cash only. ❶

➘ FOOD

Scotty's Drive-In, 618 E. 27th St. (☎308-635-3314). Bills itself as a drive-in, though you'll still have to walk in to pick up your order. Expect your entire meal to cost less than $5. Tastes cheap, is cheap: what else do you want? The truly daring can try the infamous taco burger ($1.85). Burgers $1.25-3. Fries $1.25. Open June-Aug. M-Th and Su 10am-10:30pm, F-Sa 10am-11:30pm; Sept.-May M-Th and Su 10am-10pm, F-Sa 10am-11pm. MC/V. ❶

Bush's Gaslight Restaurant & Lounge, 3315 N. 10th St. (☎308-632-7315), in Gering. Candlelit tables, a dining room fireplace, and comfortable lounge create an upscale atmosphere. Chicken, seafood, and steak entrees $9-43. Sandwiches $6-7. Open M-Th and Su 4:30-10pm, F-Sa 4:30-11:30pm. MC/V. ❸

Prime Cut, 305 W. 27th St. (☎308-632-5353). The gigantic meat cleaver sticking out from the roof tells you everything you need to know. Full steak dinners for less than $8 as well as chicken, sausage, and salad meals. Old tools and photographs lend an antique aura. Entrees $8-13. Open M-Th and Su 11am-9pm, F-Sa 11am-10pm. MC/V. ❷

◉ SIGHTS

SCOTTS BLUFF NATIONAL MONUMENT. Scotts Bluff is one of the largest and most accessible rock formations along this part of the trail. Named for a fur trader who died on its slopes, the bluff rises 830 ft. above the prairie at its highest point. The top has a small walking trail that gives visitors an unparalleled view of the prairie and the surrounding area; Chimney Rock can even be seen in the distance. At the base of the bluff, the **Scotts Bluff Visitors Center** presents the history of the Oregon Trail. The bluff itself can be scaled by car, shuttle, or the **Saddle Rock Trail** (1.6 mi.), which is steep and winding but worth the effort, cutting up the cliff face and straight through the rock to the other side of the bluff. As always, watch for rattlesnakes. For pioneers, Pony Express riders, and roadtrippers, this marks the completion of the first third of the trail. (*On Rte. 92, 3 mi. west of Gering.* ☎ *308-436-4340. Open daily 8am-7pm. $5 per vehicle. Trail maps $0.50.*)

PHOTO OP. Located east of town at Lake Minatare is a Nebraskan lighthouse—yup, a lighthouse. Built by convicts in 1939, it continues to stand watch over the prairie, though it's never had a light. Head east for 11 mi. on US 26, then north for another 9 mi. on Stone Gate Rd. Once you hit the lake, a short jaunt down The Point Rd. leads to the structure, which, needless to say, is kind of hard to miss.

NORTH PLATTE VALLEY MUSEUM. Here you can dress up in pioneer garb while you peruse the artifacts and dioramas of 19th-century pioneer life as well as Native American culture. (*At 11th and J St. Head south on 10th St. in Gering; after the sign, turn right onto Overland Trails Rd. for parking.* ☎ *308-436-5411; www.npvm.com. Open M-F 9am-4pm, Sa-Su 1-4pm. $3, ages 5-12 $1.*)

RIVERSIDE ZOO. The zoo is home to a pair of African lions, an impressive selection of primates, and an aviary where visitors can experience exotic bird droppings first hand. There's also another red panda, which should not be that impressive at this point. Wednesday admission is always $1. (*1600 S. Beltline Hwy.* ☎ *308-630-6236. Open Mar.-Nov. daily 9:30am-4:30pm; Dec.-Feb. Sa-Su 10am-4pm. $2.50, ages 5-12 $1, seniors $2.*)

⚲ THE ROAD TO LINGLE: 42 MI.

Head north on **Broadway** to its end and turn right onto **27th Street.** Follow 27th until it merges with **US 26,** heading toward Wyoming. Continue on US 26 to Lingle. Watch out here: US 26 makes a 90° turn.

The Equality State
WYOMING
Welcomes You!

LINGLE ☎ 307

Right outside of town is the **Western History Center,** 2308 US 26. A sort of archaeological display gallery, the Western History Center showcases mammoth remains, 10,000-year-old arrowheads, and fossils dating as far back as the Cretaceous Period. Temporary exhibits display everything from international doll collections to ornamental swords, providing an exciting alternative to other trail museums. (☎ 307-837-3052. Open M-Sa 9am-4pm. $2.)

⚐ DETOUR
FORT LARAMIE NATIONAL HISTORIC SITE

965 Gray Rocks Rd. Follow the signs from the town of Fort Laramie (pop. 256; according to the sign, "250 good people and 6 sore heads"). The fort is a few miles south of town along **Gray Rocks Road (Route 160).**

Fort Laramie was a critical outpost along the overland trails, serving as a central base for the US Army during its violent clashes with tribes led by Red Cloud, Crazy Horse, and Sitting Bull. Probably the best-preserved or restored fort on the trail, Fort Laramie also bustles with Union soldiers who teach everything from making campfires to firing cannons, though the illusion is sort of ruined when you see one of them driving a golf cart. Audio tours are available, although you'll probably want to explore the grounds at your own pace, as some buildings are a lot more interesting than others. A vest-clad barkeep sells sarsaparilla and ginger beer ($1.50) in the restored **Soldier's Bar.** (☎ 307-837-2221; www. nps.gov/fola. Grounds open daily sunrise-sunset. Visitors center open daily 8am-7pm. $3.)

⚲ THE ROAD TO GUERNSEY: 11 MI.

Follow **US 26** to where it becomes **Whalen Street** in the center of Guernsey.

GUERNSEY ☎ 307

Guernsey divides two different landscapes; just beyond the town, the Rocky Mountains rise suddenly into view. Nineteenth-century travelers often considered Guernsey's Register Cliff to be the real marker of the Rockies' borders. Between the names carved into the cliffs long ago and the beauty of Guernsey State Park, the town maintains the adventurous feel of something new.

ORIENTATION

US 26 runs through the center of Guernsey as **Whalen Street**. Most sights and establishments line the main drag of **Wyoming Avenue** south of its intersection with Whalen St.

VITAL STATS
Population: 1150
Tourist Office: Guernsey Visitor Center, 90 S. Wyoming Rd. (☎307-836-2715; www.townofguernseywy.us). Open M-Sa 9am-7pm, Su noon-4pm.
Library and Internet Access: North Platte County Public Library, Guernsey Branch, 108 S. Wyoming Rd. (☎307-836-2816). Open M and W noon-7pm, Tu and Th noon-5pm, F noon-4pm, Sa 9-11am.
Post Office: 401 S. Wyoming Rd. (☎307-836-2804). Open M-F 8:30am-5pm. **Postal Code:** 82214.

ACCOMMODATIONS

Bunkhouse Motel, 350 Whalen St. (☎307-836-2356). It may look and feel like a ranch, but the rooms come with all the modern conveniences (guests are still welcome to use the on-site barbecue pit if it strikes their fancy). Singles $60; doubles $65. AmEx/MC/V. ❸

Sagebrush Motel, 151 W. Whalen St. (☎307-836-2331). Somewhat lacking in the required Western decoration, it still provides microwaves and refrigerators. Free Wi-Fi. Rooms from $60. AmEx/MC/V. ❸

FOOD

Riverview Restaurant, 800 W. Laramie St. (☎307-836-2191), off US 26, at the west end of town. Has nature-inspired decor, an abrasive menu, and huge windows overlooking the North Platte. Special sandwiches like the Doc Holiday (turkey, stuffing, mashed potatoes, gravy, and cranberry; $7) and the Calamity Jane (meatloaf, sunset sauce, mashed potatoes, and onions; $7) cater to the Western theme the place tries to cultivate. Entrees $6.50-8. Open M-Sa 6am-7pm, Su 6am-6pm. AmEx/D/MC/V. ❷

Trail Inn, 37 N. Wyoming Ave. (☎307-836-2010). Offers American and Italian dishes in a friendly, local setting. Bacon cheese fries ($5) are a delicious way to start any heart attack— er, meal. Sandwiches $6.50-8. Entrees $8-19. Open Tu-Sa 11am-10pm, Su 11am-2pm. AmEx/MC/V. ❷

SIGHTS

Guernsey itself may not be much to look at, but just outside town visitors will find two awesome spots along the Oregon Trail where the presence of the pioneers is very tangible.

OREGON TRAIL RUTS STATE HISTORIC SITE. The physical scars of westward expansion are still visible in the rock and hillsides. Plaques throughout the park explain the role of the army at nearby Fort Laramie in safeguarding the trails for the westward bound. A short, paved path leads to an area overlooking several distinct sets of ruts, but it's more fun to jump off the trail and follow the ruts themselves. Two miles farther down Wyoming Ave. is **Register Cliff**, a soft, sheer face where pioneers carved their names and dates, sometimes in elaborate script. Though they spoil the aesthetic somewhat, chainlink fences point the way to some of the oldest signatures. (*Off Wyoming Ave. about a mile down a dirt road.* ☎307-836-2334. Open daily sunrise-sunset. Free.)

GUERNSEY STATE PARK. The park has 8500 acres of cliffs, forested hills, and reservoir waters. A drive through the park is rewarding, but swimming, boating, and camping are also available. The road leads to the visitors center, which has a few historical displays and explanations of the formation of the strata in the cliffs. (*Just west of town on US 26, Rte. 317 heads north. A few miles up Rte. 317.* ☎307-836-2334. Visitors center open from mid-May to Labor Day daily 10am-6pm. Park open 8am-10pm. $4 per car.)

THE ROAD TO DOUGLAS: 43 MI.

Whalen Street leads west, becoming **US 26** again outside of town. US 26 lasts another 15 mi. before ter-

OREGON TRAIL

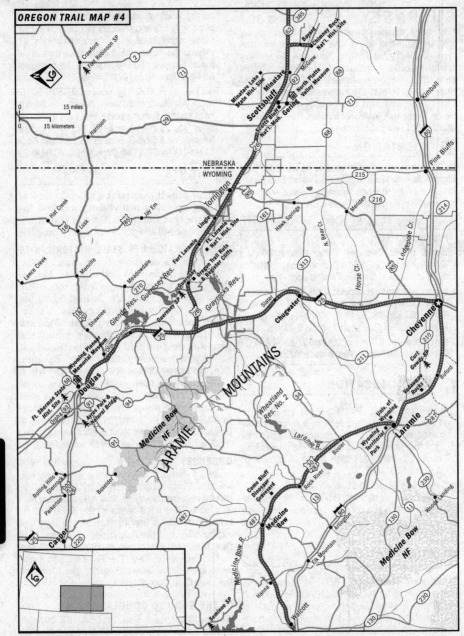

OREGON TRAIL MAP #4

OREGON TRAIL

minating at **I-25,** but the road is glorious. At the junction with I-25, turn north. **Exit 135** leads to **Business I-25;** a right from here onto **South Fourth Street** leads directly to **Center Street** and downtown Douglas.

DOUGLAS ☎307

For such a small city, Douglas carries many distinctions. Both the Oregon and Bozeman Trails passed through Douglas and nearby Fort Fetterman. Owen Wister thought enough of the town to set *The Virginian* here. Douglas casts aside the paltry mantles however, for a title of stature and substance: the home of the jackalope, a creature so elusive that some might say it doesn't exist at all. Part rabbit, part deer, the jackalope defies simple categorization. One might argue that the beast is so rare because it's been hunted to near extinction by the townsfolk who mount it on every available surface. Special jackalope hunting licenses can even be found by those with the stomach for it. Skeptics, beware: Douglas is proud of its chimeric mascot and does not take kindly to the suggestion that the creature is, just maybe, a myth.

VITAL STATS
Population: 5300
Tourist Office: Douglas Area Chamber of Commerce, 121 Brownfield Rd. (☎307-358-2950; www.jackalope.org), just off Center St., a few blocks west of downtown. Open M-F 8am-8pm, Sa-Su 10am-5pm.
Library and Internet Access: Converse County Library, 300 Walnut St. (☎307-358-3644; www.conversecountylibrary.org). Free. Open M, W, F 9am-6pm, Tu and Th 9am-8pm, Sa 9am-2pm.
Post Office: 129 N. 3rd St. (☎307-358-9358). Open M-F 8am-5pm, Sa 10am-12:30pm. **Postal Code:** 82633.

▓ ORIENTATION

Douglas is bordered by **Antelope Creek** to the west and **I-25** to the south. Numbered streets run north-south through the city, with Bus. I-25 running between **Third** and **Fifth Streets.** The downtown area, home to a pleasant combination of bookshops and barbershops, is focused around the intersection of Center St., a main east-west thoroughfare, and Third St. Most streets allow curbside parking.

▟ ACCOMMODATIONS

4 Winds Motel, 615 E. Richards St. (☎307-358-2322). Remodeled by new owners, this motel is sparkling clean and boasts free Wi-Fi. Several room sizes are available, allowing those with smaller (or larger) wallets to find something to their satisfaction. Singles from $37; doubles from $44. AmEx/MC/V. ❷

The Plains Motel, 841 S. 6th St. (☎307-358-4484). Across the street from the 4 Winds Motel. Clean and comfortable rooms at cheap rates. A veritable hodgepodge of historic Douglas buildings, the Plains is certainly the most architecturally interesting place you can spend the night in town. Mounted jackalope trophies ($70) are available in case the joke isn't worn out by the time you're ready to leave. Singles $32; doubles $34. AmEx/MC/V. ❷

▚ FOOD

Like many small towns, Douglas has its share of chain restaurants. Scattered about town, however, a few independent restaurants still have some good, cheap food to offer.

The Koop, 108 N. 3rd St. (☎307-358-3509). A mom-and-pop-style diner that's a lot tastier than you'd expect. They're not joking when they say they serve the best burgers in town ($5.60-7.60). The shakes ($3.80) are enormous. Bring a quarter for the jukeboxes attached to each booth; they still work, and everyone wants to listen to "God Bless the USA" while they eat lunch. Breakfast $4.30-8.30. Sandwiches $6.30-7.30. Open M-F 6am-3pm, Sa 7am-2pm. MC/V. ❶

La Costa, 1600 E. 2nd St. (☎207-235-6599). Offers a surprising number of seafood options, including the intriguing Chimichanga Del Mar ($7), made with crab and shrimp and topped with guacamole and sour cream. The usual dishes are present and accounted for. Check out the extensive combination menu ($10-11) to avoid ordering a la carte. Appetizers $6.25-9. Entrees $7.50-11.25. Open M-Th 11am-10pm, F-Sa 11am-10:30pm, Su 11am-9pm. Cash only. ❷

◉ SIGHTS

JACKALOPE SIGHTINGS. While the actual jackalope may only emerge in the dead of night, the residents of Douglas have erected many likenesses of the beast for the benefit of doubting Thomases everywhere. A brief tour of the most prominent jackalopes in and around Douglas will naturally start with the **Silhouetted Jackalope,** which stands sentinel on a hill overlooking I-25 and US 30. In the town proper, **Centennial Jackalope Square,** at Third and Center St., hosts the original **World's Largest Jackalope,** an 8 ft. tall beast built with more power, grace, and fiberglass than any mortal man. The surrounding park contains several nice benches for those dizzy with reverence as well as a community billboard displaying local activities. That beast's reign has recently been challenged, however, by the recently acquired **World's Even Larger Jackalope,** in front of the **Douglas Railroad Interpretive Center,** 121 Brownfield Rd. As if that weren't enough, plans are currently in the works to build an 80 ft. tall fiberglass beast to terrify sleepy morning commuters on I-25.

PIONEER MEMORIAL MUSEUM. The museum puts other local history museums to shame with its professionalism and encyclopedic scope. The museum dedicates each of its three galleries to a different side of frontier life. While the cowboy and homesteader galleries are impressive on their own, the Native American gallery stands out as more than the usual collection of arrowheads and broken pots— people especially seem to enjoy the tipi, which was featured in *Dances with Wolves. (400 W. Center St., in the state fairgrounds. ☎307-358-9288. Open M-F 8am-5pm, Sa 1-5pm. Free.)*

FORT FETTERMAN HISTORICAL SITE. It's a bit of a drive from the city itself, but Fort Fetterman tells an interesting chapter in the story begun at Fort Laramie. Fort Fetterman began as an effort to protect fortune seekers on the Bozeman Trail but eventually rose to prominence during the Native American wars. Those who've been following the story of Red Cloud and Crazy Horse will appreciate the fort's role as a staging ground for federal troops during the Great Sioux War, but those with shorter attention spans will find little of interest in the collection of old buildings and foundation markers. A short video, a few small displays, and a walking trail through the old parade grounds round out the fort's attrac-

tions. (☎307-358-2864 or 684-7629. Open daily from Memorial Day to Labor Day 9am-5pm. $2.)

◙ DETOUR
AYRES NATURAL BRIDGE

From Douglas, continue heading west along **I-25 North.** After about 10 mi., take **Exit 151** and head 5 mi. south along the road to the bridge. Be careful; the road is full of blind curves with no guard rails.

Ayres Natural Bridge is a rock wall that was slowly eroded by water to form a bridge. There's no better way to spend an afternoon than surrounded by gorgeous red cliffs and the sound of gently flowing water. Though the park is smaller than many along the trail, basic facilities and picnic tables are present. Camping is also permitted as long as it's cleared in advance with the caretaker. While the bridge itself is only accessible from a deceptively tricky "mini" trail, the view from the top is well worth the effort. (☎307-358-3532. Open Apr.-Oct. daily 8am-8pm. Free.)

> **! TRAVEL ADVISORY.** The going gets pretty rough in the not-so-distant future, and the **Alcova Backcountry Byway** is nearly impossible in winter. If your car can't handle the driving or if it's winter, head on through Douglas, continuing west on I-25 through Casper and picking up the route at Alcova (p. 631).

◤ THE ROAD TO CHEYENNE: 124 MI.
Turn around and head south on **I-25,** past the junction with **US 26.** Head through the towns of Wheatland and Chugwater to Cheyenne. Stay on I-25 through the periphery of the city until it divides: I-25 will continue straight south, while **US 85/87** will peel off to the southeast. Stay on I-25 until the exit for **Central Avenue,** which will take you across **East Pershing Avenue** and into the central downtown area.

CHEYENNE   ☎307

"Cheyenne," the name of the Native American tribe that originally inhabited this region, was once considered a prime candidate for the name of the whole Wyoming territory. The moniker was vetoed by the notoriously priggish Senator Sherman, who pointed out that the pronunciation of Cheyenne closely resembled that of the French word *chienne*, meaning "bitch." Once one of the fastest-growing frontier towns, Cheyenne has slowed down quite a bit. There are still a few places worth checking out and lots of Western style.

VITAL STATS
Population: 53,000
Tourist Office: Cheyenne Visitors Center, 121 W. 15th St. (☎307-778-3133 or 800-426-5009; www.cheyenne.org), on the 1st fl. of the Cheyenne Depot, at the end of Capitol Ave. Open May-Sept. M-F 8am-7pm, Sa 9am-5pm; Oct.-Apr. M-F 8am-5pm, Sa 9am-5pm, Su 11am-5pm.
Library and Internet Access: Laramie County Library in Cheyenne, 2200 Pioneer Ave. (☎307-634-3561. Free. Wi-Fi requires $1 guest pass. Open M-Th 10am-9pm, F-Sa 10am-6pm, Su 1-5pm.
Post Office: 4800 Converse Ave. (☎307-772-7080). Take Lincolnway east, then head north on Converse Ave. past Dell Range Blvd. Open M-F 7:30am-5:30pm, Sa 7am-1pm. **Postal Code:** 82009.

✳ ORIENTATION

Three streets run parallel to each other through downtown—**Carey Avenue, Capitol Avenue,** and **Central Avenue.** Perpendicular to these streets are a series of numbered roads,

increasing from south to north. Downtown is roughly between **Lincolnway (16th Street)** and **Pershing Avenue,** just north of **30th Street.** Free 2hr. parking is available downtown, but finding a place can be difficult. Visitors should claim a spot and walk.

🏠 ACCOMMODATIONS

As long as your visit doesn't coincide with **Frontier Days,** when rates shoot up and vacancies disappear, it's easy to land a cheap room here. While many historic buildings downtown have been converted into cheap hotels, their cleanliness and quality might be reason to opt for the more conventional motels just past the train tracks on **East Lincolnway.**

Terry Bison Ranch, 51 I-25 Service Rd. E. (☎307-634-4171). From I-25 S., take Exit 2. Go left at the bottom of the exit, then right on Terry Ranch Rd. Feel awesome when you tell your friends you camped next to a herd of bison. They don't have to know there was a fence and modern facilities. The general store also sells bison meat by the lb. Bison tours $12, ages 4-12 $6. Office open daily 8am-7pm. Tent sites $16. Bunkhouses $60; cabins $80. D/MC/V. ❶

The Ranger Motel, 909 W. 16th St. (☎307-634-7995). A no-frills sort of place with clean, comfy rooms. Singles from $30. AmEx/V. ❷

A FIELD GUIDE FOR THE NORTH AMERICAN JACKALOPE

Discovered in 1934 by a local taxidermist, the jackalope *(Lepus temperamentalus)* is one of the most intensely studied examples of western American fauna. The animal's mythological elusiveness has made a comprehensive study of its attributes and behaviors impossible. The guide that follows is a compilation of some of the fearsome creature's most commonly acknowledged features.

Field reports suggest that the jackalope is by nature very shy, relying on its speed and long jump to evade its enemies. One of the animal's most amazing attributes is its ability to mimic human voices. The beast uses this ability to confuse would-be pursuers by mimicking such phrases as, "There he goes! That way!" While such behavior may be construed as harmless or even playful, the jackalope is a creature that must be taken seriously. When cornered, the animal will not hesitate to bring its massive antlers to bear, using them to wrestle and even gore opponents.

The milk of female jackalopes is said to have medicinal qualities. In addition to its great healing potential, some reports have also identified it as a powerful aphrodisiac. As an interesting aside, the animal's powerful leaps naturally homogenize the milk, making it readily drinkable and delicious.

Seasoned jackalope hunters report that the animal displays a fondness for whiskey and can be lured out of its den by flasks left out at night. While hunters debate which variety of whiskey the beast most prefers, all agree that the resulting intoxication makes hunting the jackalope much easier.

FOOD

Unfortunately, independent restaurants seem to be a dying breed in Cheyenne. While fast-food joints sprout from almost every corner, a few local places continue to hang on.

Poor Richard's Restaurant, 2233 E. Lincolnway (☎307-635-5114). A little on the expensive side for most roadtrippers, but the variety is the best you're likely to find in Cheyenne. The walnut-crusted salmon ($15.50) is popular. Besides, 18th- century Northeastern tavern is a refreshing change from 19th- century Western saloon. Burgers and sandwiches $7-12. Entrees $11-27. Open M-Sa 11am-2:30pm, and from 5pm. MC/V. ❸

Driftwood Cafe, 200 E. 18th St. (☎307-634-5304), at Warren St. Mom-and-pop atmosphere to match dirt-cheap homestyle cooking. Try the Cheyenne Burger (2 cheeses, mushrooms, and bacon; $4.85). Slice of pie $2. Open M-F 7am-4pm. AmEx/MC/V. ❶

SIGHTS

WYOMING STATE CAPITOL BUILDING. The capitol has a gold-leafed dome (visible from every road entering the city) and beautiful stained-glass ceilings in the rotunda as well as in both legislative chambers. *(At Capitol Ave. and 24th St. ☎307-777-7220. Open M-F 8am-5pm. Tours every hr. 9am-3pm. Free.)*

NELSON MUSEUM OF THE WEST. This is Cheyenne's true Western museum. In addition to the massive collections of uniforms and firearms, the Nelson tries to focus on those aspects of life in the West that other museums would overlook—one of the most interesting displays examines the evolution of the Stetson hat. *(1714 Carey Ave. ☎307-635-7670. Open May-Oct. M-F 9am-4:30pm. $4, under 12 free, seniors $3.)*

NIGHTLIFE

Like everything else in Cheyenne, the bars are generally Western-themed.

Outlaw Saloon, 312 S. Greeley Hwy. (☎307-635-7552). A massive stage hosts live country music nightly, while the patio provides a quieter place to relax. Free dance lessons every Th 7:30-8:30pm. Open daily 11am-2am. MC/V.

Goofy's, 2801 E. Lincolnway (☎307-634-1501). An electric dance floor surrounded by dangling ornaments and glow-in-the-dark skeletons. Open M-Sa 10am-2am, Su 11am-10pm. MC/V

FESTIVALS

Every year, during the last full week of July, the population doubles as people from all over the world converge on town for **Cheyenne Frontier Days,** a 10-day celebration of all things Western. Events include nightly concerts by rock and country acts, a carnival, a frontier art show, a performance by the USAF Thunderbirds, and, perhaps most tempting, free pancake breakfasts. The main draw for most, however, will be the rodeo, which always carries the moniker "Daddy of 'Em All." While the atmosphere is certainly one-of-a-kind, 10 days of it might be a little much for even the most receptive city folk. (☎307-778-7222 or 800-227-6336; www.cfdrodeo.com. Rodeo tickets $17-23. Concert tickets $18-75.)

DETOUR
VEDAUWOO

Twenty-eight miles from Cheyenne on **Happy Jack Road,** take a left onto **Vedauwoo Road,** just past the **Medicine Bow National Forest** sign. Note that this dirt road is 8 mi. long and bumpy. It may be faster to continue down Happy Jack Rd. to I-80 and backtrack east to **Exit 329.**

Named for the towering, sculpted formations that fill it, Vedauwoo (from the Arapaho word meaning "earthborn spirits") looks more like a series of artfully arranged and balanced boulders than proper mountains. Serious rock climbers can spend all day exploring in the shadow of this red rock, but even casual hikers can find some pretty breathtaking spots. **Turtle Rock Trail** winds for 2 mi. around some of the most beautiful formations, but you should consider renting a campsite ($10) and staying the day. (☎307-745-2300. $5 per vehicle.)

DETOUR
AMES MONUMENT

Head 6 mi. east on **I-80** to **Exit 329** and follow the dirt roads over 2 mi. to the monument.

On a lonely dirt road overlooking a stretch of field sits the Ames Monument, a 60 ft. pyramid dedicated to the brothers who oversaw the construction of the Transcontinental Rail-

OREGON TRAIL

road. The site was once the highest point on the original line, at 8247 ft., until the railroad was shifted 3 mi. south. Now alone on a Wyoming hillside, the monument is kept company only by the prairie dogs and the occasional roadtripper. (Open 24hr. Free.)

⚑ THE ROAD TO LARAMIE: 51 MI.

From **I-80, Exit 313** and **316** both lead into the city; 313 opens on **Third Street** near town, while 316 leads to **Grand Avenue,** which runs past the University of Wyoming, and intersects Third St. downtown.

LARAMIE ☎307

While Laramie might be half the size of Cheyenne or Casper, the University of Wyoming provides more than its share of sights, and the downtown area, with its rare-book stores, coffeehouses, and antique shops, helps cast Laramie as more stylish than hopelessly dated.

VITAL STATS
Population: 27,000
Tourist Office: Laramie Chamber of Commerce, 800 3rd St. (☎800-445-5303; www.laramie-tourism.org). Open M-F 8am-5pm.
Library and Internet Access: Albany County Library, 310 8th St. (☎307-721-2580). Open M-Th 10am-8pm, F-Sa 1-5pm.
Post Office: 152 5th St. (☎307-721-8837). Open M-F 8am-5:15pm, Sa 9am-1pm. **Postal Code:** 82070.

✼ ORIENTATION

Laramie's two critical roads are **Third Street,** which runs north-south, and **Grand Avenue,** which runs east-west. The few blocks around their intersection comprise downtown. North of their intersection along Third St. are most motels, and east along Grand Ave. are municipal buildings and the University of Wyoming. There's free 2hr. parking along most streets.

⚑ ACCOMMODATIONS

Gas Lite Motel, 960 3rd St. (☎307-742-6616). An army of statues, including bears, horses, cowboys, and dinosaurs, monitors the entrance. The rooms

themselves are much more conventionally furnished. Singles $95; doubles $99. AmEx/MC/V. ❸

Ranger Motel, 453 3rd St. (☎307-742-6677), downtown. The rooms are spacious and have microwaves and refrigerators. Rooms from $55. MC/V. ❷

Laramie KOA, 1271 W. Baker St. (☎307-742-6553). In the middle of a trailer park. Provides clean facilities and Wi-Fi, just like your forefathers enjoyed. Camp sites $20. D/MC/V. ❶

▨ FOOD

For those who have forgotten what fresh vegetables taste like in the middle of steak country, Laramie's downtown dining options will be a great relief while also preventing scurvy.

Jeffrey's Bistro, 123 Ivinson St. (☎307-742-7046), at the corner of 2nd St. Lists a number of salads ($7.50-10) in addition to a healthy mix of American, Indian, and Italian options. Open M-Sa 11am-9pm. AmEx/D/MC/V. ❸

Sweet Melissa's, 213 1st St. (☎307-742-9607), downtown. Smells like patchouli and serves only vegetarian and vegan dishes. Nachos ($4-8) make up much of the appetizer menu, while the entrees ($6-8) include lentil loaf and eggplant parmesan. Open M-Sa 11am-9pm. MC/V. ❷

◉ SIGHTS

ABRAHAM LINCOLN'S HEAD. Before you even enter the city proper, you can see the **Abraham Lincoln Memorial Monument,** located at the rest area by Exit 323 on I-80, an embarrassingly large tribute to a president who had very little to do with Wyoming. At almost 14 ft. tall, the purposefully caricatured visage of honest Abe seems to implore you to "please drive safely."

GEOLOGY MUSEUM. Once in town, the museums at the University of Wyoming can provide a full day's entertainment by themselves. The Geology Museum may not sound like the most exciting place to spend an afternoon, but it's actually a natural history museum of some intrigue. Though small, the museum manages to cram an impressive number of skeletons into a limited space, including an enormous *Apatosaurus* skeleton, not to mention "Big Al," one of the world's most complete *Allosaurus* skeletons. (*At 11th and Lewis St.*

☎307-766-4218; www.uwyo.ede/geomuseum. Open M-F 8am-5pm, Sa-Su 10am-3pm. Free.)

UNIVERSITY ART MUSEUMS. At the opposite end of campus sits the hyper-modern and hyper-conical **Centennial Complex,** which houses two of the university's best museums. The American Heritage Center is primarily a research center, but the gallery area is filled with Western pop-culture history; exhibits on Western films and TV shows surround the saddles of Hopalong Cassidy and the Cisco Kid. (2111 Willet Dr. Take Grand Ave. to 22nd St. and head north, then east on Willet Dr. ☎307-766-4114; www.uwyo.edu/ahc. Open M 8am-9pm, Tu-F 8am-5pm. Free.) Across the lobby is the **University of Wyoming Art Museum.** Exhibits are ever-changing, drawing from both traveling selections and the university's private collection. (☎307-766-6622; www.uwyo.edu/artmuseum. Open M-Sa 10am-5pm, Su 1-5pm. Free.)

◧ NIGHTLIFE

▨ **The Library,** 1622 E. Grand Ave. (☎307-742-0500). Perhaps the best-named college bar ever sits right across the street from the university dorms and keeps one of the professors around as its brewmaster. The chocolatey Pryopysm Porter ($2.50) is a house favorite. The Library also serves sandwiches like the inscrutable, yet tasty Ulysses (chicken breast with an artichoke cheese spread and provolone; $7.50). Sandwiches $7-8.50. Entrees $8-18. Open Tu-Sa 11am-2am. AmEx/D/MC/V.

Buckhorn Bar, 114 Ivinson St. (☎307-742-3554). Hosts regional punk and alternative acts during the week while the upstairs Parlor provides hip-hop DJs Th-Sa. Ask the bartender for the story about the bullet hole in the mirror. Live music F-Sa. No cover. Open M-Sa 10am-2am, Su 10am-midnight. MC/V.

◪ THE ROAD TO MEDICINE BOW: 57 MI.

Head north along **Third Street.** Beyond the city limits, this road becomes **US 30/287,** which arcs northwest toward Sinclair and Rawlins. Five miles west of Rock River, **Marshal Road** heads north toward the **Como Bluffs** and the legendary **Dinosaur Graveyard.** After its discovery, the area seemed to be an endless source of fossilized North American dinosaurs, yielding one of the largest skeletons ever unearthed at nearly 70 ft. long. The graveyard seems to have run out of dinos, however, and today there isn't

much to see beyond the cliffs themselves. Continue on **US 30** until you reach Medicine Bow.

MEDICINE BOW ☎307

Owen Wister published his novel *The Virginian* in 1902, and Medicine Bow, population 275, suddenly became famous. In 1909, the mayor had the ▨**Virginian Hotel ❷,** 404 Lincoln Hwy., built in Wister's honor. Each of the rooms is decorated with its own style and color scheme, and highlights include thick carpets, frilled bedspreads, and a few cano-pied beds or clawed bathtubs—all available at budget prices. Those who want the full *Virginian* experience can splurge for the Owen Wister suite ($80), which contains the desk *The Virginian* was composed upon. While Wister never stayed in his eponymous suite, Teddy Roosevelt once spent the night. (☎307-379-2377. Singles with shared bath $30; doubles with private bath $55. MC/V.) **The Virginian Restaurant and Saloon ❸** serves country-style dinners ($9-10) like chicken-fried steak and calf liver. The Owen Wister Dining Room is fully furnished with Victorian-era place set-tings and decor. (☎307-379-2377. Open daily 6am-9pm. MC/V.) For true Wister enthusiasts, across the street from the Virginian is the **Medicine Bow Museum,** which contains the cabin Wister once lived in as well as exhibits on the history of Medicine Bow and lots of artifacts, including an edifying 2000-piece pen collection. (☎307-379-2383. Open M-F 10am-5pm, Sa-Su 1-5pm. Donations accepted.)

◧ DETOUR
SEMINOE-ALCOVA BACKCOUNTRY BYWAY

Continue along **US 287/US 30 West.** Get on to **I-80 West;** get off at **Exit 221.** Follow the exit past the refinery straight through the cluster of houses to **10th Street,** where you should turn off the main road. Watch carefully for signs to the Wyoming Backway.

While the winding roads and steep climbs of the byway may have been too much for the original pioneers, most of the year modern technology will allow you to conquer this formidable but beautiful stretch of road. However, during the winter, high-altitude snows can overcome even the most tricked-out yellow Hummers. Taking the byway is advisable only between May and September.

Even during the summer months, the road is rough and devoid of services; a full tank of gas and bottles of water are a must for this trip, which spans several hours and miles of dirt and gravel roads with poor (if any) cell-phone reception. The first miles of the route follow the North Platte River. To the right, the blue river rushes by, and, to the left, the red rock slants at fascinating but disconcerting angles. Up ahead, the Seminoe Mountains rise as the road descends into a gorge. After 20 mi., you'll see a huge sand dune on the right; watch for high winds that can blow sand in the roadway. About 4 mi. farther is **Seminoe State Park ❶**, which offers fishing, boating, and a serene campsite. All manner of wildlife live in and around the reservoir area, even rare mountain lions and ▉bald eagles. The park is divided into several regions, two of which—the North and South Red Hills—can be reached directly from the byway. (☎307-777-6323; http://wyoparks. state.wy.us/seslide.htm. Entrance fee $4 per car. Sites $12. Cash only.)

Beyond the park, the road becomes steep and winding. Around here, it is best to stop every so often to let your engine cool down; it'll give you a chance to enjoy the scenic vistas and will let your dirt-clogged and over-heated engine rest for a few minutes. The area is lined with places to pull off and gander. Strategically placed park benches give breathtaking views of the reservoir and Elk Mountain. After this, the road narrows and descends into deep forests for several miles. A 4 mi. downhill stretch past rock spires completes the mountainous leg of the journey. At the bottom of the slope is **Miracle Mile**, a 5 mi. stretch of stream known for its blue-ribbon trout. The fishing area is formed by the imposing **Kortes Dam,** which can be reached by following a 3 mi. detour. This side route breaks off the main road just past the bridge over Miracle Mile. The remaining 35 mi. stretch of the byway is an austere expanse of rocky plain broken only by large formations such as **Dome Rock.** At the end is the town of Alcova, which sits beneath the Alcova Dam.

◪ THE ROAD TO ALCOVA: 83 MI.
If you did not take the **Seminoe-Alcova Backcountry Byway,** you have some catching up to do. From Medi-cine Bow, head north on **Route-487** for 71 mi., then make a left onto **Route-220** and head into town.

ALCOVA ☎307
The sign marking the entrance to Alcova reads, "Alcova. Winter population: 100, summer population: 35,000. It's a dam site!", which should tell you most everything you need to know. The town is on the northern end of the Seminoe Mountains, and the surrounding lakes and rivers are full of campgrounds and fishing spots. Eight cabins with full kitchens and propane grills are highlights at the **Inn at Alcova ❹**, located right at the intersection of the Backcountry Byway and Rte. 220. The thematically decorated cabins can house up to five comfortably. (☎307-234-2066; www. sloanesatalcova.com. Office in Sloanes General Store next door. Free Wi-Fi. Cabins $90. AmEx/D/MC/V.) The **Riverview Inn ❸**, 22258 W. Rte. 220, has a magnificent view of the Gray Reef Reservoir and clean, if small, rooms. Campsites are also available; contact the manager for prices. (☎307-473-5829. Office in the Sunset Grill down the hill. Laundry. Singles $55; doubles $65. MC/V.) Locals congregate at the **Sunset Bar & Grill ❷**, 22250 W. Rte. 220, at the bottom of the Riverview Inn's hill. It's open late, so the lonely moonlight driver can stop for the ever-popular Rocky Mountain oysters ($9) or a sandwich. (☎307-472-3200. Appetizers $3-8. Sandwiches $6-7. Open M-Th 9am-midnight, F 9am-2am, Sa 8am-2am, Su 8am-midnight. AmEx/D/MC/V.)

◪ THE ROAD TO CASPER: 36 MI.
Take **Route 220 East** all the way to Casper.

CASPER ☎307
Casper is the most enjoyable of Wyoming's large cities. It combines Cheyenne's size with Laramie's sense of style and drops all delusions of Wild West grandeur. The downtown area is colorful and varied, with three old-fashioned movie houses and a string of hip restaurants, record stores, and coffee-houses. Throw in a few cool museums and some beautiful scenery, and you have a very cool, very liveable city. Like Kearney, Casper's

OREGON TRAIL

name comes from a misplaced "e" in the name of the nearby fort that preceded it.

ORIENTATION

Casper's haphazard design makes for nightmarish driving. The city is laid out around **Center Street,** which cuts a curvy line north-south through the city. **First Street** runs east-west through the downtown area, with parallel streets increasing in number as you go south. North of First St., the roads are lettered. **Yellowstone Highway** is home to a number of establishments. However, the street is almost impossible to follow, even with a map, since it does not stay in line with the city's rough grid but frequently breaks off and restarts several blocks later, only to merge and vanish again. Fortunately, downtown is very walkable, and most streets offer free curbside parking, which means you shouldn't have to drive much, anyway. Downtown Casper is worth walking around. Most of the best spots are within the area surrounding **Center** and **Second Streets,** and sculptures and statues of various sizes add a little color to any stroll.

VITAL STATS
Population: 51,000
Tourist Office: Casper Area Convention & Visitors Bureau, 992 N. Poplar St. (☎307-234-5362; www. casperwyoming.info). Open M-F 8am-6pm, Sa-Su 10am-6pm.
Library and Internet Access: Natrona County Public Library, 307 E. 2nd St. (☎307-237-4935; www. natronacountylibrary.org). Open M-Th 10am-7pm, F-Sa 10am-5pm.
Post Office: 150 E. B St. (☎307-577-6480). Open M-F 8am-6pm, Sa 9am-noon. **Postal Code:** 82604.

ACCOMMODATIONS

Sage and Sand Motel, 901 W. Yellowstone Hwy. (☎307-237-2088). Has huge comforters, lots of pillows for spontaneous battles, and thematic decor. Laundry. Singles $60; doubles $65. ❸

National 9 Showboat Motel, 100 W. F St. (☎307-235-2711), off N. Center St. Has prices just beyond the budget range, but it offers cable and a continental breakfast. Free Wi-Fi. Check-

out noon. Singles from $80; doubles from $85. AmEx/D/MC/V. ❹

Fort Caspar Campground, 4205 Fort Caspar Rd. (☎307-473-2955). Offers good rates and clean facilities, even if they're a bit of a walk from the tent sites themselves. Continental breakfast. Free Wi-Fi. Primitive sites $16. AmEx/D/MC/V. ❶

FOOD

Western Grill, 2333 E. Yellowstone Hwy. (☎307-234-7061). The prototypical roadtrip rest stop; it's cheap and tasty and has snarky, politically incorrect decor. It also provides a great service to scurvy-suffering roadtrippers by selling individual pieces of fruit. Burgers $5-7. Entrees $7-17. Open daily 6am-9pm. ❷

At Eggington's, 229 E. 2nd St. (☎307-265-8700). The extensive breakfast menu includes eggs Benedict and quiche ($7.50), while lunch features panini ($7-11) and burgers as well as a rotating soup menu. Open M-Sa 6am-2:30pm, Su 7am-2:30pm. ❷

The Sandwich Bar, 124 E. 2nd St. (☎307-266-1527). Mixes up the usual deli routine by letting you build your own sandwich from a buffet of ingredients. Impress your friends by building something that would put Scooby and Shaggy to shame. Sandwiches $7.40 per lb. Open M-Sa 8am-3pm. D/MC/V. ❷

SIGHTS

NATIONAL HISTORIC TRAILS INTERPRETIVE CENTER. Overlooking the city on an antelope-covered hill, the National Historic Trails Interpretive Center sounds like a waste of time, but is actually one of the coolest museums along the trail. The tour begins with a 20min. multimedia history of the California, Oregon, and Mormon Trails. From there, the museums curves around in a huge timeline that begins with audio recordings of Native American creation myths and proceeds through the laying of the Transcontinental Railroad. A rocking, full-motion river-fording simulation teaches you why the smart kids in elementary school always caulked their wagons. (*1501 N. Poplar St. From Center St., head west along Collins St. to Poplar St.* ☎307-261-7700. *Open Apr.-Sept. daily 8am-7pm; Oct.-*

Mar. Tu-Sa 9am-4:30pm. $6, students $4, ages 6-17 $3, ages 3-5 $1, seniors $5.)

NICOLAYSEN ART MUSEUM AND DISCOVERY CENTER. This museum shirks the standard Wild West art in favor of contemporary multimedia installations. The exhibits are constantly changing and feature mostly local artists, though a few pieces from the likes of Andy Warhol can be found floating in the collection. In the same building (through an Alice in Wonderland mini-door) is the **Discovery Center,** a workshop designed to introduce children to a variety of visual media. *(400 E. Collins Dr. ☎307-235-5247; www.thenic.com. Open Tu-Sa 10am-5pm, Su noon-4pm. Free.)*

FORT CASPAR. Named for a lieutenant killed in the Native American wars, Fort Caspar may not have the name recognition of some of its counterparts, but its museum is one of the best. Thanks to WPA reconstruction efforts during the Great Depression, the frontier fort has been restored to its 1860s size and appearance. The barracks and officers' quarters are furnished just as they would have been during the fort's heyday. A reconstruction of Brigham Young's Mormon Ferry is also on the grounds. The museum has displays on naval ship naming conventions, as the fort played a critical role in defending Wyoming's vast coastal region. *(4001 Fort Caspar Rd. ☎307-235-8462; www.fortcasparwyoming.com. Open June-Aug. daily 8am-7pm; Sept. and May daily 8am-5pm; Oct.-Apr. Tu-Sa 8am-5pm. $3, ages 6-17 $2. D/MC/V.)*

◈ DETOUR
INDEPENDENCE ROCK

The rock sits along **Route 220,** 24 mi. west of Alcova.

This huge and strangely smooth hill of stone was the halfway marker for pioneers heading toward Oregon. If the wagon train reached the rock by July 4, then the journey was on schedule to beat the winter snows—thus the name "Independence Rock." Like Register Cliff and Names Hill, Independence Rock is covered with the names of visitors past and present. A little looking will reveal names from as early as 1850. The top of the hill itself affords a great view of Mitchell Pass and Devil's Gate. As a nod to the rock's former role as a resting spot for weary travellers, the area

around the rock includes a rest stop. (Open sunrise-sunset. Free.)

◈ DETOUR
MORMON HANDCART VISITORS CENTER AND DEVIL'S GATE

47600 West Highway 220. About 5 mi. west of Independence Rock, along **Route 220.**

Sponsored by The Church of Jesus Christ Latter Day Saints, the visitors center is situated on a former ranch and tells the story of the Mormon exodus to Salt Lake City, focusing on the disasters that befell the Martin and Willie companies. Free camping is also available if you call ahead. The visitors center actually provides a better view of Devil's Gate than the actual historic site. Though the trails never passed through it, Devil's Gate was an impressive landmark associated with Independence Rock. Native legend held that a spirit had once terrorized the Sweetwater Valley in the form of a monstrous tusked beast. When daring warriors assaulted the creature, it tore the cliffs open in fury, forming the gate. (☎307-328-2953. Open daily 8am-7pm. Free.)

⚐ THE ROAD TO LANDER: 148 MI.
US 287 becomes **East Main Street** within city limits. Go straight through the intersection where **Route 789** breaks away to the east, and you'll find yourself on the western end of **Main Street,** which heads west.

LANDER ☎307

Lander is the kind of place you might want to live when you're ready to settle down. Everyone looks young, is progressive, and has their pant legs permanently rolled up and secured with bandanas, prepared for any unforseen mountain biking they that might be called for in the course of a day. The mountains provide a constant, romantic backdrop. Lander has the culture of a larger city but the charm and earnestness of a small town. It would be easy to fly through, but this is the kind of town that rewards careful exploration.

◩ ORIENTATION

Main Street is Lander's major thoroughfare, with **Third Street** providing the major intersection. The area is lined with specialty shops,

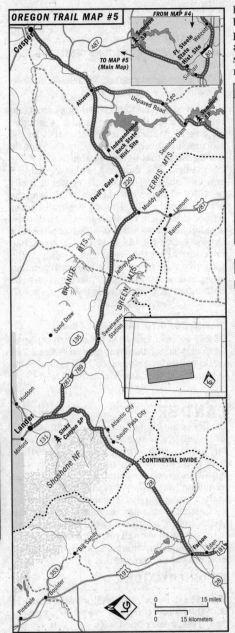

OREGON TRAIL MAP #5

FROM MAP #4

TO MAP #5 (Main Map)

Ft Steele State Hist. Site

Seminoe SP

Casper

Alcova

Unpaved Road

Seminoe SP

Seminoe Dam

Independence Rock State Hist. Site

Devil's Gate

FERRIS MTS.

Muddy Gap

Lamont

Bairoil

GRANITE MTS.

Jeffrey City

GREEN MTS.

Sand Draw

Sweetwater Station

Hudson

Lander

Milford

Sinks Canyon SP

Atlantic City

South Pass City

Shoshone NF

CONTINENTAL DIVIDE

Big Sandy

Farson

Eden

Pinedale

Bolder

0   15 miles

0   15 kilometers

OREGON TRAIL

bookstores, and outdoor outfitters. Just browsing a few blocks can take up the better part of an afternoon. Free parking is available along Main St., although stiff competition for spots between **Second Street** and **Fourth Street** might make a side street the better option.

VITAL STATS

Population: 6900

Tourist Office: Lander Chamber of Commerce, 160 N. 1st St. (☎307-332-3892 or 800-433-0662; www.landerwyoming.org). Open June-Aug. M-F 9am-5pm, Sa 9am-2pm; Sept.-May M-F 9am-5pm.

Library and Internet Access: Fremont County Public Library, 451 N. 2nd St. (☎307-332-5194). Open M-Th 10am-9pm, F-Sa 10am-4pm.

Post Office: 230 Grandview Dr. (☎307-332-2126), off E. Main St. Open M-F 8am-5pm, Sa 10am-1pm. **Postal Code:** 82520.

ACCOMMODATIONS

Free camping ❶ for up to three nights is available in **City Park,** 405 Fremont St. Follow Third St. south and then turn left at Fremont. After about half a mile, the park will be on the right. Be warned: the only facilities are soap-less, shower-less bathrooms on the opposite end of the park. Be further warned: there is no one around to tell reveling teens to settle down.

The Holiday Lodge, 210 McFarlane Dr. (☎307-332-2511), a 5min. walk from downtown. Provides large, clean rooms at the best rates in an otherwise expensive motel market. Free Wi-Fi. Singles $65; doubles $70. AmEx/D/MC/V. ❸

Blue Spruce Inn, 677 S. 3rd St. (☎307-332-8253; www.bluespruceinn.com). 2 of the 4 rooms have private baths; the others get TVs. All are individually decorated and named; the Brass Room is a classy alternative to Wyoming's ubiquitous cowboy decor. A large front porch makes for excellent lounging. Free Wi-Fi. Singles $65; doubles $75. MC/V. ❸

FOOD

Lander's best restaurants line Main St. between First St. and Fourth St.

Gannett Grill, 126 Main St. (☎307-332-8228). Reasonably priced salads and sandwiches as well as lovely outdoor patio seating. Salads

($5.50-7.25) include the "Mad Greek" and "Hail Caesar." Sandwiches $6.50-7.50. Open daily 11am-10pm. AmEx/D/MC/V. ❷

Cowfish, 128 Main St. (☎307-332-7009; www.landerbar.com). Consists of 2 main sections—Cow and Fish—though pork and poultry make guest appearances. The menu rotates regularly, though staples like Baja Fish Tacos ($18) can always be found. Cowfish is also a well-regarded microbrewery, so be sure to try a pint of one of its homebrews ($2.50) like the chocolatey "5 lb. Brown." Appetizers $6-7. Entrees $10-28. Open daily 5-9:30pm. AmEx/D/MC/V. ❹

Cooking Crow, 228 Main St. (☎307-332-5376). A relatively small but creative menu, including the delicious southwest chicken sandwich ($8), which comes with pesto and chipotle sauce on a kaiser bun, and popular walleye cakes ($10). Open Tu-Th 11am-2pm, F 11am-2pm and 5-9pm, Sa 8am-2pm and 5-9pm, Su 9am-2pm. MC/V. ❷

🔆 SIGHTS

SINKS CANYON STATE PARK. While Main St. may be the best attraction in the city itself, the wild outskirts contain Sinks Canyon State Park. From Main St., head south on Fifth St., which becomes Rte. 131. Seven miles down this road is the Rise, a calm pool into which a stream erupts to form the Popo Agie (which means "Tall Grass River" in the Crow language). Swimming against the current, dozens of rainbow and brown trout can be seen, some as large as 20 lb. Trout-food vending machines stand next to the overlook. A quarter-mile farther up the road are the Sinks, where the mighty Popo Agie disappears meekly into a hollow, only to reappear seeping from the rocks into the Rise a quarter-mile downstream. The **State Park Visitors Center** is right next to the Sinks overlook, providing an overview of the area and its wildlife, including an impressive collection of local animal skulls donated by someone named Bruce Campbell, though no evidence of shotgun or chainsaw damage can be seen. *(3079 Sinks Canyon Rd. ☎ 307-332-6333. Open daily in summer 9am-6pm.)*

WIND RIVER INDIAN RESERVATION. Beginning 4 mi. north of the town limits but extending for millions of acres beyond is the Wind River Indian Reservation of the Arapaho and Shoshone Tribes. Seeing a powwow on an actual reservation is a truly incredible experience—make every effort to catch one when you're passing through. The reservation performs powwows and sun dances throughout the summer. For specific dates, contact the Lander Chamber of Commerce (p. 633).

SHOSHONE NATIONAL FOREST. Locals and visitors alike spend a lot of time at Shoshone National Forest. Follow Rte. 131 just past Sinks Canyon State Park. Covering 2.5 million acres of forests, mountains, lakes, and plains, Shoshone is one of the most biodiverse protected areas in the country. Some of the more spectacular sights include ⬛**Gannett Glacier** and the ⬛**Cirque of the Towers,** a ring of 1000 ft. tall towers carved by retreating glaciers. Trails for hiking and biking range from 2 mi. to the epic 21 mi. **Middle Fork Trail.** Camping is available in many areas ($10-15) beginning in mid-June, although a few areas on the North Fork are restricted to hard-sided campers due to grizzly bears. *(☎307-527-6241. Supervisor's office open M-F 8am-4:30pm. Free.)*

⬛ DETOUR
GRAND LOOP ROAD

From Lander, head south on **Fifth Street.** This becomes **Route 131,** which feeds into Sinks Canyon. From there, the **Loop Road** is the only available path. It terminates on **Route 28,** 30 mi. south of Lander.

After you conquer the Seminoe-Alcova Backcountry Byway, Grand Loop Rd. won't seem like too much of a challenge, but it still demands a lot from drivers and their cars. The first stretch of road takes you past **Sinks Canyon** and the lower levels of the forest. After a few miles, **Bruce's Lot** appears on the left. Here, hikers and bikers can tackle the 21 mi. **Middle Fork Trail,** and wimpy drivers can turn back with their figurative tails between their legs. From here, the road dissolves into a dusty series of switchbacks up the slope. Keep your eyes on the road and hug the inside of the curves—there are no barriers most of the way up, and the sheer drops are not particularly forgiving. Six miles and 10 tiers later, the road levels out; take a breath and enjoy the scenery. There are a few pull-offs. The view of deep-blue **Lonely Lake** surrounded by pine trees and backed by the white-capped Wind

River Range is gorgeous. From here, you can take the left road, which leads back to Rte. 28, or take the right road, which leads to more campgrounds and great vistas.

⊠ DETOUR
FARSON MERCANTILE

4048 Highway 191. At the intersection of **Route 28** and **US 191.**

The **Farson Mercantile** ❶ is regionally famous for its ice cream and sparsely decorated 80-year-old building. The cones have been served to locals and travelers from all over the world—even astronaut training crews. Sizes range from the 6 oz. single-scoop ($1.69) to the colossal 22 oz. ($5), which is enough to give even the most hardened roadtripper a serious brain freeze. (☎307-273-9020. Sandwiches $3.50-5. Open daily 10am-7pm. MC/V.)

⚐ THE ROAD TO ROCK SPRINGS: 120 MI.

If you took **Grand Loop Road,** congratulations. Head south on **Route 28.** If you didn't, you have some catching up to do. Head southeast on **US 287 (Main Street)** for 9 mi., then get on Rte. 28 S. In Farson, take **US 191 South.** It may seem broad and flat, but the Continental Divide lies just a few miles beyond the intersection. It is announced with little fanfare but represents an important landmark, both geologically and for the Oregon Trail, indicating the completion of the 1st ascent. Rock Springs is 38 mi. ahead. Entering Rock Springs, US 191 becomes **Elk Street.**

ROCK SPRINGS ☎307

Though the arid beauty of the Red Desert surrounds the city, Rock Springs itself is not so attractive. The site of the brutal Chinese Massacre of 1885, Rock Springs now bills itself as the "Home of 54 Nationalities." While the town has gotten friendlier to outsiders, travelers may still find little going on for a town of nearly 20,000. It serves best as a break on the way to Green River or as a launching point for trips to the Flaming Gorge.

✈ ORIENTATION

The streets of Rock Springs are not easily navigable; you'll want to grab a street map from the info booth at the Chamber of Commerce. **Route 191** enters the city from the north and becomes **Elk Street,** one of the city's main drags. A little ways into the city, it intersects **Center Street (Route 30),** which runs roughly southwest-northeast. In the western half of the city, Center St. becomes **Bridger Avenue,** and then **Ninth Street.** The historic downtown district can be reached by taking Elk St. south past Center St. until it becomes **A Street.**

VITAL STATS
Population: 19,000
Tourist Office: Rock Springs Chamber of Commerce, 1897 Dewar Dr. (☎307-362-3771; www.rockspringswyoming.net). Open M-F 8am-5pm.
Library and Internet Access: Rock Springs Public Library, 400 C St. (☎307-352-6667), downtown. Open M-Th 9am-8pm, F-Sa noon-5pm.
Post Office: 2829 Commercial Way (☎307-362-9792). Open M-F 9am-5pm, Sa 9am-noon. **Postal Code:** 82901.

⌂ ACCOMMODATIONS

A glut of chain hotels surrounds I-80 on the western end of town. **The Cody Motel** ❷, 75 Center St., has clean rooms with microfridges. (☎307-362-6675. Free Wi-Fi. Singles $50; doubles $60. AmEx/D/MC/V.)

🍴 FOOD

Rock Springs is home to every imaginable type of fast-food restaurant, most of which swarm around I-80. Other options are regrettably hard to find. The **Broadway Burger Station** ❷, 628 Broadway, serves hamburgers from a menu laden with Elvis references. The final, eyebrow-raising touch comes from the animated neon sign, which endlessly raises Marilyn's skirt. (☎307-362-5858. Sandwiches $4-7. Open M-Th and Sa 11am-8pm, F 11am-9pm. AmEx/D/MC/V.)

◉ SIGHTS

WESTERN WYOMING COMMUNITY COLLEGE NATURAL HISTORY MUSEUM. The museum has one of the most impressive collections and most unusual layouts of any museum in the region. While the museum proper contains only a few fossils, full-size cast skeletons of dinosaurs are spread throughout the building, which also houses offices, the school bookstore, a theater, and a cafeteria where the *Tyrannosaurus* seems just a little out of place. A *Triceratops*, a *Stegosaurus*, and a massive *plesiosaur* round out the collection. More incongruous pieces can be found, like the replica Easter Island statue in the courtyard. *(2500 College Dr. ☎ 307-382-1666 or 382-1600. Open daily 9am-10pm. Free.)*

COMMUNITY FINE ARTS CENTER. The center showcases local artists in rotating exhibits. The permanent collection includes works by a handful of famous artists, including Salvador Dalí and Norman Rockwell. *(400 C St. In the same building as the library. ☎ 307-362-6212. Open M-Th 10am-6pm, F-Sa noon-5pm. Free.)*

ROCK SPRINGS HISTORICAL MUSEUM. Over the years, it has collected thousands of personal artifacts donated by the citizens of Rock Springs, creating a collective scrapbook. *(201 B St., at the corner of Broadway. ☎ 307-362-3138. Open M-Sa 10am-5pm. Donations accepted.)*

☒ DETOUR
FLAMING GORGE NATIONAL RECREATION AREA

Take **I-80** to **Exit 91** and get on **Route 530 South.** This will take you along the western edge of the gorge. The eastern border can be skirted via **US 191,** off **I-80 Exit 99** between Rock Springs and Green River.

Seen at sunset, the contrast between the red canyons and the aquamarine water of the Green River makes the landscape of the Flaming Gorge area appear to glow. The river was dammed in 1964, and the resulting reservoir is now the center of the Flaming Gorge National Recreation Area. The area is large enough to spill into the northern reaches of Utah, but its northern tip is just south of the town of Green River. The scenic drive south into the area is a serious undertaking, but a shorter jaunt down one edge is also possible. Elk, antelope, and bighorn sheep call the land home; these animals may not frequent the highway loop, but a turn onto one of the many side roads may lead to a sighting. Rte. 530 becomes Rte. 43 and then Rte. 44 as it meets the southern border of the area. Rte. 44 intersects with US 191 in Utah near Red Canyon. Plenty of activities, including numerous hiking and biking trails, can be found along the borders of the gorge. The Rock Springs and Green River Chambers of Commerce can provide maps of the area and phone numbers for individual campsites and marinas in the area. The Rock Springs Chamber of Commerce also sells passes required for park entrance.

☒ THE ROAD TO GREEN RIVER: 19 MI.

Head east on **I-80.** Much of Green River is along **Flaming Gorge Way,** which is a loop between **Exits 91** and **89** off I-80. Take Exit 91 to reach the city.

IN THE GORGE

The area around Flaming Gorge National Recreation Area may seem inhospitable, but a drive down into its dirt roads will reveal evidence of a tough history. Cracked and crumbling homesteads speak to the harsh existence for the sheep herders and ranchers who worked out in the gorge. If you're fortunate enough to pass one of these structures while traversing the rough, unmaintained roads, take a look inside. Most are little more than bare rooms, just big enough to fit a chair and a bed—which was often all the furniture ranchers had access to during their month-long trips down into the gorge for grazing. Honest ranchers weren't the only people who spent a lot of time in the gorge, however. The qualities that make it insufferable to most people—the heat, the dust, the inaccessibility—made it ideal for outlaws looking for a place to lie low. During Rock Springs's rougher days, hundreds of bank robbers, murderers, deserters, and convicts could be hiding in the gorge at any given time. The Hole in the Wall Gang once spent time in the gorge after an attempted robbery in the area. For some, the gorge was just another stopping place on their endless wandering. For others, it became a base of operations. And, for the unlucky ones who didn't bring enough provisions or perhaps just stayed out in the sun too long, the desolate, dusty stretch of ground became their resting place.

[the local story]

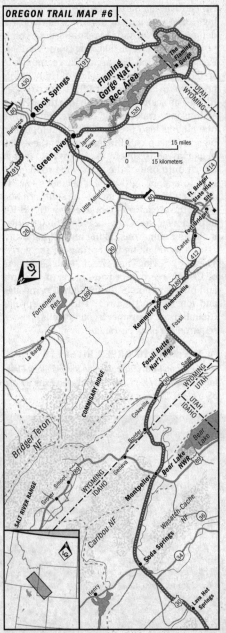

OREGON TRAIL MAP #6

GREEN RIVER ☎307

Though not overflowing with attractions, Green River is a peaceful town and a relaxing rest stop. The tip of the long Flaming Gorge National Recreation Area is just south of town, and this scenic area defines the town and much of its economy.

VITAL STATS
Population: 11,800
Tourist Office: Green River Chamber of Commerce, 541 E. Flaming Gorge Way (☎307-875-5711; www.grchamber.com). Open M-F 8:30am-5:30pm.
Library and Internet Access: Sweetwater County Library, 300 N. 1st St. E. (☎307-875-3615). Open M-Th 9am-8pm, F-Sa 9am-4pm.
Post Office: 350 Uinta Dr. (☎307-875-4920). Open M-F 9am-5:30pm, Sa 10:30am-noon. **Postal Code:** 82929.

✦ ORIENTATION

Nearly all of Green River lies along **Flaming Gorge Way,** the road that forms the loop between Exits 89 and 91 off I-80. **Uinta Drive,** which runs perpendicular to Flaming Gorge Way, is the other major road.

⌐ ACCOMMODATIONS

The Coachman Inn, 470 E. Flaming Gorge Way (☎307-875-3681). The most legit place on the main strip. Management is friendly, and the large rooms come with pleather rolling chairs. Singles $65; doubles $75. AmEx/D/MC/V. ❸

Sweet Dreams Inn, 1214 Uinta Dr. (☎307-875-2630). A nice alternative to most motels in Flaming Gorge. Large, clean bathrooms and soft beds. Singles $61; doubles $71. AmEx/D/MC/V. ❸

Tex's Travel Camp, 360 Washington St. (☎307-875-2630). Cheap tent sites with electrical hookups and cleaner than average facilities. Smores kits ($5) can be purchased in the general store. Tent sites $10. MC/V. ❶

⬟ FOOD

Flaming Gorge Way is home to Green River's best restaurants.

OREGON TRAIL

Buckaroo's Family Restaurant, 580 E. Flaming Gorge Way (☎307-875-2246). A friendly place with lots of breakfast specials ($5-10), including a set of selections "for smaller appetites" ($2.35-3.65). Made with workers and school-children in mind, sack lunches ($5.50) are also perfect for roadtrippers in a hurry. Open M-Sa 5am-4pm, Su 6am-4pm. AmEx/D/MC/V. ❸

Krazy Moose, 211 E. Flaming Gorge Way (☎307-875-5124). Chicken-fried steak ($11) is always a house favorite, although the "lonely moose," (a roast beef sandwich with green peppers and mozzarella on sourdough; $8) is also popular. The oriental chicken salad ($8.30) combines vegetables and Asian cuisine, both in short supply in western Wyoming. Omelets $6.50-7.50. Entrees $10-14. Open M-Sa 6am-9pm, Su 8am-3pm. AmEx/D/MC/V. ❷

Penny's Diner, 1170 W. Flaming Gorge Way (☎307-875-3500, ext. 550), right off the interstate. Fast, greasy, and prime roadtrip-food material. Root beer floats ($2.50) taste miraculous after a day on the dusty road. Breakfast $5-7. Sandwiches $6.50-9. Open 24hr. AmEx/D/MC/V. ❷

⑤ SIGHTS

SWEETWATER COUNTY HISTORICAL MUSEUM. A scattershot collection of artifacts ranging from dinosaur remains to Chief Washakie's drum to an altar used by the area's Chinese laborers prior to the Chinese Massacre of 1885. *(3 E. Flaming Gorge Way. ☎307-872-6435; www.sweetwatermuseum.org. Open M-Sa 10am-6pm. Free.)*

⚑ THE ROAD TO KEMMERER: 70 MI.

Get back on **I-80/US 30 West.** At Exit 66 merge onto US 30 W. Turn right on Red Canyon, and then another right back onto US 30. A short ways onward take a left and follow the road into town.

KEMMERER ☎307

Southwestern Wyoming is a pretty, peaceful place, and Kemmerer, the fossil-fish capital of the world, is no exception. The town's center has a genuine village green, and its sleepy downtown charm remains largely unblemished by corporate invasion—something of an accomplishment, since Kemmerer was the birthplace of JC Penney.

⚒ ORIENTATION

Kemmerer lies along **US 30,** which runs north-south, changing its name to **Central Avenue** in Diamondville. It becomes **Coral Street** at the Kemmerer line and then **Pine Avenue** deeper in Kemmerer. Parking is generally available on the streets or in private lots. Most of the city can be seen in a single stroll.

⌂ ACCOMMODATIONS

Kemmerer's lodgings are mostly comfortable and reasonably priced budget motels.

Antler Motel, 419 Coral St. (☎307-877-4461). Offers a range of rooms spread across 2 buildings. Little care packages with candy and toiletries are a nice touch. Reception 9am-9pm. Singles $54; doubles $60. AmEx/MC/V. ❷

Energy Inn (☎307-877-6901), right off US 30 on the Diamondville side. Has big, clean rooms with cable, complimentary lotion, and Wi-Fi. Singles $65; doubles $73. AmEx/D/MC/V. ❸

⬛ FOOD

Never mind its outlaw name; **Bootlegger's Steakhouse and Grill ❸,** 817 S. Main St., off Pine Ave., just south of Herschler Triangle Park, is a lot fancier than its trappings would suggest. Standard-issue sandwiches ($6.50) and burgers ($8-9) are supplemented by entrees ranging from spaghetti ($10) to lobster tail ($45). Several steak and shrimp combinations ($20-25) are also available. (☎307-828-3067. Open daily 5-8pm. AmEx/MC/V.)

⊙ SIGHTS

GOLDEN RULE. The Golden Rule is the mother of all JC Penney stores. Just a few storefronts down is the **Penney Homestead,** now a memorial to corporate expansion posing as a museum. The lower floor contains artifacts and photos from the founder's life, while the upstairs has been preserved in its original, unremarkable state. (107 JC Penney Dr. *At the intersection of J.C. Penney Dr. and Pine Ave.* ☎307-877-3164. *Open May-Sept. M-Sa 9am-6pm, Su 1-6pm. Free.*)

FOSSIL COUNTRY FRONTIER MUSEUM. In addition to the usual pioneer artifacts, the museum contains two stills used to keep the good times rolling during Prohibition as well as a model coal mine that recreates the previous generation's misery for the current generation's enjoyment. (400 Pine Ave. ☎307-877-6551. *Open M-Sa June-Aug. 9am-5pm; Sept.-May 10am-4pm. Free.*)

⊠ DETOUR
⊠ULRICH'S FOSSIL GALLERY

Turn off **US 30** 10 mi. west of Kemmerer. About a quarter-mile from US 30, turn left on a small dirt road.

The original Ulrich has been working in the Fossil Butte area for about 50 years, and the fossils he has on display are as much works of art as pieces of history. While the massive 69 in. gar fish fossil may not be for sale, many of the other works on display are, ranging from tiny shards of split rock with a single fish ($11) to massive pieces that offer a panoramic glimpse of life in the Middle Eocene. What really sets Ulrich's apart from the other galleries, however, are **guided fossil digs,** which allow you to dig for 3hr. at an actual quarry site—with the guarantee that you'll bring back at least a fish, though, alas, the state gets to keep anything rare or unusual. Ulrich's will prepare your fossil for presentation so you can look impress all your friends. (☎307-877-6466. Guided digs $85. Reservations required. Gallery open daily 8am-5pm. MC/V.)

⊼ THE ROAD TO MONTPELIER: 76 MI.

Follow **Pine Street** north through Kemmerer; on the outskirts of town, it becomes **US 30,** which takes you across the Idaho border to Montpelier. US 30 becomes **Fourth Street;** follow it into town.

The Gem State

IDAHO
Welcomes You!

MONTPELIER ☎208

Montpelier's mid-20th-century aura is tempered by some of its older buildings; one bank was robbed of almost $17,000 by Butch Cassidy. He escaped unscathed, though a valiant deputy gave chase on a bike. Since then, things have slowed down in Montpelier. The heavily commercialized intersection of US 30 and US 89 is balanced by the sunny downtown blocks of Washington St., which feature an old theater, an ice-cream parlor, and sidewalk benches held up by smiling bears.

VITAL STATS
Population: 2800
Tourist Office: Visitor Information Center, 320 N. 4th St. (☎208-847-3800), in the National Oregon/California Trail Center. Open May-Sept. M-Th and Su 9am-5pm, F-Sa 9am-7pm.
Library and Internet Access: Bear Lake County Library, 138 N. 6th St. (☎208-847-1664), off Washington St. Open M-Th 11am-7pm, F 9am-5pm, Sa 9am-2pm.
Post Office: 804 Grant St. (☎208-847-1894). Open M-F 9am-4pm, Sa 9am-noon. **Postal Code:** 83254.

▰ ORIENTATION

In Montpelier, **US 30** is known as **Fourth Street** and is one of the city's two main drags. The other is **Washington Street (US 89),** which runs roughly north-south, perpendicular to Fourth St. Parking is readily available in Montpelier, and most establishments have their own lots.

⌂ ACCOMMODATIONS

The busy US 30/89 intersection comes to the rescue for sleepy drivers, boasting a series of cheap but pleasant motels.

Three Sisters Motel, 112 S. 6th St. (☎208-847-2324), at the corner of Washington St. Has small rooms that manage to squeeze in refrigerators, microwaves, and comfy armchairs. Free Wi-Fi. Singles $40; doubles $50. Cash only. ❷

Park Motel, 745 Washington St. (☎208-847-1911). Clean and well furnished. Rooms from $50. AmEx/D/MC/V. ❷

⚑ FOOD

Montpelier's downtown burger and ice-cream stands are supplemented by some full-fledged restaurants on US 30.

Butch Cassidy's Restaurant, 230 N. 4th St. (☎208-847-3501). Both Old Western and cynically modern in style; the cowboy decor clashes amusingly with the satirical books and bottles of Grey Poupon left in each booth. Breakfast $4-10. Sandwiches $5.50-8. Entrees $12-22. Open daily 6am-10pm. AmEx/MC/V. ❸

Montpelier Grill, 194 N. 4th St. (☎208-847-1250). Has a simple menu that includes buffalo burgers ($8) in addition to the usual. The comfortable booths and barstools made from gnarled wood make this a place you won't mind stopping at. Burgers and sandwiches $6.50. Open M-Sa 11:30am-8:30pm. MC/V. ❷

⦿ SIGHTS

NATIONAL OREGON/CALIFORNIA TRAIL CENTER. No ordinary museum, this is a westward journey led by in-character guides. After watching a film about the trails of Idaho, a guide will take you through a gun shop, wagon yard, and mercantile, listing necessary supplies and revealing tricks of the pioneering trade along the way. From there, mount the wagons, which creak through the darkness as tales of the trail are narrated. Finally, climb out at the **Clover Creek camp** and hear more stories about life on the trail while learning how to jack a cart out of the mud. On the way out, marvel at a huge, finely detailed woodcut of the trail through Idaho that has captured the features of hundreds of people, animals, and landmarks in vivid color. *(320 N. 4th St. ☎208-847-3800; www.oregontrailcenter.org. Open May-Sept. M-Th and Su 9am-5pm, F-Sa 9am-6pm. $9, ages 8-17 $6, under 8 free.)*

⛰ THE ROAD TO SODA SPRINGS: 27 MI.
To the west, **Fourth Street** becomes **US 30** again, heading on toward Soda Springs. The road is part of the **Oregon Trail/Bear Lake Scenic Byway,** and the landscape is appropriately picturesque. In Soda Springs, US 30 is known as **Second Street.**

SODA SPRINGS   ☎208

A hundred springs once rose from these grounds until a city was built over them. The most spectacular of those remaining is, ironically, the manmade Soda Springs geyser. Parks cut through the downtown, allowing the Idaho wilderness to infiltrate the sidewalks.

VITAL STATS

Population: 3400

Tourist Office: Soda Springs Chamber of Commerce, 9 W. 2nd S. (☎208-547-4964; www.sodaspringsid.com), inside City Hall. Open M-F 8am-noon.

Library and Internet Access: Soda Springs Public Library, 149 S. Main St. (☎208-547-2606). Open M-Th 10am-8pm, F 10am-5pm.

Post Office: 220 S. Main St. (☎208-547-3794). Open M-F 8:30am-5pm, Sa noon-2pm. **Postal Code:** 83276.

✷ ORIENTATION

Whoever chose the street names in Soda Springs really dropped the ball. **Main Street** runs north-south and forms a cross with **Hooper Avenue.** All other streets are numbered: parallel to and west of Main St. is **First West,** to the east is **First East;** parallel and to the south of Hooper is **First South,** to the north is **First North.** As if this weren't confusing enough, these streets are divided in half at the axis streets, so there is W. First S. as well as S. First W., and so on. The resulting confusion might make it easier to just park along the street and stroll, asking for directions from locals.

⌂ ACCOMMODATIONS

Caribou Lodge & Motel, 110 W. 2nd S. (☎208-547-3377). Offers a range of styles and sizes, from small but comfortable singles to kitchenette suites, complete with Cold War-era wood paneling. Free Wi-Fi. Reception 7am-11pm. Singles $40; doubles $45. AmEx/D/MC/V. ❷

The JR Inn, 179 W. 2nd S. (☎208-547-3366). Fluffy carpeting straight out of the 70s, but no A/C. Microwaves and refrigerators available upon request. Singles $48; doubles $58. AmEx/D/MC/V. ❷

FOOD

Caribou Mountain Pizza and Grill, 84 S. Main St. (☎208-547-4575). Breakfast specials ($4-5) for the weak and all-you-can-eat breakfast and lunch deals ($6.50) for the iron-willed. Open M-Th 11am-9pm, F-Sa 11am-11pm. MC/V. ❷

Geyser View Restaurant, 76 S. Main St. (☎208-547-4980), in the Enders Bldg. The Geyser burger and Geyser chicken sandwich ($8.25) are good, but the chicken-fried steak ($12.50) is a sure bet. Entrees $11.50-19. Open M-Sa 7am-9pm, Su 7am-8pm. AmEx/D/MC/V. ❸

SIGHTS

SODA SPRINGS GEYSER. This geyser separates Soda Springs from all the other quaint-but-boring towns that line the highway. Created by a couple of guys who struck a pressurized chamber while trying to build a heated swimming pool, the resulting geyser (which reaches up to 70 ft. and can be seen from most roads leading into town) took a week to cap and threw Old Faithful off schedule. Today, the geyser is controlled by a timer that lets it erupt every hour on the hour.

SODA SPRINGS PATHWAY. Two miles of easy-going trails cut through downtown and then into the surrounding wetlands. The trail stops at **Octagon Park,** at the corner of Hooper Ave. and Main St. The eight-sided pavilion in the center of the park makes for good picnicking. From here, the path continues north to **Hooper Springs Park** and ends in a secluded grove. Beneath a small wood pavilion, the springs well into a low pool, easily accessible for drinking. The water is naturally carbonated and bitter but clear and cool. Wise pioneers flavored it with sugar and syrup, but the bold still knock it back straight. *(To reach Hooper Springs by car, take Hooper Ave. east to 3rd E., go north to Government Dam Rd., and head west a few hundred yards. All parks open daily sunrise-sunset.)*

◤ **THE ROAD TO LAVA HOT SPRINGS: 21 MI.** Take **Second South (US 30 West)** to Lava Hot Springs.

LAVA HOT SPRINGS ☎208

Summer turns tiny Lava Hot Springs into a crowded resort town. The streets are crammed with half-naked vacationers carrying massive inner tubes to the river before taking a dip in the town's naturally heated mineral waters.

VITAL STATS
Population: 520
Tourist Office: South Bannock County Historical Center, 110 E. Main St. (☎208-776-5254). Open M-W and F-Su 10am-5:30pm, Th noon-5pm.
Library and Internet Access: South Bannock Public Library, Lava Hot Springs Branch, 33 E. Main St. (☎208-776-5301). Open M, W, F 1-5pm; Tu, Th 1-6pm; Sa 10am-2pm.
Post Office: 45 S. Center St. (☎208-776-5680). Open M-F 9am-noon and 1-4:30pm. **Postal Code:** 83246.

ORIENTATION

Lava Hot Springs is laid out along the **Portneuf River,** south of **US 30.** Most of the town's attractions lie along **Main Street,** which runs east-west through town. In a town of Lava Hot Springs's size, parking is rarely a problem, but things can get a bit crowded when the summer tourists arrive. **Tubing** is allowed on the Portneuf River. The access point is on the eastern end of town, behind the picnic pavilion. The stream runs swiftly under Main St.'s bridge and along the highway before reaching the dismount. Stands up and down Main St. compete to rent tubes and life jackets.

ACCOMMODATIONS

Most accommodations in Lava Hot Springs are on the expensive side, though a few budget rooms can be found.

Aura Soma Lava, 196 E. Main St. (☎208-776-5800 or 800-757-1233; www.aslava.com). The most luxurious lodging option in town, with comfortable singles, entire cottages, and even a chalet. Every room has its own theme, with triple-layered sheets and huge pillows. Massages and suites with mineral-water hot tubs are available for the truly self-indulgent. Massages $60 per hr. Rooms from $79; cottage $150; chalet $225. MC/V. ❹

Lava Spa Motel, 359 E. Main St. (☎208-776-5589). A range of room sizes. For a little extra dough, you can even get one with its own hot tub. In summer singles $65; doubles $75. In winter $10 less. AmEx/D/MC/V. ❸

Home Hotel & Motel, 306 E. Main St. (☎208-776-5507; www.homehotel.com). Budget rooms within walking distance of the hot pools. Each room in the hotel proper is decorated after an early-20th-century artist. The Klimt Honeymoon Suite is one of the nicest, while the Frida Kahlo and Diego Rivera suites are connected by a walkway. Reservations recommended. Rooms from $65. AmEx/D/MC/V. ❸

🍴 FOOD

Riverwalk Cafe, 695 E. Main St. (☎208-776-5872). East of downtown, near the pavilion. You might wonder how good the pad thai ($8) can be in southern Idaho; the answer is better than you'd think. Appetizers $3-5.50. Entrees $6-15.50. Open Tu-Su 1-9pm. AmEx/D/MC/V. ❷

Ye Ole Chuckwagon Restaurant, 211 E. Main St. (☎208-776-5141). A surprising number of vegetarian options ($3-7) for a place that serves drinks in glass cowboy boots and calls its burgers "chuckwiches." The food is a little on the greasy side, but the portions are big enough to serve 2, making it a tempting option for penny pinchers. Lunch $5-7. Dinner $8-20. Open daily 6:30am-10pm. MC/V. ❸

◎ SIGHTS

LAVA HOT SPRINGS. The naturally heated waters (104-112°F) of the hot spring have been in use for centuries. Once hailed for their curative powers, there is no doubt that the springs have, at the very least, calming powers. The pools are set back from the road in a quiet, tree-strewn complex. (430 E. Main St. ☎208-776-5221 or 800-423-8597; www.lavahotsprings. com. Open Apr.-Sept. daily 8am-11pm; Oct.-Mar. M-Th and Su 9am-10pm, F-Sa 9am-11pm. Day pass M-Th $5, ages 3-11 and seniors $4.50; F-Su $7/6.50.)

⚐ THE ROAD TO POCATELLO: 38 MI.

Take **Main Street** to **Center Street,** which leads back to **US 30.** Twelve miles out of Lava Hot Springs, **US 30** meets **I-15;** take I-15 N. for another 18 mi. Take **Exit 67,** which blends conveniently into **Fifth Avenue,** the major thoroughfare at the southern tip of the city.

POCATELLO ☎208

A giant by mountain area standards, Pocatello draws students, thrill-seekers, and vacationers to see the hot springs and Yellowstone National Park. The endless flux of visitors, fused with the lively population of Idaho State University, gives Pocatello a surprisingly diverse and happening feel for a small city in the heart of the Potato State.

VITAL STATS
Population: 51,500
Tourist Office: Pocatello Convention & Visitors Bureau, 324 S. Main St. (☎208-235-7659; www.pocatellocvb.com). Open in summer M-F 9am-6pm, Sa-Su 10am-4pm; in winter M-F 10am-4pm.
Library and Internet Access: Marshall Public Library, 113 S. Garfield Ave. (☎208-232-1263; www.marshallpl.org). Open M-Th 9am-9pm, F-Sa 9am-6pm.
Post Office: 730 E. Clark St. (☎208-235-2190), off 5th Ave. Open M-F 8am-5:30pm, Sa 10:30am-2:30pm. **Postal Code:** 83201.

✥ ORIENTATION

Pocatello is long and narrow, running from the southeast to the northwest between the **Portneuf River** and **I-15.** At the southeastern end is **Ross Park,** home to a number of Pocatello's attractions. This part of the city is dominated by **Fifth Avenue,** which runs past restaurants and **Idaho State University.** Around the center of the city, Fifth Ave. ends, running into busy **Yellowstone Avenue.** The **Historic Old Town** area, Pocatello's downtown, is south of the train tracks, parallel to Fifth Ave. **Benton Street** is the most direct route from Fifth Ave. to downtown; **Center Street** is larger, but it runs one-way from downtown to Fifth Ave. This particular area is small and easily traversed by foot. North of the Pocatello is the suburb of **Chubbuck;** the two are linked by Yellowstone

Ave. Another cluster of hotels and restaurants is gathered on Chubbuck's southern border, where **I-86** divides the two cities. Most establishments have lots, so parking is easy.

ACCOMMODATIONS

Thunderbird Motel, 1415 S. 5th Ave. (☎208-232-6330; www.thunderbirdmotelid. com). Pretty much the only place around besides the chain hotels that dominate the town's 3 highway exits. The Thunderbird is also one of the best deals you're likely to find on your trip. The rooms are clean and comfortable, with high wood-beam ceilings. Cheap laundry facilities and free Wi-Fi. Singles $38; doubles $50. AmEx/D/MC/V. ❷

FOOD

Pocatello's restaurants are spread unevenly across town. The best bet is probably the downtown area, home to several ethnic eateries and student-frequented coffeehouses.

Buddy's, 626 E. Lewis St. (☎208-233-1172), just north of 5th Ave., on the edge of campus. Serves classic Italian meals to a family crowd and a few college regulars. Pasta $8-17. Pizza and calzones $10-18. Open M-Sa 11am-midnight. V. ❸

Oliver's Restaurant, 130 S. 5th Ave. (☎208-234-0672). Don't let the standard diner appearance fool you; it has a huge menu with lots of vegetarian options and reasonable prices. The southwestern lentils ($6.50) and chicken parmesan sandwich ($6.50) are great choices. Sandwiches $5.25-8.50. Entrees $8-9. MC/V. ❷

SIGHTS

FORT HALL REPLICA. The Fort Hall Replica is an exact copy of a historic trading post originally located 14 mi. north. The buildings are furnished to recall frontier life, though two of the largest rooms house mini-museums on pioneer and Native American life in the area. *(3002 Alvord Loop, north of S. 4th Ave. ☎208-234-1795. Open Tu-Sa from Memorial Day to Sept. 10am-2pm; from Sept. to Memorial Day 10am-6pm. $2.25, ages 13-17 $1.25, ages 5-11 $1.)*

BANNOCK COUNTY HISTORICAL MUSEUM. The museum displays relics from Pocatello's past. The medicinal room is especially interesting,

with jars of "dragon's blood" and "ethereal oil," but unfortunately the yellowed labels offer no further explanation. The rules for stage travel posted on the antique coach include advice applicable to your own excursion, including: "Don't discuss politics or religion. Don't point out sites where robberies or Indian attacks have taken place. Don't swear, snore, or lop over on neighbors while sleeping." *(3000 Alvord Loop, in Upper Ross Park. ☎208-233-0434. Open from Memorial Day to Labor Day daily 10am-6pm; from Labor Day to Memorial Day Tu-Sa 10am-2pm. $1, ages 12-18 and seniors $0.50, under 12 free.)*

POCATELLO ZOO. Only North American wildlife is kept at the zoo, but the lack of lions isn't a serious loss: bighorn sheep, grizzly bears, coyotes, and cougars still roam the cages. The biggest enclosure houses elk, buffalo, bison, and pronghorn antelope in something resembling a natural habitat. *(3101 Ave. of the Chiefs. ☎208-234-6264; www.pocatellozoo.com. Hours vary; call ahead. $3.75, ages 3-11 $2, seniors $2.50.)*

IDAHO MUSEUM OF NATURAL HISTORY. Bigger, scarier, and more extinct fauna can be found at the impressive Idaho Museum of Natural History. The skeleton of a monstrous *Bison latifrons* is the highlight of a display on the evolution of the bison and the museum's main prize—the 8 ft. horns are the largest horns from any bison ever recorded. The **Dinosaur Times** exhibit has partial remains of several dinosaurs indigenous to Idaho, including an as-yet-unnamed species of theropod known only as "Dinosaur Doe." *(On the Idaho State campus, at the intersection of 5th Ave. and Dillon St. ☎208-282-3317; http://imnh.isu.edu. Open Tu-Sa 10am-5pm. $5, students $3, ages 4-11 $2.)*

NIGHTLIFE

Pocatello has a tight-knit bar community. Everyone knows everyone else, and people regularly make rounds between their three or four preferred establishments. The most happening places are all concentrated along Center St. in the downtown area.

Hooligan's, 122 N. 3rd Ave. (☎208-234-0213). The ISU rugby team loves it so much that several former players have become bartenders. University students enjoy the laid-back atmosphere and taps sticking out of the front of a vintage VW bus.

Stop by at the end of July, when they rope off the surrounding streets for an old-school block party. Open daily 11am-2am. MC/V.

Club Charley's, 331 E. Center St. (☎208-239-0855). Caters to Pocatello's gay community with resident drag show "Charley's Angels" the 1st Sa of the month, while DJs take over the rest of the time with hip-hop and club beats. Karaoke M-Th. Open M-Sa 7pm-2am, Su 8pm-2am. MC/V.

The First National Bar, 232 W. Center St. (☎208-233-1516). Becomes a smokin' house of blues when there's someone around to play. Cover $5 or less. Open daily 11am-2am. AmEx/D/MC/V.

THE ROAD TO CRATERS OF THE MOON: 97 MI.
From the southern half of the city, the easiest escape is to head south on **Fifth Street** to the junction with **I-15** and head north. Take **Exit 93** to **US 26 West;** after 35 mi. it converges with **US 20.** Follow the road west, crossing the Big Lost River. From the bridge, it is 16 mi. to Arco. US 20/26 becomes **Front Street,** then makes a 90° turn, becoming **Grand Avenue** in Arco. Continue about 17 mi. to the entrance to the park.

CRATERS OF THE MOON ☎208

Walking through Craters of the Moon is a lot like walking through Mordor. An early visitor to the otherworldly landscape claimed it was "the strangest 75 sq. mi. on the North American continent." While the volcanic activity that formed the monument's 715,000 blasted and beautiful acres may be 2000 years old, the area's dry climate has left the various flows, cones, and tubes remarkably well-preserved.

VITAL STATS
Area: 715,000 acres
Tourist Offices: Craters of the Moon Visitors Center (☎208-527-1300), just inside the park. Open daily from Memorial Day to Labor Day 8am-6pm; from Labor Day to Memorial Day 8am-4:30pm. **Arco Chamber of Commerce,** 159 N. Idaho St. (☎208-527-8977). Open M-F 8am-5pm.
Gateway Town: Arco.
Fees: 7-day pass $8 per vehicle.

ORIENTATION

The only access to Craters of the Moon is about 17 mi. west of Arco on **US 20/26.** Directions are clearly marked, as if the massive expanse of black doom isn't clear enough. Several scenic overlooks allow for spectacular views of the landscape complete with interpretive signs to explain exactly what on earth you're looking at. Immediately inside the park is the visitors center, which has displays on the local geology, flora, and fauna as well as a short (10min.) video on the geologic processes responsible for Craters of the Moon. Maps of the various hiking trails are available, and the center sells flashlights to anyone wanting to explore the darker lava tubes. The park itself is divided into three areas. The first and smallest is the **developed area,** where paved roads lead past several of the more impressive craters and through some awesome and indescribable formation clusters. It may be the smallest portion of the park, but a thorough party could easily spend an entire afternoon exploring the area. The second region is the **wilderness area,** where only a few dirt paths disturb the natural order. The majority of the park is **backcountry area.** Crisscrossed by unmaintained roads, scorched in the summer, and covered with snow in the winter, the backcountry area is not hospitable to the average driver and vehicle. Anyone planning to camp in the wilderness area must obtain a free backcountry permit.

Arco, home to the nearest food and accommodations, is just 17 mi. east on US 20/26. The town is easy to spot thanks to **Number Hill,** a large hill where graduating members of every high-school class since 1920 have painted their class year onto the rockface in a show of school spirit; Arco is small-town America at its smallest. Most services are located right on the highway, which is called **Grand Avenue** and **Front Street** within city limits. The highway makes a 90° turn in the middle of town, so watch the signs carefully.

ACCOMMODATIONS

There are 51 **campsites ❶** scattered throughout the monument's single campground, located just past the entrance station. The grounds

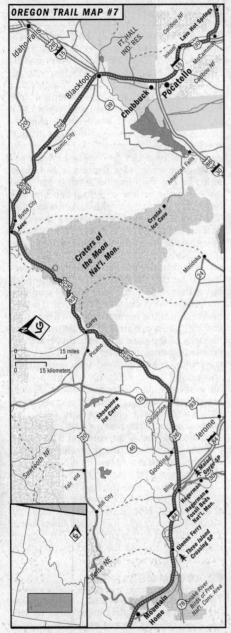

OREGON TRAIL MAP #7

are first come, first served and have toilets, water, grills, and picnic tables. A tip for tent campers: site #13 is considered one of the best, as it is private and nicely shielded from the wind. (No hookups. Open year-round. Sites in summer $10; in winter less.) Camping at unmarked **sites ●** in the dry lava wilderness of the park is possible with a free backcountry permit, available at the visitors center. Campsites are completely primitive and unmarked; it is recommended that each camper bring a gallon of water for each day spent there.

Those who think sleeping demands a solid roof will have to drive back to Arco.

> **D-K Motel,** 316 S. Front St. (☎208-527-8282). The rooms are clean and comfy, without any of the tacky decorations that spoil other small-town motels. Each room comes with a microwave, refrigerator, and coffee maker. Free Wi-Fi. Singles $38; doubles $56. AmEx/D/MC/V. ❷

> **Lost River Motel,** 405 Highway Dr. (☎208-527-3600), off Front St., near the east edge of town. Has slightly smaller but clean and comfortable rooms with recliners and access to a hot tub. Free Wi-Fi. Reception daily 8am-11pm. Singles $40; doubles $52. D/MC/V. ❷

🍴 FOOD

Besides the park's vending machines, the only food to be found in the area is in Arco. In addition to restaurants, Arco has a few grocery stores where water and other goods can be bought before any wilderness expeditions.

> **Pickle's Place,** 440 S. Front St. (☎208-527-9944). Easy to spot thanks to its deformed, boot-wearing mascot. Pickle's Place is either a down-home restaurant or a sobering reminder of the perils of the nuclear age. Home of the "world-famous" atomic burger as well as the less famous but still tasty ski bum burger ($6.50-7.75). Also serves normal breakfast options ($4-7) and sack lunches ($6.30) perfect for trips to the monument. Open daily in summer 6am-11pm; in winter 6am-10pm. MC/V. ❷

> **Deli Sandwich Shop,** 119 N. Idaho Ave. (☎208-527-375). The monster sandwiches here are delicious and reasonably priced. 20 options range in size from the small but mighty 4 in. ($4) to the imposing, if unwieldy, 24 in. ($15.50).

Yard-long (and larger) giants can be made upon request. Open daily 8am-8pm. AmEx/D/MC/V. ❷

⚪ CAVES

Some of the most popular attractions in the monument are the caves of the **Blue Dragon Flow,** which are actually lava tubes, or tunnels that formed when rivers of molten rock hardened on the surface. The four open caves are untouched by man, with no artificial lighting, pathways, or guides. **Dew Drop Cave** is actually just a deep hole scraped into the earth, and explorers are allowed to enter without a flashlight. The largest of the caves is **Indian Tunnel,** whose natural skylights also make it the most easily navigated. Hard-core spelunkers will probably enjoy **Boy Scout Cave** the most of all; after you round a bend, the light disappears entirely, while the ceiling and the floor bend to meet each other. Reaching the end requires a bright light and a bent back. Cave guides are available from a box at the start of the caves trail. If you plan to explore the caves, bring a flashlight, since you may not be allowed to proceed in some caves without one.

⚠ OTHER OUTDOORS

The easiest way to visit the attractions of the developed portions of the park is to follow the 7 mi. **loop drive,** which departs from the visitors center and winds through the major sights around the monument's northern end.

HIKING

Several trails lead to intriguing rock formations and a variety of caves. The 2 mi. **Broken Top Loop,** starting at Tree Molds parking lot, goes through **Buffalo Caves** and is a quick but comprehensive survey of the surrounding land; the short ⚪**Caves Trail,** further along the loop, leads to three large caves, each with a distinctive character. The **North Crater Flow** (1800 ft.) is a lumpy field of cooled lava that has taken on fantastic shapes. The pahoehoe ("smooth" in Hawaiian) and aa ("rough" in Hawaiian) lavas produce an unlikely variety of forms. The path here is paved and mostly flat. Just a few yards down is the **North Crater Trail** (2 mi.), a steep, rocky path that leads to three of the best-preserved **spatter cones** in the world. The insulating lava and lack of direct sunlight keep the tube of **Snow Cone** icy even on the hottest summer days. Next along the loop road is **Devil's Orchard** (½ mi.). This brief, wheelchair-accessible trail, which takes its name from the report of a minister who passed through the area and called it "a garden fit for the devil himself," passes by some spectacular cinder monoliths deposited on the plain by the advancing lava flow. When strolling through the area, the twisted husks of trees and clusters of wildflowers impose a sense of the otherworldly. At **Inferno Cone** (½ mi.), a tall, wind-ravaged hill of black cinder overlooks miles of volcanic terrain from the edge of the loop road. The hike up is short but extremely steep, and the path is unpaved. The view of the surrounding park is unparalleled. The lone tree that rises from the ash at an awkward angle must be a metaphor for something. Between Inferno Cone and the caves is a side road breaking off the main loop, leading to the **Tree Molds** trailhead. From here the **Wilderness Trail** winds into the hills and craters south of the developed area. Though not very steep, this trail is long (about 5 mi. into the wilderness before petering out), often difficult to follow through the sage brush, and brutally exposed to the sun. Sturdy shoes, water, sunscreen, and a hat are a must as there are no trees for miles.

🚗 THE ROAD TO HAGERMAN: 97 MI.

From Craters of the Moon, head southwest on **US 26/20/93** for 62 mi. Turn left on US 26/93, a.k.a. **South Greenwood Street.** Turn right onto US 26, or **South Rail Street West,** and continue for 27 mi. Turn left on **US 30** and head on for 8 mi. into Hagerman.

HAGERMAN   ☎ 208

Hagerman's main claim to fame, if you can call it that, is the **Hagerman Fossil Beds National Monument Visitors Center,** 221 N. Front St. (US 30), and the **Hagerman horse skeletons.** The visitors center itself has little to offer, but 30 full horse skeletons were found in the area. The Hagerman Horse is now the official state fossil of Idaho and is believed to have been a form of North American zebra. (☎208-837-4793. Open in summer daily 9am-5pm; in winter M and Th-Su 9am-5pm.) The only real lodging option in the area is the **Hagerman Valley Inn** ❸,

499 S. State St., where rooms have standard amenities. (☎208-837-6196. Rooms from $50. AmEx/D/MC/V.) For something to eat, try the **Snake River Grill ❸,** 611 Frogs Landing. Sandwiches ($7-9) and entrees ($13-22) feature locally caught sturgeon and catfish, along with chicken-fried steak, ribs, and alligator. A light menu featuring half-size portions is also available, but the price difference makes this menu seem a rip-off. (☎208-837-6227. Open daily 7am-9pm. D/MC/V.) For some cheaper options, head to **Larry & Mary's Restaurant ❷,** 141 N. State St. A variety of sandwiches ($5-7) is offered, including the chili buger ($6.25), a local favorite. Mini pizzas ($4.75) are a fast, tasty, and perfectly portioned meal for roadtrippers just stopping by to admire the NASCAR and religious decor. (☎208-837-6475. Open Tu-Th 11am-8pm, Sa 9am-8pm, Su 8am-2pm. MC/V.)

◪ THE ROAD TO GLENNS FERRY: 28 MI.

Follow **I-84** to **Exit 121,** which leads to **First Avenue.**

GLENNS FERRY   ☎208

Glenns Ferry is the town that time forgot. Nestled along the Snake River, the town is quiet, the people smile in passing, and going to Wal-Mart is the big excitement on weekends. On the plus side, food and lodging are loaded with small-town charm at small-town prices—reason enough to spend some time here. Besides, now you can relax, since you don't have to worry about fording the river.

VITAL STATS
Population: 1600
Tourist Office: Glenns Ferry Chamber of Commerce, 108 E. 1st Ave. (☎208-366-345; www.glennsferryidaho.org). Open Tu-F 11am-4pm.
Library and Internet Access: Glenns Ferry Public Library, 298 S. Lincoln St. (☎208-366-2045), south of the train tracks. Open M-Sa 1-5pm.
Post Office: 22 E. 2nd Ave. (☎208-366-7329). Open M-F 8am-4:30pm. **Postal Code:** 83623.

◪ ORIENTATION

Glenns Ferry lies just south of **I-84** and just north of the **Snake River.** The city's primary

street, **First Avenue,** is a loop off the interstate, running diagonally through the center of town and then joining back up with I-84. It is known as **East First Avenue** to the east of its intersection with **Commercial Avenue** and **West First Avenue** to the west of the intersection.

◪ ACCOMMODATIONS

Glenns Ferry has a handful of motels located conveniently along the First Ave. loop. Tent sites are also available at Three Island Crossing (☎888-634-3146. Sites $21.)

> **Hanson's Hotel,** 201 E. 1st Ave. (☎208-366-9933). Hidden behind trees and Hanson's Cafe, but worth finding. The 8 rooms are as comfortable as you could want and would easily cost twice as much elsewhere. Singles $35; doubles $40. MC/V. ❷

> **Redford Motel,** 525 E. 1st Ave. (☎208-366-2421). Also has clean rooms at good prices. Singles $40; doubles $50. MC/V. ❷

◪ FOOD

Dining options are limited in the city, but what's there won't disappoint.

> **Hanson's Cafe,** 201 E. 1st Ave. (☎208-366-9983). Serves good food at great prices. 1 lb. Grande Rancher burger ($8). Sandwiches $3-6. Open in summer M-Th 7am-10pm, F-Sa 7am-11pm, Su 7am-3pm; in winter M-Th 7am-9pm, F-Sa 7am-10pm, Su 7am-3pm. MC/V. ❷

> **Carmela Restaurant,** 1289 Madison Ave. (☎208-366-2313). Hard to miss due to the Godzilla-size quail out front, which abides no tomfoolery. Right on the banks of the Snake River. The restaurant prides itself on its pasta, steaks, and seafood, but lighter wrap and panino options ($7-8) are also available. Sit outside if possible and soak up the great view of the surrounding vineyard. Entrees $15-22. Open in summer M-Sa 11am-9pm, Su 10am-8pm; in winter M-F 11am-8pm, Sa-Su 11am-9pm. D/MC/V. ❹

◉ SIGHTS

THREE ISLAND CROSSING PARK. The frustrating, occasionally deadly river crossing faced by the original Oregon Trail roadtrippers is remembered at Three Island Crossing Park, right on the banks of the river. The grassy riverbanks of the park look down on three islands rising from the **Snake River** where it widens, which helped make it possible for pioneers to ford the water. While the crossers dreaded the swift and muddy river, modern transportation allows you to sit back and enjoy what's otherwise a pretty peaceful river scene. If you happen by during the second weekend of August, you can catch locals reenacting the **treacherous crossing** complete with a column of wagons and assisted by Shoshone, Bannock, and Paiute guides. The park's **Oregon Trail History and Education Center** reiterates what you've already learned about the trail from a dozen other museums and interpretive centers, but with a surprising number of interactive exhibits for such a small museum. Spin the wheel of (mis)fortune and see if your wagon makes it across the river. *(Take Commercial Ave. south from 1st Ave. and across the train tracks, turning left onto Madison when Commercial Ave. ends. The park is a short distance down the road, on the left. ☎ 208-366-2394. Open M and W-Su 9am-4pm. Call ahead for extended summer hours. $4 per car.)*

▓ THE ROAD TO MOUNTAIN HOME: 25 MI.
From downtown Glenns Ferry, continue west along **First Avenue** until it rejoins **I-84.** Head west for 25 mi. to Mountain Home. Take **Exit 95** from **I-84;** this leads onto **American Legion Boulevard,** which passes directly into the downtown area.

MOUNTAIN HOME ☎208

While Mountain Home may not have many mountains to speak of, it does have an air force base and massive sand dunes. (Those just don't roll off the tongue as easily.) While the constant flybys and battle lab tests will have conspiracy theorists giddy, the base itself is pretty inaccessible to civilians. The state park, however, provides the good people of Mountain Home with a range of activities, including fishing, sand skiing, and some unbeatable stargazing.

❄ ORIENTATION

Mountain Home's two primary roads are **American Legion Boulevard,** which runs from I-84 westward into the center of town, and **Main Street,** which runs southeast-northwest,

meeting American Legion Blvd. in the middle of town. The streets around the intersection follow a system: the first direction indicates the direction of the street, while the second indicates which half of the street you're on.

VITAL STATS

Population: 11,150

Tourist Offices: Desert Mountain Visitor Center, 2900 American Legion Blvd. (☎208-587-4464; mountain-home.org/chamber/tour/visitor.htm), off I-84 at Exit 95. Open in summer daily 9am-5pm; call for winter hours. **Mountain Home Chamber of Commerce,** 205 N. 3rd St. E. (☎208-587-4334). Open M-F 9am-5pm.

Library and Internet Access: Mountain Home Public Library, 790 N. 10th St. E. (☎208-587-4716; www.mhlibrary.org). Open M-F 10am-7pm, Sa 9am-5pm.

Post Office: 350 N. 3rd St. E. (☎208-587-1413). Open M-F 8:30am-5pm, Sa 9:30-11:30am. **Postal Code:** 83647.

▙ ACCOMMODATIONS

Mountain Home's budget lodgings are located around the downtown area, where American Legion Blvd. meets Main St. **The Towne Center Motel ❷,** 410 N. 2nd St. E., off American Legion Blvd., is a no-frills sort of motel with plain, clean rooms and a pool. (☎208-587-3373. Free Wi-Fi. Singles $40; doubles $50. AmEx/D/MC/V.) Bruneau Dunes State Park also boasts over 100 **campsites ❶.** (Tent sites $13.)

▓ FOOD

People looking for food that's new and exciting will have to hold out for Boise. However, Mountain Home's delis and cafes are pretty good at what they do.

Grinde's Diner, 550 Air Base Rd. (☎208-587-5611). Take Main St. to Rte. 51 to Air Base Rd. Boxy and covered in red, white, and blue checks. Mixes the usual 50s vintage look with some cynical gas masks hanging from the ceiling. Huge selection of sandwiches and entrees as well as 18 sundaes ($4). Burgers ($6-7) and soups ($3) are great for a quick meal. Entrees $7-20. Open daily 7am-10pm. AmEx/D/MC/V. ❷

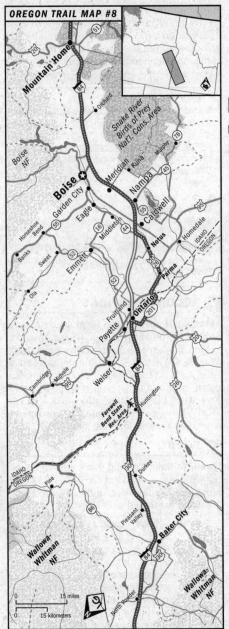

OREGON TRAIL MAP #8

The Dilly Deli, 190 E. 2nd N. (☎208-587-0885). Yet another cruelly malformed pickle mascot. Serves sandwiches with colorful names like the hearty Workin' Feller ($7.50) and the Triple Hitter ($8.50). You may want to get your meal to go, as the vibrant orange and blue interior can be nauseating. Open M-Sa 10:30am-4pm. D/MC/V. ❷

⊙ SIGHTS

⊠BRUNEAU DUNES STATE PARK. The park is Mountain Home's center for recreation. The two massive sand dunes spread over 600 acres and overlook two small picnic areas— though actual picnicking is only advisable upwind of the dunes themselves. At 470 ft., the larger dune is believed to be the tallest in North America and makes for a killer ski slope during the colder months. Sportsmen can fish for bass and bluegill in the small lakes at the base of the dunes. Those who spend the night are in for a real show. Far away from the light pollution of major urban areas, the sky around the park is some of the darkest in the country, and on clear nights the sky explodes with stars. The Bruneau Dunes Observatory provides a closer look when it's open. *(Follow Main St. south from American Legion Blvd., merging onto Rte. 51. After 14 mi., take a left onto Rte. 78; 2 mi. down that road is the turnoff for the park. ☎208-366-7919. Observatory open daily from 9pm. Donations accepted. Park gates open 7am-10pm. $4 per vehicle.)*

⛰ THE ROAD TO BOISE: 43 MI.

Follow **US 30** out of Mountain Home—just take **Main Street** northwest. US 30 merges with **I-84** en route to Boise. From I-84, **Exit 54** feeds directly onto **Broadway;** proceed through a commercial strip until you reach **Front Street** in downtown Boise.

BOISE ☎208

With a revitalized downtown brimming with great dining and nightlife options, Idaho's capital is a refreshingly cosmopolitan change of pace from the rest of the potato state. Fountains, statues, and outdoor streetside seating make the downtown area very hospitable, while beautiful parks and parkways keep the city green. The nearby foothills provide ample opportunities for camping and biking.

VITAL STATS

Population: 211,000

Tourist Office: Boise Convention and Visitors Bureau, 312 S. 9th St., Ste. 200 (☎208-344-7777 or 800-635-5241; www.boise.org). Open M-Th 8:30am-5pm, F 8:30am-4pm.

Library and Internet Access: Boise Public Library, 715 S. Capitol Blvd. (☎208-384-4076; www.boisepubliclibrary.org). Open from Memorial Day to Labor Day M-Th 10am-9pm, F 10am-6pm, Sa 10am-5pm; from Labor Day to Memorial Day M-Th 10am-9pm, F 10am-6pm, Sa 10am-5pm, Su noon-5pm.

Post Office: 750 W. Bannock St. (☎208-331-0037). Open M-F 8:30am-5pm. **Postal Code:** 83701.

ORIENTATION

Boise is fairly large, but the heart of the action is the pedestrian-only **Grove,** a segment of **Eighth Street** between **Main Street** and **Front Street,** the two main downtown thoroughfares. There are two other important downtown streets: **Grove Street,** which runs between Main and Front St., and **Capitol Boulevard,** which runs between Eighth and Sixth St. and would be named Seventh St. in a more logical city. Anyone making a trip downtown needs to allot some extra time for driving and parking. While Boise is blessed with nice, wide streets, most of them are one-ways, which can make getting around more convoluted than necessary. While driving can be frustrating, parking is downright infuriating. Boise must be relatively free of crime and civil strife, because the cops have nothing better to do than give parking tickets.

ACCOMMODATIONS

Inexpensive lodgings are hard to find around the downtown area, but a few very reasonable options are just a short drive away. Motels line Fairview Ave., the continuation of Front and Grove St. west of town. Chain motels are concentrated around Exit 53 off I-84.

☒ Hostel Boise (HI-AYH), 17322 Can-Ada Rd. (☎208-467-6858), 15min. from downtown Boise. Take Exit 38 off I-84 and turn right onto Garrity Blvd., which turns into Can-Ada Rd. A country home with 2 dormitories of 4 beds each and 1 private room. The dorms are clean, and the people are friendly, and the rates are cheaper than any motel and most campsites. Free Wi-Fi. Reception 7-10am and 5-10:30pm. Dorms $18, members $16; private rooms $35. MC/V. ●

Bond Street Motel Apartments, 1680 N. Phillippi St. (☎208-322-4407), off Fairview Ave. Flatscreen TV? Check. Huge comfy beds? Check. Fully-stocked kitchen? Check. Matching lamps and fake plants? Double check. Free Wi-Fi. Reception M-F 8am-5pm. Reservations recommended. Studios from $59. AmEx/D/MC/V. ●

Budget Inn, 2600 Fairview Ave. (☎208-344-8617). Comfy and close to downtown. Rooms are small but fit in fridges and microwaves. Singles $45; doubles $55. AmEx/D/MC/V. ●

FOOD

Although Idaho is world-renowned for potatoes, Boise offers hungry roadtrippers much more than spuds. The downtown area, centered on Eighth and Main St., bustles with delis, coffee shops, ethnic restaurants, and several stylish bistros.

☒ Zeppole Baking Company, 217 N. 8th St. (☎208-345-2149). Dispenses with all that vegetable nonsense and just puts delicious meats and cheeses on delicious bread for very little money. A simple and elegant operation. Daily specials are icing on the cake. Grab a seat outside and feel smug while you judge people who paid too much for their own lunches. Sandwiches $3-5. Soups $3.50. Fresh pastries under $2. Soup and sandwich combos $6-7. Open M-F 7am-5pm, Sa 7:30am-4pm. MC/V. ●

☒ Superb Sushi, 280 N. 8th St. (☎208-385-0123; www.superbsushidowntown.com), in the lower level of the Idaho Bldg. You have every reason to doubt that the Potato State could produce some of the best and most creative sushi you've ever tried, but it does. Expect to see macadamia nuts, jalapeño peppers, and quail eggs in addition to roe and seaweed. The Suckafish Roll is a work of genius. The patio furniture and Christmas lights keep the atmosphere cool and casual. Rolls $8-12. Open M-W 11:30am-2pm, Th-F 11:30am-2pm and 5pm-9pm, Sa 11:30am-9pm. AmEx/D/MC/V. ●

Bar Gernika, 202 S. Capitol Blvd. (☎208-344-2175). This darkened pub in the middle of the Basque Block is the place to experience authentic Basque cuisine. Every meal should begin with an order of *croquetas* ($4). Sandwiches come in pork loin, lamb, and spicy chorizo varieties. Rice pudding ($2.50) finishes meals off right. Sandwiches $7.75-9.50. Open M 11am-11pm, Tu-Th 11am-midnight, F 11am-1am, Sa 11:30am-1am. AmEx/D/MC/V. ❷

👁 🦅 SIGHTS AND OUTDOORS

JULIA DAVIS PARK. Just a few blocks from the heart of downtown, beautiful Julia Davis Park is the ideal place to take a break while exploring Boise. A paddle-boat pond, tennis courts, and a band shell mean there's always something going on, while the pavilion in the rose garden gives the adventurous a perfect opportunity to get their swerve on. (*Myrtle St. and Capitol Blvd.* ☎ *208-384-4240.*)

IDAHO HISTORICAL MUSEUM. The museum traces the history of the state from prehistoric days to the 20th century. Exhibits spotlight the experiences of Basque and Chinese immigrants in the area, although the museum's real draw is the fez-wearing, sunglasses-inside-wearing two-headed calf in the 19th-century bar and parlor. (*610 N. Julia Davis Dr.* ☎ *208-334-2120. Open May-Oct. Tu-Sa 9am-5pm, Su 1-5pm; Nov.-Apr. Tu-Sa 9am-5pm. $4, ages 6-12 $1, seniors $2.*)

BOISE ART MUSEUM. The museum features an impressive permanent collection devoted to contemporary art as well as several rotating galleries of more traditional work. (*670 Julia Davis Dr.* ☎ *208-345-8330; www.boiseartmuseum.org. Open June-Aug. M-W and F-Sa 10am-5pm, Th 10am-8pm, Su noon-5pm; Sept.-May Tu-W and F-Sa 10am-5pm, Th 10am-8pm, Su noon-5pm. $5, students and seniors $3, ages 6-18 $2, under 6 free.*)

WORLD CENTER FOR BIRDS OF PREY. Far more impressive than the average zoo, the World Center for Birds of Prey is also a research center and raptor breeding ground. Arrow-slit windows give an up-close look at 14 rare and impressive birds of prey, including California condors, harpy eagles, and bald eagles. Trained handlers regularly bring out certain birds for group demonstrations, and the recently opened Archives of Falconry details the history of the 1500-year-old sport. (*5668 W. Flying Hawk Ln. From I-84, take Exit 50, go south*

on S. Cole St., and turn right. ☎ *208-362-8687; www.peregrinefund.org. Open Mar.-Oct. daily 9am-5pm; Nov.-Feb. Tu-Su 10am-4pm. $5, ages 4-16 $3, under 4 free.*)

BASQUE MUSEUM. Dedicated to the fiercely independent and linguistically distinct people, the Basque Museum and Cultural Center attempts to explain and celebrate the history of this Iberian peninsula ethnic group. A lack of land and inconvenient inheritance laws prompted many younger Basque sons to try their luck in America, where they became sheepherders. The museum includes displays on Basque whaling and the origin of Euskara, their fascinating language, as well as Basque cultural practices, which include throwing balls against walls and lifting heavy objects at family reunions. (*611 Grove St.* ☎ *208-343-2671. Open Tu-F 10am-4pm, Sa 11am-3pm. $4, students and seniors $3, ages 6-12 $2.*)

OTHER SIGHTS. The **Museum of Mining and Geology** has displays on mining, geology, gems, and fossils. (*2455 Old Penitentiary Rd.* ☎ *208-368-9876; www.idahomuseum.org. Open W-Su noon-5pm. Free.*) Bikers, runners, and skaters enjoy the **Boise River Greenbelt,** 25 mi. of asphalt and grass pathways following the Boise River. If you look down on landlubbers, throw a tube or kayak into the river; they can be rented at **Barber Park,** at the southeast end of the Greenbelt. (☎ *208-384-4240; www.cityofboise.org/parks. Open daily sunrise-sunset.*)

🎵 NIGHTLIFE

Roadtrippers jonesing for a chance to stay out late will find a lot to love about Boise. Regular music along Main St. and street-side food carts mean there's often as much going on outside as in.

🎵 **Neurolux,** 113 N. 11th St. (☎208-343-0886). Ping-pong tables, moody red lighting, and a magic jukebox that never misses give this ultra-cool club a unique character. Many touring bands choose to play here rather than Boise's bigger venues because they like the atmosphere. Several indie rockers have been known to frequent the club and even give impromptu performances. Open daily noon-2am. AmEx/D/MC/V.

The Balcony, 150 N. 8th St. (☎208-336-1313), on the 2nd fl. of the Capitol Terrace. Nightly DJs spin the best in hip hop, techno, and 80s beats

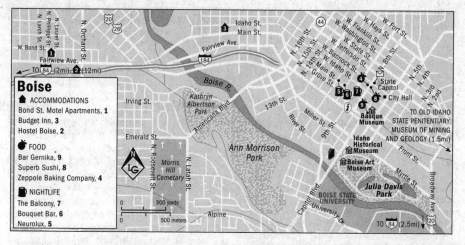

Boise

⌂ ACCOMMODATIONS
Bond St. Motel Apartments, **1**
Budget Inn, **3**
Hostel Boise, **2**

🍴 FOOD
Bar Gernika, **9**
Superb Sushi, **8**
Zeppole Baking Company, **4**

🍸 NIGHTLIFE
The Balcony, **7**
Bouquet Bar, **6**
Neurolux, **5**

---

at this gay-friendly club. The outdoor terrace is a great place to relax and soak up the night air. Karaoke on Su and drag bingo on Tu spice up the usual routine. Cover F-Sa after 9:30pm $3. Open daily 4pm-2am. MC/V.

The Bouquet Bar, 1010 W. Main St. (☎208-345-6605). A weird, fun mix of the decadent and irreverent—those in the know call it "The Bucket." Probably the only place you can find people skating on a quarterpipe inside a historic building with a 105-year-old English bar and marble countertop. Bartenders perform tricks while serving. Monthly theme parties bring in locals and college kids alike. Open M-Sa 4pm-2am, Su 6pm-2am. MC/V.

🏍 THE ROAD TO ONTARIO: 61 MI.

Take **Front Street (US 20/26)** heading west from downtown and merge left onto **I-84 West.** After 28 mi., take **Exit 26,** following US 20/26 away from the interstate. From here, the drive is all sunny fields and groves, meandering 14 mi. through the towns of Notus and Parma. From Parma, continue north along US 20/26. six miles from town, be sure to follow the road west; going straight leads into northern Idaho, away from the trail. As soon as the road has made the turn, it crosses the **Snake River** into Oregon, where you'll be greeted by the city of Nyssa, the self-proclaimed **Thunderegg Capital of the World,** in case you were wondering. About 8 mi. after crossing the border, US 20/26 veers away. Continue straight onto **Route 201.** Bear right on

Southwest Fourth Avenue, leaving Rte. 201 soon after the city limits. Turn here to reach downtown Ontario.

The Beaver State

OREGON

Welcomes You

ONTARIO ☎ 541

Ontario is as good a place as any to stop after the long haul over the Snake River. A quiet city of 11,000, Ontario is proud of its diverse heritage, which is celebrated at the **Four Rivers Cultural Center,** 676 SW Fifth St. The museum explores the complex and often turbulent relationships between the area's major ethnic groups. Visitors can walk through a replica of a **Japanese internment camp** and look at the cramped insides of a **Basque sheepherder's wagon.** The seach for water and agricultural development is another large motif explored by the museum's many exhibits. The center includes a museum, a theater, and a Japanese garden. (☎541-889-8191 or 888-211-1222; www.4rcc.com. Open M-Sa 10am-5pm. $4, ages 6-14 and seniors $3, under 6 free.) Information on other attractions in Ontario is available at the **Ontario Chamber of Commerce,**

cultural center. (☎541-889-8012 or 888-889-2012. Open M-F 8am-5pm.)

Chain lodgings can be found up and down SW 4th Ave., with some budget establishments mixed in. The **Oregon Trail Motel ❷**, 92 E. Idaho Ave., has some of the cheapest rooms in town as well as funky chairs and VCRs for anyone who brought their favorite childhood bootlegged movies to Oregon. (☎541-889-8633. Singles $40; doubles $50. AmEx/D/MC/V.) Attractive wood paneling adds some flair to the spacious rooms of the **Ontario Inn ❷**, 1144 SW Fourth Ave. (☎541-823-2556; www.theontarioinn.com. Free Wi-Fi. Singles $48; doubles $58. AmEx/D/MC/V.) After the flair and variety of Boise, Ontario's return to small-town dining is something of a letdown. Still, **DJ's Family Restaurant ❷**, 625 E. Idaho Ave., serves decent breakfasts ($7-12) named after the people behind the counter who invented them. Homegrown buffalo burgers add some spice to the usual assortment of sandwiches and pastas. (☎541-889-4386. Burgers and sandwiches $6.50-9. Entrees $9-13. Open daily 6am-11pm. AmEx/D/MC/V.)

⊠ DETOUR
FAREWELL BEND STATE PARK

From Ontario, return west on **Fourth Avenue** to **Route 201** and head north along the Snake River. Twenty five miles from Ontario, 3 mi. after the junction of Rte. 201 and **I-84**, take **Exit 353.**

After following the Snake River for more than 300 mi., pioneers had to break off here for the long overland haul across central Oregon to the Columbia River. Picnic tables and sheltering trees make for a relaxing afternoon by the river, which is much easier to appreciate when not in a moving vehicle, whether it's a Conestoga or station wagon. More than 100 campsites give the weary a chance to raise their spirits before pressing on. (☎800-551-6949. Open daily 8am-10pm. Showers $2. Entrance fee $3 per car. May-Sept. tent sites $15, with hookup $17; Oct.-Apr. $11/13. MC/V.)

⛏ THE ROAD TO BAKER CITY: 45 MI.

From Farewell Bend State Park, get back on **I-84.** Take **Exit 304,** which feeds onto the east end of **Campbell Street** in Baker City.

TIME CHANGE. Between Ontario and Baker City, Rte. 201/I-84 passes into the Pacific Time Zone, where it is 1hr. earlier.

BAKER CITY   ☎541

Baker City was a gold-boom town built by prospectors in search of the legendary Blue Bucket Mine. "Booming" may not be the appropriate adjective for Baker City anymore, but the historic downtown area is lined with little shops and businesses—some more than a century old—and the brook actually babbles as it winds through the shady park. The town tries to recapture its boomtown spirit with the annual Miners' Jubilee, held during the middle of July. The streets fill with covered wagons and live music.

VITAL STATS
Population: 10,000
Tourist Office: Baker County Chamber of Commerce and Visitors Bureau, 490 Campbell St. (☎541-523-5855 or 800-523-1235), just west of the junction with I-84. Open in summer M-F 8am-5pm, Sa 8am-4pm; in winter M-F 8am-5pm.
Library and Internet Access: Baker County Public Library, 2400 Resort St. (☎541-523-6419 or 866-297-1239; www.bakerlib.org), just south of the intersection of Campbell and Main St. Free Wi-Fi. Open M-Th 10am-8pm, F 10am-5pm, Sa 10am-4pm, Su noon-4pm.
Post Office: 1550 Dewey Ave. (☎541-523-8593). Open M-F 8:30am-5pm. **Postal Code:** 97814.

◪ ORIENTATION

There are only two roads of any importance to a Baker City visitor. **Campbell Street,** running west from **Exit 304** on **I-84,** is the city's fast-food and hotel zone. Bisecting Campbell St. is north-south **Main Street,** Baker City's downtown strip. Parking is plentiful, except during the **Miners' Jubilee,** when parking vanishes, traffic swells, roads close, and hotels fill to capacity. Ask at the visitors center about locations in Baker County where you can ⬛pan for gold.

ACCOMMODATIONS

Baker City sports the usual array of chain accommodations and budget motels on the outskirts of downtown, but it also has a few more unusual establishments.

Bridge Street Inn, 134 Bridge St. (☎541-523-6571), a 2min. walk from Main St. The walls may be a little thin, but the rooms are spacious and clean and come with refrigerators and microwaves. Breakfast included. Free Wi-Fi. Singles $40; doubles $50. AmEx/D/MC/V. ❷

Eldorado Inn, 695 Campbell St. (☎541-523-6494 or 800-537-5756; www.eldoradoinn.net). Far from a mythical motel of gold, it does have clean rooms, an indoor pool, and the Spanish flair. Continental breakfast included. Singles $69; doubles $81. AmEx/D/MC/V. ❸

FOOD

The best dining in Baker City is around Main St., while diners and fast-food places can be found on Campbell St. near the interstate.

Barley Brown's Brewpub, 2190 Main St. (☎541-523-4266), at the corner of Church St. The place to eat in Baker City. The pastas ($10-17) are delicious, and the Shrimp and Alligator Mad Pasta ($17) is something you're not likely to find elsewhere. The "Death Burger" ($11) comes with 2 patties, ham, and "killer onions." The historic building also houses a microbrewery serving 8 free-to-sample homebrews. Open M-Sa 4-10pm. AmEx/D/MC/V. ❸

Sumpter Junction Restaurant, 2 Sunridge Ln. (☎541-523-9437), at Campbell St. The breakfast menu includes large omelets ($8.50-9) and several platter options ($6-8). The dinner menu includes the usual burgers ($7-8) as well as a limited selection of Mexican dishes ($5-8). Entrees $12-17. Open daily 6am-10pm. AmEx/D/MC/V. ❷

Chamealeon Cafe, 1825 Main St. (☎541-523-7977; www.chamealeon.com). Simple but satisfying sandwich-and-salad lunches alongside the questionably quaffable $0.10 coffee. The dinner menu changes so often that it's not even listed. The signature sandwich, Aunt Caroline's Pork Loin sandwich ($8), is a secret recipe. Sandwiches

$6-8. Salads $6-8. Open M-Tu 11am-3pm, W-Th 11am-8pm, F-Sa 11am-9pm. MC/V. ❸

SIGHTS

OREGON TRAIL REGIONAL MUSEUM. The museum's name refers only to its location along the historic trail, not its actual content, which is a hodgepodge of local artifacts and exhibits. The museum is particularly proud of its scale model from the Clint Eastwood musical *Paint Your Wagon*, which was filmed nearby. The other major attraction is the Calvin-Warfel Collection, an enormous assortment of rare gems and mineral clusters weighing up to 950 lb. The thundereggs and petrified-wood selections are great, but the best room is full of minerals that glow under ultraviolet light. (*2480 Grove St. off Campbell St. ☎541-523-9308. Open daily 9am-5pm. Last entry 4:15pm. $5, under 16 free with adult, seniors $4.50.*)

NATIONAL HISTORIC OREGON TRAIL INTERPRETIVE CENTER. The entrance to the museum lets you walk through a wagon train complete with pioneers, oxen, wagons, and roadside graves. The rest of the museum traces a nameless family's journey along the trail through exhibits and video reenactments. More exciting might be the trails that wrap around the surrounding area. The 2 mi. loop trail is an easygoing hike that makes for great views of the surrounding valley, while smaller trails lead to other scenic overlooks and a set of wagon ruts. (*22267 Rte. 86. Take I-84 to Exit 302 and follow the signs. ☎541-523-1843; www.blm.gov/or/oregontrail. Open daily Apr.-Oct. 9am-6pm; Nov.-Mar. 9am-4pm. In summer $8, under 15 free, seniors $4.50; in winter $5/free/3.50.*)

THE ROAD TO LA GRANDE: 44 MI.

Head east on **Campbell Street** to **I-84** and take the westbound lane toward La Grande, 39 mi. to the north. The best way to enter town from I-84 is take the **Island Avenue Exit** and head southwest to **Adams Avenue.**

LA GRANDE ☎541

Situated between the Blue Mountains to the west and the Wallowa Mountains to the east, La Grande is a good place to stop and rest up for the long haul through the evergreen wilderness of the Pacific Northwest. Pioneers found the nearby Grande Ronde River a near paradise after roaming along the muddy North Platte and Snake Rivers. While it might be tempting to zoom through in pursuit of awe-inspiring vistas, there are some good restaurants that make La Grande worth a stop.

VITAL STATS

Population: 12,500

Tourist Office: Union County Tourism, 102 Elm St. (☎800-848-9969; www.visitlagrande.com), off Adams Ave. Open from Memorial Day to Labor Day M-F 9am-5:30pm, Sa 9am-3pm; from Labor Day to Memorial Day M-F 9am-5pm.

Library and Internet Access: La Grande Public Library, 2006 4th St. (☎541-962-1339). Open M-Th 10am-8pm, F 10am-6pm, Sa 9am-6pm.

Post Office: 1202 Washington Ave. (☎541-962-7539). Open M-F 8:30am-5pm. **Postal Code:** 97850.

ORIENTATION

Getting around is a matter of knowing your bearings relative to **Adams Avenue** and **Washington Avenue.** These two roads run parallel to each other one block apart, cutting the city in half from southeast to northwest. Most motels and restaurants are on or just off these streets, as is La Grande's downtown. Free parking is available on the edges of both streets, but most of the downtown area is pretty walkable.

ACCOMMODATIONS

There is **camping** ❶ at Hilgard Junction State Park. (☎800-551-6949, reservations 800-452-5687. Restrooms and potable water available. Sites $8. No electricity. MC/V.)

Royal Motor Inn, 1510 Adams Ave. (☎541-963-4154 or 800-990-7575). One of La Grande's better budget motels. Singles have king-size beds, and every room comes with a microwave, refrigerator, and a desk. Free Wi-Fi. Singles $45; doubles $50. AmEx/D/MC/V. ❷

Stange Manor Inn, 1612 Walnut St. (☎541-963-2400; www.stangemanor.com). Take Penn Ave. west from Washington Ave.; Walnut St. is a few blocks west of the steep hill. The numer-

ous windows and balconies let in sunlight, moonlight, and the scent of the gardens below. The elegant rooms range from singles to multi-room micro-apartments with fireplaces. Private bath. Breakfast included. Rooms $110-140. MC/V. ❺

FOOD

Fast food abounds near the highway exits, but some surprisingly good, and eclectic, options are around Adams and Washington Ave.

Ten Depot Street, 10 Depot St. (☎541-963-8766). An upscale restaurant that once served as WPA offices, a famous photographer's studio, and a brothel—at the same time. All meals start off with a cheese and vegetable relish. The emu burger ($8) should not be missed, though other sandwiches ($8-13) and pasta dishes ($11-15) are available. Appetizers $7.50-17.50. Entrees $11-45. Open M-Sa 5-10pm. AmEx/MC/V. ❷

Foley Station, 1114 Adams Ave. (☎541-963-7473). The extensive and expensive dinner menu includes Alaskan halibut with Dungeness crab princess ($37) as well as pumpkin and handmade gnocchi ($20). Those with simpler tastes will appreciate the F lunch menu, where all the pastas, salads, and sandwiches are a respectable $6. Pastas $10-17. Entrees $20-55. Open M-Th 3-9pm, F 11am-9pm, Su 9-11am and 3-9pm. D/MC/V. ❹

Cock 'n' Bull Villa Roma, 1414 Adams Ave. (☎541-963-0573), in Pat's Alley. A nice no-frills alternative to some of the fancier places in town. The entrees ($10-19) lean toward pastas and pizzas, though there is also a selection of sandwiches ($5.50-7.50), including the Turben—a frankensandwich of turkey, corned beef, and Swiss. Other menu-toppers include the Cock and Bull, which is just a fancy name for turkey and roast beef. Open M-Sa 11am-8pm. MC/V. ❷

OUTDOORS

The closest spot to experience the great outdoors is **Hilgard Junction State Park,** off I-84 Exit 252, about 8 mi. west of La Grande. A ridge hides the interstate from view, leaving the mountains on one side and the slow-moving Grande Ronde on the other. Activities at the park are limited to exploring the small grounds and wading in the river, though the peace and quiet makes for an ideal camping spot. There's more space to skip merrily among the trees a bit west of Hilgard, at **Blue Mountain Crossing Oregon Trail Interpretive Park,** which offers much more park than interpretation; trails roll through the hills, lined with panels and signs offering information on the trials of the immigrants in these parts. Some weekends feature living history actors. Head west on I-84 to Exit 248 and follow the signs for 3 mi. (☎541-963-7186. Open from Memorial Day to Labor Day daily 8am-8pm. $5.)

FORK IN THE ROAD. While the road into the Wallowa Mountains offers some of the most stunning scenery along the trail, it's a long 75 mi. drive. To skip this section and continue west, take I-84 to Pendleton (p. 659).

🚗 **THE ROAD TO ENTERPRISE AND JOSEPH: 65 MI.**

Take **Adams Avenue** to **Island Avenue** and head east. Island Ave. becomes **Route 82 (Hell's Canyon Scenic Byway)** as it heads into the **Wallowa Mountains.**

ENTERPRISE AND JOSEPH
☎ 541

When the hills of northeastern Oregon give way to the breathtaking Wallowa Mountains, one could conceivably drive right through the tiny towns of Enterprise and Joseph without batting an eyelid. This would be a huge mistake. Separated by a 6 mi. stretch of Rte. 82, these two towns, especially little Joseph, have more personality than many cities 10 times their size. While the area immediately around the mountains is consumed by tourist-trap lodges and a distasteful carnival atmosphere, these two maintain their small-town charm. Enterprise takes care of the basics—motels and general stores abound—while Joseph's main street is lined with bike-rental shops, fly-fishing stores, and outdoor outfitters. The area might be out of the way, but the scenery alone is worth the effort it takes to get there.

VITAL STATS

Population: 2000/1100

Tourist Offices: Wallowa Mountains Visitors Center, 88401 Rte. 82 (☎541-426-5546; www.josephoregon.com). Open in summer M-Sa 8am-5pm; in winter M-F 8am-5pm. **Wallowa County Chamber of Commerce,** 115 Tejaka Ln. (☎541-426-4622 or 800-585-4121), off Rte. 82 on the west edge of Enterprise, across the street from the visitors center. Open M-F 9am-5pm.

Library and Internet Access: Enterprise Public Library, 101 NE 1st St. (☎541-426-3906). Open M and F noon-6pm, Tu-Th 10am-6pm, Sa 10am-2pm.

Post Office: 201 W. North St. (☎541-426-5980), in Enterprise. Open M-F 9am-4:30pm. **Postal Code:** 97828.

LOST BUCKET BLUES

In the 1850s, hundreds of migrants, lagging behind on the trail, decided to follow a grizzled mountain man named Stephen Meek, who promised he knew a shortcut that would cut their trip time by precious weeks. Two hundred wagons set off toward what became known as Meek Cutoff. By the time the migrants realized they'd been duped, they were stranded in central Oregon, starving and dehydrated. Panicked, they began to dig for water wherever they could. In the process, the children in the party began collecting shiny pebbles that the adults had dug up in a blue bucket. In their desperation, however, the migrants tossed the children's finds aside. Eventually, the beleaguered party made its way back to the main trail, three months behind schedule. Years later, when gold was discovered in Oregon, members of the party remembered the blue bucket of shiny pebbles. Dozens of parties led by former veterans of the Meek train combed the countryside for what became known as the "Lost Blue Bucket Mine." While the activity helped develop the previously ignored central region of Oregon, the gold, and the blue bucket, remain undiscovered.

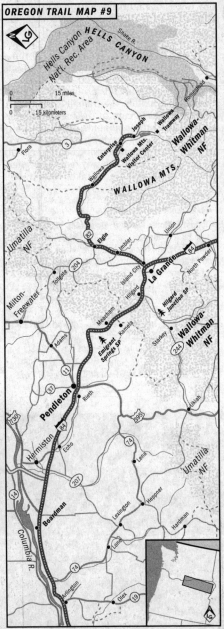

OREGON TRAIL MAP #9

ORIENTATION

Maneuvering around this two-town mountain complex is quite easy, since both cities hug **Route 82**. The road enters Enterprise from the west and runs east under the guise of **North Street**. It then turns south as **River Street** and continues 6 mi. to Joseph, where it becomes **Main Street**. At the south end of Joseph, simply follow the signs out of town, proceeding 6 mi. to **Wallowa Lake**, the main gateway to the **Eagle Cap Wilderness**. Free parking is everywhere.

ACCOMMODATIONS

Enterprise has the most conventional lodging options. The area around Lake Wallowa is crowded with tourist traps and overpriced cabins and should be avoided if possible.

Indian Lodge Motel, 201 S. Main St. (☎541-432-2651 or 888-286-5484; www.indianlodgemotel.com). One of the area's best motels, right in downtown Joseph. 16 spacious and very clean units. The vanity kits in every bathroom are icing on the cake for those used to sleeping on the ground. Singles $80; doubles $85. D/MC/V. ❹

Country Inn, 402 W. North St. (☎541-426-4986). One of Enterprise's better budget options. Small but comfy. Love seats increase sexy-time surface area. Refrigerators and coffee makers. Rooms from $65. AmEx/D/MC/V. ❸

Wallowa Lake State Park, 72214 Marina Ln. (☎541-432-4185). Campsites with access to showers, toilets, and dump station. The tent sites are nice, although those in the know will always opt for the trusty yurt. May-Sept. tent sites $17, with water and electricity $21; cabins $80; yurts $29. Oct.-Apr. tent sites $13, with water and electricity $17, cabins $58; yurts $29. MC/V. ❶

FOOD

Small eateries line both sides of the street in Joseph without even a hint of corporate infestation. Enterprise's selection is more modest, but it's still better than other towns of like size.

Friends Restaurant, 107 N. River St. (☎541-426-5929), in Enterprise. This tiny diner, hiding at the corner of Main St., serves some of the best burgers for miles. Sandwiches $4-5. Entrees $7-13. Open daily 6am-9pm. Cash only. ❷

Embers Brew House, 206 N. Main St. (☎541-432-2739), in Joseph. Stylish, with comfortable outdoor seating and plenty of vegetarian options. This place made its name on its pizzas and calzones ($10-18), although locals swear by the BLT and avocado sandwich ($9). Live rock and blues on weekends. Appetizers $5-9. Beer $3. Open daily 7:30am-11pm. MC/V. ❸

Cheyenne Cafe, 209 N. Main St. (☎541-432-6300), in Joseph. A low-priced local cafe decorated with ranch brands serving families, ranchers, and passersby. The sausages are as big as the pancakes at lesser down-home establishments, and people come from all over for the massive cinnamon rolls ($3). Just looking at the Swedish Lumberjack (a burger with beef, sausage, ham, bacon, and cheese; $10) can make your heart stop. Breakfast $8. Sandwiches $6-9. Open M-Sa 6am-2pm, Su 7am-2pm. MC/V. ❷

█ OUTDOORS

The area around Enterprise and Joseph is dominated by the **Wallowa-Whitman National Forest,** two million acres that encompass the Wallowa Mountains, the nearby Blue Mountains, and **Hell's Canyon,** the deepest gorge in North America. Most visitors will find plenty to do in the slightly more modest but still massive **Eagle Cap Wilderness,** just south of Joseph. At 360,000 acres, it is almost impossible to fully explore the area, although the **Wallowa Mountains Visitors Center** happily supplies would-be explorers with information on trailheads, car loops, camping areas, and the indigenous flora and fauna. Giant maps of the entire region are available for $6. One of the more popular, most easily accessible outdoor areas is **Wallowa Lake,** a state park nearly engulfed by the surrounding national forest. The large lake itself is open for swimming and boating, both very popular summer activities. Take Main St. south from Joseph for 6 mi., following the signs. (☎541-432-4185. Open 6am-9pm.)

Hikers can find a few of Eagle Cap's trailheads in Wallowa Lake's southern picnic grounds, leading up into the mountains along the Wallowa River. Most of these trails are for serious hikers—expect steep grades and unimproved trails. The visitors center in Enterprise provides information on current weather and trail conditions. The humble **Chief Joseph Trail** (1.4 mi.) is an easy to moderate hike through thick forests and over a bridge overlooking the bubbling east fork of the Wallowa River. The peaks around Wallowa Lake aren't the exclusive playground of battle-hardened climbers. ▣**Wallowa Lake Tramway,** 59919 Wallowa Lake Hwy., offers gondola rides to the top of Mt. Howard (8200 ft.). The 15min. ride to the top and the attendant view inspires equal parts awe and terror. The summit is relatively unspoiled except for a heinous mountaintop grill. The trails themselves are pretty easy, but the 8200 ft. gain in elevation means your lungs will be working overtime to make up for the lack of oxygen. The **summit loop trail** (30-40min.) affords an amazing view of the snow-capped Wallowas. On clear days, visitors can see four states from the **valley trail overlook** (30min.). (☎541-432-5331; www.wallowalaketramway.com. Open daily July-Aug. 10am-5pm; Sept. and May-June. 10am-4pm. $22, ages 12-17 $18, ages 3-10 $14.)

▣ THE ROAD TO PENDLETON: 125 MI.

There are two ways to get to Pendleton. You can retrace your route to La Grande via **Route 82.** From La Grande, take **I-84 West** to Pendleton. Before you descend into the Columbia River Valley, the forested campground at **Emigrant Spring State Park ❶,** off **Exit 234,** provides basic camping with showers and electrical hookups. (☎541-983-2277 or 800-551-6949. Tent sites in summer $14-16; in winter $10-12. Cabins $20-35. MC/V.) Those looking for a little more scenery should take Rte. 82 until the town of Elgin, where it branches into **Route 204.** In the town of Downing get on **Route 11** towards Pendleton.

PENDLETON ☎541

After the verdant forests surrounding the Grande Ronde, the area where Pendleton now sits is a return to the bleak high desert that defined some of the roughest stretches of trail. Like a smaller version of Cheyenne, Pendleton prides itself on its annual rodeo, even though its colorful history is much more interesting.

▣ ORIENTATION

The **Umatilla River** runs east-west through Pendleton, and the majority of the city lies south of the river. The city is bisected by north-south **Main Street**. All roads have a double designation giving their positions relative to these two dividers. The city is fairly narrow, and long east-west roads are all one-way, so expect to do a lot of looping. To prevent confusion, the streets' names are arranged alphabetically from the river toward the south: Byers, Court, Dorion, and so on.

VITAL STATS

Population: 17,000

Tourist Office: Pendleton Chamber of Commerce, 501 S. Main St. (☎541-276-7411; www.pendletonchamber.com). Open from Memorial Day to Labor Day M-Th 8:30am-5pm, F 10am-5pm, Sa 9am-4pm; from Labor Day to Memorial Day M-Th 8:30am-5pm, F 10am-5pm.

Library and Internet Access: Pendleton Public Library, 502 SW Dorion Ave. (☎541-966-0210). Open M-Th 10am-8pm, F-Sa 10am-5pm.

Post Office: 104 SW Dorion Ave. (☎541-278-4053). Open M-F 9am-5pm, Sa 10am-1pm. **Postal Code:** 97801.

ACCOMMODATIONS

Working Girls Hotel, 17 SW Emigrant Ave. (☎541-276-0730 or 800-226-6398). Euphemistically named for the former brothel it occupies. The rooms are decorated with antiques recovered from the era. Rented through Pendleton Underground Tours. Kitchen, living area, shared bath. Rooms $65; suites $75. 18+. MC/V. ❸

Knights Inn, 105 SE Court Ave. (☎541-276-3231). Though the inn is right downtown, thick walls and cleverly arranged walkways keep you away from the commotion. Free Wi-Fi. Singles $55; doubles $60. AmEx/MC/V. ❸

FOOD

Restaurants cluster around the nexus of Main St., Court Ave., and Dorion Ave.

Como's Italian Eatery, 39 SE Court Ave. (☎541-278-9142). A tiny spot at the core of downtown serving normal Italian fare as well as a few surprises, like the much-touted Banilla Wafer Shake ($6). The Prosciutto Chicken ($16) is a specialty. Sandwiches $8.50. Entrees $7.50-16. Open M-Sa 11am-9pm. MC/V. ❸

Main Street Diner, 349 S. Main St. (☎541-278-1952). Another diner that hasn't changed themes since the Eisenhower administration. Serves the usual breakfast fare ($7-8.50) as well as some slightly less conventional lunch options, like parmesan tacos ($7.50). Sandwiches $4-8. Open M-Sa 7am-2pm, Su 8am-2pm. MC/V. ❷

SIGHTS

BROTHEL TUNNELS. A system of tunnels evolved in Pendleton over the years, burrowing between the numerous brothels and saloons that sprang up here; at one point there were as many as 32 bars and 18 houses of ill repute. This whole sordid and fascinating history is told by ❧**Pendleton Underground Tours,** which leads visitors through the completely restored and redecorated underground establishments. Tours showcase a card room, ice-cream parlor, Chinese quarters and opium den, and the Cozy Rooms bordello. *(Tours located at 37 SW Emigrant Ave. ☎541-276-0730; www. pendletonundergroundtours.org. Reservations required. 1hr. tours Mar.-Oct. M-Sa 9:30am-3pm; Nov.-Feb. call for schedule. $15. MC/V.)*

TAMASTSLIKT CULTURAL INSTITUTE. The institute attempts to preserve the history and culture of the area's tribes even amid the commercial gluttony of a massive resort and casino. The circular floor plan leads visitors through the changes that have taken place in the lives of the Umatilla River tribes since the arrival of Europeans, from the introduction of the horse to the creation of treaties to the founding of the Umatilla Indian School. *(72789 Hwy. 331, off Exit 216 on I-84, east of Pendleton, on the Umatilla Reservation. ☎541-966-9748; www. tamastslikt.org. Open Apr.-Oct. daily 9am-5pm; Nov.-Mar. M-Sa 9am-5pm. $6, students and seniors $4.)*

THE ROAD TO THE DALLES: 123 MI.

Continue west on **I-84.** About 45 mi. past Pendleton, you'll pass the town of Boardman, where the highway joins with the **Columbia River.** Continue on I-84 to **Exit 85,** which feeds into **Second Avenue** in The Dalles.

THE DALLES ☎ 541

Without the cosmopolitan appeal of Portland or the rugged spirit of Hood River, The Dalles is sort of the black sheep of the three major cities situated along the Columbia. Its only real brush with fame came in 1984, when a local cult infected more than 750 residents with salmonella by contaminating local salad bars. Bioterrorism aside, The Dalles provides a few nice places to eat and sleep, but the real fun still lies farther down the river.

VITAL STATS
Population: 12,200
Tourist Office: The Dalles Area Chamber of Commerce, 404 W. 2nd St. (☎541-296-2231; www.thedalleschamber.com). Open from Memorial Day to Labor Day M-F 8:30am-5pm, Sa 10am-4pm, Su 11am-3pm; from Labor Day to Memorial Day M-F 8:30am-5pm.
Library and Internet Access: The Dalles-Wasco County Library, 722 Court St. (☎541-296-2815). Open M-Th 10am-8:30pm, F 10am-6pm, Sa 10am-5pm.
Post Office: 101 W. 2nd St. (☎541-296-1065). Open M-F 8:30am-5pm. **Postal Code:** 97058.

✳ ORIENTATION

I-84 borders the edge of town along the **Columbia River. Highway 30** passes through down as **East Third Street** and **East Second Street. Union Street** intersects the two near the center of town, heading down to the river.

🏠 ACCOMMODATIONS

Oregon Motor Motel, 200 W. 2nd St. (☎541-296-9111). Conveniently located downtown and offers clean rooms with fridges and microwaves. Singles from $55; doubles from $60. AmEx/D/MC/V. ❸

🍴 FOOD

Restaurants are clustered in the downtown area and are well advertised and easy to find.

Burgerville, 118 W. 3rd St. (☎541-298-5753). Serves the most socially and environmentally conscious fast food you'll ever eat. Eric Schlosser, author of *Fast Food Nation,* is a reported fan.

Electricity is generated by wind energy, frying oil is recycled into biodiesel, and all of the dishes use regional ingredients like Tillamook cheddar cheese and Walla Walla onions. Vegetarian options are available. Look for the seasonally rotating menu of shake flavors, including hazelnut and huckleberry. Free Wi-Fi. Burgers $2-5. Shakes $3. Open daily 7am-10pm. D/MC/V. ❶

Cottage Cafe, 111 E. 2nd St. (☎541-298-3770). Maybe not the kind of cafe where you lounge around on old couches and talk about Proust, but it serves all the normal drinks as well as ice cream ($2) and sandwiches ($6). Free Wi-Fi. Open M-F 7:30am-5pm, Sa 9am-4pm. MC/V. ❶

👁 SIGHTS

COLUMBIA GORGE DISCOVERY CENTER AND WASCO COUNTY MUSEUM. The Wasco County Museum focuses on aspects of the region's history that continue to affect people today, like the damming of the Columbia River and the loss of the salmon population. The Columbia Gorge Discovery Center contains a large exhibit on the Ice Age mega-fauna of the area, as well as a walk-through (plastic) gorge, teeming with (stuffed) wildlife and the buzz of (recorded) bird song. (*5000 Discovery Dr. Head west on I-84 to Exit 82 and follow the signs.* ☎541-296-8600; www.gorgediscovery.org. Open daily 9am-5pm. $8, ages 6-16 $4, seniors $7.)

ROCK FORT. Those jonesing for some Lewis and Clark nostalgia should head to the Rock Fort, which is exactly what it sounds like. The explorers made camp there for three days in 1805. Clark described the campground in extreme detail in his personal diary, but these days not much remains of the camp other than a few rocks. (*At Bridgeway Rd., Bridge St., and Garrison St.* ☎541-296-2231. Free.)

DALLES DOWNTOWN MURALS. The murals add a little color to an otherwise bland downtown. They provide a romanticized account of the area's history, from the fishing village of the Native Americans to Lewis and Clark's expedition to the Oregon Trail. The majority of the murals cluster around E. Federal St., between Second and Third St.

⏷ THE ROAD TO THE COLUMBIA RIVER GORGE NATIONAL SCENIC AREA: 7 MI.

Head east via **Second Street** to the **Exit 87** on-ramps, just east of town. Follow the signs toward the interstate but drive right past the ramps; the road will continue across the **Columbia River** into Washington by way of the **Dalles Bridge (US 197)**. After the bridge, go west on Rte. 14 into Washington State. Between The Dalles and Portland, you'll be driving in the heart of the Columbia River Gorge Scenic Area.

COLUMBIA RIVER GORGE NATIONAL SCENIC AREA ☎ 541

Stretching 80 stunning miles from The Dalles to Portland, the Columbia River Gorge carries the river to the Pacific Ocean through woodlands, waterfalls, and canyons. Heading inland along the gorge, heavily forested peaks give way to broad, bronze cliffs and golden hills covered with tall pines. Mt. Hood and Mt. Adams loom nearby, and breathtaking waterfalls plunge over steep cliffs into the river. While driving through offers spectacular vistas, roadtrippers should consider heading off-road via one of the area's many trails.

VITAL STATS
Area: 292,500 acres
Tourist Office: USDA Forest Service Columbia River Gorge National Scenic Area Office, 902 Wasco St., Ste. 200 (☎541-308-1700), in Hood River. Open M-F 8am-4:30pm.
Gateway Towns: The Dalles (previous page), Hood River (p. 665), Portland (p. 669).

⊕ ORIENTATION

The Columbia River Gorge is traversed by several major highways: **I-84** and **US 30** on the Oregon side and **Route 14** in Washington. Attractions on the Washington side of the Columbia can be reached by crossing the river at the **Bridge of the Gods;** 11 mi. west of Hood River, take **Exit 44** through Cascade Locks and follow the signs ($1 toll). Since it stretches for more than 80 mi. between The Dalles and Portland, there isn't a central parking location. Expect to hop between several sites spread far apart.

◉ SIGHTS

◪MULTNOMAH FALLS. The second-highest year-round waterfall in the US, dropping 620 ft. from Larch Mountain, the falls are one of the most beautiful spots in the entire scenic area. The visitors center at the base of the falls provides trail maps and other helpful information. The most popular trail is a half-mile paved path leading over a stone bridge all the way to the top of the falls. The hike can be exhausting to those not used to steep climbs, but the view from the top is worth the strain. From there, you can head back to the visitors center or continue on the 6 mi. loop trail that passes three more beautiful waterfalls and several spectacular viewpoints. (*Oregon side. 30 mi. west of Hood River.* ☎503-695-2372. *Visitors center open daily 9am-7pm.*)

HISTORIC COLUMBIA RIVER HIGHWAY. The highway provides an often terrifying, always beautiful view of the gorge below. A winding stretch that roughly parallels I-84, the River Highway hugs the cliffsides along the gorge and provides easy access to some of the gorge's most spectacular sights. (*Oregon side.*)

BEACON ROCK. Named by Louis and Clark, this titanic boulder juts out vertically from the water's edge. Across the street is **Beacon Rock State Park,** a hillside **campground ❶,** and the start of the Hamilton Mountain Trail. (*Off Rte. 14 just west of Skamania, WA, 7 mi. west of the dam.* ☎509-427-8265. *Open daily 8am-10pm for day use. Sites $19, with full hookup $26. Cash only.*)

◎ HIKING

There are tons of trails in the Gorge area. Unfortunately, they're spread out and often difficult to find. The office in Hood River sells an enormous map of all the area trails for $7. The forest service also has a comprehensive website that contains maps, descriptions, difficulty ratings, and directions to trailheads for many area trails at www.fs.fed.us/r6/columbia/recreation/trails/index.shtml.

Eagle Creek (13 mi. one-way; easy). From I-84 going east, take Exit 41 and follow the signs. The most popular trail in the gorge, Eagle Creek winds around the forests and through basalt cliffs. Tunnel Falls leads hikers behind a curtain of flowing water, and the grotto near Punch Bowl Falls is a popular resting place. Lower portion of trail open year-round; upper portion open June-Nov.

Angel's Rest (4 mi. round-trip; easy). From I-84 W., take Exit 35 onto the Historic Columbia River Hwy. and go 7 mi. west. This trail leads through mossy, fern-filled forests, past one of the last falls in the chain, and up a ridge. Open Mar.-Dec.

Catherine Creek (1 mi. round-trip; easy). From Rte. 14 in Washington, turn north on CR 1230 and proceed for 1 mi. The paved trail passes through meadows that bloom with 90 species of wildflowers Feb.-July.

Dog Mountain Trail (3 mi. round-trip; difficult). The trailhead is marked by a large sign, located off Rte. 14 about 14 mi. east of Stevenson, 1 mi. west of the Bridge of the Gods. This short trail is steep and rocky. Offers great vistas of Mt. Adams, Mt. Hood, and Mt. St. Helens. Closed in winter.

🚲 BIKING

Bike trails also lace the gorge, though info on them is not quite as readily available as it is for foot trails. **Discover Bicycles,** 116 Oak St., in Hood River, sells maps in addition to renting out bikes. (☎541-386-4820; www.discoverbicycles.com. Maps $10. Road and mountain bikes $35 per day. Open M-Sa 9am-6pm, Su 9am-5pm.) The **Post Canyon** area is home to a system of free-ride trails and has become very popular with stunt and downhill riders. To reach the canyon, go west on Cascade St. in Hood River all the way to its end and turn left. Follow Country Club Rd. for 1 mi., then turn right onto Post Canyon Rd. For more info on free riding in the canyon, visit www.gfra.org.

Mosier Twin Tunnels (4 mi., 1hr. one-way; easy to moderate). A segment of the Historic Columbia River Hwy. too narrow for cars, between Hood River and Mosier. Mainly an on-road ride, with views of the river and the tunnels. Parking $3.

Three Lake Tour (18 mi., 2-4hr. round-trip; easy to moderate). Take 13th St. in Hood River south to Rte. 281 and continue south, turning west onto Portland Dr. The road will pass through the intersection with Country Club Rd. and become Binns Hill Rd. Follow Binns Hill Rd. for 1 mi., then turn left onto Kinsley Rd. This leads to the trailhead beside Green Point Upper Reservoir. Open summer-fall.

Surveyor's Ridge (23 mi., 3-5hr. round-trip). Take Rte. 35 S. from Hood River for 31 mi., turn east onto FS 44, and follow it for 3 mi. to the trailhead. This loop rides the edge of a ridge, offering great views. The final leg of the loop is along FS 17. Open from late spring to late fall.

🚗 THE ROAD TO HOOD RIVER: 20 MI.

On the Washington side of the Columbia River, **Route 14** runs about 20 mi. west from The Dalles turnoff to Bingen. Near Bingen, take the **Hood River Toll Bridge** ($0.75) across the river to Oregon. Follow the signs

ENTERING TOWN

From the hood of my car, parked on the side of the road, I watch a wildfire devour a field. Smoke rolls across the field, over the roadways, and partway up the hillside. I'm fortunate to have avoided the interstate on the other side of the field—traffic is at a halt, backed up halfway to Hood River. People walk their dogs along the side of the road while a couple of firefighters fumble with their hose to no avail. Next to me is a nice man from the Netherlands who takes pictures of the billowing smoke and the deer that runs confusedly in front of the creeping fire. Fifteen minutes ago, a man in a pickup truck drove by. He told us that all roads into and out of The Dalles were blocked off. Then he let out a rebel yell and disappeared into the smoke. No one else has driven by; the police have our stretch of road sealed off as well. The man from the Netherlands was supposed to be on his way to a computer-science conference. He says, "I thought I would take a day or two off. Go on a little vacation, see the country a little bit. All I've seen so far is smoke." He asks what I'm doing in The Dalles. I say, "I'm supposed to go into town and review restaurants and things for a book." He says, "Now you'll never know what kind of food they have." He pauses. "Burnt deer, maybe." "Yeah," I say. "Maybe."

onto I-84 but don't go anywhere on it; the on-ramp flows right into the off-ramp that leads into Hood River. Turn left to enter the center of Hood River. From the Oregon side of the river, it's a straight shot on **I-84.**

HOOD RIVER ☎541

Built along the Oregon bank of a bend of the Columbia River, Hood River has evolved from a center for traditional sports into the windsurfing and kiteboarding capital of the Northwest. With a downtown area full of outdoor suppliers, cafes, and coffeehouses, Hood River cultivates a hip, progressive persona that makes you want to stick around.

VITAL STATS
Population: 6000
Tourist Office: Hood River County Chamber of Commerce, 720 E. Port Marina Dr. (☎541-386-2000 or 800-366-3530; www.hoodriver.org). Open M-F 9am-5pm, Sa-Su 10am-5pm.
Library and Internet Access: Hood River County Library, 502 State St. (☎541-386-2535). Open M-Th 8:30am-8:30pm, F-Sa 8:30am-5pm.
Post Office: 1795 12th St. (☎541-386-6280). Open M-F 9am-6pm, Sa 8am-5pm. **Postal Code:** 97031.

✳ ORIENTATION

Hood River is an easy city to drive in, except for the occasional busy intersection regulated only by four-way stop signs. North-south streets are numbered, increasing from east to west. The most important east-west streets are **Cascade Avenue** and **Oak Street,** both close to the interstate. Like most cities in the area, Hood River has a parking problem. Downtown spots are metered until 6pm and hard to come by, and most lots are constantly monitored. It might be worthwhile to park along the street a ways from downtown and walk.

🛏 ACCOMMODATIONS

Hood River accommodations can be expensive, and the smaller motels fill up quickly.

Columbia Gorge Hostel (☎509-493-3363; www.bingenschool.com), 1 block north of the intersection of Cedar St. and Rte. 14, in Bingen. Cheap and friendly, though it's separated by a toll bridge from Hood River. The historic building is a converted CCC schoolhouse and offers both huge private rooms and clean, dorm-style bunks. The gymnasium is open for basketball and volleyball, and the cafeteria is now a television lounge and open kitchen. Linen $3. Towel $1. Check-in M and Su by arrangement, Tu-Sa 8am-1pm and 6-9pm. Dorms $19; private doubles $49. MC/V. ❶

Praters Motel, 1306 Oak St. (☎541-386-3566). Provides clean rooms with microwaves and refrigerators. The best part is the view of Mt. Adams available from 6 of the 7 rooms. Free Wi-Fi. Rooms from $70; 5-person suites $90. MC/V. ❸

🍴 FOOD

Little cafes and lunch shops cluster in Hood River, so finding somewhere to eat after a day of windsurfing is easy.

Doppio Coffee + Lounge, 310 Oak St. (☎541-386-3000). Too hip for regular conjunctions. An open-air view of the sidewalk creates a relaxing atmosphere for windsurfer intellectuals to drink coffee and indulge in a sandwich or the homemade gelato. Free Wi-Fi. Coffee and espresso $2.25-3.25. Sandwiches $4.50-8. Gelato $2.75. Open daily 7am-10pm. MC/V. ❶

Bette's Place, 416 Oak St. (☎541-386-1880). Usual diner fare with the occasional twist. Breakfast options include fresh crab Benedict ($12) and shrimp omelets ($10). Sandwiches include ham and turkey and the Gobbler, with turkey, avocado, and cranberry sauce. Salads include shrimp and mandarin orange as well as cottage cheese and fruit. Breakfast $8-11. Open daily 5:30am-3pm. MC/V. ❷

☉ SIGHTS

MOUNT HOOD RAILROAD. The excursion train, composed of early-20th-century Pullman coaches and a ▧red caboose, winds through a valley, providing a narrated historic and scenic tour with a brief stop in the town of Parkdale. Dinner and brunch trains, in authentic restored dining cars, provide a meal to supplement the countryside ride. Specialty trips like the Train Robbery ride are occasionally offered; call for dates. (*110 Railroad St. At the intersection of Cascade Ave. and 1st St. ☎541-386-3556 or 800-872-4661; www.mthoodrr.com. Open Apr.-Dec.*

Excursion train $25, ages 2-12 $15, seniors $23. Brunch train $58, murder-mystery dinner train $80.)

NIGHTLIFE

Full Sail Brewing Co., 506 Columbia St. (☎541-386-2247). Has 3 gold-medal winners from the 2008 World Beer Championship, the Amber, Wassail, and IPA, and the lager was just voted "Best Premium Lager" at the World Beer Awards. Hourly tours from 1-4pm take you behind the scenes of the brewing process. If the overpowering brewery smell doesn't drive you away, the pub offers several burger options. Appetizers $4-10. Burgers $8-10. Open daily 11:30am-10pm.

Trillium Cafe, 207 Oak St. (☎541-386-1996). A bar and grill that serves great entrees—the parmesan-crusted chicken ($15) is especially good. Live local music on weekends keeps the atmosphere tight and friendly. Salads $5-12. Burgers $8-9. Entrees $15-17. 21+ after 10pm. Open daily 8am-1am. MC/V.

OUTDOORS

Hiking trails wrap all around Hood River in the **Columbia River Gorge National Scenic Area** (p. 662); the windsurfing and kiteboarding opportunities, however, are almost completely located in the city itself. The most important area in the windsurfing world is **Port Marina Park,** left off I-84 at Exit 64, which hosts most of the windsurfing and kiteboarding schools. North of downtown Hood River is the **Hook,** a cape the forms a windy but sheltered cove where beginners often train. Several companies rent equipment and provide instruction for all levels of windsurfers and kiteboarders. **Big Winds,** 207 Front St., at the east end of Oak St., offers 2hr. introductory windsurfing lessons to teach the basics, with an additional 1hr. of practice time per lesson. Kiteboarders have a 1hr. introductory class out of the water to learn how to control a kite; most water lessons are one on one. (☎514-386-6086; www. bigwinds.com. Windsurfing intro lesson $65. Rentals $45 full package for ½-day, $60 for full day, $40 for only board or rig. Kiteboarding intro lesson $95. Open in summer daily 8:30am-6pm.) **Hood River Water Play,** based out of Port Marina Park, provides a 6hr. windsurfing introductory class that includes free rentals for introductory-level graduates. You can sail at the beginners' beach for free after completing the intro class. Four more levels of class are available, as are private lessons. There are six levels of kiteboarding instruction: two basic, two intermediate, and two advanced. Each pair can be taken together. (☎541-386-9463 or 800-963-7873; www. hoodriverwaterplay.com. Windsurfing intro class $199, successive levels $85-95 for 2-3hr. classes. Kiteboarding intro class $99.)

THE ROAD TO MOUNT HOOD: 43 MI.

From Hood River, take **Oak Street** eastbound until it runs into **State Street.** Then drive south on **Route 35.** It's 40 mi. to the intersection with **US 26,** a central point in the arc of area campsites and trailheads.

MOUNT HOOD ☎503

At 11,249 ft., this majestic, snow-covered mountain is the highest point in Oregon and one of the most climbed mountains in the world. Covered with snow even at the height of summer, Mount Hood is also a year-round destination in the Northwest for skiers and snowboarders. Surrounded as it is by beautiful pine forests, there's no better scenery for a day on the slopes, and the hillside fruit orchards make for an unbeatable place to share a basket of cherries.

VITAL STATS
Elevation: 11,249 ft.
Tourist Office: Zigzag Ranger District Station, 70220 E. Hwy. 26 (☎503-622-3191). Open daily 7:45am-4:30pm.
Gateway Towns: Hood River (opposite page), Government Camp.
Fees: Northwest Forest Pass required for most hiking; $5 per day, $30 per year.

ORIENTATION

Route 35 connects the towns of Hood River and Government Camp northeast of Mt. Hood and is the main road for access to many trailheads and campsites. Near the southeast edge of the mountain, Rte. 35 meets **US 26,** which leads to the other major trails and camps. Government Camp, a ski village which lies on a single

BIG DETOUR

CRATERS, COUPLETS & CATHOLICS

SOUTHERN OREGON

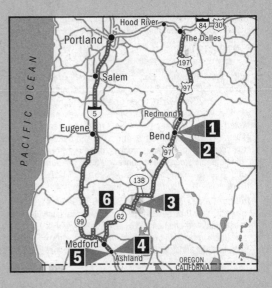

START: The Dalles

HIGHLIGHT: Oregon Shakespeare Festival

DISTANCE: 590 mi.

DURATION: 3 days

Take US 197 S. from The Dalles for 68 mi.; it will become US 97 S. Continue on US 97 for 63 mi. to Bend.

1. MCMENAMINS OLD SAINT FRANCIS SCHOOL. Built in 1936, this Catholic school was in disrepair and on the fast track to condemnation by the early 90s—until a pair of entrepreneurs saw an unlikely business venture. With much of the original architecture still intact, the school has become McMenamins Old St. Francis School, 700 NW Bond St., a combination bistro/microbrewery/historic hotel/movie theater/spa. The foyer of the school has been transformed into a full-service restaurant with great burgers ($7-10), while the auditorium has become a movie theater with huge chairs and love seats. The lower levels of the building have been turned into a motel, each room decorated with artifacts from the school and named after a former student, staffer, or faculty member. Free live music on Wednesdays means there's almost always something cool going on. (☎541-382-5174. Movie tickets $3. Appetizers $4-9. Calzones $9.50. Restaurant open daily 7am-1am. Rooms from $125. AmEx/D/MC/V.)
From Bend, take US 97 S. for about 6 mi. The entrance to the park will be on the left.

2. HIGH DESERT MUSEUM. Part zoo, part museum, the High Desert Museum, 59800 S. US 97, beats the pants off most natural history museums because the animals actually move around. Bobcats skulk around the lobby, while scorpions, turtles, and a Gila monster crawl around the desertarium. Daily live demonstrations bring out raptors and the occasional porcupine or badger. The historical exhibits are largely dioramic—visitors get to walk through replicas of a fur-trading camp, mine, and Chinese storefront, though by far the most affecting exhibit is the replica reservation home circa 1963. Living history actors keep an old sawmill running on the grounds, although occasionally they also dust off the muskets for some more exciting demonstrations. Though the museum isn't particularly large, there's so much going on that you could easily spend 3-5hr. checking everything out. (☎541-382-4754; www.highdesertmuseum.org. Open daily 9am-5pm. May-Oct. $15, ages 5-12 $9, seniors $12; Nov.-Apr. $10/9/6. MC/V.)
From Bend, get back on US 97 S. for about 73 mi. Take Rte. 138 west for about 15 mi. to the park's north entrance. The visitors center is about 15 mi. past the entrance.

3. CRATER LAKE NATIONAL PARK. The catastrophic eruption of Mt. Mazama about 7600 years ago formed Crater Lake, one of the most beautiful and amazing sights in the world. Sheer cliffs 2000 ft. high surround brilliant blue waters. With no natural inlets or outlets, the water that fills the caldera is some of the clearest and purest in the world. The visitors center provides trail maps and information about the area. The rim drive wraps for 33 mi. around the caldera's edge, offering several spectacular vantage points of the lake itself. The Cleetwood Cove Trail is steep and arduous, but it's the only trail that leads to the lake itself, which is open for fishing and swimming. It also serves as the departure point for the popular boat tours, which last 2hr. and offer a close-up view of "The Old Man of the Lake," a tree trunk that has been bobbing vertically in the lake for more than a century. (☎541-594-3100. Park open 24hr. Visitors center open daily 9am-5pm. $10 per car. Boat tours $26 per person.)

From Crater Lake, depart from the south entrance and take a right on Rte. 62 (Crater Lake Hwy.). Follow this for about 70 mi. and then merge onto I-5 S. toward Ashland. Continue for 11 mi. until Exit 19. Turn right and follow S. Valley View Rd., which becomes E. Main St., into town.

4. OREGON SHAKESPEARE FESTIVAL. The Oregon Shakespeare Festival, 15 S. Pioneer St., right off E. Main St., began in 1935, the brainchild of a local college professor who convinced city leaders to let him stage a few Shakespeare plays in a run-down building. The city agreed but insisted that the performances be preceded by amateur boxing matches to defray the losses the plays would surely incur. Ironically and thankfully, it was the plays that covered the losses of the boxing matches. Since its beginnings, the festival has staged the Bard's complete canon three times. Every season, the festival presents 11 plays, more than half of them Shakespearean, across three very different stages. Although all the stages have their own personality, the Elizabethan Stage offers an experience closest to that of the original Globe. Be sure to arrive early and catch the "Green Show," which on any given night could feature a fire dance, ballet, or a rock-and-roll reinterpretation of Shakespeare. (☎541-482-4331; www.osfashland. org. Season runs Feb.-Oct. Tickets $20-73. Backstage tours $12, ages 6-17 $6. AmEx/D/MC/V.)

5. ASHLAND GALLERIES. Downtown Ashland is packed with fantastic art galleries. More than a dozen are spread along six blocks of E. Main St., with seven clustered around the intersection of Fourth and A St. Gathering Glass Studio, 322 N. Pioneer St. (☎541-488-4738), has a vivid gallery and offers live glass-blowing demonstrations. The Hanson Howard Gallery, 82 N. Main St. (☎541-488-2562), houses an impressive collection of contemporary art of all media from Northwestern artists. The Schneider Museum of Art, 1250 Siskiyou Blvd. (☎541-552-6245), at Southern Oregon University, houses a rotating gallery of regional and national art, with an emphasis on contemporary works with a social conscience.

From Ashland, take Main St. northwest out of town and merge left onto I-5 N. Drive for 24 mi. until Exit 43 to Gold Hill. Turn right on Main St. and follow the signs to the House of Mystery at the Oregon Vortex.

6. OREGON VORTEX. Native Americans considered this half-acre of ground to be a forbidden place, but that didn't deter gold-hungry pioneers from trying to establish a mining camp in the area—until they realized none of their measurement tools worked. Within the Oregon Vortex and the House of Mystery, 4303 Sardine Creek Left Fork Rd., people appear to change heights, plumb bobs hang at unusual angles, and balls roll up inclined planes. Inside the House of Mystery, those who can remain standing do so at a precarious 7.5° angle. Short people will appreciate the chance to at least feel taller for a few minutes, while engineers and physics majors have a field day with the House of Mystery. (☎541-855-1543; www. oregonvortex.com. Open daily June-Aug. 9am-5pm; Sept.-Oct. and Mar.-May 9am-4pm. $9, ages 6-11 $7, seniors $8. MC/V.)

Back to the route. Return to I-5 N. and follow it for 257 mi. to Portland. If you want, you can then take Exit 300 to I-84 E./US 30 and follow that for 62 mi. back to Hood River.

road of highway, **Government Camp Loop,** on US 26 just east of the intersection with Rte. 35. is the closest town in proximity to the mountain and has more ski and snowboard shops than restaurants or lodgings. The town of Hood River, **Exit 63** on **I-84,** offers more options for lodging, food, coffee, and pints.

ACCOMMODATIONS

Most campgrounds in Mt. Hood National Forest cluster near the junction of US 26 and Rte. 35, though they can also be found along the length of both highways on the way to Portland or Hood River. To reach the free camping spots, take the sign toward Trillium Lake (a few miles east of Government Camp on US 26), follow a dirt road to the right 1 mi. from the entrance with the sign "2650 131," and make a left toward "Old Airstrip." Campsites with fire rings line the abandoned runway. Call the **Zigzag Ranger Station** to reserve a campsite. (☎877-444-6777. Sites $9.) For a more expensive, less outdoorsy experience (really the only option in winter), stay in a hotel or B&B in Hood River or Government Camp. If your wallet can take it, stay at the **Timberline Lodge ❺.** (Below. Rooms in summer from $105; call ahead for winter rates.)

Vagabond Lodge, 4070 Westcliff Dr. (☎541-386-2992), Exit 62 off I-84. 1 mi. west of Hood River. A nearly perfect location on 5 riverside acres, with luxurious suites, riverview rooms, and motel prices. Many of the rooms have balconies, and most have great views of the river. From the road, the modest office and street-side rooms can be deceiving; this may be one of the best-kept secrets in Hood River. Reservations recommended for the 24 riverside rooms. Rooms in summer from $46; in winter from $53. ❸

Trillium Lake, off US 26, less than 2 mi. west of the Rte. 35/US 26 intersection. The lakeside is beautiful, but the paved, popular sites are close together. Sites fill up quickly on weekends, so reserve early. Firewood $5. Sites $14-16. ❶

Still Creek, 1 mi. west of Trillium Lake, off US 26. Generally less crowded than Trillium Lake; even when full, the thickly wooded grounds are quieter, as the sites are widely spaced. Potable water, toilets, few RVs. Sites $16. ❶

FOOD

Food here is limited to **Government Camp,** which serves touristy food at touristy prices.

Ice Axe Grill, 87304 E. Government Camp Loop (☎503-272-3172). A tasty, if slightly odd, take on pub fare, such as expensive ($10-13) sandwiches including a lentil burger and the imposing Pacific Fish Taco. Appetizers include fried calamari and brie (both $10). The grill is also the home of the Mt. Hood Brewing Co., which serves several award-winning microbrews, including the "aggressively hopped" Ice Axe IPA ($4.25

LEWIS, CLARK, AND BIGFOOT

The Oregon Trail was plagued with river crossings, bad weather, and cholera. This apparently wasn't quite bad enough, though, as pioneers managed to create a special bogeyman of their own. Starr Wilkerson was a true giant, reportedly 6 ft. 8 in. tall and almost 300 lb. Unkindly nicknamed Bigfoot, Starr was something of an outcast, and, hoping to escape the region (and his nickname), he hired himself out to a pioneer family. As his journey began, he fell in love with the family's daughter— however, she was smitten with another, and trouble soon set in. Tensions mounted between Starr and his rival and broke loose one night when the two were left alone. Starr was shot during the fight but still managed to kill the other man and fled camp, joining a renegade band of Native Americans and terrorizing the region. The rest of the ill-fated party chose to spend the winter on the trail rather than proceed to Oregon. When spring came, they were heading back to the trail when they encountered Starr once more. The object of Starr's affection angrily rejected him, and, when his band slaughtered the entire party, the legend of Bigfoot was born. It is rumored that sometime later Bigfoot was slain, but legend also has it that he asked his killer not to tell anyone he was dead. With his death never certain, Bigfoot became a phantom, seen hiding behind the trees in bloodthirsty wait.

pints). Open M-Th and Su 11:30am-9pm, F-Sa 11:30am-10pm. MC/V. ❷

Huckleberry Inn, 88611 Bus. US 26 (☎503-272-3325). Serves the usual diner options in jumbo-size portions, although they're known for their ability to put huckleberries in anything, including tea ($2), pancakes ($7.50), pie ($6.25), ice cream, and milkshakes ($5.50). Burgers $8.50. Open 24hr. MC/V. ❷

👁 SIGHTS

TIMBERLINE LODGE. The historic Timberline Lodge was built in 1937 by the WPA. A popular Hollywood backdrop, you might recognize it from the opening scenes of *The Shining*, as well as a bunch of made-for-tv movies that you didn't see. The lobby is a comfortable area with a huge fireplace where visitors can relax and find information on the ski lift and surrounding trails. Daily tours take visitors through the lodge's vast collection of wood-carvings and artwork while providing a brief lesson on the edifice's history. The lift rises to within a few thousand feet of the mountain's summit. When the weather's nice, you can have lunch at the mountainside picnic tables with the clouds below you. The hike down takes about 90min., but the view is well worth the walk. *(☎503-622-7979; www.timberlinelodge.com. Magic Mile open daily 7am-1:30pm. Lift rides for walkers $15, children and seniors $9. All-day ski or snowboard pass $49.)*

🥾 HIKING

Dozens of hiking trails circle Mt. Hood and the surrounding national forest. Simple trail maps are posted around Mt. Hood and at the Hood River and Zigzag Ranger District Stations, where you can also purchase the required **Northwest Forest Pass** ($5). Trails are generally open June-November, although exceptional snowfall can leave some parts inaccessible into early August. **Timberline Mountain Guides** (☎541-312-9242; www.timberlinemtguides.com), based out of Timberline Lodge, offers two-day mountaineering classes culminating in a summit climb ($425).

Trillium Lake Loop (4½ mi., 1-2hr. round-trip; easy to moderate). The trailhead is in the day-use area of the Trillium Lake campground. One of the most popular trails in the area. Offers one of the most photographed views of Mt. Hood. Can get congested on weekends.

Mirror Lake Trail (3 mi., 1-2hr. round-trip; moderate). Trailhead at a parking lot off US 26, 1 mi. west of Government Camp. Carved by an enormous glacier, Mirror Lake is a great spot to relax.

Elk Meadows North Trail (14 mi. round-trip; moderate to strenuous). Trailhead 25 mi. south of Hood River along Rte. 35, across the highway from the Polallie parking area. Rises sharply into the meadows around Mt. Hood. Provides great views of nature's eye-candy. Start early for a day hike or make this an overnight backpacking trip.

🚗 THE ROAD TO PORTLAND: 63 MI.

Take **I-84 West** from Hood River. The Columbia Gorge provides epic vistas to the right, while seven waterfalls, including gorgeous **Multnomah Falls,** are visible on the left. The road curves up to the overlook at **Crown Point,** where **Vista House,** an octagonal stone building built in 1916. The road winds down to I-84 through Corbett. Seventeen miles farther west are the city limits of Portland. Take **Exit 1** off I-84 and continue through the stoplights. You'll reach the intersection with NE Grand Ave. and then **Northeast Martin Luther King, Jr., Boulevard.** Turn south down MLK Blvd. to **Burnside Street,** the city's central road.

PORTLAND   ☎503

Portland is a city that got it right. With a nationally renowned light-rail transit system, urban planning that has mixed parks with responsible development, and a blossoming restaurant and arts scene, Portland has hit its stride as a progressive Northwest destination. Its location on the winding Willamette River in the shadow of both Mt. Hood and Mt. Adams ensures that the city doesn't have to work hard to be beautiful, but thousands of rosebushes and landscaped riverbanks make a good thing even better. A fitting (near) end to any roadtrip, Portland embodies a fascinating integration of culture, progressivism, and the energy of a spunky teenager.

✴ ORIENTATION

Portland is divided into four manageable chunks by the **Willamette River,** which runs north-south, and **Burnside Street,** which runs

OREGON TRAIL

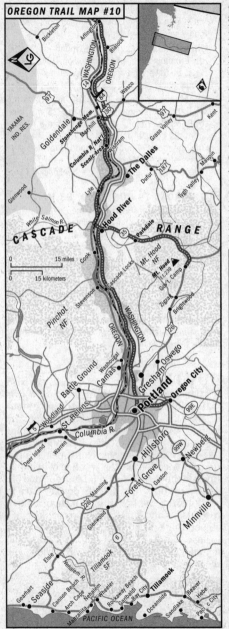

OREGON TRAIL MAP #10

east-west. The river can be crossed by a series of bridges, though the Burnside Bridge, located near **Exit 1,** is the most convenient from downtown. The city is organized as a grid, making it easy to navigate. **Old Town,** in northwest Portland, encompasses most of the city's historic sector. **ChinaTown** is located a few blocks to the east. To the north, **Nob Hill** and the **Pearl District** are swanky, revitalized areas with upscale restaurants, teashops, and art galleries. Central downtown, surrounding **Pioneer Courthouse Square,** has a rich array of cafes, theaters, and restaurants. The **University of Portland** campus is bordered by Williams Ave. on the north. The northeast side of the city has plenty of worthwhile places to check out, without the crowded streets and tourists of the downtown area. Parking around Martin Luther King, Jr., Blvd. is plentiful and free, while closer parking is best found in the neighboring Pearl District.

VITAL STATS

Population: 560,000

Tourist Office: Visitor Information Center, 701 SW 6th St. (☎877-678-5263; www.travelportland.com), in Pioneer Courthouse Sq. Open M-F 8:30am-5:30pm.

Tours: Portland Walking Tours (☎503-774-4522; www.portlandwalkingtours.com). Offers several tour options that explore different aspects of the city. The **Epicurean Excustion** tour is a 4hr. exploration of downtown Portland's best eats and drinks with more than 20 samples of cheese, tea, wine, gelato, pizza, and more. The **Underground Portland** and **Beyond Bizarre** tours are 2½hr. journeys into Portland's literal and figurative underworld. A particular highlight are the Shanghai tunnels beneath Old Town Pizza. ($19, ages 11-17 and seniors $15, ages 5-10 $5. AmEx/D/MC/V.)

Library and Internet Access: Multnomah County Library, 801 SW 10th St. (☎503-988-5234; www.multcolib.org). Open M and Th-Sa 10am-6pm, Tu-W 10am-8pm, Su noon-5pm.

Post Office: 715 NW Hoyt St. (☎503-525-5398). Open M-F 7am-6:30pm, Sa 8:30am-5pm. **Postal Code:** 97205.

▎ TRANSPORTATION

The **MAX light-rail** system is free throughout much of downtown, and trips to Portland's outer neighborhoods cost about $2 each way. (☎503-238-7433; www.trimet.org.) Bus lines run through the Portland Transit Mall (SW 5th and 6th Ave.).

♦ ACCOMMODATIONS

Those looking for high-end establishments need look no farther than the blocks around **Exit 1,** which are rife with classy chains. The best deals are located on the outskirts of town, particularly in the city's far eastern reaches. These budget lodgings, especially the few hostels, fill quickly. All accommodations in Portland fill up during the summer months, particularly during the Rose Festival, so make your reservations early.

Portland Hawthorne Hostel (HI), 3031 SE Hawthorne Blvd. (☎503-236-3380; www.portlandhostel.org), in the outskirts of Portland. A lively common space and a huge porch define this hostel. The outdoor stage with open-mike (Th) draws a crowd. Kitchen. Towels $1. Laundry. Free Wi-Fi. Reception noon-10pm. Check-out 11am. Dorms $20-25, members $17-22; private rooms $43-51. AmEx/D/MC/V. ❶

Portland Hostel, Northwest (HI), 1818 NW Glisan St. (☎503-241-2783; www.nwportlandhostel.com), at 18th Ave. Within walking distance of downtown. This snug Victorian building has a kitchen, a small espresso bar, lockers, and laundry. Free Wi-Fi. 34 dorm beds. Co-ed available. Street parking permits available. Reception 8am-11pm. Dorms $23-27, members $20-22; doubles $30-49. D/MC/V. ❶

Washington Park Inn, 840 SW King St. (☎503-226-2722). One of the best-priced hotels in the downtown area. Just a few blocks from Washington Park and Nob Hill/Pearl District. The rooms are plain but do have cable TV. Continental breakfast included. Free Wi-Fi. Rooms from $60. AmEx/D/MC/V. ❷

Lamplighter Inn, 10207 SW Park Way (☎503-297-2211). On the far southwest side of the city. Offers big, clean rooms with full-size desks and king beds. Not having to fight for parking is worth the 10min. drive. Rooms from $60. AmEx/D/MC/V. ❸

McMenamins Edgefield, 2126 SW Halsey St. (☎503-669-8610 or 800-669-8610), in Troutdale. Take I-84 to Exit 16; turn right off the ramp. A decadent 38-acre estate built upon a former farm, complete with a brewery, vineyards, 18-hole golf course, movie theater, and restaurant. Live music on summer nights. No TVs or phones; you're paying for the escape from it all. Call ahead in summer; no reservations for the hostel. Dorms $40; singles $50; doubles $85-120. AmEx/D/MC/V. ❷

♦ FOOD

The menus in Portland are a combination of the cosmopolitan and the laid-back, with plenty of ethnic, vegetarian, and eclectic offer-

WHERE THE SIDEWALK ENDS

In 1948, a hole was cut through the sidewalk at the corner of SW Taylor St. and SW Naito Pkwy. (Front St.). It was expected to accommodate a mere lamppost, but greatness was thrust upon it. The street lamp was never installed, and the 24 in. circle of earth was left empty until noticed by Dick Fagan, a columnist for the *Oregon Journal*, who grew tired of looking at the unsightly hole from his office window. Fagan used his column, "Mill Ends," to publicize the patch of dirt, pointing out that it would make an excellent park. Fagan planted flowers in the park and regularly chronicled the comings and goings of its resident leprechaun colony, with whom he frequently conversed. According to the explanatory plaque (which is bigger than the park itself), the park has hosted weddings and is presided over by an invisible leprechaun named Patrick O'Toole. The park was added to the city's roster on St. Patrick's Day, 1976, seven years after Fagan's death. At 452.16 sq. in., Mill Ends Park is officially the world's smallest. Locals have enthusiastically embraced it, planting flowers and hosting a hotly contested annual snail race on St. Patrick's Day. The park also contains a swimming pool and diving board (for butterflies) as well as a miniature Ferris wheel.

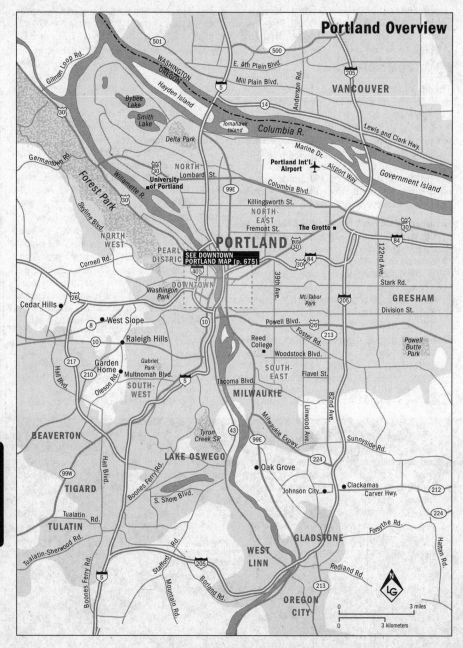

Portland Overview

ings. Recently, the city has become a mecca for tea connoisseurs, and the Pearl District is home to many a fine cup of oolong.

◼ **Voodoo Doughnut,** 22 SW 3rd Ave. (☎503-241-4704). Finally, a place that combines America's 2 great loves, Afro-Caribbean mysticism and breakfast pastries. Stand back and snicker while yuppies and the elderly ask for a Butter Fingering (devil's food cake and Butterfinger), or the glorious Triple Chocolate Penetration. The Bacon Maple Bar and Arnold Palmer are also favorites. Vegan doughnuts (I know, right?) available. Doughnuts $1-2.50. Swahili lessons daily before 9am. Open 24hr. MC/V. ❶

◼ **Pambiche,** 2811 NE Glisan St. (☎503-233-0511). One of the many gems to be found across the river on the city's northeast side. Serves awesome Cuban cuisine in a relaxed setting with street-side seating. The *empanadas* ($9.25) are a favorite among locals. Sandwiches $9.50-10.50. Entrees $11-18.50. Open M-Th 11am-10pm, F 11am-midnight, Sa 2pm-midnight, Su 2-5pm. No reservations; totally worth the wait. MC/V. ❸

Bijou Cafe, 132 SW 3rd Ave. (☎503-222-3187). Lines go out the door for weekend brunch, and finding a table in the middle of a weekday can be a challenge. Portlanders love the upscale breakfast menu, which includes an oyster omelet with bacon ($14). Gooey pecan sticky buns ($2.50), brioche french toast ($7), salads ($5-9), burgers, and sandwiches ($8-9) round out the menu. Open M-F 7am-2pm, Sa-Su 8am-2pm. MC/V. ❷

Nicholas Restaurant, 318 SE Grand Ave. (☎503-235-5123), between Oak and Pine St. The 1st real opportunity for great Mediterranean cuisine since Kansas City. The cafe itself has a casual and intimate atmosphere with comfortable sidewalk seating. The shawarma ($9) is excellent and comes with lots of fluffy pita. Vegetarian and vegan options. Sandwiches $6-8.50. Open M-Sa 11am-9pm, Su noon-9pm. Cash only. ❷

Pastini Pastaria, 1426 NE Broadway (☎503-288-4300). Something of a 1-trick pony, but the trick is delicious and reasonably priced. 12 varieties of pasta, fresh veggies, sun-dried tomatoes, authentic Italian cheeses, and bread make up a variety of pasta dishes ($6-11). A long list of gourmet salads ($5-9) is also available. Open

M-Th 11:30am-9pm, F-Sa 11:30am-10pm, Su 4-9pm. AmEx/MC/V. ❷

Old Town Pizza, 226 NW Davis St. (☎503-222-9999). In a historic hotel in the heart of downtown, this former brothel is famously haunted by one of its former ladies. Now a pizza joint serving a mostly young, cool crowd, the building retains much of its earlier ambience. The personal pizzas ($8.50) are excellent and reasonably portioned. Willem Dafoe was once a regular patron. Panini $7. Open M-Th 11:30am-11pm, F-Sa 11:30am-midnight. MC/V. ❷

◉ SIGHTS

WASHINGTON PARK

Fewer than 10 blocks west of downtown is the sprawling Washington Park, a woodland tract encompassing many of Portland's acclaimed gardens as well as an arresting Holocaust memorial. Head west on Burnside St., past 23rd Ave., take a left on Tichner, and turn right at the first intersection onto Kingston Ave. It will eventually reach a T junction, which is the center of the gardens area.

◼**INTERNATIONAL ROSE TEST GARDEN.** One of Washington Park's most striking attractions, the Rose Test Garden boasts about 550 varieties of specially bred, or hybridized, roses that appear to be named by the same people who name derby horses. When the roses are in bloom, the four-acre grounds erupt in displays of crimson, pink, yellow, and orange blooms. *(400 SW Kingston St. ☎503-823-3636. Open daily 5am-10pm. Free.)*

◼**JAPANESE GARDENS.** In a city known for its exceptional parks, the Japanese Gardens stand out. Situated high above the city, the garden actually encompasses five separate gardens designed by Professor Takuma Tono to adhere to the traditional principles of Japanese garden design. Each garden has a distinct character—from the ornate bridges and pagoda of the Strolling Pond Garden to the more abstract and suggestive Sand and Stone Garden. The view of Mt. Hood from the Tea Garden is one of the best in the city. *(611 SW Kingston Ave., across the street from the Rose Gardens.*

☎503-223-1321; www.japanesegarden.com. Open Apr.-Sept. M noon-7pm, Tu-Su 10am-7pm; Oct.-Mar. M noon-4pm, Tu-Su 10am-4pm. Tours Apr.-Oct. daily 10:45am, 2:30pm. $8, students and seniors $6.25, ages 5-18 $5.25, under 5 free.)

HOYT ARBORETUM. Forming the wooded backdrop for the rest of Washington Park's sights, the Hoyt Arboretum features 185 acres of trees, 12 mi. of trails, and flora and fauna from around the world. The visitors center has maps of Hoyt's popular hiking trails, including a 2 mi. stretch of wheelchair-accessible trail. (4000 Fairview Blvd. Take Kingston Ave. to Knights Ave. and turn right, then turn right on Fairview Blvd. ☎503-228-8733; www.hoytarboretum.org. Visitors center open M-F 9am-4pm, Sa 9am-3pm. Grounds open daily 6am-10pm. Tours Apr.-Oct. Sa-Su 2pm. Free.)

OREGON ZOO. The Pacific Northwest exhibit contains many animals your forerunners probably shot along the trail, while the African Savannah exhibit contains animals they probably did not. Their herd of Asian elephants is the most successful breeding herd in the world; Packy, the first US-born elephant in the last 40 years, is something of a local celebrity. The summer concert series fills the warm summer air with music that was cool two to 20 years ago. (4001 SW Canyon Rd. ☎503-220-2493; www.oregonzoo.com. Grounds open daily Apr. 15-Sept. 15 8am-7pm; Sept. 16-Apr. 14 9am-5pm. Last entry 1hr. before close. $9.75, ages 3-11 $6.75, seniors $8.25.)

OTHER GARDENS AND PARKS

CLASSICAL CHINESE GARDENS. The largest Ming-style gardens outside of China, the Classical Chinese Gardens occupy a full city block and were designed by Suzhou artisans. Tranquil waterfalls, a koi pond, and beautiful architecture make the garden an ideal place to retreat for a midday rest after fighting your way through densely packed downtown. The authentic teahouse serves 32 varieties of tea, presented in a traditional style. (NW 3rd Ave. and Everett St. ☎503-228-8131; www.portlandchinesegarden.org. Open daily Apr.-Oct. 9am-6pm; Nov.-Mar. 10am-5pm. $7, students $5.50, under 5 free, seniors $6. Tea $4. AmEx/D/MC/V.)

FOREST PARK. Forest Park spans 5000 acres and is the largest urban forest reserve in the US. The woods, crisscrossed by 74 mi. of trails, trace Portland's far western edge. The area makes for lovely walks, especially around midday when the sun breaks through the canopy, although hikers should be wary of mountain bikers who barrel around corners and down slopes with little warning. (At the northern edge of Washington Park. ☎503-223-5449; www.friendsofforestpark.org. Free.)

OTHER SIGHTS

◾**POWELL'S CITY OF BOOKS.** Powell's is the largest bookstore in the US and a haven for bibliophiles. A gargantuan 68,000 sq. ft., Powell's occupies an entire block of downtown Portland. Despite its Ulyssean complexity, Powell's maintains the feel of a hip neighborhood shop. In a very considerate touch, the used books are filed right with newer editions. Each room is color-coded (sort of like in Clue), and maps enable you to maraud about the store like a pro. (1005 W. Burnside St. Downtown on the edge of the northwest district. ☎503-228-4651 or 800-878-7323. Open daily 9am-11pm.)

PIONEER COURTHOUSE. Portland's most visited spot and one of the most popular outdoor venues for summer films and concerts, Pioneer Courthouse is the historic centerpiece of Pioneer Courthouse Sq. Tourists and locals of every ilk hang out in the brick quadrangle, affectionately known as "Portland's Living Room." The Noon Tunes summer concert series and Flicks on the Bricks bring music, movies, and forced rhymes to the heart of the city. (715 SW Morrison St., at 5th Ave. and Morrison St. ☎503-223-1613; www.pioneercourthousesquare.org.)

PORTLAND ART MUSEUM (PAM). PAM is the oldest art museum in the Pacific Northwest and sports an impressive, if disparate, collection ranging from Cameroonian sculpture to Japanese panel work to a collection of 17th- century silver tea and coffee vessels. The modern and contemporary art center is the region's largest. Regular discussions and panel talks mean there's almost always something going on. (1219 SW Park St., at Jefferson St. ☎503-226-2811; www.pam.org. Open Tu-W 10am-5pm,

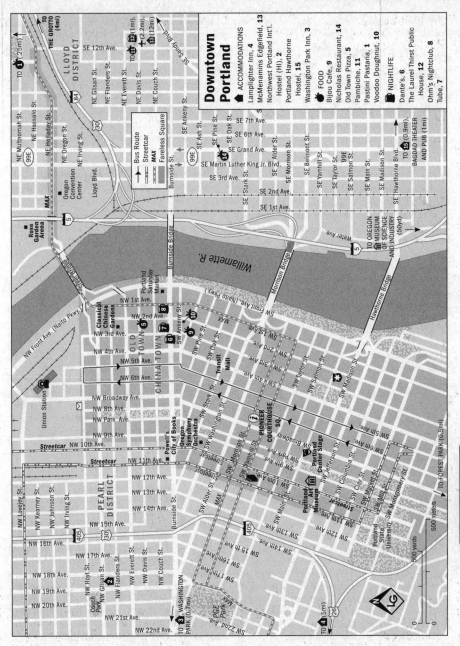

Downtown Portland

ACCOMMODATIONS
Lamplighter Inn, **4**
McMenamins Edgefield, **13**
Northwest Portland Int'l.
  Hostel (HI), **2**
Portland Hawthorne
  Hostel, **15**
Washington Park Inn, **3**

FOOD
Bijou Cafe, **9**
Nicholas Restaurant, **14**
Old Town Pizza, **5**
Pambiche, **11**
Pastini Pastaria, **1**
Voodoo Doughnut, **10**

NIGHTLIFE
Dante's, **6**
The Laurel Thirst Public
  House, **12**
Ohm's Nightclub, **8**
Tube, **7**

Bus Route
Streetcar
MAX
Fareless Square

Th-F 10am-8pm, Su noon-5pm. $10, students and seniors $9, under 18 free.)

🎵 ENTERTAINMENT

Portland's major daily newspaper, *The Oregonian*, lists upcoming events in its Friday edition, while the city's alternative weeklies, the *Willamette Week* and the *Portland Mercury*, provide a reliable guide to local music, art, and theater. *Willamette* is more comprehensive; the *Mercury* is snarkier and more fun. The **Oregon Symphony Orchestra**, 923 SW Washington St., plays from September to June. Students can buy $10 tickets starting one week before showtime. (☎503-228-1353 or 800-228-7343; www.orsymphony.org. Box office open M-F 10am-6pm.) Another piece of the McMenamins empire, the **Bagdad Theater and Pub**, 3702 SE Hawthorne Blvd., shows second-run mainstream films and has an excellent beer menu. (☎503-249-7474. 21+ after 9pm. Pub open M-Sa 11am-1am, Su noon-midnight.) **Noon Tunes**, at Pioneer Courthouse Sq., presents a plethora of rock, jazz, folk, and world music. **Flicks on the Bricks** brings classic movies to the square on Friday nights. (☎503-223-1613. July-Aug. Noon Tunes Tu and Th noon. Flicks on the Bricks F night. Free. Call ahead.) **Portland Center Stage**, in the **Portland Center for Performing Arts**, at SW Broadway and SW Main St., stages classics, modern adaptations, and world premieres. (☎503-445-3700; www.pcs.org. Tickets $25-55.) Basketball fans can watch the **Portland Trailblazers** at the **Rose Garden Arena**, 1 Center Ct. (☎503-321-3211; box office 503-224-4400; www.rosequarter.com.)

🎧 NIGHTLIFE

If you can't find someplace cool to go in Portland, that's really your own problem. A thriving, varied cultural center means every conceivable niche gets represented. Places on the northwest side of town are generally crowded and hopping; cross the river if you want a low-key evening away from the tourists. Remember, local law says every bar must serve food; some of Portland's best bars also have some of the best sandwiches and pizzas.

Laurel Thirst Public House, 2958 NE Glisan St. (☎503-232-1504), at 30th Ave. Something of a landmark in northeast Portland. Local blues acts make every night comfortable and intimate. Free of downtown barhoppers. The veggie burgers ($7) go great with beer and wine. Cover after 9:30pm $2-5. Happy hour daily 6-8pm. Open M-Th and Su 9am-1am, F-Sa 9am-2am.

Tube, 18 NW 3rd Ave. (☎503-241-8823). One of the hippest but also friendliest bars in the downtown area. Primarily a hipster hangout, but the intimate atmosphere and super-comfy couch seating make everyone feel welcome. Nightly DJs make those tight pants get up and dance. Vegetarian and vegan-friendly menu. Sandwiches and salads $7. Open daily 5pm-2:30am.

Dante's, 1 SW 3rd Ave. (☎503-226-6630). Hard to describe except as some strange cabaret-burlesque-techno-industrial club with an open fire pit and candles. Nightly DJs and live acts throw in some punk and metal for good measure. Regular events like Exotica A-Go-Go and Sinferno should be pretty illustrative. Pizza $1.50-2.50 per slice. Cover $5-15. Open daily 11am-2:30am. Pizza window open 11am-3:30am.

Ohm Night Club, 31 NW 1st Ave. (☎503-241-2916; www.ohmnightclubpdx.com), at Couch St., under the Burnside Bridge. Club dedicated to unclassifiable beats and glowing neon lights. Nationally recognized DJs spin alongside up-and-coming local talent nightly to keep the dance floor bumping. Harlem Nights on Th bring live music and spoken word poetry. Cover $10. Open W-Sa 9pm-2am.

✳️ FESTIVALS

Portland's premier summer event is the century-old **Rose Festival**, which lasts the entirety of June. The highlight is the nation's second-largest floral parade, which fills downtown Portland's streets with marching bands, horses, and lawn furniture. Seating and accommodations should be secured well in advance. (☎503-227-2681; www.rosefestival.org.) In early July, the three-day **Safeway Waterfront Blues Festival** draws some of the world's greatest blues artists to the banks of the Willamette. (☎800-973-3378; www.waterfrontbluesfest.com. Suggested donation $10 and 2 cans of imperishable food.) The **Oregon Brewers Festival,** on the last full weekend in July, is the continent's largest gathering of independent brewers, making for one enormous party at Waterfront Park and one enormous hangover the following Monday. A complimentary root-beer garden makes the kiddies and designated drivers not feel totally left out. (☎503-778-5917; www.oregonbrewfest.com. Under 21 must be accompanied by parent. Mug $5; beer tokens $1 each.) The Northwest Film Center hosts the **Portland International Film Festival,** 1219 SW Park Ave., in the last two weeks of February, with 100 films from 30 nations. (☎503-221-1156.)

THE ROAD TO OREGON CITY: 24 MI.

Head south on **Martin Luther King, Jr., Boulevard,** which becomes **Route 99.**

OREGON CITY ☎503

Oregon City was once home to the only federal land office in the Oregon Territory; travelers had little choice but to end their journey here. The **End of the Oregon Trail Interpretive Center,** 1726 Washington St., is hard to miss for its huge stylized wagon exterior. The museum itself has lots of hands-on activities for the kiddies, including the mother of all pack-your-wagon exhibits. (☎503-657-9336. Open Mar.-Oct. M-Sa 9:30am-5pm, Su 10:30am-5pm; Nov.-Feb. M-Sa 11am-4pm, Su noon-4pm. Hourly tours and films. $9, ages 5-17 $5, seniors $7.) Finish up strong at **McMenamins Oregon City,** 102 Ninth St. Traditional pub grub and great ales are served at this Oregon landmark. (☎503-655-8032. Free Wi-Fi. Open M-Th 11am-midnight, F-Sa 11am-1am, Su noon-11pm.)

THE END OF THE ROAD

Congratulations—you've reached the promised land, and in a fraction of the time it took your forerunners. You didn't have to ford the river. And Grandma didn't die of dysentery. (Hopefully.) Now head back to Portland for a well-earned night on the town and another stroll through the gardens. The pioneers blazed a long and winding road for you, and now it's time to find your own way. Drive toward the ocean to join up with the **Pacific Coast** or head north to the **Great North.**

SPEED LIMIT 65

EXIT TO

Cannon Beach, OR 79 mi.
on the pacific coast route, p. 977

Victoria, BC 254 mi.
on the great north route, p. 329

the deep south

TOP 5

1. Practice your hip swivels at **Graceland** (p. 745) in Memphis, Tennessee.
2. Remember the civil-ights movement at the **Birmingham Civil Rights Institute** (p. 732).
3. Realize that Honest Abe was one tall fella at the **Lincoln Memorial** (p. 680) in Washington, DC.
4. Head to **Stamey's Barbecue** (p. 709) for the best ribs in North Carolina.
5. Peer into a crater at the **Petersburg National Battlefield** (p. 701) in Petersburg, Virginia.

Have you watched *Gone with the Wind* hundreds of times? Do you find yourself craving hush puppies, fried okra, barbecue, and country-fried steak? Do you always wish you were in the land of cotton? The South has a storied past—the effects of slavery have not yet been washed away, and the civil-rights movement is too recent to be comfortably relegated to textbooks. But you haven't really seen America until you venture through its Southern soul. Leave your preconceptions behind and brace yourself for some serious charm—you definitely won't need Scarlett and Rhett where you're going.

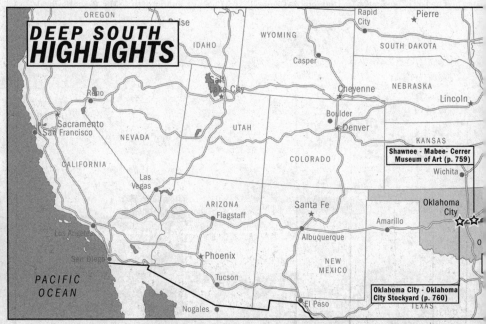

DEEP SOUTH HIGHLIGHTS

Shawnee - Mabee- Cerrer Museum of Art (p. 759)

Oklahoma City - Oklahoma City Stockyard (p. 760)

DEEP SOUTH

The route begins in **Washington, DC** (next page), the vibrant capital city and a fitting place to start a roadtrip through America's past. See a show at **Ford's Theatre** (p. 690) and take advantage of free admission to the **Smithsonian Institutions** (p. 688). From there, the road swoops into Virginia toward **Richmond** (p. 697). The **Spotsylvania Court House Battlefield** (p. 697) is only the first of many Confederate sights and Civil War battlefields that you'll encounter on your trip.

Next, the road runs to North Carolina, which brims with fields of tobacco, pastel sunsets, and rocking chairs on elegant porches. The Triangle—**Durham** (p. 703), **Raleigh** (p. 705), and **Chapel Hill** (p. 707)—is a blend of slow-paced, small-town appeal and highbrow attractions.

Take a moment to ponder the bizarre at the **Korner's Folly** (p. 710) before heading to **Winston-Salem** (p. 711). **Charlotte** (p. 713) is home to the **Levine Museum of the New South** (p. 714), a must-see for any roadtripper. The sharp ridges and rolling slopes of the southern Appalachian range create some of the most spectacular scenery in the Southeast. Cruise into **Asheville** (p. 716), the gem of western North Caro-lina, and fancy yourself a Southern belle at the spectacular **Biltmore Estate** (p. 717). See how far you've come by catching the view from **Clingman's Dome** in **Great Smoky Mountains National Park** (p. 719).

Atlanta (p. 722) isn't called "Hotlanta" for nothing—trust us, they're not just talking about the weather. Sample chicken and waffles at **Gladys Knight's and Ron Winan's Chicken and Waffles** (p. 724) and wash it all down with the samples from the **World of Coca-Cola** (p. 726). You'll know you've entered **Birmingham** (p. 732) when you see the giant statue of **Vulcan** (p. 734) and visit sights like the **Birmingham Civil Rights Institute** (p. 734).

Don't cry when you leave Alabama—save those country woes for **Nashville** (p. 739), the center of the South's country music scene and the place for barbecue, Tennessee whiskey, and glitzy entertainment. Next, the road makes a run for **Memphis** (p. 745), home of the King and all the Elvis paraphernalia to go with him. Come in May for the **World Championship Barbecue Cooking Contest** (p. 745) and definitely don't leave before hitting **Graceland** (p. 748)

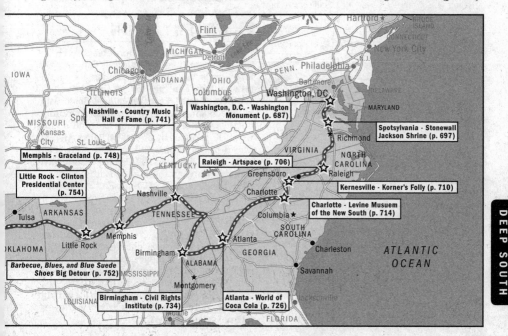

and the **Rock 'n' Soul Museum** (p. 748). Take a fun excursion into Mississippi for the **Barbecue, Blues, and Blue Suede Shoes Big Detour** (p. 752), which runs through Clarksdale, Oxford, and Tupelo and promises a rollickin' time.

Cut across Arkansas to **Little Rock** (p. 751), home to the **Clinton Presidential Library** (p. 754). Smoke a cigar, eat some fried catfish, and look at the "little rock" itself. It's only a little ways more to **Oklahoma City** (p. 759), the end of the route and the perfect time to hook onto **Route 66.** It's a long, hard road through the South, but the rewards are great. So go on; the land of cotton awaits.

ROUTE STATS
Miles: c. 2100
Route: Washington, DC, to Oklahoma City, OK.
States: 8; Virginia, North Carolina, Georgia, Alabama, Tennessee, Mississippi, Arkansas, and Oklahoma.
Driving Time: You could zoom across the South in a week, but where's the pleasure in that? Leave at least 2 or 3 weeks to hit all the sights, savor some fried okra, and develop a twang.
When To Go: Yankees beware—the South sizzles in the summer. Unless your car's A/C is something fierce, beat the heat and start the trip in late spring.
Crossroads: Route 66, in Oklahoma City, OK (p. 759).

WASHINGTON, DC ☎ 202

Visitors to the nation's capital often think they've seen it all after a tour of the White House and the Lincoln Memorial. But locals and savvy travelers know that DC is a thriving international metropolis and that monuments and museums are just the beginning of what this city has to offer. Washington's diamond-shaped borders encompass a bewildering array of world-class cultural and culinary delights, including the avant-garde galleries of Dupont Cir., the glittering mosaic of Adams Morgan nightlife, and the colonial chic of Georgetown. Now far more than just the world's most powerful city, DC has hit the bigtime, with Broadway shows at the Kennedy Center, the latest bands jamming on the "New U" St. corridor, and (finally!) major-league baseball in front of positively giddy fans at the new Nationals Stadium.

VITAL STATS
Population: 600,000 (District of Columbia); 3,500,000 (Washington metro area)
Tourist Office: DC Visitor Information Center, 1300 Pennsylvania Ave. NW (☎866-324-7386; www.dcvisit.com), in the Reagan International Trade Center. Ask for free maps of downtown DC. Open in summer M-F 8:30am-5:30pm, Sa 9am-4pm; in winter M-F 9am-4:30pm. Must have passport or driver's license to enter building.
Internet Access: Kramerbooks & Afterwords, 1517 Connecticut Ave. NW (☎202-387-1400). Free. Open M-Th and Su 7:30am-1am, F-Sa 24hr.
Post Office: Martin Luther King Jr. Station, 1400 L St. NW (☎202-523-2001), in the lobby. Open M-F 8am-5:30pm, Sa 8am-2pm. **Postal Code:** 20005.

▣ ORIENTATION

DC's diamond-shaped borders stretch in the four cardinal directions. The **Potomac River** forms the southwest border, its waters flowing between the District and Arlington, VA. **North Capitol, East Capitol,** and **South Capitol Streets** slice the city into four quadrants: northwest, northeast, southeast, and southwest. DC is ringed by the **Capital Beltway (I-495).** The Beltway is bisected by **US 1** and meets **I-395** from Virginia. The **Baltimore-Washington Parkway** connects the city to Baltimore, MD. **I-595** trickles off the Capital Beltway toward Annapolis, MD, and **I-66** heads west into Virginia. Although DC's streets are spacious and relatively easy to navigate, on-street parking is usually limited to 2hr. in the downtown area. Parking garages charge up to $25 per day downtown, though much cheaper parking can be found outside the city. A good idea is to park at a **Metro** station outside of the District of Columbia; once you're downtown, the subway and bus systems will get you everywhere you need to go.

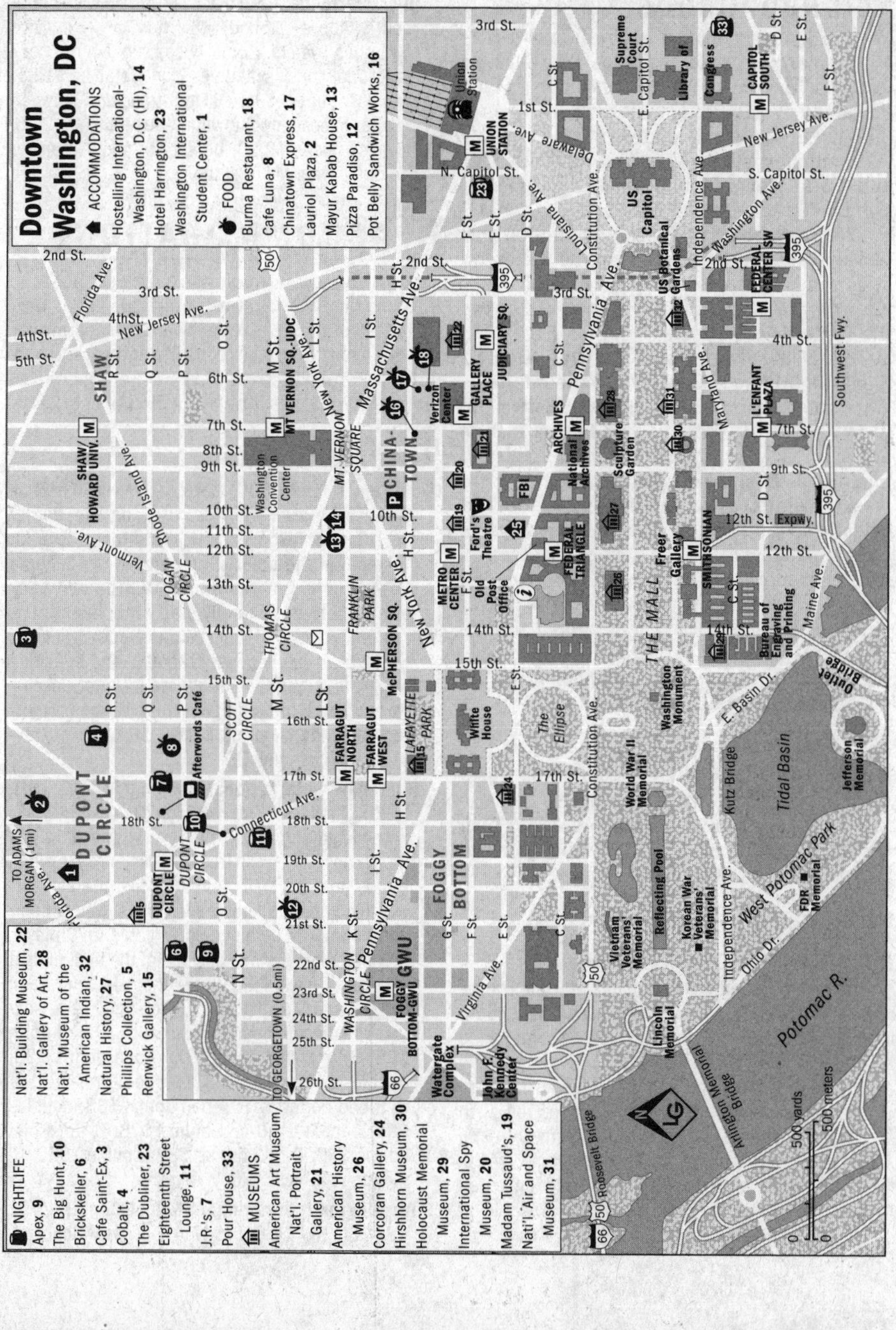

Downtown Washington, DC
ACCOMMODATIONS
Hostelling International-Washington, D.C. (HI), 14
Hotel Harrington, 23
Washington International Student Center, 1
FOOD
Burma Restaurant, 18
Cafe Luna, 8
Chinatown Express, 17
Lauriol Plaza, 2
Mayur Kabab House, 13
Pizza Paradiso, 12
Pot Belly Sandwich Works, 16
NIGHTLIFE
Apex, 9
The Big Hunt, 10
Brickskeller, 6
Cafe Saint-Ex, 3
Cobalt, 4
The Dubliner, 23
Eighteenth Street Lounge, 11
J.R.'s, 7
Pour House, 33
MUSEUMS
American Art Museum/Nat'l. Portrait Gallery, 21
American History Museum, 26
Corcoran Gallery, 24
Hirshhorn Museum, 30
Holocaust Memorial Museum, 29
International Spy Museum, 20
Madam Tussaud's, 19
Nat'l. Air and Space Museum, 31
Nat'l. Building Museum, 22
Nat'l. Gallery of Art, 28
Nat'l. Museum of the American Indian, 32
Natural History, 27
Phillips Collection, 5
Renwick Gallery, 15
TO ADAMS MORGAN (1mi)
TO GEORGETOWN (0.5mi)
0 500 yards
0 500 meters

NEIGHBORHOODS

Postcard-perfect **Capitol Hill** is home to the white marble **Capitol building,** the **Supreme Court,** and the **Library of Congress,** which all face one another. Extending west from the Capitol building is the grassy pedestrian **Mall,** which is punctuated by the Washington Monument and World War II Memorial before it ends at the Lincoln Memorial. The Mall is flanked by the **Smithsonian museums** and the **National Gallery of Art.** Cherry trees ring the Jefferson Memorial and the **Potomac River Tidal Basin,** just south and directly across the Mall from the **White House,** which is north of the Mall at 1600 Pennsylvania Ave. The State Department, the Kennedy Center, and the infamous Watergate Complex make up **Foggy Bottom,** on the west side of the city. The **Federal Triangle** area is home to a growing commercial and banking district. **Adams Morgan,** in the northwest, is a hub of nightlife and good food. In **Chinatown,** authentic Chinese restaurants bump up against the vast Verizon Center and its ring of sports bars. Though its cobblestone back streets are home to Washington's power elite, picturesque **Georgetown** pairs its high-end shops with enough nightlife to keep any college student entertained. **Dupont Circle,** the city's cultural nexus, has developed a powerful trinity of good food, trendy clubs, and cutting-edge art galleries. Another nighttime hotspot is the **U District,** with clubs that blast trance and techno until the sun rises. Be careful in this area at night. **Upper Northwest,** a residential neighborhood, is home to American University and the **National Zoo.**

TRANSPORTATION

Subway: Washington Metropolitan Area Transit Authority (☎202-637-7000; www.wmata.com). The Metrorail subway system has five color-coded lines that cover the District of Columbia and extend into Maryland and Virginia, connecting to commuter rail at several points. Trains run M-Th 5am-midnight, F 5am-3am, Sa 7am-3am, Su 7am-midnight. $1.35-4.50; 1-day pass $7.80, 7-day regional pass $26.40, 7-day unlimited pass $39. Rechargeable farecards available at most Metro stations.

Bus: Metrobus (☎202-637-7000; www.wmata.com). Above ground, DC has an extensive Metrobus system. Some buses run 24hr.; check individual bus schedules for details. $1.35; express buses $3.10. Free transfers between regular buses only. Subway-to-bus transfers $.45, express buses $2.20; be sure to take a transfer before leaving Metro station.

ACCOMMODATIONS

Except for a few reasonably priced hostels, downtown DC accommodations are uniformly expensive. Prices are more reasonable farther from downtown in Maryland and Virginia's suburban areas. Like other major US cities, DC charges a hefty 14.5% hotel tax.

HOSTELS

Hilltop Hostel, 300 Carroll St. NW (☎202-291-9591; www.hosteldc.com), on the border of DC and Takoma Park, just steps from M: Takoma. In the quiet suburban town of Takoma Park, 25min. from downtown DC. The laid-back atmosphere and friendly staff attracts an international crowd of backpackers and students. Satellite TV, kitchen, game rooms, and spacious backyard. Linen included. Free Internet access. Reception 8am-midnight. Reservations highly recommended. Dorms $22. 18+. Cash or traveler's checks only. ❶

Hostelling International-Washington, DC (HI), 1009 11th St. NW (☎202-737-2333; www.hiwashingtondc.org), 3 blocks north of M: Metro Center. In the heart of DC, 8 blocks from the White House and the Mall. Amenities like the self-service kitchen, free linens and towels, and a common room with a flatscreen TV, cable, DVD player, and free movies make this one of the best budget options in town. Free Wi-Fi. Check-in 2pm-1am; call ahead if arriving later. Check-out 11am. Reservations recommended. Mar.-Aug. 10-bed dorm $35; 6- to 8 bed dorm $37; 4-bed dorms $39; doubles $112. Sept.-Nov. 10-bed dorms $29; 6- to 8-bed dorms $31; 4-bed dorms $33; doubles $92. Dec.-Feb. 10-bed dorms $28; 6- to 8-bed dorms $30; 4-bed dorms $32; doubles $82. HI members $3 less. MC/V. ❷

Washington International Student Center, 2451 18th St. NW (☎800-567-4150; www.dchostel.

com), in the middle of Adams Morgan. Located in the heart of some of DC's finest nightlife, so not for the faint of heart or ear. Towel service, kitchen, lockers, and cable TV. No smoking. Breakfast included. Free Internet. Reception 8am-11pm. Fills up early, so book ahead. Co-ed dorms $26. Cash or traveler's checks only. ❶

HOTELS AND GUESTHOUSES

Adams Inn, 1744 Lanier Pl. NW (☎202-745-3600 or 800-578-6807; www.adamsinn.com), 2 blocks north of the center of Adams Morgan. 25 rooms with A/C, tasteful furnishings, and private sinks. Complimentary snacks. Cable TV in common area. Breakfast included. Laundry facilities. Free Internet. Limited parking $10 per night. 2-night min. if staying Sa night. Reception M-Sa 8am-9pm, Su 1-7pm. Check-in 3-9pm. Check-out noon. Singles $99, with private bath $129; doubles $109. AmEx/D/MC/V. ❹

Hotel Harrington, 436 11th St. NW (☎202-628-8140 or 800-424-8532; www.hotel-harrington.com), at E St. M: Metro Center or Federal Triangle. Simply furnished rooms with cable TV and A/C in a great location. Parking $15 per day. Singles $99-135; doubles $119-135. Student discount 10%. AmEx/D/MC/V. ❹

Kalorama Guest House, 1854 Mintwood Pl. NW (☎202-667-6369; www.kaloramaguesthouse. com). A 10min. walk from M: Woodley Park. Beautifully decorated rooms in a quiet, well-appointed townhouse near Rock Creek Park. Breakfast included. Rooms with shared bath $130, with private bath $145. 6-person suite with living room and kitchen $175. AmEx/D/MC/V. ❺

🍴 FOOD

For budget eateries, **Adams Morgan** and **Dupont Circle** are home to the *crème de la crème* of ethnic cuisine. Suburban **Bethesda, Maryland** (M: Bethesda), features over 100 restaurants within a four-block radius. For information on vegetarian- and vegan-friendly restaurants in the DC area, look for *The Vegetarian Guide* at hotels and restaurants.

ADAMS MORGAN

🏛 **Tryst,** 2459 18th St. NW (☎202-232-5500). This all-day hangout spot caters to a diverse student crowd and is the perfect "3rd place" between home and work. Enjoy a coffee and pastry in the morning or, for lunch, the Portia sandwich with prosciutto, goat cheese, and fig compote on baguette ($9). A great spot to catch up with friends over nachos ($7) or artichoke-spinach dip with tortilla chips ($6.50). Open M-Th and Su 6:30am-2am, F-Sa 6:30am-3am. 21+ F-Sa after 8:30pm. AmEx/D/MC/V. ❷

Bardia's New Orleans Cafe, 2412 18th St. NW (☎202-234-0420). If a hearty po' boy sandwich ($6.75-10.75), spicy jambalaya ($8.50-16), or rich gumbo ($4.25-10.25) is what you fancy, New Orleans Cafe delivers. Don't miss the famous beignets (3 for $2.25) and $7 daiquiris. Open Tu-F 11am-10pm, Sa 10am-10pm, Su 10am-9:30pm. AmEx/D/MC/V. ❷

The Diner, 2453 18th St. NW (☎202-232-8800). The Diner's hours and quintessential American food earn it rave reviews from families and late-night revelers alike. Omelets $7-9. Pancakes $5. Salads $5-11. Open 24hr. AmEx/D/MC/V. ❷

Meskerem Restaurant, 2434 18th St. NW (☎202-462-4100). A venerable Ethiopian restaurant, Meskerem has 2 levels of seating; upstairs under the skylight has the best atmosphere. Choose from the many stew-like beef, chicken, lamb, seafood, and vegetarian entrees that are served with *injera*, a soft flatbread for scooping up food in lieu of a fork. Entrees $7-13. Open M-Th noon-11pm, F-Sa noon-12:30am, Su noon-11:30pm. AmEx/D/MC/V. ❷

CHINATOWN/DOWNTOWN

🏛 **Chinatown Express Restaurant,** 744 6th St. NW (☎202-638-0424), between G and H St. A cut above other local eateries, Chinatown Express is often crowded, but you'll be too enthralled watching the chef to mind. In addition to standard Chinese fare (entrees $8-12), the restaurant has excellent noodle dishes made with fresh "stretched noodles" ($5.50) and delicious Shanghai soup dumplings filled with broth. The lunch special ($5) lets you mix and match 3 dishes. Open daily 10am-11pm; lunch served until 2:30pm. AmEx/D/MC/V. ❶

Potbelly Sandwich Works, 726 7th St. NW (☎202-478-0070), between G and H St. A local chain of sandwich shops with locations throughout DC. Serves cheap, filling sandwiches ($4) and not

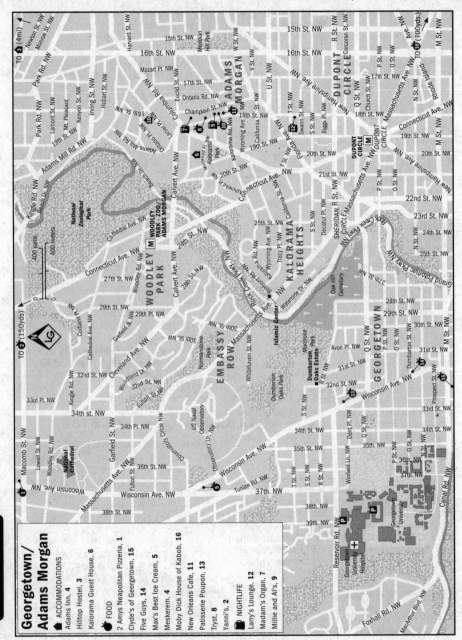

Georgetown/ Adams Morgan

⛺ ACCOMMODATIONS
Adams Inn, **4**
Hilltop Hostel, **3**
Kalorama Guest House, **6**

● FOOD
2 Amys Neapolitan Pizzeria, **1**
Clyde's of Georgetown, **15**
Five Guys, **14**
Max's Best Ice Cream, **5**
Meskerem, **4**
Moby Dick House of Kabob, **16**
New Orleans Cafe, **11**
Patisserie Poupon, **13**
Tryst, **8**
Yanni's, **2**

■ NIGHTLIFE
Larry's Lounge, **12**
Madam's Organ, **7**
Millie and Al's, **9**

much else. Despite the lack of variety, Potbelly has lightning-fast service and surprisingly high-quality ingredients. The milkshakes ($2.70) make a great dessert. Open M-Th and Su 11am-9pm, F-Sa 11am-10pm. AmEx/D/MC/V. ❶

Burma Restaurant, upstairs at 740 6th St. NW (☎202-638-1280), between G and H St. Burmese curries, unique spices, and a plethora of garnishes. Try the green-tea salad ($10) or the squid sautéed in garlic, ginger, and scallions ($11). Vegetarians will enjoy the papaya or tofu salads ($10). Open M-F 11am-3pm and 6-10pm, Sa-Su 6-10pm. AmEx/D/MC/V. ❷

Mayur Kabab House, 1108 K St. NW (☎202-637-9770), at the corner of 11th St. and K St., across from the HI-Washington, DC. Packed with hostelers looking for cheap eats, it serves a range of Indian and Pakistani dishes. Kebabs $8. All-you-can-eat lunch buffet 11am-3pm ($7.27). Open M-Sa 11am-10pm. MC/V. ❶

DUPONT CIRCLE

Pizza Paradiso, 2029 P St. NW (☎202-233-1245; www.eatyourpizza.com), 1 block west of Dupont Cir. This small Neapolitan pizzeria's thin-crust pizzas ($10-11) may not have descended from heaven, but they're outstanding nonetheless. Service is fast and friendly, and the delicious salads and antipasti ($5-6.50) are good alongside your pizza. Check out **Birreria Paradiso** in the basement for some of the world's finest beers. Open M-Th 11:30am-11pm, F-Sa 11:30am-midnight, Su noon-10pm. MC/V. ❷

Lauriol Plaza, 1835 18th St. NW (☎202-387-0035), at T St., between Dupont Cir. and Adams Morgan. Lauriol occupies half the block, with a rowdy roof deck and 3 magnificent floors of Mexican dining. Large entrees ($10-17), appetizers like fried plantains and guacamole ($3-8), and margaritas ($6, pitchers $26). Open M-Th and Su 11:30am-11pm, F-Sa 11:30am-midnight. AmEx/D/MC/V. ❸

Cafe Luna, 1633 P St. NW (☎202-387-4005), near 17th St. A popular basement restaurant serving a mix of Italian, vegetarian, and low-fat fare. Huge sandwiches ($5-10) satisfy almost any appetite. Breakfast ($3-7) served all day. Pizzas $6-8. Entrees $9-15. Open M-Th and Su 10am-11pm, F-Sa 10am-late. AmEx/MC/V. ❷

GEORGETOWN

Five Guys, 1335 Wisconsin Ave. NW (☎202-337-0400), at the corner of Wisconsin and Dumbarton Ave. An oasis of cheap surrounded by Georgetown's pricey boutiques and restaurants, Five Guys's burgers are justifiably famous and surprisingly inexpensive ($4.50-5.50). You can order your fries regular or Cajun-style ($2), but vegetarians beware: fries and grilled cheese ($2) are the only meatless items on the menu. Open M-Th and Su 11am-11pm, F-Sa 11am-4am. AmEx/MC/V. ❶

Moby Dick House of Kabob, 1070 31st St. NW (☎202-333-4400; www.mobysonline.com). A local favorite. The portions of Greek food at this tiny joint are enormous. Get salads ($2-6), gyros ($6), or kebab sandwiches ($7-11) to go and enjoy them on a quiet bench by the C&O Canal. Open M-Th 10am-11pm, F-Sa 11am-4am, Su noon-10pm. MC/V. ❶

Clyde's of Georgetown, 3236 M St. NW (☎202-333-9180), between Potomac St. and Wisconsin Ave. Pop the collar on your polo shirt and you'll blend in perfectly with the preppy clientele in Clyde's leather booths. Delicious sandwiches ($8-10), salads ($13-16), seafood ($11-19), and pasta ($13-15). Open M-Th 11am-2am, F 11am-3am, Sa 10am-3am, Su 9am-2am. AmEx/D/MC/V. ❹

Patisserie Poupon, 1645 Wisconsin Ave. NW (☎202-342-3248), near Q St. Start the day with a buttery brioche, pear danish, or croissant ($1.30-2.25). For lunch, try the "International" panino with turkey, goat cheese, onion confit, and roasted tomato. Sandwiches $4-6. Salads $7-10. Open Tu-F 8am-6:30pm, Sa 8am-5pm, Su 8am-4pm. AmEx/MC/V ❶

UPPER NORTHWEST

2Amys Neapolitan Pizzeria, 3715 Macomb St. NW (☎202-885-5700; www.2amyspiza.com), near Wisconsin Ave. Superb, Neapolitan-style pizzas ($9-13) in a pastel yellow and orange dining area. The "Norcia" pizza (tomato, salami, roasted peppers, mozzarella, and garlic; $13) is excellent. Many locals consider this Washington's best pizza, and we wholeheartedly agree. Expect a wait. "Please call ahead to make heliport arrangements," states the website. Open M

5-10pm, Tu-Th 11am-10pm, F-Sa 11am-11pm, Su noon-10pm. MC/V. ❸

Yanni's, 3500 Connecticut Ave. NW (☎202-362-8871). Find homestyle Greek cooking in this airy restaurant, adorned with classical statues and murals of Greek gods. Try charbroiled octopus, crunchy on the outside and tender within, served with rice ($13). Greek coffee ($2.50) goes well with the baklava ($4.50). Entrees $8-19. Open M-Th and Su 11:30am-11pm, F-Sa 11:30am-midnight. AmEx/D/MC/V. ❸

Max's Best Ice Cream, 2416 Wisconsin Ave. NW (☎202-333-3111), just south of Calvert St. Known in DC as the premier purveyor of homemade ice cream, Max himself dishes out old favorites and exotic flavors like spicy apple pie and chocolate honey malt. Discover what excellent homemade ice cream actually tastes like—this stuff is much better than anything you can buy at a supermarket. Single scoop $3.45, double scoop $4.65, milk shake $5.75. Open M 5-10pm, Tu-Th 11am-10pm, F-Sa 11am-11pm, Su noon-10pm. Cash only. ❶

CAPITOL HILL

Le Bon Cafe, 210 2nd St. SE (☎202-547-7200). This adorable Parisian-style cafe is surprisingly untouristy given its proximity to the Capitol. Start your day off with a pastry ($1.75-2.25) and a coffee sitting outside on the patio. For lunch, a *croque monsieur* ($7), slice of quiche ($5.25), or grilled panino ($7.25) hits the spot. Open M-F 7am-3:30pm, Sa 8am-3:30pm, Su 8:30am-3:30pm. ❷

☉ SIGHTS

CAPITOL HILL

▨US CAPITOL. The Capitol impresses visitors with a grandeur uncommon even among the city's other historic buildings and memorials. It has been the site of presidential inaugurations from Andrew Jackson's to the present day. The east front entrance, facing the Supreme Court, brings visitors on guided tours into the 180 ft. high rotunda, where soldiers slept during the Civil War. To visit the House or Senate chambers, US citizens must obtain a gallery pass from the office of their representative or senator in the House or Senate office buildings near the Capitol. Gallery passes are valid Monday through Friday 9am-4pm. You can stop by the office on the day of your visit, but it's recommended that you call in advance to make sure you can be accommodated. *(M: Capitol South or Union Station. ☎202-225-6827; www.aoc.gov. Generally open M-Sa 9am-4:30pm. Access by 30min. guided tour only. Free, but tickets are required. Same-day tickets available at the Garfield Cir. kiosk on the west front, across from the Botanic Gardens. Kiosk open from 9am until all tickets are distributed; get there by 7:30am in the spring or 8am in the summer to guarantee a ticket. Free.)* The real business of Congress, however, is conducted in **committee hearings.** Most are open to the public; check the *Washington Post*'s "Today in Congress" box for times and locations.

SUPREME COURT. In 1935, the Supreme Court justices decided it was time to take the nation's separation of powers literally and moved from their makeshift offices in the Capitol into a new Greek Revival courthouse across the street. Oral arguments are open to the public; show up early to get a seat. *(1 1st St. M: Capitol South or Union Station. ☎202-479-3221; www.supremecourtus.gov. In session Oct.-June M-W 10am-noon and open 1-3pm for 2 weeks every month; courtroom open when the justices are on vacation. The "3min. line" shuffles visitors through the standing gallery of the courtroom. Court open M-F 9am-4:30pm. Free.)*

▨LIBRARY OF CONGRESS. With over 126 million objects stored on 532 mi. of shelves (including a copy of *Old King Cole* written on a grain of rice and a Gutenberg Bible), the Library of Congress is the largest library in the world. The collection was torched by the British in 1814 and then revived using Thomas Jefferson's personal collection. Visitors of college age or older can register for a library card with a passport or driver's license in the James Madison Building, Room LM 140. For non-researchers, the library's beautiful fresco-lined Great Hall and rotating exhibits are open daily. Tours of the facilities are also available and take visitors to a balcony view of the spectacular main reading room. *(1st St. SE. M: Capitol South. ☎202-707-5000; www.loc.gov. Great Hall open M-Sa 10am-5:30pm. Visitors center and galleries open daily 10am-5pm. Tours*

M-F 10:30, 11:30am, 1:30, 2:30, 3:30pm; Sa 10:30, 11:30am, 1:30, 2:30pm. Free.)

FOLGER SHAKESPEARE LIBRARY AND THEATER. The Folger is home to the world's largest scholarly collection of Shakespeare materials, including one-third of the surviving copies of the First Folio. Visitors can view stage productions in a reconstructed Elizabethan theater (with fantastic acoustics) or explore numerous exhibits on life in Shakespeare's era. *(201 E. Capitol St. SE. M: Capitol South. ☎ 202-544-7077; www.folger.edu. Open M-Sa 10am-5pm. Box office open M-Sa noon-5pm and 1hr. prior to events. Tours 11am, 3pm.)*

MONUMENTS

The monuments lining the National Mall are beautiful during the day, but you can avoid the crowds and find plenty of on-site parking if you visit at night. All of the monuments are well lit, open for viewing 24hr., and, except for the Washington Monument, do not require tickets. The distance between monuments is deceptively long, so budget your time accordingly and consider visiting the FDR and Jefferson Memorials separately from the rest to save yourself the long walk between the Mall and the Tidal Basin.

WASHINGTON MONUMENT. With a $9.4 million restoration completed in 1999, this shrine to America's first president is in peak shape. Though determined visitors are rewarded at the top with impressive views of DC landmarks, there is almost always a long wait. Once nicknamed the "the Beef Depot monument" after the cattle that grazed here during the Civil War, the monument's location was intended to form a right angle between the White House and the Capitol Building. Unfortunately, it was built too far to the east to form a perfect 90° angle. If the water isn't too swampy, the Reflecting Pool mirrors Washington's obelisk in spectacular fashion. *(M: Smithsonian. ☎ 202-426-6841; www.nps.gov/wamo. Open daily 9am-5pm. Tours every 30min. Admission to the monument by timed ticket. Free if obtained on day of visit; arrive early. Advance ticket reservation system open 10am-10pm: ☎ 800-967-2283; www.reservations.nps. gov. Fees apply for advance tickets.)*

LINCOLN MEMORIAL. The Lincoln Memorial, at the west end of the Mall, is a must-see. It was from these steps that Martin Luther King, Jr., gave his "I Have a Dream" speech during the 1963 March on Washington. Inside, a seated Lincoln presides over his admiring visitors. Though you may find Lincoln's lap inviting, climbing on the 19 ft. president is a federal offense; a camera will catch you if the rangers don't. *(M: Smithsonian or Foggy Bottom-GWU. ☎ 202-426-6841; www.nps.gov/linc. Free.)*

VIETNAM VETERANS MEMORIAL. Maya Lin, who designed the Vietnam Veterans Memorial, received a "B" when she submitted her memorial concept for a grade as a Yale senior. She went on to beat her professor in the public memorial design competition. In her words, the monument is "a rift in the earth—a long, polished black stone wall, emerging from and receding into the earth." The wall contains the names of the 58,235 Americans who died in Vietnam, indexed in books at both ends. *(Constitution Ave. at 22nd St. NW. M: Smithsonian or Foggy Bottom-GWU. ☎ 202-634-1568; www.nps.gov/vive.)*

JEFFERSON MEMORIAL. A 19 ft. hollow bronze statue of Thomas Jefferson stands in this open-air rotunda, encircled by massive Ionic columns and overlooking the Tidal Basin. Quotes from the Declaration of Independence, the Virginia Statute of Religious Freedom, and Notes on Virginia adorn the walls. *(A long walk from M: L'Enfant Plaza or Smithsonian. ☎ 202-426-6841; www.nps.gov/thje. Free.)*

FRANKLIN DELANO ROOSEVELT MEMORIAL. Occupying a stretch of West Potomac Park, the Franklin Delano Roosevelt Memorial deviates from the presidential tributes nearby, replacing their marble statuary with sculpted gardens, cascading fountains, and thematic alcoves. Four "rooms" represent the phases of FDR's presidency. In April and May, the blooming cherry trees adjacent to the memorial are stunning. *(A long walk from M: Smithsonian. ☎ 202-426-6841; www.nps.gov/fdrm. Free.)*

KOREAN WAR MEMORIAL. The 19 colossal, polished-steel statues of the Korean War Memorial trudge up a hill, rifles in hand, expressions of weariness and fear frozen on their faces. The statues are accompanied by a black granite wall with over 2000 sand-

DEEP SOUTH

blasted photographic images from this war, in which 54,246 Americans lost their lives. *(At the west end of the Mall, near Lincoln. M: Smithsonian. ☎ 202-426-6841; www.nps.gov/kwvm. Free.)*

NATIONAL WORLD WAR II MEMORIAL. This arrangement of Neoclassical arches and pillars is the newest addition to the Mall. Two massive archways symbolize the major theaters of battle, and 56 granite pillars face a reflecting pool and represent the contribution of each of the US states and territories. *(Metro: Smithsonian or Foggy Bottom-GWU. ☎ 202-426-6841; www.wwiimemorial.com. Free.)*

THE MALL

The Smithsonian Institution's museums on the Mall constitute the world's largest museum complex. The **Smithsonian Castle**, 1000 Jefferson Dr. SW on the south side of the Mall, has an introduction to and info on all of the Smithsonian buildings. *(M: Smithsonian or Federal Triangle. ☎ 202-633-1000; www.si.edu. Castle open daily 8:30am-5:30pm.)*

◼NATIONAL AIR AND SPACE MUSEUM. This is the world's most popular museum, with 7.5 million visitors each year. Record-breaking airplanes and space vehicles hang from the ceilings. Exhibits include the Wright brothers' original biplane, which hangs in the entrance gallery, the walk-through Skylab space station, the Apollo XI command module, and a DC-7. The museum can get crowded during peak hours (11am-4pm), especially in the spring and summer. The museum also offers some costly thrills for the adrenaline or space junkie. *(On the south side of the Mall. M: Smithsonian. ☎ 202-357-2700; www.nasm.si.edu. Free. Interactive flight simulator $8. Planetarium $7.50, children $6, military $6.50. IMAX movies $8.50, children $7.)*

◼NATIONAL GALLERY OF ART. The National Gallery is not a part of the Smithsonian but is considered a close cousin because of its prime Mall-front location. The West Building, the gallery's original home, contains masterpieces by Leonardo da Vinci, El Greco, Rembrandt, Vermeer, Botticelli, and Monet as well as a collection of 19th-century American landscapes, portraits, and sculpture. The East Building is devoted to 20th-century art, from Magritte and Mondrian to Giacometti and

O'Keeffe. Don't miss the Matisse cutouts on view during limited hours in the East Tower gallery. The $5 audio tour is a good investment and guides you to the gallery's highlights. Because of its size, the gallery is rarely crowded, even during peak tourist season. The sculpture garden features a reflecting pool that serves as a skating rink during the winter and as a bandstand for jazz concerts on Friday nights in the summer. *(M: Smithsonian or Federal Triangle. ☎ 202-737-4215; www.nga.gov. Open M-Sa 10am-5pm, Su 11am-6pm. East Tower open M-Sa 10am-2pm, Su 11am-3pm. Free.)*

NATIONAL MUSEUM OF AMERICAN HISTORY (NMAH). The NMAH's plexiglas-encased clutter of old goods have earned it the nickname "the nation's attic." When the Smithsonian Institution inherits quirky pop-culture artifacts, like Dorothy's slippers from *The Wizard of Oz*, they end up here. The Hands On History Room contains a working telegraph and an interactive introduction to the Cherokee language. *(On the north side of the Mall. M: Smithsonian or Federal Triangle. ☎ 202-357-2700; http://americanhistory.si.edu. Open daily 10am-5:30pm. Free.)*

HIRSHHORN MUSEUM AND SCULPTURE GARDEN. The Hirshhorn houses DC's best collection of modern, postmodern, and post-postmodern art from around the world, with a particular emphasis on Abstract Expressionism. The slide-carousel-shaped building has outraged traditionalists since 1966. Don't miss the sculpture garden on the Mall with some of Rodin's most celebrated statues. Each floor consists of two concentric circles: an outer ring of paintings and an inner corridor of sculptures. *(On the south side of the Mall. M: Smithsonian or L'Enfant Plaza. ☎ 202-633-4674; www.hirshhorn.si.edu. Open daily 10am-5:30pm. Sculpture garden open daily 7:30am-dusk. Free.)*

NATIONAL MUSEUM OF NATURAL HISTORY (NMNH). The NMNH contains three floors of rocks, animals, gift shops, and displays selected from the museum's 124 million possessions. The Hope Diamond and dinosaur skeletons are major attractions. The museum is justly proud of its new IMAX & Jazz Cafe, which hosts live performances. Despite the updates, the museum itself remains refreshingly old-school with its life-size dioramas of Neanderthals. *(M: Smithsonian or Federal Tri-angle.* ☎ *202-633-1000; www.mnh.si.edu. Open daily 10am-5:30pm. Jazz shows F 6-10pm; $12. IMAX $8.50, seniors, youth 2-12 $7, seniors $7.50. Free.)*

NATIONAL MUSEUM OF THE AMERICAN INDIAN. The Smithsonian's newest addition to the Mall, the museum is built in the style of a Pueblo dwelling. The exhibits present the history, culture, and beliefs of Native American peoples ranging from the Inca to the Inuit. The museum's architecture may be more engaging than some of its exhibits, but it's worth a visit nonetheless. During the morning, prisms built into the wall of the museum shine rainbows onto the atrium. The museum's cafeteria features stations serving regional Native American cuisine, which is far superior to the area's standard food-court fare. *(M: Smithsonian or Federal Triangle.* ☎ *202-633-1000; www.nmai.si.edu. Open daily 10am-5:30pm. Free.)*

FREER GALLERY OF ART. The Freer, built in the style of an Italian *palazzo* with open central courtyard, houses an intriguing jumble of American and Asian art. The permanent American collection, as dictated by Charles L. Freer himself, focuses on works by James McNeill Whistler. The rotating Asian collections display pieces from 2500 BC to the present. Bronzes, manuscripts, and jade pieces make up some of the museum's most alluring exhibits. *(On the south side of the Mall. Metro: Smithsonian or Federal Triangle.* ☎ *202-357-4880; www.asia.si.edu. Open daily 10am-5:30pm. Free.)*

NATIONAL MUSEUM OF AFRICAN ART AND ARTHUR M. SACKLER GALLERY. Both museums house their exhibits in an interconnected maze of galleries in the Ripley Center, next to the Smithsonian Castle. The Museum of African Art displays artifacts from sub-Saharan Africa, such as masks, ceremonial figures, and musical instruments. *(M: Smithsonian or Federal Triangle.* ☎ *202-633-4600; www.africa.si.edu. Open daily 10am-5:30pm. Free.)* The Sackler Gallery showcases an extensive collection of manuscripts, Chinese and Japanese paintings, jade, and friezes from Egypt, Phoenicia, and Sumeria. *(M: Smithsonian or Federal Triangle.* ☎ *202-633-4880; www.asia.si.edu. Open daily 10am-5:30pm. Free.)*

NATIONAL PORTRAIT GALLERY. Paintings by Sargent and Whistler share the stage with War-

hol silkscreens at this temple to the portrait. While visages of dead white men abound, the museum also features exhibits like "Champions," which presents portraits of famous athletes, and "Bravo!" an inspiring showcase of 20th-century composers. *(8th and F St. NW M: Gallery Pl.* ☎ *202-633-8300; www.npg.si.edu. Open daily 11:30am-7pm. Free.)*

SOUTH OF THE MALL

⬛**HOLOCAUST MEMORIAL MUSEUM.** Opened in 1993, the privately funded Holocaust Memorial Museum examines the atrocities of the Holocaust. Haunting displays include a room filled with shoes taken from deportees, crematorium ovens, and a casting of the gate that greeted new arrivals at Auschwitz. Special exhibitions, which can be viewed without passes, include the Wall of Remembrance, a collection of tiles painted by American schoolchildren in memory of the 1.5 million children killed during the Holocaust, and the Wexner Learning Center, which hosts and exhibit on the genocide in Darfur, Sudan. The permanent gallery is divided into three chronologically organized floors. Arrive early to obtain tickets; during peak hours, timed-admission tickets may admit you as late as 2hr. after you pick them up. *(14th St., between C St. and Independence Ave. SW. M: Smithsonian.* ☎ *202-488-0400; www.ushmm.org. Open daily 10am-5:30pm. Free.)*

BUREAU OF ENGRAVING AND PRINTING. The buck starts here at the Bureau of Engraving and Printing, the largest producer of currency in the world. Guided tours of the presses that print $696 million in money each day are available. *(At 14th and C St. SW. M: Smithsonian.* ☎ *202-874-2330 or 866-874-2330; www.moneyfactory. gov. Ticket booth at Wallenberg Pl. on 15th St. opens Mar.-Aug. M-F at 8am to distribute free tickets for same-day tours, which run 9am-2pm. Arrive early to obtain tickets; most are gone by 9am. Tours daily Sept.-Apr. 9-10:15am and 12:30-2pm; May-Aug. 9am-7pm. Free.)*

FEDERAL TRIANGLE

⬛**NATIONAL ARCHIVES.** Visitors line up at the National Archives to view the original Declaration of Independence, US Constitution, and Bill of Rights as they make their daily appearance from the recesses of a nuclear-bomb-proof vault. This building houses 16 million pictures and posters, 18 million maps, and billions of pages of text—about 2-5% of the documents the government produces each year. During peak tourist season, the line to get in can be very long, so plan accordingly. *(8th St. and Constitution Ave. NW. M: Archives-Navy Memorial.* ☎ *202-501-5000; www.nara.gov. Open daily from Memorial Day to Labor Day 10am-9pm; from Apr. to Memorial Day 10am-7pm; from Labor Day to Mar. 10am-5:30pm. Free.)*

NEWSEUM. This recently reopened museum is a tribute to journalism, newspeople, and the importance of a free press. Highlights include the Berlin Wall gallery and a 9/11 exhibit with pieces of the Pentagon and a segment of the TV tower that stood atop the World Trade Center. Check out the views of the Capitol from the sixth-floor terrace. *(Pennsylvania Ave. and 6th St. NW M: Archives-Navy Memorial.* ☎ *888-639-7386; www.newseum.org. Open daily 9am-5pm. $20, children $13.)*

INTERNATIONAL SPY MUSEUM. Visitors navigating the movie-set-like backdrops may wonder whether this is an amusement park about to blow its museum cover, but the Spy Museum has plenty of facts and artifacts from centuries of espionage. In a city with so many free attractions, the admission price is disappointingly high unless you're a genuine espionage buff. *(800 F St. NW, at 9th St. M: Gallery Pl.* ☎ *202-393-7798; www.spymuseum.org. Open daily Apr.-Aug. 9am-8pm; Aug.-Oct. 10am-8pm; Oct.-Mar. 10am-6pm. Tickets with timed admission $18, children 5-11 $15, under 5 free, seniors and military $17.)*

FORD'S THEATRE. Having undergone renovation in 2008, a newly preserved Ford's Theatre plans to re-open in February 2009. John Wilkes Booth shot President Abraham Lincoln during a performance of *Our American Cousin* on April 14, 1865. Nonetheless, every president since 1868 has taken his chances and seen a play here at least once a year. Of course, the president's entourage always sits front-row center to avoid the unlucky box. Park rangers give a 15min. tour of the theater, but expect to wait up to an hour during tourist season. *(511 10th St. NW. M: Metro Center.* ☎ *202-637-7000; shows 347-4833. www.fordstheatre. org. Open daily 9am-5pm. Free.)*

OLD POST OFFICE. This classical masterpiece, adorned with arched windows, conical turrets, and a clock tower, no longer houses an operational post office, although it does have a food court. The city's first skyscraper is now home to the **National Endowment for the Arts,** among other organizations. If you can't make it up to the Washington Monument, the Old Post Office's soaring tower has the second-best view of the city and is rarely crowded. *(Pennsylvania Ave. and 12th St. NW. M: Federal Triangle.* ☎ *202-289-4224; www.oldpostofficedc.com. Tower open from mid-Apr. to mid-Sept. M-Sa 9am-7:45pm, Su 10am-5:45pm; from mid-Sept. to mid-Apr. M-F 9am-4:45pm, Sa-Su 10am-5:45pm. Shops open M-Sa 10am-7pm, Su noon-6pm. Free.)*

WHITE HOUSE AND FOGGY BOTTOM

◨**WHITE HOUSE.** With its simple columns and expansive lawns, the White House seems a compromise between patrician lavishness and democratic simplicity. Thomas Jefferson proposed a design for the building, but his entry lost to that of amateur architect James Hoban. Today, the president's staff works in the **West Wing,** while the first lady's cohort occupies the East Wing. Staff who cannot fit in the White House work in the nearby Eisenhower Executive Office Building. The president's official office is the **Oval Office,** site of many televised speeches. *(1600 Pennsylvania Ave. NW.* ☎ *202-456-7041; www.whitehouse.gov. Free tours of the White House can be arranged only by calling your congressional representative up to 6 months and no less than 1 month in advance. Phone numbers for representatives available at www.whitehouse.gov. Foreign visitors should inquire at their respective embassies.)* The **White House Visitor Center,** on Pennsylvania St. at 15th St. in the Commerce Department building, has a few unimpressive exhibits on White House history for those who can't get into the real thing. *(1450 Pennsylvania Ave. NW.* ☎ *202-456-7041. Open daily 7:30am-4pm. Free.)*

LAFAYETTE PARK. Historic homes surround Lafayette Park north of the White House and include the Smithsonian-owned **Renwick Gallery Craft Museum.** *(17th St. and Pennsylvania Ave. NW. M: Farragut North, Farragut West, or McPherson Sq.* ☎ *202-633-2850; www.americanart.si.edu. Open daily 10am-5:30pm. Free.)* The Neoclassical **Corcoran**

Gallery boasts an expansive collection ranging from Colonial to contemporary art. If a trip to the National Gallery of Art leaves you wanting more 19th- and 20th-century American art, the Corcoran's collection is excellent. *(17th St., between E St. and New York Ave. NW. ☎ 202-639-1700; www.corcoran.org. Open M, W, and F-Su 10am-5pm, Th 10am-9pm. $6; Th 5-9pm free.)* The **Octagon House,** designed by Capitol architect William Thornton, was home to President and Mrs. Madison after the White House was burned down by British soldiers during the War of 1812. Today it is a restored example of Federalist architecture and allegedly houses several ghosts. The Octagon is open only for prearranged group tours of 10-25 people; call in advance. *(1799 New York Ave. NW. ☎ 202-638-3221. $5, students $3.)*

KENNEDY CENTER. Completed in the late 1960s, the John F. Kennedy Center for the Performing Arts is a monument to the assassinated president, boasting four major stages, a film theater, three breathtaking halls replete with sumptuous red carpets, crystal chandeliers, and a roof deck with stunning views of the Potomac and the DC skyline. *(25th St. and New Hampshire Ave. NW. M: Foggy Bottom-GWU. ☎ 202-416-8341; www.kennedy-center.org. Open daily 10am-midnight. Free tours leave from the Level A gift shop M-F 10am-5pm, Sa-Su 10am-1pm. Free.)* Across the street is the **Watergate,** where President Richard "Tricky Dick" Nixon famously sent his "plumbers" on an ill-fated burglary attempt.

GEORGETOWN

🖼DUMBARTON OAKS ESTATE. Home to several acres of some of the most beautiful gardens in Washington, Dumbarton Oaks was the site of the 1944 Dumbarton Oaks Conference, which helped form the United Nations charter. The estate is now a museum with an impressive collection of Byzantine and pre-Columbian art as well as a gorgeous landscaped garden with numerous fountains and ornate terraces. Unfortunately, picnicking is not allowed. *(Garden entrance at 31st St. and R St. NW. Museum entrance at 1703 32nd St. NW, between R and S St. ☎ 202-339-6401, tour info 339-6409; www.doaks.org. Mansion open Tu-Su 2-5pm. Free. Gardens open daily Mar.-Oct. 2-6pm; Nov.-Mar. 2-5pm. $8, seniors and children 2-12 $5; Nov.-Mar. free.)*

GEORGETOWN UNIVERSITY. Archbishop John Carroll oversaw construction in 1788, and Georgetown University opened the following year, becoming the nation's first Catholic institution for higher learning. Today the original neo-Gothic spires overlook a bustling campus, with several stores, cafes, and sporting venues open to the public. *(37th and O St. NW on the G2 bus line from Dupont Circle. ☎ 202-687-3600; www.georgetown.edu. Campus tours through the admissions office; call for schedule and reservations.)*

UPPER NORTHWEST

🖼WASHINGTON NATIONAL CATHEDRAL. Since the cathedral's construction in 1909, religious leaders from Reverend Dr. Martin Luther King, Jr., to the Dalai Lama have preached from its pulpit. The sixth-largest cathedral in the world, the National Cathedral boasts over 200 separate stained-glass windows made from hand-blown glass, including the impressive rose window depicting the Creation. The Pilgrim Observation Gallery reveals DC from one of the city's highest vantage points. The Bishop's Garden on the cathedral grounds is worth a detour for its blooming flowers in spring and summer. *(From downtown, follow Massachusetts Ave. NW out of town to the intersection with Wisconsin Ave. NW. From M: Tenleytown, take a 30-series bus toward Georgetown or walk up Cathedral Ave. from M: Woodley Park. ☎ 202-537-6200; www.nationalcathedral. org. Open from mid-May to early Sept. M-F 10am-5:30pm, Sa 10am-4pm, Su 8am-6:30pm; from early Sept. to mid-May M-F 10am-5:30pm. Su mass 7:30am, noon, 2:30, 4pm. Organ demonstration 12:45pm. Tours M-F 10am-11:30am and 12:45-4pm, Sa 10-11:30 and 12:45-3:15pm, Su 12:45-2:30pm. Free. Guided tours $3, children $1, seniors $2.)*

NATIONAL ZOO. Founded in 1889 and designed by Frederick Law Olmsted, the mastermind behind New York City's Central Park (p. 121), the 364-acre National Zoo is rarely crowded due to its size and distance from downtown. Tigers, elephants, and gorillas await. The zoo's giant pandas are perpetual Washington celebrities; their cub, Tai Shan, began receiving visitors in 2006. The zoo also features two endangered golden lion tamarin monkeys, which wander the grounds freely. *(3001 Connecticut Ave. M: Woodley Park. ☎ 202-673-4800; www.nationalzoo.*

si.edu. Grounds open daily Apr.-Oct. 6am-8pm; Nov.-Mar. 6am-6pm. Zoo buildings open daily Apr.-Oct. 10am-6pm, Nov.-Mar. 10am-4:30pm. Free.)

DUPONT CIRCLE

PHILLIPS COLLECTION. Situated in a stately mansion, the Phillips was the nation's first museum of modern art and still turns heads with its variety of paintings by Impressionist, Post-Impressionist, and Modernist masters. Visitors gape at Renoir's masterpiece, *Luncheon of the Boating Party*, and works by Delacroix, Miró, and Turner. (1600 21st St. at Q St. NW. ☎202-387-2151; www.phillipscollection.org. Open in summer Tu-W and F-Sa 10am-5pm, Th 10am-8:30pm, Su noon-5pm; in winter Tu-W and F-Sa 10am-5pm, Th 10am-8:30pm. Permanent collection free. Special exhibitions Tu-F free; Sa-Su $12, students and seniors $10, under 19 free.)

ART GALLERY DISTRICT. The Art Gallery District contains over two dozen galleries displaying everything from contemporary photography to tribal crafts. The district galleries hold a joint open house on the first Friday of each month (6-8pm) with complimentary drinks at each venue. (Bounded by Connecticut Ave., Florida Ave., and Q St. NW.)

EMBASSY ROW. The stretch of Massachusetts Ave. between Dupont Cir. and Observatory Cir. is called **Embassy Row.** Before the 1930s, socialites lived along the avenue in extravagant townhouses; diplomats later found the mansions perfect for their purposes (and sky-high budgets). Embassy Row is too long to cover by foot but worth a detour if you're driving through this part of the city. At the northern end of Embassy Row, flags line the entrance to the **Islamic Center.** Inside the brilliant white mosque, tapestries cover the floor and ornate designs stretch to the tips of spired ceilings. (2551 Massachusetts Ave. NW. ☎202-332-3451. No shorts; women must cover their heads, arms, and legs. Open daily 10am-10pm.)

ENTERTAINMENT

MUSIC

Check the *Weekend* section in the Friday edition of the *Washington Post* for details on upcoming concerts, shows, and other events. Larger mainstream events take place at the sports arenas: **RFK Stadium,** 2400 E. Capitol St. NW, in the summer (box office ☎202-608-1119; open M-F noon-5pm) and the **Verizon Center,** 601 F St. NW, year-round (box office ☎202-628-3200; open daily 10am-5:30pm). In its 73rd season, the **National Symphony Orchestra** continues to delight DC, primarily in the Kennedy Center's concert hall. (☎202-467-4600 or 800-444-1324; www.kennedy-center.org/nso.) DC also has a diverse and thriving jazz and blues scene, with venues perfect for any budget. The **Kennedy Center** (see **Performing Arts,** below) and **Smithsonian** museums (p. 688) often sponsor free shows, especially in the summer.

PERFORMING ARTS

The Source Theatre, 1835 14th St. NW (☎202-462-1073; www.sourcetheatre.com), between S and T St., M: U St.-Cardozo. Dedicated to the local community of artists.

Woolly Mammoth Theater Company, 641 D St. NW (☎202-393-3939; www.woollymammoth.net), at 7th St. NW. M: Gallery Pl. Offers pay-what-you-can and under-25 performances of contemporary works. Tickets $28-48, under 25 $10. $10 rush tickets available 15min. before shows.

Arena Stage, 6th St. and Maine Ave. SW (☎202-488-3300; www.arenastage.org), M: Waterfront. Often called the best regional theater company in America due to its innovative takes on classics and successful productions of new works. Box office open M-Sa 10am-8pm, Su noon-8pm. Tickets $45-66. Discounts for students and seniors. A limited number of ½-price tickets is available 1hr. before show.

Kennedy Center, at 25th St. and New Hampshire Ave. NW. (☎202-416-8000, rush ticket info 467-4600; www.kennedy-center.org). Presents various balletic, operatic, symphonic, and dramatic productions. Tickets $10-75.

Shakespeare Theatre, 450 7th St. NW (☎202-547-1122 or 877-487-8849; www.shakespearetheatre.org), at Pennsylvania Ave., M: Archives-Navy Memorial. Puts on lively performances. Each summer the theater holds the "Free for All," a no-charge production of a Shakespearean work, usually one of the comedies.

Tickets $23-68, during preview week $13-59. $10 standing-room tickets available 1hr. before sold-out performances.

Folger Theatre, 201 E. Capitol St. SE (☎202-544-7077; www.folger.edu). Reproduction of Shakespeare's Globe in London. Small museum adjacent to the performance space. Box office open M-F 10am-5pm in person, M-Sa noon-4pm by phone. Student rush tickets half-price 1hr. before show.

SPORTS

The 20,000-seat **Verizon Center,** 601 F St. NW, in Chinatown, is DC's premier sports arena. (☎202-628-3200. Metro: Gallery Pl. Open daily 10am-5:30pm.) Having finally earned some respect with their 2005 season, basketball's **Wizards** are no longer the laughingstock of the NBA. (☎202-661-5065; www.washington-wizards.com. Regular season Oct.-Apr. Tickets $10-115.) The WNBA's **Mystics** play from May to September. (www.wnba.com/mystics. Tickets $8-60.) The **Capitals** are back with the rest of the NHL for the 2009 season, running from October to April. (☎202-661-5065; www. washingtoncaps.com. Tickets $10-100.) Washington's most successful and least-known pro sports team is soccer's **DC United,** with a strong local fan base and several MLS championship titles. (☎202-587-5000; http://dcunited.mlsnet. com. Tickets $16-40.) A new stadium for DC United is planned, but for now the team uses RFK Stadium, 2400 E. Capitol St. SE. Will Washington always remain a football town? Its beloved, if politically incorrect, **Redskins** still draw the faithful to FedEx Field, Raljon Dr., in Raljon, Maryland, from September to December. (☎301-276-6050; www.redskins. com. Tickets $40-200.) Baseball's **Nationals** have just moved into newly constructed Nationals Stadium. Don't miss $5 grandstand tickets! (☎888-632-6287; http://nationals.mlb. com. Tickets $5-115.)

☒ NIGHTLIFE

Don't be fooled by the sea of shirt-and-tie-clad bureaucrats who flood Washington during the day; DC is a work-hard, play-hard city. With hordes of interns, campaign staffers, journalists, and other young political types, nights and weekends in the city are anything

but quiet. If you ache for a pint of amber ale, swing by the Irish pub-laden **Capitol Hill. Dupont Circle** is home to glam GLBT nightlife, while bars in **Adams Morgan** and the **U District** stay packed well past 3am on weekend nights. For more tips, try www.dcnites.com. The *Washington Blade* (www.washblade.com) is the best source for gay news and club listings; published every Friday, it's available in virtually every store in Dupont Cir. *Metro Weekly* (www.metroweekly.com), a GLBT Washington-area magazine, is another good reference for weekend entertainment and nightlife.

DUPONT AND U DISTRICT

☒ **Brickskeller,** 1523 22nd St. NW (☎202-293-1885). Boasts the largest selection of beer in the world, with 1072 different bottled brews from which to choose ($3.25-19). Try a "beer-tail," a mixed drink made with beer ($3.25-6.50). Open M-Tu 5pm-2am, W-Th 11:30am-2am, F 11:30am-3am, Sa 6pm-3am, Su 6pm-2am. Kitchen open until 1hr. before closing. AmEx/D/MC/V.

☒ **Cobalt,** 1639 R St. NW (☎202-462-6569; www. cobaltdc.com), at 17th St. No sign marks this hot spot; look for the blue light and bouncer. Shirtless bartenders serve drinks ($4.75-5.75) to a preppy gay male and straight female crowd. Tu 70s and 80s night. Open Tu-Th 10pm-2am, F-Sa 10pm-3am, Su 8:30pm-2am. Downstairs, **30°** is a relaxed lounge. Happy hour M-F 5-8pm with ½-price martinis. Open M-Th and Su 5pm-2am, F-Sa 5pm-3am. MC/V.

Eighteenth Street Lounge, 1212 18th St. NW (☎202-466-3922). For the last decade, ESL has set the standard for the DC lounge scene with its top-shelf DJs, most of whom are signed to the lounge's own independent record label. Jazz bands often chill out on the top floor while DJs work it downstairs, spinning house, hip hop, and dance. Cover F and Sa $10. Open Tu-W 9:30pm-2am, Th 5:30pm-2am, F 5:30pm-3am, Sa 9:30pm-3am. MC/V.

Cafe Saint-Ex, 1847 14th St. NW (☎202-265-7839; www.saint-ex.com), at T St. This vintage aviation-themed bar, named after Antoine de Saint-Exupéry, author of *The Little Prince,* attracts a mixed crowd of alt-hippies and legal yuppies. It anchors an increasingly lively row of funky nightspots along 14th St. Upstairs bar and patio cafe. Downstairs Gate 54 lounge. 21+ after 10:30pm.

No cover. Happy hour daily 5-7pm with ½-price house wines and $2.50 beer. Open M-Th and Su 5pm-2am, F-Sa 5pm-3am. Kitchen open M 5-10pm, Tu-Sa 11am-4pm and 5-11pm, Su 11am-4pm and 5-10pm. AmEx/D/MC/V.

The Big Hunt, 1345 Connecticut Ave. NW (☎202-785-2333). The steam isn't a prop at this jungle-themed bar, where the khaki-and-flip-flops crowd hunts for potential mates. Notorious pickup joint for college kids and Hill workers pretending they're still in college. 24 brews on tap ($3.75-5). Solid pub fare, plus surprisingly delicious Guinness ice cream. No cover. Happy hour M-F 4-7pm. Open M-Th 4pm-2am, F 4pm-3am, Sa 5pm-3am, Su 5pm-2am. MC/V.

Cafe Citron, 1343 Connecticut Ave. NW (☎202-530-8844). This lively 2-story Latin lounge offers a number of themed nights. Sangria, mojitos, and margaritas in flavors like mango and passion fruit available by the pitcher $25-30. Live flamenco M. Live salsa, reggaeton, and merengue Tu. Samba dancing W and Sa. Salsa lessons Th. International DJ F. Happy hour M-F 4-7pm, Sa 4-8pm. Open M-Th 4-11pm, F-Sa 4pm-midnight. MC/V.

Apex, 1415 22nd St. NW (☎202-296-0505), near P St. This 2-story dance complex is one of Dupont Circle's old standbys. DJs play a mix of house, trance, and Top 40. Th college night with $3 mixed drinks. F drag karaoke 11pm. 18+. Cover Th $5, free with student ID; F and Sa $10. Open Th-Sa 9pm-4am. MC/V.

ADAMS MORGAN

🎵 **Madam's Organ,** 2461 18th St. NW (☎202-667-5370; www.madamsorgan.com), near Columbia Rd. A 4 fl. blues bar with an intimate rooftop patio serving soul food. Live band plays nightly on 1st fl. Pool tables. Redheads drink Rolling Rock for ½-price. Drafts $3.75-5.75. Mixed drinks $4.75-6.75. Cover M-Th and Su $2-4, F-Sa $5-7. Happy hour M-F 5-8pm with 2-for-1 drinks. Open M-Th and Su 5pm-2am, F-Sa 5pm-3am. AmEx/D/MC/V.

🎵 **J.R.'s,** 1519 17th St. NW (☎202-328-0090), at Church St. DC's busiest gay bar for good reason: hot bartenders, fun events like bachelor auctions, and great drink deals. Packed every night with hordes of "guppies" (gay urban professionals). Open M-Th 2pm-2am, F 2pm-3am, Sa 12:30pm-3am, Su 12:30pm-3am.

Millie & Al's, 2440 18th St. NW (☎202-387-8131). This jukebox bar draws a party-hungry, polo-shirt-wearing crew. Think pitchers, not martinis. Cheap pizza ($1.50 per slice), subs ($3.50-4.50), and $1.50 Jell-O shots. Draft beer $2-3.50; bottles $3-4.25. Nightly specials 4-7pm. DJs play rock and hip hop F-Sa. No cover. Open M-Th 4pm-2am, F-Sa 4pm-3am. MC/V.

Larry's Lounge, 1840 18th St. NW (☎202-483-1483), at the southern end of Adams Morgan. This funky bar is a long walk from the Metro, but its Singapore Slings ($6.50) are worth it. Happy hour Su-F 4-7pm with $3.75 beers, house wines, and cocktails. Be sure to check out the daily drink specials invented by the friendly and enticing bartenders. Open daily 4pm-2am. AmEx/D/MC/V.

CAPITOL HILL

The Dubliner, 4 F St. NW (☎202-737-3773), M: Union Station. Pricey and classy, this Irish pub and upscale sports bar has 2 excellent house brews, Auld Dubliner Amber Ale and Auld Dubliner Irish Lager ($5 pints). A large patio evolves into a lounge as the night goes on. Live Irish music nightly around 9pm. Open M-Th and Su 7am-2am, F-Sa 7am-3am. Kitchen open until 1am. AmEx/D/MC/V.

Pour House, 319 Pennsylvania Ave. SE (☎202-546-1001; www.politiki-dc.com), M: Capitol South. 3 levels: German *Biergarten* atmosphere downstairs, martini bar upstairs, and a typical sports bar between that stays packed with Hill staffers all week long. Nightly drink specials. Happy hour M-Th 4-7pm, F 4-9pm with $3 beers and $10 pitchers. Open M-Th 4pm-1:30am, F 3pm-2:30am, Sa-Su 10am-2:30am. MC/V.

Capitol Lounge, 229 Pennsylvania Ave. SE (☎202-547-2008), M: Capitol South. Politically themed nightspot decorated with the requisite posters and buttons. Politically themed crowd congregates for CNN and cheap drinks. Happy hour M-F 4-7pm with $4 cocktails and $3 beer. Open M-Th 4pm-2am, F 4pm-3am, Sa 10am-3am, Su 10am-2am.

🏮 THE ROAD TO TRIANGLE: 30 MI.
From downtown Washington, DC, take **I-395 South,** which becomes **I-95 South.** Follow I-95 to **Exit 150** and take **Route 619 East** to the intersection with **Route 1** in downtown Triangle. If you hit traffic or would prefer a more leisurely drive, you can take any exit between **Exit 163** and **Exit 150** off I-95 and take **Route 1 South (Jefferson Davis Highway),** which runs parallel to the Interstate. Triangle is barely outside DC, so there are more mini-malls than sweeping vistas, but it's a good time to fill up on supplies or gas.

The Old Dominion State
VIRGINIA
Welcomes You

TRIANGLE ☎703
Home to Quantico Marine Base, Triangle is a busy crossroads. **The Marine Corps Heritage Center,** 18900 Jefferson Davis Hwy., across from Quantico Marine Base on Rte. 1, provides a fascinating look at the making of Marines and the history of the Corps. With a design inspired by the iconic image of Marines raising the US flag on Iwo Jima, the museum has exhibits on recruitment and training, the global war on terrorism, and combat art. (☎877-635-1775; www.usmcmuseum.org. Open daily 9am-5pm.) One mile west of Rte. 1, off Rte. 619 (Joplin Rd.), **Prince William Forest Park,** 18100 Park Headquarters Rd., has 15,000 acres of preserved piedmont forest with 35 miles of hiking trails and 20 miles of paved roads for biking as well as a campground. (☎703-221-7181; www.nps.gov/prwi. Visitors center open daily 9am-5pm.)

For those looking to stay the night, **Best Value Inn ❸,** 4202 Inn St., across from Quantico Marine Base, is one of the only hotel options in town and offers free Wi-Fi and clean rooms. (☎703-221-1115. Singles $60; doubles $66. MC/V.) The **Oak Ridge Campground ❶,** inside Prince William Forest Park, has 100 secluded campsites in a wooded setting. (☎703-221-7181; www.nps.gov/prwi. Sites $15. Cash only.) Among the numerous food options near the intersection of Rte. 1 and Rte. 619, **El Taco Rico ❷,** 18607 Rte. 1, serves tacos, bur-

ritos, quesadillas, and other Mexican dishes. (☎703-221-7426. Combination meals $6-8. Lunch specials $5-6. Open M 11am-3pm, Tu-Sa 11am-9pm, Su 11am-8pm. AmEx/D/MC/V.)

🏮 THE ROAD TO FREDERICKSBURG: 18 MI.
Follow **Route 1 South (Jefferson Davis Highway)** for 17 mi. After crossing the Rappahannock River, turn left onto **Route 17** for 6 mi. to reach downtown Fredericksburg. Signs will point you to the downtown visitors center, which is a good place to get oriented.

FREDERICKSBURG ☎540
Due to its strategic riverfront location halfway between the capitals of the Union and the Confederacy, Fredericksburg was the site of numerous Civil War battles. Though nearly destroyed by destructive artillery fire during the war, Fredericksburg's downtown was rebuilt to approximate its antebellum appearance. Today, Fredericksburg attracts tourists interested in both its significance as a Civil War battleground and its meticulously recreated historic attractions.

VITAL STATS
Population: 19,200
Tourist Office: Fredericksburg Visitor Center, 706 Caroline St. (☎540-373-1776 or 800-678-4748; www.visitfred.com). Follow signs from Rte. 1 S. Open M-Th 9am-5pm, F-Sa 9am-7pm.
Library and Internet Access: Fredericksburg Central Rappahannock Regional Library, 1201 Caroline St. (☎540-372-1144). Open M-Th 9am-9pm, F-Sa 9am-5:30pm, Su 1-5:30pm.
Post Office: 600 Princess Anne St. (☎540-361-4235). Open M-F 8:30am-5pm. **Postal Code:** 22401.

⚔ ORIENTATION

Fredericksburg's historic downtown has two main north-south streets: **Princess Anne Street** is one-way southbound and **Caroline Street** is one-way northbound. Most historic homes and attractions are clustered around the visitors center. **Route 1** and **I-95** run north-south to the west of downtown, while **Lafayette Boulevard** runs southwest from downtown to Fredericksburg's Civil War battlefield. Fredericks-

DEEP SOUTH MAP #1

burg has some of the cheapest gas between Washington, DC and Richmond, so fill up here rather than at pricier city gas stations.

ACCOMMODATIONS

Days Inn, 5316 Jefferson Davis Hwy. (☎540-898-6800). One of many motel chains nearby. Clean, comfortable rooms. Free continental breakfast. Free Wi-Fi. Rooms M-F $57, Sa-Su $69. AmEx/D/MC/V. ❷

Fredericksburg KOA Campground, 7400 Brookside Ln. (☎540-898-7252; www.fredericksburg-koa.com), 2 mi. off Rte. 607. Excellent campsites with fishing pond, pool, showers, laundry, and free Wi-Fi. Sites M-Th and Su $30, F-Sa $32; with water and electricity $36/38. Cabins M-Th and Su $50, F-Sa $54. D/MC/V. ❷

FOOD

Sammy T's, 801 Caroline St. (☎540-371-2008; www.sammyts.com). Located in building dating from 1804. Friendly locals, a wide variety of sandwiches, and the feel of eating in a neighbor's oversized dining room. Emphasis on fresh ingredients and healthy fare, at least by Southern standards. Sandwiches $6-10. Open daily 11am-10pm. AmEx/D/MC/V. ❷

The Soup & Taco Etc..., 813 Caroline St. (☎540-899-0906). Serves delicious soup and tacos, but, contrary to the name, little else. Soup of the day $5-6. Tacos $6. Combo meals $8-9. Open Tu-Th 11am-6pm, F-Sa 11am-7pm, Su 11am-5pm. MC/V. ❷

SIGHTS

FREDERICKSBURG AREA MUSEUM. The museum displays regional crafts and artisanal works from 1730 to 1860 as well as a few rotating exhibits. (*907 Princess Anne St. ☎540-371-3037; www.famcc.org. Open Mar.-Nov. M-Sa 10am-5pm, Su 1-5pm; Dec.-Feb. M-Sa 10am-4pm, Su 1-4pm. $7, students $2, seniors $5.50.*)

FREDERICKSBURG BATTLEFIELD VISITOR CENTER. The visitors center gives a thorough summary of the region's Civil War history, offering some small exhibits and a 22min. film. A walking tour of the nearby **Sunken Road,** the site of a bloody engagement, is a good introduction to the numerous battles fought in the area during Ulysses Grant's 1864 Overland Campaign in Wilderness, Chancellorsville, Fredericksburg, and Spotsylvania. *(1013 Lafayette Blvd. ☎ 540-373-6122. Open daily 8:30am-6:30pm. Free. Film $2, under 10 free, seniors $1.)*

⚑ THE ROAD TO SPOTSYLVANIA: 10 MI.

From Fredericksburg, take **Route 1 South (Jefferson Davis Highway)** for three miles. Turn right onto **Route 208 West (Courthouse Road)** and follow it 6 miles to the intersection with **Route 608** right in downtown.

SPOTSYLVANIA   ☎ 540

The Battle of Spotsylvania Court House saw some of the most cutthroat fighting of the Civil War. At the "Bloody Angle," Union and Confederate soldiers engaged in face-to-face slaughter fierce enough to fell trees with volleys of crisscrossing bullets. All told, over 60,000 soldiers fell in the fighting. The **▣Spotsylvania Court House Battlefield** does not have a visitors center, but you can explore the grounds on your own and take walking tours led by knowledgeable historians. Follow Rte. 608 W. for 5 mi., take a right onto Rte. 613 N.; the battlefield will be on the right. (☎ 540-373-6122. Exhibit shelter open daily 10am-6pm. Bloody Angle tour in summer daily 1, 4pm; in winter Sa-Su 1, 4pm. Tours depart from stop 14 of driving tour. Free.) Although this battle was the greatest triumph of the legendary Confederate general Stonewall Jackson, it was also his last. Accidentally shot by one of his own troops at Spotsylvania, Jackson was rushed to a small house, now the **Stonewall Jackson Shrine** in the **Spotsylvania National Military Park,** where he died on May 10, 1863. Follow Rte. 608 E. for 6 mi. to Rte 1. Take Rte. 1 S. for half a mile, then turn left onto Rte. 607; continue on Rte. 607 about 5 mi. past the campground and the train tracks until it becomes Claiborne Crossing Rd. When the street ends at the stop sign, turn right on Macedonia Rd. and then take another right on Stonewall Jackson Rd. (☎ 540-373-6122. Open daily 9am-5pm. Free.)

In downtown Spotsylvania, the **Courthouse Cafe ❶,** 8955 Courthouse Rd., is a small, unpretentious diner with a wide range of American dishes. The Country Boy Special with three eggs and meat ($6.50) will keep you full all day long. (☎ 540-582-3302. Burgers $3-5. Salads $3-6.50. Open M-Sa 7am-9pm, Su 7am-3pm. AmEx/D/MC/V.) **Captain Jack's Crab Shack ❶,** 8624 Courthouse Rd., has sold crab cakes, fried shrimp, and fish for eating on the go since 1893. (☎ 540-582-5359; www.welove-crabs.com. Fish $4-6. Open Feb.-Dec. W-Su 11am-7pm. D/MC/V.)

⚑ THE ROAD TO RICHMOND: 44 MI.

From Spotsylvania, follow **Route 608 East** for 6 mi. until hitting **Route 1 (Jefferson Davis Highway).** Turn right onto Rte. 1 S. and follow it for 22 mi. Turn right onto **Route 54** to reach downtown Ashland. From Ashland, take **Highway 54 East** for three-quarters of a mile to **I-95 South.** Follow I-95 S. to **Exit 74C** in downtown Richmond.

RICHMOND   ☎ 804

Virginia's capital city has a survivor's history composed of conflicts, disasters, and triumphs. Richmond was officially chartered in 1742, but William Mayo's handiwork was decimated in 1781 in a British attack led by American traitor Benedict Arnold. The city was rebuilt and went on to become the capital of the Confederate States of America during the Civil War. Richmond today is a flourishing city, home to Virginia's state government, students at Virginia Commonwealth University, and more shopping centers per capita than any other US city.

◼ ORIENTATION

Broad Street is the city's central artery, running east-west through downtown. Both **I-95,** going north to Washington, DC, and **I-295** encircle the urban section of the city—the former to the east and north, the latter to the south and west. On the southeast edge of the city, **Shockoe Slip** and **Shockoe Bottom** overflow with partiers at night. Farther east, on the edge of town, the **Court End** and **Church Hill** districts comprise the city's historic center. **Jackson Ward,** to the north, recently underwent major construction to revamp its city center and revitalize the surrounding community—it is still wise to use caution in this area at night. The **Fan** is bounded by the **Boulevard, I-195,** the walk of statues along **Monument Avenue,** and

Virginia Commonwealth University. The pleasant bistros and boutiques of **Carytown,** west of the Fan on **Cary Street,** and the tightly knit working community of **Oregon Hill** add texture to the cityscape. Be careful in Oregon Hill at night.

VITAL STATS

Population: 200,000

Tourist Office: Richmond Metropolitan Visitor's Bureau, 405 N. 3rd St. (☎804-783-7450; www.richmondva.org), in the Richmond Convention Center. Open daily from Memorial Day to Labor Day 9am-6pm; from Labor Day to Memorial Day 9am-5pm.

Library and Internet Access: Richmond Public Library, 101 E. Franklin St. (☎804-646-4867; www.richmondpubliclibrary.org). Open M-W 9am-9pm, Th-F 9am-6pm, Sa 10am-5pm.

Post Office: 1801 Brook Rd. (☎804-775-6304). Open M-F 7am-6pm, Sa 9am-2pm. **Postal Code:** 23232.

ACCOMMODATIONS

Be My Guest Bed and Breakfast, 2926 Kensington Ave. (☎804-358-9901), in the heart of Richmond. Truly a hidden deal: neither a sign nor a Yellow Pages listing marks it. Pleasing decor, breakfast, and friendly, inviting owners make this B&B a worthwhile splurge. Rooms $115-135. Cash or check only. ❹

America's Best Value Inn, 2126 Willis Rd. (☎804-271-1281 or 877-747-6884; www.bestvalueinn.com), off I-95 at Exit 64, 10 mi. from downtown. One of the cheapest options near the city, with clean, standard rooms. Free Wi-Fi. Rooms $45-60. AmEx/D/MC/V. ❷

Pocahontas State Park, 10301 State Park Rd. (☎804-796-4255 or 800-933-7275; www.virginiastateparks.gov). Take I-95 S. to Rte. 288 (Exit 67). After 5 mi., connect to Rte. 10, exit on Ironbridge Rd. heading east, and turn right on Beach Rd. The park is 4 mi. down on the right. Biking, boating, and the 2nd-largest pool in Virginia. Rent a canoe, rowboat, kayak, or paddle boat ($6-10 per hr.). Showers. Sites with water and electricity $25. MC/V. ❶

FOOD

Zuppa, 104 N. 18th St. (☎804-249-8831; www.zuppa.org), in Shockoe Bottom. This tiny cafe serves up delicious sandwiches and salads as well as soups ranging from gazpacho to lobster bisque. Don't miss the Strawberry Margarita Chicken Salad with lime and tequila-marinated chicken in a strawberry balsamic dressing. Sandwiches $7. Open M-Th 11am-10pm, F-Sa 11am-2am, Su 11am-7pm. AmEx/D/MC/V. ❶

Strawberry Street Cafe, 421 Strawberry St. (☎804-353-6860; www.strawberrystreetcafe.com). A delicious unlimited soup and salad bar ($9), a brunch bar ($10; Sa-Su 10am-4pm), and a variety of sandwiches ($8-12) as well as a mostly gray-haired clientele. Expect a wait. Open M-Th 11am-3pm and 5-10:30pm, F 11am-3pm and 5-11pm, Sa 10am-11pm, Su 10am-10:30pm. AmEx/MC/V. ❸

La Bamba, 19 N. 18th St. (☎804-225-8883). This Mexican restaurant covers the basics and has great variations on standard tacos, burritos, and quesadillas. Lunch menu has over 40 different combos for $4-6. Dinner entrees $7-12. The giant margaritas are a must. Open M-Th 11am-10pm, F 11am-11pm, Sa noon-10pm, Su 11am-9pm. AmEx/D/MC/V. ❷

SIGHTS

SAINT JOHN'S CHURCH. St. John's Church is the site of Patrick Henry's famed "Give Me Liberty or Give Me Death" speech. In the summer, orators recreate the 1775 speech on Sundays at 2pm. The church still serves as an active house of worship. (*2401 E. Broad St. ☎804-648-5015. 25min. tours M-Sa 10am-4pm, Su 1-4pm. $6, students $4, seniors $5. Services Su 8:30 and 11am. $5, ages 7-18 $3, seniors $4.*)

EDGAR ALLAN POE MUSEUM. In Richmond's oldest standing house (c. 1737), visitors try evermore to unravel the author's mysterious death. Poe memorabilia and first editions of his works fill the museum and gardens. (*1914 E. Main St. ☎804-648-5523; www.poemuseum.org. Open Tu-Sa 10am-5pm, Su 11am-5pm. Guided tours available daily. $6, students and seniors $5, under 8 free.*)

MUSEUM OF THE CONFEDERACY. Explore the historical legacy of the Civil War at the Museum of the Confederacy. With numerous battlefield artifacts and scale models of Confederate sailing ships and "ironclad" battleships, even the most hard-boiled Yankee will

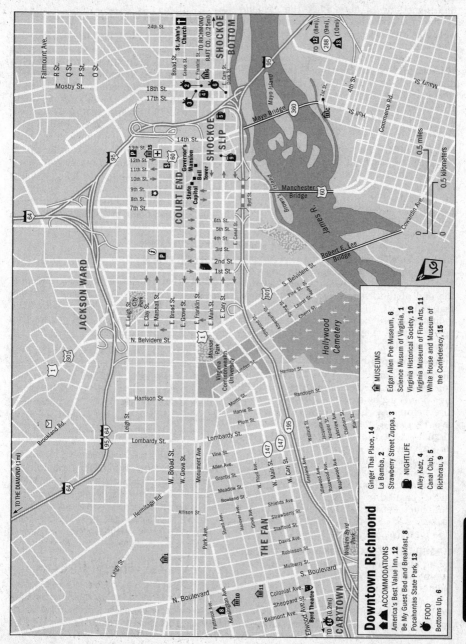

Downtown Richmond

▲ ACCOMMODATIONS
America's Best Value Inn, **12**
Be My Guest Bed and Breakfast, **8**
Pocahontas State Park, **13**

● FOOD
Bottoms Up, **6**
Ginger Thai Place, **14**
La Bamba, **2**
Strawberry Street Zuppa, **3**

♪ NIGHTLIFE
Alley Katz, **4**
Canal Club, **5**
Richbrau, **9**

MUSEUMS
Edgar Allen Poe Museum, **6**
Science Museum of Virginia, **1**
Virginia Historical Society, **10**
Virginia Museum of Fine Arts, **11**
White House and Museum of the Confederacy, **15**

find something of note. Plus, the exhibits on the crucial battles and campaigns of the Civil War will make your visits to actual Civil War battlefields much more interesting. Next door, friendly guides run tours through the **White House of the Confederacy,** Jefferson Davis's official residence during the Civil War. *(1201 E. Clay St. ☎804-649-1861; www.moc.org. Museum open M-Sa 10am-5pm, Su noon-5pm. White House guided tours Mar.-Dec. every 30-60min. Museum or White House $8, ages 7-18 $4, seniors $7; both sights $11/6/10.)*

FAN DISTRICT. This section of Richmond is home to the country's largest and best-preserved Victorian neighborhood. Stroll down Monument Ave., a boulevard lined with graceful old houses and towering statues of Virginia heroes—Richmond's memory lane. The statue of Robert E. Lee faces south toward his beloved Dixie; General Stonewall Jackson faces north so that he can scowl at the Yankees for all eternity. The statue of African-American tennis star Arthur Ashe created a storm of controversy when it was added to the end of the avenue that had previously featured only Civil War generals. Though the monuments are captivating, they're also far apart, so a drive-by tour is recommended if you're in a hurry.

VIRGINIA HISTORICAL SOCIETY. The Virginia Historical Society maintains an impressive collection in an even more impressive building. Marvel at the elegant classical architecture before moving on through the extensive "Story of Virginia" exhibit, which traces Virginia's past from prehistory all the way through the economic transformations and racial conflicts of the 20th century. The museum's showcase feature is a series of murals known as the "Four Seasons of the Confederacy," painted by the French artist Charles Hoffbauer between 1914 and 1921. *(428 N. Boulevard. ☎804-358-4901; www.vahistorical.org. Open M-Sa 10am-5pm, Su 1-5pm. $5, students $3.)*

VIRGINIA MUSEUM OF FINE ARTS. The largest art museum in the South houses a collection by some of the world's most renowned painters—Monet, Renoir, Picasso, and Warhol—as well as ancient treasures from Rome, Egypt, and Asia. *(200 N. Blvd. ☎804-340-1405; www.vmfa.museum. Open W-Su 11am-5pm. Free.)*

🎵 ENTERTAINMENT

At the marvelous old 🎭**Byrd Theatre,** 2908 W. Cary St., movie buffs buy tickets for the latest movies from a tuxedoed agent. On Saturdays, guests are treated to midnight shows and a Wurlitzer organ concert. (☎804-353-9911; www.byrdtheatre.com. Shows $2; Sa midnight movie $3.) **Friday Cheers** presents free concerts at Brown's Island on Friday evenings during the summer. Check at the visitors center for schedules. *Style Weekly,* a free magazine available at the visitors center, and *Punchline,* found in most hangouts, list concert lineups and rockin' events. Cheer on the **Richmond Braves,** Richmond's AAA minor league baseball team, at **The Diamond,** at Exit 78 off I-95. (☎804-359-4444; www.rbraves.com. Tickets $7-12.)

🌙 NIGHTLIFE

Student-driven nightlife enlivens Shockoe Slip and the Fan. After dark, Shockoe Bottom turns into college-party central, with bars pumping bass-heavy music. Be cautious in the Bottom's alleys after dark.

Alley Katz, 10 Walnut Alley (☎804-643-2816; www.alleykatzrba.com). Hosts an impressive range of alternative, jazz, R&B, and other live performances throughout the week. Cover varies. Open Tu-Su 9pm-2am. MC/V.

Richbrau, 1214 E. Cary St. (☎804-644-3018; www.richbrau.com). Part microbrewery, part pool hall, and part dance club. The downstairs restaurant has expensive food (entrees $15-25) but cheap homebrews, like the Big Nasty Porter. A rockin' dance club and a pub with pool tables split the 2nd floor. Happy hour M-F 4:30-6:30pm with discounted appetizers and drink specials like $1 pints on M. Open daily 11:30am-"past midnight"—usually around 2am on weekend nights. AmEx/D/MC/V.

🚗 THE ROAD TO PETERSBURG: 28 MI.

Get on **I-95 South** to leave the Richmond metro area. Follow I-95 for 13 mi. to **Exit 61.** Take **Hundred Road West** for half a mile to **Route 1 South.** Follow Rte. 1 for 10 mi. to downtown Petersburg.

PETERSBURG ☎804

One of the Confederacy's last strongholds during the waning months of the Civil War, Petersburg survived the longest siege in the history of North America from June 9, 1864, to April 3, 1865. The town, which dates back to 1640, is rich with history and, according to local legend, ghosts. Don't miss the **Trapezium House** at N. Market and High St., which was built in 1817 entirely without right angles based on the advice of a West Indian servant who claimed that ghosts couldn't linger in such a house. Wander the town to see old iron foundries, cotton mills, and tobacco warehouses. The **Petersburg Visitors Center,** 425 Cockade Alley, at the end of Old Towne Rd., has a parking lot for visitors as well as information about local attractions. (☎800-368-3595; www.petersburg-va.org. Open daily 9am-5pm.) From the parking lot, it's only a short walk to **Petersburg's Siege Museum,** at the corner of Bank St. and Exchange Alley. With exhibits on civilian life during the siege of Petersburg, the museum has a number of interesting artifacts, including a bullet with teeth marks from a patient undergoing emergency surgery during the siege. (☎804-733-2402. Film every 30min. Open daily 10am-5pm. $5, children and seniors $4.) At the **Petersburg National Battlefield,** 2 mi. east of downtown off Washington St. (Rte. 36), visitors can take a driving tour and view the remains of trenches and fortifications used by both Union and Confederate armies. The final stop on the driving tour is the **Crater.** (☎804-732-3531; www.nps.gov/pete. Open daily 9am-sunset. $5 per vehicle.) South of downtown Petersburg, the **National Museum of the Civil War Soldier,** 6125 Boydton Plank Rd., on Rte. 1 in Pamplin Historical Park, puts a human face on the conflict as visitors choose to follow the story of one man who served in the war. Admission also includes five sites from 19th-century America, including a military encampment, a plantation, and the Banks House, which Grant used as his headquarters. Plan to spend a couple of hours. (☎804-861-2408; www.pamplinpark.org. Open daily 9am-6pm. $15, ages 6-12 $9.)

Among Petersburg's motels, the **Super 8 ❸,** 3138 S. Crater Rd., is a little pricier, but it's worth it for the chain's reliably clean rooms and reputation. (☎804-732-6020. Singles M-F $60, Sa-Su $70; doubles $65/75. AmEx/D/MC/V.) Outside of town, the **Picture Lake Campground ❷,** 7818 Boydton Plank Rd., has some waterfront sites, a swimming pool, and showers. (☎804-861-0174; www.picturelakecampground.com. Sites with water and electricity from $28. AmEx/D/MC/V.) Downtown Petersburg has a few appealing restaurants, including **Java Mio ❶,** 322 N. Sycamore St. This fun coffeehouse serves breakfast, sandwiches, and other light fare. (☎804-861-2700; www.javamio.com. Live music F 7-10pm. Open M-Th 7am-7pm, F 7am-10pm, Sa 8am-4pm, Su 10am-4pm. AmEx/D/MC/V.) The **Dixie Diner ❷,**

THE CRATER

Siege warfare is typically boring, monotonous, and brutal, with each side waiting endlessly for the other to retreat. The Union army's 10-month siege of Petersburg during the Civil War was no exception, but it did have at least one spectacular moment. As the siege stretched into its second month, a prolonged standoff seemed inevitable, prompting Lieutenant Colonel Henry Pleasants, a former mining engineer, to suggest tunneling underneath Confederate lines. Intrigued, General Ambrose Burnside (whose exaggerated facial hair gave name to what we now call "sideburns") had the solders tunnel over 500 ft. from Union trenches into no man's land. With the tunnel complete, the miners placed barrels of gunpowder beneath a line of Confederate artillery, lit the fuse, and hurried out of the tunnel as Union forces prepared for a surprise attack. The underground explosives exploded spectacularly and created a 30 ft. deep crater in the middle of Confederate fortifications. Unfortunately for the North, the spectacle distracted the Union army, and, by the time soldiers reached the crater, the Confederates had regrouped and routed the Union troops who tried to scale the walls of the newly formed bowl. The spectacular remains of "The Crater" and the Union tunnel can be seen at Petersburg

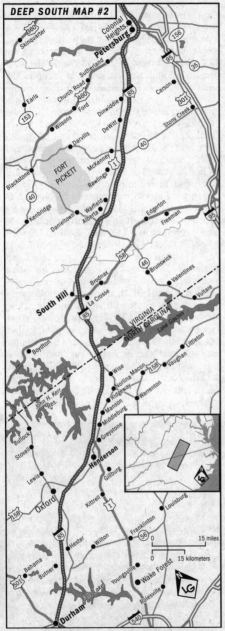

DEEP SOUTH MAP #2

250 N. Sycamore St., serves sandwiches ($4-8) and breakfast all day ($1.50-6) at booths covered with old newspaper clippings and photos. (☎804-732-7425; www.dixiediner-rocks.com. M 7am-7pm, Tu-W 7am-3pm, Th 7am-3pm and 9pm-1am, F-Sa 7am-2am, Su 9am-4:30pm and 9pm-midnight.)

⚑ THE ROAD TO SOUTH HILL: 58 MI.

From downtown Petersburg, follow signs to **Route 1 South.** Follow Rte. 1 to downtown South Hill at the intersection with **Route 47.**

SOUTH HILL ☎434

The **South Hill Visitors Center,** 201 S. Mecklenburg Ave., is home to two tiny but endearing museums, the **Model Railroad Museum** and the **Doll Museum.** The Model Railroad Museum has two working, room-size train layouts, complete with detailed landscaping, as well as a collection of antique model trains. The Doll Museum contains over 500 antique dolls. (☎434-447-4547 or 800-524-4347. Both museums and visitors center open daily 9am-4pm. Free.) A short walk from the visitors center, the **Tobacco Farm Life Museum,** 300 W. Main St., introduces visitors to the history of tobacco production in the US and explains how tobacco is grown, harvested, processed, and sold today. The 15min. video is a relic from the days of cigarette companies advertising but provides an informative look at the process of cultivating and auctioning tobacco. The two floors display artifacts and memorabilia relating to tobacco, much of which was donated by local farmers. (☎434-447-2551. Open W-Sa 10am-4pm. Free.)

Inexpensive motel rooms are available at **Budget Inn Express ❷,** 617 N. Mecklenburg Ave., near downtown. (☎434-447-8643. Singles $35; doubles $40. MC/V.) **◪Wilson Brothers Bar-B-Q ❷,** 1224 W. Danville St., specializes in pork barbecue plates and fried chicken. Fancy garnishes would only be a distraction. (☎434-447-7440. Combination plates $6-8. Open daily 5am-10pm. AmEx/D/MC/V.)

⚑ THE ROAD TO DURHAM: 73 MI.

From South Hill, follow **I-85 South.** Take **Exit 177** to downtown Durham, the first stop in the Triangle of Durham, Raleigh, and Chapel Hill.

The Tar Heel State

NORTH CAROLINA

Welcomes You

DURHAM ☎919

Durham is the economic heart of tobacco country. Its post-Civil War economic prosperity was fueled by the success of the Duke family's tobacco empire that rose to prominence in the early 20th century. The Dukes founded Duke University, a beautiful campus centered on the elegant Duke Chapel. The university's spiritual center is Cameron Stadium, home to Duke's men's basketball team, whose fierce rivalry with the nearby UNC Tar Heels is one of the most famous in college basketball history. Durham is also home to the Research Triangle Park, responsible for inventions as inspiring as the AIDS drug AZT and as down-to-earth as Astroturf.

VITAL STATS

Population: 250,000

Tourist Office: Durham Convention and Visitors Bureau, 101 E. Morgan St. (☎919-687-0288 or 800-446-8604; www.durham-nc.com). Open M-F 8:30am-5pm, Sa 10am-2pm.

Library and Internet Access: Durham County Public Library, 300 N. Roxboro St. (☎919-560-0100), near the visitors center. Open June-July M-Th 9am-9pm, F 9am-6pm, Sa 9:30am-6pm; Aug.-May M-Th 9am-9pm, F 9am-6pm, Sa 9:30am-6pm, Su 2-6pm.

Post Office: 323 E. Chapel Hill St. (☎919-683-1976). Open M-F 8:30am-5pm. **Postal Code:** 27701.

■ ORIENTATION

I-85 and **I-40** run through Durham and are connected by **Route 147 (Durham Freeway),** which runs northeast-southwest through the center of town, separating Duke University from the downtown area. Downtown is home to shopping boutiques and the **Durham Bulls Athletic Park,** while student-oriented restaurants and nightlife cluster around the Duke campus to the west of downtown. Durham lacks a walkable layout, and few sights or attractions except for those on the Duke campus are within walking distance of each other. Fortunately, most areas of Durham have ample and free on-street parking.

■ ACCOMMODATIONS

Budget lodging is scarce in Durham. Economy motels line I-85, especially between Exits 173 and 175 north of Duke, and I-40 between the Research Triangle Park and Raleigh-Durham International Airport. Midweek coupon specials can reduce the price of chain hotels, but on weekends or holidays camping may just be your best option.

Best Value Carolina Duke Inn, 2517 Guess Rd. (☎919-286-0771 or 800-438-1158), off I-85 at Exit 175. Clean rooms and an outdoor pool. Free bus service to Duke's campus. Continental breakfast included. Coin laundry. Singles $43; doubles $50. AmEx/D/MC/V. ❷

Eno River State Park, 6101 Cole Mill Rd. (☎919-383-1686; www.ncsparks.net), off I-85 at Exit 173. 10 primitive hike-in campsites. Sites each have a fire ring and a pit toilet and require a 1 mi. hike from the parking area. No water or electricity. Park open May-Aug. 8am-9pm; Sept. and Apr. 8am-8pm; Oct. and Mar. 8am-7pm; Nov.-Feb. 8am-6pm. Sites $9. AmEx/D/MC/V. ❶

■ FOOD

Duke's campus is surrounded by affordable eateries, especially along **Ninth Street.** A mile east of Ninth St. on Main St., **Brightleaf Square** has renovated warehouses that hold galleries, shops, and restaurants. The American Tobacco Historic District on Jackie Robinson St. also has several good restaurants.

The Mad Hatter's Cafe and Bake Shop, 1802 W. Main St. (☎919-286-1987; www.madhattersbakeshop.com), 1 block from 9th St. A wide selection of delectable dishes made from local, organic produce, including pizza ($8-9), grilled sandwiches ($8-9), and wraps ($8-10). The spacious and colorful restaurant has an outdoor patio and free Wi-Fi. Open M-Sa 7am-9pm, Su 8am-4pm. AmEx/MC/V. ❷

Francesca's, 706 9th St. (☎919-286-4177; www.francescasdessertcaffe.com). Durham's oldest coffeehouse serves only beverages and des-

DEEP SOUTH

serts, but the focus pays off. Sample homemade gelato for just $2.50. Milkshakes $4. Free Wi-Fi. Open M-Th 11am-11pm, F-Sa 11am-midnight, Su 11am-10pm. D/MC/V. ❶

Hog Heaven Bar-B-Q, 2419 Guess Rd. (☎919-286-7447). Hog Heaven specializes in cheap North Carolina-style barbecue served in a cafeteria-like setting. Barbecue and fried chicken meals ($6-6.75) come with a choice of 2 sides. Open M-Sa 11am-8pm. AmEx/D/MC/V. ❷

Pao Lim Asian Bistro and Bar, 2505 Chapel Hill Blvd. (☎919-419-1771; www.paolim.net), just off the US 15/501. Pao Lim pulls off Asian fusion cuisine like you've never seen it before, elegantly blending Chinese, Indian, Thai, and Korean flavors in reasonably priced dishes. Lunch specials $5-7. Dinner entrees $10-17. Open M-Th 11:30am-9:30pm, F 11:30am-10pm, Sa noon-10pm, Su noon-9:30pm. AmEx/D/MC/V. ❷

🄶 SIGHTS

DUKE UNIVERSITY. The Duke family's principal legacy, Duke University, is divided into East and West Campus. The majestic, Neo-Gothic 🄳Duke Chapel, completed in the early 1930s, looms above the center of West Campus. Over one million pieces of glass were used to make the 77 stained-glass windows depicting hundreds of figures from the Bible and Southern history. The chapel's carillonneur gives a free recital on the chapels' 50-bell carillon daily at 5pm. (☎919-681-9414; www.chapel.duke.edu. Open daily in summer 8am-8pm; during the academic year 8am-10pm. Free.) Nearby on Anderson St., the gorgeous **Sarah P. Duke Gardens** has over 55 acres divided into three segments: the Bloomington garden of native plants, the Culberson Asiatic arboretum, and the Terraces. (426 Anderson St. ☎919-684-3698, trolley tours 668-1705; www.sarahpdukegardens.org. Open daily 8am-sunset. 1hr. guided tours available from mid-Mar. to May or by appointment. Free.) The **Nasher Museum of Art** opened in 2005 to house rotating exhibitions from Duke University's art collections. Galleries radiate from an airy, glass-ceilinged atrium. (2001 Campus Dr. ☎919-684-5135; www.nasher.duke.edu. Open Tu-W and F-Sa 10am-5pm, Th 10am-9pm, Su noon-5pm. $5, students with ID $3, seniors $4.) The **Duke Lemur Center** can be seen through prearranged 1hr. private tours, which introduce visitors to about 50 different types of primates. (On Cameron Blvd./Rte. 751 past Erwin Rd. ☎919-489-3364; www.lemur.duke.edu. Reservations required for tours.)

DUKE HOMESTEAD. Visitors can explore the original farm, home, and factories where Washington Duke first planted and processed the tobacco that would become the key to the city's prosperity. The free tour includes an early factory and curing barn as well as the restored home. The adjoining Tobacco Museum explains the history of the tobacco industry. (2828 Duke Homestead Rd., off Guess Rd. ☎919-477-5498; www.dukehomestead.nchistoricsites. org. Open Tu-Sa 9am-4pm. 45min. homestead tours depart 15min. after the hour. Free.)

OTHER SIGHTS. The 1988 movie *Bull Durham* was filmed in **Durham Athletic Park,** 409 Blackwell St. The AAA farm team for the Tampa Bay Rays plays here, minus Kevin Costner. (Take the Durham Bulls Stadium exit off I-40. ☎919-687-6500, tickets 956-2855; www.durhambulls. com. Games Apr.-Sept. Tickets $6-9.) Travelers visiting the area during June and July shouldn't miss a modern dance performance by the **Paul Taylor Dance Company** at the American Dance Festival, hosted for several weeks at Duke. (☎919-684-6402; www.americandancefestival.org.)

🄲 NIGHTLIFE

Durham's nightlife runs the gamut from classy to raunchy, with most student bars and nightclubs located near Ninth St. Pick up a free copy of the weekly *Spectator* and *Independent* magazines, available at many restaurants and bookstores, for listings of Triangle events. There are numerous free concerts held in downtown Durham during the summer, such as the **Bud Light Downtown** concert series in Moore Sq. Park from June to September. (www.budlightdowntownlive.com.) The **American Tobacco Historic District,** 324 Blackwell St., also has free concerts on Thursday evenings from June to August. (www.americantobaccohistoricdistrict.com.)

George's Garage, 737 9th St. (☎919-286-4131). George's serves great sushi and drinks into the wee hours and has excellent lunch offerings. Sushi rolls $4.50-10. DJ F-Sa. Open M-Th and Su 4pm-12:30am, F-Sa 4pm-2am. AmEx/D/MC/V.

Charlie's Pub & Grill, 758 9th St. (☎919-286-4446). Since Duke bans on-campus parties, undergrads head to this no-frills bar for cheap beer. Domestic beers $2.50. Draft pitchers $10-12. Open M-Sa 11am-2am, Su noon-2am. Kitchen open until 1:30am. MC/V.

THE ROAD TO RALEIGH: 28 MI.

Follow **Route 147 South** for 7 mi. to **Exit 5A.** Take **I-40 West** for 19 mi. Take **Exit 298B** to downtown Raleigh.

RALEIGH ☎919

Home to North Carolina State University ("NC State"), Raleigh is a historic state capital with recently revamped tourist attractions. Downtown, visitors can tour the state house and numerous museums or watch artists at work in their studios at Artspace. Like Durham and Chapel Hill, Raleigh is a young city with a hot music scene, a variety of restaurants, and a college-age crowd.

VITAL STATS

Population: 370,000

Tourist Office: The Capital Area Visitor Center, 5 E. Edenton St. (☎919-715-0200 or 800-849-8499; www.visitraleigh.com), in the lobby of the North Carolina Museum of History. Open M-F 9am-4pm, Sa 9am-4pm, Su 1-4pm.

Library and Internet Access: North Regional Library, 200 Horizon Dr. (☎919-870-4000), in North Raleigh. Take Exit 8 from Rte. 440, head north on 6 Forks Rd. for 2 mi., and turn left on Horizon Dr. Open M-F 9am-9pm, Sa 10am-5pm, Su 1-5pm.

Post Office: 311 New Bern Ave. (☎919-832-1604). Open M-F 8am-5:30pm, Sa 8am-noon. **Postal Code:** 27611.

ORIENTATION

The **I-440 "Beltline"** and portions of **I-540** loop around the city through Raleigh's northern suburbs. **I-40** runs east-west to the I-440 Beltline, connecting Raleigh to the airport and Research Triangle Park to the west of the city. **Route 70** runs northwest through Raleigh toward Durham. Downtown Raleigh is constructed as a quadrant, and most of its streets are one-way.

ACCOMMODATIONS

Like Durham, Raleigh does not make it easy to find budget lodging. Shopping the chain motels with books of discount coupons from the visitors center is probably your best bet. Hotels and motels surrounds the major exits to the I-440 Beltline, especially at Glenwood Ave., Forest Rd., and Capital Blvd.

Homestead Suites, 4810 Bluestone Dr. (☎919-510-8551; www.homesteadhotels.com), off Glenwood Ave. An "extended stay" hotel designed for business travelers willing to lay out extra cash, but it offers discounted rates with hotel coupons if there are rooms available. Spacious rooms have full kitchens, refrigerators, microwaves, coffeemakers, and free Wi-Fi. Rooms $65-75. AmEx/D/MC/V. ❷

Falls Lake State Recreation Area, 13304 Creedmoor Rd. (☎919-676-1027; www.ils.unc.edu/parkproject/visit/fala/home.html), about 10 mi. north of Raleigh, off Rte. 98, 1 mi. north of Rte. 50. 4 campgrounds. The main campground, Holly Point, is adjacent to the lake and has both open lakefront sites and secluded shady sites, showers, boat ramps, 2 swimming beaches, and a dump station. 14-night max. stay. Gates close May-Aug. 9pm; Sept. and Apr. 8pm; Oct and Mar. 7pm; Nov.-Feb. 6pm. Sites $15, with hook-up $20. Day use $5 per vehicle. Cash only. ❶

FOOD

Travelers can find good dining options in **City Market's** shops, cafes, and bars.

The Rockford, 320 Glenwood Ave. (☎919-821-9020), near Hillsborough St. A trendy 2nd fl. restaurant that serves delightful, inexpensive food. Popular sandwich offerings include the grilled eggplant sandwich and the mushroom sandwich with port sauce. Bar provides ample distraction during the usual wait required for a table. Entrees $7.25. Open M-W 11:30am-2pm and 6-10pm, Th-Sa 11:30am-2pm and 6-10:30pm, Su 6-10pm. AmEx/MC/V. ❶

Marrakesh Cafe, 2500 Hillsborough St. (☎919-341-1167). North Carolina's 1st hookah bar, offering Moroccan-influenced wraps, sandwiches ($4-5.50), and salads ($3-4). Hookah $8-10. Flavors include strawberry, mango, peach, and melon. Open M-Th and Su 6pm-midnight, F-Sa 6pm-1am. D/MC/V. ❶

Caffe Luna, 136 E. Hargett St. (☎919-832-6090), downtown. Decorated in gorgeous pastels, Caffe Luna serves fresh homemade pasta that will almost melt in your mouth. Lunch pastas $7-8.50, entrees $8-12. Dinner pastas $12-17, entrees $13-17. Open M-F 11:30am-2:30pm, W-Sa 5-10pm. AmEx/MC/V. ❸

👁 SIGHTS

▨ARTSPACE. This collection of 46 artists' studios in three exhibition galleries features work by regional, national, and international artists. Watch them create art of all types, from watercolor and oil paintings to 3D fabric arts. Individual studios are open to visitors while artists are at work. You can stop by, ask questions, and learn firsthand about each artist's creative process. Call ahead or check online for guided tours and special events. *(201 E. Davie St. ☎919-821-2787; www.artspacenc.org. Open Tu-Sa 10am-6pm, 1st F of each month 10am-10pm. Studio hours vary. Free.)*

▨NORTH CAROLINA MUSEUM OF ART. One of the top art museums in the region, if not the country, it is home to a collection with staggering breadth and depth. Works by artists from Raphael to Franz Kline line the walls. An addition to be completed in early 2010 will ensure the musuem's vitality for decades to come. *(2110 Blue Ridge Rd. ☎919-839-6262; www.ncartmuseum.org. Open Tu-Th and Sa 9am-5pm, F 9am-9pm, Su 10am-5pm. Free.)*

MUSEUM OF NATURAL SCIENCES. The museum has four floors of exhibits on North Carolina's natural history, geography, and wildlife. Highlights include a 15 ft. giant ground sloth unearthed near Wilmington and other specimens of record-setting, rare, or bizarre wildlife from around the state. *(11 W. Jones St. ☎919-733-7450 or 877-462-8724; www.naturalsciences.org. Open M-Sa 9am-5pm, Su noon-5pm. Free. Audio tours $2.)*

STATE CAPITOL. North Carolina's capitol building was completed in 1840 and originally housed all three branches of state gov-

ernment. The legislature and Supreme Court have since moved out, but visitors can see the preserved House and Senate chambers on the second floor. The first floor rotunda has a collection of historic flags as well as a very unique sculpture of George Washington in the uniform of a Roman general. It's worth a quick visit, even for non-history buffs. *(1 E. Edenton St. ☎919-733-4994; www.ncstatecapitol.com. Photo ID required for entry. Open M-F 8am-5pm, Sa 9am-5pm, Su 1-4pm. Free.)* A few blocks from the capitol, the enormous **Governor's Mansion,** built in 1883, has 50 opulent rooms covering 34,000 sq. ft. *(Blount St., between Lane St. and Jones St. ☎919-807-7948; www.ncdar.gov. Call ahead for tours. Free.)*

OAKWOOD. Stretching east from the visitors center, historic Oakwood is a Victorian neighborhood featuring some of Raleigh's most notable architecture, with attractive homes constructed in the late 19th and early 20th centuries. It's a long walk from downtown, best seen as a quick detour on your way through town. This neighborhood and the adjacent Oakwood Cemetery offer visitors a sense of the town's history. *(Historic Oakwood is bordered by Franklin, Watauga, Linden, Jones, and Person St. Free walking tour guides available at the visitors center. Cemetery entrance at 701 Oakwood Ave. ☎919-832-6077. Open daily 8am-6pm. Free.)*

🍸 NIGHTLIFE

Info on happenings in Raleigh can be found at www.raleighnow.com. Nightlife options are plentiful in Raleigh; the area around Glenwood by **Hillsborough Street** is home to a number of trendy bars.

▨ The Raleigh Times, 12 W. Hargett St. (☎919-833-0999; www.raleightimesbar.com). With its 2 bars and better than average late-night grub, the Raleigh Times is the place to be for Raleigh's yuppie crowd, which likes to mingle at the tables outside. Thoughtful beer selection from around the world. Cocktails $6-8. Open M-Sa 11:30am-2am, Su 5pm-2am. AmEx/D/MC/V.

Mitch's Tavern, 2426 Hillsborough St. (☎919-821-7771; www.mitchs.com). This 2nd fl. bar is a favorite among students and locals looking for a late-night brew. The dark, smoky charm of the tavern's interior may have been what persuaded the producers of *Bull Durham* to select this as the set for 2 scenes. Pints $2.25. Pitchers $8-13. Open M-Sa 11am-2am. AmEx/D/MC/V.

The Pour House, 224 S. Blount St. (☎919-821-1120; www.the-pour-house.com). A small downtown music venue and bar with live music ranging from rock to country. 30 taps. Jazz and funk W-Sa. Cover $5-10 for some performances, others free. Call ahead for upcoming acts. Most shows start at 10pm. Open M-Sa 11am-2am. AmEx/D/MC/V.

Rum Runners, 208 E. Martin St. (☎919-755-6436; www.rumrunnersusa.com). A boisterous bar with a tropical flair. Rum Runners hosts interactive "dueling piano" shows where 2 pianists face off W-Sa nights. Open W-Th and Su 8pm-2am, F-Sa 6pm-2am. AmEx/D/MC/V.

🚗 THE ROAD TO CHAPEL HILL: 24 MI.

Take **I-440 West** for half a mile, merge onto **I-40 West,** and take **Exit 273A** onto **Route 54 West.** Follow Rte. 54 W. to downtown Chapel Hill.

CHAPEL HILL   ☎919

Chapel Hill is the smallest of North Carolina's Triangle cities, but, as the home of the University of North Carolina's main campus, it makes up for its lack of size with a vibrant college-town atmosphere. Unlike its Triangle counterparts, downtown Chapel Hill is small enough to walk and rewards pedestrians with a surprising variety of restaurants, museums, and nightlife hot spots. If you only have time to visit one city in North Carolina's Triangle area, this should be it.

🧭 ORIENTATION

I-40 runs to the north and east of downtown Chapel Hill, and **Route 54** and **US 15/501** connect the interstate to downtown. **Franklin Street** runs west of downtown and crosses into neighboring Carrboro about half a mile west of the downtown crossroads. Nightlife, restaurants, and attractions line Franklin St. all the way into Carrboro.

VITAL STATS

Population: 48,700

Tourist Office: Chapel Hill Orange County Visitors Bureau, 501 W. Franklin St. (☎919-968-2060 or 888-968-2060; www.visitchapelhill.org). Open M-F 8:30am-5pm, Sa 10am-2pm.

Library and Internet Access: Chapel Hill Public Library, 100 Library Dr. (☎919-968-2777). From UNC, go down Franklin St. toward Durham. Turn left on Estes Dr.; it's on your right. Open M-Th 10am-9pm, F 10am-6pm, Sa 9am-6pm, Su 1-8pm.

Post Office: 179 E. Franklin St. (☎919-967-6297). Open M-F 8:30am-5:30pm, Sa 8:30am-noon. **Postal Code:** 27514.

🛏 ACCOMMODATIONS

Like its companion cities, Raleigh and Durham, Chapel Hill doesn't have much in the way of discount lodging. Mid-range motels can be found at the intersection of I-40 and US 15/501 in Chapel Hill. Hillsborough is 10 mi. west of Chapel Hill on I-40 and has cheaper lodging.

Southern Country Inn, 122 Daniel Boone St. (☎919-732-8101), in Hillsborough. Take I-40 to Exit 261, then north on Rte. 86. Rooms are adequate and reasonably clean, but don't expect any extras. Key deposit $5. Singles $44; doubles $45. AmEx/D/MC/V. ❸

🍴 FOOD

Chapel Hill has numerous inexpensive restaurants along Franklin St. downtown. True to college-town form, prices are low, variety is impressive, and Wi-Fi is ubiquitous.

Mama Dip's Kitchen, 408 W. Rosemary St. (☎919-942-5837). This soul-food restaurant feels like a comfy back-porch picnic, complete with rocking chairs. From the sweet potato waffles to the fried okra to the chicken and dumplings, Mama Dip's serves some of the best regional delicacies around. Entrees $9-13. Open M-Sa 8am-9:30pm, Su 8am-9pm. D/MC/V. ❸

Foster's Market, 750 Martin Luther King, Jr., Blvd./Airport Rd. (☎919-967-3663; www.fostersmarket.com). Turn off Franklin St. onto Columbia St., which becomes Martin Luther King, Jr., Blvd./Airport Rd. This market-restaurant-coffeehouse serves tasty grilled sandwiches, wraps, and salads. Smoothies and milkshakes ($5) are a refreshing treat. Free Wi-Fi. Open daily 7:30am-8pm. AmEx/D/MC/V. ❷

Peppers Pizza, 107 W. Franklin St. (☎919-967-7766), downtown. The delicious pizza makes this a popular spot with families and students alike. Slices $2-4. Pies $11-18. Open M-Th 11am-10pm, F-Sa 11am-midnight, Su 4-10pm. AmEx/D/MC/V. ❶

👁 SIGHTS

UNIVERSITY OF NORTH CAROLINA. Chapel Hill and neighboring Carrboro are inseparable from the beautiful University of North Carolina at Chapel Hill campus. (☎919-962-1630; www.unc.edu. Tours M, W, F 1:30pm. Open M-F 9am-5pm. Free.) Until 1975, NASA astronauts trained at UNC's **Morehead Planetarium.** Of the 12 astronauts who have walked on the moon, 11 trained here. Today, Morehead gives live sky shows and presentations in the 68 ft. domed Star Theater and houses small exhibits on outer space. (250 E. Franklin St. ☎919-962-1236; www.moreheadplanetarium.org. Open from mid-June to mid-Aug. M and Su 12:30-5pm, Tu-W 10am-5pm, Th-Sa 10am-5pm and 6:30-9pm. Call for winter hours and showtimes. Shows $6; students, children, and seniors $5. Exhibits and movies free.) UNC's **Ackland Art Museum** houses an impressive collection that focuses on European painting and sculpture. (5736 S. Columbia St. ☎919-966-5736; www.ackland.org. Open W-Sa 10am-5pm, Su 1-5pm. Free.)

▨NORTH CAROLINA BOTANICAL GARDEN. These 600 acres of botanical gardens and forests operated by UNC are the largest botanical gardens in the Southeast and include an herbarium with 660,000 plants, a biological reserve with 367 acres of wetlands and woodlots, and the oldest arboretum south of the Potomac River. The gardens have walking trails through habitats that range from the seashore to the mountains. Don't miss the carnivorous plants and the giant chess set made from recycled pots and pans. (South of downtown, on Old Mason Farm Rd., off Fordham Blvd./US 15/501. ☎919-962-0522. Open Apr.-Oct. M-F 8am-5pm, Sa 9am-6pm, Su 1-6pm; Nov.-Mar. M-F 8am-5pm, Sa 9am-5pm, Su 1-5pm. Free.)

🔊 NIGHTLIFE

Popular bars line Franklin St., and several live-music clubs are clustered where Franklin St. becomes Main St. in Carrboro. **Cat's Cradle,** 300 E. Main St., in Carrboro, hosts local and national acts ranging from hip hop to country. (☎919-967-9053; www.catscradle.com. Cover varies. Only open on show nights. Doors open 7:30-9pm; shows usually begin 8pm. MC/V.) **Local 506,** 506 W. Franklin St., has mostly indie rock. (☎919-942-5506; www.local506.com. 18+. Cover $5. Open daily 2pm-2am. Shows start around 10pm. MC/V.)

🚙 THE ROAD TO GREENSBORO: 22 MI.

Follow **Route 70 West** to downtown Greensboro.

FINDERS KEEPERS

Nearly a century and a half after it was stolen during the Civil War, the state of North Carolina's long-lost copy of the Bill of Rights resurfaced in 2003. There was just one problem: one of the owners of the document wouldn't give it back. Only 14 original copies of the Bill of Rights were written in 1789, and one of them was given to the state of North Carolina, where it was housed in the capitol building in Raleigh. In 1865, troops commanded by General William Tecumseh Sherman occupied Raleigh, and the copy of the Bill of Rights disappeared, allegedly snatched by a Union soldier. The copy was bought and sold by numerous private art collectors and dealers. It finally resurfaced again in 2003 when the current owners approached the National Constitution Center in Philadelphia to sell the document. FBI agents, posing as museum buyers, arranged a sting operation and seized the copy on behalf of the state of North Carolina. One of the men relinquished his stake in the document, which he had purchased for $200,000 in 2000. The other refused, arguing that the document was legal war booty, taken from a state that seceded from the Union and therefore was not subject to constitutional protection. In 2005, the document was returned to the North Carolina state capitol after its 140-year absence. The alleged owner vowed to continue the legal battle. In March of 2008, all disputes over the ownership of the document were settled when the Wake County Superior Court ruled that the document belongs exclusively to the state of North Carolina.

GREENSBORO ☎336

Along with Winston-Salem and High Point, Greensboro forms the "Piedmont Triad" of cities in central North Carolina. Greensboro was named after Nathanael Greene, whose troops fought British forces commanded by General Earl Cornwallis at Guilford County Courthouse during the closing months of the Revolutionary War. The sit-ins in downtown Greensboro helped focus national attention on the civil-rights movement.

VITAL STATS

Population: 240,000

Tourist Office: Greensboro Visitors Information Center, 2200 Pinecroft Rd, Ste. 200 (☎336-274-2282 or 800-344-2282; www.visitgreensboronc.com). Open M-F 8:30am-5:30pm, Sa 9am-4pm, Su 1-5pm.

Library and Internet Access: Greensboro Central Library, 219 N. Church St. (☎336-373-2471; www.greensborolibrary.org). Open M-F 9am-9pm, Sa 9am-6pm, Su 2-6pm.

Post Office: 125 S. Estes St. (☎336-370-1251). Open M-F 8:30am-5:30pm, Sa 8:30am-noon. **Postal Code:** 27401.

ORIENTATION

Both **I-85** and **I-40** run south of downtown Greensboro and are connected to the downtown area by a number of wide boulevards. Most streets in the downtown area are one-way, but directions to the visitors center and other major historical attractions are clearly signposted in the downtown area. The visitors center has a helpful map of the downtown and Greensboro metro area that shows the location of attractions and some hotels.

ACCOMMODATIONS

Greensboro has plenty of discount hotels and inexpensive campgrounds along I-40 and I-85. As with other North Carolina cities, discount hotel coupons can be helpful during weekdays and off-peak times.

The Greensboro Inn, 135 Summit Ave. (☎336-370-0135). Basic, clean rooms. Singles $40; doubles $50. AmEx/D/MC/V. ❷

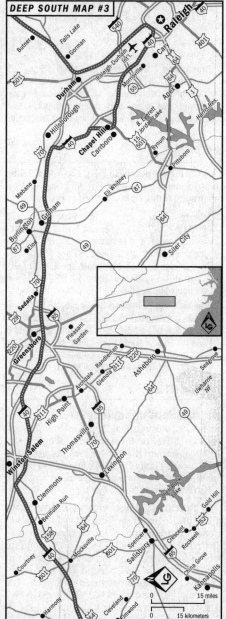

DEEP SOUTH MAP #3

DEEP SOUTH

Hagan Stone Park, 5920 Hagan Stone Park Rd. (☎336-674-0472), in Pleasant Garden, off US 421. A lovely 409-acre campground, wildlife refuge, and recreational area. 16 campsites each offer an authentic taste of nature. Free Wi-Fi. Sites $15. Open daily 8am-sunset. ❶

Greensboro Campground, 1896 Trox St. (☎336-274-4143), off I-40/I-85 at Exit 128. Swimming pool, laundry facilities, security gate, private tent sites, and clean bathrooms and showers. Sites $15, with full hookup $20. Cabins $30-35. MC/V. ❶

FOOD

Despite the preponderance of fast-food chains in strip mall complexes, Greensboro offers a surprising range of tasty dining options.

Liberty Oak, 100D W. Washington St. (☎336-273-7057). Serves excellent sandwiches, pasta, and salads in an airy, 2-level dining room. Sandwiches $9-11. Salads $9-12. Dinner entrees $17-27. Blue-plate specials $17-20. Open M-Th 11:30am-9:30pm, F 11:30am-10pm, Sa noon-10pm. AmEx/D/MC/V. ❹

Stamey's Old-Fashioned Barbecue, 2812 Battleground Ave. (☎336-288-9275; www.stameys. com). Has dished out North Carolina-style barbecue for 75 years, and the experience shows. Pork plates $4.75-5.25. Peach cobbler $1.50. Open M-Sa 11am-9pm. AmEx/D/MC/V. ❶

SIGHTS

GREENSBORO HISTORICAL MUSEUM. The Greensboro Historical Museum has a variety of exhibits on local history, including the 1960s sit-ins and the lives of famous residents such as First Lady Dolly Madison. *(130 Summit Ave. ☎336-373-2043; www.greensborohistory.org. Open Tu-Sa 10am-5pm, Su 2-5pm. Free.)*

INTERNATIONAL CIVIL RIGHTS CENTER AND MUSEUM. The International Civil Rights Center and Museum is currently under construction in the old Woolworth building where four African-American students from North Carolina A&T staged the first sit-in of the civil rights movement. Call ahead for opening information. *(134 S. Elm St. ☎336-274-9199; www.sitinmovement.org.)*

GUILFORD COURTHOUSE NATIONAL MILITARY PARK. The Guilford Courthouse National Military Park commemorates the Revolutionary War battle between General Nathanael Greene's rebels and General Earl Cornwallis's British regulars in 1781. The 230-acre park has numerous monuments along walking trails, though no water slides. *(2332 New Garden Rd. ☎336-392-8662; www.nps.gov/guco. Open daily 8:30am-5pm. Free.)*

NIGHTLIFE

After dark, college-age revelers from UNC-Greensboro and NC A&T hit the nightclubs along Elm St. downtown.

Natty Greene's, 345 S. Elm St. (☎336-274-1373). Serves microbrews in an old-fashioned pub atmosphere. 6 homemade ales, lagers, and stouts along with a full menu of salads, wraps, and sandwiches. Open M-Tu and Su noon-midnight, W-Sa 11am-2am. Kitchen open M-Sa until 11pm, Su until 10pm. MC/V.

Solaris, 125 Summit Ave. (☎336-378-0198; www.gettapas.com). A slightly upscale tapas restaurant and bar. Although it specializes in martinis, Solaris also has 8 domestic drafts on tap and a good selection of bottled beers. $4 martinis Tu. DJ or live rock and jazz F-Sa. Open Tu-Th 5-10pm, F-Sa 5pm-last customer. MC/V.

Europa Bar Cafe, 200 N. Davie St. (☎336-389-1010; www.europabarcafe.com). Serves reasonably priced food and specialty drinks in a French bistro setting. Open M-Tu and Su 11am-1am, W-Sa 11am-2am. Kitchen open until 10pm. AmEx/D/MC/V.

THE ROAD TO KERNERSVILLE: 15 MI.
From Greensboro, follow **I-40 West** and take **Exit 206** onto **Business 140 West.**

KERNERSVILLE   ☎336

Just to the east of Winston-Salem, Kernersville is home to **Korner's Folly,** 413 S. Main St., a quirky 22-room, seven-level mansion constructed by a local interior decorator. Ceiling heights range from 6 ft. to 25 ft., and rooms include everything from the unique to the improbable—there's even a theater built into the attic. (☎336-996-7922; www.kornersfolly. org. Open Th-Sa 10am-4pm, Su 1-4pm. $8.)

▞ THE ROAD TO WINSTON-SALEM: 10 MI.
Get back on **Business 140** and continue to **Exit 6** for downtown Winston-Salem.

WINSTON-SALEM   ☎336

As its name suggests, Winston-Salem was originally two different towns. Salem was founded in 1766 by the Moravians, a Protestant sect from the present-day Czech Republic. One of America's most successful utopian communities, Salem was bolstered by religious fervor, dedication to education, and the production of crafts. Winston, meanwhile, rose to prominence as a center of tobacco production and the home of famous tobacco mogul RJ Reynolds. When the two towns merged in 1913, a dynamic, bustling city was born.

VITAL STATS
Population: 232,000
Tourist Office: Winston-Salem Visitor Center, 200 Brookstown Ave. (☎336-728-4200 or 866-728-4200; www.visitwinstonsalem.com). Open daily 8:30am-5pm.
Library and Internet Access: Winston-Salem Public Library, 660 W. 5th St. (☎336-727-2264), at Spring St.. Open June-Aug. M-W 9am-9pm, Th-F 9am-6pm, Sa 9am-5pm; Sept.-May M-W 9am-9pm, Th-F 9am-6pm, Sa 9am-5pm, Su 1-5pm.
Post Office: 1500 Patterson Ave. (☎336-721-6070). Open M-F 8:30am-5pm. **Postal Code:** 27101.

▓ ORIENTATION

I-40 runs south of downtown and splits into a high-speed bypass and **Business I-40,** which runs east-west just south of downtown. The downtown streets are numbered, and wide boulevards connect downtown to Winston-Salem's surrounding suburbs. Winston-Salem offers visitors five free narrative CDs that can serve as personal tour guides. Pick them up at the Winston-Salem Visitor Center or go to www.culturalcorridors.com.

▛ ACCOMMODATIONS

There are a few reasonably priced motels in Winston-Salem, but budget travelers would probably do better to stay outside of the city, near Kernersville. Cheap motels can be found at Exit 184 off I-40. On the northern side of the city, budget motels center on Rte. 52, just past Patterson Ave.

Microtel Inn ❸, 100 Capitol Lodging Ct. (☎336-659-1994), between I-40 and Silas Creek Pkwy. A great value with free Wi-Fi, clean rooms, and a nice pool. Singles $68; doubles $79. AmEx/D/MC/V. ❸

Innkeeper, 2115 Peters Creek Pkwy. (☎336-721-0062). Near downtown and offers rooms along with a pool, free Wi-Fi, and breakfast. Singles $45; doubles $50. D/MC/V. ❸

▟ FOOD

▨ Sweet Potatoes, 529 N. Trade St. (☎336-727-4844), in the downtown arts district. Serves Southern food with an urban twist, like the wild mushroom sandwich on a sweet potato biscuit ($7.50). Lunch entrees $6-10. Dinner entrees $14-19. Open M 11am-3pm, Tu-Sa 11am-3pm and 5-10pm. D/MC/V. ❸

West End Cafe, 926 W. 4th St. (☎336-723-4774; www.westendcafe.com). A laid-back local favorite that makes every kind of sandwich under the sun ($4.50-7). Patrons line up for the curry chicken salad sandwich ($7), the Frosted Flakes-crusted brie over raspberry puree ($9), and other creative dishes. Salads $6.25-12.50. Burgers $5.25-6.75. Open M-F 11am-10pm, Sa noon-10pm. AmEx/D/MC/V. ❷

6th and Vine ❸, 209 W. 6th St. (☎336-725-5577; www.6thandvine.com). Offers salads ($5-12), panini ($8-11), and a rotating selection of entrees ($18-25). Free Wi-Fi and couches give the restaurant a lounge feel. Open Tu-Sa 11am-last customer, Su 10am-3pm. Live music F-Su. AmEx/D/MC/V. ❸

⊙ SIGHTS

▨ REYNOLDA HOUSE AND GARDENS. One of the South's most famous houses, the Reynolda House was built by tobacco tycoon RJ Reynolds and his visionary wife Katherine, who is credited with making the household completely self-sufficient and creating a working "village" on the grounds. Visitors can tour the house's lavish rooms and view its remarkable collection of American art or check out the recreation area downstairs, which includes

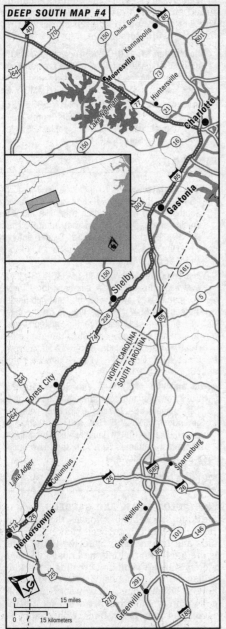

DEEP SOUTH MAP #4

a bowling alley and swimming pool. On Saturday nights in August, movies are screened on the lawn. (*2250 Reynolds Rd. ☎ 336-758-5150 or 888-663-1149; www.reynoldahouse.org. Open Tu-Sa 9:30am-4:30pm, Su 1:30-4:30pm. Last entry 4pm. $10, students and children free, seniors $9. Movies Sa 9pm. $5, students $3.*) Located on the grounds of the Reynolda House, the Reynolda Garden is gorgeous during the spring and summer. The garden's many varieties of roses are particularly impressive, making this one of the most beautiful spots in Winston-Salem. (*☎ 336-758-5593. Open daily sunrise-sunset. Free.*)

■OLD SALEM VILLAGE. Old Salem Village takes visitors back in time to a restored Moravian village, one of the best such colonial reconstructions in the country. The area stretches south from downtown and includes a visitors center, museums exhibiting the Moravian way of life, and a multitude of traditional Moravian homes and buildings, including cobbler and gunsmith shops. Tickets, which include admission to all of the museums and buildings, are pricey, but wandering the village is free. Plan on spending at least an afternoon here. (*☎ 888-653-7253 or 336-721-7300; www.oldsalem.org. Visitors center open M-Sa 9am-5:30pm, Su 12:30-5:30pm. Most attractions open Mar.-Dec. M-Sa 9am-5:30pm, Su 12:30-5:30pm.; Jan.-Feb. Tu-Sa 9am-5:30pm, Su 12:30-5:30pm. $21, ages 6-16 $10.*) Old Salem's **Frank L. Horton Museum Center** features three museums as well as one very cool echo beneath the dome in the museum lobby. The **Toy Museum** displays toys spanning 1700 years. Don't be fooled by its name—this museum is geared toward adults and older children. All of the toys are delicate antiques housed in glass cases. (*Open Mar.-Dec. M-Sa 9:30am-4:30pm, Su 1-5pm; Jan.-Feb. Tu-Sa 9:30am-4:30pm, Su 1-5pm. Free.*) The most extensive museum in the center is the **Museum of Early Southern Decorative Arts (MESDA),** which showcases furnishings from around the Southeast, representing the period from 1690-1820. The rooms are set up entirely "ropes free" to recreate the full feel of Southern homes, and all of the furnishings are original—right down to the bricks in the fireplace. (*☎ 336-721-7360. Open Mar.-Dec. M-Sa 9:30am-4:30pm, Su 1-5pm; Jan.-Feb. Tu-Sa 9:30am-4:30pm, Su 1-5pm. Free 1hr. guided tours every 30min.; reservations required.*)

OTHER SIGHTS. Winston-Salem is the birthplace of national doughnut company Krispy Kreme, and no visit to the city would be complete without stopping by the **Krispy Kreme Shop** where you can watch the famous doughnuts being made fresh on-site. Don't expect any historical exhibits here; it's just fresh doughnuts and coffee. *(259 S. Stratford Rd.* ☎ *336-724-2484. Doughnuts $1. Doughnut sundae $3.20. Open M-Th and Su 6am-11pm, F-Sa 6am-midnight; drive-through open M-Sa 6am-midnight, Su 6am-11pm. Cash only.)*

🎧 NIGHTLIFE

Look for listings of local events in the free weekly newspaper *Go Triad* or in *Relish*, the Thursday entertainment supplement to the *Winston-Salem Journal.*

The Garage, 110 W. 7th St. (☎336-777-1127; www.the-garage.ws), at Trade St. Call ahead or check online for the acts of the night, since featured bands play new grass, pop-punk, and everything in between. Beer from $2. Cover $5-15, under 21 $7-17. Open Th-Sa 7pm-2am, sometimes also W. Showtimes vary. MC/V.

Speakeasy Jazz, 410 W. 4th St. (☎336-722-6555; www.speakeasyjazz.net). Open-mic jazz jam W, cabaret-style jazz Th, and jazz bands F-Sa. The tapas bar dishes up gourmet snacks that will please any mood or palate. 21+ Cover some weekends and for big acts. Open W-Th 7pm-midnight, F-Sa 7pm-1am. MC/V.

🚗 THE ROAD TO MOORESVILLE: 59 MI.

From Winston-Salem, take **I-40 West** to **Exit 150.** Head south on **Center Street** to downtown Statesville. From Statesville, take **I-77 South** to **Exit 36.**

MOORESVILLE   ☎704

Home to numerous NASCAR race teams, NASCAR's training institute, and the Lowe's Motor Speedway, Mooresville lives up to its nickname as "Race City USA." The **North Carolina Auto Racing Hall of Fame,** 119 Knob Hill Rd., has 35 race cars driven by NASCAR champions as well as exhibits and videos on NASCAR legends. (☎704-663-5331; www.ncarhof.com. Open M-F 10am-4:30pm, Sa-Su 10am-2:30pm. $5, children $3.) Mooresville's **Lowe's Motor Speedway,** Exit 49 off I-85, hosts several major NASCAR events each year. If

there isn't an event, visitors can watch drivers practicing on the track. (☎800-455-3267; www.lowesmotorspeedway.com. NASCAR tickets $17-135; other races less expensive. Track open daily 9am-5pm. Free.) Between Mooresville and Charlotte, the **Carolina Raptor Center,** 6000 Sample Rd., is home to abandoned and injured birds of prey like falcons, owls, vultures, and bald eagles. (☎704-875-6521; www.carolinaraptorcenter.org. Bird presentations Sa 11am, 1, 3pm; Su 1, 3pm. Open M-Sa 10am-5pm, Su noon-5pm. $7, students and ages 5-18 $5, seniors $6.)

🚗 THE ROAD TO CHARLOTTE: 25 MI.

Take **I-77 South** to **Exit 11.**

CHARLOTTE   ☎704

Named in the mid-1700s after the wife of England's King George III, Charlotte is still referred to as the "Queen City." After a boy discovered a 17 lb. gold nugget near Charlotte in 1799, settlers flooded the region in the nation's first gold rush. Shortly thereafter, the first branch of the US Mint was established here in 1837. Now the biggest city in the Carolinas, Charlotte has expanded both outward and upward. For visitors, the city offers top-notch museums, ritzy clubs, and a wide variety of professional sports.

VITAL STATS
Population: 651,000
Tourist Office: Charlotte Visitors Center, 330 S. Tryon St. (☎800-231-4636; www.visitcharlotte.com). Open M-F 8:30am-5pm, Sa 9am-3pm.
Library and Internet Access: Public Library of Charlotte and Mecklenburg County, 310 N. Tryon St. (☎704-336-2572). Open M-Th 9am-9pm, F-Sa 9am-6pm, Su 1-6pm.
Post Office: 201 N. McDowell St. (☎704-333-2542). Open M-F 7:30am-6pm, Sa 10am-1pm. **Postal Code:** 28204.

🧭 ORIENTATION

The nucleus of Charlotte, the busy Uptown area, has numbered streets laid out perpendicular to named streets in a grid pattern. **Tryon Street,** which runs north-south, is the major crossroad. **I-77** crosses the city from north to south, providing access to Uptown, while **I-85** runs southwest-northeast, connecting Uptown to the UNC-Charlotte campus. Uptown is also accessible from **I-277**, which circles the city and is called the **John Belk Freeway** to the south of Uptown and the **Brookshire Freeway** to the north.

ACCOMMODATIONS

There are several clusters of budget motels in the Charlotte area: on **Independence Boulevard** off the John Belk Fwy.; off I-85 at **Sugar Creek Road** (Exit 41); off I-85 at **Exit 33** near the airport; and off I-77 at **Clanton Street** (Exit 7).

Best Value Inn, 3200 Queen City Dr. (☎704-398-3144 or 888-215-2378), off I-85 at Exit 33. This airport motel has spacious, newly renovated rooms as well as outdoor pool access and continental breakfast. Free Wi-Fi. Rooms M-F $44-54, Sa-Su $70. AmEx/D/MC/V. ❷

McDowell Nature Preserve, 15222 York Rd. (☎704-583-1284; www.parkandrec.com). Go south on Tryon St. until it becomes York Rd. RV, tent, and primitive campsites in a tranquil spot. Office open Mar.-Nov. daily 7am-sunset; Dec.-Feb. F-Su 7am-sunset. Primitive sites $15; drive-in sites with water and electricity $23; rent-a-tent sites $46; RV sites $26. MC/V. ❶

FOOD

Two areas outside Uptown offer attractive dining options at reasonable prices. **North Davidson (NoDa),** around 36th St., houses a small artists' community in a historic neighborhood. South of the city center, the **Dilworth** neighborhood, along East and South Blvd., is lined with restaurants serving everything from ethnic meals to pizza and pub fare.

Mert's Heart and Soul, 214 N. College St. (☎704-342-4222; www.mertsuptown.com). Serves outstanding soul food, ranging from soft-shell crab to pork chops, in a dining room decorated with pictures of jazz legends. Meals come with delicious cornbread. Sandwiches $6.50. Entrees $8-12. Open M-Th 11am-9:30pm, F 11am-11:30pm, Sa 9am-11:30pm, Su 9am-9:30pm. AmEx/D/MC/V. ❷

Cosmos Cafe, 300 N. College St. (☎704-372-3553; www.cosmoscafe.com), at E. 6th St. A hip spot with eclectic urban cuisine. The menu features everything from tapas ($6-9.50) to sushi and wood-fired pizzas ($8.75-10). The restaurant becomes a popular yuppie bar around 10:30pm. Swing by W nights for superb gourmet martinis at ½-price. 2-for-1 tapas M-Sa 5-7pm. Free salsa lessons Th. Open M-F 11am-2am, Sa 5pm-2am. AmEx/D/MC/V. ❸

Fuel Pizza, 1501 Central Ave. (☎704-376-3835; www.therestaurantgroup.com). New York style pizza served in a converted gas station. Slices $2-3. Pies $9-13. Open M-Th and Su 11am-10pm, F-Sa 11am-11pm. AmEx/MC/V. ❶

SIGHTS

Charlotte has a number of museums, most of which are located in the Uptown area. The **Levine Museum of the New South,** 200 E. Seventh St., explores the history of Charlotte and the Carolina Piedmont area with outstanding interactive exhibits that will engage even the most museum-weary traveler. From a working cotton gin to a recreation of a soda fountain that was occupied during the civil-rights sit-ins, the Levine shows how the "New South" developed from the end of the Civil War to the present. (☎704-333-1887. Open M-Sa 10am-5pm, Su noon-5pm. $6; students, ages 6-18, and seniors $5; under 6 free. Su free.) The **Mint Museum of Craft and Design,** 220 N. Tryon St., in Uptown, features contemporary work in glass, wood, metal, and textiles. (☎704-337-2000; www.themintmuseums.org. Open Tu-Sa 10am-5pm, Su noon-5pm. $6, college students and seniors $5, ages 6-17 $3. Tu 10am-2pm free.) The **Mint Museum of Art,** 2730 Randolph Rd., about 2 mi. southeast of downtown, focuses on American painting and decorative arts from ancient Mesoamerican civilizations to the present. A single admission fee grants entry to both museums. (☎704-337-2000; www.mintmuseum.org. Open Tu 10am-10pm, W-Sa 10am-5pm, Su noon-5pm. $6, college students and seniors $5, ages 6-17 $3. Tu 5-10pm free.)

ENTERTAINMENT

One of the newest teams to enter the NBA, the Charlotte **Bobcats** are owned by Black Entertainment Television founder Robert Johnson. The Bobcats shoot hoops in the **Time-Warner**

Cable Arena, 333 E. Trade St. (☎704-688-9000; www.timewarnercablearena.com. Box office open M-F 10am-6pm, Sa 10am-2pm.) Football fans can catch an NFL game when the Carolina **Panthers** play in **Bank of America Stadium,** 800 S. Mint St. (☎704-522-6500; www.carolinapanthers.com. Stadium tours $4, seniors $3, ages 5-15 $2. Tickets $45-70.) Ten miles south, the Charlotte **Knights** play minor-league baseball at **Knights Castle,** off I-77 S. at Exit 88. (☎704-364-6637; www.charlotteknights.com. Box office open M-F 10am-5pm, game days 10am-game time. Tickets $6-10.)

🎵 NIGHTLIFE

To check out nightlife listings, grab a free copy of *Creative Loafing* in one of Charlotte's shops or restaurants, visit www.charlotte.creativeloafing.com, or check the *Charlotte Observer.* Many of Charlotte's hippest clubs can be found Uptown.

> **Amos's Southend,** 1423 S. Tryon St. (☎704-377-6874; www.amossouthend.com). Features live rock bands, pool, and foosball. Acts often cover rock's greats, from Led Zeppelin and Pink Floyd to Journey. Call for showtimes, cover, and age restrictions. AmEx/D/MC/V.

> **The Evening Muse,** 3227 N. Davidson St. (☎704-376-3737; www.theeveningmuse.com), in NoDa. A laid-back venue for a wide variety of musical acts, from acoustic and jazz to rock. Cover around $5. Open W-Th 6pm-midnight, F-Sa 6pm-2am. MC/V.

> **Thomas Street Tavern,** 1218 Thomas Ave. (☎704-376-1622). Follow E. 10th St. out of Uptown; after E. 10th becomes Central Ave., turn right on Thomas Ave. A local favorite for its pool tables, extensive beer menu, and relaxed outdoor seating. Sandwiches $5-7. Pizzas $6-8. Open M-Sa 11am-2am, Su noon-2am. MC/V.

⛰ THE ROAD TO TRYON: 54 MI.

From Charlotte, take **I-85** to **Route 74** to Columbus. In Columbus, take **Route 108** into Tryon.

TRYON ☎828

Tryon's downtown is small but well traveled by tourists who flock to the area for its picturesque views, cool temperatures, and lovely forests. Six miles past downtown, off

Rte. 176, **🏞Pearson's Falls** is a nature preserve with a short trail to a stunning 90 ft. waterfall. Bring a camera for pictures and watch the trailside for rare wildflowers. (☎828-749-3031. Open Mar.-Oct. Tu-Sa 10am-5:15pm, Su noon-5:15pm; Nov.-Feb. Tu-Sa 10am-5pm, Su noon-5pm. $3, ages 6-12 $1.)

⛰ THE ROAD TO SALUDA: 8 MI.

Take **Route 176 West** to Saluda. The road is steep and full of switchbacks and tight turns; exercise caution.

SALUDA ☎828

Once an old railway town, Saluda is now an upscale vacation destination with antique shops, boutiques, and B&Bs clustering around its downtown area. The **Purple Onion Cafe and Coffeehouse ❷,** 16 Main St., has an inviting patio and a good selection of sandwiches ($6-9) and pizzas (from $5) in addition to fresh pastries. (☎828-749-1179; www.purpleonionsaluda.com. Live music Th and Sa. Open M-Sa 11am-3pm and 5-9pm. MC/V.) **Tosh's Whistle Stop Cafe ❶,** 173 #2 E. Main St., serves hearty breakfasts like omelets and quiches as well as muffins and sticky buns. (☎828-749-3310. Full breakfast $4.50-7. Open W-F 10am-4pm, Sa-Su 10am-5pm. MC/V.)

⛰ THE ROAD TO HENDERSONVILLE: 8 MI.

Take **Route 176 West** to Hendersonville.

HENDERSONVILLE ☎828

A medium-size vacation town in the Blue Ridge Mountains, Hendersonville is a blander version of Asheville that caters to families and retired couples. The **Hendersonville Visitors Center,** 201 S. Main St., has information about lodging and attractions throughout the region. (☎800-828-4224; www.historichendersonville.org. Open M-F 9am-5pm, Sa-Su 10am-5pm.) Three miles west of downtown, **Jump Off Rock** is an ominously-named park at the end of Laurel Park Hwy. with a phenomenal view of the Blue Ridge Mountains. (Open daily sunrise-sunset. Free.) The **Western North Carolina Air Museum,** on Wilson St. near Brooklyn Ave., off Rte. 176, has a collection of vintage airplanes on display from the "golden age of aviation" in the 1930s and 40s. (☎828-698-2482. Open

Apr.-Oct. W ans Su noon-5pm, Sa 10am-5pm, ;
Nov.-Mar. W and Sa-Su noon-5pm. Free.)

THE ROAD TO ASHEVILLE: 25 MI.

Follow **I-26 West** for 19 mi., and take the **I-240 East**
exit to Asheville/US-70/UNC Asheville. Follow I-240 E.
for 5 mi. to **Exit 3B** for Asheville.

ASHEVILLE ☎828

Hazy blue mountains, deep valleys, and spectacular waterfalls form the impressive backdrop of this small city. Once a popular retreat
for the well-to-do, Asheville hosted enough
Carnegies, Vanderbilts, and Mellons to fill a
1920s edition of *Who's Who on the Atlantic
Seaboard*. The Great Depression devastated
Asheville's high-end tourist industry, but during the past half-century Asheville has blos-
somed into a bohemian haven. With funky
restaurants, counter-culture bookstores, and
lively nightlife, Asheville is a one-of-a-kind
city that you won't want to leave.

ORIENTATION

I-40 runs east-west south of Asheville, and
the **I-240** spur connects downtown Asheville
to I-40 and **I-26**. Most streets in downtown
Asheville are one-way. **Haywood Road** runs west
across the French Broad River to Asheville's
West End. **Biltmore Avenue** runs south from
downtown to the Biltmore Estate and I-40.

VITAL STATS

Population: 70,400

**Tourist Office: Chamber of Commerce and Visi-
tor Center,** 36 Motford Ave. (☎828-258-6101 or
800-257-1300; www.exploreasheville.com). Take
Exit 4C off I-240. Open M-F 8:30am-5:30pm, Sa-Su
9am-5pm.

**Library and Internet Access: Pack Memorial
Library,** 67 Haywood St. (☎828-250-4700). Open
June-Aug. M-Th 9:30am-8pm, F 9:30am-6pm, Sa
9:30am-5pm; Sept.-May M-Th 9:30am-8pm, F
9:30am-6pm, Sa 9:30am-5pm, Su 2-5pm.

Post Office: 33 Coxe Ave. (☎828-271-6429),
off Patton Ave. Open M-F 7:30am-5:30pm, Sa
9am-1pm. **Postal Code:** 28802.

ACCOMMODATIONS

Bon Paul and Sharky's Hostel, 816 Haywood Rd.
(☎828-350-9928; www.bonpaulandsharkys.com).
A friendly, communal feel and a relaxed atmosphere. A huge TV, extensive DVD collection, outdoor hot tub, foosball table, communal kitchen,
bicycles, and free bus station and airport pickup
are just some of the perks. Free lockers. Linens.
Free Wi-Fi. Parking. Reception daily 10am-1pm
and 5-10pm. Check-in 24hr. Dorms $23; private
rooms $60. Cash only. ❶

Arthaus Hostel, 16 Ravenscroft Rd. (☎828-225-
3278; www.ashevillehostel.com). A funky, New-
Age hostel located downtown and offering brightly

BAR, BEER, AND CUES?

Barbecue may have become an American favorite, but few people know the origins of this beloved
national food. Some people claim the term "BBQ" arose when roadhouses and beer halls with pool
tables advertised "bar, beer, and cues," a phrase which was eventually shortened to "BBCue" and then
"BBQ." Others assert that the phrase came in to being when French travelers saw a pig being cooked
whole and dubbed the process *"barbe à queue,"* or "from beard to tail." Perhaps the real origins of the
word can be traced back to the Caribbean, where by the 1600s the Taino people referred to a sacred
fire pit used for cooking meat as *barabicu* or *barbicoa*. Whatever the origins of the word, barbecue
has been a staple in the Deep South since the early 19th century, when wild hogs were caught,
slaughtered, and enjoyed with neighbors and friends. Today, every region has its own barbecue, and
you better believe the showdown between the vinegar-based sauces of eastern North Carolina and
the sweet tomato sauces of Georgia and Tennessee gets fierce at Memphis's annual World Champion-

painted, spotless rooms and a communal kitchen. Linen included. Laundry $5. Free Wi-Fi. Call to arrange check-in. Restricted access noon-4pm. Dorms $20; private rooms from $60. MC/V. ❶

Powhatan Lake Campground, 375 Wesley Branch Rd. (☎828-670-5627, reservations 877-444-6777), 12 mi. southwest of Asheville off Rte. 191. In the Pisgah National Forest, with wooded sites on a lake open for swimming and fishing. Sites fill quickly in summer; call for reservations. Some sites have hookups. Showers and dump station available. Open Apr.-Oct. Gates close 10pm. Sites $18, with water and sewer $21. $5 per vehicle. Cash or check only. ❶

🍴 FOOD

🏷 **Laughing Seed Cafe,** 40 Wall St. (☎828-252-3445; www.laughingseed.com). The lineup of vegetarian dishes tastes even better when served on the patio; try the Curried Eggplant Napoleon ($13.25). Sandwiches $8-9.25. Open M and W-Th 11:30am-9pm, F-Sa 11:30am-10pm, Su 10am-9pm. AmEx/MC/V. ❸

Tupelo Honey Cafe, 12 College St. (☎828-255-4404; www.tupelohoneycafe.com). Southern home cooking with creative twists. Shrimp over goat-cheese grits $14. Sandwiches $5-8. Entrees $6-15. Open Tu-Th 9am-3pm and 5:30-10pm, F-Sa 9am-3pm and 5:30-11pm, Su 9am-3pm. AmEx/MC/V. ❸

Sunny Point Cafe and Bakery, 626 Haywood Rd. (☎828-252-0055). A popular breakfast and brunch destination. The breakfast sandwich ($7) and huevos rancheros ($7.50) are both excellent. Lunch $7-8. Open M and Su 8:30am-2:30pm, Tu-Sa 8:30am-9:30pm. D/MC/V. ❷

👁 SIGHTS

Unlike the sprawling mega-cities of Charlotte and Winston-Salem, Asheville's downtown is compact and fun to walk. Be sure to check out the varied skyline as you stroll; the city is a mix of bland glass-walled towers and glamorous Art Deco buildings from the 1920s. Highlights include City Hall, at the corner of Davidson and Marjorie St., and the tall, slender Jackson building, in Pack Sq.

BILTMORE ESTATE. George Vanderbilt's palatial Biltmore Estate was constructed in the 1890s and is the largest private home in America. A self-guided tour of the house and grounds can take all day; try to arrive early. The entrance fee includes a complimentary wine tasting at the on-site winery. (*1 Approach Rd.* ☎*828-225-1333 or 800-411-3812; www.biltmore. com. Estate open daily Apr.-Dec. 8:30am-5pm; Jan.-Mar. 9am-4pm. Winery open daily Apr.-Dec. 11am-7pm; Jan.-Mar. noon-6pm. M-F and Su $47, Sa $51; ages 9-16 $23.50/25.50. Discounted tickets available online. Audio tour $8. Rooftop tours, guided house tours, and behind-the-scenes tours $15. Estate grounds tours $17. Carriage rides $35. Horseback rides $60, ages 8-16 $50.)*

OTHER SIGHTS. The **Asheville Art Museum,** 2 S. Pack Sq., displays rotating selections of lesser-known 20th-century American artwork in an Italian Renaissance-style building. (☎*828-253-3227; www.ashevilleart.org. Open Tu-Th and Sa 10am-5pm, F 10am-8pm, Su 1-5pm. $6; students, ages 4-15, and seniors $5.)* The **Thomas Wolfe Memorial,** 52 N. Market St., between Woodfin and Walnut St., celebrates one of the early 20th century's most influential American authors with a museum and a recreation of his "old Kentucky home." (☎*828-253-8304; www.wolfememorial.com. Open Apr.-Oct. Tu-Sa 9am-5pm, Su 1-5pm; Nov.-Mar. Tu-Sa 10am-4pm, Su 1-4pm. 30min. tours every hr. at 30min. past. $1, students $0.50.)* Asheville's **Malaprops Bookstore,** 55 Haywood St., is one of the largest independent bookstores in the Southeast. With a broad selection of books, a cafe, and Internet access, Malaprops rewards both book-lovers and casual browsers. (☎*828-254-6734 or 800-441-9829. Open M-Th 8am-9pm, F-Sa 8am-10pm, Su 8am-7pm.)*

🎭 ENTERTAINMENT

The downtown area, especially the southeast end around the intersection of Broadway and College St., is a hot spot for music and movies. Indie flicks play at the **Fine Arts Theatre,** 36 Biltmore Ave. (☎828-232-1536; www.fineartstheatre.com. Ticket sales begin 30min. before showtimes. Box office open daily from 12:30pm. Tickets $8, seniors and matinees $5.75.) **Shakespeare in the Park,** 334 Pearson Dr., at the Hazel Robinson Amphitheater in Montford Park, produces four plays each summer. (☎828-254-5146; www.montfordparkplayers.org. June-Sept. F-Su 7:30pm. Free.) The Asheville **Tourists,** a minor-league

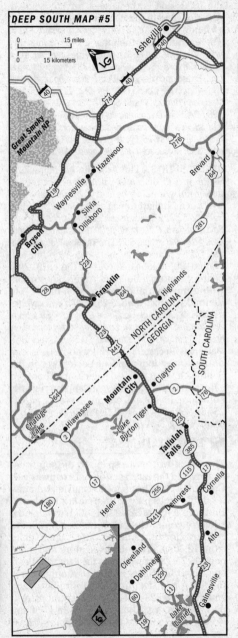

DEEP SOUTH MAP #5

0 ____ 15 miles
0 ____ 15 kilometers

Asheville

Great Smoky Mountain NP

Hazelwood

Waynesville

Silvia

Dillsboro

Bryson City

Franklin

Brevard

Highlands

NORTH CAROLINA

GEORGIA

SOUTH CAROLINA

Mountain City

Clayton

Chatuge Lake

Hiawassee

Lake Burton

Lake Tiger

Tallulah Falls

Helen

Demorest

Cornelia

Clarkesville

Cleveland

Dahlonega

Gainesville

Lake Lanier

DEEP SOUTH

baseball team, play at **McCormick Field** from April to September. (☎828-258-0428; www. theashevilletourists.com. Tickets $7; children $6.)

NIGHTLIFE

The free weekly paper Mountain Xpress has arts, events, and dining listings.

Asheville Pizza and Brewing Company, 675 Merrimon Ave. (☎828-254-1281; www. ashevillepizza.com). Shows 2nd-run movies for $2 and serves pizza (12 in. $12-16) and microbrewed beer. An Asheville institution. $2.50 pints Th. Open daily 11am-midnight. AmEx/MC/V.

Jack of the Wood, 95 Patton Ave. (☎828-252-5445; www.jackofthewood.com).Heats up at night with live celtic, bluegrass, and old-time mountain music. Fill up on corned beef and cabbage ($12) while enjoying the show. Live music daily 9pm. Trivia night M 8pm. 21+ after 9pm. Cover F-Sa $5-7. Open M-F 4pm-2am, Sa noon-2am, Su 3pm-2am. AmEx/D/MC/V.

OUTDOORS

If the Biltmore is too much for your wallet to handle, enjoy the free **Botanical Gardens,** 151 WT Weaver Blvd., which contains 10 acres of plants native to the Carolina Mountains. The best time to visit is when the wildflowers are blooming, from April to mid-May. (☎828-252-5190; www.ashevillebotanical-gardens.org. Open daily sunrise-sunset.) Twenty-five miles southeast of Asheville on US 64/74A, the scenic setting for *The Last of the Mohicans* rises up almost half a mile in **Chimney Rock Park.** After driving to the base of the chimney, take the 26-story elevator to the top or walk up for a 75 mi. view. Extend your time on the mountaintop with one of five hikes that range ½-1½ mi. in length, some of which lead to breathtaking waterfalls. (☎828-625-9611 or 800-277-9611; www.chimneyrockpark.com. Ticket office open daily Apr.-Oct. 8:30am-5:30pm; Nov.-Mar. 8:30am-4:30pm. Park open daily Apr.-Oct. 8:30am-7pm; Nov.-Mar. 8:30am-6pm. $14, ages 6-15 $6.) Two companies arrange whitewater rafting expeditions on the French Broad River. **Blue Ridge Rafting**, in Hot Springs, and **French Broad Rafting Expedi-**

tions, in Marshall, both offer a variety of trips at prices that depend on length and difficulty. (Blue Ridge Rafting ☎800-303-7238; www. blueridgerafting.com. French Broad Rafting Expeditions ☎800-570-7238; www.french-broadrafting.com. Trips from $47.)

THE ROAD TO GREAT SMOKY MOUNTAIN NATIONAL PARK: 54 MI.

From Asheville, take **Route 19/23 South** (which becomes Rte. 23 S./74 W.) to **Exit 102.** Follow **Route 276 East** for 2 mi. to Waynesville. From there, take **US 74 East** to **US 19.** Take US 19 to Cherokee and follow **US 441** into the park.

GREAT SMOKY MOUNTAINS ☎865

Great Smoky Mountains National Park encompasses over 500,000 acres of gray-green Appalachian peaks bounded by the North Carolina and Tennessee valleys, making it the largest wilderness area in the eastern US. Described by the Cherokee as "shaconage," or "blue, like smoke," the mountains are populated by black bears, wild hogs, and turkeys along with more than 1500 species of flowering plants. Spring sets the landscape ablaze with wildflowers; in June and July, rhododendrons bloom. By mid-October, the mountains have become a vibrant quilt of autumnal color.

ORIENTATION

The **Newfound Gap Road (US 441)** is the only road connecting the Tennessee and the North Carolina sides of the park. On the Tennessee side, **Gatlinburg** and **Pigeon Forge** lie just outside of the park; both are overwhelmingly touristy, especially in summer. Travelers should take the **Gatlinburg Bypass Road** off US 441 to avoid the midday mayhem of downtown Gatlinburg. **Townsend,** to the west near Cades Cove, is less crowded. The town of **Cherokee** lies near the park entrance on US 441 in North Carolina. **Bryson City,** near the Deep Creek campground, is quieter. The free *Smokies Guide* details the park's tours, lectures, activities, and changing natural surroundings. US 441 is lined with tourist info and welcome centers, but beware: these are not run by the park and they rope travelers in with deals to Dollywood and

other attractions. Travelers solely interested in the park should wait for the superior visitors centers located within the park that are run by the National Park Service.

VITAL STATS
Area: 510,086 acres
Tourist Offices: Sugarlands (☎865-436-1291), on Newfound Gap Rd., 2 mi. south of Gatlinburg, next to the park's headquarters. Open daily June-Aug. 8am-7pm; Sept.-Oct. and Apr.-May 8am-6pm; Nov. and Mar. 8am-5pm; Dec.-Feb. 8am-4:30pm. **Oconaluftee** (☎828-497-1900), on US 441, about 2 mi. north of Cherokee. Open daily 8am-6pm; low-season hours vary.
Park Info Line: (☎865-436-1200; www.nps.gov/grsm). Operates June-Aug. 8am-7pm; Sept.-Oct. and Apr.-May 8am-6pm; Nov. and Mar. 8am-5pm; Dec.-Feb. daily 8am-4:30pm. **Park Headquarters:** ☎865-436-1294.
Post Office: 130 Slope St., Bryson City, NC (☎828-488-3481). Open M-F 8:30am-5pm, Sa 10am-noon. **Postal Code:** 28713.
Gateway Towns: Gatlinburg, TN, Townsend, TN, and Bryson City, NC.

CAMPING

Ten █campgrounds ❶ lie scattered throughout the park, each with tent sites, limited trailer space, water, and bathrooms with flush toilets. There are no showers or hookups. Smokemont, Elkmont, Cosby, and Cades Cove, the largest and most popular campgrounds, accept reservations. Cades Cove is open year-round, while the other campgrounds open between March and May and close between October and December. The other campgrounds are first come, first served; visitors centers have info about availability. In summer, reserve spots as early as your travel plans allow. (☎877-444-6777; www.recreation.gov. Open daily 10am-10pm. Sites $12-23.) The river sites at Elkmont are perfect for families who are looking for an idyllic camping experience, but locals and park rangers agree that the sites at Cosby are the go-to spot for campers looking for a more rustic, solitary experience. **Backcountry camping** permits that allow access to the park's 100 primitive backcountry sites can be obtained for free at ranger stations. (☎865-436-1231. Office open daily 8am-6pm.)

⚠ OUTDOOR ACTIVITIES

HIKING

Over 900 mi. of hiking trails and 170 mi. of road meander through the park. Trail maps and a guide to area day hikes are also available at the visitors centers ($1 each; the $5 "starter pack" has all the maps you need for day hiking, fishing, auto touring, and camping). The Great Smokies are known for phenomenal waterfalls, and many of the park's most popular hikes culminate in stunning vistas or fantastic views of the surrounding mountains. Less crowded areas include **Cosby** and **Cataloochee,** both on the park's eastern edge. Wherever you go, bring water and, of course, don't feed the bears.

Laurel Falls (2½ mi., 2hr. round-trip), about 4 mi. west of Sugarlands Visitors Center on Little River Rd. One of the easier (and more crowded) hikes on the TN side of the park. Follows a paved trail through a series of cascades before reaching the 60 ft. falls; it gets crowded as the day wears on, but the path is virtually empty before 9:30am.

Clingman's Dome (1 mi., 30min. round-trip), off Clingman's Dome Rd. Ascends a steep, paved path to a viewing tower atop the highest vantage point in the park. Fantastic views of the area's spectacular sunrise and sunset.

Rainbow Falls (5½ mi., 4hr. round-trip), accessible from the trailhead on Cherokee Orchard Rd. The park's most popular hike, a moderate-to-strenuous trek that reveals the Smokies' highest single-plunge waterfall.

Albright Grove Loop (6 mi., 4hr. round-trip via Maddron Bald Trail), accessible from the Maddron Bald trailhead east of Gatlinburg. Much less crowded and passes by some gigantic, towering ancient maple trees.

Ramsay Cascades (8 mi., 5hr. round-trip), in the Greenbrier area. A strenuous hike leads to contemplative 100 ft. cascades.

Chimney Tops (4 mi., 2hr. round-trip). A steep scramble leads up to 2 4755 ft. rock spires.

BIKING

Biking is permitted along most roads within the park, with the exception of the Roaring Fork Motor Nature Trail. The best opportunities for cyclists are at the **Foothills Parkway, Cades Cove,** and **Cataloochee.** On Wednesday and Saturday mornings from May to September, the 11 mi. Cades Cove Loop is closed to car traffic to allow bicyclists full use of the road from dawn to 10am. While the Smokies have no mountain-biking trails, a few gravel trails in the park, including the **Gatlinburg Trail,** the **Oconaluftee River Trail,** and **Deep Creek** (lower section) allow bicycles. Another option is neighboring **Tsali Recreation Area,** where there are four mountain-biking loops available for a small fee. Contact the Cheoah Ranger Station in the Nantahala National Forest for more information. (☎828-479-6431. Open M-F 8am-5pm.) Bike rental is available at **Cades Cove Campground Store.** (☎828-448-9034. $4-6 per hr. Open in summer M-Tu, Th-F, Su 9am-4:30pm; W and Sa 7am-4:30pm; winter hours vary, so call ahead.)

FISHING

Forty species of fishes swim in the park's rivers and streams. The Smokies permit fishing in open waters year-round from 30min. before dawn to 30min. after sunset. Anglers over 12 (over 15 in North Carolina) must possess a valid Tennessee or North Carolina fishing license. The park does not sell licenses; check with local chambers of commerce, sports shops, and hardware stores to purchase a license or buy one online before leaving for your trip (https://www3.wildlifelicense.com/tn). Visitors centers have a free leaflet and map detailing fishing regulations.

AUTO TOURS

The park offers a number of auto tours. The **Cades Cove Loop, Newfound Gap Road,** and **Roaring Fork** tours are favorites and can get crowded in summer and on weekends. Pamphlets and maps are available in the visitors centers ($1 each). Prices for area-specific guides vary. The Cataloochee tour ($1) goes through the area where elk have been reintroduced.

THE ROAD TO BRYSON CITY: 13 MI.
From Cherokee at the east entrance to the park, take **US 441** to **US 19,** which leads into Bryson City.

BRYSON CITY ☎828
A short distance from the park, Bryson City offers food and lodging at less than astronomical rates. The **Rosewood Inn ❷**, 265 E. Main St., is an adorable motel that makes it worth staying further away from the touristy, crowded parts of the Smokies. The rooms have king-size beds with rose-patterned bedspreads and shutters on the windows. Porch rockers and flowers line the motel's front, and rooms overlook the river. (☎828-488-2194; www.greatsmokies.com/rosewoodinn. Singles from $50.) **Jimmy Mac's Restaurant ❶**, 121 Main St., has tasty American fare and friendly ambiance that makes you feel like you're eating in a relative's dining room. For lunch, choose two of soup, salad, or half-sandwich for $5.50. (☎828-488-4700. Open M 11am-9pm, W-Th 6:30am-9pm, F-Sa 6:30am-9:30pm, Su 7am-8:30pm. D/MC/V.)

THE ROAD TO FRANKLIN: 26 MI.
Take **US 19** to **Route 28,** which leads into Franklin.

FRANKLIN ☎828
Franklin has two worthwhile museums in its tiny, hilltop downtown. The **Scottish Tartans Museum,** 86 E. Main St., has exhibits on Scottish history, tartan weaving, and the interaction between Scottish settlers and Cherokee Native Americans in colonial North Carolina. The museum's mannequins are a bit odd-looking, but the collection of over 500 family and clan tartans is impressive. (☎828-524-7472; www.scottishtartans.org. Open M-Sa 10am-5pm. $2, children $1.) Just steps from Franklin's town center, the old county jail has been converted into the **Franklin Gem and Mineral Museum,** 25 Phillips St., which displays an extensive collection of gems, minerals, fossils, and Native American artifacts found in the region. Upstairs, you can walk inside a jail cell. (☎828-369-7831; www.fgmm.org. Open M-F noon-4pm, Sa 11am-3pm. Free.) The **Frog and Owl Mountain Bistro ❸**, 46 E. Main St., downtown, prepares critically acclaimed gourmet meals. The lunch entrees ($11.50-14) are delicious and significantly cheaper than dinner entrees. (☎828-349-4112. Open daily 11am-3pm and 5:30-9pm. AmEx/MC/V.)

THE ROAD TO MOUNTAIN CITY: 4 MI.
Take **Route 23/441 South** to Mountain City.

MOUNTAIN CITY ☎706
The tiny town of Mountain City is home to the **Foxfire Museum and Heritage Center,** 200 Foxfire Ln., a reconstruction of an early 1800s Appalachian mountain town. Started by students interested in Appalachian culture, the oral-history project evolved into a collection of donated artifacts housed among over 20 original log cabins. Don't miss the 1790s "tar grinder" wagon, the only remaining wagon used on the Trail of Tears. Turn right on Black Rock Mountain Pkwy., left on Down Home Ln., left on Cross St., and right onto Foxfire Ln. (☎706-746-5828; www.foxfire.org. Call in advance for guided tours. Open M-Sa 8:30am-4:30pm. $5, under 11 free.) **Black Rock Mountain State Park ❶**, Black Rock Mountain Hwy., is Georgia's highest state park, located atop the Eastern Continental Divide. The park has numerous scenic overlooks, including a stunning panorama from the visitors center, as well as 10 mi. of hiking trails and campsites. Follow the signs from US 23/411. (☎706-746-2141. Park office open daily 8am-5pm. Backcountry sites $5; primitive tent sites $12; sites with full hookup $25. MC/V.)

THE ROAD TO TALLULAH FALLS: 15 MI.
Follow **Route 23/441 South** to Tallulah Falls.

TALLULAH FALLS ☎706
The primary attraction in Tallulah Falls is **Tallulah Gorge State Park,** which surrounds a massive 1000 ft. deep gorge. The park has 20 mi. of hiking trails, campsites, and a day-use area on Tallulah Falls Lake with swimming

DEEP SOUTH

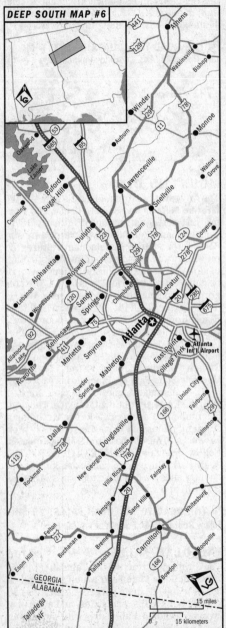

DEEP SOUTH MAP #6

DEEP SOUTH

and picnic areas. Visitors can hike to over-looks, walk across a suspension bridge 80 ft. above the gorge floor, or hike down into the gorge. (☎706-754-7970. Visitors center open daily 8am-5pm. Park open daily 8am-sunset.) For a free view, continue south on US 23/441 and turn left onto Old Hwy. 441. The **Tallulah Point Overlook Store,** 1 mi. down on Old Hwy. 441, has a free viewing platform and an exhibit about the Great Wallenda, the tightrope artist who crossed the gorge on a tightrope. (☎706-754-4318. Open daily 9am-5pm.)

THE ROAD TO ATLANTA: 48 MI.

Take **US 23/441 South** for 42 mi. and continue on US 23 when 23 and 441 split. From Gainesville, take **I-985 South** (which merges with **I-85 South**) straight in to downtown Atlanta.

ATLANTA ☎404

An increasingly popular destination for recent college grads wary of fast-paced cities, Atlanta is cosmopolitan with a smile. North-erners, Californians, the third-largest gay population in the US, and a host of ethnic groups have diversified this unofficial capital of the South, tempering its distinctly Dixie feel. An economic powerhouse, Atlanta houses offices from 400 of the Fortune 500 companies, including the headquarters of Coca-Cola, UPS, and CNN. Nineteen colleges, including Georgia Tech, Morehouse College, Spelman College, and Emory University, also call "Hotlanta" home. The city is equally blessed with hidden gems; touring Atlanta's streets reveals an endless number of delightful restaurants and beautiful old houses.

ORIENTATION

Atlanta sprawls across 10 counties in the northwest quadrant of the state at the junctures of **I-75, I-85** (the city "thruway"), and **I-20. I-285** (the "perimeter") circumscribes the city. Maneuvering around Atlanta's main thoroughfares, which are arranged much like the spokes of a wheel, challenges even the most experienced native. **Peachtree Street** (one of over 100 streets bearing that name in Atlanta) is a major north-south road; **Spring**

Street, which runs only south, and **Piedmont Avenue,** which runs only north, are parallel to Peachtree St. On the eastern edge, **Moreland Avenue** traverses the length of the city, through **Virginia Highland, Little Five Points (L5P),** and East Atlanta. **Ponce de Leon Avenue** is the primary east-west road and takes travelers to most major destinations. To the south of Ponce runs **North Avenue,** another major east-west thoroughfare.

VITAL STATS

Population: 5,100,000

Tourist Office: Atlanta Convention and Visitor's Bureau, 65 Upper Alabama St. (☎404-577-2148; www.atlanta.net), on the upper level of Underground Atlanta. MARTA: Five Points. Open M-Sa 10am-6pm, Su noon-6pm.

Library and Internet Access: Central Library, 1 Margaret Mitchell Sq. (☎404-730-1700). Open M-Th 9am-9pm, F-Sa 9am-6pm, Su 2-6pm.

Post Office: 570 Piedmont Ave. NE (☎800-275-8777), at North Ave. Open M-F 9am-5pm. **Postal Code:** 30303.

Downtown is home to **Centennial Olympic Park** as well as Atlanta's major sports and concert venues. Directly southwest of downtown, the **West End** is the city's oldest historic quarter. From Five Points, head northeast to Midtown, from Ponce de Leon Ave. to 17th St., for museums and **Piedmont Park.** East of Five Points at Euclid and Moreland Ave., the L5P district is a local haven for artists and youth subculture. North of L5P, **Virginia Highland,** a trendy neighborhood east of Midtown and Piedmont Park, attracts yuppies and college kids. The **Buckhead** area, north of Midtown on Peachtree St., greets both Atlanta's professionals and rappers, housing botiques and dance clubs.

? **DID YOU KNOW?** A law was recently passed which bans any further streets from being named "Peachtree" within Atlanta city limits.

◧ TRANSPORTATION

Navigating Atlanta requires a full arsenal of transportation strategies. Midtown and downtown attractions are best explored using the **Metropolitan Atlanta Rapid Transit Authority,** or MARTA. (☎404-848-5000; www.itsmarta.com. Trains run M-F 5am-1am, Sa-Su 5am-12:30am; bus hours vary. $1.75; weekly pass $13.) The outlying areas of Buckhead, Virginia Highlands, and Little Five Points (L5P) are easiest to get to by car; once you're there, the restaurant- and bar-lined streets encourage strolling at a leisurely pace.

◪ ACCOMMODATIONS

Hotels close to downtown Atlanta are very pricey. Stop by the Atlanta Visitors Center (opposite page) to pick up a free copy of the Georgia Travel Coupon book. Many Atlanta-area hotels have deep discounts on rooms if you use a coupon, although some do not allow coupons if you reserve a room in advance.

◪ **Atlanta International Hostel,** 223 Ponce de Leon Ave. (☎404-875-9449 or 800-473-9449; www.hostel-atlanta.com), in Midtown. From MARTA: North Ave., walk 3 blocks east on Ponce de Leon to Myrtle St. or take bus #2. Look for the "Woodruff Inn: Bed and Breakfast" sign. This family-owned establishment has clean dorms in a house with TV, pool table, and kitchen. Free coffee and muffins for breakfast. Free lockers. Towels $1. Internet $1 per 10min. Free Wi-Fi. Dorms $24; private rooms $50-70. AmEx/D/MC/V. ❶

Masters Inn, 2682 Windy Hill Rd. (☎770-951-2005), Exit 260 off I-75 in Marietta. Clean rooms with cable TV and free Wi-Fi. Singles $44; doubles $48. AmEx/D/MC/V. ❷

Red Roof Inn, 311 Courtland St. NE (☎404-659-4545). The best budget option in the heart of downtown Atlanta, with clean rooms and a pool. Free Wi-Fi and parking. Rooms start at $90. AmEx/D/MC/V. ❹

Stone Mountain Family Campground (☎770-498-5710 or 800-385-9807), on US 78. Far from the commotion of the city, this campground has more than 400 stunning sites, a free laser show, and bike rental. 2-night min. stay. Sites $23-25, with water and electricity $25-29, with hookup $32-40. AmEx/D/MC/V. ❶

FOOD

From Vietnamese to Italian, fried to fricasseed, Atlanta cooks options for any craving, but soul food nourishes the city. Head to "Chicken and Waffles" restaurants for the terrific combination. A depot for soul food's raw materials, the **Sweet Auburn Curb Market,** 209 Edgewood Ave., has an eye-popping assortment of goodies, from cow's feet to oxtails. (☎404-659-1665. Open M-Sa 8am-6pm.)

MIDTOWN

■ **Gladys Knight's and Ron Winans's Chicken and Waffles,** 529 Peachtree St. NW (☎404-874-9393; www.gladysandron.com). MARTA: North Ave. Situated on the southern border of Midtown, this upscale but reasonably priced joint screams "soul" with incredible dishes like the Midnight Train (4 fried chicken wings and a waffle; $8.75). Side dishes include collard greens, cinnamon-raisin toast, and corn muffins. Open M-Th 11am-11pm, F-Sa 11am-4am, Su 11am-8pm. AmEx/D/MC/V. ❷

■ **Chow Baby,** 1016A Howell Mill Rd. (☎404-815-4900; www.therealchowbaby.com). Offers up all-you-can-eat, create-your-own stir-fry. Start with rice or noodles, load your bowl up with a vast array of veggies and meats, and mix and match delicious sauces. There's often a wait, but once you've had one of the delicious signature cocktails ($7-8) you won't mind. Lunch $8. Dinner $12. Open M-Th 11am-2:30pm and 5-10:30pm, F 11am-2:30pm and 5-11:30pm, Su 5-10pm. MC/V ❷

■ **The Varsity,** 61 North Ave. NW (☎404-881-1706; www.thevarsity.com), at Spring St. MARTA: North Ave. Established in 1928, the Varsity is the world's largest drive-in restaurant. It was also the subject of a landmark Supreme Court ruling in the 1960s abolishing racial segregation in restaurants. The Varsity has since delighted patrons with cheap and delicious hamburgers ($1.20), frosted orange slushies ($1.40), and famous onion rings ($2). Open M-Th and Su 10am-11:30pm, F-Sa 10am-12:30am. AmEx/MC/V. ❶

Eats, 600 Ponce de Leon Ave. (☎404-888-9149). A powerful aroma of tomato sauce and walls decked out with license plates surround visitors at this restaurant that quickly whips up both terrific pasta and Southern meat-and-3 plates ($4.50-7). Pasta $4.75-5.75. Open daily 11am-10pm. MC/V. ❶

Mary Mac's Tea Room, 224 Ponce de Leon Ave. (☎404-876-1800; www.marymacs.com), at Myrtle St. MARTA: North Ave. Whether you're sipping the "table wine of the South," sweet tea ($1.25), or enjoying the Southern-style meat and vegetables, you'll appreciate the stellar service, charming tea rooms, and elegant dining hall. Entrees ($9-13) come with 2 side dishes. Open daily 11am-9pm. AmEx/MC/V. ❸

10TH STREET

The Flying Biscuit, 1001 Piedmont Ave. (☎404-874-8887; www.flyingbiscuit.com). Packed with loyal patrons, the Flying Biscuit serves breakfast feasts all day. Enjoy a MangoMosa with champagne and mango nectar ($5) alongside your scrumptious french toast with raspberry coulis ($6.60). Open M-Th and Su 7am-10pm, F-Sa 7am-10:30pm. AmEx/MC/V. ❷

Outwrite Bookstore and Coffeehouse, 991 Piedmont Ave. (☎404-607-0082; www.outwrite-books.com). Rainbow beach balls grace the windows at this bookstore and cafe that specializes in gay- and lesbian-interest books. A relaxed and stylish atmosphere with remarkably friendly service. Try the espresso specialty drink Shot in the Dark ($2.25). Answer the daily gay trivia question correctly, and your coffee is free. Open daily 10am-11pm. AmEx/D/MC/V. ❶

Zocalo, 187 10th St. (☎404-249-7576; www.zocalocreativemex.com). Woven baskets, tequila advertisements, and air-conditioned patio seating. Some of the best margaritas in Atlanta and more authentic, upscale fare than your average Mexican restaurant. Try the *molcajete carmelita,* a beef dish with grilled cactus and tomatillo salsa served in a hot lava rock. Open in summer M-Th 11am-11pm, F-Sa 1pm-1am, Su 10am-10pm; in winter M-Th 11am-10pm, F-Sa 11am-11pm, Su 10am-10pm. AmEx/D/MC/V. ❸

VIRGINIA HIGHLAND

Doc Chey's, 1424 N. Highland Ave. (☎404-888-0777; www.doccheys.com). Serves heaping mounds of noodles at super-cheap prices. This pan-Asian restaurant is popular among young locals. Try the delicious lo mein or the Thai coco-

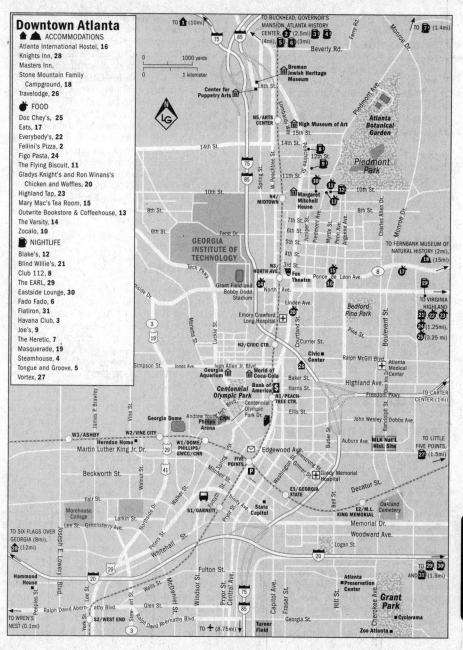

Downtown Atlanta

▲ ACCOMMODATIONS

Atlanta International Hostel, **16**
Knights Inn, **28**
Masters Inn,
Stone Mountain Family
  Campground, **18**
Travelodge, **26**

● FOOD

Doc Chey's, **25**
Eats, **17**
Everybody's, **22**
Fellini's Pizza, **2**
Figo Pasta, **24**
The Flying Biscuit, **11**
Gladys Knight's and Ron Winans's
  Chicken and Waffles, **20**
Highland Tap, **23**
Mary Mac's Tea Room, **15**
Outwrite Bookstore & Coffeehouse, **13**
The Varsity, **14**
Zocalo, **10**

■ NIGHTLIFE

Blake's, **12**
Blind Willie's, **21**
Club 112, **8**
The EARL, **29**
Eastside Lounge, **30**
Fado Fado, **6**
Flatiron, **31**
Havana Club, **3**
Joe's, **9**
The Heretic, **7**
Masquerade, **19**
Steamhouse, **4**
Tongue and Groove, **5**
Vortex, **27**

nut red curry. Entrees $6.50-8.50. Open daily 11:30am-10pm. AmEx/D/MC/V. ❷

Everybody's Pizza, 1040 N. Highland Ave. (☎404-873-4545). Receives high accolades for selling Atlanta's best pizza. Creative pizza salads (greens and chicken on a bed of, well, pizza; $14). Pizza sandwiches $9.50-10.50. Open M-Th 11:30am-11pm, F-Sa 11:30am-midnight, Su noon-10:30pm. AmEx/D/MC/V. ❸

Figo Pasta, 1021 Virginia Ave. NE (☎404-817-7728; www.figopasta.com). Italian for "cool," Figo lives up to its billing. Design your own pasta by starting with a noodle base and adding one of the delicious sauces like the rich lamb ragu. Pastas $4-6; sauces $4. M-Th 11:30am-9:30pm, F-Sa 11:30am-10pm, Su noon-9:30pm. AmEx/MC/V. ❸

BUCKHEAD

Fellini's Pizza, 2809 Peachtree Rd. NE (☎404-266-0082; www.fellinisatlanta.com). 3 watchful gargoyles and an angel welcome customers into this pizzeria, the flagship of 7 Atlanta locations, complete with a spacious deck and mouthwatering pizza. If Hotlanta has become too warm, enjoy your slice (from $1.85) or pie ($10.50-19) inside, where classic rock and romantic decor comingle. Open M-Sa 11am-2am, Su noon-midnight. AmEx/MC/V. ❶

🔄 SIGHTS

SWEET AUBURN DISTRICT

🔲**MARTIN LUTHER KING, JR., NATIONAL HISTORIC SITE.** The most moving sights in the city run along Auburn Ave. in Sweet Auburn. The Reverend Martin Luther King, Jr.'s birthplace, church, and grave are all part of the 23-acre Martin Luther King, Jr., National Historic Site. Leave your car in the parking lot at the corner of Jackson St. and John Wesley Dobbs Ave. and start your tour of the site at the visitors center, which houses poignant displays of photographs, videos, and quotations focused on King's life and the African-American struggle for civil rights. *(450 Auburn Ave. NE. MARTA: King Memorial. ☎404-331-5190; www.nps.gov/malu. Open daily June-Aug. 9am-6pm; Sept.-May 9am-5pm. Free.)* The center also gives

tours of the birth home of MLK. *(501 Auburn Ave. Tours June-Aug. every 30min.; Sept.-May every hr. Arrive early. Free.)* Across the street from the visitors center stands **Ebenezer Baptist Church,** where King gave his first sermon at age 17 and co-pastored with his father from 1960 to 1968. The church is being renovated and is expected to re-open in fall 2009. *(407 Auburn Ave. ☎404-688-7263.)* Next door, at the **Martin Luther King, Jr., Center for Nonviolent Social Change,** lies a beautiful reflecting pool with an island on which King and his wife, Coretta Scott King, have been laid to rest in a white marble tomb. The center's **Freedom Hall** contains many of King's personal articles (including his Nobel Peace Prize medal), an overview of his role model, Gandhi, and exhibits on Coretta Scott King and Rosa Parks. *(449 Auburn Ave. NE. ☎404-526-8920. Open daily June-Aug. 9am-6pm; Sept.-May 9am-5pm. Free.)*

DOWNTOWN

🔲**WORLD OF COCA-COLA.** Two blocks from the capitol, the World of Coca-Cola educates tourists on the rise of "the real thing" from its humble beginnings in Atlanta to its current position of world domination. Uncap the secrets of Coke as you walk through two floors of Coca-Cola history and memorabilia, complete with a "soda jerk" demonstration and TVs that loop old advertisements. The psychological barrage is so intense that even those with the strongest of willpowers will soon be craving a Coke. Luckily, visitors get to sample 64 flavors of Coke from around the world at the tour's end, from the long-lost "Tab" to Mozambique's "Krest." *(121 Baker St.. MARTA: Peachtree Center. ☎404-676-5151; www. worldofcoca-cola.com. Open daily June-Aug. 8am-6pm, Sept.-May 9am-5pm. $15, ages 3-12 $9.)*

🔲**GEORGIA AQUARIUM.** Brand-new in 2006, Atlanta's aquarium is the world's largest. Of the aquarium's five thematic exhibits radiating from a central atrium, the deep-sea tank is the most impressive, with a moving floor that takes visitors through a Plexiglas underwater tunnel. Keep an eye out for the 🔲**wobbegong,** one of the world's ugliest creatures. The aquarium's penguins, sea lions, and coral-reef exhibit are sure to entertain. Arrive early to avoid crowds. *(225 Baker St. at Pemberton Pl.*

MARTA: Peachtree Center. ☎ 404-581-4000; www.geor-giaaquarium.com. Open M-F 9am-6pm, Sa-Su 8am-6pm. Last entry 4:45pm. $27, ages 3-12 $22.)

CNN. Overlooking beautiful Centennial Park is the global headquarters of the Cable News Network (CNN). Check out the studio tour, which allows visitors to sit inside a replica control room, learn the secrets of the tele-prompter, and peer into the CNN newsroom. Get your tickets in advance or arrive early. (1 CNN Center at Centennial Olympic Park Dr. and Marietta St. MARTA: Omni/Dome/GWCC at W1. ☎ 404-827-2300 or 877-426-6868; www.cnn.com/tour. Tours every 10min. daily 9am-5pm. $12, ages 4-18 $9.)

STATE CAPITOL. On the corner of Washington and Mitchell St. is the Georgia State Capitol building, a Neoclassical structure built in 1889 with Georgia's own natural resources: Chero-kee marble, Georgian oak, and gold mined in Lumpkin County. Exhibits on the fourth floor detail Georgia's often tumultuous history and showcase its natural resources—don't miss the two-headed calf. (☎ 404-463-4536. Guided tours 10, 11am, 1, 2, 3pm. Open M-F 8am-5pm. Free.)

CENTENNIAL OLYMPIC PARK. Amid the com-merce and concrete of bustling downtown Atlanta, you can relax at the Centennial Olympic Park, both a 21-acre public recre-ation area and a lasting monument to the 1996 Olympic Games. Eight enormous torches and an array of flags (each representing a nation that has hosted one of the modern Olympic Games) surround the park's central feature, the **Fountain of Rings,** which enthralls (and soaks) children and adults alike. Check out one of the 20min. fountain shows (daily 12:30, 3:30, 6:30, 9pm), in which the water dances to symphonic melodies and dazzling lights. (265 Park Ave. W. NW. ☎ 404-222-7275; www.centennialpark. com. Visitors center open M-Tu and Th-Su 10am-6pm, W 10am-8pm. Park open daily 7am-11pm. Free.)

CARTER PRESIDENTIAL CENTER. Just north of L5P, a charming garden and a circle of state flags welcome visitors to an engaging museum showcasing Jimmy Carter's life and presidency. From campaign memorabilia to *Schoolhouse Rock!* video clips the center's exhibits will entertain visitors of any political persuasion. The serene 35-acre grounds are perfect for a quiet stroll. (441 Freedom Pkwy. Take bus #16 to Cleburne Ave. ☎ 404-865-7101; www.jimmy-carterlibrary.org. Museum open M-Sa 9am-4:45pm, Su noon-4:45pm. Grounds open daily Apr.-Oct. 6am-9pm; Nov.-Mar. 7am-7pm. $8, students $6, under 16 free.)

GRANT PARK CYCLORAMA. The world's larg-est painting (42 ft. tall and 358 ft. in circumfer-ence) is just next to the zoo. The 110-year-old Cyclorama takes visitors back in time on a huge revolving platform in the middle of the 1864 Battle of Atlanta. (800 Cherokee Ave. SE. Take bus #97 from Five Points. MARTA: King Memorial. ☎ 404-624-1071. Open Tu-Su 9am-4:30pm. $7, stu-dents and seniors $6, ages 6-12 $5.)

ZOO ATLANTA. With over 1000 animals, includ-ing giant pandas and Sumatran tigers, this is one of the country's premier zoos. Though the zoo is somewhat overshadowed by Atlanta's dazzling new aquarium, animal lovers will find it a rewarding experience. (800 Cherokee Ave. SE. Take bus #97 from Five Points. ☎ 404-624-5600; www.zooatlanta.org. Open M-F 9:30am-4:30pm, Sa-Su 9:30am-5:30pm. $18, students $14, ages 3-11 $13.)

WEST END

⊠HERNDON HOME. Born a slave, Alonzo F. Herndon founded Atlanta Life Insurance Co., eventually becoming Atlanta's wealthiest African-American in the early 20th century. A Beaux-Arts classical mansion, the Herndon Home was built in 1910; today it is dedicated to the legacy of Herndon's philanthropy. (587 University Pl. NW. Take bus #3 from Five Points station to the corner of Martin Luther King, Jr., Dr. and Maple St., walk 1 block west, turn right on Walnut St., and walk 1 block. ☎ 404-581-9813; www.herndonhome.org. Tours Tu and Th 10am-4pm on the hr., Sa by appointment. $5.)

WREN'S NEST. Dating from 1835, the West End is Atlanta's oldest neighborhood. A tour of the historic Wren's Nest gives a number of twists on the typical "historic home" tour. Home to author Joel Chandler Harris, who popularized the African folktale trickster Br'er Rabbit, Wren's Nest offers a glimpse into middle-class life as it was at the begin-ning of the 20th century. (1050 RD Abernathy Blvd. Take bus #71 from MARTA: West End Station/S2. ☎ 404-753-7735. Open Tu-Sa 10am-2:30pm. $8, stu-dents $7, ages 4-12 $5.)

HAMMONDS HOUSE. The home-turned gallery of Dr. Otis Hammonds, a renowned African-American physician and art lover, displays unique contemporary and older works in Georgia's only collection dedicated entirely to African-American and Haitian art. (*503 Peeples St. SW. ☎404-752-8730; www.hammondshouse.org. Open Tu-F 10am-6pm, Sa-Su 1-5pm. $4; students, children, and seniors $2.*)

MIDTOWN

HIGH MUSEUM OF ART. Within the stunning Woodruff Arts Center, the recently expanded High Museum of Art has a good collection of modern art alongside galleries devoted to American and European painting, sculpture, and design. In 2006-09, the High is hosting a series of visiting exhibitions from the collections of the Louvre, showcasing the history of its galleries and collections from its founding to the present day. (*1280 Peachtree St. NE. MARTA: Arts Center. ☎404-733-4400; www.high.org. Open Tu-W and F-Sa 10am-5pm, Th 10am-8pm, Su noon-5pm. $18, students $15, ages 6-17 $11.*)

ATLANTA BOTANICAL GARDEN. The Atlanta Botanical Garden occupies the northern end of the park and provides a peaceful refuge from everyday life. Stroll through 15 acres of gardens, a hardwood forest with trails, and an interactive children's garden. The park is also home to a rose garden, a formal Japanese garden, and the enormous glass-walled Dorothy Chapman Fuqua Conservatory, which houses an orchid collection and a tropical rainforest environment. Big-name acts like KT Tunstall perform on selected weekends during the summer. (*1345 Piedmont Ave. NE. ☎404-876-5859; www.atlantabotanicalgarden.org. Open Apr.-Oct. Tu-W and F-Su 9am-7pm, Th 9am-10pm; Nov.-Mar. daily 9am-5pm. $12, ages 3-17 $9.*)

BREMAN JEWISH HERITAGE MUSEUM. The Breman Museum has a powerful Holocaust exhibit and a collection of interviews with Holocaust survivors. The museum also has a gallery tracing the tumultuous history of Atlanta's Jewish community from 1845 to the present as well as engaging temporary exhibitions. (*1440 Spring St. NW. From MARTA: Arts Center, walk 3 blocks north to 18th and Spring St. ☎678-222-3700; www.thebreman.org. Open M-Th*

10am-5pm, F 10am-3pm, Su 1-5pm. $10, students $4, ages 3-6 $2, seniors $6.*)

MARGARET MITCHELL HOUSE. Located between the 10th St. district and Midtown is the apartment where Mitchell wrote her Pulitzer Prize-winning novel, *Gone with the Wind*. Tour the house to view her typewriter and autographed copies of the book. Included on the tour, the **Gone with the Wind Movie Museum** has memorabilia such as the portrait of Scarlett at which Clark Gable hurled a cocktail onscreen—complete with stain. The house tour will thrill *Gone with the Wind* devotees but might leave others unimpressed. (*900 Peachtree St., at 10th St., adjacent to MARTA: Midtown. ☎404-249-7015; www.gwtw.org. Open M-Sa 9:30am-5pm, Su noon-5pm. 90min. tours depart 15 min. after 1st interested visitors arrive. $12, students and seniors $9, ages 4-12 $5.*)

CENTER FOR PUPPETRY ARTS. The complexity and sophistication of puppeteering will surprise and interest even those who haven't watched *The Muppet Show* in years. Exhibits show different styles of puppets and puppeteering techniques, and visitors can try their hands at controlling an animatronic puppet. (*1404 Spring St. NW, at 18th St. ☎404-873-3391; www.puppet.org. Open Tu-Su 9am-5pm. $8, students and seniors $7, under 18 $6.*)

FERNBANK MUSEUM OF NATURAL HISTORY. Sporting outstanding dinosaur exhibits and interactive discovery centers, the Fernbank is one of the best science and natural history museums in the South. (*767 Clifton Rd. NE, off Ponce de Leon Ave.; take bus #2 from MARTA: North Ave. or Avondale. ☎404-929-6300; www.fernbankmuseum.org. Open M-Sa 10am-5pm, Su noon-5pm. Museum $15, students and seniors $14, ages 3-12 $13; IMAX film $13/12/11; both attractions $23/21/19.*) The adjacent **RL Staton Rose Garden** is small but free. The garden blossoms from spring until the middle of December.

BUCKHEAD

A drive through Buckhead, north of Midtown and Piedmont Park, off Peachtree St. near W. Paces Ferry Rd., reveals Atlanta's answer to Beverly Hills. The majority of these gaudy mansions were built by Coca-Cola bigwigs; the architectural style of this area has been aptly dubbed "Rococo-cola." The main drag along Peachtree Dr. is slowly turning from a hip, yuppie hangout to that of a younger crowd. The area, however, remains conducive to wining and dining and is strung with dance clubs and restaurants frequented by Atlanta's twenty-somethings.

ATLANTA HISTORY CENTER. The museum traces Atlanta's development from a rural area to an international urban center. In celebration of the 10th anniversary of the 1996 Atlanta Olympic Games, the museum has a new gallery on the history of the Olympics and the transformation of Atlanta into an Olympic host city. Its Civil War Gallery highlights the stories of both Confederate and Union soldiers, while the Folklife Gallery explicates Southern culture from grits to banjos. Also on the grounds are exquisite mansions from the early 20th century, including the **Swan House,** a lavish Anglo-Palladian Revival home built in 1928, and the **Tullie Smith Farm,** an 1845 yeoman farmhouse. Abutting the homes, 33 acres of trails and gardens are perfect for an afternoon stroll. *(130 W. Paces Ferry Rd. NW.* ☎ *404-814-4000; www.atlantahistorycenter.com. Open M-Sa 10am-5:30pm, Su noon-5:30pm. $15, students and seniors $12, ages 4-12 $10.)*

GOVERNOR'S MANSION. One of the most exquisite residences in the Southeast, the Greek Revival Governor's Mansion has elaborate gardens and one of the finest collections of furniture from the Federal Period. *(391 W. Paces Ferry Rd.* ☎ *404-261-1776; www.gov.state.ga.us. Tours Tu-Th 10-11:30am. Free.)*

ATLANTA METRO AREA

STONE MOUNTAIN. Sixteen miles east of the city on US 78, one of Georgia's top natural attractions, Stone Mountain Park, provides a respite from the city with beautiful scenery and the remarkable **Confederate Memorial.** Carved into the world's largest mass of granite, the 825 ft. "Mt. Rushmore of the South" profiles Jefferson Davis, Robert E. Lee, and Stonewall Jackson. On summer nights, be sure to check out the dazzling laser show that illuminates the side of the mountain. A cable car takes visitors to the top of Stone Mountain, which has a panoramic view of

the Georgia landscape and a hazy view of the Atlanta skyline. *(Take bus #120 from MARTA: Avondale.* ☎ *770-498-5690 or 800-317-2006; www.stonemountainpark.com. Park open daily 6am-midnight. $10 per vehicle. All-day pass $25, ages 3-11 $20.)*

SIX FLAGS. Six Flags Over Georgia is one of the largest amusement parks in the nation. Check out the 54 mph Georgia Scorcher roller coaster and the Superman roller coaster, with a pretzel-shaped inverted loop. *(275 Riverside Pkwy., at I-20 W. Take bus #201 from MARTA: Hamilton Homes.* ☎ *770-739-3400; www.sixflags.com/overgeorgia. Hours vary, so call ahead. $40, under 4 ft. $30.)*

ENTERTAINMENT

For hassle-free fun, buy a MARTA pass (p. 723) and pick up the city's free publications on music and events. *Creative Loafing*, the *Hudspeth Report*, and "Leisure" in the Friday edition of the *Atlanta Journal-Constitution* contain the latest info and are available in most coffee shops and on street corners. Check for free concerts in Atlanta's parks.

SPORTS

The **Philips Arena,** 1 Philips Dr. (☎404-878-3000), hosts concerts, the **Atlanta Hawks** NBA team, and the **Atlanta Thrashers** NHL team. The National League's **Atlanta Braves** play at **Turner Field,** 755 Hank Aaron Dr. (MARTA: Georgia State, or take Braves Shuttle from Five Points. ☎404-522-7630, Ticketmaster 800-326-4000. Tickets $1-53.) One-hour tours of Turner Field include views of the diamond from the $200,000 skyboxes. (☎404-614-2311. Open non-game days M-Sa 9am-3pm, Su 1-3pm; night-game days M-Sa 9am-noon; no tours on afternoon or Su game days. Tickets $10, under 14 $5.) See the **Atlanta Falcons** play football at the **Georgia Dome,** the world's largest cable-supported dome. (☎404-223-8687. Open daily 10am-3pm. Tours Tu-Sa on the hr., except during events. $6, students and seniors $4.)

THEATER

Every summer, local TV station Peachtree TV presents **"Screen on the Green,"** a series of free films shown once a week in the meadow behind the visitors center. The **Woodruff Arts Center** houses the Atlanta Symphony, the Alliance Theater Company, the Atlanta College of Art, and the High Museum of Art. Atlanta is home to a number of excellent theater groups, such as **On Stage Atlanta** (☎404-897-1802; www.onstageatlanta.com) and the **Stage Door Players** (☎770-396-1726; www.jackinthe-blackbox.org). The **Fox Theatre,** 660 Peachtree St. NE, a stunning Arabian-themed venue, hosts plays, concerts, comedy shows, and special events, including a summer film festival. (☎404-881-2100, ticket info: 249-6400 or 817-8700; www.foxtheatre.org.)

▣ NIGHTLIFE

Atlanta's rich nightlife lacks a clear focal point. Fortunately, however, it also lacks limits; young people can be found partying until the wee hours and beyond. Scores of bars and clubs along Peachtree Rd. and Buckhead Ave., in **Buckhead,** cater to a younger crowd. Pricier **Midtown** greets glamorous hipsters. Alternative **L5P** plays host to bikers and goths, while Virginia Highland and up-and-coming East Atlanta feature an eclectic mix.

Atlanta is the gay capital of the South, making Midtown the mecca of Southern gay culture. For information on gay nightlife and events, check out the free *Southern Voice,* available everywhere.

BARS AND PUBS

▣ **Blind Willie's,** 828 N. Highland Ave. NE (☎404-873-2583; www.blindwilliesblues.com). Blind Willie's is the quintessential blues club: the brick-lined interior is small and dark, and the bar serves mostly beer ($3-5) to its loyal patrons. Live blues, zydeco, and folk music daily around 9:30pm. Cover $5-10. Open daily 7pm-last customer. AmEx/MC/V.

▣ **Fado,** 273 Buckhead Ave. (☎404-841-0066). The interior of this popular bar was imported from Ireland—right down to the wood of the bar itself. The favored yuppie hangout in Buckhead, with plenty of cozy nooks and crannies for enjoying a pint of Guinness. Free Wi-Fi. Open M-Sa 11am-3am, Su 11am-midnight. AmEx/D/MC/V.

The Vortex, 438 Moreland Ave. (☎404-688-1828; www.thevortexbarandgrill.com), in L5P. With a front door that looks like a Halloween mask and bicycle-riding skeletons hanging from the ceiling, the Vortex will impress with its Applebee's-goes-to-hell ambience. With award-winning burgers like Coronary Bypass ($8.25) with a fried egg, bacon and American cheese and Elvis ($8) with peanut butter, bacon, and fried bananas, you'll need a drink from the long beer list to make it through the night. 18+. Open M-Th and Su 11am-midnight, F-Sa 11am-3am. AmEx/D/MC/V.

Joe's on Juniper, 1049 Juniper St. (☎404-875-6634; www.joesatlanta.com). Inside, gay-friendly Joe's is a classic sports bar with 32 beers on tap and 100 bottles. Stick outside on the patio for dinner and a movie M, trivia Tu and Th, and the ever-popular Crazy Bitch Bingo W 8pm. Open M-Sa 11am-2am, Su 11am-midnight.

Flatiron, 520 Flat Shoals Ave. (☎404-688-8864), in L5P. Set on the corner of Glenwood and Flat Shoals, this smoky bar caters to the edgy (and often aging) hipster crowd with cheap drinks and friendly service. 9 beers on tap (pints $2.75-5). Open M-Th 11:30am-2am, F 11:30am-3am, Sa noon-3am, Su 12:30pm-2am. AmEx/D/MC/V.

Eastside Lounge, 485A Flat Shoals Ave. SE (☎404-522-9666; www.eastsidelounge.net), in L5P. This suave hideout has a well-dressed clientele and a red-tinted decor. Couches near the bar and tables in the small upstairs offer rest for the weary, but be prepared to stand with other trendsetters in the bar area. DJ nightly. 80s night F draws the biggest crowd. Open M-Sa 9pm-2:30am. MC/V.

The EARL, 488 Flat Shoals Ave. (☎404-522-3950; www.badearl.com), in L5P. A bar and restaurant popular with hipsters, the EARL has live music most nights ranging from hip hop to country and serves burgers ($6-8) along with other late-night snacks. Open daily 11:30am-2am. MC/V.

Steamhouse, 1051 W. Peachtree St. (☎404-233-7980; www.steamhouselounge.com), in Midtown. Perfect for those who like raw oysters ($9 per dozen) with their beer. A great place on hot summer evenings. The party often spills out onto the upstairs deck and outside patio. Beer $3.50. $5 for a dozen oysters W. Open M-Sa 11am-2:30am, Su 11am-midnight. MC/V.

CLUBS

▣ **Tongue and Groove,** 565 Main St. (☎404-261-2325; www.tongueandgrooveonline.com), at the Lindbergh City Center, in Buckhead. Whether you decide to kick back at 1 of the 2 gorgeous bars or shake it on the dance floor, this popular nightclub is a lot of fun. Latin night W with free salsa lessons at 9pm. Dress code strictly enforced; no T-shirts, sneakers, or athletic apparel. Cover $10. Open M and W 9pm-3am, Th-Sa 10pm-3am. AmEx/D/MC/V.

Masquerade, 695 North Ave. NE (☎404-577-8178, concert info 577-2007; www.masq.com), in Midtown. Occupying a huge turn-of-the-century mill, this bar has 3 levels: "heaven," with live music from touring bands; "purgatory," a more laid-back pub and pool house; and "hell," a dance club catering to a largely goth crowd. Head outside for dancing or check out the 4000-seat amphitheater for your metal and punk fix. Cover varies. Usually opens at 7pm. MC/V.

Blake's, 227 10th St. (☎404-892-5786; www.blakesontheparkatlanta.com). Midtown males flock to this friendly bar, where "see and be seen" is a way of life. The popular "Hookups" allows you to send a text message that will anonymously appear on the TV screens. Shows nightly 11pm. Open M-Sa 3pm-3am, Su noon-midnight. MC/V.

Heretic, 2069 Cheshire Bridge Rd. NE (☎404-325-3061; www.hereticatlanta.com), a little outside of the center of Midtown. With no pretense to elegance, laid-back Heretic has a dress code of its own W nights when revelers have to take their shirts off and leather, latex, and military garb are de rigeur. Cover F-Sa after 11pm $5. Open M-Sa 9am-3am. MC/V.

THE ROAD TO ANNISTON: 90 MI.

Take I-20 West from Atlanta.

The Heart of Dixie
ALABAMA
Welcomes You

ANNISTON ☎256

Primarily an iron town until the cotton industry began to flourish in 1881, Anniston was awarded the All-American City Award in 1978—and they won't let you forget it. Set in Alabama's gentle hill country to the west of Talladega National Forest, Anniston is a good

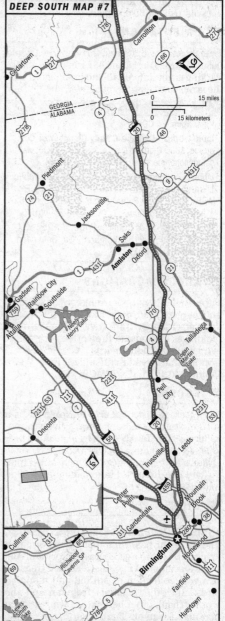

DEEP SOUTH MAP #7

DEEP SOUTH

stopping point for food or a rest before finishing your trek to Birmingham.

ORIENTATION

Tenth Street runs east-west through town while **Quintard Avenue** and **Route 431** run north-south. Parking is not difficult to find in Anniston, and the streets are easy to maneuver.

VITAL STATS
Population: 24,000
Tourist Office: Calhoun County Chamber of Commerce, 1330 Quintard Ave. (☎256-237-3536; www.calhounchamber.com). Open M-F 8am-5pm.
Library and Internet Access: Anniston Public Library, 108 E. 10th St. (☎256-237-8501). Free Wi-Fi. Open M-Th 9am-6:30pm, F 9am-5pm, Sa 10am-5pm, Su 1-5pm.
Post Office: 1101 Quintard Ave. (☎256-234-9940). Open M-F 8:30am-5pm, Sa 8am-noon.
Postal Code: 36201.

ACCOMMODATIONS

Three miles south of Anniston in Oxford, budget motels surround Exit 185 off I-20. The **Red Carpet Inn ❷,** 1007 Hwy. 215, may overlook a gas station and fireworks store, but it is a great deal nonetheless. (☎256-831-6082. Continental breakfast included. Free Wi-Fi. Rooms $40-46. AmEx/D/MC/V.)

FOOD

Damn Yankees Oyster Bar ❷, 919 Noble St., is a surf-and-turf restaurant with a lively atmosphere. Damn Yankees has fried seafood baskets ($8-10) and raw oysters. (☎256-236-7000. Oysters $5 per half-dozen. Open M 4-11pm, Tu-Th 11am-10pm, F 11am-midnight, Sa 5pm-midnight. MC/V.)

SIGHTS

ANNISTON MUSEUM OF NATURAL HISTORY. The museum has a number of kid-oriented exhibits on Earth's geological history and Alabama's ecological habitats. The real treasure is a vast collection of stuffed and mounted birds and other animals from around the world. Thanks to a benefactor who enjoyed hunting African big game, visitors can see the rare black rhino as well as lions, cheetahs, and giraffes up close. (*800 Museum Dr., 1 mi. north of downtown Anniston off McClellan Blvd. ☎256-237-6766; www.annistonmuseum.org. Open in summer M-Sa 10am-5pm, Su 1-5pm; in winter Tu-Sa 10am-5pm, Su 1-5pm. $4.50, ages 4-17 $3.50.*)

BERMAN MUSEUM OF WORLD HISTORY. Next door, this museum will enthrall aspiring cowboys and Rambos with its collection of guns and weaponry. From 15th-century hand cannons to diamond-encrusted Persian scabbards, the museum showcases more ways to die than visitors could ever have previously imagined. Don't miss the flute gun that fires when you play the right note. (*840 Museum Dr. ☎256-237-6261; www.bermanmuseum.org. Open in summer M-Sa 10am-5pm, Su 1-5pm; in winter Tu-Sa 10am-5pm, Su 1-5pm. $3.50, ages 4-17 $2.50.*)

EPISCOPAL CHURCH OF SAINT MICHAEL AND ALL ANGELS. The church was built in 1887 thanks to the patronage of John Ward Noble, one of the founders of Anniston's iron works. The majestic altar is made from Italian marble, and the stained-glass windows and ark-like wood ceiling are both gorgeous. In the entrance hall, visitors can also see an Ethiopian cross donated by Emperor Haile Selassie I. (*1000 W. 18th St. ☎256-237-4011; www.stmaaa.org. Open daily 8am-4pm.*)

WORLD'S LARGEST CHAIR. Anniston is also home to the world's largest chair, which earned its spot in the *Guinness Book of World Records* in 1982. The chair belongs to the long-established Miller's Office Furniture. (*On Noble St. between 6th St. and Rte. 202.*)

THE ROAD TO BIRMINGHAM: 56 MI.
Head west on **I-20** until you hit downtown.

BIRMINGHAM ☎205

A 180 ft. cast-iron statue of Vulcan, the Roman god of the forge, looms over the Birmingham skyline as a reminder of the city's history as an industrial powerhouse in the post-Civil War South. During the struggle for African-American civil rights, leaders like Martin Luther King, Jr., and Fred Shuttlesworth faced some of their toughest fights in what was labeled "Bombingham" after dozens of bombs rocked the city in the early 1960s. Today, industrial relics inhabit Birmingham's downtown, and the Civil Rights Institute and 16th Street Baptist Church are constant reminders of the city's tumultuous past.

VITAL STATS

Population: 1,100,000

Tourist Office: Greater Birmingham Convention and Visitors Center, 220 9th Ave. N. (☎205-458-8000 or 800-458-8085; www.thediversecity.org). Open M-F 8:30am-5pm.

Library and Internet Access: Birmingham Public Library, 2100 Park Pl. (☎205-226-3600), at the corner of Richard Arrington, Jr., Blvd. Open M-Tu 9am-8pm, W-Sa 9am-6pm, Su 2-6pm.

Post Office: 351 24th St. N. (☎202-521-7990). Open M-F 7am-8pm. **Postal Code:** 35203.

✴ ORIENTATION

Downtown Birmingham is organized in a grid, with numbered avenues running east-west and numbered streets running north-south. **Richard Arrington, Jr., Boulevard** is the one exception, running along what should have been called 21st St. Downtown is divided by railroad tracks running east-west through the center of the city—thus avenues and streets are designated "North" or "South" Avenue numbers decrease as they near the railroad tracks (with 1st Ave. N. and S. running alongside them), while street numbers increase from **11th Street** at the western edge of downtown to **26th Street** at the east. **Five Points South,** the center of nightlife, is at the intersection of 20th St. S. and 11th Ave. S., while the University of Alabama-Birmingham is northwest of Five Points South, between Sixth and 10th Ave., along **University Boulevard.** While most of the city is flat as a pancake, the southeastern edge climbs up suddenly into the bluffs, and the streets curl, wind, and become beautiful and confusing.

♜ ACCOMMODATIONS

Cheap hotels and motels dot the greater Birmingham area along the various interstates.

Delux Inn and Suites/Motel Birmingham, 7905 Crestwood Blvd. (☎205-956-4440). Take Exit 132B from I-20 E. Turn right at Montevallo Rd. and left on Crestwood Blvd. Comfortable rooms with patios and pool access. Continental breakfast included. Rooms $50. AmEx/D/MC/V. ❸

Oak Mountain State Park Campground (☎205-620-2527 or 800-252-7275), 15 mi. south of the city, in Pelham. Take Exit 246 off I-65. 10,000 acres of horseback riding, golfing, and hiking, and an 85-acre lake with a beach and fishing. Bathrooms, showers, and laundry. 2-night min. stay required for weekend reservations. Park open daily 7am-sunset. Primitive backcountry sites $3 per person; walk-in tent sites $9.50; RV sites with water and electricity $16, with full hookup $18. MC/V. ❶

🍴 FOOD

Five Points South, an old streetcar suburb at the intersection of 20th St. S. and 11th Ave. S., is the best place to find great restaurants with reasonable prices.

Niki's, 1101 2nd Ave. N. (☎205-251-1972). With 20 meats and 30 vegetable sides to choose from, this classic lunchroom keeps its faithful customers happy. There's also a tempting selection of pies ($3 per slice) and other desserts. Meat and 2-vegetable lunch $6.50-7.50. Open M-F 6am-6pm. AmEx/D/MC/V. ❷

Jim and Nick's Bar-B-Q, 1908 11th Ave. S. (☎205-320-1060), in Five Points South. Jim and Nick's began as a roadside barbecue joint over 50 years ago and has grown into a casual restaurant. The ribs are excellent (half-rack $15.50, full rack $21.50), as are the tasty cheese biscuits. Open M-Th and Su 10:30am-9pm, F-Sa 10:30am-10pm. AmEx/MC/V. ❸

Fish Market Restaurant, 622 22nd St. S. (☎205-322-3330; www.thefishmarket.net). Birmingham's oldest seafood wholesaler doubles as a no-frills joint with cheap catches. Snapper and flounder are very popular, but the frog legs ($10) are especially exciting. Open M-Th 10am-9pm, F-Sa 10am-10pm. AmEx/D/MC/V. ❸

Makarios, 940 20th St. S. (☎205-731-7414), at 10th Ave. S. Generous portions and the best falafel in town. If you're feeling more adventurous, try the quail with lemon-oregano sauce. M-Th and Su 8am-midnight, F-Sa 8am-4am. MC/V. ❷

DEEP SOUTH

◉ SIGHTS

▒BIRMINGHAM CIVIL RIGHTS INSTITUTE.
The fascinating museum looks at events
through the lens of Alabama's segregation
battle. Displays and documentary footage balance imaginative exhibits and disturbing artifacts from the Jim Crow era, like the burnt-out
shell of a torched Greyhound bus and copies
of the Birmingham segregation ordinances.
*(520 16th St. N. ☎ 205-328-9696 or 866-328-9696;
www.bcri.org. Open Tu-Sa 10am-5pm, Su 1-5pm. $10,
college students $4, under 18 free, seniors $5. Su free.)*

BIRMINGHAM CIVIL RIGHTS DISTRICT. Birmingham's commemoration of the civil-rights
struggles of the 1950s and 1960s centers on
the Birmingham Civil Rights District, at Fifth
Ave. N. between 16th and 17th St., nine blocks
dedicated to the battles and bombings that
took place there. **Kelly Ingram Park** was the site
of numerous protests, and statues and sculptures now grace the green lawns. *(Open daily
6am-10pm. Audio tours available at Civil Rights Institute
Tu-Sa 10am-3pm. $5.)*

ALABAMA JAZZ HALL OF FAME. In the heart
of the Fourth Avenue District sits the Alabama
Jazz Hall of Fame in the Carver Theater. Jazz
greats from Erskine Hawkins to Ella Fitzgerald each get a small display on their life work.
*(1631 4th Ave. N. ☎ 205-254-2731; www.jazzhall.
com. Open Tu-Sa 10am-5pm. Guided tours Tu-W and F
10am-2pm, Sa 1-5pm. Admission $2. Tours $3.)*

BIRMINGHAM MUSEUM OF ART. The largest municipal art museum in the South, this
museum contains over 18,000 works and a
sculpture garden. The gallery also houses
the **Hanson Library,** which features the largest
collection of Wedgewood china outside the
UK. *(2000 8th Ave. N. ☎ 205-254-2565. Open Tu-Sa
10am-5pm, Su noon-5pm. Free.)*

ALABAMA SPORTS HALL OF FAME. Alabama's
sports greats, from Willie "The Say Hey Kid"
Mays to speedy Carl Lewis, are immortalized
in the Alabama Sports Hall of Fame. *(2150
Richard Arrington, Jr., Blvd. N., at the corner of 22nd St. N.
☎ 205-323-6665; www.ashof.org. Open M-Sa 9am-5pm.
$5, students $3, under 6 free.)*

**SLOSS FURNACES NATIONAL HISTORIC LAND-
MARK.** Birmingham remembers its days as

the "Pittsburgh of the South" at the Sloss Furnaces National Historic Landmark. The blast
furnaces closed nearly 40 years ago, but they
are the only preserved example of 20th-cen-
tury iron smelting in the world. Visitors can
walk past the massive forges and climb down
into the cavernous tunnels below. Plays and
concerts are held in a renovated furnace shed
by the stacks. *(20 32nd St. N. ☎ 205-324-1911;
www.slossfurnaces.com. Open Tu-Sa 10am-4pm, Su
noon-4pm. Tours Sa-Su 1, 2, 3pm. Free.)*

VULCAN. The largest statue ever made in
the US and the largest cast-iron statue in
the world, the Roman god of the forge was
sculpted by Italian artist Giuseppe Moretti
to represent Alabama at the 1904 St. Louis
World's Fair. A 360° view of the region awaits
at the top, but you can also get a great view
of Birmingham from the base for free. If you
do go up the tower, the first thing you'll see as
you emerge from the elevator is Vulcan's huge
iron butt. Don't worry, the view gets better.
*(Go south on 20th St. S. and follow the signs. 1701 Valley
View Dr. ☎ 205-933-1409; www.visitvulcan.com. Grounds
open daily 7am-10pm. Museum open M-Sa 10am-6pm,
Su 1-6pm. Observation deck open M-Sa 10am-10pm, Su
1-10pm. $6, ages 5-12 $4.)*

OTHER SIGHTS. For a break from the heavy-
duty ironworks, stroll the marvelously
manicured grounds of the **Birmingham Botanical Gardens.** Spectacular floral displays, an
elegant Japanese garden, and an enormous
greenhouse occupy the 67-acre site. You can
arrange a tour if you want expert commentary on the garden's flora. *(2612 Lane Park Rd.,
off US 31. ☎ 205-414-3900. Garden center open daily
8am-5pm. Gardens open sunrise-sunset. Free.)* Prefer
cogs and grease to petals and pollen? The
Mercedes-Benz US International Visitors Center is
a 24,000 sq. ft. museum that spares no technological expense to celebrate the history of all
things Mercedes. *(On Mercedes Dr., at Vance St. Take
Exit 89 off I-20/59. ☎ 205-507-2252 or 888-286-8762.
Open M-F 8:30am-4:30pm. Free.)*

♫ ENTERTAINMENT

Opened in 1927, the **Historic Alabama Theater,**
1817 Third Ave. N., is booked 300 nights of
the year with films, concerts, and live performances. Their organ, the "Mighty Wurlitzer,"
entertains the audience before each show.
(☎ 205-251-0418. Box office open M-F

9am-4pm. Order tickets at the box office 1hr. prior to show. Shows generally M-Sa 7pm, Su 2pm. Organ plays 15min. before showtime.)

NIGHTLIFE

Nightlife centers on Five Points South, at 20th St. S. and 11th Ave. S.

The Garage, 2304 10th Terr. S. (☎205-322-3220). A cool bar tucked out of sight down 23rd St. A former architecture studio turned antique store, the Garage still has all of the original materials—customers just drink among the statues and artwork. Try a Jubel German beer in the courtyard or munch on a simple sandwich among the nymphs and Greek art. Open M 3pm-late, Tu-Sa 11am-late.

The Nick, 2514 10th Ave. S. (☎205-252-3831), at the corner of 26th St. Don't be fooled by the grungy exterior; inside, a wide range of musical acts earn The Nick a top spot in the Birmingham club scene. Nightly live rock. 21+. Cover $5-15. Open M-F 3pm-last customer, Sa-Su 8pm-6am.

THE ROAD TO CHATTANOOGA: 147 MI.

Follow **I-59 North** to **I-24 East,** just south of Chattanooga. Take **Exit 178** onto **US 27 North. Exit 1A** leads into downtown.

The Volunteer State

TENNESSEE

Welcomes You!

CHATTANOOGA ☎423

Chattanooga, once famous for being home to the legendary "Chattanooga Choo-Choo," has recently made great strides toward modernization. Although its history as a transportation hub still flavors the city, Chattanooga is now a bustling family destination, complete with a recently developed "21st Century Waterfront." Chattanooga's plot on the shores of the Tennessee River is now adorned with fountains, greenery, and cultural attractions that complement the city's old charm.

ORIENTATION

Chattanooga straddles the Tennessee-Georgia border at the junction of **I-24, I-59,** and **I-75.**

Downtown, Lookout Mountain, and the Bluff View Art District are the city's most popular areas.

VITAL STATS
Population: 496,000
Tourist Office: Visitors Center, 2 Broad St. (☎800-322-3344; www.chattanoogafun.com), next to the aquarium. Open daily 8:30am-5:30pm.
Library and Internet Access: Chattanooga Public Library, 1001 Broad St. (☎423-757-5310), at 10th St. Open M-Th 9am-9pm, F-Sa 9am-6pm, Su 2-6pm.
Post Office: 900 Georgia Ave. (☎423-267-1609), between Martin Luther King Blvd. and 10th St. Open M-F 8am-4:30pm. **Postal Code:** 37402.

ACCOMMODATIONS

Chain hotels thrive east of the city on I-24/75.

King's Lodge, 2400 West Side Dr. (☎423-698-8944 or 800-251-7702), Exit 181A off I-24 E. or Exit 181 off I-24 W. Inexpensive, clean rooms and a nice view of the city. A/C, cable TV, HBO, and Wi-Fi. Rooms $35-45. AmEx/D/MC/V. ❷

Best Holiday Trav-L-Park, 1709 Mack Smith Rd. (☎706-891-9766 or 800-693-2877; www.chattacamp.com). From Chattanooga, take I-24 E. to I-75 S. and turn off at Exit 1. Turn right at the top of the ramp, then left at the 2nd light. Occupies a Civil War battlefield. Bathrooms, a pool, showers, laundry, and Wi-Fi. Tent sites $25, with water and electricity $29; RV sites with full hookup $33; cabins $40; cottages $89-99. ❶

FOOD

Tony's Pasta Shop and Trattoria, 212 High St. (☎423-265-5033), in Bluff View District. Fresh sauces on enormous bowls of homemade pastas are a steal at $9. Deck overlooks the river. Open M-Th and Su 11am-10pm, F-Sa 11am-11pm. ❷

Rembrandt's Coffee House, 204 High St. (☎423-265-5033). Offers gourmet sandwiches and salads ($5-6.50) at great prices. The lovely brick patio is the perfect spot to relax and sample incredible pastries (under $4) or sip coffee. Open M-Th 7am-10pm, F 7am-11:30pm, Sa 8am-11:30pm, Su 8am-10pm. AmEx/MC/V. ❶

Back Inn Cafe, 412 E. 2nd St. (☎423-265-5033). Though pricier than nearby establishments, has

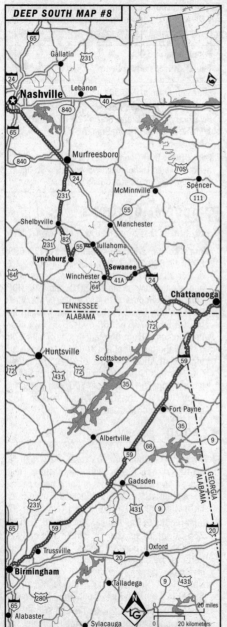

DEEP SOUTH MAP #8

Gallatin

Nashville Lebanon

Murfreesboro

McMinnville Spencer

Shelbyville Manchester

Tullahoma

Lynchburg Sewanee

Winchester

Chattanooga

TENNESSEE
ALABAMA

Huntsville Scottsboro

Fort Payne

Albertville

Gadsden

GEORGIA
ALABAMA

Trussville Oxford

Birmingham Talladega

Alabaster Sylacauga

20 miles

20 kilometers

a prime location over Bluff View. Sunset on Bluff View makes this a worthwhile splurge. Serves upscale Southern favorites like shrimp and grits ($16) and salmon with fried green tomatoes ($11). Open M-Th 7am-10pm, F 7am-11pm, Sa 8am-11pm, Su 8am-10pm. AmEx/D/MC/V. ❹

Sticky Fingers Rib House, 420 Broad St. (☎423-265-7427), in downtown. Famous for finger-lickin' ribs that come with a choice of 5 sauces of varying strengths. Half-rack $14; full rack $19. Open M-Th and Su 11am-10pm, F-Sa 11am-11pm. AmEx/D/MC/V. ❸

👁 SIGHTS

▓TENNESSEE AQUARIUM. The aquarium is home to the world's largest freshwater tank as well as exhibits like the River Gorge Explorer, which takes visitors on a 90min. tour of the 26 mi. Tennessee River Gorge and its native wildlife. The aquarium entertains visitors with an IMAX screen, mesmerizing seahorses, and some hideously ugly fish. (*1 Broad St., on Ross's Landing.* ☎ *800-262-0695; www.tennis.org. Open daily 10am-6pm. $20, ages 3-12 $13; IMAX $8.50/6; aquarium/IMAX combo pass $26/18.*)

▓HUNTER MUSEUM OF AMERICAN ART. The museum integrates three different buildings: a Neoclassical brick building from 1905, a Modernist east wing constructed of concrete, and a slick contemporary addition built in 2005. Galleries overlooking the river showcase three centuries of American art. (*10 Bluff View Ave. From downtown, take 4th St. to High St. and turn left.* ☎ *423-267-0968; www.huntermuseum.org. Open M-Tu and F-Sa 10am-5pm, W and Su noon-5pm, Th 10am-8pm. $8, ages 3-17 $4, under 3 free.*)

▓BATTLE OF CHATTANOOGA NATIONAL MILITARY PARK. Stunning panoramic views of Chattanooga and the Tennessee River dominate the park. The park's centerpiece, the New York Peace Monument, symbolizes the reconciliation between North and South. The exhibitions at the visitors center are free and include James Walker's 13 ft. by 40 ft. painting, *Battle of Lookout Mountain.* Craven's House, built in 1856, served as the headquarters for Confederate Brigadier General Edward C. Whitehall while Confederate troops occupied Lookout Mountain. The site has great views and is the trailhead for a number of short hikes. *(On Lookout Mountain, follow signs to Point Park.* ☎ *706-866-9241. Visitors center open in summer M-Th 9am-6pm, F-Sa 9am-8pm; winter hours vary, so call ahead. $3, under 16 free.)*

INTERNATIONAL TOWING AND RECOVERY HALL OF FAME AND MUSEUM. The museum chronicles the creation and life of the tow truck. Even if you're not interested in trucks, this museum is worth seeing as a testament to American ingenuity. *(3315 S. Broad St. ☎ 423-267-3132; www.internationaltowingmuseum.org. Open M-Sa 9am-5pm, Su 11am-5pm. $8, ages 6-18 and over 54 $7, under 6 free.)*

HOUSTON MUSEUM. The museum is the life work of Anna Houston, an eccentric who was married at least nine times and kept her collection of antiques strung up to the roof of a barn she built herself. Her belongings, including music boxes and an amazing glass collection, were left to a committee that started a museum on the river banks. Houston had a particular penchant for pitchers and whimsical toiletries. To see the exhibits, visitors must join a 45min. tour. *(201 High St. ☎ 423-267-7176; www.thehoustonmuseum.com. Open M-F 9:30am-4pm, Sa 11am-5pm. $9, ages 4-17 $3.50, under 4 free.)*

CHICKAMAUGA NATIONAL MILITARY PARK. Established by veterans in 1890, the park features monuments and plaques describing the battle fought here over two days during September 1863. Confederate forces successfully drove Federal troops out of northern Georgia, resulting in 34,000 casualties. ▨Retreating Union soldiers returned to Chattanooga, settling in for a two-month siege. The beautiful 8000-acre park has 60 mi. of hiking trails through rolling hills and open pastures. *(Take Exit 180 off I-24 and follow US 27 through Fort Oglethorpe to the park. ☎ 706-866-9241. Visitors center open daily June-Aug. 8:30am-6pm; Sept.-May 8:30am-5:30pm. Free.)*

INCLINE RAILWAY. Billed as "America's most amazing mile," the Incline Railway is the world's steepest passenger railway, chugging visitors up an insane 72.7% grade to an observation deck. The deck is accessible by car, allowing you to take in the incredible views for free. The railway, built in 1895, runs up Lookout Mountain. *(827 E. Brow Rd. Take S. Broad St. and follow the signs. ☎ 423-821-4224; www.ridethein-*

cline.com. Open June-Aug. daily 8:30am-9:30pm, last train 9pm; Sept.-May M-F 9am-6pm, Sa-Su 9am-7pm. $11, round-trip $14; ages 3-12 $6/7.)

ROCK CITY GARDENS. Rock City's nature trail combines scenic lookouts and narrow rock passages with singing and dancing elves and strategically placed shops. Barn roofs painted with "See Rock City" appear in 19 states. *(☎ 706-820-2531 or 800-854-0675; www.seerockcity.com. Open daily 8:30am-9pm. Last entry 8pm. $16, ages 3-12 $9.)*

♫ ENTERTAINMENT

The **Chattanooga Lookouts,** a minor-league baseball team for the Reds, play at **AT&T Field,** 201 Power Alley. *(☎ 267-2208; www.lookouts.com. Tickets $4-8, under 12 $2.)* For nine nights in June, the riverfront shuts down for live rock, country, blues, jazz, and reggae during the **Riverbend Festival.** *(☎ 423-756-2211; www.riverbendfestival.com. Tickets $35, in advance $26.)* The mountains surrounding Chattanooga offer opportunities for whitewater rafting; ask for info at the visitors center.

☕ NIGHTLIFE

For entertainment listings, check the "Weekend" section of the Friday *Chattanooga Times Free Press* or *The Pulse* and *Enigma,* two weekly alternative papers. Most nightlife options are downtown, especially in the area surrounding Jack's Alley, from Broad St. to Market St., between Fourth and Fifth St.

Taco Mac's, 423 Market St. *(☎ 423-267-8226; www.tacomac.com).* Over 40 beers on tap and over 200 bottled. Outdoor seating available. Beer from $3. Happy hour M-F 4-7pm with $2 drafts. Open M-Sa 11am-3am.

Big River Grille and Brewing Works, 222 Broad St. *(☎ 423-267-2739; www.bigrivergrille.com).* Offers 6 original beers, plus seasonal ales and lagers. Pints $4. Pool tables. Happy hour M-F 4-7pm. Open M-Th 11am-1am, F-Sa 11am-2am, Su 11am-midnight. Kitchen open M-Th until 11pm, F-Sa midnight, Su 10pm.

Rhythm and Brews, 221 Market St. *(☎ 423-267-4644; www.rhythm-brews.com).* Has hot bands most nights. 21+. Cover $5-20. Open W-Sa 8pm-late; music starts around 9:45pm.

⚑ **THE ROAD TO SEWANEE: 52 MI.**

Take **I-24** through the beautiful Tennessee River Valley to **Exit 134** for **US 41A**. In Sewanee, turn left on **University Avenue.** Travelers with time to spare should consider picking up US 41 at Exit 174 for spectacular views of the river.

SEWANEE ☎931

Nestled on top of the Cumberland Plateau, Sewanee is home to the 1400 undergraduates that attend the **University of the South.** The private liberal-arts college, owned by several southern dioceses of the Episcopal Church, dominates the town, endowing it with both traditional Southern grace and a hip, liberal vibe. The university gives tours starting at 735 University Ave. (☎931-598-1000. Tours M-F 9-11am and 2-4pm, Sa 10:30am-12:30pm. Free.) Construction began on **All Saints Chapel** in 1904, although it wasn't completed until 1957. The chapel has stained-glass windows depicting important events in Sewanee's history and a 56-bell carillon, which includes a massive 23-ton bell.

Budget motels can be found 6 mi. away in Monteagle, off I-24. Dining options reflect the presence of students. Don't miss ▨**Stirling's ❶**, 241 Georgia Ave., the kind of coffeehouse that makes you want to settle in and while away a few hours. Located in an old house with a wraparound porch, the cafe has rocking chairs for warm weather as well as computers and free Wi-Fi. If you're not in the mood for coffee, try one of the specialty drinks like the strawberry-shortcake cream soda ($2.75) or the iced Sewanee grasshopper for $3.50. (☎931-598-1885. Sandwiches $4-6; salads $4.50-6.25. Open 8am-11pm daily. D/MC/V.) Locals drive hours to splurge on dinner at **Pearl's Foggy Mountain Cafe ❺**, 15344 Sewanee Hwy. The menu changes daily to feature local ingredients and creative Southern gourmet cooking in a cozy dining room tucked back in the woods. (☎931-598-9568; www.pearlscafe. com. Open M-Sa from 5pm, Su 11am-2pm and from 5pm. MC/V.) The rustic wood tables at **Shenanigans ❶**, 12595 Sollace M. Freeman Hwy., are often crowded with students munching on made-to-order deli sandwiches ($4-5) and drinking beer. The building, constructed in 1872, leans alarmingly to the right.

(☎931-598-5774. 21+ after 9pm. Open M-Sa 11:30am-11pm, Su 11:30am-9pm.)

⚑ **THE ROAD TO LYNCHBURG: 39 MI.**

Follow **US 41A** for 26 mi. to Tullahoma. Turn right on **Route 55** and continue for 12 mi. into Lynchburg.

LYNCHBURG ☎931

Contrary to the label on bottles of Jack Daniel's Tennessee Whiskey, Lynchburg no longer has a population of 361, but the hamlet does retain a rural charm. Lynchburg's main claim to fame comes from **Jack Daniel's Distillery**, 182 Lynchburg Hwy. You can pick up souvenir glassware in town, but you'll have to cross the county line to buy a nip of Old No. 7, since Moore County is dry. Jack Daniel's, the oldest registered distillery in the US, was established in 1866, and the entire world supply of Jack is still made on site. Free tours last about an hour and take visitors through the different stages of the whiskey-making process. (☎931-759-6180; www.jackdaniels. com. Tours daily 9am-4:30pm. Free.) The ▨**Moore County Jail Museum**, 231 Main St., is a mini-Alcatraz, without the tourists. Artifacts on display include a 19th-century icebox, a hand-cranked phonograph, a 1907 vacuum cleaner, and equipment from the Lynchburg radio station in the 1950s. The cellblocks, in use from 1893 until 1990, are strikingly primitive. The sheriff's quarters on the other side of the building now house a loom, quilts, and a room filled with clothes from the turn of the century, including a complete wedding outfit. (☎931-438-8480; www.lynchburg.com/oldjail. Open from Mar. to mid-Dec. Tu-Sa 11am-3pm. Suggested donation $1, under 16 free.)

Once a boarding house, **Miss Mary Bobo's ❹**, 295 Main St., now serves family-style dinner (the noon meal) to hungry guests. The hostess, Jack's great-grandniece, stimulates conversation, shares local lore, and ensures that dishes are passed to the left. Miss Mary Bobo herself holds the record for being the oldest woman to appear in *Playboy*, shortly before her 102nd birthday–in a Jack Daniel's ad, of course. The menu ($19) changes but always includes fried chicken and ▨**fried okra**. (☎931-759-7394. Dinner M-F 1pm; 11am by demand;

Sa 11am, 1pm; 3pm by demand. Reservations required.)

THE ROAD TO NASHVILLE: 73 MI.

Return east on **Route 55** for 2 mi. before turning left onto **Route 82.** Follow Rte. 82 north to **US 231** in Shelbyville. In Murfreesboro, rejoin **I-24 North** and take it to downtown Nashville.

NASHVILLE ☎615

Nashville is often called "nouveau Dixie," with much of its wealth invested in gaudy, glitzy entertainment. Known as "the Athens of the South," the city is home to Greek—or rather, imitation-Greek—architecture. The area has also been called the "buckle of the Bible belt," a reference to its Southern Baptists. But Nashville's most popular moniker by far is "Music City, USA," and for good reason: this town has long been the banjo-pickin', foot-stompin' capital of the country's best music: country music. Whether you're seeking a pew, a preacher, or a choir of friends in low places, you're sure to have a rollicking good time—here, music (and beer) flows around the clock.

VITAL STATS

Population: 545,530

Tourist Office: Nashville Visitor Information Center, 501 Broadway (☎615-259-4747; www.nashvillecvb. com), in the Gaylord Entertainment Center, at Exit 209A off I-65 N./I-40 W. Open M-Sa 8am-5:30pm, Su 10am-5pm.

Library and Internet Access: Nashville Public Library, 615 Church St. (☎615-862-5800), between 6th and 7th Ave. Open M-Th 9am-8pm, F 9am-6pm, Sa 9am-5pm, Su 2-5pm.

Post Office: 901 Broadway (☎615-256-3088), in the same building as the Frist Center for the Visual Arts. Open M-F 8:30am-5pm. **Postal Code:** 37203.

ORIENTATION

Nashville's roads are fickle and are often interrupted by curving parkways and one-way streets. Names change without warning. **Broadway,** the main east-west thoroughfare, runs through downtown, then veers left after passing over I-40; **West End Avenue** continues

straight ahead. Broadway joins **21st Avenue** after a few blocks, passing through Vanderbilt University. In the downtown area, numbered avenues run north-south, parallel to the **Cumberland River** and divided by Broadway into north and south. The curve of **James Robertson Parkway** encloses the north end, becoming **Main Street** on the other side of the river (later Gallatin Pike) and turning into **Eighth Avenue** in the center of downtown. In the evening, parking spots become prized possessions and commercial parking costs up to $10.

ACCOMMODATIONS

Rooms in downtown Nashville can be expensive, especially in summer. The visitors center offers several deals on motel rooms, and budget motels are plentiful around **West Trinity Lane** and **Brick Church Pike,** off I-65 at Exit 87.

Music City Hostel, 1809 Patterson St. (☎615-692-1277; www.musiccityhostel.com), near Vanderbilt and Midtown. With its helpful staff, friendly mix of international travelers, and laid-back, here-for-the-party atmosphere, you couldn't ask for a better hostel experience. Full kitchen. Free Wi-Fi. Free parking. Dorms $25; private rooms $70. MC/V. ❶

Drake Inn, 420 Murfreesboro Rd. (☎615-256-7770). Close to downtown with small, clean rooms, one of which was the setting for the movie *A Thing Called Love.* Most rooms feature funky, country-music-influenced wall paintings. Pool, laundry, and free Wi-Fi. Singles $54; doubles $58. AmEx/D/MC/V. ❸

Cumberland Inn, 150 W. Trinity Ln. (☎615-226-1600). From downtown on I-65 N., take Exit 87 and turn right at the bottom of the ramp even though it says E. Trinity Ln. The inn is on the right. The rates are among Nashville's lowest and get you A/C, HBO, and laundry. Rooms $40. AmEx/D/MC/V. ❷

FOOD

The famous Nashville candy GooGoo clusters (peanuts, pecans, chocolate, caramel, and marshmallow) are sold in specialty shops throughout the city. Get that sexy stain on your white T-shirt with Nashville's other finger-lickin' traditions, barbecue and fried chicken. Restaurants catering to collegiate tastes and budgets cram 21st Ave., West End Ave., and Elliston Pl., near Vanderbilt.

Arnold's, 605 8th Ave. S. (☎615-256-4455; www. hollyeats.com). Cut a path across the blue skies to this cafeteria-style restaurant. The best meat-and-3 special ($7) for miles around. The roast beef *au jus* is delicious, and the pies are freshly made ($2). Open M-F 10:30am-2:45pm. ❷

Fido, 1812 21st St. (☎615-777-3436), in Hillsboro Village. Looks like a simple coffee shop but serves delicious sandwiches, salads, and entrees. If your previous night included 10 rounds with Jose Cuervo, try the hangover bomb, a bagel sandwich with cream cheese and bacon ($5). M-Th 7am-11pm, F 7am-midnight, Sa 8am-midnight, Su 8am-11pm. ❷

Loveless Cafe, 8400 Rte. 100 (☎615-646-9700; www.lovelesscafe.com), at the end of the Nat-chez Trace Pkwy. Follow West End Ave. to where it becomes Harding Pike/Rte. 100. A Nashville tradition since 1951. The fried chicken, country breakfasts, and delicious made-from-scratch bis-cuits are as good as ever. Breakfast served all day. Open daily 7am-9pm. AmEx/D/MC/V. ❸

Pancake Pantry, 1796 21st Ave. (☎615-383-9333). Serves stacks of delicious, fluffy pancakes, from traditional buttermilk to orange-walnut or apricot-lemon ($7.50). Don't be scared off if there's a line out the door—it always moves fast. Open M-F 6am-3pm, Sa-Su 6am-4pm. MC/V. ❶

Jack's Bar-B-Que, 416A Broadway (☎615-254-5715; www.jacksbarbque.com). A legend for both the flashing neon-winged pigs above the door and succulent, tender pork. Sandwiches $4.50. Plates $8-13. Open M-W 10:30am-8pm, Th 10:30am-9pm, F-Sa 10:30am-10pm, Su noon-7pm. AmEx/MC/V. ❷

SATCO (San Antonio Taco Company), 416 21st Ave. S. (☎615-327-4322), near Vanderbilt. Not gourmet, but crazy cheap. The outdoor patio is full of Vanderbilt students every evening. Fajitas $1.50-2. Steaming, greasy plates of enchilada $6. 6 beers for the price of 5 $13-16. Open daily 11am-last customer. AmEx/D/MC/V. ❶

Nashville, 1918 Broadway (☎615-329-6674; www.noshville.com). A New York-style deli with a menu that would please even the most die-hard Manhattanite. Noshville's selection ranges from matzah ball soup ($5-6) to pastrami on rye ($10) and smoked whitefish on a bagel ($11). Open M 6:30am-2:30pm, Tu-Th 6:30am-8:30pm, F 6:30am-9:30pm, Sa 7:30am-9:30pm, Su 7:30am-8:30pm. AmEx/D/MC/V. ❸

SIGHTS

COUNTRY MUSIC HALL OF FAME. Country music drives this city. The first stop for any traveler—country fan or not—should be the state-of-the-art Country Music Hall of Fame, where visitors can wander through well-crafted displays on the history of country,

---

"YOU ARE SO NASHVILLE IF..."

Nashville's status as the glitzy capital of country music has resulted in some awkward cultural contradictions. For the past 18 years, Nashville's *Scene* magazine has lampooned the city's image-consciousness with its annual "You are so Nashville if..." contest. In the same vein as Jeff Foxworthy's "You might be a redneck if..." jokes, the contest has poked fun at Nashville's quirky fusion of New South money and Old South tradition. The inaugural winner of the contest referred to Nashville's status as the Athens of the South with, "You are so Nashville if you think our Parthenon is better because the other one fell apart." The 1993 winner mocked Nashville's mega-churches with, "You are so Nashville if your church congregation is referred to as 'the studio audience.'" The 2006 contest prompted such entries as "you'd rather keep your quarterback and trade your senator" and "the wire holding your bumper to your car is a low E string." The 2006 winner reacted to the cultural impact of the film *Brokeback Mountain* with, "You are so Nashville if you were a gay cowboy before being a gay cowboy was cool." Perhaps the best entry of the contest's history is the 1996 winner, which sums up the Music City's perplexing but enduring appeal: "You are so Nashville if you never meant

Downtown Nashville

🏠 ACCOMMODATIONS
Cumberland Inn, **1**
Drake Inn, **9**
Music City Hostel, **5**

🍴 FOOD
Arnold's, **16**
Fido's, **15**
Jack's Bar-B-Que, **4**
Loveless Cafe, **7**
Noshville, **10**
Pancake Pantry, **12**
SATCO, **11**

🍺 NIGHTLIFE
Belcourt Theater, **13**
Big River Grille and
  Brewing Works, **3**
Bluebird Cafe, **14**
Cafe Coco, **6**
Station Inn, **8**
Wildhorse Saloon, **2**

listen to samples from greats like Johnny Cash and Patsy Cline, and watch videos of performances and interviews with modern artists. Paying $13 extra will upgrade tickets to include a guided tour of RCA's Studio B, where over 1000 Top 10 hits have been recorded. A Grayline shuttle runs between the two venues. (222 5th Ave. S. ☎615-416-2001; www.countrymusichalloffame.com. Open daily 9am-5pm. $18, students $16.15, ages 6-17 $10, under 6 free.)

RYMAN AUDITORIUM. Two-step over to the Ryman Auditorium, where the legendary Grand Ole Opry radio show was recorded for more than 30 years. Originally built to be the Union Gospel Tabernacle by a Nashville saloon owner, the Ryman began hosting the

Opry in 1943. The Opry eventually moved to a bigger studio to accommodate the growing crowd of fans, but the Ryman continues to host fantastic shows. View a short video outlining the history of the building, peruse display cases of costumes and photos, and even climb on stage. *(116 5th Ave. N. ☎615-889-3060; www.ryman.com. Open daily 9am-4pm. $12.50, ages 4-11 $6.25. Backstage tour $3.75.)*

GRAND OLE OPRY HOUSE. The nation's premier country venue is the Grand Ole Opry House. Visitors can enjoy musical performances, tour the backstage areas, or visit the free museum detailing the Opry's history. Upcoming shows are listed in *The Tennessean* and online. *(2804 Opryland Dr. Exit 11 off Hwy. 155, accessible from both I-40 and I-65. ☎615-871-6779, tickets 800-871-6779; www.opry.com. Museum open M and W-Th 10am-6pm, Tu 10am-7:30pm, F 10am-8:30pm, Sa 10am-10pm, Su noon-5pm. Tours a few times per day except concert days. Shows F 8pm, Sa 7, 9:30pm, sometimes Tu 7pm. Admission free. Tours $13.50, ages 4-11 $6.75. Tickets $34-51, ages 4-11 $24-51.)*

PARTHENON. Across West End Ave. from Vanderbilt, the pleasant **Centennial Park** stretches between 25th and 28th Ave. A visit to the park will reveal why Nashville is known as the "Athens of the South": a full-scale replica of the Parthenon sits on top of a low hill. Built as a temporary exhibit for the Tennessee Centennial in 1897, the Parthenon was so popular that it was maintained and finally rebuilt with permanent materials in the 1920s. As out of place as the structure may be, it is nonetheless impressive—especially the 42 ft. golden statue of Athena inside. In its first-floor gallery, the building contains the James Cowan Collection of American Art, a selection of 19th- and early-20th-century American art. *(☎615-862-8431; www.parthenon.org. Open June-Aug. Tu-Sa 9am-4:30pm, Su 12:30-4:30pm; Sept.-May Tu-Sa 9am-4:30pm. $5, ages 4-17 $2.50.)*

FRIST CENTER FOR THE VISUAL ARTS. Right in the heart of downtown, the Frist Center inspires both young and old with an interesting array of world-class rotating exhibits. Some of the most popular exhibitions require additional entrance fees of $5-10. *(919 Broadway. ☎615-244-3340; www.fristcenter.org. Open M-W*

and Sa 10am-5:30pm, Th-F 10am-9pm, Su 1-5:30pm. $8.50, college students with ID $6.50, under 19 free.)*

CAPITOL. At the Capitol, a stately Greek Revival building on Charlotte Ave. north of downtown, visitors can tour the Governor's Reception Room, the legislative chambers, the former Tennessee Supreme Court, and the grounds, which include the tomb of President James K. Polk. *(On Charlotte Ave., between 6th and 7th Ave. ☎615-741-0830. Open M-F 8am-4pm. Guided tours M-F 9, 10, 11am, 1, 2, 3pm. Free.)*

TENNESSEE STATE MUSEUM. Housed in the Tennessee Performing Arts Center, this museum has three floors of exhibits on state history from prehistoric times through the present. *(At 5th Ave. and Deaderick St. ☎615-741-2692 or 800-407-4324; www.tnmuseum.org. Open Tu-Sa 10am-5pm, Su 1-5pm. Free.)*

HATCH SHOW PRINT. A letterpress poster printing shop that first opened in 1879, Hatch Show Print has a collection of posters of Nashville country stars, vaudeville acts, and sporting events. The colorful posters were the leading advertising medium of their day. Go wild and decorate your car Nashville-style. *(316 Broadway. ☎615-256-2805; www.hatchshowprint.com. Open M-F 9am-5pm, Sa 10am-5pm. Free.)*

CHEEKWOOD MUSEUM. For a break from the bustle of downtown, head to the Cheekwood Botanical Garden and Museum of Art. The well-kept gardens, complete with a woodland sculpture trail, are just the place for a rendezvous on a night like this. The museum features American and contemporary sculpture and paintings and a collection of English and American decorative arts. *(1200 Forrest Park Dr., off Page Rd. ☎615-356-8000; www.cheekwood.org. Open Tu-Sa 9:30am-4:30pm, Su 11am-4:30pm. $10, students and ages 6-17 $5.)*

BELLE MEADE PLANTATION. The Belle Meade Plantation was once one of the nation's most famed thoroughbred nurseries. The lavish 1853 mansion has hosted seven US presidents, including the 380 lb. William Howard Taft, who allegedly spent some time lodged in the mansion's bathtub. Visitors can explore the charming house and grounds, including a collection of antique carriages. *(5025 Harding Rd. ☎615-356-0501 or 800-270-3991; www.*

DEEP SOUTH

bellemeadeplantation.com. Open M-Sa 9am-5pm, Su 11am-5pm. $15, ages 6-18 $7.)

HERMITAGE. The graceful manor of US president Andrew Jackson, the Hermitage holds an impressive array of its original furnishings. Admission includes a 15min. film about Jackson's life, access to the house and grounds, including the garden where Jackson is buried, and a visit to the nearby Tulip Grove Mansion and Hermitage Church. *(4580 Rachels Ln. From Exit 221 off I-40 E., continue 4 mi. on Old Hickory Blvd.; entrance is on the right. ☎615-889-2941; www.the-hermitage.com. Ticket office open daily from Apr. to mid-Oct. 8:30am-5pm; from mid-Oct. to Mar. 9am-4:30pm. $15, ages 13-18 $11, ages 6-12 $7.)*

🎵 ENTERTAINMENT

The hordes of visitors that swoop down on Nashville have turned the Grand Ole Opry (opposite page) into a grand ole American institution. However, there are other great forms of entertainment in the capital city as well. The **Tennessee Performing Arts Center,** 505 Deaderick St., at Sixth Ave. N., hosts opera, ballet, Broadway shows, and other theater productions. (☎615-255-2787; www.tpac.org. Tickets $15-75.) The **Nashville Symphony** makes its home at the recently opened **Schermerhorn Symphony Center,** a world-class acoustic environment partially modeled on Amsterdam's Concertgebouw. The **Dancin' in the District Music Festival** runs from mid-June to mid-September in Riverfront Park and features three live bands every Thursday evening. Past performers include Better Than Ezra, Cake, and Blondie. (☎800-594-8499. Tickets $5-8. Gates open at 5:30pm.) Listings for the area's music and events fill the free *Nashville Scene* and *Rage,* available at most establishments.

Although Tennesse is college football country, two professional franchises dominate the Nashville sports scene. The NFL's **Tennessee Titans** play at **LP Field,** 460 Great Circle Rd., across the river from downtown. (☎615-565-4200; www.titansonline.com. Tickets $12-52.) The NHL's **Nashville Predators** hold there own at the Gaylord Entertainment Center, 501 Broadway. (☎615-770-2040; www.nashvillepredators.com. Open M-F 10am-5:30pm. Tickets $10-85.)

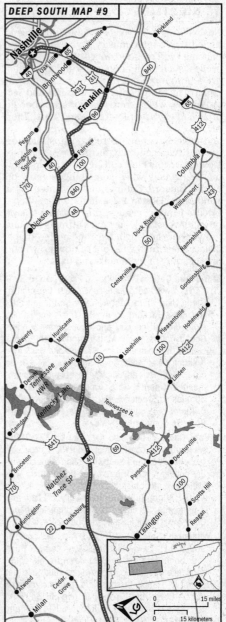

DEEP SOUTH MAP #9

DEEP SOUTH

NIGHTLIFE

Nashville has a vivacious nightlife scene fueled by country music; if you're into line dancing, you're good to go. Other, smaller scenes, such as hip-hop spots and gay clubs, are a little more out of the way. Downtown, country nightlife centers on **Broadway** and **Second Avenue,** where tourists boot-scoot boogie in Broadway's honky-tonks and bars. Bars on Broadway rarely have a cover charge, and musicians tend to rely on tips; bars on Second Ave. generally have a cover charge. Downtown parking can be difficult in summer, especially when something is going on at the Gaylord Entertainment Center. Near Vanderbilt, **Elliston Place** hops with college-oriented music venues, and **Hillsboro Village,** on 21st Ave. at Belcourt Ave., attracts a young crowd to its late-night bars and coffee shops. **Church Street** runs west out of downtown and has a variety of nightclubs and bars.

Bluebird Cafe, 4104 Hillsboro Pkwy. (☎615-383-1461; www.bluebirdcafe.com), near the mall at Green Hills. From 21st Ave., it's on the left after you cross Richard Jones Rd. This famous bird sings original country and acoustic every night. Country stars Kathy Mattea and Garth Brooks started their careers here. $7 food and drink min. if sitting at a table. Cover for shows $4-10; no cover Su or for early shows. Reservations recommended. Open M-Sa 5:30pm-last customer, Su 6pm-last customer. Early show M-Th 6pm, F-Su 6:30pm. Late show M and F-Sa 9:30pm, Tu-Th 9pm, Su 8pm. AmEx/D/MC/V.

Cafe Coco, 210 Louise Ave. (☎615-321-2626; www.cafecoco.com), off Elliston Pl. A cozy coffeehouse, bar, and sandwich shop popular with the college set. The patio and bar heat up with live music most nights starting around 7pm. Jazz 4:30-7:30pm Su. Happy hour daily 7-11am and 3-6pm with $1 coffee and $2 domestic beers. Occasional cover F-Sa $3-5. Open 24hr. MC/V.

Wildhorse Saloon, 120 2nd Ave. N. (☎615-902-8211; www.wildhorsesaloon.com). Bring your boots and 2-step until dawn in this country dance hall. It's loud and brash, but ain't that country? Dance lessons and live music most nights. Cover after 7pm M-Th and Su $4, F-Sa $6. Open M 5pm-1am, Tu-Th and Su 11am-1am, F-Sa 11am-2:30am. AmEx/D/MC/V.

Belcourt Theater, 2102 Belcourt Ave. (☎615-383-9140; www.belcourt.org), at 21st St., in Hillsboro Village. Once a silent movie theater, the Belcourt now hosts concerts, plays, foreign, independent, and classic films, and other events. Go early and enjoy a glass of wine ($6) at the bar. Films $8.50, students and over 64 $6.25, under 12 $5.75; matinees $6.25/5.75/5.75. Call or check online for showtimes. AmEx/D/MC/V.

Big River Grille and Brewing Works, 111 Broadway (☎615-251-4677; www.bigrivergrille.com). A microbrewery in the heart of downtown with plenty of wide-open spaces. The rotating choice of specialty beers ($4) and selection of salads will come as a relief to those in need of a fried-free night. Don't worry—you can still get ribs ($21). Open M-Th and Su 11am-midnight, F-Sa 11am-1am. Kitchen open M-Th and Su until 11pm, F-Sa until midnight. D/MC/V.

Station Inn, 402 12th Ave. S. (☎615-255-3307; www.stationinn.com), at Pine St. Live bluegrass nightly. The genre's very best perform at this unpretenious venue regularly. Open daily from 7pm; shows begin 9pm. AmEx/D/MC/V.

THE ROAD TO FRANKLIN: 22 MI.

Take **I-65 South** to **Exit 65.** Follow **Route 96 (Murfreesboro Road)** into Franklin.

FRANKLIN ☎615

A southern suburb of Nashville, Franklin has a small downtown that's absurdly adorable. **Franklin on Foot** arranges themed walking tours of the historic downtown, and the 90min. **Ghosts and Gore Tour** every night at 8pm exposes Franklin's darker past. It features the sites of hangings, lynchings, "activities of the night," and even some allegedly haunted buildings. (☎615-400-3808; www.franklinonfoot.com. $15.) The **Carter House,** 1140 Columbia Ave., provides an in-depth account of the 1864 Civil War battle in Franklin, including a small diorama and a guided tour of a house that was at the center of the fighting. (☎615-791-1861; www.carter-house.org. Open M-Sa 9am-5pm, Su 1-5pm. $10, ages 7-14 $6.) Franklin's Neo-classical plantation house, **Carnton Plantation,** 1345 Carnton Ln., is a majestic mansion with period furnishings. The house also served as a battlefield hospital during the Civil War, and visitors can see the Confederate cemetery on the grounds for free. (☎615-794-0903; www.carnton.org. Open M-Sa 9am-5pm, Su 1-5pm. 1hr. tours $12, ages 6-12 $5. Grounds only $5.) In downtown Franklin, **Merridee's Breadbasket** ❶, 110 Fourth Ave. S., is a cozy bakery with delicious homemade breakfasts as well as a full menu of sandwiches. (☎615-790-3755; www.merridees.com. Lunch entrees $3-6. Open M-Sa 7am-5pm. MC/V.)

⚑ THE ROAD TO MEMPHIS: 80 MI.
From Jackson, follow **I-40 West** to Memphis.

MEMPHIS ☎901

Music is the pulse of Memphis and the reason why most visitors come to the city. Still, blues, funk, soul, country, and rock are deeply entwined with the history of civil rights and social change in the United States. White farmers brought country music, black workers brought the blues, and their synthesis resulted in a mixture of contemporary musical styles. Today, most visitors make the Memphis pilgrimage to see Graceland, the former home of Elvis Presley and one of the most deliciously tacky spots in the US. There's plenty to do after you've paid your respects to the King; unusual museums, fantastic ribs, and live music are just some of the reasons you might want to stay a few days.

VITAL STATS
Population: 650,000
Tourist Office: Tennessee Welcome Center, 119 Riverside Dr. (☎901-543-6757; www.memphistravel.com), at Jefferson St. Open daily 7am-10pm.
Library and Internet Access: Cossitt Branch Library, 33 S. Front St. (☎901-526-1712), downtown at Monroe. Open M-F 10am-5pm.
Post Office: 100 Peabody Pl. (☎901-575-2054). Open M-F 8:30am-5pm, Sa 9am-1pm. **Postal Code:** 38103.

✦ ORIENTATION

Downtown, named avenues run east-west, and numbered streets run north-south. **Madison Avenue** divides north and south addresses. Two main thoroughfares, **Poplar** and **Union Avenues,** run east to west; **Second** and **Third Street**

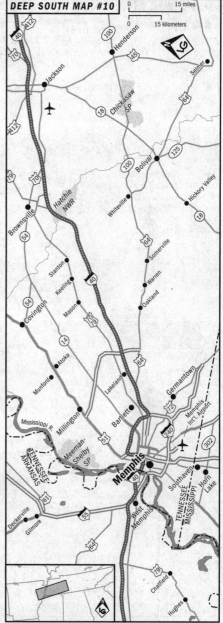

DEEP SOUTH MAP #10

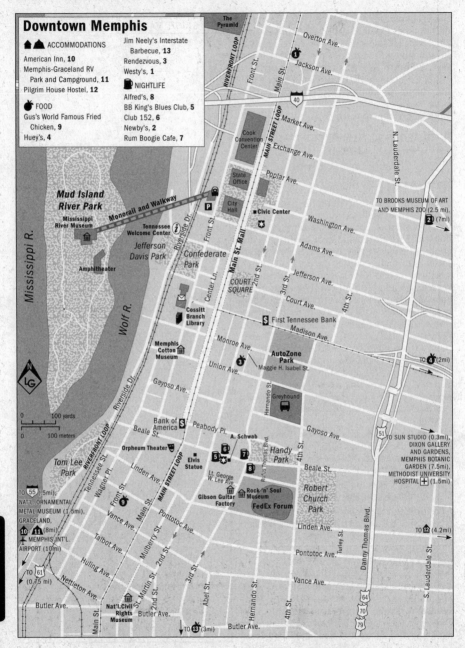

Downtown Memphis

🏠🏕 ACCOMMODATIONS

American Inn, **10**
Memphis-Graceland RV
  Park and Campground, **11**
Pilgrim House Hostel, **12**

🍅 FOOD

Gus's World Famous Fried
  Chicken, **9**
Huey's, **4**

Jim Neely's Interstate
  Barbecue, **13**
Rendezvous, **3**
Westy's, **1**

🍺 NIGHTLIFE

Alfred's, **8**
BB King's Blues Club, **5**
Club 152, **6**
Newby's, **2**
Rum Boogie Cafe, **7**

sare the major north-south routes downtown. **I-240** and **I-55** encircle the city. **Riverside Drive** takes you to **US 61,** which becomes **Elvis Presley Boulevard** and leads south straight to Graceland. **Midtown,** east of downtown, is home to a funky music scene and gay venues and is a break from the tourist attractions (and tourist traps) of **Beale Street.**

ACCOMMODATIONS

A few downtown motels have prices in the budget range; more budget lodgings are available near Graceland at **Elvis Presley Boulevard** and **Brooks Road.** Coupons from the visitors center are good for substantial discounts at many chain hotels, particularly midweek, but call ahead to confirm room availability. For the celebrations of Elvis's historic birth (Jan. 8) and death (Aug. 16) as well as for the month-long **Memphis in May** festival, book rooms six months to one year in advance.

Pilgrim House Hostel, 1000 S. Cooper St. (☎901-273-8341), in the Cooper-Young Antique District. Housed in a church. Not exactly a party scene, but the rates can't be beat, and the location is lovely, near a cluster of restaurants and bars. Chores required. Check-in 4-8pm. Dorms $15; singles $25; doubles $40. MC/V. ❶

American Inn, 3265 Elvis Presley Blvd. (☎901-345-8444), at Exit 5B off I-55, close to Graceland. One of the nicest of the motels lining Presley Blvd., with spacious, comfortable rooms,

cable TV, and free Wi-Fi. Singles $47.50; doubles $60. AmEx/D/MC/V. ❷

Memphis-Graceland RV Park and Campground, 3691 Elvis Presley Blvd. (☎901-396-7125 or 866-571-9236; www.memphisgracelandrvpark. com), beside the Heartbreak Hotel, a 2min. walk from Graceland. Very little privacy, but the location is great. Pool and laundry facilities. Reservations recommended. Sites $23, with full hookup $35. Cabins $42. D/MC/V. ❶

FOOD

In Memphis, barbecue is as common as rhinestone-studded jumpsuits; the city even hosts the **World Championship Barbecue Cooking Contest** in May. Don't fret if gnawing on ribs isn't your thing—Memphis has plenty of other Southern restaurants with down-home favorites like fried chicken, catfish, chitlins, and grits.

Jim Neely's Interstate Barbecue, 2265 S. 3rd St. (☎901-775-2304; www.interstatebarbecue. com), off I-55 at Exit 7. Great barbecue, plain and simple. The chopped pork barbecue sandwich ($4.75-5.15) is tasty, as is the rib dinner (full rack of ribs; $8.75). Open M-Th 11am-11pm, F-Sa 11am-midnight. AmEx/MC/V. ❷

Rendezvous, 52 S. 2nd St. (☎901-523-2746; www.hogsfly.com). The entrance is around back on Maggie H. Isabel St., in the alley opposite the Peabody Hotel. A Memphis legend, serving charcoal-broiled ribs (½ rack $13.75, full rack $17),

TRIBUTE TO THE KING

Sure, we may live in a celeb-obsessed culture, but few contemporary rockers or movie stars garner the same attention that Elvis still does over 30 years after his death. With more than 500 active Official Elvis Presley Fan Clubs scattered across 44 states and 45 countries worldwide, the King of Pop has not ceded his throne. *Forbes's* top-earning deceased celebrity for six of the past seven years, Elvis is far from fading into obscurity. One man from Derbyshire, in the UK, spent about £2000 getting 19 tattoos, mostly portraits of Elvis, on his back. In Vienna, Wolfgang Hahn drives a car with an ELVIS9 license plate, wears an original Elvis guitar pick around his neck, and serves as the lead singer of Little Memphis, a band that covers Elvis songs in both English and German. Elvis mania isn't limited to a small handful of individuals, though. Each year, a candlelight vigil is held at Graceland during Elvis Tribute Week in August. Over 30,000 people participated in the ceremony marking the 25th

cheese and sausages ($9), and sandwiches ($8). Open Tu-Th 4:30-10:30pm, F 11am-11pm, Sa 11:30am-11pm. AmEx/D/MC/V. ❸

Huey's, 1927 Madison Ave. (☎901-726-4327 or 866-818-8094; www.hueyburger.com). The Huey Burger ($5.25) comes with a toothpick holding the mouthwatering stack together. Look up, and you'll see a forest of these colorful wood spears stuck in the ceiling. Open M-Th 11am-1:30am, F-Sa 11am-2:30am, Su 11:30am-1am. Kitchen open M-Th until 1am, F-Sa until 1:30am, Su until 12:30am. AmEx/D/MC/V. ❷

Gus's World Famous Fried Chicken, 310 S. Front St. (☎901-527-4877). The sign out front says: "Today's Special: Chicken," and, if their fried wings, thighs, and legs aren't the world's best, they come pretty close. Chicken plates with beans and cole slaw $5.25-7.75. Open M-Th and Su 11am-9pm, F-Sa 11am-10pm. MC/V. ❶

Westy's, 346 N. Main St. (☎901-543-3278; www.westysmemphis.com), at Jackson Ave., on the trolley line, downtown. Westy's serves delicious tamales, stuffed potatoes, and creole dishes ($10-19) in a relaxed neighborhood pub atmosphere. Sandwiches on home-baked bread $5-9. Meat-and-2 lunch specials M-F 10:45am-2pm ($6.40). Happy hour daily 4-7pm. Open daily 10am-3am. AmEx/D/MC/V. ❷

🧭 SIGHTS

🏛GRACELAND. The best strategy for visiting Elvis Presley's home is to know what you want to see before you go—it's easy to be overwhelmed by the crowds once you're there. Crowds are lightest in the mornings before 10am. The **Graceland Mansion** itself can be seen in about 1½-2hr.; it takes a whole morning or afternoon to visit the array of secondary shops, museums, and restaurants. The crush of tourists swarms in a delightful orgy of gaudiness around the tackiest mansion in the US. The faux-fur furnishings, mirrored ceilings, green shag-carpeted walls, ostrich-feather pillows, and yellow-and-orange decor of Elvis's 1974 renovations are not easily forgotten. The blinding sheen of hundreds of gold and platinum records illuminates the **Trophy Building,** where exhibits detail Elvis's stint in the army and his more than 30 movie roles. The King is buried in the adjacent **Meditation Gardens.** Be sure to check out the thousands of inscriptions carved on the stone wall next to the sidewalk in front of the mansion. (*3763 Elvis Presley Blvd. Take I-55 S. to Exit 5B or bus #43 "Elvis Presley." ☎901-332-3322 or 800-238-2000; www.elvis.com. Ticket office open Mar.-Oct. M-Sa 8:30am-5pm, Su 9:30am-4pm; Nov.-Feb. daily 9:30am-4pm. Attractions open Mar.-May M-Sa 9am-5pm, Su 10am-4pm. June-Oct. M-Sa 9am-5pm, Su 9am-4pm; Nov. daily 10am-4pm; Dec.-Feb. M and W-Su 10am-4pm; tour $27, students, ages 13-18, and seniors $24.30, ages 7-12 $10.*)

🎸SUN STUDIO. For rock and roll fans, no visit to Memphis is complete without a visit to Sun Studio, where rock and roll was conceived. In this legendary one-room recording studio, Elvis rocked the jailhouse, Johnny Cash walked the line, and Jerry Lee Lewis was consumed by great balls of fire. Tours go through a small museum area and proceed to the studio itself, where visitors listen to the recording sessions that earned the studio its fame. (*706 Union Ave. ☎800-441-6249 or 901-521-0664; www.sunstudio.com. Open daily 10am-6:15pm. 35min. tours every hr. at 30min. past $9.50, under 12 free.*)

🏛NATIONAL CIVIL RIGHTS MUSEUM. On April 4, 1968, Dr. Martin Luther King, Jr., was assassinated at the Lorraine Motel in Memphis. Today, the powerful National Civil Rights Museum occupies the original building. Relive the courageous struggle of the civil-rights movement through photographs, videos, and interviews in this moving exhibit, which ends in Dr. King's motel room. The main exhibition's presentation is comprehensive, engaging, and among the best of the South's many similar museums. Across the street, in the house where the fatal shot was fired, the annex offers visitors a fascinating look at the criminal investigation process and the trial of James Earl Ray. (*450 Mulberry St. ☎901-521-9699; www.civilrightsmuseum.org. Open June-Aug. M and W-Sa 9am-6pm, Su 1-6pm; Sept.-May M and W-Sa 9am-5pm, Su 1-5pm. $12, students and seniors $10, ages 4-17 $8.50. M after 3pm free. Audio tour $2.*)

🎵ROCK 'N' SOUL MUSEUM. Memphis's musical roots run deep into the fertile cultural soil of the Mississippi Delta region. During the early and mid-1900s, Memphis's musical scene blended jazz, soul, and folk traditions to create a new, unique blues sound. Downtown Memphis's historic Beale St. saw the invention of the blues and the soul hits of the Stax label. At the must-see Rock 'n' Soul Museum, the numerous artifacts on display include celebrity stage costumes and BB King's famous guitar, Lucille. Best of all, the audio tour contains 99 complete songs. The museum also provides an account of rock and roll's origins, from the cotton fields to the blending of black and white musical styles in Memphis recording studios. *(191 Beale St., across from the Gibson Guitar factory. ☎ 901-205-2533; www.memphisrocknsoul.org. Open daily 10am-7pm. Last entry 6:15pm. $10, ages 5-17 $7.)*

ELVIS PRESLEY AUTOMOBILE MUSEUM AND CUSTOM JETS. If you love him tender, love him true, visit the peripheral Elvis attractions across the street from the mansion. The Elvis Presley Automobile Museum houses a fleet of Elvis-mobiles, including pink and purple Cadillacs and motorized toys aplenty. *(☎901-332-3322 or 800-238-2000; www.elvis.com. $8, students and seniors $7.25, ages 7-12 $4.)* Visitors to Elvis Custom Jets can walk through the King's private plane, complete with a blue suede bed and gold-plated seat belts, and peek into the tiny *Hound Dog II Jetstar. (☎901-332-3322 or 800-238-2000; www.elvis.com. $7, children $3.50.)*

GIBSON GUITAR FACTORY. Long before Sam Phillips and Sun Studio produced Elvis and Jerry Lee Lewis, the Gibson Guitar Factory was lovingly constructing the quintessential rock instrument. The factory only produces about 35 instruments each day; tours detail the various stages of the guitar-making process. Visit during the week in the morning or early afternoon to see the craftsmen at work. Gibson's factory store is stocked with its entire lineup of guitars and will leave aspiring rock stars drooling. *(145 Lieutenant George W. Lee Ave. ☎901-544-7998; www.gibsonmemphis.com. 35-45min. tours M-Sa 11am-4pm, Su noon-4pm. $10.)*

BROOKS MUSEUM OF ART. The Brooks Museum of Art, in the southwest corner of Overton Park, east of downtown, showcases a diverse collection of paintings and decorative art and features visiting exhibits throughout the year. On the first Wednesday of each month, the museum hosts a celebration (6-9pm, $5) with food, films, live music,

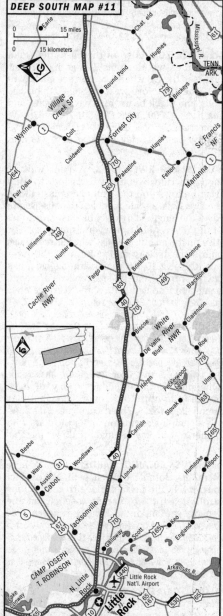

DEEP SOUTH

and drinks. *(1934 Poplar Ave. ☎901-544-6200; www.brooksmuseum.org. Open Tu-W and F 10am-4pm, Th 10am-8pm, Sa 10am-5pm, Su 11:30am-5pm. $7, students and ages 7-17 $3, seniors $6. W free.)*

MEMPHIS ZOO. Also in the park, the small but impressive Memphis Zoo is one of four places in the US where you can see giant pandas. The new Northwest Passage exhibit has polar and black bears, bald eagles, seals, and sea lions. *(2000 Prentis Pl. ☎901-276-9453; www.memphiszoo.org. Open daily Mar.-Oct. 9am-6pm; Nov.-Feb. 9am-5pm. Last entry 1hr. before close. $13, ages 2-11 $8. Tram tour $2. Parking $3.)*

MUD ISLAND RIVER PARK. A quick walk or monorail ride over the Mississippi to Mud Island allows you to stroll and splash along the **River Walk,** a scale model of the Mississippi River the length of five city blocks. Free tours of the River Walk run several times per day. Also on the island, the **Mississippi River Museum** charts the history and culture of the river over the past 10,000 years with videos, musical recordings, and life-size replicas of steamboats and ironclad battleships. *(Monorail leaves from 125 N. Front St. every 10min. ☎901-576-7241 or 800-507-6507; www.mudisland.com. Park open Tu-Su June-Aug. 10am-6pm; Sept.-Oct. and Apr.-May 10am-5pm. Last entry 1hr. before close. 3-5 tours per day. River Museum, round-trip monorail, and guided River Walk tour package $8, ages 5-11 $5.)* The newest feature is the **Sleep Out on the Mississippi,** scheduled for the second Friday of each month from April to October. Though it may sound like a form of political protest, it's actually a camping excursion under the stars with dinner, music, kayaks, and breakfast. *(Reservations ☎901-576-7241 or 800-507-6507. $40.)*

MEMPHIS BOTANIC GARDEN. The 96-acre Memphis Botanic Garden, with 23 distinct gardens, is the perfect place to take a long stroll. Relish the 57-variety rose garden, the sensory garden, or the Japanese garden. *(750 Cherry Rd., in Audubon Park off Park Ave., 12 mi. east of downtown Memphis. ☎901-576-4100; www.memphis-botanicgarden.com. Open Apr.-Oct. M-Sa 9am-6pm, Su 11am-6pm; Nov.-Mar. M-Sa 9am-4pm, Su 11am-4pm. $5, ages 3-12 $3, under 2 free, seniors $4.)*

DIXON GALLERY AND GARDENS. Across Park Ave., the Dixon Gallery and Gardens flaunts an impeccable garden accented with an impressive range of sculptures and a collection of Impressionist art with works by Renoir, Degas, and Monet. *(4339 Park Ave. ☎901-761-2409 or 901-761-5250. Open Tu-F 10am-4pm, Sa 10am-5pm, Su 1-5pm. $7, students and seniors $5, ages 7-17 $3, under 6 free. Sa 10am-noon. Free.)*

OTHER SIGHTS. South of downtown, the **National Ornamental Metal Museum,** the only institution of its kind in the US, displays fine metalwork from artists around the world. Get a better idea of the artistic process at the working blacksmith shop behind the museum and check out the front gate as you walk in. *(374 Metal Museum Dr. Exit 12C from I-55. ☎901-774-6380; www.metalmuseum.org. Open Tu-Sa 10am-5pm, Su noon-5pm. $5, students $3, ages 5-18 free, seniors $4.)* A general store, antique museum, and clothing shop rolled into one, **A. Schwab** has stood on Beale St. since 1876. Used clothing, toys, gadgets, and miscellaneous treasures abound for the bargain hunter. *(163 Beale St. ☎901-523-9782. Open M-Sa 9am-5pm.)*

ENTERTAINMENT

The majestic **Orpheum Theatre,** 203 S. Main St., hosts Broadway shows and big-name performers. On Fridays during the summer, the grand old theater shows classic movies with an organ prelude and a cartoon. *(☎901-525-3000; www.orpheum-memphis.com. Movies $6, under 12 $5. Concerts and shows $15-55. Box office open M-F 9am-5pm and 2hr. before shows.)* Just as things are really beginning to heat up in the South, the legendary **Memphis in May** celebration hits the city with concerts, art exhibits, food contests, and sporting events throughout the month. *(☎901-525-4611; www.memphisinmay.org.)* One such event is the **Beale Street Music Festival,** featuring some of the biggest names from a range of musical genres. There's also the **World Championship Barbecue Cooking Contest** and the **Sunset Symphony,** a concert near the river given by the Memphis Symphony Orchestra. In August, **Elvis Week** commemorates the King with events ranging from film festivals to impersonator contests. For more info, see www.elvis.com.

NIGHTLIFE

WC Handy's 1917 "Beale St. Blues" claims that "you'll find that business never closes 'til somebody gets killed." Today's visitors are more likely to encounter the Hard Rock Cafe and all the mega-commercialism that comes with it than the rough-and-tumble juke joints of old. Despite all the change, the strip between Second and Fourth St. is still the place to go for live music. The free *Memphis Flyer* and the "Playbook" section of the Friday *Memphis Commercial Appeal* can tell you what's goin' down in town. For a collegiate climate, try the **Highland Street** strip near Memphis State University or the intersection of **Young** and **Cooper Avenue** in Midtown. The city's gay bars are also in Midtown. For info on gay clubs and happenings, *Triangle Journal News* can be found in any gay venue. Memphis can be unsafe after dark outside the Beale St. area and downtown, so be careful and ask any bar to call you a cab.

Rum Boogie Cafe, 182 Beale St. (☎901-528-0150; www.rumboogie.com). One of the 1st clubs on Beale St., Rum Boogie still rocks with homegrown blues and a friendly ambience. Check out the celebrity guitars hanging from the ceiling. Nightly live music. 21+. Happy hour M-F 4-7pm. Open M-Th and Su 11am-midnight, F-Sa 11am-1am. AmEx/D/MC/V.

BB King's Blues Club, 143 Beale St. (☎901-524-5464; www.bbkingsclub.com). Live blues makes this place popular with locals, visitors, and celebrities. Drinks are expensive, even for Beale St. BB himself occasionally plays a show, though tickets can reach $200 and typically sell out. Entrees $13-24. Music starts Sa-Su 2pm; M-F 6pm, house band starts at 8:30pm. 21+ after 8pm. Cover from 7pm $5-7. Open daily 11am-3am. AmEx/D/MC/V.

Club 152, 152 Beale St. (☎901-544-7011). One of the most popular clubs on Beale, offering 3 floors of dancing and drinks. Live music acts range from blues to techno. On weekends DJs spin upstairs. Check out the "mood elevator," a wildly painted elevator that takes you to hip hop (F, 2nd fl.), techno (Sa, 3rd fl.), and beyond. Beer from $3.50. Cover F-Sa after 10pm $5. Open M 4pm-3am, W-Su 11am-5am. MC/V.

Alfred's, 197 Beale St. (☎901-525-3711; www.alfreds-on-beale.com). Known for its karaoke, live music, and DJs spinning into the wee hours. Upstairs patio overlooks Beale St.'s nightly debauchery. Live music daily 6-10pm. 21+ after

10pm. Cover some Th and F-Sa after 9:30pm $10. Open M-Th and Su 11am-3am, F-Sa 11am-5am. AmEx/D/MC/V.

Newby's, 539 S. Highland St. (☎901-452-8408; www.newbysmemphis.com). A lively college bar with pool tables, comfy red booths, and an outdoor patio. Live bands play everything from rock to reggae almost every night beginning at 10pm. Cover usually $3-5. Happy hour daily 3-10pm. Open M and Sa-Su 3pm-3am, Tu-F 11am-3am.

BIG DETOUR. Explore the Southern soul in Mississippi on the **Barbecue, Blues, and Blue Suede Shoes Big Detour,** next page.

THE ROAD TO LITTLE ROCK: 135 MI. Take **I-40 West** to **Exit 153B** for **I-30 West,** which leads to downtown Little Rock.

The Natural State ARKANSAS *Welcomes You!*

LITTLE ROCK ☎501

Located squarely in the middle of the state along the Arkansas River, Little Rock became a major trading city in the 19th century. A small rock served as an important landmark for boats pushing their way upstream. Though this "little rock" is still visible today, it doesn't loom as large as the historic Central High School, where, in 1957, Governor Orval Faubus and local white segregationists resisted the entrance of nine black students under the protection of the National Guard. Today, this and other events are remembered in the many museums in the downtown area. The main attraction is the Clinton Presidential Library, which overlooks the Arkansas River.

ORIENTATION

Little Rock lies at the intersection of **I-40** and **I-30,** 140 mi. west of Memphis. Downtown, numbered streets run east-west, while named

BIG DETOUR

BBQ, BLUES, BLUE SUEDE SHOES
NORTHERN MISSISSIPPI

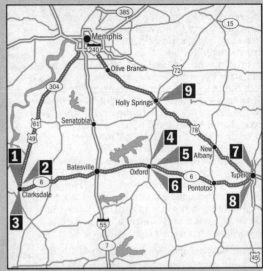

START: Memphis

HIGHLIGHT: Graceland Too

DISTANCE: 229 mi.

DURATION: 2 days

From downtown Memphis, take Third St. S., which becomes US 61 S., for 70 mi. to the Clarksdale/US 278/Rte. 6 exit. At the bottom of the exit ramp, turn right and follow US 278/Rte. 6 W. for half a mile. Turn left onto Rte. 161 S. to the intersection with DeSoto Ave. This is the Crossroads.

1. THE CROSSROADS. According to legend, the pioneering blues guitarist Robert Johnson sold his soul to the devil at the **Crossroads** in Clarksdale, Mississippi. Johnson's legendary guitar playing may or may not have benefited from satanic intervention, but the story lives on in Delta folklore, and the former intersection of US 49 and 61 is marked with two blue guitars to commemorate the alleged event.

From the intersection, take DeSoto Ave. north and turn left onto Third St. Turn left onto Blues Alley. The Delta Blues Museum will be on your left.

2. DELTA BLUES MUSEUM. Housed in an old train depot, the Delta Blues Museum displays regional artwork, photographs, and rare Delta artifacts, including harmonicas owned by Sonny Boy Williamson and a guitar fashioned by ZZ Top from a log cabin Muddy Waters once lived in. (☎662-627-6820; www.deltabluesmuseum.org. Open Mar.-Oct. M-Sa 9am-5pm; Nov.-Feb. M-Sa 10am-5pm. $7, students $3, ages 6-12 $5.)

From the Delta Blues Museum, just head straight across the street to Ground Zero.

3. GROUND ZERO. Head to Ground Zero, 0 Blues Alley, for a plate lunch ($7), complete with beverage, cornbread, and dessert. Wednesday through Saturday, stay late for local tunes. You might even catch a glimpse of co-owner and actor 🎬**Morgan Freeman.** (☎662-621-9009; www.groundzerobluesclub.com. Plate lunch special M-F 11am-2pm. Open M-Tu 11am-2pm, W-Th 11am-11pm, F-Sa 11am-1am. AmEx/D/MC/V.)

From Blues Alley in Clarksdale, backtrack to US 278/Rte. 6 and follow it east to the Lamar Ave./Downtown Oxford exit. Turn left on Lamar Ave. and follow it to Courthouse Sq. in downtown Oxford.

4. SQUARE BOOKS. Square Books, 160 Courthouse Sq., is one of the best independent bookstores in the nation. The owner also happens to be the city's mayor. Expand your belly and your mind—coffee drinks and pastries are just $1-2 at the coffee shop upstairs. (☎662-236-2262. Open M-Th 9am-9pm, F-Sa 9am-10pm, Su 10am-6pm.)

Take Lamar Ave. back toward Rte. 6, then turn right on University Ave. Follow University Ave. to Lyceum Cir. Park anywhere on the circle and walk toward the Lyceum, the building with six white columns on the far side of the circle from University Ave. The Civil Rights Memorial and Ole Miss Blues Archive are behind the Lyceum building.

5. CIVIL RIGHTS MEMORIAL AND OLE MISS BLUES ARCHIVE.
Opened in 2006, the Civil Rights Memorial commemorates racial equality in higher education. A large stone doorway celebrates the successful struggle of James Meredith, the first African-American to enroll at the University of Mississippi. Next to the memorial in the main library, the Ole Miss Blues Archive will delight blues fans with one of the largest collections of blues memorabilia in the world. (☎662-915-7753. Open M-F 8am-5pm. Free.)

From Lyceum Cir., follow University Ave. toward Lamar Ave. Turn right on Lamar Ave. and follow it until Old Taylor Rd. Turn right on Old Taylor Rd. and follow it to the parking area for Rowan Oak.

6. ROWAN OAK.
Entranced by the house's history (it once belonged to a Confederate general), William Faulkner bought the place in 1930 and named the property after the rowan tree, a symbol of peace and security. The plot outline of his 1954 novel *A Fable* is etched on the walls of the study. (☎662-234-3284. Mansion open for self-guided tours Tu-Sa 10am-4pm, Su 1-4pm. Grounds open sunrise-sunset. $5.)

Backtrack on Old Taylor Rd., turning right on Lamar Ave. and following it to Rte. 6. Take Rte. 6 E. for 52 mi. Rte. 6 becomes Main St. near Tupelo. After passing through downtown Tupelo, turn left onto Franklin St. The Tupelo Automobile Museum will be on your right.

7. TUPELO AUTOMOBILE MUSEUM.
Antique car fanatics will be in heaven at the Tupelo Automobile Museum, 1 Otis Blvd., off E. Main St., which includes hot rides like a gullwing DeLorean and a customized Corvette. (☎662-842-4242. Open Tu-Su 10am-6pm. $10, children $5.)

Follow Rte. 6 E. (Main St.) to the intersection with Veterans Blvd. Turn right on Veterans Blvd. and take the first right onto Reese St. The Elvis Presley Birthplace will be on the right.

8. ELVIS PRESLEY BIRTHPLACE.
The Elvis Presley Birthplace, 306 Elvis Presley Blvd., is definitely worth a visit. There's also a museum, a memorial chapel, a fountain, and a statue of 13-year-old Elvis. (☎662-841-1245; www.elvispresleybirthplace.com. Open M-Sa 9am-5pm, Su 1-5pm. House and museum $10, ages 7-12 $5. House only $4/2. Museum only $8/4.)

Head back on Reese St., turn right onto Veterans Blvd., and follow it to US 78. Take US 78 W. to Rte. 4 E./7 N. Follow it to E. Gholson Ave. and turn right. Graceland Too is on your left. You really can't miss it.

9. GRACELAND TOO.
Part museum and part Elvis shrine, Graceland Too is home to Paul MacLeod, the self-proclaimed "World's Number One Elvis Fan," and his son, Elvis Aaron MacLeod. The house's expansive collection of Elvis memorabilia is mind-boggling, but Paul's enthusiastic tours and encyclopedic knowledge of everything Elvis are equally stupefying. Tours can last anywhere from 1hr. to 4hr.; Paul's longest was 12hr. (☎601-252-7954. Open 24hr. If it's nighttime, just knock louder. $5.)

Back to the route. From Graceland Too, backtrack to US 78 and follow it west for 33 mi. to Memphis.

streets run north-south. The four major thoroughfares are **I-630, Cantrell Road, University Avenue,** and **Rodney Parham Road.** The east side of **Markham Street** is now **President Clinton Avenue** and moves through the lively **Riverwalk** district. **North Little Rock** is linked to downtown by three bridges spanning the **Arkansas River.**

VITAL STATS

Population: 184,500

Tourist Office: Little Rock Visitor Information Center, 615 E. Capitol Ave. (☎501-370-3290 or 877-220-2568; www.littlerock.com), in Curran Hall. Take the 6th or 9th St. exit off I-30 and follow the signs. Free Wi-Fi. Open M-Sa 9am-5pm, Su 1-5pm.

Library and Internet Access: Main Library, 100 Rock St. (☎501-918-3000), near River Market. Open M-Th 9am-8pm, F-Sa 9am-6pm, Su 1-5pm.

Post Office: 600 E. Capitol Ave. (☎501-375-5155). Open M-F 7am-5:30pm. **Postal Code:** 72701.

ACCOMMODATIONS

Budget motels crowd around I-30 southwest of town and off I-40 in North Little Rock.

America's Best Value Inn, 2508 Jackson Hwy. (☎501-945-4167), off I-40 at Exit 157, in North Little Rock. Newly renovated and spacious rooms. Free coffee and Internet in the lobby. Rooms from $40. AmEx/D/MC/V. ❷

Cimarron Inn, 10200 I-30 (☎501-565-1171), off Exit 130 on the west access road. Offers clean and basic rooms with fridges and microwaves. Singles $35; doubles $40. AmEx/MC/V. ❷

Maumelle Park, 9009 Pinnacle Valley Rd. (☎501-868-9477), on the Arkansas River. From I-430, take Rte. 10 (Exit 9) west 2 mi., turn right on Pinnacle Valley Rd., continue for 2 mi., and look for the sign. 129 RV sites near Pinnacle Mountain State Park. Reception daily 9am-9pm. Sites $18-20. MC/V. ❶

FOOD

The city has revamped the downtown area starting with **River Market,** 400 President Clinton Ave. The downtown lunch crowd heads here for a wide selection of food shops, coffee stands, delis, and an outdoor farmers' market. (☎501-375-2552; www.rivermarket. info. Market Hall open M-Sa 7am-6pm; many shops open only for lunch. Farmers' market open May-Oct. Tu and Sa 7am-3pm.)

The Flying Fish, 511 President Clinton Ave. (☎501-375-3474), near Market Hall. Has quickly become downtown's most popular hangout because of its unpretentious atmosphere and walls covered with photos of fish caught by patrons. Hungry diners clamor for platters of fried catfish, shrimp, and oysters ($4-16). Open daily 11am-10pm. AmEx/D/MC/V. ❷

Cotham's in the City, 1401 W. 3rd St. (☎501-370-9177). Popularized by then-Governor Bill Clinton and other political types during the 80s and 90s, which explains the campaign signs and posters that decorate the walls. Cotham's onion rings are enormous and delicious, but the restaurant is best known for its "Hubcap Hamburgers," grilled underneath a hubcap ($9.50). Open M-F 11am-2pm. MC/V. ❸

Whole Hog Cafe, 2516 Cantrell Rd. (☎501-664-5025; www.wholehogcafe.com), in the Riverdale Center strip mall. Eat like a hog at this award-winning barbecue restaurant. Pulled pork plates come with 2 sides for $6-7. Open M-Sa 11am-8pm. AmEx/D/MC/V. ❶

Pizza D'Action, 2919 W. Markham St. (☎501-666-5403), just past the Hillcrest area. Boasts some of the tastiest pizzas and liveliest crowds in the neighborhood. Large pies from $12. Burgers and sandwiches $4.75-6.50. Nightly live music. Open M-F 11am-2am, Sa 11am-1am, Su 11am-10pm. Kitchen open M-Sa until 10pm, Su until 9pm. D/MC/V. ❶

SIGHTS

CLINTON PRESIDENTIAL CENTER. The Clinton Presidential Center was hailed by admirers as a metaphor for Clinton's "Bridge to the 21st Century" and lampooned by critics as a gigantic glass-walled mobile home. Highlights include Clinton's presidential limo, replicas of the Oval Office and Cabinet Room, and a compilation of humorous White House television moments. *(1200 E. President Clinton Ave. ☎501-374-4242. Open M-Sa 9am-5pm, Su 1-5pm. $7, students $5, ages 6-17 $3.)*

ARKANSAS INLAND MARITIME MUSEUM. At the Arkansas Inland Maritime Museum, visitors can tour the *USS Razorback,* a WWII-era submarine. Quarters in the submarine are not for the claustrophobic, but this is a rare and undeniably cool chance to see the inside of a submarine. Don't push any of the buttons; the 95% operational submarine can submerge, but she can't rise. *(Off Riverfront Dr. in North Little Rock, accessible from I-30 at the Broadway exit. ☎501-371-8320; www.aimm.com. Open May-Aug. W-Sa 10am-6pm, Su 1-6pm; Sept.-Apr. F-Sa 10am-6pm, Su 1-6pm. $6, children $4.)*

HISTORIC ARKANSAS MUSEUM. In the middle of downtown, the Historic Arkansas Museum showcases rotating exhibits of art and artifacts from Arkansas. The museum also contains a small outdoor village that recreates life in 19th-century Little Rock using period actors who show off old-time frontier living. *(200 E. 3rd St. ☎501-324-9351; www.arkansashistory. com. Open M-Sa 9am-5pm, Su 1-5pm. Free. 1hr. tour of historic homes $2.50, under 19 $1, seniors $1.50.)*

OLD STATE HOUSE. The Old State House, a Greek Revival-style building built in 1833, is the oldest standing state capitol building west of the Mississippi River and was the site of Clinton's election-night speeches and celebrations in '92 and '96. Today, the museum houses exhibits on Arkansas's first families, replica period parlors, and the original 1836 legislative chamber. *(300 W. Markham St. ☎501-324-9685; www.oldstatehouse.com. Open M-Sa 9am-5pm, Su 1-5pm. Free.)*

CENTRAL HIGH SCHOOL. The aftermath of Little Rock's civil-rights struggle is manifest at the corner of Daisy L. Gatson Bates Dr. (formerly 14th St.) and Park St., where Central High School remains a fully functional school. It is therefore closed to visitors, but a visitors center across the street contains an excellent exhibit on the Little Rock Nine. *(2125 Daisy L. Gatson Bates Dr. ☎501-374-1957; www.nps.gov/chsc. Open daily 9am-4:30pm. Free.)*

OTHER SIGHTS. The **State Capitol,** at the west end of Capitol St., which is modeled after the US Capitol in Washington, DC, allows visitors surprising freedom to wander the governor's reception room, the old Supreme Court chamber, the Senate chamber, and the House of Representatives chamber with its beautiful stained-glass ceiling. *(☎501-682-1010. Open M-F 8am-5pm. Free.)* Tourists can visit **"Le Petite**

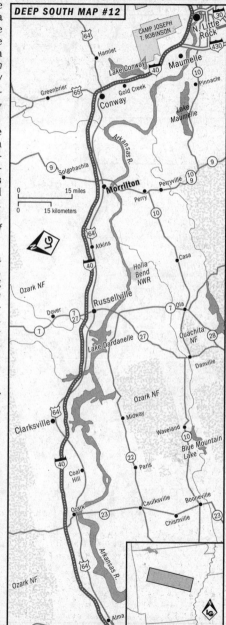

DEEP SOUTH MAP #12

DEEP SOUTH

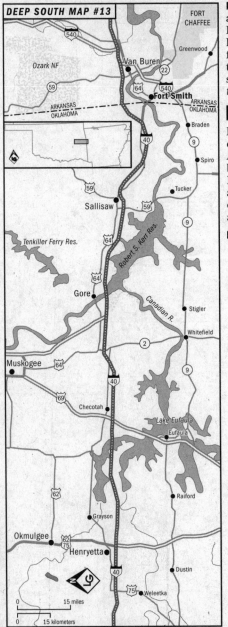

DEEP SOUTH MAP #13

Roche," the actual "little rock" of Little Rock, at Riverfront Park. From underneath Junction Bridge, the railroad bridge at the north end of Louisiana St., look straight down. Look carefully; the rock is part of the embankment (it's that small), and it's been covered in graffiti since its plaque was stolen. *(At Riverfront Park, at the north end of Rock St.)*

NIGHTLIFE

Little Rock's growing nightlife scene centers on the **River Market District** on President Clinton Ave. West of downtown, a number of bars can be found in the **Hillcrest** neighborhood along Kavanaugh Blvd. For listings of shows, bands, and events, pick up a free copy of *Nightflying* or *Free Press*, available at most restaurants and bars around Little Rock.

The Flying Saucer, 322 President Clinton Ave. (☎501-372-7468; www.beerknurd.com). A beer-lover's paradise, with 75 beers on tap and 130 bottled beers. Settle into a cozy sofa or relax at a table in the main tap room, which is decorated with—of course—UFOs. Most beers $2.75-4. $2.75 pints M. Live music F-Sa. Open M-W and Sa 11am-1am, Th-F 11am-2am. AmEx/D/MC/V.

Vino's, 923 W. 7th St. (☎501-375-8468; www.vinosbrewpub.com), at Chester St. Little Rock's original microbrewery-nightclub, with a clientele ranging from lunchtime's corporate businessmen to midnight's younger set. Pizza slices $1.40-3.30. Live rock music Th-Sa nights and some Tu and Su nights. 18+ at night. Cover $5-13. Open M-W 11am-10pm, Th 11am-11pm, F 11am-midnight, Sa 11:30am-midnight, Su 1-9pm. MC/V.

Sticky Fingerz, 107 S. Commerce St. (☎501-372-7707; www.stickyfingerz.com), across President Clinton Ave. from the River Market. Serves its signature chicken fingers ($6.50) with a side of alt-rock. 21+ after 7pm. Cover from 8pm $3-20. Open M-F 11am-1:30pm and 4pm-last customer, Sa 11am-1am. MC/V.

The Underground Pub, 500 President Clinton Ave. (☎501-707-2537). Offers British fare like fish and chips ($8) to go with your Guinness. Enjoy music, darts, pool, foosball, and British soccer on big-screen TVs or head to the outdoor patio overlooking the Arkansas River. Happy hour M-F 4-7pm with $2 drafts, $3 well drinks, $3 house wines. Open M-Sa 11am-2am. AmEx/D/MC/V.

OUTDOORS

Just a 15min. drive to the west of the city is **Pinnacle Mountain State Park,** 11901 Pinnacle Valley Rd., in Roland, home to the **Arkansas Arboretum.** The 71-acre arboretum highlights the different natural regions and flora in Arkansas with interpretive exhibits and a half-mile paved trail. Visitors can walk down to the Little Maumelle River on the **Kingfisher Trail** (½ mi.) and see birds and giant cypress trees. For a more strenuous hike, visitors can climb to the top of the **Pinnacle Mountain** via the West Summit Trail. From Little Rock, take I-430 to Exit 9 and follow Rte. 10 W. for 7 mi. Take Rte. 300 N. for 2 mi. and follow the signs to the park. (☎501-868-5806; www. arkansasstateparks.com/pinnaclemountain. Open M-F 8am-5pm, Sa-Su 8am-6pm. Free.)

THE ROAD TO MORRILTON: 60 MI.

Take **I-40 West** for 45 mi. to **Exit 108.** Follow **Route 9 South** for 7 mi., then turn right onto **Route 154 West** to head into Morrilton.

MORRILTON   ☎501

The **Museum of Automobiles,** 8 Jones Ln., off Rte. 154, is Morrilton's main attraction, with over 50 restored classic cars. Highlights include Bill Clinton's '67 Mustang convertible, Elvis's Ranchero pickup, and antique vehicles dating back to the Model T era. (☎501-727-5427; www.museumofautos.com. Open daily 10am-5pm. $7, ages 6-17 $3.50.) Just down Rte. 154, **Petit Jean State Park,** 1285 Petit Jean Mountain Rd., is one of the largest state parks in Arkansas. Visitors can enjoy 20 mi. of hiking trails, drive to an overlook at the summit of Petit Jean Mountain, explore the 95 ft. **Cedar Falls,** and fish or boat on Lake Bailey. The park also has a campground with 125 sites with water, electricity, and showers. (☎501-727-5441; www.petitjeanstatepark. com. Open sunrise-sunset. Sites with water and electricity $17, with full hookup $27. Lodge rooms $65-70; cabins $75-175. MC/V.)

THE ROAD TO FORT SMITH: 109 MI.

Follow **I-40 West** to **Exit 7** onto **I-540 South.** Take Exit 7 onto **Rogers Avenue (Highway 22 West)** towards downtown Fort Smith.

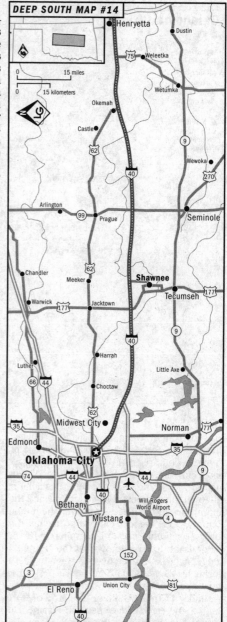

DEEP SOUTH MAP #14

DEEP SOUTH

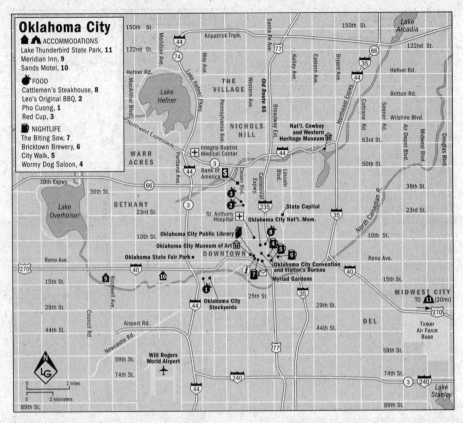

Oklahoma City

🏠🏕 **ACCOMMODATIONS**
Lake Thunderbird State Park, **11**
Meridian Inn, **9**
Sands Motel, **10**

🍎 **FOOD**
Cattlemen's Steakhouse, **8**
Leo's Original BBQ, **2**
Pho Cuong, **1**
Red Cup, **3**

🍸 **NIGHTLIFE**
The Biting Sow, **7**
Bricktown Brewery, **6**
City Walk, **5**
Wormy Dog Saloon, **4**

FORT SMITH ☎479

An old frontier town, Fort Smith's biggest draw is the **Fort Smith National Historic Site,** Third St., comprised of two preserved military posts built on America's western frontier during the 1830s. The visitors center has a short video on the settlement of Oklahoma and the importance of the fort in enforcing the Indian Removal Act. Visitors can walk through the fort's basement jail and the chambers of Judge Isaac Parker, known as the "Hanging Judge," who sentenced over 160 men to death during his 21 years in office. (☎479-783-3961; www.nps.gov/fosm. Open daily 9am-5pm. $4, under 17 free.) Dubbed "the attic of Fort Smith," the **Fort Smith Museum of History,** 320 Rogers Ave., chronicles the growth of the city around the fort from its beginnings as a small outpost during the Trail of Tears to its boomtown days as a gateway to America's western territories. The museum also has a working 1920s-era soda fountain with fountain sodas and ice-cream floats. (☎479-783-7841; www.fortsmithmuseum.org. Open June-Aug. Tu-Sa 10am-5pm, Su 1-5pm. $5, ages 6-15 $2.)

A few blocks north of downtown, the **Inn Towne Lodge ❷,** 301 N. 11th St., has clean rooms with refrigerators, microwaves, coffeemakers, and free local calls. (☎479-783-0271; www.stay3rdnightfree.com. Rooms $45-65. 3rd night free. AmEx/D/MC/V.) In downtown Fort Smith, **◪Leoncia's New Orleans Cafe ❷,** 1000 Garrison Ave., has cheerful, Mardi Gras-colored walls, friendly service, and delicious

Cajun food. The crab cakes are some of the best anywhere. (☎479-783-6500. Live music Th-Sa. Open M-W 11am-2pm and 5-8pm, Th-Sa 11am-2pm and 5-9pm. AmEx/D/MC/V.) **Tammy's Tamales ❶**, 115 N. 10th St., has cheap, delicious tamales. A plate of two tamales with a side will set you back just $5. (☎479-783-8045. Open M-F 11am-2pm. MC/V.)

⚲ THE ROAD TO SHAWNEE: 57 MI.

Take **I-40 West** to **Exit 185.** Head south on **Kickapoo Street** to **MacArthur Street.**

SHAWNEE ☎405

Shawnee is home to two universities as well as the ◪**Mabee-Gerrer Museum of Art,** 1900 W. MacArthur St. This gem of a museum contains artistic treasures collected by the Benedictine monk Father Gregory Gerrer during a lifetime of world travel. In addition to a fine collection of European and American art from the Renaissance to the 20th century, the museum has ancient Greek and Roman objects, an Egyptian mummy, and a pair of shrunken heads from South America. From Kickapoo St., follow MacArthur St. West to the entrance of St. Gregory University, on the right. (☎405-878-5300; www.mgmoa.org. Open Tu-Sa 10am-5pm, Su 1-4pm. $5, students and ages 6-17 $3.) At the intersection of Kickapoo and MacArthur St., **Abuelita Rosa's ❷**, 2613 N. Kickapoo St., serves authentic and delicious Mexican food. (☎405-214-5500. Lunch

entrees $6.25-8.50. Dinner entrees $8.65-10.60. Open M-Th 11am-10pm, F-Sa 11am-10:30pm, Su 11am-9:30pm. AmEx/D/MC/V.)

⚲ THE ROAD TO OKLAHOMA CITY: 39 MI.

From Shawnee, follow **I-40 West.** Take **Exit 150C** to reach downtown Oklahoma City.

OKLAHOMA CITY ☎405

For years, Oklahoma City was just a dusty stop for cattle drives and railroad trains. That all changed with the land run of 1889 when the city's population exploded from a few dozen people to 15,000 virtually overnight. The city remained relatively quiet until the tragic bombing of the Federal Building in 1995 suddenly thrust this self-proclaimed "cow town" into the spotlight. As the site of the infamous terrorist attack, Oklahoma City became a symbol of American patriotism and solidarity around the world.

■ ORIENTATION

Oklahoma City is constructed as a nearly perfect grid. **Santa Fe Avenue** divides the city east-west, and **Reno Avenue** slices it north-south. Cheap and plentiful parking makes driving by far the best way to get around. Some areas of the city are unsafe at night; be careful around **Sheridan Avenue** and **Walker Street.**

THE BUDGET MOTEL: BARGAIN OR BOOBY TRAP?

Independently owned motels are a staple of the long-distance vacation, with neon signs, convenient locations, and comfortable—if sometimes tacky—accommodations. Independent motels can be a great value—costing $10-20 less per night than brand-name motels of similar quality—but, without the brand name, you can't be sure what you're paying for.

Well-run motels typically have evidence of consistent upkeep such as neatly trimmed landscaping, a sealed or recently paved parking lot, and recent improvements to the rooms such as Wi-Fi or electronic keycard locks. Friendly staff and a full parking lot are also both good signs; an empty motel is usually empty for good reason. Look to see where truck drivers are staying; these frequent travelers will know good value better than most. If the motel's sign, facade, facilities, or lobby are dilapidated, the rooms are probably not much better. If the motel's office has a window between you and the clerk, it may be worried about being robbed. Always ask to see a room before you decide to stay at a motel that you're not sure about. Examine the furniture, carpet, television, and walls for damage, which could be charged to you if you stay there. Look at the bathroom—it should be spotless. Check the towels and bedsheets to see if they're stained or worn. With a little investigation, you can be reasonably confident that you're getting a good deal. If ever in doubt, just stick to this mantra: you

VITAL STATS

Population: 506,000

Tourist Office: Oklahoma City Convention and Visitors Bureau, 189 W. Sheridan Ave. (☎405-297-8912 or 800-225-5652; www.okccvb.org), at Robinson St. Open M-F 8:30am-5pm.

Library and Internet Access: Oklahoma City Public Library, 300 Park Ave. (☎405-231-8650). Open M-Th 9am-9pm, F 9am-6pm, Sa 9am-5pm, Su 1-6pm.

Post Office: 305 NW 5th St. (☎405-232-2198). Open M-F 7am-9pm, Sa 8am-5pm. **Postal Code:** 73102.

ACCOMMODATIONS

Meridian Inn, 1224 S. Meridian Ave. (☎405-948-7294; www.meridianinnokc.com). Large, clean rooms in a convenient location off Exit 145 on I-40. Singles from $45; doubles from $50. AmEx/D/MC/V. ❷

Sands Motel, 721 S. Rockwell Ave. (☎405-787-7353), off Exit 143 on I-40. The cheapest of the cheap. RV sites $16; private rooms $32.50-39.50. AmEx/D/MC/V. ❶

Lake Thunderbird State Park (☎405-360-3572). Take I-40 E. to Exit 166 and go south 10 mi. until the road ends. Make a left and drive 1 mi. Campsites near a beautiful lake fit for swimming and fishing. Rent canoes at the marina or a horse at the riding stables. Showers available. Office open M-F 8am-5pm; call for late or weekend arrivals. Sites $10, with water and electricity $16-23. Huts $45. AmEx/D/MC/V. ❶

FOOD

Oklahoma City contains the largest cattle market in the US, and beef tops most menus. Restaurants with longer hours lie east of town on Sheridan Ave., in the Bricktown district, and north of downtown along Classen Blvd. and Western Ave. Asian restaurants cluster around Classen and NW 23rd St.

Cattlemen's Steakhouse, 1309 S. Agnew Ave. (☎405-236-0416; www.cattlemensrestaurant.com), in the heart of Stockyards City. Established in 1910, this famous restaurant was the prize in a craps game played in 1945. Steaks

$10-26. Open M-Th and Su 6am-10pm, F-Sa 6am-midnight. AmEx/D/MC/V. ❹

Pho Cuong, 3016 N. Classen Blvd. (☎405-524-5045). Serves up delicious, heaping bowls of pho, a traditional Vietnamese noodle based soup served with basil leaves, bean sprouts, and lime, for a mere $5. If you're feeling adventurous, try the pho with either tripe or tendon. Open daily 8:30am-9pm. ❶

Leo's Original BBQ, 7 N. Harrison St. (☎405-236-5367). A classic hickory-smoking barbecue outfit downtown. Beef sandwich and baked potato ($5). Open M 11am-2pm, Tu-Sa 11am-8pm. AmEx/D/MC/V. ❷

Red Cup, 3122 N. Classen Blvd. (☎405-525-3430; www.redcupok.com). Giant red cup on the outside and brightly colored decor. Local coffee house serving breakfast and sandwiches ($3.65-5.25). Open M-W 7am-5pm, Th-F 7am-10pm, Sa 9am-10pm, Su 9am-5pm. MC/V. ❶

SIGHTS

OKLAHOMA CITY NATIONAL MEMORIAL. The memorial is a haunting tribute to the victims of the bombing of the Murrah Federal Building. Outside lies the Field of Empty Chairs (one for each of the 168 victims), a stone gate, and a reflecting pool. Indoors, a museum tells the story of the bombing and the world's response through photographs, videos, and testimonials. (620 N. Harvey St. at 5th St. ☎405-235-3313; www.oklahomacitynationalmemorial.org. Open M-Sa 9am-6pm, Su 1-6pm. $10, students and ages 6-17 $6, under 6 free.)

NATIONAL COWBOY AND WESTERN HERITAGE MUSEUM. A popular tourist attraction, the museum features an extensive collection of Western art and exhibits on rodeos, Native Americans, and raucous frontier towns. (1700 NE 63rd St. ☎405-478-2250; www.nationalcowboymuseum.org. Open daily 9am-5pm. $10, students $8.50, ages 6-12 $4.50, under 5 free.)

OKLAHOMA CITY STOCKYARDS. Monday is the time to visit the Oklahoma City Stockyards, the busiest in the world. Visitors enter via a catwalk over cow pens and cattle herds northeast of the auction house. The auction is as Old West as it gets. (2500 Exchange

Ave. ☎*405-235-8675; www.onsy.com. Auctions M-W 8am-last cow. Free tours M starting at 8am.)*

OKLAHOMA CITY MUSEUM OF ART. The museum has a standard collection of modern and classical art, but the dazzling and wildly inventive ◼**Dale Chihuly glass pieces** are alone worth the price of admission. *(415 Couch Dr.* ☎*405-236-3100; www.okcmoa.com. Open Tu-W and Sa 10am-5pm, Th-F 10am-9pm, Su noon-5pm. $12, students and children $10, under 6 free.)*

MYRIAD GARDENS. Plant lovers should make a beeline for Myriad Gardens, which has 17 acres of vegetation from deserts and rainforests. Cross the Crystal Bridge, a 70 ft. diameter glass cylinder perched over a tropical ravine. *(301 W. Reno Ave.* ☎*405-297-3995; www.myriadgardens.com. Gardens open daily 7am-11pm. Free. Crystal Bridge open M-Sa 9am-6pm, Su noon-6pm. $6, students and ages 13-18 $5, ages 4-12 $3.)*

🎭 NIGHTLIFE

Oklahoma City nightlife is growing by leaps and bounds—head to **Bricktown** to get into the thick of it all.

Wormy Dog Saloon, 311 E. Sheridan Ave. (☎405-601-6276). Bricktown's best beer specials ($10 buckets). Hear Oklahoma's "red dirt" country music firsthand. Cover varies. Open W-Th 8pm-2am, F-Sa 6pm-2am. AmEx/D/MC/V.

The Bricktown Brewery, 1 N. Oklahoma St. (☎405-232-2739), at Sheridan Ave. Brews 6 beers. Live music F-Sa 9pm. Upstairs 21+. Cover $5-15 for shows. Open M-Th 11am-11pm, F-Sa 11am-1am, Su noon-10pm. AmEx/D/MC/V.

The Biting Sow, 1 E. California Ave. (☎405-232-2639). The best place in town for live blues and jazz. Cover $5. Open daily from 4pm. AmEx/D/MC/V.

City Walk, 70 N. Oklahoma St. (☎405-232-9255; www.citybrickwalk.com). Houses 7 clubs. Enjoy the tropical Tequila Park, line dance inside the City Limits, or sing along at Stooge's piano bar. No athletic wear or excessive tattoos or piercings. Cover for men $10, for women $8. Ladies free until 10pm F-Sa. Open F-Sa 8pm-2am, Su 9pm-2am. AmEx/D/MC/V.

THE END OF THE ROAD

You've eaten your way through mounds of barbecue, hit every blues and country joint in the South, gained a new appreciation for Elvis's pelvis, and, dare we say it, developed a bit of a twang. Congratulations on your journey through the Deep South, but don't let the comfort food slow you down—you've seen one part of America, and it's time to see the rest. Stay in Oklahoma City to try out **Route 66** or drive north to explore the **National Road.**

EXIT TO

Tulsa, OK   106 mi.
on route 66, p. 528

SPEED LIMIT 65

St. Louis, MO   499 mi.
on the national road route, p. 379

southern border

TOP 5

1. Get classy at a **live jazz** show in New Orleans, Louisiana (p. 789).
2. **Cajun dance** with the locals in Houma, Louisiana (p. 799).
3. Gorge yourself on **barbecue** and **watermelon** in Luling, Texas (p. 818).
4. Commando-crawl your way through passages while **caving** in Carlsbad Caverns (p. 824).
5. Perfect your tan and feel an oh-so-welcome breeze on San Diego's **beaches** (p. 887).

Only the strong survived in the Old West, but you won't need spurs and a rifle to make it through this route—just a lot of water and a working air-conditioner. You'll experience both a wet heat and a dry heat as you gallop across eight states on your way from the semi-tropics of the South to the arid deserts of the Wild West. On the way, you'll visit all the gator-filled swamps, historic antebellum mansions, starkly beautiful monuments, and national parks that the borderlands have to offer.

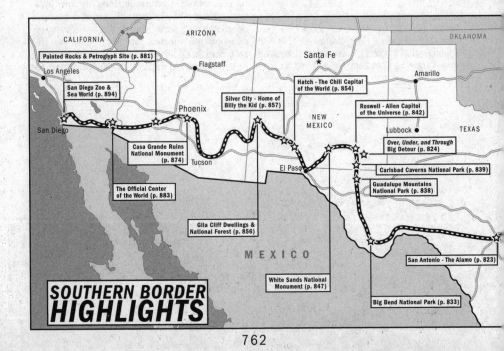

SOUTHERN BORDER HIGHLIGHTS

- Painted Rocks & Petroglyph Site (p. 881)
- San Diego Zoo & Sea World (p. 894)
- Casa Grande Ruins National Monument (p. 874)
- The Official Center of the World (p. 883)
- Gila Cliff Dwellings & National Forest (p. 856)
- Silver City - Home of Billy the Kid (p. 857)
- Hatch - The Chili Capital of the World (p. 854)
- Roswell - Alien Capitol of the Universe (p. 842)
- Over, Under, and Through Big Detour (p. 824)
- Carlsbad Caverns National Park (p. 839)
- Guadalupe Mountains National Park (p. 838)
- White Sands National Monument (p. 847)
- San Antonio - The Alamo (p. 823)
- Big Bend National Park (p. 833)

CALIFORNIA · ARIZONA · Santa Fe · OKLAHOMA · Los Angeles · Flagstaff · Amarillo · Phoenix · NEW MEXICO · Lubbock · TEXAS · San Diego · Tucson · El Paso · MEXICO · San Antonio

SOUTHERN BORDER

Your journey begins in the mangrove swamps of the **Everglades** (next page), where you'll meet alligators, dolphins, and sea turtles. Tracing Florida's coastline, you'll visit the mermaids of **Weeki Wachee** (p. 775) and the "Redneck Riviera" of **Panama City Beach** (p. 777). Continuing west across Florida's (not-so) "Forgotten Coast," you'll soon brush across coastal Alabama and Mississippi on your way to the French Quarter of resilient **New Orleans** (p. 789). Louisiana has more good things in store, from bayous and crawfish to **Avery Island** (p. 801), home of the McIlhenny Company's spicy Tabasco empire.

You can have your steak and eat it, too, as the road leads deep into the heart of Texas. Learn about the Buffalo Soldiers in **Houston** (p. 811). Jam to live music in alternative, liberal **Austin** (p. 819). Remember the **Alamo** (p. 823) in San Antonio and continue west through the Lone Star State, where the oil derricks are big and the steakhouses are bigger. In western Texas, see roadrunners, wily coyotes, and the mighty Río Grande at **Big Bend National Park**

(p. 834), then chill out at **Guadalupe Mountains National Park** (p. 838).

Head north into New Mexico and the cool limestone grottoes of **Carlsbad Caverns** (p. 840), where at dusk 16 species of bat swarm out of the caves at a rate of 6000 bats per minute (BPM). That's a lot of bats. Don't get carried away at the UFO Festival in **Roswell** (p. 842)— you still have miles to go. Ascend the 12,000 ft. peak of Sierra Blanca outside of **Ruidoso** (p. 845) for some of the most beautiful vistas of the trip, then duck test missiles and surf down the snowy dunes of **White Sands National Monument** (p. 847). Fall in love with the west Texas town of **El Paso** (p. 849), then bid it goodbye as you re-cross the border into New Mexico.

Back in the "land of enchantment," stop for a fiery bite in **Hatch** (p. 855), the "Chili Capital of the World." Head north to marvel at the 700-year-old **Gila Cliff Dwellings** (p. 857), then chase Billy the Kid through ▧**Silver City** (p. 857) before slipping across the border into Arizona. Don't miss the otherworldly rock spires of **Chiricahua National Monument** (p. 859) as you make your way across the

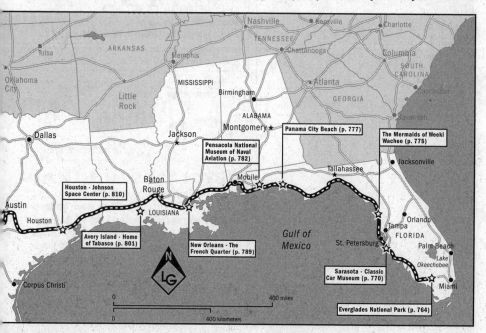

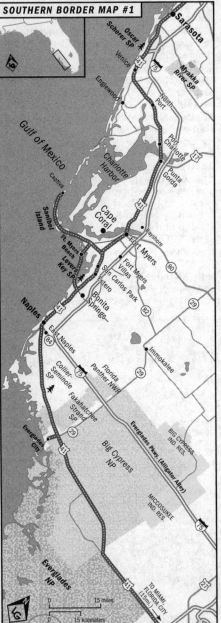

SOUTHERN BORDER MAP #1

Arizona desert to the Wild West town of **Tombstone** (p. 864. Next up is laid-back **Tucson** (p. 865), then it's on to the mysterious **Casa Grande Ruins** (p. 874) and hip **Phoenix** (p. 875). Ponder ancient spirals and pictographs at **Painted Rocks Petroglyph Site** (p. 881), then stop for some lettuce head bowling in **Yuma** (p. 882), the mother of all truck stops.

At long last, you'll find yourself in southern California, home to movie stars and the "Official Center of the World" (p. 883). Follow the road less traveled through small towns on your way to the mellow beaches of **San Diego** (p. 887) where, if you're still feeling adventurous, you can pick up the **Pacific Coast route** (p. 888). Bring a Texas-sized appetite for adventure and ditch your winter coat, because the Southern Border is hot, hot, hot!

ROUTE STATS
Miles: c. 2700
Route: The Everglades, FL, to San Diego, CA
States: 8; Florida, Alabama, Mississippi, Louisiana, Texas, New Mexico, Arizona, and California
Driving Time: Two weeks will get you there, but you'll want four to catch all the best sights.
When to Go: Prices will be higher in winter, but the weather will be much, much hotter in summer.
Crossroads: The **Pacific Coast** in San Diego, CA (p. 887), The **East Coast** in the Everglades, FL (this page).

The Sunshine State

FLORIDA

Welcomes You

EVERGLADES ☎ 239

Encompassing the entire tip of Florida and dipping into Florida Bay, **Everglades National Park** (the country's second-largest national park) spans 1.6 million acres and includes nine unique and fragile ecosystems. Vast prairies of sawgrass cut through broad expanses of shallow water, creating the park's famed river of grass, and tangled mazes of mangrove swamps wind up and down the western coast. To the south, delicate coral reefs lie below the shimmering blue waters of the bay. Keep your eyes open for American alligators, dolphins, sea turtles, birds, and fish—and particularly for the endangered American crocodile, Florida manatee, and Florida panther.

VITAL STATS

Area: 1.6 million acres

Tourist Offices: Ernest Coe Visitors Center, 40001 Rte. 9336 (☎305-242-7700; www.nps.gov/ever), located at the eastern edge of the Everglades. Open daily 9am-5pm. **Flamingo Visitors Center** (☎239-695-2945), on Rte. 9336, 40 mi. into the park. Open daily 9am-4:30pm. **Gulf Coast Visitors Center,** 815 Copeland Ave. S. (☎239-695-3311), in Everglades City. Open daily 9am-4:30pm.

Gateway Towns: Everglades City (p. 768), Florida City.

Fees: $10 per vehicle, $5 per person or bicycle. Cypress National Preserve free.

ORIENTATION

Everglades National Park stretches across the entire southern end of Florida. **Florida City** is the real gateway to the Everglades and leads to **US 41,** also known as the **Tamiami Trail,** which stretches along the northern border of the park and is the only way across it. **Everglades City** lies on the western edge of the park, some distance from other towns, and leads to just one visitors center and a few hiking trails and boating routes. Other visitors centers are scattered throughout the park. To reach the sights, food, and accommodations in Florida City and Homestead, take US 41 W to **Route 997. Homestead** lies about 20 mi. south along Rte. 997. Florida City is just southwest of Homestead; go south on Rte. 997 and then take **Route 9336 West** to reach it. The main entrance to the park, **Ernest Coe Visitors Center,** is just inside the eastern edge of the Everglades, near Florida City. From here, Rte. 9336 cuts 40 mi. through the park past campgrounds, trailheads, and waterways to the Flamingo Visitors Center. Approaching from the north, **Florida's Turnpike** is a scenic and relatively easy route to Florida City, but be prepared to pay hefty tolls.

ACCOMMODATIONS

Campgrounds ❶ (☎877-444-6777; www.reservations.nps.gov) line Rte. 9336 inside the park. All sites have drinking water, grills, dump sites, and restrooms, but none have hookups. Flirt with a fellow camper while roasting marshmellows, though, and you might. (Reservations required Nov.-Mar. Sites $16. AmEx/D/MC/V.) **Backcountry** camping (☎239-695-3311) inside the park is accessible primarily by boat, although some campgrounds can be reached by foot or bike. Required permits are available on a first come, first served is accessible primarily by boat, although some campgrounds can be reached by foot or on bike.

Everglades Hostel and Tours, 20 SW 2nd Ave. (☎305-248-1122 or 800-372-3874; www.evergladeshostel.com), off Rte. 9336 (Palm Dr.). A backpacker's delight, with modern rooms and a friendly staff. After venturing into the Everglades, hang out with fellow travelers in the gazebo, gardens, or kitchen. The house has a big-screen TV, a piano, and an extensive video collection. Bicycles $15 per day. Canoes $30 per day. Free Internet, Wi-Fi $5. Breakfast included. Linen $2. Dorms $22 without reservation, $25 with reservation. Private rooms $65. MC/V. ❶

The Inn of Homestead, 1020 N. Homestead Blvd. (☎305-248-2121). Large, clean rooms. Pool access. Rooms $70. AmEx/D/MC/V. ❸

FOOD

Robert Is Here, 19200 SW 344th St. (☎305-246-1592; www.robertishere.com), off Palm Dr. In 1959, 6-year-old Robert sold his 1st bunch of cucumbers in Florida City and Robert Is Here was born. Today Robert sells tropical fruit, vegetables, local honey, and out-of-this-world key lime milkshakes ($4.40). While waiting for your shake, check out the emus or the golden macaw parrot out back. Wheelchair-accessible. Open Nov.-Aug. daily 8am-7pm. AmEx/D/MC/V. ❶

Rosita's, 199 Palm Dr. (☎305-246-3114), across the street from the hostel in Florida City. Rosita's has some of the best Mexican food in the area. Fire up your jets with a plate of hot tamales for $6.50. Wheelchair-accessible. Open daily 8:30am-9pm. AmEx/MC/V. ❷

Farmer's Market Restaurant, 300 N. Krome Ave. (☎305-242-0008), at the southern end of Homestead. The restaurant delivers "good home cooking" alongside a variety of seafood dishes, all of which are completely prepared—even breaded—in-house. Enjoy the delicious two eggs, ham, and grits ($6.25) or fried fish fingers ($9.50). Open daily 5:30am-9pm. MC/V. ❷

🅖 SIGHTS

CORAL CASTLE. After his fiancée changed her mind the day before the wedding, Latvian immigrant Ed Leedskalnin spent the next 29 years constructing this monument to lost love, singlehandedly turning 1100 tons of coral rock into a sculpture garden. The site has since been studied by anthropologists (though a team of psychiatrists might have been more appropriate), who think it might explain how humans built the Egyptian pyramids. (28655 S. Dixie Hwy., in Homestead. ☎305-248-6345; www.coralcastle.com. Open M-Th and Su 8am-7pm, F-Sa 8am-9pm. Self-guided tours. $9.75, ages 7-12 $5, seniors $6.50.)

EVERGLADES ALLIGATOR FARM. Though touristy, this is the place to see thousands of gators, from little hatchlings clambering for a bit of sunlight to 18-footers clambering for a bit of you. The farm is also home to crocs, snakes, and even the rare Florida panther. (40351 SW 192 Ave., 4 mi. south of Palm Dr., in Florida City. ☎305-247-2628; www.evergaldes.com. Open daily 9am-6pm. Alligator feeding noon and 3pm. Alligator shows daily at 11am, 2, 5pm. $13.50, ages 4-11 $8.50. Boat tours $5.50, children $3.50.)

COOPERTOWN AIRBOAT TOURS. Coopertown Airboat has been running tours for over 50 years. When you're pressed for time, this is the quickest way to get to the gators. The company not only leads 8 mi. tours, but also shelters a 14 ft. gator and serves up gator-tail samplers for $12. (52388 Tamiami Trail. ☎305-226-6048. Open daily 8am-6pm. Tours $19.)

LOOP ROAD DETOUR. Travelers seeking to commune more intimately with fauna can drive the deserted dirt road that once led to Al Capone's headquarters to see alligators, birds, and the occasional turtle or deer. The 18 mi. detour takes about 2hr. and is well worth the trip. For a really close look at wildlife, hardcore naturalists can head down one of the rough trails off the road.

CLYDE BUTCHER'S GALLERY AND STUDIO. The gallery exhibits photographs of the Everglades, the Western US, and Cuba. (22700 Tamiami Trail, 5 mi. after the sign for Bear Lake Campsite. ☎239-695-2428. Open daily 10am-5pm. Free.)

SCHNEBLY REDLAND'S WINERY. Schnebly's is only 3 years old, but its delicious tropical fruit wines will have you refilling your glass—and coming back with friends. Bring a picnic lunch and eat your baguette with a bottle of wine in the well-maintained backyard garden. (30205 SW 217th Ave. ☎305-242-1224; www.schnebly-winery.com. Open M-F 10am-5pm, Sa 10am-6pm, Su noon-5pm. Tastings daily. Tours $7. AmEx/MC/V.)

🅧 OUTDOORS

The park is swamped with fishing, hiking, canoeing, biking, and wildlife-watching opportunities. From November through April, the park sponsors amphitheater programs, canoe trips, and ranger-guided Slough Slogs (swamp tours). Just don't think about swimming; alligators (there are estimated to be over a million of them in the park), sharks, and barracuda patrol the waters. The air is swimming with carnivores, too: around sunrise and sunset, mosquitos are unavoidable, particularly in swampy areas. Unless you're a willing blood donor, the best time to visit is winter or spring, when animals congregate in and around shrinking pools of water, and heat, humidity, storms, and bugs are at a minimum. Wear long sleeves and bring insect repellent, but even then don't expect to escape unscathed. Warm oatmeal baths can provide welcome relief from itching.

HIKING

The Everglades is accessible via a series of well-developed short trails, the trailheads for which are located at the eastern entrance to the park. If you haven't picked up on this already, however, do note that in the 'Glades

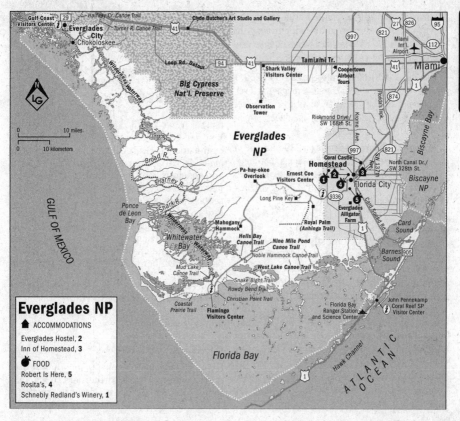

Everglades NP

🏠 ACCOMMODATIONS

Everglades Hostel, **2**
Inn of Homestead, **3**

🍴 FOOD

Robert Is Here, **5**
Rosita's, **4**
Schnebly Redland's Winery, **1**

it's always best to verify that a log is indeed a log (check for teeth) before, say, sitting on it.

Pa-hay-okee Overlook, 12.5 mi. from the main entrance off Rte. 9336. This overlook rewards visitors with a stunning view of wide-open sawgrass prairie after only a hundred yards or so.

Anhinga Trail, in the Royal Palm area inside the park, just 4 mi. from the main entrance. On this moderately difficult trail, explorers are likely to encounter anhinga birds and turtles.

Long Pine Key Trail, 16 mi. from the main entrance. For a more strenuous trek through 10 mi. of slash pine forest, try this trail.

Mahogany Hammock Trail, 20 mi. from the main entrance. This half-mile boardwalk offers incredible glimpses of both freshwater prairies and pine

forests. The Mahogany Hammock is at its best in the winter, when mosquitos are superbly absent.

BOATING

The best way to get your feet wet when traveling in the Everglades is to start paddling. Rent a canoe and take it to **Hell's Bay Canoe Trail,** about 29 mi. from the entrance—by all accounts a good place to push off. At **Nine Mile Pond,** you can paddle through vast mangrove trails and sawgrass prairies. The 99 mi. **Wilderness Waterway** winds its way from the northwest entrance to the Flamingo Visitors Center in the far south. Consult the rangers at the **Flamingo Visitors Center** for more information on navigating the park's waterways. **Everglades National Park Boat Tours,** at the Gulf Coast

Visitors Center, offers guided boat tours, but if you want to travel in your own canoe, your only options are the **Flamingo Visitors Center** and **Everglades Hostel and Tours** in Florida City.

> **Ten Thousand Island Cruise** (☎239-695-2591). The cruise is a 1½hr. tour through the Everglades's myriad tiny islands; visitors often see bald eagles, dolphins, and manatees. (Tours $26.50, $13.25 children.)

> **Mangrove Wilderness Cruise** (☎239-695-2591). A 2hr. cruise through inland swamps that brings its six passengers face-to-face with alligators. (Tours 9, 9:15, 11, 11:15am, 1, 1:15, 3, 3:15pm. $35, children $17.50.)

BIKING

While the Everglades mostly caters to those with walking sticks and canoe paddles, it also offers some excellent biking trails. The most popular route is a paved 15 mi. loop at the **Shark Valley Visitors Center** (☎305-221-8776). The trail peaks at an observation tower that offers incredible views of the park's rivers of grass, alligators, and deer. In the winter months, guided bike tours are available. (Tram tours daily May-Nov. 9:30, 11am, 1, 3pm; Dec.-Apr. every hr. 9am-4pm. $15.25. Reservations recommended. Bike rental ☎305-221-8455 available daily 8:30am-3pm. $6.50 per hr.)

⛴ THE ROAD TO EVERGLADES CITY: 94 MI.

Roll down **US 41 West (Tamiami Trail)** across the northern border of Everglades National Park and through the Big Cypress National Preserve. Take the exit for Everglades City after cruisin' through Ochopee.

EVERGLADES CITY ☎239

Everglades City is a bit of a waterlogged fishing town, but it contains the Gulf Coast Visitors Center, the main western visitors center for the Everglades. The **Everglades City Motel** ❹, 310 Collier Ave. (Rte. 29), has clean and spacious rooms that look as if they were just renovated. (☎800-695-8353. Reservations recommended. Rooms $79-109. MC/V.) For a bite to eat, the **Seafood Depot** ❸, 102 Collier Ave., cooks up tasty seafood dishes and may be your last chance to turn the food-chain tables and munch on some alligator. (☎239-695-0075. Dinner entrees $11-20. Open daily 10:30am-9pm. AmEx/D/MC/V.)

⛴ THE ROAD TO NAPLES: 36 MI.

Continue gliding north on **US 41 (South Tamiami Trail)** until you reach Naples.

NAPLES ☎239

Quiet and affluent, Naples is mostly a retirement community for Northerners (a.k.a Yankees). Although the city is starting to diversify, a stroll down the ritzy main drag (5th Ave. S.)

TIME TRAVEL IN THE EVERGLADES

What we see of the Everglades now is a shadow of what they once were. Before humans moved to the region, Lake Okeechobee would flood every year, allowing water to flow hundreds of miles through sawgrass plains down to the tip of Florida. The use of land for farming and industry in the region has stopped this water flow and reduced the Everglades to less than half of its original size.

On June 25, 2008, the state of Florida announced a $1.75 billion deal to buy back 187,000 acres of land between Lake Okeechobee and the park by 2012. This deal, which marks the state of Florida's largest land acquisition ever, will allow the natural flow of water to resume. Assuming the deal progresses, water will saturate the park during its dry seasons, preventing fires and protecting wildlife.

Unfortunately, the deal is not without its complications. The land is being purchased from US Sugar, a company that is going out of business. Thousands of workers will lose their jobs as a result of the purchase, and the land may be damaged from years of fertilizer use.

These concerns, however, have not proved deal-breakers: in about 20 years, the Everglades will

reveals just what you would expect: beautifully kept buildings, high-end chain stores, expensive restaurants, and hand-holding octogenarians. The budget traveler will appreciate Naples's beautiful white sand beaches lined with palm trees. Head down to the **Naples Pier** (at the westernmost end of 12th Ave. S) to see pelicans and the occasional dolphin family. The pier can get crowded; try to visit in the evening, when the crowds head home. The streets of Naples are lined with chain food options. If you want something to cool you off on a hot day, stop by **Amalfi Italian Ice ❶**, 51 9th St. N. (Ices $3-4. ☎239-659-5600.) When life gives you lemons, head to the **Lemon Tree Inn ❹**, 250 9th St. S. (US 41), which has lovely rooms, a pool, garden, gazebo, and free lemonade in the lobby. Some rooms even have screened-in porches to save you from the ravages of bloodthirsty local mosquitoes. (☎239-262-1414. Breakfast included. Rooms Apr.-Dec. $89; Jan.-Mar. $129-179. AmEx/D/MC/V.) The **Tamiami Motel ❷**, 2164 Tamiami Trail E., about 2 mi. before downtown Naples and the beach, offers simple and clean rooms. (☎239-774-4626. Rooms $55-90. AmEx/D/MC/V.)

◪ THE ROAD TO LOVERS KEY STATE PARK: 21 MI.

Head north on **US 41 (South Tamiami Trail)** and turn left at **Bonita Beach Boulevard,** which becomes **Estero Boulevard.** Follow the road 5mi. until you see signs for Lovers Key. Turn left into the park.

LOVERS KEY STATE PARK   ☎239

An exploration of ◪**Lovers Key State Park,** 8700 Estero Blvd., is one of Florida's most romantic adventures. You can take short hikes in the park or rent a kayak at the concession stand in Parking Area One and paddle through the brackish streams between the narrow keys. The shell-covered beaches are the highlight of the park and are generally not too crowded. For real seclusion, walk about 30-45min. north or south along the beach. (☎239-463-4588. Kayaks $40 per day. Canoes $50 per day. Open daily sunrise-sunset. $3 for 1 person, $5 per vehicle with 2+ people.)

◪ THE ROAD TO FORT MYERS BEACH: 6 MI.

Turn left out of Lovers Key State Park and continue on **Estero Boulevard (US 41).** After a few miles, you'll

cross a bridge and enter Fort Myers Beach. From US 41, turn right on **Route 865 West,** then left on **Route 869 West** and left again onto **Route 865 South,** following signs for Fort Myers Beach. Rte. 865 S. crosses the bridge over the San Carlos Bay as Estero Blvd.

FORT MYERS BEACH   ☎239

Fort Myers is famous for its happening beach scene. The beach is accessible on nearly every block, and young children, spring break partiers, and hand-holding octogenarians mingle on its hot sand. Just over the bridge is the town square, where most action takes place. The newly renovated **Beacon Motel ❸**, 1240 Estero Blvd., is a good deal and right on the beach—the staff sports Hawaiian shirts. (☎239-463-5264; www.thebeaconmotel.com. Reservations recommended. Rooms from $70. AmEx/D/MC/V.) ◪**Dusseldorf's ❷**, 1113 Estero Blvd., has over 140 imported beers and serves a wide variety of excellent German and American dishes. Be sure to try the quarter-pound hot dog ($5.25). (☎239-463-5251. Sandwiches $6-9. Sausage sampler $12. Accordion music F-Su 3-7pm. Open daily 11am-2am. AmEx/D/MC/V.) If you want a quick bite right by the beach, head to **Chiller's ❶**, 1190 Estero Blvd. The blended fruit smoothies ($4-5) are delicious. (☎239-463-4747. According to the sign: "Open early, closed late." AmEx/D/MC/V.)

◪ DETOUR
SANIBEL ISLAND

Take Estero Blvd. over the bridge out of Fort Myers and take a left on **Summerlin Road.** Continue 8 mi., crossing over a **toll bridge** ($6) to Sanibel.

A quiet, affluent community of lounging vacationers and hand-holding octogenarians, Sanibel Island is famous for its seashells and for the **JN "Ding" Darling Wildlife Refuge,** 1 Wildlife Dr. The refuge, established in 1976 to protect one of the world's largest mangrove ecosystems, has many good short hikes and offers tram rides. (Refuge visitors' information ☎239-472-1100. Open M-Th and Sa-Su sunrise-sunset. $5 per vehicle.) **Tarpon Bay Explorers** has kayak and canoe rentals for $20 per 2hr. (☎239-472-8900). Head to **Billy's Rentals,** 1509 Periwinkle Way, if you want to explore the island's 25 mi. of bike paths. (☎239-472-5248; www.billysrentals.com. Bikes $15 per day. Open daily 8:30am-5pm.) A 15 mi. drive to the end of the island will take you to **Captiva Beach,** where fabulous sunsets light up the sky.

THE ROAD TO OSPREY: 86 MI.

Head back west along **Summerlin Road** and follow signs to **I-75 North.** Take I-75 N. until **Exit 195,** then turn left and drive 6 mi. to Oscar Scherer State Park.

OSCAR SCHERER STATE PARK ☎941

Osprey is most notably home to **Oscar Scherer State Park ❶,** 1843 S. Tamiami Trail, which has beautiful creekside **camping ❶,** fishing, swimming, and canoeing (rentals $5 per hr., $25 per day) amid trees draped with Spanish moss. (☎941-483-5956. Open daily sunrise-sunset. $4 per vehicle. Sites with water and hookup $24.20. AmEx/D/MC/V.) For slightly cheaper camping, head 8 mi. east to **Myakka River State Park,** State Rd. 72, Exit 205, which has a few **campsites ❶** about 2 mi. from the parking lot. (☎941-361-6511. Sites $22. AmEx/D/MC/V.)

THE ROAD TO SARASOTA: 13 MI.

US 41 runs parallel to Oscar Scherer State Park. Press on 13 mi. north and you'll run directly into Sarasota.

SARASOTA ☎941

The self-proclaimed "cultural capital" of Florida, Sarasota doesn't disappoint. The city has a beautiful harbor, a premier arts scene, and the stunning white sand beaches that make Florida's Gulf Coast famous.

VITAL STATS
Population: 53,000
Tourist Office: Sarasota Convention and Visitors Bureau, 701 N. Tamiami Trail (☎941-957-1877; www.sarasotafl.org). Open M-Sa 10am-4pm, Su noon-3pm.
Library and Internet Access: Fruitville Library, 100 Coburn Rd. (☎941-861-2500). Free. Open M-Th 9am-8pm, F-Sa 9am-5pm.
Post Office: 1661 Ringling Blvd. (☎941-331-4221). Open M-F 8am-5:30pm, Sa 9am-noon. **Postal Code:** 34236.

ORIENTATION

US 41 runs right into the center of town, where it changes into **Bay Shore Drive** and

passes through Sarasota's lush harbor-front area. Turn right on major streets like **Ringling Boulevard, Main Street,** or **Fruitville Road** to reach downtown. I-75 is a little to the west of town and runs north to Tampa or south to Naples.

ACCOMMODATIONS

The Cadillac Motel, 4021 N. Tamiami Trail (☎941-355-7108). Has clean rooms and access to a swimming pool. Rooms June-Sept. $40-54; Oct.-May $60. AmEx/D/MC/V. ❷

FOOD

Yoder's Restaurant, 3434 Bahia Vista St. (☎941-955-7771; www.yodersrestaurant.com). This Amish restaurant is in the heart of the Amish 'hood. Meals come with homemade bread and butter, and Mrs. Yoder's pie (slice $4) is divine. Open M-Sa 6am-8pm. AmEx/MC/V. ❸

Phillippi Creek Village Oyster Bar, 5353 S. Tamiami Trail (☎941-925-4444; www.creekseafood.com). In addition to oysters, Phillippi serves up sandwiches ($8) and seafood platters. Open-air dockside seating with nautical decor aplenty. Entrees $13-20. Open M-Th 11am-10pm, F-Sa 11am-10:30pm. AmEx/D/MC/V. ❹

Sierra Station Cafe, 400 N. Lemon Ave. (☎941-906-1400; www.sierrastation.com). This cafe is creatively painted to resemble a 19th-century train station. A little pricey, but a good place to grab breakfast or lunch downtown. The turkey train sandwich ($8.75) and the eggs benedict ($9) come highly recommended. Open daily 8am-3pm. AmEx/MC/V. ❸

SIGHTS

JOHN AND MABLE RINGLING MUSEUM OF ART. Built by circus baron John Ringling in an attempt to promote Sarasota (most of which he owned), the expansive, three-part museum is now Florida's official state art museum. The **Art Museum** houses an impressive collection of work by Rubens. The **Circus Museum** features all sorts of colorful circus relics and a model circus painstakingly assembled over 50 years by circus enthusiast Howard Tibbals. But the star of the show is the **Ca d'Zan Mansion,** the one-time Ringling winter quarters. Evoking Ringling's fondness for Venetian-Gothic palaces, the mansion has marble pillars, cathedral ceilings, and the historic Asolo Theater, built in Italy in 1798 and moved to the museum piece by piece—and boasts an unbeatable Gulf view. *(5401 Bay Shore Dr., off US 41. ☎941-359-5700; www.ringling.org. Open daily 10am-5:30pm. $19, students and Florida teachers $6.)*

■**SARASOTA CLASSIC CAR MUSEUM.** This world-class collection is comprised of nearly 100 classic cars that span automotive history. From Ford Model Ts to a 1974 Bentley Formula One racer and everything in between, these cars deserve a look from both avid enthusiasts and curious roadtrippers. The collection is as amusing as it is astounding. Featured vehicles change frequently but include such cars as Paul McCartney's humble Mini, John Lennon's funky "psychedelic roadster," and the 1982 Delorean from *Back to the Future*. *(5500 N. Tamiami Trail, across the street from Ringling. ☎941-355-6228; www.sarasotacarmuseum.org. Open daily 9am-6pm. $8.50.)*

◪ THE ROAD TO BRADENTON: 13 MI.
From Sarasota, head north on **US 41.**

BRADENTON   ☎941

Take a left on Manatee Ave. and an immediate right at 10th St. to visit the **South Florida Museum,** 201 10th St., which chronicles southwestern Florida's history from the Pleistocene to the present. The **Parker Manatee Aquarium,** which is but one part of the museum, houses Manatee County's official mascot, 59-year-old Snooty. Mornings at the museum are often devoted to programs for delightful but screaming children. (☎941-746-4131; www.southfloridamuseum.org. Open Jan.-Apr. and July M-Sa 10am-5pm, Su noon-5pm; May-June and Aug.-Dec. Tu-Sa 10am-5pm, Su noon-5pm. $16, ages 4-12 $12, 60+ $14.)

◪ THE ROAD TO ST. PETERSBURG AND CLEARWATER: 30 MI.
Continue on **US 41 North** and hang a left at **US 19,** which will take you to I-275 N. The view crossing the **Sunshine Skyway Bridge** into Clearwater and St. Petersburg is well worth the $1 toll.

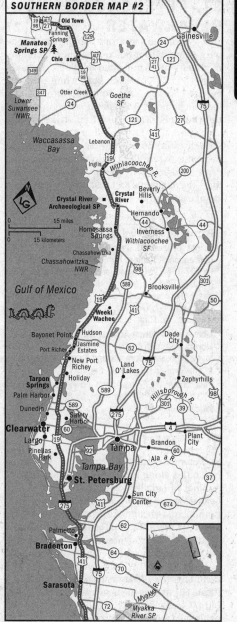

SOUTHERN BORDER MAP #2

ST. PETERSBURG AND CLEARWATER ☎727

Just across the bay from Tampa, St. Petersburg is home to a relaxed beach community of young singles and hand-holding octogenarians. The town basks in soft, white beaches, emerald water, and about 361 days of perfect sunshine every year (if you don't count the thunderstorms that often strike around 4 or 5pm). The St. Petersburg-to-Clearwater stretch caters to beach bums and city slickers alike. While the outdoor scenery draws crowds, indoor activities are equally captivating—the museums and restaurants rival even orange-and-purple sunsets.

VITAL STATS
Population: 248,000/108,000
Tourist Offices: St. Petersburg/Clearwater Area Convention & Visitors Bureau, 14450 46th St. N. (☎727-464-7200; www.floridasbeach.com). Open M-F 8am-5pm, Sa 10am-5pm, Su noon-5pm. **Suncoast Welcome Center,** 3350 Courtney Campbell Cswy. (☎727-726-1547), in Clearwater. Open M-Sa 9am-5pm, Su 10am-5pm.
Library and Internet Access: St. Petersburg Main Library, 3745 9th Ave. N. (☎727-893-7724). Open M, W, F-Sa 9am-6pm, Tu and Th 11am-8pm, Su 10am-6pm.
Post Office: 3135 1st Ave. N. (☎727-322-6696), at 31st St. Open M-F 8am-6pm, Sa 8am-12:30pm. **Postal Code:** 33730.

ORIENTATION

St. Petersburg and Clearwater are two separate cities along a peninsula connected by a number of smaller towns. In St. Petersburg, **Central Avenue** parallels numbered avenues, running east-west in the downtown area. **34th Street (US 19), I-275,** and **Fourth Street** are major north-south thoroughfares. The beaches line a strip of barrier islands on the far west side of town facing the Gulf. Several causeways, including the **Clearwater Memorial Causeway (Route 60),** access the beaches from St. Petersburg. Clearwater sits at the far north of the peninsula. **Gulf Boulevard** runs down the coastline, connecting St. Petersburg, Clearwater, and all the towns in between.

You'll find a parking garage at the corner of 2nd Ave. N and 2nd St. N that costs $1 per hr., or at most $6 per day. There's free parking in abundance in downtown St. Petersburg and all street parking is free after 6pm.

ACCOMMODATIONS

Cheap motels line **Fourth Street North** and **US 19** in St. Petersburg. To avoid the worst neighborhoods, stay on the north end of 4th St. and the south end of US 19. Several inexpensive motels are located on the beaches along **Gulf Boulevard** in the towns of **Madeira Beach** and **Indian Rocks Beach.**

☑ Gram's Place, 3109 N. Ola Ave (☎813-310-3447; www.grams-inn-tampa.com). Across the bay from St. Petersburg, Gram's is the place to meet fellow travelers from all corners of the globe. Sleep in rooms whose decor evokes a railroad station and sleeper cars. Check out a phenomenal view of Tampa and the surrounding areas from the Crow's Nest atop the hostel. Cable TV, A/C, and outdoor hot tub. Dorms $25. D/MC/V. ❶

☑ Fort De Soto County Park, 3500 Pinellas Bayway S (☎727-893-9185 or 582-2267; www.pinellascounty.org/park). Fort De Soto, which is composed of 5 islands jutting into the Gulf of Mexico, was rated the top beach in the US by *Dr. Beach* in 2005. North Beach can get crowded during peak hours, but there are plenty of deserted beach areas along the Gulf side. If you're planning to visit, check out the park's website; you can view pictures of every campsite and make reservations in advance. Park office open daily 8am-9pm. Tyrannical curfew 10pm. Sites $34. MC/V. ❷

Suncoast Motel, 10264 Gulf Blvd. (☎727-360-9256). A hop, skip, and jump from the beach; go splash about to your heart's content in the surf. Quaint. Has basic rooms with small kitchens and free Wi-Fi. Singles $39-51. MC/V. ❷

FOOD

St. Petersburg has a wide variety of restaurants, but you'll do best if you have a penchant for seafood. Night owls are out of luck—not much stays open after 9pm.

Fourth Street Shrimp Store, 1006 4th St. N. (☎727-822-0325; www.theshrimpstore.com). Purveyor of all things shrimp, the Shrimp Store is full of seafaring memorabilia and license plates. ½ lb. jumbo shrimp $11. Chipotle shrimp salad $8. Open M-Th and Su 11am-9pm, F-Sa 11am-9:30pm. MC/V. ❷

Frenchy's Cafe, 41 Baymont St. (☎727-446-3607; www.frenchysonline.com). Though neither a cafe nor French, this place attracts tons of tourists from Clearwater Beach. The tasty fish sandwiches are made from fish caught by Frenchy's own fleet. Be sure to try the shrimp sandwich ($8) with some of Frenchy's own habañero sauce. Open M-Th 11am-11pm, F-Sa 11am-midnight, Su noon-11pm. AmEx/MC/V. ❷

Tangelo's Bar and Grille, 226 1st Ave. N. (☎727-894-1695). A Cuban restaurant with fabulously fruity sangria ($3 per glass). Variety of filling sandwiches $5-8. Open M 11am-4pm, Tu-Th 11am-8pm, F-Sa 11am-9pm. MC/V. ❷

The Chattaway Drive-In, 358 22nd Ave. S (☎727-823-1544). No longer a drive-in, this old school establishment's entrance features a bridge spanning a fish pond and a patio lit by twinkling lights. Fish and chips $13.50. Live blues F-Sa night. Open daily 11am-9:30pm. Cash only. ❸

Chiang Mai Thailand Restaurant, 1100 Central Ave. (☎727-895-4851). Famous among locals, Chiang Mai offers amazing Thai cuisine at reasonable prices. For a change from grouper, try some tofu red curry or a great Panang curry ($9). Open M-Sa 11am-3pm and 4-10pm. AmEx/MC/V. ❷

◉ SIGHTS

Grab a copy of *TBT* or **Creative Loafing** at many restaurants in downtown St. Petersburg for the lowdown on area events. *Creative Loafing* includes alternative news stories about upcoming festivals, art exhibits, and forums that are open to the public. The *St. Petersburg Official Visitor's Guide* also has information about tourist attractions, hands out coupons, and provides maps.

MUSEUM OF FINE ARTS. This is St. Petersburg's premier museum, featuring over 4600 objects from such big-name artists as Cézanne, Monet, and Gaugin. A spectacular glass conservatory connects the older wing of the museum with a recently constructed wing. The contemporary art halls, which feature Georgia O'Keefe's *Poppy*, are especially worthwhile. The museum also has a small gallery with rotating exhibits of works by the likes of Ansel Adams. (*255 Beach Dr. NE. ☎727-896-2667; www.fine-arts.org. Open Tu-Sa 10am-5pm, Su 1-5pm. Free 45min. tours daily 11am, 1:30, 2:30pm. $12, seniors $8, students $6, under 7 free.*)

BEACHES. Beaches are one of the most worthwhile attractions along the coast. Although **Pass-a-Grille Beach's** parking meters eat quarters by the bucket ($0.25 per 15min.), it is the most beautiful beach in the area. For cheaper options, drive down to **Fort De Soto Park,** where parking is free, or check out **Clearwater Beach,** located at the northern end of Gulf Blvd. The touristy but fun **Sunsets at Pier 60 Festival** brings arts and entertainment to Clearwater Beach in the form of souvenir booths and buskers. (☎727-449-1036; www.sunsetsatpier60.com. Festival daily from 2hr. before sundown to 2hr. after.)

SALVADOR DALÍ MUSEUM. St. Petersburg got lucky: avid Dalí collectors Mr. and Mrs. A. Reynolds Morse were looking for a tourist-oriented town to give their collection public exposure, and St. Petersburg fit the bill. Since it opened in 1982, the Salvador Dalí Museum (now the property of the city itself) has housed the largest collection of Dalí's work in the world, featuring a stunning array of oil paintings, prints, sculptures, and drawings that span over 50 years of the maestro's life work. Be sure to check out his first Surrealist painting, the spectacular *Hallucinogenic Toreador.* Informative tours are offered throughout the day. (*1000 3rd St. S. ☎727-823-3767; www.salvadordalimuseum.org. Open M-W and Sa 9:30am-5:30pm, Th 9:30am-8pm, F 9:30am-6pm, Su noon-5:30pm. Free tours every hr. Admission $15, students $6, under 10 $4, seniors $12.50.*)

FLORIDA INTERNATIONAL MUSEUM. Closed for the summer of 2008, the museum plans to unveil itself anew in fall 2008. It has no permanent exhibits but rather hosts excellent traveling displays. Topics touch on history, anthropology, archaeology, and a little bit of everything in between. Tickets can be expensive (up to $25), so make sure to call ahead before making the trip. *(244 2nd Ave. N. ☎ 727-341-7900; www.floridamuseum.org. Call ahead for prices. Open Tu-Sa 10am-5pm, Su noon-5pm.)*

HASLAM'S BOOK STORE. A local landmark since 1933, Haslam's is the biggest bookstore in Florida and has a loyal contingent of shoppers and over 300,000 new and used books. It even has roadtripper cred—Jack Kerouac used to hang here. Pick up a 10-cent romance novel to entertain you on the road. *Let's Go* does not recommend reading while driving. *(2025 Central Ave. ☎ 727-822-8616; www.haslams.com. Open M-Sa 10am-6:30pm.)*

SUNKEN GARDENS. The Gardens are home to some of the oldest tropical plants in the region; like Florida's inhabitants, many have lived more than 100 years. The gardens were originally dug out of a large sink hole by plumber George Turner. The city later took over, adding 6000 plants and even constructing a butterfly garden. *(1824 4th St. N. ☎ 727-551-3100. Open M-Sa 10am-4:30pm, Su noon-4:30pm. $8, children $4, seniors $6.)*

DERBY LANE. If museums aren't your thing, or if you just want to kick back and relax after a long day, check out Derby Lane. You can wager any amount on greyhounds in any one of about 15 daily races or just grab a seat and watch the action. Derby Lane also features a poker room upstairs, with a variety of different games running weekdays 1pm-1am and

weekends 2pm-2am. *(10490 Gandy Blvd. ☎ 727-812-3339. Greyhound races begin at 7:30pm M-Sa with additional 12:30pm matinees W, Sa. Free admission. 18+ to wager or play poker.)*

🚗 **THE ROAD TO TARPON SPRINGS: 18 MI.** Leave St. Petersburg by jetting north on **34th Street (US 19).** Follow US 19 until **US 19A,** and then swing a left toward the Gulf. Turn onto **Dodecanese Boulevard** and continue onward to reach Tarpon Springs.

TARPON SPRINGS   ☎ 727

Sponge harvesters used hooks to retrieve the sponges off the coast of Tarpon Springs until Greek immigrant John Corcoris introduced Greek sponge-diving technology in 1905 (revolutionizing life for sponge-divers across the nation). Unfortunately, a red algae bloom in 1947 wiped out massive amounts of sponge and forced the waterfront to change its focus from industry to tourism. Tarpon Springs subsequently emerged as a little piece of Greece in Florida, with a close-knit, Greek-speaking community and a thriving Greek Orthodox church. In early January, the bayou just south of the docks on Tarpon Ave. hosts an **Epiphany Festival** in which young Greek Orthodox men dive into the chilly waters to retrieve a ceremonial cross. Whoever recovers the cross is said to be blessed for one year. Having capitalized on the local culture, the waterfront "sponge district" is now touristy, but it's still

RUN AND DONE

In the United States, animal rights are protected by the government—in most cases. However, the Animal Welfare Act does not apply to greyhound racing. Greyhound races can be a thrill to watch, but few people realize how the dogs are treated or that, after greyhounds stop being profitable to their owners, they are often euthanized.

Several organizations, such as the Greyhound Pets of America (GPA) and the National Greyhound Adoption Program (NGAP), have sprung up in the past 20 years to save the lives of greyhounds after their racing careers are over by putting them up for adoption. These organizations neuter the dogs and provide them full medical care before putting them up for people like you to adopt.

Greyhounds put up for adoption are generally only two to five years old, and they can live for a full 12 years with adequate medical care. They are a friendly and social breed by nature, good with children, and thrive on the attention and affection of humans. For more information on adoption, contact GPA (☎ 800-366-1472) or NGAP (☎ 215-331-9718).

worth a stop. Buy a souvenir sponge and sample Greek food at **Mama's Greek Cuisine ❸**, 735 Dodecanese Blvd. (☎727-944-2888. Gyros $6. Broiled octopus $12. Open daily 11am-10pm. MC/V.) For a more friendly encounter with Tarpon Springs's marine life, head to **Tarpon Springs Aquarium,** 850 Dodecanese Blvd. At the aquarium, you can get close to a variety of sharks and rays—and even pet them. (☎727-938-5378. $5.75, children $3.75, seniors $5. Open M-Sa 10am-6pm, Su noon-6pm.)

THE ROAD TO WEEKI WACHEE: 26 MI.

Continue on **US 19 North.** Drive carefully; while this road is unquestionably the most direct route between Tarpon Springs and Weeki Wachee, it also has an average of 52 fatalities each year and is the single most dangerous stretch of road in the US.

WEEKI WACHEE ☎352

Since 1947, Weeki Wachee has been famous for the **Weeki Wachee Springs Park,** 6131 Commercial Way (US 19 N.), where professional **mermaids** hold underwater spectacles and then pose for pictures with landlubbers. Nowadays the park's bread and butter are wilderness river cruises and a water park, which is often filled with kids. The mermaids, though, remain the real draw. The 1:30pm show is fantastic; mermaids demonstrate underwater eating, drinking, and dancing. Once a month, retired mermaids from decades past come back to relive their underwater glory days. (☎352-596-2062; www.weekiwachee.com. Open daily 10am-4pm. Shows 11am, 1:30, 3pm. Parking $3. $25, ages 3-10 $20.)

THE ROAD TO CRYSTAL RIVER: 26 MI.

Follow **US 19 North** to Crystal River.

CRYSTAL RIVER ☎352

The **Crystal River Archaeological State Park,** on Museum Point, preserves the remains of a Native American mound complex and village that stood on the riverbank 1600 years ago. Because the inhabitants left no written record, the purpose of the mound complex remains unknown. The small **visitors center** displays artifacts found on site, and there are tranquil fishing and picnic spots on the riverbanks. (☎352-795-3817. Park open daily 8am-sunset.

Visitors center open daily 9am-5pm. $2 per vehicle, $1 per pedestrian.) The park is surrounded by the **Crystal River Preserve State Park,** which offers a number of short hiking trails. In the winter, wear a hat; over 350 types of migratory birds frequent the area. (☎352-795-3817. Open daily 8am-sunset. Free.)

THE ROAD TO CHIEFLAND: 50 MI.

Continue on **US 19** to the town of Chiefland, turn left on **Route 320,** and drive 7 mi.

CHIEFLAND ☎352

The giant spring at **Manatee Springs State Park** gushes forth water at a rate of 50 to 150 million gallons per day, providing excellent swimming on hot summer afternoons. The park is absolutely beautiful for canoeing and kayaking—paddle through the serene Suwannee River and look out for manatees, the gentle creatures for which the park is named. **Camping ❶** is also available. (☎352-493-6072; www.floridastateparks.org. Open daily 8am-sunset. $4 per vehicle. Sites $17. AmEx/D/MC/V.)

THE ROAD TO OLD TOWN: 13 MI.

Continue on **US 19 North** to reach Old Town.

OLD TOWN ☎352

The village of Old Town sits on the Suwannee River, where the lazy flow of the dark waterway creates an aura of tranquility along its banks. Enjoy long afternoons and warm, peaceful evenings at the **Suwannee Gables Motel ❸,** 27659 SE US 19. Each room in this tiny motel has a great river view, pool access, and a gorgeous wooded backyard above the Suwannee's banks. Feel free to loll around the dock, but don't try to swim—the current is too strong in this section of the river. (☎352-542-7752; www.suwanneegables.com. Rooms from $75; cabins $180. AmEx/MC/V.)

THE ROAD TO CROSS CITY: 10 MI.

10 mi. after leaving Old Town on **US 19 North,** you'll hit Cross City, the seat of tiny Dixie County.

CROSS CITY ☎352

Though "Cross Village" might be an apter name, you'll find a drugstore, a grocery store, a gas station, and a few restaurants. The **Car-**

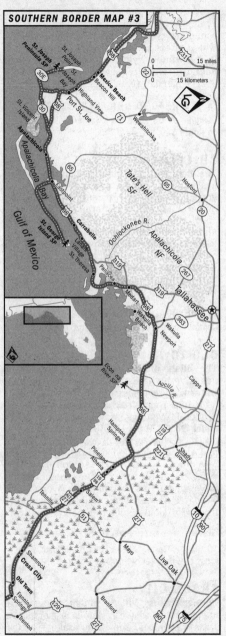

SOUTHERN BORDER MAP #3

riage Inn Motel and Restaurant ❷, 16782 SE Hwy. 18, serves hearty breakfast fare. Try the Big Bear Special—a plentiful serving of hash browns and eggs ($5) that will leave you wanting to hibernate it off in one of the motel's comfy rooms—or an equally hearty country buffet for just $8. (☎352-498-3910. Open M-Th and Su 7am-9pm, F-Sa 7am-10pm. Free Internet. Rooms $52-65. AmEx/D/MC/V.)

⚐ THE ROAD TO CARRABELLE: 85 MI.

At the edge of Perry, turn left onto **US 98 West.** Follow it for 85 mi. through several small towns and forested areas and along the Gulf. Notice that the houses on the shore are perched on stilts—an attempt to keep them above hurricane flooding. Pass over the Ochlockonee River and into Carrabelle.

CARRABELLE   ☎850

Life in this quiet fishing village is as slow and steady as the tides. Stop at the **World's Smallest Police Station**—a single telephone booth off US 98. The phone was previously located outside of the police station in town, but there it was used by tourists to make unauthorized long-distance calls. The new and more remote location was intended to prevent abuse of the phone—unfortunately, the plan didn't work because the tourists just moved with it. Take a load off at **Carrabelle Junction ❶**, 88 Tallahassee St., for some of the only espresso ($1.50-2) you'll find along the coast. The little cafe has wicker chairs, an old-time jukebox, ice cream, and gloriously cheap coffee. Look for Tallahassee St. right as you enter Carrabelle, then turn right. (☎850-697-9550. Open M-F 8am-4pm, Sa-Su 9am-3pm. Cash only.)

◨ DETOUR

ST. GEORGE ISLAND STATE PARK

Continue 16 mi. down **US 98** through the ominous Tate's Hell Forest to Eastpoint and go left over the **Bryant Grady Patton Bridge.** The state park is 4 mi. down US 98, at the east end of the island.

▨**St. George Island State Park's** nine miles of undeveloped beaches and sand dunes are right at the end of St. George Island. The park is the place to go if you are looking for waves, few people, and an extremely dry climate. Amid the sandy coves, salt marshes, shady pines, and oak forests of the pristine island sanctuary, you may hear the call of an American bald eagle or the rustle of a loggerhead turtle, raccoon, or ghost crab. If you really love it, set up **camp ❶**. (☎850-927-2111. Open daily sunrise-sunset. $5 per vehicle. Tent sites $21.)

☖ THE ROAD TO APALACHICOLA: 23 MI.
Head west on **Highway 98.**

APALACHICOLA   ☎850

Located on the shores of a peaceful bay, this romantic fishing port has an inviting (and mostly red-brick) historic downtown. Apalachicola is part of the Forgotten Coast that is not too forgotten—as indicated by the **Forgotten Coast Outfitters,** 94 Market St. (☎850-653-9669. Open M and W-Sa 11am-4pm.) Head to the 100-year-old **Apalachicola Seafood Grill ❹**, 100 Market St., to enjoy the best oysters in town. Entrees $15-20. (☎850-653-9510. Open M-Sa 11am-4pm. AmEx/D/MC/V.) The **Rancho Inn ❸**, 240 US 98 W., has large, well-equipped rooms with access to a pool and barbecue grill. (☎850-653-9435. Reception 8am-11pm. Rooms M-F $85, Sa-Su $95. AmEx/D/MC/V.) If you feel like splurging, the **Coombs House Inn ❺**, 80 Sixth St., is the place to do it. The inn features amazing wood paneling and floral decor, four poster beds, flatscreen TVs, free Wi-Fi, and complementary bicycles and deck chairs. (☎850-653-9199. Rooms from $119.)

⧉ DETOUR

ST. JOSEPH PENINSULA STATE PARK

Follow **US 98** out of Apalachicola for about 5 mi. until you reach the fork in the road at **State Road 30A** (there is a small sign indicating the park on the right). Bear left and follow 30A for 12 mi. to **Cape San Blas Road (30E).** Turn left, and continue another 10 mi.

Here on the edge of the world sits the astoundingly beautiful **St. Joseph Peninsula State Park.** Miles of white sand beaches, sea-oat-covered dunes, and a forested interior provide an incredible backdrop for campers, snorkelers, and fishermen. Nearly two-thirds of the park is protected wilderness and serves as a sanctuary for brown pelicans, horseshoe crabs, sea turtles, peregrine falcons, and monarch butterflies. St. Joseph offers phenomenal

birdwatching opportunities; 240 different species of birds have been spotted in the park to date. **Camping ❶** is available at primitive sites. (☎850-227-1327. Open 8am-sunset. $4 per vehicle. Sites $20. Cabins, currently under renovation, usually $90. AmEx/D/MC/V.) For rentals, check out **Scallop Cove BP,** 4310 Cape San Blas Rd., just outside of the park. (☎850-227-1573. Bikes $8 per 4hr. Canoes and kayaks $35 per 4hr. Open daily 8am-sunset.)

☖ THE ROAD TO MEXICO BEACH: 34 MI.
From Apalachicola, head northwest on **US 98/Route 30** and continue to Mexico Beach.

MEXICO BEACH   ☎850

Most of the town is contained on a small stretch of US 98. The town has of late built condos to attract Panama City Beach tourists looking for sandy seclusion. With many shores located no more than 50 ft. from the road, Mexico Beach is a good place to get your daily dose of sun and sand without getting too far off-route. If you're feeling peckish, head to **Sharon's Cafe ❶**, 1100 US 98, for pancakes, eggs, sandwiches, and a huge helping of happy faces. (☎850-648-8634. Breakfast $3-6. Open daily 6am-2pm. Cash only.) If you insist on stopping for the night, try the **Buena Vista Motel ❸**, 903 Hwy. 98, which has huge rooms right on the beach. (☎850-648-5323. $55-$135. AmEx/D/MC/V.)

☖ THE ROAD TO PANAMA CITY BEACH: 37 MI.
Continue on **US 98,** passing through Panama City, to Panama City Beach.

> **TIME CHANGE.** At the eastern border of Mexico Beach, US 98 enters the Central Time Zone, where it is 1hr. earlier.

PANAMA CITY BEACH   ☎850

It doesn't matter whether you're in college or not; the Panama City Beach (PCB) experience is the epitome of the spring-break rampage.

Here at the heart of the "Redneck Riviera," there is no pretension or high culture—just 27 mi. of hot sand obscured by thousands of tourists, miles of parties, and loud, thumping bass. Bath-temperature turquoise water, roaring roller coasters, surf shops, and water parks round out the city's entertainment possibilities—no octogenarians here.

VITAL STATS

Population: 8000

Tourist Office: Panama City Visitors Center, 17001 Panama City Beach Pkwy. (☎800-722-3224; www. thebeachloversbeach.com), at the corner of US 98 and Rte. 79. Open daily 8am-5pm.

Library and Internet Access: Panama City Beach Library, 110 S. Arnold Dr. (☎850-233-5055), in Panama City Beach. Free. Open M 10am-8pm, Tu-F 10am-5pm, Sa 10am-4pm.

Post Office: 1336 Sherman Ave. (☎850-747-4890). Open M-F 8:30am-6pm, Sa 9:30am-12:30pm. **Postal Code:** 32401.

⊞ ORIENTATION

PCB is essentially two roads: **US 98 (Panama City Beach Parkway)** runs parallel to **Alternate US 98 (Front Beach Road),** which runs along the beach. Front Beach Rd. becomes the glorious, tourist-crammed beachfront known as the "Miracle Strip," PCB's main drag. As you enter PCB from the east, turn south (left) onto Thomas Dr. This will take you to the beach, where it joins up with Front Beach Rd.

⊞ ACCOMMODATIONS

Finding an affordable hotel on the beach in PCB is no picnic. Call well in advance for summer reservations. Cheap motels can be found in Panama City on US 98, just over the bridge from PCB. Though these rooms are rarely worth the $50 they average, they are the best bargain in town.

🏨 **Monterey Motel,** 5501 Thomas Dr. (☎850-234-5062). Has large singles with living rooms. Rooms from $60. AmEx/D/MC/V. ❸

Treasure Cove Motel, 2603 Thomas Dr. (☎850-230-0712). Closer to PCB proper. The rooms

are simple but the price is right. Key deposit $5. Doubles $55. AmEx/D/MC/V. ❷

St. Andrews State Recreation Area, 4607 State Park Ln. (☎850-233-5140, reservations 800-326-3521), at the east end of Thomas Dr. Here you'll find 1000 acres of parkland that include nature trails, good fishing, and beaches. You can also camp on beautiful Shell Island with special permission from a ranger. Kayak rentals $20 per 4hr., $35 per day. Open daily 8am-sunset. Reservations recommended. Entrance fee $5. Sites $24. AmEx/D/MC/V. ❶

Seafoam Motel, 6010 Thomas Dr. (☎850-234-3830). 14 affordable rooms located right by the beaches, but some staff members are less than friendly. Singles from $50; doubles from $95. Varies by season. AmEx/D/MC/V. ❸

⊞ FOOD

Along **Thomas Drive** and the **Miracle Mile** you can have your fill at numerous buffets—most of which offer "early bird" half-price specials from 4-6pm.

🍴 **Liza's Kitchen,** 7008 Thomas Dr. (☎850-233-9000). All breads and sauces made from scratch. The roasted chicken with red pepper, goat cheese, and spinach on homemade focaccia ($7) is delicious. Breakfast $4-6.50. Sandwiches $5-8. Open M-F 10am-6pm, Sa 8am-4pm, Su 9am-2pm. D/MC/V. ❷

Scampy's, 4933 Thomas Dr. (☎850-235-4209). Serves tasty seafood in a less harried atmosphere than many of the other mega-troughs along this strip. Lunch specials $5-10. Entrees $12-21. Open M-Th and Su 11am-10pm, F-Sa 11am-11pm. AmEx/D/MC/V. ❹

Schooners Bar and Grill, 5121 Gulf Dr. (☎850-235-3555). Calls itself "the last local beach club," and it's no surprise why—it features lively, open-air dance floors that look well-traveled, all perched right on the beach. In the evenings, R&B bands croon tunes to a crowd of locals and tourists of all ages. Entrees $11-20. 21+ after 9pm. Open M-Th 11am-11pm, F-Su 11am-1am. Live music M-Th 9-11pm, F-Sa 9pm-1am. AmEx/D/MC/V. ❹

Sharky's, 15201 Front Beach Rd. (☎850-235-2420). Adventurous souls can savor "shark bites" (fried shark cubes $10), Sharky's signature appetizer. A Hurricane or a Sharkbite cocktail ($6.50) will make eating shark seem even cooler. Happy hour M-F 4-6pm with ½-price drinks. Live music Th-Su, in summer W-Su. Open daily 11am-2am. AmEx/D/MC/V. ❸

👁 SIGHTS

MUSEUM OF MAN IN THE SEA. Nearly a dozen submarines of various sizes are parked outside the museum, making this roadside attraction hard to miss. Inside the tiny museum, colorful displays trace the history of man's exploration of the ocean from more than 5000 years ago to the present day. The museum also features treasure pulled from shipwrecks and allows visitors to crawl inside a small scientific submarine. *(17314 Panama City Beach Pkwy., on the left side of US 98 E. ☎850-235-4101. Open daily 10am-4pm. $5, ages 6-16 $2.50.)*

LIGHTHOUSE MARINA. "The world's largest speed boat," the Sea Screamer, cruises the Grand Lagoon at a cool 40 mph for 1½hr., showing you dolphins along the way. *(5325 N. Lagoon Dr. ☎850-233-9107. 4 cruises per day; call for times in spring and fall. $17, ages 4-12 $12.)*

ISLAND TIME SAILING CRUISES. Island Time offers 3hr. snorkel-and-swim-with-dolphins tours ($25) and a 2hr. sail and dolphin watch ($15) cruise as the sun goes down. *(3605 Thomas Dr., at Treasure Island Marina. ☎850-234-7377. Call ahead for specific dates and times.)*

LET'S FLY. Let's Fly has seaplane rides starting at only $25 and also offers waverunner rentals and tours of the backwater that will bring you close to alligators and dolphins. *(Located off Rte. 79 by the Boondocks Restaurant. ☎850-234-1532. Call ahead for reservations.)*

🎸 NIGHTLIFE

Club La Vela, 8813 Thomas Dr. (☎850-234-3866). The largest club in the US (capacity 8000) and an MTV favorite, La Vela has 14 different themed rooms and 48 bar stations under one jammin' roof, with new rooms and bars added every year. Live bands work the Rock Pavilion every night, and the "Kyrogenics Room" freezes suddenly when the DJ presses a magic button. Wet T-shirt, bikini, and hardbody contests occur

on weekends and every night during spring break. Playboy bunnies, models, and famous actors have been known to hang out in the Pussykat Lounge, so look your best and cross your fingers. Dress code "sexy chic" in VIP rooms. Cover generally $5-15. 18+. Open daily 10am-5pm and 7pm-4am. AmEx/D/MC/V.

Spinnaker, 8795 Thomas Dr. (☎850-234-7882, ext. 10), located next door to La Vela. A slightly more laid-back PCB mainstay. Ten bars, DJs, and live bands entertain partygoers all night long. Cover varies. 21+ after 9pm. Open daily 11am-4am. AmEx/D/MC/V.

🚗 **THE ROAD TO FORT WALTON BEACH: 52 MI.**

Take **Route 30A** out of Panama City Beach. Continue past the hidden entrance to **Topsail Hill State Preserve,** just outside of **Destin.** At this secluded area, roadtrippers can take a short drive down a dirt road through scrub pines to isolated white sand dunes. Continue along Rte. 30A to rejoin **US 98/Route 30** heading toward Fort Walton Beach. If you prefer speed to scenery, skip Rte. 30A and take **US 98** out of town.

FORT WALTON BEACH ☎850

The Fort Walton area was first settled around 12,000 BC by prehistoric peoples who left their mark in the form of large mounds and middens. The bay was also a safe harbor to pirate ships in need of a break from the "Arr!" life. Tales of the notorious Billy Bowlegs are among the area's most famous pirate legends and are celebrated in the city's annual Billy Bowlegs Festival in June.

VITAL STATS
Population: 20,000
Tourist Office: Emerald Coast Convention and Visitors Bureau, 1540 Miracle Strip Pkwy. (☎800-322-3319; www.destin-fwb.com). Open M-F 8am-5pm, Sa-Su 9am-4pm.
Library and Internet Access: Fort Walton Beach Library, 185 Miracle Strip Pkwy. SE (☎850-833-9590). Free. Open M-Th 9am-9pm, F-Sa 9am-5pm.
Post Office: 21 Walter Martin Rd. NE (☎850-244-2625). Open M-F 8:30am-4:45pm, Sa 10am-1pm. **Postal Code:** 32548.

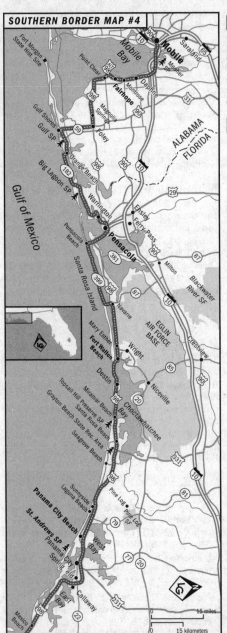

SOUTHERN BORDER MAP #4

ORIENTATION

Fort Walton Beach is small and easy to navigate. **US 98/Route 30** runs east-west along the coast as the **Miracle Strip Parkway.** The other east-west thoroughfare is **Hollywood Boulevard,** which divides **Memorial Parkway** and **Wright Parkway** into northern and southern halves.

ACCOMMODATIONS

Dolphin Inn, 207 Miracle Strip Pkwy. (☎850-244-2443). Spotless, comfortable, and reasonably priced rooms. Reservations recommended. Rooms from $50. AmEx/D/MC/V. ❸

FOOD

Maas Coffee Roasters, 150 Miracle Strip Pkwy. (☎850-585-0496). For a quick cup of coffee, live blues, or poetry readings, stop by Maas. Reasonably priced coffee and espresso drinks, a cool little backyard area to enjoy your beverage, and very friendly staff. Poetry readings every other W, alternating weeks with live blues F-Sa nights. Opens M-Th at 8am, Sa 9am, Su 10am. Closing time is often around 6pm but varies with showtimes, so call ahead. AmEx/D/MC/V. ❶

Brooks Bridge BBQ and Cafe, 240 Miracle Strip Pkwy. (☎850-244-3003). A homey little place with daily specials on a blackboard and delectable barbecue dinners ($6-12). Open M-F 11am-8pm. AmEx/D/MC/V. ❷

SIGHTS

GULFARIUM. Dolphin stars Princess, Delilah, and Lily play comedic soccer games and perform 18 ft. skyward leaps daily at the **Gulfarium,** 1010 Miracle Strip Pkwy. You'll also find sea lions, scuba divers, and acts that include more than one species. The grounds feature many aquariums, a shark moat, a stingray pool, a monstrous 14 ft. alligator, bottlenose dolphins, and penguins. *(On the left side of US 98 W., just before the bridge. ☎850-243-9046; www.gulfarium.com. Dolphin shows 10am, noon, 2, 4pm. Open in summer daily 9am-4pm. $18.75, ages 4-11 $10.50.)*

INDIAN TEMPLE MOUND MUSEUM. Explore the museum to see a reconstruction of the

Chief's Temple, the ancient political and ceremonial center of the area. The museum holds one of the finest collections of Southeastern Native American ceramics and artifacts in the country, most of which were obtained over the 60-year excavation of this site. *(139 Miracle Strip Pkwy./US 98, on the right side of US 98 W., after Rte. 85. ☎850-833-9595. Open M-Sa 10am-4:30pm. $5, ages 6-17 $3, seniors $4.50.)*

📷 THE ROAD TO PENSACOLA: 38 MI.

From Fort Walton Beach, head west on **US 98/Route 30** to reach Pensacola.

PENSACOLA   ☎850

Pensacola's military population and reputation for conservatism have been a part of the city since the antebellum period, when three forts on the shores of Pensacola formed a triangular defense to guard its deep-water ports. For roadtrippers, Pensacola has a small historic downtown, noteworthy diners and barbecue joints, and the wacky TT Wentworth Museum. Pensacola is a bit run-down, so don't plan to spend too much time at this last stop in Florida, but do take a moment to bid farewell to the Sunshine State.

VITAL STATS

Population: 56,000

Tourist Office: Pensacola Visitors Center, 1401 E. Gregory St. (☎800-874-1234; www.visitpensacola.com). Open daily 8am-5pm.

Library and Internet Access: Pensacola Public Library, 200 W. Gregory St. (☎850-436-5060). Open Tu-Th 9am-8pm, F-Sa 9am-5pm, Su 2-7pm. Free.

Post Office: 101 S. Palafox St. (☎850-439-0171). Open M-F 8am-5pm. **Postal Code:** 32502.

◼ ORIENTATION

Follow the Pensacola Bay Bridge 3 mi. into town, where it becomes **Bayfront Parkway** to the left and **Gregory Street** to the right. Both streets will lead you into Pensacola's historic downtown district. **Cervantes Street** is the main east-west artery, while **Palafox Street, Davis Highway, Pace Boulevard,** and **Ninth Street** are major

north-south routes. Traveling east, Cervantes St. becomes **Scenic Highway (US 90),** which hugs the coast of Pensacola Bay. The 11 mi. drive, high on some of the Gulf Coast's bluffs, has unforgettable views of the quiet bay below.

> **WALDO WISDOM.** This section of the Gulf Coast is famous for its sugar-white sand and emerald water. In fact, that fine, white sand is neither sugar nor sand: it's mostly quartz runoff from the Appalachian Mountains. The sun reflecting off the quartz gives the water its emerald tint.

◤ ACCOMMODATIONS

Hotels along the beach cost at least $65 and get significantly more expensive during the summer. Cheaper options lie inland, north of downtown. Motels line Cervantes St. for about $40 per night, but, at these, you get what you pay for. The **Red Roof Inn ❷,** 7340 Plantation Rd., is close to the airport and offers tidy rooms with Internet access. (☎850-476-7960. Reservations recommended. Singles from $50; doubles from $60. AmEx/D/MC/V.)

◰ FOOD

◼ **McGuire's Irish Pub and Brewery,** 600 E. Gregory St. (☎850-433-6789). Built in the building of Pensacola's original firehouse. Has dollar bills hanging from the ceiling, Irish music playing, and huge portions. Simple slogan says it all: "Feasting, Imbibing, Debauchery." Signature steaks are some of Florida's best but can get a bit pricey ($25-30). 25 varieties of hamburger ($10)—add on Senate bean soup for only $0.18 extra. Open daily 10am-10pm. AmEx/D/MC/V. ❹

King's BBQ, 2120 N. Palafox St. (☎850-433-4479), 1 mi. north of Cervantes St., at Maxwell Rd. The owner of King's built this drive-up stand with his own hands 29 years ago and is often around to tell you about it. Rib sandwiches $7.50. Open M-F 11am-6:30pm. MC/V. ❷

Jerry's Drive-In, 2815 E. Cervantes St. (☎850-433-9910). This roadside grill dishes out standard diner fare with frosty milkshakes. Open M-F 10am-10pm, Sa 7am-10pm. Cash only. ❶

SOUTHERN BORDER

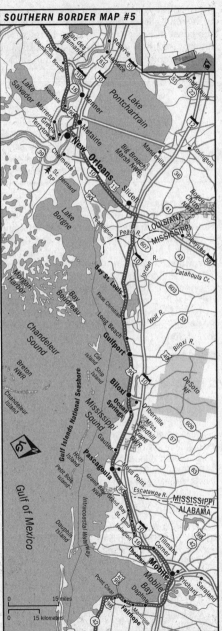

SOUTHERN BORDER MAP #5

Tu-Do Restaurant, 7130 N. Davis Hwy. (☎850-473-8877), a 10min. drive north on Davis Hwy. Serves Vietnamese food, including a wealth of vegetarian options. Entrees $5-7. Open daily 10:30am-9:30pm. AmEx/D/MC/V. ❷

🔍 SIGHTS

◾**NATIONAL MUSEUM OF NAVAL AVIATION.** Here, more than 130 planes will have pilot wannabes soaring on natural highs. The museum covers American aviation from WWI through 1989, and, for $25, you and a friend can spend 30 min. inside a real F-14 simulator pretending that you're Maverick and Goose from *Top Gun.* Touching and climbing in and around many of the planes is encouraged, and the museum is full of interactive displays. *(Inside the Naval Air Station, at Exit 2 off I-10. ☎850-452-3604. Open daily 9am-5pm. Tours daily 9:30am, 11am, 1pm, 2:30pm. Must show picture ID to enter. No cell-phone use on the naval base. Free.)*

NAVAL LIVE OAKS AREA. For more grounded fun, escape to the relaxing paths that meander through the Live Oaks Area. John Quincy Adams established this as the first and only naval tree reservation in the US and set apart its oaks to make pre-Civil War-era warships. Hiking trails now cover the reservation, and some provide visitors with stunning views of Pensacola Bay. *(1801 Gulf Breeze Pkwy. Head across the Pensacola Bay Bridge. ☎850-934-2600. Open daily 8am-5:30pm. Free.)*

TT WENTWORTH MUSEUM. In the 1980s, millionaire junk collector TT Wentworth donated his eccentric collection to the city of Pensacola. The resulting museum has one exhibit hall dedicated to Wentworth's collection, which includes oddities like a petrified cat, a shrunken head, and a gigantic shoe that belonged to the world's tallest man (who stood 8 ft., 8 in. tall). The rest of the museum includes exhibits on Spanish explorers, model trains, sports, African-American history, and the area's shipwrecks. *(330 S. Jefferson St. ☎850-595-5990. Open M-Sa 10am-4pm. Free.)*

PHOTO OP. The 3 mi. World's Longest Fishing Pier shadows the Pensacola Bay Bridge.

◈ DETOUR
BIG LAGOON RECREATION AREA

Located on **Route 292A (Gulf Beach Highway)**, 30min. west of Pensacola. Take **Garden Street** and hang a left when it splits. Follow **Route 292 (Barrancas Avenue)** to **Route 173,** turn left, and then take a right on **292A** after about a mile or so. You'll find the recreation area on your left.

Sandpine scrub grows on dunes while gnarled underbrush testifies to the harsh coastal environment of this state recreation area. The park's trails and **campsites ❶** are situated alongside the lake, off Pensacola Bay. Several beaches line the lagoon, and in addition to hiking trails there are opportunities for fishing, boating, and canoeing throughout the area. Quiet visitors may get a glimpse of one of the many threatened or endangered species of bird, tortoise, and snake that call the area home. (☎850-492-1595. Park open daily 8am-sunset. $4 per vehicle. Sites $16. Electric hookups. AmEx/D/MC/V.)

◪ THE ROAD TO FAIRHOPE: 45 MILES

From Pensacola, head north and follow signs to **I-10 West** Drive for about 40 mi., crossing the Florida-Alabama border, and take Exit 35 south to **Alternate US 98** into the oh-so-cute town of Fairhope.

FAIRHOPE   ☎251

Fairhope was founded by a group of Midwesterners seeking utopia—whether or not it lives up to their goals, you can decide. Downtown's second stoplight is **Fairhope Avenue,** and a right here leads to a panoramic view of Mobile Bay from the Fairhope pier. The **Down By the Bay Cafe ❸,** 4 Beach Rd., offers a wide variety of seafood dishes on a patio overlooking the pier. Peek through the large bay windows to look for whales. (☎251-928-4363. Entrees $8-14. All-you-can-eat shrimp F nights $14. Open M and Sa-Su 11am-3pm, Tu-F 11am-2pm and 5-8pm. Cash only.)

◪ THE ROAD TO MOBILE: 33 MI.

Head back the way you came on **Alternate US 98,** get back onto **I-10 West,** and continue straight on through the heart of Mobile.

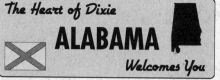

The Heart of Dixie **ALABAMA** *Welcomes You*

MOBILE   ☎251

Although Bob Dylan lamented being stuck here, Mobile (MO-beel) has had plenty of fans in its time. French, Spanish, English, Sovereign Alabama, Confederate, and American flags have each flown over the city since its founding in 1702. This historical diversity is manifested not only demographically but also architecturally; antebellum mansions, Italianate dwellings, Spanish and French forts, and Victorian homes border the city's azalea-lined streets. The site of the country's very first Mardi Gras, Mobile still hosts a three-week-long Fat Tuesday celebration without the hordes that plague its Cajun counterpart; the city feels like a less touristy New Orleans.

VITAL STATS
Population: 200,000
Visitor Info: Fort Conde Welcome Center, 150 S. Royal St. (☎251-208-7304), in a reconstructed French fort near Government St. Open daily 8am-5pm.
Library and Internet Access: Mobile Public Library, 701 Government St. (☎251-208-7076). Free. Open M-Th 9am-9pm, F-Sa 9am-6pm.
Post Office: 168 Bay Shore Ave. (☎251-478-5639). Open M-F 9am-4:30pm. **Postal Code:** 36607.

◪ ORIENTATION

Mobile is surrounded by three major highways: **I-10** runs north-south to the south of downtown; **I-65** runs north-south near the airport; and **I-165** east of the city heads north. Downtown Mobile is a grid, surrounded by **Broad Street** to the west, **Canal Street** to the south, **Water Street** to the east, and **Beauregard Street** to the north. **Dauphin Street,** which is one-way downtown, and **Government Boulevard (US 90),** which becomes **Government Street** downtown, are the major east-west routes. **Airport Boulevard, Springhill Avenue,** and **Old Shell Road** are secondary east-west roads. **Royal Street** and **Broad Street** are major north-south byways. Free daytime parking is available in the lot across from the Welcome Center on S. Royal St.

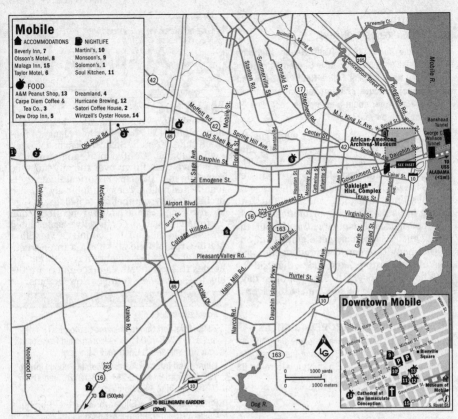

Mobile

ACCOMMODATIONS
Beverly Inn, **7**
Olsson's Motel, **8**
Malaga Inn, **15**
Taylor Motel, **6**

NIGHTLIFE
Martini's, **10**
Monsoon's, **9**
Solomon's, **1**
Soul Kitchen, **11**

FOOD
A&M Peanut Shop, **13**
Carpe Diem Coffee &
Tea Co., **3**
Dew Drop Inn, **5**
Dreamland, **4**
Hurricane Brewing, **12**
Satori Coffee House, **2**
Wintzell's Oyster House, **14**

Downtown Mobile

ACCOMMODATIONS

There are few budget options in the historic part of Mobile, but a 15-20min. drive from downtown will take you to the cheaper motels lining I-65 and Government Blvd. Pick up the Alabama Travel Coupons at the visitors center for discounts on a variety of chain motels.

Olsson's Motel, 4137 Government Blvd. (☎251-661-5331). Though it's far from downtown, Olsson's offers the most spacious, comfortable, and well-decorated rooms you'll find on a budget. Singles $45; doubles $59. AmEx/D/MC/V. ❷

Malaga Inn, 359 Church St. (☎251-438-4701; www.malagainn.com), at Claiborne St., in front of the Civic Center. Occupying 2 townhouses dating from 1862, the pink stucco hotel boasts a central

courtyard. Continental breakfast included. Rooms from $94. AmEx/D/MC/V. ❹

Taylor Motel, 2598 Government Blvd. (☎251-479-5481), a 10min. drive from downtown. Decent rooms with A/C and TVs. Singles $45; doubles $58. AmEx/D/MC/V. ❷

Beverly Motel, 4384 Government Blvd. (☎251-661-0331). Fresh-smelling rooms for cheap. Singles $45; doubles $50. AmEx/MC/V. ❷

FOOD

Mobile's Gulf location means fresh seafood, tasty barbecue, and good, old-fashioned Southern cookin'. But, unwilling to be pigeonholed, Mobile hosts restaurants serving a wide variety of cuisines.

Wintzell's Oyster House, 605 Dauphin St. (☎251-432-4605; www.wintzellsoysterhouse. com). Wintzell's is a longtime local favorite; oysters are served "fried, stewed, or nude" amid wall decorations that range from the highly profound to the nearly profane. Beat the 1hr. oyster-eating record of 31 dozen (held by "Big Joe" Evans) to gain fame and $25. Happy hour M-F 4-7pm with ½-price raw oysters and $1 draft beer. $8.50 for a dozen oysters any way you like 'em. Open M-Th 11am-10pm, F-Sa 11am-11pm. AmEx/MC/V. ❸

Dreamland, 3314 Old Shell Rd. (☎251-479-9898). As soon as you catch sight of Dreamland, you'll also catch a whiff of its famous barbecue. The restaurant's hickory ribs, cooked over an open fire in the dining room, will stick to yours. Don't expect much flora with your fauna, though; the restaurant's only vegetarian option is the house salad. ½-rack $10. Open M-Sa 10am-10pm, Su 11am-9pm. AmEx/D/MC/V. ❷

Dew Drop Inn, 1808 Old Shell Rd. (☎251-273-7872). Mobile's oldest restaurant serves hot dogs, hamburgers, and seafood. Mull over your options as you sip a Coke from a classic green bottle—and then admire whoever coined the restaurant's punny name. Open M and Sa 10am-3pm, Tu-F 10am-8pm. AmEx/D/MC/V. ❷

A&M Peanut Shop, 209 Dauphin St. (☎251-438-9374). This candy shop is solely responsible for the extreme obesity of the local squirrels, who snack on the leftover hot peanuts. Also serves other sweet, sticky, and chocolate-covered things, with a little bit of health food just for show. Open M-Sa 9am-6pm. AmEx/D/MC/V. ❶

Satori Coffee House, 5460 Old Shell Rd. (☎251-343-6677; www.satoricoffee.com). Satisfies all your hippie cravings for acoustic folk music, veggie food, and handmade pottery mugs. Lounge as long as you'd like on the snug couches, enjoying a full complement of wraps ($6-9) and salads ($3-7). Live music frequently; call for dates and times. Free Wi-Fi. Open M-F 7am-10pm, Sa 10am-10pm. Open later for special events. AmEx/MC/V. ❷

Carpe Diem Coffee & Tea Co., 4072 Old Shell Rd. (☎251-304-0448). Because this locally adored coffeehouse has its own roaster, the beans used to make your coffee are never more than 2 weeks old. Enjoy the venue's free Wi-Fi (and good company) on a comfy couch in front of the fireplace, at a table, or out on the airy back patio. Coffee from $1.75. Open M-F 6am-11pm, Sa 7am-11pm, Su 8am-11pm. D/MC/V. ❷

Hurricane Brewing, 225 Dauphin St. (☎251-245-2544). This modern-style pub brews 7 of its own varieties of beer, which are stored in gigantic tanks set up right behind the bar. Located in downtown Mobile, it's a great place to grab a sandwich ($7-10) and a drink with friends. Hurricane also features flatscreen TVs, a friendly staff, and a happy hour from 4-7pm with $0.50 wings. Open daily 11am-10pm. D/MC/V. ❷

👁 SIGHTS

USS ALABAMA BATTLEFIELD MEMORIAL PARK. The *USS Alabama* earned nine battle stars, each of which signifies a valiant operation, in WWII. Open passageways let civilians explore the ship's depths, and the park around the ship houses airplanes, tanks, a Vietnam river patrol boat, and the submarine *USS Drum*. Not only is the ship open, but also everything in the park can is open to exploration by anyone with a sense of adventure and a lot of time. *(In Battleship Park, just east of town, accessible from I-10 or by driving through the Bankhead tunnel at the east end of Government St. ☎251-433-2703. Open daily Mar.-Oct. 8am-6pm; Nov.-Feb. 8am-4pm. $10, ages 6-11 $5, under 6 free.)*

BIENVILLE SQUARE. With its oak trees, white gazebo, and cast-iron fountain, Bienville Sq. is the picture of Southern charm. While visually impressive, the square is not just for show; the shade of the tall oaks offers pedestrians real and welcome relief on a hot day. Eight historic districts, marked by signs, showcase the city's architectural and cultural influences. *(On Dauphin St., between Conception and St. Joseph St.)*

MUSEUM OF MOBILE. This museum celebrates and documents 300 years of Mobilian history in all its glory. Exhibits cover the founding of Mobile, the fate of the slave ship *Clotilda*, and the private collections of prominent Mobile families. *(111 S. Royal St. ☎251-208-7569. Open M-Sa 9am-5pm, Su 1-5pm. $5, students $3, seniors $4. 1st Su of each month free.)*

AFRICAN-AMERICAN ARCHIVES MUSEUM. The museum is housed in what was the first African-American library in the US. The museum contains portraits, books, and other artifacts pertaining to the lives of African-Americans from the Mobile area and beyond. *(564 Dr. Martin Luther King, Jr., Ave. ☎251-433-8511. Open M-F 8am-4pm. Free.)*

OAKLEIGH HISTORICAL COMPLEX. This complex contains the grandiose **Oakleigh House Museum,** the working-class **Cox-Deasy House Museum,** and the **Mardi Gras Cottage Museum.** The complex features 19th- and 20th-century art collections, and each house portrays the lives of a different class of Mobilians in the 1800s. All visits are chaperoned by costumed guides. *(350 Oakleigh Pl., 2 blocks south of Government St., at George St. ☎251-432-1281; www.historic-mobile.org. Open daily 10am-4pm. Tours every 30min. 9am-2pm. $7, ages 6-11 $5, seniors $6.50.)*

BELLINGRATH GARDENS. The gardens on Mr. Bellingrath's estate-turned-museum were voted one of America's top five formal gardens for the 900 acres of lush roses, oriental displays, and bayou boardwalk. Visitors can also tour the richly decorated **Bellingrath Museum Home** or take a narrated 45min. cruise on the *Southern Belle* riverboat. While the long drive and steep admission price may deter some, rose lovers should make visiting the mildly fragrant gardens a priority. *(12401 Bellingrath Gardens Rd. Take Exit 15A off I-10 in Theodore. ☎800-247-8420. Open daily 8am-5pm. Gardens $10, with home $18, with home and cruise $26.)*

CATHEDRAL OF THE IMMACULATE CONCEPTION. Completed in 1850 and recently renovated, the cathedral's architecture and decor fuse practical American red brick with the dramatic splendor of European churches. Stunning red-and-white marble columns and an enormous suspended crucifix highlight the altar, while detailed stained-glass windows and a beautiful organ complete the artistic panorama. *(400 Government St. ☎251-434-1565. Open 24hr.)*

NIGHTLIFE

At night, Mobile's hottest district is the **Lower Dauphin Street Entertainment District,** which runs along Dauphin St. between Conception and Lawrence St. On weekdays most places close around 2 or 3am, but bars can be open on weekends until 4am or later—often until the last patrons straggle out. For the latest events, check out the free weekly *Lagniappe.* For more staid entertainment, the **Mobile Symphony** plays in the historic 1927 **Seanger Theatre,** 6 S. Joachim St., most Saturdays over the summer at 8pm, with encore performances Sundays at 2:30pm. (☎251-432-7080; www.mobilesymphony.org. Tickets from $15, students $8. Call ahead or check the website for dates.)

Soul Kitchen, 219 Dauphin St. (☎251-433-5958; www.soulkitchenmobile.com). Attracts an energetic and hip college-age crowd. Live music and DJs. Call for showtimes. AmEx/D/MC/V.

Martini's, 250 Dauphin St. (☎251-433-9920). Martini's draws a slightly older crowd of young professionals to its chic, dimly lit atmosphere. Sample 1 of 35 different martinis ($9-11), each named for a different musical icon. No cover. Open W-F 4pm-last customer, Sa 6pm-last customer. AmEx/D/MC/V.

Monsoon's, 9 N. Jackson St. (☎251-438-5500). A bit more laid-back than other live music venues, Monsoon's has folk and bluegrass performances throughout the week. Call ahead for show dates and times. Cover varies.

Solomon's, 5753 Old Shell Rd. (☎251-344-0380), at University Rd. Reminiscent of "the Emporium" in *Dazed and Confused* and located right across the street from the University of Southern Alabama, this warehouse-sized space with 18 pool tables, darts, and video games caters to a college-age crowd. 21+. Happy hour 11am-7pm. Open 24hr. AmEx/MC/V.

THE ROAD TO PASCAGOULA: 42 MI.

Take **Government Boulevard (US 90 W)** out of Mobile. After 20 mi., you will cross from "sweet home" Alabama into Mississippi, which, according to the road sign, is like "coming home."

The Magnolia State
MISSISSIPPI
Welcomes You

PASCAGOULA ☎228

The city of Pascagoula is a mess of oil rigs and shipping ports, and there's not much of interest here unless you're looking to get into the oil or shipbuilding industry. The city does, though, have a few places to sleep. The **King's Inn Motel ❸**, 2303 Denny Ave., offers clean, basic rooms. (☎228-762-8110. Singles $55; doubles from $65. AmEx/D/MC/V.)

🏕 THE ROAD TO GULF ISLANDS NATIONAL SEASHORE: 13 MI.

Ocean Springs is 13 mi. past Pascagoula on **US 90**—although it's somewhat difficult to tell where one town ends and the other begins. The turnoff for the Gulf Islands National Seashore is in eastern Ocean Springs. Turn left (south) at the signs and head about 4 mi. to arrive at the park visitors center.

GULF ISLANDS NATIONAL SEASHORE ☎228

Sheltered woods, palmetto groves, and grassy bayous make up the **Davis Bayou** segment of the Gulf Islands National Seashore, Mississippi District. Although **Hurricane Katrina** destroyed a substantial number of trees, this park is still covered in rich foliage and in many places seems nearly untouched by the hurricane's destruction. The small visitors center provides park info on the wildlife and geographic features of the area as well as a wide variety of hiking, fishing, picnicking, and boating opportunities. Refugees were housed here in the aftermath of Katrina, but now the park and main campground are fully re-opened, as are primitive **campsites ❶** on Horn, Petit Bois, Cat, and East Ship Islands, though visitors must arrange their own transportation. (☎228-875-9057; www.nps.gov/guis. Park open 8am-sunset. Campsites $15.)

🏕 THE ROAD TO OCEAN SPRINGS: 3 MI.

Exit the Gulf Islands National Seashore and head left (west) on **US 90**. Continue 3 mi. and take a left on **Washington Avenue** to reach Ocean Springs.

OCEAN SPRINGS ☎228

The heart of Ocean Springs is oak-lined **Washington Avenue**. Life may move at a slower pace, but price tags still run high. Visitors can experience the bohemian flavor of the town at the **Walter Anderson Museum of Art**, 510 Washington Ave. Anderson was a schizophrenic and was committed to a mental institution twice, which explains why some of his work looks like the cover of a late-60s Beatles album. The true masterpieces of the museum are the murals that line the walls of the attached community center, which Anderson created in 1951 and gave to the community for $1. (☎228-872-3164; www.walterandersonmuseum.org. Open M-Sa 9:30am-4:30pm, Su 12:30-4:30pm. $7, ages 16-24 $6, under 16 $3.)

Bayview Gourmet ❷, 1010 Robinson St., serves upscale dishes like smoked-salmon omelets and portobello mushroom sandwiches. (☎228-875-4252. Breakfast $5-12. Lunch $8-12. Open Tu-W and Sa-Su 7:30am-2:30pm, Th-F 7:30am-8pm. AmEx/D/MC/V.)

🏕 THE ROAD TO BILOXI AND GULFPORT: 5 MI.

From Ocean Springs, head back on **Washington Avenue** to **US 90** and head west, passing over the newly completed **Biloxi Bay Bridge** into downtown Biloxi, where **US 90** becomes **Beach Boulevard**.

BILOXI AND GULFPORT ☎228

Once known for towering resort casinos, Biloxi and its neighbor Gulfport were flattened by Hurricane Katrina. The towns have since, however, begun to rebuild. Along the beach are empty lots, pieces of construction equipment, and beat-up signs advertising places that no longer exist. Yet the rubble from the hurricane has been cleared away, and an increasing number of restaurants, hotels, and resort casinos are returning to life. While Biloxi and Gulfport undeniably have several years of hard work still ahead, it is impressive how quickly and bravely these two cities have responded to a natural disaster of such massive proportion.

VITAL STATS
Tourist Office: Mississippi Gulf Coast Convention and Visitors Bureau (☎228-575-4297; www.gulfcoast.org).

✈ ORIENTATION

US 90 runs right along the shoreline as **Beach Boulevard.** Some restaurants, gas stations, and residential services line **Pass Road,** which parallels Beach Blvd. one block inland and is most easily accessible by turning on **Beauvoir Road,** next to the **Coliseum** in central Biloxi.

🏠 ACCOMMODATIONS

Options for motels, hotels, and B&Bs are limited in the Biloxi area, but more places are being rebuilt every day.

Star Inn, 1716 Beach Blvd. (☎ 228-374-8688). One of the cheapest options in the area. Brand new, clean rooms with A/C and cable TV. Rooms from $59. AmEx/D/MC. ❸

Jubilee Inn, 1876 Beach Blvd. (☎228-432-1984). Offers A/C, TV, free Wi-Fi, continental breakfasts, and access to a pool that overlooks the ocean. Rooms from $80. 21+. ❹

🍴 FOOD

Most restaurants in Biloxi were obliterated by the hurricane, but many have already reopened and more will continue to do so. Chain restaurants and hotels have been some of the fastest to rebuild; many are located amid the vacant lots inland of Beach Blvd.

Mary Mahoney's Old French House Restaurant, 116 rue Magnolia (☎228-436-6000; www.mary-mahoneys.com). One of the only local restaurants open on Beach Blvd. The beautiful courtyard (home to a 2000 year-old-tree) and cozy interior seem worlds away from the rubble outside. Entrees cost $20-45. Open daily 11am-9pm. Reservations recommended. AmEx/D/MC/V. ❺

Port City Cafe, 2418 14th St. (☎228-868-0037), right off Hwy. 49. Big windows, exposed brick, and a friendly owner who is extremely generous with pickles. Open M-F 7am-3pm. D/MC/V. ❷

Shady's New World Cuisine, 1795 Pass Rd. (☎228-432-8424). Shady's offers a unique mixture of Thai, Italian, Creole, and soul food; the menu includes everything from ribs to crab rangoon. Be sure to try the down-south fried pickles ($5). Open M-F 11am-9pm, Sa-Su noon-10pm. Entrees $8-20. D/MC/V. ❸

Ben's Deli, 1412 Pass Rd. (☎228-214-4099). An intimate place with a takeout window, picnic tables, and huge portions. The deli serves burgers, po' boys, chicken dinners ($4-7), and Chinese dishes including a mean lo mein. Chinese dishes $4-6. Open M-Sa 10am-7pm. Cash only. ❶

👁 SIGHTS

SHIP ISLAND. This island, one of the many barrier islands located 12 mi. off the coast of Biloxi, can be reached from Gulfport via a ferry run by the National Park Service. The marvelous white sand beaches of this large island are as pure as they were when the Spanish discovered them in the 1500s. The Civil War-era **Fort Massachusetts** is also located on Ship Island. Free tours are offered every time a boatload of tourists docks. (*Departs from Gulfport Yacht Harbor, adjacent to the intersection of US 90 and Rte. 49. ☎866-466-7386; www.msshipisland. com. Ferries depart from mid-May to mid-Aug. daily 9am, noon; from mid-Aug. to late Oct. W-Sa 9am, Su noon; from late Mar. to mid-May. W-F 9am, Sa 9am, noon, Su noon.*)

SAILFISH. This boat takes guests on 70min. tours during which the crew drops its shrimping nets and discusses its catch. Don't worry—they throw all the sea critters back alive. (*Departs from the Main St. Harbor. ☎800-289-7908; www.gcww.com/sailfish. Tours Feb.-Nov. Call for times. $15, ages 4-12 $12. Cash only.*)

BEAU RIVAGE. One of Biloxi's most upscale casinos, the Beau Rivage rebuilt after Katrina and has re-opened its doors to gamblers. Come to try your luck—or skip gambling and attend concerts, golf, go to the spa, and dance it up at Club Tiki. This casino is the picture of self-indulgence. (*875 Beach Blvd. ☎888-595-2534; www.beaurivage.com. Open 24hr.*)

ISLE OF CAPRI. By all accounts a good place to work the slots, this casino offers themed nights such as "maniac Mondays," when gamblers earn double points. The Isle of Capri boasts a hotel, several restaurants, and live entertainment in its LAVA bar every Friday and Saturday night. (*151 Beach Blvd. ☎228-435-5400; www.isleofcapricasino.com. Open 24hr.*)

THE PALACE CASINO RESORT. This is a popular casino that features slots aplenty, a hotel, a buffet, a cafe, and more. (*158 Howard Ave. ☎800-725-2239; www.palacecasinoresort.com. Open 24hr.*)

MARITIME AND SEAFOOD INDUSTRY MUSEUM. The museum is no longer open, but will be rebuilt at its original location (115 1st St.) with intended completion scheduled for summer 2010. It is, however, still offering 2hr. tours in the Gulf Bay on full-scale replicas of 19th-century oyster schooners. (☎228-435-6320; www.maritimemuseum.org. Call ahead for times and reservations. $25.)

⚑ THE ROAD TO BAY ST. LOUIS: 17 MI.
From Biloxi/Gulfport, stay on **US 90 West** and follow it for 17 mi. until it runs right into Bay St. Louis.

BAY ST. LOUIS ☎228
Bay St. Louis sustained a lot of damage in the hurricane, but the town still retains a quaint charm. Locals have worked diligently to rebuild the shops and cafes that once lined the shopping district, and the town seems to be nearly back to its pre-hurricane condition. The posh **Sycamore House ❹**, 210 Main St., offers romantic candlelit dining and fabulous desserts, like chocolate torte. (☎228-469-0107; www.thesycamorehouse.com. Entrees $15-29. Brunch/lunch $6-12. Open W 5-8:30pm, Th-Sa 11:30am-2pm and 5-9:30pm, Su 11am-2pm. AmEx/D/MC/V.) To stay the night, a good bet is the **Economy Inn ❷**, 810 US 90, which offers clean rooms at the best rate in the area. (☎228-467-8441. Singles $35; doubles $40. AmEx/D/MC/V.)

⚑ THE ROAD TO NEW ORLEANS: 58 MI.
From Bay St. Louis, follow **US 90 West** for 17 mi. to the junction with I-10. Get on **I-10 West,** and continue 37 mi. to New Orleans. Take the **Canal Street/Superdome** exit to head directly into the French Quarter.

NEW ORLEANS ☎504
First explored by the French, La Nouvelle Orléans was secretly ceded to the Spanish in 1762, but its citizens didn't find out until 1766. Spain returned the city to France just in time for the US to grab it in 1803. Centuries of cultural cross-pollination have resulted in a vast melange of Spanish courtyards, Victorian verandas, Cajun jambalaya, Creole gumbo, and French beignets, to name but a few unique hallmarks of New Orleans. Life hasn't been easy since the city was devastated by Hurricane Katrina, but the city has rebuilt impressively, making the Big Easy well worth an extended stay.

⬙ ORIENTATION

Most sights in New Orleans are located within a central area. The city's main streets follow the curve of the **Mississippi River**—hence its nickname, "the Crescent City." Directions from locals are usually relative to bodies of water—"lakeside" means north, and "riverside" means south. Uptown lies west and downtown is towards the east, although "The East" usually refers to areas further east than downtown.

Tourists flock to the small **French Quarter,** bounded by the Mississippi River, **Canal Street, Rampart Street,** and **Esplanade Avenue.** Streets in the Quarter follow a grid pattern, making navigation easy. Just northeast of the Quarter, across Esplanade Ave., **Faubourg Marigny** is a residential neighborhood that has trendy nightclubs, bars, and cafes, with its nightlife centered around Frenchmen St.. Northwest of the Quarter, across from Rampart St., the African-American neighborhood of **Tremé** has a storied history. Its appearance has been marred by the encroaching highway overpass and the housing projects lining its Canal St. border. Be careful in Tremé and in **Central City** (the area southwest of the Superdome) at night. It is generally inadvisable to walk anywhere in New Orleans alone at night; play it safe and take a cab. Uptown, the residential **Garden District,** bordered by **Saint Charles Avenue** to the north and **Magazine Street** to the south, is distinguished by its elegant homes.

VITAL STATS

Population: 275,000.

Visitor Info: New Orleans Convention and Visitors Bureau, 529 St. Anne St. (☎504-568-5661). Open daily 9am-5pm.

Library and Internet Access: New Orleans Public Library, 219 Loyola Ave. (☎504-529-7323). Open M-Th 10am-6pm, F-Sa 10am-5pm.

Post Office: 701 Loyola Ave. (☎800-275-8777). Open M-F 7am-7pm, Sa 8am-5pm. **Postal Code:** 70113.

TRANSPORTATION

Parking in New Orleans is relatively easy, with the notable exception of the French Quarter, where it is borderline impossible (parking info ☎337-299-3700). Throughout the French Quarter (and in most other residential neighborhoods), signs along the streets designate 2hr. parking. Many streets throughout the city have meters (M-F before 9am and after 6pm, weekends, and holidays free). Parking lots along Rampart St. sell day-long spaces ($5-12), but many lots within the French Quarter charge upwards of $15 for anything over 3hr. However, if you manage to wake up early and drive into the French Quarter before 8 or 9am, many lots have early bird specials where you can park all day for around $8. Another viable option is to park for free in the Garden District; just take the **Saint Charles Streetcar** along St. Charles Ave. into downtown and the French Quarter. As a general rule, avoid parking on deserted streets at night. After sunset, it's often best to take a cab or the St. Charles or Canal St. Streetcars, which cost $1.25 and accept only exact change.

The St. Charles St. streetcar route picks up at Canal St. and Carondelet St., passes through parts of the Central Business District ("CBD" or "downtown"), the Garden District, and the Uptown and Carrollton neighborhoods along South Carrollton Avenue and passes Tulane and Loyola University. Plan ahead for a night out, as streetcar service ends at midnight.

ACCOMMODATIONS

Finding inexpensive, decent rooms in the **French Quarter** can be as difficult as staying sober during Mardi Gras. Luckily, other parts of the city compensate for the absence of cheap lodging downtown. Several hostels cater to the young and almost penniless, as do guesthouses near the **Garden District.** With streetcar and bus routes that thoroughly cover most of the city and an abundance of cabs, staying far away from the French Quarter is no big deal. Accommodations for Mardi Gras and the Jazz Festival are booked solid up to a year in advance. During peak times, proprietors will rent out any extra space, so be sure you know what you're paying for.

▦ **St. Charles Guest House,** 1748 Prytania St. (☎504-523-6556; www.stcharlesguesthouse. com), off Jackson St. Located in the heart of the beautiful Garden District, this large 19th-century home is luxury without the hefty price tag. Caring and quirky owner Dennis Hilton is the traveler's personal encyclopedia of all things New Orleans and the South. Large courtyard and beautiful pool, in addition to A/C and private bath in each room. Located right on the St. Charles St. Streetcar line, so getting downtown from here is hassle-free. No phones or TVs. Continental breakfast included. Free Wi-Fi. Singles with shared bath $45, with private bath $65-75; doubles $65/75-85; triples with private bath $85-95; quads with private bath $100-105. Cash only. ❸

▦ **India House,** 124 S. Lopez St. (☎504-821-1904; www.indiahousehostel.com), at Canal St. This bohemian haunt has all the character you'd expect from a former brothel and more—in the best possible way. Big TVs, comfy couches, and a backyard patio as well as a kitchen, pool, and turtle pond. Linen deposit $5. Free Wi-Fi. 6-bed dorms $17; 3- to 4-bed dorms $22.50. Singles and doubles $45. Cash only. ❶

Marquette House New Orleans International Hostel, 2249 Carondelet St. (☎504-523-3014), in the Garden District. This hostel does not allow alcohol inside, ensuring a quiet stay. 150 beds, A/C, kitchen (without stove), reading rooms, a big lounge area with comfy couches, and lovely outdoor courtyards. Linen included. Key deposit $10. Dorms $25; private rooms $70. D/MC/V. ❶

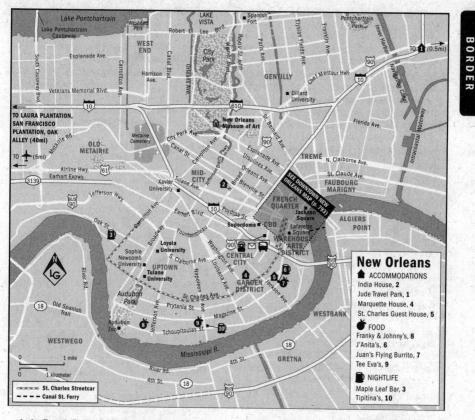

New Orleans

▲ ACCOMMODATIONS
India House, 2
Jude Travel Park, 1
Marquette House, 4
St. Charles Guest House, 5

🍴 FOOD
Franky & Johnny's, 8
J'Anita's, 6
Juan's Flying Burrito, 7
Tee Eva's, 9

🎷 NIGHTLIFE
Maple Leaf Bar, 3
Tipitina's, 10

Jude Travel Park, 7400 Chef Menteur Hwy./US 90 (☎504-241-0632), at Exit 240B, 5 mi. from the French Quarter. Jude Travel Park is the closest place you're going to find to the city if you want to camp out, but it caters mostly to RVs. The travel park is fairly sociable for a campground; activity is centered on the hot tub, though, so don't worry—you'll still sleep soundly in your tent. 47 sites. Electricity, showers, and 24hr. security. Laundry $2. Sites $25. AmEx/D/MC/V. ❶

St. Peter House Hotel, 1005 St. Peter St. (☎888-604-6226). Located right in the French Quarter, this hotel puts you in the thick of the action at a reasonable price. The clean, spacious rooms— some of which have 4-poster beds—are far enough from the street that you won't have to worry about all-night partying consuming your stay in the Big

Easy (unless you want it to). Cable, A/C, and some wrought-iron balconies. Rooms $49-79; cheapest on weeknights. AmEx/D/MC/V. ❸

🍴 FOOD

If the eats in the Quarter prove too trendy, touristy, or tough on the wallet, there are plenty of options on **Magazine Street** and in the Tulane area. Residents of New Orleans take a special pride in their food, so be sure to hit up as many local restaurants as you can.

🍴 **Coop's Place,** 1109 Decatur St. (☎504-525-9053). A cozy neighborhood bar with wooden interior decor and a stained glass window that reads "Coop's." Some of the Quarter's best

Southern cooking. The gumbo ($6.75) is thick and spicy, the shrimp creole ($9.50) will leave you stuffed for hours, and the jambalaya ($6.50) has a flavor found nowhere else. Open daily 11am-last customer. D/MC/V. ❸

🔲 **Tee Eva's,** 4430 Magazine St. (☎504-899-8350). Eva used to sell her scrumptious pies from a basket around town. Now she has a more permanent home—a brightly painted food counter. Soul-food lunches ($4-7) change daily. Creole pralines $2. Crawfish pie $4. Sweet potato or pecan pie $2. Open daily 11am-7pm. Cash only. ❶

Juan's Flying Burrito, 2018 Magazine St. (☎504-569-0000). These crunchy burritos may be the best on the planet. Get the "gutter punk" burrito ($7), a meal the size of your head, and wash it down with some Mexican beer. Open M-Sa 11am-10pm, Su 4-9pm. AmEx/D/MC/V. ❷

Clover Grill, 900 Bourbon St. (☎504-598-1010). Open since 1950, Clover serves greasy and delicious burgers ($5+) grilled under an American-made hubcap. Breakfast ($7) served all day. Open 24hr. AmEx/MC/V. ❷

Franky and Johnny's, 321 Arabella St. (☎504-899-9146), southwest of downtown at the corner of Tchoupitoulas St. A noisy and popular bar that specializes in seafood; you can sample alligator soup ($4) or fried crawfish ($10). The stuffed artichokes ($8) are fantastic. Open daily 11am-last customer. AmEx/D/MC/V. ❷

Johnny's Po' Boys, 511 St. Louis St. (☎504-524-8129), near the Decatur St. corner. This French Quarter institution has 40 varieties of the classic po' boy ($4-7.50) and almost as many choices for a hearty breakfast. Open M-F 9am-3pm, Sa-Su 9am-4pm. AmEx/MC/V. ❷

Acme Oyster House, 724 Iberville St. (☎504-522-5973). A touristy spot with excellent oysters (6 for $5, 12 for $8). Get your oysters shucked before your eyes by Hollywood, the senior shucker. Open M-Th and Su 10am-10pm, F-Sa 10am-11pm. AmEx/D/MC/V. ❸

Croissant d'Or, 617 Ursulines Ave. (☎504-524-4663). French pastries, sandwiches, and quiches are served to a crowd that comes to leisurely nurse a cup of coffee over the morning paper. Open daily 6:30am-2pm. AmEx/MC/V. ❷

Café du Monde, 800 Decatur St. (☎504-587-0833). Picture old school tables, a sprawling patio, and a bustling waitstaff, and you have it. This people-watching paradise, open since 1862, only does 2 things—hot café au lait and scrumptious beignets ($2)—and it does them well. Open 24hr. Cash only. ❶

Mother's Restaurant, 401 Poydras St. (☎504-523-9656), at the corner of Tchoupitoulas St. Mother's is a deli-style restaurant frequently packed with locals and tourists—not because this is a touristy restaurant, but because the food is just that good. While you munch the "world's best baked ham po' boy" ($8), take a minute to appreciate the decor. The walls are covered with framed newspaper clippings and awards that attest to Mother's greatness. Open M-Sa 6:30am-10pm, Su 7am-10pm. AmEx/MC/V. ❷

The Market Cafe, 1000 Decatur St. (☎504-527-5000). With open-air dining and a live 5-piece jazz band every day, you can take in both the culture and the cuisine of New Orleans at once. Sample alligator tail if you've missed out so far ($9) or grab a salad, po' boy, or another local staple, all prepared directly from the cafe's own recipes. AmEx/D/MC/V. ❷

J'Anita's, 1906 Magazine St. (☎504-373-5337). J'Anita's specializes in serving only the most artery-clogging types of foods. There is a heavy focus on BBQ, sandwiches, and nachos here, but you can also grab one of the many salads offered if you're into that whole health thing. Get the triple-bypass nachos (loaded with cheese, jalapeño, sour cream, and guacamole; $7.50), pulled pork, BBQ brisket, or crawfish ... and a cardiologist's number. Open M and F-Su 9am-9pm, Tu-Th 10:30am-9pm. MC/V. ❷

🔘 SIGHTS

FRENCH QUARTER

Allow a full day in the Quarter. The oldest section of the city is famous for its ornate wrought-iron balconies—French, Spanish, and uniquely New Orleans architecture—and raucous atmosphere. Known as the **Vieux Carré** (vyuh ca-RAY), or Old Square, the historic district of New Orleans encompasses dusty used bookstores, voodoo shops, museums, art galleries, bars, and tourist traps. **Bourbon Street** is packed with touristy bars, strip clubs,

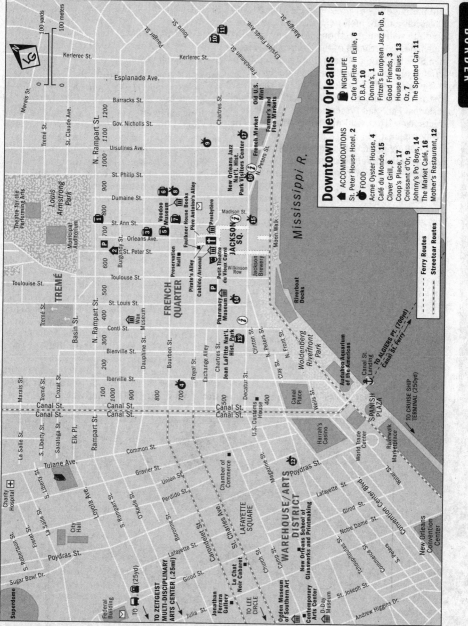

Downtown New Orleans

ACCOMMODATIONS
St. Peter House Hotel, **2**

FOOD
Acme Oyster House, **4**
Café du Monde, **15**
Clover Grill, **8**
Coop's Place, **17**
Croissant d'Or, **9**
Johnny's Po' Boys, **14**
The Market Café, **16**
Mother's Restaurant, **12**

NIGHTLIFE
Cafe LaFitte in Exile, **6**
D.B.A., **10**
Donna's, **1**
Fritzel's European Jazz Pub, **5**
Good Friends, **3**
House of Blues, **13**
Oz, **7**
The Spotted Cat, **11**

— Ferry Routes
----- Streetcar Routes

Mississippi R.

TREMÉ

FRENCH QUARTER

WAREHOUSE/ARTS DISTRICT

Louis Armstrong Park

JACKSON SQ.

Moon Walk

Riverboat Docks

Woldenberg Riverfront Park

Audubon Aquarium of the Americas

SPANISH PLAZA

New Orleans Convention Center

New Orleans Jazz Nat'l Hist. Park Visitors Center

French Market

Old U.S. Mint

Farmer's and Flea Markets

Theatre for the Performing Arts

Municipal Auditorium

Wax Museum

Voodoo Museum

Faulkner House Books

Père Antoine's Alley

Presbytere

Pirate's Alley

Preservation Hall

Petit Theatre du Vieux Carré

Cabildo/Arsenal

Pharmacy Museum

Jackson Brewery

Wilkinson Row

Jean LaFitte Nat'l Hist. Park

Exchange Alley

U.S. Customs House

Canal Place

Harrah's Casino

World Trade Center

Riverwalk Marketplace

Canal St. Landing

TO ALGIERS PT. (700yd)
Canal St. Ferry

TO CRUISE SHIP TERMINAL (250yd)

Superdome

Charity Hospital

City Hall

Federal Building

Sugar Bowl Dr.

TO ZEITGEIST MULTI-DISCIPLINARY ARTS CENTER (.25mi)

TO LEE CIRCLE

Le Chat Noir Cabaret

Jonathan Ferrara Gallery

Ogden Museum of Southern Art

New Orleans School of Glassworks and Printmaking

Contemporary Arts Center

D-Day Museum

LAFAYETTE SQUARE

Chamber of Commerce

100 yards
100 meters

VG

and panhandlers disguised as clowns; **Decatur Street** has a more mellow version of the same. If you're searching for bona fide New Orleans tunes, head northeast of the Quarter to **Frenchmen Street,** a block of bars that locals claim is what Bourbon St. was like 20 years ago.

If you're really curious about the Quarter's history and culture, the **Jean Lafitte National Historical Park and Preserve Visitors Center** conducts free 1hr. walking tours through the French Quarter. (419 Decatur St. ☎504-589-2636. Office open daily 9am-5pm. Tours daily 9am.) Alternatively, Robert Batson, "history laureate" of New Orleans, gives a politically insightful and lively **Gay Heritage Tour** that highlights GLBT happenings in and around New Orleans. (Leaves from 909 Bourbon St. ☎504-945-6789. 2½hr. tours W 4pm and Sa 1pm. Reservations required. $20.)

NEW ORLEANS JAZZ NATIONAL HISTORICAL PARK VISITORS CENTER. This is your destination for all things jazz. The center has a jovial environment, tons of information, and frequent jazz jam sessions between park rangers. Professional musicians have also been known to make frequent appearances. *(916 N. Peters St., in the French Market. ☎504-589-4841. Open Tu-Sa 9am-5pm. Live performances every Sa at 11am. Call ahead for afternoon concert schedule. Free.)*

ROYAL STREET. A streetcar named *Desire* once rolled down **Royal Street,** one of the French Quarter's most aesthetically pleasing avenues. Pick up the free *French Quarter Self-Guided Walking Tour* from the visitors center on St. Ann St.; they may be hiding it behind the counter.

JACKSON SQUARE. During the day, much of the activity in the French Quarter centers Jackson Sq., a park dedicated to General Andrew Jackson, victor in the Battle of New Orleans. The square swarms with artists, mimes, musicians, psychics, magicians, and con artists. Those with cash to burn can take a 30min. horse-drawn tour of the Quarter here for $60. The oldest Catholic cathedral in the US, **Saint Louis Cathedral,** possesses a simple beauty and has been fully operational since 1718. Some afternoons, tour guides hang around the cathedral and will be happy to talk to you about the paintings, the architecture, or even the cathedral's function as a mausoleum. *(615 Père Antoine Alley. ☎504-525-9585. Open daily between masses, which take place at 7:30am and 5pm.)* Behind the cathedral lies **Cathedral Garden,** also known as St. Anthony's Garden, bordered by **Pirate Alley** and **Père Antoine Alley.** Legend has it that Pirate Alley was the site of covert meetings between pirate Jean Lafitte and Andrew Jackson as they drafted their plans for the Battle of New Orleans. In reality, the alley wasn't even built until 16 years later. Pirate Alley is also home to **Faulkner House Books,** where the late American author wrote

RAGIN' CAJUN: EATIN' WELL IN N'AWLINS

Cajun country is well known for its fearsome alligators, endless bayous, and jovial music. Ask any Cajun, and he'll tell you the key to the easygoing spirit of the region is a hearty enjoyment of good food. Here's a quick guide to get you started:

Gumbo: The most famous Cajun dish, gumbo consists of an extremely salty and thick stock known as roux, which contains flour and fat. This roux is then packed with "the holy trinity" of vegetables: celery, bell pepper, and onion. Seafood gumbo, the most popular variety, includes crab, shrimp, oyster, and crawfish, but different varieties of gumbo use different types of meats. The whole mixture is served over rice.

Jambalaya: The second-in-command to gumbo, jambalaya is a smorgasbord of vegetables, meat, and rice in a broth. Unlike gumbo, the rice is cooked in with the whole mixture, and the broth is usually less thick, meaning that jambalaya is considered a solid, rice dish, whereas gumbo is a soup.

Boudin: A thick sausage, made from pork, green onion, rice, and garlic, boudin is readily available throughout Louisiana and is usually eaten with some sort of bread.

Andouille: A very coarse, smoked sausage made of pork, pig intestines, pepper, wine, and

his first novel, *Soldier's Pay*. The bookshop is a treasure trove of Faulkner's books, which sit alongside an extensive catalogue of other Southern writers. *(624 Pirate Alley. ☎504-524-2940. Open daily 10am-5:30pm.)*

FRENCH MARKET. The historic French Market takes up several city blocks east of Jackson Sq., toward the water along N. Peters and Decatur St. The market begins at the famous **Café du Monde** (p. 792) and for the first few blocks is a strip mall of touristy shops in a historic building. By Governor Nicholls St., it becomes the outdoor **farmers' market,** which never closes and has been selling "most anything that grows" since 1791. Beyond the farmers' market is the **flea market,** where vendors offer everything from feather boas to woodcarvings to touristy souvenirs of questionable taste. Since Hurricane Katrina, these markets have specialized exclusively in trinkets—perfect if you want to buy your mother a "N'awlins" salt-and-pepper shaker set. *(☎504-522-2621. Most shops open daily 9am-8pm.)*

WATERFRONT. For an up-close view of the Mississippi River and a unique district of New Orleans, take the **Canal Street Ferry** to **Algiers Point.** Once called "The Brooklyn of the South," Algiers was home to much of New Orleans's African-American population as well as the city's most famous jazz musicians. Nowadays there's not much to do there, but,

if you're hankering for a pretty neighborhood and a glimpse of a few brightly painted bungalows, it might be worth visiting. At night, the ferry's outdoor observation deck affords a panoramic view of the city's sights. *(Ferry departs from the end of Canal St. daily every 30min. 5:45am-midnight. $1 per vehicle.)*

WAREHOUSE ARTS DISTRICT

The **Warehouse Arts District,** at the intersection of Julia and Camp St., contains several contemporary art galleries in revitalized warehouse buildings. Many galleries have exhibition openings on the first Saturday of every month. On **White Linen Night,** the first Saturday in August, thousands take to the streets in their fanciest white finery.

CONTEMPORARY ARTS CENTER. In an old brick building with a modern, glass-and-chrome facade, the center mounts exhibits of local and national artists' works, ranging from puzzling to positively cryptic. It also hosts music and performance art. *(900 Camp St. ☎504-528-3805; www.cacno.org. Open Th-Su 11am-4pm. $5, students and seniors $3, under 12 free.)*

OGDEN MUSEUM OF SOUTHERN ART. Across the street, the Ogden contains a huge collection of modern art and sculpture created in the Southern US. *(925 Camp St. ☎504-539-9600; www.ogdenmuseum.org. Open W-Su 11am-4pm. Live jazz Th 6-8pm. $10, students and seniors $8, under 17 $5.)*

◪ Beignets: Chunks of fried dough topped off with confectioner's sugar.
◪ Crawfish: Crawfish resemble little lobsters and are boiled in much the same way, but eating them can be tricky. First, you want to grab the head with one hand and the underside of the tail with the other. Snap the crawfish apart at the midsection and toss the head. Then pinch the top and bottom of the base of the tail and yank a strip of juicy meat out.
◪ Catfish: Catfish can be described as "the fishiest-tasting of fish." People have also said that they have a sweet and sometimes earthy taste that defies classification.
◪ Frog Legs: Close your eyes, and you'll swear you're eating chicken.
◪ Muffuletta: Invented in 1906 by Salvatore Lupo, the owner of the Central Grocery on Decatur St., the muffuletta sandwiches ham, salami, provolone cheese, and olive relish between slices of round muffuletta bread. These can get messy to eat, but they're worth the extra napkins.
◪ Po' boy: A New Orleanian pronunciation of "poor boy," this is basically New Orleans's version of the grinder, hoagie, submarine, or hero sandwich. The name originates from the Great Depression, when oyster po' boys were the cheapest meal you could buy in the city. Served on french bread, today's po' boy may feature oysters, catfish, shrimp, or more traditional lunchmeats.

NEW ORLEANS SCHOOL OF GLASWORKS. In the rear studio of the New Orleans School of Glassworks and Printmaking, you can watch students and instructors transform molten glass into artistic vases and sculptures. *(727 Magazine St. ☎504-529-7277. Open in summer M-Sa 10am-5pm; in winter M-F 10am-5pm Free.)*

JONATHAN FERRARA GALLERY. The gallery hosts local and regional artists, focusing on contemporary art. *(843 Carondelet St. ☎504-522-5471. Open Tu-Sa noon-6pm. Free.)*

ZEITGEIST MULTI-DISCIPLINARY ARTS CENTER. Just west of the Warehouse District, this venue has films, art exhibits, and theatrical and musical performances. *(1618 Oretha Castle Haley Blvd. ☎504-592-3220. Recommended donation $7, students and seniors $6.)*

OUTSIDE NEW ORLEANS

Across from downtown New Orleans, River Rd. curves along the Mississippi River. If you follow it 40 mi. west (or take I-10 W. to Exit 194), you can access several plantations preserved from the 19th century. *Great River Road Plantation Parade: A River of Riches*, available at the New Orleans Visitors Center, contains a good map and descriptions of the houses. Choose wisely, since tours of the privately owned plantations are quite expensive, ranging from $50 to $90.

LAURA PLANTATION. The plantation was owned and operated by slave-owning Creoles whose lives were not like those of white antebellum planters. Br'er Rabbit hopped into his first briar patch here, the site of the first recorded "Compair Lapin" West African stories. The tours are fantastic. *(2247 Rte. 18/River Rd. ☎225-265-7690. Tours daily at 10, 11:15am, 1:30, 1:45, 3, 4pm. $10, students $5. Open for tours only.)*

SAN FRANCISCO PLANTATION. This building is an example of the Creole style, with its bright blue, peach, and green exterior; it also points to the aesthetic tastes of its Bavarian mistress. The inside features lavish furnishings and beautiful painted ceilings, all of which are original. *(2646 Hwy. 44. ☎985-535-2341; www.sanfranciscoplantation.org. Open daily Apr.-Oct. 9:30am-4:40pm, Nov.-Mar. 9am-4pm. $15, students and seniors $7.)*

OAK ALLEY. The name Oak Alley refers to the magnificent lawn alley bordered by 28 evenly spaced oaks that correspond to the 28 columns surrounding the Greek Revival house. The Greeks wouldn't have approved, though—the mansion is bright pink. *(3645 Rte. 18, between St. James and Vacherie St. ☎225-265-2151; www.oakalleyplantation.com. Open M-F 9am-4pm, Sa-Su 9am-5pm. $15, students and seniors $7.50.)*

🏛 MUSEUMS

NATIONAL WORLD WAR II MUSEUM. This gargantuan building opened in 2000 as the National D-Day Museum, but it was recently designated by Congress the National World War II Museum. It lives up to its hype as an engaging, exhaustive, and moving study of WWII. Through photos, recorded footage, and personal testimony, the museum explains how the US entered WWII and how D-Day was planned and executed. It also showcases authentic equipment, from soldiers' rations to warplanes. The museum deals in great depth with the Pacific theater of the war and discusses propaganda that fueled hate against the Japanese and Japanese-Americans. *(945 Magazine St., at the corner of Andrew Higgins Dr. ☎504-527-6012; www.ddaymuseum.org. Open M-Sa 9am-5pm. $14, students and seniors $8, ages 5-12 $6.)*

NEW ORLEANS PHARMACY MUSEUM. This enthralling look into medical history is housed in an apothecary shop built by America's first licensed pharmacist in 1923. Among the exhibits are 19th-century "miracle drugs" like cocaine and opium, voodoo powders, a collection of old spectacles, a rare 1855 soda fountain, and live leeches. A little-known fact: soda got its start as a chaser for the nasty medicines that pharmacists used to cook up. *(514 Chartres St., between St. Louis and Toulouse St. ☎504-565-8027. Open Tu-Th 10am-2pm, W, F and Sa 10am-5pm. $5, students $4, under 12 free.)*

LOUISIANA STATE MUSEUM. Eight separate museums are overseen by the "State Museum," six of which have now fully rebuilt and re-opened following Katrina. The **Cabildo** presents the history of Louisiana and houses Napoleon's death mask. *(701 Chartres St. ☎504-*

488-2631. *$6, students and seniors $5, under 12 free. Open daily 9am-5pm.*) The **Arsenal** recounts the history of the Mississippi River and New Orleans as a port city. (*615 St. Peter St. Enter through the Cabildo. ☎504-488-2631. $6, students and seniors $5, under 12 free. Open daily 9am-5pm.*) The **Presbytère** features a gigantic exhibit on Mardi Gras, which allows visitors to try on costumes and clamber onto floats. (*751 Chartres St. ☎800-568-6968. $6, students and seniors $5, under 12 free. Open daily 9am-5pm.*) The **Old US Mint** opened in 1835 and is the only mint in the country to have served as both a Confederate mint during the Civil War and a US Mint in later years. See a wide variety of historic coins at this national landmark. (*400 Esplanade Ave. ☎504-568-6968. $6, students and seniors $5, under 12 free. Open daily 9am-5pm.*) **Madame John's Legacy,** an 18th-century building complex, has been around since 1795 and offers visitors a real sense of what the city looked like in its early days. (*632 Dumaine St. ☎504-568-6968. $3, students and seniors $2, under 12 free. Open daily 9am-5pm.*) Finally, the **1850 House,** originally the product of a rich colonial landowner, has been furnished to look exactly like a middle-class house would have looked in, you guessed it, 1850. (*523 St. Anne St. ☎504-568-6968. $3, students and seniors $2, under 12 free. Open daily 9am-5pm.*)

NEW ORLEANS MUSEUM OF ART (NOMA). This magnificent museum houses art from North and South America, a phenomenal glass collection, opulent works by the jeweler Fabergé, a strong exhibit of French paintings, and some of the best African and Japanese work in the country. The inspiring new sculpture garden sprawls over acres of walkways. (*1 Collins Diboll Cir. ☎504-488-2631; www.noma.org. Open F-Su 10am-4:30pm. $8, students and seniors $7, ages 3-17 $4. Louisianans free. Sculpture garden free.*)

VOODOO MUSEUM. Learn why all those dusty shops in the Quarter sell gris-gris and alligator teeth at this quirky haunt. What this museum lacks in size it makes up for in spookiness, with all sorts of relics, things in jars, and animal skulls lining the hallways and rooms. It's not for the faint of heart, but, in a spooky way, it's very New Orleans. (*724 Dumaine St. ☎504-680-0218. Open daily 10am-6pm. $7, students and seniors $5.50, under 12 $3.50.*)

AUDUBON AQUARIUM OF THE AMERICAS. If you like aquariums, you'll love this one. The 110,000 sq. ft. facility has state-of-the-art exhibits, including sharks from the Gulf Coast, penguins, and a coral reef. Look for the 10 ft. albino alligator. (*1 Canal St. ☎800-774-7394; www.auduboninstitute.org/aoa. Open Tu-Su 10am-5pm. $17.50, children $10.50, seniors $13.50.*)

🎵 ENTERTAINMENT

Uptown houses authentic Cajun dance halls and university hangouts, while the **Marigny** is home to New Orleans's alternative and local music scenes. There are good bars along **Frenchmen Street** that often have live music and are less touristy than the French Quarter equivalents. Check out *Off Beat*, free in many restaurants, *Where Y'At*, another free weekly, or the Friday *Times-Picayune* to find out who's playing where. The Warehouse Arts District (p. 795) is also a source for constant performance options.

Le Petit Théâtre du Vieux Carré, 616 St. Peter St. (☎504-522-2081; www.lepetittheatre.com). One of the city's most beloved historic theaters and the oldest continuously operating community theater in the US, the building replicates the early 18th-century abode of Louisiana's last Spanish governor. Approximately 5 musicals and plays are produced each year. Tickets $35, students $30. Call for box office hours, though shows are generally limited to weekends.

Preservation Hall, 726 St. Peter St. (daytime ☎504-522-2841, after 8pm 504-523-8939). Traditional New Orleans jazz was born at the turn of the century, and it's still alive and well here. With only 2 small ceiling fans to cool the place, most people only stay for 1 set, so you can usually find a spot. $10, except special events. Open W-Su 8-11pm with shows every hr.

Le Chat Noir, 715 St. Charles Ave. (☎504-581-5812; www.cabaretlechatnoir.com). In a turn-of-the-century house on St. Charles, Le Chat Noir prides itself on being a "European-style cabaret" (dark interior and little white-tableclothed tables with candles). The venue seats 125 and hosts all sorts of shows. Ticket prices and showtimes vary; call ahead or check online.

NIGHTLIFE

Life in New Orleans is and always will be a party. On any night of the week, at any time of the year, the masses converge on Bourbon St. to drift in and out of bars and strip joints. Ask any local what to do on a weekend, and he'll probably tell you to avoid Bourbon at all costs; the street has become increasingly touristy of late. **Decatur Street,** near the French market, is a quieter, though still touristy, nightlife area. To experience what the Quarter was like before the tourist traps took over, head southeast to **Frenchmen Street,** which offers eclectic bars and clubs. Another good place to find nightlife is around Tulane University on **Oak Street.** While the French Quarter has no **open container law,** this law does not technically extend to the rest of the city (which includes Frenchmen St.), so be careful.

BARS

Bars in New Orleans stay open late, and few keep a strict schedule; in general, they open around 11am and close around 3am, but many go all night when there's a crowd or a party. Most blocks, especially in the Quarter, feature at least one venue with cheap draft beer and "Hurricanes" (sweet juice and rum).

■ **Donna's,** 800 N. Rampart St. (☎504-596-6914), on the edge of the French Quarter. As 1 fan says, this is "the place where you can sit and watch New Orleans roll by." Brass and jazz bands play inside, the smell of ribs and chicken wafts out, and customers sit on the sidewalk and take it all in. Cover $10. Open M and Th-Su 6:30pm-last customer. AmEx/MC/V.

■ **The Spotted Cat,** 623 Frenchmen St. (☎504-943-3887). This is what you might have imagined most New Orleans bars would be like: a small, dim place with passionate trumpet and piano solos that pour out onto the sidewalk. Caters to the local music community; call ahead if you want to know who's playing the following week. Blues, jazz, ragtime, and swing. Live bands Sa-Su 2pm-2am. No cover but a 1-drink min. Open M-Sa 1pm-3am, Su 1pm-midnight. MC/V.

d.b.a., 618 Frenchmen St. (☎504-942-3731; www.drinkgoodstuff.com). Modeled after the original in New York City, **d.b.a.** has a yuppie urban vibe with a great selection of beers from around the world, Wi-Fi, and a delightfully dark interior. Bands play jazz, rock, or blues every night. Cover $5-10. Open M-Th and Su 4pm-4am, F-Sa 4pm-5am. AmEx/D/MC/V.

Fritzel's European Jazz Pub, 733 Bourbon St. (☎504-566-0176). On Bourbon St., many of the bars look and sound the same, with loud music, expensive drinks, and flashy, eye-catching decor. Fritzel's has all of the above but stands apart from the others in the quality of its live jazz W-Su night. Good company and reasonably priced drinks, all things considered. 18+. No cover. Open daily 1pm-last customer. AmEx/D/MC/V.

DANCE CLUBS

■ **Tipitina's,** 501 Napoleon Ave. (☎504-895-8477; www.tipitinas.com). The best local bands and some big national names play so close you can almost touch them. Bars line the sides of the room and serve domestic beer at a reasonable $3. A 2nd fl. balcony offers the best viewing spots at packed concerts, but it can be hard to spot the staircase that will take you there. (It's past the bar, by the door on your left.) Su 5-9pm. Music usually W-Su 9pm-3am; call ahead for times and prices. Cajun *fais do-dos*. 18+. Cover up to $20. AmEx/MC/V.

■ **Maple Leaf Bar,** 8316 Oak St. (☎504-866-9359; www.themapleleafbar.com), off Carrollton Ave. A staple of the New Orleans jazz, blues, zydeco, and brass-band scene, the Maple Leaf features live music 7 nights a week, from local groups to national acts. An open-air backyard patio, a wood dance floor, and a massive piano bring this place to life. 21+. Cover $5-15. Open daily 3pm-last customer. AmEx/D/MC/V.

House of Blues, 225 Decatur St. (☎504-310-4999). A sprawling complex with a large dance hall and a balcony and bar overlooking the action. Concerts most nights. Showtimes 7-10pm. Cover from $12. AmEx/D/MC/V.

GLBT NIGHTLIFE

The New Orleans gay scene is more inclusive than that of many other urban centers, and straight people often visit gay venues because the drinks are cheap and strong. The majority of gay establishments are located toward the northeast end of **Bourbon Street** ("downriver"), and along **Saint Ann Street,** known to some as the **"Lavender Line."** A good point of reference is the intersection of St. Ann and Bourbon St. To get the lowdown on gay nightlife, pick up a copy of *Ambush Magazine.*

Cafe LaFitte in Exile, 901 Bourbon St. (☎504-522-8397). Banished from LaFitte's Blacksmith Shop in 1953 when the shop came under new management, the ousted gay patrons trooped up the street to found the oldest gay bar in America. On the opening night, surrounded by patrons dressed as their favorite exiles, Cafe Lafitte in Exile lit an "eternal flame" (it still burns today) that represents the soul of the gay community in New Orleans. Two floors of bars, video screens, pool tables, and a rockin' dance scene. Happy hour M-F 4-9pm. Open daily 24hr. MC/V.

Good Friends, 740 Dauphine St. (☎504-566-7191). Entering this bar is like stepping into a gay *Cheers* episode. A cozy, friendly neighborhood bar full of locals happy to welcome refugees from Bourbon St. Domestic beers $2.75. Don't miss sing-along Su 4-9pm. Happy hour daily 4-9pm. Open M-Th and Su 1pm-2am, F-Sa 1pm-5am. MC/V.

Oz, 800 Bourbon St. (☎504-593-9491; www.ozneworleans.com). So you wanted a N'awlins party? Well, here it is. Oz, with 2 floors and a balcony, has something crazy every night of the week. Strippers dance on the bar from time to time, laser lights fill up the place, and the music dominates Oz's section of Bourbon St., which is no easy task. M and W drag shows. Th strip contest. F drag bingo. Happy hour M-F 4-10pm, Sa-Su 4-8pm with ½-price domestic beers. Open M-F 1pm-3am, Sa-Su 24hr. D/MC/V.

🚗 THE ROAD TO HOUMA: 56 MI.

To leave the Big Easy, head west on **Claiborne Street (US 90)** for 48 mi. Take **Exit 210 (Route 182 West)** and continue 8 mi. to Houma.

HOUMA   ☎985

Fishing boats line the waterways here in the heart of Cajun country at the confluence of seven bayous. Don't be surprised if one of them glides alongside as you meander down one of the swamp-hugging streets. Alligators,

wandering from their bayou homes, have been known to approach humans on the sidewalks. One of the nicest ways to get a feel for Houma is to wander the historic downtown. You can pick up a self-guided tour at the **Houma Area Visitor Information Center,** 114 Tourist Dr. (☎985-868-2732. Open M-F 9am-5pm, Sa-Su 9:30am-3:30pm.) To learn more about the bayou, check out the **Bayou Terrebonne Waterlife Museum,** 7910 Park Ave. The museum features interactive displays focusing on almost every aspect of southern Louisiana, from its history, culture, and economy to the geography that makes this place so unlike any other. (☎985-580-7200. Open Tu-F 10am-5pm, Sa noon-4pm. Free. Live Cajun music 5:30-7pm $1.) Houma also has numerous swamp tours run by locals. Bill Munson of **Munson's Swamp Tours,** 979 Bull Run Rd., is an expert in all things swamp-related and offers marvelous 2hr. excursions to see alligators, otters, and nutria. His tours are also the only ones run entirely on private property, ensuring that the swamp you see remains unaltered by hunting, fishing, or real-estate development. (☎985-851-3569. Tours leave daily 10am, 1:30pm. $20, under 12 $15.)

On the right side of Rte. 182, half a mile east of downtown, **A-Bear's Motel ❷,** 342 New Orleans Blvd., has small, decent rooms with cable TV at the lowest prices you'll be able to find in Houma. (☎985-872-4528. Singles $40; doubles $45. AmEx/D/MC/V.)

The residents of Houma two-step to the rhythms of Cajun music, zydeco, and swamp pop at the 🏆**Jolly Inn Dance Hall,** 1507 Barrow St. The rambunctious hall boasts live bands, a wood dance floor, and a cafe that serves up sizzling Cajun dishes. A jovial group of locals frequents the place, and they're always up for showing out-of-towners the right dance steps. (☎985-872-6114. Cafe open M-F 10:45am-2pm. Dance hall open F 8pm-midnight, Su 4-7pm. $3, under 12 free.) **Big Al's Seafood Restaurant ❸,** 1226 Grand Caillou Rd., boasts some of the best seafood in town. Get a heaping plate of catfish, crawfish, crabs, or oysters. (☎985-876-7942. Open Tu-Th 11am-10pm, Sa 11am-10pm, Su 4-9pm. AmEx/D/MC/V.)

◥ **THE ROAD TO MORGAN CITY: 36 MI.**
From Houma, get back on **US 90 West** and follow it into Morgan City.

MORGAN CITY ☎985

Following the Civil War, Charles Morgan, a steamship and railroad tycoon, dredged the Atchafalaya Bay Channel to make Morgan City a bustling trade center. The halfway point between New Orleans and Lafayette, the city remains an important crossroads at the edge of the swamp. Although the city isn't too active, there are some worthwhile stops along your way. Some may be interested in making the trek to the **International Petroleum Museum and Exposition,** also known as the "Rig Museum" because it's located on an old oil rig known fondly as "Mr. Charlie." The so-called museum is actually a guided tour of Mr. Charlie, but it's the only place in the world members of the public can walk aboard an offshore drilling rig, so jump at the chance. (☎985-384-3744; www.rigmuseum.com. Tours 10am, 2pm. $5, under 12 $3.50, seniors $4.)

The **Morgan City Motel ❷,** 505 Brashear Ave., has surprisingly large and comfy rooms. (☎985-384-6640. Singles $40; doubles $60. Cash only.) For a food stop, check out **Manny's Restaurant ❷,** 725 Rte. 90, on the left just before the underpass, a diner with little decor but one that's packed full of locals. Hearty American breakfasts like pork chops and eggs ($9), roast-beef dinners ($10), and an all-you-can-eat lunch buffet ($10-12) mean no one goes home hungry. (☎985-384-2359. Open M-Sa 6:30am-8pm, Su 7am-2pm. Buffet daily 11am-2pm. AmEx/D/MC/V.)

◥ **THE ROAD TO FRANKLIN: 22 MI.**
From Morgan City, take **US 90 West** for 17 mi. to the junction with **Route 182.** Take Rte. 182 W. for 4 mi.

FRANKLIN ☎337

Franklin's gas lamps, oak canopies, and antebellum mansions suggest the elegance of years gone by even while its preserved slave quarters stand as constant reminders of the price of such opulence. The rooms at the **Billmar Motel ❷,** 1520 Main St., are clean and

comfortable. (☎337-828-5130. Singles $40; doubles $55. AmEx/D/MC/V.)

◥ **THE ROAD TO JEANERETTE: 17 MI.**
Route 182 follows the 125 mi. **Bayou Teche,** one of the longest of Louisiana's swampy waterways. It is easy to imagine the frustration of the steamboat captains who often navigated these sinuous waters.

JEANERETTE ☎337

Ivy climbs the lofty heights of the lonely brick spire in Jeanerette. The town was once home to a large cypress logging operation; the solitary tower is all that remains of the industry. Otherwise, life in Jeanerette remains much the same as it was a century ago, and decaying brick buildings still line Main St. (Rte. 182). Jeanerette's other name is Sugar City, and its sugarcane industry survives to this day. In the fall, the cane is harvested and brought to mills while the stalks burn in the fields and fill the air with sweet smoke. The **Jeanerette Museum,** 500 Main St., shows a 13min. video on sugarcane history that also indoctrinates viewers on the importance of sugar as part of a "balanced diet." *Let's Go* is glad that someone is getting out this true and important message. The museum's real treasures are its knowledgeable guides, who can tell you all about the sugar biz. (☎337-276-4408. Open M-F 10am-4pm. Last tour 1hr. before close. $3, students $1.)

Just before you reach Jeanerette, look for the **Yellow Bowl Restaurant ❸,** 19478 Rte. 182 W., which derives its name from the use of "bowl" as a code word for speakeasy during prohibition. But alcohol is not its major claim to fame; a Cajun family acquired it in the 1950s and began serving crawfish and soon the crustacean was on every menu in the state. Try a crawfish étouffée ($13) or a cup of crawfish bisque ($4) for an authentic Cajun delight. (☎337-276-5512. Po' boys $6-8. Open W-F 11am-9:30pm, Sa 5-9:45pm, Su 11am-2:30pm. AmEx/D/MC/V.) The folks at **LeJeune's Bakery ❶,** 1510 W. Main St., bake French bread in an old-fashioned brick oven, just like they've been doing since 1884. The bakery is still family-owned, run by the fifth generation of LeJeunes. They don't have a storefront, but they'll gladly sell the bread straight from the kitchen. Enter through the door on the left side of the building to get a delicious hot loaf for $2.50. (☎337-276-5690. Open daily 7am-5pm or whenever they run out of bread. Cash only.)

DID YOU KNOW? Cajun legend holds that when the French Acadians left Nova Scotia for Louisiana, the local lobsters grew lonely and swam after them. The long journey left them so exhausted that they shrank to the size of shrimp, becoming the "mud bugs" (crawfish) that inhabit the waters of Louisiana today.

THE ROAD TO NEW IBERIA: 12 MI.

Continue west on **Route 182** to New Iberia.

NEW IBERIA ☎337

The "Queen City" of the Bayou Teche, New Iberia was the only Spanish settlement in Acadiana. Later, it was the home to many wealthy sugar plantation owners during the antebellum period. No trace of Spanish culture remains, but New Iberia is still the major city in these parts—at least compared to the other towns in New Iberia Parish—and it has many boutiques and restaurants as well as a beautiful, oak-lined Main St.

VITAL STATS

Population: 33,000

Tourist Office: Iberia Parish Visitors Bureau, 2513 Rte. 14 (☎337-365-1540). Open daily 9am-5pm.

Library and Internet Access: Iberia Parish Library, 445 E. Main St. (☎337-364-7024). Open M-Th 8:30am-8pm, F-Sa 8:30am-5:30pm, Su 1:30-5:30pm.

Post Office: 817 E. Dale St. (☎337-364-6972). Open M-F 8am-5pm, Sa 8:30am-noon. **Postal Code:** 70560.

ORIENTATION

Main Street (Route 182 West) runs westward through town, while **Saint Peter Street (Route 182 East)** handles the eastbound traffic one

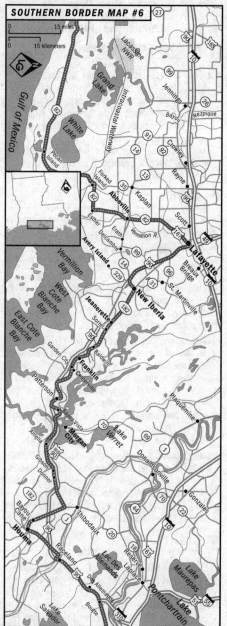

SOUTHERN BORDER MAP #6

block south. **Center Street (Route 14),** which runs perpendicular to Main St., is lined with fast-food restaurants and chain motels.

ACCOMMODATIONS

Teche Motel, 1830 E. Main St. (☎337-369-3756). Makes up half of a cabin that sits underneath an oak canopy on the sleepy bayou's edge. Guests have access to the beautiful Bayou Garden, which includes a dock, a gazebo, a rope swing, and even a trampoline. The friendly hosts aim to please; they might even lend you their barbecue grill for bayou-side grilling. Rooms $40. Cash only. ❷

FOOD

New Iberia has many cheap eateries and a few classy establishments.

Steve's Drive Inn, 1218 W. Main St. (☎337-365-0566). A drive-in (not an inn) that has quick burgers, seafood, and po' boys. Hang out in the parking lot with locals, who sit in and on cars while chowing down. Sandwiches $3-8. Open M-Th 10am-2:15pm and 5-9pm, F 10am-2:15pm and 5-10pm, Sa 10am-4pm. MC/V. ❷

Clementine, 113 E. Main St. (☎337-560-1007), located in downtown New Iberia, is named after the late folk artist Clementine Hunter. The gourmet eatery has a Cajun slant. Lunches include seafood gumbo, po' boys, and entrees like blackened tilapia. Dinners are quite a bit more expensive, but, if you're willing to splurge, try the crab meat au gratin. Open M-F 11am-2pm, Tu-Th 6-9pm, F-Sa 6pm-10pm. AmEx/D/MC/V. ❸

Duffy's Diner, 1106 Center St. (☎337-365-2326). A 50s-style diner that offers food at (almost) 50s-era prices. The place is frequently packed and offers such local favorites as seafood, po' boys, and hamburgers. Grab a big hot dog and fries for $3.25. Open M-Sa 10am-9:30pm. MC/V. ❶

SIGHTS

AVERY ISLAND. Perhaps the most visited sight around New Iberia is Avery Island, home of Tabasco hot sauce. Over 130 years ago, EA McIlhenny planted a crop of capsicum peppers and combined their fiery juices with the island's natural salt to create the now-famous pepper sauce known as Tabasco. Today there is a $1 toll for the island, located 11 mi. southwest of New Iberia, but the charge is quickly made up in free samples, if you can handle the heat. On the **Tabasco Factory Tour,** visitors are exposed to 15min. of hard-core pro-Tabasco propaganda before viewing the assembly lines and bottlers. The next stop is the Tabasco Country Store, which sells Tabasco items ranging from kitchenware to neckties. The store also offers free samples of everything from Tabasco Habanero to Tabasco Dill Pickles. (*Take Rte. 14 to Rte. 329 and follow it for 5 mi. to the tollbooth.* ☎337-365-8173. *Tours every 20min. daily 9am-4pm. Store hours 9am-4:30pm. Free.*)

JUNGLE GARDENS. Avery Island's natural beauty also rewards explorers. Drivers can take a 4 mi. tour of the beautifully landscaped Jungle Gardens, which contain over 250 acres of plants from across the world, such as Chinese lotuses and azaleas. There is also a bird sanctuary that attracts some 20,000 snowy egrets to platforms in a pond nicknamed "Bird City." Just don't picnic too close to the ponds—impolite alligators lurking in the waters are known to take without asking. (*☎337-369-6243. Open daily 8am-5pm. $6.25, ages 6-12 $4.50.*)

OTHER SIGHTS. The rest of New Iberia's sights are primarily historical. Surrounded by dazzling flower gardens and shaded by massive oaks draped in Spanish moss, **Shadows-on-the-Teche,** 317 E. Main St., is a lovely Classical Revival plantation built by sugarcane planter David Weeks in 1834. (*☎337-364-6446. Open daily 9am-4:30pm. $10, children $6.50, seniors $8.*) The **Konriko Rice Mill,** 301 Ann St., is the oldest functioning rice mill in the US. Tours highlight the mill's old equipment, which is still in use, and also explain Cajun culture. (*☎800-551-3245; www.conradricemill.com. Open M-Sa 9am-5pm. $3.*)

FESTIVALS

The visitors bureau has information on New Iberia's annual festivals, including the **Cajun Hot Sauce Festival** of early April, **Hi Sugar!,** a sugarcane festival in late September, and the

World Championship Gumbo Cookoff Contest in mid-October.

⚶ THE ROAD TO LAFAYETTE: 24 MI.

From New Iberia, follow signs to **Route 14 West.** Stay on **Route 14 West** for 3 mi., then merge onto **US 90 West,** which will take you 21 mi. into Lafayette.

LAFAYETTE ☎ 337

At the center of bayou land, Lafayette is the two-stepping, crawfish-eating heart of Acadiana. Although Lafayette advertises itself as a French-speaking oasis and many of the roads have French names, very few people under the age of 65 actually speak French. Cajuns remain extremely proud of their Acadian heritage, however, and have started importing French teachers from Quebec, France, Belgium, and even Martinique to experiment with French immersion programs in Lafayette elementary schools. The jury's out on a French revival in the area, but Cajun culture reigns supreme in the music and food.

VITAL STATS
Population: 114,000
Tourist Office: Lafayette Convention and Visitors Commission, 1400 NW Evangeline Throughway (☎800-346-1958; www.lafayettetravel.com). Open M-F 8:30am-5pm, Sa-Su 9am-5pm.
Library and Internet Access: Lafayette Public Library, 301 W. Congress St. (☎337-261-5775). Open M-Th 8:30am-8pm, F 8:30am-6pm, Sa 9am-5pm, Su 1-5pm.
Post Office: 1105 Moss St. (☎337-269-7111). Open M-F 8am-5:30pm. **Postal Code:** 70501.

◤ ORIENTATION

Lafayette is a crossroads at the center of the swamp. **I-10** leads east to New Orleans and west to Lake Charles; **US 90** heads south to New Iberia and the Atchafalaya Basin and north to Alexandria and Shreveport; **US 167/ I-49** runs north into central Louisiana. Most of the city is west of the **Evangeline Throughway** (I-49 in the north, US 90 in the south), where budget motels are located. **Johnston Street**

marks the eastern border of downtown and has many fast-food restaurt.

⌂ ACCOMMODATIONS

☒ **Blue Moon Guest House & Saloon,** 215 E. Convent St. (☎337-234-2422; www.bluemoonhostel.com). Driving south on Evangeline Throughway (US 90), take a left on Johnston St. and a left on Convent St. Located in downtown Lafayette. A large dorm and comfy private rooms are accompanied by an inviting common area, a deck, and a "saloon" where bands whoop it up W-Sa. Guests get free concert access and a complimentary drink at the bar. Free breakfast and coffe/tea. Linens $5 deposit. Free Wi-Fi. Check-in 5-10pm. Late check-in $6. Dorms $18; private rooms $40-80. AmEx/MC/V. ❶

Travel Host Inn South, 1314 N. Evangeline Throughway (☎337-233-2090). Sweet-smelling rooms and pictures on the wall make it feel a bit more like home than your average motel does. Continental breakfast included. Singles $45; doubles $55. AmEx/D/MC/V. ❷

Plantation Motor Inn, 2810 NE Evangeline Throughway (☎337-232-7285). The inn has clean and spacious rooms with big windows. Rooms $45. AmEx/D/MC/V. ❷

Acadiana Park Campground, 1201 E. Alexander St. (☎337-291-8388), off Louisiana Ave. On the site of a former plantation, just a stone's throw from the center of Lafayette. 75 shaded sites near a stream. Access to tennis courts and a soccer field. Reception M-Th and Sa-Su 8am-5pm, F 8am-8pm. Sites $15. Cash only. ❶

KOA Lafayette, 537 Apollo Rd. (☎337-235-2739), in Scott, 5 mi. west of town, on I-10 at Exit 97. This lakeside campground has over 200 sites, a store, a minigolf course, and 2 pools. Water, electricity, and bathrooms. Reception M-Th and Su 7:30am-8pm, F-Sa 7:30am-9pm. Reservations recommended. Sites $24-34. MC/V. ❷

▤ FOOD

It's not hard to find reasonably priced Cajun and Creole cuisine in Lafayette, a city that prides itself on its food. Of course, it also prides itself on music, which can be found live in many restaurants at night. Make sure to get to restaurants relatively early, since it is hard to find anything other than a chain that stays open after 10pm.

Dwyer's Cafe, 323 Jefferson St. (☎337-235-9364). Since 1927, this brick-and-white-table diner has been a local favorite for breakfast or lunch. It serves a bang-up breakfast special (grits, eggs, ham, biscuits, juice, and coffee; $6). At lunch and dinnertime, locals saunter in for plates of gigantic proportions ($7-9). Open M and Su 6am-2pm, Tu-Sa 6am-8pm. AmEx/D/MC/V. ❷

The Judice Inn, 3134 Johnston St. (☎337-984-5614; www.judiceinn.com). A roadside time warp with booths and a wood bar, the inn is almost always presided over by a member of the Judice family. While the Judice Inn serves a variety of sandwiches, the phenomenal burgers ($3), which come covered in the Judice Inn's own sauce, are definitely the main attraction. Open M-Sa 10am-10pm. AmEx/D/MC/V. ❶

Old Tyme Grocery, 218 W. St. Mary Blvd. (☎337-235-8165; www.oldtymegrocery.com). Serves some of the best po' boys in town. Home to a convenience store, a takeout counter, and a charming dining area with wood paneling and checkered tablecloths. Don't expect variety—the only menu items are po' boys ($4-7) and the occasional salad ($7). Open M-F 8am-10pm, Sa 9am-7pm. Cash only. ❷

Poor Boy's Riverside Inn, 240 Tubing Rd. (☎866-837-6650; www.poorboysriversideinn.com). A standby since 1932 without the touristy schlock that plagues other Cajun restaurants in Lafayette. Lunch specials M-F 11am-2pm $9.25. Veggie options $9-14. Entrees $14-30 Open M-Th 11am-10pm, F 11am-11pm, Sa 5-11pm, Su 11am-last customer. AmEx/D/MC/V. ❸

Guamas, 302 Jefferson St. (☎337-267-4242; www.guamas.com). The friendly Reuben and Julieta cook meals that combine a variety of Caribbean and Latin American dishes in this bright restaurant. The coconut shrimp ($18) are mouthwatering, as are the specialty mixed drinks. Entrees $13-19. Happy hour Tu-F 4-7pm. Salsa dancing Sa 11pm-2am. Open Tu-Th 11am-10pm, F 11am-11pm, Sa 5pm-2am. Kitchen open until 10pm. AmEx/D/MC/V. ❸

Randol's, 2320 Kaliste Saloom Rd. (☎337-981-7080). One of many large, barn-like establishments in Lafayette. Cajun bands, a crowd of adorable elders dancing the two-step, and checkered tablecloths. Order drinks, hang out and listen to the bands, or get food and sit at the tables. Entrees $10-18. Live music nightly 6:30-9:30pm. Open M-Th and Su 5-10pm, F-Sa 5-11pm. AmEx/D/MC/V. ❸

Borden's, 1103 Jefferson St. (☎337-235-9291). Serving yummy sundaes ($3-4) and banana splits ($4.50) since 1940. All, from grandparents to teen couples, indulge. Open Tu-Th 1-8pm, F-Sa noon-9pm, Su noon-8pm. Cash only. ❶

◎ SIGHTS

ACADIAN CULTURAL CENTER. The center is a unit of the **Jean Lafitte National Historic Park and Preserve,** which runs throughout the delta region of Louisiana. The Acadian Center has a dramatic 35min. documentary chronicling the arrival of the Acadians in Louisiana as well as a 15min. film on conservation efforts in the Atchafalaya swamp. Check out the terrific exhibits on Cajun history and culture and learn a tiny bit of French in the process. (501 Fisher Rd. Take Johnston St. to Surrey, then follow the signs. ☎337-232-0789, ext. 11. Open daily 8am-5pm. Shows every hr. 9am-4pm. Free.)

VERMILIONVILLE. A "living museum" re-creates the Acadian settlement of Vermilionville with music, crafts, food, and dancing on the Bayou Vermilion banks. The sheer size of Vermilionville is impressive; it takes a mile to walk the length of the village. Take the perhaps once-in-a-lifetime opportunity to chat with in-character historical actors. Most of the buildings date from 1790-1890, though a few, like the church, are reproductions. (300 Fisher Rd. ☎337-233-4077. Live bands Su 1-4pm. Cajun cooking demos daily. Open Tu-Su 10am-4pm. Last entry 3pm. $8, ages 6-18 $5, seniors $6.50.)

ACADIAN VILLAGE. The village features 19th-century Cajun homes that house displays of artifacts. Highlights include the **Thibodeaux House,** a collection of 19th-century medical paraphernalia at the Doctor's House, and the small replica 1850 chapel. (200 Greenleaf Rd. Take Johnston St. to Ridge Rd., turn left on Broussard, and follow the signs. ☎337-981-2489 or 800-962-9133. Open daily 10am-4pm. $8, ages 6-14 $5, seniors $7.)

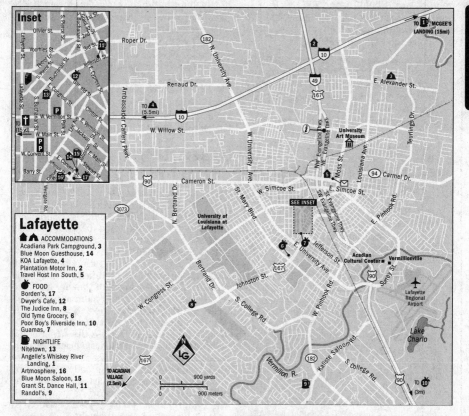

Lafayette

🏠🏕 ACCOMMODATIONS
Acadiana Park Campground, 3
Blue Moon Guesthouse, 14
KOA Lafayette, 4
Plantation Motor Inn, 2
Travel Host Inn South, 5

🍴 FOOD
Borden's, 17
Dwyer's Cafe, 12
The Judice Inn, 8
Old Tyme Grocery, 6
Poor Boy's Riverside Inn, 10
Guamas, 7

📷 NIGHTLIFE
Nitetown, 13
Angelle's Whiskey River
    Landing, 1
Artmosphere, 16
Blue Moon Saloon, 15
Grant St. Dance Hall, 11
Randol's, 9

MCGEE'S LANDING. Follow signs to McGee's Landing, which features live music 12:30-3:30pm on Sundays and sends three 1hr. boat tours into the basin daily. *(1337 Henderson Rd. ☎337-228-2384. Tours daily 10am, 1, 3pm. Sunset tours by reservation. $20, under 12 $15, seniors $18.)*

OTHER SIGHTS. Closer to downtown, the University of Louisiana's **University Art Museum** houses both temporary and permanent exhibits of sculpture, photography, ancient art, and paintings in a gorgeous building. *(710 E. St. Mary Blvd. ☎337-482-2278; www.museum.louisiana. edu. Open Tu-Sa 10am-5pm. $5, Over 49 $4, ages 3-17 $3. Free and Sa 10am-noon.)* The **Cathedral of Saint John the Evangelist** is worth a peek for its stunning 19th-century architecture. *(515 Cathedral St. ☎337-232-1322. Open daily 6am-6pm. Free.)*

PHOTO OP. Skip the church museum and check out the nearby **Saint John's Cathedral Oak,** 914 St. John St., which has a trunk 19 ft. in circumference. No matter where you're standing on the lawn, you're sure to get some shade.

🎵 NIGHTLIFE

To find the best zydeco in town, pick up a copy of *The Times,* free at restaurants and gas stations. There is also a variety of local music festivals throughout the year. The best of these is **Downtown Alive!,** a 12-week annual concert series held on the 700 block of Jefferson St., showcasing everything from New Wave to Cajun and zydeco. (☎337-291-5566. Apr.-June and Sept.-Nov. F 6-8:30pm.)

☒ **Angelle's Whiskey River Landing,** 1365 Henderson Levee Rd. (☎337-228-8567), in Breaux Bridge. On Su afternoons, this is the place to be. Live Cajun music has people dancing on the very lip of the levee overlooking the swamp. Boatmen pull ashore right outside and come in to join the party—it sometimes feels like the whole floor could collapse into the swamp with all the stamping. Su live music 4-8pm.

Artmosphere, 902 Johnston St. (☎337-233-3331). Artmosphere has just about everything: live music nightly, hookahs ($5), free Internet, and food seasoned with herbs from the backyard garden. Music generally starts around 9:30pm and finishes around 2am or whenever the performers feel like stopping. Cover $3-5 after 8:30pm. Open daily 11am-2am or later. AmEx/D/MC/V.

Grant St. Dance Hall, 113 W. Grant St. (☎337-237-8513; www.grantstreetdancehall.com). This former United Fruit warehouse is now a venue for live music, playing everything from zydeco to metal, from local acts to big-name groups. 18+. Cover usually $5-15, up to $50 depending on the act. Open only on show days; call ahead or check online. D/MC/V.

Blue Moon Saloon, 215 E. Convent St. (☎337-234-2422). Area bands play in this backyard bar, which is conveniently attached to the Blue Moon Guest House. W cajun jam with lots of locals and often dancing. Cover $5. Open W-Su 5pm-midnight. AmEx/MC/V.

Nitetown, 524 Jefferson St. (☎337-593-8551). Nitetown hosts some of the biggest acts to come through Lafayette in a wide-open, festive environment. Th night is always ladies' night, with free wine and margaritas for women and 2-for-1 mixed drinks for the whole crowd. Cover and hours vary based on acts. AmEx/D/MC/V.

❋ FESTIVALS

The **Festival International de Louisiane** is the largest free outdoor Francophone festival in the US. It transforms Lafayette into a gigantic French-speaking fairground for one wild weekend in April. (☎337-232-8086; www. festivalinternational.com.) The **Breaux Bridge Crawfish Festival,** in nearby Breaux Bridge, 10 mi. east on I-10 at Exit 109, features crawfish races, live music, dance contests, cook-offs, and a crawfish-eating contest. (☎337-332-6655; www.bbcrawfest.com.)

◤ THE ROAD TO ABBEVILLE: 21 MI.

Take **Johnston Street** west out of Lafayette. The road becomes **Route 167.** Take Rte. 167 S., and turn right on **Concorde Street** to reach downtown Abbeville.

ABBEVILLE   ☎337

Abbeville is a rice mill town with a pretty downtown center, friendly locals, and a different festival almost every week. The quirkiest (and perhaps best) of these festivals is the **Giant Omlette Celebration,** on the first Sunday in November, when the town makes a 5000-egg omelet. Many of the historic buildings that line S. State St. (Rte. 82) in downtown Abbeville date back to the mid-19th century, when French immigrants settled here. Picturesque buildings form the heart of the city and lead up to the Greek Revival columns of the **Vermilion Parish Courthouse.** Next to Magdalen is the Romanesque **Saint Mary Magdalen Catholic Church,** built in 1911. Across the street is the **Abbeville Cultural and Historical Alliance Museum and Art Gallery,** 208 N. Magdalen Sq. Despite its formidable name, it's actually a charming museum with displays of art and antiques as well as exhibits on the history of the town and the Cajun people. (☎337-898-4114. Open Tu and Sa 10am-3pm, W-F 10am-5pm.)

On the main drag of Abbeville, the **Sunbelt Lodge ❷,** 1903 Veterans Dr., has large, bright rooms and free Wi-Fi. (☎866-299-1480; www. sunbeltlodge.com. Continental breakfast included. Singles $47; doubles $52. AmEx/D/MC/V.) **Dupuy's Oyster Shop ❸,** 108 S. Main St., has served oysters since 1869 and also prepares other scrumptious seafood dishes, such as gumbo ($4.80). (☎337-893-2336. Entrees $12-19. Open Tu-Sa 11am-2pm and 5-9pm, F-Sa 5-10pm. AmEx/D/MC/V.) The nearby **Riverfront Grill ❸,** 503 W. Port St., has a lovely riverside patio and specializes in seafood. The crab and corn bisque ($4.50) is famous in Abbeville. (☎337-898-9218; www.riverfrontlouisianagrill.com. Open M-Th 11am-9pm, F 11am-10pm, Sa 5-10pm, Su 11am-3pm.

AmEx/D/MC/V.) For a quick lunch with a side of town gossip, Abbevillians head to **Comeaux's Cafe ❷**, 106 S. State St. A laid-back diner, CC's serves po' boys ($4-7), sandwiches ($2.50-5), and burgers ($3-5). Don't be afraid to join the senior-citizen set for the all-you-can-eat lunch buffet for just $6-10. (☎337-898-9218. Buffet daily 11am-2pm. Open M-F 5:30-10am and 11am-2pm, Sa 5:30-11am. MC/V.)

⚑ THE ROAD TO CAMERON: 93 MI.

From Abbeville, continue straight on **Route 167,** which becomes **Route 82** and eventually joins up with **Route 27.** The rice paddies outside Abbeville quickly give way to miles of marsh and swamp. Keep your eyes peeled for the elusive American alligators that lurk in these waters. There are few gas stations along these roads, so be sure to fill up in Abbeville.

CAMERON   ☎337

The tiny town of Cameron is the first real sign of life in this swampy area. Getting gas isn't impossible between Cameron and Port Arthur, but you should fill up here if you're getting low. Look for the sign for the **Hurricane Cafe ❶**, a small trailer that sells hot dogs ($1.25), a variety of chicken dishes, and burgers ($3.50). They sometimes have fresh shrimp. (☎337-775-2801. Open daily 6:30am-5pm. Cash only.) At the intersection of Rte. 82 and Rte. 27 lies **Hunt Brothers Pizza ❶**, which offers the weary traveler hot slices of pizza ($2.80) as well as snacks and gas. (Open M-Sa 5am-7pm, Su 6am-7pm. AmEx/MC/V.)

⚑ THE ROAD TO PORT ARTHUR: 50 MI.

After Cameron, it's a short 3 mi. trip to the **Calcasieu Ferry,** which shuttles cars across a small channel to the continuation of **Route 82.** Service costs $1 and runs continually. While the jump across the canal is only a few hundred yards, the ferry is as slow as it is small—waits can exceed 30min. Continue on Rte. 82 until you cross the towering **Martin Luther King, Junior, Bridge.** As you emerge on the other side, you are greeted by a sign welcoming you to Texas, "the proud home of President George W. Bush," and the sight of looming oil refineries belching smoke into the air.

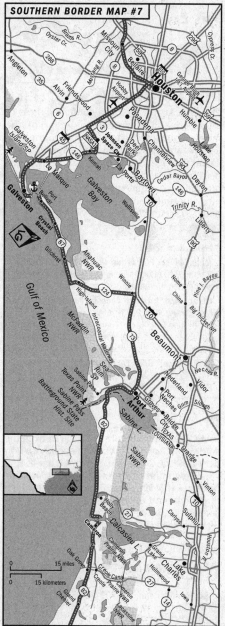

SOUTHERN BORDER MAP #7

The Lone Star State

TEXAS

Welcomes You!

PORT ARTHUR ☎409

The Port Arthur area is a confusing mess of intersecting highways, reminiscent of the miles of pipelines that wind around the endless natural gas and oil refineries that surround the city. This is the heart of the Texas petroleum industry, and natural gas fires burn high into the night. Other than the jaw-dropping enormity of the refineries, there isn't much to see in Port Arthur.

VITAL STATS

Population: 58,000

Tourist Office: Port Arthur Convention and Visitors Bureau, 3401 Cultural Center Dr. (☎800-235-7822; www.portarthurtexas.com). Open M-F 9am-5pm.

Library and Internet Access: Port Arthur Public Library, 4615 9th Ave. (☎409-985-8838). Open June-Aug. M-Th 10am-9pm, F 10am-6pm, Sa 10am-5pm, Sept.-May M-Th 10am-9pm, F 10am-6pm, Sa 10am-5pm, Su 2-5pm.

Post Office: 345 Lakeshore Dr. (☎409-983-3423). Open M-F 9am-5pm, Sa 9am-1pm. **Postal Code:** 77640.

✳ ORIENTATION

Route 73 enters the Port Arthur area from the southwest. **Route 82** defines the southern border of the area, running perpendicular to Rte. 73; a few miles north on Rte. 73 is **Memorial Boulevard (US 69),** which runs through much of downtown Port Arthur from northwest to southeast. Farther north on Rte. 73, **Twin City Highway (Route 347)** runs parallel to Memorial Blvd. between Port Arthur and Groves; this road is home to many attractions.

⌂ ACCOMMODATIONS

Southwinds Inn, (☎409-962-3000). 5101 E. Parkway St. All rooms at the Inn are large and have TVs, microwaves, fridges, and pool access. Free Wi-Fi. Rooms $54. AmEx/D/MC/V. ❷

🍴 FOOD

There are numerous fast-food chains lining Twin City Hwy. If you do end up here for the night, note that Vietnamese food is also usually a dining option, courtesy of Port Arthur's large population of Vietnamese immigrants.

Tony's BBQ, 4700 Twin City Hwy. (☎409-963-1005). Serves tantalizing meats slow-cooked with hickory; it has a drive through for those in a rush. Sandwiches $3-7. Dinner entrees $7-19. Open M-Sa 11am-9pm. AmEx/D/MC/V. ❷

👁 SIGHTS

MUSEUM OF THE GULF COAST. At the Museum of the Gulf Coast, Port Arthur displays its pride in some of its famous residents, including Jimmy Johnson and Janis Joplin. Aside from large exhibits dedicated to football and music, the two-story museum also features excellent displays on the petroleum industry, mariners, and prehistoric animals as well as a large collection of paintings by Robert Rauschenberg. *(700 Procter St. Take Memorial Blvd. all the way to its southeastern end at the intercoastal canal. Head right onto Lakeshore Dr., which becomes 4th St. The museum is hidden on the right, across the street from the police station. ☎409-982-7000. Open M-Sa 9am-5pm, Su 1-5pm. $4, children $2.)*

OTHER SIGHTS. The rest of Port Arthur's old downtown core is a ghost town—everyone has moved into the suburbs that are closer to the refineries. Built in 1900 as a winter home for the barbed-wire king Isaac Ellwood, the pink **Pompeiian Villa** is modeled after a house built in Pompeii, Italy. *(1953 Lakeshore Dr. ☎409-983-5977. Call ahead for hours. $2.)* The **Queen of Peace Shrine & Gardens** is a picturesque Asian garden with a huge statue of the Virgin Mary flanked by several minor statues. Built in the 1980s by Catholic Vietnamese who relocated to Port Arthur after the Vietnam War, the shrine is a tranquil place for contemplation. *(801 9th Ave. ☎409-983-7676. Open 24hr. Free.)*

⚐ THE ROAD TO CRYSTAL BEACH: 68 MI.

From Port Arthur, head west on **Route 73** for 25 mi. Take **Route 124 South** for 43 mi. Rte. 124 will become **Route 87** through the **Bolivar Peninsula.**

CRYSTAL BEACH   ☎409

If Bolivar's beaches strike your fancy or you just can't make it to Galveston Island before nightfall, Crystal Beach is a good place to stop. Lodgings are available at the **Joy Sands Motel ❸**, 1020 Rte. 87. The rooms at this coastal dwelling each have A/C, TV, fridge, microwaves, and cheerful flowers. (☎409-684-6152. Singles M-F $55, Sa-Su $65; doubles $70/90. AmEx/D/MC/V.) **The Outrigger Grill ❷**, 1035 Rte. 87, offers typical breakfast, lunch, and dinner fare for the region served up on tables with homey red-checkered tablecloths. Bacon, eggs, pancakes, omelets, and biscuits and gravy run about $4-6. Lunch options ($6-9) include burgers, sandwiches, po' boys, steaks, and chicken. For dinner, expect to pay $11-16 if you hope to eat steaks, seafood, or salads. (☎409-684-6212. Open M-Th 7am-8:30pm, F-Su 7am-9pm. AmEx/D/MC/V.)

⚐ THE ROAD TO GALVESTON: 8 MI.

Follow **Route 87** until it ends. Take the free ferry across the water. The ride is about 15min., but waits can exceed 1hr. on weekends.

GALVESTON   ☎409

This island is infamous as the base for swashbuckler Jean Lafitte's pirate fleet. In the 19th century, Galveston was the "Queen of the Gulf," the wealthiest city in Texas, a claim to which over 6000 historic buildings stand testament. Things changed in 1900, when a devastating hurricane ripped through the city and claimed 6000 lives. Today, the 27 mi. island is powered mainly by tourism, its cool sea breezes offering a much-needed respite from Houston's heat.

◢ ORIENTATION

The Bolivar Peninsula ferry deposits you on the eastern end of the island. From there, you can head west (right) on **Broadway Street (Avenue J)**, which runs east-west in the center of the island, or on **Seawall Boulevard,** the main beachfront drag, which also runs east-west. On the far eastern edge of the island sits **Apffel Park,** the only beach in Galveston that permits alcoholic beverages ($8 entrance for cars). Downtown, most establishments and some beaches are located east along Seawall Blvd., while the western side of the island is more sparsely populated. Nine miles to the west lies **Galveston Island State Park.** Away from the waterfront, Galveston sports a revitalized downtown, known as **The Strand,** where five blocks of gas lamps evoke the 19th-century "Queen of the Gulf" era. **Strand Street** runs east-west along the north side of the island and is most easily accessible from **Rosenberg Street (25th Street),** which crosses north-south from Seawall Blvd. to Strand St. Another major north-south street is **61st Street,** which connects Seawall Blvd. to Broadway. Galveston is a grid, with streets running north-south and labeled by number (numbers rise as you head west) and avenues running east-west, labeled by letters (A is in the north).

With regards to parking, there is a municipal lot at 25th St. and Mechanics Row ($5 per day) and free parking along Seawall Blvd. Parking is allowed on most streets and is not difficult, except on Strand St.

VITAL STATS
Population: 57,000
Tourist Office: Galveston Island Visitors Information Center, 2428 Seawall Blvd. (☎888-425-4753; www.galveston.com). Open daily 8:30am-5pm.
Library and Internet Access: Rosenberg Library, 2310 Sealy Ave. (☎409-763-8854). Open M-Th 9am-9pm, F-Sa 9am-6pm.
Post Office: 601 25th St. (☎409-763-6834). Open M-F 8:30am-5pm. **Postal Code:** 77550.

◤ ACCOMMODATIONS

On summer weekends, even the shabbiest accommodations can get away with charging upward of $100, but cheaper deals can be found during the week and in the winter.

Rosenberg Inn, 2027 Rosenberg St. (☎409-765-7632). Although it's not very well lit from the outside, the inn has huge rooms with full kitchens only a few blocks from the beach. Try to get rooms on the 2nd floor for better light. Key deposit $2. Rooms $45. AmEx/D/MC/V. ❷

Driftwood Motel, 3128 Seawall Blvd. (☎409-763-6431). This motel has large, decent rooms with comfy beds and great views of the beach. Singles M-F $40, Sa-Su $50-70; doubles $50/80-120. AmEx/D/MC/V. ❸

Economy Inn, 2008 Seawall Blvd. (☎409-762-0664). As far as the glut of $40-per-night motels on Galveston Island goes, this should be your choice. The inn has clean and new-looking rooms, and the staff is friendly. Singles $40; doubles $55. AmEx/D/MC/V. ❷

🍴 FOOD

Benno's, 1200 Seawall Blvd. (☎409-762-4621). It can be crowded with tourists, but the food makes up for it. Try the Cajun platter with a cup of jambalaya. The key lime pie is the perfect dessert. Entrees $8-16. Open M-Th and Su 11am-10pm, F-Sa 11am-11pm. AmEx/D/MC/V. ❸

Original Mexican Cafe, 1401 Market St. (☎409-762-6001). Go east from Rosenberg St.; it's on the right. The cafe cooks up Tex-Mex meals with homemade tortillas. Lunch specials $7-10. Open M-Th 11am-9:30pm, F 11am-10pm, Sa-Su 8am-10pm. AmEx/D/MC/V. ❷

The Diner, 1017 61st St. (☎409-744-3223). Locals head to the Diner for its cheap but award-winning breakfasts. Expect to be called "baby doll" and "sugar" repeatedly. Breakfast $3-8. Open M-Tu and Th-Su 6am-2pm. MC/V. ❷

Java's 213, 213 Tremont St. (☎409-762-5282). For a jolt of joe, head to the island's hippie-student-European cafe par excellence. Lounge on the couches, surf the Internet, or just revel in the stained-glass windows. Smoking is permitted inside, and you can purchase a cigar from the cafe's surprisingly good selection on hand. Open daily 7:30am-midnight. AmEx/D/MC/V. ❶

👁 SIGHTS

SEAWALL BOULEVARD. Galveston Island's main attraction is Seawall Blvd., which brims with hotels, minigolf, and chain restaurants. Driving down this strip can be difficult with all the SUVs circling to score a parking spot.

Making left turns going east on this road is also borderline impossible.

THE STRAND. On The Strand, in the **historic downtown,** you can find boutiques and outdoor vendors selling local art and kitschy souvenirs. The **Galveston Railroad Museum** pays homage to Texas railroad history with displays, model trains, and dozens of actual trains spanning an entire century. With no off-limits areas, visitors are free to explore every corner of the trains, from the luxurious Pullman car parlors to the kitchen galleys to the locomotive cabs. *(123 Rosenberg St., at the west end of The Strand. ☎409-765-5700; www.galvestonrrmuseum. com. Open Mar.-Dec. daily 10am-4pm; Jan.-Feb. Tu-Su 10am-4pm. $6, ages 4-12 $3, seniors $5.)*

OCEAN STAR OFFSHORE ENERGY CENTER. The one-of-a-kind Ocean Star Offshore Energy Center demystifies the oil drilling rigs that dot the Gulf of Mexico horizon but with a predictably corporate bias. The museum is located on a retired oil rig anchored just offshore and accessible by a causeway. *(Pier 19, on Harborside Dr. at 20th St. ☎409-766-7827; www.oceanstaroec.com. Open June-Aug. daily 10am-6pm; Sept.-May 10am-5pm. $8, ages 7-18 and seniors $5.)*

OTHER (MOODY) SIGHTS. Most of the historic Victorian buildings in the city are private homes, but a few are open to public tours. The elegant **Moody Mansion** is the former home of Galveston's leading family and contains original furnishings and stunning stained glass. *(2618 Broadway. ☎409-762-7668; www.moodymansion.org. Open M-Sa 10am-3pm, Su noon-3pm. $6, ages 4-18 $3, seniors $5.)* Three glass pyramids house a tropical rainforest, aquarium, water park, science museum, and IMAX theater at **Moody Gardens,** a tourist-oriented theme park. The manicured grounds are beautiful and free. *(1 Hope Blvd. Take the West Beach exit onto 61st St. and follow the signs south. ☎800-582-4673. Open in summer daily 10am-9pm; in winter M-Th and Su 10am-6pm, F-Sa 10am-9pm. Aquarium $16, ages 4-12 $10, seniors $11; rainforest $10/8/9; IMAX $10/8/9. Day pass to all attractions $45; after 6pm everything ½-price.)*

⚑ THE ROAD TO HOUSTON: 52 MI.

Take **61st Street,** stopping along the way as you cross **Offatts Bayou** (the only bit of water you'll see) to look for pelicans, herons, and other water birds. Hang a left at **Broadway** and follow it as it turns into **I-45.** Follow the interstate for 50 mi. north to Houston.

HOUSTON   ☎ 713

Houston is the fourth most populous city in the US. Like many big cities, it has miles of strip malls and, often, gridlocked traffic—a combination of features that have earned it the nickname "the city with millions of people and nothing to do." Though infamous for sprawl and lack of urban planning, Houston also has a revitalized downtown with a light-rail line, glorious modern architecture, stadiums, and top-notch performing-arts centers. Contrary to the city's unfortunate nickname, the wealth of Houston's oil and maritime industries has resulted in a downtown with immaculate streetscapes, parks, and public buildings—and a vibrant cultural life to boot.

VITAL STATS

Population: 2,100,000

Tourist Office: Houston City Hall (☎ 713-437-5200 or 800-446-8786; www.cityofhouston.gov), at Walker and Bagby St. Open daily 9am-4pm.

Library and Internet Access: Houston Public Library, 500 McKinney St. (☎ 713-236-1313), at Bagby St. Open M-Th 9am-9pm, F-Sa 9am-6pm, Su 1-5pm.

Post Office: 701 San Jacinto St. (☎ 713-223-4402). Open M-F 8am-5pm. **Postal Code:** 77052.

✳ ORIENTATION

Houston's freeway system is a traffic nightmare; the more you avoid it, the happier you'll be. Major interstates **I-45** and **I-10** intersect at the city's downtown and are constantly clogged with angry Texans. The **Sam Houston Tollway (Beltway 8),** an effort to alleviate traffic congestion, wraps around the outer edge of the city. **I-610** forms a tighter belt around the city closer to downtown. **US 59** and **290,** as well as **Routes 225** and **288,** also turn into large freeways as they approach the city.

Though the flat Texan terrain has sprouted several mini-downtowns, true downtown Houston borders the **Buffalo Bayou** between

the intersections of **I-10, I-45,** and **US 59.** A grid of interlocking one-way streets centers on **Main Street.** The **Museum District** sits just southwest of Midtown, centered at Bissonnet St. and Main St. To get to the **Rice Village** area, which has lots of shopping and restaurants, continue west on Bissonnet and go south (left) down Kirby Dr. The **Montrose** area (along Westheimer St. around Montrose St.) is filled with antique shops, piercing studios, vintage clothing stores, and cafes. It's one of the only places in Houston where people stroll around. A light-rail line runs along Main St. and San Jacinto St. through downtown, Midtown, and the Museum District. Buses run on all major streets, although service on weekends is very slow. For $2 you can get a day-long pass for all modes of public transport.

TIP **TRAFFIC? NO THANKS.** When driving in Houston, if you have a GPS device, select the "Off Freeways" option. Otherwise, you're sure to get stuck in horrendous gridlock.

ACCOMMODATIONS

Near downtown, US 59 is rife with budget motels. If you forgo the freeways and approach Houston via Alt. US 90 on Main St., you'll find the south Main St. area is also full of options, although some stretches may be unsafe at night. Motels around the Houston area are generally cheap, with prices ranging $35-45 per night.

Perry House Houston International Hostel, 5302 Crawford St. (☎ 713-523-1009). From Main St., turn east on Binz St. and north on Crawford St. Just past Hermann Park and near downtown, this beautiful 1920s home is tucked away in a quiet neighborhood. Minor chores. No alcohol. Internet $5 per hr. Reception 8-10am and 5-11pm. Lockout 10am-5pm. Dorms $15. Cash only. ❶

YMCA, 1600 Louisiana St. (☎ 713-758-9250; www.ymcahouston.org), between Pease and Leeland St., downtown. Small, spartan rooms—all singles—with daily maid service and cable TV. Towel deposit $2.50. Key deposit $10. Reception 24hr. Singles $39. AmEx/D/MC/V. ❶

Southwest Inn, 6855 Southwest Fwy. (☎713-771-0641). Exit at Hillcroft Ave./W. Park Dr., and take the access road on the east side of the freeway. Cheaper than most hotels of its quality, this hotel offers rooms adjacent to a lovely courtyard with a playground. All rooms have TVs, A/C, and pool access. Free Wi-Fi. Singles $49; doubles $58. AmEx/MC/V. ❷

Brazos Bend State Park, 21901 FM 762 (☎512-389-8900). From Houston, take Rte. 288 to Rosharon. Head west on FM 1462 and then north on FM 762. This nature-lover's paradise is less than 1hr. from downtown. Among the diverse flora and fauna, visitors are sure to see American alligators, some over 12 ft. long. Sites have water and electricity, and the park offers fishing, picnicking, wildlife observation towers, and 22 mi. of trails. $5 per person. Primitive sites $12, with electricity and water $20. D/MC/V. ❶

🍴 FOOD

As a city by the sea, Houston has harbored many immigrants, and their cultures are well represented in the city's eclectic ethnic cuisine. Along with the more indigenous barbecue and Southern soul food, you'll find Mexican, Cajun, and Asian fare. Search for reasonably priced restaurants along the chain-laden streets of Westheimer Rd. and Richmond Ave., especially where they intersect with Fountainview Ave. Houston has two Chinatown/Little Vietnam areas. The older one is the district south of the George R. Brown Convention Center along Main St.; the newer one, called DiHo, is on Bellaire Blvd., west of downtown. For authentic Mexican fare, try Houston's East End. Rice Village, near the Museum District in the southwest of Houston, offers a variety of restaurants and bars geared toward a college-age crowd.

🍴 **Brasil,** 2604 Dunlavy St. (☎713-528-1993), at Westheimer Rd. This hip and inconspicuous coffee shop houses a bar, restaurant, and bakery. Munch on California-style salads and pizzas with toppings like goat cheese, spinach, eggplant, and basil. Sit inside, where the walls are adorned with local art, or head to the foliage-enclosed patio. Breakfast $3-7. Sandwiches, pizza, and salads $7-9. Open daily 8am-2am. AmEx/MC/V. ❷

🍴 **House of Pies,** 3112 Kirby Dr. (☎713-528-3816). Little has changed in this classic 60s diner. 30 kinds of pies and cakes grace Formica countertops. Try the Bayoo Goo pie with pecans, cream cheese, custard, and whipped cream ($3.25). Slice of pie $2.50-4. Breakfast $4-8. Sandwiches $5-8. Open 24hr. AmEx/D/MC/V. ❶

Goode Company BBQ, 5109 Kirby Dr. (☎713-522-2530), near Bissonnet St. Decorated with memorabilia, license plates, and a bison head, this little restaurant serves mouthwatering mesquite-smoked brisket, ribs, and sausage links all smothered in homemade sauce. If you're in the mood for a different kind of food but the same price range, the Goode Company also operates a taqueria, burger shop, and seafood restaurant, all within a block or 2 of each other on Kirby Dr. Sandwiches from $5. Dinners $9-12. Open daily 11am-10pm. AmEx/D/MC/V. ❷

Buffalo Grille, 3116 Bissonnet St. (☎713-661-3663). 2nd location at 1201 S. Voss Rd. One of the best and biggest breakfasts in town. Try the pancakes with fruit ($4-5), which are bigger than the plates on which they're served. The huevos rancheros ($5.75) satisfy even the most ravenous appetite. Open M 7am-2pm, Tu-F 7am-9pm, Sa 8am-9pm, Su 8am-2pm. AmEx/D/MC/V. ❷

Ragin' Cajun, 4302 Richmond Ave. (☎713-623-6321). Scarf down buckets of crawfish, surrounded by walls chock-full of postcards while zydeco plays in the background. You can't get more cajun. Po' boys $8-10. Gumbo $5. Entrees $12-17. Open M-Th 11am-10pm, F-Sa 11am-11pm, Su 11am-9pm. AmEx/D/MC/V. ❷

Black Walnut Cafe, 5510 Morningside Dr. (☎713-526-5551). Located in Rice Village, the Black Walnut Cafe has a variety of hamburgers, sandwiches, pasta, and salads, all made with a number of different ingredients and all delicious. The cafe features indoor and outdoor seating, which is enjoyed by the younger crowd that fills the cafe before heading to bars across the street. Entrees $9-13. Open M-Th 8am-10pm, F-Sa 8am-11pm, Su 8am-9pm. AmEx/D/MC/V. ❸

👁 SIGHTS

JOHNSON SPACE CENTER. The city's most popular attraction, the Johnson Space Center is technically not even in Houston

Houston Overview

White Oak Dr.
North Loop
Shepherd Dr.
Memorial Dr. ■ Beer Can House
DOWNTOWN
West Loop
MUSEUM DISTRICT
Bellaire Blvd.
Main St.
South Loop
Bellfort St.
TO SAN JACINTO BATTLEGROUND (12mi)
TO JOHNSON SPACE CENTER (10mi)

Houston

▲ ACCOMMODATIONS
Brazos Bend State Park, **15**
Perry House, **10**
Southwest Inn, **16**
YMCA, **2**

● FOOD
Brasil, **4**
Buffalo Grille, **18**
Goode Company BBQ, **17**
House of Pies, **5**
Ragin' Cajun, **14**
Black Walnut Café, **19**

● NIGHTLIFE
Poison Girl, **3**
Sambuca Jazz Cafe, **1**
Valhalla, **21**
The Ginger Man, **20**

🏛 MUSEUMS
Buffalo Soldiers
  National Museum, **9**
Byzantine Fresco
  Chapel Museum, **8**
Contemporary Arts
  Museum, **11**
Menil Collection, **6**
Museum of Fine Arts, **12**
Museum of Natural
  Science, **13**
Rothko Chapel, **7**

Map labels

Buffalo Bayou
Ruiz St.
Commerce St.
HISTORIC DISTRICT
Franklin St.
Congress St.
Preston St.
Prairie St.
Minute Maid Park
Market Square Park
Alley Theatre
Texas Ave.
Houston Symphony
Rusk St.
Capitol St.
Sam Houston Park
Walker St.
City Hall
McKinney St.
George R. Brown Conv. Ctr.
Houston Center Gardens
DOWNTOWN
Lamar St.
Dallas St.
Polk St.
Clay St.
Basketball Arena
Bell St.
Leeland St.
Pease St.
Jefferson St.
St. Joseph Pkwy.
Hadley St.
McGowen St.
Tuam St.
Emancipation Park
Elgin St.
Holman St.
Alabama St.
Cleburne St.
High School for the Performing & Visual Arts
Wheeler St.
Blodgett St.
MUSEUM DISTRICT
Southmore St.
Oakdale St.
Binz St.
The Houston Zoological Gardens
Hermann Dr.
Sam Houston Monument
Miller Outdoor Theatre
Sunset Blvd.
Rice University
Hermann Park
Zoo

Westheimer Rd.
Montrose Blvd.
Richmond Av.
Southwest Frwy.
Bissonnet St.

TO UPTOWN,
MORE SHOPPING,
DINING

TO 14 (3mi)
TO 15 (45mi)
16 (4mi)
17 (2mi)
TO 18 (0.5mi)
TO 19, 20 (250m),
JOHNSON SPACE
CENTER (16mi)

but 21 mi. away in Clear Lake. The Mission Control Center is fully operational; when today's astronauts say, "Houston, we have a problem," these people answer. Admission includes tours of the Mission Control Center and astronaut training facilities, which take about 90min. and can have waits that are even longer. Among the attractions are exhibits of astronaut suits from the past 30 years, simulator rides, lunar rocks, and out-of-this-world harnesses; strap in and bounce around like a real space explorer. The complex also houses models of the Gemini and Apollo crafts. To fully explore everything at the space center, be sure to set aside at least 3-4hrs. or even a full day if you have the time. (*1601 NASA Rd. 1. Take I-45 S. to the NASA Rd. exit and head east for 3 mi. ☎ 281-244-2100 or 800-972-0369; www.spacecenter. org. Open M-F 10am-5pm, Sa-Su 10am-6pm. $19, ages 4-11 $15, seniors $18. Parking $5.*)

▨ MUSEUM OF FINE ARTS. The museum features paintings of the American West by artists such as Frederic Remington, as well as the largest collection of African gold pieces to be found outside of Africa. The two large buildings also hold Impressionist and Post-Impressionist art and works from Asia, Africa, and Latin America. The museum is huge and well funded and holds a staggering number and variety of pieces, ranging from Botticellis to artifacts from Ancient Egypt. The museum's Sculpture Garden includes pieces by Matisse and Rodin. (*1001 Bissonet St. ☎ 713-639-7300; www.mfah.org. Open Tu-W 10am-5pm, Th 10am-9pm, F-Sa 10am-7pm, Su 12:15-7pm. $17, students and seniors $13. Th free. Sculpture garden, 5101 Montrose St., open daily 9am-10pm. Free.*)

BUFFALO SOLDIERS NATIONAL MUSEUM. Between the end of the Civil War in 1865 and the integration of the armed forces in 1944, the US Army had several all-black units. During the Native American wars of the late 1800s, the Cheyenne warriors nicknamed these troops "Buffalo Soldiers," both because of their naturally curly hair and as a sign of respect for their fighting spirit. Learn the history of the Buffalo Soldiers and African-Americans in the military and NASA from the Revolutionary War to the present. Many exhibits provide interesting tidbits about historical contri-

butions by African-American soldiers—for example, there's a feature on the man who introduced jazz to the French in WWI. (*1834 Southmore Blvd. ☎ 713-942-8920. Open M-F 10am-5pm, Sa 10am-4pm. $2.*)

SAN JACINTO STATE PARK. The San Jacinto Battleground State Historical Park is the most important monument to Lone Star independence. On this battleground in 1836, Sam Houston's outnumbered Texan Army defeated Santa Anna's Mexican forces, thereby earning Texas its freedom from Mexico. The San Jacinto Monument, the world's tallest memorial tower, honors all those who fought for Texas's independence. Riding to the top of the 50-story tower yields a stunning view of the area. The museum inside the monument celebrates the state's history with relics like the battleship *Texas*, the only surviving naval vessel to have served in both World Wars and the last remaining dreadnought. (*21 mi. east of downtown on Rte. 225, then 3 mi. north on Rte. 134. ☎ 281-479-2421. Park open daily 9am-6pm. $1 per vehicle. Monument and museum open daily 9am-6pm. Free. Battleship ☎ 281-479-2431. Open daily 10am-5pm. $10, under 12 free, seniors $5.*)

HERMANN PARK. The 388 acres of Hermann Park, near Rice University and the Texas Medical Center, encompass the **Miller Outdoor Theater,** sports facilities, a mini-train ($2.25), and a pond with paddle boats ($8 per 30min.). It's a pretty area to wander, especially if you want some shade in the midday heat. (*Open daily 10am-6pm. Free.*) Near the northern entrance of the park, the **Houston Museum of Natural Science** has formidable-looking dinosaur fossils and a splendid display of gems and minerals. The museum also has a six-story glass butterfly center with 50 species, a planetarium, and an IMAX theater. (*1 Hermann Circle Dr. ☎ 713-639-4629; www.hmns.org. Open M and W-Sa 9am-5pm, Tu 9am-8pm, Su 11am-5pm. $10, under 12 and seniors $7. Butterfly center $8/6. Planetarium $6/5. IMAX $10/8. Main exhibit free Tu 2-8pm.*) At the southern end of the park, crowds flock to see the gorillas, hippos, and reptiles in the **Houston Zoological Gardens.** (*1513 N. MacGregor St. ☎ 713-533-6500. Open Mar.-Oct. 9am-7pm, Nov.-Feb. 9am-6pm. $10, ages 3-12 $5, seniors $5.75.*)

BEER CAN HOUSE. Many a Bacchanalian feast must have preceded the construction of the Beer Can House. Adorned with 50,000 beer cans, strings of beer-can tops, and a beer-can fence, the house was built by the late John Milkovisch, who followed a six-pack-a-day regimen for 18 years to achieve the look. At $0.05 per can, the tin abode has a market price of $2500. *(222 Malone St., between Washington St. and Memorial Dr. Open Sa-Su noon-5pm. $1.)*

HOUSTON TUNNEL SYSTEM. Earthly pleasures can be found underground in the downtown area. Hundreds of shops and restaurants line the 7 mi. Houston Tunnel System, which connects all the major buildings extending from the Civic Center to the Tenneco Building and the Hyatt Regency. Duck into the air-conditioned passageways via any major building or hotel or through designated staircases/escalators at street level. Note that the entrances are closed Saturday and Sunday.

OTHER SIGHTS. The small **Contemporary Arts Museum** has two galleries with frequently changing exhibits featuring well-known artists from around the world. *(5216 Montrose St. ☎ 713-284-8250; www.camh.org. Open Tu-W and F-Sa 10am-5pm, Th 10am-9pm, Su noon-5pm. Free.)* The **Menil Foundation** exhibits an array of artwork in four buildings grouped within a block of one another. The **Menil Collection** has a fabulous assortment of Surrealist paintings and modern art, one highlight of which is the Warhol room. This eclectic collection has Byzantine, medieval, African, and Oceanic art and artifacts as well. *(1515 Sul Ross St. ☎ 713-525-9400. Open W-Su 11am-7pm. Free.)* A block away, the **Rothko Chapel** houses 14 of the artist's paintings in a nondenominational sanctuary. Worshippers of modern art will delight in Rothko's ultra-simplicity; others will wonder where the paintings are. *(3900 Yupon St. ☎ 713-524-9839. Open daily 10am-6pm. Free.)* The **Byzantine Fresco Chapel Museum** displays the ornate dome and apse from a 13th-century Byzantine chapel in Cyprus. They were rescued in 1983 before being sold on the black market and are now the only intact Byzantine frescoes in the Western Hemisphere. *(4011 Yupon St. ☎ 713-521-3990. Open W-Su 11am-6pm. Free.)*

🎵 ENTERTAINMENT

From March to October, orchestras, dance companies, and theater companies stage free performances at the **Miller Outdoor Theatre,** in Hermann Park. (☎713-284-8350; www.milleroutdoortheatre.com.) The **Alley Theatre,** 615 Texas Ave., puts on excellent productions at moderate prices. (☎713-228-8421; www.alleytheatre.org. Tickets $40-95; student rush tickets 1hr. before show M-Th and Su $13.) The **Houston Symphony,** 614 Louisiana St., performs from September to May. (☎713-227-2787; www.houstonsymphony.org. Tickets $25-85.) Various festivals are held throughout the year. Check out the **Texas Music Festival** in June. (☎713-743-3313; www.uh.edu.tmf. Locations vary. $10, students and seniors $5.)

🎵 NIGHTLIFE

There are a number of bars in **Rice Village,** near Rice University. The once (in)famous **Richmond Strip,** along Richmond St., has quieted down, though some bars remain. In the last few years, the downtown core's nightlife has been revitalized; there are numerous bars along **Main Street,** accessible by transit rail. For indie-kid hangouts, head to the area around **Westheimer Road** and **Montrose Street.** To find out what's going on where, grab a copy of the free weekly *Houston Press* or the free magazines *Envy* and *002houston,* all of which can be found at cafes and restaurants.

🍸 **Poison Girl,** 1641B Westheimer Rd. (☎713-527-9929). A trendy place whose pink walls are covered with beautiful "poison girls," vixens with sultry stares. Poison Girl lends its name to its signature shot, a mixture of bourbon, vodka, sweet and sour, and raspberry ($3). The indie-cool clientele hangs out on old furniture on the patio, while the inside features a number of old-school pinball machines drawn from the owner's personal collection. 1st Su of the month all profits go to charity. 21+. No cover. Happy hour daily 5-8pm with $2.50 draft beer. Open daily 5pm-2am. AmEx/D/MC/V.

🍸 **Valhalla,** 6100 Main St. (☎713-348-3258). For "gods, heroes, mythical beings, and cheap beer," students, locals, and travelers descend to the depths of Keck Hall in the center of the Rice campus. Beer $0.95. (Yes, you read that right.) A remarkable find. Open M-F 11:30am-1pm and 4pm-2am, Su 7pm-2am. Cash only.

The Ginger Man, 5607 Morningside Dr. (☎713-526-2770). This bar in Rice Village has a phenomenal selection of beers on tap from all over the world, a backyard patio, and a few sporting events usually on the TV. Open M-F 2pm-2am, Sa-Su 1pm-2am. 21+. No cover. AmEx/D/MC/V.

Sambuca Jazz Cafe, 909 Texas Ave. (☎713-224-5299). This bar hosts live music daily from 7pm. Business casual attire. No cover. Happy hour M-F 4-7pm; $2 appetizers and $4 martinis. Open M-W 11am-midnight, Th 11am-1am, F-Sa 11am-2am, Su 11am-3pm. AmEx/D/MC/V.

THE ROAD TO HALLETTSVILLE: 119 MI. Houston has miles of sprawling suburbs, which becomes painfully apparent as you head out through stop-and-go traffic along **Alternate US 90 West,** the continuation of **Wayside Street.** Once you pass through Richmond and Rosenberg, the suburbs give way to rolling hills. Continue 72 mi. to Hallettsville.

HALLETTSVILLE ☎361

Hallettsville is the first stop in Lavaca County, a section of Texas settled by German and Czech immigrants in the 1880s. Nowadays, the people of Lavaca County know only smatterings of their grandparents' native tongues,

but a European influence remains—especially in the region's cooking. Hallettsville is famous for its yearly **Kolache Festival** (2nd weekend in Sept.), which features beer gardens, raucous dancing, and kolache-eating contests. Kolache is a type of pastry that can come with fillings ranging from fruits to cheeses. In town, the impressive clock tower of the **Lavaca County Courthouse** looms over the square. The **Hallettsville Chamber of Commerce,** 1614 N. Texana St., is located a half-mile north and provides more info on area attractions. (☎361-798-2662. Open M-F 9am-2pm.)

The **Hallettsville Inn ❷,** 608 W. Fairwinds Rd., offers the best combination of good rooms and good prices in town. (☎361-798-3257. Singles $50; doubles $55. AmEx/D/MC/V.) If you're hungry, head to **Werner's Steakhouse ❸,** 101 Rte. 77 S. Be on the lookout for a sign for "The Smokehouse," since Werner's has just purchased this place and doesn't have much of a sign up yet. A huge menu features Italian, Mexican, seafood, and steak entrees, with prices ranging from $3 for a burger to $24 for a steak. Right by the entrance, an old piano and jukebox keep the atmosphere definitively country. (☎830-672-8300. Open daily 10am-9pm. AmEx/D/MC/V.)

THE ROAD TO SHINER: 14 MI. Continue on **US 90A** until you reach Shiner.

WHERE (BUDGET-MINDED) VIKINGS PLAY

If you've ever woken up after a long night out and checked your wallet, that morning-after headache and nausea may have suddenly gotten a lot worse. At many establishments, especially touristy ones, patrons can expect to pay between $3 and $6 for a beer. Some travelers report that adds up fast.

Not so if you head to Valhalla, a nonprofit pub located under the chemistry building (Keck Hall) on Rice University's campus, where beers range from $0.95 to a staggering $1.50 for a premium lager. Valhalla is staffed entirely by volunteers (mostly graduate students), and despite its location anyone is welcome within this hallowed hall. People do come in numbers, especially on Thursday and Friday nights.

The real trick is finding the place. Though its address is technically 6100 Main St., going to this address will lead to nothing but confusion. Valhalla is located at about the midpoint of Loop Rd. which makes a short loop through Rice's campus. Your best bet is to look up #35 on a Rice campus map, ask someone, or drive around aimlessly looking for groups of people sitting outside a wood door drinking cold, refreshing beer paid for with the change they found in their sofas. Valhalla literally

SHINER ☎361

Shiner is known as the "cleanest little city in Texas," though the "littlest clean city in Texas" would have been equally accurate; Shiner's population of 2100 warrants the title "hamlet" rather than "city." The stunning **Saints Cyril and Methodius Church,** 306 S. Ave. F, is the first thing that grabs your attention as you head into Shiner. The church, named after the saints who brought Catholicism to Bohemia, was built in 1921 and features a majestic altar, murals, beautiful statues, and stained-glass windows—all imported from Bavaria. Be sure to check out the **Spoetzl Brewery,** 603 E. Brewery St., founded in 1909 by a Bavarian immigrant and the oldest independent brewery in the state. (☎361-594-3383; www.shiner.com. Tours M-F 11am, 1:30pm. Free.) The ◙**Shiner Country Inn ❷,** 1016 N. Ave. E, greets visitors with quaint rooms with a ranch-house feel. All rooms include coffeemakers, cable, huge bathrooms, and four comfy pillows per bed. (☎361-594-3335; www.shinertx.com. Singles $50; doubles $65. AmEx/D/MC/V.) **Werner's Restaurant ❷,** 317 N. Ave. E, has excellent steaks, barbecue, burgers, and sandwiches. There is also an 18 ft. salad bar. (☎361-594-2928. Entrees $8-15. Open daily 6-10pm. MC/V.)

⛰ THE ROAD TO GONZALES: 18 MI.

Head west on **Alternate US 90.** After 16 mi., turn left onto **Route-146.**

GONZALES ☎830

On October 2, 1835, the first shot of the Texas Revolution was fired at Mexican troops who were marching into Gonzales demanding that the citizens hand over their cannon. The townsfolk rebelled and defeated the Mexicans, and the famous cannon still sits in the **Gonzales Memorial Museum,** 414 Smith St. The museum complex resembles a miniature version of the Washington Monument's mall and reflecting pool and honors those who took part in the revolution. It also houses an eclectic collection of objects, from dolls to wedding dresses to muskets that help to illustrate the way of life of early settlers. (☎830-672-6532. Open Tu-Sa 10am-noon and 1-5pm, Su 1-5pm. Free.) The **Gonzales County Jail Museum,**

414 St. Lawrence St., is a great little museum that gives a sense of the town's Wild West roots. You can wander the old cellblocks and gallows of the jail, constructed in 1887. (Watch your footing.) The last hanging took place in 1921, before the electric chair came into fashion. Legend has it that Albert Howard, the last man hanged here, swore that the clock on the nearby courthouse would prove his innocence and that after he was hanged the four faces of that clock would never tell the time correctly. Sure enough, after he was hanged, the clocks went haywire. On the ground floor of the museum, small exhibits show the tools of prisons, such as balls and chains, weapons, and wanted posters. Don't miss the cell for "women and lunatics" and the solitary confinement cell. (☎888-672-1095. Open M-F 8am-5pm, Sa 8am-4pm, Su 4pm. Donation suggested.) A great place to stop in town is the **Sandy Fork Trading Post ❶,** 2100 Water St. (US 183 N.), a family-run cafe that has perky flower arrangements on every table. (☎888-672-5900. Sandwiches $4.50-5.50. Open M-F 10am-2pm. MC/V.)

⛰ THE ROAD TO PALMETTO STATE PARK: 13 MI.

To leave Gonzales, get on **Route 183** and head north past **Alternate US 90,** toward Luling. Ten miles down Rte. 183, look for signs for **Palmetto State Park.** Turn left and continue for 2 mi. to the park headquarters.

PALMETTO STATE PARK ☎512

This lush tropical oasis in the middle of the Texas grassland feels like the jungle of southern Florida. The dwarf palms of the park's namesake grow abundantly in the underbrush, where armadillos, deer, and other fauna make their homes. The San Marcos River and small Oxbow Lake run through the park and are perfect for swimming and fishing. The park also features nature trails, picnic areas, a playground, and **campsites ❶.** Most of the hiking around Palmetto State Park is not very challenging. Try the Lake Trail, which runs two-thirds of a mile around Oxbow Lake and offers great views of the park and its animal inhabitants. (☎512-389-8900; www.tpwd. state.tx.us. Entrance fee $3 per vehicle. Primi-

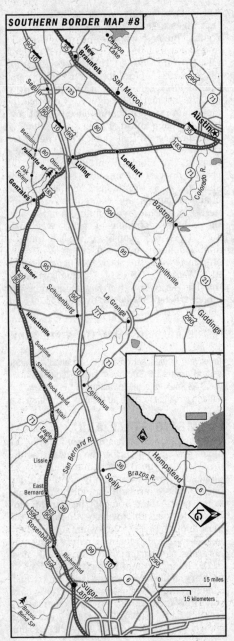

SOUTHERN BORDER MAP #8

tive sites with water $10, with electricity $16. Visitors center open daily 8am-5pm.)

◤ THE ROAD TO LULING: 6 MI.
Get back on **Route 183** and continue north to Luling.

LULING ☎ 830

Luling is the name, and watermelons are the game. During the last weekend of June, the town hosts the **Luling Watermelon Thump.** Watermelon lovers from all over the state come for country music, street dancing, car rallies, seed-spitting competitions, and the crowning of the Watermelon Queen. (☎830-875-3214, ext. 2; www.watermelonthump.com.) Even if you're not around for the Thump, you can still see watermelons everywhere you look. The water tower is painted like one, and the oil drills feature amusing watermelon-y scenes. The most famous is a boy eating a watermelon in the parking lot of the Dollar General Store. Ask anyone to point the way. You can also buy delicious watermelons at outdoor stalls all over town ($2.50-3.50 per melon). No one in the town actually grows watermelons anymore, however; they are (somewhat ironically) imported from nearby towns. Luling is right in the heart of barbecue country, so if you're hungry for something a different type of pink and juicy check out **J-R BBQ ❶**, 806 Rte 183. Little more than some tables next to an impressive barbecue setup, J-R specializes in giving you succulent meat at dirt-cheap prices. (☎512-376-8327. Pulled pork sandwich $3.50. Open Tu-Su 8am-7pm. Cash only.)

◤   THE ROAD TO LOCKHART: 15 MI.
From Luling, cruise another 15 mi. on **Route 183 North,** and you'll wind up in Lockhart.

LOCKHART ☎ 512

Some argue that Lockhart is the barbecue capital of Texas. The title is contested by many other towns, including Luling (which already has the watermelon title anyway), but Lockhart is certainly an earnest and worthy competitor. The red-brick buildings have a real "Old West" feel; oddly, the county court-house in the center of town looks as though it was transplanted straight from Russia. **Black's BBQ ❶**, 708 N. Main St., is the self-proclaimed oldest family barbecue joint in Texas. That declaration may be as truthful as its claim to be open eight days a week, but, either way, Black's is delicious and cheap. Follow the signs from Rte. 183 and try the beef brisket or the pork ribs, both $2.50 for a ¼-lb. (☎512-398-2712; www.blacksbbq.com. Lunch special $5. Open M-Th and Su 10am-8pm, F-Sa 10am-8:30pm. AmEx/D/MC/V.)

🚗 THE ROAD TO AUSTIN: 30 MI.

Take **Route 183 North** to **Bastrop Highway.** Take the **Airport Boulevard** exit and bear left on the **First-Fifth Street** ramp into Austin.

AUSTIN   ☎ 512

Austin breaks with the Lone Star State's stereotypical images of rough-and-tumble cattle ranchers riding horses across the plains. Very much a young people's town, many dot-com millionaires made their fortunes here around 2000. Nowadays, Fortune 500 companies and Internet startups play second fiddle to Austin's reputation for musical innovation as the "Live Music Capital of the World." For roadtrippers, Austin's live music scene won't disappoint; no matter what day you arrive, there are bound to be plenty of venues with great bands and DJs. With funky vintage stores, zesty restaurants, and a happening cafe scene, Austin is a vibrant, liberal, and alternative oasis in an otherwise conservative state.

🏙 ORIENTATION

The road around Austin, like life, features steep climbs and sharp curves and demands the driver's full attention. Most of the city lies between **MoPac Expressway (Route 1)** and **I-35,** which both run north-south. Students at the University of Texas inhabit central **Guadalupe Street ("The Drag"),** where music stores and cheap restaurants thrive. The state capitol governs the area a few blocks to the southeast. South of the capitol dome, **Congress Avenue** has upscale eateries and shops. The many bars and clubs of Sixth St. hop at night. Away

from the urban sprawl, **Town Lake** is a haven for joggers, rowers, and cyclists.

Parking is easy to find outside the center of downtown for $4-5 per day. Streets downtown are lined with parking meters, which cost $1.25 per hr. The closer you get to Congress Ave., the harder spaces will be to find. If you can't find parking, drive either east or west from Congress Ave. until you see a spot—there are generally plenty available. There are free Park 'n' Ride lots on Toomey Rd. at Lamar or on MoPac Expwy. at César Chavez St. (☎512-474-1200).

VITAL STATS
Population: 710,000
Tourist Offices: Austin Visitors Center, 209 E. 6th St. (☎866-GO-AUSTIN/462-87846). Open M-F 8:30am-5pm, Sa-Su 9am-5pm. **Capitol Visitors Center,** 112 E. 11th St. (☎512-305-8400). Open M-Sa 10am-5pm, Su noon-5pm.
Library and Internet Access: Austin Public Library, 800 Guadalupe St. (☎512-974-7400). Open M-Th 10am-9pm, F-Sa 10am-6pm, Su noon-6pm.
Post Office: 510 Guadalupe St. (☎512-494-2210), at 6th St. Open M-F 8:30am-6:30pm. **Postal Code:** 78701.

🛏 ACCOMMODATIONS

Chain motels lie along I-35, which runs north-south of Austin. This funkified city, however, is a great place to find cheap options with character. Co-ops at UT offer rooms and meals to hostelers. Only a 10-20min. drive separates Austin from the nearest campgrounds.

🏨 **Hostelling International Austin (HI-AYH),** 2200 S. Lakeshore Blvd. (☎512-444-2294 or 800-725-2331), 3 mi. from downtown. From I-35, exit at Riverside, head east, and turn left at Lakeshore Blvd. Beautifully situated, quiet, and clean hostel with a 24hr. common room overlooking Town Lake. 42 dorm-style beds in mostly single-sex rooms. Full kitchen and barbecue. No alcohol. Free computer and Internet. Free Wi-Fi. Rents bikes, kayaks, and canoes ($10 per day). Reception 8-11am and 5-10pm; arrivals after 10pm must call ahead to check in. Dorms $22, members $19. AmEx/D/MC/V. ❶

🏚 **The Austin Motel,** 1220 S. Congress Ave. (☎512-441-1157; www.austinmotel.com). Look for the oddly phallic sign. Bright, airy rooms are individually decorated with themes like "Zen" and "California Greenhouse." Access to a big, modern pool. Reservations recommended. Singles from $70; doubles from $87. AmEx/D/MC/V. ❸

UT Co-ops (☎512-476-5678), at various locations around the University of Texas campus. UT co-ops house students during the year and will usually accept summer hostelers for a nominal fee ($10-20 per night, including food). The 21st St. Co-op (707 W. 21st St.) and the Pearl St. Co-op (2000 Pearl St.) are 2 of the best. Call ahead to make arrangements. Ask for the membership coordinator upon arrival. Cash only. ❶

McKinney Falls State Park, 5808 McKinney Falls Pkwy. (☎512-243-1643), southeast of the city. Turn right on Burleson off Rte. 71 E., then right on McKinney Falls Pkwy. Caters to RV and tent campers. Sites with ample shade and privacy near excellent swimming and 6 mi. of hiking trails. Reception daily 8am-10pm. Primitive sites $12, with water and electricity $16. Screened shelters for up to 8 $35; no linen provided. Day use $4 per person, under 13 free. D/MC/V. ❶

🍴 FOOD

Downtown, patrons often get free or cheap appetizers with drinks during happy hour and, as night falls, vendors appear on the streets, selling pizza, barbecue, and burgers. Near UT, along Guadalupe St., there are a number of inexpensive restaurants. Though a bit removed from downtown, **Barton Springs Road** offers a diverse selection of eateries, including Mexican restaurants and Texas-style barbecue joints. If you want to cook or snack on free samples, head to the flagship store of **Whole Foods Market,** at 525 N. Lamar Blvd. The organic food chain started in Austin. (☎512-476-1206. Open daily 8am-10pm.)

🍴 **Polvos,** 2004 S. 1st St. (☎512-441-5446). Scrumptious Mexican food and an extensive salsa bar. The ceviche (fresh, cold whitefish with tomato, cilantro, lemon, and spice; $9) is a must. The *chile relleno al nogal* (poblano pepper stuffed and topped with pecan cream sauce; $11) will take you out of your taco-and-burrito

comfort zone. Open M-F and Su 7am-10pm, Sa 7am-11pm. AmEx/D/MC/V. ❸

🍴 **Bouldin Creek,** 1501 S. 1st St. (☎512-416-1601), at Elizabeth St. A hip cafe with murals, funky couches, and delicious vegan and vegetarian food. Try the portobello tacos ($7) or the vegan blueberry cornbread ($3). Free Wi-Fi. Open M-F 7am-midnight, Sa-Su 9am-midnight. MC/V. ❷

🍴 **Hut's Hamburgers,** 807 W. 6th St. (☎512-472-0693). "God Bless Hut's" has been the motto since 1981, when a flood destroyed everything in the area but inexplicably spared Hut's. Hut's has over 20 different varieties of burgers ($5-7) from which to choose. The Fats Domino ($6.50) comes with lettuce, tomatoes, pickles, onions, mayo, jalapenos, cheddar cheese, and New Orleans seasonings, making it the only meal you'll need all day. Open M-Sa 11am-10pm, Su 11:30am-10pm. AmEx/MC/V. ❷

Hoover's Cooking, 2002 Manor Rd. (☎512-479-5006), east of I-35. Also known as "the good taste place" or as "the smoke, fire, and ice house," Hoover's will suck you in with cooking that's darn good. Chipotle chicken salad sandwich $8.50. Open daily 8am-10pm. AmEx/D/MC/V. ❸

Ruby's BBQ, 512 W. 29th St. (☎512-477-1651; www.rubysbbq.com). Ruby's barbecue is good enough to be served on silver platters, but that just wouldn't seem right in this cow-skull-and-butcher-paper establishment. The owners order only hormone-free meat from Colorado farm-raised, grass-fed cows. Lean and juicy brisket sandwich $5.50; brisket dinner $11. Open daily 11am-midnight. MC/V. ❸

The Kerbey Lane Cafe, 3704 Kerbey Ln. (☎512-451-1436; www.kerbeylanecafe.com). An Austin institution. The pancakes ($2.75-5.25) are renowned and come in buttermilk, gingerbread, blueberry, or apple whole wheat. Open 24hr. AmEx/D/MC/V. ❷

🔆 SIGHTS

If Austin were an armadillo, the **University of Texas at Austin (UT)** would be its backbone. The university is both the wealthiest public university in the country, with an annual budget of over a billion dollars, and one of the largest, with over 50,000 students. Not surprisingly, it's also the city's cultural center. A number of

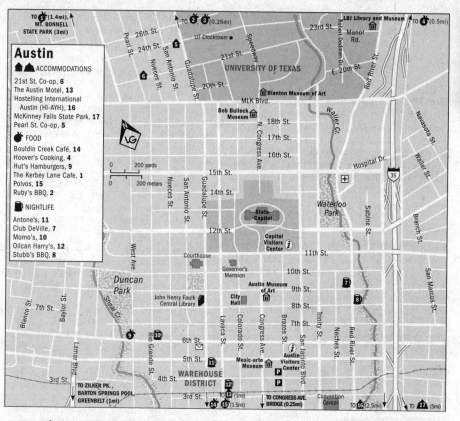

TO (1.4mi),
MT. BONNELL
STATE PARK (3mi)

TO (0.25mi)

LBJ Library and Museum

TO (0.5mi)

23rd St.

Manor
Rd.

26th St.

Pearl St.

24th St.

UT Clocktower

Speedway

Robert Dedman Dr.

21st St.

E. 20th St.

Red River St.

Austin

ACCOMMODATIONS

21st St. Co-op, 6
The Austin Motel, 13
Hostelling International
Austin (HI-AYH), 16
McKinney Falls State Park, 17
Pearl St. Co-op, 5

FOOD

Bouldin Creek Café, 14
Hoover's Cooking, 4
Hut's Hamburgers, 9
The Kerbey Lane Cafe, 1
Polvos, 15
Ruby's BBQ, 2

NIGHTLIFE

Antone's, 11
Club DeVille, 7
Momo's, 10
Oilcan Harry's, 12
Stubb's BBQ, 8

San Antonio St.
Nueces St.
Guadalupe St.

UNIVERSITY OF TEXAS

20th St.

Blanton Museum of Art

MLK Blvd.

Bob Bullock
Museum

Waller Ct.

Navasota St.

18th St.

17th St.

16th St.

N. Congress Ave.

Hospital Dr.

Waller St.

0   200 yards

0   200 meters

15th St.

14th St.

Nueces St.

Guadalupe St.

San Antonio St.

35

Sabine St.

Branch St.

12th St.

State
Capitol

Waterloo
Park

West Ave.

Capitol
Visitors
Center

11th St.

San Marcos St.

Courthouse

Governor's
Mansion

10th St.

Duncan
Park

Shoal Cr.

John Henry Faulk
Central Library

City
Hall

Austin Museum
of Art

9th St.

Blanco St.

Bouldin St.

7th St.

Lamar Blvd.

8th St.

Trinity St.

Neches St.

Red River St.

7th St.

Rio Grande St.

6th St.

Lavaca St.

Colorado St.

Congress Ave.

Brazos St.

San Jacinto Blvd.

5th St.

Mexic-arte
Museum

Austin
Visitors
Center

3rd St.

4th St.

WAREHOUSE
DISTRICT

TO ZILKER PK.,
BARTON SPRINGS POOL,
GREENBELT (1mi)

3rd St.

TO (1mi)

TO (1.5mi)

TO CONGRESS AVE.
BRIDGE (0.25mi)

Convention
Center

TO (2.5mi)

TO (5mi)

noteworthy attractions, like the LBJ Library and Museum, are affiliated with the school. Austin is, further, Texas's capital and the "bat capital" of the world.

CONGRESS AVENUE BRIDGE. Just before dusk, head to the Congress Ave. Bridge near the Austin American Statesman parking lot and join thousands of others to watch the massive swarm of **Mexican free-tailed bats.** When the bridge was reconstructed in 1980, the engineers unintentionally created crevices that formed ideal homes for the migratory bat colony. The city exterminated the night-flying creatures until **Bat Conservation International** moved to Austin to educate people about the bats' harmless behavior and the benefits of

their presence—the bats eat up to 3000 lb. of insects each night. Stand on the bridge itself to see the bats fly out from underneath or on the southern riverbank under the bridge for a more panoramic view. (For flight times, call the hotline at ☎ 512-416-5700, ext. 3636. Bats Mar.-Nov.)

STATE CAPITOL. Proving that everything is bigger in Texas, Texans built their state capitol 7 ft. taller than its federal counterpart. Its pink hue comes from Texas red granite, which was used instead of more-traditional limestone. The capitol, its dome, the legislature chambers, and the underground extension are all open to the public. (At Congress Ave. and 11th St. ☎ 512-463-0063. Open M-F 7am-10pm, Sa-Su 9am-8pm. 45min. tours every 15min. M-F

8:30am-4:30pm, Sa 8:30am-3:30pm, Su noon-3:30pm. Tours depart from the capitol steps. Free.) The visitors center has exhibits on the capitol's history and construction as well as general visitor info. (112 E. 11th St. ☎512-305-8400. Open M-Sa 10am-5pm. 2hr. parking on 12th and San Jacinto St.)

LYNDON B. JOHNSON LIBRARY AND MUSEUM. This destination explores not only the life and times of Lyndon B. Johnson, Texas native, but also of the American presidency in general. A life-size animatronic LBJ tells jokes and anecdotes on the second floor, while the 10th floor features a scale model of the Oval Office that you can explore and an exhibit on Lady Bird Johnson, a great leader in her own right. (2313 Red River St. ☎512-721-0200; www.lbjlib. utexas.edu. Open daily 9am-5pm. Free.)

BOB BULLOCK TEXAS STATE HISTORY MUSEUM. The museum traces nearly 500 years of Western settlement. Its worship of Travis, Houston, and Austin is tempered by its exhibits on the lives of minorities and on the state's historical economy and culture. (1800 N. Congress Ave. ☎512-936-8746; www.thestoryoftexas. com. Open M-Sa 9am-6pm, Su noon-6pm. $7, ages 5-18 $4, seniors $6.)

AUSTIN MUSEUM OF ART. This downtown museum displays traveling exhibits of 20th-century and contemporary art, from photography to painting. A second branch, housed in a Mediterranean-style villa, has exhibits that focus on nature. (823 Congress Ave. ☎512-495-9224; www.amoa.org. Branch at 3809 W. 35th St. ☎512-458-8191. Open Tu-W and F-Sa 10am-6pm, Th 10am-8pm, Su noon-5pm. $5, students and seniors $4, under 12 free. Tu $1.)

MEXIC-ARTE MUSEUM. This small museum features traveling exhibits by Mexican-American and Latino artists. (419 Congress Ave. ☎512-480-9373. Open M-Th 10am-6pm, F-Sa 10am-5pm, Su noon-5pm. $5, students $4, under 12 $1.)

BLANTON MUSEUM OF ART. This recently built museum is a giant in Austin, with over 17,000 works and an eclectic focus on European, American, and Latin American art. (MLK Blvd. at Congress St., across from the Bob Bullock Museum. ☎512-471-7324; www.blantonmuseum.org.

Open Tu-F 10am-5pm, Sa 11am-5pm, Su 1-5pm. $7, ages 13-25 $3, under 13 free, seniors $5. Th free.)

OTHER SIGHTS. Covert Park at Mt. Bonnell offers a sweeping view of Lake Austin and Westlake Hills from the highest point in the city, 785 ft. above sea level. (3800 Mt. Bonnell Rd., off W. 35th St.) Flanked by walnut and pecan trees in **Zilker Park,** just south of the Colorado River, the 1000 ft. long ⬛**Barton Springs Pool** is a spring-fed swimming hole that stays around 68°F. Families crowd the shores by day, while many young people make a splash here at night. (2201 Barton Springs Rd. ☎512-499-6700. Pool open M-W and F-Su 5am-10pm. $3, ages 12-17 $2, under 12 $1. Free daily 5-8am and 9-10pm.) The **Barton Springs Greenbelt** offers more outdoorsy types challenging hiking and biking trails.

◼ NIGHTLIFE

Austin has replaced Seattle as the nation's underground music hot spot, so keep an eye out for rising indie stars as well as blues, folk, country, and rock favorites. Downtown, Sixth St. is lined with warehouse nightclubs and fancy bars. The mellow, cigar-smoking, night-owl set gathers in the **Fourth Street Warehouse District.** The bars and clubs along **Red River Street** have all of the grit and glamor of Sixth St., with more parking. The Austin coffee-house scene provides a low-key alternative. The weekly *Austin Chronicle* and *XL-ent* have details on current music performances, shows, and movies. The *Gay Yellow Pages* is free at stands along **Guadalupe Street.**

◼ **Antone's,** 213 W. 5th St. (☎512-320-8424; www. antones.net). A blues paradise for all ages. Shows 7-9pm almost every night; call for details. Cover $5-25. Open daily 7pm-2am. AmEx/D/MC/V.

◼ **The Alamo Drafthouse Cinema,** 409B Colorado St. (☎512-476-1320; www.originalalamo.com). 2nd runs, cult classics, and other offbeat films that you're sure to remember are shown at the Alamo. Revel in 1980s horror classics and sing-alongs while you chow down at the full-service restaurant and bar. Tickets up to $10. MC/V.

Club DeVille, 900 Red River St. (☎512-457-0900). Chandeliers cast a mellow glow over the funky furniture and black walls of this slick cocktail lounge. The patio is carved out of the side of a cliff. Occasional live music outdoors. Try its signature cucumber shot, made with plum ice wine ($6). Cover inexpensive but varies. Happy hour M-F 5-8pm with $1 off all drinks and drafts. Open daily until 2am. AmEx/D/MC/V.

Momo's, 618 W. Sixth St. (☎512-479-8848; www.momosclub.com), above Katz's. This laid-back 2nd fl. bar hosts local bands every night of the week and has a terrific wood patio overlooking the city. Music ranges from bluegrass to rock to acoustic. Music from 8pm. M-Th and Su $2 Lonestar beer. Cover $5-10. Open daily 7:30pm-2am. AmEx/D/MC/V.

Stubb's BBQ, 801 Red River St. (☎512-480-8341; www.stubbsaustin.com). Has a fabulous all-you-can-eat buffet that includes live gospel for $18 (reservations recommended; seatings 11am, 1pm). BBQ $10-16. Downstairs, an all-ages club hosts acts 3-4 nights per week, starting at around 8pm. Cover $5-20. Restaurant open M 5-10pm, Tu-Th 11am-10pm, F-Sa 11am-11pm, Su 11am-9pm. Nightclub open Tu-Th 7pm-midnight, F-Sa 7pm-1am. AmEx/D/MC/V.

BIG DETOUR. Explore the mountains and caves of this area in the **Over, Under, and Through** Big Detour (next page).

⚐ THE ROAD TO NEW BRAUNFELS: 48 MI.
Take **I-35 South** for 46 mi. to **Exit 187.**

NEW BRAUNFELS   ☎830
If you like waterslides, you'll love the **Schlitterbahn Waterpark Resort** in New Braunfels. Schlitterbahn is one of the largest water parks in the US and has received accolades from the Travel Channel, which called it the best water park in America. It features 65 acres of slides, tube chutes, wave pools, and uphill "water coasters," which you'll appreciate all the more after making the long walk from wherever you can find parking. (☎830-625-2351. $38, ages 3-11 $30. Open daily 10am-between 6 and 8pm; varies by day.) If you're looking to grab some food on the way to San Antonio, drop by the **Crosswalk Coffeehouse ❶,** 489 Main Plaza. This neighborhood sandwich and

coffee place offers modestly priced fare, with an inventive sandwich list and prices ranging $5-7. (☎830-620-7200. Free Wi-Fi. Open daily 6:30am-7:30pm. MC/V.)

⊠ DETOUR
NATURAL BRIDGE CAVERNS

From **I-35,** take **Exit 175** to **Route 3009** and follow the signs to get to the caverns.

The Natural Bridge Caverns are Texas's largest underground cave system and maintain a pleasant 70°F. Don't miss the famed Watchtower, an amazing 50 ft. rock formation that resembles a crystallized flower. Guided tours of two different routes are available; tours leave every half hour and generally last about 75min. (☎210-651-6101; www.naturalbridgecaverns.com. Open daily 9am-4pm. Each tour $17, ages 3-11 $10. Both tours $27/15.)

⚐ THE ROAD TO SAN ANTONIO: 33 MI.
Continue south on **I-35,** which will take you into downtown San Antonio. Exit at **Alamo/Commercial Drive.**

SAN ANTONIO   ☎210
Once the stomping ground of Santa Anna and Davy Crockett, San Antonio is still fiercely proud of its fused Hispanic and Anglo-American culture. The city revels in its Mexican heritage, with missions, mariachis, and margaritas around every corner. Still, there are enough 10-gallon hats and barbecue joints to remind travelers that they're, as the song goes, deep in the heart of Texas.

▣ ORIENTATION

Commerce, Guadalupe, and **Market Streets** are major east-west arteries—they run by the city's vital organs, like the **Riverwalk, Market Square,** and **La Villita. Durango Boulevard** stretches from east to west in the south end of the city. Major north-south streets are **Alamo,** which runs alongside the Alamo in the center of downtown, **San Pedro Avenue,** and **Saint Mary's**—this last one runs down to the missions. **Flores Street** runs north-south on the east side. The two major north-south highways are **I-35** and **I-37.** I-37 (also called US 281) heads north toward Brackenridge Park, the second-largest

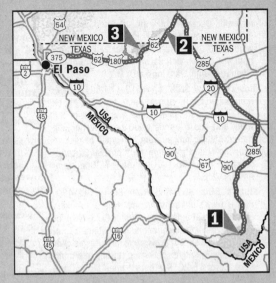

BIG DETOUR

OVER, UNDER & THROUGH

GET OUTDOORS IN NEW MEXICO

START: Big Bend National Park

HIGHLIGHT: Carlsbad Caverns' Spider Cave

DISTANCE: 275 mi.

DURATION: 3 days

1. OVER: BIG BEND NATIONAL PARK. In Big Bend, you're right in the middle of the desert, where clouds are scarce and the views are unparalleled. You can meander along the roads of Big Bend in your car or four-by-four, but that would be an insult to this beautiful landscape. The **Lost Mine Peak** hiking trail (4¾ mi. round-trip) takes visitors up 1300 ft. to the top of Lost Mine Peak. Lost Mine Peak is the second-highest peak in the park—the highest being Emory Peak, which is difficult. Unless you're a diehard, Lost Mine is as good as it gets. You can find the well-marked trailhead about a mile before the Chisos Basin campground, and there's plenty of parking. At the trailhead, guides that give information on 24 different markers placed all the way up the mountain are sold. The trail guide is informative, but use it too much, and you'll miss the trail's fantastic views. The Lost Mine Peak trail starts off gently enough, making its way gradually uphill past deer, lizards, and more prickly pear than you will ever see again. About a mile in, the trail becomes a mess of switchbacks leading up the side of the mountain. If you're not up to the trek, the view from marker 10 is spectacular and comparatively easy to get to. Once you hit the top of the mountain and the trail peters out into a big, flat plain of rock, you can see a full 360°—all the way to Mexico. If you want to go a bit more off the beaten path but don't want to climb a mountain, the seldom-used **Ward Spring** trail is a hidden gem. Half of the difficulty in the Ward Spring trail is just locating the trailhead. From the junction at the northern end of the Ross Maxwell Scenic Drive, head 5½ mi. south toward Castolon. On your left, there should be a paved pullout, and, although the trailhead has no sign, you will be able to see a well-worn path. The trail itself leads over the harsh desert ground and becomes hard to find during its last third, when you need to look for rock cairns on the ground or simply fragments of trail. After a 1¾ mi. hike (one-way), with an elevation gain of 480 ft., visitors reach a rewarding destination—several trees at the bottom of the volcanic formation and a cool spring.

Take Rte. 385 north until it intersects I-10. At this point, take Rte. 285 N. Follow Rte. 285 N. into Carlsbad. From town, take Rte. 180 S. to the caverns.

2. UNDER: CARLSBAD CAVERNS NATIONAL PARK. While the **Big Room** of the caverns is more than 750 ft. underground, it is well paved and well lit, which makes you feel like a tourist. If you want to see parts of the caves that most visitors can't access and have the physical ability to do so, try your luck in **Spider Cave.** (Only one tour is offered a week, and they fill up fast, so be sure to call months in advance.) The tour of Spider Cave begins with a 20 ft. descent down a ladder. When you get to the bottom, you may be wondering where the cave is. It turns out that the cave is about 40 ft. away from you, and you're going to have to crawl commando-style through a tight tunnel with only the light of your helmet to guide you. If you don't like tight spaces or worry about your ability to fit in such spaces, you're going to have trouble right from the start. Once you get off your belly, the hike through the cave isn't too taxing—although there are some small but very deep pits you need to maneuver around and the floor can be slippery. Spider Cave is much smaller than the main cavern, and as such it lacks the enormous pillars of the Big Room. However, it has its own unique features, such as a mace room, where one spectacular stalagmite has grown to resemble a medieval mace. About halfway through your 4hr. hike, the ranger leading the tour asks everyone to turn off their headlamps and be quiet. It's ultimate darkness and silence (as well as the ultimate opportunity to scare your more jittery companions). Off to one side of the Big Room is the so-called "bottomless pit," which may appear never-ending from the paved path. The Lower Cave tour begins with a brief walk to a big gate marked "Do Not Enter" along the main path. After the ranger unlocks this gate, cavers must descend backward down a steep slope with the aid of a rope. Following the rope is a series of three twisting and turning ladders, which are attached to the cave wall but can be wet and slippery. At the bottom of these ladders lies an easy walk underneath the Big Room in an area known as Lower Cave. The floor in Lower Cave is extremely slippery because the cave is still active, so bring good hiking shoes. Your tour guide will guide you past rare "cave pearls" and through many specacular limestone and crystal formations that tourists have damaged less than those in the Big Room. Over the course of the trip, you will also learn about the very first explorers of the cave, who, 100 years ago, dared to venture down this far in small buckets. At the very end of the 3hr. tour, there is an optional crawling section for those who want a more rough-and-tumble experience. There is something spectacular about caves when they're illuminated with a single headlamp instead of a plethora of fluorescent lights and signs. For anyone truly interested in seeing Carlsbad Caverns, Lower Cave, Spider Cave, and the Hall of the White Giant are must-sees.

From the caverns, take Rte. 180 S. to Guadalupe Mountains National Park.

3. THROUGH: THE SLOT CANYONS OF THE GUADALUPE MOUNTAINS. The king of all hikes in the Guadalupe Mountains is the **Guadalupe Peak** trail, which climbs 3000 ft. over the course of a 4¼ mi. (one-way) hike. Although the park is in the desert, its wet season comes in the summer, when it occasionally sees days of heavy fog and rain, which can make hiking to the peak a wasted effort. A great little hike that keeps you close to the ground is the **Devil's Hall** trail, which is 4¼ mi. round-trip. The trail starts out following the same route as the Peak trail, and, after a while, signs direct you straight ahead into a canyon, while the Peak trail heads off to the left. The first mile or so of Devil's Hall is flat, with a few hundred feet of elevation gain and some amazing views of the desert if you turn around. After a mile, the trail descends into a dried up-wash, where it barely seems like a trail at all. Although there is a route marked out, it is often hard to find. As long as you stay in the creek bed and keep moving, you're doing something right. Boulders litter this part of the "trail"; you will need to use your legs, your arms, and your balance, so don't attempt this one if you have lingering injuries. As soon as it seems like the wash will never end, a beautiful, naturally carved staircase appears on your left. It's almost so perfect that it could have come out of someone's house, and it leads up into a slot canyon. No more than 20 ft. wide, with sheer cliffs leading up to the mountains above, this canyon winds along before a sign marks the end of the trail. Since the trail isn't developed, feel free to explore the canyon to your heart's content; just listen (and look!) for the rattlesnakes that call this cool little place home.

Continue southwest on Rte. 180 into El Paso and pick back up the route!

urban municipal park in the country. **Highway 410** circles the downtown area, connecting all highways that run into the city. Watch for traffic jams on I-37 and Hwy. 410, especially at rush hour. Parking lots dot the downtown region and all cost about $6-8 for the day. If you're staying only a short time or moving about the city, meters are cheap ($0.10 per 30min.). Outside the small downtown core, free parking is easy to find.

VITAL STATS

Population: 1,300,000

Tourist Office: San Antonio Convention and Visitors Bureau, 317 Alamo Plaza (☎210-207-6748; www.sanantoniovisit.com), across from the Alamo. Open daily 9am-5pm.

Library and Internet Access: San Antonio Public Library, 600 Soledad St. (☎210-207-2500). Open M-Th 9am-9pm, F-Sa 9am-5pm, Su 11am-5pm.

Post Office: 615 E. Houston St. (☎210-212-8046), 1 block from the Alamo. Open M-F 9am-5pm. **Postal Code:** 78205.

ACCOMMODATIONS

For cheap motels, try **Roosevelt Avenue,** a southern extension of **Saint Mary's Street,** and Fredericksburg Rd. Inexpensive motels also line Broadway between downtown and Brackenridge Park. Follow I-35 N. or the Austin Hwy. to find cheaper lodging outside town.

San Antonio International Hostel, 621 Pierce Ave. (☎210-223-9426), off Grayson St. Friendly management, a pool, and a rec room. 42 beds in a ranch-style building. Check-in for the hostel is located inside the adjacent Bullis House B&B. Breakfast ($6) served in an elegant dining room. Reception 8am-noon and 4-10pm. Dorms $25; private rooms $45. AmEx/D/MC/V. ❷

Alamo Lodge, 1126 E. Elmira St. (☎210-222-9463), off Grayson St. This budget motel provides basic rooms in a neighborhood as quiet as the starry Texan desert at night. Outdoor pool, A/C, and 5 free local calls. Cable TV. Key deposit $2. Rooms $49. AmEx/D/MC/V. ❷

Roosevelt Inn, 2122 Roosevelt Ave. (☎210-533-2514), a few minutes south of downtown. Clean, no-frills rooms with A/C and TV. You'll feel oh

so retro borrowing VHS movies from the office. Rooms M-F $45, Sa-Su $50. AmEx/D/MC/V. ❷

Alamo KOA, 602 Gembler Rd. (☎210-224-9296 or 800-833-7785), 6 mi. from downtown. From I-10 W., take Exit 580, drive 2 blocks north, and take a left onto Gembler Rd. Well-kept grounds with lots of shade and security. Each site has a grill and a patio. Pool, hot tub, and free movies. Showers and laundry. Reception 8am-8:30pm. Sites $24, with full hookup $33. D/MC/V. ❷

FOOD

Be prepared to pay dearly for dining along the Riverwalk. North of town, Asian restaurants line Broadway across from Brackenridge. On weekends, hundreds of carnival food booths crowd the walkways of Market Sq. If you come late in the day, prices drop and some travelers report that vendors will haggle.

Mi Tierra, 218 Produce Row (☎210-225-1262), in Market Sq. A huge restaurant filled with shining ceiling decorations. Features a bakery, a bar, and a very long wait for a table. Mariachi musicians serenade diners while they munch on delicious Mexican fare, like chicken enchiladas with mole sauce ($9). Lunch plates $7-8. Dinner plates $10-14. Open 24hr. AmEx/MC/V. ❷

Rosario's, 910 S. Alamo St. (☎210-223-1806), at S. Saint Mary's St. Rosario's is known as the best Tex-Mex eatery in town and has the awards to prove it. Scrumptious chicken quesadillas ($6.25) and *relleno de pascado* ($11.25) uphold its reputation. Live Latin-infused music F starting at around 9:30pm. Open M-Th 11am-10pm, F-Sa 11am-11pm, Su 11am-8pm. AmEx/D/MC/V. ❸

Liberty Bar, 328 E. Josephine St. (☎210-227-1187). Friendly service. You'll feel classy just being here. Napa Valley-inspired daily specials ($12-20) and sandwiches ($7-10). Try the karkade, an iced hibiscus and mint tea with fresh ginger and white grape juice. Open M-Th 11am-10:30pm, F-Sa 10:30am-midnight, Su 10:30am-10:30pm. Bar open M-Th and Sa until midnight, F-Sa until 2am. AmEx/D/MC/V. ❸

Ruta Maya, 107 E. Martin St. (☎210-223-6292; www.rutamayariverwalk.com), at Soledad. Serves organic Chiapas-grown coffee ($1.50) along with homemade sandwiches and salads. Try the chicken on sourdough with olive tapenade

($6.75). Relaxed, lounging-friendly atmosphere. Free Wi-Fi. Frequent live music or DJs at night. Open M-Th 7:30am-10pm, F 7:30am-2am, Sa 9am-2am. AmEx/D/MC/V. ❷

Josephine St. Steaks/Whiskey, 400 Josephine St. (☎210-224-6169), at Ave. A. The specialty is thick steak, but Josephine St. offers a wide array of other tasty dishes for less voracious carnivores. Of course, nothing goes quite as well with steak as a glass of whiskey—Josephine's impressive selection has you covered there too. Nice shaded patio. Entrees $7-13. Open M-Th 11am-10pm, F-Sa 11am-11pm. AmEx/D/MC/V. ❸

Twin Sisters, 124 Broadway and 6322 N. New Braunfels Ave. (☎210-354-1559). Some of the best vegetarian food in San Antonio and great ambience. The tofu quesadillas—against all odds—are delicious. Open M-F 7am-9pm, Sa 7am-2pm, Su 9am-2pm. AmEx/MC/V. ❷

Madhatter's Tea House and Cafe, 302 Beauregard St. (☎210-212-4832). A tea lover's wonderland, with over 50 different varieties of tea. An eclectic selection of sandwiches and salads complements your beverage of choice. Lounge around in the relaxed atmosphere and enjoy free Wi-Fi as long as you like; refills of your tea are only $1. Open M-F 7am-9pm, Sa 9am-9pm, Su 9am-6pm. AmEx/MC/V. ❶

⊙ SIGHTS

ALAMO. Built as a Spanish mission during the colonization of the New World, the Alamo has come to serve as the symbol of Texas's break from Mexico and thus a touchstone of Lone Star pride. For 12 days in 1836, a motley crew of Americans (including 🏠**Davy Crockett**), Europeans, and Hispanic Tejanos defended the Alamo against the army of Mexican General Santa Anna, who was determined to reclaim the land for Mexico. The morning of the 13th day saw the end of their defiant stand, and all 189 men were killed. However, the massacre united Texans behind the independence movement, and "Remember the Alamo!" became the rallying cry for Sam Houston's ultimately victorious forces. After languishing for decades, the mission was put under the care of the Daughters of the Republic of Texas in 1905 and has since been transformed

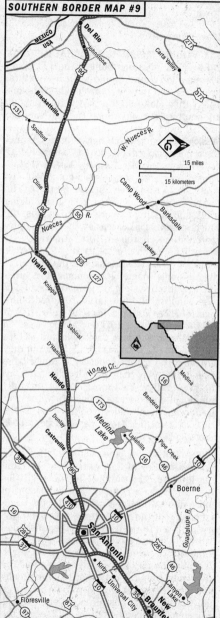

SOUTHERN BORDER MAP #9

into a museum and the focus of the city's downtown. *(At the center of Alamo Plaza. ☎ 210-225-1391; www.thealamo.org. Open M-Sa 9am-5:30pm, Su 10am-5:30pm. Free.)*

SAN ANTONIO MISSIONS NATIONAL HISTORIC PARK. Four missions built in the 1720s and 30s supplied San Antonio with agricultural products and newly converted Catholics. Today they make up the park. Stretching 23 mi. south of the city along the San Antonio River, they are connected by the brown-signed **Mission Trail** road, which begins at the Alamo. *(Visitors Center located at Mission San José. ☎ 210-932-1001; www.nps.gov/saan. Open daily 9am-5pm.)* Stopping at every mission takes a good half-day; some may wish to see only the first two. The missions are connected by biking and hiking trails, and the first two are served by Bus #42. The first is **Mission Concepción,** the oldest unrestored stone church in North America. *(807 Mission Rd., 4 mi. south of the Alamo off E. Mitchell St. ☎ 210-534-1540.)* **Mission San José,** the "Queen of the Missions," contains remnants of its original irrigation system, a gorgeous sculpted rose window, and numerous restored buildings. *(6701 San José Dr., off Roosevelt Ave. ☎ 210-922-0543. Mass Su 7:45, 9, 10:30am; "Mariachi Mass" Su noon.)* **Mission San Juan Capistrano** and **Mission San Francisco de la Espada** are smaller, but they surround the **Espada Aqueduct,** a remarkable engineering feat that provided irrigation to the river valley. Visitors can view the fully functional aqueduct as it carries water over the streams and valleys below. *(San Juan at 9101 Graf St. ☎ 210-534-0749. San Francisco at 10040 Espada Rd. ☎ 210-627-2021.)*

RIVERWALK. After the Alamo, the most famous symbol of San Antonio is its 2 mi. long **Riverwalk (Paseo del Rio),** built in the 1930s by the WPA as a combination flood control and real-estate project. Following the original course of the San Antonio River, the Riverwalk is a 3 ft. deep river lined with shaded pathways, picturesque gardens, shops, and cafes, all of which are below street level. Recently, the city has decided to expand the Riverwalk 13 mi., a plan that will drastically affect the Riverwalk and downtown San Antonio. Construction has already begun and is expected to be completed by 2012. Along the southern arm of Riverwalk is **La Villita,** a preserved section of historic houses and streets that has been turned into a Spanish-style artisan village where the public can watch artists at work. *(418 Villita. ☎ 210-207-8612; www.lavillita.com. Open daily 10am-6pm. Free.)*

MARKET SQUARE. The square is a part open-air, part enclosed market where customers can haggle with vendors. Weekends feature the upbeat tunes of Tejano bands and the sweet backbeat of buzzing frozen margarita machines. *(Between San Saba and Santa Rosa St. ☎ 210-207-8600. Vendors and indoor market area open daily May-Sept. 10am-8pm; Sept.-May 10am-6pm.)*

HEMISFAIR PARK. The site of the 1968 World's Fair, HemisFair Plaza still draws tourists with museums, historic houses, and generally impressive architecture. *(Plaza located between S. Alamo St., E. Market St., Bowie St., and Durango Blvd.)* The view is beautiful from the **Tower of the Americas,** which rises 750 ft. above the Texas hill country and boasts a revolving restaurant. *(600 HemisFair Park. ☎ 210-233-3101. Open M-Th and Su 10am-10pm, F-Sa 10am-11pm. $11, ages 4-11 $9, seniors $10.)* Inside the park, the **Institute of Texan Cultures** documents the histories and contributions of 27 different ethnic groups in Texas, from Czech to Chinese to Swedish. *(☎ 210-458-2300; www.texancultures.utsa.edu. Open Tu-Sa 10am-5pm, Su noon-5pm. $7.)*

BUCKHORN SALOON & MUSUEM. In continuous operation since 1881, this museum displays objects from the Old West as well as a huge collection of preserved animals from around the world, an interactive wax museum of Texas history, and exhibits on ranching and gunfights. Stop in for a drink and a bite to eat at the saloon. *(318 Houston St. ☎ 210-247-4000. Museum $10, children 3-11 $7.50, seniors $9. Open daily from Memorial Day to Labor Day 10am-6pm; from Labor Day to Memorial Day 10am-5pm.)*

SAN ANTONIO MUSEUM OF ART. Housed in the former Lone Star Brewery, the museum showcases a nice collection of pre-Columbian, Egyptian, Oceanic, Asian, and Islamic folk art. In 1998, the museum established the **Nelson A. Rockefeller Center for Latin American Art,** the first of its kind in the US. Highlights include works by Diego Rivera. *(200 W.*

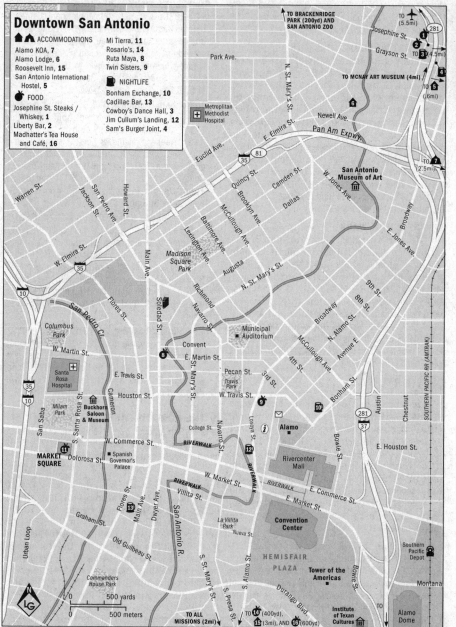

Downtown San Antonio

ACCOMMODATIONS
Alamo KOA, **7**
Alamo Lodge, **6**
Roosevelt Inn, **15**
San Antonio International Hostel, **5**

FOOD
Josephine St. Steaks / Whiskey, **1**
Liberty Bar, **2**
Madhatter's Tea House and Café, **16**

Mi Tierra, **11**
Rosario's, **14**
Ruta Maya, **8**
Twin Sisters, **9**

NIGHTLIFE
Bonham Exchange, **10**
Cadillac Bar, **13**
Cowboy's Dance Hall, **3**
Jim Cullum's Landing, **12**
Sam's Burger Joint, **4**

Jones Ave. ☎210-978-8100. Open Tu 10am-9pm, W-Sa 10am-5pm, Su noon-6pm. $8, students $5, ages 3-11 $3, seniors $7. Tu 4-9pm free.)

MCNAY ART MUSEUM. This museum displays the collection of Impressionist, Post-Impressionist, and Expressionist masterpieces accumulated by Mrs. McNay, who stirred up controversy in the early 20th century by promoting experimental modern art in otherwise conservative Texas. The 23-acre grounds are free to the public, but the museum has recently built a new 45,000 sq. ft. exhibition center and now charges admission. (6000 N. New Braunfels Ave. ☎210-805-1756; www.mcnayart. org. Open Tu-W and F 10am-4pm, Th 10am-9pm, Sa 10am-5pm, Su noon-5pm. Grounds open daily 7am-7pm. $8, students and seniors $5.)

BRACKENRIDGE PARK. To escape San Antonio's urban congestion, amble down to Brackenridge Park. The 343-acre grounds include plenty of picnic tables along the river, playgrounds, a miniature train, and a driving range. The main attraction in the park is a lush, perfumed Japanese tea garden with pathways weaving in and out of a pagoda and around a goldfish pond. No fishing is allowed. (3853 N. St. Mary's St., 5 mi. north of the Alamo. ☎210-223-9534. Open daily 5am-11pm. Train daily 9am-6:30pm. Free. Train $2.75, children $2.25.)

▶ NIGHTLIFE

In late April, the 10-day **Fiesta San Antonio** (☎210-227-5191) ushers in spring with concerts, carnivals, and hoopla in honor of Texas's many heroes and cultures. Clusters of funky, independent bars can be found in the residential areas of **King William, North Saint Mary's Street** (around Woodlawn Ave.), and **Josephine Street.** The *Friday Express* and the weekly *Current* (available at the visitors center and in many bars and businesses) are guides to the city's nightlife.

> **Cadillac Bar,** 212 S. Flores St. (☎210-223-5533). This restaurant and bar fills to the brim after 9pm with local yuppies who dance between the tables to authentic Tejano music. It's not exactly a taste of old-style San Antonio culture, but it's still a good time. No cover. Open M-Th and Su 11am-11pm, F-Sa 11am-2am. AmEx/MC/V.

Sam's Burger Joint, 330 E. Grayson St. (☎210-223-2830; www.samsburgerjoint.com). Brightly painted restaurant with a huge bar and performance area in a separate building. Sam's has something going on every night of the week, from karaoke to Americana music to blues jams. The burgers ($5-7) are tasty. Cover free-$15. Open M-Sa 11am-2am. AmEx/D/MC/V.

The Bonham Exchange, 411 Bonham St. (☎210-271-3811), around the corner from the Alamo. This 1200-person-capacity club is the place to be on weekend nights. 8 bars, 3 stories, and a huge backyard patio mean you can spend an entire night just getting situated. Gay-friendly. College night W. Cover up to $20; free before 10pm. Open W-Th 4pm-2:30am, F 4pm-3am, Sa 8pm-3am, Su 8pm-2:30am. MC/V.

Cowboy's Dance Hall, 3030 US 410 NE (☎210-646-9378). Both types of music—country and Western. With a mechanical bull and 2 dance floors, you'd best bring your cowboy hat. Friends can't tell your bull-riding and dance moves apart? No worries: most evenings begin with free lessons at 7pm. Live bull riding every F night. 18+. Cover varies. Open W and F 8pm-2am, Th 7pm-2am, Sa 7pm-3am. AmEx/D/MC/V.

Jim Cullum's Landing, 123 Losoya St. (☎210-223-7266; www.landing.com). Located deep in the Hyatt Regency. Dixieland, bluegrass, jazz, and swing nightly, including Cullum and his band, who play 5 nights a week. Cover $6. Open M-F 4pm-midnight, Sa-Su noon-midnight. D/MC/V.

▶ THE ROAD TO CASTROVILLE: 25 MI.

To leave San Antonio, hop on **I-10** and follow it west. Take **Exit 153** to **US 90 West** and continue on it for 23 mi. in order to get to Castroville.

CASTROVILLE   ☎ 830

Just outside San Antonio, on the sleepy banks of the Medina River, sits Castroville, "the little Alsace of Texas." In the mid-19th century, the town's founder, Henri Castro, a gentleman of French birth, Portuguese ancestry, Jewish faith, and American citizenship, began recruiting settlers from the Rhine Valley and especially from the French province of Alsace. As the French families flocked to their new Texas home, they constructed their houses in the same style as those they had left behind: little cottages with asymmetrical roof lines. Many of these quaint Alsatian-style structures still stand, and you can pick up a pamphlet for a self-guided walking tour at one such building: the **Chamber of Commerce**, 100 Karm St., on the left when you enter town from US 90 W. (☎830-538-3142. Open M-F 9am-5pm.) At the **Castroville Regional Park ❶**, 816 Alsace St., camping, picnicking, athletic fields, and an Olympic-size swimming pool are available year-round. You can also swim in the **Medina River.** Turn left onto Alsace St. and look for the signs. (☎830-931-4070. Park open daily in summer 5am-10pm; in winter 6am-9pm. Entrance fee $5 per vehicle. Picnic fee $5. Tent sites $10. Cash only.) If you'd like to splurge on lodgings, try the **Landmark Inn ❸**, 402 Florence St., where you can stay in a 19th-century building with antique furnishings and few modern distractions. The inn has bikes and canoes for guests. You can also tour the beautiful five-acre grounds or see the small museum. The entire inn is designated a state historical site. (☎830-931-2133. Museum open daily 8am-6pm; $3. Continental breakfast included. Reservations recommended. Rooms with shared bath $75, with private bath $80. AmEx/D/MC/V.)The denizens of a little Alsatian cottage serve excellent French cuisine at **La Normandie Restaurant ❹**, 1302 Fiorella St. Favorites include the beef medallions in bearnaise sauce with artichoke hearts and roast duck. (☎830-538-3070. Champagne brunch Su 11:30am-3pm $17. Dinner F-Sa 3-9pm. Reservations required for dinner.)

▥ THE ROAD TO HONDO: 17 MI.
Take **US 90 West** toward Hondo.

HONDO ☎830
Picturesque gas lamps and old brick buildings line the railroad tracks running through the town of Hondo. As you enter town, you'll see a sign for the Hondo train depot, where you can imagine gunslingers hanging out over 100 years ago. At the **Regency Inn ❷**, 401 US 90 E., you'll find comfortable country living in clean rooms. (☎830-426-3031. Pool and picnic area. Reservations recommended. Singles from $40; doubles from $55. AmEx/D/MC/V.)Try ▨**El Restaurante Azteca ❷**, 1708 Ave. K. This family-owned restaurant has a no-tip policy—they believe that "good service comes at no extra charge." From US 90 E., take a left on Ave. K and cross the tracks. (☎830-426-4511. Lunch specials $6-7. Combination plates $8-10. Open M-Sa 11am-9pm. AmEx/D/MC/V.)

▥ THE ROAD TO UVALDE: 43 MI.
Continue on **US 90 West** to Uvalde.

UVALDE ☎830
Uvalde sits at the intersection of the two longest highways in the continental United States (US 90 and US 83). On the east side of town stands the former home of lawless lawman Pat Garrett, who killed Billy the Kid. Wild West blood once flowed freely through the streets at the heart of the town, but at the turn of the century Uvalde became as civilized as it once had been wild. The town is proud of its most famous resident, John Nance Garner, the vice president who served for two terms under Franklin D. Roosevelt. The **Garner Museum,** 333 N. Park St., preserves his home and displays his papers and some memorabilia. Turn right onto Park St. from US 90. (☎830-278-5018. Open Tu-Sa 9am-5pm. Free.)

The large rooms of the **Amber Sky Motel ❸**, 2005 E. Main St., are the cheapest option in Uvalde and look almost new. All rooms have TVs, microwaves, and fridges. (☎830-278-5602. Free Wi-Fi. Singles $55; doubles $65. AmEx/D/MC/V.) In a log cabin on the east side of town, **Jack's Steakhouse ❸**, 2500 E. Main St., serves good steaks, burgers, and chicken to hungry travelers and locals. (☎830-278-9955. Entrees $12-17. Open M-Th and Su 11am-9:30pm, F-Sa 11am-11pm, Su 11am-3pm. AmEx/D/MC/V.)

▥ THE ROAD TO BRACKETTVILLE AND FORT CLARK SPRINGS: 40 MI.
Once you leave Uvalde on **US 90,** you enter Texas scrub brush country, and the scenery looks dramatically more like desert. Forty miles along sit the old white brick buildings of Brackettville.

SOUTHERN BORDER

BRACKETTVILLE AND FORT CLARK SPRINGS ☎830

Once the support town of Fort Clark, Brackettville had little left to offer after the Army withdrew. An impressive courthouse stands in the center of town, accessible by turning north onto Rte. 674. The best attraction in Brackettville is the **Alamo Village Movie Location**—the self-proclaimed "movie capital of Texas"—7 mi. north of Brackettville on Rte. 674. The Alamo Village was constructed for the 1960 John Wayne epic *Alamo*, and has since provided a backdrop for several other films and TV shows. See the Old West-style buildings and, in the summer, daily music and rodeo shows. Lots of employees have been extras in films—ask them about their experiences with stardom. (☎830-563-2580; www.alamovillage.com. Open daily in summer 9am-6pm; in winter 9am-5pm. Shows in summer 10:30am, 12:30, 2:30, 4:30pm. Tickets $10.75, under 11 $5.) To your left as you enter Brackettville on US 90 West, the once-abandoned Fort Clark base has been revitalized as a residential community, run collectively by an association of homeowners. Driving tours of the former barracks, parade grounds, guardhouses, and depots are available from the visitors center if you call in advance. Otherwise, you can wander around the lovely grounds by yourself. There is also a small museum about the barracks. (☎830-563-9150.Visitors center open M-F 8am-6pm, Sa-Su 8am-1pm. Museum open Sa-Su 1-4pm. $2, children free.) The fort also boasts a ▧**motel ❷** renovated from cavalry barracks. You get access to the spring-fed pool and the chance to sleep in a former barracks without emptying your wallet. The rooms look brand-new. Wood furniture, comfy beds, and TVs. (☎800-937-1590. Rooms M-Th $38, Sa-Su $62. AmEx/D/MC/V.)

▧ THE ROAD TO DEL RIO: 32 MI.

From Brackettville, continue on **US 90 West** for 32 mi. to Del Rio. Once in town, turn right onto **Veterans Boulevard** to reach motels and restaurants (many of them chains) or turn left to get to the historic downtown. Veterans Blvd. is also the continuation of US 90, so to leave town you'll head west until the chains fade away and you're back in the open country.

DEL RIO ☎830

Many colorful personalities have passed through Del Rio since it was founded in 1883. The **Whitehead Memorial Museum,** 1308 S. Main St., is the burial site of self-made lawman Judge Roy Bean, who held court in the saloon and infamously once fined a dead man for carrying a concealed weapon. **Perry House** is one of the oldest buildings in town; built as a general store, it later served as a courthouse, a Masonic hall, a church, and a post office. Now a museum, it houses a collection of exhibits about Bean and the town's history. Go straight when US 90 turns at Gibbs St. (☎830-774-7568. Open Tu-Sa 9am-4:30pm, Su 1-5pm. $5, children $2, seniors $4.) The nearby **San Felipe Springs** was a watering hole for the US Army Camel Corps, a short-lived pre-Civil War cavalry experiment. The town was also home to Dr. John R. Brinkley, whose inventions included goat-gland implants (to improve the sex lives of men) and autographed pictures of Jesus Christ.

Lodging in Del Rio is inexpensive in general, and budget motels line Veterans Blvd. The **Motel 6 ❷,** 2115 Veterans Blvd., has very clean, basic rooms with pool access, cable TV, and air-conditioning. (☎830-774-2115. Singles $30; doubles $36. AmEx/D/MC/V.) **Don Marcelinos ❷,** 1110 Veterans Blvd., offers Mexican food in a festive environment. Dinner options involve a huge variety of combination plates ($6-8), and the service is exceptionally quick. (☎830-775-6242. Open M-Sa 11am-10pm, Su 10am-8pm. AmEx/D/MC/V.)

◪ DETOUR
AMISTAD NATIONAL RECREATION AREA

On **US 90,** 13 mi. west of Del Rio, on the right-hand side. Look for the signs.

Amistad ("friendship") is an international recreation area on the US-Mexico border. The reservoir was created by the 6 mi. long dam on the Rio Grande, and the water always appears strikingly blue by virtue of the area's limestone rock and exceptionally clear water. Run by the National Park Service, this area is renowned for its watersports, but it also protects prehistoric pictographs (accessible only by boat) and a diverse animal population.

SOUTHERN BORDER

You can fish, snorkel, swim, kayak, or canoe in the river, but bring your own equipment. Great touristy photos await if you drive onto the reservoir dam (on the 349 spur, left off US 90, just past the visitors center): between two bronze eagles, you can stand with one foot in Mexico and the other in the US. If you don't have a boat, get a phenomenal panoramic view of the reservoir by driving to the end of the Diablo East spur off of US 90 and hiking the quick quarter-mile nature trail out onto a peninsula. **Camping ❶** is available at Governor's Landing. (☎830-775-7491; www.nps.gov/amis. Visitors center open daily 8am-5pm. Campsites with water $8. Cash only.)

✄ DETOUR
SEMINOLE CANYON STATE PARK

Off **US 90,** 33 mi. past the Amistad visitors center.

Inspired by ancient peoples, the museum showcases small, well-executed exhibits about the Native Americans who left pictographs on the canyon walls thousands of years ago. Despite the years of harsh sun, these paintings are still in phenomenal condition. The park features 10 mi. of trails, although a guided tour ($5) is required for the canyon trail, the only way to see the pictographs up close. Otherwise, you can walk the 6 mi. **Rio Grande River Trail** to catch a glimpse of some pictographs from across the canyon. If you're in a hurry, a nature trail runs two-thirds of a mile from the visitors center toward the canyons and is the best way to get a quick feel for the park. (☎432-292-4464. Open daily 9am-4:45pm. Canyon tour W-Su 10am. $3. Tour $5.) **Camping ❶** is also available. (Showers and toilets. Sites $10, with hookup $14.)

✄ DETOUR
PECOS RIVER CANYON

Off **US 90,** 3 mi. past Seminole Canyon State Park. Don't blink, or you might miss it.

The awe-inspiring Pecos Canyon was formed by the eponymous river. The only real way to explore the canyon is by canoe, but you can still get some worthwhile views from the road. Take the high road for beautiful views or the low road to get down to the boat launch area. A few feet along the high road is a lovely picnic spot with shelters. From there, you can look down to the old river roads that have now been washed out by floods.

🚗 THE ROAD TO LANGTRY: 62 MI.
From **Pecos River Canyon,** drive down **US 90.**

LANGTRY ☎432

As the erstwhile home of Judge Roy Bean, who embodied "the law west of the Pecos," this town has one of the most colorful histories in the West. Judge Bean dispensed hard liquor and harsh justice—since Langtry had no jail, all offenses were punished by fines payable to Bean. To learn more about the good judge and his pet bear, stop by the impressive **Judge Roy Bean Visitor Center,** off US 90, at W. Loop 25. The center houses a small museum dedicated to Bean, the original saloon/courtroom, the judge's house, and a labeled cactus garden. There are also state-of-the-art holographic history exhibits designed by Disney. Follow the signs and take a left off US 90. (☎432-291-3340. Free Wi-Fi. Open daily 8am-6pm. Free.)

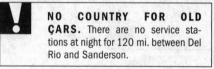

NO COUNTRY FOR OLD CARS. There are no service stations at night for 120 mi. between Del Rio and Sanderson.

🚗 THE ROAD TO SANDERSON: 61 MI.
Head back on **US 90** to reach Sanderson.

SANDERSON ☎432

Sanderson bills itself as the "Cactus Capital of Texas." Despite the slogan, there are surprisingly few cactuses in the area; despite the designation "town," there are surprisingly few people. Until recently, trains changed crews in Sanderson, and local businesses housed and fed resting workers. When crews began to switch at Alpine, businesses folded. The town still plays a role as the only stop on an otherwise long and barren stretch of road, but only a few (pop. 891) diehards remain.

The accommodations at the **Outback Oasis Motel ❷,** 800 US 90, are spacious and have been remodeled in fine Southwestern style. The pool has been converted into a koi pond,

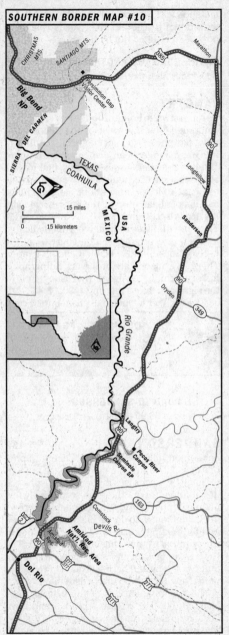

SOUTHERN BORDER MAP #10

and there's a fine reptile exhibit by the lobby. (☎888-466-8822; www.outbackoasismotel. com. Cable, A/C, and free Wi-Fi. Singles $39; doubles $59. AmEx/D/MC/V.) Get a meal with friendly service at **Mi Tierra Mexicana ❷**, at US 90, on your right as you enter town. A little place run by Delores Rodriguez, Mi Tierra serves "authentic border Tex-Mex." Get a breakfast taco for $2 or a burger and fries for $5.25. (☎432-345-2266. Dinners $5-8. Steaks $8-14. Open daily 6:30am-8pm, but sometimes closed for siesta. AmEx/D/MC/V.)

◤ THE ROAD TO BIG BEND: 144 MI.

Seventy two miles past Marathon on **Route 385** is the park's first entrance. From there, it's another 30 mi. to **Panther Junction,** the visitors center and park head-quarters. The drive is beautiful, as the grasslands give way to rocky mountains of volcanic debris.

BIG BEND NATIONAL PARK ☎432

❗ NOT A DROP TO DRINK. Always carry at least one gallon of water per person per day in the desert. Many of the park's roads can flood during the "rainy" late summer months. In summer (May-Sept.) it can be very uncomfortable, and potentially dangerous, to hike during the middle of the day. Consult a ranger if you have any uncertainty about weather conditions—hot or cold—when you head out.

Roadrunners, coyotes, wild pigs, black bears, and a few mountain lions make their home in Big Bend National Park, a tract of land about the size of Rhode Island that is cradled by the mighty Rio Grande. Spectacular canyons, vast stretches of the Chihuahua Desert, and the airy Chisos Mountains occupy this spot. At night, Big Bend has some of the best star-gazing you will find, which is due to the lack of ambient light and the park's distance from any sizable city. The high season for tourism is in the early spring—in the summer, the park (though still beautiful) is excruciatingly hot.

ORIENTATION

There are only five paved roads in the park. Of these, the best sightseeing is along the **Ross Maxwell Scenic Drive**, a 30 mi. paved route from the western edge of the **Chisos Mountains** that leads down to the **Rio Grande** and **Santa Elena Canyon.** From this drive on a clear day, you can see far into Mexico and through the beautiful Santa Elena Mountains. The 8 mi. drive that winds its way up into the Chisos Basin is also quite rewarding. However, the most spectacular drives in the park are unimproved, accessible only to four-wheel-drive jeeps and trucks: **River Road** (51 mi.) skirts along the Rio Grande from Castolon to the Rio Grande Village, and the 26 mi. old **Ore Road** travels along the western edge of the **Sierra del Caballo Muerto.** Those interested in driving the back roads of Big Bend should purchase the *Guide to Backcountry Roads* ($2) at the visitors center and check at the visitors center for the most current road information.

VITAL STATS
Area: 800,000 acres
Tourist Office: Park Headquarters (☎432-477-2251; www.nps.gov/bibe), 29 mi. inside the park, in Panther Jct. Open daily 8am-6pm. Ranger stations located at Rio Grande Village, Persimmon Gap, Castolon, and Chisos Basin. Castolon and Rio Grande Village closed in summer.
Emergency: ☎432-477-2251 until 5pm—or 911.
Gateway Towns: Marathon (north) or Study Butte/Terlingua (west).
Fees: Weekly entrance pass $20 per vehicle, $10 per pedestrian, bicycle, or motorcycle.

ACCOMMODATIONS

There is a budget motel outside of the park and three campsites within the park. **Backcountry camping ❶** is permitted as long as you have a permit ($10), which can be obtained at the Panther Jct. Visitors Center.

Chisos Mining Co. Motel, (☎432-371-2254), on Rte. 170, west of Rte. 118. The nearest budget motel. Singles $50; doubles from $65; 6-person cabins $70-90. AmEx/D/MC/V. ❸

Chisos Basin Campground (☎877-444-6777; www.reserveusa.com). At 5400 ft. Stays about 20° cooler than the other campgrounds do in the summer. Has sites with running water and flush toilets. Sites $14. ❶

Rio Grande Village Campground (☎877-444-6777; www.reserveusa.com). Tent sites and an RV park with 25 full hookups ironically (if you know what we're talking about) near the only showers in the park. Tent sites $14; RV sites $26. ❶

FOOD

If you're going into Big Bend for any length of time, you probably do not want to rely on restaurants to feed you. Go to a grocery store before you get into the park and bring cooking equipment. The stores adjacent to many of the visitors centers sell basic provisions.

Chisos Mountains Lodge, (☎432-477-2291), in the Chisos Basin. The only restaurant in the park, which serves 3 meals per day. Lunch sandwiches $7-9. Dinner entrees $9-17. Open daily 7-10am, 11am-4pm, 5-8pm. AmEx/D/MC/V. ❸

Starlight Theater Bar and Grill, 631 Ivey Rd. (☎432-371-2326), off Rte. 170 in Terlingua Ghost Town. Serves healthy portions of Tex-Mex ($10-19), plays live music, and boasts the only pool table south of Alpine. Open M-F and Su 5pm-midnight, Sa 5pm-1am. Kitchen open until 10pm. AmEx/MC/V. ❸

OUTDOORS

Big Bend encompasses several hundred miles of hiking trails, ranging from 30min. nature walks to backpacking trips of several days. Pick up the *Hiker's Guide to Big Bend* ($2) or grab a ranger and ask about the kind of hike you're looking for; the rangers are knowledgeable about the area and lead free nature hikes throughout the year, schedules for which are usually posted outside of any visitors center. In the middle of the park are the Chisos Mountains, where you'll find cooler hiking and camping. The Chisos are also home to a number of species that are found nowhere else in North America, such as the drooping juniper and several cactuses.

In the Chisos, there are several good hikes. The **Lost Mine Trail** (4.8 mi. round-trip) takes

[the big splurge]

about 3hr. to complete and is one of the most popular trails in the park. **Emory Peak** (9 mi.) is an intense climb with 40% grades at some points but is widely regarded as the park's best hike. Pick up a guide ($1) at the trailhead. The easier **Santa Elena Canyon** trail (1 mi.) ambles along the Rio Grande.

Though upstream damming has decreased the river's pace, rafting is still big fun on the Rio Grande. **Far-Flung Outdoor Center,** on Rte. 170, 2 mi. west of Rte. 118, in Terlingua, organizes one- to seven-day trips. (☎432-371-2633 or 800-839-7238; www.farflungoutdoorcenter. com. From $129 per person.) Across Hwy. 170, **Big Bend River Tours** rents canoes and inflatable kayaks and organizes rafting and paddling trips. (☎915-371-3033 or 800-545-4240; www. bigbendrivertours.com. Canoes $50 per day. Inflatable kayaks $40 per day.)

▥ THE ROAD TO ALPINE: 80 MI.

Route 118 runs west out of the park. Almost immediately you pass through the tiny, tourist-oriented town of **Study Butte**. If you're ready to press on to Alpine, stay on Rte. 118 as it curves northward for 80 mi. The desert mountains slowly give way to green shrublands, grassy foothills, and finally, mountains. This part of Texas doesn't receive enough water to support tree growth, but occasional storms bring enough rain for a golden, hay-like grass to blanket the ground.

ALPINE   ☎432

With a population of 5900, Alpine is this area's big metropolis. High above town on the eastern hills, **Sul Ross State University** is Alpine's main attraction and has one of the nation's best rodeo teams. Sul Ross also houses the **Museum of the Big Bend,** a collection of colorful displays depicting artifacts representing the Big Bend region of Texas. Exhibits detail the history of Native Americans, Texan cowboys, and Mexicans—with a heavy focus on Mexican Revolutionary General Pancho Villa. (☎432-837-8143. Open Tu-Sa 9am-5pm, Su 1-5pm. Free.) Quietly set against the blossoming foothills, the ▨**Antelope Lodge ❸,** 2310 US 90 W, 1 mi. west of Alpine, is a friendly Texas ranch at a budget motel price. The best lodging in town, each room occupies half a small cottage and opens onto a beautiful courtyard with a fountain and some old barbecues. (☎800-880-8106; www.antelopelodge.com. Singles $50; doubles $59. AmEx/D/MC/V.) The **Motel Bien Venido ❷,** 809 E. Holland Ave., is located near the university, and its rooms have air-conditioning, microfridges, and free Wi-Fi. (☎432-837-3454. Singles $38; doubles $42. AmEx/D/MC/V.) For a quick breakfast or lunch, head to **Alicia's Restaurant ❷,** 708 E. Gallego St. Alicia's is a cramped little box right by the university, but it's a good value and even has a drive-through window for travelers in a rush. (☎432-837-2802. Breakfast burritos

ROUGH AND RUGGED: OFF-ROAD JEEPS IN BIG BEND

With only five paved roads in Big Bend National Park and over 800,000 acres of ground, there's a lot you're going to miss unless you leave the beaten (read: paved) track. Explore the area a bit more thoroughly by getting in a jeep and hitting all of the ominous-looking unpaved roads characterized by jagged rocks sticking up out of the ground and little maintenance.

Over 1100 mi. of unpaved roads cover the park, awaiting those with a sense of adventure. Far Flung Outdoor Center, 2 mi. south of Terlingua on Rte. 170 (☎800-839-7238; www.farflungoutdoorcenter.com), rents two-door jeeps for $100 per day (8:30am-5pm) or four-door variants for $125. One of the best drives is the 51 mi. River Rd., which follows the Rio Grande through largely untouched desert from Castolon to the Rio Grande Village. The Old Ore road is a tougher drive, taking drivers 26 mi. from the Dagger Flat Auto Trail to Rio Grande Village.

For those who don't want to navigate the harsh conditions, Far Flung also offers guided jeep tours. The Camp 360 tour (the most popular) lasts 3hr. and takes visitors over four-by-four terrain to one of the best views in the Big Bend area. Tours depart daily at 9am and 2pm and cost $64 per person.

$3-4. Burgers and mexican food $5-7. Open M-F 8am-3pm, Sa-Su 9am-3pm. MC/V.)

◪ THE ROAD TO MARFA: 26 MI.
Follow **US 90 West** 25 mi. to Marfa.

MARFA   ☎432

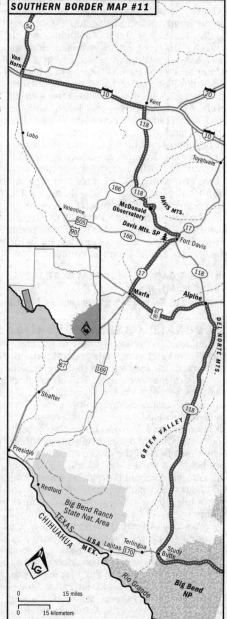

SOUTHERN BORDER MAP #11

Billboards on the way to Marfa declare that "Marfa is what the West was." If the West was a thriving artist colony, then they hit the nail right on the head. At the end of Highland St. stand the gargantuan peach stucco walls and elaborate dome of the **Presidio County Courthouse.** The **Marfa and Presidio County Museum,** 110 W. San Antonio St., possesses a fine collection of Old West knick-knacks and antiques. The museum also supplies excellent advice to tourists and shows a 7min. film on the region's enigma—the spooky Marfa lights. (☎432-729-4140. Open Tu-Sa 1-5pm. Free.)

Lodging in Marfa will cost you dearly wherever you hang your hat; one option is the **Riata Inn ❸**, US 90 E, which has big, airy rooms. (☎432-729-2900. Pool. Free Wi-Fi. Rooms $65. AmEx/D/MC/V.) **The Brown Recluse ❷**, 111 W. San Antonio St., is in an old house with a large patio and porch. It sells used books and serves organic coffee and breakfast plates ($7.70). (☎432-729-1811. Open Th-M 7:30am-1pm. MC/V.) In the marble lobby of the Paisano Hotel, **Jett's Grill ❹**, 207 N. Highland St., is a high-end restaurant. Try the pistachio-encrusted fried steak for $19. (☎432-729-3838. Salads $6-10. Open M-Th 5-9pm, F-Su 2-10pm. Reservations required. AmEx/D/MC/V.) **Mando's ❷**, US 90 W., is a casual Mexican restaurant that serves "trans-Pecos-style" Mexican food. Try the *botanas* or the burritos. (☎432-729-3291. Entrees $5-18. Open Tu-F 11am-2pm and 5-9pm, Sa 11am-10pm, Su 11am-3pm. AmEx/D/MC/V.)

◪ THE ROAD TO DAVIS MOUNTAINS: 25 MI.
From Marfa, follow signs north onto **Route 17.** Stay on Rte. 17 for 21 mi. until you hit the town of Fort Davis, then obey signs that instruct you to take a slight left onto **Route 118 North.** After 3 mi., you'll reach the entrance to Davis Mountains State Park on your left.

DAVIS MOUNTAINS ☎432

While sometimes overshadowed by Big Bend to the south and the Guadalupe Mountains to the north, the Davis Mountains—which make up the most extensive mountain range in Texas—are certainly worth a visit. Davis Mountains State Park is located in a beautiful little valley nestled among the mountains; the park's main entrance is also the starting point for scenic drives and hikes, and the park offers **camping ❶** in well-developed sites that are shaded by oak trees. (☎432-426-3337. Park gates open 24hr. Office open 8am-10pm. Entrance fee $5 per person. Sites $10, with full hookup $20.) Visitors can take the **Skyline Drive** (1 mi.) from the park entrance up to the top of a nearby mountain, where there is a flat, paved area that offers spectacular views of the landscape from Fort Davis on down past Van Horn. This spot is also popular at night; visitors bring up blankets and lay out in the desert with a billion stars all around.

THE ROAD TO MCDONALD OBSERVATORY: 10 MI.

Get back onto **Route 118 North** and follow it 10 mi.

MCDONALD OBSERVATORY ☎432

If you want to get even closer to the stars, check out McDonald Observatory, 10 mi. north on Route 118 from the Davis Mountains State Park main entrance. The observatory features exhibits on the sun and starlight during its normal operating hours and offers guided tours led by a professional researcher at 11am and 2pm daily. Of course, the observatory is used more meaningfully at nighttime, when members of the public are allowed to attend "Star Parties" in which researchers educate guests about the many constellations and galaxies visible through the observatory's telescopes. Once a month, the observatory opens up its behemoth 82 in. and 107 in. telescopes to public viewing, which is a once-in-a-lifetime stargazing opportunity. Call a month in advance to reserve a spot. (☎432-426-3640; www.mcdonaldobservatory.org. Visitors center open daily 10am-5:30pm. Star Parties every Tu and F-Sa. Precise times of Star Parties and special telescope viewing sessions vary by season, so check online in advance. Visitors center $8 adults, $7 children. $10, children $8.)

THE ROAD TO VAN HORN: 75 MI.

Continue north on **Route 118** until it runs into **I-10.** Take the ramp to **I-10 West** and follow it to Van Horn.

VAN HORN ☎432

Van Horn was originally established as a support center for area ranchers—and now also serves as a support center for roadtrippers. There are dozens of budget motels along Broadway Blvd. that are inexplicably cheaper than the motels in any neighboring cities. Most of them advertise their prices and amenities on roadside signs, allowing you to shop around for the best price without leaving your car. The recently remodeled **Village Inn Motel ❷**, 403 W. Broadway Blvd., offers good value, with air-conditioning, TVs, microwaves, and fridges. (☎432-283-7213. Continental breakfast included. Wi-Fi. Singles $32; doubles $50. AmEx/D/MC/V.) If you're looking for a bite to eat and the plentiful fast-food options aren't up your alley, try **Papa's Pantry ❷**, 515 Van Horn Dr. The little roadside grill, right on US 90 as you enter town from the south, serves up everything from burritos ($2-4) to steak, salads, and chicken dinners ($6-10). Chicken-fried steak ($7.50) is the specialty. (☎432-283-2302. Open M-Sa 7am-9pm. MC/V.)

THE ROAD TO GUADALUPE MOUNTAINS NATIONAL PARK: 64 MI.

To continue on to **Guadalupe Mountains National Park,** go to the stoplight on the eastern side of town and follow signs to **Route 54 North.** Follow Rte. 54 for 53 mi. along a lonely stretch of asphalt until it merges with **Route 180/62.** Continue 16 mi. on Rte. 180 to the entrance to Guadalupe Mountains National Park.

GUADALUPE MOUNTAINS NATIONAL PARK ☎915

The Guadalupe Mountains are the highest and most remote of the major Texas ranges. The peaks are remnants of the ancient Capitan Reef that formed 265 million years ago along the edge of a vast inland sea and covered much of what is now western Texas and southeastern New Mexico. After the sea receded, the reef was buried under layers of sediment until major block faulting and erosion excavated and exposed the petrified remains 26 million years ago. Drivers can glimpse the park's best sights from Rte. 180/62: **El Capitan,** a 2000 ft. high limestone cliff, and **Guadalupe Peak,** the highest point in Texas at 8749 ft.

☀ ORIENTATION

Beautiful roadside vistas notwithstanding, **Guadalupe Mountains National Park** belongs to the hikers. The road to **McKittrick Canyon Visitors Center** is the only paved road that strays far from Rte. 180. The **Williams Ranch Road** ventures deepest into the park, but this trail has soft sands and rocky sections that are only passable by four-by-four, high-ground-clearance vehicles. The 7 mi. journey lies behind two locked gates, the keys to which may be checked out free of charge at the visitors center. The desert trail ends in **Bone Canyon** at the historic **Williams ranch house.** Just up the highway from the visitors center, there is a 1.5 mi. unpaved road up to **Frijole Ranch,** which houses a history museum and is the location of several trailheads. Even this road may be difficult at some times of year, so consult with rangers at the visitors center.

VITAL STATS
Area: 86,500 acres
Tourist Office: Headquarters Visitor Center (☎915-828-3251; www.nps.gov/gumo), in Pine Springs. Accessible by US 62/180 between Carlsbad and El Paso. Open daily 8am-6pm.
Fees: $5 per person.

⚑ CAMPING

Free **backcountry camping ❶** permits are available at the visitors center. None of the backcountry sites in the park has water or toilets. **Pine Springs ❶,** just past park headquarters, and **Dog Canyon ❶,** at the north end of the park, have water and bathrooms but no hookups or showers. Wood and charcoal fires are not allowed. Keep in mind that Dog Canyon is nearly 100 mi. by road from Pine Springs and is nowhere near the park's highlights. You'll probably need a hammer to peg down your tent in the hard-packed desert ground.

(☎915-828-3251. Reservations for groups of 10-20 only. Tent sites $8. Cash only.)

◆ HIKING

There are many rewarding day hikes that highlight the park's best features. A beautiful, moderate hike is **Devil's Hall** (4.2 mi.), which winds through the desert and then descends into a dried-up wash in Pine Springs Canyon among deer, velvet ash, and juniper. Smith **Spring Trail** (2 mi.) is a short, easy trail. **McKittrick Canyon Trail** (4.8-6.8 mi.) is the most popular hike in the park and meanders through thick vegetation alongside McKittrick Stream. The **Bowl Loop** (9 mi.) takes hikers through a conifer forest located high above the road. **Guadalupe Peak** (8 mi.), at 8749 ft., is the highest mountain in Texas and the trail that runs up it is strenuous (3000 ft. elevation gain) but marked by outstanding views. One lengthy hike (24 mi.) follows the **Tejas Trail** from Pine Springs all the way to the Dog Canyon Campground and then returns via the **Bush Mountain Trail.**

> **❓ DID YOU KNOW?** Hikers in the high Guadalupe Mountains are treading on the same rock that forms the underground Carlsbad Caverns.

⛰ THE ROAD TO WHITE'S CITY: 34 MI.

The 34 mi. on **Route 180** between Guadalupe Mountains National Park and the Carlsbad Caverns is also known as the **Texas Mountain Trail.** As you leave, look westward to see the monolithic El Capitan peak thrusting out from the heart of the mountains, a 2000 ft. cliff formed by a Permian limestone reef deposit. Sixteen miles from the Guadalupe Mountains National Park Visitors Center, you will pass into New Mexico, where the speed limit drops to 55 mph.

Land of Enchantment
NEW MEXICO
Welcomes You!

WHITE'S CITY   ☎ 505

The sign at the state line promises that New Mexico is the Land of Enchantment, but the first "city" on this route is anything but. To reach Carlsbad Caverns, you must make a left through White's City, which should perhaps better be called "The Caverns Tourist Trap." White's City consists of a hotel, a restaurant, an RV park, a general store (filled with souvenirs), a museum, and no real populace aside from the tourists. The **Million Dollar Museum,** 17 Carlsbad Caverns Hwy., under the grocery store, feels like being inside a video arcade fortune-telling machine. The museum houses a collection of antiques from the 19th and 20th centuries. The highlights are four grotesque skulls, a two-headed rattlesnake, an "alien baby," and two 6000-year-old mummies believed to have been natives of the area. (☎505-785-2291. Open daily 8am-8pm. $5, ages 6-12 $2.50, under 6 free.) If you're too hungry to make it to Carlsbad, grab a bite at **Velvet Garter/Jack's Restaurant ❸,** 26 Carlsbad Caverns Hwy., which serves burgers, ribs, steaks, and Tex-Mex (entrees $10-11, steaks $15-20) in the evening and breakfast staples ($4-9) in the mornings. (☎505-785-2291. Open daily 7am-8:30pm. AmEx/D/MC/V.)

CARLSBAD CAVERNS NATIONAL PARK ☎505

Imagine the surprise of European explorers in the middle of the New Mexico desert when 250,000 bats appeared out of nowhere. Following the swarm led to the discovery of the Carlsbad Caverns. By 1926, the National Park Service had built trails and installed lights, and colonies of tourists were competing with the bats for space in the caves. Carlsbad Caverns National Park contains one of the world's largest and oldest known cave systems, and even the most experienced caver will be struck by its phenomenal geological formations.The bats reside in a different part of the cavern from that which visitors explore, but you can still witness them flying out of the cave's natural entrance by the thousands each day just before the sun goes down.

▨ ORIENTATION

To check out the oft-forgotten aboveground areas of the park, the only way to go is the

Walnut Canyon Desert Drive, a 9 mi., one-way auto tour on dirt roads (passable to all vehicles). A road guide is available at the beginning of the road (½ mi. from the visitors center). The guide mostly points out plant features and the surface geology of the park, taking note of the fossilized coral reefs that cover the area. The road offers excellent views of the basin below the park and follows a creek bed back to the main road. If you only have a limited amount of time to spend in the park, you might want to skip the road and head straight underground.

VITAL STATS

Area: 47,000 acres

Tourist Office: Visitors Center (☎505-785-2232 or 800-967-2283; www.nps.gov/cave). Open daily from June to mid-Aug. 8am-7pm; from mid-Aug. to May 8am-5:30pm. Last entrance via natural entrance 3:30pm; Last entrance via elevator in summer 5pm; in winter 3:30pm.

Gateway towns: White's City (previous page), Carlsbad (opposite page).

Fees: Entrance $6, ages 6-15 $3. Audio tour $3.

⌂ ACCOMMODATIONS

There are no accommodations in Carlsbad Caverns National Park, but camping is close by in Guadalupe Mountains National Park, and motels line the street in Carlsbad.

◢ CAVES

The most accessible section of the caverns (and the only area that you can enter without reservations) is the **Big Room,** which you can enter at any time either by the natural entrance (a 1 mi. hike descending 750 steep ft. into the cave) or by elevator. Self-guided audio tours are available. The Big Room houses beautiful and skillfully illuminated natural formations, such as a 62 ft. pillar and every kind of stalagmite and stalactite out there. It is circled by a flat, paved 1.2 mi. path and generally takes a little over an hour to complete. Those with severe asthma may have difficulty breathing the moist cave air. Guided tours of caves near the Big Room include a lantern tour though the **Left Hand Tunnel** and a climbing tour of the **Lower Cave.** The guided **King's Palace** tour passes through four of the cave's lowest rooms and some of the most awesome subterranean sights. (Big Room open daily from June to mid-Aug. 8:30am-5pm; from mid-Aug. to May 8:30am-3:30pm. Left Hand Tunnel tour $7. Lower Cave tour M-F $20. King's Palace tour $8, ages 6-15 $4; reservations required.) Plan your visit to the caverns for late afternoon and stick around for the bat flight. Watching the hungry bats storm out of the cavern at dusk is a major tourist draw but hasn't been quite as impressive in the last few years; the colony, which once numbered 300,000-500,000, has dwindled to 24,000 because of pollution and drought. (May-Oct. daily just before sunset.)

Tours of the undeveloped **Slaughter Canyon Cave** offer a unique caving experience. The parking lot is 18 mi. down Rte. 418, an unpaved road several miles south of the park's main entrance on US 62/180. The cave entrance is a steep, strenuous half-mile walk from the lot. While there are no paved tours in the cave, the terrain is fairly flat and mild— and only occasionally slippery. (2hr. tours June-Aug. daily 2 per day; Sept.-May Sa-Su 2 per day. $15, ages 6-15 $7.50. Call the visitors center at least 2 days ahead to reserve. Bring a flashlight.) Tours of **Hall of the White Giant** and **Spider Cave** are the most challenging in the park and require crawling and climbing through tight passages. These tours are not for claustrophobes and should only be undertaken by those in good physical shape. (4hr., 1 per week $20, call at least a month in advance to reserve.) **Backcountry hiking** is permitted aboveground, but a free permit (available at the visitors center), a map, and massive quantities of water are required.

🚗 THE ROAD TO CARLSBAD: 21 MI.

After you exit the park, head north along **US 62/180** until you eventually reach Carlsbad.

CARLSBAD ☎ 505

In 1899, townsfolk decided to name their riverside agricultural settlement after the Karlsbad Spa in the modern Czech Republic, hoping to attract tourists to the area's natural springs. In a weird twist of fate, their wish came true when the splendors of the Carlsbad

Caverns became widely known in the 1920s. Courtesy of Carlsbad Cruiselines, you can rent pedal boats and kayaks or take a 40min. narrated tour aboard the *George Washington* historic paddle boat. (☎505-302-7997; www.carlsbadcruiselines.com. Open from Mar. to Labor Day M-F 11am-dark, Sa-Su 10am-dark. All rentals $12 per hr. Paddle boat tour $5.) If you're in town for the evening, don't miss a movie at the **Fiesta Drive-In ❶**, 401 W. Fiesta Dr. Look for signs on Canal St. Do it 1950s-style by ordering dinner from the concession stand. (☎505-885-4126; www.fiestadrivein.com. 3 screens playing 3 movies nightly at 8:30pm. Gates open at 8pm. Showings F-Sa 11pm. $5 per person or $10 per car.)

The **Stage Coach Inn ❷**, 1819 S. Canal St., is the best of the budget motels and features an outdoor pool, laundry, and clean, comfortable rooms. (☎505-887-1148. Free Wi-Fi. Singles $48; doubles $62. AmEx/D/MC/V.) The **Caverns Motel ❷**, 844 S. Canal St., has some of the cheapest, most respectable accommodations in town. (☎505-887-6522. Free Wi-Fi. Singles $40; doubles $55. Some travelers report that room rates are negotiable. AmEx/D/MC/V.) You can pay to pitch a tent in the **Carlsbad RV Park and Campground ❶**, 4301 National Parks Hwy., 4 mi. south of town. The RV park actually has a surprising number of amenities, including a pool, hot tub, and free Wi-Fi. (☎505-885-6333 or 888-878-7275; www.carlsbadrvpark.com. Rates vary by day and season; call ahead. AmEx/D/MC/V.) Rules and helpful hints pervade the **No Whiner Diner ❸**, 1801 S. Canal St., a classic roadside stop. The menu suggests you tell your waitress what kind of bread you want because "she can't read minds," while the sign out front reminds customers that: "history is a better guide than good intentions." Don't whine, and you'll enjoy huge dinner plates, pastas, and sandwiches. (☎505-239-2815. Entrees $5-9. Open M-Th 11am-2pm and 5-8pm, F 11am-2pm and 5-9pm. AmEx/D/MC/V.) **Mi Casita ❷**, 309 N. Main St., serves great New Mexican food and is often so packed with locals that you'll need to take your meal to the nearby beach. (☎505-628-1393. Huge burritos $3.75. Dinner $9-12. Open Tu-F 10:30am-1:30pm and 5-7:30pm, Sa 7am-1pm. MC/V.) **Red Chimney Pit BBQ ❸**, 817

N. Canal St., does the best barbecue dinners in town. It also 'serves amazing fruit cobblers for dessert. (☎505-885-8744. Open M-F 11am-2pm and 4:30-8:30pm. MC/V.)

⚑ THE ROAD TO ARTESIA: 37 MI.

To leave Carlsbad, head north on **Canal Street** as it veers westward and becomes **Route 285.** Follow Rte. 285 for 35 mi. to Artesia.

ARTESIA   ☎505

The city's slogan is "Artesia: Smells like Success." This might seem funny to a tourist struck by the stench of oil refineries, but Artesians mean it literally: oil is the town's raison d'être. Even the name of the town comes from the nearby Artesian oil wells. On the left as you enter town, the **visitors center,** 107 N. First St., has info and hosts the **Dairy Museum,** a room dedicated to Artesia's other export. (☎505-746-2744. Open M-F 9am-5pm.)

On the way into town, the **Starlite Motel ❷,** 1018 S. 1st St., has decent rooms for those who can't make it to Roswell for the night. (☎505-746-9834. Free Wi-Fi. Continental breakfast included. Singles $45. AmEx/D/MC/V.) The **Wellhead Restaurant ❸,** 332 W. Main St., has everything an oil tycoon could want, including tasty sandwiches, country-fried steak, catfish, salads, and handmade burgers ($6-7), but some travelers report slow and unfriendly service. If you're feeling ignored, drown your sorrows with the homemade beers by brewmaster Diane Riley at the on-site microbrewery; $3.50 buys you a sampler of three of her favorites. (☎505-746-0640; www.thewellhead. com. Entrees $8-15. Open daily 11am-2pm and 5-9pm. Pub open M-Sa 11am-midnight, Su 11am-10pm. AmEx/D/MC/V.) For a place to chill, try **Jahva House ❷,** 105 N. Fifth St., which has modern decor, late hours, and good espresso that will keep you awake during all of 'em. Try the Artesian sandwich with smoked turkey, guacamole, and Havarti. (☎505-746-9494; www.thejahvahouse.com. Open M-Th 7am-8pm, F 7am-10:30pm, Sa 10am-10:30pm. AmEx/D/MC/V.)

⚑ THE ROAD TO ROSWELL: 40 MI.

Follow **First Street** out of Artesia, where it turns back into **US 285** and takes you to Roswell.

ROSWELL   ☎505

Roswell was a small town known only for its dairy industry until July 1947, when an alien spacecraft reportedly crashed on a ranch. The official press release reported that the military had recovered pieces of a "flying saucer," but a retraction followed the next day—the wreckage, the government claimed, was actually a weather balloon. The incident was the birth of Roswell's permanent craze and the beginning of multiple government-conspiracy theories.

WHITE'S CITY: YOUR PERSONAL UTOPIA?

If you liked Carlsbad Caverns more than the average nature area and have a lot of money to throw around, you're in luck. How about owning the caverns' entire gateway city? At press time, White's City, New Mexico, was being put up for sale on the auction site eBay. With a minimum bid set at $1 million and no one currently taking, you still have a chance to make this hamlet your own.

Want to capitalize on high gas prices? White's City comes with the only gas station between Van Horn and Carlsbad. Like food? All of the city's restaurants and the grocery store are included in the deal. Museums? Hotels? Even those get thrown in. They mean it when they say that you're buying the whole city.

Although White's City looks like it has seen better days, it's in your power to change all that. And with 500,000 people coming to visit Carlsbad Caverns every year, there's no shortage of opportunity for capitalistic innovation. The next time *Let's Go* comes through, we could be writing about the booming economy of a little town that used to be known only as the gateway to Carlsbad Caverns. We could be writing about a town that some imaginative reader decided to turn into a nudist colony or the home

Today, traveling skeptics and alien enthusiasts have made tourism a far more lucrative industry than dairy cows. Contrary to expectations, however, aliens do not land on every corner, and there is a disappointing lack of spacecraft debris littering the highways into town.

◈ ORIENTATION

Second Street (US 70/US 380) runs east to west through the middle of town, with intersections at **Sycamore Avenue, Union Avenue, Main Street (US 285),** and **Atkinson Avenue (Route 93).** The main streets parallel to the highway are **Country Club Road, College Boulevard,** and **Eighth Street** to the north and **McGaffey Street, Poe Street,** and **Brasher Road** to the south. Numbered streets begin a bit south of the highway and ascend heading north. Roswell also has some close encounters of the natural kind, with a large park and a trail system that runs parallel to Second St.

VITAL STATS

Population: 45,000

Tourist Office: Roswell Visitors Center, 426 N. Main St. (☎505-624-7704; http://roswell-usa.com), at 5th St. Free Wi-Fi. Open M-F 8:30am-5:30pm, Sa-Su 10am-3pm.

Library and Internet Access: Roswell Public Library, 301 N. Pennsylvania Ave. (☎505-622-7101). Open M-Tu 9am-9pm, W-Sa 9am-6pm, Su 2-6pm.

Post Office: 5904 S. Main St. (☎505-347-2262). Open M-F 8:30am-1pm and 2-4:30pm. **Postal Code:** 88201.

⌂ ACCOMMODATIONS

Budget Inn, 2200 W. 2nd St. (☎800-806-7030). Definitely the best place to crash in Roswell. Recently remodeled rooms. Refrigerators, microwaves, A/C, HBO, coffee, and pool access. Singles $40; doubles $48. AmEx/D/MC/V. ❷

Belmont Hotel, 2100 W. 2nd St. (☎505-623-4522). Smallish rooms. Clean and well-furnished. Singles $50. AmEx/D/MC/V. ❷

Crane Motel, 1212 W. 2nd St. (☎505-623-1293). An awesome illuminated sign. Clean, comfy rooms with fridges, microwaves, A/C, TV, and pool access. Singles $55; doubles $70. AmEx/D/MC/V. ❷

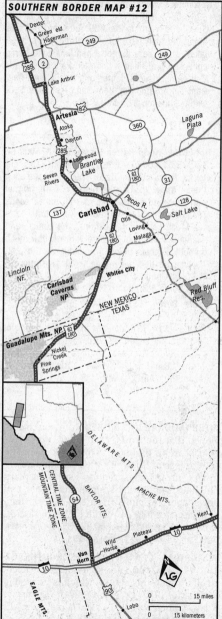

SOUTHERN BORDER MAP #12

Bottomless Lakes State Park, Union Ave. (☎505-624-6058), 12 mi. east of Roswell on US 70/US 380; head south on Rte. 409. You can camp here along the high red bluffs that border 7 pristine lakes, which were formed when limestone caves collapsed and filled with water. Park open daily 7am-9pm. Visitors center open daily June-Aug. 9am-6pm; Sept.-May 8am-5pm. Tent sites $10, with full hookup $18. MC/V. ❶

🍴 FOOD

Not of This World Coffee Bistro, 209 N. Main St. (☎505-627-0077). Props to the management for the flashy outdoor decor; they've got the alien theme down. Inside, the bistro is fairly normal and has good sandwiches ($6-7), baked goods ($1-3), and coffee. Try the heavenly turtle latte ($4), with chocolate, caramel, hazelnuts, and whipped cream, but be sure you ask how much something costs before you order, as the pricing can be deceptive. Free Wi-Fi. Live music F 8-10pm. Open M-Th 7:30am-5:30pm, F 7-11pm, Sa 8:30am-5:30pm. D/MC/V. ❶

Cattle Baron, 1112 N. Main St. (☎505-622-2465). Famous across New Mexico for its steaks ($14-30), though the pasta, chicken, and fish are superb as well. Can be packed at times, so call ahead. Entrees $14-24. Open M-Th 11am-9:30pm, F-Sa 11am-10pm, Su 11am-9pm. AmEx/D/MC/V. ❹

👁 SIGHTS

INTERNATIONAL UFO MUSEUM. If you're convinced that the truth is out there, make this your search's first stop. This museum is the centerpiece of Roswell's UFO-oriented downtown. Surprisingly no-nonsense, it displays timelines, photographs, signed affidavits, and newspaper clippings from the historic incident. Expect lots of reading. *(114 N. Main St., at the corner of 2nd St. ☎800-822-3545. Open daily 9am-5pm. $5, children $2, seniors $3.)*

HISTORICAL CENTER OF THE SOUTHEAST-ERN NEW MEXICO. For something less alien, stroll through this center, which is housed in a beautiful 1910 home and tells the history of Roswell and the county. *(200 N. Lea Ave. ☎505-622-8333. Open daily 1-4pm. Free.)*

🚩 THE ROAD TO LINCOLN: 68 MI.

Take **Second Street** westbound as it turns into **US 380.** After 50 mi. you'll pass through the hamlet of Hondo, which has gas and minimal eats. When the road splits 1 mi. from Hondo, veer right, staying on **US 380,** now called the **Billy the Kid Scenic Byway.**

LINCOLN ☎505

The town of Lincoln, first settled by Mexicans around 1800 and then later by Americans in the 1850s, put the wild in Wild West. Its (in)famous inhabitants have included Kit Carson, Victorio, the last powerful Apache chief, cattle baron John Chisum, and Civil War general Lew Wallace, author of *Ben Hur.* Perhaps the two best known residents of Lincoln, thanks to Hollywood and dime-store novels, are Sheriff Pat Garrett and his nemesis, William H. Bonney (a.k.a. Billy the Kid). These two lived at a time when Lincoln was so lawless that from 1876 to 1879 the area erupted in combat known as the "Lincoln County War." The town itself looks much as it did at the time of the county war, and its buildings have been maintained in close-to-original state. Six of the buildings are open to the public and feature museum-quality exhibits preserving the Lincoln of yore. The **Lincoln State Monument Visitors Center and Museum,** on your right as you enter town, tells the story of the county war and sells one ticket ($5) that includes all of the other buildings and museums. Make sure to see the **Tunstall Museum and the Courthouse,** featuring the bullet hole that, according to legend, Billy made when he escaped Garrett's jail. (☎505-653-4025. Open daily 8:30am-4:30pm. Cash only.)

🚩 THE ROAD TO SMOKEY BEAR HISTORI-CAL PARK: 12 MI.

Follow **US 380** out of Lincoln as it winds its way to the junction with **Route 48.** The park is to the right.

SMOKEY BEAR HISTORICAL PARK ☎505

Smokey the Bear was found in May 1950, orphaned by a raging fire in the Lincoln National Forest. After the badly burnt black bear cub healed, he was sent to the National

Zoo in Washington, DC, where he became the spokesbear for preventing forest fires. This park is not a park in the sense of a state or national park. Instead, it is a walled-in area landscaped to represent the six different ecological zones found in New Mexico. A path guides you along a guided walk that eventually winds up at Smokey's final resting place. Smokey is buried within view of the mountain where he was originally found. The gateway village to the park is the village of Capitan, where half of the establishments are named for Smokey. (☎505-354-2748. Open daily 9am-5pm. $2, children $1.)

THE ROAD TO RUIDOSO: 19 MI.

From Capitan, follow signs to **Route 48** and head southwest for 19 mi. to Ruidoso. Rte. 48 turns into **Mechem Drive,** which takes you through the outskirts of town until it dead-ends at **Sudderth Drive.** Head left to see the full extent of Ruidoso's mountain-tourist paradise and also to get to **US 70.**

RUIDOSO   ☎505

During ski season, the mountain hideaway of Ruidoso turns into a bustling tourist hub. Do not leave town without taking the scenic drive up **Sierra Blanca.** Towering at 12,000 ft., the peak of Sierra Blanca looms over Ruidoso's sprawl of expensive hotels and cabins, and the 11 mi. winding ascent offers views that only birds wouldn't envy. Switchbacks snake their way through pine forests and aspen groves up to the **Windy Point Vista,** where you can stare hundreds of miles eastward. Those fit enough to handle the demanding climb through thin air should take the **Lincoln National Forest Scenic Trail,** which departs from just outside the Ski Apache valley and connects with the crest trail; it heads above the treeline to wildflower meadows at the mountain's summit. After 3 mi., hikers are rewarded with a 360° panorama that encompasses everything from Mexico to White Sands to Texas. Follow the signs for skiing and recreation just outside Ruidoso on Rte. 48.

During the peak summer and winter seasons, it may be difficult to find an affordable room in town. A few budget motels can be found along US 70, but most of the action is on Sudderth Dr. The **Alpine Lodge ❷,** 2805 Sudderth Dr., has small but clean rooms for decent prices. Jeanne, the owner, dispenses advice both in person and on her business cards. (☎505-257-4423. Singles $45; doubles $50. MC/V.) The **Arrowhead Motel ❸,** 616 US 70, west of town, has large rooms with recliners and queen-size beds as well as a friendly staff. (☎888-547-6652; www.ruidoso.net/arrowhead. Singles from $49; doubles from $59. D/MC/V.) A lively 20-something crowd enjoys pool, video games, a back patio, and 17 beers on tap at **Farley's ❸,** 1200 Mechem Dr., which doubles as a family restaurant serving burgers,

ROSWELL, NEW MEXICO: OUT OF THIS WORLD

Something crashed onto Mac Brazel's ranch on July 4, 1947, but what it was is still up for debate. Most Roswell residents believe it was a flying saucer and have collected much evidence—and even created a museum—to prove it. Others, guffawing at the extraterrestrial hype, theorize that the object was merely a weather balloon or physics experiment gone awry. Either way, the series of events that took place are worthy of note. The perplexed Brazel took a sackful of debris to Fort Worth, where US Army Intelligence took possession of it. Brazel was told to step out of the room and claims that, when he returned, the original debris had been replaced with different material. Later, Roswell undertaker Glenn Davis claims to have received a strange call from the Army asking how many "hermetically sealed" child-size caskets he had. Believers maintain that a Roswell nurse was brought in to the Army air base hospital to examine alien bodies; legend holds that she was transferred to England the next day but, before leaving, gave Davis hand-drawn pictures of the alien forms she had examined. In 1994 the US military released a hefty report explaining that the alleged alien debris was in reality part of Project Mogul, a top-secret American Cold War-era effort to search high in the atmosphere for reverberations from Soviet nuclear test blasts. Many maintain, though, that this report is but an extension of the earlier cover-up and, their beliefs encouraged by popular movies such as *Independence Day*, continue to argue that the government is in secret communication with aliens.

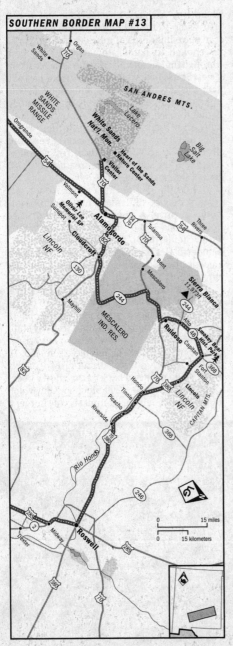

SOUTHERN BORDER MAP #13

hot dogs, chicken strips, and fajitas during the day. The menu at Farley's devotes almost three pages to drinks. (☎505-258-5676. Open M-Th 11:30am-midnight, F-Sa 11:30am-1am, Su 11am-11pm. AmEx/D/MC/V.)

THE ROAD TO CLOUDCROFT: 37 MI.
Leave town on **US 70 West,** and a few miles down you'll pass a sign indicating that you're in the **Mescalero Indian Reservation.** During the First week of July, the Mescalero hold a traditional Apache coming-of-age ceremony; visitors are welcome to attend, but you must call the **Mescalero Cultural Center** (☎505-464-4494) beforehand for instructions regarding proper etiquette. Make a left turn and head southeast on **Route 244** for 30 mi. to reach Cloudcroft.

CLOUDCROFT ☎505

Perched above 8500 ft., this mountaintop village is in a drastically different environment than the desert valley below; Cloudcroft promises both heady altitudes and heady prices. The "playland of the four seasons" lures visitors with a climate ranging from snowy flurries to breezy summer days. The premier budget accommodation in the area is the ■Cloudcroft **Mountain Park Hostel ❶,** 1049 US 82, which opened in October 2005 and stands on 27 acres next to the Lincoln National Forest. It is quiet and clean, with a living room, TV, kitchen, and large front porch. The private rooms are especially nice and should be reserved in advance. Six miles west of town, look for the oil drum with "hostel" painted across it. (☎505-682-0555; www.cloudcrofthostel.com. Free Wi-Fi. Dorms $17; private rooms $30. Cash only.) The **Aspen Motel ❷,** 1315 US 82, features remodeled rooms nestled into the hillside. (☎505-682-2526. Rooms $45. AmEx/D/MC/V.) Camping opportunities abound among the majestic pines of Lincoln National Forest. The **Apache Campground ❶,** 3 mi. northeast of Cloudcroft along Rte. 244, has 24 wooded sites with hot showers and many cross-country ski trails. (☎505-682-2551. Showers $3. Sites $11. Cash only.) In the costly **Lodge Hotel** (☎800-395-6343), **Rebecca's ❹** is named for the hotel ghost, who may well be sticking around for the gourmet food. The stately dining room serves delicious (if pricey) meals, with excellent fish and steak selections. Take the last left as you exit Cloudcroft on US 82 and look for the sign. (☎505-682-3131. Entrees $20-25. Dress code "resort casual." Open daily 7-10:30am, 11:30am-2:30pm, and 5:30-9pm. AmEx/D/MC/V.)

⛰ THE ROAD TO ALAMOGORDO: 20 MI.

Head west on **US 82.** As you depart, notice the old trestles in the gorges; these are remnants of the 19th-century tourist railroad that transported the summer's overheated Texans from El Paso to Cloudcroft. The road makes its way down 4312 ft. in these 16 mi., so exercise caution. (If that doesn't convince you, note that speeding fines are doubled in this area.) Halfway down the mountain, the road passes through New Mexico's only tunnel. **Route 82** intersects with **US 70/US 54;** take a left (south) on US 70 to enter Alamogordo.

ALAMOGORDO   ☎505

Alamogordo is Spanish for "fat poplar," but there are few trees in the town. Instead, there is a forest of motel, fast-food, and gas-station signs along **US 70 (White Sands Boulevard).** While sights in the town may be scarce, Alamogordo does provide plenty of eating and sleeping opportunities and is a good base for exploring the area. Head to the **Satellite Inn ❷,** 2224 N. White Sands Blvd., for clean rooms with Internet access and a pool. (☎800-221-7690; www.satelliteinn.com. Continental breakfast included. Internet. Singles $38; doubles $42. AmEx/D/MC/V.) **Memories ❸,** 1223 New York Ave., is a beautiful restaurant in a restored historic home that serves good seafood—a precious commodity in the desert. (☎505-437-0077. Burgers $4.50. Seafood dishes $11-15. Steaks $14-17. Open M-Sa 11am-9pm. MC/V.) **Maximinos ❷,** 2300 N. White Sands Blvd., has breakfast burritos for $3.75; chicken mole runs $7. (☎505-443-6102. All-you-can-eat lunch buffet Tu and Th-Su 11am-2pm; $6.50. Open Tu-F 8am-2pm and 5-9pm, Sa 8am-9pm, Su 8am-3pm. AmEx/D/MC/V.) The **Lincoln National Forest Office,** 1101 New York Ave., provides info on hiking or camping trips in the Sacramento Mountains. (☎505-434-7200. Open M-F 7:30am-4:30pm.) **Outdoor Adventures,**

1516 10th St., rents good bikes and provides advice on trails in the area. (☎505-434-1920; www.outdooradventuresnm.com. Bikes $20 per day. Open M-F 10am-6pm, Sa 10am-5pm.)

⛰ THE ROAD TO WHITE SANDS NATIONAL MONUMENT: 13 MI.

To get to **White Sands National Monument,** take **White Sands Boulevard (US 70/Route 54)** southwest out of town. Thirteen miles on your right you'll find the National Monument Visitors Center.

WHITE SANDS NATIONAL MONUMENT   ☎505

Perhaps the world's greatest beach (minus the water), the white gypsum dunes of White Sands National Monument inspire awe both for their purity and for their bleakness. The Tularosa Basin, bordered by the Sacramento and San Andres Mountains, lacks any outlet to the sea, so rainwater collects at the low point, known as Lake Lucero. As the desert heat evaporates the lake water, gypsum crystals collect on the dry bed and are swept away by the wind, transforming them into blindingly white sand that collects as dunes. In these forbidding and treacherous conditions, only a few highly adaptive species can survive. The white lizards and fast-growing plants are nearly as astounding as the dunes.

VITAL STATS
Area: 144,000 acres
Tourist Office: White Sands Visitor Center (☎505-479-6124; www.nps.gov/whsa), on US 70. Open daily June-Aug. 8am-7pm; Sept.-May 8am-6pm. Park open daily June-Aug. 7am-9pm; Sept.-May 7am-sunset.
Gateway Town: Alamogordo (this page).
Fees: $3, under 16 free.

◾ ORIENTATION

The **Dunes Drive** is the only real way to access the park. Beginning at the visitors center, the scenic road (16 mi. round-trip) winds from the edge of the dunes to the **Heart of the Sands drive.**

Exhibits along the way provide information about geology and natural history. The park is occasionally closed for missile testing at the nearby **White Sands Missile Range**, so call ahead or check the website for closure times.

> **? DID YOU KNOW?** Why is a sand dune, like White Sands, a "monument"? Since the days of Teddy Roosevelt, presidents have been able to declare a site a "monument" in order to preserve it in a jiffy. A more lengthy process is required for Congress to declare a site a "national park."

CAMPING

There are no established campgrounds available in the park, but 10 daily permits for the primitive **backcountry camping ❶** are available on a first come, first served basis. ($3 per person. Cash only.) The sites have no water or toilet facilities and are not accessible by any road; to reach them, you must hike 1-2 mi. through the sand dunes. Campers must register in person at the visitors center and be in their sites before dark.

OUTDOORS

The most popular activity at White Sands is sand surfing (though careening down the incredibly steep sides of 25 ft. dunes via sled is more akin to tobogganing than surfing). You can purchase a surfing disc (a saucer-shaped sled) from the gift shop for $9.50; they'll buy it back from you for $3.50, so keep your receipt. Although the dunes are steep, the sand puts up a good fight; be sure to grab some sled wax from the gift shop so that you can have a decent ride. Roadtrippers who are around for one of the monthly ranger-led auto caravans have the chance to travel across the open dunes to Lake Lucero. (3hr. advance reservations required; contact the visitors center for information.) Informative ranger-led walks are held daily at sunset, which is a particularly beautiful time to be out on the dunes. Walks begin 1hr. before sunset. At any time, you can walk along the **Interdune Boardwalk** (½ mi.), which carves an easy route above

the sands. Another easy but rewarding walkway is the **Dune Life Nature Trail** (1 mi.), which makes a loop through the edges of the dunes where plants and wildlife are more abundant. The strenuous **Alkali Flat Trail** (4 mi.) loops from the Heart of the Sands to the edge of the salty lakebed of **Lake Otero**. Even if there isn't enough time or it's too hot for the whole Alkali trail, it's worth your while to hike just a short distance—you'll be struck by the sheer vastness of the seemingly interminable dunes. Off-trail hiking is permitted anywhere along the eastern edge of the park. On full-moon nights in the summer, the park stays open until 11pm (last entrance 10pm). Ask the rangers about stargazing activities, including the yearly ✦**star party** held in late September.

THE ROAD TO OLIVER LEE MEMORIAL: 25 MI.

Head back east on **US 70**. Pass through the outskirts of Alamogordo and take **US 54** 10 mi. to the entrance of Oliver Lee Memorial State Park. Turn left into the park gate and drive 4 mi. to the visitors center.

OLIVER LEE MEMORIAL STATE PARK ☎ 505

Perched at the mouth of a vast canyon at the edge of the Sacramento Mountains, the Oliver Lee Memorial State Park provides a panoramic view of the canyon and the desert below. Those up for a challenge should think about trekking at least a half-mile up the mountain's face on the ludicrously steep **Dog Canyon Trail** (5.5 mi. round-trip) to behold an astonishing vista of the Tularosa Basin. A less strenuous way to see some of the park is by walking the **Riparian Nature Trail** (½ mi.) through a stream-fed canyon. The park has excellent **camping ❶** with clean showers, but make sure you watch out for rattlesnakes, especially the venomous western diamondback, which calls Oliver Lee home. (☎505-437-8284; www.emnrd.state.nm.us/nmparks. Visitors center open daily 9am-4pm. Entrance $5 per vehicle. Sites $10, with hookup $14. Cash only.)

THE ROAD TO EL PASO: 77 MI.

Head back to **US 54** and go west. The only civilization that intrudes on the desert vistas is the busted mining town of Orogrande, which exists today only as a gas station strategically placed to save the lives of those who forgot to fill up in Alamogordo. Enter El Paso by following US 54 until it branches into **I-10.** Follow I-10 to downtown and take **Exit 19A (Mesa Street)** or **19B.**

The Lone Star State
TEXAS
Welcomes You!

EL PASO ☎ 915

Since it was first established in the 17th century, this Texas city has always been "the pass." It is a gateway to Mexico, the Rio Grande, the western deserts, and the eastern Texas rangeland. As Americans have begun to worry increasingly about the Mexican border, El Paso's reputation and the tourism industry have suffered. Residents are more than aware of the politics at stake, and aren't afraid to engage the issue while proudly promoting the city's reputation as "second-safest city in the US" (Honolulu is safer.) The truth is that El Paso is a lively town with a world-class art museum, a historic downtown core, excellent Mexican restaurants, and fabulous desert scenery just minutes away.

VITAL STATS

Population: 560,000

Tourist Office: El Paso Convention and Visitors Bureau, 1 Civic Center Plaza (☎915-534-0600 or 800-351-6024; www.visitelpaso.com), at Santa Fe and Mills Ave. Open M-F 8am-5pm.

Library and Internet Access: El Paso Public Library, 501 N. Oregon St. (☎915-543-5401). Open M-Th 9am-8pm, F 11am-6pm, Sa 9am-6pm, Su 1-5pm.

Post Office: 219 E. Mills Ave. (☎915-532-8824), between Mesa and Stanton St. Open M-F 8:30am-5pm, Sa 8:30am-noon. **Postal Code:** 79901.

✈ ORIENTATION

While El Paso and Ciudad Juárez, its Mexican sister city, sprawl across the valley floor, the downtown districts of both cities are relatively small and easily navigable. **San Jacinto Plaza,** at the corner of **Main** and **Oregon Street,** is the heart of El Paso. **I-10** runs east-west through the city and intersects with north-south **US 54** in a mess of tangled concrete fondly dubbed "the spaghetti bowl." **US 85** becomes **Paisano Drive** as it enters downtown. Paisano Dr. and **San Antonio Avenue** are two of the city's major east-west arteries. **Santa Fe Avenue, Stanton Street,** and **El Paso Street** run north-south, with El Paso St. continuing to the border crossing. The main north-south artery is Mesa St., which connects to the **Trans Mountain Road,** leading through Franklin State Park. Streetside parking all over El Paso could not be easier, since the city is so spread out. Tourists should be wary of the streets between San Antonio Ave. and the border late at night.

> **? DID YOU KNOW?** Some of the South's larger border crossings see hundreds of senior citizens making a run for the border every day. What do they come for? The drugs. Mexican border towns often have discount pharmacies, where regular prescription drugs are much cheaper than in the US. *Let's Go* does not recommend drug-running.

⌂ ACCOMMODATIONS

There are motels along Dyer and Alameda St. Beautifully situated camping is available in the **Franklin Mountains State Park ❶.** Four of the five sites have shelters and, while there are clean outhouses, there is no water or electricity. The sites are reached from the park entrance along the Trans Mountain Rd., but, if you're planning to arrive after the park closes, you must contact the rangers in advance to get the gate combination. (☎915-566-6441. Reservations recommended. Sites $8. Cash only.)

Gardner Hotel, 311 E. Franklin Ave. (☎915-532-3661; www.gardnerhotel.com), between Stanton and Kansas St. Has housed weary travelers since 1922. El Paso's oldest hotel. John Dillinger, the famous bank robber, stayed here in 1934. Make calls from a wood phone booth and take the cage elevator up from the ornate lobby. Singles $48, with private bath from $54. MC/V. ❷

El Paso International Hostel, 311 E. Franklin Ave. (☎915-532-3661). Takes great pride in meeting the needs of backpackers, offering clean, 4-bed, single-sex rooms with a full kitchen and a large lounge. Unfortunately, the hostel has no parking of its own, so you have to park on the street, and the city begins ticketing parking meters M-Sa at 8am. Pool table free. HI, HA, ISIC, student, or teacher ID required. Towels $0.50. Laundry $1.50. Internet $1 per 15min. Check-out noon. 4-bed dorms $20; 2-bed $25. MC/V. ❶

Gold Star Inn, 1401 N. Mesa, (☎915-533-2220). Clean, spacious rooms. Located in a relatively safe area. Singles $34; doubles $43. AmEx/D/MC/V. ❷

🍴 FOOD

There's no shortage of good Mexican food in downtown El Paso, and prices are generally cheap. El Paso's fast-food joints cluster around Stanton and Texas St. Be aware that many downtown restaurants close at 5pm and on the weekends.

The Tap Bar and Restaurant, 408 E. San Antonio Ave. (☎915-532-1848). The burritos ($2-3.25), chicken tacos ($6), and *chiles rellenos* ($8) are delicious. Open M-Sa 9am-2am, Su 10am-2am. Kitchen open until 10pm. AmEx/D/MC/V. ❷

Carlos and Mickey's, 1310 Magruder St. (☎915-778-3323), off Montana St. Sit at the bar and get a bowl of fried ice cream, an El Paso specialty, for $3.50. A full selection of Mexican and American food and a wide variety of vegetarian options. Entrees $10-15. Open daily 11am-10pm. Bar open M-Th and Su 11:30am-11pm, F-Sa 11:30am-1:30am. AmEx/D/MC/V. ❶

👁 SIGHTS

Self-guided walking tours of the historic downtown and its restored buildings are a great way to spend a few hours. The visitors center has pamphlets with the route laid out.

EL PASO MUSEUM OF ART. This is the undisputed jewel of El Paso's museums and features over 5000 works in a nicely renovated building. Particularly impressive are the 19th- and 20th-century Southwestern and Mexican colonial collections. The museum also features a collection of Mexican-American art donated to the museum by none other than Cheech Marin, of Cheech and Chong fame. *(1 Arts Festival Plaza. ☎915-532-1707. Open Tu-Sa 9am-5pm, Th 9am-9pm, Su noon-5pm. Free.)*

NATIONAL BORDER PATROL MUSEUM. Regardless of your politics, this museum gives a sense of the very real issues at stake in El Paso. The exhibits, which span history from the Old West to the present and include vehicles, guns, paintings, and photos, will leave you rolling your eyes or applauding the bravery of the border guards and vigilantes. *(4315 Trans Mountain Rd. ☎915-759-6060; www.borderpatrolmuseum.com. Open Tu-Sa 9am-5pm. Free.)*

CHAMIZAL NATIONAL MEMORIAL. If you're interested in the more peaceful side of US-Mexico relations, check out this memorial, which commemorates the diplomatic resolution of a centuries-old border dispute, and was created to help illustrate the history of friendship and cooperation between the two countries. Visitors can lounge on the beautifully kept grounds, located right on the shore of the Rio Grande, or check out several art galleries featuring art that somehow ties into the spirit of the memorial. *(800 S. San Marcial St. ☎915-532-7273. Park open daily 5am-10pm. Visitors center and galleries open Tu-Sa 10am-5pm. Free.)*

WYLER AERIAL TRAMWAY. The tramway takes visitors to the top of Ranger Peak (5632 ft.). The third tramway of its kind in the US, it was built in 1960 to service TV and radio antennas. On a clear day, you can see 7000 sq. mi. from the top—all the way to the Guadalupe Mountains and Ruidoso. If you're around for the night, go up just before sunset—you won't regret it. *(1700 McKinley Ave. ☎915-562-9899. Open M and Th noon-6pm, F-Su noon-9pm. $7, children $4.)*

🎵 ENTERTAINMENT

For shows and events around town, leaf through the free weekly *What's Up.* If you're in town on Sunday, don't miss **Music Under the Stars,** the hugely popular free summer concert series in Chamizal National Memorial Park. Shows range from Brazilian jazz to flamenco to symphonic, and there is always dancing and food. (☎915-541-4481; www.elpasotexas. gov/mcad. Shows June-Aug. Su 7:30pm.) Free concerts, dubbed **Alfresco Fridays,** are held every Friday in summer at Arts Festival Plaza, near the El Paso Museum of Art. You'll hear local bands that represent a wide variety of genres. (☎915-541-4481; www.elpasotexas. gov/mcad. June-Aug. F 5:30pm.)

> ⚠ **BORDER ALERT.** For anyone traveling around the southern border, be aware that the United States Supreme Court has ruled it constitutional for border control checkpoints to be set up within 100 mi. of the US-Mexico border. At these checkpoints, every single car is required to stop and answer a few simple questions. Border Patrol agents then ask to check the trunks of any cars they would like; such an inspection is usually very brief. However, it is within your constitutional rights to refuse such a request. These checkpoints exist to look for the presence of illegal immigrants or drugs being smuggled into the country. Many larger checkpoints have drug-sniffing dogs at them, which can detect even a very small amount of any illegal substance. Border checkpoints should generally be nothing more than a minor hassle or delay for you, but realize that there are between 35 and 40 of them out there at any given time.

🎵 NIGHTLIFE

Most would-be partiers cross the border in order to take advantage of the lower drinking age and cheaper prices at bars in Ciudad Juárez. Still, there remain a number of good options north of the Rio Grande.

Cincinnati Bar, 207 Cincinnati Ave. (☎915-532-5592). One of the most happening places to be on F night if you're college-aged. All drinks $2 Tu. Open mike Th. Happy hour daily 2-7pm; all drinks $1 off. Open daily 2pm-2am. AmEx/D/MC/V.

El Paso

▲ ♠ **ACCOMMODATIONS**
El Paso International Hostel, 4
Franklin Mountains State Park, 3
Gardner Hotel, 5
Gold Star Inn, 1

🍴 **FOOD**
Carlos and Mickey's, 6
The Tap Bar and Restaurant, 9

🍸 **NIGHTLIFE**
Cincinnati Bar, 2
Dome Bar, 8

Dome Bar, 101 S. El Paso St. (☎915-534-3000, ext. 5012), in the Camino Real Hotel downtown. Serves martinis and mojitos in the aesthetically appealing lobby of a restored 1912 hotel. It's worth dropping by for the gorgeous decor—if not for the chocolate cake and raspberry sauce martini ($9). Mixed drinks $8-10. Beers on tap $5. Live music (salsa, jazz, and instrumental) plays Th-Sa nights at 9:30pm. Open M-Th and Su 3pm-midnight, F-Sa 3pm-2am. AmEx/D/MC/V.

🏔 OUTDOORS

North of downtown, **Franklin Mountains State Park** covers 24,000 acres, making it the largest urban wilderness park in the US. The park's visitors center is located in McKelling-

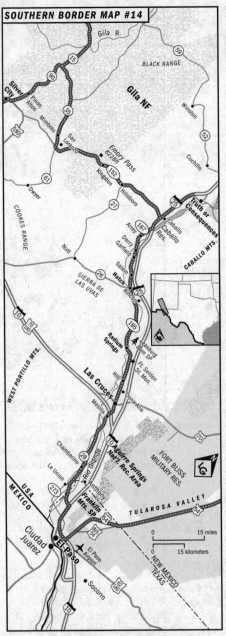

SOUTHERN BORDER MAP #14

ton Canyon on the east side of the Franklin Mountains. From downtown, take Scenic Dr. east, and turn left onto Alabama St., following it for a couple of miles. Turn left at McKellington Canyon Rd. (Visitors center open daily 8am-4pm. Park open June-Sept. M-F 8am-8pm, Sa-Su 8am-6:30pm; Oct.-May daily 8am-5pm. Park entrance $4.) Franklin Mountains is reserved almost exclusively for the use of hikers, and there is a wide variety of routes that weave throughout the park. The most popular hike is **West Cottonwood Spring** (1½ mi. one-way), which begins at Sneed's Cory and makes a loop leading to a spring with a breathtaking view of the valley. Also starting at Sneed's Cory, the **North Franklin Peak Trail** (8 mi. round-trip) is a difficult hike to the top of 7200 ft. Mt. Franklin. The **Aztec Caves Trail** (1¼ mi. one-way) is a steep 2hr. workout. To reach the trailhead, take the second right after the fee station. For those who don't feel like sweating profusely, **Upper Sunset** (1½ mi. one-way), which runs along the western edge of the mountain, is an easier but still popular hike. The trail begins just after the fee station on the left side of the road. The Tom Mays section of the park is a perfect setting for hiking, mountain biking, and rock climbing and is accessible only from the west side of the Franklin Mountains. Ask at the park's main gate for trail maps.

🚗 THE ROAD TO LAS CRUCES: 46 MI.

From El Paso, hop on **I-10 West** to get to Las Cruces.

Land of Enchantment
NEW MEXICO
Welcomes You!

LAS CRUCES ☎ 505

Las Cruces was named for the many crosses in the area that marked the graves of early pioneers. Perhaps the heat killed them: the city gets 350 days of sunshine per year. To make the most of your visit, bypass the car dealerships, strip malls, and chain motels that make up the city and take advantage of the good weather by heading outdoors; take a walking tour of historic Mesilla or go hiking in the beautiful Organ Mountains.

ORIENTATION

Las Cruces is framed by **I-25** to the east and **I-10** to the south. East to west, the major north-south streets are **Telshor Boulevard** (I-25), **Main Street,** and **Valley Drive. Lohman Avenue, Amador Avenue,** and **Picacho Avenue** run east-west through the city, while **University Avenue** forms the southern boundary. This road leads east to the Organ Mountains and is the easiest route to the Mesilla plaza. Parking in Las Cruces is generally free and easy to locate.

VITAL STATS

Population: 86,000

Tourist Office: Las Cruces Convention and Visitors Bureau, 211 N. Water St. (☎505-541-2444; www.lascrucescvb.org). Free Wi-Fi. Open M-F 8am-5pm.

Library and Internet Access: Thomas Branigan Memorial Library, 200 E. Picacho Ave. (☎505-528-4000). Open June-July M-Th 8am-9pm, F 8am-6pm, Sa 10am-6pm; Aug.-May. M-Th 8am-9pm, F 8am-6pm, Sa 10am-6pm, Su 1-5pm.

Post Office: 201 E. Las Cruces Ave. (☎505-524-2903). Open M-F 8am-6pm, Sa 8-11:30am. **Postal Code:** 88001.

ACCOMMODATIONS

Cheap motels line Picacho Ave. to the west of Valley Dr. This area can be unsafe at night, so exercise caution when alone. Other motels cluster around the I-10 and I-25 exits, and motels in Las Cruces are rather inexpensive.

Lundeen Inn of the Arts Bed and Breakfast, 618 S. Alameda Blvd. (☎505-526-3327 or 888-526-3326; www.innofthearts.com). Located in a beautifully decorated 100-year-old adobe mansion. Serves as both a guesthouse and local art gallery and is worth the premium price. The spacious rooms are named after local artists, are well decorated, and have luxurious baths. Reception 8am-10pm. Reservations required. Singles $79-89; doubles $82-125. AmEx/D/MC/V. ❸

Day's End Lodge, 755 N. Valley Dr. (☎505-524-7753). Offers clean accommodations with free popcorn and morning coffee. A/C and cable TV. Singles $37. AmEx/D/MC/V. ❷

FOOD

Culinary options in Las Cruces revolve around chain restaurants, but there are a number of interesting places to dine in Mesilla.

La Posta, 2410 Calle de San Albino (☎505-524-3524; www.laposta-de-mesilla.com), off Avenida de Mesilla. Located in an adobe structure that once housed road-weary travelers from the Butterfield Trail, including Billy the Kid, Kit Carson, and Pancho Villa. Now it houses a large water fountain, a gift shop, and a collection of parrots. Combination plates run $9. Entrees cost $7-14. Open M-Th and Su 11am-9pm, F-Sa 11am-9:30pm. AmEx/D/MC/V. ❸

El Comedor, 2190 Avenida de Mesilla (☎505-524-7002). An understated restaurant that serves up big Mexican specialty plates. Try the Doña Ana Fajitas ($9.75) or the tacos al pastor ($7.50). Entrees $7-10. Open M-Th 9am-8pm, F-Sa 9am-9pm, Su 9am-3pm. AmEx/D/MC/V. ❷

The Chocolate Lady, 2379 Calle de Guadalupe (☎575-526-2744), located right across from the Mesilla plaza. The shop is so small that you may not be able to stay out of the sun for very long, but at least you can grab one of over 30 different varieties of ice cream ($2-4) to take your mind off it. Open M-F 10:30am-5pm, Sa 10:30am-5:30pm, Su noon-5pm. MC/V. ❶

International Delights, 1245 El Paseo (☎505-647-5956), in the corner of the Albertson's shopping center. A comfortable haven away from the city's suburban sprawl. Has a relaxed atmosphere and a full selection of coffee drinks ($1-3.50) and sandwiches. Falafel $5. Turkey and Swiss $7.50. Open M-Sa 7am-midnight, Su 8am-midnight. AmEx/D/MC/V. ❶

High Desert Brewing Co., 1201 W. Hadley Ave. (☎505-525-6752), off Valley Rd. The only local brewery in town. Serves up an award-winning selection of beers. The sampler, which isn't on the menu, includes 4.5 oz. glasses for $5. You can also taste up to 2 shots of beer for free. Pints $3.50. Burgers $6-7. Burrito plate $7. Th and Sa Live music Th and Sa 8-11pm. Open M-Sa 11am-midnight, Su noon-10pm. Kitchen open M-Sa until 10pm, Su until 9pm. D/MC/V. ❷

👁 SIGHTS

▓GIANT ROADRUNNER MADE OF RECYCLED TRASH. Las Cruces has its own roadside oddity: a giant roadrunner made from recycled trash, perched high on a hillside rest stop. The roadrunner was made in the mid-1990s by a resident in protest of recyclable material being thrown into the city's dump. First displayed in the dump, the roadrunner was such a hit that he was moved to this more visible hilltop perch. From the 20 ft. tall, 42 ft. long roadrunner, you can see the entire Mesilla Valley. *(Take I-10 W. out of Las Cruces to Exit 135. The bird can be seen from the westbound lanes, but the rest stop can only be visited from the eastbound lanes.)*

MESILLA. Though Las Cruces is the demographic center of the area, Mesilla, 3 mi. southwest, is the cultural center. When the US acquired the land in 1854 with the Gadsden Purchase, Mesilla became an important stop for traders and travelers en route to San Francisco. By the 1880s, the town was as wild as any in the West; it was in Mesilla that Billy the Kid was tried for murder and sentenced to hang in 1881. Mesilla looks much the same as it did in the 1880s, and most of the adobe buildings around the central plaza date back 150 years. While the shops are very touristy, selling arts and crafts, postcards, and t-shirts, the adobe-ringed plaza is lovely. The majestic **San Albino Church,** originally built as an adobe structure in 1855, presides over the square. Inside are an array of woodcarvings, paintings, and relief paintings as well as a small display room showing the development of the church. *(2250 Calle Principal. ☎505-526-9349. Open M-Tu and Th-F 1-3pm. Su mass 8, 11am. Free.)*

🏔 OUTDOORS

Las Cruces provides decent mountain biking opportunities. The **"A" Mountain Trail** (3.5 mi. loop) is a moderately difficult ride around the base of the hill at the east end of New Mexico State University's campus that has some technical sections. The trail takes its name from the "A" formed by the white stones that adorn the mountain's east face, visible from most of Las Cruces. The length of the **Sierra Vista Trail** (14 mi. round-trip) makes it somewhat more difficult, and, although it is not particularly steep, it includes some rolling hills. The most technically challenging trail is the **SST Trail** (6 mi. one way). Check with the bike shop **Outdoor Adventures,** 1424 Missouri Ave., for more information on these and other trails. (☎505-521-1922. Bikes $20 per day. Open M-F 10am-7pm, Sa 10am-5pm.)

☒ DETOUR
ORGAN MOUNTAINS

Drive east on **US 70** for 15 mi. Turn left on **Aguirre Spring Road** to camp or follow **Dripping Springs Road** 11 mi. east of the city to reach the visitors center.

East of Las Cruces, the jagged Organ Mountains provide opportunities for hiking, mountain biking, and rock climbing. On the western slope of the Organ Mountains, the **Dripping Springs Trail** leads you 1½ mi. uphill past the Dripping Springs to the ruins of an old resort. Half a mile west of the visitors center, the **La Cueva Trail** is an easy half-mile walk to a cool, small cave that has housed countless inhabitants throughout history. For more info, check at the **AB Cox Visitors Center.** Follow the signs from University Blvd. (☎505-522-1219. Open daily 8am-5pm. Park open until 7pm in the summer.) On the eastern slope of the Organ Mountains, Aguirre Springs is farther from Las Cruces and offers challenging hiking opportunities. The **Aguirre Springs National Recreation Area** is an idyllic place to pitch your tent, with isolated, quiet camping against a background of gorgeous mountains and desert valleys. Each site has a grill and is near an outhouse. (☎505-644-9143. Open daily from mid-Apr. to mid-Oct. 8am-8pm; from mid-Oct. to mid-Apr. 8am-6pm. Vault toilets. Water available at campground host's site. $3 per vehicle. Sites $3. Cash only.) To reach hiking trails, follow **Aguirre Spring Road** through the campground and look for the trail markers leading off the road. You can park your car at the pull-offs.

☒ THE ROAD TO RADIUM SPRINGS: 19 MI.

From Las Cruces, go north on **Valley Road** until it turns into **Route 185.** Follow Rte. 185 for 15 mi. and turn at the sign for Fort Selden. For a less scenic but quicker route, hop on **I-25 North** and take it to **Exit 19.**

RADIUM SPRINGS   ☎505

While you'll be hard-pressed to find any radium or springs here, you can find intriguing ruins at the old **Fort Selden State Monument,** 1280 Fort Selden Rd. The fort marks the beginning of the *jornada del muerto* (journey of death), where the era's longest highway, **El Camino Real,** curved away from the Rio Grande. The combination of desert and vulnerability to Apache raids made this 90 mi. stretch particularly deadly. The fort was commissioned to protect this area in 1865 and was in operation until just before the turn of the century. It features a small but excellent collection of historic military artifacts. (☎505-526-8911. Open M and W-Su 8:30am-5pm. Activities such as cooking demonstrations, military reenactments, and lectures occur in summer most Sa-Su 1-4pm. $3, under 17 free.)

⛰ THE ROAD TO HATCH: 21 MI.

From Radium Springs, head back out to **Route 185** and follow it north 21 mi. to the village of Hatch. **I-25 North** also leads right into Hatch, for those in a hurry.

HATCH   ☎505

All kinds of produce are grown in the fertile Rio Grande Valley. As you approach Hatch, Rte. 185 meanders through orchards, green fields, and cropland devoted to the most famous of all New Mexico exports: the chili. During the right season, these farms offer freshly picked chilies to passersby, and in the low season, dried chilies hang for sale on most houses, trailers, and stores. In fact, Hatch lays claim to the title of "Chili Capital of the World." Every Labor Day weekend, the town celebrates its status at the annual **Chili Festival,** when it crowns two queens: one for red chilies and one for green. The **Pepper Pot ❷,** 207 W. Hall St., is on the main (and only) road through town. They serve up chili classics like *relleno* ($6.50). To taste several dishes, try the combo plate for $7.50. (☎505-267-3822. Open daily 6am-3pm. Cash only.)

⛰ THE ROAD TO TRUTH OR CONSEQUENCES: 43 MI.

Follow **I-25 North** for 38 mi. and then take **Exit 79** toward Truth or Consequences.

TRUTH OR CONSEQUENCES   ☎505

In 1950, Ralph Edwards's popular radio game show "Truth or Consequences" celebrated its 10th anniversary by announcing that the program would be broadcast from the first town to rename itself after the show. Formerly known as "Hot Springs," Truth or Consequences (sometimes fondly known as "T or C") jumped at the opportunity. Every year on the first weekend of May, residents celebrate the rechristening with a town-wide fiesta. Events include parades, rodeos, country music, high-energy drum circles, and canoe races. Day-to-day life in T or C is as quirky as one would expect it to be, and many artists have recently opened studios in the area.

VITAL STATS
Population: 7300
Tourist Office: T or C Visitors Information Center, 205 Main St. (☎505-894-1968). Open M-Sa 9am-5pm, Su 11am-4pm.
Library and Internet Access: Truth or Consequences Public Library, 325 Library Ln. (☎505-894-3027). Follow the signs from Main or 2nd St. northbound onto Foch St., then take a right at 3rd Ave.; the library is on the left. Open M-F 9am-7pm.
Post Office: 1507 N. Date St. (☎505-894-0876). Open M-F 8:30am-5pm. **Postal Code:** 87901.

◧ ORIENTATION

Taking the first exit off **I-25 North** into T or C puts you on **Broadway Street.** The road turns into **Date Street** on the east side of town, leading up to **Elephant Butte State Park** and to the numbered streets. Right before turning into Date St., **Broadway Street** becomes one-way. **Main Street** runs one-way in the other direction a few blocks over and curves to combine with Broadway St., circling a small downtown area. **Foch Street** and **Austin Street** lead down southward to the Rio Grande.

⌂ ACCOMMODATIONS

The mineral baths in T or C add a touch of luxury to accommodations. Campsites at the **Elephant Butte Lake State Park ❶,** north of T or

C, have access to restrooms and hot showers. (☎505-744-5421 or 877-664-7787. Primitive beach camping $8; tent sites $10, with water and electricity $14. D/MC/V.)

Riverbend Hot Springs Hostel and Resort, 100 Austin St. (☎505-894-7625; www.riverbendhotsprings.com). Stay on the banks of the Rio Grande and spend your days soaking in an outdoor mineral bath that overflows into the river. Riverbend is an eclectic place with brightly tiled courtyards, lots of plants, and mineral baths, which are free for guests. All dorms have common rooms and kitchens. Free Wi-Fi, although coverage can be spotty. Reception 8am-10pm. Tent sites and tipi $20. Single-sex dorms $24; 2-bed semi-private rooms $45; semi-private singles $49; doubles $58. AmEx/D/MC/V. ❶

Charles Motel and Spa, 601 Broadway St. (☎505-894-7154 or 800-317-4518; www.charlesspa.com). Simple, clean accommodations with free mineral baths on the premises (in bathtubs, not pools). Massages, reflexology, mud baths, and a host of other splurge-worthy spa treatments ($50 per hr.) are available on-site. Most rooms have kitchenettes. Singles $41; doubles $47. AmEx/D/MC/V. ❷

🍴 FOOD

Nearly all of T or C's restaurants are easy on the wallet, but some of the best ones close up shop pretty early.

Happy Belly Deli, 313 Broadway St. (☎505-894-5555). A small deli with a few tables, brightly painted walls, and a laid-back artist clientele. Locals claim that its sandwiches ($5-8) and salads ($5-7) are some of the tastiest in town. Breakfast served until 11am. Open M-F 7am-3pm, Sa 8am-3pm. MC/V. ❶

Hacienda Mexican Restaurant, 1615 S. Broadway St., (☎505-894-1024). Cozy and unassuming. Dishes like *arroz con pollo* (rice with chicken; $9) and breakfast *chorizo con huevos* (sausage with eggs; $6) are excellent. Open Tu-Sa 11am-9pm, Su 11am-8pm. D/MC/V. ❷

👁 🎿 SIGHTS AND OUTDOORS

T or C is proud of its status as an artist colony in the making. Inquire at the visitors center for a studio map or just wander down Broadway between Daniels and Pershing St. to visit many of the artists' studios. Every second Saturday of the month, all the studios are open 6-9pm and serve refreshments.

HOT SPRINGS. T or C's mineral baths are the town's other main attraction; locals claim that they heal virtually everything. *($10 per hr.; private pool on the water's edge $15 per hr. Open 8am-10pm.)* The only outdoor tubs are located at the **Riverbend Hot Springs Hostel and Resort,** where five tubs abut the Rio Grande.

GERONIMO SPRINGS MUSEUM. The museum showcases Native American history, military history, 1950s television history, and more. The highlight of the museum is the Native American pottery collection, which has intricately designed pots in pristine condition. *(211 Main St. ☎575-894-6600. Open M-Sa 9am-5pm, Su 11am-4pm. $5, ages 6-18 $1.50, under 6 free.)*

ELEPHANT BUTTE LAKE STATE PARK. Five miles north of T or C, Elephant Butte Lake State Park features New Mexico's largest lake, created by the construction of a dam on the Rio Grande in 1916. The park offers sandy beaches and a marina. Fishing is another key attraction of the park—there are so many bass, walleye, and catfish by the docks that you can almost grab them with your bare hands (like Mulan). There is a visitors center at the entrance of the park with a small museum on the natural history of the area. Although the park has little hiking, there is an easy nature trail (1 mi.) that begins in the nearby parking lot. *(Head north on Date St. to a sign for Elephant Butte; turn right onto Rte. 181 and follow the signs. ☎505-784-5421. Open M-F 7:30am-4pm, Sa-Su 7:30am-11pm. Front gate never closes. $5 per vehicle.)*

🎵 NIGHTLIFE

Pine Knot Saloon, 700 E. 3rd Ave. (☎505-894-2714), just past the curve on 3rd St. toward Elephant Butte. A vintage Western saloon festooned with photos of John Wayne. Locals in cowboy hats listen to live music weekend nights. According to the bartender, the music is "whatever the crowd wants ... but they always want country and Western." Karaoke Th. Open M-Th 10am-midnight, F-Sa 10am-2am, Su noon-midnight. AmEx/D/MC/V.

Dam Site (☎505-894-2073), just past the Elephant Butte Dam on Rte. 51. Features a bar and restaurant above a marina. The bar has a deck with spectacular views of the end of the lake and surrounding mountains. Entrees $7-19. Bottles $3. Open M-Th and Su 11am-7pm, F-Sa 11am-9pm. AmEx/D/MC/V.

◪ DETOUR
◪GILA CLIFF DWELLINGS NATIONAL MONUMENT

From Truth or Consequences, follow **I-25 South** to **Route 152 West**. After 49 mi., turn right onto **Route 35**. Follow Rte. 35 until it meets **Forest Road 15**, then turn north (right). Although these roads are all paved, the speed limits are generally low, and it is practically impossible to go much above 25 mph on significant parts of Rte. 35 and Forest Rd. 15.

The mysterious Gila Cliff Dwellings National Monument is set amid the mountains and pines of Gila National Forest. The monument preserves over 40 stone-and-timber rooms, which were constructed on top of the cliff's natural caves by the Mogollon tribe during the late 13th century. About a dozen families lived here for 20 years, farming on the mesa top and along the river. In the early 14th century, the Mogollon abandoned their homes for unknown reasons. Today, visitors can explore inside the ruins using traditional ladders. A 1 mi. loop hike takes visitors through the dwellings, and, although the trail features about 150 ft. of elevation gain, it is fairly easy. Rangers are scattered at the entrance to the loop trail as well as by the dwellings and will generally take you on a tour at your request. Mogollon ruins are scattered throughout the area, and rangers can direct you to more remote sites. (☎505-536-9461; www.nps.gov/gicl. Visitors center open daily 8am-5pm. Dwellings open daily from Memorial Day to Labor Day 8am-6pm; from Labor Day to Memorial Day 8am-4pm. $3, under 16 free, families $10.)

At the intersection of Rte. 35 and Forest Rd. 15, the **Breathe Inn ❷** is a quiet retreat in the middle of the great Gila wilderness. The lodge has cozy rooms and the cafe serves home-cooked meals, but the real attraction is its location in the path of the annual ◪humming-bird migration. From mid-July to mid-August, 3000-4000 hummingbirds visit the lodge's feeders each day. Each comfy room in the lodge is named after a Wild West figure, and there's a great deck out back where guests can sit by the fire and watch the sun set. (☎505-536-3206; www.breatheinnlodge.com. Breakfast $4-7. Sandwiches $7-9. Cafe open M-Tu and Sa 8am-4:30pm, W-Sa 8:30am-4:30pm and 5-9pm. Singles $50; doubles $60.) From here, the road climbs to a peak above the Gila River, where red, pine-covered rocks extend into endless vistas. Soon you'll pass the infinitesimally small hamlet of Gila Hot Springs, where gas and food are available at **Doc Campbell's Post Vacation Center**. Like many of the buildings in Gila Hot Springs, Doc Campbell's is geothermally heated. Four miles past Gila Hot Springs, Forest Rd. 15 enters the Gila National Forest. The area encompasses hundreds of miles of hiking trails through mountains, canyons, and forest interspersed with hot springs and is ideal for backpacking, mountain biking, and rock climbing.

◪ THE ROAD TO SILVER CITY: 92 MI.

Take **I-25 South** for 11 mi. to **Exit 63 (Hillsboro)**. Take **Route 152 West** for 17 mi. to the little town of Hillsboro. At one time, gold chunks as heavy as 240 lb. attracted prospectors from all over the West to Hillsboro. The road climbs up into the pristine, pine-covered mountains. It's a mere 35 mi. to reach the turn-off for Rte. 35, which will take you north into the **Gila Wilderness Area**, or, if you want to continue to Silver City directly, follow the forested road another 15 mi. to Santa Clara, where it meets **Route 180**. A short 9 mi. drive westward on Rte. 180 brings you to Silver City.

◪ SILVER CITY   ☎505

In its heyday, Silver City was a rough and wild place that spawned the infamous outlaw Billy the Kid. Brown historical markers strewn about town point out the sites of his home, his school, his first bank robbery, his first jailbreak, and other typical landmarks of a Wild West childhood. Today, Billy would be more likely to find a latte in Silver City than a brawl. The very quaint Bullard St., in the heart of Silver City's historic downtown, has one civilized cafe and gallery after another—it is yet another artists' community in the making.

Population: 10,500

Tourist Office: 201 N. Hudson St. (☎505-538-3785), near Broadway. Open M-Sa 9am-5pm.

Library and Internet Access: Silver City Public Library, 515 W. College Ave. (☎505-538-3672). Open M and Th 9am-8pm, Tu-W 9am-6pm, F 9am-5pm, Sa 9am-1pm.

Post Office: 500 N. Hudson St. Open M-F 8:30am-5pm, Sa 10am-noon. **Postal Code:** 88061.

✈ ORIENTATION

Hudson Street (Route 90) and **Silver Heights Boulevard (US 180)** are the major routes through town and run north-south and east-west, respectively. Around the center of town, **College Avenue** bisects Hudson St. and leads to the University of Western New Mexico on the west side of town. Most of the action in Silver City is along **Bullard Street,** which runs parallel to Hudson St. and is accessible from **Broadway.** Free parking is easily available along Bullard St. and all over town.

⌂ ACCOMMODATIONS

◪ **Palace Hotel,** 106 W. Broadway St. (☎505-288-1811; www.zianet.com/palacehotel), at Bullard St. Est. 1882. Captures the grandeur of years gone by. Spacious sky lit common room. Continental breakfast. Reservations recommended. Singles $48; doubles $65. AmEx/D/MC/V. ❷

Drifter Motel and Cocktail Lounge, 711 Silver Heights Blvd. (☎800-853-2916, lounge 505-538-2916). A solid budget option with a diner upstairs and a lounge with live music downstairs. Don't worry about the lounge if you just need a good night's sleep—the motel rooms are far enough away that noise isn't an issue. Live music Th-Sa. Lounge open daily 5pm-2am. Singles $42; doubles $53. D/MC/V. ❷

🍴 FOOD

◪ **Java the Hut,** 611A N. Bullard St. (☎505-534-4103). Far from the dusty deserts of Tatooine, this coffee shop is made almost entirely of windows and looks unlike any other building you've seen. Lounge on the sofas, at 1 of the 2 Formica tables, or on the patio. Serves sandwiches, salads, and coffee. Open M-F 8am-4pm, Sa 9am-3pm. Cash only. ❶

Javalina, 201 N. Bullard St. (☎505-388-1350). Local artwork and hard-to-find magazines are for sale in this spacious cafe that caters to a younger crowd while maintaining a very homey feel. Try some of the fresh-baked goods or the Karma Latte (caramel, vanilla, espresso) for $4.25. Free Wi-Fi and comfy chairs make it easy to while away a few hours here. Open Tu-F 6am-9pm, Sa-Su 6am-10pm. MC/V. ❶

Jalisco Cafe, 100 S. Bullard St. (☎505-388-2060). The chefs here put the New Mexican chile pepper to good use. The jalapeño guacamole ($7) is delicious in a masochistic sort of way. The menu warns people to ask for samples of their specialty red and green chile sauce before ordering—many guests just can't take the heat. Entrees $8-12. Open M-Sa 11am-8:30pm. D/MC/V. ❷

Diane's, 510 N. Bullard St. (☎575-538-8722). Diane's is a small, upscale restaurant with pricey dinners but surprisingly affordable breakfast and lunch options. If you do stick around for dinner, try the signature lemon-caper chicken ($18). Breakfast and lunch $5-8. Dinner $16-23. Open Tu-F 11am-2pm and 5:30-9pm, Sa 9am-2pm and 5:30-9pm, Su 9am-2pm. ❸

☉ ⚲ SIGHTS AND OUTDOORS

Silver City contains the main forestry station of the **Gila National Forest,** 3005 E. Camino del Bosque. The station provides excellent maps of the forest and local wilderness areas as well as info on various outdoor activities in the region. All sorts of passes and permits for parks or backcountry camping are also available here, on the 32nd Bypass Rd. off US 180, east of town. (☎505-388-8201. Open M-F 8am-4:30pm.) Rent mountain bikes with which you can explore Gila and the surrounding foothills at the **Gila Hike and Bike Shop,** 103 E. College Ave. They also repair bikes, sell outdoor equipment, and provide maps of the area. (☎505-388-3222. $20 for 1st day, $15 for 2nd, $10 for 3rd, $5 thereafter. Helmets included. Open Apr.-Dec. M-F 9am-5:30pm, Sa 9am-5pm, Su 10am-4pm.) For a "wilderness" experience just off Bullard St., walk along the town's famed **Big Ditch,** a lush, tree-filled ditch that was created when the original Main St. washed away in a 1902 flood. Art enthusiasts will find an impressive collection of local **art galleries** on Bullard St. and Yankie St.

◨ THE ROAD TO PORTAL: 97 MI.

A drive southwest on **Route 90** connects Silver City with Lordsburg. The only excitement on this road is cresting the **Continental Divide** at 6300 ft. From Lordsburg, take **I-10 West** and pass through a true dust bowl, where high winds can reduce visibility to almost zero. Use extreme caution when driving through dust storms. Drive 16 mi. and exit at **Route 80.** Head south for 28 mi. along flat desert roads and turn right (west) on **Route 533.** Continue for 7 mi. to Portal.

 TIME CHANGE. Most of Arizona does not observe Daylight Saving Time, so those traveling between April and October will need to set their clocks back 1hr. From November to March, there is no change—yet.

The Grand Canyon State
ARIZONA
Welcomes You!

PORTAL   ☎520

The village of Portal consists almost entirely of the **Portal Peak Lodge ❹,** cafe, and attached store. (☎520-558-2223; www.portalpeaklodge.com. Office and store open daily 9:30am-7:30pm. Cafe open daily 7:30am-3:30pm and 5-7pm. Rooms $75-$85. AmEx/MC/V.) Its diminutive size aside, Portal is a welcome bit of civilization before the road begins a steep ascent into the Chiricahua Mountains.

◨ THE ROAD TO CHIRICAHUA NATIONAL MONUMENT: 25 MI.

Drive 25 mi. west along **Pinery Canyon Road** to reach the entrance to Chiricahua National Monument. The road passes through the beautiful Chiricahua Mountains and is extremely bumpy and poorly maintained— it's impossible to exceed 15 mph for most of the drive. If you have doubts about the condition of your car or if it has been raining heavily, it is advised that you do not try to drive up to Chiricahua and instead continue on Rte. 80 south to Douglas. On the right 3 mi. past Portal is the **Cave Creek Visitors Information Center,** which welcomes you to the mountains and has an excellent view of the boulder-topped canyon walls. (☎520-558-2221. Open Sa-Su 8am-noon and 12:30-4pm.) Monday through Friday, contact the **Coronado Forest Douglas Ranger District** (☎520-364-6800) for info on the Cave Creek area.

> ⚠ **BUMPS AHEAD.** The road through the Chiricahua Mountains is not maintained for winter travel, so check with the **Coronado Forest Douglas Ranger District Office** (☎520-364-6800) for information on road conditions and safe driving.

CHIRICAHUA NATIONAL MONUMENT   ☎504

Over 25 million years ago, the Turkey Creek Caldera spewed forth thick, white-hot ash that settled over the Chiricahua area. Since then, erosion has sculpted the fused-ash rock into peculiar formations that loom over the landscape and awe those who walk among them. The massive stone spires weigh hundreds of tons and are often perched precariously on small pedestals; because of this, the Apaches called the area "Land of the Standing-Up Rocks," and pioneers dubbed it "Wonderland of Rocks." The geological magnificence here could be the cousin of Zion or Bryce Canyons, yet the park happily lacks their popularity.

◼ ORIENTATION

Extending from the park's entrance station to **Massai Point** at the back of the park is the

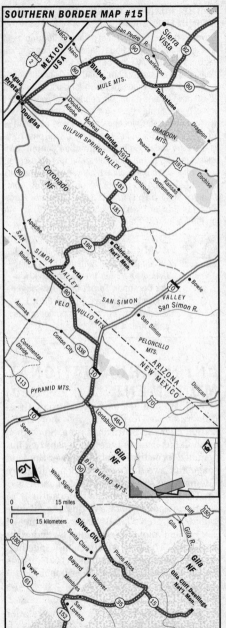

SOUTHERN BORDER MAP #15

Bonita Canyon Drive, a scenic 8 mi. road that is the only way to get through the monument. At the end of Bonita Canyon Dr., the road squeezes through the narrow gap between the towering granite walls of Bonita Canyon and then ascends to pine-studded Massai Point (elevation 6870 ft.) at the mountain's crest. Keep an eye out for the **Organ Pipe** formation on your left as you're driving up the canyon, a mile or two from the visitors center. A short interpretive nature trail encircles the peak and also serves as the starting point for the more demanding Echo Canyon Trail and other trails into the wilderness. All of the park, except for a strip around the main road, is federally designated wilderness; no biking or climbing is permitted.

VITAL STATS

Area: 12,000 acres

Tourist Office: Chiricahua Visitors Center, 13063 E. Bonita Rd. (☎504-824-3560; www.nps.gov/chir), on your right 2 mi. beyond the entrance station. Open daily 8am-4:30pm.

Entrance Fees: $5 per person, under 15 free; valid for 7 days.

CAMPING

No backcountry camping is allowed along the trails but there is one established campground inside the park. The well-equipped **Bonita Canyon Campground ❶** has toilets, picnic grounds, water, and easy access to the park trails, but no showers. (☎504-824-3560. 22 sites. 14-day max. stay. No reservations. Sites $12. D/MC/V.) There are several campgrounds in the Cave Creek area along Pinery Rd. between Portal and the monument. The first of these, **Idle Wilde ❶,** has grills, outhouses, a water pump, and shaded sites. (Open 24hr. Sites $10. Cash only.) The road forks a few times, so keep a close eye on the well-marked signs for the National Monument. You will pass many other well-developed campsites and short hiking or birding trails in the National Forest, as you begin the steep, switch-back laden trip up into the mountains. The picturesque canyons and boulder formations are worth exploring before continuing to the

National Monument. The road is in extremely poor condition from the Idle Wilde, so make sure your car is durable—and that you really like rock formations—before committing to the drive. Reaching **Pinery Canyon Camp ❶** seems like a reward for those who've stuck it out: the campground has amenities like picnic tables and fire rings. (Open 24hr. Free.)

🏔 HIKING

There is a terrific selection of day hikes in the monument. Many combinations are possible, since several loops and spurs provide flexibility, but most trails either lead to **Echo Canyon** or to the remote and more-spectacular **Heart of Rocks**. From the parking lot on Massai Point, the moderate 📷**Echo Canyon Loop** (2.7 mi., 2-3hr.) is the best way to see many formations in a short period of time. The trail runs through an impressive cluster of formations, including rock grottoes, before descending into the wooded **Echo Park** area and then out through a more desert-like trail. For hikers with more time, an excellent route is the **Echo Canyon to Heart of Rocks Trail** (7 mi.) that passes by the most spectacular formations in the park. The route follows the **Ed Riggs Trail** from the Echo Canyon trailhead through the forest and up to the top of the canyon, where you hike along the ridge on the **Big Balanced Rock Trail**. From there, follow the **Heart of Rocks Loop** to see the most unusual rock formations in the monument. The trail is strenuous, mostly because of its length, and it requires about half of a day to complete. For info and trail maps, check the visitors center.

🚗 THE ROAD TO ELFRIDA: 40 MI.

From **Chiricahua National Monument,** drive 3 mi. to the junction of **Route 186/181** and turn left on Rte. 181 toward Douglas. Follow the road for 23 mi. until the junction with **US 191** and take a left (south). Fourteen miles down the road is the tiny village of Elfrida.

ELFRIDA ☎ 520

A smattering of houses, a motel, and a gas station make up the tiny town of Elfrida. The **Longhorn Steakhouse ❷,** 10348 Hwy. 191, offers lunch, including a veggie burger ($6), steak dinners ($15-25), and draft beer. (☎520-642-3496. Open daily 8am-10pm. MC/V.)

🚗 THE ROAD TO DOUGLAS: 26 MI.

Continue on **US 191** for 24 mi. to the junction of **Route 80** and turn left into Douglas.

DOUGLAS ☎ 520

The quiet border town of Douglas sits at the intersection of **Route 80** and **US 191.** While Rte. 80 runs through the center of town, US 191 makes a run for the border toward the Mexican sister city of **Agua Prieta.** Stores swarm around Rte. 80 (rechristened **G Avenue** for municipal purposes), and most city services lie off either this route or **10th Street.**

The city's main attraction is the **John Slaughter Ranch,** 6153 Geronimo Trail. The ranch's eponymous owner was a Confederate soldier, rancher, and lawman who was voted the marshal of Tombstone. He proceeded to shoot or prosecute (in no particular order) Tombstone's worst. Slaughter's ranch buildings are now a museum where visitors can get a sense of the Wild West and get a great view of the town below. Visitors can also watch a 2hr. long Disney rendition of the life and times of John Slaughter. The ranch is located 15 mi. east of the city on an unpaved, bumpy road that takes about 45min. each way, so make sure you really like ranches before setting out. Follow 15th St. east until it becomes the Geronimo Trail, which leads to the ranch. (☎520-558-2474; www.slaughterranch.com. Open W-Su 10am-3pm. $8, children free.)

The **Gadsden Hotel ❸,** 1046 G Ave., is an extravagant yet inexpensive hotel. Established in 1907, this opulent palace hails itself as "the last of the grand hotels," and the white marble staircase, 14-karat-gold-topped marble pillars, and ridiculously ornate lobby support the claim. While the rooms may not be as luxurious as the great hall, they are still nicely decorated, with big, bright windows. (☎520-364-4481; www.hotelgadsden.com. Rooms $60-150. AmEx/D/MC/V.) The **Grand Cafe ❶,** 1119 G Ave., has walls filled with pictures of Marilyn Monroe, an obsession of the first owner's wife. It also offers hot Mexican food for

$6-9. (☎520-364-2344. Open M-Th 10am-8pm, F 10am-9pm, Sa noon-9pm. D/MC/V.)

The well-marked **Visitor Information Center**, 1125 Pan American Hwy., is off Rte. 80 on your right as you enter town, located behind the city's police station. (☎888-315-9999. Open M-F 8am-5pm, Sa 8am-1pm.)

⊠ DETOUR
AGUA PRIETA

Your best bet is to park your car in Douglas and walk across the border—Mexico requires foreign drivers to carry Mexican liability insurance (your existing American policy won't cover it), and those caught without it face stiff penalties. Due to recently implemented security measures, you'll need your passport or driver's license and birth certificate to cross the border.

The 10-block area of Agua Prieta close to the border with Douglas, while not as visually appealing as the American side of the city, is still safer than other border cities like Juárez or Acuña. A quick hop over the border into the lively Mexican side of the city is worthwhile, though. Street vendors sell *helado* (ice cream), *fruta* (fresh fruit), and *agua fresca* (juice and soda). Don't worry about exchanging money if you're only going to be in Mexico for a few hours; vendors will accept dollars or pesos, overcharging tourists either way. The city is laid out with *avenidas* running north-south and *calles* running east-west. The best Mexican food can be found on Avenida 4. Don't miss the plaza at Calle 5 and Avenida 4, site of many a fiesta. The town also has beautiful churches, like the Iglesia de Guadalupe, at Avenida 4 and Calle 6. The border crossing is located on Calle 3. It is easiest to park your car on the American side of Third St., at Pan American, and walk across. If you decide to drive, be prepared to wait in long lines returning through the crossing. If you're planning on roadtripping through Mexico, this is a great place to start; Agua Prieta marks the beginning of the Janos Hwy., the shortest route to Mexico City from the US. For more coverage of Mexico, see ⊠**Let's Go: Mexico.**

⚑ THE ROAD TO BISBEE: 25 MI.

From Douglas, take **Route 80 West** for 25 mi. to Bisbee across more desert.

BISBEE   ☎520

This rough-and-tumble mining town turned artist colony is famous for its eccentricity. Old miners give tours of prosperous shafts while bohemians hang out at cafes and galleries. The Victorian-style houses that line the narrow streets of the historic district could as easily be part of a European town as part of this Old West settlement. Some hail Bisbee as a land where time stands still, but in truth it seems more a community where time accumulates; the Western frontier, the Gold Rush, the 1950s, the summer of love, and the postmodern age are all alive and well here.

VITAL STATS
Population: 6100
Visitor Info: Bisbee Visitors Center, 2 Copper Queen Plaza (☎520-432-3554; www.discoverbisbee.com), on Main St. Open M-F 9am-5pm, Sa-Su 10am-4pm.
Library and Internet Access: Copper Queen Library, 6 Main St. (☎520-432-4232). Open M noon-7pm, Tu-W 10am-7pm, Th-F 10am-5pm, Sa 10am-2pm.
Post Office: Copper Queen, 6 Main St. (☎520-432-2052). Open M-F 8:30am-4:30pm. **Postal Code:** 85603.

⊠ ORIENTATION

The streets of Bisbee are almost entirely unnavigable, as they wind uphill and downhill at sharp angles and are only wide enough for one car. However, **Main Street** is drivable, and the downtown area is small and easy to walk. Get a map—you'll still be lost, but you'll feel better. The town's tiny alleys were designed for hooved travel, so the sooner you ditch your car and take to your own feet, the better off you'll be. Most restaurants and galleries lie along Main St., which curves and turns into **Tombstone Canyon Road.**

⚑ ACCOMMODATIONS

Lodging in Bisbee is expensive. If you're on a budget and in between Bisbee and Tombstone, your best bet may be a 20 mi. drive west on Rte. 80 to Rte. 90 to Sierra Vista, where motels are often $30-40 cheaper. However, the places to stay in Bisbee are cool enough that they may be worth the splurge.

🏨 **The Shady Dell,** 1 Douglas Rd. (☎520-432-3567; www.theshadydell.com). Just before historic Bisbee, take a left after the rotary by the Chevron station. Stay in 1 of 11 restored vintage trailers, complete with period furnishings including propane stoves, refrigerators, and electric percolators. Each of the sleek aluminum trailers is unique; some even have original black-and-white TVs. Trailers range in luxury from a basic place to crash for a night to a 38 ft. boat fully restored and worthy of a honeymoon. Reservations recommended. Trailers $45-145. Ages 10+. MC/V. ❷

🏨 **School House Inn,** 818 Tombstone Canyon Rd. (☎520-432-2996 or 800-537-4333), at the south end of town. Located in a remodeled 1918 schoolhouse. Has beautifully decorated rooms named to go along with the inn's theme, a balcony, and an oak-shaded patio for guest use. Check out the working 1950s soda machine. All rooms have private baths. Ironically, no children under 10 are allowed. Hot breakfast included. Singles $74; doubles from $79. AmEx/MC/V. ❸

Jonquil Motel, 317 Tombstone Canyon Rd. (☎520-432-7371 or 866-432-7371). Clean, smoke-free rooms, and a backyard that is perfect for barbecues or just for lounging. Free Wi-Fi. Rooms $70-105. D/MC/V. ❸

🍴 FOOD

Eateries line the main drags downtown, many of which have patio seating and great views. Most places close pretty early, so make sure you get dinner early, or you may find yourself hungrily eyeing the desert cactuses.

🍴 **Dot's Diner** (☎520-432-1112), in a 1957 trailer. You'll have to fight the walls for elbow room, but the cozy family kitchen evokes the original atmosphere of diner eating. Classic breakfasts ($3-5) are served all day along with hamburgers, sandwiches, and Southwestern food. Lunch $4-6. Open Aug.-May W-Su 7am-2:30pm. ❶

Cafe Cornucopia, 14 Main St. (☎520-432-4820). Hollowed out of a turn-of-the-century structure. Fresh sandwiches and salads. The chicken-salad sandwich will knock your socks off, and don't miss the tangy cilantro coleslaw. Also serves smoothies and soups in a bread bowl. Open Th-Su 10am-5pm. Cash only. ❷

Rosa's Little Italy, 7 Bisbee Rd. (☎520-432-1331), 1 mi. from the historic district. So popular (and small) that you'll need reservations. Adorably romantic, it has small, candlelit tables inside and a beautiful vine-shaded courtyard with a fountain outside. The Peasant's Pasta ($16) is great, as is the extensive vegetarian menu ($15-17). Bring your own wine or beer at no charge. Open Th-Sa 5-9pm, Su 5-8pm. MC/V. ❸

The Bisbee Grill (☎520-432-6788), at Copper Queen Plaza, right next to the visitors center. Offers an upscale yet casual environment, and is open later than many other places around town. The menu mainly focuses on burgers, ribs, and pasta, but there is also a good selection of salads available. Entrees $8-18. Salads $6-10. Open daily 11am-9pm. D/MC/V. ❷

👁 SIGHTS

QUEEN MINES. Copper mining built Bisbee, and, although the mine became unprofitable and shut down in the mid-1970s, you can still learn about it on educational 1¼hr. tours at the Queen Mines, on the Rte. 80 interchange as you enter town. Tours are led by former miners and require headlamps and safety gear. The miners also offer van tours of the town's historical sights. (☎866-432-2071. Mine tours daily 9, 10:30am, noon, 2, 3:30pm. $12, ages 4-15 $5. Van tours daily 10:30am, noon, 2, 3:30pm. $10.)

CHIHUAHUA HILL SHRINES. After exploring the lows of Bisbee's mines, you'll welcome the heavenly experience of the Chihuahua Hill Shrines. A 15min. steep uphill hike over rocky ground leads to two shrines, the first Buddhist and the second Catholic. The Catholic shrine is exceptional in its complexity and was erected in the 1950s by a grieving family who lost their son at war. The more understated Buddhist shrine features several works of rock art in addition to innumerable prayer flags and pictures of the last two Dalai Lamas. (Head up Brewery Ave.; there is a grocery store on the right. Behind the store are 2 staircases; take the left one. Next, turn left and briefly follow a concrete driveway. Before the private property sign, turn right off the paved road. At the cross, follow the trail up.)

MINING AND HISTORICAL MUSEUM. This museum gives a retrospective view on the area. The Smithsonian-affiliated museum has exhibits that highlight the discovery of Bisbee's copper surplus and the lifestyle of the fortune-seekers who extracted it. The newest exhibit features a realistic faux mine, and treats of how copper affects our present-day lives. *(5 Copper Queen. ☎520-432-7071. Open daily 10am-4pm. $7.50, under 16 $3.)*

THE ROAD TO TOMBSTONE: 27 MI.

From Bisbee, head northwest on **Route 80** out of town and continue 27 mi. to Tombstone.

TOMBSTONE ☎520

Long past its glory days as a silver-mining town that was also the largest city between the Mississippi River and the Pacific, Tombstone has abandoned its dangerous Old West history for a more sanitized Disney version of cowboy living. Despite its touristy feel, it's a fun place to spend a few hours; it gives you a real sense of how a Western town was built in the late-1800s, not to mention tons of cheesy but fabulous photo ops. The city offers a little bit of everything touristy and a lot of rotgut and gunfight reenactments.

VITAL STATS

Population: 1600

Tourist Office: City of Tombstone Visitor and Information Center, 317 E. Allen St. (☎520-457-3929; www.cityoftombstone.org), at 4th St. Open daily 9am-4pm.

Library and Internet Access: Tombstone Public Library, 337 S. 4th St. (☎520-457-3612), at Toughnut St. Open M-F 8am-noon and 1-5pm.

Post Office: 100 N. Haskell Ave. (☎520-457-3479). Open M-F 8:30am-4:30pm. **Postal Code:** 85638.

ORIENTATION

Historic Tombstone is basically two streets: **Route 80** rolls through town one block north of **Allen Street,** which is closed to traffic between **Sixth** and **Third Streets** and is the main historic drag. Numbered streets run perpendicular to Allen St. and attractions lie in the pedestrian-only section. Parking is not a problem.

ACCOMMODATIONS

Larian Motel, 410 E. Fremont St./Rte. 80 (☎520-457-2272; www.tombstonemotels.com). Spacious, clean rooms named for famous outlaws, vigilantes, and ruffians. All rooms have A/C, TVs, and coffee; some have fridges and microwaves. Free Wi-Fi. Singles $70; doubles $75. MC/V. ❸

FOOD

Food in Tombstone is a one-trick pony consisting of hamburgers and other grilled items.

Longhorn Restaurant, 501 E. Allen St. (☎520-457-3405). Once the "Bucket of Blood Saloon" where Virgil Earp was shot from the 2nd-story window. Now a boisterous family restaurant. Try the "too tough to die burger" ($11). Less legendary burgers and sandwiches cost $6-8, while dinner plates like roast beef or meatloaf are $13. Open daily 7:30am-9pm. AmEx/MC/V. ❷

Big Nose Kate's Saloon, 417 Allen St. (☎520-457-3107). Named for the girl who loved Doc Holliday and everyone else, the saloon is done up in an Old West style and has live honky-tonk music daily. The ghost of "the swamper" is said to haunt these halls searching for his lost cache of silver, left when the building was still the Grand Hotel. Lunch from $7. Open daily 11am-10pm. AmEx/MC/V. ❸

Nellie Cashman's Restaurant, 402 S. 5th St. (☎520-457-2212), off Allen St. Named after the "angel of the mining camps" who devoted her life to clean living and public service. Less Old West than modern casual. Hamburgers $5-8. Entrees $11-15. Open daily 7:30am-9pm. D/MC/V. ❸

SIGHTS

OK CORRAL. Tombstone has turned the shootout at the OK Corral into a year-round tourist industry, inviting visitors to view the vacant lot where Wyatt Earp and his posse showed outlaws who was boss. Besides a reenactment of the shootout daily at 2pm, the OK Corral has good exhibits on the history of the site, the town, and on legal prostitution in Tombstone in the 1880s. Attached to the Corral is the Tombstone Historama, where Vincent Price narrates the town's history as a plastic mountain revolves on stage and a dramatization of the gunfight is shown on a movie screen. Visitors can also grab a free copy of the *Tombstone Epitaph* from the day after the gunfight. (*308 E. Allen St. ☎520-457-3456. Open daily 9:30am-5pm. Historama shows every 30min. Ticket for Corral, Historama, and gunfight $9.*)

BIRD CAGE THEATER. The site of the longest poker game in Western history (8 years, 5 months, and 3 days), the Bird Cage Theater, at Sixth and Allen St., is named for the upper-level booths that once held "soiled doves" (prostitutes) with feathers in their hair. Men would pay $25 for 8hr. of "negotiable affection" with the lady of their choice. When the mines went bust in 1889, the Bird Cage was shut and left as it was—a time capsule preserving the history of Tombstone's men and the women who serviced them. It is unrestored today; the original 1881 curtains, piano, tables, and chairs have been left essentially undisturbed. The museum also houses artifacts, including a 100-year-old "merman," original show posters, and the "crib" (bordello room) of Sadie Jo, Wyatt Earp's famous actress-lover. The Bird Cage is said to be haunted, with 26 violent deaths in its nine-year run. (*☎505-457-3421. Open daily 8am-6pm. $10, ages 8-18 $8, under 8 free.*)

TOMBSTONE COURTHOUSE STATE HISTORIC PARK. If hype and tall tales are not your style, then head here. The impressive old building that tried to bring law to the lawless is now a museum offering the most accurate account of what really happened at high noon at the OK Corral. The most interesting part of the museum may be the historic gallows. (*At 3rd and Toughnut St. ☎520-457-3311. Open daily 8am-5pm. $3, under 13 free. MC/V.*)

BOOTHILL GRAVEYARD. The actual tombstones of Tombstone—the results of all that gunplay—stand in the Boothill Graveyard. Look for the graves of the OK Corral losers (the McLaury brothers and Billy Clanton) and other Tombstone notables like Dutch Annie, "queen of the red light district." Pick up a map

of the graveyard at the entrance. (*Just outside of town on Rte. 80 N. ☎800-457-3423. Open daily 7:30am-5:30pm. Suggested donation $2.*)

PHOTO OP. For something a little less high-noon and a little more horticulture, the **Rose Tree Museum,** at Fourth and Toughnut St., shelters the **world's largest rose tree,** which was planted in 1885 and is now over 8,700 sq. ft. Its annual flowering in April is a sight to behold. (☎520-457-3326. Open daily 9am-5pm. $3, under 14 free. Cash only.)

THE ROAD TO SONOITA: 37 MI.
Head north on **Route 80** for 3 mi. to **Route 82.** Head west 34 mi. to the town of Sonoita, located in Arizona's wine country, where a few scattered wineries offer wine tastings down back roads.

SONOITA   ☎520
You might be surprised to learn that Sonoita is located in Arizona's wine country—the area is mostly open prairie. The town, situated at the crossroads of Rte. 82 and 83, has little to offer but an expensive hotel, gas, and a couple of restaurants. The aptly named **Sonoita Crossroads Cafe ❶,** 3172 Hwy. 83, fuels up passersby with gourmet coffees and classic American cuisine with the Madera Canyon and mountains as a backdrop. (☎520-455-5189. Open M and Th-Sa 8am-3pm, Su 8am-noon. MC/V.)

THE ROAD TO TUCSON: 51 MI.
Take **Route 82 West** to **Route 83 North.** Here, you'll see your first saguaro, the tall, standing cactus that makes the Arizona landscape famous. Get on **I-10 West** and take **Exit 265** to downtown Tucson.

TUCSON   ☎520
A little bit country, a little bit south of the border, Tucson is a melting pot of culture, history, and contradictory influences. Mexican property until 1854, the city retains much of its Mexican influence while also championing the rugged individualism of the American West. Home to the students of the University

of Arizona, the soldiers of the Davis-Monthan Air Force Base, ranching cowboys, downtown artists, and suburban retirees, Tucson is the colorful fusion of a seemingly disparate variety of folk. Somehow, though, add just a few desert sunsets and half-empty margarita glasses, and the war machines and creative photography, honky-tonk, and Latin techno all harmoniously combine.

VITAL STATS

Population: 490,000

Tourist Office: Tucson Convention and Visitors Bureau, 100 S. Church Ave. (☎520-624-1817 or 800-638-8350; www.visittucson.org). Open M-F 9am-5pm, Sa-Su 9am-4pm.

Library and Internet Access: Joel D. Valdez Main Public Library, 101 N. Stone Ave. (☎520-791-4393). Open M-W 9am-8pm, Th 9am-6pm, Sa 10am-5pm, Su 1-5pm.

Post Office: 1501 S. Cherrybell Stra. (☎520-791-5043). Open M-F 8:30am-8pm, Sa 9am-1pm. **Postal Code:** 85726.

⚡ ORIENTATION

Just east of I-10, Tucson's downtown area surrounds the intersection of **Broadway Boulevard** and **Stone Avenue.** The **University of Arizona** lies 1 mi. northeast of downtown between **Euclid Avenue, Campbell Avenue, and Speedway Boulevard.** Avenues run north-south, streets east-west; because some of each are numbered, intersections such as "Sixth and Sixth" exist. **Speedway Boulevard, Broadway Boulevard,** and **Grant Road** are the quickest east-west routes through town, but they get very clogged during rush hour. To go north-south, follow **Stone Avenue** through the heart of the city or **Campbell Avenue** east of downtown. A younger crowd hangs out around **Fourth Avenue** and on **Congress Street,** both of which are home to small shops, quirky restaurants, and a slew of bars. Tucson is accustomed to bustle, and, as in most of the Southwest, parking is not an issue. If you want to ditch your car downtown, ride the free TICET buses that circulate downtown between **Tools Avenue** and I-10 and Sixth and 12th St. On weekends, a $1 electric trolley runs up and down **University Boulevard**

and **Fourth Street.** Tucson is very spread out, so plan ahead and make sure to leave enough time to travel between places.

🏨 ACCOMMODATIONS

There's a direct correlation between the temperature in Tucson and the warmth of its lodging industry to budget travelers; expect the best deals in summer, when rain-cooled evenings and summer bargains help to ease the midday scorch. The Tucson Gem and Mineral Show, which falls mid February, drives prices up. Cheap motels can be found along I-10 between Exits 260 and 262, but there are also plenty of fun budget options.

🏨 Roadrunner Hostel, 346 E. 12th St. (☎520-628-4709). Exceptionally clean, with a friendly staff. All rooms have A/C or are swamp-cooled. Amenities such as a full kitchen, giant TV, a formidable movie collection, coffee, tea, and breakfast. Lockers, linen, towels, and laundry soap included. Laundry $1. Free internet. Lockout noon-3pm. Reservations recommended in winter. Dorms $24; private rooms $48. Cash only. ❶

Hotel Congress, 311 E. Congress St. (☎520-622-8848; www.hotelcongress.com). Conveniently located in the center of downtown, this hotel offers superb lodging to night owls. Downstairs, Club Congress booms until 3am on weekends; for quieter rooms, reserve in advance. Private rooms come with bathtubs, phones, vintage radios, ceiling fans, and swamp cooling. Outdoor patio accessible from the club. The cafe downstairs serves great salads ($5-12) and sandwiches ($7-12). Cafe open M-F 7am-11pm, Sa-Su 7am-midnight. TV and free Internet in lounge. Free Wi-Fi. Reception 24hr. Singles $69-99; doubles $89-119. AmEx/D/MC/V. ❸

The Flamingo Hotel, 1300 N. Stone Ave. (☎520-770-1910; www.flamingohoteltucson.com). Houses Arizona's largest collection of Western movie posters, many of them signed by Hollywood's greatest cowboys. Rooms are spacious, with large windows, plants, and movie-poster decorations. All rooms have A/C, TVs, coffee, and pool access. Continental breakfast included. Laundry $1. Reception 7am-midnight. Singles from $55; doubles from $65. Prices can rise in winter. AmEx/D/MC/V. ❷

Loews Ventana Canyon Resort, 7000 N. Resort Dr. (☎520-299-2020). 5 mi. north of downtown off Oracle Rd. A quintessential 5-star hotel. At the base of an 80 ft. waterfall, this incredible resort delivers on every level, from its relaxing spa to its championship golf course to the beautiful Catalina Mountain foothills. If you want luxury and are traveling with some friends, it's not a bad deal in the low season. Rooms from mid-May to mid-Sept. from $149; from mid-Sept. to mid-May from $280. AmEx/D/MC/V. ❺

Gilbert Ray Campground, McCain Loop Rd. (☎520-883-4200), just outside Saguaro West. An easy drive from the city. Toilets and drinking water, but no showers and little shelter from the desert sun. No reservations. No fires. Tent sites $10, RV sites $20. Cash only. ❶

🍴 FOOD

Like any good college town, Tucson brims with inexpensive, tasty eateries, and, as in any good Southwestern town, Mexican fare dominates the culinary scene.

Elle, 3048 E. Broadway Blvd. (☎520-327-0500). Cool jazz reverberates throughout this elegant eatery. Spoil yourself with a satisfying meal of butternut squash ravioli ($17.25) and a glass of cool Arizona wine (from $5). Entrees $17-24. Open M-Th 11:30am-9pm, F-Sa 11:30am-10pm, Su 4-9pm. AmEx/D/MC/V. ❸

El Charro, 311 N. Court Ave. (☎520-622-5465), near the corner of Franklin and Court St. Opened in 1922, El Charro is Tucson's oldest Mexican restaurant owned continuously by the same family. It is so popular that the *USS Tucson* submarine has named its galley "El Charro Down Under." The most famous dish is the *carne seca,* beef dried for 48hr. on the roof and then thinly sliced and grilled with tomatoes, onions, chilies, and spices ($16). Entrees $9-14. Open M-Th and Su 11am-9pm, F-Sa 11am-10pm. AmEx/D/MC/V. ❷

La Indita, 622 N. 4th Ave. (☎520-792-0523). A small, colorful restaurant that delights customers with traditional and delicious Mexican cuisine ($4-10) served on tortillas. The food is prepared by the charismatic Indita herself, who will undoubtedly spice up your dining experience. Free Wi-Fi. Open M-F 11am-3pm and 6-10pm, Sa-Su 9am-9pm. AmEx/D/MC/V. ❷

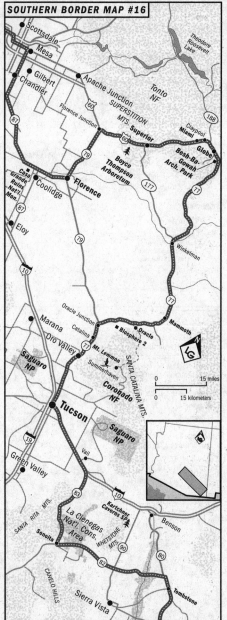

SOUTHERN BORDER MAP #16

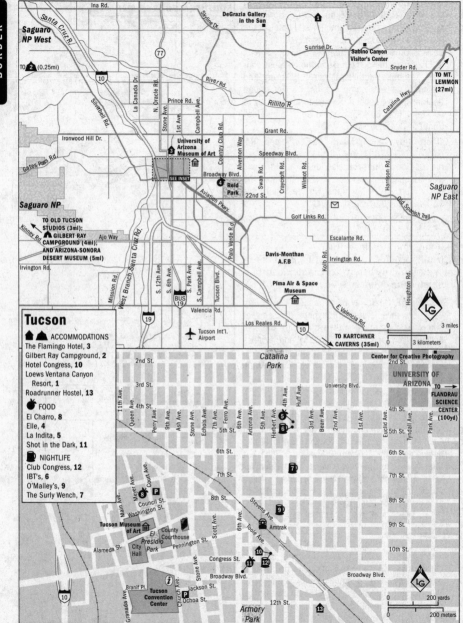

Ina Rd.

Saguaro NP West

DeGrazia Gallery in the Sun

Santa Cruz R.

Sunrise Dr.

Sabino Canyon Visitor's Center

Skyline Dr.

TO 2 (0.25mi)

River Rd.

Snyder Rd.

TO MT. LEMMON (27mi)

Silverbell Rd.

La Canada Dr.

N. Oracle Rd.

Stone Ave.

1st Ave.

Campbell Ave.

Prince Rd.

Rillito R.

Catalina Hwy.

Ironwood Hill Dr.

Gates Pass Rd.

Country Club Rd.

Grant Rd.

University of Arizona Museum of Art

Alvernon Way

Speedway Blvd.

Swan Rd.

Craycroft Rd.

Wilmot Rd.

Harrison Rd.

Saguaro NP East

Broadway Blvd.

Reid Park

22nd St.

Aviation Pkwy.

Old Spanish Trail

Saguaro NP

TO OLD TUCSON STUDIOS (3mi); GILBERT RAY CAMPGROUND (4mi); AND ARIZONA-SONORA DESERT MUSEUM (5mi)

Kinney Rd.

Ajo Way

West Branch Santa Cruz Rd.

Golf Links Rd.

Escalante Rd.

Irvington Rd.

Mission Rd.

S. 12th Ave.

S. 6th Ave.

S. Park Ave.

S. Campbell Ave.

Tucson Blvd.

Palo Verde Rd.

Davis-Monthan A.F.B

Kolb Rd.

Irvington Rd.

E. Valencia Rd.

Houghton Rd.

BUS 19

Pima Air & Space Museum

Valencia Rd.

19

Los Reales Rd.

Tucson Int'l. Airport

10

TO KARTCHNER CAVERNS (35mi)

N LG

0   3 miles

0   3 kilometers

Tucson

ACCOMMODATIONS
The Flamingo Hotel, **3**
Gilbert Ray Campground, **2**
Hotel Congress, **10**
Loews Ventana Canyon
  Resort, **1**
Roadrunner Hostel, **13**

FOOD
El Charro, **8**
Elle, **4**
La Indita, **5**
Shot in the Dark, **11**

NIGHTLIFE
Club Congress, **12**
IBT's, **6**
O'Malley's, **9**
The Surly Wench, **7**

Catalina Park

Center for Creative Photography

2nd St.

2nd St.

3rd St.

UNIVERSITY OF ARIZONA

TO FLANDRAU SCIENCE CENTER (100yd)

University Blvd.

11th Ave.

Queen Ave.

Perry Ave.

9th Ave.

Ash Ave.

Stone Ave.

7th Ave.

Ferro Ave.

6th Ave.

Arizona Ave.

5th Ave.

Herbert Ave.

4th Ave.

Huff Ave.

3rd Ave.

Bean Ave.

2nd Ave.

1st Ave.

Euclid Ave.

4th Ave.

Tyndall Ave.

Park Ave.

4th St.

5th St.

5th St.

6th St.

6th St.

7th St.

7th St.

8th St.

Mountain Ave.

Stevens Ave.

8th St.

9th Ave.

9th St.

Amtrak

Toole Ave.

6th Ave.

10th St.

Broadway Blvd.

Mever Ave.

Court Ave.

Council St.

Washington St.

Tucson Museum of Art

El Presidio Park

County Courthouse

Pennington St.

Scott Ave.

10th St.

Congress St.

Broadway Blvd.

Alameda St.

City Hall

Stone Ave.

Church Ave.

Main Ave.

Granada Ave.

Bráñif Pl.

Tucson Convention Center

Jackson St.

Ochoa St.

12th St.

13

Armory Park

N LG

0   200 yards

0   200 meters

Shot in the Dark Cafe, 121 E. Broadway Blvd. (☎520-882-5544). This cafe has phenomenal sandwiches ($4-6), comfy couches, and an artsy, laid-back atmosphere. Thanks to the cafe's long hours, free Wi-Fi, and separate room for smokers, you can drop by for a bite to eat or spend hours just lounging about. The tuna salad sandwich ($6) is especially good. Live music frequently in the evenings. Open 24hr. MC/V. ❶

👁 SIGHTS

UNIVERSITY OF ARIZONA. Lined with cafes, restaurants, galleries, and vintage clothing shops, Fourth Ave. is an alternative magnet and a great place to take a stroll. Between Speedway and Broadway Blvd., the street becomes a shopping district with increasingly touristy shops. Lovely for its varied and elaborately irrigated vegetation, the University of Arizona's mall sits where E. Third St. should be.

CENTER FOR CREATIVE PHOTOGRAPHY. The center is home to the archives of over 50 great 20th-century photographers, including Ansel Adams, Edward Weston, and W. Eugene Smith. The museum also hosts temporary exhibits. (*1030 N. Olive Rd. ☎520-621-7968. Open M-F 9am-5pm, Sa-Su noon-5pm. Archives available to the public by appointment. Free.*)

FLANDRAU SCIENCE CENTER. The center dazzles visitors with a public observatory and a laser light show. A new exhibit features an enormous representation of parts of Mars's surface that visitors can check out up close. (*1601 E. University Blvd. ☎520-621-7827. Open Th-F 9am-3pm and 6-9pm, Sa noon-9pm, Su noon-5pm. $3, under 4 free; with planetarium show $5/free.*)

UNIVERSITY OF ARIZONA MUSEUM OF ART. The museum displays modern American and 18th-century Latin-American art and has an entire floor devoted to sculptures, with a focus on artist Jacques Lipchitz. On the second floor, there is a great exhibit of outer-space-related artwork, done by Robert McCall, the artist responsible for artwork in the movie *2001: A Space Odyssey*. The museum also exhibits student art. (*☎520-621-7567. Open Tu-F 9am-5pm, Sa-Su noon-4pm. Free.*)

TUCSON MUSEUM OF ART. This major museum presents impressive traveling exhibits in all media to supplement its permanent collection of American, Mexican, and European art. Housed in the surrounding and affiliated Presidio Historic Block, it boasts an impressive collection of pre-Columbian and Mexican folk art as well as art of the American West. (*140 N. Main Ave. ☎520-624-2333. Open Tu-Sa 10am-4pm, Su noon-4pm. $8, students $3, under 13 free. 1st Su of each month free.*)

DEGRAZIA GALLERY IN THE SUN. Stepping through the ornate iron doors of this old-fashioned pueblo home reveals the artistic world of Ettore "Ted" DeGrazia. The home itself, wonderfully spacious and colorful, breathes life into the paintings that adorn the walls. DeGrazia's artwork shows its Western and cowboy influences, with a focus on the Wild West, Native Americans, and conquistadors. Wander the grounds before entering the gallery; wood sculptures and sun-bleached metalwork are scattered throughout the cactus garden. Don't miss the chapel, dedicated to the Virgin Guadalupe. (*6300 N. Swan Rd., about ¼ mi. north of Sunrise Rd. ☎520-299-9191 or 800-545-2185; www.degrazia.org. Open daily 10am-4pm. Free.*)

OLD TUCSON STUDIOS. As Speedway Blvd. works its way west from Tucson's city center, it passes by a variety of sights. After winding through a mountain pass, it eventually ends at Kinney Rd. Turning left leads you to Old Tucson Studios, an elaborate Old West-style town constructed for the 1938 movie *Arizona* and used as a backdrop for Westerns ever since, including many John Wayne films and the 1999 Will Smith blockbuster *Wild Wild West*. It's open year-round to tourists, who can walk around the Old West mockup, watch comedy and musical shows, view gunfight reenactments, and maybe catch a filming. (*201 S. Kinney Rd. ☎520-883-0100; www.oldtucson.com. Open daily 10am-4pm. Occasionally closed for group functions; call ahead. $17, Ages 4-11 $11, under 4 free.*)

ARIZONA-SONORA DESERT MUSEUM. Those opting to turn right will eschew the *Wild Wild West* for the merely Wild West; less than 2 mi. from the fork lies the Arizona-Sonora Desert Museum, a first-rate zoo and nature preserve.

The living museum recreates a range of desert habitats and features over 300 kinds of animals. A visit requires at least 2hr.; it's most fruitful to come in the morning before the animals take their afternoon siestas. Be prepared to walk a lot—the museum contains over 2 mi. of trails. (*2021 N. Kinney Rd. Follow Speedway Blvd. west of the city as it becomes Gates Pass Rd., then Kinney Rd. ☎520-883-1380; www.desertmuseum. org. Open daily Mar.-Sept. 7:30am-5pm; Oct.-Feb. 8:30am-5pm. $9.50, ages 6-12 $2.25.*)

PIMA AIR AND SPACE MUSEUM. Affiliated with the nearby Davis-Monthan Air Force Base, this museum chronicles aviation history from the days of the Wright brothers to its modern military incarnations. While exhibits on female and African-American aviators are interesting, the museum's main draw is a fleet of decommissioned warplanes. The amazing size of this collection alone makes the place worth a visit. (*6000 E. Valencia Rd. ☎520-574-0462. Open daily 9am-5pm. Last entry 4pm. June-Oct. $11.75, ages 7-12 $8; Nov.-May $13.50/9.*)

■ NIGHTLIFE

The free weeklies *Tucson Weekly* and *Caliente* are the local authorities on nightlife, while the weekend sections of the *Star* or the *Citizen* also provide good coverage. Throughout the year, the city of the sun presents **Music Under the Stars,** a series of sunset concerts performed by the **Tucson Pops Orchestra** at the bandstand in Reid Park. (☎520-722-5853 or 791-0479. Concerts generally May-June Su evening in May and June. Free.) The **Tucson Jazz Society** holds free concerts every Sunday evening from April to May and from September to October. (☎520-903-1265; www.tucsonjazz.org. Venue varies.) Every Thursday, the **Thursday Night Art Walk** lets you mosey around downtown galleries and studios. For more info, call **Tucson Arts District** (☎520-624-9977). U of A students rock and roll on Speedway Blvd., while others do the two-step in clubs on N. Oracle Rd. Young locals hang out on Fourth Ave., where most bars have live music and a low cover.

Club Congress, 311 E. Congress St. (☎520-622-8848). This is the venue for most of the indie music coming through town, including alt-country, alt-rock, and blues. The friendly hotel staff and a cast of regulars make it an especially good time. Pabst Blue Ribbon $1.25. 80s night M. DJs M and Th and live bands the rest of the week. Cover $3-10. Open daily 9pm-3am. Bar open until 2am. AmEx/D/MC/V.

O'Malley's, 247 N. 4th Ave. (☎520-623-8600). A large bar with decent bar food, pool tables, and pinball. Usually a better place to nurse your pint of Guinness than it is to get your groove on, although the dance floor gets packed on Th and Sa for 80s and 90s cover bands. No cover. Open daily 11am-1am. AmEx/D/MC/V.

Surly Wench Pub, 424 N. 4th Ave. (☎520-882-0009). If there's one thing you notice about the pub, it's the decor. Scandalous pictures, a cool lighting scheme, and colorful bartenders make this place what it is. Located on the popular 4th Ave., the venue frequently hosts live shows and draws a crowd every night of the week. No cover. Open M-F 5pm-2am, Sa-Su 2am-2am. MC/V.

IBT's, 616 N. 4th Ave. (☎520-882-3053). The single most popular gay venue in Tucson, IBT's pumps dance music in a lively club to a mixed weekend crowd. Karaoke Sa-Su. Pints of Bud Sa-Su $1. Hip-hop DJs F-Sa. No cover. Happy hour daily noon-8pm with $2 domestic beers and mixed drinks. Open daily noon-2am. Cash only.

▲ CAVES

Kartchner Caverns State Park, 9 mi. off I-10 at Exit 302, is enormously popular, filled with magnificent rock formations and home to thousands of bats. This is a "living" cave, which contains water and is still experiencing the growth of its formations. Kartchner Caverns was only discovered in 1974 and opened to the public in 1999, so relatively few people have seen the magnificent formations inside. The damp conditions cause the formations to shine and glisten in the light. Taking a tour is the only way to enter the cave. Two different tours are offered, although one is closed during the summer to allow the bats inhabiting the cave to give birth undisturbed. The park is located about 50 mi. from Tucson, and camping is available on-site. (☎520-586-4100, reservations 586-2283. Open daily 7:30am-6pm. 90min. tours every 20min. 8:30am-4:30pm. Reservations strongly recommended. Entrance fee $5 per vehicle, free with reservation. Tours $19-23, ages 7-13 $10-13.) Near Saguaro National Park East, **Colossal Cave** is one of the only dormant (no water or new formations) caves in the US. A variety of tours are offered; on Saturday evenings, a special ladder tour through otherwise sealed-off tunnels, crawl spaces, and corridors can be arranged. (☎520-647-7275. Open daily from mid-Mar. to mid-Sept. 8am-5pm; from mid-Sept. to mid-Mar. 9am-5pm. Entrance fee $5 per vehicle. Guided tours $8.50, ages 6-12 $5. Ladder tour $15, including dinner $35.)

🏔 OUTDOORS

North of the desert museum, the western half of **Saguaro National Park (Tucson Mountain District)** has hiking trails and an auto loop. The **Bajada Loop Drive** runs about 6 mi. on an ungraded dirt road, but passes through some of the most striking desert scenery the park has to offer. The paved nature walk (¼ mi.) near the **visitors center,** 2700 N. Kinney Rd., has some of the best specimens of saguaro cactus in the Tucson area. (☎520-733-5158. Open daily 7am-sunset. Visitors center open daily 9am-5pm. Entrance fee $10 per vehicle; good for 7 days.) There are a variety of hiking trails through **Saguaro West; Sendero Esperanza Trail** (3 mi.), beginning at the Ez-Kim-In-Zin picnic area, is the mildest way to approach to the summit of Wasson Peak (4687 ft.), the highest in the Tucson Mountain Range. The **Hugh Norris Trail** (5 mi.) is a slightly longer, more strenuous climb to the top but has great views of unique rock formations, while gaining over 2100 ft. in elevation. The eastern half of Saguaro National Park, known as the **Rincon Mountain District,** has more hiking. Mountain biking is permitted only around the **Cactus Forest Loop Drive** (6 mi.) and **Cactus Forest Trail** (2 mi.), at the eastern end of the park near the visitors center. The trails in Saguaro East can be much longer than those in the western segment of the park.

Northeast of downtown Tucson, the cliffs and desert pools of **Sabino Canyon** provide an ideal backdrop for picnics and day hikes. Locals beat Tucson heat by frolicking in the water holes. No cars are permitted, but a narrated 45min. bus makes trips through the canyon. A great day hike idea is to take the shuttle one-way from the visitors center through the canyon to stop #9 and then walk back along the **Phoneline Trail** (5 mi.), a picturesque route along the ridge of the canyon. The visitors center is at the park's entrance. Take Speedway Blvd. to Swan Rd. to Sunrise Dr. The entrance is at the cross of Sunrise Dr. and Sabino Canyon Rd. (☎520-749-8700. Park open 24hr. Visitors center open daily 9am-4:30pm. Shuttle runs July-Nov. every hr. 9am-4pm; Dec.-June every 30min. sunrise-sunset. Entrance fee $3, ages 3-12 $1. Shuttle $7.50, ages 3-12 $3.)

◪ DETOUR
SKY ISLAND SCENIC BYWAY

From downtown, follow **Grant Road** east until it meets up with **Tanque Verde Road.** Hop on Tanque Verde Rd., still headed east, and follow it to signs for the **Catalina Highway.** The highway itself comes out of the northeast corner of the city limits and then runs through the scenic **Coronado National Forest.**

The beautiful 27 mi. Sky Island road leads up steep inclines and switchbacks through the Coronado National Forest (☎520-388-8300; $5 per vehicle) up to **Mount Lemmon** and a great ski area. For those who don't wish to stop off at any points located in Coronado National Forest, there is no fee to drive the road. From there, you must backtrack to get back to Tucson. The entire adventure, not including any hiking, takes several hours, but fortunately the road is paved and in very good condition. In both temperature and terrain, the nearly mile-high climb can be compared to a transcontinental journey from Mexico to Canada. Every 1000 ft. change in elevation witnesses a metamorphosis that parallels a 300 mi. drive northward. As the road blasts through impressive granite formations and snakes along canyon walls, the temperature drops nearly 30° and the Sonoran desert gives way to forest.

Nearing the summit, the highway hugs the ridgeline, and the impressive vistas of the surrounding desert valleys are visible on both sides of the roadway. Stopping at one of the many turnoffs or picnic areas for a picture is a must. At 8000 ft., **Inspiration Rock Picnic Ground** offers the brave a chance to take a few (cautious) steps out onto a giant granite precipice and gaze down at the miniature Tucson Valley below. At the top lies the teensy hamlet of Summerhaven, where a public restroom makes up half of the buildings in the town, and **Mount Lemmon Ski Valley** (☎520-576-1321). The Forest Service offers campgrounds along the way **Rose Canyon Campground ❶**, on the shores of a lovely lake, is the most popular. **Spencer Canyon Campground ❶** is closer to the summit, so it stays cooler than many other sites. Both campgrounds have toilets and potable water but no showers. (☎520-749-8700. Sites $18. Each additional vehicle $8.) Other campgrounds have primitive sites and cost $10. **Molino Basin ❶** and **General Hitchcock ❶** have toilets but no potable water. (Open Apr.-Oct. Sites $10.) Call the **Santa Catalina Ranger District** (☎520-749-8700) for more info.

THE ROAD TO ORACLE: 30 MI.

Once you've seen or passed **Catalina State Park,** continue north on **Route 77** past the town of Oro Valley, essentially a suburb of Tucson, to Biosphere 2.

ORACLE ☎520

Biosphere 2, 32540 S. Biosphere Rd., an "earth-bound spaceship," is a massive three-acre laboratory that looks and feels like it is, indeed, independent of planet Earth. Concrete, glass, and 500 tons of steel make up and close off this sealed ecosystem, which houses five biomes: a desert, a marsh, a savanna, a rainforest, and even an ocean. Ultra-high technology powers Biosphere 2, from the two dome-like "lungs" that manage air pressure to the wave machine that keeps 700,000 gal. of water moving through the reefs of the ocean biome. Perhaps best known for a 1991 experiment that examined whether humans could survive in a closed environment, the center now focuses on education and research. There is a small visitors center by the entrance to the Biosphere, but the only way to really explore the place is by taking a guided tour. (☎520-838-6200; www.bio2.com.Open daily 9am-4pm. Last tour 3:30pm.

Visitors center free. Tours $20, ages 12-17 $13, under 12 free. AmEx/D/MC/V.)

THE ROAD TO MAMMOTH: 17 MI.

Continue on **Route 77** for 17 mi. to reach Mammoth.

MAMMOTH ☎520

The prairies and foothills that surround the self-proclaimed wildflower capital of Arizona explode with color in springtime with adequate rainfall—which unfortunately hasn't happened in a few years. For those in search of a meal, **Los Michoanos ❷**, 337 Rte. 77, serves up authentic Mexican food and also a few American dishes. Breakfast plates ($5-7) come with a tortilla or toast and hash browns or beans. For lunch, it offers hamburgers ($3.50), burritos ($3-6), and tacos ($4-6). Though the restaurant isn't much to look at, the food hits the spot. (☎520-487-2380. Open Tu-Sa 7:30am-8pm, Su 7:30am-3pm. D/MC/V.)

THE ROAD TO GLOBE-MIAMI: 59 MI.

From Mammoth, continue on **Route 77** until it joins up with **US 70.** Hang a left and follow US 70 into Globe. Once in Globe, US 70 meets **US 60** and becomes **Willow Street.** Turn right at the signs for the "Historic District" to reach **Broad Street,** the town's main drag.

GLOBE-MIAMI ☎928

The history of these two small conjoined mountain towns is inextricably tied to the mineral deposits that lace the surrounding mountain walls. A quick stop at the **Gila County Historical Museum,** 1330 N. Broad St., reveals the impact mining has had on this community. (☎928-425-7385. Open M-F 10am-4pm, Sa 11am-3pm. Free.) Globe is also home to the **Besh-Ba-Gowah Archaeological Park,** a reconstructed pueblo that once featured over 400 rooms. Few artifacts remain at the site, but, if you don't mind the facsimile, you'll enjoy the intricate walls, multistoried buildings, and recreated settings. The adjoining **Besh-Ba-Gowah Museum** houses actual artifacts, tons of pottery, and two large models of the giant pueblo. The name means "place of metal" and was given to the early mining towns of Globe and Miami by the Apache. From US 60, take Broad St. until it ends at the railroad tracks, then go left on Jesse Hayes Rd. The park is up the hill on the left. (☎928-425-0320. Museum open daily 9am-5pm. Park open daily 6am-6pm. $3, under 12 free, seniors $2.)

Inexpensive rooms are located right on US 60 at the **Budget Motel ❶**, 792 N. Willow St. Rooms show some wear, but are generally clean and decorated with a ragtag assortment of old-school furniture. (☎928-425-4573. Singles $34; doubles $39. AmEx/D/MC/V.) **Joe's Broad Street Grill ❷**, 247 S. Broad St., sits in the heart of Globe's historic district, in the building that was once Globe's first schoolhouse. This classic diner full of American flags serves tasty Italian food and handmade burgers hot off the grill. (☎928-425-6269. Open M-F 6am-2:30pm, Sa 6am-1pm. D/MC/V.)

⚑ THE ROAD TO SUPERIOR: 22 MI.

Leave Globe on **US 60** and continue toward Superior. The road to Superior takes you into the heart of the Superstition Mountains, where the barren landscape gives way to oaks as the road winds through a rust-colored canyon. The aptly named **Oak Flat Campground ❶** is near the red boulder formations and oak groves of these heights. Turn left 16 mi. after Globe. (☎928-402-6200. Picnic tables and grills. No water or toilets. Open 24hr. Free.) When the climb levels off, the road finds itself in a high-altitude valley dotted with oaks. The impressive scenery ends as you cruise into the mining town of Superior.

SUPERIOR ☎ 520

At the base of the Superstition Mountains sits the still-active mining community of Superior. The local copper smelter looms over the village, an imposing monument to the ore that runs this city. Superior has seen better days, but classic Old West facades maintain its mining-town character. The biggest attraction in Superior is, ironically, the ⬛**World's Smallest Museum,** 1111 W. US 60. This 15 ft. long museum displays everything from mining equipment to guns and a 1984 Compaq computer to a Barry M. Goldwater bobble-head. Outside, the museum has an assortment of fountains made from old junk. One fountain is made from wheelbarrows and miscellaneous rusted farming equipment, while another is constructed entirely from tires. The museum

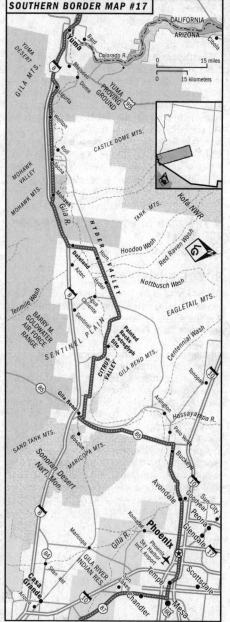

SOUTHERN BORDER MAP #17

SOUTHERN BORDER

is on the left as you leave Superior on W. US 60, attached to the Buckboard City Cafe. Look for signs for the cafe. (☎520-689-5857; www. smallestmuseum.com. Open M and W-Su 8am-1:30pm. Suggested donation $1-2.)

The **Copper Mountain Motel ❷**, 70 W. Hwy. 60, has clean, well-decorated rooms with large windows against the backdrop of the Superstition Mountains. (☎520-689-2886. Laundry $1. Free Wi-Fi. Rooms both $60. AmEx/D/MC/V.) Next door, the **Buckboard City Cafe ❷**, 1111 W. US 60, serves traditional breakfast fare, hamburgers, sandwiches, salads, soups, and Mexican food. Try the "sweat-hog" (spicy wrap with sausage and jalapeño; $7) or the "Southwesty burger," a $6 heap of chili, bacon, and cheese. (☎520-689-5800. Open M and Th-Su 6am-2pm. D/MC/V.)

⚐ THE ROAD TO BOYCE THOMPSON ARBORETUM: 3 MI.

Continue on **US 60** for 3 mi. past Superior.

BOYCE THOMPSON ARBORETUM   ☎520

Nestled in the gorge created by Queen Creek lies the shady hollow of the ⚑**Boyce Thompson Arboretum State Park**, 37615 US 60. Founded in the mid-1920s, the botanical garden features plants from the world's deserts in Arizona's oldest and largest botanical garden. Just a bunch of cactuses? Think again. In addition to a large selection of domestic and exotic cactuses, the gardens exhibit flora from the Australian Outback to the tropics to the native Sonoran desert. In total, over 3200 species of plants and 72 species of animals are represented in the park. The tall trees ensure that the trails will be pleasant in just about any season, but avoid walking the 1 mi. trail through the park at midday in summer. (☎520-689-2811; www.arboretum.ag.arizona. edu. Open daily May-Sept. 6am-3pm; Oct.-Apr. 8am-5pm. $7.50, ages 5-12 $3.)

⚐ THE ROAD TO FLORENCE: 25 MI.

Continue on **US 60** for 13 mi. to Florence Junction. From here, you can continue directly to Phoenix on US 60 or dip south on **Route 79** to reach Florence.

FLORENCE   ☎520

As Rte. 79 rolls into Florence, it passes a sign that reads "State Prison: do not stop for hitch-hikers." That, in a nutshell, is Florence. Home to Arizona's largest state prison, the town has a long penal history, having housed WWII internment camps for Japanese-Americans and German POWs. The **Pinal County Historical Museum**, 712 S. Main St., documents the town's penal history in grisly detail, displaying a collection of hangman's nooses, a two-seater from a gas chamber, and photos of criminals put to death. (☎520-868-4382. Open from Sept. to mid-July Tu-Sa 11am-4pm, Su noon-4pm. Donation suggested.) Quietly meditate on all you've learned about the penal system at **Saint Anthony's Greek Orthodox Monastery**, 4784 N. St. Joseph Way, a peaceful compound framed by the gold domes of the Eastern Rite. Built in 1995 by five Orthodox fathers from Greece, the monastery houses 40 fathers who take visitors to see the ornate and beautifully groomed grounds on monk-led tours. Find it 10 mi. south of Florence, off Rte. 79, at mi. 124. (☎520-868-3188; www.stanthonysmonastery. org. Open daily 10:30am-2:30pm. Appropriate dress required: men must wear long pants and long sleeves; women must wear skirts below the knee, long sleeves, and scarves. Free.)

The outrageously teal **Blue Mist Motel ❸**, 40 S. Pinal Pkwy., off Rte. 79, has clean and comfortable rooms. All rooms have HBO and pool access, and fortunately are not painted teal. (☎520-868-5875. Wi-Fi. Singles $55; doubles $65. AmEx/D/MC/V.) For good eats day or night, head to **Don Francisco's ❷**, 981 S. Main St., which offers Mexican dishes of generous portions. (☎520-868-0200. Entrees $5-7.50. Super Nachos $7. Open 24hr. Cash only.)

◤ DETOUR
CASA GRANDE RUINS NATIONAL MONUMENT

Go west on **Route 287** for 9 mi. toward Coolidge. Follow Rte. 287 for 2 mi. as it curves southward and look for signs for Casa Grande. The ruins are on your right.

The nation's first archaeological preserve, the Casa Grande Ruins National Monument is also one of the most perplexing. Built around 1350 by the Hohokam people, the four-story structure is almost all that remains of one of North America's most advanced civilizations. The structure, which mystified Spanish explorers called Casa Grande ("great house"), was part of a vast, innovative civilization. The walls of the house face the cardinal directions, and a circular hole in the upper west wall aligns with the setting sun during the summer solstice. The park has a visitors center with a small museum and offers self-guided tours through the ruins. (☎520-723-3172. Open daily 8am-5pm. $5, under 15 free.)

⚑ THE ROAD TO PHOENIX: 63 MI.

From Casa Grande, go back to **Route 287** and retrace your route 2 mi. toward Florence. When the road splits, turn left and follow **Route 87 West** for 7 mi. to **Route 387.** Turn left on Rte. 387 W. and follow it another 7 mi. west to **I-10.** Although you're already technically in the greater Phoenix area, it takes another 30-45min. to drive into the center of town.

PHOENIX   ☎602

Anglo settlers named their small farming community Phoenix, believing that their oasis had risen from the ashes of ancient Native American settlements. The 20th century has seen this unlikely metropolis live up to its name. The expansion of water resources, the proliferation of the railroad, and the introduction of air-conditioning have fueled Phoenix's ascent to the ranks of America's leading urban centers. Shiny high-rises now crowd the business district, while a vast web of six-lane highways and strip malls surrounds the downtown area. During the balmy winter, tourists, golfers, and businessmen flock to enjoy perfect temperatures, while in summer the visitors flee and the city crawls into its air-conditioned shell as temperatures exceed 100° F.

◼ ORIENTATION

The intersection of **Central Avenue** and **Washington Street** marks the center of downtown. Central Ave. runs north-south and Washington St. east-west. One of Phoenix's peculiarities is that numbered avenues and streets both run north-south. Avenues are numbered sequentially west from Central Ave., while streets are numbered east. Standing on Central Ave. facing north, the first road to your right is **First Street,** and the first to your left is **First Avenue.** East-west streets in the downtown area are named after US presidents. Large north-south thoroughfares include **Seventh Street, 16th Street, Seventh Avenue,** and **19th Avenue,** while **McDowell Road, Van Buren Street, Indian School Road,** and **Camelback Road** are major east-west arteries. Greater Phoenix includes smaller independent municipalities that sometimes have different street-naming schemes. If you park and want to get around the downtown area (Adams, Washington, and Jefferson St.), look for the free Dash buses and jump aboard (M-F 6:30am-8pm). Phoenix rush-hour traffic is some of the worst in the country—you'll be happy if you stay off the roads between 4 and 6pm. Parking is not a problem anywhere in the city; most roads have metered spots.

Once a series of independent communities, the numerous townships of "the Valley of the Sun" now bleed into one another in a continuous chain of strip malls, office parks, slums, and super-resorts. Just to the east of downtown Phoenix and south of the Salt River lies **Tempe,** with the third-largest university in the US and the nightlife to prove it. Don't make the mistake of leaving town without experiencing at least one night as a Sun Devil. East of Tempe, the suburban paradise of **Mesa** stretches out along Rte. 202. Tamer than its collegiate neighbor, Mesa is home to one of the largest Mormon populations outside of Utah as well as a bevy of cheap eats and chain motels. **Scottsdale,** north of Mesa and northeast of downtown, is the playground of the rich and is filled with world-class resorts.

VITAL STATS
Population: 1,500,000
Tourist Office: Greater Phoenix Visitors and Convention Bureau, 125 N. 2nd St. (☎602-254-6500 or 877-225-5749, recorded info 602-252-5588; www.visitphoenix.com), at Adams St. Open M-F 8am-5pm.
Library and Internet Access: Burton Barr Central Library, 1221 N. Central Ave. (☎602-262-4636). Open M-Th 10am-9pm, F-Sa 9am-6pm, Su noon-6pm.
Post Office: 522 N. Central Ave. (☎602-253-5045). Open M-F 9am-6pm. **Postal Code:** 85034.

▚ ACCOMMODATIONS

Budget travelers should consider visiting Phoenix during July and August, when motels slash their prices by as much as 70%. In the winter, when temperatures drop, the number of vacationers rises, vacancies are few, and prices go up; make reservations early. The reservation-less should cruise the rows of motels on Van Buren St. east of downtown, toward the airport. Parts of this area can be unsafe; guests should examine a motel thoroughly before checking in. Although more distant, the areas around Papago Fwy. and Black Canyon Hwy. are loaded with motels and can present some safer options. Downtown itself has very few options, but if you head out of town on a big road there should be plenty of inexpensive places to crash. Suburbs to the east such as Mesa and Tempe are full of inexpensive options. Chandler and Scottsdale are both significantly more expensive. Another alternative is to contact **Mi Casa Su Casa Advanced Reservations Arizona,** which arranges stays in B&Bs throughout Arizona, New Mexico, Utah, Nevada, and Southern California. (☎800-456-0682; www.azres.com. Open daily 6am-9pm. From $50.)

Metcalf House (HI-AYH), 1026 N. 9th St. (☎602-254-9803), a few blocks northeast of downtown. The ebullient owner gives helpful advice about the area and fosters a lively community in this decorative house. Evening gab sessions are common on the front porch. The neighborhood has seen better days, so using a coin lockers available in the dorms is probably a good idea. Closed July-Aug. Check-in 7-10am and 5-10pm. Lockout from kitchen 10am-5pm. Open Sept.-June. Single-sex dorms $18, members $16; private rooms $30-35. Cash only. ❶

YMCA Downtown Phoenix, 350 N. 1st Ave. (☎602-253-6181). Another option in the downtown area with small, clean, single-occupancy rooms with shared bathrooms for both men and women. Temporary gym memberships $5. Reception daily 7am-10pm. Call 24-48hr. in advance. Rooms $25. 18+. AmEx/D/MC/V. ❶

Lost Dutchman Comfort Lodge, 560 S. Country Club Dr. (☎480-969-2200), in Mesa. A good location near restaurants. Very clean rooms. Kitchenettes are available for a small extra charge. Check-in after 3pm. Check-out noon. Rooms in summer $49; in winter, rates vary, so call ahead. AmEx/D/MC/V. ❸

Days Inn Tempe, 1221 E. Apache Blvd. (☎480-968-7793; www.daysinn.com), in Tempe. A chain with tidy rooms and reasonable prices. Located right by Arizona State, near all of the collegiate action. TVs, pool, and hot tub. Breakfast included. Free Internet. Singles from $50; doubles from $60. AmEx/D/MC/V. ❸

Sunland Motel, 2602 E. Main St. (☎480-833-1713), in Mesa. One of many motels along E. Main St., this is a solid option with clean, standard rooms. Some kitchenettes. Singles from $49; doubles from $54. AmEx/MC/V. ❷

Motel 6 Phoenix East, 5315 E. Van Buren St. (☎602-267-8555), by the airport. Although it isn't located in the greatest neighborhood, this chain motel is on a major street and offers rooms, clean to the point of sterility, at some of the cheapest prices you can find. Cable TV and A/C. Check-in after 3pm. Check-out by noon. Singles from $36; doubles from $41. MC/V. ❷

Mission Palms, 60 E. 5th St. (☎480-894-1400; www.missionpalms.com). At the base of the Tempe's Hayden Butte, this deluxe hotel is a steal in the summer, though prices more than double in the winter. Indulge in luxury (2 hot tubs, a pool, health club, and tennis center) with the knowledge that raucous Mill Ave. is just a minute's walk away. Singles and doubles in summer from $139; in winter $279. AmEx/D/MC/V. ❺

🍴 FOOD

While much of the Phoenix culinary scene seems to revolve around shopping-mall food courts and expensive restaurants, quality budget eateries can be found. McDowell and Camelback Rd. offer a (small) variety of Asian restaurants. The **Arizona Center,** an open-air shopping gallery at Third Avenue and Van Buren St., features food venues amid fountains and palm trees. Downtown, cafes and restaurants can be found interspersed between parking lots, while in Tempe you can fill up on bar food in the hybrid "resto-bars" that cater to college students around Mill and University St.

Los Dos Molinos, 8646 S. Central Ave. (☎602-243-9113). From downtown, go 8 mi. south on Central Ave. Lively, colorful, and with chilies hotter than hell, it's worth the trip. The food is authentic, and they don't know mild, so be ready to swallow fire. For those who need something to douse the flames, the margaritas are phenomenal. Enchilada dinner $7-9. Burritos $3-7. Open

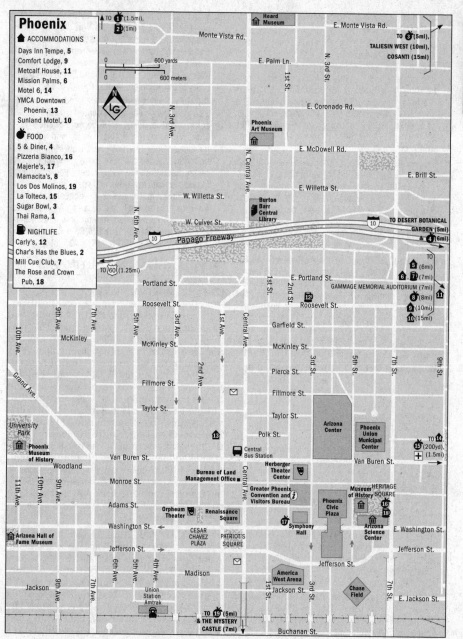

Phoenix

ACCOMMODATIONS

Days Inn Tempe, **5**
Comfort Lodge, **9**
Metcalf House, **11**
Mission Palms, **6**
Motel 6, **14**
YMCA Downtown
  Phoenix, **13**
Sunland Motel, **10**

FOOD

5 & Diner, **4**
Pizzeria Bianco, **16**
Majerle's, **17**
Mamacita's, **8**
Los Dos Molinos, **19**
La Tolteca, **15**
Sugar Bowl, **3**
Thai Rama, **1**

NIGHTLIFE

Carly's, **12**
Char's Has the Blues, **2**
Mill Cue Club, **7**
The Rose and Crown
  Pub, **18**

Tu-F 11am-2:30pm and 5-9pm, Sa 11am-9pm. AmEx/D/MC/V. ❷

La Tolteca, 1205 E. Van Buren St. (☎602-253-1511; www.latoltecamex.com), at 12th St. A local favorite. This cafeteria-style restaurant and Mexican grocery, with brightly painted murals, serves up uncommercialized Mexican fare in *grande* portions. Familiar dishes are offered alongside specialties like *cocido* soup (sausage, chickpeas, and tomatoes; $6) and *pozole* ($6). Big burritos $5-7. Dinner plates $6-10. Open daily 7am-8pm. AmEx/MC/V. ❶

Pizzeria Bianco, 623 E. Adams St. (☎602-258-8300; www.pizzeriabianco.com), in Copper Sq. A delightful restaurant where the roaring wood oven takes up a sizable chunk of the floor space. The just-made pizzas are superb, particularly The Rosa (pistachio, red onion, and rosemary; $11). Salads $6-9. Open Tu-Sa 5-10pm. Bar open 4-11pm. AmEx/MC/V. ❷

Thai Rama, 1221 W. Camelback Rd. (☎602-285-1123). Combines cool, modern decor with cozy booths and Thai decorations. Try a delicious coconut curry dish ($10), a stuffed pork omelet ($9), or one of the many vegetarian options. For dessert, sample homemade coconut ice cream with black sweet rice ($5). Open M-Th 11am-2:30pm and 5-9:30pm, F 11am-2:30pm and 5-10:30pm, Sa noon-10:30pm, Su 5-9:30pm. AmEx/MC/V. ❷

Mamacita's, 216 E. University Dr. (☎480-967-7744), in Tempe. Located right by the ASU campus, Mamacita's skirts the line between restaurant and nightspot. Laid-back day-drinking mentality and tasty Mexican dishes. Patio seating with both indoor and outdoor bars. Huge burritos $5-8. No cover. Happy hour M-F 3-6pm, Sa-Su all day with $2 bottles. Open daily M-Th and Su 11am-midnight, F-Sa 11am-2am. AmEx/D/MC/V. ❶

5 & Diner, 5220 N. 16th St. (☎602-264-5200), with branches dotting the greater metro area. Vinyl booths, a smiley waitstaff, and innumerable jukeboxes playing sock-hop favorites will give you a sense of what the 50s could have been. Outdoor seating under misters that blow a cool, damp breeze onto patrons. Some of the best milkshakes in town ($4.50). Burgers $8-10. Sandwiches $8-9. Open 24hr. AmEx/MC/V. ❷

Sugar Bowl Ice Cream Parlor & Restaurant, 4005 N. Scottsdale Rd. (☎480-946-0051), in Scottsdale. Get out of the heat and into this old-time ice-cream parlor, where everything is super cutesy and super pink. The sundaes are piled thick and high ($3-5), and the milkshakes ($4.25) are a meal in themselves. Still hungry? Sandwiches and salads ($5-7) are available. Be sure to check out the ice-cream-themed arcade before you leave. Open M-Th and Su 11am-10pm, F-Sa 11am-midnight. AmEx/D/MC/V. ❷

Majerle's Sports Grill, 24 N. 2nd St. (☎602-253-0118), downtown. Located in the oldest commercial building in Phoenix, Majerle's is a sports-themed restaurant owned and operated by former Phoenix Suns great Dan Majerle (pronounced "Marley"). Unlike many gimmicky sports restaurants, the food here is really good, and Dan Majerle himself has been known to come in to chat with customers. Burgers, sandwiches, and salads are mostly what you'll find here—try Mama Majerle's Burger with grilled mushrooms and onions ($9). Entrees $7-10. Open M-Sa 11am-2am, Su 11am-midnight. AmEx/D/MC/V. ❷

🔵 📷 SIGHTS AND OUTDOORS

🏛HEARD MUSEUM. Renowned for its presentation of ancient Native American art, the Heard Museum also features exhibits on contemporary Native Americans. The permanent collection includes fabulous modern Southwestern art and photography, an exhibit devoted to the government's forced residential school system, and a gallery with artifacts from the region's native peoples, including the Hohokam, builders of Casa Grande. The museum itself is a graceful adobe building with Spanish tiles, fountains, and beautifully landscaped gardens. Due to its close ties with the local art community, the museum is constantly adding new art and features five temporary exhibitions at any given time. (*2301 N. Central Ave., 4 blocks north of McDowell Rd. ☎602-252-8840, recorded info 252-8848; www.heard.org. Open daily 9:30am-5pm. Tours noon, 1:30, 3:30pm. $10, students $5, under 6 free.*)

PHOENIX ART MUSEUM. This museum showcases art of the American West, including paintings from the Taos and Santa Fe art colonies. The permanent collection is a mix of European, Asian, and American art and houses pieces by the Tres Grandes of Mexican art (Orozco, Siqueiros, and Rivera), works by Jackson Pollock and Georgia O'Keeffe, and a fashion gallery. Don't miss Yayoi Kusama's

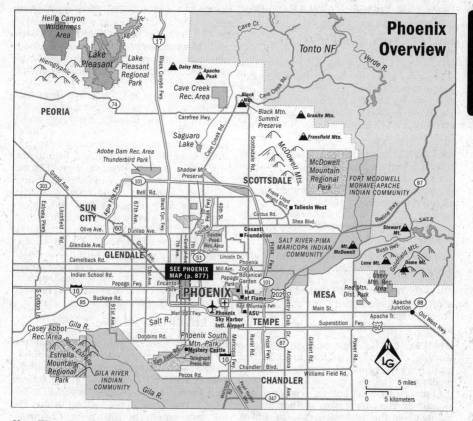

Phoenix Overview

You Who Are Getting Obliterated in the Dancing Swarm of Fireflies, a new mixed-media installation with LED lights in a mirrored room. *(1625 N. Central Ave., at McDowell Rd. ☎ 602-257-1880. Open Tu 10am-9pm, W-Su 10am-5pm. Free guided tours daily noon, 1, 2pm. $10, students and seniors $8, ages 6-17 $4. Tu 3-9pm free.)*

DESERT BOTANICAL GARDEN. To reach Papago Park from downtown, take Van Buren St. east and head left at the well-marked exit. From the south or east, take Apache Blvd. and, as it turns left, exit right at Galvin Rd.; there is no sign for the park. The garden showcases colorful cactuses, plants native to the Sonoran Desert, and several breeds of endangered or threatened species. Walk up to the Mountain Vista for great views of the desert valley below or to Ullman Terrace for scenic outlooks on the mountains and saguaro forests. It's best not to hit the park at midday in the summer, since the garden can be excruciatingly hot. *(1201 N. Galvin Pkwy. ☎ 408-941-1225; www.dbg.org. Open daily 7am-8pm. $10, students $5, ages 3-12 $4.)*

PHOENIX ZOO. If you spot an orangutan amid the cactuses, you must be at the Phoenix Zoo, which has over 1300 critters from South America, Africa, and the Southwest. Attractions include massive 100-year-old tortoises, over 200 endangered species, and the zoo's newest exhibit, dubbed "Monkey Village." Zoo employees give daily talks on different animals and their roles in the wild. *(455 N. Galvin Pkwy. ☎ 602-273-1341; www.phoenixzoo.org. Open*

June-Sept. M-F 7am-2pm, Sa-Su 7am-4pm; Oct.-May daily 9am-5pm. $14, ages 3-12 $6.)

HALL OF FLAME MUSEUM OF FIREFIGHTING. This museum, just outside the southern exit of Papago Park, features antique fire engines and other firefighting equipment spread throughout a large, open building. The museum also includes a memorial to firefighters who have died in the line of duty. (6101 E. Van Buren St. ☎602-275-3473. Open M-Sa 9am-5pm, Su noon-4pm. $6, ages 6-17 $4, ages 3-5 $1.50.)

SALT RIVER. East of the city, in Mesa, the Salt River is one of the last remaining desert rivers in the Southwest. **US Salt River Recreation,** 15 mi. north of the city on US 60, arranges tubing trips and rents tubes to those who want to lay back and float away the day. (☎408-984-3305; www.saltrivertubing.com. Tube rental $14 per day, including shuttle service to the river. Open daily 9am-7pm.)

ARIZONA SCIENCE CENTER. At the center, interactive science exhibits exist alongside an IMAX theater and planetarium. Galleries discuss topics like electricity and space technology. (600 E. Washington St., in Copper Sq. ☎602-716-2000. Open daily 10am-5pm. $9, students and ages 3-12 $7. IMAX $8/7. Planetarium $8/7.)

MYSTERY CASTLE. The striking castle is worth the 5 mi. trip from downtown. Built in small increments over 15 years (c. 1930), this modern-day castle is a spectacular example of the creative architectural use of space. Laugh along with the tour guides as they provide tidbits about the masterpiece's peculiarities. (800 E. Mineral Rd. Head south on Central Ave. and take a left on Mineral Rd. just before the South Mountain Park entrance. ☎602-268-1581. Open from Oct. to mid-June Th-Su 11am-4pm. $5, ages 5-15 $3.)

OTHER SIGHTS. Taliesin West was built as the winter camp of Frank Lloyd Wright's architectural collective; in his later years, he lived there full-time. It is now a campus for an architectural college run by his foundation. The beautiful compound, entirely designed by the master, seems to blend naturally into the surrounding desert and includes a studio, a Chinese cinema, and a performance hall. (12621 Frank Lloyd Wright Blvd. Head east off the Cactus St. exit from Rte. 101. ☎480-860-2700; www. franklloydwright.org. Open Sept.-June daily 9am-4pm. Guided tours required. 1hr. tours $27, students and

seniors $23, ages 4-12 $10. 90min tours, offered every hr. $32, students $29, ages 4-12 $20.) One of the last buildings Wright designed, the **Gammage Memorial Auditorium** is a standout with its unique rotunda shape and pink-and-beige earth tones in harmony with the surrounding environment. (At Mill Ave. and Apache Blvd., on the ASU campus in Tempe. ☎408-965-0458. 30min. tours Sept.-Apr. M 1-4pm, when auditorium is not in use. Call ahead for times. Free.) **Cosanti** is a working studio and bell foundry designed by the architect and sculptor Paolo Soleri, one of Wright's students and the mastermind behind the utopian community **Arcosanti,** located 70 mi. north of Phoenix. The buildings here fuse with the natural landscape even more strikingly than those at Taliesin West, and visitors are allowed to wander the grounds freely and observe artists working. Arrive early in the day (10:30am-12:30pm) to watch the casting of Cosanti's famous bronze wind bells. (6433 Doubletree Ranch Rd. Traveling north on Scottsdale Rd., turn left on Doubletree Ranch Rd.; it will be on your left in about 5 blocks. ☎800-752-3187. Open M-Sa 9am-5pm, Su 11am-5pm. Suggested donation $1.)

♫ ENTERTAINMENT

Phoenix is stacked with stadiums, and the large facilities make it easy to get last-minute tickets. NBA basketball action rises with the **Phoenix Suns** (☎602-379-7867) at the **America West Arena,** while the **Arizona Cardinals** (☎602-379-0101) migrate to the football field in the fall and winter. The 2001 Series-Champion **Arizona Diamondbacks** play at the state-of-the-art **Chase Field,** complete with a retractable roof, an outfield swimming pool, and "beer gardens." (☎602-514-8400. Tickets from $10. $1 tickets available 1st come, 1st served 2hr. before games.) The **Phoenix Symphony,** 225 E. Adams St., plays regularly from September to June and holds the occasional summer concert. (☎602-495-1999; www.phoenixsymphony.org. Tickets $20-60. Student discount 25%. Student rush tickets $10 1hr. before showtime.) For theater of all types from musicals to Shakespearean tragedies, check out the historic 1364-seat **Orpheum Theatre,** 203 W. Adams St., which was built in 1929 as a movie house. (☎602-262-7272. Tickets $15-70. Box office open M-F 10am-4pm.)

NIGHTLIFE

The free *New Times Weekly*, available on local magazine racks, lists club schedules for Phoenix's after-hours scene (www.phoenix-newtimes.com). The *Cultural Calendar of Events* covers area entertainment in three-month intervals. The *Western Front*, found in bars and clubs, covers gay and lesbian nightlife. Happening bars are easy to find if you walk up Mill St. around ASU. Downtown, there are a few gems scattered about if you know where to look.

Char's Has the Blues, 4631 N. 7th Ave. (☎602-230-0205; www.charshastheblues.com). Intimate, laid-back bar with excellent live music. While shows are generally blues, music can range from jazz to R&B to Motown. The 30-something crowd grooves on the small dance floor or sits with style at tables. Live music nightly from 9pm. Cover Su $1. Open daily 7:30pm-1am. AmEx/D/MC/V.

Carly's, 128 E. Roosevelt St. (☎602-262-2759). There's no doubt that Carly's is hip: cool, modern decor, funky, well-dressed waitstaff, and indie kids playing music most nights. Often acoustic, always eclectic. Eat gourmet grilled panini and salads ($7-9) or nurse a drink as you listen. Happy hour daily 4-7pm with $2 beers and discounts on selected wines. Open M-Th 11am-midnight, F-Sa 11am-2am, Su 4-10pm. D/MC/V.

Mill Cue Club, 607 S. Mill Ave. (☎480-858-9017), in Tempe. For those looking to mingle in a casual place that still exudes some class. The leather sofas in the corner complement the dark-paneled walls and the rows of pool tables in the back. Long Island iced tea $4-5. The club gets packed for "reverse happy hour" W 7:30pm-midnight. Some nights 21+. Generally no cover. Happy hour 2-7pm. Open daily 2pm-2am. AmEx/D/MC/V.

The Rose and Crown Pub, 628 E. Adams St. (☎602-256-0223). A classic British pub located in Copper Sq., this place has a substantial group of regulars and draws a huge crowd on days of Diamondbacks or Suns games. Pool tables, classy leather furniture, and good outdoor seating. Punk rock M with $2 well drinks and $2 Pabst Blue Ribbon from 8:30pm to close. 80s movie night W with $2 domestic beer. No cover. Open M-Th 11am-1am, F-Sa 11am-2am, Su 11am-11pm.

THE ROAD TO GILA BEND: 69 MI.

Get on **I-10 West** to **Exit 112** to **Route 85.** Follow Rte. 85 S. toward **I-8** for 36 mi. Gila Bend lies at the junction of Rte. 85 and I-8.

GILA BEND   ☎928

Gila Bend has definitely seen better days. Once the proud crossroads joining Yuma, Phoenix, and Tucson, today the old town doesn't get a passing glance from motorists whizzing by on I-8. Gila Bend features a fine assortment of gas stations, a mechanic, and a laundromat, but otherwise it has little to offer. The one attraction that seems to have withstood the test of time is the **Space Age Outer Limits Hotel and Restaurant,** 401 E. Pima St., built in 1964-65 by Al Stovall, a rich industrialist with a thing for the NASA program—the building features a 28 ft. spaceship with a space-themed mural, and even the pool heater is shaped like a crash-landed satellite. After a change of ownership, the motel is now the **Best Western Space Age Motel ❹** and has basic, clean rooms that thankfully do not follow the spaceship theme. (☎928-683-2273. Continental breakfast included. Rooms $89-99. AmEx/D/MC/V.) For a less cosmic experience, it's best to check out one of the other motels along the E. Pima strip. The **Yucca Motel ❷,** 836 E. Pima St., promises "service with a smile" and has clean rooms with pool access, microwaves, fridges, and HBO. (☎928-683-2211. Singles $48; doubles $60. AmEx/D/MC/V.) The **Outer Limits Restaurant ❸** offers the best (and only) Mexican and American cuisine in town. (☎928-683-2273. Entrees $8-11. Open daily 5am-9pm. AmEx/D/MC/V.)

DETOUR
PAINTED ROCKS PETROGLYPH SITE

From Gila Bend, take **I-8 West** for 13 mi. to **Exit 102** and turn right (north). Continue a very lonely 11 mi. down **Painted Rock Dam Road** to the site.

This national monument showcases one of the best collections of prehistoric Native American art in existence. Centuries ago, Native Americans in the area found a pile of boulders standing alone on the flat desert land and concluded that it must be of spiritual importance. They inscribed hundreds of spirals and unique figures, whose complex meanings can be loosely interpreted using guides available at the site. De Anza, the Mormon Battalion, Kit Carson, and many other pioneers passed by and left their own inscriptions. A very short trail runs around the rock mound, and, while visitors can't get too close to the petroglyphs, the best views can be seen by heading left on the trail from the parking area. The site is run by the **Phoenix Bureau of Land Management** but has no visitors center, just a shaded picnic area. (☎602-580-5500. $2 per vehicle.) Next to the petroglyph site, the **Petroglyph Campground ❶** offers the chance to spend the night under the incredible desert stars at this sacred site, but it has no running water and only one pit toilet. As with the petroglyphs, the campground is entirely self-serve. The area is dangerously hot in the summer, and there are no services nearby, so be cautious when deciding to camp here. (☎602-580-5500. Free.)

⛰ THE ROAD TO DATELAND: 35 MI.

To get to Dateland, head back to **I-8** and continue west for 35 mi. Get off at **Exit 67** for Dateland.

DATELAND   ☎928

One might assume that Dateland is named after the numerous date trees scattered throughout the town. But here, as often happens on the back roads of America, logic fails. The name is derived from WWII-era General Datelan, who commanded a military base in the area. The dates came later, and with their arrival the second "D" was added to the name. The gift shop tells about the wonders of the palm-tree fruit, but visitors should seek to actually experience it firsthand, in the form of the Dateland date milkshake. **⛱Dateland Palms Village Restaurant ❷**, which basically constitutes the entire town of Dateland, serves up both date and cactus shakes ($3) as well as other date treats and a full diner menu. (☎928-454-2772; www.dateland.com. Entrees $6-8. Open M-Tu and Sa 8am-6pm, W-Th 8am-7pm, F and Su 8am-10pm. MC/V.)

⛰ THE ROAD TO YUMA: 67 MI.

Take **I-8 West** to Yuma. You can't miss it.

YUMA   ☎928

The mother of all truck stops, Yuma sits smack-dab in the middle of nowhere, as far as modern-day travelers are concerned. For travelers of old, however, Yuma had the important distinction of being at the narrowest point on the Colorado River, which made it an ideal place to cross into California. The crossing at Yuma was first used by Native American traders and nomads, then by Spanish explorers, the US Army, and gold miners. Nowadays, Yuma has a range of motels and restaurants to give respite to travelers before they cross the state line into California.

▣ ORIENTATION

To hit **Fourth Avenue,** Yuma's main drag, exit I-8 at Fourth Ave. and head south. Most hotels and fast-food chains are on Fourth Ave., while the **Yuma Crossing State Historic Park** lies east on **Giss Parkway.** A small downtown area with a restaurant and store-filled pedestrian walkway lies on **Main Street** between **Second** and **Third Streets.** Parking is easy. Beyond downtown and the major thoroughfares, Yuma seems to blend into a sprawl of housing developments, trailer parks, and gas stations.

⛺ ACCOMMODATIONS

Knights Inn, 2655 S. 4th Ave. (☎928-344-0082). The inn has huge, nicely-furnished rooms with king beds, A/C, TVs, microwaves, refrigerators, and pool access to boot. Singles $30; doubles $40. AmEx/D/MC/V. ❷

Yuma Cabana, 2151 S. 4th Ave. (☎520-783-8311). This tropically themed motel is a resort by motel standards. Spacious and clean rooms come with fridges, microwaves, HBO, A/C, and a pool. Continental breakfast included. Internet. Singles $44; doubles $59. AmEx/D/MC/V. ❸

FOOD

Lutes Casino, 221 S. Main St. (☎928-782-2192). Pool and dominoes are still played in the casino, as they have been since 1920; this is the state's oldest pool hall. Grab a burger and check out the decor, which features everything from a hanging pterodactyl with boots to a tin-can robot. Entrees $3-5.50. Pool $6 per hr. Open M-Th 9am-8pm, F-Sa 9am-9pm, Su 10am-6pm. Cash only. ❶

Spanky's Cafe, 202 S. 1st Ave. (☎928-782-0818). For something healthful, check out this pretty little cafe. Serves sandwiches like grilled portobello and snazzy salads. Open M-F 7am-4pm, Sa 7am-1pm. AmEx/D/MC/V. ❷

SIGHTS

YUMA TERRITORIAL PRISON STATE HISTORIC PARK. The infamous prison in the park was home to some of the West's most ruthless bandits. In 1876, the inmates were forced to construct the walls that would confine them in the heart of the scorching desert. After the local high school burned down, the unlucky prisoners were transferred east to Florence. The jail was used as a school in 1910-14; Yuma High School's sports teams are still called "the Criminals" as a tribute. Tour what remains of the cell blocks and guard tower and visit the museum, which perches on a hill overlooking the Colorado River. If you don't want to pay for jail time, visit the free park below the prison, where there are shaded picnic tables and nice paths that meander along the river. (*1 Prison Hill Rd. Take I-8 to Exit 1, head east on Giss Pkwy., and turn at Prison Hill Rd. ☎928-783-4771. Open daily 8am-5pm. $4, under 14 free.*)

SAIHATI CAMEL FARM. This camel farm specializes in the breeding of one-humped camels, also known as dromedaries. These animals' natural home is Central Asia, and they are well-mannered; unlike two-humped camels and llamas, they do not spit. Another fun fact: baby camels are born with no hump. Twenty other species of animals, including Arabian wild cats, Watusi cattle, Go-bex, an African spurred tortoise, and Turkens also share the farm's premises. Why breed camels in the middle of the Arizonan desert, one might ask? These camels are available for parades and special events; the farm also hosts school groups and special tours. (*15672 S. Ave. 1 E. ☎928-627-7511. Open Nov.-May M-Sa 10am-5pm. $3, under 3 free, seniors $2.50.*)

TIME CHANGE. If you're traveling from November to March, set your clock back 1hr. as you enter California and the Pacific Time Zone. If it's between April and October, don't do a thing.

DETOUR
OFFICIAL CENTER OF THE WORLD

Go 10 mi. west of Yuma on **I-8.** Exit at **Sidewinder Road,** then go north and take your first left to find the spot. There are no signs once you leave the interstate.

Your first stop in California looks suspiciously like the Arizona desert. Well, cheer up: you've reached both the center of the world and one of the kitschiest roadside attractions on the trip. The title Official Center of the World was originally made up by the writer of a children's book, but it was officially set in stone in 1985, and tours are now given of the granite pyramid where this point resides. Admission comes with a photograph and a commemorative certificate. Outside, stare in wonder at a span of wall (in a pink that matches the pyramid) that commemorates great moments in French aviation, casualties of the Korean War, the entire 1949 class of Princeton University, and the genealogical history of the Taylor family. Michelangelo's **Arm of God** (from the Sistine Chapel) sets the local solar time at a giant sundial, while stairs from the Eiffel Tower sit nearby, awkwardly leading to nowhere but the desert sky. If the center is not open, you can still wander the grounds—you just won't get a certificate or a peek inside the pyramid. (☎760-572-0100. Open Thanksgiving-Easter daily. Suggested donation $5.)

DETOUR
IMPERIAL SAND DUNES

Continue another 9 mi. west on **I-8.** Take **Exit 156 (Grays Wells Road)** and you will soon enter the **Imperial Sand Dunes Recreation Area.**

If the shifting sands and rolling slopes of the Imperial Dunes remind you of another planet, they should. These sands appeared as the desert planet Tatooine in the classic movie *Star Wars: A New Hope* and have been featured in many other films. Hundreds of buggies and motorcycles zip across the dunes each year, but before it served as a racing grounds the area presented a formidable obstacle for cross-country travelers. Winds and migrating dunes quickly erased any trail, while soft sands slowed travelers to a crawl—if they didn't stop them entirely.

With the invention of the automobile, people became even more interested in finding a passage over the sands. The answer came in 1916, with a piece of desert ingenuity—the **plank road.** Thousands of wood boards held together by metal bands traversed the dunes, effectively creating a boardwalk for Model Ts. This innovation lasted until 1926, when the paved road that became US 80 was constructed, though a piece of the historic old plank road still remains in the desert. Today, there is still very little to do at the dunes except drive on through, unless you had the foresight to bring a dune buggy along with you. Permits ($25) are required to park your car for any significant period of time at the dunes. For info and permits, contact the Bureau of Land Management, El Centro, 1661 Fourth St. (☎760-337-4400. You can also buy permits at ☎800-278-0165 or www.icso.org.)

⚐ THE ROAD TO HOLTVILLE: 52 MI.

Continue west on **I-8.** Take **Exit 131 (Holtville/Route 115),** turn right (north), and make another right (east) immediately onto **Evan Hewes Road.** Follow the road 1 mi. over an aqueduct until you see the palm trees of a desert oasis on the right. Geothermal activity warms the water, and a fountain caps the source, shooting the hot water into a spa area. The oasis is a fun break from the road, and the palm-ringed pond next to it makes for the perfect for an oasis-in-the-desert photo to send home to Mom. To continue on to Holtville, retrace your steps and head north on Rte. 115.

HOLTVILLE   ☎760

The little farming town of Holtville doesn't see much action, nor will you while you're there. There is, however, a central square that is quite pretty and a few great Mexican food places, and it's a perfect place to grab a bite to eat after frolicking in the oasis. Stop at **Nueva Mexico Lindo ❶,** 411 E. Fifth St., where the food is made with handmade tortillas in a friendly, family atmosphere. (☎760-356-2197. Open daily 8am-9pm. AmEx/D/MC/V.)

⚐ THE ROAD TO EL CENTRO: 11 MI.

Make your way through Holtville along the main street until you see a sign for El Centro. This is the continuation of **Route 115** and runs directly into El Centro.

EL CENTRO   ☎760

El Centro's motto, "where the sun spends its winters," is a preferable alternative to the perhaps more accurate "where the sun burns so hot you'll wish you were dead." El Centro is the center of the Imperial Valley, but there is little to do in town.

The main reason to stop in El Centro is that the city boasts an abundance of cheap accommodations on Adams Ave. Many of these are rented out during the week by nomadic farmhands or county officials. The **Ranch House Motel ❷,** 808 Adams Ave., welcomes visitors to a lush oasis in the surrounding concrete jungle. The clean and comfortable 15 units are often filled up and include pool access, air conditioning, and TVs. (☎760-352-5571. Singles $30; doubles $35. AmEx/D/MC/V.) Located near the courthouse, **La Hacienda Family Restaurant ❶,** 841 W. Main St., serves a filling dinner for under $8 and also gives religious advice in the form of wall adornments ("Try Jesus—you might like him!"). You might also like the taco plate with three homemade tacos, rice, and beans. (☎760-353-8118. Open M-F 8am-8pm, Sa 8am-2pm. MC/V.)

⚐ THE ROAD TO JACUMBA: 44 MI.

Get on **I-8 West** and continue for 38 mi. After you pass **Exit 87,** the road sheds all semblance of normality: red boulders appear on all sides, becoming increasingly dense and forming spectacular hills. In the middle of these boulders, take **Exit 77** to **Old Highway 80** and continue 6 mi. to Jacumba.

JACUMBA   ☎619

In 1922 Bert Vaughn, the mayor of San Diego, got insider info that Jacumba would be getting a border crossing, so he bought the town. Jacumba never got its crossing, but it did get one of the decommissioned US 80's most interesting sights: the **Desert View Tower** (a.k.a. the Mystery Cave, or Boulder Park), 1 In-Ko-Pah Rd. Vaughn built a 70 ft. tower on the edge of the mountains overlooking the desert floor and, in the 1930s, artist WT Ratliffe decided to add to it. After noticing how nearby boulders resembled actual and mythological creatures, he spent the next two years with a mallet and chisel carving mysterious creatures into the surrounding rock. Visitors can wander through carvings of Ratliffe's fantasy and climb Vaughn's tower. The gift store and the friendly owner offer a wealth of roadtrip info. To get to the tower, don't head to the town of Jacumba; head right after you get off of the interstate and continue to the end of the county road. (☎619-766-4612. Open daily 9am-5pm. $3.50, children $1.)

? DID YOU KNOW? The reason for the abundance of sparsely populated towns in this region goes back to the days when steam engines used to roar across the tracks that now parallel the freeway. In the desert heat, trains needed to stop for water about every 6 mi., and every stop required a new town. Today, the towns still appear on the map, but you'll be hard-pressed to find anything in them.

◪ DETOUR
SUNRISE HIGHWAY

From Jacumba, continue 8 mi. on **Old Highway 80** until it joins back up with **I-8.** Go west on I-8 for 15 mi. to **Exit 47.** Head north on **Scenic Route 1** for 25 mi. through the Laguna Mountains.

This scenic drive carves through the oak canyons and pine peaks of the Cuyamaca and Laguna Mountains, which stand as a formidable barrier between the coast and the desert. Ten miles in, you'll come to **Laguna Mountain Village,** which is the highest point on the drive at 6000 ft. and contains a grocery store, an overpriced restaurant, and the **Cleveland Forest Visitor Center,** which is staffed by volunteers. (☎619-473-8824. Visitors center open F-Su 8am-4pm.) To park your car, picnic, hike, or camp, you must purchase an **Adventure Pass** ($5), which can be obtained at any of the three

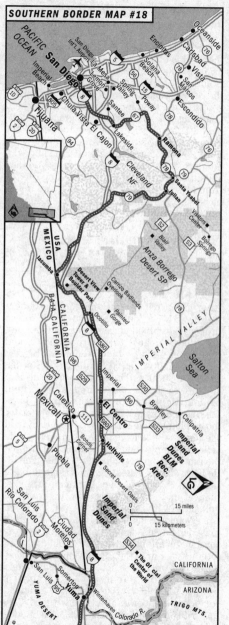

SOUTHERN BORDER MAP #18

establishments in **Laguna Mountain Village.** Continue 200 ft. past the village to Desert View Picnic Area, which has a beautiful view of the desert valley below. Just 2 mi. farther down the road is an even better lookout with panoramic views and a wood viewing platform. Continue on the winding highway through the ashen wasteland remaining from a 2002 wildfire, and then into beautiful desert fields where agaves and wildflowers grace the rolling hills. **Camping** is available in the Cleveland Forest at many sites just off of the highway. After 25 long and winding miles, the highway connects with Rte. 79 and will carry you into Julian. For those in a hurry, following Rte. 79 from I-8 to Julian is slightly faster, but, if you have even a little time to spare, the Sunrise Highway is well worth your time.

⚐ THE ROAD TO JULIAN: 57 MI.

From Jacumba, head west on **I-8** for 25 mi. Take **Exit 40** onto **Route 79** and continue for 23 mi. to Julian.

JULIAN   ☎ 760

After the Civil War, Confederate soldiers wandered west looking for land and, in the process, stumbled across gold. Understandably, they decided to put roots down and established Julian, which became the biggest gold-producing area in Southern California. In the late 1800s, the reserves dried up and Julian's residents discovered a new kind of gold: apples. Soon Julian's apples were famous across the US. Now the main industry in the picturesque little town is tourism, and the townspeople have gone from mere apple sellers to apple bakers—making fresh apple pie that has tourists coming for miles. The little **Julian Pioneer Museum,** 2811 Washington St., off Main St., has Native American artifacts, pioneer and mining tools, and the best lace collection in the state. (☎760-765-0227. Open Apr.-Thanksgiving Tu-Su 10am-4pm; Christmas-Mar. Sa-Su 10am-4pm. $3.) Those looking for an educational adventure should take an interactive tour of the **Eagle and High Peak Mine,** at the end of C St., where visitors can take a 1hr. guided tour through 1000 ft. of tunnels and pan for gold. (☎760-765-0036. Call ahead for hours of operation and tour times. $10, under 16 $5.) The **Town Hall,** 2129 Main St., distributes helpful information about the town

and shows local art. (☎760-765-1857. Open daily 10am-4pm.) For food in Julian, visit the **Miner's Diner & Soda Fountain ❷,** 2134 Main St. Housed in an 1886 building, this old-fashioned soda shop holds true to its roots with brickwork still visible behind the 1928 soda fountain. Grab a burger while you check out its displays of license plates. (☎760-765-3753. Breakfast $5.50-9. Lunch $7-11. Open M-Th 10:30am-5pm, F 10:30am-6pm, Sa 8am-6pm, Su 8am-5pm. MC/V.) For the bison-obsessed and the bison-curious, the bison-themed **Buffalo Bill's ❷,** at the corner of Third and B St., serves up bison burgers ($8.25). Bison meat has one-fourth the fat of beef, so chow down guilt-free. (☎760-765-1560. Sandwiches $5-9. Open M-F 7am-2pm, Sa-Su 7am-4pm. MC/V.) It would be a tragedy to leave town without a slice of Julian's apple pie, and many places on Main St. serve the all-American dessert by the slice for under $3. **Apple Alley Bakery ❷,** 2122 Main St., is one of the better-known pie purveyors ($3 per slice). For something different, try apple-boysenberry or apple-cherry mixes. (☎760-765-2532. AmEx/D/MC/V.)

⚐ THE ROAD TO SANTA YSABEL: 7 MI.

Continue west on **Route 78/79,** which becomes **Julian Road,** for 7 mi.

SANTA YSABEL   ☎ 760

It may be a tiny pit stop, but Santa Ysabel offers some of the world's best baked goods. Half of the town is ▣**Dudley's Bakery ❶,** 30218 Rte. 78, at Rte. 79, which is known across San Diego County for its fresh bread. Stop and buy a loaf ($2.75) or try the tasty fruit bars ($3) and other assorted pastries. (☎800-225-3348. Open Th-Su 8am-5pm. AmEx/D/MC/V.)

⚐ THE ROAD TO RAMONA: 15 MI.

Continue along **Route 78/79 (Julian Road).**

RAMONA   ☎ 760

This ranching community in the foothills of the Cuyamaca Mountains centers on horses. Don't miss the **Ramona Rodeo** in May and the **Country Fair** days in August. For more info, contact the **Ramona Chamber of Commerce/ Information Center,** 960 Main St. (☎760-689-1311; www.ramonachamber.com. Open M-F 8:30am-4:30pm, Sa 9am-2pm.) The **Woodward**

Museum, 645 Main St., has displays on horses and horse-related gear, a memorial exhibit to a local championship rodeo rider, and a rose garden. (☎619-789-7644. Open Th-Su 1-4pm. $3, under 12 $0.50.) Ramona is also known for its wine and antiques. You can taste the former at **Schwaesdall Winery,** 17677 Rancho de Oro Rd., at Rte. 67, the only licensed taster in the Ramona Valley. (☎760-789-7547, tasting room 789-7542. Tastings Sa-Su 10am-6pm.) Ramona has many antique stores, but the biggest is **Charlotte's,** 969 Main St., which features 6000 sq. ft. of antiques, including cool vintage clothing. (☎760-788-2784. Open M-Sa 9am-3pm or by appointment.) The other antique warehouses, which comprise "Antique Row," line a drab stretch of Main St. in the 700-1000 blocks.

In Ramona, the best (and basically only) place to sleep is the clean, hospitable, and by budget standards somewhat pricey **Ramona Valley Inn ❸,** 416 Main St. The bright rooms have pool access, free coffee, and TVs. (☎760-789-6433 or 800-648-4618. Singles $68; doubles $74. 21+. AmEx/D/MC/V.) Grab a home-cooked meal at the **Kountry Kitchen ❷,** 826 Main St., where they've been serving all-American favorites and misspelling "country" since 1939. (☎760-789-3200. Open M-W and Su 5am-3pm, Th-Sa 5am-8:30pm. D/MC/V.)

 THE ROAD TO SAN DIEGO: 36 MI.

From Ramona, head southwest on **Route 67** to the **Scripps Poway Parkway.** Make a right on the Scripps Poway Pkwy. and take it west to **I-15 South,** which leads you downtown. If you want to visit **Escondido's Wild Animal Park** first, continue west on **Route 78** for 17 mi. through Escondido and go south on I-15. Follow the highway another 25 mi. into central San Diego.

SAN DIEGO   ☎619

The natives call it "America's Finest City," and visitors pulling into this picturesque port will soon understand why. In a state where every other town has staked its claim as paradise, San Diego may be Southern California's best return on the promises of the Golden State. Year-round sunny weather makes for abundant flower-filled gardens and inviting beaches—but an ocean breeze makes the city cooler than some other stops along your route have been. A strong collegiate presence in the city makes for a friendly, take-you-in-as-family sort of nightlife scene. In short, San Diego is just the eldorado that you've been searching for all this time: it's vibrant, cosmopolitan and chill.

> **PAGE TURN.** See the **Pacific Coast** route (p. 890) for complete coverage of San Diego.

THE END OF THE ROAD

Gawk at the beasties in the San Diego Zoo, build a huge sand castle on the beach, and take a well-deserved surfing break. You survived the Southern Border, enduring desert heat, prickly cactuses, lonely tumbleweed, and the occasional spicy chili while keeping your roadtripping spirit intact. Cool your fiery heels in the ocean, then head north along the Pacific Coast or meet up with Rte. 66 in L.A.

EXIT TO

Laguna Beach, CA 73 mi.
on the pacific coast route, p. 902

Los Angeles, CA 120 mi.
on route 66, p. 595

pacific coast

TOP 5

1. Dip away to your heart's content at the **Giant Artichoke Restaurant** (p. 939) in Castroville.

2. Get thee to the **Shakespeare Room** (p. 972) of the Sylvia Beach Hotel in Newport, Oregon.

3. Drink a glass of Riesling at the **Nehalam Bay Winery** (p. 977) in Nehalam, Oregon.

4. Toss a Frisbee and admire the Golden Gate Bridge at **Crissy Field** (p. 483) in San Francisco.

5. Eat a cup of gelato at **Pioneer Square** (p. 998) in Seattle after finishing your route.

Crashing waves, sheer coastal bluffs, monumental redwoods, expansive ocean sunsets—exhilaration doesn't begin to describe the way it feels to be poised on the western edge of the country. On the Pacific Coast, every cliff-hugging turn ahead promises a brighter future (or at least a sparkling sea view), and the past recedes in your rearview mirror. The coast has a way of winning over even the stodgiest skeptic, usually with avocado sandwiches, vanilla-scented Jeffrey pines, and beach bonfires. Our route takes you from San Diego, the southernmost of California's major cities, all the way to Seattle, on the foggy edge of Pudget Sound.

From **San Diego** (p. 890), you'll cruise through California beach culture; unassuming beach communities begin near San Diego and dot the coast all the way to San Francisco. You'll pass by (or stop and surf) the mythical swells of **Huntington Beach** (p. 904) before reaching laid-back **Hermosa,** carnivalesque **Venice,** and **Santa Monica,** all of which bow year-round to the gods of sun and surf. Of course, you'll have to venture into **Los Angeles** (p. 906); visit the Getty Museum, see the silver-screen sights in Hollywood, and party on **Sunset Strip** before heading through **Zuma Beach** (p. 920), which has the best surfing and softest sand.

Continuing north, the 400 mi. stretch of coast between L.A. and San Francisco embodies all that is this route—rolling seas, an oceanside highway built for cruising, and dramatic bluffs topped by weathered pines. You'll pass through **Santa Barbara** (p. 922), home to stunning sunsets and Spanish architecture, before reaching **Big Sur** (p. 933), where the magnificence that inspired John Steinbeck's novels and Jack Kerouac's musings lives on and clear skies, dense forests, and old seafaring towns beckon. The landmarks along the way—**Hearst Castle** (p. 933), the **Monterey Bay Aquarium** (p. 937), the historic missions—are well worth visiting, but the highlight of this stretch is the road itself.

Give yourself ample time to explore **San Francisco** (p. 948)—wander the streets and cross the **Golden Gate Bridge** before continuing north. Windswept and larger than life, the coast then winds from the Bay Area to the Oregon border. Redwoods tower over undiscovered black sand beaches, and otters frolic next to jutting rock formations—the untouched wilderness is simply stunning. From the **Marin Headlands** (p. 948), the road snakes along craggy cliffs between pounding surf and monolithic redwoods. You'll drive along the **Avenue of the Giants,** home of the redwoods that make the region famous, and back to the coast where more redwoods tower, protected within the long strip of **Redwood National and State Parks** (p. 964).

From there, it's on to **Oregon,** where a string of touristy resort towns and small, unspoiled fishing villages line the route. The road winds through the scenic **Oregon Dunes National Recreation Area,** and, for those brave enough for the bone-chilling waves, some of the most pristine beaches along the entire coast. Finally,

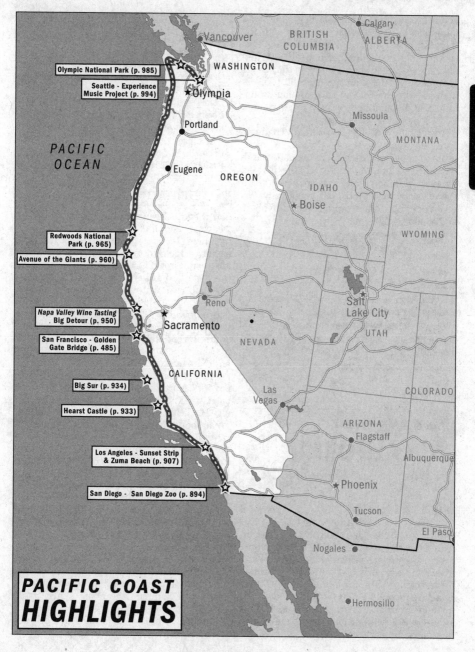

Olympic National Park (p. 985)

Seattle - Experience Music Project (p. 994)

Redwoods National Park (p. 965)

Avenue of the Giants (p. 960)

Napa Valley Wine Tasting Big Detour (p. 950)

San Francisco - Golden Gate Bridge (p. 485)

Big Sur (p. 934)

Hearst Castle (p. 933)

Los Angeles - Sunset Strip & Zuma Beach (p. 907)

San Diego - San Diego Zoo (p. 894)

PACIFIC OCEAN

BRITISH COLUMBIA

Vancouver

Calgary

ALBERTA

WASHINGTON

Olympia

Portland

Eugene

OREGON

Missoula

MONTANA

IDAHO

Boise

WYOMING

Reno

Sacramento

NEVADA

Salt Lake City

UTAH

CALIFORNIA

Las Vegas

COLORADO

ARIZONA

Flagstaff

Albuquerque

Phoenix

Tucson

El Paso

Nogales

Hermosillo

PACIFIC COAST HIGHLIGHTS

you'll cross into **Washington;** here, the road loops around the **Olympic Peninsula,** skirting the vast, lush forests of **Olympic National Park** (p. 985), before ending in **Seattle**—the Emerald City, where skyscrapers tower, the streets are nearly spotless, and every hilltop offers impressive views of the surrounding mountains and the glinting waters of Puget Sound. Don't forget to try the **coffee.**

The Pacific Coast is no ordinary roadtrip; it's neither lonely nor especially kitschy. You'll probably end up eating more avocado sandwiches than burgers (although the **In-N-Out Burgers** of Southern California are hands down the ultimate road food), but you'll return to wherever you came from relaxed, refreshed, and significantly tanner.

ROUTE STATS
Miles: c. 1500
Route: San Diego, CA, to Seattle, WA.
States: 3; California, Oregon, and Washington.
Driving Time: At least 1 week; allow 2-3 weeks to take in the coast at a more leisurely pace.
When To Go: California is pleasant year-round, but a summer roadtrip will find warm days and decreased precipitation in the perpetually rainy Northwest.
Crossroads: Southern Border, in San Diego, CA (this page); **Route 66,** in Santa Monica, CA (p. 595); **National Road,** in San Francisco, CA (p. 477).

The Golden State

CALIFORNIA

Welcomes You!

SAN DIEGO   ☎ 619

The natives call it "America's Finest City," and visitors pulling into this picturesque port will soon understand why. In a state where every other town has staked its claim as paradise, San Diego may be Southern California's best return on the promises of the Golden State. Year-round sunny weather makes for abundant gardens, inviting beaches, friendly smiles, and a vibrant city that is simultaneously cosmopolitan and chill.

VITAL STATS
Population: 1,400,000
Tourist Office: International Visitors Information Center, 1040 W. Broadway (☎619-236-1212; www.sandiego.org), at Harbor Dr. Open daily in summer 9am-5pm; in winter 9am-4pm.
Library and Internet Access: San Diego Public Library, 820 E St. (☎619-236-5800). Open M and W noon-8pm, Tu and Th-Sa 9:30am-5:30pm, Su 1-5pm.
Post Office: 2535 Midway Dr. (☎619-758-7101). Open M 7am-5pm, Tu-F 8am-5pm, Sa 8am-4pm. **Postal Code:** 92186.

☀ ORIENTATION

San Diego is beautiful, but it's also a city of freeways and highways—there's no avoiding them. **I-5** runs north-south, skirting the eastern edge of downtown on its way to the Mexican border. **I-15** runs northeast through the desert to Las Vegas, and **I-8** runs east-west along downtown's northern boundary, connecting the desert with Ocean Beach. To get to downtown from I-5, take the **Civic Center exit** or **Fourth Avenue exit.** Downtown is just south of the interstate, and its grid layout is extremely easy to navigate—one-way streets alternate every block.

The epicenter of San Diego tourism is **Balboa Park.** Northwest of the park is stylish **Hillcrest,** which centers on Fifth Ave. and University Blvd. It's the city's gay enclave and has great shopping and the most diverse restaurants in the city. The **Gaslamp Quarter** sits in the southern section of downtown between Fourth and Sixth St. and contains signature theaters, restaurants, and nightclubs. Just north of downtown in the southeast corner of the I-5 and I-8 junction lies a little slice of old Mexico known as **Old Town.** Along the coast, San Diego Bay opens up south of downtown, bounded by classy **Coronado Island.** Northwest of town sits the collection of shiny beaches and man-made inlets known as **Mission Bay,** home to several laid-back, sun-soaked communities including **Ocean, Mission,** and **Pacific Beaches.** A jaunt up the coast leads to the swanky haven of **La Jolla.**

Parking lots scattered throughout the downtown area charge up to $5 per hour, although

TO [1][2][3][4][5], MISSION BEACH (5mi),
[6][7] (25mi), ESCONDIDO (30mi),
LA JOLLA (8mi), PACIFIC BEACH (6mi)

↑ TO OLD TOWN,
AND [8] (2mi)

↑ TO [9], HILLCREST (0.5mi)
[10] (20mi), [11] (1mi)

TO [13][14]
OCEAN BEACH (4mi),
SEA WORLD (2mi)
←

SEE BALBOA
PARK INSET

San Diego
Int'l. Airport

Maple St.
Laurel St.   El Prado
Kalmia St.
Juniper St.
Ivy St.
Hawthorn St.
Grape St.
Fir St.
Elm St.

Laurel St.
Pacific Hwy.
India St.
Kettner Blvd.
San Diego Fwy.
Union St.
Front St.
Albatross St.
Brant St.
Curlew St.

Balboa Dr.
6th Ave.
8th Ave.
Pan-American E.
Cabrillo Fwy.
Heathside Wy.
Park Blvd.

San Diego
Air and Space
Museum

Balboa Park

US Naval
Medical
Center

LITTLE ITALY

Date St.
Cedar St.
Beech St.
Ash St.
A St.
B St.
C St.

Medea
Berkeley
Star of
India
Maritime
Museum

Harbor Dr.
Pacific Hwy.

1st Ave.
2nd Ave.
3rd Ave.
4th Ave.
5th Ave.
6th Ave.
7th Ave.
8th Ave.
9th Ave.
10th Ave.
11th Ave.
12th Ave.

Balboa
Stadium

Russ Blvd.
San Diego
City College

Copley
Symphony
Hall

EMBARCADERO

B Street
Pier

Broadway
Pier

Navy Pier

Santa Fe
Amtrak
Depot

Museum of
Contemporary
Art

City
Hall
Balboa
Theater

International Visitor
Information Center

Greyhound
Broadway

Ferry to
Coronado

Kettner Blvd.
State St.
Union St.

Pantajo
Park

Horton
Plaza
Center

E St.
F St.
G St.

13th St.
14th St.
15th St.
16th St.
17th St.

Tuna Harbor
Park

Tuna Harbor

**GASLAMP
QUARTER**

SEE GASLAMP
QUARTER INSET

Market St.
Island Ave.

8th Ave.

J St.
K St.
L St.

Seaport
Village

Embarcadero
Marina Park

Horton
Grand
Theater

Harbor Dr.

Imperial Ave.

TO CORONADO ISLAND (1mi)

*Coronado
Island*

*San Diego
Harbor*

San Diego

▲▲ ACCOMMODATIONS
Banana Bungalow, **2**
Ocean Beach International (OBI), **13**
Mission Beach International Hostel, **3**
San Diego Downtown Hostel
   (HI-AYH), **17**
San Elijo Beach State Park, **6**
South Carlsbad Beach State Park, **7**
USA Hostels San Diego, **16**

FOOD
The Corvette Diner, **9**
Casa Guadalajara, **8**
Newport Pizza and Ale House, **14**
Kono's Surf Club, **1**
La Especial Norte, **10**

NIGHTLIFE
Bourbon St., **11**
Canes Bar and Grill, **5**
The Casbah, **12**
Croce's Top Hat Bar and Grill
   & Croce's Jazz Bar, **15**
Pacific Beach Bar and Grill
and Club Tremors, **4**

Balboa Park

San Diego Zoo

Spanish Village
Art Center

The Old Globe
Theater

Botanical
Building

Balboa
Park
Gardens

Museum of Man
Museum
of Art

Timkin Museum
of Art

Visitor Info Center

Museum of
Photographic
Arts

Reuben H.
Fleet Space
Theater and
Science Center

Gaslamp Quarter

E St. →

Horton
Plaza
Center

F St.

G St.

3rd Ave.
4th Ave.
5th Ave.
6th Ave.
7th Ave.

Market St.

**GASLAMP
QUARTER**

Horton
Grand
Hotel

Gaslamp
Quarter
Foundation

Island Ave.

some are cheaper than others. The cheapest lot downtown ($1 per hr.; max. $8 per day) can be found between Sixth Ave. and Seventh Ave. on Market St. For those who plan to shop, parking at **Horton Plaza,** San Diego's gigantic outdoor mall at Broadway and Fourth Ave., is free with validation in one of the mall's stores (3hr. max.). **Balboa Park** has numerous parking lots, and from there you can take the free narrated park tram around to all the museums.

▐ TRANSPORTATION

Although most San Diegans seem content to battle traffic on the freeways, buses run throughout downtown and the suburbs, and electric trolleys run in the downtown core. Buy a **Daytripper Pass** for unlimited rides in one day. (☎619-233-3004 or 800-COMMUTE; www.sdcommute.com. Passes available at the **West Broadway Visitors Info** center or at the **Transit Store** at 1st St. and Broadway. Day passes also sold from ticket vending machines, found at many trolley stops. $5.)

▐ ACCOMMODATIONS

Finding a place to stay in San Diego requires one of two things—a lot of planning or a lot of money. San Diego is littered with generic chain motels, which are generally clean and safe. There is a cluster of motels and hotels known as **Hotel Circle** (2-3 mi. east of I-5 along I-8), where you'll be lucky to find a room for under $80-90 per night in the summer, even during the week. Hostels in San Diego tend to fill up as much as four to six weeks in advance, so be sure to plan your stay in San Diego well ahead of time. Several beaches in North County, as well as one on Coronado, allow camping, but these too fill up very early. For info call the **San Diego and North County Coast Rangers Headquarters** (☎619-688-3260) or, for advance reservations, contact **ReserveAmerica** (☎800-444-7275).

▩ **Banana Bungalow,** 707 Reed Ave. (☎858-273-3060; www.bananabungalowsandiego.com), in the center of Pacific Beach. Smack-dab on the beach, this hostel is like one big beach party with an open courtyard and gorgeous deck overlooking the water. Communal dinners cooked by friendly, travel-savvy hostel staff: free barbecue Su, $1 cheeseburgers W. Tons of beach acces-

sories available to borrow, such as coolers, volleyball net, and boogie boards. Must have out-of-state ID, international passport, or proof of travel. Breakfast included. Lockers available. Linen included. Laundry $1.50. Free Wi-Fi. In summer dorms $25; private rooms $105. In winter dorms $20; private rooms $65. Private rooms $105/65. MC/V. ❷

▩ **San Diego Downtown Hostel (HI-AYH),** 521 Market St. (☎619-525-1531; www.sandiegohostels.org), in the Gaslamp Quarter. Quiet, impeccably clean, and close to popular attractions and clubs. Airy common rooms, big kitchen, and pretty courtyard. No alcohol. Full breakfast. Dinner $5. Laundry. Free Wi-Fi. Bike rental $10. 4- to 6-bed dorms in summer $23-26; in winter $19-22. Singles from $47. . AmEx/D/MC/V. ❷

USA Hostels San Diego, 726 5th Ave. (☎619-232-3100 or 800-438-8622; www.usa-hostels.com), between F and G St. This colorful European-style fun house fits in with the happening atmosphere of the Gaslamp Quarter, hosting frequent parties, several weekly pub crawls, and Tijuana trips. Hang out with fellow travelers in the "party room" and waste the night away on leather couches. Bottom-floor rooms can be very loud. International passport, out-of-state ID. Pancake breakfast included. Lockers, linen, and laundry ($1.50). Free Wi-Fi; Internet terminals $2 per 20min. Bike rental $10. Dorms in summer $25-28, except during special events; in winter $20-23. Private rooms $50-70. MC/V. ❷

Lucky D's Hostel, 615 8th Ave. (☎619-595-0000; www.luckyds.com). Between G and Market St. Lucky D's is another San Diego hostel with a great downtown location and tons of fun activities. Recently opened, so the facilities are all new, and it's a few minutes from the Gaslamp Quarter, while far enough away that you can still get a good sleep. Breakfast included. Free phone calls anywhere in the US and Canada. Free Gaslamp pub crawls and walking tours. Internet and free Wi-Fi. In summer 4-bed dorms $25; private rooms $65. In winter 4-bed dorms $20; private rooms $49. AmEx/D/MC/V. ❶

Ocean Beach International (OBI), 4961 Newport Ave. (☎619-223-7873 or 800-339-7263; www.californiahostel.com). Clean rooms in a social area right by the most laid-back beach in San Diego. Proof of international travel in the last 6 months required. Pancake breakfast included daily. Internet $1 per 20min. Free transport to hostel from train/bus station or airport. Lockout daily 11am-2pm. In summer 4- to 6-bed dorms $24; doubles $54. In winter 4- to 6-bed dorms $17; doubles $44. MC/V. ❶

Mission Beach International Hostel, 3204 Mission Blvd. (☎858-539-0043), across the street from Mission Beach roller coaster. Intimate hostel with over 2000 DVDs and videotapes lining the walls. Rooms painted according to theme—check out the cardboard palm trees. Small common room, coffee, microwave, and fridge. Free movies and popcorn nightly. Internet $1 per 10min. Dorms $15-24; singles $45; doubles $64. ❷

San Elijo Beach State Park (☎760-753-5091), off Rte. 101 south of Cardiff-by-the-Sea. Over 170 sites on seaside cliffs. Both this campground and South Carlsbad Beach fill up as much as 6 months in advance for weekend sites, so plan way, way ahead. Showers and laundry. Tent sites $16-35, with hookup $29-44. ❶

South Carlsbad Beach State Park (☎760-438-3143), off Carlsbad Blvd. near Leucadia. Over 100 sites near beautiful beaches with good surfing. Showers. Laundry. Sites $16-35. ❶

🍴 FOOD

San Diego has a large Hispanic population and is darn close to Mexico; not surprisingly, its Mexican cuisine can't be beat. The city also offers an assortment of ethnic and more traditional eateries. Classy restaurants cluster downtown along C St., Broadway Blvd., and in the historic Gaslamp Quarter. The best food near Balboa Park and the zoo is in nearby Hillcrest and University Heights. Beachfront areas like Ocean Beach proffer pizzas, hamburgers, and beer.

Casa Guadalajara, 4105 Taylor St. (☎619-295-5111), in Old Town. With its brightly painted tiles, heavy wood furniture, and lush, shady patio, you'll feel like you're in a pristine version of Mexico. Colossal combo plates ($10-12) and soft taco fajitas ($12.50) are overshadowed only by the selection of margaritas ($5-14). Open M-Th 11am-10pm, F 11am-11pm, Sa 7am-11pm, Su 7am-10pm. AmEx/D/MC/V. ❷

The Corvette Diner, 3946 5th Ave. (☎619-542-1476; www.corvettediner.signonsandiego.com), in Hillcrest. This 50s-style diner has more chrome

than Detroit and more neon than Las Vegas. Greasy-spoon classics and unique creations like the Rory Burger (with peanut butter and bacon; $9). A DJ spins oldies nightly 6-9pm while costumed waitstaff give as much lip as service. Make sure you reserve early; this place gets packed nightly. Open M-Th and Su 11am-10pm, F-Sa 11am-11pm. AmEx/MC/V. ❷

Kono's Surf Club, 704 Garnet Ave. (☎858-483-1669), across from the Crystal Pier in Pacific Beach. Identifiable by the line stretching out the door, Kono's is a surfer's shrine that serves up legendary burritos. Mostly takeout, so you can eat on the beach. Try the huge Egg Burrito #3, which includes bacon, cheese, potatoes, and sauce ($4.75). Open M-F 7am-3pm, Sa-Su 7am-4pm. D/MC/V. ❶

La Especial Norte, 664 N. Coast Hwy. 101 (☎760-942-1040), 25 mi. north of San Diego, in Leucadia. A great place to stop for well-made Mexican food. This family-run restaurant has huge portions, friendly service, and food so good that the Diego lifeguards rent the restaurant for their annual banquet. *Bistek ranchero* $13. Open M-F 10am-9pm, Sa-Su 8am-9pm. AmEx/D/MC/V. ❷

Newport Pizza and Ale House, 5050 Newport Ave. (☎619-224-4540), in Ocean Beach. Right by the beach. Draws a packed house of young surfer-types every night of the week. The pizza ($2.50-3.50 per slice) is some of the best you will find anywhere, and there's a huge selection of domestic beers and microbrews on tap. The perfect place to kick back after a long day of trying to surf. Drop by late for major discounts on pizza that's still left. Open M-Th and Su 11am-11pm or midnight, F-Sa 11pm-2am. MC/V. ❶

👁 SIGHTS

San Diego's world-class attractions are extremely varied, and there are enough of them to keep any traveler engaged. Pick up the free weekly *Reader* for local event listings. Special ticket deals, like the **Go San Diego Card** (3 days for $108) are available online (www.gosandiegocard.com) or at the attraction ticket counters.

DOWNTOWN

San Diego's downtown attractions are concentrated in the corridor that includes its business, Gaslamp, and waterfront districts—all testaments to San Diego's continuing renaissance. Travelers should be careful outside of this area; in particular, the neighborhood to the southeast may not be safe.

GASLAMP QUARTER

The Gaslamp Quarter houses antique shops, Victorian buildings, trendy restaurants, and many nightclubs. The streets, especially Fifth Ave., get packed on Friday and Saturday nights with well-dressed, well-tanned folks out to see and be seen. The **Gaslamp Quarter Foundation**, 410 Island Ave., at William Heath Davis House, offers guided walking tours as well as a small museum about San Diego's oldest house, its occupants, and their amusing stories. (☎619-233-4692; www.gaslampquarter.org. Museum open Tu-Sa 10am-6pm, Su 9am-3pm. $5, seniors $4. 2hr. walking tours Sa 11am. Tours $10, students and seniors $8, under 12 free. Self-guided tour maps $2.)

HORTON PLAZA. The plaza is the jewel of San Diego's redevelopment. This pastel-hued urban creation is an open-air shopping center covering seven blocks. (At Broadway and 4th Ave.)

SAN DIEGO MUSEUM OF CONTEMPORARY ART. The steel-and-glass museum shows rotating exhibits of 20th-century works, generally post-1950. Exhibits are nicely curated and always interesting. (1001 Kettner Blvd. ☎619-234-1001. Open M, W, F-Su 11am-5pm, Th 11am-7pm. $10, under 25 free. Th 5-7pm free.)

SAN DIEGO MARITIME MUSEUM. Displays at this museum showcase San Diego's rich maritime history. The museum also maintains the magnificently restored 1863 sailing vessel *Star of India*, along with nautical exhibits and a replica of an old naval frigate with a cool pirate exhibit. (1492 N. Harbor Dr. ☎619-234-9153; www.sdmaritime.org. Open daily from Memorial Day to Labor Day 9am-9pm; from Labor Day to Memorial Day 9am-8pm. $14, ages 6-17 $8.)

EMBARCADERO. Spanish for "dock," the Embarcadero has boardwalk shops and museums that face moored windjammers, cruise ships, and the occasional naval destroyer. To get out on the water, you can opt for a 1hr. harbor cruise that will take you around the bay for beautiful views of the cityscape and the Coronado Bridge. (☎619-234-4111 or 800-442-

7847; www.sdhe.com. Tours leave approximately every hr. in summer 10am-5:30pm; in winter 10am-4:15pm. $18, ages 4-12 $9.)

SEAPORT VILLAGE. At the southern tip of the Embarcadero area lies Seaport Village, a cute Spanish village-like area filled with 57 touristy boutiques and restaurants. (☎619-235-4014; www.seaportvillage.com. Shops open daily 10am-9pm.)

BALBOA PARK

Balboa Park was created from the baked dirt of an abandoned pueblo tract when pioneering horticulturists planted its first redwood seedlings in 1889. Today, the park nurtures these spectacular trees, a profusion of flora, and many museums and cultural attractions. The **Balboa Park Visitors Center**, 1549 El Prado St., sells maps and the Passport to Balboa Park, which allows admission into 13 of the parks and museums. (From I-5, merge onto Rte. 163 N. and take the Balboa Park exit. ☎619-239-0512; www.balboapark.org. Open daily in summer 9am-4:30pm; in winter 9am-4pm. Passport $39, children $21.)

■**SAN DIEGO ZOO.** With over 100 acres of exquisite fenceless habitats, this zoo deserves its reputation as one of the finest in the world. Its unique "bioclimatic" exhibits group animals and plants by habitat. The panda exhibit is the most famous feature of the park, and the zoo invests over $1 million a year on panda habitat preservation in China. The most thorough way to tour the zoo is on foot, though visitors can board an educational 40min. double-decker bus tour that races across 75% of the zoo. Seats on the upper deck are popular, but trees can obstruct views, so the lower deck is a better bet. Plan to spend several hours at the zoo—there's a lot to see. Show up in the morning to catch the animals before their afternoon siestas. (2920 Zoo Dr. ☎619-234-3153; www.sandiegozoo.org. Open daily from late June to early Sept. 9am-9pm; from early to late Sept. 9am-6pm; from late Sept. to late June 9am-5pm. Last entry 1hr. before close. $24.50, with 45min. bus tour and 2 tickets for the aerial tramway $34; ages 3-11 $16.50/24.)

MUSEUM OF MAN. Creationists, beware: the Museum of Man dedicates an entire floor to the 98.4% of DNA we share with chimpanzees. Downstairs has rotating exhibits focused on the history of various cultural groups and also a section dedicated to Mexico. The real treat, however, is the museum's exterior, which features gleaming Spanish mosaic tiles on its much-photographed tower and dome. *(On the west end of the park. ☎ 619-239-2001; www.museumofman.org. Open daily 10am-4:30pm. $10, ages 13-17 $7.50, ages 3-12 $5.)*

SAN DIEGO AIR AND SPACE MUSEUM. The museum displays 24 full-scale replicas and 44 original planes as well as information on aviation history and the International Space Station project. Exhibits focus on military aviation, the "golden age" of air travel, and an ever-expanding display of space-age technology. The museum also has a GPS satellite and flight simulators. *(2001 Pan American Plaza. ☎ 619-234-8291; www.aerospacemuseum.org. Open daily in summer 10am-5:30pm; in winter 10am-4:30pm. . $15, students $12, ages 3-11 $6.)*

REUBEN H. FLEET SPACE THEATER AND SCIENCE CENTER. The Fleet houses the world's very first Omnimax theater, complete with 153 speakers and a dome-shaped planetarium. The science center has interactive exhibits about the five senses, aging, and more. Although it's filled with kids, it can be fun if you like science centers. Don't miss the aging machine, where you can see what you'll look like at age 70. *(1875 El Prado Way. ☎ 619-238-1233; www.rhfleet.org. Open M-Th and Sa-Su 9:30am-8pm, F 9:30am-9pm. $8, with Omnimax show $12.50; ages 3-12 $9.75/6.75. 1st Tu of each month free.)*

SAN DIEGO MUSEUM OF ART. This museum has a collection ranging from ancient Asian to contemporary Californian works, and also rotating exhibits. Its collection of paintings by old Spanish masters is renowned. *(☎ 619-232-7931. Open Tu-W and Sa-Su 10am-6pm, Th 10am-9pm. $10, students $7, ages 6-17 $4.)*

MUSEUM OF PHOTOGRAPHIC ARTS (MOPA). The small, ultramodern museum features excellent rotating exhibits. It occasionally shows films, which range from ultra-artsy to more traditional. *(☎ 619-238-7559; www.mopa.org. Open Tu-Su 10am-5pm. $6, students and seniors $4. 2nd Tu of each month free.)*

TIMKEN MUSEUM OF ART. Right next to the Botanical Gardens is the small but impressive Timken Museum of Art. The collection, sus-

tained by the wealthy Timken family, includes a few choice pieces by European masters and an excellent collection of Russian icons. *(☎ 619-239-5548. Open Tu-Sa 10am-4:30pm, Su 1:30-4:30pm. Guided tours Tu-F 10am-noon. Free.)*

BALBOA PARK GARDENS. The Botanical Building is a giant wood structure filled with the scent of jasmine and the murmur of fountains; the orchid collection is particularly striking. The Desert Garden and the award-winning Inez Grant Parker Memorial Rose Garden offer a fascinating contrast of flora. The Desert Garden contains more than 1300 plants within its two acres and is in full bloom from January to March. The Rose Garden has approximately 2500 roses of nearly 200 varieties and is at its peak between April and May. *(2200 Park Blvd. ☎ 619-235-1100, tour info 235-1121. Open M-W and F-Sa 10am-4pm. Free.)*

OLD GLOBE THEATER. Constructed in 1937, this is the oldest professional theater in California and a Tony Award-winning institution. *(☎ 619-234-5623; www.theoldglobe.org. Ticket prices vary but average $50-60. Limited number of $29 tickets available for students and seniors. Call ahead.)*

OLD TOWN

In 1769, supported by a brigade of Spanish infantry, Father Serra established the first of 21 missions that would line the California coast in the area now known as Old Town. The remnants of this early settlement have become one of San Diego's tourist mainstays. Old Town is centered around **State Park,** where seven original buildings still stand, along with 21 reconstructed ones. *(To reach Old Town, take the Old Town exit from I-5 N.)*

STATE PARK. The most popular of the area's attractions, the park's early-19th-century buildings contain museums, shops, and restaurants. On the square, **Seeley Stable,** once the Yuma-San Diego stagecoach stop, now houses a huge museum of 19th-century transportation, namely of the horse and carriage variety. *(☎ 619-220-5427. Open daily 10am-5pm. Tours every hr. 11am-2pm. Free.)* The **Whaley House Museum** stands on the site of San Diego's first gallows, and the house itself was the site of several deaths. Not all of the condemned went quietly, and after over 100 years of reported ghost sightings the house is now one of two

PACIFIC COAST MAP #1

haunted houses officially recognized by the state of California. Tours cover aspects of the Victorian era in San Diego, the Whaley family, and, of course, ghosts. *(2482 San Diego Ave. ☎619-298-2482, tours 293-0117. Open in summer daily 10am-10pm. Reduced hours in winter. Before 5pm $6, ages 3-12 $4; after 5pm $10/5.)*

HERITAGE PARK. Up the street from State Park is Heritage Park, a group of 150-year-old Victorian buildings that was transported to Old Town as part of preservation effort in the 1970s. Most of the buildings are now private offices, but you can tour tiny **Senlis Cottage,** an 1896 home, and **Temple Beth Israel,** the first synagogue in San Diego. *(9001 Towne Centre Dr. ☎619-291-9784. Open daily 9am-5pm. Free.)*

COASTAL SAN DIEGO

BEACHES. San Diego's younger population flocks to these communities by the surf for the hopping nightlife. **Ocean Beach** (OB) is the most hippie-flavored of the beaches, in large part because community groups have fought to keep out condo rental developers and chain restaurants. OB has a great farmers' market every Wednesday 4-7pm on the 4900 block of Newport Ave., the beach's main thoroughfare. Farther north, at the corner of W. Mission Bay Dr. and Mission Blvd., **Mission Beach** is a people-watcher's paradise. **Belmont Park,** a combination amusement park and shopping center, draws a youthful crowd. To find it, look for the roller coaster ($6 per ride). **Pacific Beach** and its boisterous **Garnet Avenue** are home to the best nightlife. Ocean Front Walk is packed with joggers, cyclists, and the usual beachfront shops. Rent a bike from **Cheap Rentals Mission Beach,** 3221 and 3685 Mission Blvd., to cruise the strip and work on your tan. *(☎619-488-9070 or 800-941-7761; www.cheap-rentals.com. In-line skates, bikes $12 per day.)*

SEA WORLD. Since the 190-acre park opened in 1964, Sea World has welcomed more than 100 million guests. The A-list star here is the behemoth killer whale Shamu, whose signature move is a cannonball splash that soaks anyone in the first 20 rows. The original Shamu died long ago, but the name is proudly carried as a stage name by all of Sea World's performing killer whales. In addition, there are animals from all walks of sea life in their natural habitats, including penguins, polar bears, and sharks. Try the ray-petting pool and Shipwreck Rapids, Sea World's first adventure ride, but be prepared to spend big; even parking at Sea World will cost you $12. *(From I-5, take the Sea World Dr. exit and turn west toward the park. ☎619-226-3901. Open in summer daily 9am-11pm; call ahead for winter hours. $61, ages 3-9 $51.)*

LA JOLLA

The Spanish named this area La Jolla ("The Jewel") for its physical beauty. More recently, the craggy promontory developed as the exclusive hideaway for wealthy Easterners, and today it remains true to its tony roots. Despite the snobbery, you'll find good shopping, great eating, and beautifully constructed buildings here, so it's worth a look. To reach La Jolla, take the Ardath exit west from I-5.

◼BIRCH AQUARIUM. The Birch Aquarium at the **Scripps Institute of Oceanography** has great educational exhibits, including a tank of eerily lit jellyfish, a large collection of sea horses, and a 70,000 gal. kelp and shark tank. Just outside, you'll find a tide-pool exhibit, tons of information on sharks, and fabulous views of the ocean. *(2300 Expedition Way. ☎858-534-3474; http://aquarium.ucsd.edu. Open daily 9am-5pm. Last entry 4:30pm. $11, students $8, ages 3-17 $7.50.)*

BEACHES. La Jolla claims some of the finest beaches in the city. **La Jolla Cove** is popular with scuba divers, snorkelers, and brilliantly colored Garibaldi goldfish. Wander south along the cliffs to a semicircular inlet known as the **Children's Pool.** Established in 1931 by wealthy philanthropist Ellen Scripps, the inlet became the preferred sunbathing spot for a community of sea lions. Some of the best breaks in the county can be found at **Tourmaline Beach** and **Windansea Beach.** However, these are notoriously territorial spots, so outsiders might be advised to surf elsewhere. **La Jolla Shores** has gentle swells ideal for inexperienced surfers, boogie boarders, and swimmers. Learn to hang ten from **Surf Diva,** one of the area's most famous surf schools that caters primarily to women, but is willing to show guys a thing or two if they reserve far enough in advance. *(2160 Ave. de la Playa. ☎858-454-8273. Private lessons $82.50 per hr. group lessons $85 per 2hr.)*

GEISEL LIBRARY. If you've got time, go see the terraces and buttresses of Geisel Library at the **University of California San Diego (UCSD),** a space-age structure endowed by La Jolla resident Theodore Geisel, better known as the late and beloved author Dr. Seuss. Twice a year (usually in March and July or August), a revealing collection of his original sketches and notes are on display. *(The library is in the center of campus. ☎858-534-3339. Open M-F 8am-6pm, Sa-Su 10am-6pm. Free.)*

SAN DIEGO MUSEUM OF CONTEMPORARY ART. The museum shares its rotating collection of pop, minimalist, and conceptualist

KAYAK THE SEA CAVES OF LA JOLLA

Park the car for a day, hop in a kayak, and explore the seven north-facing sea caves of La Jolla. Check out the majestic scenery and marine life on a guided tour at La Jolla Kayak or paddle around on your own. While the westernmost cave, known as Sunny Jim, is easily accessible by foot, the other six can be explored only by kayak. They encompass four marine environments: sandy beach, rocky coast, kelp forest, and open ocean. In the spring, you might have the chance to see sea lions or cormorants on the rocks, and in the summertime harmless leopard sharks and rays linger near shore. You can satisfy the appetite you're sure to work up by purchasing one of the meal-package trips. On the Brunch Paddle tour, top off your weekend workout with a delicious omelet at nearby Piatti restaurant. (Single $75, double $110. Sa-Su 10am.) On the El Charro Taco and Beer paddle, kayak after work, then treat yourself to a drink and Mexican food at El Charro restaurant. (Single $30, double $50. M-F after 3pm, Sa-Su after 4pm.) La Jolla Kayak also rents snorkeling gear (fins $7, mask and snorkel $12), wetsuits ($15), boogie boards ($20), and surfboards ($50) for the full day.

La Jolla Kayak, 2199 Avenida de la Playa (☎858-459-1114; www.lajollakayak.com). 1½hr. kayak tours ($50) at 9, 11am, 1, 3pm, sunset. Single kayak rental $28 per 2hr., $38 per 4hr.; double

art with the downtown branch. The museum is as visually stunning as the art it contains, with gorgeous ocean views and high-ceilinged, light-filled spaces. *(700 Prospect St.* ☎*858-454-3541. Open M-Tu and F-Su 11am-5pm, Th 11am-7pm. $10, under 25 free. Th 5-7pm free.)*

ESCONDIDO

Escondido lies 30 mi. north of San Diego amid rolling, semi-arid hills that blossom with wildflowers in the spring. Because Escondido is farther from the ocean than many parts of the city, lodging is comparatively cheaper here than it would be elsewhere.

SAN DIEGO WILD ANIMAL PARK. The real reason to head to Escondido is to see the free-roaming animals at the 1800-acre wild animal park, a sister to the San Diego Zoo. Rhinos, giraffes, gazelles, and tigers roam the grounds. One of the park's highlights is the █giraffe-feeding station. The open-air **Wgasa Bush Line Railway,** a 1hr. monorail safari, travels through four created habitat areas; sit on the right if possible ($10). Another option is a **Photo Caravan Safari,** which takes you close enough to the animals to touch them. *(From I-15, take the Via Rancho Pkwy.* ☎*619-747-8702; www. wildanimalpark.org. Open daily in summer 9am-9pm; in winter 9am-5pm. Last entry 1hr. before park closes. Rail tours June-Aug. 9:30am-9pm; Sept.-May 9:30am-4pm. $34, ages 3-11 $24. Safaris $90 per person.)*

🎭 ENTERTAINMENT

The definitive source of entertainment info is the free *Reader*, found in shops, coffeehouses, and visitors centers. Listings can also be found in the San Diego *Union-Tribune*'s Thursday *"Night and Day"* section or the *What's Playing* pamphlet from the visitors center. If cruisin' and boozin' isn't your idea of fun, you can spend a more sedate evening at one of San Diego's excellent theaters, such as the **Balboa Theatre,** 854 4th Ave. (☎619-570-1100) or the **Horton Grand Theatre,** 444 4th Ave. (☎619-234-9583). The **La Jolla Playhouse,** 2910 La Jolla Village Dr., is an award-winning theater that presents shows on the UCSD campus. (☎858-550-1010; www.lajollaplayhouse.com. Tickets from $25.) The **San Diego Symphony** plays from the standard repertorie throughout the year. (☎619-235-0804; www.sandiegosymphony.com.)

🎵 NIGHTLIFE

Nightlife in San Diego is scattered across distinct pockets of action. Posh locals and party-seeking tourists flock to the **Gaslamp Quarter.** The **Hillcrest,** next to **Balboa Park,** draws a young, largely gay crowd to its clubs and eateries. Away from downtown, the beach areas (especially **Garnet Avenue** in **Pacific Beach**) are loaded with clubs, bars, and cheap eateries.

Pacific Beach Bar and Grill and Club Tremors, 860 Garnet Ave. (☎858-272-1242; www.pbbarandgrill.com). One of the best (and only) dance clubs in Pacific Beach. Live DJ spins hip hop, house, and retro for a packed 2-level dance floor filled with a young crowd. Respectable food, more than 20 beers on tap, and live music (generally rock) on Su from 6pm. 21+ after 4pm. Cover varies, but is generally not too expensive. Enter through the bar instead of Club Tremors Th-Sa to avoid the cover. Dress code in the club: no flip-flops. Club open Tu and Th-Sa 9pm-1:30am. Bar open Tu-Su 11am-1:30am. Kitchen open until midnight. AmEx/D/MC/V.

Canes Bar and Grill, 3105 Ocean Front Walk (☎858-488-1780; www.canesbarandgrill.com), in Mission Beach. In addition to being a huge live music venue, this beachside bar has unbeatable sunset views from the terrace. Music is usually rock, but check the website for schedule. Cover $5-15. Open daily 11am-2am; grill open until 10pm. AmEx/D/MC/V.

The Casbah, 2501 Kettner Blvd. (☎619-232-4355; www.casbahmusic.com). Intimate show venue with black walls, bar, and stage. Famous for attracting alt-rock greats before they became great: Pearl Jam, Nirvana, and The White Stripes have all played here. Music is generally alt-rock but can lean toward punk. Nightly shows are sometimes sold out, so call ahead or purchase tickets online. Cover $5-15. Cash only.

Croce's Top Hat Bar and Grille and Croce's Jazz Bar, 802 5th Ave. (☎619-233-4355; www.croces.com), at F St. in the Gaslamp Quarter. Ingrid Croce, widow of singer Jim Croce, created this blues and jazz bar in memory of her late husband. Bypass the pricey restaurant and head to the wood-paneled piano bar with huge pictures of Jim adorning the walls. The live music is top-notch and the crowd is composed of jazz connoisseurs (most of whom are over 40). Don't wear your dirty backpacker gear. Music nightly from 8:30pm. 21+. Cover M-Th and Su $5, F-Sa $10. Restaurant and bar open M-F 5:30pm-midnight, Sa-Su 10am-midnight. AmEx/D/MC/V.

Bourbon St., 4612 Park Blvd. (☎619-291-4043), in University Heights. Happening gay bar that's open nightly. Have a stiff drink in the front, but most of the fun is in the back, where a covered patio is decorated to look like a street from the New Orleans French Quarter. The entire place is made up of 3 bars and 3 buildings that are usually packed. Music is generally Top 40 and retro dance. Karaoke Tu from 9pm. Th 4-7pm $3 martinis. Su $3 pitchers, $2 drafts. No cover. Open daily 4pm-2am. MC/V.

🚗 THE ROAD TO TORREY PINES: 18 MI.

Head north on **Ninth Avenue,** turn right onto **Broadway,** and hang a left onto **11th Avenue.** Merge onto **I-5 North (San Diego Freeway).** Take **Exit 29** onto **Genesee Avenue West** and follow it north as it becomes **Torrey Pines Road.**

TORREY PINES ☎858

The closest you'll get to the great outdoors just outside of San Diego, **Torrey Pines State Park,** 12600 N. Torrey Pines Rd., is often crowded, but the hiking trails and beach are lovely. Be sure to watch for the frolicking dolphins along the coast. The park is also home to the scrub jay bird and the rarest kind of pine tree in the US; it's the only place you can find the torrey pine tree other than the Channel Islands in Santa Barbara. (☎858-755-2063; www.torreypine.org. Open daily 7:30am-7:30pm. $8 per vehicle.) The **Torrey Pines Lodge,** 11480 N. Torrey Pines Rd., provides info on hiking trails as well as an exhibit on why the torrey pines are so unique. (☎858-453-4420. Open daily 9am-5:30pm.)

🚗 THE ROAD TO DEL MAR: 3 MI.

Torrey Pines Rd. becomes **Camino Del Mar** north of the park and leads into Del Mar.

DEL MAR ☎858

The affluent suburb of Del Mar is home to racehorses and famous fairgrounds as well

as small shops and some good eats along Camino Del Mar. During June and early July, Del Mar hosts the **San Diego County Fair,** one of the largest fairs in California. To the north, Solana Beach boasts the **Cedros Design District,** which is chock-full of warehouses converted into specialty boutiques. Here, shoppers wander through everything from salvage yards to upscale clothing stores. The celebrity-studded **Del Mar Thoroughbred Club,** at the corner of Via de la Valle and Jimmy Durante Blvd., fills with racing fans in late July and August. Founded in 1937 by Bing Crosby and Pat O'Brien, the racetrack is one of the most beautiful in the world. (☎858-755-1141; www.delmarracing.com. At least 8 races daily. Post time 2pm. Gates open M-F at noon, Sa-Su at 11:30am.)

Surf-weathered locals favor **Board and Brew ❷,** 1212 Camino Del Mar, for its cheap beer ($3) and delicious sandwiches. Try the Board Master ($5.50), a roast beef and turkey combination with cheddar and sweet-and-sour dressing. (☎858-481-1021. Open M-Th and Su 10am-7pm, F-Sa 10am-8pm. Cash only.) Relax on the patio at the **Beach Grass Cafe ❷,** 159 S. Hwy 101., in Solana Beach, as you enjoy tasty soups and fresh salads. Come for music-themed dinners like samba or Hawaiian country, or enjoy brunch on the weekend. (☎858-509-0632; www.beachgrasscafe.com. Open M-Th 7am-3:30pm and 5-9pm, F 7am-3:30pm and 5-10pm, Sa 7am-3:30pm and 5-10pm, Su 7am-3:30pm and 5-9pm. Breakfast and lunch $8-11. Dinner entrees $16-25. Beer $4.50-5.50. AmEx/D/MC/V.) **Pizza Port ❷,** 135 N. US 101, in Solana Beach, has awesome deep-dish pizza and "grub and grog." Expect a wait at dinnertime; the place is usually packed. (☎858-481-7332. Pizzas from $6. Pints $4.25-5.25. Open M-Th and Su 11am-11pm, F-Sa 11am-midnight. AmEx/MC/V.)

🚗 THE ROAD TO CARLSBAD: 17 MI.

Camino Del Mar becomes **Old US 101** and then **Carlsbad Boulevard** as it heads north along the coast. Turn right onto **Carlsbad Village Drive.**

CARLSBAD ☎760

Farther up the rocky coast is the charming lagoon hideaway of Carlsbad, where US 101, known here as Carlsbad Blvd., winds past silky sands and shingled homes adorned with stunningwild rosebushes.

PACIFIC COAST

VITAL STATS

Population: 92,000.

Tourist Office: Carlsbad Convention and Visitors Bureau, 400 Carlsbad Village Dr. (☎760-434-6093; www.visitcarlsbad.com). Open M-F 9am-5pm, Sa 10am-4pm, Su 10am-3pm.

Library and Internet Access: Georgina Cole Library, 1250 Carlsbad Village Dr. (☎760-434-2870), downtown. Open M-Th 9am-9pm, F-Sa 9am-5pm. Su 1-5pm.

Post Office: 2772 Roosevelt St. (☎760-729-1244). Open 7:30am-5pm, Sa 9am-12:30pm. **Postal Code:** 92008.

ORIENTATION

Carlsbad Boulevard (US 101) is the major north-south route and runs mostly parallel to **I-5. Carlsbad Village Drive** runs inland toward **I-5.**

ACCOMMODATIONS

Surf Motel, 3136 Carlsbad Blvd. (☎760-729-7961; www.surfmotelcarlsbad.com). The motel offers decent value across the street from the beach. Rooms in summer $139-359; in winter $89-199. AmEx/D/MC/V. ❹

Motel 6, 1006 Carlsbad Village Dr. (☎760-434-7135), just east of Carlsbad Village. Wi-Fi in certain rooms $3 per 24hr. Singles $54-70; doubles $60-76. AmEx/D/MC/V. ❸

San Elijo Beach State Park, 2050 S. Coast Hwy. (☎760-753-5091), in Cardiff. Over 170 sites on seaside cliffs. Showers and laundry. Sites $25-35, with hookup $34-44. ❷

South Carlsbad Beach State Park, off Carlsbad Blvd. (☎760-438-3143). 222 sites near beautiful beaches with good surfing. Showers and laundry. Sites $25-35. ❶

FOOD

There are a variety of great beachfront restaurants along the Pacific Coast Hwy.

Trattoria I Trulli, 830 S. Coast Hwy. (☎760-943-6800.), in Encinitas. Locals and tourists alike cram the trattoria's intimate dining area for good reason: the Italian cuisine is delicious and the restaurant's beige-stucco decor is charmingly chic. Dinner entrees run $13-24. Open M-Th and Su 11:30am-2:30pm and 5-10pm, F-Sa 11:30am-2:30pm and 5-10:30pm. AmEx/D/MC/V. ❸

Coyote Bar and Grill, 300 Carlsbad Village Dr. (☎760-729-4695). The place to karaoke your heart out or to warm up as you dine around one of the fire pits. Live music on the patio and Southern cuisine make this a popular local hangout. Entrees $10-16. Beer $4.25-5. Happy hour M-F 4-6pm. Open M-Th and Su 11am-12:30am, F-Sa 11am-2am. AmEx/MC/V. ❸

Honey's Bistro and Bakery, 632 S. Coast Hwy., (☎760-942-5433). Blackboards and tile floors create an intimate coffeehouse atmosphere. Enjoy

TRY SOMETHING NEW: AÇAÍ SMOOTHIES

For a yummy pick-me-up, skip the coffee and order an açaí-infused smoothie. The açaí (ah-sah-ee) berry grows on the açaí palm tree, native to the swamps of Central and South America. Brazilians mix the pulp of the berries, which are round, dark purple, and about 1 in. in diameter, with granola or with other fruit to make juices. Studies have proven açaí to contain high levels of antioxidants, which improve the body's defense system against diseases like heart disease and certain cancers. So, naturally, the health-conscious population of Southern California has jumped at the chance to pour another beneficial ingredient into its fruit-and-granola diet. Smoothie shops throughout California are jumping on the açaí bandwagon, offering a variety of smoothie-like products. Açaí Energy Shots (1 oz. $2.50, 2 oz. $4) at Beach City Smoothies, 594 Carlsbad Village Dr. (☎760-729-0011), blend açaí juice with 18 other fruits. If your açaí appetite is the size of a meal, try the Açaí Energy Bowl ($4-6.50), açaí sorbet topped with granola, mixed fruit, honey, and coconut

a fresh salad ($5-8), sandwich ($4-7), or soup ($4-6) and grab one of the mouthwatering baked goods for dessert. Open daily 5:30am-3:30pm and 5pm-last customer. MC/V. ❶

Beach City Smoothies, 594 Carlsbad Village Dr. (☎760-729-0011). The place to satisfy your smoothie craving. Owned and operated by Mary Jacobson and her daughter, Jamie, this cozy shop also serves coffee drinks, gourmet pretzels, and adds no dairy or sugar to its 100% fresh-fruit smoothies ($3.50-4.50). Try the Acai Energy Bowl ($4-6.50), an antioxidant blend of sorbet made from the Brazilian Acai berry, banana, granola, honey, and coconut. Open M-Sa 8:30am-7pm, Su 8:30am-6pm. ❶

🅖 SIGHTS

MUSEUM OF MAKING MUSIC. Shake, rattle, and roll at this museum, where over 450 innovative musical instruments showcase and symbolize 20th-century American music in its totality. (*5790 Armada Dr. ☎ 760-438-5996; www. museumofmakingmusic.org. Open Tu-Su 10am-5pm. $5; students and ages 4-18 $3; under 3 free.*)

LEGOLAND. This theme park is a fun, goofball tribute to the interlocking kiddie blocks that have inspired countless junior architects. Visitors who pay the hefty admission price might be disappointed to find no gem-studded Legos. (*1 Legoland Dr., south of town. Head east on Cannon Rd. ☎ 760-918-5346. Open in summer daily 10am-8pm; in fall M and Th-Su 10am-5pm; in spring daily 10am-5pm. Hours vary in winter. $60, ages 3-12 $50.*)

🅜 FESTIVALS

Carlsbad has one major festival, the **Carlsbad Village Street Faire.** It is the largest one-day fair in California and attracts over 80,000 people on the first Sunday in May and Nov.

🅑 BEACHES

The California state park system maintains a number of breathtaking beaches, including Carlsbad State Beach. This 4-mile-long gem is marred only slightly by the mammoth power plant that occupies the coast to the south. **Offshore Surf Shop,** 3179 Carlsbad Blvd., offers surfing lessons and rents boogie boards and 6-8 ft. "soft" foam surfboards for beginners.

(☎760-729-4934. www.offshoresurfshop.com. Boogie boards $4 per hr., $15 per day. Credit card or deposit of $60. Surfboards $7/25. Wetsuits $4/15. Credit card or deposit of $150. 2hr. lessons, including board and wetsuit, $90. Open daily 9am-7pm.)

🅝 THE ROAD TO OCEANSIDE: 5 MI.

Carlsbad Boulevard becomes **Coast Highway** as it heads north toward Oceanside.

OCEANSIDE ☎760

Oceanside is the largest and least glamorous of San Diego's coastal resort towns. Neighbor to **Camp Pendleton,** a Marine Corps base, as well as one of the world's greatest surfing beaches at Oceanside Harbor, Oceanside is part military order, part surfer chill. The pier gets crowded during the **World Body Surfing Championships** in mid-August. Call the **Oceanside Special Events Office** (☎760-435-5540) for info. Get a taste of surf culture at the 🅒**California Surf Museum,** 223 N. Coast Hwy., where the exhibit changes yearly. (☎760-721-6876. Open daily 10am-4pm. Free.) Catch your own dinner by renting gear at **Helgren's Sportfishing Trips,** 315 Harbor Dr. S. (☎760-722-2133; www. helgrensportfishing.com. 1-day license $14. Rod rental $14, shark rod $16. ½-day trips on the fishing boat $45, ¾-day $65, full-day $75. Shark trips F-Sa 5:30-11:30pm; $70. Non-fishing harbor cruise daily $14, ages 5-12 $7. Whale-watching excursions $25, ages 13-16 $20, under 13 $15.) Find California's first pepper tree (and God) at **Mission San Luis Rey de Francia,** 4050 Mission Ave., founded by Father Lausen in 1798. The only original building still standing is the church and the five adjoining arches. Follow Mission Ave. E. from N. Coast Hwy. (☎760-757-3651; www.sanluisrey.org. Open daily 10am-4pm. $6, ages 6-18 $4, families $25. Tours $7. Cemetery free. Cash only.)

Power up before hitting the waves at 🅒**The Longboarder ❷,** 228 N. Coast Hwy., which serves juicy burgers ($7-12) and heaping omelets ($7-10) to hungry surfers. (☎760-721-6776. Open M-W 7am-2pm, Th-Sa 7am-9pm, Su 7am-4pm. MC/V.)

PACIFIC COAST

PACIFIC COAST

THE ROAD TO SAN CLEMENTE AND DANA POINT: 24 MI.
Head east on **Mission Avenue** to **I-5 North.** Follow I-5 N. through the Camp Pendleton Marine Base.

SAN CLEMENTE AND DANA POINT ☎949

Ole Hanson, who bought the area and started building here in 1925, called San Clemente a "small Spanish village by the sea." Indeed, San Clemente provides the waves of bigger beach towns without all the noise and antics. San Clemente's downtown is a mecca for antique hunters. The historic buildings lining the town's streets house many shops. Just south of town, **San Onofre State Beach** is a prime surfing zone for experienced thrill-seekers. Neighboring Dana Point's spectacular bluffs were popularized in namesake Richard Henry Dana's 1841 account of Southern California's sailing culture, *Two Years Before the Mast.* The harbor holds nearly 3000 yachts and serves as a point of departure for Catalina Island. If you're in the mood for a swim, ask for Dana Point's **swimming beach,** which lies at Green Lantern Cove and Ensenada Place.

◄ DETOUR
SAN JUAN CAPISTRANO

From San Clemente or Dana Point, take **I-5 North** to Exit 82. Turn left on **Ortega Highway.**

The **Mission San Juan Capistrano,** founded in 1776 by Father Serra, is the birthplace of Orange County. Full of romance and beauty, the mission stands as a monument to Native American, Mexican, and European cultures. Although most of the original structure collapsed in an earthquake in 1812, this is the oldest used building in California and the only standing site where Serra himself is known to have given mass. Mass is still celebrated daily at 7am in the beautiful **Serra Chapel,** whose crumbling walls are adorned by a 17th-century Spanish altar and Native American designs. With its lily-pad fountain, blossoming trees, and benches hidden among flower bushes, the courtyard garden is perhaps the most charming part of the mission. On March 19 each year, the city of San Juan Capistrano gathers here for the famous **"Return of the Swallows,"** a celebration of the flock of birds that always migrates back to the mission. Throughout the year, the courtyard is host to various art receptions, dinners, and concerts. (☎949-234-1300; www.missionsjc. com. Open daily 8:30am-5pm. $9, ages 4-11 $5, under 4 free. Audio tour included with adult and senior tickets, $2 with child ticket.) Bras and neckties hanging from the rafters add to the intimidatingly grungy feel of **The Swallows Inn,** 31786 Camino Capistrano, the favorite local pub for over 50 years. Home to one of the country's largest chili cook-offs each May, it's also the best place to catch the **Swallows Day Parade** in March. (☎949-493-3188. Open M 10am-10pm, Tu-W 8am-midnight, Th-F 8am-2pm, Sa 7am-2am, Su 7am-10pm.)

THE ROAD TO LAGUNA BEACH: 14 MI.
From the **Pacific Coast Highway (Route 1),** turn right onto **Forest Avenue** and right again onto **Glenneyre Street** to reach Laguna Beach.

LAGUNA BEACH ☎949

A sign at the corner of Forest and Ocean Ave. sums up the industry-free pleasantness of Laguna with this message: "This Gate Hangs Well and Hinders None, Refresh and Rest, Then Travel On." Recent television fame has popularized this oceanside town, though its bustling beaches, rocky cliffs, coves, and lush hillside foliage don't need the extra publicity to appeal to visitors. Much of the town's charm is visible along the coastal highway, including dozens of displays of public art.

✦ ORIENTATION

Ocean Avenue, at the Pacific Coast Hwy., and **Main Beach** are the prime hangout spots in Laguna Beach. **Westry Beach,** which spreads south of Laguna just below Aliso Beach Park, and **Camel Point,** between Westry and Aliso, form the hub of the local gay community. You'll know you've reached the town center when you see the seaside Main Park; the main drags of **Forest Avenue** and Ocean Ave. run perpendicular to it. Parking downtown can be a problem; meters gobble quarters for 15min. of legality 8am-6pm. For beach access, park on streets to the east and look for "Public Access" signs between private properties.

VITAL STATS

Population: 25,000

Tourist Office: 252 Broadway (☎800-877-1115; www.lagunabeachinfo.org). Open daily 10am-4pm.

Library and Internet Access: Laguna Beach Library, 363 Glenneyre St. (☎949-497-1733), 1 block south of Forest Ave. Open M-W 10am-8pm, Th 10am-6pm, F-Sa 10am-5pm.

Post Office: 24001 Calle de la Magdalena (☎949-837-1848). Open M-F 7:30am-6pm, Sa 9am-3pm.

Postal Code: 92654.

ACCOMMODATIONS

Seacliff Laguna Inn, 1661 S. Coast Hwy. (☎949-494-9717; www.seaclifflaguna.com). A cut above the average motel with some rooms overlooking the ocean (over other roofs) and a heated pool. Coffee and pastries included. Rooms $85-180. AmEx/D/MC/V. ➎

FOOD

Orange Inn, 703 S. Coast Hwy. (☎949-494-6085). Dates back to 1931. Serves sandwiches ($5-8.75), smoothies ($4.25), baked goods, and assorted fresh fruit and veggie juices. Check out the pictures of old Laguna Beach along the back wall. Open daily 6:30am-5pm. D/MC/V. ➋

The White House, 340 S. Coast Hwy. (☎949-494-8088), across the street from the park. Has been serving upscale American food since 1918. The "twilight dinner" (M-Th and Su 4-6pm) is a steal: only $12 for a 2-course meal with choices like seafood pasta and peppered steak. Entrees $11-29. Open M-Th and Su 11am-10pm, F-Sa 9am-11pm. AmEx/MC/V. ➍

Laguna Village Market and Cafe, 577 S. Coast Hwy. (☎949-494-6344). Ritzy. Sits atop a cliff and houses an open-air gazebo market, though the oceanfront terrace is the real draw. Mixed drinks $11. Open M-F 8:30am-8:30pm, Sa-Su 8:30am-9:30pm. ➌

SIGHTS

WYLAND GALLERY. A native of Laguna Beach, the artist Wyland has distinguished himself in the art world by capturing the enchant-ing spirit of whales and other underwater life forms. He has completed more than 100 murals worldwide; he painted the most recent one at the Great Wall of China for the 2008 Olympics. You can see one, in tiles, on the side of the Gallery. His sculptures, paintings, and other artistic creations are on display inside. *(509 S. Coast Hwy.)*

PACIFIC MARINE MAMMAL CENTER. The center rescues and rehabilitates sick sea lions and seals, which you can visit as they recover. *(20612 Laguna Canyon Rd. ☎ 949-494-3050; www.pacificmmc.org. Open daily 10am-4pm. Free.)*

FESTIVALS

Pageant of the Masters (☎949-494-1145; www.foapom.com). The highlight of Laguna Beach's Festival of Arts. People in costumes faithfully recreate famous works of art as "living pictures." July-Aug. daily 8:30pm.

Sawdust Art Festival (☎949-494-3030). Showcases the work of 200 local artists in a beautiful three-acre setting. Open July-Aug. 10am-10pm. $7, ages 6-12 $3, under 6 free.

OUTDOORS

Thousand Steps Beach may be missing 800 of the steps it claims, but the beauty of the arched descent is enough to make you lean toward poetic exaggeration. The (extremely) inconspicuous entrance (think hidden!) is one block south of the medical center on Ninth St.; park your car inland. **Crystal Cove State Park**, 8471 Rte. 1, 3 mi. north of Laguna Beach, is a beautiful nature preserve with a rocky shoreline. El Moro Canyon extends up the hills east of Rte. 1, offering hikes with coastal views. Choose one of the better hikes: a comfortable 2.5 mi. loop around **No Dogs Road, Poles Road,** and **El Moro Canyon Road** or the strenuous 10 mi. ascent up **Moro Ridge Road.** (Open daily 6am-sunset. $10 per vehicle.)

THE ROAD TO NEWPORT BEACH: 12 MI.
Continue along **Route 1 North.**

NEWPORT BEACH   ☎949

Multi-million-dollar homes share the oceanfront with beach bums along the Newport

Beach shore. Bicyclists pedal lazily around the residential Balboa Peninsula, while out-of-towners play beach volleyball and surf alongside locals. Newport's **Harbor Nautical Museum,** 600 E. Bay Ave., in the Balboa Funzone, has exhibits on maritime history and model ships as well as educational and family activities. (☎949-675-8915; www.nhnm.org. Open M and W-Su 10am-6pm. Free.) Get a dose of OC style at **Fashion Island,** just inland from the Pacific Coast Hwy., between MacArthur Blvd. and Jamboree Rd. Surrounded by circular Newport Center Dr., this outdoor mall divided into seven courts is the Orange County version of a regular mall but lets you get a tan while you shop. (☎949-721-4000. Open M-F 10am-9pm, Sa 10am-7pm, Su 11am-6pm.)

The **Balboa Inn** ❺, 105 Main St., is a renovated landmark built in 1929 that offers rooms with ocean views and access to a hot tub. (☎949-675-3412; www.balboainn.com. Continental breakfast included. Parking $8 in a nearby lot, $28 valet. Rooms $189-500. AmEx/D/MC/V.) **Joe's Crabshack** ❷, 2607 Pacific Coast Hwy., has brightly colored chairs, neon beer signs on the walls, and a fantastic view of the harbor. Happy hour (M-F 3-7pm) has discounted eats and dirt-cheap drinks. (☎949-650-1818; www.joescrabshack.com. Entrees $8-20. Open M-Th and Su 11am-10pm, F-Sa 11am-11pm. AmEx/D/MC/V.) **Ho Sum Bistro** ❷, 3112 Newport Blvd., at 32nd St., is a quintessentially Southern California mix of healthfulAsian-influenced food and neon-lit white decor. Among your choices of "califoriental cuisine," the Ho Sum chicken salad ($8.80) will definitely fill you up. (☎949-675-0896. Entrees $6-10. Open M-Th and Su 11am-10pm, F-Sa 11am-1am. AmEx/MC/V.)

⚂ THE ROAD TO HUNTINGTON BEACH: 6 MI. Take the **Pacific Coast Highway/Route 1 North**.

HUNTINGTON BEACH ☎714
The prototypical Surf City of the US, Huntington Beach is a playground for beach bums. This town has surf lore galore, and the proof is on the **Surfing Walk of Fame** (the sidewalk along PCH at Main St.) and in the **International Surfing Museum,** 411 Olive St. Plans are in the works for the museum to move to a new building, to be built near the pier. (☎714-960-3483; www.surfingmuseum.org. Open M-F noon-5pm, Sa-Su 11am-6pm. $2, students $1.) Check out **Corky Carroll's Surf School** at Bolsa Chica State Beach, lifeguard station 18, where you can have a 1hr. lesson and then practice with the school's equipment for another hour. (☎714-969-3959; www.surfschool.net. Private lesson $60, group lesson $45.) The pier is the best place to watch the cavalcade of official surfing contests that occur periodically throughout the summer. Browse the stalls at the **Huntington Beach Pier Plaza,** right at the foot of the pier, where vendors sell everything from glass jewelry to watercolor paintings.

Though it's far from the beach, the **Beach Inn Motel** ❹, 18112 Beach Blvd., is the cheapest option around and has a pool and hot tub. Follow Main St. 3mi. inland to Beach Blvd. (☎714-841-6606. Singles $89; doubles $99-120.) Turn off Rte. 1 onto Main St. for six blocks, and on your left you'll find **Jan's Health Bar** ❷, 501 Main St. This wholesome hole in the wall sells scrumptious sandwiches ($5-7), salads, and smoothies. (☎714-536-4856. Open M-Sa 8am-7pm, Su 8am-6pm. Cash only.) **Ruby's** ❸, at the end of the Huntington Beach Pier, is a flashy white and neon-red 50s-style diner with burgers ($9) and a fabulous ocean view. (☎714-969-7829. Open M-Th and Su 7am-10pm, F-Sa 7am-11pm. AmEx/D/MC/V.)

⚄ DETOUR
DISNEYLAND

From Huntington Beach, take **Beach Boulevard (Route 39) North** for 11 mi. Turn right on **Ball Road** and continue for 4 mi to the park.

Disneyland calls itself the "Happiest Place on Earth," and everyone's inner child agrees. (☎714-781-4565; www.disneyland.com. Open daily 8am-10pm; hours may vary. $66, ages 3-9 $56, under 3 free. 2- and 3-day passes also available. Park Hopper ticket permits access to both parks. $91, ages 3-9 $81.)

⚄ DETOUR
KNOTT'S BERRY FARM

Stay on **Route 39 North** 1 mi. after the turnoff for Disneyland on Ball Rd.

Knott's Berry Farm gave up a long time ago on being the happiest place on Earth—it settles for "America's First Theme Park." (☎714-220-5200. Open M-F and Su 10am-10pm, Sa 10am-11pm; hours may vary. $50, print-at-home tickets $43; ages 3-11 and over 61 $20; under 3 free.) Neighboring **Soak City USA** is Knott's 13-acre effort to make a splash in the already drenched water-park scene. (☎714-220-5200. Open daily 10am-7pm; hours may vary. $29, print-at-home tickets $24; ages 3-11 and over 61 $18; under 3 free.)

THE ROAD TO LONG BEACH: 19 MI.

Take the **Pacific Coast Highway/Route 1 North.** In Long Beach, turn left on **Alamitos Avenue** to head for the shore at Long Beach.

LONG BEACH ☎562

Long Beach is an industrial shipping center—massive, hulking, and impersonal. The fifth-largest city in California has less coastal charm than its neighbors. There are two main attractions on the coast: the Queen Mary luxury liner and the aquarium. Every April, Long Beach hosts a Grand Prix, and world-class racecar drivers and celebrities alike come to careen around the downtown track.

VITAL STATS
Population: 475,000
Tourist Office: Long Beach Visitors Bureau, 1 World Trade Center, Ste. 300 (☎800-452-7829), at Ocean Blvd. Open M-F 8am-5pm.
Library and Internet Access: Long Beach Library, 101 Pacific Ave. (☎562-570-7500), between Broadway and Ocean Blvd. Open M and W 10am-6pm, Tu and Th 10am-8pm, F-Sa 10am-5pm, Su noon-5pm.
Post Office: 300 N. Long Beach Blvd. (☎562-628-1303), on the corner of 3rd St. Open M-F 8:30am-5pm, Sa 9am-2pm. **Postal Code:** 90802.

ORIENTATION

Long Beach's main tourist attractions lie by the bay. **Pine Avenue,** the backbone of downtown, runs north from the bay. **Ocean Boulevard** runs west to the boutiques of Belmont Shore. As Tupac has warned, steer clear of the inland areas of industrial Long Beach.

ACCOMMODATIONS

The Beach Inn Motel, 823 E. 3rd St. (☎562-437-3464), right off the water. Affordable and has all the standard amenities. Singles $60; doubles $80. AmEx/D/MC/V. ❸

Beach Plaza Hotel, 2010 E. Ocean Blvd. (☎562-437-0771), at Cherry Ave. Is by no stretch of the imagination a "budget" hotel but has spacious rooms right on the beach. Pool and beach access. Reservations recommended. Doubles $95-180, with ocean view and kitchenette $150-250. AmEx/MC/V. ❺

FOOD

Shorehouse Cafe, 5271 E. 2nd St. (☎562-433-2266), in Belmont Shore. Don't be scared off by the huge shark painted with a fiery decal hanging from the ceiling—satisfy any craving at any time by ordering off the restaurant's expansive menu. Huge burgers $8-9. Entrees $15-17. Omelets $7-10. Beer $4. Open 24hr. AmEx/D/MC/V. ❸

The Omelette Inn, 108 W. 3rd St. (☎562-437-5625). A restaurant where the health-conscious roadtripper can chow down on egg-white omelets, brown rice, and veggie bacon strips. After a night of partying on the beach, try the Hangover Omelette (black forest ham, Ortega chile, green onion, and cheddar; $6.75). Open daily 7am-2:30pm. AmEx/D/MC/V. ❷

SIGHTS

QUEEN MARY. The legendary 1934 Cunard luxury liner has been transformed into a hotel with art exhibits, historical displays, and upscale bars. During WWII, the "Grey Ghost" (as she was known) carried 765,429 military personnel and sailed a total of 569,429 mi. The ship was so crucial to the Allied war effort that Hitler offered highest honors to anyone who sank her. Spookify the scene with the Haunted Encounters Passport or the Ghosts and Legends Special Effects Show or explore a Russian submarine from the Cold War era. Call to reserve a spot at the **Champagne Sunday Brunch** aboard the ship. (*At the end of Queen's Way Dr. ☎562-435-3511, brunch reservations 499-1606; www.queenmary.com. Open daily 10am-6pm. Paranormal Ship Walk Th-F and Su 8pm. Dining with the Spirits*

Sa 7pm. Paranormal Investigation 1st and 3rd F of the month at midnight. Twilight Historical Tour Th-Su 6:45pm. $25, ages 5-11 $13. Scorpion Submarine tour $11/10. "1st class," including guided tour $33/20. Haunted Encounters Passport $28/16.)

OTHER SIGHTS. The **Aquarium of the Pacific,** 100 Aquarium Way, is a celebration of the world's largest and most diverse body of water. Meet the dazzling creatures of the deep that struggle to coexist with the harbor's flotsam, jetsam, and effluvium. Among over 500 species, the seals, sea lions, otters, sharks, and jellyfish are sure to please. (☎562-590-3100; www.aquariumof-pacific.org. Open daily 9am-6pm. $21, seniors $18, ages 3-11 $12.) Just south of Ocean Blvd. and east of the Convention and Entertainment Center is an enormous **life-size mural of whales,** cited by locals as the largest in the world. Ready your game face and head to **Gameworks,** in The Pike at Rainbow Harbor. With bowling lanes and "Two-for-Thursdays" ($2 domestic drafts and specialty shots), you can play the night away. (10 Aquarium Way. ☎562-308-7529; www.game-works.com. Open M-Th 11am-midnight, F 11am-2am, Sa 10am-2am, Su 10am-midnight. 18+ if unaccompanied by a 21+ adult. AmEx/MC/V.)

◪ **THE ROAD TO LOS ANGELES: 25 MI.**
Take **Atlantic Avenue North** to **I-405 North.**

LOS ANGELES ☎213

In a city where nothing seems to be more than 30 years old, the latest trends command more respect than tradition. People flock to this historical vacuum in an effort to live like the stars—and what better place to do so? Bring your sense of style and an attitude; both are mandatory in this city of celebrities. Cruise through the city and watch the sun set over the Pacific in Santa Monica or stay to see the stars; either way, it's one hell of a show.

✦ ORIENTATION

Five major freeways connect California's vainest city to the rest of the state: **I-5 (Golden State Freeway), US 101 (Hollywood Freeway), the Pacific Coast Highway (PCH or Route 1), I-405 (San Diego Freeway),** and **I-10 (Santa Monica Freeway).**

I-5, I-405, I-110 (Harbor Fwy.), US 101, and the Pacific Coast Hwy. all run north-south. I-10 runs east-west. I-5 intersects I-10 just east of downtown and is one of the two major north-south thoroughfares. I-405, which goes from Orange County in the south all the way through L.A., parallels I-5 closer to the coast and separates Santa Monica and Malibu from L.A.'s less appealing Westside.

A legitimate downtown L.A. exists, but few go there except to work. The heart of downtown is relatively safe on weekdays, but avoid walking there after dark and on weekends. **Monterey Park** is one of the few cities in the US with a predominantly Asian-American population. The **University of Southern California (USC), Exposition Park,** and the districts of **Inglewood, Watts,** and **Compton** stretch south of downtown. **South Central,** as this area is called, suffered the brunt of the 1992 riots, is known for crime, and holds little for tourists. The predominantly Latino section of the city is found east of downtown and is comprised of **Boyle Heights, East Los Angeles,** and **Montebello.**

Sunset Boulevard has virtually everything L.A. has to offer the food- and fashion-conscious. The Sunset Strip, the hot seat of L.A.'s nightlife, is the West Hollywood section of Sunset Blvd. closest to **Beverly Hills.** The region known as the **Westside** encompasses prestigious **West Hollywood, Westwood, Bel Air, Brentwood, Beverly Hills, Pacific Palisades, Santa Monica** (p. 595), and **Venice.** A good portion of the city's gay community resides in West Hollywood, while Beverly Hills and Bel Air are home to the rich and famous. West L.A. is a municipal distinction that refers to Westwood and the no man's land that includes **Century City.** The area west of downtown and south of West Hollywood is known as the **Wilshire District.**

Eighty miles of beaches line L.A.'s coastal region. **Long Beach** is the southernmost. North across the Palos Verdes Peninsula is **Venice,** followed by **Santa Monica, Malibu,** and **Zuma Beach.** The **San Fernando Valley** sprawls north of the Hollywood Hills and the Santa Monica Mountains. The basin is bounded to the north and west by the **Santa Susana Mountains** and **Route 118 (Ronald Reagan Freeway),** to the south by **Route 134 (Ventura Boulevard),** and to the east by I-5. The **San Bernardino Valley,** home to about two million people, stretches eastward from

L.A., south of the San Gabriel Mountains. In between these two valleys lie the affluent foothills of **Pasadena** (p. 593).

VITAL STATS

Population: 10,000,000

Tourist Office: L.A. Convention and Visitor Bureau, 685 S. Figueroa St. (☎213-689-8822; www.visitlanow.com), between Wilshire Blvd. and 7th St., in the Financial District. Open M-F 8:30am-5pm.

Library and Internet Access: Los Angeles Public Library, Central Library, 630 W. 5th St. (☎213-228-7000; www.lapl.org). Free. Open M-Th 10am-8pm, F-Sa 10am-6pm, Su 1-5pm.

Post Office: 7101 S. Central Ave. (☎323-586-4414). Open M-F 7am-7pm, Sa 7am-3:30pm.

Postal Code: 90001.

ACCOMMODATIONS

When choosing where to stay, location should be the first consideration. Those looking for a tan should choose lodgings in Venice, Santa Monica, or the South Bay. Sightseers will be better off in Hollywood or the more expensive Westside. Chain motels can be found along Hollywood Blvd. south of Fairfax Ave. Listed prices do not include L.A.'s 14% hotel tax.

USA Hostels Hollywood, 1624 Schrader Blvd. (☎323-462-3777 or 800-524-6783; www.usa-hostels.com), south of Hollywood Blvd. The young travelers hanging out on the patio fill this green-and-yellow chain hostel with energy. Special events nightly. Passport or proof of travel required. Breakfast included. M, W, F all-you-can-eat dinner barbecue $5. Lockers and linen included. 6- to 8-bed dorms with private bath $27; private rooms $95. MC/V and traveler's checks. ❶

Orbit Hotel and Hostel, 7950 Melrose Ave. (☎323-655-1510 or 877-672-4887; www.orbit-hotel.com), 1 block west of Fairfax Ave. in West Hollywood. Opened by 2 young locals several years ago, Orbit sets new standards for swank budget living. Retro furniture, spacious kitchen, TV lounge, small courtyard, and late-night party room. Dorms only accept international students with passport. Free TV-show tickets. Breakfast and lockers included. 6-bed dorms $27; private quads from $119. MC/V. ❶

Los Angeles Surf City Hostel, 26 Pier Ave. (☎310-798-2323), in Hermosa Beach's Pier Plaza. A young international clientele enjoys the beach by day and the downstairs club by night. Kitchen and TV lounge. Boogie boards, breakfast, showers, and linen included. Internet. Key deposit $10. No parking. 3-night max. stay for US citizens. Reservations recommended. 4-bed dorms $25; private rooms $60. AmEx/MC/V. ❶

Claremont Hotel, 1044 Tiverton Ave. (☎310-208-5957 or 800-266-5957), in Westwood Village near UCLA. Still owned by the Quilico Family, who built it in 1939, this hotel is pleasant and inexpensive. Clean rooms, ceiling fans, private baths, and a well-kept Victorian-style TV lounge. Free Wi-Fi. Reservations recommended, especially in June. Singles $65; doubles $72; quads $82. AmEx/D/MC/V. ❸

Venice Beach Hostel, 1515 Pacific Ave. (☎310-452-3052; www.caprica.com/venice-beach-hostel), just north of Windward Ave., in Venice. Central location with friendly staff and a lively atmosphere. A full kitchen, 2 enormous lounges, and a pool table encourage mingling. Lockers, storage rooms, and linen included. Laundry $2. Computers in every room with free Internet access. Free Wi-Fi. Security deposit $25-100. 4- to 12-bed dorms $29.50-31.50; private rooms from $75. AmEx/MC/V. ❶

FOOD

Los Angeles elevates chain restaurants to heights unknown. For the supreme burger-and-fries experience, try the beloved **In-N-Out Burger.** (☎800-786-1000; www.in-n-out.com.) If you're looking for a healthful snack, **Trader Joe's** specializes in budget gourmet food. (☎800-746-7857. Most open daily 9am-9pm.) The **Farmers' Market,** 6333 W. Third St., at Fairfax Ave., attracts three million people every year and has over 160 produce stalls as well as international food booths, handicraft shops, and a juice bar. (☎323-933-9211; www.farmersmarketla.com. Open M-F 9am-9pm, Sa 9am-8pm, Su 10am-7pm.)

HOLLYWOOD

The Griddle Cafe, 7916 Sunset Blvd. (☎323-874-0377; www.thegriddlecafe.com), in West

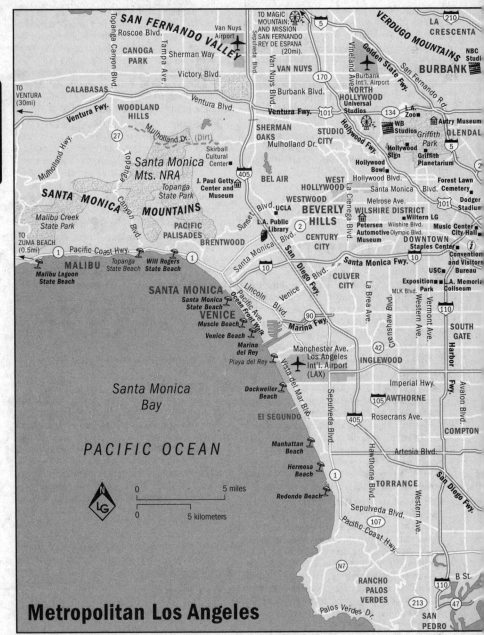

Metropolitan Los Angeles

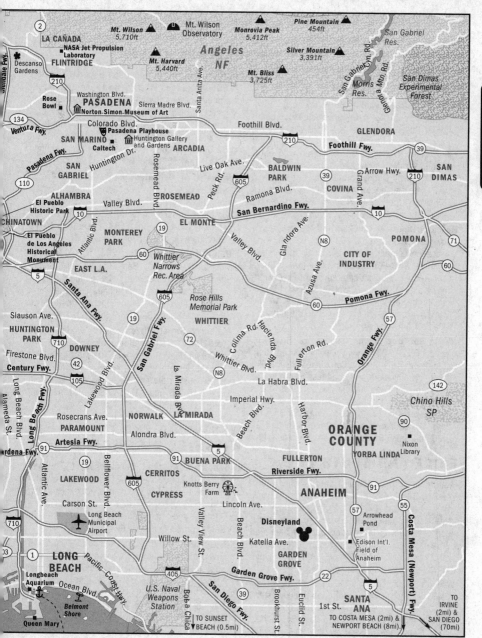

Hollywood. A popular brunch spot. Prides itself on breakfast creativity and the most attractive waitstaff around. The Apple Cobbler French Toast ($11) and Black Magic (Oreo-crumb-filled flapjacks; $10) are especially popular. A 45min. wait is not uncommon on weekends. Open M-F 7am-4pm, Sa-Su 8am-4pm. AmEx/D/MC/V. ❷

✉ **Duke's Coffee Shop,** 8909 Sunset Blvd. (☎310-652-3100; www.dukescoffeeshop.com), in West Hollywood. Legendary Duke's is the best place to see hungry, hungover rockers slumped over tables. The walls are plastered with autographed album covers and movie memorabilia. Try the Howdy Doody (orange juice, hot cakes, fried eggs, and bacon or sausage; $7). Entrees $5.50-15. Open M-F 7:30am-8:30pm, Sa-Su 8am-3:30pm. MC/V. ❷

Roscoe's House of Chicken and Waffles, 1514 Gower St. (☎323-466-7453 or 466-9329; www.roscoeschickenandwaffles.com), at the corner of Sunset Blvd. A down-home feel makes this a popular spot; we even spotted Flavor Flav (wearing his clock). Try the Carol C. Special, "1 succulent chicken breast and 1 delicious waffle" ($8.50). Open M-Th and Su 8:30am-midnight, F-Sa 8:30am-4am. AmEx/MC/V. ❷

Pink's Hot Dog Stand, 709 N. La Brea Ave. (☎323-931-4223; www.pinkshollywood.com), at Melrose Ave. An institution since 1939, Pink's serves up chili-slathered goodness in a bun. The aroma of chili and freshly cooked dogs draws crowds far into the night. Try the special "Martha Stewart Dog (It's a good thing)" for $5. Chili dogs $3. Chili fries $3.20. Open M-Th and Su 9:30am-2am, F-Sa 9:30am-3am. Cash only. ❶

VENICE AND SOUTH BAY

✉ **Meditrina Cafe,** 1029 Abbot Kinney Blvd. (☎310-396-5000; www.meditrinacafe.com). Enjoy breakfast ($7-12), lunch, or dinner in this Mediterranean-infused cafe or relax with a cup of coffee on the garden patio in back. Top off a delicious sandwich ($9-12) with a scoop of gelato ($3.25) for dessert. Free Wi-Fi. Open M-Sa 8am-5pm, Su 9am-5pm. ❷

Wahoo's Fish Tacos, 1129 Manhattan Ave. (☎310-796-1044), in Manhattan Beach. A small but quality chain, each Wahoo's pays homage to surfing and serves cheap and flavorful Mexican grub. Many locals swear by the teriyaki steak

Maui Bowl ($8). Open M-Sa 11am-10pm, Su 11am-9pm. AmEx/MC/V. ❷

BEVERLY HILLS

✉ **Al Gelato,** 806 S. Robertson Blvd. (☎310-659-8069), between Wilshire Blvd. and Olympic St. Popular among the theater crowd, this authentic gelateria also does pasta with a delicious basil tomato sauce ($10). If gelato isn't your thing, try the made-to-order cannoli ($5.25). Gelato $3.50-6.50. Open Tu-Th and Su 11am-midnight, F-Sa 11am-12:30am. ❶

Nate 'n' Al Delicatessen, 414 N. Beverly Dr. (☎310-274-0101; www.natenal.com), near Little Santa Monica Blvd. This deli has been serving up hand-pressed latkes ($9), blintzes ($10), and reubens ($14.50) since 1945. Beer from $3.75. Open daily 7am-9pm. AmEx/MC/V. ❸

Belwood Bakery Cafe, 246 N. Beverly Dr. (☎310-274-7500). Here, baked delights and panini ($10) refuel weary shoppers. Yellow-and-green mosaic tables and chairs create a warm, Italian kitchen-like atmosphere. Open M-Sa 8:30am-6:30pm, Su 9am-4:30pm. MC/V. ❷

Mulberry Street Pizzeria, 240 S. Beverly Dr. (☎310-247-8100). Additional location at 347 N. Canon Dr., in Beverly Hills. The wide, flat pizzas, like the Tomato and Artichoke ($26), are some of the best in the city. Slices $3.25-4.25, whole pies $19-28. Open M-Th and Su 11am-11pm, F-Sa 11am-midnight. MC/V. ❶

WESTWOOD AND THE WILSHIRE DISTRICT

✉ **Sandbag's Gourmet Sandwiches,** 1134 Westwood Blvd. (☎310-208-1133), in Westwood. A cheap, healthful lunch comes with a chocolate cookie. Try the Sundowner (turkey, herb stuffing, lettuce, and cranberries; $6.45). Open daily 9am-5pm. AmEx/MC/V. ❷

Gypsy Cafe, 940 Broxton Ave. (☎310-824-2119; www.gypsycafe.com). Modeled after a sister spot in Paris, this cafe's fare is more Italian than French (penne cacciator $11), and its mood is more Turkish than Italian (hookahs $12). The tomato soup ($7) is famous throughout Westwood and beyond. Open M-W 9am-3am, Th-Sa 9am-5am. AmEx/D/MC/V. ❸

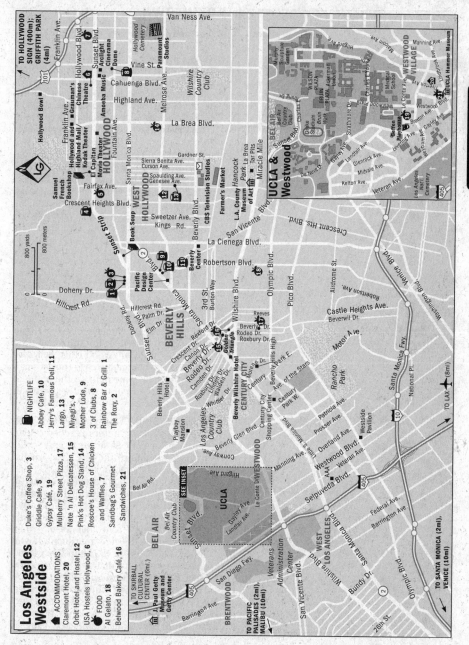

Los Angeles Westside

ACCOMMODATIONS
Claremont Hotel, **20**
Orbit Hotel and Hostel, **12**
USA Hostels Hollywood, **6**

FOOD
Al Gelato, **18**
Belwood Bakery Café, **16**
Duke's Coffee Shop, **3**
Griddle Café, **5**
Gypsy Café, **19**
Mulberry Street Pizza, **17**
Nate 'n Al Delicatessen, **15**
Pink's Hot Dog Stand, **14**
Roscoe's House of Chicken
   and Waffles, **7**
Sandbag's Gourmet
   Sandwiches, **21**

NIGHTLIFE
Abbey Cafe, **10**
Jerry's Famous Deli, **11**
Largo, **13**
Miyagi's, **4**
Mother Lode, **9**
3 of Clubs, **8**
Rainbow Bar & Grill, **1**
The Roxy, **2**

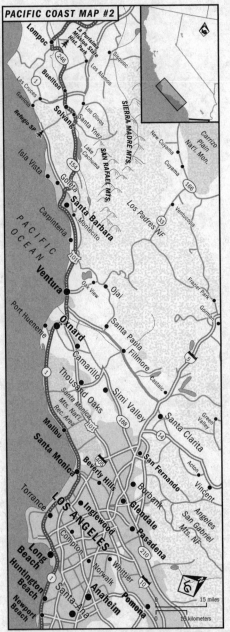

PACIFIC COAST MAP #2

(Map shows Lompoc, Buellton, Solvang, Santa Barbara, Ventura, Oxnard, Malibu, Santa Monica, Los Angeles, Long Beach, Anaheim, and surrounding areas with highways and landmarks.)

DOWNTOWN

The Pantry, 877 S. Figueroa St. (☎213-972-9279). Since 1924, it hasn't closed once—not for the earthquakes, not for the 1992 riots (when it served as a National Guard outpost), and not even when a taxicab punched through the front wall. There aren't even locks on the doors. Owned by former L.A. mayor Richard Riordan, this spot is known for its large portions and carnivore-friendly menu. Giant ham, steak, and eggs platter $15.50. Burgers $11. Open 24hr. Cash only. ❷

Philippe, The Original, 1001 N. Alameda St. (☎213-628-3781; www.philippes.com), 2 blocks north of Union Station. Sawdust covers the floor of this 100-year-old lunch eatery. Chow down on a pork, beef, ham, or turkey dip ($5.25). Top it off with pie ($3.25) and quite quaffable coffee (**$0.09**—no, that's not a typo). Open daily 6am-10pm. Cash only. ❶

👁 SIGHTS

HOLLYWOOD

Exploring the Hollywood area requires a pair of sunglasses, a camera, some cash, and a whole lot of patience. Running east-west at the foot of the Hollywood Hills, **Hollywood Boulevard** is the center of L.A.'s tourist madness. Thousands come daily to the home of the Walk of Fame, famous theaters, souvenir shops, and museums.

HOLLYWOOD SIGN. Those 50 ft. high, 30 ft. wide, slightly erratic letters perched on Mt. Lee in Griffith Park stand as a universally recognized symbol of the city. The original 1923 sign read "HOLLYWOODLAND" and was not intended to be permanent; it was an advertisement for a new subdivision in the Hollywood Hills. The sign has been a target of many college pranks, which have made it read everything from "**Hollyweed,**" when California adopted a new marijuana law in 1976, to "GO UCLA" in 1993 and "**Hollyweird.**" A fence keeps you at a distance of 40 ft. from the sign. For more information about the sign and its history, visit www.hollywoodsign.org. *(To get as close to the sign as possible requires a strenuous 2½ mi. hike. Take the Bronson Canyon entrance to Griffith Park and follow Canyon Dr. to its end, where park-*

PACIFIC
COAST

ing is free. The Brush Canyon Trail starts where Canyon Dr. becomes unpaved. At the top of the hill, follow the road to your left. For those satisfied with driving, go north on Vine St., take a right on Franklin Ave. and a left on Beachwood, and drive up until you are forced to drive down.)

GRAUMAN'S CHINESE THEATRE. Loosely modeled on a Chinese temple, this monumental, eye-catching theater is a Hollywood icon that frequently rolls out the red carpet for movie premieres. The sculptures on the exterior columns—"Heaven Dogs"—were imported from China, where they once supported a Ming Dynasty temple. The theater, which opened in 1927, houses a collection of celebrity foot- and handprints pressed into cement as well as other star trademarks, including Whoopi Goldberg's dreadlocks and R2-D2's wheels. (6925 Hollywood Blvd., between Highland and Orange St. ☎323-461-3331. 7-12 tours per day; call ahead. $12.25, children $8, under 2 free.)

WALK OF FAME. Tourists along Hollywood Blvd. stop mid-stride to gawk at the sidewalk's over 2000 bronze-inlaid stars, which are inscribed with the names of the famous, the infamous, the obscure, and even some fictional characters. Inside each star, a bronze symbol indicates for which category it was awarded: movies, radio, TV, audio recording, or live performance. Only Gene Autry has all five stars. To catch today's stars in person, call the Chamber of Commerce for info on star-unveiling ceremonies. (☎323-469-8311; www.hollywoodchamber.net. Free.)

WEST HOLLYWOOD. Bring your walking shoes and spend a day on the 3 mi. strip of **Melrose Avenue** from Highland Ave. west to the intersection of Doheny Dr. and Santa Monica Blvd. This strip began to develop its funky flair in the late 1980s when art galleries, designer stores, lounge-like coffee shops, used clothing and music stores, and restaurants began to take over. Now it is home to the hip, with the choicest stretch lying between La Brea and Fairfax Ave. While much sold here is used ("vintage"), none of it is cheap. North of the Beverly Center is the **Pacific Design Center,** a royal-blue complex nicknamed the Blue Whale and constructed in the shape of a rippin' wave. The GLBT scene here is always happening; gay or bisexual men make up about 40% of the population. (8687 Melrose Ave. ☎310-657-0800; www.pacificdesigncenter.com.)

OTHER SIGHTS. The hillside **Hollywood Bowl** is synonymous with picnic dining and classy summer entertainment. All are welcome to listen to the L.A. Philharmonic's free rehearsals; call the box office for info. (2301 N. Highland Ave. ☎323-850-2000; www.hollywoodbowl.com. Open Tu-Sa July-Sept. 10am-8pm; Nov.-June 10am-4:30pm. Free. Parking $14-30.) The sprawling **Hollywood and Highland Mall** centers on two monstrous elephant sculptures and contains ritzy shops, high-profile restaurants, and the impressive **Kodak Theatre,** built specifically to host the Academy Awards. (6801 Hollywood Blvd. Mall ☎323-467-6412, box office 308-6363. Box office open M-Sa 10am-6pm, Su 10am-2:30pm. Tours daily every 30min. Daily 10:30am-2:30pm. $15, under 18 $10.)

VENICE AND SOUTH BAY

Ocean Front Walk, Venice's main beachfront drag, is a seaside circus of fringe culture. In-line skaters, skateboarders, and almost anything else that moves can be seen along this strip of beach. Find the city's biggest bodybuilders at **Muscle Beach,** 1800 Ocean Front Walk, closest to 18th St. and Pacific Ave. Vendors sell everything from beach blankets to fake tattoos and define the colorful culture of this playground population.

About 20 mi. southwest of downtown L.A., the PCH passes through the heart of the beach scene at **Redondo Beach, Hermosa Beach,** and **Manhattan Beach.** Most visit Redondo Beach for its harbor, pier, and seafood-rich boardwalk. Hermosa Beach, the most popular urban beach in L.A. County, has a reputation for cleanliness. Manhattan Beach is favored for surfing. Both Manhattan and Hermosa beaches host elite beach volleyball and surf competitions. (☎310-426-8000; www.avp.com or www.surffestival.org.) **The Strand** is a concrete bike path crowded with bikers and in-line skaters that runs along the beach from Santa Monica to Hermosa Beach.

BEVERLY HILLS

Conspicuous displays of wealth border on the vulgar in this center of extravagance. Residential ritz reaches its peak along Beverly Dr., where the mansions are bigger than most city libraries. If stories of the rich and famous intrigue you, hop in a cab and ask for an informal tour of this street.

The greedy heart of the city, **Rodeo Drive** is known for its clothing boutiques and jewelry shops and is in the **Golden Triangle,** a wedge formed by Beverly Dr., Wilshire Blvd., and Santa Monica Blvd. (413 N. Rodeo Dr. ☎310-858-6545.)

DOWNTOWN

EL PUEBLO HISTORIC PARK. The historic birthplace of L.A. is now known as El Pueblo de Los Angeles Historical Monument and is bordered by César Chavez Ave., Alameda St., Hollywood Fwy., and Spring St. In 1781, 44 settlers started a pueblo and farming community here; today, 27 buildings from the eras of Spanish and Mexican rule are preserved, 11 of which are open to the public. Established in 1825, **The Plaza** is the center of El Pueblo and hosts festivals like the **Mexican Independence** celebration (Sept. 16), **Dia de los Muertos** celebrations (Oct. 25-Nov. 2), and **Cinco de Mayo** (May 5). Treat yourself to the cheapest churros around (2 for $1) as you walk down historic **Olvera Street,** or bargain with *puestos* (vendors) selling everything from Mexican crafts to food and personalized knick-knacks. The **Avila Adobe** (c. 1818) is the "oldest" house in the city. (10 E. Olvera St. ☎213-485-6855. Open W-Su 10am-3pm. Free.)

MUSIC CENTER. The beautiful Music Center is easily identified by the sweeping silver curves of the Frank Gehry-designed Walt Disney Concert Hall. Since it opened in 2003, this gleaming 2265-seat structure has become home to the **Los Angeles Philharmonic** and the **Los Angeles Master Chorale.** (135 N. Grand Ave. ☎213-972-7211; www.disneyhall.org.) The **Dorothy Chandler Pavilion,** on the south side of the plaza, houses the **Los Angeles Opera** and is the former site of the Academy Awards. (☎213-972-8001; www.laopera.org.) Also part of the Music Center are the **Mark Taper Forum** and the intimate **Ahmanson Theatre,** both known for world-class shows. (☎213-628-2772; www.taperahmanson.com. Open daily 10am-2pm as performance schedules permit. Self-guided tours $12, students and seniors $10.)

OTHER SIGHTS. One of the most recognizable buildings in southern California, **City Hall** has starred in more movies than most actors. (200 N. Spring St.) Bargain hounds can haggle to their hearts' delight in the **Fashion District,** between Sixth and Ninth St., along Los Angeles St. At 1018 ft., the **Library Tower** has a distinctive glass crown and is the tallest building between Chicago and Hong Kong. (633 W. 5th St.) The **Museum of Contemporary Art (MOCA)** features an extensive and varied collection of American and European art dating from 1940 to the present, including the work of Abstract Expressionists and photography. (250 S. Grand Ave. ☎213-626-6222; www.moca.org. Open M and F 11am-5pm, Th 11am-8pm, Sa-Su 11am-6pm. $10, students and seniors $5, under 12 free.)

NEAR DOWNTOWN

UNIVERSITY OF SOUTHERN CALIFORNIA (USC). North of Exposition Park, USC's 30,000 students bring a youthful character to downtown. The alma mater of celebrities such as astronaut Neil Armstrong, the school has had a gold-medal-winning athlete in every summer Olympics since 1912. L.A. sports fans go wild when the burnished USC Trojans clash with the blue-and-gold UCLA Bruins in annual football and basketball games. (From downtown, head south on Figueroa St. and turn right on 35th St. ☎213-740-2311; www.usc.edu. Campus tours M-F every hr. 10am-3pm. Free.)

GRIFFITH PARK AND GLENDALE. For fresh air and a respite from city life, take to the slopes of **Griffith Park,** the nation's largest municipal park, nestled between US 101, I-5, and Rte. 134. A stark contrast to the concrete of downtown and the star-studded streets of Hollywood, the park is a refuge from the city and the site of outdoor diversions. Fifty-two miles of hiking and horseback-riding trails, three golf courses, several museums, and a 6000-person Greek theater are contained within its 4107 rolling acres. (4730 Crystal Spring Dr. ☎323-913-4688, emergency 913-7390. Park open daily 6am-10pm.) The park has numerous equestrian trails and places to saddle up, such as **JP Stables.** No riding experience is necessary; guides are provided. (1914 Mariposa St., in Burbank. ☎818-843-9890. Open daily 8am-6pm. No reservations. $25 for 1st hr., $20 thereafter.) The world-famous white stucco and copper domes of the **Griffith Observatory and Planetarium** would be visible from nearly any point in L.A. were it not for the smog. The observatory parking lot lends a terrific view of the Hollywood sign. You may remember the planetarium from the James Dean film *Rebel Without A Cause*. (*2800 E. Observatory Rd. ☎213-473-0800; www.griffithobs.org. Open Tu-F noon-10pm, Sa-Su 10am-10pm.*) Rare animals from around the world are on display throughout the **Los Angeles Zoo's** 113 well-kept acres. The zoo's five sea lions are a big hit, as are the red apes and chimps. (*5333 Zoo Dr. ☎323-644-4200; www.lazoo.org. Open daily July-Aug. 10am-6pm; Sept.-June 10am-5pm. Animals are tucked into bed starting 1hr. before closing. $12, 2-12 $7, under 2 free, seniors $9.*) A rather twisted sense of celebrity sightseeing may lead some to Glendale's **Forest Lawn Cemetery,** where you can gaze upon stars of past generations. Among the illustrious dead are Clark Gable, George Burns, and Jimmy Stewart. The cemetery has a 30 ft. by 15 ft. stained-glass reproduction of Leonardo da Vinci's *The Last Supper*. (*1712 S. Glendale Ave. ☎800-204-3131. Open daily 8am-5pm.*)

SAN FERNANDO VALLEY

TV and movie studios redeem the Valley (somewhat) from its bland warehouses, blonde "Valley girls," and strip malls. Passing Burbank on Rte. 134, you might catch glimpses of the Valley's most lucrative trademark studios: **Universal, Warner Brothers, NBC,** and **Disney.** To best experience the industry, attend a free TV show taping or take one of the tours offered by most studios.

█UNIVERSAL STUDIOS. A movie and television studio with the world's first and largest movie-themed amusement park, Universal Studios Hollywood is the most popular tourist spot in Tinseltown. The park is located in its very own municipality, Universal City, which has its own police and fire stations. (*Take US 101 to the Universal Studios Blvd. exit. ☎800-864-8377; www.universalstudios.com. Open July-Aug. M-F 9am-8pm, Sa-Su 9am-9pm; Sept.-June M-F 10am-6pm, Sa-Su 10am-7pm. $64, under 48' in. $54, under 2 free.*)

MISSION SAN FERNANDO REY DE ESPAÑA. Founded in 1797, the San Fernando Mission is the largest adobe structure standing in California. The grounds are beautifully kept and definitely worth a visit. (*15101 San Fernando Mission Blvd. ☎818-361-0186. Open daily 9am-4:30pm. Mass M-Tu and Th-Sa 7:25am, Su 9 and 10:30am. $4, ages 7-15 $3.*)

PASADENA

The excellent **Convention and Visitors Bureau,** 171 S. Los Robles Ave., is a useful first stop in Pasadena, with numerous promotional materials and guides to regional events. (☎626-795-9311 or 800-307-7977; www.pasadenacal.com. Open M-F 8am-5pm, Sa 10am-4pm.)

ROSE BOWL. In the gorge that forms the city's western boundary, this sand-colored, 90,000-seat stadium is home to "the granddaddy of them all." The annual Rose Bowl game is a college football clash on January 1 between the champions of the Big Ten and Pac 10 conferences. A Bowl Championship Series game takes place annually; every four years, contending teams vie for the national championship title. Additionally, the UCLA Bruins play regular-season home games here. (*1001 Rose Bowl Dr. ☎626-577-3100; www.rosebowlstadium.com. Bruins info ☎310-825-2946; www.cto.ucla.edu.*) The bowl also hosts a monthly flea market that attracts 2000 vendors selling nearly one million items. (☎323-560-7469. 2nd Su of each month 5am-4:30pm. Admission after 9am $8, under 12 free. Express admission 8-9am $10. Early admission from 7-8am $15. VIP admission 5-7am $20.)

CALIFORNIA INSTITUTE OF TECHNOLOGY (CALTECH). Some of the world's greatest scientific minds do their work at the California Institute of Technology (Caltech). Founded in 1891, Caltech has amassed a faculty that includes several Nobel laureates and a student body that prides itself on both its staggering collective intellect and its loony practical jokes. In the Great Rose Bowl Hoax of 1961, students from Caltech orchestrated a stunt in which fans of the Washington Huskies and the Minnesota Golden Gophers unknowingly held up placards that collectively spelled out "CALTECH" across the stadium stands. (*1200 E. California Blvd., about 2 mi. southeast of Old Town. Take I-110 N. until it becomes the Arroyo Pkwy. Turn right on California Blvd. and go 1 mi. Turn left on Hill Ave., left on San Pasqual St., and right on Holliston Ave. Register your car at 370 S. Holliston Ave.; $1 per hr., $5 per day, $15 per week. ☎626-395-6327; www.caltech.edu. Tours M-F*

2pm. Free.) The **NASA Jet Propulsion Laboratory,** 5 mi. north of Old Town, sent the Mars Pathfinder on its way. Ask to see pictures of the face of Mars. *(4800 Oak Grove Dr. ☎818-354-9314; www.jpl.nasa.gov. Free tours by appointment.)*

🏛 MUSEUMS

▥J. PAUL GETTY CENTER AND MUSEUM. Above Bel Air and Brentwood in the Santa Monica Mountains shines a modern Colosseum, The Getty. Wedding classical materials to modern designs, renowned architect Richard Meier designed the stunning $1 billion complex, which consists of five pavilions overlooking the Central Garden. The pavilions contain the world-class Getty collection of Impressionist paintings. *(1200 Getty Center Dr. Exit I-405 (San Diego Fwy.). ☎310-440-7300; www.getty.edu. Open Tu-Th and Su 10am-6pm, F-Sa 10am-9pm. $8 per vehicle.)*

▥LOS ANGELES COUNTY MUSEUM OF ART (LACMA). Opened in 1965, the LACMA is the largest museum on the West Coast and holds several of Steve Martin's Dada and Surrealist works. (This explains why Steve was able to rollerskate LACMA's halls in *L.A. Story.*) The newest of the museum's buildings is the Broad Contemporary Art Museum, which opened in February 2008. *(5905 Wilshire Blvd. ☎323-857-6000; www.lacma.org. Jazz F 5:30-8:30pm. Chamber music Su 6-7pm; free with museum admission. Open M-Tu and Th noon-8pm, F noon-9pm, Sa-Su 11am-8pm. $12, students and seniors $8, under 18 free. Film tickets $10, students and seniors $6.)*

▥NORTON SIMON MUSEUM OF ART. Rivaling the Getty in quality, this private collection chronicles Western art from Italian Gothic to 20th-century abstract. The Impressionist and Post-Impressionist hall, the Southeast Asian sculptures, and the 79,000 sq. ft. sculpture garden by Nancy Goslee Power are particularly impressive. *(11 W. Colorado Blvd. ☎626-449-6840; www.nortonsimon.org. Open M, W-Th, Sa-Su noon-6pm, F noon-9pm. $8, students and under 18 free, 62+ $4.)*

▥PETERSEN AUTOMOTIVE MUSEUM (PAM). Petersen's is the world's largest car museum, showcasing over 150 classic cars, hot rods, motorcycles, and celebrity cars, not to mention a 1920s service station, 50s body shop, and 60s suburban garage. There's also a

Children's Discovery Center on the third floor. *(6060 Wilshire Blvd., at Fairfax Ave. ☎323-930-2277; www.petersen.org. Open Tu-Su 10am-6pm. $10, students $5, ages 5-12 $3, under 5 free.)*

UCLA HAMMER MUSEUM OF ART. This museum houses the world's largest collection of works by 19th-century French satirist and painter Honoré Daumier. The gem of the collection is Van Gogh's *Hospital at Saint Rémy.* *(10899 Wilshire Blvd., at the corner of Westwood Blvd. ☎310-443-7000; www.hammer.ucla.edu. Open Tu-W and F-Sa 11am-7pm, Th 11am-9pm, Su 11am-5pm. Free tours of traveling exhibits Tu 1pm, Th 1, 6pm. Jazz concerts in summer Th 8pm. $5, under 17 free, seniors $3.)*

AUTRY MUSEUM OF WESTERN HERITAGE. City slickers and lone rangers may discover that the West is not what they thought—the museum insists that the real should not be confused with the reel, drawing the line between Old West fact and fiction. *(4700 Western Heritage Way, in Griffith Park. ☎323-667-2000; www.autrynationalcenter.org. Open Tu-W and F-Su 10am-5pm, Th 10am-8pm. $9, students $5, ages 2-12 $3, under 2 free.)*

🎦 ENTERTAINMENT

There are many ways to sample the silver-screen glitz created and peddled by the entertainment capital of the world. Shopping is, like, a major pastime in the L.A. area. For after-hours fun, L.A. features some of the trendiest, most celeb-frenzied nightlife imaginable. For amusement parks, check out nearby giants **Disneyland** (p. 904), **Knott's Berry Farm** (p. 904), and **Universal Studios** (previous page).

TELEVISION STUDIOS

A visit to L.A. isn't complete without exposure to the actual business of making a movie or TV show. Fortunately, most production companies oblige. **Paramount** (☎323-956-5000), NBC, and Warner Bros. offer 70min., 2hr., and 2hr. (respectively) guided tours that take you onto sets and through back lots. Tickets to a taping are free, but studios tend to overbook, so holding a ticket doesn't guarantee you'll get in; show up early. **NBC,** 3000 W. Alameda Ave., at W. Olive Ave., in Burbank, is your best bet for getting in. Studio tours run on the hour. (☎818-840-3537. M-F 9am-3pm. Tickets $7.50, ages 5-12 $4.) Many of NBC's other shows are taped at **Warner Brothers,** 4000 Warner Blvd. (☎818-954-6000), in Burbank. A **CBS** box office, 7800 Beverly Blvd., next to the Farmers' Market in West Hollywood, hands out free tickets to *The Price is Right* (taped M-Th) up to one week in advance. (☎323-575-2458. Box office opens at 7:30am on days with show tapings. 18+. Open M-F 9am-5pm.) You can request up to ten tickets by sending a self-addressed, stamped envelope to *The Price is Right* Tickets, 7800 Beverly Blvd., Los Angeles, CA 90036 several weeks in advance.

MOVIES

It would be a cinematic crime not to partake of L.A.'s moviegoing experiences. The city's movie palaces show films the way they were meant to be seen: on a big screen, in plush seats, with gut-rumbling sound, and with top-quality air conditioning. The gargantuan theaters at **Universal City,** as well as those in Westwood Village near UCLA, are incredibly popular. In Santa Monica, there are 22 screens within the three blocks of the Third St. Promenade. Devotees of second-run, foreign-language, and experimental films can get their fix at the eight **Laemmle Theaters** in Beverly Hills, West Hollywood, Santa Monica, and Pasadena. (☎310-478-1041; www.laemmle. com. $10, students $8.50, children, seniors, and matinee $7.) For info on what's playing around town, call ☎323-777-3456 or read the "Calendar" section of the *Los Angeles Times*.

▨ **Arclight Cinerama Dome,** 6360 Sunset Blvd. (☎323-464-4226), in Hollywood, between Vine St. and Ivar Ave. The ultimate cineplex for the serious moviegoer. 14 movie screens surround a gigantic dome that seats 850 people. The screen is 32 by 86 ft. Recent releases only. Don't be late—doors close 7min. after movies begin. Tickets range $7.75-14.

▨ **Grauman's Chinese Theatre,** 6925 Hollywood Blvd. (☎323-464-8111), between Highland and La Brea Ave., in Hollywood. Hype to the hilt. See **Sights** (p. 912). Tickets M-Th $11.25, F-Su $12.75; children $8; over 64 $8.50.

El Capitan, 6838 Hollywood Blvd. (☎800-347-6396). The cineplex your inner child has always dreamed of. Shows Disney films and nothing else. Tickets $10-18; varies by movie.

Mann Village Theater, 961 Broxton Ave. (☎310-208-5576), in Westwood Village. Built to resemble a Spanish mission in 1931, this theater hosts some of Hollywood's biggest premieres. Tickets $11, students $9, ages 3-12 $8.

LIVE THEATER AND MUSIC

L.A.'s live-theater scene does not have the reputation of New York City's Broadway, but its 115 "equity-waiver theaters" (under 100 seats) offer dizzying, eclectic choices for theatergoers, who can also view small productions in art galleries, universities, parks, and even garages. Browse listings in the *L.A. Weekly* to find out what's hot. L.A.'s music venues range from small clubs to massive amphitheaters. The **Hollywood Palladium,** 6215 W. Sunset Blvd., seats 3500 (☎323-962-7600.). Mid-sized acts head for the **Gibson Ampitheatre,** 100 Universal City Plaza (☎818-622-4440). Huge indoor sports arenas like the **Staples Center,** 1111 S. Figueroa St., double as concert halls for big acts (☎213-742-7100). Few dare to play at the 100,000-seat **Los Angeles Memorial Coliseum and Sports Arena,** 3911 S. Figueroa St.; only U2, Depeche Mode, Guns N' Roses, and the Warped Tour have filled the stands in recent years. Call **Ticketmaster** (☎213-480-3232) to purchase tickets for any of these venues.

▨ **Hollywood Bowl,** 2301 N. Highland Ave. (☎323-850-2000), in Hollywood. The premier outdoor music venue in L.A. Free open-house rehearsals by the L.A. Philharmonic and visiting performers usually Tu and Th; call the box office for info. Parking is limited and pricey ($14-30). It's better to park at one of the lots away from the bowl and take a shuttle. Depending on the lot, shuttles depart every 10-20min. starting 2½hr. before the concert. Round-trip $3.

Wiltern LG, 3790 Wilshire Blvd. (☎213-380-5005). Seating 2200, this midsize music venue has hosted acts like Belle & Sebastian, Sufjan Stevens, T.I., and Good Charlotte. Shows 3 nights per week. Tickets $25-85. Box office opens 3hr. before showtime.

Geffen Playhouse, 10886 LeConte Ave. (☎310-208-5454; www.geffenplayhouse.com), in Westwood. Off-Broadway and Tony Award-winning shows. Ticket prices vary by show. Student rush tickets 10min. before shows $15. Box office open M-F 10am-6pm, Sa-Su 11am-6pm.

SPORTS

Exposition Park and the often dangerous city of Inglewood, southwest of the park, are home to many sports teams. The **USC Trojans** play football at the **Los Angeles Memorial Coliseum**, 3911 S. Figueroa St., which seats over 100,000 spectators. It is the only stadium in the world to have hosted the Olympic Games twice (☎213-740-4672). Basketball's doormat, the **Los Angeles Clippers** (☎213-742-7500), and the recent NBA Champion **Los Angeles Lakers** (☎310-426-6000) play at the new **Staples Center**, 1111 S. Figueroa St. (☎213-742-7100, box office 742-7340), along with the **Los Angeles Kings** hockey team (☎888-546-4752) and the city's WNBA team, the **Los Angeles Sparks** (☎213-929-1300). Call **Ticketmaster** (☎213-480-3232) for tickets. **Elysian Park,** about 3 mi. northeast of downtown, curves around the northern portion of Chavez Ravine, home of **Dodger Stadium** and the popular **Los Angeles Dodgers** baseball team. Single-game tickets ($6-200) are a hot commodity during the April-October season, especially if the Dodgers are playing particularly well. (☎866-DODGERS; www.dodgers.com.)

SHOPPING

In L.A., shopping isn't just a practical necessity; it's a way of life. Rodeo Dr. may be too much for the average budget traveler's wallet, but you can't brag that you've shopped L.A. without taking a trip down the ritzy strip. The downtown **Fashion District** is home to designers, wholesalers, retail stores, and guys hawking "Gucci" bags from suitcases. The hub of the shop-until-you-drop spots is the **Westside**.

- **Book Soup,** 8818 Sunset Blvd. (☎310-659-3110; www.booksoup.com), in West Hollywood. A maze of new books, with especially strong film, architecture, poetry, and travel sections. Open M-Th and Su 9am-9pm, F-Sa 9am-10pm.
- **Amoeba Music,** 6400 Sunset Blvd. (☎323-245-6400; www.amoebamusic.com), in Hollywood. Carries all genres and titles, including DVDs, LPs, and underground music. Take advantage of daily $1 clearance sales. Open M-Sa 10:30am-11pm, Su 11am-9pm.

Samuel French Bookshop, 7623 Sunset Blvd. (☎323-876-0570), in Hollywood. This wealth of entertainment-industry wisdom is filled with acting directories, TV and film reference books, trade papers, a vast selection of plays, and screenplays. Open M-F 10am-6pm, Sa 10am-5pm.

NIGHTLIFE

LATE-NIGHT RESTAURANTS

Given the rapidly changing nature of L.A.'s club scene, late-night restaurants are often more reliable hangouts than clubs.

- **Canter's,** 419 N. Fairfax Ave. (☎323-651-2030), in Fairfax, north of Beverly Blvd. The soul of historically Jewish Fairfax since 1931. Walk past the delicious baked goods to the Kibitz Room for nightly free rock, blues, jazz, and a chance to spot L.A.'s finest in the audience. Grapefruit-size matzah balls in chicken broth $4.50. Sandwiches $7.50-14. Beer from $3.75. Open 24hr. MC/V.
- **Fred 62,** 1850 N. Vermont Ave. (☎323-667-0062; www.fred62.com), between Hollywood and Franklin, in Los Feliz. "Eat now, dine later," and look for a booth with headrests. Hip, edgy East L.A. crowd's jukebox selections rock the house. Try the "French toast ($7). Open 24hr. AmEx/D/MC/V.
- **The Rainbow Bar and Grill,** 9015 Sunset Blvd. (☎310-278-4232; www.rainbowbarandgrill.com), in West Hollywood. Dark red, vinyl booths, dim lighting, loud music, and colorful characters set the scene. Marilyn Monroe met Joe DiMaggio on a blind (and apparently rather silent) date here. Calamari $10. Brooklyn-quality pizza $15. Open M-F 11am-2am, Sa-Su 5pm-2am. Cover M-Th and Su $5; includes 1 drink. Cover F-Sa $10; includes 2 drinks. AmEx/D/MC/V.
- **Jerry's Famous Deli,** 8701 Beverly Blvd. (☎310-289-1811), at the corner of San Vicente Ave., in West Hollywood. An L.A. deli with red leather and sky-high prices. There are more than 600 items on the menu—Jerry reportedly wanted "the longest menu possible while still maintaining structural integrity." Something here is bound to satisfy your 4am craving, whether you're in the mood for an omelet ($8-12), a specialty pizza ($12-18), or "nosh" (toasted bagel with cucumber, tomato, and choice of spread). Entrees $11-30. Mixed

Drinks from $10. Beer $4.50. Open 24hr. AmEx/MC/V.

BARS

The 1996 film *Swingers* has had a homogenizing effect on L.A.'s hipsters. Grab your retro polyester shirts, sunglasses, and throwback Cadillac convertibles, 'cause if you can't beat them, you have to swing with them, daddy-o.

- **Miyagi's,** 8225 Sunset Blvd. (☎323-650-3524), on the Sunset Strip. With 3 levels, 5 sushi bars ($8-14), 6 liquor bars, waterfalls, and streams, this Japanese restaurant/bar/lounge/hip-hop dance club is a hot spot. Hot sake $6. No cover. Happy hour daily 5:30-7:30pm with 2-for-1 drinks. Open daily 5pm-2am. AmEx/D/MC/V.

- **3 of Clubs,** 1123 N. Vine St. (☎323-462-6441; www.threeclubs.com), in Hollywood. In a small strip mall beneath a "Cocktails" sign, this bar made a famous appearance in *Swingers*. Live bands Th. DJ F-Sa. Happy hour M-F 6-8pm. Open daily 6pm-2am. Knock before 8pm. AmEx/MC/V.

- **Beauty Bar,** 1638 Cahuenga Blvd. (☎323-464-7676; www.beautybar.com), in Hollywood. Where else can you get a manicure and henna tattoo while sipping a mixed drink and schmoozing? It's like getting ready for the prom again, except that the drinking starts earlier. Drinks around $8. DJ nightly 10pm. Martinis and Manicures Th-Sa. Open M-W and Su 9pm-2am, Th-Sa 6pm-2am. AmEx/MC/V.

CLUBS

With the highest number of bands per capita in the world and more streaming in every day, L.A. is famous for its (often expensive) club scene. Coupons in *L.A. Weekly* and those handed out by the clubs can save you a bundle. To enter the club scene, it's best to be at least 21 (and/or beautiful). While the Sunset Strip features all the nightlife any Jack and Jill could desire, gay men and lesbians may find life more interesting a short tumble down the hill on Santa Monica Blvd. Still, many ostensibly straight clubs have gay nights; check *L.A. Weekly*. The free weekly magazine *fab!* lists events in the gay and lesbian community.

- **The Derby,** 4500 Los Feliz Blvd. (☎323-663-8979; www.the-derby.com), at the corner of Hillhurst Ave., in Los Feliz. Still jumpin' and jivin' with the kings of swing. Ladies, grab your snoods; many dress the 40s part. Italian fare from Louise's Trattoria next door. Full bar. Swing lessons Su 6:30, 7:30pm free with cover. Cover $7-15. Open daily 6pm-2am. AmEx/MC/V.

- **Largo at the Coronet,** 366 N. La Cienega Blvd. (☎310-855-0350; www.largo-la.com), 1 block north of Beverly Blvd. at Oakwood St. Intimate sit-down (or, if you get there late, lean-back) club. Rock, pop, folk, and comedy acts. Cover varies. Open M-Sa 8:30pm-2am.

- **Abbey Cafe,** 692 N. Robertson Blvd. (☎310-289-8410), at Santa Monica Blvd., in West Hollywood. 6 candlelit rooms, 2 huge bars, a large outdoor patio, and a hall of private booths make this beautiful GLBT lounge and dance club the best place around. On hot days they turn the mister on. Open daily 8am-2am. AmEx/D/MC/V.

- **Roxy,** 9009 Sunset Blvd. (☎310-278-9457; www.theroxyonsunset.com), on the Sunset Strip. One of the best-known Sunset Strip clubs, a great option for all ages, including under 21. Bruce Springsteen got his start here. Live rock, blues, comedy, and occasional hip hop. Many big touring acts. Cover $10-30. Open 8pm-last customer. AmEx/D/MC/V.

- **Mother Lode,** 8944 Santa Monica Blvd. (☎310-659-9700). A friendly and popular GLBT bar that steers clear of the surrounding West Hollywood trendiness. Pool, pinball machines, and cheap drinks are sure to delight. Open M-F 3pm-2am, Sa-Su noon-2am. Cash only.

- **Eleven,** 8811 Santa Monica Blvd. (☎310-855-0800). Exposed brick and tile walls and a high, woodbeam ceiling give this popular GLBT restaurant and bar a classy feel. Enjoy a cocktail ($11) on the patio, decorated with strings of lights. Happy hour 4-8pm, with 2-for-1 mixed drinks, $3 beer, and ½-price appetizers.

⚑ THE ROAD TO SANTA MONICA: 16 MI.

Hop on **I-10 West**, which drops off in Santa Monica at the junction with **Route 1**.

SANTA MONICA   ☎310

Santa Monica is safe, clean, and unpretentious—and you can usually find a parking spot here. The city's residential areas, once populated by screen superstars, are just blocks away from its main districts. The area on and around the carnival pier is filled with hawkers, and street performers and a farmers' market add a bit of spice to the pedestrian-only Third St. Promenade. Farther inland, along Main St. and beyond, a smattering of galleries, design shops, and museums testify to the city's love of art and culture.

> **PAGE TURN.** See p. 595 in **Route 66** for complete coverage of Santa Monica.

THE ROAD TO MALIBU: 21 MI.
From **Route 1,** turn right onto **Malibu Canyon Road.**

MALIBU ☎310

North of Santa Monica along the Pacific Coast Highway, the cityscape gives way to appealing stretches of sandy, sewage-free shoreline. Stop along the coast, and you may see dolphin pods swimming close to shore—or at least pods of surfers trying to catch a wave. Malibu's beaches are clean and relatively uncrowded—easily the best in L.A. County for surfers and sunbathers.

VITAL STATS

Population: 13,300

Tourist Office: Malibu Chamber of Commerce, 23805 Stuart Ranch Rd., Ste. 100 (☎310-456-2489; www.ci.malibu.ca.us). Follow signs to City Hall; it's in the same complex. Open M-F 9am-5pm.

Library and Internet Access: Malibu Public Library, 23519 W. Civic Center Way (☎310-456-6438). Open M-Tu 10am-8pm, W-Th 10am-6pm, F-Sa 10am-5pm.

Post Office: 23648 Pacific Coast Hwy. (☎310-317-0328). Open M-F 9am-5pm, Sa 9:30am-1:30pm.
Postal Code: 90265.

ACCOMMODATIONS

Motels in Malibu pay the same prices for real estate as the multi-million-dollar stars, so the best budget option is to head to L.A. or to camp. A good option is **Sycamore Canyon ❶**, on the beach 19 mi. northwest of Malibu in Point Mugu State Park. (☎805-488-5223. Sites $25. Cash or check only.) Alternatively, **Leo Carrillo State Park ❶** has 139 sites (and free Wi-Fi)

in a lot across the highway from the beach. (☎805-488-1827. Sites $25.)

FOOD

Cheap eats are hard to come by at Malibu's waterfront restaurants, which charge as much for their view as for their food.

Neptune's Net Seafood, 42505 Pacific Coast Hwy. (☎310-457-3095). Offers baskets of fried seafood. Dine at one of the outdoor picnic tables or cross the street and eat overlooking the ocean. Open M-Th 10:30am-8pm, F 10:30am-8:30pm, Sa-Su 10am-8:30pm. MC/V. ❷

Howdy's Taqueria, 3835 Cross Creek Rd. (☎310-456-6299). Serves simple, delicious Mexican food. Try the Famous Mexican Pizza ($9), with organic beans, jack and parmesan cheese, tomatoes, cilantro, and onions on a baked tortilla. Open M-Th 10am-7pm, F-Su 10am-8pm. ❷

SIGHTS AND OUTDOORS

The prime beach spot in Malibu is **Zuma,** L.A. County's largest beach. For a more intimate Malibu experience, check out **Escondido Beach**—look for the small brown coastal access sign 2 mi. north of Pepperdine. **Will Rogers State Beach** hosts an annual volleyball tournament. You can jet through the wave tubes at **Surfrider Beach,** 23000 Pacific Coast Hwy., a section of **Malibu Lagoon State Beach** north of the pier. Walk there via the **Zonker Harris Access Way** (named after the Doonesbury character), 22700 Pacific Coast Hwy. **Malibu Surf Shack,** 22935 Pacific Coast Hwy., across from the pier, rents surfboards, kayaks, boogie boards, and wetsuits. The store, which sells bathing suits and sandals, also offers surfing lessons and tours. (☎310-456-8508; www.malibusurf-shack.com. Surfboards $15-25 per hr. Single kayaks $15 per hr., $35 per day; doubles $20/50. Boogie boards $12 per day. Wetsuits $10 per day. 1hr. lesson and full-day gear rental $100. 2hr. tour Sa 10am $59. Open M-Tu 10am-6pm, W-Su 9am-6pm.)

Hike at **Leo Carrillo State Park,** 35000 W. Pacific Coast Hwy., which has beautiful trails on hills above the ocean. (☎818-880-0350; www.parks.ca.gov. $10.) **Pepperdine University,** 24255 Pacific Coast Hwy., rising above the coast in sunny conservative glory, offers free tours of

PACIFIC COAST

the campus as well as the **Weisman Museum of Art.** (Pepperdine ☎310-506-4000; www.pepperdine.edu. Museum ☎310-506-4851. Open Tu-Su 11am-5pm. Free.) The red-roofed **Malibu Lagoon Museum and Adamson House,** 23200 Pacific Coast Hwy., overlooks the Pacific in classic Californian style. The home, now owned by the state, serves as a museum and is open for tours. (☎310-456-8432. Open W-Sa 11am-3pm; last tour 2pm. $5, ages 6-16 $2, under 6 free. Cash only.)

🎫 **THE ROAD TO OXNARD: 28 MI.**
Once again, take **Route 1 North.**

OXNARD   ☎805

A sanctuary of sand awaits at **Oxnard State Beach Park,** about 5 mi. south of Ventura, an urban beach backed by dunes and a jogging trail that is usually quiet and peaceful—but not on weekends. Oxnard celebrates its farming roots and 8500 berry acres each May with a delightful **Strawberry Festival.** (☎888-288-9242; www.strawberry-fest.org.)

🎫 **THE ROAD TO VENTURA: 11 MI.**
Route 1 and US 101 merge heading into Ventura. Exit and turn right onto **South California Street,** following it three blocks to **Main Street.**

VENTURA   ☎805

The Central Coast's southernmost city, Ventura is Southern in image and mentality, and is blessed with great weather and easygoing charm. Visitors to "California's Rising Star" flock to the revitalized downtown, home to numerous restaurants, shops, museums, galleries, and thrift stores. The locals come out at night and fill nearly every bar in town. Ventura Harbor is a bustling center of activity with over 30 restaurants and shops, as well as many concerts and festivals.

🔲 ORIENTATION

Ventura lies 30 mi. south of Santa Barbara and 70 mi. north of L.A., off **US 101. Main Street** runs east-west in the historic downtown area on the east side of town, intersecting with **California Street,** which runs to the pier. **Ventura Harbor** lies south of downtown along the

coast; from downtown, take Harbor Blvd. to Spinnaker Dr. To locate all that Ventura has to offer, pick up the historical walking tour map from the visitors bureau.

VITAL STATS
Population: 106,000
Tourist Office: Ventura Visitors Bureau, 89 S. California St. (☎805-648-2075 or 800-333-2989; www.ventura-usa.com). Open M-F 8:30am-5pm, Sa-Su 10am-4pm.
Library and Internet Access: EP Foster Library, 651 E. Main St. (☎805-648-2716). Free. Open M-Th 10am-8pm, F-Sa 10am-5pm.
Post Office: 675 E. Santa Clara St. (☎805-643-3057). M-F 8:30am-5:30pm, Sa 9am-3pm. **Postal Code:** 93001.

🛏 ACCOMMODATIONS

Prior to its rejuvenation, Ventura was exclusively a stopover point along the coastal routes. As a result, the city has a number of budget motels, particularly along **East Thompson Avenue,** though many are decades old and in need of renovation. During summer months, the area's campgrounds on and near the beach fill up quickly, so reserve your site with **Reserve America** (☎805-654-4744; www.reserveamerica.com) well in advance.

Clocktower Inn, 181 E. Santa Clara St. (☎805-652-0141). From Main St., go south 1 block on California St. and turn right on Santa Clara. Located in the heart of the city and formerly a firehouse, the inn offers an outdoor hot tub. Some rooms have balconies and fireplaces. Rooms from $169. AmEx/D/MC/V. ❺

Mission Bell Motel, 3237 E. Main St. (☎805-642-6831), near Pacific View Mall. Your best bet for basic lodging. Rooms M-F from $60, Sa-Su from $109. AmEx/D/MC/V. ❸

🍴 FOOD

Affordable restaurants cluster along Main St. in the heart of historic downtown.

Savory Cafe and Bakery, 419 E. Main St. (☎805-652-7092). Serves Italian-inspired breakfast ($6-14), lunch ($9-12), and delicious baked goods on mosaic tables in a bustling location. Open M-Sa 6:30am-5pm, Su 7am-3pm. ❸

Top Hat, 299 E. Main St. (☎805-643-9696), at Palm St. A roadside shack that's been serving chili cheeseburgers ($2.50), hot dogs ($1.50), and fries ($1) to a local crowd since 1966. Open Tu-Sa 10am-6pm. Cash only. ❶

Jonathan's at Peirano's, 204 E. Main St. (☎805-648-4853; www.jonathansatpeiranos. com). A popular Mediterranean spot. The beautiful patio is adjacent to a well-manicured park and large fountain. Lunch entrees $9-15. Dinner entrees $12-25. Open Tu-Su 5:30pm-last customer. AmEx/D/MC/V. ❹

Wine Lovers Wine Bar, 1067 E. Thompson Ave. (☎805-652-1810; www.wineloversbar.com). Gourmet pizza and nightly live music. On Reggae Wine Splash nights (Th 7pm-1am), you can enjoy music in the wine garden. Open daily Tu-Sa 5pm-1am. AmEx/MC/V. ❸

Winchester's Grill, 632 E. Main St. (☎805-653-7446), is a Western bar and grill where the locals go for beer variety. With 37 beers, 3 ciders, and 1 root beer on tap, this is a bar for some serious drinkers. Burgers and sandwiches $8-12. Entrees $17-21. Happy hour daily 4-6pm. Open M-F 4pm-last customer, Sa-Su 11am-last customer. AmEx/D/MC/V. ❷

🎭 🎆 SIGHTS AND FESTIVALS

OLIVAS ADOBE. Inland from Ventura Harbor on Olivas Park Dr. is the Olivas Adobe. The restored 1847 home sits on 5000 acres of land that the Mexican army gave to Raymundo Olivas for services rendered. The nine-room house is decorated in period furnishings and is a tribute to the early rancho period of Ventura's history. Olivas was not only one of the richest ranchers in California but also an early friend of the budget traveler; next to visitors' beds, Raymundo placed bowls of coins from which guests could draw some pocket change. As if that weren't enough, the house now also boasts 110-year-old fuchsias. (4200 Olivas Park Dr. ☎805-658-4728; www.olivasadobe.org. Tours Sa-Su 11am-4pm. Last tour begins 3pm. $5, children under 12 and seniors $3.)

MUSIC UNDER THE STARS. Enjoy the summer music series Music Under the Stars, which features live performances of swing, jazz, R&B, and blues at 7:30pm on Saturday nights. (From US 101, take the Telephone Ave. exit south to Olivas Park Ave. and turn right. ☎805-658-4728; www. olivasadobe.org. Open Tu-Su noon-4pm. Free.)

MISSION SAN BUENAVENTURA. Mission San Buenaventura still functions as a parish church. It also houses a tiny museum of treasures from Father Junípero Serra's order. A small and colorful courtyard lies between the church and gift shop. (211 E. Main St. ☎805-643-4318. Open M-F 10am-5pm, Sa 9am-5pm, Su 10am-4pm. $2, under 16 $0.50.)

🏖 BEACHES

Billed as California's "Gold Coast," the clean beaches near Ventura roar with surf. **Emma Wood State Beach,** on Main St. (take the State Beaches exit off US 101), and **Oxnard State Beach Park,** about 5 mi. south of Ventura, are quiet except on weekends. **San Buenaventura State Park,** at the end of San Pedro St., entertains families and casual beachgoers with its volleyball courts and nearby restaurants. Surfer's Point, at the end of Figueroa St., has the best waves around, but novices should start at **McGrath State Beach,** about 1 mi. south of Ventura down Harbor Blvd. Be forewarned that surfers can be territorial. Pick up insider surfing tips and Patagonia outlet gear at **Real Cheap Sports,** 36 W. Santa Clara St. From Main St., go one block south on Ventura Ave. and turn right onto Santa Clara St. (☎805-648-3803. Open M-Sa 10am-6pm, Su 11am-5pm.)

🛣 THE ROAD TO SANTA BARBARA: 27 MI.

From Ventura, take **US 101 North (Ventura Freeway)** for about 27 mi.; exit at **Garden Street** to access downtown Santa Barbara.

SANTA BARBARA ☎805

If L.A. and Santa Cruz had a baby, her name would be Santa Barbara. The town is an enclave of wealth and privilege, true to its soap-opera image, but in a less aggressive and flashy way than its SoCal counterparts. Santa Barbara's golden beaches, museums, missions, and scenic drives make it a weekend escape for the rich and famous and an attractive destination for surfers, artists, shoppers, and backpackers.

VITAL STATS

Population: 94,000

Tourist Office: Santa Barbara Visitor Information Center, 1 Garden St. (☎805-965-3021; www.santabarbaraca.com), at Cabrillo Blvd. across from the beach. Open M-Sa 9am-5pm, Su 10am-4pm.

Library and Internet Access: Santa Barbara Public Library, 40 E. Anapamu St. (☎805-962-7653). Free. Open M-Th 10am-9pm, F-Sa 10am-5:30pm, Su 1-5pm.

Post Office: 836 Anacapa St. (☎805-564-2202), 1 block east of State St. Open M-F 8am-6pm, Sa 9am-5pm. **Postal Code:** 93102.

ORIENTATION

Santa Barbara is 92 mi. northwest of L.A. and 27 mi. from Ventura on **Ventura Freeway (US 101).** Since the town is built along an east-west expanse of shoreline, its street grid is skewed. The beach lies at the south end of the city, and **State Street,** the main drag, runs northwest from the waterfront. All streets are designated "east" and "west" from State St. The major east-west arteries are US 101 and **Cabrillo Boulevard;** US 101, normally north-south, runs east-west between **Castillo Boulevard** and **Hot Springs Road.**

ACCOMMODATIONS

A 10min. drive north or south on US 101 will reward you with cheaper lodging than that in Santa Barbara proper. Trusty **Motel 6** is always

an option. All Santa Barbara accommodations are more expensive on the weekends (peaking July-Aug. and on holidays).

Hotel State Street, 121 State St. (☎805-966-6586; www.statestreethotel.com), 1 block from the beach. Welcoming, comfortable, and meticulously clean, this European-style inn offers a good (and relatively cheap) night's sleep. Common bathrooms are pristine. Rooms have sinks and cable TV; a few have private bathrooms, and others have skylights with origami cranes dangling from them. Reservations recommended. Rooms $79-139. MC/V. ❹

Santa Barbara International Tourist Hostel, 134 Chapala St. (☎805-963-0154; www.sbhostel.com). Great location near the beach and State St. Bike ($6-15) and boogie-board rentals ($5-8). Laundry. Free Wi-Fi. Internet $1 per 10min. Dorms $30; private rooms $69-89. MC/V. ❶

Haley Cottages, 227 E. Haley St. (☎805-963-0154; www.haleycottages.com), at Garden St. Run by the same folks as the International Hostel, these 12 private cottages have a comfortable, carefree spirit. Each cottage has its own kitchen and bathroom and is a 5min. walk from the beach. Rooms in summer $64-84; in winter $54. MC/V. ❸

Carpinteria Beach State Park, at the end of Palm Ave. (☎805-684-2811 or Reserve America at 800-444-7275). 12 mi. south of Santa Barbara; follow signs from US 101. 216 developed sites with hot showers, fire rings, and picnic tables.

CRAFTS ON THE BEACH

For more than 40 years, locals and tourists alike have been enjoying the Santa Barbara Arts and Crafts Show. Artists from the area established the show in 1965, inspired by European sidewalk art shows. Today over 250 Santa Barbara County artists display their work here each Sunday at the only continuous, non-juried arts festival in the country. Ask the artists about their work—most of them love to explain it, and the informal atmosphere encourages conversation. The show extends along the waterfront to the left of Stearns Wharf, facing the water. Arts, including sculpture, acrylic paintings, and photography, are displayed between the Chase Palm Park Recreation Center and the wharf. Crafts, like clothing, jewelry, and wood products, are beyond the recreation center. Parking is available on Garden St. and at parking lots on Garden St. or Cabrillo Blvd.

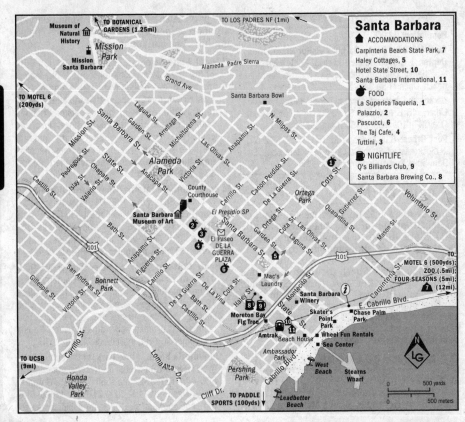

Santa Barbara

ACCOMMODATIONS
Carpinteria Beach State Park, **7**
Haley Cottages, **5**
Hotel State Street, **10**
Santa Barbara International, **11**

FOOD
La Superica Taqueria, **1**
Palazzio, **2**
Pascucci, **6**
The Taj Cafe, **4**
Tuttini, **3**

NIGHTLIFE
Q's Billiards Club, **9**
Santa Barbara Brewing Co., **8**

Reservations recommended. Sites $25, with hookup $34-44. Day use 7am-sunset $8. ❶

FOOD

Palazzio, 1026 State St. (☎805-564-1985). The reproduction of the Sistine Chapel ceiling is as impressive as the enormous pasta dishes ($24-26, ½-portion $16-18; lunch $9.75) and the serve-yourself wine bar. Open M-Th and Su 11:30am-3pm and 5:30-10pm, F-Sa 11:30am-3pm and 5:30-11pm. AmEx/MC/V. ❺

Tuttini, 10 E. Carrillo St. (☎805-963-8404), off State St. The friendly staff, as well as the restaurant's fresh, satisfying dishes, make this a great spot for breakfast, lunch, or Su brunch. Try the PBCB (peanut-butter-chocolate-banana panino;

$7) or polenta and poached eggs ($9.25). Open M-Sa 7am-2:30pm, Su 8am-2pm. MC/V. ❸

Pascucci, 729 State St. (☎805-963-8123), in Paseo Nuevo. A neighborhood Italian spot that uses local ingredients in true California style. Panini come on garlic cheese bread with salads ($10). The macadamia-crusted halibut salad is great ($10). Open M-Th and Su 11:30am-9pm, F-Sa 11:30am-10pm. AmEx/MC/V. ❸

La Super Rica Taqueria, 622 Milpas St. (☎805-963-4940). Rumored to have been Julia Child's favorite for Mexican. Maybe the culinary icon came for the freshest tortillas around (made while you watch), tamales, and excellent *pozole* on Su. Be prepared to wait. Entrees under $10. Open M-Tu, Th, Su 11am-9pm, F-Sa 11am-9:30pm. Cash only. ❸

The Taj Cafe, 905 State St. (☎805-564-8280). Enjoy low-fat, village-style Indian cooking with natural ingredients. Tandoori chicken in a sweet, tangy mango sauce $11. Lunch specials $6.50-11. Many vegetarian entrees $8.50-13. Open M-Th and Su 11:30am-10pm, F-Sa 11:30am-11pm. Lunch buffet 11:30am-2:30pm. AmEx/D/MC/V. ❸

👁 📷 SIGHTS AND BEACHES

Santa Barbara is best explored in three sections—the coast, swingin' State St., and the mountains. Essential to discovering local events and goings-on is the *Independent*, published every Thursday and available at city newsstands.

COASTAL SANTA BARBARA

Recently revamped, Santa Barbara's supreme coastal drive is Cabrillo Blvd., the first leg of the city's scenic drive. Follow the green signs as they lead you on a loop into the mountains and around the city, winding through the hillside bordering the town along Alameda Padre Serra. This part of town is known as the "American Riviera" for its high concentration of wealthy residents.

SANTA BARBARA ZOO. This delightfully open, leafy habitat gives visitors the feeling of wandering around the animals' natural homes. A miniature train provides park tours and views of the "cats of Africa" and the western lowland gorilla area. There's also a miniaturized African plain where giraffes stroll lazily, silhouetted against the Pacific. Ask the admissions window for special biscuits ($4) to hand-feed the giraffes. *(500 Niños Dr., off Cabrillo Blvd. from US 101. ☎805-962-5339. Open daily 10am-5pm. $10, children $8, under 2 free. Train $2, children $1.50.)*

TY WARNER SEA CENTER. Stearns Wharf, at the foot of State St., is the oldest working pier on the West Coast, housing the newly renovated Sea Center, restaurants, and shops. The center, affiliated with the Santa Barbara Museum of Natural History, is now a working lab with hands-on exhibits for visitors. Crawl through a 1500 gal. tide-pool-tank tunnel to observe wildlife in its natural state. *(At State St. and Cabrillo Blvd. ☎805-682-4711; www.sbnature.org. Open daily 10am-5pm. $8, ages 2-12 $5, under 2 free.)*

OTHER SIGHTS. Santa Barbara's beaches are breathtaking, with sailboats bobbing around the local harbor and breeze-rustled palm trees lining the shore. **West Beach** and **Leadbetter Beach** flank the wharf. **Skater's Point Park,** along the waterfront on Cabrillo Blvd., south of Stearns Wharf, is a free park for skateboarders. Helmets and gear are required. **Wheel Fun Rentals** rents out retro surreys, covered Flintstone-esque bicycles with bench seats that look a bit like buggies. You and up to eight friends can cruise in style. *(23 E. Cabrillo Blvd. ☎805-966-2282. Surreys $25-45 per 2hr., depending on number of riders. Open daily 8am-8pm.)* **SurfnWear's Beach House** rents surfboards and body boards plus all the necessary equipment. *(10 State St. ☎805-963-1281; www.surfnwear. com. Softboard surfboard $7 per hr., soft-top surfboard $12 per hr. Bodyboards $4 per hr. Full wetsuit $4 per hr., spring suit $3 per hr. Credit card required.)* **Paddle Sports** offers kayak rentals and lessons. *(117B Harbor Way. ☎805-899-4925; www.kayaksb.com. Rentals $20-35 per 2hr., $40-55 per day. Open in summer M-F 10am-6pm, Sa-Su 9am-6pm.)* Across the street from the visitors center is idyllic **Chase Palm Park,** complete with a perfectly manicured lawn, a fountain, and a vintage 1916 Spillman carousel. *(Open daily in summer 10am-9pm; in winter 11am-6pm. $2. Parking $1.50 per hr.)* For the best sunset around, have a drink ($8-18) at the bar at the **Four Seasons Biltmore Hotel.** This five-star lodging, from $550 per night, is off-limits to budget travelers, but the view of the Pacific is priceless (and free), and there's often free evening music. *(1260 Channel Dr., in Montecito. Take US 101 towards Montecito and exit at Olive Mill. ☎805-969-2261. Complimentary valet parking.)*

STATE STREET

State St., Santa Barbara's tree-lined monument to city planning, runs 2 mi. through the center of the city. Among the countless shops and restaurants are some cultural and historical landmarks that should not be missed. Everything that doesn't move—malls, mailboxes, telephones, even the restrooms at the public library—is slathered in Spanish tile.

SANTA BARBARA MUSEUM OF ART. This art museum has an impressive collection of classical Greek, Asian, American, and European works that spans 3000 years. The 20th-century and Hindu collections are particularly good. Come the third Thursday of the month (May-Sept.) for "Nights: Culture with a Twist" performances for $35. *(1130 State St. ☎ 805-963-4364; www.sbma.net. Open Tu-Su 11am-5pm. Tours Tu-Su noon and 1pm. $9, students, and ages 6-17 $6. Tu and Th 1-5pm and all day Su free.)*

MISSION SANTA BARBARA. Praised as the "Queen of Missions" in 1786, the mission was restored after the 1812 earthquake. Towers containing splayed Moorish windows around a Greco-Roman temple and facade while a Moorish fountain bubbles outside. The museum contains items from the mission archives, and visitors may attend mass in the colorful but solemn main chapel. The mission is also an infirmary and friary. *(2201 Laguna St., at the end of Las Olivas St. ☎ 805-682-4149. Open daily 9am-5pm. $5, ages 6-15 $1. Mass M-F 7:30am, Sa 4pm, Su 7:30, 9, 10:30am, noon.)*

SANTA BARBARA MUSEUM OF NATURAL HISTORY. Unlike your typical museum, the only way to get from one exhibit to the next here is to go outside. The founder's wish to establish a museum of comparative oology (no, not zoology) was overturned by a Board of Trustees that thought devoting the space to the study of eggs was silly. So they hatched the current exhibitions, which include the largest collection of Chumash artifacts in the West, a natural-history gallery, and a planetarium. *(2559 Puesta del Sol Rd. Follow signs to parking lot. ☎ 805-682-4711. Open daily 10am-5pm. Planetarium shows in summer M-F 1:15, 2, 3pm. $10, ages 12-19 $7, 3-12 $6, under 3 free. Planetarium $4.)*

SANTA BARBARA BOTANICAL GARDEN. Far from town but close to Mission Santa Barbara and the Museum of Natural History, the botanical garden boasts non-native flora planted along easy, meandering paths. The 1 mi. main trail winds through 85 acres of native Californian trees, wildflowers, and cactuses. The garden's dam and aqueduct were built in 1807 by the Chumash and are now some of the last vestiges of the region's native heritage. Make sure to visit the Redwood Exhibit, where the oldest tree was planted in 1930. *(1212 Mission Canyon Rd. ☎ 805-682-4726; www.sbbg.org. Open daily Mar.-Oct. 9am-6pm; Nov.-Feb. 9am-5pm. Tours M-F 2pm, Sa-Su 11am, 2pm. Special demonstrations F and Su 2pm, Sa 10:30am. $8, students $6, ages 13-17 and military $4, ages 2-12 $4, under 2 free.)*

UNIVERSITY OF CALIFORNIA AT SANTA BARBARA (UCSB). This beautiful outpost of the UC system is stuck in Goleta, a shapeless mass of suburbs, gas stations, and coffee shops, but the beachside dorms and gorgeous student body more than make up for the town. The outstanding **University Art Museum** is worth visiting. It houses the Sedgwick Collection of 15th- to 17th-century European paintings. *(Museum off US 101. ☎ 805-893-2951. Open W-Su noon-5pm. Free.)*

OTHER SIGHTS. At the corner of Montecito Ave. and Chapala St. stands the notable **Moreton Bay Fig Tree.** Brought from Australia by a sailor in 1877, the tree's gnarled branches now span 167 ft.; it can provide shade for more than 1000 people at once. If you'd rather drink than stand in the shade with 999 other people, sample award-winning wine at the **Santa Barbara Winery.** *(202 Anacapa St. ☎ 805-963-3633. Open daily 10am-5pm. Tastings $5 for 6 wines.)*

🥾 HIKING

The popular **Inspiration Point** is a 4 mi. round-trip hike that climbs 3000 ft. Half of the hike is an easy walk on a paved road. The other half is a series of mountain switchbacks. The reward on a clear day is an extensive view of the city, the ocean, and the Channel Islands. To reach the point, take a left off the road leading into the chaparral, then continue 300 ft. farther to the field of boulders. The late afternoon's shade and golden lighting make it the best time of day for this hike. Following the creek upstream will lead to **Seven Falls.** (From Mission Santa Barbara, drive toward the mountains and turn right onto Foothill Rd. Turn left onto Mission Canyon Rd. and continue 1 mi. Bear left onto Tunnel Rd. and drive 1 mi. to its end.) **Rattlesnake Canyon Trail** is a moderate 3 mi. round-trip hike to the **Tunnel Trail** junction with a 1000 ft. elevation. It passes waterfalls, pools, and secluded spots, but it is highly popular—expect company. (From Mission Santa Barbara, drive toward the mountains and turn right onto Foothill Rd. Turn left onto Mission Canyon Rd. and continue until Las Conas Rd.; make a sharp right onto this road and travel 1 mi. Look for a large sign on the left side of the road.) The treks from the **Cold Springs Trail** to Montecito Peak (7 mi. round-trip, 2462 ft. elevation gain) or to Camino Cielo (9 mi. round-trip, 2675 ft.

elevation gain) are more strenuous but offer great views. (From US 101 S., take the Hot Springs Rd. exit and turn left. Travel 2 mi. to Mountain Dr. Turn left, drive 1 mi., and stop by the creek crossing.) For a more extensive listing of trails, try the botanical garden gift shop or the visitors center in town. Another option is to join the local **Sierra Club** on one of its group hikes. (☎415-977-5500. Free.)

NIGHTLIFE

Every night of the week, the clubs on State St., mostly between Haley St. and Canon Perdido St., are packed. This town is full of people who love to eat and drink. Consult the *Independent* to see who's playing.

Q's Billiards Club, 409 State St. (☎805-966-9177). Patrons enjoy a 3-level bar, 8 pool tables, and dancing. Sample the sushi ($5-19), and wash it all down with sake ($3-6). M-Tu and Th-Sa 21+, W 18+. Cover Sa after 10pm $5. Happy hour M-Sa 4-7pm with 20% off sushi plates, ½-price drinks and appetizers, and free pool. Open M-Sa 4pm-2am. AmEx/D/MC/V.

Santa Barbara Brewing Company, 501 State St. (☎805-730-1040). Caters to those looking for drinks that hail from the US. Try the Rincon Red or the Santa Barbara Blonde. Entrees $10-15. Mixed drinks $6-8. Happy hour M-F 3-6pm and 10pm-last customer with $2.50 pints and $5 Kamikaze shots. Open M-F and Su 11am-10pm or last customer, Sa 11am-midnight or last customer. AmEx/D/MC/V.

DETOUR

LAKE CACHUMA COUNTRY PARK
From **US 101,** take **Route 154.**

If Lake Cachuma's clean, deep-blue waters placidly filling the crooks of the Santa Ynez Mountains are so stunning they seem almost unreal, that's because they are—they come from a manmade dam. The lake is nevertheless an unbelievably beautiful spot for hiking, boating (rentals from $15 per hr., $35-310 per day), fishing, wildlife observation, and camping. No swimming is allowed. Campers enjoy more than 400 **sites ❶**—first come, first served—with a general store, gas station, nature center, outdoor theater, pool, and marina. (☎805-686-5055; www.cachuma.com. Sites $20. Yurts $60-70. Day use $8 per car, $5 per hiker or biker. D/MC/V.)

THE ROAD TO SOLVANG: 14 MI.

Take **Route 154** to **Route 246 West** to Solvang. Along Rte. 154 is the lovely **Santa Ynez Valley,** home to acres of vineyards, hundreds of ostriches, and Michael Jackson's Wonderland Ranch (next to Disneyland, reputedly the second-happiest place on Earth). Clydesdale horses pull tourist-packed trolleys down the street in Solvang ("sunny field" in Danish).

SOLVANG   ☎805

Established in 1911, this former Danish colony will remind you of Disneyland's "Small World" ride. The town trumpets its Danish heritage—every shop and motel has a watered-down pitch related to Copenhagen or Hans Christian Anderson. Ironically, the Danish population has dwindled to a minority, even as the town's Danish thrust has become more concerted. In a formerly Mexican territory, this enclave is interesting simply for its novelty.

VITAL STATS
Population: 5300
Tourist Office: Solvang Conference and Visitors Bureau, 639 Copenhagen Dr. and 1511A Mission Dr. (☎800-468-6765). Open daily 10am-4pm.
Library and Internet Access: Solvang Branch Library, 1745 Mission Dr. (☎805-688-4214). Free. Open M 2-7:30pm, Tu-Th 10am-7:30pm, F-Sa 10am-5:30pm.
Post Office: 430 Alisal Rd. (☎805-688-9309). Open M-F 9am-5pm, Sa 9am-2pm. **Postal Code:** 93463.

ORIENTATION

Activity centers on **Mission Drive,** the town's main drag, neighboring **Copenhagen Drive,** and the intersecting **Alisal Road,** which features a turning windmill.

ACCOMMODATIONS

Viking Motel, 1506 Mission Dr. (☎805-688-1337). The lowest prices in town, depending on the time of year. Bear in mind that the cost can skyrocket up to $150 on summer weekends. Breakfast included. Rooms from $49. AmEx/D/MC/V. ❸

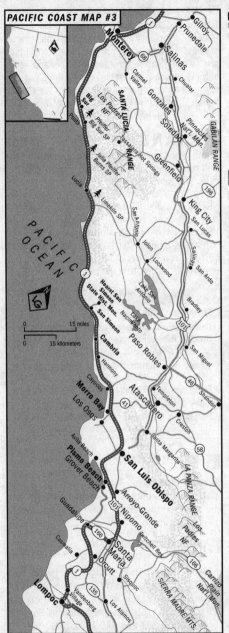

PACIFIC COAST

FOOD

Olsen's Village Bakery and Coffee Shop, 1529 Mission Dr. (☎805-688-6314; www.olsendanishbakery.com). The most authentic Danish bakery in town. Goods are delivered fresh every day by a 3rd-generation Dane. The Kringle is particularly scrumptious. The Danish breakfast is a terrific value, with bread, cheese, pastry, coffee, and orange juice for $7.50. Open in summer daily 7am-7pm; in winter M-F 7am-6pm, Sa-Su 7am-8pm. AmEx/MC/V. ❶

SIGHTS

Stroll around the themed streets and admire the elements of Scandinavian design—a thatched roof is at First St. and Copenhagen Dr.—and enjoy the cutesy storefronts, wine-tasting shops, and bakeries. The **Elverhoj Museum,** 1624 Elverhoy Way, off Second St., has displays and artifacts from Danish-American pioneer life. (☎805-686-1211; www.elverhoj.org. Open W-Th 1-4pm, F-Su noon-4pm. Suggested donation $3.) The **Hans Christian Anderson Museum,** 1680 Mission Dr., upstairs in the Book Loft, pays homage to Hans Christian Anderson, the children's author of such tales as *The Ugly Duckling*, *The Emperor's New Clothes*, and *The Little Mermaid*, with a modest display of his valuable books as well as his paper cutouts. (☎805-688-6010. Open daily 10am-5pm. Free.) Bike buffs will enjoy the **Vintage Motorcycle Museum,** 320 Alisal Rd. (☎805-686-9522; www.motosolvang.com. Open Sa-Su 11am-5pm. $5.)

THE ROAD TO BUELLTON: 4 MI.

Go west on **Mission Drive (Route 246)**.

BUELLTON ☎805

At the intersection of Rte. 246 and US 101 is the town of Buellton, home of **Andersen's Pea Soup ❷**, an I'll-drive-to-LA-just-to-stop-there institution where split-pea soup has been sold thick, hot, and fresh since 1924. (☎805-688-5581. Soup $5. Soup and milkshake $9. Open daily 7am-10pm. AmEx/D/MC/V.)

THE ROAD TO LOMPOC: 18 MI.

Continue on **Route 246 West**.

LOMPOC ☎805

The nation's largest producer of flower seed, Lompoc consists of every chain convenience you could imagine alongside flower fields and a mission. The acres upon acres of blooms, which peak near the end of June, are both a visual and olfactory explosion. Lompoc holds a **Flower Festival** (☎805-735-8511; www.flow-erfestival.org) at the season's peak, usually the last weekend in June. Stretch out at **La Purisima Mission State Park**, 2295 Purisima Rd. This mission, worked on by the CCC after the Great Depression, is the most fully restored of California's missions. Ten buildings stand alongside 25 mi. of hiking, biking, and eques-trian trails. (☎805-733-3713; www.lapurisi-mamission.org. Open daily 9am-5pm. Free guided tours daily 1pm. $4, seniors $3.)

THE ROAD TO PISMO BEACH: 49 MI.

Take **Route 246 West** to **Route 1 North;** follow Rte. 1 N. to Pismo Beach.

PISMO BEACH ☎805

Pismo Beach is a honky-tonk town situated around one of California's longest and widest beaches. At the **Pismo Dunes,** the loveliness of the broad, white sand is enjoyed by the all-terrain vehicles (ATV) that cruise around like insects on a picnic spread. Rent ATV equip-ment from **Steve's ATV**, 1206 W. Grand Ave., in Grover Beach. (☎805-474-6431; www.steve-satv.com. 2hr. ATV rental including helmet $48-140. Open daily 8am-6pm.) Those sur-passing the speed limit of 15 mph risk a hefty fine and their lives, as careless driving on the dunes can be deadly. For more informa-tion, head to the **Pismo Beach Chamber of Com-merce,** 581 Dolliver St. (☎805-773-4382; www. classiccalifornia.com.) **Pismo SB North Beach Campground ❶,** on Dolliver St., on Rte. 1, has the nicest campsites in Pismo, though even these are in a parking lot. (☎800-444-7275. Sites $15-20.) Another option is **Pismo Beach State Park ❶,** on Rte. 1, just south of scenic Pismo Beach. The huge campground is split into two areas; North Beach has 103 tent sites with showers and restrooms, while Oceano has 40 tent sites and 84 RV hookups with water, flush toilets, and showers. North Beach sites are larger and closer to the beach.

(☎805-489-1869. Reservations recommended. Tent sites $25; RV sites $34. Cash only.)

THE ROAD TO SAN LUIS OBISPO: 13 MI.

Follow **Route 1 North** to San Luis Obispo.

SAN LUIS OBISPO ☎805

Amid sprawling green hills close to the rocky coast, San Luis Obispo (frequently condensed to "SLO," pronounced like "slow") is a town that lives up to its nickname. The mission, which has reigned as the center of local life since 1772, saw SLO become a full-fledged town after the Southern Pacific Railroad laid tracks here in 1894. Ranchers and oil-refinery employees comprise a large percentage of today's population, and **California Polytechnic State University (Cal Poly)** students add a young, energetic component to the mix. Along the main downtown roads, hip students mingle with laid-back locals in outdoor eateries, trendy shops, and music-filled bars.

VITAL STATS
Population: 44,360
Tourist Office: Visitors Center for the Chamber of Commerce, 1039 Chorro St. (☎805-781-2777). Watch for signs on US 101. Open M-W and Su 10am-5pm, Th-Sa 10am-7pm.
Library and Internet Access: San Luis Obispo Branch Library, 995 Palm St. (☎805-781-5989). Open Tu 10am-8pm, W-Sa 10am-5pm.
Post Office: 893 Marsh St. (☎805-541-9138). Open M-F 8:30am-5:30pm, Sa 9am-3pm. **Postal Code:** 93401.

🔁 ORIENTATION

Downtown, **Monterey,** and **Higuera Streets** (north-south) and **Broad** and **Garden Streets** (east-west) are the main drags. Walking here is easy, and there is plenty of cheap parking.

🏠 ACCOMMODATIONS

Los Padres Inn, 1575 Monterey St. (☎805-543-5017). Conveniently located just a few blocks out of downtown. Though there's no A/C, little touches like flowers draped over the bedposts give this motel a cozy feel. Rooms from $55. AmEx/D/MC/V. ❸

Montaña de Oro State Park, Pecho Rd. (☎805-528-0513), 15 mi. from SLO via Los Osos Valley Rd. Pitch a tent in one of this gorgeous park's 50 primitive sites. Gray whales, seals, otters, dolphins, and the occasional orca frequent Montaña de Oro, whose 8000 acres and 7 mi. of shoreline remain relatively secluded. Outhouses and running water. Bring your own drinking water. Reservations recommended, especially in summer. Sites from mid-May to mid-Sept. $15; from mid-Sept. to mid-May $11. Cash only. ❶

▓ FOOD

Higuera St. and its cross streets are lined with restaurants and cafes.

▓ **Big Sky Cafe,** 1121 Broad St. (☎805-545-5401; www.bigskycafe.com). Voted "Best Restaurant in SLO" and winner of many other awards, the outdoor cafe serves up vegetarian-friendly food under the stars. Sandwiches $8.50-11. Open daily 7am-9pm. AmEx/D/MC/V. ❸

▓ **Oasis,** 675 Higuera St. (☎805-543-1155). Lavish surroundings and belly dancers add to the Mediterranean and Moroccan atmosphere. The "feast" (appetizer, soup or salad, entree, and baklava or cup of mint tea; $30) satisfies even the weariest desert traveler. Lunch $7-15. Open Tu-Su 11am-3pm and 4-9pm. D/MC/V. ❹

▓ **Mother's Tavern,** 725 Higuera St. (☎805-541-8733). A Yukon-inspired bar and restaurant that attracts mostly Cal Poly students. Try the Mother's Club (chicken, bacon, cheddar, and avocado on sour dough; $13) and top the evening off with karaoke, live music, and DJs. Sandwiches $11-13. Mixed drinks $7-10. Open M-F 11:30am-1:30am, Sa-Su 8am-2am. Kitchen open until 10pm. AmEx/D/MC/V. ❷

Woodstock's Pizza Parlour, 1000 Higuera St. (☎805-541-4420). A local hangout that invariably sweeps annual "best pizza" awards. Young crowds keep it lively all night. Lunch specials include all-you-can-eat pizza and bottomless soda for $8. Single slices $2.30. Beer $3-7.50. Trivia Tu. Open M-W and Su 11am-midnight, Th-Sa 11am-1am. AmEx/D/MC/V. ❶

◉ SIGHTS

APPLE FARM MILL. A gurgling 14 ft. water wheel and shady deck await visitors at the Apple Farm Mill. Alternately churning ice cream and flour, the mill provides free samples of homemade ice cream, popcorn, and cider from a local farm. The mill is also home to a restaurant, bakery, gift shop, and inn. (2015 Monterey St. ☎805-544-2040. Open M-Th and Su 7am-9pm, F-Sa 7am-10pm.)

COVES. Spooner's Cove, across from the campground, is a great day hangout. Up the coast to the north, **Coralina Cove** has tide pools and whale-watching spots at **Bluff's Trailhead.**

FARMERS' MARKET. Every Thursday night, rain or shine, downtown SLO is transformed into a block party of sorts. Locals flock to the Farmers' Market for fresh fruit and produce or to pick up a hot meal from one of the food stands. (On Higuera Street.)

MISSION SAN LUIS OBISPO. San Luis Obispo grew around the Mission San Luis Obispo de Tolosa, and the city continues to hold celebrations and socialize around its front steps and at the creek that runs through its courtyard. The mission was built in 1772 to resemble a steepled New England church, but its appearance has changed over the years. In the late 1800s, the town began reviving the mission's Spanish origins; by the 1930s it was fully restored. It still serves as the Catholic parish church for SLO. The mission houses a small museum, which displays objects from the early days of the mission and a small collection of Chumash artifacts. (☎805-543-6850. Open daily Apr.-Oct. 9am-5pm; Nov.-Mar. 9am-4pm.) The mission faces beautiful **Mission Plaza,** where Father Serra held the area's first mass.

SAN LUIS OBISPO HISTORICAL SOCIETY MUSEUM. The city recently dropped a cool $1 million to transform the public library into this museum. The exhibits tell the story of SLO's past and change several times a year. (696 Monterey St. ☎805-543-0638; www.slochs.com. Open W-Su 10am-4pm.)

⚑ THE ROAD TO MORRO BAY: 14 MI.

Follow **Route 1 North** to Morro Bay.

MORRO BAY   ☎805

The Nine Sisters, a chain of small ex-volcanoes, are remnants of a time when SLO County was hot with volcanic activity. The lava that once flowed here formed the dramatic shorelines along Rte. 1 from Morro Rock to SLO. The northernmost sister, Morro Rock, and three large smokestacks from an electric company shadow tiny Morro Bay, just north of the park that shares its name.

Morro Bay State Park is home to coastal cypresses that are visited by monarch butterflies from November to March. (☎800-444-7275.) The park's modern, hands-on **Museum of Natural History** flexes its curatorial muscle on the aquatic environment and wildlife of the coastal headlands. A bulletin board near the entrance lists free nature walks led by park docents. (☎805-772-2694. Reserve campsites year-round. Open daily 10am-5pm. $2, under 16 free.) South Bay Blvd., which links the town and the park, winds through the **Morro Bay National Estuary,** a sanctuary for great blue herons, egrets, and sea otters. Take the trail or rent a kayak or canoe to explore. Pack a basket and paddle out to the sand dunes for a picnic lunch. Check tide schedules at **Kayak Horizons,** 551 Embarcadero, or ask at the marina to avoid (or take advantage of) numerous sandbars. Kayak Horizons rents kayaks and offers instruction. (☎805-772-6444; www.kayakhorizons.com. $9-16 per hr., $23-49 for up to 4 hr. Open daily 9am-5pm. MC/V.)

Along the beach, the **Embarcadero** is the locus of Morro Bay activity and fish-and-chips bargains. The modest **Morro Bay Aquarium,** 595 Embarcadero, is a rehabilitation center for distressed marine animals. Family-owned by Dean and Bertha Tyler since 1960, it is home to over 100 ocean critters. The seal-feeding station is a rare opportunity to see these animals from only feet away. (☎805-772-7647. Open daily in summer 9am-6:30pm; in winter 9:30am-5:30pm. $2, ages 5-11 $1, under 5 free. Cash only.) Morro Bay's pride and joy is the **Giant Chessboard,** 800 Embarcadero, in Centennial Park across from Southern Port Traders. The board is 256 sq. ft., with 18-30 lb. carved redwood pieces. The chess club plays on Saturday and you can join them for free. You must fill out a form and leave a credit card or driver's license in exchange for a key. (Call the Morro Bay Recreation office at ☎805-772-6278 to set up a game or watch for free M-F 8am-5pm. $38 per game.)

⚑ THE ROAD TO CAMBRIA AND SAN SIMEON: 21 MI.

Follow **Route 1 North** to Cambria.

CAMBRIA AND SAN SIMEON   ☎805

The original settlers of the southern end of the Big Sur coast were awestruck by the stunning pastoral views and rugged shoreline, reminiscent of the eastern coast of England. In homage to the natural beauty of their homeland, they named this equally impressive New World area Cambria, the ancient Roman name for Wales. Ten miles north of Cambria, neighboring New San Simeon is a strip town along Rte. 1 with few roads and many motels near spectacular beaches. Old San Simeon is north of New San Simeon and consists of the 150-year-old Sebastian Store and the homes of Hearst Corporation ranchers.

VITAL STATS
Population: 6232
Tourist Offices: Cambria Chamber of Commerce, 767 Main St. (☎805-927-3624). Open M-F 9am-5pm, sometimes Sa 11am-3pm. **San Simeon Chamber of Commerce,** 250 San Simeon Dr. (☎805-927-3500; www.sansimeonchamber.com), on the west side of Rte. 1. Look for signs. Open daily 10am-4pm.
Library and Internet Access: Cambria Branch Library, 900 Main St. (☎805-927-4336), in Cambria. Free. Open Tu-F 11am-5pm, Sa noon-4pm.
Post Offices: Cambria, 4100 Bridge St. (☎805-927-8610). Open M-F 9am-5pm. **Postal Code:** 93428. **San Simeon** (☎805-927-4156), on Rte. 1, in the back of Sebastian's General Store; take the road opposite the entrance to Hearst Castle. Open M-F 8:30am-5pm. **Postal Code:** 93452.

◢ ORIENTATION

For a quick stop, turn off **Route 1** at the **Burton Drive** exit, which takes you straight to **Main Street.** Drive north up Main St. through the town center to the **West Village,** where most of the action is. There (after passing the wonderful **Robin's** restaurant), in a one-block radius you'll find an ATM, a gas station, and old-timey **Soto's Market & Deli.** (☎805-927-4411. Open M-Sa 7am-8pm, Su 8am-6pm.)

ACCOMMODATIONS

Cambria has lovely but pricey B&Bs. Budget travelers will have better luck in San Simeon. The arrival of Motel 6 set off a pricing war that has led to wildly fluctuating rates, so it is always a good idea to call ahead. Beware of sky-high prices in summer.

San Simeon State Beach Campground (☎800-444-7275), just north of Cambria on Rte. 1. San Simeon Creek has 134 developed sites near the beach. Reservations recommended. Sites $25. Cash only. ❶

Washburn (☎800-444-7275). Neighbors San Simeon State Beach and sits on a breezy hill overlooking the ocean. Primitive camping, pit toilets, and cold running water. Reservations recommended. Sites $15. Cash only. ❶

Bridge Street Inn, 4314 Bridge St. (☎805-927-7653), in Cambria. Originally built in the 1890s for the preacher at the church next door. Includes sunny clean rooms with sturdy bunks and a volleyball net in the yard. Continental breakfast and linen included. Reception 5-9pm. Dorms $22; private rooms $50-70. MC/V. ❶

FOOD

Robin's, 4095 Burton Dr. (☎805-927-5007). Many San Luis Obispo residents consider Robin's to be the only reason to drive the 30 mi. to Cambria. International cuisine and daily deli salads are served in a arts-and-crafts-style bungalow with outdoor gardens. Dinner entrees $14-25. Open M-Th and Su 11am-9pm, F-Sa 11am-10pm. Reservations recommended. MC/V. ❹

Creekside Gardens Cafe, 2114 Main St. (☎805-927-8646). Locals frequent the cafe, at the Redwood Shopping Center, for a burger ($7-9.25) or hearty breakfast scramble ($8.75). Dine outside on the patio to the sounds of the garden fountains. At night, Creekside turns up the Mexican flavor with dishes, like spinach and mushroom quesadillas, from $8. Su brunch 10am-2:30pm. Open M-Sa 7am-2pm and 5-9pm, Su 7am-1pm. Cash only. ❸

SIGHTS

San Simeon marks the beginning of Big Sur's dramatic coastline. Sea otters, once near extinction, live in the kelp beds of **Moonstone Beach,** on Moonstone Dr., off Rte. 1, toward San Simeon. Along this stretch of coast, surfers are occasionally nudged off their boards by playful seals (and, far more rarely, by not-so-playful great white sharks). Scenic **Leffingwell's Landing** is the best spot for whale watching. (Open Apr.-Dec. daily 8am-sunset.) Call **Virg's Landing** for info. (☎805-772-1222.) In

THE ELEPHANT SEAL: A FRIEND IN NEED

As you drive along Rte. 1 north from Cambria, you will see signs for the Friends of the Elephant Seal rookery at Piedras Blancas. Turn off the road and park in the lot, then observe the seals from a distance of 50-100 ft. Protected by the point from storms and by a kelp forest from predators, here huge numbers of elephant seals relax on the beach and frolic in the waves. The long noses of the males gave these seals their name; females lack the distinctive nose and are much smaller. Harvested by whalers for their blubber, elephant seals were thought to be extinct by the 1880s. A small group survived the hunts, and today the population of about 170,000 is protected by the 1972 Marine Mammal Protection Act. Although elephant seals are solitary creatures while at sea, when they come on land to breed and give birth, they live in harems of one male and a group of females. If you plan to be in the area for an extended period of time, you can apply to be a volunteer docent. Docents learn about not only elephant seals but also about sea otters, sea lions, and harbor seals, then educate

addition to providing the best swimming for miles, **San Simeon** and **Hearst State Beaches,** just across from **Hearst Castle** (below), are ideal for cliff climbing and beachcombing.

◤ DETOUR
HEARST CASTLE

The castle is located on **Route 1,** 3 mi. north of San Simeon and 9 mi. north of Cambria.

Newspaper magnate and multi-millionaire owner William Randolph Hearst casually referred to it as "the ranch," or, in his more romantic moments, "La Cuesta Encantada" (the enchanted hill). The hilltop estate is an indescribably decadent dreamland castle of limestone, shaded cottages, pools almost too exquisite to swim in, fragrant gardens, and Mediterranean *esprit.* Hearst spent most of his life gathering Renaissance sculpture, tapestries, and ceilings and telling his architect to incorporate them into his castle's design. Scores of celebrities and luminaries such as Charlie Chaplin, Charles Lindbergh, and Winston Churchill visited the castle (by invitation only) to bask in Hearst's legendary hospitality. Take the garden tour (Tour 4) to stroll along the azalea walk that Cary Grant nicknamed "Lovers' Lane." The castle is impressive, and the colorful stories told by the tour guides are not to be missed.

The **State Parks Department** runs five different tours, all of them strictly hands-off experiences. (☎805-927-2020, reservations 800-444-4445; www.hearstcastle.com. Call in advance, as tours often sell out. 4 different daytime tours leave frequently 8:20am-3:20pm. 1hr. tours from mid-May to mid-Sept. $24-30, ages 6-17 $12-15; from mid-Sept. to mid-May $20-30/$10-15. Theater ☎805-927-6811. Films daily every 45min. 8:15am-5:15pm. $8, under 12 $6; after purchasing Tour 1 $6/4.)

◤ THE ROAD TO BIG SUR: 74 MI.

Follow **Route 1 North** to Big Sur. Big Sur is a stretch of highway that was left as wilderness, and you need to make preparations in advance. That means getting food, camping equipment, and gas before you hit the Sur Grande. There are few services in Big Sur and the ones that do exist are exorbitantly priced. Pick up a free copy of the newspaper leaflet *El Sur Grande,* which includes a good map of the stretch.

BIG SUR   ☎831

Monterey's Spanish settlers called the entire region below their town El Sur Grande—the Big South. Today, Big Sur is a more explicitly defined 90 mi. coastal stretch, bordered on the south by San Simeon and on the north by Carmel. Cutting the road into the cliff, whose wending ways and tremendous views make a spectacular driving experience, was quite a lot of work: the entire highway, completed in 1937, took 18 years to build and cost $10 million to finish. More of a region than a precise destination, the area draws a curious mix of hippies, rich folk, and outdoor enthusiasts who come for its enchanting wilderness. Outdoorsy travelers will find too much to do in Big Sur. River and creek water is swimmable in the summer months, and there are more hiking trails than year-round inhabitants. Even in this coastal area, there isn't always enough water, however. Summer 2008 saw forest fires rage through Big Sur in early July. At press time, much of Big Sur was still closed and recovering from the blazes. After what many are calling the worst forest fires in the state's history, no one knows if and how much Big Sur will rebound; research before your trip.

VITAL STATS

Tourist Offices: Big Sur Station (☎831-667-2315), north of Pfeiffer Big Sur entrance on Rte. 1. Multi-agency station includes the **State Park Office,** the **US Forest Service (USFS) Office,** and the **CalTrans Office.** Provides permits, maps, and info on hikes and campfires. Also serves as the trailhead to a hike that leads to hot springs. Open June-Sept. daily; Oct.-May reduced hours.

Road Conditions: ☎800-427-ROAD/7623.

Post Office: 47500 Rte. 1 (☎831-667-2305). Open M-F 8:30am-4pm. **Postal Code:** 93920.

◤ DETOUR
POINT LOBOS RESERVE

The reserve is located on **Route 1,** three miles south of Carmel. Park on Route 1 before the tollbooth, and walk or bike in for free.

This extraordinary 550-acre, state-run wildlife sanctuary calls itself "the greatest meeting of land and water in the world" and is popular with skin divers and day hikers. Bring binoculars to view otters, sea lions, seals, brown pelicans, gulls, or migrating whales from the paths along the cliffs. At the water, Point Lobos offers tide pools and scuba access. (☎831-624-4909, reservations 624-8413. Open daily 8am-½hr. past sunset. Free daily nature tours; call for times. Map $1. Reservations required. Dive fee $10. $10 per vehicle, with a senior $9, disabled $6.)

THE ROAD TO CARMEL: 28 MI.

Go northwest on **Route 1** toward Carmel.

CARMEL ☎831

Moneyed Californians migrate to Carmel (officially Carmel-by-the-Sea) to live out their fantasies of small-town life. Carmel has beautiful beaches, a multitude of boutiques and art galleries, and an aura of quaintness. Local ordinances forbid address numbers, parking meters, high heels, billboards, chain stores ,and, at one time, eating ice-cream cones outside—all considered undesirable symbols of encroaching urbanization.

VITAL STATS
Population: 4081
Tourist Office: Carmel-by-the-Sea Chamber of Commerce and Visitor Information Center (☎831-624-2522 or 800-550-4333; www.carmel-california.org), next to the Eastwood Bldg., on San Carlos St., between 5th and 6th Ave. Open daily 10am-5pm.
Internet Access: Mail Mart (☎831-624-4900), at Dolores St. and 5th Ave. Open M-F 8:30am-5:30pm, Sa 9am-3pm. $3 per 15min.
Post Office: (☎831-624-3630), on 5th Ave., between San Carlos and Dolores St. Open M-F 9am-4pm. **Postal Code:** 93921.

ORIENTATION

Carmel lies at the southern end of the Monterey Peninsula off Rte. 1, 126 mi. south of San Francisco. The town's main street, **Ocean Avenue,** cuts west from the freeway to— you guessed it—the ocean. All other east-west avenues are numbered; numbers ascend as you head south. **Junípero Avenue** crosses Ocean Ave. downtown and leads south to the

mission at **Rio Road.** Free town maps are available at most hotels and at the visitors center. Free parking can be found on the corner of Junípero Ave. and Third Ave.

ACCOMMODATIONS

The expensive inns and lodges in Carmel usually offer only double-occupancy rooms (which fall below $90 only midweek or in winter) and usually include full breakfasts. A 15min. drive to Monterey will yield lower rates at places with less charm.

Carmel Lodge, (☎831-624-1255 or 800-252-1255), on San Carlos St., between 4th and 5th Ave. The upscale lodge has rooms with cable TV, phones, and private baths. Some have fireplaces, wet bar, or balcony. Pool access. Parking $10. Rooms from $169. AmEx/D/MC/V. ❺

Carmel Inn and Suites (☎831-624-1900 or 800-325-8515; www.carmelinnandsuites.com), at the northeast corner of Junípero and 5th. With free parking and antique furniture, the inn is one of the cheapest options right in town. Breakfast included. Rooms $119-299. ❺

FOOD

Food, like everything else in Carmel, is overpriced. It is, however, occasionally good enough to justify the expense.

Em Le's (☎831-625-6780), on Dolores St., between 5th and 6th Ave. Known for its fabulous breakfasts, including omelets with cottage cheese and toast ($9-15) and unique French toast ($10). For dinner, early birds (4-6pm) can get an entree with soup or salad for $13. Open daily 7am-3pm and 4:30-10pm. D/MC/V. ❸

Forge in the Forest (☎831-624-2233), at the southwest corner of 5th Ave. and Junípero St. Has been voted best outdoor dining in Monterey County since 1992. The popular restaurant serves pasta, seafood, grill items (from $23), and gourmet pizza (roasted duck and caramelized onion; $14.50) on a garden patio complete with open-fire forge. Open M-Th and Su 11:30am-9pm, F-Sa 11:30am-10pm. AmEx/MC/V. ❹

Tuck Box English Tea Room (☎831-624-6365), on Dolores Ave., between Ocean and 7th Ave. Housed in a historic building dating from 1927, the Tea Room is famous for scones ($4.75), preserves, and a fairy-tale-esque facade. Omelets $8. Open daily 7:30am-2:30pm. Cash only. ❸

👁 SIGHTS

🏛MISSION BASILICA SAN CARLOS BOR-ROMEO DEL RIO CARMELO. Established at its present site in 1771 by Father Serra, "the great conquistador of the cross," the Carmel Mission "welcomed" 4000 converted Native Americans before it was abandoned in 1836. Fastidiously restored in 1931, the mission's marvels are still astounding. With a stone courtyard, a bell tower, lavish gardens, and a daily mass, the mission is one of the most elaborate in California. Father Serra and many Native Americans are buried here. The three museums display the original silver altar furnishings, handsome vestments, and the first library in California. *(3080 Rio Rd., at Lasuen Dr., off Rte. 1. ☎831-624-1271. Open M-Sa 9:30am-5pm, Su 10:30am-5pm. $5, children $1.)*

SUNSET CULTURAL CENTER. The Sunset Cultural Center, which once housed Ansel Adams and Edward Weston's photography, is now home to the **Center for Photographic Art,** on San Carlos St. between Eighth and Ninth Ave. The center exhibits top-notch work by local and international artists and offers workshops. Recently, photographer Kenneth Parker was exhibited here. *(East side of San Carlos between 8th and 9th in downtown Carmel-by-the-Sea. ☎831-625-5181. Open Tu-Su 1-5pm. Free.)*

🏖 BEACHES

The northern Big Sur coast begins at the end of Ocean Ave. at **Carmel City Beach,** a white, sandy crescent framing a cove of chilly waters. The beach ends abruptly at the base of red cliffs, which make a fine grandstand for sunsets. **Carmel River State Beach,** just south of Carmel City Beach, is windier and colder than its neighbor, but it is blessed with better surf, parking, and smaller crowds. Bring a jacket or sweater, even in summer. To get to Carmel River State Beach, walk about one mile along Scenic Road, or drive to the end of Carmelo Street off Santa Lucía.

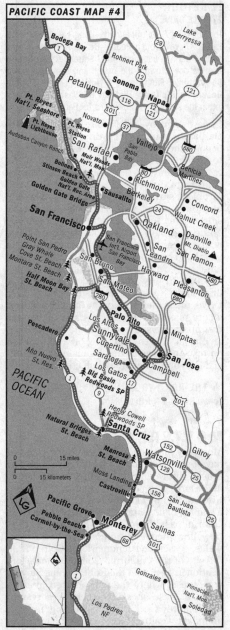
PACIFIC COAST MAP #4

⊠ DETOUR
17-MILE DRIVE

The 17-Mile Drive meanders along the coast from Pacific Grove through Pebble Beach and the forests around Carmel. For the Carmel entrance, take **Ocean Avenue** down toward the beach and turn right down **San Antonio**. From **Route 1 North,** take the **Pebble Beach/Pacific Grove Highway 68 West** exit and turn left at the stoplight. Follow signs for Pebble Beach.

Once owned by Del Monte Properties, **Pebble Beach**—which you'll drive through—has become the playground of the fabulously well-to-do. Its enormous, manicured golf courses creep up almost to the shore's edge in bizarre contrast to the dramatically jagged cliffs and turbulent surf. The drive is rolling, looping, and often spectacular, though plagued by slow-driving tourists and a hefty toll ($8.50). To drive in and out as you please over the course of a day, present your receipt to the guard and have him record your license-plate number. Save money by biking it (bicyclists and pedestrians are allowed in for free) or drive along Sunset Dr. instead. Along 17-Mile Drive, make sure to stop at **Fanshell Overlook,** where massive harbor seals and their pups rest up on the shore, and at the **Lone Cypress,** an old, gnarled tree growing on a rock promontory. An image of this tree is now the official logo of the Pebble Beach community.

⊠ THE ROAD TO MONTEREY: 8 MI.
Follow **Route 1 North** to Monterey.

MONTEREY   ☎831

Monterey makes good on its public claim to have preserved more of its heritage than any other Californian city. Although luxury hotels and tourist shops abound and the "Cannery Row" of Steinbeck fame has all but vanished, a number of important sites testify to the city's colorful past. The "Path of History," marked by yellow medallions embedded in the sidewalks, passes such landmarks as Colton Hall, the site of the California Constitutional Convention in 1849, and the Robert Louis Stevenson House, where the author lived in 1879. Most of these sites owe their preservation to Monterey's other distinguishing feature: abundant wealth. Multi-million-dollar homes

and golf courses line the rocky shoreline, and luxury cars cruise the city streets.

⊠ ORIENTATION

The **Monterey Peninsula,** 116 mi. south of San Francisco, consists of **Monterey,** residential **Pacific Grove,** and **Pebble Beach,** a nest of mansions and golf courses. **Alvarado Street** runs north-south through Old Monterey and hosts most nightlife. Parallel to it is **Pacific Street.** At Alvarado St.'s northern end stand luxury hotels and the giant Double Tree Conference Center; beyond the plaza lie a parking lot, the marina, and Fisherman's Wharf. Perpendicular to Alvarado St., **Del Monte Avenue** runs northeast to the coast; on the other side, **Lighthouse Avenue** leads northwest through Pacific Grove, where it becomes **Central Avenue** and veers back to Lighthouse Ave., ending at the **Point Piños Lighthouse.**

VITAL STATS
Population: 33,000
Tourist Office: Monterey Peninsula Visitor and Convention Bureau, 401 Camino El Estero (☎831-657-6400 or 888-221-1010; www.montereyinfo.org). Open in summer M-Sa 9am-6pm, Su 9am-5pm.
Library and Internet Access: Monterey Public Library, 625 Pacific St. (☎831-646-3930), across from City Hall. Free. Open M 1-9pm, Tu-W 10am-9pm, Th-F 10am-6pm, Sa-Su 1-5pm.
Post Office: 686 Lighthouse Ave. (☎831-375-8545). Open M-F 9:30am-3:30pm. **Postal Code:** 93940.

⊠ ACCOMMODATIONS

Inexpensive hotels line the 2000 block of Fremont St. in Monterey. Others cluster along Munras Ave. between downtown Monterey and Rte. 1. The cheapest hotels in the area are in the less appealing towns of Seaside and Marina, just north of Monterey. Prices fluctuate depending on the season, day of the week, and events. In Monterey, camping is an excellent option for the budget traveler. Call **Monterey Parks** (☎831-755-4895) for camping information and **ReserveAmerica** (☎800-444-7275) for reservations.

Monterey Carpenter's Hall Hostel (HI-AYH), 778 Hawthorne St. (☎831-649-0375), 1 block west of Lighthouse Ave. This 45-bed hostel is fairly new and well located. Modern facilities and a large living room with a piano, library, and games. Make-your-own-pancake breakfast with tea, hot chocolate, and coffee. Limited shower time: visitors get 2 tokens per day, each good for 3min. of hot water. Towels $0.50. Linen and parking included. Lockout 10:30am-5pm. Curfew 1am. Reservations essential June-Sept. Dorms $25.50, members $22.50, ages 7-17 with adult $15.50; under 7 $11.50; doubles $59. MC/V. ❶

Sea Breeze Lodge, 1101 Lighthouse Ave. (☎800-575-1805), minutes from Monterey and the ocean. 30 clean and comfortable rooms are set in the residential area of Pacific Grove. Outdoor pool. Continental breakfast included. Rooms $59-139. AmEx/D/MC/V. ❹

Veterans Memorial Park Campground (☎831-646-3865), 1 mi. from downtown. From Rte. 68, turn left onto Skyline Dr. From downtown, go south on Pacific St., turn right on Jefferson St., and follow the signs. Located on a hill with a view of the bay. 40 sites. No hookups. Playground, barbecue pits, and hot showers. 3-night max. stay. No reservations; in summer and Sa-Su arrive before 3pm. Sites $25. Cash only. ❶

Monterey Bay Lodge, 55 Camino Aguajito (☎831-372-8057; www.montereybaylodge.com), off Del Monte Ave. Modern, brightly colored rooms steps from the beach. Pool and hot tub. Free Wi-Fi. Rooms $119-230. AmEx/D/MC/V. ❺

▅ FOOD

Once a hot spot for the sardine industry, Monterey Bay now yields crab, red snapper, and salmon. Seafood is often expensive; look for free chowder samples or early-bird specials (usually 4-6pm). Stroll along the wharf, where most restaurants give out free samples of chowder. **Old Fisherman's Grotto** has some of the best (☎831-375-4606). Nibble on free samples at the **Old Monterey Market Place,** on Alvarado St. between Pearl St. and Del Monte Ave. (☎831-655-2607. Open Tu 4-8pm.)

▨ **Thai Bistro II,** 159 Central Ave. (☎831-372-8700), in Pacific Grove. Graced with a flower-encircled patio, this bistro offers top-quality Thai cuisine in a comfy atmosphere. Lunch combos ($7-9)

come with soup, salad, egg roll, and rice. Vegetarian menu. Tuk-Tuk Delight $9. Open daily 11:30am-3pm and 5-9:30pm. AmEx/MC/V. ❸

▨ **Tillie Gort's,** 111 Central Ave. (☎831-373-0335), in Pacific Grove. This cozy restaurant has been in business since 1969 and has won many awards for its outstanding vegetarian options. Large portions of dishes like Mexican fiesta salad ($11.50), eggplant francese ($9.50), or spinach ravioli ($12.25), and sweet treats like berry cheesecake or chocolate cake ($5) please even carnivores. Open daily 8am-10pm. MC/V. ❸

Bagel Bakery, 452 Alvarado St. (☎831-372-5242). Has been making delicious bagel sandwiches since 1976, this local chain has several additional locations in the area. Open M-Sa 6am-6pm, Su 7am-4pm. AmEx/MC/V. ❶

Austino's Patisserie, 851 Cannery Row, across from the Monterey Bay Aquarium. This simple yellow structure was the inspiration for La Ida Cafe in Steinbeck's *Cannery Row,* back when it housed Edith's Restaurant. Huge sandwiches from $6. Pizza $4.50 per slice. Ice cream $3-4. In addition to an assortment of pastries, Austino's serves beach-town snacks like candy apples ($5), pretzels, and hot dogs. Open daily 9am-6pm. ❶

◎ SIGHTS

▨ **MONTEREY BAY AQUARIUM.** The largest of Monterey's attractions, this extraordinary aquarium benefits from the area's superb marine ecology. Gaze through the world's third-largest window at an enormous marine habitat containing green sea turtles, giant ocean sunfish, large sharks, and yellowfin and bluefin tuna in one million gallons of water. Don't miss the provocative exhibit connecting the shape, movement, and beauty of jellyfish to various art forms or the new exhibit exploring the myth and mystery of sharks. Kids and adults love watching the sea otters during feeding time, walking through the shorebird aviary, perusing the living kelp forest housed in a two-story glass aquarium, and checking out the touch pool of bay creatures (bat rays included). Be patient; the lines can be unbelievably long. Save 20-40min. by picking up tickets the day before. *(886 Cannery Row.* ☎*831-648-4888 or 800-756-3737. Open daily June-*

Aug. 9:30am-6pm; Sept.-May 10am-6pm. $25, students, and ages 13-17 $23, ages 3-12 $16.)

CANNERY ROW. Lying along the waterfront east of the aquarium, Cannery Row was once a dilapidated street crammed with languishing sardine-packing plants. The row has since been converted into tourist-packed minimalls, bars, and a pint-size carnival complex. All that remains of the earthiness and gruff camaraderie celebrated by John Steinbeck in *Cannery Row* and *Sweet Thursday* are a few building facades: 835 Cannery Row was the Wing Chong Market, the bright yellow building next door is where *Sweet Thursday* took place, and Doc Rickett's lab, 800 Cannery Row, is now closed to the public. Take a peek at the Great Cannery Row Mural; local artists have covered a construction-site barrier on the 700 block with depictions of 1930s Monterey and what "The Row" was like in its heyday. The **Wine Visitors Center,** on the second floor of the 700 building, offers a well-priced bottles and winery maps. *(700 Cannery Row. ☎888-646-5446. Open daily M-Th 11am-5pm, F-Sa 11am-6pm, Su 11am-4pm. $5 for 6 tastings.)*

SUNSET DRIVE. West of Monterey in Pacific Grove, Sunset Dr. provides a free, 6 mi. scenic alternative to 17-Mile Drive. Appropriately, Sunset Dr. is the best place in the area to watch the sun go down. People arrive a full 2hr. before sunset in order to secure front-row seats along the road, also known as Ocean Blvd. At the western tip of the peninsula stands **Point Piños Lighthouse,** the oldest continuously running Pacific Coast lighthouse, which has exhibits on Coast Guard history. *(☎831-648-5716. Open Tu-Sa 10am-5pm. Free.)*

PACIFIC GROVE. Pacific Grove took root as a Methodist enclave over 100 years ago, and many of the Victorian houses are still in excellent condition. This unpretentious town (which falls eerily quiet at night) has a beautiful coastline, numerous lunch counters, and lots of antique and artsy home-furnishing stores. Browse secondhand-clothing, book, and music stores along Lighthouse Ave. or outlet-shop until you drop at the American Tin Cannery, on Ocean View Blvd., near New Monterey. Thousands of monarch butterflies winter in Pacific Grove from October to

March. Look but don't touch; bothering the butterflies is a $1000 offense. The **Pacific Grove Museum of Natural History** has exhibits on monarchs and local wildlife. The stuffed birds are top-notch. *(At Forest and Central Ave., one block west of Lighthouse Ave. ☎831-648-5716; www.pgmuseum. org. Open Tu-Sa 10am-5pm. Free.)*

MARITIME MUSEUM OF MONTEREY. This haven for sea buffs illustrates the maritime history of Monterey with ship models, photos, navigation tools, logs, and a free 14min. film. The museum's centerpiece is the original Fresnel lens of Point Sur Lighthouse. The lens is a two-story structure of gears and cut glass later replaced by the electric lighthouse. *(5 Custom House Plaza, across from Fisherman's Wharf. ☎831-372-2608. Open Tu-Su 10am-5pm. Free.)*

PATH OF HISTORY. The early days of Monterey spawned a unique architectural trend that combined flourishes from the South, like wraparound porches, with Mexican adobe features like 3 ft. thick walls and exterior staircases. The Path of History Walking Tour, marked by yellow sidewalk medallions, snakes through **Monterey State Historic Park** downtown, passing numerous historic buildings, including the **Royal Presidio Chapel,** built in 1794, and the **Larkin House,** home to the US consul to Mexico during the 1840s. Use the visitors center brochure to walk the path unguided or join a free tour led by state-park guides. *(☎831-649-7118. Tour times and starting locations vary; call for details.)*

☕ NIGHTLIFE

Monterey knows how to cut loose at night, but some areas of the peninsula quiet down early. The main action is downtown along Alvarado St.; there are also a few Lighthouse Ave. bars. Those under 21 have few options.

Mucky Duck British Pub, 479 Alvarado St. (☎831-655-3031). Empty front window booths might fool you—many patrons are in the back beer garden, listening to music or staying warm around a coal-burning fire. Come early to avoid waits. Live music, karaoke, or DJ from around 9pm; some live music during the day. Open daily noon-2am. AmEx/MC/V.

The Hippodrome, 321D Alvarado St. (☎831-646-9244; www.hippclub.com), on the 2nd fl., at Del Monte Ave. Strobe lights and smoke machines throb like teenage hormones. 14 bars and 4 dance floors with different DJs. Pool tables and a smoking deck. Nightly drink specials. Male and female burlesque M 9:30pm. Live music Th-Sa. No hats, tennis shoes, or beach flip-flops. Cover M $7, F-Sa $5. Open M and Th-Su 9pm-1:45am. AmEx/D/MC/V.

◤ OUTDOORS

There are several bike paths in the area. The best is the **Monterey Peninsula Recreation Trail,** which follows the coast for approximately 20 mi. from Castroville to Asilomar St. in Pacific Grove. Bikers can then continue through Pacific Grove to Pebble Beach along the famous 17-Mile Drive. Sea kayaking above kelp forests and among otters can be a heady experience. Companies on Fisherman's Wharf offer critter-spotting boat trips around Monterey Bay. The best time to go is during gray whale migration season (Nov.-Mar.), but the trips are hit or miss year-round.

   Chris's Fishing Trips, 48 Fisherman's Wharf (☎831-375-5951; www.chrissfishing.com). Has offered daily whale-watching tours and fishing boat charters since the 1940s. 2-3hr. whale-watching tours May-Nov. 11am, 2pm. $25, children $20. 2hr. gray whale migration tours Dec.-Apr. $22. Boat charters for tuna, salmon, rock cod, halibut, sea bass and others also available. Open daily 4am-5pm.

   Monterey Bay Kayaks, 693 Del Monte Ave. (☎831-373-5357 or 800-649-5357; www.montereybaykayaks.com). Provides rentals and tours. Call for lesson info. Rentals $30 per person; includes gear, wetsuit, and instruction. 3hr. natural history guided tour $50-60. Open M-Th and Su 9am-7pm, F-Sa 9am-8pm.

◥ DETOUR
SAN JUAN BAUTISTA

Take **Route 1 North** to **Route 156 East.**

A historic mission town founded in 1797, San Juan Bautista has retained the tranquility of a bygone era by adopting slow-growth policies and by rejecting chain stores. **San Juan Bautista Mission** was the largest of the missions built in the 18th century to bring Catholicism to the "savage natives." The area around the town square—the mission, cemetery, garden, hotel, town hall, and stable—has been preserved in a historical park, and the buildings function like museums, although the mission still holds daily mass. At the end of the green lies a portion of **El Camino Real** ("the royal road"), the path that connected the 21 missions from San Diego to San Francisco, each a day's journey on horseback from the next. On the first Saturday of every month, San Juan Bautista hosts a **Living History Celebration** with displays of spinning, weaving, candle-making, and dancing. Pick up an events calendar at the mission or around town for other festivals. (☎831-623-2127. Mass in English M-F noon, Sa 5pm, Su 8:30, 10am, noon; in Spanish Su noon. $4, under 3 free, ages 4-12 $3.)

◤ THE ROAD TO CASTROVILLE: 18 MI.
Take **Route 1 North** toward Castroville.

CASTROVILLE   ☎831
Though it's not worth more than a quick stop, Castroville distinguishes itself as "the artichoke center of the world" and hosts the **Castroville Artichoke Festival** in May. For a taste, head to the **Giant Artichoke Restaurant ❶,** 11261 Merritt St., which is easy to spot with its enormous statue of an artichoke outside. A small order of deep-fried artichoke hearts runs $5.30. The produce store next door sells exceptionally fresh local fruit. (☎831-633-3501. Open daily 6am-9pm. AmEx/MC/V.)

◤ THE ROAD TO SANTA CRUZ: 28 MI.
Continue on **Route 1 North** toward Santa Cruz. Cruise past Watsonville, a chain-store center where the only sight of interest is the **Sunset State Beach ❶,** 201 Sunset Beach Rd. Wind through eucalyptus-lined roads and end up by a stunning beach. Take the San Andreas Rd. exit and turn right onto Sunset Beach Rd. (☎831-763-7063. 90 sites with fire rings. Food lockers, picnic tables, and coin-operated showers. Reserve 3 months in advance for staying in summer. Sites $25. Day use $6. Cash only.)

SANTA CRUZ   ☎831
One of the few places where the 1960s catch phrase "do your own thing" still applies, Santa Cruz embraces sculpted surfers, aging hippies,

free-thinking students, and same-sex couples. The atmosphere here is fun-loving but far from hedonistic, intellectual but nowhere near stuffy. Friendly and unpretentious, Santa Cruz offers a mix of Southern California's surf culture and Northern California's laid-back vibe. Pacific Ave. teems with independent bookstores, cool bars, trendy cafes, and pricey boutiques. Be careful about visiting on Saturday or Sunday, since the town's population virtually doubles on summer weekends, clogging area highways as daytrippers make their way to and from the Bay Area.

VITAL STATS

Population: 55,717

Tourist Offices: Santa Cruz County Conference and Visitor Council, 1211 Ocean St. (☎831-425-1234 or 800-833-3494; www.santacruz.org). Publishes the free *Santa Cruz County Traveler's Guide.* Open M-Sa 9am-5pm, Su 10am-4pm. **Downtown Info Center,** 1126 Pacific Ave. (☎831-459-9486). Open daily; hours vary.

Library and Internet Access: Central Library, 224 Church St. (☎831-420-5730). $3 per hr. Open M-Th 10am-8pm, F-Sa 10am-5pm, Su 1-5pm.

Post Office: 850 Front St. (☎831-426-0144). Open M-F 9am-5pm. **Postal Code:** 95060.

✴ ORIENTATION

Santa Cruz is on the northern tip of Monterey Bay, 65 mi. south of San Francisco. Through west Santa Cruz, **Route 1** becomes **Mission Street.** The **University of California at Santa Cruz (UCSC)** stretches inland from Mission St. Southeast of Mission St. lie the waterfront and the downtown. By the ocean, **Beach Street** runs roughly east-west. The narrow **San Lorenzo River** runs north-south, dividing the Boardwalk scene from the quiet residences of the affluent. **Pacific Avenue** is the main street downtown. Along with **Cedar Street,** Pacific Ave. carves out a nightlife niche accessible from the beach motels. Resident-traffic-only zones, one-way streets, and dead ends can make Santa Cruz frustrating to navigate.

🏠 ACCOMMODATIONS

Santa Cruz gets jam-packed during the summer, especially on weekends. Room rates sky-rocket; reservations are always recommended. Surprisingly, the nicer motels tend to have more reasonable summer weekend rates. Reservations for state campgrounds are available through ReserveAmerica (☎800-444-7275) and should be made three months in advance.

▨ Big Basin Redwoods State Park, 21600 Big Basin Way (☎831-338-8860), in Boulder Creek, 23 mi. from Santa Cruz. Go north on Rte. 9 to Rte. 236 through Boulder Creek. Big Basin offers the best camping in the region, with 80 mi. of cool, breezy trails, including the 2-day, 30 mi. Skyline to the Sea Trail (trailhead parking $6), and 145 campsites with showers. Reservations required. Reservation fee $5. Sites $25, backcountry $10. Tent cabins $65. Day use $6. ❶

▨ Carmelita Cottage Santa Cruz Hostel (HI-AYH), 321 Main St. (☎831-423-8304), 2 blocks from the beach. A 40-bed Victorian house centrally located in a quiet neighborhood. Linen and towels included. Overnight parking free; day permits $1. July-Aug. 3-night max. stay. Reception 8-11am and 5-8pm. Lockout 11am-5pm. Strict curfew 11pm. Reservations recommended, but no refunds after 48hr. prior to reservation date. Dorms $28, members $25, ages 12-17 $14, ages 4-11 $10, under 4 free. MC/V. ❶

Santa Cruz Beach Inn, 600 Riverside Ave. (☎831-458-9660), off Laurel St. Close to the Boardwalk. Rooms are upscale but surprisingly budget-friendly. Outdoor pool and 2 hot tubs. All rooms have patio or balcony. Continental breakfast and Wi-Fi included. Rooms from $90. AmEx/D/MC/V. ❹

Capri Motel, 337 Riverside Ave. (☎831-426-4611). This little motel is the cheapest option in town, located right near the action. Within walking distance of the Boardwalk, wharf, and downtown. Pool, Wi-Fi, and free parking. Rooms from $40. ❷

Manresa Uplands State Beach Park, 205 Manresa Rd. (☎831-761-1795), in La Selva Beach, 13 mi. south of Santa Cruz. Take Rte. 1 and exit at San Andreas Rd. Veer right and follow San Andreas Rd. for 4 mi., then turn right on Sand Dollar Rd. Located in farm country, away from the hustle and bustle of Santa Cruz. Walk-in tent sites $25. Day use $6. Cash only. ❶

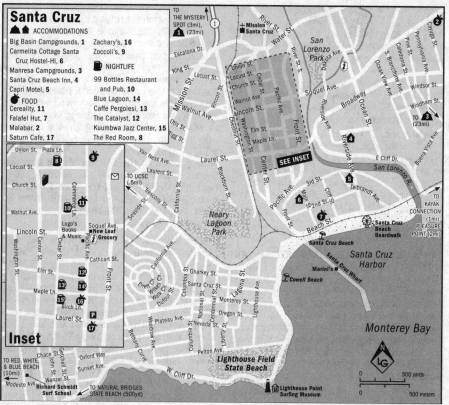

Santa Cruz

▲▲ **ACCOMMODATIONS**

Big Basin Campgrounds, **1**
Carmelita Cottage Santa
  Cruz Hostel-HI, **6**
Manresa Campgrounds, **3**
Santa Cruz Beach Inn, **4**
Capri Motel, **5**

🍴 **FOOD**
Cereality, **11**
Falafel Hut, **7**
Malabar, **2**
Saturn Cafe, **17**

Zachary's, **16**
Zoccoli's, **9**

🍺 **NIGHTLIFE**
99 Bottles Restaurant
  and Pub, **10**
Blue Lagoon, **14**
Caffe Pergolesi, **13**
The Catalyst, **12**
Kuumbwa Jazz Center, **15**
The Red Room, **8**

Inset

🍴 FOOD

Santa Cruz offers an astounding number of budget eateries. The restaurant community goes out of its way to embrace vegans—tofu can be substituted for just about anything. **New Leaf Grocery,** 1134 Pacific Ave., offers healthful snacks and fresh produce in Santa Cruz's first ozone-friendly store—the store has a refrigeration system that is free of all ozone-depleting gases. (☎831-425-1793. Open daily 9am-9pm.)

🍴 **Zoccoli's,** 1534 Pacific Ave. (☎831-423-1711). This phenomenal deli uses only fresh ingredients in its sandwiches. Daily pasta specials ($5.50-8) come with salad and bread. Sandwiches $5-6.50. Open M-Sa 9am-6pm, Su 10am-6pm. MC/V. ●

🍴 **Cereality,** 1315 Pacific Ave. (☎831-425-1997; www.cereality.com). This cereal bar and cafe provides the ingredients for you to create that perfect bowl of cereal, from brand-name cold cereals to fruit toppings and oatmeal. Try the Chocolate Banana (oatmeal with Nutella, chocolate chips, bananas, and strawberries; $4). This classy, comfortable budding franchise also offers smoothies, parfaits, and coffee drinks. Free Wi-Fi. Open M-Th 6am-10pm, F 6am-11pm, Sa 7am-11pm, Su 7am-10pm. AmEx/D/MC/V. ●

Zachary's, 819 Pacific Ave. (☎831-427-0646). Savory potatoes, fresh bread, and enormous omelets will give you a reason to laze about for the rest of the day. Basic breakfast (2 eggs, oatmeal-molasses toast, and hash browns) for

$5.75. Eat at the counter to avoid the wait. Open Tu-Su 7am-2:30pm. MC/V. ❶

Saturn Cafe, 145 Laurel St. (☎831-429-8505; www.saturncafe.com), at Pacific Ave. At this planetary-punk-themed restaurant, the hard-working waitstaff serves a 100% vegetarian menu. Try the Saturn Spuds (organic eggs and home fries scrambled with mushrooms, onions, and bell peppers; $7.50). The Spartacus Salad ($9.25) is also delicious. Open daily 10am-3am. MC/V. ❷

Falafel Hut, 309 Beach St. (☎831-423-0567), across the street from the Boardwalk. A good place for a quick late-night snack, the Hut serves Middle Eastern and American dishes. The owners pride themselves on their falafel sandwiches ($5), but the chicken ($6.25) is hard to beat. Open daily 11am-11pm. MC/V. ❷

🄶 SIGHTS

SANTA CRUZ BEACH BOARDWALK AND WHARF. Transport yourself to the 1950s of the movies by strolling the Santa Cruz Boardwalk in the evening. The Giant Dipper roller coaster, built in 1924, has been featured in the films *Sudden Impact* and *Dangerous Minds*. From the 1911 carousel to the arcade games and minigolf at Neptune's Kingdom, the Boardwalk offers good old-fashioned fun for all ages. *(www.beachboardwalk.com. Minigolf $5. Boardwalk open from June to Labor Day daily. Tickets $0.75, 60 tickets $40; all-day pass $30.)* Wander onto the Santa Cruz Wharf to explore the many souvenir shops, rental booths, and restaurants. *(At the convergence of Beach St. and W. Cliff Dr. ☎831-423-7258.)* Enjoy the spectacular view while snacking on the signature saltwater taffy at **Marini's,** Municipal Wharf #55A. A mecca of all things sweet, Marini's also sells carmel apples ($4.25) and ice cream ($3-4.50) at two other locations, one downtown on Pacific Ave. and the original 1915 location on the Boardwalk. *(☎831-425-7341. Open M-Th and Su 10am-9:30pm, F-Sa 10am-10pm.)*

UNIVERSITY OF CALIFORNIA AT SANTA CRUZ. This sprawling, 2000-acre campus lies within a mile of downtown. Governor Ronald Reagan's plan to make UCSC a "riot-proof campus" (free of a central point where radicals could inflame a crowd) resulted in the university's decentralized and beautiful for-

ested layout. Although the campus appears to be tranquil amid rolling hills and redwood groves, UCSC is famous (or infamous) for its leftist politics and conspicuous drug culture. If driving, make sure you have a parking permit on weekdays, available at the kiosk inside the main campus entrance, the police station, or the parking office. *(Parking office on the right, past the entrance kiosk. ☎831-459-3799; www.ucsc.edu. Permit $5.)* Be sure to visit the university's gorgeous **Arboretum,** which contains over 45 colorful kinds of flowers. *(1156 High St. ☎831-427-2998. Open daily 9am-5pm. Free.)* UCSC is also home to the **Seymour Marine Discovery Center,** which overlooks the Monterey Bay National Marine Sanctuary. Take a tour that includes an on-site laboratory. *(100 Shaffer Rd. ☎831-459-3800. Open Tu-Sa 10am-5pm, Su noon-5pm. $6, students and ages 4-16 $4.)*

OTHER SIGHTS. The **Mission Santa Cruz** was founded by Father Serra's successor, Father Fermin Francisco de Lasuen, in 1791. Its peaceful garden is a quiet place to relax for an afternoon. *(130 Emmett St., off Mission St. ☎831-426-5686. Open Tu-Sa 10am-4pm, Su 10am-2pm. Donation suggested.)* Two miles into the Santa Cruz Mountains lies a warped cabin where the trees grow twisted: the **Mystery Spot.** Tour guides perform magic tricks in this house of illusions where you'll struggle to find your center of balance. Why don't the laws of nature apply to the Mystery Spot? It's a mystery, duh. *(Head north on Branciforte Dr., then make a left onto Mystery Spot Rd. ☎831-423-8897. Open daily from Memorial Day to Labor Day 9am-7pm; from Labor Day to Memorial Day 9am-5pm. $5.)*

🅝 NIGHTLIFE

There are comprehensive weekly events listings in the free *Good Times* and *Metro Santa Cruz* as well as in the *Spotlight* section of Friday's *Sentinel* (all available at cafes and bookstores). The Boardwalk bandstand offers free summer concerts, usually by oldies bands on Friday evenings. The Santa Cruz Parks and Recreation Department publishes info in the free *Summer Activity Guide.* Pacific Ave. is home to a host of bustling coffee shops and laid-back bars.

🄼 **99 Bottles of Beer on the Wall Restaurant and Pub,** 110 Walnut Ave. (☎831-459-9999). This modest but lively bar in the heart of downtown offers standard bar meals and 99 different types of beer. Check the wall to see who has tried them all. Karaoke M. Quiz night W. Happy hour M-F 4-6pm, Tu-W 10pm-1:30am, Th 11:30am-10pm with $1 off pints. Open M-Th 11:30am-1:30am, F-Sa 11:30am-2am, Su 11:30am-midnight. Kitchen open until midnight. AmEx/D/MC/V.

Caffe Pergolesi, 418A Cedar St. (☎831-426-1775). A relaxed coffeehouse and bar with small rooms and a patio for both reading and socializing. Three types of hot chocolate. Open M-Th and Su 7am-11pm, F-Sa 7am-midnight. Cash only.

The Red Restaurant and Lounge, 1003 Cedar St. (☎831-425-1913). You'll be seeing red everywhere you look as you mingle on plush couches. Downstairs, The Red Room is its rock and roll counterpart. Jazz band Su. Happy hour 5-7pm. Open daily 4pm-2am. AmEx/MC/V.

Blue Lagoon, 923 Pacific Ave. (☎831-423-7117). This mega-popular club has won all kinds of awards and is known as the city's best dance club. Bar in front, 2 pool tables, and dancing everywhere. Stronger-than-the-bouncer drinks $3-4. Live music Su. Cover $2-5. Open daily 4pm-2am. Cash only.

The Catalyst, 1011 Pacific Ave. (☎831-423-1338). The town's primary music and dance venue draws national, college, and local bands. Pool and arcade games upstairs, pizza and bar downstairs. Cover and age restrictions vary with show. Upstairs bar area is strictly 21+. Shows daily $5-30. Open M-Th and Su noon-last customer, F-Sa noon-2am. MC/V.

Kuumbwa Jazz Center, 320 Cedar St. (☎831-427-2227; www.kuumbwajazz.org, tickets www.ticketweb.com). Known throughout the region for great jazz and innovative off-night programs. Big-name bands M. All ages welcome. Tickets $10-35. Shows M 7, 9pm, Th 7pm. MC/V.

BEACHES

For information on Santa Cruz's many beach facilities, head to the **California Parks and Recreation Department,** 600 Ocean St. (☎831-429-2850. Open M-F 8am-5pm.) The **Santa Cruz Beach** (officially named Cowell Beach) is broad, reasonably clean, and packed with volleyball players. If you're seeking solitude, you'll have to venture farther afield. Away from the main

drag, beach access points line Rte. 1. Railroad tracks, farmlands, and dune vegetation make several of these access points difficult to reach, but the beaches are correspondingly less crowded. Around the point at the end of W. Cliff Dr. is **Natural Bridges State Beach.** Only one natural bridge remains, but the park offers a pristine beach and awe-inspiring tide pools. In November and December, thousands of stunning monarch butterflies swarm along the beach and blanket the nearby groves with their orange hues. (☎831-423-4609. Open daily 8am-sunset. Free.)

The best vantage points for watching surfers are along W. Cliff Dr. To learn more about the activity, stop in at **Steamer's Lane,** the deep water off the point where surfers have flocked since Hawaiian "Duke" Kahanamoku kick-started California's surf culture here 100 years ago. Surfers also gather at the more remote "Hook" along Pleasure Point, north of Santa Cruz in Live Oak. **Lighthouse Field State Beach,** on W. Cliff Dr., a surfing haven, is home to Lighthouse Point and the **Santa Cruz Surfing Museum,** housed in the **Mark Abbott Memorial Lighthouse,** which displays surfing artifacts from 100 years of Santa Cruz wave riding. (☎831-420-6289. Open M and W-Su noon-4pm. Free.) For surfing lessons, contact **Richard Schmidt Surf School,** 236 San Jose Ave., or ask for him at the beach. Locals boast that Schmidt can get anyone up and riding. (☎831-423-0928; www.richardschmidt.com. 1hr. private lesson $80-100; 2hr. group lesson $80. Lessons include equipment.)

KAYAKING

Outdoor sports enthusiasts will find ample activities in Santa Cruz. Parasailing and other pricey pastimes are popular on the wharf, but kayaking is a more accessible option. You must provide ACA certification for a closed-deck kayak unless you go to **Elkhorn Slough,** a beautiful estuary that is safe for inexperienced kayakers. **Kayak Connection,** 413 Lake Ave., offers tours of Elkhorn Slough (9:30am, 1:30pm; $40) and the Santa Cruz Harbor ($30-45) and rents ocean kayaks at decent rates. (☎831-479-1121. $35 per 4hr. $45 per day. Paddle, life jacket, brief instruction, and wetsuit included. Open M-F 10am-5pm, Sa-Su 9am-6pm.) Beware of rental agencies that don't include instruction sessions; closed-deck ocean kayaking can be dangerous.

◄ DETOUR
AÑO NUEVO STATE RESERVE
Find it 20 mi. north of Santa Cruz on **Route 1.**

This wildlife reserve has several hiking trails that offer views of Año Nuevo Island, the site of an abandoned lighthouse now taken over by birds, seals, and sea lions. Free hiking permits are available at the ranger station by the entrance and at the visitors center (though seal-viewing permits are only issued until 3:30pm). From mid-December to late March, the reserve is the mating place of 15 ft., 4500 lb. elephant seals. Thousands of fat seals crowd the shore where, like frat boys looking to score, the males fight each other for dominance over a herd of females. Before mid-August, you can still see the last of the "molters" and the young who have yet to find their sea legs. Don't get too close—if the seals don't get you, the cops might; the law requires that visitors stay 25 ft. away. (☎831-879-0227. No pets. Open daily 8am-sunset. Visitors center open daily 10am-3:30pm.)

⚐ THE ROAD TO PESCADERO: 14 MI.
Follow **Route 1 North** toward Pescadero.

PESCADERO ☎650
Twenty-seven miles north of Santa Cruz, turn off Rte. 1 at the lighthouse to reach the **Pigeon Point Hostel ❶.** This secluded white house right on the water has 41 dorm beds and four private rooms. (☎650-879-0633; www.pigeonpointhostel.org. Hot tub $7 for 30min. Linen and Wi-Fi included. Lights out 11pm. Lockout 10am-3:30pm. Dorms $22-27, under 11 $10.)

The town of Pescadero is a one-horse town, but **Duarte's ❷,** is the place to go for awesome green chili soup ($7.50) or homemade pie. The simple wood restaurant and tavern has been run by the Duarte family since 1894. Sound like a local by asking for a cup of "half and half." (202 Stage Rd. ☎650-879-0464. Open daily 7am-9pm. AmEx/MC/V.)

⚐ THE ROAD TO HALF MOON BAY: 14 MI.
Follow **Route 1 North.** Turn right on **Main Street.**

HALF MOON BAY ☎650
The sleepy town of Half Moon Bay is a lovely place to stop for lunch. Browse the specialty shops and galleries along historic Main St. or stop in at the **Chamber of Commerce and Visitors' Bureau,** 235 Main St., for ideas. (Open M-F 9am-5pm.) Relax in the gorgeous garden before resting your head at **San Benito House ❺,** 356 Main St., built in 1905. This B&B owned by Greg Regan offers breakfast in bed at your request. (☎650-726-3425; www.sanbenitohouse.com. Rooms $90-175.)Dig into a huge, fresh sandwich like the curried chicken and apple ($9.25) at **Moonside Bakery and Cafe ❷,** 604 Main St. Indulge in a fruit tart, cake, or pastry for dessert. (☎650-726-9070. Open daily 6:30am-5pm.) If it's an Internet fix you need to satisfy, visit **Coastside Net,** 345 Main St. (☎650-712-5900; www.coastside.net. $10 per hr. Wi-Fi $6 per day. Open 8am-5pm.)

⚐ THE ROAD TO SAN JOSE: 57 MI.
Take **Route 1 North** to **Route 92 East.** Follow Rte. 92 E. to **I-280 South,** toward San Jose. Take the **Route 87/Guadalupe Parkway** exit on the left.

SAN JOSE ☎408
Founded in 1777 in a bucolic valley of fruit and walnut orchards, San Jose was California's first civilian settlement. In 1939, the first computer company, Hewlett-Packard, had its modest beginnings here in Dave Packard's garage. By the early 1970s, many of San Jose's orchards had been replaced by offices, and the moniker "Silicon Valley" began to take hold. In recent years, San Jose residents have broadened their one-track focus on the high-tech to include other industries. Museums, restaurants, hotels, and vineyards have all sprouted up as part of an effort to expand San Jose beyond the world of microchips and barefoot office techies.

▦ ORIENTATION

San Jose is centered on the convention-hosting malls and plazas near the intersection of east-west **San Carlos Street** and north-south **Market Street.** Numbered streets run north-south and alternate one-way directions. The **Transit Mall,** the center of San Jose's transit system, runs along First and Second St. in the downtown area. **The Alameda** lies at the east end of **Santa Clara Street** and leads to Santa Clara University and Santa Clara Mission.

VITAL STATS

Population: 945,000

Tourist Office: Convention and Visitors Bureau, 150 W. San Carlos St. (☎408-792-4173; www.sanjose.org), in the San Jose McEnerny Convention Center. Open M-F 9am-5pm.

Library and Internet Access: Martin Luther King, Jr., Public Library (☎408-808-2000; www.sjlibrary.org), at the intersection of E. San Fernando and 4th St. Open M-W 8am-8pm, Th-Sa 9am-6pm, Su 1-5pm.

Post Office: 105 N. 1st St. (☎408-292-0487). Open M-F 8:30am-5pm. **Postal Code:** 95110.

ACCOMMODATIONS

County parks with campgrounds surround the city, as do chain motels.

Sanborn Park Hostel (HI-AYH), 15808 Sanborn Rd. (☎408-741-0166), in Sanborn County Park. This hostel features clean rooms and 39 beds for travelers in search of peace and quiet. Volleyball, badminton, and croquet. Only open F-Sa nights. Linen included. Reception 5-10:30pm. Check-out 9am. Curfew 11pm. Dorms $17, members $14, under 18 $6. Cash only. ●

Santa Clara Inn, 2188 The Alameda (☎408-244-8860), just before Santa Clara University. Rooms with cable TV, kitchens, and complimentary breakfast. Free Wi-Fi. Rooms from $55. AmEx/D/MC/V. ●

Mount Madonna County Park, on Pole Line Rd. (☎408-842-2341, reservations 355-2201), off Hecker Pass Hwy. 117 sites in a beautiful setting, available by reservation or on a first come, first served basis. Tent sites $15; RV sites $25. ●

Sanborn County Park, 16055 Sanborn Rd. (☎408-867-9959, reservations 355-2201). From Rte. 17 S., take Rte. 9 to Big Basin Way, and turn left onto Sanborn Rd. This densely forested park features miles of horse and hiking trails. Open from late Mar. to mid-Oct. for camping. Tent sites $12; RV sites $25. D/MC/V. ●

FOOD

Familiar fast-food franchises and pizzerias surround San Jose State University. More

international cheap eats lie along **South First Street** and near **San Pedro Square,** at St. John and San Pedro St.

Bill's, 1115 Willow St. (☎408-294-1125), at Lincoln Ave. Friendly waitstaff serves hearty omelets ($6-9.45) and burgers ($8-9) on a cozy patio. Start the day off sweetly with the bread pudding french toast ($9), topped with fried banana. Open daily 7am-3pm. AmEx/D/MC/V. ●

The Mini Gourmet, 599 S. Bascom Ave. (☎408-275-8973.) Voted "best after-hours coffee shop." Huge pizza omelette with Italian sausage, meat sauce, and jack cheese $9.60. Half a sandwich and soup $6. Dinner entrees $11.50-16.50. Open 24hr. MC/V. ●

Sonoma Chicken Coop, 31 N. Main St. (☎408-287-4083), at San Pedro Sq. Quality food at inexpensive prices. Standard Italian-American fare with a few quirks like butterscotch bread pudding ($6.50) and surf-and-turf pizza ($11). Appetizers $4-11. Open M-Th and Su 11am-9pm, F-Sa 11am-10pm. AmEx/MC/V. ●

Morocco's Restaurant, 86 N. Market St. (☎408-998-1509). This fusion restaurant puts a California spin on traditional Moroccan dishes. Create your own *tagine,* a slowly braised stew of meats or vegetables ($13-19). Sandwiches $7-8. Open daily 11am-11pm.

SIGHTS

TECH MUSEUM OF INNOVATION. Curious kids and their parents love the hands-on, cutting-edge science exhibits and IMAX theater at this tourist-savvy attraction. Grow your own jellyfish DNA and watch it glow. The museum is underwritten by high-tech firms and housed in a sleek geometric building. (*201 S. Market St. ☎408-795-6224; www.thetech.org. Open Apr.-Sept. daily 10am-5pm; Oct.-Mar. Tu-Su 10am-5pm. $8; includes 1 IMAX ticket. Additional IMAX $4.*)

WINCHESTER MYSTERY HOUSE. This enormous Victorian house is the creation of Sarah Winchester, of the family famous for its rifles. After the death of her six-week-old daughter, followed by that of her husband, Sarah visited a Boston occultist for insight into her bad fortune. She was convinced that, in order to appease the spirits of all those killed by Winchester rifles, she needed to move west and begin never-ending construction on her new home. Sarah communed with the spirits nightly in her séance room, then attempted to confuse them by ordering the building of a bizarre maze of rooms including a staircase to the ceiling and a door to nowhere. Work on the mansion continued 24 hr. a day for 38 years, and today you can get lost in the 160-room result. (*525 S. Winchester Blvd., near the intersection of I-880 and I-280. ☎408-247-2101. Open June-Aug. daily 9am-7pm; from Sept. to mid-Oct. M-Th and Su 9am-5pm, F-Sa 9am-7pm; from mid-Oct. to May daily 9am-5pm. 65min. Mansion Tour $24, ages 6-12 $18. Behind the Scenes Tour of stables, basement, and grounds $21, ages 10-12 $20; under 9 not allowed. 2½hr. Estate Tour that includes Mansion and Behind the Scenes $29, ages 10-12 $26.*)

ROSICRUCIAN EGYPTIAN MUSEUM AND PLANETARIUM. Rising out of the suburbs, this grand structure houses the largest exhibit of Egyptian artifacts in the western US. The museum has a collection of over 4000 ancient pieces that includes a walk-in tomb and spooky animal mummies. This collection belongs to the ancient and mystical Rosicrucian Order, whose past members include Amenhotep IV, Pythagoras, Sir Francis Bacon, René Descartes, Benjamin Franklin, and Sir Isaac Newton. (*1342 Naglee Ave. ☎408-947-3635; www.egyptianmuseum.org. Open M-F 10am-5pm, Sa-Su 11am-6pm. $9, students $7, ages 5-10 $5.*)

MISSION SANTA CLARA DE ASIS AND SANTA CLARA UNIVERSITY. The first California mission to honor a woman as its patron saint, Mission Santa Clara de Asis was established on the Guadalupe River in 1777 and moved to its present site in 1828. (*Mass M-F noon, Su 10am.*) Santa Clara University, built around the mission, was established in 1851, making it California's oldest university. Subsequent restorations have refitted the structures to match the beauty of the surrounding rose gardens and 180-year-old olive trees. (*500 El Camino Real, 5 mi. northwest of downtown San Jose off The Alameda. ☎408-554-4000; www.scu.edu.*)

GREAT AMERICA. Paramount's Great America theme park is a jungle of roller coasters, log rides, and fiendish contraptions designed to spin you, flip you, drop you, and generally separate you from your stomach. (*☎408-988-*

1776; www.pgathrills.com. Off US 101 at Great America Pkwy. in Santa Clara, 8 mi. northwest of downtown San Jose. Open June-Aug. M-F and Su 10am-8pm, Sa 10am-9pm; Sept.-Oct. and Mar.-May Sa-Su 10am-6pm. $45, ages 3-6 $35, under 3 free. Parking $10.*)

RAGING WATERS. The area's best collection of waterslides is at Paramount's Raging Waters. Just don't expect to be the only one seeking a soaking. (*Off US 101 at the Tully Rd. exit, about 5 mi. east of downtown San Jose. ☎408-238-9900; www.rwsplash.com. Open June-Aug. M-F 10am-6pm, Sa-Su 10am-7pm; Sept. Sa-Su 10am-5pm. $30, under 48 in. $22; after 3pm $19/14.*)

NIGHTLIFE

Fahrenheit Ultra Lounge, 99 E. San Fernando St. (☎408-998-9998; www.fultralounge.com). This plush lounge is the destination of choice for young professionals looking to unwind. The college crowd takes over Th night. Karaoke Tu. Jazz W. DJs Th-Sa. Open Tu-F 11:30am-2:30pm and 5pm-2am, Sa 5pm-2am. AmEx/MC/V.

Voodoo Lounge, 14 S. 2nd St. (☎408-286-8636; www.voodooloungesj.com). A popular local spot with drinks like the Voodoo Child ($6) and Black Magic Margarita ($6). This club also hosts art exhibits and Mario Kart racing tournaments. Open M, W, F-Sa 10pm-2am, Th 9:30pm-10am.

THE ROAD TO PALO ALTO: 17 MI.

Take **Route 87 North** to **US 101 North.**

PALO ALTO   ☎650

Dominated by the beautiful 8000-acre Stanford University campus, Palo Alto is an upscale university town populated by affluent homeowners and elite college students. Stanford's perfectly groomed grounds, sparkling lake, and Spanish mission-style buildings have a manufactured quality that suits the university's speedy rise to international acclaim. The city that Stanford calls home is equally manicured, with a tidy downtown strip of restaurants, bookstores, and boutiques. Its nightlife caters to students and suburbanites, while weekday happy hours help singles unwind.

VITAL STATS

Population: 60,000

Tourist Offices: Palo Alto Chamber of Commerce, 122 Hamilton Ave. (☎650-324-3121), between Hude and Alta St. Open M-F 9am-5pm. **Stanford University Information Booth** (☎650-723-2560), across from Hoover Tower in Memorial Auditorium. Open M-F 8am-5pm, Sa-Su 9am-5pm.

Library and Internet Access: Palo Alto Main Library, 1213 Newell Rd. (☎650-329-2436). Open M-W 10am-9pm, Th noon-9pm, F-Sa 10am-6pm, Su 1-5pm.

Post Office: 2085 E. Bayshore Rd. (☎650-321-1423). Open M-F 8:30am-5pm. **Postal Code:** 94303.

✴ ORIENTATION

Residential Palo Alto is not easily distinguished from the Stanford campus. **Stanford University** spreads out from the west end of **University Avenue,** the main thoroughfare off **US 101.** Despite its name, University Ave. belongs much more to the town than to the college. Cars coming off US 101 onto University Ave. pass very briefly through East Palo Alto and into the university's side of town. **El Camino Real (Route 82)** abuts University Ave. and runs northwest-southeast through town. From there, University Ave. turns into **Palm Drive,** which leads to Stanford's campus.

▐ ACCOMMODATIONS

Motels are plentiful along El Camino Real, but rates can be steep. In general, rooms are cheaper farther away from Stanford and to the north. Many Palo Alto motels cater to business travelers and are actually busier on weekdays than on weekends.

Hidden Villa Ranch Hostel (HI-AYH), 26870 Moody Rd. (☎650-949-8648), about 10 mi. southwest of Palo Alto in the Los Altos Hills. The first hostel on the Pacific Coast (opened in 1937), it functions as a working ranch and farm in a wilderness preserve. Recent renovations have completely rebuilt the dorms and extended the living room, kitchen, and dining room. Reception 8am-noon and 4-9:30pm. Reservations required for weekends and groups. Open Sept.-May. Dorms $24, children $10.50; private cabins $41-58. ❶

Stanford Inn, 115 El Camino Real (☎650-325-1428), in Menlo Park. Offers something a little ritzier. Full of character and charm, this yellow building dates back to 1937, when it was built as an upscale apartment complex. Printing, faxing, copying, scanning, and laminating. Free Wi-Fi. Singles from $65; doubles from $70. AmEx/D/MC/V. ❸

▤ FOOD

Dining in Palo Alto is centered on posh restaurants downtown. Those who are watching their wallets should stay on University Ave.

Café Borron, 1010 El Camino Real (☎650-327-0830), in Menlo Park. A bustling, brasserie-style cafe that spills onto a large patio and serves freshly baked bread, sinful *gâteaux* ($2-4), coffee drinks, Italian soda, wine ($5-6), and beer (pints $4). Check the chalkboard for specials or choose from a wide range of salads, sandwiches, and quiches for $4-10. Open M-Th 7am-10pm, F 7am-11pm, Sa 8am-11pm, Su 8am-4pm. MC/V. ❷

Mango Caribbean Restaurant and Bar, 435 Hamilton Ave. (☎650-324-9443). Offers reggae music and Caribbean cuisine, like seriously spicy Aruban-style "jerk joints" ($6.50) and tropical smoothies ($4). Veggie options are available. Delicious bread pudding $6. Live steel drums Sa night. Open M-W and Su 11am-10pm, Th-Sa 11am-11pm. AmEx/D/MC/V. ❷

Oasis Burgers and Pizza, 241 El Camino Real (☎650-326-8896; www.theoasisbeergarden. com), in Menlo Park. Known as "The O." Burgers ($6.50-8) and pizza ($14.50-24) are served amid tables and walls crudely carved by past patrons or on long picnic tables outside. Open daily 11am-2am. AmEx/D/MC/V. ❷

◉ SIGHTS

Palo Alto's main tourist attraction, **Stanford University,** was founded in 1885 by Jane and Leland Stanford to honor their son, who died of typhoid fever. The Stanfords loved Spanish colonial mission architecture and collaborated with Frederick Law Olmsted, designer of New York City's Central Park, to create a red-tiled campus of uncompromising beauty. The school has produced such eminent conservatives as Chief Justice William Rehnquist and Herbert Hoover, and the campus has been called "a hotbed of social rest."

MAIN QUADRANGLE. The oldest part of campus is the Main Quadrangle, the location of most undergraduate classes. The walkways are dotted with diamond-shaped, gold-numbered stone tiles that mark the locations of time capsules put together by each year's graduating class. (*On Serra St. ☎650-723-2560. Tours depart from the information booth in Memorial Auditorium daily 11am, 3:15pm. Free.*)

MEMORIAL CHURCH. Just south of the Main Quad, at Escondido Mall and Duena, Memorial Church is a non-denominational gold shrine with stained-glass windows and glittering mosaic walls like those of an Eastern Orthodox church. (*☎650-723-3469. Open M-F 8am-5pm. Tours F 2pm. Free.*)

HOOVER TOWER. The Hoover Tower's observation deck has views of campus, the East Bay, and San Francisco. (*☎650-723-2053. Open daily 10am-4:30pm; closed during finals and academic breaks. $2, under 13 and seniors $1.*)

IRIS AND B. GERALD CANTOR VISUAL ARTS CENTER. The museum displays an eclectic collection of painting and sculpture. (*328 Lomita Dr., at Museum Way off Palm Dr. ☎650-723-4177. Open W and F-Su 11am-5pm, Th 11am-8pm. Free.*)

RODIN SCULPTURE GARDEN. The extensive Rodin Sculpture Garden contains a stunning bronze cast of Rodin's 1880-1900 *Gates of Hell*, among other larger figures. Enjoy a picnic lunch here while contemplating the next life. (*At Museum Way and Lomita Dr. ☎650-723-4177. Tours M-F 2pm, Sa 11:30am, Su 3pm. Free.*)

▣ NIGHTLIFE

Though Palo Alto can't compete with San Francisco's wild nightlife, it still has a couple of hot spots and bars perfect for sitting back and having a few beers. There's a fiesta every day in the vibrant, super-popular **Nola**, 535 Ramona St. Colorful strings of lights and patio windows open onto a cool courtyard dining area. The late-night New Orleans-themed menu offers barbecue shrimp ($10), pulled-pork quesadilla ($9.50), and steak-and-crab gumbo ($3-8) to accompany mixed drinks. (*☎650-328-2722. Happy hour daily 4-6pm. Open M-F 11:30am-2am, Sa-Su 5:30pm-2am. Kitchen open M-Th until 10pm, F-Sa until 11pm, Su until 9pm. AmEx/MC/V.*)

◪ THE ROAD TO SAN FRANCISCO: 34 MI. Follow **US 101 North** to downtown San Francisco.

SAN FRANCISCO ☎415

If California is a state of mind, then San Francisco is euphoria. Welcome to the city that will take you to new highs, leaving your mind spinning, your tastebuds tingling, and your calves aching. The dazzling views, daunting hills, one-of-a-kind neighborhoods, and laid-back, friendly people fascinate visitors. Though smaller than most "big" cities, the city manages to pack an incredible amount of vitality into its 47 sq. mi., from its thriving art communities and bustling shops to the pulsing beats in some of the country's hippest nightclubs and bars.

PAGE TURN. See p. 477 in **National Road** for complete coverage of San Francisco.

◪ THE ROAD TO MARIN HEADLANDS: 10 MI. From San Francisco, follow **US 101 North** across the Golden Gate Bridge. Take the first exit (Alexander Ave.) off 101, veer right off the ramp onto **Alexander Avenue** and then left on **Bunker Road** through a one-lane tunnel. For the most scenic drive and best view of the city, take your first left onto **McCullough Road** and turn right along **Conzelman Road**. For the visitors center, from Bunker Rd., take a left onto **Field Road**.

MARIN HEADLANDS ☎415

The fog-shrouded hills just west of the Golden Gate Bridge constitute the Marin Headlands. Formerly a military installation charged with defending the San Francisco harbor, the Headlands are dotted with machine-gun nests, missile sites, and soldiers' quarters dating from the Spanish-American War to the 1950s. These windswept ridges, precipitous cliffs, and hidden sandy beaches offer superb hiking and biking minutes from downtown. For more info, contact the **Marin Headlands Visitors Center**, Building 948, at Bunker and Field Rd., Fort Barry. The center is also a museum and a store with artifacts. The visitors center hosts many events and activities through-the year, including bird-watching, lighthouse tours, and all kinds of nature walks. (☎415-331-1540. Open daily 9:30am-4:30pm.)

For instant gratification, drive up to any of the lookout spots and pose for your own post-card-perfect shot of the Golden Gate Bridge and the city skyline. One of the best short hikes is to the lighthouse at Point Bonita, a prime spot for seeing sunbathing California sea lions in summer and migrating gray whales in the cooler months. The lighthouse at the end of the point doesn't seem up to guarding the whole San Francisco Bay, but it has stood vigilant since 1855; in fact, its original glass lens is still in operation. At the end of a narrow, knife-like ridge lined with purple wildflowers, the lighthouse is reachable by a short tunnel through the rock and a miniature suspension bridge that will quicken your heart rate. Even when the lighthouse is closed, the short walk provides gorgeous views on sunny days. The visitors center hosts **Full Moon Walks** to the lighthouse along a half-mile trail every full moon 7:30-10pm. Make reservations, as the trips are limited to 40 people. (No dogs or bikes through tunnel. Open M and Sa-Su 12:30-3:30pm. Guided walks M and Sa-Su 12:30pm. Free.) **Battery Spencer,** on Conzelman Rd. immediately west of US 101, offers one of the best views of the city skyline and the Golden Gate Bridge, especially around sunset on a (rare) clear day. Tourists are known to wait for hours to catch a fogless shot of the Golden Gate Bridge.

To get to the **Marin Headlands Hostel (HI) ❶,** follow the signs from the visitors center. This charmingly secluded hostel offers a kitchen, large common room with multiple inviting couches, piano, fireplace, and picnic tables as well as a basement game room with pool, foosball, and ping-pong tables. There are eight private rooms and 76 dorm beds. (☎415-331-2777; www.norcalhostels.org. Soap $0.50. Dorms $21, children $10; private rooms $60. AmEx/D/MC/V.) Accessible by car, **Kirby Cove ❶,** off Conzelman Rd. west of the Golden Gate Bridge, consists of four campsites in a grove of cypress and eucalyptus trees on the shore, with fire rings, food lockers, and pit toilets. (☎800-365-2267. Bring your own water. No pets. 3-day max. stay. Open Apr.-Nov. Sites $25. D/MC/V.)

⚐ **THE ROAD TO SAUSALITO: 7 MI.**
Sausalito is a few miles north of the Golden Gate Bridge on **US 101.**

SAUSALITO   ☎415

Originally a fishing center full of bars and bordellos, the city at Marin's extreme southeastern tip has long since traded its sea-dog days for retail boutiques and overpriced seafood restaurants. The palm trees and 14 ft. elephant statues of Plaza de Vina del Mar Park look out over a wonderful view of San Francisco Bay, making for a sunny, seaside tourist distraction. The sheer number and variety of quality art galleries in the small town make it worth checking out in spite of its touristy feel. Half a mile north of the town center is the **Bay Model and Marinship Museum,** 2100 Bridgeway, a massive working model of San Francisco Bay. Built in the 1950s to test proposals to dam the bay, the water-filled model recreates tides and currents in great detail. (☎415-332-3871. Open Tu-Sa 9am-4pm. Free.) Those tired of Rice-A-Roni should venture to the **Venice Gourmet Delicatessen ❶,** 625 Bridgeway, which serves sandwiches ($5.50-7.50) and side dishes ($2-5) in a Mediterranean-style marketplace; cross the street and eat by the water. (☎415-332-3544; www.venicegourment.com. Open daily 9am-6pm. MC/V.)

> ♟ **WALDO WISDOM.** While staying on a houseboat in Sausalito, Otis Redding wrote his greatest hit, "The Dock on the Bay."

⌦ **DETOUR**
🌲**MUIR WOODS**

Muir Woods is 5 mi. west of US 101 on **Route 1.**

At the center of **Mount Tamalpais State Park** is Muir Woods National Monument, a 560-acre stand of old coastal redwoods. William and Elizabeth Thacher Kent bought this land in 1905 in order to protect it and requested that it be named for conservationist John Muir. These massive, centuries-old trees are shrouded in silence. The level, paved trails along the canyon floor are lined with wood fences, but a hike up the canyon's sides will soon put you far from the tourists, face to

CHABLIS, CHAMPAGNE & CHARDONNAY

NAPA VALLEY, CALIFORNIA

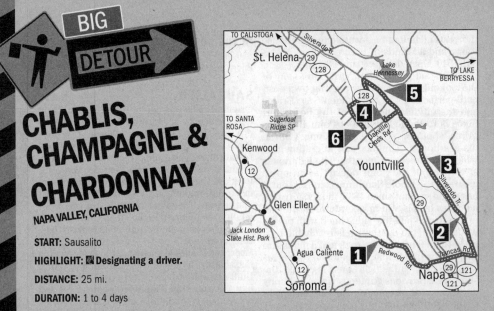

START: Sausalito

HIGHLIGHT: 🎨 Designating a driver.

DISTANCE: 25 mi.

DURATION: 1 to 4 days

From Sausalito, follow US-101 N. for 15 mi. Take Exit 460A to Rte. 37 E. After 7.5 mi., bear left onto Rte. 121 N. After 15 mi., turn left onto Rte. 121 N./Rte. 29 N. Follow Rte. 29 N.

1. HESS COLLECTION. Donald M. Hess is said to have turned water into wine; he came to the Mt. Veeder summit looking to expand his Swiss sparkling mineral water company, but instead he bought this 310-acre vineyard, located at 4411 Redwood Rd. This ivy-covered, grand estate with a lily-pad pond was built in 1903 but has a surprisingly chic interior. The open floor plan of light wood and stone includes Hess's art collection on the second and third floors. Take a free self-guided audio tour of the gallery, which includes modern photography, sculpture, and paintings by international artists like Rolf Iseli, Theodoros Stamos, and Armando. The king of the Hess Collection, though, is The Lion, a red wine that has been "the credo" of the Hess family for nine generations. (☎707-255-8584; www.hesscollection.com. Choose 4 of the current releases to taste for $10. Cheese and wine pairing with local artisan cheeses $35. Reservations required. Free showing of "A Year in the Vineyard" every 30min. Open daily 10am-5:30pm.)
Take Rte. 29 N. to Redwood Road.

2. BLACK STALLION WINERY. This 32-acre estate, at 4089 Silverado Trail, was an equestrian center until the mid-90s. Two brothers from Minnesota purchased the property in 2005, switching their business from wine importing to wine making. Visitors sample wines inside the cavernous tasting room with a huge, circular bar made of dark Douglas fir or outside at tables surrounded by trellises. This winery's claim to fame is its red wine, Bucephalus, named for the horse Alexander the Great rode into battle—not coincidentally, a black stallion. (☎888-BSW-NAPA; www.blackstallionwinery.com. Choose 4 of 3 whites, a *rosé*, and 3 reds to taste for $10. Open daily 10am-5pm.)
Take Rte. 29 N. through Yountville and St. Helena. Turn right on Conn Valley Rd. and left on Silverado Trail.

3. STAG'S LEAP WINE CELLARS. Inside this cozy, yellow stucco building at 5766 Silverado Trail, two tasting tables are crowded in amid huge tanks of wine. Established in 1972 by Warren Winiarski, this vineyard is renowned for its Cabernet Sauvignons. The Winiarski family

focuses on a balance of "fire and water": the fire of volcanic rock and the water of alluvial soils that contribute to the flavors of the grapes grown here. (☎866-422-7523; www.cask23.com. 4 pre-selected wines from the collection to taste for $15. Open daily 10am-4:30pm.)
Take Rte. 29 N. Turn right on Yountville Cross Rd. and right on Silverado Trail.

4. PLUMPJACK WINERY. Drive down a long, winding driveway to the secluded cottage that is PlumpJack's tasting room. PlumpJack, 620 Oakville Cross Rd., took its name from Queen Elizabeth's nickname for Falstaff, a chubby character in Shakespeare's *Henry IV* known for his wit and irreverence. If you hate uncorking pesky wine bottles, thank PlumpJack, the first luxury producer to introduce the screw cap. Surrounded by 50 acres of Cabernet Sauvignon grapevines, this winery offers panoramic views of the Mayacamas and Vaca Mountains. Enjoy a tasting on the patio or at the wood, copper, and brass bar in the casual interior. (☎707-945-1220; www.plumpjack.com. 4 pre-selected wines to taste for $10. Open daily 10am-4pm.)
Take Rte. 29 N. Turn right on Oakville Cross Rd.

5. MUMM CUVÉE NAPA. Mumm, 8445 Silverado Trail, was recently named "Best of Napa Valley" for its tasting room, an airy gallery with views of the vineyard and mountains beyond. Relax on the patio in a wicker chair under a yellow umbrella. Wander through the white-washed gift shop to explore the photography galleries in back. Founded in 1987, this winery has the relaxed feel of a farmhouse. Its goal is to create the finest sparkling wines in the country, using the traditional French *méthode champenoise*. (☎707-942-3434; www.mummnapa.com. Flights—slightly fuller glasses of wine—$14-25 for 3 wines. 45min. tours 10am-3pm.)
Take Rte. 29 N. Turn right on Oakville Cross Rd. and left on Silverado Trail.

6. ROBERT MONDAVI WINERY. In 1966, Robert Mondavi designed this sand-colored stucco building, 7801 St. Helena Hwy., with a thatched roof to resemble a mission. It was the first major winery built in Napa Valley after the 1933 repeal of Prohibition. Situated around an expansive green lawn, this winery has the open feel of a museum. Come for the Summer Festival in July for music from the likes of Pat Benatar, David Benoit, and UB40 while enjoying a wine tasting at intermission that costs $55-90. (☎888-766-6328; www. robert-mondaviwinery.com. Guided 45min. lesson about how to read labels and how to smell, taste, and describe wine Tu-Su 10am; $15. 75min. To Kalon Tour includes a tasting of 3 top wines; $25. Open daily 10am-5pm.)
To make this detour more than just a daytrip, stay overnight in the pleasant city of Napa. Stop in at the helpful **Conference and Visitors Bureau,** 1310 Napa Town Center (☎707-226-5813) for ideas about accommodations or just stay at **The Chardonnay Lodge ❹,** 2640 Jefferson St., an unbelievable value. Friendly proprietress Karen designed each room with a distinct inspiration, from the romantic Champagne room to the cozy Tuscany room, and has paired each with a personalized poem. (☎707-224-0789; www.chardonnaylodge.net. Complimentary water and snacks. Free Wi-Fi. Rooms $75-170.)

PACIFIC COAST

face with nature. There are 6 mi. of trails, including unpaved routes out of the canyon that connect with trails in the nearby Mt. Tamalpais State Park. (☎415-388-7368. Open daily in summer 8am-5pm; in winter 9am-6pm. $3, under 15 free.) Avoid the fee by starting your hike 2 mi. from the **Pantoll Ranger Station.** It's also worth a detour to check out the **Muir Beach Overlook.**

⚐ THE ROAD TO STINSON BEACH: 10 MI.
Take **US 101 North,** switching to **Route 1 North.** Three miles after the turnoff onto Rte. 1, you can choose to go to Muir Woods or Mt. Tamalpais.

STINSON BEACH   ☎415

A younger, rowdier, and better-looking surfer crowd is attracted to Stinson Beach, although cold and windy conditions often leave them languishing on dry land. The Bard visits Stinson Beach from July to October during **Shakespeare at Stinson.** (☎415-868-1115; www.shakespeareatstinson.org. Tickets $25, under 17 $18.) Bring a jacket, as the town chills down after the sun sets. Turn west at the only stop sign in town to reach the **Parkside Cafe ❸,** 43 Arenal Ave., where a light interior and garden patio complement an American menu that edges toward the gourmet. Pick your favorite from the wine list to accompany your Parkside burger and apple-wood-smoked chicken salad. (☎415-868-1272; www.parksidecafe. com. Mexican night M. Spaghetti night $7.50 Tu. 2 soups and 2 salads $7.50 W. Live jazz Sa. Open M-F 7:30am-4pm and 5-9:30pm, Sa-Su 8am-4pm and 5-9:30pm. MC/V.)

⚐ THE ROAD TO BOLINAS: 7 MI.
Continue along **Route 1 North** until you reach the exit for Olema Bolinas Rd. Travel south to reach the city.

BOLINAS   ☎415

Bolinas, a tiny colony of hippies, artists, and writers, is perhaps the mellowest place on earth—it's certainly one of the hardest to find. For years, locals have tried to discourage tourist traffic by tearing down any and all signs marking the Bolinas-Olema road. Press coverage of the "sign war" won the people of Bolinas exactly the publicity they wanted to avoid, but for now, at least, the town remains

unspoiled in ways that Sausalito is not—and they intend to keep it that way. But who needs signs anyway? Generations of locals walk and bike through town, mostly ignoring the tourist presence that creeps in on weekends. Restaurants and shops open and close at whim, which exemplifies the town's laid-back attitude. At the end of Olema-Bolinas Rd. is the **Bolinas Gallery,** 52 Wharf Rd. Colorful paintings are displayed throughout the gallery, even hanging from the ceiling. (☎415-868-0782. Open Sa-Su 1-5pm.)

Turn right, and you can see the convergence of the lagoon and the ocean. Take the next-to-last right off Olema-Bolinas Rd. to reach **The Grand Hotel ❷,** 15 Brighton Ave., which has two cozy rooms that share a bathroom and kitchen above a secondhand shop. (☎415-868-1757. Rooms $60. MC/V.) To graze while you gaze at the locals, try Northern California cuisine at **Coast Cafe ❷,** 46 Wharf Rd., open for breakfast, lunch, and dinner, but don't tell them we sent you. Try "The Unusual" (2 eggs, potatoes, biscuits, and gravy; $8) if you're feeling feisty or stick to "The Usual" (2 eggs, potatoes, and meat; $8.50) if you fear change. (☎415-868-2298. Open Tu-Th 11:30am-3pm and 5-8pm, F 11:30-3pm and 5-9pm, Sa-Su 7:30am-3pm and 5-9pm. AmEx/D/MC/V.)

⚐ THE ROAD TO POINT REYES: 12 MI.
Follow **Route 1 North** for about eleven miles. Turn left onto **Bear Valley Road,** which leads to the Point Reyes Visitor Center. To reach Point Reyes Station, continue north on Route 1.

POINT REYES   ☎415

A near island surrounded by nearly 100 mi. of isolated coastline, the Point Reyes National Seashore is a wilderness of pine forests, chaparral ridges, and grassy flatlands. Five million years ago, this outcropping was a suburb of LA, but it hitched a ride on the submerged Pacific Plate and has been creeping northward along the San Andreas Fault ever since. In summer, colorful wildflowers attract crowds of gawking tourists, but with hundreds of miles of amazing trails, it's quite possible to gawk alone.

PACIFIC COAST

VITAL STATS

Population: 350

Tourist Office: Point Reyes National Seashore Headquarters (also referred to as Bear Valley Visitor Center; ☎415-464-5100; www.nps.gov/pore), on Bear Valley Rd. Open M-F 9am-5pm, Sa-Su 8am-5pm.

Library and Internet Access: Point Reyes Station Library, 11431 Rte. 1 (☎415-663-8375). Open M 10am-6pm, Tu and Th 2-9pm, F-Sa 10am-2pm.

Post Office: 11260 Rte. 1 (☎415-663-1761). Open M-F 8am-4:30pm. **Postal Code:** 94950.

ACCOMMODATIONS

Point Reyes Hostel (☎415-663-8811; www.norcalhostels.org), just off Limatour Rd., 2 mi. from Limatour Beach. Miles from civilization, this excellent hostel provides shelter in the wilderness. The surrounding landscape is still scarred from a major forest fire that scorched the region in 1995. Linen included. Towels $1. Check-in 4:30-9:30pm. Check-out 10am. Dorms $20, under 17 $10. MC/V. ❶

Sky Camp (☎415-663-8054). 12 sites with views of Drakes Bay on the western side of Mt. Wittenberg, a 1.5mi. walk from Sky Trailhead on Limantour Rd. **Wildcat Camp** has 7 sites with ocean views 6 mi. from the Coast Trail. Picnic tables, charcoal grills, pit toilets, and food lockers. Bring water. Sites $15-30. AmEx/D/MC/V. ❶

FOOD

Bovine Bakery, 11315 Rte. 1 (☎415-663-9420). Proffers caffeinated drinks and vegan-friendly gooey treats like the morning bun ($2.75). Sandwiches are $6.50 when fresh (Tu and F) and 30% off other days. Open M-F 6:30am-5pm, Sa-Su 7am-5pm. Cash only. ❷

The Station House Café, 11180 Rte. 1 (☎415-663-1515). Serves classic American food. The heavenly bread pudding costs $7. Come on Th for pub night, with $3 beer and $5 wine, or on the 3rd Su of the month for foot-stomping bluegrass at 5pm. Open M-Tu, Th, Su 8am-9pm, F-Sa 8am-10pm. AmEx/MC/V. ❸

OUTDOORS

Before you do anything, make sure you've picked up a map from the **Bear Valley Visitor Center.** The center has extensive exhibits about the environment and animals living in the area and offers field seminars like "Mono Lake: A Natural History Tour" and "Butterfly Watching." Three types of terrain are distinguishable on the hiking trails of Point Reyes: the pasture lands of Pierce Point and the Estero, the chaparral and California laurel to the east and west of Limantour Rd., and forests and meadowlands in the southeast. The Earthquake Trail is a paved half-mile walk along the infamous San Andreas Fault, which starts right at Bear Valley. Lovely **Limantour Beach** sits at the end of Limantour Rd., 8 mi. west of the park headquarters. Nearby Estero de Limantour is a great place for birdwatching. Both Limantour and Point Reyes Beaches have high, grassy dunes and long stretches of sand, but strong ocean currents along the point make swimming very dangerous. Swimming is safest at **Hearts Desire Beach,** north of the visitors center on sheltered Tomales Bay at **Tomales Bay State Park.** (No dogs. Open daily 8am-8pm. Day use $6 per vehicle.) To reach the dramatic **Point Reyes Lighthouse** at the very tip of the point, follow Sir Francis Drake Blvd. to its end (20 mi. from the visitors center) and head right along the stairway to Sea Lion Overlook. From January to April, migrating gray whales can be spotted from the overlook. (☎415-669-1534. Open M and Th-Su 10am-4:30pm.) To hike from the Coast Trail to **Bass Lake Swimming Hole,** take the unmarked Olema-Bolinas Rd. 2 mi. north of Stinson. Take a left at the fork and then a right onto Mesa Rd., which will curve around for several miles past the bird observatory to the Palomarin Trailhead. The hike will take you along the Pacific into the rocky cliffs, through trees, and finally to a secret swimming spot. Bring a picnic and take a dip. Two miles south of the Russian River, turn west for **Goat Rock Beach** where, from late May to early September, you can see newborn baby seals; harbor seals and elephant seals are currently in a silent war over the territory.

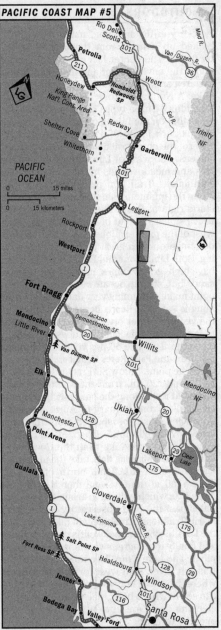

PACIFIC COAST MAP #5

THE ROAD TO VALLEY FORD: 32 MI.
Follow **Route 1/Shoreline Highway.**

VALLEY FORD ☎707

The only reason to stop in Valley Ford is to go to ◪**Dinucci's Italian Dinners** ❹, 14485 Valley Ford Rd., an old-school, family-oriented, and unpretentious restaurant with brown-checkered cloths on the table. Don't expect any delicate olive oil on the table here. Hearty five-course meals of spaghetti, lasagna, or ravioli come with antipasto, fabulous minestrone, a starch (baked potato, rice pilaf, or french fries), and salad, all from $14.75. Top it off with cheesecake or chocolate mousse for $4. (☎707-876-3260. Live music some Sa nights. Open M and Th-Sa 4-9pm, Su noon-8pm. AmEx/D/MC/V.)

THE ROAD TO BODEGA BAY: 9 MI.
Follow **Route 1/Shoreline Highway** to Bodega Bay.

BODEGA BAY ☎707

The small town of Bodega Bay shows its seafaring roots in the incredibly fresh salmon and crab served at oceanside restaurants. Both the towns of Bodega Bay and Bodega, 1 mi. away, were featured in Alfred Hitchcock's 1963 film *The Birds*. The **Bodega Bay Visitors Center**, 850 Rte. 1, has info on the North Coast. (☎707-875-3866; www.bodegabay.com. Open M-Th and Sa 9am-5pm, F 9am-6pm, Su 10am-5pm.) On the Sonoma coast, west of Bodega Bay, the **Bodega Head Loop** is a short coastal hike with pristine beach and ocean views. To reach the 1 mi. trail from the town, turn left on E. Shore Rd., turn west on Bay Flat Rd., and continue around the bay past Spud Point Marina to Bodega Head parking for the trailhead. **Sonoma Coast State Beach** begins just north of Bodega Bay off Rte. 1. Unfortunately, unpredictable currents make the water unsafe (see **Sleeper Waves**, p. 961) for swimming. The 5000 acres of land offer 16 mi. of beautiful beach, spectacular views, and places to picnic, hike, and camp. One popular coastal campground is **Bodega Dunes** ❶, with 99 campsites. (☎707-875-3483. Hot showers. Sites $25. Cash only.) Another very popular spot is **Wright's Beach** ❶, with 27 sites. (☎707-875-3483. Sites $25. Cash only.) Call ReserveAmerica (☎800-444-

7275) for reservations. If the campsites are full, the clean rooms at **Bodega Harbor Inn ❸**, 1345 Bodega Ave., off Rte. 1 in Bodega Bay, are your cheapest bet. (☎707-875-3594; www.bodegaharborinn.com. Breakfast included. Rooms $80-135. MC/V.)

⛰ THE ROAD TO JENNER: 11 MI.
From Bodega, follow **Route 1 North** and then turn right onto **Old State Highway.**

JENNER   ☎707

Heading north from Bodega Bay, Rte. 1 hits Jenner at the mouth of the Russian River. **Goat Rock Beach,** with its astounding waves and coast, is the site of a famous harbor seal rookery. **Reef Campground ❶,** 10 mi. north of Jenner, is part of **Fort Ross State Historic Park** and provides 20 sites in a wooded gulch, a 5min. walk from a rocky secluded beach. (☎707-847-3286. No showers. Sites $15. Cash only.) **Salt Point State Park,** 20 mi. north of Jenner, is a 6000-acre park for the hiker or horseback rider with an inland campsite surrounded by woods, **Woodside Creek ❶,** and a coastal campground, **Gerstle Cove ❶,** on a bluff among scattered pines overlooking the sea. Gerstle Cove is a good spot for mushroom gathering (5 lb. per day) and abalone diving. (☎707-847-3221, reservations 800-444-7275. Drinking water and toilets. Open for day use sunrise-sunset. Sites $25. Cash only.)

⛰ THE ROAD TO GUALALA: 38 MI.
From Jenner, follow **Route 1** for 37 mi. and then turn right onto **Old State Highway.**

GUALALA   ☎707

Stop in at **Bones Roadhouse ❸,** 38920 S. Hwy. 1, where you can dine on barbecued oysters amid roadtripping memorabilia. The food has a Southwestern flair. The Big Johnson (kielbasa with mustard; $9) will satisfy a craving for something simple. (☎707-884-1188. Open daily 11am-9pm. MC/V.)

⛰ THE ROAD TO POINT ARENA: 14 MI.
Turn right onto **Route 1/Shoreline Highway.**

POINT ARENA   ☎707

Point Arena's central attraction is the **Point Arena Lighthouse,** 2 mi. north of town. The 115 ft. structure is the tallest lighthouse in the country accessible to the public. The current lighthouse was built after the San Francisco earthquake of 1906 demolished the 1870 original. Although no longer in commission, it contains a Fresnel lens, an intricate array of prisms, and a magnifying glass worth $3.5 million—an optician's paradise. The downstairs exhibit includes a whale-watching information room. (☎707-882-2777; www.pointarenalighthouse.com. Open daily 10am-3:30pm. $5, under 12 $1.) **CityArt,** 284 Main St., is a nonprofit community arts gallery in the former home of a teacher who murdered her lover. It shows changing exhibits of works by local artists and hosts a poetry reading the third Thursday of every month. (☎707-882-3616. Open Th-Su noon-4pm.) Surfers like swells at **the cove** (take the coastal access sign from Rte. 1), although there's not much to speak of in terms of beauty.

◪The Record ❷, 265 Main St., a cafe and natural gourmet market, is the best place to meet the town locals—mostly artists whose work decorates the walls. The chicken curry sandwich ($8) is particularly good. (☎707-882-3663. Sandwiches $4.50-10. Open M-Sa 7am-7pm, Su 8am-6pm. MC/V.) **Carlini's Cafe ❸,** 206 Main St., a cozy little diner full of regulars, serves breakfast all day. (☎707-882-2942. Omelets $9-12. Burgers $9. Open daily 7am-2pm.)

⛰ THE ROAD TO ELK: 19 MI.
Take **Route 1** toward Elk.

ELK   ☎707

Fans of Jack London should stop in Elk, where the famed author often stayed to write in a hotel room overlooking the ocean. The town is little more than a charming rest stop with a quaint inn and a few walking trails. Poor drainage, thin soil, and ocean winds have created an unusual bonsai garden 3 mi. south of Mendocino at the **Pygmy Forest** in **Van Damme State Park ❶.** (Sites $25. Day use $6. Cash only.) The forest, off Rte. 1 past the park, is free to hikers. Take the 3 mi. **Fern Canyon Trail** to see the bonsai trees.

🔺 THE ROAD TO MENDOCINO: 17 MI.
From **Route 1,** turn left onto **Little Lake Road.**

MENDOCINO ☎707

Teetering on bluffs over the ocean, isolated Mendocino is a charming coastal community of art galleries, craft shops, bakeries, and B&Bs. The town's weathered shingles, white picket fences, and clustered homes seem out of place on the West Coast; maybe that's why Mendocino was able to masquerade for years as the fictional Maine village of Cabot Cove in the TV series *Murder, She Wrote.*

VITAL STATS

Population: 1100

Tourist Office: Mendocino Headlands State Park Visitor Center, 735 Main St., at the Ford House. Open daily 11am-4pm.

Library and Internet Access: Regional Branch Library of Mendocino, 499 Laurel St. (☎707-964-2020), in Fort Bragg. Open Tu-W 11am-7:45pm, Th-F 11am-5:45pm, Sa 10am-4:45pm.

Post Office: 10500 Ford St. (☎707-937-5282). Open M-F 7:30am-4:30pm. **Postal Code:** 95460.

🔳 ORIENTATION

Mendocino sits on **Route 1,** right on the Pacific coast, 30 mi. west of US 101 and 12 mi. south of Fort Bragg. Once you're in Mendocino, exploring is best done on foot. All shops, restaurants and hotels are on **Main Street, Lansing Street,** and **Ukiah Street.**

🏠 ACCOMMODATIONS

Sweetwater Spa & Inn, 44840 Main St. (☎707-937-4076 or 800-300-4140). If you're arriving after 10pm, you can crash in the "late night" room, where you'll get free exclusive use of the hot tub and sauna all night. Check-in 3pm. Check-out 11am. Rooms from $70. MC/V. ❹

Medocino Hotel, 45080 Main St. (☎707-937-0511). Luxurious to say the least. Relax by the fireside in the sitting room, where newspapers and Wi-Fi are available. Rooms from $95. AmEx/MC/V. ❹

Jug Handle Creek Farm, (☎707-964-4630), 5 mi. north of Mendocino off Rte. 1, across the street from the Jug Handle State Reserve. A beautiful old house with 40 acres of gardens. 1 hr. of chores earns you a $5 discount per night. Reservations highly recommended in summer. Sites $12, students $10. Private rooms $35/28; cabins $40/33. ❷

🍴 FOOD

All of Mendocino's breads are freshly baked, all vegetables locally grown, all wheat unmilled, and almost all prices inflated.

Harvest at Mendosa's Market, 10501 Lansing St. (☎707-937-5879). A must before any picnic on the Headlands. Open daily 7:30am-10pm. ❶

Moody's Cafe, 10450 Lansing St. (☎707-937-4843). An organic coffee bar with a modern vibe. The cafe has free Wi-Fi, an adjoining Internet cafe ($6 per hr.), and tasty treats like spiced apple cider and cookies. Open daily 6am-8pm. D/MC/V. ❶

Tote Fête, 10450 Lansing St. (☎707-937-3383). Delicious takeout food. An asiago cheese, pesto, and artichoke heart sandwich ($6) on fresh bread hits the spot. Open M-F 8am-7pm, Sa 8am-8pm, Su 8am-6pm. MC/V. ❶

Lu's Kitchen, 45013 Ukiah St. (☎707-937-4939), west of Lansing St. A local favorite featuring leafy vegetarian cuisine. Students get a break here; ask for the Mendo student burrito for $5. Entrees $6-10. Open Apr.-Dec. W-Su 11:30am-5pm; closed rainy days. Cash or check only. ❷

Frankie's, 44951 Ukiah St. (☎707-937-2436). Free Wi-Fi and homemade ice cream ($3.50). Bizarre flavors like mushroom, make this little cottage popular. Open daily 11am-9pm. ❷

🔆 SIGHTS

🔳MENDOCINO HEADLANDS. Mendocino's greatest natural feature lies 900 ft. to its west, where the earth comes to a halt and falls off into the Pacific, forming the impressive coastline of the Mendocino Headlands. The windy quarter-mile stretch of land that separates the town from the rocky shore remains an undeveloped meadow of tall grass and wildflowers despite its obvious value as a site for multimillion-dollar vacation homes.

JUG HANDLE STATE PARK. The ecological staircase at Jug Handle State Park, 5 mi. north of town, is a terrace of five different ecosystems formed by a combination of erosion and tectonic uplift, with each ecosystem roughly 100,000 years older than the one below it.

ORR HOT SPRINGS. An abundance of hot springs in the Mendocino area proves once again that the region is a natural paradise. Orr Hot Springs is an hour's drive east of Mendocino. The sauna, steam room, and gardens make the world disappear at this clothing-optional resort. *(13201 Orr Springs Rd., in Ukiah, off US 101. ☎707-462-6277. 18+ or accompanied by an adult. Open daily 10am-10pm. $25.)*

⚐ THE ROAD TO FORT BRAGG: 10 MI.
Continue on **Route 1 North/Shoreline Highway** for 10 mi. Turn onto **East Laurel Street** to reach downtown.

FORT BRAGG ☎707

Fort Bragg is a little rougher around the edges than its genteel sibling Mendocino. The town's major industry, the lumber mill, was shut down in August 2002 and the town now relies on tourism as well as smaller fishing and logging operations.

VITAL STATS
Population: 6963
Tourist Office: Fort-Bragg-Mendocino Coast Chamber of Commerce, 332 N. Main St. (☎707-961-6300). Open M-F 9am-5pm, Sa 9am-3pm.
Library and Internet Access: Regional Branch Library of Mendocino, 499 Laurel St. (☎707-964-2020). Open Tu and Th 10am-6pm, W noon-8pm, F-Sa 10am-5pm.
Post Office: 203 N. Franklin St. (☎800-275-8777). Open M-F 8:30am-5pm. **Postal Code:** 95437.

▟ ACCOMMODATIONS

Colombi Motel, 647 Oak St. (☎707-964-5773), 5 blocks east of Main St. Clean single and double units with cable TV, phones, and private bath; some units also have full kitchens. Free Wi-Fi. Check-out 11am. In summer singles $55-60; doubles $70-75. In winter singles $35-40; doubles $65-70. MC/V. ❷

MacKerricher State Park (☎707-937-58042), 2 mi. north of Fort Bragg. Excellent views of tidepool life, passing seals, sea lions, and migratory whales as well as 9 mi. of beaches and a murky lake for trout fishing. Around this lake is Lake Cleone Trail, an easy 1 mi. hike that features thick cypress trees and a pretty marsh. Access the trail from Cleone Camp or Surfwood Camp. Showers, bathrooms, and potable water. Reservations necessary in summer. Sites $25. Cash only. ❶

▤ FOOD

Eggheads, 326 Main St. (☎707-964-5005). Offers omelets ($8-13) stuffed with ingredients like cheese, bacon, and Dungeness crab, along with vegetarian specialties. Open M-Tu and Th-Su 7am-2pm. AmEx/MC/V. ❷

◉ SIGHTS

▨NORTH COAST BREWING COMPANY. The much-lauded North Coast Brewing Company makes 11 of its own brews on site. The excellent ▨**Old Rasputin** (9% alcohol) or Old Stock (a whopping 13% alcohol!) will get you tipsy faster than you can destabilize tsarist Russia—at the bar they'll only serve you two. The food is good too, with salads, seafood, burgers, and steak made with delicious all-natural Brandt Beef. Across the street, you can peek in at the enormous brewing vats behind the store or take a free tour. *(44 N. Main St. ☎707-964-3400. Open M-Th and Su noon-4pm and 5-9:30pm, F-Sa 5-10:30pm. Tours Sa 12:30pm.)*

TRIANGLE TATTOO AND MUSEUM. There are only six tattoo museums in the world, and Fort Bragg has one of them. Triangle Tattoo and Museum functions as a tattoo parlor and museum. Founded by the infamous Madame Chinchilla and Mr. G, the museum displays multicultural tattoo art from around the world. If you have an old tattoo, let them know; they document tattoos inked between 1920 and 1960. *(356B N. Main St., in downtown. ☎707-964-8814. Open daily noon-6pm.)*

SKUNK TRAIN. The California Western Railroad, also called the Skunk Train, has offered a jolly, child-friendly diversion since 1885. A steam engine, diesel locomotive, and vintage motorcar take turns running between

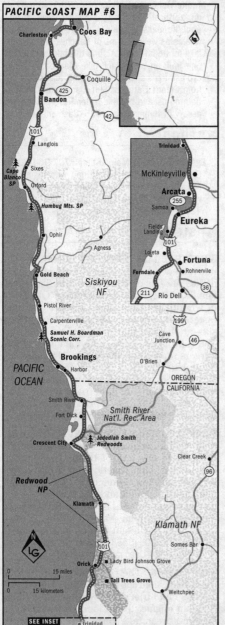

PACIFIC COAST MAP #6

Fort Bragg and Northspur. *(At Rte. 1 and Laurel St. ☎707-964-6371 or 800-45-SKUNK; www.skunktrain.com. 3hr. round-trip. Reservations recommended. Departs Fort Bragg daily 10am. $47, children $22.)*

🚗 **THE ROAD TO WESTPORT: 16 MI.**
Continue on **Route 1/Shoreline Highway.**

WESTPORT ☎707

Blink and you'll miss Westport, a town with only a general store (gas available) and a couple of inns. Despite its size, however, it still manages to display a lot of tie-dye. If this kind of seclusion appeals to you, try the lovely **De Haven Valley Farm ❺**, housed in an 1875 Victorian ranch house, 1 mi. north of town at 39247 Rte. 1 N. The owners plan on turning the old barn into an artists' cooperative. (☎707-961-1660; www.dehavenvalleyinn.com. Rooms $115-155.)

🚗 **THE ROAD TO GARBERVILLE: 51 MI.**
The **Pacific Coast Highway** north of Westport becomes exceedingly curvy and therefore slow. North of Rockport, it turns inland to Leggett; there is no possible way to continue along the coast here. Road-builders decided to circumvent the formidable King Range, abandoning this portion of land, the mysterious Lost Coast. Where **Route 1** turns inland and snakes around the Lost Coast, stay on smoothly paved, speedy **US 101** toward Garberville and the **Avenue of the Giants** for some of the most beautiful redwoods in the world.

GARBERVILLE ☎707

Garberville is a good jumping-off point for Humboldt State Park. The **Garberville-Redway Chamber of Commerce,** 728 Main St., in the Redwood Drive Center, offers information on local events and attractions. (☎707-923-2613. Open M-F 10am-5pm.) **Ray's Food Place,** on Redwood Dr., is the largest supermarket for miles. (☎707-923-2279. Open daily 7am-10pm.) Locals highly recommend **Calico's Cafe ❷**, on Redwood Dr. next to Sherwood Forest Motel, for its homemade pastas, salads, and burgers as well. Try the garlicky fettuccine gorgonzola ($10) made from scratch. (☎707-923-2253. Open M-Th and Su 11am-9pm, F-Sa 11am-10pm. Cash only.) If you don't feel like getting out of the car, swing by **Getti Up Drive Thru Coffee and Cafe ❶**, on Redwood Dr. at Sprowel Creek Dr. This little building in front of Ray's Food Place sells healthful smoothies ($3) and bagels ($2), too. (Open daily 6am-6pm.)

▓ THE ROAD TO HUMBOLDT REDWOODS STATE PARK: 35 MI.

Take **US 101 North** for 24 miles. Take the ramp to **South Fork/Honeydew**, then quickly make a left onto **Route 254/Redwood Highway/Avenue of the Giants.** Turn left onto **Mattole Road** and continue on Mattole Road to reach the park.

HUMBOLDT REDWOODS
STATE PARK   ☎707

About 24 mi. north of Garberville on US 101 in the Humboldt Redwoods State Park, the **Avenue of the Giants** (the actual name of the road) splits off the highway and winds its way through 31 mi. of redwoods, the world's largest living organisms above ground level. Garberville is the main town along the avenue and is connected to its smaller neighbor, Redway, by Redwood Dr., the main street in both towns. Moving north up the avenue, drivers encounter the tiny towns of Phillipsville, Miranda, Myers Flat, Weott, Redcrest, and Pepperwood. The **Humboldt Redwoods State Park Visitors Center,** just south of Weott on Ave. of the Giants, has a very knowledgeable staff who can direct you to the avenue's groves, facilities, and trails while providing safety tips on camping. (☎707-946-2263. Open Apr.-Oct. daily 9am-5pm; Oct.-Apr. Th-Su 10am-4pm.) Hiking, swimming, fishing, biking, and rafting opportunities abound in this rugged area. The **Bull Creek Trail North** is a moderate, 2hr. hike of 3.7 mi. in each direction. The trail starts at Lower Bull Creek Flats, 1 mi. west of Ave. of the Giants on Mattole Rd. In summer when bridges are installed, you can make a loop by returning via **Bull Creek Trail South.** The south section traverses the forest floor and creek bank, with stunning views of the Rockefeller Forest. For an easier hike, take a 30min. walk along the **Gould Grove Nature Trail,** which is only half a mile long. This trail, directly across the street from the visitors center, has signs leading to a self-guided tour.

Developed campsites offer coin-op showers, flush toilets, and fire rings. (☎707-946-2409. Sites $15.) The wildlife-filled **Albee Creek ❶,** on Mattole Rd. 5 mi. west of US 101, near Rockefeller Forest, has access to biking and hiking trails and is open year-round. (☎707-946-2409. Sites $20. Cash only.) **Hidden Springs ❶,** near Myers Flat, is situated on a hillside in a mixed forest and has 154 semi-secluded sites with hot showers. Few hiking trails start directly at the campground, but the South Fork of Eel River is a 10min. hike away. (☎707-943-3177. Open from mid-May to mid-Oct. Sites $20.)

▓ THE ROAD TO PETROLIA: 35 MI.

Continue on **Mattole Road** toward Petrolia.

[the hidden deal]

A HOLE-Y TREE

It's all very well to view the redwood forests from the road, but, if you're looking for a new angle, try marveling at these giants from the inside. Three trees turned tunnels remain of the many such attractions that cropped up during the tourist boom of the 1920s.

With a diameter of 21 ft., the Shrine Drive-Thru Tree, in Myers Flat on the Ave. of the Giants, is one of California's oldest tourist attractions. A natural tunnel was formed within the tree by fire generations ago. From inside, one catches an epic glimpse of the Pacific Coast's blue sky.

The 900-year-old Tour-Thru Tree, in Klamath, was hollowed out in 1976. After driving through this 9 ft. wide, 7 ft. high tunnel, have lunch at the picnic table nearby. Feel free to use the restroom—located inside the trunk of an 8 ft. diameter redwood.

The Chandelier Drive-Thru Tree in Leggett is 315 ft. tall, with a diameter of 21 ft. The 6 ft. wide by 9 ft. tall tunnel was created in the 1930s. It gets its name from the huge branches, themselves as wide as an average tree, that begin about 100 ft. up the trunk. Watch for deer grazing under the apple

PETROLIA
☎707

Named for being the site of the first oil drilling in California, Petrolia is now one of the few outposts for the region's farmers. Stop for a bite at the cozy and authentic **Petrolia General Store**. After Petrolia, the road passes by a stretch of the coast that is made all the sweeter by its remoteness. Chances are you'll be one of the few cars on this beautiful stretch, with only the wildflowers, dark sea rocks, and grazing cows for company.

⚲ THE ROAD TO FERNDALE: 30 MI.
From Petrolia, follow **Mattole Road (Route 211)** to reach downtown Ferndale.

FERNDALE
☎707

The northern end of the Lost Coast, Ferndale exemplifies small-town perfection. The amphitheater-like cemeteries near Russ Park on Ocean Ave. give a sense of the town's history and provide a breathtaking view of grazing dairy cattle. The entire village is designated a State Historical Landmark, and, as a result, there's not a franchise in sight. The atmosphere is honest enough to allow for an unattended jam shop, **Jackie Jett Jam,** with a box for payments. The jams ($6) are delicious, too! One of the area's oddest features, the annual **Arcata Kinetic Sculpture Race** (p. 962) ends at the studio of the event's founder, **Hobart Galleries,** 393 Main St., at Brown St. (☎707-786-9259; http://hobartgalleries.com. Open M-Sa 11am-5pm, Su noon-5pm. $1.) See kooky contraptions from past races in the form of a raccoon, dragon, bumblebee, flying saucer, and purple crayon at the **Ferndale Kinetic Sculpture Museum,** inside the **Arts and Cultural Center,** 580 Main St., at Shaw Ave. (☎707-786-9634; www.ferndaleartgallery.com. Open daily 10am-5pm.) The **Ferndale Museum,** on Shaw Ave., around the corner from Main St., is worth a stop for its exhibits on local history. (☎707-786-4466; www.ferndale-museum.org. Open June-Sept. Tu-Sa 11am-4pm, Su 1-4pm; Oct.-Dec. and Feb.-May. W-Sa 11am-4pm, Su 1-4pm. $1.) **Ferndale Repertory Theatre,** on Main St., hosts live productions and an art gallery showcasing local work. (☎707-786-5483; www.ferndale-rep.org. Performances F-Sa 2, 8pm. Tickets $12-15; seniors and students $10-15.)

Accommodations in Ferndale tend to be exorbitantly priced B&Bs, but if you've been saving for a splurge, this is the time. The ▨**Francis Creek Inn ❹**, 577 Main St., offers quaint rooms with lush carpets and lace curtains at the edge of downtown. (☎707-786-9611. Free Internet. Rooms $73-83. MC/V.) Another option is California's oldest B&B, the **Shaw House ❺**, 703 Main St. Built in 1854, the Carpenter Gothic Revival-style home has seven opulent rooms, a sit-down hot breakfast, and afternoon tea. (☎707-786-9958; www.shawhouse.com. Check-in 4-6pm. Check-out 11am. Rooms in summer from $135. MC/V.) ▨**The Wild Blackberry Cafe ❶**, 468 Main St., is worth a stop. Try the grilled goat cheese and caramelized onions ($6.25) and top it off with a sticky cinnamon roll for $3. (☎707-786-9440. Open daily 8am-4pm. MC/V.)

> **?** **DID YOU KNOW?** The films *The Majestic* and *Outbreak* were filmed in Ferndale.

⚲ THE ROAD TO EUREKA: 20 MI.
Follow **Route 211** out of Ferndale, then merge onto **US 101 North** and continue to Eureka.

EUREKA
☎707

Eureka was born out of the demands of mid-19th-century gold prospectors who wanted a more convenient alternative to the tedious overland route from Sacramento. Humboldt Bay provided a landing spot, and Eureka was founded as its port. Its rugged beginnings resulted in a town less appealing than its neighbors to the north, but Old Town in Eureka is regaining some of its historic attraction. Next to the harbor are quaint shops, restaurants, and art galleries in period Victorian-style buildings. Don't judge Eureka only by driving through; the city's perimeter may reek of fish matter, but the city center has a pleasant, old-time charm.

◢ ORIENTATION

Eureka straddles **US 101**, 7 mi. south of Arcata and 280 mi. north of San Francisco. To the south, US 101 is referred to as **Broadway.** In town, US 101 is called **Fourth Street** (heading south) and **Fifth Street** (heading north).

VITAL STATS
Population: 28,606
Tourist Office: Eureka/Humboldt Visitors Bureau, 1034 2nd St. (☎707-443-5097 or 800-346-3482). Open M-F 9am-5pm.
Library and Internet Access: Eureka Public Library, 202 S. Main St. (☎309-467-2922). Open M-Tu and Th 9am-8pm, W and F 9am-6pm.
Post Office: 337 W. Clark St. (☎707-442-1768), near Broadway St. Open M-F 8:30am-5pm, Sa noon-3pm. **Postal Code:** 95501.

⚑ ACCOMMODATIONS

Travelers will find many budget motels off US 101, but most are unappealing, so be selective. Walking alone at night, especially along Broadway, is not recommended.

Motel 6, 1934 Broadway (☎707-445-9631), south of town off US 101. Offers satellite TV and standard amenities. Singles $48-54; doubles $54-60. AmEx/D/MC/V. ❸

Big Lagoon County Park (☎707-445-7652), 20 mi. north of Eureka on US 101. 25 sites with flush toilets, drinking water, and a big lagoon for swimming, canoeing, and kayaking. Arrive early to beat the rush. No hookups. Sites $15. Cash only. ❶

🍴 FOOD

Old Town Coffee and Chocolates, 211 F St. (☎707-445-8600). Makes fresh fudge in house ($2.50 per ¼ lb.). In addition to all kinds of delicious confections, there are huge waffles with sweet toppings like bananas and pecans ($3.50-6.50) and hearty bagel sandwiches. Free Internet and Wi-Fi. Open M-W and Su 7am-9pm, Th-Sa 7am-11pm. ❶

Ramone's Bakery and Cafe, 209 E St. (☎707-445-2923), between 2nd and 3rd St. Specializes in homemade truffles, fresh-baked pies, and the ever-popular "Chocolate Sin"—a chocolate and liqueur torte. Sandwiches ($5.25-5.75), soups ($3-4), and salads ($3.75) are also available. Open M-Sa 7am-6pm, Su 8am-4pm. AmEx/D/MC/V. ❶

Los Bagels, 403 2nd St. (☎707-442-8525). Combines Mexican and Jewish baking traditions with tasty results. Open M and W-F 6:30am-5pm, Sa 7am-5pm, Su 7am-4pm. MC/V. ❶

Cafe Marina, 601 Startare Dr. (☎707-443-2233), off US 101 at the Samoa Bridge Exit. Take the Woodley Island exit north of town and across the bridge. Outdoor dining is the perfect way to enjoy fresh seafood, like the spicy blackened snapper ($19). The polished bar is a popular nightspot for local fishermen. Sandwiches $8-11. Entrees $13-25. Open daily in summer 7am-10pm; in winter 7am-9pm. AmEx/D/MC/V. ❹

🔘 SIGHTS

CARSON MANSION. Eureka is very proud of its Victorian homes, several of which are worth driving past. Many are now expensive B&Bs. If you do drive by, don't miss the much-photographed Carson Mansion, which belonged to a logger in the 1850s. *(143 M St.)*

FIRST STREET GALLERY. Art galleries, Eureka's main claim to fame, cluster downtown. Ask at the visitors center for information on specific exhibits around town. Check out First Street Gallery, which features cultural, artistic, and educational exhibits. Rotating shows go up every four to six weeks, so it's best to call ahead. *(422 1st St. ☎707-443-6363. Open Tu-Su noon-5pm. Free.)*

INK PEOPLE GALLERY. The gallery is a cultural development organization that offers exhibitions, workshops, poetry readings, and even free Internet. *(411 12th St. ☎707-442-8413. Open Tu-Sa 11am-4pm.)*

> **❗ SLEEPER WAVES.** Sleeper waves are overpowering waves that crash ashore and then forcefully pull back whatever or whomever they happen upon. Many beaches have posted warnings about such dangerous currents, and it is safest to simply stay out of treacherous waters. However, if a sleeper wave yanks you into the surf, do not swim toward shore. Doing so will only tire you out in a futile battle against the current. Instead, swim parallel to the beach until you're out of the wave's clutches.

◻ DETOUR

SAMOA

From **US 101**, take **Route 255** over the Samoa Bridge, turn left on **Samoa Boulevard**, and take the first left onto **Cookhouse Road**.

Built in 1893 to feed the lumberjacks of the mill company that owned the town, the **Samoa Cookhouse** ❸ opened to the public in the 60s. It remains a great place to roll up your sleeves and pack down some solid food. A set meal (no menu) is served for breakfast (7-11am; $10), lunch (11am-3:30pm; $11), and dinner (5-9pm; $14). People enjoy the likes of pot roast and baked ham on picnic tables. Seconds are served for free. The building also houses a logging exhibit. (☎707-442-1659; www.samoacookhouse.net. AmEx/D/MC/V.) The **dunes recreation area,** in Samoa off Rte. 255 (past the cookhouse and left at the Samoa Bridge, on the north end by the jetty), was once a thriving dune ecosystem. Now, the peninsula has beach access and dune hiking.

◩ THE ROAD TO ARCATA: 8 MI.

Follow **US 101 North** and take the **Route 255/Samora Boulevard** exit toward Arcata.

ARCATA   ☎707

Arcata (ar-KAY-ta) is like a transplanted slice of Berkeley in a remote northern corner of California. At the intersection of US 101 and Rte. 299, Arcata typifies the laid-back existence characteristic of the state's northern coast. Check out the town's murals and Victorian homes. Arcata's neighbor, Humboldt State University, focuses on forestry and marine biology (Earth First! was founded here). All over Humboldt County, students get baked in the sun—and on the county's not-quite-legal cash crop.

VITAL STATS
Population: 15,700
Tourist Office: Arcata Chamber of Commerce, 1635 Heindon Rd. (☎707-822-3619). Open daily 9am-5pm.
Library and Internet Access: Humboldt County Library, Arcata Branch, 500 7th St. (☎707-822-5954). Open Tu and F noon-5pm, W and Sa 10am-5pm, Th noon-8pm.
Post Office: 799 H St. (☎707-822-3370). Open M-F 8:30am-5pm. **Postal Code:** 95521.

◩ ACCOMMODATIONS

Arcata has many budget and chain motels off US 101 at the Giuntoli exit.

Motel 6, 4755 Valley W. Blvd. (☎707-822-7061). Clean and quiet with cable TV, a pool, and A/C. Rooms $57. AmEx/D/MC/V. ❸

Clam Beach County Park (☎707-445-7651), on US 101, 7 mi. north of Arcata. Dunes and a huge

TOP 10 PLACES TO SELF-ACTUALIZE, OR, *TO THE LIGHTHOUSE*

1. Yaquina Head Lighthouse (☎541-574-3100). 3 mi. south of Newport, off US 101. 93 ft. high. Stands 162 feet above sea level. The tallest on Oregon's coast. Automated light aids navigation along the coast and entrance to Yaquina Bay. Trails to tide pools accessible year-round. $5 per vehicle.

2. Haceta Head Lighthouse. 12 mi. north of Florence, on the west side of Heceta Head. Illuminated in 1894. Has the strongest light on the Oregon coast. Assistant keeper's house, built in 1893, is now a B&B. Sea birds nest on offshore rocks and headlands. Open daily May-Sept. 11am-5pm; Oct. and Mar.-Apr. M and F-Su 11am-5pm. $3 per vehicle.

3. Coquille River Lighthouse (☎541-756-0100). In Bullards Beach State Park, 2 mi. north of Bandon on the north bank of Coquille River. 40 ft. tall octagonal tower. Commissioned in 1896 to lead boats across a dangerous bar; after improvements to the channel, it was decommissioned in 1939. Restored in 1979 and now operated by solar power. Open May-Oct. daily; Apr. W-Su.

4. Cape Blanco Lighthouse. 9 mi. north of Port Orford, off US 101. 59 ft. On the westernmost point in Oregon. Oldest standing lighthouse on the state's coast—built in 1870 to guide ships related to the gold-mining and lumber industries. Open Apr.-Oct. daily 10am-3pm.

5. Point Arena Lighthouse (☎707-882-2777). In Port Arena, 1 mi. west of Hwy. 1. 115 ft. Strong currents and reefs made Point Arena difficult to traverse for ships bringing lumber from the redwood

beach with seasonal clam digging. Sites with water and pit toilets $10. Cash only. ❶

Patrick's Point State Park (☎707-677-3570, reservations 800-444-7275), 15 mi. north of Arcata on US 101. An excellent spot for whale watching and seals. The 124 sites feature terrific ocean views, lush vegetation, and treasure hunting in the beach's tide pools. Showers and flush toilets. No hookups. Reservations recommended. Sites $20. Day use $6. Cash only. ❶

🍜 FOOD

A **farmers' market** offering tie-dyed dresses, candles, and the usual fresh produce livens up the Arcata Plaza (Apr.-Nov. Sa 9am-2pm).

🍕 **Live From New York Pizza,** 670 9th St. (☎707-822-6199). Pies to die for. A cheese slice costs a well-spent $2, but try something more exciting, like the Godfather, with ricotta, fresh tomatoes, sun-dried tomatoes, pesto, and mozzarella. Open M-Tu and Su 11:30am-9pm, W-Sa 11:30am-10pm. MC/V. ❶

Tomo's, 708 9th St. (☎707-822-1414). Fresh and affordable sushi, with occasional jazz accompaniment. Seek out the specials or any of the mango rolls. Open daily 5pm-last customer. MC/V. ❸

Golden Harvest Cafe, 1062 G St. (☎707-822-8962). Options for vegetarians and vegans like the California Cristo ($11), a grilled french toast sandwich. Entrees $6-12. Open M-F 6:30am-3pm, Sa-Su 7:30am-3pm. MC/V. ❷

Crosswinds, 860 10th St. (☎707-826-2133). A number of hearty breakfast and lunch options in a beautifully restored Victorian home. Come during the week for the weekday special: breakfast for $4 and lunch for $5.50. Open W-Su 7:30am-2pm. D/MC/V. ❶

🔄 SIGHTS

ARCATA PLAZA. Experience Arcata by taking a short stroll around the Arcata Plaza, in the center of town near the intersection of Eighth and H St. The plaza hosts folk and acoustic music on the weekends and is a great place for people-watching.

NATURAL HISTORY MUSEUM. A brief walk from the plaza, the museum is home to a modest collection of prehistoric fossils and whale skulls. (*At 13th and G St. ☎707-826-4479. Open Tu-Sa 10am-5pm. Suggested donation $3.*)

KINETIC SCULPTURE RACE. Held annually over Memorial Day weekend, the race is Humboldt County's oddest festival. A few dozen insane and artsy adventurers attempt to pilot homemade vehicles (like the squash-shaped "Gourd of the Rings") on a grueling three-day, 42 mi. trek from Arcata to Ferndale over road, sand, and water. Vehicles from previous competitions are on display in Ferndale (p. 960).

forests to San Francisco. First lit in 1870, but entirely rebuilt after the 1906 quake. Was the setting for the 1992 film *Forever Young*. Open in summer M-F 11am-2:30pm, Sa-Su and holidays 10am-3:30pm; in winter daily 11am-2:30pm.

6. Point Reyes Lighthouse (☎415-464-5100). 30 mi. northwest of the entrance to San Francisco Bay. Intense fog at Point Reyes necessitated building the lighthouse 275 ft. down the bluff so it wouldn't be obscured. In early 2003, the tower was repainted and the 308 steps leading down to it rebuilt. Open M and Th-Su 10am-4:30pm.

7. Alcatraz Lighthouse. Known as "The Rock." The site of a famous former high-security prison and California's 1st lighthouse. Day and evening island tours from Pier 41, near Fisherman's Wharf.

8. Pigeon Point Lighthouse. On Rte. 1, 20 mi. south of Half Moon Bay. Named for the clipper ship *Carrier Pigeon*, which crashed on the rocks in 1853, this lighthouse was first lit in 1872. HI hostel in former residences. Grounds open 8am-sunset. Guided tours F-Su 10am-4pm.

9. Point Loma. Follow Rte. 209 south from I-5. Completed in 1855. Visible for 39 mi. Spectacular view of San Diego. Natural history and military history exhibits, trails, and tide pools. Open daily 9am-5pm. $5 per vehicle.

10. Cape Disappointment (☎360-642-3078). On the grounds of Cape Disappointment State Park, in Ilwaco, WA. Originally lit in 1856. Joined by a 2nd lighthouse at North Head in 1937. Hike 1.5 mi.

OUTDOORS

Redwood Park, at 14th and Union St., contains lots of nooks for picnicking among giant trees. Behind the park lies **Arcata Community Forest,** which has picnic spaces, meadows, redwoods, and hiking trails. A former "sanitary" landfill, the 307-acre **Arcata Marsh and Wildlife Sanctuary** lies at the foot of I St., across from Samoa Blvd. Visitors can wander around the lake or take a tour to see how this saltwater marsh and converted sewer system treats waste. The **Sanctuary Trail** (2 mi., 1hr.), along Humboldt Bay, offers great birdwatching opportunities. (☎707-826-2359. Open daily 9am-5pm. Tours Sa 8:30am, 2pm.)

THE ROAD TO TRINIDAD: 13 MI.

Continue on **US 101 North,** and take the exit toward Trinidad. Turn left onto **Westhaven Drive/Main Street,** and continue to follow Main St.

TRINIDAD   ☎707

Originally founded as a port during the gold-rush era, Trinidad's main attraction is the unofficially named **College Cove.** The beach provides sandy shores for the clothed to the north and the nudists to the south. From the Trinidad exit, follow signs for the Trinidad Beach on Stagecoach Rd., then take the second left onto a gravel road at the Elk Head Park sign. **Patrick's Point State Park,** 5 mi. north of Trinidad, is worth a stop for the 2 mi. walk along the **Rim Trail,** which sweeps by Agate Beach, Mussel Rocks, Patrick's Point, and **Wedding Rock,** a tremendous boulder that juts out into the ocean. On the beach, you can hunt for semi-precious agate stones. Sharing the 640-acre park is also a model **Yurok village** for visitors and a nice **campground ❶** with water and coin-operated showers. (☎707-677-3570. Sites $20. Day use $4. Cash only.)

THE ROAD TO REDWOOD NATIONAL AND STATE PARKS: 23 MI.

Continue on **US 101 North/Redwood Highway.** The park's south entrance is a few miles up the road.

REDWOOD NATIONAL AND STATE PARKS   ☎707

With ferns that grow to the height of humans and redwood trees the size of skyscrapers, Redwood National and State Parks will leave an impression. The redwoods are the last remaining stretch of the old-growth forest that used to blanket two million acres of Northern California and Oregon. Wildlife runs free here, with black bears and mountain lions roaming the backwoods and Roosevelt elk grazing in the meadows. While a short tour of the big sights and the drive-through trees certainly provides visitors with ample photo opportunities, a more memorable experience of the redwoods may require heading down a trail into the quiet of the forest, where you can see the trees as they have stood for many thousands of years.

VITAL STATS
Area: 112,613 acres
Tourist Office: Redwood National Park Head-quarters and Information Center, 1111 2nd St. (☎707-464-6101), in Crescent City. Open in summer daily 9am-5pm; in winter M-Sa 9am-5pm.
Gateway Towns: Orick, Klamath, Crescent City.
Fees: Fees vary by park and are different for parking, camping, and hiking. There is usually no entrance fee. Day use fees ($4 per car) for parking and picnic areas are typical.

ORIENTATION

"Redwood National and State Parks" is an umbrella term for four contiguous parks. The parks span 40 mi. of coast and two counties, with information centers and unique attractions throughout. **Redwood National Park** is the southernmost of the four; the others, from south to north, are **Prairie Creek Redwoods State Park, Del Norte Coast Redwoods State Park,** and **Jedediah Smith Redwoods State Park.**

Orick and **Klamath** border the national forest to the south and north, respectively. **US 101** traverses most of the parks. The slower but more scenic **Newton Drury Parkway** runs parallel to US 101 for 31 mi. from Klamath to Prairie Creek (watch for bikers).

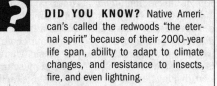

DID YOU KNOW? Native American's called the redwoods "the eternal spirit" because of their 2000-year life span, ability to adapt to climate changes, and resistance to insects, fire, and even lightning.

ACCOMMODATIONS

Redwood Hostel (HI), 14480 US 101 (☎707-482-8265 or 800-295-1905; www. redwoodhostel.com), at Wilson Creek Rd., 7 mi. north of Klamath. This family-friendly hostel has a prime beach location and great sunset views. Linen included. Check-in 8-10am and 5-9pm. Check-out 8-10am. Reservations highly recommended in summer. Dorms $21, under 12 $10.50; doubles $52. MC/V. ❶

Hiouchi Motel, 2097 Rte. 199 (☎707-458-3041; www.hiouchimotel.com), 8 mi. east of Crescent City. Offers basic amenities near the park. Singles $50; doubles $65. D/MC/V. ❷

Gold Bluffs Beach Campground (☎707-464-6101). Turn west on Davison Rd., 3 mi. north of Orick. The campsites sit among tall, yellow grass on a sandy shore that is surprisingly sheltered from the wind. This former port is now one of the best spots for beach camping along the coast. Sites $12. Cash only. ❶

Jedediah Smith Redwoods State Park Campground (☎707-464-6101). Nestled in among old-growth redwoods. Flush toilets and water. No hookups. Sites $20. MC/V. ❶

FOOD

There are more picnic tables than restaurants in the area, so the best option for food is probably the supermarket. In Crescent City, head to the 24hr. **Safeway,** 475 M St. (☎707-465-3353).

Palm Cafe, 21130 Hwy. 101 (☎707-488-3381), in Orick. Famous for its Paul Bunyan rolls ($8), enormous cinnamon rolls that can feed 5. Entrees $5-11. AmEx/D/MC/V. ❷

Glen's Bakery and Restaurant, 722 3rd St. (☎707-464-2914), at G St. in Crescent City. A family affair since it opened in 1947. Dedicated regulars love the plate-size pancakes ($5).

Breakfast served all day. Open Tu-F 5am-6:30pm, Sa 5am-2pm. MC/V. ❶

OUTDOORS

All plants and animals in the park are protected—even feathers dropped by birds of prey are off-limits. California **fishing licenses** ($10 per day) are required for freshwater and saltwater fishing off any natural formation, but fishing is free from any manmade structure (check out Battery Point in Crescent City). There are minimum-weight and maximum-catch requirements specific to both. Call the **Fish and Game Department** (☎707-445-6493; www.dfg.ca.gov) for more information.

The redwoods are best experienced on foot. Hikers should take particular care to wear protective clothing—ticks and poison oak thrive in the dark undergrowth. Roosevelt elk roam the woods and are interesting to watch but dangerous to approach, as those who encroach on their territory are promptly circled and trampled. You can observe them from a distance at **Elk Prarie** (south of the entrance to Prarie Creek Redwoods State Park), **Davison Road** (just west of Hwy. 101), or at **Gold Bluffs Beach** (4 mi. down an unpaved section of Davison Rd.). Also look out for the black bears and mountain lions that inhabit the park. Before setting out, get advice and trail maps at the visitors center.

ORICK AREA

The Orick area covers the southernmost section of Redwood National and State Parks. The **visitors center** lies on US 101, 1 mi. south of Orick and half a mile south of the Greyhound bus stop. A popular sight is the **Tall Trees Grove,** accessible by car to those with permits (free from the visitors center) when the road is open. Allow at least 3-4hr. for the trip. From the trailhead at the end of Tall Trees Access Rd., off Bald Hills Rd. from US 101 north of Orick, it's a 1 mi. hike down to some of the tallest trees in the world. The return hike up is steep. If the road is closed, hardy souls can see these giants by hiking the 16 mi. round-trip from **Dolason Prairie Trail** to **Emerald Ridge Trail,** which connects with Tall Trees Trail.

Orick is a somewhat desolate town overrun by cows (which outnumber the people) and souvenir stores selling burl sculptures (over-crafted and expensive wood carvings). However, those needing to stock up on the essentials will find a post office and a market for groceries. The rodeo, held every July, is the biggest event of the year.

PRAIRIE CREEK AREA

The Prairie Creek area, equipped with a ranger station, visitors center, and state park campground, is perfect for hikers, who can explore 70 mi. of trails in the 14,000-acre park. Be sure to pick up a trail map ($1) at the ranger station before heading out; the loops of crisscrossing trails can be confusing. Starting at the **Prairie Creek Visitors Center,** the **James Irvine Trail** (4 mi. one-way) snakes through a prehistoric garden of towering old-growth redwoods. Winding past small waterfalls that trickle down 50 ft. fern-covered walls, the trail ends at **Fern Canyon** on Gold Bluffs Beach. **Rhododendron** (7 mi. one-way) is another choice pick because of its beautiful blossoms and many possibilities; if you get tired, just take the convenient switchback, **South Fork Trail.** The less ambitious can elk-watch on the meadow in front of the ranger station or cruise part of the **Foothill Trail** (½ mi. one-way) to the 1500-year-old 306 ft. high **Big Tree.** This behemoth is a satisfying alternative for those who don't want to trek to Tall Trees Grove (above).

KLAMATH AREA

The Klamath area to the north consists of a thin stretch of parkland connecting Prairie Creek with Del Norte State Park. The town itself has only a few stores stretched over 4 mi., so the main attraction here is the spectacular coastline. The **Klamath Overlook,** where Requa Rd. meets the steep **Coastal Trail** (8 mi.), is an excellent whale-watching site with a view (provided the fog doesn't obscure it).

The mouth of the **Klamath River** is a popular commercial fishing spot in fall and spring, when salmon spawn, and in winter, when steelhead trout do the same. (Permit required; contact the Redwood Visitors Info Center, ☎541-464-6101.) In spring and summer, sea lions and harbor seals congregate along **Coastal Drive,** which passes by the remains of the Douglas Memorial Bridge and continues along the ocean for 8 mi. of incredible views.

Kitsch meets high-tech at **Trees of Mystery,** 15500 US 101 N., just north of Klamath. It's a three-quarter-mile walk through a maze of curiously shaped trees and elaborate chainsaw sculptures that talk and play music. There is also a small, free Native American museum that displays ornate costumes, baskets, and tapestries. The tourist trap's latest addition, the **Sky Trail,** is a multi-million-dollar gondola snaking up the hill to offer an exclusive bird's-eye view of the towering trees. A 49 ft. tall Paul Bunyan and his blue ox Babe mark the entrance to the sight. (☎800-638-3389; www. treesofmystery.net. Trail and museum open daily 8am-6:30pm. $13.50, children $6.50.)

CRESCENT CITY AREA

An outstanding location from which to explore the parks, Crescent City calls itself the city "where the redwoods meet the sea." The **Battery Point Lighthouse** is on a causeway jutting out from Front St.; turn left onto A St. at the top of Front St. The lighthouse contains a museum open only during low tide. (☎707-464-3089. Open Apr.-Sept. W-Su 10am-4pm, tide permitting. $3, students and children $1.) From June through August, the national park offers **tidepool walks,** which leave from the Enderts Beach parking lot. The trailhead is at the **Crescent Beach Overlook** on Enderts Beach Rd., just off US 101. Turn 4 mi. south of Crescent City. (Schedules ☎707-464-6101.) A scenic drive from Crescent City along Pebble Beach Dr. to **Point Saint George** snakes past coastline that looks transplanted from New England; craggy cliffs, lush prairies, and an old lighthouse add to the atmosphere. The **World Championship Crab Races,** on the third Sunday in February, features races and crab feasts. The **Sea Cruise,** a parade of over 500 classic cars, occurs over three days on the first or second weekend in October. (Both ☎800-343-8300.)

North of Crescent City, the **Smith River,** the state's last major un-dammed river, rushes through rocky gorges on its way from the mountains to the coast. This area offers the best salmon, trout, and steelhead fishing around, and excellent camping awaits on the riverbanks. There are also numerous hiking trails in the surrounding forest.

HIOUCHI AREA

This inland region, known for its rugged beauty, sits in the northern part of the park region along **US 199** and contains some excellent hiking trails, most of which are in **Jedediah Smith Redwoods State Park.** Several trails lie off **Howland Hill Road,** a dirt road accessible from both US 101 and US 199. From US 199, turn onto South Fork Rd. in Hiouchi and right onto Douglas Park Rd., which then turns into Howland Hill Rd. From Crescent City, go south on US 101, turn left onto Elk Valley Rd., and veer right onto Howland Hill Rd. Drive through **Stout Grove,** which some say surpasses even the Ave. of the Giants. From here, you can take the **Stout Grove Trail** (½ mi.) and admire the ancient redwoods up close. The trailhead is near the eastern end of Howland Hill Rd. The **Mill Creek Trail** (4 mi.; moderate) provides excellent swimming, accessible from the Mill Creek Bridge on Howland Hill Rd. and from the footbridge in the Jedediah Smith campground during summer. The more strenuous **Boy Scout Trail** off Howland Hill Rd. splits after 3 mi.; the right-hand path goes to the monstrous and impressive Boy Scout Tree, and the left ends at Fern Falls.

THE ROAD TO BROOKINGS: 26 MI.
Continue on **US 101** and cross into Oregon.

The Beaver State
OREGON
Welcomes You

BROOKINGS ☎541

In Brookings, one of the few coastal towns that remains relatively tourist-free, hardware stores are easier to find than trinket shops, and the beaches are among Oregon's least spoiled. The city also sits in Oregon's "banana belt"; warm weather is not rare in January, and some Brookings backyards even boast scraggly palm trees. Brookings is known statewide for its flowers. In downtown's **Azalea Park,** azaleas encircle pristine lawns and bloom at intervals year-round; call ahead to make sure the flowers are out. The pride of Brookings is its **Azalea Festival** (☎541-469-3181), held in Azalea Park over Memorial Day weekend. **South Beach** is just north of town and offers soft sand as well as haunting vistas of angular volcanic rocks strewn about the sea. **Harris Beach,** a bit farther north, has an equally excellent view of the rock formations and less obstructed views.

The **Pacific Sunset Inn ❸,** 1144 Hwy. 101 N., is one of many cheap motels with basic amenities along the section of Hwy. 101 called Chetco Ave. (☎541-469-2141. Rooms $50-70.) **Harris Beach State Park Campground ❶,** at the north edge of Brookings, has 63 tent sites set back in the trees. (☎541-469-2021 or 800-452-5687. Free showers. Sites $17, with electricity and water $21; RV sites $22. Yurts $29. MC/V.) A number of seafood spots can be found near the harbor. The local favorite is **Oceanside Diner ❷,** 16403 Lower Harbor Rd. Regular customers and their orders are featured on the menu. (☎541-469-7971. Open daily 4am-1:30pm. Cash only.)

THE ROAD TO GOLD BEACH: 29 MI.
Continue on **US 101/Oregon Coast Highway.** At **Samuel Boardman State Park,** explore 15 mi. of trails, some leading to beaches covered in volcanic rocks. Don't be surprised if an exploratory hike unexpectedly ends at an intimate seaside cove.

GOLD BEACH ☎541

Thirty miles north of Brookings, in Gold Beach, you can ride a jet boat up the Rogue River. **Mail Boat Hydro-Jets,** 94294 Rogue River Rd., offers 6-7hr. whitewater daytrips. Longer trips get more whitewater, but all trips offer many wildlife-viewing opportunities. (☎541-247-7033 or 800-458-3511. Trips May-Oct. $45-87, ages 4-11 $20-40. D/MC/V.) **Oregon Trail Lodge ❸,** 29855 Hwy. 101, has charming and rustic rooms near restaurants and shops at affordable rates. (☎541-247-6030. Free Wi-Fi. Rooms $45-71.)

THE ROAD TO BANDON-BY-THE-SEA: 56 MI.
Continue on **US 101/Oregon Coast Highway.** Bandon is 27 mi. north of Port Orford. **Humbug Mountain State Park ❶,** 6 mi. south of Port Orford along US 101, surrounds the heavily forested mountain. A moderate 3 mi. trail ascends the 1700 ft. peak, with lush

ferns on the trail and amazing views from the top. The trail is accessible from a campground at the foot of the mountain, which has 95 tightly packed sites with toilets. (☎541-332-6774. Sites $14, with hookup $16. MC/V.) **Cape Blanco State Park,** just north of Port Orford, offers a long stretch of empty beach; it is the farthest point west on the Oregon Coast, and its **lighthouse** is the coast's oldest, with views that stretch for miles. Take a tour of the lighthouse and its mesmerizing lens, located at the end of the road leading into the park. (Open Apr.-Oct. Tu-Su 10am-3:30pm. $2, under 16 free.) Few stop at the **Cape Blanco State Park campground ❶** a few miles back from the lighthouse; it offers exceptional seclusion between hedges, plus a quarter mile walk to a beautiful isolated beach. (☎541-332-2973. Toilets and showers. RV sites $16. Cabins $35. MC/V.)

BANDON-BY-THE-SEA ☎541

Despite a steady flow of summer tourists, the fishing town of Bandon-by-the-Sea has refrained from catering to kitsch. A few outdoor activities make Bandon worth a stop on a lengthy coastal tour.

VITAL STATS
Population: 2800
Tourist Office: Bandon-by-the-Sea Visitors Center, 300 2nd St. SE (☎541-347-9616), in Old Town. Open daily in summer 10am-5pm; in winter 10am-4pm.
Library and Internet Access: Bandon Public Library, Hwy. 101 (☎541-347-3221). Open Tu-Th 10:30am-8pm, F-Sa 10:30am-5pm.
Post Office: 105 12th St. SE (☎541-347-1160). Open M-F 8:30am-4:30pm. **Postal Code:** 97411.

⚓ ORIENTATION

Ocean Drive runs along the Pacific before heading inland through downtown Bandon. After it intersects with **US 101,** Ocean Dr. becomes **Second Street. First Street** runs parallel to Second St. along the waterfront.

🏠 ACCOMMODATIONS

Sea Star Guest House, 375 2nd St. (☎541-347-9632; www.seastarbandon.com). Several elegant rooms overlook the marina. For a bargain, ask for one of the bare dorm rooms, which you'll likely have to yourself. Dorms $25; private rooms $65-115. AmEx/D/MC/V. ❶

Bullard's Beach State Park (☎541-347-2209), 2 mi. north of town and across the bridge. Houses the Coquille River Lighthouse, built in 1896. 185 sites. Showers. Sites $20. Yurts $27. MC/V. ❶

🍴 FOOD

Bandon Baking Co. and Deli, 160 2nd St. (☎541-347-9440; www.bandonbakingco.com). Offers soups and breads like sunflower, hazelnut, and the regionally ubiquitous cranberry-nut. Open M-Sa 7am-4pm. Cash only. ❶

Alloro Wine Bar & Restaurant, 375 2nd St. (☎541-347-1850; www.allorowinebar.com). Extensive collection of wines focuses on Oregon and Italy. The pricey Italian fare is worth a splurge. Try the Caesar *con gancho* (with crab; $11). Open daily 4-9:30pm. AmEx/D/MC/V. ❹

👁 SIGHTS

In September, the town holds the **Cranberry Festival** (☎541-347-9616; www.bandon.com).

OLD TOWN. The Old Town actually just dates from 1936, when a giant fire swept through and destroyed all the living quarters, but not the industry, in Bandon. People were living in tents and hurried to put up "temporary" buildings, many of which are still standing today.

FABER FARMS. The ▧cranberry bog at Faber Farms showcases the floating berries bobbing on the water as they're harvested. (*54982 Morrison Rd. At the traffic light, turn onto Hwy. 42 S. for 1 mi. and then right on Morrison Rd. for 1 mi. ☎866-347-1166; www.faberfarms.com. Open M-Sa 10am-4pm.*)

HISTORICAL SOCIETY MUSEUM. A visit to the Museum is like leafing through a grandmother's scrapbook filled with the area's Native American, industrial, maritime, and pioneer heritage. (*270 Fillmore Ave., at US 101. ☎541-347-2164; www.bandonhistoricalmuseum.org. Open M-Sa 10am-4pm. $2, under 12 free.*)

🚗 THE ROAD TO CHARLESTON: 22 MI.

Go north on **US 101/Oregon Coast Highway,** turn left onto **Seven Devils Road,** and continue west.

CHARLESTON ☎ 541

Tiny Charleston sits peacefully on the coast, with a string of state parks along the coastline and a pristine estuary near its bay. Four miles south of Charleston up Seven Devils Rd., the ■**South Slough National Estuarine Research Reserve** ("slough" is pronounced like "slew") is one of the most fascinating and under-appreciated sights on the central coast. Spreading out from a small interpretive center, almost 4779 acres of saltwater and freshwater estuaries nurture all kinds of wildlife, from sand shrimp to blue herons. Head to the interpretive center first to check if there are any guided hikes (free) or paddles going out ($10 per boat) or to begin one of the short trails starting at the center. A great way to observe wildlife by canoe or kayak is to start from the **Charleston Marina** (near the Charleston Bridge) at low tide. Paddle into the estuary with the tide and out as it subsides; the estuary turns into a wasteland of mud flats at low tide. (☎541-888-5558; www.southsloughestuary.com. Open June-Aug. daily 10am-4:30pm; Sept.-May M-Sa 10am-4:30pm. Trails open daily sunrise-sunset.)

⛰ THE ROAD TO COOS BAY: 9 MI.

From Charleston, head on to the **Cape Arago Highway,** then follow **Empire Coos Bay Highway** into town.

COOS BAY ☎ 541

The largest city on the Oregon Coast, Coos Bay still has the feel of a down-to-earth working town. For two weeks in mid-July, Coos Bay hosts the **Oregon Coast Music Festival,** the most popular summer music event in the region. A week of jazz, blues, and folk is followed by a week of performances by the renowned festival orchestra. Art exhibits and a free classical concert in Mingus Park make the festival a worthwhile attraction for the ticketless. (☎541-267-0938. Tickets $5-20.)

Akin to camping in a well-landscaped parking lot, **Sunset Bay State Park ❶,** 89814 Cape Arago Hwy., 12 mi. south of Coos Bay and 3 mi. west of Charleston, has 138 sites. The Loop B sites are a bit more secluded. (☎541-888-4902, reservations 800-452-5687. Tent sites $16; RV sites $20. Yurts $27. MC/V.) Three miles north of North Bend, off US 101,

the **Bluebill Campground ❶** offers 18 sites among sandy scrub half a mile from the ocean. Follow the signs to the Horsfall Beach area, then continue down the road. (☎541-271-3611. Open Apr.-Oct. Sites $20. Cash only.)At the **Blue Heron Bistro ❸,** 100 Commercial Ave., at Broadway, German cuisine like sauerbraten ($14) and bratwurst ($11.50) complements the memorabilia on the walls. (☎541-267-3933. Sandwiches $7.50-10. Dinner $14-18. Open M-F 11am-9:30pm, Sa 5-9:30pm. MC/V.) **Cranberry Sweets ❷,** 1005 Newmark Ave., near the corner of Ocean Blvd., is a far-from-average candy factory with numerous original offerings such as beer *pâtés* and cheddar-cheese fudge. The Vineyard Sweets *pâtés* are made with real wine, like White Zinfandel and Cabernet Sauvignon. Cheapskates can load up on free samples. (☎541-888-9824. Open M-Sa 9am-5:30pm, Su 11am-4pm. AmEx/D/MC/V.)

⛰ THE ROAD TO WINCHESTER BAY: 23 MI.

Continue on **US 101 North/Oregon Coast Highway.** Along the way, nature's ever-changing sculpture, the **Oregon Dunes National Recreation Area,** presents sand in shapes and sizes unequaled in the Northwest. Perhaps the only hotbed of "reverse conservation," the dunes are actually greening rapidly. European beachgrass, planted in the 1920s, has spread its tenacious roots and sparked concerns that the dunes may disappear in as few as 100 years. Get them while they're hot: everyone, from the hard-partying buggy or ATV rider to the hiker seeking solitude, enjoys the endless expanses of windblown sand. For an unmuffled and undeniably thrilling dune experience, venture out on wheels. Plenty of shops on US 101 between Coos Bay and Florence rent and offer tours, and most either transport ATVs to the dunes or are located on them. The visitors center in Reedsport (below) also offers a list of places that rent ATVs.

WINCHESTER BAY ☎ 541

The vast stretches of sand south of Winchester Bay and around Eel Creek represent Oregon Dunes at their most primal. The experience of any day hike is heightened by solitude, so go early or late to avoid other tourists. With little to guide you besides an occasional marking pole, the **John Dellenback Dunes Trail** (1 mi.), located off US 101, wanders through unparalleled beauty in the sand slopes, wind cornices,

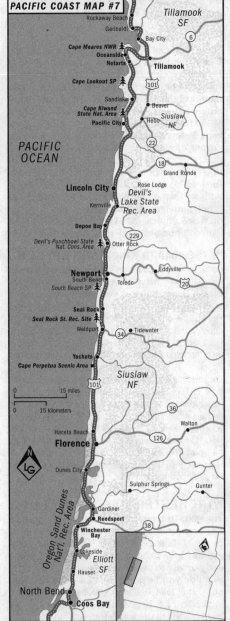

PACIFIC COAST MAP #7

Tillamook SF

Rockaway Beach
Garibaldi
Bay City
6
Cape Meares NWR
Oceanside
Netarts
Tillamook
101
Cape Lookout SP
Sandlake
Beaver
Cape Kiwanda
State Nat. Area
Pacific City
Hebo
Siuslaw NF
22
18
Grand Ronde
Lincoln City
Rose Lodge
Devil's
Lake State
Rec. Area
Kernville
Depoe Bay
229
Devil's Punchbowl State
Nat. Cons. Area
Otter Rock
Newport
Eddyville
South Beach
South Beach SP
Toledo
20
Seal Rock
Seal Rock St. Rec. Site
Waldport
34
Tidewater
Yachats
Cape Perpetua Scenic Area
Siuslaw NF
101
0   15 miles
0   15 kilometers
36
Haceta Beach
Walton
126
Florence
Dunes City
Sulphur Springs
Gunter
Gardiner
Reedsport
Winchester
Bay
38
Lakeside
Elliott SF
Hauser
North Bend
Coos Bay

PACIFIC OCEAN

Oregon Sand Dunes Nat'l. Rec. Area

PACIFIC COAST

and rippled surfaces of the dunes. Access the trailhead off US 101. The area is ATV-free, and you'll probably find yourself wandering along the ridges of the dunes while exploring an occasional patch of vegetation. The views are best when the sun is low in the sky and the shadows highlight the precise transitions between slopes and other wind-sculptured features. The trail goes 6 mi. to the ocean over soft sand, requiring several hours of hiking.

The **Harbor View Motel ②**, 540 Beach Blvd., is so close to the marina that there are boats in the parking lot. A robotic frog welcomes guests to the office. Rooms are comfortable and clean, with striking color schemes. (☎541-271-3352. Rooms with TVs and refrigerators $47-55, with kitchen $60-65. D/MC/V.) For well-sheltered campsites, **William M. Tugman State Park ①**, 8 mi. south of Reedsport on US 101, is close to gorgeous Eel Lake. (☎541-759-3604, reservations 800-452-5687. Water and electricity. Sites in summer $16, in winter $12. Yurts $27. MC/V.) Rent crab traps to try to capture the elusive creatures; even if you can't get one, cheap meal options abound here. The **Anchor Grill ③**, 208 Bayfront Loop, is a classy but casual choice on the waterfront. Try the halibut fish and chips for $16. (☎541-271-2104. Lunch $7-11. Dinner $15-23. Open M-F 10am-9pm, Sa 8am-9pm, Su 8am-8pm. AmEx/D/MC/V.)

◤ THE ROAD TO REEDSPORT: 5 MI.

Follow **US 101/Oregon Coast Highway**, then turn right and follow **Route 38** into Reedsport.

REEDSPORT   ☎541

A popular stopover by the dunes, Reedsport has excellent camping and is a great place to rest between runs on the sand. Birdwatching is popular around town; lists of species and their seasons are available at the **Oregon Dunes National Recreation Area Visitors Center**, 855 US 101, at Rte. 38, just south of the Umpqua River Bridge. The center has a 10min. video on dune ecology and essential info on fees, regulations, hiking, and camping. (☎541-271-3611. Open June-Oct. daily 8am-4:30pm; Nov.-May M-F 8am-4:30pm.) Most tourists enjoy stopping at the **Oregon Dunes Overlook**, between Reedsport and Florence. Several 1-3hr. walks depart from the overlook and explore the dunes amid the constant barrage of bird calls from nearby shrubs.

Harbor Lights Family Restaurant ❸, at US 101 and Rte. 38, offers American food in a comfortable, unpretentious setting. Regulars rave about the rotating seafood specials. (☎541-271-3848. Salmon burger $10. Open daily 7am-9pm. AmEx/D/MC/V.) **Carter Lake Campground ❶**, 12 mi. north of Reedsport on US 101, has boat access to the lake, and some sites are lakeside. The well-screened spots are about as quiet as it gets out here. (☎541-271-3611. 23 sites. No ATVs. Open May-Sept. Sites $17.)

◢ THE ROAD TO FLORENCE: 23 MI.
Continue on **US 101/Oregon Coast Highway.** Take the **Old Town Loop** off US 101.

FLORENCE   ☎ 541

Florence is home to the most photographed lighthouse in the US as well as a cormorant rookery. The **Siuslaw Pioneer Museum,** 278 Maple St., housed in a 1905 schoolhouse, displays historic pictures and artifacts as well as information about the Siuslaw River area. (☎541-997-7884. Open Tu-Su noon-4pm. $3, children free.) Up the road, the picturesque, red-topped **Heceta Lighthouse,** built in 1894, is another worthy photo op. The surrounding **Heceta Head Lighthouse State Scenic Viewpoint** is a 549-acre park with beaches, trails, and tide pools. On the north side of Heceta Head, a challenging 2 mi. route winds upward to ocean views. (☎541-547-3416. Tours from Memorial Day to Labor Day daily 11am-5pm; Oct. and Mar.-Apr. M and F-Su 11am-3pm. $3.)

Siltcoos Station Retreat ❷ is a 15min. drive from Old Town on Siltcoos Lake, the largest lake on the Oregon coast. Each of the four heated cabins has a bath and kitchen. (☎541- 997-8444; www.lanecc.edu/florence/siltcoos. Proceeds from rooms fund scholarships at Lane Community College. Rooms $50.) If that's not close enough to camping for you, head to the **Jessie M. Honeyman Memorial State Park,** 84505 Hwy. 101, 3 mi. south of Florence. There are flush toilets and showers for the 121 electrical sites with water, 47 full hookup sites, 187 tent sites, and 10 yurts.

(☎541-997-3641. May-Sept. tent sites $17, with full hookup $22; yurts $29. Oct.-Apr. tent sites $13.) **Lovejoy's ❸**, 195 Nopal St., is a casual English tearoom that also offers lunch. Royal Tea ($15 for 1, $26 for 2) includes sausage rolls, two salads, two crustless and quartered sandwiches, fresh-baked scones, an English biscuit, and a petite dessert. (☎541-902-0502. Lunch $7-9. Open Tu-Sa in summer 11am-4pm, in winter 11am-3pm.) For dinner, stop in at **Curve's ❷**, 294 Maple St., across from the Siuslaw Pioneer Museum. This restaurant and tapas bar claims to serve "the best food on the central Oregon coast," from baked brie (in phyllo dough; $8) to ahi tuna tartare for $10. (☎541-997-3154. Open M and Th-Sa 4-11pm, Su 4-9pm. D/MC/V.)

◣ DETOUR
ALPHA FARM

Drive 14 mi. east of Florence to the tiny community of **Mapleton.** Press on 30min. farther along **Route 36** and then 7 mi. up **Deadwood Creek Road.**

Alpha Farm offers a 280-acre communal alternative to the coast's bourgeois tourism. Members farm and produce gift-shop-type craft items to support the communal purse. Anyone willing to lend a hand with the chores is welcome to camp out or stay in the beautiful, simple bedrooms. Visitors can stay up to three days; afterward, a long-term commitment to the farm is required. (☎541-964-5102.) The **Alpha Bit Cafe ❶**, in Mapleton on Rte. 126, is staffed by the very chill members of Alpha Farm. (☎541-268-4311. Open M-Th and Sa-Su 10am-6pm, F 10am-9pm. Cash only.)

◢ THE ROAD TO CAPE PERPETUA: 22 MI.
Continue on **US 101/Oregon Coast Highway.**

CAPE PERPETUA   ☎ 541

Cape Perpetua is the highest point on the coast that you can drive to (803 ft.), and it's certainly a high point for scenic beauty. In the fall and winter, hundreds of boisterous sea lions make their home at the Cape Perpetua Scenic Area in the **world's largest sea cave,** 91560 US 101, which accounts for the smell. In spring and summer, the creatures prefer to sun themselves just outside on the rookery. (☎541-547-3111; www.sealioncaves.com.

Open daily 8am-6pm. $8, ages 6-15 $4.50.)Even if you're only passing through, drive to the top of the **Cape Perpetua Viewpoint** (2 mi.) and walk the quarter-mile loop. Gaze out at the ocean as well as the headlands to the north and south. Those looking for a more challenging hike can take the difficult 1 mi. **Saint Perpetua Trail** up to the same viewpoint. The trail departs from **Cape Perpetua Visitors Center**, 2400 US 101, just south of the viewpoint turnoff, which has hilarious rangers and informative exhibits about the surrounding area. (☎541-547-3289. Open May-Nov. daily 9am-5pm.) At high tide, witness an orgy of thundering spray in the **Devil's Churn** (¼ mi. north of the interpretive center down Restless Water Trail) and **Spouting Horn** (¼ mi. south down Captain Cook Trail). The two sites, as well as the tidal pools, are connected; the tidal pools can also be reached from the interpretive center. The **Cape Perpetua Campground ❶**, at the turnoff for the viewpoint, is an excellent place to sleep, with 37 sites alongside a tiny, fern-banked creek. (☎877-444-6777. Water and toilets. Firewood $5. Sites $20. Cash only.) The **Rock Creek Campground ❶**, 8 mi. farther south, has 15 sites under mossy spruces half a mile from the sea. (☎877-444-6777. Drinking water and toilets. Sites $20. Cash only.)

⛆ **THE ROAD TO YACHATS: 4 MI.**
Follow **US 101/Oregon Coast Highway.**

YACHATS ☎541

Billing itself as the "Gem of the Oregon Coast," Yachats (YAH-hots) comes from the Native American word meaning "dark water between timbered hills." There's not much to do in this small resort town but stroll around and enjoy. **Silver Surf Motel ❹**, 3767 US 101, at the north end of town, features sliding glass doors overlooking a grassy hill that rolls 120 ft. to the sea. Rooms have kitchenettes and access to a pool and hot tub. (☎800-281-5723 or 541-547-3175; www.silversurf-motel.com. Rooms $79-189. AmEx/D/MC/V.) Stop in at the **Green Salmon Coffee and Tea House ❶**, off US 101 at Third St., where the menu is written on coffee bags, the cash register uses solar power, and the outdoor tables are giant tree stumps. (☎541-547-3077. Raspberries on toast

$4.50. Open Tu-Su 7:30am-4pm. Cash only.) The cozy **Grand Occasions Deli ❸**, 84 Beach St., off US 101, at Third St., offers a delightful Dungeness crab melt ($13) as well as fresh pies, cookies, cobblers, and scones. (☎541-547-4409. Open in summer M-Th 10am-6pm, F-Su 10am-8pm; in winter daily 10am-5pm. D/MC/V.) A local favorite for jazz, blues, rock, and folk as well as tasty cuisine, the **Drift In ❹**, 124 US 101, showcases live music almost every night around 6:30pm. Sit in the classy Victorian parlor or drink and dine near the bar. (☎541-547-4477; www.the-drift-inn.com. Open daily 8am-last customer. MC/V.)

The **Yachats Visitors Center**, 241 US 101, next to the supermarket, is extremely helpful for information on local attractions. (☎800-929-0477. Open daily 10am-4pm.)

⛆ **THE ROAD TO SEAL ROCK: 14 MI.**
Head north on **US 101/Oregon Coast Highway.**

SEAL ROCK ☎541

Home to striking yellow cliffs, Seal Rock has some terrific sights. The **Triad Art Gallery**, at milepost 153, shows distinctly interesting pieces. Look for the neon horse out front. (☎541-563-5442. Open daily 10am-5pm.) **South Beach**, 2 mi. south of town on US 101, offers haunting views of angular volcanic rocks strewn about the sea plus sand that's soft on bare feet. Near the gallery, **Yuzen ❸**, on US 101, has fantastic Japanese food. There's no sign, but look for the huge wood man shoving forward a plate of sushi. (☎541-563-4766. Open Tu-Su 11:30am-2pm and 4:30-9pm. MC/V.)

⛆ **THE ROAD TO NEWPORT: 10 MI.**
Continue north on **US 101/Oregon Coast Highway.**

NEWPORT ☎541

After the miles of malls along US 101, Newport's renovated waterfront area dotted with pleasantly kitschy restaurants and shops can be a delight. Newport's claim to fame, however, is the world-class Oregon Coast Aquarium. This, in addition to the Mark Hatfield Marine Science Center and loads of inexpensive seafood, make Newport a star attraction for marine lovers.

VITAL STATS

Population: 9500

Tourist Office: Chamber of Commerce, 555 SW Coast Hwy. (☎541-265-8801 or 800-262-7844; www.discovernewport.com). Open in summer M-F 8:30am-5pm, Sa 10am-2pm; in winter M-F 8:30am-5pm.

Library and Internet Access: Newport Public Library, 35 Nye St. NW (☎541-265-2153), at Olive St. Open M-W 10am-9pm, Th-Sa 10am-6pm, Su noon-5pm.

Post Office: 310 SW 2nd St. (☎541-867-3986). Open M-F 8:30am-5pm, Sa 10am-noon. **Postal Code:** 97365.

ORIENTATION

Newport is bordered on the west by the foggy Pacific Ocean and on the south by **Yaquina Bay. US 101,** known in town as the **Coast Highway,** runs north-south through town. **US 20,** known as **Olive Street,** bisects the north and south sides of town. Just north of the bridge, **Bay Boulevard** circles the bay and runs through the heart of the port. Historic **Nye Beach,** bustling with tiny shops, is on the northwest side of town, between **Third** and **Sixth Street.**

ACCOMMODATIONS

Motel-studded US 101 provides affordable but sometimes noisy rooms.

Sylvia Beach Hotel, 267 NW Cliff St. (☎541-265-3707; www.sylviabeachhotel.com). By far the best option around, with a variety of rooms devoted to famous authors and literary themes. Owners Sally Ford and Goody Cable serve breakfast (included) and dinner family-style at the **Table of Content** restaurant as well as hot spiced wine at 10pm in the 3rd Fl. library. Stay in one of the luxurious Classics overlooking the ocean like the Agatha Christie room, a mid-range Bestseller like the Edgar Allan Poe room, complete with a stuffed raven and bricked-up door frame, or a Novel, like the forested Tolkien room, fun but without a view. Novels $68-94; Bestsellers $94-131; Classics from $183. AmEx/MC/V. ❹

City Center Motel, 538 SW Coast Hwy. (☎541-265-7381 or 800-627-9099). Spacious rooms

in a convenient location. Singles $40; doubles $60. AmEx/D/MC/V. ❷

Beverly Beach State Park, 198 NE 123rd St. (☎541-265-9278, reservations 800-452-5687), 7 mi. north of Newport and just south of Devil's Punch Bowl. A campground of gargantuan proportions. Sites $4-22. Yurts $29. MC/V. ❶

FOOD

Food in Newport is surprisingly varied, but seafood is the dining option of choice.

Mo's Restaurant, 622 SW Bay Blvd. (☎541-265-2979). Famous for its clam chowder ($4.25) since 1942. Just about always filled to the gills. If "Old Mo's" is packed, head across the street to **Mo's Annex,** 657 Bay Blvd. (☎541-265-7512). Dishes up the same food in a less historic atmosphere. Open daily 11am-10pm. AmEx/D/MC/V. ❷

April's, 749 NW 3rd St. (☎541-265-6855), by Nye Beach. The pinnacle of local dining. The serene ocean view and exceptional food are worth every penny. Entrees $18-24. Towering chocolate eclairs $5. Open W-Su 5pm-last customer. Reservations recommended. D/MC/V. ❺

SIGHTS

MARK O. HATFIELD MARINE SCIENCE CENTER. The center is the hub of Oregon State University's coastal research. The 300 scientists working here maintain rigorous intellectual standards for the exhibits, which explore fascinating topics ranging from chaos—demonstrated by a paddle wheel/water clock—to climate change and a behavioral analysis of Wile E. Coyote's causality. While you can't play with the live octopus, a garden of sea anemones, slugs, and bottom-dwelling fish awaits you in the touch tanks. (At the south end of the bridge on Marine Science Dr. ☎541-867-0100. Open in summer daily 10am-5pm; in winter M and Th-Su 10am-4pm. Donations accepted.)

OREGON COAST AQUARIUM. More famous, less serious, and much more expensive than the Science Center is the Oregon Coast Aquarium. This aquarium housed Keiko, the much-loved *Free Willy* Orca, during his rehabilitation before he returned to his childhood waters near Iceland. The Passages of the Deep exhibit features a 200 ft. tunnel surrounded by sharks, rays, and fish. *(2820 SE Ferry Slip Rd., at the south end of the bridge. ☎541-867-3474; www.aquarium.org. Open daily from late June to early Sept. 9am-6pm; from late Sept. to early June 10am-5pm. $14.25, ages 3-12 $8.75, under 3 free.)*

ROGUE ALE BREWERY. The brewery has won more awards than you can shake a pint at. Cross the bay bridge and follow the signs to the aquarium. Twenty brews, including Oregon Golden, Shakespeare Stout, and Dead Guy Ale, are available upstairs at **Brewers by the Bay**, where taster trays of four beers are $5.25. *(2320 Oregon State University Dr. SE. Brewery ☎541-867-3660. Brewers by the Bay ☎541-867-3664. Pints $4.50. Open M-Th and Su 11am-10pm, F-Sa 11am-11pm. Tours daily noon, 4, 6pm. Free.)*

⚐ THE ROAD TO DEPOE BAY: 13 MI.
Continue on **US 101/Oregon Coast Highway.** Consider taking a detour on the renowned **Otter Crest Loop,** a twisting 4 mi. excursion high above the shore that affords spectacular views at every bend, including vistas of **Otter Rock** and the **Marine Gardens.** A lookout over the aptly named **Cape Foulweather** has telescopes ($0.50) for spotting sea lions lazing on the rocks. The **Devil's Punch Bowl,** formed when the roof of a seaside cave collapsed, is also accessible off the loop. It becomes a frothing cauldron during high tide when waves crash through an opening in the side of the bowl. **Otter Rocks Beach** is a great place to learn to surf; beginners can try out breaks closer to shore.

DEPOE BAY   ☎541
Depoe Bay, the smallest harbor in the world, has whale watching along the town's low seawall at the **Depoe Bay State Park Wayside and the Observatory Lookout,** 4 mi. to the south. Go early in the morning on a cloudy day during the annual migration (Mar.-Dec.) for your best chance of spotting the gray giants. **Tradewinds Charters,** off US 101, downtown, has 6hr. fishing and crabbing trips and 1-2hr. whale-watching trips. (☎541-765-2345 or 800-445-8730. 5hr. bottom-fishing and crabbing trips $85, children and seniors $80. Whale-watching trips $18, ages 13-19 $16, ages 5-12 $9.)

⚐ THE ROAD TO LINCOLN CITY: 12 MI.
Take **US 101/North Oregon Coast Highway** directly into downtown Lincoln City.

LINCOLN CITY   ☎541
Lincoln City is actually five towns wrapped around a 7 mi. strip of oceanfront motels, gas stations, and souvenir shops along US 101. Most budget travelers (and *Let's Go*) will tell you that the Three Capes area to the north is far superior as a destination. As one of the largest "cities" on the North Coast, Lincoln City can, however, be used as a gateway to better points north and south. Four miles north of Lincoln City, lifelong Oregon resident and author Ken Kesey *(One Flew Over the Cuckoo's Nest; Sometimes a Great Notion)* is memorialized in the Sometimes a Great Notion house on the Siletz River.

Pets are welcome in the beautiful, small rooms at the **Captain Cook Inn ❹,** 2626 US 101 NE. A quaint New England-style exterior hides clean and charmingly adorned rooms. (☎541-994-2522 or 800-994-2522; www.captaincookinn.com. Rooms $49-69, with kitchen $69-99. AmEx/D/MC/V.) **Lil' Sambo's,** 3262 Hwy. 101, serves excellent pancakes ($6), steak ($10.50-14.75), and seafood ($8.50-16). This casual restaurant was inspired by author Helen Bannerman's 1899 story of the same name. (☎541-994-3626. Open daily 6am-8:30pm. AmEx/D/MC/V.)

⚐ THE ROAD TO PACIFIC CITY: 23 MI.
Follow **US 101/South Oregon Coast Highway** and turn left onto **Brooten Road** (BRAW-ten).

PACIFIC CITY   ☎503
The nearest town to Cape Kiwanda, Pacific City is a hidden gem that most travelers on US 101 never see. The **Anchorage Motel ❸,** 6585 Pacific Ave., offers nine homey rooms on a quiet street just blocks from the beach. (☎541-965-6773 or 800-941-6250. Singles $42-59; doubles $59-99. D/MC/V.) If the Anchorage is booked up, try the **Inn at Pacific City ❹,** 32515 Brooten Rd. Rustic, well-furnished rooms are worth the cost. (☎503-965-6366. Free Wi-Fi. Rooms in summer $100-130; in winter $60-80. D/MC/V.) Local youth have been known to camp near the beach or on more secluded beaches north of Cape Kiwanda, but camping on Oregon beaches is illegal. The town contains some surprisingly good restaurants. At the **Grateful Bread Bakery ❸,** 34805 Brooten

Rd., enjoy vegetarian stuffed focaccia ($9) or sample one of the many excellent omelets for $8-10. (☎503-965-7337. Open M and Th-Su 8am-4pm. $5 meals Th 4:30-6pm. MC/V.)

DETOUR
CAPE KIWANDA STATE PARK
Along the **Three Capes Loop,** north of Lincoln City.

Cape Kiwanda State Park (☎800-551-6949; open 24hr.), 1 mi. north of Pacific City, is the jewel of the Three Capes Loop's triple crown. This sheltered cape draws beachcombers, kite-flyers, volleyball players, surfers, and windsurfers, not to mention the odd snow-boarder out to ride a giant sand hill. A walk up the sculptured sandstone on the north side reveals a hypnotic view of swells rising over the rocks, forming crests, and smash-ing into the cliffs. If the surf is up, head to **Seven Surfboards,** 33310 Cape Kiwanda Dr., a little ways off the beach, where the walls are lined with handcrafted surfboards and local artwork. Buy a pair of "Locals" (flip-flops) for $5. (☎503-965-7873. Surfboard rental $20 until 5pm. Boogie boards $10. Wetsuits $20. Pack-age deal $45. Lessons $35 per hr. Open in sum-mer daily 9am-6pm; hours vary in winter.)

DETOUR
CAPE LOOKOUT STATE PARK
Go 12 mi. southwest of **Cape Meares.**

Cape Lookout State Park offers a small, rocky beach with incredible views of the sur-rounding sights. From here, the **Cape Trail** (2 mi.) heads past the 1943 crash site of a mili-tary plane to the end of the lookout, where a spectacular 360° view featuring **Haystack Rock** awaits. The **Cape Lookout Campground ❶** offers lovely camping near the dunes and the forests behind them, although sites with better privacy tend to go far in advance. (☎503-842-4981 or 800-551-6949. 216 sites. Sites May-Sept. $16, with hookup $20; Oct.-Apr. $12/16. Day use $3. Yurts $27. MC/V.)

DETOUR
CAPE MEARES STATE PARK
At the tip of the promontory jutting out from **Tillamook** 6 mi. south of Tillamook.

Cape Meares State Park protects one of the few remaining old-growth forests on the Oregon coast. The mind-blowing **Octopus Tree,** a gnarled Sitka spruce with six candelabra trunks, looks like the imaginative scribbles of an eight-year-old. The **Cape Meares Lighthouse** operates as an illuminating on-site interpre-tive center. (☎503-842-2244. Open Apr.-Oct. daily 11am-4pm. Free.) If you walk down to the lighthouse, bring binoculars or use the $0.25 viewer to look at the amazing seabird colony on the giant volcanic rock. As you drive south of Cape Meares, a break in the trees reveals a beach between two cliffs; this is a beautiful place to pull off and explore.

The towns of **Oceanside** and **Netarts** lie a cou-ple of miles south of Cape Meares and offer overpriced gas, a market, and a few places to stay. The **Terimore ❸,** 5103 Crab Ave., in Netarts, has decent, clean rooms, some with ocean views. (☎541-842-4623 or 800-635-1821. Rooms in summer $56-77, with views $69-79, with kitchen and/or fireplace $87-125; in win-ter $10 less. AmEx/D/MC/V.) **Olmedo's Family Dining ❸,** 6060 Whiskey Creek Rd., in Netarts, is a popular Italian restaurant. Create your own pasta for $14. (☎541-842-5117. Pizza $13-15. Twice-baked lasagna $14. Open daily 11am-9:30pm. AmEx/MC/V.)

THE ROAD TO TILLAMOOK: 35 MI.
Between Lincoln City and Tillamook, **US 101** wanders east into wooded land, leaving the coast. The **Three Capes Loop** is a 35 mi. circle that connects a trio of spectacular promontories—**Cape Kiwanda, Cape Look-out,** and **Cape Meares State Parks**—that will almost certainly make you linger longer than you expect; plan accordingly. The loop leaves US 101 10 mi. north of Lincoln City and rejoins at Tillamook. Unless time is of the utmost importance, the loop is a far better choice than driving straight up US 101.

TILLAMOOK ☎503

Although the word Tillamook (TILL-uh-muk) translates to "land of many waters," to those in the Northwest it is synonymous with cheese. Tourists come by the hundreds to gaze at blocks of cheese being cut into smaller blocks on a conveyor belt at the Tillamook Cheese Factory. The dairy cows themselves give the town a rather bad odor; still, two good muse-ums, hiking and biking in the nearby coastal mountains, and the Three Capes Loop redeem Tillamook for the adventurous traveler.

ORIENTATION

Tillamook's main drag, **US 101,** splits into two one-way streets downtown; **Pacific Avenue** runs north, and **Main Avenue** runs south. The cross streets are labeled numerically and increase as you head south.

VITAL STATS

Population: 4400

Tourist Office: Tillamook Chamber of Commerce, 3705 US 101 N. (☎503-842-7525), in the big red barn near the Tillamook Cheese Factory, 1 mi. north of town. Open daily M-F 9am-5pm.

Library and Internet Access: Tillamook County Library, 210 Ivy Ave. (☎503-842-4792). Open M-Th 9am-9pm, F-Sa 9am-5:30pm.

Post Office: 2200 1st St. (☎503-842-2517). Open M-F 9am-5pm. **Postal Code:** 97141.

CAMPING

Motel prices in Tillamook are steep, with a 7% city lodging tax–in other words, camp.

Kilchis River Park (☎503-842-6694), 6 mi. northeast of town at the end of Kilchis River Rd. 36 sites between a mossy forest and the Kilchis River. The campground itself is geared toward families, with a baseball field, volleyball court, horseshoes, and swimming. Water and toilets. Open May-Oct. Sites $12-15. MC/V. ❶

FOOD

Dekunsam's 2nd St. Coffee House, 1912 2nd St. (☎503-842-2299). A colorful cafe serving delicious drinks and food. Free Wi-Fi. Open daily 9am-5pm. Cash only. ❶

Blue Heron French Cheese Company, 2001 Blue Heron Rd. (☎503-842-8281), 1 mi. south of the Tillamook Cheese Factory. Tasty deli sandwiches ($6), a wine tasting station, and a petting zoo. Still craving dairy? It also has plenty of free cheese samples. Open daily in summer 8am-8pm; in winter 8am-6pm. Deli open daily 11am-3:30pm. AmEx/D/MC/V. ❶

SIGHTS

TILLAMOOK CHEESE FACTORY. The factory gives out cheese samples and lets visitors take a free guided tour. (4175 US 101 N. ☎800-542-7290; www.tillamookcheese.com. Open daily in summer 8am-8pm; in winter 8am-6pm. Free.)

TILLAMOOK NAVAL AIR STATION MUSEUM. Aviation buffs and all who celebrate mechanical marvels will appreciate this impressive museum. This hulking seven-acre former blimp hangar is the largest wood clear-span structure in the world. The airy cavern is home to over 38 fully functional war planes, including WWII beauties like the P-38 Lightning and a PBY-5A Catalina. (2 mi. south of town. ☎503-842-1130; www.tillamookair.com. Open daily 9am-5pm. $11.50, ages 6-17 $7, under 6 free.)

TILLAMOOK COUNTY PIONEER MUSEUM. The museum features an exceptionally thorough collection of WWII artifacts and displays the head-turning work of taxidermist and big-game hunter Alex Walker. (2106 2nd St. ☎503-842-4553; www.tcpm.org. Open Tu-Sa 9am-5pm, Su 11am-5pm. $3, ages 12-17 $2, under 12 $0.50.)

THE ROAD TO WHEELER: 23 MI.

Continue on **US 101/Oregon Coast Highway.**

WHEELER   ☎503

Eight miles north of Rockaway Beach lies this quaint community that runs alongside Nehalem Bay. The ▨**Old Wheeler Hotel** ❹, 495 Hwy. 101, is a warm and welcoming B&B with antique furniture and a collection of the "greatest movies ever made." Proprietors Winston and Maranne encourage their guests to get comfortable in the piano room or cozy living room, which has a bay view. (☎503-368-6000; wwwoldwheelerhotel.com. Continental breakfast included. Free Wi-Fi. Rooms in summer from $90; in winter from $65. AmEx/D/MC/V.) The **Sea Shack** ❸, 380 Marine Dr., serves delightfully fresh seafood right on the waterfront. (☎503-368-7897. Halibut sandwich $9.50. Open M-Th and Su 11am-9pm, F-Sa 11am-10pm. AmEx/D/MC/V.)

THE ROAD TO NEHALEM: 2 MI.

Head north on **US 101/Oregon Coast Highway.**

NEHALEM ☎ 503

Just north of Wheeler, a cluster of shops along US 101 make up Nehalem. The **Nehalem Bay Winery,** 34965 Rte. 53, 2 mi. south of town, has free tastings of local cranberry and blackberry vintages. The winery sponsors performances in a small theater and an annual reggae and bluegrass festival, providing a forum for bacchanalian revelry. (☎503-368-9463; www.nehalembaywinery.com. Open daily 9am-6pm.) Outside of town, **Nehalem Bay State Park ❶** has several camping options. (☎503-368-5154, reservations 800-452-5687. Sites May-Sept. $8-20; Oct.-Apr. $5-16. Day use $3.)

⚑ DETOUR
OSWALD WEST STATE PARK
Located off **US 101,** 3 mi. south of Arch Cape.

Oswald West State Park is a tiny headland rainforest of hefty spruce and cedars. With a first-rate break and camping close by, **Short Sands Beach,** or Shorty's, is a premier surf destination. The beach and woodsy campsites are only accessible by a trail off US 101, but the park provides wheelbarrows for transporting gear from the parking lot to the 30 sites. The campground fills quickly; call ahead. (Open Mar.-Nov. Sites $14. Cash only.) From the south side of the park, a segment of the Oregon Coast Trail leads over the headland to 1661 ft. **Neahkahnie Mountain.**

⚑ THE ROAD TO CANNON BEACH: 8 MI.
Go north on **US 101/Oregon Coast Highway.** Along the way, you'll pass **Hug Point,** famous for tidal caves that are accessible only at low tide.

CANNON BEACH ☎ 503

Many moons ago, a rusty cannon from a shipwrecked schooner washed ashore at Arch Cape, giving this town its name. Today, home to a veritable army of boutiques, bakeries, and galleries, Cannon Beach is a more refined alternative to nearby Seaside's crass commercialism. Arguably the most desirable location on the entire Oregon coast because of its amazing ocean views and interesting shops, Cannon Beach is always crowded with Port-

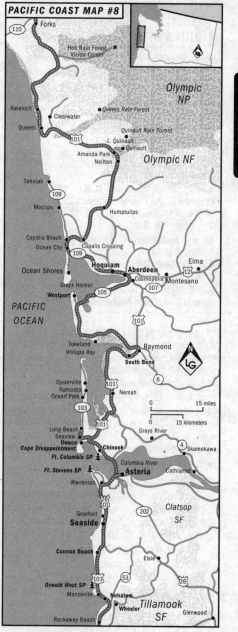

PACIFIC COAST MAP #8

landers and other tourists. Still, it's well worth the stop to take in the view.

ORIENTATION

Cannon Beach lies 8 mi. south of **Seaside** and 42 mi. north of **Tillamook** on **US 101.** Lovely Ecola and Oswald State Parks lie just to the north and a few miles south of the town, respectively. The four exits into town from US 101 all lead to **Hemlock Street,** which is lined with restaurants and galleries.

VITAL STATS
Population: 1588
Tourist Office: Cannon Beach Chamber of Commerce and Tourist Office, 207 N. Spruce St. (☎503-436-2623), at 2nd St. Open M-Sa 10am-5pm, Su 11am-4pm.
Library and Internet Access: Cannon Beach Library, 131 N. Hemlock St. (☎503-436-1391). $6 per hr. Open M-Tu and F 1-5pm, W-Th 1-7pm, Sa 10am-5pm.
Post Office: 163 N. Hemlock St. (☎503-436-2822). Open M-F 9am-5pm. **Postal Code:** 97110.

ACCOMMODATIONS

During the winter months, inquire about specials; many motels offer two-for-one deals. In the summer, however, it's a seller's market, so most motels have two-night minimum stays if you want a reservation. Real budget deals are a short drive away: the **Seaside International Hostel** is 7 mi. north (opposite page), and the stunning **Oswald West State Park** is 10 mi. south (previous page).

McBee Cottages, 888 S. Hemlock St. (☎800-238-4107; www.cannonbeachhotellodgings. com). Bright and cheerful rooms a few blocks from the beach. Kitchen units and cottages available. Rooms in summer from $140; in winter from $70. AmEx/D/MC/V. ❹

Wright's for Camping, 334 Reservoir Rd. (☎503-436-2347), off US 101. 19 sites offer a relaxing retreat from RV mini-cities. Toilets and showers. Reservations recommended in summer. Sites $21-30. MC/V. ❶

FOOD

The deals are down Hemlock St., in midtown. If you're looking to stock up, **Mariner Market,** 139 N. Hemlock St., holds grocery items on its expansive shelves. (☎503-436-2442. Open July-Sept. M-Th and Su 8am-10pm, F-Sa 8am-11pm; Oct.-June M-Th and Su 8am-9pm, F-Sa 8am-10pm. MC/V.)

Lazy Susan's Cafe, 126 N. Hemlock St. (☎503-436-2816), in Coaster Sq. A Cannon Beach favorite with an intimate, woodsy interior. Excellent homemade scones cost $2.50. Omelets $8-10. Open in summer M and Su 8am-3pm, W-Sa 8am-8pm; in winter M, W-Th, Su 8am-3pm, F-Sa 8am-8pm. Cash only. ❷

Bill's Tavern, 188 N. Hemlock St. (☎503-436-2202). Brews beer upstairs that flows on tap downstairs. Basic pub grub $3-8.25. Pints $3.75. Open M-Tu and Th-Su 11:30am-last customer, W 4:30pm-last customer. Kitchen open until 10pm. D/MC/V. ❷

ENTERTAINMENT

Coaster Theater, 108 N. Hemlock St., is a small playhouse that stages theater productions, concerts, dance performances, comedy, and musical revues throughout the year. (☎503-436-1242; www.coastertheater.com. Tickets $8-17. Box office open W-Sa 1-5pm.)

OUTDOORS

Cannon Beach has expensive, sporadically elegant galleries and gift shops. A stroll along the 7 mi. stretch of flat, bluff-framed beach suits many better. The best place to enjoy the dramatic volcanic coastline of Cannon Beach is at **Ecola State Park,** which attracts picnickers, hikers, and surfers alike. Have a look at Ecola Point's views of hulking **Haystack Rock,** which is spotted with seagulls, puffins, barnacles, anemones, and the occasional sea lion. Follow signs from US 101. **Indian Beach** is a gorgeous surfing destination where you can catch waves between volcanic rock walls before rinsing off in the freshwater stream that runs down the beach. Rent boards from **Cleanline Surf,** 171 Sunset Blvd. (☎503-436-9726. Surfboards and boogie boards $15 per day. Wetsuits $20 per day. Wetsuit and board $35, children $25. Open in summer daily 8am-8pm; in winter M-F 10am-6pm, Sa-Su 9am-6pm.)

Indian Beach Trail (2 mi.) leads to the Indian Beach tide pools, which teem with colorful sea life. Follow signs to "Ecola" to reach the trailhead. **Tillamook Head Trail** (12 mi. round-trip) leaves from Indian Beach and hugs the coast to the mini-cape that separates Seaside Beach from Cannon Beach. The trail passes the top of Tillamook Head (2 mi. up the trail), where five campsites await those willing to make the trek for free camping. Fourteen miles east of Cannon Beach, **Saddle Mountain Trail** (5 mi. round-trip) climbs the highest peak in the Coast Range. The trail leads to the mountain's 3283 ft. summit and ends with astounding views of the Pacific Ocean, Nehalem Bay, and the Cascades.

THE ROAD TO SEASIDE: 8 MI.

Continue to follow **US 101/Oregon Coast Highway.**

SEASIDE ☎503

In the winter of 1805-06, explorers Lewis and Clark made their westernmost camp near Seaside. While the amenities were few and far between at the time, the development of a resort in 1870 brought in hordes of tourists. The town center, replete with indoor minigolf and barrels of saltwater taffy, has transformed Seaside from a remote coastal outpost to a bustling beachfront. For those uninterested in video arcades, Seaside still has merit as a base for exploring the beautiful Oregon coast. Seaside is also less expensive than its nearby neighbors, and its hostel is one of the best in the whole of the Northwest.

ORIENTATION

Seaside lies 17 mi. south of Astoria and 8 mi. north of Cannon Beach along **US 101.** The **Necanicum River** runs north-south through Seaside, two blocks from the coastline. In town, US 101 becomes **Roosevelt Drive,** and another major road, **Holladay Drive,** splits off from it. **Broadway,** a tourist-dollar black hole, runs perpendicular to the two and is the town's main street. Streets north of Broadway are numbered, and those south of Broadway are let-

tered. The **Promenade** (or "Prom") is a footpath that hugs the beach for the length of town.

VITAL STATS
Population: 5900
Tourist Office: Seaside Visitor Bureau (☎503-738-3097 or 888-306-2326; www.seasideor.com). Open June-Aug. M-Sa 8am-5pm, Su 10am-4pm; Oct.-May M-F 9am-5pm, Sa-Su 10am-4pm.
Library and Internet Access: Seaside Library, 60 N. Roosevelt Dr. (☎503-738-6742). Open Tu-Th 9am-8pm, F-Sa 9am-5pm, Su 1-5pm.
Post Office: 300 Ave. A (☎503-738-5190), off Columbia Ave. Open M-F 8:30am-5pm, Sa 8:30-10:30am. **Postal Code:** 97138.

ACCOMMODATIONS

Seaside's expensive motels are hardly a problem for the budget traveler, thanks to the large hostel on the south side of town. Motel prices are directly proportional to their proximity to the beach and start at $50.

Seaside International Hostel (HI), 930 N. Holladay Dr. (☎503-738-7911). Offers free nightly movies, a well-equipped kitchen, an espresso bar, and a grassy yard along the river. Kayak and canoe rental. Reception 8am-11pm. Reservations recommended. Dorms $26, members $23; private rooms $39-65/36-42. D/MC/V. ❶

Saddle Mountain (☎800-551-6949), 10 mi. east, off US 26. Drive 8 mi. northeast of Necanicum Jct., then another 7 mi. up to the base camp. Offers sites with drinking water. Sites Oct.-Apr. $5; May-Sept. $9. Cash only. ❶

FOOD

Prices on Broadway, especially toward the beach, are outrageous.

Morning Star Cafe, 280 S. Roosevelt Dr. (☎503-717-8188). Comfy couches and aging board games will remind you of your old basement rec room. Enjoy a sandwich ($5-8.25) or quiche ($6.25) with a mocha. Get the grilled cheese royale ($8.75) for a dairy fix. Wi-Fi or Internet $2.50 per 15min. Open in summer M-F 7am-7pm, Sa-Su 7am-2 or 4pm; in winter M-F 7am-6pm, Sa-Su 7am-2 or 4pm. D/MC/V. ❷

The Stand, 101 N. Holladay Dr. (☎503-738-6592). Serves the cheapest Mexican meals around to a local crowd. Burritos $3-5. Open M-Sa 11am-8pm. Cash only. ❶

👁 ⚠ SIGHTS AND OUTDOORS

Seaside's tourist population (which often outnumbers that of locals) swarms around Broadway, a carnival-esque strip of arcades and shops running the half-mile from Roosevelt Dr. (US 101) to the beach. "The Arcade," as it is called, is the focal point of downtown and attracts a youthful crowd. Bumper cars, basketball games, and other tourist trappings abound. The turnaround at the end of Broadway signals the end of the Lewis and Clark Trail.

Perhaps the premier recreational road race in the US, the **Hood to Coast Relay** is the ultimate team running event. Held annually at the end of August, runners tear up the trails between Mt. Hood and Seaside (195 mi.) to the cheers of 50,000 spectators. About 750 twelve-person teams run three five mile shifts in this one- to two-day relay race. For more info, call ☎503-292-4626.

SEASIDE AQUARIUM. Though smaller than its companion in Newport, the aquarium makes up for its size by giving visitors the chance to feed playful harbor seals. *(200 N. Promenade. ☎503-738-6211; www.seasideaquarium.com. Open Mar.-June daily 9am-7pm; hours vary in winter. $7, ages 6-13 $3.50, under 6 free, seniors $5.75.)*

PROM. If it's a bright day, you might want to take a stroll down the beach or bike or skate along the wood walkway known as the Prom. Get into the spirit by renting a beach bike, tossing back your hair, and eating an ice-cream cone by the sea.

SALT CAIRNS. Although pots in piles of stones are traditionally none too exciting, the Salt Cairns mark the spot where members of Lewis and Clark's party boiled seawater for two months, supplying the explorers with the salt required to preserve their food for the journey home. *(8 blocks south of Broadway.)*

GEARHART BEACH. Seaside's beachfront is sometimes crowded despite the bone-chilling water and strong undertows that preclude swimming. For a slightly quieter beach, head to Gearhart, where stretches of dunes await exploration. *(2 mi. north of downtown off US 101.)*

🛣 THE ROAD TO FORT CLATSTOP NATIONAL MEMORIAL: 10 MI.

Continue north on **US 101.** Turn right at **Southeast Marlin Avenue** and follow the signs to the memorial.

FORT CLATSTOP NATIONAL MEMORIAL ☎503

This memorial reconstructs Lewis and Clark's winter headquarters from journal descriptions. The fort contains exhibits about the explorers' quest for the Pacific Ocean. In summer, rangers in feathers and buckskin demonstrate quill writing, moccasin sewing, and musket firing. (☎503-861-2471. Open daily from June to Labor Day 9am-6pm; from Labor Day to May 9am-5pm. $3, under 16 free.)

🛣 THE ROAD TO FORT STEVENS STATE PARK: 1 MI.

Head north on **Fort Stevens Highway** to the park.

FORT STEVENS STATE PARK ☎503

Fort Stevens was constructed in 1863 to prevent attack by Confederate naval raiders. The fort was significantly upgraded in 1897 with the addition of eight concrete artillery batteries. The remaining batteries are the focus of a 2hr. self-guided walking tour that begins up the road from the campground area. The **Military Museum** has exhibits on Fort Stevens's role from the Civil War through World War II. Great places to surf or kayak await at the South Jetty, near the northern tip of the peninsula in the park. Waves get big when wave refraction off the jetty kicks in. Everyone loves catching a wave in front of the **Wreck of the Peter Iredale** that sticks out of the sand, even though the breaks are nothing special. (☎503-861-2000. Get a map and pass from the camp registration. Open 8am-6pm. Museum open 10am-6pm. Entrance fee $3.) Rugged, empty beaches and hiking and bike trails surround the **campground ❶,** though the 287 cramped sites don't offer much in the way of privacy. (☎503-861-1671, reservations 800-452-5687. Toilets and water. Reservations recommended; $6 fee. Tent sites $18; RV sites $22; hiker sites $4. Yurts $30. MC/V.)

ⓘ THE ROAD TO ASTORIA: 9 MI.
Follow **Fort Stevens Highway (Alternate US 101)** out of Fort Stevens Park and turn left to follow **US 101.**

ASTORIA ☎503

Established in 1811 by John Jacob Astor's trading party, Astoria is the oldest US city west of the Rocky Mountains. Originally built as a fort to guard the mouth of the Columbia River, it quickly became a port city for ships heading to Portland and to Longview, Washington. A more pleasant and less expensive destination than the resort cities to the south, Astoria offers the same beautiful views of the Pacific Ocean. Its Victorian homes, energetic waterfront, rolling hills, and persistent fog suggest a smaller-scale San Francisco. However, Astoria has a microclimate with wicked winter storms; gale-force winds aren't uncommon, and many travelers come to watch storms roll into the Columbia River outlet.

VITAL STATS
Population: 9800
Tourist Office: Astoria-Warrenton Area Chamber of Commerce, 111 W. Marine Dr. (☎503-325-6311), just east of Astoria Bridge. Open daily 9am-5pm.
Library and Internet Access: Astoria Library, 450 10th St. (☎503-325-7323). Open Tu-Th 10am-7pm, F-Sa 10am-5pm.
Post Office: 750 Commercial St., Ste. 104 (☎503-338-0316). Open M-F 8:30am-5pm. **Postal Code:** 97103.

✴ ORIENTATION

Astoria is a peninsula that extends into the **Columbia River,** approximately 7 mi. from the ocean beaches in Fort Stevens and Washington. Two bridges run from the city: the **Youngs Bay Bridge** leads southwest when **Marine Drive** becomes **US 101,** and the **Astoria Bridge** spans the Columbia River into Washington. All streets parallel to the water are named in alphabetical order, except for the first one.

⌂ ACCOMMODATIONS

Motel rooms can be extremely expensive and elusive during summer. US 101, both north and south of Astoria, is littered with clean and scenic campgrounds.

Grandview B&B, 1574 Grand Ave. (☎503-325-0000 or 325-5555; www.grandviewbedandbreakfast.com). Intimate, cheery, and luxurious rooms. Breakfast included. Rooms $66-129. D/MC/V. ❸

Lamplighter Motel, 131 W. Marine Dr. (☎503-325-4051 or 800-845-8847), near the tourist office. Recently remodeled, spotless, and well-lit rooms with cable TV, large bathrooms, and Internet. Rooms in summer $78-102; in winter $46-78. AmEx/D/MC/V. ❸

🍴 FOOD

A small but growing farmers' market convenes each summer Sunday downtown at 12th St. from 10am to 3pm.

Columbian Cafe, 1114 Marine Dr. (☎503-325-2233; www.columbianvoodoo.com). Offers local banter, wines by the glass, and fantastic pasta and seafood. Try "Seafood Mercy" or "Vegetarian Mercy"—name the heat your mouth can stand and chef Uriah Hulsey will design a meal for you. Lunch entrees $6-14. Dinner entrees $12-24. Open W-Th 8am-2pm and 5-8pm, F 8am-2pm and 5-9pm, Sa-Su 9am-2pm and 5-9pm. Cash only. ❸

T. Paul's Urban Cafe, 1119 Commercial St. (☎503-338-5133). Check out the Meat Lover weekends (F-Sa), when pork loin, prime rib, and lamb rotate. The veggie burger ($8) is exceptional. Open daily for coffee 9-11am. Kitchen open M-Th 11am-9pm, F-Sa 11am-10pm. MC/V. ❸

Danish Maid Bakery (☎503-325-3657), across the street from Paul's. Offers delicious sweets for pocket change. Crazy Coolies ($0.25) and Chocolate Chews ($0.75) are particularly popular. Open M-Sa 4am-5:30pm. AmEx/MC/V. ❶

👁 SIGHTS

◼ASTORIA COLUMN. On the rare clear day, Astoria Column, cradled between Saddle Mountain to the south and the Columbia River Estuary to the north, grants climbers a stupendous view of Astoria. Completed in 1926, the column on Coxcomb Hill Rd. encloses a dizzying 164 steps past newly repainted friezes depicting local history; picture something like an exceptionally well-decorated barber's pole jutting into the sky, albeit one that (luckily) doesn't spin. *(Follow signs from 16th Ave. and Commercial St. Open sunrise-10pm.)*

COLUMBIA RIVER MARITIME MUSEUM. The cavernous, wave-shaped museum is packed with marine lore, including displays on the fisheries that once dominated Astoria. Among the model boats is the 1792 vessel that Robert Gray first steered into the mouth of the Columbia River. *(1792 Marine Dr., on the waterfront. ☎503-325-2323; www.crmm.org. Open daily 9:30am-5pm. $8, ages 6-17 $4, under 6 free.)*

◼ NIGHTLIFE

◼ **Voodoo Room** (☎503-325-2233; www.columbianvoodoo.com), adjacent to Columbian Cafe. A hot venue for live music, known by many as an artists' hang. Egyptian sarcophagi complete the scene. Bluegrass Th. Funk, jazz, and every other kind of music F-Sa. Cover F-Sa $3-5. Open daily 5-10pm or later. Cash only.

Wet Dog Cafe & Pacific Rim Brewing Co., 144 11th St. (☎503-325-6975). Youthful crowds flock here for hip hop and Top 40 on weekends. Burgers $8. Seafood burgers $10. DJs Th-F. 21+ after 10pm. Open M-F 11:30am-11pm, F-Sa 11:30am-2am. AmEx/D/MC/V.

⚐ THE ROAD TO CHINOOK: 10 MI.
Follow the **US 101/Oregon Coast Highway** across the border into Washington.

The Evergreen State

WASHINGTON

Welcomes You

CHINOOK   ☎360
As you stop in the **Country Store,** 775 US 101, for some candy or a bottle of juice, check out the photographs of Chinook from days of yore with dirt streets and horses pulling in the fishing catch. (☎360-777-2248. Open M-

Th and Su 5am-7:30pm, F-Sa 5am-8pm.) One of the few intact coastal defense sites in the US, **Fort Columbia State Park** offers 5 mi. of hiking trails, an interpretive center, and wildlife viewing. (Center open daily 10am-5pm. Park open daily in summer 6:30am-9:30pm; in winter 8am-5pm. Donations accepted.)

⚐ THE ROAD TO ILWACO: 7 MI.
Head north on **US 101** to Ilwaco.

ILWACO   ☎360
The best thing to do once you've set foot in the beautiful, wet state of Washington is to traipse around its southernmost tip in Ilwaco, at ◼**Cape Disappointment State Park.** The confluence of the Columbia and Pacific is breathtaking, and along the way you'll stumble over some unexpected beaches tucked into the jetty. The cape was named for that "aw, shucks" feeling felt by the British explorer Captain John Meares in 1788 when he missed the passage over the main sandbar. The 1882-acre park has 6 mi. of hiking trails and 2 mi. of beachfront. North Head is one of the windiest places on the west coast: Wind speeds have reached 120 mph. Follow the signs to the **Lewis and Clark Interpretive Center,** park your car, and wander; you can't go too far without coming to the water's edge. If the weather turns on you (which is a frequent occurrence in Washington), you can pop into the center, which has excellent displays about the famous duo's journey as well as on maritime and Native American history. (☎360-642-3078. Open daily 10am-5pm. $5, children $2.50, families $15.) A three-quarter-mile trail leads to the **Cape Disappointment Lighthouse,** one of the oldest operating lighthouses on the West Coast.

Like most towns along the bay, Ilwaco was devastated when depleted salmon stocks required a shutdown of the fishery for several years. Salmon steaks are plentiful along the waterfront, where the industry is beginning to recover. **Pacific Salmon Charters** leads 8hr. fishing tours. (☎360-642-3466 or 800-831-2695. From $83.50. Open daily at 4:30am.)

⚐ THE ROAD TO WILLAPA BAY: 15 MI.
Follow **US 101** as it heads north toward Willapa Bay.

WILLAPA BAY ☎360

Willapa Bay stretches between the Long Beach Peninsula and the Washington mainland. Home to the last unpolluted estuary in the nation, this is an excellent place to birdwatch, especially in late spring and early fall. From the north, stop at the headquarters of the **Willapa National Wildlife Refuge,** 12 mi. north of the junction between US 101 and Rte. 13, just off US 101, by Chinook. The headquarters has info on Canada geese, loons, grebes, cormorants, and trumpeter swans. (☎360-484-3482. Open M-F 7:30am-4pm.) Rent a kayak or canoe and travel down the **Willapa Bay Water Trail** through Willapa Bay to Tokeland; there's a boat ramp at the refuge.

⚐ THE ROAD TO SOUTH BEND: 37 MI.

Continue on **US 101** to the tiny town of South Bend.

SOUTH BEND ☎360

South Bend grew into a township as the location of the Northern Pacific Railway terminus. As you drive through, pull over into the harbor for a closer view of the wood statues dedicated to fishermen. Don't miss the beautiful **1910 Courthouse,** 300 Memorial Dr., one block east of US 101, set in stunning landscaped gardens. Take a look up at the kaleidoscopically colored glass dome. (☎360-875-9320. Open M-F 8:30am-5pm.)

⚐ THE ROAD TO TOKELAND: 26 MI.

Continue on **US 101** to Raymond and follow **Route 105** out of Raymond along the coast; it's worth it to take the little extra time to loop around the coastal Rte. 105 instead of staying inland on US 101. Be careful of the low speed limits here, especially the 25 mph of the Shoalwater Reservation, which are enforced with particular diligence.

TOKELAND ☎360

A stop in Tokeland is worth it for the **Tokeland Hotel ❸.** Isolated on the Willapa Bay, the gracious 1889 hotel has pretty whitewashed rooms with quilts and shared bathrooms. The downstairs living room and restaurant are open from 8am to 8pm. From Rte. 105, take the Tokeland exit. The hotel is 2 mi. down on the left. (☎360-267-7006; www.tokelandhotel.

com. Reservations required. Rooms in summer $55-65; in winter $44-49. D/MC/V.)

⚐ THE ROAD TO WESTPORT: 14 MI.

Continue on **Route 105** to Westport.

WESTPORT ☎360

Westport is a pleasant town, but aside from the fishing there's not much going on here. The highlight is the beautiful **Westhaven State Park,** northeast of town on Rte. 105, where a 1 mi. trail along the coast leads to the lighthouse. (☎360-268-9717. Donations accepted.) Charter a fishing boat or surf the cove; you can rent equipment from **Steepwater Surf,** 1200 N. Montesano St. (☎360-268-5527; www.steepwatersurfshop.com. Board and wetsuit $36 per day. Open in summer daily 9am-5pm; in winter M and Th-Su 10am-4pm.)

⚐ THE ROAD TO ABERDEEN AND HOQUIAM: 22 MI.

Continue on **Route 105** for about 18 mi., then turn left to approach Aberdeen and Hoquiam on US 101 N.

ABERDEEN AND HOQUIAM ☎360

From Olympic National Park to the north, US 101 passes Grays Harbor and the industrial cities of Aberdeen and Hoquiam at the mouth of the Chehalis River. The two towns, once deeply embedded in the largely defunct fishing and timber industries, are now focusing on tourism. Aberdeen is best known as the hometown of Nirvana frontman Kurt Cobain

✈ ORIENTATION

Aberdeen is at the eastern side of **Grays Harbor,** on the banks of the Wishkah and Chehalis Rivers. **US 101** runs through Aberdeen as two one-way streets a block apart. Hoquiam is west of Aberdeen, on the banks of the **Hoquiam River.** Both cities can be extremely confusing to navigate, so be sure to pick up a map from the Grays Harbor Chamber of Commerce.

PACIFIC COAST

▲ ACCOMMODATIONS

Olympic Inn Motel, 616 W. Heron St. (☎360-533-4200 or 800-562-8681), on US 101 N. Flashing neon torch on the sign out front means you can't miss it. Rooms in summer $56-80; in winter $46-54. AmEx/D/MC/V. ❸

Hoquiam's Castle, 515 Chenault Ave. (☎360-533-2005; www.hoquiamcastle.com). Not a castle at all, but a charming 1897 Victorian inn with 5 rooms built by the lumber baron who started the town. Dolls crowd the windowsill in the Princess room, and some bathrooms have vanity tables and claw-footed tubs. Rooms $145-195. MC/V. ❺

▓ FOOD

Billy's Bar & Grill, 322 E. Heron St. (☎360-533-7144), at G St. Crosses a rugged Old West saloon with a Howard Johnson. It's named for a sailor who used to keep his seafaring pals' money in his safe and then, when they came back from the sea, would pull a trap door and drop them into the ocean. Entrees $8-19. Mixed drinks $4.25-6.75. Beer $3.75. Free Wi-Fi. Open M-Th 8am-11pm, F-Sa 8am-midnight, Su 8am-9pm. AmEx/D/MC/V. ❸

◎ SIGHTS

HUBB'S MUFFLER. Head across the street from the visitors center to Hubb's Muffler, not to fix your car but to see a small statue and homemade shrine to Kurt Cobain. The statue is hidden in the corner. Aberdeen has a fraught relationship with its most famous resident, and controversy has raged over whether the statue should be displayed publicly; many residents have reservations about honoring a heroin addict who committed suicide. The sculptor, Randy, is married to the mechanic who runs the shop. *(☎360-533-1957. Open M-F 8am-5pm, Sa 10am-noon. Free.)*

GRAYS HARBOR HISTORIC SEAPORT. Now slightly obscured by a gigantic Wal-Mart, the seaport occasionally harbors the *Lady Washington*. Launched in 1750, the vessel was the first American ship to round Cape Horn and dock in the Northwest. The boat that exists today is a 1989 replica of the historic brig and has recently appeared in Disney's *Pirates of the Caribbean*. The boat offers a selection of 3hr. tours: a sunset sail, a "sailing adventure" where you can pull the ropes and navigate yourself, or the most exciting—an 18th-century sea battle. *(☎800-200-5239 or 360-532-8611; www.ladywashington.org. Open daily 10am-1pm. $3, students and seniors $2, children $1. Trips $35-50.)*

POLSON MUSEUM. The museum has an extensive collection of local artifacts, photographs, and period clothing. *(1611 Riverside Ave., in Hoquiam. ☎360-533-5862. Open in summer W-Sa 11am-4pm, Su noon-4pm; in winter Sa-Su noon-4pm or by appointment. $4, students $2, under 12 $1.)*

◪ THE ROAD TO OCEAN SHORES: 22 MI.

Follow **US 101**, then turn left onto **Route 109**. About 16 mi. later, turn left on **Route 115**.

OCEAN SHORES ☎360

Declared "the richest little city in America" in 1969 because of its lucrative real estate, Ocean Shores remains an enviable destination for its antiquing, boating, and gambling. Grab your shillelagh and head to **Galway Bay Irish Pub** ❸, 880 Point Brown Ave. NE, for live music every Friday and Saturday night. Try the traditional corned beef sandwich ($8), or the Irish breakfast—two eggs, two rashers, one banger, two black puddings, one white pudding, fried tomatoes, and toasted soda bread—for $13. (☎360-289-2300; www.galwaybayirishpub.com. Open M-Th and Su 11am-10pm, F-Sa 11am-1am. AmEx/D/MC/V.)

THE ROAD TO OLYMPIC NATIONAL PARK: 109 MI.

Continue north on **US 101** through Amanda Park and Queets toward Olympic National Park.

OLYMPIC NATIONAL PARK ☎360

North of Aberdeen, US 101 loops around the Olympic Peninsula, a remote backpacking paradise, before heading back south toward Seattle. To the west, the Pacific Ocean stretches to a distant horizon; to the north, the Strait of Juan de Fuca separates the Olympic Peninsula from Vancouver Island; and to the east, Hood Canal and the Kitsap Peninsula isolate this sparsely inhabited wilderness from Seattle's urban sprawl. Olympic National Park, sheltering one of the most diverse landscapes in the world, is certainly the centerpiece of the Olympic Peninsula. Roads lead to many corners of Olympic National Park, but they only hint at the depths of its wilderness. A dive into the backcountry leaves summer tourists behind and reveals the park's richness and diversity.

VITAL STATS

Area: 922,610 acres

Tourist Office: Olympic National Park Visitors Center, 3002 Mt. Angeles Rd. (☎360-565-3130), off Race St. in Port Angeles. Open daily in summer 9am-4:30pm; in winter 9am-4pm.

Gateway Towns: Forks and Port Angeles.

Fees: $15 per vehicle.

ORIENTATION

US 101 encircles the park in the shape of an upside-down U. Farthest south is **Forks,** a gateway to the park's rainforested western rim. Separate from the rest of the park, much of the Pacific coastline comprises a gorgeous coastal zone. The much-visited northern rim extends eastward to **Port Angeles,** the major gateway to the park and home to many food and lodging options. The park is huge, and US 101 passes through far more than you could experience in one roadtrip; don't be in any hurry to get to Seattle.

ACCOMMODATIONS

Thor Town International Hostel, 316 N. Race St. (☎360-452-0931; www.thortown.com), in Port Angeles. A friendly, family-owned refuge located in a big red house. Helpful staff. Backpacker-friendly. Laundry $2. Bike rental $8 per day. Dorms $15; private rooms $30. Cash only. ❶

Town Motel, 1080 S. Forks Ave. (☎360-374-6231), in Forks. Offers a garden, comfortable rooms with dark wood paneling, and an activities room with a tanning bed and exercise equipment. Singles from $47; doubles from $57. AmEx/D/MC/V. ❷

South Beach Campground, 3 mi. south of the ranger station. Every site has an ocean view, meaning that it can get windy. 50 sites 1st come, 1st served. No water. Sites $10. Cash only. ❶

FOOD

Pacific Pizza, 870 S. Forks Ave. (☎360-374-2626), in Forks. The Italian dinner menu at this inexpensive choice features classic spaghetti and meatballs ($7.65) as well as delicious slices of pizza ($3-4) and sandwiches ($6.50). Open daily 11am-10pm. AmEx/D/MC/V. ❶

The Veela Cafe, 133 E. 1st St. (☎360-452-5040; www.veela-cafe.com), in Port Angeles. This chic yet comfy cafe offers soups, sandwiches, coffee drinks, and delicious smoothies ($4.25). Internet $6 per hr. Free Wi-Fi. Open M and W-Th 8am-7pm, Tu 8am-9:30pm, F-Sa 8am-11:30pm, Su 9am-5pm. ❶

The Lyre's Club, 229 W. 1st St., in Port Angeles. A casual Cajun restaurant that becomes a popular hangout after dark, complete with a dance floor. Texas Caviar (black-eyed peas, white corn, red peppers, tomatoes, and celery) $4.75. Free Wi-Fi. Entrees $9-13. Live music. Open M-F 11:30am-2am, Sa 3pm-2am, Su 6pm-2am.

SIGHTS

Port Angeles is the gateway to the Olympic National Park and has the most attractions to show for it. Near town, a trail (5 mi., 2hr.) leads out on the **Dungeness Spit,** the world's longest natural sand spit, which extends 6 mi. into the Strait of Juan de Fuca. The trail winds all the way to **New Dungeness Light-**

PACIFIC COAST

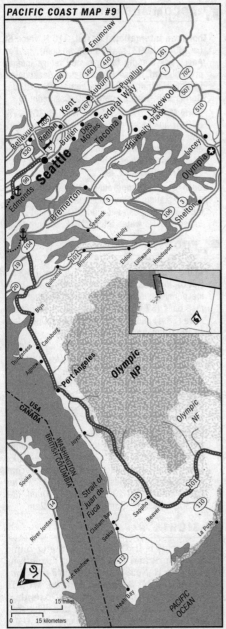

PACIFIC COAST MAP #9

house, once at the tip of the spit, now half a mile from the end. (☎603-683-9166; www.newdungenesslighthouse.com. Open daily from 9am to 2hr. before sunset. Free.) Over 200 species of birds inhabit this area, which is part of the **Dungeness National Wildlife Refuge.** Offshore, indigenous crabs, clams, seals, and sea lions populate the waters. When passing through Forks, take time to visit the **Forks Timber Museum.** (☎360-374-9663. Open June-Sept. Tu-Sa 10am-4pm. Logging and mill tours M, W, F 9am. Free.) East on US 101 on the northern rim, 13 mi. of paved road penetrate the park's interior to the popular **Sol Duc Hot Springs Resort,** where retirees de-wrinkle in the springs and eat in the lodge. (☎360-327-3583; www.visitsolduc.com. Open daily from late May to Aug. daily 9am-9pm; Sept.-Oct. and Mar.-Apr. 9am-7pm. Suit and towel rental available. $11, ages 4-12 $8.)

▲ OUTDOORS

EASTERN RIM

The eastern rim stuns visitors with its canals and grand views of the peninsula and Puget Sound. Steep trails lead up **Mount Ellinor,** 5 mi. past Staircase Campground on Rte. 119. Hikers can choose the 3 mi. path or an equally steep but shorter journey to the summit; look for signs to the Upper Trailhead along Forest Rd. #2419-04. In the nearby national forest, a 3 mi. hike goes to **Lena Lake,** 14 mi. north of Hoodsport off US 101; follow Forest Service Rd. 25 off US 101 for 8 mi. to the trailhead. The Forest Service charges $3 per trailhead pass. The **West Forks Dosewallip Trail** (10 mi.) to Mount Anderson Glacier is the shortest route to any glacier in the park. The road to **Mount Walker Viewpoint,** 5 mi. south of Quilcene on US 101, is spectacular but has sheer dropoffs and shouldn't be attempted in bad weather or with an unreliable car. A view of Hood Canal, Puget Sound, Mt. Rainier, and Seattle awaits travelers at the top.

NORTHERN RIM

The most developed section of Olympic National Park lies along its northern rim, near Port Angeles, where glaciers, rainforests, and sunsets over the Pacific are only a short drive away. Farthest east off US 101 lies **Deer**

Park, where trails tend to be uncrowded. Past Deer Park, the **Royal Basin Trail** meanders 6 mi. to the Royal Basin Waterfall. The 17 mi. road up **Hurricane Ridge** is a curvy drive, so be cautious. Before July, walking on the ridge usually involves snow. Clear days provide splendid views of Mt. Olympus and Vancouver Island set against a foreground of snow and indigo lupine. From here, the uphill **High Ridge Trail** is a short walk from Sunset Point. On weekends from late December to late March, the Park Service organizes snowshoe walks on the ridge. The **Sol Duc** trailhead is a starting point for those heading up, but crowds thin dramatically above Sol Duc Falls. The **Eagle Ranger Station** has info. (☎360-327-3534. Open in summer daily 8am-4:30pm.) Farther west, off US 101 past Lake Aldwell, lies **Elwha Valley.** A wheelchair-accessible trail leads along Madison Creek through a mountainside cleft to Madison Falls, which flows 100 ft. down basalt cliffs. In January, the falls often freeze solid, while in July this is a great place to find wild strawberries. A massive body of water located in the north-central region of the peninsula, just off US 101, **Lake Crescent** is often ignored by travelers. The glacial lake offers brisk swimming, blissful picnicking, and frequent sunshine. **Storm King Ranger Station** is on a small peninsula in the center of the lake and offers standard services. (☎360-928-3380. Open in summer daily 10am-5pm.) The **Lake Crescent Lodge,** next to the Storm King Ranger Station, rents rowboats to summertime romantics. (☎360-928-3211. $9 per hr., $25 per ½-day. Rentals 7am-8pm.)

NEAH BAY AND CAPE FLATTERY

At the westernmost point on the Juan de Fuca Strait and north of the park's western rim is **Neah Bay,** known as the "Pompeii of the Pacific." The only town in the **Makah Reservation,** Neah Bay is a 500-year-old village that was buried in a landslide at Cape Alava. The Makah Nation, whose recorded history goes back 2000 years, still lives here. Just inside the reservation, the **Makah Cultural and Research Center,** on Rte. 112, in Neah Bay, has artifacts from the archaeological site. (☎360-645-2711; www.makah.com/mcrchome.htm. Open from June to mid-Sept. daily 10am-5pm; from mid-Sept. to May W-Su 10am-5pm. Free tours W-Su noon-4pm. $5, students and seniors $4.) For over 80 years, Native Americans from around the region have come for canoe races, dances, and bone games during **Makah Days,** a festival held the last weekend of August. (☎360-645-2711; www.makah.com/makahdays.htm. $10 per vehicle.) ◪**Cape Flattery,** the northwesternmost point in the contiguous US, lies just outside Neah Bay. Head out of town on Neah Bay Rd., then take the right fork onto Arrow Head Rd. This will turn into Cape Loop Rd., which will lead you to the trailhead. A half-mile trail leads to breathtaking views along the cape.

COASTAL ZONE

Pristine coastline traces the park's far western edge for 57 mi. and is separated from the

WEASELING THEIR WAY OUT OF EXTINCTION

A long-lost native of the Washington forests has finally returned home: the fisher. Contrary to its name, this small, reclusive member of the weasel family doesn't actually catch fish. Rather, it hunts for snowshoe hares, grouse, voles, birds, and mice on the forest floor or chases squirrels up in the canopy. Over-trapping in the late 1800s and early 1900s, in addition to habitat loss and fragmentation, led to the fisher's disappearance a few decades ago. Recently, biologists determined that Olympic National Park would be an optimal site for restoration of the fisher population in Washington. On January 27, 2008, 11 fishers from British Columbia were deposited in remote sites within the Elwha and Morse Creek valleys; on March 2, 7 more were released. They are equipped with small radio transmitters so that biologists can track them. Over the next three years, about 100 fishers will be restored to the park; watch for their five-toed tracks on the trails as you explore.

rest of Olympic National Park by US 101 and non-park forest. Eerie fields of driftwood, sculptured arches, and dripping caves frame flaming sunsets, while the waves are punctuated by rugged sea stacks. Between the Quinalt and Hoh Reservations, US 101 hugs the coast for 15 mi. with parking lots a short walk from the sand. North of where the highway meets the coast, **Beach #4** has abundant tide pools plastered with sea stars. **Beach #6,** 3 mi. north at mi. 160, is a favorite whale-watching spot. Near mi. 165, sea otters and eagles hang amid tide pools and sea stacks at **Ruby Beach,** a magical spot where lovers and photographers tend to congregate. Day hikers and backpackers adore the 9 mi. loop that begins at **Ozette Lake.** The trail leads along boardwalks through the rainforest. One heads toward sea stacks at Cape Alava, and the other goes to a beach at Sand Point.

⎇ THE ROAD TO SEATTLE: 84 MI.

Leave Port Angeles on **US 101;** continue east and then south. Thirty five miles beyond Port Angeles, bear right onto **Route 104 South.** Twenty five miles later, take the **ferry to Edmonds,** leaving the Olympic Peninsula, and take **I-5 South** into Seattle.

SEATTLE ☎ 206

Seattle's serendipitous mix of mountain views, clean streets, espresso stands, and rainy weather was the magic formula of the 90s, attracting transplants from across the US. The droves of newcomers provide an interesting contrast to the older residents who remember Seattle as a town, not a thriving metropolis bubbling over with millionaires. Software and coffee money have helped drive rents sky-high in some areas, but grungy ·street culture prevails. At the end of the day, there is a nook or cranny for almost anyone in Seattle. The city is shrouded in cloud 200 days a year, but when the skies are clear Seattleites rejoice that "the mountain is out" and head for the countryside.

VITAL STATS
Population: 594,000
Tourist Office: Seattle Convention and Visitors Bureau (☎206-461-5840; www.seeseattle.org), at 8th and Pike St. Open M-F 9am-5pm.
Library and Internet Access: Seattle Public Library, 1000 4th Ave. (☎206-386-4636), at Madison St. Photo ID required. Open M-Th 10am-8pm, F-Sa 10am-6pm, Su noon-6pm.
Post Office: 301 Union St. (☎206-748-5417), at 3rd Ave., downtown. Open M-F 7:30am-5:30pm. **Postal Code:** 98101.

◪ ORIENTATION

Seattle stretches from north to south on an isthmus between **Puget Sound** to the west and Lake Washington to the east. Get to downtown (including **Pioneer Square, Pike Place Market,** and

MEALS ON WHEELS

Roadtrips and good food are not generally synonymous terms, at least in the history of the American roadtrip. Roadtrippers spend the majority of their money on gas, cheap motels, and kitschy roadside attractions, leaving pittance for food. In an effort to save money, roadtrippers limit meal options to the three sandwiches (or rather two slices of bread plus condiment) on the menu for under $5. Worse, they sometimes skip the restaurant altogether and simply munch on honey-roasted peanuts and $1 gas station burritos between highway exits. But just because you're driving from coast to coast doesn't mean that your meals should be anything less than square. All you need for a dinner that will make your grandmother proud is your car engine. For every wad of cash you pour into your gas tank, a huge amount of heat is produced under the hood. In order to harness this engine cooking power, you need heavy-duty aluminum foil and some space next to the manifold (hint: it's metal and hot). Then head to a local grocery store and pick up your meal of choice; if you're still tied to your microwave oven, start off with a pre-prepared frozen meal. Otherwise, pick up some fish or chicken (other meats tend to get tough) and a few vegetables. Wrap these morsels tight in the foil and secure them on a hot (i.e., metal) part of the engine with wire. By the time you reach your destination of choice, the meal will be steamed through, perfect for your dining delight. Cooking by engine is not an exact science

the **waterfront**) from **I-5** by taking any of the exits from **James Street** to **Stewart Street.** Take the Mercer St. exit to the **Seattle Center.** The Denny Way exit leads to **Capitol Hill,** and, farther north, the 45th St. exit heads toward the **University District.** The city is easily accessible via I-5, which runs north-south through the city, and **I-90** from the east, which ends at I-5 southeast of downtown. The less crowded **Route 99** (also called Aurora Ave. and Aurora Hwy.) runs parallel to I-5 and skirts the western side of downtown, with great views from the **Alaskan Way Viaduct.** Rte. 99 is often the better choice driving downtown or to Queen Anne, Fremont, Green Lake, and the northwestern part of the city. Street parking creates many blind pullouts in Seattle, so be extra careful when turning onto crossroads. Downtown, avenues run northwest to southeast and streets run southwest to northeast. Outside downtown, everything is simplified: with few exceptions, avenues run north-south and streets east-west. The city is divided into quadrants: 1000 1st Ave. NW is a long walk from 1000 1st Ave. SE.

When driving in Seattle, yield to pedestrians. Locals drive slowly, calmly, and politely, and the police ticket mercilessly. Downtown driving can be a nightmare: parking is expensive, hills are steep, and one-way streets are ubiquitous. Read the street signs carefully, as many areas have time restrictions, and ticketers know them by heart. Prepare yourself for heavy traffic at almost any hour of the day.

ACCOMMODATIONS

Seattle's hostel scene is not amazing, but there are plenty of choices and establishments to fit all types of personalities. **Pacific Reservation Service** (☎800-684-2932) arranges B&B singles for $50-65. For inexpensive motels farther from downtown, drive north on Aurora Ave.

Green Tortoise Backpacker's Hostel, 105 Pike St. (☎206-340-1222), at 1st Ave. A young party hostel downtown. Kitchen and library. Breakfast (6-9:30am) and dinner (Tu, Th, Su) included. Towel $1. Laundry. Internet access. Key deposit $20. Reception 24hr. Dorms $31-35; private rooms $85. MC/V. ❷

Moore Hotel, 1926 2nd Ave. (☎206-448-4851 or 800-421-5508), at Virginia St. 1 block from Pike Place Market. Built in 1907, the Moore Hotel has a swanky lobby, cavernous hallways, and attentive service. Rooms from $59, with bath from $72. MC/V. ❸

Panama Hotel, 605 S. Main St. (☎206-223-9242), in the International District. Opened in 1910. This hotel's rooms reflect its history. All rooms have shared bath and come with a *yukata* (Japanese robe). Breakfast pastry and coffee included. Singles from $70; doubles from $80. MC/V. ❹

The College Inn, 4000 University Way NE (☎206-633-4441; www.collegeinnseattle.com). The friendly

and can be dangerous to both you and your car if done incorrectly. Odds are that your first meal will not meet with Martha Stewart's approval, but don't worry—you have 3000 mi. to perfect it.

Salmon with Lemon and Soy Sauce

- ¼ lb. salmon fillet
- 1 lemon, sliced
- 2 tsp. olive oil
- 2 soy sauce packets

Cut the salmon filet in half. Tear two squares of tin foil and spread the dull side evenly with olive oil. Place a salmon portion on each square and place lemon slices on it. Pour contents of one soy sauce packet over each portion and wrap up into a tight packet. Tuck each packet next to the manifold. Drive 40 mi. at 65 mph. If the salmon does not flake easily, replace and drive another 5 mi. Delish!

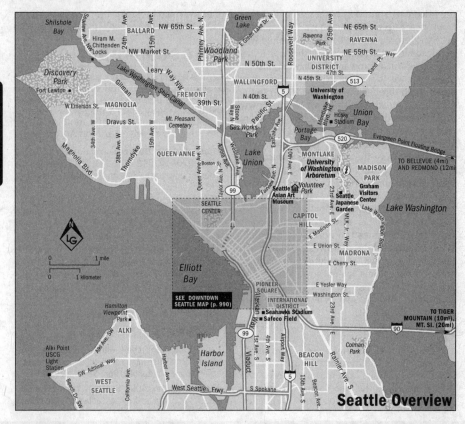

Seattle Overview

great views from the **Alaskan Way Viaduct.** Rte. 99 is often the better choice driving downtown or to Queen Anne, Fremont, Green Lake, and the northwestern part of the city. Street parking creates many blind pullouts in Seattle, so be extra careful when turning onto crossroads. Downtown, avenues run northwest to southeast and streets run southwest to northeast. Outside downtown, everything is simplified: with few exceptions, avenues run north-south and streets run east-west. The city is divided into quadrants: 1000 1st Ave. NW is a long walk from 1000 1st Ave. SE.

When driving in Seattle, yield to pedestrians. Locals drive slowly, calmly, and politely, and the police ticket mercilessly. Downtown driving can be a nightmare: parking is expensive, hills are steep, and one-way streets are ubiquitous. Read the street signs carefully, as many areas have time restrictions, and ticketers know them by heart. Prepare yourself for heavy traffic at almost any hour of the day.

ACCOMMODATIONS

Seattle's hostel scene is not amazing, but there are plenty of choices and establishments to fit all types of personalities. **Pacific Reservation Service** (☎800-684-2932) arranges B&B singles for $50-65. For inexpensive motels farther from downtown, drive north on Aurora Ave.

Green Tortoise Backpacker's Hostel, 105 Pike St. (☎206-340-1222), at 1st Ave. A young party hostel downtown. Kitchen and library. Breakfast

$6. Open in summer M-Th and Su 8am-6pm, F-Sa 8am-8pm; in winter daily 7:30am-8pm. AmEx/D/MC/V. ❸

Emmett Watson's Oyster Bar, 1916 Pike Pl. (☎206-448-7721). The Oyster Bar Special (2 oysters, 3 shrimp, bread, gazpacho, and chowder; $8.50) will delight. Beer bottles line the shelves. Open M-Th 11:30am-7pm, F-Sa 11:30am-8pm, Su 11:30am-6pm. MC/V. ❸

THE WATERFRONT

Budget eaters should steer clear of Pioneer Sq. Instead, take a picnic to **Waterfall Garden Park,** on the corner of S. Main St. and Second Ave. S. The garden has tables and a manmade waterfall that masks traffic outside. (Open daily sunrise-sunset.)

Mae Phim Thai Restaurant, 94 Columbia St. (☎206-624-2979), a few blocks north of Pioneer Sq., tucked between 1st Ave. and Alaskan Way. Slews of pad thai junkies crowd in for cheap, delicious Thai cuisine. All dishes $6. Open M-Sa 11am-7pm, Su noon-7pm. Cash only. ❷

Ivar's Fish Bar, Pier 54 (☎206-467-8063; www.ivars.net), north of Pioneer Sq. A fast-food window serves the definitive Seattle clam chowder ($3). Clam and chips $5.75. For a more upscale meal, try Ivar's Restaurant next door. Fish Bar open daily 10am-midnight. Restaraunt open M-Th 11am-10pm, F-Sa 11am-11pm, Su 9am-10pm. MC/V. Fish Bar ❶/Restaraunt ❸

INTERNATIONAL DISTRICT

Along King and Jackson St., between Fifth and Eighth Ave., Seattle's International District is packed with great eateries.

▨ **Uwajimaya,** 600 5th Ave. S. (☎206-624-6248). The Uwajimaya Center—the largest Japanese department store in the Northwest—is a full city block of groceries, gifts, videos, and CDs. There is even a food court, plying Korean barbecue and Taiwanese-style baked goods. Open M-Sa 9am-10pm, Su 9am-9pm. ❷

Tai Tung, 655 S. King St. (☎206-622-7372). Authentic Mandarin dishes and a comprehensive menu. Entrees $5-12. Open M-Th and Su 10am-11pm, F-Sa 10am-1:30am. MC/V. ❸

Ho Ho Seafood Restaurant, 653 S. Weller St. (☎206-382-9671). Eat generous portions of fresh seafood inside Bruce Lee's old kung fu studio. Lunch $4.75-6.50. Dinner $7-14. Open M-Th and Su 11am-1am, F-Sa 11am-3am. MC/V. ❸

CAPITOL HILL

With bronze dance steps emblazoned on the sidewalks and neon storefronts, Broadway Ave. is a land of espresso houses, imaginative shops, elegant clubs, and good eats.

Ristorante Machiavelli, 1215 Pine St. (☎206-621-7941), across from Bauhaus. A small, bustling Italian place. The gnocchi ($10) are considered to be the best in town. Pasta $8.50-15. Open M-Sa 5am-2am. MC/V. ❸

HaNa, 219 Broadway Ave. E. (☎206-328-1187). Packed quarters testify to the popularity of the sushi here. Lunch sushi combo platter with rice and soup $8.25. Dinner $6-19. Open M-Sa 11am-10pm, Su 4-10pm. MC/V. ❸

Honey Hole Sandwiches, 703 E. Pike St. (☎206-709-1399). Primary colors and veggie-filled sandwiches will make you feel healthy and happy. Try the pork and pineapple-filled Buford T. Justice ($8). Open daily 11am-2am. MC/V. ❷

UNIVERSITY DISTRICT

The neighborhood around the immense University of Washington ("U-Dub"), north of downtown between Union and Portage Bay, supports funky shops, international restaurants, and coffeehouses. The best of each lies within a few blocks of University Way, known as locally as **"the Avenue."**

Flowers Bar & Restaurant, 4247 University Way NE (☎206-633-1903). This 1920s landmark was once a flower shop; now, the mirrored ceiling tastefully reflects an all-you-can-eat vegan buffet ($8). Great daily drink specials. $3 sour night Th. $3 margarita night Sa. Open M-Sa 11am-2am, Su 11am-midnight. AmEx/MC/V. ❷

Star Life on the Oasis, 1405 50th St. NE (☎206-729-3542). A secret gem, tucked in next to the Grand Illusions Cinema. Mostly sandwiches and other treats to snack on. Get the vegan open faced ($6.50). Free Wi-Fi. Open M-W and F-Sa 8am-11pm, Su 10am-10pm. MC/V. ❷

Costa's Restaurant, 4559 University Way NE (☎206-633-2751). Everything from souvlaki ($12) to burgers ($7.50-9.50). Try the combina-

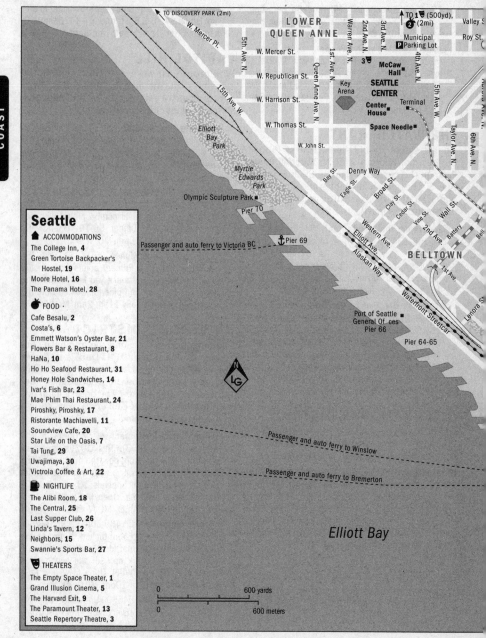

Seattle

ACCOMMODATIONS
The College Inn, **4**
Green Tortoise Backpacker's
  Hostel, **19**
Moore Hotel, **16**
The Panama Hotel, **28**

FOOD
Cafe Besalu, **2**
Costa's, **6**
Emmett Watson's Oyster Bar, **21**
Flowers Bar & Restaurant, **8**
HaNa, **10**
Ho Ho Seafood Restaurant, **31**
Honey Hole Sandwiches, **14**
Ivar's Fish Bar, **23**
Mae Phim Thai Restaurant, **24**
Piroshky, Piroshky, **17**
Ristorante Machiavelli, **11**
Soundview Cafe, **20**
Star Life on the Oasis, **7**
Tai Tung, **29**
Uwajimaya, **30**
Victrola Coffee & Art, **22**

NIGHTLIFE
The Alibi Room, **18**
The Central, **25**
Last Supper Club, **26**
Linda's Tavern, **12**
Neighbors, **15**
Swannie's Sports Bar, **27**

THEATERS
The Empty Space Theater, **1**
Grand Illusion Cinema, **5**
The Harvard Exit, **9**
The Paramount Theater, **13**
Seattle Repertory Theatre, **3**

tion plate, which offers the tastiest Greek specialties (moussaka, spanakopita, gyros, and dolmas served with rice and fresh veggies; $15). Open daily 7am-10pm. MC/V. ❸

☕ CAFES

The coffee bean is Seattle's first love; you can't walk a single block without passing an institution of caffeination. The city's obsession with Italian-style espresso drinks has even gas stations pumping out the dark, soupy java.

Victrola Coffee & Art, 411 15th Ave. (☎206-326-6520; www.victrolacoffee.com). This cafe possesses atmosphere in abundance, balancing private sitting space with inviting sofas. Coffee beans are roasted in house. Open daily 5:30am-11pm. Cash only.

Cafe Besalu, 5909 24th Ave. NW (☎206-789-1463). The coffee is good, but the real draw is the delectable pastries—from artisan bread to croissants and brioches—baked fresh in the open kitchen. Open W-Su 7am-3pm. MC/V.

◎ SIGHTS

Most of the city's major sights are within walking distance. Seattle taxpayers spend more per capita on the arts than do any other Americans, and the investment pays off in unparalleled public art installations throughout the city. The investments of Seattle-based millionaires have brought startlingly new and bold architecture in the **Experience Music Project** and **International Fountain.** Outside cosmopolitan downtown, Seattle boasts over 300 parks with well-watered greenery.

DOWNTOWN AND THE WATERFRONT

SEATTLE AQUARIUM. The star attraction of the Seattle Aquarium is a huge underwater dome, and the harbor seals, fur seals, otters, and endless supply of fish won't disappoint. Touch tanks and costumes delight kids, while a million-dollar salmon exhibit teaches about the state's favorite fish. Exciting feedings occur throughout the day. (Pier 59, near Pike St. ☎206-386-4320. Open daily in summer 9:30am-7pm; in fall and winter 10am-5pm; in spring 9:30am-6pm. Last entry 1hr. before closing. $15, ages 4-12 $10.)

PIKE PLACE MARKET. In 1907, angry citizens demanded the elimination of the middleman, and local farmers began selling produce by the waterfront, creating the Pike Place Market. Business thrived until an enormous fire burned the building in 1941. The early 1980s heralded a Pike Place renaissance, and today thousands of tourists mob the market daily. In the Main Arcade, on the west side of Pike St., fishmongers compete for audiences as they hurl fish from shelves to scales. (1531 Western Ave. ☎206-682-7453; www.pikeplacemarket.com. Open M-Sa 10am-6pm, Su 11am-5pm.) The **Pike Place Hillclimb** descends from the south end of Pike Place Market past chic shops and ethnic restaurants to the Alaskan Way.

THE SEATTLE CENTER

The 1962 World's Fair demanded a Seattle Center to herald the city of the future. Now the Center houses everything from carnival rides to ballet. The center is bordered by Denny Way, W. Mercer St., First Ave., and Fifth Ave. and has six gates, each with a model of the center and a map of its facilities. The anchor point is the **Center House,** which holds a food court, stage, and info desk. (☎206-684-8582. Info desk open daily 7am-9pm.)

EXPERIENCE MUSIC PROJECT (EMP). Undoubtedly the biggest and best attraction at the Seattle Center is the futuristic, abstract, and technologically brilliant EMP. The museum is the brainchild of Seattle billionaire and Microsoft cofounder Paul Allen, who originally wanted to build a shrine to his music idol and Seattle native Jimi Hendrix. The project eventually ballooned to include dozens of ethnomusicologists and multimedia specialists, a collection of over 80,000 musical artifacts, the world-renowned architect Frank Gehry, and enough money to make the national debt appear small (fine, it was only $350 million). The result? In 2000, the rock and roll museum of the future opened. Even if you don't go inside, the building alone—sheet metal molded into abstract curves and then acid-dyed gold, silver, purple, light blue, and red—is spectacular. Inside, check out the guitar Hendrix smashed on a London stage and

On Stage, a karaoke stage gone haywire. *(325 5th Ave., at Seattle Center. From I-5, take Exit 167 and follow signs to Seattle Center. ☎ 206-367-5483 or 877-367-5483. Open daily in summer 10am-7pm; in fall, winter, spring 10am-5pm. First Th of each month free. $15, ages 5-17 $12, under 5 free.)*

SPACE NEEDLE. Built in 1962 for the World's Fair, this 607 ft. rotating building was hailed as avant-garde and daring. Today, the EMP has stolen part of the Space Needle's glory, but it is still internationally recognized as a symbol of Seattle. On a clear day, it provides a great view and an invaluable landmark for the disoriented. The elevator ride itself is a show—operators are hired for their unique talents. The Space Needle houses an observation tower and a high-end 360° rotating restaurant. *(At Seattle Center. ☎ 206-905-2100. $16, ages 4-13 $8, under 4 free.)*

PIONEER SQUARE

ELLIOT BAY BOOKS. Taking up an entire block in Pioneer Sq., Elliot Bay Books houses more books than you could ever read (a whopping 150,000 titles) and, of course, the omnipresent Seattle coffee shop. With expansive children's and fiction sections, you can find almost any title imaginable. The bookstore employees detail their personal favorites on sticky notes in the store. *(101 S. Main St. ☎ 206-624-6600. Open M-Sa 9:30am-10pm, Su 11am-7pm.)*

SEATTLE UNDERGROUND. Originally, downtown Seattle stood 12 ft. lower than it does today. The Seattle Underground Tour guides visitors through the subterranean city of old. Be prepared for lots of company, comedy, and toilet jokes. The tour begins in **Doc Maynard's Public House,** where a guide gives a brief and oh-so-witty overview of the history of Seattle and its famous resident, Crapper, before leading you into the dark depths of the underground. *(610 1st Ave. ☎ 206-682-4646; www.undergroundtour.com. 1hr. tours daily roughly every hr. 10am-6pm. No reservations—arrive early on weekends. $15, students $12, ages 7-12 $7. Cash only.)*

INTERNATIONAL DISTRICT AND CHINATOWN

█SEATTLE ASIAN ART MUSEUM. What do you do when you have too much good art to exhibit all at once? Open a second museum. This is just what the Seattle Museum of Art did, creating a wonderful stand-alone attraction. The museum displays a particularly strong collection of Chinese art, but the rest of East Asia is admirably represented. *(In Volunteer Park, just beyond the water tower. ☎ 206-654-3100. Open Tu-W and F-Su 10am-5pm, Th 10am-9pm. Suggested donation $5, ages 13-17 $3, under 12 free.)*

█WING LUKE ASIAN MUSEUM. This museum gives a thorough description of life in an Asian-American community, investigates different Asian nationalities in Seattle, and shows work

DANCING IN THE DARK

What better way to celebrate the summer in Seattle than to kick off your Sunday shoes and join in the outdoor dancing? Thursday nights from mid-July to August, Freeway Park offers free dance parties on a floor rolled out across the tree-lined plaza. Whether you prefer blues, swing, waltz, Latin, country western, or line dancing, there's an evening for you. There's even a special night of zydeco, a fast-tempo American folk style usually dominated by the button accordion and washboard. The swinging and waltzing starts in August every Tuesday at Westlake Park, right by the walk-through fountain. If you're no pro, show up early for a free dance lesson courtesy of Dance for Joy. Lessons start at 6pm, and the dancing lasts 7-9pm. "No partner" is no excuse, since many people come to meet someone new. To participate, head to Freeway Park, Sixth Ave. and Seneca St., Westlake Park, across from the Westlake Center at 400 Pine St. More information is available at www.danceforjoy.biz.

by local Asian artists. One permanent exhibit is Camp Harmony, a replica of barracks from a Japanese internment camp during WWII. *(719 S. King St. ☎206-623-5124; www.wingluke.org. Open Tu-Su 10am-5pm. $8, students $6, ages 5-12 $5. 1st Th and 3rd Sa of the month free.)*

UNIVERSITY OF WASHINGTON ARBORE-TUM. The University of Washington Arboretum nurtures over 4000 species of trees, shrubs, and flowers and maintains superb trails. Tours depart the Graham Visitors Center, at the southern end of the arboretum. *(8 blocks east of Volunteer Park. Visitors center on Arboretum Dr. E., off Lake Washington Blvd. ☎206-543-8800. Open daily sunrise-sunset. Visitors center open daily 10am-4pm. Tours 1st and 3rd Su of the month. Free.)*

SEATTLE JAPANESE GARDEN. This tranquil three-acre park is a retreat of sculpted gardens, fruit trees, a reflecting pool, and a traditional teahouse. The original teahouse, a gift from Tokyo, was hand-constructed in Japan and reassembled on site. It was destroyed by fire in 1973 but rebuilt in 1981 and given the name "Shoseian," or "Arbor of the Murmuring Pines." *(At the south end of the UW Arboretum; entrance on Lake Washington Blvd. ☎206-684-4725. Open Mar.-Nov. daily 10am-sunset. $5, students, ages 6-18, and seniors $3, under 6 free.)*

UNIVERSITY DISTRICT, FREMONT, AND BALLARD

HENRY ART GALLERY. Specializing in modern and contemporary art, the Henry reflects its curators' enthusiasm with unconventional installations and rarely exhibited artists. *(NE 41st St. and NE 15th Ave. ☎206-543-2280; www.henryart.org. Open Tu-W and F-Su 11am-5pm, Th 11am-8pm. $10, students free, seniors $6. Th free.)*

THOMAS BURKE MUSEUM OF NATURAL HISTORY AND CULTURE. Savor the chance to see the only dinosaur bones on display in Washington as well as a superb collection on Pacific Rim cultures. Across the street, the astronomy department's old stone observatory is open to the public. *(NE 45th St. and 17th Ave. NE, in the northwest corner of the University of Washington campus. ☎206-543-5590; www.washington.edu/burkemuseum. Observatory ☎206-542-0126. Open daily 10am-5pm. $8, students $5, under 5 free, seniors $6.50. Special exhibits occasionally cost more.)*

FREMONT. This area is home to residents who pride themselves on their love of art and antiques and the liberal atmosphere of their self-declared "center of the universe" under Rte. 99. Twice in the past 15 years, Fremont has applied to secede from the United States. The immense **Fremont Troll,** beneath the Aurora Bridge on 35th St., grasps a Volkswagen Bug, a confounded expression on his face. Some say kicking the Bug's tire brings good luck; others say it hurts. A **flamin' Vladimir Lenin** resides at the corner of N. 36th St. and N. Fremont Pl.; this work from the USSR will be around until it is bought by a permanent collection.

NORDIC HERITAGE MUSEUM. Just east of the University District, the primarily Scandinavian neighborhood of Ballard offers a wide variety of Scandinavian eateries and shops along Market St. The museum presents realistic exhibits on the history of Nordic immigration and influence in the US. Stumble over cobblestones in old Copenhagen or visit the slums of New York City that turned photographer and Danish immigrant Jacob Riis into an important social reformer. The museum also hosts a series of Nordic concerts by national and international musicians throughout the year. *(3014 NW 67th St. ☎206-789-5707; www.nordicmuseum.org. Open Tu-Sa 10am-4pm, Su noon-4pm. $6, students and seniors $5, ages 6-18 $4.)*

WOODLAND PARK AND WOODLAND PARK ZOO. Woodland Park is mediocre at best, but the zoo has won a bevy of AZA awards (the zoo Oscars, if you will) for best new exhibits. The African Savannah and the Northern Trail exhibits are both full of zoo favorites: grizzlies, wolves, lions, giraffes, zebras, and flamingoes. *(Entrances at 5500 Phinney Ave. and 750 N. 50th St. ☎206-684-4800. Park open daily 4:30am-11:30pm. Zoo open daily May-Sept. 9:30am-6pm; Oct.-Apr. 9:30am-4pm. In summer $15, ages 3-12 $10; in winter $11/8.)*

🎵 ENTERTAINMENT

Seattle has world-renowned underground music scenes and a bustling theater community. In summer, the free **Out to Lunch** series (☎206-623-0340; www.downtownsummer.com) brings everything from reggae to folk-dancing into parks, squares, and office buildings. Check the free weekly *The Stranger* for thorough event listings.

CINEMA

Seattle is a cinephile's paradise. Most of the theaters that screen non-Hollywood films are on Capitol Hill and in the University District. On summer Saturdays, outdoor cinema in Fremont begins at dusk at N. 35th St., at Phinney Ave., in the U-Park lot by the bridge, behind the Red Hook Brewery. (☎206-781-4230. Entrance 7:30pm. Suggested donation $5.) **TCI Outdoor Cinema** shows everything from classics to cartoons at the Gasworks Park. (Live music 7pm-sunset. Free.) The **Paramount Theatre,** 911 E. Pine St., is best known for hosting the **Seattle International Film Festival** in the last week of May and first two weeks of June. (☎206-467-5510. Tickets $10. Box office open M-F 10am-6pm.) The **Harvard Exit,** 807 E. Roy St., on Capitol Hill, near the north end of the Broadway business district, has its own ghost, an enormous antique projector, and quality classic and foreign films. (☎206-323-8986. $9.25, under 12 $6.25.) **Grand Illusion Cinema,** 1403 NE 50th St., in the U District at University Way, is one of the last independent theaters in Seattle and often shows old classics and hard-to-find films. (☎206-523-3935. $7, children and seniors $5.50.)

MUSIC

The **Seattle Opera** performs from August to May in **McCaw Hall,** 321 Mercer St. The culmination of a 10-year renovation, the **Opera House** re-opened in 2003 with a glass facade, decked-out lobbies, and a modernized auditorium. Opera buffs should reserve well in advance, although rush tickets are sometimes available. (☎206-389-7676; www.seattleopera. com. Tickets from $35. Students and seniors can get ½-price tickets 2hr. before the performance. Box office open M-Tu and Th-F 9am-5pm, W 9:30am-5pm.) The **Seattle Symphony** performs in the new **Benaroya Hall,** 200 University St., at Third Ave., from September to June. (☎206-215-4747; www.seattle-symphony.org. Tickets from $15-39, seniors ½-price. Same-day student tickets $10. Box office open M-F 10am-6pm, Sa 1-6pm.)

SPORTS

The Mariners, or "M's," play baseball (or try to) in the $500 million, hangar-like **Safeco Field,** at First Ave. S. and Royal Brougham Way S., under an enormous retractable roof. (☎206-622-4487; www.mariners.com. Tickets from $7.) Seattle's football team, the **Seahawks,** play in **Qwest Field.** The University of Washington **Huskies** football team has contended in the Pac-10 for years. Call the **Athletic Ticket Office** (☎206-543-2200) for schedules and prices.

THEATER

The city hosts an exciting array of first-run plays and alternative works, particularly by talented amateur groups. Rush tickets are often available at nearly half-price on the day of the show from **Ticket/Ticket.** (☎206-324-2744. Cash only.) **⧉The Empty Space Theatre,** 901 12th Ave., in the **Lee Center for the Arts,** presents comedies and bold dramatic works from April to December. (☎206-547-7500. Tickets $10-30.) **The Seattle Repertory Theater,** 155 Mercer St., at the wonderful **Bagley Wright Theater** in the Seattle Center, presents contemporary and classic winter productions. (☎206-443-2222; www.seattlerep.org. Tickets $15-48, under 25 $10. Rush tickets 30min. before curtain $20.)

⧉ NIGHTLIFE

Seattle has moved beyond beer to a new nightlife frontier: the cafe-bar. The popularity of espresso bars in Seattle might lead one to conclude that caffeine is more intoxicating than alcohol, but often an establishment that poses as a diner by day brings on a band, breaks out the disco ball, and pumps out the microbrews by night. The best spot to go for guaranteed good beer, live music, and big crowds is **Pioneer Square,** where UW students from frat row dominate the bar stools. You may prefer to go to Capitol Hill or up Rte. 99 to Fremont, where the atmosphere is usually more laid-back than in the square.

DOWNTOWN

▨ **The Alibi Room,** 85 Pike St. (☎206-623-3180; www.seattlealibi.com), across from the Market Cinema in the Post Alley off Pike Pl. A remarkably friendly local indie filmmaker hangout. Bar

PACIFIC COAST

with music. Downstairs dance floor F-Sa. Brunch Sa-Su. No cover. Happy hour 4-6pm. Open daily 4pm-2am. AmEx/D/MC/V.

PIONEER SQUARE

Most bars participate in a joint cover (M-Th and Su $5, F-Sa $10) that will let you wander from bar to bar to sample the bands. The larger venues are listed below. Two smaller venues, **Larry's,** 209 First Ave. S. (☎206-624-7665), and **New Orleans,** 114 First Ave. S. (☎206-622-2563), feature great blues and jazz nightly. Most clubs close at 2am on weekends and at midnight on weekdays.

> **The Central,** 207 1st Ave. S. (☎206-622-0209; www.centralsaloon.com). Established in 1892, Seattle's oldest saloon became one of grunge's early venues in the late 1980s and is now a favorite for bikers. Live rock nightly. Punk music Tu. Joint cover. Open daily 11:30am-2am. Kitchen open until 9pm. AmEx/MC/V.

> **Last Supper Club,** 124 S. Washington St. (☎206-748-9975; www.lastsupperclub.com), at Occidental. 3 levels, 4 bars, and 2 dance floors, DJed with everything from 70s disco to funky house, drum and bass, and trance. Open W-Su 6pm-2am. AmEx/MC/V.

> **Swannie's Sports Bar,** 222 S. Main St. (☎206-622-9353). Share drink specials with pro ballplayers who stop by post game. Any Seattle sports junkie will swear this is the place to be. Drink specials change daily. Happy hour M-F 3-6pm. Open daily 11:30am-2am. AmEx/MC/V.

CAPITOL HILL

East of Broadway, travelers can sit back in a cool lounge on **Pine Street.** West of Broadway, **Pike Street** has the clubs that push the limits (punk, industrial, fetish, dance) and break the sound barrier in the process.

> ▣ **Linda's Tavern,** 707 Pine St. E. (☎206-325-1220). A very chill post-gig scene for Seattle rockers. DJ plays jazz and classic rock Tu. Movie night W. No cover. Open daily 4pm-2am. MC/V.

> **Neighbors,** 1509 Broadway Ave. (☎206-324-5358; www.neighborsnightclub.com). Enter from the alley on Pike St. A gay dance club for 24 years, Neighbors prides itself on techno slickness. Mark "Mom" Finley Tu. Drag nights Th-Sa. Cover $3-6.

Happy hour F 9-11pm. Open Tu-Su 6:30pm-last customer. MC/V.

✳ FESTIVALS

Pick up the visitors center's **Calendar of Events** (www.seeseattle.org/events) for coupons and listings. The first Thursday of each month, the art community sponsors **First Thursday,** a free gallery walk where galleries and art cafes open to the city. The **Fremont Fair** (☎206-694-6706; www.fremontfair.com) honors the summer solstice in mid-June with the **Fremont Solstice Parade,** led by dozens of bicyclists wearing only body paint. **Bumbershoot** is a massive four-day festival that caps off Labor Day weekend with major rock bands, street musicians, and a young, exuberant crowd. (☎206-281-7788; www.bumbershoot. org. 1-day pass $18-30; 3-day pass $50-80. Some events require additional tickets.) Puget Sound's yachting season starts in May. **Maritime Week,** in the third week of May, and the **Shilshole Boats Afloat Show** (☎206-748-0012; www.boatsafloatshow.com), in mid-September, let boaters show off their craft. Over the July 4 weekend, the Center for Wooden Boats sponsors the free **Wooden Boat Festival and Classic Speedboat Show** (☎206-382-2628; www.cwb. org) on Lake Union, which includes a demonstration of boat-building skills. The finale is the **Quick and Daring Boatbuilding Contest,** in which competitors sail wood boats that they built in the previous 24hr. using limited tools and materials.

⚠ OUTDOORS

BIKING

Seattle has more bike commuters than any other American city. The city prides itself on 30 mi. of bike-pedestrian trails, 90 mi. of signed bike routes, and 16 mi. of bike lanes on city streets. Over 1000 cyclists compete in the 190 mi. **Seattle to Portland Race** in mid-July. Call the **Cascade Bicycle Club** for more info. (☎206-522-3222; www.cascade.org.) On **Bicycle Saturdays/Sundays** from May to September, Lake Washington Blvd. is open only to cyclists 10am-6pm (usually on the 2nd Sa and the 3rd Su of each month). Contact the **Seattle Parks and Recreation Activities Office** for more info. (☎206-684-4075.)

HIKING

The 4167 ft. **Mount Si** is the most climbed mountain in the state of Washington, and with good reason. From downtown Seattle, hikers can reach a lookout that showcases Mt. Rainier, the Olympic Mountains, and Seattle in just a few hours (1 mi. one-way). A 4hr. hike (4 mi. one-way) brings you to **Haystack Basin,** the false summit. Don't try climbing higher unless you have rock-climbing gear, though. To get to Mt. Si, take I-90 E. to SE Mt. Si Rd. Cross the Snoqualmie River Bridge to the trailhead parking lot. **Tiger Mountain** (2522 ft.) is another great day hike near Seattle. A 4hr. hike (5 mi. round-trip) leads to the summit. Take I-90 to Tiger Mountain State Forest. From the Tradition Plateau trailhead, walk to Bus Road Trail and then to West Tiger Trail.

WHITEWATER RAFTING

Although the rapids are hours away by car, over 50 whitewater rafting outfitters are based in Seattle and are often willing to undercut one another with merciless abandon. **Washington State Outfitter and Guides Association** provides advice and sends out info. (☎509-997-1080.) The **Northwest Outdoor Center,** 2100 Westlake Ave., on Lake Union, gives $50-70 instructional programs in whitewater and sea kayaking. (☎206-281-9694; www.nwoc.com. Kayak rentals $13-18 per hr. Wetsuit $15 per day. Reservations recommended. Hours vary; call ahead.)

THE END OF THE ROAD

Head over to the Pike Place Market for some hard-core fish-throwing, wander among the vintage shops on Capitol Hill, or spend a quiet afternoon at Elliot Bay Books. You've made it all the way up the sunny coast, the road of a thousand beaches and avocados. Do you think you've quenched your thirst for the road? You ain't seen nothing yet. Grab a cup of coffee (there's no better place than Seattle) and continue your adventures in the **Great North** (p. 195) or on the **Oregon Trail** (p. 599).

EXIT TO

Portland, OR	174 mi.
on the oregon trail route, p. 669	
Victoria, BC	108 mi.
on the great north route, p. 329	

SPEED LIMIT 65

APPENDIX

CLIMATE

AVG. TEMP.(LOW/ HIGH), PRECIP.	JANUARY		APRIL		JULY		OCTOBER	
	°F	in.	°F	in.	°F	in.	°F	in.
Atlanta	36/52	5	52/72	3.6	70/88	5.1	54/72	3.1
Chicago	18/32	1.8	39/55	3.4	66/81	3.6	46/61	2.7
Dallas	36/55	1.9	55/75	2.5	75/93	2.4	57/79	4.7
Miami	61/73	2	66/81	3	75/88	6	72/82	7
New York City	25/37	3.7	42/57	4	66/82	4.1	48/70	3.5
San Francisco	45/55	4.1	48/63	1.5	53/64	0	53/68	1.1
Seattle	36/45	5.1	42/57	2.6	53/72	0.8	46/59	3.2

MEASUREMENT

Like the rest of the rational world, the US uses the standard system of measurement. The basic unit of length is the foot (ft.), which is divided into 12 inches (in.). Three feet make up a yard (yd.), and 5,280 feet make up a mile (mi.). Fluids are measured in fluid ounces (fl. oz.), and 128 fluid ounces make a gallon. A pint is 16 ounces. The basic unit of weight is the pound (lb.), and 2,000 pounds make a ton.

MEASUREMENT CONVERSIONS	
1 inch (in.) = 25.4mm	1 millimeter (mm) = 0.039 in.
1 foot (ft.) = 0.305m	1 meter (m) = 3.28 ft.
1 yard (yd.) = 0.914m	1 meter (m) = 1.094 yd.
1 mile (mi.) = 1.609km	1 kilometer (km) = 0.621 mi.
1 ounce (oz.) = 28.35g	1 gram (g) = 0.035 oz.
1 pound (lb.) = 0.454kg	1 kilogram (kg) = 2.205 lb.
1 fluid ounce (fl. oz.) = 29.57mL	1 milliliter (mL) = 0.034 fl. oz.
1 gallon (gal.) = 3.785L	1 liter (L) = 0.264 gal.

To convert from degrees Fahrenheit to degrees Celsius, subtract 32 and multiply by 5/9. To convert from Celsius to Fahrenheit, multiply by 9/5 and add 32.

°CELSIUS	-5	0	5	10	15	20	25	30	35	40
°FAHRENHEIT	23	32	41	50	59	68	77	86	95	104

LANGUAGE

FRENCH PHRASEBOOK

Both English and French are official languages in Canada. Roadtrippers should have no trouble getting around in English, but a basic familiarity with French is helpful, especially in Quebec, where attempts to use French words will be much appreciated.

ENGLISH	FRENCH	PRONUNCIATION
hello/good day	bonjour	bohn-zjhoor
good evening	bon soir	bohn-swah
Hi!	Salut!	sah-lu
goodbye	au revoir	oh ruh-vwahr
good night	bonne nuit	bon nwee
yes/no/maybe	oui/non/peut-être	wee/nohn/puh-tet-ruh
please	s'il vous plaît	see voo play
thank you	merci	mehr-see
you're welcome	de rien	duh rhee-ehn
Excuse me!	Excusez-moi!	ek-sku-zay-mwah
Go away!	Allez-vous en!	ah-lay-vooz on
Where is...?	Où se trouve...?	oo s'trhoov
closed/open	fermé/ouvré	ferh-may/oo-vray
Help!	Au secours!	oh-sk-oor
I'm lost.	Je suis perdu(e).	zh'swee pehr-du
I'm sorry.	Je suis désolé(e).	zh'swee day-zoh-lay
Do you speak English?	Parlez-vous anglais?	par-lay-vooz ahn-glay
It's just one step from the sublime to the ridiculous. (Napoleon)	Du sublime au ridicule il n'y a qu'un pas.	doo soo-bleem oh ree-dee-cule eel nee ah khun pas

SPANISH PHRASEBOOK

Although Spanish is not an official language in the US, it is widely spoken in California and the states bordering Mexico.

ENGLISH	SPANISH	PRONUNCIATION
hello	hola	OH-la
goodbye	adios	ah-dee-OHS
good day/night	buenas días/noches	bweh-nos DEE-ahs/NO-ches
yes/no/maybe	si/no/tal vez	SEE/no/tal VEHS
please	por favor	POHR fa-VOHR

thank you	gracias	GRA-see-ahs
you're welcome	de nada	DEH NAH-da
Excuse me!	¡Perdón!/¡Disculpe!	pehr-DOHN/dees-SKOOL-pay
Go away!	¡Váyase!	VAH-yah-say
Love is so short, and forgetting is so long. (Neruda)	Es tan corto el amor, y es tan largo el olvido.	ess tan CORT-o el AM-or ee ess tan lar-go el ol-BEED-o
Where is...?	¿Dónde está...?	DOAN-day eh-STAH
closed/open	cerrado(a)/abierto(a)	sehr-RAH-doh/ah-BYEHR-toh
Help!	¡Auxilio!	ow-SEE-lee-yoh
I'm lost.	Soy perdido.	soy payr-DEE-doh
I'm sorry.	Lo siento.	low SYEN-toh
Do you speak English?	¿Habla inglés?	AH-blah een-GLAYS

INDEX

INDEX

INDEX

INDEX

map index

MAP LEGEND

⚲	Beach	⚓	Police	▬▬▬	Pedestrian Zone
Hotel or Hostel		Ferry Landing	Post Office	▬▬▬	Roadtrip Route
Camping		✚ Hospital	Theater	(70)	Interstate Highway
Food		Internet Access	ⓘ Tourist Office	(56)	State Highway
Nightlife		Library	Train Station	(73)	Other Highway
Park		✝ Church	℞ Pharmacy	14	Local Road
Mountain		$ Bank	P Parking	▬ ▬ ▬	Unpaved Road
Site or Point of Interest		Museum	Border Crossing		River
Airport		Observatory	Ranger Station		Wash

Abbreviations Key:
BLM - Bureau of Land Management
Cons. - Conservation
Hist. Park - Historic Park
Ind. Res. - Indian Reservation
Nat'l. Mon. - National Monument
NWR - National Wildlife Refuge
SP/NP - State/National Park
SF/NF - State/National Forest
Rec. Area - Recreation Area

Cities and attractions in **B O L D**
are stops along the route.

The Let's Go compass
always points **N O R T H**.